Plant Finder 2025

Devised by Chris Philip and Realised by Tony Lord

Editor-in-Chief
Janet Cubey

RHS Editors
Jordan Bilsborrow Richard Dee Dawn Edwards
Jonathan Gregson Kálmán Könyves Neil Lancaster

Compiler
Lindsay Durrant

Published and compiled by
Royal Horticultural Society
80 Vincent Square
London SW1P 2PE

Reg charity no: 222879/SC038262

© Royal Horticultural Society 2024
First edition 1987
Thirty-seventh edition 2024

All rights reserved. No part of this publication may be reproduced, stored in a retrieval system, or transmitted in any form or by any means, electronic, mechanical, photocopying, recording or otherwise, without the prior written permission of the copyright owner.

British Library Cataloguing Publication Data
A catalogue record for this book is available from the British Library

ISBN 9781911666363

RHS Books Publisher – Helen Griffin

RHS Art Editor – Mark Timothy

RHS Prepress Designer – Anthony Masi

RHS Workflow Manager – Ally Page

RHS Head of Editorial – Tom Howard

Designer – Peter Cooling

Printed and bound by CPI WILLIAM CLOWES, Copland Way, Ellough, Beccles, Suffolk NR34 7TL

The compiler and editors of the *RHS Plant Finder* have taken every care, in the time available, to check all the information supplied to them by the nurseries concerned. Nevertheless, in a work of this kind, containing as it does hundreds of thousands of separate computer encodings, errors and omissions will inevitably occur. The RHS, the Publisher and Editors, cannot accept responsibility for any consequences that may arise from such errors.

If you find any mistakes, we hope that you will let us know so that the matter can be corrected in the next edition.

Front cover photograph: *Dahlia* 'Dikara Jodie' (© Anthony Masi)

Back cover photographs from top:
Heliopsis helianthoides Loraine Sunshine ('Helhan'[PBR])
Nigella damascena
Geum 'Totally Tangerine'[PBR] AGM
Echinops bannaticus (all © Anthony Masi)

The Royal Horticultural Society is the UK's leading gardening charity dedicated to advancing horticulture and promoting good gardening. Its charitable work includes providing expert advice and information, training the next generation of gardeners, creating hands-on opportunities for children to grow plants and conducting research into plants, pests and environmental issues affecting gardeners.

For more information visit rhs.org.uk or call 020 3176 5810.

LUX UNIQUE

Bespoke Steel Landscaping Products

hello@luxunique.co.uk

www.luxunique.co.uk

MADE IN BRITAIN

The ALPINE GARDEN SOCIETY

Join the AGS
and enjoy all these benefits
while supporting our charitable aims

- Access to our quarterly high quality digital journal
- Option to buy our print biannual journal
- Access our national network of local groups
- Access to one of the largest seed exchanges in the world
- Free entry to over 20 AGS national shows & plant fairs
- Free zoom lectures throughout the year
- Member discounts on books
- Member discounts on tours run by the AGS

Membership of the AGS starts from as little as £36 a year
Visit the AGS website for more details
www.alpinegardensociety.net

Limited-time offer for UK members joining by Direct Debit

Digital Journal ~ Half price for the first 12 months £18 (normally £36)
Digital & Paper Journal ~ Half price for the first 12 months £38 (normally £56)

To join by Direct Debit call us on **01386 554790**
(Monday - Thursday, 10am - 4pm)

Contents

New Plant Highlights
Janet Cubey   *page 7*

Perfecting Peat Free
Claire Thorpe and Nikki Barker   *page 25*

General Information   *page 33*

Introduction   *page 34*
New in this Edition
List of nurseries for plants with more than 30 suppliers
Plants last listed in earlier editions
RHS Online
Application for entry
Acknowledgements   *page 35*
Symbols and Abbreviations   *page 36*

Extended Glossary   *page 37*

Conservation and the Environment   *page 42*

Supplementary Keys to the Directory   *page 45*
Collectors' References   *page 45*
Nomenclature Notes   *page 49*
Classification of Genera   *page 50*

How to Use the Plant Directory   *page 55*

Using the Plant Directory   *page 56*

Plants   *page 57*

The Plant Directory   *page 58*
AGM Fruit   *page 739*
AGM Vegetables   *page 751*
RHS Plants for Pollinators   *page 767*

Nurseries   *page 775*

Using the Nursery Listings   *page 777*

How to Use the Nursery Listings   *page 778*

Nursery Details by Code   *page 780*

Nursery Index by Name   *page 841*
Display Advertisements   *page 845*
Index of Advertisers   *page 846*

Perfect plants for every garden direct to your door

SHOP ONLINE TODAY

Gardens come in all sorts of shapes and sizes, from window boxes to country gardens. RHS Plants has something to suit every space. Shop over 3,000 varieties of quality plants, plus garden equipment, accessories and more.

Visit **rhsplants.co.uk** or scan the **QR code**.

Your purchase supports our work as a charity.

rhsplants.co.uk

New plant highlights 2025

The *RHS Plant Finder* is both a celebration and an education on the diversity of plants available for UK gardeners. Each year, after I've finished proof-reading, I like taking time to reflect on the plants that are being included in the publication for the first time. I'd like to thank our nurseries who have taken the time to tell us about their new plants; I always appreciate hearing about them. So here's my personal selection of new plants in this edition; I hope you enjoy reading about these and finding your own new plants in the Plant Directory.

Author: **Janet J Cubey,** Editor-in-Chief, *RHS Plant Finder 2025*

Anemone ROYAL CANDY ('Ifrocan')

One of the Japanese anemones, ROYAL CANDY (right) grows to around 70cm tall and flowers from late summer through autumn. The abundant, semi-double, waterlily-form flowerheads are the palest pink with each of the numerous tepals tipped with darker rose pink, drawing the eye inwards to the large central boss of golden stamens. Although occasionally attributed to *A. tomentosa*, it is more likely to be of hybrid origin.

Another Japanese anemone marketed under the Royal banner is also new in this edition. ROYAL BLUSH ('Ifroblu') has darker pink flowers with a prominent white line around the edge of each tepal.

Aster amellus 'Paul Picton'

Raised at Old Court Nurseries, Herefordshire, in 2019 and introduced in 2024, this one caught my attention so we asked nursery owner Helen Picton to tell us more about it.

"There are very few new *Aster amellus*; to my knowledge the last was 'Forncett Flourish' AGM in 1996. Dad always said that he would only ever have a plant named after him if it was an *Aster amellus* (I suspect under the illusion there wouldn't be one!). But lo and behold we have managed to raise a lovely unique plant from *Aster amellus* 'Veilchenkönigin' seed."

Helen says that 'Paul Picton' has good-sized flowers with many narrow lavender-blue rays, ageing to purple-blue from late August into October and an upright growth with dark-green almost purple tinted stems. It grows to 60cm tall and is mildew resistant. While its habit is similar to its parent cultivar 'Veilchenkönigin' AGM, 'Paul Picton' differs by having larger and more robust flowers of a unique shade among this species.

Astilbe 'Dark Side of the Moon'

Jumping into this edition with several suppliers we have the striking *Astilbe* 'Dark Side of the Moon'. It was bred by Hans Hansen of Walters Gardens in Michigan, US and is notable for having both dark leaves and purple flowers.

The tall, robust and architectural flower spike is densely covered in dark raspberry-coloured flower buds, which open a brighter rosy purple. These spikes are held above a broad mound of coarsely textured foliage. The leaves emerge in yellow-bronze-green tones with a darker margin, darkening as they mature to a rich dark chocolate-purple. With adequate soil moisture it is said to perform best in a sunny situation, though it will grow in shade too.

Begonia sutherlandii 'Saunders's Legacy'

Begonia sutherlandii AGM is a winter-dormant, tender perennial with a trailing habit that can produce orange flowers from early summer all the way through to late autumn. Growing to 30cm tall, it's suitable for growing in a range of situations including hanging baskets, patio containers and as a houseplant.

'Saunders's Legacy' is an attention-grabbing dissected leaf form of this species that was named to honour the British-South African plant collectors, the late Rod and Rachel Saunders of Silverhill Seeds.

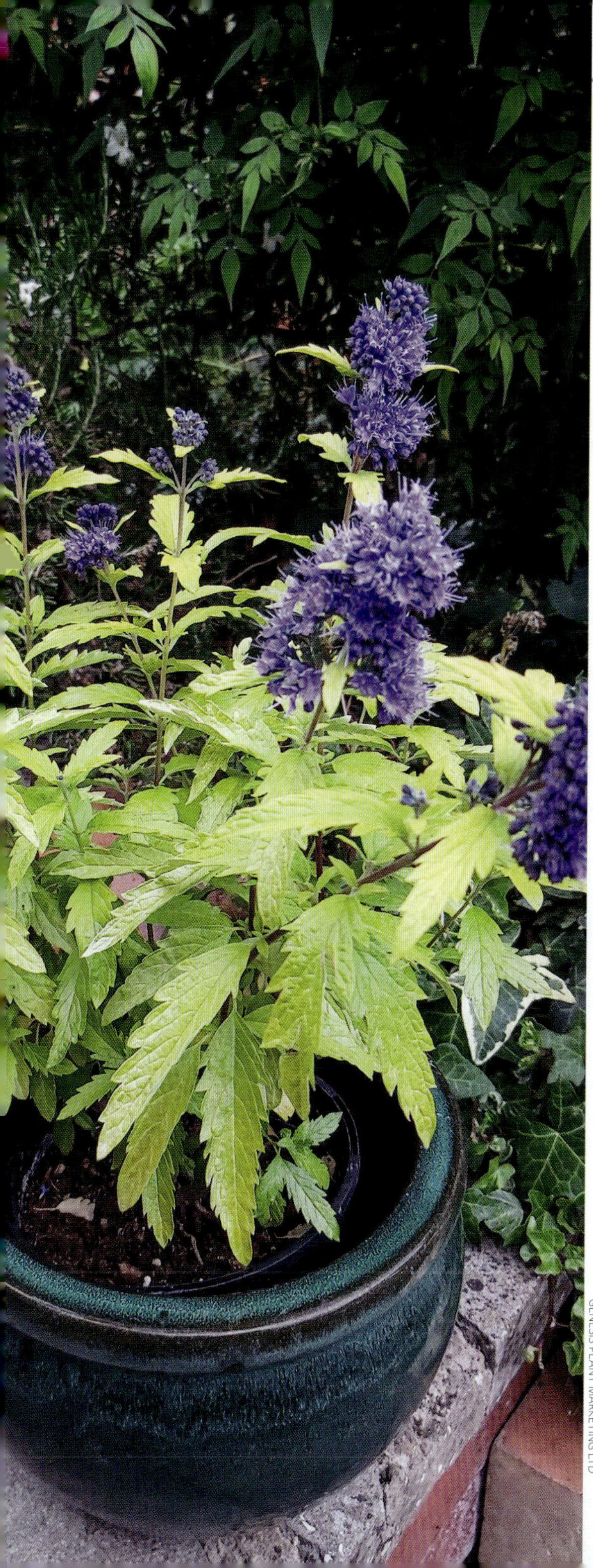

GENESIS PLANT MARKETING LTD

GENESIS PLANT MARKETING LIMITED

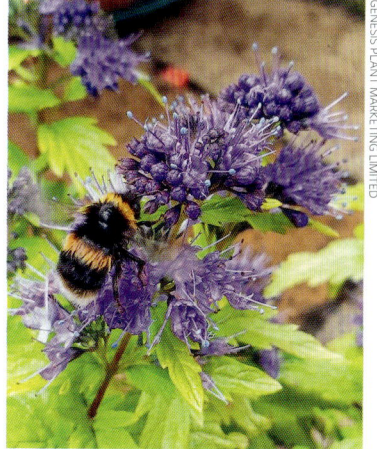

Caryopteris × clandonensis Sapphire Dream ('Lissmiv')

The latest *Caryopteris* bred by Peter Catt of Liss Forest Nursery, Hampshire, is Sapphire Dream, which has been launched by Genesis Plant Marketing Ltd. With a compact, well-branched habit, reaching around 40cm in height, it would make an ideal small shrub for a patio container or for the front of a border.

The combination of golden foliage and deep blue flower buds makes it a particularly eye-catching plant. Being repeat flowering, first in June and then again in late August or early September, it provides a double hit of this vibrant colour contrast.

Corylus avellana RED GHOST ('Bwm 01')

RED GHOST is a selection of the purple-leaved hazel. Jack Williams of Frank P Matthews, Worcestershire, told us about this new hazel (or filbert, depending on which common name you use) that they're selling.

"The leaves retain their dark purple-red colour all the way through the summer and into the autumn. Most purple-leaved hazels do turn green-leaved in the summer but this one is very special, retaining its colour throughout the season."

A productive cropper, its pink catkins in spring are a precursor to edible nuts in autumn. Having fringed red husks to the nuts adds to the ornamental appeal of this plant that was bred by Brigitta van Zoelen of Breederplants, Boskoop, Netherlands.

Dahlia 'Octopus Sparkle'

Growing to 1.2m tall, 'Octopus Sparkle' is classified as a Miscellaneous dahlia. All this means is that the flowerheads don't fit into any of the existing classifications; it looks a bit different.

The outer, ray florets are eight in number and roll in on themselves so that the outer red is more visible than the inner yellow-orange. They resemble those of the Single Orchid (or Star) cultivars. However, this is a double-flowered dahlia with an anemone-flowered centre. The tubular central florets develop more as the flowerheads mature, often causing the ray florets to recurve. They are also red on the outside and yellow-orange on the inside, showing clearly at their star-like tip.

Delosperma DESERT DANCERS RED ('Fsdd2112') (Desert Dancers Series)

This edition has a relatively large number of new *Delosperma* cultivars for the size of the genus.

Niamh Mullally of Southwold Succulent Co, Suffolk, told us DESERT DANCERS RED (right), with both red foliage and bright red flowers, was named for its likeness to the tones of desert sunset. It is one of the latest ice plants bred by Nishikawa Koichiro of FlorSAIKA Delosperma Breeding.

Delosperma 'PEACH PASSION'

Bred by D'Arcy & Everest, Cambridgeshire, *Delosperma* 'Peach Passion' (bottom right) is one that they are introducing in this 2025 edition. Partner Luke Whiting says it has a compact habit with two-toned vibrant orange-pink flowers and narrow, dark green leaves.

Both these cultivars are described as being easy to grow, drought-tolerant, low-maintenance, have a long flowering period, are good for pollinators and are suitable for planting in a range of situations including border edges and containers.

Hosta 'Silly String'

Some genera have a good number of new cultivars in every *RHS Plant Finder* and hosta is one of these. This year, it was the cultivar 'Silly String' (left and inset) that made me look twice. Coincidentally, this is the second cultivar in this year's selection bred by Hans Hansen at Walters Gardens in Michigan.

It's the long, lance-shaped, narrow leaves with their wavy margins that I particularly like. They remind me more of streamers than silly string, but the name does make me smile. Forming a neat mound, these arching leaves are glaucous blue-green and said to have their greatest blue hue in spring. Spires of pale purple flowers are a bonus.

Other cultivars to look out for include 'Golden Falls' (leaves bright yellow in spring) and 'Sister Act' (leaves yellow-green with a wide green border), both of which have entered this edition with three nursery suppliers.

Hydrangea CLOUD NINE ('Tmhy18-1')

Hydrangea CLOUD NINE caught my attention while I was checking plant names. Its lace-cap flowers are produced over a long flowering period on an upright plant, to 1.2m tall, with a neat habit. The outer, sterile flowers are large and clearly serrated; starting lime green they open fully to white and then can mature with a pink hue.

According to the US Plant Patent, it sprang from a breeding programme to create more floriferous cultivars with large flowers and upright habits. Its female parent is *H. macrophylla* 'Mariesii Lilacina' AGM and the male parent, *H. chinensis* f. *macrosepala* 'Golden Crane' (though the latter is often seen attributed to f. *angustipetala*).

Introduced by Thompson & Morgan (a division of Branded Garden Products Ltd), it was bred by Charles Valin of Valin Genetics.

Hydrangea serrata 'Gotemba Nishiki'

If more colourful hydrangeas are for you, then how about this one that was bred in Japan: *Hydrangea serrata* 'Gotemba Nishiki' (also seen sold as Euphoria Pink). It was runner-up to the RHS Chelsea Plant of the Year 2023, so I am pleased to see it entering *RHS Plant Finder 2025*.

A cultivar of *H. serrata*, it has a bushy, compact habit, lace-cap flowers and variegated leaves. The foliage is, for the most part, shades of green with a white edge. But the newly emerging leaves are tinged with pink too, as are the new shoots later in the season. The flowers are typically bright vibrant pink grading through to a small pale white-pink centre, though if grown in acid soils the predominant colour is violet-blue, with a white centre. A veritable kaleidoscope of colour.

Hypericum RADIANCE ('Methyra')

Introduced through Plantipp, *Hypericum* RADIANCE was bred in Europe by Marc Etienne and, as the name suggests, it has radiant golden yellow flowers in summer. However, its foliage is the stand-out feature: mature leaves mottled in shades of green explode with white and salmon pink on red stems when they emerge in spring. It's described as a compact shrub, ultimately growing up to 1m tall and a bit more in width.

When I first saw images of the spring foliage, I was reminded of the marble-leaved *Salix integra* 'Hakuro-nishiki' AGM and how popular that cultivar rapidly became. If I was growing this hypericum in my garden I'd be monitoring it to see if it needed pruning to maximise the number of spring shoots and therefore the tricolour foliage effect.

Malus domestica
QUEEN OF THE REALM

Released to celebrate the Platinum Jubilee of Queen Elizabeth II in 2022, apple QUEEN OF THE REALM was selected by Frank P Matthews from their trials programme in Worcestershire.

Delicate white spring flowers are followed by apples with a beautiful purple-blushed skin with white undertones, resembling HM The Queen's resplendent purple robes. The apple flesh is white, crisp and juicy with sweet, aromatic flavours. It can either be eaten straight from the tree or stored for a couple of months and is considered good for eating, juicing and cooking. It is in Pollination Group 3.

A nomenclatural note: QUEEN OF THE REALM has been trademarked in the UK for this apple, which is why the name is styled as a trade epithet rather than a cultivar. We aren't currently aware of a true cultivar name for this plant, so it seems that there isn't a name that is freely available to use.

Massonia hirsuta & *M. latebrosa*

Our entries for the genus *Massonia* (aka the hedgehog lilies) have more than doubled in this edition, thanks to some wonderful new additions from Jacques Amand International. These unusual bulbous plants from South Africa typically have just two leaves that lie flat with flowers emerging between the leaves. But there is a diverse range of colours, textures and variations to both the foliage and the flowers.

I've selected just two of them to highlight here: *M. hirsuta* (right, top), the dune hedgehog lily, enchants with its white fragrant flowers, black stamens and bracts with hairs on the margins. The rounded leaves are smooth to hairy.

M. latebrosa (right, bottom) is distinguished by the purple streaks and markings on the pustulated leaves and green and reddish flowers.

As a general rule in the UK, *Massonia* are best suited to cultivation in a cool glasshouse or alpine house. This helps to fulfil their wish for a period of dry dormancy following their spring flowering.

Osteospermum Summersmile Series

The Summersmile Series of *Osteospermum* is marketed by InnovaPlant GmbH and was bred in Germany by Silvia Hofmann. Raised to be bushy, well-branched plants with good flower coverage they aim to flower non-stop, all summer long. They've jumped into this edition in three different colour ways:

- SUMMERSMILE ORANGE ('Inostorang') with yellow-orange flowers (pictured)
- SUMMERSMILE SUNRISE with pink flowers overlaid with yellow, giving a blush effect that changes as the flowers age
- SUMMERSMILE YELLOW ('Inostyellow') with vibrant yellow flowers.

I'm sure we'll see more colours listed in the Plant Directory in future years.

Papaver (Oriental Group) Red Rumble ('Hg01')

Growing to 90cm tall, the oriental poppy Red Rumble was bred by Herbert Oudshoorn in the Netherlands and is marketed through Plantipp.

Flowers are a deep classic red poppy colour with dark petal blotches on the multiple layers of ruffled petals. Flowering in late spring and early summer, the flower stems are said to be particularly strong and don't become leggy or floppy.

This cultivar was short-listed for the RHS Chelsea Flower Show Plant of the Year 2024, where it was described as a reliable garden poppy that performs year after year with super-sized vibrant flowers.

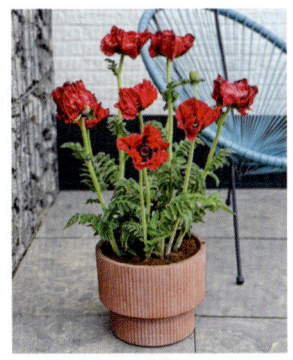

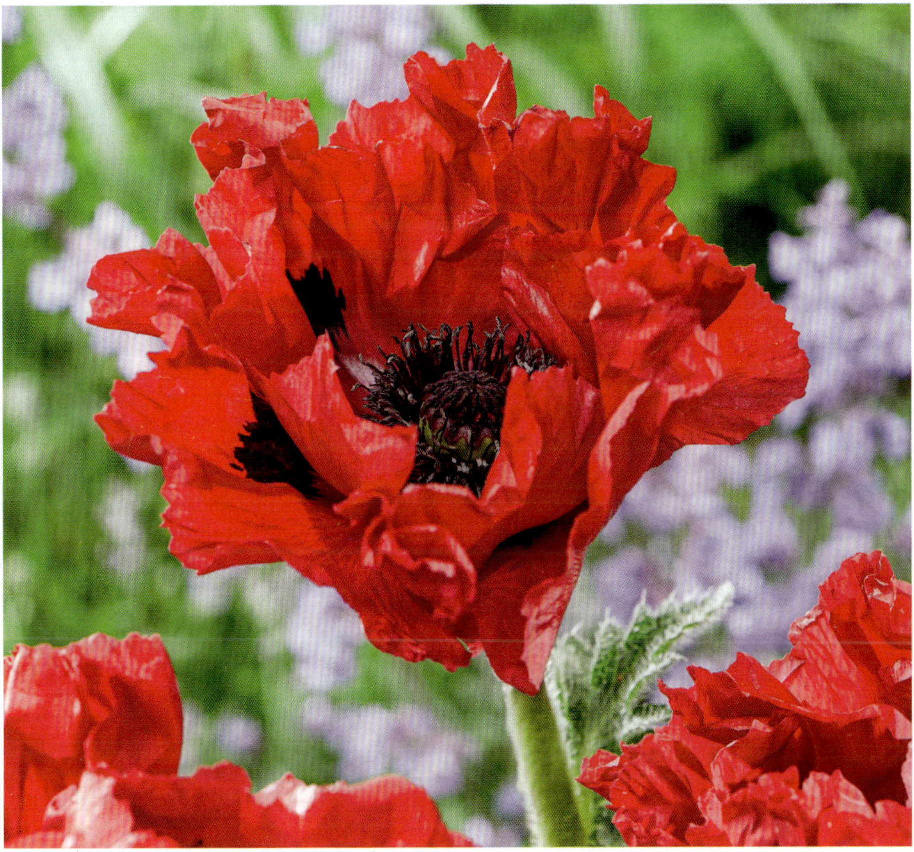

BURNCOOSE NURSERIES

VISIONS BV, NETHERLANDS / PLANTIPP

Petunia AMAZONAS PLUM COCKATOO ('Dpetampluc')

Part of the Amazonas Series from Danziger, AMAZONAS PLUM COCKATOO (right) is a truly eye-catching petunia. The flowers are large and ruffled, the base colour a pale lilac that is layered on each petal with a prominent vibrant green overlay and dark purple veins that become more intense and dense as they lead your eye towards the purple centre. Flowering from early in the season with a neat habit, it is said to have good drought tolerance. More in this Series will follow soon, no doubt.

The Capella Series is also new in this edition from Danziger. A slightly smaller flower and without the ruffles, I can see the bright yellow flowers of CAPELLA HELLO YELLOW ('Dpethloylw') adding a sunny splash to any summer patio container.

Sanguisorba officinalis 'Jam Session'

New from Future Plants in the Netherlands, comes great burnet 'Jam Session' (left). While the species is often more typically thought of as deep red-flowered, this cultivar has creamy-white flowers packed in the typical tight flowerheads on airy stems. These flower spikes dance up to 50cm tall above low-growing dark green foliage.

A second new burnet cultivar, 'Plum Drops', from Intrinsic Perennial Gardens in Illinois, has deep wine-red flower spikes on taller stems to 90cm tall.

Thalictrum Purple Wings ('Macthapuwi')

Continuing the light and airy theme, *Thalictrum* Purple Wings (above) is a new hybrid from Elizabeth MacGregor in Scotland. A hybrid of *T. delavayi* and *T. rochebruneanum* AGM, it is very floriferous with its branched, dark wiry stems laden with flowers from midsummer onwards.

The four-petalled flowers are lilac-purple with a central creamy-white stamen cluster and it is said to flower for much longer than *T. delavayi*. Favouring fertile soils, it will grow to 1.2–1.5m tall.

Another new cultivar that is popular with our nurseries is *T. aquilegiifolium* 'The Cloud' bred by Thierry Delabroye in France. It is the stamens that you notice most with the flowers of this species, and it is very aptly named, for its neat cloud of palest pink flowers.

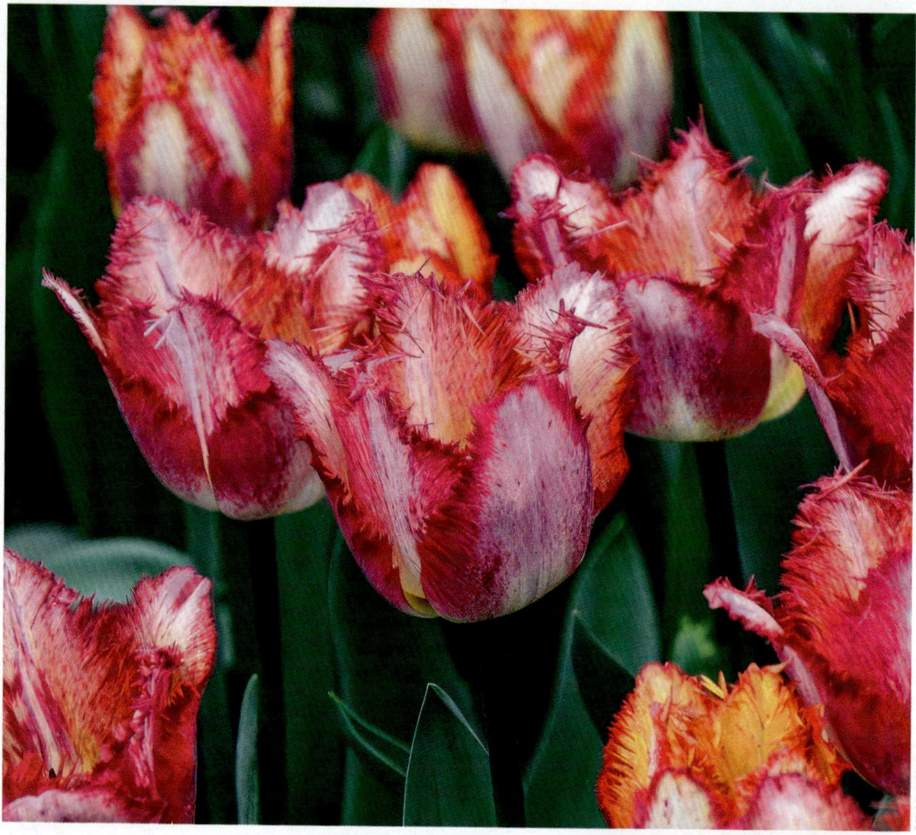

NIJSSENBULBS

Tulipa 'Cabanna' & *T.* 'Colour Fusion'

I'm concluding my selection of new plants with some colourful tulips. I love the pops of colour that tulips bring to the garden in spring (and enjoy cutting them to enjoy in the house) and having moved to a garden without tulips, I've been planting...lots!

'Cabanna' (above) is a Parrot Group tulip that arose as a sport of the Triumph Group tulip 'First Class'. It grows to 40cm tall with long-lasting flowers around 8cm in length. They are creamy-white, tipped with various intensities of rose pink through their life, puckered and curled with frayed edges and irregularly touched with green.

'Colour Fusion' (right) is a Fringed tulip. It grows to 45cm with flowers around 5.5cm in length. The fabulously fringed flowers start out egg-shaped and cream, boldly streaked with deep raspberry and flushed with pale yellow. As they mature they turn darker with more intense colours and the flowers open to be riotous fringed bowls of colour.

PETER NYSSEN

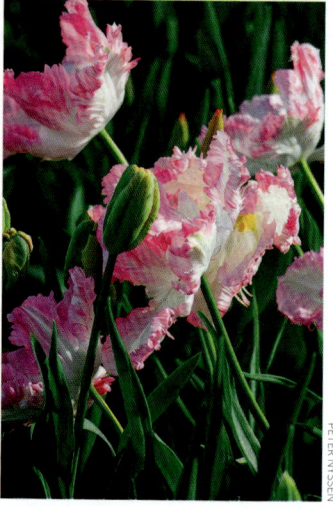

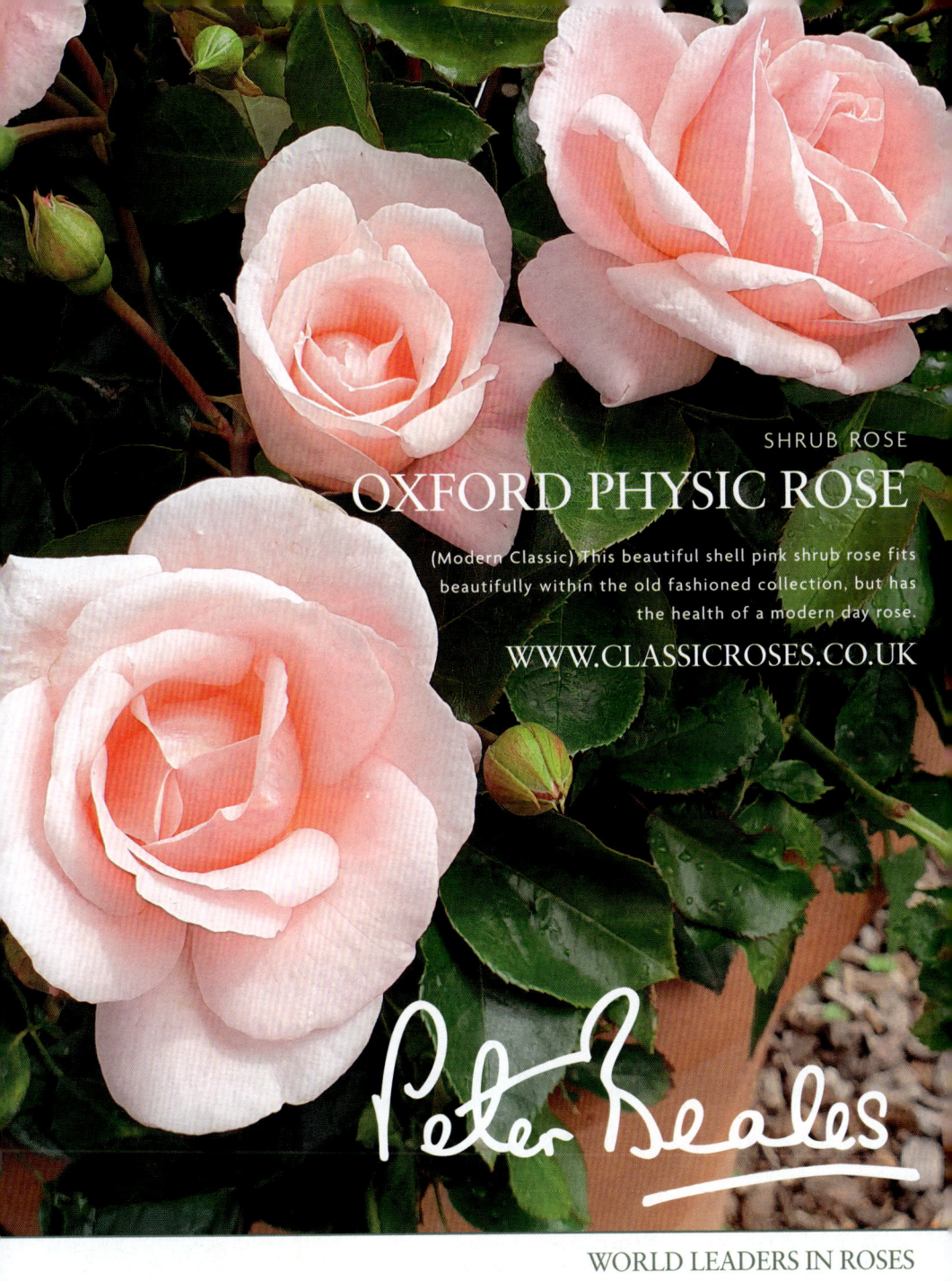

Perfecting Peat Free

Growing without peat has never been easier, and new research shows that there is a peat-free mix for every plant and situation, plus many plants grown without peat that are newly available to buy. **Claire Thorpe** and **Nikki Barker** share news from the RHS peat-free campaign trail

Peatlands are unique ecosystems that globally store a third of the world's carbon

Why protect peatlands?

Peatlands are unique places, brimming with rare and specialised wildlife, and covering nearly three million hectares in the UK, which is roughly 12 per cent of the land area. These diverse habitats, from lowland fens in East Anglia to the bogs covering much of the uplands, are all formed on peat soils.

Peat forms as vegetation decays under wet conditions; it's a slow process and it can take up to 1,000 years for a metre of peat to accumulate. Peatland stores large amounts of carbon in its soil – globally, peatlands store twice as much carbon as all the world's forests combined.

Peatlands provide many benefits to climate, nature and people, which are lost when peat is damaged. In extracting peat for use in horticulture, thousands of years of peat formation is lost in minutes, releasing carbon back into the atmosphere and contributing to the climate crisis.

The RHS is committed to removing peat from all its operations by the end of 2025, and to helping gardeners and growers to go peat-free. The RHS online peat-free hub at **rhs.org.uk/peat** helps both commercial growers and amateur gardeners find information to help them make the transition to peat-free.

RHS Peat-Free Transition Co-ordinator Nikki Barker explains: "Sharing your peat-free success stories, whether that's with friends, your local gardening club or on social media, helps inspire others to go peat-free and gives people the confidence to try a peat-free compost if they weren't sure where to start."

Going peat-free: top tips to achieve expert results

Drawing from more than 100,000 gardening questions that the RHS advisory service answers each year, here are the top tips and adjustments to help ensure successful peat-free growing.

Buying peat-free compost

Peat-free mixes vary widely between brands because they contain a broader range of ingredients than peat-based composts. The most common components are wood fibre, bark and coir, with smaller amounts of additional materials, such as green waste and anaerobic digestate.

You might need to test a few brands to find the one that works for you, your plants and your growing environment. It can help on cost to share a bag with a friend while you're trying it out.

Before you buy, look for a production date on the bag, which some brands include – the newer the better. And ensure the product meets your needs; for example, for best results in your garden, use soil improvers and mulches for beds and borders rather than multipurpose mixes. Look for a specific growing use on the packaging, such as seed sowing, cuttings, potting on and ericaceous plants. (For more tips on growing seeds and cuttings peat-free, visit **rhs.org.uk/peatfreepropagation**)

Store your peat-free compost in a cool, dry place – under cover if possible – and use it all in the growing season you bought it to avoid the components breaking down and adversely affecting plant performance.

The RHS and the Garden Centre Association have created a list of retailers stocking only peat-free bagged products because it can be hard to tell from the packaging whether something is peat-free: **rhs.org.uk/peatfreestockists**

Test different brands of peat-free compost to find which works best for you and choose mixes formulated for specific growing use, such as seed compost for sowing or cuttings compost for plants such as pelargoniums (top)

Peat-free plants

Peat-free plants are becoming more widely available, but you might need to ask the retailer whether plants were grown in peat because this is not always stated on the labelling. The RHS has created a list of 100% peat-free nurseries, listed by location, available on the peat-free hub: rhs.org.uk/peatfreenurseries

Adjustments to growing

When growing peat-free the watering regime is key. Peat-free mixes tend to need watering little and often and can look dry on top but be moist lower down in the pot, so check with a finger to see if the soil is damp under the surface, or lift the pot and test by weight.

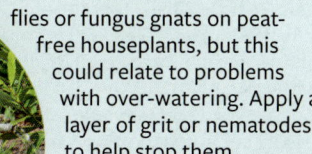

Plants grown peat-free often need a little more feed than those in peat. Follow the manufacturer's instructions and make sure you buy the right feed for the type of plants you are growing, especially more specialised plant groups.

Sam Gallivan, Team Leader for Propagation at RHS Garden Wisley, advises: "It's especially important to check before you water plants growing in peat-free composts to make sure you don't wash out the feed as this can cause plants to look poor." Many new feeds on the market are especially designed to be used with peat-free compost.

Peat-free composts often have more microbial activity, but if you notice small mushrooms popping up, just pluck off the fungi and put them in the compost; some mycorrhizae below the surface are great for soil and plant health.

Some gardeners notice more sciarid flies or fungus gnats on peat-free houseplants, but this could relate to problems with over-watering. Apply a layer of grit or nematodes to help stop them.

Wholesale changes

Charles Carr, Head of Hillier Wholesale Nurseries, suggests growers test different suppliers and learn which changes you need to make to crop husbandry. He says: "Plants grown in peat-free require a very different approach and a relearning of many practices that are ingrained in growers!".

Growers should also ask suppliers whether their plug plants are peat-free. In 2024, the RHS surveyed UK plug plant producers and found few customers asked whether the plugs they were buying were peat-free, and most suppliers did not state in catalogues whether these plants were peat-free.

Peat-free grown *Dianthus* Tickled Pink ('Devon Pp 11') at Golden Valley Plants in Herefordshire

The RHS road to peat-free

As part of its sustainability strategy, the RHS is committed to removing the use of peat from all our operations by December 2025, and to sharing this journey with its members, the nursery trade and gardeners.

Alistair Griffiths, RHS Director of Science and Collections, says: "The RHS is committed to its shows, gardens and retail being peat-free by the end of 2025. We will use this as an opportunity to diversify our offering and we are working in collaboration with many growers on the transition to peat free. An increasing number of UK plug producers, particularly Kernock Park Plants and Seiont, are well on their way to 100% peat-free, while growers in Europe are also starting that journey. This is partly due to pressure from the UK, as well as to Belgium, Holland, Switzerland, Germany and France starting to develop their own peat-free legislative goals. Any growers looking for help should get in touch and we can explore what kind of support the RHS can offer."

Showing up peat-free

One of the stand-out show gardens created for the 2024 RHS Hampton Court Palace Garden Festival in July was entirely peat-free, created by the RHS and sustainable designer Arit Anderson. In her garden Arit showcased 2,000 different peat-free plants from many UK growers, and provided peat-free advice for 100,000 visitors through garden signage and workshops at the six-day event. As a result of the information they received, visitors felt empowered to try peat-free. Some had previously experienced poor germination and cultivation problems, but Arit's advice was that mixes are much better than five years ago and to give peat-free another go to find a compost that suits.

The RHS-led Peat-Free Fellowship collaborative research project unites government, growers and growing-media manufacturers to move to sustainable peat alternatives. Led by Dr Raghavendra Prasad, the Fellowship researches peat alternatives in growing media and shares advice on best practice through trials for a wide range of ornamental plants, peat-free plug plant production and developing evidence-based growing protocols for nurseries. Research findings are shared with partners and the wider industry and will provide advice for the UK's 30 million gardeners on successful peat-free growing.

Dr Prasad said: "We are encouraged by the initial findings from the peat-free trials, which focused on irrigation in 2024. Once analysed, results will be shared to assist growers."

To view the latest information and access workshops and events for growers, visit: **rhs.org.uk/science/transition-to-peat-free**

Clockwise from top: Plant Trials from the Fellowship research; Dr Raghavendra Prasad presenting at RHS Garden Harlow Carr; RHS Peat-Free Garden at RHS Hampton Court Palace Garden Festival 2024; numbers of peat-free seedlings

The Responsible Sourcing Scheme

This industry-led initiative aims to promote environmentally responsible sourcing of materials used in growing media. It assesses the environmental impact of each component, providing a transparent rating system for consumers. By evaluating factors, such as energy usage, water usage and biodiversity impact, the scheme helps manufacturers, retailers and consumers make informed, sustainable choices in their gardening and horticultural practices. Gardeners can look out for the logo on bags of compost, and a QR code that takes them to the product rating or visit: **responsiblesourcing.org.uk**

MINI GREENHOUSES AND GROWHOUSES

Ideal where space is limited

- Toughened Safety Glass
- Extra Strong Aluminium
- Adjustable Shelving
- Mist Watering

Call for a FREE 40 page brochure   **0800 298 6284**

Ref: RHP24 • Crick, Northampton NN6 7XS   www.garden-products.co.uk

Dingle Nurseries & Garden

We have one of the largest ranges of trees and shrubs in the country, including native trees, hedging, conifers, roses, perennials and fruit. Semi mature and standard trees are also available, as well as specimen shrubs and many rarities all at competitive prices.

DINGLE NURSERIES & GARDEN
Welshpool, Powys, Wales SY21 9JD
T: 01938 555145 E:info@dinglenurseryandgarden.co.uk

Open 7 days a week 9am to 5pm.

WINTERLING

Botanical labelling

winterling.co.uk

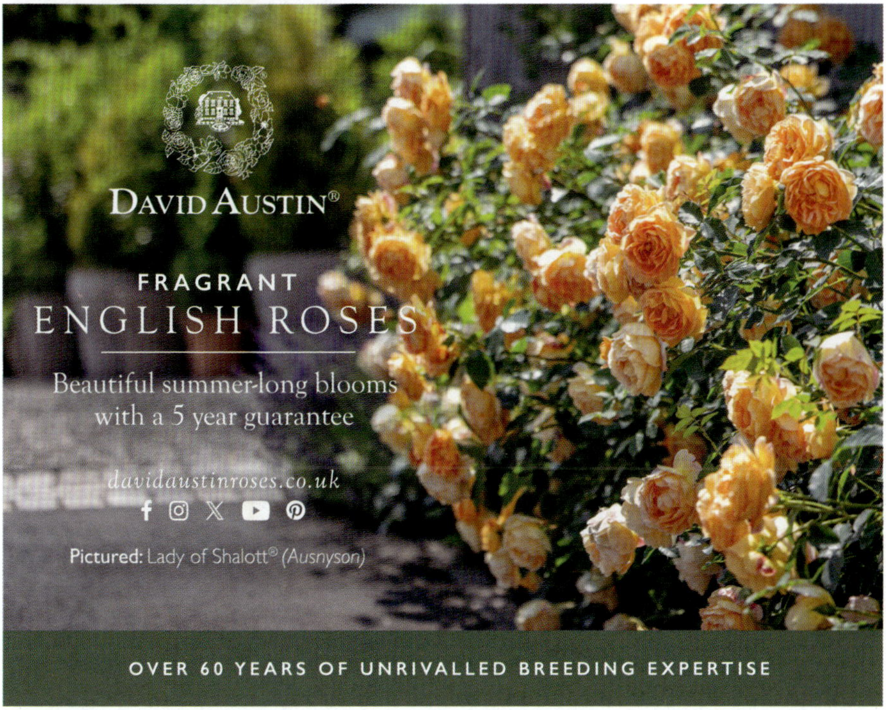

DAVID AUSTIN®

FRAGRANT ENGLISH ROSES

Beautiful summer-long blooms with a 5 year guarantee

davidaustinroses.co.uk

Pictured: Lady of Shalott® *(Ausnyson)*

OVER 60 YEARS OF UNRIVALLED BREEDING EXPERTISE

I
GENERAL INFORMATION

Introduction

The *RHS Plant Finder* exists to put enthusiastic gardeners in touch with suppliers of plants. It is comprehensively updated every year.

The book is divided into two related sections: **Plants** and **Nurseries**.

Plants includes an A–Z Directory of over 64,000 plant names, against which are listed a series of nursery codes. These codes point the reader to the full nursery details contained in the **Nurseries** section towards the back of the book.

New in this Edition

After much discussion with our publications team, we have taken the decision to publish the *RHS Plant Finder* directory in the autumn of 2024 to test the potential for pre-Christmas sales of the directory. The book will be labelled as the 2025 edition. If successful, we will continue this pattern going forward. The online RHS Find-a-plant website, which holds the suppliers and plants information from the directory, is published in the Spring as usual. With traffic to this website reaching nearly half a million enquiries in 2023, this continues to be a primary source for gardeners to find plants and potential suppliers, check horticultural nomenclature and link through to the 40,000 plant profiles we currently have available on the RHS website.

This is the sixth Editor's choice of new plant highlights, illustrating just some of the plants that are appearing for the first time in this edition.

The plant names used in the 2025 edition reflect the decisions made by the RHS Nomenclature and Taxonomy Advisory Group (NATAG). Nomenclature Notes (p.49) give a brief overview of the changes made since the compilation of the previous edition.

As of last year, banned, invasive, non-native plants will not show suppliers and will be marked with the text 'Prohibitive Invasive' in the directory. From this year, those that are not banned but considered to be a potential nuisance will be marked at species level with a '?' and we recommend that an alternative is chosen where possible.

Please see https://www.rhs.org.uk/prevention-forprotection/garden-thugs-potential-nuisance-plants for further advice on nuisance plants. For a full list of invasive, non-native plants, please visit our RHS advice guide at https://www.rhs.org.uk/prevention-protection/invasive-non-native-plants. For further information see Conservation and the Environment section p.42.

It is important to remember when ordering plants that many of the nurseries listed in this book are small, family-run businesses which propagate their own material. They cannot, therefore, guarantee to hold large stocks of the plants they list. Some will, however, propagate to order.

Nurseries appearing in the *RHS Plant Finder* for the first time or re-entering after an absence are printed in bold type in the **Nursery Index by Name** (pp.841–844).

Lists of Nurseries for Plants with more than 30 Suppliers

To prevent the book from becoming too big, we do not print nursery codes where more than 30 nurseries offer the same plant. The plant is then listed as being 'widely available'. See **How to Use the Plant Directory** (p.55).

Plants Last Listed in Earlier Editions

Plants cease to be listed for a variety of reasons. For more information, turn to **How to Use the Plant Directory** (p.55). Please contact Lindsay Durrant, Plant Finder Compiler, if searching for long-lost plants.

RHS Online

The plant data from the *RHS Plant Finder* is available at www.rhs.org.uk/plants under the RHS Find-a-plant section.

Application for Entry

If you would like your nursery to be considered for inclusion in the next edition of the *RHS Plant Finder*, please contact the Compiler. Entries to the book are free. The deadline for nursery entries is the 31st December 2024.

Contact details
Lindsay Durrant – Compiler, *RHS Plant Finder*
Ⓣ (01483) 226577
Ⓔ plantfinder@rhs.org.uk

Acknowledgements

This edition was compiled by Lindsay Durrant. Richard Sanford managed the editing of plant names in the database, and prepared the text of the AGM sections and Plant Directory. Julia Barclay and Rupert Wilson administered the RHS Horticultural Database using Brahms. BRAHMS is developed at the Department of Plant Sciences, University of Oxford, and managed and licensed by Oxford University Innovation. We would like to acknowledge the work of Denis Filer and Andrew Liddell from the Brahms team at the University of Oxford and assistance from RHS IT and digital teams.

We give our grateful thanks to the following: RHS botanists Dawn Edwards, Kálmán Könyves, Neil Lancaster, Richard Dee, Jordan Bilsborrow and Jonathan Gregson.

RHS Books Publisher Helen Griffin and all her team for their various contributions including Louise Bowering, Louise Tee, Ally Page, Mark Timothy, Tom Howard, Simon Maughan and the Peterborough Media team.

Science & Collections colleagues for their support with either the book itself, or in enabling others to help, Jane Rowlands, Sharon McDonald, Melanie Underwood, Sarah Holme and John David.

Thank you to Claire Thorpe, RHS Peat-Free Campaign Manager, and Nikki Barker, RHS Peat-Free Transition Co-ordinator, for their assistance in putting together the article 'Perfecting Peat Free'.

We would also like to thank those who have kindly provided plant images featuring in the book this year, especially our Plant Finder nurseries.

Finally, we are greatly indebted to Peter Cooling for his skill in turning our data into a publishable form.

Our colleagues on the RHS Nomenclature and Taxonomy Advisory Group, along with the RHS International Cultivar Registrars, have all provided valuable guidance and information. Many nurseries have supplied useful details on new plants and have suggested corrections to existing entries. Some of these remain to be checked and will be entered in the next edition, although those that contravene the Codes of Nomenclature may have to be rejected. We appreciate your patience while these checks are made. We are also grateful to our regular correspondents and to all those readers who have made helpful comments.

Clematis	Sarah Holme, Int. Cultivar Registrar
Chrysanthemum	J. Barker
Conifers	S. McDonald, Int. Cultivar Registrar
Dahlia	S. McDonald, Int. Cultivar Registrar
Dianthus	S. McDonald, Int. Cultivar Registrar
Delphinium	M.R. Underwood, Int. Cultivar Registrar
Ilex	S. Andrews
Lilium	Sarah Holme, Int. Cultivar Registrar
Narcissus	M.R. Underwood, Int. Cultivar Registrar
Nerine	Dr J.C. David
Orchids	J.M.H. Shaw, Int. Cultivar Registrar
	C. Pritchard, Int. Cultivated Plant Registrar
Rhododendron	S. McDonald, Int. Cultivar Registrar
Sorbus	Dr H. McAllister
Thymus	M. Easter, Int. Cultivar Registrar

Janet Cubey
RHS Editor-in-Chief
May 2024

Symbols and Abbreviations

Symbols Appearing to the Left of the Name

* *   Name not validated. Not listed in the International Plant Names Index or the appropriate International Registration Authority checklist and not yet found in printed matter. For fuller discussion see p.37
* I   Invalid name. See *International Code of Botanical Nomenclature 2018* and *International Code of Nomenclature for Cultivated Plants 2016*. For fuller discussion see p.37
* §   Plant listed elsewhere in the Plant Directory under a synonym
* ×   Hybrid genus
* +   Graft hybrid genus
* ?   Invasive but not banned from sale. It is an offence to plant or cause these to grow in the wild. We recommend alternatives are chosen

Symbols Appearing to the Right of the Name

* ✿   Plant Heritage National Plant Collection® exists for all or part of this genus. Further details can be found by searching the National Plant Collections online or in the Plant Heritage Directory available from www.plantheritage.org.uk or by phone (01483) 447540.
* ♀H4   The Royal Horticultural Society's Award of Garden Merit, see p.37
* (d)   double-flowered
* (F)   Fruit
* (f)   female
* (m)   male
* (v)   variegated plant, see p.41
* PBR   Plant Breeders' Rights see p.39
* **new**   New plant entry in this edition

For abbreviations relating to individual genera see **Classification of Genera** p.50

For **Collectors' References** see p.45

For symbols used in the **Nurseries** section see p.777

Symbols and Abbreviations used as Part of the Name

* ×   hybrid species
* aff.   affinis (akin to)
* agg.   aggregate, a single name used to cover a group of very similar plants, regarded by some as separate species
* ambig.   ambiguous, a name used by two authors for different plants and where it is unclear which is being offered
* cf.   compare to
* cl.   clone
* f.   forma (botanical form)
* gx   grex
* *sensu stricto*   in the narrow sense
* sp.   species
* subsp.   subspecies
* subvar.   subvarietas (botanical subvariety)
* var.   varietas (botanical variety)

It is not within the remit of this book to check that nurseries are applying the right names to the right plants or to ensure nurseries selling plants with Plant Breeders' Rights are licensed to do so.

We recommend that you use the latest edition of the *RHS Plant Finder*

Extended Glossary

This glossary combines some of the helpful introductory sections from older editions in an alphabetical listing. A fuller, more discursive account of plant names, *Guide to Plant Names*, and a detailed guide to the typography of plant names, *Recommended Style for Printing Plant Names*, are both available as leaflets. To request a copy of either please send an A4 sae to The Compiler at the contact address given on page 34.

Authorities

In order that plant names can be used with precision throughout the scientific world, the name of the person who coined the name of a plant species (its author, or authority) is added to the plant name. Usually this information is of little consequence to gardeners, except in cases where the same name has been given to two different plants or a name is commonly misapplied. Although only one usage is correct, both may be encountered in books, so indicating the author is the only way to be certain about which plant is being referred to. This can happen equally with cultivars. Authors' names, where it is appropriate to cite them, appear in a smaller typeface after the species or cultivar name to which they refer and are abbreviated following Brummitt and Powell's *Authors of Plant Names*.

♀ Award of Garden Merit

The Award of Garden Merit (AGM) is intended as a practical guide for the gardener and is therefore awarded only after a period of assessment by the RHS Standing and Joint Committees. The AGM is awarded only to plants that are:
- excellent for ordinary use in appropriate conditions
- available
- of good constitution
- essentially stable in form and colour
- reasonably resistant to pests and diseases

The AGM symbol is cited in conjunction with the **hardiness** rating. A full list of AGM plants may be found on the RHS website at www.rhs.org.uk/plants/trials-awards/award-of-garden-merit.

The AGM list was originally reviewed every ten years, to ensure that every plant still merited the award. The last review took place in 2012; since 2013, the list has been subject to a "rolling review", and AGMs may now be rescinded at any time.

Botanical Names

The aim of the botanical naming system is to provide each different plant with a single, unique, universal name. The basic unit of plant classification is the species. Species that share a number of significant characteristics are grouped together to form a genus (plural **genera**). The name of a species is made up of two elements; the name of the genus followed by the specific epithet, for example, *Narcissus romieuxii*.

Variation within a species can be recognised by division into subspecies (usually abbreviated to subsp.), varietas (or variety abbreviated to var.) and forma (or form abbreviated to f.). Whilst it is unusual for a plant to have all of these, it is possible, as in this example, *Narcissus romieuxii* subsp. *albidus* var. *zaianicus* f. *lutescens*.

The botanical elements are always given in italics, with only the genus taking an initial capital letter. The rank indications are never in italics. In instances where the rank is not known it is necessary to form an invalid construction by quoting a second epithet without a rank. This is an unsatisfactory situation, but requires considerable research to resolve.

In some genera, such as *Hosta*, we list the cultivar names alphabetically with the species or **hybrid** to which they are attributed afterwards in parentheses. For example, *Hosta* 'Reversed' (*sieboldiana*). In other situations where the aim is not to create a list alphabetically by cultivar name we would recommend styling this as *Hosta sieboldiana* 'Reversed'.

Classification of Genera

Genera that include a large number of species or with many cultivars are often subdivided into informal horticultural classifications or more formal Cultivar Groups, each based on a particular characteristic or combination of characteristics. Colour of flower or fruit and shape of flower are common examples and, with fruit, whether a cultivar is grown for culinary or dessert purposes. How such groups are named differs from genus to genus.

To help users of the *RHS Plant Finder* find the plants they want, the classifications used within cultivated genera are listed using codes and plants are marked with the appropriate code in brackets after its name in the Plant Directory. To find the explanation of each code, simply look it up under the genus concerned in the **Classification of Genera** starting on p.50. The codes relating to edible fruits are also listed here, but these apply across several genera.

Collectors' References

Abbreviations (usually with numbers) following a plant name refer to the collector(s) of the plant. These abbreviations are expanded, with a collector's name or expedition title, in the section **Collectors' References** starting on p.45.

A collector's reference may indicate a new, as yet unnamed range of variation within a species. The inclusion of collectors' references in the *RHS Plant Finder* supports the book's role in sourcing unusual plants.

The Convention on Biological Diversity calls for conservation of biodiversity, its sustainable use and the fair and equitable sharing of any derived benefits. Since its adoption in 1993, collectors are required to have prior informed consent from the country of origin for the acquisition and commercialisation of collected material.

Common Names

In a work such as this, it is necessary to refer to plants by their botanical names for the sake of universal comprehension and clarity. However, at the same time we recognise that with fruit and vegetables most people are more familiar with their common names than their botanical ones. Cross-references are therefore given from common to botanical names for fruit, vegetables and the commoner culinary herbs throughout the Plant Directory.

Cultivar

Literally meaning cultivated variety, cultivar names are given to denote variation within species and that generated by hybridisation, in cultivation. To make them easily distinguishable from botanical names, they are not printed in italics and are enclosed in single quotation marks. Cultivar names coined since 1959 should follow the rules of the International Code of Nomenclature for Cultivated Plants (**ICNCP**).

Descriptive Terms

Terms that appear after the main part of the plant name are shown in a smaller font to distinguish them. These descriptive elements give extra information about the plant and may include the **collector's reference**, **authority**, or what colour it is. For example, *Clematis henryi* B&SWJ 3402, *Penstemon* 'Sour Grapes' M. Fish, *Akebia quinata* cream-flowered.

Families

Genera are grouped into larger groups of related plants called families. Most family names, with the exception of eight familiar names, end with the same group of letters, *-aceae*. While it is still acceptable to use these eight exceptions, the modern trend adopted in the *RHS Plant Finder* is to use alternative names with *–aceae* endings. The families concerned are *Compositae* (*Asteraceae*), *Cruciferae* (*Brassicaceae*), *Gramineae* (*Poaceae*), *Guttiferae* (*Clusiaceae*), *Labiatae* (*Lamiaceae*), *Leguminosae* (*Fabaceae*), *Palmae* (*Arecaceae*) and *Umbelliferae* (*Apiaceae*).

Apart from these exceptions we now follow *Mabberley's Plant-book* (4th edition).

Genus (plural – genera)

Genera used in the *RHS Plant Finder* were originally based on Brummitt's *Vascular Plant Families and Genera* but are now based on a range of sources. For spellings and genders of generic names, Greuter's *Names in Current Use for Extant Plant Genera* has also been consulted. See **Botanical Names**.

Grex

Within orchids, hybrids of the same parentage, regardless of how alike they are, are given a grex name. Individuals can be selected, given cultivar names and propagated vegetatively. For example, *Pleione* Versailles gx 'Bucklebury', where Versailles is the grex name and 'Bucklebury' is a selected **cultivar**.

Group

This is a collective name for a group of cultivars within a genus with similar characteristics. The word Group is always included and, where cited with a cultivar name, it is enclosed in brackets, for example, *Actaea simplex* (Atropurpurea Group) 'Brunette', where 'Brunette' is a distinct cultivar in a group of purple-leaved cultivars.

Another example of a Group is *Rhododendron concinnum* Pseudoyanthinum Group. In this case *Rhododendron pseudoyanthinum* was a species that is now "botanically sunk" within *Rhododendron concinnum*, but is still recognised horticulturally as a Group.

Group names are also used for swarms of hybrids with the same parentage, for example, *Rhododendron* Polar Bear Group. These were formerly treated as **grex** names, a term now used only for orchids. A single clone from the Group may be given the same cultivar name, for example, *Rhododendron* 'Polar Bear'.

Extended Glossary

Hardiness

Hardiness ratings are shown for **Award of Garden Merit** plants. To assist gardeners to determine more clearly which plants are hardy in their local area, the RHS introduced a new, enhanced, hardiness rating scheme in 2013, to coincide with the publication of the new **Award of Garden Merit** plant list. The categories now used are as follows: Temperature ranges given are intended to be absolute minimum winter temperatures (°C).

H1a = Heated greenhouse – tropical >15
H1b = Heated greenhouse – subtropical 10 to 15
H1c = Heated greenhouse – warm temperate 5 to 10
H2 = Tender – cool or frost-free greenhouse 1 to 5
H3 = Half-hardy – unheated greenhouse/mild winter –5 to 1
H4 = Hardy – average winter –10 to –5
H5 = Hardy – cold winter –15 to –10
H6 = Hardy – very cold winter –20 to –15
H7 = Very hardy <–20

Further definition of these categories can be found on the RHS website and in the *RHS Plant Finder 2013* essay.

Hybrids

Some species, when grown together, in the wild or in cultivation, are found to interbreed and form hybrids. In some instances a hybrid name is coined, for example hybrids between *Primula hirsuta* and *P. minima* are given the name *Primula* × *forsteri*, the multiplication sign indicating hybrid origin. Hybrid formulae that quote the parentage of the hybrid are used where a unique name has not been coined, for example *Tulbaghia cominsii* × *T. violacea*. In hybrid formulae you will find parents in alphabetical order, with the male (m) and female (f) parent indicated where known. Hybrids between different genera are also possible, for example × *Mahoberberis* is the name given to hybrids between *Mahonia* and *Berberis*.

There are also a few special-case hybrids called graft hybrids, where the tissues of two plants are physically rather than genetically mixed. These are indicated by an addition rather than a multiplication sign, so *Laburnum* + *Cytisus* becomes + *Laburnocytisus*.

ICNCP

The ICNCP is the International Code of Nomenclature for Cultivated Plants. First published in 1959, the 9th edition was published in 2016.

Cultivar names that do not conform to this Code, and for which there is no valid alternative, are flagged I (for invalid). This code states that the minimum requirement is for a cultivar name to be given in conjunction with the name of the genus. However, in the *RHS Plant Finder* we choose to give as full a name as possible to give the gardener and botanist more information about the plant, following the Recommendation in the Code.

Nomenclature and Taxonomy Advisory Group

This Group advises the RHS on individual problems of nomenclature regarding plants in cultivation and, in particular, use of names in the *RHS Horticultural Database*, reflected in the annual publication of the *RHS Plant Finder*.

The aim is always to make the plant names in the *RHS Plant Finder* as consistent, reliable and stable as possible and acceptable to gardeners and botanists alike, not only in the British Isles but around the world. Recent proposals to change or correct names are examined with the aim of creating a balance between the stability of well-known names and botanical and taxonomic correctness. In some cases the conflicting views on the names of some groups of plants will not easily be resolved. The Group's policy is then to wait and review the situation once a more obvious consensus is reached, rather than rush to rename plants only to have to change them again when opinions have shifted.

As we start in 2024, Dr John David is Chairman of the Group, with Dr Dawn Edwards as Secretary. The Group also includes Susyn Andrews, James Armitage, Dr James Compton, Dr Alastair Culham, Rafaël Govaerts, Mark Griffiths, Dr John Grimshaw, Dr Stephen Jury, Dr Tony Lord, Prof David Mabberley, Helen Picton and Chris Sanders, with Björn Aldén, Dr Ross Bayton, Chris Brickell, Dr Janet Cubey, Dr Marco Hoffman, Dr Alan Leslie, Yoko Otsuki, Svengunnar Ryman and Julian Sutton (corresponding members) and Richard Dee, Mike Grant and Julian Shaw (in attendance).

Nomenclature Notes

The **Nomenclature Notes**, p.49, highlight where significant changes have been made to the names we use, since the last edition of the book, by the **Nomenclature and Taxonomy Advisory Group**.

Plant Breeders' Rights

Plants covered by an *active* grant of Plant Breeders' Rights (PBR) are indicated throughout the Plant Directory. Grants indicated are those awarded by the Plant Variety Office in the UK, as well as those from the EU prior to 1 January 2021 (which now have a corresponding Right in the UK). Because grants can both come into force and lapse at any time, this book can only aim to represent the situation at one point in time, but it is hoped that this will act as a useful guide to growers and gardeners. New grants included represent the published position as of the end of January 2024. We do not give any indication where PBR grants may be pending.

To obtain PBR protection, a new plant must be registered and pass tests for distinctness, uniformity and stability under an approved name. This approved name, under the rules of the **ICNCP**, established by a legal process, has to be regarded as the cultivar name. Increasingly however, these approved names are a code or "nonsense" name and are therefore often unpronounceable and meaningless, so the plants are given other names designed to attract sales when they are released. These secondary names are often referred to as selling names but are officially termed **trade designations**. We do our best to link PBR names to their trade descriptions but if you spot any we've missed, do let us know.

On the odd occasion the name for a plant with Plant Breeders' Rights in the UK differs from the name by which it is known outside of the UK and indeed may be different to that given in the relevant International Cultivar Registration Authority (ICRA) register. As the *RHS Plant Finder* has to use the correct name for the plant within the UK, on these occasions this may not be the same name given as the accepted name in the relevant RHS Cultivar Register and Checklist which, being international provides the name that complies with the **ICNCP**.

For further information on UK PBR contact:
**Plant Variety Rights Office,
Animal and Plant Health Agency,
Eastbrook, Shaftesbury Road,
Cambridge CB2 8DR**
Ⓔ pvs.helpdesk@apha.gov.uk
Ⓦ www.gov.uk/plant-breeders-rights

The *RHS Plant Finder* takes no responsibility for ensuring that nurseries selling plants with PBR are licensed to do so.

Selling Names

See **Trade Designations**

Series

With seed-raised plants and some popular vegetatively propagated plants, especially bedding plants and pot plants such as *Petunia* or *Glandularia*, Series have become increasingly popular. A Series contains a number of associated cultivars, differing in one or more characters. It differs from a **Group** in that it is a marketing device. Additionally, individual elements within a Series may be represented by slightly different cultivars over the years.

The word Series is always included and, where cited with a cultivar name it is enclosed in brackets, for example *Aquilegia* 'Robin' (Songbird Series). The Series name usually follows the rest of the plant name, but sometimes in this book we list it before the cultivar name in order to group members of a Series together when they occur next to one another on the page.

Species

See under **Botanical Names**

Subspecies

See under **Botanical Names**

Synonyms

Although the ideal is for each species or cultivar to have only one name, anyone dealing with plants soon comes across a situation where one plant has received two or more names, or two plants have received the same name. In each case, only one name and application, for reasons of precision and stability, can be regarded as correct. Additional names are known as synonyms. Further information on synonyms and why plants change names is available in *Guide to Plant Names*. See the introduction to this glossary for details of how to request a copy.

Trade Designations

A **trade designation** is the name used to market a plant when the cultivar name is considered unsuitable for selling purposes. It is distinguished typographically (see below) from a cultivar name, and is not enclosed in single quotation marks.

In the case of **Plant Breeders' Rights** it is a legal requirement for the cultivar name to appear with the trade designation on a label at the point of sale. Most plants are sold under only one trade designation, but some, especially roses, are sold under a number of names, particularly when cultivars are introduced from other countries. Usually, the correct cultivar name is the only way to ensure that the same plant is not bought unwittingly under two or more different trade designations. The *RHS Plant Finder* follows the recommendations of the **ICNCP** when dealing with trade designations and PBR. These are always to quote the cultivar name and trade designation together and to style the trade designation in small capitals, for example *Choisya* × *dewitteana* GOLDFINGERS ('Limo'PBR). Here GOLDFINGERS is the trade designation and 'Limo' is the cultivar name that has been granted **Plant Breeders' Rights**.

Extended Glossary

Translations

When a cultivar name is translated from the language of first publication, the translation is regarded as a **trade designation** and styled accordingly. We endeavour to recognise the original cultivar name in every case and to give an English translation where it is in general use.

Variegated Plants

Following a suggestion from the Variegated Plant Group of the Hardy Plant Society, a (v) is cited after those plants which are "variegated". The dividing line between variegation and less distinct colour marking is necessarily arbitrary and plants with light veins, pale, silver or dark zones, or leaves flushed in paler colours, are not shown as being variegated unless there is an absolutely sharp distinction between paler and darker zones.

Further details of the Variegated Plant Group can be found at www.hardy-plant.org.uk.

Variety

See under **Botanical Names** and **Cultivar**

Conservation and the Environment

Invasive/non-native Plants
As the *RHS Plant Finder* demonstrates, gardens in Britain have been greatly enriched by the diversity of plants introduced to cultivation from abroad. While the vast majority of those introduced have enhanced our gardens, a few have proved to be highly invasive and to threaten native habitats. Once such plants are established it is very difficult, costly and potentially damaging to native ecosystems to eradicate or control the invasive "alien" species. Gardeners can help by choosing not to buy or distribute non-native invasive plants and by taking steps to prevent them escaping into the wild and by disposing of them in a responsible way.

Invasive non-native species are controlled by two pieces of legislation in the UK. The EU Invasive Alien Species Regulation has been translated into UK Law and is backed up by the Alien Invasive Species (Enforcement and Permitting) Order which came into force in 2019, sets out the financial penalties and other enforcement measures for breaches of the Regulation. Species of Special Concern are banned from sale under the regulation. These are listed below and are included in the *RHS Plant Finder* as a "Prohibited invasive" and no suppliers are given.

Acacia saligna – Golden wreath wattle
Ailanthus altissima – Tree of heaven
Alternanthera philoxeroides – Alligator weed
Andropogon virginicus – Broomsedge
Asclepias syriaca – Milkweed
Baccharis halmifolia – Tree groundsel
Cabomba caroliniana – Carolina fanwort
Cardiospermum grandiflorum – Balloon vine
Cortaderia jubata – Purple pampas grass
Ehrharta calycina – Purple veldgrass
Eichhornia crassipes – Water hyacinth
Elodea nuttallii – Nuttall's water weed
Gunnera tinctoria – Chilean rhubarb
Gymnocoronis spilanthoides – Senegal tea
Heracleum mantegazzianum – Giant hogweed
Heracleum persicum – Giant hogweed (Tromso palm)
Heracleum sosnowskyi – Giant hogweed
Humulus scandens – Japanese hop
Hydrocotyle ranunculoides – Floating pennywort
Impatiens glandulifera – Himalayan balsam
Lagarosiphon major – Curly waterweed
Lespedeza cuneata – Chinese shrub clover
Ludwigia grandiflora – Water primrose
Ludwigia peploides – Water primrose
Lygodium japonicum – Climbing fern
Lysichiton americanus – American skunk cabbage
Microstegium vimineum – Japanese stiltgrass
Myriophyllum aquaticum – Parrot's feather
Myriophyllum heterophyllum – Broadleaf watermilfoil
Parthenium hysterophorus – Parthenium weed
Pennisetum setaceum – Crimson fountain grass
Persicaria perfoliata – Asiatic tearthumb
Prosopis juliflora – mesquite
Pueraria montana var. *lobata* – Kudzu
Salvinia molesta – Giant salvinia
Triadica sebifera – Chinese tallow tree

Following the UK's departure from the EU, any further changes to the EU Regulation will not apply in England, Wales and Scotland, but they will in Northern Ireland.

A further four species have been added to the list of species of Union Concern in 2022:
Celastrus orbiculatus – Staff vine
Hakea sericea – Silky hakea
Koenigia polystachya – Himalayan knotweed
Pistia stratiotes – Water lettuce

Celastrus orbiculatus and *Pistia stratiotes* are subject to a transition period and the ban comes into effect in the EU and Northern Ireland in August 2024 and August 2027 respectively.

Gardeners in possession of any of the listed species may dispose of the plants through composting, burning or in local authority green waste recycling as provided for in the Environment Agency's Regulatory Position Statement 178: https://www.gov.uk/government/publications/treatment-and-disposal-of-invasive-non-native-plants-rps-178/treatment-and-disposal-of-invasive-non-native-plants-rps-178

The second piece of legislation is the Wildlife and Countryside Act (1981). This legislation lists the species for which it is an offence to plant or cause to grow in the wild (Schedule 9). An amendment to the Act in 2014 brought in a ban of sale for the most serious aquatic invasive plants (indicated by a *). Those not covered by the EU Regulation are listed below. In addition we have decided to add Japanese knotweed (on Schedule 9) as it is such a serious invasive species.

**Azolla filiculoides* – fairy fern
*Crassula helmsii – New Zealand pygmy weed
Reynoutria japonica – Japanese knotweed

In Scotland the Wildlife and Natural Environment Act (2011) makes it an offence to release any non-native plant into the wild without a permit.

All plants on Schedule 9 are considered as invasive, but some are not currently banned from sale. However, it is still an offence to plant or cause these to grow in the wild in all or part of the UK and the Republic of Ireland, and we strongly recommended that alternatives are chosen. These are marked with a

? in the left hand margin in the main directory.
Ⓦ www.nonnativespecies.org/non-native-species
Large-leaved gunneras
Research recently published by the RHS indicates that plants widely grown in the UK as *Gunnera manicata* are the hybrid of *G. manicata* with *G. tinctoria* (*G.* × *cryptica*), or *G. tinctoria*. Under the IAS Regulation, a species is defined as including any hybrid of that species. As a consequence, the hybrid gunnera is also considered to be a Species of Special Concern subject to the same restrictions as *G. tinctoria* and is indicated as such in this Directory. While *Gunnera manicata* is not subject to these restrictions, due to the lack of certainty over the identification of plants in cultivation as this species, it is not recommended to use these plants in exhibits, or offer them for sale, at shows.

Species control provisions
The UK Government introduced new provisions in the Infrastructure Act (2015) to control invasive non-native species in England and Wales. There are two levels of control: a species control agreement and a species control order. In the former the owner of land where an invasive non-native species is present, when approached by the relevant environmental authority, agrees to take action to limit or remove the species. If the landowner fails to do so, or does not agree, or where it is not known who the landowner is, then the environment authority can take action to enforce the control of the species. This may involve entry of the property by the authority to carry out the control if the owner fails to comply. In the case of an emergency then a species control order may be issued without going through the previous steps.

Importing Plants
Travelling can be a great source of inspiration for gardeners and often provides an opportunity to encounter new and interesting plants. Anyone wishing to bring plants – a term which includes any living part of a plant (seeds, cuttings, seedlings, bulbs, flowers, etc) into Britain from abroad must realise, however, that this comes with a risk of introducing a plant pest or disease. In January 2021 the regulations for plants being brought into Britain changed for both amateur gardeners and commercial nurseries. Both rules and processes in the UK continue to change so those planning to import live plant material are advised to check well in advance of the event.

If collecting plants, including seed, from the wild in an EU member state (including Switzerland or Liechtenstein) or any other country you are required, by law, to obtain a phytosanitary certificate before bringing the plants into Britain. The phytosanitary certificate can only be issued by the National Plant Protection Organisation (NPPO) in the country where the plants are being collected. Material, including seeds, of some plant species pose such a high risk to plant health that they are prohibited. Before travelling to collect wild plants you must notify the Animal and Plant Health Agency (APHA) of your intentions via planthealth.info@apha.gov.uk. In addition it is advised that you contact the NPPO in the country of travel to check if permits to collect wild plants and seeds and export them are required. The following webpage can be used to contact the NPPO in the country you are travelling to: www.ippc.int/en/countries/nppos/list-countries/. Please ensure that you contact the APHA or the relevant NPPO well in advance of travel.

If bringing cultivated plants into Britain from an EU member state (including Switzerland or Liechtenstein) or any other country similar rules apply. You will need to obtain a phytosanitary certificate from the NPPO before bringing the plants into Britain, and will need to notify the APHA of your intentions before travel. It is important to note that EU plant passports are no longer valid in Britain. If bringing cultivated plants from a country other than the UK or EU member state you must check with the APHA, before travel, if additional import documents are required.

Depending on the risk category, material may be subject to documentary, physical and identity checks on entry to the UK. There are costs associated with these checks. Bringing plants into Britain without the required documentation is an illegal activity, and will result in plants being confiscated as a minimum penalty.

Plant Health Regulations. Since 2019 the UK and EU member states have been tightening regulations concerning the movement and trade of many plant species. These regulations aim to prevent the introduction and spread of plant pests and diseases which, if established, could have an unacceptable economic and environmental impact.

On March 4th 2021 the UK government introduced strict import regulations for plant species identified as posing a 'high-risk' of introducing the bacterium *Xylella*. This bacterium, not yet present in the UK, causes severe disease and has the potential to infect and kill over 690 plant species. *Xylella* is considered to be the most concerning disease threat to UK horticulture, please visit the RHS *Xylella* information webpage for guidance on 'high-risk' plant species.
Ⓦ www.rhs.org.uk/disease/xylella-fastidiosa

Additionally, other plant species which pose a risk of introducing pests and diseases of concern into Britain are subject to import regulations and movement restrictions. In January 2021 the UK government introduced changes to legislation concerning plant imports from EU member states. The extent of legislation is significant and primarily only relevant to commercial nurseries and professional operators. Understanding phytosanitary certificates and other import documentation is only relevant to amateur gardeners if bringing plants into Britain from abroad, see first section of Importing Plants.

The UK government regularly reviews the regulatory status of plant pests and diseases present and not yet present. This ensures that legislation keeps pace with potential new introductions and changing situations, i.e. increase in spread of a pest. The Department for Environment, Food and Rural Affairs (Defra) provides an online portal where comprehensive information on regulated plant pests and diseases can be found: planthealthportal.defra.gov.uk. The portal allows you to search by plant name for information on regulated pests or diseases a plant may be at risk from. There are also links to current legislation and guidance on how to report a suspected regulated pest or disease.

The Convention on International Trade in Endangered Species (CITES) affects the transport of animal and plant material across international boundaries. Its aim is to prevent exploitative trade and thereby to prevent harm and the ultimate extinction of wild populations. A tighter regime on trade in species of wild fauna and flora exists in the EU that requires export permits for any plants listed in Appendices A, B & C and import permits for Appendices A & B. There is a further Appendix D for non-CITES listed species that the EU considers to be endangered and potentially at risk from trade. A broad range of plants is covered in these Appendices, including aloes, succulent euphorbias, carnivorous plants, cycads, *Cactaceae* and *Orchidaceae*. Although species are mentioned in the convention title, the restrictions cover all cultivars and hybrids of listed species too, except for specific exclusions, where there are annotations in the Appendices.

With the completion of the UK's withdrawal from the European Union, CITES permits are now required to import and export listed species to countries in the EU and Northern Ireland, which was not previously the case. EU CITES regulation was translated into UK law, and therefore the requirements of that legislation continue to apply in the UK.

Ⓦ www.gov.uk/cites-imports-and-exports#cites-species

The Convention on Biological Diversity (CBD) or the "Rio Convention") recognises the property rights of individual countries in relation to their own biodiversity. It exists to enable access to that biodiversity, but equally to ensure the sharing of any benefit derived from it. In principle it is possible to collect plant material from other countries that have asserted their rights under the CBD, by ensuring that you have obtained documentary evidence of prior informed consent on the basis of mutually agreed terms for any uses that the material will be put to in the future. In practice the legal requirements for collecting plant material vary from country to country and it is advisable to contact the National Focal Point for further information.

Ⓦ www.cbd.int

The **Nagoya Protocol**, is a supplementary agreement of the CBD which entered into force in 2015, and provides a framework for Access and Benefit Sharing. In the UK this is implemented by the retained European Union Regulation, as amended by Statutory Instrument in 2018. From 12 October 2014 anyone utilising genetic resources collected after that date from another country which is a signatory of the Nagoya Protocol, collected after 12 October 2014, is required to carry out due diligence to ensure that the material was collected in accordance with national laws, the Protocol and the CBD. While the most likely examples of utilisation are the development of new products or medicines from plants, breeding programmes to raise new plants for horticulture would also be covered. Although the burden to prove legitimate use of the genetic resource lies with the person or organisation utilising the genetic resource, anyone providing the source of the genetic resource (such as wild collected plants) will need to be able to provide the relevant paperwork, such as a Material Transfer Agreement and Prior Informed Consent.

Ⓦ http://www.cbd.int/abs/about/

In March 2015 the UK Government put in place the scheme of penalties for failure to comply with the EU Regulation which includes a range of both civil and criminal penalties, with the ultimate sanction of a two-year prison sentence. The Office of Product Safety and Standards is reponsible for monitoring compliance and enforcing the legislation in the UK.

Ⓦ https://www.gov.uk/guidance/abs

Contact addresses
Plant Health
Animal and Plant Health Agency
The National Agri-food Innovation Campus
Sand Hutton
York
YO41 1LZ
Ⓣ 01904 405 138
Ⓔ planthealth.info@apha.gov.uk

CITES
Animal & Plant Health Agency (APHA)
Centre for International Trade – Bristol
2 The Square
Temple Quay
Bristol
BS1 6EB
Ⓣ 0117 372 8774
Ⓔ wildlife.licensing@apha.gov.uk
Ⓦ www.gov.uk/plant-health-controls

SUPPLEMENTARY KEYS TO THE DIRECTORY

Collectors' References

Abbreviations following a plant name, refer to the collector(s) of the plant. These abbreviations are expanded below, with a collector's name or expedition title. For a fuller explanation, see p.38.

A&JW	Watson, A. & J.
A&L	Ala, A. & Lancaster, Roy
AB&S	Archibald, James; Blanchard, John W. & Salmon, M.
AC	Clark, Alan J.
AC&H	Apold, J.; Cox, Peter & Hutchison, Peter
AC&W	Albury; Cheese, M. & Watson, J.M.
ACE	AGS Expedition to China (1994)
ACL	Leslie, Alan C.
AER	Robinson, Allan
AGS/ES	AGS Expedition to Sikkim (1983)
AGSJ	AGS Expedition to Japan (1988)
AH	Hoog, A.
AIM	Avent, Tony Mexico (1994)
Airth	Airth, Murray
Akagi	Akagi Botanical Garden
AL&JS	Sharman, Joseph L. & Leslie, Alan C.
APA	Cox, K.; Hootman, S.; Hudson, T.; et al, Expedition to Arunchal Pradesh (2005)
ARG	Argent, G.C.G.
ARGS	Alaska Rock Garden Society trip to China
ARJA	Ruksans, J. & Siesums, A.
B	Blanchard, John
B&F MA	Brown, Robert & Fisher, Rif & Middle Atlas (2007)
B L.	Beer, Len
B&L	Brickell, Christopher D. & Leslie, Alan C.
B&M & BM	Brickell, Christopher D. & Mathew, Brian
B&S	Bird P. & Salmon M.
B&SWJ	Wynn-Jones, Bleddyn & Susan
B&V	Burras, K. & Vosa, C.G.
BB	Bartholomew, B.
BBJMT	Boland, Brownless, Jamieson & McNamara
BC	Chudziak, W.
BC&W	Beckett; Cheese, M. & Watson, J.M.
Beavis	Beavis, Derek S.
Berry	Berry, P.
Berry & Brako	Berry, P. & Brako, Lois
BKBlount	Blount, B.K.
BKN	Bis, J., Kupčák, P. & Novak, H.
BL&M	University of Bangor Expedition to NE Nepal
BM	Mathew, Brian F.
BM&W	Binns, David L.; Mason, M. & Wright, A.
BO	Olsen, Bjornar
BOA	Boardman, P.
Breedlove	Breedlove, D.
BR	Rushbrooke, Ben
BS	Smith, Basil
BSBE	Bowles Scholarship Botanical Expedition (1963)
BSSS	Crûg Expedition, Jordan (1991)
Bu	Bubert, S.
Burtt	Burtt, Brian L.
BWJ	Wynn-Jones, Bleddyn
C	Cole, Desmond T.
C&C	Cox, P.A. & Cox, K.N.E.
C&Cu	Cox, K.N.E. & Cubey, J.
C&H	Cox, Peter & Hutchison, Peter
C&K	Chamberlain & Knott
C&R	Christian & Roderick
C&S	Clark, Alan & Sinclair, Ian W.J.
C&V	K.N.E. Cox & Vergera, S.
C&W	Cheese, M. & Watson, J.M.
CC	Chadwell, Christopher
CC&H	Chamberlain, David F.; Cox, Peter & Hutchison, P.
CC&McK	Chadwell, Christopher & McKelvie, A.
CC&MR	Chadwell, Christopher & Ramsay
CCH&H	Chamberlain, D.F.; Cox, P.; Hutchison, P. & Hootman, S.
CD&R	Compton, J.; D'Arcy, J. & Rix, E.M.
CDB	Brickell, Christopher D.
CDC	Coode, Mark J.E.; Dockrill, Alexander
CDC&C	Compton; D'Arcy; Christopher & Coke
CDPR	Compton; D'Arcy; Pope & Rix
CE&H	Christian, P.J.; Elliott & Hoog
CEE	Chengdu Edinburgh Expedition China (1991)

CGG	Glendoick Gardens Expedition to Guizou (2009)	Farrer	Farrer, Reginald
CGV	Vosa, Canio	FK	Kinmonth, Fergus W.
CGW	Grey-Wilson, Christopher	FMB	Bailey, F.M.
CH	Christian, P. & Hoog, A.	FMWJ	A. Floden, T. Mitchell & B. Wynn-Jones, Vietnam 2011
CH&M	Cox, P.; Hutchison, P. & Maxwell-MacDonald, D.	FO	Otiery, Felix
CHB	Boulanger, Charles	FSYNI	Furse, Paul. & Synge, Patrick. 1700m in the Elburz Mountains, Iran October 1977
CHP&W	Kashmir Botanical Expedition	G	Gardner, Martin F.
CL	Lovell, Chris	GEY125	Nielsen, Jens. Seed from China
CLD	Chungtien, Lijiang & Dali Exped. China (1990)	G&K	Gardner, Martin F. & Knees, Sabina G.
		G&P	Gardner, Martin F. & Page, Christopher N.
CM&W	Cheese M.; Mitchel J. & Watson, J.	GDJ	Dumont, Gerard
CN&W	Clark; Neilson & Wilson	GG	Gusman, G.
CNDS	Nelson, C. & Sayers D.	GS	Sherriff, George
COLA	Costin, J.J. & Lancaster, R., Japan (1990)	Green	Green, D.
Cooper	Cooper, R.E.	Guitt	Guittoneau, G.G.
Cox	Cox, Peter A.	Guiz	Guizhou Expedition (1985)
CPC	Cobblewood Plant Collection	GWJ	Goddard, Sally; Wynne-Jones, Bleddyn & Susan
CPN	Compton, James		
CS	Stapleton, Christopher	G-W&P	Grey-Wilson, Christopher & Phillips
CSE	Cyclamen Society Expedition (1990)	H	Huggins, Paul
CT	Teune, Carla	H&B	Hilliard, Olive M. & Burtt, Brian L.
CW&T	Clark, A., Wilson, H. & Taggart, J., North Vietnam	H&D	Howick, C. & Darby
		H&M	Howick, Charles & McNamara, William A.
CWJ	Colley, Finlay; Wynn-Jones, Bleddyn, Taiwan (2007)	H&W	Hedge, Ian C. & Wendelbo, Per W.
Dahl	Dahl, Sally	Harry Smith	Smith, K.A.Harry
DBG	Denver Botanic Garden, Colorado	Hartside	Hartside Nursery
DC	Cheshire, David	HCM	Heronswood Expedition to Chile (1998)
DF	Fox, D.	HECC	Hutchison; Evans; Cox, P.; Cox, K.
DG	Green, D.	HEHEHE	Zetterlund, H. et al, Gothenburg Botanic Gardens Expedition to northern China
DHTU	Hinkley, D., Turkey (2000)		
DJF	Ferguson, Dave	Hird	Hird
DJH	Hinkley, Dan	HH&K	Hannay, S & S & Kingsbury, N.
DJHC	Hinkley D., China	HK	Kuenzler, Horst
DJHS	Hinkley, D., Sichuan	HLMS	Springate, L.S.
DJHT	Hinkley, Dan in Taipingshan, Taiwan	HM&S	Halliwell, B.; Mason, D. & Smallcombe
DJHV	Hinkley, D., Vietnam	HOA	Hoog, Anton
DM	Millais, David	HOLUB	Holubec, V.
Doleshy	Doleshy, F.L.	HRS	Hers, J.
DS&T	Drake, Sharman J. & Thompson	Hummel	Hummel, D.
DWD	Rose, D.	HW&E	Wendelbo, Per; Hedge, I. & Ekberg, L.
DZ	Zummell, D.	HWEL	Hirst, J.Michael; Webster, D.
ECN	Nelson, E. Charles	HWJ	Crûg Heronswood Joint Expedition
EDHCH	Hammond, Eric D.	HWJCM	Crûg Heronswood Expedition
EGM	Millais, T.	HWJK	Crûg Heronswood Expedition, East Nepal (2002)
EKB	Balls, Edward K.		
EM	East Malling Research Station	HZ	Zetterlund, Henrik
EMAK	Edinburgh Makalu Expedition (1991)	ICE	Instituto de Investigaciónes Ecológicas Chiloé & RBGE
EMR	Rix, E.Martyn		
EN	Needham, Edward F.	IDS	International Dendrological Society
ENF	Fuller, E. Nigel	ISI	Int. Succulent Introductions
ETE	Edinburgh Taiwan Expedition (1993)	J&JA	Archibald, James & Jennifer
ETOT	Kirkham, T.S.; Flanagan, Mark	J. Jurasek	Jurasek, J.
F	Forrest, G.	JCA	Archibald, James
F&M	Fernandez & Mendoza, Mexico	JE	Jack Elliott
F&W	Watson, J. & Flores, A.	JJ	Jackson, J.

JJ&JH	Halda, J. & Halda, J.
JJH	Halda, Joseph J.
JL	Lode, Joel
JLS	Sharman, J.L.
JMH	Hoog, J. & M.
JM-MK	Mahr, J.; Kammerlander, M.
JMT	Mann Taylor, J.
JN	Nielson, Jens
JR	Russell, J.
JRM	Marr, John
JW	Watson, J.M.
K	Kirkpatrick, George
K&LG	Gillanders, Kenneth & Gillanders, L.
K&Mc	Kirkpatrick, George & McBeath, Ronald J.D.
K&P	Josef Kopec & Milan Prasil
K&T	Kurashige, Y. & Tsukie, S.
KC	Cox, Kenneth
KEKE	Kew/Edinburgh Kanchenjunga Expedition (1989)
KGB	Kunming/Gothenburg Botanical Expedition (1993)
KM	Marsh, K.
KMR	Kupčák, M.
KR	Rushforth, K.D.
KRW	Wooster, K.R. (distributed after his death by Kath Dryden)
KW	Kingdon-Ward, F.
KWJ	Crûg-World of Ferns Joint Expedition, Vietnam (2007)
L	Lancaster, C. Roy
L&S	Ludlow, Francis & Sherriff, George
LA	Long Ashton Research Station clonal selection scheme
LB	Bercht, L. (*Cactaceae*)
LB	Bird P.; Salmon, M.
LEG	Lesotho Edinburgh/Gothenburg Expedition (1997)
Lismore	Lismore Nursery, Breeder's Number
LM&S	Leslie, Mattern & Sharman
LP	Palmer, W.J.L.
LS&E	Ludlow, Frank; Sherriff, George & Elliott, E. E.
LS&H	Ludlow, Frank; Sherriff, George & Hicks, J. H.
LS&T	Ludlow, Frank; Sherriff, George & Taylor, George
LZ	Lutz, Eberhard
M&H	Rickard, Martin & Hayward, Richard
M&PS	Mike & Polly Stone
M&T	Mathew & Tomlinson
Mac&W	McPhail & Watson
McB	McBeath, R.J.D.
McLaren	McLaren, H.D.
MCW	Michael Wickenden
MDM	Myers, Michael D.
MECC	Scottish Rock Garden Club, Nepal (1997)
MESE	Alpine Garden Society Expedition, Greece (1999)
MF	Foster, Maurice
MH	Heasman, Matthew T.
MK	Kammerlander, Michael
MP	Pavelka, Mojmir
MPF	Frankis, M.P.
MS	Salmon, M.
MS&CL	Salmon, M. & Lovell, C.
MSF	Fillan, M.S.
MUG	Uhlig, M.
NAPE	Expedition to Naglaland and Arunachal Pradesh (2003)
NICE	North India Expedition (1997)
NJM	Macer, N.J.
NMWJ	Taiwan National Museum of Natural Science; Wynn-Jones, B. & S. (2015)
NN	Nielsen & Nielsen (2009)
NNS	Ratko, Ron
NS	Turland, Nick
NVD	Expedition to Vietnam
NVFDE	Northern Vietnam First Darwin Expedition
Og	Ogisu, Mikinori
ORO	Oron, Peri
OS	Sonderhousen, O.
P. Bon	Bonavia, P.
P&C	Paterson, David S. & Clarke, Sidney
P&W	Polastri & Watson, J. M.
PAB	Barney, P.A.
PB	Bird, Peter
PBR	Bruggeman, Pascal
PC&H	Pattison, G.; Catt, P. & Hickson, M.
PD	Davis, Peter H.
PDM	Purdom, William
PF	Furse, Paul
PG	Pichler, G.
PJC	Christian, Paul J.
PJC&AH	P.J. Christian & A. Hogg
PNMK	Nicholls, P.; Kammerlander, M.
Polunin	Polunin, Oleg
Pras	Prasil, M.
PS&W	Polunin, Oleg; Sykes, William & Williams, John
PW	Wharton, Peter
R	Rock, J.F.C.
RB	Brown, R.
RBS	Brown, Ray, Sakharin Island
RCB AM	Brown, Robert, Expedition to Armenia
RCB/Arg	Brown, Robert, Argentina, (2002)
RCB E	Brown, Robert, Expedition to Spain (Andalucia)
RCB/Eq	Brown, Robert, Ecuador, (1988)
RCB RA	Brown, Robert
RCB RL	Brown, Robert, Expedition to Lebanon
RCB/TQ	Brown, Robert, Turkey (2001)
RE	Evans, Ron
RH	Hancock, R.
RJN	Neilsen, R.

RKMP	Ruksans, J.; Krumins, A.; Kitts, M.; Paivel, A.	SS&W	Stainton, J.D. Adam; Sykes, William & Williams, John
RM	Ruksans, J. & Kitts, M.	SSNY	Sino-Scottish Expedition to NW Yunnan (1992)
RMRP	Rocky Mountain Rare Plants, Denver, Colorado	SSSE	Sino-Scottish Sichuan Expedition 2002
RS	Suckow, Reinhart	T	Taylor, Nigel P.
RSC	Richard Somer Cocks	T&K	Taylor, Nigel P. & Knees, Sabina
RV	Richard Valder	TCM	Mitchell, Thomas Carly
RWJ	Crûg Farm-Rickards Ferns Expedition to Taiwan (2003)	TG	Thomas, H-P. & Gilmer, K.
		TH	Hudson, T.
S&B	Blanchard, J.W. & Salmon, M.	TJR	Roberts, Tim
S&F	Salmon, M. & Fillan, M.	TS&BC	Smythe, T. & Cherry, B.
S&L	Sinclair, Ian W.J. & Long, David G.	TSS	Spring Smyth, T.L.M.
S&SH	Sheilah & Spencer Hannay	TW	Weston, Tony
Sandham	Sandham, John	USDAPI	US Department of Agriculture Plant Index Number
SB	Brack, Steven		
SB&L	Salmon, Bird & Lovell	USDAPQ	US Dept. of Agriculture Plant Quarantine Number
SBEC	Sino-British Expedition to Cangshan		
SBEL	Sino-British Lijiang Expedition	USNA	United States National Arboretum
SBQE	Sino-British Expedition to Quinghai	VdL	Van de Laar, Harry
Sch	Schilling, Anthony D.	VHH	Vernon H. Heywood
SD	Sashal Dayal	VV	Victor, David
SDR	Rankin, Stella & David	W	Wilson, Ernest H.
SEH	Hootman, Steve	W&B	Watkins, D. & Brown, R., Bulgaria (2012)
SEP	Swedish Expedition to Pakistan		
SF	Forde, P.	W&O	Wu, August & Olsen, Bjornar
SG	Salmon, M. & Guy, P.	WJC	Wynn-Jones, B. & S. & Colley, F.
SH	Hannay, Spencer	WM	McLewin, William
Sich	Simmons, Erskine, Howick & Mcnamara	Woods	Woods, Patrick J.B.
SJ	Johansson, Stellan	Wr	Wraight, David & Anke
SLIZE	Swedish-Latvian-Iranian Zagros Expedition to Iran (May 1988)	WWJ	Wharton, Peter & Wynn-Jones, Bleddyn, Vietnam 2006–7
SOJA	Kew/Quarryhill Expedition to Southern Japan	Yu	Yu, Tse-tsun
		ZE&S	Zetterlund, H., Eriksson, A-I. & Strid, A.

Nomenclature Notes

Since the publication of the 2023 edition of the *RHS Plant Finder* the following changes have been made to the names used. These changes are based upon the decision of the RHS Nomenclature and Taxonomy Advisory Group (NATAG). If you have any suggestions for other plant name changes with the *RHS Plant Finder*, then please write, stating your reason in full to:

The Secretary,
Dr Dawn Edwards
Nomenclature and Taxonomy Advisory Group
Royal Horticultural Society
RHS Garden Wisley
Woking
Surrey
GU23 6QB

- *Acer* 'Red Flamingo' corrected to *Acer* 'Esk Flamingo'
- *Campsis* × *tagliabuana* corrected to *Campsis* × *tagliabueana*
- Some species of *Caryopteris* moved to other genera: you will find *Tripora* in this edition
- *Chenopodium* updated. In this edition you will see species transferred to *Blitum* and *Dysphania*
- *Dendroseris* transferred to *Sonchus*
- *Dypsis* updated with some species transferred to other genera. The species listed in this edition have moved to *Chrysalidocarpus*
- *Euphorbia* expanded to include *Monadenium*, *Pedilanthus* and *Synadenium*
- *Greenovia* now included in *Aeonium*
- *Halimium* (and × *Halimiocistus*) transferred to *Cistus*
- *Homalocladium* now incorporated within *Muehlenbeckia*
- *Hylotelephium* Herbstfreude Group changed to *Hylotelephium* × *mottramianum*
- *Leptosiphon* segregated from *Linanthus*
- *Micranthes* segregated from *Saxifraga*
- *Nomocharis* moved into *Lilium*
- Some species of *Papaver* transferred to *Oreomecon* and *Roemeria*, and *Stylomecon* moved into *Papaver*
- Some species of *Scorzonera* transferred to other genera. In this edition you will see *Pseudopodospermum*
- *Selinum wallichianum* transferred to *Ligusticopsis wallichianum*
- *Tibouchina* updated, with horticulturally familiar species transferred to *Pleroma* and *Chaetogastra*
- *Zigadenus* reduced to a single species (*Z. glaberrimus*); other species moved to *Anticlea*, *Stenanthium* and *Toxicoscordion*

This is not intended to be an exhaustive list of the changes made to the RHS Horticultural Database, reflected in the *RHS Plant Finder*; many more changes are made during the year by the RHS botanical team. This list just highlights some of the NATAG changes.

You'll find some of these have had explanatory articles, or will have been mentioned in the *Classification Corner* of *The Plant Review* (previously *The Plantsman*). Watch out for articles in the coming year on future changes.

Classification of Genera

Genera including a large number of species, or with many cultivars, are often subdivided into informal horticultural classifications, or formal cultivar groups in the case of *Clematis* and *Tulipa*. The breeding of new cultivars is sometimes limited to hybrids between closely related species, thus for *Saxifraga* and *Primula*, the cultivars are allocated to the sections given in the infrageneric treatments cited. Please turn to p.37 for a fuller explanation.

ACER PALMATUM

(A)	Amoenum Group
(D)	Dissectum Group
(Dw)	Dwarf Group
(L)	Linearilobum Group
(M)	Matsumurae Group
(P)	Palmatum Group

ACTINIDIA

(s-p)	Self-pollinating

BEGONIA

(C)	Cane-like
(R)	Rex Cultorum
(S)	Semperflorens Cultorum
(T)	× *tuberhybrida* (Tuberous)

BRUGMANSIA

(Breeding History Sets, from the International *Brugmansia* Register, for hybrid combinations with no corresponding hybrid binomial)

(AI)	Aurinsi (*B. aurea* & *B. insignis*)
(AVS)	Arbovulsa (*B. arborea*, *B. vulcanicola* & *B. sanguinea*)
(SA)	Saurea (*B. suaveolens* & *B. aurea*)
(SI)	Suavinsi (*B. suaveolens* & *B. insignis*)
(SIA)	Suavinsaurea (*B. suaveolens*, *B. insignis* & *B. aurea*)
(SIVA)	Siva (*B. suaveolens*, *B. insignis*, *B. versicolor* & *B. aurea*)
(SV)	Suaver (*B. suaveolens* & *B. versicolor*)
(SVI)	Suaverinsi (*B. suaveolens*, *B. versicolor* & *B. insignis*)
(VA)	Vularbo (*B. vulcanicola* & *B. arborea*)
(VI)	Verinsi (*B. versicolor* & *B. insignis*)
(VIA)	Verinsaurea (*B. versicolor*, *B. insignis* & *B. aurea*)
(VS)	Vulsa (*B. vulcanicola* & *B. sanguinea*)

CHRYSANTHEMUM

(By the National Chrysanthemum Society)

(1)	Indoor Large (Exhibition)
(2)	Indoor Medium (Exhibition)
(3a)	Indoor Incurved: Large-flowered
(3b)	Indoor Incurved: Medium-flowered
(3c)	Indoor Incurved: Small-flowered
(4a)	Indoor Reflexed: Large-flowered
(4b)	Indoor Reflexed: Medium-flowered
(4c)	Indoor Reflexed: Small-flowered
(5a)	Indoor Intermediate: Large-flowered
(5b)	Indoor Intermediate: Medium-flowered
(5c)	Indoor Intermediate: Small-flowered
(6a)	Indoor Anemone: Large-flowered
(6b)	Indoor Anemone: Medium-flowered
(6c)	Indoor Anemone: Small-flowered
(7a)	Indoor Single: Large-flowered
(7b)	Indoor Single: Medium-flowered
(7c)	Indoor Single: Small-flowered
(8a)	Indoor True Pompon
(8b)	Indoor Semi-pompon
(9a)	Indoor Spray: Anemone
(9b)	Indoor Spray: Pompon
(9c)	Indoor Spray: Reflexed
(9d)	Indoor Spray: Single
(9e)	Indoor Spray: Intermediate
(9f)	Indoor Spray: Spider, Quill, Spoon or Any Other Type
(10a)	Indoor, Spider
(10b)	Indoor, Quill
(10c)	Indoor, Spoon
(11)	Any Other Indoor Type
(12a)	Indoor, Charm
(12b)	Indoor, Cascade
(13a)	October-flowering Incurved: Large-flowered
(13b)	October-flowering Incurved: Medium-flowered
(13c)	October-flowering Incurved: Small-flowered
(14a)	October-flowering Reflexed: Large-flowered
(14b)	October-flowering Reflexed: Medium-flowered
(14c)	October-flowering Reflexed: Small-flowered
(15a)	October-flowering Intermediate: Large-flowered
(15b)	October-flowering Intermediate: Medium-flowered
(15c)	October-flowered Intermediate: Small-flowered
(16)	October-flowering Large
(17a)	October-flowering Single: Large-flowered
(17b)	October-flowering Single: Medium-flowered
(17c)	October-flowering Single: Small-flowered
(18a)	October-flowering Pompon: True Pompon
(18b)	October-flowering Pompon: Semi-pompon

(19a)	October-flowering Spray: Anemone
(19b)	October-flowering Spray: Pompon
(19c)	October-flowering Spray: Reflexed
(19d)	October-flowering Spray: Single
(19e)	October-flowering Spray: Intermediate
(19f)	October-flowering Spray: Spider, Quill, Spoon or Any Other Type
(20)	Any Other October-flowering Type
(21a)	Korean: Anemone
(21b)	Korean: Pompon
(21c)	Korean: Reflexed
(21d)	Korean: Single
(21e)	Korean: Intermediate
(21f)	Korean: Spider, Quill, Spoon, or any other type
(22a)	Charm: Anemone
(22b)	Charm: Pompon
(22c)	Charm: Reflexed
(22d)	Charm: Single
(22e)	Charm: Intermediate
(22f)	Charm: Spider, Quill, Spoon or Any Other Type
(23a)	Early-flowering Outdoor Incurved: Large-flowered
(23b)	Early-flowering Outdoor Incurved: Medium-flowered
(23c)	Early-flowering Outdoor Incurved: Small-flowered
(24a)	Early-flowering Outdoor Reflexed: Large-flowered
(24b)	Early-flowering Outdoor Reflexed: Medium-flowered
(24c)	Early-flowering Outdoor Reflexed: Small-flowered
(25a)	Early-flowering Outdoor Intermediate: Large-flowered
(25b)	Early-flowering Outdoor Intermediate: Medium-flowered
(25c)	Early-flowering Outdoor Intermediate: Small-flowered
(26a)	Early-flowering Outdoor Anemone: Large-flowered
(26b)	Early-flowering Outdoor Anemone: Medium-flowered
(27a)	Early-flowering Outdoor Single: Large-flowered
(27b)	Early-flowering Outdoor Single: Medium-flowered
(28a)	Early-flowering Outdoor Pompon: True Pompon
(28b)	Early-flowering Outdoor Pompon: Semi-pompon
(29a)	Early-flowering Outdoor Spray: Anemone
(29b)	Early-flowering Outdoor Spray: Pompon
(29c)	Early-flowering Outdoor Spray: Reflexed
(29d)	Early-flowering Outdoor Spray: Single
(29e)	Early-flowering Outdoor Spray: Intermediate
(29f)	Early-flowering Outdoor Spray: Spider, Quill, Spoon or Any Other Type
(29Rub)	Early-flowering Outdoor Spray: Rubellum
(30)	Any Other Early-flowering Outdoor Type

CLEMATIS

(Cultivar Groups as per Matthews, V. (2002) *The International Clematis Register & Checklist 2002*, RHS, London.)

(A)	Atragene Group
(Ar)	Armandii Group
(C)	Cirrhosa Group
(EL)	Early Large-flowered Group
(F)	Flammula Group
(Fo)	Forsteri Group
(H)	Heracleifolia Group
(I)	Integrifolia Group
(LL)	Late Large-flowered Group
(M)	Montana Group
(T)	Texensis Group
(Ta)	Tangutica Group
(V)	Viorna Group
(Vb)	Vitalba Group
(Vt)	Viticella Group

DAHLIA

(Classification according to The International Dahlia Register (1969), 22nd Supp. (2012) formed through consultation with national dahlia societies.)

(Sin)	1	Single
(Anem)	2	Anemone-flowered
(Col)	3	Collerette
(WL)	4	Waterlily
(D)	5	Decorative
(Ba)	6	Ball
(Pom)	7	Pompon
(C)	8	Cactus
(S-c)	9	Semi-cactus
(Misc)	10	Miscellaneous
(Fim)	11	Fimbriated
(SinO)	12	Single Orchid (Star)
(DblO)	13	Double Orchid, including Stellar
(P)	14	Peony-flowered
(B)		Botanical
(DwB)		Dwarf Bedding
(Lil)		Lilliput

DIANTHUS

(By the RHS)

(b)	Carnation, border
(M)	Carnation, Malmaison
(p)	Pink
(p,a)	Pink, annual
(pf)	Carnation, perpetual-flowering
(pt)	Carnation, pot

EPILOBIUM

(Z)	previously in the genus *Zauschneria*

Fruit

(B)	Black (*Vitis*), Blackberry (*Rubus*), Blackcurrant (*Ribes*)
(Ball)	Ballerina (*Malus*)
(C)	Culinary (*Malus, Prunus, Pyrus, Ribes*)
(Cider)	Cider (*Malus*)
(D)	Dessert (*Malus, Prunus, Pyrus, Ribes*)
(F)	Fruit
(G)	Glasshouse (*Vitis*)
(O)	Outdoor (*Vitis*)
(P)	Pinkcurrant (*Ribes*)
(Perry)	Perry (*Pyrus*)
(R)	Red (*Vitis*), Redcurrant (*Ribes*)
(S)	Seedless (*Citrus, Vitis*)
(s-p)	Self-pollinating
(W)	White (*Vitis*), Whitecurrant (*Ribes*)

Fuchsia

(E)	Encliandra
(T)	Variants and hybrids of *F. triphylla*

Gladiolus

(B)	Butterfly
(E)	Exotic
(G)	Giant
(L)	Large
(M)	Medium
(Min)	Miniature
(N)	Nanus
(P)	Primulinus
(S)	Small
(Tub)	Tubergenii

Hepatica nobilis

(Adapted from the International Hepatica Society classification for Hepatica nobilis)

(1)	Hyoujun (normal)
(2)	(degenerated anther)
(3)	Otome (degenerated stamen)
(4)	Henka (petal deformity)
(5/d)	Herashibe (semi-double, primitive)
(5A/d)	Choji (semi-double, primitive)
(6/d)	Nidan (semi-double, advanced)
(7/d)	Sandan (double, primitive)
(8/d)	Karako (double, advanced)
(9/d)	Sene-e (double, completed)

Hydrangea macrophylla

(H)	Hortensia
(L)	Lacecap

Impatiens

(NG)	New Guinea Group

Iris

(Adapted from the American Iris Society Classification)

(AB)	Arilbred
(BB)	Border Bearded
(Cal-Sib)	Series *Californicae* × Series *Sibiricae*
(CH)	Californian Hybrid
(DB)	Dwarf Bearded (not assigned)
(Dut)	Dutch (can be assigned to *I.* × *hollandica*)
(IB)	Intermediate Bearded
(J)	Juno (subgenus *Scorpiris*)
(La)	Louisiana Hybrid
(MDB)	Miniature Dwarf Bearded
(MTB)	Miniature Tall Bearded
(Rc)	Regeliocyclus (Section *Regelia* × Section *Oncocyclus*)
(Reticulata)	
(SDB)	Standard Dwarf Bearded
(Sib)	Siberian
(Sino-Sib)	Series *Sibiricae*, chromosome number 2n=40
(SpH)	Species Hybrid
(Spuria)	Spuria
(TB)	Tall Bearded

Lilium

(Classification according to *The International Lily Register* (ed. 4, 2007))

(I)	Asiatic hybrids derived from *L. amabile, L. bulbiferum, L. callosum, L. cernuum, L. concolor, L. dauricum, L. davidii, L.* × *hollandicum, L. lancifolium, L. lankongense, L. leichtlinii, L.* × *maculatum* and *L. pumilum, L.* × *scottiae, L. wardii* and *L. wilsonii.*
(II)	Martagon hybrids derived from *L. dalhansonii, L. hansonii, L. martagon, L. medeoloides* and *L. tsingtauense*
(III)	Euro-Caucasian hybrids derived from *L. candidum, L. chalcedonicum, L. kesselringianum, L. monadelphum, L. pomponium, L. pyrenaicum* and *L.* × *testaceum.*
(IV)	American hybrids derived from *L. bolanderi, L.* × *burbankii, L. canadense, L. columbianum, L. grayi, L. humboldtii, L. kelleyanum, L. kelloggii, L. maritimum, L. michauxii, L. michiganense, L. occidentale, L.* × *pardaboldtii, L. pardalinum, L. parryi, L. parvum, L. philadelphicum, L. pitkinense, L. superbum, L. vollmeri, L. washingtonianum* and *L. wigginsii.*
(V)	Longiflorum lilies derived from *L. formosanum, L. longiflorum, L. philippinense* and *L. wallichianum.*
(VI)	Trumpet and Aurelian hybrids derived from *L.* × *aurelianense, L. brownii, L.* × *centigale, L. henryi, L.* × *imperiale, L.* × *kewense, L. leucantheum, L. regale, L. rosthornii, L. sargentiae, L. sulphureum* and *L. sulphurgale* (but excluding hybrids of *L. henryi* with all species listed in Division VII).
(VII)	Oriental hybrids derived from *L. auratum, L. japonicum,*

CLASSIFICATION OF GENERA 53

	L. nobilissimum, *L.* × *parkmanii*, *L rubellum* and *L. speciosum* (but excl. all hybrids of these with *L. henryi*).
(VIII)	Other hybrids not covered by any of the previous divisions (I-VII)
(IX)	Species and cultivars of species
a/	upward-facing flowers
b/	outward-facing flowers
c/	downward-facing flowers
/a	trumpet-shaped flowers
/b	bowl-shaped flowers
/c	flat flowers (or with only tepal tips recurved)
/d	recurved flowers

MALUS *SEE* FRUIT

NARCISSUS

(By the RHS, revised 1998)

(1)	Trumpet
(2)	Large-cupped
(3)	Small-cupped
(4)	Double
(5)	Triandrus
(6)	Cyclamineus
(7)	Jonquilla and Apodanthus
(8)	Tazetta
(9)	Poeticus
(10)	Bulbocodium
(11a)	Split-corona: Collar
(11b)	Split-corona: Papillon
(12)	Miscellaneous
(13)	Species

NYMPHAEA

(H)	Hardy
(D)	Day-blooming
(N)	Night-blooming
(T)	Tropical

OENOTHERA

| (G) | previously in the genus *Gaura* |

PAEONIA

| (S) | Shrubby |

PELARGONIUM:

(Based on the International *Pelargonium* Register)

(A)	Angel
(B)	Bird's egg (in combination)
(C)	Coloured foliage (in combination)
(Ca)	Cactus (also known as Quilled) (in combination)
(Dec)	Decorative
(Dw)	Dwarf (in combination)
(Fr)	Frutetorum
(I)	Ivy-leaved
(Mic)	Micro-minature (in combination)
(Min)	Minature (in combination)
(R)	Regal
(Ros)	Rosebud (in combination)
(Sc)	Scented-leaved
(St)	Stellar (in combination)
(T)	Tulip (in combination)
(U)	Unique
(Z)	Zonal
(Za)	Zonartic

PRIMULA

(Classification by Section evolved from Richards. J. (2002) *Primula* (2nd edition). Batsford, London)

(Ag)	*Auganthus*
(Al)	*Aleuritia*
(Am)	*Amethystinae*
(Ar)	*Armerina*
(Au)	*Auricula*
/A	Alpine Auricula
/B	Border Auricula
/S	Show Auricula
/St	Striped Auricula
(Bu)	*Bullatae*
(Ca)	*Capitatae*
(Cf)	*Cordifoliae*
(Ch)	*Chartaceae*
(Co)	*Cortusoides*
(Cr)	*Carolinella*
(Cu)	*Cuneifoliae*
(Cy)	*Crystallophlomis*
(Da)	*Davidii*
(De)	*Denticulatae*
(Dr)	*Dryadifoliae*
(F)	*Fedtschenkoanae*
(G)	*Glabrae*
(Ma)	*Malvaceae*
(Mi)	*Minutissimae*
(Mo)	*Monocarpicae*
(Mu)	*Muscarioides*
(Ob)	*Obconicolisteri*
(Or)	*Oreophlomis*
(Pa)	*Parryi*
(Pe)	*Petiolares*
(Pf)	*Proliferae*
(Pi)	*Pinnatae*
(Pr)	*Primula*
/Poly	Polyanthus (can be assigned to *P.* × *polyantha*)
/Prim	Primrose
(Pu)	*Pulchellae*
(Py)	*Pycnoloba*
(R)	*Reinii*
(Si)	*Sikkimenses*
(So)	*Soldanelloides*
(Sp)	*Sphondylia*
(Sr)	*Sredinskya*
(Su)	*Suffrutescentes*
(Y)	*Yunnannenses*

PRUNUS *SEE* FRUIT

PYRUS *SEE* FRUIT

Rhododendron

(A)	Azalea (deciduous, species or unclassified hybrid)
(Ad)	Azaleodendron
(EA)	Evergreen azalea
(G)	Ghent azalea (deciduous)
(K)	Knap Hill or Exbury azalea (deciduous)
(M)	Mollis azalea (deciduous)
(O)	Occidentalis azalea (deciduous)
(R)	Rustica azalea (deciduous)
(V)	Vireya rhododendron
(Vs)	Viscosa azalea (deciduous)

Ribes see Fruit

Rosa

(A)	Alba
(Bb)	Bourbon
(Bs)	Boursault
(Ce)	Centifolia
(Ch)	China
(Cl)	Climbing (in combination)
(D)	Damask
(DPo)	Damask Portland
(F)	Floribunda or Cluster-flowered
(G)	Gallica
(Ga)	Garnette
(GC)	Ground Cover
(HM)	Hybrid Musk
(HP)	Hybrid Perpetual
(HT)	Hybrid Tea or Large-flowered
(Min)	Miniature
(Mo)	Moss (in combination)
(N)	Noisette
(Patio)	Patio, Miniature Floribunda or Dwarf Cluster-flowered
(Poly)	Polyantha
(Ra)	Rambler
(RH)	Rubiginosa hybrid (Hybrid Sweet Briar)
(Ru)	Rugosa
(S)	Shrub
(SpH)	Spinosissima Hybrid
(T)	Tea

Rubus see Fruit

Salvia

(Pe)	previously in the genus *Perovskia*
(Ro)	previously in the genus *Rosmarinus*

Saxifraga

(Classification by Section from Gornall, R.J. (1987). *Botanical Journal of the Linnean Society*, 95(4): 273–292)

(1)	*Ciliatae*
(2)	*Cymbalaria*
(3)	*Merkianae*
(4)	*Micranthes*
(5)	*Irregulares*
(6)	*Heterisia*
(7)	*Porphyrion*
(8)	*Ligulatae*
(9)	*Xanthizoon*
(10)	*Trachyphyllum*
(11)	*Gymnopera*
(12)	*Cotylea*
(13)	*Odontophyllae*
(14)	*Mesogyne*
(15)	*Saxifraga*

Streptocarpus

(AV)	African violets (previously in the genus *Saintpaulia*)

Tulipa

(Classification by Cultivar Group from *Classified List and International Register of Tulip Names* by Koninklijke Algemeene Vereniging voor Bloembollencultuur 1996)

(1)	Single Early Group
(2)	Double Early Group
(3)	Triumph Group
(4)	Darwin Hybrid Group
(5)	Single Late Group (including Darwin Group and Cottage Group)
(6)	Lily-flowered Group
(7)	Fringed Group
(8)	Viridiflora Group
(9)	Rembrandt Group
(10)	Parrot Group
(11)	Double Late Group
(12)	Kaufmanniana Group
(13)	Fosteriana Group
(14)	Greigii Group
(15)	Miscellaneous
(16)	Coronet Group

Veronica

(H)	previously in the genus *Hebe*
(P)	previously in the genus *Parahebe*

Viola

(C)	Cornuta Hybrid
(dVt)	Double Violet
(ExVa)	Exhibition Viola
(FP)	Fancy Pansy
(P)	Pansy
(PVt)	Parma Violet
(SP)	Show Pansy
(T)	Tricolor
(Va)	Viola
(Vt)	Violet
(Vtta)	Violetta

Vitis see Fruit

How to Use the Plant Directory

Nursery Codes

Look up the plant you require in the alphabetical Plant Directory. Against each plant you will find one or more four or five letter codes, for example WCru, each code represents one nursery offering that plant. The first letter of each code indicates the main area of the country in which the nursery is situated. For this geographical key, refer to the **Nursery Codes and Symbols** on p.776.

Turn to the **Nursery Details by Code** starting on p.780 where, in alphabetical order of codes, you will find details of each nursery which offers the plant in question. For a fuller explanation of how to use the nursery listings please turn to p.778. **Always check that the nursery you select has the plant in stock before you visit.**

Plants with more than 30 Suppliers

In some cases, against the plant name you will see the term 'Widely available' instead of a nursery code. If we were to include every plant listed by all nurseries, the *RHS Plant Finder* would become unmanageably bulky. We therefore ask nurseries to restrict their entries to those plants that are not already well represented. As a result, if more than 30 nurseries offer any plant the Directory gives no nursery codes and the plant is listed instead as being 'Widely available'.

You should not have difficulty in locating these in local nurseries or garden centres. If, however, you are unable to find such plants, please contact the compiler for further assistance. See the Introduction (p.34).

Finding Fruit, Vegetables and Herbs

You will need to search for these by their botanical names. Common names are cross-referenced to their botanical names in the Plant Directory.

If you have Difficulty Finding your Plant

If you cannot immediately find the plant you seek, look through the various species of the genus. You may be using an incomplete name. The problem is most likely to arise in very large genera such as *Phlox* where there are a number of possible species, each with a large number of cultivars. A search through the whole genus may well bring success. For space reasons, we are not able to list in the Plant Directory annuals or orchids (except hardy terrestrial orchids), or non-ornamental vegetables. For fruit and vegetables with an RHS Award of Garden Merit please see the relevant sections on p.740 and p.752.

Cross-references

It may be that the plant name you seek is a synonym. Our intention is to list nursery codes only against the correct botanical name. Where you find a synonym you will be cross-referred to the correct name.

Plants Last Listed in Earlier Editions

It may be that the plant you are seeking has no known suppliers and is thus not listed.

The loss of a plant name from the Directory may arise for a number of reasons – the supplier may have gone out of business, or may not have responded to our latest questionnaire and has therefore been removed from the book. Such plants may well be available but we have no knowledge of current suppliers. Alternatively, some plants may have been misnamed by nurseries in previous editions and are now appearing under their correct name.

For further information on plants last listed in earlier editions please see the Introduction (p.34).

Non-Native Banned Plants

Plants listed as non-native and banned from sale under Schedule 9 of the Wildlife and Countryside Act (1981) will be shown without suppliers listed and with a note 'Prohibited invasive' in the right hand column. Plants that are not banned from sale but have the potential to become a nuisance are shown with a ? symbol.

Using the Plant Directory

The purpose of the Plant Directory is to help the reader correctly identify the plant they seek and find stockists. Each nursery has a unique code which appears to the right of the plant name. **Nursery Details by Code** (p.780) gives details about each nursery. The first letter in each code denotes its geographical region. Turn to the **Nursery Codes and Symbols** (p.776) to find the correct code for an area.

The Plant Directory provides information about plants through symbols and notes. For example: if a plant has an alternative name; is new to the book; or has received the RHS Award of Garden Merit.

PLANT HERITAGE SYMBOL
Plant Heritage National Plant Collection exists for all or part of this genus.

SYMBOLS TO THE LEFT OF THE NAME
Provides information about the name of the plant. See p.36 for the key.

ABBREVIATIONS
To save space a dash indicates that the previous heading is repeated. If written out in full the name would be Hydrangea quercifolia 'Harmony'.

SYMBOLS TO THE RIGHT OF THE NAME
Tells you more about the plant itself, e.g. (d) indicates that the plant is double-flowered, (F) = fruit. See p.36 for the key.

TRADE DESIGNATION
See p.40.

Hydrangea ❀ (Hydrangeaceae)

§ *platyarguta*	CBcs EBee EGrl EWld SChF WCru WPGP
– B&SWJ 6266	WCru
'Preziosa' ♕H4	Widely available
PRINCESS BRIDE	see *H.* CLOUD NINE
quercifolia	Widely available
– 'Alice'	CBcs CDoC CMac CMCN EBee ELan EPfP ESwi LMil LRHS LSRN MAsh NLar SGol WCot WLov WPGP
– 'Alison'	SGol
– 'Amethyst' Dirr	NLar SGol
– 'Applause'	CDoC ELan EPfP LRHS NLar SGol WPGP
– 'Back Porch'	NLar SGol
– 'Burgundy'	CBcs ESwi IArd MBlu NLar SGol WPGP WSpi
– 'Flore Pleno'	see *H. quercifolia* SNOWFLAKE
– 'Harmony'	CMac EBee ELan ELon EPfP ESwi MGos SGol SVen WPGP
– ICE CRYSTAL ('Hqopr010'^{PBR})	CAbb CDoC EAri EBee ELan EPfP ESwi LBom SGol WPGP WSpi
– JETSTREAM ('Piihq-i')	MGos MPri SGol
– 'Lady Anne'	WPGP
– LITTLE HONEY ('Brihon')	CWGN EBee LCro MAsh SGol SMad WPGP
– 'Munchkin'	CDoC CWnw LCro LRHS MBlu MGos SGol
– 'Pee Wee'	CDoC CMac CSpe EBee EGren ELan EPfP SAko SGol SPoG WPGP
– 'Queen of Hearts'	ESwi MGos
– 'Ruby Slippers'	CDoC ESwi IArd LCro LRHS MBlu MGos MPri SGol SMad WSpi
– 'Sike's Dwarf'	ELon NLar SGol
– 'Snow Giant' (d)	SGol
– SNOW QUEEN ('Flemygea') ♕H5	CBcs CDoC CMCN CSpe EAri EGren ELan EPfP LCro LMaj LMil LRHS LSRN MAsh MGos NLar SGol SPoG SVen WFar WPGP WSpi
– 'Snowcicle' **new**	SMad
§ – SNOWFLAKE ('Brido') (d) ♕H5	CBcs CDoC CEnd CMac CWGN ELan EPfP LCro MAsh MGos NCth NLar SGol SMad SPoG WPGP WSpi
– 'Tennessee Clone'	NLar SGol
– RUNAWAY BRIDE SNOW WHITE ('Ushyd0405'^{PBR})	CBcs CDoC CWGN CWnw EPfP LCro LRHS MSwo NLar SAth SGol SMad WCha
sargentiana	see *H. aspera* subsp. *sargentiana*
scandens	NBro
scandens	NBro
– B&SWJ 5448	WCru
– B&SWJ 5481	WCru
– B&SWJ 5496	WCru

WIDELY AVAILABLE
Indicates that more than 30 Plant Finder nurseries supply the plant, and it may be available locally. See p.55.

DESCRIPTIVE TERM
See p.38.

CROSS-REFERENCES
Directs you to the correct name of the plant and the nursery codes. See p.55.

NURSERY CODE
A unique code identifying each nursery. Turn to p.780 for details of the nurseries.

♕H5
This plant has received the RHS Award of Garden Merit. See p.37.

NEW
Plant new to this edition.

PBR
Plant Breeders' Rights. See p.39.

II
PLANTS

THE PLANT DIRECTORY

A

Abelia (Caprifoliaceae)
- **chinensis** misapplied — see *A.* × *grandiflora* 'Lake Maggiore'
- § **chinensis** R. Br. — CBcs CExl CMac CMCN EBee ELan EPfP LRHS MMuc SEND SRms
  - AUTUMN FESTIVAL ('Minabaut01') — EHeP ELan EPfP LRHS
  - 'Edward Goucher' ♀H5 — CBcs CBrac CCps CDoC CEnd CMac CWnw EBee EGren EHeP ELan EPfP ERom LBom LRHS LSRN LSto MGos MSwo NCth SEND SGol SPlb SRms WFar WLov WSpi
- ***floribunda*** — see *Vesalea floribunda*
- × ***grandiflora*** 'Aurea' — see *A.* × *grandiflora* 'Gold Spot'
  - 'Brockhill Allgold' — EPfP SPoG
  - common clone — see *A.* × *grandiflora* 'Lake Maggiore'
  - 'Compacta' — MSwo WFar
  - CONFETTI ('Conti'PBR) (v) — CBcs CDoC CMac CTsd EGren ELan ERom MGos MPri NLar SEND SNig SPoG WCha
- § - 'Francis Mason' (v) — CBcs CBrac CMac CSBt EBee EHeP ELan EPfP LRHS MAsh MBlu MSwo NCth NQui SEND SGol SPoG SRms WCot WFar WHtc
  - GOLD JEWEL ('Abhfgold') — CBcs LRHS MPri
- § - 'Gold Spot' (v) — CDoC ELon EPfP LRHS LSou
  - 'Gold Strike' — see *A.* × *grandiflora* 'Gold Spot'
  - 'Goldsport' — see *A.* × *grandiflora* 'Gold Spot'
  - 'Hopleys'PBR (v) ♀H4 — CBcs CMac CSBt EBee ELan ELon EPfP LRHS MAsh MGos SEND SPoG WHtc
  - 'Kaleidoscope'PBR (v) — CBcs CDoC CMac CSBt CWnw EBee EGren ELan EPfP ERom LBom LCro LRHS LSou LSRN LSto MAsh MBros MGos MPri SGol SOrN SPoG WCot WFar WHtc
  - LADY LIBERTY ('Keylib') — LRHS
- § - 'Lake Maggiore' ♀H5 — CBrac CCoa CDoC CMac CSBt EGren EHeP ELan EPfP ERom GKev LBom LCro LRHS LSRN LSto MBlu MGos NLar MAsh SDix SEND SFol SNig SOrN SPoG SSta WFar WLov
  - LUCKY LOTS ('Wevo2') (v) — EBee ELan ERom LCro NCth
  - MAGIC DAYDREAM ('Opstal103') — LCro LRHS LSou MGos NEoE WFar
  - MYSTIC DAYDREAM ('Opstal40') — EBee
  - 'Panache' (v) — WCot
  - 'Prostrate White' — CMac ELan GKev LRHS LSou SPoG
  - 'Radiance' (v) — CWnw EBee MBlu NEoE SHar
  - 'Semperflorens' — CWnw LRHS WFar
  - 'Sherwoodii' — EBee EHeP EPfP MGos MHtn
  - 'Sparkling Silver' (v) — CDoC CWnw ELan GKev LRHS LSRN MGos SEND
  - SUNNY CHARMS ('Mindu01'PBR) — CBcs
  - SUNSHINE DAYDREAM ('Abelops'PBR) (v) — CEnd EBee EGren LCro LRHS MGos SRms WFar WSpi
  - TRICOLOR CHARM ('Mincautri'PBR) (v) — CSBt LCro LRHS LSou MHtn
  - 'Variegata' — see *A.* × *grandiflora* 'Francis Mason'
- § 'Lynn'PBR — LRHS MGos SPoG
- **macrotera** — CExl MBlu
  - var. **engleriana**
- **mosanensis** — see *Zabelia tyaihyonii*
- **parvifolia** — CBcs CExl CMac CMCN CSBt ELan EPfP LRHS SPoG WKif
  - 'Bumblebee' — LRHS MAsh MGos NLar SPoG
  - PETITE GARDEN ('Minedward'PBR) — CDoC ELan GKev
  - PINKY BELLS — see *A.* 'Lynn'
  - 'Raspberry Profusion'PBR — MPri
- **rupestris** misapplied — see *A.* × *grandiflora*
- **rupestris** Lindl. — see *A. chinensis* R. Br.
- **triflora** — see *Zabelia triflora*
- **umbellata** — see *Zabelia umbellata*

Abeliophyllum (Oleaceae)
- **distichum** — CBcs EBee EGren EGrI ELan EPfP LCro LRHS LSto MAsh MBlu WCFE WCot
  - Roseum Group — CBcs CExl CMac CMCN ELan LCro LRHS MAsh MMuc NQui SPoG

Abelmoschus (Malvaceae)
- **esculentus** — SVic
  - 'Clemson Spineless' — MCtn

Abies ✿ (Pinaceae)
- **alba** — CAco MMuc WHtc
  - 'Barabits' Star' — CAco
  - 'Fastigiata' — CAco NLar
  - 'Green Spiral' — CAco
  - 'Minaret' — CAco NLar
  - 'Pendula' — CAco
  - 'Pyramidalis' — CAco CWnw LRHS
  - 'Scarabantia' — CAco
- **amabilis** — CAco
  - 'Spreading Star' — CAco
- **arizonica** — see *A. lasiocarpa* var. *arizonica*
- × **arnoldiana** — CAco
- **balsamea**
  - 'Bruce's Variegated' (v) — NLar
  - 'Eugene Gold' — NLar
  - Hudsonia Group — GArf
  - - 'Nana' — CAco LCro
  - var. **phanerolepis** 'Bear Swamp' — LRHS
  - 'Piccolo' — CAco
  - 'Tyler Blue' — LRHS
  - 'Verkade's Prostrate' — LRHS
- **borisii-regis** — CAco
- * - 'Pendula' — CAco
  - 'Spring Delight' — CAco NLar
- **bracteata** — CAco LRHS
- **cephalonica** — CAco
  - 'Barabits' Gold' — CAco

Abies 59

- 'Greg's Broom'	CAco NLar	
§ - 'Meyer's Dwarf'	CAco	
- 'Nana'	see *A. cephalonica* 'Meyer's Dwarf'	
chensiensis	CAco	
cilicica	CAco	
concolor	CAco CBcs EUrb IPap LMaj LRHS MMuc SEND	
- 'Archer's Dwarf'	CAco NLar	
- 'Bedoń'	CAco	
- 'Blue Cloak'	CAco	
- 'Clarence'	NLar	
§ - 'Compacta' ♀H7	CAco MGos NLar	
- 'Glauca'	see *A. concolor* (Violacea Group) 'Violacea'	
- 'Glauca Compacta'	see *A. concolor* 'Compacta'	
- 'Globosa'	CAco	
- Lowiana Group	CAco	
- - 'Creamy'	NLar	
- 'Pendula'	CAco	
- 'Piggelmee'	MAsh	
- 'Scooter'	LRHS	
- 'Sherwood's Blue'	CAco	
§ - (Violacea Group) 'Violacea' ♀H7	CAco ELan WMat	
- - 'Violacea Prostrate' ♀H7	CAco LRHS NLar	
- 'Wintergold'	CAco MBlu NLar	
delavayi	WPGP	
- var. *delavayi*	CExl	
- - Fabri Group	see *A. fabri*	
- 'Green Giant'	CAco NLar	
- 'Midnight Blue'	CAco LRHS	
durangensis	CAco	
var. *coahuilensis*		
§ *fabri*	CAco	
fanjingshanensis	CAco	
fargesii var. *faxoniana*	CAco	
- 'Headfort'	NLar	
firma	CAco	
forrestii	CAco	
- var. *ferreana*	CAco	
- var. *georgei*	CAco	
fraseri	CAco CBcs EBar EWhm MCtn MMuc MPri	
- 'Blue Bonnet'	CAco EUrb NLar	
- 'Kline's Nest'	CAco	
- 'Piglet's WB'	CAco LRHS	
- 'Raul's Dwarf'	CAco NLar	
grandis	CAco CMac IPap MMuc	
- 'Van Dedem's Dwarf'	LRHS NLar	
guatemalensis	CAco	
holophylla	CAco	
* - 'Glauca'	CAco	
homolepis	CAco	
- 'Prostrata'	CAco	
- var. *umbellata*	CAco	
× *insignis*	CAco	
kawakamii	CAco	
koreana ♀H7	CAco CBcs CBrac CCVT CHll CLnd CMac EHeP ELan EPfP GKin IPap LRHS MBlu MCtn MGos MMuc NPip SGol SPad SPlb WHtc WMat WMou	
- 'Alpin Star'	CAco LRHS MAsh	
- 'Aurea'	see *A. koreana* 'Flava'	
- 'Blauer Eskimo' ♀H7	CAco LRHS MAsh NLar SArc	
- 'Blauer Pfiff'	CAco EUrb NLar	
- 'Blue Emperor'	CAco EUrb LRHS MBlu NLar	
- 'Blue Magic'	CAco NLar	
- 'Blue 'n' Silver'	CAco	
- blue-leaved	CDoC	
- 'Bonsai Blue'	CAco	
I - 'Brevifolia'	NLar	
- 'Brilliant'	CAco	
- 'Cis' ♀H7	CAco EUrb NLar	
- 'Compact Dwarf'	CAco	
- Crystal Globe	see *A. koreana* 'Kristallkugel'	
- 'Dark Hill'	CAco NLar	
- 'Discus'	CAco NLar	
- 'Eisregen'	NLar	
§ - 'Flava'	CAco	
- 'Frosty'	CAco NLar	
- 'Gait'	CAco NLar	
- 'Goldener Traum'	NLar	
- 'Green Carpet'	CAco NLar	
- 'Green 'n' Cream'	CAco	
- 'Grübele'	LRHS	
- 'Grüne Spinne'	CAco MBlu	
- 'Kleiner Prinz'	NLar	
- 'Kohout'	CAco	
- 'Kohout's Ice Breaker'PBR ♀H7	CAco LRHS MAsh MGos NLar	
§ - 'Kristallkugel'	CAco MAsh MBlu NLar	
- 'Luminetta'	CAco NLar	
- 'May'	CAco	
- 'Molli'	CAco	
- 'Nadelkissen'	CAco	
- 'Nisbet'	CAco	
- 'Oberon'	CAco CWnw LRHS NLar	
- 'Pinocchio'	CAco	
- 'Ry'	LRHS NLar	
- 'Schwedenkönig'	CAco	
- 'Shorty'	NLar	
- 'Silberkugel'	CAco	
- 'Silberlade' ♀H7	CAco	
- 'Silberlocke' ♀H7	CAco CCVT CDoC LRHS MBlu MGos NLar NPip WMat	
- 'Silbermavers'	CAco LRHS	
- 'Silberperl'	CAco NLar	
- 'Silberzwerg'	LRHS	
- 'Silver Show'	CAco CWnw SArc	
- 'Silver Star'	CAco	
- 'Super Bush'	CAco	
- 'Tundra'	CAco NLar	
- 'Verdener Dom'	CAco NLar	
- 'Žehušice'	CAco	
lasiocarpa	CAco CCVT IPap	
§ - var. *arizonica*	CAco	
- - 'Argentea'	CAco	
- - 'Compacta' Hornibr. ♀H7	CAco CWnw EUrb LRHS MAsh MGos MPri NLar NPip SPoG WMat	
- - 'Kenwith Blue'	CAco	
- 'Glacier'	see *A. lasiocarpa* 'Logan Pass'	
- 'Green Globe'	CAco NLar	
- var. *lasiocarpa*	CAco	
§ - 'Logan Pass'	CAco	
- 'Mikolaš'	CAco EUrb NLar	
- 'Prickly Pete'	CAco NLar	
magnifica	CAco IPap	
- 'Glauca'	CAco	
- 'Mount Si'	NLar	
- var. *shastensis*	CAco	
marocana	see *A. pinsapo* var. *marocana*	
nebrodensis	CAco	
- 'Sicilian Gold'	NLar	
nephrolepis	CAco	
nobilis	see *A. procera*	
nordmanniana	CAco CBcs CBrac CCVT CMac CMCN CSBt EBar ELan EWhm IPap LBuc LMaj LSto MMuc MNHC MPri NLar NTrD SPoG WCha WHtc WMou WRjT	
- 'Ambrolauri'	CAco	

Abies

- subsp. ***equi-trojani***	CAco
- 'Filip's Gold Heart'	NLar
- 'Geusert'	CAco
- 'Hasselt'	see *A. nordmanniana*
	subsp. *nordmanniana* 'Pévé Hasselt'
- 'Kilian'	CAco
- subsp. ***nordmanniana***	CAco
'Aurea'	
- - 'Barabits' Compact'	CAco
- - 'Dobřichovice'	CAco NLar
- - 'Golden Spreader' ♀H7	CAco LRHS MAsh MBlu MGos MPri NLar
- - 'Kbng'	CAco
- - 'Midwinter Gold'	CAco NLar
- - 'Münsterland'	CAco
- - 'Pendula'	CAco MBlu
§ - - 'Pévé Hasselt'	CAco
- - 'Saerling'	CAco
- 'Robusta'	CAco
numidica	CAco
- 'Delicado'	CAco
- 'Glauca'	CAco LRHS
pindrow	CAco
- var. ***brevifolia***	CAco
pinsapo	CAco IPap
- 'Atlas'	CAco
- 'Aurea' ♀H6	CAco LCro LMaj NLar
- 'Fastigiata'	CAco EUrb NLar SAko
- 'Glauca' ♀H6	CAco CDoC LMaj MBlu NLar
I - 'Horstmann'	CAco EUrb LRHS NLar
- 'Kelleriis'	CAco NLar
§ - var. ***marocana***	CAco LRHS
- 'Pendula'	CAco
- var. ***pinsapo***	CAco
- 'Serenade'	CAco NLar
- 'Soltau'	CAco
- var. ***tazaotana***	CAco
§ ***procera***	CAco IPap MMuc
- 'Bizarro'	CAco NLar
- 'Blaue Hexe'	CAco
- 'Delbar Cascade'	CAco NLar
- Glauca Group	GKin MBlu
- - 'Glauca' ♀H7	CAco LMaj
I - - 'Glauca Pendula'	CAco
- 'Glauca Prostrata' ♀H7	CAco EUrb MAsh
- 'Hupp's Dwarf'	CAco NLar
- 'Hupp's Single Snake'	CAco
- 'La Graciosa'	CAco NLar
- 'Prostrata'	LRHS
- 'Rat Tail'	CAco EUrb NLar
- 'Rick's Foxtail'	CAco
recurvata	CAco
sachalinensis	CAco
sibirica	CAco
veitchii	CAco
- 'Drevenack'	CAco
- 'Glauca'	CAco
- 'Heddergott'	CAco NLar
- 'Kramer'	CAco NLar
I - 'Pendula'	CAco
- 'Rumburk'	CAco
vejarii	CAco
× ***vilmorinii***	CAco

'Canary Bird' ♀H2	CBcs CHll CSde EAri LCro LRHS MGos SPad WFar WJun WKif
'Cannington Carol' (v) ♀H2	CCps CHll SEND
'Cerise Queen'	SPad
'Cloth of Gold'	CMac SPad
dark yellow-flowered	CHll
'Emperor'	SPad
'Estella's Little Bird'	CBcs ELan SChF SPad WPGP
'Feuerwerk'	SPad
'Fool's Gold'	EAri SPad
'Gerdemann's Red'	CBcs SPad WMal WPGP
'Giant Orange'	SPad
globosum	see *A.* × *hybridum*
'Golden Terracotta'	SPad
'Himbeere'	SPad
'Hinton Seedling'	CHll CRHN EAri LRHS SEND SPad
§ × ***hybridum***	LBom SAth
- apricot-flowered	WFar WJun
- Giant Flowering Mixed **new**	EAri
'Isabella'	SPad
'John Thompson'	CBcs EPfP SEND SPad
'Kentish Belle' ♀H3	CAbb CBcs CBrac CCps CHll CMac CRHN CSBt CSde CWGN EBee ELan ELon EPfP EUrb LRHS LSRN MGos MPri SEND SIvy SPad SPlb SPoG SRkn SRms SVen WCot WJun WSpi
'Kleine Schönheit'	SPad
'Lachskönigin'	SPad
'Leila Jackson'	EAri EBee SEND SPad WJun
'Lemon Queen'	WJun
'Lilac Jewel'	SPad
'Lilac Wonder'	SPad
'Lilli'	SPad
'Lillian'	SPad
'Linda Vista Peach' ♀H2	SPad WMal
'Lisa Roja'	SVen
'Louis Marignac'	CHll
Lucky Lantern Tangerine ('Nuabtang')	EAri SPad
'Marion' ♀H2	CRHN SPad SPlb WJun WKif
'Master Michael'	CMac SPad
megapotamicum ♀H3	CAbb CBcs CCps CDoC CHll CMac CRHN CSde ELan EPfP EUrb LCro LRHS MAsh MGos MSCN SDix SEle SPad SPoG SRms SVen WFar WJun WTHo
- 'Big Bell'	LRHS WFar
- 'Ines'	CHll EBee ELon SPad WFar WPGP
- 'Variegatum' (v) ♀H3	CBcs CCps CDoC CMac EAri ELon EPfP EUrb LRHS MAsh MPri SPoG SVen WJun
- 'Wisley Red'	CAbb CRHN EAri ELan ELon EPfP SEle SPad WJun WLov
× ***milleri*** hort. ♀H3	CMac CRHN EBee ELon SPad WCot WJun
- 'Variegatum' (v)	CMac EAri EBee SVen WCot WFar
- 'Ventnor Gold'	SEle SEND SPad SVen
'Mrs Trimmer'	SRkn
'Nabob' ♀H2	CBcs CCoa CCps CExl CHll CRHN CSde EAri EBee ELan EPfP EUrb LRHS SEND SPad SVen WCot WFar WJun
'Old Rose Belle'	SPad
'Orange Hot Lava'	CBcs CExl CMHG EAri EBee EUrb SChF SPad WPGP
'Paddy's Nephew'	EBee WFar WJun
'Patrick Synge' ♀H2	CBcs CExl CHll EAri EBee SChF SEle SPad SPhx WPGP
pictum	SPad
- 'Thompsonii' (v) ♀H2	CHll EAri EMdy SEND SPad WJun

Abutilon ✿ (Malvaceae)

'Apfelsine'	SPad
'Aphrodite'	CSde EMdy SPad WCot
'Ashford Red'	CBcs CHll CMac GQue SPad SVen WKif
Bella Series	CDoC
'Buttercup'	SPad

'Pink Charm'	CWGN EAri EBee ELon EShb SPad WJun
pink-flowered	EAri
'Red Bells'	SVen
'Red Dragon'	MGos
'Red Hot Lava'	CBct EAri
RED TIGER ('Atn Rt5')	EAri SEle SPad WFar WKif
RED TRUMPET ('Oostredtrump'^PBR)	EAri LRHS SEND WCot
'Redisch'	WJun
'Rose Glow'	WCot
'Roter Vulkan'	SPad
'Russels Dwarf'	SPad
'Satin Pink Belle'	SPad
'Schneeflocke'	SPad
'Snowfall'	SPad
'Sonnenkind'	SPad
'Souvenir de Bonn' (v) ♀H2	CHll EUrb NQui SPad WCot WJun
'Sunny'	SPad
× *suntense*	see *Corynabutilon* × *suntense*
'Sydney Belle'	SPad
'Tango'	CCps EAri ELan SPad WJun
'Thomas Jackson'	SPad
'Tinkerbell'	CHll
'Versicolor'	SPad
'Victorian Lady' (d)	CHll SPad WJun
'Victory'	CSde
'Violet Melody'	SPad
vitifolium	see *Corynabutilon vitifolium*
'Waltz'	CCps EAri EBee ELan EUrb LRHS SIvy SPad WCot WFar
WHITE TRUMPET ('Oostwhitru'^PBR)	EAri
YELLOW TRUMPET ('Oosttrump'^PBR)	EAri WFar

Acacia (Fabaceae)

acinacea	SPlb
adunca	SPlb
alpina	SArc
angustissima	SPlb
armata	see *A. paradoxa*
axillaris	SPlb
baileyana ♀H3	CBcs CDoC CMac CSBt LRHS LSRN MCtn MGos SPlb
- var. *aurea*	SPlb
- 'Purpurea' ♀H3	CBcs CBct CDoC CEnd CExl CMac CMHG CSBt CSpe ELan EPfP EShb EUrb LRHS LSRN MGos NPip SBig SChF SIvy SPlb SPoG WPGP
- 'Songlines'	LRHS
boormanii	CDoC EGrI SPlb WPGP
cassioides	see *A. peruviana*
cognata 'Limelight'^PBR	LRHS
cultriformis	SAth
dealbata ♀H3	Widely available
- 'Gaulois Astier'	CDoC CSBt EPfP LSRN MGos SPoG WCha
- 'Le Gaulois'	CWnw LRHS
'Exeter Hybrid'	CSBt
farnesiana	WJur
glaucoptera	SPlb
gregorii	SPlb
jibberdingensis	SPlb
julibrissin	see *Albizia julibrissin*
karroo	see *Vachellia karroo*
longifolia	CBcs CDoC CDTJ CMac ELan
macradenia	SPlb
mearnsii	EBee ELan
melanoxylon	CAgr CBcs CDTJ CWnw ELan EUrb SArc SPlb
minuta	see *Vachellia farnesiana*
nanodealbata	SPad
obliquinervia	EBee SChF WPGP
§ *paradoxa*	WCha
pataczekii	CSBt WPGP
pendula	SPlb
§ *peruviana*	WJur
podalyriifolia	SPlb
pravissima ♀H3	CBcs CDoC CExl CMac CTsd CWnw EGrI ELan EPfP EUrb GBin LSRN SArc SBig SEle SPlb WJun
- 'Bushwalk Baby'	SEle
- 'Lemon Twist'	EAri LCro
retinodes	CAgr CBcs CDTJ ELan EUrb SBig SEND SPad
- blue-leaved	EUrb
rubida	SPlb
saligna	Prohibited invasive. See Conservation and the Environment, p.42
sentis	see *A. victoriae*
spectabilis	SPlb
suaveolens	SPlb
truncata	SPlb
verticillata	CBcs CDoC CDTJ LRHS
- riverine form	CDoC EPfP EUrb SEle
§ *victoriae*	SPlb

Acaena (Rosaceae)

adscendens misapplied	see *A. affinis*, *A. saccaticupula* 'Blue Haze'
? *adscendens* ambig. 'Glauca'	NBir
? *affinis*	ECha EGrI
anserinifolia misapplied	see *A. novae-zelandiae*
? *buchananii*	EBee GAbr LRHS NLar SRms
caerulea hort.	see *A. caesiiglauca*
? *caesiiglauca*	GQue
? *inermis*	SPlb
- 'Purpurea'	CoPl EBee ECha ELan EPPr GArf GKev GMaP GQue MMrt MMuc NDov NLar SDix SLee SPlb WCav WIce
? *magellanica*	GKev
? *microphylla*	CoPl EBee GArf GQue MBel MCtn NLar SLee SPlb SRms
- COPPER CARPET	see *A. microphylla* 'Kupferteppich'
- 'Dichte Matte'	NLar
- 'Glauca'	see *A. caesiiglauca*
- 'Grüner Zwerg'	NLar
§ - 'Kupferteppich'	EGrI ELan EPPr GAbr GMaP LRHS NBir NBro NLar NSti SLee SMHy SRms
? *minor* var. *antarctica*	GBin
? *novae-zelandiae*	GKev SDix
? *ovalifolia*	GKev
'Pewter'	see *A. saccaticupula* 'Blue Haze'
'Purple Carpet'	see *A. microphylla* 'Kupferteppich'
? *saccaticupula*	GKev
§ - 'Blue Haze'	EBee ECha EGrI LRHS NBir SPlb SRms

Acanthocalyx see *Morina*

Acanthopanax see *Eleutherococcus*

ricinifolius	see *Kalopanax septemlobus*

Acanthophyllum (Caryophyllaceae)

§ *cerastioides*	CSpe EPfP EPot GAbr LBar LRHS LShi MHol MWlw NGdn NLar SLee SPlb SRms SRot WAbe WFar WIce
- 'Border Belle'	SHar

- Pretty Maid ('Yatgyp')	EGren EHeP EPfP LBar LCro LRHS MHtn MMrt MPnt NEoE	Arctic Jade ('Isiaj')^{PBR} (Jack Frost Series)	CBTr MPkF NLar
- 'Rosy Stripe'	WAbe	*argutum*	WJur
		'Asian Queen'	CJun

Acanthus ✿ (*Acanthaceae*)

balcanicus misapplied	see *A. hungaricus*	*buergerianum*	CAco CLnd CMen EBee IPap MMuc NLar SMil WJur
caroli-alexandri	see *A. spinosus* L.		
'Colin's Folly'	ECha ESgI	- B&SWJ 12676 from South Korea	WCru
dioscoridis	CDor NLar WHil		
- var. *perringii*	CDor ECha NLar WCot WFar WMal	- var. *formosanum* CWJ 12477	WCru
- - JCA 109.700	WHil	- 'Integrifolium'	see *A. buergerianum* 'Subintegrum'
eminens	WCot	- 'Naruto'	CMCN
hirsutus	CDor MAvo WCot WHil	§ - 'Subintegrum'	CMCN
- subsp. *syriacus*	ECha EPPr SBig SMrm	*caesium* subsp. *giraldii*	WPGP
'Hollande du Nort'	EBee WHil	*campbellii*	MBlu
§ *hungaricus*	CDoC CDor CMac EBee ELan LCro MBel NLar SDix SHar WCot WFar	- 'Exuberance'	CJun
		* - var. *fansipanense*	WJur
- MESE 561	EPPr	*campestre*	Widely available
- 'White Lips'	LCro MNrw NLar WCot WFar	- 'Anny's Globe'	LMaj MBlu
longifolius Host	see *A. hungaricus*	- 'Arends'	EBar
mollis	Widely available	- 'Carnival' (v) ♀^{H6}	ELan MBlu NOra NPip SPoG WMat
- from Turkey	WHil	- 'Elegant'	see *A. campestre* 'Huibers Elegant'
- 'Fielding Gold'	see *A. mollis* 'Hollard's Gold'	- 'Elsrijk'	CAco CBTr CCVT CLnd EBar IPap LMaj
- free-flowering	ESwi		
§ - 'Hollard's Gold'	CBct CDor CExl CMac EBee ECha ELan EMor EPPr EWhm GKin GMaP LBar LRHS MNrw NGdn NWbg SDix SPoG SRms WCAu WCot WFar	- 'Evelyn'	see *A. campestre* 'Queen Elizabeth'
		- 'Evenley Red' ♀^{H6}	EBee LRHS MBlu WHtc
		- 'Fastigiatum'	CCVT CMac
		- 'Green Column'	CAco
		§ - 'Huibers Elegant'	CAco CBTr EBar EHeP ELan LMaj
- 'Jefalba'	see *A. mollis* (Latifolius Group) 'Rue Ledan'	- 'Lienco'	EBar
		- 'Louisa Red Shine'	EBar
- Latifolius Group	CDor SRms	- 'Nanum'	CAco MBlu
§ - - 'Rue Ledan' ♀^{H6}	CBcs EBee ELan EPfP EPPr GBin GMaP LCro LRHS LSto MAvo MBel MNrw NGdn NLar NSti SHor SNoN WCAu WCot WHil WTre	- 'Pendulum'	CEnd
		- 'Postelense'	MBlu
		- 'Pulverulentum' (v)	EBee
		§ - 'Queen Elizabeth'	CAco EBar LMaj MGos SGol
- 'Long Spike'	EPPr	- 'Red Shine'	CAco CBcs CBTr EBar LMaj LRHS SGol
- 'Tasmanian Angel' (v)	CDor CWGN LBar LRHS MBNS NWbg SPoG WCot WFar		
		- 'Royal Ruby'	CLnd MGos
montanus	WHil	- 'Ruby Glow'	CEnd
'Morning's Candle'	EBee ECha ELan ELon LBar MMrt MNrw NGdn NLar WFar	- 'Streetwise'	EHeP
		- 'William Caldwell' ♀^{H6}	CAco CEnd EBar MAsh MBlu WMat
polystachius	WHil	*capillipes*	CAco CBcs CLnd CMCN EBee ELan LMaj LRHS MMuc SMil SPlb WJur WMat
'Ruth's Gold'	WFar		
sennii	CWnw EBee ECha ESwi LRHS NCth NLar SMad SPhx SVen WCot WPGP	- 'Antoine'	CJun MBlu
		- 'Candy Stripe'	see *A.* × *conspicuum* 'Candy Stripe'
spinosus misapplied	see *A. spinosus* Spinosissimus Group	- 'Honey Dew'	SSta
		cappadocicum	CAco CMCN WHtc WJur
§ *spinosus* L.	Widely available	- 'Aureum' ♀^{H6}	CAco CBcs CLnd CMCN CNWT EBee EGrI ELan EPfP GKin IArd LMaj MBlu NLar NOra NPip WMat
- Ferguson's form	EBee MAvo WCot		
- 'Lady Moore' (v)	CDor NLar NWbg		
§ - Spinosissimus Group	CBct CBWd CDor EBee ECha GBin LEdu MGos NLar WCot WFar	- var. *mono*	see *A. pictum*
		- 'Rubrum' ♀^{H6}	CAco CBcs CLnd CMCN CNWT EBar EBee ELan EPfP IArd LCro LMaj LRHS MBlu NOra NPip SGol WMat
- 'Typ Wichmann'	LBar		
'Summer Beauty'	EBee EWes NLar WCot WFar		
'Whitewater' (v)	CBcs CBct CDor CWGN EBee ELan EPfP GKin LBar LBom LCro LRHS MPro NLar SMad SPad SPeP SPoG SRms WCot WFar WHil	- subsp. *sinicum*	WJur
		carpinifolium	CAco CMCN MBlu WJur
		- B&SWJ 10955	WCru
		- B&SWJ 11124	WCru
		§ *caudatifolium*	WJur

Acca ✿ (*Myrtaceae*)

sellowiana	see *Feijoa sellowiana*	- NMWJ 14459	WCru
		§ *caudatum* HWJK 2240	WCru

Acer ✿ (*Sapindaceae*)

		- HWJK 2338	WCru
albopurpurascens NMWJ 14455	WCru	- subsp. *ukurunduense* B&SWJ 12602	WCru
amoenum	WJur	*circinatum*	CAco CCVT CJun CMCN EGrI MBlu MMuc SEND SPlb
- B&SWJ 10916	WCru		
- 'Firecracker'	see *A. palmatum* 'Firecracker'	- B&SWJ 9565	WCru
- 'Ample Surprise'^{PBR}	MBlu	- 'Burgundy Jewel'	CJun MPkF

Acer 63

- 'Gee's Witch's Broom'	MPkF	
- 'Monroe'	CJun	
- 'Pacific Fire'	CJun NLar	
cissifolium	WJur	
- B&SWJ 10801	WCru	
'Cobhay Ruby'	CJun	
§ × *conspicuum*	CJun	
'Candy Stripe'		
- 'Elephant's Ear'	CJun MBlu NLar	
- 'Phoenix'	CEnd CJun EPfP MBlu NCth NLar NOra NPip SPoG WMat	
§ - 'Silver Vein'	CAco CEnd CJun CMCN ELan EPfP NLar SGol SSta WHtc WMat	
crataegifolium	SSta WJur WPGP	
- B&SWJ 11036	WCru	
- 'Ittai-san-nishiki'	SSta	
- 'Meuri-no-ōfu' (v)	SSta	
- 'Veitchii' (v)	CMCN EPfP MBlu SSta	
creticum misapplied	see *A. sempervirens*	
dasycarpum	see *A. saccharinum*	
davidii	CAco CBcs CCVT CTsd EGrI EHeP IPap LCro LMaj MBlu MGos MMuc SGol SSta WHtc	
§ - 'Canton'	CJun SSta	
- 'Cantonspark'	see *A. davidii* 'Canton'	
- 'Cascade'	MBlu	
- 'Diamondback'	LRHS MPri	
- 'George Forrest' ♀H5	CMac CMCN ELan LCro MGos MMuc NLar NOra NPip SPoG SSta WMat	
- 'Hagelunie'	SSta	
- 'Hansu-suru' (v)	SSta	
- 'Karmen'	CJun SSta	
- 'Madeline Spitta'	CAco	
- 'Purple Bark'	CJun SSta	
- 'Rosalie'	CJun MBlu SSta	
- 'Sekka'	SSta	
- 'Silver Vein'	see *A.* × *conspicuum* 'Silver Vein'	
- VIPER ('Mindavi')	CAco CBTr CCVT EBee ELan EPfP IArd LCro LMaj LMil LRHS LSRN MPri NOra NPip SAth SPoG WMat	
duplicatoserratum	WCru	
NMWJ 14599		
erythranthum	WCru	
FMWJ 13157		
§ 'Esk Flamingo' (v)	CAco CJun CMac CWnw EUrb LCro LRHS MBlu NOra NPip SGol SMad SPoG WMat	
fabri	WPGP	
flabellatum	CJun	
forrestii	CMCN MBlu MMuc SChF WJur WPGP	
- 'Alice'	CEnd CJun SSta	
- 'Inoense'	SSta	
- 'Sirene'	SSta	
- 'Sparkling'	CJun	
× *freemanii*	CMCN LMaj	
- 'Armstrong'	CAco EBar EHeP IPap LMaj LSRN MBlu	
- AUTUMN BLAZE ('Jeffersred') ♀H4	Widely available	
- AUTUMN FANTASY ('Dtr 102')	EBar SEWo	
- CELEBRATION ('Celzam')	CCVT CLnd EBee EHeP IPap LMaj MGos NPip	
- 'Indian Summer'	see *A.* × *freemanii* 'Morgan'	
§ - 'Morgan'	CBTr CMac EPfP LCro MGos WHtc WMat WMou	
ginnala	see *A. tataricum* subsp. *ginnala*	
glabrum B&SWJ 14119	WCru	
globosum	see *A. platanoides* 'Globosum'	
grandidentatum	see *A. saccharum* subsp. *grandidentatum*	
griseum ♀H5	Widely available	
grosseri	CMCN	
- var. *hersii*	EGrI ELan LSRN MMuc NOra SArc SSta WHtc WMat	
heldreichii	CMCN	
heptaphlebium FMWJ 13369	WCru	
ICE DRAGON ('Isiid' PBR) (Jack Frost Series)	MPkF NLar WMat	
japonicum	MMuc SEWo	
- B&SWJ 12847	WCru	
- CWJ 12840	WCru	
§ - 'Aconitifolium' ♀H6	Widely available	
- 'Akame hauchiwa'	MPkF	
- 'Meu-jutan'	CJun	
- 'Attaryi'	MBlu WLov	
- 'Aureum'	see *A. shirasawanum* 'Aureum'	
- 'Emmit's Pumpkins'	CJun	
- 'Filicifolium'	see *A. japonicum* 'Aconitifolium'	
- 'Green Cascade' ♀H6	CEnd CJun CMac MGos MPkF NCth	
- 'King's Copse'	CJun MPkF	
- 'Laciniatum'	see *A. japonicum* 'Aconitifolium'	
- 'Ogurayama'	see *A. shirasawanum* 'Ogurayama'	
- 'Ō-taki'	CJun	
- 'Ruby'	MBlu	
- 'Vitifolium' ♀H6	CAco CCVT CDoC CEnd CJun CMac CMCN EGrI ELan LMaj LRHS MBlu MGos NLar SArc SMil SPoG SSta WCha WFar WLov	
kawakamii	see *A. caudatifolium*	
laevigatum FMWJ 13378	WCru	
- FMWJ 13439	WCru	
§ - var. *reticulatum*	SArc	
- var. *salweenense*	WPGP	
laurinum FMWJ 13412	WCru	
laxiflorum	LRHS SSta	
macrophyllum	CAco CBcs CMCN MBlu MMuc SMil WJur	
- B&SWJ 13183	WCru	
§ *maximowiczianum*	MMuc MPkF WJur	
metcalfii	SMil	
micranthum ♀H6	CMCN MBlu WJur WPGP	
- CWJ 12843	WCru	
miyabei	SMil	
mono	see *A. pictum*	
monspessulanum	CAco CMCN LEdu LMaj SEND WJur	
morifolium	WJur	
- B&SWJ 11473	WCru	
morrisonense Hayata	see *A. caudatifolium*	
negundo	CAco CMCN EBar	
- B&SWJ 14060	WCru	
- 'Aureomarginatum' (v)	CAco	
- 'Aureovariegatum' (v)	WCha	
§ - 'Elegans' (v)	CEnd CMCN SArc	
- 'Elegantissimum'	see *A. negundo* 'Elegans'	
- 'Flamingo' (v)	CAco CCVT CEnd CMac CMCN EBar EGren ELan IPap MGos NLar NOra NPip SArc SEWo SGol SPoG WCha WFar WHtc WMat	
- 'Kelly's Gold'	CAco CBcs CBTr CEnd ELan EUrb LRHS NLar NPip SPoG SReu WFar WMat	
- subsp. *mexicanum*	WJur	
- 'Sensation'	NLar	
- 'Variegatum' (v)	CAco EGren LMaj LRHS SAth WCha	
- var. *violaceum* ♀H6	CEnd ELan EPfP SReu SVen	
nikoense misapplied	see *A. maximowiczianum*	
nipponicum	WJur	

NORTH WIND ('Isinw'PBR) (Jack Frost Series)	CBTr MPkF NLar WMat
oblongum	WJur
oliverianum	MBlu WJur
- subsp. *formosanum* NMWJ 14460	WCru
- - NMWJ 14514	WCru
- - NMWJ 14521	WCru
opalus	CAco CMCN SEND
orientale misapplied	see *A. sempervirens*
ORIENTALIA ('Minorient')	CAco LRHS MGos SArc
PACIFIC SUNSET ('Warrenred')	CAco EBar LMaj LRHS NLar SAth SEWo
palmatum	Widely available
- (D)	CAco CCVT CEnd CJun CMac EpfP LCro LMaj LRHS LSRN MAsh MGos NLar SGol SSta WFar WMat
- 'Abigail Rose' (Dw/v)	NWbg
- 'Akane' (P)	EBee NWbg WFar WLov
§ - 'Aka-shigitatsu-sawa' (M)	CAco CJun CMac CMen MGos MPkF NLar NWbg WFar
- 'Akegarasu' (M)	CJun CMCN
- 'Akishino' (A)	MPkF
- 'Alloys' (D)	MPkF
- 'Alpenweiss' (P)	CJun MPkF NWbg
- 'Alpine Surprise' (Dw)	SAko
- 'Amagi-shigure' (M)	CJun LCro MPkF NLar NWbg
- 'Amber Ghost' (M)	CJun NWbg
- 'Andras'	MPkF
- 'Anne Irene'PBR (P)	EBee EGren LBuc LRHS MPkF NCth
- 'Annick'	CJun
- 'Aoba-jo' (Dw)	CJun CMen NWbg SMil
- 'Ao-kanzashi' (P/v)	MPkF
- 'Ao-shidare' (D)	CJun
- 'Aoshime-no-uchi'	see *A. palmatum* 'Shinobuga-oka'
- 'Aoyagi' (P)	CAco CEnd CJun CMCN CMen GKin MPkF MSwo NCth NLar SMil WFar
- 'Aoyagi-gawa' (L)	CJun
§ - 'Arakawa' (P)	CAco CMac MGos MPkF NLar NWbg SArc
- 'Arakawa-ukon'	CJun
- 'Aratama' (Dw)	EMac LRHS MPkF NWbg SMil
- 'Ariadne' (M/v) ♀H6	CEnd CJun EGrI MGos NWbg SArc SMil SPoG WCha
- 'Ariake-nomura' (A)	MPkF
- 'Asahi-zuru' (P/v)	CAco CMCN CMen EGren LBuc MGos NWbg WMat
- 'Atrolineare' (L)	CAco CMen LRHS MPkF SArc WCha WFar
- 'Atropurpureum' (A)	Widely available
- 'Attraction' (P)	CMac NTrD NWbg
- 'Aureum' (P)	CAco CMCN CMen EGren ELan EpfP LMaj LMil LRHS MAsh MBlu MGos MPkF MSwo NLar SPoG WFar
- 'Autumn Fire' (D)	CJun
- 'Autumn Glory' (M)	CEnd CJun CMac EGrI LRHS MBlu NWbg WFar
- 'Autumn Red' (M)	NWbg
* - 'Autumn Showers'	CEnd CJun
- 'Azuma-murasaki' (M)	CJun EGrI MPkF SMil
- 'Baby Lace' (Dw)	SAko
- 'Baldsmith' (D)	CAco CJun CWnw EMac LRHS MPkF
- 'Barrie Bergman' (D)	CJun NLar
- 'Bell Green' (A)	MPkF
- 'Beni-gasa' (M)	MPkF
- 'Beni-hime' (Dw)	CCVT NWbg
- 'Beni-hoshi' (Dw)	MPkF NWbg
- 'Beni-kagami' (M)	CAco CJun MPkF
- 'Beni-kawa' (P)	CJun CMCN LRHS MPkF
- 'Beni-komachi' (P)	CAco CDoC CEnd CMac CMCN CMen EGrI LBuc MGos MPkF NWbg WSpi
- 'Beni-kosode' (Dw/v)	NLar
- 'Beni-maiko' (P) ♀H6	CAco CDoC CEnd CJun CMCN CMen CSBt CWnw EGren EGrI EUrb LBuc LCro LRHS MGos MPkF NWbg SOrN SReu SRms WCFE WCha WFar WLov
- 'Beni-otake' (L)	CJun ESMi LMaj LRHS MGos NWbg SAko SMil WFar
- 'Beni-otome'	MPkF NWbg
- 'Beni-schichi-henge' (P/v)	CAco CMCN CMCN CWGN MAsh MPkF NOra NWbg SAko SSta WMat
- 'Beni-shidare' (D)	SArc
- 'Beni-shidare Tricolor'	see *A. palmatum* 'Toyama-nishiki'
- 'Beni-shidare Variegated'	see *A. palmatum* 'Toyama-nishiki'
- 'Beni-shi-en' (P)	CJun
- 'Beni-shigitatsu-sawa'	see *A. palmatum* 'Aka-shigitatsu-sawa'
- 'Beni-tsukasa' (P/v) ♀H6	CAco CEnd CJun CMCN NWbg SSta
- 'Beni-tsukasa-shidare' (D)	MBlu
- 'Beni-tsuru'	MPkF
- 'Beni-yubi-gohon' (P)	MPkF
- 'Berrima Bridge' (D)	CJun MPkF
- 'Berry Broom'	CAco LBuc MPkF
- 'Berry Dwarf' (Dw)	CJun
- 'Bewley's Red' (D)	CJun
- 'Bi Hō' (P)	CAco CCVT CDoC CJun CMac CWnw EGren ELan EpfP EUrb LBom LBuc LCro LMil LSRN MPkF MPri NLar NWbg SAth SGol WCha WFar
- BLACK LACE ('Jww2') (M)	CAco EpfP GKin LBuc MGos MPkF MPri NTrD WCha
- 'Blackbeard's Gold'	MPkF
- 'Bloodgood' (A) ♀H6	Widely available
- 'Bonfire' ambig.	CJun
- 'Bonnie Bergman'	LRHS SMil WFar
- 'Boskoop Glory' (A)	GKin
- 'Brandt's Dwarf' (Dw)	EGrI MPkF
- 'Brocade' (D)	CJun MPkF
- 'Bronzewing' (D)	CJun
- BROWN SUGAR ('Jww7'PBR)	WCha WSpi
- 'Bultinck' (M)	MPkF
- 'Burgundy Lace' (M) ♀H6	CAco CEnd CJun CMCN CWnw ELan EMac EUrb GKin LMil MAsh MGos MPkF NWbg SMil SOrN SPoG SSta WCha
- 'Butterfly' (P/v)	CAco CBcs CJun CMac CMCN CMen CWGN ELan ELon LBom LCro LMaj LMil LRHS LSRN MAsh MBlu MGos MPkF NCth NLar NTrD NWbg SArc SGol SReu WCha WFar
- BUTTERSCOTCH ('Jww8'PBR)	CAco CWGN
- 'Calico' (P)	CJun
- 'Caperci Dwarf' (Dw)	MPkF NWbg
- 'Carlis Corner' (Dw)	MPkF
- 'Carminium'	see *A. palmatum* 'Corallinum'
- 'Cascade'	LBuc LRHS
- CASCADE EMERALD ('Sonkoot8')	LBuc MPkF
- 'Cascade Gold' (P)	LBuc MPkF NLar WCha
- CASCADE RUBY ('Sonkoot6')	LBuc MPkF
- 'Chantilly Lace' (D)	CJun MPkF
- 'Chikuma-no' (A)	MPkF
- 'Chiri-hime' (M)	NWbg
- 'Chirimen-nishiki' (P/v)	MPkF

	Cultivar	Codes
	- 'Chishio' (P)	CAco CMCN CMen ESMi LRHS MPkF NWbg
	- 'Chishio Improved' (P)	CDoC CJun CMac CMCN MGos NLar NWbg SArc
	- 'Chitose-yama' (M) ♀H6	CJun CMac CMCN EGrI GKin LRHS MAsh MGos MSwo NLar SMil SSta WFar WLov
§	- 'Chiyo-hime' (Dw)	CAco CDoC CWnw EGren LBuc LRHS MPri NTrD NWbg WCFE WCha WFar
	- 'Cobhay Beacon'	CJun
	- 'Cobhay Copper Cloud' **new**	CJun
	- 'Cobhay Eclipse'	CJun
	- 'Cobhay Flare'	CJun
	- 'Cobhay Glow'	CJun
	- 'Cobhay Salmon'	CJun
	- 'Cobhay Splendour' **new**	CJun
	- 'Cobhay Yeti'	CJun
	- 'Coonara Pygmy' (Dw)	CMac CMCN EMac GKin LRHS MPkF
	- 'Coral Pink' (Dw)	MPkF
§	- 'Corallinum' (P) ♀H5	CAco CJun CMCN CMen EGren EGrI EUrb LRHS NLar NWbg SAth SPoG
	- var. *coreanum* B&SWJ 8606	WCru
	- 'Cosmos' (v)	MPkF
	- 'Crimson Carol' (M)	CJun
	- 'Crimson Prince'	CJun EMac
	- 'Crimson Princess' (D)	CDoC CWnw EGrI LMil MPkF NPip NWbg WMat
	- 'Crimson Queen' (D) ♀H6	CAco CBcs CBrac CEnd CJun CMac CMen ELan EMac EPfP GKin LBom LBuc LMaj LMil MAsh MGos NLar NPip NTrD NWbg SArc SMil WCFE WCha WFar WMat
	- 'Crippsii' (D)	CMac MPkF NWbg SArc
§	- 'Crumple Leaf' (M)	CJun MPkF
	- 'Cynthia's Crown Jewel'	NWbg
§	- 'Daimyō' (A)	CAco
	- 'Daimyō-nishiki'	see *A. palmatum* 'Taimin-nishiki'
	- 'Deshōjō' (P)	CAco CMCN CMen EGren LBuc LMaj MBlu MGos MPkF NCth NLar NWbg SArc WMat WSpi
	- 'Diana' (Dw)	CJun CMen NTrD
	- 'Dissectum' (D)	CAco CBTr CDoC CWnw EGren EGrI EHeP LBuc LCro LRHS MSwo NCth NOra NPip SOrN WCha WFar WJur WMat
	- 'Dissectum Atropurpureum' (D)	CAco CCVT EGrI LMil SOrN
	- 'Dissectum Flavescens' (D)	CAco CBcs CEnd CJun CMac EMac LBuc MBlu MGos MPkF NPip NWbg SArc WMat
§	- 'Dissectum Nigrum' (D)	CJun CMac LBuc MAsh SArc WFar
	- 'Dissectum Palmatifidum' (D)	CAco CMen EMac MPkF NWbg
	- 'Dissectum Rubrifolium' (D)	CAco CCVT MPkF
	- 'Dissectum Viride Group	Widely available
	- 'Dixie Delight'	MPkF NLar
	- 'Doctor Baker' (D)	MPkF
	- 'Doctor Tilt' (P)	CAco
	- 'Dolly Hill'	MPkF
	- 'Donzuru-bo'	CJun
	- 'Dormansland'	CEnd
	- 'Dr Seuss' (L)	MPkF NLar
	- 'Dragon King' (D)	MPkF
	- 'Dragon Master'	MPkF
	- 'Dragon's Fire'	CJun
	- 'Earthfire'	MPkF
I	- 'Ebbingei'	CMac
	- 'Eddisbury' (P) ♀H6	CAco CJun MBlu SMil
	- 'Edna Bergman' (M)	CJun
	- 'Effegi'	see *A. palmatum* 'Fireglow'
	- 'Eimini' (Dw)	MPkF
§	- 'Elegans' (M) ♀H6	CAco MAsh SArc SMil
	- 'Elizabeth' (Dw)	CJun
	- 'Ellen' (D)	CJun LRHS MPkF SMil WLov
	- 'Elmwood Spreader' (D)	MPkF
	- 'Emerald Isle'	MPkF
	- 'Emerald Lace' (D) ♀H6	CAco CBcs CDoC CJun CSBt CWnw EBee EGren EMac EPfP EUrb GKin IPap LBom LBuc LCro LMil LRHS MGos MPkF NLar NTrD SArc SHor SPoG SRms WCFE WCha WFar
	- 'Emma' (D)	LRHS
§	- 'Emperor 1' (A)	CAco CJun CWnw EBar EBee EGren EMac LRHS MAsh MBlu MPkF NPip SMil WCha WFar WLov WMat
	- 'Englishtown' (Dw)	LRHS
	- 'Enkan' (L)	CBTr CDoC CEnd CJun CSBt CWGN CWnw EPfP LBuc LMil LRHS MAsh MGos MPkF MPri NLar NOra NPip NTrD SPoG WMat
	- 'Ever Autumn'	CJun
	- 'Ever Red'	see *A. palmatum* 'Dissectum Nigrum'
	- 'Extravaganza' (v)	LBuc LCro LRHS MPri
	- 'Fascination' (M)	CJun
	- 'Felice' (D)	CJun MPkF NWbg
	- 'Festival'	EBee LBuc LRHS MPkF
	- 'Filigree' (Dw/v)	CAco CJun CMCN MPkF NWbg
	- 'Fior d'Arancio' (M)	CAco CJun EGren MPkF NLar
§	- 'Firecracker' PBR (D)	CAco CCVT CDoC EBee EGren EPfP GKin LBom LBuc LMil MPkF NCth NLar NTrD SArc WCha WFar WSpi
§	- 'Fireglow' (A)	CAco CCVT CDoC CJun CMCN CWnw EBar EGren EGrI EMac LBom LBuc LMaj LRHS LSRN MGos MPkF NCth NTrD SAko SArc SAth SMil WFar
	- 'First Ghost' (M/v)	CJun NWbg
	- 'Fujinami'	NLar
	- 'Furu-kawa' (A)	MPkF
	- 'Garnet' (D) ♀H6	Widely available
	- 'Garnet Tower' (D)	MPkF
	- 'Garyū' (Dw)	MPkF
	- 'Geisha' (Dw)	NWbg
	- 'Geisha Gone Wild' (P/v)	CJun NWbg
	- 'Gentaku'	CJun
	- 'Germaine's Gyration' (D)	CJun
	- 'Ginko-san'	LRHS
	- 'Glowing Embers' (P)	CJun NWbg
	- GOING GREEN ('Sonkootgre' PBR)	CAco EGren EUrb LCro MPkF MPri NLar WCha
	- 'Golden Falls'	NLar
	- 'Golden Pond' (A)	CJun MPkF NWbg
	- 'Goshiki-kotohime' (Dw/v)	CJun LBuc NWbg
	- 'Goshiki-shidare'	see *A. palmatum* 'Toyama-nishiki'
	- 'Grandma Ghost' (M)	CJun NWbg
	- 'Green Fingers' (D)	MPkF NLar
	- 'Green Flag'	CJun
	- 'Green Globe' (D)	CAco CJun MPkF SArc
	- 'Green Hornet' (D)	CJun
	- 'Green Lace' (D)	MPkF
	- 'Green Mist' (D)	CJun CWnw LRHS

- 'Green Star' (A) — MPkF
- 'Green Trompenburg' (M) — CAco CJun LRHS MBlu MPkF SMil
- 'Green Ueno-Yama' — CAco CJun MPkF
§ - 'Gwen's Rose Delight' (P/v) — CAco CDoC CMac CWGN EMac GKin LBuc LMaj LMil LSRN MAsh MGos MPkF NLar NOra NTrD NWbg SMil WCha WMat
§ - 'Hagoromo' — CMac
- 'Hamaotome' (A) — MPkF
- 'Hanabi-no-mai' (M/v) — MPkF
- 'Hanami-nishiki' (Dw) — NWbg
- 'Hanzel' (D) — MPkF
- 'Happy Corallinum' (A) — CJun
- 'Harusame' (P/v) — MPkF
- 'Heartbeat' (D) — CDoC CJun MPkF
- 'Heffner's Red' — CJun
- 'Heguri' (M) — MPkF
- 'Heiwa' — MPkF
- 'Hemelrijt' (M) — MPkF
- var. *heptalobum* — CMCN
- 'Heptalobum Elegans Purpureum' — see *A. palmatum* 'Hessei'
- 'Herbstfeuer' (P) — CJun LRHS
§ - 'Hessei' (M) — LRHS MBlu MPkF SMil
- 'Hida-hanabi' (M) — CJun
- 'Higasa-yama' (P/v) — CAco CEnd CMCN CWGN NWbg SArc
- 'Highland Sunset' — CEnd
- 'Hime-shōjō' — CAco LBuc MGos MPkF NLar
- 'Hi-no-tsukasa' — MPkF
- 'Hippy-fin-mo' (Dw) — MPkF
- 'Hiryū' (P) — CAco SArc
- 'Hōgyoku' (A) — CAco CJun CMCN MPkF
- 'Hondo-ji' (M) — MPkF
- 'Hoshi-kuzu' (Dw) — MPkF NWbg
- 'Hupp's Dwarf' (Dw) — MPkF
- 'Hupp's Red Willow' — MPkF NLar NPip WMat
- 'Hyōtei' — MPkF
- 'Ibo-nishiki' (P) — CMen MPkF
- 'Ichigyōji' (A) — CEnd CJun CMen SMil
- 'Iijima-sunago' (M) — MPkF
- 'Ijoshi' (v) **new** — WFar
- 'Ikandi' (P/v) — NWbg
- 'Inaba-shidare' (D) ♀H6 — Widely available
- 'Inazuma' (M) — CAco CJun CMCN EGrI MPkF
- 'Irish Lace' — CJun
- 'Isobel' — NTrD
- 'Iso-chidori' (Dw) — MPkF
- 'Issai-nishiki' — CMen MPkF
- 'Itami-nishiki' — MPkF
- 'Jane' — CCVT CJun NTrD
- 'Japanese Sunrise' (P) — CCVT CJun EMac MPkF NLar NPip NTrD NWbg WMat
- 'Jeddeloh Orange' (D) — MPkF NWbg
- 'Jerre Schwartz' (Dw) — CAco CCVT CDoC CEnd CWnw EGren LBuc MGos MPkF MPri NCth NWbg SBig SOrN SPoG WCha WFar
- 'Jirō-shidare' (P) — LRHS NLar
- 'JJ' — CJun
- 'Johnnie's Pink' (P) — NWbg
- 'Julia D.' — CJun
- 'Kaba' (Dw) — MPkF SPoG
- 'Kaga-shidare' — MPkF
- 'Kagero' (A/v) — MPkF
§ - 'Kagiri-nishiki' (P/v) — CJun CMac CMen EGren MPkF NWbg SMil
- 'Kamagata' (Dw) — CAco CEnd CJun CMCN CMen ESMi MAsh MPkF NLar NWbg
- 'Karaori-nishiki' (P/v) — MPkF
- 'Karasu-gawa' (P/v) — CWGN MPkF NWbg WFar
- 'Kasagiyama' (M) — CEnd CJun NWbg
- 'Kasen-nishiki' (P) — MPkF
- 'Kashima' (Dw) — CJun CMCN CMen MBlu MPkF NWbg
- 'Katja' — CJun
- 'Katsura' (P) ♀H6 — Widely available
- 'Katsura-hime' (P) — MPkF
- 'Kawahara Rose' — MPkF NWbg
- 'Kegon' (M) — MPkF
- 'Keiden' — MPkF
- 'Kenko-nishiki' — MPkF
- 'Kenzan' (M) — CJun
- 'Ki-hachijō' (M) — CAco CJun EGren LRHS MPkF SMil WCha WFar
- 'Killarney' (M) — CJun
- 'Kinky Krinkle' (P) — CJun
- 'Kinran' (M) — CAco CJun MPkF
- 'Kinshi' (L) ♀H6 — CBTr CEnd CJun CMCN EBee EPfP LRHS MPkF NOra NPip NWbg SAko WLov WMat
- 'Kiri-nishiki' (D) — CJun CMen MPkF
- 'Ki-shuzan' (M) — CJun
- 'Kiyohime' (Dw) ♀H6 — CAco CMCN CMen EGrI ESMi NWbg
- 'Koba-shōjō' (M) — MPkF
- 'Kogane-sakae' (A) — CJun
- 'Kokobunji-nishiki' (v) — MPkF NWbg
- 'Komachi-hime' (Dw) — MPkF NWbg
- 'Komon-nishiki' (P/v) — MPkF NWbg
- 'Korean Gem' (M) — CJun MPkF
- 'Koriba' (P) — CJun MPkF
- 'Koshibori-nishiki' (P) — MPkF
§ - 'Koshimino' — CMac
- 'Kotohime' (Dw) — CAco CMCN CMen CWnw MPkF NLar SPoG
- 'Koto-ito-komachi' (Dw/L) — CJun CMen MPkF NWbg
- 'Koto-maru' (Dw) — CAco LBuc MPkF NLar NWbg
- 'Koto-no-ito' (L) — CAco CMCN EGren LBuc LRHS MAsh MBlu MGos MPkF NCth NLar SAko SMil SPoG WCha WFar WLov
- 'Koyamadani-nishiki' (M) — MPkF
- 'Koya-san' (Dw) — MPkF
- 'Kōyō-ao-shidare' — MPkF
- 'Koyuki' — MPkF NWbg
- 'Kurabu-yama' (M) — MPkF
- 'Kurenai-jishi' (Dw) — MPkF
- 'Kuro-hime' (Dw) — LRHS MPkF SMil WFar
- 'Kurui-jishi' (Dw) — MPkF
- 'Kyōryū' — MPkF
- 'Kyra' — MPkF
- 'Laura's Love' (D) — MPkF
- 'Lemon Lime Lace' (D) — MPkF
- 'Limelight' (P) — CDoC
§ - 'Linearilobum' (L) — CAco CBTr CDoC CMen EMac EPfP LBuc LMaj LRHS LSRN MGos MPkF NLar NOra NPip SArc SMil WLov WMat
* - 'Lionheart' (D) — CAco CJun CWGN MGos NLar SArc
- 'Lisa' (v) — MPkF
- 'Little Margie' (Dw) — MPkF
- 'Little Princess' — see *A. palmatum* 'Chiyo-hime'
- 'Little Red' (Dw) — LBuc MPkF MPri
- 'Livy' (Dw) — LBuc
- 'Lucky Star' (P) — CJun MBlu
- 'Lutescens' (A) — MPkF
- 'Lydia' — MPkF
- 'Maiko' (P) — MPkF
- 'Mallet' — NLar
- 'Mama' (P) — NWbg
- 'Manyō-no-sato' (P/v) — CAco LRHS MPkF NLar NWbg

- 'Mapi-no-machi-hime' (Dw)	CEnd CJun CMCN CMen LRHS	- 'Octopus' (D)	CJun MPkF
- 'Marakumo' (P)	MPkF	- 'Ōgi-nagashi' (P/v)	MPkF
- 'Marasaki-yama'	MPkF	- 'Ōgon-sarasa' (A)	CJun MPkF
- 'Margaret Bee' (A)	CJun	- 'Ojishi' (Dw)	MPkF
- 'Marjan' (M)	CJun MPkF NLar	- 'Ō-kagami' (P)	CAco CJun CMac CWnw EGrI
- 'Marlo'^PBR (D)	MAsh MGos		EMac LRHS MAsh MPkF NWbg
- 'Masamurasaki'	MPkF		WFar
- 'Masukagami' (P/v)	CAco CJun MPkF NWbg	- 'Okken'	MPkF
- 'Matsu-ga-e' (P/v)	MPkF	- 'Okukuji-nishiki' (P)	CAco
- 'Matsukaze'	CJun	- 'Okushimo' (P)	CEnd CJun CMac CMCN CMen
- var. *matsumurae* B&SWJ 11100	WCru		LBuc MPkF NLar NWbg
- 'Olsen's Frosted Strawberry' (P)			NWbg
- 'Matsuyoi' (A)	CJun MPkF	- 'Omato' (A)	CJun MPkF
- 'Meihō-nishiki' (A/v)	CJun	- 'Omure-yama' (M)	CAco CEnd CJun CMac CMCN
- 'Melanie'	MPkF		ESMi MPkF NWbg SGol
- 'Mendip Fantasy'	CMen	- 'Orange Dream' (P) ♀H6	Widely available
- 'Meoto'	CJun	- ORANGE LACE ('Sonkoot9'^PBR)	LCro MPkF WFar
- METAMORPHOSA ('Arjos1'^PBR)	CBcs CWnw LRHS NCth NLar WCha WFar	- 'Orangeola' (D) ♀H6	CAco CJun CWnw EGren EGrI
- 'Michiko'	MPkF		GKin LBom LBuc LRHS MAsh
- 'Midore-mure-hibari'	MPkF		MGos MPkF NLar NWbg SArc SMil
- 'Midori-no-teiboku' (Dw)	CJun MPkF		SPoG SRms WFar WLov WMat
- 'Mika' (P)	MPkF SMil	- 'Oranges and Lemons' (M)	CJun
- 'Mikawa-yatsubusa' (Dw)	CAco CMac CMCN CMen CWnw EMac LBuc LMil MGos MPkF NLar NWbg SAko	- 'Oregon Sunset' (M)	CJun MPkF NPip SMil WMat
- 'Oridono-nishiki' (P/v)			CAco CEnd CJun CMac CMCN CWGN EGren ESMi LBuc LRHS
- 'Mikazuki' (M/v)	CJun LRHS MPkF		MBlu MGos MPkF NLar NWbg SBig
- 'Mila' (M)	MPkF NWbg		SMil SPoG SSta WCha WFar
- 'Mimaye'	CJun	- 'Oriental Lace' (D)	MPkF
- 'Mini Mondo'	MPkF	- 'Oriental Mystery'	MPkF NWbg
- 'Mioun' (D)	MPkF	- 'Ori-zuru'	MPkF
- 'Mira'	MPkF	- 'Ornatum' (D) ♀H6	CAco CMCN EGren EGrI LBuc LMaj
- 'Mirte' (M)	CAco CJun		LRHS LSRN MAsh MGos MPkF
- 'Mischa'	MPkF		MSwo NCth NLar NWbg SMil
- 'Miss Piggy'	NWbg	- 'Ōsakazuki' (A) ♀H6	Widely available
- 'Misty Moon'	MPkF	- 'Ōshio-beni' (A)	CJun EGrI WSpi
- 'Miwa'	MPkF	- 'Ōshū-beni' (M)	CJun
- 'Mizuho-beni' (P)	CJun NLar	- 'Ōshū-shidare' (M)	CJun MPkF
- 'Mizu-kuguri' (A)	CJun MPkF	- 'Oto-hime' (Dw)	CJun EGrI
- 'Momiji-gawa' (A)	LRHS MBlu SMil	- 'Otome-zakura' (P)	CJun MPkF NWbg
- 'Momoiro-koya-san' (Dw)	CJun MPkF	- 'Otto's Dissectum' (D)	CJun
- 'Mon Papa' (M)	CJun MPkF NLar NWbg	- 'Peaches and Cream' (M/v)	CJun NWbg SArc
- 'Monzukushi' (A)	CJun MPkF	- 'Pendulum Julian' (D)	CAco
- 'Moonfire' (M)	CAco CJun CMCN EMac LMil LRHS MAsh MPkF NLar WFar	- 'Péve Chameleon'	MPkF NLar
- 'Péve Dave'			CDoC CEnd LBuc LRHS LSRN MPkF NCth
- 'Moonglow'	CJun	- 'Péve Multicolour'	MPkF NLar
- 'Mugiwara-nishiki' (L/v)	MPkF	- 'Péve Ollie'	MPkF NLar
- 'Murasaki-hime' (Dw)	MPkF	- 'Péve Stanley'	MPkF
- 'Murasaki-iroha' (A)	MPkF	- 'Péve Starfish'	NLar
- 'Murasaki-kiyohime' (Dw)	CJun CMCN MPkF	- 'Phoenix' (P)	CAco CBcs CJun CSBt CWnw
- 'Murasaki-shikibu'	MPkF		EGren EGrI EUrb IPap LBuc LMil
- 'Mure-hibari' (M)	CJun MPkF		LRHS MGos MPkF NLar NTrD
- 'Murogawa' (A)	CJun		NWbg WCha WFar
- 'Musashino' (M)	CJun	- 'Pine Bark Maple'	see *A. palmatum* 'Nishiki-gawa'
- 'Mutsu-beni-shidare' (D)	NLar	- 'Pink Ballerina' (Dw/v)	CJun
- 'Mystic Jewel' (P)	LBuc MPkF	- 'Pink Filigree' (D)	CAco CJun
- 'Nagisa-hime' (M)	MPkF	- 'Pink Passion' (v)	CAco MPkF WFar
- 'Nakakamado Weeping'	NLar	- 'Pixie' (Dw)	CAco CBTr CWnw EGren LBuc
- 'Nanase-gawa' (A)	MPkF		LRHS MGos MSwo NOra NPip
- 'Nathan'	MPkF		NWbg SAko SArc SBig SMil WCha
- 'Nicholsonii' (M)	CAco LRHS MPkF		WFar WLov WMat
- 'Nigrum' (A)	NOra	- 'Princetown Gold'	LRHS MPri
- 'Nimura Princess'	MPkF	- 'Pung-kil' (L)	LRHS MBlu MPkF NLar NWbg SAko
§ - 'Nishiki-gawa' (P)	CJun CMen MPkF NWbg SMil WFar		SMil WFar
- 'Nishiki-momiji' (P)	LRHS WFar	- 'Purple Ghost' (M)	CJun NWbg
- 'Nomura'	CJun	- 'Radiant' (v)	MPkF
- 'Nomurishidare' misapplied	see *A. palmatum* 'Shōjō-shidare'	- 'Rainbow' (M/v)	MPkF NLar
- 'Noto' (A)	MPkF	- 'Raraflora' (D)	CJun
- 'Nuresagi' (M)	CAco CEnd CJun MPkF		

Cultivar	Codes
- 'Red Autumn Lace' (D)	CJun
- 'Red Baron' (A)	CJun
- 'Red Cloud' (L)	CJun MPkF
- 'Red Dragon' (D)	CAco CJun CWGN LBuc LRHS MAsh NWbg SAko SMil
- RED EMPEROR	see *A. palmatum* 'Emperor 1'
- 'Red Feather' (D)	CJun LBuc LRHS MGos MPkF
- 'Red Filigree Lace' (D)	CJun MPkF
- 'Red Flash' (A)	CJun MPkF
- 'Red Jonas'	CAco
- 'Red Pygmy' (L) ♀H6	CAco CJun CMac CMCN CWGN EGren EPfP GKin LMil LRHS MAsh MBlu MGos MPri NLar NWbg SAko SMil SPoG WLov
- 'Red Select' (D)	MPkF
- 'Red Spider' (L)	CJun MPkF
- 'Red Wood' (P)	CJun SArc
- 'Redwine'PBR (P)	CDoC EPfP LBuc MPkF
- 'Relish' (M/v)	MPkF
- 'Reticulatum'	see *A. palmatum* 'Shigi-tatsu-sawa'
- 'Reticulatum Como' (v)	NWbg
- 'Reticulatum Purple'	MPkF
- 'Rhode Island Red' (Dw)	LBuc MPkF NLar
- 'Ribesifolium'	see *A. palmatum* 'Shishi-gashira'
- 'Rising Sun'	CJun
- 'Roseomarginatum'	see *A. palmatum* 'Kagiri-nishiki'
- 'Rough Bark Maple'	see *A. palmatum* 'Arakawa'
- 'Royle' (Dw)	MPkF
I - 'Rubrum Kaiser'	CJun
- 'Ruby' (P)	MPkF
- 'Ruby Ridge'	see *A. palmatum* 'Crumple Leaf'
- 'Ruby Star'	MPkF
- 'Rufescens' (P)	MPkF
- 'Ruslyn-in-the-Pink' (Dw)	MPkF NWbg
- 'Ryokū-ryū' (P)	MPkF
- 'Ryusen'	CAco LBuc MBlu MPkF NLar SArc SPoG SWCha WMat
- 'Ryuzu' (Dw)	CJun MPkF
- 'Sagara-nishiki' (v)	CEnd NWbg
- 'Sai-ho'	MPkF
- 'Samidare' (A)	CJun
§ - 'Sango-kaku' (P) ♀H6	Widely available
- 'Sanguineum' (P)	LBuc NLar
- 'Saoshika' (A)	CAco CJun MPkF NLar
- 'Sa-otome' (P)	MPkF
- 'Satsuki-beni' (M)	CJun CMen EGrI MPkF NWbg
- 'Sawa-chidori' (M)	MPkF NWbg
- 'Sazanami' (M)	CEnd CJun MPkF NWbg
- 'Scolopendriifolium'	see *A. palmatum* 'Linearilobum'
- 'Seigen' (Dw)	CMCN CMen MBlu
- 'Seiryū' (D) ♀H6	Widely available
- 'Seiun-kaku' (P)	CJun MPkF NWbg
- 'Sekimori' (D)	CJun MPkF
- 'Sekka-yatsubusa' (P)	CMCN CMen MPkF NWbg
- 'Senkaki'	see *A. palmatum* 'Sango-kaku'
- 'Septemlobum Elegans'	see *A. palmatum* 'Elegans'
- 'Septemlobum Purpureum'	see *A. palmatum* 'Hessei'
- 'Sessilifolium' dwarf	see *A. palmatum* 'Hagoromo'
- 'Sessilifolium' tall	see *A. palmatum* 'Koshimino'
- 'Shaina' (P)	CAco CBcs CDoC CWGN EBee EGren EGrI ELom LBuc LCro LMaj LRHS MBlu MGos MPkF NCth NLar NPip NWbg SPoG SRms WFar
- 'Sharp's Pygmy' (P)	CJun LMil MPkF NWbg
- 'Sherwood Elfin' (Dw)	MPkF
- 'Sherwood Flame' (M)	CAco CJun EGren EGrI MAsh MBlu MGos MPkF MSwo NLar WFar
- 'Shidava Gold' (Dw)	CJun EMac
- 'Shigarami' (P)	CJun
§ - 'Shigi-tatsu-sawa' (A/v)	CAco CCVT CEnd CJun CMac CMCN LRHS LSRN NWbg
- 'Shigure-bato' (M)	CJun MPkF NLar
- 'Shigurezome' (M)	MPkF
- 'Shikageori-nishiki' (P)	CJun MPkF
- 'Shime-no-uchi' (L)	CJun
- 'Shimofuri-nishiki'	MPkF
- 'Shin-chishio' (P)	CJun
§ - 'Shin-deshōjō' (P) ♀H5	CAco CBcs CEnd CJun CMac CMCN CMen CWGN EBee EMac EPfP LBuc LMil LRHS LSRN MAsh MGos MPkF MPri NCth NLar NWbg SBig SPoG SSta WSpi
- 'Shin-nyo'PBR	CAco LBuc MBlu MPkF
§ - 'Shinobuga-oka' (L)	CJun CMCN EMac MPkF
- 'Shinonome' (M)	CAco CJun MPkF SArc
- SHIRAZZ	see *A. palmatum* 'Gwen's Rose Delight'
- 'Shiro-fu-nishiki'	MPkF
§ - 'Shishi-gashira' (P) ♀H6	CAco CJun CMac CMCN CMen CWnw ESMi LBuc LMaj LRHS MBlu MGos MPkF NCth NLar NWbg SHor WFar
- 'Shishio-hime' (Dw)	MPkF
- 'Shishi-yatsubusa'	CJun MPkF
- 'Shōjō' (A)	CJun CMCN
- 'Shōjō-nomura' (A)	CEnd LRHS MPkF
§ - 'Shōjō-shidare' (D)	CEnd CJun NOra WMat
- 'Shu-shidare' (D)	CJun
- 'Silhouette'PBR	CCVT LMaj NLar
- 'Sister Ghost' (M)	CJun NWbg
- 'Skeeter's Broom' (Dw)	CAco CBcs CCVT CDoC CWnw EBee EGren ELan EPfP IArd LBom LBuc LMaj LMil LRHS MGos MPkF NCth NLar NWbg SArc SBig SHor SPoG SReu WCha WFar
* - 'Sode-nishiki' (P)	CJun
- 'Spring Delight' (D)	CJun MPkF SAko
- 'Spring Surprise' (P/v)	MPkF
- 'Stanley's Jewel' (Dw)	MPkF
- 'Starfish'PBR	CAco LBuc MGos MPkF WLov
- 'Stella Rossa' (D)	CAco CJun LBuc NLar NWbg
- 'Sumi-nagashi' (D)	CAco CJun CWnw EGrI LBuc LCro LRHS MAsh MPkF MPri NLar NOra NWbg SMil WFar WMat
- 'Sumi-shidare' (D)	NLar
I - 'Summer Gold' (P)	CAco CBcs CDoC CJun CWnw EGren EUrb LBuc LRHS MPkF MPri NLar NTrD SArc SAth SMil WCha WFar WLov
- 'Sunshine' (D)	CCVT MPkF NTrD
- 'Super Ruby' (L)	MPkF NLar
- 'Susan'	MPkF
- 'Taima' (A)	NWbg
- 'Taimin'	see *A. palmatum* 'Daimyō'
§ - 'Taimin-nishiki' (M)	CAco
- 'Tama-hime' (Dw)	CMen MPkF NWbg
- 'Tamukeyama' (D)	CAco CBTr CJun CMCN CMen CWnw EBee EGren EMac LBom LBuc LCro LMaj LRHS MAsh MGos MPkF NLar NOra NPip NWbg SArc SMil WCha WMat WSpi
- 'Tana' (A)	CJun MPkF
- 'Tanabata' (M)	MPkF
- 'Tarō-yama' (Dw)	CJun MPkF NWbg
- 'Tatsuta'	MPkF
- 'Taylor'PBR (P/v)	CAco CWGN LCro LMil MAsh MGos MPkF NCth SMad SPoG WCha WFar
- 'Tennyo-no-hoshi' (P)	CMen MPkF NWbg
- 'Tess'	MPkF

Acer 69

- 'Tiger Rose' (M) — CJun NWbg
- 'Tiny Tim' — MPkF
- 'Tobiosho' (P) — CJun
- § 'Toyama-nishiki' (Dw/v) — CAco CMac CMCN CWGN NWbg
- 'Trompenburg' (M) ♀H6 — Widely available
- 'Tsuchigumo' (P) — CJun LRHS MPkF
- 'Tsuma-gaki' (A) — CAco CMCN LBuc MPkF SMil WFar
- 'Tsuri-nishiki' (M) — CJun
- 'Twombly's Red Sentinel' — CJun EGren LBuc LCro LMil LRHS MBlu MGos MPkF NLar NWbg SMil WFar WLov
- 'Ueno-homare' (P) — NWbg SArc
- 'Uki-gumo' (P/v) — CAco CEnd CMac CMCN CMen LBuc LCro LRHS MGos MPkF NWbg SPoG SSta
- 'Umegae' (A) — CJun
- 'Uncle Ghost' (M) — CJun NWbg
- 'Uncle Red' (P) — MPkF
- 'Usu-midori' — CJun
- 'Uta-fuku' — MPkF
- 'Utsu-semi' (A) — CJun MPkF
- 'Van der Akker' — CJun
- 'Van der Maat' (D) — MPkF
- 'Vens Red' — MPkF
- 'Versicolor' (P/v) — CMCN
- 'Vic Pink' (D) — CJun
- 'Villa Taranto' (L) ♀H6 — CAco CEnd CJun CMCN EPfP LBuc LRHS MBlu MGos NLar NOra NPip NWbg WCFE WLov WMat
- 'Volubile' (P) — CMen EGrI MPkF
- 'Wabito' (P) — CJun MPkF
- 'Waka-momiji' (P/v) — CJun LBuc
- 'Wakehurst Pink' (M/v) — LRHS MPkF NOra
- 'Waterfall' (D) — CJun
- 'Watnong' (D) — CJun
- 'Wendy' (P) — CJun LRHS MPkF NWbg
- 'Werner's Pagoda' (P) — MPkF
- 'Westonbirt Orange' (A) — MPri
- 'Westonbirt Red' (M) — CJun LRHS MPri
- 'Westonbirt Spreading Star' **new** — MPri
- 'Wetumpka Red' — CJun
- 'Wild Goose' (P) — CJun LRHS MBlu MPkF NWbg WFar
- 'Wildfire' — MPkF
- 'Will's Devine' — CJun MPkF
- 'Wilson's Pink Dwarf' (Dw) — CAco CCVT CEnd CJun CWnw LBuc LCro MGos MPkF MPri NLar NWbg SPoG WCha WFar
- 'Winter Flame' (P) — CJun MPri
- 'Wou-nishiki' — MPkF NWbg
- 'Yadawara' (A) — CJun
- 'Yana-gawa' — MPkF
- 'Yasemin' (M) — CCVT CJun CWGN LBuc MPkF NWbg WFar
- 'Yatsubusa' (Dw) — MPkF
- 'Yellow Cascade' — NLar
- 'Yezo-nishiki' (A/v) — MBlu MPkF WFar
- 'Yoshimizu' (M) — MPkF
- 'Yūba-e' (M) — CAco MPkF NOra
- 'Yū-fuji' — MPkF
- 'Yūgure' (M) — MPkF
- 'Zoë' (Dw) — MPkF
- *papilio* — see *A. caudatum*
- *pauciflorum* 'Blaze Away' — CJun
- *pectinatum* — MMuc WJur WPGP
- - GWJ 9354 — WCru
- - 'Mozart' — CJun MBlu SSta
- - subsp. *pectinatum* — WPGP
- - - HWJ 569 — WCru
- - - HWJ 944 — WCru
- *pensylvanicum* — CAco CBcs CMCN MMuc NPip SSta WJur
- - 'Erythrocladum' — CEnd CJun CMCN LBuc
- *pentaphyllum* — IArd SMil
- § *pictum* — CMCN WJur
- - B&SWJ 12737 — WCru
- - subsp. *dissectum* — NCth
- - subsp. *macropterum* — WPGP
- - subsp. *okamotoanum* — CMCN
- - - B&SWJ 12623 — WCru
- - 'Shufu-nishiki' — CMCN
- *platanoides* — CAco CBcs CBrac CBTr CCVT CLnd CMac CMCN CSBt EBar EGren EGrI EHeP IPap LCot MCtn MGos MMuc NPip SEWo WMat WRjT
- - 'Cleveland' — CAco EBar IPap
- - 'Columnare' — CAco EBar EHeP IPap LMaj
- - 'Crimson King' ♀H7 — Widely available
- - 'Crimson Sentry' — CAco CBTr CCVT CEnd CLnd CMac CWnw EBar EBee EGren EHeP ELan EPfP IPap LMaj LSRN MAsh MGos SArc SAth SGol WCha WMat
- - 'Deborah' — CAco CLnd EBar IPap LMaj
- - 'Dissectum' — CAco IArd
- - 'Drummondii' (v) — Widely available
- - 'Emerald Queen' — CAco CBTr CCVT EBar IPap LMaj
- - 'Faassen's Black' — EHeP
- - 'Fairview' **new** — LMaj
- - 'Farlake's Green' — CAco EBar
- § - 'Globosum' — CAco CCVT EBar EGren LMaj NLar SArc WCha
- - 'Olmsted' — CAco EBar
- - Princeton Gold ('Prigo'PBR) ♀H7 — Widely available
- - 'Royal Red' — CAco CBTr CLnd CMCN EBar EGren EPfP LMaj NLar NPip SArc SEWo WFar
- - 'Schwedleri' ♀H7 — CAco
- - Sensation — see *A. platanoides* 'Ulmers Sensation'
- - subsp. *turkestanicum* — SSta
- § - 'Ulmers Sensation'PBR (v) — SPoG
- *pseudoplatanus* — CBcs CBrac CBTr CCVT CHab CLnd CMCN LCot WRjT
- - 'Atropurpureum' — EBar EHeP IPap SEWo
- § - 'Brilliantissimum' ♀H7 — CBTr CCVT CEnd CLnd CMac CMCN EBar EGren EHeP ELan EPfP GKin IPap LBuc LCro LRHS LSRN MAsh MGos NLar NOra NPip SEND SPoG WCha WHtc WMat
- - 'Bruchem' — EBar LMaj
- - 'Gadsby' — CAco
- - 'Negenia' — EBar
- - 'Prinz Handjéry' — CBTr CEnd CMCN MGos NLar NOra NPip WHtc WMat
- - 'Spaethi' misapplied — see *A. pseudoplatanus* 'Atropurpureum'
- § - f. *variegatum* (v) — EBar MMuc
- - - 'Esk Sunset' (v) — CLnd ELan MGos NLar NOra NPip SAth SPoG WMat
- - - 'Leopoldii' misapplied — see *A. pseudoplatanus* f. *variegatum*
- - - 'Leopoldii' ambig. (v) — CBTr SEND
- - - 'Simon-Louis Frères' (v) — CCVT CLnd CMCN EGren LRHS MAsh MGos NLar NOra NPip WHtc WMat
- - 'Worley' — CMCN EBar EHeP
- *pseudosieboldianum* — CMCN MBlu MPkF
- - B&SWJ 8769 — WCru

- var. *microsieboldianum* B&SWJ 8766	WCru
- subsp. *takesimense*	MBlu
- - B&SWJ 8500	WCru
- - B&SWJ 8540	WCru
'Red Flamingo'	see *A.* 'Esk Flamingo'
'Red Wings' (*A. palmatum* hybrid)	CJun
reticulatum	see *A. laevigatum* var. *reticulatum*
rubescens	EBee MBlu SChF SMil WPGP
- NMWJ 14525	WCru
rubrum	CAco CAgr CBcs CLnd CMCN EBee EGrI IPap LCot LMaj MGos SEWo SGol WMat
- 'Autumn Flame'	CCVT LBuc WMat
- 'Autumn Spire'	CJun
- 'Bowhall'	EBar SEWo
- 'Brandywine'	CAco CBcs CBTr CEnd CJun CLnd CMac CMCN EPfP LBuc LMaj LRHS LSRN LSto MAsh MBlu MGos MPri NLar NOra NPip SArc SPoG WHtc WMat WMou
- var. *drummondii*	SAth
- 'Embers'	CJun
- FAIRVIEW FLAME	see *A. rubrum* 'Pete's Fairview'
- 'Firedance'	CJun
- 'Joseph'	NLar
- 'Karpick'	CAco
- 'October Glory' ♀H6	Widely available
§ - 'Pete's Fairview'	CAco CCVT IPap LRHS MMuc NLar
- 'Red King'	CJun
- RED SUNSET ('Franksred') ♀H6	CAco CBcs CCVT CEnd CMCN EBar EBee ELan EPfP IPap LCro LMaj MMuc NLar SGol SPoG WMat
- REDPOINTE ('Frank Junior')	CCVT LMaj
- 'Scanlon'	CAco CBcs CBTr CEnd CJun CMCN EBar EBee EPfP LCro LMaj LSto NOra NPip WMat
- 'Schlesingeri'	CMac CMCN
I - 'Sekka'	MBlu
- 'Somerset'	CJun NPip WMat
- SUMMER RED ('Hosr')	CAco EBee SAth WCha WMat
- 'Sun Valley'	CAco CBTr CCVT CJun CLnd CMac LCro LRHS MAsh NOra NPip WCha WMat
§ *rufinerve*	CAco CBcs CMCN EGrI LRHS MPri NLar NPip SGol SMil SSta WHtc WJur WMat
- 'Albolimbatum' (v)	CJun LRHS NLar
- 'Erythrocladum'	CJun MBlu
- 'Ko-fuji-nishiki'	SSta
I - 'Sunshine'	SSta
- 'Winter Gold'	CJun SSta
§ *saccharinum*	CAco CBcs CCVT CLnd CMCN EGrI EHeP EPfP NPip WMat
- 'Born's Gracious'	CAco
- 'Fastigiatum'	see *A. saccharinum* 'Pyramidale'
- f. *laciniatum*	CAco MBlu
- - 'Laciniatum Wieri'	CAco CCVT CMCN EBar IPap MMuc
§ - 'Pyramidale'	CAco EHeP IPap LMaj
saccharum	CAco CAgr CBcs CLnd CMCN EPfP IPap LMaj MBlu MCtn NPip WJur WMat
§ - subsp. *grandidentatum*	CMCN
§ *sempervirens*	EBee WJur WPGP
'Sensu'	CJun
'Serendipity'	SSta
'Serpentine'	CAco CBcs CJun CMCN ELan IArd MAsh MBlu SSta
serrulatum NMWJ 14521	WCru
- hybrid NMWJ 14548	WCru
shenkanense	WPGP
§ *shirasawanum*	Widely available
'Aureum' ♀H6	
- 'Autumn Moon'	CAco CJun CMCN CMen CWGN EGrI EMac EPfP GKin LBuc LRHS MAsh MPkF NCth NLar NPip SMil SPoG WMat
- 'Blue Moon'	MPkF
- 'Gloria'	CJun EGrI MPkF
- 'Green Snowflake'	MPkF
- 'Johin'	MPkF
- 'Jordan'	CAco CBcs CDoC CEnd CMac CWGN CWnw EBee ELan EPfP IArd LBuc LCro LMil LRHS MAsh MGos MPkF MPri NCth NLar SPoG WCha WFar WLov
- 'Kakure-gasa'	CJun
- 'Lovett'	CJun
- 'Microphyllum'	SArc
- MOONRISE ('Munn 001'PBR)	CBcs EBee EGrI EPfP LBuc LCro LRHS MPkF MPri NCth NLar WCha WLov
- 'Mr Sun'	CJun
§ - 'Ogurayama'	CJun
- 'Ookisa'	MPkF
- 'Palmatifolium'	CJun
- 'Red Dawn'	CJun MPkF
- 'Seasons of Change'	CJun
- 'Susanne'	CJun NLar
- var. *tenuifolium* B&SWJ 11073	WCru
sieboldianum ♀H6	CMen MBlu
- B&SWJ 10849	WCru
- B&SWJ 11049	WCru
- B&SWJ 11090	WCru
- 'Katsura-gisan'	CAco
- 'Miyama-nishiki'	MPkF
- 'Sode-no-uchi'	CJun CMen
- var. *tsushimense* B&SWJ 10962	WCru
sikkimense B&SWJ 11689	WCru
- B&SWJ 11703	WCru
- FMWJ 13166 from northern Vietnam	WCru
- WJC 13674 from Sikkim	WCru
- WWJ 11601	WCru
- WWJ 11613	WCru
- WWJ 11853	WCru
'Silver Cardinal' (v)	CEnd CJun MBlu SSta WJur
'Silver Vein'	see *A.* × *conspicuum* 'Silver Vein'
sinense	CMCN WJur
- 'Rogov'	CJun
spicatum	CMCN NLar
stachyophyllum W&O 8014	GGro
- W&O 8015	GGro
- subsp. *betulifolium*	WJur
§ *sterculiaceum*	EGrI WJur
- cf. subsp. *franchetii*	WPGP
- subsp. *sterculiaceum* NJM 13.087	WPGP
§ *tataricum* subsp. *ginnala*	CAco CBcs CMCN CNWT EBar EGrI EHeP IPap LRHS MBlu NLar SGol WJur
- - 'Flame'	CAco EBee EPfP LRHS MMuc SPoG
- HOT WINGS ('Gar Ann')	LCro
tegmentosum ♀H5	CJun CMac MBlu WJur
- 'Cobhay Ghost'	CJun
- subsp. *glaucorufinerve*	see *A. rufinerve*

Achillea

tonkinense subsp. *liquidambarifolium* DJHV 6173	WCru
triflorum ♀H7	CAco CCVT CMCN LMaj MBlu NLar WJur WMat
truncatum 'Akikaze'	WFar
- 'Akikaze-nishiki' (v)	MPkF
- 'Volcano'	NLar
tschonoskii	GKin
- subsp. *koreanum*	MPkF
- - B&SWJ 12596	WCru
- - B&SWJ 12603	WCru
turkestanicum from Kyrgyzstan	WPGP
velutinum	CMCN
villosum	see *A. sterculiaceum*
'White Tigress'	CJun EBee EPfP MCtn NLar NPip SSta WMat
wilsonii	WJur
× *zoeschense*	MPkF
- 'Annae'	CAco CMCN MMuc

Achillea ✿ (Asteraceae)

ageratifolia ♀H5	EDAr ELan SRms
§ *ageratum*	CCBP CGHo ENfk EWhm GQue LShi MHer MHoo MMuc MNHC MWIw NAts SEdi SRms SVic WCot WFar WGwG WJek WTre
'Alabaster'	CBcs
ANTHEA ('Anblo')	EBee MPro SRms WCAu WFar
§ 'Apfelblüte' (Galaxy Series)	EBee ECha ECul ELan LRHS LSRN MArl MHtn MMuc MPro NGdn SEND SHar SRms WCAu WFar
APPLEBLOSSOM	see *A.* 'Apfelblüte' (Galaxy Series)
'Apricot Beauty'	ECul
'Apricot Seduction' (Seduction Series)	ECul
arabica from Kyrgyzstan	GGro
argentea misapplied	see *A. clavennae, A. umbellata*
aurea	see *A. chrysocoma*
§ *chrysocoma*	WIce
- 'Grandiflora'	ECha GQue LShi MNrw NGdn WBrk
§ *clavennae*	EDAr NBir SPlb SRms WAbe
clypeolata Sm.	SRms
coarctata	ECha NBir WMal
Colorado Group	ECul EPfP LRHS MCtn MSCN
'Coronation Gold' ♀H7	EBee EBlo ECul EGren ELan EPfP GQue LRHS MArl MAsh MAvo MSwo NDov SAth SOrN SRms WCAu WCot WFar WSpi
'Credo' ♀H7	CBcs CBWd CDor ECha ECul EGren ELan ELon EPfP GBin GQue LCro LRHS LSto MArl MHol NBir NCth NGdn NLar NSti NWbg SAth SPel WCAu WFar WSpi
decolorans	see *A. ageratum*
DESERT EVE LIGHT YELLOW (Desert Eve Series)	SRms
'Dwarf Taygetea'	WCot
falcata	GKev
§ 'Fanal'	CAby CGHo EBee ECha ECul ELan EPfP ESgI LRHS Midl MWlw NBir NWbg SMrm WCAu WFar
'Faust'	CDor ELon
'Feuerland'	EBee ECha ELon ESgI MHol NBir NCth NDov NGdn NWbg SPoG WFar WSpi
filipendulina 'Cloth of Gold' ♀H7	CBcs EBee ECul EGren EHeP ELan ELon EPfP GBin GMaP GQue LBar LCro LRHS LShi LWaG MAsh MBNS MGos NBir NLar SPlb SRms WBrk WCav WFar WTre
- 'Gold Plate' ♀H7	CAby CBWd CEnd CKno CMac CMHG EBee EBlo ECha ELan EPfP ESgI GMaP GQue LRHS LSto MAvo MBel MHer NLar SEND SPoG SRms WCAu WCot WFar WHoo WSpi
- 'Parker's Variety'	CWal EBee MCtn
'Fleur van Zonneveld'	NDov
FLOWERS OF SULPHUR (Forncett Series)	see *A.* 'Schwefelblüte'
'Forncett Citrus'	WFar
- 'Forncett Fletton'	ECul MArl MBel MBNS NGdn SPel WCAu WFar
'Gloria Jean'	SHar
grandifolia misapplied	see *Tanacetum macrophyllum* (Waldst. & Kit.) Sch.Bip.
§ *grandifolia* Friv.	GGro MArl MHol NBro SMrm WFar
'Great Expectations'	see *A.* 'Hoffnung'
'Hella Glashoff' ♀H7	EUrb LRHS NDov NLar SBeP WGoo
§ 'Hoffnung'	NLar WCAu WFar
× *huteri*	EDAr GKev LShi MMuc NRya SEND SRms WFar
'Inca Gold'	CBcs ECha ECul EPPr ESgI LRHS NCth NDov SRms WCAu WFar WHoo WSpi
× *kellereri*	LRHS
'King Alfred'	GKev LCro LRHS SRms
× *kolbiana*	EWes SRms WFar
§ 'Lachsschönheit' (Galaxy Series) ♀H7	CDor CGHo ECha ELan EPfP ERCP GMaP LBom LRHS MArl MBNS Midl NDov NLar NSti NWbg SAth SBeP SRms WCAu WFar WTor
× *lewisii* 'King Edward' ♀H5	EDAr ELan ESgI GKev LShi SRms WFar WIce
'Lucky Break' ♀H7	EBee ECha SDix WCot
macrophylla	MBNS
'Marmalade'	CDor NDov SMrm
'Martina' ♀H7	ESgI GBin MBel MBNS NGdn NWbg WCAu WCot WHoo
millefolium	CBWd CCBP CGHo CGwi CHab ECul ENfk GJem GQue IDun LCro LShi LSto MAsh MCtn MHoo MNHC NAts NMir SRms StAn SVic WHer WJek WKit WOrg WSpi
- 'Angie' (Song Siren Series)	ECul
- 'Apricot Delight' (Tutti Frutti Series)	ECul ELan GKev LRHS
- 'Bloodstone'	EWes
- 'Carla Hussey'	WFar
- 'Cassis'	CSpe CWal ECul EGren EPfP GKev GQue MArl MCtn NLar WFar WHil WKit WTre
§ - 'Cerise Queen'	Widely available
- 'Chamois'	MNrw
- 'Cherry King'	NBir
- 'Circus'	ECul
- 'Crazy Little Thing'	NCth
- 'Darcies Cherry Red' **new**	EDAr
- 'Dark Lilac Beauty'	ECul
- 'Ending Blue' (Rainbow Series)	LBar
- KIRSCHKÖNIGIN	see *A. millefolium* 'Cerise Queen'
- 'Lansdorferglut' ♀H7	CKno EBlo ECha LRHS NDov
- 'Laura' (Song Siren Series)	CWGN MNrw NLar NWbg WFar
- 'Lavender Beauty'	see *A. millefolium* 'Lilac Beauty'
- 'Layla' (Song Siren Series)	CAby CGHo ECul Midl
§ - 'Lilac Beauty'	CGHo EBee ECha EGren ELon EPfP ERCP ESgI GBin GMaP LCro LRHS LSRN LSto MMuc MPro NBir NLar NWbg SAth SMrm SPel SRms

	WCAu WCav WFar WHoo WSpi WTor
- LITTLE MOONSHINE ('Acbz0002'^{PBR})	EBee ECul EPfP LRHS MHol MMrt SPel
- 'Little Susie' (Song Siren Series)	CWGN ECul NLar
- (Milly Rock Series) MILLY ROCK RED ('Florachre1'^{PBR})	LCro WHil
- - MILLY ROCK ROSE ('Florachro1'^{PBR})	MPro WHil
- - MILLY ROCK YELLOW TERRACOTTA ('Florachye1')	MPro
- (New Vintage Series) NEW VINTAGE LILAC	see *A. millefolium* (New Vintage Series) NEW VINTAGE VIOLET
- - NEW VINTAGE RED ('Balvinred')	ECul EGren LBar LBom LRHS LSou MHol Midl MPri MPro WHil
- - NEW VINTAGE ROSE ('Balvinrose')	ECul EGren LBar LRHS LSou Midl MPri MPro
§ - - NEW VINTAGE VIOLET ('Balvinviolet')	ECul EGren EPfP ERCP LBar LRHS LSou MAsh MHol MPri MPro SBeP WNPC
- - NEW VINTAGE WHITE ('Balvinwite')	ECul EGren LBar LRHS Midl MPri MPro
- 'Old Brocade'	NDov
- pastel shades	WFar
- 'Peggy Sue'	CWGN EGren EPfP MArl MPro WFar WHil
- 'Pink Grapefruit' (Tutti Frutti Series)	CWGN ECul EPfP GBin LRHS Midl MPro NLar WCAu WTor
- 'Pomegranate' (Tutti Frutti Series)	CAby CWGN ECul EGren EPfP ESgI LBar LCro LRHS Midl MPro NDov NLar SHar WCot WTor
- 'Pretty Woman' (Song Siren Series)	CWGN
- 'Proa' **new**	StAn
- Raspberry Ripple'	GBin
- 'Red Beauty'	EBee EPfP SRms
- 'Red Velvet' ♀^{H7}	Widely available
- (Ritzy Series) RITZY ROSE ('Acbz0003'^{PBR})	ECul
- - RITZY RUBY ('Acbz0004'^{PBR})	ECul
- 'Rose Madder'	ECul GMaP LSto MArl MHtn MNrw NBir NCth NGdn NLar NWbg SMrm SPel SPoG WCot WFar
- 'Ruby Port'	WFar
- 'Salmon Queen'	WFar
- 'Sammetriese'	ELon MNrw MWlw
- (Sassy Summer Series) 'Sassy Summer Lemon'	ECul EGren EPfP LBar LRHS MPro WHil
- - 'Sassy Summer Sangria'	ECul EGren EPfP LBar LRHS Midl MPro
- - 'Sassy Summer Sunset'	ECul EGren LBar LRHS MPro
- - 'Sassy Summer Taffy'	ECul EGren LBar MHol Midl MPro
- 'Schneetaler'	ECul ELon
- (Summer Fruits Series) 'Summer Fruits Carmine'	ELan EPfP
- - 'Summer Fruits Lemon'	ELan Midl WFar WSpi
- - 'Summer Fruits Salmon'	ELan SPoG WFar
- 'Summertime'	WFar
- 'White Beauty'	ECul GBin LRHS WCAu
- 'White Queen'	EGren
- 'Wonderful Wampee' (Tutti Frutti Series)	ECul ELan SPoG
'Mondpagode' ♀^{H7}	NGdn
MOON DUST ('Novaachdus')	ECul EGren MArl
* 'Moonbeam'	SEND
'Moonlight'	CTtf
'Moonshine' ♀^{H7}	Widely available
'Moonwalker'	ECul WCot
nobilis subsp. *neilreichii*	ECha LShi WFar
'Paprika' (Galaxy Series)	Widely available
'Petra'	EBee EUrb NCth NLar
pindicola subsp. *integrifolia*	EWes
'Pretty Belinda'	CDor EGren ELon EPfP ERCP ESgI EUrb EWhm GBin LRHS MBel MHer MPro NLar NWbg SPoG SRms WCAu
'Prospero'	WCot
ptarmica	CBWd CGwi CPud GBin MCtn MHer MNHC NAts NMir SRms WOrg
* - 'Ballerina'	NDov
- 'Double Diamond' (d)	LShi LSto
- 'Marshmallow' (d)	CWnw MMrt SRot WHil
- 'Nana Compacta'	CMac NBir SPlb SPoG WCAu
- 'Noblessa' (d)	EDAr NLar
- 'Perry's White' (d)	ECha MBNS MNrw WCAu WCot
- 'Peter Cottontail'^{PBR}	ECul EGren LBar LCro LRHS MBel Midl MNrw MPri MPro NCth WHil
- 'Stephanie Cohen'	see *A. sibirica* 'Stephanie Cohen'
- (The Pearl Group) 'Boule de Neige' (clonal) (d)	ELan NPer SHar WFar WSpi
- - seed-raised (d)	ECul ELan MMuc SPlb WFar
- - 'The Pearl' (clonal) (d)	CMac CoPl EBee ECha ELin EPfP GMaP GQue LCro LRHS LSto MAsh MBel MCtn NBid NBir NBro NLar NWbg SMrm SRms WBrk WCAu WCot WFar WOld WTre XFar
'Rougham Salmon'	CDor
'Ruby Wine'	SHar WFar
'Safran'	EBee ECul EWes MPro NLar
salicifolia	WFar
- 'Silver Spray'	NLar SDix
- 'Sally'	CKno
SALMON BEAUTY	see *A.* 'Lachsschönheit' (Galaxy Series)
'Sandstone'	see *A.* 'Wesersandstein'
'Saucy Seduction' (Seduction Series)	ECul ELan EPfP LBar LRHS SPoG WFar
'Saucy Sensation'	ECul MPro
§ 'Schwefelblüte'	NBir
'Schwellenburg'	ECha WCot WFar
sibirica	GGro
subsp. *camschatica*	
- - 'Love Parade'	EBee EPfP GQue LCro MAsh MCtn MNrw NLar WTor
§ - 'Stephanie Cohen' Song Siren Series	SMrm Midl
SUMMER BERRIES (mixed)	ECul EGren LRHS MAsh MCtn SAth SMrm WFar
Summer Pastels Group	GKev LRHS MCtn NLar SRms WFar WKit XFar
- (Seduction Series) 'Peachy Seduction'^{PBR}	CWal ECul NLar WCAu
- - 'Strawberry Seduction'	ECul EHeP EPfP LBar Midl MPro NLar SMrm
'Summerwine' ♀^{H7}	Widely available
'Sunbeam'	SHar
'Sunny Seduction' (Seduction Series)	ECul LBar LRHS Midl MPro NLar WTor
I 'Taygetea'	EBee ECul LCro SPoG WCAu WCot WFar WSpi
'Terracotta'	Widely available
'The Beacon'	see *A.* 'Fanal'
'Tissington Old Rose'	MNrw

tomentosa ♀H5	LWaG
§ - 'Aurea'	ECha LShi NBro WCAu
- 'Maynard's Gold'	see *A. tomentosa* 'Aurea'
'Tri-colour'	MBNS NGdn
§ ***umbellata***	StAn
'Walther Funcke'	Widely available
'W.B. Childs'	MNrw NDov SHar
§ 'Wesersandstein'	MNrw NBir
'Wilczekii'	SRms

× *Achimenantha* (*Gesneriaceae*)

'Cool Inferno'	WDib
'Golden Jubilee'	WDib
'Himalayan Sunrise'	WDib
'Inferno' ♀H1b	WDib
'Pisces'	WDib
'Star of Stars'	WDib

Achimenes (*Gesneriaceae*)

admirabilis	WDib
'Aimee Saliba'	WDib
'Ambroise Verschaffelt' ♀H1c	LAma WDib
'Apple Cider'	WDib
'Apricot Glow'	WDib
'Ballerina'	WDib
'Beautiful Fire'	WDib
'Big Weiss'	WDib
'Boheme'	WDib
'Caligula'	WDib
'Cameo Rose'	WDib
'Caprice'	WDib
'Cascade Fairy Pink'	WDib
'Cascade Fashionable Pink'	WDib
'Cattleya'	LAma
cettoana	WDib
'Charm'	WDib
'Clouded Yellow Stone'	EAri
'Crummock Water'	WDib
'Dale Martens'	WDib
'Dot'	WDib
'Double Pink Rose' (d)	WDib
erecta	WDib
'Erlkönig'	WDib
'Escheriana'	LAma
'Extravaganza'	WDib
'Femme Fatale'	WDib
'Firefly'	WDib
'Forget Me Not'	WDib
'George Houche'	WDib
'Glory'	WDib
'Golden Butterfly'	WDib
'Golden Lady'	WDib
'Harry Williams'	EAri LAma WDib
'Hilda Michelssen' ♀H1c	WDib
'Himalayan Mandarin' (Himalayan Series)	LAma WDib
'Honey Queen'	WDib
'Hugues Aufray'	WDib
'Ice Tea'	WDib
'Imperial Light'	WDib
'Jay Dee Large White' (Jay Dee Series)	WDib
'Jennifer Goode'	WDib
'Konrad Michelssen'	WDib
'Lady in Black'	WDib
'Lavender Fancy'	WDib
'Lemon Orchard'	WDib
'Light Lilac'	WDib
'Little Beauty'	WDib
'Little Lulu'	WDib
longiflora var. ***alba***	EAri
- - 'Snow Queen'	LAma
- 'Major'	WDib
'Magnificent'	WDib
'Mauve Delight'	WDib
'Melon Ice Cream'	WDib
mexicana	LAma
misera	WDib
'Nocturne'	WDib
'Old Rose Pink'	WDib
'Orange Delight'	WDib
'Orange Orchard'	WDib
'Patens Major' ♀H1c	WDib
'Peach Blossom'	LAma WDib
'Peach Cascade'	WDib
'Peach Glow'	WDib
pedunculata	WDib
'Petite Fadette'	WDib
'Poil de Carotte'	WDib
'Primadonna'	WDib
'Pulcherrima'	EAri LAma
'Purple Kimono'	WDib
'Purple King'	WDib
'Rai'	WDib
'Rainbow Warrior'	WDib
'Rozi Roza'	WDib
'Santa Claus'	WDib
'Schneewittchen'	WDib
'Serge Saliba'	WDib
'Serge's Fantasy'	WDib
'Shy Sun'	WDib
skinneri	WDib
'Stan's Delight' (d) ♀H1c	WDib
'Sterntaler'	WDib
'Sugarland'	WDib
'Sun Dance'	WDib
'Sun Wind'	WDib
'Sweet and Sour'	WDib
'Tetra Himalayan Purple' (Tetra Series)	LAma WDib
'Valse Bleu'	WDib
'Veronika Gotmanova'	WDib
'Vivid'	EAri LAma
'Weinrot Elfe'	WDib
'Wetterlow's Triumph'	WDib
'Yellow Beauty'	WDib
'Yellow English Rose' (d)	WDib

Achimenes × *Smithiantha* see × *Achimenantha*

Achnatherum see *Stipa*

Acidanthera see *Gladiolus*

Aciphylla (*Apiaceae*)

aurea	GKev SPlb
crosby-smithii	GKev
glaucescens	GKev SPlb
kirkii	GKev
subflabellata	GKev

Acis (*Amaryllidaceae*)

§ ***autumnalis*** ♀H5	CBro CElw CSpe CTtf EBlo ECha EDAr EGrl EPot EWes GEdr GKev LAma LEdu LRHS LSto MCtn MMuc MNrw NBir NLar SMHy SRms SRot WAbe WHoo WPGP
- var. ***oporantha***	CMiW CWCL GKev
- - f. ***dispathacea***	GEdr GKev
- var. ***pulchella***	GKev
- 'September Snow'	EBee ELan GKev LAma NLar
ionica	GKev WMal

Acis

	nicaeensis	CTtf
§	*rosea*	CTtf EDAr WAbe
§	*tingitana*	CBro GKev
	trichophylla	WCot
	f. *purpurascens*	
§	*valentina*	CTtf WCot

Acmella (Asteraceae)
§ *oleracea* — MCtn

Acmena see *Syzygium*

Acnistus see *Iochroma*
australis — see *Eriolarynx australis*

Acoelorrhaphe (Arecaceae)
wrightii — NPlm

Acokanthera (Apocynaceae)
oblongifolia — CRHN

Aconitum ✿ (Ranunculaceae)

	ACE 1449	EPPr
	from Russia	EPPr
	altissimum	see *A. lycoctonum* subsp. *vulparia*
	anglicum	see *A. napellus* subsp. *napellus* Anglicum Group
§	*anthora*	GKev WCot
	arcuatum	see *A. fischeri* var. *arcuatum*
	austroyunnanense BWJ 7902	WCru
	autumnale misapplied	see *A. carmichaelii* Wilsonii Group
	autumnale Rchb.	see *A. fischeri* Rchb.
	× *bicolor*	see *A.* × *cammarum* 'Bicolor'
	'Blue Opal'	EPPr MAvo SPel
	'Blue Sceptre'	SRms
§	'Blue Sparrow'	ELon MHol WCAu
	'Bressingham Spire' ♀H7	ELan GKin NGdn NPer SRms WCAu WSpi
§	× *cammarum* 'Bicolor' ♀H7	EBee ELan ELon EMor GAbr GMaP GQue LBar LCro MMrt MNrw MPro NBro NCth NPer SPoG SRms WCAu WCot WFar WSpi
	- 'Eleanora'	ECha EWld MHol SRms
	- 'Grandiflorum Album'	MNrw WGoo
§	*carmichaelii*	GKev GKin LBar MMuc MNrw NBro NGdn SEND SRms WCot WFar WSpi
	- B&SWJ 8809	ESwi
	- Arendsii Group	CAby EBee GKev LEdu WCAu
	- - 'Arendsii' ♀H7	Widely available
	- - 'Cloudy' PBR	EBee EMor EPfP MArl NGdn NLar WCot WFar WSpi XFar
	- 'Moody Blues'	EBee
	- 'Redleaf'	see *A. carmichaelii* 'Royal Flush'
	- 'River Finn'	WCot
	- 'River Lugg'	WCot
	- 'River Medway'	WCot
	- 'River Nene'	WCot
	- 'River Ouse'	WCot
	- 'River Spey'	WCot
	- 'River Teifi'	WCot
	- 'River Trent'	WCot
	- 'River Welland'	WCot
§	- 'Royal Flush' PBR	EMor MNrw NLar SPoG WCot
	- var. *truppelianum*	WCot
§	- Wilsonii Group	CMac EBee EGrI NDov NQui SMHy SPel
	- - 'Barker's Variety'	EBee ELon GKev MCtn NGdn NLar NSti SRms WCot WSpi
	- - 'Kelmscott' ♀H7	LCro SDix WFar WSpi

	- - 'Spätlese'	EBee MHol NBir NGdn NLar SMHy SPoG WCot
§	*chasmanthum*	EBee
	- GWJ 9393	WCru
	chiisanense B&SWJ 4446	ESwi WCru
	cilicicum	see *Eranthis hyemalis* Cilicica Group
	confertiflorum	see *A. anthora*
	episcopale	WCru
	ferox	EBee
	fischeri misapplied	see *A. carmichaelii*
§	*fischeri* Rchb.	EBee GKev NBid NCth NLar
	- B&SWJ 8809	WCru
§	- var. *arcuatum*	EBee
	- - B&SWJ 774	WCru
	formosanum B&SWJ 3057	WCru
	fukutomei B&SWJ 337	WCru
	grossedentatum	NLar
	- subsp. *paniculatum*	see *A. variegatum* subsp. *paniculatum*
§	*hemsleyanum*	CExl CRHN GKev NBid WCru
	- dark blue-flowered	WSpi
	- 'Red Wine'	CSpe
	heterophylloides	WCot
	hyemale	see *Eranthis hyemalis*
	'Ivorine'	EBee EPfP LCro MHol NGdn NLar WFar WPnP
	jaluense	EPPr
	- B&SWJ 8741	WCru
	japonicum	GQue NLar WCot
	- var. *hakonense*	CExl
	- var. *montanum* B&SWJ 5507	WCru
§	- subsp. *napiforme*	EWes
	- B&SWJ 943	WCru
§	- subsp. *subcuneatum* B&SWJ 6228	WCru
	kitadakense B&SWJ 11173	WCru
	krylovii	EWld GKev NQui
	lamarckii	see *A. lycoctonum* subsp. *neapolitanum*
	lasianthum	see *A. lycoctonum* subsp. *vulparia*
	loczyanum	WCot
	lycoctonum	GKev NLar NSti StAn WFar WSpi WTre
	- 'Darkeyes'	WCot
	- subsp. *lycoctonum*	SRms
§	- subsp. *moldavicum*	SBrt WCot
§	- subsp. *neapolitanum*	CDor GKev GMaP LBar MMuc NLar SDix SEND WSpi
	- 'Russian Yellow'	ESwi EWld
§	- subsp. *vulparia*	ESwi LShi MHol NGdn SRms
	mairei	see *A. vilmorinianum*
	moldavicum	see *A. lycoctonum* subsp. *moldavicum*
	nagarum	WCot
	napellus	CCBP EGrI EPfP EPPr GAbr GJos GKev LBar LCro MBel MHol MMuc MNHC NAts SEND SPoG SRms WCot WFar WHoo WPnP WShi WTre
	- 'Bergfürst'	SPel
	- 'Blue Valley'	ELan
§	- subsp. *napellus* Anglicum Group	MHol MMuc SEND WCot
	- - - 'Spring Yellow'	WCot
	- 'Rubellum'	EMor GKev NBro NLar
	- 'Schneewittchen'	EWes
	- subsp. *vulgare* 'Albidum'	CSpe EGrI GKev GMaP LBar MBel MHol NBid NLar NQui SPoG WCAu WShi

napiforme see *A. japonicum* subsp. *napiforme*
neapolitanum see *A. lycoctonum* subsp. *neapolitanum*
'Newry Blue' CBcs EBee ELan LBar LSto MBNS MHol SRms WSpi
orientale misapplied see *A. lycoctonum* subsp. *vulparia*
paniculatum misapplied see *A. variegatum* subsp. *paniculatum*
paniculatum Lam. see *A.* × *cammarum*
piepunense EBee GKev
proliferum WCot
- B&SWJ 4107 WCru
'Purple Sparrow' see *A.* 'Blue Sparrow'
pyrenaicum misapplied see *A. lycoctonum* subsp. *neapolitanum*
ranunculifolium see *A. lycoctonum* subsp. *neapolitanum*
sachalinense NLar WCot
  subsp. *yezoense*
scaposum GKev
senanense var. *incisum* WCru
  B&SWJ 11032
seoulense B&SWJ 694 WCru
- B&SWJ 864 WCru
'Spark's Variety' ♀H7 CBcs EBee ECha ELan EPfP GAbr GMaP LBar LBom LCro LRHS LSto MBNS MMuc NBid NCth NLar SAko SDix SPoG SRms WCAu WFar WSpi
'Stainless Steel' ♀H7 CExl EBee EPfP LCro LSto MHol NGdn SAko SDix SPoG WCAu WCot WFar WSpi
subcuneatum see *A. japonicum* subsp. *subcuneatum*
'Surprise' WCot
× *tubergenii* see *Eranthis hyemalis* Tubergenii Group
uchiyamae B&SWJ 1005 WCru
- B&SWJ 1216 ECha WCru
- B&SWJ 4446 NLar
§ *variegatum* EPPr WCot
  subsp. *paniculatum*
§ *vilmorinianum* BWJ 8055 WCru
violaceum var. *robustum* see *A. chasmanthum*
volubile misapplied see *A. hemsleyanum*
vulparia see *A. lycoctonum* subsp. *vulparia*
yamazakii WCru
zigzag var. *ryohakuense* WCru
  B&SWJ 8906

Aconogonon see *Koenigia*

Acorus (Acoraceae)
calamus CBen CLil CPud CWat ELin EPfk GQue LRHS NPer WMAq
- 'Argenteostriatus' (v) CBen CLil CWat ECha ELin MMuc SEND SRms WMAq
* *christophii* CBen ELon EPPr
gramineus EGren ELin NPer
- 'Albovariegatus' (v) **new** CLil
- 'Golden Delight' LCro LRHS LSou SRms WFar
- 'Golden Edge' (v) CKno ELon
- 'Hakuro-nishiki' (v) GQue SRms WFar
- 'Licorice' WBrk
- 'Oborozuki' misapplied see *A. gramineus* 'Ōgon'
- 'Oborozuki' (v) LCro
§ - 'Ōgon' (v) CBen CKno CLil CoPl CWCL ELan ELin ELon EMor EPot EPPr EUrb GMaP GQue LCro LRHS MGos MMuc MWts NBir NSti SArc SEND SPlb SPoG SRms WFar
- var. *pusillus* ELin NBro

- 'Variegatus' (v) CBcs CBen CBWd CKno CoPl CWat EGren ELan ELin ELon EMor EPPr GMaP GQue IDun LRHS MGos MMuc MWts NBid NBro SArc SEND SPoG SRms
- 'Intermedius' NPer

Acradenia (Rutaceae)
franklinae CBcs CMac EBee EPfP IArd MBlu SPlb WPGP

Actaea ✿ (Ranunculaceae)
alba misapplied see *A. pachypoda, A. rubra* f. *neglecta*
arizonica EBee
asiatica B&SWJ 616 WCru
- B&SWJ 6351 from Japan WCru
- B&SWJ 8694 from Korea WCru
- BWJ 8174 from China WCru
biternata SDix
- B&SWJ 8917 NLar WCru
- B&SWJ 11190 IPot WCru
aff. *cimicifuga* WJC 13720 WCru
§ *cordifolia* EBee GMaP NLar
dahurica B&SWJ 8426 WCru
- B&SWJ 8573 WCru
erythrocarpa see *A. rubra*
§ *japonica* ECha NLar
- B&SWJ 5828 WCru
- B&SWJ 11136 WCru
- B&SWJ 11526 WCru
- from Jejudo, South Korea MNrw
- var. *acutiloba* WCru
  B&SWJ 6257
- 'Cheju-Do' EBee EMor GGro GKev LRHS MHol MMrt NLar
- compact B&SWJ 8758A WCot WCru
- 'Silver Blush' EBee EMor IPot LBar
- 'Silver Dance' EBee EMor LRHS NLar WTor
mairei BWJ 7635 WCru
- BWJ 7939 WCru
§ *matsumurae* NLar
- B&SWJ 11133 WCru
- B&SWJ 11528 WCru
- 'Elstead Variety' ♀H7 CExl ECha
- 'Frau Herms' EBlo LRHS
- 'High Rise' WCru
- 'White Pearl' ♀H7 CBcs CDor CExl EBee EBlo ECha EGren EPfP GKev GMaP GQue MBel MPro NBid NSti SPoG SRms WCAu
§ *pachypoda* CExl EBee GKev MBel MMrt NAts NBid NLar WCru
- Misty Blue ('Lk05'PBR) CWGN EBee ECha ELan EMor ESwi GKev LRHS MAvo MHol MPro NSti SMad SMrm SPoG WCot WFar
- 'Silver Leaf' CFis EBee EMor GKev
§ *podocarpa* EBee SPlb SRms WCru
'Queen of Sheba'PBR CWGN EBee EMor IPot LBar LCro MAvo MBel MPri MPro NDov NLar SDix WTor XFar
racemosa ♀H7 CMac EBee ELan LRHS MCtn MHoo MPri NGdn NLar NSti SHor WCAu WFar WTre XFar
§ *rubra* EBee ECha EWld NBid SPoG WCru
- B&SWJ 9555 WCru
- *alba* see *A. pachypoda, A. rubra* f. *neglecta*
§ - f. *neglecta* GKev MCtn WCot WCru
simplex LRHS WCot
- B&SWJ 8653 WCru
- B&SWJ 8664 WCru

Actaea

- B&SWJ 10957	WCru	
§ - Atropurpurea Group	EBee EBlo ECha EGrI ELan ELon EMor GMaP LBar LCro LRHS MCtn MGos MHoo Midl NBir NGdn NLar SPel SRms WCAu WFar WPnP	
- - 'Black Negligee'	Widely available	
- - 'Brunette' ♀H7	Widely available	
- - 'Carbonella'	CWGN EMor NLar WFar	
- - 'Chocoholic'	CWGN EBee ELan ELon EMor EPfP EUrb IPot LRHS LSou MArl MAsh MAvo MHol Midl MMrt MPro NCth NLar SPel SRkn WFar WHil WNPC	
- - 'Hillside Black Beauty' ♀H7	CBWd CDor CTtf EAri EBee EMor EPfP GKin GMaP LBar MAvo MBel MHol Midl NLar NWbg SPel SPeP WFar WHil WNPC	
- - 'James Compton' ♀H7	CDor EBee EBlo ECha EMor GBin GMaP IPot LRHS MAvo MBel MPro NDov NGdn NLar SHar SHor WCAu WCot WFar	
- - 'Mountain Wave'	Midl NDov	
- - 'Satin Darkness' **new**	IPot	
- - 'Pink Spike'	Widely available	
§ - 'Prichard's Giant'	CLil EBlo ECha ELon EMor LBar LRHS NDov WFar	
- *ramosa*	see *A. simplex* 'Prichard's Giant'	
- variegated (v)	WCot	
spicata	WCru	
yesoensis	NLar	
- B&SWJ 6355	WCru	
- B&SWJ 10860	ESwi WCru	

Actinella see *Tetraneuris*

Actinidia (Actinidiaceae)

BWJ 8161 from China	WCru
arguta	EBee WJur
- (f/F)	CAgr
- (m)	LWaG
- B&SWJ 4455 from Jejudo, South Korea	WCru
- B&SWJ 4823 from Japan	WCru
- B&SWJ 8529 from Ulleungdo, South Korea	WCru
- 'Ambrosia Grande' (f/F)	NLar
- 'Ananasnaya' (f/F)	CAgr WJur
- 'Bayern' (f/F)	CAgr
- 'Cornell' (m)	WJur
- 'Geneva 2' (f/F)	CAgr
- 'Honigbeere' (m)	NLar
- 'Issai' (s-p/F)	CAgr CBcs CMac CRHN EPom LBuc MBlu SAth SVic WFar WJur WKor WSpi
- 'Jumbo' (f/F)	CAgr SVic
- 'Ken's Red' (f/F)	CAgr CDoC EPom LEdu MGos SVic WSpi
- 'Kokuwa' (s-p/F)	CAgr
- 'Meader' (m)	CAgr
- 'Missionario Chiandetti' (f/F)	WJur
- var. *purpurea* 'Hardy Red' (f/F)	CAgr
- - 'Purpurna Sadowa' (f/F)	NLar
- 'Rogow' (f/F)	CAgr
- SCARLET SEPTEMBER KIWI ('Mirzan') (f/F)	CAgr
- 'Unchae' (m)	WCru
- 'Weiki' (m)	CAgr SVic WJur WPGP
chinensis var. ***setosa*** B&SWJ 3563	WCru

coriacea WWJ 11895	WCru	
deliciosa (m)	MCtn	
- 'Atlas' (m)	NLar SVic	
- 'Hayward' (f/F)	CBcs CMac EGren EPom ERom SVic	
- 'Jenny' (s-p/F)	CAgr CBcs CDoC CEnd CMac EAri EGren ELan EPfP EPom LBuc LCro MGos NLar NTrD SBmr SNig SPoG SPre SSFr SVic WFar WMat	
- 'Oriental Delight' (s-p/F)	CRHN	
- SOLISSIMO ('Renact'[PBR]) (s-p/F)	CDoC EPom SSFr	
- 'Solo' (s-p/F)	CMac CRHN LRHS NLar	
- 'Tomuri' (m)	CBcs CMac EPom	
hypoleuca B&SWJ 5942	WCru	
kolomikta ♀H5	CBcs CBrac CMac EBee EGren ELan EPfP GKin LCro LRHS LSRN LSto MAsh MGos MHtn MMuc MNrw NCth NLar SBmr SDix SNig SPlb SPoG SRms SWor WFar WTHo	
- (m)	CDoC CWnw MBlu SAth	
- B&SWJ 4243	LSRN WCru	
- 'Doctor Szymanowski' (s-p/F)	CAgr	
- 'Sentyabraskaya' (f/F)	NCth	
- 'Tomoko' (f/F)	WCru	
- 'Yazuaki' (m)	WCru	
melanandra	SPlb	
pilosula misapplied	see *A. tetramera* var. *maloides*	
pilosula (Finet & Gagnep.) Stapf ex Hand.-Mazz.	CDoC IArd MBNS SIvy SPoG SRms	
polygama	WJur	
- B&SWJ 5444	WCru	
- B&SWJ 8525 from Korea	WCru	
- B&SWJ 8923 from Japan	WCru	
- B&SWJ 12564 from Korea	WCru	
strigosa WJC 13662	WCru	
§ ***tetramera*** var. ***maloides*** ♀H5	CExl CWGN CWnw EPfP LCro LRHS MPri NLar WCru WPGP	

Actiniopteris (Pteridaceae)

australis	LRHS LWaG

Acystopteris (Woodsiaceae)

taiwaniana	WPGP

Adansonia (Malvaceae)

digitata	MCtn NPlm SPlb WJur
grandidieri	NPlm SPlb
madagascariensis	SPlb
perrieri	NPlm
rubrostipa	SPlb
za	SPlb

Adelocaryum see *Lindelofia*

Adenium (Apocynaceae)

obesum ♀H1a	CDoC EAri LBom MCtn NPlm SPad

Adenocarpus (Fabaceae)

decorticans	SPlb

Adenophora (Campanulaceae)

bulleyana	GKev NBid SPlb WCot WFar
capillaris	NLar
subsp. ***leptosepala***	
- - BWJ 7986	WCru
coelestis	NBid
confusa 'Hemelstraling'	EMor EPPr

Aegopodium 77

FAIRYBELLS	see *A.* 'Gaudi Violet'
§ 'Gaudi Violet'	CBWd CWnw EMor LBar LSou MHer MHol NCou SMrm SPoG WCot
khasiana	EMor GKev MCtn WHil
latifolia misapplied	see *A. pereskiifolia*
liliifolia	EBee NPer WFar
maximowicziana B&SWJ 11008	WCru
morrisonensis RWJ 10008	MHol WCru
- subsp. *uehatae*	GEdr GKev
- - B&SWJ 126	WCru
§ *nikoensis*	NBid WCot
§ *pereskiifolia*	SHar SPlb WCot
- 'Alba'	SRms
- 'White Blaze'	CWnw LBar LCro LSou NSti SHar
polyantha	SRms
polymorpha	see *A. nikoensis*
remotiflora	EBee MHol
- B&SWJ 8714	WCru
- B&SWJ 10825	ESwi
- B&SWJ 11016	WCru
stricta subsp. *confusa*	GKev
- subsp. *sessilifolia*	EBee
takedae	EBee
taquetii	GEdr
tashiroi	EBee GKev
triphylla	GKev
- B&SWJ 10916	WCru
- var. *japonica*	SBrt
- - B&SWJ 10933	WCru

Adenostyles (Asteraceae)
alpina	GKev

Adesmia (Fabaceae)
longipes	SPlb

Adiantum (Pteridaceae)
§ *aleuticum* ♀H6	CLAP CMiW EWld LCro NBro SPlb
- 'Imbricatum'	CAbb CDor CElw CLAP CMiW CSde CSpe CSta EBee ECha ELan EMor EUrb GBin GEdr GKev Isha LCro LEdu NAlc NBid NBro NLar SDix SPoG SRms
- 'Miss Sharples'	CDTJ CElw CLAP LEdu SRms WCot
§ - 'Subpumilum' ♀H5	CLAP EBlo MWlw NBro WCot
capillus-veneris	EBee ISha
- 'Mairisii'	see *A.* × *mairisii*
caudatum	CDoC EShb ISha LRHS
cuneatum	see *A. raddianum*
fulvum	CDoC
hispidulum ♀H4	CDoC EBee ELan LEdu LRHS LWaG MAsh SPlb WFar WPGP
- 'Bronze Venus'	CDoC EShb ISha SRms
§ × *mairisii* ♀H5	CLAP ISha MAsh WCot WPGP
pedatum misapplied	see *A. aleuticum*
pedatum ambig.	CExl EGrI SHor
pedatum L.	CBcs CDor CLAP CLil CSpe ELan ELon EUrb GAbr GBin GKev GMaP ISha LBom LEdu NAlc NBro NLar SPlb WCot WFar
- var. *subpumilum*	see *A. aleuticum* 'Subpumilum'
poiretii	LEdu
pubescens	LRHS
§ *raddianum*	CDoC LBom LInT WFar
- 'Fragrans'	see *A. raddianum* 'Fragrantissimum'
§ - 'Fragrantissimum'	CDoC LCro LRHS NHrt
- 'Fritz Lüthi'	CDoC LRHS

- 'Lisa'	LRHS
- 'Misty Cloud'	LRHS NAlc
- 'Monocolor'	LRHS
tenerum	LWaG
× *tracyi*	ISha LEdu MWlw WPGP
venustum ♀H7	Widely available
- 'Microphyllum'	LRHS
- 'Texas'	LEdu

Adlumia (Papaveraceae)
fungosa	CSpe

Adonis (Ranunculaceae)
aestivalis	MCtn
amurensis misapplied	see *A.* 'Fukujukai', *A. multiflora*
amurensis ambig.	EBee GEdr
- 'Pleniflora'	see *A. multiflora* 'Sandazaki'
- 'Ryokuho'	GEdr
annua	SPhx
brevistyla	GEdr
'Chichibu-beni'	GEdr
§ 'Fukujukai'	GEdr
multiflora 'Beni-nadeshiko'	GEdr
- 'Hakuju'	GEdr
- 'Hanazono' (d)	GEdr
§ - 'Sandazaki' (d)	GEdr
'Sado-no-maboroshi' (d)	GEdr
vernalis	EDAr

Adoxa (Viburnaceae)
moschatellina	EBee LEdu LShi MNrw NRya WHer WShi

Adromischus (Crassulaceae)
caryophyllaceus	SPlb
cooperi ♀H2	CDoC CPic EShb NTro SIvy
cristatus	CPic
filicaulis	SIvy
maculatus ♀H2	CDoC
marianiae	NTro
schuldtianus	CDoC
trigynus	NTro SPlb

Aechmea ✿ (Bromeliaceae)
candida	NCft
coelestis	NCft
'Covata'	CExl
distichantha	CExl EAri SChr
var. *schlumbergeri*	
filicaulis	NCft
gamosepala	CDTJ CExl
lindenii	NCft
'Nigre' ambig.	NCft
nudicaulis var. *nudicaulis*	NCft
'Flavomarginata' (v)	
pineliana var. *minuta*	see *A. triticina*
recurvata	CBlu SChr
- var. *recurvata*	SBig SBrt
'Red Bands'	NCft
§ *triticina*	NCft
victoriana var. *discolor*	EAri

Aegle (Rutaceae)
sepiaria	see *Citrus trifoliata*

Aegopodium (Apiaceae)
podagraria gold-margined (v)	EPPr
- 'Variegatum' (v)	EBee ECha EPPr GMaP GQue MHoo NBid NSti SEND SIvy WCot WFar WHil

Aeonium

Aeonium ✿ (*Crassulaceae*)

aizoon	SPlb
'Anna' (v)	CPic
appendiculatum	NCft
arboreum	CDTJ CHll CPic EAri ELan EShb MSwo NCft SAth SBig SChr SEND SIvy SMrm WCor
- 'Albovariegatum' (v)	SIvy
- 'Atropurpureum'	CAbb CDTJ CPbh CPic CSde ELan EShb EUrb LWaG NCft NPer SEND SIvy WCor WCot
- subsp. **holochrysum**	CAbb CPbh NCft
I - 'Magnificum'	NCft SArc
- 'Rosie P' **new**	WCor
- 'Tip Top'	CoPl CPbh CPic CSpe EGren MSwo WCor WFar WOld
- 'Variegatum' (v)	CoPl CPic NPer
§ **aureum**	SPlb
balsamiferum	CDoC CDTJ CoPl CPbh CPic EAri EUrb NCft NSti SChr SEND SIvy WCor WCot
'Black Cap'	WOld
'Black Magic'	CPic NCft WOld
'Blushing Beauty' ♀H1c	CAbb CPic EAri EGrl EShb NCft SIvy SMrm WCor WCot WOld
'Bronze Medal'	CPbh CPic EAri NCft SMrm WCor WCot WOld
'Bronze Teacup'	WOld
* **calderense**	NCft
canariense	SEND SIvy
- Californian selection	EAri
- var. **palmense**	EAri
- var. **virgineum**	CDTJ CPic EAri SPlb
castello-paivae	EUrb NCft SChr WCor WFar
ciliatum	CPbh CPic NCft SArc SPlb WCot
'Copper Kettle'	CPic
'Cornish Pixie'	CPic WCor
'Cornish Rose'	WOld
'Cornish Tribute'	CoPl CPbh CPic WCor WOld
'Cristata Sunburst'	CDTJ WCot
cuneatum	CDTJ CoPl CPbh CPic CSde EAri NCft SEND WCor
- blue-leaved	SChr
'Cyclops'	CAbb CPbh CPic NCft WCor WCot WOld
davidbramwellii	CWal NCft
decorum	CPic
* - 'Variegatum' (v)	EShb WCot
diplocyclum	CPbh NCft
- 'Gigantea'	SPlb
dodrantale	CPic
× **domesticum**	see *Aichryson × aizoides* var. *domesticum*
'Du Rozzen'	CPbh
'Durango'	WOld
'Emerald Flame'	CPic WFar WOld
'Emerald Ice' (v)	WOld
* **escobarii**	SPlb
'Feng Ling'	CPic
'Fire Glow'	WOld
'Firecracker'	CAbb CPic EAri EShb WOld
- variegated (v)	WOld
'Floresens' (v)	NCft SIvy WCor
'Garnet'	CPic
glutinosum	CPic EAri
'Goblin'	CPic WOld
gomerense	CPic WFar
goochiae 'Ballerina' (v)	CPic EUrb NCft SIvy WCor WCot WFar
gorgoneum	NCft
'Green Jade'	WOld
'Green Lemon' (v)	CPic
'Green Tea' (v)	CPic
'Halloween'	CPic
haworthii ♀H1c	CDoC CDTJ CPic EShb NCft SEND WCor
- 'Bicolor'	MSwo
- 'Dream Color' (v) ♀H1c	CDTJ CoPl CPbh CPic CSBt EAri EGrl EShb MHer NCft SBig SIvy SMrm WBrk WCor WCot WOld
hierrense	CPbh SPlb
× **holospathulatum**	WCor
× **hybridum**	CPic
'Ice Warrior'	WOld
'Kilimanjaro' (v)	CPic WOld
korneliuslemsii	CExl EAri WOld
lancerottense	SIvy WFar
leucoblepharum	CPic EShb NCft WCor
'Lily Pad'	CPic WCor
lindleyi	NCft
× **loartei**	SIvy WCor WFar
'Logan Rock'	CPbh EShb WCor WCot WOld
'Mardi Gras' (v)	CPbh CPic WOld
'Marnier-Lapostolle' (v)	NCft
'Mary Ann Kunkel'	CPic
'Maximus'	CPic MSCN NCft WCor
'Medusa' (v)	CPbh CPic
'Merry Maiden'	CPbh
* **multiflorum** 'Variegatum' (v)	CDTJ
nobile	WCor
'Pembrokeshire Promise'	WCor
'Phoenix Flame'	CPbh CPic NCft WCor WCot WOld
'Pink Witch' (v)	WOld
'Plum Pudding'	WOld
'Plum Purdy'	CoPl CPic WOld
'Plum Thumb'	CPic EShb WCor WOld
'Poldark'	CPbh CPic SIvy
'Pomegranate'	WCor WOld
I 'Pygmaeum'	NCft WOld
'Red Glow'	WOld
'Rock Hopper'	WCor
'Rosa Catlin'	WOld
rubrolineatum	WCot
'Saturn'	CPic
sedifolium	CPbh CPic CSBt NCft SPlb WAbe WCor
'Simply Scarlet'	CPic
simsii	CDTJ CoPl CTsd NCft SArc WCor
- variegated (v)	EShb
simsii × 'Zwartkop'	NCft SChr WFar
smithii	SChr
spathulatum	CDTJ EDAr NCft WAbe WCot
'Starburst' (v)	EAri NPlm
'Sunburst' (v) ♀H1c	CPbh EAri NCft SIvy WCor
'Suncup'	CPic
'Superbang' (v)	CPic WOld
tabulaeforme ♀H1c	CDTJ CPbh CPic CSde NCft SPlb WCot WOld
'Torchbearer'	CPbh CPic WCor WCot
'Trewidden'	WCot WOld
undulatum	CDTJ CPic NCft SBig SEND SPlb
- 'Poseidon' (v)	WOld
urbicum	SEND
'Velour'	CDoC CDTJ CPbh CPic CTtf CWal EAri EPfP EUrb LCro MSCN NCft NPer SIvy SMrm WCor WOld
'Voodoo'	CAbb CPic EAri EGrl ELan EUrb NCft SBig SEND SIvy WCot WOld
'Zwartkop' ♀H1c	Widely available

Aeschynanthus ✿ *(Gesneriaceae)*

sp.	CDoC EHap NHrt
Black Pagoda Group	WDib
buxifolius ⚑H1a	SBrt WAbe
- KR 9978	WMal
'Fire Wheel'	WDib
'Hot Flash'	WDib
'Japhrolepis'	LBom LCro
'Little Tiger'	WDib
§ ***longicaulis*** ⚑H1a	CDoC EAri LBom LCro WDib
marmoratus	see *A. longicaulis*
'Mona Lisa'	LBom LCro
'Pink Polka'**new**	NHrt
pulcher ⚑H1a	WCot
radicans ⚑H1a	WDib
'Rasta'^PBR	LBom NHrt
rhododendron	WDib
'Scooby Doo'	WDib
speciosus ⚑H1a	WDib
'Twister'^PBR	LCro

Aesculus ✿ *(Sapindaceae)*

arguta	see *A. glabra* var. *arguta*
× ***arnoldiana***	CCVT
assamica	MBlu WPGP
'Autumn Splendor'	CAco CBcs
§ × ***bushii***	MBlu
californica	CMCN SBrt WJur WPGP
- 'Blue Haze'	NPip
- 'Canyon Pink'	CMCN
× ***carnea***	CAco
- 'Briotii'	CAco CBrac CCVT CDoC CEnd EBar EHeP ELan EPfP IPap LMaj MMuc NLar NPip SEWo SHor WFar WHtc WMat
* - 'Variegata' (v)	CMCN
chinensis	CBcs CMCN LMaj SArc
'Dallimorei' (graft-chimaera)	CAco
flava ⚑H5	CAco CBcs CMCN ELan EPfP LMaj MMuc SEND SHor WJur
- 'Burning Gold'	MBlu
- f. ***vestita***	LMaj MBlu
georgiana	see *A. sylvatica*
glabra	CMCN MMuc SEND WJur
- 'April Wine'	MBlu
- var. ***arguta***	NLar
- 'October Red'	EPfP
glaucescens	see *A.* × *neglecta*
hippocastanum	CAco CBcs CBrac CWal CWnw EBar EHeP ELan IPap MMuc NLar NPip SEWo WFar WMat
- 'Baumannii' (d)	CAco EBar ELan
- 'Digitata'	IPap
- 'Flore Pleno'	see *A. hippocastanum* 'Baumannii'
- 'Globosa'	see *A. hippocastanum* 'Umbraculifera'
- f. ***laciniata***	CAco CMCN NLar
§ - 'Umbraculifera'	CAco
- 'Wisselink'	CMCN
indica	CMCN ELan EPfP MMuc SEND SHor WJur
- 'Sydney Pearce' ⚑H5	CAco CBcs CEnd CMCN ELan EPfP MBlu MGos WMat
× ***mississippiensis***	see *A.* × *bushii*
× ***mutabilis*** 'Induta'	CAco CMCN EPfP WMat
§ × ***neglecta***	CMCN
- 'Autumn Fire'	CAco CBcs CMCN WMat
- 'Erythroblastos' ⚑H5	CBcs CEnd CMCN MBlu WMat
parviflora ⚑H5	CAco CBcs CMCN ELan EPfP GKin MBlu MMuc NLar NPip WJur WMat
pavia	CAco CBcs CMCN MMuc WJur
- 'Atrosanguinea'	CAco CEnd CMCN
- var. ***discolor***	LMaj
- - 'Koehnei'	CAco CMCN ELan SPoG WMat
- 'Purple Spring'	EPfP
§ - Splendens Group	CMCN
splendens	see *A. pavia* Splendens Group
§ ***sylvatica***	CMCN
turbinata	CAco LMaj MMuc WJur
wilsonii	CExl MBln

Aethionema *(Brassicaceae)*

sp.	GArf
armenum	GKev
§ ***grandiflorum*** ⚑H5	ECha EDAr EPot GKev MHol SRms
- Pulchellum Group ⚑H5	CSpe
* ***kotschyi*** hort.	EDAr WAbe
membranaceum	GKev
pulchellum	see *A. grandiflorum*
'Warley Rose' ⚑H5	ECha ELan EPot MAsh MNrw SRms
'Warley Ruber'	EDAr EPot WAbe

Agapanthus ✿ *(Amaryllidaceae)*

'African Queen'	EBee EPfP LRHS Midl SBeP
'African Skies' ⚑H3	CPbh IBal LBuc LRHS MPri NLar SFai
africanus misapplied	see *A. praecox*
- 'Albus' misapplied	see *A. praecox* 'Albiflorus'
'Aimee'	CBro
'Alan Street' ⚑H4	IBal SNoN
'Albatross'	ECha
'Albus' ambig.	GMaP
I 'Albus Nanus'	IBal
I 'Albus Roseus'	IBal
'Alice Double' (d)	CPbh
'Allisio'	IBal
Amourette Blue	see *A.* 'Romeo' (Amourette Series)
Amourette White	see *A.* 'Juliet' (Amourette Series)
'Amsterdam'	ELon IBal WTre
'Angela'	ELon IBal
'Ankara'	IBal
'Anneke'	IBal
'Antibe'	IBal
'Aquamarine'	IBal WHoo
'Arctic Star' ⚑H4	CBcs CBdn CDoC CExl CKno CMac CWnw EAri EBee ELan ELon EPfP IBal LRHS LSou LSRN NLar SFai SPoG SVen WTor
'Ardernei'	IBal
'Ardernei Hybrid'	ECha EWes WCot
'Ascona'	IBal
'Autumn Mist'	IBal
'Azure Blue'	IBal
§ 'B in B'^PBR	CBro ECha IBal MBNS NBid NLar SMrm SPel WFar
'Baby Blue'	see *A.* 'Blue Baby' Rom.
'Baby Pete'	IBal
Back in Black	see *A.* 'B in B'
'Ballerina' ⚑H3	IBal
'Ballyrogan'	IBal
'Barcelona'	IBal
'Barnfield Blue'	IBal
'Beeches Dwarf'	IBal
'Ben Hope'	CBro IBal NWbg
'Berlin'	IBal
I 'Best in Show'	ELan MPro
'Beth Chatto'	see *A. campanulatus* 'Albovittatus'
'Bicton Bell'	IBal
'Big Ben'	IBal
'Big Blue'	CAby CEnd CKit CMac CoPl CSde CWCL MSwo SEND SRkn WSpi

Agapanthus

'Big Dutch Blue'	IBal
BINGO BLUE	see *A.* EVER SAPPHIRE (Everpanthus Series)
BINGO WHITE	see *A.* EVER WHITE (Everpanthus Series)
'Black Beauty'	EBee IBal LRHS MAsh WSpi
'Black Buddhist'	EBee EPfP EsgI ESwi GKev IBal LAma MAvo NGdn NSti SMad XFar
BLACK JACK ('Dwaghyb02') (Everpanthus Series)	IBal LCro LRHS MPri SFai SHor WNPC XFar
'Black Magic'	CAbb CBdn CPbh EBee EGrI ELan EsgI ESwi IBal LBar LRHS MHol MNrw NSti SFai SPoG WCot WFar WTor
'Black Pantha'^PBR	CBcs CBro CExl CPbh CWGN EBee ELan EPfP EUrb EWes GKin GMaP IBal LCro LRHS MBNS MHol Midl MNrw NGdn NLar NSti SFai SIvy SPoG SVen WCot WSpi WTor
BLITZ PRESTIGE ('Allprestige'^PBR)	IBal
'Blitzza'	IBal
'Bloemfontein'	IBal
§ 'Blue Baby' Rom.	ELan ELon IBal
'Blue Beauty'	CBdn
'Blue Brush'	SEND
'Blue Flare'	IBal
'Blue Formality'	IBal
'Blue Fox'	SMHy
'Blue Giant'	CBro EGrI ELan IBal MGos NLar WSpi
'Blue Globe'	GMaP IBal
'Blue Heaven'^PBR	CWGN EWes IBal SMad
'Blue Horizons'^PBR (v)	IBal
'Blue Ice' ♀H3	CBdn IBal LCro LRHS SAko
'Blue Imp'	CBro IBal
'Blue Jay'	IBal
'Blue Magic' ♀H4	IBal
'Blue Moon'	CBro ECha IBal MHol SEND WCot
'Blue Nile'	IBal
'Blue Pixie'	IBal
'Blue Prince'	ELon
'Blue Ribbon'	ECha IBal
'Blue Skies' ambig.	IBal
'Blue Spear'	IBal
'Blue Steel'	IBal
BLUE STORM ('Atiblu'^PBR) (Storm Series)	EGren EPfP ERom IBal LBuc LRHS SArc SBig SEND
BLUE THUNDER ('Sdb002'^PBR) (Everpanthus Series)	CAbb CPbh EBee IBal LRHS LSou MHol MPri NCth NLar SFai
'Blue Triumphator'	CDor EGren EGrI EPfP GKev GMaP IBal LRHS MAvo MSwo SAth WSpi
'Blue Umbrella'	CDor LRHS LShi WSpi
'Blue Velvet'	IBal
BLUE VELVET ('Malan Don')	WFar
'Bluety'^PBR	IBal SVen
'Boleyn Blue'	ECha
'Border Blue'	IBal
'Bressingham Blue'	CBro CDoC EBlo EPPr EWes IBal
'Bressingham Bounty'	EBee EBlo IBal
'Bressingham White'	CDoC EBlo EGren IBal
'Bridal Bouquet'	EBee IBal LBar LBuc LRHS LSRN MPri SAko SFai
'Bright Blue'	IBal
BRILLIANT BLUE ('Aga04051'^PBR)	CAbb CBdn CBWd CCht CEnd CKno CTsd EAri EGren ELan EPfP IBal LBom LRHS LSou MHol MPri NCth NLar SFai SOrN SRkn WHoo
'Bristol'	IBal SVen
'Broadleigh Babe'	CBro
'Buckingham Palace'	CBro ECha EWes GAbr IBal WCot
'Calimero'	IBal
'Cally Blue'	EPPr IBal
'Cally Pale Blue'	IBal
campanulatus	CMac ELan ELon EPfP ESgI GKev GKin IBal LRHS MArl WCot WFar WSpi
- var. *albidus*	CDor ECha EPfP GKev GKin IBal MArl MHer MMuc NBid NGdn SEND WGwG WHoo WSpi
§ - 'Albovittatus' (v)	CTtf
- 'Cobalt Blue'	ECha EGrI ELan EPfP GKin IBal LRHS MArl MMuc NGdn
- subsp. *patens*	EPfP IBal
- 'Profusion'	CBro ECha IBal
- 'Ultramarine'	IBal
- variegated (v)	NPer
- 'Wedgwood Blue'	IBal
- 'Wendy'	EBlo
- 'White Hope'	EBlo
'Castle of Mey'	CBro CExl ELon GAbr IBal LCro WSpi
'Catharina'	IBal
§ *caulescens*	EBlo IBal
- subsp. *angustifolius*	ELon SEND
'Cedric Morris'	ESgI IBal
'Celebration' ♀H4	CBdn IBal LCro
'Chandra'	IBal
'Charlie Morrell'	IBal
'Charlotte'^PBR	CAbb CMac EBee EGren ELan EPfP IBal LBar LBom LBuc LCro LRHS LSou MHol MPri MPro SFai SOrN SPad SPel SPoG SVen WCot WFar WTor
'Cheney's Lane'	SMHy
'Cherbours'	IBal
'Cherry Holley'	ELon
'Chika's Blue'	EBee IBal
'Clarence House'	IBal
'Cloud Burst' **new**	IBal
'Cloudy Days'	IBal
coddii	IBal MHer WCot
'Columba'	EGren ELon IBal LAma NBid SVen
comptonii	see *A. praecox* subsp. *minimus*
DANUBE	see *A.* 'Donau'
'Dark Silk'	CBdn CPbh EPfP IBal LBar LCro LRHS MHol SFai
I 'Darkest of All'	MPro
'Dart Valley'	CBdn
'Dawn Star'	ECha
'Debbie'	IBal
'Delft'	IBal
'Delft Blue'	IBal NLar
'Devon Dawn'	IBal
'Dnjepr'	CBro EBee IBal
'Dokkum'	IBal
'Dokter Brouwer'	EGren EPfP IBal LAma LCro LRHS NLar SVen WCha
§ 'Donau'	CBro GKev IBal NBir
DOUBLE DIAMOND ('Rfdd'^PBR) ♀H3	CBdn CDor CPbh EBee EPfP EWes IBal LBuc NLar NWbg SFai SPoG WNPC WSpi WTor
'Dublin'	IBal
'Duivenbrugge Blue'	IBal
'Durban'	IBal
'Dutch Seaside'	IBal
dwarf blue	IBal
dyeri	see *A. inapertus* subsp. *intermedius*
'Early Blue'	EBee ELon IBal
'Eggesford Sky' ♀H5	IBal
'Elaine'	IBal
'Elisa'	IBal

Agapanthus

'Elizabeth Salisbury'	IBal
'Enigma'	CBro CDor CExl EAri EBee ECha ELan ELon EPfP EsgI EWhm IBal LBar LBom LRHS MHol Midl NCth NLar SAth SEND SPel WCot WSpi
'Essence of Summer'	IBal
'Ethel's Joy'	IBal
'Evening Eclipse'	CBlu EPfP IBal LBar LRHS
'Evening Star'	ECha
(Everpanthus Series)	see *A.* POPPIN' PURPLE (Everpanthus Series)
EVER AMETHYST	
§ - EVER SAPPHIRE ('Andbin'^{PBR})	IBal LBom LBuc LRHS LSou MPri SFai
§ - EVER WHITE ('Wp001'^{PBR}) ♀H5	CBro EGren IBal LBom LBuc LRHS LSou MHtn MPri MPro NCth SFai
'Exmoor' ♀H4	CBdn IBal
'Finnline' (v)	SRms
'Fiona'	IBal
FIREWORKS ('Mdb001'^{PBR}) ♀H3	Widely available
'First Love'	IBal
'Flore Pleno' (d)	CDor CExl CMac ECha GKin IBal MHol NGdn WFar
'Flower of Love' ♀H4	CBdn CWGN EGren EPfP IBal LBom LCro LRHS LSou MPri NCth NLar SFai SPoG WNPC
'Fluor'	IBal
I 'Forma'	IBal
FRAGRANT GLEN	see *A.* 'Glen Avon'
FRAGRANT SNOW	see *A.* 'Snow Cloud'
'Full Moon' ♀H3	CBdn IBal LBar LRHS LSou MHol SFai WNPC
'Gail's Purple'	IBal
'Galgery'	IBal
'Gayle's Lilac'	CBcs CExl EGren ELan ELon EPfP GKin LRHS MPie NGdn SMrm WFar WGwG
'Gem'	CBdn ELon
'Gentian'	IBal
'Genua'	IBal
'Getty White'	LRHS
'Glacier'	IBal
'Glacier Stream'	CBro CDor EsgI IBal NLar
§ 'Glen Avon'	CBdn CPbh CWCL IBal LBar LRHS SFai
'Gold Strike'^{PBR} (v)	IBal SPoG
'Golden Drop'^{PBR} (v)	CBcs EPfP ESwi IBal LBar LCro LRHS NSti SBig SRms WCot
'Gothenburg'	IBal
GRAPHITE BLUE ('Turk8'^{PBR})	CBcs
'Greenfield'	IBal
'Hamar'	IBal
'Hanneke'	IBal SAko SFai WNPC
'Hannover'	IBal
'Happy Blue' ♀H3	IBal
'Harvest Blue'	IBal
§ Headbourne hybrids	Widely available
'Helsinki'	IBal
'His Majesty'	IBal MPro
'Hole Park Blue'	WMal
'Hoyland Blue' ♀H4	IBal WFar
'Ice Blue Star' ♀H5	CBro ELon IBal
'Ice Lolly'	CBro IBal
ICICLES ('Duivenbrugge White')	CBlu IBal MHol NSti
inapertus	CAby CPbh CSpe CWnw EWes IBal SMHy WPGP
- 'Avalanche' ♀H4	WSpi
- 'Cascade Crystal'	IBal
- 'Crystal Drop'	CExl IBal
- subsp. *hollandii*	IBal
- - 'Sky' ♀H4	CBro CDor IBal NBid SRms
- 'Ice Cascade'	IBal
- 'Icicle'	CSpe SPoG
- subsp. *inapertus* 'White'	IBal
§ - subsp. *intermedius*	IBal
I - - 'August Bells'	CBro IBal
- 'Little Black Number'	EsgI
- 'Midnight Cascade'	CExl CSpe EBee EGrI NBid SRms
- 'Mood Indigo'	IBal
- subsp. *pendulus*	EGrI
- - 'Black Magic'	CBdn CDor CWnw IBal SPeP WFar
- - 'Graskop'	CBro CExl CSpe EBee IBal LCro MPro SMrm SRms
- 'Summer Blue Bells'	EBlo
- tall, pale blue-flowered	WPGP
- 'Tempest'	WPGP
- 'White Cloud'	IBal
'Indigo Dreams'	CBdn CBlu CKno CPbh CWnw EBee ELon IBal LRHS MHol NLar SFai SVen
INDIGO FROST	see *A.* TWISTER
'Inkspots'	CMac ELon IBal SPoG
I 'Intermedius' van Tubergen	IBal LAma NBid
'Isis'	CBro CSde ECha ELon IBal
'Jacaranda' ♀H4	CBcs CBdn CMac CPbh IBal NWbg SFai WNPC
'Jack's Blue'	CBro EBee ELan GAbr IBal LRHS MHol MPro NGdn NLar SEND WCot WFar WSpi
'James'	CBdn IBal
'Jersey Giant'	IBal
'Jessica' ♀H4	IBal LRHS LSou
'Jodie'	ELon IBal SMHy
'Johanna'	IBal
'Johannesburg'	IBal
Johannesburg hybrids	ECha
'Jolanda'	IBal LAma
'Jonie' ♀H3	IBal
'Jonny's White' ♀H4	IBal
§ 'Juliet' (Amourette Series)	LRHS SVen
'Kalmthout Blue'	IBal
'Kew White'	SMHy SPel
'Kilmurry Blue'	IBal
'Kilmurry White'	IBal
'Kingston Blue'	ECha NBid
'Kirsty'	IBal
'Kobold'	CBro IBal WFar
'Lady Thumb'	IBal
§ 'Lapis'	CDoC CMac CSde EBee EPfP EUrb LRHS MHol MPri NLar SFai SVen
'Lapis Lazuli'	see *A.* 'Lapis'
'Lavender Haze'	CDoC CMac CPbh EBee EPfP IBal LCro MPri SFai SPoG
'Leanne'	CBdn IBal
'Leicester' ♀H4	IBal
'L'Esprit'	IBal
'Liam's Lilac'	CBdn CDoC CExl ELon IBal LCro LRHS NLar WFar WTre
'Lilac Flash'	CPbh EsgI IBal SVen
'Lilac Lullaby'	IBal MPro NLar
'Lilac Time'	ELon IBal
'Lilliput'	CBcs CBro CMac CSpe EBlo ECha ELan ELon EPot GArf GMaP IBal MAsh NGdn NLar SMHy SRms WFar
'Lissabon'	IBal
'Lisse'	IBal
'Little Boy Blue'	IBal
LITTLE DUTCH BLUE ('Ldb 14'^{PBR})	IBal LCro MHol
'Little Dutch White'^{PBR}	IBal LCro MHol
'Little White'	IBal

Name	Sources
'Littlecourt'	CBro IBal
'Loch Hope' ♀H5	CBro CElw EBee EBlo ELon IBal MArl MHol NGdn WCot WSpi
'Lorna'	CBdn
'Los Angeles'	IBal
'Luly' ♀H3	IBal
'Luna'	IBal
'Lydenburg'	IBal WPGP
'Lyn Valley'	CBdn IBal
'Madurodam'	IBal
'Magnifico'	IBal
'Malaga'	IBal
'Malmo'	IBal
'Marchants Cobalt Cracker'	ECha SMHy
'Marchants Night Sky'	SMHy
'Marcus'	EGren IBal LAma
'Margaret'	ELon IBal WFar
'Maria'	CBdn
'Marianne'	IBal
'Marjorie' ♀H4	IBal
'Martine'	IBal
'Maureen' ♀H5	CBdn EBee IBal
'May Snow' (v)	WCot
'Medan'	IBal
'Medusa'	IBal
'Megan's Mauve' ♀H4	CBcs CBdn CBro EBee ELon IBal LBar LCro MPri MPro NSti SFai
'Meibont' (v)	WCot
'Melbourne'	IBal
'Messina'	IBal
MI CASA ('Aaopr017'PBR)	IBal Midl SEND
'Michelle'	IBal
'Middelburg'	IBal
MIDKNIGHT BLUE ('Monmid')	EWes SEND
'Midnight'	EWes IBal
'Midnight Blue' ambig.	CDoC ELan IBal MHer NLar WFar WTre
'Midnight Dream'	EBee IBal WFar
'Midnight Madness'	IBal LCro MHol
MIDNIGHT SKY ('Dwaghby01') (Everpanthus Series)	CBdn EBee IBal LBar LCro LRHS SFai SOrN
§ 'Midnight Star' ♀H5	Widely available
'Mini Blue'	IBal
'Misty Dawn' (v)	CWGN EBee ELon EWhm IBal MHol SPeP
'Mole Valley'	CBdn IBal
'Molly Howick'	ELon
'Monique' ♀H4	EGren IBal
'Montreal'	IBal
'Moonlight Star'	EBee IBal MHol WFar
'Moonshine'	IBal WFar WTre
I 'Mooreanus' misapplied	EBee IBal NBid
'Morning Star'	IBal
'Mount Stewart'	IBal
'Nancy'	IBal
'Napoli'	IBal
'Navy Blue'	see A. 'Midnight Star'
'Neverland' (v)	CBdn LCro LRHS MHol NWbg SOrN
'Newcastle'	IBal
'Nghia'**new**	CBdn
'Night Sky'	CBdn IBal LRHS MHol
'Nikki'	CBdn IBal
'Nocturnal Horizons'	MPro
'Northern Light'	IBal WTre
'Northern Star'PBR ♀H4	CBcs CBlu CDoC CExl CKno CWnw EAri EBee ELan ELon EPfP EUrb EWes IBal LBar LBom LCro LRHS LSou LSRN MHol Midl MPri NSti SFai SPoG SRkn SRms WNPC
nutans	see A. caulescens
'Odessa'	IBal
'Oslo'	ELon IBal
I 'Ovatus'	ERom
'Oxford'	IBal
'Pacific Blue'PBR	CDoC IBal
Palmer's hybrids	see A. Headbourne hybrids
'Patent Blue'	IBal
'Patricia'	MPro
'Patriot'	IBal
'Pavlova'	CSde EPfP IBal
'Penelope Palmer'	IBal
'Penny Slade'	IBal
'Peter Franklin' ♀H4	IBal
'Peter Pan' ambig.	CBcs CBlu CDor EBee ECha EGren ELan ELon EPfP IBal LBar LRHS MCtn NLar NWbg SAth SPoG SRkn SRms WCAu
'Peter Pan American'	GKev
'Phantom'	CBdn EBee IBal LBar LRHS NLar SAko SFai WCot
'Picton Blue'	WFar
'Pink Cloud'	IBal
'Pino' ♀H4	CAbb CBdn CBro CKno IBal LRHS MHol MPri NWbg SFai SRkn
'Pinocchio'	EGren IBal MPri
'Pirame'	IBal
PITCHOUNE BLUE ('Scrarey09'PBR)	IBal LRHS
PITCHOUNE WHITE ('Tur161'PBR)	EGren LRHS WTor
'Plas Merdyn White'	IBal
'Podge Mill'	IBal
'Polar Ice'	EGren ELon EPfP IBal LAma LCro MNrw SVen WCAu WSpi
'Polar Star'	EBee EPfP IBal LRHS WCAu
§ POPPIN' PURPLE ('Pm003'PBR) (Everpanthus Series)	CBdn CBlu CPbh CSde CWGN EAri EBee EHeP ELan EPfP EUrb IBal LBar LBom LBuc LCro LRHS LSou MAvo MHol MPri NCth NLar SFai SMrm SOrN XFar
POPPIN' STAR ('Amdb002'PBR) (Everpanthus Series)	IBal LBar LRHS
'Porcelain'	IBal
§ *praecox*	CBcs CBlu CTsd CWal EAri EGren EPfP EUrb IBal LCro SArc SBig SVic SWor WCha XFar
§ - 'Albiflorus'	CBcs CBro CBWd CSde CTsd EGren EHeP EPfP ERom EUrb IBal LBom LCro LSRN MGos MSwo SAth SEND SHor SRms SWor XFar
§ - subsp. *minimus*	IBal SEND
- - 'Adelaide'	IBal
§ - subsp. *orientalis*	CBro MCtn
- - 'Weaver'	IBal
- 'Storms River'	IBal
'Pretty Heidy'	LRHS LSou MHol NLar SFai
'Pretty Wendy'	IBal
'Pride of Bicton'	CBdn
'Princess Margaret'	IBal
§ 'Purple Cloud'	CBcs CBro CBWd CExl EBee EGren EGrI ELan EPfP LCro MArl MHer MHol NBid NGdn NLar NSti SBig SMad WCot WSpi
'Purple Delight' ♀H3	CPbh EPfP IBal LBuc LCro SAko SVen WNPC
'Purple Emperor'	CPbh IBal LBar MHol
'Purple Fountain'	IBal SRms
'Purple Heart'	CAbb CBdn IBal MPri MPro SFai
'Purple Magic'	IBal
'Purple Prince'	CBdn
'Queen Anne'	IBal

Agapanthus

Name	Suppliers
'Queen Mother'	IBal Midl WSpi
QUEEN MUM ('Pmn06'PBR)	Widely available
'Queen of the Ocean'	IBal
'Quink Drops'	SMHy
'Radiant Star'	IBal
'Regal Beauty'	CBdn CBro CPbh IBal LBar LSRN NBid SAko SFai
'Rhapsody in Blue' ♀H4	CBdn IBal
'Rhone'	CBro IBal
'Rob Cole'	WCot
'Robin'	IBal
§ 'Romeo' (Amourette Series)	SVen
'Rosemary'	CDor
'Rosewarne'	CBcs CDoC CExl
'Rotterdam'	IBal
'Roxanne'	EGren IBal
'Royal Blue' ♀H4	CBro GMaP IBal WCot WSpi
'Royal Jubilee'	IBal
'Royal Purple'	CWnw
'Royal Velvet' ♀H4	CAbb CBdn CBlu CKno EPfP IBal LBar LCro LRHS MHol MMrt MPri SFai SVen WFar WNPC
'Sabang'	IBal
'Saint Paul's Walden Bury'	IBal
'Sally Anne'	CBdn
'San Remo'	IBal
'Sandringham' ♀H5	CBcs CWnw EBee ELon EWes IBal LBar LRHS LSRN Midl NBid NLar SEND
'Sandy'PBR ♀H4	CKno IBal LSou MHol
'Sapphire'	IBal
'Sarah'PBR	IBal NLar
SEA BREEZE ('Breag2')	XFar
'Sea Coral'	CMac EBee ESgI IBal LRHS MArl NSti SBig SEND SPoG
'Sea Foam'	CMac
'Sea Spray'	WFar
SEA STORM ('Atisea'PBR) (Storm Series)	EGren EPfP WLov
'Second Chance'	IBal
'Selma Bock'	CPbh IBal
'Semarang'	IBal
'Senna'PBR	IBal
'Septemberhemel'	IBal WTre
'Shooting Stars'	IBal LRHS MPro
'Silberpfeil'	IBal NLar
'Silver Anniversary'	IBal
'Silver Baby' ♀H3	CAbb CBcs CBdn CBro CDoC CKno CWGN EBee ELon EPfP IBal LBar LEdu LRHS LSou MPri MPro NLar SFai SPoG SRms WNPC
'Silver Lining'	CBlu CSde EPfP IBal LBar MPro NLar SMrm SPel WLov
'Silver Mist'	CDor IBal
SILVER MOON ('Notfred'PBR) (v) ♀H5	CBcs CBdn CBro EBee EBlo ELan GKev IBal LCro LRHS LSou MGos MHol MHtn NLar NSti SFai SPeP SPoG WCot XFar
'Sky Rocket'	IBal
'Sky Star'	IBal
'Skyscraper'	IBal
§ 'Snow Cloud' ♀H4	CBcs CBdn CExl EBee LBar LRHS NLar SAko SEND SFai SOrN SPoG WSpi
'Snow Crystal' ♀H3	CBro CPbh EPfP IBal LCro SFai SPoG
'Snow Pixie'	CSpe EBee EBlo IBal SArc WSpi
'Snow Princess'	ELon IBal
'Snow Shadows'	CBro IBal
'Snowball'	EGren
'Snowstorm'PBR (Storm Series)	CCht ERom IBal SArc
'Sofie'PBR	CWnw IBal
'Sorento'	IBal
'Sosua'	IBal
'Southern Cross'	IBal
'Spanish Lady'	IBal
SPARKLE ('Dwaghyb05') (Everpanthus Series) new	SFai
'Star Quality'	CSde EGren ELan IBal LRHS LSou MPri MPro
'Starburst Blue'	IBal
'Starburst White'	IBal
'Stardust'	CSde EBee EGren EPfP IBal MPri MPro NLar
'Stargazer'	EGren IBal MPro
'Starry Night' new	IBal LSou
'Stellenbosch'	LEdu
'Stéphanie'	ELan
'Stéphanie Charm'	ELan IBal
'Stephanie's Beauty'	IBal
'Stockholm'	IBal LAma XFar
'Storm Cloud' Reads	see A. 'Purple Cloud'
'Storm Cloud' (d)	CBro IBal
'Strawberry Ice'	EBee EPfP IBal IPot LBar LCro LRHS NWbg SFai WSpi
'Streamline'	CBcs CEnd CKno EBee EGrI ELon EPfP EsgI GAbr GKin GMaP IBal LRHS MArl SEND SVen
'Su Casa'	IBal
'Summer Blue'	EGren
'Summer Clouds'	ELan IBal
'Summer Days' ♀H5	CBdn ELon IBal
'Summer Delight' ♀H4	IBal
Summer Love Series	CSde
- SUMMER LOVE BLUE ('Corag02bl'PBR)	CBlu EGren ELan EPot IBal LRHS
'Summer Skies'	ELon IBal
'Summer Snow'	IBal
'Sunfield'	IBal LAma MNrw NLar NPer
'Super Star'	CBro IBal MPro
'Suzan'	IBal
'Sweet Dreams'	CBdn
'Sweet Surprise'	CWCL EPfP IBal LBar LBuc MPri SFai SVen
'Sylvia'PBR	EGren IBal LBuc MPro
'Sylvine'	CWnw IBal WTre
'Tarka'	ELon ESgI IBal
'Taw Valley'	CKno EBee ELon EPfP EPPr IBal LRHS
'Thorn'	IBal
'Three Times'	IBal
'Thumbelina'	CMac ELan IBal
THUNDER STORM ('Dunaga02') (Storm Series) (v)	CWGN SPeP
'Timaru'	CBro ELan ELon GAbr GMaP MHol NGdn WCot WTre
'Tinkerbell' (v)	EBlo ELan EPfP IBal MHol NPer SPoG SRms
'Tiny Tim'	IBal
'Tom Thumb'PBR	CBlu CDoC CExl CKit CSde EPot EUrb IBal SArc SVen
'Top Slice' (v)	WCot
'Torbay'	EBee ELon EPfP GAbr GKin IBal LRHS MArl MNrw NCth NLar SEND
'Tornado'	ELan ELon IBal NLar
'Tresco Select'	IBal
'Triangle'	IBal
'Tripoli'	IBal
'Tsolo'	IBal
'Turquoise Princess'	LBar MPro

Agapanthus

	'Twilight Zone'	IBal LBar
§	TWISTER ('Ambic001'^{PBR}) ♀^{H4}	Widely available
	umbellatus Redouté	see *A. praecox* subsp. *orientalis*
	'Underway'	ELon EWes IBal
	'Valencia'	IBal LBar
	'Vallée Blanche'	IBal
	'Vallée d'Azur' **new**	IBal
	'Vallée de la Loire'	IBal LBar
	'Vallée de la Sarthe'	IBal LBar
	'Vallée de l'Authion'	IBal
	'Vallée du Cap'	IBal LBar
	'Vallée du Lathan'	IBal LBar
	Ventnor hybrid	SVen
	'Virginia'	IBal
	'Volendam'	IBal
	'Washington'	IBal
	'Wavy Navy'	IBal
	'Wedding Day'	EBee IBal
	'Wembworthy'	IBal
	'White Baby'	IBal
	'White Century'	CBdn
	'White Dwarf'	see *A.* white-flowered, dwarf
	'White Giant'	EGrI EPfP WSpi
	'White Heaven'^{PBR}	CAby EBee EWes IBal LRHS MHol Midl SEND SMad SPel WSpi WTre
	'White Ice'	CPbh IBal
	'White Pixie'	CBdn CPbh IBal LRHS SFai
	'White Superior'	EBee GMaP IBal WTre
	'White Umbrella'	ELan
§	white-flowered, dwarf	CBro ECha EPfP IBal NBir NGdn
	'Whitney'^{PBR}	IBal SVen
	'Windlebrooke'	ECha IBal NLar
	'Windsor Grey'	Widely available
	'Winsome'	IBal
	'Winter Sky'	CBdn
	'Wolga'	CBro IBal
	'Yellow Tips'	IBal
	'Zachary'	ELon IBal
	'Zeal Thomas'	IBal
	'Zigzag White' ♀^{H3}	WCot
	'Zomba'	IBal

Agapetes (Ericaceae)

	'Ludgvan Cross' ♀^{H2}	CBcs CTsd
	serpens ♀^{H2}	CBcs CTsd
	- 'Scarlet Elf'	CTsd LRHS

Agastache (Lamiaceae)

	'After Eight'	CMiW CSpe LBar
	anethiodora	see *A. foeniculum* (Pursh) Kuntze
	anisata	see *A. foeniculum* (Pursh) Kuntze
	APADANA ORANGE	MPro
	APADANA ROSE	MPro
	'Arcado Pink'	MCtn SPhx
	aurantiaca	CAgr GKev SPhx SPlb
	- 'Apricot Sprite'	CSpe CWnw EGren LRHS LShi MCtn MHol MHoo MPro NGdn SPeP SRkn StAn WKit
	- FRAGRANT CARPET (mixed) **new**	SPhx
	- 'Navajo Sunset'	CWal MCtn
	- 'Tango'	CAby CFis EDAr EUrb GElm LRHS MHoo SPad SPhx WFar
	'Blackadder'	Widely available
	'Blue Boa'^{PBR}	CDor CKno CWGN CWnw EAri EBee ECha EGren EUrb LCro LSRN MHol Midl MPro NBir NLar NSti NWbg SAth SDix SIvy SPoG SRms WCAu WCav WFar WHoo WSpi WTor

*	'Blue Bonnet'	CSpe
	'Blue Fortune' ♀^{H6}	CBcs ECha EGren ELan EPfP GMaP LCro LRHS NDov NLar SPhx SRms WCAu WNPC WSpi WTor
	'Bolero'	CSpe MHoo SPhx
	cana 'Heatwave'^{PBR}	LCro WNPC
	'Cotton Candy'^{PBR}	LCro
	'Crazy Fortune' (v)	CWGN
	'Firebird'	CWGN EBee ELan MArl MHol SRms WFar
	'Fleur'	GKev WGoo
	foeniculum misapplied	see *A. rugosa*
§	*foeniculum* (Pursh) Kuntze	CCBP CGHo ELan ENfk GJem IDun MCtn MHer MHoo MNHC SPhx SRms SVic WFar WJek WKit WRBe WTre
	- 'Alabaster'	CBcs EWes LCro NLar NSti SPhx XFar
*	'Fragrant Delight'	EDAr
	'Globetrotter'	CAgr CFis SHor SPhx WFar
	'Heather Queen'	MCtn
	'Kolibri'	NDov WGoo
	(Kudos Series) 'Kudos Ambrosia'^{PBR}	ELan MAsh SHor SPoG
	- 'Kudos Coral'^{PBR}	CWnw EBee EPfP LBar MHol NWbg SRkn WFar WNPC
	- 'Kudos Gold'^{PBR}	EBee EPfP LRHS MCtn MHol NWbg SPoG
	- 'Kudos Mandarin'^{PBR}	ELan EPfP LBar LCro MPro SPoG
	- 'Kudos Red'^{PBR}	LBar MPro WHil
	- KUDOS SILVER BLUE ('Kudos Sb'^{PBR})	EBee ELan EPfP NWbg
	- 'Kudos Yellow'^{PBR}	ELan EPfP LBar MPro NWbg WHil
	'Linda'	CWGN WCot
	'Mango Tango'	GKev MPri
	mexicana	CAgr
	- 'Red Fortune'^{PBR}	CBcs CWGN EBee ELan EPfP EUrb LCro MAsh MHol SPoG WNPC
	- 'Sangria'	CWGN MHoo NGdn SPhx SRms
	- 'Morello'	LBar LBom LCro LRHS MHtn NWbg
	nepetoides	CAgr CBWd CSpe EMor EPPr MCtn
	pallidiflora	CAgr
	- var. *neomexicana*	SPlb
	- - 'Rose Mint'	CSpe WKit
	'Peachie Keen'	LRHS
	'Pink Pearl'	LBar
	'Pink Pop'	MHoo
	(Poquito Series) POQUITO BUTTER YELLOW ('Tnagapby'^{PBR})	EPfP LRHS
	- POQUITO DARK BLUE ('Tnagapdb'^{PBR})	LBar LRHS
	- POQUITO LAVENDER ('Tnagapl'^{PBR})	LBar LRHS
	- POQUITO ORANGE ('Tnagapo'^{PBR})	LBar LRHS
	'Purple Haze'	CDoC EBee EBlo LRHS MAvo MWlw NDov WCAu WCav
	'Raspberry Summer'^{PBR}	MHtn
	'Rosie Posie'^{PBR}	LBar MPri
§	*rugosa*	CFis EPPr IDun MEar MHoo SPlb SRms WJek
	- f. *albiflora*	CCBP IDun SDix WCAu
	- - 'Alabaster'	CDor EMor NDov XFar
	- - 'Liquorice White'	CBWd ELan EPfP GQue MArl MBel MCtn MHoo SPlb SPoG SRms WKit
	- BEELICIOUS PURPLE ('Agapd'^{PBR})	EBee ELan LBar LCro MArl MAsh Midl MPie
	- 'Golden Jubilee'	CSpe EBlo ECha ELan EMor EUrb LBar MArl MCtn MHol NGdn NLar SDix SRms WFar WJek WKit WMal

Agave 85

– 'Korean Zest'	ESwi SPhx WCru	*bovicornuta*	WCot
– 'Liquorice Blue'	CDor EGrl ELan EPfP GQue LRHS MArl MBel MCtn MHol NGdn SMrm SPoG SRms StAn WFar WHoo WKit	*bracteosa*	CAco CBlu CDTJ EUrb NPlm SBig WCot
		celsii	see *A. mitis* var. *mitis*
		cerulata subsp. *nelsonii*	CDTJ
– 'Little Adder'	CBcs CBWd CMiW CSpe EGren EUrb LBar LCro LRHS MBNS MHol MidI MPie MPro NCth SPad WHoo WNPC	'Chia Nong Pink Sapphire'ᴾᴮᴿ	WCot XFar
		'Chia Nong Sensation'ᴾᴮᴿ	LCro XFar
		'Chia Nong Yellow Baby'ᴾᴮᴿ	WCot
rupestris	CSpe EDAr MHoo SPhx	*chrysantha*	CAco CBlu CDTJ SBig WCot
– 'Apache Sunset'	CAgr GKev MCtn SPlb	– 'Black Canyon'	WCot
'Sandstone' (Arizona Series)	CBlu	*chrysoglossa*	CDTJ
'Serpentine'	EBee NLar	*colimana*	see *A. ortgiesiana*
'Summer Glow'	CWGN NDov SPoG WCot	*colorata*	CBlu CDTJ CJun NPlm WCot
'Summer Sunset'ᴾᴮᴿ	CDor CWGN LCro	'Cornelius'	NCft WCot
'Tangerine Dreams'	CSpe MAsh	*cupreata*	CDTJ
urticifolia	EMor	*decipiens*	SPlb
– 'Alba'	WFar	*demeesteriana* variegated (v)	NPlm
'Violet Vision'ᴾᴮᴿ	CWGN EPfP LCro		
		deserti	CAco CDTJ CJun CPic WCot
		– var. *simplex*	WCot

Agathaea see *Felicia*

Agathis (Araucariaceae)

australis	CAco	*difformis*	CDTJ
		durangensis	CCht SPad SPlb
		elongata	see *A. angustifolia*
		ensifera	CJun

Agathosma (Rutaceae)

capensis	CBcs SEle	'Falling Waters'	EUrb NPlm
pulchella **new**	CBcs	*ferdinandi-regis*	see *A. victoriae-reginae*
		ferox	see *A. salmiana* var. *ferox*
		filifera ♀ᴴ²	CDoC CDTJ CJun CPbh SBig SChr SPlb WCot

Agave ✿ (Asparagaceae)

albomarginata	CDTJ	*flexispina*	SPlb
americana ♀ᴴ²	CAbb CBcs CCht CPbh CPic CTsd EGren EShb EUrb NPlm SArc SAth SBig SChr SEND SFol SPlb SVen WCot	*funkiana*	SBig
		garciae-mendozae	CDTJ
		geminiflora	CDTJ CJun CPbh EShb EUrb NPlm SBig
– subsp. *franzosini*	EUrb NPlm SAth SBig	*gentryi*	CDTJ CExl EUrb NPlm SBig SPlb WCot
– 'Marginata' (v) ♀ᴴ²	CAco CDTJ NQui SAth SEND SVen WCot		
– 'Mediopicta' misapplied	see *A. americana* 'Mediopicta Alba'	– 'Jaws' **new**	EUrb
– 'Mediopicta' (v) ♀ᴴ²	CDTJ SArc SWor	*ghiesbreghtii*	CPbh EUrb NCft
§ – 'Mediopicta Alba' (v) ♀ᴴ²	CDTJ CJun CPbh CPic ELan EUrb LRHS NCft NPlm SBig SPlb WCot	*gracilipes*	CExl
		gracilis	see *A. atrovirens* var. *atrovirens*
– 'Mediopicta Aurea' (v)	CTtf NPlm WCot	*gracillima*	SPlb
– subsp. *protamericana*	CDTJ NCft	*guadalajarana*	CDTJ CPbh NCft NPlm SBig
– – blue	CExl SPlb	*guiengola* 'Crème Brûlée' (v)	CPic
– 'Striata' (v)	CDTJ EShb WCot		
– 'Variegata' (v) ♀ᴴ²	CAbb CBcs CPbh CPic CSde CTsd CWal ELan EPfP EShb EUrb LWaG NCft NPer NPlm SArc SBig SChr SFol SPlb SWor WFar	*guttata*	EAri WCot
		gypsophila 'Ivory Curls'	see *A. pablocarrilloi* 'Ivory Curls'
		havardiana	CBlu CDTJ CExl CPbh CPic NPlm SBig
amica	EPfP LCro	*horrida*	CDTJ NPlm SBig
– 'Super Gold'	XFar	– subsp. *horrida*	SPlb
– 'The Pearl' (d)	EGren GKev LAma LCro XFar	– 'Perotensis'	CDTJ EShb
§ *angustifolia*	WCot	*impressa*	WCot
– 'Marginata'	NPlm WCot	'Inkblot'ᴾᴮᴿ	ELan EUrb
applanata	CJun NPlm SPlb	*isthmensis*	SBig SPlb
× *arizonica*	SBig	*kerchovei*	WCot
asperrima	CDTJ	'Lavender Lady'ᴾᴮᴿ	CAbb ELan LCro WFar
§ – subsp. *maderensis*	SPlb	*lechuguilla*	CDTJ CPic SBig SChr WCot
§ – subsp. *zarcensis*	CBlu	*lophantha*	see *A. univittata*
atrovirens	CExl WCot	– var. *caerulescens*	see *A. univittata*
§ – var. *atrovirens*	CExl	'Macho Mocha'	WCot
– var. *mirabilis*	CDTJ CExl	*macroacantha* ♀ᴴ¹ᶜ	CDTJ EUrb NPlm
attenuata	CDTJ CPic NPlm SArc SBig SPlb	*maculata*	WCot
'Bad Hair Day' **new**	EUrb	*maximilliana*	SPlb
'Blazing Saddles'	LCro	*mckelveyana*	CPic WCot
'Bloodspot'	WCot	– DJF 1575 from Bagdad, Arizona	WCot
'Blue Brian'	NPlm SArc SBig		
'Blue Flame'	SBig	'Mission to Mars'ᴾᴮᴿ	CAbb ELan EUrb LCro WCot WFar
§ 'Blue Glow'	EUrb LCro NHrt SBig	*mitis* var. *albidior*	SBig
boldinghiana	WCot	§ – var. *mitis*	CDTJ ESwi SPlb

Agave

montana	CBlu CDTJ CExl CPbh EUrb NCft NPlm SArc SBig SPlb	
- 'Blue Ocean'	NPlm SBig	
'Moonglow'[PBR]	CAbb NPlm WFar	
× *nigra* hort.	SBig	
§ *obscura*	CDTJ WCot	
§ *ortgiesiana*	WCot	
ovatifolia	CBlu CDTJ CExl CJun EAri NPlm SBig SPlb WCot WPGP	
- 'Emerald' **new**	EUrb	
- 'Iced Heart' **new**	EUrb	
- 'Vanzie'	EUrb NPlm	
§ *pablocarrilloi* 'Ivory Curls' (v)	NPlm	
palmeri	CDTJ NPlm SPlb WCot	
panamana	see *A. angustifolia*	
parrasana ♀H2	CDTJ EUrb NPlm SBig WCot	
- 'Meat Claw'	EUrb	
parryi ♀H2	CDTJ CExl CPbh CPic SPlb WCot	
- var. *couesii*	CDTJ	
- 'Cream Spike' (v)	SMrm WCot	
- var. *huachucensis*	CBlu CDTJ SBig WCot	
- subsp. *neomexicana*	CDTJ CPic EUrb NPlm SBig SPlb WCot	
- - SB 948 from W of Artesia, New Mexico	WCot	
- 'Ohi-kissho-ten-nishiki' (v)	WCot	
- subsp. *parryi*	CBlu CDTJ SBig SBrt WCot	
- small	EShb	
- var. *truncata*	CBlu CDTJ EUrb NPlm SBig SPlb WCot	
- - variegated (v)	WCot	
parviflora ♀H2	WCot	
pedunculifera	NPlm	
'Pineapple Express'[PBR]	ELan EUrb LCro WFar	
polyacantha	see *A. obscura*	
var. *xalapensis*		
potatorum ♀H2	CPbh WCot	
- 'Gary Fisher'	WCot	
- 'Kichijokan' (v)	NCft EUrb	
- 'Shoji-rasin'	NCft	
- var. *verschaffeltii*	NCft NPlm	
'Red Edge'	NPlm	
'Red Wing'	CAbb WFar	
'Royal Spine'	NPlm	
salmiana	CDTJ CExl SPlb	
- subsp. *crassispina*	SPlb	
§ - var. *ferox*	CDTJ EUrb SArc SBig SChr SPlb	
scabra	NPlm WCot	
- subsp. *maderensis*	see *A. asperrima* subsp. *maderensis*	
- subsp. *zarcensis*	see *A. asperrima* subsp. *zarcensis*	
schidigera	EUrb NPlm WCot	
- 'Shira-ito-no-ohi' (v)	EUrb NPlm WCot	
- 'White Stripe' (v)	CBlu EShb	
schottii	CDTJ WCot	
seemanniana	CDoC	
'Shaka Zulu'	see *A.* 'Blue Glow'	
'Sharkskin Shoes'	NPlm WCot	
shrevei subsp. *magna*	CCht SPlb	
sileri	WCot	
'Silver Fox'[PBR]	EUrb NPlm	
sisalana	CDTJ CPic	
'Snow Leopard' (v)	NPlm	
stictata	WCot	
striata subsp. *falcata*	WCot	
* - 'Rubra'	CDTJ SPlb WCot	
stricta ♀H2	CDTJ NPlm WCot	
- 'Nana'	CDTJ	
- 'Rubra'	WCot	
titanota ♀H1c	CPbh SPlb WCot	
toumeyana ♀H2	CPbh SPlb WCot	
- var. *bella*	CDTJ
triangularis	CDTJ
undulata	WCot
- 'Cherry Chocolate Chip'[PBR] **new**	EUrb NPlm WFar
- 'Chocolate Chips'	WCot
§ *univittata*	CBlu CDTJ CJun CPic SBig WCot WFar
- 'Quadricolor' (v) ♀H2	CDoC CDTJ CPbh NCft SChr SPlb WCot WFar
I - 'Splendida' (v)	NCft
utahensis ♀H3	CDTJ SEND SPlb WCot
- DJF 1521 from Peach Springs, Arizona	WCot
- var. *eborispina*	WCot
- subsp. *kaibabensis*	CBlu WCot
variegata	EAri WCot
- B&SWJ 10234	WCru
§ *victoriae-reginae* ♀H2	CDTJ CJun CPbh NPlm SBig SPlb WCot
- dwarf	CBlu WCot
- variegated (v)	CTtf
vilmoriniana	EUrb NPlm
virginica	WCot
weberi	NPlm
'Whale Tale'	EUrb NPlm
wocomahi	WCot
xylonacantha	CDTJ SBig SChr SPlb WCot

Ageratina (Asteraceae)

§ *altissima*	CDor CMac EAri GJos SMrm StAn
- 'Braunlaub'	NBir NLar NSti WCAu
- 'Chocolate'	Widely available
- LUCKY MELODY ('Allmelody'[PBR])	EBee LBar LRHS MMrt MPro WFar
- LUCKY SYMPHONY ('Allsympho')	IPot LBar LRHS MPro SHar
aromatica	GJos SDix
§ *ligustrina*	CBcs CCoa CDoC CMCN CRHN CSpe EBee ELan EPfP MBlu SDix SEND SPoG SRkn SRms

Ageratum (Asteraceae)

'Blue Champion'	EGren MPri WFar
corymbosum	CHll CSpe EAri EShb WFar WJun
houstonianum	MCtn
'Blue Horizon' ♀H2	
- 'Dondo White'	MCtn
- 'High Tide Blue'	MPri
- 'Timeless Mixed'	MCtn
petiolatum	SHar WFar

Aglaomorpha (Polypodiaceae)

coronans ♀H1b	LCro NTro

Aglaonema (Araceae)

'Christina'	NHrt
commutatum **new**	NTro
- KEY LIME ('Uf25712kl') **new**	NHrt NTro
'Crete'	LBom LCro NHrt
'Cutlass'	LBom LCro NHrt
'Diamond Bay' (v) **new**	NHrt
'Freedman'	NHrt
'Jubilee' (v) **new**	NTro
'Jubilee Compacta'[PBR] (v)	LCro
'King Of Siam'[PBR]	LBom
LEMON MINT ('Supag2203') (v) **new**	NHrt
'Light Pink Star' (v)	LBom LCro
'Maria'	NHrt
'Maria Christina'	NHrt

'Orange Star' (v)	LCro		- 'Blue Ensign'	LShi
'Peacock'^PBR	LBom		'Little Court Pink'	see *A. reptans* 'Purple Torch'
pictum 'Tricolor' (v) **new**	NTro		*lupulina*	GEdr
'Red Star' (v)	LCro		- BO 15-009	GGro
'Silver Bay' (v)	LBom LCro NHrt NTro		*metallica* hort.	see *A. pyramidalis*
'Silver Queen' ♀H1b	NHrt NTro		NOBLE NIGHTINGALE ('Nobnig')	LBar
'Silver Queen Compact'	NHrt		(Feathered Friends Series)	
'Spotted Star' (v)	LCro		*ovalifolia* W&O 9044	GGro
'Stripes' (v)	NHrt		'Pink Lightning' (v)	ELan MWlw SRms WCot WFar
'Tigress' (v)	LCro		'Pink Spires'	WFar
WHITE KIWI	NHrt		§ *pyramidalis*	EGrI ELin
('Kk9004'^PBR) (v) **new**			- 'Metallica Crispa'	ELan ELin EWes EWld GBin GJos
'White Lance'^PBR **new**	NTro			GKev LRHS MPri NBir NEoE NLar
				SRms WCav WFar

Agrimonia (Rosaceae)

eupatoria	CBWd CGwi CHab ENfk IDun		- 'Metallica Crispa Rubra'	CoPl
	MCtn MHer MHoo MNHC NAts		*reptans*	CGHo CGwi CHab EGren EHeP
	NMir SRms WHer WOrg WTre			ENfk GKev IDun LCro LWaG MBel
* - var. *alba*	IDun MHoo NLar			MCtn MHer MHoo MNHC NAts
- 'Cambridge Lace' (v)	WCot			NMir SRms StAn WKit
odorata misapplied	see *A. procera*		- f. *albiflora*	CDor ISha
§ *procera*	GQue SPhx		- - 'Alba'	EBee EGrI LCro MBel NBro SRms
				WCAu WFar

Agropyron (Poaceae)

glaucum	see *Elymus hispidus*		- 'Arctic Fox' (v)	GEdr NBro
magellanicum	see *Elymus magellanicus*		- 'Argentea'	see *A. reptans* 'Variegata'
pubiflorum	see *Elymus magellanicus*		§ - 'Atropurpurea'	ECha EGrI EHeP ELan IDun LBom
				LCro MGos MMuc SEND SPlb SRms
			- BLACK SCALLOP	Widely available
			('Binblasca'^PBR)	

Agrostemma (Caryophyllaceae)

coronaria	see *Silene coronaria*		- 'Blueberry Muffin'	EGren LCro LRHS MHol Midl MPro
githago	CBWd CHab EHet ELan GJem LCro			MSCN NWbg
	MCtn MNHC NBir SRms		- 'Braunherz'	EBee ECha EGren EHeP ELan
- 'Milas'	MCtn			EPfP GMaP LBar LRHS LSto
- 'Ocean Pearl'	CSpe			MAsh MBros MPri MSwo NBir
- 'Purple Queen'	CSpe NClf			NLar SRms WBrk WCav WCot
				WFar

Agrostis (Poaceae)

alba misapplied	see *A. stolonifera*		- 'Burgundy Glow' (v)	Widely available
calamagrostis	see *Stipa calamagrostis*		§ - 'Catlin's Giant' ♀H7	Widely available
capillaris	CHab		- 'Chocolate Chip'	see *A. tenorei* 'Valfredda'
nebulosa	MCtn WCot		- 'Dixie Chip'	see *A. tenorei* 'Dixie Chip'
stolonifera 'Julia Ann' (v)	WCot		- 'Evening Glow'	EBee GJos LWaG WIce
			§ - 'Gold Chang'^PBR	WTor

Aichryson ✿ (Crassulaceae)

§ × *aizoides*	CPic		- 'Golden Beauty' (v)	EGren LBar LSou SRms
var. *domesticum*			- 'Golden Glow' (v)	EBee ELan EPfP
- - 'Variegatum' (v) ♀H1c	CDTJ CoPl CPbh CPic LWaG NCft		- GOLDEN TREASURE	see *A. reptans* 'Gold Chang'
	SIvy WCot		- 'Julia'	EPPr
laxum	CoPl		- 'Lemon and Lime'	EHeP LBuc MHtn
tortuosum subsp.	EAri		- 'Macrophylla'	see *A. reptans* 'Catlin's Giant'
bethencourtianum			- 'Mahogany'	EMor NLar SRms
			§ - 'Multicolor' (v)	ELan GPSL LRHS LWaG MAsh MPri
				SPlb SPoG SRms WFar

Ailanthus (Simaroubaceae)

§ *altissima*	Prohibited invasive. See Conservation and		- 'Pink Delight'	CoPl
	the Environment, p.42		- 'Pink Elf'	CDor NBro
glandulosa	see *A. altissima*		- 'Pink Surprise'	MHer NRya WFar
			- 'Purple Brocade'	NLar
			§ - 'Purple Torch'	NLar SHar SRms

Ainsliaea (Asteraceae)

acerifolia	EWld		- 'Purpurea'	see *A. reptans* 'Atropurpurea'
apiculata	MAsh		- 'Rainbow'	see *A. reptans* 'Multicolor'
dissecta **new**	EWld		- 'Rosea'	GKev WCAu WFar
			- 'Tricolor'	see *A. reptans* 'Multicolor'
			§ - 'Variegata' (v)	CoPl ELin LShi MBel MMuc SPoG
				SRms WBrk

Ajania see *Chrysanthemum*

SUGAR PLUM	LBar NEoE NGdn
('Binsugplu'^PBR) (v)	

Ajuga (Lamiaceae)

chamaepitys	NLit		§ *tenorei* 'Dixie Chip'	LRHS WFar
FANCY FINCH ('Fanfin')	LBar		- PRINCESS NADIA	EGren ELan LBar LCro LRHS NEoE
(Feathered Friends Series)			('Piotrek01') (v)	NLar SPeP WHil WIce
genevensis	GEdr GKev		§ - 'Valfredda'	EGren ELin GBin GQue LCro LRHS
incisa 'Bikun' (v)	NEoE SPoG WCot WFar			LWaG MPri NLar SLee SRms WCav
- 'Blue Enigma'	CExl LBar NLar WFar			WFar
			TROPICAL TOUCAN ('Trotou')	LBar
			(Feathered Friends Series)	

Akebia (Lardizabalaceae)

longeracemosa	CBcs CRHN CWGN EPfP MBlu SBrt
- B&SWJ 3606	CExl WCot WCru WPGP
× *pentaphylla*	CBcs EPfP MAsh
quinata	Widely available
- B&SWJ 4425	WCru
- 'Amethyst Glow'	CDoC ELan EPfP LBom LRHS SMrm SPoG WHtc
- cream-flowered	CRHN CWnw EBee EPfP LCro LRHS MGos MHtn SMrm SRms WPGP
- 'Shirobana'	CBcs CWGN LRHS MBlu WCru WHtc
- 'Silver Bells'	CWGN EBee LRHS SWCr
- variegated (v)	SWCr
- 'White Chocolate' ♀H6	ESwi WCru
trifoliata	CBcs CRHN ELan MGos WJur WPGP
- B&SWJ 5063	WCru
- B&SWJ 14570	WCru
- 'Big Fruit'	NLar

Alangium (Cornaceae)

platanifolium	SBrt WPGP

Albizia ✿ (Fabaceae)

chinensis	LRHS
distachya	see *Paraserianthes lophantha*
§ *julibrissin*	CAco CBlu CCht CDTJ CHab CMac CMCN CTsd EAri EBee EGrI EPfP IPap MCtn SAth WJur
- Chocolate Fountain ('Ncaj1')	CAco EUrb NPip WMat
- 'Evy's Pride'	CAco CDoC EUrb LRHS NPip WMat
- 'Evy's Purple'	ELan SArc
- Leonidas	see *A. julibrissin* 'Summer Chocolate'
- Ombrella ('Boubri'PBR)	CAco CBcs CDoC CMCN EGren ELan EUrb LCro LRHS MGos NPip WMat
- f. *rosea* ♀H4	CAco CBcs CMCN CWGN EAri EBee ELan EPfP EUrb LRHS SArc SAth SEND SIvy SPad SPlb SPoG WLov
I - 'Rouge Selection'	EPfP LRHS SPoG
- 'Shidare'	ELan EUrb NPip WMat
§ - 'Summer Chocolate'PBR ♀H4	CAco CBcs CMCN CWGN EAri ELan EPfP LCro LRHS LSRN MAsh NPip NPlm SPoG WFar WMat
- Tropical Dream ('Pos 1')	CAco
kalkora	SPlb
lophantha	see *Paraserianthes lophantha*

Albuca ✿ (Asparagaceae)

G&L 13 from Sentinel Peak, South Africa	EPPr
canadensis (L.) F.M. Leight.	WHil
clanwilliamigloria	WHil
cooperi	WHil
corymbosa	WHil
decipiens new	WHil
fastigiata	EDAr
flaccida	WHil
fragrans	WHil
glauca	MPie
grandis new	WHil
humilis	EDAr EPot GKev MCtn MHer WHil
juncifolia	WHil
kirstenii new	WHil
longipes new	WHil
rupestris JCA 15856	WHil
setosa	WHil
shawii	CSpe EBee EDAr EPfP EWld GEdr LRHS MArl MCtn MHer MHol SBeP SChr SMrm SPel SPoG SRms WGwG WKif
spiralis	WCot
- 'Frizzle Sizzle'	CDoC MHer

× *Alcalthaea* (Malvaceae)

suffrutescens 'Freedom'	WFar
- 'Parkallee' (d)	CDor EBee LBar LCro MNrw MPro NLar SPel WCot WTor
- 'Parkfrieden' (d)	ERCP MPro NLar WTor
- 'Parkrondell' (d)	CDor CSpe LCro MAvo MNrw MPro NLar SPel
- 'Poetry'	MPro

Alcea ✿ (Malvaceae)

'Apple Blossom' (d)	EPfP
ficifolia	LShi MCtn WFar WSpi
- pink-flowered	LShi
- white-flowered	LShi
- yellow-flowered	LShi
froloviana	GGro
'Las Vegas'	WFar
litvinovii	GGro
nudiflora	GGro
§ *rosea*	EPfP WFar
- 'Blacknight' (Spotlight Series)	EDAr ELan EPfP LRHS MHer
- Chater's Double Group (d)	EGren EHeP MCtn SPoG SRms SVic WFar
- - chestnut-brown-flowered (d)	EPfP
- - maroon-flowered (d)	EGren EPfP LRHS MPri MPro SPoG
- - pink-flowered (d)	ELan EPfP LBom MPro
- - purple-flowered (d)	EGren EPfP MPro
- - red-flowered (d)	ELan EPfP SPoG
- - rose-pink-flowered (d)	EGren MPri NLar
- - salmon-pink-flowered (d)	EGren EPfP LRHS MPro
- - scarlet-flowered (d)	EGren EPfP LRHS MPri MPro SPoG
- - violet-flowered (d)	EPfP
§ - - white-flowered (d)	EGren ELan EPfP LCro LRHS MPri MPro NLar SPoG
- - yellow-flowered (d)	EGren EPfP LRHS MPri MPro NLar SPoG SRms
- 'Crème de Cassis'	ELan EPfP MCtn
- double pink-flowered (d)	LRHS
- - scarlet-flowered (d)	LRHS
- - yellow-flowered (d)	LBom LRHS
- Halo Series	EGren MPri WFar
- - 'Halo Apricot'	EPfP LRHS MCtn SPoG
- - 'Halo Blossom'	MCtn
- - 'Halo Blush'	EPfP LRHS MCtn SPoG
- - 'Halo Cerise'	EPfP LRHS SPoG
- - 'Halo Cream'	EPfP LRHS SPoG
- - 'Halo Red'	SPoG
- - 'Halo White'	EPfP LRHS MCtn SPoG
- 'Mars Magic' (Spotlight Series)	EBee EDAr ELan EPfP MHer MPri
- 'Nigra'	CSpe ELan EPfP LBom LCro LShi LSRN MCtn NGdn SHar SRms WCAu
- 'Polarstar' (Spotlight Series)	EBee EDAr ELan EPfP MPri SPel
- 'Purple Rain' (Spotlight Series) new	EDAr MHer
- 'Radiant Rose' (Spotlight Series)	EDAr ELan EPfP MHer MPri

- single-flowered	GJem MCtn MMuc SRms	***Allagoptera*** (Arecaceae)	
- (Spring Celebrities Series)	MCtn MPro	*arenaria*	NPlm
'Spring Celebrities Apricot' (d)		***Alliaria*** (Brassicaceae)	
- - 'Spring Celebrities Carmine Rose'	MPro	*petiolata*	MAsh MCtn MNHC WHer
- - 'Spring Celebrities Crimson' (d)	MPro	***Allium*** ✿ (Amaryllidaceae)	
- - 'Spring Celebrities Lemon' (d)	MPro	RCB AM 21	WCot
- 'Sunshine' (Spotlight Series)	MPro	SSSE 250	GEdr
- - 'Spring Celebrities White' (d)	MPro	*acutiflorum*	GKev LAma
- Summer Carnival Group	MCtn SRms	*aflatunense* misapplied	see *A. hollandicum*
- 'Sunshine' (Spotlight Series)	EBee EDAr EPfP MHer MPri	*aflatunense* ambig.	EGren EGrI LSRN SDix
§ ***rugosa***	EBee StAn	*aflatunense* B. Fedtsch.	MCtn NNys
THE BRIDE	see *A. rosea* Chater's Double Group white-flowered	*albopilosum*	see *A. cristophii*
		altaicum	CAgr
		altissimum	LAma

Alcea × ***Althaea*** see × *Alcalthaea*

Alchemilla ✿ (Rosaceae)

		- 'Goliath'	EGren WCot
		amabile	see *A. mairei* var. *amabile*
		'Ambassador' ♀H5	ECul EGren ELan ERCP GKev LAma LCro LRHS MArl MHtn NBir NNys SDix SHar WCot WFar XFar
alpina misapplied	see *A. conjuncta, A. plicatula*		
alpina ambig.	EGrI		
alpina L.	EBee EMor EWld GMaP GQue LRHS MBel MMuc NBir NLar SEND SRms StAn WFar WPGP		
§ *conjuncta*	CDor CMac EBee ECha EGrI EMor EWld GAbr GMaP LEdu MHer NBid NRya SMHy SPlb SRms WCAu WFar WKif WTre	*amethystinum*	EGren ELan EPot ERCP GKev LAma MArl MNrw WCot WHoo XFar
		'Red Mohican' PBR	
		ampeloprasum	ECha MCtn SPlb WShi
		- var. *babingtonii*	CAgr CGwi CWRo LEdu MEar NBac SRms WHer WKor WPGP WShi
ellenbeckii	GAbr		
epipsila	EGren ELan LRHS LSto NLar SHar SHor	- - 'Green Drops'	XFar
		- 'Purple Mystery'	WCot
erythropoda ♀H7	Widely available	- 'White Cloud'	ELan ERCP
- from Turkey	ECha NCIf SPel	*amphibolum*	GKev
- 'Alma'	EMor LRHS WHoo	*amplectens* 'Graceful Beauty'	CBro CBWd EGren ELan EPfP EPot ERCP ETay GKev LAma LCro LRHS MNrw NLar SHor XFar
faeroensis var. *pumila*	GKev WAbe		
glabra	EBee	§ *angulosum*	CMiW EBlo ELin GKev MHol MMuc SNoN WCot WMal
hoppeana misapplied	see *A. plicatula*		
'Irish Silk'	EGren EPfP LBar LRHS MPri	*aschersonianum*	WCot
mollis ♀H7	Widely available	*atropurpureum*	CBWd ECha ECul EGren ELan EPfP ERCP ETay GKev LAma LCro LSto SHor WCot XFar
- 'Cream Dream' (v)	WCAu		
- 'Robustica'	LBar LSou MCtn MMuc NLar SEND SMad SPlb WFar		
- 'Thriller'	ELan EPfP	*atroviolaceum* W&B BG A-5	WCot
'Mr Poland's Variety'	see *A. venosa*	'Avatar'	LBar XFar
pectinata	CBcs	*azureum*	see *A. caeruleum*
peristerica	EBee	*backhousianum*	LAma
§ *plicatula*	GKev LBar NLar	'Green Craze'	
saxatilis	EMor NLar SHar StAn	'Beau Regard' ♀H7	LRHS NLar
sericata 'Gold Strike'	EBee ELan EPfP LSto SHar	*beesianum* misapplied	see *A. cyaneum*
valdehirsuta	EBee	*beesianum* W.W. Sm.	CMiW CTtf LEdu NBir
§ *venosa*	EBee SHar	- from Sichuan, China	CMiW
vetteri	EBee WHrl	*bodeanum*	see *A. cristophii*
vulgaris misapplied	see *A. xanthochlora*	'Bubble Bath'	CKno CWGN LBar LSou MPro NWbg
vulgaris L. agg.	GQue MNHC		
§ *xanthochlora*	MHoo NLar SRms SVic	*bucharicum*	ETay
		bulgaricum	see *A. siculum* subsp. *dioscoridis*

Alchornea (Euphorbiaceae)

davidii	EPfP LCro	§ *caeruleum*	CBro CTtf EBee EGren EGrI EPfP EPot ERCP ETay GAbr GKev LAma LCro MNrw NBir NLar NPer NRya WCAu XFar

alecost see *Tanacetum balsamita*

Alectryon (Sapindaceae)

excelsus	CBcs	- *azureum*	see *A. caeruleum*
		caesium ♀H5	ELan ERCP GKev LAma WCot XFar
		- AQUAMARINE	see *A. caesium* 'Pskem's Beauty'

Alisma (Alismataceae)

		§ - 'Pskem's Beauty'	WCot
		callimischon	GKev
		subsp. *callimischon*	
lanceolatum	ELin	- subsp. *haemostictum*	EDAr EWld WAbe WCot WFar
plantago-aquatica	CBen CGwi CHab CLil CPud CTtf CWat ELin MWts NPer WMAq	'Caméléon'	ERCP GKev LAma LCro WCot XFar
		canadense	MCtn SHar WKor
subcordatum	CBen CLil CWat ELin SPlb	§ *carinatum*	LAma WHer

Allium

§ - subsp. *pulchellum* ♀H5 — CSpe CTtf ECha EGrI ELan EPot EPPr GKev GQue LAma MMuc MNrw NBir SPhx
- - f. *album* ♀H5 — CSpe CTtf ECha EDAr EGrI ELan EPPr GKev LAma LEdu MNrw NBir SPhx WFar
carolinianum
  'Rosy Beauty' — XFar
- 'Rosy Dream' — EGren GKev
'Catweazle' — XFar
cepa — SVic
- Aggregatum Group — CWRo NBac SRms
cernuum — CBro CSpe ECha EGren EGrI ELan EPot EPPr EWhm GArf GKev GMaP GQue LAma LEdu MCtn MHoo MNrw NQui SPhx SRms StAn WCAu WJek WKor
§ - 'Hidcote' ♀H6 — CAby EDAr LRHS MHol MHoo Midl MPro SPeP WKif
- 'Major' — see *A. cernuum* 'Hidcote'
- 'White Dwarf' — ELan EPot LAma SPhx
chinense — CAgr LEdu SMHy WFar WKor
cirrhosum — see *A. carinatum* subsp. *pulchellum*
convallarioides
  yellow-flowered — LCro
cowanii — see *A. neapolitanum* Cowanii Group
§ *cristophii* ♀H5 — Widely available
curtum RCB RL 13 — WCot
§ *cyaneum* ♀H7 — CMiW CTtf EPot GArf GEdr LRHS NRya WCot WFar
cyathophorum — CSpe
§ - var. *farreri* — CBro CMiW CSpe CTtf ECha EPot EPPr GKev LAma LEdu MHer MNrw NRya SBeP WCot
'Dallas' **new** — XFar
'Darcies Purple' **new** — EDAr
darwasicum — WCot
'Dutchman' — EGren ERCP GKev LAma
ericetorum — WCot
- PAB 1009 — LEdu
'Eros' — CTtf EGren EPfP ERCP GKev LAma LCro LRHS XFar
falcifolium — LAma WCot
farreri — see *A. cyathophorum* var. *farreri*
'Firmament' — ERCP GKev LAma SHor WCot
fistulosum — CAgr CCBP CGwi CHby EHet ENfk EWhm GKev GQue IDun LCro MCtn MHer MHoo MNHC MPri NBac SRms SVic WCot WJek WKit WKor WRBe
- 'Red Welsh' — MNHC SRms WJek WKit
flavum ♀H5 — CTtf ECha EDAr EGren ELan EPot EPPr LAma SPhx WFar
- subsp. *flavum* — GKev
- - var. *minus* — see *A. webbii*
- - var. *nanum* — EDAr
- subsp. *tauricum* — EPPr WCot
'Forelock' — EGren ERCP GKev LAma MHtn MNrw SHor WCot XFar
forrestii — WCot
giganteum — EBee EGren ELan EPfP ERCP ETay GKev LAma LBom LCro LRHS LSRN MBros NLar SHor SPoG SRms WFar XFar
'Gladiator' ♀H6 — EGren ERCP GKev GMaP LAma LCro LRHS MArl NLar NNys XFar
glaucum — see *A. senescens* subsp. *glaucum*
'Globemaster' ♀H6 — CAby CBro EBee EGren EGrI EHeP ELan EPfP EPot ERCP ETay GKev LAma LCro LEdu LRHS LSRN MArl NLar NNys SArc SAth SDix WCot WFar WHoo XFar
goodingii — GKev
'Guardsman' ♀H3 — MCtn
guttatum — GKev
  subsp. *dalmaticum*
- subsp. *sardoum* — GKev
haemanthoides — WCot
'Hair' — see *A. vineale* 'Hair'
§ *hollandicum* — ECha EPfP LCro SPlb WFar
- 'Purple Sensation' ♀H6 — Widely available
- 'Purple Surprise' — WCot
hookeri — LEdu
- ACE 2430 — GGro LEdu WCot
- var. *muliense* — EDAr EPPr GEdr LEdu
- 'Zorami' — CAgr ELan LEdu WMal
humile — GEdr
hyalinum pink-flowered — LRHS LSou MHol NCth NWbg
'In Orbit' — LRHS LSou MHol NCth NWbg
§ *insubricum* ♀H5 — EDAr GEdr MNrw NBir
'Jackpot' — ERCP GKev LAma
jesdianum 'Early Emperor' ♀H5 — GKev LAma
- 'Michael Hoog' — see *A. rosenorum* 'Michael H. Hoog'
- 'Shing' — EGren GKev LAma
- 'Judith' — WCot
'Judith's Findling' — WCot
kansuense — see *A. sikkimense*
karataviense — CAby ECha EGren ELan EPot GKev LAma LCro NBir NLar SBig
- 'Ivory Queen' — ECha EGren ERCP GKev LAma LSRN NLar SPlb XFar
- 'Red Giant' — EGren ELan ERCP GKev LAma LRHS XFar
komarovianum — see *A. thunbergii*
'Lavender Bubbles' — CKno LBar LBom LCro LEdu LRHS MHtn MPro NCth SHar SOrN SPel WNPC
ledebourianum — CAgr WFar
lenkoranicum — WCot
LITTLE SAPPHIRE ('Ifalls') — LBar LRHS MPro
litvinovii — WCot
loratum 'Marshmellow' — LRHS
'Lucky Balloons' — ERCP XFar
'Lucy Ball' — EGren LAma NLar
lusitanicum — Widely available
- 'Lisa Blue' — LBar LEdu
- 'Lisa Green' — LBar LEdu SHar
macleanii 'His Excellency' — EGren ERCP LAma LCro LRHS NLar
macranthum — LAma SBrt
- S&L 5369 — GGro
mairei — NRya
- var. *amabile* — GEdr NRya
maximowiczii — LAma
'Medusa's Hair'^PBR — WMal
'Mercurius'^PBR — LAma LCro WCot
'Metallic Shine' — GKev LAma
meteoricum — LAma WCot
'Miami' — CBro EGren EPfP ERCP GKev LAma LCro LRHS MHtn
'Millennium' — Widely available
moly — CAgr EGren EGrI EWld GKev GQue LAma LCro LRHS LShi NRya SRms XFar
- 'Jeannine' ♀H6 — CBro EPot GKev LAma LBar MPie NClf SDix
- 'Mont Blanc' — EGren ELan GKev LAma LCro MSwo NLar SAth SMrm
multibulbosum — see *A. nigrum*
murrayanum misapplied — see *A. unifolium*
myrianthum — GKev

Allium

	narcissiflorum misapplied	see *A. insubricum*	'Round 'n' Purple' ♀H5	LAma LCro XFar
§	*narcissiflorum* Vill.	CSpe LEdu MNrw	*rupestre*	GKev
	neapolitanum	CAgr EGren EPfP GKev LAma WKor	*sativum*	CGHo ENfk MPri SPoG SRms
§	- Cowanii Group	EGrI GKev LAma LCro SPhx WCot XFar	- var. *ophioscorodon*	MCtn SPlb WKor
	neriniflorum	WAbe	*saxatile*	WCot
	nevskianum	GKev WCot XFar	*schoenoprasum*	Widely available
§	*nigrum*	CBro ECha EGren EGrI EPfP EPot ERCP GKev LAma LCro LRHS NBir NPer WCot XFar	- f. *albiflorum*	CCBP EWhm LEdu MHer MNHC NBir SRms WTre
			- 'Black Isle Blush'	MHer WGoo
	- pink-flowered	LAma	- 'Cassis Ice' **new**	LEdu
	nutans	CGwi EWhm GKev LAma LEdu MHer MHoo SRms WHil WJek WMal	- 'Curly Mauve'	LBar
			- dwarf, white-flowered	SRms
	- 'Caroline'	LEdu WGoo	- 'Elbe'	LEdu
	- 'Isabelle'	LEdu	- fine-leaved	CCBP
§	*obliquum*	CBro CSpe ECha EGrI EPpr ERCP GEdr GKev GQue LAma MCtn SPhx WCot WKit WTre XFar	- 'Forescate'	ECha EGren EWhm LEdu NBir SRms
			- medium-leaved	MNHC MPri
	ochotense	GKev WCot	- 'Pink Bere'	LEdu WPGP
	odorum L.	see *A. ramosum* L.	- 'Pink One' (One Series)	MPro
	oleraceum	WHer	- 'Pink Perfection'	LEdu MHer
§	*oreophilum*	EGren EGrI GKev LAma LCro MNrw SRms XFar	- 'Polar Bere'	LEdu WPGP
			- 'Polystar'PBR	MNHC
	- 'Samur'	WCot	- 'Purple One' (One Series)	MPro
	- 'Zwanenburg' ♀H6	EPot	- 'Rising Star'	GKev LAma LBar
	orientale	GKev	- var. *sibiricum*	SDix WShi
	'Ostara'	EGren ERCP GKev LAma LRHS MHtn WFar XFar	- 'Silver Chimes'	EPPr EWhm MHoo
			- thick-leaved	SRms
	ostrowskianum	see *A. oreophilum*	- 'White One' (One Series)	MPro
	ovalifolium	GEdr	*schubertii*	CBro CSpe EGren EGrI ELan EPfP EPot ERCP ETay GKev LAma LCro LRHS MArl MPie NCIf SHor SMrm WCAu WCot WFar XFar
	var. *leuconeurum*			
	pallens	NBir		
§	*paniculatum*	GKev LAma WCot		
	- 'Yellow Fantasy'	GKev	- 'Arctic Snow'	ERCP GKev LAma NCIf XFar
P	*paradoxum*	LEdu NBir	- 'Magic'	EGren GKev LAma
	- var. *normale* ♀H6	CBro CTtf EPot EWld MWlw NBir WCot	*scorodoprasum*	CoPl
			- B&SWJ 15921	WCru
	parciflorum	GKev	- 'Art'	ERCP GKev LAma MHtn XFar
	'Party Balloons'	GKev LAma XFar	- 'Passion'	MCtn
	pedemontanum	see *A. narcissiflorum* Vill.	*senescens* ♀H6	CAgr CBro CTca EBee EPot GJos LAma LEdu LRHS LSto MBel MHoo SAth SRms StAn WCAu
	pendulinum	GKev		
	'Pinball Wizard'	EGren EPfP GKev LAma LRHS MMrt NLar		
			§ - subsp. *glaucum*	CBro CCBP CMiW CSpe EBlo ECha EDAr EPfP GQue LCro LEdu LRHS MHer MHol MMuc NDov NGdn NLar NRya NWbg SEND SMHy SOrN SPel WBrk WCot WHoo
	'Ping Pong'	EGren GKev LAma LRHS MArl MHtn NLar XFar		
	'Pink Jewel'	ECha ERCP GKev WCot XFar		
	'Pink Planet'	LBar		
	platycaule	WCot	- subsp. *senescens*	EGrI LEdu SArc WPGP
	'Powder Puff' ♀H5	LAma LCro	'Serendipity'	CWGN LSou MPro
	prattii	EBee WCot	*sibthorpianum*	see *A. paniculatum*
	× *proliferum*	CAgr CGHo CGwi EWhm GQue LEdu MHer MHoo MNHC SRms WHer WJek WKor	*siculum*	CBro CSpe EGren ELan EPfP ERCP GKev LCro LRHS LShi LSRN LSto MArl MCtn NBir NSti SDix SPoG XFar
	przewalskianum	EBee	- subsp. *bulgaricum*	see *A. siculum* subsp. *dioscoridis*
	pskemense	GKev LAma LEdu NLar WCot	§ - subsp. *dioscoridis*	CAby ECha EGrI EPot GKev LAma MNrw NNys SPhx WCot
	pulchellum	see *A. carinatum* subsp. *pulchellum*		
	'Purple Rain' ♀H5	CAby CBro ECha EGren ELan ERCP GKev LAma LCro LRHS LShi MArl MPro SHor WCot	§ *sikkimense*	EDAr GEdr GQue MHer MMuc MNrw WAbe WCot WFar
			- 'Tiny Blue' **new**	EDAr
	pyrenaicum misapplied	see *A. angulosum*	'Silver Spring'	EGren EPot ERCP ETay GKev LAma LCro XFar
	pyrenaicum Costa & Vayr.	MMuc		
	ramosum Jacq.	see *A. obliquum*	*sphaerocephalon* ♀H6	Widely available
§	*ramosum* L.	CAgr MHoo	- subsp. *arvense*	WCot
	'Red Eye'	XFar	'Spider'	see *A.* 'Toabago'
	rosenbachianum misapplied	see *A. stipitatum*	*stamineum* W&B BGF-2	WCot
			'Statos'	EGren GKev LAma LRHS SArc WCot XFar
	rosenbachianum Regel 'Album'	WCot		
§	*rosenorum* 'Michael H. Hoog' ♀H5	EPot	*stellatum*	WGwG WHer
			stellerianum var. *kurilense*	NRya WAbe
	roseum	EGren LAma LCro XFar	§ *stipitatum*	LAma LCro LRHS WCot

Allium

- 'Mount Everest' ⚥H5	CBro ECha EGren EPfP EPot ERCP ETay GKev GMaP LAma LCro LRHS LSRN LSto MArl MHtn NLar SHor SPhx WFar XFar
- 'Violet Beauty' ⚥H5	EGren EPfP ERCP GKev LAma LBom LCro LRHS MHtn NLar SHor WCot
- 'White Giant'	EGren GKev LAma LRHS MSwo NLar SArc XFar
stracheyi	WCot
suaveolens	MMuc
subhirsutum	EPPr
'Sugar Melt'	GKev LAma LBar
'Summer Beauty'	see *A. lusitanicum*
'Summer Drummer'	ECha EGren ELan EPfP ERCP GKev LAma MArl MHtn WCot XFar
taquetii	see *A. thunbergii*
§ *thunbergii* ⚥H5	EPot NBir NRya WAbe
- PAB 3821	LEdu
- 'Album'	LEdu NRya WAbe WFar
- 'Ozawa'	GEdr SMHy SPel WAbe WCot WFar
tibeticum	see *A. sikkimense*
§ 'Toabago'	EGren ELan EPot ERCP WCot
tolmiei var. *platyphyllum*	GKev
trifoliatum	GKev
tripedale	CSpe GKev LAma LCro MCtn XFar
P *triquetrum*	CoPl ELan GQue LAma LEdu MHoo NBir WCot
tuberosum	Widely available
- B&SWJ 8881	WCru
- Cliffs of Dover ('Ifalcod')	GKev LBar LRHS MPro SHar
- purple/mauve-flowered	CHby
- 'White Dwarf'	WCot
tuncelianum	WCot
§ *unifolium* ⚥H5	ETay LAma LCro NBir NPer NQui WCot WGwG
'Universe' ⚥H5	ERCP GKev LAma LCro XFar
ursinum	Widely available
- 'Golden Fleece'	EPPr WCot
victorialis 'Cantabria'	EBee
vineale	WHer WJek
- 'Dready'	LAma
§ 'Hair'	EGren EGrI ELan ERCP GKev LAma LShi MCtn MHtn NBir NPer XFar
violaceum	see *A. carinatum*
virgunculae	EDAr WAbe
wallichii	CSpe EPot EWes GArf GMaP GQue LEdu NBir WCot WFar
- CLD 1500	GGro LEdu NBid
- PAB 2976	LEdu WPGP
- PAB 9191	LEdu
- dark-flowered	CTtf WCot WFar
- - W&O 9049	GGro
§ *webbii*	CTtf MMuc
zaprjagajevii	WCot
zebdanense	EBee SHar

Alluaudia (Didiereaceae)

procera	NPlm

almond see *Prunus dulcis*

Alniphyllum (Styracaceae)

eberhardtii FMWJ 13121	WCru
fortunei FMWJ 13013	WCru

Alnus ✿ (Betulaceae)

§ *alnobetula*	CAgr CSto
- subsp. *sinuata*	CAgr
cordata ⚥H6	CBcs CBTr CCVT CLnd CMac CMCN CNWT EBar EHeP ELan LBuc LMaj LRHS MMuc NLar SEND SEWo SPlb WHtc WMat WMou WRjT
glutinosa	CBcs CBTr CBWd CCVT CHab CLnd CMac EBar EHeP GQue IPap LBuc LCot LMaj LRHS MCtn MGos MSwo NLar NTrD SEWo WHnu WHtc WMat WMou WRjT
- 'Aurea'	CCVT CEnd MGos WCot
- 'Imperialis' ⚥H7	CBTr CCVT CDoC CEnd CMac CMCN ELan EPfP IPap LCro LMaj MBlu MMuc NOra NPip SEND SHor WHtc WMat WMou
- 'Laciniata'	CCVT EHeP IPap MGos NLar WFar
- 'Pyramidalis'	MBlu
incana	CAco CBcs CBTr CCVT CLnd EBar EGren EHeP LBuc LCro LMaj MGos SFoI SHor WHtc WMat WRjT
- 'Aurea' ⚥H7	CCVT CEnd CLnd CMac EHeP ELan EPfP IPap MBlu MGos NLar NOra NPip SEWo SPoG WFar WHtc WMat
- 'Pendula'	WMou
japonica	CSto MBlu
maximowiczii	CSto
- from Ulleungdo, South Korea	WCru
oregana	see *A. rubra*
pendula B&SWJ 10895	WCru
§ *rubra*	CLnd CMCN ELan WHtc WMat
- f. *pinnatisecta*	CMCN MBlu
serrulata	CMCN
sieboldiana	WCru
× *spaethii*	EBar LMaj MBlu MMuc NPip WMat
subcordata	MMuc
- NJM 13.009	WPGP
viridis	see *A. alnobetula*

Alocasia (Araceae)

× *amazonica* ⚥H1a	LBom NPlm NTro
- (Bambino Series) 'Bambino'	LRHS NHrt
- - Bambino Arrow ('Ruhe 1'PBR)	CDoC LRHS NHrt NTro
- 'Polly'	CDoC LBom LCro LRHS LWaG NHrt NTro
- 'Polly Bambino'	LBom NTro
azlanii	LCro NTro
'Black Velvet'	LBom LCro LRHS NTro WFar
brisbanensis	NPlm
'Calidora'	CDTJ LRHS
× *chantrieri*	NTro
cucullata	EAri LBom LRHS NHrt NTro
cuprea	NTro WFar
- 'Red Secret'	LBom LCro NHrt NTro
'Dragon Scale'	LBom LCro NTro WFar
'Frydek' misapplied, green	see *A. micholitziana* 'Maxkowskii'
'Frydek' variegated	see *A. micholitziana* 'Freydyk'
gageana	EAri LBom LRHS
'Green Velvet'	see *A. micholitziana* 'Maxkowskii'
lauterbachiana	LCro LRHS NPlm
macrorrhizos	CDoC CDTJ CTsd EAri LBom LCro LDro LInT NPlm SBig WFar
- 'Lutea'	EAri
- 'Variegata' (v) ⚥H1a	SBig
micholitziana	EAri LBom
§ - 'Freydyk' (v) **new**	NTro
- 'Maxkowskii'	LCro
odora	CDTJ EAri LAma XFar
'Pink Dragon'	LBom LCro NTro
portei	NTro
'Portodora'	EAri LBom LCro LRHS NHrt NPlm

'Regal Shields' **new**	LInT	
reversa **new**	NTro	
sarawakensis 'Yucatan Princess'	LBom LCro LRHS NHrt NPlm NTro	
'Sarian'	LBom LCro	
scabriuscula **new**	NTro	
scalprum **new**	NTro	
× *sedenii*	NTro	
'Silver Dragon'	LBom LCro NTro	
sinuata **new**	NTro	
'Stingray'	LBom LCro LInT LRHS LWaG NHrt	
'Tigrina Superba'	NTro	
watsoniana	NTro	
wentii	EArí LBom LRHS NHrt NPlm NTro	
zebrina	CDoC LBom LCro LRHS LWaG NHrt NPlm NTro	

Aloe ✿ (Asphodelaceae)

arborescens	CDoC CDTJ CPbh EShb EUrb LBom LCro LWaG NCft NPlm SEND SIvy SPlb
- 'Variegata' (v) ♀H1c	CPbh EShb SChr SRms
aristata	see *Aristaloe aristata*
bainesii	see *Aloidendron barberae*
bakeri ♀H1b	EShb LCro SRms
barbadensis	see *A. vera*
barberae	see *Aloidendron barberae*
'Bedford's Beau'	NCft
'Brass Hat'	NCft
brevifolia ♀H2	EShb LWaG SArc WCor
broomii	SPlb
camperi	CoPl
- 'Maculata'	SEND
castanea	CPbh
'Christmas Carol'	Midl SPad
ciliaris	see *Aloiampelos ciliaris*
'Cleopatra'	CAbb CBlu SBig SEND SMrm WCot
cooperi	CDTJ EShb NCft
davyana	see *A. greatheadii* var. *davyana*
dawei	EShb
* *delaetii*	SEND
deltoideodonta	NCft SPlb
dichotoma	see *Aloidendron dichotomum*
dorotheae	CPic
dorotheae × *jucunda*	NCft
ecklonis	SPlb
ferox	CPbh SPlb SPoG
glauca **new**	SBig
globuligemma	CPbh
§ *greatheadii* var. *davyana*	SChr SPlb
haworthioides ♀H1c	NCft
humilis	CDoC CPic NCft SChr
- variegated (v)	SPlb
imalotensis	SPlb
jucunda	NCft SPlb
juvenna	CoPl NCft SEND SPlb SRms WCor WFar
kedongensis	NTro SEND
maculata	CCht SBig SChr
margaritifera	see *Tulista pumila* var. *pumila*
marlothii	SBig SPlb
melanacantha	SBig
microstigma	CPbh
'Midnight Exchange'	NCft
mitriformis	see *A. perfoliata*
mutabilis	SEND
ngobitensis	SPlb
× *nobilis*	SChr SEND WCor
- variegated (v)	SPlb
I *paradisicum*	MPri NHrt
peglerae	NCft SRms
'Pepe'	NCft
§ *perfoliata*	CoPl LCro NCft
'Pink Blush'	CPic
plicatilis	see *Kumara plicatilis*
polyphylla ♀H2	CBlu CDTJ CPbh MCtn SArc SBig WCot
rauhii ♀H1b	CPbh NCft SRms
rauhii × *somaliensis*	NCft
reitzii	CBlu CPbh SBig SPlb
rivierei	SPlb
Safari Sunrise ('X5'PBR)	CBcs ESuc LCro SBig
sinkatana	CPic
'Snowflake'	SPad
somaliensis ♀H1b	NCft NTro
× *spinosissima*	NPlm SBig
squarrosa	CDoC MPri SEND WFar
'Stingray'	CPic
striata	CBcs CBlu CoPl CPbh EShb EUrb SPlb
striatula	see *Aloiampelos striatula*
- var. *caesia*	see *Aloiampelos striatula* var. *caesia*
suprafoliata	CBlu
tenuior	see *Aloiampelos tenuior*
variegata	see *Gonialoe variegata*
§ *vera* ♀H1c	Widely available
'White Beauty'	EShb Midl
wickensii	SPlb
yavellana	SPlb
zebrina 'Dannyz'	LCro NCft SPad

Aloe × *Haworthia* see × *Alworthia*

Aloiampelos (Asphodelaceae)

§ *ciliaris*	CHll EShb SArc SChr SEND
§ *striatula* ♀H3	CBrP CDTJ CPbh CSde CTca CTsd EArí ElAn EShb LWaG SArc SAth SBig SChr SEND SPlb SPoG SVen WCor WCot WJun WMal
- var. *caesia*	WPGP
§ *tenuior*	EShb

Aloidendron (Asphodelaceae)

§ *barberae*	CPbh NPlm SBig
§ *dichotomum*	CPbh SPlb

Aloinopsis (Aizoaceae)

spathulata	GEdr SPlb

Alonsoa (Scrophulariaceae)

acutifolia var. *candida*	LBar
- coral	WFar
'Bright Spark'	CSpe LBar
meridionalis	LBar
- 'Rebel'	MCtn SRkn
- 'Salmon Beauty'	MCtn
- 'Shell Pink'	LBar WFar
warscewiczii	WFar
- 'Peachy-keen'	CSpe

Alopecurus (Poaceae)

pratensis	CHab
- 'Aureovariegatus' (v)	GElm SRms
- 'Aureus'	NBro SPlb

Alophia (Iridaceae)

lahue	see *Herbertia lahue*

Aloysia (Verbenaceae)

chamaedryfolia	SEND
citriodora	see *A. citrodora*

Aloysia

§	*citrodora* ♀H3	Widely available		
	- 'Goliath' **new**	MNHC		
	- 'Spilsbury Mint'	ELan EPfP LRHS MHer MHoo SEND SPhx		
	gratissima	MHoo WJek		
	triphylla	see *A. citrodora*		
	virgata **new**	WJek		

Alpinia (Zingiberaceae)

caerulea	NPlm	
galanga	ELan SBig	
japonica	LEdu	
- B&SWJ 8889	ESwi	
- PAB 6441	LEdu	
nutans misapplied	see *A. zerumbet*	
speciosa	see *A. zerumbet*	
§ *zerumbet*	SBig	
- 'Variegata' (v)	EAri LCro SBig	

Alsobia (Gesneriaceae)

dianthiflora	WDib
'San Miguel'	WDib

Alsophila (Cyatheaceae)

§	*australis*	CBrP CDTJ LRHS SBig SPlb
§	*dregei*	SPlb
§	*spinulosa*	SBig
§	*tricolor*	CDTJ SBig

Alstonia (Apocynaceae)

yunnanensis **new**	SBrt

Alstroemeria ✿ (Alstroemeriaceae)

'Aimi'	EGrI ELon
'Andez Rose'	CDor
'Andez Vanilla'	CDor
'Apollo' ♀H4	CTsd
'Aubance' (Garden Series)	SEND
aurea	MCtn SRms
- 'Apricot'	EPPr
- 'Lutea'	SPlb WFar
- 'Orange King'	EGrI ELan EPfP
'Avanti'	ELon
'Blushing Bride'	CTsd
'Bodega'PBR	LRHS
'Bolero'	ELon
brasiliensis	CTsd WCot
- 'Cally Star' (v)	EBee EPPr
'Brissac' (Garden Series)	NLar XFar
'Cahors' (Planet Series) ♀H4	LCro
'Candy'	MPro
'Cardinal Purple'	SPel
'Caroline' (Midi Series)	EGrI
'Charles' (Maxi Series)	LBar SEND
'Charlotte' (Mini Series)	EGrI
'Charm'	CTsd ELon
'Christina'PBR (Little Miss Series)	EGrI ELan LRHS MPro
'Dandy Candy'	EPfP MCtn MHol WCot
'Davina'PBR (Little Miss Series)	EPfP LRHS MPro
Doctor Salter's hybrids	SRms
ELIZABETH ('Stamutro')	EGrI
'Evening Song'	SMHy
exserens	WCot
'Flaming Star'	ELon SPel
'Frances' (v)	CBro
'Freedom'	CWGN ELon MHol SPoG WCot
'Friendship' ♀H5	CTsd SMHy WMal
Garden Series	NLar
'Gina'PBR (Little Miss Series)	EGrI

'Golden Delight'	ELon
I 'Hatch Hybrid'	EPPr
'Henri' (Maxi Series)	MHol
HOLIDAY VALLEY ('Tessumholid'PBR) (Summer Paradise - Valley Series)	LRHS
hookeri	WAbe WFar WHil
(Inca Series) INCA BANDIT ('Koncaband')	LBuc
- INCA BATTLE	LBuc
- INCA FIRE ('Koncafire')	SPoG
- INCA FLAMINGO ('Koncaflamo')	LBuc
- INCA GLOW ('Koglow')	EGrI ELan ELon MHol SRms
- INCA GOAL ('Koncagoal')	CWnw ELan Midl MPro SDix WHil
- INCA GOLD	LBuc
- INCA HUSKY ('Koncahusky'PBR)	CWnw EBee ELon LRHS MHol Midl MPro SDix
- INCA ICE ('Koice')	NLar
- INCA MOONLIGHT ('Komolight')	NLar
- INCA NOBLE ('Koncanoble')	LBar MSwo
- INCA PULSE ('Konpulse'PBR)	ELan ELon NLar
- INCA RIO ('Koncario')	LBar
- INCA SUNDANCE ('Koncasunda'PBR)	CWnw EBee ELan ELon LRHS Midl MPro SDix SPad
- INCA SUNSET ('Kosunset')	EGren
- INCA SWEETY ('Koncasweet'PBR)	CWnw ELan LBar LRHS Midl MPro
- INCA VITO ('Koncavito'PBR)	CWnw ELon MHol Midl MPro SDix SPoG
- INCA YUKO ('Koncayuko'PBR)	LBuc MHol WSpi
INDIAN SUMMER ('Tesronto'PBR) (Summer Paradise - Summer Series)	Widely available
(Inticancha Series) INTICANCHA BRYCE ('Tesbryce'PBR)	EGren LRHS MHol NLar NWbg WFar
- INTICANCHA CABANA ('Tescaban')	MBros MHol MPro SPoG
- INTICANCHA DARK PURPLE ('Tesdarklin'PBR)	EGren LRHS MPro WFar
- INTICANCHA DOBA ('Tesdoba'PBR)	EGren LRHS MAsh MPro NLar
- INTICANCHA HULA ('Teshula') **new**	LSou MPri
- INTICANCHA INDIGO ('Tesindig'PBR)	EGren LRHS MAsh MPri MPro NLar
- INTICANCHA MACHU ('Tesmach'PBR)	LRHS MAsh MPro NLar WFar
- INTICANCHA MAGIC WHITE ('Tesmagwhi'PBR)	EBee MHol MPro
- INTICANCHA MALAGA ('Tesmala') **new**	MPri
- INTICANCHA MAYA ('Tesmaya'PBR)	EGren LRHS MAsh MPri MPro NLar WFar WHil
- INTICANCHA MOON (Inticancha Series)	see *A.* INTICANCHA MOONLIGHT
§ - INTICANCHA MOONLIGHT ('Tesmoonli'PBR)	EGren MSCN
- INTICANCHA NAVAYO ('Tesnava'PBR)	LRHS MHol MPri MPro WFar
- INTICANCHA PARAÍSO ('Tesparai')	EBee LRHS MAsh
- INTICANCHA PASSION ('Tespassion'PBR)	EGren LRHS MPro WFar
- INTICANCHA PURPLE ('Tespurplin'PBR)	WFar
- INTICANCHA RED ('Tesrobin'PBR)	EGren LRHS MBros MHol MPro WFar WHil

Alstroemeria

– Inticancha Sunlight ('Tessunlight'^{PBR})	WFar	– Princess Lisa ('Zaprilisa'^{PBR})	CBcs CWGN
– Inticancha Sunstar ('Tessunstar') **new**	LSou	– Princess Louise ('Zaprilou'^{PBR})	CBcs
– Inticancha White Pink Blush ('Tesblushin'^{PBR})	LRHS MPro WFar	– Princess Mulan ('Zaprimu'^{PBR})	CBcs
(Inticancha Sun Series) Inticancha Havana ('Tessunhava')	EGren LRHS MSCN	– Princess Ninon – Princess Paola ('Stapripal'^{PBR})	LRHS CBcs CWGN SPoG
– Inticancha Sunday ('Tessunday'^{PBR})	MPro	– Princess Sara ('Staprisara'^{PBR})	EPfP SPoG
– Inticancha Sunset ('Tessunse')	LSou MPro WHil	– Princess Tamara ('Zapritama'^{PBR})	CBcs CWGN SPoG
– Inticancha Sunshine ('Tesshine'^{PBR})	EGren EPfP LRHS MHol MPri NLar WFar	– Princess Zavina ('Staprivina'^{PBR})	SPoG
§ *isabellana*	WCru	Princess Victoria	see *A.* 'Victoria'
'Junon' (Planet Series)	LCro	*pseudospathulata*	WCot
'Jupiter' (Planet Series)	LCro NLar	§ *psittacina*	CAby CBro CTsd ECha EPPr GBin
'Layon' (Garden Series)	EBee LRHS		SHar SMHy SRms WFar
ligtu hybrids	ECha EPfP LCro LRHS MCtn MNrw NPer SRms WBrk	– 'Royal Star' (v)	CBro CExl CWCL EArl EPfP EPPr LRHS MHol MPie SBea
– subsp. *simsii*	SPlb		SHar SPoG SRms WCot WFar
'Liré' (Garden Series)	EBee MHol		WHoo WSpi
'Louis' (Maxi Series)	LRHS	*pulchella* Sims	see *A. psittacina*
'Lucas' (Mini Series)	LRHS	'Purple Rain'	ELon
'Marcé' (Garden Series)	LRHS	'Red Beauty' (v)	see *A.* 'Spitfire'
'Marguerite' (Midi Series)	LRHS XFar	'Red Beauty'	GMaP
'Marissa'	GMaP	'Red Elf' ♀^{H4}	CTsd SMHy SPel
'Mars' (Planet Series)	CWnw ELon EUrb	'Regina'	see *A.* 'Victoria'
'Mathilde' (Midi Series)	LRHS	River Valley ('Tessumriver') (Summer Paradise - Valley Series)	MHol MPro
'Mauve Majesty'	ELon LRHS NSti SPoG WCot		
'Mazé' (Garden Series)	SPel	Rock 'n' Roll ('Alsdun01'^{PBR}) (v)	CDor EBee MHol MHtn SPoG SRms WCot WFar
'Natalie'^{PBR} (Little Miss Series)	MPro		
		'Roselind' (Little Miss Series)	EGrI ELan LRHS MPri MPro
'Neptune'	LCro	'Rosie' (Mini Series)	LBar
'Nicolas' (Maxi Series)	LBar SEND XFar	'Royal Velvet'	SPel
'Orange Glory' ♀^{H4}	ELon MNrw	'Saturne' (Planet Series)	CDor LCro
pallida	SPlb	'Selina'	MNrw
'Phoenix' (v) ♀^{H4}	ELon	'Serrant' (Garden Series)	MMrt
Planet Series	EGrI	Silvester ('Gasilves')	CWGN WFar
presliana RB 94103	WCot	'Sirius' (Planet Series) ♀^{H4}	LCro
(Princess Series) Princess Amina ('Zapriamin'^{PBR})	CBcs SPoG	'Sophie'^{PBR} (Little Miss Series)	CWGN ELan EPfP LRHS MPri MPro
– Princess Beatrix ('Stadoran')	SChr	§ 'Spitfire' (v) ♀^{H4}	ELon LCro LRHS MNrw WCot
– Princess Camilla ('Stapricamil')	SPoG	Spring Valley ('Tesvalsprin') (Summer Paradise - Valley Series)	CWGN LRHS MAsh MHtn MPro NLar
– Princess Claire ('Zapriclair'^{PBR})	CBcs CWGN	Summer Paradise Series	MHol
– Princess Diana ('Zapridapal'^{PBR})	CBcs CWGN EPfP SPoG	– Summer Ice – Summer Party ('Tessumpar')	CWGN MAsh MHtn MPro NLar WFar
– Princess Eliane ('Zaprielia'^{PBR})	CBcs	– Summer Red ('Tessumred'^{PBR})	CWGN EGren LRHS LSou MHol WFar
– Princess Eliane Light Pink ('Zaprieliali')	LRHS	– Summer Relieve ('Gasumrelie')	MHol
– Princess Eliane Orange ('Zapriliarange'^{PBR})	MBNS	(Summer Paradise - Summer Series) Summer Break ('Tessumbreak'^{PBR})	CAbb CWGN EPfP LRHS MArl MHol MPri MPro WFar
– Princess Fabiana ('Zaprifabi'^{PBR})	CWGN SPoG	– Summer Breeze ('Teshunte'^{PBR})	CAbb LBom LRHS MAsh MPri MPro SPoG SRms WFar
– Princess Ivana ('Staprivane'^{PBR})	SPoG	– Summer Chic ('Tessumchi') **new**	LSou
– Princess Kate ('Zaprikate'^{PBR})	CBcs CWGN EPfP	– Summer Heat ('Tessumheat') **new**	MPro
– Princess Katiana ('Zaprikatia')	CBcs LRHS	– Summer Pepper ('Tessumpep')	MPro NLar
– Princess Letizia ('Zaprilet')	SPoG	– Summer Rose ('Tessumrose') **new**	LSou
– Princess Leyla ('Stapriley'^{PBR})	EGrI	– Summer Saint ('Tessumsaint')	CAbb EGren EPfP LRHS LSou MHol MPro WFar
– Princess Lilian ('Zaprilian'^{PBR})	EPfP		

Alstroemeria

- SUMMER SKY ('Tessumsky')[PBR] — CWGN EGren LRHS LSou MHol MPri MPro WFar
- SUMMER SNOW ('Gasumsnow') — EGren LRHS WFar
'Sunstar' — GMaP
'Sweet Laura'[PBR] — CWnw ELan ELon MHol NSti SPoG WCot
'Tanya' — MNrw
'Tara'[PBR] (Little Miss Series) — ELan LRHS MPro
'Tessa' ♀[H4] — CDor MNrw
'Tiercé' (Garden Series) — LRHS XFar
TIMES VALLEY ('Tessvaltime') (Summer Paradise - Valley Series) — CWGN MPro
'Uranus' (Planet Series) — LCro
VALLEY GIRL ('Tesvalgirl') (Summer Paradise - Valley Series) — CWGN LRHS MAsh MPro
'Vanessa'[PBR] (Little Miss Series) — EGrI LRHS MPri MPro
'Venus' (Planet Series) — LCro
§ 'Victoria' — EGrI
'White Buttons' — LBar LBom MPro
WILD VALLEY ('Tesvalwild') (Summer Paradise - Valley Series) — MPro
'Yellow Friendship' ♀[H4] — CTsd MNrw
'Zoë'[PBR] (Little Miss Series) (v) — LRHS MPro

Alternanthera (Amaranthaceae)
dentata — LRHS
philoxeroides — Prohibited invasive. See Conservation and the Environment, p.42
reineckii — ELin
- 'Cardinalis' — ELin
- 'Lilacina' — ELin

Althaea (Malvaceae)
armeniaca — EPPr MCtn SHar WCot
cannabina — CAby CCBP CDor CSpe CTtf EBee ECha EPPr LRHS LSto MAvo MBel MCtn MHer MNrw SBeP SDix SHar SMHy SMrm SNoN SPel SPhx StAn WCav WChS WCot WOld WTor WTre
officinalis — CCBP CGHo CGwi CHab CPud EBee ELan ENfk EPPr GJem GQue IDun MAsh MCtn MEar MHer MHoo MMuc MNHC NAts NLar SRms SVic WHer WJek WSpi
* - alba — SMHy
§ - 'Romney Marsh' — WFar WKif WMal
rosea — see *Alcea rosea*
rugosostellulata — see *Alcea rugosa*

Altingia see Liquidambar

× Alworthia (Asphodelaceae)
'Black Gem' — CoPl EShb NCft SEND SMrm WCor WCot WFar

Alyogyne (Malvaceae)
§ huegelii — CWal EAri EUrb SEle SEND SPlb
- 'Santa Cruz' — CHll EShb LRHS WFar
MAGIC MOMENTS ('Hutwow') — SPoG

Alyssoides (Brassicaceae)
utriculata — MCtn

Alyssum (Brassicaceae)
aizoides Boiss. — EDAr
montanum — MAsh SPlb SRms
§ - 'Berggold' — ECha ELan EPfP
- 'Luna' — EGren
- MOUNTAIN GOLD — see *A. montanum* 'Berggold'
- subsp. *pluscanescens* — WCot
saxatile — see *Aurinia saxatilis*
- 'Summit' — EDAr SRms
serpyllifolium — EDAr
'Snowcloth' — WFar
wulfenianum — GKev WIce

Amaranthus (Amaranthaceae)
caudatus — LCro MCtn
- 'Green Cascade' — LCro
- 'Viridis' — MCtn
cruentus 'Autumn's Touch' — CSpe MCtn
- 'Hot Biscuits' — MCtn
- 'Oeschberg' ♀[H2] — MCtn
- 'Red Spike' — CSpe
- 'Velvet Curtains' ♀[H2] — LCro
hypochondriacus 'Green Thumb' ♀[H2] — CSpe MCtn
- 'Pygmy Torch' ♀[H2] — CSpe MCtn
'Opopeo' — MCtn
'Red Army' — EHet
tricolor — SRms
- 'Early Splendor' — CSpe
- 'Red Leaf' — MNHC

× Amarcrinum (Amaryllidaceae)
'Dorothy Hannibal' — WCot
memoria-corsii — GKev LAma MHtn WCot
'Howardii'

× Amarine (Amaryllidaceae)
tubergenii — SMrm
- Belladiva Series — CBlu CBro EBee ELan EPfP GKev LAma LCro WHil
- - 'Anastasia'[PBR] ♀[H4] — CBro EGren ELan ERCP GKev LAma LCro LRHS NBir XFar
- - 'Aphrodite'[PBR] — CBro GKev LAma LCro WFar WHil XFar
- - 'Elvi' — LAma
- - 'Emanuelle'[PBR] ♀[H4] — CBro ELan ERCP GKev LAma LCro LRHS SEND WHil XFar
- - 'Paris' — CBro ELan ERCP GKev SMad
- - 'Smilla' — CBro LAma
- - 'Tomoko'[PBR] — CBro ELan ERCP GKev XFar
- 'Fletcheri' — WCot
- 'Zwanenburg' — CBlu LAma SEND WCot

× Amarygia (Amaryllidaceae)
§ bidwillii 'Alba' — CBro
- 'Rosea' — WCot

Amaryllis (Amaryllidaceae)
§ belladonna ♀[H4] — CBcs CBro CPbh CTca EBee EGrI EPfP EShb GKev LAma LCro MNrw SEND SMrm WCot WFar XFar
- 'Beacon' — GKev LAma
- 'Hathor' — CBro WCot
- 'Johannesburg' — CBro WCot
- 'Major' — SChr
- 'Parkeri Alba' — see × *Amarygia bidwillii* 'Alba'
- 'Purpurea' — WCot
- 'White Queen' — GKev LAma
- white-flowered — XFar

Amaryllis × *Brunsvigia* see × *Amarygia*

Amaryllis × *Crinum* see × *Amarcrinum*

Amaryllis × *Nerine* see × *Amarine*

Amberboa (Asteraceae)
- 'Desert Star' — MCtn
- *moschata* 'Imperialis' — MCtn
- - 'The Bride' — MCtn

Ambrosina (Araceae)
- *bassii* — WCot

Amelanchier ✿ (Rosaceae)
- *alnifolia* — SBmr StAn WKor
- - 'Forestburg' (F) — MBlu
- - 'Honeywood' (F) — CAgr MBlu NOra
- - 'Jb30' (F) — CAgr NOra
- - 'Martin' (F) — CAgr NOra
- - 'Northline' (F) — CAgr EBee LCro NOra SBmr WMat
- - 'Obelisk'^{PBR} — CAco CAgr CBcs CDoC CMac EBee EGren ELan EPfP GKin LBom LBuc LCro LMaj LRHS LSRN MAsh MGos MPri NLar NOra NPip SPoG WHtc WMat
- § - var. *pumila* — WCot
- - 'Regent' (F) — CAgr
- - 'Smokey' (F) — CAco CAgr EBee MBlu MPri NOra SPoG WKor WMat
- - 'Thiessen' (F) — NOra SBmr
- * *alpina* — SSta
- *arborea* 'Robin Hill' — see *A.* × *grandiflora* 'Robin Hill'
- *bartramiana* — SSta
- - 'Eskimo' — NLar
- *canadensis* K. Koch — see *A. lamarckii*
- *canadensis* ambig. — CAco CBTr CDoC CTsd EGrI EHeP ERom IPap LMaj LSto MPri NOra SEWo SPoG WFar WKor WLov
- *canadensis* (L.) Medik. — CAgr CBrac CLnd CMac CSpe EBee ELan EPfP EUrb LMaj SArc SAth WHnu WMat
- § - 'Glenn Form' — CAco CCVT EBee EGren EHeP ELan EPfP LCro LRHS MPri NLar NOra NPip SEWo SPoG WMat
- - 'October Flame' — CCVT EBee EPfP LRHS
- - 'Prince William' — CAgr MBlu SGol
- - 'Rainbow' — see *A. canadensis* 'Glenn Form'
- - RAINBOW PILLAR — see *A. canadensis* 'Glenn Form'
- - SPRING GLORY ('Sprizam') — SRms
- × *grandiflora* — EHeP
- - 'Autumn Brilliance' — CEnd LRHS MBlu SGol
- - 'Ballerina' — Widely available
- - 'Cole's Select' — EBee
- - 'Princess Diana' ♀^{H7} — SSta
- § - 'Robin Hill' ♀^{H7} — Widely available
- - 'Rubescens' — CEnd SSta
- 'La Paloma' ♀^{H6} — EBee ELan EPfP LRHS LSRN MAsh MGos NOra NPip SSta WHtc WMat
- *laevis* — CBcs EPfP LRHS SHor
- - 'R.J. Hilton' ♀^{H7} — CBTr CDoC CLnd EBee ELan EPfP LRHS MAsh NOra NPip SRms SSta WMat
- - 'Snow Cloud' — LRHS
- - 'Snowflakes' — CAco CBTr CDoC CEnd EBee EPfP LBom LCro LRHS MAsh MPri NLar NOra NPip SEWo SOrN SPoG SSta WMat WMou

- § *lamarckii* ♀^{H7} — Widely available
- - 'Snowberry' — SBmr
- *obovalis* 'Jennybelle' (F) — SSta
- *ovalis* misapplied — see *A. spicata* (Lam.) K. Koch
- *ovalis* Medik. — SPlb
- - 'Edelweiss' — CAco EPfP LRHS MGos
- - 'Helvetia' — NLar
- *pumila* — see *A. alnifolia* var. *pumila*
- *rotundifolia* ambig. — CAgr
- § *spicata* (Lam.) K. Koch — CAgr MCtn

Amelanchier × *Sorbus* see × *Amelasorbus*

× *Amelasorbus* (Rosaceae)
- *raciborskiana* — MBlu NLar

Amentotaxus (Taxaceae)
- *argotaenia* — WPGP
- var. *argotaenia*

Amianthium (Melanthiaceae)
- *muscitoxicum* — LRHS

Amicia (Fabaceae)
- *zygomeris* — CBcs CDTJ CExl CHll CSde CSpe EAri EBee ELan EPfP EWes EWld LRHS SChF SDix SHor SMrm SPel SPoG WCot WPGP
- - 'John's Big Splash' (v) — WCot

Ammi (Apiaceae)
- *majus* ♀^{H6} — CSpe EPfP LCro LSto MAvo MCtn MNHC SDix SHor SMHy SPhx WJek WSpi WTor
- - 'Graceland' ♀^{H6} — LCro MCtn NClf
- *visnaga* — see *Visnaga daucoides*

Ammobium (Asteraceae)
- *alatum* — MCtn SPlb
- *calyceroides* — SPlb

Ammocharis (Amaryllidaceae)
- *coranica* — WCot

Ammophila (Poaceae)
- *arenaria* — CKno EBee

Amomyrtus ✿ (Myrtaceae)
- § *luma* — CBcs CMHG EBee ELon LEdu LRHS SEND SPoG WJek WPGP
- *meli* — WPGP

Amorpha (Fabaceae)
- *canescens* — CSpe EGrI MNrw SPlb WSpi
- *fruticosa* — IArd MBlu MMuc SEND SPlb WJur

Amorphophallus ✿ (Araceae)
- *albus* — CDTJ SPlb WCot
- *bulbifer* — CDTJ EAri EGren ESwi GKev LAma SPlb XFar
- *dunnii* — LEdu
- *henryi* — WCot
- *konjac* — CDTJ CExl LEdu NGKo SChr SPlb WCot WJun
- *napalensis* — EAri GKev LAma SBig WCot
- *paeoniifolius* — LAma
- *stipitatus* — LEdu WCot
- *yuloensis* — WCot

Ampelaster (Asteraceae)
- *carolinianus* — EShb

Ampelodesmos (Poaceae)
mauritanicus ♀H3	CExl CKno ECha EWes SDix SEND SPlb StAn WCot WSpi

Ampelopsis (Vitaceae)
aconitifolia	NLar WJur
- B&SWJ 12982	WCru
- 'Chinese Lace'	LRHS WCot
arborea B&SWJ 4711	WCru
brevipedunculata	ELan MMrt WJur
- 'Elegans' (v)	CBcs CDoC CMac EBee ELan EPfP LCro LRHS LSto MGos SDix SPoG WCot WJur WLov
- var. **maximowiczii**	SBig
delavayana	MMuc
glandulosa	WCru
var. **hancei** B&SWJ 1793	
- var. **heterophylla**	WJur
- - 'Monozuki' (v)	GGro
henryana	see *Parthenocissus henryana*
sempervirens hort. ex Veitch	see *Clematicissus striata*
tricuspidata 'Veitchii'	see *Parthenocissus tricuspidata* 'Veitchii'

Amphicome see *Incarvillea*

Amsonia (Apocynaceae)
'Blue Ice'	Widely available
ciliata	EMor GKev MNrw NLar SHar WPGP
- 'Halfway to Arkansas'	EMor LBar SHor
§ **elliptica**	EBee EMor EPPr
'Ernst Pagels'	EBee ECha EMor EPPr GBin LBar MAvo SHar SPel WCot WGoo WHil
hubrichtii	CBWd CDor CKno CSpe CTtf EBee ECha EGrI EMor EPfP EPPr GKev LEdu LSto MAvo MBel NClf NLar SDix SHor SPeP StAn WCAu WFar WPGP WSpi WTre
illustris	CSpe EBee EMor EPPr LEdu NLar SHar SMHy SPel WHoo WPGP
§ **orientalis**	CSpe EBee ECha EGrI ELan EMor LEdu LRHS LShi MAvo NDov NLar SHor SMHy SMrm SPel SPeP SPhx WCAu WCot WFar WKif WTre
- from Turkey	CSpe SMHy
- 'Cally Dark Stem'	SPel WMal
sinensis	see *A. elliptica*
tabernaemontana	Widely available
* - **galacticifolia**	EGrI
- var. **salicifolia**	CBWd CSpe EBee EMor LCro NBir SHor WCAu WPGP
- 'Stella Azul'	EMor MNrw
- 'Storm Cloud'	GBin LCro MMrt NCth

Amydrium (Araceae)
medium new	NTro

Amygdalus see *Prunus*
nana	see *Prunus tenella*

Anacampseros (Portulacaceae)
papyracea new	NTro
retusa	SPlb
telephiastrum 'Sunrise'	see *A. telephiastrum* 'Variegata'
§ - 'Variegata' (v)	NCft WOld

Anacamptis (Orchidaceae)
pyramidalis	CHab

Anacyclus (Asteraceae)
pyrethrum	EBee ELan EPfP GKev LRHS MAsh
var. **depressus** ♀H4	SPlb
- - 'Garden Gnome'	SRms
- - 'Silberkissen'	EDAr GKev

Anagallis (Primulaceae)
arvensis	MCtn
monellii	CSpe
subsp. **linifolia** 'Blue Light'	
- 'Skylover'	LCro
tenella	CBen CoPl CWat ELin EWat
- 'Studland'	EPot WAbe

Ananas (Bromeliaceae)
comosus (F)	MPri NTrD SPre
- 'Champaca' (F) ♀H1a	EGren SPre
- CORONA ('Duranas2'PBR) (F)	LCro LRHS

Anaphalis (Asteraceae)
margaritacea	CBcs ECha GMaP NLar SRms WCAu WFar
§ - 'Neuschnee'	EBee EPfP GJos LShi NLar StAn WFar
- NEW SNOW	see *A. margaritacea* 'Neuschnee'
- var. **yedoensis**	SDix
§ **nepalensis**	NSti SRms
var. **monocephala**	
nubigena	see *A. nepalensis* var. *monocephala*
subumbellata	EBee
transnokoensis	EWes
triplinervis ♀H7	EBee EBlo ELan EWld GMaP GQue NBid NLar NWbg SHar StAn WCAu WFar
- CC 1620	NBir
- 'Schwefellicht'	NLar
- 'Silberregen'	SAko
- 'Silver Wave'	ELon LRHS NLar
§ - 'Sommerschnee' ♀H7	CMac ECha EPfP MHol NLar WHoo WTre
- SUMMER SNOW	see *A. triplinervis* 'Sommerschnee'

Anaphaloides (Asteraceae)
§ **bellidioides**	ECha

Anchusa (Boraginaceae)
§ **azurea**	NLar
- 'Dropmore'	CDor CSpe EBee EPfP LCro MCtn NLar SRms WHil
- 'Feltham Pride'	ELan MNrw SRms
- 'Little John'	SRms
- 'Loddon Royalist'	CAby CBcs CMac EBee EGren ELan EPfP GMaP LBom LCro LRHS MArl MAsh MPri MPro MSCN NDov NLar SMHy SMrm SOrN SPoG SRms WCAu WFar WTor WTre
- 'Opal'	CFis MArl WCAu
caespitosa Lam.	LRHS MNrw
capensis	GKev
- 'Blue Angel'	MCtn WFar
italica	see *A. azurea*
laxiflora	see *Borago pygmaea*
myosotidiflora	see *Brunnera macrophylla*
officinalis	MCtn SRms
sempervirens	see *Pentaglottis sempervirens*

Ancylostemon see *Oreocharis*

Andrachne (Phyllanthaceae)
    colchica   see *Leptopus chinensis*

Androcymbium see *Colchicum*

Andromeda (Ericaceae)
polifolia	SPlb
- 'Alba'	GArf
- 'Alisa'	GKev
- 'Blue Ice'	CBcs CDoC ELan EPot GAbr GArf GKev LRHS MAsh MHtn NBir NLar SPad SPoG WFar
- 'Blue Lagoon'	CBcs CDoC ELan LCro LRHS MAsh NLar WFar
- 'Compacta' ♀H6	CDoC ELan EPot LCro LRHS MAsh NLar WFar
- 'Grandiflora'	GKev
- 'Kirigamine'	GArf
- 'Macrophylla' ♀H6	EPot
- 'Nikko'	CMac NLar
- 'Shibutsu'	EPot GArf

Andropogon (Poaceae)
gerardii	GQue
- 'Darkhawks'PBR	IPot
- 'Prairie Sommer'	NDov
- 'Red October'	EBee ELan IPot WCot
- 'Weinheim Burgundy'	IPot MNrw NDov
hallii 'JS Purple Konza'PBR	IPot
ischaemum	see *Bothriochloa ischaemum*
scoparius	see *Schizachyrium scoparium*
ternarius	EDAr
virginicus	Prohibited invasive. See Conservation and the Environment, p.42

Androsace (Primulaceae)
bulleyana	WAbe
carnea	GEdr
- subsp. **brigantiaca**	GKev
- var. **halleri**	see *A. carnea* subsp. *rosea*
- subsp. **laggeri** ♀H5	EDAr
- - 'Andorra'	GArf
§ - subsp. **rosea**	EDAr GArf
carnea × pyrenaica	GArf WIce
cylindrica	WAbe
cylindrica × hirtella	LRHS
ENF strain	
delavayi	WAbe
geraniifolia	GKev SRms
globifera	WAbe
halleri	see *A. carnea* subsp. *rosea*
hedraeantha	WAbe
himalaica	EPot WAbe
hirtella	WAbe
jacquemontii	see *A. villosa* var. *jacquemontii*
kosopoljanskii	EPot GKev
lactea	WAbe WIce
laevigata	GArf
- 'Gothenburg'	WFar
lanuginosa ♀H5	EDAr GKev SLee SRms SRot WIce
- 'Leichtlinii'	GKev
limprichtii	see *A. sarmentosa* var. *watkinsii*
× marpensis	EPot MWlw WAbe
mathildae	EDAr WAbe
microphylla	see *A. mucronifolia* G.Watt
montana	WAbe
mucronifolia misapplied	see *A. sempervivoides*
§ **mucronifolia** G.Watt	EPot GArf WAbe
muscoidea	WAbe
- 'Breviscapa'	EPot
- 'Dolpo Lilac'	WAbe
- Schacht's form	WAbe
nivalis	SPlb
primuloides	see *A. sarmentosa* subsp. *primuloides*
pyrenaica	SPlb
robusta subsp. **purpurea**	WAbe
- - 'Dolpo Dwarf'	WAbe
rotundifolia	GArf
sarmentosa misapplied	see *A. sarmentosa* subsp. *primuloides*
sarmentosa ambig.	SPlb
sarmentosa Wall.	SRms WHoo
- from Namche, Nepal	EPot WAbe
- Galmont's form	see *A. sarmentosa* subsp. *primuloides* 'Salmon's Variety'
§ - subsp. **primuloides** ♀H5	GKev WAbe
- - 'Chumbyi'	EPot SRms WIce
- - 'Conwy Gem'	EPot WAbe
- - 'Doksa' ♀H5	EPot WAbe WIce
§ - - 'Salmon's Variety'	EDAr
- - 'Sherriffi'	GArf GKev MMuc SRms WIce
- var. **watkinsii**	EPot
- var. **yunnanensis** misapplied	see *A. sarmentosa* subsp. *primuloides*
selago	WAbe
- 'Red Eye'	WAbe
§ **sempervivoides**	EDAr ELan EPot GArf GKev GMaP SLee SPlb SRms
- 'Susan Joan'	EPot GKev MWlw WAbe
septentrionalis	CSpe
- 'Stardust'	CFis EDAr ELan EPfP LRHS SPoG
strigillosa	GKev
vandellii	GArf WAbe
villosa	GArf WAbe
§ - var. **jacquemontii**	CTtf
- - lilac-flowered	EPot
- - pink-flowered	EPot WAbe
vitaliana	see *Vitaliana primuliflora*
watkinsii	see *A. sarmentosa* var. *watkinsii*

Andryala (Asteraceae)
    lanata   see *Hieracium lanatum*

Aneilema (Commelinaceae)
    beniniense   WTra

Anemanthele (Poaceae)
§ **lessoniana** ♀H4	Widely available
- 'Gold Hue'	ELon
- 'Sirocco'	EGren EMor EPfP EUrb ISha MAvo SMrm WCot WFar

Anemarrhena (Asparagaceae)
    asphodeloides   WCot

Anemia (Schizaeaceae)
mexicana	WCot
tomentosa	LRHS

Anemonastrum see *Anemone*

Anemone ✿ (Ranunculaceae)
altaica	EWld GKev NLar SRms
'Annerose'	ECha NLar
apennina ♀H6	GEdr LEdu
- var. **albiflora**	ECha GKev SPlb
- double-flowered (d)	CTtf ECha
- 'Petrovac'	GKev LEdu WCot
baldensis	GKev SRms

Anemone

barbulata	CExl CTsd EBee EWes GPSL LEdu SHar
blanda ♀H6	CAby EGren EGrI EPfP ETay LAma LCro LRHS MAsh NLar NNys SEND SRms WCav WFar
- 'Alba'	LRHS
- blue-flowered	CBro CTtf EGren ELan EPfP EPot ERCP GAbr GKev GMaP LAma LBom LCro LRHS MPie SPoG SRms XFar
- 'Charmer'	EGren EPfP EPot GKev LAma LCro NLar WCot XFar
- 'Ingramii'	GKev MNHC WCot
- var. *rosea*	SPoG
- - 'Pink Star'	CBro EBee EGrI EPot GKev LAma LBar NBir
- - 'Radar'	EPot GKev LAma NBir
- 'Violet Star'	GKev LAma MPie
- 'White Splendour' ♀H6	CBro CTtf ECha EGren ELan EPfP EPot ERCP ETay GKev GQue LAma LBar LCro LRHS NBir SPhx SPoG SRms WCot XFar
- white-flowered	LRHS
'Bowles's Mauve'	GEdr LRHS
caerulea	LEdu
canadensis	GEdr LEdu LShi SBrt WCot WFar
coronaria De Caen Group	EPfP GKev LAma LCro LRHS SPoG XFar
- - 'Bicolor'	EGren GKev LAma LRHS WCot XFar
- - 'Bordeaux'	ETay GKev LAma LCro LRHS WCot WFar
§ - - 'Die Braut'	EPfP ERCP GKev LAma LCro LRHS NBir XFar
- - 'His Excellency'	see *A. coronaria* (De Caen Group) 'Hollandia'
§ - - 'Hollandia'	EGrI ERCP GKev LAma LCro LRHS XFar
- - 'Mister Fokker'	EGrI ERCP GKev LAma LCro LRHS SHor XFar
- - pink-flowered	LRHS
- - 'Rainbow Blue and White'	XFar
- - 'Rainbow Jaguar' **new**	XFar
- - 'Rainbow Lavender' **new**	XFar
- - 'Rainbow Pink and White' **new**	XFar
- - THE BRIDE	see *A. coronaria* (De Caen Group) 'Die Braut'
- - 'The Governor'	ERCP GKev WCot XFar
- Full Star Series	LCro XFar
- - 'Full Star Albino' (d)	XFar
- - 'Full Star Blue' (d)	XFar
- - 'Full Star Pink' (d)	XFar
- - 'Full Star Red and White' (d)	XFar
- - 'Full Star Red' (d)	XFar
- GALILEE PASTEL MIX	LCro XFar
- (Harmony Series) 'Harmony Blue'	LCro
- - 'Harmony Double White' (d)	EPfP
- - 'Harmony Orchid'	EPfP LCro LRHS
- - 'Harmony Pearl'	EPfP LCro LRHS
- - 'Harmony Scarlet'	EPfP LCro LRHS
- (Mistral Series) 'Mistral Bordeaux'	XFar
- - 'Mistral Rosa Chiaro'	XFar
- - 'Mistral Tigre'	XFar
- (Mistral Plus Series) 'Mistral Plus Azzurro'	XFar
- - 'Mistral Plus Bianco Centro Nero'	XFar
- - 'Mistral Plus Blu'	XFar
- - 'Mistral Plus Edge'	XFar
- - 'Mistral Plus Fucsia'	XFar
- - 'Mistral Plus Grape'	XFar
- - 'Mistral Plus Rarity'	XFar
- - 'Mistral Plus Rosa Shocking'	XFar
- - 'Mistral Plus Vinato'	XFar
- Saint Bridgid Group (d)	GKev LCro XFar
- - 'Lord Lieutenant' (d)	ERCP GKev LAma NBir WCot XFar
- - 'Mount Everest' (d)	ERCP GKev LAma NBir XFar
- - 'Saint Bridgid' (d)	EGren NNys
- - 'The Admiral' (d)	GKev LAma NBir
- 'Sylphide' (Mona Lisa Series)	EGrI ERCP ETay GKev LAma LCro LRHS MCtn NBir XFar
crinita	GKev
cylindrica	CElw EMor
DAINTY SWAN ('Macane005'^{PBR})	CWGN EBee EMor EPfP GEdr ISha LBar LRHS Midl MNrw MPro NCth NLar WFar WTor
'Danish White'	MNrw WCot
decapetala	MHer
DREAMING SWAN ('Macane004'^{PBR})	CMiW CWGN EBee ELan EMor EPfP GMaP ISha LBar LRHS MBel MBNS MHol MPri MPro NLar NSti SPoG WCAu WFar WHil WNPC WPnP
drummondii	GKev
ELFIN SWAN ('Macane017'^{PBR})	CWGN EMor EPfP ISha LRHS MHol MPri MPro NLar SPoG WCot WFar WTor
'Elite Pure White'	Midl
FALL IN LOVE	see *A.* × *hybrida* 'Sweetly'
fasciculata	GKev
filisecta	GGro MHol WCot
flaccida	CBro CMiW EPPr GEdr LEdu MNrw SHar WCot WFar
- 'Futabazuru' (d)	GEdr LEdu MNrw WFar
- 'Ginpai' (d)	GEdr LEdu WFar
FRILLY KNICKERS ('Fp007'^{PBR}) (d)	CWGN CWnw EBee EMor LBar LBom LBuc LCro LRHS LSou MHol MHtn MPri MPro NCth NWbg SHar SPad WCot WFar WHil WNPC WPnP
× *fulgens* 'Multipetala'	SBrt
GISELLE ('Macane015'^{PBR})	LRHS
globosa	see *A. multifida* Poir.
'Guernica'	EWes
hepatica L.	see *Hepatica nobilis*
hortensis	SBrt
subsp. *heldreichii*	
§ *hupehensis*	CExl CWal EGren GMaP WTre
- BWJ 8190	WCru
- BWJ 16191	WCru
- BWJ 16215	WCru
- NJM 11.068	WPGP
- (Alando Series) ALANDO DOUBLE ROSE	Midl
- - ALANDO ROSE	Midl
- - ALANDO WHITE **new**	MPri
- f. *alba*	CExl CSpe MCtn
- ARIEL ('Ifanfa') (Fantasy Series)	LBar LRHS MPro
- BELLE ('Ifanfb'^{PBR}) (Fantasy Series)	LBar LBom LRHS MPri MPro
§ - 'Bowles's Pink' ♀H7	CDor CExl EBee SMHy WCAu WFar
- 'Cinderella'^{PBR} (Fantasy Series)	LBar LRHS Midl MPro NCth NLar
- 'Crispa'	see *A.* × *hybrida* 'Lady Gilmour' Wolley-Dod

- ELSA ('Ifanels')   LBar MPri MPro
  (Fantasy Series)
- 'Hadspen Abundance' ♀H7   CBcs CDor CExl CMac ECha EGren EGrI ELan ELon EPfP GAbr GKin GMaP LBom LCro LShi LSRN MBNS NBir NLar SRms WCAu WSpi WTre
- var. *hupehensis*   WFar
§ - var. *japonica*   MCtn SRms
- - B&SWJ 4886   WCru
- - 'Bodnant Burgundy'   EBee EMor SMHy
§ - - 'Bressingham Glow'   CExl CMac EBee ELan EMor EPfP EPot GKin LRHS LShi LSto Midl NBir WCAu WFar WHil
§ - - 'Pamina' ♀H7   Widely available
- - 'Pink Saucer'   EGren WFar WHil
- - PRINCE HENRY   see *A. hupehensis* var. *japonica* 'Prinz Heinrich'
§ - - 'Prinz Heinrich'   Widely available
§ - - 'Rotkäppchen' ♀H7   CDor GKin GQue NLar NSti WCot
- - 'Splendens'   EBlo EGren ELan EPfP LRHS MPro NLar SPoG SReu SRms WFar WSpi
- - 'Tiki Sensation' PBR   CWGN EMor WCot
- JASMINE ('Ifanfj' PBR)   LBar LRHS MPri MPro WFar
  (Fantasy Series)
- (Little Breeze Series)   Midl
  LITTLE BREEZE CANDY **new**
- - LITTLE BREEZE KISS   see *A. hupehensis* (Little Breeze Series) LITTLE SUMMER BREEZE
- - LITTLE SUMMER BREEZE ('Anem081' PBR)   NLar
- 'Little Princess' PBR   LRHS MNrw NLar
- 'Pocahontas' PBR   EPfP GEdr LBar LRHS MNrw MPri NCth NLar WCot
  (Fantasy Series)
- 'Praecox'   LBar LRHS LSto MBNS MBros MPro NBir SRms WCAu WHoo
- RAPUNZEL ('Ifanfrap')   LBar LRHS
  (Fantasy Series)
- RED RIDING HOOD ('Apanfarrh' PBR)   LBar LBom LRHS MPri MPro NLar WCot WHil
  (Fantasy Series)
- 'September Charm'   see *A.* × *hybrida* 'September Charm'
- SNOW ANGEL ('Ifansa' PBR)   CWGN EBee EMor EPfP LBom LRHS Midl MPri MPro
  (Fantasy Series)
§ - SUMMER BREEZE ('Anem080' PBR)   EBee Midl WHil
  (Little Breeze Series)
- (Summer Breeze Series)   Midl WHil
  SUMMER BREEZE SNOW
- - SUMMER BREEZE VIBRANT PINK   LBar
- 'Superba'   WSpi
§ × *hybrida*   LRHS
- 'Alba' misapplied (UK)   see *A.* × *hybrida* 'Honorine Jobert'
- 'Albert Schweitzer'   see *A.* × *hybrida* 'Elegans'
- 'Andrea Atkinson'   CDor EBee EGren ELan EMor EPfP GElm LRHS LSRN MArl Midl MPro NGdn NLar NSti SPoG SRms WCot WFar WSpi WTre
- 'Bowles's Pink'   see *A. hupehensis* 'Bowles's Pink'
- 'Bressingham Glow'   see *A. hupehensis* var. *japonica* 'Bressingham Glow'
- 'Carmen'   LRHS MHol NLar
- 'Cloudy Abundance'   MNrw
- 'Coupe d'Argent'   EBee LRHS NLar SPeP
§ - 'Elegans' ♀H7   GMaP LCro MArl MMuc NBir NLar SEND
- 'Géante des Blanches'   SMHy
§ - 'Honorine Jobert' ♀H7   Widely available
§ - 'Königin Charlotte' ♀H7   Widely available
- 'Lady Gilmour' misapplied   see *A.* × *hybrida* 'Montrose'
- 'Lady Gilmour' Wolley-Dod   EBee NBir SRms WSpi
- 'Leather and Lace'   EBee
- 'Loreley'   CBWd EGren EPfP GPSL LCro LRHS LShi NCth NLar NWbg WCot WFar
§ - 'Margarete' Kayser & Seibert   ELan EMor WFar
- 'Max Vogel'   see *A.* × *hybrida* 'Elegans'
- 'Monterosa'   see *A.* × *hybrida* 'Montrose'
§ - 'Montrose'   EBee ELan EMor EPfP EWes GMaP MPro NBir SPeP SRms WCAu
- 'Pamina'   see *A. hupehensis* var. *japonica* 'Pamina'
§ - PINK CLOUD ('Pkan' PBR)   EGren LSou WFar
- PINK KISS   see *A.* × *hybrida* PINK CLOUD
- (Pretty Lady Series)   EBee LBar NLar
  'Pretty Lady Diana' PBR
- - 'Pretty Lady Emily' PBR   GEdr LBar LRHS NLar
- - 'Pretty Lady Julia' PBR   EBee GEdr LBar NLar
- - PRETTY LADY MARIA ('Aneplaria' PBR)   EBee LBar LRHS NLar
- - 'Pretty Lady Susan'   EBee LBar LCro
- PRINCE HENRY   see *A. hupehensis* var. *japonica* 'Prinz Heinrich'
- 'Profusion'   LBuc
- QUEEN CHARLOTTE   see *A.* × *hybrida* 'Königin Charlotte'
- 'Richard Ahrens'   EPfP GMaP LSto MGos NGdn NLar
§ - 'Robustissima'   CBWd CWnw EBee EGren EPfP GMaP LBar LCro LRHS LSRN MAsh MHol MMuc MNrw MSwo NBir NGdn NLar SEND SRms WCAu WFar
- 'Rosea'   WFar
- 'Rosenschale'   EWes NLar
- 'Rotkäppchen'   see *A. hupehensis* var. *japonica* 'Rotkäppchen'
§ - 'September Charm' ♀H7   Widely available
- 'Serenade'   EGren ELan EPfP LBom LRHS LSRN Midl MPro NBir NLar SPoG WBrk WCAu WFar WTor
- 'Sweetly' PBR   ELan LBar LRHS MPro NCth WCot
- TOURBILLON   see *A.* × *hybrida* 'Whirlwind'
- 'Whirlwind'   Widely available
- 'White Queen'   see *A.* × *hybrida* 'Géante des Blanches'
- WIRBELWIND   see *A.* × *hybrida* 'Whirlwind'
  japonica   see *A. hupehensis, A. hupehensis* var. *japonica, A.* × *hybrida*
  japonica ambig. 'Crustata'   CMac
§ × *lesseri*   ECha GEdr GKev SRms WKif
- SPRING BEAUTY PINK ('Anem078')   LRHS
- SPRING BEAUTY WHITE ('Anem079')   NLar
  leveillei   Widely available
- BWJ 7919   WCru
§ × *lipsiensis*   CBro CTtf EBee ENun GBin GEdr GMaP GQue LBar LEdu LShi MNrw NLar NQui WCru WFar WHoo WSpi
- 'Pallida' ♀H5   CMiW CSpe GEdr GKev GQue LEdu WCot WFar WIce
- 'Schwefelfeuer'   EPPr LEdu
- 'Sioux'   EPPr
- 'Vindobonensis'   EPot GEdr SMHy WCot
  lithophila   EDAr GKev
  LITTLE BREEZE PINK   see *A. hupehensis* SUMMER BREEZE (Little Breeze Series)
  magellanica hort. ex Wehrh.   see *A. multifida* Poir.
  'Margarette'   see *A.* × *hybrida* 'Margarete' Kayser & Seibert
  matsudae B&SWJ 1452   WCru
- NMWJ 14517   WCru

multifida misapplied   see *A.* × *lesseri*
   red-flowered
§ ***multifida*** Poir.   ECha EDAr EGrI EPfP EPPr GEdr
     GKev LRHS MCtn NBir NSti StAn
     WFar WHoo
- Annabella Series   GKev
- - 'Annabella White'   EDAr
- 'Major'   CSpe EDAr WIce
- 'Rubra'   EDAr EPfP GEdr LCro MPie NBir
     NLar SPoG WFar
- white-flowered   LRHS
- yellow-flowered   GArf GEdr
narcissiflora   EDAr GKev NBir
nemorosa   Widely available
- 'Alba'   CMiW EGrI WFar
- 'Alba Plena' (d)   ECha EPPr GKev MWlw NGdn
     NLar WFar
- 'Allenii' ♀H5   CBro CElw CMiW CSpe EBlo ELon
     EPfP EPot EPPr GEdr GKev GMaP
     LRHS MBel NRya WFar
- 'Amelia'   EPPr
- 'Apuseni'   LEdu
- 'Atley'   GEdr MAvo MWlw WCot WFar
I - 'Atrocaerulea'   ELon GArf NLar
- 'Atrorosea'   EPPr
- 'Axel'   EPPr
- 'Ballyrogan Blue'   MWlw
- 'Behemoth Blue'   LEdu
- 'Blue Beauty'   CMiW ELon GMaP
- 'Blue Bonnet'   LEdu MWlw
- 'Blue Eyes' (d)   CBro CMiW CSpe CTca EMor
     EPot EPPr EWld GBin GEdr GKev
     GMaP IPot LAma LBar LCro LEdu
     LShi NBir NCth NLar SMHy SPeP
     WCot WFar WHoo WPnP
- 'Blue Queen'   ELon
- blue-backed double (d)   CBro
- 'Blush'   LEdu
- 'Bowles's Blue'   ELon
- 'Bowles's Purple'   CMiW ELon GBin GEdr GMaP LSto
     NBid NHar NRya SMHy WCot WFar
- 'Bracteata'   CMiW GEdr GKev LAma
- 'Bracteata Pleniflora' (d)   CLAP CMiW CTtf EPot GKev GMaP
     LBar LEdu LShi MAvo MNrw NBir
     WCot WFar
- 'Bressingham Blush'   EBlo LRHS
- 'Buckland'   EPot
- 'Cedric's Pink'   CMiW ECha EPPr WFar
- 'Celestial'   EPPr
- dark blue-flowered   GKev
- 'Dark Leaf'   EPPr
- 'Dee Day'   EPPr MWlw
- 'Dell Garden'   EPPr
- 'Elizabeth'   EPPr
- 'Flore Pleno' (d)   LShi NBir WFar
- 'Flushing'   EPot GEdr WFar
- 'Frenzy'   WCot
- 'Frühlingsfee'   EPPr MWlw NLar
- 'Gerda Ramusen'   CBro ELan EPot LEdu WHoo
- 'Gerry'   GKev
I - 'Gigantea Rubra'   WCot
- 'Glyncoch Gold'   WCot
- 'Green Fingers'   CMiW EMor EPPr GEdr GMaP ISha
     LBar NHar NLar
- 'Hakumane Senjuizaki'   WCot
- 'Hannah Gubbay'   EPot
- 'Helsinki'   MWlw
- 'Hilda'   EBee ELan EMor GEdr GKev IPot
     LAma LBar LEdu NBir NCth NLar
     NRya SPeP WFar WPnP
- 'Ice and Fire'   GKev LEdu

- 'Kentish Pink'   GMaP
- 'Knightshayes Vestal' (d)   CExl CMiW
- 'La Rochanne'   MNrw MWlw
- 'Lady Doneraile'   CTca ELon EPot LEdu NBir WFar
- 'Latvian Pink'   EPot GEdr WFar
- 'Leeds'Variety'   CMiW ELon EPot GKev GMaP LEdu
- 'Lionel Bacon'   LEdu
- 'Lismore Blue'   CTca EPPr
- 'Lismore Pink'   GEdr WFar
- 'Lucia'   GEdr GKev LEdu WCot WFar
- 'Lychette'   CTca ECha EPPr GEdr GKev MAvo
     SHar
- 'Marie Rose'   EPot GKev WFar
- 'Mart's Blue'   WCot WFar
- 'Monstrosa'   EMor GBin IPot LBar
- 'Multiplicity'   EPPr
- 'Parlez Vous'   CExl CTca ELon EPPr GEdr LBar
     LEdu MNrw SMHy WFar
- 'Pentre Pink'   EPot
- 'Pink Carpet'   GEdr LEdu
- 'Pink Delight'   LEdu
I - 'Plena'   CSpe
- 'Ploeger's Plena' (d)   ECha
- 'Robinsoniana' ♀H5   Widely available
- 'Rosea'   GKev LEdu NLar
- 'Royal Blue'   CBro CMiW CTca EBee ECha ELon
     EPPr GAbr GEdr GKev GMaP LAma
     LBar LEdu NCth NLar WCot WFar
     WHoo WPnP
- 'Salt and Pepper'   LEdu
§ - 'Stammerberg' (d)   EPot EPPr
- 'Stammheim'   see *A. nemorosa* 'Stammerberg'
- 'Tinney's Blush'   CLAP
- 'Tomas'   ELon EPot GBin GEdr LEdu NRya
     WFar
- 'Tups'   LEdu
- 'Vestal' (d) ♀H5   Widely available
- 'Virescens' ♀H5   CMiW CTtf CWCL EGrI ELon EMor
     EPPr GEdr GKev GMaP LEdu LShi
     NHar SMHy
- 'Viridiflora'   CExl CLAP GBin GQue MNrw NBir
     NSti WCot WFar
- 'Westwell Pink'   EPPr MNrw MWlw WCot WFar
- 'Wilks' Giant'   EPPr
- 'Wilks' White'   ELon EPPr GEdr WFar
- 'Wisley Pink'   EPot LEdu WFar
I - 'Wisley White Form'   ENun LRHS NLar
- 'Wyatt's Pink'   CDor EPot GMaP LEdu WHoo
- 'Yerda Ramusem'   EPPr LEdu MNrw MWlw WFar
nemorosa   see *A.* × *lipsiensis*
   × ***ranunculoides***
obtusiloba   GBin GEdr MWlw WAbe
- CLD 1549   GEdr
- 'Alba'   GEdr WAbe
- 'Large Blue'   GEdr LEdu WAbe
- 'Pradesh'   GBin GEdr GKev NHar
palmata   LEdu
parviflora   GKev WHil
patens   see *Pulsatilla patens*
pavonina   CAby CMiW CSpe CTsd ECha LRHS
     MHol SMHy SPoG WFar
polyanthes   EBee GKev
prattii   CExl GEdr MNrw
pseudoaltaica   LEdu
- double pink-flowered (d)   GEdr
- pink-flowered   GEdr
- 'Yuki-no-sei' (d)   GEdr
pulsatilla   see *Pulsatilla vulgaris*
* ***raddeana*** f. ***rosea***   GEdr
ranunculoides ♀H6   CBro CMiW CTtf EBee EBlo EPfP
     EPot GAbr GArf GEdr GKev GMaP

	LAma LBar LEdu LRHS MBel MMrt NBid NHar NLar NQui NRya NSti WFar WPnP
- 'Bill Baker'	LEdu
- 'Crazy Vienna'	EPPr WCot
- 'Ferguson's Fancy'	EPPr
- 'Frank Waley'	MAvo WCot
- 'Fuchsis Traum' (d)	MAvo WCot
- 'Hiiumaa' (d)	WCot
- 'Kai' (d)	EPPr
* _laciniata_	WCot
- 'Muku' (d)	WCot
- 'Pleniflora' (d) ♀H6	ECha EPPr GKev NLar WCot WFar
- subsp. _ranunculoides_	GKev
- 'Semi-Plena'	CTtf GEdr LEdu
- subsp. _wockeana_	EPot LEdu
reflexa	GKev
REGAL SWAN ('Macane044')	EBee EMor LBar MHol Midl WHil
rivularis	CSde CSpe CTsd CTtf EBee EBlo EMor EPfP EWld GArf GKev LEdu MCtn MNrw NBir NLar SMad SRms WCAu WCru WKif WSpi
- BWJ 7611	WCru
- 'Glacier'	GMaP MHol
- semi-double aff. _rivularis_	WCot WSpi
ROYAL BLUSH ('Ifroblu') **new**	Midl
ROYAL CANDY ('Ifrocan') **new**	LBar Midl MPri WTor
RUFFLED SWAN ('Macane007'PBR)	CWGN EBee EMor EPfP GEdr ISha LBar LRHS MBNS MHtn Midl MPri MPro NCth NLar SPoG WHil WNPC
rupicola	GEdr GKev NBir WCot
'Satin Doll Blush'	EGren LSou MBros Midl
'Satin Doll Rosé'	Midl
× _seemannii_	see _A._ × _lipsiensis_
stolonifera double-flowered (d)	LShi WCot
sylvestris	Widely available
- 'Madonna'	MPro
- 'Snow White'	LRHS
tetrasepala	WCot
§ _tomentosa_	MArl MPie SDix SRms
- 'Robustissima'	see _A._ × _hybrida_ 'Robustissima'
- 'September Glanz'	EBee
trifolia L.	CMiW EPPr GEdr LEdu LShi NLar WCot
trullifolia	GArf GEdr NHar NQui
- var. _linearis_	GEdr WAbe
udensis	GEdr WCot
vernalis	see _Pulsatilla vernalis_
virginiana	EDAr LEdu
vitifolia misapplied	see _A. tomentosa_
vitifolia Buch.-Ham. ex DC.	WPGP
WILD SWAN ('Macane001'PBR)	Widely available

Anemonella (Ranunculaceae)

thalictroides	CElw CTtf ECha EMor ENun EPot GEdr GKev LAma LRHS LShi MBel MTha NLar NRya SHor SMHy SPlb WAbe WFar WPnP WSpi
- 'Amelia'	CElw GEdr MTha NBro WFar
- 'Babe'	WCot
- 'Betty Blake' (d)	ESwi GEdr MTha NBro WCot WFar
- 'Blushing Bride' (d)	GEdr NBro WCot
- 'Cameo'	ESwi GEdr MNrw MTha WCot WFar
- 'Charlotte'	GEdr MTha WFar
- dark-flowered **new**	MTha
- 'Diamante'	CElw WCot
- 'Double Diamante' (d)	WCot
- 'Flore Pleno' (d)	MTha
- 'Green Dragon'	see _A. thalictroides_ 'Jade Feather'
- 'Green Hurricane'	see _A. thalictroides_ 'Jade Feather'
- 'Hakikomi-fu' (v)	GEdr
§ - 'Jade Feather'	GEdr LShi MTha WCot
- 'Kikuzaki Pink' (d)	GEdr MTha WFar
- 'Kikuzaki White' (d)	GEdr MTha WFar
- f. _rosea_	ELan EMor MAvo MTha NLar WAbe WFar
- - 'Oscar Schoaf' (d)	GArf GEdr MTha WCot WFar
- - semi-double pink-flowered (d)	CElw
- 'Rosea Plena' (d)	GArf MTha
- semi-double white-flowered (d)	CElw
- 'Shiozaki' (d)	GEdr
- 'Snowflake' (d)	GEdr
- 'Tairin'	GEdr MTha WCot WFar

Anemonopsis (Ranunculaceae)

macrophylla	CDor CExl CMiW CSpe EBee EDAr EMor EWes EWld GArf GEdr GKev LEdu MCtn MNrw MPie MPro NLar SHor StAn WPGP WSpi
- 'Alba'	CSpe EWld GKev
- double-flowered (d)	EWld GEdr IPot
- 'White Swan'	CExl GEdr MNrw

Anemopsis (Saururaceae)

californica	CLil CPud CWat ELin EPfk LCro MWts WCot

Anethum (Apiaceae)

graveolens	CCBP CGHo EHet ENfk IDun LCro MCtn MEar MHer MHoo MNHC MPri SRms SVic WCot WKit
- 'Domino' ♀H2 **new**	MNHC
- 'Dukat'	LCro MCtn MHoo
- fern-leaved	MHoo
- 'Mariska'	MCtn SHor SPhx

angelica see _Angelica archangelica_

Angelica (Apiaceae)

acutiloba	WFar
anomala B&SWJ 10886	ESwi WCru
- BSWJ 10968	WCot
archangelica	Widely available
- subsp. _archangelica_	ELin
- subsp. _decurrens_	LEdu
arguta B&SWJ 14115	WCru
- B&SWJ 14162	WCru
atropurpurea	MHoo MNrw
breweri B&SWJ 14083	WCru
dahurica	CAgr GGro MHoo SPhx
decursiva B&SWJ 5746	WCru
- B&SWJ 14605	WCru
edulis	WPGP
- B&SWJ 10968	WCru
genuflexa B&SWJ 14109	WCru
gigas	Widely available
- B&SWJ 4170	WCru
hendersoni	EBee SPhx WPGP
hispanica	see _A. pachycarpa_
japonica B&SWJ 11480	WCru
'Loushan Filigree'	NDov SDix WPGP
montana	see _A. sylvestris_
§ _pachycarpa_	EBee EPPr GBin GMaP LBar MHer MHoo MPro NLar SBig WFar
pubescens	NDov
- B&SWJ 5593	LEdu WCru
purpurascens **new**	SDix
sachalinensis	GBin

Angelica

sinensis	GGro MHoo
'Summer Delight'	see *Ligusticum scoticum*
§ *sylvestris*	CGwi CHab MCtn MNHC NAts SArc SPhx
- B&SWJ 15332	WCru
- 'Ebony' ♀H5	CBct CSpe CTtf CWnw EPfP GAbr LBar LEdu LShi MBNS MCtn MHer MHol MHoo MNrw MPro SHor SPoG WCot WFar
- 'Purple Giant'	EBee
* - 'Purpurea'	CDor CElw CSpe EWes MAsh StAn
- 'Vicar's Mead'	EAri EBee ECha ELan EPfP LBar MCtn MPro MSwo NBir NLar SBig SPhx StAn WCAu WTor
taiwaniana	CDTJ EBee ESwi LWaG WCot WPGP
triquinata B&SWJ 15429	WCru
ursina	WCru

Angelonia (Plantaginaceae)

(Adessa Series) ADESSA PINK ('Adepin')	MPri
- ADESSA WHITE ('Adewit') (Adessa Series)	MPri
(Angelface Series) ANGELFACE BLUE BICOLOUR ('Anstern')	LRHS
- ANGELFACE PINK IMPROVED ('Anpinkim'PBR)	MHol
- ANGELFACE WEDGWOOD BLUE ('Anwedg')	LRHS MHol

Anigozanthos (Haemodoraceae)

sp.	CDoC
flavidus	SPlb
manglesii	SPlb
'Red Beauty'PBR	LRHS
rufus	SEle

anise see *Pimpinella anisum*

Anisodontea (Malvaceae)

§ *capensis* ♀H2	CAbb CTtf GBin SEle SPel SPlb SRkn SRms SVen
- (African Rose Series) AFRICAN ROSE MARSHMALLOW **new**	WLov
- - AFRICAN ROSE RUFARO **new**	WLov
- ELEGANS PRINCESS ('Oostani'PBR)	CAbb CWGN LBom **LRHS** WLov
'Crystal Rose'	**MGos**
'El Rayo' ♀H2	**Widely available**
huegelii	see *Alyogyne huegelii*
× *hypomadara* misapplied	see *A. capensis*
§ × *hypomadara* (Sprague) D.M.Bates	WCot
julii	CSpe SVen
LADY IN PINK ('Nuanilaninp')	LBar LRHS MBros MHol
'Orchard Pink'	SEND

Anisodus (Solanaceae)

§ *luridus*	EAri
- HWJK 2252	GGro
tanguticus	GGro

Anisotome (Apiaceae)

imbricata var. *imbricata*	WAbe
lyallii	GKev

Annona (Annonaceae)

cherimola (F)	WJur
muricata (F)	WJur

squamosa (F)	SPlb WJur

Anoiganthus see *Cyrtanthus*

Anomalesia see *Gladiolus*

Anomatheca see *Freesia*

cruenta	see *Freesia laxa*

Anredera (Basellaceae)

§ *cordifolia*	CRHN EShb

Antennaria (Asteraceae)

aprica	see *A. parvifolia*
dioica	GKev LRHS SPlb SRms WAbe
- 'Alba'	ECha GQue LRHS MPro
- 'Alex Duguid'	GMaP LRHS MPro
- 'Aprica'	see *A. parvifolia*
- 'Minima'	GMaP NBro WAbe
- 'Nyewoods Variety'	SRms
- var. *rosea*	see *A. rosea*
- 'Rotes Wunder'	ECha MMrt WAbe WHoo
- 'Rubra'	ECha EDAr GJos MWIw NBir SRms WCav WIce
§ *parvifolia*	LRHS SRms
- 'Alba'	EDAr MSwo
§ *rosea* ♀H5	EDAr GArf GKev GMaP MAsh SPlb SRms WIce

Antenoron see *Persicaria*

Anthemis ✿ (Asteraceae)

from Turkey	EWes
arvensis	CHab EHet GJem LCro MCtn MNHC SRms
- subsp. *sphacelata*	WCot
'Beauty of Grallagh'	see *Cota tinctoria* 'Beauty of Grallagh'
'Cally Cream'	ELon LSto SDix SPel
'Cally White'	GBin
cretica	GKev
- subsp. *carpatica*	NBro
- - 'Karpatenschnee'	EPfP LRHS SRms
- subsp. *leucanthemoides*	WAbe
- subsp. *tenuiloba*	EWes
cupaniana ♀H4	CBcs CExl CTtf ECha EGrl ELan GAbr GBin GElm GMaP MHer MMuc MWIw NCth NDov NLar NPer SDix SEND SMrm SPoG SRms WBrk WCAu WChS WCot WFar WKif WSpi
- 'Nana'	NBir NPer WCot
frutescens Voss	see *Argyranthemum frutescens*
'Grallagh Gold'	see *Cota tinctoria* 'Grallagh Gold'
marschalliana	see *Archanthemis marschalliana*
nobilis	see *Chamaemelum nobile*
'Orange Dream'	see *Cota tinctoria* 'Orange Dream'
sancti-johannis	see *Cota tinctoria* subsp. *sancti-johannis*
spruneri	EWes
'Tetworth'	see × *Cotanthemis* 'Tetworth'
tinctoria	see *Cota tinctoria*
'Tinpenny Sparkle'	EWes EWhm MHol MMrt WFar WHoo
triumfettii	see *Cota triumfettii*

Anthemis × Cota see × *Cotanthemis*

Anthericum (Asparagaceae)

algeriense	see *A. liliago*
* *bovei*	CBro

§ **liliago** CMac CSpe ESwi EWld GKev
GMaP GQue MHer NLar SBeP
SMad
- 'Major' ♀H5 CBro ECha GKev MHol
plumosum see *Trichopetalum plumosum*
ramosum CAby CCBP CSpe EBee ECha EPfP
EPPr GJos CSpe GKev LEdu MBrN NBid
NBir NLar SMHy SPel WCot

Antholyza see *Gladiolus*
coccinea see *Crocosmia paniculata*
paniculata see *Crocosmia paniculata*

Anthoxanthum (Poaceae)
odoratum CHab GQue

Anthriscus (Apiaceae)
cerefolium CGHo CHby EHet ENfk LCro MCtn
MEar MHer MHoo MNHC SEdi
SPhx SRms
nemorosa LEdu
sylvestris CGwi CHab GQue LCro LRHS
MCtn MNHC SHor SPhx
- 'Dial Park' CSpe LRHS MNrw
- 'Going for Gold' CTtf EWes MHol MNrw WCot WHil
- 'Golden Fleece' EBee ELan MArl MHoo NSti SPhx
WFar
- 'Ravenswing' Widely available

Anthurium (Araceae)
sp. EHap
andraeanum ♀H1a LBom
(Andraeanum Group) NTrD
  'Anthdebyk'**new**
- BLACK LOVE ('Rijn200643') LBom LRHS NTro
- CORAL CHAMPION LCro LRHS
  ('Anthdotfan'^PBR)
- LILLI ('Anthdosdoh'^PBR) LCro
- MILLION FLOWERS RED LCro
  ('Ryn2010043'^PBR)
- ORANGE CHAMPION LBom
  ('Antion')
- PRINCE OF ORANGE LBom
  ('Ryn2006109'^PBR)
- RED CHAMPION LCro LRHS
  ('Anthbnena'^PBR)
- ROYAL CHAMPION NHrt
  ('Antholodoj') **new**
- VANILLA ('Anthlepam'^PBR) LBom LCro
'Baby Red' LCro
CHERRY LOVE IMPROVED LCro
  ('Ryn2007042')
clarinervium LBom LRHS
crystallinum ♀H1a LBom LCro NTro
JOLI ('Anthucoen'^PBR) LRHS NHrt
JUNGLE BUSH ('Antingo') LRHS
magnificum NTro
PINK CHAMPION ('Antinkeles') LBom LCro LRHS
RED HEART ('Rijn200469') LInT
regale new NTro
scherzerianum ♀H1a NTro
vittariifolium new NTro
warocqueanum NTro
WHITE CHAMPION LCro LRHS
  ('Anthefaqyr'^PBR)

Anthyllis (Fabaceae)
hermanniae 'Compacta' see *A. hermanniae* 'Minor'
§ - 'Minor' ELan EPot
montana LRHS
  subsp. **atropurpurea**

- 'Rubra' ♀H5 CSpe EDAr EPot LShi SPhx StAn
- 'Rubra Compacta' WAbe
vulneraria CBWd CGwi CHab GEdr GJos
MCtn NAts NMir NRya SPhx StAn
WOrg
- var. **coccinea** CAby EDAr EWld GJos MBel SPhx
WIce
- dark red-flowered CSpe

Anticlea (Melanthiaceae)
§ **elegans** EAri EBee EDAr EPfP GKev LEdu
LRHS MHer WFar

Antigonon (Polygonaceae)
leptopus CSpe EShb MCtn
- 'Album' MCtn

Antirrhinum (Plantaginaceae)
ANTIRINCA BRONZE APRICOT LRHS
  (Antirinca Series)
asarina see *Asarina procumbens*
barrelieri SEND
braun-blanquetii WCot
- 'Lemon Sherbet' SVic
- 'Canarybird' LSto MCtn
- 'Defiance' MCtn
- 'Eva Grey' ELan
glutinosum see *A. hispanicum*
  subsp. *hispanicum*
§ **hispanicum** CSpe
  subsp. **hispanicum**
  majus 'Admiral White' LCro MCtn
- APPEAL BICOLOUR MIX EGren
- 'Appleblossom' LCro LSto MCtn
- 'Black Prince' CSpe ELan LSto MCtn WCot
- 'Chantilly Bronze' MCtn
  (Chantilly Series) **new**
- 'Giant Rust Resistant' MCtn
  (mixed)
- 'Liberty Classic Lavender' MCtn
  (Liberty Classic Series)
- 'Madame Butterfly' MCtn
  (mixed) (d)
- Monarch Series MCtn
- 'Night and Day' CSpe LCro MCtn
- 'Purple Twist' MCtn
- 'Rocket White' CSpe MCtn
  (Rocket Series)
- (Sonnet Series), formula LCro MBros MPri WFar
  mixed
- - 'Sonnet Crimson' WFar
- - 'Sonnet Orange Scarlet' LRHS
- - 'Sonnet Pink' WFar
- - 'Sonnet Rose' LRHS
- - 'Sonnet White' LRHS
- - 'Sonnet Yellow' LRHS WFar
- subsp. **tortuosum** WHil
molle CSpe EBee EPot GKev NPer SChF
- pink-flowered SChF WSpi
- white-flowered SEND
nanum 'Twinny Peach' MCtn
'Oh That's Cute' NCth
'Opus Appleblossom' MCtn
  (Opus III/IV Series) **new**
PRETTY IN PINK CCps CSBt LBar LCro MHol MPro
  ('Pmoore07'^PBR) WNPC
RICH RUBY ('Yaby') MCtn
sempervirens WAbe
'The Rose' LSto MCtn

añu see *Tropaeolum tuberosum*

Anubias (Araceae)
barteri var. *nana*   ELin

Aphananthe (Cannabaceae)
aspera **new**   WJur

Aphelandra (Acanthaceae)
squarrosa   LRHS NTro
- 'Dania' (v)   LRHS
- 'White Wash'^{PBR}   LRHS NTro

Apios (Fabaceae)
§ *americana*   EArl EGrl EWes LEdu NBir SBrt WCot WCru WKor
- 'Nutty'   CAgr
tuberosa   see *A. americana*

Apium (Apiaceae)
graveolens   CGHo CGwi CHab CoPl ENfk MHer MHoo MNHC SRms SVic WJek
- Secalinum Group   EHet ELan IDun
- - 'Par-cel'   MCtn MHer MNHC SRms
nodiflorum   see *Helosciadium nodiflorum*

Apodasmia (Restionaceae)
similis   LRHS SPlb

Aponogeton (Aponogetonaceae)
desertorum   CLil EWat
distachyos   CBen CLil CPud CWat ELin EPfk EWat LCro MWts NPer WMAq
madagascariensis   ELin

Aporocactus see *Disocactus*

apple see *Malus domestica*; also AGM Fruit Section

apricot see *Prunus armeniaca*

Aptenia (Aizoaceae)
cordifolia   CoPl CPic NPer SChr SPlb
- 'Variegata' (v)   CoPl CPic LRHS

Aquilegia (Ranunculaceae)
akitensis misapplied   see *A. flabellata* var. *pumila*
'Alaska' (State Series)   EBee LRHS
alpina   CDor CWal EBee ECha EPfP GJos GKev LRHS LWaG MAsh MCtn MNHC NBir NGdn SRms WFar WSpi
amaliae   see *A. ottonis* subsp. *amaliae*
atrata   EBee EMor GKev MCtn
atrovinosa from Kazakhstan   GGro
bertolonii ♀^{H5}   GEdr MCtn SRms WAbe
Biedermeier Group   EPfP LRHS NGdn NLar WFar
'Blue Star' (Star Series)   ELan EPfP GMaP MCtn
'Bluebird' (Songbird Series)   LBuc MCtn NBir NPer WFar
buergeriana   ECha EPPr GKev StAn
- 'Calimero'   EDAr NLar
- var. *oxysepala*   see *A. oxysepala*
canadensis   CSpe EBee GJos MCtn NBir NBro SRms StAn WFar WSpi
- 'Corbett'   WAbe WFar
- 'Little Lanterns'   EDAr EMor MCtn MPro NLar SMrm WIce
- 'Nana'   GKev
- 'Pink Lanterns'   MPro
'Cardinal' (Songbird Series)   LBuc
chaplinei   GKev NBir XFar

chrysantha   GJos MCtn SRms
- 'Denver Gold'   CDor CSpe SHor
- 'Yellow Queen'   CAby CExl EMor EPPr GBin GMaP LCro MCtn MHer MPnt NClf NGdn SHor WCFE WFar
clematiflora   see *A. vulgaris* var. *stellata*
coerulea   MCtn SRms StAn
'Crimson Star'   ELan EMor EPfP GBin MPro SPoG
desertorum   EWld GKev
§ 'Dove' (Songbird Series)   LBuc SHar SMrm
I 'Dragonfly'   ELan SPoG
Earlybird Series   EGren
- Earlybird Blue White ('Pas1258485')   EGren LBar MPro
- Earlybird Purple Blue ('Pas1258487')   LBar
- Earlybird Purple White ('Pas1258486')   LBar MHol
- Earlybird Red White ('Pas1258484')   LBar
- Earlybird Red Yellow ('Pas1258483')   LBar MPro
- Earlybird White ('Pas1258490')   LBar
ecalcarata   see *Semiaquilegia ecalcarata*
flabellata f. *alba*   EGren
- 'Blackcurrant Ice'   MPro
- Cameo Series   LRHS MHer
- - 'Cameo Blue and White'   EDAr SRms WTor
- - 'Cameo Pink and White'   EDAr
- - 'Cameo Red and White'   EDAr
- - 'Cameo Rose and White'   WTor
- - 'Cameo White'   EDAr
- 'Ministar'   EDAr LRHS
- 'Nana Alba'   see *A. flabellata* var. *pumila* f. *alba*
§ - var. *pumila* ♀^{H5}   NGdn SRms
§ - - f. *alba*   LRHS
- - 'Atlantis'   EPot GKev LRHS MPri
I - - f. *kurilensis* 'Rosea'   WAbe
- 'Vermont' (State Series)   EBee
'Florida' (State Series)   MPro WFar
formosa   GKev GQue MCtn
§ *fragrans*   GKev
'Fruit and Nut Chocolate'   WCot
glandulosa   EDAr
glauca   see *A. fragrans*
§ 'Goldfinch' (Songbird Series)   LBuc NBir
'Heavenly Blue'   CDor MPro
'Hensol Harebell'   ELan SHar SRms WSpi
japonica   see *A. flabellata* var. *pumila*
jonesii   GEdr SPlb
'Koralle'   CDor
'Kristall'   LRHS MCtn MHtn
* *kuhistanica*   GGro GKev
'Leprechaun Gold' (v)   EPfP NGdn
'Lime Sorbet' (d)   ELan SRms
'Little Plum'   EBee
longissima   EPPr GKev GQue SHar WHoo
'Louisiana' (State Series)   WFar
'Magpie'   see *A. vulgaris* 'William Guiness'
McKana Group   EHeP ELan EPfP GJos LRHS MCtn MGos MPro NGdn NLar SMrm SPlb SPoG SRms SVic WCAu WCav WFar
'Montana' (State Series)   CDor
Mrs Scott-Elliot hybrids   EGren EPfP
Music Series   SRms
olympica   GKev
'Oranges and Lemons'   WFar
(Origami Series) 'Origami Blue and White'   LRHS
- 'Origami Red and White'   LRHS

§ *ottonis* subsp. *amaliae* WAbe
§ *oxysepala* CExl GGro LCro
- var. *kansuensis* GKev
Perfumed Garden Group GAbr
pyrenaica dwarf WAbe
'Red Hobbit' CSpe ELan EPfP EPot MSwo NGdn NLar WFar
'Red Star' (Star Series) SPoG
'Rhubarb and Custard' MPri
rockii EPPr GKev
- W&O 9057 GGro
'Rose Queen' MCtn
§ 'Schneekönigin' NLar
scopulorum WFar
sibirica EBee SHor
'Silver Queen' CBcs
skinneri WKif
- 'Tequila Sunrise' CSpe ELan EPfP MHer MPnt MPro NClf
Snow Queen see *A.* 'Schneekönigin'
Spring Magic Series LBom MPri WCav
- Spring Magic Blue and White CWCL LBuc LRHS MPri
- Spring Magic Navy and White LRHS MPri
- Spring Magic Rose and Ivory LRHS MPri
- Spring Magic Rose and White LBuc MPri
- Spring Magic White LBuc LRHS MPri
- Spring Magic Yellow LBuc LRHS
stellata see *A. vulgaris* var. *stellata*
Swan Series EGren MPro
- 'Swan Lavender' WFar
- 'Swan Pink and Yellow' MPro
- 'Swan Red and White' MPro WFar
- 'Swan Violet and White' WFar
'Virginia' (State Series) EGren WFar
viridiflora EDAr GGro NClf WCot
- 'Chocolate Soldier' CDor CSpe LRHS MCtn MPnt MPro WSpi
Volcano! (mixed) GQue
vulgaris CBWd CHab CoPl EGren EPfP GJem GQue LCro MCtn MHer MNHC NBro NGdn SEND SPlb StAn WCAu WOrg WShi
- 'Adelaide Addison' ECha
- var. *alba* ECha EPfP MMuc WCAu
- 'Aureovariegata' see *A. vulgaris* Vervaeneana Group
- 'Blackbird' (Songbird Series) (d) CWCL
- *clematiflora* see *A. vulgaris* var. *stellata*
- Clementine Series MPro
- - 'Clementine Blue' (d) ECha LRHS SPoG WCot
- - 'Clementine Dark Purple' (d) SPoG
- - 'Clementine Rose' (d) EPfP SPoG
- - 'Clementine Salmon Rose' (d) EPfP SPoG
- - 'Clementine White' (d) SPoG WSpi
- 'Dove' see *A.* 'Dove' (Songbird Series)
- 'Eyecatcher' WCot
- var. *flore-pleno* black-flowered (d) MMuc WCot
- - purple-flowered (d) WSpi
- 'Gold Finch' see *A.* 'Goldfinch' (Songbird Series)
- 'Heidi' WSpi
- 'Mellow Yellow' EPfP
- Munstead White see *A. vulgaris* 'Nivea'
§ - 'Nivea' CDor CSpe EBee ELan EMor EPPr LCro MPro SHor SPoG WCot WSpi WTor
- 'Pink Petticoat' (d) XFar
- 'Pom Pom Crimson' (Pom Pom Series) WCot

§ - var. *stellata* CDor MPnt NBir NBro
- - (Barlow Series) CBcs CDor CSpe ECha EGren ELan EMor EPfP EUrb GBin GMaP LBom LCro LRHS LShi LSRN LSto LWaG MCtn Midl MNrw MPnt MPri NGdn NLar SBeP SRms WCot WKif WSpi
- - - 'Blue Barlow' (d) CDor CSpe EBee EMor EPfP ERCP GBin GMaP LCro LSRN MHtn SAth SBeP WCot WSpi WTor XFar
- - - 'Bordeaux Barlow' (d) EPfP MCtn MPri
- - - 'Christa Barlow' (d) EBee EPfP MCtn NLar SHar
- - - 'Nora Barlow' (d) Widely available
- - - 'Rose Barlow' (d) EPfP LSRN MPro WSpi
- - - 'White Barlow' (d) CDor CWal ECha EMor EPfP GMaP LCro LRHS MCtn MPro NLar SAth WCAu XFar
- - blue-flowered MMuc NBir
- - 'Greenapples' (d) CBcs CDor EMor EWhm MMuc NLar SHor
- - 'Ruby Port' (d) CBcs CDor CWal ECha EGren ELan EMor EPfP EPPr ERCP GBin GMaP LCro LSRN LSto MCtn MMuc MNrw MSwo NGdn NLar SBeP SMHy SPhx WCAu XFar
- - white-flowered MPnt NBir
- variegated foliage see *A. vulgaris* Vervaeneana Group
§ - Vervaeneana Group (v) CDor LRHS NBir NPer SPlb SRms WFar WHoo
- - 'Woodside White' (v) NBir
§ - 'William Guiness' CBcs CDor CMHG CSpe EBee ELan EMor EPfP EPPr ERCP GBin LBom LCro LRHS MCtn MGos MMuc MPnt MPri MPro NBir NLar SPoG WCAu WSpi
'White Star' (Star Series) CDor EBee ELan EPfP GBin GMaP SPoG WTor
'White Swan' WFar
Winky Series EGren WFar
- 'Winky Blue-White' NLar SPoG
- 'Winky Double Blue' LRHS
- 'Winky Double Red-White' (d) EPfP LRHS MPro
- 'Winky Early Sky Blue' LRHS
- 'Winky Rose-Rose' LRHS
- 'Winky White-White' LRHS
yabeana EBee
- W&O 7020 GGro
'Yellow Star' (Star Series) CBcs CDor EPfP MHol NLar

Arabis (Brassicaceae)

allionii MCtn
alpina GQue SPlb
- subsp. *caucasica* GKev
- - 'Arctic Joy' (v) WCot WHoo
- - 'Douler Angevine' (v) SPoG SRms
- - 'Flore Pleno' (d) ♀H6 ELan EPfP GAbr GMaP SRms WBrk WFar
- - Little Treasure Deep Rose ('Ararosa') LRHS
- - Little Treasure White ('Aralba') EPfP LCro LRHS SPoG
- - 'Lotti Deep Rose' EGren
- - 'Lotti White' EGren WFar
- - 'Pink Pearl' WFar
- - 'Pinkie' WFar
- - 'Pixie Cream' EPfP NGdn SRms
- - 'Rosea' EPfP GJos NBir SRms
§ - - 'Schneehaube' ♀H6 EPfP GMaP GQue LRHS MCtn NBir NGdn SPoG SRms
- - Snowcap see *A. alpina* subsp. *caucasica* 'Schneehaube'

Arabis

- - 'Snowdrop'	WFar
- - 'Variegata' (v)	ELan LRHS SPoG SRms WFar
androsacea	GKev SRms
× **arendsii** 'Compinkie'	SPlb SRms
- 'Pinkie'	LRHS
blepharophylla	EPfP LRHS MPri
- (Barranca Series) BARRANCA DEEP ROSE ('Pas1213796')	EGren
- - BARRANCA PINK ('Pas1374881')	EGren
§ - 'Frühlingszauber' ♀H5	ELan EPfP GJos GKev LRHS MAsh NGdn SPoG SRms WFar
- 'Rose Delight'	EPfP GJos LRHS SPoG
- 'Rote Sensation'	ELan EPfP NGdn
- SPRING CHARM	see *A. blepharophylla* 'Frühlingszauber'
ferdinandi-coburgi	SRms WCav
- 'Aureovariegata' (v)	ELan
- 'Old Gold' (v)	CoPl ECha EPfP GJos GQue LRHS LShi MAsh MHer NBir NRya SLee SPoG SRms SRot WFar
- 'Variegata'	see *A. procurrens* 'Variegata'
koehleri	WHil
procurrens	MWlw WCot
§ - 'Variegata' (v) ♀H6	ECha ELan EUrb EWes GKev GPSL MAsh MBrN MWlw SLee SPlb SRms WCot WFar

Arachis (Fabaceae)

hypogaea	MCtn
- JUSTPINK (Not Just Peanuts Series)	SPre

Arachniodes (Dryopteridaceae)

aristata	CTsd
davalliaeformis	MAsh SPlb WCot WPGP
§ **simplicior**	CCht CLAP CSpe EBee EHeP EMor EPfP ESwi LBom LBuc LCro LEdu LRHS MAsh NAlc SBig SHor SPlb WCot WHil WPGP
standishii	CLAP LEdu MAsh MWlw SPlb WCot WPGP
tripinnata	WCot

Araiostegia (Davalliaceae)

faberiana	CExl
hymenophylloides	WCot
parvipinnata	see *A. perdurans*
§ **perdurans**	CExl GEdr LEdu SPlb WCot WPGP
- B&SWJ 1608	WCru
pulchra HWJ 1007	ESwi WCru

Aralia ✿ (Araliaceae)

apioides EDHCH 9720	ESwi WCru
armata B&SWJ 6916	WCru
bipinnata Blanco	WPGP
- CWJ 12407	WCru
cachemirica	CDTJ ESwi NBid SPlb
- HWJK 2120b	WCru
californica	ESwi NLar SBrt WCru
castanopsidicola CWJ 12411	WCru
chapaensis B&SWJ 11812	WCru
- HWJ 1013	WCru
chinensis misapplied	see *A. elata*
chinensis L. BWJ 8102	WCru
continentalis	NLar
- pink-flowered B&SWJ 8437	ESwi WCru
§ **cordata** Thunb.	CAgr LEdu LRHS MBlu MCtn NClf WTre
- B&SWJ 5596	WCru

- B&SWJ 8524 from Ulleungdo, South Korea	WCru
- var. **sachalinensis** B&SWJ 4773	WCru
- 'Sun King'	CBcs EBee EPfP EUrb LBar LCro MBlu MHol NBid NEoE SPoG WFar
dasyphylla	LEdu
decaisneana	LEdu
- NMWJ 14531	WCru
- NMWJ 14542	WCru
- RWJ 9910	WCru
§ **elata**	CBcs CDoC CMac CTsd EBar EBee EHeP ELan EUrb IPap LMaj MBlu MHtn SArc SGol SPoG WFar WJur WSpi
- B&SWJ 5480	WCru
- 'Albomarginata'	see *A. elata* 'Variegata'
- 'Aureo-marginata' (v)	WSpi
- 'Aureovariegata' (v) ♀H5	CBcs IArd NLar
- 'Golden Umbrella' (v)	NLar
- 'Silver Umbrella' (v)	NLar
§ - 'Variegata' (v) ♀H5	CBcs EUrb IArd NLar
foliolosa	MBlu
- B&SWJ 8360	WCru
kansuensis B&SWJ 9515	ESwi
- BWJ 7650	WCru
leschenaultii B&SWJ 9515	WCru
- B&SWJ 11789	WCru
nudicaulis Blume	see *A. cordata* Thunb.
papyrifera	see *Tetrapanax papyrifer*
racemosa	LEdu WJek
- B&SWJ 9570	WCru
searelliana BWJ 8131	WCru
sieboldii de Vriese	see *Fatsia japonica*
spinosa misapplied	see *A. elata*
spinosa L.	MBlu SPlb
subcordata HWJK 2385	WCru
- WJC 13833	WCru
verticillata B&SWJ 11797	WCru
vietnamensis B&SWJ 12349E	WCru

Araucaria (Araucariaceae)

angustifolia	CAco CDTJ
§ **araucana**	Widely available
bernieri	CAco
bidwillii	CAco WJur
biramulata	CAco
columnaris	CAco
cunninghamii	CAco LRHS WJur
excelsa misapplied	see *A. heterophylla*
§ **heterophylla** ♀H2	CAco CDoC ERom LBom LCro LInT LRHS LWaG NHrt SArc SEND WJur
imbricata	see *A. araucana*
laubenfelsii	CAco
luxurians	CAco
montana	CAco
muelleri	CAco
nemorosa	CAco
rulei	CAco SBig

Araujia (Apocynaceae)

sericifera	CBcs CHll CRHN CSde CSpe LRHS SChF SNig SVen WJur

Arbutus ✿ (Ericaceae)

andrachne	CBcs WJur
× **andrachnoides** ♀H4	CBrP CJun EBee ELan EPfP EUrb SArc SPoG SSta WPGP WSpi
× **androsterilis**	EBee WPGP

glandulosa	SArc
menziesii	MBlu SPlb
× *reyonii* 'Marina'	CJun EBee ELan EPfP MBlu MPri SPoG WPGP
× *thuretiana*	WPGP
unedo	Widely available
- 'Atlantic' ♀H5	CCoa CDoC CJun EBee EPfP LRHS LSRN MBlu MGos NLar SBig WLov
- 'Compacta'	CBcs CMac CSBt CSpe EBee EGren EGrI ELan EPfP EUrb LCro LRHS MAsh MHtn SGol WFar WLov
- 'Elfin King'	SPoG
- MERCURIUS ('Bocarm') **new**	NLar
- 'Quercifolia'	CJun NLar
- 'Red Grange'	CMHG EBee SChF SMad WPGP
- f. *rubra* ♀H5	CAgr CBcs CDoC CJun EGrI ELan EPfP LRHS LSRN MAsh MBlu SBig SGol SPoG SSta WMat
- - ROSELILY ('Minlily'PBR)	CDoC CWnw ELan EPfP LRHS LSRN MPri
xalapensis	SPlb

Archanthemis (Asteraceae)
§ *marschalliana*	EPot SMrm SPlb SRms WCot

Archontophoenix (Arecaceae)
alexandrae	NPlm SPlb
cunninghamiana	NPlm

Arctanthemum (Asteraceae)
§ *arcticum*	NLar
- 'Polarstern'	EBee MNrw WFar

Arctium (Asteraceae)
from Asia	GGro
lappa	MCtn SEdi SRms WHer
minus	NMir

Arctostaphylos (Ericaceae)
pringlei	SPlb
uva-ursi	GArf LCro SPlb
- 'Snowcap'	MAsh
- 'Vancouver Jade'	GArf GKin MAsh SPoG

Arctotis (Asteraceae)
fastuosa var. *alba* 'Zulu Prince'	MCtn
§ HANNAH ('Archnah'PBR) ♀H2 (The Ravers Series)	CCht ELan
'Holly'	MHol
'Hope'	ELan
× *hybrida* hort. 'Flame' ♀H2	ELan SRkn
- 'Red Devil'	CTsd SPoG
- 'Wine'	ELan SPoG SRkn
PUMPKIN PIE (The Ravers Series)	see *A.* HANNAH (The Ravers Series)

Ardisia (Primulaceae)
crenata	MPri
- 'Queen Star'PBR	LCro
japonica	WCot
- B&SWJ 1032	WCru
- var. *angusta*	WCot
- 'Houkan' (v)	CDTJ CExl EBee
- 'Ito-fukurin' (v)	CDTJ EBee SHor WFar
- var. *minor*	GEdr
- - B&SWJ 1841	WCru
- - B&SWJ 3809	WCru
- variegated (v)	CBct

Argyranthemum 109

Arecastrum see *Syagrus*

Arenaria (Caryophyllaceae)
§ *alfacarensis*	EPot NLar SPlb
balearica	EWes MAsh SPlb SRms
festucoides	GKev WAbe
montana ♀H5	ECha EPfP GKev LRHS MGos NBir SDix SPlb SRms SRot WAbe WCav WFar WIce WKif
- 'Avalanche'	EGren LRHS MCtn MHol
- 'Blizzard'	LRHS SPoG
- 'Lemon Ice'	EGren GKev LCro LRHS
- 'Snow White'	EGren GKev LCro MHol
- SUMMER WHITE COMPACT ('Amoz0002'PBR)	LRHS
pulvinata	see *A. alfacarensis*
purpurascens	EGren EPot EWes LCro LRHS MWlw SRms
serpens Kunth	SPlb
tetraquetra	EDAr
- subsp. *amabilis*	EPot

Arenga (Arecaceae)
engleri	NPlm

Argemone (Papaveraceae)
grandiflora	CSpe
mexicana	ELan
platyceras	MCtn

Argyranthemum (Asteraceae)
'Cornish Gold' ♀H2	CBcs
double pink-flowered (d)	SVen
'Everest' (Angelic Series)	LRHS SPoG
foeniculaceum	NPer
'Royal Haze' ♀H2	
§ *frutescens*	EGren LCro LRHS MBros WKif
- 'Nelia'	LRHS
- pink-flowered	SEND
gracile 'Chelsea Girl' ♀H2	MBNS WKif
Grandaisy Series	see × *Argyrimelia* Grandaisy Series
'Jamaica Primrose' ♀H2	CElw CSpe EAri EShb SDix
aff. 'Jamaica Primrose'	ELan
(LaRita Series) LARITA BANANA SPLIT ('Kleaf10067') ♀H2	LRHS SPoG
- LARITA RED ('Kleaf15097')	LRHS
'Lemon Cupcake' **new**	LSou MBNS MSwo
'Levada Cream' ♀H2	CSpe
'Lolly'	ELan MBNS MSwo
(Madeira Series) MADEIRA CRESTED HOT PINK ('Bonmad 11277')	LSou MPri
- MADEIRA CRESTED IVORY ('Bonmadcivy') (d)	SPoG
- MADEIRA CRESTED MERLOT ('Bonmadmerlo') (d)	LRHS
- MADEIRA CRESTED PINK ('Bonmadcink')	LRHS SPoG
- MADEIRA CRESTED YELLOW ('Bonmadcrel'PBR)	LRHS MPri SPoG
- MADEIRA DEEP PINK ('Bonmadepi')	LRHS MPri
- MADEIRA PINK IMPROVED ('Bonmadpinkim')	LRHS
- MADEIRA RED ('Bonmadre'PBR)	LRHS MPri SPoG
- MADEIRA WHITE ('Ohmadleva')	LRHS MPri
- MADEIRA WHITE IMPROVED ('Bonmadwitim'PBR)	LRHS SPoG

MARGARITA **new**	MSwo
METEOR RED ('Supa742')	CWGN ELan
(Daisy Crazy Series)	
(Molimba Series) MOLIMBA	LRHS
M YELLOW ('Argyminyel')	
- MOLIMBA MINI DOUBLE WHITE	LRHS
('Argymidowi') (d)	
- MOLIMBA PINK ('Argymip')	LRHS
- MOLIMBA XL PASTEL YELLOW	LRHS SPoG
('Argyrayesi')	
PACIFIC GOLD	CWGN
('Pacargone'^{PBR}) (d)	
POLLY ('Innpolly')	CBcs MSwo
'Raspberry Ruffles' (d)	CBcs ELan MSwo
'Vanilla Latte'	LSou MSwo
white-flowered, single	SEND

Argyranthemum × *Glebionis*
see × *Glebianthemum*

Argyranthemum × *Ismelia* see × *Argyrimelia*

× *Argyrimelia* (Asteraceae)

(Aramis Series)	LRHS
'Aramis Apricot'	
- 'Aramis Bicolor Rose'	LRHS
(Aramis Series)	
- 'Aramis Deep Rose'	LRHS
(Aramis Series)	
(Grandaisy Series)	LCro MBros
GRANDAISY PINK HALO	
('Bonmax 9163'^{PBR}) ♀H3	
- GRANDAISY RED	MBros
('Bonmax 1472'^{PBR})	
- GRANDAISY YELLOW	see × *Glebianthemum* GRANDAISY
	YELLOW (Grandaisy Series)

Argyrocytisus (Fabaceae)

§ battandieri	CBcs CDoC CWnw EAri EGren
	EHeP ELan ELon EPfP LCro LRHS
	LSRN MAsh MBlu MGos MPri NLar
	SAth SEND SPlb SPoG SRkn SRms
	SVen WCot WHtc
- 'Yellow Tail' ♀H5	LRHS MGos NLar NPip SPoG SSta
	WMat

Ariocarpus (Cactaceae)

elongatus	see *A. retusus*
§ retusus	SBig

Arisaema ✿ (Araceae)

amurense	EPfP MCtn
candidissimum ♀H4	CDor EAri ECha ENun EPPr EWld
	GEdr GKev LAma LCro LRHS NLar
	WAbe WCot
- pink-flowered	NGKo
- white-flowered	GEdr
ciliatum ♀H4	ECha GEdr ISha LAma NLar
- var. *liubaense*	EAri EWld WCot
- - CT 369	GEdr
concinnum	EWld GKev LAma NGKo SBig
consanguineum	CMiW EBee GEdr GKev LAma
	MAvo MCtn SBig SPeP WCot WFar
- subsp. *kelung-insulare*	ESwi WCru
B&SWJ 256	
- 'Siren's Song' (v)	WCot WJun
- 'The Perfect Wave'	WCot
- variegated (v)	WCot
costatum	EPfP GKev LAma WFar WPGP
dracontium	EBee GKev LAma
exappendiculatum	SBig

fargesii	CExl GKev WCot
flavum	CMiW EAri EBee EPPr ESwi GArf
	GKev ISha LAma MCtn NGKo SPlb
	WHil
galeatum	LAma
§ griffithii	EBee GKev ISha LAma NLar
- var. *pradhanii*	CAby GKev LAma
helleborifolium	see *A. tortuosum*
intermedium	EBee GKev LAma
jacquemontii	MCtn
japonicum Komarov	see *A. serratum*
kishidae	GEdr
kiushianum	GKev
- 'Kikkou-fu'	WCot
murrayi **new**	CExl
§ nepenthoides	CAby EBee EGrI GKev LAma SBig
ochraceum	see *A. nepenthoides*
propinquum	EBee GKev LAma
ringens ambig.	CDTJ EBee EPfP GEdr GKev
aff. ringens	LAma
sazensoo	GEdr
§ serratum	EBee GKev LAma
- var. *mayebarae*	GEdr LAma
sikokianum	CMiW EBee GKev ISha LAma NLar
speciosum	EGren EGrI GEdr GKev ISha LAma
	LCro SPlb
* - var. *magnificum*	CAby EBee GKev LAma NLar
- var. *mirabile*	EBee GKev LAma
taiwanense B&SWJ 269	WCru
- NMWJ 14541	WCru
- f. *cinereum*	WMal
- - NMWJ 14530	WCru
- silver-leaved	WCot WFar
thunbergii	EPPr GEdr
- subsp. *urashima*	LAma
- - red-flowered	LAma
- - white-flowered	LAma
§ tortuosum	CBro EBee ECha EWld GKev ISha
	LAma LEdu MAvo NLar WFar
- 'Black Rod'	CExl
tosaense	LAma
triphyllum	GKev LAma LRHS SPlb
§ utile	GKev LAma
verrucosum	see *A. griffithii*
- var. *utile*	see *A. utile*

Arisarum (Araceae)

proboscideum	CBcs CDoC CDor CExl CMac CTsd
	CTtf EBee ECha EDAr ELon EPfP
	EPot GEdr GKev GQue LEdu MHer
	NAts NBir NBro NQui NRya NSti
	SPlb SRms WCot WShi
vulgare	ESwi GKev

Aristaloe (Asphodelaceae)

§ aristata ♀H2	CBcs CBct CBen CBlu CCht CPic
	CSde ELan EShb ESuc LWaG NCft
	SArc SChr SEND SIvy SPlb WCor
	WFar
- 'Cathedral Peak'	SChr
- 'Green Pearl'^{PBR}	CoPl EPfP LCro NHrt SEND SPad
- ZAMBEZI ('Amial1809')	MPri

Aristea (Iridaceae)

§ capitata	CDoC EAri WJun
ecklonii	CBcs CExl CPbh CTsd EAri EWld
	MHol WJun
- GWJ 9469	CDoC MHol WCru
ensifolia	MMuc SEND
platycaulis	MCtn
thyrsiflora	see *A. capitata*

Aristolochia (Aristolochiaceae)
baetica B&SWJ 14001	WCru
- B&SWJ 15071	ESwi WCru
californica	LEdu SBrt WPGP
chilensis	SPlb
clematitis	EPPr LEdu
cucurbitifolia B&SWJ 7043	WCru
cymbifera	MCtn
durior	see *A. macrophylla*
elegans	see *A. littoralis*
fimbriata	EPPr
- B&SWJ 13612	WCru
grandiflora	CHll
griffithii B&SWJ 2118	WCru
- DJH 16082	WCru
kaempferi	CHll
- B&SWJ 14674	ESwi WCru
- NMWJ 14565	WCru
§ **littoralis**	EAri
§ **macrophylla**	CBcs EAri LCro MCtn WSpi
manshuriensis B&SWJ 12557	WCru
- B&SWJ 16071	WCru
rotunda	LEdu
sempervirens	LEdu WCru
- B&SWJ 13600	ESwi WCru
- from Carqueiranne, Toulon	SBrt
sipho	see *A. macrophylla*

Aristotelia (Elaeocarpaceae)
§ **chilensis**	CBcs LEdu WJur WKor WPav
- 'Variegata' (v)	CMCN SEND
macqui	see *A. chilensis*
serrata	CTsd ESwi SVen

Armeria (Plumbaginaceae)
'Abbey Deep Rose' (Abbey Series)	EPfP LRHS MPri
alliacea f. *leucantha*	SRms
§ **alpina**	GKev
'Brutus'	WMal
§ **caespitosa** ♀H5	EDAr EGrI ELan EPfP EPot GArf GJos GKev MAsh MHer NAts SLee SPlb SRms WAbe WIce
- 'Alba'	ELan GJos GKev GMaP MHer SLee SRms SRot WAbe WHoo
- 'Babi Lom'	NLar
- 'Bevan's Variety' ♀H5	CAby ECha EGrI ELan ELon EPfP EPot GEdr LRHS MHer NLar NRya SHar SPoG SRms SRot WCav WHoo
- dark-flowered	WAbe
- spiny, dwarf	EPot
§ - 'Sugar Baby'	LBar LRHS NLar SRms
'Darcies Pink' **new**	EDAr
§ **girardii**	EPot
(Joystick Series) 'Joystick Lilac Shades'	ELan LRHS SPoG
- 'Joystick Red'	ELan LRHS SPoG
- 'Joystick White'	ELan LRHS SPoG
juniperifolia misapplied	see *A. caespitosa*
- 'New Zealand Form'	see *A. caespitosa* 'Sugar Baby'
§ **maritima**	CBWd CHab EHet ELan EPfP GJos LWaG MBel SRot StAn WBrk WFar WOrg
§ - 'A Little in the Red'	WFar
- 'Abbey White'	LRHS MPri
- 'Alba'	CBcs ECha ELan EPfP GJos GMaP LSto MAsh MCtn MMuc NRya SEND SLee SPlb SPoG SRms StAn WIce
- (Armada Series) 'Armada Rose'	EPfP LCro LRHS MPri SRms
- - 'Armada White'	EPfP LRHS MBel WHil
- 'Bloodstone'	ELan
- 'Candy Floss' **new**	EDAr
- 'Corsica'	NBir NRya WIce
- DÜSSELDORF PRIDE	see *A. maritima* 'Düsseldorfer Stolz'
§ - 'Düsseldorfer Stolz'	CElw CSde ECha ELan EPfP EPot GKev GMaP LCro LRHS MBros MPro NLar SPoG WCav WIce
§ - 'In the Red'	CAby CSde ECha EGren ELon EUrb GEdr LRHS MHer MMuc NLar NRya SLee SPad SRms SRot WFar WHoo WIce
- 'Laucheana'	MCtn WHoo
- 'Morning Star White'	CSde EDAr EGren ESgI LCro LRHS
- 'Nifty Thrifty' (v)	ELan GJos LCro LRHS MHer SPoG SRms
- 'Nodwood Pink'	GJos
- 'Pomegranate' **new**	EDAr
- 'Rubrifolia'	see *A. maritima* 'In the Red'
- 'Rubrifolia Compacta'	see *A. maritima* 'A Little in the Red'
- 'Splendens'	CBcs EDAr EHeP EPfP LCro LShi LSto LWaG MAsh MBel MMuc SLee SPoG WFar
pseudarmeria	EPfP
- (Ballerina Series) 'Ballerina'	NBir
- - 'Ballerina Lilac'	EGren EPfP LRHS LShi MHol MPro SLee SPoG WFar
- - 'Ballerina Purple Rose'	MPro
- - 'Ballerina Red'	CAby CBcs EGren EPfP LRHS LShi MCtn MPro SLee SPad SPoG SRms WFar WTor
- - 'Ballerina White'	CBcs EGren EPfP LRHS LShi MCtn MPro SLee SPoG WFar WTor
- (Dreameria Series) 'Daydream' PBR	EGren LBar LSou MHol Midl MPri
- - 'Dream Clouds' PBR	LBar LSou MPri
- - 'Dreamland'	EGren LBar LSou Midl MPri
- - 'Sweet Dreams' PBR	EGren EPfP LBar LRHS LSou Midl MPri
- hybrids	SMrm
pubinervis	see *A. alpina*
pungens	ECha
setacea	see *A. girardii*
vulgaris	see *A. maritima*

Armoracia (Brassicaceae)
§ **rusticana**	CCBP CGHo CGwi EHet ELan ENfk GAbr GJos GQue IDun LCro MEar MHer MHoo MNHC NBac NPer SPoG SRms SVic WHer WHrl WSpi
- 'Variegata' (v)	ELan LEdu MHoo NSti SRms WHer

Arnebia (Boraginaceae)
echioides	see *A. pulchra*
longiflora	see *A. pulchra*
§ **pulchra**	EDAr

Arnica (Asteraceae)
angustifolia subsp. *iljinii*	NBir
chamissonis Less.	CCBP ENfk MNHC NLar SRms
montana	MHer MHoo MNHC SRms

Aronia (Rosaceae)
arbutifolia	EPfP LSRN MBlu SPlb WJur WKor
- 'Erecta'	CCVT ELan MBlu MMuc SPoG SRms
melanocarpa	CMCN CSpe EGrI EHeP EPfP EWld GKin LRHS MAsh WHtc WJur WKor

Aronia

- 'Hugin'	CAgr CCVT ELan GKin LRHS MMuc NLar SVic WFar
* - 'Red Viking'	NOra
× *prunifolia*	WJur WKor
- 'Aron' (F)	CAgr
- 'Autumn Magic' ♀H6	CBcs MAsh WFar
- 'Brilliant'	CBcs CCVT CDoC EBee ELan EPfP LCro LRHS NLar NPip SGol WMat
- 'Nero' (F)	CAgr CBcs ELan NLar SVic WMat
- 'Viking' (F)	CAgr CCVT CDoC EBee ELan EPom LBuc LCro LRHS MBlu MMuc NLar SGol SVic WFar WMat

Aronia × Sorbus see × Sorbaronia

Arrhenatherum (Poaceae)

elatius	CHab
- var. *bulbosum* 'Variegatum' (v)	ELan EPPr GBin MMuc NBid SEND

Artemisia ✿ (Asteraceae)

from Taiwan	WHer
§ *abrotanum*	CCBP CEls CGHo EBee ECha EGrI ENfk EWhm GJos GMaP GQue LEdu LRHS LShi MHer MHoo MMuc NLar NSti SDix SMad SRms WCot WHer WHoo WJek WKit WTre
- 'Courson'	ECha
absinthium	CEls CGHo CGwi CHab EBee ENfk GBin GJos GQue IDun LRHS LShi MCtn MHer MHoo MNHC NAts NLar SRms SVic WFar WHer WJek WKit
- 'Lambrook Mist'	CEls CFis CMac CMHG EPfP SMrm WCAu
- 'Lambrook Silver'	CDor CEls EBee ECha ELon GMaP LSRN MHer MPri NBro NLar SMrm SRms
- 'Silver Ghost'	CEls
- 'Silverado' **new**	StAn
afra	CEls
§ *alba*	CEls MHer SRms WJek
§ - 'Canescens' ♀H5	CEls EBee ECha EGrI LRHS LShi MAsh NLar WMal
alcockii	CEls
§ *alpina* ♀H7	CEls EPot EWes GBin GKev SRms
annua	CEls MCtn
anomala	CEls
§ *arborescens* ♀H4	CEls GAbr LBom LWaG SRms
- 'Brass Band'	see A. 'Powis Castle'
- 'Faith Raven' ♀H4	CEls GBin NLar
arbuscula	CEls
argentea misapplied	see A. *arborescens*
argentea L'Hér.	CEls
argyi	CEls
§ *armeniaca*	CEls WHer
assoana	see A. *alpina*
caerulescens subsp. *cretacea*	CEls WCot
- subsp. *gallica*	CEls
californica	CEls
- 'Canyon Gray'	CEls
- 'Montara'	CEls
campestris subsp. *borealis*	EUrb
- subsp. *campestris*	CEls
- subsp. *glutinosa*	CEls
- subsp. *maritima*	CEls
camphorata	see A. *alba*
cana	CEls

canariensis	see A. *thuscula*
canescens misapplied	see A. *alba* 'Canescens'
canescens Willd.	see A. *armeniaca*
carruthii	CEls
caucasica	see A. *alpina*
chamaemelifolia	CEls SRms
cretacea	see A. *nutans*
discolor Dougl. ex Besser	see A. *michauxiana*
douglasiana	CEls
- 'Valerie Finnis'	see A. *ludoviciana* 'Valerie Finnis'
dracunculus	CoPl ECha LCro LShi MCtn MNHC SDix SPlb SRms SVic WBrk WKit WTre
- French	CCBP CEls CGHo EHet ELan ENfk EWhm GJos IDun LCro MHer MHoo MPri SEND WCav WFar WJek WKit
- Russian	CEls ENfk SVic WKit
- VIENCO **new**	MNHC
filifolia	CEls
fragrans	CEls
frigida	CEls
glacialis	CEls
gmelinii	CEls
gnaphalodes	see A. *ludoviciana*
gorgonum	CEls SEND
herba-alba	CEls WTre
indica var. *momiyamae*	CEls WCot
japonica	CEls
keiskeana	CEls
kitadakensis 'Guizhou'	see A. *lactiflora* Guizhou Group
laciniata	CEls
lactiflora ♀H7	CEls CElw EBee ECha GMaP MHoo NGdn SBea SDix SMrm SRms StAn WTre
- NJM 11.01	CEls
- 'Elfenbein'	CEls EMor EPPr LBar MNrw NDov SMHy
§ - Guizhou Group	CBWd CDor CEls EBee ELan EMor EPfP GElm GKev GMaP LBar LRHS LSto MHol MNrw NBid NBro NGdn NLar NSti SRms WCAu WFar
- - 'Dark Delight'	EBee ECha EWes
- 'Jim Russell'	CDor CEls CElw EBee
- *purpurea*	see A. *lactiflora* Guizhou Group
- 'Weisse Dame'	CEls MNrw
lanata Willd.	see A. *alpina*
laxa	see A. *umbelliformis*
'Little Mice'	CEls LBar
§ *ludoviciana*	CEls CGHo MHoo NLar NPer SMrm SRms WFar
- subsp. *ludoviciana* var. *incompta*	CEls
- - var. *latiloba*	CEls NBro
- subsp. *mexicana* var. *albula*	CEls
- 'Silver Queen'	CBcs CDor CEls CMac EBee EHeP ELan EPfP ESgI GBin GMaP GQue LCro LRHS MAvo NBir NLar NSti SPoG SRms WCAu WFar
§ - 'Valerie Finnis' ♀H6	CBcs CCBP CDor CEls CMHG EBee ECha ELan EPfP GBin GMaP LBar LCro LRHS LShi MHer MHol NLar SMad SMHy SRms WCAu WCot WFar WMal
MAKANA SILVER ('Tnartms')	EUrb
maritima 'Coca-Cola'	CEls EBee GBin LBar LRHS MNHC SRms WKit
- var. *maritima*	CEls
mauiensis	CEls
§ *michauxiana*	CEls

molinieri　CEls
mutellina　see *A. umbelliformis*
nova　CEls
§ *nutans*　CEls WMal
　ORIENTAL LIMELIGHT　CEls CGHo LRHS MHoo MPri NLar
　　('Janlim') (v)　NSti SDix SMrm WCAu WHrl
palmeri hort.　see *A. ludoviciana*
pedemontana　see *A. alpina*
pontica　CEls EBee ECha EGrI GMaP GQue
　　LShi MMuc NBro NLar NSti SRms
　　WFar WHoo
§ 'Powis Castle' ♀H3　Widely available
princeps　CEls EBee
procera Willd.　see *A. abrotanum*
purshiana　see *A. ludoviciana*
pycnocephala　CEls
　'David's Choice'
'Rosa Schleier'　CEls GQue SHar
rupestris　CEls
schmidtiana ♀H5　CEls ECha SDix SRms
- 'Nana' ♀H5　CBcs CEls EBee EBlo EGrI ELan
　　EPfP EPot GMaP LRHS LShi MAsh
　　MHer NLar SPlb SPoG SRms WAbe
　　WFar WJek
- 'Nana Attraction'　CGHo EGren EUrb LRHS MBNS
　　SRot
selengensis　CEls
somai var. *batakensis*　WCru
　　NMWJ 14559
splendens misapplied　see *A. alba* 'Canescens'
stelleriana　CEls CGHo ECha ELan LShi MHol
　　NBro SRms StAn
§ - 'Boughton Silver'　CBcs CCBP CDor CEls CFis EBee
　　ELan EPfP GKev GMaP LBar LRHS
　　MAsh MHer SRms WCAu WHil
　　WMal
- 'Mori'　see *A. stelleriana* 'Boughton Silver'
- 'Nana'　CEls
- 'Prostrata'　see *A. stelleriana* 'Boughton Silver'
- 'Shemya'　CEls
- 'Silver Brocade'　see *A. stelleriana* 'Boughton Silver'
suksdorfii　CEls
§ *thuscula*　CEls
tilesii　CEls
tridentata　CEls
　subsp. *tridentata*
- subsp. *wyomingensis*　CEls
§ *umbelliformis*　EWes
vallesiaca　CEls WMal
verlotiorum　CEls
vulgaris　CAgr CEls CGwi GJos LShi MCtn
　　MNHC WHer
- 'Variegata' (v)　ELan SRms
× *wurzellii*　CEls

Arthropodium (Asparagaceae)
candidum　WCot
- 'Little Lilia' (v)　WCot
- 'Maculatum'　MPie SPlb
- 'Purpureum'　CTtf ECha WFar
cirratum　CTsd ESwi EWld MPie WFar
- 'Matapouri Bay'　SEND
milleflorum　SBrt

artichoke, globe see *Cynara cardunculus*
　　Scolymus Group

artichoke, Jerusalem see *Helianthus tuberosus*

Artocarpus (Moraceae)
heterophyllus　WJur

Arum ❀ (Araceae)
byzantinum　EAri GKev
'Chameleon' ♀H7　CDor EBee EMor EPPr ISha MCor
　　NBir NLar SEND WCot
concinnatum 'Mount Ida'　ESwi LEdu
cornutum　see *Sauromatum venosum*
creticum　CBro CMiW EAri GEdr GKev LAma
　　MNrw
- 'Karpathos'　CExl EAri EBee WAbe WCot WMal
- 'Marmaris White'　WCot WMal
- white-spotted　ECha EWes
cyrenaicum　EAri
dioscoridis　ESwi GKev ISha
- var. *dioscoridis*　GKev
- var. *syriacum*　GKev
dracunculus　see *Dracunculus vulgaris*
hygrophilum　LEdu
- B&SWJ 15277　WCru
italicum　CoPl ELin GKev LAma LRHS LWaG
　　MHol SPlb WCot WShi XFar
- 'Badsey Giant'　WCot
- 'Black Spot'　EPPr
- 'Crocodile'　WCot
- 'Curtis Giant'　ESwi
- 'Edward Dougal'　WCot
- 'Godzilla'　LEdu
- 'Green Marble' (v)　LShi WFar
- 'Indubitable'　WCot
- subsp. *italicum*　MHer WBrk
- - 'Angelique'　WCot
§ - - 'Marmoratum' ♀H6　Widely available
- - 'Sandy McNab'　WCot
- - 'Spotted Jack'　WCot
- - 'Tiny'　SMHy
- - 'Uniquity'　WCot
§ - - 'White Winter' ♀H6　WBrk WCot WMal
- - 'XXL'　EPPr
- 'Nancy Lindsay'　WCot
- subsp. *neglectum*　SChr
- - 'Maculate Monksilver'　WCot
- - 'Miss Janey Hall' (v)　ESwi WCot
§ - - 'Monksilver'　WCot
- 'Pamela Harper'　WCot
- 'Pictum'　see *A. italicum* subsp. *italicum*
　　'Marmoratum'
- 'Van Gogh'　WCot
- 'Yarnells'　WCot
aff. *italicum*　CMiW
korolkowii　WCot
maculatum　EPot NLar WHer WShi
- 'Golden Joy'　ESwi
- 'Painted Lady' (v)　WCot
pictum　CExl CMac EAri EWes GKev LEdu
　　WMal
- B&SWJ 15276　WCru
- 'Taff's Form'　see *A. italicum* subsp. *italicum*
　　'White Winter'
purpureospathum　EPPr
rupicola var. *virescens*　LEdu
'Streaked Spectre'　LEdu
'The Patch'　see *A. italicum* subsp. *neglectum*
　　'Monksilver'

Aruncus (Rosaceae)
aethusifolius ♀H7　CSpe CToG ECha EDAr ELan ELon
　　EMor EPfP GKev GKin GMaP GQue
　　LBar LSto MBel MPnt NBir NGdn
　　NLar NRya SPlb SPoG SRms WAbe
　　WFar WPnP
- 'Filigran'　EBee

114 *Aruncus*

- 'Little Gem'	WCru
- 'Porzellan'	EBee
- 'Snowflurries'	EBlo
asiaticus B&SWJ 8624	WCru
'Chantilly Lace'	LBar WChS WFar WTor
§ *dioicus*	Widely available
§ - (m) ♀H6	CBen CMac MBNS MWts NBro NSti SRms
- var. *astilboides*	LEdu
- CHILD OF TWO WORLDS	see *A. dioicus* 'Zweiweltenkind'
- 'Glasnevin'	ECha WFar
- var. *kamtschaticus*	NLar WHrl
- - RBS 208	NGdn
- 'Kneiffii'	CLil CSpe EBee ECha ELan EMor GKin GMaP LBar LCro LSto MHol MPnt SPlb SPoG SRms WCAu WFar WKif
- 'Sommeranfang'	ECha
- 'Whirlwind'	EWhm MPie NLar
§ - 'Zweiweltenkind'	NLar WCot
'Fairy Hair'	EMor LBar NCth SPad
GUINEA FOWL ('Perlhuhn')	ELon GKev GQue MAvo MHol MWlw NBid NBir NGdn NLar WCAu WFar
'Horatio'	CBWd CDor CElw CWnw ECha EMor GMaP LCro LEdu LRHS LSto MAvo MBel MHol MPie NBid NDov NLar NSti NWbg SEND SPhx SPoG WCAu WChS WCot WHoo
'Johannifest'	ECha WCot
'Misty Lace'	CWnw EBee ELan GBin GKev LBar LRHS NGdn NLar NWbg SPel WCAu
'Noble Spirit'	MPie NGdn NLar WChS
plumosus (m)	see *A. dioicus*
'Sparkles'	ELan IPot LBar
sylvestris (m)	see *A. dioicus*
'Woldemar Meier'	NLar WCot

Arundinaria (Poaceae)

anceps	see *Yushania anceps*
auricoma	see *Pleioblastus viridistriatus*
disticha	see *Pleioblastus pygmaeus* 'Distichus'
falconeri	see *Himalayacalamus falconeri*
fargesii	see *Borinda fargesii*
fastuosa	see *Semiarundinaria fastuosa*
fortunei	see *Pleioblastus variegatus*
hookeriana Munro	see *Himalayacalamus hookerianus*
japonica	see *Pseudosasa japonica*
jaunsarensis	see *Yushania anceps*
marmorea	see *Chimonobambusa marmorea*
murielae	see *Fargesia murielae*
nitida	see *Fargesia nitida*
palmata	see *Sasa palmata*
pumila	see *Pleioblastus argenteostriatus* f. *pumilus*
pygmaea	see *Pleioblastus pygmaeus*
quadrangularis	see *Chimonobambusa quadrangularis*
simonii	see *Pleioblastus simonii*
tessellata	see *Bergbambos tessellata*
vagans	see *Sasaella ramosa*
variegata	see *Pleioblastus variegatus*
veitchii	see *Sasa veitchii*
viridistriata	see *Pleioblastus viridistriatus*

Arundo (Poaceae)

ᵽ *donax*	CAbb CBen CKno CLil EArl EBee ELan ELon EUrb EWes MAvo MBlu MMuc MNrw SArc SDix SEND SPlb SPoG SSta
- 'Ely' (v)	LCro SNoN WHil
- 'Golden Chain' (v)	CKno EArl EPPr EShb EUrb EWes LRHS SNoN
- 'Macrophylla'	CKno EArl EBlo EPPr EWes LEdu LRHS SBig WPGP
- 'Peppermint Stick' (v)	SNoN
- 'Variegata'	see *A. donax* var. *versicolor*
§ - var. *versicolor* (v)	CBcs CBen CKno CLil EArl EBee EBlo ELan ELon EUrb EWes MMuc SArc SAth SBig SDix SEND SMad SPlb SPoG SSta
I - - 'Aureovariegata' (v)	CDTJ CLil MMuc SEND
formosana	CKno EArl EPPr

Asarina (Plantaginaceae)

barclayana	see *Maurandya barclayana*
erubescens	see *Lophospermum erubescens*
§ *procumbens*	GElm GKev MCtn NBir NRya SPhx SRms WFar WKif
scandens 'Snowwhite'	MCtn

Asarum (Aristolochiaceae)

albomaculatum B&SWJ 1726	WCru
arifolium 'The Giant'	NLar
canadense	CDor EBee GKev LAma
caudatum	CDTJ EBee ECha EMor EPfP EPPr ESwi GKev ISha LEdu NBro NLar SRms WCot WFar WPGP WSpi
- white-flowered	GGro
caulescens	GGro
Chen Yi 5	ESwi
epigynum	CDTJ ESwi MHol WCot
- 'Silver Web'	NSti WCot
europaeum ♀H6	Widely available
- PAB 4377	LEdu WPGP
- Pontic	WPGP
hypogynum B&SWJ 3628	WCru
infrapurpureum B&SWJ 1694	WCru
longirhizomatosum	GEdr
macranthum B&SWJ 1691	WCru
maculatum B&SWJ 1114	WCru
maximum	ISha
- 'Green Panda'	CDTJ
- 'Ling Ling'	CDTJ EBee EMor EUrb ISha MAvo MMrt SBig WHil
- 'Silver Panda'	CDTJ EArl ESwi MNrw WCot WFar
nipponicum B&SWJ 2839	WCru
petelotii B&SWJ 11755	WCru
pulchellum	ESwi LEdu WPGP
splendens	CBro CDTJ EBee EMor ISha LEdu LRHS MAvo MHol MNrw NLar NSti SMHy SPlb SPoG WCot WCru WFar
taipingshanianum B&SWJ 1688	WCru

Asclepias ✿ (Apocynaceae)

asperula	SIvy
'Cinderella'	EArl ELan SPeP
curassavica	CSpe EArl EShb SBig SRkn WFar
- 'Apollo Orange'	MCtn
- 'Silky Gold'	EShb
- 'Silky Red'	EShb
exaltata	SBrt WHil
§ *fascicularis*	WPGP
fasciculata	see *A. fascicularis*
fruticosa	see *Gomphocarpus fruticosus*

incarnata	CSpe CTtf ECha ELin SBrt SMHy SMrm SPeP SPlb WTre
- 'Alba'	MCtn WTre
- 'Ice Ballet'	EAri EBee ELan ELin LBar MBel NEoE NLar WCAu
- 'Soulmate'	EPfP GQue LBar MAsh MCtn MHol MMrt SMad
- 'White Superior'	SPeP
purpurascens	EDAr
speciosa	EAri SBea SIvy
syriaca	Prohibited invasive. See Conservation and the Environment, p.42
tuberosa	CBcs CSpe EAri EBee EDAr LBar LCro LShi MCtn MHer MHol MNHC MPie NBir SPoG SRms WCot WFar
- Gay Butterflies Group	MCtn
- 'Hello Yellow'	EAri LBar
- subsp. *interior*	MHol
verticillata	WHil
viridis	WHil

Asimina (Annonaceae)

triloba (F)	CBcs CDTJ CMCN MBlu NLar SPlb WJur WKor
- 'Sunflowers' (F)	SAko

asparagus see also AGM Vegetables Section

Asparagus (Asparagaceae)

acutifolius	LEdu SBrt
asparagoides ♀H3	EShb
densiflorus	NHrt WCot
- 'Mazeppa'	EShb
- 'Myersii' ♀H1c	EShb LBom LCro LWaG MPri NHrt SEND
- 'Myriocladus'	EShb MPri SPlb
- Sprengeri Group ♀H1c	EShb LBom LCro MPri NHrt SEND
falcatus	CDoC EShb LBom LCro MPri NHrt SEND
filicinus	LEdu
- NJM 12.024	WPGP
- var. *giraldii*	WCot
aff. *meioclados* B&SWJ 8309	WCot WCru
officinalis	CWRo
plumosus	see *A. setaceus*
pseudoscaber 'Spitzenschleier'	WCot
retrofractus	WCot
scandens	EShb WCot
§ *setaceus* ♀H2	CDoC EGren EShb LBom LCro LInT LWaG MCtn MPri NHrt SPlb SPre WCot
- 'Nanus'	MNHC
- 'Pyramidalis' ♀H1c	CDoC
tenuifolius	WPGP
verticillatus	MCtn
virgatus	EBee EShb LEdu SPlb WPGP

Asperula (Rubiaceae)

§ *arcadiensis* ♀H3	EPot SPlb
aristata subsp. *scabra*	ECha MMuc WCot
- subsp. *thessala*	see *A. sintenisii*
boissieri	SPlb
daphneola	ELan EPot EWes GKev
gussonei	EPot WAbe WHoo
hexaphylla	EDAr
lilaciflora	see *A. lilaciflora* subsp. *lilaciflora*
var. *caespitosa*	
§ - subsp. *lilaciflora*	ELan WIce

nitida	ELan EPot WIce
- subsp. *puberula*	see *A. sintenisii*
odorata	see *Galium odoratum*
orientalis	MCtn
§ *sintenisii*	EPot WAbe WHoo
suberosa misapplied	see *A. arcadiensis*
taurina	EBee
- subsp. *caucasica*	NLar
tinctoria	GQue MHer SRms

Asphodeline (Asphodelaceae)

liburnica	CBro CFis CSpe ECha LCro SMHy SNoN WCAu
§ *lutea*	Widely available
§ - 'Gelbkerze'	EAri EBee EPfP
- YELLOW CANDLE	see *A. lutea* 'Gelbkerze'
taurica	CSpe EDAr

Asphodelus (Asphodelaceae)

acaulis	WAbe WCot
§ *aestivus*	EPPr MBel WCot
albus	CBro EBee ECha EGrI EPPr GBin MCtn NBid SBeP SPlb SRms
cerasiferus	see *A. ramosus*
fistulosus	CBro CSpe EBee ECha SBeP SVen
lusitanicus	see *A. ramosus*
luteus	see *Asphodeline lutea*
microcarpus	see *A. aestivus*
§ *ramosus*	WCot

Aspidistra ✿ (Asparagaceae)

Chen Yi 135	ESwi
attenuata 'Dungpu Dazzler'	ESwi WCru
- 'Small 'n' Smart'	WCru
- 'Xitou Starlet'	WCru
caespitosa	WCru
- 'Jade Ribbons'	see *A. hainanensis* 'Jade Ribbons'
daibuensis 'Taiwan Stars'	ESwi WCot WCru
- 'Tidy Trim'	ESwi WCot WCru
- 'Totally Dotty' (v)	EShb ESwi WCru
- 'Yuli Yummy'	ESwi WCot WCru
- 'Yushan Galaxy'	ESwi
ebianensis 'Flowing Fountains'	ESwi WCru
elatior ♀H3	CBct CDTJ EShb ESwi LBom LCro LDro LInT LWaG SChr SEND SHor SMad SPlb WCot WFar
- 'Akebono' (v)	WCot
- 'Asahi' (v)	CDTJ ESwi WCot
- 'Hoshi-zora' (v)	WCot
- 'Lennon's Song' (v)	CDTJ EShb ESwi SEND WCot
- 'Milky Way' (v)	EShb ESwi SEND
- 'Morning Frost' (v)	WCot
- 'Okame' (v)	WCot
- 'Oshima'	WCru
- 'Variegata' (v) ♀H3	CDTJ EShb
fasciaria	WCru
fungilliformis 'China Star' misapplied	see *A. zongbayi* 'China Moon'
§ *hainanensis* 'Jade Ribbons'	CDTJ EShb ESwi WCot WCru
hekouensis BWJ 15207	WCru
leshanensis CBCH 768 (v)	WCru
- CBCH 769/70 (v)	WCru
linearifolia	WCru
- 'Leopard' (v)	CDTJ ESwi WCot WCru
- 'Skinny Dippin'	WCru
lurida	EShb GKev LAma
- 'Ginga'	see *A. sichuanensis* 'Ginga'
- 'Ginga Giant' (v)	ESwi WCot WCru
minutiflora	ESwi WCot

Aspidistra

- 'Spangled Ribbons'	WCru
mushaensis	WCru
'Purple Picket'	
- 'Wushe Wacky'	WCru
'Mystery Man'	WCru
neglecta 'Soft Spot'	WCru
oblanceifolia	ESwi WCot WCru
'Nagoya Stars'	
omeiensis	CDTJ WCot
- 'Ogisu'	WCru
'Opium Hit'	WCru
'Pha-Hom Pok-adot'	WCru
pulchella	WCru
- 'Spiderman' **new**	WCru
- 'Stretch Marks'	WCru
punctata B&SWJ 14629	WCru
retusa 'Nanjing Green'	WCru
saxicola 'Uan Fat Lady'	see *A. zongbayi* 'Uan Fat Lady'
sichuanensis	WCru
- CBCH 281 from Emei Shan, China	WCru
- CBCH 603 from Sichuan, China	WCru
- 'Beauty Spot'	WCru
- 'Despot'	WCru
- 'Giant'	WCru
§ - 'Ginga' (v)	CDTJ ESwi WCot
- 'Gold Lancer' (v)	WCru
- 'Golden Freckles' (v)	WCru
- 'Kinboshi' (v)	WCot WCru
- 'Misty Spot'	WCru
- 'Qipao'	WCot
- 'Rarely Spotted'	CDTJ WCru
- 'Spotlight' **new**	WCru
- spotted selection	WCru
- 'Spotty'	WCru
- 'Well Spotted'	WCru
'Spotty Dotty'	ESwi WCru
sutepensis 'Chiang-dao Chace'	WCru
- 'Chiang-dao Dappled'	WCru
tonkinensis	ESwi WCot WCru
- var. *compacta* BWJ 15525	WCru
typica 'China Sun'	ESwi WCot
vietnamensis	WCru
- 'Garden Gallery' (v)	ESwi
- 'Seiun' (v)	WCru
zongbayi	WCot
§ - 'China Moon' (v)	CExl ESwi SMad WCot WCru
- 'Dotty Dan'	WCru
§ - 'Uan Fat Lady'	EBee ESwi WCot WCru WPGP
- 'Yunnan Sunbeam' (v)	WCot
- 'Crispy Wave' PBR	CDoC LBom LCro LRHS LWaG NHrt NTro WFar
- 'Osaka'	NHrt
nitidum	SPlb
'Parvati'	CDoC LCro LRHS NHrt
scolopendrium ♀H6	Widely available
- 'Angustatum' ♀H6	Widely available
- Crispum Group ♀H6	CLAP ELan EMor NBid SRms WAbe WFar
- - 'Crispum Bolton's Nobile'	CLAP
- - 'Golden Queen'	CDor
- Crispum Fimbriatum Group Nobile'	CLAP
- Cristatum Group	CAby CDor CLAP CMHG CSpe CWnw EBee ELan ELon EMor EPfP ISha LBom LCro LRHS MGos MMuc NAlc NBro NLar SRms SRot WBrk WCAu
- Fimbriatum Group	LRHS
- 'Furcatum'	CDTJ ELan NLar
- 'Muricatum'	NBid
- 'Sagittatoprojectum Sclater'	WCot
- Undulatum Group	CDTJ EBee ECha EPfP GBin LSto MAsh MHer MHol NBir NLar SHor SRms WAbe WCot WFar
trichomanes ♀H6	Widely available
- Cristatum Group	MAsh NLar
- Incisum Group ♀H6	WAbe

Astelia (Asteliaceae)

banksii	CBcs CBct CTsd EGren EPfP LCro MGos NLar SEND
§ *chathamica* ♀H3	CCht CWnw EArl EGren LBom LRHS MHol MPri MSwo SArc SBig SChF SEND SPlb SPoG WCot WSpi
- 'Silver Spear'	see *A. chathamica*
fragrans	LEdu
grandis	LEdu WPGP
nervosa	SArc WHil
- 'Westland'	CAbb CBcs CCht CTsd EBee EUrb LCro LSRN MGos SEND StAn
'Red Devil'	CBcs MGos MHol MHtn SBig SEND SPoG WSpi
RED SHADOW ('A1')	CBcs EUrb LCro LRHS SBig SHor
'Silver Shadow' PBR	CBcs CWnw EBee EGren EPfP EUrb LCro LRHS LSou SBig WFar WSpi

Aster ✿ (Asteraceae)

acris	see *Galatella sedifolia*
'Afternoon Delight'	EBee
ageratoides	SPel WCot
- 'Adustus Nanus'	ELon MPro
- 'Ashvi'	CKno CSpe ELon EMor ESgI GBin GElm LRHS MBel MHol MMuc MPro NSti SPoG WCot WFar WOld
- 'Asmo'	MPro
- 'Asran'	ELon EPPr EWes EWhm LRHS MHer MHol MMuc MPie MPro NLar SEND SMHy WBrk WCAu WCot WFar WOld
- 'Ezo Murasaki'	CDor CMHG CSpe ECha ELon EMor ESgI GBin GMaP LEdu LRHS MAvo MNrw NDov SAko SDix SMHy SNoN SPel SPoG WCot WFar WKif WOld
- var. *firmus*	WPGP
- 'Harry Smith'	NSti SPoG WCAu WCot WFar WOld
- 'Stardust'	EBlo GMaP LRHS MPro

Aster

- 'Starshine' PBR	CBcs CKno CWGN LBar LCro LRHS MAvo MPro WCot
§ **albescens**	EAri
× **alpellus**	WOld
alpinus ♀H7	GArf GKev MHol SRms StAn WFar
- var. **albus**	EDAr ELan EPfP GKev LBar LRHS LShi MPro
- Dark Beauty	see *A. alpinus* 'Dunkle Schöne'
- var. **dolomiticus**	GKev
§ - 'Dunkle Schöne'	EDAr MCtn SRms WFar
- 'Goliath'	EAri EBee EDAr ELan EUrb LBar Midl SPlb StAn WFar
- 'Happy End'	EPfP LRHS MPro NBir SPoG SRms
- 'Pinkie'	EBee EDAr ELan EPfP
- 'Trimix'	NBir SRms
- violet-flowered	LRHS MPro
- 'White Beauty'	MCtn
amelloides	see *Felicia amelloides*
amellus	ELon StAn
- 'Blue King'	EWes NLar SMrm WFar WSpi
- 'Brilliant'	CMHG ELon EPPr LSto MArl MAvo MBNS NBir NLar NSti SAko SRms WCAu WHoo WOld WSpi
- 'Butzemann'	WCot
- 'Danzig'	NLar
- 'Doktor Otto Petschek'	ELon NLar WCot
- 'Forncett Flourish' ♀H7	EBee EBlo EPPr LRHS SPel WCot WHoo WMal WOld
- 'Framfieldii' ♀H7	SMHy WCot WOld
- 'Gründer'	WCot WOld
- 'Jacqueline Genebrier' ♀H7	WOld
- 'King George' ♀H7	CDor CMac EBee ECha ELan ELon EPfP GBin GMaP LBar LCro LSto MArl MHol MMuc NLar SEND SRms WCFE WCot WHoo WMal WOld
- 'Lac de Genève'	WCot
- 'Lady Hindlip'	NLar WCot WMal
- 'Louise'	MBrN
- 'Mira'	ELon
- 'Moerheim Gem'	WCot WOld
- 'Mrs Ralph Woods'	WOld
- 'Nocturne'	ELon WCot WOld
- 'Paul Picton' **new**	WOld
- Pink Zenith	see *A. amellus* 'Rosa Erfüllung'
§ - 'Rosa Erfüllung' ♀H7	CDor CKno EBee EPPr EWes GBin GMaP LSto MAvo MNrw NLar SPhx SPoG WCAu WHoo WOld WSpi
- 'Rotfeuer'	WSpi
- 'Rudolph Goethe'	EBee EGren EHeP ELan EPfP LSto MCtn NLar WCAu WOld WSpi
- 'September Glow'	SHar
- 'Silbersee' ♀H7	ELon MNrw
- 'Sonia'	ECha ELon
- 'Sonora' ♀H7	EGren MAsh MNrw SHar SPhx WKif WOld
- 'Sternkugel'	WOld
- 'Ultramarine'	WOld
- 'Vanity'	WOld
§ - 'Veilchenkönigin' ♀H7	Widely available
- Violet Queen	see *A. amellus* 'Veilchenkönigin'
× **amethystinus**	see *Symphyotrichum* × *amethystinum*
asperulus misapplied	see *A. peduncularis*
baccharoides W&O 0026	GGro
'Betel Nut'	ECha
capensis 'Variegatus'	see *Felicia amelloides* variegated
'Cassandra'	NCth
'Chilly Fingers'	ESgI MAvo MNrw MWlw SPel
ciliolatus	see *Symphyotrichum ciliolatum*
'Climax' misapplied	see *Symphyotrichum laeve* 'Arcturus', 'Calliope'
'Climax' ambig.	see *Symphyotrichum laeve* 'Climax'
'Climax' Vicary Gibbs	see *Symphyotrichum* 'Climax' Vicary Gibbs
coelestis	see *Felicia amelloides*
corymbosus	see *Eurybia divaricata*
'Cotswold Gem'	EBee EBlo LRHS SPel WCot WMal WOld
diffusus	see *Symphyotrichum lateriflorum*
diplostephioides	EWhm GArf GEdr SPlb
divaricatus	see *Eurybia divaricata*
'Eleven Purple' PBR	MNrw MPro
ericoides	see *Symphyotrichum ericoides*
falcatus	see *Symphyotrichum falcatum*
× **frikartii**	CMac EBee EPfP
- 'Eiger'	WOld
- 'Flora's Delight'	EBlo ELon EMor EPfP LBar NLar SPoG SRms WCAu WSpi
- 'Jungfrau'	CWGN EBee ELan EPPr GMaP MBNS NLar SPeP SPhx SRms WOld
- 'Mönch' ♀H7	Widely available
- Wonder of Stafa	see *A.* × *frikartii* 'Wunder von Stäfa'
§ - 'Wunder von Stäfa' ♀H7	CCps CEnd CKno EBee ELon EPfP GBin GElm GMaP LCro LSto MArl MAsh MBel MBNS NBir NGdn NLar SRGP WCAu WCot WOld WSpi
glehnii	WCAu
- 'Aglenii'	MNrw NDov SAko
greatae	see *Symphyotrichum greatae*
× **herveyi**	see *Eurybia* × *herveyi*
himalaicus	GArf GKev
hybridus luteus	see *Solidago* × *luteus*
'Ice Cool Pink'	ECha ESgI IPot MNrw
'JS El Macho'	MNrw
koraiensis	GGro MMrt
* **kotarimus**	MHol
laevis	see *Symphyotrichum laeve*
lateriflorus	see *Symphyotrichum lateriflorum*
linosyris	see *Galatella linosyris*
macrophyllus	see *Eurybia macrophylla*
mongolicus	see *Kalimeris mongolica*
natalensis	see *Felicia rosulata*
novae-angliae	see *Symphyotrichum novae-angliae*
novi-belgii	see *Symphyotrichum novi-belgii*
Octoberlight	see *Symphyotrichum* 'Oktoberlicht'
§ **peduncularis**	EBlo ECha EMor LBar MHol NSti SHar WCot WFar WOld
petiolatus	see *Felicia petiolata*
pilosus	see *Symphyotrichum pilosum*
puniceus	see *Symphyotrichum puniceum*
pyrenaeus 'Lutetia'	CBWd CKno CTtf ECha EPfP EPPr ESgI GMaP LBar LSto MArl MNrw NLar SPel SRms WCAu WCot WFar WOld
radula	see *Eurybia radula*
rotundifolius 'Variegatus'	see *Felicia amelloides* variegated
rugulosus 'Asrugo'	CKno
savatieri	SHar
§ **scaber**	CAgr WCot
- W&O 9268	GGro
- 'Ki Hakikomi-fu'	GGro
schreberi	see *Eurybia schreberi*
sedifolius	see *Galatella sedifolia*
sibiricus	see *Eurybia sibirica*
'Snow Flurry'	see *Symphyotrichum ericoides* var. *prostratum* 'Snow Flurry'
souliei	GArf
spathulifolius	WCot
spectabilis	see *Eurybia spectabilis*
stracheyi	GKev
subcaeruleus	see *A. tongolensis*
tataricus 'Jindai'	EBee SNoN SPeP WCAu

thomsonii GBin SHar SPel WCot WOld WSpi WTre
- 'Nanus' GMaP SPoG WOld WSpi
§ *tongolensis* GKev
- 'Berggarten' LRHS MHol MNrw WHil
- 'Napsbury' WCot
- 'Wartburgstern' EPfP LRHS
tradescantii misapplied see *Symphyotrichum pilosum* var. *pringlei*
tradescantii L. see *Symphyotrichum tradescantii*
trinervius var. *harae* WFar WOld
tripolium see *Tripolium pannonicum*
'Triumph' WCot
turbinellus ambig. see *Symphyotrichum turbinellum* ambig.
vimineus Lam. see *Symphyotrichum lateriflorum*

Asteranthera (Gesneriaceae)
ovata CExl EBee GGGa WAbe WPGP

Asteromoea (Asteraceae)
mongolica see *Kalimeris mongolica*
pinnatifida see *Kalimeris pinnatifida*

Asterotrichion (Malvaceae)
discolor CTsd EBee LRHS SBrt SHor SPlb

Astilbe ✿ (Saxifragaceae)
'Alive and Kicking' CMHG WFar
'Amerika' (× *arendsii*) CMHG LRHS NWbg SRms
'Amethyst' (× *arendsii*) CLil CMac CMHG EGren LBuc MBel NBir WFar
'Angel Wings' (× *arendsii*) CMHG NEoE
'Anita Pfeifer' (× *arendsii*) CMHG EGren ELon LRHS NLar
× *arendsii* LBuc
(Astary Series) 'Astary Light Rose' (× *arendsii*) EGren
- 'Astary Red' (× *arendsii*) MPro
- 'Astary Rose' (× *arendsii*) MPro WFar
- 'Astary White' (× *arendsii*) EGren MPro NWbg WFar
astilboides CMHG
- 'Bonn' LRHS MPri
'Avalanche' CAby CMHG CoPl ELin NBir NEoE WSpi
'Bakker's Beauty' CMHG
§ 'Beauty of Ernst' (× *arendsii*) CMHG ECha ELon EMor MAsh MNrw NLar SPoG SRms WFar
§ 'Beauty of Lisse' (× *arendsii*) ELon EMor LBom LRHS MNrw NLar
'Bergkristall' (× *arendsii*) CMHG
'Betsy Cuperus' CMHG WCAu
(*thunbergii* hybrid)
'Bonn' (*japonica* hybrid) CWat NLar SRms
'Boogie Woogie' PBR CMHG
(× *arendsii*)
§ 'Brautschleier' CMac CMHG EGren ELan GKev
(× *arendsii*) ♀H7 LCro LSRN NGdn NLar WPnP
'Bremen' (*japonica* hybrid) CMHG
'Bressingham Beauty' CMHG EBee EGren EHeP ELan
(× *arendsii*) ♀H7 EMor EPfP GKev GMaP GQue LCro LRHS NEoE NSti SPoG SRms WFar WSpi
BRIDAL VEIL (× *arendsii*) see A. 'Brautschleier' (× *arendsii*)
§ 'Bronce Elegans' CMHG ECha GMaP NLar SRms
(*simplicifolia* hybrid) ♀H7 WSpi
'Bronzelaub' (× *arendsii*) CMHG
'Brunhilde' CMHG EGren
'Bumalda' (× *arendsii*) EGrI GMaP NBid NGdn SPlb WFar
'Burgunderrot' (× *arendsii*) CMHG ELin LRHS MNrw NLar SRms WFar
'Cappuccino' (× *arendsii*) CMHG EWld MAsh MBel MPri WTre XFar

* 'Carmine King' MMuc
  'Carminea' CMHG
  'Catherine Deneuve' see A. 'Federsee' (× *arendsii*)
  'Cattleya' (× *arendsii*) CMHG LRHS NLar WFar WSpi
  'Cattleya Dunkel' CMHG
  (× *arendsii*)
  'Ceres' (× *arendsii*) CMHG
  'Cherry Ripe' see A. 'Feuer' (× *arendsii*)
  chinensis EPfP MBros
  - B&SWJ 8178 WCru
  - BLACK PEARLS see A. *chinensis* 'Dunes Future'
  - 'Brokat' CMHG
  - var. *davidii* B&SWJ 8583 WCru
  - - B&SWJ 8645 WCru
  - 'Diamonds and Pearls' PBR CMHG CWGN LBom WFar
  § - 'Dunes Future' NEoE NSti
  - 'Dunes Glory' NEoE
  § - 'Dunes Victory' NEoE
  - 'Finale' CMHG GKev
  - 'Frankentroll' CMHG
  § - 'Harvandermeerrubyred' NEoE
  § - 'Harvandermeerwhite' NEoE
  - HOT PEARLS see A. *chinensis* 'Dunes Glory'
  - 'Intermezzo' CMHG GMaP NLar
  - IVORY PEARLS see A. *chinensis* 'Dunes Victory'
  - 'Little Vision in Pink' PBR WFar
  - LOWLANDS RUBY RED see A. *chinensis* 'Harvandermeerrubyred'
  - LOWLANDS WHITE see A. *chinensis* 'Harvandermeerwhite'
  - 'Milk and Honey' PBR CMHG CWGN NEoE WFar WSpi
  § - var. *pumila* ♀H7 CPud EBee ECha EGren EHeP ELan EPfP GArf GKev GMaP GQue LShi NBid NLar NQui SPlb SRms StAn WCAu WCot WFar WPnP WTor
  - - 'Serenade' CMac CMHG NGdn
  - 'Purple Glory' CMHG
  - 'Spätsommer' CMHG
  - var. *taquetii* CMac ELan LRHS MCtn NSti SRms
  - - PURPLE LANCE see A. *chinensis* var. *taquetii* 'Purpurlanze'
  § - - 'Purpurlanze' ♀H7 CBWd CKno ECha GMaP GQue LSRN MBel NBir NBro NDov NGdn NLar SPoG WCAu WFar WSpi
  § - - 'Superba' ♀H7 CMac CMHG ECha MWIw NBro SDix SRms WFar
  - 'Veronika Klose' CMHG LSou NLar WHoo
  - 'Vision in Pink' PBR CLil CMHG EMor LRHS MNrw NCth WFar XFar
  - 'Vision in Red' PBR CMHG EGrI EMor EPfP EUrb LRHS MNrw NBir NLar SPoG SRkn WCAu WFar XFar
  - 'Vision in White' EPfP LBom LCro NEoE SAko SPoG SRkn WFar XFar
  - 'Visions' CBWd CMac CMHG LRHS NBro NEoE NGdn SPoG
  - 'White Cloud' NQui
  - white-flowered WTre
  'Chocolate Cherry' PBR CMHG EMor LCro LRHS MSCN
  (Mighty Series) NEoE SPeP XFar
  'Chocolate Shogun' CBcs CElw CSpe CWGN EMor
  (*thunbergii* hybrid) GMaP IPot ISha LRHS MHol MNrw NSti SMad SPad SPoG WCot WFar XFar
  COLOGNE see A. 'Köln' (*japonica* hybrid)
  COLOR FLASH see A. 'Beauty of Ernst' (× *arendsii*)
  COLOR FLASH LIME see A. 'Beauty of Lisse' (× *arendsii*)
  'Cotton Candy' (× *arendsii*) XFar
  'Country and Western' PBR NEoE
  (× *arendsii*)
  'Cream of Marwood' CMHG

Astilbe

'Crimson Feather' — see *A.* 'Gloria Purpurea' (× *arendsii*)
× *crispa* 'Lilliput' — NBir NEoE NLar NRya
§ - 'Perkeo' ♀H5 — GMaP NBir NEoE NLar SRms WFar
- 'Peter Pan' — see *A.* × *crispa* 'Perkeo'
- 'Red Rog' — NEoE
- 'Snow Queen' — NBir NEoE
'Dark Side of the Moon' **new** — CKno MHtn Midl WTor XFar
'Darwin's Dream' — CMHG MNrw NEoE NLar
'Delft Lace' — CLil EBee LBom LBuc LSou MBel MHol MMrt MPri NCth SRms WSpi
'Deutschland' (*japonica* hybrid) ♀H7 — CBcs CMHG CPud EBee EHeP ELan EPfP GMaP LRHS LSRN LSto MAsh MBNS MGos NBid NBir NEoE NLar SAth SDix SPoG SRms WSpi
§ 'Diamant' (× *arendsii*) — CMHG LRHS LSRN MMuc MNrw NBir NGdn WFar
DIAMOND — see *A.* 'Diamant' (× *arendsii*)
'Donna' (× *arendsii*) — CMHG
'Drayton Glory' (× *arendsii*) — see *A.* × *rosea* 'Peach Blossom'
'Drum and Bass'[PBR] — CMHG NLar
'Dusseldorf' (*japonica* hybrid) — CMHG NGdn NWbg
'Eden's Odysseus' — CMHG
'Elegans' (*simplicifolia* hybrid) — CMac CMHG
'Elisabeth' van Veen (× *arendsii*) — CMHG
ELIZABETH BLOOM ('Eliblo') (× *arendsii*) — CMHG LRHS NGdn WFar
'Ellie' (× *arendsii*) — CLil CMac CMHG CTsd ELan EPfP GQue LBuc LRHS MArl MBel MBNS MHol MPri NCth NGdn NLar NWbg SOrN SPoG WFar WTor
'Else Schluck' (× *arendsii*) — CMHG ECha
'Emden' (*japonica* hybrid) — CMHG
'Erica' (× *arendsii*) — CAby CMHG EGrI ELin GQue LRHS NEoE NLar SHar WFar
'Etna' (*japonica* hybrid) — CBcs CMHG CPud NGdn NLar SRms WFar WHoo
'Europa' (*japonica* hybrid) — CMac CMHG CoPl CPud EMor GPSL GQue LRHS MMuc MSwo NGdn NLar SPoG SRms WCAu WFar WTor
'Fanal' (× *arendsii*) ♀H7 — Widely available
'Fata Morgana' (× *arendsii* hybrid) — CMHG
§ 'Federsee' (× *arendsii*) — CBcs CMHG EBee ECha LRHS MBNS NBro NEoE NGdn WFar
§ 'Feuer' (× *arendsii*) — CMac CMHG NEoE NGdn NLar WFar
FIRE — see *A.* 'Feuer' (× *arendsii*)
'Fireberry'[PBR] (Short 'n' Sweet Series) — CMHG NLar
'Fireworks Pink' — MAsh NEoE
'Fireworks White' — NEoE XFar
'Flamingo'[PBR] (*simplicifolia* hybrid) — CMHG MBel NLar
'Freya' (× *arendsii*) — LBuc LRHS MPri
'Gertrud Brix' (× *arendsii*) — CMHG MMuc NBir NGdn
§ *glaberrima* — NBid
§ - var. *saxatilis* ♀H5 — CMHG GArf GBin GEdr WAbe WFar
- - 'Candy Floss' — NEoE
'Gladstone' (× *arendsii*) — see *A.* 'W.E. Gladstone' (*japonica* hybrid)
'Gloria' (× *arendsii*) — CMac CMHG LRHS
§ 'Gloria Purpurea' (× *arendsii*) — CMHG NQui
GLOW — see *A.* 'Glut' (× *arendsii*)
§ 'Glut' (× *arendsii*) — CMHG EBee MMuc NGdn SRms WFar

'Granat' (× *arendsii*) — CMac CMHG EGren LRHS NBir NGdn NLar
grandis BWJ 8076A — NLar
'Grete Püngel' (× *arendsii*) — ECha SRms WFar
'Happy Spirit' — EPfP LRHS LSou MHol MPri NLar WFar
'Harmony' (× *arendsii*) — CMHG
'Heart and Soul'[PBR] — CWGN MHol MPri
'Hennie Graafland' (*simplicifolia* hybrid) — CBcs CMHG EGren ELan EMor EPfP LRHS NLar SHar WFar
'Henry Noblett' — CMHG
'HonkyTonk'[PBR] — NEoE
HYACINTH — see *A.* 'Hyazinth' (× *arendsii*)
§ 'Hyazinth' (× *arendsii*) — CMHG EBee GMaP
'Icecream' (× *arendsii*) — CMHG MAsh NEoE
'Inshriach Pink' (*simplicifolia* hybrid) — CMHG GAbr NBir NLar SRms WKif
'Irene Rottseiper' (× *arendsii*) **new** — CMHG
'Irrlicht' (× *arendsii*) — CMac CMHG EBee LRHS MHol SRms WHoo WPnP
* *japonica* 'Pumila' — NBir NGdn
- var. *terrestris* — see *A. glaberrima*
'Jo Ophorst' (*davidii* hybrid) — GQue NGdn NLar WFar
'Jump and Jive'[PBR] — CMHG WFar
'Juno' — CMHG
'Key West' (*simplicifolia* hybrid) — LBom LRHS
'Koblenz' (*japonica* hybrid) — CMHG
§ 'Köln' (*japonica* hybrid) — CMHG
koreana — WCot
- B&SWJ 8611 — WCru
- B&SWJ 8680 — WCru
'Kvĕle' (× *arendsii*) — CMHG EBlo LRHS WFar
'Lakeland Mist' — CMHG
'Lara' (× *arendsii*) — CMHG
'Lilli Goos' (× *arendsii*) — CMHG
'Lola' — CMHG
'Lollipop' — CMHG NEoE SRms
longicarpa B&SWJ 6711 — WCru
'Look at Me'[PBR] (× *arendsii*) — CWGN EPfP LCro LSou NWbg SPoG WFar
'Magenta' — CMHG
'Maggie Daley' (× *arendsii*) — CMHG LSto NBro NEoE SRms
'Mainz' (*japonica* hybrid) — CMHG EBee
'Mars' (× *arendsii*) — CMHG
'Martha Illing' (× *arendsii*) **new** — CMHG
'Marwood Dark Beauty' **new** — CMHG
microphylla — CMHG
- B&SWJ 11085 — WCru
'Midnight Arrow' (*davidii* hybrid) — CMHG
'Mighty Plonie' (Mighty Series) — CMHG
'Moccachino' (× *arendsii*) — LRHS MAsh MSCN NEoE NGdn
'Moerheim Glory' (× *arendsii*) — CMHG NGdn NLar
'Moerheimii' (*thunbergii* hybrid) — CMHG
'Mojito' (× *arendsii*) — NEoE
'Mont Blanc' (× *arendsii*) — CMHG
'Montgomery' (*japonica* hybrid) ♀H7 — LSRN MBel MBNS MNrw MPri NGdn NLar SPoG
'Nemo' — CMHG
'Nikki' — CMHG NEoE NLar
§ *okuyamae* B&SWJ 10975 — WCru
'Opal' (× *arendsii*) — CMHG
OSTRICH PLUME — see *A.* 'Straussenfeder' (*thunbergii* hybrid)
'Peaches and Cream' — CMHG NBro NLar

'Peter Barrow' (*glaberrima* hybrid) — CMHG SRms
'Pink Lightning'^PBR (*simplicifolia* hybrid) — CMHG LRHS NLar WFar
PINK PEARL (× *arendsii*) — see A. 'Rosa Perle' (× *arendsii*)
'Plumet Neigeux' **new** — CMHG
'Poschka' — NEoE
'Professor van der Wielen' (*thunbergii* hybrid) — CMHG ECha NLar SRms WCAu WSpi
pumila — see A. chinensis var. *pumila*
'Purple Rain'^PBR (× *arendsii*) — CMHG EGren LBuc LRHS LSou MPri WFar XFar
'Queen of Holland' (*japonica* hybrid) — CMHG NLar
'Radius' (× *arendsii*) — CMHG EGrI ELon NGdn NLar
'Raspberry' (Short 'n' Sweet Series) — EPfP LRHS
'Red Baron' — CAby CMHG ELin NEoE
RED LIGHT — see A. 'Rotlicht' (× *arendsii*)
'Red Quin'^PBR (Mighty Series) — CMHG
'Red Sentinel' (*japonica* hybrid) — CBcs CMHG CPud CWat EPfP GMaP LRHS MArl MHol MPri NBro NEoE NGdn NLar WFar
'Rheinland' (*japonica* hybrid) ♀H7 — CBcs CLiI CMHG CPud EGren MArl NGdn NLar SAth SEND WPnP
'Rhythm and Blues'^PBR — CMHG NLar
rivularis — ESwi LSto SDix WCot
- CC 5201 — GKev
- GWJ 9366 — WCru
- PAB 9763 — LEdu
§ - var. *myriantha* — WPGP
- - BWJ 8076a — WCru
- - SICH 757 — CExl
'Robinson's Pink' — NGdn
'Rock and Roll'^PBR — NEoE NWbg
§ 'Rosa Perle' (× *arendsii*) — CMHG SMrm
'Rosalind de Wesselow' **new** — CMHG
§ × *rosea* 'Peach Blossom' — CBcs CLiI CMHG CWnw EHeP EMor LRHS MArl MSwo NBir NEoE NGdn NWbg SOrN SPoG WFar WHoo
- 'Queen Alexandra' — CMHG
§ 'Rotlicht' (× *arendsii*) — CMac CMHG NEoE NGdn NLar
'Rubella' **new** — CMHG
'Rubin' **new** — CMHG
'Salmonea' (*simplicifolia* hybrid) — CMHG
'Saxosa' — see A. *glaberrima* var. *saxatilis*
'Sheila Haxton' (*chinensis*) — CMHG
Showstar Group (× *arendsii*) — MCtn SRms
simplicifolia ♀H5 — WFar
- BRONZE ELEGANCE — see A. 'Bronce Elegans' (*simplicifolia* hybrid)
- 'Darwin's Snow Sprite' — CMac CMHG NLar WFar
- 'Isa Hall' — CMHG ECha NEoE
- 'Jacqueline' — CMHG
* - 'Nana Alba' — NEoE
- 'Praecox' — CMHG
- 'Praecox Alba' — CMHG
- 'Pretty in Pink' **new** — XFar
- 'Rose of Cimarron' — CMHG GPSL NEoE
- 'White Sensation'^PBR — CMHG ELan NLar
'Snowdrift' (× *arendsii*) — CMHG CPud CWat EGren GMaP LRHS MBNS NBir NEoE
'Solferino' (× *arendsii*) — CMHG
'Spartan' (× *arendsii*) — see A. 'Rotlicht' (× *arendsii*)
'Spinell' (× *arendsii*) — WFar WPnP
'Spotlight'^PBR — CMHG EMor LBuc LRHS MPri NEoE NLar WFar
'Sprite' (*simplicifolia* hybrid) ♀H7 — CBcs CMac CMHG CPud CToG ECha EHeP GKev GMaP GQue LRHS LShi LSto MArl MBel MPie NBid NLar NQui SDix SMad SPlb SRkn SRms WCFE WFar WHoo WKif WPnP
'Stand and Deliver' — CMHG
§ 'Straussenfeder' (*thunbergii* hybrid) ♀H7 — CMac CMHG GBin GKev GMaP GQue NBro NGdn NLar SPoG SRms WCAu WFar
'Sugar Plum' (*simplicifolia* hybrid) — CMHG NGdn
'Sugarberry'^PBR (Short 'n' Sweet Series) — CMHG EGren NLar
'Superba' — see A. *chinensis* var. *taquetii* 'Superba'
thunbergii — LRHS
- var. *congesta* B&SWJ 10961 — WCru
- var. *hachijoensis* B&SWJ 5622 — WCru
- var. *okuyamae* — see A. *okuyamae*
- var. *sikokumontanum* B&SWJ 11164 — WCru
- - B&SWJ 11534 — WCru
- var. *terrestris* B&SWJ 6125 — WCru
'Thunder and Lightning' (*chinensis* hybrid) — NEoE
'To Have and To Hold' — MNrw
'Touch of Pink' (*simplicifolia* hybrid) — CMHG
'Venus' (× *arendsii*) — ECha GMaP LSto MBNS MMuc NGdn SEND WFar
'Vesta' **new** — CMHG
'Vesuvius' (*japonica* hybrid) — CMHG NBro NLar
virescens — see A. *rivularis* var. *myriantha*
'Vision'^PBR — WFar
'Vision Inferno'^PBR (× *arendsii*) — CAby NEoE
'Vision Vulcano' (× *arendsii*) — XFar
'Walküre' (× *arendsii*) — CMHG
'Washington' (*japonica* hybrid) — CWnw EMor EPfP LRHS MSwo NGdn WCAu
§ 'W.E. Gladstone' (*japonica* hybrid) — CMHG EGren EMor LRHS NLar
§ 'Weisse Gloria' (× *arendsii*) — CLiI CMac CMHG CPud CToG ECha EMor EPfP LBom LRHS MMuc MSwo NBro SMrm WCAu WFar WTor
'Weisse Perle' (× *arendsii*) — CMHG
'White Diamond' (× *arendsii*) — WFar
WHITE GLORIA — see A. 'Weisse Gloria' (× *arendsii*)
'White Wings'^PBR (*simplicifolia* hybrid) — CMHG NLar
'Whiteberry'^PBR (Short 'n' Sweet Series) — EGren NGdn NLar
'William Reeves' (× *arendsii*) — CMHG
'Willie Buchanan' (*simplicifolia* hybrid) — CBcs CMHG CToG GBin GKev GMaP LRHS LSou MArl NCth SLee SRms WAbe WFar
(Younique Series) — MAsh
  YOUNIQUE CARMINE ('Verscarmine'^PBR)
- YOUNIQUE CERISE ('Verscerise'^PBR) — WFar
- YOUNIQUE LILAC ('Verslilac'^PBR) — EGrI ELin
- YOUNIQUE PINK ('Verspink'^PBR) — LRHS WFar
§ - YOUNIQUE RED ('Versred'^PBR) — LRHS WFar

Astrantia 121

- Younique Ruby Red	see *A.* (Younique Series) Younique Red		MPro NGdn NLar NWbg SDix SHor
- Younique Silvery Pink ('Versilverypink'PBR)	NLar WFar		SPel SRkn SRms WCAu WKif
		- 'Côte d'Azur'	WSpi
- Younique White ('Verswhite'PBR)	MAsh	- 'Cottage Herbery'	MNrw WFar
		- 'Dark Desire'	NDov WGoo
'Zuster Theresa' (× *arendsii*)	CMHG EPfP LRHS MNrw NLar	- deep red-flowered	CAby
		- 'Elaine's Pink'	WHoo

Astilboides (Saxifragaceae)

		- 'Elmblut'	WFar
§ *tabularis*	CLil CMac EAri EBee ECha ELan	- 'Florence'PBR	Widely available
	EMor EPfP EUrb GKev GMaP	- Gill Richardson Group	Widely available
	GQue LEdu MBel MNrw NGKo	- 'Gracilis'	EBee EPfP Midl SPel WFar
	NLar SHor SPlb WCAu WCFE	- 'Green Tapestry' (v)	WCot
	WFar WPnP WSpi	- 'Gwaun Valley'	WFar
		- subsp. *involucrata*	CElw MBel WGoo

Astragalus (Fabaceae)

		- - 'Barrister'	NLar
glycyphyllos	NAts WCot	- - 'Canneman'	MNrw SMHy WCot
		- - 'Jumble Hole'	NDov WFar WGoo WHoo

Astrantia ❀ (Apiaceae)

		- - 'Margery Fish'	see *A. major* subsp. *involucrata* 'Shaggy'
'Arno's Surprise' **new**	EBee	- - 'Mayroyd Memories'	NDov
'Atomic Sunburst'	GQue	- - 'Moira Reid'	CExl
bavarica	CKno LBar MBNS MHol Midl MPro	- - 'Orlando'	SPel WFar
	SHar WFar	§ - - 'Shaggy'	Widely available
'Berendien Stam'	CElw NLar WFar	- 'Snape Cottage'	WFar
'Bloody Mary'	MNrw NGdn	- 'Jade Lady'	WFar
'Buckland' ♀H7	Widely available	- 'Jitse'	MNrw WFar
'Bullseye'	MNrw	- 'Large White'	LCro SRms
'Burgundy Manor' ♀H7	CMiW CWnw ECha ELan EMor	- 'Lars'	NGdn NLar SPoG SRms WCAu WFar
	EPfP ISha LCro LRHS LSou MAvo	- 'Little Flowerer'	LBar
	MHol Midl MPri MPro NCth NLar	- 'Lola'	CDor EBee MPro SMrm
	SHar SHor SPeP WTor	§ - 'Madeleine van Bennekom'	WFar
'Bury Court'	CSpe NDov		
carniolica major	see *A. major*	- Magical Diamonds Pink ('Ruiastpi')	LBar
- 'Rubra'	GMaP WCAu WSpi		
- 'Variegata'	see *A. major* 'Sunningdale Variegated'	- 'Midnight Owl'	EBee EMor LBar MNrw NLar NSti WFar
'Censation Milano'	CWGN LRHS NLar WFar	- 'Penny's Pink'	EBee EWhm LCro Midl MNrw
'Dark Shiny Eyes'	CExl EDAr NLar		MWlw NCth SPel WFar WSpi
'Glebe Cottage Crimson' **new**	SPel	- Pink Button ('Noastone')	CMiW EGren LBar Midl MPro NCth
'Hadspen Blood'	CDor CElw CExl CWGN CWnw	- 'Pink Crush'	EBlo ECha EPfP LRHS
	EBee ECha EGren EWhm GKin	- 'Pink Joyce'	MNrw NGdn
	LCro LEdu LRHS LSRN LSto MAsh	- 'Pink Pride'	ELan EMor GPSL LBar LRHS
	MCtn MHol MMuc NBid NBir		MArl MBNS Midl MPro NLar
	NGdn SPoG SRms WCAu WCot		SHar SPel WCAu WFar WKif
	WFar WHoo WSpi		WTor XFar
'Harvington Adrian's Choice Pink'	LRHS	- 'Pink Sensation'	EBee NCth
		- 'Pink Surprise'	NLar WFar
'Helen'	NLar WFar	- 'Pisa'	NLar
helleborifolia	see *A. maxima*	- 'Primadonna'	EBee EBlo EDAr EMor EPfP GMaP
'Larch Cottage Clear Pink'	NLar WFar		LRHS MCtn NLar SPlb SRms
'Larch Cottage Magic'	WFar	- 'Princesse Sturdza'	WFar
'Madeleine'	see *A. major* 'Madeleine van Bennekom'	- 'Purple Joyce'	MNrw NGdn
		- 'Red Joyce'	IPot LBar LSto WCAu
§ *major*	Widely available	- 'Red Promise'	IPot LBar
- 'Abbey Road'PBR	CDor CExl ELan EGren LBar LBom	- 'Reverse Sunningdale Variegated' (v)	WFar
	LRHS MHol Midl NGdn NLar SHor		
	SRms WFar XFar	- 'Rosa Lee'	CElw NLar
I - 'Alba'	CBcs EGren GKev GMaP LRHS	- var. *rosea*	NGdn SHar WCAu WFar
	MCtn MHed MSwo NBir NGdn	- George's form	EPPr WFar
	NPer WFar WSpi	- 'Rosensinfonie'	CBWd CFis EBee GJos GMaP GPSL
- 'Apple Blossom'	NDov		LBar LSou MCtn MHer NBro StAn
- 'April Love'	LBar LCro Midl MNrw		WHoo WPnP
- subsp. *biebersteinii*	NBir WFar	§ - 'Rubra'	EGren EPfP GKin LCro MGos
- 'Bo-Ann'	NLar WFar		MHed MSwo NBir NPer SRms
- 'Can Candy' ♀H6	MNrw		WCAu WTre
- 'Capri'PBR	IPot LBar NCth NLar	- 'Ruby Cloud'	EGren EMor EPfP LRHS NBro NGdn
- Cerise Button ('Noastwo')	EGren IPot LBar LSou Midl MPro		NLar WFar WSpi
	NCth NLar WHil	- Ruby Flame ('Hyrume')	LBar MPro
- 'Claret'	CBcs CDor CEnd CMac ECha	- 'Ruby Giant'	EBee GKin LBar NSti WHil
	EGren EGrI ELan EPfP GKev GMaP	- 'Ruby Wedding'	Widely available
	GQue LCro LRHS LSto MHol Midl	- Sparkling Stars Series	Midl

- - Sparkling Stars Pink ('Westarpin')	LBar LCro LRHS LSou MAvo MHol Midl MNrw MPri NCth NEoE NLar SMrm XFar	
- - Sparkling Stars Red ('Westarr')	IBal LBar LBom LRHS MPri MPro NCth SMrm WHil XFar	
- - Sparkling Stars White ('Westarwit')	CWCL LBar LSou MPri NCth SMrm XFar	
- 'Star of Beauty'^PBR	EGren ELan EMor EPfP LBar LEdu LRHS MHol MHtn MNrw MPri MPro NLar NSti SPoG SRkn SRms WFar WSpi	
- 'Star of Billion'^PBR	CWnw EBee EGren ELan EMor EPfP LBar LBom LRHS MHol Midl MNrw MPri MPro NLar SOrN SPoG SRkn WCAu WCot WFar	
- 'Star of Fire'^PBR	CWGN EMor LRHS Midl NLar SPel WFar	
- 'Star of Love'^PBR	CKno CWCL CWnw EBee EMor EPfP LRHS MHol Midl MPri MPro NWbg SOrN SPoG WFar WSpi	
- 'Star of Magic'^PBR (v)	CWGN LRHS NCth SPoG WCot	
- 'Star of Royals'^PBR	Midl SPoG WFar	
- 'Starburst'	WFar	
- 'Sue Barnes' (v)	WFar	
§ - 'Sunningdale Variegated' (v) ♀^H7	CBro CDor CElw CExl CWGN EBee ECha EWhm GKin GMaP GQue LShi LSto NBid NBir NGdn NLar NSti NWbg SPeP SPlb SPoG SRms WCAu WCot WFar	
- 'Titoki Point'	WCot	
- 'Venice'^PBR	CBcs CDor CKno CWGN EBee EGren EGrI ELon EPfP LRHS LSou MAvo MHol MHtn Midl MNrw MPro NLar NSti SPad SPoG SRms WCAu WCot WFar WPnP WSpi	
§ maxima ♀^H7	CMiW CSpe EBee ECha EDAr ELon EMor GAbr GMaP LRHS LSto MBel NBid NSti SPlb SRms WCAu WFar	
- 'Mark Fenwick'	NBir	
I - 'Rosea'	CDor MNrw NGdn	
'Millwood Crimson'	CMiW	
'Miss Elly'	LBar	
'Moulin Rouge'^PBR	Widely available	
§ 'Mrs MacGregor'	MNrw WFar	
'Old Warwickshire Pink'	see A. 'Mrs MacGregor'	
'Purple Happiness'^PBR	LBar Midl	
'Queen's Children'	CDor	
'Rainbow'	NLar WFar	
'Roma'^PBR ♀^H7	Widely available	
rubra	see A. *major* 'Rubra'	
'Ruby Star'^PBR	CDor EMor EPfP GMaP MHol Midl MNrw NLar WCAu WCot WFar WSpi	
'Sheila's Red'	MNrw	
'Snow Star'^PBR	EBee ELan EMor EPfP LRHS MAvo Midl MNrw MPro NCth NLar SHar SPel XFar	
'Star of Flame'^PBR	EBee EMor	
'Star of Heaven'	NLar	
'Star of Passion'^PBR	EBee ELan EMor EPfP ISha LBar LBuc LRHS Midl MPro WFar	
'Star of Treasure'^PBR	ELan EMor EPfP MPro NLar	
'Supernova'	NDov	
'Superstar'^PBR	CDor CWCL EBee ELan EMor EPfP GElm IPot LBar MArl MBel MHol Midl MMuc MNrw NDov SPel WCAu WCot WFar WSpi WTor	
'Warren Hills'	GMaP WFar	
'Washfield'	EGrI GPSL NDov SPel WFar	
'White Angel'	CKno CWGN EBee LBar Midl MPro NCth	

Astrodaucus (Apiaceae)
littoralis — WPGP

Astrolepis (Pteridaceae)
sinuata — LRHS MAsh SPlb WCot

Astroloba ❀ (Asphodelaceae)
spiralis — CPic

Astrophytum (Cactaceae)
myriostigma ♀^H2 — LBom SBig SPad

Asyneuma (Campanulaceae)
campanuloides — GKev
limonifolium — GKev
§ *prenanthoides* — SMrm
pulvinatum — SPlb WAbe

Asystasia (Acanthaceae)
bella — see *Mackaya bella*

Athamanta (Apiaceae)
cretensis — GKev SPhx
turbith — CSpe EWld WSpi
- subsp. *haynaldii* — CMiW
vestina — SPhx

Athanasia (Asteraceae)
§ *parviflora* — SPlb

Atherosperma (Atherospermataceae)
moschatum — CExl EBee WPGP

Athrotaxis (Cupressaceae)
cupressoides — WJur
selaginoides — CAco WJur

Athyrium ❀ (Woodsiaceae)
badium **new** — WPGP
'Branford Beauty' — CLAP ISha LEdu
'Branford Rambler' — CLAP ISha LEdu NBro SPel
filix-femina — CBcs CLil CMac CPud CWCL ECha EGren EHeP ELan EMor GMaP ISha LBom LCro LRHS LSRN LSto MHtn MMuc NBro SHor SRms SRot WCav WCot WPnP WShi
§ - subsp. *angustum* ♀^H6 — NGdn
- - f. *rubellum* 'Lady in Red' ♀^H6 — CDor CLAP CSta EBee EGrI ELan EMor EUrb LCro LEdu LRHS MAvo MGos NAlc NLar NWbg SPoG WCot XFar
- 'Clarissimum Jones' — WCot
- 'Crispum Grandiceps Kaye' — NGdn
- Cristatum Group — CLAP ELan LSRN NGdn WCot
- 'Dre's Dagger' — CLAP CMiW EUrb LCro LEdu NBro SPoG WPGP
- 'Frizelliae' ♀^H6 — CDor CElw CLAP CMiW CSta EBee ELan EMor EUrb GMaP ISha LBom LEdu LRHS NAlc NLar SMHy SPlb SPoG SRms SRot WCAu WCot WFar WGwG WPnP
- 'Frizelliae Cristatum' — CLAP
- 'Howardii' — NBro
- 'Minutissimum' — EBee EBlo LRHS SPel WCot
- 'Plumosum Axminster' — CLAP WCot WFar
- 'Plumosum Cristatum Drueryi' — WCot
- 'Plumosum Divaricatum' — WCot

Aubrieta 123

- 'Plumosum Percristatum'	WCot
- RED STEM	see *A. filix-femina* 'Rotstiel'
§ - 'Rotstiel'	CLAP ELan NBro NLar WCot
- 'Setigerum Cristatum'	WFar
- 'Vernoniae' ♀H6	CLAP
- 'Vernoniae Cristatum'	CLAP
- 'Victoriae'	CDor EBee ELan EMor GMaP LCro LEdu LRHS NAlc NBid NLar WFar WPGP WSpi
- 'Victoriae' seedling	EWld
- aff. 'Victoriae'	CLAP CSta ISha MAsh
- Victoriae Group	see *A. filix-femina* subsp. *angustum*
'Ghost' ♀H5	CDor CLAP EBee EMor LEdu MAsh NAlc NBro NLar SPel SPlb SPoG WCot
goeringianum 'Pictum'	see *A. niponicum* var. *pictum*
minimum	EMor LCro LEdu NBro NLar WCot WPGP
niponicum	CLAP CLil CPud EGren SPel
- 'Crested Surf'	EMor LRHS
- 'Godzilla'	CLAP LEdu LRHS NBro WPGP
- f. *metallicum*	see *A. niponicum* var. *pictum*
§ - var. *pictum* ♀H5	Widely available
- - 'Apple Court'	CLAP EBee EMor ESwi ISha LEdu LRHS MAsh NBro SPel WPGP
- - 'Burgundy Lace'	CAby CDor CLAP CMiW CSta EAri EBee EGrI EMor ESwi MHer MPnt MPro NAlc NBro NLar NWbg SMrm WCot WFar
- - 'Cristatoflabellatum'	EBlo LRHS
- - 'Pearly White'	ISha LEdu LRHS MAsh NBro SPel
- - 'Pewter Lace'	CDor CLAP CMiW CSta EBee EMor ISha LEdu NAlc NBro NLar SPad SPeP WFar WKif WSpi
- - 'Red Beauty'	Widely available
- - 'Regal Red'	CLAP ISha MAsh NAlc
- - 'Silver Falls' ♀H5	CBcs CLAP CLil CSta EBee EGren EMor ESwi ISha LCro LEdu LRHS LWaG MAsh NAlc NBro NLar SMad SPoG WCot WFar
- - 'Ursula's Red'	CElw CMiW CSta EBee EGrI ELan EMor LCro MHol NLar SPel SPoG WCAu WCot WPGP
'Ocean's Fury'	CLAP SPoG WCot WFar
otophorum ♀H4	WPGP
- var. *okanum* ♀H4	Widely available
palustre	WCot
pycnocarpon	LRHS
vidalii	CLAP CSta EGrI EMor GMaP LEdu MHer NBro NLar SMad

Atocion (Caryophyllaceae)

§ *armeria*	WHil
- 'Electra'	CSpe CTtf WCot
§ *compactum*	GJos
§ *rupestre*	NDov

Atragene see *Clematis*

Atriplex (Amaranthaceae)

canescens	CAgr EPPr
halimus	CAgr CBcs CCoa CWnw ECha EPPr LRHS LShi MEar NLar SEND SPlb WCot
- 'Cascais'	WCot
- 'Limelight' (v)	ECha EPPr LShi
hortensis	ENfk
* - var. *purpurea*	MCtn
- var. *rubra*	CBgR CSpe ELan MNHC SPhx SRms
nummularia 'Silver Holly'	SMad
'Scarlet Emperor'	MCtn

Atropa (Solanaceae)

mandragora	see *Mandragora officinarum*

aubergine see AGM Vegetables Section

Aubrieta (Brassicaceae)

albomarginata	see *A.* 'Argenteovariegata'
§ 'Argenteovariegata' (v) ♀H6	EPfP
(Audrey Series) 'Audrey Blue'	SRGP
- 'Audrey Light Blue'	LCro
- 'Audrey Purple Shades'	EGren LCro
- 'Audrey Red'	LCro
- 'Audrey Red and Purple'	LRHS
- 'Audrey Sky Blue'	GAbr LCro
§ 'Aureovariegata' (v) ♀H6	NPer
(Axcent Series)	EPfP WTor
AXCENT ANTIQUE ROSE ('Audelanro')	
- AXCENT BURGUNDY ('Abrz0004'PBR)	EPfP GBin LCro LRHS MPri WTor
- AXCENT DEEP PURPLE ('Audelpur')	EPfP LCro LRHS
- AXCENT DEEP RED ('Abrz0001')	SRms
- AXCENT GLACIER LIGHT BLUE	see *A.* (Axcent Series) AXCENT LIGHT BLUE
§ - AXCENT LIGHT BLUE ('Abrz0002'PBR)	EPfP LCro LRHS
- AXCENT LILAC ('Audelip')	EPfP LCro SPoG
- AXCENT WHITE	EPfP LCro Pro
BLAUE SCHÖNHEIT	see *A.* 'Blue Beauty'
'Blaumeise'	EGren LRHS MHol WFar
§ 'Blue Beauty'	NLar
'Blue Cascade' (Cascade Series)	EGrI GBin GMaP LShi SPlb SPoG SRms
'Blue Whale'	LBuc NLar SRms
'Bressingham Pink' (d) ♀H6	SRms
'Bressingham Red'	EBee EPfP SRms
Cascade Series	MAsh MCtn SPoG
× *cultorum*	SVic
deltoidea	StAn
- Variegata Group (v)	EGren MAsh MHol WFar
'Doctor Mules' ♀H6	SRms
'Doctor Mules Variegata' (v)	ELan EPfP LRHS MHer MPro NLar SPoG SRot WIce
double pink-flowered (d)	EGren ELan MHol
'Elsa Lancaster'	EPot
(Florado Series) FLORADO ROSE RED ('Floag17361')	EPfP LRHS
- FLORADO WHITE ('Floauq1618')	MPro
glabrescens	EPot SPlb WAbe
'Gloria'	EPot NLar
'Golden King'	see *A.* 'Aureovariegata'
gracilis 'Kitte'	ELan MHer NLar SPoG SRms WTor
- 'Kitte Blue'	EGren ELan EPfP LBuc LCro LRHS MPri MPro SPoG SRms WIce
- 'Kitte Blue Blush Bicolour'	ELan
- 'Kitte Purple'	ELan SPoG
- 'Kitte Rose'	EPfP LBuc SPoG
- 'Kitte Rose Blush Bicolour'	ELan
- 'Kitte Rose Red'	ELan
- 'Kitte White'	EPfP
'Hamburger Stadtpark'	ELan EPfP GMaP LRHS SRms
'Hendersonii'	WFar
'Ida'	WIce
JUST SPRING BLUE ('Yataub43')	EGren LBar MPro
JUST SPRING RED ('Yataub17')	EGren LBar LRHS MPro
KATIE MIX	EGren

'Leichtlinii'	WFar
'Lilac Cascade' (Cascade Series)	SPoG SRms
'Purple Cascade' (Cascade Series)	GBin GJos LCro LShi LSRN SPlb SPoG SRms WFar
'Purple Charm'	SRms
'Red Carpet'	MAsh SRms WIce
'Red Cascade' (Cascade Series) ♀H6	EGrI ELan EPfP GAbr GBin LSRN SPlb SPoG
REGADO WHITE ('Loauq1262') (Regado Series)	LRHS LShi
Royal Series ♀H6	SHar
- 'Royal Blue'	ELan MPro NLar SRms WFar
- 'Royal Lilac'	WFar
- 'Royal Red'	ELan GBin MCtn MPro SRms WCav
- 'Royal Violet'	ELan WFar
'Silberrand' (v)	ECha LBuc
'Snow Maiden'	SPoG
'Somerfield Silver'	ELan EPfP
'Somerford Lime' (v)	EBee ELan EPfP SRms
'Valerie'	EWes
'Westacre Gold' (v)	EGren EWes LBar MHol MSCN WFar
'Whitewell Gem'	MCtn

Aucuba ✿ (*Garryaceae*)

chlorascens	CExl
filicauda B&SWJ 11820	WCru
- B&SWJ 11826	WCru
himalaica	CExl
- var. dolichophylla	CDTJ CExl EUrb GGro IArd SBrt
japonica	CCVT CDoC EHeP NLar SEWo WCru WFar
- B&SWJ 14602	WCru
- 'Angelon' (f/v)	LRHS
- var. borealis CWJ 12898 (f)	WCru
- 'Clent Wortley Hall' (m)	WCFE
- 'Crassifolia' (m)	EPfP SArc SMad
- 'Crotonifolia' (f/v) ♀H5	CAco CBcs CBrac CCVT CDoC CEnd CSBt EBee EGren EHeP ELan ELon EPfP GArf IBal LCro LRHS LSRN LSto MGos MMuc MPri NLar SArc SBig SEND SPlb SPoG WCFE WFar
- - (m/v)	CMac MAsh SDix SRms
- 'Dentata' (f)	SRms WCru WHtc
- 'February Star' (f/v)	ESwi SDix
- 'Golden Girl' (v)	CBrac CEnd LRHS MAsh Midl WHtc
- 'Golden King' (m/v) ♀H5	CAco CCVT CDoC CMac CSBt CWnw EBee EGren ELan ELon EPfP LBom LRHS LSto MAsh MGos NLar WFar
- 'Golden Spangles' (f/v)	CBcs EPfP
- 'Leucocarpa' (f)	ELon
- f. longifolia	CMac EHeP SArc SBig WCru
- - 'Salicifolia' (f) ♀H5	EBee EHeP ELon EPfP ESwi SMad WCru WFar WPGP
- 'Maculata' misapplied	see A. japonica 'Variegata'
- 'Marmorata' (v)	MAsh WFar
- 'Mr Goldstrike' (m/v)	CEnd EPfP LRHS MAsh MPri WFar
- PEPPER POT ('Shilpot') (m/v) ♀H5	EPfP LRHS MAsh WCFE
- 'Pepperspot' PBR (m/v)	EHeP EUrb LCro
- 'Picturata' (m/v)	CMac ELan ELon ESwi LCro LRHS MAsh NLar SEND WFar
- 'Rozannie' (f) ♀H5	CBcs CBrac CDoC CEnd CMac EBee EGren EHeP ELan ELon EPfP GArf LBom LCro LRHS LSRN LSto MAsh MBlu MGos NLar NLit SAth SBig SEND SPoG WFar
- 'Sulphurea Marginata' (f/v)	CMac CMCN ESwi NLar WFar
§ - 'Variegata' (f/v)	CBrac CCVT CMac CSBt EBee EGren EHeP ELan ELon EPfP LBuc LRHS LSto MAsh MGos MPri NHrt NLit SOrN SRms WCha WFar WHtc
omeiensis	CBcs CDTJ CExl CMCN
- B&SWJ 2864	ESwi WCru
- BWJ 8048	WCru
- L 614	WPGP

Aulax (*Proteaceae*)

cancellata	SPlb

Auranticarpa (*Pittosporaceae*)

§ rhombifolia	WJur

Aurinia (*Brassicaceae*)

§ saxatilis ♀H5	ELan EPfP MMuc SHar SPlb WFar
- 'Citrina' ♀H5	ECha EGrI SRms
- 'Compacta'	WIce
- GOLD BALL	see A. saxatilis 'Goldkugel'
- 'Gold Cushion'	EPfP LRHS
- 'Gold Dust'	MCtn SRms
§ - 'Goldkugel'	EGren SPoG SRms WFar
- 'Sulphurea'	GKev WFar
- 'Variegata' (v)	SPoG SRms

Austrocedrus (*Cupressaceae*)

§ chilensis	CAco

Austrocylindropuntia (*Cactaceae*)

§ cylindrica	CBlu SBig
subulata	SEND
§ verschaffeltii	NPlm
§ vestita	NPlm

Avena (*Poaceae*)

candida	see Helictotrichon sempervirens

Avenula see *Helictotrichon*

Averrhoa (*Oxalidaceae*)

carambola (F)	WJur

avocado see *Persea americana*

Azalea see *Rhododendron*

Azara ✿ (*Salicaceae*)

dentata	CBcs CMac ELan WFar WPav
- 'Variegata'	see A. integrifolia 'Variegata'
integrifolia	WPav
§ - 'Variegata' (v)	LRHS
lanceolata	ELan LRHS WPav
microphylla ♀H4	CBcs CBct CDoC CMac EBee ELan ELon EPfP EUrb GKev LSRN MMuc NQui SArc SEND SPlb WFar WPav WPGP WSpi
* - 'Albovariegata' (v)	WPav
- 'Gold Edge' (v)	MSwo WPav
- 'Variegata' (v)	CBcs CCoa CMac CTsd EBee ELan EPfP EUrb GKev LSto NLar SEND SPoG WFar WPav
* patagonica	MBlu WPav
petiolaris	WPav
- G&P 5026	WPGP
serrata ♀H4	CBcs CCoa CEnd CMCN CoPl CSde CTsd EPfP EUrb LCro LRHS LSto MMuc NLar SDix SEND SPoG SRms SVen WFar WKif WPav WSpi

uruguayensis GBin WPav

Azolla (Salviniaceae)
filiculoides Prohibited invasive. See Conservation and the Environment, p.42

Azorella (Apiaceae)
filamentosa EPot GEdr
glebaria misapplied see *A. trifurcata*
glebaria A. Gray see *Bolax gummifer*
gummifer see *Bolax gummifer*
lycopodioides SPlb WAbe
patagonica SPlb
* *speciosa* LRHS
§ *trifurcata* EDAr GAbr GKev LRHS MMuc NBir SPlb WAbe
- 'Nana' ECha GArf GEdr GMaP

Azorina (Campanulaceae)
§ *vidalii* MCtn SPlb WFar

B

Babiana (Iridaceae)
fragrans CPbh
nana XFar
patersoniae SPlb
stricta ♀H2 GKev XFar
- Kew hybrids EGren
- 'Purple Star' CExl
thunbergii CPbh
tubulosa GKev

Baccharis (Asteraceae)
genistelloides CWnw SEND
halimifolia Prohibited invasive. See Conservation and the Environment, p.42
patagonica MMuc SArc SVen

Backhousia (Myrtaceae)
citriodora MHer

Bacopa (Plantaginaceae)
caroliniana ELin
monnieri ELin
'Snowflake' see *Chaenostoma cordatum* 'Snowflake'

Baeckea (Myrtaceae)
linifolia SEle SPlb
virgata SPlb

Baldellia (Alismataceae)
ranunculoides CBen CLil CPud CWat ELin EWat WMAq

Ballota (Lamiaceae)
acetabulosa see *Pseudodictamnus acetabulosus*
'All Hallow's Green' see *Marrubium bourgaei* var. *bourgaei* 'All Hallows Green'
nigra MHer MHoo NMir SRms
- 'Upper Moor' WCot
pseudodictamnus see *Pseudodictamnus mediterraneus*

Baloskion (Restionaceae)
§ *tetraphyllum* ♀H3 CPbh CTsd SPlb SPoG
- 'Cornish Gold' (v) CPbh

Balsamita see *Tanacetum*

Bambusa (Poaceae)
bambos SPlb
pubescens see *Dendrocalamus strictus*

banana see *Ensete, Musa*

Banksia ✿ (Proteaceae)
ashbyi CPbh
attenuata CPbh
blechnifolia CPbh
caleyi CPbh
canei SPlb
coccinea CPbh
elderiana CPbh
ericifolia CPbh
- var. *macrantha* SPlb
formosa CPbh SPlb
'Giant Candles' CPbh
grandis CPbh SPlb
§ *heliantha* SPlb
integrifolia CBcs CDTJ CPbh LRHS SEle SPlb
marginata EUrb LRHS SEle SPlb
media CPbh SPlb
menziesii CPbh
- shrubby CPbh
oblongifolia SPlb
paludosa SPlb
petiolaris CPbh
praemorsa CPbh
quercifolia CPbh
repens CPbh
robur SPlb
seminuda SPlb
serrata CPbh LRHS SPlb
speciosa SPlb
spinulosa CPbh
- 'Birthday Candles' CPbh SEle
- var. *collina* CPbh SPlb
- var. *spinulosa* CPbh
victoriae CPbh
violacea SPlb

Baptisia (Fabaceae)
§ *alba* EBee EGren ELan EMor GKev LSto MBel MNrw NSti StAn
- var. *alba* WCAu
§ - var. *macrophylla* LRHS MNrw
'American Goldfinch' EBee LRHS NCth
australis ♀H7 Widely available
- 'Blueberry Sundae' CDor CSpe CWGN CWnw EBee
  (Decadence Series) ECha ELan EMor GMaP LEdu LRHS LSou NCth NWbg SHar SMrm
- 'Caspian Blue' CExl EPfP GKev LEdu MArl MHol MMrt MNrw StAn WHil WHoo
- 'Exaltata' ♀H7 EBee NLar WCot
- var. *minor* CSpe MBel SPhx
- 'Nelson's Navy' SMHy
× *bicolor* 'Starlite' CDor
  (Prairieblues Series)
'Blue Bubbly' (Decadence LBar
  Deluxe Series)
'Brownie Points' EBee
'Burgundy Blast' EBee LBar LRHS NCth
'Carolina Moonlight' CBcs EBee ECha NSti
'Chocolate Chip' EBee SHar SPeP
'Dark Chocolate' NClf NWbg WHil
  (Decadence Series)

Baptisia

'Dutch Chocolate' (Decadence Series)	CBcs CDor CWGN EBee ELan ELon EPfP ERCP EWes LBar LCro LRHS MNrw NSti SDix SHar SMrm SPad SPel SPoG WCot WPGP
'Grape Taffy'	LCro
'Indigo Spires'	EBee LRHS MBel WCot
lactea	see *B. alba* var. *macrophylla*
'Lemon Meringue' (Decadence Series)	CBcs CDor CWGN EBee ECha ELan EMor EPfP ESwi GMaP LBar LCro LRHS MAvo MNrw NCth SDix SMrm SPoG WCot
leucantha	see *B. alba* var. *macrophylla*
'Nachthemel'	ECha IPot
pendula	see *B. alba*
'Pink Lemonade' (Decadence Deluxe Series)	EBee LBar LCro LRHS NWbg WCot
'Pink Truffles'^{PBR} (Decadence Deluxe Series)	EBee ECha GMaP LBar LCro LSou MMrt NCth NSti NWbg WCot
'Plum Rosy'	LBar
'Purple Smoke'	CBcs CExl CSpe EBee ECha EGren GKev LCro MBel SPel WPGP
'Solar Flare' (Prairieblues Series)	MBel SHar SMad WHil
'Sparkling Sapphires'^{PBR} (Decadence Series)	LBar LRHS NCth
sphaerocarpa	EBee SPlb
tinctoria	CAgr
'Vanilla Cream' (Decadence Series)	CWnw EBee EMor EPfP LBar LCro LEdu MBel NSti NWbg SMrm WCot
× *varicolor*	CWGN EBee LCro LRHS WCot
'Cherries Jubilee' (Decadence Series)	
- 'Twilite' (Prairieblues Series)	EBee GMaP SPel WCAu
'Violet Dusk'	LBar

Barbarea (Brassicaceae)

praecox	see *B. verna*
§ *verna*	CWRo MCtn MEar MHer SVic WKit
vulgaris 'Variegata' (v)	EPPr NBro WKit
- 'Variegated Winter Cream' (v)	EPfP IDun

Barleria (Acanthaceae)

obtusa	EShb
suberecta	see *Dicliptera sericea*

Barnardia (Asparagaceae)

japonica	WHil

Barosma see *Agathosma*

Bartlettina (Asteraceae)

sordida	CBct CExl EAri EShb EUrb

Basella (Basellaceae)

alba	CAgr CWRo MCtn

Bashania (Poaceae)

§ *fargesii*	MMuc MWht SEND
I *qingchengshanensis*	MWht

basil see *Ocimum basilicum*

Bauhinia (Fabaceae)

alba hort.	see *B. variegata*
brachycarpa	WJur
natalensis	SPlb
purpurea L.	SPlb
§ *variegata*	CAco CSpe
yunnanensis	MCtn SPlb

Baumea see *Machaerina*

bay see *Laurus nobilis*

beans see AGM Vegetables Section

Beaucarnea (Asparagaceae)

recurvata ♀^{H1c}	CDoC EGren LCro MCtn NHrt SPad SPlb WFar

Beaufortia (Myrtaceae)

squarrosa	SEle SPlb

Beaumontia (Apocynaceae)

grandiflora	MCtn

Bedfordia (Asteraceae)

linearis	SPlb

Beesia (Ranunculaceae)

§ *calthifolia*	CDor CDTJ CSpe EBee ESwi EWes EWld GEdr LCro LEdu WCot WCru
- DJHC 98447	CExl
deltophylla misapplied	see *B. calthifolia*

beetroot see AGM Vegetables Section

Begonia ✿ (Begoniaceae)

from Cally Gardens (C)	ESwi
from Siam	ESwi GGro
from Taiwan	GGro
'Abel Carrière' (R)	WDib
aconitifolia (C)	EAri EShb
ALASKA CREEK ('Krbelac01'^{PBR}) (Beleaf Series) (R)	LBom WFar
albopicta 'Rosea' (C)	CSpe EShb WDib WFar
AMAZON RIVER ('Krbelar01'^{PBR}) (Beleaf Series) (R)	WFar
AMOUR ('Yamour') (Million Kisses Series)	MBros
amphioxus	LBom NTro
'Angelique' (T/d)	XFar
aff. *angularis*	SPlb
§ *annulata* ♀^{H1b}	LEdu WPGP
- HWJK 2424	ESwi GGro WCru WFar
- 'Karma Khonoma'	LEdu WFar WPGP
'Arctic Breeze'^{PBR} (Beleaf Series) (R)	LBom
'Argenteo-guttata'	EShb
'Aya' (C)	WDib
balansana	CBct
Balcony Series (T/d)	XFar
- 'Balcony Pink' (T/d)	XFar
baviensis BWJ 15651	GGro WCru
'Beatrice Haddrell'	CBct WFar
BELLECONIA SOFT ORANGE ('Innbellpea'^{PBR}) (Belleconia Series)	ELan
'Benitochiba' (R) ♀^{H1b}	CBct CDTJ CExl CSpe CTsd ESwi GGro SPoG WDib
'Bethlehem Star'	WDib
'Betulia Double Red' (d) (Bewitched Series)	LAma MPri
'Bewitched Night Owl' (R) **new**	
- 'Bewitched White' (R) **new**	MPri
'Black Fang' ♀^{H1b}	WDib

Begonia

'Black Knight' (R)	WDib
'Blackberry Swirl' (R)	WDib
'Blue Sky Appleblossom'	MBros
boliviensis 'Firecracker'	WDib
- 'San Francisco' (T)	XFar
- 'Santa Barbara' (T)	XFar
- 'Santa Cruz' (T)	XFar
BONFIRE ('Nzcone'^PBR) ♀H1b (T)	SPoG
'Bouton de Rose' (T)	LAma
bowerae LIME FEVER ('Krbellf01') **new**	ESwi
burkillii	GGro
'Candy Floss'	see *B. labordei* 'Candy Floss'
carolineifolia ♀H1b	EShb ESwi SIvy WDib WFar
'Cascade Pink' (Cascade Series) (T/d)	XFar
- 'Cascade Red' (T/d)	XFar
- 'Cascade Yellow' (T/d)	XFar
'Casey Corwin' (R)	WDib
cathayana B&SWJ 8315	WCru
§ *chapaensis* HWJ 642	WCru
CHARDONNAY ('Inbegchard'^PBR) (T)	ELan
'China Curl' (R) ♀H1b	WDib
chitoensis	GGro WFar
- B&SWJ 1954	WCru
× *chungii* DJHT 99168	GGro
chuyunshanensis	CExl
- PB 07-1111	GGro WFar
circumlobata	GGro
- SHANGRI-LA ('Monshayne') (Tectonic Series)	WPGP
'Cleopatra' ♀H1b	WDib WFar
cleopatrae **new**	NTro
'Comte de Lesseps' (C)	WDib
conchifolia **new**	WFar
- f. *rubrimacula*	WFar
'Connee Boswell' ♀H1c	WDib
'Crestabruchii'	ESwi WCot
Crispa Marginata Group white-flowered (T)	XFar
- yellow-flowered (T)	XFar
cucullata var. *arenosicola* (S)	EPPr ESwi MCtn SEND
'Curly Cherry Mint' (R) **new**	MPri
'Curly Fireflush' (R) ♀H1b	WDib WFar
'Dark Eyes' (C)	WDib
'David Blais' (R) ♀H1b	WDib
'Dawnal Meyer' (C)	WDib
I 'De Elegans'	WDib
Devil Series (S)	EGren
- 'Devil Rose' (S)	EGren
- 'Devil White' (S)	EGren
- DEVIL'S DELIGHT (mixed) (S)	EGren
'Dewdrop' (R) ♀H1b	WDib
'Dibleys Pink Showers' ♀H1b	WDib
discolor	see *B. grandis* subsp. *evansiana*
'Doublet White' (Doublet Series) (S/d)	LAma
'Doublonia Rose' (Doublonia Series) (S/d)	LAma
'Down Home' (W&O)	WDib
DRAGON WING RED ('Bepared'^PBR) ♀H1b	MBros
§ *dregei* (T) ♀H1b	CSpe EShb SPlb
edulis **new**	WPGP
elatior 'Carmen'	MPri
emeiensis	CBct CSpe EBee EPPr ESwi WFar WJun WPGP
- DJHC 98479	EWld
'Emerald Giant' (R)	WDib
'Erythrophylla' ♀H1b	EShb LWaG
'Escargot' (R) ♀H1b	LBom LCro WDib
'Evening Glow'^PBR (Beleaf Series) (R)	LBom
fangii BWJ 16171 from northern Vietnam	WCru
ferox **new**	WFar
Fimbriata Group pink-flowered (T/d)	XFar
- red-flowered (T/d)	XFar
- white-flowered (T/d)	XFar
- yellow-flowered (T/d)	XFar
'Fireworks' (R) ♀H1b	CTsd WDib
'Flo'Belle Moseley' (C)	WDib
§ *foliosa* var. *miniata* ♀H1b	CBct CTsd EWld SDix SIvy WCot WDib WFar
formosana f. *albo-maculata* B&SWJ 6881	WCru
Fragrant Falls Improved Series (T)	SPoG
fuchsioides	see *B. foliosa* var. *miniata*
'Funky Pink' (Funky Series) (T/d)	MPri
fusca	ESwi WPGP
GARDEN ANGEL BLUSH ('Tnbeggab') (Garden Angel Series)	WCot
'Glowing Embers' ♀H1b	LBuc MBros MPri SPoG WFar
'Golden Balcony' (Balcony Series) (T/d)	XFar
grandis	SBig
- PB 03-718 (T)	WFar
§ - subsp. *evansiana* ♀H2	CAby CBct CElw CMiW CTsd CWal EAri EBee ELan EPfP EPPr EShb EUrb EWld ISha LEdu SBig SDix SEND SIvy SPlb WCot WCru WFar WJun WOld
- - B&SWJ 11188	WCru
- - var. *alba* hort. ♀H2	CAby CBlu CDor CMiW EAri EBee ELon EPPr EShb ESwi EWld LEdu SDix SPel WCot WJun WPGP
- - - CMB JP2143	GGro
- - 'Bells and Whistles'	EAri EPPr ESwi WPGP
- - 'Claret Jug'	CExl EAri EPPr ESwi
- - 'Pink Parasol'	ESwi
- - pink-flowered	WFar
- - 'Simsii'	WFar
- - 'Sublime'	LEdu WFar
- 'Heron's Pirouette'	EAri EPPr ESwi GGro WCru WFar
- subsp. *holostyla* 'Nnjiang Silver'	EAri EPPr GGro SPlb WFar WPGP
- 'Sapporo'	EAri EPPr ESwi GGro SBeP SChr WCru WFar
§ - subsp. *sinensis* (T)	EUrb WFar
- - BWJ 8011A (T)	GGro WFar
§ - - 'Red Undies'	CBct CExl EAri ESwi GGro WCru WFar
- - 'Snowpop'	CExl EAri EBee EPPr ESwi GGro SBeP WFar WPGP
- - aff. var. *villosa* W&O 9305	GGro
- aff. subsp. *sinensis* BWJ 8133 (T)	GGro WCru WFar
'Green Gecko' (C)	WDib
'Green Gold' (R) ♀H1b	WDib WFar
'Green Sparkles' (R)	WDib
griffithii	see *B. annulata*
'Gryphon'	LSou WFar
§ *guaniana* 'Pink Lady'	GGro WCru
hatacoa	LEdu

Begonia

- var. *meisneri* — GGro
- 'Silver' — GGro WDib
- Heaven Series (S) — EGren
- 'Heaven White' (S) — MBros
- 'Helen Teupel' (R) — WDib
- *hemsleyana* — GGro
- (Hiemalis Group) — MPri
  - 'Catrin' **new**
- – Dreams Esmay Peach — MPri
  - ('Bkpbeesm') (Indoor Dreams Series) **new**
- – Glory Bicolour **new** — MPri
- – MacaRose ('Bkpbemcrs') — MPri
  - (Garden Dreams Series) **new**
- – MacaRouge ('Bkpbemcrg') — MPri
  - (Garden Dreams Series) **new**
- – Sunpleasure White **new** — MPri
- – Sunpleasure Yellow **new** — MPri
- 'Hilo Holiday' (R) ♀H1b — WDib
- *homonyma* — see *B. dregei*
- Honeymoon ('Yamoon'PBR) — MBros
  - (Million Kisses Series)
- Hula Series **new** — LSou
- *humilis* **new** — NTro
- Illumination Series (T/d) — MBros MPri
- – 'Illumination Apricot' (T/d) — LCro
- 'Immense' — ESwi WFar
- 'Inca Fire'PBR (R) — WFar WMal
- Inca Night ('Krbelin02'PBR) — LBom
  - (Beleaf Series) (R)
- *incarnata* 'Metallica' — see *B. metallica*
- 'Indian Summer'PBR — LBom
  - (Beleaf Series) (R)
- × *intermedia* 'Bertinii' (T) — LCro XFar
- 'Jolly Noel' — WDib
- *josephii* (T) — SBrt
- 'Joyful Blaze' (R) — WDib
- * *koelzii* — CDTJ ESwi LEdu SPlb
- * – NJM 12.077 — GGro WFar WPGP
- 'La Paloma' (C) — WDib
- *labordei* W&O 9079 — GGro
- § – 'Candy Floss' — GGro WCru WFar
- Large-flowered — XFar
  - Double Group
  - pink-flowered (T/d)
- – red-flowered (T/d) — XFar
- – yellow-flowered (T/d) — XFar
- 'Lime Green' — GGro
- 'Limeade' ♀H1b — WDib
- *listada* ♀H1b — WDib
- 'Little Brother — WDib WFar
  - Montgomery' ♀H6
- 'Little Miss Mummey' (C) — WFar
- 'Lois Burks' (C) — WDib
- 'Looking Glass' (C) — EAri LBom
- 'Lucerna' (C) — CBlu EAri EShb WDib
- *luxurians* ♀H1b — CAbb CBct CDTJ CHIl CSpe CTsd EAri EBee EPPr ESwi EWld SBig SIvy SPlb WCot WFar
- *maculata* (C) — CDoC LBom LWaG NTro SBig
- – 'Wightii' (C) — CTsd LBom LInT WDib
- *malipoensis* — GGro
- 'Maori Haze'PBR (R) — LBom
- 'Marie Reed' — WDib
- 'Marmaduke' ♀H1b — WDib
- 'Martin Johnson' (R) ♀H1b — WDib
- *masoniana* ♀H1b — ESwi GGro LBom WDib
- – Rock ('Ec-bego-1901') **new** — WFar

- 'Merry Christmas' (R) — LBom WDib
- 'Merrymaker' (R) — WDib
- 'Metallic Mist'PBR — ESwi
- § *metallica* ♀H1b — CBct EShb WFar
- 'Midnight Magic' (R) ♀H1b — WDib
- Million Kisses Series — MPri
- 'Mishmi Silver' — CBct CExl GGro LEdu WFar
- 'Mother's Day' (T) — LCro
- 'Munchkin' ♀H1b — WDib
- 'My Best Friend' — WDib
- 'Namur' (R) ♀H1b — WDib
- *nantoensis* NMWJ 14461 — GGro WCru
- (Narcissiflora Group) — XFar
  - 'Daffodil Salmon' (T)
- *natalensis* — see *B. dregei*
- Nonstop Series (T/d) — MBros
- – 'Nonstop Pink' (T/d) — EGren
- – 'Nonstop Red' (T/d) — MBros
- – 'Nonstop Rose Petticoat' (T/d) — MBros
- – 'Nonstop White' (T/d) — EGren MBros
- – 'Nonstop Yellow' (T/d) — EGren MBros
- (On Top Series) — XFar
  - On Top Fandango ('Pas1384150')
- – On Top Pink Halo ('Pas1384154') — XFar
- – On Top Sun Glow ('Pas1384156') (T) — XFar
- 'Orange Rubra' (C) — WDib
- Organdy (mixed) — MBros
- *palmata* — CBct CDTJ GGro WFar
- – CMB TW1566 — GGro
- – DJHM — SVen
- – 'Dark Star' — GGro WFar
- – 'Snow Splash' — CBct WMal
- *panchtharensis* — SPlb WFar
- – B&SWJ 2692 — GGro WCot WCru WFar
- *partita* — see *B. dregei*
- *pavonina* — NTro
- *pedatifida* — CSpe GGro WFar
- – DJHC 98473 — ESwi EWld WCru WFar
- – 'Apalala' — WFar WPGP
- Pendula Group (T) — LAma
- – pink-flowered (T) — XFar
- – 'Pink Giant' (T) — LCro
- – red-flowered (T) — EGren XFar
- – 'Red Giant' (T) — LCro
- – salmon-flowered (T) — XFar
- – white-flowered (T) — EGren XFar
- – 'White Giant' (T) — LCro
- – yellow-flowered (T) — EGren XFar
- 'Picotee Lace Red' (T/d) — XFar
- 'Picotee Sunburst' (T/d) — EGren XFar
- *picta* Sm. (T) — WFar
- 'Pink Champagne' (R) ♀H1b — WDib
- 'Pink Delight' (T) — XFar
- 'Pink Flamingo' (T) — LCro
- 'Pink Gin' (R) — WDib
- 'Pink Spirit' (R) — WDib
- 'Pink Twist' — WDib
- 'Pollux' ♀H1b — WDib
- 'Princess of Hanover' (R) ♀H1b — WDib
- *putii* B&SWJ 7245 — WCru
- 'Queen Olympus' — WDib
- *radicans* Vell. ♀H1b — SPlb
- 'Raspberry Swirl' (R) — WDib
- *ravenii* (T) — CDTJ WFar
- 'Red Glory' (T) — LCro XFar
- 'Red Robin' (R) ♀H1b — WDib

'Red Tempest'	WDib
'Red Undies' (*grandis*)	see *B. grandis* subsp. *sinensis* 'Red Undies'
'Regal Minuet' (R) ♀H1b	WDib
rex (R)	CWal EGren NHrt
rhytidophylla BWJ 15544 from northern Vietnam	WCru
'Richmondensis' (S)	EShb WFar
'Ricinifolia'	ESwi WJun
'Rocheart' (R) ♀H1b	WDib
'Rosebud' (T/d)	XFar
'Rosebud Tutu' (T/d)	LCro
'Rosy Jewel' (R)	WDib
'Ruby Celebration' (C)	WDib
'Saint Kew' (R)	WCot
'Sal's Comet' (R) ♀H1b	WDib
SAMBA (mixed) (T/d)	XFar
'Sangria' (T/d)	XFar
'Satin Starburst' (R)	WDib
'Scherzo'	WDib
schmidtiana (S)	WFar
'Sea Urchin'	ESwi WDib
'Senator White' (Senator Series)	MBros
serratipetala ♀H1b	WDib
'Shamus'	WDib
* *shepherdii*	EShb EWld WDib WFar
sikkimensis	ESwi GGro WFar
- var. *kamengensis*	GGro WFar
silletensis	WCot
- subsp. *mengyangensis*	ESwi WCot WFar
'Silver Cloud' (R) ♀H1b	WDib
'Silver Jewell' ♀H1b	WDib
'Silver Lace'	WDib WFar
'Silver Spirit' (R)	WDib
'Silver Splendor'	CSpe WFar
sinensis	see *B. grandis* subsp. *sinensis*
sizemoreae	GGro NTro WDib WMal
'Smooch'	WFar
'Snow Storm'	WDib
I 'Snowcap' (C) ♀H1b	EShb WDib
solananthera A. DC. ♀H1b	WCot WDib
'Solid Silver' (R)	WDib
soli-mutata ♀H1b	ESwi LWaG WDib
'Splendide Alifra' (T/d)	LCro
'Splendide Apricot' (T/d)	XFar
'Splendide Ballerina' (T)	LCro XFar
'Stained Glass'	WDib
'Star Bright'	WDib
'Star Light'	WDib
'Starshine Calypso' (Starshine Series) **new**	MPri
'Sugar Plum'	MAsh
(Summerwings Series)	CBlu CSpe SPoG
SUMMERWINGS DARK ELEGANCE ('Insumdaele'^PBR)	
- SUMMERWINGS EBONY AND ORANGE ('Inbegebo 16'^PBR)	CBlu
- SUMMERWINGS WHITE ('Innbolwhi'^PBR)	ELan
'Sunny Dream' (T)	XFar
I 'Superba Red' (T/d)	XFar
I 'Superba Salmon' (T/d)	XFar
I 'Superba White' (T/d)	XFar
I 'Superba Yellow' (T/d)	XFar
'Supercascade Apricot Shades'	LCro
sutherlandii (T) ♀H2	CBct CBlu EAri EBee EPPr EShb ESwi EWld MCtn NPer SAdn SBeP
	SIvy WCot WDib WFar WMal WPGP
- 'Papaya' (T)	CSpe EPPr WFar
- 'Saunders's Legacy' (T) **new**	CBct EAri SIvy
(Sweet Spice Series)	MBros
SWEET SPICE CITRUS ('Kerbespicit'^PBR) (T/d)	
- SWEET SPICE ENGLISH ROSE ('Kerbespiros'^PBR) (T/d)	MBros
'Switzerland' (T)	XFar
taiwaniana	GGro
var. *albomaculata*	
taliensis	SPlb
- EDHCH 42	CExl GGro WCot WCru WFar
- W&O 8043	GGro
- W&O 9083	GGro
tengchiana PB 07-1110	GGro
'Thurstonii' ♀H1b	EShb WFar
'Tiger Paws' ♀H1b	EShb ESwi
'Tiny Gem'	WDib WFar
'Torsa'	CExl CSpe EAri GGro LEdu WCot WFar WMal WPGP
* *tripartita* (T)	WDib
'Truffle Cream'	MBros
'Two Face'	WDib
'Tye Dye'	CBct WFar
U614	GGro
undulata (C)	WFar
versicolor BWJ 15726	WCru
'Vesuvius' (R)	WDib
'Wavy Green'	CBct EBee GGro WFar
'White Cascade'	XFar
'Wild Swan'	GGro WCru WFar
Wummi Series (T/d)	XFar
wynn-jonesiae 'Pink Lady'	see *B. guaniana* 'Pink Lady'

Belamcanda see *Iris*

Bellevalia ✿ (*Asparagaceae*)

'Cream Pearl'	WCot
cyanopoda	GKev
dubia	WCot
forniculata	WCot
hyacinthoides	WCot
kurdistanica	GKev
longistyla	GKev
nivalis	GKev
§ *paradoxa*	CAby EGren ERCP GKev LAma MNrw WCot
pycnantha misapplied	see *B. paradoxa*
pycnantha ambig.	XFar
pycnantha (K. Koch) Losinsk. 'Green Pearl'	XFar
romana	WCot XFar
sarmatica	GKev
tabriziana	WCot
trifoliata	GKev

Bellis (*Asteraceae*)

§ *caerulescens*	GAbr LShi
perennis	EHet MCtn MNHC SVic
- 'Alba Plena' (d)	LShi
- Bellissima Series	EGren LCro MBros
- 'Big Bob' (d)	WCot
- 'Dresden China'	LShi WIce
- 'Miss Mason'	WCot
- 'Monstrosa'	MCtn
- old strain	WCot
- 'Prolifera' double-flowered (d)	WCot
- 'Rob Roy' (d)	LShi

130 *Bellis*

- 'Single Blue'	see *B. caerulescens*	- subsp. *insignis*	WCru
- Tasso Series (d)	MCtn	var. *insignis*	
- - 'Tasso Strawberries and Cream' (d)	MCtn	B&SWJ 2432	
- 'The Pearl'	LShi WCot	§ × *interposita*	EHeP WFar
rotundifolia	see *B. caerulescens*	'Wallich's Purple'	
'Caerulescens'		*jamesiana*	ELan
		julianae	CBcs CBrac CEnd CMac EHeP ELan LBuc MGos MMuc SEND WFar WHtc WSpi

Belloa (Asteraceae)
chilensis SPlb

'Jytte' LRHS
koreana NLar
linearifolia 'Orange King' see *B. trigona* 'Orange King'
'Little Favourite' see *B. thunbergii* f. *atropurpurea* 'Atropurpurea Nana'

Beloperone see *Justicia*

× *lolotensis* 'Apricot Queen' ♀H5 CBcs CMac ELan EPfP MGos NLar SPoG

Benthamiella (Solanaceae)

azorella	WAbe
graminifolia	WAbe
patagonica	SPlb WAbe
- F&W 9345	WAbe
- white-flowered	WAbe
- yellow-flowered	WAbe

- 'Mystery Fire' IArd NLar
- 'Stapehill' CBrac CMac EPfP LRHS SPoG
× *media* 'Parkjuweel' SRms
- 'Red Jewel' ♀H5 CDoC CMac EGren MGos MMuc SPoG WFar

microphylla 'Pygmaea' EBee EHeP EPfP
nigricans **new** CExl
× *ottawensis* f. *purpurea* CMac
- - 'Silver Miles' (v) WFar
§ - - 'Superba' CBcs CDoC CEnd CSBt EBee EHeP ELan EPfP ERom MMuc NLar SEND SRms WFar

Berberidopsis (Berberidopsidaceae)
corallina CBcs CDoC CMac CRHN EGrI EPfP EWes IArd MGos NLar SPoG

- 'Silver Bells' (v) LRHS
panlanensis 'Cally Rose' see *B. triacanthophora* 'Cally Rose'
'Red Tears' WFar
× *rubrostilla* 'Cherry Ripe' CMac
- 'Wisley' LRHS
sargentiana ELan
sieboldii WPav WSpi
× *stenophylla* Lindl. ♀H5 CMac CSBt EPfP LBuc MMuc SRms WFar

Berberis (Berberidaceae)

aggregata	NBir WKor
amurensis var. *latifolia* B&SWJ 8539	WCru
aquifolium	see *Mahonia aquifolium*
- 'Fascicularis'	see *Mahonia* × *wagneri* 'Pinnacle'
asiatica	WPGP
bealei	see *Mahonia bealei*
calliantha	SBrt WFar
candidula C.K. Schneid.	MMuc NLar SEND
× *carminea* 'Buccaneer'	WSpi
- 'Pirate King'	LRHS SPoG
'Coral'	EBee WFar
darwinii ♀H5	CBcs CBen CBrac CDoC CEnd CSBt CTsd CWnw EBee EGren EHeP ELan ELon EPfP LBuc LCro LRHS LSRN LSto MAsh MGos MHed MMuc NLar SAth SPoG WFar WHtc WKor WLov
I - 'Compacta'	CDoC CMac CSBt EBee ELan EPfP LBuc LRHS MAsh MGos MPro NLar SPoG WCot WFar
densa B&SWJ 14873	WCru
aff. *densa* B&SWJ 14880	WCru
dictyophylla	MMuc WSpi
dulcis 'Nana'	see *B. microphylla* 'Pygmaea'
empetrifolia	WAbe WPav WSpi
exigua	GKev
'Fireball'	ELan
× *frikartii* 'Amstelveen' ♀H5	CDoC EBee EHeP EPfP LRHS MMuc
gagnepainii misapplied	see *B. gagnepainii* var. *lanceifolia*
gagnepainii C.K. Schneid.	CMac
§ - var. *lanceifolia*	EHeP MMuc SEND
- - 'Fernspray'	EBee EPfP LRHS SRms
- 'Purpurea'	see *B.* × *interposita* 'Wallich's Purple'
'Georgei' ♀H6	EPfP
'Goldilocks'	EBee EPfP LRHS MBlu SPoG SReu
goudotii B&SWJ 10769	WCru
- B&SWJ 14721	WCru
- B&SWJ 14892	WCru
hamiltoniana H&M 1919	EBee
hypokerina	CMac WPGP
insignis	CBcs WPGP

- 'Brilliant' **new** SReu
- 'Claret Cascade' EBee ELan LRHS SPoG SReu WFar
- 'Corallina Compacta' ♀H5 CMac EBee EDar ELan EPfP EPot GKev MAsh MHer SPoG WCot
- 'Cornish Cream' see *B.* × *stenophylla* 'Lemon Queen'
- 'Cream Showers' see *B.* × *stenophylla* 'Lemon Queen'
- 'Etna' ELan LRHS MAsh SPoG
- 'Irwinii' CMac WFar
§ - 'Lemon Queen' SReu WSpi
- 'Nana' CWnw LRHS
subacuminata FMWJ 13290 WCru
taliensis CExl
temolaica ♀H5 WSpi
thunbergii CBcs CEnd CMac EHeP LBuc LMaj LSto WFar
- f. *atropurpurea* CBcs CBrac CDoC CMac EBee EGren EGrI ELan LBuc LCro LRHS MGos MHed NLar SPlb SRms WFar
- - 'Admiration'[PBR] ♀H7 CBcs CDoC CSBt ELan EPfP LCro LRHS LSou LSRN MAsh MGos MMrt NLar SPoG WFar WHtc WLov
§ - - 'Atropurpurea Nana' ♀H7 CBcs CBrac CDoC CMac CSBt EBee EGrI EHeP EPfP LRHS LSto MGos MPri NLar SGol SNig SPoG WFar
- - 'Bagatelle' CDoC EGrI ELan EPfP IArd LRHS LSRN MAsh NLar
- - 'Chocolate Summer'[PBR] LRHS WFar
- - 'Concorde' ♀H7 ELan EPfP LRHS MAsh
- - 'Dart's Red Lady' ♀H7 CDoC CSBt ELan NLar WFar
- - 'Golden Ring' (v) ♀H7 CDoC CMac EGren ELan EPfP EUrb LRHS MAsh MGos SPoG WFar

Bergenia 131

- - 'Harlequin' (v) ♀H7	CDoC CEnd EGren ELan EPfP LCro LRHS LSRN MAsh MGos SPoG SRms WFar	§ *triacanthophora* 'Cally Rose'	EBee ELan EPfP EPPr GBin SBrt WCot WPGP
- - 'Helmond Pillar'	CDoC CMac CSBt EBee EGren EGrI ELan EPfP LCro LRHS MAsh MGos NLar SOrN SPoG WFar WHtc	§ *trigona* 'Orange King'	CBcs ELan LRHS MAsh MGos NLar SPoG
- - 'Maja'PBR	EUrb	*valdiviana* ♀H5	CBcs CExl IArd MBlu MMuc SChF SMad WPGP
- - 'Pink Queen' (v)	EGren EHeP ELan EPfP WFar WHtc	*verruculosa* ♀H5	CBcs CBrac CDoC EHeP LSto MBlu SRms WFar
- - 'Red Chief'	CBcs CMac EHeP ELan LRHS MGos SGol SPoG SRms WFar	aff. *verticillata* B&SWJ 10672	WCru
- - 'Red Pillar'	CDoC CMac ELan LRHS MAsh MGos SReu WFar WLov	*vulgaris*	CAgr GQue MCtn WKor
- - 'Red Rocket'	EBee EGrI ERom NLar WFar	*wilsoniae*	CMac ELan MMrt WFar WHtc WSpi
- - 'Red Tower'	EGren	- blue-leaved	WFar
- - 'Rose Glow' (v) ♀H7	CBcs CBrac CDoC CMac CSBt EBee EHeP ELan EPfP LRHS MAsh MGos SGol SPoG WFar WHtc WSpi	- var. *guhtzunica*	EWes
		aff. *wilsoniae*	CBrac
- - 'Rosea'	EHeP	*yingjingensis*	WPGP

Berberis × *Mahonia* see × *Mahoberberis*

- - 'Rosy Rocket'PBR (v)	CBrac CWGN EBee ELan NLar SPoG WFar
- 'Atropurpurea Superba'	see *B.* × *ottawensis* f. *purpurea* 'Superba'

Berchemia (Rhamnaceae)

racemosa	NLar WCru

- 'Aurea'	CBcs CBrac CDoC CMac EGrI EHeP ELan LCro MBlu MGos NLar SPlb SRms WFar

bergamot see *Citrus* × *limon* Bergamot Group

Bergbambos (Poaceae)

§ *tessellata*	MMuc SEND

- BONANZA GOLD ('Bogozam'PBR)	EHeP ELan EPfP LRHS MAsh NLar WFar

Bergenia ❀ (Saxifragaceae)

- 'Chiquita'PBR	LRHS MHtn	'Abendglocken'	CMac ECha EGrI NSti WCot WFar
- 'Crimson Pygmy'	see *B. thunbergii* f. *atropurpurea* 'Atropurpurea Nana'	§ 'Abendglut'	CBcs CMac EBee ECha ELan ELon GKev GKin GMaP LCro LRHS MHol NGdn NLar SPoG SRms WCAu WCot WHoo WSpi
- 'Desperados' (Neon Series)	WLov		
- 'Diabolic'	EGrI MAsh SPoG WFar		
- 'Erecta'	CMac EPfP	'Admiral'	CMac ECha EGrI WCot
- 'Fireball'PBR ♀H7	EPfP LRHS MAsh	'Andrea'	WCot
- 'Florence'PBR	LRHS WFar	'Angel Kiss' (Dragonfly Series)	ELan LCro LRHS Midl MPri NLar SMrm WCot
- 'Glowing Embers'	LRHS		
- 'Golden Carpet'	LRHS	'Apple Blossom'	ELon EPfP LRHS Midl WCAu
- 'Golden Dream'PBR	LRHS MGos	'Autumn Magic'	EGrI ELon EPfP EUrb LRHS NCou WFar
- GOLDEN HORIZON ('Hoho 2'PBR)	WFar		
- 'Golden Rocket'PBR	CSBt EBee EGren ELan EPfP LRHS MAsh MGos NLar SPoG WFar WLov	'Baby Doll'	CDor CMac CMHG EBee ECha EGren EGrI ELon LBom LCro LRHS LSRN MAsh MBel MHer Midl MMuc NBir NEoE NGdn NLar NPer NSti NWbg SEND StAn WCAu WCot WFar WSpi
- 'Golden Torch'	CDoC EHeP ELan LRHS MAsh		
- 'Green Carpet'	CMac EGren EGrI EHeP MBlu SPoG		
- 'Kobold'	CMac EPfP NLar WFar		
- 'Lutin Rouge'PBR	LCro LRHS		
- 'Maria'PBR ♀H7	CWGN EGrI EPfP LCro LRHS MGos MPri NLar SGol SPoG WFar	'Bach'	CDor EPfP LRHS LSto Midl MMuc NLar NSti SHar SRms WCAu WCot WFar
- 'Neon' (Neon Series) **new**	WFar WLov		
- 'Orange Dream'PBR	CDoC MGos	§ 'Ballawley' clonal	EBlo ECha LRHS WCot WMal
- 'Orange Ice'PBR	CSBt EUrb IArd LRHS LSou MPri	Ballawley hybrids	CMac WSpi
- 'Orange Rocket'PBR	CDoC EBee EGren EGrI ELan EPfP LCro LRHS MAsh MGos MPri SPoG WFar WLov	'Barcock'	ECha
		'Bartók'	Midl SRms WCAu WCot WTor
		beesiana	see *B. purpurascens*
- 'Orange Sunrise'PBR (v)	CWnw EPfP GBin LCro LRHS MAsh SPad	'Beethoven'	ECha EGrI NBir WCAu WCot
		'Biedermeier' ♀H7	ECha
- 'Orange Torch'	LRHS	'Bressingham Bountiful'	WCAu
- 'Pow-wow'	ELan LRHS NLar SPoG	'Bressingham Ruby'	CWCL EBee EBlo ECha EGren ELon EPfP GQue LRHS LSto MAvo MGos NBir NLar SArc WCAu WCot WHoo WSpi
- 'Ruby Star'PBR	LRHS		
- 'Silver Mile'	see *B.* × *ottawensis* f. *purpurea* 'Silver Miles'		
- 'Silver Pillar'PBR	NLar	'Bressingham Salmon'	EBlo ECha ELon LBar NLar SRms WCAu WCot
- 'Somerset'	CMac		
- 'Starburst'PBR (v)	CSBt LRHS LSou MAsh MGos NEoE SRms WHtc	'Bressingham White' ♀H6	Widely available
		'Britten' ♀H7	CMac
- 'Summer Sunset'PBR	EBee LRHS MHtn WFar WLov	*ciliata*	CBct CDor CMac ECha EGrI LEdu NLar SDix SHar SPlb WCAu WFar WKif WPGP WSpi
- 'Tiny Gold'PBR	ELan LCro LRHS MAsh SOrN WFar		
* - 'Tricolor' (v)	CMac WFar		
- 'Venice'PBR	LRHS NWbg WLov	- 'Dumbo'	CBct IBal LBom LEdu LRHS NLar SPoG WCAu
- 'Volcano' (Neon Series)	WLov		
'Thunderbolt'	LRHS	- f. *ligulata*	see *B. pacumbis*

Bergenia

- 'Wilton'	CBct ESwi EWld LEdu SHar WCot WPGP
ciliata × *crassifolia*	see *B.* × *schmidtii*
'Claire Maxine' ♀H7	EPPr GBin NLar SRms WCAu WCot
cordifolia	CAgr CMac EBee EGren EHeP ELan EPfP GBin GMaP LSto LWaG MGos MMuc NLar SEND SPlb SRms WMal XFar
- 'Jelle'	EUrb NLar WCAu
- 'Lunar Glow'	SRms WFar
- 'Michael's Jungle Leaf' **new**	ESwi
- 'Purpurea'	CBcs CMac EBee ECha EGren EGrI EHeP ELan EPfP GQue LBuc LCro LRHS NBir SRms WFar
- 'Rosa Schwester'	ECha
- 'Rosa Zeiten' ♀H7	GBin
- 'Tubby Andrews' (v)	CBct CMac CTtf ECha LEdu NEoE NLar NSti SRms WHrl
- 'Vinterglöd'	EDAr EGren EHeP EPfP GMaP LBom LRHS MBel MPri NLar SRms
crassifolia	EPfP GKev SRms
- 'Autumn Red'	ECha
- 'Orbicularis'	see *B.* × *schmidtii*
* *cyanea*	WCot
'Dark Damsel'	CMHG EHeP IBal LBar LRHS LSRN MPro
'David'	ECha LBar
'Delbees'	see *B.* 'Ballawley' clonal
'Diamond Drops'	CWCL EArI ELan GKev IBal LBar LBom LRHS Midl MPri MPro NCou NEoE NSti
'Eden's Dark Margin'	EBee ELon EPfP LBar LBuc LRHS MHol Midl MNrw NLar WCot WFar
'Eden's Magic Giant' ♀H7	CToG EBee ELan ELon EPfP EUrb GQue LBar MHol Midl NLar SRms WCot
emeiensis	CBct CDor EPfP GKev LEdu SDix WCot
'Eric Smith' ♀H7	CDor ECha EGrI WCAu
'Eroica' ♀H7	CAby ECha EGren EGrI ELan ELon EPfP EUrb GBin LRHS Midl MMuc MPri NLar NSti SEND WCAu WHoo WSpi
'Evening Glow'	see *B.* 'Abendglut'
'Fire and Ice'	CBcs EPfP LBar LBom LBuc LRHS LSRN MPri MPro NCth SMrm
'Flirt'PBR	CDor EGren ELan LBar Midl WFar
'Godfrey Owen'	EBee WMal
'Harzkristall'	CAby CDor CMac CWCL ELan EPfP EUrb GBin GKev LRHS Midl MPro NCou SHar SPoG WSpi
'Helen Dillon'	see *B. purpurascens* 'Irish Crimson'
'Herbstblute'	NLar WCAu
'Ice Queen'	EBee ELan GBin GKev LCro Midl NLar WCAu WCot WGwG
'Kerstin'	Midl WGwG
'Lambrook'	see *B.* 'Margery Fish'
'Little Pine'	WCot
§ 'Margery Fish'	ECha StAn
'Memelinks Pride'	NLar WCAu
milesii	see *B. stracheyi*
'Miss Piggy'	LBar
§ 'Morgenröte' ♀H6	CBcs CMac ECha EGrI ELon GMaP LRHS NLar NSti SRms WCAu WCot
MORNING RED	see *B.* 'Morgenröte'
'Mrs Crawford'	ECha WMal
'Oeschberg'	GBin WCAu
'Opal'	EBee
'Overture'	CBcs CDor CMac CMHG EBee EBlo EGren ELan ELon EPfP GAbr GQue LBom LCro LRHS LSRN MBel MHed
	MHer MHol NGdn NLar SDix SPoG SRms WCot WGwG WMal
§ *pacumbis*	ECha EPPr ESwi EWld GQue NBid NSti SPlb
- B&SWJ 2693	WCru
- CC	GGro
- CC 1793	WCot
- 'Bouncing Babe'	WCot
'Pink Dragonfly'	CBWd CMac EBee ELon EWes GKev LRHS LSou Midl MPri NLar SMrm WCAu WCot WFar
'Pink Ice'	CDor LBar LCro MHtn WCAu
'Pugsley's Pink' ♀H7	ECha WMal
§ *purpurascens* ♀H5	CMac EBee EBlo EPfP GMaP LBuc LRHS LWaG MCtn WSpi
- SDR 4548	GKev
- var. *delavayi* ♀H5	GKev LRHS SRms
- 'Irish Crimson' ♀H7	ECha EGrI WCot
aff. *purpurascens*	CoPl NGdn
'Rietheim'	GBin
'Rosenkristall'	EPfP LRHS
'Rosi Klose'	CDor ECha EGrI ELon EPfP GBin LRHS MHol MPri NGdn WCot WFar
'Rotblum'	EGren ELon EPfP GMaP LBuc LSto NBir NGdn SPoG SRkn SRms
'Sakura' (Dragonfly Series)	LBar LRHS Midl MPri NWbg
§ × *schmidtii*	CMac EGren NBir NLar
'Schneekissen'	CMac WCAu WGwG
'Schneekoenigin'	ECha EGrI WCot
§ 'Silberlicht' ♀H6	CBcs CMac ECha EGren EGrI EHeP ELan ELon EPfP GKev GKin GMaP LCro LRHS MGos Midl NLar SPoG SRms StAn WCAu WCot WFar WSpi
SILVERLIGHT	see *B.* 'Silberlicht'
'Simply Sweet'	WCot
SNOW QUEEN	see *B.* 'Schneekoenigin'
'Spring Fling'PBR (Dragonfly Series)	EBee LBar LRHS Midl WFar
§ *stracheyi*	ECha NBid NLar WCot
- Alba Group	ECha EGrI SMHy
- 'Sunningdale' ♀H7	CMac ECha GMaP NBir NGdn WCAu
WINTER FAIRY TALES	see *B.* 'Wintermärchen'
§ 'Wintermärchen' ♀H7	ECha EGrI ELan ELon Midl MMuc SEND SHar SPoG SRms WCot
'XXL'	WCot WMal

Bergenia × Mukdenia see × *Mukgenia*

Bergera (Rutaceae)

§ *koenigii*	SPre SVen WJek

Bergeranthus (Aizoaceae)

sp.	SPoG
multiceps	EArI
scapiger	SRot

Berkheya (Asteraceae)

cirsiifolia	EDAr GGro WHil
macrocephala	SPlb
multijuga	GGro GKev SPlb
purpurea	CDor CSpe ECha EDAr ELon EPfP GElm SHor SNoN SPhx SPlb StAn WCot WFar WKif
- 'Silver Spike'	EGrI
- 'Zulu Warrior'	EGrI LShi MCtn MHer SMHy SMrm
radula	GGro WCot

Berneuxia (Diapensiaceae)

thibetica	EPot

Betula 133

Berula (Apiaceae)
   erecta   CAco NPer

Berzelia (Bruniaceae)
   galpinii   SPlb

Beschorneria (Asparagaceae)
albiflora	CExl LRHS SBig WCot
calcicola	CCht CDTJ EUrb WCot
'Red Bells'	WCot
rigida	WCot
septentrionalis ♀H3	CAbb CBcs CDTJ CExl CMac CTsd EUrb MHol SPeP WCot
- 'Bob Brown' (v)	WCot
tubiflora	CDTJ WPGP
wrightii	CExl WCot
yuccoides ♀H3	CCht CExl CHll CMac CPic CSpe ELan EPfP EShb EUrb LRHS NPlm SArc SChr SEND SPad SPlb WPav
- FLAMINGO GLOW ('Besys'^{PBR}) (v)	CBcs CBlu CCht CDTJ CMac CSBt CTsd CWGN EArl ELan EUrb LSou SBig SMrm SPeP WCot
- 'Quicksilver'	CEnd MHtn SPoG WPav

Bessera (Asparagaceae)
   elegans   CAby EPot WCot XFar

Besseya see *Veronica*
   alpina   see *Veronica besseya*

Beta (Amaranthaceae)
vulgaris	CGHo CWRo WHer WKit
- subsp. *cicla* var. *cicla*	LCro
- - var. *flavescens*	LCro
- subsp. *maritima*	CAgr NBac

Betonica (Lamiaceae)
§ *macrantha*	CAby CDor CMac EBee ECha EGrl GAbr GJos GKev LEdu LRHS MCtn NBir NLar NSti SPhx WCAu WCot WHil WKif WTre
* - 'Alba'	CCBP ECha EPot WCAu
- 'Ben' (v)	LEdu
- 'Morning Blush'	LBar SPhx WCAu WCot WFar WHil
- 'Robusta' ♀H7	CKno ELan GAbr LEdu NBro NGdn WCot
- 'Rosea'	CElw ELan GMaP LRHS SPlb WCAu
- 'Superba' ♀H7	CSpe EBee EBlo ECha EGren EPfP GMaP LBar LEdu LRHS MHol NLar SMHy SRms WCAu WCot WFar
- 'Violacea' ♀H7	GKev WCot WFar
§ *nivea*	LRHS MWlw NLar WCAu WCot
- subsp. *ossetica*	GEdr
officinalis	Widely available
- 'Alba'	CBWd CMiW LEdu NBro SMHy WCAu
- 'Blush'	SMHy
- 'Cally Bicolor'	GBin
§ - 'Hummelo' ♀H7	Widely available
- 'Pink Cotton Candy'	CKno LBar LSRN
- 'Rosea'	CBWd CCBP CMiW EGrl MBel NBro WCAu WFar
- 'Rosea Superba'	CTtf ECha WCot
- 'Saharan Pink'	CKno EBee ELon MHol NLar
- 'Summer Grapes'	LBar XFar
- 'Summer Snowcone'**new**	LBar XFar
- 'Summer Sweets'^{PBR}	LBar LRHS XFar
- 'Ukkie'	CoPl EBee GElm LBar LRHS NDov NLar WCAu

Betula ✿ (Betulaceae)
alba	see *B. pendula*, *B. pubescens*
albosinensis	see *B. utilis* subsp. *albosinensis*
- var. *septentrionalis*	see *B. utilis* subsp. *albosinensis*
§ *alleghaniensis*	CMCN CSto LMaj MMuc NLar WCru
ashburneri	CAco EBee WPGP
austrosinensis	see *B. kweichowensis* subsp. *kweichowensis*
bomiensis	GKev
'Charlotte'	CJun
chichibuensis	GKev
chinensis 'Rhinegold'	MBlu
'Cobhay Cream Spire'	CJun
'Cobhay Snow Spire'	CJun
'Conyngham'	CJun MBlu
cordifolia 'Clarenville'	CJun
costata misapplied	see *B. ermanii* 'Grayswood Hill'
costata ambig.	CAco CMCN LMaj SGol
'Crimson Frost'	see *B. pendula* 'Crimson Frost'
cylindrostachya	WPGP
dauurica	WJur
- 'Maurice Foster'	CBcs CSto EBee MBlu WPGP
- 'Stone Farm'	CJun
'Edinburgh'	CBTr CJun MBlu NOra NPip WMat
ermanii	CAco CBcs CCVT CLnd CMCN CSto EBar EGrI ELan IPap LMaj MBlu StAn
- B&SWJ 8801 from South Korea	WCru
- B&SWJ 10852 from Aomori, Japan	WCru
- B&SWJ 12600 from South Korea	WCru
- from Hokkaido, Japan	CAco
- 'Blush'	CJun MBlu
- 'Cobhay Mount Hakkoda'**new**	CJun
- 'Daleside'	NOra NPip WMat
- 'Fincham Cream'	CJun
§ - 'Grayswood Hill' ♀H7	CEnd CJun CMCN EBee EPfP LRHS MBlu WPGP
- 'Hakkoda Orange'	CExl CJun CMCN CSto EBee EPfP WPGP
- 'Kwanak Weeping' ♀H7	CJun MBlu
- 'Mount Zao'	CBcs CExl CJun CSto EBee EPfP WMou WPGP
- WHITE CHOCOLATE ('Wvo2f2'^{PBR}) **new**	CBTr EBee
fargesii	GKev
'Fascination' ♀H6	Widely available
'Fetisowii'	CJun MBlu NOra NPip WMat
glandulifera	see *B. pumila*
globispica	CJun
§ *gmelinii* 'Mount Apoi' ♀H7	CJun CLnd EBee NPip WMat
'Hergest'	CJun EPfP LRHS NOra NPip WMat
'Holland'	EGren IArd LMaj
'Hoseri'	CAco
insignis	see *B. kweichowensis*
jacquemontii	see *B. utilis* subsp. *jacquemontii*
'Kerscott Charm'	CSto
§ *kweichowensis*	WPGP
- subsp. *fansipanensis*	IArd
- - B&SWJ 11751	WCru
- - FMWJ 13169	WCru

§	- subsp. **kweichowensis**	GKev	
	lenta	CAgr CMCN MBlu MMuc StAn WJur	
	'Long Trunk'	CCVT EHeP LRHS MBlu SGol	
	luminifera	EBee MBlu WPGP	
	lutea	see *B. alleghaniensis*	
	maximowicziana	CMCN IArd MBlu SGol WSpi	
	medwediewii	CAco CMCN GKev WJur WPGP	
	- from Winkworth	MBlu	
	- 'Gold Bark'	CJun CMCN MBlu	
	megrelica	CSto GKev	
	michauxii	NLar WAbe WCru WJur	
	'Mount Apoi'	see *B. gmelinii* 'Mount Apoi'	
	nana	CAco ELan	
	- 'Glengarry'	EPot GKev	
	neoalaskana	see *B. pendula* subsp. *mandshurica*	
	nigra	CAco CBcs CCVT CLnd CMac CMCN CNWT EBar ELan IPap LCro LMaj MCtn MMuc SArc SEWo SFol SGol SHor WCha	
	- 'Black Star'	ELan LMaj NOra NPip WMat	
§	- 'Cully'	CLnd EBee MBlu NOra NPip SArc WFar WMat	
	- HERITAGE	see *B. nigra* 'Cully'	
	- 'Peter Collinson'	CJun	
	- 'Shiloh Splash'	CAco EBee LRHS SSta WMat	
	- 'Summer Cascade' PBR	CAco ELan LMaj LRHS LSRN NPip SAth WMat	
	- 'Wakehurst'	SPoG WPGP WSpi	
	papyrifera	CAco CCVT CMac CMCN EBar EHeP ELan IPap LBuc LCro NPip SGol WMat	
	- subsp. *humilis*	see *B. pendula* subsp. *mandshurica*	
	- 'Saint George'	CAco CBTr EBee EPfP NPip WMat	
§	**pendula**	Widely available	
§	- 'Crimson Frost'	CDoC EBee NCth	
	- subsp. *mandshurica*	CSto MCtn	
§	- subsp. *pendula*	CBTr EGren NPip SAth	
	- - 'Dalecarlica' misapplied	see *B. pendula* subsp. *pendula* 'Laciniata'	
	- - 'Darlecarlica' ambig.	CAco EBar EHeP LMaj LRHS MPri NPip WMat	
	- - 'Fastigiata'	CAco CCVT CSBt EBar EBee EGren EHeP IPap LMaj MGos WFar	
	- - FASTIGIATA JOES (Jolep 1' PBR)	CWnw EBee ELan LCro LRHS MAsh NPip SPoG WMat	
§	- - 'Globe' PBR	CAco LRHS	
	- - 'Golden Beauty'	CEnd CMac MGos NPip NTrD SGol WMat	
	- - 'Golden Cloud'	see *B. pendula* subsp. *pendula* 'Schneverdinger Goldbirke'	
	- - 'Golden Fountain'	NPip WMat	
	- - 'Karaca' PBR	CAco ELan LRHS	
§	- - 'Laciniata' ♀H7	CAco CBcs CBTr CMac EBee ELan LMaj MBlu MGos SGol WMou	
	- - MAGICAL GLOBE	see *B. pendula* subsp. *pendula* 'Globe'	
	- - 'Obelisk'	LMaj	
	- - 'Purpurea'	CAco CCVT CMac CMCN EGren EHeP ELan IPap LRHS LSRN MGos SFol SGol SMad WFar	
§	- - 'Schneverdinger Goldbirke'	CAco LMaj NPip	
	- - 'Silver Grace'	CJun MBlu	
§	- - 'Spider Alley' PBR	CAco ELan LRHS NPip WCha WMat	
	- - 'Tristis' ♀H7	CAco CBcs CBTr CCVT CEnd CLnd CMCN EBar EBee EHeP ELan EPfP IPap LMaj LRHS LSRN LSto MGos NPip SGol WFar WMat WMou	
	- - 'Trost Dwarf'	CAco	
	- - 'Youngii'	Widely available	
	- - 'Zwitsers Glorie'	CAco EBar LMaj	
	- 'Swiss Glory'	see *B. pendula* subsp. *pendula* 'Zwitsers Glorie'	
	- subsp. **szechuanica**	MBlu	
	'Liuba White'		
	platyphylla	see *B. pendula* subsp. *mandshurica*	
	× **plettkei** 'Golden Treasure' PBR	CAco EGren GKev LRHS MGos	
	'Polar Bear'	CJun CSto EBee MBlu NPip WMat WPGP	
	potaninii	GKev	
§	**pubescens**	CAco CBTr CCVT CHab CLnd EBar EGren EHeP IDun IPap LCot LMaj MMuc SEND WCha WHtc WRjT	
	- 'Embla'	GKev	
§	**pumila**	CBcs	
	raddeana	GKev	
	resinifera Britton	see *B. pendula* subsp. *mandshurica*	
	'Royal Frost'	CAco CBcs CBTr ELan LCro LMaj LSRN MBlu NOra NPip SGol WHtc WMat WMou	
	'Silver Trestles'	see *B. pendula* subsp. *pendula* 'Spider Alley'	
	tianschanica	WPGP	
	utilis	CMCN LMaj SAth SHor SSta WCha	
	- GWJ 9259	WCru	
	- HWJK 2250	WCru	
	- HWJK 2345	WCru	
	- S&L from Nepal	CAco	
§	- subsp. **albosinensis**	CAco CCVT CEnd CLnd EPfP IPap MBlu SGol WMou WPGP WSpi	
	- - PDM 752	WPGP	
	- - 'Bowling Green' ♀H7	CExl CJun EBee ELan MBlu WPGP	
	- - CACAO ('C1' PBR) **new**	ELan	
§	- - 'China Rose'	CBcs CExl CJun CSto EBee EPfP EUrb WMat WMou WPGP	
	- - 'China Ruby' K.Ashburner	see *B. utilis* subsp. *albosinensis* 'China Rose'	
	- - 'China Ruby' ambig.	CBcs CJun EPfP NPip	
	- - 'Chinese Garden'	CBcs CExl CJun CSto MBlu WPGP	
	- - clone F	see *B. utilis* subsp. *albosinensis* 'Ness'	
	- - 'Jim Russell'	WPGP	
	- - 'Joseph Rock'	CJun	
	- - 'K.Ashburner'	CAco CJun	
	- - 'Kansu' ♀H7	CJun CLnd MBlu NPip WMat	
§	- - 'Ness'	CJun	
	- - 'Pink Champagne'	CBcs CExl CJun CSto ELan EPfP MBlu MGos NCth WMat WPGP	
	- - 'Purdom'	CJun	
	- - 'Red Lady' **new**	EBee	
	- - 'Red Panda' ♀H7	CAco CBcs CExl CJun CSto EBee EPfP EUrb NCth NPip WMat WPGP	
	- 'Cinnamon' **new**	CBTr LRHS	
*	- 'Fastigiata'	CJun SSta	
§	- subsp. **jacquemontii**	Widely available	
§	- - Polunin	WPGP	
§	- - 'Doorenbos' ♀H7	Widely available	
	- - 'Grayswood Ghost' ♀H7	CBcs CBTr CEnd CJun CMCN CSto EBar EBee EGren ELan EPfP LCro LRHS LSRN MBlu NLar NPip SChF SMad SSta WMat WPGP WSpi	
	- - 'Himalayan Spirit' **new**	CSto	
	- - 'Inverleith'	CJun CMCN WPGP	
	- - 'Jermyns' ♀H7	CEnd CJun CLnd CMCN EGren EPfP LSRN MBlu NPip SSta WMat WPGP	
	- - 'Knightshayes'	CJun EBee EPfP WPGP	
	- - 'Kyelang'	CJun	
	- - 'McBeath'	LRHS MGos NPip	

- - 'Moonbeam'	CJun CSto EBee EPfP LRHS NPip SBig SEWo SPoG WMat	*Bidens* (Asteraceae)	
§ - - 'Ramdana River'	CJun EBee MBlu WPGP	*atrosanguinea*	see *Cosmos atrosanguineus*
- - 'Sacred Scroll'	CSto	§ *aurea*	CCBP EAri EPPr EWes LEdu MAsh MHol MMrt NPer SIvy SMrm WFar WMal WPGP
- - 'Silver Shadow' ♀H7	CBTr CCVT CEnd CJun CLnd CMCN EBee EPfP LBom LCro LRHS LSRN MAsh MBlu NPip SPoG SSta WMat WSpi	- cream-flowered	CFis MNrw WChS WMal
		- 'Hannay's Lemon Drop'	CCBP CKno CTtf EAri ELan ELon EMor EPPr ESgl LEdu LShi MAsh
- - 'Snow Leopard'	CJun CSto EBee ELan WPGP	- 'Mellow Yellow'	WCot
- - 'Snow Queen'	see *B. utilis* subsp. *jacquemontii* 'Doorenbos'	- 'Super Nova'	EAri EPPr ESgl SPel WFar
- - 'Trinity College'	CBTr CDoC CJun CLnd EBee ELan LBom MAsh MGos NPip WMat WPGP	- white-flowered	EBee EPPr GElm GMaP GPSL LShi NSti WFar
- - 'Werrington'	CBcs	**Campfire Nice 'N' Spicy** (Campfire Series) **new**	LSou
- Melony Sanders' **new**	CBTr	- 'Efraim's Gold'	LCro
- subsp. *occidentalis*	WPGP	*ferulifolia*	NPer
- - 'Kyelang'	see *B. utilis* subsp. *jacquemontii* 'Kyelang'	- 'Bee Alive' (Bee Series)	MBros
- var. *prattii*	see *B. utilis* subsp. *utilis*	- **Bee Happy Red** ('Baleehedi') (Bee Happy Series)	LSou
- 'Silver Queen'	MPri WSpi		
§ - subsp. *utilis*	CJun MBlu	- **Beedance Painted Red** ('Sunbidevb 2'PBR)	SPoG
- - 'Bhutan Sienna'	CJun CSto EBee WPGP		
§ - - 'Buddha' ♀H7	CJun MBlu WPGP	- **Beedance Painted Yellow** ('Sunbidevb 4'PBR)	SPoG
- - 'China Bronze'	CExl EBee MBlu WPGP		
- - 'Chris Lane'	CJun EBee WPGP	- 'Golden Empire'	LSou MPri
- - 'Chris Sanders'	CJun EBee WPGP	- 'Golden Eye'	LSou MBros SPoG
- - 'Cobhay Amber'	CJun	- 'Golden Glory'	MBros
- - 'Cobhay Sentinel'	CJun	- 'Hot and Spicy'	MSwo
- - 'Dark-Ness'	CJun EBee EPfP EUrb LSto MBlu NPip WMat WPGP	- **Pretty in Pink new**	MPri
		- 'Rising Sun' (Brazen Series)	EWes
- - 'Forest Blush' ♀H7	CExl CJun CSto EBee ELan EPfP WPGP	- (Taka Tuka Series) **Taka Tuka Double Yellow Red Center** (d) **new**	MPri
- - 'Himalayan Pink'	see *B. utilis* subsp. *utilis* 'Nepalese Orange'	- - **Taka Tuka Red Glow new**	MPri
- - 'Mount Luoji'	CExl CJun CSto EBee EUrb WPGP	- - **Taka Tuka Red Yellow Center new**	MPri
§ - - 'Nepalese Orange'	CAco CBcs CJun CSto EBee ELan EPfP EUrb MGos NLar SGol WMat WPGP WSpi	*heterophylla* Ortega	see *B. aurea*
		'Spicy Ice'	MSwo
- - 'Park Wood'	CAco CJun EBee MBlu WPGP	*triplinervia* 'Sunny Days'	WCru
- - 'Ramdana River'	see *B. utilis* subsp. *jacquemontii* 'Ramdana River'	*Bigelowia* (Asteraceae)	
- - 'Schilling'	see *B. utilis* subsp. *utilis* 'Buddha'	*nuttallii*	CSpe WHil
- - 'Sichuan Red'	CJun	*Bignonia* (Bignoniaceae)	
- - 'Wakehurst Place Chocolate' ♀H7	CBcs CBTr CJun CSbt EBee EPfP LRHS MBlu NPip WMat WSpi	*capreolata*	CBcs CRHN EGrl
		- 'Dragon Lady'	CRHN WCot
- - 'White-Ness'	MBlu NLar WMat	*lindleyana*	see *Clytostoma calystegioides*
cf. *utilis*	SGol	*tweedieana*	see *Dolichandra unguis-cati*
verrucosa	see *B. pendula* subsp. *pendula*	*unguis-cati*	see *Dolichandra unguis-cati*
Biancaea (Leguminosae)		*Bijlia* (Aizoaceae)	
§ *decapetala*	WJur	*tugwelliae*	CPic
Biarum (Araceae)		*Bilderdykia* see *Fallopia*	
S&L 604	WCot	*Billardiera* (Pittosporaceae)	
SB&L 597	WCot	*heterophylla*	CAbb CBcs CBrac CDoC CMac CRHN CSBt CSpe CTsd CWGN EAri EGrl ELan EPfP EShb LBom LCro LRHS LSRN MAsh MGos MPri SEle SPoG SWCr WCot WPGP WTHo
carratracense from Spain	WCot		
davisii	WCot		
ditschianum from Turkey	WCot		
marmarisense	WCot		
tenuifolium	WCot	- 'Alba'	CBcs EPfP LBom LCro SEle SPoG WTHo
- LB 295	WCot		
- PB 357	WCot	- 'Pink Charmer'	CBcs SEle SPoG WTHo
- S&L 174	WCot	- **Ultra Blue** ('Tuisol')	CWnw EUrb LCro
- subsp. *abbreviatum* MS 974	WCot	*longiflora*	CAbb CBcs CHll CMCN CSBt EPfP LCro LRHS MAsh MGos MPri SPoG
- subsp. *arundanum*	WCot		
- subsp. *galianii* PB 435	WCot		
- subsp. *zelebori*	WCot	- 'Cherry Berry'	LRHS MGos SPoG
- - CRL 502	WCot	- 'Fructu-albo'	LRHS SPoG
- - LB 300	WCot		

Billbergia ✿ (Bromeliaceae)

'Fosters Striate'	CDTJ SChr
'Hallelujah'	NCft
nutans	CDTJ CHll CoPl EShb EUrb LEdu LWaG SChr SEND SNoN SPlb StAn WJun
- var. *schimperiana*	EShb
* - 'Variegata' (v)	CHll ELan EShb EUrb NCft SChr SNoN WCot WJun
'Santa Barbara' (v)	CDTJ SChr
× *windii* ♀H1b	CDTJ CoPl EShb LWaG NCft

Billbergia × *Cryptanthus* see × *Cryptbergia*

Biophytum (Oxalidaceae)

sensitivum	CDoC NTro

Biserrula (Fabaceae)

pelecinus	LShi

Bismarckia (Arecaceae)

nobilis	NPlm

Bistorta (Polygonaceae)

§ ***affinis***	CBcs EGren GAbr LCro NBro WFar
- 'Darjeeling Red' ♀H7	Widely available
- 'Dimity'	see *B. affinis* 'Superba'
- 'Donald Lowndes' ♀H7	CMac EBee EGrI EHeP ELan ELon EPfP GBin GMaP GQue LRHS LSRN MBel MHer MPro SAko SPoG SRms WCAu WChS WCot WFar WPnP WSpi
- 'Kabouter'	EBee LBar NLar
§ - 'Superba' ♀H7	EBee ECha EGren EHeP ELan ELon EPfP GBin GKev GMaP GQue LCro LRHS LSto MBel MGos MMuc MWlw NBir NBro NGdn SMrm SPoG WBrk WCAu WFar WHoo WPnP WSpi
§ Alba Junior ('Ifperaj')	LBar MPro SHar
§ ***amplexicaulis***	EAri EGren EHeP EWes GMaP MBel WBrk WFar WJun
- 'Alba' ♀H7	Widely available
- 'Amethyst'	CKno WCAu
- 'Amethyst Summer'	CWnw IPot LBar LSou MBel WCAu
- 'Ample Pink'	MAvo MNrw
- 'Anne's Choice'	LRHS
- 'Arends Pride'	SDix
- 'Arends Stolz'	ECha
- 'Atrosanguinea'	CMac EBee ECha ELan ELon GQue LRHS LSto MMuc NBir NLar SEND SMrm SRms WBrk WFar WHoo
- 'Avondale Sparkler'	MAvo
- 'Betty Brandt'	GQue
- 'Blackfield' PBR ♀H7	Widely available
- 'Bloody Mary'	LBar LRHS MPro
- 'Blotau'	see *B. amplexicaulis* Taurus
- 'Blush Clent' ♀H7	SNoN WCot
- Bonfire ('Bokrafire' PBR)	LBar
- 'Clent Charm'	WCot
- 'Cottesbrooke Gold'	EWhm MWlw
- dark red-flowered	EGren ESwi LRHS
- 'Dikke Floskes'	CKno ELon EPPr MHol SRms WBrk WCot WFar
- 'Early Pink Lady' ♀H6	EPPr SNoN
- 'Elworthy Candy' **new**	SHar
- 'Fascination'	CBWd CDor ELon SRkn WCot
- 'Fat Domino' PBR ♀H7	Widely available
- 'Fat White'	GBin
- 'Fine Pink' ♀H6	LSto
- 'Finy Tiny'	LBar
- 'Firedance'	CAby CKno ELon EPPr NDov SMHy SMrm SPel SPhx SRms WCot WFar
- 'Firetail'	Widely available
- 'Flamingo Feathers' **new**	LBar XFar
- 'Golden Arrow' (v)	CMac CTtf ELon EUrb LBar LRHS LShi LSto MPri MPro NBid NEoE NLar NSti SPeP SPoG SRms WCAu WCot WFar WTor
- 'High Society'	CBWd CKno GBin SPoG SRms WCAu
- 'Inverleith'	ECha ELon GBin GMaP GQue MMuc NBid NBir SMHy SPel SPoG WCAu WPnP
- 'Janet' ♀H6	SNoN
I - 'Jo and Guido's Form'	ELon EPPr NLar WCAu WFar
- 'JS Caliente' PBR	ELon LRHS MHol Midl MNrw SAko SHar SRms WCot WPnP WSpi
- 'JS Calor' PBR	EBee
- 'JS Delgado Macho' PBR ♀H6	EBee ESwi MNrw SRms
- 'JS Misty Morning' ♀H6	LBar LRHS
- 'Keep Smiling' **new**	LBar
- 'Lisan'	EPPr MNrw NLar WCAu WCot
- 'Marchants Red Devil'	SMHy
- 'October Pink'	EPPr SNoN
- Orange Field ('Orangofield' PBR) ♀H7	CKno CSpe CTtf EBee ELan EMor EUrb GBin GMaP LCro LRHS LSto MArl MHol MNrw MPie NCth NEoE NGdn NLar SAko WCAu WFar WHoo WTor
- var. *pendula*	ELon MBel NBir WFar
- - HWJK 2255	WCru
- 'Pink Knot'	LRHS
- 'Pink Mist' ♀H6	CWnw SPel WGoo WHil
- 'Pinkfield' **new**	IPot
- 'Red Baron' ♀H6	EBee EPPr Midl WFar
- 'Rosea'	Widely available
- 'Rosy Clent'	WCot
- 'Rowden Gem'	CCBP CKno ECha SNoN WCAu
- 'Rubie's Pink'	ECha
- 'September Spires'	CKno WGoo
- 'Spotted Eastfield' (v)	EPPr WCot WFar
- 'Summer Dance'	CKno ELon EPPr WCAu
§ - Taurus ('Blotau')	CDor EBlo ECha ELon EPPr ESwi LRHS NLar NSti SMHy SRkn SRms WCAu WFar
- 'White Eastfield' ♀H6	CDor CKno EBee ECha ELan EMor GElm GPSL NCth NDov NLar SAko WCAu WFar
carnea	CBWd CToG CTtf EBee ECha ELon EPPr EWhm GPSL MArl MBNS MMuc NBir NBro WCot
§ 'Ellie's Pink'	WCot
§ ***macrophylla***	GArf WCot
§ ***milletii***	EBlo NDov WCru
§ ***officinalis***	EGren IDun LCro LRHS LSto MHer MMuc MPro NBir NLar SRms WFar WKit WShi
- dwarf, shell-pink-flowered	WCot
- 'Hohe Tatra' ♀H7	CBWd CDor EBlo EPPr GMaP LBar LRHS MHol NDov NLar SDix SPoG WBrk WCot WFar WHil
- subsp. *pacifica*	LRHS
- 'Superba' ♀H7	Widely available
§ 'Pink Elephant' ♀H5	CDor CTtf EBee ECha ELon EPfP EPPr GBin LRHS MBel Midl MNrw MPro NDov NLar SAko SHor SRkn SRms WCAu WFar WMal WNPC WSpi WTor
§ ***tenuicaulis***	CMiW ECha ESwi GBin SBrt WCru

§ *vacciniifolia* ♀H7 CBcs EAri EBee ECha GAbr GBin
GEdr GKev GMaP MHer NBid NBir
NLar SLee SPlb SRms WAbe WFar
WHoo WIce WSpi
- 'Harran' GArf

Bituminaria (Fabaceae)
bituminosa SPhx WCot

blackberry see *Rubus fruticosus*; also AGM Fruit Section

blackcurrant see *Ribes nigrum*; also AGM Fruit Section

Blechnum (Blechnaceae)
alpinum see *B. penna-marina* subsp. *alpinum*
appendiculatum CAbb
auratum SBig
brasiliense ♀H1a CBrP ESwi SPlb
- 'Volcano' CBcs CSde CTsd EAri ELan LBuc
LCro LWaG MBlu NAlc NPlm NWbg
SBig SPoG
cartilagineum CDTJ CExl
§ *chilense* ♀H4 CDTJ CExl CLAP CSpe ECha EGren
EWes GKev LCro LEdu MAsh MWht
NBro SArc SBig SPlb SRms WCru
cycadifolium CBrP CDTJ CExl
discolor CBrP
- 'Silver Lady' CDoC
fluviatile CBrP CDTJ
gibbum ♀H1a CDoC LWaG SPlb
- 'Silver Lady' ISha LBom LCro LRHS LWaG NPlm
SBig
longicauda CBrP
magellanicum misapplied see *B. chilense*
magellanicum CExl SPlb
(Desv.) Mett.
minus LEdu
§ *niponicum* CExl CSta
novae-zelandiae CBrP CTsd
nudum CBrP CDTJ
penna-marina CBcs CDor CElw CLAP CSta CTsd
EGren ELan ELon EMor GAbr GEdr
GKev GMaP ISha LEdu LRHS LSto
MAsh NAlc NBir NBro NHar NRya
SAko SHor SPlb WCot
§ - subsp. *alpinum* EBee ECha EPfP GEdr GKev LEdu
SHar WAbe
- - BR 68 GEdr
- - Paradise Centre form ECha
- 'Cristatum' CLAP GEdr NBro NHar
spicant ♀H6 Widely available
tabulare misapplied see *B. chilense*
tabulare (Thunb.) Kuhn CBdn CDTJ SPlb

Blepharocalyx ✿ (Myrtaceae)
cruckshanksii see *Temu cruckshanksii*

Bletilla (Orchidaceae)
hyacinthina see *B. striata*
ochracea EAri EBee LAma XFar
§ *striata* ♀H4 CAby CBct CDoC CTsd EAri EBee
EDAr EGren EMor GKev LAma
LCro LEdu MBel MHer MNrw
MSCN NWbg SIvy SPlb WCot
WFar WPGP
- *alba* see *B. striata* f. *gebina*
- 'Albostriata' EAri ELan EMor ESwi NWbg WCot
- BLUE DRAGON see *B. striata* 'Soryu'

§ - f. *gebina* EAri ELan EMor GKev LAma LCro
LEdu NWbg SIvy WCot WFar
- - variegated (v) LAma LEdu
- 'Kuchi-beni' EMor LAma NWbg
- 'Lips' LAma
- pink-flowered LAma
§ - 'Soryu' EBee EMor LAma MHol NWbg
SEle
- variegated (v) CTtf EMor

Blitum (Amaranthaceae)
§ *bonus-henricus* CAgr CHab CHby ENfk EWhm
GQue IDun MCtn MEar MHer
MNHC NBac SRms SVic WHer
WJek WKor
§ *californicum* **new** NBac
§ *capitatum* MHoo SVic
§ *virgatum* MCtn

blueberry see *Vaccinium corymbosum*; also AGM Fruit Section

Blumea (Asteraceae)
balsamifera CHab

Blyxa (Hydrocharitaceae)
japonica ELin

Bocconia (Papaveraceae)
cordata see *Macleaya cordata* (Willd.) R. Br.
frutescens EAri SPlb
- B&SWJ 10654 WCru
integrifolia **new** EAri
microcarpa see *Macleaya microcarpa*

Boehmeria ✿ (Urticaceae)
CMBJP 1941 GGro
CMBJP 1961 GGro
from Kyushu, Japan LEdu
from Shikoku, Japan LEdu SMad SPlb
biloba EMor GGro SPlb
cylindrica EMor GGro
× *dura* GGro
gigantea GGro
holosericea CMBJP 2095 GGro
japonica **new** LEdu
§ - var. *tenera* EMor LEdu SDix SIvy SMad
- - CMBJP 1906 GGro
- - H2MD 057 WPGP
- 'Kyushu Rikishi' **new** WPGP
aff. *nipononivea* GGro
CMBJP 1924
nivea LEdu WCot WPGP
platanifolia EWld MNrw SBrt SDix SIvy SPhx
SPlb
aff. *platanifolia* GGro
CMBJP 1909
sieboldiana CSpe EAri EBee EPPr GGro SBrt
SDix SPhx SPlb WFar
silvestrii GGro
spicata see *B. japonica* var. *tenera*
splitgerbera GGro LEdu SPhx
tricuspis EPPr LEdu SBrt SPlb
- PB 96.976 WPGP
- var. *unicuspis* EWld GGro LEdu
- - CMBJP 1907 GGro
virgata var. *rotundifolia* EAri
- - PB 2.53 WPGP

Boenninghausenia (Rutaceae)
albiflora B&SWJ 1479 WCru

Bolanthus (Caryophyllaceae)
cherlerioides   GKev

Bolax (Apiaceae)
glebaria   see *B. gummifer*
§ *gummifer*   EPot GEdr SPlb WAbe WFar

Bolbitis (Lomariopsidaceae)
heteroclita   ELin

Boltonia (Asteraceae)
asteroides   ECha GQue MArl SMrm WHil
- var. *latisquama*   GMaP MHol NLar SHar
- - 'Snowbank'   EBee ELan EMor SDix WCAu WGoo
incisa   see *Kalimeris incisa*

Bomarea (Alstroemeriaceae)
acuminata   see *B. andreana*
acutifolia   EAri WCot
- B&SWJ 14291   WCru
- F&M 104   WPGP
§ *andreana* B&SWJ 14376   ESwi WCru
aff. *andreana* B&SWJ 10617 WCru
boliviensis misapplied   see *Alstroemeria isabellana*
boliviensis Baker   EAri
aff. *bredemeyerana* B&SWJ 14706   WCru
- B&SWJ 14725   WCru
caldasii   see *B. multiflora*
§ *edulis* ♀H3   CHll CRHN EAri SBeP WCot WPav
- B&SWJ 9017   WCru
'Fiesta'   WCot
frondea   see *B. multiflora*
hirsuta   EAri
- B&SWJ 14442   WCru
- B&SWJ 14902   WCru
hirtella   see *B. edulis*
§ *multiflora* ♀H2   EAri EBee LEdu MBlu MCtn WCot WCru WFar WPGP
- B&SWJ 14347   WCru
- B&SWJ 14354   WCru
- B&SWJ 14406   WCru
- B&SWJ 14419   EAri WCru
- B&SWJ 14847   WCru
aff. *multiflora* B&SWJ 14730 WCru
'Orange Sunset'   EAri
patacocensis JCA 13987   WCot
§ *patinii* B&SWJ 14213   WCru
- B&SWJ 14310   WCru
- B&SWJ 14946   WCru
puracensis B&SWJ 14705   WCru
- B&SWJ 14729   WCru
racemosa   see *B. patinii*
setacea   EAri
- B&SWJ 14875   WCru

Bombax (Malvaceae)
ceiba   SPlb

Bonia (Poaceae)
§ *solida*   MMuc SEND

Boophone (Amaryllidaceae)
disticha   CBlu LAma

Boquila (Lardizabalaceae)
trifoliolata   WCru

borage see *Borago officinalis*

Borago (Boraginaceae)
laxiflora   see *B. pygmaea*
officinalis   CCBP CGHo CHby EHet ENfk EPfP GJem IDun LCro LSto LWaG MCtn MHer MHoo MNHC MPri NBir SEdi SPhx SRms SVic WKit
- 'Alba'   ENfk LCro LSto LWaG MCtn MHoo MNHC SEdi SPhx SRms SVic WJek
§ *pygmaea*   CCBP CSpe ECha EWld MHer MHoo MNrw NBir NSti SRms WHer WJek

borecole see AGM Vegetables Section

Borinda (Poaceae)
KR 5287   MWht
KR 5600   MWht
KR 6438   MWht
KR 6439   MWht
KR 7346   MWht
KR 7613   MWht
KR 7662   MWht
albocerea ♀H4   MWht
- Yunnan 2   CDTJ
- Yunnan 3a   CDTJ
angustissima   CDTJ LRHS MMuc NLar
frigida   CDTJ
- KR 4059   MWht
grossa   CDTJ EUrb
- KR 5931   MWht
'Harlequin'   WCot
lushuiensis   WCot
- Yunnan 4   CDTJ MWht
macclureana   WCot
- KR 5051   MWht
- KR 5177 from Gyala, Nepal   MWht
aff. *macclureana* KR 6900   MWht
nujiangensis   CDTJ WPGP
papyrifera   EUrb MWht WCot WPGP
- CS 1046   CJun MWht
- KR 3968   MWht
perlonga   EUrb
- Yunnan 6   MWht

Boronia (Rutaceae)
crenulata   SEle
heterophylla   CAbb CBcs CSde CTsd EGrI SEle WCot

Bossiaea (Fabaceae)
riparia   SPlb
scolopendria   SPlb

Bothriochloa (Poaceae)
§ *bladhii*   CKno EPPr SRms
caucasica   see *B. bladhii*
§ *ischaemum*   EPPr

Bougainvillea (Nyctaginaceae)
'Alexandra'   LCro SPre
§ × *buttiana* 'Poulton's Special' ♀H2   CHll
'Fuchsia Rosea'   SAth
glabra ♀H1c   CWal SPre
§ - 'Sanderiana'   NPlm
'Poultonii Special'   see *B.* × *buttiana* 'Poulton's Special'
'Sanderiana'   see *B. glabra* 'Sanderiana'
spectabilis 'Vera Deep Purple'PBR   LCro

Boussingaultia (Basellaceae)
   baselloides Hook.   see *Anredera cordifolia*

Bouteloua (Poaceae)
§ **gracilis**   CBWd MCtn SMHy
    - 'Bad River' **new**   EDAr
    - 'Blonde Ambition' **new**   NClf

Bouvardia (Rubiaceae)
   ternifolia   WCot

Bowiea (Asparagaceae)
   volubilis   GKev LAma LBom SPlb

Bowkeria (Stilbaceae)
   cymosa   SPlb SVen

Boykinia (Saxifragaceae)
   aconitifolia   CMac GEdr GKev NRya WCru
   elata   see *B. occidentalis*
   lycoctonifolia   LEdu NLar
   major   WFar
§ **occidentalis**   WCru
   rotundifolia   GKev LShi NBir WCru
   tellimoides   see *Peltoboykinia tellimoides*

boysenberry see *Rubus* 'Boysenberry'

Brachychiton (Malvaceae)
   acerifolius   SPlb WJur
   discolor   EShb WJur
   populneus   SPlb WJur
§ **rupestris**   EShb

Brachyglottis (Asteraceae)
§ **bidwillii**   EBee WCot
    - 'Basil Fox'   WAbe
§ **compacta**   MAsh
   Dunedin Group   CWal
    - 'Drysdale'   ELan EPfP LRHS
§ - 'Sunshine' ♀H4   CAgr CoPl CSBt EBee EGren EHeP
                                         ELan EPfP GArf LCro LRHS LSto
                                         LWaG MGos MHtn MMuc NPer
                                         SDix SEND SPlb SRms WFar
   greyi misapplied   see *B.* (Dunedin Group) 'Sunshine'
§ ***greyi*** (Hook. f.) B. Nord.   CMac EBee
   huntii   SVen
   laxifolia misapplied   see *B.* (Dunedin Group) 'Sunshine'
   'Menthe Glaciale'   CBcs
§ **monroi**   CBcs CMac CSBt CWal SVen WFar
                                         WMal
§ **rotundifolia**   WCot
I 'Sunshine Improved'   CBcs CBrac MAsh
   WALBERTON'S SILVER DORMOUSE   CBcs CSBt EBee ELan EPfP LRHS
   ('Walbrach'PBR) ♀H4   MGos NSti SPoG

Brachypodium (Poaceae)
   pinnatum   EPPr MMuc
   sylvaticum   CHab MMuc SEND

Brachyscome (Asteraceae)
   angustifolia 'Billabong   LSou
      Mauve Delight'PBR
    - BRASCO VIOLET   WHil
      ('Dbrasc9'PBR)
      (Brasco Series)
   iberidifolia   MCtn
    - 'White Splendour'   MCtn
   'Magenta Delight'   LRHS LSou
   'Mini Mauve Delight'   LRHS

   'Royal Blue'   LCro
   'Strawberry Mousse'   LRHS

Brachystelma see *Ceropegia*

Bracteantha see *Xerochrysum*

Brahea ✿ (Arecaceae)
   armata ♀H1c   CDTJ EOli EUrb NPlm SArc SBig
                               SPlb
   calcarea   NPlm
   decumbens   NPlm
   dulcis   SPlb
   edulis   NPlm SBig SChr
   'Super Silver'   NPlm

Brassaiopsis (Araliaceae)
   bodinieri new   CExl
    - FMWJ 13495 **new**   WCru
   dumicola KWJ 12217   WCru
   hispida   CDTJ CExl
   mitis   CDTJ

Brassica (Brassicaceae)
   juncea   SVic WKit
   napus Napobrassica   SVic
      Group
   oleracea   CAgr NBac
    - Alboglabra Group   LCro SVic
    - Capitata Group   SVic
    - Gemmifera Group   SVic
    - Gongylodes Group   LCro SVic
    - Italica Group   SVic
    - var. ***ramosa***   CCps LEdu MEar NBac
    - - 'Cotswold Cream' (v)   WCot
    - - 'Luigi Leopold' (v)   WCot
   rapa Chinensis Group   SVic WKit
    - subsp. ***nipposinica***   LCro SVic
      var. ***laciniata***

× *Brigandra* see *Oreocharis*

Briggsia see *Oreocharis*

Brighamia (Campanulaceae)
   insignis   LCro SPad

Brillantaisia (Acanthaceae)
   kirungae   EShb SDix Slvy
   owariensis   WCot

Brimeura (Asparagaceae)
§ **amethystina** ♀H5   EGrl EPPr LEdu WPGP
    - 'Alba'   EGrl
   fastigiata   GKev

Briza (Poaceae)
   maxima   CTtf ECha LCro LWaG MCtn NClf
                             NGdn SPhx
   media   Widely available
    - 'Golden Bee'   CKno EPfP EPPr LEdu LRHS MMrt
                                SMad SPel WMal
    - 'Limouzi'   CElw CSpe EPfP EPPr GBin LEdu
                              MMrt MNrw NLar NSti SMad SMHy
                              SPel SPhx SPoG WPnP
    - 'Romany Silver'   LEdu
    - 'Russells'PBR   CDor CTtf EBee ELan GElm LEdu
                              LRHS MGos SPoG SRms
   minor   MCtn
   subaristata   EPPr
   triloba   ECha SPhx

broccoli see AGM Vegetables Section

Brodiaea (Asparagaceae)
§ *californica* — CSpe EBee
  – NNS 00-109 — WCot
  – 'Babylon' — EAri ERCP
  – 'Corrina' — see *Triteleia* 'Corrina'
  ida-maia — see *Dichelostemma ida-maia*
  laxa — see *Triteleia laxa*
§ *minor* — GKev
  peduncularis — see *Triteleia peduncularis*
  purdyi — see *B. minor*

Bromus (Poaceae)
  erectus — CHab
  – W&B BG B-5 — WCot
  inermis 'Skinner's Gold' (v) — EPPr WCot

Broussonetia (Moraceae)
  papyrifera — CMCN ESwi LMaj WJur WKor WLov
  – 'Laciniata' — SMad

Browningia (Cactaceae)
  hertlingiana — MCtn

Brugmansia ✿ (Solanaceae)
§ *arborea* ♀H1c — CBcs CDTJ EAri MCtn WFar
* – 'Rosea' variegated (v) — ELan
  × *candida* 'Angels Phänomena' (d) — EAri
  – 'Angels Sunbeam' (d) ♀H1c — ELan EShb
  – 'Creamsickle' (d) ♀H1c — NGKo
  – 'Double White' (d) — CHll
  – double-flowered (d) — EUrb
  – 'Flowerdream' (d) — EUrb
  – 'Grand Marnier' ♀H1c — CHll WKif
§ – 'Knightii' (d) ♀H1c — CDTJ
  – 'Maya' (v) — NGKo
  – 'Plena' — see *B.* × *candida* 'Knightii'
  – 'Snowbank' (v) — EAri EUrb
§ – 'Variegata' (v) — CDTJ EAri
  cream-flowered — CHll
  × *cubensis* 'Baby Doll' (d) — CHll
  – 'Charles Grimaldi' — EAri EShb NGKo
  double orange-flowered (d) — CHll
  pink-flowered — EAri
  rosei — see *B. sanguinea*
§ *sanguinea* ♀H2 — EAri EShb EUrb LWaG SAth SEND SPlb WFar
§ *suaveolens* ♀H1c — CBcs EAri LWaG MSwo WFar
  – 'Variegata' (v) — EShb
  – white-flowered **new** — EUrb
  – yellow-flowered — EShb EUrb
  'Triple A' (d) — EAri
  'USA Rosa' — NGKo SEND
  'Variegata Sunset' — see *B.* × *candida* 'Variegata'
  versicolor misapplied — see *B. arborea*
§ *versicolor* Lagerh. — WFar
  – 'Grand Marnier' — see *B.* × *candida* 'Grand Marnier'
  white-flowered — CPic
  yellow-flowered — CPic EAri

Brunfelsia (Solanaceae)
  calycina — see *B. pauciflora*
§ *pauciflora* ♀H1c — EShb

Brunia (Bruniaceae)
  albiflora — SPlb

Brunnera ✿ (Boraginaceae)
§ *macrophylla* — Widely available
  – 'Alba' — see *B. macrophylla* 'Betty Bowring'
  – ALCHEMY SILVER ('Tnbruas') (Alchemy Series) — EGren EMor EPfP LBar MBel Midl WFar
  – 'Alexanders Great'^{PBR} — Widely available
  – 'Alexandria' — EGren GAbr LBar MPnt NCth SPad
§ – 'Betty Bowring' — CBcs CBWd CMac CMHG CTtf ECha EMor EPfP GBin GKev GMaP LBar LCro LEdu LRHS MArl MPie NBir NGdn NLar NSti SBeP SPoG WCAu WCot WFar WPnP WTor XFar
  – 'Blaukuppel' — EWes LRHS MArl
  – 'Dawson's White' (v) — CBcs CDor EAri ECha ELan EMor EPfP EUrb GMaP LRHS LSto MPri NBid NBir NLar SRms WCAu WCot WFar WTor XFar
  – 'Diane's Gold'^{PBR} — CBcs EBee ELan EMor LBar LRHS LSou LSto MHol Midl MNrw NBid NLar SPeP WFar
  – 'Emerald Mist'^{PBR} (v) — EBee EMor MPnt NLar SHar WSpi
  – 'Golden Jack Frost' — LRHS MPnt
  – 'Gordano Gold' (v) — EWld WCot
  – 'Green Gold' (v) — WFar
  – 'Hadspen Cream' (v) ♀H6 — CBcs CDor CExl CMac ECha ELan EMor EUrb GAbr GMaP LBar LCro MBel MPnt NBid NBir NGdn NLar SPoG WCAu WChS WCot WFar WNPC WSpi
  – 'Henry's Eyes' — WFar
  – 'Jack Frost'^{PBR} ♀H6 — Widely available
  – 'Jack of Diamonds'^{PBR} — CWGN EAri EBee LBar LBom LSou MPnt MPri MPro WFar
  – 'Jack's Gold'^{PBR} — EMor GKev LBar MArl Midl NSti SMrm WNPC
  – 'Jennifer' — EBee EMor LBar MBel NLar NSti WCAu
  – 'King's Ransom'^{PBR} (v) — CWGN EMor GPSL NLar NSti WFar
  – 'Langtrees' — CBct CMac EBee ECha GAbr MArl MMuc NBir NGdn SEND WSpi
  – 'Little Jack' (v) — EBee EBlo EPfP SPoG
  – 'Looking Glass'^{PBR} ♀H5 — Widely available
§ – 'Mister Morse'^{PBR} (v) ♀H6 — CBWd CDor CExl CWGN CWnw EMor GMaP LCro LRHS MAvo Midl MNrw MPnt NBir NGdn NLar NSti SPel WCAu WCot WNPC WSpi
  – 'Mrs Morse' — see *B. macrophylla* 'Mister Morse'
  – 'Queen of Hearts'^{PBR} — EBee NCth
  – 'Sea Heart'^{PBR} — CSpe EBee ECha EPfP IPot LCro MBel Midl MMrt MPro NCth NGdn NLar NSti WCAu WFar
  – 'Silver Heart'^{PBR} — CCht CDor CWGN ELon EMor GPSL LBar LBuc MArl MAvo MPri NCth SBig SMad SPad SPel WCAu
  – 'Silver Spear' — CCps CDor EBee EPfP GElm IPot MGos NSti SPoG WCAu WCav WCot WNPC
  – 'Silver Wings' — GKev MGos NBir NGdn NLar NSti WCAu WFar
  – 'Sterling Silver'^{PBR} — LBuc LRHS MPnt MPri MPro NCth WTor
  – 'White Zebra' — EMor
  sibirica — EAri EBee EMor EPPr EWes NAts NBid NLar

Brunsvigia (Amaryllidaceae)
  bosmaniae — LAma WCot
  elandsmontana — WCot
  gariepensis **new** — LAma

grandiflora	LAma		– B&SWJ 8083	WCru
josephinae	WCot		– ADONIS BLUE ('Adokeep'^{PBR})	CBcs CBrac CCps CSBt SPoG WLav
– LAV 30394	WCot		– 'African Queen'	EPfP LRHS WLav
litoralis	LAma		– var. *alba*	CoPl LShi
marginata	WCot		– 'Apollonaria'	WLav
multiflora	see *B. orientalis*		– 'Autumn Beauty'	CCps WLav
§ *orientalis*	WCot		– 'Beijing'	see *B. davidii* 'Autumn Beauty'
pulchra	WCot		– 'Billy's Blue'	WLav
radulosa	LAma WCot		– 'Black Knight' ♀^{H6}	Widely available
– 'Barkley East' **new**	LAma		– 'Blue Eyes'	WLav
rosea 'Minor'	see *Amaryllis belladonna*		– 'Blue Horizon' ♀^{H6}	ELon SRGP WCot WLav
striata 'Oorlogskloof' **new**	LAma		– 'Border Beauty'	WLav

Brussels sprouts see AGM Vegetables Section

Bryonia (*Cucurbitaceae*)
dioica GGro

Bryophyllum see *Kalanchoe*

Buckinghamia (*Proteaceae*)
celsissima CPbh

Buddleja ✿ (*Scrophulariaceae*)

from Arunchal Pradesh	WPGP
agathosma	CExl EAri WCFE WLav WPGP
albiflora	WLav
– BO 15-041	EPPr GGro
alternifolia ♀^{H6}	CBcs CDoC CMac CMCN EBee ECha ELan EPfP EUrb LCro LRHS LSto MAsh MBlu MGos NLar NQui SPoG SRms WFar WSpi WTre
– 'Argentea'	CDoC ELan EPfP MBNS MMuc NLar SPoG WCot WLav
ARGUS VELVET ('Ilvoargus2'^{PBR})	EGren
ARGUS WHITE ('Ilvoargus01'^{PBR})	EGren
asiatica B&SWJ 11278 ♀^{H3}	WCru
auriculata	CBcs CExl CMCN CSde EPfP EPPr LRHS SDix SPlb SVen WLav
BERRIES AND CREAM ('Pmoore14'^{PBR})	CCps CDoC CoPl CSBt EBee EHeP LBuc LCro LRHS MHtn MSCN WNPC
'Blue Chip'^{PBR} (Lo and Behold Series)	EPfP LBuc SGol SRms WCot WFar WLav
'Blue Chip Junior' (Lo and Behold Series)	LBom SPoG
'Blue Knight' (Monarch Series)	LRHS MPri
* 'Blue Trerice'	CExl
'Bressingham Bountiful' **new**	EBee EBlo
caryopteridifolia	SEND
colvilei	CBcs CCps CMCN EAri EBee ELan EPfP EUrb GKin IArd WSpi
– B&SWJ 2121	WCru
– GWJ 9399	WCru
– WJC 13760	WCru
– 'Kewensis'	CCps CExl CHll CRHN EBee EGrI EPfP EWes SVen WCFE WLav
– pink-flowered	GBin MBNS NLar WSpi
– 'Tregye'	WPGP
cordata	SVen
– B&SWJ 10433	WCru
§ *crispa*	CBcs CDoC CExl EBee ECha ELan EPfP SVen WFar WKif WPGP WSpi
– var. *farreri*	SPoG
– – Farrer 44	WPGP
– 'Stone House Cottage'	LRHS
curviflora Hook. & Arn.	WPGP
davidii	CDoC CoPl MCtn

– BUTTERFLY TOWER ('Tobud1305')	EBee LRHS MHtn Midl NLar WLov WNPC
– Buzz Series	LBuc SOrN
– – BUZZ CANDY PINK ('Tobudsopin'^{PBR})	CCps CDoC ELan EPfP LRHS LSou MPro MSwo NLar SPoG WFar WLav
– – BUZZ HOT RASPBERRY ('Tobud1202')	CCps CSBt ELan Midl MPri MPro MSwo NBir NPer SPad WFar WLav
§ – – BUZZ INDIGO ('Tobudmidni'^{PBR})	CCps CDoC EBee ELan EPfP LBom LRHS LSou LSRN Midl MPri MPro WFar WLav
– – BUZZ IVORY ('Tobudivory'^{PBR})	CCps CMac ELan LSRN MGos Midl MMrt MPro MSwo SPoG WCot WLav WSpi
– – BUZZ LILAC	ELan MGos
– – BUZZ MAGENTA IMPROVED ('Tobudmagen'^{PBR})	CCps CDoC CMac CSBt ELan EUrb LBom LSou LSRN MGos MPri MPro NLar SPoG SRms WFar WLav WSpi
– – BUZZ MIDNIGHT	see *B. davidii* (Buzz Series) BUZZ INDIGO
– – BUZZ SKY BLUE ('Tobudskybl'^{PBR})	CCps CDoC CMac EGrI LBom MGos MPri MPro NLar SPoG SRms WFar WLav
– – BUZZ VELVET ('Tobudvelve'^{PBR})	CCps EGrI ELan EPfP LBom MPri MPro WLav
– – BUZZ VIOLET ('Tobudviole')	CCps CDoC EGrI ELan EPfP MGos MPro NLar SPoG WFar WHtc WLav
– – BUZZ WINE **new**	EUrb
– CAMBERWELL BEAUTY ('Camkeep') (English Butterfly Series) ♀^{H6}	WLav
– 'Castle School'	WLav
– 'Clive Farrell'	see *B. davidii* 'Autumn Beauty'
– 'Corinne Tremaine'	WHer
– 'Cotswold Blue'	WLav
– 'Cotswold Twilight'	WLav
– 'Crown Jewels' (Monarch Series)	LRHS NWbg
– 'Darent Valley' ♀^{H6}	LRHS
– 'Dark Dynasty' (Monarch Series)	LRHS
– 'Dartmoor' ♀^{H6}	CCoa CCps CDoC CEnd CExl CMac CSBt EBee EGren ELan EPfP LRHS MAsh NLar NPer SDix SPlb SPoG SRGP SRms WFar WLav WSpi
– 'Dart's Ornamental White'	WLav
– 'Dart's Papillon Bleu'	see *B. davidii* 'Pixie Blue'
– 'Dart's Purple Rain'	WLav
– 'Dubonnet'	WLav
– 'Ecolonia'	WLav
– 'Empire Blue'	CBcs CCps CDoC CSBt EAri EGren EPfP GKin LBom LRHS LSRN MAsh MGos NBir NPer SPlb SPoG SRms WTre
– 'Fair Lady'	WLav
– 'Fascinating'	NBir WLav
– 'Flaming Violet'	WLav
§ – FLORENCE ('Watflor')	MAsh WLav
– 'Foxtail'	WLav

Buddleja

- 'Glasnevin Hybrid'	EPfP NLar SDix WLav
- 'Gonglepod'	WLav
- 'Grand Cascade'	EBee LCro LRHS WNPC
- 'Grey Dawn'	WLav
- 'Griffin Blue'	WLav
- GROOVY GRAPE ('Piibd-i')	LRHS NCth
- 'Gulliver'[PBR]	LCro LRHS SGol WFar WLav
- 'Harlequin' (v)	CBcs CCps CMac CoPl CTsd ELan EPfP LRHS MGos NLar SEND SPlb SPoG SRms WFar WHtc WTre
- 'Île de France'	EGren SRms WLav
- 'Les Kneale'	WLav
- LILA SWEETHEART ('Botex 002') (Butterfly Candy Series)	CSBt EGren LBuc WNPC
- 'Lilac Moon'	WLav
- LITTLE LILA ('Botex 004') (Butterfly Candy Series)	CMac EGren EUrb LBuc LCro MBNS WFar WLov
- LITTLE PINK ('Botex 005') (Butterfly Candy Series)	CMac EUrb LBuc LCro LSou MBNS WFar WLov
- LITTLE PURPLE ('Botex 001') (Butterfly Candy Series)	LCro LSou MBNS WLov WNPC
- LITTLE RUBY ('Botex 006') (Butterfly Candy Series)	CSBt CWGN EUrb LBuc LCro LSou WFar WLov WNPC WTor
- LITTLE WHITE ('Botex 003') (Butterfly Candy Series)	CSBt EGren LBuc LCro LRHS
- 'Loganberry Jam'	WLav
- 'Longstock Autumn Delight'	LRHS
- MAGDA'S GOLD KNIGHT ('Elstb1') **new**	MBNS
- MARBLED WHITE ('Markeep') (English Butterfly Series)	NEoE WLav
- 'Midnight Skies'	LBuc
- 'Miss Violet'[PBR]	LBom
- MOONSHINE ('Buddma'[PBR])	NEoE WFar
§ - NANHO BLUE ('Mongo')	CBcs CMac CSBt EGren EHeP GKev GKin LRHS MAsh MGos NBir NLar WSpi
- 'Nanho Petite Indigo'	see B. davidii NANHO BLUE
- 'Nanho Petite Plum'	see B. davidii NANHO PURPLE
- 'Nanho Petite Purple'	see B. davidii NANHO PURPLE
§ - NANHO PURPLE ('Monum') ♀H6	CBcs CMac EPfP LRHS LSRN MGos NLar SPlb SRms
- NANHO WHITE ('Monite') ♀H6	CMac EPfP LRHS SRms
- var. nanhoensis	WFar WLav
- - BO 15-043	GGro
- 'Orchid Beauty'	WLav
- 'Orpheus'	CCps EPfP WLav
- 'Panache'	EPfP LRHS MAsh WLav
- 'Peace'	CMac LSRN NLar SPoG WLav
- PEACOCK ('Peakeep'[PBR]) (English Butterfly Series)	CSBt EGren MAsh NWbg WLav
- 'Persephone'	WLav
- 'Petite Indigo'	see B. davidii NANHO BLUE
- 'Pink Beauty'	LSRN MBlu SRGP WFar
- 'Pink Cascade'	CBrac LRHS MMrt
- PINK PANTHER ('Rutbu2016') **new**	LRHS
- 'Pink Pearl'	WLav
- 'Pink Spreader'	WLav
§ - 'Pixie Blue'	LBuc NLar WLav
- 'Pixie Red'	see B. davidii 'Royal Red'
- 'Pixie White'	LBuc MAsh NLar WLav
- 'Prince Charming'[PBR] (Monarch Series)	CoPl EPfP LRHS MAsh WLov
- 'Purple Champion'	CCps
- PURPLE EMPEROR ('Pyrkeep') (English Butterfly Series)	NBir WLav
- 'Purple Friend'	WLav
- 'Raspberry Wine'	MPro
- 'Red Admiral'	see B. davidii 'Royal Red'
- RÊVE DE PAPILLON ('Minpap')	MAsh WLav
- RÊVE DE PAPILLON BLUE ('Minpap3')	WLav
§ - 'Royal Red' ♀H6	Widely available
- 'Sage Blue'	WLav
- 'Santana' (v)	CCps CMac ELon EWes MAsh NWbg SPoG SRms WSpi
- 'Shire Blue'	WLav
- 'Son of Orpheus'	WLav
- 'Sophie'[PBR]	EBee MBlu NLar
- 'Summer Beauty'	MBlu WLav
- 'Summerhouse Blue'	CoPl LBuc LRHS WLav
- 'Twotones'	WLav
- 'Variegata'	see B. davidii FLORENCE
- 'White Ball'	ELan NLar WLav
- 'White Bouquet'	CSBt EPfP GKin NLar WFar WLav
- 'White Cloud'	EPfP SRms
- 'White Profusion' ♀H6	CBcs CBrac CCoa CDoC EBee EGren ELan EPfP LCro LRHS LShi LSto MBlu NBir NEoE SOrN SPoG SRms WFar WHtc
- 'White Wings'	CCps WLav
- 'Wisteria Lane'	CBcs EBee ELan LBom LRHS LSou WLov
§ delavayi	CExl SEND
DREAMING PURPLE ('Hinebud4'[PBR])	NLar WNPC
DREAMING WHITE ('Hinebud3'[PBR])	NLar WNPC
'Ellen's Blue'	ELon EPfP LRHS WLav
fallowiana misapplied	see B. 'West Hill'
fallowiana Balf. f. & W.W. Sm.	LRHS WLav
- BWJ 7803	WCru
- var. alba ♀H5	CMac ELan EPfP EPPr LRHS MBNS NLar SEND
- 'Bishop's Violet'	CTsd
'Flower Power'	see B. × weyeriana 'Bicolor'
(Flutterby Petite Series)	LCro
FLUTTERBY PETITE BLUE HEAVEN ('Podaras 8'[PBR])	
- FLUTTERBY PETITE DARK PINK ('Podaras 10'[PBR])	EGren LCro
- FLUTTERBY PETITE PINK ('Podaras 16')	EBee
- FLUTTERBY PETITE SNOW WHITE ('Podaras 15'[PBR])	LCro NLar
- FLUTTERBY PETITE TUTTI FRUITTI PINK ('Podaras 13'[PBR])	LCro LSou SRms
forrestii	WCru
- BWJ 8020	WCru
- W&O 7061	GGro
FUNKY FUCHSIA ('Piibd-ii')	LRHS NCth
'Glass Slippers' (Monarch Series)	LRHS
globosa ♀H5	Widely available
- RCB/Arg C-11	WCot
- 'Lemon Ball'	CCps MBlu NPer WLav
glomerata	EShb LRHS SPlb
- 'Silver Service'	WFar
heliophila	see B. delavayi
HIGH FIVE PURPLE ('Podcept1')	Midl
indica	WLav
INSPIRED PINK	see B. × weyeriana 'Pink Pagoda'
japonica B&SWJ 8912	WCru
'Lavender Cupcake' (Humdinger Series)	LRHS NWbg

Bulbocodium 143

'Lilac Chip' (Lo and Behold Series)	CDoC NLar
lindleyana	CBcs CCBP CCoa CCps CExl CMac CMCN CSde CTsd EAri EBee ECha EPfP LRHS NLar NQui SBrt SPoG SRms WFar WLav
- 'Floral Fanfare' (d)	CCps
aff. *lindleyana*	EShb WSpi
- B&SWJ 11478	WCru
'Lochinch' ♀H5	CBcs CBrac CCps CDoC CMac EBee ELan EPfP GBin GKin LBom LCro LRHS LShi LSto MGos MPri NLar SDix SPlb SRms WFar WSpi WTre
longiflora	WPGP
'Longstock'	CCps
'Longstock Gem'	CCps LBuc
loricata	CBcs CExl CMCN EAri EPfP EPPr LRHS LShi SBrt SEND SPlb WLav WSpi
macrostachya	WCot WPGP
- PAB 4198	WCot
- WWJ 12016	WCru
§ *madagascariensis* ♀H2	CRHN EShb NLar SPlb SVen
'Magenta Munchkin' (Humdinger Series)	WLov
marrubiifolia × *saligna*	WPGP
megalocephala	EAri SPlb
- B&SWJ 9106	WCru WPGP
'Miss Ruby'PBR ♀H5	CCps CDoC EBee LBuc MAsh WLav
§ 'Morning Mist'PBR	CBcs CCps CDoC CExl CMac CSBt EGren EPfP GBin LCro LRHS LSRN SRms WCot
myriantha	CExl
- 'Sikkim Snow'	WCru
nicodemia	see *B. madagascariensis*
nivea	CExl CMCN EBee SEND WLav WSpi
- B&SWJ 2679	WCru
aff. *nivea*	WSpi
officinalis ♀H3	CExl WLav
'Orange Sceptre'	EBee SChF WPGP
paniculata BWJ 16321 from northern Vietnam	WCru
parvifolia MPF 148	WLav
× *pikei* 'Hever'	SRms
- Unique ('Pmoore12'PBR)	CCps CDoC CMac LCro LRHS NLar SPoG SRkn WCot
'Pink Delight' ♀H5	Widely available
'Pink Micro Chip' (Lo and Behold Series)	NLar SPoG
'Pink Perfection'	WFar
'Pride of Longstock'	CCps LRHS SPoG
Psychedelic Sky ('Piibd-iii')	LRHS
pterocaulis	EBee
'Purple Punk'	WCot
Purple Splendour ('Hinebud2'PBR)	Midl
'Queen of Hearts' (Monarch Series)	WFar
'Red Chip' (Lo and Behold Series)	SGol
(Rocketstar Series)	LBuc LRHS
Rocketstar Flamingo ('Smnbdpt'PBR)	
- Rocketstar Indigo ('Smnbdbt'PBR)	LBuc LRHS
- Rocketstar Orchid ('Smnbdo'PBR)	LBuc LRHS
- Rocketstar Snow ('Smnbdw')	LBuc
'Salmon Spheres'	CCps WLav
salviifolia	CBcs CCoa CExl CHll CMac CSde EBee EPfP ESgl EUrb MBlu MPri NLar SChF SEND SPlb SVen WKif WLav WPGP
Silver Anniversary	see *B.* 'Morning Mist'
speciosissima	EAri EBee EUrb SBrt WPGP
stachyoides	WLav WPGP
stenostachya	CBcs CExl
sterniana	see *B. crispa*
Sugar Plum ('Lonplum'PBR)	CBrac CCps CSBt EGrl EPfP LBuc LCro LRHS MAsh SPoG WNPC
Summer Bird Series	EGren
tibetica	see *B. crispa*
True Blue ('Bostulu'PBR)	NLar
tubiflora	WLav
venenifera f. *calvescens*	LRHS
- - B&SWJ 895	ESwi
× *wardii* KR 4881	CExl WPGP
§ 'West Hill' ♀H5	EPfP WLav
× *weyeriana*	CMac EGren EPPr EWld MNrw NBir SIvy SPlb WFar
- 'Bee Balm Beauty'	WCot
§ - 'Bicolor'	CoPl CWal ELon EPPr LCro LRHS LSRN MNHC MNrw NCth NLar NQui SRms WCot WLav WMal
- 'Boy Blue'	CCps WLav
- 'Golden Glow'	CCps WLav
- 'Honeycomb'	ELon EPPr MGos NLar
- 'Lady de Ramsey'	NLar SEND
- 'Moonlight'	CBcs CCps CDoC CExl EPfP GBin MPri WCot WLav WSpi
§ - 'Pink Pagoda'PBR	CCps CSBt NLar SPoG
- 'Pink Sundae'	WLav
§ - 'Sungold' ♀H6	CBcs CCps CMac EAri ELan EPPr ESgl GBin LCro LRHS LShi LSRN MAsh MBlu NBir NLar SPoG SRGP SRms WCot WFar WLav WMal WSpi WTre
'White Chip' (Lo and Behold Series)	SGol
yunnanensis	CBcs GGro LRHS NLar SBrt
- B&SWJ 8146	WCru

Buglossoides (Boraginaceae)

§ *purpurocaerulea*	ECha EPfP EWld LShi MNrw NBid WCot WFar

Bukiniczia (Plumbaginaceae)

cabulica	EDAr GKev

Bulbine (Asphodelaceae)

caulescens	see *B. frutescens*
§ *frutescens*	CAgr CoPl CTtf EDAr EGrl LWaG MHer SEND SIvy SVen SVic WJek
- (Avera Sun Series) 'Avera Sunrise Yellow'	MPro
- - 'Avera Sunset Orange'	CSpe MPro SMad SMrm
- 'Hallmark'	CWnw EShb
- orange-flowered	SIvy
narcissifolia	WCot

Bulbinella (Asphodelaceae)

angustifolia	GKev
gibbsii var. *balanifera*	GKev
hookeri	CExl EWld GEdr GKev WCot

Bulbinopsis see *Bulbine*

Bulbocodium see *Colchicum*

bullace see *Prunus insititia*

Bunias (Brassicaceae)
orientalis — CAgr LEdu MEar NBac WKor

Bunium (Apiaceae)
bulbocastanum — CAgr GBin SHor SMHy WTre
ferulaceum — MHol MPie NSti SHar

Buphthalmum (Asteraceae)
salicifolium — EBee ELan EPfP LRHS MMuc NBro NGdn SRms StAn WFar WHil
- 'Alpengold' — ECha
- 'Dora' — WCot WFar
- 'Sunwheel' — SRms
speciosum — see *Telekia speciosa*

Bupleurum (Apiaceae)
angulosum — NBir SDix
- copper-leaved — see *B. longifolium*
candollei — LEdu SAng WPGP
falcatum — ECha GMaP NDov SDix SPhx WCot
- tall — CSpe
fruticosum — CBcs CCoa CDoC CSpe EBee ECha ELan EPfP EWes GKev MCtn MNrw SDix SHor SPoG WCot WLov
griffithii 'Decor' — CSpe
§ *longifolium* — CSpe EBee EWes LEdu MNrw NBir NCth WPGP
- subsp. *aureum* — GGro SPhx
- 'Bronze Beauty' — ELan GEdr MCtn SBrt SHor
- lime-green-flowered — WPGP
- subsp. *longifolium* — WPGP
ranunculoides — CSpe LShi MNrw
rotundifolium — CSpe LEdu SAng SPhx WCot
- 'Copper' — NClf NDov
- 'Garibaldi' — MCtn
- 'Griffithii' — MCtn

Bursaria (Pittosporaceae)
spinosa — WHil

Butia ✿ (Arecaceae)
archeri — NPlm
capitata ♀H3 — CDTJ EGren EOli EUrb NPlm SArc SAth SBig SFol
§ - var. *odorata* — SArc SBig SPlb
eriospatha — NPlm SBig
odorata — see *B. capitata* var. *odorata*
paraguayensis — NPlm
yatay — NPlm

Butomus (Butomaceae)
umbellatus — CBen CLil CPud CToG CTtf CWat ECha ELin EPfk EWat MNrw MWts NBir NPer WMAq
- f. *albiflorus* — CLil ECha
- 'Rosenrot' — EWat
- 'Schneeweisschen' — ELin EWat MWts

butternut see *Juglans cinerea*

butternut squash see AGM Vegetables Section

Buxus (Buxaceae)
aurea 'Marginata' — see *B. sempervirens* 'Marginata'
balearica — IDun SBrt WSpi
bodinieri — LTop
harlandii misapplied — CMen SRiv
macowanii — LTop
macrophylla — WSpi
microphylla 'Badsey Kingsville' — WCot
§ - 'Compacta' — CMen WCot
- 'Faulkner' ♀H6 — LBuc MGos MSwo WSpi
- 'Green Pillow' — WSpi
- 'Herrenhausen' — WSpi
- var. *japonica* 'National' — WSpi
rugulosa var. *prostrata* — SBrt
sempervirens — Widely available
- 'Angustifolia' — SMad
- 'Argenteo-variegata' (v) — SGol WFar
- 'Aurea' — see *B. sempervirens* 'Aureovariegata'
- 'Aurea Maculata' — see *B. sempervirens* 'Aureovariegata'
- 'Aurea Marginata' — see *B. sempervirens* 'Marginata'
§ - 'Aureovariegata' (v) — LTop NLar SRiv SRms
- 'Bentley Blue' — LTop
- 'Blauer Heinz' — GQue LTop SRiv WSpi
- clipped ball — EGren EPfP LTop MGos NLar SRiv
- clipped bird — LTop SRiv
- clipped cone — EGren LTop SRiv SRms
- clipped pyramid — EGren EPfP LTop MGos NLar SRiv SRms
- clipped spiral — EGren LTop NLar SRiv SRms
- 'Elegans' — LTop
§ - 'Elegantissima' (v) ♀H6 — ELan EPfP LTop MAsh MGos MMuc NLar SGol SPoG SRiv SRms WCFE WSpi
- 'Fiesta' — SRms
- 'GoldTip' — see *B. sempervirens* 'Notata'
§ - 'Graham Blandy' ♀H6 — SAko SGol SRiv WSpi
- 'Green Balloon' — LBuc
- 'Greenpeace' — see *B. sempervirens* 'Graham Blandy'
- 'Handsworthensis' — LTop SRms WCFE WSpi
- 'Ickworth Giant' — WSpi
- 'Japonica Aurea' — see *B. sempervirens* 'Latifolia Maculata'
- 'Kensington Gardens' — WSpi
- 'King Midas' — SAko
- 'Kingsville' — see *B. microphylla* 'Compacta'
- 'Kingsville Dwarf' — see *B. microphylla* 'Compacta'
§ - 'Latifolia Maculata' (v) ♀H6 — EPfP LTop NPer SPoG SRiv WSpi
- 'Longifolia' — see *B. sempervirens* 'Angustifolia'
§ - 'Marginata' (v) — LTop WSpi
- 'Memorial' — LTop WSpi
- 'Myosotidifolia' — SRiv WCot WSpi
- 'Myrtifolia' — WSpi
§ - 'Notata' (v) — WSpi
- 'Pendula' — WSpi
- 'Prostrata' — WSpi
- 'Pylewell' — WSpi
- 'Rotundifolia' — CNWT LTop WSpi
- 'Silver Variegated' — see *B. sempervirens* 'Elegantissima'
- 'Suffruticosa' — CBrac CSBt EHeP LBuc LTop MGos MHed NLar SRms WCFE WSpi
- 'Suffruticosa Variegata' (v) — SRms
- 'Vardar Valley' — WSpi
- 'Variegata' (v) — CWal SArc WHtc
- 'Wisley Blue' — LTop WSpi
sinica — LTop WSpi
- var. *insularis* — LTop
- - 'Filigree' — WSpi
- - 'Justin Brouwers' — SRiv WSpi
- - 'Tide Hill' — LTop SRiv WSpi
wallichiana — LTop

C

cabbages see AGM Vegetables Section

Cabomba (Cabombaceae)
aquatica	ELin
caroliniana	Prohibited invasive. See Conservation and the Environment, p.42

Cacalia see *Adenostyles*
suaveolens L.	see *Hasteola suaveolens*

Cachrys (Apiaceae)
alpina	LEdu SBrt SPhx WCot

Caesalpinia (Fabaceae)
decapetala	see *Biancaea decapetala*
gilliesii	see *Erythrostemon gilliesii*
spinosa	see *Tara spinosa*

Cajanus (Fabaceae)
cajan	CAgr

calabrese see AGM Vegetables Section

Caladium (Araceae)
'Aaron' (v)	XFar
bicolor 'Bottle Rocket' (Heart to Heart Series) (v)	LCro
- 'Limelite' (v)	XFar
- 'Party Punch' (v)	XFar
- 'Pink Splash' (v)	LCro
- 'Scarlet Flame' (v)	LCro
'Candidum' (v)	XFar
'Carolyn Whorton' (v)	LBom XFar
'Cranberry Star' (v)	XFar
Fancy Mix	XFar
'Fannie Munson' (v)	XFar
'Festivia' (v)	XFar
'Flash Rouge' (v)	LBom XFar
'Florida Elise' (v)	XFar
'Florida Moonlight' (v)	XFar
'Florida Sweetheart'	XFar
'Frieda Hempel'	LCro XFar
'Frog in a Blender' (v)	XFar
'Galaxy' (v)	XFar
'Gingerland' (v)	XFar
'Kathleen' (v)	XFar
§ **lindenii** (v)	LBom
'Miss Muffet' (v)	XFar
praetermissum	LBom XFar
'Hilo Beauty'	
'Rosebud' (v)	XFar
'Sizzle' (v)	XFar
'Spring Fling'	XFar
'White Christmas' (v)	LCro XFar
'White Queen' (v)	LCro XFar
'White Wonder' (v)	LCro

Calamagrostis (Poaceae)
× **acutiflora** 'Avalanche'	CBWd CCps CKno CWnw EBee ECha ELon EMor EPfP EPPr EWes GKev GQue LRHS MArl MAsh MBel MMrt NClf NGdn SPoG SRot WFar WHoo WTor
- 'Eldorado' (v)	CKno ECha ELan EMor EPPr MAsh MMuc SEND WCot
- 'England' (v)	EBee ECha EMor EPPr GBin MAvo MNrw NCth WFar
- 'Karl Foerster' ♀H6	Widely available
- 'Overdam' (v)	Widely available
- 'Stricta'	EPPr
- 'Waldenbuch'	CKno ECha ELon EPPr LEdu LRHS WCAu
argentea	see *Stipa calamagrostis*
arundinacea	CMac EGren EMor SPlb
§ **brachytricha** ♀H6	Widely available
- 'Mona'	NCth NDov SPel
canadensis	EMor
effusiflora	CElw EPPr
emodensis	CAby CElw CSpe EMor EPPr ESwi GQue LEdu MMrt MMuc NBid WChS WPGP
epigejos	EMor EPPr WPGP
'Glenorchy Fireworks'	EPPr
'Kyrgyz Giant'	WPGP
ophitidis	SPlb
splendens misapplied	see *Stipa calamagrostis*
varia	CKno EMor NClf SMHy

Calamintha (Lamiaceae)
alpina	see *Clinopodium alpinum*
clinopodium	see *Clinopodium vulgare*
§ **grandiflora**	CCBP ECha EGrl GJos LShi MHoo NBir NLar NPer NQui SPlb SRms WCAu WKif
- 'Camlihemsin'	WCru
- 'Variegata' (v)	MHoo SRms WCAu
§ **nepeta**	CCBP CHab ECha EGren EGrl ENfk GBin LCro LSto MArl MHer MHol MHoo MMrt MNHC NBro SEND SMHy SMrm SPlb SPoG SRms StAn WCAu WHer WHoo WKit
- subsp. **glandulosa** 'White Cloud'	ELan EPfP LRHS LSto MArl MBel MHol MPie NBir NDov SRms WCAu WHil
- 'Gottfried Kuehn'	SNoN
- 'Marvelette Blue'	GBin LRHS MCtn NLar SPel SPhx WHil WTor
- 'Marvelette White'	LRHS MCtn SPhx
§ - subsp. **nepeta**	CBlu CBWd ELan EPfP GMaP MHer MMuc NDov
- - 'Blue Cloud'	CSpe EBee ECha EPfP GBin GElm GMaP MBel MCtn NBir NDov NLar SHor SMHy SPhx SPoG SRms WCAu WFar WHil WRBe WTor
- 'Triumphator'	WGoo
- 'Weisse Riese'	EBee NDov
- white-flowered	ECha SMHy
nepetoides	see *C. nepeta* subsp. *nepeta*
vulgaris	see *Clinopodium vulgare*

calamondin see *Citrus* × *microcarpa*

Calandrinia (Montiaceae)
caespitosa	EDAr
fuegiana	SPlb
grandiflora	CPbh LShi
sibirica	see *Claytonia sibirica*
umbellata	EDAr WIce

Calanthe (Orchidaceae)
aristulifera	LAma WFar
§ **Atsushi Hasegawa gx**	GKev
bicolor misapplied	see *C.* Atsushi Hasegawa gx
bicolor Lindl.	see *C. striata*
discolor	LAma

- var. *flava*	see *C. striata*
Kozu gx	LAma LEdu
reflexa	LAma
sieboldii	see *C. striata*
§ *striata*	LAma
Takane gx	see *C.* Atsushi Hasegawa gx
tricarinata	WFar

Calathea (Marantaceae)

crocata	see *Goeppertia crocata*
lancifolia	see *Goeppertia insignis*
makoyana	see *Goeppertia makoyana*
orbiculata	see *Goeppertia truncata*
ornata	see *Goeppertia ornata*
roseopicta	see *Goeppertia roseopicta*
stromata	see *Ctenanthe burle-marxii*
zebrina	see *Goeppertia zebrina*

Calceolaria (Calceolariaceae)

acutifolia	see *C. polyrhiza* Cav.
andina	EDAr SPlb
arachnoidea	SPlb
- 'Darcies Velvet'	EDAr
* × *banksii*	WMal
§ *biflora*	EDAr EWes LShi
- 'Goldcap'	GEdr
'Camden Hero' ♀H2	CSpe WMal
cavanillesii	SPlb
fothergillii	EDAr WAbe
(Fruticohybrida Group)	EBee EDAr ELan ESgI LCro LShi
'Kentish Hero' ♀H2	MHer SAdn SHor SPel WAbe WMal
§ *integrifolia* ♀H2	CDTJ CFis CRHN ELan SPoG
paralia 'Lemon Drops'	EDAr
aff. *pavonii*	CRHN
perfoliata B&SWJ 14742	WCru
plantaginea	see *C. biflora*
§ *polyrhiza* Cav.	EDAr
rugosa	see *C. integrifolia*
tenella	WAbe
thyrsiflora	LShi
trilobata subsp. *trilobata* B&SWJ 14896	WCru
'Walter Shrimpton'	WAbe WIce

Calendula (Asteraceae)

arvensis	MCtn
'Bronze Beauty'	CSpe
Everdaisy Series	see *C.* Winter Wonders Series
officinalis	CCBP CGHo EGren EHet ENfk GJem LCro MHer MHoo MNHC SRms SVic WKit
- 'Apricot Twist'	LSou
- 'Art Shades'	MCtn
- 'Candyman Orange' (d)	MCtn
- 'Double Lemon' (d)	MCtn
- Fiesta Gitana Group ♀H5	LCro MPri
- 'Greenheart Orange' (Greenheart Series)	MCtn
- 'Indian Prince' (Prince Series)	LCro LSto MCtn NClf
- 'Lemon Twist' (d)	LCro
- 'Neon' (d)	MCtn
- Oopsy Daisy (mixed)	MCtn MHoo MPro
- 'Orange King'	LCro
- 'Orange Porcupine'	MCtn
- 'Pacific Beauty Apricot'	MCtn
- 'Radio Extra Selected'	MCtn
- 'Sherbert Fizz'	LCro
- 'Snow Princess'	LCro LSto MCtn MHoo
- 'Sunset Buff' **new**	SHor
- Touch of Red Series	MCtn
- - 'Touch of Red Buff'	MCtn
- - 'Touch of Red Orange'	MCtn
'Orange Flash'	MCtn
PowerDaisy Series	MPro
- PowerDaisy Sunny ('Kercalsun') **new**	MPro
- PowerDaisy Tango ('Kercaltan'^{PBR})	MHol MPro
suffruticosa subsp. *tomentosa*	SEND
'Tarifa'	SNoN
(Winter Wonders Series)	LCro MPro
Winter Wonders Amber Arctic ('212372d')	
- Winter Wonders Banana Blizzard ('2012357d'^{PBR})	LCro
- Winter Wonders Golden Glaze ('2012329d')	LCro
- Winter Wonders Peach Polar ('2012391d'^{PBR})	LCro MPro

Calibrachoa (Solanaceae)

(Cabaret Series) Cabaret Deep Blue ('Balcabdebu'^{PBR})	LSou
- Cabaret Good Night Kiss ('Balcabooni'^{PBR})	LCro
- Cabaret Hot Pink ('Balcabhopi')	LCro
- Cabaret Light Pink ('Balcablitpi')	LCro
- Cabaret Light Pink Kiss ('Balcablipism')	LSou
- Cabaret Yellow ('Balcabyelow')	LCro
(Calitastic Series)	MPri
Calitastic Cappuccino ('Wescacacap') **new**	
- Calitastic Merry Cherry ('Wescacalimerc') **new**	MPri
(Can-can Series) Can-can Black Cherry	LCro MBros
- Can-can Coral Reef ('Balcanoree')	MBros
- Can-can Double Apricot (d)	LCro
- Can-can Double Blue (d)	MBros
- Can-can Double Dark Yellow (d)	MBros
- Can-can Double Provence Blue (d)	LCro
- Can-can Orange ('Balcanoran')	LCro MBros
- Can-can Oriental **new**	LSou
- Can-can Pink Punch **new**	LSou
- Can-can Sunlight	LSou
- Can-can Sunrise	LSou
Celebration Deep Red ('Wescacherryno')	LCro
(Dream Kisses Series)	
(Chameleon Series)	LCro
Chameleon Double Pink Yellow ('Wescachadpiyecheba') (d)	
- Chameleon Tart Deco ('Wescachatade') **new**	MPri
Kabloom Denim ('Pas1122759')	LCro
(Kabloom Series)	
(Superbells Series)	MSwo
Superbells Blackcurrant Punch ('Bbcal81801')	

- Superbells Evening Star ('Bbcal87705') **new**	MSwo
- Superbells Honey Peach **new**	LSou MSwo
- Superbells Lemon Slice ('Uscal5302m'^{PBR})	MSwo
- Superbells Strawberry Punch ('Uscal58205')	MBros
Trixi Hot Petticoat (mixed) (d)	MPri
(Unique Series) Unique Golden Yellow **new**	MSwo
- Unique Orange **new**	MSwo

Calibrachoa × *Petunia* see × *Petchoa*

Calla (Araceae)

aethiopica	see *Zantedeschia aethiopica*
palustris	CLil CPud CWat ELin EWat LWaG NPer SRms WMAq

Calliandra (Fabaceae)

'Dixie Pink'	SEle
surinamensis	CBcs LBom SMad

Callianthemum (Ranunculaceae)

§ *anemonoides*	EDAr GEdr WAbe WCot
§ *coriandrifolium*	GKev
kernerianum	WAbe
rutifolium	see *C. anemonoides*, *C. coriandrifolium*

Callicarpa (Lamiaceae)

CW&T 6228	CMCN
americana var. *lactea*	CMCN
bodinieri	EGrl EHeP WJur
- var. *giraldii*	CBrac NLar
- - 'Profusion' ♀^{H6}	Widely available
- 'Imperial Pearl'	CWnw ELan LRHS
- Magical Purple Giant ('Kolmapurgi') **new**	LSou
- Magical Snowqueen ('Kolmsqueen'^{PBR})	WHil
- Magical Snowstar ('Kolmsnostar')	ELan EPfP LCro LRHS MMrt NLar
cathayana	NLar
dichotoma	CBcs LRHS NLar NLit WJur
- f. *albifructa*	NLar
- 'Issai'	EBee EGrl ELan EPfP LCro MBlu NLar WLov
formosana NMWJ 14553	WCru
japonica	CMen NLar SBrt
- B&SWJ 12621	WCru
- f. *albibacca*	LMaj NLar
- 'Heavy Berry'	ELon NLar
- 'Koshima-no-homate'	NLar
- 'Leucocarpa'	CBcs CMac EBee ELan EPfP LRHS NLar SPoG WJur
- var. *luxurians* B&SWJ 8521	WCru
kwangtungensis	CBcs EBee EPfP NLar
Pearl Glam ('Nccx2') **new**	ELan
pilosissima NMWJ 14508	WCru
psilocalyx NJM 13.057	WPGP
rubella	WJur
shikokiana	NLar
× *shirasawana*	NLar
aff. *tikusikensis* B&SWJ 7127	WCru
Van den Broek selection	NLar
yunnanensis	NLar

Callirhoe (Malvaceae)

involucrata	CSpe MCtn SBrt
- var. *tenuissima*	EBee SBrt

Callisia (Commelinaceae)

elegans	see *C. gentlei* var. *elegans*
fragrans	EShb WJun
- 'Infinity' (v)	WTra
- 'Melnickoff' (v)	WTra
§ *gentlei* var. *elegans*	EShb WTra
- var. *macdougallii*	WTra
§ *navicularis* ♀^{H1c}	CPic
repens	CoPl EShb LWaG
- 'Bianca' (v)	WTra
- 'Bianca' big leaf (v)	WTra
- 'Gold'	WTra
- 'Gold Variegated' (v)	WTra
- 'Green Turtle'	WTra
- 'Kribo' (v)	WTra
- 'Rosato' big leaf	WTra
soconuscensis	WTra
- 'Variegata' (v)	WTra
'Turtle'	CDoC WFar

Callistemon (Myrtaceae)

acuminatus	EBee
Amarette ('Hutnik')	CAbb MHtn Midl
brachyandrus	SVen
citrinus	EGrl EPfP MPro MSwo SEND SPlb
- 'Albus'	see *C. citrinus* 'White Anzac'
- 'Angela'	EUrb
- 'Firebrand'	LRHS
- 'Splendens' ♀^{H3}	CBcs CBrac CCoa CDoC CMac CoPl CSBt CSde CWnw EGrl ELan ELon EPfP EUrb IArd LCro LRHS MGos MPri SEND SIvy SPoG SVen SWor WCot WFar
§ - 'White Anzac'	CCoa CDoC CMac CSBt CSde CTsd ELan ELon EPfP SEND SIvy SPoG
glaucus	see *C. speciosus*
'Havering Gold'	EUrb
Hot Pink ('Kkho1'^{PBR})	CBcs CWnw EGrl LRHS MGos SEle WCot
Inferno ('Yanferno')	CAbb CBcs CWnw EGrl LCro LSou Midl SPad
'Injune'	EUrb
laevis hort.	see *C. rugulosus*
linearifolius	LSRN
linearis ♀^{H2}	CBrac CCoa CMac CSde ELan EPfP LRHS LSRN MGos SEND SIvy SPlb
macropunctatus	SPlb SVen
'Masotti'^{PBR}	EGrl LRHS SEle SPoG
'Mauve Mist'	CDoC CMac EBee ELan ELon EPfP EUrb LRHS SEND SIvy SPad SPoG SVen WFar
pallidus	CBcs CBrac CCoa CDoC CMac CTsd EBee EGrl ELan ELon EPfP EUrb LRHS SEle SEND SPlb SVen WFar
- 'Father Christmas'	EUrb
paludosus	see *C. sieberi* DC.
'Perth Pink'	CBcs CCoa CDoC CSBt CSde CTsd EBee EGrl ELan ELon EPfP EUrb LRHS SEle SEND SIvy SPad SVen
pinifolius	SPlb SVen
'Pink Champagne'	EUrb
§ *pityoides* ♀^{H5}	CTsd EGrl ELan ELon EUrb NLar SEle SIvy SVen
'Red Clusters'	CBcs CBrac CCoa CDoC CMac CSde ELan WFar

Callistemon

'Red Rocket'	CDoC LRHS
rigidus	CBcs CDoC EBee EGrI EHeP ELan LRHS LSRN MGos MMuc MPro NLar NLit SAth SVen
§ *rugulosus*	CBrac EBee EPfP LCro SAth SFol SVen
salignus ♀H2	CBcs CCoa CMac ELon SEle SVen
- BEEZNEEZZ	see *C. salignus* HONEY POT
- FLAMING FIRE ('Flaipp')	EGren
§ - HONEY POT ('Hutneezz')	LSou Midl WFar
sieberi misapplied	see *C. pityoides*
§ *sieberi* DC.	CBcs CCoa CDoC ELon EPfP MMuc NLar SEle SPlb
- purple-flowered	ELon EUrb
- 'Widdicombe Gem'	LRHS WCot
§ *speciosus*	GBin SEND SPlb
subulatus	IDun SArc SPlb
- 'Crimson Tail'	MMuc
I - 'Packer's Selection'	EUrb
'Taree Pink'	EUrb
viminalis	CBcs SPlb
- 'Captain Cook'	CMac LCro SAth SVen WFar
- 'Endeavour'	NLit
- 'Hannah Ray'	WFar
- 'Little John'	CAbb CBcs CSde EGrI SEle SPad
'Violaceus'	SPlb SVen
viridiflorus	CTsd EGrI SEND SPlb WGwG
'White Anzac'	see *C. citrinus* 'White Anzac'
'Woodlanders Hardy'	SChF WPGP

Callistephus (Asteraceae)

chinensis	SVic
- DUCHESS MIXED (Duchess Series) (d)	LCro
- 'Hulk'	CSpe MCtn
- 'King Size Apricot' (d)	LCro
- 'Matsumoto' (d)	MCtn
- 'Matsumoto Blue' (d)	CSpe
- Nova Series (d) **new**	MCtn
- 'Paeony Silver-Blue' (d)	CSpe
- POMPOM DARK RED (Pompom Series) (d)	MCtn
- Princess Series (d) **new**	MCtn
- 'Tower Chamois' (d)	MCtn
'Sun Ball Light-Blue'	LCro

Callitriche (Plantaginaceae)

§ *palustris*	CBen CLil
stagnalis	CPud ELin EWat
verna	see *C. palustris*

Callitris (Cupressaceae)

endlicheri	CBrP

Callitropsis see *Chamaecyparis*

× *leylandii*	see × *Cuprocyparis leylandii*
nootkatensis	see *Xanthocyparis nootkatensis*

Calluna ✿ (Ericaceae)

vulgaris	EGren MCtn
- 'Alba Rigida'	CFst
- 'Alexandra'PBR (Garden Girls Series)	SPoG
- 'Alicia' (Garden Girls Series) ♀H7	SPoG
- 'Allegro'	MAsh
- 'Amethyst'PBR (Garden Girls Series)	MAsh SPoG
- 'Amilto'	CFst
- 'Angie' (Garden Girls Series)	CFst
- 'Annemarie' (d) ♀H7	SPlb
- 'Aphrodite'PBR (Garden Girls Series)	CBcs ELan
- 'Athene'PBR (Garden Girls Series)	CFst LCro
- 'Beoley Gold' ♀H7	MAsh
- 'Beoley Silver'	MAsh
- 'Blazeaway'	MAsh
- 'Boskoop'	MAsh
- 'County Wicklow' (d) ♀H7	ELan MAsh
- 'Crimson Glory'	MAsh
- 'Dark Beauty'PBR (d) ♀H7	CBcs CFst ELan LCro MAsh
- 'Dark Star' (d) ♀H7	MAsh
- 'Darkness' ♀H7	CBcs CFst
- 'Dunnet Lime'	SPlb
- 'Elsie Purnell' (d) ♀H7	CFst ELan SPlb
- 'Firefly' ♀H7	CFst
- 'Flamingo'	MAsh
- 'Forest Fire'	CFst
- 'Fred J. Chapple'	MAsh
- 'Galaxy'PBR	CFst
- 'Gold Charm'	MAsh
- 'Gold Haze'	MAsh
- 'Gold Mist'	MAsh
- 'Golden Angie' (Garden Girls Series)	CFst
- 'Hammondii Aureifolia'	MAsh SPlb
- 'Hammondii Rubrifolia'	MAsh
- 'Hannover'	CFst
§ - 'H.E. Beale' (d)	ELan MAsh
- 'Highland Rose'	SPlb
- 'Hilda'PBR (Garden Girls Series)	CFst
- 'Hookstone'	MAsh
- 'Jana' (d)	CFst
- 'J.H. Hamilton' (d)	MAsh
- 'Kerstin' ♀H7	CFst SPlb
- 'Kinlochruel' (d) ♀H7	CBcs CFst MAsh SPlb
- 'Kirby White'	MAsh SPlb
- 'Klaudine'PBR (Garden Girls Series)	CFst
- 'Melanie' (Garden Girls Series)	LCro MAsh
- 'Mrs Pat'	CFst
- 'Multicolor'	MAsh
- 'Peter Sparkes' (d) ♀H7	CBcs CFst MAsh
- 'Pink Beale'	see *C. vulgaris* 'H.E. Beale'
- 'Red Beauty'	CBcs CFst
- 'Red Favorit' (d)	CFst
- 'Red Haze'	MAsh
- 'Robert Chapman' ♀H7	CFst MAsh
- 'Ronas Hill'	CFst
- 'Rosita'PBR (Garden Girls Series)	CFst ELan
- 'Sandy'PBR (Garden Girls Series)	CBcs SPoG
- 'Scholje's Super Star' (d)	NBir
- 'Seestern'	CFst
- 'Silvana'PBR (Garden Girls Series)	CFst
- 'Silver Fox'	CFst
- 'Silver Knight'	ELan MAsh SPlb
- 'Silver Queen' ♀H7	CFst MAsh
- 'Spring Cream' ♀H7	CBcs MAsh
- 'Spring Torch'	CBcs MAsh
- 'Strawberry Delight' (d)	ELan
- 'Summer Gold'	MAsh
- 'Sun Sprinkles'	CFst
- 'Sunrise'	MAsh
- 'Theresa' (Garden Girls Series)	LCro
- 'Tib' (d) ♀H7	CFst MAsh

Camassia 149

- 'Waquoit Brightness'	MAsh
- 'White Coral' (d) ♀H7	ELan
- 'Wickwar Flame' ♀H7	CBcs CFst ELan MAsh SPlb
- 'Winter Chocolate'	MAsh
- 'Yellow Beauty'PBR	CFst
- 'Yvette's Gold'	CFst
- 'Zoe'PBR (Garden Girls Series)	CFst

Calocedrus (Cupressaceae)

§ *decurrens* ♀H7	CAco EBar EUrb IPap LMaj MBlu WJur
- 'Aureovariegata' (v) ♀H7	CAco NPlm
- 'Berrima Gold' ♀H7	CAco NLar
- 'Columnaris'	CAco
- 'Maupin Glow' (v)	CAco NLar
- 'Pillar'	NLar
formosana	WPGP

Calocephalus (Asteraceae)

brownii	see *Leucophyta brownii*

Calochortus (Liliaceae)

'Cupido'PBR	EPot XFar

Calonyction see *Ipomoea*

Caloscordum see *Allium*

Calothamnus ✿ (Myrtaceae)

quadrifidus	CBcs SEle
rupestris	SPlb
validus	SPlb
villosus	SPlb

Calotropis (Apocynaceae)

gigantea	SBig
procera	SBig

Calpurnia (Fabaceae)

aurea	SPlb

Caltha (Ranunculaceae)

howellii	see *C. leptosepala* subsp. *howellii*
laeta	see *C. palustris* var. *palustris*
leptosepala	EBee ELin ELon GArf GEdr NLar WFar
§ - subsp. *howellii* NNS 31959	GKev
palustris	Widely available
- var. *alba*	CLil CMac CPud CSpe CWat EBee ECha ELan ELin ELon EPfk EUrb GEdr GKev GKin LCro LRHS LWaG MMuc NBid NBir NGdn NLar SRms WCAu WChS WFar WHil WMAq
- 'Bronze Age'	CDor
- 'Flore Pleno' (d) ♀H7	CBen CLil CMac CTtf EBee ELon EWat GKin GMaP GQue MMuc NBir NGdn NLar NPer NRya SEND SPlb SRms WFar
- 'Himalayan Snow'	WFar
- var. *himalensis*	GKev
- 'Honeydew'	CDor ELon MNrw WCot WFar
- var. *major*	CLil
- 'Multiplex' (d)	CDor WFar
§ - var. *palustris*	CBen CToG ECha EGren ELin EUrb NCth
- - 'Plena' (d)	CPud CToG CWat EHeP LShi MArl WHil
- var. *radicans*	EWat
- 'Stagnalis'	CTtf MWts
- 'Yellow Giant'	CLil
polypetala Hochst. ex Lorent	CDor CLil CPud CWat ELin NPer WCAu WMAq
- 'Moonshine'	WCot

Calycanthus ✿ (Calycanthaceae)

'Aphrodite'	CBcs CJun CMCN CWGN CWnw ELan EPfP GKin LRHS MAsh MGos NLar SHor SMad WMat
chinensis	CBcs CMCN EGrI EPfP MBlu MCtn NLar WJur
floridus	CAgr CBcs CDoC CMCN CWnw EBee EGren EPfP EUrb IArd LRHS MBlu MCtn NLar SPad SPlb SPoG WJur
- 'Athens'	EBee EPfP NLar WPGP
- var. *glaucus* 'Purpureus'	CJun EGrI MBlu NLar
- 'Michael Lindsay'	EBee WPGP
occidentalis	CMCN MAsh MBlu SBrt
- NNS 02-93	WCot
× *raulstonii* 'Hartlage Wine' ♀H5	CBcs CDoC CJun CMCN CWGN CWnw EGrI ELan EPfP EUrb GBin GKin IArd LCro LMil LRHS LSRN MAsh MBlu MGos MMrt MPri NCth NLar SMad SPoG WCot WFar WKif
'Venus'	CBcs CJun CMCN CWnw EBee EGrI ELan EPfP LCro LMil LRHS LSRN MAsh MBlu MPri NLar SHor SMad WFar
'White Dress'	NLar

Calystegia (Convolvulaceae)

§ *hederacea* 'Flore Pleno' (d)	SMad
japonica 'Flore Pleno'	see *C. hederacea* 'Flore Pleno'

Calytrix (Myrtaceae)

tetragona	SPlb

Camassia ✿ (Asparagaceae)

'Blue Candle'	ERCP GKev LAma LRHS
'Blue Heaven'	EGren ELan ERCP ETay GKev GMaP LAma LRHS MAvo NLar
Broadleigh Belle Group	CBro
cusickii	CBro CoPl CWCL EAri EBee EGren EGrI ELan EPfP EPot ERCP EWhm GKev LAma LCro LRHS MArl NBir NLar NNys SDix SPeP WPnP
- 'Zwanenburg'	EPot ERCP GKev LAma WCot
esculenta Lindl.	see *C. quamash*
'Lavender Mist'	MAvo
leichtlinii misapplied	see *C. leichtlinii* subsp. *suksdorfii*
leichtlinii (Baker) S.Watson	NNys
- 'Alba' misapplied	see *C. leichtlinii* subsp. *leichtlinii*
* - 'Alba Plena'	LAma MHol MNrw NBir
- BLUE DANUBE	see *C. leichtlinii* subsp. *leichtlinii* 'Blauwe Donau'
§ - subsp. *leichtlinii*	Widely available
- 'Pink Star'	ECha XFar
- 'Plena' (d)	ECha
- 'Sacajawea' (v)	CTtf EAri ECha EPfP ERCP GBin GKev GPSL LAma MArl NLar SMrm WCot WFar XFar
- 'Semiplena' (d)	CBro CTtf EBee EPfP EPot ERCP ETay GKev LAma MNrw NSti SPhx WCot WPnP WShi XFar
- 'Silk River'	ERCP GKev LAma LRHS SPeP XFar
§ - subsp. *suksdorfii*	EGrI LCro MCtn WCot
- - 'Alba'	EGrI EPot GMaP LCro LRHS LSto NSti
§ - - 'Blauwe Donau'	XFar
- - Caerulea Group	Widely available

- - - 'Maybelle' ERCP LRHS MPri
- - - 'Electra' CBro ECha MAvo WCot
- - - 'Lady Eve Price' CBro MAvo WCot
§ *quamash* Widely available
- 'Blue Melody' (v) CoPl EAri EBee ERCP GKev GMaP LAma MPie NSti XFar
- 'Orion' EBee EGren ERCP GBin GKev LAma NSti WCot
- var. *quamash* CBcs ELin MHol

Camelina (Brassicaceae)
sativa **new** MCtn

Camellia ✿ (Theaceae)
'Admiral Spry' CSgt
'A.L. Rowse' CSgt
'Arbutus Gum' (*japonica* × *reticulata*) CSgt
'Auburn White' see *C. japonica* 'Mrs Bertha A. Harms'
'Autumn Jewel' LRHS
'Baby Bear' LRHS
'Barbara Clark' (*reticulata* × *saluenensis*) CDoC CSgt
'Bertha Harms Blush' see *C. japonica* 'Mrs Bertha A. Harms'
'Betty Ridley' CMHG
'Black Lace' ♀H5 CBcs CDoC CMHG CSgt CTrh CWnw EGrI ELan ELon LBom LCro LMil LRHS MAsh SArc WCha
'Blissful Dawn' CBcs CTrh
'Bonnie Marie' CBcs EGren SCam
brevistyla WJur
'California Sunset' CBcs
'Canterbury' EGrI
'Cinnamon Cindy' CBcs LRHS SCam SRot
'Cinnamon Scentsation' CBcs LRHS SRot
'Congratulations' CSBt
'Contessa Lavinia Maggi' see *C. japonica* 'Lavinia Maggi'
'Cornish Snow' (*cuspidata* × *saluenensis*) ♀H4 CDoC LRHS SCam
'Cornish Spring' (*cuspidata* × *japonica*) ♀H4 CBcs CSBt CSgt CTrh CTsd EGrI LRHS MAsh SCam
costei **new** CBcs
'Crimson Candles' ♀H5 CSgt EPfP LRHS
cuspidata CMac WJur
'Czar' see *C. japonica* 'The Czar'
'Doctor Clifford Parks' (*japonica* × *reticulata*) ♀H4 LMaj
'Donckelaeri' see *C. japonica* 'Masayoshi'
'Dream Castle' (*japonica* × *reticulata*) CBcs
'Duchess of York' CSgt
'Extravaganza' (*japonica* hybrid) ♀H5 IArd
'Fairy Blush' LCro MGos NLar SPoG SWCr WFar
'Festival of Lights' CTrh LRHS
'Fire 'n' Ice' CBcs
forrestii GKev WPGP
'Forty-niner' (*japonica* × *reticulata*) CSgt
'Fragrant Pink' CBcs
'Francie L' ♀H4 CMac LRHS
'Frau Minna Seidel' see *C. japonica* subsp. *rusticana* 'Otome'
'Free Spirit' CBcs CTrh
'Freedom Bell' ♀H5 CDoC CSgt CTrh EGrI GKin SCam
'Frosted Star' LRHS
'Gay Baby' CBcs LRHS
'Golden Anniversary' see *C. japonica* 'Dahlohnega'
grijsii CBcs LRHS SCam
'Happy Anniversary' CSBt
§ *hiemalis* 'Bonanza' ♀H4 CTrh LRHS

- 'Chansonette' CDoC CSgt CTsd LMil LRHS SCam
§ - 'Dazzler' SCam SRot
- 'Elfin Rose' ♀H4 LRHS
- 'Interlude' LRHS
- 'Kanjirō' CSgt CWnw EBar LMaj LRHS SCam SRot
I - 'Maiden's Blush' LMil SCam SRot
- 'Shōwa-no-sakae' LRHS
'High Fragrance' CBcs CSgt EGrI LRHS
'Highlight' (*reticulata* hybrid) CSgt
'Hooker' CDoC CSgt SCam
'Imbricata Rubra' see *C. japonica* 'Imbricata'
'Innovation' CDoC CSgt MAsh
'Inspiration' (*reticulata* × *saluenensis*) ♀H5 CDoC CMac CSgt CTrh MGos
'Interval' (*reticulata* hybrid) CSgt
'Isabel Cordelia' **new** CTrh
japonica EGren EUrb LMaj SEWo SFol SPre WJur
- 'Aaron's Ruby' CSgt
- 'Ace of Hearts' CAco CMHG CWnw LRHS
- 'Ada Pieper' CBcs
- 'Adelina Patti' ♀H5 CBcs CDoC CMHG CSgt CTrh ELon LMil
- 'Adeyaka' CSgt EGren LCro LRHS
- 'Adolphe Audusson' ♀H5 CBcs CDoC CEnd CSBt CSgt CTrh EGrI EPfP LCro LMil LRHS LSRN MAsh MGos MPri SPoG SRms SRot SSta WFar
- 'Aitonia' CMac
§ - 'Akashigata' ♀H5 CBcs CMac LRHS LSRN SCam
§ - 'Akebono' CBcs
- 'Alba Plena' ♀H5 CAco CTrh EGren SReu WFar
- 'Alba Simplex' CBcs CMac CSgt CTrh EPfP SSta
- 'Alexander Hunter' ♀H5 CSgt
- 'Anemoniflora' EPfP
- 'Angel' CBcs
- 'Ann Sothern' CBcs
- 'Annette Riddle' **new** CMHG
- 'Annie Wylam' ♀H5 CBcs CTrh
- 'Apollo' ambig. CBcs CSgt MAsh
- 'Apollo' Paul, 1911 SCam
§ - 'Apple Blossom' CBcs CSgt
- 'April Blush' CSgt LRHS
- 'April Kiss' LRHS
- 'April Remembered' CDoC CSgt EGrI LRHS
- 'April Rose' LRHS
- 'April Tryst' EGrI
- 'Arajishi' misapplied see *C. japonica* subsp. *rusticana* 'Beni-arajishi'
- 'Augustine Supreme' CMac
- 'Ave Maria' ♀H5 CTrh ELon MGos
- 'Baby Pearl' SCam
- 'Baby Sis' CMHG CSgt CWnw LRHS
- 'Ballet Dancer' ♀H5 EGren ELon
- 'Berenice Boddy' ♀H5 CTrh
- 'Berenice Perfection' CMHG
- 'Betty Foy Sanders' CTrh EPfP
- 'Betty Robinson' CSgt
- 'Betty Sheffield' CMHG
- 'Betty Sheffield Pink' LMil SCam
- 'Betty's Beauty' LRHS
- 'Binda' CSgt
- 'Black Magic' CDoC CSgt CTrh CTsd LMil MAsh
- 'Black Tie' CMHG CSgt ELon EPfP LRHS MGos WFar
§ - 'Blood of China' CAco CBcs CSBt CSgt CWnw EGren LBom LSRN MGos MPri NLar
- 'Bob Hope' ♀H5 CAco CBcs CDoC CMHG
- 'Bob's Tinsie' ♀H5 CSBt EPfP SBig SPoG

Camellia

§ - 'Bokuhan' ♀H5	CSgt
- 'Bonomiana'	CAco EGren EGrI LCro LRHS WFar
- 'Bright Buoy'	CMac CSgt
- 'Brushfield's Yellow'	CAco CBcs CDoC CSBt CSgt CTrh CWnw EGren EGrI ELan ELon EPfP IArd LBom LCro LRHS LSRN MAsh MGos MPri NLar SArc SRot SSta WCha
- 'Bush Hill Beauty'	see *C. japonica* 'Lady de Saumarez'
- 'Campsii Alba'	CAco CTsd EGrI SCam
- 'Candy Apple'	CBcs
- 'Carolyn Tuttle'	CSgt
- 'Carter's Sunburst' ♀H5	CBcs
- 'Cécile Brunazzi'	CBcs
- 'Centifolia Alba'	LRHS
- 'Chandleri Elegans'	see *C. japonica* 'Elegans'
- 'Charlotte de Rothschild'	CTrh
- 'Cheryll Lynn'	LMaj
- 'Cinderella'	CSgt
- CLASSIQUE ('Kerguelen'PBR) (v)	LRHS SRot WCot WFar
- 'Cleopatra'	LMaj
§ - 'C.M. Hovey' ♀H5	CMac CSgt LMil
- 'C.M. Wilson'	CMac CSgt EPfP LRHS
- 'Colonel Firey'	see *C. japonica* 'C.M. Hovey'
- 'Colonial Dame'	CAco
- 'Commander Mulroy' ♀H5	CBcs
- 'Conspicua'	CBcs
§ - 'Coquettii' ♀H5	CAco CSgt LMil MAsh
- 'Curly Lady'PBR	CAco LRHS SReu
§ - 'Dahlohnega'	CSgt CTrh EPfP LMil LSRN SRot WFar
- 'Daitairin'	see *C. japonica* 'Dewatairin'
- 'Daphne du Maurier'	CSgt MAsh
- 'Dear Jenny'	CBcs
- 'Debutante'	CBcs CMac
- 'Deep Secret' ♀H5	CSgt
- 'Desire' ♀H5	CBcs CMHG CSgt CTrh ELon EPfP LCro LMil LSRN MGos SPoG SRot WFar
- 'Devonia'	CBcs CSgt SCam
§ - 'Dewatairin' (Higo)	LRHS SCam
- 'Dobreei'	CMac
- 'Doctor Burnside'	CBcs CSgt CTrh CWnw EGren LRHS
- 'Doctor King'	CAco CDoC CEnd CSgt CWnw EGren EPfP LBom LCro LMil LRHS MPri SArc SOrN SPoG WCha WFar
- 'Doctor Tinsley' ♀H5	CDoC CSgt CTsd EPfP LMil LRHS MAsh
- 'Dona Jane Andresson'	SCam
- 'Donckelaeri'	see *C. japonica* 'Masayoshi'
- 'Donnan's Dream'	CBcs CTrh
- 'Drama Girl' ♀H5	CBcs CSgt LMaj SCam
- 'Duchesse Decazes'	SCam
§ - 'Elegans'	CSgt EGrI EPfP LCro LMil LRHS MGos SCam SPoG SRot
- 'Elegans Champagne'	CSgt
- 'Elegans Supreme'	CSgt
- 'Elizabeth Cooper'	CTrh
- 'Elizabeth Hawkins'	CDoC CSgt CTrh
- 'Elizabeth Weaver'	CTrh
- 'Ellen Sampson'	CSgt
- 'Emperor of Russia'	CBcs
- 'Eric Baker'	SCam
- 'Erin Farmer'	**CMHG CSgt**
- 'Eximia'	**CWnw**
- 'Faith'	CBcs CSgt
- 'Fanny'	MHtn
- 'Festival'	LCro
- 'Finlandia Variegated' (v)	ELon
- 'Firebird'	CBcs
- 'Flashlight'	CMHG CSgt
§ - 'Fleur Dipater'	CBcs LRHS
- 'Forest Green'	MAsh SRot
- 'Fred Sander'	CSgt
§ - 'Général Lamoricière'	CBcs
- 'Giardino Santarelli'	CAco
- 'Glen 40'	see *C. japonica* 'Coquettii'
- 'Gloire de Nantes' ♀H5	CTrh EGrI
- 'Golden Wedding' (v)	LRHS NTrD
- 'Grace Bunton'	CBcs ELon
- 'Grand Prix' ♀H5	LMaj NLar
- 'Grand Slam' ♀H5	CMac CMHG CSgt
- 'Guest of Honor'	CSgt EGrI
- 'Guilio Nuccio' ♀H5	CAco CBcs CSgt SCam
- 'Gwenneth Morey'	CBcs SCam
§ - 'Hagoromo' ♀H5	CBcs CTrh CWnw LRHS
§ - 'Hakurakuten' ♀H5	CTrh
- 'Hanafuki'	CSgt SCam
- 'Hanatachibana'	CMHG
- 'Happy Birthday'	EGrI LSRN
- 'Happy Higo'	SCam
- 'Haru-no-utena'	CTrh
- 'Hatsuzakura'	see *C. japonica* 'Dewatairin'
- 'Hawaii'	CMac CSgt
- 'Hinomaru'	CMac
- 'Holly Bright'	CTrh LRHS
§ - 'Imbricata'	CSgt LRHS
- 'In the Pink'	CMHG CSgt
- 'Incarnata'	SCam
- 'Italiana Vera'	CDoC CSgt MAsh
- 'Janet Waterhouse'	CBcs
- 'Jennifer Turnbull'	CSgt
- 'Jingle Bells'	CBcs
- 'J.J. Whitfield'	CMac
- 'Joseph Pfingstl' ♀H5	CSgt EPfP LMil MAsh NLar
- 'Jovey Carlyon'	CBcs CDoC CSgt MAsh
- 'Joy Sander'	see *C. japonica* 'Apple Blossom'
- 'Julia Drayton'	MAsh
- 'Juno'	CBcs LRHS
- 'Jupiter' Paul, 1904 ♀H5	CMac CSgt EGrI LMil LSRN MAsh SCam
- 'K. Sawada'	SCam
- 'Kick-off'	CTrh EGren LRHS
- 'Kimberley'	CBcs EGrI LCro SRot
- 'King's Ransom'	CDoC CMac CSgt LMil
- 'Kingyoba-shiro-wabisuke'	SCam
- 'Kingyo-tsubaki'	LMaj SSta
- 'Kitty'	CBcs
- 'Kitty Berry'	CTrh
§ - 'Konronkoku' ♀H5	CBcs CSgt LMil
- 'Kouron-jura'	see *C. japonica* 'Konronkoku'
- 'Kramer's Beauty'	CBcs
- 'Kramer's Supreme' ♀H5	CAco CBcs CDoC CSgt LBom LMil LSRN WFar
- 'Kumasaka'	CSgt
- 'Lady Campbell'	CAco EGren EGrI EPfP LBom LCro LMil LRHS MPri SOrN WCha WFar
- 'Lady Clare'	see *C. japonica* 'Akashigata'
§ - 'Lady de Saumarez'	CBcs CMac CSgt
- 'Lady Loch'	CTrh
- 'Lady Marion'	see *C. japonica* 'Kumasaka'
- 'Lady McCulloch'	CWnw LRHS
- 'Lady Vansittart'	CDoC CSgt CTrh EPfP LCro LMil LSRN MAsh MGos SCam SPoG SRot SSta
§ - 'Lady Vansittart Pink'	CMac
- 'Lady Vansittart Red'	see *C. japonica* 'Lady Vansittart Pink'
- 'Lady Vansittart Shell'	see *C. japonica* 'Yours Truly'

Camellia

- 'Laurie Bray'	CAco CMHG
§ - 'Lavinia Maggi' ♀H5	CAco CBcs CSgt CTsd EPfP LCro LMaj LRHS LSRN MPri SPoG SRms SSta
- 'Lemon Drop'	CBcs CTrh
- 'Lily Pons'	CTrh
- 'Lipstick'	LRHS
- 'Little Bit'	ELon SSta
- 'Look-away'	SBig
- 'Louise Allstrop' **new**	CMHG
- 'Lovelight' ♀H5	CMHG CSgt CTrh WCot
- 'L.T. Dees'	CBcs
- 'Ludvgan Red'	LRHS
- 'Mabel Blackwell'	SCam
- 'Madame de Strekaloff'	CMac CSBt SCam
- 'Madge Miller'	CSgt
- 'Magnoliiflora'	see *C. japonica* 'Hagoromo'
- 'Maiden's Blush'	CMac
- 'Margaret Davis' ♀H5	CDoC CMHG CSgt CTrh CWnw ELan ELon EPfP LCro LMil LRHS MAsh MGos SCam WFar
- 'Margaret Davis Picotee'	CBcs EGren
- 'Margherita Coleoni'	CAco CBcs
- 'Marguérite Gouillon' Drouard-Gouillon	CMHG
- 'Marian Mitchell'	SCam
- 'Marie Williams'	EGren
- 'Marie-Galante'	LRHS
- 'Mariottii Rubra'	CMac
- 'Marjorie Magnificent'	CSgt SCam
- 'Mark Alan'	SCam
- 'Mars' ♀H5	CBcs SCam
- 'Marshmallow'	LRHS
- 'Mary Costa'	CBcs CTrh SCam
§ - 'Masayoshi' ♀H5	CSBt CSgt CTsd
- 'Mathotiana'	CBcs
- 'Mathotiana Alba'	CAco CBcs CMac EPfP LRHS LSRN SCam WSpi
- 'Mathotiana Supreme'	SCam
- 'Matilija Poppy'	SCam
- 'Matterhorn'	CTrh
- 'Mercury' ♀H5	CMac CSgt
- 'Midnight'	CBcs CDoC CSgt CTsd EGrI LRHS
- 'Midnight Magic'	CBcs CSgt CTrh
- 'Midnight Serenade'	CSgt SCam
- 'Midnight Variegated' (v)	LRHS
- 'Midsummer's Day'	CBcs
- 'Mikado'	CDoC CSgt
§ - 'Mikenjaku'	CAco CBcs CDoC CSgt LRHS MAsh
- 'Miss Charleston'	CMHG CSgt
- 'Miss Lyla'	CAco SCam
- 'Miss Universe'	CMHG
- 'Montironi'	LMaj
- 'Morning Glory'	CSgt
- 'Moshe Dayan'	CDoC CSgt LMil MAsh
§ - 'Mrs Bertha A. Harms'	CBcs
- 'Mrs Charles Cobb'	MPri
- 'Mrs D.W. Davis'	EPfP
- 'Mrs Swan'	EPfP LRHS
- 'Mrs Tingley'	MPri
- 'Myrtifolia'	CSgt
- 'Nagasaki'	see *C. japonica* 'Mikenjaku'
- 'Nigra'	see *C. japonica* 'Konronkoku'
- 'Nina Avery'	SCam
- 'Nobilissima' ♀H5	CAco CBcs CMac CSgt CWnw EGrI LCro MAsh MBlu SCam SOrN SPoG SRot WFar
- 'Nokogiriba-tsubaki'	SCam
- 'Nuccio's Amigo'	MAsh
- 'Nuccio's Cameo' ♀H5	CDoC CSgt CTrh EPfP LCro LMil LRHS MAsh
- 'Nuccio's Gem' ♀H5	CDoC CMHG CSgt EPfP LCro LMil LRHS
- 'Nuccio's Jewel' ♀H5	CBcs CDoC CSBt CSgt CWnw EPfP LMil LRHS MAsh SCam
- 'Nuccio's Pearl' ♀H5	CAco CBcs CEnd CSgt CTsd ELon EPfP LMil LRHS LSRN SArc
- 'Nuccio's Pink Lace'	CBcs CDoC CSgt LRHS
- 'Onetia Holland'	CBcs LSRN WFar
- 'Oo-La-La'	CTrh
- 'Optima'	CBcs ELon
- 'Orandakō'	CAco
- 'Pat La Motte Jones'	CSgt
- 'Peachblossom'	see *C. japonica* 'Fleur Dipater'
- 'Pearl Maxwell'	EGrI
- 'Pink Clouds'	CBcs
- 'Pink Perfection'	see *C. japonica* subsp. *rusticana* 'Otome'
- 'Pompone'	SCam
- 'Pope John Paul XXIII'	SCam
- 'Powder Puff'	CAco
- 'Preston Rose'	CBcs CSgt
- 'Primavera'	CBcs CTrh
- 'Prince Murat'	CSgt
- 'Princess Baciocchi'	CAco SReu
- 'Princess du Mahe'	CMac
- 'Red Dandy'	SCam
- 'Reg Ragland'	SCam
- 'R.L. Wheeler' ♀H5	CBcs CDoC CMHG CSBt CSgt EPfP LCro LMil LRHS MGos MPri SRot
- 'Roger Hall'	CBcs CDoC CSgt CTrh EPfP LRHS LSRN SPoG
- 'Rōgetsu'	CBcs
- 'Rosularis'	ELon
- 'Royal Velvet'	CBcs CTrh
- 'Rubescens Major'	CBcs
- 'Ruddigore'	CTrh SCam
- subsp. ***rusticana*** 'Arajishi' misapplied	see *C. japonica* subsp. *rusticana* 'Beni-arajishi'
- - 'Arajishi' Ko'emon	SCam
§ - - 'Beni-arajishi'	CBcs CMac CSgt
§ - - 'Otome'	LMaj
- - 'Reigyoku' (v)	CBcs LRHS
- 'Sacco Nova'	CWnw
- 'Saint André'	CMac CSgt
- 'Sally Harrell'	SCam
- 'San Dimas' ♀H5	CMHG CTrh LRHS SCam
- 'Sanpei-tsubaki'	LRHS
- 'Saturnia'	CDoC CSgt LMil SCam
- 'Scented Red'	CSgt
- 'Scentsation' ♀H5	CMHG CSgt
- 'Sea Foam'	CWnw
- 'Seiji'	CMac
- 'Shikibu'	CTrh
- 'Shin-akebono'	see *C. japonica* 'Akebono'
- 'Silver Anniversary' ♀H5	CBcs CDoC CEnd CSBt CWnw EGrI EPfP LCro LMil LRHS LSRN MAsh MGos MHtn NLar SPoG SRot WFar
- 'Silver Ruffles'	CBcs CTrh
- 'Snow Chan'	CMHG
- 'Snow White'	CAco LRHS
- 'Souvenir de Bahuaud-Litou' ♀H5	CBcs
- 'Splendens Carlyon'	CSgt LMil MAsh
- 'Spring Fling'	CBcs CTrh LRHS SPoG
- 'Spring Formal'	CTrh LRHS
- 'Spring Sonnet'	CMHG
- 'Strawberry Parfait'	CBcs
- 'Strawberry Swirl'	CBcs WFar
- 'Sugar Babe'	CMHG CSgt SCam
- 'Sundae'	CBcs

Camellia

- 'Sunny Side'	LRHS	
- 'Susan Stone'	EPfP MPri	
- 'Sylva' ♀H5	SCam	
- 'Sylvia'	CMac	
- 'Takanini'	CBcs CTrh LRHS SCam	
- 'Tammia'	LRHS	
§ - 'The Czar'	CBcs CSgt	
- 'Tiffany'	CAco CBcs CSgt EGrI SCam	
- 'Tom Thumb' ♀H5	CTrh ELon SRms	
- 'Tomorrow'	CSgt EGrI MAsh	
- 'Tomorrow's Dawn'	SCam	
- 'Tregye'	CBcs	
§ - 'Tricolor' ♀H5	CBcs CMac CSgt CTsd LMil LRHS SCam SRot	
- 'Tricolor Red'	see *C. japonica* 'Lady de Saumarez'	
- 'Trinity House' **new**	CMHG	
- 'Triumphans'	WFar	
- 'Turandot'	CSgt	
- 'Variegata'	CMac	
- 'Victor Emmanuel'	see *C. japonica* 'Blood of China'	
- 'Ville de Nantes'	CDoC CSgt	
- 'Virginia Carlyon'	CBcs CSgt	
- 'Vittorio Emanuele II'	CDoC CSgt CTrh LRHS MAsh	
- 'Volunteer'	LCro LMil LRHS MGos	
- 'White Nun'	LMaj	
- 'White Swan'	CDoC CMac CSBt CSgt CWnw EGren MAsh	
- 'Wilamina' ♀H5	CMHG	
- 'William Bartlett'	CAco CBcs CTrh LCro SReu	
- 'Winter Perfume Pearl'	LCro NLar	
- 'Winter Perfume Pink'	WCha	
- 'Wisley White'	see *C. japonica* 'Hakurakuten'	
- 'Witman Yellow'	CTrh	
- 'Wonderland'	CMHG CSgt	
§ - 'Yours Truly'	CDoC CMac CSgt CTrh EPfP LMil LRHS	
'Jury's Yellow'	see *C. × williamsii* 'Jury's Yellow'	
'Koto-no-kaori' (*lutchuensis* hybrid)	LRHS	
'Leonard Messel' (*reticulata* × (× *williamsii*)) ♀H5	CDoC CMac CSgt LRHS MGos NLar SCam	
lutchuensis	LRHS	
maliflora	CBcs	
'Marguérite Gouillon' misapplied	see *C. japonica* 'Général Lamoricière'	
'Maud Messel' (*reticulata* × (× *williamsii*))	SCam	
'Mimosa Jury'	LRHS	
'Minato-no-akebono' **new**	LRHS	
'Nicky Crisp' (*japonica* × *pitardii*)	CSgt CTrh LMil LRHS SPoG	
'Nijinski' (*reticulata* hybrid)	CSgt SCam	
'Nikisi Kerin'	CWnw EGren	
oleifera	CTrh	
- 'Sasanqua Fragrans'	SArc	
'Paper Dolls'	EGrI	
'Pink Goddess' (*hiemalis* hybrid)	EGrI LRHS	
'Pink Icicle' (*oleifera* hybrid)	CBcs LCro SCam	
pitardii WWJ 11925 from Vietnam	WCru	
'Polar Ice'	CBcs	
'Quintessence' (*japonica* × *lutchuensis*)	LRHS	
reticulata 'Kerdalo'	LRHS	
- 'Mary Williams'	CAco EGrI LCro SPoG	
- 'Rosemary Sawle'	LRHS	
rosthorniana 'Beauty Blush'	LCro WFar	
- Cupido	see *C. rosthorniana* 'Elina'	
§ - 'Elina'PBR	ELan LCro LRHS SPoG	
'Royalty' (*japonica* × *reticulata*) ♀H5	CSgt	
saluenensis	CMac GKev	
'Salutation' (*reticulata* × *saluenensis*)	SCam	
sasanqua Thunb.	GKev SAth SPre WCha	
I - 'Alba'	CDoC CMac CSgt CTsd LMil	
- 'Blush'	LRHS SRkn	
- 'Bonanza'	see *C. hiemalis* 'Bonanza'	
- 'Cleopatra'	CSgt EBar EGrI ELan EPfP LBom LMil SEWo	
- 'Crimson King' ♀H4	CDoC CSgt CTrh CTsd CWnw EGrI LMil	
- 'Dazzler'	see *C. hiemalis* 'Dazzler'	
- 'Early Pearly'	EGrI	
- 'Fuji-no-yuki'	LRHS	
- 'Gay Border'	CBcs	
- 'Gay Sue' ♀H4	CSgt CTrh EGrI	
- 'Hinode-gumo'	LMaj LRHS SEWo	
- 'Hiryū'	EGrI LRHS MHtn WCot	
- 'Hugh Evans' ♀H4	CBcs CSgt CTrh EGrI ELan EPfP GKev LMil LRHS SCam SSta	
- 'Île Wrac'h' **new**	LRHS	
- 'Jean May' ♀H4	ELon EPfP	
- 'Jennifer Susan'	CTrh LMaj	
- 'Mahe' **new**	LRHS	
- 'Maiden's Blush'	CSgt EGrI SCam	
- 'Mignonne'	CTrh	
- 'Mine-no-yuki'	CTrh	
I - 'Narcissiflora'	CWnw LRHS	
- 'Narumigata' ♀H4	CBcs CMac CTrh CTsd EGrI ELan ELon EPfP LCro LMaj LRHS MBlu MGos SCam SPoG SSta	
- 'Navajo'	CTrh EGrI	
- 'New Dawn'	SRot	
- 'Nyewoods'	CMac	
- 'Paradise Audrey'	SCam SPoG	
- 'Paradise Belinda'	ELan SCam SPoG	
- 'Paradise Blush'	CBcs	
- 'Paradise Glow'	CBcs	
- 'Paradise Hilda'	CBcs	
- Paradise Illumination ('Parillumination')	EGren	
- 'Paradise Pearl'	CBcs SCam	
- 'Paradise Petite'	SCam	
- 'Paradise Venessa'	LBom	
- 'Peach Blossom'	EGrI	
- 'Plantation Pink' ♀H4	CSgt CTrh CTsd EBee EGrI LCro LMil	
- 'Rainbow'	CBcs CDoC CSgt CTrh CWnw EGrI ELan ELon EPfP LCro LMil SCam SRot SSta	
- 'Rosea'	CMac CTsd ELon SCam	
- 'Sasanqua Rubra'	CMac	
- 'Sasanqua Variegata' (v)	CTrh	
- 'Sekiyō'	CBcs	
- 'Setsugekka'	LRHS	
- 'Shinonome'	CBcs	
- 'Sparkling Burgundy'	see *C.* 'Sparkling Burgundy'	
- 'Tanya'	CTrh	
- 'Versicolor' ♀H4	CDoC CSgt CTsd LCro LRHS	
- 'Waterfall Pink' **new**	LRHS	
- 'Waterfall White' **new**	LRHS	
- 'Winter's Joy'	CBcs	
'Satan's Robe' (*reticulata* hybrid)	CBcs	
'Scented Sun'	CTrh	
'Scentuous' (*japonica* × *lutchuensis*)	CBcs SCam	
§ *sinensis*	CBcs CDoC LWaG MCtn MHtn NTrD SPlb SPre WJur WPGP	

- var. *assamica* — CTsd SPre
- var. *sinensis* — CSgt LCro
- 'Snow Flurry' ♀H5 — CBcs CSgt CTrh LCro
§ 'Sparkling Burgundy' ♀H4 — CSgt CTsd LCro MGos
- 'Spring Festival' (*cuspidata* hybrid) ♀H4 — CAco CBcs CTrh EGrI ELan EPfP LBom LCro LMil MGos NLar SCam WCha WFar
- 'Spring Mist' (*japonica* × *lutchuensis*) — CSgt
- 'Superscent' — CTrh
- 'Survivor' — LRHS
- 'Swan Lake' — EPfP LBom LMil LRHS MGos MPri
- 'Sweet Emily Kate' (*japonica* × *lutchuensis*) — LRHS
- 'Sweet Jane' — LRHS
- 'Sweet Olive' — LRHS
- 'Tarōkaja' (*wabisuke*) — SCam
- *thea* — see *C. sinensis*
- 'Tinsie' — see *C. japonica* 'Bokuhan'
- 'Tiny Princess' (*fraterna* × *japonica*) — CMac
- *transnokoensis* ♀H4 — CMac CTrh LRHS WAbe
- 'Transtasman' — LRHS
- 'Tricolor Sieboldii' — see *C. japonica* 'Tricolor'
- 'Tristrem Carlyon' (*reticulata* hybrid) — CBcs CDoC CSgt EPfP LRHS MAsh SCam
- *tsaii* — CSgt LRHS
- 'Usu-ōtome' — see *C. japonica* subsp. *rusticana* 'Otome'
- 'Valley Knudsen' (*reticulata* × *saluenensis*) — LMaj
- 'Vanilla Moon' **new** — CTrh
- × *vernalis* 'Yuletide' — CBcs CDoC CSgt CTrh EGrI LBom LCro LMil LRHS LSRN MGos NTrD WFar
- 'Volcano' — LRHS
- × *williamsii* — CBcs CDoC CEnd CMac CSBt CSgt
  - 'Anticipation' ♀H5 — CTrh CWnw EGrI EPfP GKin LBom LCro LMil LRHS MAsh MGos SPoG WFar
  - 'Ballet Queen' — CBcs CSBt
  - 'Bartley Number Five' — CMac
  - 'Beatrice Michael' — CBcs CMac
  - 'Bernadine' — MPri
  - 'Blue Danube' — CBcs
  - 'Bow Bells' — EPfP
  - 'Bowen Bryant' ♀H5 — CTrh EPfP LRHS
  - 'Brigadoon' ♀H5 — CBcs CDoC CSgt CTrh GGGa SCam
  - 'Burncoose' — CBcs
  - 'Buttons 'n' Bows' — LRHS
  - 'Caerhays' — CBcs
  - 'Carolyn Williams' — CBcs
  - 'Celebration' — CBcs CSBt
  - 'Charles Michael' — CBcs
  - 'China Clay' ♀H5 — CBcs CDoC CSgt CTsd LMil
  - 'Citation' — CMac
  - 'Contribution' — CTrh
  - 'Crinkles' — CMHG SCam
  - 'Debbie' ♀H5 — CAco CBcs CDoC CEnd CMac CSBt CSgt CTrh CWnw EGrI ELon EPfP LBom LCro LMil LRHS LSRN MAsh MBlu MGos MPri NLar SCam SReu SRot SSta WFar
  - 'Debbie's Carnation' — CSgt
  - 'Desmond Haydon' **new** — CTrh
  - 'Doctor Ralph Watkins' — LRHS
  - 'Donation' ♀H5 — CBcs CDoC CMac CSBt CTrh EGrI ELan EPfP GGGa GKin LCro LMil LRHS LSRN MGos MPri SPoG SSta WFar
  - 'Edward Carlyon' — CSgt
  - 'E.G. Waterhouse' — CAco CBcs CSgt CTrh CWnw EGrI ELan EPfP GKin LBom LCro LMil LRHS MAsh MGos SCam SSta WFar
  - 'Elegant Beauty' ♀H5 — CBcs CDoC CSgt CTrh ELon LMil NLar SRot
  - 'Elizabeth Anderson' — CTrh
  - 'Ellamine' — CBcs
  - 'Elsie Jury' ♀H5 — CBcs CDoC CMac CSgt CWnw ELon GKin MGos NLar SCam
  - 'E.T.R. Carlyon' ♀H5 — CBcs CSgt CTrh ELon EPfP LMil LRHS MGos NLar
  - 'Exaltation' — CBcs SCam
  - 'Francis Hanger' — CBcs CTrh
  - 'Galaxie' — CBcs
  - 'Gay Time' — WFar
  - 'George Blandford' ♀H5 — CMac
  - 'Glenn's Orbit' ♀H5 — CMHG NLar
  - 'Golden Spangles' (v) — CMac SPoG
  - 'Gwavas' — CBcs CDoC CSgt CTrh SCam
  - 'Jamie' — LRHS
  - 'J.C. Williams' ♀H5 — CBcs CMac
  - 'Jenefer Carlyon' — CSgt
  - 'Jennifer Trehane' — CTrh
  - 'Jill Totty' — CTrh
  - 'John Pickthorn' — CBcs CSgt
  - 'Julia Hamiter' ♀H5 — CBcs CSgt LRHS
§ 'Jury's Yellow' ♀H5 — CBcs CDoC CSBt CSgt CTrh EBee EGrI EPfP GGGa LBom LCro LMil LRHS MAsh MGos SPoG SRot SSta
  - 'Lady's Maid' — CBcs
  - 'Laura Boscawen' — CBcs CTrh
  - 'Les Jury' ♀H5 — CBcs CDoC CSBt CTrh LCro LMil LRHS MGos SRot WFar
  - 'Lucky Star' — LRHS
  - 'Margaret Waterhouse' — CDoC CSgt LMil SCam
  - 'Marjorie Waldegrave' — CSgt
  - 'Mary Larcom' — CMHG
  - 'Mary Phoebe Taylor' ♀H5 — CBcs LMaj NLar SCam
  - 'Monica Dance' — CBcs
  - 'Muskoka' ♀H5 — CBcs
  - 'New Venture' — CBcs
  - 'Night Rider' — CSgt EBee EPfP LRHS SBig WPGP
  - 'November Pink' — CBcs
  - 'Philippa Forward' — CMac
  - 'Pink Wave' — CSgt
  - 'Red Dahlia' — CBcs
  - 'Rendezvous' — CBcs CTrh
  - 'Rose Bouquet' — CSgt
  - 'Rose Parade' — CSgt
  - 'Rose Quartz' — CSgt
  - 'Rosemary Williams' — CBcs CMac
  - 'Ruby Wedding' ♀H5 — CBcs CDoC CSBt CSgt CTrh EBee EGrI ELon EPfP LBom LCro LMil LRHS LSRN MAsh MGos MHtn NTrD SPoG WFar
  - 'Saint Ewe' ♀H5 — CBcs CSgt CTrh LRHS MGos SCam WFar
  - 'Saint Michael' — CBcs
  - 'Señorita' ♀H5 — CSgt EGrI LCro LRHS NLar SRot
  - 'Taylor Maid' **new** — CMHG
  - 'The Duchess of Cornwall' — CSgt
  - 'Toni Finlay's Fragrant' — CTrh
  - 'Tregrehan' — CSgt CTsd
  - 'Tulip Time' — LRHS
  - 'Twinkle Star' — CSgt
  - 'Water Lily' ♀H5 — CBcs CSgt EPfP LMil NLar
  - 'Wilber Foss' — CBcs
  - 'William Carlyon' — CSgt
  - 'Winter Gem' — LRHS
  - 'Wynne Rayner' — CMHG LRHS
  - 'Yesterday' — CSgt LMil

Campanula   155

'Winter's Charm'	CBcs CDoC CSgt LMil
'Winter's Interlude'	CBcs CDoC CSgt LMil
'Winter's Snowman' ♀H5	CBcs LCro NLar
'Winter's Toughie'	CBcs CSgt LCro LMil SCam
'Winton' (*cuspidata* × *saluenensis*)	CBcs CSgt
'Yoimachi' (*fraterna* × *sasanqua*)	LRHS
'Yume' ♀H5	LRHS

Campanula (*Campanulaceae*)

ADANSA WHITE COMPACT ('Psw 09102'PBR)	LCro
'Albert Kirkham'	WCot
§ *alliariifolia*	CDor CWal CWnw EBee ECha ELan EPfP LRHS LShi MCtn NBro NGdn NLar NSti SEND SRms WCAu WCot WFar WSpi
- B&SWJ 15316	WCru
- 'Ivory Bells'	see *C. alliariifolia*
- 'Ivory Towers'	EBee
- 'Minor'	GKev
§ - subsp. *ochroleuca*	EPPr WCot
- - B&SWJ 16351 from Abkhazia	WCru
- 'Snow Dune'	LSou NCth
AMBELLA PINK ('Skl1800302')	LCro LRHS
americana	WFar
arvatica	EPot SRms WAbe WFar
aucheri	see *C. bellidifolia* subsp. *aucheri*
§ 'Balchiniana' (v)	EShb
'Barbara Valentine'	EBee
'Belinda'	EPot WHoo
§ *bellidifolia*	GEdr
subsp. *aucheri*	
- subsp. *besenginica*	GEdr
- subsp. *saxifraga*	EDAr GEdr
§ *betulifolia* ♀H5	GEdr GKev WFar
'Birch Hybrid'	ELan EPfP SRms WFar
BLUE OCTOPUS ('Jls0504m'PBR)	CWGN SRms WSpi
bononiensis	SRms
'Burghaltii'	NLar SHar
carpatha white-flowered	EGren
carpatica ♀H5	GAbr GQue LShi MCtn NGdn SPlb SRms StAn WFar
- f. *alba*	EPfP LRHS NGdn SPlb
§ - - 'Weisse Clips'	CBcs EPfP GMaP LCro MAsh NGdn SPoG SRms WFar
§ - 'Blaue Clips'	CBcs EPfP GMaP LCro MAsh MGos NGdn SPoG SRms WFar
- BLUE CLIPS	see *C. carpatica* 'Blaue Clips'
- 'Blue Uniform'	EDAr
- dark blue-flowered **new**	LRHS
- 'Jingle Bells'	LRHS
- 'Kathy'	EPot
- 'Pearl White'	EPfP LRHS
- 'Rapido Blue'	EGren LBar MHol
- 'Rapido White'	EGren LBar
- var. *turbinata*	SRms
- WHITE CLIPS	see *C. carpatica* f. *alba* 'Weisse Clips'
- 'White Uniform'	EDAr EPfP
§ *cashmeriana*	WAbe
§ *chamissonis*	EPot GKev
- 'Alba'	WFar
- 'Major'	EWes
§ - 'Superba' ♀H5	EDAr WAbe WIce
'Chloe'	CMiW WFar
choruhensis	EDAr GEdr SPlb
ciliata	GEdr

§ *cochlearifolia* ♀H5	ELan GJos GMaP GQue LRHS MAsh MCtn MPri SLee SPoG StAn WCav WFar WHoo
- var. *alba*	EDAr ELan LShi SLee SRms WAbe WFar WHoo
- - 'Advance White'	WFar
- - double white-flowered (d)	WFar
- - 'White Baby' (Baby Series)	EPot LRHS SPoG SRms WFar
- 'Bavaria Blue'	GJos
- 'Bells Blue'	LRHS SAth
- 'Blue Baby' (Baby Series)	SPoG SRms SRot
- 'Elizabeth Oliver' (d) ♀H5	CSpe ELan EPot GArf GEdr LShi MHer MPro NBir SLee SPlb SRms WAbe WFar WIce
- 'Flore Pleno' (d)	WFar
- 'R.B. Loder' (d)	MHer
- 'Silver Bells'	LSou
- 'Tubby'	ELan EPot MHer MWlw SRms WIce
collina	GEdr
'Country Bells Pink'	LBar
'Covadonga'	WAbe
'Cremewit'	EPot
'Crystal'	MAvo MHol NLar WCot WFar
dasyantha	see *C. chamissonis*
dolomitica	EGrI
'E.K.Toogood'	EPot SRms WFar
erinus	MHol
'Faichem Lilac'	MCtn WCot
fenestrellata	EPot SLee
finitima	see *C. betulifolia*
fragilis subsp. *cavolinii*	WAbe
garganica ♀H5	EPfP GKev GMaP LRHS MAsh SRms SVic WFar
- 'Alba'	WFar
- 'Aurea'	see *C. garganica* 'Dickson's Gold'
- 'Blue Diamond'	EPot NLar
§ - 'Dickson's Gold'	CMac EDAr ELan EPfP EPot GMaP LBar LRHS MAsh MHer NLar SLee SPlb SPoG SRms SRot WAbe WFar WHoo WIce
- 'Filigree'	WCot WFar
- 'Major'	LRHS SPoG WFar
- 'Mrs Resholt'	EGren LRHS LWaG MHol NBir NLar SRms WFar WIce
- 'W.H. Paine' ♀H5	GKev WAbe WCav WFar WHoo
'Glandore'	SAko
glomerata	CGwi EGren GJos LShi LSRN MAsh MHer NAts NBir NMir WFar
- var. *acaulis* hort.	EPfP LRHS MPri NLar NRya SRms WFar
- var. *alba*	CBcs CDor CMHG CSpe ECha EDAr ELan EMor EPfP GJos GMaP LCro LRHS MArl MBel SPlb SPoG WCAu XFar
§ - - 'Schneekrone'	ECha LCro LRHS NBir WFar
- 'Angel Bells' (Bells Series)	LBar WHil
- Bellefleur Series	EHet
- - BELLEFLEUR BLUE	CDor
- 'Caroline' ♀H7	CDor CWGN EBee ECha EMor EPfP EPot GMaP LEdu LRHS MHol MMrt MNrw NCou NCth NLar NSti WCAu WCot WFar WHil WTre XFar
- CROWN OF SNOW	see *C. glomerata* var. *alba* 'Schneekrone'
- var. *dahurica*	CSpe EBee NLar SHar
- 'Emerald'	EBee EMor LRHS MHer MNrw NLar SRms WFar
- 'Freya'PBR ♀H7	LRHS MAsh Midl MNrw MPro WCot WFar WHil

Campanula

- (Genti Series) GENTI BLUE ('Allgentibl'PBR) — ELan EPfP LRHS MPri WFar
- - GENTI TWISTERBELL ('Allgentitwist'PBR) — EMor EPfP MHol MPro NEoE
- - GENTI WHITE ('Allgentiw'PBR) — CWGN ELan EPfP LRHS MPri WFar
- 'Joan Elliott' — EBee ECha LEdu MHol
- 'Purple Pixie' — LRHS SRms
- subsp. *speciosa* **new** — NClf
- 'Superba' ♀H7 — CBcs CMHG EBee EGren EHeP ELan EMor EPfP EPot GMaP GQue LCro LEdu LRHS MArl MCtn MPie NBir NCou NPer SPlb SPoG SRms WCAu WFar WSpi
- × *haylodgensis* misapplied see *C.* × *haylodgensis* 'Plena'
§ × *haylodgensis* W. Brockbank 'Marion Fisher' (d) — WAbe WFar
§ - 'Plena' (d) — EPot SRms WAbe WFar
- 'Yvonne' — ELan GKev LRHS WFar
hercegovina 'Nana' — WAbe
hofmannii — GJos
hypopolia — WAbe
§ *incurva* — CSpe EDAr GEdr MCtn
IRIDESCENT BELLS ('Iribella'PBR) — CWGN EBee EMor LBar LCro LRHS MHol MNrw MPro NSti SAth WCAu
isophylla ♀H2 — EShb
- 'Alba' ♀H2 — EShb WMal
- 'Mayi' misapplied — see *C.* 'Balchiniana'
- 'Variegata' — see *C.* 'Balchiniana'
JENNY ('Harjen') — CWGN SHar
'Joan Beeston' — WAbe
'Joe Elliott' — WAbe
kemulariae — ESwi WCot
'Kent Belle' ♀H7 — CBro CDor EBee ELon EMor EPfP GElm GMaP GQue LRHS LSRN MAsh MBel MNrw NLar NSti SPoG SRms WCAu WCot WFar WHoo WKif
kirpicznikovii — EBee GEdr
komarovii — WCot
lactiflora — CAby CElw CMac CSpe CWal EBee ECha GAbr GJos LCro LRHS LSto MCtn MNrw WCAu WFar WSpi
- 'Alba' ♀H7 — EBee ECha ELan EPfP GBin GMaP MBel SDix WCAu WCot WFar WSpi
- 'Assendon Pearl' ♀H7 — ELon LCro MHol MWlw SHar WCot
- AVALANCHE ('Camblo') — LCro
- 'Border Blues' — ECha LBar MHol NDov NLar WFar
- dwarf, pink-flowered — WFar
- 'Favourite' ♀H7 — NGdn SHar
- 'Gloaming' — NCth
- 'Loddon Anna' ♀H7 — Widely available
- 'Monica's Dream' — EBee LBar MAvo MMuc NDov SEND WCAu WCot WHoo
- 'Platinum' ♀H7 — EPPr SPel
- 'Pouffe' — EBee NGdn
- 'Prichard's Variety' ♀H7 — Widely available
- tall, dark blue-flowered — MMuc
- 'Violet' — WSpi
- 'White Pouffe' — EPfP GMaP LBar MArl NSti SPoG WFar
- white-flowered — CWal EHeP NBir WCAu WCav
latifolia — ECha EPfP GQue LShi MCtn NBid NMir NSti SRms WCAu WSpi
- B&SWJ 15326 — WCru
- var. *alba* — EBee EMor MAsh SRms WFar WSpi
* - 'Amethyst' — WSpi
- blue-flowered — SEND
- 'Brantwood' — WSpi
- 'Gloaming' — WSpi
- var. *macrantha* — CAby EBee EMor EPfP LRHS NSti
- - 'Alba' — CAby ECha EMor GMaP MPro NLar WBrk WCAu
latiloba — WCot
§ - 'Alba' — EBee MNrw NLar WBrk
- 'Hidcote Amethyst' — CDor CWGN GMaP LBar NBir NGdn NLar WCAu WCot WSpi
- 'Highcliffe Variety' ♀H7 — EBee EPfP LRHS NLar SPoG WCAu WCot WSpi
- 'Percy Piper' ♀H7 — LRHS WSpi
- 'Splash' — MNrw
'Lilac Time' **new** — EBlo
makaschwilii — CWal ELan EWhm GArf GKev MCtn WHil
'Margaret Brine' — WAbe
'Marion Fisher' — see *C.* × *haylodgensis* W. Brockbank 'Marion Fisher'
medium — EPfP LRHS MPro
§ - var. *calycanthema* hort. — WSpi
- 'Cup and Saucer' — see *C. medium* var. *calycanthema* hort.
- single blue-flowered — GJos MCtn
- - white-flowered — MCtn
'Mevr. V. Vollenhove' — CSpe EBee LBar MHol
'Misty Dawn' ♀H7 — NLar WCot
moesiaca — GKev
'Moonlight' — EBlo LRHS
muralis — see *C. portenschlagiana*
'Napoli'PBR **new** — LRHS
nitida — see *C. persicifolia* var. *planiflora*
'Norman Grove' — EPot
ochroleuca — see *C. alliariifolia* subsp. *ochroleuca*
odontosepala — EBee
- from Iran — EPPr NLar
olympica misapplied — see *C. rotundifolia* 'Olympica'
pallida subsp. *tibetica* — see *C. cashmeriana*
patula — CSpe LCro SMHy WKif
'Paul Furse' — NSti SHar WCot WFar
pendula — EDAr EPfP GJos LRHS
peregrina — ESwi
(Perla Series) 'Perla Blue' — LRHS
- 'Perla White' — LRHS
persicifolia — CBcs CCBP CMac CWal EBee ECha EPfP GAbr GKev GMaP GQue LCro LRHS LSto MBel MPri NBro NMir SDix SPoG SRms WCAu WCot WFar WHoo WTor WTre
- var. *alba* — CBcs CDor CSpe EBee EPfP GAbr GMaP LCro LRHS MAsh MBel MMuc NMir SEND SPlb SPoG WCAu WCot WFar WHoo WTor WTre
§ - 'Alba Coronata' (d) — GAbr LShi SRms
- 'Alba Plena' — see *C. persicifolia* 'Alba Coronata'
- 'Azure Beauty' — NLar WCot WSpi
- 'Beau Belle' — EWld
- blue and white-flowered — SRms
- 'Blue Bell' — EGren MCtn
- 'Blue Bloomers' (d) — CDor EWes LRHS NQui SRms WCot
- blue-flowered — LRHS SPlb SRms
- 'Boule de Neige' (d) — CDor WSpi
§ - 'Chettle Charm' — CDor GAbr LRHS MBel NBir NLar NWbg SRms WCot WFar
- 'Cornish Mist' — CDor EBee EPfP WSpi
- double silver-blue-flowered (d) — LShi
- 'Frances' (d) — WCot
- 'Gawen' — CMiW
- 'George Chiswell' — see *C. persicifolia* 'Chettle Charm'
- 'Grandiflora' — CDor

Campanula

- 'Grandiflora Alba' NLar SDix
- 'Hampstead White' (d) CDor WSpi
- 'Kelly's Gold' SRms
- 'La Belle' (d) LBar NLar WHil
- 'La Bello'^PBR MNrw NLar
- 'La Bonne Amie' (d) EBee EPfP LBar LSou MNrw NLar SPoG
- 'Moerheimii' (d) WSpi
- 'Perry's Boy Blue' NPer
§ — var. *planiflora* WAbe
- — f. *alba* GKev WAbe
- 'Pride of Exmouth' (d) ♀H7 CDor CMiW WSpi
- subsp. *sessiliflora* 'Alba' see *C. latiloba* 'Alba'
- 'Snowdrift' SRms
- (Takion Series) 'Takion Blue' EGren ELan EPfP GBin LBar LRHS LSou Midl MPri SPoG SRms
- — 'Takion White' EGren ELan EPfP LBar LRHS LSou Midl MPri SPoG SRms
- 'Telham Beauty' ambig. EHeP WSpi
- 'Telham Beauty' misapplied EBee EPfP LRHS MArl SRms
- 'Telham Beauty' D.Thurston MCtn NLar
- 'Tinpenny Blue' WCot
- 'White Bell' EGren
- 'Wortham Belle' ambig. LBar LRHS MArl MHol
- 'Wortham Belle' Blooms CFis
- *petrophila* WAbe
- *pilosa* see *C. chamissonis*
- - 'Superba' see *C. chamissonis* 'Superba'
- 'Pink Octopus'^PBR CAby CSde CTtf CWGN EGren ELan EMor EPfP ERCP LBar MBNS MHol MSCN NCth NLar SEle SPoG SRms WFar WKif WSpi
- *planiflora* see *C. persicifolia* var. *planiflora*
§ *portenschlagiana* ♀H5 CMac CWal EBee EGren EHeP ELan EPfP GAbr GBin GJos GMaP LCro LRHS LShi MAsh MCtn MHer MMuc NRya SDix SEND SPoG SRms StAn WAbe WFar
- 'Alba' WFar
- AMBELLA INTENS PURPLE ('Ptdb141301'^PBR) LCro LRHS SPoG
- AMBELLA LAVENDER ('Ptb11701'^PBR) LCro LRHS
- AMBELLA WHITE ('Ptw1101'^PBR) LCro LRHS SPoG
- 'Blue Magic' EDAr LBar
- 'Blue Sky' LRHS
- 'Catharina' EPfP LBar LRHS MPro SPoG SRms WFar
- Clockwise Series EPfP LRHS SRot
- — CLOCKWISE DEEP BLUE EPfP NBir WTor
- 'Lieselotte' EPot SAko WFar
- 'Major' GJos NCou
- 'Planet'^PBR **new** LRHS
- 'Porto1' **new** LRHS
- 'Resholdt's Variety' ELan EPot GKev LRHS MBel SAko SLee SRms WAbe WCot
- 'Sago' EGren LBar LRHS LSou MHol MPri MPro
- *poscharskyana* CMac CoPl ELan EPfP GAbr GJos GKev GQue ISha LBuc LCro LSRN LWaG MCtn MHer MHol MMuc NBid NBro NGdn NLar SEND SHor SPlb SPoG SRms WCAu WFar
- 'Blauranke' EWes WFar
- 'Blue Gown' WIce
- BLUE WATERFALL ('Camgood') CWGN EPfP LRHS MBNS NCth NDov SPoG WCot
- 'E.H. Frost' CElw ECha ELan EPfP EPPr GKev GMaP ISha LBar LRHS MArl MMuc
- 'Frühlingszauber' WCot
- 'Garden Star' LRHS MHol
- 'Hirsch Blue' LRHS MPri SRms
- 'Lilacina' EPPr
- 'Lisduggan Variety' EPPr EWes GMaP LRHS LSto MAvo NLar SLee SRms WFar WIce
- 'Nana Alba' WBrk
- 'Pinkins'^PBR GJos LRHS LSou MArl
- 'Purple Fountain' EBlo LRHS
- 'Silberregen' EPPr GJos GKev LRHS LShi SAko
- 'Stella' ♀H5 ECha EGrI ELan EPfP GMaP LRHS LSou LSRN MAvo NDov WCav WCot WHoo
- 'Trollkind' EPPr SAko
- 'Weissranke' WFar
- white-flowered WFar
- *prenanthoides* see *Asyneuma prenanthoides*
- *pulla* ELan GKev SPoG SRms WAbe WIce
- 'Alba' WAbe
- × *pulloides* hort. EPot GEdr GMaP NLar SRkn WFar
  'G.F.Wilson' ♀H5
- *punctata* EAri EPfP GArf GJos NBro NSti WFar
- B&SWJ 7436 GGro
- f. *albiflora* WFar
- 'Alina's Double' (d) NLar
- var. *hondoensis* EAri GGro GKev
- 'Hot Lips' CMac
* — var. *howozana* GKev
- — var. *microdonta* B&SWJ 5553 WCru
* — 'Nana' WFar
- 'Pantaloons' (d) CDor CMac CWGN MHer NLar SRms
- 'Pink Chimes' CDor EMor GJos NWbg SMrm
- purple-flowered EPfP
- f. *rubriflora* CDor CSde CSpe EAri EBee EGrI ELan EMor EPfP LRHS SRms WCAu WKif WTre
- — 'Beetroot' EMor GKev GQue LBar MHer MHol WFar
- — 'Bowl of Cherries' SRms
- — 'Cherry Bells' EAri EPfP LRHS
I — 'Silver Bells' EMor LBar NLar NSti SRms WCot WFar WHil
- 'Wedding Bells' CDor LBar LRHS LSou MBel NWbg SMrm SRms WCAu WHil
I — 'White Bells' MHol
- 'Purple Sensation'^PBR CMiW CWGN MNrw NLar WCot
- *pusilla* see *C. cochlearifolia*
- *pyramidalis* CSpe EBee EGrI ELan EPfP GJos MCtn MMuc SPlb
- 'Alba' CSpe ELan EPfP GJos MCtn SPlb
- variegated (v) LRHS
- *raddeana* SBrt
- *raineri* WAbe
* — 'Alba' WAbe
§ *rapunculoides* EGrI MCtn SRms
- 'Alba' WFar
- *rapunculus* MCtn MNHC WKit
- *recurva* see *C. incurva*
- *rhomboidalis* Gorter see *C. rapunculoides*
- *rhomboidalis* L. GKev WCot
  (Ringsabell Series) ELan EPfP SPoG
  'Ringsabell Indigo Blue'
- 'Ringsabell Mulberry Rose' ELan EPfP SRms
- 'Ringsabell Opal White' ELan
- *rotundifolia* CMac ELan EPfP GAbr GJos GQue LRHS LShi MAsh MCtn MHer

	MNHC NAts NMir SHor SPhx SPlb SRms StAn WOrg
- 'Jotunheimen'	WAbe
§ - 'Olympica'	WHoo
- 'White Gem'	ELan GJos GKev LRHS
'Royal Wave'	NLar
'Samantha'	GEdr LRHS SHar WFar
'Sarastro'	Widely available
sarmatica	EWld GKev SRms WFar
- 'Hemelstraling'	GElm MHer MHol
sartorii	WAbe
scheuchzeri	WAbe
'Senior'	EPPr LRHS WCot WGoo
sibirica 'Royal Wedding'	EMor LBar MAsh NCth NEoE
'Spring Bell White'	LRHS
subramulosa	see *C. cochlearifolia*
'Summer Pearl'	LRHS
'Summertime Blues'PBR	EBee ELan MHol NLar WCot
'Swannables'	MWlw NCth WFar
takesimana	CSpe CTtf ELan EPfP GKev GKin GQue LRHS LShi LSou MAsh MCtn NLar SPoG SRms WSpi
I - 'Alba'	WFar
- 'Beautiful Trust'	CDor MHol
- 'Elizabeth'	EBee EBlo EGrI EMor EPfP ERCP ESgI GMaP LRHS MHol NGdn SHar SPlb WCAu WFar WKif
- 'Elizabeth II' (d)	SHar WFar
- 'White Giant'	SHar
thyrsoides	CSpe GKev
'Timsbury Chimes'	WAbe
'Timsbury Perfection'	EDAr WAbe
tommasiniana ♀H5	WAbe
trachelium	CBWd CCBP CGwi EBee EHep ELon EMor GJem GJos LCro MCtn MHer MNHC NAts NMir WCot WFar WHer WHil WOrg WShi WSpi
- B&SWJ 15057	WCru
- f. *alba*	EMor NLar WCot WFar
- 'Bernice' (d)	CDor EBee ELan EMor GMaP MHol MNrw NSti WCot WFar WSpi WTre
- 'Purple Break'	MHol WCot
- 'Van-Houttei'	NLar WCot
versicolor	CDoC SRms
vidalii	see *Azorina vidalii*
'Viking'PBR	LBar LRHS SHar SRms
waldsteiniana	GKev WAbe
wanneri	EDAr GKev
× *wockei* 'Puck'	EDAr WAbe
zangezura	EDAr ELan EPfP WHil
zoysii	WAbe

Campanula × *Symphyandra* see *Campanula*

Campanumoea see *Codonopsis*

Campomanesia (Myrtaceae)
schlechtendaliana	WJur

Campsis (Bignoniaceae)
'Fire Light'	LCro
grandiflora	CBcs CWGN ELan EPfP LSRN
- 'Tropical Summer'	CDoC MPri SPoG
radicans	CBcs CMac CRHN EGren EGrI ELan EPfP EUrb LRHS MCtn MHtn SPlb WJur
- 'Atrosanguinea'	SVen WCot
- 'Flamenco'	CBcs CBrac CDoC CMac CWCL EBee EGren ELan EPfP EUrb LRHS LSRN SAth SEND SPoG SVen

§ - f. *flava* ♀H4	CBcs CMac EBee EGrI ELan ELon EPfP EUrb LRHS LWaG MBlu MGos MPri SPoG SVen SWor
- 'Stromboli'	EBee EPfP LRHS
- 'Yellow Trumpet'	see *C. radicans* f. *flava*
× *tagliabueana*	CWCL CWGN LRHS MPri
DANCING FLAME ('Huidan'PBR)	
- GOLDEN TRUMPET ('Mincamja3'PBR) new	LRHS
- GRENADINE ('Rutcam') new	CBcs
- INDIAN SUMMER ('Kudian'PBR)	CBcs CDoC CWGN CWnw EPfP LBom LCro LRHS LSRN MGos SPoG
- 'Madame Galen' ♀H4	CBcs CDoC CWCL CWGN CWnw EBee ELan EPfP LCro LRHS LSRN LWaG MAsh MBlu MGos MPri MSwo SArc SBig SEND SPoG SRms SSta SVen SWor WCot
- ORANGEADE ('Tracamp')	EBee ELan
- Summer Jazz Series	LRHS
- - SUMMER JAZZ FIRE	see *C.* × *tagliabueana* (Summer Jazz Series) 'Takarazuka Fresa'
§ - - 'Takarazuka Fresa'PBR	LCro

Camptosorus see *Asplenium*

Camptotheca (Nyssaceae)
acuminata	CBcs

Campylandra see *Tupistra*

Canarina (Campanulaceae)
abyssinica new	EAri
canariensis ♀H2	CTsd EAri EShb
- from Los Silos, Tenerife	WCot
eminii	WCot

Candollea see *Hibbertia*

Canna ✿ (Cannaceae)
'Admiral Aurellan'	SEND
'Alaska'	LRHS SHaC
'Alberich'	SHaC
altensteinii	CDTJ SAth SHaC SNoN SPlb
'Ambassadour'	SHaC
'Angie Summers'	CLil
'Annaeei' ♀H3	SAth SHaC SPlb
'Anthony and Cleopatra' (v)	WCot
'Argentina'	SHaC
'Assaut'	SHaC
I 'Australia'	CCps CDTJ EPfP SHaC SWor
'Banana Punch'	WFar
'Bethany'	SHaC SNoN
'Bird of Paradise'	SHaC
'Black Knight'	SHaC
'Bonfire'	CDTJ
brasiliensis	EShb SHaC
'Brillant'	CLil LAma SHaC SNoN
'Burbank'	CDTJ
'Caballero'	LAma SHaC XFar
'Carnaval'	SHaC
'Centenaire de Rozain-Boucharlat'	SHaC SNoN
'Champion'	SHaC
'Cherry Red' misapplied	see *C.* 'Pfitzer's Cherry Red'
'Chocolate Sunrise'	EPfP LCro
'Chouchou'	SHaC
§ 'City of Portland'	SHaC
§ 'Cleopatra' ♀H3	CCht LRHS SBig SHaC SNoN SPlb
coccinea	SArc
compacta	SHaC

Canna 159

'Corail'	SHaC		- 'Kreta' (Island Series)	LRHS
'Corsica' (Island Series)	SHaC		- 'Purpurea'	CDTJ EUrb SHaC SPlb
'Crimson Beauty'	CWnw		- 'Russian Red' ♀H3	EUrb SBig SHaC SIvy SNoN
dark red	EGren		- TROPICANNA GOLD	CBcs CSBt EGren LCro SEND SHaC
'Délibáb'	SHaC		('Mactro')PBR	SWor WCot WLov
'Durban' Hiley, orange-flowered	see *C*. 'Phasion'		'Intrigue'	EUrb SHaC
			iridiflora misapplied	see *C*. × *ehemanii*
'Durban' ambig.	CBen CWGN EGren SArc SWor		'Italia'	CDTJ
'E. Neubert'	ELan SHaC SWor		*jacobiniflora*	SHaC
edulis	CDTJ LRHS SArc SBig		*jaegeriana*	SHaC
- green-leaved	EGren		'Jivago'	SHaC
§ × *ehemanii* ♀H3	CCps CDTJ CWnw SBrt SHaC SPlb	I	'King Humbert' (blood-red)	CDTJ SEND
'Emblème'	SHaC		KING HUMBERT (orange-red)	see *C*. 'Roi Humbert'
'En Avant'	SHaC		'King Midas'	see *C*. 'Richard Wallace'
'Endeavour'	CLil EUrb SHaC	§	'Königin Charlotte'	CWnw SHaC XFar
'Erebus' ♀H3	CBen CLil SHaC		*latifolia*	SHaC
'Ermine'	SHaC	I	'Leopoldii'	SHaC
'Extase'	SHaC		'Lesotho Lil'	SHaC
'Fantasy'	XFar		'Liberté'	see *C*. 'Wyoming'
'Fatamorgana'	SHaC		'Lolita'	SHaC
'Feuerzauber'	SHaC		'Louis Cayeux' ♀H3	SHaC
'Fiesta'	SHaC		'Louis Cottin'	LAma XFar
FIREBIRD	see *C*. 'Oiseau de Feu'		'Lucifer'	LAma NPer
'Firebird'	SHaC XFar		'Lucy Steele'	SHaC
flaccida	CLil SHaC		LUSH LEAVES (mixed) (v)	XFar
'General Eisenhower' ♀H3	SHaC		*lutea*	SHaC
× *generalis* Cannova Series	SHaC		'Madame Paul Casaneuve'	SHaC
- - CANNOVA BRONZE ORANGE	CCht MPri SHaC WFar		'Madeira' (Island Series)	SHaC
('Fcaa33')			'Malawiensis Variegata'	see *C*. 'Striata'
- - CANNOVA BRONZE PEACH	MPri SHaC		MANDELA (mixed) (v)	XFar
('Fcaa43')			'Marabout'	SBig SHaC
- - CANNOVA BRONZE SCARLET	CAbb CCht EGren LCro MPri SHaC		'Marlena'	SHaC
('Fcaa35') ♀H3	WFar		'Marshmallow'	SHaC
- - CANNOVA LEMON	LRHS SHaC		'Monique' (v)	XFar
('Fcaa15')			'Montaigne'	SHaC
- - CANNOVA MANGO	CAbb CCht LRHS SHaC		'Moonshine'	LCro WFar
('Fcaa10')			'Musifolia' ♀H3	CDTJ EAri ESwi EUrb NGKo SHaC
- - CANNOVA ORANGE SHADES	LRHS SHaC			SIvy
('Fcaa17')			'Mystique' ♀H3	SHaC
- - CANNOVA RED SHADES	CCht SHaC	§	'Oiseau de Feu'	NGKo
('Fcaa23') ♀H3			'Oiseau d'Or'	SHaC
- - CANNOVA ROSE	LRHS SHaC		'Orange Chocolate'	SHaC
('Fcaa05') ♀H3			'Orange Punch'	SHaC
- - CANNOVA YELLOW	CCht LCro SHaC		'Orchid'	see *C*. 'City of Portland'
('Fcaa02') ♀H3			'Panache'	CDTJ SHaC
- 'Pink Princess'	XFar		'Panama'	SHaC
- 'Red Tiger' (v)	SHaC		*paniculata*	SHaC
- 'Regal Red'	SHaC		'Perkeo'	SHaC
glauca	SHaC	§	'Pfitzer's Cherry Red'	XFar
'Golden Orb'	SHaC SNoN	§	'Pfitzer's Salmon Pink'	LRHS
'Gran Canaria'	SHaC	§	'Phasion' (v) ♀H3	CAbb CCps CLil CSBt CTsd
'Grand Duc'	SHaC			EGren ELan EUrb LCro LRHS
'Grande'	EShb ESwi SHaC SPlb			LSou MSwo NPer SEND SHaC
'Grandiose'	SHaC			SNoN SPeP SPoG SWor WCot
'Happy Carmen' (CannaSol Series)	EGren ELan LRHS SAth SIvy WFar		'Picasso' ♀H3	WLov XFar LAma SEND SHaC
'Happy Cleo' (CannaSol Series)	EGren ELan SAth SHaC WFar	*	'Pink Paradise' 'Pink Perfection'	XFar SHaC
'Happy Emily' (CannaSol Series)	EGren ELan SHaC		'President' 'Pretoria'	SHaC see *C*. 'Striata'
'Happy Isabel' (CannaSol Series)	EGren LRHS SHaC WFar		'Pretoria Variegata' 'Prince Charmant'	see *C*. 'Striata' SHaC
'Happy Julia' (CannaSol Series)	EGren LRHS SHaC		'Pringle Bay' (v) 'Professor Lorentz'	SHaC see *C*. 'Wyoming'
'Happy Wilma' (CannaSol Series)	EGren SArc SHaC		'Queen Charlotte' 'Ra' ♀H3	see *C*. 'Königin Charlotte' CBen CLil SHaC
Henlade hybrids	CDTJ		'Red Giant'	CWnw SEND
'Herman'	SHaC		'Red Stripe'	XFar
'Indiana'	SHaC	§	'Richard Wallace'	SHaC SPlb
indica	CDTJ CTsd EShb NGKo SArc SAth SHaC SMHy SPlb	§	'Robert Kemp' 'Roi Humbert'	SHaC EUrb SHaC

'Roi Soleil'	SHaC
'Roma'	SHaC
'Rosa Fuerta'	SHaC
'Rose Futurity' (Futurity Series)	XFar
'Rosemond Coles'	SHaC
'Saladin'	SHaC
'Salmon Pink'	see *C.* 'Pfitzer's Salmon Pink'
'Salsa'	SHaC
'Sémaphore'	LRHS SEND SHaC WCot
'Shenandoah' ♀H3	CCps SHaC
'Singapore Girl'	SHaC
'Society Belle' ♀H3	SHaC
'South Pacific'	SHaC
'South Pacific Ivory'	SHaC
'South Pacific Orange'	SHaC
'South Pacific Rose'	SHaC
'South Pacific Scarlet'	SHaC
speciosa	CBcs SPlb
'Strasbourg'	NPer
'Striata' misapplied	see *C.* 'Stuttgart'
§ 'Striata' (v) ♀H3	CBen CCps CDTJ CWGN EUrb SHaC SIvy SWor WCot XFar
'Striped Beauty' (v)	CDTJ CLil SBig SHaC
§ 'Stuttgart' (v)	CDTJ CLil ESwi EUrb EWes LCro SBig SHaC SNoN XFar
'Sunset'	WCot
'Tali'	SHaC
'Talisman'	LAma
'Taney'	CLil EUrb SHaC
'Tangerine' **new**	CSBt
'Taroudant'	SHaC
'Triomphe'	SHaC
(Tropical Series) 'Tropical Bronze Scarlet'	EShb SHaC
- 'Tropical Red'	SHaC
- 'Tropical Rose'	SHaC
- 'Tropical Salmon'	SHaC
- 'Tropical White'	SHaC
- 'Tropical Yellow'	SHaC
TROPICANNA	see *C.* 'Phasion'
TROPICANNA BLACK ('Lon01' PBR)	CAbb CBcs CCht CSBt CSpe CTsd CWnw EAri EGren ELan EPfP EUrb LCro LRHS LSou MBros MPie SEND SHaC SPeP SPoG SWor WCot
tuerckheimii	SHaC
'Valentine'	WCot
'Vanilla Cream'	XFar
'Velvet Red'	EGren SNoN
'Verdi' ♀H3	CLil LAma SHaC
warscewiczii	CDTJ EShb SHaC
'Whithelm Pride' ♀H3	SHaC SNoN
'Wilma'	LRHS SNoN
'Wintzer's Colossal'	SHaC
§ 'Wyoming' ♀H3	CDTJ CWnw EUrb LAma LCro LRHS SEND SHaC SWor XFar
'Yara'	SHaC
'Yellow Humbert' misapplied	see *C.* 'Cleopatra', 'Richard Wallace'

Cannomois (Restionaceae)

grandis ♀H4	CPbh SPlb

Cantua (Polemoniaceae)

buxifolia ♀H3	CCoa CTsd EAri EShb LRHS SEND SIvy
- 'Alba'	CTsd EAri EShb
- 'Dancing Oaks'	SVen

Cape gooseberry see *Physalis peruviana*

Capeochloa (Poaceae)

§ *cincta*	WCot

Capnoides see *Corydalis*

Capparis (Capparaceae)

spinosa	WJur
- subsp. *rupestris*	MCtn SPlb WJek

Capsicum (Solanaceae)

annuum	SVic WKit
- 'Anaheim'	MCtn
- 'Ancho'	SVic
- var. *annuum* 'Black Hungarian'	MCtn
- - (Cerasiforme Group) 'Piccante Calabrese'	SVic
- - (Conioides Group) 'Super Chili' ♀H1c	SPre SVic
- - (Grossum Group) 'Almapaprika'	SVic
- - - 'Bell Boy'	LCro MCtn
- - - 'Bendigo'	MBros
- - - 'Corno di Toro Rosso' ♀H1c	CHby LCro MCtn
- - - 'Friggitello' ♀H1c	MCtn
- - - 'Gourmet' **new**	EKin
- - - 'Mini Bell Red'	SVic
- - - 'Mini Bell Yellow'	SVic
- - - 'Mohawk' ♀H1c	EKin
- - - 'New Ace'	LCro
- - - 'Popti' **new**	MCtn
- - - 'Redskin' ♀H1c	EKin LCro
- - - 'Thor'	MCtn
- - - 'Topepo Rosso' ♀H1c	MCtn
- - (Longum Group) 'Bolivian Rainbow' ♀H1c	SVic
- - - cayenne	LCro
- - - 'Fish'	SVic
- - - 'Hot Thai' ♀H1c	EKin
- - - jalapeño	EHet LCro MCtn SVic
- - - 'Joe's Long Cayenne'	SVic
- - - 'Long Red Cayenne'	LCro
- - - 'Piccante Di Cayenna'	LCro
- - - 'Ring of Fire'	SEdi SVic
- - - 'Serrano'	SVic
- - - 'Tokyo Hot'	SVic
- - 'Marconi Rosso'	LCro SVic
- - 'Midas'	EKin
- - 'Prairie Fire' ♀H1c	LCro SVic
- - 'Red King'	EKin
- - 'Sweet Banana'	LCro
- - SWEETONIA MIX	EKin
- 'Apache' ♀H1c	EHet EKin MBros MPri SPre
- 'Apple Crisp'	SVic
- 'Basket of Fire' ♀H1c	EDel EHet EKin LCro SPre SVic WKit
- 'Cayenne Long Slim'	MCtn
- 'Cayenne Purple'	SVic
- 'Cayenne Red'	EHet SEdi SPre SVic
- 'Cayenne Sweet'	SVic
- 'Cayennetta'	EKin
- 'Cow Horn'	SVic
- 'Cozumel'	SVic
- 'Demon Red' ♀H1c	EHet EKin MCtn SPre SVic
- 'Etna'	MCtn
- 'Explosive Ember'	MCtn SVic
- 'Fat Bird'	SVic
- 'Fiery Flames' **new**	EKin

Cardamine   161

- var. *glabriusculum* — SVic
- 'Granova' **new** — EKin
- 'Holy Mole' — SVic
- 'Hungarian Hot Wax' ♀H1c — CHby EKin LCro MCtn SVic
- 'Hungarian Yellow Wax' — SVic
- 'Jalapeño Farmer's Market Potato' — SVic
- 'Jalapeño Fooled You' — SVic
- 'Jazz' **new** — EKin
- 'Jigsaw' — SVic
- Kashmiri chilli — SVic
- 'Las Cruces Cayenne' — SVic
- 'Nosferatu' — SVic
- 'Numex April Fools' Day' — SVic
- 'Numex Centennial' — SVic
- 'Numex Cinco de Mayo' — SVic
- 'Numex Garnet' — SVic
- 'Numex Heritage Big Jim' — SVic
- 'Numex Lemon Spice' — SVic
- 'Numex Orange Spice' — SVic
- 'Numex Piñata' — SVic
- 'Numex Primavera' — SVic
- 'Numex Pumpkin Spice' — SVic
- 'Numex Sweet' — SVic
- 'Numex Twilight' — SPre SVic
- 'Padron' — LCro MCtn SVic
- 'Pasilla Bajio' — SVic
- 'Peter Pepper' — SVic
- 'Pinocchio's Nose' — SVic
- 'Pot Black' ♀H1c — EDel SVic WKit
- 'Red Cherry Small' — SEdi
- 'Serrano Purple' — SVic
- 'Spaghetti' — SVic
- 'Toofan' **new** — MCtn
- 'Trinidad Perfume' — LCro
- 'Turkish Pickling' — EKin
- 'Uchu Cream Red' (v) — SVic
- 'Vampire' — MCtn SVic
- *baccatum* 'Aji Delight' — EKin
- 'Aji Omnicolor' — SVic
- 'Brazilian Starfish' — SVic
- 'Christmas Bell' — SVic
- 'Havana Gold' — EKin
- 'Lemon Drop' — SVic
- var. *pendulum* 'Bishop's Crown' — MCtn
- 'Spangles' ♀H1c — LCro
- *chinense* — SVic WKit
- 'Aribibi Gusano' — SVic
- 'Bhut Jolokia' — SVic
- 'Carolina Reaper' — EHet LCro SVic
- 'Cheiro Roxa' — SVic
- 'Golden Ghost' — EHet
- Habanero Group — EKin
- - 'Caribbean Antillais' ♀H1c — SVic
- - 'Habanero Caribbean Red' — SVic
- - 'Naga Morrich' — SVic
- - 'Turtle Claw' — SVic
- 'Hot Paper Lantern' — SVic
- 'Machu Pichu' — EKin
- 'Numex Suave Orange' — SVic
- 'Numex Suave Red' — SVic
- 'Numex Trick or Treat' — SVic
- 'Peito de Moca' — SVic
- 'Scotch Bonnet' — EHet LCro MBros SPre
- 'Seven Pod Brain Strain Yellow' — SVic
- 'Shabu Shabu' — SVic
- 'Trinidad Moruga Scorpion' — EKin LCro SVic
- 'Trinidad Scorpion' **new** — EKin
- 'Zing' — SVic
- *frutescens* 'Adorno' — LCro
- Tabasco Group — MCtn SVic
- 'Goan Button' — SVic
- 'Goan Hot Sweet' — SVic
- *pubescens* — CAgr
- 'Pumpkin' — MCtn
- 'Quickfire' — EKin MCtn
- 'Rodeo' — SVic
- Tenerife — SVic

Caputia (Asteraceae)
§ *scaposa* — LWaG
§ *tomentosa* ♀H1c — CPic LCro SIvy WCot

Caragana (Fabaceae)
- *arborescens* — CAgr EPfP MCtn SPlb WSpi
- - 'Lorbergii' — MBlu
- - 'Pendula' — CMac ELan LRHS MBlu NLar WSpi
- - 'Walker' — CMac ELan MAsh MBlu MGos NLar
- *aurantiaca* — NLar SBrt SPlb
- *halodendron* — MBlu

carambola see *Averrhoa carambola*

caraway see *Carum carvi*

Cardamine ❀ (Brassicaceae)
- *asarifolia* misapplied — see *Pachyphragma macrophyllum*
- *bipinnata* — WCot
- *bulbifera* — CCBP EBee ELon EPPr ESwi GGro GQue LEdu NAts NRya WCru
- *californica* — EBee EPPr LEdu LShi NRya WCot WCru
- *concatenata* — GEdr WCru
- - 'Fine Lace' **new** — WCru
- *digitata* — EWld
- *diphylla* — LSto WCot WCru WFar
- - 'American Sweetheart' — CExl CMiW
- - 'Eco Cut Leaf' — CExl CMiW LEdu SHar WCru
- - 'Eco Moonlight' — WCru
- *enneaphyllos* — NBid
- *glanduligera* — CTtf EBee ECha EPPr GKev LEdu MNrw NLar WCot WCru WFar
§ *heptaphylla* — CMiW ECha EWld GAbr GEdr GQue LEdu WCru
- - 'Big White' — EBee EPPr GAbr MNrw WFar
- - 'Guincho form' — EPPr GEdr LEdu WCot
- - 'Helen Myers' — GEdr
§ *kitaibelii* — CMiW EPPr EWld NLar WCot WCru WFar
- - B&SWJ 15919 — WCru
- *latifolia* Vahl — see *C. raphanifolia*
- *macrophylla* — CTtf LEdu WCot
- - 'Bright and Bronzy' — CExl WCru
- *maxima* — SHar WCot
- *pentaphyllos* ♀H5 — CSpe ECha EPPr EWld GKev GMaP GQue LEdu NLar SBeP SPhx WCru WFar
- *pratensis* — CBcs CBWd CCBP CDor CoPl CPud CTtf CWat ELin EMor GJos LCro MCtn MHer MNHC NAts NMir SRms WCAu WHer WOrg WShi
- - 'Flore Pleno' (d) — CDor CTtf ECha EGren EMor GArf GQue LEdu NBid NBir NBro NRya
- - - white-flowered (d) — LEdu SHar
- - white-flowered — CDor

Cardamine

– 'William' (d)		LEdu
quinquefolia		CCBP CDor CElw CMiW CTtf ECha ELon GAbr LEdu LSto MBel MNrw NCth SBeP SDix SMrm WBrk WCot WCru WFar
– PAB 9992		LEdu
§ **raphanifolia**		CExl ECha GAbr LSto NBid NBro NRya WFar
– PAB 204		LEdu
trifolia		CCBP CMac CoPl EBee ECha ELon EMor EPPr GEdr GMaP LEdu LShi MNrw MPnt NBir NBro NRya WCot WCru WFar
waldsteinii		CExl EBee EPPr GArf GEdr IPot LEdu NBro NLar WCru WFar
yezoensis		LEdu
– B&SWJ 4659		EBee EPPr ESwi GGro WCru

cardamon see *Elettaria cardamomum*

Cardiandra see Hydrangea

formosana	see *Hydrangea densifolia*

Cardiocrinum ✿ (Liliaceae)

cordatum B&SWJ 2812	WCru
– B&SWJ 4841	WCru
– B&SWJ 5427	WCru
– B&SWJ 6336	WCru
– B&SWJ 11069	WCru
– var. **glehnii**	GEdr
– – B&SWJ 10827	WCru
– – B&SWJ 10843	WCru
– red-flowered	SBrt
giganteum	CBcs CWnw EBee EGren GAbr GEdr GKev IDun LAma LCro LRHS NBid NLar SBig WAbe WCru WPnP XFar
– B&SWJ 2419	WCru
– HWJK 2158 from Nepal	WCru
– GWJ 9219 from Sikkim	WCru
– WJC 13661 from Sikkim	WCru
– WJC 13698 from Sikkim	WCru
– var. **giganteum**	CSpe
– var. **yunnanense**	EBee EPPr GEdr LRHS NBid SChF WCru WPGP
– – NJM 11.023 from Guizhou	WPGP
– – 'Big and Pink' seedlings	WCru
– – brown-leaved	GEdr

Cardiospermum (Sapindaceae)

grandiflorum	Prohibited invasive. See Conservation and the Environment, p.42
halicacabum	MCtn

cardoon see *Cynara cardunculus*

Carduus (Asteraceae)

nutans	GGro SPhx

Carex (Cyperaceae)

from Kyoto, Japan	GGro
from Rwenzori Mountains, Africa	EPPr
acuta	CHab CPud ELin
– 'Variegata' (v)	CBen CLil CMac CWat GMaP NBro
acutiformis	ELin MMuc MWts NMir
'Amazon Mist'	LBom LRHS NLar NWbg SRms WFar
arenaria	CKno
aurea	WChS
berggrenii	SPlb
brunnea	CMac
– 'Jenneke' (v)	EBee GKev LCro LRHS WFar
– 'Lady Sunshine'	NLar
– 'Variegata' (v)	WSpi
buchananii	CAby CBWd CDoC CoPl EBee EHeP ELan EPPr GMaP GQue LCro LRHS MAsh MGos NBir NBro NLar NRya SAth SDix SPlb SPoG SRms StAn WSpi
– 'Firefox'	SHor
– 'Green Twist'	EPfP NLar
– 'Red Rooster'	EHeP EPfP LBuc LCro LRHS NBir NLar NWbg SAth SMrm WFar WNPC
chathamica	SVen
'China Blue'	LRHS
ciliatomarginata 'Treasure Island' (v)	EBee EMor NLar
comans	NBro SAth
– 'Bronco'	LBuc WFar
– bronze-leaved	CBWd CDoC EAri EGren EHeP ELan EPfP GArf LRHS LSto MAsh NBir NSti SRms WCha
– 'Bronzita'	LRHS NWbg WFar
– 'Frosted Curls'	Widely available
– red-leaved	NLar SRms
conica 'Hime-kan-suge'	see *C. conica* 'Snowline'
– 'Kiku-sakura' (v)	EPPr
§ – 'Snowline' (v)	CMac ELan GMaP NBro NLar
dipsacea	CMac CWCL GMaP GQue
– 'Dark Horse'	MMuc
divulsa	CKno ELan LCro
– subsp. **leersii**	EPPr
§ **dolichostachya** 'Kaga-nishiki' (v)	NLar
elata	CBen
– 'Aurea' ♀H6	Widely available
– 'Bowles's Golden'	see *C. elata* 'Aurea'
– 'Knightshayes'	WCot WFar
elongata	CHab
'Evergold'	see *C. oshimensis* 'Evergold'
'Feather Falls' (v)	EPfP LRHS SMad
firma 'Variegata' (v)	EDAr WAbe
flacca	CHab CKno ELin EPPr GBin
– 'Blue Zinger'	CAby CKno ELan EPfP GBin GMaP LRHS NCth NLar SAth SHor SPeP
§ – subsp. **flacca**	EBee NSti
flagellifera	CMac CSpe EBee EGren EHeP ELan ELon EPfP EPPr GMaP GQue LRHS MMuc NBir SEND SPlb SPoG
– 'Kiwi'	EAri
– 'Toffee Twist'	LBuc
flava	EBee
fraseri	see *Cymophyllus fraserianus*
fraserianus	see *Cymophyllus fraserianus*
glauca Scop.	see *C. flacca* subsp. *flacca*
'Gold Fountains'	see *C. dolichostachya* 'Kaga-nishiki'
grayi	ELin GQue LEdu LShi MBlu Midl NLar SPlb
'Ice Dance' (v)	CBcs CKno CSBt CWCL EBee EGren EHeP ELan EMor EPfP GMaP GQue LBuc LRHS LWaG MAsh MMuc MPro NClf SEND WCha WChS WFar WHoo
laxiculmis 'Bunny Blue'PBR	CKno NLar
maorica	EPPr
MILK CHOCOLATE ('Milchoc'PBR) (v)	CBWd EBee ELan EPfP LRHS MAsh NGdn SRms
montana	StAn

Carpinus 163

morrowii misapplied	see *C. oshimensis*
morrowii Boott 'Everglow'PBR (EverColor Series) (v)	CKno EGren EMor LCro LRHS
I - 'Fisher's Form' (v)	CBen CBrac EPPr WFar WOld
- 'Gilt' (v)	EPPr
- 'Irish Green'	EBee EGren ELan GBin LRHS MBel
- 'Pinkie'	CDoC
- VANILLA ICE ('Vanice'PBR) (v)	CKno EGren EMor EUrb LCro MAsh
- 'Variegata' (v)	EHeP ELan EPPr GKev GMaP LRHS NBir NSti SRms WFar
* *multifida*	EGrI
muskingumensis	CKno EGren ELan ELin EPfk EPPr GBin LCro LEdu LRHS LSto NBro NLar SDix WChS
- 'Little Midge'	CKno CMac LEdu NLar
- 'Oehme' (v)	CKno CWCL NBid SNoN
- 'Silberstreif' (v)	CKno EMor EPPr MMuc
No 1, Nanking (Greg's broad leaf)	ESwi
No 4, Nanking (Greg's thin leaf)	EPPr
§ *oshimensis*	SAth WCot
- (EverColor Series)	CKno LBom LRHS SPoG WCha
EVERCREAM ('Ficre'PBR) (v)	
- - EVEREST ('Fiwhite'PBR) (v)	CAby CBcs CKno EBee EBlo EGren ELon EMor EUrb GKev LBom LCro LRHS LSRN LSto MArl MAsh NBir NEoE SAth SPoG SRms WCot WFar
- - 'Everillo'PBR	CBcs CKno EBee EGren ELan EMor EPfk EPfP EUrb GBin LBom LBuc LCro LRHS MAsh Midl NLar SDix SPeP SPoG SRms WCha WCot WHoo WNPC
- - 'Everlime'PBR	CKno EBee EGren EUrb LRHS MAsh WCha WNPC
- - 'Everlite' (v)	LCro
- - 'Everoro' (v)	CKno EUrb LRHS MHol WCot
- - 'Eversheen'PBR (v)	EGren LCro LRHS
§ - 'Evergold' (v) ♀H7	Widely available
- 'Evergreen'	LRHS WCha
otrubae	CHab CPud
panicea	CWat EBee ELin
paniculata	SHor
pendula	CBen CGwi CHab CKno CoPl CPud CWat ECha EHeP GAbr GMaP MCtn MMuc NBro NLar NSti SEND SHor WCAu
- 'Cool Jazz' (v)	EPPr
- 'Moonraker' (v)	ESwi WCot
petriei	ECha
phyllocephala 'Sparkler' (v)	SPad SPoG WCot
plantaginea	EPPr LEdu WPGP
pseudocyperus	CPud ELin EPfk NPer
remota	CKno EPPr
RIBBON FALLS ('Et Crx02'PBR)	LCro LRHS SMad
riparia	CHab CLil CPud ELin LCro MMuc NPer
- 'Bowles's Golden'	see *C. elata* 'Aurea'
scaposa	CExl ESwi WCot
- KWJ 12304	ESwi EWld LEdu WCru
secta - from Dunedin, New Zealand	EPfP GMaP SHor SRms EPPr
sideristicta 'Banana Boat'	see *C. sideristicta* 'Golden Falls'
§ - 'Golden Falls' (v)	LEdu SMad
- 'Nakafu'	ESwi
- 'Shiro-nakafu'	EMor ESwi LCro
- 'Variegata' (v)	LEdu NBir NClf NLar NSti
- 'Silver Sceptre' (v)	CBrac CKno EGren EMor GMaP LRHS LWaG MBel MGos NClf NSti SIvy SPlb WFar
spicata	CHab
stricta Gooden. 'Bowles's Golden'	see *C. elata* 'Aurea'
stricta Lam.	MMuc
strictissima	SPlb
strigosa	CBct
sylvatica	CHab LRHS
tenuiculmis	NSti WCot
testacea	Widely available
- LIMESHINE ('Wilshine')	WFar
- 'Old Gold'	SPlb
- 'Prairie Fire'	CSpe EGren EHeP EMor GMaP LBom LBuc LCro LRHS LSRN LWaG MMrt MMuc MPri NClf NLar SBig SRms WCot WTor
texensis	EPPr
'The Beatles'	LRHS NBir NGdn WCAu
trifida	EPPr
- 'Chatham Blue'	MMuc SEND
- 'Rekohu Sunrise'PBR (v)	EMor EPfP MMuc NWbg SEND SPoG WCot

Carica (Caricaceae)
papaya (F) ♀H1b	EAri MCtn NPlm SPre
pubescens	see *Vasconcellea pubescens*
quercifolia	WJur

Carissa (Apocynaceae)
grandiflora	see *C. macrocarpa*
§ *macrocarpa* (F)	EShb WJur WKor

Carlina (Asteraceae)
acanthifolia	GGro
acaulis	SPlb
- var. *caulescens*	see *C. acaulis* subsp. *simplex*
§ - subsp. *simplex*	ECha LRHS
vulgaris 'Silver Star'	SPhx

Carmichaelia (Fabaceae)
arborea	SArc
australis	EBee LRHS
stevensonii	CSpe MBlu WPGP

× *Carmispartium* see *Carmichaelia*

Carnegiea (Cactaceae)
gigantea	NPlm

Carpenteria (Hydrangeaceae)
californica	EBee EPfP LCro LRHS MGos NLar WSpi
- 'Bodnant' ♀H4	CBcs LRHS LSRN MAsh MGos NLar WPGP WSpi
- 'Elizabeth' ♀H4	CSBt CWGN MAsh SPoG
- 'Eskimo'	CDoC WSpi
- 'Ladhams' Variety'	CBcs CMac CWnw EPfP WSpi

Carpinus ✿ (Betulaceae)
betulus	Widely available
* - 'A. Beeckman'	CCVT LMaj WFar
- CHARTREUSE ('Carpsim') **new**	CBTr LCro
- 'Columnaris'	CAco CLnd EBee LMaj
§ - 'Fastigiata' ♀H7	CAco CBcs CBTr CCVT CDoC CEnd CLnd CMac CMCN CNWT CWnw EBar EHeP ELan ERom EUrb IPap LBuc LMaj MGos NPip SArc

Carpinus

		SEWo SFol SGol SSta WFar WHtc WMat
I	- 'Folis Argenteovariegatis Pendula' (v)	MBlu
	- 'Frans Fontaine'	CAco CBTr CCVT CLnd CMac CMCN EBar EBee EHeP EPfP EUrb IArd IPap LMaj LSRN LSto MBlu MGos NLar NOra NPip SArc SEWo SFol SGol SPoG WHtc WMat WMou
	- 'Globus'	MBlu
	- 'Lucas' ♀H7	CBTr CCVT CMac EBar IPap LMaj MBlu NOra NPip SArc SGol WMat
	- 'Monument'	SArc
I	- 'Monumentalis'	CAco LMaj
	- 'Orange Retz' PBR	CWnw EPfP LMaj
	- 'Pendula'	CAco CEnd EBee MBlu WHtc
	- 'Purpurea'	CAco CEnd LMaj MBlu
	- 'Pyramidalis'	see C. betulus 'Fastigiata'
	- 'Quercifolia'	ELan IPap
	- ROCKHAMPTON RED ('Lochglow') ♀H7	CBcs CBTr CCVT CLnd EBee ELan IPap LCro MBlu NOra NPip SGol WCha WMat WMou WReH
	- 'Stegemanns Primus' PBR	LSRN NPip
	caroliniana	CAco CLnd CMCN EBee LMaj WJur
	- from Mexico	WPGP
	- 'Autumn Fire'	NLar
	- 'Red Fall'	CBcs LRHS MBlu
	- 'Sentinel Dries'	MBlu
	cordata	MBlu SSta
	coreana	CMCN
	fangiana	CBcs CJun EBee EPfP MBlu NPip SHor WPGP
	fargesiana	EBee EPfP LMaj MBlu WPGP
	- KR 8780	WPGP
	fargesii	see C. viminea
	henryana var. simplicidentata	CMCN MBlu
	japonica ♀H6	CAco CBcs CMen EBar IPap LMaj LRHS MBlu NOra NPip SSta WMat
	- B&SWJ 10803	WCru
	- B&SWJ 11072	WCru
	- 'Chinese Lantern'	CBTr LRHS WMat
	kawakamii	CBcs WPGP
	- CWJ 12412	WCru
	- CWJ 12449	WCru
	laxiflora	CMen
	- B&SWJ 10809	WCru
	- B&SWJ 11035	WCru
	- var. macrostachya	see C. viminea
	omeiensis	EBee MBlu
	- KR 280	WPGP
	orientalis	WJur
	polyneura	CBcs EBee MBlu SSta WPGP
	pubescens	EBee WPGP
	rankanensis	MBlu SSta
	- NMWJ 14544	WCru
	shensiensis	EBee WPGP
	tschonoskii B&SWJ 10800	WCru
	- BBJMT 197	WPGP
	turczaninowii	CMCN CMen EBee IPap LMaj MBlu SSta
	- var. turczaninowii Farrer 331	WPGP
§	viminea	CEnd SSta

Carpobrotus (Aizoaceae)

	acinaciformis	SVen
P	edulis	CDTJ CoPl CSde CWal EUrb LWaG MCtn SArc SAth SBig SEND SVen WCor
	- 'Gugh Dawn' (v)	SVen

	- var. rubescens	CPic SAth
	- white-flowered	SAth
	muirii	SVen

Carpoxylon (Arecaceae)

macrospermum	NPlm

Carrierea (Salicaceae)

calycina	WPGP

carrot see *Daucus carota* for species; also AGM Vegetables Section for cultivars

Carthamus (Asteraceae)

mitissimus	EDAr
tinctorius	MNHC SRms
- 'White Grenade' (Grenade Series)	MCtn

Carum (Apiaceae)

carvi	EHet ENfk MCtn MHer MHoo MNHC SRms SVic WJek
- pink-flowered **new**	SDix
petroselinum	see Petroselinum crispum

Carya ✿ (Juglandaceae)

cordiformis	MBlu WJur
illinoinensis (F)	CAgr CBcs EBar LRHS MBlu WJur
- 'Carlson No 3' seedling (F)	CAgr
- 'Colby' seedling (F)	CAgr
- 'Cornfield' (F)	CAgr
- 'Lucas' (F)	CAgr
laciniosa (F)	IArd
- 'Henry' (F)	CAgr
- 'Keystone' seedling (F)	CAgr
ovata (F)	CAgr CBcs ELan MBlu
- 'Grainger' seedling (F)	CAgr
- 'Neilson' seedling (F)	CAgr
- 'Weschcke' seedling (F)	CAgr
- 'Yoder No 1' seedling (F)	CAgr

Caryophyllus see *Syzygium*

Caryopteris (Lamiaceae)

× clandonensis	CMac EHeP
- 'Arthur Simmonds' ♀H4	CCps ECha
- aff.'Arthur Simmonds'	CCps
- BLUE BALLOON ('Korball')	WHil WLov
- BLUE EMPIRE ('Elst33'PBR)	EBee LRHS WFar WLov
- 'Dark Knight'	CCoa CCps CDoC CSpe EBee EGrl ELan EPfP LBuc LCro LRHS LShi MAsh Midl NCth NLar SPel SPoG SRkn WFar WHil WHoo WHtc
- 'Ferndown'	NLar SEND SRms
- aff.'Ferndown'	CBrac
- 'First Choice' ♀H4	CBrac EPfP LSRN MAsh SPel SRkn
- 'Gold Crest' PBR	MArl WHil
- 'Gold Giant'	EPfP LRHS
- GOOD AS GOLD ('Novacargol')	LRHS
- GRAND BLEU ('Inoveris'PBR)	CMac EBee EGren ELan ELon EPfP LCro LRHS LSRN MGos MHtn
- 'Heavenly Baby' ♀H4	EPfP LRHS MAsh
- 'Heavenly Blue'	CBcs CBrac CCps CDoC EBee ECha EGren EGrl EHeP ELan ELon EPfP LCro LRHS LSRN MAsh MGos MHol MSwo NLar SBeP SEND SOrN SPlb SSta WFar WTor
- HINT OF GOLD ('Lisaura'PBR) ♀H4	CSBt ELan EPfP LCro LRHS MAsh MPri NLar WFar WHil WTor
- 'Katie'	CCps

- 'Kew Blue'	CBcs CSBt EBee ELan ELon EPfP LRHS MAsh MGos MHer Midl NLar SRms SSta	- var. *saxolmontana*	GKev
		wardii	GArf
		- 'George Taylor'	GArf
- 'Longwood Blue'	ECha EPfP LRHS		
- Pink Perfection ('Lisspin'^{PBR})	CSBt ELan EPfP LCro LRHS MMrt NEoE SPel SPoG WHil WLov	*Castanea* ✿ (*Fagaceae*)	
- Sapphire Dream ('Lissmiv') **new**	CSBt MBNS Midl	'Bouche de Bétizac' (F)	CAgr
		crenata	CAgr
- Stephi ('Lissteph'^{PBR})	CBcs ELan EPfP LCro LRHS MAsh SPoG WTor	*henryi* CBS 755.04	WPGP
		'Maraval' (F)	CAgr WMat
- Sterling Silver ('Lissilv'^{PBR}) ♀H4	CCps CMac CSBt EBee EGren ELan EPfP LCro LRHS LSRN MAsh NCth NEoE SPoG SRkn SRms SSta WHil WHtc	'Maridonne' (F)	CAgr
		'Marigoule' (F)	CAgr EPom WMat
		'Marsol' (F)	CAgr CHab LMaj WMat
		'Précoce Migoule' (F)	CAgr
		sativa	CAco CBrac CBTr CCVT CDoC CHab CLnd CMCN CWal EBar EGren EHeP ELan EPfP EPom IPap MGos MMuc NOra NPip SEWo SGol SVic WFar WHtc WJur WMat WRjT
- 'Summer Gold'	CMac MAsh		
- 'Summer Sorbet'^{PBR} (v) ♀H4	CMac CWGN ELan EPfP LRHS MAsh MGos Midl NLar SRms WCot WFar WHil WTor		
- weeping	ELan EPPr		
- 'White Surprise'^{PBR} (v)	CCps CMac CWGN EPfP LCro LRHS MAsh SGol SPoG WFar WHil WTor	§ - 'Albomarginata' (v) ♀H6	CEnd NOra NPip SPoG WMat
		- 'Argenteovariegata'	see *C. sativa* 'Albomarginata'
		- 'Aureomarginata'	see *C. sativa* 'Variegata'
- 'Worcester Gold' ♀H4	CBcs CCps CMac CSBt ECha EHeP ELan LRHS MAsh MGos MHer MMrt SPlb SRms	- 'Belle Epine' (F)	CAgr
		- 'Bournette' (F)	CAgr
		* - 'Doré de Lyon' (F)	CAgr
		- 'Marlhac' (F)	CAgr CHab NOra WMat
divaricata	see *Tripora divaricata*	- 'Marron Comballe' (F)	CAgr
§ *incana*	WJur	- 'Marron de Goujounac' (F)	CAgr
- 'Blue Cascade'	ELan EPfP SRms	- 'Marron de Lyon' (F)	CAgr CEnd CHab EPfP EPom
- 'Delft Blue'	EPfP	- 'Regal' (F)	EPom
§ - 'Jason'^{PBR}	CBrac CCps EGrI LRHS LSou SPoG WHil	§ - 'Variegata' (v)	CAco
- Sunshine Blue	see *C. incana* 'Jason'	*Castanospermum* (*Fabaceae*)	
mastacanthus	see *C. incana*	*australe*	LCro NHrt
Caryota (*Arecaceae*)		*Castilleja* (*Orobanchaceae*)	
mitis	LBom LCro LDro NHrt	*integra*	SPlb
- 'Himalaya'	NPlm	*latifolia*	WAbe
Casimiroa (*Rutaceae*)		*miniata*	SPlb WAbe WIce
edulis	WJur	*sessiliflora*	SPlb
Cassia (*Fabaceae*)		*Casuarina* (*Casuarinaceae*)	
corymbosa Lam.	see *Senna corymbosa*	*cunninghamiana*	CAco SPlb
fistula	MCtn	*equisetifolia*	WJur
marilandica	see *Senna marilandica*	*glauca*	SVen
nemophila	SPlb WJur		
Cassinia (*Asteraceae*)		*Catalpa* ✿ (*Bignoniaceae*)	
fulvida	SVen	*bignonioides* ♀H6	Widely available
'Ward Silver'	CWal	- B&SWJ 15090	WCru
		- 'Aurea' ♀H6	Widely available
Cassiope ✿ (*Ericaceae*)		- 'Nana'	EBar ELan ERom LRHS SAth WCha WLov
* 'Askival'	GArf		
'Askival Snow-wreath'	see *C.* Snow-wreath Group	- 'Purpurea'	see *C.* × *erubescens* 'Purpurea'
'Badenoch'	GArf	- 'Variegata' (v)	CLnd WLov
'Edinburgh'	EPot GArf	*bungei* misapplied	see *C. ovata*
lycopodioides	GArf	*bungei* ambig.	CAco EGren LMaj MBlu SArc WCha WJur
- 'Beatrice Lilley' ♀H6	GArf		
- 'Jim Lever'	WAbe	§ *bungei* C.A. Mey. Duclouxii Group ♀H6	CAco CBcs CEnd MBlu SHor WPGP
- 'Rokujō'	GArf WAbe		
mertensiana	GArf	- 'Purpurea'	SBig
- 'California Pink'	GKev	§ × *erubescens*	CAco CBcs CBrac CCVT CEnd
- subsp. *californica*	EPot GArf WAbe	'Purpurea' ♀H6	CMac CMCN EBee ELan EPfP EUrb LCro LMaj LRHS MBlu NLar NOra NPip SArc SEND SPoG WFar WMat
- var. *gracilis*	GArf		
'Muirhead'	GArf WAbe		
'Randle Cooke'	EPot	*fargesii* f. *duclouxii*	see *C. bungei* Duclouxii Group
selaginoides	GArf	§ *ovata*	CMCN EGrI SEND WJur
- LS&E 13284	EPot WAbe	*speciosa* ♀H6	CAco CMCN EUrb LMaj SVen
§ Snow-wreath Group	EPot	- 'Frederik'	NLar
'Suzuki'	GArf	- 'Pulverulenta' (v)	CAco MBlu
tetragona	GArf		

Catalpa × *Chilopsis* see × *Chitalpa*

Catananche (Asteraceae)
caerulea	CCBP CSpe CWal EBee ECha EGrI ELan EPfP ESgI GKev GMaP LCro LShi LSto MArl MBel MCtn MHol MMuc MNrw MPie MSCN NClf SMHy SMrm SPoG StAn WCAu WChS WTre
- 'Alba'	CSpe EBee ECha ELan EPfP ESgI GMaP LRHS LShi MArl MBel MCtn MNrw SMrm SPoG WCAu
- 'Amor Blue'	CFis EPfP LRHS SPoG
- 'Major' ♀H5	GQue LBom LCro SRms

Catharanthus (Apocynaceae)
roseus ♀H1c	CSpe

Cathaya (Pinaceae)
argyrophylla	CAco

Cathcartia (Papaveraceae)
§ chelidoniifolia	EWld GKev NBid

cauliflower see AGM Vegetables Section

Caulokaempferia (Zingiberaceae)
petelotii	EAri
- B&SWJ 11818	WCru
- HWJ 541	WCru
sikkimensis	EAri SBig

Caulophyllum (Berberidaceae)
thalictroides	EBee EMor EPPr GKev MBel WCru WPGP
- subsp. *robustum*	EBee WCru

Causonis (Vitaceae)
§ japonica B&SWJ 6636	WCru

Cautleya ✿ (Zingiberaceae)
cathcartii 'Tenzing's Gold'	EPPr ESwi LEdu WCru WPGP
§ gracilis	CBlu CDTJ EBee EWld GKev LAma WCru
- from Manipur, India	WPGP
- 'Crûg Gold'	WCru WPGP
- 'Crûg's Cangshan **new**	WCru
- 'Dzoukou'	LEdu
- 'Purple Emperor'	EAri LEdu
- 'Purple Splendour'	WPGP
- var. *robusta* 'Mighty Mewa'	WCru
lutea	see *C. gracilis*
spicata	CBlu CDTJ CSpe EAri ELon GKev LAma NGKo SBig
- 'Arun Flame'	CBct CDTJ EBee ESwi LEdu SChF WCru WPGP
- 'Bleddyn's Beacon'	EPPr ESwi WCru
- 'Crûg Canary'	CBct ELon ESwi LEdu NGKo WCru WPGP
- 'Crûg Compact'	WCru
* - var. *lutea*	CDTJ LEdu WPGP
- 'Robusta' ♀H3	CBcs EAri EBee ELan EPPr LEdu LRHS MNrw WCot WPGP

Cayratia (Vitaceae)
japonica	see *Causonis japonica*
thomsonii	see *Yua thomsonii*

Ceanothus ✿ (Rhamnaceae)
arboreus	SArc

- 'Trewithen Blue' ♀H4	CBcs CBrac CBTr CDoC CMac CSBt CTsd CWnw ELan EPfP LBom LCro LRHS LSRN MGos MHtn MPri MSwo NLit SEND SEWo SPoG WHtc WKif WMat
'A.T. Johnson'	EHeP SRms WHtc
'Autumnal Blue' ♀H4	CAco CBcs CBrac CDoC CEnd CMac CSBt EBee EGren EHeP ELan EPfP EUrb LCro LRHS MAsh MGos NLar SChF SSta WFar WHtc
'Blue Cushion'	EPfP MGos
'Blue Diamond'PBR	CWGN LSou
'Blue Jeans'	LRHS MMuc NLar
'Blue Mound' ♀H4	CAco CBcs CBrac CDoC CEnd CMac EGren EHeP ELan EPfP LBom LRHS LSou LSto MAsh MGos MSwo NCth NLar SNig SPoG WFar WLov
'Blue Sapphire'PBR	CWGN EGren EHeP EUrb LSou LSRN MAsh Midl SPoG
'Blue Sensation'	NLar
'Burkwoodii' ♀H4	CBcs CBrac CEnd CSBt EGren ELan EPfP LRHS MAsh
'Cascade' ♀H4	CBcs
'Cielo Blue'	WPGP
'Comtesse de Paris'	see *C.* × *delileanus* 'Comtesse de Paris'
'Concha' ♀H4	Widely available
'Cynthia Postan'	EPfP LRHS MHer NLar
'Dark Star' ♀H4	CBcs CSBt CWGN ELan EPfP EUrb LRHS LSRN MAsh MPri SEND SPoG SSta
'Delight'	CBcs LRHS
§ × *delileanus* 'Comtesse de Paris'	LRHS
- 'Gloire de Versailles' ♀H4	CBcs EPfP MSwo NLar SPoG WSpi
- 'Henri Desfossé'	EGren EPfP LSRN NLar SPoG WSpi
- 'Topaze' ♀H4	EPfP NLar WSpi
dentatus Torr. & A. Gray	SPlb
- var. *floribundus* (Hook.) Trel.	EHeP
'Diamond Heights'	see *C. griseus* var. *horizontalis* 'Diamond Heights'
'Edinburgh'	CCoa EHeP
EL DORADO ('Perado') (v)	CSBt ELan LRHS Midl SGol
gloriosus 'Emily Brown'	CBcs
§ *griseus* var. *horizontalis* 'Diamond Heights' (v)	LRHS MAsh MPri NLar
- - - 'Silver Surprise'PBR (v)	LBuc LCro LRHS NLar
- - - 'Yankee Point'	CBcs CBrac CDoC CMac EGren EPfP LBom LBuc LDro LRHS LSRN MGos MPri NLar SEND SEWo SPoG WHtc
impressus	EHeP EPfP MPri WFar
'Italian Skies'	CBrac CEnd CSBt EGren EHeP ELan ELon EPfP LBom LRHS LSRN MGos MPri NLar SEWo SPoG WFar WHtc
'Lemon and Lime'PBR	LBuc LCro LRHS
× *lobbianus*	EHeP
'Madagascar'	LRHS MPri SPoG
MARIE-ROSE ('Minmarose')	EPfP LCro
× *pallidus* 'Marie Simon'	CBcs EGren EGrI ELan EPfP GKev SPoG WKif WSpi
- 'Perle Rose' ♀H4	CBcs NLar WSpi
papillosus	IArd WPav
§ 'Pershore Zanzibar'PBR (v)	CMac EPfP LRHS MGos MPri SPoG SRms
'Pin Cushion'	CDoC EPfP MPri
'Point Millerton'	see *C. thyrsiflorus* 'Millerton Point'
'Puget Blue' ♀H4	CBcs CBrac CDoC CEnd CMac EGren ELan EPfP LBom LCro LRHS LSRN MAsh MGos MHed MPri

Celastrus 167

		MPro MSwo NLit SAth SPoG WFar WTHo	‡ - 'Aurea Pendula'	CAco
	purpureus 'Mill's Glory' **new**	LRHS	- 'Blue Globe'	CAco NLar
			- 'Blue Surprise'	CAco
	repens	see *C. thyrsiflorus* var. *repens*	- 'Blue Triumph'	WCha
	'Skylark' ♀H4	CBcs CBrac CDoC CEnd CMac EGren EHeP ELan EPfP LBom LCro LRHS LSRN MAsh MGos MPri NLar SEND SEWo SWor WFar WHtc WTHo	- 'Bush's Electra'	CAco MBlu
			- 'Cascade of Cream' **new**	MPri
			- 'Cream Puff'	CAco CCVT
			- 'Eisregen'	CAco
			- 'Feelin' Blue' ♀H6	CAco EGren ELan LMaj LRHS MAsh NLar NPlm WCha WMat
	'Snow Flurries'	see *C. thyrsiflorus* 'Snow Flurry'		
	'Snow Showers'	CBcs	- FEELIN' SUNNY ('Monkinn')	CAco NLar
	'Southmead' ♀H4	CSpe EHeP ELan EPfP LRHS MGos MPri MSwo	- 'Gold Cascade'	CAco
			- 'Golden Horizon'	CAco CCVT LCro LRHS MAsh SPoG WMat
	thyrsiflorus	LRHS SRms		
	- 'Cool Blue'	CWGN EGren ELan EPfP LBuc LRHS LSou	- 'Karl Fuchs'	CAco EPfP EUrb LRHS NLar WMat
			- 'Kelly's Gold'	EBee ELan
§	- 'Millerton Point'	ELan LRHS MPri NLar	- 'Klondyke'	CAco EPfP LRHS MAsh NPip WMat
	- 'Oregon Mist'	EBee WPGP		
§	- var. *repens* ♀H4	CBcs CBrac CDoC CEnd CMac CSBt EBee EGren EHeP ELan EPfP LBom LCro LRHS LSRN LSto MAsh MGos MSwo NCth NLar SPoG SRms SSta WFar WHtc WKif	- 'Lime Glow'	CAco NLar
			- 'Miles High'	CAco
			- 'Mr Blue'	CAco SPoG
			- Paktia Group	CAco
			- 'Pendula' ♀H5	CAco SArc
			- 'Polar Winter'	CAco
			- 'Robusta'	CAco WPGP
§	- 'Snow Flurry'	ELan MSwo	- 'Roman Candle'	CAco
	'Tuxedo' PBR	LCro NLar	- 'Shower of Silver' **new**	MPri
	× *veitchianus*	CSBt	- 'Silver Spring'	CAco
	'Victoria'	CEnd EBee EGren ELan LRHS MSwo NCth NLar	- 'White Imp'	CAco
			libani ♀H6	CAco CBrac CCVT CLnd CMac CMCN ELan EPfP EUrb IPap LCro LMaj MBlu MCtn MMuc MPri NLar NOra NPip SArc SEND SFol SGol SPlb WCha WHtc WMou
	'Zanzibar'	see *C.* 'Pershore Zanzibar'		

Cecropia (Urticaceae)

	sp.	EAri		
	polystachya **new**	EAri	- 'Blue Angel'	CAco NLar
			- 'Blue Fountain'	CAco LRHS NLar

Cedrela (Meliaceae)

	sinensis	see *Toona sinensis*	- 'Comte de Dijon'	CAco NLar
			- 'Dino'	CAco NLar

Cedronella (Lamiaceae)

			- 'Glauca'	CAco CCVT EHeP WCha
§	*canariensis*	CCBP CGHo ENfk EShb IDun MHer MNHC WJek	- 'Gold Tip'	CAco MAsh
			- 'Green Prince'	CAco NLar
	triphylla	see *C. canariensis*	- 'Hedgehog'	CAco NLar
			- 'Italie'	CAco NLar

Cedrus (Pinaceae)

			- 'May'	CAco
	atlantica	CAco ERom EUrb LMaj MMuc SEND WJur WMat	- 'Minitaur'	CAco
			- Nana Group	CAco
	- 'Aurea' ♀H6	CAco NLar	- 'Pendula'	CAco
	- 'Fastigiata'	CAco LMaj NLar	- 'Sargentii'	CAco ELan MBlu
	- Glauca Group	CCVT CMen ELan EPfP ERom IPap LRHS MBlu MGos MPri NLar NPip NPlm SPlb SPoG WMat	- subsp. *stenocoma* **new**	CAco
			- 'Taurus'	CAco
	- - 'Glauca' ♀H6	CAco CBcs CLnd LCro LMaj MAsh NOra WHtc		

Ceiba (Malvaceae)

	- - 'Glauca Pendula' ♀H6	CAco CCVT EPfP ERom EUrb LCro LRHS MAsh MBlu MGos NLar NOra NPip WCha WMat	*pentandra*	SPlb
			speciosa	SPlb

Celastrus (Celastraceae)

	- - 'Horstmann's Silberspitz'	CAco MAsh NLar	*angulatus*	WJur
	- 'Green Wave' **new**	NLar	*dependens* CWJ 12478	WCru
	- 'La Fontaine'	CAco EUrb	- NMWJ 14556	WCru
	- 'Pendula'	NOra	*flagellaris* B&SWJ 8572	WCru
	- 'Sahara Frost'	CAco	*gemmatus* **new**	WJur
	- 'Sapphire Nymph'	CAco NLar	*glaucophyllus*	WJur
	brevifolia	CAco LRHS	*hookeri* B&SWJ 11667	WCru
	- 'Epstein'	CAco	*kusanoi*	ESwi
	- 'Hillier Compact'	NLar	- CWJ 12445	WCru
	- 'Jade Medusa'	CAco NLar	*orbiculatus*	CBcs WJur
	- 'Kenwith'	CAco NLar	- 'Diana' (f)	CMac MBlu
	deodara ♀H6	Widely available	- 'Hercules' (m)	CMac MBlu
	- 'Aurea' ♀H6	CAco CCVT EPfP LMaj LRHS MGos NOra NPip WCha WMat	- Hermaphrodite Group ♀H6	MMuc SDix

- var. *papillosus* B&SWJ 591	WCru
- var. *punctatus* CWJ 12439	WCru
scandens	CMac SPlb
- (m)	GKev
stephanotiifolius B&SWJ 4727	WCru
stylosus WJC 13746	WCru

celeriac see AGM Vegetables Section

celery see AGM Vegetables Section

Celmisia (Asteraceae)

allanii	GArf GKev WAbe
alpina	WAbe
argentea	EPot GArf NHar WAbe
bellidioides	EPot GArf GKev WAbe
coriacea misapplied	see *C. semicordata*
discolor	WAbe
'Eggleston Silver'	NBir
'Garth Merelie' **new**	EPot
gracilenta	GKev NHar WAbe
hectorii	EPot GArf WAbe
ramulosa	GEdr WAbe
§ *semicordata*	GKev
sessiliflora	EPot GArf WAbe
spedenii	GKev

Celosia (Amaranthaceae)

argentea var. *cristata* (Cristata Group)	MCtn
'Act Vida' **new**	
- - 'Act Zara'^{PBR} **new**	MCtn
- - (Plumosa Group)	LSou
'Dragon's Breath' ♀^{H2}	
- - - Kimono Series	SPoG
- - (Spicata Group)	MCtn
'Flamingo Feather' ♀^{H2}	
DEEP PURPLE CARACAS	LCro

Celsia see *Verbascum*

× **Celsioverbascum** see *Verbascum*

Celtica see *Stipa*

Celtis (Cannabaceae)

australis	CBcs EBee IPap LEdu MBlu
biondii	NLar
occidentalis	IPap WJur
sinensis	WJur
tenuifolia	WJur
tetrandra	WPGP

Cenolophium (Apiaceae)

denudatum ♀^{H6}	Widely available

Centaurea ✿ (Asteraceae)

alba	NWbg
alpestris	GKev NLar
americana 'Aloha Blanca'	CSpe MCtn
- 'Aloha Rosa'	CSpe MCtn
'Amethyst on Ice'	CMac LBuc LRHS SRms WCav
atropurpurea	see *C. calocephala*
babylonica RCB/TQ 18	WCot
bella	EBee ECha EDAr NBro NSti SHar SMHy WMal
benoistii misapplied	see *C. calocephala*
benoistii ambig.	SPel
'Blue Carpet'	MCtn
§ *calocephala*	CSpe EBee EDAr EGrl ELan EWes GQue LBar MBNS MHol NLar NSti SPhx SPlb WCAu WCot
cana	see *C. triumfettii* subsp. *cana*
candidissima misapplied	see *C. cineraria*
'Caramia'	EBee ELan EPfP LBar MHol MNrw NBid NLar WCAu
carniolica SDR 5443	EBee
cheiranthifolia	EDAr EPPr GKev LRHS MHol MNrw NBid NBir NLar SHar
§ *cineraria*	WSpi
- subsp. *cineraria* ♀^{H3}	SEND WCot WMal
cyanus	CBWd CHab CSpe EHet GArf GJem LCro MCtn MHer MHoo MNHC SVic WKit
- 'Black Ball'	CSpe LCro LSto MCtn MHoo MNHC SPhx
- 'Blue Ball' (d)	CSpe LCro
- 'Blue Diadem'	MCtn
- (Classic Series) CLASSIC MAGIC (mixed)	LCro MCtn MHoo
- - CLASSIC ROMANTIC (mixed)	LSto MCtn MHoo
- 'Mauve Ball'	MCtn
- 'Pinkie' (d)	MNHC
- Polka Dot Series	GJem LCro MCtn MHoo
- 'Red Ball'	MCtn
- 'Snowman'	LRHS MCtn MNHC
- 'White Ball' (d)	LCro
cynaroides Link	see *Rhaponticum centaureoides*
dealbata	CBcs CWal EBee EPfP LRHS LShi MBel MCtn MHol MMuc NBro NLar SEND SRms StAn WCAu
- 'Steenbergii'	NBid NGdn NPer NSti SPoG WCAu WCot
declinata RCB UA 18	WCot
gigantea	WHer
glastifolia	EBee
gymnocarpa	see *C. cineraria*
jacea	GAbr GKev MCtn MMuc NLar SEND SPhx StAn WCot WPGP
'John Coutts'	EBee ECha EPfP GMaP LRHS MArl MMuc NBid NLar NSti SEND SHar SPoG SRms WCAu
'Jordy'	CBcs CCBP CSpe CWGN EBee EPfP ESgI GAbr GBin GQue LBar LCro LSto MBel MHol MMuc MNrw MPnt NLar NSti SBeP WBrk WCAu WCot WKif WMal WTre XFar
karabaghensis	EBee GKev
macrocephala	CMac CWal ECha ELan EPfP EPPr GAbr LEdu MBel MCtn MMrt NBid NBro NLar SDix SPoG SRms WCAu
marschalliana W&B BGB-1	WCot
mollis	NBid
montana	CAby CBWd CElw CWal EBee EGrl ELan EPfP GJos GMaP LRHS LShi LSto MBel MCtn MSwo NBro NGdn NLar SDix SPlb SPoG SRms WBrk WCAu WCav WFar WTre
- 'Alba'	CBcs CHab ECha ELan EPfP ERCP GMaP LCro MBel NBid NGdn NLar NSti SPlb SPoG SRms WCAu WFar
- 'Amethyst Dream'^{PBR}	ELan EPfP LBar LRHS MNrw MPnt MPri MPro NLar SPel SPoG WCAu
- 'Amethyst in Snow'	CAby CElw ELan EPfP LBar LRHS LShi MBNS MHol MPnt MPri MPro NBid NLar SPoG WPGP WTor
- 'Black Sprite'	CWGN EBee ELan EPfP GMaP LShi MBNS MPnt MWlw NLar NSti SPoG WFar

- 'Blewit'	NLar
§ - 'Carnea'	CElw ERCP GAbr GMaP LBar MBel MNrw NBir NLar NSti SBeP SHar WCAu WFar
- 'Crinita'	LShi WCAu
- 'Elworthy Glacier'	CElw WMal
- 'Gold Bullion'	CWGN NBid SMrm
- 'Grandiflora'	EBee LBar MBel
- 'Joyce'	CElw NBid NLar SHar WMal
- 'Lady Flora Hastings'	CElw CSpe MMuc NBid SEND
- lilac-flowered	NBid NLar
- 'Ochroleuca'	CElw NBid
- 'Parham'	GAbr GQue MArl MWlw NLar NSti SPlb WCAu
- 'Purple Heart'	CBcs CMHG CWGN EBee EPfP LCro LRHS LShi MArl MAsh MBel MBNS MNrw MPnt MWlw NLar SBeP SRms WCAu WCot WFar WHoo
- 'Purpurea'	CElw
- 'Rosea'	see *C. montana* 'Carnea'
- 'Tini's Pink'	LBar
- 'Violetta'	CElw LCro MBel MPnt NBir WCAu
nervosa	NBro
nigra	CBWd CGwi CHab CWal EBee ELan EPfP GJem GJos GQue LCro LRHS LShi MCtn MNHC NLar NMir SPhx SRms WCav WOrg
- subsp. *rivularis*	MMuc
- 'Waterfall White'	MHol WPGP
orientalis	CCBP CSpe LBar MBel MHol SPhx SRms
phrygia	GGro WCot
- subsp. *abbreviata*	GKev
- - B&SWJ 15321	WCru
pindicola	GKev
pulcherrima	EDAr MNrw
'Pulchra Major'	see *Rhaponticum centaureoides*
ragusina 'Snowy Owl'	LBar LSou
ruthenica	MCtn SPhx SPlb
salicifolia	NBir
scabiosa	CBWd CGwi CHab CWal GJem GQue LCro LRHS LShi MCtn MHer MNHC NBir NMir SPhx SRms WOrg WRBe WShi
- subsp. *adpressa*	GGro
'Silver Feather'	CAby CBcs LBar LRHS MBel MBNS MHol NLar NSti SPoG SRms WNPC
simplicicaulis	EBee NBir SHar SRms WHoo
stoebe	SPhx
thracica	WCot
triumfettii	MMuc
§ - subsp. *cana*	GMaP NBid
- subsp. *stricta*	GKev SHar

Centaurium (Gentianaceae)
erythraea	EDAr MCtn MHoo WOrg
scilloides	WAbe

Centella (Apiaceae)
§ *asiatica*	CGHo LCro LEdu SPre WJek

Centradenia (Melastomataceae)
inaequilateralis 'Cascade'	MBros

Centranthus (Caprifoliaceae)
§ *lecoqii*	ECha EPPr LCro SHor SPhx WCAu WMal
macrosiphon	CMac
§ *ruber*	Widely available

§ - 'Albus'	CBcs ECha ECul EGren ELan EPfP GMaP IDun LBar LCro LRHS LWaG MArl MAsh MBel MHer MNrw NBir NDov NPer SDix SEND SOrn SPel SPoG SRms WCAu WCot WFar
- 'Atrococcineus'	ECha LBar MAsh MMuc
- var. *coccineus*	CBcs EBee EHeP ELan EPfP GAbr GBin GKin GMaP LBuc LRHS LWaG MArl MBel MSwo SDix SEND SOrn WCot WFar
- mauve-flowered misapplied	see *C. lecoqii*
- 'Roseus'	IDun WFar
- 'Snowcloud'	EBee ENfk GJem MCtn SRms WTre

Centratherum (Asteraceae)
punctatum	CSpe

Cephalanthus (Rubiaceae)
occidentalis	LRHS MBlu MMuc NQui SPoG
- MAGICAL MOONLIGHT ('Kolmoon')	CDoC LCro NPlm

Cephalaria (Caprifoliaceae)
§ *alpina*	ELan EPPr GJos MNrw SDix SEND SHar SRms WBrk WFar
ambrosioides	WPGP
balansae	CDor CSpe LRHS SHor SMHy SPhx SRms WGoo
caucasica	see *C. gigantea*
§ *gigantea*	Widely available
leucantha	MMuc NLar SEND WBrk
radiata	SPhx
tatarica hort.	see *C. gigantea*
tchihatchewii	WCot
transsylvanica	SPhx WSpi
- W&B BGJ-1	CSpe WCot

Cephalophilon see Persicaria

Cephalotaxus (Taxaceae)
fortunei	CAco WCru WJur
- var. *fortunei*	CAco
harringtonia	CAco CMCN WJur WPGP WSpi
- var. *drupacea*	see *C. harringtonia* var. *harringtonia*
- 'Duke Gardens'	LRHS
- 'Fastigiata'	CAco CDoC CWnw ERom IArd LCro LRHS MAsh MGos MPri SPoG
- 'Gimborn's Pillow'	CAco
§ - var. *harringtonia*	CAco CAgr
- 'Korean Gold'	CAco MGos
sinensis	CAco MCtn WJur
wilsoniana	WJur

Cerastium (Caryophyllaceae)
alpinum	SRms
- var. *lanatum*	EWes
candidissimum	EWes
fontanum	CHab
tomentosum	CWCL EBee EGren ELan EPfP LCro LRHS LSto MHol MMuc NBir SEND SLee SPlb SPoG StAn WFar
- var. *columnae*	ECha EWes GMaP WIce
- 'Silberteppich'	StAn

Ceratonia (Fabaceae)
siliqua	SPlb WJur

Ceratophyllum (Ceratophyllaceae)
demersum	CBen CHab CLil CPud CWat ELin EPfk EWat LCro MWts WMAq

Ceratopteris (Pteridaceae)
thalictroides — ELin

Ceratostigma ✿ (Plumbaginaceae)
abyssinicum — EGrI
asperrimum B&SWJ 7260 — WCru
'Autumn Blue' — LRHS
* *capensis* — CMac
griffithii — CBcs CBrac CDoC CEnd CMac CSde EBee EGren EGrI EHeP ELan EPfP EUrb LRHS LSto MAsh MSwo NLar SEND SPoG SRms SSta SVen WFar
§ *plumbaginoides* ♀H5 — Widely available
'Summer Skies' — CBcs LBom
willmottianum ♀H4 — Widely available
- BWJ 8140 — WCru
- DESERT SKIES ('Palmgold') — CMac EPfP NLar
- FOREST BLUE ('Lice') ♀H4 — CBcs CBrac CDoC CEnd CMac CSBt EGren ELan EPfP GKev LBom LCro LRHS LSRN MAsh MGos MPri MSwo SAth SNig SPoG SSta WFar WLov
- SAPPHIRE RING ('Lissbrill') PBR — CBcs CDoC EBee ELan EPfP LRHS LSRN MAsh MGos SPoG WFar WHil

Ceratotheca (Pedaliaceae)
triloba — CSpe MCtn SBeP

Cercidiphyllum ✿ (Cercidiphyllaceae)
japonicum ♀H5 — Widely available
- 'Boyd's Dwarf' — CJun MBlu NLar SPoG
- 'Chameleon' (v) — MBlu
- GLOWBALL ('Jww4') PBR — CAco LRHS MBlu NPip
- 'Herkenrode Dwarf' — MBlu
- 'Heronswood Globe' ♀H5 — CAco CJun CMCN MBlu NLar SSta
- 'Kreukenberg Dwarf' — CJun
- 'Morioka Weeping' — CJun NLar SChF SSta WPGP
- 'Peach' — NLar
§ - f. *pendulum* ♀H5 — CAco CEnd CJun CMHG ELan EPfP IArd MAsh MBlu MGos NLar NPip SHor SPoG SSta WMat
- - 'Amazing Grace' — MBlu SSta
- 'Plum Custard' — WPGP
- RA ('Jww3') PBR — CAco MBlu
- 'Raspberry' — CJun MBlu
- RED FOX — see *C. japonicum* 'Rotfuchs'
§ - 'Rotfuchs' — CAco CBcs CEnd CJun CLnd CMac CMCN EBee EGrI ELan EPfP LRHS MAsh MBlu NCth NLar NPip SChF SGol SPoG SSta WMat
- 'Ruby' — CJun MBlu
- 'Strawberry' — CJun MBlu SSta
- 'Tidal Wave' — CJun MBlu SSta
- 'Titania' — SSta
magnificum — CEnd MBlu NLar
- f. *pendulum* — see *C. japonicum* f. *pendulum*

Cercis ✿ (Fabaceae)
canadensis — CAco CAgr CMac CMCN CTsd CWGN EGren EGrI EPfP EUrb LMaj MGos MMuc NLar SFol WJur WLov
- 'Ace of Hearts' PBR — EUrb NLar
- f. *alba* — LSRN
- - 'Royal White' — CAco CWnw MBlu
- 'Alley Cat' (v) — CAco EBee EUrb LCro NPip WMat
- 'Appalachian Red' — LMaj LRHS MBlu
- CAROLINA SWEETHEART ('Nccc1') — EBee ELan LRHS NPip WMat
- 'Cascading Hearts' — WFar
- ETERNAL FLAME ('Nc2016-2') — CBcs CMac EBee ELan EPfP LCro LRHS LSRN SEWo SMad SPoG SWCr
- 'Flame' — LRHS SSta
- 'Forest Pansy' ♀H5 — Widely available
- GOLDEN FALLS ('Nc2015-12') — CBTr CDoC EBee ELan LCro LRHS MPri NPip WMat WNwn
- 'Hearts of Gold' PBR — CAco CBTr CDoC CLnd CWGN CWnw EBee ELan LCro LRHS LSRN MGos NOra NPip SPoG WMat
- LAVENDER TWIST ('Covey') — CAco CBTr CMac EBee ELan LBom LCro LMaj LRHS LSRN MBlu MGos MPri NLar NOra NPip SPoG WMat
- LITTLE WOODY ('Litwo') PBR — NLar
- 'Melon Beauty' — MBlu
- 'Merlot' — CAco CBTr EBee EGrI EUrb IArd LRHS MBlu MGos MPri NLar NPip SEWo SMad SWCr WFar WMat
- var. *mexicana* NJM 9.024 — WPGP
- 'Pink Pom Poms' — CAco CBTr EBee ELan MAsh NLar NPip WMat
- RED FORCE ('Minrouge3') PBR — CDoC CWGN CWnw ELan LMaj LRHS LSRN NLar WCot
- 'Ruby Falls' PBR ♀H5 — CAco CBcs CBTr CLnd CMac CWnw EBee ELan EPfP IArd LBom LCro LMaj LRHS MAsh MBlu MGos MPri NOra NPip SMad SPoG SWCr WCha WHtc WMat
- 'Rubye Atkinson' — NLar
- var. *texensis* 'Oklahoma' — CAco CBcs CBTr CMHG EBee ELan EPfP LCro NPip WMat WPGP
- - 'Texas White' — CAco CBcs CMac EBee ELan EPfP LCro LMaj LRHS MBlu NPip WMat
- - 'Traveller' — CAco
- THE RISING SUN ('Jn2') — CAco CBTr CDoC CWGN EBee ELan EUrb IArd LMaj LRHS MBlu MGos NPip SHor WFar
- 'Vanilla Twist' PBR — CAco CMac EBee ELan LRHS NLar NPip SPoG WFar WMat
chinensis — CAco CTsd EGrI NLar WJur WMou
- 'Avondale' ♀H5 — CAco CBcs CBTr CCVT CJun CMac CMCN EBar EGren EGrI ELan EPfP EUrb EWes IArd LCro LMaj LRHS LSRN MAsh MBlu MGos MPri NLar NPip SPoG SWCr WCot WMat
- 'Diane' — EBee MAsh MPri
- 'Don Egolf' ♀H5 — CJun MBlu NLar
- 'Shirobana' — CAco CJun NPip WMat
gigantea — CAco
glabra — CBcs
griffithii — WJur WPGP
orbiculata — WPGP
racemosa — WPGP
siliquastrum — Widely available
- f. *albida* — CLnd WJur
- 'Bodnant' ♀H5 — CBcs CMac ELan EPfP IArd LCro LRHS LSRN LSto MAsh MBlu MGos MPri NLar NPip SSta WMat

Cereus (Cactaceae)
azureus — NHrt
repandus — CBlu LWaG NPlm SBig
- 'Monstruosus' — NPlm
- 'Spiralis' — CDoC LBom LCro LWaG NHrt NPlm SBig

Cerinthe (Boraginaceae)
major 'Purpurascens' — CSpe CWCL ELan EPfP LCro LSto LWaG MCtn MNHC MPro NClf SHor SPhx SPoG WCav WFar WKif
- 'Rhubarb and Custard' — MPro

Chaenostoma 171

Ceropegia (Apocynaceae)
ampliata	EShb
dichotoma	NTro
linearis	EShb NTro
§ - subsp. woodii ♀H1c	CDoC ELan EShb LBom LCro LWaG MPri NHrt NTro WFar
§ - - 'Lady Heart' (v)	LInT LWaG NHrt NTro
- - 'Variegata'	see C. linearis subsp. woodii 'Lady Heart'
sandersonii ♀H1c	CDoC NTro SPre
woodii	see C. linearis subsp. woodii

Ceroxylon (Arecaceae)
parvifrons	NPlm

Cestrum (Solanaceae)
aurantiacum	SEND
buxifolium	SBig
- B&SWJ 14385	WCru
× cultum 'Cretan Pink'	CCoa WJun
- 'Cretan Purple'	CBcs CHll EBee ELan EPfP EShb EUrb LRHS SEND WJun WKif
§ elegans	CCoa CSde CTsd EArl ELon EPfP EWld MSCN SEle SEND SIvy
fasciculatum	SDix
'Newellii' ♀H3	CBcs EGrI ELan ELon EPfP SEle SEND SIvy SPlb SVen WJun
nocturnum ♀H2	CBcs CHll EArl EShb SPre WCFE WJun
parqui ♀H3	CBcs CCoa CHll CMCN EBee EGrI ELan EPfP LRHS SBeP SDix SEND SIvy SMad SPlb WKif
purpureum (Lindl.) Standl.	see C. elegans
roseum B&SWJ 10255 from Oaxaca State, Mexico	WCru
- 'Crûg's Crimson' **new**	WCru
- 'Ilnacullin'	CSde EBee

Ceterach see Asplenium
officinarum	see Asplenium ceterach

Chaenomeles ✿ (Rosaceae)
cathayensis	CAgr LEdu LSto MMuc WCru WFar WJur WKor WPGP
§ japonica	CAco EHeP LSto MMuc SEND SPre WJur WKor
- 'Chojubai'	CMen
- 'Cido'	CAco CAgr NLar WSpi
- 'Orange Beauty'	LRHS
- 'Rising Sun'	NLar
- 'Sargentii'	CAco EGren MBlu NLar SGol
'Kurokoji' **new**	WSpi
MADAME BUTTERFLY ('Whitice')	EBee ELan EPfP LRHS LSRN MAsh SGol SPoG SRms
maulei	see C. japonica
'Orange Star'	CEnd SGol
sinensis	see Pseudocydonia sinensis
speciosa	LRHS WJur
- 'Apple Blossom'	see C. speciosa 'Moerloosei'
- 'Contorta'	WFar
I - 'Contorta Rosea'	WFar
- 'Falconnet Charlet' (d)	LRHS SGol SRms
- 'Flocon Rose'	SGol
- 'Geisha Girl' (d) ♀H6	CBcs CDoC CEnd CMac CSBt CWnw EBee EGrI ELan EPfP LCro LRHS LSRN MAsh MGos MMrt MPri SGol SPoG SRkn SRms WFar WLov
- 'Grayshott Salmon'	WSpi
- HOT FIRE ('Minvesu')	CDoC WCot WSpi
- 'Kinshiden'	CWnw EBee ELan EPfP LRHS LSRN MPri NCth NLar SGol WSpi
- MANGO STORM ('Mincha01' PBR)	CAco CDoC CWnw EBee ELan EPfP LBom LCro LRHS MAsh MBNS NLar SGol
§ - 'Moerloosei' ♀H6	CBcs CBrac CDoC CMac CSBt CSpe ELan ELon EPfP IArd LCro LEdu LRHS LSRN MAsh MBlu MMuc MPri NLar SEND SGol SPoG SRkn SRms WCot WFar WHtc WLov WSpi
- 'Nivalis'	CAco CAgr CBcs CBrac CDoC CMac CTsd EBee EGren EHeP ELan EPfP LCro LRHS LSto MAsh MGos MMuc MPri SGol SPoG SRms WFar WHtc WSpi
- 'Orange Storm' PBR	CAco EBee ELan EPfP LBom LCro LRHS LSRN SGol
- 'Pink Storm' PBR	CAco EBee ELan EPfP LBom LCro LRHS MAsh MBNS SGol
- RED KIMONO ('Ainoomoi' PBR)	CAco NLar SGol
- 'Rubra Grandiflora'	CAco WSpi
- 'Scarlet Storm' PBR	CAco EBee EPfP LBom LCro LRHS MAsh MBNS SGol
- 'Simonii' (d)	WSpi
- 'Snow'	SRms
- 'Umbilicata'	MBlu SRms
- 'Yukigotan' (d)	CDoC EBee ELan MBNS NLar SGol WFar WLov WSpi
× superba 'Cameo' (d)	CAco CEnd EGrI IArd NLar SGol SRms WCot WFar WHtc WSpi
- 'Clementine'	CAco
- 'Crimson and Gold' ♀H6	Widely available
- 'Elly Mossel'	CAco CMac EHeP SGol SRms
- 'Etna'	CAco WFar
- 'Fascination'	EGren WFar
- 'Fire Dance'	CAco SGol WCot WFar WLov WSpi
- 'Fusion'	CAgr
- 'Hollandia'	CAco SRms
- 'Jet Trail'	CAco CBcs CMac CSBt EGren EHeP ELan EPfP LBom LRHS LSto MAsh MGos NLar SGol SRms WFar
- 'Knap Hill Scarlet'	EBee ELan EPfP LRHS MGos MMuc MPri SPoG SRms WCot
- 'Lemon and Lime'	CBcs CMac CSBt LRHS LSto MGos MPri NLar SRms WFar WLov WSpi
- 'Nicoline' ♀H6	CAco CBcs EGren EGrI ELan EPfP WFar
- 'Orange Trail'	CAco EBee LRHS LSto WLov
- 'Pink Lady' ♀H6	CAco CBcs CBrac CMac EGren EGrI EHeP ELan EPfP IArd LCro LRHS LSRN LSto MBlu MGos MMuc MSCN MSwo NLar SGol SPoG SRms WFar WSpi
- PINK TRAIL ('Interpitra')	CAco NLar SRms
- 'Red Joy'	LRHS NLar SRms
- 'Salmon Horizon'	CAco ELan SGol
- 'Texas Scarlet'	CAco SRms
- 'Tortuosa'	LRHS MBNS NLar WCot
- 'Toyo-nishiki'	MBlu WFar

Chaenorhinum (Plantaginaceae)
§ origanifolium	SPlb SRot StAn
- 'Blue Dream'	CSpe ELan EPfP LRHS LShi MAsh SPoG WFar WIce
villosum 'Little Dragons'	SPhx

Chaenostoma (Scrophulariaceae)
cordatum (Abunda Series) ABUNDA COLOSSAL BLUE ('Balabolue')	LSou

Chaenostoma

- - Abunda Colossal White ('Balabowite'PBR)	LSou MPri
- Scopia Golden Leaves White ('Dancop15') (Scopia Series)	MBros
§ - 'Snowflake'	LCro MBros MSwo NPer SPoG
- Snowtopia ('Pas430726')	MCtn

Chaerophyllum (Apiaceae)

aromaticum	LEdu
aureum	NAts
azoricum	CSpe ECha ELan LEdu LShi MNrw SDix WCot WPGP
hirsutum 'Roseum'	Widely available
temulum	CGwi

Chaetogastra (Melastomataceae)

§ grossa B&SWJ 10758	WCru
§ paratropica	CBcs CoPl CRHN SIvy WCot

Chamaecrista (Fabaceae)

fasciculata	CSpe SPhx

Chamaecyparis ✤ (Cupressaceae)

funebris	see Cupressus pendula Thunb.
lawsoniana	CAco CBrac IPap
- 'Allumii Aurea'	see C. lawsoniana 'Alumigold'
§ - 'Alumigold'	CAco
- 'Alumii'	CAco CBrac
- 'Aurea'	CBrac
§ - 'Aurea Densa' ♀H6	CSBt LRHS MGos MPri
- 'Aurea Nana'	see C. lawsoniana 'Aurea Densa', 'Minima Aurea'
- 'Bleu Nantais' ♀H6	MGos SPoG
- 'Blue Surprise'	MPri
- 'Brégeon'	CAco
- 'Broomhill Gold' ♀H6	CSBt MGos MPri SPoG
- 'Burford Gold'	MPri
§ - 'Chilworth Silver' ♀H6	CBrac MAsh
- 'Columnaris'	CAco CBrac CMac EBar EPfP MGos SPoG WCha WFar
- 'Columnaris Aurea'	see C. lawsoniana 'Golden Spire'
- 'Cream Glow'	LRHS MAsh
- 'Dik's Weeping' ♀H6	CAco NLar
- 'Drooping Solo'	CAco NLar SMad
- 'Dutch Gold'	LRHS MPri
- 'Elegantissima' ambig.	CMac
- 'Ellwoodii' ♀H6	CAco CBrac CMac CSBt EGren ELan LRHS LSto MAsh MGos NLar WFar
- 'Ellwood's Empire'	CAco
- 'Ellwood's Gold' ♀H6	CAco CBcs CBrac CMac CSBt ELan EPfP LRHS MAsh MGos SPlb SPoG WFar
- 'Ellwood's Gold Pillar' ♀H6	LRHS MAsh NLar WHtc
- Ellwood's Pillar ('Flolar') ♀H6	CMac LCro LRHS MAsh MGos SPoG WHtc
- 'Ellwood's Pygmy'	CMac
- 'Ellwood's Variegata'	see C. lawsoniana 'Ellwood's White'
§ - 'Ellwood's White' (v)	CMac SPoG
- 'Emerald Spire'	LRHS MPri
- 'Erecta Aurea'	CAco LRHS
- 'Erecta Viridis'	CAco CBrac CMac
- 'Filip's Golden Sprinklers' (v) **new**	NLar SMad
- 'Filip's Golden Tears'	CAco ELan NLar
- 'Filip's Twinkle Tails' sport **new**	NLar
- 'Fleckellwood'	LRHS
- 'Fletcheri' ♀H6	CBrac CMac
- 'Forsteckensis'	CBrac NLar
- 'Gimbornii' ♀H6	MPri
- 'Glauca Pendula'	CAco
- 'Globosa'	CAco EGren
- 'Gnome'	CMac MPri SPoG
§ - 'Golden Pot'	CSBt LSto
§ - 'Golden Spire'	CAco
- 'Golden Wonder' ♀H6	MPri
- 'Grayswood Feather' ♀H6	LRHS MPri
- 'Green Globe' ♀H6	MAsh NLar
§ - 'Green Pillar'	EPfP LRHS
- 'Green Spire'	see C. lawsoniana 'Green Pillar'
- 'Ilona'	CAco
- 'Imbricata Pendula' ♀H6	CAco EPfP EUrb MBlu NLar WPGP
- 'Ivonne' ♀H6	CAco EBar EGren LCro LRHS MAsh MGos MPri NLar SPoG WCha
- 'Jackman's Variety'	see C. lawsoniana 'Green Pillar'
- 'Jeanette'	LRHS
- 'Karaca'	CAco NLar
- 'Kilmacurragh' ♀H6	CAco
- 'Knowefieldensis'	CMac
- 'Lane' den Ouden	CBrac LRHS MPri
- 'Lanei Aurea' ♀H6	ELan
- 'Little Spire' ♀H6	CAco EUrb
§ - 'Lutea Nana'	CBrac CMac
- 'Lycopodioides'	LRHS WCha
- 'Minima Argentea'	see C. lawsoniana 'Nana Argentea'
§ - 'Minima Aurea' ♀H6	CAco CBrac CMac CSBt LCro LRHS MAsh MGos SPoG
- 'Minima Glauca' ♀H6	CAco CBrac CMac EPfP LCro LRHS WFar WHtc
- 'Moonsprite' ♀H6	LRHS MAsh SPoG
- 'Nana'	CBrac
§ - 'Nana Argentea'	SPoG
- 'Nana Lutea'	see C. lawsoniana 'Lutea Nana'
- 'Nicole'	LRHS MAsh MPri
- 'Nyewoods'	see C. lawsoniana 'Chilworth Silver'
- Pearly Swirls ('Spicwirl') (v)	LRHS MPri SPoG
§ - 'Pelt's Blue'	CAco CBrac CSBt NLar
- 'Pembury Blue' ♀H6	CBrac CCVT EPfP LCro LRHS LSto MGos MPri SPoG
- Pot of Gold	see C. lawsoniana 'Golden Pot'
- 'Pottenii'	CBrac LRHS MPri NLar
- 'Pygmaea Argentea' (v) ♀H6	CBrac CMac ELan MGos SPoG
- 'Pygmy'	CMen
- 'Robusta Glauca'	CAco
- 'Romana'	NLar
- 'Silver Threads' (v)	MPri SPoG
- 'Snow White' (v) ♀H6	CAco EPfP LCro LRHS MAsh MGos MPri SPoG WFar WHtc
- 'Somerset'	CMac
- 'Stardust' ♀H6	CAco CBcs CSBt EBar EGren ELan MGos MPri NLar
- 'Summer Snow' (v) ♀H6	LRHS
- 'Sunkist'	CAco EGren LRHS
- 'Susan'	NLar
- 'Tharandtensis Caesia'	CAco NLar
- 'Twisted Ball'	NLar
- 'Uschi's Curtain'	CAco
- 'Van Pelt'	see C. lawsoniana 'Pelt's Blue'
- 'Waterfall'	CAco
- 'White Spot' (v)	CAco LRHS
- 'Wisselii' ♀H6	CAco CWnw ELan MGos MPri
- 'Wissel's Saguaro' ♀H6	CAco ELan EUrb LRHS MPri NLar
× leylandii	see × Cuprocyparis leylandii
nootkatensis	see Xanthocyparis nootkatensis
obtusa	SArc
- 'Aurea'	CAco
- 'Aurora' ♀H7	CAco ELan LRHS SPoG

Chamaemelum 173

- 'Bambi'	WAbe	- 'Baby Blue'	CWnw EGren ELan EPfP LRHS SPoG WCha WFar
- 'Birgit'	CAco	- 'Blue Moon' PBR	EPfP LCro LRHS MGos WSpi
- 'Blue Feathers'	see *C. obtusa* 'Ivan's Column'	- 'Blue Planet' PBR	EPfP LRHS WFar
- 'Brigitt'	CAco SPoG	- 'Boulevard' ♀H7	CBcs CBrac CMac CSBt EGren ELan EPfP LRHS MAsh MGos MMuc MPri WFar
- 'Caespitosa'	WAbe		
- 'Chabo-yadori'	CAco		
- 'Chirimen'	CAco CMen		
- 'Clarke's Seedling'	NLar	- 'Curly Top' ♀H7	LRHS MAsh SPoG
- 'Confucius'	MPri	- 'Filifera'	CMac MMuc
§ - 'Coralliformis'	CMac	- 'Filifera Aurea' ♀H7	CMac CWnw EGren ELan EPfP LRHS MAsh MGos MPri WFar
§ - 'Crippsii' ♀H7	CMac	- 'Filifera Nana'	EGren EPfP LCro LRHS MAsh SPoG WFar
- 'Crippsii Aurea'	see *C. obtusa* 'Crippsii'		
- 'Dainty Doll'	NLar		
- 'Densa'	see *C. obtusa* 'Nana Densa'	- 'Filifera Nana Aurea'	see *C. pisifera* 'Golden Mop'
- 'Draht'	CAco EGren	- 'Filifera Sungold'	see *C. pisifera* 'Sungold'
- 'Elf'	GKev	- 'Gold Dust'	see *C. pisifera* 'Plumosa Aurea'
- 'Fernspray Gold' ♀H7	CAco CCVT LRHS MGos SPoG	- 'Gold Spangle'	CBrac
- 'Filiformis Aurea'	CAco	§ - 'Golden Mop'	CBrac
- 'Gitte'	CAco SPoG	- 'Hime-sawara'	CMen
- 'Gnome'	CMen	- 'Nana'	CBrac CMen
- 'Gold Nugget'	NLar	I - 'Nana Compacta'	CMac
- 'Golden Sprite'	WAbe	- 'Nana Variegata' (v)	CMac
- 'Gracilis'	CAco	§ - 'Plumosa Aurea'	MAsh
- 'Gracilis Aurea'	CMen	- 'Plumosa Aurea Nana'	MAsh
- 'Hannah'	NLar	I - 'Plumosa Aurea Nana Compacta'	CMac
- 'Intermedia'	WAbe		
§ - 'Ivan's Column'	LRHS	- 'Plumosa Aurescens'	CMac
- 'Juniperoides Compacta'	WAbe	- 'Plumosa Compressa' ♀H7	CBrac
- 'Kamarachiba' ♀H7	CAco EGren EPfP LSRN NLar SPoG	- 'Plumosa Densa'	see *C. pisifera* 'Plumosa Compressa'
- 'Kerdalo'	CAco	- 'Pompom'	MAsh
- 'Kojolcohiba'	NLar	I - 'Squarrosa Lombarts'	CMac
- 'Konijn'	NLar	- 'Squarrosa Sulphurea'	CAco MPri
- 'Kosteri' ♀H7	CAco CMac ELan EUrb LRHS NLar WFar	§ - 'Sungold' ♀H7	CWnw EGren ELan GKev LCro LRHS MAsh MGos SMad SPoG WFar
- 'Leprechaun'	WAbe		
- 'Little John'	NLar	- 'True Blue'	EPfP
- 'Lucas' PBR	CAco LRHS	- 'White Beauty' (v)	LRHS
- 'Lutea Nova'	CAco	*thyoides* 'Andelyensis'	CMac
- 'Lycopodioides'	CAco CWnw LRHS	- 'Conica'	MAsh
- 'Lycopodioides Aurea'	CAco NLar	- 'Ericoides'	SPlb
- 'Marian'	NLar	- 'Red Star'	see *C. thyoides* 'Rubicon'
- 'Maureen'	CAco	§ - 'Rubicon'	CMac EPfP LRHS MAsh MPri SPoG
- 'Melody'	CAco NLar	- 'Top Point'	GKev LRHS MAsh MPri SPoG
- 'Meroke'	CAco		
- 'Nana' ♀H7	CMac CMen		
- 'Nana Aurea' ♀H7	CAco CBrac CMac EGren EPfP MPri		

Chamaecytisus see *Cytisus*

Chamaedaphne (Ericaceae)

§ - 'Nana Densa'	CMac
- 'Nana Gracilis' ♀H7	CAco CBrac CCVT CMen CWnw EGren ELan EPfP EUrb LCro LRHS MAsh MGos MPri NLar SMad SPoG WFar
calyculata 'Nana'	SSta

Chamaedorea (Arecaceae)

elegans ♀H1a	EGren LBom LCro LWaG NHrt NTrD WFar
I - 'Nana Gracilis Aurea'	CMen
I - 'Nana Lutea' ♀H7	CAco ELan MGos MPri
- 'Nana Pyramidalis'	NLar
erumpens	see *C. seifrizii*
- 'Pagoda'	CAco NLar
metallica misapplied	see *C. microspadix*
- 'Petite Minorette'	CAco
metallica O.F. Cook ex H.E. Moore ♀H1a	NHrt
- 'Pygmaea'	CBrac LRHS
- 'Rezek'	see *C. obtusa* 'Rezek Dwarf'
§ *microspadix* ♀H3	NPlm SChr
§ - 'Rezek Dwarf'	CMen
plumosa	NPlm
- 'Saffron Spray'	CAco NLar
radicalis	NPlm SArc
- 'Sparkles'	NLar
§ *seifrizii*	NHrt NPlm
- 'Spirited'	CAco
- 'Stoneham'	CMen

× *Chamaelobivia* see *Echinopsis*

- 'Teddy Bear'	CAco CCVT WCha
- 'Tempelhof'	CAco LRHS SPoG

Chamaemelum (Asteraceae)

- 'Tetragona Aurea'	CAco CMac NLar
- 'Timothy'	CMac
§ *nobile*	CAgr CCBP CGHo CHby EGren EHet ENfk EPfP LCro LRHS MCtn MEar MHer MHoo MMuc MNHC MPri NGdn SEND SPlb SRms SVic WKit WSpi WTre
- 'Torulosa'	see *C. obtusa* 'Coralliformis'
- 'Tsatsumi Gold' ♀H7	CAco ELan EPfP LRHS SPoG WFar
- 'Villa Marie'	LRHS NLar
- 'Wiels Baby'	NLar
pisifera	CAco
- dwarf	SMor SVic
- - double-flowered (d)	LEdu

- 'Flore Pleno' (d) — ECha EHet ENfk EPfP GElm MHer MHoo MMuc MNHC NBro NGdn SRms WChS WFar WJek WKit WTre
- 'Treneague' — CGHo ECha EHet ELan ENfk EPfP EWhm GAbr GQue IDun MHer MHoo MNHC SMor SPlb SRms WFar WJek WKit WTre

Chamaenerion (Onagraceae)
§ **angustifolium** — LBar
§ - 'Album' — CAby CMHG CSpe CTtf EBee ECha GMaP GQue LBar LCro LEdu LRHS LShi LSto MBel MMuc MNrw NBid NSti SMHy SPoG WCAu WCot WFar WPGP
- 'Isobel' — CSpe CTtf WCot
- 'Stahl Rose' — EWes LBar LEdu LRHS MBel NLar NSti SMHy WCot WHrl
§ **dodonaei** — EWes LBar MCtn SMHy WCot

Chamaerops ✿ (Arecaceae)
excelsa misapplied — see *Trachycarpus fortunei*
excelsa Thunb. — see *Rhapis excelsa*
humilis ♀H4 — CAbb CAco CBcs CBrP CDoC EGren EPfP EUrb LRHS LWaG MGos MPri NHrt SArc SAth SBig SChr SEND SFol SIvy SPlb SPoG WCha WJur
§ - var. **argentea** — CBlu CDTJ EOli MGos NPlm SBig SEND SPlb WCot WPGP
- var. **cerifera** — see *C. humilis* var. *argentea*
I - 'Compacta' — EOli
- var. **humilis** — EOli ERom NPlm
- 'Vulcano' — CDTJ EGren EOli EUrb LWaG NPlm SArc SBig WPGP

Chamaespartium see *Genista*

Chamaesphacos (Lamiaceae)
ilicifolius misapplied — see *Siphocranion macranthum*

Chambeyronia (Arecaceae)
macrocarpa — NPlm

Chamelaucium (Myrtaceae)
uncinatum — SPre

Chamerion see *Chamaenerion*

chard see AGM Vegetables Section

Charybdis (Asparagaceae)
§ **maritima** — GKev LAma MHol SPeP WCot XFar

Chasmanthe (Iridaceae)
aethiopica — SChr
bicolor — CTca CWal EWld
floribunda — XFar
- var. **duckittii** — GKev LAma XFar
- 'Saturnus' — EGrl GKev LAma XFar

Chasmanthium (Poaceae)
§ **latifolium** — CAby CKno CSde CSpe CWal EBee ECha ELan EMor LSto MBel MCtn MPnt SDix SHor SMHy SPel SPoG StAn WCot WTre
- 'Little Tickler' — EMor SPel
- 'River Mist' (v) — EBee EMor SPoG

Cheilanthes (Pteridaceae)
distans — WCot

eckloniana — WCot
grisea — WCot
lanosa — CCht CDoC CMiW CSde CTsd EBee EGren EUrb GKev LBuc LRHS NAlc SAth SPlb SPoG SRot WFar
lindheimeri — WCot
myriophylla — WCot
tomentosa — CAby LEdu LSRN MAsh
wootonii — WCot

Cheiranthus see *Erysimum*

Cheirolophus (Asteraceae)
benoistii misapplied — see *Centaurea calocephala*
sempervirens — WCru
B&SWJ 15321

Chelidonium (Papaveraceae)
hylomeconoides — GEdr
japonicum — see *Hylomecon japonica*
majus — CGwi LRHS MCtn NBir NMir
- 'Flore Pleno' (d) — NBid NBir NBro
- var. **grandiflorum** — GGro
  W&O 7061
- var. **laciniatum** — LShi WCot
- 'Laciniatum Flore Pleno' (d) — LShi

Chelone (Plantaginaceae)
barbata — see *Penstemon barbatus*
§ **glabra** — CBWd CMac EAri EBee ECha GMaP LBar LRHS LShi MHol MMuc MPie NBid NBro NGdn NLar NSti SBrt SPlb SRms WCot WFar WTre
lyonii — EBee
- 'Hot Lips' — LBar
- 'Pink Temptation' — EBee ELan
obliqua — CAby CBWd CMac CMHG EAri EBee ECha ELan GJos GMaP GQue LCro LEdu LRHS LShi MArl MHol NBir NGdn NLar NSti SPlb SRms StAn WCAu WFar WKif WNPC WOld WTre
- var. **alba** — see *C. glabra*
- 'Pink Sensation' — WFar
- Pink Turtle ('Arturtle'PBR) — LRHS MHol

Chelonopsis (Lamiaceae)
moschata — EAri EBee EGrl EWld LEdu SPlb
- white-flowered — EWld GGro WFar
yagiharana — WFar WTre

Chengiopanax (Araliaceae)
sciadophylloides — WCru
B&SWJ 14633

Chenopodium (Amaranthaceae)
ambrosioides — see *Dysphania ambrosioides*
bonus-henricus — see *Blitum bonus-henricus*
californicum — see *Blitum californicum*
capitatum — see *Blitum capitatum*
foliosum — see *Blitum virgatum*
giganteum — EHet ELan LCro MNHC SRms WJek
quinoa — MCtn

cherimoya see *Annona cherimola*

cherry, Duke see *Prunus* × *gondouinii*

cherry, sour or morello see *Prunus cerasus*; also AGM Fruit Section

cherry, sweet see *Prunus avium*; also AGM Fruit Section

chervil see *Anthriscus cerefolium*

chestnut, sweet see *Castanea sativa*

Chiastophyllum see *Umbilicus*
   simplicifolium   see *Umbilicus oppositifolius*

chicory see *Cichorium intybus*; also AGM Vegetables Section

Chiliotrichum (Asteraceae)
   diffusum   GAbr GArf MMuc

chilli pepper see *Capsicum*; also AGM Vegetables Section

Chimonanthus ✿ (Calycanthaceae)
   fragrans   see *C. praecox*
   nitens   CMCN NLar
   - B&SWJ 13616   WCru
  § *praecox*   CBcs CDoC CJun EBee EGren EGrI EHeP ELan EPfP LCro LRHS LSRN LSto MAsh MBlu MCtn MGos MMuc NLar NQui SDix SEND SGol SPlb SSta WCot WFar WJur
   - 'Cobhay Sunshine'   CJun
   - 'Grandiflorus' ♀H5   CJun CWnw LRHS MAsh SPoG WCot
   - 'Luteus' ♀H5   CJun LRHS MAsh MGos NLar SPoG WCot
   - 'Moonlight'   EPfP
   yunnanensis W.W. Sm.   NLar

Chimonobambusa (Poaceae)
   KR 7592   MWht
  § *marmorea*   CDTJ MMuc
   - 'Variegata' (v)   CDTJ
  § *quadrangularis*   CBcs CDTJ MWht
   - 'Suow' (v)   CDTJ
   tumidissinoda   CBcs CDTJ ESwi MWht SPlb WCot WFar WPGP

Chinese cabbage see AGM Vegetables Section

Chinese chives see *Allium tuberosum*

Chiogenes see *Gaultheria*

Chionanthus (Oleaceae)
   retusus   CBcs LMaj MBlu MCtn MMuc NLar SBrt WJur
   - 'China Snow'   NCth NLar
   - 'Norfolk Weeper'   NLar
   virginicus   CBcs CMCN ELan MBlu MMrt MMuc NLar SPlb WHtc WJur WSpi

Chionochloa (Poaceae)
   conspicua   CElw EBee GAbr NBid NBir WHoo WPGP
   - subsp. *conspicua*   WCot
   - 'Rubra'   see *C. rubra*
   flavescens   CTsd WPGP
   flavicans   CSpe EPfP
  § *rubra* ♀H7   CBcs CElw CMHG CSpe EBee EPfP EWes GQue MBlu MCtn SHor WCot WHoo WPGP
   - PAB 67   LEdu

Chionodoxa see *Scilla*
   gigantea   see *Scilla luciliae* Gigantea Group

Chionohebe see *Veronica*

Chiranthodendron (Malvaceae)
   pentadactylon   SPlb

Chirita see *Primulina*
   sinensis   see *Primulina dryas*
   speciosa   see *Henckelia speciosa*
   tamiana   see *Deinostigma tamiana*

Chironia (Gentianaceae)
   baccifera   SPlb

× ***Chitalpa*** (Bignoniaceae)
   tashkentensis   CBcs CEnd CTsd ESwi SBrt
   - 'Morning Cloud'   MBlu
   - 'Pink Dawn'   CBcs IPap LMaj MBlu
   - SUMMER BELLS ('Minsum')   CDoC CMCN EBar EBee EGrI EUrb NCth SPad WCot WFar WLov WMal

chives see *Allium schoenoprasum*

Chlidanthus (Amaryllidaceae)
   fragrans   SEND XFar

Chloranthus (Chloranthaceae)
   fortunei   CMiW ESwi WCot
   glaber   see *Sarcandra glabra*
   henryi   GEdr SIvy WCot
   - NMWJ 14496   WCru
   japonicus   EMor ESwi GEdr WHil
   oldhamii   EWld WPGP
   - B&SWJ 2019   ESwi LEdu WCru
   serratus   EMor GEdr
   sessilifolius 'Domino'   ESwi WCot WCru WFar

Chlorogalum (Asparagaceae)
   pomeridianum   SBrt

Chlorophytum ✿ (Asparagaceae)
   comosum   CoPl EShb EUrb LInT LWaG SEND SVic WFar
   - 'Aureomarginata' (v)   SEND
   - 'Bonnie'[PBR] (v)   CDoC EShb LCro MPri NHrt
   - 'Lemon'   LCro
   - 'Ocean'[PBR]   LCro NHrt
   - 'Variegatum' (v) ♀H2   CoPl CPic EGren EShb LCro MPri NHrt SEND SMrm SPre
   - 'Vittatum' (v) ♀H2   CDoC EShb NHrt
   graminifolium   EBee
   krookianum   WCot
   laxum   LBom
   nepalense   WPGP
   - B&SWJ 2528   WCru
   - PAB 13.034   LEdu
   orchidastrum ♀H1b   NHrt
   - 'Green Orange'   NHrt
   saundersiae   CPbh
   - 'Starlight'[PBR] (v)   LCro

Choisya (Rutaceae)
   × *dewitteana*   SAth
   - APPLE BLOSSOM ('Pmoore09'[PBR])   CBcs CCps CEnd EBee EGrI LCro NCth SPoG
   - 'Aztec Gold'[PBR]   CBcs CDoC CWnw EBee EGrI LCro LRHS MGos

- 'Aztec Pearl' ♀H4 — Widely available
- GOLDFINGERS ('Limo') — CBcs CBrac CCps CMac CWGN EBee EGren ELan EPfP EUrb LBom LCro LRHS LSRN MGos Midl MPri SPoG
- LITTLE BEE ('Ap Cg001') — LBuc LSou
- SNOW FLURRIES ('Lisflurry'PBR) — ELan SPoG
- WHITE DAZZLER ('Londaz'PBR) ♀H4 — Widely available
- *dumosa* var. *arizonica* 'Whetstone' — EBee WMal WPGP
- GREENFINGERS ('Lissfing') — CSBt CWnw EBee ELan EPfP EUrb LCro LRHS MAsh MPri NLar
- ROYAL LACE ('Pmoore06'PBR) — CCps LBuc MHtn
- *ternata* ♀H4 — Widely available
  - GOLD STAR ('Lisstar') — CBcs EBee EPfP LRHS
  - MOONSHINE ('Walcho'PBR) — CBcs
  - MOONSLEEPER — see *C. ternata* SUNDANCE
  - SCENTED GEM ('Lissbrid') — CBcs EPfP LRHS LSou MAsh
§ - SUNDANCE ('Lich') ♀H4 — Widely available

Chondrosum (Poaceae)
gracile — see *Bouteloua gracilis*

Chordospartium see *Carmichaelia*

Chorisia see *Ceiba*

Chorizema (Fabaceae)
cordatum — SVen
dicksonii — SPlb
diversifolium — CSpe

Chromolaena (Asteraceae)
arnottiana RCB RA 2 — EBee

Chrysalidocarpus (Arecaceae)
§ *decaryi* — NPlm SPlb
§ *decipiens* — NPlm
§ *lanceolatus* — NPlm
§ *leptocheilos* — NPlm
§ *lutescens* ♀H1a — CDoC EGren LCro LDro LWaG MCtn NHrt SPlb
§ *pembanus* — NPlm
§ *pilulifer* — NPlm

Chrysanthemopsis see *Rhodanthemum*

Chrysanthemum ✿ (Asteraceae)
E.H.Wilson s.n. — EPPr ESgI EWes EWoo LShi MHer MNrw SMHy WCot WFar WHoo WMal
'Agnes Ann' (21d) — ESgI MNrw
'Ahlemer Rote' (21) — MNrw SAko
'Alan Foxall Yellow' (3b) — MCms
'Alex Young' (25b) — MCms
'Alfredo Mauve' (12) — MCms
'Alfredo Orange' (12) — MCms
'Alice Jones' (24b) — MCms
'Aline' (21) — MNrw
'Alison' (29c) — EWoo MNrw WFar
'Alison's Dad' — EPPr MNrw
'Allouise' (25b) ♀H3 — NHal
'Allouise Orange' (25b) — MCms NHal
'Allouise Pink' (25b) — MCms
'Allyson Peace' (14a) — MCms NHal
'Amber Matlock' (24b) — MCms
'Amelia Rose' (7a) — MCms
'American Beauty Lemon' (5b) — MCms
'American Beauty Snowball' (5b) — MCms
'American Beauty White' (5b) — MCms
'Anastasia' ambig. — GAbr SAko
'Anastasia'PBR (10a) — MWlw
'Anastasia' (21c) — ELon EWoo MCms MNrw SRms
'Anderton' (6b) — MCms
'Andrew' — MNrw
'Angela Blundell' (19b) — MNrw WCot WFar
'Angelic' (21b) ♀H4 — EWoo
'Ann Dickson' (25b) — MCms
'Anne, Lady Brocket' (21d) — MNrw
'Anne Ratsey' (21) — EWoo MNrw MWlw WFar
'Anthony Peace' (25b) — MCms
'Antigua'PBR — MCms
'Apollo' H. Shoesmith — MNrw
'Apollo' (21) — LShi MCms MWlw WFar
'Apricot' — see *C.* 'Cottage Apricot'
'Apricot Chessington' (25a) — MCms
'Apricot Courtier' (24a) — MCms NHal
'Apricot Enbee Wedding' — see *C.* 'Bronze Enbee Wedding'
'Apricot Mundial' (6b) — MCms
'Arctic Beauty' (4b) — MCms
arcticum L. — see *Arctanthemum arcticum*
'Arthur Ellis' (15b) — MCms
'Astro' (25b) — MCms NHal
'Aunt Millicent' (21d) ♀H4 — EPPr EWoo MHCG NHal WCot
'Balcombe Perfection' (5a) — MCms NHal
balsamita — see *Tanacetum balsamita*
BARBARA ('Yobarbara') (22) ♀H3 — NHal
'Barbara Dakin' (25b) — MCms NHal
'Barbara Lambert' (21) — MNrw
'Beacon' (5a) ♀H2 — MCms
'Beechcroft' (29Rub) — LShi MNrw MWlw SPeP WFar
'Belle' (21d) — ESgI MNrw MWlw
'Beppie Bronze' (29e) — MCms
'Beppie Purple' (29e) — MCms
'Beppie Red' (29e) — MCms
'Beppie Rose' (29e) — MCms
'Beppie Yellow' (29e) — MCms
'Betty Wiggins' (25b) — MCms
'Bienchen' — WFar
'Bill Holden' (14a) — MCms
'Bill Wade' (25a) — MCms
'Billy Bell' (15a) — MCms NHal
'Blanche Poitevene' (12c) — EMal MCms
'Bob Green' (13b) — MCms
'Boulou Pink' (12) — MCms
'Boulou White' (12) — MCms
'Boulou Yellow' (12) — MCms
'Bounty Blanc' — LShi WFar
'Branbeach Orange' — LRHS
'Branbeach Sunny' — LRHS
'Branbeach White' — LRHS
'Brancrown' — LRHS
'Brandream' — LRHS
'Branhalo' — LRHS
'Branmaya' — LRHS
'Bransky Lilac' — LRHS
'Bransky Plum' — LRHS
'Bransound Pink' — LRHS
'Branspice' — LRHS
BRAVO ('Yobra') (22c) — NHal
* 'Breitner's Supreme' — MNrw WFar
'Brennpunkt' — EPPr MNrw
'Bretforton Road' — EPPr LShi MCms MNrw MWlw WCot WFar WHoo WMal WOld
'Bronze Cassandra' (5b) ♀H2 — MCms NHal

'Bronze Dee Gem' (29c)	MCms NHal		NPer SEND SMrm SPoG SRms WCAu WFar
§ 'Bronze Elegance' (21b) ♀H4	CDor ELan EPPr ESgI MHCG MWlw NBir NGdn SEND SHor SRms	'Clare Louise' (24b)	MCms
§ 'Bronze Enbee Wedding' (29d) ♀H3	MCms NHal	'Clarksdale' (15b)	MCms
		coccineum	see *Tanacetum coccineum*
'Bronze Fleece' (12b)	MCms	'Cochinelle'	MNrw
'Bronze Matlock' (24b)	MCms NHal	'Colsterworth' (21a)	MNrw MWlw
'Bronze Max Riley' (23b) ♀H3	MCms NHal	'Connie Mayhew' (5a)	MCms
		'Coral Reef' (10b)	MCms NHal
'Bronze Mayford Perfection' (5a) ♀H2	MCms	'Corinna' (21d)	CDoC ELan MWlw
		'Cornetto' (25b)	MCms NHal
'Bronze Mei-kyo'	see *C*. 'Bronze Elegance'	'Corsair' (9d)	MCms
'Bronze Talbot Parade' (29c) ♀H3	MCms	*corymbosum*	see *Tanacetum corymbosum*
		§ 'Cottage Apricot' (21)	CDor EBee ELan EPfP MBNS SHor SPeP SRms WFar
'Bronze William Florentine' (15a)	MCms	'Cottage Bronze'	MNrw MWlw
'Brown Eyes' (21b) ♀H4	ESgI MNrw	'Cottage Lemon'	EPPr ESgI MNrw MWlw WFar WHoo
'Bryony Wade' (13b)	MCms NHal		
'Bryony Wade White' (13b)	MCms	'Cottage Pink'	see *C*. 'Emperor of China'
'Buff William Florentine' (15a)	MCms	'Courtier' (24a)	MCms NHal
		'Cousin Joan' (21d) ♀H4	CAby CDor ELan ELon MCms MWlw SHor SPhx WCot WFar WMal
burnt-orange-flowered	CDor CFis ESgI EWoo LShi MNrw MWlw WCot WFar WMal		
		'Cream Dorridge Crystal' (24a)	MCms
'Burntwood Belle' (3b)	MCms		
'Buxton Ruby'	EWoo LShi MNrw	'Cream John Hughes' (3b)	MCms
'Cameo' (28a)	MNrw	'Cream Talbot Maid' (29c)	MCms
'Candy John Wingfield' (14b)	MCms	'Cream Talbot Parade' (29c) ♀H3	MCms
'Capel Manor'	LShi MNrw WCot		
'Capella' (10a)	MCms	'Cream West Bromwich' (14a)	MCms
'Capri Orange'	WFar		
'Carlene Welby' (25b)	MCms	'Cricket' (25b)	MCms
'Carmine Blush' (21d) ♀H4	CDor ELan ESgI LShi MNrw MWlw WCot WFar	'Crimson Purple Glow' (5a)	MCms
		DANCE ('Fidance'[PBR]) (9f)	MCms
'Casablanca' (25a)	MCms NHal	'Dance Red' (9f)	MCms
'Cassandra' (5b) ♀H2	MCms NHal	DANCE SALMON ('Fidancesal') (9f)	MCms
'Cawthorne' (29d)	WFar		
'Ceres' (6b)	MCms	'Dance Sunny' (9f)	MCms
'Cerisa' (29d)	MCms NHal	'Dance White' (9f)	MCms
'Charles Tandy' (5a)	MCms	'Daniel Cooper' (21d) ♀H4	ELan MNrw WFar
'Charles Tandy Primrose' (15a)	MCms	'Daphne Davis' (29d)	NHal
		'Darren Pugh' (3b)	MCms NHal
'Charles Tandy Yellow' (15b)	MCms	'Darren Pugh Primrose' (3b)	MCms
'Charlie' (24b)	MCms		
'Chatsworth' (29c)	NHal	'David Shoesmith' (25a)	MCms
'Chelsea Physic Garden' (21)	CDor EPPr ESgI EWoo GAbr LShi MNrw MPie MWlw SMad SPeP SPhx WCot WFar WMal	'Dawn Charlton' (14a)	MCms
		'Dee Gem' (29c) ♀H3	MCms NHal WFar
		'Denise Oatridge' (5a)	MCms
'Cherry Chessington' (25a)	MCms	'Dernier Soleil'	MNrw
'Cherry Tracey Waller' (24b)	MCms	'Disco Club'	MCms
		'Dixter Orange'	CCBP EBee ELan ESgI EWes GElm LShi MHer MNrw NDov SDix SHar SMad SMHy SPel SPhx WCot WHoo WMal
CHESAPEAKE ('Yochesapeake'[PBR]) (10a)	MCms NHal		
'Chesapeake Primrose' (10a)	MCms	§ 'Doctor Tom Parr' (21c)	EPfP EWoo MCms MNrw MWlw
		'Domingo' (14b)	MCms
'Chessington' (25a)	MCms	'Doreen Statham' (14b)	MCms NHal
'Chessington Oyster' (25a)	MCms	'Doris Ozols' (25a)	MCms
'Chestnut Talbot Maid' (29c)	MCms	'Dorothy Stone' (25b)	NHal
		'Dorridge Crystal' (24a)	MCms NHal
'Chestnut Talbot Parade' (29c) ♀H3	MCms WFar	'Dorridge King' (4b)	MCms
		'Downpour' (10a)	MCms
'Chloe Ball' (13b)	MCms	'Duchess of Edinburgh' (21d)	CDor ELan ELon EWoo GBin LRHS LShi MNrw NLar WCAu WFar WMal
'Christmas'	MNrw WFar		
'Christopher Lawson' (24b)	MCms NHal	'Dulwich Pink' (21d) ♀H4	MNrw NHal WCot WFar
cinerariifolium	see *Tanacetum cinerariifolium*	'Dunnettii'	MCtn
'Citronella'	MNrw WFar	'Early Yellow'	EBee ELan ELon EWoo MNrw WCot WFar
'Clapham Delight' (23a)	MCms		
'Clara Curtis' (21d)	CDor CMac CWal EBlo ECha ELan EPfP GKev LCro LRHS LShi MArl MHol MNrw MPie MPri MWlw	'Edelweiss' (21d)	EPPr MNrw
		'Edina' (29d)	NHal
		'Edmund Brown'	EPPr WCot WFar

Chrysanthemum 177

'Egret' (23b)	MCms NHal	
'Elaine's Hardy White'	MNrw MWlw WCot WFar WHoo WMal	
'Eliška'	MNrw	
'Elizabeth Lawson' (5b)	NHal	
'Elspeth' (6b)	LShi	
§ 'Emperor of China' (21)	CDor CElw ECha EPPr EWoo LShi LSto MHer MNrw SMad SRms WFar WMal	
'Enbee Wedding' (29d) ♀H3	MCms NHal	
'Energy'PBR (9)	MCms	
'Erntekranz'	MNrw WMal	
'Esther' (21d)	CElw ESgI MHer MNrw MWlw NDov WFar	
'Etna' **new**	ESgI SMad WMal	
'Etta Dakin' (15b)	MCms	
'Eugen's Messingknopf'	SAko	
'Fairweather' (3b)	MCms	
'Fairweather Cream' (3b)	MCms	
'Fairweather Peach' (3b)	MCms	
'Feeling Green Dark'PBR	MCms	
'Feeling Sunny'PBR	MCms	
'Finn Lyttle' (29d)	NHal	
'Fleur de Lis' (10a)	MCms	
'Folk Song' (4b)	ESgI MNrw	
'Fred Shoesmith' (5a)	EMal	
'French Rose'	WFar	
'Frizbee' (29d)	NHal	
'Froggy'PBR (9)	MCms	
frutescens	see *Argyranthemum frutescens*	
'Gambit' (24a)	MCms	
'Geoff Amos' (3b)	MCms	
'Geoff Brady' (5a)	MCms NHal	
'George Griffiths' (24b)	MCms NHal	
'George Simons'	WHoo	
'Gillette' (23b)	MCms	
'Ginger Nut' (25b)	MCms	
'Ginger Nut Yellow' (25b)	MCms	
I 'Gladys' (12a)	NHal	
'Gladys Emerson' (3b)	MCms	
'Gold Enbee Wedding' (29d) ♀H3	MCms	
'Gold Mundial' (6b) ♀H2	MCms	
'Golden Cassandra' (5b) ♀H2	MCms NHal	
'Golden Chalice' (12a)	NHal	
'Golden Courtier' (24a)	MCms NHal	
'Golden Masons' (7b)	MCms	
'Golden Mayford Perfection' (5a) ♀H2	MCms	
'Golden Rain' (10a) ♀H2	MCms NHal	
'Golden Shoesmith Salmon' (4a)	MCms	
'Golden Splendour' (10a)	MCms NHal	
'Golden William Florentine' (15a)	MCms	
'Goldengreenheart' (21d) ♀H4	EBee ELon ESgI MHCG MHer MNrw MWlw SPeP SRms WFar WHoo	
'Goldmarianne' (21)	WFar	
'Goldtopas'	WFar	
'Goodlife Sombrero' (29a) ♀H3	MCms	
'Gordon Dowson' (25b)	MCms	
'Goshu Penta' (10a)	MCms	
'Gräfenhausen'	WFar	
'Granatapfel'	MNrw WFar	
'Grandchild' (21c) ♀H4	MNrw NHal	
'Green Goddess' (2)	MCms	
'Hana-no-yume' (12b)	MCms	
'Hanenburg' (25b)	MCms NHal	
haradjanii	see *Tanacetum haradjanii*	
* 'Harry Lawson'	MCms	
'Harry Woolman' (13b)	MCms	
'Hatsuhikari' (12b)	MCms	
'Heather James' (3b)	MCms NHal	
'Hebe' (21d)	MNrw	
'Heda'	MNrw SMHy SPeP	
'Heide' (29c) ♀H4	NHal	
'Helen Harrison'	MWlw	
'Helen Louise' (25b)	MCms NHal	
'Helen Ward'	MNrw	
'Herbstbrokat'	ESgI GBin WFar	
'Herbstfeuer' (21)	MNrw	
'Herbstkuss'	SPel WMal	
'Hillside Apricot'	SHor	
'Hoagy' (29d)	MCms NHal	
HOLLY ('Yoholly') (22b)	NHal	
'Honey Enbee Wedding' (29d)	MCms NHal	
hosmariense	see *Rhodanthemum hosmariense*	
indicum	SVic	
'Innocence' (21d) ♀H4	CDor CFis ELan ELon ESgI GAbr LShi MBNS MCms MNrw NGdn SHar SHor WFar	
'Jan Jones' (29d)	NHal	
'Janet South'	MNrw	
'Jante Wells' (21b) ♀H4	MCms MNrw	
'Jasoda Dark Orange'PBR	LCro	
'Jasoda Mauve'PBR	LCro	
'Jasoda Pink'PBR	LCro	
'Jasoda White'PBR	LCro	
'Jasoda Yellow'PBR	LCro	
'Jeanette McCauley' (23b)	NHal	
'Jennie Atkinson' (7b)	MCms	
'Jessie Cooper' misapplied	see *C.* 'Mrs Jessie Cooper'	
'Jill Anderton' (6b)	MCms	
'Jimmy Tranter' (14b)	NHal	
'John Hughes' (3b)	MCms NHal	
'John Riley' (14a)	NHal	
'John Wingfield' (14b)	MCms NHal	
'John Wingfield Honey' (14b)	MCms	
'John Wingfield Pearl' (14b)	MCms	
'Jolie Rose'	MHCG MWlw SHar WCot WFar	
'Joyce Fountain' (24a)	MCms	
'Joyce Frieda' (13b)	MCms NHal	
'Julia' (28)	MNrw	
JULIA ('Yojulia')	NLar	
'Julia Arnold'	WHoo	
'Julia Peterson'	ESgI MHCG MHer MNrw MWlw SRms WCot WFar	
'Julie Lagravère' (28)	MWlw WFar	
'June Peace' (25b)	MCms	
'Karen Taylor' (29c) ♀H3	NHal	
'Kay Woolman' (13b)	MCms NHal	
'Kay Woolman Cream' (13b)	MCms	
'Kay Woolman Primrose' (13b)	MCms	
'Kay Woolman Yellow' (13b)	MCms	
'Killerton Tangerine'	MNrw WFar WMal	
'Kimberley Marie' (15b)	MCms NHal	
'Kiyomi-no-meisui'	MCms NHal	
'Kleiner Bernstein'	MNrw MWlw	
'Kurume' (12b)	MCms	
'La Damoiselle'	WCot	
§ 'Lady in Pink' (21)	MNrw	
'Lakelanders' (3b)	MCms NHal	
'Laura Jayne' (25a)	MCms	
'Lava' (10a)	MCms	

leucanthemum	see *Leucanthemum vulgare*	'Mrs Jessie Cooper No 2'	EPPr MNrw MWlw
'Lexy'^PBR (9)	MCms	'Mundial' (6)	MCms
'Lexy Red'^PBR (9)	MCms	'Mundial Peach' (6b/9a)	MCms
'Lighthouse'	NHal	'Mundial Rose' (6b)	MCms
'Lilac Chessington' (25a)	MCms	'Mundial Ruby' (6b)	MCms
'Lily Anderton' (6b)	MCms	'Music' (23b)	MCms NHal
'Liverpool Festival' (23b)	MCms	'Myss Dorothy' (29c)	MCms NHal
'Lollipop'^PBR (9e)	MCms	'Myss Eliza' (29c)	MCms
LOLLIPOP PURPLE ('Filollipop Purple'^PBR) (9e)	MCms	'Myss Goldie' (29c)	MCms
		'Myss Rihanna' (29c)	MCms NHal
'Long Island Beauty' (6b)	MCms	'Myss Saffron' (29c) ♀H3	MCms NHal
'Lorna Wood' (13b)	MCms NHal	'Nantyderry Sunshine' (28b) ♀H4	CDor EBee ELon EPfP EPPr ESgI EWld EWoo LRHS LShi MNrw MPie SRms WCot WFar WOld
'Lucy' (29a)	MCms NHal		
LYNN ('Yolynn') (22c) ♀H3	NHal		
'Lynn Johnson' (15a)	MCms	'Nell Gwynn' (21d)	MNrw NHal
macrophyllum	see *Tanacetum macrophyllum* (Waldst. & Kit.) Sch.Bip.	'Neue Kokarde'	MNrw
		'NHS Rainbow' (25b)	MCms
'Mancetta Symbol' (5a)	MCms	NICOLE ('Yonicole') (22c)	NHal
'Mandarin' (5b)	NLar SAko	*nipponicum*	see *Nipponanthemum nipponicum*
'Manito'	MNrw	'Nutcracker' (23b)	MCms
maresii	see *Rhodanthemum hosmariense*	'Old Norwell'	MNrw MWlw WHoo WMal
'Margery Fish'	MNrw WFar	'Orange Enbee Wedding' (29d)	NHal
'Marion' (25a)	MNrw MWlw WCot WFar WHoo		
'Marion Couchman' (25b)	NHal	*pacificum*	EUrb LShi WFar
'Martin Bell' (29d)	WFar	*parthenium*	see *Tanacetum parthenium*
MARTINA ('Dlfmart12'^PBR) (24b)	MCms	'Pat Bahn' (29c)	NHal
		'Patricia Millar' (14b)	MCms
'Mary' (21f)	NHal	'Patricia Millar Cerise' (14b)	MCms
'Mary Aldred' (29d)	MCms	'Patricia Millar Coral' (14b)	MCms
'Mary Stoker' (21d)	CDor EBee ELan EPPr LShi MBNS MNrw MPie NHal NLar SPel WCAu	'Patricia Millar Orange' (14b)	MCms
		'Patricia Millar Peach (14b)	MCms
'Mason's Bronze' (7b)	MCms	'Patricia Millar Salmon' (14b)	MCms
'Matlock' (24b)	NHal		
'Mauve Gem' (21f) ♀H3	NHal	'Patricia Millar Yellow' (14b)	MCms
'Mavis' (21)	ESgI MNrw		
'Mavis Smith'	LShi MNrw MWlw	'Paul Boissier' (30)	CDor CFis ESgI MCms MNrw WFar
'Max Riley' (23b) ♀H3	MCms NHal	'Pauline White' (15a)	MCms
maximum misapplied	see *Leucanthemum × superbum*	'Peach Courtier' (24a)	NHal
maximum Ramond	see *Leucanthemum maximum* (Ramond) DC.	'Peach Enbee Wedding' (29d) ♀H3	MCms
		'Peach John Wingfield' (14b)	MCms NHal
'Maxine Charlton' (24b)	NHal		
'Maxine Johnson' (25b)	MCms	'Peach Southway Sheeba' (29d)	NHal
'May Shoesmith' (5a) ♀H2	MCms		
'Mayford Perfection' (5a) ♀H2	MCms	'Pearl Celebration' (24a)	MCms
		'Pearl Dorridge Crystal' (24a)	MCms
'Megumi' (12b)	MCms		
'Mei-Kyō' (28b) ♀H4	CDor CMHG EBee ELan EPfP EPPr EWoo LShi MCms MNrw NSti SRms WCAu WFar	'Pearl Enbee Wedding' (29d)	MCms
		'Peggy' (28a)	MCms
		'Pennine Bullion'	NHal
'Membury' (24b)	NHal	'Pennine Gambol' (29a)	MCms
'Mezzo Bronze Red' (Poppins Series) ♀H3	MCms	'Pennine Jude' (29a)	MCms
		'Pennine Oriel' (29a) ♀H3	MCms NHal
'Mezzo Gold' (Poppins Series)	MCms	'Pennine Point' (19c)	NHal
		'Pennine Polo' (29d)	NHal
'Mezzo Magenta' (Poppins Series) ♀H3	MCms	'Pennine Punch' (29a)	MCms
		'Pennine Swan' (29c)	MCms
'Mezzo Pink' (Poppins Series)	MCms	'Penny's Yellow'	MCms MNrw
		'Percy Salter' (24b)	MCms NHal
'Migdale' (24b)	MCms NHal	'Perry's Peach' (21d) ♀H4	ELan ELon EPPr MCms MNrw NHal NPer SHor
'Milkshake'	MNrw		
'Millennium' (25b) ♀H3	MCms	'Peter Jolley' (25b)	MCms
'Misty Cream' (25b)	MCms	'Peter Rowe' (23b)	MCms NHal
'Misty Golden' (25b)	MCms	'Peterkin'	CMac ELon EPPr
'Misty Lemon' (25b)	MCms	'Picasso'	LShi WCot WFar
'Morning Star' (12a)	NHal	'Pink Progression'	see *C.* 'Lady in Pink'
'Mount Fuji' (10b)	MCms	'Pocahontas' (10a)	MCms
'Mr Mappie' (21c)	WCot	'Poesie'	EPPr MHCG MHer MNrw MWlw NLar SAko WCot WFar WMal
§ 'Mrs Jessie Cooper' (21d) ♀H4	EBee ELan ELon ESgI EWoo MCms MNrw SHor SMrm SRms WCot WFar WHoo		
'Mrs Jessie Cooper No 1'	MWlw SHar		

'Polar Gem' (3a) — MCms
'Pomander' (25b) — MCms
'Pot Black' (14b) — MCms
'Prelude Apricot' (Poppins Series) — MCms
'Prelude Autumn Bronze' (Poppins Series) — MCms
'Prelude Popcorn' (Poppins Series) — MCms
'Prelude Rose Pink' (Poppins Series) — MCms
'Prelude White' (Poppins Series) — MCms
'President Osaka' — MNrw
'Primrose Allouise' (24b) ♀H3 — MCms NHal
'Primrose Billy Bell' (15a) — NHal
'Primrose Chessington' (25a) — MCms
'Primrose Courtier' — see C. 'Yellow Courtier'
'Primrose Cricket' (25b) — MCms
'Primrose Dorridge Crystal' (24a) — MCms
'Primrose Egret' (23b) — MCms
'Primrose Enbee Wedding' (29d) ♀H3 — MCms NHal
'Primrose Fairweather' (3b) — MCms
'Primrose John Hughes' (3b) — MCms
'Primrose Mayford Perfection' (5a) ♀H2 — MCms
'Primrose Pauline White' (15a) — MCms
'Primrose Pennine Oriel' (29a) — MCms
'Primrose West Bromwich' (14a) — MCms
'Princess Anne' (4b) — MCms
'Promise' (25a) — MCms NHal
'Purleigh White' (28b) — EPPr ESgI LShi MNrw WFar
'Purple Dee Gem' (29c) — NHal
'Purple Glow' (5a) — MCms
'Rafia Rouge' — WFar
'Raquel' (21) — MNrw
'Ray's Red' — EPPr MNrw
'Rebecca Read' (7b) — MCms
'Red Balcombe Perfection' (5a) — MCms NHal
'Red Goodlife Sombrero' (29a) — MCms
'Red Mayford Perfection' (5a) — MCms
'Red Regal Mist' (25b) — MCms NHal
'Red Shirley Model' (3a) — MCms NHal
'Redbreast' (12a) — NHal
'Reg Lawrence' (25a) — MCms
'Regal Mist' (25b) — NHal
'Regal Mist Purple' (25b) — MCms
'Regent' (5b) — MCms
'Rehauge' — SAko
I 'Rhumba' — MNrw WCot
'Riley's Dynasty' (14a) — MCms
'Rita Fox' (15a) — MCms NHal
'Rita McMahon' (29d) ♀H3 — NHal
ROBIN ('Yorobi') (22c) — NHal
'Roen Sarah' (29c) — NHal
'Romantica' — EWoo MNrw
'Rose Enbee Wedding' (29d) — MCms NHal
'Rose Madder' — EWoo GAbr WCot WFar
'Rose Mayford Perfection' (5a) ♀H2 — MCms
'Rose Patricia Millar' (14b) — MCms
'Rose Talbot Parade' (29c) — MCms
'Rosedew' (25b) — MCms
'Rosetta' — MNrw
roseum — see *Tanacetum coccineum*
'Rosie Lyttle' (29c) — NHal
'Roter Spray' — WHoo
'Rotes Julchen' — SAko
'Roy Bevan' (29d) — MCms
'Royal Command' (21a) — ELon EPPr ESgI MNrw WCot WHoo
'Royal Sport' — MNrw
rubellum — see *C. zawadzkii*
'Ruby Enbee Wedding' (29d) ♀H3 — MCms WFar
'Ruby Mound' (21c) ♀H4 — CDor ELon ESgI EWoo LShi MCms MNrw NHal SHar SPhx WCot WFar WMal WOld
'Ruby Raynor' (21c) ♀H4 — MNrw NHal WFar
'Rumpelstilzchen' (21d) — CFis ELon LShi MHer MNrw WMal
'Rusty Margaret' (29c) — MNrw
'Saint Stephan' — WFar
'Salhouse Dream' (10a) — MCms
'Salhouse Joy' (10a) — MCms NHal
'Salmon Allouise' (25b) — MCms NHal
'Salmon Enbee Wedding' (29d) ♀H3 — NHal
'Salmon Fairweather' (3b) — MCms
'Salmon John Wingfield' (24b) — MCms
'Salmon Pauline White' (15a) — MCms
'Salmon Talbot Maid' (29c) — MCms
'Salmon Talbot Parade' (29c) ♀H3 — MCms WFar
'Salmon Tracey Waller' (24b) — MCms
'Salmon Venice' (24b) — MCms
'Samba' — WCot WFar
'Samson' — MCms
'Samson Orange' — MCms
'Samson Purple' — MCms
'Sarah Louise' (25b) — NHal
'Satomi Orange' (12b) — MCms
'Savanna Charlton' (25a) — NHal
'Schaffhausen' — WFar
'Schweizerland' — WFar
'Sea Urchin' (21f) ♀H3 — NHal
'Seaton's Galaxy' (10a) — MCms
'Seizan' (12b) — MCms
'Senkyo Karyu' (10a) — MCms
'Senkyo Kenshin' (10a) — MCms NHal
'Shamrock' (10b) — MCms
'Sheila Coles' (7b) — MCms
'Sheila Harris' (3b) — MCms
'Shenley Orange' — ELon
'Shining Light' (21f) — WCot WFar
'Shoesmith Salmon' (4a) — MCms
'Shoesmith Salmon Bright Bronze' (4a) — MCms
'Shoesmith Salmon Crimson' (4b) — MCms
'Shoesmith Salmon Purple' (4a) — MCms
'Skomer' (9f) — MCms
'Skomer Pink' (9f) — MCms
'Skomer Yellow' (9f) — MCms
'Šlapanická Vladěnka' — MNrw
'Soir d'Orient' — WFar
'Somerset Gold' — WCot WMal

Chrysopogon

'Sonya' (21)	MNrw
'Sound' (9d)	MCms
'Southway Sheba' (29d) ♀H3	MCms NHal
'Southway Sheba Apricot' (29d)	MCms
'Southway Sheba Bronze' (29d)	MCms
'Southway Sheba Chestnut' (29d)	MCms
'Southway Sheba Salmon' (29d)	MCms
'Southway Shimmer' (29d)	MCms NHal WFar
'Southway Shiraz' (29d)	MCms WFar
'Southway Sloe' (29d)	NHal
'Southway Spectacular' (29d)	MCms
'Southway Strontium' (29d)	MCms NHal
'Spartan Canary' (21d) ♀H4	LShi
'Spartan Display'	MHer MNrw
'Spartan Seagull' (21d)	ESgI MNrw
'Stallion' (9)	MCms
'Stallion Yellow'	MCms
'Starburst'	MCtn
'Starlet' (21f) ♀H4	LShi NHal
'Steve Packham' (23b)	NHal
'Stockton' (3b)	MCms
'Stratford Pink' (21d)	MNrw
'Suffolk Pink' (21d)	EPPr ESgI MNrw
'Sunny John Wingfield' (14b)	MCms NHal
'Super-Bronze Shoesmith Salmon' (4a)	MCms
SWAN ('Fiswan'^PBR) (9)	MCms
'Swan Cream'	MCms
'Swan Sunny'	MCms
'Sweetheart Pink'	MNrw MWlw WFar WMal
'Syllabub' (21f) ♀H3	ESgI MNrw
'Symphony' (10a)	MCms NHal
'Talbot Maid' (29c)	MCms
'Talbot Parade' (29c) ♀H3	MCms
'Talbot Parade Pink' (29c)	MCms
'Tapestry Rose' (21d)	ESgI MNrw SRms WFar WHoo WMal WOld
'Terry Brook' (29e)	WFar
'Thomas Russell' (7b)	MCms
'Thoroughbred' (24a)	NHal
'Tickle Pink' (29f/K)	MHer MNrw
'Tom Parr'	see *C.* 'Doctor Tom Parr'
'Tom Snowball' (3b)	MCms
'Tonto' (29d)	NHal
'Topsy' (21d) ♀H4	MNrw
'Tracey Waller' (24b)	MCms
TRIUMPH ('Yotri') (22)	NHal
uliginosum	see *Leucanthemella serotina*
'Uri'	CFis EBee ELon ESgI MHCG MNrw SAko WFar
'Vagabond Prince'	ELon EPPr ESgI EWoo MHCG MNrw SRms WFar
'Venice' (24b)	MCms
'Venice Peach' (24b)	MCms
'Venice Rose' (24b)	MCms
'Venus' (21d)	MWlw WCot WMal
'Venus One'	MNrw NHal
'Vysočina'	MNrw
'Wedding Day' (29K)	MNrw
'Wedding Sunshine' (21)	MNrw WFar
welwitschii	see *Glebionis segetum*
'Wembley' (24b)	MCms
'Wendy Tench' (21d)	ESgI MCms MNrw WCot WMal
'West Bromwich' (14b)	MCms
weyrichii	EDAr EPfP EPot GKev LRHS LShi MHol NRya SRms WFar WIce
'White Allouise' (25b)	MCms NHal
'White Beppie' (29e)	MCms WFar
'White Bouquet' (28)	WFar
'White Cassandra' (5b)	MCms NHal
'White Enbee Wedding' (29d)	MCms NHal
'White Fairweather' (3b)	MCms
'White Gem' (21f)	NHal
'White Gloss' (21e)	MNrw
'White Pearl Celebration' (24a)	MCms
'White Tower' (21d)	MNrw
'Wilder Charms'	MNrw
'William Florentine' (15a)	MCms NHal
'Will's Wonderful' (21d) ♀H4	MNrw WMal
'Wind Dancer' (10a)	MCms
'Winning's Red' (21)	SMad WCot WFar
'Winter Queen' (5b)	MCms
'Winter Queen Yellow' (5b)	MCms
'Woolley Globe' (15b)	MCms
'Woolman's Glory' (7a)	MCms
'Woolman's Glory Red' (7a)	MCms
'Woolman's Star' (3a)	MCms NHal
'Woolman's Venture Red' (14b)	MCms
'Yellow Allouise' (25b)	MCms
'Yellow American Beauty' (5b) ♀H2	MCms
'Yellow Billy Bell' (15a)	NHal
'Yellow Chessington' (25a)	MCms
'Yellow Clapham Delight' (23a)	MCms
§ 'Yellow Courtier' (24a)	MCms NHal
'Yellow Egret' (23b)	MCms
'Yellow Enbee Wedding' (29d)	MCms NHal
'Yellow Goodlife Sombrero' (29a)	MCms
'Yellow Heide' (29c) ♀H3	NHal
'Yellow Jewel' (Poppins Series) ♀H4	MCms
'Yellow John Hughes' (3b) ♀H2	MCms NHal
'Yellow John Wingfield' (14b)	MCms
'Yellow Mayford Perfection' (5a) ♀H3	MCms
'Yellow Pennine Oriel' (29a) ♀H4	MCms
'Yellow Percy Salter' (24b)	MCms
'Yellow Talbot Parade' (29c)	MCms
'Yellow Woolman's Glory' (7a)	MCms
yezoense	CDor ESgI MNrw SRms
- B&SWJ 10872	WCru
aff. *yezoense*	MHol
§ *zawadzkii*	CMac SRms
'Zoe Russell' (7a)	MCms

Chrysogonum (Asteraceae)

virginianum	EBee EWes LShi WFar
- var. *australe*	SBrt
- - 'Andre Viette'	ECha
- 'Pierre'	ELon EMor MAvo MWlw WFar

Chrysopogon (Poaceae)

gryllus	CAby EBee EDAr SHor

Chrysoplenium (Saxifragaceae)

alternifolium	EBee EMor GBin
davidianum	GJos GKev NBid WCru
- SBEC 233	CExl
aff. *hebetatum*	GGro
B&SWJ 9835	
lanuginosum	GGro WCru
var. *formosanum*	
B&SWJ 6979	
macrophyllum	CExl ECha EGrI EPfP EPPr EWld
	GKev GMaP LSto MWlw NBid SDix
	WCot WCru WFar WKif
- green-flowered	GGro LSto WFar
oppositifolium	CTtf GQue WShi

Chusquea (Poaceae)

breviglumis misapplied	see *C. gigantea*
culeou	CBcs MAvo MWht SArc SSta WCot
	WPGP
- 'Purple Splendour'	WPGP
delicatula from Machu Picchu, Peru	CDTJ
§ *gigantea* ♀H4	CDTJ CExl LEdu SBig
montana	CDTJ
nigricans	CDTJ

Cicer (Fabaceae)

arietinum	MCtn

Cicerbita (Asteraceae)

BO 16-085	GGro
§ *alpina*	GAbr NBid SPlb
bourgaei	GBin MHol
macrophylla	CTtf
subsp. *macrophylla*	
macrorhiza B&SWJ 2970	WCot
plumieri	GAbr SBrt WCot
- 'Blott' (v)	WCot

Cichorium (Asteraceae)

endivia 'Pancalieri' ♀H3	CHby EKin MCtn
intybus	CCBP CHby CSpe CTtf EDAr
	EHet ELan ENfk GJem GQue
	LShi MBel MCtn MHer MHoo
	MNHC NCth NMir SPlb SPoG
	SRms WFar WKit
- f. *album*	CCBP CTtf ECha LShi LSto MArl
	MHoo
- 'Brussels Witloof'	SVic
- 'Palla Rossa' ♀H5	CHby MCtn SRms
- 'Pan di Zucchero' ♀H5	CHby
- 'Red Rib'	SRms
- 'Roseum'	CCBP CTtf ECha ELan LEdu LShi
	MArl MBel MHol MHoo SPoG
- 'Rossa Di Treviso'	LCro

Cimicifuga see *Actaea*

acerina	see *Actaea japonica*
americana	see *Actaea podocarpa*
cordifolia (DC.) Torrey & A. Gray	see *Actaea cordifolia*
cordifolia Pursh	see *Actaea podocarpa*
racemosa var. *cordifolia*	see *Actaea cordifolia*
- 'Purpurea'	see *Actaea simplex* Atropurpurea Group
ramosa	see *Actaea simplex* 'Prichard's Giant'
rubifolia	see *Actaea cordifolia*
simplex	see *Actaea matsumurae*
var. *matsumurae*	

Cineraria (Asteraceae)

maritima	see *Jacobaea maritima*

Cinnamomum (Lauraceae)

camphora	CBcs IArd
japonicum B&SWJ 14627	WCru
- BCJMMT 327	WPGP

Circaea (Onagraceae)

lutetiana	WHer
- 'Caveat Emptor' (v)	WCot

Cirsium (Asteraceae)

aomorense	GGro
botryodes W&O 9092	GGro
canum	CDor CSpe GGro MHol WTre
chlorolepis W&O 9309	GGro
eriophorum	GGro
erisithales	GGro
handelii W&O 0030	GGro
helenioides	see *C. heterophyllum*
§ *heterophyllum*	CDor GAbr GGro GJos MCtn MHol
	NAts NLar SHar WHil WRBe
- PAB 67	LEdu
- 'Pink Blush'	LBar LCro LRHS MHol NSti
japonicum	GGro
- 'Rose Beauty'	MCtn WSpi
- 'Mount Etna'	EBee EMor EPfP GGro GKin LBar
	LRHS MBel MBNS MMuc MWlw
	NCth NDov NGdn WCAu
oleraceum	GGro LEdu NBac NBid NLar SBrt
	WKor
rivulare	Widely available
'Atropurpureum' ♀H7	
- FROSTED MAGIC	CBWd CDor EBee ELan EPfP LBar
('Lowcir')PBR	LCro MBNS MHol Midl MPro NBir
	NLar SPoG WCAu WFar WHil
- 'Trevor's Blue Wonder'	see *C. rivulare* 'Trevor's Felley Find'
§ - 'Trevor's Felley Find'PBR	Widely available
setidens	GGro
tuberosum	ECha GGro LEdu SDix WCot

Cissus (Vitaceae)

amazonica	LCro LWaG
antarctica ♀H1c	EShb
discolor	LBom
nodosa	EShb
quadrangularis	EAri LBom SPlb
rhombifolia ♀H1c	EShb LWaG
- 'Ellen Danica' ♀H1c	EGren EShb LBom NHrt SEND
- 'Mandaiana'	SEND
rotundifolia	EShb LBom
striata	see *Clematicissus striata*

Cistus ✿ (Cistaceae)

acutifolius misapplied	see *C. inflatus*, *C.* × *pulverulentus*
× *aguilarii*	WMal
- 'Maculatus' ♀H4	CBcs CDoC EGrI ELan EPfP LRHS
	LSRN NLar SPoG WKif WSpi
albidus	CWal
algarvensis	see *C. ocymoides*
'Anne Palmer'	see *C.* × *fernandesiae* 'Anne Palmer'
'Anya'	CExl
'April Snow'	LCro
'April Sun'	LCro LRHS
× *argenteus* 'Blushing Peggy Sammons'	LRHS NLar
- 'Paper Moon'	NLar
§ - 'Peggy Sammons'	CBrac ECha EGren EHeP ELan EPfP
	MAsh MSwo NLar

Cistus 183

- 'Silver Ghost'	CDoC		- var. *petiolatus*	WMal
- 'Silver Pink' misapplied	see *C.* × *lenis* 'Grayswood Pink'		'Bennett's White'	
- 'Silver Pink' ambig.	CBcs CBrac CDoC CSpe EBee EGren EHeP ELan EPfP LCro LRHS LSto MAsh MGos MNHC MSwo NBir SPoG WFar WKif WSpi	§	- var. *sulcatus*	ELan LRHS WKif
			lasianthus	CMac CSBt LCro LRHS
			- 'Concolor' ♀H4	MAsh
		§	- 'Formosus'	WKif
- 'Silver Pink' Hillier	LCro		- 'Sandling' ♀H4	EPfP LRHS MAsh SChF SPoG SRms WPGP
'Blanche'	see *C. ladanifer* 'Blanche'			
× *bornetianus* 'Jester' ♀H4	CBrac CSBt ECha ELan EPfP LRHS NLar SEND		*laurifolius*	EPfP NQui StAn WJur WMal WSpi
			× *laxus* 'Snow White' ♀H4	CWGN EBee ECha NLar NPer
§	*calycinus*	CBcs CDoC EBee EGrl ELan EPfP LCro LRHS LSou MAsh SPoG WLov	× *lenis* 'Grayswood Pink' ♀H4	CBrac CCoa CDoC EBee ELan EPfP EUrb LCro LRHS LSRN LSto MAsh MSwo SEND SPlb SPoG
§	× *candidus* 'Susan' ♀H4	EBee ELan WAbe	*libanotis* misapplied	see *C.* × *calycinus*
§	× *cheiranthoides* var. *pauanus*	MMuc	× *loretii* misapplied	see *C.* × *dansereaui*
	commutatus	see *C.* × *calycinus*	× *loretii* Rouy & Foucaud	see *C.* × *stenophyllus*
	× *corbariensis*	see *C.* × *hybridus*	× *lusitanicus* Maund	see *C.* × *dansereaui*
	creticus	CBcs CCoa CDoC CSde CWal LBom LCro LRHS MAsh MPri SNig SPoG SRms WSpi	'Merrist Wood Cream'	see *C.* × *revolii* H.J. Coste & Soulié subsp. *grandiflorus* 'Merrist Wood Cream'
	- subsp. *corsicus*	LBom	*monspeliensis*	CMac EBee SPoG WJur
§	- subsp. *creticus*	ECha EGren ELan EPfP WLov	- 'Vicar's Mead'	WMal
§	× *crispatus* 'Warley Rose'	WKif	*monspeliensis* × *salviifolius*	see *C.* × *florentinus* Lam.
	crispus misapplied	see *C.* × *pulverulentus*, *C.* × *purpureus*	× *obtusifolius* ambig.	EPfP WSpi
§	*crispus* L.	CBcs ELan SEND	§	× *obtusifolius* Sweet 'Thrive' ♀H4	CBcs CSBt LCro LRHS MGos MSwo WLov
	- 'Prostratus'	see *C. crispus* L.	*ocymoides*	WFar
	- 'Sunset'	see *C.* × *pulverulentus* 'Sunset'	× *pagei*	WMal
§	× *cyprius* ♀H4	CBrac EBee ELan LRHS SDix SRms WKif WSpi	'Paladin'	see *C. ladanifer* 'Paladin'
§	- var. *ellipticus* 'Elma' ♀H4	ELan EPfP NLar	*palhinhae*	see *C. ladanifer* var. *sulcatus*
§	× *dansereaui*	CMac EGren WSpi	*parviflorus* misapplied	see *C.* × *lenis* 'Grayswood Pink'
	- 'Decumbens' ♀H4	CBcs CCoa CDoC CSde CTtf CWnw EBee EGren EHeP ELan EPfP LRHS MAsh MSwo NLar SArc SPoG WSpi	*parviflorus* Lam.	WMal
			aff. *parviflorus*	GMaP
			'Peggy Sammons'	see *C.* × *argenteus* 'Peggy Sammons'
	- 'Jenkyn Place' ♀H4	CDoC EBee ELan EUrb GMaP LRHS MMuc NLar SPoG WKif	× *picardianus*	WMal
			'Pink Gin'	WSpi
	'Elma'	see *C.* × *cyprius* var. *ellipticus* 'Elma'	× *platysepalus*	SDix
§	× *fernandesiae* 'Anne Palmer'	CDoC LRHS NLar WKif WSpi	*populifolius*	CMac ECha LRHS NLar SArc WKif
	× *florentinus* misapplied	see *C.* × *ingwersenii*	- var. *lasiocalyx*	see *C. populifolius* subsp. *major*
	× *florentinus* ambig.	EGren LWaG WSpi	- subsp. *major*	WSpi
§	× *florentinus* Lam.	GMaP	§	× *pulverulentus*	ECha LRHS LWaG
	- 'Fontfroide'	SEND		- (Delilei Group) 'Fiona'	WMal
	formosus	see *C. lasianthus* 'Formosus'	§	- 'Sunset' ♀H4	Widely available
	'Gordon Cooper' ♀H4	ECha ELan MMuc NLar SPoG WMal WSpi		- 'Warley Rose'	see *C.* × *crispatus* 'Warley Rose'
	halimifolius misapplied	see *C.* × *cheiranthoides* var. *pauanus*	§	× *purpureus* ♀H4	Widely available
			- 'Alan Fradd'	CBcs CDoC CMac EGren EHeP ELan EPfP LBom LCro LRHS LSou LSRN LSto MAsh MGos MHtn MSwo NLar SEND SNig SPoG SRGP WFar WLov
	halimifolius L.	WMal			
	× *heterocalyx* 'Chelsea Bonnet'	GMaP NLar SPoG			
§	× *hybridus*	Widely available	- 'Betty Taudevin'	see *C.* × *purpureus*
	- 'Gold Prize' (v)	CWGN ECha LCro LRHS NLar	- f. *stictus*	LRHS
	- LITTLE MISS SUNSHINE ('Dunnecis'PBR) (v)	MGos NLar	× *revolii* misapplied	see *C.* × *sahucii*
	- ROSPICO ('Rencis'PBR) (v)	NLar	× *revolii* H.J. Coste & Soulié subsp. *grandiflorus* 'Merrist Wood Cream' ♀H4	CBcs CCoa CDoC CSBt CSde EBee EGrl ELan EPfP LRHS MAsh SPoG WFar WKif WSpi
	inflatus	MMuc			
§	× *ingwersenii* ♀H4	CCoa CSde ELan LRHS SRms			
	ladanifer misapplied	see *C.* × *cyprius*	- - 'Wintonensis' ♀H4	EGrl EPfP GMaP LRHS MAsh NLar SRms
	ladanifer ambig.	CMac ECha WKif			
	ladanifer L.	CBcs CCoa CSBt CSde CSpe CWal EBee ELan EPfP MAsh MSwo WMal WSpi	× *rodiaei* 'Jessabel'	EPfP NLar
			'Ruby Cluster'	CDoC MMuc
	- B&SWJ 15064	WCru	§	× *sahucii* ♀H4	CBcs CDoC CSBt CSpe ECha ELan EPfP LCro LRHS LSou MAsh MMuc MSwo NLar SPoG SRms WLov
§	- 'Blanche'	LSRN MMuc NLar WSpi			
§	- 'Paladin'	SArc WSpi			
	- Palhinhae Group	see *C. ladanifer* var. *sulcatus*	- ICE DANCER ('Ebhals') (v)	EBee MAsh WFar
	- 'Pat'	CDoC EPfP MAsh NLar SPoG WMal WSpi	*salviifolius*	CWal ECha WMal
			- B&SWJ 15066	WCru
			- 'Avalanche'	WAbe
			- 'Gold Star'	CDoC NLar
			- 'May Snow'	MAsh

184 *Cistus*

	- 'Prostratus'	CCoa CDoC CSde ELan EPfP WSpi
§	× **skanbergii**	CBcs CCoa CDoC CEnd CMac CSde ECha ELan EPfP NLar SAth SDix SEND WSpi
	'Snow Fire' ♀H4	CBrac CSpe EBee EGren ELan EPfP LBom LRHS MAsh SNig WLov WMal
§	× **stenophyllus**	CMac
	'Susan'	see *C.* × *candidus* 'Susan'
	'Thrive'	see *C.* × *obtusifolius* Sweet 'Thrive'
	tomentosus	see *Helianthemum nummularium* subsp. *tomentosum*
	villosus	see *C. creticus* subsp. *creticus*
	× **wintonensis**	see *C.* × *revolii* H.J. Coste & Soulié subsp. *grandiflorus* 'Wintonensis'

Citharexylum (Verbenaceae)
	quadrangulare	see *C. spinosum*
§	**spinosum**	WFar

× *Citrofortunella* see *Citrus*
	limequat	see *Citrus* × *floridana*
	mitis	see *Citrus* × *microcarpa*

citron see *Citrus medica*

Citronella (Icacinaceae)
§	**gongonha**	SVen
	mucronata	see *C. gongonha*

Citrullus (Cucurbitaceae)
	lanatus 'Charleston Gray'	SVic
	- 'Little Darling'	EKin MCtn
	- 'Mini Love'	LCro

Citrus ✿ (Rutaceae)
§	× **aurantiifolia** (F)	SFol SPre WFar
	- key lime	see *C.* × *aurantiifolia*
§	× **aurantium** (F)	LBom SFol WJur
	- subsp. **bergamia**	see *C.* × *limon*
	- 'Bigaradier Apepu' (F)	EPom
	- 'Bouquet de Fleurs'	see *C.* × *aurantium* (Sour Orange Group) 'Bouquet'
	- Grapefruit Group (F)	EUrb NPlm NTrD SFol SPre
	- - 'Star Ruby' (F/S)	SPre
	- var. **myrtifolia**	see *C.* × *aurantium*
	- 'Pursha' (F)	SPre
§	- (Sour Orange Group) 'Bouquet' (F)	SBig
	- - 'Chinotto' (F)	NTrD SPre
	- - 'Seville' (F)	EPom LSRN SFol SPre
	- Sweet Orange Group (F)	CoPl EUrb NPlm NTrD SArc SBig SFol SPre
	- - 'Chislett Summer Navel'^PBR (F)	NPlm
	- - 'Lane Late' (F)	SPre
	- - 'Navelina' (F/S)	LCro SPre
	- - 'Newhall' (F/S)	NLar
	- - 'Sanguinelli' (F)	EUrb NPlm SPre
	- - 'Spanish Sanguinelli'	see *C.* × *aurantium* (Sweet Orange Group) 'Sanguinelli'
	- - 'Valencia' (F)	SPre
	australasica (F)	EPom NPlm SPre
	bergamia	see *C.* × *limon*
	- bergamot	see *C.* × *limon* Bergamot Group
	'Buddha's Hand'	see *C. medica* 'Fingered'
	calamondin	see *C.* × *microcarpa*
§	× **floridana** (F)	LCro NTrD WJur
	- 'Eustis' (F)	SPre
	- 'Lakeland' (F)	SBig SPre
	fortunella 'Lemon'	WCha
§	**hystrix**	CDoC ELan EPom LBom LSRN NLar NPlm NTrD SBig SFol SPre WJur
	jambhiri	see *C.* × *taitensis*
§	**japonica** (F) ♀H1c	CBcs ELan LCro NTrD SPre WJur
	- 'Nagami' (F)	SFol SPre
	- 'Reale'^PBR (F)	SPre
§	× **junos**	EPom NPlm SBig SPre WJur
	kinokuni	see *C. japonica*
	kotokan	see *C.* × *aurantium*
	'Kucle' (F)	SPre
	kumquat	see *C. japonica*
	× **latifolia** (F/S)	EGren ELan EPfP EPom NPlm SBig SPre
	- 'Bearss' (F)	LCro
	- variegated (F/v)	SPre
	latipes Hook.f. & Thomson ex Hook.f.	see *C. hystrix*
	limetta (F)	CHll EPom SFol SPre WJur
	limettioides (F)	SPre
§	× **limon** (F)	EGren EPfP EUrb LCro LSRN NPlm SBig SFol SPre WFar
§	- Bergamot Group (F)	EPom LBom NPlm SPre
	- 'Eureka'	see *C.* × *limon* 'Garey's Eureka'
	- 'Eureka Pink Variegated' (v)	NPlm
	- 'Four Seasons'	see *C.* × *limon* 'Garey's Eureka'
§	- 'Garey's Eureka' (F)	ELan LCro NLar NPlm SPre WCha
	- 'Improved Meyer'	see *C.* × *limon* 'Meyer'
	- 'Lunario' (F) ♀H2	EPom
§	- 'Meyer' (F)	CBcs CDoC ELan EOli EPfP EPom LDro LSRN NLar NTrD SPoG SPre
	- 'Quatre Saisons'	see *C.* × *limon* 'Garey's Eureka'
	- 'Rangpur' (F)	EPom SPre
	- 'Variegata' (F/v)	ELan NPlm SPre
	- 'Zagara Bianco' (F)	SPre
	× **limonia**	see *C.* × *limon*
	'Lipo' (F)	SPre
	madurensis	see *C. japonica*
§	**medica** (F)	CHll EPom NPlm
	- 'Cedra' (F)	SPre
	- 'Cidro Digitado'	see *C. medica* 'Fingered'
	- var. **digitata**	see *C. medica* 'Fingered'
	- 'Ethrog' (F)	SPre
§	- 'Fingered' (F)	CHll EPom NPlm NTrD SPre
*	- 'Rubra'	SPre
	- var. **sarcodactylis**	see *C. medica* 'Fingered'
	× **meyeri**	see *C.* × *limon*
§	× **microcarpa** (F) ♀H3	CDoC EPom LBom LCro LWaG NLar NTrD SFol SPre WFar
	- Philippine lime	see *C.* × *microcarpa*
	- 'Tiger' (F/v)	SPre
	- 'Variegata'	see *C.* × *microcarpa* 'Tiger'
	× **mitis**	see *C.* × *microcarpa*
	natsudaidai	see *C.* × *aurantium*
	× **nobilis** var. **inermis**	see *C. japonica*
	- Ortanique Group	see *C.* × *aurantium* Sweet Orange Group
	× **obovata** (F)	SPre
	× **paradisi**	see *C.* × *aurantium* Grapefruit Group
	reshni	see *C.* × *aurantium*
§	**reticulata** (F)	CHll EGren EPom NTrD SFol SPre
	- Mandarin Group (F)	NPlm NTrD SPre
	- - 'Clementine' (F)	SPre
	- Satsuma Group	see *C. reticulata*
	sinensis	see *C.* × *aurantium* Sweet Orange Group
	sudachi	see *C. medica*
§	× **taitensis** (F)	SPre
	- 'Otaheite' (F)	SPre
§	**trifoliata**	CAgr CBcs CDoC EBee ELan ELon LCro LRHS MBlu MMuc SArc SBig

Clematis 185

	SEND SMad SPlb SVic WFar WJur WKor
- 'Flying Dragon'	WJur
unshiu	see *C. reticulata*
volkameriana	see *C.* × *limon*
wilsonii	see *C.* × *junos*

Cladrastis (Fabaceae)
§ *delavayi*	MBlu WPGP
§ *kentukea*	CAgr CBcs CLnd CMCN EBar EBee ELan ESwi EUrb IPap MBlu NLar SChF SFol WJur WMat WPGP
- 'Perkins Pink'	MBlu
- 'Rosea'	see *C. kentukea* 'Perkins Pink'
lutea	see *C. kentukea*
sinensis	see *C. delavayi*
wilsonii	WPGP

Clarkia (Onagraceae)
amoena	MCtn
- 'Memoria'	MCtn
Crown Double Mixed (d)	SVic
pulchella	MCtn
unguiculata	MCtn
- 'Appleblossom' (d) **new**	MCtn

Claytonia (Montiaceae)
alsinoides	see *C. sibirica*
§ *perfoliata*	CWRo MCtn MNHC WHer
§ *sibirica*	CAgr CCBP CTtf EUrb LEdu WKor
- f. *albiflora*	EWld MPie SPlb WCot
virginica	EBee EPot GKev LAma WFar

Cleistocactus (Cactaceae)
samaipatanus ♀H2	LWaG
straussii ♀H2	NPlm
winteri ♀H2	LWaG

Clematicissus (Vitaceae)
§ *striata*	CBcs CDoC CMac CWCL EBee EShb LCro LWaG SBrt SEND
- 'Sugar Vine' PBR **new**	NHrt

Clematis ✿ (Ranunculaceae)
'Abigail' (Vt)	CRHN NHaw
Abilene ('Evipo027' PBR) (Boulevard Series) (EL)	CWCL ELan EPfP LCro LRHS MAsh MGos NTay SPoG
'Abundance' (Vt) ♀H6	CBcs CDoC CWCL ELan LCro LRHS LSRN MAsh MGos NTay SDix SNig WFar WSpi WTHo
Acropolis ('Evipo078' PBR) (Boulevard Series)	ELan EPfP LBom LCro LRHS MGos NTay SNig SPoG WTHo
'Ada Moon' (V)	NHaw
addisonii	NHaw
'Advent Bells' (C)	CWGN LCro NTay WSpi WTHo
'Ai-Nor' (EL)	SNig
'Akaishi' (EL)	WTHo
'Akane no tsubo' (V)	NHaw
akebioides	GKev
Alabast ('Poulala' PBR) (EL) ♀H6	MGos WSpi WTHo
Alaina ('Evipo056' PBR) (Boulevard Series) (EL)	LCro LRHS NTay SNig SPoG WTHo
'Alba Luxurians' (Vt)	CBcs CDoC CRHN EGren ELan LCro LRHS LSRN MGos NTay SNig SPoG WTHo
'Albiflora' (A)	NTay
'Albina Plena' (A/d)	LCro LRHS NTay WTHo
'Alice Fisk' (EL)	LCro LRHS LSRN WTHo
'Alionushka' (I) ♀H6	CRHN ELan EPfP LCro LRHS NTay SPoG WTHo
'Allanah' (LL)	LSRN MGos WSpi WTHo
alpina	EHeP GKev LCro LSRN MAsh NPer SEWo SOrN SPlb SPre StAn WFar
- 'Columbine White'	see *C.* 'White Columbine'
§ - 'Pamela Jackman' (A) ♀H6	CMac ELan LSRN MAsh MMuc SPoG WFar WTHo
- 'Stolwijk Gold' (A)	CWGN MBlu NTay SRms WTHo
alternata	CWGN
'Amanda Marie' (Vt)	NHaw
'Amethyst' (EL)	WTHo
'Amethyst Beauty' (A)	CWCL CWGN EPfP LRHS MGos SNig SPoG
Amethyst Beauty ('Evipo043' PBR) (LL)	LCro MAsh NTay SPoG WTHo
'Andante' (I)	CWGN WSpi WTHo
'Andromeda' (EL)	CDoC EBee EPfP LCro MGos NLar SNig WTHo
Aneta ('Evipo055' PBR) (Vt)	CWGN
Angela ('Zoang' PBR) (EL)	LRHS LSRN WTHo
Angelique ('Evipo017') (Boulevard Series) (EL)	CWGN ELan EPfP LRHS MAsh MGos WTHo
angustifolia 'Mongolian Snowflakes' (F) **new**	WHil
'Anissa' (V)	NHaw
'Anita' (Ta)	EPfP NHaw NTay WTHo
Anna Louise ('Evithree' PBR) (EL) ♀H6	CWCL EPfP LRHS LSRN MGos NTay SNig WTHo
'Annabel' (EL)	LSRN MAsh
Annabella ('Zo08169') (V)	CWGN LRHS WTHo
'Annette's Seedling'	WCot
'Anniseed' (M)	NHaw
Anniversary ('Pynot') (EL)	LSRN
Ansley ('Evipo103') (EL)	LRHS MGos WTHo
'Aotearoa' (LL)	NHaw WTHo
'Aphrodite' (I)	MAsh
'Aphrodite Elegafumina' (I)	CWGN
apiifolia	WSpi
- 'Hakikomi Fu'	GGro
'Apollonia'	CWGN
'Apple Blossom' (Ar) ♀H4	CBcs CDoC CWCL EArl EGren EHeP ELan EPfP LBom LBuc LCro LRHS LSRN LSto MAsh MGos NBir NCth NLar NTay SBig SPoG SRms SWor WFar WTHo
'Arabella' (I) ♀H6	CRHN CWCL CWGN ELan EPfP LBom LCro LRHS LSRN MGos NLar NTay SDix SNig SPoG WCAu WFar WSpi WTHo
'Archie' (EL)	LCro LRHS WTHo
§ Arctic Queen ('Evitwo' PBR) (EL) ♀H6	LRHS SPoG
armandii	CBcs CBrac CDoC CWCL EArl EBee EGren EGrI EHeP ELan EPfP EUrb LBom LCro LRHS LSRN MAsh MGos NCth NLar NTay SArc SAth SBig SEWo SRms WFar WSpi WTHo
- 'Enham Star' (Ar)	LBom MGos WFar
§ - 'Little White Charm' (Ar)	ELan EPfP LCro NTay SPoG SWCr WTHo
- 'Meyeniana'	see *C. armandii* 'Little White Charm'
§ - 'Snowdrift' (Ar)	CBcs CWCL EBee ELan EPfP LCro LRHS LSRN MAsh MGos NLar NTay SPoG SRms WFar WTHo
× *aromatica*	CWGN ELan LCro MMrt NHaw NTay SPoG WCot WSpi WTHo
'Asao' (EL)	EBee EPfP MGos SPoG WTHo
'Ascotiensis' (LL) ♀H6	WTHo
'Ashva' (LL)	CWGN SNig
Astra Nova ('Zo09085' PBR) (Vt)	CWGN EPfP LBom LRHS NTay WSpi WTHo
'Aureolin' (Ta)	CDoC LRHS NLar

Avant-Garde ('Evipo033'PBR) (Vt)	CDoC CWCL CWGN EPfP LCro LRHS MGos NTay SPoG WTHo	
Aztek	see *C.* 'Helios'	
Baby Doll ('Zobadol') (EL)	WSpi WTHo	
Baby Star ('Zobast'PBR) (EL)	SPoG WTHo	
§ 'Bagatelle' (LL)	LRHS WTHo	
'Bal Maiden' (Vt)	CRHN	
'Barbara' (LL)	LSRN NHaw	
'Barbara Dibley' (EL)	LRHS MAsh WTHo	
'Barbara Harrington'PBR (LL)	CWCL	
'Barbara Jackman' (EL)	LSRN MAsh MGos SNig SPoG WTHo	
'Beautiful Bride'PBR (EL)	LCro LRHS MGos WTHo	
'Beauty of Worcester' (EL)	CDoC ELan EPfP LSRN MAsh MGos SNig WTHo	
Becca ('Evipo104') (Tudor Patio Series) (EL)	WTHo	
'Bees' Jubilee' (EL)	CBcs CMac CWCL EGren EHeP ELan EPfP LBom LCro LRHS LSRN LSto MAsh MGos NLar NTay SNig SPoG WTHo	
'Belle Nantaise' (EL)	SRms	
Bellissima ('Zo10075') (EL)	LCro NTay	
Bernadine ('Evipo061'PBR) (Boulevard Series) (EL)	EBee EPfP LBom LCro LRHS LSou MSwo NTay SNig WTHo	
'Best Wishes'	WSpi WTHo	
§ 'Beth Currie' (EL)	ELan LRHS	
'Betty Corning' (Vt)	CRHN CWCL CWGN ELan EPfP IPot LRHS LSRN MGos NLar NTay SDix SNig SPoG SRms WTHo	
'Bieszczady' (LL)	SPoG	
Bijou ('Evipo030'PBR) (Tudor Patio Series) (EL)	EPfP LCro LRHS MGos NTay SNig SPoG WTHo	
'Bill MacKenzie' (Ta) ♀H6	CBcs CDoC CMac EGren ELan EPfP GBin LCro LRHS LSRN MGos NLar NTay SDix SPoG SRms SWCr WTHo WTre	
'Black Prince' (Vt)	CRHN CWGN ELan EPfP IPot LCro LRHS LSRN MGos NLar NTay SPoG SRms WTHo	
'Black Tea' (EL)	SNig	
§ 'Błękitny Anioł' (LL) ♀H6	CRHN CWGN EBee EPfP LCro LRHS MAsh MGos NLar NTay SNig SPoG WTHo	
Blue Angel	see *C.* 'Błękitny Anioł'	
'Blue Belle' (Vt)	CRHN LRHS NLar WFar	
'Blue Bird' (A/d)	CBcs ELan LRHS MAsh MGos SRms	
Blue Blood	see *C.* 'Königskind'	
Blue Boy	see *C.* 'Elsa Späth'	
'Blue Boy'	see *C.* × *diversifolia* 'Blue Boy'	
'Blue Carillon' (I)	NHaw	
'Blue Dancer' (A)	CBcs CDoC CWCL EPfP LBom LCro LRHS LSto MGos NLar NTay SDix WTHo	
'Blue Eclipse' (A)	CWGN LCro LRHS NLar SPoG WTHo	
'Blue Explosion' (EL)	SPoG	
'Blue Eyes' (EL)	LSRN NLar SNig WTHo	
§ 'Blue Light'PBR (EL/d)	CWGN ELan LBom LRHS MGos NLar SPoG WTHo	
Blue Moon ('Evirin'PBR) (EL)	EPfP LRHS LSRN WTHo	
Blue Pirouette ('Zobluepi'PBR) (I)	ELan NTay SPoG WTHo	
Blue River ('Zoblueriver'PBR) (I)	CWGN ELan LCro NTay WTHo	
'Blue Tapers' (A)	LRHS WTHo	
'Bolam Belle' (Vt)	CRHN NHaw	
Bonanza ('Evipo031'PBR) (Vt)	EPfP SPoG	
× *bonstedtii* 'Crépuscule' (H)	CWGN LBar WSpi	
Bourbon ('Evipo018'PBR) (EL)	CWCL ELan EPfP LBom LCro LRHS MGos NTay SNig SWCr WTHo	
'Bredon Blue' (A)	LCro LRHS NTay	
'Brianna' (Vt)	NHaw	
'Brocade' (Vt)	CRHN NHaw	
'Broughton Bride' (A)	CBcs CDoC CWGN LCro LRHS NTay SRms WTHo	
'Broughton Star' (M/d) ♀H5	CDoC CMac CRHN CSBt EGrI ELan EPfP LBom LCro LRHS LSRN LSto MAsh MBlu MGos NBir NLar NTay SDix SPoG SRms WTHo	
'Brunette' (A)	ELan LRHS NTay WTHo	
buchananiana Finet & Gagnep.	see *C. rehderiana*	
'Buckland Beauty' (V)	CWGN NHaw	
'Buckland Pixie' (Vt)	NHaw	
'Burford Bell' (V)	NHaw	
'Burford Princess' (Vt)	CRHN NHaw	
'Burford White' (A)	LRHS	
'Burma Star' (EL)	CWGN NHaw WTHo	
Burning Love ('Vitiwester'PBR) (Vt)	CWGN NTay SNig WTHo	
'By the Way' (M)	LRHS	
Caddick's Cascade	see *C.* 'Semu'	
calycina	see *C. cirrhosa* var. *balearica*	
§ *campaniflora*	CRHN GGro MCtn NHaw NTay WTHo	
'Candy Stripe'	SPoG	
'Capitaine Thuilleaux'	see *C.* 'Souvenir du Capitaine Thuilleaux'	
'Cardinal Wyszynski'	see *C.* 'Kardynał Wyszyński'	
'Carlien' (Vt)	CRHN	
'Carmencita' (Vt)	CRHN IPot LSRN NHaw NTay	
'Carnaby' (EL)	EBee ELan EPfP LBom LCro LRHS LSRN SPoG WSpi WTHo	
'Carol Klein' (I)	NHaw	
'Carol Leeds' (Vt)	NHaw	
'Caroline' (LL)	CWGN LSRN	
× *cartmanii* 'Avalanche'PBR (Fo/m)	CWCL EGren ELan EPfP LBom LCro LRHS MGos MPri NLar NTay SNig SPoG WFar WTHo	
- 'Joe' (Fo/m) ♀H4	CBcs CDoC ELan EPfP LCro LRHS LSRN MAsh MPro NTay SPoG WFar WIce WTHo	
- Michiko ('Evipo044'PBR) (Boulevard Series) (Fo)	CWCL EPfP LCro LRHS SDix SNig SPoG WTHo	
- 'White Abundance'PBR (Fo/f)	NLar WCha	
Cassis ('Evipo020'PBR)	LCro SPoG WTHo	
'Catherine Clanwilliam' (T)	NHaw	
'Catherine Penny' (Vt)	NHaw	
Cézanne ('Evipo023'PBR) (Boulevard Series) (EL)	CDoC ELan EPfP LCro LRHS MAsh MGos NLar NTay SNig WTHo	
'Chacewater' (Vt)	CRHN	
Champagne Truffle ('Hyfatis04') (Truffle Series) (M/d) **new**	WNPC	
'Change of Heart' (EL)	CWGN EBee SNig	
Chantilly ('Evipo021'PBR) (Boulevard Series) (EL)	ELan LSRN NTay WTHo	
'Charissima' (EL)	CWGN	
'Charlie Brown' (LL)	CRHN NHaw	
Charmaine ('Evipo022'PBR) (EL)	CWGN EPfP LBom LCro LRHS NLar NTay SPoG WTHo	
'Chatsworth' (Vt)	CRHN CWGN NHaw	
Chelsea ('Evipo100'PBR) (Boulevard Series)	CDoC LBom NTay SPoG WTHo	
Cherokee	see *C.* Ooh La La (Boulevard Series)	
Chevalier ('Evipo040'PBR) (Boulevard Series) (EL)	CWCL EPfP LRHS MAsh NLar SNig SPoG WTHo	

chinensis misapplied — see *C. terniflora*
CHINOOK ('Evipo013'^PBR) — SRms
chrysantha — see *C. tangutica*
chrysocoma misapplied — see *C. spooneri, C. × vedrariensis*
chrysocoma Franch. — WSpi
'Cicciolina' (Vt) — CRHN NHaw
cirrhosa — CHll MAsh
§ — var. *balearica* — CBcs CDoC CMac ELan EPfP LCro LRHS LSRN MAsh MGos NTay SDix SEND SPoG WTHo
— 'Christmas Surprise' (C) — LCro SPoG SWCr WTHo
— 'Jingle Bells' (C) — CBcs CBrac CDoC CMac CWCL EBee EGren ELan EPfP LBom LCro LRHS LSRN LSto MAsh MGos MPri NLar NTay SNig SRms SWCr WFar WTHo
— 'Ourika Valley' (C) — CWGN EPfP LCro LRHS MAsh NLar NTay SPoG WTHo
— var. *purpurascens* — CBcs CDoC CMac CWCL
'Freckles' (C) ♀^H4 — EGren ELan EPfP LBom LCro LRHS LSto MGos MPri NLar NTay SEND SPoG SRms SWCr WFar WTHo
— — 'Lansdowne Gem' (C) — CWGN IArd LCro NLar NTay SPoG WFar WSpi WTHo
— 'Winter Parasol' (C) — EBee NTay
— 'Wisley Cream' (C) ♀^H4 — CBcs CBrac CDoC CMac CWCL EBee EGren ELan EPfP LCro LRHS LSRN LSto MAsh MGos MPri NLar NTay SNig SPoG SRms WHtc WTHo
clarkeana misapplied — see *C. urophylla* 'Winter Beauty'
columbiana — WAbe
var. *tenuiloba* 'Ylva' (A)
'Columella' (A) — CWGN
'Comtesse de Bouchaud' — CWCL EBee ELan EPfP LBom LCro
(LL) ♀^H6 — LRHS LSRN LSto MAsh MGos NTay SNig SPoG WTHo
'Congratulations' (EL) — SPoG
connata W&O 7066 — GGro
'Consort' (LL) — CWGN
'Constance' (A) ♀^H6 — CWCL EBee EPfP LCro LRHS LSRN LSto NLar NTay SRms WFar WTHo
'Continuity' (M) — LRHS
'Cora' (I) — CWGN
'Coralie' (T) — NHaw
CORINNE ('Evipo063'^PBR) — LCro LRHS MAsh NLar NTay SNig
(Boulevard Series) (EL) — SPoG WTHo
'Cornish Spirit' (Vt) — CRHN
'Côte d'Azur' (H) — CCps ELan LRHS WCAu WCot
'Countess of Lovelace' (EL) — CBcs LSRN MGos WTHo
COUNTRY ROSE ('Zocoro'^PBR) — NTay SWCr WSpi
(A)
'Cragside' (A) — LRHS NTay SPoG SWCr
§ — 'Crimson King' (LL) — WTHo
'Crinkle'^PBR (M) — LRHS
§ *crispa* — CWGN NHaw
'Crispa Angel' (V) — NHaw
'Crispa Niccy' (V) — NHaw
§ CRYSTAL FOUNTAIN — CDoC CWCL CWGN ELan EPfP
('Evipo038'^PBR) (EL) — LBom LBuC LCro LRHS LSRN MGos NTay SNig SPoG SRms WTHo
DAIYU ('Evipo083'^PBR) — LCro MSwo NTay SNig WLov
'Danae' (Vt) — CRHN NHaw
DANCING KING ('Zodaki'^PBR) — SWCr WTHo
(EL)
DANCING QUEEN — WSpi WTHo
('Zodaque'^PBR) (EL)
'Daniel Deronda' (EL) ♀^H6 — CDoC CWGN EBee ELan EPfP LBom LCro LRHS LSRN MAsh MGos NTay SNig SPoG WTHo

DARCY ('Evipo106') — LCro LRHS NTay SNig WTHo
(Tudor Patio Series)
'Darius' (EL) — SPoG
'Dark Eyes' (Vt) — CBcs CRHN CWGN IPot LCro NLar NTay WTHo
'Dark Secret' (A) — LRHS NLar
dasyandra NJM 11.075 — WPGP
'Dawn' (EL) — LSRN WSpi WTHo
'Dazzle' (EL) — LCro LRHS WTHo
'De Vijfhoeven' (Vt) — NHaw
'Débutante' (EL) — NHaw
'Dedication' (V) — NHaw
'Denny's Double' (EL/d) — CWGN IPot
'Destiny' (EL) — SPoG
DIAMANTINA ('Evipo039'^PBR) — CDoC CWCL EPfP LCro LRHS
(EL) — MGos NLar NTay SPoG WTHo
'Diamond Anniversary' (A) — EPfP LCro LRHS MGos WTHo
'Diamond Ball'^PBR (EL) — CWGN EBee NTay SPoG
DIANA'S DELIGHT — CWCL EPfP LCro LRHS MAsh NTay
('Evipo026'^PBR) — SNig SPoG WTHo
(Boulevard Series) (EL)
dioscoreifolia — see *C. terniflora*
§ × *diversifolia* — CRHN LSto NHaw WCot
§ — 'Benedikt' (I) — CWGN WSpi
§ — 'Blue Boy' (I) — CRHN LRHS NHaw WSpi
— 'Heather Herschell' (I) — CRHN SNig
§ — 'Hendersonii' (I) — EPfP LSRN LSto MAsh MBNS MHol MMrt NSti SMHy WCot
— 'Olgae' (I) — NHaw
'Doctor Mary' (V) — NHaw
'Doctor Ruppel' (EL) — CDoC CMac CWCL EBee EHeP EPfP LCro LRHS LSRN MAsh MGos SNig SPoG WFar WTHo
'Dominika' (LL) — NHaw
'Dorath' — CWCL CWGN LRHS NLar
'Dorothy Tolver' (EL) — WTHo
'Dorothy Walton' — see *C.* 'Bagatelle'
DOUBLE DELIGHT — CWGN EHeP NTay
('Doudeli'^PBR) (M)
DOUBLE RASPBERRY TRUFFLE — WNPC
('Hyfatis08') (Truffle Series) (M/d) **new**
DOUBLE STRAWBERRY TRUFFLE — WNPC
('Hyfatis06') (Truffle Series) (M/d) **new**
'Duchess of Albany' 1897 — CDoC CWCL ELan EPfP LRHS LSRN
(T) — MGos WTHo
DUCHESS OF CORNWALL — CWGN EPfP LCro LRHS NTay
('Evipo118') (LL)
'Duchess of Edinburgh' — CBcs CDoC CMac ELan EPfP LSRN
(EL) — MAsh MGos NTay SPoG WTHo
× *durandii* ♀^H6 — CBcs CRHN ELan EPfP IPot LCro LSRN MAsh MGos SPoG WCAu WSpi WTHo
'Dutch Sky' (LL) — CWGN WTHo
'Early Sensation' (Fo/f) — CBcs CDoC EGren ELan LCro LRHS LSRN MAsh MPro NTay SPoG SPre SWCr WFar WTHo
EAST RIVER ('Zoeastri'^PBR) (I) — LCro NTay
EDDA ('Evipo074'^PBR) — CWCL EPfP LCro LRHS NTay SNig
(Boulevard Series) (EL) — WTHo
'Edith' (EL) ♀^H6 — WTHo
'Édouard Desfossé' (EL) — WTHo
'Eetika' (LL) — CRHN NHaw
'Ekstra' (LL) — NHaw
'Eleanor' (Fo/f) — EPot GEdr
'Elf' (Vt) — CWGN NHaw
'Elgar' — see *C.* 'Sir Edward Elgar'
'Elizabeth' (M) ♀^H5 — CBcs CBrac CDoC CMac CRHN CWCL EGren EPfP LBom LCro LRHS LSRN MBlu MGos MPri NLar

Clematis

			NTay SAth SNig SPoG SRms SSta WFar WTHo
'Elly Elisabeth' (I)	NHaw	'Fond Memories' (EL)	CWGN EPfP LCro LRHS LSRN MAsh MGos NLar WTHo
ELODI ('Evipo115') (Tudor Patio Series)	LCro LRHS NTay	'Forever' (EL)	LRHS WTHo
§ 'Elsa Späth' (EL)	CBcs CMac CWCL ELan EPfP LBom LCro LRHS LSRN MAsh MGos NLar NTay SNig SPoG WTHo	FOREVER FRIENDS ('Zofofri'PBR) (LL) 'Forget-me-not' New Leaf Plants	CWGN LCro NTay SPoG WTHo see C. 'Forget-me-not NLP1'
'Elvan' (Vt)	CRHN NHaw	§ 'Forget-me-not NLP1'	LCro LRHS LSRN LSto NLar WTHo
'Ember' (I)	CWGN NHaw	*forrestii*	see C. *napaulensis*
'Emerald Dream'PBR (Fo)	LCro LRHS NTay	'Foxtrot' (Vt)	CRHN
'Emilia Plater' (Vt)	CRHN CWGN EPfP IPot LRHS NHaw NTay SNig WTHo	'Foxy' (A) ♀H6 FRAGRANT OBERON ('Hutbron'PBR) (Fo)	WTHo LCro LRHS WTHo
EMPRESS ('Evipo011'PBR) (EL)	CWCL ELan EPfP LBom LCro LRHS MGos NLar SWCr WTHo	'Fragrant Spring' (M)	CDoC CWGN EBee EGren EHeP LRHS MGos NCth NLar NTay SNig SPoG SWCr WFar WTHo
ENDELLION ('Evipo076'PBR) (Boulevard Series) (EL)	WTHo	'Frances Rivis' (A) ♀H6	CDoC ELan LCro LRHS LSRN MAsh MBlu MCtn NLar NTay SPoG SRms WTHo
'Entel' (Vt)	CRHN NHaw		
× *eriostemon*	see C. × *diversifolia*		
'Ernest Markham' (LL) ♀H6	CBcs CDoC CMac EHeP ELan EPfP LBom LCro LRHS LShi LSRN MAsh MGos NLar NTay SPoG WFar WSpi WTHo	'Frankie' (A) ♀H6 FRANZISKA MARIA ('Evipo008') (EL)	ELan EPfP LCro LRHS MAsh MGos MHer NTay WTHo EPfP LCro LRHS MGos WTHo
ESME ('Evipo048'PBR)	NLar WTHo	'Freda' (M) ♀H6	CRHN CWGN ELan EPfP LBom LCro LRHS LSRN MBlu MGos NTay SPoG SRms WFar WTHo
'Étoile de Malicorne' (EL)	LRHS SNig WTHo		
ETOILE NACRÉE	see C. 'Sakurahime'		
'Étoile Rose' (Vt)	CRHN ELan EPfP IPot LCro LRHS LSRN NHaw NTay SDix WTHo	*fremontii* *fruticosa* W&O 0129	SBrt WPGP GGro
'Étoile Violette' (Vt) ♀H6	CDoC CMac CRHN EGren ELan EPfP IPot LCro LRHS LSRN LSto MAsh MBlu MGos NLar NTay SDix SNig SPoG SRms WFar WTHo	'Fujimusume' (EL) ♀H6 'Fukuzono' (I) *fusca* misapplied *fusca* Turcz.	CWGN IPot LRHS MAsh MGos NTay SPoG WTHo EGrI SNig see C. *japonica* NHaw
EXCITING ('Zoexci'PBR) (EL)	WTHo	- dwarf	CWGN
'Fair Rosamond' (EL)	LRHS MGos WTHo	- var. *coreana* **new**	WTHo
'Fairy Bells' (Vt)	NHaw	- large-flowered B&SWJ 8431	WCru
FAIRY BLUE	see C. CRYSTAL FOUNTAIN	'Fuyu-no-tabi' (EL)	EBee
'Fairy Dance' (Vt)	NHaw	GAZELLE ('Evipo014'PBR) (I)	MAsh SRms
'Fairy Slippers' (Vt)	NHaw	'Generał Sikorski' (EL)	CBcs CDoC ELan EPfP LCro LRHS LSRN MAsh MGos NTay SNig SPoG WSpi WTHo
'Fairydust' (Vt)	NHaw		
× *fargesioides*	see C. 'Paul Farges'		
fasciculiflora L 657	CExl WCru WPGP		
'Fascination'PBR (I)	CWGN WCot WSpi WTHo	*gentianoides*	WAbe
FAUN ('Evipo108')	LRHS WTHo	'Geoffrey Tolver' (LL)	CWGN
'Fay' (Vt)	NHaw	GIANT STAR ('Gistar'PBR) (M)	EHeP EPfP LRHS NLar NPer NTay SPoG WFar WNPC
'Fenna' (EL)	CWGN		
FILIGREE ('Evipo029'PBR) (Tudor Patio Series) (EL)	EPfP LBuc LCro LRHS MGos NLar NTay WTHo	'Gillian Blades' (EL) ♀H6	ELan EPfP LBuc LRHS MAsh MGos SPoG WTHo
finetiana misapplied	see C. *paniculata* J.F. Gmel.	GINA ('Evipo092'PBR) (Garland Series) (LL)	CWGN
'Fireworks' (EL)	CWGN EGren LSRN MAsh MGos NLar NTay SPoG WTHo	'Ginny' (V)	NHaw
FLAMENCO DANCER ('Bfccfla'PBR) (LL)	LCro	§ 'Gipsy Queen' (LL) ♀H6	CBcs CWCL ELan EPfP LSRN MAsh MGos NTay SNig SPoG WTHo
flammula	CDoC ELan EPPr LCro LSRN MAsh MBlu MCtn NBid NLar SPoG SRms WSpi WTHo	GISELLE ('Evipo051'PBR)	EPfP LBom LCro LRHS NLar SNig SPoG WTHo
- B&SWJ 15041	WCru	'Gladys Picard' (EL)	EGren
- 'Rubra Marginata'	see C. × *triternata* 'Rubromarginata'	*glauca* Turcz.	see C. *intricata*
FLEURI ('Evipo042'PBR) (Boulevard Series) (EL)	EPfP LCro LRHS LSRN NTay SNig SPoG WSpi WTHo	*glaucophylla* GLORIOUS DAY ('Zo23020') (Vt) **new**	NHaw IPot LCro
florida	CWGN	GLORIOUS RED ('Zo23015') (Vt) **new**	IPot LCro
- 'Bicolor'	see C. *florida* var. *florida* 'Sieboldiana'	'Gojōgawa' (EL) 'Golden Harvest' (Ta)	WTHo EPfP LRHS NLar WTHo
- var. *flore-pleno* 'Plena' (d)	CWCL EPfP LCro LRHS LSRN NTay SAth SNig SPoG WTHo	GOLDEN TIARA ('Kugotia'PBR) (Ta) ♀H6	CWGN LRHS LSRN MGos NTay SRms WCot WTHo
§ - var. *florida* 'Sieboldiana' (d)	CBcs CWCL CWGN ELan EPfP LCro LRHS LSRN MAsh NTay SNig SPoG SWCr WTHo	'Gothenburg' (M) 'Grace' (Ta) *gracilifolia* BWJ 8002	LRHS WTHo NHaw WCru
- var. *normalis* PISTACHIO ('Evirida'PBR) (LL)	CWCL CWGN ELan EPfP LCro LRHS MAsh MGos NTay SPoG WTHo	I 'Grandiflora' (F) 'Grandiflora Sanguinea' (Vt) *grata* misapplied	CDoC StAn WFar WTHo NHaw see C. × *jouiniana*
'Floris V' (I)	CWGN EGrI NLar		

188

Clematis 189

'Gravetye Beauty' (T)	CDoC CRHN CWCL EBee EGren ELan EPfP LCro LRHS LSRN MGos NTay SNig SPoG SRms WTHo
'Grażyna' (LL)	WTHo
GREEN PASSION ('Zo11050'^PBR) (EL/d)	CWGN LCro WTHo
GREFVE ERIK RUUTH ('Kbk02'^PBR) (EL)	CWGN
'Guernsey Cream' (EL)	CBcs CDoC CWCL EPfP LBom LCro LRHS LSRN LSto MAsh MGos NLar NTay SOrN SPoG WTHo
GUERNSEY FLUTE ('Evigsy153')	LCro WTHo
GUIDING PROMISE ('Evipo053'^PBR) (Boulevard Series)	LCro LRHS NTay SNig
'Guiding Star' (EL)	LRHS
'Hågelby Pink' (Vt) ♀H6	CRHN CWGN ELan NHaw
'Hågelby White' (Vt)	CRHN CWGN ELan NHaw WTHo
'Hagley Hybrid' (LL)	CBcs CMac CWCL EBee EGren EHeP ELan EPfP LBom LCro LRHS LSRN MAsh MGos NLar NTay SNig SOrN SPoG SRms WFar WTHo
'Hakuōkan' (EL)	LRHS LSRN SNig WSpi WTHo
I 'Hakuree' (LL)	NHaw WTHo
'Halina Noll' (EL)	SNig
'Hanaguruma' (EL)	IPot LRHS LSRN SNig WTHo
'Hanajima' (I)	NHaw
'Hania' (EL)	IPot WTHo
'Happy Anniversary' (EL)	EPfP LBuc LCro LRHS LSRN NLar NTay WTHo
§ HAPPY BIRTHDAY ('Zohapbi'^PBR) (LL) ♀H6	LCro LSRN NTay SPoG WSpi
'Happy Diana' (T)	CWGN NHaw
HARLOW CARR ('Evipo004'^PBR)	SRms
'Haru Ichiban' (EL)	WTHo
'Hayate'	CWGN
§ 'Helios' (Ta)	NTay WTHo
'Helsingborg' (A) ♀H6	CDoC ELan EPfP LBom LRHS MGos NLar NTay SPoG SRms WTHo
aff. 'Helsingborg' (A)	NTay
hendersonii Koch	see *C.* × *diversifolia* 'Hendersonii'
hendersonii Stand.	see *C.* × *diversifolia*
§ 'Hendersonii' (I)	GElm LRHS LSRN
I 'Hendersonii Rubra' (Ar)	LBom LCro LRHS SPoG SWCr WTHo
'Hendryetta'^PBR (I)	CWGN WTHo
henryi	LSRN MAsh NTay
- B&SWJ 3402	WCru
- var. *morii* B&SWJ 1668	WCru
'Henryi' (EL)	CDoC CMac EBee ELan EPfP LCro LRHS LSRN SPoG WTHo
heracleifolia	ELan GKev
- 'Blue Dwarf' (H)	CWGN WTHo
- 'Cassandra' (H) ♀H5	CMac CSpe CWGN ELan EWld LRHS LSRN MHer MHol SRms WCot WTHo WTre
- 'China Purple' (H)	CWGN EMor GKev LBar LSto MAsh MBNS MHol
- 'Pink Dwarf' (H)	CWGN WTHo
'H.F.Young' (EL)	ELan EPfP LBom LCro LRHS LSRN MGos NLar NTay SNig SPoG WTHo
hirsutissima var. *scottii*	SBrt
'Honora' (LL)	CWGN
'Hope' (A)	LRHS
'Horn of Plenty' (EL)	WTHo
'Hoshi-no-flamenco' (T)	CWGN WTHo
huchouensis	NHaw
HUDSON RIVER ('Zo06137'^PBR) (I)	LCro NTay WTHo
'Huldine' (LL) ♀H6	CBcs CRHN CWGN ELan EPfP LCro LRHS LShi LSRN LSto NTay SNig SPoG WTHo
'Huvi' (LL)	CWGN NHaw
'Hybrida Sieboldii' (EL)	EHeP
HYDE HALL ('Evipo009'^PBR) (EL)	CMac CWGN ELan EPfP LRHS MAsh MGos SNig SPoG SRms
'Hythe Egret' (Fo)	EPot WIce
I AM A LITTLE BEAUTY ('Zolibe') (Vt)	CRHN
I AM HAPPY ('Zoiamha') (Vt)	CWGN ELan NTay SWCr
I AM LADY J ('Zoiamlj') (Vt)	ELan NTay
I AM LADY Q ('Zoiamladyq'^PBR) (Vt)	CWGN NTay WTHo
I AM RED ROBIN ('Zorero'^PBR) (A)	CWGN
ianthina	IPot
- var. *kuripoensis*	SBrt
- - B&SWJ 700	WCru
'Ibi' (EL)	WSpi
ICE BLUE ('Evipo003'^PBR) (Prairie Series) (EL)	ELan EPfP LCro LRHS MAsh NLar NTay WTHo
'Ice Queen' (EL)	MAsh
ICE TRUFFLE ('Hyfatis09') (Truffle Series) (M) **new**	WNPC
indivisa Willd.	see *C. paniculata* J.F.Gmel.
INES ('Evipo059'^PBR) (Boulevard Series)	CWCL LRHS SNig WTHo
'Ingrid Biedenkopf' (Vt)	NHaw
'Innocent Blush'^PBR (EL)	CWGN EBee SNig SPoG WTHo
'Innocent Glance'^PBR (EL)	CWGN EBee LRHS SNig SPoG WTHo
INSPIRATION ('Zoin'^PBR) (I)	LRHS NLar SPoG WTHo
integrifolia (I)	EAri EGrI ELan EPfP EUrb GQue LCro NHaw NLar NPer NTay SRms StAn WHoo WTHo
§ - 'Alba' (I)	EPfP LCro LRHS NHaw NLar NTay SRms WTHo
- 'Baby Blue' (I)	NHaw
- 'Baby Rose' (I)	NHaw
- 'Baby White' (I)	NHaw
- 'Blue Ribbons' (I)	CSpe LBar NLar WFar
- 'Gletschereis' (I)	CCBP LBar
- 'Hendersonii' hort.	see *C.* 'Hendersonii'
- 'Hendersonii' Koch	see *C.* × *diversifolia* 'Hendersonii'
- MONGOLIAN BELLS ('Psharlan') (I)	CSpe NHaw
- 'Ozawa's Blue' (I)	CWGN WTHo
- white-flowered	see *C. integrifolia* 'Alba'
§ *intricata* W&O 0130	GGro
- 'Harry Smith' (Ta)	NHaw WSpi
ISABELLA ('Zo12220'^PBR) (EL)	LRHS
ispahanica	NHaw
ISSEY ('Evipo081'^PBR) (LL)	EPfP LCro LRHS WTHo
'Iubileinyi-70' (LL)	NHaw
'Ivan Olsson' (EL)	LCro SNig SPoG WTHo
'Jackmanii' (LL) ♀H6	CBcs CMac EBee EGren EPfP LBom LCro LRHS LSRN LSto MAsh MGos NTay SNig SPoG WTHo
'Jackmanii Alba' (EL)	LSRN MAsh SPoG WTHo
JACKMANII PURPUREA ('Zojapur'^PBR) (LL)	LCro LRHS NTay WTHo
'Jackmanii Superba' misapplied	see *C.* 'Gipsy Queen'
'Jackmanii Superba' ambig. (LL)	CDoC CWCL ELan EPfP LCro LRHS MAsh MGos NPer NTay SNig SPoG WTHo
'Jacqueline du Pré' (A) ♀H7	CDoC ELan
'James Mason' (EL)	EPfP LRHS WTHo
'Jan Fopma'^PBR (I)	CWGN

'Jan Lindmark' (A/d)	CDoC EPfP LBom LCro LRHS MAsh NLar NTay SPoG SPre WTHo
§ 'Jan Paweł II' (EL)	ELan LRHS MGos SNig WTHo
'Jane Ashdown' (M)	NHaw
§ *japonica*	WFar
'Jean Caldwell' (Vt)	NHaw
'Jean Cumpston' (C)	NHaw
'Jeanne's Pink' (EL)	LRHS WTHo
I 'Jenny' (Cedergren) (LL)	WTHo
'Jenny' (M/d)	LRHS SPoG WSpi WTHo
'Jenny Caddick' (Vt)	NHaw
JEWEL OF MERK	see *C.* HAPPY BIRTHDAY
'Joan Baker' (Vt)	CRHN
JOHN HOWELLS ('Zojohnhowells'PBR) (Vt)	CWGN LCro NTay WSpi WTHo
'John Huxtable' (LL)	LCro WSpi WTHo
JOHN PAUL II	see *C.* 'Jan Paweł II'
'John Treasure' (Vt)	CRHN NHaw
JOLLY GOOD ('Zojogo'PBR) (LL)	SPoG
JOSEPHINE ('Evijohill'PBR) (EL)	CDoC CWCL CWGN EPfP LBom LCro LRHS LSRN MAsh MGos NLar NTay SPoG WSpi WTHo
'Josie's Midnight Blue' (V)	NHaw
§ × *jouiniana*	NHaw SEND
JULIANE ('Evipo049'PBR) (Boulevard Series)	LBom LRHS NTay WTHo
'Julka' (EL)	CDoC EPfP LRHS NHaw WSpi WTHo
'Justa' (Vt)	LRHS NHaw NLar SPoG WTHo
'Juuli' (I)	LSRN NHaw
'Kaaru' (LL)	CRHN NHaw
'Kaiser'PBR (EL)	EBee SNig WTHo
'Kaiu' (V)	CWGN NPot NHaw NTay WTHo
§ 'Kakio' (EL)	LRHS LSRN NLar SNig SPoG WTHo
I 'Kamilla' (EL)	CWGN
§ 'Kardynał Wyszyński' (EL)	LRHS
'Kasmu' (Vt)	NHaw
'Kathleen Dunford' (EL)	LSRN
'Kathryn Chapman' (Vt)	CRHN NHaw
'Ken Donson' (EL) $\mathbb{Q}$H6	WTHo
'Kermesina' (Vt) $\mathbb{Q}$H6	CBcs CDoC CRHN EBee ELan EPfP LCro MGos NTay SNig SPoG SRms WTHo
'Kiev' (Vt)	CRHN NHaw
'Killifreth' (Vt)	CRHN NHaw
KIMIKO ('Evipo066'PBR) (Boulevard Series) (Fo)	LRHS SNig SPoG
KINGFISHER ('Evipo037'PBR) (EL)	ELan EPfP LCro SPoG SWCr WTHo
'Kiri Te Kanawa' (EL)	EPfP NLar WSpi WTHo
kirilowii	NHaw
KITTY ('Evipo097') (Boulevard Series) (EL)	LRHS NTay SNig SPoG WSpi WTHo
'Kokonoe'PBR (d)	CWGN EBee EPfP LBom LCro LRHS MHtn NTay SNig SPoG WLov WTHo
'Kommerei' (LL)	NHaw
KÖNIGIN MAXIMA ('Wellmax'PBR) (T)	CWGN NHaw
§ 'Königskind' (EL)	NLar WTHo
koreana	MAsh
– AMBER ('Wit141205'PBR) (A)	CWGN ELan IPot LCro NTay SPoG SWCr WTHo
– var. *carunculosa*	CRHN NSti
– – 'Lemon Bells' (A)	SPoG
– 'Love Child' (A)	NTay
'Krakowiak'PBR (Vt)	EBee NHaw SNig
ladakhiana	NHaw
– CC 7135	GGro
'Lady Betty Balfour' (LL)	WTHo
'Lady Kyoko' (d)	LCro
'Lady Northcliffe' (EL)	LRHS MAsh WTHo
'Lambton Park' (Ta) $\mathbb{Q}$H6	CRHN NTay WTHo
lasiandra	NHaw
'Last Dance' (Ta)	CRHN
'Lasurstern' (EL) $\mathbb{Q}$H6	CBcs EGren ELan EPfP LCro LRHS LSRN MAsh NTay SNig SPoG WFar WTHo
'Laura Denny' (EL)	LRHS WTHo
LAVALLEE No 1 ('Utop012') new	WTHo
'Lavender Twirl' (Vt)	CRHN
'Lemon Beauty' (A)	CWGN LRHS
'Lemon Dream'PBR (A)	CWGN LRHS
LIBERATION ('Evifive'PBR) (EL)	NLar WSpi
LIBERTY ('Zo08095'PBR) (EL)	LRHS WTHo
ligusticifolia	NHaw
'Lilac Wine' (I)	NHaw
'Lilacina Floribunda' (EL)	LRHS
'Lily the Pink' (Vt)	NHaw
'Lincoln Star' (EL)	CMac MAsh WTHo
'Lisboa' (Vt)	CRHN NHaw
'Little Bas' (Vt)	CDoC CRHN CWGN ELan NHaw NTay WTHo
'Little Butterfly' (Vt)	CRHN
LITTLE LEMONS ('Zo14100'PBR) (Ta)	CDoC CWGN GKev LCro LRHS LSou MHtn SPoG WFar WTHo
'Little Mermaid' (EL)	LCro SNig
'Little Nell' (Vt)	CRHN ELan LRHS LSRN MGos NLar NTay WTHo
'Liviana' (V)	NHaw
'Lord Herschell'	CWGN NHaw
'Louise Rowe' (EL)	ELan WTHo
LUCKY CHARM ('Zo09067'PBR) (LL)	CWGN LBom NTay
LULA ('Evipo057'PBR) (Boulevard Series)	LBom LRHS
'Lunar Lass' (Fo/f)	GArf LRHS
'Luxuriant Blue' (Vt)	CRHN NHaw
'M. Koster' (Vt)	CDoC CRHN NHaw SNig SRms WTHo
macropetala (d)	CDoC EHeP ELan EPfP LBom LCro LRHS MAsh MCtn MMuc WTHo
– 'Blue Lagoon'	see *C. macropetala* 'Lagoon' Jackman 1959
– 'Lagoon' Jackman 1956	see *C. macropetala* 'Maidwell Hall' Jackman
– 'Lagoon' ambig.	LCro WTHo
§ – 'Lagoon' Jackman 1959 (A/d) $\mathbb{Q}$H6	LCro LSRN MAsh NTay WTHo
– 'Maidwell Hall' ambig.	MGos WTre
§ – 'Maidwell Hall' Jackman (A/d)	EPfP LCro LSRN
– 'Maidwell Hall' O.E.P.Wyatt (A)	CBcs
– 'Wesselton' (A/d) $\mathbb{Q}$H6	CBcs CDoC LCro LRHS MAsh NLar NTay SPoG SPre SRms WTHo
– 'White Moth'	see *C.* 'White Moth'
'Madame Baron-Veillard' (LL)	WTHo
'Madame Édouard André' (LL)	MGos SNig WTHo
'Madame Grangé' (LL)	NHaw
'Madame Julia Correvon' (Vt) $\mathbb{Q}$H6	CDoC CRHN EBee ELan EPfP IPot LBom LCro LRHS LSRN LSto MAsh MGos MPri NLar NTay SDix SPoG SSta SWCr WTHo
'Madame le Coultre'	see *C.* 'Mevrouw Le Coultre'
'Majojo' (Fo)	GEdr
MANDY ('Zo12153') (EL)	NTay
'Manju' (d)	CWGN SNig WLov

'Manon' ('Evipo054'PBR) (Boulevard Series) (EL)	EPfP SNig		– var. *montana*	CBcs EGren LCro LRHS LSto NBir NTay SNig SPoG WFar WTHo
'Margaret Hunt' (LL)	LRHS SDix SWCr WTHo		– var. *rubens* misapplied	see *C. montana* var. *montana*
'Margaret Jones' (M/d)	SPoG SWCr		– var. *rubens* E.H.Wilson	CDoC ELan SPlb WTHo
'Maria Cornelia'PBR (Vt)	CWGN IPot LCro NTay WTHo	I	– – 'Odorata' (M)	EPfP GKin LCro LRHS NCth WTay WTHo
'Maria Skłodowska-Curie'PBR (EL)	MGos NTay		– – 'Pink Perfection' (M)	CDoC CMac CRHN EGren ELan EPfP GKin LCro LRHS LSRN MAsh NTay SOrN SPoG WFar WTHo
'Marie Boissellot' (EL) ♀H6	CBcs CMac ELan EPfP LBom LCro LRHS LSRN MAsh MGos MPri NLar NTay SNig SPoG WTHo	§	– – 'Rubens Superba' (M)	EPfP GKin LBom LRHS MGos NTay SRms WFar WTHo
'Marinka'	CWGN		– – 'Tetrarose' (M) ♀H5	CBcs CBrac CDoC CMac CRHN EGren ELan EPfP LBuc LCro LRHS LSRN MGos NTay SEND SOrN SPlb SPoG SRms WFar WTHo
'Marjorie' (M/d)	CBcs CBrac CDoC CMac EAri EGren ELan EPfP GKin LBom LCro LRHS LSRN LSto MAsh MGos NLar NTay SDix SNig SPoG SRkn SRms WFar WTHo		– var. *sericea*	see *C. spooneri*
'Markham's Pink' (A/d) ♀H6	CBcs CDoC CWCL ELan EPfP LBom LCro LRHS LSRN MAsh MGos NLar NTay SPoG SRms WFar WTHo		– var. *wilsonii*	CMac CWCL ELan EPfP GKin LCro LRHS LSRN MMuc NTay SDix SNig SPoG SRms WFar WTHo
marmoraria	EPot SPlb SRms WAbe		'Monte Cassino' (EL)	CWGN SNig
– (m)	EDAr GKev		'Moonfleet' ('Evipo046'PBR) (LL)	LRHS
marmoraria × *petriei*	EPot		'Moonglow' (EL)	LCro LRHS WTHo
'Marmori' (LL)	CWGN NHaw	§	'Moonlight' (EL)	MAsh
'Mary Habberley' (Vt)	NHaw		× *morelii* 'Boulevard' (V)	EGren
'Mary Rose'	see *C. viticella* 'Flore Pleno'		'Morning Cloud'	see *C.* 'Yukikomachi'
'Mary Whistler' (A)	LRHS		'Morning Heaven' (Vt)	CRHN NHaw
'Mary-Claire' (EL/d)	SPoG		'Morning Sky' (LL)	SNig
'Masa' ('Evipo089'PBR) (Garland Series)	CWGN LCro LRHS WTHo		'Morning Star' ('Zoklako'PBR) (EL)	CWGN
maximowicziana	see *C. terniflora*		'Morning Yellow' ('Cadmy'PBR) (M)	EHeP LRHS NLar SPoG SWCr WNPC
'Mayleen' (M) ♀H5	CMac EGren EHeP EPfP LBom LCro LRHS MAsh MMuc NTay SNig SPoG SRkn SRms SWCr WFar WTHo		'Mrs Cholmondeley' (EL) ♀H6	CWCL EHeP ELan EPfP LBom LCro LRHS LSRN MAsh MGos MPri NLar NTay SNig SPoG WFar WTHo
'Mazurek' (Vt)	NHaw		'Mrs George Jackman' (EL) ♀H6	LCro NLar WSpi WTHo
'Mazury' (LL)	SNig			
'Meghan' (EL)	EPfP LCro LRHS WTHo		'Mrs N.Thompson' (EL)	CDoC CMac EHeP ELan LBom LCro LRHS LSRN LSto MAsh NPer NTay SNig SPoG WTHo
I 'Melodie' (Vt)	NHaw			
§ 'Mevrouw Le Coultre' (EL)	EHeP NTay SNig			
'Mia' (EL/d)	CWGN		'Mrs P.B.Truax' (EL)	LRHS WTHo
'Midori' (EL/d) new	SNig		'Mrs Robert Brydon' (H)	CWGN LBar LRHS SRms WTHo
'Mienie Belle' ('Zomibel'PBR) (T)	CWGN		'Mrs Spencer Castle' (EL)	LRHS
'Mikelite' (Vt)	NHaw		'Mrs T.Lundell' (Vt)	CRHN LRHS MGos NHaw WTHo
'Miniseelik' (LL)	NHaw		'Multi Blue' (EL)	CBcs EGren EHeP ELan EPfP EUrb LBom LCro LRHS LSRN MAsh MGos NBir NLar NTay SNig SPoG SRms SWCr WSpi WTHo
'Minuet' (Vt) ♀H6	CDoC CRHN LCro LRHS MAsh MGos NTay SNig SPoG WTHo			
'Mirabelle' ('Evipo072'PBR) (Boulevard Series)	SNig			
'Miranda' ('Floclemi'PBR) (I)	CWGN NHaw		'Multi Pink' ('St17333'PBR) (LL/d)	CWGN LCro NTay WTHo
'Miss Bateman' (EL)	CDoC CMac CWCL EBee EGren ELan EPfP LBom LCro LRHS LSRN MAsh MGos NTay SNig SOrN SPoG WTHo		'My Angel'PBR (Ta)	ELan LCro LRHS MGos NTay WSpi WTHo
			'My Darling' (EL)	CWGN LRHS NTay SNig SPoG WTHo
'Miss Christine' (M)	CDoC ELan LCro LRHS LSRN SPoG WTHo	§	*napaulensis*	CDoC ELan EPfP LCro LRHS MNrw WCru WSpi WTHo
'Mon Amour' ('Zomoa'PBR) (EL)	CWGN	I	'Natacha' (EL)	NLar
'Mon Cherry' ('Zomonch') (EL)	CWGN		'Natascha' (EL)	LRHS WTHo
			'Negritianka' (LL)	NHaw
montana	EAri EHeP MAsh SEWo WHtc WJur		'Nelly Moser' (EL) ♀H6	CBcs CDoC CMac CWCL EGren ELan EPfP LBom LCro LRHS LSRN MAsh MGos MPri NLar NTay NWbg SNig SPoG SRms WFar WSpi WTHo
– W&O 7064	GGro			
– W&O 7065	GGro			
– var. *alba*	see *C. montana* var. *montana*			
– 'Alexander' (M)	SPoG			
– 'Da Yun' (M)	CWGN		'Neva' ('Evipo050'PBR) (Boulevard Series) (EL)	NLar
– var. *grandiflora* (M) ♀H5	CBrac CMac CWCL EGren EHeP ELan EPfP GKin LBom LBuc LCro LRHS MMuc MPri NLar NTay SAth SEND SNig SOrN SPoG SRms WCha WTHo WTre		'New Dawn' (M)	NTay
			'New Love'PBR (H)	CWGN LCro LRHS LSou LSRN SPoG WTHo XFar
I – 'Lilacina' (M)	NLar		'Night Veil' (Vt)	CDoC LRHS MGos NHaw NTay WTHo

Clematis

NINON ('Evipo052'PBR) (Boulevard Series) — EAri EPfP EUrb LCro LRHS LSou SNig WLov

'Niobe' (EL) ♀H6 — CBcs CDoC CMac CWCL EBee EHeP ELan EPfP EUrb IPot LBom LCro LRHS LSRN MAsh MGos NLar NTay NWbg SDix SNig SPoG SRms WFar WSpi WTHo

'North Star' (EL) — LRHS WTHo

NUBIA ('Evipo079'PBR) (Boulevard Series) (LL) — CWCL CWGN EAri EPfP EUrb LBom LCro LRHS LSou MGos NLar NTay SNig WLov WTHo

nutans var. *thyrsoidea* — see *C. rehderiana*, *C. veitchiana*

'Oberek' (Vt) — CRHN NHaw SNig

'Ocean Pearl' (A) — LSRN NTay SPoG WTHo

ochroleuca — NHaw

OCTOPUS ('Zooct'PBR) (A) — CWGN LRHS NTay SPoG SWCr

'Odoriba' (V) — CRHN CWGN NHaw WTHo

OLYMPIA ('Evipo099'PBR) (Boulevard Series) — CWCL EAri EPfP EUrb LCro LRHS LSou MGos MSwo NTay SPoG WTHo

'Omoshiro' (EL) — CWGN NTay SNig WTHo

§ OOH LA LA ('Evipo041'PBR) (Boulevard Series) (EL) — CWCL EPfP LBom LCro LRHS MAsh MGos NTay SPoG SWCr WSpi WTHo

orientalis misapplied — see *C. tibetana* subsp. *vernayi*

- 'Orange Peel' — see *C. tibetana* subsp. *vernayi* var. *vernayi* 'Orange Peel'

orientalis ambig. — SRms

orientalis L. — EBee EHeP GKev SEND
- PAB 13.731 — LEdu
- var. *orientalis* — LRHS WTHo

otophora — NHaw SBrt

'Ovation'PBR (Fo) — LCro

'Pagoda' (Vt) — CRHN SRms

'Pamela' (F) — NTay

'Pamela Jackman' (A) — see *C. alpina* 'Pamela Jackman'

'Pamiat Serdtsa' (I) — NHaw

'Pamina' (EL) — LRHS NLar WTHo

'Pangbourne Pink' (I) ♀H6 — LCro LRHS NHaw WTHo

paniculata Thunb. — see *C. terniflora*

§ *paniculata* J.F. Gmel. — MCtn MNrw
- var. *lobata* — WSpi

'Panther' (I) — NHaw

'Paradise Queen' (EL) — LRHS WTHo

PARADISO ('Zo11154') (EL) — LCro

PARISIENNE ('Evipo019'PBR) (Boulevard Series) (EL) — CDoC CWCL CWGN EPfP LRHS MAsh NLar NTay SPoG WTHo

parviflora DC. — see *C. campaniflora*

parviloba var. *bartlettii* — WPGP
- - B&SWJ 6788 — WCru

'Pastel Blue' (I) — NHaw

'Pastel Pink' (I) — NHaw

'Pastel Princess' (EL) — WTHo

'Pat Coleman' (EL) — CWCL LRHS WTHo

patens 'Korean Moon' (EL) — WCru
§ - 'Manshuu Ki' (EL) — EPfP LCro LRHS SNig SWCr WTHo
- 'Ruriokoshi' (EL) **new** — SPoG
- 'Yukikoshi' (EL) — IPot WTHo

'Paul Farges' (Vb) ♀H6 — CDoC CWGN IPot LRHS MNrw NHaw NLar NTay WTHo

§ PAULIE ('Evipo058'PBR) (EL) — CWCL WTHo

'Pauline' (A/d) ♀H6 — LRHS LSRN

'Pendragon' (Vt) — CRHN NHaw

PEPPERMINT ('Evipo005'PBR) (d) — ELan LCro

'Perida' (LL) — CWGN NHaw

'Perle d'Azur' (LL) ♀H6 — CBcs CDoC CRHN ELan LBom LCro LSRN MAsh MGos NTay SPoG SRms WFar WSpi WTHo

PERNILLE ('Zo09113'PBR) (Vt) — CWGN LCro NTay WTHo

PETIT FAUCON ('Evisix'PBR) (I) ♀H6 — CWCL EPfP LCro LRHS LSRN MGos NLar SNig SRms WTHo

'Peveril Pendant' — NHaw
'Peveril Pristine' (Vt) — CWGN NHaw
'Peveril Profusion' (T) — NHaw

PICARDY ('Evipo024'PBR) (Tudor Patio Series) (EL) — EPfP LRHS MAsh SNig SPoG WSpi WTHo

PICOTEE ('Zo09124'PBR) (EL) — CWGN LRHS NTay WSpi WTHo

I 'Picton's Variety' (M) — LRHS SPoG WTHo

'Piilu' (EL) — CDoC CWGN EGren EHeP ELan EPfP LBom LCro LRHS LSRN MAsh MBNS MGos NBir NLar NTay SNig SPoG WCha WCot WTHo

PINK CHAMPAGNE — see *C.* 'Kakio'

'Pink Dream' (A) — CWGN LRHS
'Pink Fantasy' (LL) — LCro LRHS MAsh NLar SNig WTHo
'Pink Flamingo' (A) ♀H6 — CWCL ELan EPfP LCro LRHS LSto NTay SPoG WTHo

'Pink Ice' (I) — EPfP
'Pink Swing' (A) — LRHS WTHo
'Pirko' (Vt) — NHaw

§ *pitcheri* — CWGN NHaw WTHo
'Pixie' (Fo/m) — CDoC ELan LCro NLar SPoG WFar WTHo

§ 'Plum Beauty' (A) — NTay
pogonandra — NHaw
POLAR BEAR — see *C.* ARCTIC QUEEN
'Poldice' (Vt) ♀H6 — CRHN
'Polish Spirit' (LL) ♀H6 — CBcs CDoC CMac CRHN EGren EHeP ELan EPfP LCro LRHS LSRN LSto MGos MSwo NLar NTay SAth SNig SPoG SWCr WFar WSpi WTHo

'Polonez' (Vt) — NHaw
POMPEII ('Evipo116') (Boulevard Series) — LCro NTay

potaninii — WFar
- 'Summer Snow' — see *C.* 'Paul Farges'

'Praecox' (H) ♀H6 — CDoC CFis CRHN EBee EPfP GElm GPSL LRHS LSto NQui SDix SEND WCot WTHo

'Prairie River' (A) — LRHS MGos WSpi
'Primrose Star' — see *C.* 'Star'
'Prince Charles' (LL) ♀H6 — CDoC CRHN CWCL ELan EPfP IPot LCro LRHS LSRN MGos NHaw NLar NTay SDix SNig WTHo

'Prince George' (LL) — CDoC EPfP IPot LCro LRHS LSRN MGos NLar NTay SWCr WTHo

'Prince Louis' (EL) — LCro LRHS MGos
'Prince Philip' (EL) — EGren LCro LRHS

PRINCE WILLIAM ('Zo08171'PBR) (EL) — CWGN EBee IPot LCro NTay SNig SWCr WTHo

'Princess Charlotte' (EL) — LCro LRHS MGos WTHo

§ 'Princess Diana' (T) ♀H5 — CBcs CRHN CWGN EAri EBee EGrI ELan EPfP IPot LBom LBuc LCro LRHS LSRN MBlu MGos MSwo NTay SNig SOrN SPoG SRms WTHo

PRINCESS KATE ('Zoprika'PBR) (T) — CWGN EAri EBee EPfP LBom LCro MBlu MGos MPri NTay SPoG SWCr WCot WSpi WTHo

§ 'Princess of Wales' 1875 (EL) — CDoC CWCL LRHS LSRN NLar
'Princess Red' (V) — NHaw
'Prinsesse Alexandra'PBR (EL) — LRHS

'Propertius' (A) — CDoC CWGN EPfP LCro LRHS NLar NTay SNig SPoG WSpi WTHo

'Prosperity' (M) — CRHN WTHo
'Proteus' (EL) — EPfP LCro LRHS MAsh MGos NLar SNig SPoG SWCr WTHo

'Pruinina' — see *C.* 'Plum Beauty'
pseudopogonandra W&O 7068 — GGro

Clematis

psilandra CWJ 12377	WCru
'Purple Dream'^{PBR} (A)	LRHS
'Purple Haze' (Vt)	CRHN
'Purple Princess' (H)	CDoC SPoG
'Purple Rain' (A)	CDoC LRHS NLar
'Purple Spider' (A/d)	MAsh MBlu MGos NTay WTHo
'Purpurea Plena Elegans' (Vt/d) ♀H6	CBcs CDoC CMac CRHN CWCL EBee EGren ELan EPfP IPot LCro LRHS LSRN MGos NLar NTay SDix SPoG WTHo
QUEEN MOTHER ('Zoqum') (Vt)	CWGN EAri LCro LRHS NTay SWCr WTHo
'Radar Love' (Ta)	LSto MCtn
'Radiance'	CWGN NHaw NLar
'Rahvarinne' (LL)	IPot SPoG SWCr
ranunculoides W&O 7069	GGro
'Rapture' (T)	NHaw
'Raspberry Ripple' (V)	NHaw
'Rasputin' (LL)	CWGN WTHo
REBECCA ('Evipo016'^{PBR}) (Boulevard Series) (EL)	CDoC CWCL CWGN ELan EPfP LBom LCro LRHS LSRN MAsh MGos NTay SPoG WSpi WTHo
recta	GKev MCtn MNrw NHaw NLar WOld
- PAB 9005	LEdu
- 'Purpurea' (F)	CDor CWGN ELan EMor EPfP LRHS MHol MNrw SEND WTHo WTre
- 'Velvet Night' (F)	MHol NLar NSti WCot
'Red 5' (T)	NHaw
'Red Cooler'	see *C.* 'Crimson King'
RED PASSION ('Zo11056'^{PBR}) (EL/d)	CWGN WTHo
'Red Pearl' (EL)	LSRN
RED VELVET TRUFFLE ('Hyfatis02') (Truffle Series) (M) new	WNPC
REFLECTIONS ('Evipo035') (LL)	CWCL EPfP LCro LRHS NTay SNig
§ *rehderiana* ♀H5	CDoC EGrI ELan EPfP LCro LRHS MBlu NHaw NLar NTay SDix WCot WFar WTHo
aff. *rehderiana*	MCtn
- BO 16-026	GGro
REIKO ('Evipo088'^{PBR}) (Garland Series)	CWGN
REMBRANDT ('Zo16356') (M)	CWGN
'Remembrance' (LL) ♀H6	CWGN EPfP LCro LRHS LSRN WTHo
reticulata	NHaw
'Retrousse' (V)	NHaw
'Reverie' (T)	CRHN NHaw
'Rhapsody' ambig.	CDoC EPfP LBuc MAsh MGos
'Rhapsody' B. Fretwell (EL)	LBom LCro LRHS LSRN LSto NHaw SNig WTHo
'Ribble Red' (V)	NHaw
'Richard Pennell' (EL) ♀H6	CDoC WTHo
'Richard's Picotee' (Vt)	CRHN NHaw
'Rising Star'	NHaw
'Ristimägi' (LL)	NHaw
'Rituaal' (LL)	NHaw
'Roelie' (Vt)	NHaw
'Roko' (LL)	CWGN
'Roko-Kolla' (LL) ♀H6	LRHS NHaw SNig WTHo
ROLLERCOASTER ('Zo16170') (EL/d)	IPot LCro NTay SWCr
'Romantika' (LL)	CBcs ELan EPfP LCro LRHS LSRN MAsh NHaw NTay WTHo
'Rooguchi' (I)	CDoC CWCL CWGN LCro NHaw SPoG WTHo
'Rosa Königskind' (LL)	LRHS NLar WTHo
ROSALYN ('Zo09087'^{PBR}) (Vt)	CWGN IPot LCro NTay WTHo
'Rosamunde' (LL)	SNig
ROSE TRUFFLE ('Hyfatis07') (Truffle Series) (M) new	WNPC
I 'Rosea' (I)	LRHS LSRN NTay WHoo WTHo
I 'Rosea' Westphal (Vt)	CRHN NHaw
ROSEBUD ('Robud'^{PBR}) (M/d)	LCro NPer NTay
ROSEMOOR ('Evipo002'^{PBR}) (EL)	CWGN EPfP LRHS MAsh
'Rosy O'Grady' (A) ♀H6	MAsh NLar SRms
'Rosy Pagoda' (A)	ELan LRHS NLar WTHo
'Rouge Cardinal' (LL)	CBcs CDoC EBee EGren ELan EPfP LBom LCro LRHS LSRN LSto MAsh MGos NTay SNig SPoG SRms WFar WHtc WTHo
'Royal Velours' (Vt)	CBcs CRHN ELan EPfP LCro LRHS LSRN MAsh MGos NLar NTay SNig SPoG WSpi WTHo
ROYAL VELVET ('Evifour'^{PBR}) (EL)	LSRN
'Royal Wedding' (EL)	LCro NTay WTHo
'Royalty' (EL)	CDoC ELan LCro LSRN MAsh MGos WSpi WTHo
'Rubens Superba'	see *C. montana* var. *rubens* 'Rubens Superba'
'Rubra' (Vt)	NTay
'Ruby' (A)	ELan LRHS LSRN MGos NTay SRms
'Ruby Celebration' (A)	CDoC LRHS
'Ruby Glow' (EL)	LSRN
'Ruby Tuesday' (V)	NHaw
'Ruby Wedding' New Leaf Plants (EL)	see *C.* 'Ruby Wedding NLP2'
'Ruby Wedding' Fretwell (T)	CWGN LRHS NHaw WSpi
§ 'Ruby Wedding NLP2' (EL)	EPfP LBuc LCro LSRN LSto MGos NLar NTay WTHo
'Rüütel' (EL)	LRHS MAsh MGos NHaw SNig WTHo
'Saalomon' (LL)	NHaw
SABINE ('Bfccsab'^{PBR}) (LL)	CWGN
SACHA ('Evipo060') (EL)	CWCL EPfP LCro LRHS NLar NTay SPoG WTHo
'Sakala' (EL)	WSpi
§ 'Sakurahime' (EL)	LBom
SALLY ('Evipo077'^{PBR}) (Boulevard Series) (EL)	CWCL ELan EPfP LBom LCro LRHS MAsh NLar NTay SNig SPoG WTHo
SAMARITAN JO ('Evipo075') (Boulevard Series)	CWGN EPfP LBom LCro LRHS LSou MAsh NLar NTay SNig SPoG SWCr WTHo
SAPHYRA DOUBLE ROSE ('Cleminov 29'^{PBR}) (LL)	NHaw
SAPHYRA ESTRELLA ('Cleminov27'^{PBR}) new	WTHo
SAPHYRA INDIGO ('Cleminov 51'^{PBR}) (I)	NHaw WTHo
SAPHYRA NANCY ('Cleminov15') new	WTHo
SAPHYRA VIOLETTA ('Cleminov32') (I) new	WTHo
SARAH ELIZABETH ('Evipo098') (Boulevard Series)	CWGN ELan EPfP LCro LRHS NLar NTay SNig SPoG WTHo
§ 'Scented Clem'^{PBR} (Vt)	LCro LRHS NTay WTHo
SEA BREEZE ('Zo09063'^{PBR}) (Vt)	CWGN EGren LCro NTay WSpi WTHo
§ 'Semu' (LL)	CWGN NHaw NLar WTHo
serratifolia	CBcs NHaw SDix SPlb
- B&SWJ 8458 from Korea	WCru
'Sherriffii' (Ta)	NLar
'Shikoo' (EL)	EPfP LRHS LSRN NLar WTHo
SHIMMER ('Evipo028'^{PBR}) (LL)	EPfP LRHS MAsh NTay SWCr

sibirica from Kazakhstan	GGro
'Silver Moon' (EL)	NLar WSpi WTHo
simsii Small	see *C. pitcheri*
simsii Sweet	see *C. crispa*
'Sinii Dozhd' (I)	NHaw
§ 'Sir Edward Elgar' (A)	NLar
'Sir Eric Savill' (M)	CWGN WTHo
'Sir Trevor Lawrence' (T)	NHaw
'Skyfall' (LL)	CWGN EBee LRHS WTHo
smilacifolia	WPGP
'Snow Queen' (EL)	CDoC EPfP SNig SOrN SPoG SRms WTHo
'Snowbird' (A/d)	NTay SPoG
'Snowdrift'	see *C. armandii* 'Snowdrift'
So Many Red Flowers ('Zo06178'[PBR]) (EL)	NTay WTHo
socialis	NHaw
'Södertälje' (Vt)	CRHN NHaw WTHo
'Solidarność' (EL)	SNig
'Solina' (Vt)	NHaw
songarica	GKev NHaw SBrt
'Sonnette' (V)	CRHN CWGN NHaw
'Sophie' (V)	CWGN NHaw
Sorbet ('Zosor'[PBR]) (A)	NTay SWCr
§ 'Souvenir du Capitaine Thuilleaux' (EL)	SNig SPoG WTHo
'Sparkler' (EL)	NTay
'Special Occasion' (EL)	CWGN LCro MGos NLar WTHo
Spiky ('Zospi'[PBR]) (A/d)	LCro NTay SPoG SWCr
§ *spooneri*	LCro LRHS LSto MGos SDix WLov WSpi WTHo
Spotlight ('Zo08160'[PBR]) (EL)	LCro NTay WTHo
Spring Joy ('Zo12053'[PBR]) (M)	NTay SPoG
stans	CDoC GGro LRHS MGos WTHo
- B&SWJ 5073	WCru
- B&SWJ 6345	WCru
§ 'Star'[PBR] (M/d)	CDoC EPfP LCro NLar SPoG WTHo
'Star of India' (LL)	EGren EHeP ELan EPfP LCro LRHS MGos NTay SPoG SWCr WTHo
Star of Pakistan ('Zostapa') (LL)	CWGN SPoG
Star River ('Zostarri'[PBR]) (I)	ELan LCro NTay
'Starlight' (M)	CWCL SNig
'Stasik' (LL)	NHaw
'Stefan Franczak' (EL)	WTHo
Still Waters ('Zostiwa'[PBR]) (EL)	WTHo
'Strawberry Splash' (V)	NHaw
'Sue Reade' (V)	NHaw
Sugar Candy ('Evione'[PBR]) (EL)	NLar
Sugar Sweet	see *C.* 'Scented Clem'
Summer Snow	see *C.* 'Paul Farges'
'Sundance' (Ta)	NHaw
Sunny Sky ('Zosusk'[PBR]) (Vt)	EGren NTay SWCr WTHo
'Sunrise' (M/d)	CDoC CWGN EPfP LCro LRHS NLar NTay SWCr WTHo
'Sunset' (EL) ♀H6	EPfP LBom LRHS MGos NLar WTHo
Super Cute ('Zo09122') (Vt)	CWGN LCro NTay
Super Night ('Zo11112') (Vt)	CWGN LRHS NTay WTHo
Super Nova ('Zo09088'[PBR]) (Vt)	ELan IPot LCro NTay WTHo
'Swedish Bells' (I)	CWGN NHaw WTHo
'Sweet Scentsation' (F)	CDoC EGren LCro LRHS NTay WSpi WTHo
'Sweet Summer Love'[PBR] (F)	CDoC CWGN EPfP LCro LRHS MGos NTay WTHo
Sweetheart ('Witswe'[PBR]) (I)	ELan
'Sylvia Denny' (EL)	EPfP MAsh WSpi WTHo
'Sylviorna' (v)	NHaw
szuyuanensis CWJ 12455	WCru
'Tae'	see *C.* 'Toltae'
'Tage Lundell' (A)	LRHS WTHo
'Taiga'[PBR] (d)	CBcs CWGN EGren ELan LCro LRHS MGos NTay SNig SPoG WLov WTHo
'Tamakazura' (V)	CWGN NHaw
'Tango' (Vt)	CRHN NHaw
§ *tangutica*	CBcs CDoC CMac EAri ELan GKev LCro LRHS LShi LSRN MAsh MCtn MGos NBir NLar NTay SDix SEND SNig SPlb SPoG SRms StAn WFar WJur WTHo
tashiroi	SBrt
- 'Yellow Peril'	WCru
Tekla ('Evipo069'[PBR]) (LL)	LCro NTay SPoG WSpi WTHo
Temptation ('Zotemp'[PBR]) (EL)	IPot WTHo
'Tentel' (LL)	NHaw
§ *terniflora*	EPfP NHaw NTay WTHo
- B&SWJ 5751	WCru
- var. *mandshurica*	LCro NHaw NTay SDix StAn WSpi WTHo
- - dwarf	CWGN
- 'Early Snow' (F) **new**	LRHS
texensis	NHaw StAn
'The Bride' (EL)	CWGN LRHS LSRN SWCr WTHo
The Countess of Wessex ('Evipo073') (Boulevard Series) (EL)	CWCL EPfP LCro LRHS NTay SNig SPoG WTHo
'The First Lady' (EL)	LCro LRHS WTHo
'The President' (EL) ♀H6	CDoC CMac EHeP ELan EPfP LBom LCro LRHS LSRN MGos NLar NTay SNig SPoG SRms WCha WFar WSpi WTHo
'The Princess of Wales' (EL)	see *C.* 'Princess of Wales' (1875)
'The Princess of Wales' (T)	see *C.* 'Princess Diana'
'The Vagabond' (EL)	CWGN ELan EPfP LCro LRHS LSRN MAsh NLar SNig WSpi WTHo
thunbergii misapplied	see *C. terniflora*
'Thyrislund' (EL)	EBee SNig WTHo
tibetana	NHaw
- 'Black Tibet' (Ta)	CWGN NHaw
- subsp. *vernayi*	IArd
'Glasnevin Dusk' (Ta)	
- - 'Lorcan O'Brien' (Ta)	IArd
- - 'Marmalade' (Ta)	NHaw
§ - - var. *vernayi* 'Orange Peel' (Ta)	IPot LCro LRHS MGos WTHo
'Tie Dye' (LL)	CDoC CWGN ELan EPfP LCro NTay SPoG SRms SWCr WTHo
'Tim's Passion' (Vt)	CRHN
'Titipu' (V)	NHaw
'Toki' (EL)	CWGN WTHo
'Toltae'[PBR] (EL)	CDoC CWGN LRHS
Tranquilité ('Evipo111') (Boulevard Series)	CDoC EPfP LCro LRHS NTay SNig WTHo
'Tranquility' Fretwell	CRHN CWGN
trichotoma	NHaw
'Triinu' (Vt)	NHaw
Triomphe ('Evipo117') (Boulevard Series)	LSou
§ × *triternata*	CDoC CMac CRHN CWCL CWGN EAri ELan EPfP IPot LCro LRHS LSRN MAsh MGos NLar NTay SDix SPoG SRms SWCr WTHo
'Rubromarginata'	

Clerodendrum 195

Tsukiko ('Evipo110'PBR) (Garland Series)	CWGN EPfP LCro LRHS NTay WTHo	'Warszawska Nike' (EL) ♀H6	CRHN CWCL EGren ELan EPfP LBom LCro LRHS LSto MAsh MGos NTay SPoG WCha WTHo
tubulosa B&SWJ 8852	WCru	'Warwickshire Rose' (M)	CDoC CMac CRHN CWCL CWGN ELan EPfP LCro LRHS LSRN MAsh MGos NTay SDix SPoG SWCr WTHo
- 'Wyevale' (H)	CMac CRHN WTHo		
'Tuchka' (EL)	CWGN		
'Tudor' (EL)	SNig WTHo		
Tumaini ('Evigsy151')	EPfP LCro LRHS WTHo	'Wedding Day' (EL)	LCro LRHS LSRN NLar WTHo
'Tutti Frutti' (V)	NHaw	'Wee Willie Winkie' (M)	SRms
'Twilight' (EL)	MAsh WTHo	'Westerplatte' (EL)	CBcs CWGN EPfP IPot LCro LRHS MGos NHaw NTay SNig SPoG SWCr WSpi WTHo
Twinkle ('Zotwi') (I)	CWGN NTay WTHo		
'Uno Kivistik'PBR (LL)	NHaw		
§ *urophylla* 'Winter Beauty'	CDoC CWCL EGren ELan EPfP IArd IPot LCro LRHS LSRN MAsh NTay SDix SHor SPoG SWCr WSpi WTHo	White Arabella ('Zo14089')	CWGN LBom LCro LRHS WTHo
		§ 'White Columbine' (A) ♀H6	EGren ELan NTay SNig
urticifolia B&SWJ 8651	WCru	'White Heart' (Vt)	NHaw
'Utopia' (EL)	CWGN NHaw	§ 'White Moth' (A/d)	LSRN MAsh
'Valge Daam' (LL)	CWGN NHaw	White Pearl ('Zo08080') (EL)	NTay
'Valour' (Vt)	LCro LRHS NHaw NLar NTay WTHo		
'Van Gogh' (M)	CWGN LRHS WTHo	'White Prince Charles' (LL)	CWGN EBee NHaw NTay SNig
'Vanessa' (LL)	CRHN NHaw	'White Satin' (A)	LRHS SRms
'Vanso'	see *C.* 'Blue Light'	'White Swan' (A/d)	MAsh NTay
'Varenne' (EL)	WTHo	'White Wings' (A/d)	LRHS
§ × *vedrariensis*	WSpi	'Wildfire' (EL)	CWGN LCro SNig WTHo
§ *veitchiana*	NHaw	'Will Goodwin' (EL) ♀H6	EPfP SRms
'Venosa' (Vt)	LCro	'William Kennett' (EL)	SNig
'Venosa Violacea' (Vt) ♀H6	CBcs CDoC CRHN ELan LCro LRHS LSRN MAsh NHaw NTay SNig SPoG SRms WTHo	'Willy' (A)	EHeP ELan EPfP LCro LRHS LSto MAsh MGos NLar NTay SPoG SRms WTHo
'Vera' (M)	EPfP LRHS LSRN NTay WTHo	Wisley ('Evipo001'PBR) (Vt) ♀H6	LCro MGos NLar
'Veronica's Choice' (EL)	ELan LRHS MGos SNig WTHo		
Vicki ('Evipo114') (EL)	EPfP LCro LRHS NTay WTHo	Wonderful ('Zo09073'PBR) (Vt)	CWGN LCro LRHS NTay SPoG WTHo
'Vicky' (A/d)	LRHS		
Victor Hugo ('Evipo007'PBR) (LL)	NLar	'Xerxes' misapplied	see *C.* 'Elsa Späth'
		Xiu ('Evipo065'PBR) (Boulevard Series) (Fo)	EGren LRHS
'Victoria' (LL)	NHaw WTHo		
Viennetta ('Evipo006'PBR) (d)	CWGN EPfP LCro LRHS NTay SRms WTHo	'Yellow Queen' Holland	see *C. patens* 'Manshuu Ki'
		'Yellow Queen' Lundell/ Treasures (Boulevard Series)	see *C.* 'Moonlight'
'Ville de Lyon' (LL)	CBcs CDoC CRHN EGren EHeP ELan EPfP LCro LRHS LSRN LSto MAsh MGos NBir NTay NWbg SNig SPoG WTHo		
		Yuan ('Evipo082'PBR) (Boulevard Series) (EL)	LRHS WLov
vinacea	NHaw WPGP	§ 'Yukikomachi' (EL)	IPot WSpi
'Vince Denny' (Ta)	NHaw	Zara ('Evipo062'PBR) (Boulevard Series) (EL)	EPfP LCro LRHS NTay WTHo
Vino ('Poulvo'PBR) (EL)	IPot		
'Viola' (LL)	IPot LSRN NHaw SDix WTHo		
viorna	CWGN MCtn NHaw		

Clematopsis see *Clematis*

Cleome (Cleomaceae)

virginiana misapplied	see *C. vitalba*
§ *vitalba*	CHab EAri LWaG MCtn NHaw NTay WHer WSpi
viticella	CRHN EHeP MCtn NHaw NTay SMHy
- subsp. *campaniflora*	see *C. campaniflora*
§ - 'Flore Pleno' (Vt/d)	CRHN CWCL ELan IPot LCro LRHS LSRN NHaw NLar NTay SPoG WTHo
- 'Hanna' (Vt)	CRHN IPot LSRN NHaw WTHo
- 'Mary Rose'	see *C. viticella* 'Flore Pleno'
'Vivienne'	see *C.* 'Beth Currie'
Volcano ('Mazowsze') (LL)	NHaw SNig
'Voluceau' (Vt)	CWCL ELan EPfP LRHS SRms
Volunteer ('Evipo080'PBR) (Boulevard Series) (EL)	LCro LRHS NTay SNig WTHo
'Vostok' (LL)	NHaw
'Vyvyan Pennell' (EL)	CBcs CDoC CMac ELan LBom LCro LSRN MAsh NLar SNig SPoG WFar WSpi WTHo
Wada's Primrose	see *C. patens* 'Manshuu Ki'
'Walenburg' (Vt) ♀H6	CRHN CWGN NHaw NTay WTHo
'Warsaw' (Ta)	LBom NLar

angustifolia	MCtn
Clio Magenta ('Dcleo2') (Clio Series)	LSou
hassleriana	see *C. houtteana*
houtteana 'Cherry Queen'	MCtn
- 'Helen Campbell' ♀H2	CSpe LCro WSpi
- 'Pink Queen'	MCtn
- 'Rose Queen'	CSpe
- 'Violet Queen'	CBlu LCro MCtn
Señorita Rosalita ('Inncleosr'PBR)	CTsd MHol
spinosa 'Violet Queen'	CSpe
viridiflora	SIvy

Cleretum (Aizoaceae)

bellidiforme Harlequin Mix new	MNHC
- Magic Carpet Series new	EGren

Clerodendrum (Lamiaceae)

bungei	CBcs CDoC CMac CMHG EAri EBee EGrI ELan EPfP EUrb IArd LMaj LRHS LWaG MBlu MGos MMuc

Clerodendrum

	MNrw MPri NLar NSti SBig SDix SPoG WFar WJur WKif WTre
- 'Pink Diamond' (v)	CMac EPfP EWes MGos NCth SPoG
§ *chinense* var. *chinense* (d)	CHll
- 'Pleniflorum'	see *C. chinense* var. *chinense*
colebrookianum B&SWJ 6651	WCru
fragrans var. *pleniflorum*	see *C. chinense* var. *chinense*
laevifolium 'Prospero'	CDoC LCro
myricoides 'Ugandense'	see *Rotheca myricoides* 'Ugandense'
philippinum	see *C. chinense* var. *chinense*
× *speciosum*	CHll
aff. *subscaposum* WWJ 11735	WCru
trichotomum	CBcs CMCN CSpe EGrI EPfP EUrb IArd LRHS NLar WJur WMat
- var. *fargesii* ♀H5	CBcs CDoC CHll CMac CTsd ELan EPfP EUrb LRHS MBlu MBNS MMuc MNrw NLar SBrt SMad SPoG SVen WCot WFar
- - 'Carnival' (v) ♀H5	CDoC CMac EBee EPfP EWes LRHS NLar SMad SPoG WCot WFar
- 'Purple Blaze'	LRHS WFar
- 'Shiro'	LRHS WCru

Clethra (Clethraceae)

acuminata	NLar
alnifolia	CBcs CCVT CMCN EBee SRms WFar
- 'Anne Bidwell'	MBlu NLar
- 'Creel's Calico' (v)	NLar
- 'Fern Valley Pink'	CDoC CMac EPfP NLar SRms WFar
- 'Hokie Pink'	NLar
- 'Hummingbird' ♀H5	CDoC CEnd CMac CWnw ELan ELon EKin LSou MAsh MBlu NLar SPad SPoG WFar
- 'Paniculata'	CCVT EBee
- 'Pink Spires'	CBcs EGrI GKin LRHS NLar
- 'Rosea'	CMCN GKin
- 'Ruby Spice' ♀H5	CBcs CDoC CEnd CJun CMac EBee ELan ELon GKin LSou LSRN MAsh MBlu NQui SPad SPoG WFar
- 'September Beauty'	NLar
- 'Sixteen Candles'	GGGa GKin NLar
- Vanilla Spice ('Caleb')	NLar
- White Spire ('Darwish'PBR)	EGren
barbinervis ♀H5	CBcs CExl EBee GGGa MBlu NLar WJur WPGP
- B&SWJ 11562	WCru
- Great Star ('Minbarb')	LRHS WPGP
- 'White Star'	CJun CMac NLar
delavayi Franch.	CBcs CDoC CMCN EBee EGrI NLar WPGP
- SBEC 1513	CExl
fabri B&SWJ 11702	WCru
- FMWJ 13037	WCru
fargesii	CExl CMHG EBee MBlu NLar SChF WPGP
kaipoensis NJM 11.02	WPGP
- NJM 11.058	WPGP
- PAB 8571	LEdu
mexicana	CExl
monostachya	CExl EBee SHor WPGP
pachyphylla	WPGP
petelotii FMWJ 13041	WCru
pringlei	EBee NLar
tomentosa 'Cottondale'	CBcs CJun NLar

Cleyera (Pentaphylacaceae)

fortunei	see *C. japonica* 'Fortunei'
- 'Variegata'	see *C. japonica* 'Fortunei'
japonica	CBcs
§ - 'Fortunei' (v)	CMac EBee SSta WFar
- var. *japonica*	WPGP
- var. *wallichii*	EBee
pachyphylla	WPGP

Clianthus ❀ (Fabaceae)

maximus	CTsd
- 'Kaka King'	LRHS
§ *puniceus* ♀H3	CAbb CBcs CDoC CSpe CTsd EAri EUrb LCro MCtn SPlb SPoG WKif
§ - 'Albus' ♀H3	CBcs CTsd EAri EPfP LRHS SPoG
- 'Flamingo'	see *C. puniceus* 'Roseus'
- 'Red Admiral'	see *C. puniceus*
- 'Red Cardinal'	see *C. puniceus*
§ - 'Roseus' ♀H3	CBcs EPfP EUrb MPri SPoG
- 'White Heron'	see *C. puniceus* 'Albus'

Clinopodium (Lamiaceae)

§ *alpinum*	ECha EDAr GJos GKev SRms
calamintha	see *Calamintha nepeta*
chinense var. *parviflorum*	GGro
grandiflorum	see *Calamintha grandiflora*
§ *vulgare*	CAgr CGwi CHab EBee EHet GPSL LShi MAsh MHer MHol MNHC NAts NMir SEND SRms WOrg
- PAB 7562	LEdu

Clintonia (Liliaceae)

andrewsiana	GKev
borealis	GKev

Clitoria (Fabaceae)

ternatea	CSpe
- double-flowered (d)	MCtn

Clivia ❀ (Amaryllidaceae)

caulescens	WCot
- pink-flowered	WCot
caulescens × *miniata* 'Vico Yellow'	WCot
'Coral and Cream'	WCot
gardenii	LAma MCtn SEND WCot
'Judith Shields'	WCot
miniata ♀H1c	CAbb CBcs CBlu CDoC CTca CTsd LAma LCro SBig SEND SPlb WCot WFar
- 'Anshan Variegated' (v)	WCot
- 'Arturo's Yellow'	WCot
- 'Aurea'	CSpe
- Belgian hybrids	WCot
- 'Beverley's Delight'	WCot
- broad-leaved, variegated (v)	WCot
- var. *citrina* ♀H1c	CBlu CTca LAma LCro MCtn WCot
- - variegated (v)	WCot
- Daruma Group	WCot
- 'Framed Coral' (v)	WCot
- 'Green Throat'	WCot
- green-centred	WCot
- 'Hirao'	MCtn
- 'Light of Buddha' (v)	WCot
- 'Milk White'	WCot
- 'Mitsuhashi Multipetal'	WCot
- pastel shades	WCot
- 'Patrick'	WCot
I - 'Patsy' (v)	WCot
- 'Paul'	WCot
- 'Peach Clusters'	WCot
- 'Peggy'	WCot

- 'Percy' WCot
- 'Persephone' WCot
- 'Peter' WCot
- 'Philip' WCot
- 'Pink Perfection' WCot
- 'Pip' WCot
- 'Pru' WCot
- 'Steven's Striped' (v) WCot
- 'Striata' (v) WCot
- 'Terracotta Treasure' (v) WCot
- 'Vico Shima' WCot
- 'Wide Leaf Monk' WCot
nobilis ♀H1c SPlb WCot
'Pale Quail' WCot
'Peaches and Cream' WCot
'Pedro' (v) WCot
'Posy' WCot
'Richard' WCot
'Spring Song' WCot
'Sweet Undress' WCot

Clusia (Clusiaceae)
rosea LCro NHrt
- 'Green Magic' LCro
- 'Princess'^PBR LCro

Clytostoma (Bignoniaceae)
§ **calystegioides** CRHN

Cnicus (Asteraceae)
benedictus MCtn

Cnidium (Apiaceae)
silaifolium LEdu

Cobaea (Polemoniaceae)
pringlei ♀H3 CRHN EAri WPGP
scandens ♀H2 CDTJ CSpe EAri ELan EShb LCro LWaG MCtn
- f. **alba** CSpe EAri EShb LCro MCtn

cobnut see *Corylus avellana*; also AGM Fruit Section

Coccothrinax (Arecaceae)
borhidiana NPlm

Cocculus (Menispermaceae)
laurifolius WCot
§ **orbiculatus** B&SWJ 535 WCru
trilobus see *C. orbiculatus*

Cochlearia (Brassicaceae)
armoracia see *Armoracia rusticana*
danica CAgr
glastifolia CAgr
officinalis CAgr MCtn WHer

Cochliasanthus (Fabaceae)
caracalla MCtn

Cocos (Arecaceae)
plumosa see *Syagrus romanzoffiana*

Codiaeum ✿ (Euphorbiaceae)
variegatum var. **pictum** LCro
  'Banana' (v)
- - 'Excellent' (v) EGren LCro
- - 'Gold Star' (v) LCro
- - 'Gold Sun' (v) LCro
- - 'Mammi' (v) LCro
- - 'Mrs Iceton' (v) LCro NHrt

- - 'Petra' (v) LCro NHrt
- - 'Sunny Star' (v) LBom
- - 'Tamara' (v) LCro

Codonanthe (Gesneriaceae)
gracilis WDib
'Paula' WDib

Codonanthe × *Nematanthus* see × *Codonatanthus*

× *Codonatanthus* (Gesneriaceae)
'Golden Tambourine' WDib
'Sunset' WDib
'Tambourine' WDib

Codonopsis ✿ (Campanulaceae)
affinis HWJK 2151 WCru
benthamii GWJ 9352 WCru
canescens EDAr GKev
cardiophylla EBee GArf
clematidea CCBP CSpe CWal EAri EBee ECha EPPr GKev MCtn MNrw SPlb StAn WKif
convolvulacea misapplied see *Pseudocodon grey-wilsonii*
convolvulacea Kurz see *Pseudocodon convolvulaceus*
'Dangshen' see *C. pilosula*
forrestii misapplied see *Pseudocodon grey-wilsonii*
forrestii Diels see *Pseudocodon convolvulaceus* subsp. **forrestii** (Diels) D.Y. Hong
grey-wilsonii see *Pseudocodon grey-wilsonii*
inflata GWJ 9442 WCru
kawakamii RWJ 10007 WCru
lanceolata EPPr
nepalensis Grey-Wilson see *Pseudocodon grey-wilsonii*
ovata NBro
§ **pilosula** EPPr
- var. **modesta** GArf
- subsp. **tangshen** ambig. SBrt
§ - subsp. **tangshen** (Oliv.) EBee
   D.Y. Hong
silvestris see *C. pilosula*
subscaposa GArf
tangshen see *C. pilosula* subsp. **tangshen**
thalictrifolia NBro
   subsp. **mollis**

Coffea (Rubiaceae)
arabica LCro NHrt SPre WJur
- 'Nana' MCtn

coffee see *Coffea*

Coix (Poaceae)
lacryma-jobi MCtn

Colchicum ✿ (Colchicaceae)
× **agrippinum** ♀H4 ECha EPot GBin NBir SPel WAbe WCot WHoo
'Antares' ECha
§ **autumnale** CHab EPot GKev LAma NRya SEND WShi
- 'Alboplenum' ELan ERCP LAma NBir SPel XFar
- 'Album' ♀H5 ELan EPfP EPot GAbr LAma LCro NBir SPeP WShi XFar
- 'Karin Persson' GKev
- var. **minor** hort. see *C. autumnale*
§ - 'Nancy Lindsay' ♀H5 CBro EPot LAma
- 'Pannonicum' see *C. autumnale* 'Nancy Lindsay'
§ - 'Pleniflorum' (d) EGrI LAma NBir
- 'Roseum Plenum' see *C. autumnale* 'Pleniflorum'

Colchicum

bivonae	ECha	
- 'Apollo'	GKev	
- 'Mount Giona'	LAma	
bornmuelleri misapplied	see *C. speciosum* var. *bornmuelleri* hort.	
bornmuelleri Freyn	EGrl NBir	
× *byzantinum* ambig.	LAma	
× *byzantinum* Ker Gawl.	EGren	
- *album*	see *C.* × *byzantinum* 'Innocence'	
§ - 'Innocence' ♀H5	EPot LAma WCot	
cilicicum	EGrl NBir SPel	
- from Turkey	EPot	
- 'Purpureum' ♀H5	EPfP LAma	
confusum **new**	GKev	
corsicum	GKev	
cupanii	GKev	
davisii	GKev	
'Dick Trotter'	EPfP LAma	
'Disraeli'	GKev	
'Giant'	ECha EGren EPfP EPot LAma LCro XFar	
§ *giganteum*	LAma	
'Glory of Heemstede'	ECha EPot ERCP LAma	
'Hannibal'	GKev	
'Harlekijn'	EPot ERCP LAma	
hungaricum	GKev LAma	
illyricum	see *C. giganteum*	
kurdicum	EPot	
'Lilac Bedder'	LAma	
'Lilac Wonder'	ECha EGren EGrl ELan EPot LAma LCro NBir WCot WHoo	
macrophyllum	GKev LAma WMal	
§ *montanum* L.	EPot	
'Oktoberfest'	EPot	
'Pink Goblet' ♀H5	GKev	
'Poseidon'	GKev	
'Rosy Dawn' ♀H5	CBro ECha SPel	
soboliferum	WCot	
'Spartacus'	LAma	
speciosum	ELan EPot GAbr GBin LAma NBir	
- 'Album' ♀H5	ECha EGren EPot ERCP LAma LEdu NBir	
- 'Atrorubens' ♀H5	ECha EPot	
§ - var. *bornmuelleri* hort.	SPel	
- var. *illyricum* hort.	see *C. giganteum*	
× *tenorei* ♀H4	NBir	
triphyllum	GKev	
'Violet Queen'	GAbr LAma	
'Waterlily' (d) ♀H5	ECha EGren EGrl ELan EPfP EPot ERCP GKev LAma LCro NBir SPeP WCot XFar	

Coleonema (Rutaceae)

§ *pulchellum*	CCoa CSde CSpe NLit SVen
§ - 'Pink Fountain'	CAbb CCoa CSde CTsd ELan EPfP LRHS SEle SEND SPoG WCot
pulchrum misapplied	see *C. pulchellum*
§ 'Sunset Gold'	CBct CCht CCoa CDoC CSBt CSde ELan EPfP LRHS SEle SEND SPlb SPoG

Coleus (Lamiaceae)

§ *amboinicus*	CCBP CGHo CPic ELan LWaG MNHC WJek
§ *argentatus* ♀H1c	CBct CDTJ CSpe EAri EUrb LWaG SDix SEND SPel SRkn WKif WOld
- 'Hill House' (v) ♀H1c	CHll EAri EShb SNoN
- 'Limelight' (v) **new**	SNoN
- 'Silver Shield' ♀H1c	EShb MPie WFar
§ *calycinus*	SPlb
caninus misapplied	CBct

§ *caninus* (B. Heyne ex Roth) Vatke	SPoG WFar
Cuban oregano	ENfk
§ *hadiensis*	CPic EShb
- 'Penge' (v)	EAri EShb
I - 'Variegata' (v)	CoPl
madagascariensis 'Lothlorien' (v)	SNoN
- 'Lynne' (v)	WDib WKif WOld
§ - 'Variegated Mintleaf' (v) ♀H1c	EUrb MNHC SRms
§ *neochilus*	CCBP CSpe EAri EShb
paniculatus	LCro
prostratus	EShb
scutellarioides 'Angel of the North'	WDib
- 'Autumn Rainbow'	WDib
- 'Beauty of Lyon' (v)	WDib
- 'Brilliant' (v)	WDib
- 'Bronze Pagoda' (v)	WDib
- BURGUNDY WEDDING TRAIN ('Kakegawa Ce10') (v)	WDib
- CAMPFIRE ('Uf12823')	EAri MBros MPri
- 'Chamaeleon' (v)	WDib
- 'Chocolate Covered Cherry' (v)	LCro MPri
- 'Chocolate Mint' (v)	LCro
- 'City of Sunderland'	WDib
- 'Combat' (v) ♀H1c	WDib
- 'Coral Candy' (Premium Sun Series) **new**	LSou
- 'Crimson Ruffles' (v) ♀H1c	WDib
- 'Dazzler' (v)	WDib
- 'Durham Gala' (v) ♀H1c	WDib
- 'Firelight' (v)	WDib
- GIANT EXHIBITION PALISANDRA (Giant Exhibition Series)	CSpe
- HENNA ('Balcenna'PBR) (v) ♀H1c	MBros MPri
- 'Illumination' (v)	WDib
- 'Inky Fingers' (v)	WDib
- 'Juliet Quartermain' ♀H1c	WDib
- 'Jupiter'	WDib
- 'Kentish Fire' (v)	WDib
- 'Kiwi Fern' (Stained Glassworks Series) (v)	WDib
- (Kong Series) KONG RED ('Kakegawa Ce12') (v)	MPri
- - KONG ROSE ('Kakegawa Ce14') (v)	MPri
- 'Lemon Chiffon' (v)	WDib
- 'Lime Delight'	LCro
- 'Lord Falmouth' (v) ♀H1c	WDib
- 'Mrs Pilkington' (v)	WDib
- 'Muriel Pedley' (v)	WDib
- 'Paisley Shawl' (v)	WDib
- 'Peter Wonder' (v)	WDib
- 'Pineapple Beauty' (v) ♀H1c	WDib
- 'Pineapplette' (v) ♀H1c	WDib
- 'Pink Chaos' (v) ♀H1c	WDib
- RAINBOW CHOICE MIXED	MCtn
- 'Red Angel' (v)	WDib
- 'Red Velvet' (v)	WDib
- REDHEAD ('Uf0646'PBR) ♀H1c	EAri MPri
- 'Rose Blush' (v)	WDib
- 'Roy Pedley' (v) ♀H1c	WDib
- 'Royal Scot' (v) ♀H1c	WDib
- 'Saturn' (v)	MBros WDib
- 'The Flume' (v)	WDib

- 'Timotei' (v)	WDib
- TRUSTY RUSTY ('Uf06419') (v) ♀H1c	MPri
- 'Walter Turner' (v) ♀H1c	WDib
- 'Winsome' (v) ♀H1c	WDib
- 'Winter Sun' (v)	WDib
- 'Wisley Tapestry' (v) ♀H1c	WDib
- WIZARD SUNSET ('Pas2030') CSpe (Wizard Series) **new**	
§ *venteri*	EAri EShb

Colignonia (Nyctaginaceae)
ovalifolia B&SWJ 10644	WCru

Colletia (Rhamnaceae)
armata	see *C. hystrix*
cruciata	see *C. paradoxa*
§ *hystrix*	CMac CMCN ELon EPfP SArc SPlb
- RCB RA S3	WCot
- 'Rosea'	CMac MBlu SArc
§ *paradoxa*	EPfP EUrb NLar SArc SPlb SPoG WFar WPav
ulicina	SVen

Collinsia (Scrophulariaceae)
heterophylla	MCtn

Collinsonia (Lamiaceae)
canadensis	SBrt WPGP

Collomia ❀ (Polemoniaceae)
grandiflora	CSpe WCot

Colobanthus (Caryophyllaceae)
canaliculatus	EPot

Colocasia (Araceae)
affinis var. *jenningsii*	CAbb
antiquorum	see *C. esculenta*
§ *esculenta* ♀H1b	CAbb CDTJ CLil EAri ISha LAma LCro NTrD SAth SBig SDix SPlb XFar
- B&SWJ 6909	ESwi WCru
- 'Black Magic'	CHll CLil CTsd ISha LAma LCro LWaG NTro SBig XFar
- 'Black Sapphire Gecko'	ISha LRHS
- burgundy-stemmed	CAbb CBlu CDTJ EAri LAma
- 'Coco'	SMrm WFar
- 'Emerald'	CBct CBlu LAma
- 'Fontanesii'	CBct CDTJ EAri LRHS
- 'Illustris'	CAbb CDTJ CLil EAri NPlm SBig XFar
- 'Jack's Giant'	CDTJ EAri LRHS SBig
- 'Mammoth'	CDTJ EAri
- 'Metallica'	EUrb LRHS
- 'Mojito' (v)	EAri LCro XFar
- 'Pink China'	CAbb CBct EAri ISha LRHS SAth SBig SNoN SPlb
- (Royal Hawaiian Series) 'Aloha'	CAbb EGren XFar
- - 'Black Coral'	CAbb CBlu LRHS SDix SMrm SPad WFar XFar
- - 'Blue Hawaii'	CAbb CBlu CDTJ CTsd LRHS SAth SDix XFar
- - 'Diamond Head'	EGren LBar WFar XFar
- - 'Hawaiian Punch'	ISha LCro LRHS SMrm WFar XFar
- - 'Kona Coffee'	SBig
- - 'Maui Gold'	CBct LRHS SMrm XFar
- - 'White Lava' (v)	LAma LRHS XFar
- 'Ruffles'	EUrb
- 'Sangria'	LRHS
- 'Tea Cup'	ISha XFar
fallax	MCtn
gaoligongensis	CBct CDTJ EAri SBig SBrt SPlb WPGP
gigantea	CLil ISha LRHS
- 'Thailand Giant'	EAri
'Painted Black Gecko' **new**	LRHS
PHARAOH'S MASK ('Cophama')	XFar
'Red Eyed Gecko' **new**	LRHS
REDEMPTION ('Corede') **new**	XFar

Colquhounia (Lamiaceae)
coccinea	CHll CSde EAri EShb LEdu LRHS MBlu MPri NQui SIvy SPoG WFar
- Sch 2458	EBee EPfP WPGP
§ - var. *coccinea*	SMad
§ - var. *mollis* B&SWJ 7222	WCru
- var. *vestita* misapplied	see *C. coccinea* var. *coccinea*, *C. coccinea* var. *mollis*
- var. *vestita* ambig.	CBcs EBee EPfP LRHS SEND

Colutea (Fabaceae)
arborescens	CAgr CBcs EAri ELan ESwi MBlu MCtn MMuc SEND SPlb
§ *buhsei*	CSpe
× *media* 'Copper Beauty'	CBcs EBee ELan LRHS MMrt SEND
orientalis	EBee WJur
persica misapplied	see *C. buhsei*

Colvillea (Fabaceae)
racemosa	SPlb

Colysis (Polypodiaceae)
elliptica	WCot

Combretum (Combretaceae)
indicum	EAri NPlm

Commelina (Commelinaceae)
coelestis	see *C. tuberosa* Coelestis Group
dianthifolia	CAby EDAr EPPr GEdr LEdu LShi SBrt WFar
- 'Electric Blue'	ELan SVic
robusta	EShb WCot WFar
tuberosa	CWCL ESwi
- B&SWJ 10353	WCru
§ - Coelestis Group	CAby CCBP CTtf ECha EGrI LShi WKif
- - 'Alba'	EPPr LShi
- - 'Hopleys Variegated' (v)	WTra
- - 'Rhapsody'	WFar
- - 'Sleeping Beauty'	MCtn

Commersonia (Malvaceae)
hermanniifolia	WAbe

Comptonia (Myricaceae)
peregrina	WPGP

Conandron (Gesneriaceae)
ramondoides B&SWJ 8929	WCru

Coniogramme (Pteridaceae)
emeiensis	CBcs CCht ESwi LCro LEdu LRHS MHtn NAlc SBig SPlb WCot
gracilis	LEdu
intermedia	LEdu WPGP
- 'Yoroi Musha'	SPlb WPGP
japonica	LEdu WCot WPGP
- 'Flavomaculata'	CCht EBee LEdu SPlb WCot WFar WPGP

Conoclinium (Asteraceae)
§ **coelestinum** EBee EShb LRHS
  - 'Cori' LBar

Conopodium (Apiaceae)
majus SPhx WOrg WShi

Consolea (Cactaceae)
rubescens NHrt NPlm SBig

Consolida (Ranunculaceae)
§ **ajacis** CSpe
  - 'Fancy Purple Picotee' **new** LCro
  - Giant Imperial Series (d) SVic
  ambigua see *C. ajacis*
  regalis MCtn
  - 'Blue Cloud' CSpe MCtn

Convallaria ✿ (Asparagaceae)
japonica see *Ophiopogon jaburan*
keiskei EPPr WFar
I - 'Marginata' (v) WCot
  - 'Shiro-shima-fu' (v) GEdr NWbg WFar
  majalis ♀H7 Widely available
  - from Tatra Mountains EPPr
  - 'Albostriata' (v) CBct CTtf EBee EBlo EPPr ESwi
    GKev GMaP LEdu LRHS MHer
    MHol MNrw NBir NWbg WCAu
    WCot WFar WHer WHoo WPnP
  - 'Aurea' WFar
  - 'Berlin Giant' EPPr NRya WFar
  - 'Blush' WFar
  - 'Bordeaux' CBro CDor CExl ELan EMor EPPr
    ESwi MAvo NLar WCot WPnP
  - 'Bridal Choice' EBee EPot NLar WFar
  - 'Cream da Mint' (v) WFar
  - 'Dorien' EPPr WFar
  - 'Fernwood's Golden EWld GEdr WCot WFar
    Slippers'
  - 'Flore Pleno' (d) EMor GEdr GKev MNrw WFar
  - 'Géant de Fortin' ♀H7 CBro EPPr GEdr NBir NLar WCot
    WFar
  - 'Gérard Debureaux' see *C. majalis* 'Green Tapestry'
  - 'Golden Jubilee' CBct EPPr ESwi LEdu MNrw WCot
    WFar
  - 'Grandiflora' WFar
§ - 'Green Tapestry' (v) EPPr WCot WFar
  - 'Haldon Grange' (v) CMiW EPPr WFar
  - 'Hardwick Hall' (v) CBct CDor CExl CTtf EBee EBlo
    ECha ESwi GEdr GKev LBar LEdu
    LRHS MAvo NCth NSti NWbg
    SMHy SPeP WCot WFar
  - 'Heitmann' WFar
  - 'Hitscherberger WFar
    Riesenperle'
  - 'Hofheim' (v) CBct CMiW EBee ELon EMor ESwi
    LEdu SPeP WCot WFar
  - 'Landgraaf' (v) WFar
  - 'Lineata' (v) WFar
  - 'Marcel' (v) WFar
  - 'Mary Brooks' EBee EBlo LRHS WFar
  - 'Plant Pips' XFar
  - POLISH BEAUTY see *C. majalis* 'Polska Piękność'
§ - 'Polska Piękność' (v) WFar
  - 'Prolificans' CDor EBee EPPr ESwi GEdr
    GKev LAma LCro NBir NLar
    NSti NWbg WCot WFar WPnP
    XFar
  - var. **rosea** Widely available
  - 'Rosea Plena' (d) EGrI LAma SPeP

  - 'Silberconfolis' (v) WCot WFar
  - 'Variegata' (v) LAma WFar
  - 'Vic Pawlowski's Gold' (v) CBct CBro CDor CExl CMac
    CMiW EPPr GEdr MNrw WFar
    WPGP
  - 'Vierländer Glockenspiel' WFar
  - 'Viktor' WFar
* - 'Viridistriatus' WFar
  transcaucasica GKev

Convolvulus (Convolvulaceae)
althaeoides CFis
§ - subsp. **tenuissimus** EWes WCot
§ **boissieri** WAbe
  cantabrica SPhx
  cneorum ♀H4 Widely available
  dorycnium SPhx
  elegantissimus see *C. althaeoides*
    subsp. *tenuissimus*
  mauritanicus see *C. sabatius*
  nitidus see *C. boissieri*
§ **sabatius** ♀H3 CCht EBee ELan ELon EPfP EPot
    EShb LShi SDix SEND SMrm SPlb
    SPoG SVen WKif
  tricolor 'Blue Ensign' ♀H3 CSpe LCro
  - 'Royal Ensign' MCtn

× *Cooperanthes* see *Zephyranthes*

Cooperia see *Zephyranthes*

Copernicia (Arecaceae)
alba NPlm
hospita NPlm

Copiapoa ✿ (Cactaceae)
humilis SPlb
hypogaea ♀H2 **new** SPlb
- subsp. **laui** SPlb
marginata SPlb

Coprosma (Rubiaceae)
acerosa 'Hawera' CBcs SEle
- 'Red Rocks' SEle
baueri misapplied see *C. repens*
'Beatson's Gold' (f/v) CBcs ELan IDun SEND
'Black Cloud' ELon SEND
brunnea SEle
'Chocolate Soldier' (m) SAth
'City Knights' (v) MHtn
'Clearwater Gold' SIvy
'Dark Spire' SEle
'Evening Glow'PBR (f/v) CCht CDTJ CSBt MBlu MGos MHtn
  Midl SEle WNPC
'Fire Burst'PBR (f/v) CBcs Midl WNPC
'Inferno'PBR (f/v) CAbb CBcs CCht CDoC CMHG
  ELan LCro Midl
× **kirkii** CBcs
- 'Variegata' (f/v) CBcs CMHG ELan SEND
'Lemon and Lime'PBR (f/v) CSBt LCro LRHS SAth SPoG SVen
  WFar
macrocarpa (f) CCoa
petriei GArf
propinqua SEle
'Rainbow Surprise'PBR (f/v) CDoC CSBt LRHS MGos WFar
  WNPC
§ **repens** EShb SPlb SVen
- 'County Park Plum' (v) SVen
- ECLIPSE ('Aldawn') (v) CSBt LSou
- 'Marble Queen' (m/v) EShb
- 'Midnight Martini' (v) WFar WNPC

Coreopsis 201

- 'Pacific Dawn'	CCht CSBt LBom LCro LRHS Midl SAdn SEle WCot WNPC		- 'Mambo'	LCro NHrt
- Pacific Night ('Hutpac'PBR) (m)	CDoC CSBt EHeP LBom LRHS MBNS MGos Midl WFar WNPC		'Green Goddess'	WCha
- Pacific Sunset ('Jwncopps') (m/v)	CDoC CMHG CSBt ELan LBom LCro LRHS LSRN SEle		§ *indivisa*	CDTJ CTsd ESwi LRHS LWaG SArc SAth SBig SFol WCha
- 'Painter's Palette' (m)	SVen		'Jive'PBR (Dancing Series) (v)	CCht CSBt EBee EUrb LBuc LCro LRHS SEND
- 'Picturata' (m/v)	SEND		§ Lime Fountain ('Corjur08') **new**	EUrb
- 'Pina Colada'PBR (v)	CAbb CCht CDoC CSBt LRHS LSou SEle SPoG WFar		Lime Passion ('Alcorlipa') (v)	CDoC CMac EGren EUrb MPri WFar
- 'Tequila Sunrise'	CAbb CBcs CCht CDoC CSBt LCro LRHS LSou LSRN SAdn		Little Red Star ('Filiresta')	MHtn WFar
rigida (f)	WJur		*obtecta* 'Albatross'PBR	EUrb LCro LRHS
robusta	CTsd		'Pacific Sunset'PBR	CKit WFar
'Scarlet O'Hara'	CCht LRHS SPoG		'Pink Champagne' (v)	EGren EUrb LRHS
'Walter Brockie'	CCoa CSde		Pink Passion ('Seipin'PBR)	CKit CMac CTsd ELan LBom LBuc LCro NPlm SPoG WCha WFar

Coptis (Ranunculaceae)

japonica var. *dissecta*	GEdr
- var. *major*	GEdr WFar
quinquefolia	WAbe

Corallospartium see *Carmichaelia*

Cordyline ❀ (Asparagaceae)

australis ♀H3	Widely available
- 'Albertii' (v) ♀H3	SArc
- 'Atlantic Green'	CBrac LRHS MPri
- 'Atropurpurea'	CBrac
- 'Black Night'	LRHS
- Charlie Boy ('Ric01'PBR) (v)	CDoC EGren ELon EUrb LBom LCro LRHS MBros MPri WFar
- 'Coral'	LRHS NPlm
- 'Karo Kiri'	SArc
- Paso Doble'PBR (Dancing Series)	EUrb NPlm
- 'Peko'PBR	CDoC EGren EPfP LRHS
- Pink Star ('Tus019'PBR) (v)	LCro LRHS
- Purpurea Group	CDoC CDTJ ELan MCtn MGos SEND SPlb WFar
- 'Red Sensation'	CBcs
- 'Salsa'PBR (Dancing Series)	CWnw EUrb MHtn WFar
- 'Sparkler' (v)	EPfP SEND
- 'Torbay Dazzler' (v) ♀H3	CAbb CBcs CBrac CCht CDoC CEnd CKit CSBt CTsd CWnw EGren ELan EPfP EUrb LBom LCro LRHS LSRN MAsh MGos MPri NPlm SAth SBig SPoG WCha WFar
- 'Torbay Sunset'	EGren WFar
- 'Variegata' (v)	CDoC
banksii	ESwi EUrb SPlb
- Electric Flash ('Sprilecflash'PBR)	CWnw LBom LRHS WCha
- Electric Pink ('Sprilecpink')	EGren ELan LRHS
- Electric Star ('Sprilecstar'PBR)	CWnw LBom LRHS
'Can Can'PBR (Dancing Series) (v)	CDoC EUrb LBuc NPlm WFar WLov
'Cha Cha'PBR (Dancing Series) (v)	CCht CDoC EBee LRHS SEND WCot
'Cherry Sensation' (v)	LRHS NPlm WFar
§ *congesta*	SPlb
'Dark Star'	CDTJ CMac
Festival Burgundy	see *C.* 'Red Fountain'
Festival Grass	see *C.* 'Red Fountain'
Festival Lime	see *C.* Lime Fountain
fruticosa	NHrt
- 'Chocolate Queen' (v) **new**	SPre
- 'Conga' (v)	LCro
- 'Kiwi'	LCro LRHS

'Pink Stripe' (v)	EGren LSRN
'Polka'	WFar
pumilio	ESwi
'Purple Tower' ♀H3	NPlm
§ 'Red Fountain'PBR	EGren EUrb WLov
'Red Heart'	WFar
'Red Star'	CAbb CBcs CDoC CEnd CKit CSBt CTsd EGren EHeP EPfP LCro LRHS NPer NPlm SAth SBig SEND SPoG WCha WFar
Renegade	see *C.* 'Tana'
'Rumba'	NHrt
'Southern Splendour' (v)	CBcs CDoC EGren ELan LCro LRHS NPlm SPoG WFar
'Sundance' ♀H3	MGos NPer NPlm SPoG SRms WFar
'Sunrise' (v)	LRHS
§ 'Tana'PBR **new**	LBom
'Tango'	LCro
'Torbay Red' ♀H3	CBrac EPfP LRHS LSRN MAsh MPri SPoG
'Verde'PBR **new**	LRHS

Coreopsis (Asteraceae)

'Astolat'	CFis MMrt
auriculata Cutting Gold	see *C.* 'Schnittgold'
- 'Elfin Gold'	ELan LRHS
- 'Zamphir'	CDor MWlw
'Baby Gold'	see *C. lanceolata* 'Sonnenkind' (unblotched)
Baby Sun	see *C.* 'Sonnenkind' (red-blotched)
Bloomsation Chameleon ('Uribl02'PBR)	LCro
Bloomsation Dragon ('Uribl01')	LCro
'Buttermilk'PBR	CDor MPro NLar
'Calypso' (v)	LRHS SPoG
'Center Stage'	CWnw ELan
'Cherry Pie'PBR (Pie Series)	EUrb
'Citrine'PBR (Hardy Jewel Series)	CWGN
Corey Yellow ('Core Yel'PBR)	LRHS
'Cosmic Evolution' (Big Bang Series)	ELan SPoG
'Cosmic Eye' (Big Bang Series)	ELan SPoG WFar
'Cranberry Ice'	LRHS
'Daybreak' (Li'l Bang Series)	LCro LRHS SHar
'Desert Coral'PBR (Hardy Jewel Series)	MPro
'Enchanted Eve'PBR (Li'l Bang Series)	LRHS WFar
'Fool's Gold'	EBee LSto
'Full Moon'PBR (Big Bang Series)	ELan NLar SPoG WFar
'Galaxy' (Big Bang Series)	ELan WFar

Coreopsis

gigantea — SPlb
'Golden Gain' — see *C.* 'Schnittgold', *C. verticillata* 'Golden Gain'

grandiflora — GJos LRHS
- 'Bernwode' (v) — CMac
- CASTELLO POMPON YELLOW ('Csgz0005'^{PBR}) — LBuc
- COREY SINGLE GOLD ('Csgz0002'^{PBR}) — LRHS NBir
- 'Domino' — LRHS
- 'Double the Sun' — EGren LBar LCro LRHS MHol
- 'Early Sunrise' ♀H5 — EGren EPfP LBuc LCro LRHS MPri NBir NPer SPoG WFar WPnP
- FLYING SAUCERS ('Walcoreop'^{PBR}) — LRHS SPoG
- 'Heliot' — SMrm
- 'Illico' — LRHS
- 'Mayfield Giant' — EBee EHeP ELan MAsh MNHC SRms
- 'Presto' (d) — EGren ELan LRHS NLar WFar
- 'Rising Sun' — ELan EPfP LRHS
- 'Santa Fe' — EBee EPfP LRHS
- (Solar Series) SOLAR FANCY ('Mvnc1904') **new** — XFar
- - SOLAR JEWEL ('Mvnc1902') **new** — LBar WTor XFar
- - SOLAR MELLOW ('Mvnc1823') **new** — XFar
- - SOLAR MOON ('Mvnc1906') **new** — XFar
- 'Sunburst' — EHeP ELan
- 'Sunfire' — EHeP LRHS WFar
- SUNKISS ('M8867p'^{PBR}) — EGren LBar LBuc LCro LRHS MPri WFar
- 'Sunray' — CBcs LRHS NGdn SHar SOrN SPlb SPoG SRms
'Ladybird' — EGren EUrb LCro LRHS MAvo MPro SRot WFar

lanceolata — CMac CWal EPot ESgl
- 'Goldfink' — SRms
§ - 'Sonnenkind' (unblotched) — EPfP GMaP
- 'Walter' — SPoG WFar
'Lightning Bug' — MMrt NCth
'Limerock Ruby'^{PBR} — LCro MHol SPoG WFar

major — WFar
MANGO PUNCH ('Rp5') — CAby LCro LRHS
(Punch Series)

maximiliani — see *Helianthus maximiliani*
'Mercury Rising'^{PBR} — EPfP LRHS SHar
(Big Bang Series)

palmata — SPhx
'Pink Lady'^{PBR} — LRHS
pubescens 'Sunshine Superman' — ELan LRHS
'Red Elf'^{PBR} (Li'l Bang Series) — LCro
'Red Satin' (Permathread Series) — LRHS WTor
'Redshift' — LCro NLar SPoG

rosea — MCtn
- 'American Dream' — ELan EPfP GKev GMaP GPSL LRHS MArl MAsh MHol MPro NBir NBro NGdn NLar SPlb SRms WCav WFar
- 'Heaven's Gate'^{PBR} — EGrI MHol WFar
- 'Sweet Dreams' — NLar SBig
'Route 66'^{PBR} — NCth WFar
'Ruby Frost' (Hardy Jewel Series) — CBcs NLar SPoG
'Rum Punch'^{PBR} (Punch Series) — CAby LRHS

§ 'Schnittgold' — SHar
'Sienna Sunset' — ELan

(Solanna Series) — EGren EPfP LRHS SPoG
SOLANNA GOLDEN SPHERE ('Dcoreo16'^{PBR})
- SOLANNA SUNSET BURST ('Dcorsosb') — MPro
'Solar Dance' — CWGN LBar NLar SMad
'Solena Double Gold' (Solena Series) (d) — LRHS
§ 'Sonnenkind' (red-blotched) — LRHS
'Star Cluster' (Big Bang Series) — CWGN ELan EPfP LEdu SMad SPoG WFar
'Starbright'^{PBR} (Li'l Bang Series) — LRHS MMrt
'Starlight' (Li'l Bang Series) — EPfP WFar
'Starstruck'^{PBR} (Li'l Bang Series) — LCro
'Sterntaler' — EBlo ELon EMor GJos LRHS LSou MCtn
SUN CHILD — see *C.* 'Sonnenkind' (red-blotched)
SUNNY DAY ('Balcorsunay') — WFar
(Sunstar Series) — LCro
SUNSTAR ORANGE ('Tncorso'^{PBR})
- SUNSTAR ROSE ('Tncorsr'^{PBR}) — EGren LCro MPro
'Sweet Marmalade'^{PBR} — EPfP LRHS

tinctoria — MEar MNHC SRms
- 'Amulet' — CSpe
- 'Mahogany Midget' — LRHS MNHC
- 'Red River Valley' **new** — CSpe

tripteris — CAby EAri ELan EMor EPPr MHol SPhx
- 'Red November' — MNrw
TWINKLEBELLS PURPLE ('Uritw01'^{PBR}) — LRHS
(Twinklebells Series)
(UpTick Series) UPTICK CREAM & RED ('Balupteamed'^{PBR}) — MPro MSCN WFar
- UPTICK CREAM ('Balupteam'^{PBR}) — WFar
- UPTICK GOLD AND BRONZE ('Baluptgonz'^{PBR}) — EGren LBar LRHS LSou WFar
- UPTICK RED ('Baluptred'^{PBR}) — EGren LBar LSou MPro
- UPTICK YELLOW AND RED ('Baluptowed'^{PBR}) ♀H3 — LBar WFar

verticillata — CMac EGrI MBrN NLar NPer SRms WCAu
- 'Bengal Tiger'^{PBR} — CAby EUrb MPro SBig SMad
- CRÈME BRÛLÉE ('Crembru'^{PBR}) — ELan NLar
§ - 'Golden Gain' — EPfP LRHS MArl MAsh NGdn WFar
- 'Golden Shower' — see *C. verticillata* 'Grandiflora'
§ - 'Grandiflora' ♀H5 — CBcs ECha ELan ELon EPfP GMaP LRHS LSto MArl MBel MHer MPie NGdn SHar SOrN WCAu WFar
- 'Moonbeam' — Widely available
- 'Old Timer' — SDix
- 'Red Hot Vanilla' — EPfP LRHS
- 'Ruby Red' — LRHS
- (Sizzle and Spice Series) — EPfP
'Crazy Cayenne'
- - 'Curry Up' — EPfP LBuc WFar
- - 'Hot Paprika' — EPfP
- - 'Zesty Zinger' — LRHS
- 'Tweety'^{PBR} — WFar
- 'Zagreb' ♀H5 — CAby CBWd CDor EBee ELan ELon EPfP EWhm GMaP LRHS MArl MAvo MBel MHol MNrw MPro NCth NLar SBeP SMrm SOrN SPoG WCAu WCav WFar

Corethrodendron (Fabaceae)
§ **multijugum**   MBlu

coriander see *Coriandrum sativum*

Coriandrum (Apiaceae)
'Lemon Coriander'   IDun
sativum   CGHo EGren EHet ENfk EWhm
                               LCro MCtn MEar MHer MHoo
                               MNHC MPri SPoG SRms WKit
- 'Calypso'^{PBR} ♀^{H2}   EKin MCtn WKit
- 'Confetti' ♀^{H5}   EKin LCro MCtn MHoo MNHC
- 'Cruiser'^{PBR} ♀^{H2}   EDel MCtn MNHC WKit
- 'Leisure'   LCro MCtn SVic

Coriaria (Coriariaceae)
from Cally Gardens   ESwi
arborea   ESwi
intermedia B&SWJ 19   ESwi
japonica   CTsd ESwi NLar SVen WCru
- subsp. **intermedia**   WCru
  B&SWJ 3877
kingiana   WCru
§ **microphylla** B&SWJ 14702 WCru
myrtifolia   WCru
- B&SWJ 14003   WCru
nepalensis   NLar
pteridoides   WCru
ruscifolia HCM 98178   WCru
terminalis   EWld WCru
  var. *xanthocarpa*
- - HWJK 2112c   WCru
thymifolia   see *C. microphylla*

Cornopteris see *Athyrium*

Cornus ✿ (Cornaceae)
alba L.   CBTr CCVT CLnd EBar GArf LMaj
                               SAth SEWo SRms WHnu WMou
                               WRjT
- 'Argenteovariegata'   see *C. alba* 'Variegata'
- 'Aurea' ♀^{H7}   CBcs CMac CMCN CSBt EBee
                               EGren EHeP ELan ELon EPfP LCro
                               LRHS LSto MAsh MBlu MGos NCth
                               NLar SDix SPoG WFar
- BATON ROUGE ('Minbat'^{PBR}) CDoC CWnw EBee ELan ELon EPfP
                               LBom LRHS LSRN MAsh SPoG
                               WCot WFar WLov
- 'Elegantissima' (v)   Widely available
- 'Gouchaultii' (v)   CMac EBee GKin LRHS LSto MGos
                               NLar SRms WFar
- 'Hessei' misapplied   see *C. sanguinea* 'Compressa'
- IVORY HALO   EGren EPfP LSRN MAsh NLar WCha
  ('Bailhalo'^{PBR}) ♀^{H7} WLov
- 'Kesselringii'   Widely available
- MIRACLE ('Verpaalen2'^{PBR}) EBee EGren LCro LRHS NCth NLar
  (v)   WFar
- NEON BURST   ELon LRHS NCth
  ('Byboughen'^{PBR})
- RED GNOME ('Regnzam')   ELon NLar
- 'Siberian Pearls'   CBcs EGren ELan GKin LRHS MBlu
                               NLar SPoG
§ - 'Sibirica'   Widely available
- 'Sibirica Variegata' (v) ♀^{H7} CBcs CMac EBee EHeP ELon EPfP
                               GKin LRHS LSRN MAsh MBlu MGos
- 'Spaethii' (v)   CBcs CBrac CMac CSBt EBee EGren
                               EHeP ELan ELon EPfP GKin LSto
                               MGos MMuc NLar SPlb SRms SSta
                               WFar
§ - 'Variegata' (v)   EGren WFar

- 'Westonbirt'   see *C. alba* 'Sibirica'
alternifolia   CCVT EGrI LMaj SSta
§ - 'Argentea' (v) ♀^{H6}   Widely available
- 'Brunette'   MBlu
- GOLDEN SHADOWS   CWGN LRHS MGos NCth NLar
  ('Wstackman'^{PBR}) (v) SHor WMat
- 'Goldfinch' (v)   CJun MBlu
- 'Illusion' (v)   CJun
- 'Moonlight' (v)   CJun
- PINKY SPOT ('Minpinky')   LRHS NLar
- 'Silver Giant' (v)   CJun NLar WSpi
- 'Variegata'   see *C. alternifolia* 'Argentea'
amomum   NLar
- 'Blue Cloud'   EBee EPfP MBlu
- 'Lady Jane'   NLar
'Ascona'   CBcs CEnd CJun EPfP LMil LRHS
'Blooming Merry Tetra'   CJun LRHS NCth NLar
'Blooming Pink Tetra'   CJun LRHS NCth NLar
'Blooming White Tetra'   CJun LRHS NCth NLar
canadensis   CAgr CBcs CBct CDoC CEnd CMac
                               CTsd EBee EGren EHeP ELan EPfP
                               GEdr GElm GKev GMaP LBuc LCro
                               LRHS MBel MBlu MCtn MGos MPnt
                               MPri MSwo NLar SHor SPoG WFar
candidissima Marshall   see *C. foemina* Mill.
capitata   CBcs CCVT CExl CJun CMac CTsd
                               EBee EGrI EPfP ESwi EUrb LRHS
                               SEND SPoG WCru WJur WKor
                               WPGP
- subsp. **emeiensis**   CJun
- 'Kilmacurragh Rose'   CJun IArd NLar
- 'Celestial Shadow'   see *C. × rutgersensis* 'Michael
                               Steinhardt'
chinensis   SSta
'Cobhay Titan'   CJun
§ **controversa**   CAco CBcs CCVT CMCN EBar EGrI
                               IPap LCro LMaj LRHS MBlu MMuc
                               NLar SEND SEWo SGol SHor SSta
                               WCha
I - 'Aurea'   MAsh
- 'Candlelight'   MBlu
- 'Frans Type' (v)   CJun
- 'Gosia'^{PBR} (v)   LRHS
- 'Green Carpet'   NLar
- 'Laska'   CJun MBlu NLar
- 'Lucia'   CJun NLar
I - 'Marginata Nord'   NLar
- 'Pagoda'   CJun LCro MBlu
- 'Variegata' (v) ♀^{H5}   Widely available
'Dorothy'   CJun
'Eddie's White Wonder' ♀^{H5} CDoC CEnd CJun EBar EBee EGrI
                               ELan EPfP LCro LMaj LMil LRHS
                               LSRN MAsh MBlu MGos MPri NCth
                               NLar NPip SGol SPoG WCot WMat
                               WPGP WSpi
elliptica   WPGP
- EMPRESS OF CHINA ('Elsbry') CBcs ELan EPfP LRHS LSRN MMrt
                               NCth NLar SMad
- 'First Choice'   CJun
- 'Full Moon'   CJun
× **elwinortonii** (Jersey   NCth NLar
  Star Series) STARLIGHT
  ('Kn4 43'^{PBR})
- - VENUS ('Kn30 8'^{PBR}) ♀^{H5} CWGN EBee ELan LCro LRHS MAsh
                               MBlu SEWo WPGP
excelsa   EBee MBlu SChF WJur
- F&M 57   WPGP
florida   CBcs CLnd EGren EGrI IPap LCro
                               LRHS MMuc NPip SSta WCha WHtc
                               WJur WMat
- 'Alba Plena' (d)   CMac

Cornus

- 'Autumn Gold'	SSta
- CHEROKEE BRAVE ('Comco No 1')	LMil LRHS MAsh SPoG
- 'Cherokee Chief'	CBcs CBTr CEnd CJun EBee EGrI LCro LMaj LRHS LSRN NLar WSpi
- 'Cherokee Daybreak'	see *C. florida* 'Daybreak'
- 'Cherokee Princess'	CBTr LMil LRHS MAsh NLar NPip WMat
- 'Cherokee Sunset'	see *C. florida* 'Sunset'
- 'Cloud Nine'	EGrI ERom GKin NLar WMat
§ - 'Daybreak' (v)	CBcs LRHS MAsh NPip SGol SPoG WMat
- 'Granary Gold'	SSta
- 'Junior Miss'	CEnd
- 'Rainbow' (v)	CBcs LMil LRHS MAsh NPip SGol SPoG WMat
- f. *rubra*	CBcs CMac EGrI GKin LCro LMaj LRHS NPip SPoG WCha WMat
- - 'Red Giant'	CBcs
- - 'Spring Song'	CMac EGrI
- 'Spring Day'	CMac
- 'Stoke's Pink'	CEnd
§ - 'Sunset' (v)	CBTr CEnd EGrI LCro LMaj LMil MAsh NPip WMat
- 'Sweetwater'	EGrI NLar
- subsp. ***urbiniana***	SChF WPGP
- 'Variegata' (v)	GKin
- 'White Cloud'	CBTr ERom NPip WMat
§ ***foemina*** Mill.	SBrt
'Gloria Birkett' ♀H5	CJun LMil NLar
hessei misapplied	see *C. sanguinea* 'Compressa'
hongkongensis	CBcs ESwi NLar
- HWJ 1033	EPfP
- aff. subsp. ***gigantea*** FMWJ 13379	WCru
'Jerry Mundy'	CMac
'Kelsey Dwarf'	see *C. sericea* 'Kelseyi'
'Kenwyn Clapp'	CJun
kousa	CBcs CCVT CDoC CMac CMCN CWnw EGrI GKev GKin LMaj NLar SAth SHor SOrN SPlb WFar WJur WKor
- B&SWJ 12610 from Korea	WCru
- B&SWJ 14620 from Japan	WCru
- 'Akabana'	CJun
- 'Akatsuki' (v)	MAsh
- 'All Summer'	CJun
- 'Angyo Issai'	NLar
- 'Autumn Rose'	CJun
- 'Beni-fuji' ♀H6	MBlu NCth NLar SMad
- 'Big Apple'	CJun EPfP LMil LRHS LSRN NLar
- 'Blue Shadow'	CJun MBlu NLar
- 'Blue Spark'	NLar
- 'Bonfire' (v)	CDoC NLar
- 'Bultinck's Giant'	CDoC CJun MBlu MPkF NLar
- 'Cappuccino' ♀H6	CBTr CDoC CJun EPfP LRHS MAsh NCth NLar SHor WPGP
- 'Cherokee'	CJun NLar
- 'China Dawn' (v)	CJun NLar
- var. ***chinensis***	Widely available
- - 'Barmstedt'	SAko
- - 'Bodnant Form'	CEnd CJun EGrI NLar
- - 'China Girl' ♀H5	Widely available
- - 'Claudia'	IArd NLar
- - CROWN JEWEL	see *C. kousa* var. *chinensis* 'Madison'
- - 'Great Star'	CWnw EPfP LSRN MAsh
- - 'Greta's Gold' (v)	CJun
- - 'Ikone'	SAko SHor
- - 'Kea'	NLar
§ - - 'Madison'	NLar
- - 'PVG'	CJun LMaj
- - 'Schmetterling'	CBTr CJun EPfP MBlu MPkF NLar WMat
- - 'Snowflake'	CJun NCth NLar
- - 'Summer Stars'	CJun
- - 'White Dusted' (v)	MBlu
- - 'White Fountain'	CBTr CJun EPfP LRHS LSRN MGos NPip WMat
- - 'Wieting's Select'	CJun MBlu MPkF NLar SAko
- - 'Wisley Queen' ♀H6	CJun LMil NLar SChF SPoG WPGP
- 'Claudine'	CJun
- 'Copacabana'	CJun LRHS MBlu
- 'Doubloon'	CJun
- 'Dwarf Pink'	CJun MAsh NCth NLar
- 'Ed Mezitt'	CDoC CJun MAsh NLar
- 'Elizabeth Lustgarten'	CJun MBlu
- 'Eurostar'	MBlu
- 'Fanfare'	CJun
- 'Fernie's Favourite'	CJun
- FLOWER TOWER ('Zuilb1')	CWnw EBee SMad
- GALILEAN ('Galzam')	CDoC LMil NLar
- 'Gay Head'	CJun
- giant-flowered	MPkF
I - 'Girard's Nana'	CJun MPkF NLar
- 'Gold Cup' (v)	CJun
- 'Gold Star' (v)	CBcs CEnd CJun EBee EPfP LMil LRHS MBlu NLar SPoG
- 'Greensleeves'	CJun EPfP LMil
- HEART THROB ('Schmred')	MPkF NLar
- 'Helena' PBR	SMad
- 'Highland'	CJun
- 'John Slocock' ♀H6	CJun IArd NLar
- 'Kim'	MAsh NLar
- 'Koree'	NLar
- 'Kreuzdame'	CJun LRHS MBlu
- 'Laura'	CWGN MAsh MBlu NLar
- 'Lizzie P'	NLar
- 'LT Délicatesse'	NLar
- 'Lustgarten Weeping'	CJun
- 'Madame Butterfly'	CJun MBlu NCth NLar SPoG
- 'Marwood Dawn'	CMHG MBlu WPGP
- 'Marwood Twilight'	CMHG EPfP MBlu SChF
- 'Milky Way'	CBTr CCVT CDoC CJun CLnd CMCN EBar EBee EPfP ERom IPap LMil LRHS LSRN MAsh MBlu MGos MPkF NCth NLar SGol SHor WCha WMat WSpi
- 'Milky Way Select'	CBcs CJun EPfP LRHS
- 'Miss Petty'	CJun
- 'Miss Satomi' ♀H6	CBcs CDoC CJun CNWT CWGN CWnw EBee EGrI ELan EPfP GKin IArd LCro LMil LRHS LSRN MAsh MBlu NCth NLar SChF SEWO SGol SHor SMad SPoG WPGP
- 'Moonbeam'	CDoC CJun NLar SGol
- 'Mount Fuji'	MBlu NLar
- 'National'	CDoC CJun EGrI LMil
- 'Nicole'	CJun MPkF NLar SReu
- 'Ohkan'	CJun
- 'Pévé Foggy'	CDoC NLar
- 'Pévé Limbo' (v)	CJun
- 'Pévé Sammy' (v)	NLar
- 'Pink Lips'	MAsh
- 'Polywood'	CJun
- RADIANT ROSE ('Hanros')	MAsh NCth NLar SSta
- 'Rasen'	CJun
- 'Rel Whirlwind'	CJun MBlu
* - 'Robert'	NLar
- 'Rosea'	CJun
- 'Rosemoor Pink'	CJun NLar
- 'Rosy Teacups' PBR	WMat

Corokia 205

– Samaritan ('Samzam') (v)	CBcs CDoC CEnd CMHG LRHS LSRN MAsh	*oblonga*	CExl LRHS
– Scarlet Fire ('H 3 Dr 11 P21'^PBR)	LRHS	*officinalis*	CAgr CJun CMac CMCN CWnw EBee EGren EPfP LRHS MBlu NLar SAth WJur WSpi
– 'Sluis Slim'	CJun MBlu MPkF	– 'Kintoki' ♀H6	NLar
– 'Snowbird'	CJun	– 'Robin's Pride'	LMaj NLar
– 'Snowboy' (v)	MBlu	– 'Ormonde' ♀H5	CJun EBee EGrI WPGP
– 'Snowflurries'	CJun LRHS	'Pink Blush'	CJun
– 'Southern Cross'	CJun	'Porlock' ♀H5	CJun CMCN NLar SHor
– 'Square Dance'	CJun	*pumila*	CBcs CMCN NLar
– 'Steeple'	CJun	§ × *rutgersensis* 'Michael Steinhardt' (v)	CDoC NPip WMat
– 'Summer Flair'	CJun		
– 'Summer Fun' (v)	CJun LMil MAsh NLar SPoG	– (Stellar Series) Aurora ('Rutban')	CJun MBlu
– 'Summer Gold' (v)	LRHS MAsh		
– 'Summer Majesty'	CJun MAsh	– – Celestial ('Rutdan') ♀H5	CJun NLar WMat
– 'Sunsplash' (v)	SPoG	– – Celestial Shadow	see *C.* × *rutgersensis* 'Michael Steinhardt'
– 'Temple Jewel' (v)	CJun		
– 'Teresa' (v)	NLar	– – Constellation ('Rutcan')	CJun CMac
– 'Teutonia' ♀H5	CBTr CJun ELan IArd LCro LSto MGos NCth NLar SAko WMat	– – Galaxy	see *C.* × *rutgersensis* (Stellar Series) Celestial
– 'Trinity Star'	CJun	– – Hyperion ('Kf111 1')	NLar
– 'Tsukuba No Mine'	CJun	– – Ruth Ellen ('Rutlan') ♀H5	CJun CMac MPkF
– 'Weaver's Weeping'	CJun MPkF	– – Stardust ('Rutfan')	CMac SMad
– 'Weisse Fontäne'	MAsh MBlu MPkF NCth NLar SHor SMad WMat	– – Stellar Pink ('Rutgan')	CBcs CJun EPfP LRHS MGos NLar SAko SGol SHor SMad WPGP
– 'White Dream'	CJun MPkF NLar	*sanguinea*	CBcs CBrac CBTr CBWd CCVT CHab CLnd CMac EGren EHeP EPfP LBuc LSto MMuc MSwo SEWo SVic WHnu WMat WMou WRjT
– 'White Giant'	CJun		
– 'Willy Boy'	MAsh NLar		
– Wolf Eyes' (v) ♀H5	CJun ELan LMaj LMil MAsh MBlu MPkF NLar SHor SPoG		
		– 'Anny'	MBlu
macrophylla Koehne	see *C. controversa*	– 'Anny's Winter Orange' ♀H5	CDoC CLnd CMac CSBt CSpe EBar EGren ELan EPfP LRHS LSou MAsh MPri MSwo NCth SEWo SHor SMad SPoG WBrk WCot WFar WTor
macrophylla Wall.	EBee EGrI EPfP LEdu MBlu WPGP		
– B&SWJ 14646	WCru		
– MSF 821	WPGP		
– var. *macrophylla*	SSta	– 'Compressa'	GKev MBlu NLar
mas	Widely available	– 'Magic Flame' ♀H5	CDoC CWnw EPfP LRHS MAsh MPri SPoG WCot
– 'Aurea' (v) ♀H6	CBcs LMil MAsh MBlu NLar SSta WCot		
§ – 'Aureoelegantissima' (v)	CMac NLar WCot	– 'Midwinter Fire'	Widely available
– 'Elegant' (F)	CAgr CJun	– 'Sifa'^PBR	WCha
– 'Elegantissima'	see *C. mas* 'Aureoelegantissima'	– 'Winter Beauty'	CSBt EBee LRHS LSto MAsh MBlu NLar SHor
– 'Golden Glory' ♀H5	CJun EBee ELan MGos MPri NLar NPip WMat	– Winter Flame 'Saudade'	see *C. sanguinea* 'Anny' CJun
– 'Gourmet' (F)	CAgr	*sericea* 'Bud's Yellow' ♀H7	EGren EPfP LCro LRHS MBlu NLar SHor
– 'Happy Face'	NLar		
– 'Hillier's Upright'	CJun	– 'Cardinal'	CDoC EBee EPfP LRHS LSto MAsh MGos
– 'Jolico' (F) ♀H6	CAgr CJun ELan MBlu NLar WMat		
– 'Kazanlak' (F)	CAgr CJun LRHS MBlu NLar NPip	– 'Flaviramea' ♀H7	Widely available
– 'Macrocarpa'	WJur	– 'Hedgerows Gold' (v) ♀H7	EBee ELan ELon EPfP LRHS LSto MGos NEoE SPoG WFar WLov
– 'Pancharevo' (F)	CAgr		
– 'Pioneer' (F)	CJun	§ – 'Kelseyi'	CMac EBee EPfP LRHS NLar SBrt SPoG WFar
– Redstar ('Vidubetskii) (F)	NLar		
– 'Redstone' (F)	CJun	– Kelsey's Gold ('Rosco') ♀H7	CMac LRHS SPoG
– 'Shan' (F)	CAgr		
– 'Shumen' (F)	CAgr NLar	– subsp. *occidentalis* 'Sunshine'	NEoE
– 'Spring Glow'	CJun		
– 'Variegata' (v) ♀H6	CAco CJun ELan MAsh MBlu MGos NLar	– 'White Gold' (v) ♀H7	EBee ELon EPfP LRHS LSRN NLar SPoG SRms WFar
– 'Vraća Kaštel' (F)	CAgr	– 'White Spot'	see *C. sericea* 'White Gold'
– 'Xanthocarpa' (F)	CAgr CJun	*stricta*	see *C. foemina* Mill.
– 'Norman Hadden' ♀H5	CBcs CDoC CEnd CJun CMCN EBee ELan EPfP GKin LEdu LMaj LMil LSRN MAsh MBlu MGos MPkF NCth NLar NPip SHor SPoG SSta WAbe WCot WMat WPGP WSpi	– 'Summer Glassy'	CJun LRHS NLar
		– 'Summer Passion'	NLar
		– 'Summer Sky Tree'	CJun LRHS
		× *unalaschkensis*	GKev
nuttallii 'Colrigo Giant'	CJun	*wilsoniana*	CJun EBee EPfP MBlu SChF WPGP
– 'Monarch'	CJun	– 'Winter Orange'	CDoC NLar
– 'North Star'	CJun NLar		
– 'Osmunda'	CEnd	# *Corokia* ✿ (Argophyllaceae)	
– 'Portlemouth'	CEnd CJun	*buddlejoides*	CBcs CCoa CSde LRHS NLar SEND WFar
– 'Zurico'	CJun		
		Clover ('Tg4')	EUrb LRHS WLov

cotoneaster	CBcs CBrac CCoa CEnd CMac CSBt CSde ELan EPfP LRHS LWaG MAsh NLar SArc SEle SIvy SPoG WCot WFar WJur WLov
'Geenty's Ghost'	SEle
× *virgata*	ELan EPfP LBom LRHS NLar SArc
- 'Banana Royal'	CBct CDoC SIvy
- 'Bronze King'	ELan LRHS SPlb
- 'Cheesemanii'	SPlb
- 'Coppershine'	CBcs CCoa
- 'Envy'	SEle
- 'Frosted Chocolate'	CBcs CBct CCht CCoa CDoC CSde EAri ELan ELon EPfP LRHS SArc SEND SIvy SPoG SSta WFar WLov
- 'Limey'	LSou WFar
- 'Mangatangi'	CBcs SArc
- MAORI GREEN ('Ruycomagre'^{PBR})	LBom LRHS
- MAORI SILVER ('Ruycomasil'^{PBR})	LRHS
- 'Pink Delight'	ELan LRHS
- 'Red Wonder'	CBct CMac ELan ELon EPfP LRHS SEND SPoG SVen WFar WLov
- 'Sunsplash' (v)	CBcs CBct CCoa CDoC CMac ELan EPfP LRHS MMrt NLar SAdn SArc SEle SEND SPoG SSta WFar
- 'Welsh Whiskey'	CDoC SEle WCot
- 'Yellow Wonder'	CBcs ELan EPfP GAbr NLar SEND SPlb

Coronilla (Fabaceae)

comosa	see *Hippocrepis comosa*
emerus	see *Hippocrepis emerus*
glauca	see *C. valentina* subsp. *glauca*
valentina	CRHN
- 'Cotswold Cream' (v)	SPoG WCot
§ - subsp. *glauca* ♀^{H4}	CBcs CCoa CDoC CMac CSde CWal EAri EBee ELan EPfP EShb EWld LSRN SEND SRms SVen WFar
- - 'Brockhill Blue'	EPfP SVen WCot
- - 'Citrina' ♀^{H4}	Widely available
- - 'Lauren Stevenson'	MHol SMrm SPel WCot WMal
* - - 'Pygmaea'	SRms WCot
- - 'Variegata' (v)	CBcs CDoC CMac EBee ELan EPfP EShb LRHS MAsh MHtn MPri SMrm SPoG SRms SVen WCot WFar
- - 'XXS'	WCot
varia	see *Securigera varia*

Corpuscularia (Aizoaceae)

taylorii	CPic WCor

Correa ❀ (Rutaceae)

alba	CWal EPfP SEle
- 'Pinkie' ♀^{H3}	CExl CTsd SEle SPlb
alba × *backhouseana*	CCoa
backhouseana ♀^{H3}	CAbb CBcs CCoa CMac CSBt CSde ELan EPfP GAbr SEle SRkn SVen
- 'Peaches and Cream'	SEle SRkn
'Canberra Bells'^{PBR}	SEle
decumbens	SEle
'Dusky Bells' ♀^{H3}	CAbb CBcs CCoa CSde CTsd ELan MAsh SEle SPad SPlb SPoG SRkn SVen WMal
'Federation Belle'	SEle
glabra	SEle
- var. *glabra*	SEle SPlb
'Harrisii'	see *C.* 'Mannii'
'Ivory Bells'	LRHS
lawrenceana	EUrb LRHS SChF SEle SEND WPGP
- var. *genoensis*	WPGP
- var. *grampiana*	SVen
§ 'Mannii' ♀^{H3}	LRHS
'Marian's Marvel' ♀^{H3}	CBcs CCoa CSde CTsd ELan EPfP IArd LRHS MAsh SEle SEND SRkn SVen WFar
'Peachy Cream'	CSBt LRHS
'Poorinda Mary'	CBcs SEle
pulchella ♀^{H3}	CMac SEle
- orange-flowered	SEle WAbe
- 'Pink Mist'	EPot SEle WAbe
reflexa	CBcs CCoa LRHS MAsh MHtn SEle
var. *nummulariifolia*	WCot WPGP
- var. *reflexa*	WCot
schlechtendalii	SEle
'Starlight'	SEle

Corryocactus (Cactaceae)

brevistylus	SPlb

Cortaderia (Poaceae)

araucana	ELan
argentea	see *C. selloana*
fulvida misapplied	see *C. richardii* (Endl.) Zotov
§ *fulvida* (Buchanan) Zotov ♀^{H5}	EUrb IArd WCot
jubata	Prohibited invasive. See Conservation and the Environment, p.42
richardii misapplied	see *C. fulvida* (Buchanan) Zotov
richardii ambig.	MMuc NBir NLar SMad WSpi
§ *richardii* (Endl.) Zotov ♀^{H5}	CAby CBcs CDoC CKno ESwi EUrb GBin SArc SDix SRms WPGP
- Brown's strain	WCot
§ *selloana*	CBcs EHeP LRHS MCtn MGos NBir SAth SPlb WCha
§ - 'Albolineata' (v)	CBcs ELon MWht
§ - 'Aureolineata' (v) ♀^{H6}	CBcs CMac CSde ELan GMaP MWht SEND SPoG
- 'Evita'^{PBR} ♀^{H6}	LRHS NLar SPoG WCot
- 'Gold Band'	see *C. selloana* 'Aureolineata'
- 'Golden Comet'	WCha
- 'Golden Goblin'^{PBR}	CKno MPri NLar WFar
- 'Green Goblin'^{PBR} **new**	MPri
- 'Icalma'	CSde EPPr
- MINIGOLDENPAMPAS ('Vercor 5'^{PBR}) (v)	EGren LRHS WCha
- MINIPAMPAS ('Vercor3'^{PBR}) (v)	EGren WCha
- MINISILVERPAMPAS ('Vercor 6'^{PBR}) (v)	EGren
- 'Monstrosa' ♀^{H6}	SEND
- 'Patagonia' ♀^{H6}	EBlo EPPr
- 'Pink Feather'	EBee EHeP EPfP NLar WFar
- 'Pumila' ♀^{H6}	CBcs CKno CMac CSBt CSde EBlo ECha EGren ELan ELon EPfP EUrb EWhm GMaP LCro LRHS MAsh MGos MPri NLar SArc SDix SEND SMHy SPoG SRms WFar
- 'Rendatleri'	CBcs
- 'Rosea'	EGren EHeP LRHS MCtn WCha WFar
- 'Silver Comet'	LRHS
- 'Silver Fountain' (v)	ELan EPfP MAsh SPoG
- 'Silver Goblin'^{PBR} **new**	MPri
- 'Silver Star' (v)	LRHS
- 'Silver Stripe'	see *C. selloana* 'Albolineata'
- 'Splendid Star'^{PBR} (v)	LBuc LRHS MAsh MGos SPoG
- 'Sunningdale Silver' ♀^{H6}	CBcs CMac ECha ELan ELon MGos NLar SEND SMad SPoG
- TINY PAMPA ('Day1'^{PBR})	CKno CSBt EGren EHeP EUrb LCro LRHS MHtn MPri NCth
* - 'White Feather'	LCro LRHS NLar WFar
- 'White Plume'	LRHS
Toe Toe	see *C. richardii* (Endl.) Zotov

Cortusa (Primulaceae)
* **caucasica** — GKev
* -'Alba' — GKev
§ **matthioli** — CFis GPSL LBar WFar
  - var. **congesta** — GKev
  - subsp. **pekinensis** — GKev
  - - var. **sachalinensis** — GKev

Corydalis ✿ (Papaveraceae)
angustifolia — WCot
anthriscifolia — CElw
'Blackberry Wine' — EMor LCro NCth SPoG
BLUE LINE ('Couriblue') — CWGN NCth NHar SPoG
'Blue Panda' — see *C. flexuosa* 'Blue Panda'
brunneovaginata — MMrt
bulbosa misapplied — see *C. cava*
bulbosa (L.) DC. — see *C. solida*
buschii — NHar
calycosa — CAbb CSpe EBee ECha EMor IPot LBar MPro NClf NCth SPel SPeP
'Canary Feathers'^PBR — CBcs LRHS
cashmeriana — GArf
-'Kailash' — EBee
caucasica var. **alba** misapplied — see *C. malkensis*
§ **cava** — GKev LAma MCtn WShi
chaerophylla — EWld
cheilanthifolia — ECha EGrI EWld GGro LEdu SRms WMal
'Craigton Blue' — CDor EMor EPPr EUrb EWld GKev GMaP GQue MNrw MPnt NHar NLar NSti WAbe WFar WMal
'Craigton Purple' — CSpe EWld GMaP NHar WMal
curviflora — GKev
- subsp. **rosthornii** 'Blue Heron' — CAby CWCL CWGN EGren EUrb GEdr LBar MAvo MBNS MHol Midl MPnt MPri MPro NBir NCth NLar SPad SRkn WFar
densiflora — GKev
'Dzkou Mousse' — WPGP
elata — CSpe CTtf EMor EWes GArf MArl MBel MNrw MBid NBir SHar SPoG StAn
-'Blue Summit' — EPPr WFar
elata × **flexuosa** — SPeP
flexuosa — EPfP MNrw StAn WCAu
-'Blue Dragon' — see *C. flexuosa* 'Purple Leaf'
§ -'Blue Panda' ♀^H5 — CSpe EPPr
-'Blue Panther' — LEdu
-'China Blue' — CAby CBcs ECha ELan EMor EPfP EWes GKev GMaP LCro LEdu LRHS Midl NBir NLar SPoG SRms WCAu WFar
-'Hale Cat' — EPPr
-'Nightshade' — WCot
I -'Norman's Seedling' — EPPr WFar
-'Père David' — CDor CMac EBee ECha EMor EPfP EPPr GKev GQue LEdu LRHS NBir NCth SPlb SPoG SRms
-'Porcelain Blue'^PBR — EMor EPot GJos LBar LCro MHol MHtn Midl MPnt MPri MPro MSCN NBir SPad WPnP
§ -'Purple Leaf' ♀^H5 — CAby CBcs CDor CElw CMac CMiW CTtf EBee ECha ELan EMor EPfP EPPr GKev GMaP LEdu LSto Midl NCth NLar SDix SHor SPlb SPoG SRms WAbe WCot WFar
glauca — see *C. sempervirens*
'Golden Spinners' — EMor LRHS NCth

'Heavenly Blue' — EPot GKev
integra — GKev
'Kingfisher' — CDor NBir WAbe
'Korn's Purple' — CElw CWnw EBee ECha EMor EPPr EWes GKev IPot LSto NClf NCth NHar
'Lentune Rouge' — NHar
leucanthema DJHC 752 — CExl
-'Silver Spectre' (v) — CExl ECha
§ **lutea** — LBar MCtn MMuc NBir NPer SEND SRms WCot
§ **malkensis** ♀^H5 — CTtf EMor NRya
microflora — GGro GKev
mucronipetala — GKev
- W&O 9038 — GGro
nobilis — MCtn NCth SPhx
§ **ochroleuca** — CMac CSpe MCtn
omeiana ♀^H5 — EPPr LEdu NLar SHor WCot
ophiocarpa — ECha ELan
pachycentra — WAbe WCot
paczoskii — GKev
petrophila — GGro
pseudofumaria alba — see *C. ochroleuca*
'Rainier Blue' — EPot WFar
SAPPHIRES AND GOLD ('Tuialis') — EWes
scandens — see *Dactylicapnos scandens*
scouleri — CTtf
§ **sempervirens** — MCtn
shimienensis 'Berry Exciting'^PBR — EGren GJos LBar MBNS MPro NPer SPoG
siamensis B&SWJ 7200 — GGro WCru
§ **solida** — CElw EGrI GKev LAma LEdu MHtn NBir NRya WBrk WCot WShi
-'Bird of Paradise' — GKev
- subsp. **incisa** 'Lentune Snow' — NHar
-'Lentune Red' — NHar
-'Purple Bird' — CBro EPot ERCP GKev LAma NBir SPhx XFar
- RAINBOW (mixed) — GKev
§ - subsp. **solida** — NBir NRya WCot
- -'Beth Evans' — CBro CTtf ECha EMor EPot ERCP GKev LAma LEdu LRHS MAvo MNrw NBir SBeP SPhx WBrk XFar
- -'George Baker' — CAby GKev LAma LEdu MCtn MNrw MPie NBir NLar SPhx
- -'Nettleton Pink' — GKev
- -'White Knight' — GKev LAma NLar SPhx WCot
- f. **transsylvanica** — see *C. solida* subsp. *solida*
- -'White King' — WCot
- -'White Swallow' — EMor GEdr LEdu
'Spinners' — CCBP CDor EBee EMor EPPr ESwi GKev GPSL LRHS NQui WFar WKif
stipulata B&SWJ 2951 — WCru
taliensis — CExl GKev
tauricola — GEdr
temulifolia 'Chocolate Stars' — CSpe CWGN EBee EGrI ESwi EWld MHol SPoG WCot WTre
tomentella — GKev
'Tory MP' — CDor CExl CMiW CSpe EBee EPPr LBar LEdu MNrw NCth WFar WPGP
transsylvanica hort. — see *C. solida* subsp. *solida*
vivipara — EPPr WMal
'Wildside Blue' — EPPr NHar
wilsonii — CExl GKev

Corylopsis (Hamamelidaceae)
glabrescens — CBcs CJun EGrI NLar WJur
- B&SWJ 14636 — WCru

- var. **gotoana**	CJun EPfP MAsh NLar	- 'Scooter'	LRHS NLar WFar
- - 'Chollipo'	CJun	- 'Tonda di Giffoni' (F)	MLod NOra WMat
- 'Lemon Drop'	CJun	- 'Tonda Gentile delle Langhe' (F)	WJur
glandulifera	CJun		
himalayana	WAbe	- 'Twister'	CDoC LRHS WCha
multiflora	WJur	- 'Webb's Prize Cob' (F)	CAco CAda CAgr CBTr CDoC
pauciflora ♁H5	CBcs CDoC CEnd CJun EBee		EBee ELan IArd LCro MBlu
	EPfP LCro LRHS LSRN LSto		MLod MNHC NLar SBmr SGol
	MAsh NLar SGol SPoG WCha		SSFr SVic WMat
	WSpi	**chinensis**	MBlu
platypetala	see *C. sinensis* var. *calvescens*	**colurna** ♁H6	CAgr CBcs CBTr CCVT CDoC
- var. **laevis**	see *C. sinensis* var. *calvescens*		CMCN EBar EBee EHeP ELan
sinensis	CBcs EBee GKev WJur		EPfP IArd IPap LMaj LRHS MBlu
§ - var. **calvescens**	CJun EPfP GKev		MPri NLar SGol SRms WJur
§ - - f. **veitchiana** ♁H5	CJun EPfP MAsh		WMat WMou
§ - var. **sinensis** ♁H5	CDoC CJun EBee EPfP LRHS MAsh	× **colurnoides** 'Chinoka' (F)	CAgr
	WSpi		
- - 'Spring Purple'	CMac MGos NLar SPoG WPGP	- 'Freeoka' (F)	CAgr
	WSpi	EARLY LONG ZELLER	see *C. avellana* 'Lang Tidlig Zeller'
- 'Veitch's Purple'	NLar	**fargesii**	WPGP
spicata	CBcs CMCN EGrl MBlu SGol SHor	**ferox**	CJun
	WJur	- WJC 13655	WCru
- 'Red Eye'	NLar	**maxima** (F)	CBTr CLnd EPom
veitchiana	see *C. sinensis* var. *calvescens*	- 'Butler'	see *C. avellana* 'Butler'
	f. *veitchiana*	- 'Ennis'	see *C. avellana* 'Ennis'
willmottiae	see *C. sinensis* var. *sinensis*	- 'Fertile de Coutard'	see *C. maxima* 'White Filbert'
		- 'Grote Lambertsnoot'	see *C. maxima* 'Kentish Cob'

Corylus ✿ (Betulaceae)

		- 'Gunslebert' (F) ♁H6	CCVT CMac NOra SPoG SRms SSFr WMat
avellana (F)	Widely available	- HALLE GIANT	see *C. maxima* 'Halle'sche Riesennuss'
- 'Anaconda'	MBlu		
- 'Anny's Purple Dream'PBR	MBlu	§ - 'Halle'sche Riesennuss' (F)	CAda CAgr CMac ELan LCro MMuc
- 'Anny's Red Dwarf'	NLar		MNHC NLar SBmr SSFr WMat
- 'Aurea'	CBcs CEnd EHeP ELan MBlu NLar	§ - 'Kentish Cob' (F) ♁H6	CAda CAgr EBee EGren ELan EPfP
	SPoG SSta WFar		EPom IArd LBuc LCro MSwo NLar
- 'Bollwylle'	see *C. maxima* 'Halle'sche Riesennuss'		SBmr SEdi SEWo SPoG SRms SSFr
			SVic WMat WMou
§ - 'Butler' (F)	CAgr CMac LCro SRms WMat	- 'Lambert's Filbert'	see *C. maxima* 'Kentish Cob'
- 'Casina' (F)	CAgr	- 'Longue d'Espagne'	see *C. maxima* 'Kentish Cob'
- 'Contorta' ♁H6	Widely available	- 'Monsieur de Bouweller'	see *C. maxima* 'Halle'sche Riesennuss'
- 'Corabel' (F)	CAgr MLod NLar NOra SRms WMat		
- 'Cosford' (F)	CAda CAgr CCVT CEnd CMac	- 'Nottingham Cobnut' (F)	CDoC LRHS NOra SBmr SVic WMat
	EPom IArd LBuc LCro MBlu NLar	- 'Purple Filbert'	see *C. maxima* 'Purpurea'
	NOra SEWo SRms WFar WMat	§ - 'Purpurea' (F)	Widely available
- Emoa Series	WMat	- 'Red Filbert' misapplied	see *C. avellana* 'Rotblättrige Zellernuss'
§ - 'Ennis' (F)	CAgr NOra WMat		
- 'Feriale' (F)	CAgr	- 'Red Zellernut'	see *C. avellana* 'Rotblättrige Zellernuss'
§ - 'Fuscorubra' misapplied	see *C. avellana* 'Rotblättrige Zellernuss'		
		- 'Spanish White'	see *C. maxima* 'White Filbert'
- 'Gustav's Zeller' (F)	NOra WMat	§ - 'White Filbert' (F)	CHab WJur
§ - 'Heterophylla'	CEnd EBee NLar SSta	- 'White Spanish Filbert'	see *C. maxima* 'White Filbert'
- 'Laciniata'	see *C. avellana* 'Heterophylla'	- 'Witpit Lambertsnoot'	see *C. maxima* 'White Filbert'
§ - 'Lang Tidlig Zeller' (F)	CAda CAgr CBTr MLod NLar NOra	'Nottingham Early' (F)	NLar
	WMat	**sieboldiana**	MBlu
- 'Lewis' (F)	CAgr	var. **mandshurica**	
- 'Lombardii' (F)	CLnd	'Te Terra Red'	CMCN EBar EPfP LRHS MBlu NPip
- MEDUSA ('Jww9')	NLar		SRms WMat
- 'Merveille de Bollwyller'	see *C. maxima* 'Halle'sche Riesennuss'	**tibetica**	LEdu WPGP
		× **vilmorinii**	WPGP
- 'Nottingham Prolific'	see *C. avellana* 'Pearson's Prolific'		
- 'Pauetet' (F)	CAgr NLar		

Corymbia (Myrtaceae)

§ **citriodora**	LWaG SPlb WGrf WKit
§ **eximia**	SPlb
- 'Nana'	SPlb
ficifolia	SAth WGrf

§ - 'Pearson's Prolific' (F)	CAgr IArd LBuc LCro NLar SSFr		
- 'Pendula'	LMaj MBlu NOra SRms WCot		
- 'Red Dragon'	MBlu		
- RED GHOST ('Bwm 01') (F) **new**	MNHC		

Corynabutilon (Malvaceae)

§ × **suntense**	CSBt EGren LCro LRHS LShi MAsh MPri MSCN NPer WMal
- 'Jermyns' ♁H4	CExl MGos SEle SPoG
- 'Violetta'	WSpi

- 'Red Majestic'PBR ♁H6	Widely available
§ - 'Rotblättrige Zellernuss' (F) ♁H6	CEnd CHab EBar EPfP EPom LCro LMaj MBlu MLod NLar NOra SBmr SGol SPoG SRms SSta WCot
- 'Rouge de Zeller'	see *C. avellana* 'Rotblättrige Zellernuss'

§	*vitifolium*	CDTJ EAri LShi SPad SPoG WCot WFar WKif WSpi
	-'Album'	CExl LRHS LShi WSpi
	-'Tennant's White' ♀H4	CExl EPfP WCot
	-'Veronica Tennant' ♀H4	CExl EBee EPfP SChF

Corynephorus (Poaceae)
canescens   NBir

Corynopuntia (Cactaceae)
§ *invicta*   SPlb

Coryphantha (Cactaceae)
elephantidens   SPlb

Cosmos ✿ (Asteraceae)

§	*atrosanguineus*	CBcs CSpe CTsd CWGN EGren ELan EPfP EShb LAma LCro LSRN MPro NLar SPoG WHoo WTre
	-'Black Magic'	EDAr MCtn
	- CHOCAMOCHA ('Thomocha' PBR)	CBcs CSpe CWGN EBee EUrb GMaP LCro LRHS MBros MGos MHol NLar SAth SPeP SPoG XFar
	- ECLIPSE ('Hamcoec' PBR)	IPot LBar LCro MPro
	bipinnatus 'Antiquity'	LCro LSto MCtn
	- (Apollo Series) 'Apollo Carmine' ♀H3	LCro LSou MPri
	- -'Apollo Pink' ♀H3	LCro LSou MPri
	- -'Apollo White' ♀H3	LCro LSou MPri
	-'Apricot Lemonade'	CSpe MCtn WSpi
	-'Apricotta'	LCro LSto
	- BRIGHT LIGHTS (mixed) (d)	MCtn
	-'Candy Stripe'	MCtn
	-'Capriola'	MCtn
	- (Casanova Series) 'Casanova Pink'	EPfP LCro SPoG
	- -'Casanova Red'	EPfP SPoG
	- -'Casanova Violet'	SPoG
	- -'Casanova White'	SPoG
	- (Cosimo Series) 'Cosimo Collarette'	LCro MCtn
	- -'Cosimo Red-White' new	LCro
	- (Cupcakes Series) 'Cupcakes Blush'	CSpe MCtn
	- -'Cupcakes White'	CSpe LSto MCtn
	-'Daydream'	MCtn
	-'Dazzler'	LCro LSto MCtn
	- Double Click Series (d)	MCtn
	- -'Double Click Bicolour Rose' (d)	MCtn
	- -'Double Click Cranberries' (d)	CSpe LCro MCtn
	- -'Double Click Rose Bonbon' (d)	CSpe LCro MCtn WSpi
	- -'Double Click Snow Puff' (d)	CSpe LCro MCtn
	- (Fizzy Series) 'Fizzy Rose Picotee'	LCro LSto MCtn
	- -'Fizzy White'	LCro MCtn
	-'Gazebo Red'	MCtn
	-'Gazebo White'	MCtn
	-'Hummingbird Lilac' (Hummingbird Series) new	LCro
	-'Lemonade'	CSpe
	-'Picotee'	MCtn
	-'Pied Piper Blush White'	MCtn
	-'Pied Piper Red'	MCtn
	-'Pink Popsocks'	MCtn
	- PSYCHE MIXED	MCtn
	-'Psyche White'	CSpe
	-'Purity'	CSpe LCro LSto MCtn SPhx WSpi
	- Razzmatazz Series	LCro MBros
	-'Rosetta'	MCtn
	-'Rubenza' ♀H3	CSpe LCro LSto MCtn SPhx
	- SEA SHELLS (mixed)	MCtn
	- Sensation Series	GJem MCtn
	- -'Sensation Picotee'	LCro
	- -'Sensation Pinkie' ♀H3	LCro
	- Sonata Series	LCro MBros MCtn
	- - SONATA CARMINE ('Pas1786')	MPri
	- - SONATA PINK ('Pas1787')	LSto MPri
	- - SONATA PINK BLUSH ('Pas1788')	MCtn
	- - SONATA WHITE ('Pas1789')	CSpe LCro MBros MCtn MPri
	-'Velouette' ♀H3	LCro MCtn
	-'White Popsocks'	MCtn
	-'Xanthos'	LCro LSto MBros MCtn
	peucedanifolius	CSpe MCtn
	-'Flamingo'	EShb LAma LCro XFar
	sulphureus BUNTE LICHTER MIXED	LCro
	- (Cosmic Series) 'Cosmic Orange'	MCtn
	- -'Cosmic Red'	CSpe MCtn WSpi
	- LADYBIRD (mixed)	SVic
	-'Limara Lemon'	MCtn
	-'Mandarin' new	CSpe
	- POLIDOR MIXED	MCtn

Cosmos × *Dahlia* (Asteraceae)
'Mexican Black'   see *Dahlia* 'Mexican Black'

costmary see *Tanacetum balsamita*

Costus (Costaceae)
	arabicus	SBig
	-'Bicolor Variegated' (v)	WCot
	barbatus	NGKo
	speciosus	MCtn

Cota (Asteraceae)
§	*tinctoria*	CGHo CHby CMac ENfk GJem IDun LShi MCtn MEar MHer MHoo MNHC NAts NPer SRms SVic WJek WRBe
	-'Alba'	EBee IDun MHoo WFar
§	-'Beauty of Grallagh'	ESgI WSpi
	-'Charme'	SPoG SRms
	-'Compacta'	EWes MWlw
	- dwarf	LBar MMrt NCth NLar
	- E.C. Buxton ♀H6	Widely available
	-'Eva'	IDun NDov
I	-'Golden Rays'	GBin SDix
	-'Grallagh Gold' misapplied, orange-yellow	see *C. tinctoria* 'Beauty of Grallagh'
§	-'Grallagh Gold'	ECha NPer WFar
	-'Hall Farm Frilly'	ELon
	-'Kelwayi'	EBee EPfP GQue MBNS NLar SRms StAn WFar
	-'Lemon Ice'	EBee LBar MBel MPro NLar WHil
	-'Lemon Maid'	ELon
	-'Mieke'	EWes
§	-'Orange Dream'	LRHS
	-'Pom Pom'	EWes
§	- subsp. *sancti-johannis*	EPfP LBar MCtn NPer SRms
	-'Sauce Hollandaise'	Widely available
	- subsp. *tinctoria*	SMrm
	-'Top Gold'	EWes
	-'Wargrave Variety'	CMac ECha ELan GBin LBar MHol NBir NGdn NLar SDix WCAu WFar
§	*triumfettii*	NDov NPer

× *Cotanthemis* (Asteraceae)
SUSANNA MITCHELL ('Blomit') CDor CTtf EBee EBlo ECha ELon GAbr GMaP LBar MHol MNrw NDov NLar SMrm WFar WKif WMal
§ 'Tetworth' ECha ELan EPfP

Cotinus ✿ (Anacardiaceae)

americanus	see *C. obovatus*
'Candy Floss'	EBee LCro LRHS MBNS
§ *coggygria*	CBcs CBrac CMac CMCN EGren EGrI EHeP ELan LRHS MMuc NLar SAth SEND SRms WFar WJur
- FLAMISSIMO ('Mincofla20'PBR)	CWnw EPfP LRHS MPri
- GOLDEN LADY ('Mincojau3'PBR)	CWnw LRHS MAsh MPri NCth WFar
- GOLDEN SPIRIT ('Ancot'PBR) ♀H5	Widely available
- GREEN FOUNTAIN ('Kolcot'PBR)	EBee
- 'Kanari'	NLar
- 'Lilla'PBR	CBcs CWGN CWnw EPfP LRHS MAsh MBlu NLar
- 'Notcutt's Variety'	EGrI
- 'Old Fashioned'PBR	CBcs EBee EPfP NLar
- 'Pink Champagne'	NLar SSta
- Purpureus Group	SRms
- RED SPIRIT ('Firstpur')	NLar
- 'Royal Purple' ♀H5	Widely available
- Rubrifolius Group	SEND
- SMOKEY JOE ('Lisjo'PBR)	CBcs EBee LRHS MAsh SPoG SSta
- 'Velvet Cloak'	MGos
- 'Westonbirt Orange'	NLar
- 'Young Lady'PBR ♀H5	CBcs CDoC CMac EBee ELan EPfP EUrb EWes IArd LBom LRHS LSou LSto MAsh MBlu MCtn NLar WFar WMat
DUSKY MAIDEN ('Londus'PBR)	CCps CMac CSBt EGren EGrI ELan EPfP IArd LMaj LRHS MAsh MGos NEoE SFol WFar WHtc
'Flame' ♀H5	CBcs CDoC EBee EGrI ELan EPfP EUrb MAsh MGos SPoG WFar
'Grace'	Widely available
§ *obovatus*	EGrI MBlu SSta WPGP
'Ruby Glow'	CSpe EPfP LBom LCro LRHS MBNS MGos MHtn

Cotoneaster ✿ (Rosaceae)

acuminatus	NLar
acutifolius	see *C. laetevirens*
var. *laetevirens*	
§ *adpressus* 'Little Gem'	GQue NHar
- 'Tom Thumb'	see *C. adpressus* 'Little Gem'
ambiguus Rehder & E.H.Wilson	NLar
amoenus	NLar SRms
§ *apiculatus*	NLar
§ *astrophoros*	CMac MBlu NLar
atropurpureus	NLar SRms
§ - 'Variegatus' (v) ♀H6	CBcs CDoC CMac EBee EHeP ELan EPfP LRHS MGos NLar NPer SPoG SRms WFar
aurantiacus	NLar SHor
beimashanensis	ELan NLar
boisianus	NLar
bradyi	NLar
brickellii	ELan NLar
℗ *bullatus*	EHeP EPfP NLar WHtc WJur
- 'Firebird'	see *C. ignescens*
- f. *floribundus*	see *C. bullatus*
- var. *macrophyllus*	see *C. rehderi*
bumthangensis	NLar
buxifolius blue-leaved	see *C. lidjiangensis*
- f. *vellaeus*	see *C. astrophoros*
canescens	NLar
chadwelli	NLar
chuanus	NLar
chungtiensis	NLar
§ *cochleatus*	EHeP LRHS NHar SRms
§ *congestus*	CSBt EHeP NLar SPlb SRms WPGP
- 'Nanus'	LRHS MPri
conspicuus	CBcs EHeP LRHS SRms
- 'Decorus' ♀H6	CBrac CDoC CSBt LRHS MGos MPri MSwo SArc SPlb SPoG
- 'Red Glory'	CMac
cooperi 'Nicolette'	MBlu NLar
cordifolius	MBlu NLar
§ 'Cornubia' ♀H6	CBrac CCVT CDoC CLnd CMac CSBt EBar EBee EHeP ELan EPfP IPap LCro LMaj LRHS LSRN MGos MMuc MPri NBir SArc SEND SEWo SFol SOrN SPoG WFar WHtc WMat WMou
crispii	NLar
cuspidatus	MBlu NLar
§ *dammeri*	CBcs CDoC CEnd CMac CSBt EBee EHeP ELan EPfP MAsh MGos MSwo SGol SPoG SRms WFar WHtc
§ - 'Major'	EHeP LBuc
§ - 'Mooncreeper'	CDoC
- 'Oakwood'	see *C. radicans*
- var. *radicans* misapplied	see *C. dammeri* 'Major'
- var. *radicans* (Dammer ex C.K.Schneid.) C.K.Schneid.	see *C. radicans*
delavayanus	IArd
distichus	see *C. rotundifolius* Wall. ex Lindl.
duthieanus	NLar
- 'Boer'	see *C. apiculatus*
elatus	NLar
elegans	SHor
emeiensis	NLar
encavei	NLar
'Erlinda'	see *C. × suecicus* 'Erlinda'
'Exburiensis'	CBrac CBTr EBee EPfP LCro LRHS MAsh MMuc NLar NPip SEND WMat
flinckii	NLar
floccosus	IArd SEND
forrestii	GKev NLar
franchetii	CBcs CCoa CCVT CDoC CEnd CMac CSBt CWnw EBee ELan EPfP LBuc LCro LRHS MGos MMuc MSwo NLar SArc SEND SHor SPoG SRms WFar
frigidus	CMCN SRms
* - 'Cornubia' misapplied	CBTr LRHS NPip
froebelii	SHor
fulvidus	NLar
ganghobaensis	CMCN NLar
- B&L 12234	WCru
glabratus	SHor
glacialis	GKev
glaucophyllus	IArd
§ *glomerulatus*	NLar
harrovianus	SHor SRms
harrysmithii	NLar
hebephyllus	NLar
I *hedegaardii* 'Fructu Luteo'	SRms

Cotoneaster

'Herbstfeuer'	see *C. salicifolius* 'Herbstfeuer'
'Highlight'	see *C. pluriflorus*
hillieri	NLar SHor
§ *hjelmqvistii*	LBuc NLar SHor
- 'Robustus'	see *C. hjelmqvistii*
- 'Rotundifolius'	see *C. hjelmqvistii*
P *horizontalis*	CBcs CDoC CMac CSBt CWnw EBee EGren EHeP ELan EPfP LBom LCro LRHS LSto MAsh MGos NLar SDix SPlb SPoG SReu SRms WFar WHtc
- 'Variegatus'	see *C. atropurpureus* 'Variegatus'
hualiensis	NLar
- B&SWJ 3143	WCru
humifusus	see *C. dammeri*
§ 'Hybridus Pendulus'	CBcs CBrac CBTr CCVT CDoC CMac CSBt IPap LCro LRHS LSRN MAsh MGos MPri NLar NPip SPoG SRms WHtc WMat
§ *hylmoei*	ELan NLar
§ *ignescens*	NLar
incanus	NLar
insolitus	NLar
P *integrifolius*	ELan EPfP NLar SHor
kingdonii	NLar
kitaibelii	NLar
konishii	NLar
kweitschoviensis	NLar
lacteus ♥H6	CAco CBcs CCVT CDoC CEnd EBee EGren EHeP ELan EPfP GArf LBuc LCro LRHS LSto MGos MMuc MPri NLar SEND SPoG SRms WFar
- F 10419	ELan
- 'Milkmaid' (v)	NLar
§ *laetevirens*	NLar
lancasteri	ELan
§ *lidjiangensis*	ELan NLar
lucidus	WJur
§ *mairei*	NLar
§ *marginatus* 'Blazovice'	NLar
marquandii	NLar
§ *meiophyllus*	MBlu NLar
melanotrichus misapplied	see *C. cochleatus*
meuselii	NLar
P *microphyllus* ambig.	CBcs CSBt EBee LRHS LSto
P *microphyllus* Wall. ex Lindl.	EPfP
- NICE 4	WCFE
- 'Donard Gem'	see *C. astrophoros*
- 'Teulon Porter'	see *C. astrophoros*
- var. *thymifolius* (Lindl.) Koehne	see *C. integrifolius*
- var. *thymifolius* ambig.	NLar
mirabilis	NLar
'Mooncreeper'	see *C. dammeri* 'Mooncreeper'
morrisonensis	GKev NLar
moupinensis	CBcs WJur
- BWJ 8167	WCru
mucronatus	NLar
nanshan 'Boer'	see *C. apiculatus*
naoujanensis	NLar
- 'Berried Treasure'	LBom LCro LRHS MGos
nepalensis	NLar
newryensis	NLar
nitens	NLar
nitidifolius	see *C. glomerulatus*
nohelii	NLar
* *obrienii*	GKev
ogisui	LEdu SHor
- Og 95.105	GKev WPGP
parkeri	NLar
permutatus	see *C. pluriflorus*
§ *pluriflorus*	GKev
poluninii	NLar
praecox 'Boer'	see *C. apiculatus*
procumbens	SReu
- 'Needham'	NLar
- 'Queen of Carpets' ♥H6	CBrac CDoC EBee ELan EPfP LBuc LRHS LSRN LSto MAsh MGos NLar SPoG SRms
- 'Streib's Findling'	MAsh NLar SGol
prostratus	SRms
- 'Arnold-Forster'	ELan
* *psikangensis*	NLar
pyrenaicus misapplied	see *C. congestus*
qungbixiensis	NLar
raboutensis	NLar
racemiflorus	SRms
§ *radicans*	CMCN
§ *rehderi*	NLar
reticulatus	NLar
rhytidophyllus	ELan
rokujodaisanensis	NLar
roseus	NLar
'Rothschildianus' ♥H6	CBcs CCVT CMac CSBt EBee ELan EPfP LRHS MAsh MBlu MGos MPri MSwo NLar SRms SSta
§ *rotundifolius* Wall. ex Lindl.	NLar
rubens W.W. Sm.	NLar
rugosus E. Pritz. ex Diels	NLar
'Saint Andrews Blaze'	ELan SHor
'Saint Monica'	ELan EPfP LRHS MBlu
salicifolius	NLar SRms WFar
- AUTUMN FIRE	see *C. salicifolius* 'Herbstfeuer'
§ - 'Avonbank'	CEnd
- 'Gnom' ♥H6	CDoC CMac EHeP ELan EPfP LRHS MAsh MHtn NBir SPoG SRms
§ - 'Herbstfeuer'	SRms
- 'Pendulus'	see *C.* 'Hybridus Pendulus'
- 'Pink Champagne' ♥H6	CMac ELan EPfP LRHS
- 'Repens'	CBrac EBee EHeP EPfP LCro NPip SPoG WMat
- var. *rugosus*	see *C. hylmoei*
salwinensis	NLar
sandakphuensis	NLar
schantungensis	NLar
schlechtendalii **new**	SHor
- 'Blazovice'	see *C. marginatus* 'Blazovice'
'Seattle'	NLar
I *sengorensis*	NLar
serotinus misapplied	see *C. meiophyllus*
shannanensis	ELan
shansiensis	NLar
sherriffii	NLar
P *simonsii*	CEnd CLnd CMac EHeP ELan LBuc LRHS MGos NLar SArc SRms WFar
§ *splendens*	ELan NLar SHor
- 'Sabrina'	see *C. splendens*
sternianus ♥H6	EPot SHor SRms
submultiflorus	NLar
× *suecicus* 'Coral Beauty' ♥H6	CBcs CBrac CBTr CDoC CEnd CSBt EGren EHeP EPfP LBom LBuc LCro LRHS LSto MGos MHtn MPri MSwo NLit NPip SGol SPoG SRms WHtc WMat
§ - 'Erlinda' (v)	CEnd SPoG
- 'Ifor'	SRms
- 'Juliette' (v) ♥H6	CBTr CMac LRHS LSRN MAsh NPip SPoG WMat
- 'Royal Carpet' **new**	EBee

Cotoneaster

- 'Skogholm'	CBcs EHeP SArc SRms
svenhedinii	NLar
tardiflorus	NLar
teijiashanensis	NLar
thimphuensis	NLar
transcaucasicus	NLar
turbinatus	NLar
vandelaarii	ELan NLar SHor
veitchii	NLar
vestitus	NLar
vilmorinianus	SHor
wardii misapplied	see *C. mairei*
× *watereri*	CCVT EGren
- 'Avonbank'	see *C. salicifolius* 'Avonbank'
- 'Cornubia'	see *C.* 'Cornubia'
- 'John Waterer'	SPoG
- 'Pendulus'	see *C.* 'Hybridus Pendulus'

Cotula (Asteraceae)

coronopifolia	CBen CWat ELin NPer
hispida ambig.	ECha EPfP EPot GKev SLee SRot
§ *hispida* (DC.) Harv.	EDAr EUrb GMaP MAsh MHer NPer NRya SPoG SRms
perpusilla	see *Leptinella pusilla*
'Platt's Black'	see *Leptinella squalida* 'Platt's Black'
potentilloides	see *Leptinella potentillina*
pyrethrifolia	see *Leptinella pyrethrifolia*
squalida	see *Leptinella squalida*
'Tiffindell Gold'	EWes

Cotyledon (Crassulaceae)

chrysantha	see *Rosularia chrysantha*
gibbiflora var. *metallica*	see *Echeveria gibbiflora* 'Metallica'
oppositifolia	see *Umbilicus oppositifolius*
orbiculata	CPbh CPic EShb SPlb WCot
- 'Cedric Morris'	EMal SChr
- var. *oblonga*	CDoC LCro WCot
- var. *orbiculata*	CPbh EShb
- silver	CAbb
- 'Staghorn'	EShb
pendens	EShb
simplicifolia	see *Umbilicus oppositifolius*
tomentosa subsp. *ladismithensis* ♀H1c	EShb
- - 'Variegata' (v)	CPic EShb

courgette see AGM Vegetables Section

Crambe (Brassicaceae)

cordifolia ♀H5	Widely available
- 'Morning's Snow'	ESwi NLar
fruticosa **new**	WHil
maritima	CCBP CEls CSpe CTtf EBee ECha ELan EPfP GJos GMaP LRHS MCtn MHol MNrw NBac NLar SBrt SEND WCAu WCot WFar WJek WSpi WTor WTre
- 'Lilywhite'	CAgr ESwi MCtn SVic
orientalis	ESwi NLar

cranberry see *Vaccinium macrocarpon*, *V. oxycoccos*

Craspedia (Asteraceae)

globosa	MCtn
- GOLF BEAUTY ('Dcragolfby'^{PBR}) **new**	EGren
* *hispidula*	GArf

Crassothonna (Asteraceae)

§ *capensis*	CPic EShb

Crassula ✿ (Crassulaceae)

alba	CPbh
anomala	see *C. atropurpurea* var. *anomala*
arborescens	CPbh EShb LBom LWaG SChr SPlb WFar
- subsp. *undulatifolia*	CDoC CPic EUrb NCft
argentea	see *C. ovata*
§ *atropurpurea* var. *anomala*	SChr
- subsp. *arborescens* 'Blue Mist'	SEND
'Baby's Necklace'	CoPl CPic CSBt LBom LCro LWaG NHrt SPlb WCot
barklyi ♀H2	WOld
'Blue Waves'	SIvy
brevifolia	CPic
'Buddha's Temple'	CoPl LBom LCro NCft SPoG WOld
capitella 'Campfire'	EShb LRHS SPoG WCor
- subsp. *thyrsiflora*	CPic
'Celia'	CPic
cephalophora	see *C. nudicaulis* var. *nudicaulis*
coccinea	CPbh EAri EShb SPlb WCot WMal
* *coralloides*	SPlb
cordata	EShb WCor
cultrata	WCor
dejecta	CPbh
elegans	SEND
'Estagnol'	EShb
exilis subsp. *picturata*	CPic
'Garnet Lotus' **new**	EShb
helmsii	Prohibited invasive. See Conservation and the Environment, p.42
lycopodioides	see *C. muscosa*
- *variegata*	see *C. muscosa*
marginata	see *C. pellucida* subsp. *marginalis*
mesembryanthoides 'Tenelli'^{PBR}	LWaG
multicava	CoPl EShb SChr
- 'Ngabara'	CPbh
§ *muscosa*	CSBt EShb LRHS NCft NHrt SIvy SPlb WCor WFar
§ *nudicaulis* var. *nudicaulis*	NCft
orbicularis	LWaG WCot
§ *ovata* ♀H2	CHll CoPl CPic CWal EUrb LBom LCro LWaG MPri NCft NHrt NPer NPlm SArc SChr SEND SIvy SPlb SPre WCor WFar
- 'Blue Bird'	WCor
- 'Gollum' ♀H2	CPbh CPic EShb EUrb LBom LCro LWaG NCft NHrt SEND SIvy WCor WFar
- 'Gollum Minor'	CPic
- 'Horn Tree'	LBom NHrt
- 'Hummel's Sunset' (v) ♀H2	CAbb CoPl EShb LBom LWaG NCft NHrt WOld
- 'Minima'	CPic EShb NCft SIvy
- 'Red Horn Tree'	WOld
- 'Undulata'	CoPl CPic NHrt WCot
- 'Variegata' (v)	CPic EShb SIvy WCot
§ *pellucida* subsp. *marginalis*	CDoC SPoG WCor
- - 'Little Missy' (v)	ESuc LRHS
- - f. *rubra*	CDoC EShb WFar
- - 'Variegata' (v)	CoPl CPic WFar WOld
perfoliata	WOld
- var. *falcata* ♀H2	CPic EShb WCot
perforata ♀H2	CDoC CPic NCft NHrt NPlm SIvy WCor WFar
- giant	WCor

- 'Variegata' (v)	CDoC CPic NCft WCot
portulacea	see *C. ovata*
pubescens subsp. **radicans**	CoPl CPic ESuc SPoG
pyramidalis	NCft WOld
rogersii	LWaG
rubricaulis 'Candy Cane' (v)	CPbh
rupestris ♀H2	CDoC CPic NCft
- subsp. **marnieriana**	CDoC LCro NCft SIvy
sarcocaulis misapplied	see *C. sarcocaulis* Eckl. & Zeyh. 'Ken Aslet'
§ **sarcocaulis** Eckl. & Zeyh. 'Ken Aslet' ♀H3	CPic CTtf EAri ELan GEdr LRHS MAsh SBrt SEND SIvy SLee SPlb SPoG SRms SRot WAbe WCor WHoo WIce WMal
- var. **parvisepala** 'Alba'	SBrt
sarmentosa 'Comet' (v)	CoPl CPic
sedifolia	see *C. setulosa* 'Milfordiae'
sediformis	see *C. setulosa* 'Milfordiae'
setulosa	ESuc SPlb
§ - 'Milfordiae'	GBin NRya WAbe
socialis	ELan WAbe
'Springtime'	CoPl CPic NCft
streyi	WCot
swaziensis 'Money Maker' PBR	CPic EShb WCor
- 'Money Maker Variegata' (v)	WCor
tetragona	CoPl CPic CSBt EShb NCft SEND WCor
* **tomentosa** 'Variegata' (v)	EShb

× *Crataegosorbus* (Rosaceae)

§ 'Granatnaja'	CAgr

Crataegus (Rosaceae)

ambigua	CBcs
anomala 'Zbigniew'	CAgr
arnoldiana	CAgr CLnd ELan LRHS NLar SPoG WHtc WMat
'Autumn Glory'	CEnd CLnd
azarolus	LEdu WJur
coccinea misapplied	see *C. intricata*
§ **coccinea** L.	CAgr CCVT CLnd CNWT WJur WMat
cordata	see *C. phaenopyrum*
crus-galli misapplied	see *C. persimilis* 'Prunifolia'
crus-galli L.	CCVT CLnd EHeP EPfP MAsh WJur
× **durobrivensis**	CAgr MBlu
ellwangeriana	CAgr SDix WCot
- 'Fire Ball'	IArd LRHS MBlu
eriocarpa	CLnd
gemmosa	CAgr
× **grignonensis** ♀H7	CLnd EHeP MBlu
harbisonii	IArd WJur
§ **intricata** new	WJur
jonesiae	EPfP
laciniata misapplied	see *C. orientalis*
laevigata 'Coccinea Plena'	see *C.* × *media* 'Paul's Scarlet'
- 'Gireoudii'	WLov
- 'Rosea'	GKin
- 'Rosea Flore Pleno'	see *C.* × *media* 'Punicea Flore Pleno'
× **lavalleei**	CCVT CLnd CMCN EBar ELan LMaj NLar
- 'Aurora'	NLar
- 'Carrierei' ♀H7	CMac CNWT EBar EPfP IArd LCro LMaj LRHS LSRN MMuc MPri NPip SEND SEWo SPoG WHtc WMat WMou
× **media** 'Crimson Cloud' ♀H6	CBrac CBTr CCVT CMac EGren EPom LBuc LCro LRHS MLod NPip WMou
- 'Mutabilis'	CWnw
§ - 'Paul's Scarlet' (d) ♀H7	Widely available
- 'Pink Corkscrew' (d)	MBlu
- 'Plena' (d) ♀H7	CCVT CLnd CMac CWnw EHeP ELan EPom LCro LRHS MGos MLod NOra NPip SEWo WHtc WMat
- 'Princesse Sturdza'	MBlu
- 'Punicea' ♀H7	CBcs CBrac CCVT CDoC CLnd EHeP ELan EPfP IPap LSRN MLod MMuc MPri NLar NOra SEND SEWo SPoG WFar WMat WMou
§ - 'Punicea Flore Pleno' (d) ♀H7	Widely available
§ **mexicana**	WJur
mollis	CAgr WSpi
monogyna	Widely available
§ - 'Biflora'	CEnd CLnd EBee MGos MLod WMat WSpi
- 'Compacta'	MBlu
- 'Praecox'	see *C. monogyna* 'Biflora'
- 'Stricta'	CCVT EBar EHeP IPap LMaj WFar
× **mordenensis** 'Toba' (d)	CLnd
nigra	WJur
§ **orientalis** ♀H6	CCVT CDoC CEnd CMCN ELan IArd NPip WMat WMou WSpi
oxyacantha 'Rosea Plena'	see *C.* × *media* 'Punicea Flore Pleno'
pedicellata	see *C. coccinea* L.
pentagyna	WJur
persimilis	LMaj WJur
§ - 'Prunifolia' ♀H7	Widely available
- 'Prunifolia Splendens'	CAgr CBTr CCVT EBar EBee IPap LBuc LCro LMaj NOra NPip WMat
§ **phaenopyrum**	CLnd CMCN
pinnatifida	CCVT WJur
- 'Big Ball'	CCVT
- var. **major**	CEnd EPfP MMuc
- - 'Big Golden Star' ♀H7	CAgr EBee EPfP MBlu MNHC NOra NPip WHtc WMat WMou
pojarkovae	CAgr
pontica 'Poltzi'	CAgr
'Praecox'	see *C. monogyna* 'Biflora'
prunifolia	see *C. persimilis* 'Prunifolia'
pubescens f. **stipulacea**	see *C. mexicana*
punctata f. **aurea**	EPfP MBlu
schraderiana ♀H6	CAgr CLnd CSpe ELan LCro MBlu MNHC NPip WHtc WMat
submollis	CLnd WJur
succulenta	CAgr
- 'Jubilee' PBR ♀H7	CBTr CCVT LCro LMaj NOra NPip WMat
- 'Long Thorn'	MBlu
- var. **macracantha**	WJur
tanacetifolia	CAgr MBlu
viridis 'Winter King'	CAgr CLnd EPfP
wattiana	ELan

Crataegus × *Sorbus* see × *Crataegosorbus*

Cremanthodium (Asteraceae)

arnicoides	GKev
lineare	GKev

Cremastra (Orchidaceae)

variabilis	WCot

Crepis (Asteraceae)

aurea	LShi

incana ♀H5   EWld MNrw SRms WAbe
rubra   CSpe

Crinitaria see *Aster*

Crinodendron (Elaeocarpaceae)
hookerianum ♀H4   Widely available
- 'Ada Hoffmann'   CBcs CBrac CCoa CEnd CMac CMCN CSde CTsd EBee EGrI EPfP EUrb EWld GEdr GKin LCro MBlu MGos NLar SEle
- 'Alf Robbins'[PBR]   CBcs CCoa CSde EBee EGrI GBin IArd LCro LSou NCth NLar
- 'Ashmount'   EUrb GBin IArd MGos MHtn NCth NLar
patagua   CMac CMCN CTsd EAri EBee EPfP ESwi EUrb NLar SEle SEND SPlb SVen WFar WJur WPav

Crinum (Amaryllidaceae)
americanum   CLil
amoenum   GKev LAma
asiaticum   GKev LAma
* - 'Purpureum'   EAri XFar
'Carolina Beauty'   WCot
'Cintho Alpha'   XFar
'Elizabeth Traub'   WCot
'Ellen Bosanquet'   ELan GKev LAma WCot XFar
'Emma Jones'   WCot
moorei   CBro SChr
- f. *album*   CBcs CTsd EGren GKev LAma
- hybrid   WCot WMal
'Ollene'   WCot
§ × *powellii*   CAby CBcs CBct CBlu CBro ECha EGren ELan EPfP GBin GKev LAma LCro LEdu MNrw SEND SRms WCot WHil XFar
- 'Album'   CAby CBlu CBro EBee ECha ELan EPfP EWes GKev LAma LEdu SEND SMad SMrm SRms WCot WFar WPGP XFar
- 'Harlemense'   EBee WCot
- 'Krelagei'   EBee WMal
- 'Roseum'   see *C.* × *powellii*
'Sangria'   WCot
'Summer Nocturne'   WCot
'White Queen'   WCot

Criogenes see *Cypripedium*

Crithmum (Apiaceae)
maritimum   CCBB CEls IDun LCro MCtn MNHC SPhx SPlb SRms WHil WJek WKit WKor

Crocosmia ✿ (Iridaceae)
'Abundant Joy'   EBee ECrc IBal
'African Beauty'   ECrc IBal
'Anna Marie'   CBro ELan ERCP GAbr GKev LAma WCot WFar
'Antique Gold'   SHar
'Apricot'   IBal
'Ashburnham Red' **new**   SMHy
aurea misapplied   see *C.* × *crocosmiiflora* 'George Davison' Davison
aurea (Pappe ex Hook.f.) Planch.   LRHS
- from Swaziland   IBal
- subsp. *aurea*   CTca ECrc
- 'Golden Ballerina'[PBR]   EBlo LRHS SPoG
'Auricorn'   IBal WPGP
'Aurora'   NGdn
'Bee's Delight'   CTca
'Beth Chatto'   CTca ECrc IBal
'Big Top'   ESgI IBal LRHS
'Blaze'   IBal
'Bowland Blaze'   ESgI IBal
'Bressingham Blaze'   CMHG CTca EBee IBal NGdn
'Bressingham Dark Fires'   EBlo IBal LBar NCth
'Bressingham Flare'   EBlo
BRIGHT EYES ('Walbreyes'[PBR]) ♀H5   EBee EPfP IBal LBar LRHS NCth
'Buttercups'   ELan WCAu
'Cadenza'   IBal
'Caistor Sunset'   IBal
'Carnival'   IBal
'Cascade'   IBal
'Chinatown'   IBal
'Chrome Spray'   CTca
'Citrone Spray'   CTca
'Comet' Knutty   CTca EPPr IBal MNrw
'Cornish Copper'   CTca
'Cornish Red'   CTca
'Cornish Sunset'   CTca
P × *crocosmiiflora*   CTca EHeP LCro SPlb SRms WBrk WShi
- 'African Glow'   IBal
- 'Amberglow'   IBal NPer WFar
- 'Baby Barnaby'   WFar
- 'Babylon'   CAby CBlu CDor CoPl CTca ECrc EGren ELan EPfP GKev IBal LAma LBom LCro LRHS LSto MNrw NBid NLar SAth SPel SRms WCAu WFar
- 'Bicolor' ♀H4   CTca
- 'Burford Bronze'   IBal
- 'Burnt Umber'   IBal
- 'Buttercup'   CBro CDor CTca ECrc ELon EPfP IBal LRHS MPri WFar WSpi
- 'Canary Bird'   CBro ECrc IBal NGdn WSpi
§ - 'Carmin Brillant' ♀H4   CBlu CBro CDor CTca EBee EGrI ELon EPfP EPPr GKev LAma LBom LCro LRHS LSto MGos MPie MPri NGdn SPoG SReu SRms WFar WOld WSpi
- 'Challa'   ECrc IBal
- 'Citrina'   WSpi
- 'Citronella' misapplied   see *C.* × *crocosmiiflora* 'Honey Angels'
- 'Citronella' J.E. Fitt   CoPl EBee ELon EPfP GMaP LSou MBel NGdn SDix WCAu
§ - 'Coleton Fishacre'   CoPl CTca ECha EHeP EPfP GMaP LRHS LSto MMuc NCth SEND WFar WOld WSpi
§ - 'Columbus' ♀H4   CBro CoPl CTca EPfP ERCP EWhm GKev IBal LAma LCro LRHS MPro SIvy SRms WCAu WFar
- 'Colwall'   IBal
- 'Comet'   IBal
- 'Constance' ♀H4   CBro CDor CTca EPPr ERCP GAbr IBal LAma LCro NBid NGdn WCAu WFar
- 'Corona'   IBal
- 'Custard Cream'   ECrc
- 'David Fitt'   IBal WFar
- 'Debutante' ♀H4   CTca ECrc IBal WHoo
§ - 'Diadème'   CTca IBal
- 'Dragonfire' (Nova Series)   LBar MMrt
- 'Dusky Maiden'   CDor CMac GKin GMaP IBal SRms WTre
- 'Dwarf Gold'   IBal
§ - 'E.A. Bowles'   ECrc
- 'Eastern Promise'   IBal

Crocosmia

	Name	Availability
	- 'Elegans'	ECrc IBal
§	- 'Emily McKenzie' ♀H4	Widely available
	- 'Fantasie'	IBal
	- 'Fire Jumper'	CTca IBal LBar LRHS MPro SMad WHoo
	- 'Fireglow'	EGren
	- 'George Davison' misapplied	see *C.* × *crocosmiiflora* 'Golden Glory' ambig., *C.* 'Sulphurea'
§	- 'George Davison' Davison	Widely available
	- 'Gloria'	IBal
	- 'Golden Glory' misapplied	see *C.* × *crocosmiiflora* 'Diadème'
§	- 'Golden Glory' ambig.	CDor EHeP ELan ELon
	- 'Goldfinch'	EBee ELon SMrm
	- 'Goldie'	WFar
	- 'Hades'	IBal
	- 'Harlequin'	CBcs CElw CoPl CTca ECrc EPPr IBal LBar LRHS LSou MAsh MHol MPro SPoG WCAu WFar WHoo WSpi
	- 'His Majesty'	ECrc WFar
	- 'Hoey Joey'	ECrc
§	- 'Honey Angels'	CBcs CElw CTca ECha ECrc ELon EPfP ESgl EWhm GAbr GKin GMaP GQue IBal LRHS MHer MMuc NBir SEND SPoG WCot WFar WSpi
	- 'Irish Dawn'	ECrc IBal
§	- 'Jackanapes'	ELon EPfP IBal MHtn SRms WSpi XFar
	- 'Jackanapes VI'	IBal
	- 'James Coey' misapplied	see *C.* × *crocosmiiflora* 'Carmin Brillant'
	- 'James Coey' J.E. Fitt	ECha EPfP GKin IBal SMrm SPoG
§	- 'Jessie'	CElw
	- 'Judith'	IBal
	- 'Kiautschou'	IBal
	- 'Lady Hamilton'	CDor EPPr IBal
	- 'Lady McKenzie'	see *C.* × *crocosmiiflora* 'Emily McKenzie'
	- 'Lambrook Gold'	CFis ECrc IBal
	- 'Lord Nelson'	IBal
	- 'Loweswater'	IBal
	- 'Lutea'	IBal
	- 'Marjorie'	IBal
	- 'Mars'	ECrc NGdn
	- 'Mephistopheles'	CTca WFar
	- 'Merryman'	ECrc EPPr IBal
	- 'Météore'	LRHS WFar
	- 'Morgenlicht'	IBal WFar
	- 'Mount Usher'	CTca ECrc EPPr IBal MNrw
§	- 'Mrs Geoffrey Howard'	IBal WCru
	- 'Mrs Morrison'	see *C.* × *crocosmiiflora* 'Mrs Geoffrey Howard'
	- 'Newry Seedling'	see *C.* × *crocosmiiflora* 'Prometheus'
	- 'Nimbus'	IBal
§	- 'Norwich Canary'	ECha EGrI ELon GAbr IBal MBNS NBir NGdn WCAu WSpi WTre
	- 'Plaisir'	IBal NBid
	- 'Polo'	IBal LRHS
	- 'Princess'	see *C. pottsii* 'Princess'
	- 'Prolificans'	IBal
§	- 'Prometheus'	IBal
§	- 'Queen Alexandra' J.E. Fitt	ECha EWes
	- 'Queen Charlotte'	IBal
	- 'Queen Mary II'	see *C.* × *crocosmiiflora* 'Columbus'
	- 'Queen of Spain'	ELon IBal
	- 'Rayon d'Or'	IBal
	- 'Red David'	WFar
	- 'Red King'	CDor CoPl EGren EPfP GKev IBal LAma LBom LCro NLar WFar
	- 'Red Knight'	IBal
	- 'Rheingold' misapplied	see *C.* × *crocosmiiflora* 'Diadème'
	- 'Saracen'	CMac CoPl CTca EBee EWhm GKin LEdu MHol Midl SPoG WCot WFar
	- 'Sir Mathew Wilson'	IBal
	- 'Solfatare'	CDor CMac CMHG ECha EGrI EPfP GKin IBal LRHS MBel NBid SRms WCAu WCot WFar WSpi
	- 'Solfatare Coleton Fishacre'	see *C.* × *crocosmiiflora* 'Coleton Fishacre'
	- 'Star of the East' ♀H4	CDor CMac CTca EBee EBlo ECha ELan EPPr GKin GMaP IBal LBar LBom LEdu MPro SRms WCAu WCru WFar WPGP
	- 'Sultan'	WFar
	- 'Sunglow'	CAby CoPl IBal LAma MNrw WSpi
	- 'Twilight Fairy Gold'	EBee ECha MNrw WCot WCru WFar WSpi
	- 'Venus'	CDor IBal MHer WSpi
	- 'Vesuvius'	EPPr IBal
	- 'Vic's Yellow'	IBal
	- 'Voyager'	EGren IBal LAma LRHS NBir
	- 'Wasdale strain'	IBal
	- 'ZealTan'	CBro CMHG EBee EPfP EPPr ESgl EWhm IBal LEdu MNrw NLar NSti SMrm SPoG WCAu WCot WFar
	× *crocosmioides* 'Castle Ward Late' ♀H4	CBro CTca ECha EPfP IBal LBar LEdu LSto SPel WCAu WCot WFar WSpi
	'Crowing Rooster'	LBar
	'Darkleaf Apricot'	see *C.* × *crocosmiiflora* 'Coleton Fishacre'
	'Diablo' (Firestars Series)	IBal LBar
	'Disco Dancer'	NCth
	'Doctor Marion Wood'	IBal
	'Eldorado'	see *C.* × *crocosmiiflora* 'E.A. Bowles'
	'Ellenbank Canary'	ECha IBal
	'Ellenbank Firecrest'	CTca ECrc ELon IBal
	'Ellenbank Skylark'	IBal
	'Emberglow' ♀H4	CBcs CDor CoPl CTca EAri EBee EGren ELon EPfP EPPr ERCP ESgl EUrb GKev GKin GMaP IBal LAma LBar LCro LEdu LRHS LSto MBel MHer NBid NLar SPoG WCAu WSpi
	'Fandango'	ESgl IBal
	'Fever Pitch'	LBar
	'Fire King' misapplied	see *C.* × *crocosmiiflora* 'Jackanapes'
	'Fire King' ambig.	GKev IBal LAma NLar NSti
	'Firebird'	CDor ELon MHol SRms WCot
	'Firefly'	SPel
	(Firestars Series) 'Firestars Firestarter'	IBal LBar LRHS MAsh NCth SHar SMad
	- 'Firestars Hot Spot' ♀H5	ECrc LBar NCth SMad
	- 'Firestars Scorchio' ♀H5	ECrc IBal LBar LRHS NCth SHar SMad
	'Fleuve Jaune'	IBal
	'Forbidden City'	LBar
	'Forest Fire'	IBal
	fucata	CTca
	'Fugue'	CTca IBal SMad
	'Gold Dragon' (Nova Series) **new**	Midl
	'Golden Dew'	IBal WCot WFar
	GOLDEN FLEECE *sensu* Lemoine	see *C.* × *crocosmiiflora* 'Coleton Fishacre'
	'Harmonia'	CTca
	'Hellfire' ♀H5	Widely available
	'Highlight'	IBal
	'Jennine'	IBal
	'Jenny'	IBal
	JENNY BLOOM ('Blacro')	EBee IBal

'John Boots'	ELon MPri NBid
'Jupiter'	CTca IBal NBir SPel WHil
'Karin'	CTca ECrc LBar WFar
'Kathleen'	ECrc
'Kilmurry Orange'	IBal
'Krakatoa'	ECrc MHer WFar
'Lady Ann'	CBlu CBro ECrc LAma
'Lady Jane'	CTca ECrc LAma
'Lady Wilson' misapplied	see *C.* × *crocosmiiflora* 'Norwich Canary'
'Lana de Savary' ♀H4	EPPr EWes IBal NBid WCot
'Late Cornish'	see *C.* × *crocosmiiflora* 'Queen Alexandra' J.E. Fitt
'Late Lucifer'	IBal
'Late Yellow'	IBal
'Lava' (Firestars Series)	LRHS
'Lemon Spray'	CTca
'Limpopo' ♀H5	CBcs CBro CMac CMHG CSpe CTca EBee ECha ELon EPfP IBal LEdu MArl MAvo MBNS MNrw MPro NLar SDix WCAu WCot WFar WPGP
'Lincolnshire Gold'	ECrc
'Lucifer' ♀H5	Widely available
LUCIFER'S CHILDREN	ELan
§ 'Marcotijn'	CTca IBal
masoniorum misapplied	see *C.* 'Marcotijn'
masoniorum (L. Bolus) N.E. Br.	CBcs CMac ECha EGren EGrI EHeP ELan GMaP IBal LAma LCro LRHS MSCN NBir NGdn SPlb StAn SVen WCot
– from Satan's Nek, South Africa	IBal
– 'African Dawn'	CTca
– 'Dixter Flame'	ECha SDix
– 'Golden Swan'	SRms
– hybrid	ECrc
– 'Rowallane Orange'	IBal
– 'Rowallane Yellow'	CTca EPPr IBal MNrw WPGP
– 'Sherbert Orange'	IBal
– Slieve Donard selection	IBal
mathewsiana	CTca
aff. *mathewsiana*	IBal
'Mex'	ECha IBal MPro WPGP
'Ministar'	ECrc WFar
'Minotaur'	IBal
'Miss Scarlet' ♀H4	EPfP IBal NCth SAko
'Mistral'	CBlu GAbr IBal LBom LCro NLar WFar XFar
'Moorland Sunset'	IBal
'Mount Stewart'	see *C.* × *crocosmiiflora* 'Jessie'
'Okavango'	CBcs CBro CMac CoPI CTca ELon IBal LRHS LSou MAvo MBNS MHol MNrw MPro NLar NSti SMHy SMrm WCAu WCot WFar WSpi
OLD HAT	see *C.* 'Walberton Red'
'Orange Devil'	EPfP ESgI EWes GKin IBal MBNS SPel WGoo
ORANGE PEKOE ('Pek Or'PBR)	EUrb IBal LCro LRHS MPro NSti
'Orange River'	ECha IBal WCot WFar
'Orangeade'	IBal SRms
'Pageant'	IBal
§ *paniculata*	CFis CMac GAbr NBid WPGP
– 'Cally Greyleaf'	EBee EPPr GBin IBal MNrw WCot WMal
– 'Cally Sword'	CSpe EPPr IBal
– 'Natal'	CTca IBal
– red-flowered	IBal
'Paul's Best Yellow' ♀H4	Widely available
'Peach Melba'	XFar
'Peach Spray'	CTca
'Peach Sunrise'	IBal LRHS MPro SMrm
'Phillipa Browne'	IBal NLar WCot
'Ping Pong'	CTca
'Plancheon'	IBal
pottsii 'Culzean Pink'	CTca EPPr EWhm GBin IBal MNrw NBid NBir WFar
– 'Grandiflora'	IBal
§ – 'Princess'	CoPI IBal LAma LRHS
– tall	IBal
'Pride of Plantion'	CTca ECrc LBar
'Prince of Orange'	CBro CTca EBee ERCP GKev LAma LBar LCro LRHS WCAu WFar XFar
'Queen Alexandra'	WFar
'Red Star'	IBal
rosea	see *Tritonia disticha* subsp. *rubrolucens*
'Rowden Bronze'	see *C.* × *crocosmiiflora* 'Coleton Fishacre'
'Rowden Chrome'	see *C.* × *crocosmiiflora* 'George Davison' Davison
'R.W. Wallace'	IBal
'Sampford Yellow'	IBal
'Saturn'	see *C.* 'Jupiter'
'Scarlatti'	IBal
'Severn Sunrise' ♀H5	CMac CTca EGrI EWhm GKin GMaP IBal MArl MHer MMuc NBir NGdn SMHy SRms WCAu WFar WSpi WTre
'Shocking'	IBal
'Short Apricot' **new**	IBal
'Sonate'	ECrc
'Spitfire' ♀H4	CCps CTca IBal WFar
'Splash of Claret'	WCot
§ 'Sulphurea'	IBal LCro LSto
'Sun Flare'	CTca
'Sunset'	XFar
'Sunzest'	IBal
'Suzanna'	CTca ECrc ERCP ESgI GKev LAma MPro NLar XFar
'Tai Pan'	IBal MPro
'Tamar Bronze'	CTca
'Tamar Double Red' (d) ♀H4	CTca
'Tamar Glow'	CTca WOld
'Tamar Gold'	CTca
'Tamar Golden Ring'	CTca
'Tamar New Dawn'	CTca
'Tangerine Queen'	IBal
'Tanllyd'	WCot
'Twilight Fairy Crimson'	CTsd CWGN ECrc NCth NLar SMrm WFar WSpi
I 'Vulcan' A. Bloom	CTca IBal
§ 'Walberton Red'	CTca EBee IBal LRHS MArl
WALBERTON YELLOW ('Walcroy') ♀H4	CBro IBal LRHS
'Yellow Emberglow'	EGren
'Zambesi'	CBro CMac ELon IBal LRHS MBNS MNrw WCAu WCot
'Zeal Giant' ♀H4	CTca IBal SChr
'Zeal Unnamed' ♀H4	CBro CTca IBal

Crocus ❀ (Iridaceae)

'Advance'	CBro EGren EPot GKev LAma LCro
ancyrensis 'Golden Bunch'	LAma
§ *angustifolius* ♀H6	EPot GKev LAma
– 'Minor'	ERCP
'Aqua' **new**	GKev LAma
'Ard Schenk'	CBro EGren EPfP ETay GKev LAma XFar
asturicus	see *C. serotinus* subsp. *salzmannii*
aureus	see *C. flavus* subsp. *flavus*
banaticus ♀H6	GArf NHar

Crocus

Name	Suppliers
biflorus 'Blue Pearl' ♀H6	CBro EGren EPfP EPot ERCP ETay GKev LAma LCro SPhx WCot WShi XFar
- 'Miss Vain'	EPot ERCP GKev LAma
- subsp. *weldenii* 'Albus'	LAma
- - 'Fairy'	EPot GKev LAma
- 'Blue Bird'	EGren
- 'Blue Ocean' **new**	GKev LAma
boryi	EPot
§ *cancellatus*	LAma
subsp. *cancellatus*	
- var. *cilicicus*	see *C. cancellatus* subsp. *cancellatus*
candidus var. *subflavus*	see *C. olivieri* subsp. *olivieri*
cartwrightianus 'Albus' misapplied	see *C. hadriaticus*
chrysanthus	CHab
- 'Blue Marlin'	ERCP
- 'Buttercup'	LAma
- 'Cream Beauty' ♀H6	CBro EGren EPfP EPot ERCP ETay GKev LAma LCro WShi
- var. *fuscotinctus*	EGren EPot GKev LAma LCro
'Cloth of Gold'	see *C. angustifolius*
corsicus ♀H6	EPot GKev LAma
§ × *cultorum*	XFar
'Dorothy'	EGren EPot GKev LAma WShi
'Dutch Yellow'	see *C.* × *luteus* 'Golden Yellow'
etruscus 'Zwanenburg'	EPot GKev LAma
§ *flavus* subsp. *flavus* ♀H6	WShi
fleischeri	EPot GKev LAma
'Flower Record'	EGren EGKev LAma LCro XFar
gargaricus	GKev LAma
'Gipsy Girl'	EPot ERCP GKev LAma LCro XFar
'Golden Mammoth'	see *C.* × *luteus* 'Golden Yellow'
'Goldilocks' ♀H6	EPot ETay GKev LAma
goulimyi ♀H6	EPot WCot
- subsp. *leucanthus*	GKev
* *gramensis* **new**	GKev
'Grand Maître'	EGren ETay GKev LAma LCro NNys
§ *hadriaticus*	LAma NDry
- var. *chrysobelonicus*	see *C. hadriaticus*
'Herald'	ETay GKev LAma XFar
§ *heuffelianus*	LAma
- 'Michael's Purple'	GKev
'Ice Queen' **new**	GKev LAma
imperati	ERCP GKev LAma
subsp. *suaveolens* 'De Jager'	
'Ivory Princess' **new**	GKev LAma
'Jeanne d'Arc'	CAby CBro EGren EPot ETay GKev LAma LCro LRHS NNys XFar
karduchorum	EPot LAma
'King of the Striped'	EPot GKev LAma LCro
korolkowii	GKev LAma LRHS XFar
- 'Kiss of Spring'	EPot GKev LAma
kosaninii	GKev
- 'April View'	LAma
kotschyanus ♀H6	EGrI LAma MBros
'Ladykiller'	EGren EPot ERCP GKev LAma
laevigatus ♀H4	GKev LAma
- 'Fontenayi'	EPot ERCP LAma
- 'Large Yellow'	see *C.* × *luteus* 'Golden Yellow'
× *leonidii* 'Early Gold'	LAma
ligusticus ♀H6	LAma
§ × *luteus* 'Golden Yellow' ♀H6	CBro EGren EPot ETay GKev LAma LCro LRHS NNys
malyi ♀H6	GKev LAma
mathewii	EPot GKev LAma NDry
- 'Dream Dancer'	EPot
minimus	EPot ERCP GKev LAma
- 'Spring Beauty'	EGren ERCP LCro XFar
niveus	EPot LAma
nudiflorus	GKev
ochroleucus	LAma
olivieri subsp. *balansae*	EPot
§ - - 'Orange Monarch'	EGren ERCP ETay GKev LAma XFar
- - 'Zwanenburg'	GKev LAma
§ - subsp. *olivieri*	LAma
'Orange Monarch'	see *C. olivieri* subsp. *balansae* 'Orange Monarch'
'Panda' **new**	ERCP
'Pickwick'	CAby CBro EGren ETay GKev LAma LCro XFar
'Polar Bear' **new**	ERCP
'Prins Claus'	EGren EPot ERCP GKev LAma LCro MBros XFar
pulchellus ♀H6	LAma
- 'Albus'	LAma
- 'Inspiration'	GKev
puringii	GKev
'Remembrance'	CAby CBro EGren EPot ETay GKev LAma LCro NBir
'Romance'	EGren EPot GKev LAma LCro XFar
'Ruby Giant'	CBro EGren EPfP EPot ERCP ETay GKev LAma LCro LRHS NNys XFar
rujanensis	GKev
salzmannii	see *C. serotinus* subsp. *salzmannii*
sativus	EGren ELan EPot ERCP LAma LCro LRHS MHtn NBir NNys SVic XFar
scepusiensis	see *C. heuffelianus*
§ *serotinus*	GKev LAma MNrw
subsp. *salzmannii*	
sieberi subsp. *atticus* 'Firefly'	EGren EPot GKev LAma XFar
- 'Ronald Ginns'	EPot GKev
'Snow Bunting' ♀H6	EGren ELan LAma LCro WShi
speciosus ♀H6	LAma LCro NBir WShi XFar
- 'Albus' ♀H6	EGrI EPot ERCP LAma LCro
- 'Cassiope'	LAma
- 'Conqueror'	ELan ERCP LAma LCro NBir
- 'Oxonian'	ELan EPot LAma
- subsp. *speciosus*	EPot NBir
- subsp. *xantholaimos*	GKev
striped	EPfP
sublimis 'Tricolor' ♀H6	CBro EGren EPfP EPot ETay GKev LAma LCro NBir XFar
susianus	see *C. angustifolius*
suterianus	see *C. olivieri* subsp. *olivieri*
tommasinianus ♀H6	CBro CHab ELan EPot GKev LAma LCro LRHS LSto MCtn NBir NNys SRms WShi XFar
- 'Albus'	EPot GKev LAma
- 'Barr's Purple'	CAby EGren EPot ETay GKev LAma LCro NBir NNys
- 'Lilac Beauty'	EPot GKev LAma
- 'Pictus'	GKev
- 'Roseus'	EPot GKev LAma
- 'Whitewell Purple'	CBro EGren EPot ERCP ETay GKev LAma LCro LSto NBir
tournefortii ♀H4	EPot
vallicola	GKev
'Vanguard' ♀H6	EGren GKev LAma LCro WCot
veluchensis	GKev
§ *vernus*	GKev WShi
- subsp. *albiflorus*	see *C. vernus*
- garden hybrids	see *C.* × *cultorum*
- 'Lavender Symphony'	GKev
- subsp. *vernus* 'Silver Coral' **new**	ERCP
- 'Whale Shark' **new**	ERCP
versicolor 'Picturatus'	EPot ERCP GKev LAma
yalovensis	GKev

Crocus

'Yalta'	GKev LAma SPhx WCot XFar
'Yellow Mammoth'	see *C.* × *luteus* 'Golden Yellow'
yellow-flowered	XFar
'Zenith'	GKev
'Zephyr' ♡H6	EPot GKev LAma

Crossyne (Amaryllidaceae)
flava	WCot

Crucianella (Rubiaceae)
stylosa	see *Phuopsis stylosa*

Cruciata (Rubiaceae)
glabra	MAsh
laevipes	NAts

Crusea (Rubiaceae)
coccinea	GEdr WCot

Cryptanthus (Bromeliaceae)
bivittatus ♡H1a	NCft
- 'Pink Starlite' (v) ♡H1a	NCft
- 'Red Star'	MPri

× *Cryptbergia* (Bromeliaceae)
'Rubra'	SChr

Cryptocarya (Lauraceae)
alba	SVen

Cryptocoryne (Araceae)
beckettii 'Angustifolia'	ELin
blassii	ELin

Cryptomeria ✿ (Cupressaceae)
fortunei	see *C. japonica*
§ *japonica*	CAco CMen IPap LMaj LRHS MBlu MCtn MMuc SEND WJur WMou
- Araucarioides Group	CAco CBcs
- 'Bandai-sugi' ♡H6	CAco CMac CMen MGos NLar
- 'Barabits Gold'	CAco IArd LRHS
- 'Carmel'	MBlu
- 'Compressa'	CAco EPfP LRHS MAsh
§ - 'Cristata'	CAco CCVT CMac ELan MGos
- 'Dacrydioides'	CAco NLar
- 'Dinger'	CAco NLar
- 'Elegans Aurea'	CCVT ELan MMuc SPoG WFar
- 'Elegans Compacta' ♡H6	CMac CSBt ELan EUrb LRHS MAsh MMuc MPri NLar SRms WSpi
- Elegans Group	CBcs CMac CSBt EGren ELan EPfP LRHS LSto MGos MMuc NLar SEND SPoG WFar WMat
- - 'Elegans' ♡H6	CBrac CCVT EBar SAth SEWo
- 'Elegans Nana'	LCro SRms
- 'Elegans Viridis' ♡H6	CAco EGren LRHS MPri SArc WMat
I - 'Elegantissima'	CCVT
- 'Globosa Nana' ♡H6	CAco CDoC ERom MGos MPri SArc SPoG WCha
- 'Golden Promise' ♡H6	CAco CBcs LRHS LSto MAsh
- Gracilis Group	CAco LRHS WMat
- 'Green Pearl'	CAco
- 'HB Bandai'	MBlu
- 'Hide' **new**	NLar
- 'Jindai-sugi'	CAco CMac
- 'Kamasan'	NLar
- 'Kitayama-dai'	CAco
- 'Kyara Gold'	NLar
- 'Little Champion'	CAco ELan MAsh NLar SArc
- 'Little Sonja'	CAco
- 'Lobbii Nana' hort.	see *C. japonica* 'Nana'
- 'Magic Bonsai'	NLar
- 'Midare'	CAco
- 'Monstrosa Nana'	CAco EGren
- 'Mushroom'	GKev LRHS MAsh SPoG
§ - 'Nana'	CMac SEWo SRms
- 'Pipo'	CAco MBlu
- 'Pygmaea'	CAco SRms
- 'Rasen-sugi'	CAco NLar SBig SMad
- 'Sekkan-sugi' ♡H6	CAco CBcs CBrac CCVT CMac ELan EPfP ESwi EUrb GKin IArd LCro LRHS MAsh MGos MPri NLar SBig SMad SPoG WFar WMat
- 'Sekka-sugi'	see *C. japonica* 'Cristata'
- SERAMA ('Fm5')	CAco
- 'Shigyoku' **new**	NLar
§ - 'Spiralis' ♡H6	CAco CMac ELan EPfP EUrb LCro MAsh MGos SAko SPoG WFar
- 'Spiraliter Falcata'	CAco NLar
- 'Tansu'	CAco
- 'Tenzan-sugi' ♡H6	CAco EPfP WAbe
- 'Tenzan-yatsubusa'	CMen
- 'Tilford Gold'	LRHS NLit
- 'Tomahawk' **new**	NLar
- 'Twinkle Toes'	CAco LRHS MBlu
- 'Vilmorin Gold'	CAco WCha
- 'Vilmoriniana' ♡H6	CAco CWnw EGren ELan EPfP GKin LCro LRHS LSRN MAsh MGos SPoG WFar
- 'Yatsubusa'	see *C. japonica* 'Tansu', 'Yokohama'
§ - 'Yokohama'	CAco LRHS
- 'Yore-sugi'	see *C. japonica* 'Spiralis', 'Spiraliter Falcata'
sinensis	see *C. japonica*

Cryptostegia (Apocynaceae)
grandiflora	MCtn

Cryptotaenia (Apiaceae)
canadensis	SPhx
japonica	CAgr CHby EHet MCtn MHoo MNHC WHer WJek
- f. *atropurpurea*	CDor CSpe ECha EWhm MCtn

Ctenanthe (Marantaceae)
§ *amabilis* ♡H1b	LBom NHrt
§ *burle-marxii*	CDoC LBom NHrt
- var. *burle-marxii*	LBom
lubbersiana	LBom
oppenheimiana	LBom LCro
- 'Amagris' PBR	LBom NHrt
pilosa 'Golden Mosaic' (v)	LBom

Cucubalus see *Silene*

cucumber see AGM Vegetables Section

Cucurbita (Cucurbitaceae)
pepo	LCro

Cudrania see *Maclura*

cumin see *Cuminum cyminum*

Cuminum (Apiaceae)
cyminum	MCtn MNHC SRms SVic

Cumulopuntia (Cactaceae)
§ *boliviana*	SPlb
subsp. *boliviana*	
§ - subsp. *dactylifera*	SBig

Curio   219

§	*sphaerica*	SPlb

Cunninghamia (*Cupressaceae*)

§	*lanceolata*	CAco CMac SArc WJur WPGP
	- 'Glauca'	CAco CJun
	- 'Samurai'	CAco
	sinensis	see *C. lanceolata*
	unicaniculata	see *C. lanceolata*

Cuphea (*Lythraceae*)

	caeciliae	EShb SEle
	cyanea	CSpe SDix
	'David Verity'	SHar
	'Harlequin'	EShb
	hyssopifolia ♀^{H2}	EShb
	- 'Alba'	EShb
	- 'Rosea'	EShb
§	*ignea* ♀^{H2}	CTsd MCtn SEle WJun
	- 'Matchless'	SVic
	- 'Roxy'	EPPr SHar
	lanceolata 'Purple Passion' ♀^{H2}	MCtn
	'Lilac Belle'	CSpe
I	*macrophylla* hort.	CHll
	maculata	CHll
	platycentra	see *C. ignea*
	procumbens SWEET TALK LAVENDER SPLASH ('Pas11697l2') **new**	LSou
	× *purpurea* 'Firecracker'	SPoG
	'Torpedo'	LCro MBros
	VERMILLIONAIRE ('Cupver')	WCot
	viscosissima	CSpe MCtn

Cupressus (*Cupressaceae*)

	arizonica	CAco EUrb NPlm SArc
I	- 'Fastigiata Aurea'	NPlm
§	- var. *glabra*	CAco
	- - 'Aurea'	CAco
	- - 'Blue Ice'	CAco CMac LCro LRHS MAsh
	- - 'Fastigiata'	CCVT EPfP
	- - 'Glauca'	CAco EBar LRHS
	- var. *nevadensis*	CAco
	- 'Pyramidalis' ♀^{H5}	SEND
	- 'Réka'	CAco
	- var. *stephensonii*	CAco
I	- 'Sulfurea'	CAco
	austrotibetica KR 5528E	WPGP
	bakeri	CAco
	cashmeriana ♀^{H3}	CAco SHor
	- KR 8688A	WPGP
	- 'Blue Wave'	CAco
	chengiana	CAco
	duclouxiana	CAco
	dupreziana	CAco
	- var. *atlantica*	CAco WPGP
	funebris	see *C. pendula* Thunb.
	gigantea	CAco
	- KR 3353	WPGP
	glabra	see *C. arizonica* var. *glabra*
	goveniana	CAco
	- var. *abramsiana*	CAco
	- var. *goveniana* **new**	WPGP
	guadalupensis	CAco
	- var. *forbesii*	CAco
	- var. *guadalupensis*	CAco
	× *leylandii*	see × *Cuprocyparis leylandii*
	lusitanica	CAco
	- var. *benthamii*	CAco
	- 'Brice's Weeping'	CAco
	macnabiana	CAco
	macrocarpa	CAco CBcs CCVT CMCN IPap MCtn SEND SPlb WCha
	- 'Crippsii'	MAsh
	- 'Goldcrest' ♀^{H4}	CAco CBcs CCVT CMac EBar EGren ELan MGos MPri NBir SEWo WCha WHtc
	- 'Golden Pillar'	CMac
I	- 'Pendula'	SArc
	- 'Wilma' ♀^{H4}	CBTr CMac CSBt EGren ELan EPfP LCro LRHS MAsh MGos SFol SPoG WMat
	nootkatensis	see *Xanthocyparis nootkatensis*
§	*pendula* Thunb.	CAco
	sargentii	CAco
	sempervirens	CBrP ELan EPfP ERom EUrb LCro LMaj LRHS LWaG MPri SAth SBig SFol SPlb WCha WFar WMat
	- 'Agrimed'	LSRN
	- 'Bolgheri'	LSRN
	- 'Garda'	CWnw WMat
	- 'Karaca Fastigiata Aurea'	CAco
	- 'Pyramidalis'	see *C. sempervirens* Stricta Group
	- var. *sempervirens*	see *C. sempervirens* Stricta Group
§	- Stricta Group	CBcs CBrac CCVT EBar EGren EPfP EUrb LMaj NLar SArc SAth SEND SEWo WCha WSpi
	- 'Stricta Blue'	CAco
	- 'Totem Pole'	CAco CCVT CSBt ELan EOli EPfP EUrb IPap LCro LMaj LRHS MGos NLit NPlm SAth SHor SPoG WCha WMat
	torulosa	CAco

Cupressus × *Xanthocyparis* see × *Cuprocyparis*

× *Cuprocyparis* ✿ (*Cupressaceae*)

§	*leylandii*	Widely available
§	- '2001'	CCVT SGol
	- 'Blue Jeans'^{PBR}	NLit SEND
§	- 'Castlewellan'	CMac EBar EHeP LBuc LSRN MAsh MGos MPri NHed SEND SGol SPoG WFar
	- 'Ferngold'	MAsh
	- 'Galway Gold'	see × *C. leylandii* 'Castlewellan'
	- 'Gold Rider' ♀^{H6}	CCVT CMac ELan MAsh SEND SPoG WCha WFar
	- 'Green Ornament'	SMad
	- 'Haggerston Grey'	SEND
§	- 'Harlequin' (v)	CMac SEND
	- 'Naylor's Blue'	CMac SEND
	- 'Pyramidalis'	see × *C. leylandii* '2001'
	- 'Robinson's Gold'	CMac SGol
	- 'Variegata'	see × *C. leylandii* 'Harlequin'

Curculigo (*Hypoxidaceae*)

	crassifolia	CExl EUrb
	- B&SWJ 2318	WCru
	- NJM 10.123	WPGP

Curcuma ✿ (*Zingiberaceae*)

	alismatifolia	XFar
	longa	SPlb SPre
	ornata	EAri
	roscoeana	SBig
	zedoaria 'Pink Wonder'	LAma
	- 'White Wonder'	LAma

Curio (*Asteraceae*)

§	*articulatus*	EShb NCft NGKo
	- 'Candlelight' (v) ♀^{H1c}	WCor
§	*ficoides*	EShb NCft

220 *Curio*

- 'Mount Everest'^{PBR}	EShb	
radicans	CoPl CPic EShb SIvy	
§ repens	CDoC CoPl EShb SArc SEND SIvy SPlb	
§ rowleyanus ♀H2	CDoC CoPl CPic EShb LBom LCro LWaG MPri NCft SMrm WCor WOld	
talinoides 'Himalayan Blue'	WCot	
§ - subsp. mandraliscae	CPic EAri	
- - 'Blue Finger'	WCot	

Cussonia ✿ (Araliaceae)

paniculata	CDTJ CWGN SPlb
sphaerocephala	SPlb
spicata	CDTJ SPlb
transvaalensis	CDTJ

custard apple see *Annona cherimola*

Cyananthus (Campanulaceae)

integer misapplied	see *C. microphyllus*
lobatus ♀H5	EPot WAbe
- 'Albus'	NHar WAbe
- giant	GEdr NHar
microphyllus ♀H5	GEdr GKev NHar WAbe
sherriffii	WAbe

Cyanotis (Commelinaceae)

arachnoidea	WTra
beddomei 'Coeruleus'	WCot
ceylanica	WTra
ciliata 'Hijau Baru'	WTra
somaliensis ♀H1b	EShb
villosa	WTra

Cyathea (Cyatheaceae)

australis	see *Alsophila australis*
cooperi	see *Sphaeropteris cooperi*
dealbata	see *Alsophila tricolor*
dregei	see *Alsophila dregei*
felina	see *Sphaeropteris felina*
medullaris	see *Sphaeropteris medullaris*
podophylla	see *Gymnosphaera podophylla*
spinulosa	see *Alsophila spinulosa*
tomentosissima	see *Sphaeropteris tomentosissima*

Cyathodes (Ericaceae)

colensoi	see *Leucopogon colensoi*

Cycas (Cycadaceae)

circinalis	NPlm
panzhihuaensis	NPlm SPlb
revoluta ♀H3	CBrP CDoC EBee EGren EOli EShb LCro LWaG MCtn NHrt NPlm SArc SAth SBig SEND SFol SPlb
§ rumphii	CBrP
taitungensis	CBrP
thouarsii	see *C. rumphii*

Cyclamen ✿ (Primulaceae)

africanum	MAsh WHil
§ alpinum	GKev LAma MAsh
- f. leucanthum **new**	GKev
- 'Nettleton White'	MAsh
balearicum	LAma
cilicium ♀H3	EGrI EPPr ETay GKev LAma LCro MAsh MHtn WHil
- f. album	EGrI EPot EPPr GKev LAma MAsh
colchicum	GKev LAma MAsh
confusum	MCtn
§ coum ♀H5	Widely available
- subsp. coum	GKev MAsh
f. albissimum	
- - - 'Golan Heights'	MCtn
- - f. coum Nymans Group	MAsh
- - - Pewter Group ♀H5	CTtf GEdr WCot
- - - - 'Maurice Dryden'	EPot LAma LEdu MHer WHoo
- - - - 'Tilebarn Elizabeth'	MAsh NBir WHoo
- - - Silver Group	EPot GKev LAma LRHS WFar WHoo
- - - - magenta-flowered	WHoo
- - - - pink-flowered **new**	WHil
- - - - red-flowered	WHoo
- - f. pallidum 'Album'	CDor EGrI EWhm GEdr GKev GMaP ISha LAma LCro MCtn WCAu WHil WHoo WPnP WShi
- - - 'Marbled Moon'	LAma
- (Cyberia Series) 'Cyberia Red'	LRHS
- - 'Cyberia White'	LRHS
- dark pink-flowered	WHoo
- marble-leaved	SBea WHoo
- 'Meaden's Crimson'	CBro EPot GKev
- red-flowered	EGrI GKev
I - 'Rubrum'	LCro
- 'Ruby Star'	ELan GEdr
- selected leaf form	EPot GEdr LRHS
cyprium	GKev MAsh
- 'Galaxy'	MAsh
× drydeniae	WHil
europaeum	see *C. purpurascens*
graecum	EPPr GKev LAma MCtn MHer SRot WAbe WHil
- subsp. graecum f. album	GKev LAma MAsh WAbe
- - f. graecum 'Glyfada'	EPot GKev LAma
§ hederifolium ♀H5	Widely available
- S&L 175/1	WCot
- 'Amazeme' (Amazeme Series)	ISha WCot
- arrow leaf **new**	LAma
- arrow-head	GKev
- subsp. crassifolium	WHil
- var. hederifolium	CBcs CBro CDor EBee ECha EGrI ELan GKev LAma LCro LEdu LShi LSto SBea SEND WCAu WHoo WPnP
f. albiflorum ♀H5	
- - - 'Album'	CWCL WShi
- - - 'Discovery'	WCot
- - - 'Nettleton Silver'	see *C. hederifolium* var. hederifolium f. albiflorum 'White Cloud'
- - - 'Perlenteppich'	GMaP
§ - - - 'White Cloud' ♀H5	MAsh
- - f. hederifolium 'Fairy Rings'	MAsh
- - - 'Rosenteppich'	CMiW
- - - 'Ruby Glow'	LRHS MAsh NBir
- - - Silver Cloud Group ♀H5	CBro CDor MAsh NBir WHoo
- - - 'Silver Shield'	MAsh
- - - 'Stargazer'	MAsh
- island scented strain	WCot
- 'Lysander'	GKev MAsh
- Red Sky	CBro EPot GKev LAma MAsh WPGP
- 'Rosy Pink'	EGrI
- Silver-leaved Group	CSpe CTtf ECha EPot GEdr GKev LAma LRHS WFar WHil
- - 'Silver Leaf Pink'	GBin GMaP
- - 'Silver Leaf White'	GMaP
- - 'Silverme Pink'	EPPr LRHS
- - 'Silverme White'	LRHS
- 'Indiaka Violet'	LRHS
intaminatum	GKev LAma MAsh
latifolium	see *C. persicum*

libanoticum	GKev LAma MAsh MCtn WHil		- 'Seibosa' (F)	SKee
maritimum	WHil		- 'Serbian Gold' (F) ♀H5	CAda CBTr CCVT CEnd CMac
mirabile ♀H4	EGrI EPot GKev LAma MAsh WAbe WHil			EGren ELan EPom LCro MLod MNHC NLar NOra SKee WMat
- 'Alba'	EGrI GKev LAma		- 'Shams' (F)	SKee
- f. *mirabile* 'Tilebarn Anne'	MAsh		- SIBLEY'S PATIO QUINCE (F)	EPom
- - 'Tilebarn Nicholas'	MAsh		- 'Smyrna' (F)	NOra WMat
neapolitanum	see *C. hederifolium*		- 'Sobu' (F)	SKee
orbiculatum	see *C. coum*		- 'Vranja' misapplied	see *C. oblonga* 'Bereczki'
§ *persicum*	LWaG MAsh WCot		- 'Vranja' ambig. (F)	CBcs CBTr CDoC IPap LMaj MAsh MLod MSwo SBmr SEdi SPoG
- ABSOLU DE MOREL	LSou			
- 'Ashwood Silver Leaf'	MAsh		- 'Vranja' Nenadovic (F)	CAgr CEnd CHab CLnd CMac EBee ELan EPfP EPom LBuc LCro LSRN MGos MMuc NLar NOra SEND SKee SSFr WMat WWct
- var. *persicum*	MAsh			
f. *puniceum*				
'Tilebarn Karpathos'				
- (Super Verano Series)	LCro		*Cylindropuntia* (Cactaceae)	
VERANO DARK VIOLET			§ *fulgida*	NCft NPlm
- - VERANO NEON PINK	LCro		*imbricata*	CBlu NCft SPlb WJur
- - VERANO RED	LCro		*kleiniae*	SBig
- WINFALL WHITE	LCro		*leptocaulis*	NCft
('Synwinfwhi')			*whipplei*	NCft
(Winfall Series)				
pseudibericum ♀H4	GKev LAma MAsh WCot		*Cymbalaria* (Plantaginaceae)	
- f. *roseum*	MAsh		*aequitriloba* 'Alba'	NRya
§ *purpurascens*	EPot GKev LAma MAsh		§ *hepaticifolia*	SPlb
'Rainier Scarlet' (Rainier Series)	LCro		§ *muralis*	CoPl GAbr GJos LShi MCtn MHer NRya SPhx WHer WIce
repandum	CTtf GKev LAma MAsh		- 'Albiflora'	see *C. muralis* 'Pallidior'
- subsp. *repandum*	LAma LRHS		- 'Kenilworth White'	WCot
f. *album*			- 'Nana Alba'	MWlw WAbe WIce
rohlfsianum	GKev LAma MAsh		- 'Pallidior'	SPhx
× *schwarzii*	MAsh		§ *pallida*	EBee EPfP GQue MAsh MMuc SEND SPlb WAbe WFar
trochopteranthum	see *C. alpinum*			
			I - 'Alba'	EPfP WFar
Cyclanthera (Cucurbitaceae)			§ *pilosa*	NLar
pedata	NGKo			
			Cymbopogon (Poaceae)	
Cyclea (Menispermaceae)			*citratus*	CAgr CGHo CWal EHet ENfk IDun LCro MHoo MNHC SEdi SPlb SPre SRms SVic
polypetala KWJ 12157	WCru			
Cyclosorus (Thelypteridaceae)			*flexuosus*	CAgr MCtn SRms WJek WKit
falcilobus	LRHS			
tottoides	LEdu WPGP		*Cymophyllus* (Cyperaceae)	
			§ *fraserianus*	SBrt
Cydonia ✿ (Rosaceae)				
japonica	see *Chaenomeles japonica*		*Cynanchum* (Apocynaceae)	
oblonga (F)	LMaj MCtn SPre WJur		*ascyrifolium*	EAri EBee
- 'Agvambari' (F)	SKee		*decorsei*	EAri
- 'Aromatnaya' (F)	CBTr MLod NOra SKee WMat		*stoloniferum*	EAri
- 'Bereczcki'	see *C. oblonga* 'Bereczki'			
§ - 'Bereczki' (F)	EGren NOra		*Cynara* (Asteraceae)	
- 'Champion' (F)	CAgr CHab CLnd EBee ELan EPom LBuc LCro LMaj NOra SEdi SKee SVic WMat		*cardunculus* ♀H5	Widely available
			- 'Bianco Avorio'	SVic
- 'Early Prolific' (F)	SEdi SEND		- dwarf	SDix
- 'Ekmek' (F)	SKee		- subsp. *flavescens*	EPPr IDun
- 'Gamboa' (F)	SKee		- - from La Gomera	WCot
- 'Iranian' (F)	CAgr SKee		I - 'Florist Cardy'	NLar
- 'Isfahan' (F)	SKee WMat		- 'Gobbo di Nizza'	SRms
- 'Krymsk' (F)	CAgr WWct		- 'Porto Spineless'	CAgr LShi MCtn
- 'Leskovac' (F)	CAgr CLnd EPom LCro LMaj NOra SBmr WWct		§ - Scolymus Group	CBcs CTsd EGrI EWes LCro LRHS LSRN MNHC MPro SHar SPoG WHer WKit
§ - 'Lusitanica' (F)	CAgr CHab EPom LCro MLod SSFr WMat			
- 'Meech's Prolific' (F)	CAda CAgr CBTr CHab CLnd EBee EGren ELan EPfP EPom LBuc LCro LSRN MGos MLod MMuc NLar NOra SBmr SEdi SKee SSFr WMat		- - 'Gros Camus de Bretagne'	WCot
			- - 'Gros Vert de Láon' ♀H5	CBcs ELan LEdu WCot
			- - 'Monica Lynden-Bell'	WCot
			- - 'Purple Globe'	SRms
- pear-shaped (F)	CHab		- - 'Romanesco'	LCro MCtn MHer MNHC SRms SVic
- PORTUGAL	see *C. oblonga* 'Lusitanica'		- - 'Rouge d'Alger'	CAgr MCtn
- 'Rea's Mammoth' (F)	CHab NLar		- - 'Tavor'	LRHS SEND SVic

Cynara

- - 'Vert Globe'	ENfk IDun LCro MCtn MNHC NLar NPer SRms SVic WFar WKit
- - 'Violet de Provence'	IDun SRms WKit
- - 'Violet Globe'	WCot
- - 'Violetto Precoce'	WCot
* **gomerensis**	WCot
scolymus	see *C. cardunculus* Scolymus Group
syriaca	SPhx WPGP

Cynodon (Poaceae)

aethiopicus	EBee EPPr ESwi

Cynoglossum (Boraginaceae)

amabile ♀H5	CSpe LCro LSto
- 'Firmament'	MCtn
- 'Mystic Pink'	MCtn
- f. *roseum* 'Mystery Rose'	CSpe
grande	MCtn
nervosum	CAby CFis EBee EPPr GGro MArl MHol MMuc SEND WCAu WCot
officinale	MCtn

Cynosurus (Poaceae)

cristatus	CHab NMir

Cypella (Iridaceae)

aquatilis	CLil EWat

Cyperus (Cyperaceae)

§ albostriatus	EShb
alternifolius misapplied	see *C. involucratus*
alternifolius L.	CBen CLil ELin LCro LWaG SArc WMAq
- 'Compactus'	see *C. involucratus* 'Nanus'
diffusus misapplied	see *C. albostriatus*
§ eragrostis	EPPr MWts NSti SDix SPlb WMAq
esculentus	CAgr
fuscus	WFar
§ giganteus	CLil EWat
glaber	LRHS
haspan misapplied	see *C. papyrus* 'Nanus'
haspan L.	CLil WCot
§ involucratus	CWal ELin EShb EWat MWts SEND WJun
- 'Gracilis'	ELin
§ - 'Nanus'	EShb
longus	CAgr CBen CGwi CLil CPud CWat LWaG MMuc MWts NPer NSti SEND SMad SPlb WMAq
papyrus ♀H1c	CDTJ EAri EGren ELin EShb LCro LWaG MCtn SArc SPlb WCot
- 'Mexico'	see *C. giganteus*
§ - 'Nanus' ♀H1c	SBig
- 'Perkamentus' PBR	ELin
vegetus	see *C. eragrostis*
'Zumila'	EShb

Cyphostemma (Vitaceae)

mappia	SPlb

Cypripedium (Orchidaceae)

Bernd gx	LAma
calceolus	LAma
fasciolatum	LAma
flavum	GKev
formosanum ♀H5	LAma
Gabriela gx 'Kentucky Maxi'	LAma
Ivory gx ♀H5	LAma
kentuckiense	LAma
Lucy Pinkepank gx	LAma
- 'Kentucky Pink Blush'	LAma
parviflorum var. *parviflorum*	LAma
§ - var. *pubescens*	LAma
Philipp gx 'Kentucky Pink'	GKev LAma
pubescens	see *C. parviflorum* var. *pubescens*
reginae ♀H5	LAma WCot
Sabine Pastel gx	LAma
× ventricosum pink-flowered	LAma
- white-flowered	LAma

Cyrilla (Cyrillaceae)

racemiflora	CMac

Cyrtanthus (Amaryllidaceae)

§ brachyscyphus	EGrI
breviflorus	CPbh WCot
§ elatus ♀H2	CTsd NSti WCot
epiphyticus	WCot
falcatus ♀H2	WCot
mackenii	CBlu
- cream-white-flowered	XFar
- 'Himalayan Pink'	XFar
montanus	WCot
parviflorus	see *C. brachyscyphus*
purpureus	see *C. elatus*
sanguineus	WCot
speciosus	see *C. elatus*

Cyrtomium (Dryopteridaceae)

§ caryotideum	CLAP SPlb
devexiscapulae	LEdu LRHS NLar SBig WPGP
§ falcatum ♀H3	CDoC CLAP CSde CSpe EPfP EUrb EWld GKev GMaP ISha LBom LEdu LRHS LWaG MAsh MMrt NAlc NBir NLar SBig SDix SEND SPlb SPoG SRms SRot WCot WFar
- 'Rochfordianum'	ISha LRHS MAsh
§ fortunei ♀H3	CLAP CSpe CSta CTsd EGren EPfP EUrb LBom LCro LRHS MAsh MGos NBid NBro NLar SAth SBig SPoG SRms SRot WPnP
- var. *clivicola*	CBdn CMHG CSpe EBee EPfP EUrb EWld GKev ISha LBom LCro LRHS LWaG MGos NAlc NBro NLar SBea SHor WBrk WCot WFar WPnP
macrophyllum	CLAP EBee ISha WPGP
tukusicola	EBee

Cystopteris ✿ (Woodsiaceae)

bulbifera	EWld NAlc
dickieana	LEdu
fragilis	EWld GKev LEdu WCot
moupinensis	CLAP WPGP
- B&SWJ 6767	WCot WCru

Cytisus (Fabaceae)

battandieri	see *Argyrocytisus battandieri*
× beanii ♀H5	ELan EPfP
'Boskoop Glory'	NLar
× boskoopii 'Apricot Gem'	CSBt EGren ELan LRHS MAsh NLar
- 'Boskoop Ruby' ♀H5	CBcs CBrac CDoC CMac CSBt EGren ELan ELon EPfP GKin LCro LRHS LSRN MAsh MPri
- 'Dukaat'	NLar
- 'Hollandia' ♀H5	CBcs ELan GKin LRHS MSCN NBir NLar
- 'La Coquette'	CDoC EPfP SPlb
- 'Windlesham Ruby'	EHeP ELan LSRN NLar WFar
- 'Zeelandia' ♀H5	CMac ELan EPfP LRHS NLar

'Burkwoodii' ♥H5   CBcs EHeP ELan EPfP LRHS LSRN MSCN SPoG WFar
§ *decumbens*   GArf GKev
demissus ♥H5   WAbe
'Golden Cascade'   ELan MAsh
'Goldfinch'   ELan EPfP NLar WFar WLov
§ *hirsutus*   SBrt
   × *kewensis* ♥H5   MGos
   - 'Niki'   LRHS
   'Killiney Salmon'   GKin LSRN
   'Lena' ♥H5   CMac CSBt EHeP ELan EPfP GKin LCro LRHS LSRN MAsh MGos NCth NLar SPoG WFar
   'Luna'   EPfP
   maderensis   see *Genista maderensis*
   'Moyclare Pink'   LCro NCth
   'Newry Seedling'   CMac
   nigricans 'Cyni' ♥H5   ELan SPoG
   'Porlock'   see *Genista* 'Porlock'
   × *praecox*   CMac EHeP EPfP LRHS MAsh SPlb SPoG WFar
   - 'Albus'   CBcs CDoC CMac EGren EHeP ELan EPfP LCro LRHS LSRN MAsh MGos MMuc WFar
   - 'Allgold' ♥H5   CBcs CDoC CMac CSBt EGren EHeP ELan ELon EPfP LCro LRHS LSRN MAsh MPri SPoG SRms WFar
   - 'Frisia'   WFar
   - 'Lilac Lady'   EPfP MAsh
   - 'Warminster' ♥H5   GKin MMuc
procumbens   EHeP
purpureus   MMrt
racemosus   see *Genista* × *spachiana*
'Red Wings'   NCth
scoparius   CAgr EHeP
   - 'Cornish Cream'   ELan
   - 'Firefly'   CBcs CMac
   - 'Fulgens'   EPfP
   - 'Golden Sunlight'   MSwo
§   - subsp. *maritimus*   CMac
   - var. *prostratus*   see *C. scoparius* subsp. *maritimus*
   × *spachianus*   see *Genista* × *spachiana*
supinus   see *C. hirsutus*
'White Lion'   CMac EGren

D

Daboecia ✿ (Ericaceae)
cantabrica f. *alba*   MAsh
   - - 'Alberta White'   CBcs CFst
   - 'Andrea'   CFst
   - 'Angelina'PBR   CFst
   - f. *blumii* 'Pinky Perky'   CFst
   - - 'Purple Blum'   CFst
   - - 'White Blum'   CFst
   - 'Glamour'   CFst
   - 'Heather Yates'   CFst
   - 'Lilac Osmond'   CFst
   - 'Romantic Muxoll' (d)   CFst
   - 'Rosella'PBR   CBcs CFst
   - 'Stardust Muxoll'   CFst
   - 'Sun Seeker'   CFst
   - 'Vanessa'PBR   CFst
   × *scotica* 'Goscote'   MGos
   - 'Jack Drake'   CFst
   - 'Katherine's Choice'   CFst
   - 'Silverwells' ♥H5   MAsh
   - 'William Buchanan' ♥H5   GAbr MAsh MHtn

Dacrydium (Podocarpaceae)
franklinii   see *Lagarostrobos franklinii*

Dactylicapnos (Papaveraceae)
'Golden Tears'   GEdr
macrocapnos   CSpe WCru
§ *scandens*   CRHN CSpe GEdr NSti SBrt WCot
   - GWJ 9438   WCru
   - WJC 13793   WCru
§ *ventii* GWJ 9376   WCru
   - WJC 13786   WCru

Dactylis (Poaceae)
glomerata   CHab SVic
   - 'Variegata' (v)   MMuc

Dactylorhiza (Orchidaceae)
§ *foliosa* ♥H4   CTtf
§ *fuchsii*   CHab CTtf EWld GKev LEdu MCtn MNrw NBir WHer
   × *grandis* Blackthorn hybrid   CTtf
incarnata   NBid
§ *maculata*   EDAr
maderensis   see *D. foliosa*
mascula   see *Orchis mascula*
praetermissa   CHab EWat
purpurella   CHab GAbr GJos NRya

Dahlia ✿ (Asteraceae)
'Abbie' (D)   NHal
'AC Ben' (S-c)   NHal
'AC Casper' (D)   NHal
'AC Dark Horse' (D)   XFar
'Addison June' (Ba)   LCro
'Admiral Rawlings' (D)   ERCP
'Aggie White' (D) ♥H3   NHal
'Aitara Diadem' (D)   LSou
'Akita' (Misc)   LAma LCro MPri
'Alauna Clair-Obscur' (Fim)   ERCP LCro XFar
'Alfred Grille' (S-c)   LAma LCro
'All Directions' (D)   ERCP LCro SHor
'Allan Sparkes' (WL) ♥H3   WKif
'Alloway Cottage' (D)   NHal
'Alva's Doris' (S-c) ♥H3   LAyl
'Alva's Supreme' (D) ♥H3   LAyl NHal
'Alyshia' (Anem) **new**   XFar
'Amante' (D)   LCro
I   'Amazone' (Sin/DwB)   SPoG
'Ambition' (Fim)   EBee ERCP LAma LCro LRHS
'American Dawn' (D) ♥H3   ERCP LCro LRHS XFar
'American Dream' (S-c)   LRHS
'American Sun' (D)   ERCP
'American Sunset' (Misc)   ERCP
'Amy Cave' (Ba)   NHal
I   'Andrea' (D)   LCro
'Andrea Clark' (D)   NHal
'Andrew Mitchell' (S-c)   NHal
'Ann Breckenfelder' (Col) ♥H3   NHal SMrm
'Anna Mari US' (Fim)   LAma
'Anne Cornelia' (D)   ERCP
'Another Pet'   see *D.* 'Mystic Enchantment'
'Antique'PBR (Sin)   LRHS
'Apache' (Fim)   ERCP LAma LCro SMrm WFar
apiculata B&SWJ 10222   WCru
'April Heather' (Col) ♥H3   NHal
'Arabian Night' (D)   CAby EAri EBee EGren ELan ERCP LCro LSRN MAsh NLar SEND SHor WCot WSpi XFar
'Arbatax' (D)   EBee ELan ERCP LAma WFar

Dahlia

'Ariko Aphrodite' (D) **new**	XFar
'Ashpire Fancy' (Col)	NHal
'Askwith Edna' (D)	NHal
'Askwith Josephine' (D) ♀H3	NHal
'Askwith Minnie' (D)	NHal
'Audacity' (D)	LAyl
'Aurora's Kiss' (Ba)	NHal
'Aurwen's Violet' (Pom)	NHal
australis	EAri
- B&SWJ 10358	WCru
I 'Autumn Fairy' (S-c)	LRHS
'Autumn Orange' (C)	ERCP
'Avignon' (D)	EGren
'Avoca Amanda' (D)	NHal
'Babylon' (D)	EAri
§ 'Babylon Brons' (D)	EAri ERCP LCro LRHS XFar
'Babylon Bronze'	see *D.* 'Babylon Brons'
§ 'Babylon Paars' (D)	ERCP
'Babylon Purple'	see *D.* 'Babylon Paars'
'Bacardi' (D)	ERCP LRHS XFar
'Bantling' (Pom)	ERCP
'Barbarry d'Amour' (D)	NHal
'Barbarry Glamour' (Ba)	ERCP
'Barbarry Pip' (D)	NHal
'Barbarry Primrose Hall' (D)	NHal
'Bargaly Blush' (D)	NHal
'Bayou'PBR (Anem)	CAby ELan ERCP LAma LCro LRHS LSou NHal SHor
'Bednall Beauty' (P) ♀H3	ELan SNoN WSpi
'Belfloor' (D)	ERCP LCro XFar
'Belle of Barmera' (D)	ERCP XFar
'Ben Huston' (D)	XFar
'Berger's Rekord' (S-c)	XFar
'Berner Oberland' (D)	ERCP
'Berwick Wood' (D)	NHal
'Best Bett'	see *D.* MYSTIC SPIRIT
'Beth's Chaplet' (Sin)	WCot
'Big Bro' (D)	XFar
'Big Hailstone' (D)	EPfP SEND WFar
'Bilbao'PBR (D)	EGren
'Bishop of Auckland'PBR (Sin)	CAby CWGN CWnw ELan EPfP ERCP LAma LCro LRHS MGos MPro WCot
'Bishop of Canterbury'PBR (P)	CAby EAri ELan EPfP ERCP LAma LCro LRHS LSou MGos MPro MSwo SAth SPoG
'Bishop of Dover' (Sin)	EGren LAma LCro SAth WFar XFar
'Bishop of Lancaster' (Sin)	NLar
'Bishop of Leicester' (P)	CAby EPfP LAma LCro LRHS NLar SEND SHar WFar XFar
'Bishop of Llandaff' (P) ♀H3	Widely available
'Bishop of Oxford' (Sin)	CAby CCht CWnw ELan LAma LCro LRHS MGos MPro SEND SHor SPoG WHoo XFar
'Bishop of York' (Sin)	CAby CWnw EAri EPfP LAma LCro LRHS LSou MGos MPro MSwo NLar SAth SHor SPoG WFar XFar
BISHOP'S CHILDREN (mixed) (Sin)	LCro MCtn SMrm WFar
'B.J. Beauty' (D)	MArl NHal
'Black Beauty' ambig.	CSpe EAri
'Black Jack' (S-c)	EPfP ERCP LCro LRHS LSRN MArl NHal XFar
'Black Lars' (D) **new**	ERCP
'Black Monarch' (D)	NHal
'Black Narcissus' (C)	ERCP LCro
'Black Touch' (Fim)	ERCP LAma
'Blue Bell' (D)	MPri
'Blue Boy' (D)	ERCP LCro LRHS LSou XFar
'Blue Wish' (WL)	LCro
'Blueberry Hill' (Col)	LAyl
'Blues Bird' (D)	ERCP
'Bluesette' (D)	XFar
'Blutiful' (D)	ELan ERCP XFar
'Blyton Everest' (D)	NHal
'Blyton Golden Girl' (D)	NHal
'Blyton Lady in Red' (D)	NHal
'Blyton Red Ace' (D)	NHal
'Blyton Softer Gleam' (Ba) ♀H3	LAyl NHal
'Blyton Stella' (D)	NHal
'Bob's Bonaventure' (D)	NHal
'Bohemian Spartacus' (D)	EBee ERCP LAma LCro LRHS XFar
'Bold Accent' (C) **new**	XFar
'Bon Odori' (Anem) **new**	XFar
'Boom Boom Red' (Ba)	EPfP WFar
'Boom Boom White' (Ba)	ERCP LCro
'Bora Bora' (S-c)	EPfP LRHS XFar
'Boy Scout' (Ba)	EGren
'Brabo' (D) **new**	MPri
'Brackenridge Ballerina' (WL)	NHal
BRAVEHEART ('Vdtg67'PBR) (Dark Angel Series) (Sin)	LCro
'Break Out' (D) **new**	LCro
'Bride's Bouquet' (Col)	LRHS
'Bright Eyes NL' (Sin)	ERCP LRHS
'Brigitta Alida' (S-c)	ERCP
'Brindisi' (Anem)	LRHS
'Bristol Stripe' (D)	XFar
'Brown Sugar FDM' (Ba)	ERCP XFar
'Bryn Terfel' (D)	MArl NHal
'Burlesca' (Ba)	ERCP LCro
'Cabana Banana' (S-c)	LAma XFar
'Café au Lait' (D)	CAby ELan EPfP ERCP LAma LAyl LCro LRHS MArl MAsh MPri NHal WFar WSpi XFar
'Cafe au Lait Rosé' (D)	ERCP LAma LCro XFar
'Cafe au Lait Royal' (D)	ERCP LAma LCro LRHS XFar
CAFÉ AU LAIT SUPREME ('Calemerpus') (D)	XFar
'Cafe au Lait Twist' (D)	ERCP LAma XFar
'Café de Paris' (S-c) **new**	ERCP XFar
'Caitlin's Joy' (Ba)	ERCP XFar
'Cambridge' (D)	EGren
I 'Cameo' (WL)	ELan LAyl NHal
campanulata	CBlu EShb SChr WFar
- B&SWJ 14901b	WCru
- white-flowered B&SWJ 14340	WCru
'Canary Fubuki' (Fim)	ERCP
CANDY EYES	see *D.* 'Zone Ten'
'Caproz Josephine' (Fim)	EPfP
'Caramel Antique' (D)	ERCP
'Cardinal Star' (Sin)	SMHy
'Caribbean Fantasy' (D)	LAma
'Carolina Moon' (WL)	MArl NHal
'Carstone Firebox' (Col)	LAyl
'Carstone Ruby' (D)	NHal
'Carstone Valiant' (Ba)	NHal
'Catching Fire' (Misc)	LAma
'Catherine Deneuve' (Misc)	CWGN
'Charlie Two' (D)	NHal
'Chat Noir' (S-c) ♀H3	ERCP LAma LCro XFar
'Cherry Cake' (D) **new**	LAma
'Cherwell Goldcrest' (S-c)	NHal
'Cherwell Linnet' (Ba)	NHal
'Chick A Dee US' (Pom) **new**	ERCP
'Chimacum Davi' (Ba)	XFar
'Chimborazo' (Col)	EWes LAyl SDix

Dahlia

'Christine' (D)	EPfP
'Christopher Taylor' (WL)	NHal SHar
'Citron du Cap' (Fim)	NHal
'City of Leiden' (S-c)	LCro LRHS
'Clair de Lune' (Col) ♀H3	MArl NHal WCot WSpi
I 'Clarion' (Sin)	MPro
'Classic Rosamunde' (Misc) ♀H3	NHal
§ 'Classic Swanlake' (Misc)	LCro
'Clearview Cameron' (C)	MArl NHal
'Clearview Daniel' (Ba) ♀H3	NHal
'Clearview Edie' (S-c)	NHal
'Clearview Louise' (S-c)	NHal
'Clearview Tammy' (S-c)	NHal
'Cleo Laine' (S-c)	MArl NHal
coccinea	CSpe CTtf EAri EShb SDix SMHy WPGP
- B&SWJ 9126	WCru
- var. *palmeri*	CBlu CSpe MCtn WPGP
'Color Spectacle' (S-c)	LAma
'Contraste' (D)	XFar
'Copperboy' (Ba)	ERCP LRHS SHor XFar
'Coral Jupiter' (S-c)	MArl NHal
'Cornel' (Ba)	ERCP LCro
'Cornel Brons' (Ba) ♀H3	ERCP LCro XFar
'Cornish Ruby' (Sin)	EBee EPfP LRHS
'Cornwall Island' (Fim)	ERCP
'Corson George' (S-c)	NHal
'Corson Gold' (S-c)	NHal
'Cranberry Classic' (Misc) **new**	ERCP XFar
'Crazy 4 Don' (D)	NHal
'Crazy Love' (D)	LCro MBros XFar
'Cream Diane' (D)	NHal
'Cream Moonlight' (S-c)	NHal
'Creme de Cassis' (D) ♀H3	CAby CWnw EPfP ERCP LCro NHal XFar
'Creme de Cognac' (D) ♀H3	ERCP LCro XFar
'Crème Silence' (D) **new**	LAma XFar
'Cryfield Harmony' (Ba)	ERCP
(Dahlegria Series)	ERCP XFar
DAHLEGRIA BICOLORE ('Dahlgr128'^PBR) (Sin)	
- **DAHLEGRIA TRICOLORE** ('Dahlgr85'^PBR) (Sin) ♀H3	ERCP LCro LRHS XFar
- **DAHLEGRIA WHITE** ('Dahlgr95') (Sin) ♀H3	ERCP LRHS
(Dahlietta Surprise Series)	MBros
DAHLIETTA BECKY (Col)	
- **DAHLIETTA LILY** (D)	LRHS
(Dahlightful Series)	ERCP
DAHLIGHTFUL CRUSHED CRIMSON ('G14402dahl') (P)	
- **DAHLIGHTFUL MAGENTA** ('G16-216') (P)	ERCP
'Daisy Duke' (D)	ERCP XFar
(Dalaya Meena Series)	LSou
DALAYA MEENA SANYA (D)	
- **DALAYA MEENA YOGI** ('Kledh11031'^PBR) (D)	LRHS
'Daleko Jupiter' (S-c)	MArl NHal
Dalina Maxi Series	MBros
- **DALINA MAXI COZUMEL** (D/DwB)	LRHS
- **DALINA MAXI EMILIO** ('Datyve'^PBR) (D)	LRHS
- **DALINA MAXI TOPIA** ('Da12'^PBR) (D/DwB)	LRHS
- **DALINA MAXI TAMPICO** ('Datretten'^PBR) (D/DwB)	LRHS
- **DALINA MAXI ROMERO** ('Danitten'^PBR) (D)	LRHS
- **DALINA MAXI SALINAS** ('Dasyvogtyve'^PBR) (D)	LRHS
'Dana US' (D)	LRHS
I DANDY (mixed) (Col)	MCtn SVic WHil
'Danique' (D)	ERCP
'Dark Butterfly' (D)	LCro
'Dark Hero' (Ba) **new**	ERCP
§ 'Dark Side of the Sun'^PBR (Sin)	EPfP LCro LRHS LSou MPro SPoG
'Dark Spirit' (D)	ERCP LCro MPri XFar
'Darkarin' (Misc)	ERCP
'David Howard' (D) ♀H3	CAby EAri EBee EGren ELan EPfP ERCP LAyl LCro LRHS LSou MHol MSwo NHal SDix WCot WFar WSpi
'Dawn Sky' (D)	LAyl
'Dazzling Magic' (D)	XFar
'Dazzling Sun' (D)	MAsh
'Deborah's Kiwi' (C)	NHal
'Debra Anne Craven' (S-c)	NHal
'De-la-Haye' (S-c)	NHal
'Destinys Teachers' (SinO)	EPfP ERCP LCro LRHS XFar
DIABLO MIXED (Misc/DwB)	MBros
'Diana's Memory' (D)	ERCP LAma LCro LRHS LSRN MPri
'Dikara Jodie' (D)	NHal
'Dikara Superb' (D)	LAyl NHal
'Dilys Ayling' (Col)	NHal
'Diva US' (D) ♀H3	ERCP
'Doris Day' (C)	NHal
'Doris Duke' (D)	ERCP
'Double Dream Fantasy' (Dreamy Series) (Misc)	LRHS
'Dovegrove' (Sin) ♀H3	ERCP SNoN
'Downham Peggy' (Ba)	NHal
'Downham Royal' (Ba)	ERCP LCro
'Drama Queen' (D)	XFar
'Dream Seeker' (Col)	LRHS MPro
(Dreamy Series) DREAMY EYES (Misc)	MPri
- DREAMY FANTASY (P)	ELan LCro MPri MPro
- DREAMY HOT CHOCOLATE (P)	LRHS MBNS
- DREAMY KISS (P)	LCro MPri MPro MSwo
- DREAMY LIPS (P)	MPro MSwo
- DREAMY NIGHTS (Misc) ♀H3	LCro LRHS MBNS MPri MPro MSCN
- DREAMY SUNSET (P) **new**	ERCP
'Duet' (D)	EGren LAma XFar
'Dutch Explosion' (S-c)	LRHS XFar
I 'Dutch Pearl' (D) **new**	ERCP
'Early Bird' (D)	MCtn WHil
'Eastwood Essex' (S-c)	NHal
'Eastwood Jane' (C)	NHal
'Eastwood Moonlight' (S-c)	NHal
'Edge of Joy' (D)	ELan LCro LRHS SMrm WFar
'Edinburgh' (D)	CDoC EBee EGren ELan EPfP ERCP LAma NHal WFar
'Edith Jones' (Col)	NHal
'Edmund' (Sin)	WCot
'El Paso' (D)	MBros
'Electric Flash' (S-c)	LAma
'Electric Light' (S-c) **new**	LAma
ELECTRO PINK ('71853-09'^PBR) (C)	LRHS
'Ellen Huston' (D/DwB) ♀H3	MPri
'Ellen Nauta' (D) **new**	ERCP
'Elma E.' (D)	NHal
'Embassy' (D)	LAma

	'Emory Paul' (D)	ERCP SDix	'Gipsy Night' (Ba)	ERCP LCro
I	'Encore' (Fim)	ERCP	'Glorie van Heemstede' (WL) ♀H3	ELan ERCP LAyl LCro NHal XFar
	'Engelhardts Matador' (D)	ERCP MPri WCot	'Glorie van Noordwijk' (S-c)	LCro LRHS SHor WFar
	'Esli' (D)	ERCP XFar	'Go American' (D)	NHal
	'Espacio' (D)	ERCP SHor	'Golden Crown' (C)	CAby
	'Eternal Snow'^PBR (WL)	ERCP LRHS	'Golden Scepter' (Ba)	ERCP LAma WFar XFar
	'Ethereal' (Sin)	LRHS	'Golden Torch' (Ba)	EGren
	'Evanah' (D) ♀H3	LCro	'Great Hercules' (D)	ERCP LCro LRHS MPri SHor
	'Eveline NL' (D)	CAby EGren ERCP LAma LCro	'Great Silence' (D)	ERCP LSRN XFar
	excelsa (B)	CHll SNoN	'Greenways Zoe' (S-c)	NHal
	- B&SWJ 10238 (B)	ESwi	'Grenadier' (D) ♀H3	WCot
	- 'Penelope Sky' (Sin)	ESwi SNoN WCru	'Grenidor Pastelle' (S-c)	MArl NHal
	'Excentrique' (Misc)	SNoN	'Gurtla Twilight' (Pom)	NHal
	'Explosion' (S-c)	MPri	'Gwyneth' (WL)	MArl NHal
	'Extase' (S-c)	LAma	'Hadrian's Bubblegum' (Sin)	NHal
	'Eye Candy' (Sin)	NHal	'Hadrian's Glowing Embers' (Sin/DwB)	NHal
	'Fabula' (Col)	LCro LRHS MPri	'Hadrian's Midnight' (Sin)	LAyl NHal
	'Fairway Pilot' (D)	NHal	'Hadrian's Summerwine' (Sin)	NHal
	'Fairway Spur' (D)	MPri NHal XFar	'Hadrian's Sunlight' (Sin) ♀H3	LAyl NHal SNoN
	'Famoso' (Col)	ERCP LCro XFar	'Hadrian's Sunset' (Sin)	NHal
	'Fancy Pants' (Misc)	ERCP XFar	'Hallmark' (Pom)	NHal
	'Fantastico' (Col)	LCro	'Hamari Accord' (S-c) ♀H3	LAyl
	'Fascination' (P) ♀H3	CAby CCht ERCP LAyl LSRN NLar WHoo WSpi	'Hamari Girl' (D)	MArl NHal
	'Fashion Monger' (Col)	CAby ERCP LCro NHal XFar	'Hamari Gold' (D) ♀H3	MArl NHal
	'Feline Yvonne' (D)	ERCP LCro SHor XFar	'Hamari Rosé' (Ba) ♀H3	NHal SHar
	'Fenna Baaij' (Anem)	ERCP XFar	'Hapet Blue Sea' (WL) ♀H3	NHal
	'Ferg's Best White' (Sin) **new**	SDix	'Hapet Champagne' (Fim)	NHal
	'Fern Ridge Painted Lady' (D)	XFar	'Hapet Daydream' (D) ♀H3	ERCP
	'Ferncliff Illusion' (D)	LAma	'Hapet P' (Fim)	NHal
	'Festivo' (Col)	LRHS	'Happy Butterfly' (D)	ERCP XFar
	'Fidalgo Supreme' (D)	LAyl	(Happy Days Series)	MBros MPri MPro
	Figaro Series (Misc/DwB)	MBros	HAPPY DAYS BICO ('Hdbic34'^PBR) (Sin)	
	'Finchcocks' (WL) ♀H3	ERCP LAyl	- HAPPY DAYS CHERRY RED ('Hdchr23'^PBR) (Sin)	MPri
	'Fire Mountain' (D)	LBom LRHS MPro NHal	- HAPPY DAYS FUCHSIA HALO (Sin)	LRHS MPri MPro
	'Firepot' (D)	ERCP LRHS	- HAPPY DAYS LEMON ('Hdle105'^PBR) (Sin)	ERCP LCro MPri MPro WHil
	'Fleur'	see *D.* 'Fleurel'	- HAPPY DAYS PINK ('Hdpi117'^PBR) (Sin) ♀H3	MPri MPro WFar
§	'Fleurel'^PBR (Fim)	EBee ERCP LRHS MPri	- HAPPY DAYS PURPLE ('Hdpu165') (Sin) ♀H3	EPfP MPri
	'Floorinoor' (Anem)	LCro LRHS	- HAPPY DAYS RED FLAME ('Hdrf 155') (Sin)	EPfP
	'Formby Art' (D)	LAyl	- HAPPY DAYS SCARLET ('Hdsc18'^PBR) (Sin)	MBros MPri MPro
	'Franz Kafka' (Pom)	ERCP LAma MBros NHal XFar	'Happy Halloween' (D)	ERCP
	'French Cancan' (D)	LCro XFar	(Happy Single Series)	EGren LCro
§	'Freya's Paso Doble' (Anem) ♀H3	ELan EPfP ERCP LAyl WFar XFar	HAPPY SINGLE DATE ('HS Date'^PBR) (Sin)	
	'Fringed Star' (S-c)	LAma	- HAPPY SINGLE FIRST LOVE ('HS First Love'^PBR) (Sin)	ERCP
	'Fusion' (D) ♀H3	WCot	- HAPPY SINGLE FLAME ('HS Flame'^PBR) (Sin) ♀H3	ERCP LAma
	'Fuzzy' (Fim)	XFar	- HAPPY SINGLE JULIET ('HS Juliet'^PBR) (Sin)	EGren ERCP
	(Gallery Series) 'Gallery Art Deco' (D) ♀H3	NHal XFar	- HAPPY SINGLE KISS ('HS Kiss'^PBR) (Sin)	CWnw LCro XFar
	- 'Gallery Art Fair' (D) ♀H3	ELan LCro MPro NLar XFar	- HAPPY SINGLE PARTY ('HS Party'^PBR) (Sin)	ERCP
	- 'Gallery Art Nouveau' (D) ♀H3	LRHS NHal WFar	- HAPPY SINGLE PRINCESS ('HS Princess'^PBR) (Sin) ♀H3	ERCP LRHS
	- 'Gallery Leonardo' (D) ♀H3	LCro		
	- 'Gallery Pablo' (D) ♀H3	EGren MPro XFar		
	- 'Gallery Rembrandt' (D) ♀H3	LCro XFar		
	- 'Gallery Rivera' (D)	NLar XFar		
	- 'Gallery Valentin'^PBR (D)	WFar		
	'Garden Wonder' (D)	EGren LRHS		
	Gardenetta Series	MPri		
	'Geerlings Indian Summer' (S-c)	NHal		
§	'Geerlings Sorbet' (S-c)	CAby LAyl		
	'Gelber Vulcan' (S-c)	LRHS		
	'Genova' (Ba)	ERCP LCro LRHS		
	'Gerrie Hoek' (WL)	LAma WSpi		
	'G.F. Hemerik' (Sin)	LCro		
	'G.H. Lammerse' (D)	LRHS		

– Happy Single Romeo ('HS Romeo'^PBR) (Sin)	LRHS WFar
– Happy Single Wink ('HS Wink'^PBR) (Sin) ♀H3	ERCP LAma LCro
'Haresbrook' (Sin/DwB)	SHar WSpi
'Hartenaas' (Col/DwB)	XFar
§ 'Harvest Samantha' (Sin/Lil) ♀H3	NHal
'Hawaii' (Misc)	LBom
'Hawaiian Dreams'^PBR (Sin)	EPfP LRHS MPro
'Hawaiian Sunrise' (Sin)	LCro LRHS MPro
'Hayley Jayne' (C)	EGren LSou
I 'Henriette' (S-c)	ERCP
'High Fidelity' (D) **new**	XFar
'Hillcrest Candy' (S-c) ♀H3	NHal
'Hillcrest Charlie' (S-c)	NHal
'Hillcrest Delight' (D)	NHal
'Hillcrest Firecrest' (D)	LAyl NHal
'Hillcrest Jersie' (C)	NHal
'Hillcrest Jonathan' (D)	NHal
'Hillcrest Kismet' (D)	MArl NHal
'Hillcrest Royal' (C) ♀H3	LAyl NHal
'Hollyhill Dark Beauty' (D) **new**	LCro
'Hollyhill Lemon Ice' (P)	EPfP
'Hollyhill Serenity' (WL)	NHal
'Hollyhill Spiderwoman' (Misc)	CAby EPfP ERCP LAma LCro LRHS XFar
'Honka' (SinO) ♀H3	LAyl LCro LRHS NHal WCot WFar
'Honka Black' (SinO)	CBlu LAma WFar XFar
'Honka Crème' (SinO) **new**	ERCP
'Honka Dark' (SinO) **new**	ERCP
'Honka Fragile' (SinO)	CAby ERCP LCro LRHS MPri
'Honka Pink' (SinO)	MPri
'Honka Red' (SinO)	CAby CBlu ERCP LCro LRHS MPri
'Honka Rose' (SinO)	ERCP XFar
'Honka Surprise' (SinO)	CAby LCro MPro WCot
'Honor Francis' (Misc)	WCot
'Hootenanny - Swan Island' (Col) ♀H3	ERCP XFar
'Hy Trio' (S-c)	XFar
(Hypnotica Series)	MPri
Hypnotica Electric Pink ('Dodahhypelpin') (D) **new**	
– Hypnotica Rose Bicolor ('Fidahhyprobico') (D) **new**	MPri
'Ice Crystal' (Fim)	CAby LAma LCro LSou
'Ice Tea' (D)	ERCP XFar
'Icoon'^PBR (D)	LRHS
imperialis (B)	CBlu CDTJ CHll EAri ERCP ESwi EUrb EWes LAma LCro SBig SMrm SPlb WFar XFar
– B&SWJ 8997 (B)	WCru
– 'Alba' (Sin)	EBee LAma SNoN WFar XFar
– dark-leaved (B)	ESwi
– white-flowered (B)	ERCP
– – B&SWJ 14341 (B)	WCru
aff. ***imperialis***	EShb SNoN
'Impression Flamenco' (Col/DwB)	ERCP
'Innocent Silence' (D)	XFar
'Irish Pinwheel' (Misc)	ERCP LRHS XFar
'Isa Candy' (D)	ERCP
I 'Isabel' (Ba)	ERCP
'Islander' (D)	ERCP LCro XFar
'Ivanetti' (Ba)	ERCP LCro NHal
'Ivor's Rhonda' (Pom)	NHal
'Izarra' (SinO) **new**	EUrb
'Janal Amy' (S-c)	NHal
'Janny P' (Fim) **new**	NHal
'Jean Marie'^PBR (D)	LRHS
'Jennifer Mary Ellen' (D)	ERCP SHor XFar
'Jescot Julie' (DblO)	LAyl LCro
'Jim Branigan' (S-c)	NHal
'Jive' (Anem)	LCro
'Jocondo' (D)	NHal
'Jodie Wilkinson' (Ba) ♀H3	NHal
'Joel's Favourite' (D) **new**	ERCP
'John Hill' (D)	NHal
'John Street' (WL)	WSpi
'Jomanda' (Ba) ♀H3	NHal
'Josudi Andromeda' (C) ♀H3	MArl NHal
'Josudi Aurora' (C)	NHal
'Josudi Hercules' (S-c) ♀H3	NHal
'Josudi Mercury' (S-c)	NHal
'Josudi Neptune' (S-c)	NHal
'Jowey Frambo' (Ba)	ERCP LCro XFar
'Jowey Linda' (Ba)	ERCP XFar
'Jowey Marilyn' (Misc)	LCro
'Jowey Merel' (D) **new**	LCro
'Jowey Mirella' (Ba)	ERCP LCro
'Jowey Nicky' (D)	ERCP
'Jowey Veronique' (D)	ERCP
'Jowey Winnie' (Ba)	ERCP LCro XFar
'Joyful Investment' (Col)	ERCP
'JS Dorothy Rose' (D)	NHal
'Jubilee Boy' (S-c)	NHal
'Karenglen' (D) ♀H3	NHal
'Karma Amanda' (D)	LRHS
'Karma Amora'^PBR (D)	LRHS
'Karma Bon Bini'^PBR (C)	CAby LSou
'Karma Choc'^PBR (D) ♀H3	CAby CSpe EPfP LCro SDix SEND WCot WFar WHoo
'Karma Corona'^PBR (C)	EAri LRHS
'Karma Fiesta'^PBR (D)	EAri LSRN
'Karma Fuchsiana' (D)	LCro
'Karma Lagoon'^PBR (D)	EAri ERCP LRHS
'Karma Maarten Zwaan'^PBR (WL)	ERCP LRHS
'Karma Naomi' (D)	EAri ERCP LRHS
'Karma Pink Corona'^PBR (C)	LCro LRHS
'Karma Prospero'^PBR (D)	EAri ERCP LCro LRHS
'Karma Red Corona'^PBR (C)	LRHS
'Karma Sangria' (C)	LCro LRHS
'Karma Serena' (D)	EAri LSRN
'Ka's Cloud' (D) **new**	ERCP
'Kelsey Annie Joy' (Col)	ERCP LCro XFar
'Kelsey Sunshine' (Col)	ERCP XFar
'Kelvin Floodlight' (D)	EAri EBee LAma LRHS MAsh MPri XFar
'Kennemerland' (S-c)	LCro LRHS
'Kenora Challenger' (S-c)	NHal
'Kenora Macop-B' (Fim)	LAyl NHal SNoN
'Kenora Sunset' (S-c) ♀H3	MArl NHal
'Kenora Valentine' (D) ♀H3	LAyl NHal
'Kenora Wow' (S-c)	MArl NHal
'Ken's Rarity' (WL)	LAyl NHal
'Kick Off' (D)	ERCP XFar
'Kidd's Climax' (D) ♀H3	ERCP LCro
'Kiev' (D)	EGren LCro
'Kilburn Glow' (WL)	LAyl MArl NHal
'Kilmorie' (S-c)	NHal
'Kiwi Gloria' (C)	NHal
'Knockout' (S-c)	LSou
§ 'Knockout'^PBR (Sin) ♀H3	CAby CBcs EAri EGren LRHS MBNS MPri MPro SPoG
'Kogane Fubuki' (Fim)	EBee LAma XFar
'Kordessa' (D)	EBee EPfP LAma

Dahlia

'La Belle Epoque' (D) **new** — ERCP
'La Corbière' (Ba) — NHal
LABELLA MAGGIORE FUN CHOCOLATE YELLOW ('Bkdamagfcy') (D) **new** — LRHS MPri
'Labyrinth' (D) ♀H3 — ERCP LCro XFar
'Labyrinth Twotone' (D) **new** — ERCP SHor XFar
'Lady Darlene' (D) — ERCP LRHS LSou
'Lady Kate' (D) — LAma LCro
'Lady Liberty' (D) — ERCP LRHS
'Lake Carey' (D) — LCro
'Lake Tahoe' (D) — XFar
'L'Ancresse' (Ba) — LAyl NHal
'L.A.T.E.' (Ba) — LAyl
'Laughing Lizza' (D) — ERCP
'Lavender Perfection' (D) — ERCP LRHS XFar
'Lavender Ruffles' (D) — LRHS
'Le Baron' (D) — ERCP LRHS
'Le Feu du Soleil' (Fim) — NHal
'Lemon Elegans' (S-c) ♀H3 — LRHS NHal
'Lemon Sherbet' (Sweet Candy Series) (Col) — LRHS MPro
'Lilac Bull' (D) — EPfP WFar
'Lilac Marston' (D) ♀H3 — NHal
I 'Lilac Time' (D) — ERCP
'Linda's Baby' (Ba) — ERCP LCro XFar
'Lindsay Michelle' (Fim) — LAma XFar
'Liquid Desire' (Col) — ERCP LAma SHor SMrm XFar
'Lismore Carol' (Pom) — NHal
'Lismore Moonlight' (Pom) — NHal
'Little Robert' (D) — EBee ERCP LAma LRHS WFar
'Little Swan' (P) — ERCP
'Louis White' (D) — NHal
'Love of my Life' (D) — ERCP LRHS
'Lovelife' (D) — LRHS
(Lubega Series) LUBEGA BURGUNDY (D) — LRHS
- LUBEGA SCARLET (D) — LRHS MPro
- LUBEGA WHITE (D) — LRHS
- LUBEGA YELLOW (D) — LRHS
(Lubega Dark Series) LUBEGA DARK BICOLOR ORANGE (P) **new** — MPro
- LUBEGA DARK ORANGE (P) **new** — MPro
- LUBEGA DARK RED GLOW (Sin) **new** — MPro
- LUBEGA DARK VELVET (Sin) **new** — MPro
(Lubega Power Series) LUBEGA POWER BRONZE BICOLOR (D) — LRHS
- LUBEGA POWER BURGUNDY (D/DwB) — EPfP LRHS
- LUBEGA POWER ORANGE (D) **new** — MPro
- LUBEGA POWER SCARLET-WHITE (D) — LRHS
- LUBEGA POWER TRICOLOR ('Voldah5612') — LRHS MPro
- LUBEGA POWER TROPICAL PUNCH (D) **new** — MPro
- LUBEGA POWER WHITE LILAC FROST (D) **new** — MPro
- LUBEGA POWER YELLOW ORANGE (D) — LRHS MPro
(Lubega Special Series) LUBEGA SPECIAL BICOLOR BURGUNDY (Misc) **new** — MPro

(Lubega XL Series) LUBEGA XL BURGUNDY (D/DwB) — MPro
- LUBEGA XL YELLOW (D) **new** — MPro
'Lucky Number' (D) — MPri XFar
'Ludwig Helfert' (S-c) — LRHS
'Maaike' (D) **new** — ERCP
'Mabel Ann' (D) — LAyl
'Madame Simone Stappers' (P) — LAyl WSpi
'Magenta Magenta' (D) — LAyl
'Magenta Magic' (Sin/DwB) — NHal
'Magenta Star' (Sin) ♀H3 — ERCP SDix WHoo
'Maiko Girl' (DblO) ♀H3 — LAyl
'Maldini' (D) — XFar
'Mambo NL' (Anem) — ERCP
'Mango Madness' (D) **new** — XFar
'Manhattan Island' (D) — EGren LAma MAsh MPri
'Manoa' (D) — ERCP
'Marble Ball' (D) — EPfP LRHS
'Marcel Dassault' (D) — ERCP
'Maroon Fox'^PBR (Ba) — ERCP
'Marshmallow Baby' (D) **new** — ERCP
'Marston George' (Ba) — NHal
'Marston Suzanne' (D) — NHal
'Marta' (S-c) — LRHS MPri
'Martin's Yellow' (Pom) — NHal
'Mary Eveline' (Col) — CAby NHal
'Mary Hammett' (D) — WSpi
'Mary Margaret Row' (D) — MArl NHal
'Mary's Jomanda' (Ba) ♀H3 — NHal
'Matilda Huston' (S-c) — NHal
'Maxime' (D) — LAma
'Maya' (D) — ERCP XFar
'Mayan Pearl' (DblO) ♀H3 — LAyl NHal
'Maya's Rhonda' (Pom) — NHal
'Mediterrannee' (D) — LAma
'Megan Dean' (Ba) — ERCP NHal
'Melchior' (D) **new** — ERCP
'Melissa Anna Marijke' (D) — ERCP
'Melody Allegro'^PBR (D) — WFar
'Melody Bolero'^PBR (D) — WFar
'Melody Dixie'^PBR (D) — WFar
'Melody Dora'^PBR (D) — LCro
'Melody Harmony'^PBR (D) ♀H3 — XFar
'Melody Lizza'^PBR (D) — LRHS
'Mel's Orange Marmalade' (Fim) — LCro
'Menorca' (D) — LCro
merckii (B) — CExl CFis CSpe CTtf EAri ECha EPPr EShb EWes LCro MNrw NClf SDix SHar SIvy SMHy SNoN SPlb WFar WTre
- 'Alba' (Sin) — CSpe WFar
- compact — WPGP
- dark-flowered — SChr
'Meteorite' (D) — ERCP
§ 'Mexican Black' (Misc) — CSpe SDix SIvy
'Mexican Star' (Sin) — EAri ELan ERCP LAma LCro XFar
'Mick's Peppermint' (S-c) — CAby
'Midnight Star' (SinO) — NHal
'Mignon Rose Shades' — MCtn
'Mignon White Shades' — MCtn
'Milena F' (D) — ERCP LCro XFar
I 'Milly' (D) — NHal
'Mingus Joshua' (Fim) **new** — LAma
* 'Mingus Max' — ERCP
'Mingus Randy' (S-c) — MPri
'Mingus Toni' (D) — ERCP

'Minley Carol' (Pom)	NHal
'Miss Trucella' (D)	ERCP SHor
'Missis Dutch' (Misc) **new**	ERCP
'Mister Frans' (D) ♀H3	ERCP
'Mister Optimist' (D)	MPri
'Mondriaan' (D) **new**	ERCP LAma LCro
'Montenegro' (D)	ERCP
'Moonfire' (Sin) ♀H3	CAby CBcs CCht CWGN CWnw EAri ELan EPfP ERCP EUrb LAyl LCro LRHS NHal NLar WCot WHil WHoo WKif WSpi
'Moor Place' (Pom)	ERCP NHal
'Morning Kissis' (D) **new**	ERCP LAma
'Motto' (D)	MPri
'Ms Kennedy' (Ba)	LAyl NHal
'Muchacha' (D) **new**	LRHS
'Murdoch' ambig. (D)	WCot WKif WSpi
'Murillo' ambig. (Sin)	LAyl
'My Love' (S-c)	EPfP ERCP LAma LCro LRHS SHor XFar
'Myama Fubuki' (Fim)	ELan ERCP LAma
'Myrtle's Folly' (Fim)	ERCP XFar
'Mystery Day' (D)	LAma LRHS MAsh
MYSTIC DREAMER	see *D.* 'Zone Ten'
§ 'Mystic Enchantment'^{PBR} (Sin)	EGren ELan EPfP LRHS LSou MPro SPoG
'Mystic Haze'	see *D.* 'Dark Side of the Sun'
MYSTIC ILLUSION	see *D.* 'Knockout'
'Mystic Sparkler'^{PBR} (Sin)	EGren LSou MPro WHil
§ **MYSTIC SPIRIT** ('Hamspirit'^{PBR}) (Sin)	EGren ELan EPfP LSou MPro
'Mystic Wonder' (Sin)	ELan LRHS
'Myth' (D) **new**	LAma
'Nadia Ruth' (Fim)	ERCP NHal
'Nargold' (Fim)	LAyl
'Narrow's Tricia' (S-c)	LRHS
'Natal' (Ba)	ERCP LAma
'Natalie G' (D)	ERCP XFar
'Nenekazi' (Fim)	LAyl
'Neon Splendor' (D)	ERCP
'Nescio' (Pom)	LSou MPri
I 'New Baby' (Ba)	LCro
'Newfield Maggie' (D)	NHal
'Nicholas' (D)	ERCP
'Night Butterfly' (Col)	EPfP LCro WFar XFar
I 'Night Queen' (Ba)	EPfP WFar XFar
'Night Silence' (D)	ERCP XFar
'Nonette' (WL)	WCot
'Normandie Delight' (Fim)	NHal
'Normandie Frills' (Fim)	NHal
'Normandie Memories' (S-c)	NHal
'Normandie Wedding Day' (Fim)	NHal
§ 'Nuit d'Eté' (C)	ELan ERCP LAma LCro
'Nuland's Josephine' (Ba)	ERCP NHal
'Oakwood Goldcrest' (S-c)	NHal
'Octopus Sparkle' (Misc) **new**	ERCP LAma NHal SHor
'Offshore Dream' (D)	LCro
'Omega' (Fim)	LCro
'Onesta' (D)	ERCP LRHS MPri
'Orange Fubuki' (Fim)	ERCP LCro
'Orange Girl' (D)	LCro LRHS
'Orange Nugget' (Ba)	XFar
'Oreti Bliss' (C)	LAyl
'Orfeo' (C)	EPfP LCro MNrw
'Otto's Thrill' (D) ♀H3	ERCP LRHS SHor
'Pacific Jewel' (Misc)	LRHS XFar
'Pacific Ocean' (WL) ♀H3	ERCP
'Painted Girl' (D)	ERCP LAma LSou
'Palmares' (D)	LSou
'Pam Howden' (WL)	MArl NHal
'Paradise City' (D)	XFar
'Park Princess' (C/DwB)	ELan LAyl LRHS NHal
'Park Record' (S-c)	LCro LRHS
'Parkland Glory' (D)	LSou
'Paso Doble' misapplied	see *D.* 'Freya's Paso Doble'
'Paso Doble Dancer' (D) **new**	ERCP LAma MPri
'Peach and Vanilla' (D) **new**	XFar
I 'Peaches' (Ba)	ERCP
'Peaches and Cream'^{PBR} (D)	EBee
'Pearl of Heemstede' (WL) ♀H3	NHal
'Penhill Dark Monarch' (D) ♀H3	ERCP XFar
'Penhill Watermelon' (D)	ERCP LCro XFar
'Penny Lane' (D)	MBros
'Pepita Pink' (Col) **new**	ERCP
'Petra's Wedding' (D)	EGren ERCP LCro
'Phyllis Farmer' (WL)	ERCP
'Piano'	LRHS
'Pink Jupiter' (S-c)	NHal
'Pink Pat and Perc' (Col)	NHal
'Pink Perception' (WL)	ERCP
'Pink Runner' (D)	ERCP
'Pink Spur' (D)	NHal
'Piper's Pink' (S-c/DwB)	LRHS MHol
'Platinum Blonde' (Anem)	ERCP LCro
'Playa Blanca' (C/DwB)	ELan LRHS XFar
'Polar Ice' (D)	ERCP
'Polka NL' (Anem)	XFar
'Polventon Kristobel' (D)	NHal
'Polventon Supreme' (Ba)	ERCP
'Poodle Skirt' (Anem) ♀H3	ERCP LRHS MPri
'Pooh' (Col)	see *D.* 'Pooh - Swan Island'
§ 'Pooh - Swan Island' (Col) ♀H3	CAby ESwi LAma LAyl LRHS NHal WCot XFar
'Porcelain' (WL)	WSpi
'Preference' (C)	CAby ERCP LAma LCro XFar
'Preston Park' (Sin/DwB) ♀H3	LAyl NHal
PRETTY WOMAN ('Vdtg43'^{PBR}) (Dark Angel Series) (Sin) ♀H3	EPfP LCro
'Priceless Pink' (Misc)	ERCP LRHS
PRIDE OF BERLIN	see *D.* 'Stolz von Berlin'
'Pride One' (Misc) **new**	ERCP
'Princess Nadine' (Misc)	ERCP SHor
'Procyon' (D)	LRHS XFar
'Profundo' (D)	SNoN
pteropoda B&SWJ 10240	WCru
PULP FICTION ('Vdtg61'^{PBR}) (Dark Angel Series) (Sin)	EAri
'Purple Explosion' (D)	LRHS
'Purple Flame'^{PBR} (D)	LCro
'Purple Fox'^{PBR} (Ba)	ERCP
'Purple Gem' (S-c)	EGren EPfP ERCP LCro LRHS
'Purple Haze' (Anem)	EGren ERCP LCro LRHS
'Purple Pearl' (D)	NHal
'Purple Posy' (Anem)	LRHS
'Purple World' (D) **new**	ERCP
aff. *purpusii* B&SWJ 10321	WCru
'Quin' (Misc) **new**	ERCP
'Radegast' (D)	ERCP
'Ragged Robin' (Misc)	CSpe WTre
'Rancho' (WL)	ERCP LCro
I 'Rawhide' (WL)	EPfP XFar
'Rebecca's World' (D)	ELan EPfP LCro MPri XFar
'Red and White Fubuki' (Fim)	XFar

	'Red Cap' (D)	LCro	'Sheer Heaven' (D) **new**	ERCP
	'Red Diamond' (D)	NHal	'Sheval Megan' (D)	LAyl NHal
	'Red Fox'^{PBR} (Ba)	LCro	'Shiloh Noelle' (D)	ERCP XFar
	'Red Fubuki' (D)	LRHS XFar	'Shirwell Greta' (D)	NHal
	'Red Labyrinth' (D)	ERCP LRHS XFar	'Short Track' (D) **new**	XFar
	'Red Pygmy' (S-c)	LRHS XFar	'Show 'n' Tell' (Fim)	EPfP WFar XFar
	'Red Silence' (D) **new**	CAby	'Siberia'^{PBR} (D)	LRHS SHor
I	'Redskin'	MCtn	'Sights of Summer' (D)	LRHS
	'Reginald Keene' (S-c)	NHal	'Silver Years' (D)	LCro
	'Rejman's Firecracker' (Fim)	EPfP	SINCERITY ('Dahsc226'^{PBR}) (D) ♀H3	EGren LRHS XFar
	'Rhonda' (Pom)	NHal	'Sir Alf Ramsey' (D)	LAma LAyl NHal
	'Rhubarb and Custard' (Sweet Candy Series) (Col)	LRHS MPro	'Skyfall' (Col)	ERCP
			'Small World' (Pom) ♀H3	ERCP LAyl NHal
	'Richards Fortune' (Anem)	ERCP LRHS XFar	I 'Smokey' (D)	EGren LAma
	'Rip City' (S-c)	ERCP LCro	'Sneezy' (Sin/DwB)	LAma
	'Rocco' (Pom)	ELan ERCP LCro LRHS LSou	'Snow Cap' (S-c)	EBee EGren LAma
	'Rose Jupiter' (S-c)	NHal	'Snowbound' (D)	LCro
	'Rosemary Dawn' (Ba)	NHal	I 'Snowflake' (Pom)	ERCP LAma LRHS SHor
	'Rosemary's Blush' (Ba)	NHal	'Sorbet' (S-c)	see *D.* 'Geerlings Sorbet'
	'Rossendale Natasha' (Ba)	NHal	'Soulman' (Anem)	ERCP LCro LRHS
	'Rothesay Herald' (D/DwB)	EGren	'Souvenir d'Eté' (Pom)	EPfP LRHS MPri
			'Spanish Conquest' (D)	NHal
I	'Roxy' (Sin/DwB)	CAby CBcs CWnw ELan ERCP EUrb LAyl LRHS MHol MPie WCot WSpi	'Spartacus' Senior (D)	ERCP LAma LAyl LCro LRHS NHal SHor
			'Speech' (Anem) **new**	XFar
	'Royal Blood' (Misc)	ELan LAyl	STAR WARS ('Vdtg14'^{PBR}) (Dark Angel Series) (Sin)	LCro LRHS
	rudis	WPGP		
	'Ruskin Andrea' (S-c)	NHal	'Star's Favourite' (C)	LAma
	'Ruskin Diane' (D)	NHal	§ 'Stolz von Berlin' (Ba)	ERCP LRHS
	'Ruskin Marigold' (S-c)	NHal	'Strawberry Bon Bon' (Sweet Candy Series) (Col)	LRHS MPro
	'Ruskin Michelle' (S-c)	NHal		
	'Ruskin Tangerine' (Ba)	NHal		
I	'Ruth Ann' (Ba)	NHal	'Strawberry Cream' (D) **new**	EBee LCro XFar
	'Ryecroft Bella' (Ba)	NHal	'Striped Emory Paul' (D)	ERCP
	'Ryecroft Blackberry' (Pom)	NHal	'Striped Vulcan' (S-c)	CAby
			'Sturm Sweet Nicole' (D) **new**	XFar
	'Ryecroft Brenda T' (D)	NHal		
	'Ryecroft Caroline's Beauty' (WL)	NHal	'Suffolk Punch' (D)	ELan LAyl
			'Summer Flame' (D)	LCro
	'Ryecroft Gold' (D)	NHal	'Summer Haze' (D)	LRHS
	'Ryecroft Helen' (S-c)	NHal	'Summer Night' (C)	see *D.* 'Nuit d'Eté'
	'Ryecroft Huntsman' (D)	NHal	'Summit Festival' (WL)	MArl NHal
	'Ryecroft Jan' (Ba) ♀H3	NHal	'Sunlady' (D)	LSou
	'Ryecroft Jill' (Ba)	NHal	'Sunny Boy' (Ba)	EGren MBros
	'Ryecroft Jim' (Anem)	LAyl	I 'Sunset Glow' (Sin)	LRHS MPri MPro
	'Ryecroft Laura' (Ba)	LAyl NHal	'Susan Gilbert' (Col) ♀H3	NHal
	'Ryecroft Misty' (D)	NHal	'Susan Gilliott' (S-c)	NHal
	'Ryecroft Pixie' (C)	NHal	'Swan Lake'	see *D.* 'Classic Swanlake'
	'Ryecroft Porcelain' (D)	NHal	'Sweet Love' (D)	ERCP LCro LSRN
	'Ryecroft Zoe' (S-c)	NHal	'Sweet Nathalie' (D)	ERCP XFar
	'Sakura Fubuki' (Fim)	LRHS XFar	'Sweet Sanne' (D) **new**	ERCP
	'Salmon Runner' (D) ♀H3	ERCP LCro XFar	'Sweet Surprise' (D)	ERCP LCro
	'Sam Hopkins' (D)	ERCP LCro MArl NHal	'Sweet Suzanne' (Ba)	LCro XFar
	'Samantha'	see *D.* 'Harvest Samantha'	I 'Sylvia' (Ba)	EPfP ERCP LCro WFar
	'Sandia Flirt' (WL)	NHal	'Table Dancer' (Fim)	LAma LCro
	'Sandia Gold' (WL) **new**	NHal	'Tahiti Sunrise' (S-c)	ELan EPfP LSou MAsh WFar
	'Sandra' (D)	ERCP LCro LRHS XFar	'Tahoma Moonshot' (SinO)	CWnw LRHS
	'Santa Claus US' (D)	ELan	'Take Off' (Anem)	ERCP LAma LCro LRHS
I	'Sarah' (S-c)	LRHS MHol	'Tally Ho' (Sin) ♀H3	EPfP LRHS WCot
	'Sascha' (WL) ♀H3	NHal	'Tam Tam' (Ba)	XFar
	'Schippers Bronze' (Sin) **new**	CSpe	*tamaulipana* – F&M 312	EAri SNoN SPlb WFar WPGP
	'Seattle' (D)	EGren MPri XFar	'Tamburo' (S-c)	EPfP ERCP LCro
	'Sebastian' (D)	ERCP LAma XFar	'Tangerine Gem' (Sin)	MPro
	'Seduction' (D)	ERCP	'Taratahi Ruby' (WL) ♀H3	MArl NHal
	'Seniors Darkness' (D)	LCro	'Tartan' (D)	ELan ERCP LCro LSou XFar
	'Seniors Dream' (D) **new**	LAma	'Tee Set' (D)	WFar
	'Seniors Hope' (Misc)	ERCP LCro	'Teesbrooke Audrey' (Col)	CAby LCro NHal XFar
	'Shaggy Chic' (Fim)	ERCP	'Temple of Beauty' (Misc)	LCro
	'Shandy' (S-c)	LAyl SHar	*tenuicaulis*	CDTJ

'Thomas A. Edison' (D)	CAby ERCP LCro LRHS MAsh MBros MPri SHor WSpi XFar	'Woodbridge' (Sin)	SNoN
'Tiger Eye' (D)	MPro	'X Factor' (D)	LAma LRHS
'Tirza' (Misc)	ERCP	'Yellow Hammer' (Sin/DwB) ♀H3	NHal
'Tomo' (D)	LAyl	'Yellow Happiness' (S-c)	XFar
'Topmix White' (Sin/DwB)	XFar	'Yellow Jill' (D)	LCro
'Totally Tangerine' (Anem) ♀H3	CSpe CWnw EPfP ERCP LAma LCro LRHS MPro NHal XFar	'Yellow Perception' (WL)	ERCP
		'Yellow Sneezy' (Sin/Lil)	LAma
'Tracy Diane' (D)	NHal	'Yellow Star' (S-c)	EGren ERCP LAma LRHS MPri
'Trelyn Kiwi' (S-c) ♀H3	NHal	'York and Lancaster' (D)	ESwi WFar
'Trelyn Seren' (SinO)	LAyl	'Zahra' (Anem) **new**	ERCP XFar
'Tricolor' ambig.	LSou	'Zingaro' (D)	LCro
'Trooper Dan' (S-c)	LRHS MPri	'Zippity Do Da' (Pom)	ERCP LAma
'Tsuki-yori-no-shisha' (Fim)	LCro XFar	§ 'Zone Ten'PBR (Sin/DwB)	CAby EGren EPfP LCro LRHS LSou MPro SPoG WHil
'Twiggy' (WL)	ERCP		
'Twyning's After Eight' (Sin) ♀H3	CSpe CWGN EPfP LAyl LCro LRHS MArl MPro NHal WCot WHoo	'Zorro' (D) ♀H3	NHal
		'Zundert Mystery Fox'PBR (Ba) ♀H3	ERCP LCro
'Twyning's Revel' (Sin) ♀H3	MPro WMal		

Daiswa see *Paris*

Dalea (Fabaceae)

candida	EBee
purpurea	CWal EBee MCtn StAn
- 'Stephanie'	CSpe

damson see *Prunus insititia*

Danae (Asparagaceae)

§ **racemosa** ♀H5	CBcs CMac EBee EPfP EWes LEdu LRHS MGos SAko SEND WCot WCru WJur WPGP WSpi

Daphne (Thymelaeaceae)

from Burma	CJun
acutiloba	WSpi
- 'Fragrant Cloud'	CExl CJun EBee EPfP EWes WPGP
albowiana	WSpi
alpina	GKev MCtn
arbuscula ♀H5	WIce
aurantiaca	GKev IArd
bholua	CJun ESwi GKev LEdu SChF WSpi
- B&SWJ 8275 from Fansipan, Vietnam	WCru
- GWJ 9436 from India	WCru
- NJM 13.115	WPGP
I - 'Alba'	SSta WPGP WSpi
- 'Cobhay Coral'	CJun
- 'Cobhay Debut'	CJun
- 'Cobhay Snow'	CJun
- 'Darjeeling'	CBct CExl CJun EBee EPfP LRHS WPGP WSpi
- 'Garden House Enchantress'	CJun WPGP
- 'Garden House Ghost'	CJun EBee EPfP WPGP
- 'Garden House Red Stem'	WPGP
- 'Garden House Sentinel'	CJun WPGP
- var. **glacialis** 'Gurkha' ♀H4	CExl CJun EPfP WPGP
- 'Hazel Edwards'	LRHS SHor SSta
- 'Jacqueline Postill' ♀H4	CDoC CExl CHll CJun CMac CSpe EBee EGren EGrI ELan EPfP EUrb GKev LCro LRHS LSRN MAsh MBlu MGos NCth SChF SHor SSta WFar WPGP WSpi
- 'Limpsfield'	CJun EBee EPfP SSta WPGP
- 'Mary Rose'	CJun EBee EPfP WPGP
- 'Penwood'	CJun
- 'Peter Smithers'	CExl CJun EBee MPri SChF SSta WPGP

'Twyning's Smartie' (Sin)	LCro XFar		
'Twyning's White Chocolate' (Sin)	LRHS XFar		
'Uniquity' (Sin)	WCot		
'Val's Candy' (S-c)	NHal		
'Vancouver' (Misc)	LAma LCro WFar		
'Vassio Meggos' (D)	ERCP LRHS NHal XFar		
'Vectra' (D)	EGren EPfP LAma		
'Veritable' (S-c)	LCro		
'Verrone's Obsidian' (SinO)	CAby CBlu CSpe CWnw ELan EPfP ERCP LCro SHor WFar		
I 'Viking' (Pom)	EGren XFar		
'Vivian Russell' (WL)	NHal		
'Waltzing Mathilda' (Misc) ♀H3	EPfP ERCP LCro		
'War of the Roses' (D)	EWes SIvy		
I 'Waterlily' (Sin)	LRHS		
'Westerton Ella Grace' (D)	NHal		
'Westerton Folly' (Ba) ♀H3	NHal		
'Westerton Gatehouse' (D)	NHal		
'Westerton Harry' (D)	NHal		
'Westerton J.W.H.' (D)	NHal		
'Westerton Lilian' (D)	NHal		
'Westerton Pearl' (Ba)	NHal		
'Weston Pirate' (C) ♀H3	LAyl NHal SNoN		
'Weston Spanish Dancer' (C) ♀H3	NHal		
'White Alva's' (D) ♀H3	LAyl NHal		
'White Aster' (Pom)	ELan ERCP XFar		
'White Ballerina' (WL)	NHal		
'White Ballet' (D) ♀H3	LAyl		
'White Charlie Two' (D)	NHal		
'White Cockatoo' (D)	MPri MPro		
'White Isa' (D)	LCro		
'White Onesta' (D)	ERCP		
I 'White Perfection' (D)	LAma WSpi		
'White Star' (S-c)	EGren LAma LCro		
'White Swallow' (S-c)	LAyl NHal		
'Willo's Borealis' (Pom)	NHal		
'Willo's Violet' (Pom)	NHal		
'Windmill' (C)	LRHS		
'Wine Eyed Jill' (D)	ELan EPfP ERCP LCro LRHS XFar		
'Winholme Diane' (D)	NHal		
'Winkie Lambrusco' (Pom)	NHal		
'Winston Churchill' (WL)	WSpi		
'Wishes n Dreams' (Sin) ♀H3	XFar		
'Wittem' (D)	EBee XFar		
'Witteman's Best' (S-c)	EGren LRHS MPri		
'Witteman's Superba' (S-c) ♀H3	NHal		
'Wizard of Oz' (Ba)	ELan EPfP ERCP LCro XFar		

- 'Tashi'	WPGP	*pontica*	CJun EPfP LRHS MAsh SChF SPoG WPGP WSpi
blagayana	GKev	*retusa*	see *D. tangutica* Retusa Group
- 'Brenda Anderson'	EPot SChF WAbe	'Richard's Choice'	CJun
'Bramdean'	see *D.* × *napolitana* 'Bramdean'	× *rollsdorfii* 'Arnold Cihlarz'	SChF WAbe
× *burkwoodii*	EGren	- 'Wilhelm Schacht' ♀H5	CMac LRHS SChF SSta
- 'Astrid' (v)	EGren	'Rosy Wave'	CJun SChF
I - 'Gold Sport'	CJun	× *schlyteri* 'July Glow'	GEdr SChF WIce
- 'Marjolein'PBR	NLar	- 'Lovisa Maria'	GEdr
- 'Somerset' ♀H4	CJun LCro	§ *sericea* Collina Group	CMac SSta WIce
cneorum	EWes GKev NBir NLar	'Spring Beauty'	CJun EBee EPfP IArd LRHS LSRN MAsh MPri NCth NLar SHor WPGP WSpi
- 'Variegata' (v)	EWes GEdr		
'Cobhay Pink Delight'	CJun		
'Cobhay Purple Clouds'	CJun	'Spring Herald'	CJun EBee EGrl MPri NLar WPGP WSpi
'Cobhay Purple Pillar'	CJun		
collina	see *D. sericea* Collina Group	*sureil*	LEdu WPGP
domini	GKev	× *susannae* 'Anton Fahndrich'	GKev NLar
§ *gemmata*	CBcs IArd		
- 'Royal Crown'	EBee ELan LCro LRHS LSou MAsh SMrm WSpi	- 'Cheriton' ♀H5	CMac EPot GEdr GKev LRHS MPri SChF SSta
giraldii	GKev		
× *hendersonii*	WAbe	- 'Tichborne'	CMac EWld GEdr GKev LRHS SChF SSta WIce
'Fritz Kummert'			
- 'Kath Dryden'	GEdr	*tangutica* ♀H5	CBcs CExl CJun ELan EPfP EWld GArf GKev IArd LCro LRHS MAsh MGos MMrt NBid NCth NLar SRkn SRms WKif WPGP WSpi
'Hinton'	CJun		
japonica 'Striata'	see *D. odora* 'Aureomarginata'		
jasminea	SChF		
jezoensis	SSta		
kosaninii	GKev	§ - Retusa Group ♀H5	CExl EWes GAbr GKev SRms WSpi
kurdica	EWld	× *transatlantica*	GEdr
× *latymeri* 'Spring Sonnet'	SChF	'Beulah Cross' (v)	
laureola	EBee GKev NBir NPer WSpi	- ETERNAL FRAGRANCE ('Blafra'PBR) ♀H5	Widely available
- 'Margaret Mathew'	SChF		
- subsp. *philippi*	CMac EBee EGrl EPfP EWes GEdr LCro MBlu NBir NLar WCot WPGP WSpi	§ - PINK FRAGRANCE ('Blapink'PBR)	CBcs CDoC CEnd EBee EGren ELan EPfP LCro LRHS MAsh MGos MPri NCth NLar SHor SMrm SOrN SPoG WFar WSpi
longilobata	CJun		
× *mantensiana* 'Manten'	CJun	- SPRING PINK ETERNAL FRAGRANCE	see *D.* × *transatlantica* PINK FRAGRANCE
'Meon'	see *D.* × *napolitana* 'Meon'		
mezereum	EWld GKev MCtn WFar	- 'Summer Ice' (v)	CBcs EBee ELon EPfP LCro LRHS NCth NLar SMrm WSpi
- f. *alba*	GKev LRHS SRms WSpi		
- - 'Bowles's Variety'	NBid	'Valerie Hillier'	NCth SMrm
- 'Rosea'	SRms	'White Queen'	EPfP LCro NCth NLar WSpi
- var. *rubra*	CBcs CDoC EGren EGrl ELan GKin LRHS WFar WSpi	× *whiteorum* 'Beauworth'	CMac LRHS SSta WAbe WOld
modesta	WAbe	- 'Kilmeston'	SChF
× *napolitana* ♀H4	CJun	*wolongensis*	GKev
§ - 'Bramdean'	SChF	- 'Guardsman'	GEdr GKev
- 'Enigma'	CJun	- 'Kevock Star'	CExl GKev
§ - 'Meon'	SChF		

Daphniphyllum (Daphniphyllaceae)

odora	CBcs CJun EGren EPfP LCro SWor WFar WPGP WSpi
aff. *angustifolium* WWJ 12020	WCru
- f. *alba* 'Sakiwaka'	CExl WCot WMal
chartaceum KWJ 12244	WCru
- KWJ 12313	WCru
- 'Aureomarginata' (v)	Widely available
glaucescens	WCru
I - 'Aureomarginata Alba' (v)	WSpi
subsp. *oldhamii*	
- 'Mae-jima' (v)	CExl WSpi
var. *oldhamii* CWJ 12351	
- 'Marginata'	see *D. odora* 'Aureomarginata'
humile	see *D. macropodum* var. *humile*
- MARIANNI ('Rogbret') (v)	CBcs CEnd EBee EGren IArd LRHS MPri NLar SHor SMrm
aff. *longeracemosum* B&SWJ 11788	WCru
- REBECCA ('Hewreb') (v)	EBee ELan EPfP LCro LRHS MAsh MGos SPoG WSpi
macropodum	CMCN EPfP LEdu SArc SBig SDix WCru WJur WPGP
- 'Rogald' Or'	LRHS		
- 'Rogalski' (v)	NLar	- B&SWJ 581	WCru
- var. *rubra*	CMac	- B&SWJ 2898	WCru
- 'Sweet Amethyst'PBR	LCro	- B&SWJ 6809 from Taiwan	WCru
- 'Variegata' (v)	SWor WFar	- B&SWJ 8507 from Ulleungdo, South Korea	WCru
- 'Walberton' (v)	EPfP LRHS		
papyracea	CExl WPGP	- B&SWJ 8763 from Jejudo, South Korea	WCru
PERFUME PRINCESS ('Dapjur01')	Widely available		
PERFUME PRINCESS WHITE ('Dapjur02'PBR)	LCro	- B&SWJ 11489 from Yakushima, Japan	WCru

Delosperma 233

- B&SWJ 12691	WCru		*solida* var. *fejeensis*	LCro
- dwarf	WCru		*trichomanoides*	CLAP
§ - var. *humile* B&SWJ 11232	WCru		- f. *barbata*	CMen
majus B&SWJ 11744	WCru		*tyermannii*	see *Humata tyermanii*
paxianum B&SWJ 9755	WCru			
pentandrum B&SWJ 3805	WCru			

Davidia (Nyssaceae)

involucrata ♀H5	Widely available
- 'Crimson Spring'	CAco
- 'Kylee's Columnar'	CAco NLar
- 'Sonoma' ♀H5	CAco ELan LMaj MBlu NLarWMat
- var. *vilmoriniana* ♀H5	CAco ELan MBlu NLar SHor

- B&SWJ 6888 WCru
- RWJ 9836 WCru
teysmannii B&SWJ 14626 WCru
  from Japan
aff. *teysmannii* CWJ 12350 WCru
  from Taiwan

Darlingtonia (Sarraceniaceae)
californica ♀H3   MCtn SPlb WFar WSSs

Daviesia (Fabaceae)
cordata	SPlb
pectinata	SPlb

Darmera (Saxifragaceae)
peltata ♀H6	Widely available
- 'Nana'	EBee ECha NBid NLar SDix WFar

Debregeasia (Urticaceae)
longifolia	SVen
- WWJ 11686	ESwi WCru

Darwinia (Myrtaceae)
taxifolia   WCot

Decaisnea (Lardizabalaceae)
fargesii	CAgr CBcs CDoC CExl CMCN ELan EPfP EUrb GAbr GEdr IArd MBlu MGos NGKo SArc SChF SPlb SPoG StAn WJur WKor
insignis	WJur

Dasylirion (Asparagaceae)
§ *acrotrichum*	CDTJ CExl EShb EUrb SArc
berlandieri	CExl
cedrosanum	CDTJ CJun SPlb
glaucophyllum	CJun NPlm
gracile Planchon	see *D. acrotrichum*
leiophyllum	SPlb
longissimum	EOli EUrb NPlm SBig
miquihuanense	CBlu CCht CExl CTsd
quadrangulatum	EUrb SArc SPlb
serratifolium	CDoC EOli ERom EUrb NPlm SAth SBig SFol
wheeleri ♀H2	CBlu EUrb MCtn NPlm SPlb

Decumaria see Hydrangea
sinensis   see *Hydrangea obtusifolia*

Deinanthe see Hydrangea

Deinostigma (Gesneriaceae)
§ *tamiana*   WDib

Delairea (Asteraceae)
§ *odorata* Lem.   CExl EShb WPGP

Delonix (Fabaceae)
decaryi	SPlb
* *grandiflora*	SPlb
regia	SPlb

Dasyphyllum (Asteraceae)
diacanthoides   WPGP

date see *Phoenix dactylifera*

Datisca (Datiscaceae)
cannabina   CDTJ CSpe EAri ECha IPot LEdu LShi MHoo StAn WFar

Datura (Solanaceae)
arborea	see *Brugmansia arborea*
cornigera	see *Brugmansia arborea*
rosei	see *Brugmansia sanguinea*
sanguinea	see *Brugmansia sanguinea*
stramonium	CBgR MCtn
suaveolens	see *Brugmansia suaveolens*
versicolor	see *Brugmansia versicolor* Lagerh.

Daubenya (Asparagaceae)
alba	MCtn
aurea	MCtn

Daucus (Apiaceae)
carota	CBWd CGwi CHab GJem GQue LCro LShi LSto MCtn SPhx WHer WOrg WTre
- 'Dara'	CSpe LCro LSto MCtn MPro NClf SHar SHor SPhx WHil
- 'Dara Dark Red'	CSpe
- subsp. *maximus*	SPhx WFar WPGP

Davallia (Davalliaceae)
bullata	LEdu WPGP
canariensis ♀H1c	LEdu

Delosperma (Aizoaceae)
from Graaf Reinet, South Africa	EPot ESuc
§ *aberdeenense* ♀H3	ESuc SLee
alpinum	see *Ectotropis alpina*
ashtonii	EPot ESgI ESuc SLee
basuticum	ESuc MAsh
'Beaufort West'	EDAr
bosserianum **new**	ESuc
'Candy Floss'	EDAr
congestum misapplied	see *Malotigena frantiskae-niederlovae*
congestum ambig.	CTsd EDAr EPfP EPot ESuc GEdr GKev LRHS SAth SLee SMad WAbe WIce WJur
cooperi	CPbh CWal EAri EGren ELan EPfP EPot ESgI GArf GKev LRHS LWaG MCtn MHer SIvy SPlb SRms SVen WCor WIce WJur
- (Ice Cream Series) Ice Cream Fire ('Deloredcu7')	ESuc WFar
- - Ice Cream Orange ('Delooran3')	ESuc LRHS WFar
- - Ice Cream Salmon ('Delorasb1')	ESuc WFar
- - Ice Cream Yellow ('Delolemo12')	LRHS WFar

Delosperma

- (Jewel of Desert Series) JEWEL OF DESERT AMETHYST ('Dsam131'PBR)	EPfP ESuc WIce
- - JEWEL OF DESERT CANDYSTONE ('18can62'PBR)	ESuc
- - 'Jewel of Desert Garnet'PBR	EHeP GEdr LCro LRHS SLee SPoG WIce
- - JEWEL OF DESERT GRENADE ('Dsaa131'PBR)	ESuc LCro SPoG
- - 'Jewel of Desert Moon Stone'PBR	ELan EPfP LRHS SLee SPoG WIce
- - JEWEL OF DESERT OPAL ('Dsab131'PBR)	ESuc EUrb GEdr SLee WIce
- - 'Jewel of Desert Peridott'PBR	EPfP GEdr SLee SPoG WIce
- - 'JEWEL OF DESERT ROSEQUARTZ ('12Rosk1'PBR)	EHeP ESuc LBar LRHS SLee SPoG
- - 'Jewel of Desert Ruby'PBR	ELan ESuc LRHS WIce
- JEWEL OF DESERT SUNSTONE ('18sun52'PBR)	ESuc SLee SPoG WIce
- - 'Jewel of Desert Topaz'PBR	ELan EPfP ESuc EUrb LRHS SLee SPoG WIce
- (Wheels of Wonder Series) FIRE WONDER ('Wowday2'PBR)	EPfP ESuc LBar
- - GOLDEN WONDER ('Wow20111'PBR)	ESuc LBar LCro SPoG
- - HOT PINK WONDER ('Wowdry1'PBR)	ESuc LBar LCro
- - ORANGE WONDER ('Wowdoy3'PBR)	ESuc LBar SPoG
- - VIOLET WONDER ('Wowdrw5'PBR)	EPfP ESuc LBar SPoG
- - WHITE WONDER ('Wowdw7'PBR)	ESuc LBar LCro SPoG
'Darcies Smile'	EDAr
* *deschampsii*	ESuc
DESERT DANCERS RED (Desert Dancers Series) **new**	ESuc
dyeri RED MOUNTAIN ('Psdold')	EDAr ELan EPot ESuc LRHS SPoG WIce
echinatum	CoPl CPic LCro LRHS LWaG SIvy WCor
ecklonis	ESuc
esterhuyseniae	CPic
FIRE SPINNER ('P001s')	EDAr ESuc WIce
floribundum	ESuc
- 'Starburst'	CPic EPfP
harazianum	ESuc
'Hot Pink'	ESuc
§ 'John Proffitt'	EDAr ESuc GKev LRHS SRot WMal
LAVENDER ICE ('Psfave') **new**	ESuc LRHS
lavisiae ♀H6	EWes SPlb
'Lesotho Pink'	ESuc EWes
lydenburgense	ESuc
'Mountain Dew' **new**	ESuc
nubigenum	CPic EDAr ELan EPfP EPot GAbr GArf GKev LRHS SIvy SLee SPlb SPoG
- (Wheels of Wonder Series) HOT ORANGE WONDER ('W1813')	ESuc
- - HOT RED WONDER ('W1811')	ESuc
- - PURPLE WONDER ('P15r1'PBR)	ESuc LBar
- - SALMONY PINK WONDER ('P15py4'PBR)	ESuc LBar
'Orange Crush' **new**	ESuc
'Peach Passion' **new**	EDAr
'Pink Flame'	EDAr
'Pink Sherbet' **new**	EDAr
(Ranger Series) 'Royal Ranger Neon' **new**	ESuc
- 'Royal Ranger Red' **new**	ESuc
- 'Royal Ranger White' **new**	ESuc
'Ruby Coral'	see *Ectotropis seanii-boganii*
sphalmanthoides	EDAr EPot ESuc GEdr SPlb SRot WJur
(Sundella Series) SUNDELLA APRICOT	ESuc MPro
- SUNDELLA LAVENDER	ESuc MPro
- SUNDELLA NEON	ESuc MPro
- SUNDELLA ORANGE	MPro
- SUNDELLA RED	ESuc MPro
(Suntropics Series) SUNTROPICS COPPER	ESuc LRHS MPro SPoG
- SUNTROPICS CREAM **new**	MPro
- SUNTROPICS HOT PINK	EPfP ESuc LRHS MPro SPoG
- SUNTROPICS PURPLE	ESuc LRHS MPro SPoG
- SUNTROPICS RED	ESuc LRHS MPro
sutherlandii ♀H4	CPic CTsd EAri EBee EDAr EPfP ESuc GKev LRHS SPoG
- 'Peach Star'	CPic EBee EDAr ESuc WIce
TABLE MOUNTAIN	see *D.* 'John Proffitt'
'Violet Honey'	ESuc

Delphinium ✿ (Ranunculaceae)

'After Midnight'	LHom
'Alice Artindale' (d)	LHom
'Amadeus'	ENun LRHS
ambiguum	see *Consolida ajacis*
'Angela Harbutt'	LHom
'Angela Rowe'	LHom
'Ann Woodfield'	LHom
'Apple Blossom' **new**	Midl
Astolat Group	ELan EPfP GMaP LBom LBuc LCro MGos NLar SPoG WCAu WTor
(Aurora Series) 'Aurora Dark Blue'	EGren LBom MHol Midl
- 'Aurora Deep Purple'	EGren LBom LCro LRHS Midl MPri MPro NCth
- 'Aurora Lavender'	EGren LCro Midl MPro
(Belladonna Group) 'Atlantis'	ECha ELan NLar WSpi
- 'Bellamosum'	ELan EPfP GMaP WSpi
- 'Casa Blanca'	ELan EPfP GMaP MCtn NLar WSpi
- 'Cliveden Beauty'	ELan EPfP GMaP NLar SPoG WSpi
- 'Moerheimii'	WSpi
- 'Oriental Blue'	MCtn
- 'Piccolo'	ECha NLar SPoG
- 'Pink Sensation'	see *D.* × *ruysii* 'Pink Sensation'
- 'Völkerfrieden'	MNrw NLar WSpi
Black Knight Group	CBcs EGren ELan EPfP GMaP GQue LBom LCro LSRN LSto MCtn MGos MPro NGdn NLar SPlb SPoG WCAu WFar WTor
'Black Velvet'	see *D.* (Paramo Series) PARAMO BLACK VELVET
'Black-eyed Angels' (New Millennium Series)	CDor ELan IPot
'Blue Arrow'	see *D.* 'Blue Max Arrow'
Blue Bird Group	CBcs CWal ELan EPfP GMaP LBuc LShi MCtn MGos MPri MPro MSwo SPoG WCAu WTor
'Blue Butterfly'	see *D. grandiflorum* 'Blue Butterfly'
'Blue Dawn' ♀H5	LHom

Delphinium

Blue Fountains Group	SPoG SRms
Blue Jade Group	LHom
'Blue Jay'	CFis ELan EPfP LRHS MHtn MPro WSpi
'Blue Lace'	CDor IPot
I 'Blue Lace'	ELan EPfP LCro LRHS LSRN MPro
(New Millennium Series)	NLar WSpi
'Blue Nile' ♀H5	ESgI LCro LHom LRHS MPro SPoG
Blue Springs Group	NGdn
'Blue Tit'	LHom
'Bolero'	EPfP LRHS MPri SPoG
'Boudicca'	LHom
'Bruce' ♀H5	ENun LHom LRHS
brunonianum	GKev
'Butterball'	LHom
Cameliard Group	CBcs ELan EPfP LBom LCro NLar SPoG
'Cameliard' (Pacific Hybrid Series)	LRHS
cashmerianum	EBee
'Cassius'	LHom
'Celebration'	ELan LHom
(Centurion Series)	LCro
'Centurion Sky Blue' ♀H5	
- 'Centurion White'	LCro
'Cha Cha'	CBcs EBee ELan EPfP LRHS MHol MPri WCot WTor
'Chelsea Star'	LHom
'Cherub' ♀H5	ENun LRHS
chinense	see *D. grandiflorum*
'Christel'	LSRN NLar WSpi
'Cinderella'	LRHS MPro
'Clifford Sky' ♀H5	ENun LRHS
'Coadelbol'PBR (d)	CBcs ELan Midl
'Coadelfla'PBR (d)	LBom LCro MHtn Midl MPro
'Coadelpsur' (d)	ELan LRHS XFar
'Cobalt Dreams' (New Millennium Series)	CDor
'Conspicuous' ♀H5	LHom
'Constance Rivett'	LHom
'Cupid'	LHom
'Dark Blue Black' (Excalibur Series)	EPfP LRHS
'Dark Blue Black Bee' (Excalibur Series)	EGren LRHS SPoG
'Dark Blue White Bee' (Excalibur Series)	EGren EPfP LRHS SPoG
'Darling Sue'	LHom
(Delgenius Series)	MPri
DELGENIUS BLUE FABULOSA	
- DELGENIUS BREEZIN ('Et Dlp 17 11')	LBom LRHS MPri MPro NCth
- DELGENIUS CHANTAL ('Et Dlp 827') **new**	MPro SPad
- DELGENIUS GLITZY ('Et Dlp 17 10')	ELan LRHS MPri MPro NCth
- DELGENIUS JULIETTE ('Et Dlp 17 14')	LBom LRHS MPri MPro NCth
- DELGENIUS KINGSLEY ('Et Dlp 807') **new**	MPro
- DELGENIUS NEVA ('Et Dlp 824') **new**	MPro
- DELGENIUS SHELBY ('Et Dlp 17 03')	ELan LRHS MPri MPro
'Delphi's Evening Light'	NLar
'Delphi's Pink Power'PBR	NCth
'Dreaming Spires'	SRms
'Dunsden Green'	LHom
Dusky Maidens Group	CDor ELan EPfP LCro MBNS MPro MSwo NLar SPoG
elatum	EGren StAn
- (Aurora Series) 'Aurora Blue'	LCro LRHS MBros MHol MPri MPro
- - 'Aurora Light Blue'	EGren LBom LCro LRHS MPri MPro
- - 'Aurora White'	LCro MPro
- 'Austin's Dawn Chorus'	LHom
- CINDERELLA ('Dd2011')	LCro
- 'Delphi's Hollands Glorie'	NLar
- (New Millennium Series) 'Blushing Brides'	EBee ELan SPoG
- - 'Double Innocence' (d)	CDor ELan MBNS MPro NLar WSpi
- - 'Morning Lights'	CDor EPfP MPro NLar SPoG
- - 'Sweethearts' ♀H5	EBee EPfP LCro LRHS MPro
- 'Regal Splendour'	LHom
'Elisabeth Sahin' ♀H5	LHom
'Elizabeth Cook' ♀H5	LHom
'Elmfreude'	WSpi
'Emily Hawkins' ♀H5	LHom
exaltatum	CSpe GKev
'Fanfare'	LHom
'Faust' ♀H5	ELan ENun IPot LCro LHom LRHS MPri SPoG WSpi
'Fenella' ♀H5	ENun LHom LRHS
'Finsteraarhorn'	WCot WSpi
'Flamenco'	CBcs EPfP LBom LRHS MHol MPri SPoG WCot WTor
'Flocrysdel'PBR (d)	ELan MHol MPri SPoG
'Flodelpie'PBR (d)	LRHS MPri SPoG
'Foxhill Nina' ♀H5	LHom
'Frosted Skies Improved'	MCtn
Galahad Group	CBcs ELan EPfP GMaP NGdn SHar SPlb SPoG WCAu WTor
'Galahad' (Pacific Hybrid Series)	LBom LCro LShi LSto MCtn MGos MPro NLar
'Gemini'	LHom
'Gemma'	LHom
'Gillian Dallas'	LHom
'Gordon Forsyth'	LHom
'Gossamer'	LHom NLar
§ *grandiflorum*	EBee
§ - 'Blue Butterfly'	CSpe MCtn SPlb SPoG
- 'Diamonds Blue'	EGren
§ - 'Fantajisuta'	MPro
§ - 'Miyotia Blue'	EGren
- OCEAN PINK	see *D. grandiflorum* 'Fantajisuta'
- OCEAN TIARA BLUE	see *D. grandiflorum* 'Miyotia Blue'
- (Summer Series) 'Summer Blues'	EDAr
- - 'Summer Colors'	MCtn
- - 'Summer Morning'	EDAr MPro
- - 'Summer Nights'	EDAr LBom MPro SPoG
- - 'Summer Stars'	EDAr
'Green Twist' (New Millennium Series)	EPfP
Guardian Series	WFar
- 'Guardian Blue'	EGren LBar Midl MPro SPoG
- 'Guardian Lavender'	EGren LBar MHol Midl MPro SPoG
- 'Guardian White'	EGren LBar Midl MPro SPoG
Guinevere Group	EPfP LRHS LShi MPro SPoG
- 'Lady Guinevere'	MPro
hotulae	EBee
'Innocence'	WSpi
'Jill Curley' ♀H5	ENun LCro LRHS
(Jupiter Series) 'Jupiter Blue'	MPro
- 'Jupiter Pink'	MPro
- 'Jupiter Purple'	MPro
- 'Jupiter Sky Blue'	MPro
- 'Jupiter White'	MPro
'Kennington Classic' ♀H5	LHom
'Kestrel' ♀H5	LHom
King Arthur Group	CBcs ELan EPfP LCro LRHS LSRN MGos MPro NLar SHar SPoG

Delphinium

'La Bohème'	NCth WSpi
'Langdon's Orpheus'	LHom
§ 'Langdon's Royal Flush'	ENun LRHS
'Lanzenträger'	LRHS
'Light Blue' (Excalibur Series)	LRHS
'Light Blue White Bee' (Excalibur Series)	LRHS SPoG
'Lillian Basset'	LHom
'Loch Leven'	ENun
'Loch Nevis'	LHom
'Lord Butler' ♀H5	EBee LHom
'Lucia Sahin' ♀H5	LHom
maackianum	GKev WCot
Magic Fountains Series	EHeP MBros MCtn MPri SPlb SPoG SVic
- 'Magic Fountains Blue/White Bee'	EPfP LRHS MBros Midl SRms
- 'Magic Fountains Bright Eye'	SRms
- 'Magic Fountains Cherry Blossom'	EGren EPfP LRHS MHtn Midl NLar SPoG SRms
- 'Magic Fountains Dark Blue'	CWCL EGren GMaP MCtn NLar SPoG SRms WFar
- 'Magic Fountains Dark Blue/Dark Bee' **new**	MPro
- 'Magic Fountains Dark Blue/White Bee'	EPfP MPro WTor
- 'Magic Fountains Deep Blue'	Midl SRms
- 'Magic Fountains Deep Rose/White Bee'	LRHS MPro SRms
- 'Magic Fountains Lavender'	EGren ELan EPfP Midl MPro SRms
- 'Magic Fountains Lavender/White Bee'	MPro
- 'Magic Fountains Lilac Pink'	ELan EPfP LRHS Midl SPoG SRms WFar WTor
- 'Magic Fountains Lilac Rose'	LRHS MPro SPoG SRms
- 'Magic Fountains Pure White'	CWCL EGren ELan EPfP LBuc LRHS MBros Midl MPro SRms WFar WTor
- 'Magic Fountains Sky Blue'	EGren ELan EPfP LRHS Midl SPoG SRms WFar
- 'Magic Fountains Sky Blue/White Bee'	MPro WTor
- 'Magic Fountains The Blues'	SRms
- 'Magic Fountains White Dark Bee'	EPfP MPro
- 'Magic Fountains White Pixie'	Midl SRms
'Margaret' ♀H5	LHom
'Melanie Avery'	LHom
'Michael Ayres' ♀H5	LHom
'Mighty Atom'	ELan LCro LHom LSRN
'Min' ♀H5	ENun LHom
'Misty'PBR	NCth
'Misty Mauves' (New Millennium Series) (d)	ELan EPfP WSpi
'Moon Light'PBR (Highlander Series) (d)	CBcs LRHS MHol MPri SPoG WCot
'Moonbeam'	LBom LCro LRHS LSRN NCth SPoG
'Morgentau'	NLar
'Morning Sunrise'PBR (Highlander Series) (d)	Midl SPoG
'Mydark'	LHom
MYSTERY SENSATION ('Coadelpnk') (Highlander Series) (d)	ELan XFar
'Neon Sensation' (Highlander Series) (d)	XFar
New Zealand hybrids	WFar
'Nimrod'	ESgI
'Norfolk White'	LHom
nudicaule	GKev SPlb
- 'Fox'	EDAr
- 'Laurin'	EDAr MCtn
'Olive Poppleton' ♀H5	LHom
'Oliver' ♀H5	LHom
'Our Deb' ♀H5	LHom
oxysepalum	GKev
Pacific hybrids	EPfP LCro LSRN MHer SRms
'Pagan Purples' (New Millennium Series) (d)	ELan EPfP LCro LSRN MBNS MPro MSwo NLar WSpi
(Paramo Series) 'Paramo Azul'	LRHS MPri
§ - PARAMO BLACK VELVET ('Barthirty'PBR)	IPot LRHS MPri WNPC
- 'Paramo Blanca'	LRHS MPri
- 'Paramo Celeste'	MPri
- 'Paramo Lavanda'	LRHS MPri
- 'Paramo Púrpura'	MPri
- 'Paramo Rosa'	MPri
Percival Group	LRHS LShi LSto
'Pericles'	LHom
'Pink' (Excalibur Series)	LRHS SPoG
'Pink Punch' (New Millennium Series)	ELan EPfP
'Pink Ruffles'	LHom
'Plagu Blue'	WSpi
'Polar Sensation' (Highlander Series) (d)	XFar
polycladon	GKev
PRINCESS CAROLINE ('Odabar')	LRHS MPro
'Princess Charlotte'	LCro
'Pure White' (Excalibur Series)	LRHS SPoG
'Purple Passion' (New Millennium Series)	CDor ELan EPfP SPoG WSpi
'Purple Velvet' ♀H5	ENun
RAINBOW SENSATION ('Coadelchmo') (Highlander Series) (d)	XFar
RED CAROLINE ('Bartwentyfive'PBR)	LRHS MPro
'Red Lark'PBR	EGren ELan EPfP LCro LRHS MHtn MPro WNPC
requienii	CBgR CCBP CSpe ESwi MCtn SMHy
'Rose Butterfly' (d)	LRHS
'Rosemary Brock' ♀H5	ENun LCro LHom LRHS
'Royal Aspirations' (New Millennium Series)	CDor ELan SPoG
'Royal Flush'	see *D.* 'Langdon's Royal Flush'
'Ruby Wedding'	LHom
§ × *ruysii* 'Pink Sensation'	NLar WSpi
SAMBA ('Coadelsam') (Highlander Series) (d)	LBom LRHS
'Sandpiper'	ENun LHom LRHS
'Secret'PBR	LRHS
semibarbatum	MCtn
'Sherbet Lemon'	EBee LRHS MPro
'Shimmer'	ENun LRHS
'Sky Sensation'	NLar
'Spindrift' ♀H5	ENun LHom LRHS
'Strawberry Fair'	ELan LCro MPri NCth NLar SPoG
Summer Skies Group	CBcs ELan EPfP LCro MCtn MGos MPro SPoG WCAu
'Summerfield Oberon'	LHom
'Sungleam' ♀H5	ENun EWes LHom MPro NLar WSpi
'Sunkissed' ♀H5	LHom

'Sunny Skies' (New Millennium Series)	ELan		§	- 'Goldstaub'	EPPr
			§	- 'Goldtau' ♀H5	Widely available
'Sweet Sensation'PBR (Highlander Series) (d)	LCro LRHS MHol MPri SPoG WCot WTor			- 'Mill End'	CKno LEdu SPel WPGP
				- 'Morning Dew'	WFar
'Tiddles' ♀H5	ENun LRHS			- 'Northern Lights' (v)	ELan EPfP LRHS SPhx SPoG SRms
'Tiger Eye'	LHom			- 'Palava'	EPPr LRHS MPro NDov
'Titania'	LHom			- 'Pixie Fountain'	ELan EPfP GKev LRHS MNrw MPro NClf WFar
tricorne	SBrt WCot				
'Turkish Delight'	ELan LCro LHom			- 'Schottland'	CKno EBee ECha EPPr GBin LEdu MBel SPel
uliginosum	SPlb				
'Vanessa Mae'	LHom			- 'Tardiflora'	EBee LRHS SMHy
'Walton Benjamin'	LHom			- 'Tauträger'	ELon GQue
'Walton Gemstone' ♀H5	LHom		§	- var. *vivipara*	EPPr NBro
				- 'Waldschatt'	EBee ECha EPPr
				- 'Yunnan'	EPPr

Dendranthema see Chrysanthemum

Dendriopoterium see Sanguisorba

Dendrocalamus (Poaceae)

calostachys	SPlb			*flexuosa*	GQue LRHS MBel NBir SHor SPhx
§ *strictus*	SPlb			- AMILIME ('Amilim'PBR)	LRHS
				- 'Tatra Gold' ♀H6	ECha EHeP GMaP NBir NBro NLar NSti SPeP SPoG SRot
				'Silver Mist'	EBee EBlo LRHS

Dendromecon (Papaveraceae)

rigida	LRHS WPGP

Desfontainia (Columelliaceae)

§ *spinosa* ♀H4	CBcs CDoC CMac EBee ELon EPfP GAbr GArf GBin GKev GKin IArd MBlu MMuc NLar SPad SPoG SRms
- 'Harold Comber'	CMac
- f. *hookeri*	see *D. spinosa*

Dendropanax (Araliaceae)

trifidus	WPGP
- B&SWJ 11230	WCru

Desmanthus (Fabaceae)

illinoensis	MCtn

Dendroseris see Sonchus

litoralis see *Sonchus brassicifolius*

Desmodium (Fabaceae)

callianthum	CMac SBrt
canadense	CAby EPPr NLar StAn WHil
§ *elegans*	CBcs CExl EBee EPfP NLar NSti SVen WJun
- dark-flowered	EBee EPfP WPGP
nudiflorum	ESwi
praestans	see *D. yunnanense*
tiliifolium	see *D. elegans*
§ *yunnanense*	CExl

Dennstaedtia (Dennstaedtiaceae)

davallioides	WPGP
glauca	SPlb WPGP

Dentaria see Cardamine

pinnata	see *Cardamine heptaphylla*
polyphylla	see *Cardamine kitaibelii*

Deparia (Woodsiaceae)

japonica	ESwi WCot WPGP

Deuterocohnia (Bromeliaceae)

brevifolia ♀H2	NCft WCot WPGP
longipetala	CPic
lorentziana	NCft
lotteae	NCft WCot

Dermatobotrys (Scrophulariaceae)

saundersii	EAri EWld WCot

Derwentia see Veronica

Deutzia ✿ (Hydrangeaceae)

bhutanensis HWJK 2180	WCru
'Bright Eyes'	WPGP
calycosa	MBlu
- BWJ 8007	WCru
- DS 18	GGro
- 'Dali'	CBcs CExl EBee EPfP IArd
chunii	see *D. ningpoensis*
compacta	CMCN WPGP
- 'Lavender Time'	CDoC CExl CMac ELan EPfP GKev LRHS NLar
cordatula B&SWJ 6917	WCru
corymbosa GWJ 9202	WCru
- GWJ 9203	WCru
- GWJ 9339	WCru
- var. *corymbosa*	WSpi
crenata B&SWJ 8886	WCru
- B&SWJ 8896	WCru
- B&SWJ 8924	WCru
- 'Flore Pleno'	see *D. scabra* 'Plena'
- var. *heterotricha* B&SWJ 5805	WCru
- - B&SWJ 8879	WCru

Deschampsia (Poaceae)

cespitosa	CBWd CKno EGren EHeP EPPr LCro LRHS MBel MCtn SPhx SPlb WCot
- BRONZE VEIL	see *D. cespitosa* 'Bronzeschleier'
§ - 'Bronzeschleier'	CBWd CDor CMHG EBee EGrI ELan ELon EMor EPfP EPPr GMaP GQue LRHS LSto MAsh MHol NGdn NLar SAth SRms WCAu WFar WPGP
- 'Cabana Buta'	LEdu WPGP
- 'Coral Cloud'	GQue
- 'Fairy's Joke'	see *D. cespitosa* var. *vivipara*
- 'Garnet Schist'	EPPr GQue LEdu WPGP
- GOLD DUST	see *D. cespitosa* 'Goldstaub'
- GOLDEN DEW	see *D. cespitosa* 'Goldtau'
- GOLDEN PENDANT	see *D. cespitosa* 'Goldgehänge'
- GOLDEN SHOWER	see *D. cespitosa* 'Goldgehänge'
- GOLDEN VEIL	see *D. cespitosa* 'Goldschleier'
§ - 'Goldgehänge'	CKno EPPr NBir NLar
§ - 'Goldschleier' ♀H6	CBWd CKno EBee ECha EGren ELon EMor EPPr GMaP LRHS MAsh MBel NGdn NLit SAth SPeP WFar WSpi

Deutzia

- var. *nakaiana* B&SWJ 11184	WCru
- - 'Nikko'	see *D. gracilis* 'Nikko'
§ - 'Pride of Rochester' (d) ♀H5	CBcs CDoC CMCN ELan EPfP GKin LRHS LSto MBlu MMuc NLar SPoG WFar
'Dark Eyes'	CBcs CExl EBee EPfP GBin SChF
discolor 'Major'	CExl WCru
× *elegantissima*	SRms
- Fasciculata'	ELan ELon EPfP LRHS NLar WSpi
- 'Rosealind' ♀H5	CBcs CDoC CMac ELan EPfP GKin IArd LRHS LSRN NCth SRms WHtc WKif WSpi
glabrata B&SWJ 617	WCru
- B&SWJ 8427	WCru
- W&O 0039	GGro
glomeruliflora	CMCN EBee MBlu
- BWJ 7742	WCru
gracilis	CBcs EHeP GKin LRHS MGos NLar SOrN WFar WHtc WSpi
- B&SWJ 8927	WCru
- 'Aurea'	CMac LRHS
- 'Carminea'	see *D.* × *rosea* 'Carminea'
§ - 'Nikko' ♀H5	CBcs CDoC CMac CMCN CTsd EGren ELan ELon EPfP EWes GKev GKin LCro LRHS MGos MHer MMrt MPri MSwo NLar SGol SPad SPlb SRms WFar WKif WLov
- var. *ogatae* B&SWJ 8911	WCru
- 'Rosea'	see *D.* × *rosea*
hookeriana	EPfP LSRN SBrt
× *hybrida*	MSwo
- 'Contraste' ♀H5	CMac
- 'Iris Alford'	EPfP MGos WPGP WSpi
- 'Joconde' ♀H5	WFar WKif
- 'Magicien' misapplied	see *D.* × *hybrida* 'Strawberry Fields'
- 'Magicien' ambig.	EGrI WSpi
- 'Magicien' Lemoine	CMac ELan EPfP LRHS MAsh NBir SRms WFar WLov WSpi
- 'Mont Rose' ♀H5	CBrac CDoC CMac EGren EHeP ELan EPfP GKin LBuc LCro LRHS LSto MAsh MGos MMuc MSwo NCth NLar SEND SGol SPoG WFar WHtc WKif
- 'Perle Rose'	EHeP NLar
§ - 'Strawberry Fields' ♀H5	Widely available
× *kalmiiflora*	CBrac CMac EHeP ELan GKev GKin MAsh NLar SRms WFar WLov
× *lemoinei*	EGren WHtc
longifolia	CMCN EBee WPGP
- 'Veitchii'	WSpi
× *magnifica*	EGren LMaj MMrt SRms WFar
- 'Rubra'	see *D.* × *hybrida* 'Strawberry Fields'
maximowicziana B&SWJ 11567	WCru
monbeigii ♀H5	CExl EBee ELan EPfP MBlu WKif WSpi
- BWJ 7728	WCru
multiradiata	CExl EBee MBlu NLar WPGP
§ *ningpoensis*	EBee MBlu NLar WLov WPGP WSpi
paniculata B&SWJ 8562	ESwi WCru
parviflora var. *barbinervis* B&SWJ 8478	WCru
'Pink Pompon'	see *D.* 'Rosea Plena'
prunifolia B&SWJ 8588	WCru
pulchra	CBcs CDoC CEnd CMCN EBee ELan EPfP EWld LCro MMuc NLar SPoG WPGP WSpi
- B&SWJ 1738	WCru
- B&SWJ 3870	WCru
- B&SWJ 3948 from the Philippines	WCru
- B&SWJ 6908	WCru
- pink-tinged	WPGP
purpurascens BWJ 7859	WCru
Raspberry Sundae ('Low 18'PBR)	LCro LRHS MAsh MPri NLar WFar
§ × *rosea*	WLov CEnd EGrI GJos LRHS MAsh SRms WKif
- 'Carminea'	EGren LRHS SDix SPlb SRms WFar
- Yuki Cherry Blossom ('Ncdx2')	CBcs EPfP LBuc LCro LMil LRHS MAsh MMrt MPri NLar SGol SMad
- Yuki Snowflake ('Ncdx1')	EPfP LCro LRHS MAsh MPri NLar SMad
§ 'Rosea Plena' (d)	CEnd CMac CSBt ELan EPfP GKin LBuc LRHS MGos NLar SNig SPoG SRms WFar WLov
scabra	CBrac
- B&SWJ 11127	WCru
- B&SWJ 11168	WCru
- B&SWJ 11178	WCru
§ - 'Candidissima' (d) ♀H5	EHeP MMuc SEND WFar
- 'Codsall Pink' ♀H5	ELan NLar
§ - 'Plena' (d)	CBcs CBrac EPfP GKin NLar SPoG
- 'Pride of Rochester'	see *D. crenata* 'Pride of Rochester'
- 'Punctata' (v)	MAsh SRms WCot
- 'Robert Fortune'	SPlb
- 'Variegata' (v)	CMac WFar
setchuenensis	CMac
- PAB 7449	LEdu
- var. *corymbiflora* ♀H5	CBcs CExl CMCN EBee ELan EPfP GKev MSwo NLar SChF SPoG WFar WKif WPGP WSpi
- - NJM 11.096	WPGP
- - 'Kiftsgate'	CExl MPri WPGP
taiwanensis	CMCN WPGP
- CWJ 12443	WCru
- CWJ 12459	WCru
× *wellsii*	see *D. scabra* 'Candidissima'
× *wilsonii*	SRms

Dianella (Asphodelaceae)

caerulea	CMac CTsd EBee EWld NBir NLar SMrm
- Cassa Blue ('Dbb03'PBR)	CBcs CCht CKit ELan EPfP EUrb LBom MHol SArc
- Little Jess ('Dcmp01'PBR)	EBee
- 'Variegata'	see *D. tasmanica* 'Variegata'
nigra	LEdu WFar
- 'Margaret Pringle' (v)	GAbr
§ *revoluta* 'Allyn Citation'PBR	CBcs ELan LBom LCro LRHS WFar
- 'Blue Stream'	ELan LBom LRHS MHtn NLar
- Coolvista	see *D. revoluta* 'Allyn Citation'
- Little Rev ('Dr5000'PBR)	CCht EBee LCro SArc
'Silver Streak' (v)	WFar
tasmanica	CAbb CBro CElw CKno CMac CWal LEdu SArc SRms SVen
- Destiny ('Tas100') (v)	CCht CKit ELan MBNS MPri SMrm WCot
- Tasred ('Tr20'PBR)	CBcs CCht CKit CTsd EPfP EUrb LRHS
- 'Variegata' (v)	CDTJ LCro
- Wyeena ('Tas300')	LRHS SArc

Dianthus ❀ (Caryophyllaceae)

from Uzbekistan	EPPr GGro
'Alan Titchmarsh' (p)	SPoG
'Alice Lever' (p)	WAbe
'Allen's Maria' (p)	LShi
'Allspice' (p)	LShi

Dianthus

Allwoodii Alpinus Group (p)	NGdn SRms
- 'Alyson' (p)	LShi
- 'Bobby' (p)	LShi
- 'Bovey Belle' (p)	LShi
- (Cocktails Series)	EGren EPfP LBar LRHS MPri SRGP
CHERRY DAIQUIRI ('Wp15 Pie42'PBR) (p)	WCot WTor
- - COSMOPOLITAN ('Wp15 Pie43'PBR) (p)	EGren EPfP LBar LCro LRHS MPri WTor
- - SHIRLEY TEMPLE ('Wp15 Pie44'PBR) (p)	EGren EPfP LBar LCro LRHS
- - TEQUILA SUNRISE ('Wp15 Pie45'PBR) (p)	EGren LBar LCro LRHS MPri SRGP WTor
- 'Doris' pre-1932 (p)	LBar LShi
- 'Doris' pre-1954 (p) ♀H6	CBcs EGren EGrI EPfP GQue LCro LRHS LShi LSto MGos MHer MHol MPro SPlb SPoG SRGP SRms WCAu WTor
- 'Doris Majestic' (p)	LShi
- 'Eileen' (p)	LShi
I - 'Fiona' (p)	LShi
- 'Hope' Allwood, pre-1932 (p)	LShi
- 'Hope' Allwood, 1946 (p)	LShi
- 'Purple Jenny' (p)	LShi
alpinus 'Albus' (p)	GArf
- 'Darcies Love' (p)	EDAr
- 'Joan's Blood' (p) ♀H6	WFar
- 'Millstream Salmon' (p)	WFar
amurensis	EPPr GGro
- 'Siberian Blue' (p)	EPPr
anatolicus	GQue LRHS MBel MCtn MHer NGdn
'Anders Fay Seagrave' (p)	LShi
'Anders Melody' (p)	LShi
'Anders Patricia Griffiths' (p)	LShi
'Annette' (p)	EDAr NGdn SLee SRot
ARCTIC STAR	see *D.* 'Devon Arctic Star' (Early Bird Series)
arenarius	GKev NGdn SPlb
- 'Little Maiden' (p)	CSpe EDAr MCtn NGdn SLee
'Argus' (p)	LShi
armeria	CBgR CTtf GQue MNHC NAts WHer
arpadianus	GKev
- var. *pumilus*	EDAr EPot GKev
§ × *arvernensis* (p) ♀H6	ECha EPot StAn
'Aurora' (b)	MCtn
'Auvergne' (p)	see *D.* × *arvernensis*
'Averiensis'	see *D.* 'Berlin Snow'
AZTEC STAR ('Wp19 Nam02'PBR) (p)	EPfP LRHS NBir
'Bailey's Celebration' (p)	LRHS SRms
barbatus	CoPl GQue MPri StAn
- *albus*	LSto MCtn
- AURICULA EYED MIXED (p,a)	LSto MCtn
- Dash Series (p,a)	EGren MHol
- - DASH CRIMSON ('Pas889166') (p,a)	MHol
- - DASH MAGICIAN ('Pas889167') (p,a)	MHol WHil
- double-flowered (p,a/d)	LSto
- EXCELSIOR MIXED (p,a)	LSto
- Festival Series (p,a)	SPoG
- GREEN TRICK ('Temarisou'PBR) (p,a)	LCro
- 'Heart Attack' (p,a)	WCot WMal
- HOLLANDIA (mixed) (p,a)	MCtn
- Indian Carpet Group (p,a)	EGren LCro
- Messenger Group (p,a)	SVic
- 'Monksilver Black' (p,a)	CSpe ESwi EUrb LShi NWbg SMrm WCot WMal
- 'Newport Pink' (p,a)	MCtn
- Nigrescens Group (p,a) ♀H6	CSpe
- - 'Sooty' (p,a)	CWal LSto MCtn WFar WHer
- 'Oeschberg' (p,a)	MCtn
- SUPER DUPLEX MIXED (p,a/d) **new**	MCtn
§ 'Bat's Double Red' (p)	LShi WFar
'Becky Robinson' (p) ♀H6	LShi
§ 'Berlin Snow' (p)	EDAr EPot GArf LShi
BERRY BLUSH ('Wp21 Min01') (p) **new**	EPfP
'Betty Morton' (p) ♀H6	LRHS
'Black Cherry Frost' (Fruit Punch Series) (p) **new**	MMrt
'Blue Hills' (p)	GKev
'Blush'	see *D.* 'Souvenir de la Malmaison'
BLUSHING STAR ('Wp19 Nam01'PBR) (p)	WIce WTor
'Bombardier' (p)	GMaP
BRIDAL STAR ('Wp18 Cas06') (p)	EGren EPfP LBar LCro LRHS MArl MHol MPro
'Bridal Veil' (p)	LShi SRGP WFar WHer
'Brilliant'	see *D. deltoides* 'Brilliant'
'Brilliant Star' (p) ♀H6	LRHS
'Brympton Red' (p)	ECha LShi
caesius	see *D. gratianopolitanus*
'Calypso Star' (p)	SPoG
'Can-can' (pf)	LRHS
CANDY FLOSS	see *D.* 'Devon Flavia' (Scent First Series)
'Capitán Marco' (Capitán Series) (pt)	EPfP
§ 'Carmine Letitia Wyatt'PBR (p) ♀H6	LRHS SPoG
CARMINE VALDA	see *D.* 'Devon Louise'
carthusianorum	Widely available
- W&B BGL-1	WCot
- subsp. *carthusianorum*	GElm
I - 'Rupert's Pink' (p)	ECha LSto MCtn NDov NGdn SHar WCAu
caryophyllus	EGren ENfk SVic
'Charcoal'	MHer
'Charles' (p)	LShi
'Charles Edward' (p)	LShi
'Charles Musgrave'	see *D.* 'Musgrave's Pink'
'Chastity' (p)	LShi WHoo
Cheddar pink	see *D. gratianopolitanus*
CHERRY BURST ('Wp19 Mou01'PBR) (p)	EPfP LCro LRHS WTor
'Cheryl'	see *D.* 'Houndspool Cheryl'
chinensis (p,a)	MCtn
- 'Black and White' (p,a)	MCtn
- 'Chomley Farran' (b)	CSpe
'Clare' (p)	LShi
'Claret Joy' (p) ♀H6	LShi MMuc SEND
'Cleopatra' (pf)	EMal
§ 'Cockenzie Pink' (p)	LShi WHer
COCONUT SUNDAE ('Wp 05 Yves'PBR) (Scent First Series) (p) ♀H6	ELan ELon EPfP LBar LCro LRHS MPro
'Constance' (p)	LShi
'Constance Finnis'	see *D.* 'Fair Folly'
'Conwy Silver' (p)	WAbe

240 *Dianthus*

'Conwy Star' (p)	WAbe		'Duke of Norfolk' (pf)	EMal
'Coral Reef'^PBR (Scent First Series) (p)	ELan EPfP LBar SPoG		'Earl Kelso' (pf)	EMal
			'Earl of Essex' (p)	LShi WFar
'Coronation Ruby' (p) ♀H6	LShi		'Edenside Scarlet' (b)	LShi
'Cranmere Pool' (p) ♀H6	CBcs ELan ESgI GQue LBar LCro LRHS LShi MPro SEND SPoG WCAu WFar		'Eileen Lever' (p)	GArf SRot WAbe WIce
			'Eleanor Parker' (p)	WAbe
			'Eleanor's Old Irish' (p)	CFis LShi WCot WFar WHer
cruentus	CSpe CTtf ECha EDAr ELan EPPr EWes GElm LCro LRHS LShi LSto MBel MHol MMrt NClf NDov SDix SHar SHor SPhx WCAu WCot WTor		'Elizabethan' (p)	CFis WFar WTor
		*	'Elizabethan Pink' (p)	LShi NClf
			'Emile Paré' (p)	LShi
			'Emperor'	see *D.* 'Bat's Double Red'
			erinaceus	EPot GArf LShi StAn
'Dad's Favourite' (p)	LShi WFar		- var. *alpinus*	EPot LShi MWlw
'Dainty Dame' (p) ♀H4	CSpe SPoG		- Duguid's	WAbe
Dancing Geisha (mixed) (p)	EDAr GGro GQue MPro SBrt SVic		'Evening Star' (p) ♀H6	SPoG
'David' (p)	EHeP LShi	§	'Fair Folly' (p)	LShi WFar WHer
'D.D.R.'	see *D.* 'Berlin Snow'		'Farnham Rose' (p)	LShi
'Dedham Beauty' (p)	SEND WCot		*ferrugineus*	EPPr SPhx
deltoides ♀H6	CBWd CoPl EGrl ENfk EPfP GQue LCro MCtn MNHC SDix SPlb SRms StAn WFar		'Fettes Mount' (p)	MWlw WCot WMal
			'Fimbriatus' (p)	WHoo
- 'Albus' (p)	CoPl ECha EGren EPfP GKev LRHS LShi NGdn WFar		Fire Star	see *D.* 'Devon Xera'
			Fizzy ('Wp08 Ver03'^PBR) (Early Bird Series) (p)	ELan EPfP
- 'Arctic Fire' (p)	EGren EPfP MPro NGdn WFar		Flutterburst ('Wp18 Zor01') (p)	LCro LRHS NBir WTor
§ - 'Brilliant' (p)	LRHS LShi NGdn SRms StAn WFar			
- 'Broughty Blaze' (p)	LShi		'Flutterby' (p)	EPfP SPoG WIce
- Flashing Light	see *D. deltoides* 'Leuchtfunk'		'Fragrant Ann' (pf) ♀H6	EMal
§ - 'Leuchtfunk' (p)	EAri ECha EDAr EPfP GBin LRHS LShi LSto NBir SMHy SPoG WFar		'Frances Isabel' (p)	LShi
			'Freda Woodliffe' (p)	WAbe WHoo
I - 'Luneburg Heath Maiden Pink' (p)	EPfP NGdn		French Red (pf)	EMal
			freynii	EPot GKev LShi
- 'Nelli' (p)	NGdn	*	- var. *nana*	GKev
- 'Roseus' (p)	WFar		fringed pink	see *D. superbus*
- 'Shrimp' (p)	NGdn		*furcatus*	GKev
- 'Vampir' (p)	MPro		'Fusilier' (p)	EPfP LRHS LShi MAsh SPoG WIce WTor
- 'Zing Rose' (p)	MCtn			
§ 'Devon Arctic Star' (Early Bird Series) (p)	ELan EPfP GMaP LCro SPoG SRms WIce WTor		*giganteus*	GBin SPhx WCot
			'Gingham Gown' (p)	EPot LShi NBir
'Devon Cream' (p)	ELan SPoG		'Gold Dust' (p)	EPot GArf LShi MWlw
'Devon Dove' (p) ♀H6	ELan EPfP		'Grandma Calvert' (p)	LShi
'Devon Esther'	see *D.* Pop Star		'Gran's Favourite' (p) ♀H6	CBcs EGren EGrl ELan EPfP LBar LCro LShi LSRN MArl MHer MHol MMuc MPro SEND SPlb SPoG SRGP SRms WCAu WTor
'Devon Fatima'	see *D.* Iced Gem (Scent First Series)			
§ 'Devon Flavia'^PBR (Scent First Series) (p) ♀H6	LBar LRHS MPro SPoG WTor			
'Devon Flores'	see *D.* Shooting Star			
'Devon Haytor'	LRHS	§	*gratianopolitanus* ♀H6	CBWd EDAr ENfk GKev GQue LShi MHer MNHC
§ 'Devon Louise'^PBR (p)	WFar		- 'Babi Lom' (p)	LShi
'Devon Sapphire'	see *D.* Mystic Star		- Babylon ('Morbyl') (p)	MPro
'Devon Wizard' (p) ♀H6	CMHG EGren EPfP LBar LCro LRHS MHol MPro SEND SPoG WCAu		- dwarf	WAbe
		*	- 'Karlik' (p)	GKev GQue
§ 'Devon Xera' (p) ♀H6	ELan EPfP LRHS MAsh SEND WTor	§	- 'Tiny Rubies' (p)	EDAr LShi MWlw WAbe
§ 'Devon Yolande'^PBR (Scent First Series) (p)	EPfP LRHS MPro SPoG WCav		'Greensides' (p)	LShi
			'Gypsy Star' (p)	SPoG
'Dewdrop' (p)	EPot LRHS LShi MMuc NBir SEND		*haematocalyx*	GArf
'Diane' (p) ♀H6	LShi MPri SPoG SRGP WFar		- 'Alpinus'	see *D. haematocalyx* subsp. *pindicola*
'Dianne' (pf)	SRms WFar			
Diantica Purple Wedding ('Kledg18274'^PBR) (pt)	LCro LRHS	§	- subsp. *pindicola*	WAbe
			'Hannah Gertsen' (p)	LShi
Diantica Strawberry Cream ('Kledg15176'^PBR) (pt)	EPfP		'Harlequin' (p)	LShi
			Haytor	see *D.* 'Haytor White'
'Dinetta Pink' (p)	LRHS		'Haytor Rock' (p) ♀H6	EPfP LShi
'Dinetta Purple' **new**	LRHS	§	'Haytor White' (p) ♀H6	CBcs EGrl EHeP LCro LShi LSto NBir WCAu WFar
'Dinetta Soft Pink' **new**	LRHS			
'Doreen Hodgson' (p)	LShi		'Heath' (p)	LShi
'Doris Allwood' (pf)	EMal		'Helen' (p)	LShi
'Doris Elite' (p)	LShi		'Helena Allwood' (pf)	EMal WMal
'Doris Ruby'	see *D.* 'Houndspool Ruby'		'Hot Spice' (p)	SPoG
'Doris Supreme' (p)	LShi	§	'Houndspool Cheryl' (p) ♀H6	CBcs EPfP LShi SPoG SRms WCAu
'Duchess of Roxburghe' (pf)	EMal			
'Duchess of Westminster' (M)	EMal LShi	§	'Houndspool Ruby' (p) ♀H6	CBcs LShi SRGP
			hyssopifolius	GQue LShi MCtn

Dianthus

I Love U ('Kledp20383'PBR) (pt)	LCro	*microlepis*	GKev LShi NGdn
§ Iced Gem ('Wp06 Fatima'PBR) (Scent First Series) (p)	ElAn EPfP SPoG	- f. *albus*	GKev
		- ED 791562	NGdn
'Icomb' (p)	WHoo	'Miss Farrow' (p)	SHar SPhx
'Inchmery' (p)	LShi	Mojito ('Wp15 Pie41'PBR) (p)	EGren EPfP LBar LCro LRHS MPri WCot
'Ine' (p)	MPro	'Mondriaan' (pt)	LRHS
'Inshriach Dazzler' (p) ♀H6	EDAr EPot GAbr GArf GEdr GMaP MAsh MHer MSwo SLee SRot WIce	'Monica Wyatt' (p) ♀H6	SPoG
		'Montrose Pink'	see D. 'Cockenzie Pink'
'James Muir' (M)	EMal	'Monty Allwood' (p)	LShi MWlw
japonicus	CSpe	'Monty's Pink' (pf)	EMal
'Joy' (p) ♀H6	LShi SPoG	Morello Star ('Wp24 Jap01') (p) **new**	WTor
'Kahori' (p)	EGren LRHS SPoG		
'Kessock Rose Blush' (p)	LShi	'Moulin Rouge' (p) ♀H6	CBcs ElAn LBar LCro MPro SPoG SRms
'Kesteven Kirkstead' (p) ♀H6	LShi MNrw		
		(Mountain Frost Series)	MPro
'King of the Blacks' (p,a)	LSto	- Mountain Frost Red Garnet ('Kond1335k1') (b)	
knappii	CCBP ECha EDAr LSto SDix SHar SPhx		
- 'Yellow Harmony' (p,a)	MCtn	- Mountain Frost Ruby Glitter ('Kond1400k6') (b)	MPro
kuschakewiczii from Kazakhstan	GGro		
'La Bourboule' (p) ♀H6	GMaP LShi WIce	- Mountain Frost Ruby Snow ('Kond1400k4') (b)	MPro
'La Bourboule Alba' (p) ♀H6	LShi MAsh		
'Laced Joy' (p)	LShi	'Mrs McBride's Old Irish' (p)	LShi
'Laced Monarch' (p)	CBcs EGrI ElAn EPfP LRHS LShi SPlb SPoG SRGP SRms	'Mrs Sinkins' (p)	CBcs ECha EGrI ElAn EPfP GArf GKev GMaP LShi LSRN LSto MHer MNrw SBeP SEND SMrm SPoG SRms WCAu WFar WKif
'Laced Mrs Sinkins' (p)	LShi		
'Laced Prudence'	see D. 'Prudence'		
'Laced Romeo' (p)	LShi		
'Laced Treasure' (p)	LShi	'Murray Douglas' (p)	LShi
'Lady Granville' (p)	LShi MWlw	§ 'Musgrave's Pink' (p)	ECha LShi WHer
Lady in Red ('Wp04 Xanthe'PBR) (p)	ElAn EPfP LCro NBir SPoG SRms	'Musgrave's White'	see D. 'Musgrave's Pink'
		myrtinervius	GPSL NGdn
'Lady Windermere' (M)	EMal	§ Mystic Star ('Wp05 Saphire') (p) ♀H6	ElAn
'Lancing Supreme' (p)	LShi WHer		
'Lawley's Red' (p)	LShi	'Napoléon III' (1840) (p)	LShi WMal
'Lemsii' (p) ♀H6	NGdn	'Nautilus' (b)	LShi
'Letitia Wyatt' (p) ♀H6	EGrI EPfP LBar LShi MPro SPoG SRms WTor	*neglectus* misapplied	see D. *pavonius*
		'Neon Star'PBR (p) ♀H6	ElAn GEdr GKev LRHS SPoG
'Leuchtkugel' (p)	EPot	'Night Star' (p) ♀H6	EDAr ElAn LShi
Lily the Pink ('WP05 Idare'PBR) (p) ♀H6	SRGP	*nitidus*	LShi
		nivalis	GKev
'Linfield Dorothy Perry' (p) ♀H6	LShi	*noeanus*	see D. *petraeus* subsp. *noeanus*
		'Northland' (pf)	EMal
'Little Ben' (p)	LShi	'Nyewoods Cream' (p)	EPfP EPot GArf GMaP LShi MHer NGdn
'Little Jock' (p)	EPot LRHS LShi LSto MAsh MWlw SPlb SRms		
		'Oakwood Sweet-heart' (p)	LShi
'London Brocade' (p)	LShi	'Odessa Red' (Odessa Series) (pt)	LRHS SRms
'London Delight' (p)	LShi		
'London Glow' (p)	LShi	'Old Blush'	see D. 'Souvenir de la Malmaison'
* 'London Joy'	LShi	'Old Dutch Pink' (p)	CFis
'London Lovely' (p)	LShi	'Old Red Clove' (p)	WCot WKif
'London Poppet' (p)	LShi	'Old Rose' (pf)	EMal
'Loveliness' (p,a)	CTtf	§ 'Old Square Eyes' (p)	EPPr LShi MNrw SHar WMal
lummitzeri	GKev LShi	'Old Velvet' (p)	LShi WFar
'Mandy' (p)	LShi	'Owston Third Avenue' (p)	LShi
'Mandy Gamble' (p)	LShi	'Oxford Magic' (p)	LShi
'Marchioness of Headfort'	EMal	'Painted Lady' (p)	LShi
'Maria'	see D. 'Allen's Maria'	'Paisley Gem' (p)	LShi
'Marian Allwood' (pf)	EMal	Passion ('Wp Passion'PBR) (Scent First Series) (p)	EBee ElAn EPfP LBar LCro LRHS MHer MPro SEND SPoG WCot WTor
'Marmion' (pf)	EMal LShi		
'Ma's Choice' (p)	LShi		
'Matthew' (p)	WHoo	§ *pavonius*	EWes NGdn
'Megan' (pf)	EPfP	'Peach' (p)	SEND
Memories ('WP11 Gwe04'PBR) (Scent First Series) (p)	CBcs EBee ElAn EPfP GBin LBar LBuc LCro LRHS MPri MPro SPoG WCot WFar WTor	Peach Party ('Kledg18305'PBR) (pt)	EPfP LCro LRHS MPri
		'Pendle Doris Delight' (p)	LShi
Mendlesham Minx ('Russmin'PBR) (p)	ElAn LRHS WTor	*petraeus*	NGdn
		§ - subsp. *noeanus*	GEdr
'Messines Pink' (p)	LShi	'Petticoat Lace' (p)	LShi

Dianthus

'Pheasant's Eye' (p)	LShi WHer
* 'Picton's Propeller' (p)	EPPr MNrw MWlw
'Pike's Pink' (p) ♀H6	EPfP LShi MAsh MWlw NBir NGdn SEND SPoG
PINBALL WIZARD ('Wp15mow08') (p)	EPfP SPoG
pindicola	see *D. haematocalyx* subsp. *pindicola*
pinifolius	EDAr LShi
PINK CELEBRATION	LBar
'Pink Jewel' (p)	ECha EGren EPot MAsh SLee
PINK KISSES ('Kledg12163'PBR) (pt)	EGren LCro MPri SPoG SRGP
'Pink Mrs Sinkins' (p)	LShi
PINK PANTHER ('Hilpinkpan'PBR) (pt)	MPro
PINK RUFFLES ('Wp18 Mow09'PBR)	EPfP LCro MPro
'Pixie' (b)	EPot
'Pixie Star'PBR (p) ♀H6	SPoG
plumarius	LShi StAn
- 'Maischnee' (p)	ECha
pontederae 'Dear Kim'	NDov
§ POP STAR ('Wp04 Esther'PBR) (p)	LCro WIce WTor
PRETTY FLAMINGO	see *D.* 'Carmine Letitia Wyatt'
'Prince Charming' (p)	MAsh
'Princess of Wales' (M)	EMal LShi
'Priory Pink' (p)	LShi
§ 'Prudence' (p)	LShi
'Pudsey Prize' (p)	EPot
'Purple Frosted' (pf)	EMal
pygmaeus CMBTW 1678	GGro
- NMWJ 14561	WCru
§ 'Queen of Henri' (p)	LShi
'Queen of Sheba' (p)	LShi WHer
'Rachel' (p)	LShi MPro
'Rainbow Loveliness' (p,a)	MCtn SDix
'Raspberry Parfait' (p,a)	MBros
RASPBERRY SUNDAE	see *D.* 'Devon Yolande' (Scent First Series)
REBEKAH ('Wp09 Mar05'PBR) (Early Bird Series) (p) ♀H6	ELan LRHS
RED CARPET ('Wp18 Rlw15'PBR)	LBar MPro
'Red Dwarf'	see *D.* 'Red Star'
§ 'Red Star'PBR (p) ♀H6	MAsh
'Reine de Henri'	see *D.* 'Queen of Henri'
'Robert Allwood' (pf)	EMal
'Robina's Daughter' (p)	GAbr
(Rockin' Series)	MSCN
ROCKIN' PURPLE ('Pas1350219') (p,a)	
- ROCKIN' RED ('Pas1141436') (p,a)	MSCN
'Romance' (pf)	MPri
ROMANCE ('Wp09 Wen04'PBR) (Scent First Series) (p) ♀H6	EPfP LRHS
'Rose de Mai' (p)	CFis LShi WHer WHoo
'Royal Crimson' (pf)	EMal
'Royal Salmon' (pf)	EMal
'Ruby'	see *D.* 'Houndspool Ruby'
'Ruby Doris'	see *D.* 'Houndspool Ruby'
rupicola	CSpe
'Russian Skies'	GQue
'Sam Barlow' (p)	LShi
SCARLET BEAUTY ('Hilbeau')	LSto MCtn
serotinus	EPot LShi WCot
SHERBET ('Wp08 Nik03'PBR) (Early Bird Series) (p)	EPfP WIce
'Shire Delight' (p)	LShi
§ SHOOTING STAR ('Wp04 Flores'PBR) (p)	ELan SPoG SRms
'Shot Silk' (pf)	EMal
'Show Aristocrat' (p)	LShi
'Show Harlequin' (p)	LShi
SHOWGIRL ('Wp08 Uni02') (Scent First Series) (p)	EPfP
SILVER STAR ('Wp10 Hel01'PBR) (p)	EPfP
simulans	SRot
SLAP 'N' TICKLE ('Wp 05 Pp 22'PBR) (Scent First Series) (p) ♀H6	EPfP SPoG
'Snowshill Manor' (p)	LShi
'Solomon' (p)	LShi
'Sops-in-wine' (p)	LShi
'Sops-in-wine 2' (p)	LShi
§ 'Souvenir de la Malmaison' (M)	EMal LShi WFar
spiculifolius	CFis EDAr EPot LShi MMuc
'Sprint Violetta'	LRHS
'Square Eyes'	see *D.* 'Old Square Eyes'
squarrosus	LShi SRot WAbe
- 'Nanus'	see *D.* 'Berlin Snow'
'Starburst'PBR (p)	LRHS WTor
STARGAZER ('Wp13 Gil05'PBR) (Whetman Stars Series) (p)	LCro LRHS SPoG WTor
STARLIGHT ('Hilstar') (pf)	SRms
'Starry Eyes' (p) ♀H6	ELan GBin SRms
'Storm' (pf)	EMal
'Strawberries and Cream' (p)	SPoG
strictus	WCot
* - subsp. *pulchellus*	EPot GEdr WFar
subacaulis	MMuc
suendermannii	see *D. petraeus*
SUGAR PLUM ('Wp08 Ian04'PBR) (Scent First Series) (p)	EBee ELan EPfP LBar LCro LRHS MPri MPro
'Summerfield Blaze' (p)	LShi
'Summerfield Blush' (p)	LShi
'Summerfield Jo' (p)	CFis
§ *superbus*	CWal ECha EPPr GQue MCtn SBrt SMrm SPhx WHer
- BO 15-070	GGro
- from Japan	GGro SMrm
- var. *longicalycinus*	GGro
- - dark-flowered	GGro
- - white-flowered	GGro
I - 'Primadonna' (p)	SHar
- 'Spooky'	MCtn SBeP
SUPERNOVA ('Wp11 Tyr04'PBR) (pf) ♀H6	LRHS WHil WTor
SUPERTROUPER SOPHIE	LRHS
SUPERTROUPER SORBET ('Kledc06080') (pt)	LRHS
SUPERTROUPER WHITE	LRHS
SUPERTROUPER WHITNEY ('Kledp18255'PBR) (pt)	LRHS SPoG
SUPERTROUPER WITTA ('Kledp08098'PBR) (pt)	LRHS
'Sway Lass' (p)	SEND
'Tatra' (pf)	NQui
'Tatra Blush' (p)	EPPr GBin LShi MWlw
'Tatra Fragrance' (p)	EPPr LShi SMHy
'Tayside Red' (M)	EMal
'Telhouet' (b)	SMHy

Diascia 243

'Thora' (M)	EMal
tianschanicus	GGro GKev
TICKLED PINK ('Devon Pp 11'PBR) (Scent First Series) (p) ♀H6	EBee ELan LCro LRHS MPri MPro SPoG WTor
'Tiny Rubies'	see *D. gratianopolitanus* 'Tiny Rubies'
'Treasure' (p)	LShi
'Tudor'	MNrw
'Unique' (p)	CFis LShi
'Valda Wyatt' (p) ♀H6	CBcs EPfP LRHS SEND SPoG WFar WTor
'Velvet Pelargonium' (pf)	EMal
'W.A. Musgrave'	see *D.* 'Musgrave's Pink'
'Waithman Beauty' (p)	CFis LShi WHoo
'Warden Hybrid' (p)	EPfP LShi SPoG
'Whatfield Brilliant' (p)	LShi
'Whatfield Cancan' (p) ♀H6	ELan EPfP GMaP LRHS LShi NGdn SPoG WTor
'Whatfield Cyclops' (p)	LShi
'Whatfield Dorothy Mann' (p)	WIce
'Whatfield Gem' (p)	EDAr ELan EPot LRHS LShi WCav WIce
'Whatfield Joy' (p)	ELan EPfP LShi NGdn
'Whatfield Magenta' (p) ♀H6	ELan EPot LRHS LShi SPoG SRms
'Whatfield Mini' (p)	LShi SRot
'Whatfield Miss' (p)	LShi
'Whatfield Peach' (p)	LShi
'Whatfield Pom-pom' (p)	LShi
'Whatfield Ruby' (p)	LShi
'Whatfield White' (p)	LShi
'Whatfield Wisp' (p)	GArf LShi NBir
'White Ladies' (p)	LShi
'Widecombe Fair' (p) ♀H6	LShi SPoG

Diapensia (Diapensiaceae)

lapponica var. *obovata*	GArf

Diarrhena (Poaceae)

japonica	EPPr
obovata	EPPr

Diascia (Scrophulariaceae)

'Apricot'	see *D. barberae* 'Hopleys Apricot'
'Aurora Apricot' (Towers of Flowers Series)	EPfP LCro
'Aurora Cherry Blossom' (Towers of Flowers Series)	LSou
barberae	MBros
- 'Belmore Beauty' (v)	EWes
- 'Blackthorn Apricot' ♀H4	ECha NDov NQui SPoG SRms
§ - 'Fisher's Flora'	LSto WFar
§ - 'Hopleys Apricot'	EBee
- 'Pink Queen'	SPhx
§ - 'Ruby Field'	EBee ECha LShi SMad SPoG SRms
BLUE BONNET ('Hecbon')	CSpe
'Bluebelle' (Maritana Series)	ECha NDov
'Blush'	see *D. integerrima* 'Blush'
(Breezee Series) BREEZEE APPLE BLOSSOM	ELan NLar
- BREEZEE APRICOT ('Diaspritwo')	MMrt NLar
- BREEZEE ORANGE	LRHS
- BREEZEE PLUS PINK	LRHS
- BREEZEE RED	LRHS NLar
- BREEZEE SNOW ('Indiabzsno')	ELan NLar
'Coldham'	SMHy WGoo WMal
CORAL BELLE ('Hecbel') ♀H3	NQui
cordata misapplied	see *D. barberae* 'Fisher's Flora'
cordata ambig.	WFar
cordifolia	see *D. barberae* 'Fisher's Flora'
'Diamond Fuchsia'	LCro
'Diamond Light Pink'	LCro
'Diamond White Blush'	LCro
'Divara Blush' (Divara Series)	NLar
'Divara Deep Red' (Divara Series)	NLar
elegans misapplied	see *D. fetcaniensis, D. vigilis*
'Emma'	NDov SMHy WGoo WMal
felthamii	see *D. fetcaniensis*
§ *fetcaniensis*	EBee EPfP GBin GElm NDov SIvy
- 'Daydream'	ESgI LRHS LShi MMrt MNrw MPie WFar
flanaganii misapplied	see *D. vigilis*
Flying Colours Series	MPri
- FLYING COLOURS ANTIQUE ROSE ('Diastu')	MPri SPoG
- FLYING COLOURS APPLEBLOSSOM ('Diastara')	MPri SPoG
- FLYING COLOURS APRICOT ('Diastina')	SPoG
- FLYING COLOURS DEEP SALMON IMPROVED ('Dala Depsam')	SPoG
- FLYING COLOURS RED ('Diastonia')	MPri SPoG
- FLYING COLOURS ROSE	MPri
- FLYING COLOURS UPRIGHT ORANGE	MPri
- FLYING COLOURS WHITE	MPri
'Hector Harrison'	see *D.* 'Salmon Supreme'
§ 'Hopleys'	CCps CSpe ECha ESgI LCro LRHS LShi LSto MAvo MPie MSCN NDov NLar SHar SPel WCot WFar
ICE CRACKER ('Hecrack')	ELan SRms
§ *integerrima*	ECha LShi
- 'Alba'	see *D. integerrima* 'Blush'
§ - 'Blush'	CSpe NDov SMHy
- 'Ivory Angel'	see *D. integerrima* 'Blush'
integrifolia	see *D. integerrima*
'Jacqueline's Joy'	NPer
'Joyce's Choice' ♀H3	SRms
'Katherine Sharman' (v)	EWes
'Lilac Belle' ♀H3	EDAr SPoG SRms
'Lilac Mist'	NPer
LITTLE DANCER ('Pendan')	ELan LCro LRHS NLar
LITTLE DREAMER ('Pender')	NLar
LITTLE DRIFTER ('Pendrif')	NLar
LITTLE MAIDEN ('Penmaid')	NLar
LITTLE TANGO ('Pentang')	NLar SRms
personata	CCBP CCps CDor CTtf CWCL EBee EMor EPfP EWhm GBin GElm GMaP LCro MHol MNrw SDix SIvy SNoN SRkn WCot WFar WMal
- 'Coral Spires'	CCps CDor CSpe EBee ESgI NDov WCot
- 'Hopleys'	see *D.* 'Hopleys'
- orange-flowered	CTtf ESgI GBin WMal
'Peter'	NDov
PICCADILLY DENIM BLUE ('Kledb06039')	EDAr WFar
RED ACE ('Hecrace')	NPer
rigescens ♀H3	LRHS NPer SChF SPlb SPoG WSpi
'Ruby Field'	see *D. barberae* 'Ruby Field'
'Rupert Lambert' ♀H3	ESgI MNrw WCot
§ 'Salmon Supreme'	NPer SPoG SRms
'Twinkle' ♀H3	NBir NPer SRms

244 *Diascia*

§	*vigilis* ♀H3	EBee EPot NBro NCth NLar SRms
	- 'Jack Elliott'	SDix

Dicentra (Papaveraceae)

	'Adrian Bloom'	CDor WFar
	(Amore Series) 'Amore Pink'	CWGN
	- 'Amore Rose'^{PBR}	CWGN LSou MPro SPeP
	- 'Amore Titanium' **new**	lPot LSou SPeP
	'Aurora'	CBcs CMiW CoPl ECha EMor GMaP LCro LSto MNrw NGdn NLar SPoG WBrk WCAu WHil
	'Boothman's Variety'	see *D.* 'Stuart Boothman'
	'Bountiful'	CMac NGdn
	'Burning Hearts'^{PBR}	CWGN EGrI MHol SPoG WCAu
	canadensis	CMiW LEdu WAbe WPGP
	'Candy Hearts'^{PBR}	ELan EMor
	cucullaria	CMiW EMor EPot EPPr GArf GEdr GKev LAma LEdu NBir SPeP StAn WAbe WFar
	- 'Carl Gehenio'	GEdr
	- 'Pink Punk'	EPPr
	- 'Pittsburg'	CMiW EPPr LEdu
	eximia misapplied	see *D. formosa*
	eximia ambig.	CMac GPSL MCtn StAn WFar
	eximia (Ker Gawl.) Torr. 'Alba'	see *D. eximia* (Ker Gawl.) Torr. 'Snowdrift'
§	- 'Snowdrift'	CDor EHeP SRms WFar WTre
	'Filigree'	CSpe ECha LEdu SMad
§	*formosa*	CBcs CToG ECha EGrI GGro LSto NBro SPlb SRms WCAu WTre
	- f. *alba*	ECha NBir SBeP SRms WCru WFar WKif
	- 'Bacchanal' ♀H5	CElw EBee EGren EGrI EPfP ERCP GMaP LCro MBel MNrw NBid NBir NLar SPel SPeP SPoG SRms WCAu WHil WKif WPnP WSpi WTre
	- 'Cox's Dark Red'	GMaP LEdu
	- 'Langtrees' ♀H5	CMac ECha LCro NBro SRms WCru WFar WSpi
	- 'Moorland Mist'	WFar
	- subsp. *oregana*	EGrI EPPr LEdu
	- 'Spring Gold'	EGrI EPPr NLar WFar
	- 'Spring Magic'	CTsd EPPr NLar WSpi
	'Ivory Hearts'^{PBR}	CWGN ELan EMor MPro NLar SMad
	'King of Hearts'	CDor CMac CWGN EGren EMor EPfP MGos MHol SPoG SRkn WCAu WCot WHil WSpi
	'Love Hearts'^{PBR}	MHol
	'Luxuriant' ♀H5	CBcs CMac CoPl EBee ELan EMor EPfP GBin LAma LRHS MAsh MGos SBeP SPoG SRms WCAu WFar
	macrantha	see *Ichthyoselmis macrantha*
	'Pearl Drops'	MMrt NBid SRms
	'Pink Diamonds'	MPri
	'Red Fountain'^{PBR}	NCth
	scandens	see *Dactylicapnos scandens*
	spectabilis	see *Lamprocapnos spectabilis*
	'Spring Morning'	CDor CElw EPPr LEdu NGdn WSpi
§	'Stuart Boothman' ♀H5	ELan EPfP MAsh NBro NGdn NLar NQui SPoG SRms WBrk WCAu WFar WKif
	'Sulphur Hearts'	CWGN XFar
	thalictrifolia	see *Dactylicapnos scandens*
	ventii	see *Dactylicapnos ventii*

Dichelostemma (Asparagaceae)

	capitatum 'Ginny's Giant'	CSpe
	congestum	LCro XFar
§	*ida-maia*	CAby EPot GKev LAma XFar
	- 'Pink Diamond'	EPot GKev LAma XFar
	volubile	GKev

Dichondra (Convolvulaceae)

	argentea 'Silver Falls'	EShb LSou MBros SPoG
§	*micrantha*	EShb
	repens misapplied	see *D. micrantha*

Dichorisandra (Commelinaceae)

*	*pendula*	EAri SBrt

Dichroa see *Hydrangea*

cyanea	see *Hydrangea wallichii*
yunnanensis	see *Hydrangea hwangii*

Dichromena see *Rhynchospora*

Dichrostachys (Fabaceae)

cinerea	SPlb

Dicksonia (Dicksoniaceae)

antarctica ♀H3	Widely available
fibrosa ♀H3	CDTJ MCtn SBig
sellowiana	CDTJ WPGP
squarrosa ♀H3	CBrP CDTJ SBig
youngiae	CDTJ

Dicliptera (Acanthaceae)

§	*sericea*	EAri EShb EWld SEND SRkn
	suberecta	see *D. sericea*

Dicranostigma (Papaveraceae)

leptopodum	MCtn

Dictamnus (Rutaceae)

	albus	CSpe EBee ECha EGrI ELan EPfP ERCP GKev GMaP LCro LRHS LSto MBel MHoo MNrw SMHy SPoG WCAu WSpi
§	- var. *albiflos*	EAri
§	- var. *albus* ♀H6	CDor CSpe EAri EBee ECha EGren EGrI EPfP GKev MBel MHoo MNrw StAn WCAu WSpi
	- purple-flowered	see *D. albus* var. *albus*
	- white-flowered	see *D. albus* var. *albiflos*
	fraxinella	see *D. albus* var. *albus*

Dictyosperma (Arecaceae)

album var. *rubrum*	NPlm

× *Didrangea* see *Hydrangea*

Didymochlaena (Dryopteridaceae)

	lunulata	see *D. truncatula*
§	*truncatula*	CDoC LCro

Dieffenbachia (Araceae)

'Camille' (v) ♀H1a	EGren LCro
'Compacta' (v)	LCro NHrt
'Maroba'	NHrt
'Reflector' (v)	LCro
'Summer Style'^{PBR}	LCro
'Tropic Snow' (v) ♀H1a	LCro NHrt

Dierama ✿ (Iridaceae)

adelphicum	CElw GAbr GKev
ambiguum	CElw
'Archangel' **new**	NLar
argyreum	CBcs CElw CMiW EWoo LRHS NLar SPoG
'Autumn Sparkler'	GKev WHil
Barr hybrids	CBro WHil

Digitalis 245

'Blackberry Bells'	CDor CLil CTsd CWCL CWGN ELan EPfP GKev LBar LCro MAvo MBel MHol NLar SChF SPad SPoG WHil WSpi
'Blood Drops'	WHil
BLUE BELLE ('Rowbluy'^PBR)	IBal
'Candy Stripe'	EBee
'Champagne Fairy' **new**	CBro
'Cinnamon Fairy'	IBal
cooperi	NBir
'Coral Belle'	IBal
'Coral Bells'	IBal WPGP
'Cosmos'	LShi
'Dark Angel'	EBee NLar
§ *dracomontanum*	CBcs CBro CElw CExl CWCL ECha GKev GMaP LRHS NBir NLar NSti SPeP WFar WHoo
- dwarf, pink-flowered	GArf
ensifolium	see *D. pendulum*
erectum	CTsd CWCL LBar LRHS LSou NLar SPeP
galpinii	CWCL WHil
'Guinevere'	CCBP CDor CWCL CWGN EBee GMaP LEdu LShi NBir NGdn NQui SPoG SVen WFar WGwG WHoo
igneum	Widely available
insigne	EPPr MHtn
jucundum	WCot
'Kilmurry White'	IBal
'Lancelot'	GMaP IBal NBir WFar
luteoalbidum	GKev
'Miranda'	CLil IBal NLar
mossii	CWCL LEdu NLar NQui SPlb SPoG SVen WPGP
'Painted Lady'	IBal
pauciflorum	CWCL EWld NBir NLar WAbe
- 'Luana'	SPeP
§ *pendulum*	CBro CElw CExl EPfP LRHS LSto MArl SPeP WCot WFar
- 'Album'	WHil WPGP
'Perky'	CBro
'Pink Rocket'	CMiW ELan LBar LCro MHer MHtn SPad
'Pizzazz'	CBro
PLANT WORLD JEWELS	WFar
pulcherrimum	Widely available
- var. *album*	CBcs CSpe CWCL ElAn EWes GKev LBar LCro LRHS MAvo MBel MHer MHol MNrw NCth SPeP
- 'Blackbird'	CBcs CoPl CSpe CWCL EBee ElAn LSRN MBel MCtn MHer NLar SChF SPeP SPoG WFar WHil WPGP WTre
- dark cerise-flowered	EBee IPot
- 'Merlin'	CDor IBal NBir SVen WFar
- pale-flowered	ECha ESgI
- purple-flowered	CSpe ESgI
- Slieve Donard hybrids	CWCL CWnw WCot WFar
pumilum misapplied	see *D. dracomontanum*
pumilum hybrid	NCth
reynoldsii	EWoo GAbr NLar SPlb SPoG SVen WFar WSpi
robustum	CLil CTsd CWCL EBee EWes WCot WFar WPGP
sertum	WHil
'Spring Dancer'	GKev MHer SPlb
'Tiny Bells'	EDAr GBin IBal
'Titania'	IBal
trichorhizum	CBro CElw CWCL GKev WHil
'White Eyes'	CBro
white-flowered	MBel
Wildside hybrids	WHil
'Wind Sprite Dusty Rose' **new**	SPeP
'Wind Sprite Lavender' **new**	SPeP

Diervilla ✿ (*Caprifoliaceae*)

middendorffiana	see *Weigela middendorffiana*
rivularis HONEYBEE ('Diwibru01'^PBR)	CSBt EBee EGren LCro LRHS MMrt NEoE NLar SPoG WHtc WLov
- 'Troja Black'	EPPr MBlu NLar
§ *sessilifolia*	CBrac CMac MBlu WCot
- 'Butterfly'	CMac LCro LRHS MBlu NLar WFar
- COOL SPLASH ('Lpdc Podaras'^PBR) (v)	CMac LRHS NEoE SPoG
× *splendens*	CBrac EBee EGren EPPr MBlu MSwo NLar SIvy SPoG
- DIVA	see *D.* × *splendens* 'El Madrigal'
§ - 'El Madrigal'^PBR	EBee LCro LRHS MMrt NEoE NSti
- HONEY SURPRISE ('Diwibru02') (v)	LCro
- KODIAK RED ('G2x885411')	MMuc

Dietes (*Iridaceae*)

bicolor	CExl CPbh CSpe EAri EBee ESgI ESwi EWoo LBar LCro LEdu SChr SPoG
grandiflora	CAbb CExl CPbh ESwi EWoo SChr SVen WCot
§ *iridioides*	ESwi
robinsoniana	WCot

Digitalis ✿ (*Plantaginaceae*)

ambigua	see *D. grandiflora*
apricot hybrids	see *D. purpurea* 'Sutton's Apricot'
canariensis	CDTJ CHll CSpe CTsd EAri EShb LRHS LWaG SEle SIvy SPad SPlb SVen
ciliata	GKev LShi WHil
'Elsie Kelsey'	EPfP SRot
eriostachya	see *D. lutea*
ferruginea ♀^H6	CCBP CDor CElw CSpe CWal CWnw EBee ECha EGren ELan EPPr GArf GKev GQue LSto LWaG MCtn MPie NBir NClf NGdn SMHy SRms StAn SVen WBrk WCAu WKif WPGP WTre
- B&SWJ 15395	WCru
- 'Gelber Herold'	CDor CWnw GMaP LRHS MCtn WFar WSpi
- 'Gigantea' ♀^H7	CWnw EAri EDAr ELan EPfP GAbr LBuc LEdu LShi MBNS MCtn MNrw MPro NDov SDix SPlb WPGP
× *fulva* ARCTIC FOX ROSE ('Balroxose'^PBR)	EGren EPfP LBar LBuc LSou MPro
'Glory of Roundway' ♀^H6	CDor EBee EPfP LCro MHol MNrw NLar WCot
§ GOLDCREST ('Waldigone'^PBR)	CBcs CWGN EPfP LBuc LRHS LSou MBNS MHol MPri SHar SPoG WNPC
§ *grandiflora* ♀^H6	Widely available
- 'Carillon' ♀^H5	EBee EDAr ELan EPfP MPro NBir WCAu WCav
- 'Dwarf Carillon'	EMor LRHS
heywoodii	see *D. purpurea* subsp. *heywoodii*
Illumination Series	see *D.* × *valinii* Illumination Series
isabelliana	LRHS
- BELLA ('Isob007')	CSpe LCro LRHS
'John Innes Tetra'	CTtf MNrw
kishinskyi	see *D. parviflora* Jacq.

Digitalis

laevigata	CTtf LShi NBro
- white-flowered	MHol WCot
lamarckii misapplied	see *D. lanata*
§ *lanata*	CSpe EAri EDAr ELan EPfP MArl MBNS MHol MPie NGdn SPlb SRms
- 'Café Crème'	CDor MCtn MMrt NLar
'Lucas'	LRHS Midl MPro
'Lucas Light Pink'	LBar MPro WTor
'Lucas White'	Midl MPro
§ *lutea* ♀H6	Widely available
- subsp. *australis*	MCtn
× *mertonensis* ♀H5	Widely available
- 'Strawberry Summer' **new**	CWnw
- 'Summer King'	CDor CWnw ELan GJos LSRN MPro SMrm WFar
minor	LShi
obscura	CDor CSpe SPlb
I - 'Dusky Maid'	MPro
- 'Sunset'	EDAr MCtn
orientalis	see *D. grandiflora*
§ 'Panther'	EGren EPfP LBuc LCro LRHS LSou MHol Midl MPri MPro WHil
§ *parviflora* Jacq. ♀H5	CElw ECha EDAr EGren EPfP EPPr GAbr GEdr GKev LCro LShi MBNS MCtn NBir NBro WCAu
- 'Milk Chocolate' ♀H5	CDor CMHG CSpe CTtf CWnw EAri ELan EPfP ERCP GJos GKev GMaP LSRN MPnt MPro NLar SHor
PINK PANTHER	see *D.* 'Panther'
'Polkadot Polly' (Polkadot Series)	MCtn MPro WHil
purpurea	Widely available
- 'Alba'	see *D. purpurea* f. *albiflora*
§ - f. *albiflora*	Widely available
- 'Apricot Delight'	EBee WCAu
- Camelot Series	MBros SVic
- - 'Camelot Cream' ♀H5	ELan EPfP LRHS MCtn MNHC SPoG
- - 'Camelot Lavender' ♀H5	ELan EPfP LRHS MCtn
- - 'Camelot Rose' ♀H5	EGren ELan EPfP LRHS
- - 'Camelot White' ♀H5	ELan EPfP LRHS
- 'Campanulata'	LShi
- 'Candy Mountain'	MPro
- 'Cream Carousel' (Carousel Series)	EBee
- (Dalmatian Series)	EGren EPfP LBar LBuc LRHS MCtn MPri MPro WFar
'Dalmatian Crème' ♀H7	
- - 'Dalmatian Peach' ♀H7	CWnw EGren ELan EPfP LBar LCro LRHS MBros MCtn MNHC MPro
- - 'Dalmatian Purple' ♀H7	EGren ELan EPfP LBar LBuc LCro LRHS MCtn MPri MPro WFar
- - 'Dalmatian Rose' ♀H5	EGren ELan EPfP LBar LBuc LCro LRHS MCtn MPri WFar
- - 'Dalmatian White' ♀H5	EGren ELan EPfP LBar LBom LBuc LCro LRHS MBros MCtn MPri MPro
- Excelsior Group	CBcs CDor EGren EPfP GJos LBom LCro MArl MAsh MCtn MPro NMir SMrm SPoG SRms SVic
- Foxy Group	EPfP SMrm SPoG
- Giant Spotted Group	SPoG
- Gloxinioides Group	EDAr EGren
- - 'The Shirley' ♀H7	MCtn
§ - subsp. *heywoodii*	CSpe LRHS
- - 'Silver Fox'	LRHS MCtn
- subsp. *mariana*	CSpe
- 'Monstrosa'	LRHS
- 'Pam's Choice' ♀H7	CAby CBcs CCps CDor CSpe EBee EDAr EGren ELan EPfP ERCP GBin GJos LCro LRHS LSRN LSto MCtn MPro MSwo NLar
- 'Pink Gin'	MCtn
- 'Primrose Carousel' (Carousel Series)	NLar
- 'Serendipity'	LCro
- 'Snow Thimble'	CBcs CCps CDor EDAr ELan EPfP LRHS MBros MCtn NLar
- 'Sugar Plum'	MHtn MPro
§ - 'Sutton's Apricot'	CBcs CCps CDor ECha ELan EPfP GMaP LBom LCro LRHS LSto MArl MAsh MBel MCtn MHol MPro MSwo NGdn NLar SDix SPoG WCot
- 'Virtuoso Rose' (Virtuoso Series)	MAsh
- 'White Carousel' (Carousel Series)	LRHS
- William Series **new**	EGren
sceptrum	SPlb
'Silver Cub'	MPro SMrm
'Spice Island'	CBWd EBee EWes LCro MHer MNrw NLar SPel WCot WSpi WTor
* *stewartii*	CElw EWes
thapsi	EPfP
- 'Spanish Peaks'	LRHS
trojana	GKev LShi NBir
- 'Helen of Troy'	MPro WSpi
× *valinii*	LBuc
- 'Berry Canary'	EAri EPfP LBar LBuc LRHS Midl MPro SPoG WCot WHil
- 'Falcon Fire'	EAri EPfP LBuc Midl MPro WHil
- 'Firebird'PBR	CBcs CCht CWnw EHeP EPfP LBuc LCro LRHS LSou MPnt
- 'Firecracker'	EAri LBar LBuc LRHS Midl MPri MPro WHil
- Foxlight Series	LBuc Midl MPri
- - FOXLIGHT PLUM GOLD ('Takfoplgo'PBR)	CWGN EGren LBom LBuc LCro LRHS LSou Midl MPri MPro NWbg WHil
- - FOXLIGHT ROSE IVORY ('Takforoiv'PBR)	EGren LRHS MHol Midl MPri NWbg WHil
- - FOXLIGHT RUBY GLOW ('Takforugl'PBR)	EGren EPfP LBom LCro LRHS MBros Midl MPri MPro NWbg WFar WHil
§ - Illumination Series	EAri
§ - - 'Harkstead Apricot'	EMdy LBuc LRHS Midl
§ - - 'Harkstead Flame'PBR	CWnw EAri EMdy LRHS LSou Midl SPoG
- - 'Harkstead Red'	EPfP LRHS
- - ILLUMINATION APRICOT	see *D.* × *valinii* (Illumination Series) 'Harkstead Apricot'
- - ILLUMINATION CHERRY BRANDY ILLUMINATION RUBY SLIPPERS	see *D.* × *valinii* (Illumination Series)
- - ILLUMINATION FLAME	see *D.* × *valinii* (Illumination Series) 'Harkstead Flame'
- - ILLUMINATION PINK ('Tmdgfp001'PBR)	CAbb EBee EPfP LBuc LCro SPoG WCot
§ - - ILLUMINATION RUBY SLIPPERS ('Tmdg1204'PBR)	CWnw EAri EBee EMdy LBar LBuc LRHS Midl
- 'Rising Phoenix'	EPfP LBar LRHS Midl
- Vesuvius Group	LShi
- 'Walberton's Goldcrest'	see *D.* GOLDCREST

dill see *Anethum graveolens*

Dimocarpus (Sapindaceae)

longan	WJur

Dionaea ✿ (Droseraceae)

muscipula	ISha LBom LCro LWaG MCtn MPri SPlb WSSs
- 'Akai Ryū' ♀H3	WSSs

– 'B52'	WSSs
– 'Bohemian Garnet'	WSSs
– 'Darwin'	WSSs
– (Dentate Traps Group) 'Dentate Traps'	WSSs
– FUNNEL TRAP	see *D. muscipula* 'Trichterfulle'
– 'Mk1979'	WSSs
– 'Royal Red'	WSSs
– 'Sawtooth'	WSSs
– 'South West Giant' ♀H3	WSSs
– 'Tiger Fangs'	WSSs
§ – 'Trichterfulle'	ISha

Dionysia (Primulaceae)

'Adora' **new**	WAbe
'Annielle'	WAbe
archibaldii	WAbe
aretioides ♀H4	WAbe
– 'Bevere'	WAbe
bryoides	WAbe
'Charlson Emma'	WAbe
'Charlson Petite'	WAbe
'Charlson Pip'	WAbe
'Corona'	WAbe
curviflora	WAbe
'Emmely'	WAbe
'Eric Watson'	WAbe
gaubae	WAbe
'Geist'	WAbe
'Inka Gold'	WAbe
'Lycaena'	WAbe
'Mike Bramley'	WAbe
'Monika'	WAbe
revoluta	WAbe
sarvestanica	WAbe
'Schneeball'	WAbe
tapetodes	WAbe
– 'Brimstone'	WAbe
'Tess'	WAbe
'Yellowstone'	WAbe

Dioon (Zamiaceae)

argenteum	CBrP
edule	CBrP SPlb
merolae	CBrP
spinulosum	CBrP NPlm

Dioscorea (Dioscoreaceae)

BO 15-072	GGro
bulbifera	SPlb
elephantipes ♀H1c	LBom
japonica	CAgr ESwi EWld GGro LEdu WPGP
oppositifolia	EAri GGro
polystachya	CAgr CRHN EAri LEdu SPlb
sylvatica	SPlb
villosa	LEdu

Diosma (Rutaceae)

hirsuta	SEND
– 'Silver Flame'	EGrI
'Pink Fountain'	see *Coleonema pulchellum* 'Pink Fountain'
'Sunset Gold'	see *Coleonema* 'Sunset Gold'

Diosphaera see *Campanula*

Diospyros (Ebenaceae)

austroafricana	SPlb
glabra	SVen
* *hyrcanum*	NLar
kaki (F)	CBcs CMCN NPlm WJur
– 'Fuyu' (F)	CAgr
– 'Kostata' (F)	CAgr
– 'Mazelii' (F)	CAgr
– 'Pendula' (F)	NPlm
lotus	CAgr CBcs CMCN NLar SPlb WJur WKor
– FMWJ 13164	WCru
– (f)	LMaj
– (m)	SEND
– 'Albert' (m)	CAgr
– 'Browny' (f/F)	CAgr
lycioides	CPbh SPlb WJur
'Mount Goverla' (F)	CAgr
nigra **new**	WJur
'Nikita's Gift' (F)	CAgr
'Nikita's Russian' (F)	CAgr
'Nikshoo' (F)	CAgr
rhombifolia	NLar
'Russian Beauty' (F)	CAgr
'Russian Red' (F)	CAgr
virginiana (F)	CBcs CMCN SPlb WJur WKor
– 'Morris Burton' (F)	CAgr
– 'Nc-10' (F)	CAgr
whyteana	WJur

Dipcadi (Asparagaceae)

serotinum	EPot

Dipelta (Caprifoliaceae)

floribunda ♀H5	CExl EBee LRHS MBlu WJur WPGP
ventricosa	CExl MBlu SBrt SPoG WPGP
yunnanensis	CExl EPfP LRHS NLar SPoG WPGP

Diphylleia (Berberidaceae)

cymosa	ECha GEdr LEdu MCtn WCot WCru WOld
grayi	GEdr LEdu
sinensis	LEdu WCru

Diplacus see *Mimulus*

Diplarrena (Iridaceae)

§ *latifolia*	NCth
moraea	CDor CElw CMac EGrI GAbr MNrw SPlb
– West Coast form	see *D. latifolia*

Diplazium (Woodsiaceae)

caudatum	WPGP

Diplopanax (Cornaceae)

stachyanthus B&SWJ 11803	WCru

Diplotaxis (Brassicaceae)

erucoides 'Wasabi'PBR	LCro
tenuifolia	CAgr ENfk EWhm LCro MHoo MNHC NBac SRms WKit

Dipogon (Fabaceae)

§ *lignosus*	CTsd

Dipsacus (Caprifoliaceae)

asper	WCot
– PAB 8884	LEdu
– from Ghangzhou, China	ESwi SNoN
asperoides	GGro
dipsacoides	WPGP
§ *fullonum*	CBWd CGwi CHab CMac CTtf ECha EHet ENfk EPfP GAbr GJem GJos GQue LCro LRHS MAsh MCtn

Dipsacus

	MNHC MPro NBir NLar NMir SRms WHer
inermis	CAby CTtf ECha EPPr GGro MCtn NBid
laciniatus	CGwi SPhx
pilosus	CBgR CGwi NDov
pinnatifidus PAB 2845	LEdu
sativus	MCtn NAts
strigosus	SPhx
sylvestris	see *D. fullonum*

Dipteracanthus see *Ruellia*

Dipteronia (Sapindaceae)

sinensis	CBcs CMCN MBlu WJur

Disanthus (Hamamelidaceae)

cercidifolius ♀H5	CJun CMac EBee EGrI EPfP MBlu SPoG WMat WPGP
- 'Ena-nishiki' (v)	MBlu
ovatifolius	WPGP
- B&SWJ 11706	WCru
- FMWJ 13365	WCru
- WWJ 11933	WCru
- WWJ 11994	WCru

Dischidia (Apocynaceae)

nummularia	LCro
'Pangolin Kisses'	LCro
ruscifolia	CDoC

Disepalum (Annonaceae)

petelotii FMWJ 13375	WCru

Disocactus (Cactaceae)

crenatus	EAri
flagelliformis ♀H1c	EShb
phyllanthoides **new**	EShb

Disphyma (Aizoaceae)

? *crassifolium*	CoPl EAri

Disporopsis ✿ (Asparagaceae)

arisanensis	see *D. pernyi*
aspersa	CBro CTtf EPPr ESwi EWld LEdu MNrw NBir WCot WCru WFar WPGP
- tall	CBct ESwi EWld WCru
bodinieri FMWJ 13277	WCru
- FMWJ 13457	WCru
- KWJ 12240	WCru
- KWJ 12277	ESwi WCru
fuscopicta	EPPr EWld LEdu WCru
'Lily Pads' **new**	ESwi
luzoniensis	WPGP
- B&SWJ 3891	CBct EPPr ESwi GEdr LEdu WCru
* *nova*	EBee EPPr ESwi MAvo
§ *pernyi*	Widely available
- B&SWJ 229	ESwi WCru
- B&SWJ 1864	EPPr GEdr WCru
- 'Bill Baker'	CBct EPPr ESwi LEdu
aff. *pernyi*	EAri
taiwanensis	LEdu
- B&SWJ 3388	CBct GEdr WCru
undulata	CSpe EBee EPPr ESwi LEdu NBid SHar WCru WPGP
- 'Jade Point' **new**	ESwi

Disporum ✿ (Colchicaceae)

bodinieri	CAbb CDor CTtf EBee EMor EPfP GKev IPot LAma LRHS MMuc SBea WFar
- DJHC 765	WCru
aff. *bodinieri*	EAri
cantoniense	CBct CSpe LEdu SPlb WFar WHil WJur
- B&L 12512	CExl
- B&SWJ 9715	WCru
- DJHC 98485	LEdu WOld WPGP
- PAB 8339	LEdu
I - 'Aureovariegata' (v)	CBct ESwi LEdu WCot
- 'Blueberry Bere'	IPot LEdu
- 'Leigong'	WPGP
- 'Leigong Chocolate'	EAri LEdu
- 'Moonlight' PBR (v)	EBee ELan ELon EMor ESwi LBar LEdu LRHS NLar WFar
- var. *sikkimense* B&SWJ 2337	WCru
- - B&SWJ 2358	LEdu WCru
- - PAB 13.1711	LEdu
hookeri	see *Prosartes hookeri*
kawakamii RWJ 10103	WCru
lanuginosum	see *Prosartes lanuginosa*
leschenaultianum B&SWJ 9484	WCru
leucanthum	EBee ECha WCru
- B&SWJ 2389	WCru
'Lisu Bells'	LEdu
longistylum	EBee LEdu
- B&SWJ 2859	WCru
- BWJ 8128	WCru
- L 1564	CBct EPfP ESwi EWld WCru WOld
- 'Bagheera'	WPGP
- 'Green Giant'	CBct CDor CExl CMiW CSpe CTtf EAri EBee EPfP GEdr GKev LCro LEdu LRHS NLar SBea SHar WFar WHil
- 'Night Heron' ♀H6	CDor CExl CSpe CTtf EAri EBee ECha ENun EWld GEdr IPot LCro LEdu LRHS LSto MNrw SHar SHor WCot WFar
- 'Night Lark' **new**	LEdu
aff. *longistylum* NJM 11.011	WPGP
lutescens	LEdu WCru WPGP
maculatum	see *Prosartes maculata*
megalanthum	CAbb CBct CCBP CExl CMiW EAri EBlo ECha EPfP ISha LRHS WFar WPGP
- CD&R 2412B	CDor CExl EBee IPot MMrt
menziesii	see *Prosartes smithii*
nantouense B&SWJ 359	LEdu WCru
- B&SWJ 6812	WCru
oreganum	see *Prosartes hookeri* var. *oregana*
sessile	EAri EBee GKev LEdu MAvo NBir WCru
- B&SWJ 2824	WCru
I - 'Aureovariegatum' (v)	EPPr WFar
- 'Kinga' (v)	EAri LEdu
- f. *macrophyllum* B&SWJ 4316	WCru
I - 'Robustum Variegatum' (v)	SHar
- 'Snow Stream' (v)	GEdr WFar
- 'Variegatum' (v)	CDor CExl CMiW CTtf EAri EBee EBlo ECha ELon EMor EPfP EPPr ESwi LEdu LSto MNrw NBir NLar NQui NWbg WFar WHil WPGP
smilacinum	NLar WCru
- B&SWJ 713	WCru
* - 'Aureovariegatum' (v)	LEdu
- 'Dai-setsurei' (v)	WCot
- 'Ki-naka-fu' (v)	WFar
- 'Koutei' (v)	WFar
- 'Moonshine' (v)	GEdr

– pink-flowered	LEdu WCot WCru	
smithii	see *Prosartes smithii*	
taiwanense	LEdu	
– B&SWJ 1513	WCru	
tonkinense B&SWJ 11814	WCru	
trabeculatum	CBct CDor ESwi MMuc SVen WCru	
– 'Nakafu' (v)	WCru	
– 'Pu Ta Leng'	WPGP	
uniflorum	CBct CMiW EArl EBlo ECha EMor ENun EPfP EPPr GKev IPot ISha LEdu LRHS MBel MNrw NBid NWbg	
– B&SWJ 651	ESwi LEdu WCru	
– B&SWJ 872	WCru	
– B&SWJ 4100	WCru	
– MSF 800	LEdu	
viridescens	EBee EBlo ECha EPPr LEdu LRHS WCru	
– B&SWJ 4598	ESwi WCru	

Distictis (Bignoniaceae)
buccinatoria	CHll

Distyliopsis (Hamamelidaceae)
tutcheri	CJun

Distylium (Hamamelidaceae)
BLUE CASCADE ('Piidist-ii')	CBcs CDoC EBee LRHS MMuc NLar SEND
LINEBACKER ('Piidist-iv') **new**	CWnw
racemosum	CBcs CMac EBee LMaj MBlu NLar SSta WJur

Dittrichia (Asteraceae)
viscosa	WCot

Diuranthera see *Chlorophytum*

Dobinea (Anacardiaceae)
vulgaris B&SWJ 2532	WCru

Dodecatheon (Primulaceae)
alpinum	GKev
'Aphrodite'^{PBR}	NLar
austrofrigidum	GEdr LEdu SBrt
clevelandii	EDAr GEdr GKev
'Comet'	WFar
conjugens	GKev
cusickii	see *D. pulchellum* subsp. *cusickii*
dentatum	CDor GEdr LEdu NHar NRya SBrt WAbe WFar
– subsp. *utahense*	GEdr NHar NRya WFar
frigidum	EDAr GEdr
§ *jeffreyi*	EDAr GEdr GKev MHol MNrw MPnt NLar StAn WFar
latilobum **new**	GKev
§ *meadia* ♀H5	Widely available
– from Cedar County, USA	WAbe
– f. *album* ♀H5	CBro CTtf ECha EDAr ELan GKev ISha LAma LEdu MPie WFar WPnP WSpi
– 'Aphrodite'	EPfP LBar WFar
– 'Goliath'	CSpe StAn
– membranaceous	WAbe
– 'Queen Victoria'	GKev LBar NLar WFar
'Meteor'	WFar
pauciflorum misapplied	see *D. pulchellum*
pauciflorum (Dur.) E. Greene	see *D. meadia*
poeticum	EPPr SPlb
§ *pulchellum* ♀H5	EBee EGrI LEdu MNrw NRya WIce
– subsp. *cusickii*	ECha
– subsp. *pulchellum*	CTtf EBee EGrl ELan GKev ISha LEdu MPnt NHar NLar WCav
'Red Wings'	
§ – Radicatum Group	GEdr
– 'Sooke Variety'	GEdr GKev WAbe
radicatum	see *D. pulchellum* Radicatum Group
'Stellar Pink'	GEdr
tetrandrum	see *D. jeffreyi*

Dodonaea (Sapindaceae)
viscosa	SPlb
– (f)	ESwi WJur
– 'Purpurea'	CBcs CCht CSgt CTsd ELon MCtn MHtn SArc SEle SIvy SPoG SVen

Doellingeria (Asteraceae)
scabra	see *Aster scaber*
umbellata	CFis CKno ECha EPPr GQue LCro LRHS LSto MMuc NBir NDov NLar SEND SHar SPel WCAu WCot WOld WTre
– 'Weisser Schirm'	MNrw

Dolichandra (Bignoniaceae)
§ *unguis-cati* ♀H3	CRHN EShb MCtn WJur

Dolichos (Fabaceae)
lignosus	see *Dipogon lignosus*

Dolichothele see *Mammillaria*

Dombeya (Malvaceae)
calantha	EShb
rotundifolia	EShb

Dondia see *Sanicula*

Doodia (Blechnaceae)
aspera	CLAP
– 'Rough Ruby'	CBcs CTsd EBee ELan LCro LRHS MAsh MHtn WCot
media	CBrP CLAP CMiW EBee EPfP GQue LCro LEdu LRHS MAsh MBlu NAlc NBro SBig SPlb WCot

Dorema (Apiaceae)
ammoniacum	SPhx

Doronicum (Asteraceae)
austriacum	GJos MSCN
caucasicum	see *D. orientale*
§ *columnae*	CBcs
cordatum	see *D. columnae*
§ × *excelsum* 'Harpur Crewe'	EBee EWes LEdu LShi NPer SHar
'Finesse'	GJos MCtn SRms
'Little Leo'	ELan EMor EPfP GMaP LShi MMrt MPro SPoG SRms WFar WHil
§ *orientale*	EHeP ELan GJos MPri SPoG
– 'Leonardo'	EGren EMor EPfP WFar
– 'Leonardo Compact'	LRHS MPri WCot
– 'Magnificum'	SPoG SRms WCAu WFar
pardalianches	GJos MMuc MNHC SEND WBrk
plantagineum	MMuc
– 'Excelsum'	see *D.* × *excelsum* 'Harpur Crewe'

Dorotheanthus see *Cleretum*

Dorstenia (Moraceae)
foetida	SPlb

Dorstenia

gigas	SPlb
hildebrandtii	SPlb
var. *hildebrandtii*	

Dorycnium see *Lotus*

Doryopteris (Pteridaceae)
pedata	LWaG

Douglasia see *Androsace*
vitaliana	see *Vitaliana primuliflora*

Doxantha see *Dolichandra*

Draba (Brassicaceae)
aizoides	SPlb SRms
alpina	GKev
arabisans	GKev
bruniifolia	EDAr
'Buttermilk'	WAbe
dedeana	EPot
'John Saxton'	WAbe
kotschyi	SPlb
longisiliqua ♀H5	WAbe
mollissima	SPlb WAbe
nivalis	SPlb
norvegica	SPlb
oligosperma	EDAr SPlb
- subsp. *subsessilis*	WAbe
ossetica	WAbe
rigida var. *bryoides* compact	EPot WAbe
rosularis	EPot WAbe
× *salomonii*	EPot
sphaeroides	EDAr SPlb
yunnanensis	WAbe

Dracaena ✿ (Asparagaceae)
cochinchinensis	SPlb
congesta	see *Cordyline congesta*
draco ♀H1c	MCtn NPlm SIvy SPlb
fragrans	LWaG NHrt
- Compacta Group	LCro NHrt
- - 'Compacta'	LBom NHrt
- - 'White Jewel'^{PBR}	LBom LCro NHrt
- - (Deremensis Group)	EGren LBom LCro NHrt NPlm
'Lemon Lime' (v) ♀H1b	
- - 'Limelight'	LCro
- - 'Warneckei' (v) ♀H1b	NHrt NPlm
- 'Janet Craig'	LBom LCro NHrt
- 'Janet Lind' (v)	LCro NHrt
- 'Massangeana' (v) ♀H1b	NHrt
- 'Paloma'^{PBR}	LBom
'Green Jewel'^{PBR}	LBom
indivisa	see *Cordyline indivisa*
'Jade Jewel'^{PBR}	LBom
marginata (v) ♀H1b	EGren LBom LCro NHrt
- 'Bicolor' (v)	LBom LCro LInT MPri NHrt
- 'Colorama' (v)	LBom
- 'Magenta' (v)	LBom LCro LWaG
- 'Sunray'^{PBR} (v) new	LBom LCro
- 'Tricolor' (v) ♀H1b	LBom
'Red Edge'	NHrt
reflexa 'Anita'^{PBR}	LBom
I - 'Song of India' (v)	LCro
- 'Song of Jamaica' (v)	LBom LCro
steudneri CINTHO	NHrt
('Stedneri Cintho'^{PBR})	
surculosa	LCro NHrt
- 'Florida Beauty' (v) ♀H1b	LCro
- 'Mike' (v)	LCro

Dracocephalum (Lamiaceae)
argunense	LShi SRms
- 'Blue Carpet'	EBee
- 'Fuji Blue'	EDAr ELan EPfP EWes GKev LRHS MHol SPhx SPoG WIce
- 'Fuji White'	EDAr SPhx
botryoides	SPhx
calophyllum	GKev
grandiflorum	WCot
- 'Altai Blue'	EDAr
moldavica	LRHS SPhx
nutans	SPhx
peregrinum 'Blue Dragon'	EDAr
rupestre	EMor GKev MHol
ruyschiana	SPhx
- 'Blue Moon'	MHol MMrt
sibiricum	see *Nepeta sibirica*
virginicum	see *Physostegia virginiana*

Dracunculus (Araceae)
canariensis	EBee ESwi WCot
muscivorus	see *Helicodiceros muscivorus*
§ *vulgaris*	EAri EBee EGren EPfP EPot ERCP ESwi EUrb GKev IsHa LAma SEND SPlb WCot XFar

Drapetes (Thymelaeaceae)
dieffenbachii	GArf

Dregea (Apocynaceae)
sinensis	CBcs CExl CHII CRHN EAri EBee EGrI ELan EPfP EWes MPri SEND SNig SPoG WPGP
- 'Brockhill Silver'	LRHS SPoG SVen

Drepanostachyum (Poaceae)
hookerianum	see *Himalayacalamus hookerianus*

Drimiopsis (Asparagaceae)
maculata	EShb ESwi

Drimys (Winteraceae)
andina	MMuc
aromatica	see *Tasmannia lanceolata*
colorata	see *Pseudowintera colorata*
granadensis	WCru
var. *grandiflora* B&SWJ 10777	
winteri ♀H4	CBcs CCoa CMac CSBt CSde CTsd EGrI ELan EPfP EUrb GKin LSRN MBlu MGos NQui SArc SEle SPlb SPoG WFar WJur WPav
§ - var. *chilensis*	CBcs EPfP LRHS SVen WCru WPGP
- Latifolia Group	see *D. winteri* var. *chilensis*

Drosanthemum (Aizoaceae)
bellum	WCor
candens new	WCor
eburneum	WCor
flammeum	ESuc
floribundum	EShb WCor
hispidum	ELan ESuc MAsh SPlb SPoG SRot WIce
micans	ESuc
* *sutherlandii*	SRot

Drosera ✿ (Droseraceae)
aliciae ♀H3	LCro SPlb WFar

Dryopteris 251

australis salmon-pink-flowered	WFar
binata	CoPl WFar
- T form	WFar
capensis	CoPl ISha LCro SPlb WFar
- 'Albino' ♀H3	CoPl ISha WFar
× *carbarup*	WFar
filiformis	CoPl
- var. *filiformis*	SPlb
gibsonii	WFar
helodes red	WFar
'Marston Dragon'	WFar
nivea	WFar
omissa Diels × *pulchella*	WFar
paleacea subsp. *trichocaulis*	WFar
pulchella	WFar
scorpioides	WFar
sewelliae	WFar
× *sidjamesii*	WFar
spatulata	CoPl
stelliflora	WFar

Dryandra see *Banksia*

quercifolia	see *Banksia beliantha*

Dryas (Rosaceae)

caucasica	GKev
drummondii	EDAr GEdr GKev
integrifolia 'Greenland Green'	WAbe
octopetala ♀H7	EDAr GArf GBin GJos GKev MCtn MMrt SPoG SRms WAbe WHoo
§ - 'Minor' ♀H7	EPot GArf WAbe WHoo
× *suendermannii* ♀H7	EPot GArf GEdr GMaP LRHS NHar WAbe
tenella misapplied	see *D. octopetala* 'Minor'

Drynaria (Polypodiaceae)

baronii	LEdu SBrt WCot WPGP
propinqua	SPlb

Dryopteris ✿ (Dryopteridaceae)

aemula	EWld LEdu
§ *affinis* ♀H5	Widely available
- 'Angustata Crispa'	EBee ISha LRHS MAsh SRms
- 'Congesta Cristata'	CCps CWCL EMor LEdu LRHS SRot
- Crispa Group	CLAP CSta EGren ISha LCro LRHS LWaG WFar
§ - 'Crispa Gracilis' ♀H5	CLAP CMiW CSta ELan GMaP ISha LRHS NAlc NBir NLar WFar
* - 'Crispa Gracilis Congesta'	EUrb NGdn
§ - 'Cristata' ♀H5	Widely available
- 'Cristata Angustata' ♀H5	CLAP LRHS MAvo NBid NBro NGdn WCot
- 'Cristata The King'	see *D. affinis* 'Cristata'
- 'Pinderi'	CDor CLAP EBee EMor EPfP GBin ISha LEdu LRHS MAsh MPnt NLar WSpi
- Polydactyla Group	ISha SPlb
- - 'Polydactyla Dadds'	CLAP CSta EBee EMor LRHS NLar WCot
atrata misapplied	see *D. cycadina*
atrata (Wall. ex Kunze) Ching	CAby CDTJ CSde ELan EUrb LCro LRHS MAvo MPri NLar SPoG StAn
× *australis*	CLAP ISha
austriaca	see *D. dilatata*
buschiana	EMor EUrb NLar WCot
carthusiana	EBee EMor WSpi
celsa	ISha
championii	CLAP EBee ELan ELon EMor ISha LEdu LRHS NBid NBro NCth SRot WCot
clintoniana	EMor ISha LRHS
× *complexa*	CLAP ISha
- 'Stablerae' ♀H7	CLAP
coreanomontana	LRHS NLar
crassirhizoma ♀H6	CLAP EBee ELan ISha NLar SPoG WCot WPGP WSpi
cristata	CLAP EBee EPfP ISha
§ *cycadina* ♀H4	CBcs CBdn CLAP EGren ELan EMor EPfP EWld ISha LBom LCro LEdu LRHS MAsh MGos MPri NAlc NBid NBir NLar SPlb
§ *dilatata* ♀H6	CLAP ELan EMor EPfP ISha LCro LRHS WShi
- 'Crispa Whiteside' ♀H6	CDor CLAP CMiW CSta CWCL EBee ELan EMor EPfP EWld ISha LRHS MAsh MPri NBid NBro NLar SPlb SPoG SRot
- 'Grandiceps'	CMac
- 'Jimmy Dyce'	CLAP ISha NBro
I - 'Lepidota Crispa'	LRHS
- 'Lepidota Crispa Cristata'	CLAP EBee
- 'Lepidota Cristata' ♀H6	CMiW CWCL EWld ISha LEdu LRHS NAlc NBro NWbg
* - 'Recurvata'	CLAP
erythrosora ♀H4	Widely available
- 'Brilliance' ♀H5	CBcs CDoC CDor CLAP EBee ELon EPfP GAbr ISha LBom LWaG MAsh MPie MPri NAlc NCou NWbg SBig WCot
- dwarf	CMiW LEdu
- var. *koidzumiana*	GBin LEdu LRHS
- var. *prolifica*	CDor CLAP CLiL CSta CWnw ELan EPfP EUrb GMaP ISha LBom LCro LEdu LRHS MAsh MAvo MGos MHer MPri NAlc NBir NLar SPoG SRot WBrk WCot WFar WLov
filix-mas ♀H7	Widely available
- 'Barnesii'	CCps CLAP CWCL EGren ELan EMor EPfP EUrb LBom LCro LRHS NLar SEND SPlb WFar WLov
- 'Crispa'	ISha LBom LEdu MAsh MPnt WFar
- 'Crispa Congesta'	see *D. affinis* 'Crispa Gracilis'
- 'Crispa Cristata' ♀H7	CBWd CLAP CSta CWCL EBee ELan EMor GMaP ISha LEdu LRHS MAsh NBid NBir NBro SPoG WCot
- 'Crispatissima'	EBee
- 'Cristata' ♀H7	CLAP EBee ELan LBom LCro NBro SEND WCAu
- (Cristata Group) 'Cristata Jackson'	SPlb
- - 'Cristata Martindale'	CLAP NBid
- 'Depauperata'	CLAP
- 'Furcans'	EBee LRHS NAlc
- Grandiceps Group	EWld
- 'Grandiceps Wills' ♀H7	NBid
- 'Linearis'	EMor EWld MGos WCha
- 'Linearis Polydactyla' ♀H7	CDor CLAP CMac CSta CWCL EGren ELan EPfP EUrb EWld ISha LCro LEdu LRHS MMuc MPri NAlc NBid NLar SEND SPoG WBrk WCAu WPnP
- 'Parsley'	CLAP NBro
formosana	LRHS WPGP
goldieana	CDTJ CLAP ECha EMor EUrb GMaP ISha LCro NBid NBir NLar SPlb WFar WPnP WSpi

Dryopteris

hirtipes misapplied	see *D. cycadina*
kuratae	CCht CSde EMor LEdu LRHS NBro NLar WBrk WCot WLov WPGP
labordei	LRHS
lepidopoda	CBcs CDoC CDor CLAP EBee EMor EUrb GBin ISha LEdu LRHS MAsh NAlc NBro NCth NLar SBig SPoG WCot WPGP WSpi
ludoviciana	EBee WSpi
marginalis	EGren ISha LRHS NLar
namegatae	WCot
pseudofilix-mas	ISha
pseudomas	see *D. affinis*
pycnopteroides	CLAP
× *remota*	CLAP
sabaei	CSta
sichotensis	EMor SPlb
sieboldii ♀H6	CBcs CDor CLAP CSta CTsd ECha ELon EMor EUrb ISha LEdu LRHS NAlc NBid NBir NBro NLar SEND SPad SPlb SRot WCot WPGP
sinofibrillosa	see *D. xanthomelas*
stewartii	CLAP CSde EMor ESwi ISha LCro LEdu NBro NLar
tokyoensis ♀H6	CDTJ LRHS WSpi
uniformis	SBrt WCot
varia	SBrt
wallichiana ♀H5	Widely available
– JURASSIC GOLD ('Hollasic')	Widely available
§ *xanthomelas*	SPlb

Duchesnea (*Rosaceae*)

chrysantha	see *D. indica*
§ *indica*	SEND WKor

Dudleya (*Crassulaceae*)

brittonii ♀H3	CPbh
calcicola	SPlb
cymosa	SPlb
lanceolata	SPlb

Dugaldia see *Hymenoxys*

Dumasia (*Fabaceae*)

truncata	LEdu WPGP

Dunalia (*Solanaceae*)

australis	see *Eriolarynx australis*

Duranta (*Verbenaceae*)

§ *erecta*	CBcs CHll SEle
§ – 'Geisha Girl'	EShb
– 'Sapphire Swirl'	see *D. erecta* 'Geisha Girl'
– 'Variegata' (v)	SEle
– white-flowered	EShb
plumieri	see *D. erecta*
repens	see *D. erecta*

Duvernoia see *Justicia*

Dyckia (*Bromeliaceae*)

brevifolia	WCot
'Brittle Star' **new**	EUrb
'Burgundy Ice'	EUrb NPlm WCot
'Cherry Coke'	WCot
floribunda	EShb
frigida	WCot
goehringii	WCot
'Grand Marnier'	EUrb NPlm SBig
jonesiana	WCot
leptostachya	EAri SEND SPlb WCot

marnier-lapostollei	SPlb
'Morris Hobbs'	WCot
remotiflora	SChr
yellow American hybrid	WCot

Dypsis (*Arecaceae*)

decaryi	see *Chrysalidocarpus decaryi*
decipiens	see *Chrysalidocarpus decipiens*
lanceolata	see *Chrysalidocarpus lanceolatus*
leptocheilos	see *Chrysalidocarpus leptocheilos*
lutescens	see *Chrysalidocarpus lutescens*
pembana	see *Chrysalidocarpus pembanus*
pilulifera	see *Chrysalidocarpus pilulifer*

Dysphania (*Amaranthaceae*)

§ *ambrosioides*	SEdi SVic

Dystaenia (*Apiaceae*)

takeshimana	CAgr EBee GGro LEdu SPhx
– B&SWJ 12627	WCru

E

Ecballium (*Cucurbitaceae*)

elaterium	CDTJ LWaG SNoN WCot

Eccremocarpus (*Bignoniaceae*)

scaber	CWCL EAri EShb EUrb NBir NPer SPlb SPoG WJur
– orange-red-flowered	MCtn
– 'Pink Lemonade'	EPPr
– red-flowered	CSpe EPPr
– 'Tangerine'	CSpe
– Tresco Series	MCtn
– – 'Tresco Cream'	EPPr MCtn

Echeveria ❀ (*Crassulaceae*)

from Huautla, Mexico	CPic
from Mexico	LRHS
affinis	CDTJ CoPl MHer SPlb WCot
agavoides ♀H2	CDoC CDTJ CPic LCro SIvy
– from Tuxpan, Mexico	CPic
– 'Cosari'	CPic
– 'Ebony'	CPic WCot WOld
– 'Lipstick'	CPic EAri WCot WOld
– 'Romeo'	EAri WCot
§ – TAURUS	see *E. agavoides* 'Romeo'
agavoides × *colorata* f. *colorata*	CoPl LCro
'Alabaster Magic'	WOld
albicans	see *E. elegans* var. *elegans*
alpina	see *E. secunda*
amoena	CSBt EAri LRHS
'Apollo'	CPic
'Apus' PBR	EAri
bicolor B&SWJ 14388	WCru
'Black Knight'	EGrI LCro MSwo SIvy SMrm
'Black Prince'	CDoC CDTJ CPic CSBt EGrI LCro NCft NPer SArc SPlb SRms WCor WCot WOld
'Blondie'	CPic
'Blue Bird'	CDoC NCft
'Blue Curls'	CPic
I 'Blue Minima'	CPic
'Blue Prince'	CPic NCft
'Blue Waves'	WCot
× *bombycina* ♀H2	SIvy WCot
'Bradburyana'	CPic

'Briar Rose'	NCft		'Lepus'	WOld
- cristate	NCft		*lilacina* ♀H2	CBlu CDoC CPic CSBt CSpe EAri EShb LCro LRHS MHol NCft SMrm SPlb SRms
'Campfire'	SIvy			
cante ♀H2	CPic SPlb			
'Chantilly'	WOld		*lilacina* × *setosa* var. *oteroi*	CPic
chihuahuaensis ♀H2	CAbb CBlu CPic CSBt MSwo NCft SPoG SRms			
			'Linguas'	WOld
- 'Raspberry Dip'	WCot WOld		'Lola'	CPic EAri
chihuahuensis × *pulidonis*	CPic		*macdougallii*	CoPl
			'Magic Red'	LRHS
'Chrissy 'n' Ryan'	CPic		'Mahogany'	WCot
'Christmas'	CPic		'Mandala'	CPic
'Chroma'	CPic		MARROM ('Tsaech1606'PBR)	CPic
coccinea	ELan		'Marzipan'	NCft
colorata ♀H2	EAri LRHS NCft		'Mauna Loa'	MHol WCot WOld
- from Tapalpa, Mexico	CPic		*maxonii* B&SWJ 10536	WCru
- f. *colorata* 'Mexican Giant'	CPic		'Melaco'	NCft
			'Meteor'	WOld
- f. *colorata* × *elegans* var. *elegans*	CPic		*meyraniana*	CPic
			minima ♀H2	SPlb
colorata × *desmetiana*	SMrm		'Mira'PBR	EShb
compressicaulis	CPic WOld		'Miranda'	LRHS NHrt
'Corymbosa'	WCot		'Monroe'	CPic
crassicaulis	SPlb		*montana* B&SWJ 10277	WCru
'Cubic Frost'	CPic EUrb NCft WCot WOld		'Moon Goddess'	WOld
'Curly Locks'	NCft WCot		*moranii*	NCft
'Dagda'	CPic		'Neon Breakers'	NCft NPlm WOld
'Dark Vader'	CPic		*nodulosa*	CPic LRHS SIvy SPoG WCot
'Deresina'	CPic		'Orion'PBR	CPic NCft WOld
× *derosa*	CDTJ		*pallida*	CPic
- 'Worfield Wonder'	WHil		'Paul Bunyon'	CPic
§ *desmetiana*	LRHS MCtn SPlb WCor WCot		'Perle von Nürnberg' ♀H2	CDoC EShb EUrb LCro NCft NHrt
'Dick's Pink'	CPic		'Pink Edge'	CPic
diffractens	CPic		'Pollux'	CPic LRHS NCft
'Dondo'	SPoG		*prolifica*	CPic NCft
'Doris Taylor'	CoPl CPic		*pulidonis* ♀H2	CPic LCro
'Duchess of Nuremberg'	CBlu CPbh CPic EAri LBar LCro MHol SIvy SMrm SPlb WCor		*pulvinata* ♀H2	LRHS
			- DEVOTION ('Bcec12001'PBR)	LCro LSou
'Eastoft Aura Sings'	CPic		- 'Frosty'	CoPl CPic NCft SRms
'Eastoft Giulia'	WOld		I - 'Rubra'	SPlb
'Eastoft Harlecina'	CPic		'Purple Pearl'PBR	LCro NCft NHrt
elegans ♀H2	CDoC CDTJ CoPl CPic ELan EShb EUrb EWes LCro LRHS MSwo NCft SEND SIvy SMrm SPlb SPoG SRms		*purpusorum*	CDoC CoPl SPlb
			quitensis B&SWJ 14393	WCru
			'Ramillete'	CPic WMal
§ - var. *elegans*	SPlb		- cristate	CPic
'Etna'	WOld		'Red Prince'	CDoC CPic
'Fabiola'	NCft		*rosea* ♀H2	MHer SPlb WCot WMal
fimbriata	CPic		'Rubella'	CPic
- cristate	CPic		*runyonii* ♀H2	CDoC SRms
'Fireball'	WOld		- 'Topsy Turvy' ♀H2	CDTJ CPic CSBt LRHS MHer MHol NCft SIvy SRms WCor WCot
'Fred Wass'	CPbh			
'Ghost Buster'	NHrt		'Scorpio'	CPic WOld
'Giant Blue'	CDoC		§ *secunda*	CAbb CoPl EUrb SPlb
§ *gibbiflora* 'Metallica'	EShb LRHS SMrm SRms		- var. *glauca*	see *E. secunda* f. *secunda*
gigantea	CPic		§ - f. *secunda*	CDoC CDTJ CPic ELan EShb GAbr LCro NCft SIvy SMrm WFar
× *gilva* ♀H2	CPic SChr			
- 'Blue Surprise'	CPic		- - 'Compton Carousel' ♀H2	SArc WCot WOld
* - 'Red'	CAbb CBlu CPic WCot		* - - 'Gigantea'	NPer
glauca Baker	see *E. secunda* f. *secunda*		'Serrana'	CPic NCft
'Green Abalone'	CPic		'Set-Oliver'	CSBt EShb LRHS SMrm
'Green Pearl'PBR	LCro		*setosa* ♀H2	CAbb CDTJ CoPl CPic LCro LWaG NCft SPlb
'Grey Prince'	EUrb NCft			
halbingeri var. *sanchez-mejoradae*	NCft		- var. *ciliata*	EShb
			- cristate	NCft
harmsii	WCor		- var. *deminuta*	NCft
'Hercules'PBR	NCft SPoG		- var. *oteroi*	SPlb
humilis	WOld		*shaviana* ♀H2	CDTJ CPic EAri LRHS NCft SRms WCot
hyalina from San Luiz de la Paz, Mexico	CPic			
			'Son of Pearl'	MHtn
'Imbricata'	MSwo SEND SRms		*subcorymbosa*	NCft
'Joan Daniel'	CPic		*subsessilis*	see *E. desmetiana*

Echeveria 253

'Tarantula'	WOld
tolimanensis	CPic SPlb
'Vampire Red Ball'	WOld
'Van Breen'	CPic
'Violet Queen'	EShb
'Zodiac'	CPic
'Zonnestraal'	EGrI

Echeveria × *Graptopetalum* see × *Graptoveria*
Echeveria × *Pachyphytum* see × *Pachyveria*
Echeveria × *Sedum* see × *Sedeveria*

Echinacea (Asteraceae)

§ 'After Midnight'^{PBR} (Big Sky Series)	EGrI
'Aloha'^{PBR}	
'Amazing Dream'^{PBR}	CMHG SPoG WCAu
angustifolia	LCro NCth WSpi
APRICOT RAINBOW MARCELLA (Butterfly Series)	CAgr ENfk MHoo SHor WKit
Artisan Series	MHtn Midl
§ – ARTISAN RED OMBRE ('Pas1257973')	LBuc
§ – ARTISAN SOFT ORANGE ('Pas1308374')	MPro
§ 'Art's Pride'^{PBR}	MHoo MPro
'Big Kahuna'^{PBR}	EGrI
'Blackberry Truffle' (Cone-fections Series) (d)	CBcs CWGN NCth SPeP WSpi
BLUEBERRY CHEESECAKE ('Blu481') (d) **new**	LRHS XFar
BLUSHING MEADOW MAMA ('Blus302') (Meadow Mama Series) **new**	XFar
'Butterfly Kisses'^{PBR} (Cone-fections Series) (d) ♀H5	LBar LCro LRHS MPri SPeP WSpi XFar
'Cantaloupe'^{PBR} (Supreme Series) (d)	CWGN MAsh XFar
CARA MIA SPICY (Cara Mia Series) **new**	Midl
CARROT CAKE ('Carrot489') (Cone-fections Series) (d)	LBar MPri
CHERRY FLUFF ('Echcher298'^{PBR}) (Cone-fections Series) (d)	CWGN XFar
CHEYENNE SPIRIT (mixed)	CDoC CDor EBlo EGren ELan EPfP LEdu LRHS MCtn MHoo MPro WFar WSpi WTor
'Chiquita'^{PBR} (Prairie Pixie Series)	SPoG
'Choco Green' **new**	SHar
'Cinnamon Cupcake'	SPoG
'Cleopatra'^{PBR} (Butterfly Series)	LBom SPoG WCot
'Dark Pink Pearl' (Pearl Series)	CAbb
'Daydream'^{PBR}	WSpi
DELICIOUS CANDY ('Noortdeli'^{PBR}) (d)	CWGN LBar LBom LCro LRHS MAsh MHol MHtn Midl MMrt MPri MPro NCth WCot WTor
DELICIOUS ICE ('Mvne167') (d)	MPri
DELICIOUS NOUGAT ('Noecthree'^{PBR}) (d)	LRHS MAsh Midl MPri SPeP WTor
(Dixie Series) 'Dixie Belle'	WSpi
– 'Dixie Scarlet'^{PBR}	MPro
(Double Scoop Series) DOUBLE SCOOP CRANBERRY ('Balscanery'^{PBR}) (d)	EGren Midl MPro MSCN
– DOUBLE SCOOP MANDARIN ('Balscandin') (d)	LRHS
'Eccentric'^{PBR} (d)	EMor LBar MHoo MNrw WSpi WTor XFar
'Elegance'^{PBR} (Supreme Series) (d)	LRHS
'Emily Saul'	see *E.* 'After Midnight' (Big Sky Series)
'Evan Saul'	see *E.* 'Sundown' (Big Sky Series)
EVENING GLOW ('Eglow'^{PBR})	CWGN WSpi
EVOLUTION COLORIFIC ('Balevoeen')	LCro LRHS XFar
'Fantastic Pink' (SunMagic Series)	EGren LBar
'Fantastic Red' (SunMagic Series)	CAbb EGren LBar LSou
'Fantastic Yellow' (SunMagic Series)	CAbb EGren LBar LSou
'Ferris Wheel' (Carnival Series)	WSpi
FIERY MEADOW MAMA (Meadow Mama Series)	LBar
'Flame Thrower'^{PBR}	LCro
FLAMINGO (Fine Feathered Series)	MPro
(Fountain Series) 'Fountain Pink Eye'	CAbb Midl WHil
– 'Fountain Red'	Midl WSpi
'Funky White'	CWGN EPfP LRHS MPro
'Funky Yellow'	CWGN LBar WCot
GOLDEN SKIPPER ('Echgol243'^{PBR}) (Butterfly Series)	EMor NLar XFar
'Green Envy'^{PBR}	ELan EMor GMaP LCro MNrw
'Guava Ice' (Cone-fections Series) (d)	LBar MSwo
Halo Series	see *E.* Sombrero Special Series
§ 'Harvest Moon'^{PBR} (Big Sky Series)	EBee EGrI LCro LRHS MPro WCAu
HONEY SKIPPER (Butterfly Series)	Midl
'Honeydew'^{PBR} (Cone-fections Series) (d)	XFar
'Hot Lava'^{PBR}	CWGN EBee EUrb LCro NLar
'Hot Papaya'^{PBR} (Cone-fections Series) (d)	CWCL ELan EMor EUrb LCro MHol Midl MSwo SPoG XFar
'Hot Summer'^{PBR}	EGrI EUrb MPro WTor
'Irresistible'^{PBR} (d)	EGren EMor LBar LCro LRHS XFar
'JS Stiletto'	LBar WTor
§ 'Jsengeltje'^{PBR}	EBee LBar LCro LRHS MBNS Midl MNrw MPro SHar WTor XFar
(Kismet Series) KISMET INTENSE ORANGE ('Tnechkio')	EGren
– KISMET RASPBERRY ('Tnechkr')	CWGN EGren LSou
– KISMET RED ('Tnechkrd')	EGren LRHS SPeP
– KISMET WHITE ('Tnechkw')	EGren
– KISMET YELLOW ('Tnechky')	EGren LBar
LAKOTA ORANGE	see *E.* ARTISAN SOFT ORANGE (Artisan Series)
LAKOTA RED	see *E.* ARTISAN RED OMBRE (Artisan Series)
'Leilani'^{PBR} ♀H5	WCAu
'Mac 'n' Cheese'^{PBR}	EBee
'Magenta Pearl' (Pearl Series)	CAbb LRHS
'Mama Mia'^{PBR}	CWGN LCro
'Marmalade'^{PBR} (Cone-fections Series) (d)	EMor EUrb MHol MSwo SPoG WCAu XFar
'Matthew Saul'	see *E.* 'Harvest Moon' (Big Sky Series)

Echinacea 255

Name	Sources
Meadow Farm selection (mixed)	WHoo
'Meditation'PBR	WCot
'Meditation Cerise'	CAbb LBar
'Meditation Lime'	LBar
MEDITATION ORANGE ('Mvne177')	LBar LRHS
MEDITATION WHITE'PBR	CBcs CKno EGren EPfP LRHS MBNS MPri SOrN SPoG
'Mellow Yellow'	see *E. paradoxa* 'Yellow Mellow', *E. purpurea* 'Mellow Yellows'
MINI BELLE ('Minbel252'PBR)	XFar
(Cone-fections Series) (d)	
(Mooodz Series) MOOODZ COSY ('Hilmooocosy'PBR)	LRHS MPri
- MOOODZ COURAGE ('Hilmoocour')	LBom LRHS MPri
- MOOODZ DEVOTION ('Hilmoodevot') **new**	MPri NWbg
- MOOODZ DREAM ('Hilmoodrea')	LBar
- MOOODZ FUNNY ('Hilmoofun')	LRHS
- MOOODZ GLORY ('Hilmooglor')	LBar LBom LRHS
- MOOODZ IMAGINATION ('Hilmooimag') **new**	MPri
- MOOODZ JOY ('Hilmooojoy')	EGren
- MOOODZ MEDIATION ('Hilmoomedi')	EGren LBar LRHS Midl
- MOOODZ MOTIVATION ('Hilmoomotiv')	LBar LBom LRHS Midl MPri
- MOOODZ PEACE ('Hilmoopea')	LBar LRHS MPri NWbg
- MOOODZ SATISFY ('Hilmoosati')	LRHS
- MOOODZ SHINY ('Hilmooshin')	MPri
- MOOODZ SYMPATHY ('Hilmoosymp')	LRHS MPri
MYSTIC (Dark Shadows Series) **new**	Midl
'Now Cheesier'PBR	LCro
ORANGE MEADOWBRITE	see *E.* 'Art's Pride'
ORANGE PASSION ('Orpass'PBR)	EGrI WCAu
ORANGE PEARL ('Pearl495') (Pearl Series)	LBar
ORANGE SKIPPER ('Echor273') (Butterfly Series)	EGrI LRHS
'Pacific Summer'	WSpi
pallida	Widely available
- 'Hula Dancer'	CDor EDAr LRHS MCtn MNrw MPro NClf NDov NGdn SHor SPel StAn WTre
- 'Satin Lights'	MNrw
(Papallo Series) 'Papallo Classic Orange'	LRHS
- 'Papallo Classic Rose'	EPfP LRHS
- 'Papallo Semi-double Cherry' (d)	LBar
- 'Papallo Semi-double Peach' (d)	LBar LRHS Midl
- 'Papallo Semi-double Pink' (d)	EPfP LRHS Midl
- 'Papallo Semi-double White' (d)	Midl
paradoxa	CTsd ECha ELan EPfP GPSL LRHS MCtn MHoo MPro SPlb WCAu WFar
§ - 'Yellow Mellow'	LRHS
'Parrot' (Fine Feathered Series)	CAbb LBar LCro LRHS Midl MPri MPro SHar WHil XFar
POSTMAN ('Post301'PBR) (Butterfly Series)	SPoG WSpi XFar
PRAIRIE BLAZE GOLDEN YELLOW	LRHS
PRETTY PARASOLS	see *E.* 'Jsengeltje'
(Prima Series) PRIMA BERRY **new**	LBar LSou Midl
- PRIMA RUBY ('Tnechpr')	LBar Midl
- PRIMA SAFFRON ('Tnechps')	LBar LSou Midl MPro
'Purple Emperor'PBR (Butterfly Series)	LCro LRHS Midl WSpi
§ *purpurea*	Widely available
I - 'Alba'	ECha EGren EPfP LWaG WCot WFar
- 'Augustkönigin'	WCAu WCot
- 'Avalanche'PBR (Butterfly Series)	MBNS MSwo NLar
- 'Baby Swan Pink'	CWnw
- 'Baby Swan White'	CBWd CWnw EBee EBlo EDAr ELan EPfP LRHS LSto MCtn NLar
- Bressingham hybrids	EBee EBlo EPfP GPSL LRHS LSou MArl MAsh MPie
- CHUNKY PURPLE ('Noecone'PBR)	LRHS MPri
- 'Coconut Lime' (Cone-fections Series) (d)	LCro WCAu
- DOPPELGANGER	see *E. purpurea* 'Doubledecker'
§ - 'Doubledecker'	EDAr EGren ELan EPfP LRHS MPro NGdn
- ELTON KNIGHT ('Elbrook'PBR) ♀H5	WCot
- 'Fatal Attraction'PBR	CAby CBcs CWGN ELan GMaP LRHS MBNS MPro NLar SHar SPoG WCAu WCot WTor XFar
- 'Firebird'PBR	SPoG
- 'Fragrant Angel'PBR	NLar
- 'Green Eyes'	EGren
- 'Green Jewel'PBR ♀H5	CAby CBcs CWnw EBee EGren EGrI EMor EPfP EUrb LBar LBom LCro LRHS MNrw MPro NCth NLar SPeP WCAu WCot WFar WSpi WTor XFar
- 'Green Twister'	CBcs CDor CWGN CWnw EBee EDAr EMor EPfP LRHS LSto MAsh MAvo MBel MBNS MCtn MHoo MPro SIvy WFar XFar
- 'Happy Star'	CDor EBee EDAr EPfP MPro SPel SPoG
- 'Hope'PBR	LRHS NLar WCAu
- 'Kim's Knee High'PBR	NLar SPoG
- 'Kim's Mop Head'	NLar
- LEMON DROP ('Drop352'PBR) (Cone-fections Series) (d)	XFar
§ - 'Leuchtstern'	CKno ELan EPfP GQue LRHS NBir NGdn
- 'Little Magnus'PBR	MPro NLar SPoG
- 'Lucky Star'	ELan EPfP MPro
- 'Magnus'	Widely available
- 'Magnus Superior'	CBWd CDor CSpe EBee EDAr EPfP EUrb GAbr GPSL LRHS LSou LSto MAvo MBel MHer MHoo MPel StAn
§ - 'Mellow Yellows'	CDor CWnw EArI EDAr EPfP ESgI LBuc LRHS LSto MPro WFar XFar
- 'Meringue' (Cone-fections Series) (d)	LRHS
- 'Milkshake'PBR (Cone-fections Series) (d)	EMor MSwo WSpi XFar
- 'Pink Double Delight'PBR (Cone-fections Series) (d)	EGrI EHeP LCro LRHS Midl NGdn XFar

Echinacea

- 'Pink Shimmer' ♀H5 **new**	LCro MBel
- (PowWow Series) POWWOW WHITE ('Pas709018')	CWGN EAri EGren LRHS MPro SPoG WCAu WFar WTor
- - - POWWOW WILD BERRY ('Pas702917'PBR)	CWGN CWnw EGren EPfP MCtn MHol MPro SPoG WFar WTor
- (Prairie Splendor Compact Series) PRAIRIE SPLENDOR COMPACT ROSE	WTor
- - PRAIRIE SPLENDOR COMPACT WHITE	LRHS WTor
- (Prairie Splendor Series) PRAIRIE SPLENDOR DEEP ROSE **new**	WTor
- - PRAIRIE SPLENDOR	LRHS SRkn
- (Primadonna Series) 'Primadonna Deep Pink'	EPfP LRHS
- - 'Primadonna Deep Rose'	ELan MCtn MPro SVic
- 'Primadonna White'	CSpe EAri EPfP LRHS SRms
- 'Profusion'	WSpi
- 'Purity'PBR	SPoG
- RAINBOW MARCELLA ('Rainb299'PBR) (Butterfly Series)	LBar NLar WSpi XFar
- 'Razzmatazz'PBR (d)	CMac SPoG WCot
- 'Red Rocket'	LRHS MPro
- 'Robert Bloom'	NBir WSpi
- ROBIN HOOD ('Jsroho'PBR)	LBar
- 'Rubinglow'	LCro NBir
- 'Rubinstern'	CBWd CKno EAri EBee ECha ELan EPfP EUrb LCro LRHS LSou LSRN LSto MAvo MBel NLar NSti SDix SMHy SPel SPoG SRkn SRms WCAu WCot WFar WHoo WSpi
- 'Ruby Giant'	ELan GMaP LRHS WCot
- 'Sensation Pink'PBR	CAby CKno CWGN EGren EPfP LRHS MBNS MPri WSpi
- 'Southern Belle'PBR (Cone-fections Series) (d)	ELan EMor MBNS MHol MSwo WSpi XFar
- 'Summer Salsa'PBR	CWGN WCot
- 'The King'	NGdn WSpi
- 'Vanilla Cupcake'PBR (d)	SPoG
- 'Verbesserter Leuchtstern'	MCtn
- 'Vintage Wine'PBR	EGrI ELan LCro MAsh SPoG
- 'Virginia'PBR ♀H5	LCro MAvo MBel MPro SPel WCAu WCot WTor XFar
- 'White Lustre'	SRms
- 'White Swan'	Widely available
'Raspberry Truffle'PBR (Cone-fections Series) (d)	XFar
'Red Pearl' (Pearl Series)	LBar LRHS WSpi
RED SKIPPER (Butterfly Series)	Midl
'Secret Passion'PBR (Secret Series) (d)	WSpi
(Sensation Series) SENSATION HONEYGOLD	XFar
- SENSATION WILD ROMANCE **new**	Midl
simulata	CWal LSto MCtn MPro
'Solar Flare'PBR (Big Sky Series)	WSpi
(Sombrero Series) SOMBRERO ADOBE ORANGE ('Balsomador'PBR)	EGren LRHS Midl MPro
- SOMBRERO BLANCO	EGren LRHS
- SOMBRERO FLAMENCO ORANGE ('Balsomenco'PBR)	LRHS
- SOMBRERO GRANADA GOLD ('Balsomold'PBR)	LRHS
- SOMBRERO LEMON YELLOW ('Balsomemy')	EGren Midl
- SOMBRERO LEMON YELLOW IMPROVED ('Balsomemyim'PBR)	Midl MPro
- SOMBRERO ROSADA ('Balsomrosa')	MPri
- SOMBRERO SALSA RED ('Balsomsed'PBR)	CBcs CWGN EGren LRHS MPri MPro NLar
- SOMBRERO SANGRITA ('Balsomanita'PBR)	EGren LRHS Midl MPri MPro NLar
- SOMBRERO TRES AMIGOS ('Balsomtresgo')	EGren LRHS Midl MPro
(Sombrero Special Series) SOMBRERO SPECIAL HALO YELLOW RED	WHil
- SOMBRERO SPECIAL WHITE PURPLE ('Abha547')	LRHS Midl MPri
- SOMBRERO SPECIAL YELLOW RED ('Abha685')	Midl MSCN
'Starlight'	see *E. purpurea* 'Leuchtstern'
'Strawberry and Cream' (d)	LRHS Midl XFar
'Summer Cloud'	LCro NLar
'Summer Cocktail'PBR	CWGN ELan LBar LCro LRHS Midl SPoG WSpi WTor
'Summer Sun'PBR	SPoG
'Sundown'PBR (Big Sky Series)	EPfP LCro NLar WCAu
(Sunny Days Series) SUNNY DAYS LEMON ('Tnechsdl')	LBar
- SUNNY DAYS RUBY ('Tnechsdr') (d)	LBar
'Sunrise'PBR (Big Sky Series)	ELan GMaP LBar NLar SPoG WCAu
(SunSeekers Series) SUNSEEKERS APPLE GREEN ('Ifecssag')	LBar LRHS MPri MPro
- SUNSEEKERS BLUSH ('Ifecssblus')	LBar LRHS MPro
- SUNSEEKERS BUBBLELICIOUS	LBar LRHS Midl MPri
- SUNSEEKERS CITRUS ('Ifecsscitr')	LBar MPri
- SUNSEEKERS CLEMENTINE ('Ifecsscle')	LBar LRHS MPri MPro WTor
- SUNSEEKERS CORAL ('Ifecssc')	LRHS MPri
- SUNSEEKERS GOLDEN SUN ('Ifecssgold')	LBar Midl MPri
- SUNSEEKERS HOT PINK **new**	LBar Midl MPri
- SUNSEEKERS LIGHT PINK	LRHS MPri
- SUNSEEKERS MAGENTA ('Apecssima'PBR)	CWnw LBar LRHS MPri
- SUNSEEKERS MANGO SUNRISE **new**	MPri
- SUNSEEKERS MELLOW ('Apecssime')	EPfP LBar LRHS MPri
- SUNSEEKERS MINEOLA ('Ifecssmin') **new**	Midl WTor
- SUNSEEKERS ORANGE ('Apecssior'PBR)	EGren EPfP LRHS MPri MPro WSpi WTor
- SUNSEEKERS PINK ('Ifecssrs')	LRHS MPri
- SUNSEEKERS POMEGRANATE ('Ifecsspom')	LBar LRHS MPro
- SUNSEEKERS PURPLE ('Apecssipu')	LBar
- SUNSEEKERS PURPLELICIOUS ('Ifecsspur')	MPro
- SUNSEEKERS RAINBOW ('Ifecssra')	LBar LCro LRHS Midl MPri MPro WTor
- SUNSEEKERS RED ('Apecssired'PBR)	CKno LCro LRHS MHtn MPri
- SUNSEEKERS ROSY **new**	Midl

Echium 257

– SunSeekers Salmon ('Ifecsssal'PBR)	EGren LCro LRHS MAsh MHol Midl MPri MPro WFar WTor	*commutatus*	see *E. exaltatus*
– SunSeekers Sweet Fuchsia ('Ifecssswfu')	LCro LRHS Midl MPri MPro SPad	§ *exaltatus*	NBid
		gmelinii 'Snow King'	MSwo
– SunSeekers Tequila Sunrise ('Ifecssts')	LRHS MPri MPro WTor	*maracandicus*	WCot
		niveus	GJos
– SunSeekers White ('Apecssiwh')	EPfP LRHS MPri WFar	*ritro* misapplied	see *E. bannaticus*
– SunSeekers White Perfection ('Ifecsswp') (d)	Midl	§ *ritro* L.	CBWd CCBP CMac CSpe CWal EAri EBee ECha EGren EHeP ELan ELon EPfP GJos LRHS LSto LWaG MBel MCtn MMuc MPro NBro SEND SPlb SPoG SRms WBrk WCAu WFar WTre
– SunSeekers Yellow ('Apecssiye'PBR)	LRHS MPri	– 'Blue Cloud'	EBee
'Sunset'PBR (Big Sky Series)	ELan LRHS LSRN	– subsp. *ruthenicus* ♀H7	WCot
'Sweet Chili' (Cone-fections Series) (d)	WCAu	– – 'Platinum Blue'	CDor EBee EDAr ELan ELon GJos MBNS MNrw MPro NLar SRms WFar WHil WHoo
Sweet Meadow Mama ('Sweet342'PBR) (Meadow Mama Series)	WFar XFar	– 'Veitch's Blue' misapplied	see *E. ritro* L.
		– 'Veitch's Blue'	CBcs CDor ECha EGren ELon EWhm GAbr GMaP LBom LCro LSRN LSto MAsh MAvo MBel MGos MHol MPri MSwo NLar SOrN SPel SPoG SRms WCAu WFar WHoo WTre XFar
Sweet Sandia ('Tnechss')	Midl MPri MPro WFar		
'Tangerine Dream'PBR	EBee EPfP MPro NLar WSpi		
tennesseensis 'Rocky Top'	EBlo LRHS SHor WKit		
'Tiki Torch'PBR	CAby LCro MArl MPro SPoG WCot WTor	*sphaerocephalus*	GJos NBir SPlb
'Tomato Soup'PBR	CAby CBcs EBee ELan EPfP GMaP LCro MNrw NLar SPoG WCAu WCot WHil WTor	– 'Arctic Glow'	CBcs CDor EBee ECha EGren ELan EPfP EPPr ESgl GKev LSto MAsh NGdn NLar SPlb SPoG WFar XFar
'Twilight'PBR (Big Sky Series)	EGrI	*spinosissimus*	WCot
Unica Cherry on Ice **new**	Midl	*tjanschanicus*	GJos GPSL MMuc SEND
Vintage Red ('Bullechi 01'PBR) (SunMagic Series)	EGren LBar Midl MPri		

Echinopsis ✿ (*Cactaceae*)

§ *ancistrophora* ♀H2	LCro LWaG NCft
arachnacantha ♀H2	SPlb
atacamensis subsp. *pasacana*	CBlu NPlm
chamaecereus ♀H3	SIvy
chiloensis	SPlb
'Damisa'	SPlb
'Dark Melody'	SPlb
huascha	NPlm
'Kawinai'	SPlb
multiplex	NCft
oxygona ♀H2	NCft
pachanoi	MCtn NPlm
peruviana	CBlu NPlm
'Pink Flamingo'	SPlb
pygmaea	see *Rebutia pygmaea*
red-orange-flowered	SPlb
subdenudata	see *E. ancistrophora*
tanjensis subsp. *bertramiana*	NPlm
terscheckii	NPlm
tubiflora	SBig

Vintage Ruby (SunMagic Series) | LBar
'Yellow Passion' | WCAu
'Yellow Pearl' (Pearl Series) | LRHS
'Yellow Rainbow' (Butterfly Series) **new** | XFar

Echinocactus (*Cactaceae*)

grusonii ♀H1c	LBom LWaG NHrt NPlm SBig
– var. *brevispinus*	NPlm
– var. *inermis*	NPlm
– spineless	NHrt

Echinocereus (*Cactaceae*)

pectinatus	MCtn
viridiflorus	SPlb

Echinodorus (*Alismataceae*)

bleheri	see *E. grisebachii*
§ *grisebachii*	ELin

Echinops ✿ (*Asteraceae*)

§ *bannaticus*	CBcs CWal
* – 'Albus'	WCAu
– 'Blue Globe'	CMHG EGrI ELan EPfP LBar LRHS LShi LSRN MBel MGos MHol MPro NGdn NLit SMHy SPoG WCAu WFar WHoo
– 'Blue Glow'	CDor EGren EPPr GJos MBNS NLar WFar
– 'Star Frost'	CBWd EBee EDAr ELan EPfP EPPr GJos LBar MCtn MMuc NLar SMrm SRms WFar WHil WTor
– 'Taplow Blue'	CBcs CBWd CDor CMac CMHG EBee ECha EGren ELan ELon EPfP GMaP LBar LCro LRHS LSto MBNS MHol MPri MSwo NBir NLar NPer SEND SOrN SPoG SRkn WCAu WFar

Echium ✿ (*Boraginaceae*)

amoenum	CSpe EPfP EWes LRHS MCtn SPhx
'Blue Steeple'	CWCL MEch SAth WCor
boissieri	WPGP
callithyrsum	MEch
candicans ♀H1c	CAbb CBcs CPbh CTsd CWal ELan EShb EUrb LCro LRHS LWaG MEch SAth SBig SVen
decaisnei subsp. *decaisnei*	MEch
gentianoides	MEch SPlb
giganteum	MEch
hierrense	MEch
italicum	MEch
maculatum	see *Pontechium maculatum*
nervosum	MEch
onosmifolium	MEch

Echium

'Pearce's Grey'	SVen
pininana ♀H3	CAbb CBcs CCht CDoC CPbh CSpe CTsd CWal EArl EGren ELan EUrb LRHS LWaG MCtn MEch SArc SAth SChr SEND SPhx SVen WCor WJun
- 'Snow Tower'	CAbb CDTJ CWCL ELan MCtn MEch SAth
'Pink Fountain' ♀H3	CAbb CDTJ CWCL ELan MEch
'Red Rocket'	CDTJ
russicum	see *Pontechium maculatum*
sabulicola	MEch
simplex ♀H2	MEch
strictum	CCht CDoC MCtn MEch SArc SEND
sventenii	SPlb
tuberculatum	MEch SPhx
virescens	MEch
vulcanorum	MEch
vulgare	CBWd CCBP CGHo CHab CSpe CTtf EGren EHet ELan ENfk GJem LCro LRHS LWaG MCtn MEch MHer MHoo MNHC NMir SBig SHor SPhx WOrg WRBe WShi WTre
- from Armenia	WCot
- 'Blue Bedder' ♀H7	CSpe MCtn MNHC SPhx
- 'Pink Bedder'	MCtn
- 'White Bedder'	MCtn
webbii	MMrt
wildpretii ♀H2	CCht CDoC CDTJ CPbh CTsd EArl ESgl LRHS LWaG MEch SPlb SVen
- subsp. *wildpretii*	MEch

Ectotropis (Aizoaceae)

§ *alpina*	GEdr LRHS
§ *seanii-hoganii*	EPot ESuc GEdr SPlb WAbe

Edgeworthia (Thymelaeaceae)

§ *chrysantha*	CBcs CDoC CMCN EBee EGren ELan LCro LMil LRHS MGos MHtn NCth SArc SEWo SPoG WFar
- 'Frederic'	LSRN
I - 'Grandiflora'	CBcs CDoC ELon EPfP IArd LCro LMaj LRHS MGos MMrt NCth NLar SBig SMad SWor WCha WCot WFar WPGP
- 'Nanjing Gold'	LRHS
§ - 'Red Dragon'	CMCN LCro LRHS
- f. *rubra* hort.	see *E. chrysantha* 'Red Dragon'
- 'Winter Liebe'	LMaj LRHS NLar
gardneri BWJ 15170	WCru
papyrifera	see *E. chrysantha*

Edraianthus (Campanulaceae)

dalmaticus	GKev
graminifolius	GEdr MWlw
jugoslavicus	GKev
niveus	GEdr
§ *pumilio* ♀H5	GArf GEdr SRms WAbe
sutjeskae	GKev

Egeria (Hydrocharitaceae)

P *densa*	ELin
najas	ELin

Ehretia (Boraginaceae)

§ *acuminata*	WPGP
dicksonii	WPGP
ovalifolia	see *E. acuminata*
rigida	SPlb
thyrsiflora	see *E. acuminata*

Ehrharta (Poaceae)

calycina	Prohibited invasive. See Conservation and the Environment, p.42

Eichhornia (Pontederiaceae)

crassipes	Prohibited invasive. See Conservation and the Environment, p.42

Elaeagnus (Elaeagnaceae)

angustifolia	CAgr CBcs EHeP LSto MCtn SFol SRms WJur WKor
- Caspica Group	see *E.* 'Quicksilver'
argentea Pursh	see *E. commutata*
§ *commutata*	CMac MBlu
I - 'Aurea'	NLar
- 'Zempin'	NLar
× *ebbingei*	see *E.* × *submacrophylla*
macrophylla	CMac EBee WJur
multiflora	MBlu NLar WJur WKor
- 'Sweet Scarlet'	CAgr
parvifolia	ELan LRHS
pungens	see *E. pungens* 'Variegata'
'Argenteovariegata'	
- 'Aureovariegata'	see *E. pungens* 'Maculata'
- 'Dicksonii' (v)	EPfP LRHS NLar SRms WFar
- 'Frederici' (v)	CCoa CDoC CEnd CMac ELon LRHS MAsh NLar
- 'Hosoba-fukurin' (v)	ELan ELon EPfP LRHS NLar WHtc
§ - 'Maculata' (v)	CBrac CDoC CMac EGren EHeP ELan EPfP LRHS LSRN MAsh MGos NLar SGol SHor SPoG SRms SSta WFar WHtc
§ - 'Variegata' (v)	CBcs CMac
§ 'Quicksilver'	CBcs CCoa CDoC CEnd CMac CMCN EBee ELan EPfP IArd LCro LRHS LSto MAsh MGos MMrt NLar NLit NPip SArc SChF SEND SHor SPoG SSta WFar WHtc WLov WMat
× *reflexa*	CBcs
§ × *submacrophylla* ♀H5	Widely available
- 'Coastal Gold' (v)	CCoa CDoC EBee EHeP EPfP LSRN MGos SRms WFar WHtc
I - 'Compacta'	CCoa CCVT CSBt CWnw EBee EGren ELan EPfP LCro LRHS LSRN MGos NHed SArc SBig SEWo WCha WFar WHtc WReH
- 'Gilt Edge' (v) ♀H5	CAco CBcs CBrac CCoa CDoC CMac EGren EHeP ELan ELon EPfP LRHS LSRN MAsh MGos NLar SPoG WFar WHtc
- GOLD SPLASH ('Lannou') (v)	CMac EPfP LRHS SGol
- 'Limelight' (v)	CAgr CBcs CBrac CCoa CCVT CDoC CEnd CMac CSBt EGren EHeP ELan EPfP GKin LBuc LCro LRHS LSto MAsh MGos MHed NLar SEND SFol SGol SPoG WFar WHtc
- MARYLINE ('Abrela') (v)	EPfP LRHS MAsh NLar SEWo
- 'Moonlight'	EPfP LRHS
- 'Svelte Edge'	NLar
- 'Viveleg' PBR (v)	CCVT CDoC EGren ELan LRHS MAsh MGos MHed NLar SAth WCha WHtc
umbellata	CBcs CEnd CNWT EBee LMaj MBlu NLar SArc WFar WJur WKor
- 'Amber' (F)	CAgr NLar
- 'Big Red' (F)	CAgr
- var. *borealis* 'Polar Lights'	NLar
- 'Brilliant Rose' (F)	CAgr
- 'Garnet' (F)	CAgr
- 'Hidden Springs' (F)	CAgr

Enkianthus   259

- 'Jewel' (F)	CAgr
- 'Late Scarlet' (F)	CAgr
- 'Le Vasterival'	MAsh
- 'Newgate' (F)	CAgr
- POINTILLA SWEET'N'SOUR (Pointilla Series) (F)	EGrI
- 'Red Cascade' (F)	CAgr MBlu NLar
- var. *rotundifolia* CWJ 12835	WCru
- 'Ruby' (F)	CAgr NLar
- 'Sweet 'n' Tart' (F)	CAgr

Elatostema (Urticaceae)

CHB from Yunnan	GGro
CHB 14	GGro
CHBMV 1511	GGro
brevifolium PB 04-307	GGro
umbellatum 'Dents de Kyoto'	EAri EWld GGro WFar
- 'Ogon'	GGro

elderberry see *Sambucus nigra*

Elegia (Restionaceae)

capensis ♀H3	CDTJ CPbh SPlb
elephantina ♀H4	CPbh LCro SArc
equisetacea ♀H3	CPbh
grandis	SPlb
macrocarpa	CPbh SPlb
tectorum ♀H2	CAbb CPbh CTsd LRHS SEND SPlb SPoG
- dwarf	CPbh
- 'Fish Hoek'	CPbh

Eleocharis (Cyperaceae)

acicularis	CLil CPud CWat
palustris	CPud CWat ELin
vivipara	ELin

Elettaria (Zingiberaceae)

cardamomum	EAri EShb LEdu SBig SPre WJek

Eleutherococcus ✿ (Araliaceae)

divaricatus B&SWJ 5027	WCru
giraldii BWJ 8091	WCru
henryi	WJur
hypoleucus B&SWJ 5532	WCru
leucorrhizus	WJur
aff. *leucorrhizus*	EBee
pictus	see *Kalopanax septemlobus*
senticosus B&SWJ 4568	WCru
septemlobus	see *Kalopanax septemlobus*
sessiliflorus	WJur
- B&SWJ 4528	ESwi WCru
- B&SWJ 8457	WCru
- B&SWJ 8618	WCru
sieboldianus	LCro
'Aureovariegatus' (v)	
- 'Variegatus' (v)	ESwi EUrb NLar SPoG
spinosus misapplied	see *E. sieboldianus*
trifoliatus RWJ 10108	WCru

Ellisiophyllum (Plantaginaceae)

pinnatum B&SWJ 197	WCru

Elmera (Saxifragaceae)

racemosa var. *puberulenta*	GKev

Elodea (Hydrocharitaceae)

P *canadensis*	NBir WMAq
densa	see *Egeria densa*
nuttallii	Prohibited invasive. See Conservation and the Environment, p.42

Elsholtzia (Lamiaceae)

flava	CExl EAri EBee
- PAB 13.012	WPGP
stauntonii	CAgr CBcs ECha EPPr LCro LRHS MCtn MHer NLar NQui WJek
- 'Alba'	MCtn

Elymus (Poaceae)

arenarius	see *Leymus arenarius*
canadensis	EPPr
- 'Icy Blue'	CAby EPPr
glaucus misapplied	see *E. hispidus*
§ *hispidus* ♀H6	MBlu NDov WCot
§ *magellanicus*	CDoC CKno CMHG CSpe CWnw EBee ECha EGrI ELan EPfP EShb GArf GElm GKev GQue MArl MAsh NBir NLar NSti SMHy SPeP SPlb SPoG SRms WCot WPav
- 'Blue Sword'	ELan MGos SRkn SRms
villosus	EPPr
- var. *arkansanus*	EPPr
virginicus	EPPr

Embothrium ✿ (Proteaceae)

coccineum	GKev IArd NCth SPlb WJur
- Lanceolatum Group	CEnd GAbr LRHS MBlu SArc SSta WAbe

Emilia (Asteraceae)

coccinea	CSpe
sonchifolia var. *javanica* 'Irish Poet'	LWaG MCtn

Emmenopterys (Rubiaceae)

henryi	CBcs CMCN MBlu SArc

Empetrum (Ericaceae)

nigrum	WKor
- 'Bernstein'	GArf

endive see AGM Vegetables Section

Endymion see *Hyacinthoides*

Engelhardia (Juglandaceae)

spicata HWJK 2421	WCru

Engelmannia (Asteraceae)

peristenia	EPPr ESgI

Enkianthus ✿ (Ericaceae)

campanulatus ♀H5	CBcs CDoC CEnd CMac EBee EGren EGrI ELan EPfP GKev GKin LCro LRHS MAsh MGos MHtn MMuc NLar NPip SGol SPoG SSta WFar WMat
- var. *campanulatus* f. *albiflorus*	GKev GKin NLar
I - 'Hollandia'	NLar
- 'Miyama-beni'	NLar
I - 'Pagoda'	CBcs IArd LCro LRHS NLar SMrm
- var. *palibinii*	EPfP GKev GKin LRHS MAsh NLar
- PRETTYCOAT ('Jww10'PBR)	CBcs ELan LCro MMrt
- 'Red Bells'	CBcs CTsd EGrI GKin MAsh MSCN NLar SGol SPad WFar
- 'Red Velvet'	GKin

- 'Ruby Glow'	CBcs EGrI NLar SAko	*acuminatum*	EMor GEdr GPSL LEdu MNrw NCth NLar WFar WPGP
- 'Showy Lantern'	NLar		
- 'Tokyo Masquerade' (v)	LRHS SPoG	- L 575	CDor CElw CExl CSta
- 'Venus'	CBcs GKin NLar	- 'Galaxy'	CExl LEdu
- 'Wallaby'	CBcs GKev NLar	- 'Night Mistress'♀H6	CSta CTtf ESMi GPSL LEdu WPGP
cernuus f. *rubens* ♀H5	CMac LRHS NLar	- 'Persian Carpet'	CSta ESMi EWld
chinensis	EPfP LRHS MAsh SPoG	- 'Quinquin'	CSta
deflexus	LRHS WPGP	- white-flowered	CDor
perulatus ♀H5	CEnd	- yellow-flowered	WPGP
		- - CC 1141	CSta

Ensete (Musaceae)

glaucum	CDTJ MCtn	'Akebono'	CBcs CDor CMHG CTtf EBee EGrI EMor EPfP EPPr GElm IPot LSto MHol MNrw NLar NWbg SDix SPoG SReu SRms WCAu WCot WFar WGwG WPnP WSpi
§ *ventricosum* ♀H2	CDTJ EShb LWaG MCtn SArc		
§ - 'Maurelii' ♀H2	CBlu CCht CDoC CDTJ CSBt CTsd EAri ELan ELon EUrb LCro MHtn MPri NPlm SAth SBig SDix SEND SMrm SPoG SWor		
		ALABASTER ('Conalba')	EBee GEdr GPSL LRHS WFar
		alpinum	CMac EAri EBee EMor GKev LEdu SRms WFar WHil
- 'Rubrum'	see *E. ventricosum* 'Maurelii'	- 'Samobor'	LEdu
- 'Tandarra Red'	CAbb	'Amanogawa'	CoPl CSta CTtf ESMi GEdr LEdu WCot

Entelea (Malvaceae)

arborescens	EAri EShb SPlb	'Amber Freckles'	ESMi
		'Amber Queen'PBR ♀H6	Widely available

Eomecon (Papaveraceae)

chionantha	CExl CMiW CTtf EAri EBlo EPfP EPPr EWld GAbr GEdr GKev LEdu LRHS NBro NQui NSti WCru WFar WPGP	'Anardil'	CSta
		'André Charlier'	CDor CElw CSta WCAu
		'Arctic Wings'PBR	CSta CTtf GEdr LEdu NGdn
		'Asiatic Hybrid'	CTsd EUrb LRHS WCAu WFar
		'Astrid'	CSta

Epacris (Ericaceae)

paludosa	GArf GKev	'Beni-goromo'	GEdr
		'Beni-kujaku'	EMor GEdr GPSL LRHS SHar WCot WFar

Ephedra (Ephedraceae)

chilensis	SEND	'Beni-yushima'	GEdr
distachya	WKor	'Bieke'	SMHy
equisetina RCB/TQ K-1	WCot	'Black Sea'	CDor CElw CSpe EBee EMor EPPr GMaP MNrw NLar SPel WFar
fedtschenkoi	GKev		
gerardiana	EAri LEdu	*brachyrrhizum*	CDor CExl CTtf NLar
- CC 3925	WCot	*brevicornu*	CSta GEdr WPGP
- var. *sikkimensis*	GGro	- Og 82.01	CExl
monosperma	WCot	- Og 88.01	CDor
		brown-leaved	CSta
		'Buckland Spider'	CFis CSta EBee EPPr GEdr LEdu MNrw SPeP WCot WFar WPGP

Epilobium (Onagraceae)

angustifolium	see *Chamaenerion angustifolium*	'Buff Beauty'	CSta ECha ESMi
- f. *leucanthum*	see *Chamaenerion angustifolium* 'Album'	'Calisto'	CSta
		campanulatum	CDor
californicum misapplied	see *E. canum*	- Og 93.087	CExl
§ *canum* (Z)	EDAr LRHS MBrN MCtn SRms WAbe	× *cantabrigiense*	CBro CDor CMac CWCL EGrI EPPr GMaP GPSL NLar SRms WCAu WFar
- 'Albiflorum' (Z)	ECha	*chlorandrum*	CDor EBee EPPr LEdu WPGP
§ - 'Dublin' (Z) ♀H4	CAby CBcs ECha EPot EUrb LBar LRHS LShi LSRN MAsh SPlb SPoG SRms SRot WAbe WCFE WHoo WKif WOld	creeping yellow	CDor EBee ELan NLar WFar WHil
		cremeum	see *E. grandiflorum* subsp. *koreanum*
		'Cyrion'	CSta
- 'Ed Carman' (Z)	ECha EPfP LShi WMal	'Dark Secret'	CSta ESMi
- 'Glasnevin'	see *E. canum* 'Dublin'	'Darrell's Pink'	EBee NCth
- 'Olbrich Silver' (Z)	ECha MNrw WAbe WKif WMal	'David Barker'	ESMi
- 'Solidarity Pink' (Z)	WMal	*davidii*	CDor CSta CTtf EPfP EPPr ESMi GEdr LEdu NLar StAn WPGP
- 'Western Hills' (Z) ♀H4	CFis ECha EPot LRHS MMuc SChF SEND SRms WPGP	- CPC 960079	CExl LEdu
		- EMR 4125	CElw CExl
dodonaei	see *Chamaenerion dodonaei*	- dwarf	CExl
glabellum G. Forst.	CSpe	*diphyllum*	CExl EMor WPGP
'Merriments Orange' (Z)	SMrm	- subsp. *kitamuranum*	NCth
I 'Pumilio' (Z)	EPot	*dolichostemon*	CElw ECha EMor EPfP ESMi GPSL WFar
rosmarinifolium	see *Chamaenerion dodonaei*		
septentrionale (Z)	WAbe WIce	- Og 81.01	WPGP
villosum	see *E. canum*	'Domino' ♀H6	CTtf ELan EMor ESMi GPSL ISha LBar LEdu MAvo MWlw NClf NCth NLar SDix WCAu WFar WPGP

Epimedium ✿ (Berberidaceae)

from Jian Xi, China	GEdr	'Double Cream' (d)	CSta ECha
from Yunnan, China	GEdr WPGP	*ecalcaratum*	EBee GEdr LEdu WCot WPGP

Epimedium

– Og 93.082	CExl
– spurred	CSta
'Egret'	CSta CTtf EBee LEdu SMHy WCot WPGP
'Elessar'	CSta
elongatum	ESwi
'Emperor'	see *E*. 'Phoenix'
'Enchantress'	CDor CMiW CSta EPPr ESmi MNrw NLar
epsteinii	CDor CSta EPPr ESmi EWld GEdr LEdu MNrw SBrt SMad WCot WPGP
– CPC 940347	CElw CExl
fangii	CExl
fargesii	CDor CExl CSta EBee ESmi EWld GEdr LEdu MNrw WCAu WPGP
– 'Pink Constellation' ♀H6	CDor CExl CSta CTtf EBee GEdr LEdu MNrw SPel WCot WPGP
'Fire Dragon'PBR	MNrw NCth NLar SPoG WFar
flavum	EBee WPGP
– Og 92.036	CExl EBee
'Flowers of Sulphur'PBR	CDor CSta EBee GEdr LRHS WFar WSpi
franchetii	CElw CExl CSta GEdr
– 'Brimstone Butterfly' ♀H6	CDor CExl CFis CTtf ECha EMor EPPr ESmi GEdr GPSL LEdu NLar WCAu WCot WPGP WSpi
'Fukujuji'	GEdr
'Ghent Orange' **new**	ESmi
'Golden Eagle'	CElw CExl CSta MNrw WCot
§ *grandiflorum*	CBcs CElw CSta CWCL EAri EGrI ELan ELon GKev NBir NLar WCAu WFar WPnP
– 'Akagi-Zakura' ♀H6	CSta
– 'Akakage'	CExl
– 'Beni-chidori'	GEdr
– 'Bicolor Giant'	CSta
– 'Chris Norton'	CSta
– 'Circe' ♀H6	CSta ESmi
– 'Cranberry Sparkle'	EBee
– 'Crimson Beauty'	CTtf ECha WHoo
– 'Elfenkönigin'	EBee NLar
– 'French Braid'	EBee
– 'Freya'	CExl EBee EBlo ECha LEdu
§ – var. *higoense*	GEdr WCot WPGP
– – 'Bandit'	CSta EMor EUrb GEdr GPSL LBar NCth WCAu
– – speckled-leaved	GEdr
– 'Jennie Maillard'	ELon ESmi WCot
– 'Koji'	EBee EMor GKev
§ – subsp. *koreanum*	ECha ESmi GEdr
– 'Kourin'	CSta GEdr
– 'La Rocaille'	CElw CSta
– 'Lilafee'	Widely available
– 'Mount Kitadake'	WAbe
– 'Nanum'	EBee ESmi GArf MNrw NHar SMHy SPlb WAbe WHoo WPGP
– 'Pierre's Purple'	LBar
– 'Purple Pixie'PBR	CDTJ CWnw ELan GPSL LRHS LSou NLar SMrm WFar
– 'Purple Prince'	CExl CSta WCot WPGP
– 'Queen Esta'	CExl CSta ECha ESmi LEdu MNrw WPGP
– 'Red Beauty'	CMac CMiW CSpe CSta CWCL CWnw EGren ELon EMor EPfP GEdr IPot LBar LEdu LSou MAsh MGos MNrw NBir NCth SMrm WFar WPGP
– 'Red Queen'	WCAu
– 'Rose Queen'	EGrI ELan EMor EPfP ESmi LBar LEdu MNrw NBir NSti WCAu WFar WPGP
– 'Roseum'	CMac GMaP GPSL
– 'Rubinkrone'	GMaP MNrw
– var. *thunbergianum*	CSta
– f. *violaceum*	CElw EBee LRHS WCFE
– 'Waterfall'	CSta
– 'White Queen'	EBee ELon EMor EPfP EPPr LBar MBel NClf WCot WFar
– 'Wildside Red'	WCot
– 'Yellow Princess'	EBee
– 'Yubae'	CSta EMor GEdr NLar
'Hagoromo'	GEdr
§ 'Hakubai'	GEdr NLar WCAu XFar
'Harugasumi'	GEdr
higoense	see *E. grandiflorum* var. *higoense*
'Hina Matsuri'	GEdr
ilicifolium	CDor CSta CTtf LEdu WCot WPGP
'Jean O'Neill'	CDor CElw CSta ECha EPPr ESmi WCot WPGP
'Jenny Pym'	EBee
'Jinto Shan'	LEdu
'Kaguyahime'	CDor CElw CSta EPPr GPSL
'King Prawn'	CSta EPPr ESmi IPot LEdu MWlw WPGP
'Knight Star'	CSta ESmi
'Kodai Murasaki' ♀H6	CSta ESmi GPSL
'Koki'	GEdr
'Kotobuki'	GEdr
latisepalum	EBee ESmi GEdr LEdu MNrw WCot
'Lemon Zest'	EBee ESmi LBar
leptorrhizum	CDor CElw CExl CSta EBee EMor EPPr ESmi EWld GEdr GKev LEdu MNrw NLar SBrt WAbe WCot
– Og Y44	CExl
– 'Mariko'	CExl CSta CTtf LEdu
lishihchenii	CExl CMiW ESmi GEdr WPGP
'Little Shrimp'	EBee EPfP GMaP GPSL LRHS NLar
macranthum	see *E. grandiflorum*
macrosepalum	GEdr GPSL WPGP
'Madame Butterfly'PBR	GEdr
'Mandarin Star'	CWCL ESmi GEdr GPSL WHil
'Marchants Twin Set'	CSta EAri SMHy
'Marion Courdoisy'	CSta MWlw
'Marion Sisley'	ESmi
membranaceum	CSta EGrI ESmi GEdr LEdu WAbe WCot WPGP
– Og 93.047	CExl EPPr GEdr LEdu
mikinorii	CExl CSta GEdr
– CC 990001	LEdu WPGP
'Mine-no-fubuki'	GEdr
'Moonlight'	CSta
'Myojo'	EBee GEdr
myrianthum	CDor CSta EBee GEdr GPSL LEdu WPGP
'Never the Red Rooster'	CSta IPot
ogisui	CDor CSta CTtf ESmi LEdu WPGP
– Og 91.001	CExl MNrw
– 'Diane'	LEdu
§ × *omeiense* 'Akame'	CExl CWnw EMor EPPr ESmi LBar LEdu MNrw
– 'Emei Shan'	see *E*. × *omeiense* 'Akame'
– 'Myriad Years'	WPGP
– 'Pale Fire Sibling'	GEdr
– 'Stormcloud'	CDor CElw CExl CMiW CSta CTtf EPPr LEdu
'Parfum des Elfes' **new**	CSta
parvifolium	LEdu
'Pathfinder'	CSta CTtf ESmi GEdr
pauciflorum	EBee EPPr ESmi GEdr LEdu WPGP
– Og 92.123	CExl
'Peachy'	CSta SMHy
× *perralchicum*	CBro EBlo LRHS NLar WCAu

Epimedium

Name	Availability
- 'Fröhnleiten'	Widely available
- 'Lichtenberg'	EBee
- 'Wisley'	CDor CElw EWes LBar
perralderianum	CMac CSta CWCL EBee EHeP GMaP MBel MNrw SRms WCAu
- 'Weihenstephan'	CDor CWCL LEdu NLar WFar WPnP WCot
'Perrine's Pink' (Magique Elfes Series)	
§ 'Phoenix'	CDor CExl CSta CTtf WCot
'Pink Champagne' ♀H6	CSta CTtf ECha EMor ESMi GEdr GKev GPSL LBar LEdu MWlw NCth NWbg WCAu WCot WFar WMal WPGP
'Pink Elf' PBR	CBWd CDor CSta CWCL CWGN CWnw EBee EMor GEdr GPSL IPot LBar LSou MHol MNrw NGdn NLar NSti SPad SRms WCAu WFar WPnP XFar
'Pink Panther'	CSta
pinnatum	GMaP SAth
§ - subsp. *colchicum* ♀H7	CTsd CTtf CWCL ELan EMor EPfP GQue LEdu LRHS MAvo MBel NGdn SDix WCAu WCot WFar WPnP WSpi
- - - L 321	WPGP
- - - light, No1 Olga B	GEdr
- - - No2 Olga B	GEdr
- - 'Thunderbolt'	EBee MWlw WCot
- *elegans*	see *E. pinnatum* subsp. *colchicum*
platypetalum	CDor ESMi SBrt WCot
- Og 93.085	CExl EBee
'Pretty in Pink'	CSta ELon EMor ESMi GElm MAvo NCth WCAu WFar
pubescens CC 22556 from Shaanxi, China	CSta
- Og 91.003	CExl EBee WPGP
- from Shaanxi, China	ESMi LEdu
pubigerum	CBWd CDor EBee ECha EGrI EMor ESMi GAbr LEdu MMuc MWlw NLar SEND SRms WCAu WFar WSpi
- 'Talsprudel'	CSta
qingchengshanense	CSta
'Red Maximum' ♀H6	CSta EMor ESMi LBar LEdu WCot WPGP
reticulatum	GEdr
rhizomatosum	CDor CTtf EPPr ESMi GEdr WPGP
- Og 92.114	LEdu WCot WPGP
'Rhubarb and Custard'	ESMi
'Rik'	ECha ESMi
'Roadside Red'	WCot
'Royal Purple' ♀H6	CSta ESMi LEdu
× *rubrum* ♀H7	Widely available
- 'Galadriel'	CDor ECha ELon EMor EPfP ESMi ESwi GPSL LBar LRHS LSto MAvo NLar SPad SPeP WCAu WFar WHoo
- 'Sweetheart'	GEdr
sagittatum	CSta
- 'Warlord'	CSta ESMi WPGP
'Sakura-maru'	GEdr
'Sam Taylor'	CSta
'Sasaki'	CWCL EAri ESMi ESwi GKev GPSL LBar NLar
sempervirens 'Candy Hearts'	CSta WCot
- 'Creamsickle' (v)	GEdr WCot
- 'Okuda's White'	EBee
× *setosum*	ESMi NLar SPlb
'Shiho'	CWCL EMor GKev GPSL NLar
'Shiro-chiri-fu' (v)	CSta
shuichengense	GEdr
- CC 30175	CSta
'Simple Beauty'	CSta MWlw
small-white-flowered, French origin	CSta
'Space Wagon'	MWlw
'Sparkler'	ESMi
'Sphinx Twinkler'	see *E*. 'Spine Tingler'
§ 'Spine Tingler' ♀H6	Widely available
'Spinners'	EBee ESMi WCot
'Starcloud'	EBee
stellulatum	GEdr
- long-leaved	CSta EAri EMor ESMi EUrb
- 'Wudang Star'	CDor CExl EMor ESMi EWes GEdr GPSL LEdu LRHS NLar SDix WFar
sulphureum 'Plena'	see *E*. × *versicolor* double-flowered
'Sunny and Share'	ELan ELon LBar NCth NLar WHil
'Sunshowers'	CSta MWlw
sutchuenense CC 990394	CSta
'Suzuka'	GEdr LEdu MWlw WPGP
'Tama-no-genpei'	CSta GEdr LEdu WCot
'Tanima-no-yuki'	GEdr
'The Giant'	CSta WCot WPGP
'Togen'	WCot
'Tokiwa-gozen'	GEdr
'Totnes Turbo'	CDor CSta EBee ELon ESMi NCth WCot
trifoliolatobinatum CC 950046	LEdu
truncatum	CSta
'Valor'	ECha GQue WCot
× *versicolor*	CExl
- 'Cherry Tart'	CDor EPPr ESMi IPot LBar
- 'Cupreum'	CDor EGrI EMor EPfP GPSL LEdu SHar WCAu WFar
§ - 'Discolor'	CDor CElw CMiW CoPl CSta ECha EPPr NBir WCot
§ - double-flowered (d)	MHol
- 'Neosulphureum'	CBro CDor CTtf CWCL EBee EPPr WFar WPGP
- 'Sulphureum' ♀H7	Widely available
- 'Versicolor'	see *E*. × *versicolor* 'Discolor'
× *warleyense*	Widely available
- 'Orangekönigin'	Widely available
'White Hart'	see *E*. 'Hakubai'
'Wildside Amber'	CSta
'Wildside Ruby'	CSta CTtf EPPr
'William Stearn'	CExl CSta EWld GEdr WCot WPGP
'Windfire'	EBee
'Winter's End' ♀H6	CSta ESMi GEdr GQue LBar WHoo
wushanense	EBee EPPr ESMi GEdr LCro LEdu
- CC 14193	WPGP
- Og 93.019	CDor CExl WPGP
- 'Caramel'	CExl CSpe CSta CTtf EMor GEdr GPSL LEdu MWlw NLar WCot
- 'Cardiff Star'	CSta
- nova	EAri ESMi
- 'Sandy Claws'	CSta WCot
- spiny-leaved	ESMi LSou WCot WFar
- - CC 14631	WPGP
'Yachimata-hime'	GEdr
'Yokihi'	CSta
× *youngianum* 'Beni-kujaku'	IPot WFar
- 'Grape Fizz'	EBee
- 'Merlin'	CDor CElw EBee EMor EPPr GEdr GPSL LBar LRHS MGos NLar NSti WFar
- 'Niveum'	Widely available
- 'Roseum'	CDor CSta EGren EMor EUrb GKev GKin LSRN MAsh NLar NSti SPlb SRms WFar WPnP
- 'Ruby Tuesday'	EBee

Eremurus 263

Epipactis (Orchidaceae)

- 'Shikinomai'	CExl
- 'Tamabotan'	CSta EMor EPPr GEdr MNrw WHil
§ - 'Typicum'	CElw
- 'Youngianum'	see *E. × youngianum* 'Typicum'
zhushanense	EBee ESMi GEdr GQue LEdu WCot WPGP
- dark-flowered CC 22403	CSta

Epipactis (Orchidaceae)

Catalina gx	EAri EDAr GEdr
gigantea	EAri EBee ECha EGrI ELan EWld GEdr GKev
- 'Serpentine Night'	LRHS
Lowland Legacy gx	GEdr
- 'Edelstein'	WFar
palustris	EAri EBee
Passionata gx Light Royals Group	GEdr
royleana	GEdr
Sabine gx 'Frankfurt'	EWld GEdr

Epiphyllum ✿ (Cactaceae)

ackermannii	EAri EShb NTro SBig
anguliger	CDoC CoPl LBom LCro LWaG NHrt NTro SBig
'Beavertail'	EShb
hookeri	EShb
- subsp. *guatemalense*	NPlm
oxypetalum	EAri EShb NTro WCot
pumilum	EShb NPlm
purple-flowered	EShb
'Red Tip'	CoPl EAri EShb LCro

Epipremnum (Araceae)

§ *aureum* ♀H1b	EGren LBom LCro LDro LInT LWaG MPri NHrt NPlm WFar
- 'Neon'	EHap LBom LWaG NHrt
N'JOY ('Hansoti12'PBR) (v)	EHap LBom LCro NHrt WFar
pinnatum	EHap
- 'Cebu Blue' **new**	LInT
- HAPPY LEAF ('Ad260664'PBR) (v)	EHap LBom
- MARBLE PLANET ('Ppiepi003'PBR)	LBom LCro NTro
- 'Marble Queen' (v)	EHap LBom LCro LWaG NHrt

Equisetum ✿ (Equisetaceae)

'Bandit' (v)	GGro WPGP
* *camtschatcense*	EShb SArc SMad SPlb
fluviatile	CLil CWat ELin
giganteum 'El Tabacal'	GGro
hyemale	CBen CDor CLil CWal CWat EGren ELin EPfk EWat GQue LWaG MMuc NBro NLit NPer NSti SBig SPlb WCot
§ - var. *affine*	ELan SBig WPGP
- var. *robustum*	see *E. hyemale* var. *affine*
ramosissimum	CLil CToG CWat EUrb LCro SBig
var. *japonicum*	WFar WPGP
scirpoides	CLil CWat ELin LWaG MWts NPer WCot WFar WMAq
telmateia	LEdu SMad WPGP
variegatum	EBee GGro

Eragrostis (Poaceae)

curvula	CElw ECha EPfP EPPr NBir NGdn SEND
- S&SH 10	CElw EPPr SMHy WPGP
- 'Totnes Burgundy'	CAby CElw CKno CSde ELan EPfP EPPr LEdu LRHS MAsh SHor SRms WPGP

Eranthis (Ranunculaceae)

cilicica	see *E. hyemalis* Cilicica Group
§ *hyemalis* ♀H6	CBWd CSpe EGren ELan EPfP GKev LAma LCro LShi MCtn MNHC MPri NBir NClf SPoG WCot WHoo WShi WTor XFar
- Cilicica Group	EPot ETay GEdr GKev GMaP LAma LRHS NBir NLar SPlb WCot
- 'Flore Pleno' (d)	GEdr LAma WCot
- 'Grünling'	WCot
- 'Grünspecht'	GEdr
- 'Orange Glow'	GEdr LAma
- 'Pauline'	LAma
- 'Schwefelglanz'	GEdr LAma WCot
§ - Tubergenii Group	LAma
- - 'Guinea Gold' ♀H6	GEdr
× *tubergenii*	see *E. hyemalis* Tubergenii Group

Ercilla (Phytolaccaceae)

volubilis	CHIl CRHN CWGN EGrI EWld LRHS SBrt WCru WSpi

Eremophila (Scrophulariaceae)

longifolia	SPlb

Eremurus (Asphodelaceae)

'Apricot Yellow'	LAma
bungei	see *E. stenophyllus* subsp. *stenophyllus*
'Charleston'	GKev LAma SPhx
'Foxtrot'	ERCP GKev LAma
'Helena'	GKev LAma SPhx
himalaicus	ECha EPot ERCP GBin GKev GMaP LAma LCro NLar XFar
× *isabellinus* 'Cleopatra'	ECha EGren EGrI ELan EPot ERCP GBin GKev GMaP LAma LCro LRHS MBNS MHer MSwo NLar SPhx SPoG WCot XFar
- 'Obelisk'	EPfP
- 'Pinokkio'	EGren ETay GKev LAma LCro SPhx XFar
- Ruiter hybrids	ELan GKev LAma MGos NLar SPhx XFar
'Jeanne-Claire'	GKev LAma
'Joanna' ♀H6	GKev LAma LCro
'Lemon Fizz'	GKev LAma NLar
'Line Dance'	EGren EPfP ERCP ETay GKev LAma SPhx
'Moneymaker'	GKev LAma
'Oase'	EPfP LRHS
'Pink Fizz'	LAma NLar
robustus ♀H6	CBcs EGren EPot ERCP GBin GKev LAma LCro MCtn NLar SPlb WCot XFar
'Romance'	EGren ELan ETay LAma LRHS SPhx XFar
'Rumba'	GKev LAma NLar
'Samba'	GKev LAma
'Sandy's White' **new**	EGren
'Sarah Cato'	GKev LAma
stenophyllus ♀H6	EPfP ERCP ETay LAma LCro NLar SPoG WCot
- subsp. *stenophyllus*	EGren GMaP LRHS MNrw MSwo NPer

'Tap Dance' GKev NBir XFar
'White Beauty Favourite'^{PBR} EPfP LCro MHer
'White Sensation' GKev LAma NLar

Erepsia (Aizoaceae)
lacera SPlb

Erianthus see *Saccharum*

Erica ✿ (Ericaceae)
aestiva SPlb
alopecurus SPlb
andevalensis f. **albiflora** CFst
arborea CTsd SPlb
§ - var. **alpina** f. **aureifolia** CBcs CDoC ELan EPfP GAbr GArf
 'Albert's Gold' ♀^{H4} LCro LRHS MAsh MGos MPri SPoG
 - 'Arbora Gold' see *E. arborea* var. *alpina*
 f. *aureifolia* 'Albert's Gold'
 - 'Arnold's Gold' see *E. arborea* var. *alpina*
 f. *aureifolia* 'Albert's Gold'
 - f. **aureifolia** 'Estrella CBcs CDoC CSBt ELan EPfP LCro
 Gold' ♀^{H4} LRHS MAsh SPoG
 - - 'Golden Smile' CFst ELan LRHS
australis f. **albiflora** LCro
 'Polar Express'
 - 'Holehird' CDoC LRHS
 - 'Rivierslea' ♀^{H4} CDoC LRHS SPoG
canaliculata ♀^{H3} CBcs
carnea 'Adrienne SRms
 Duncan' ♀^{H6}
 - f. **alba** 'Golden CFst CSBt MAsh SRms
 Starlet' ♀^{H6}
 - - 'Ice Princess' ♀^{H6} ELan MAsh SRms
 - - 'Isabell' ♀^{H6} MAsh SRms
 - - 'Rosalinde Schorn' SRms
 - - 'Schneesturm' SRms
 - - 'Snow Queen' SRms
 - - 'Snowbelle'^{PBR} CFst ELan
 - - 'Springwood White' ♀^{H6} CFst CSBt ELan MAsh MMuc SRms
 - - 'Whitehall' CFst LCro MAsh SRms
 - - 'Winter Snow' ♀^{H6} CBcs CFst ELan SRms
 - 'Ann Sparkes' ♀^{H6} CBcs CFst ELan MAsh SRms
 - f. **aureifolia** 'Aurea' MAsh SRms
 - - 'Barry Sellers' SRms
 - - 'Bell's Extra Special' SRms
 - - 'Dorset Sunshine' CFst
 - - 'Foxhollow' ♀^{H6} CBcs CFst IArd MAsh SRms
 - - 'Gelber Findling' SRms
 - - 'Hilletje' SRms
 - - 'January Sun' SRms
 - - 'Westwood Yellow' MAsh SRms
 - 'Aztec Gold' CFst
 - 'Beoley Pink' SRms
 - 'Branton Bamford' CFst
 - f. **carnea** 'March CFst ELan MAsh MPri SRms
 Seedling' ♀^{H6}
 - - 'Tanja' CFst
 - 'Challenger' ♀^{H6} ELan MAsh SRms
 - 'C.J. Backhouse' SRms
 - 'Clare Wilkinson' SRms
 - 'Claribelle' CFst
 - 'Corinna'^{PBR} CFst
 - 'December Red' CBcs CFst ELan MAsh MMuc SEND
 SRms
 - 'Dømmesmoen' SRms
 - 'Early Red' SRms
 - 'Eileen Porter' MMuc
 - 'Eva' ♀^{H6} CBcs CFst SRms
 - 'Foxhollow Fairy' SRms
 - 'Gracilis' SRms
 - 'Heathwood' SRms

 - 'James Backhouse' CFst
 - 'Jason Attwater' SRms
 - 'Jennifer Anne' SRms
 - 'John Kampa' SRms
 - 'John Pook' SRms
 - 'King George' MAsh SRms
 - 'Lohse's Rubin' SRms
 - 'Loughrigg' ♀^{H6} MAsh SRms
 - 'Margery Frearson' SRms
I - 'Martin' SRms
 - 'Myretoun Ruby' ♀^{H6} CBcs CFst LCro MAsh SRms
 - 'Nathalie' ♀^{H6} CFst CSBt ELan MAsh SRms
 - 'Pink Cloud' CFst
 - 'Pink Mist' SRms
 - 'Pink Pearl' CFst
 - 'Pink Spangles' ♀^{H6} CBcs CFst CSBt MAsh SRms
 - 'Pirbright Rose' SRms
 - 'Polden Pride' SRms
 - 'Praecox Rubra' SRms
 - 'Queen Mary' SRms
 - 'Queen of Spain' SRms
 - 'R.B. Cooke' SRms
 - 'Robert Jan' SRms
 - 'Rosalie' ♀^{H6} CFst ELan IArd MAsh SRms
 - 'Rosantha' SRms
 - 'Rosea' SPlb
 - 'Rosy Morn' SRms
 - 'Rotes Juwel' SRms
 - 'Rubinteppich' SRms
 - 'Sally' CFst
 - 'Saskia' CFst
 - 'Scatterley' SRms
 - 'Schatzalp' SRms
 - 'Sherwood Creeping' SRms
 - 'Smart's Heath' SRms
 - 'Springwood Pink' MAsh SRms
 - 'Viking' MAsh
 - 'Vivellii' MAsh SRms
 - 'Walter Reisert' SRms
 - 'Weisse March Seedling' CFst
 - 'Wentwood Red' SRms
 - 'Winter Rubin' ♀^{H6} CFst NBir SRms
 - 'Winterfreude' CFst
 - 'Wintersonne' ♀^{H6} SRms
cerinthoides ♀^{H2} CBcs CPbh
ciliaris f. **albiflora** CFst
 'Stoborough'
 - 'Corfe Castle' CFst
 - 'David McClintock' CFst
 - 'Wych' CFst
cinerea EGren
 - f. **alba** 'Alba Minor' CFst MAsh
 - - 'Hookstone White' CFst
 - - 'White Dale' CFst
 - f. **aureifolia** 'Fiddler's MAsh
 Gold'
 - - 'Golden Drop' CFst
 - - 'Goldilocks' CFst
 - 'C.D. Eason' ♀^{H7} CFst
 - 'Champs Hill' CFst
 - 'Creepy Crawly' CFst
 - 'Discovery' CFst
 - 'Eden Valley' CFst
 - 'John Ardron' CFst
 - 'Joseph Murphy' CFst
 - 'Katinka' CBcs CFst
 - 'Lady Skelton' CFst
 - 'Lilac Time' CFst
 - 'Mrs E.A. Mitchell' SPlb
 - 'My Love' CFst
 - 'Pink Ice' ♀^{H7} CFst MAsh

- 'Providence'	CFst
- 'Rosita'	CFst
- 'Sandpit Hill'	CFst
- 'Stephen Davis' ♀H7	CFst
- 'Vivienne Patricia'	CFst
cooperi	SPlb
curviflora	SPlb
× **darleyensis**	EGren
- 'Alba'	see *E.* × *darleyensis* f. *albiflora* 'Silberschmelze'
- f. ***albiflora*** 'Ada S. Collings'	MAsh SRms
- - 'N.R. Webster'	SRms
§ - - 'Silberschmelze'	CSBt CWnw ELan MAsh MMuc SRms WFar
- - 'White Glow'	MAsh SRms
- - 'White Perfection' ♀H5	CBcs CDoC CFst ELan IArd LSto MAsh MPri SPoG SRms WFar
- 'Archie Graham'	SRms
- 'Arthur Johnson' ♀H5	CFst MAsh SRms
§ - f. ***aureifolia*** 'Eva Gold'PBR	CBcs CFst MPri
- - 'Golden Perfect'	CFst
- - 'Jack H. Brummage'	CSBt MAsh SRms
- - 'Mary Helen'	CSBt ELan MAsh SRms WFar
- - 'Moonshine'	CFst SRms
- - 'Tweety' ♀H5	CSBt MAsh SRms
- 'Aurélie Brégeon'	SRms
- 'Cherry Stevens'	see *E.* × *darleyensis* 'Furzey'
§ - 'Darley Dale' ♀H5	CBcs CSBt CWnw ELan MAsh MMuc NBir SPoG SRms WFar
- 'Epe'	SRms
- 'Eva'	see *E.* × *darleyensis* f. *aureifolia* 'Eva Gold'
§ - 'Furzey'	CSBt LCro MAsh SRms
- 'George Rendall'	MAsh SRms
- 'Ghost Hills' ♀H5	CBcs CSBt LCro LSto MAsh SPoG SRms WFar
- 'Irish Treasure'	CFst
- 'James Smith'	SRms
- 'Jenny Porter' ♀H5	ELan
- 'J.W. Porter'	MAsh SRms
- 'Katia'PBR (Winter Belles Series)	CFst
- 'Kramer's Rote' ♀H5	CBcs CFst CSBt CWnw ELan LSto SPoG SRms WFar
- 'Lucie'PBR (Winter Belles Series)	CFst MPri
- MOLTEN SILVER	see *E.* × *darleyensis* f. *albiflora* 'Silberschmelze'
- 'Phoebe'PBR (Winter Belles Series) ♀H5	CBcs CFst
- 'Pink Perfection'	see *E.* × *darleyensis* 'Darley Dale'
- 'Spring Surprise'PBR ♀H5	CFst CWnw
- 'W.G. Pine'	SRms
- 'Winter Surprise' ♀H5	CFst
- 'Winter Treasure' ♀H5	CFst
erigena f. ***alba***	CBcs MAsh SRms
'W.T. Rackliff' ♀H5	
- f. ***aureifolia*** 'Golden Jubilee'	CFst
- - 'Golden Lady'	MAsh SRms
- - 'Thing Nee'	SRms
- 'Irish Dusk' ♀H5	CBcs CSBt MAsh MMuc SRms
- 'Superba'	SRms
glauca var. **glauca**	SPlb
gracilis	CDoC
§ × ***griffithsii*** 'Elegant Spike'	CFst
- 'Jacqueline'	CFst
- 'Valerie Griffiths'	CFst
lusitanica ♀H4	CBcs LRHS
- GREAT STAR	see *E. lusitanica* 'Le Vasterival'
§ - 'Le Vasterival'	LRHS MMrt
- 'Sheffield Park'	ELan EPfP LRHS SPoG
mackayana f. ***eburnea***	CFst
'Shining Light'	
mammosa ♀H2	SPlb
manipuliflora 'Elegant Spike'	see *E.* × *griffithsii* 'Elegant Spike'
nana LIMONCELLO ('Nico1'PBR) **new**	CBcs
× **oldenburgensis** 'Ammerland' ♀H5	LRHS SRms
- 'Oldenburg'	LRHS
patersonia	SPlb
perspicua	SPlb
spiculifolia f. ***albiflora***	GKev
straussiana	SPlb
× **stuartii** 'Irish Lemon' ♀H5	CFst
- 'Irish Orange'	CBcs EPot
tetralix f. ***alba*** 'Alba Mollis' ♀H6	CFst MAsh
- 'Con Underwood'	CFst
- 'Hookstone Pink'	CFst
- 'Ken Underwood'	CFst
- 'L.E. Underwood'	CFst
- 'Riko'	CFst
- f. ***stellata*** 'Pink Star' ♀H6	CFst
vagans f. ***alba*** 'Diana's Gold'	SRms
- - 'Golden Triumph'	CFst
- - 'Lyonesse' ♀H5	MAsh MMuc
- f. ***aureifolia*** 'Yellow John'	CFst MAsh SRms
- 'Birch Glow' ♀H5	CFst
- 'Keira'	SRms
- 'Mrs D.F. Maxwell' ♀H5	CBcs CFst MMuc
- 'Mrs Donaldson'	CFst
- 'Saint Keverne'	CFst IArd MAsh MMuc
- 'Summertime'	CFst
× **veitchii** 'Exeter' ♀H4	CDoC CFst CSBt ELan EPfP MAsh SPoG
- 'Gold Tips' ♀H4	CFst CSBt EPfP LCro LRHS
versicolor ♀H2	CPbh SPlb
verticillata	CPbh
× **watsonii** 'Cherry Turpin'	CFst
× **williamsii** 'Ken Wilson'	CFst
'Winter Fire'	CDoC LRHS
woodii	SPlb

Erigeron (Asteraceae)

acris	GKev
'Adria'	MBel MHol WFar
§ **alpinus**	ESgI SLee
annuus	CSpe ECha LRHS LSto LWaG MHol MNrw NDov SDix SHar SPel SPhx WBrk WChS WMal
aurantiacus	CSpe ELan EPfP GKev
aureus 'Canary Bird' ♀H4	EPot WAbe
- 'The Giant'	WAbe
'Azure Beauty'	EGren LRHS NLit
AZURE FAIRY	see *E.* 'Azurfee'
§ 'Azurfee'	ELan EPfP GKev GMaP GPSL LRHS MCtn NBir NLar SBeP SMrm SPoG WFar
BLACK SEA	see *E.* 'Schwarzes Meer'
'Blue Beauty'	SRms
chrysopsidis	GKev
- 'Grand Ridge'	EPot WAbe
compositus	EDAr SRms
§ - var. ***discoideus***	SPlb
DARKEST OF ALL	see *E.* 'Dunkelste Aller'
'Dignity'	EBee ELan LBar LRHS LSto MArl MBrN SMHy WCAu WFar

266 *Erigeron*

'Dimity'	ECha NBir WFar
'Dominator'	CWGN LBar MHer MHol WCot
§ 'Dunkelste Aller'	CBcs CFis ELan EPfP EUrb GElm LBar MArl MAsh MHol MWIw NLar SPoG SRms WCAu WFar
elegantulus	EDAr
flettii	GKev
'Foersters Liebling' ♀H5	LBar MBel WCAu
'Four Winds'	ELan EWes GKev NGdn WIce
glaucus	CWal GJos GQue MCtn NGdn SBeP SEND StAn WBrk
- 'Albus'	ELon NLar WFar
- 'Elstead Pink'	ELan NQui WFar
- large-flowered	ELon
- 'Roger Raiche'	CFis MHol
- 'Roseus'	SEND
- 'Sea Breeze'	Widely available
- 'Viewpoint Blue'	ELon
grandiflorus	MHol
howellii	MHol
'Karminstrahl'	LBar
§ *karvinskianus* ♀H5	Widely available
- 'Kew Profusion'	LCro
- 'Lavender Lady'	Widely available
- 'Sea of Blossom'	CCht CWnw EAri EPot EUrb LBom LRHS LSou MHol MPri MSwo NCou SPoG
- 'Stallone'	EGren LBar LRHS MHol NLar
leiomerus	EDAr GEdr
linearis	EDAr GEdr
'Mrs F.H. Beale'	EBlo ELon GBin LBar WCot WHoo
mucronatus	see *E. karvinskianus*
'Nachthimmel'	LBar NGdn
nanus	GEdr
philadelphicus	CElw NBro
PINK JEWEL	see *E.* 'Rosa Juwel'
pinnatisectus	GArf
'Profusion'	see *E. karvinskianus*
pumilus	WGoo
pyrenaicus misapplied	see *E. alpinus*
'Quakeress'	CTtf ERCP ESgI GMaP GQue LBar MBel MHol MNrw NGdn SBeP SHar SMHy SMrm StAn WFar
§ 'Rosa Juwel'	EHeP ELan EPfP EUrb GMaP LRHS MCtn NBir SBeP SPoG SRms WCAu WFar
'Rotes Meer'	CMac EBee LBar
rotundifolius	see *Bellis caerulescens*
'Caerulescens'	
salsuginosus misapplied	see *Eurybia sibirica*
§ 'Schneewittchen' ♀H5	CCBP EBee ELan EPfP LRHS MArl MBel MBNS MHol NCth SRms
§ 'Schwarzes Meer'	ELon WCot
scopulinus	EDAr EPot GEdr WAbe
SNOW WHITE	see *E.* 'Schneewittchen'
'Sommerabend'	LBar NSti
'Sommerneuschnee'	EBee LBar MNrw NDov WCAu
'Synehurst'	WCot WFar
trifidus	see *E. compositus* var. *discoideus*
uniflorus	SRms
vagus	WHil
'Violetta'	SPoG
'Wayne Roderick'	EGren ELan LSou LSto MHol MPro WFar
'White Quakeress'	CFis ESgI LSto SBeP SMrm WCot WFar

Erinacea (Fabaceae)

§ *anthyllis*	EDAr GArf
pungens	see *E. anthyllis*

Erinus (Plantaginaceae)

alpinus ♀H6	EDAr EPot GAbr GJos GKev MAsh NBir SLee SRms WIce
- var. *albus*	EDAr GJos SRms
- 'Doktor Hähnle'	EDAr GJos SRms WHil

Eriobotrya (Rosaceae)

from northern Vietnam	WPGP
'Coppertone'	see × *Rhaphiobotrya* 'Coppertone'
deflexa	EUrb WJur
elliptica var. *petelotii* BWJ 16323	WCru
japonica (F) ♀H4	CBct CDoC CMCN CTsd EGren EGrI ELan EPfP EUrb LMaj MGos MMuc NPlm SArc SFol SPlb SSta WJur WKor WPGP
- 'Mrs Cookson' (F)	CAgr WMat
- 'Oliver' (F)	CAgr WMat
- 'Rose-Anne' (F)	LEdu SChF WPGP

Eriobotrya × *Rhaphiolepis* see × *Rhaphiobotrya*

Eriocapitella see *Anemone*

Eriocephalus (Asteraceae)

africanus	SPlb WJek

Eriogonum (Polygonaceae)

caespitosum	WAbe
fasciculatum	GKev WMal
ovalifolium Wellington form	GEdr
umbellatum	GKev
- var. *humistratum*	SLee WAbe
wrightii var. *subscaposum*	GKev

Eriolarynx (Solanaceae)

§ *australis* ♀H3	CBcs CSpe EAri ELan LSRN NGKo NSti SAth SDix SEND SIvy SPlb SPoG WCot WFar WPGP
§ - 'Andean Snow'	CHll CSpe EShb NGKo WPGP
§ - 'Bill Evans'	CHll
- blue-flowered	see *E. australis* 'Bill Evans'
- white-flowered	see *E. australis* 'Andean Snow'

Eriophorum (Cyperaceae)

angustifolium	CBen CLil CoPl CPud CTtf CWat ELin EWat LCro MWts SPlb WMAq
- subsp. *angustifolium*	ELin
chamissonis	CWat ELin
rousseauianum	CTtf
vaginatum	EWat MCtn

Eriophyllum (Asteraceae)

lanatum	ECha EPfP SHar WMal

Eriostemon (Rutaceae)

myoporoides	see *Philotheca myoporoides*

Eriosyce (Cactaceae)

napina **new**	SPlb
taltalensis violet-flowered	SPlb

Eritrichium (Boraginaceae)

aretioides	SPlb

Erodium ✿ (Geraniaceae)

absinthoides	EPot
- var. *amanum*	see *E. amanum*

Eryngium

§	*acaule*	ECha EPPr		
	'Almodovar'	WCot WFar	'Robertino'	WAbe
§	*amanum*	GMaP MPnt	*romanum*	see *E. acaule*
	'Anna's Fairy'	EDAr	*rupestre*	SRms WIce
	'Ardwick Redeye'	MNrw	'Spanish Eyes'	EPfP LRHS LShi MPnt MPri NDov SLee SMad SRot WAbe WCot WFar
	balearicum	see *E.* × *variabile* 'Joe Elliott'	'Special Rose'	ECha EDAr EPot MNrw SLee WFar
	'Caroline'	WHoo	'Stephanie'	ELan EWes LShi MHer MMuc MNrw NLar WAbe WIce
	carvifolium	GKev		
§	*castellanum*	SMrm	'Tiny Kyni'	WFar
	- 'La Féline'	MNrw	'Toni's Surprise'	EDAr
	celtibericum	EPot	*trichomanifolium* misapplied	see *E. cheilanthifolium*
	chamaedryoides	see *E. reichardii*		
	- 'Roseum'	see *E.* × *variabile* 'Roseum'	§ *trifolium*	CWal MHer
§	*cheilanthifolium*	SLee SRot	× *variabile*	WFar
	- 'White Pearls'	EPot	- 'Album'	see *E.* × *variabile* 'Joe Elliott'
	chrysanthum	CAby ECha EDAr EGrI ELan EPot EWoo LShi MMuc MPnt NLar SEND SLee WKif WMal	- 'Bishop's Form'	see *E.* × *variabile* 'William Bishop'
			- 'Candy'	MHer
	- (f)	EPot GQue LBar MNrw SRot WFar	- 'Flore Pleno' (d)	EDAr ELan EPfP EPot EWes LRHS MHer SLee SPoG SRms SRot WFar
	- (m)	NRya		
	'County Park'	ECha SHar SRms WFar	§ - 'Joe Elliott'	EDAr EGren EPfP EPot GKev GMaP LRHS LShi MHer SRms SRot WAbe
	daucoides misapplied	see *E. castellanum*		
	daucoides ambig.	GKev	§ - 'Roseum' ♀H5	EGren ELan EWoo LRHS SLee SPlb SRms StAn
	'Felicity'	SHar		
	foetidum hybrids	SRot	§ - 'William Bishop'	CSpe ECha EDAr EGren EPfP EPot GJos GMaP LCro LRHS LShi MAsh MHol MPri NQui SPoG SRms SRot WAbe WFar WHoo WIce
	'Fran's Delight'	EDAr EPot MNrw MPnt WAbe WFar WHoo		
	'Freedom'	WFar		
	'Fripetta'	WIce		
	'Gini's Choice'	WCot		

Erpetion see *Viola*

Eruca (Brassicaceae)

§	*glandulosum* ♀H5	EBee MMuc SEND SLee SRms WAbe WFar WKif
	'Grey Blush'	WKif
	guttatum misapplied	see *E.* 'Katherine Joy'
	guttatum (Desf.) Willd.	CWGN ESgI EWoo GMaP MPnt NLar SRms WFar

	vesicaria	EHet ENfk MCtn
	- subsp. *sativa*	EHet LCro MHer MNHC SRms SVic
	- - 'Astra'	MCtn
	- - 'Dragon's Tongue'	MCtn
	- - 'Victoria' **new**	MNHC
	- - 'Wild'	EHet MCtn

Eryngium ✿ (Apiaceae)

	hymenodes L'Hér.	see *E. trifolium*
	'Jen's Jewel' **new**	EDAr
	'Julie Ritchie'	WHoo
§	'Katherine Joy'	EDAr LShi MHer MWlw SRot WFar
	× *kolbianum*	SMHy WAbe WCot WFar WHoo
	- 'Natasha'	ELan EPot EWes MHer MMuc MNrw SRot WIce WKif
	'Las Meninas'	WCot
	'Linda's Love'	EDAr
	× *lindavicum*	MHer
	macradenum	see *E. glandulosum*
	'Maisey'	EDAr
	manescavii ♀H5	Widely available
	'Marchants Mikado'	WKif
	'Maryla'	ESgI MPnt WFar WIce
	'Matilda's Purple'	EDAr
	'Merstham Pink'	SRms
	'Milly'	EDAr
	'Oliver's Cup'	EDAr
	pelargoniiflorum	CAby CCht CSpe ELan EMor EWoo GKev LShi NCou SAko SBeP SDix SMrm SRms SRot WFar WHil WTor
	'Peter Vernon'	MHer MNrw
	petraeum subsp. *crispum* misapplied	see *E. cheilanthifolium*
	-subsp. *petraeum*	EPot
	'Pickering Puzzle'	EDAr
	'Pippa Mills'	EDAr MNrw WAbe
	'Princesse Marion'	MNrw
	'Purple Haze'	ELan EMor EPfP LRHS SLee SRms WFar
§	*reichardii*	MBrN SPoG SRms WCav
	- 'Album'	EPfP LCro LRHS MAsh SLee SPoG WFar WHoo
	- 'Bianca'	ELan EPfP

§	*agavifolium*	CAby CBcs CBWd CDoC CDor CSde CSpe EBee ECha ELan EMor EPfP EPPr EUrb GKev GMaP GQue LRHS MArl MHol NLar SDix SEND SNoN SPlb SPoG SRms WCAu WCot WFar
	- giant	WPGP
	alpinum	CSpe ECha EGren EMor GBin GMaP LBar NBir SRms WCAu WFar
	- 'Blue Jackpot'	EBee EWes MNrw
	- 'Blue Star'	ELan GJos GPSL MBel NLar StAn WCAu WFar WSpi XFar
§	- 'Donard Variety'	MAvo
	- 'Slieve Donard'	see *E. alpinum* 'Donard Variety'
	- 'Superbum'	SRms
	amethystinum	ELan SPhx
	biebersteinianum	see *E. caeruleum*
	bourgatii	CDor EArl EBee ECha EDAr ELan ELon EMor EPfP EWhm GJos GKev GMaP LBom LCro LRHS LSto MCtn Midl MSwo NBro NGdn NLar SEND SHor SMHy SRms StAn WCAu WMal
	- 'GST Selected'	CDor CSpe EBee GAbr NBir SRms WCAu WCot WHoo WSpi
	- 'Lapis Blue'	CBcs IPot LRHS NSti SHar
	- Picos Amethyst ('Mackpam'PBR)	CBcs CSde EBee EGren EMor EPfP LBar LCro LRHS LSto MArl MAvo MHol Midl NLar SRkn SRms WCAu WNPC
	- 'Picos Blue'PBR ♀H5	CAby CBcs EBee EGren ELan EMor EPfP EUrb LBom LCro MBel MHer

Eryngium

		MHol Midl NDov NLar SAth WCAu WKif WPGP		MHol Midl MSwo NLar SPad SPoG SRms WCot
bromeliifolium misapplied	see *E. agavifolium*, *E. eburneum*		- (Magical Series) MAGICAL ANITA ('Kolmanita'^{PBR})	LRHS MBNS MHol NLar
§ *caeruleum*	GQue		- - MAGICAL BLUE FALLS ('Kolmbufa'^{PBR})	NCth
campestre	GKev SPhx		- - MAGICAL BLUE GLOBE ('Kolmaglo')	LRHS NCth NLar
caucasicum	see *E. caeruleum*		- - MAGICAL PURPLE FALLS ('Kolmapufa'^{PBR})	MHol NCth NLar
cymosum	ELan		- - MAGICAL SILVER ('Kolmagsil'^{PBR})	NCth NLar XFar
- B&SWJ 10267	WCru		- - MAGICAL SYMPHONY ('Kolmasy')	EPfP MHol NCth NLar
decaisneanum misapplied	see *E. pandanifolium*		- - MAGICAL WHITE FALLS ('Kolmwhifal')	LRHS MHol NLar
ebracteatum	CSpe EPPr WPGP		- 'Paradise Jackpot'^{PBR}	SRms
- var. *poterioides*	LCro SMHy		- 'Seven Seas'	MArl MAsh MBNS
§ *eburneum*	CFis CSde ECha EGrI EPfP EWes GMaP SHor SMHy WTre		- 'Silver Salentino'	GPSL
- 'Fromefield Rapier'	ELan		- 'Silver Stone'	SRms
foetidum	MCtn WJek		- 'Tetra Petra'	SRms WMal
§ *giganteum* ♀^{H6}	CBcs CDor CSpe EAri EBee ECha EGren EGrI ELan EPfP LCro LEdu LSto MCtn MNrw MPri NBir NGdn NLar SDix SMHy SPhx SRms WCAu WFar WSpi WTre		- 'Tiny Jackpot'	NLar
			- 'Victory Blue'	XFar
			- 'White Glitter'	ELan EPfP EPPr MCtn SPoG
			proteiflorum	CDor SPlb WFar
- 'Silver Ghost' ♀^{H6}	CDor CSpe CTtf EPfP GBin GMaP GQue LBom LCro MCtn Midl MPro NDov NGdn NLar SMrm SPhx WCot WFar WSpi		*serbicum*	GBin
			serra	CBcs LRHS
			spinalba	GKev
'Grumpy'	LBar Midl		*tricuspidatum*	CDoC EPfP
guatemalense B&SWJ 10397	ESwi WCru		× *tripartitum* ♀^{H5}	EBee ECha EGren LSRN MArl MNrw NBro WCAu WHoo
horridum misapplied	see *E. eburneum*		*variifolium*	Widely available
horridum ambig.	ECha NLar SArc		- 'Miss Marble'	EPfP IPot LShi SRms WFar
horridum Malme	WCot		*venustum*	EUrb GGro SPhx WPGP
humboldtii B&SWJ 14342	WCru		*vesiculosum*	SPlb
humile	MHol		*yuccifolium*	CBWd CSpe CTtf EBee ECha EMor GKev LCro MAvo MCtn NLar SDix SHor SMHy SPeP SPhx SPlb WCAu WTor
- var. *brevibracteatum* B&SWJ 14735	WCru			
longifolium B&SWJ 14786	WCru			
(Magical Series) MAGICAL BLUE LAGOON ('Kolmblula'^{PBR})	LBar LRHS MHol NLar SRkn		- 'Kershaw Blue'	WPGP
- MAGICAL WHITE LAGOON ('Kolmwhila'^{PBR}) **new**	Midl		- MAGICAL GREEN GLOBE ('Kolmgrobe'^{PBR}) (Magical Series)	LRHS NCth
maritimum	CSpe EGren MCtn SPlb SRms		× *zabelii*	ECha
Miss Willmott's ghost	see *E. giganteum*		- BIG BLUE ('Myersblue'^{PBR}) ♀^{H5}	Widely available
× *olivierianum* ♀^{H5}	NBir SPoG WCot		- 'Blue Waves'	LRHS WHoo
§ *pandanifolium* ♀^{H4}	EAri EBee EWes MNrw SArc SMad SMHy SNoN SPlb SPoG WPGP		- 'Cobalt Star'	SMHy
- 'Physic Purple'	CAby CDor CSpe EBee IPot SDix SHor SMrm SNoN WCot WPGP WSpi		- 'Forncett Ultra'	MNrw
			- 'Jos Eijking'	CBcs CDor EBee ELon EMor EPfP GMaP IPot LBar LCro LRHS LSou LSRN LSto MArl MAvo MBel NCth NLar NSti SMHy SPel SPoG WCAu WCot WHoo
paniculatum	ECha EWes			
- B&SWJ 14367	WCru			
- B&SWJ 14826	WCru			
planum	CBcs CDor CGHo CSde CWal EBee ECha EGren ELan EPfP GJos GMaP LRHS LSto MCtn MGos MHer NLit NMir SBeP SMHy SMrm SPlb SPoG SRms WCAu WCav WFar WRBe WTre		- 'Neptune's Gold'^{PBR}	CBcs CDoC CWGN EBee EPfP GMaP LBar LCro LSou MArl MHol Midl MSwo NBro NCou NEoE NLar NSti SHar SPeP SPoG WNPC
§ - 'Blauer Zwerg'	EGren GMaP LRHS NLar WFar		- 'Pen Blue'	CBWd CDor CSpe EPfP LBar LRHS MBel MGos MHol Midl MNrw NLar SAko SPel SPoG WCAu WCot WFar WHoo WTor
- 'Blaukappe'	EBee ECha ELan EPfP GJos LSto MMuc SDix SEND SRms WFar			
- BLUE DWARF	see *E. planum* 'Blauer Zwerg'		- 'Violetta'	CDor CSpe EBee ECha ELon EMor EPfP LBar Midl MNrw NLar SPel WCAu WFar WTor
- 'Blue Glitter'	CDor CWal EPPr GElm GJos MCtn MPie WHil			
- 'Blue Hobbit'	EBee EDAr EGren ELan EPfP GJos LBuc LRHS LShi MCtn MGos MNrw MPro NGdn NLar NQui NRya SMad SRms WCAu WFar			

Erysimum (Brassicaceae)

- 'Flüela'	CCBP EPfP EWes GPSL LRHS LSRN MArl SMrm SPel WFar
- 'Jade Frost'^{PBR} (v)	CBcs CDor CWGN EBee ELan EMor EWes GJos LBar LCro LRHS MBNS

allionii misapplied	see *E.* × *marshallii*
alpinum misapplied	see *E. hieraciifolium*
'Apricot Delight'	see *E.* 'Apricot Twist'

Erysimum 269

§ 'Apricot Twist'	CBcs CWCL CWGN EGren ELan EPfP GElm GMaP LBar LRHS LShi MAsh Midl MPri MPro NLar SPoG SRms WCav WFar WHoo WMal	'Moonlight'	GMaP SRms SRot WHoo
		§ 'Mrs L.K. Elmhirst'	NPer
		mutabile	ECha EPfP LRHS LShi LWaG MCtn LBar NLar
		'Night Skies' (Sky Series)	LBar NLar
		'Orange Flame'	ECha EPot GArf LShi NPer WHoo
arkansanum	see *E. helveticum*	Orange Zwerg ('Inneryoz'PBR)	LRHS WIce
'Audrey's Pink'	CCBP ESgI WCot WMal		
'Bowles's Mauve' ♀H4	Widely available	'Paint Box' (Artist Series)	LBar LRHS Midl MPro
'Bowles's Purple'	SRms	'Parish's'	CCBP CElw CFis CSpe ESgI LShi WChS WMal
'Bowles's Yellow'	LShi WCot		
'Bredon'	LShi NPer WKif WMal	'Pastel Patchwork'	ECha LCro MPro
'Canaries Yellow'	LRHS LShi	Perry's hybrid	NPer
'Caribbean Island'	LShi	'Perry's Peculiar'	NPer
cheiri	EHet LShi MCtn MHer MPri	'Perry's Surprise'	NPer
- from Prospect Cottage **new**	CSpe	'Perry's Variegated' (v)	NPer
- 'Baden-Powell' (d)	EPPr	*pieninicum*	LShi
- 'Bedder Primrose' (Brilliant Bedder Series)	MCtn	'Plant World Lemon'	LBar Midl MMrt MPro NLar
		Poem Lavender ('Inerypolav'PBR)	LRHS MPri
- 'Blood Red'	LCro		
- 'Bloody Warrior' (d)	EBee ESgI WCot WKif WMal	Poem Lilac ('Inerypolil'PBR)	LRHS MPri
- 'Cloth of Gold'	MCtn	§ *pulchellum*	ECha GKev
- Fair Lady Mixed	MCtn	*pumilum* DC.	see *E. helveticum*
- 'Fire King'	LCro	'Red Jep'	CDoC EGren ELan EPfP GBin LCro LRHS LShi MPro SAdn WCot WFar WKif WTor
- 'Gold Dust'	LRHS		
- 'Harpur Crewe' (d)	CFis EBee ESgI LShi NPer SRms WHer WMal		
		rupestre	see *E. pulchellum*
- 'Ivory White'	GQue MCtn	'Ruston Royal'	ESgI
- Persian Carpet (mixed) ♀H5	EGren LCro MCtn	Rysi Copper	EPfP LRHS SPoG
- 'Scarlet Bedder'	CWal MCtn	Rysi Moon ('Inneryrysimoon')	MPro
- Sunset Series	MPri		
- 'Vulcan'	CWal LCro MCtn	*scoparium*	LShi WMal
'Chelsea Jacket'	MMrt	'Sissinghurst Variegated'	see *E. linifolium* 'Variegatum'
Colour Vibe Red ('Cdcery1')	EGren MPro	'Spring Breeze Copper'	EGren Midl MPro
'Constant Cheer'	CBcs ELan LBar LRHS LShi MAvo MPro NDov NLar NPer NQui SPoG SRGP SRms WHoo WMal WSpi	'Spring Breeze Sunglow'	Midl MPro
		'Spring Breeze Sunset'	EGren EPfP LCro MHtn Midl MPro
		'Sprite'	NPer SEND
Coral ('Er0509-01') (Glow Series)	LRHS	Sugar Rush Series	EGren MCtn SPoG
		- 'Sugar Rush Orange' **new**	LCro
'Cotswold Gem' (v)	MHer NPer	- 'Sugar Rush Primrose'	LCro
'Desert Island'	LShi	- 'Sugar Rush Purple Bicolor'	MCtn
'Dorothy Elmhirst'	see *E.* 'Mrs L.K. Elmhirst'		
'Early Sunrise' (Sky Series)	MPro	- 'Sugar Rush Red'	CSpe LCro MCtn
'Gogh's Gold' (Artist Series)	LRHS LShi NLar WMal	Sunburst ('Listrace') (v)	CWCL LShi WCot
'Gold Shot'	MCtn	'Sweet Sorbet'	NLar
'Golden Jubilee'	LRHS SRms WCav WIce	* 'Tricolor'	LWaG
§ *helveticum*	LShi SRms	'Variegatum' ambig. (v)	SRot
§ *hieraciifolium*	LShi	Walberton's Fragrant Star ('Walfrastar'PBR) (v)	EGren EPfP LRHS MAsh SPoG SRms
'Jacob's Jacket'	LSto NPer		
'John Codrington'	LShi NPer WSpi	Walberton's Fragrant Sunshine ('Walfrasun')	EGren EPfP LRHS MPri MPro SPoG WCot
kotschyanum	GEdr LShi SRms WAbe WIce		
'Lady Roborough'	NQui	(WallArt Series) WallArt Berry Lemonade ('Doerywaberlem')	LRHS MPri
'Lemon Light'	EPot WHoo		
linifolium	SRms	- WallArt Pearl ('Doerywape')	LRHS MPri
- 'Bowles me Away'	LBar LRHS MPro		
- 'Little Kiss Lilac'	MCtn	- WallArt Pink Lemonade ('Doerywapilem')	LRHS MPri
- Stars 'N' Stripes ('Yastrip'PBR) (v)	EGren LRHS MHol MPro		
		'Wenlock Beauty'	CFis SRms
- (Sunstrong Series) 'Sunstrong Bicolor Purple'	EGren	Winter Charme ('Inerywicha')	EPfP SRot
- - 'Sunstrong Violet'	MPro	'Winter Joy'	ELan
- Super Bowl Mauve ('Erfz0001')	LBar LRHS	'Winter Light'	MPro
		Winter Orchid ('Innerywinorch')	CWGN EPfP GMaP LCro LRHS MPri MPro
- Super Bowl Sunset ('Erfz0002')	LRHS		
		'Winter Party'	LCro
§ - 'Variegatum' (v)	CFis EDAr ELan EPfP LShi NPer SHar SMad SPoG	'Winter Passion'	CWCL EPfP LCro LRHS MPri MPro NLar SPoG
- - peach-flowered (v)	LRHS		
§ × *marshallii*	LShi	Winter Power ('Inerywipow')	MPri
'Monet's Moment' (Artist Series)	LShi Midl SPoG	Winter Sorbet ('Inneryws'PBR)	ELan Midl

Erythraea see *Centaurium*

Erythrina (Fabaceae)
abyssinica	SPlb
amazonica	SPlb
arborescens	SPlb
crista-galli ♀H3	CBcs CDTJ CHll CSpe EAri ELan
	EPfP EShb LRHS SArc SChF SEND
	SPlb
flabelliformis	SPlb
guatemalensis	SPlb
herbacea	SPlb
§ *humeana*	SPlb
latissima	SPlb
lysistemon	SPlb
madagascariensis new	SPlb
princeps	see *E. humeana*
rubrinervia	SPlb
speciosa	SPlb
vespertilio	SPlb

Erythronium ✿ (Liliaceae)
americanum	EPot GKev LAma WAbe
'Bryn Meifod'	WAbe
californicum	EBee ENun GKev LEdu MAvo
- 'White Beauty' ♀H5	Widely available
caucasicum	GKev
'Citronella'	CMiW MAvo
'Craigton Cover Girl'	GMaP
dens-canis	CAby CBro CTtf ECha EGren ELan
	EMor EPot ETay GEdr GKev GMaP
	ISha LCro LEdu MCtn MNrw NBir
	SBeP SDix WAbe WShi
- 'Charmer'	GEdr MNrw
- 'Frans Hals'	GEdr GKev LAma LEdu WAbe
- 'Lilac Wonder' ♀H5	EBee EGrl EPot GEdr GKev GMaP
	LAma MNrw MPie XFar
- var. *niveum*	GEdr
- 'Old Aberdeen' ♀H5	EBee ENun LRHS MAsh
- 'Pink Perfection'	EBee GEdr GKev LAma LEdu MNrw
	WAbe
- 'Purple King'	EBee EGren EPot GEdr GKev GMaP
	LAma LEdu MNrw
- 'Rose Queen'	EGrl EPot GKev GMaP MNrw
- 'Snowflake'	EMor ENun EPot GEdr GKev LAma
	LRHS MAsh MNrw NBir WAbe
- 'Valerie Wollaston'	MAvo
- 'White Splendour'	MNrw
'Harvington Elizabeth'	ENun
'Harvington Imogen'	ENun
'Harvington Lilli'	ENun
'Harvington Snowgoose'	ENun MAsh
'Harvington Sunshine'	ENun LRHS MAsh
hendersonii ♀H5	CTtf ENun SPlb
'Hidcote Beauty'	ENun
howellii	ENun LRHS
'Janice' ♀H5	GEdr
japonicum	CMiW EMor LAma
'Jeannine'	CMiW WAbe
'Joanna' ♀H4	CMiW CTtf LAma MNrw WAbe
'Kinfauns Pink'	EBee GEdr GKev GMaP LAma
'Kondo'	EPfP ETay NBir LAma
'Margaret Mathew'	MAvo
'Minnehaha'	MAvo
oregonum	ENun EPot GKev LRHS MAsh MCtn
	MNrw
'Pagoda' ♀H5	Widely available
revolutum	CBro CTtf EPot GEdr GMaP MCtn
	MNrw NHar
- from God's Valley, Oregon	MAvo MNrw

- Johnsonii Group	MCtn
- 'Knightshayes'	LRHS MAsh
- 'Knightshayes Pink'	ENun MAsh WShi
- 'Pink Beauty'	GKev
- 'Wild Salmon'	ENun MAsh
sibiricum	LAma
subsp. *altaicum*	
'Sundisc' ♀H4	CBro ECha EPot
'Susannah'	ENun
tuolumnense	CBro CMiW EAri EPPr GEdr GKev
	GMaP LAma MCor MNrw
- 'Spindlestone'	CMiW ENun GEdr LRHS MAsh

Erythrostemon (Fabaceae)
§ *gilliesii* ♀H3	CBcs SPlb WCot WJur

Escallonia (Escalloniaceae)
'Apple Blossom' ♀H4	Widely available
§ *bifida* ♀H3	CMCN ELan EPfP EWes LRHS MAsh
	SDix WPGP
'C.F. Ball'	LRHS SRms
'Dart's Rosy Red'	MSwo
'Donard Beauty'	CBrac SRms
'Donard Brilliance'	SRms
'Donard Radiance' ♀H4	CBrac CEnd CMac EHeP ELan EPfP
	NLar SPoG SRms WFar
'Donard Seedling'	CBrac EGren EHeP EPfP GArf LRHS
	LSto MAsh MGos MMuc MSCN
	NPer SRms WFar
'Donard Star'	NLar
'Donard White'	SPoG
'Edinensis'	NLar SRms WSpi
× *exoniensis*	SRms
Glowing Embers	EPfP LCro LRHS MAsh MPri WHtc
('Lowat21'PBR)	
Golden Carpet	ELan EPfP LRHS MHtn SPoG
('Alcaura'PBR)	
'Good as Gold'	LSou NLar
'Hopleys Gold'	see *E. laevis* 'Gold Brian'
'Iveyi' ♀H4	CBcs CBrac CCoa CDoC CEnd
	CMac CMCN CSBt CSpe EGren
	ELan EPfP GKin LCro LRHS LSRN
	MAsh MMuc MSwo SAth SEND
	SPlb SPoG SRms WKif
§ *laevis*	NLar
§ - 'Gold Brian'	CMac MAsh MGos
- 'Gold Ellen' (v)	CDoC CSBt EGren ELan ELon EPfP
	LRHS MAsh MGos MPri NLar NLit
	SNig SPoG SRms
- Pink Elle ('Lades'PBR)	CDoC CSBt EGren ELan EPfP LCro
	LRHS LSou MAsh MGos NLit NWbg
	SPoG WFar
'Langleyensis' ♀H4	SRms
montevidensis	see *E. bifida*
myrtilloides	WCru
B&SWJ 14329	
organensis	see *E. laevis*
'Peach Blossom' ♀H4	CBcs CDoC CEnd EHeP ELan EPfP
	LRHS MAsh MMuc SRms WFar
'Pink Carpet'	NLar
'Pride of Donard' ♀H4	CSBt EHeP SRms
'Red Dream'	CSBt EGren EHeP ELan EPfP LRHS
	MAsh MGos MHed NWbg SPoG
	SRms WFar
'Red Elf'	CMac EHeP ELan GKin LRHS MAsh
	MGos NLar SPlb SRms WFar
'Red Hedger'	CTsd EHeP LRHS SRms
'Red Knight'	NLar
resinosa	CExl CMCN CTsd SPlb SRms SVen
	WPav
revoluta	WPav

Eucalyptus 271

rubra 'Crimson Spire' ♀H4	CBcs CBrac CEnd CSBt EHeP GKin LRHS LSRN MAsh MGos MMuc MPri SEND SNig SPlb SRms		*dalrympleana* ♀H5	CDoC ELan EUrb IPap MMuc NPer SEND SPlb WGrf WPGP
- 'Ingramii'	EHeP SEND		*deanei*	WGrf
- var. *macrantha*	CBcs CBrac CDoC CEnd CMac CSBt EHeP ELan EPfP GArf GKin IArd LRHS MHed SNig SPoG SRms		*debeuzevillei*	see *E. pauciflora* subsp. *debeuzevillei*
			deglupta	WGrf
- 'Woodside'	SRms		*delegatensis*	NPer WGrf
SHOWSTOPPER ('Pmoore20')	ELon LSou NLar		*denticulata*	SVen WGrf
'Silver Anniversary'	MSwo		*deuaensis*	WGrf
'Slieve Donard'	CBrac CMac EHeP SRms		*divaricata*	see *E. gunnii* subsp. *divaricata*
tucumanensis	CBcs SPlb		*elliptica*	WGrf
'Ventnor'	SPlb SVen		*erythrocorys*	SPlb
virgata	WPav		*eximia*	see *Corymbia eximia*
			fastigiata	WGrf
			fraxinoides	SPlb

Eschscholzia (Papaveraceae)

caespitosa 'Sundew'	MCtn		*gamophylla*	SPlb
californica	LWaG MBel MCtn NClf		*glaucescens*	CAbb LRHS SArc WGrf
- 'Alba'	CSpe MCtn		- from Mount Franklin, Australia **new**	WGrf
- 'Apricot Chiffon' (Thai Silk Series) ♀H3	LCro MCtn		- 'Guthega' **new**	WGrf
- 'Carmine King'	MCtn		- 'Tinderry' **new**	WGrf
- 'Ivory Castle'	LCro MCtn SHor SPhx		*globulus* ♀H3	SPlb WKit
- var. *maritima*	CSpe WHil		- subsp. *bicostata*	WGrf
- 'Mikado'	MCtn		- coastal	WGrf
- 'Milkmaid' (Thai Silk Series)	MCtn		*goniocalyx*	WGrf
- 'Mission Bells'	GJem LCro		§ *gregsoniana*	CTsd EBee EPfP SPlb WGrf WPGP
- 'Orange King'	LCro MCtn SPhx		*gunnii* ♀H5	Widely available
- 'Peach Sorbet'	CSpe LCro		- AZURA ('Cagire'PBR)	CBTr CDoC CMac CSBt EPfP LCro LRHS LSRN NLar NPip SEWo WGrf WMat
- 'Purple Gleam'	MCtn			
- 'Red Chief'	CSpe MCtn MNrw SHor SPhx		- 'Blue Ice'	CAbb EGren
'Jelly Beans'	MCtn		§ - subsp. *divaricata*	CTsd EBee ELan WGrf
			- FRANCE BLEU ('Rengun'PBR)	CBcs CDoC CWnw EBee EGren ELan LBom LRHS LSRN MPri NLar SAth SBig WGrf

Escobaria (Cactaceae)

roseana	SPlb		* - 'Silver Drop'	CSBt SWor WFar
sneedii	SPlb		- SILVERANA ('Lon40')	CBcs CMac CWnw EBee ELan EPfP LBom LRHS MPri WCha WGrf
- subsp. *leei*	NCft			
zilziana	SPlb		*johnstonii*	WGrf
			kitsoniana	WGrf

Espostoa (Cactaceae)

blossfeldiorum	NCft		*kruseana*	SPlb
guentheri	see *Vatricania guentheri*		*kybeanensis*	WGrf
lanata ♀H2	LWaG NPlm SPlb		*lacrimans*	WGrf
melanostele subsp. *nana*	NPlm		*leucoxylon*	SAth
			- subsp. *megalocarpa*	SPlb WGrf
			ligustrina	WGrf

Esterhuysenia (Aizoaceae)

alpina	EAri SPlb		'Little Boy Blue'	WGrf
			macrocarpa	SPlb WGrf
			mitchelliana	WGrf

Eucalyptus ✿ (Myrtaceae)

aggregata	SArc WGrf		'Moon Lagoon'	WGrf
alpina	SPlb		*moorei*	ELan
amygdalina	SPlb WGrf		- var. *moorei*	WGrf
apiculata	WGrf		*neglecta*	WGrf
approximans	WGrf		- 'Dargo Plains'	WGrf
archeri	CAbb CDoC CTsd MHtn WGrf		*nicholii*	CAbb CBcs CDoC CSpe CTsd ELan EUrb SPoG WGrf
badjensis **new**	WGrf			
boliviana	WGrf		*niphophila*	see *E. pauciflora* subsp. *niphophila*
§ *bridgesiana*	MHtn WGrf		*nitens*	EUrb SArc SPlb SVen WGrf
caesia ♀H2	SPlb		*nitida*	WGrf
- subsp. *magna*	WGrf		*nova-anglica*	WGrf
camaldulensis	SPlb WCha WGrf		*obliqua*	WGrf
camphora	WGrf		*ovata*	WGrf
chapmaniana **new**	WGrf		*paliformis*	WGrf
cinerea	MCtn SFol SPlb WGrf		*parvula* ♀H5	GAbr LRHS MCtn MMuc SEND WGrf
citriodora	see *Corymbia citriodora*			
coccifera	CDoC EBee EPfP EUrb NPer SArc SPlb SVen WGrf		*pauciflora*	EBee MCtn NPip SAth
			- subsp. *acerina*	WGrf
cordata	CDoC EBee EPfP WGrf		§ - subsp. *debeuzevillei* ♀H5	CTsd EBee EPfP EUrb SArc WGrf WPGP
crenulata	WGrf			
crucis subsp. *crucis*	SPlb		- subsp. *hedraia*	WGrf
cypellocarpa	SPlb		- var. *nana*	see *E. gregsoniana*

§ - subsp. **niphophila** ♀H5	CBcs CDoC CEnd EBee EHeP ELan EPfP IPap LCro LRHS LSRN MBlu MGos MHtn SPlb SPoG WGrf WMat WPGP
- - from Mount Bogong, Australia	WGrf
- subsp. **pauciflora**	WGrf
- - from Mount Buffalo, Australia	WGrf
perriniana	CBcs EHeP ELan EUrb MGos MHtn NPip SPlb SPoG WGrf WMat
pulchella	EBee WGrf
pulverulenta	SPlb WGrf
- 'Baby Blue'	CBcs CBrac ELan EUrb LCro LRHS MCtn MHtn WGrf WKit
regnans	WGrf
risdonii	CTsd SAth WGrf
robusta	SFol WGrf
rodwayi	SVen WGrf
rossii	SPlb
rubida	WGrf
saligna	WGrf
saxatilis	WGrf
scoparia	WGrf
'Shannon Blue'	WGrf
sideroxylon	SPlb WGrf
- 'Rosea'	SPlb
smithii	WGrf
stellulata	WGrf
stricta	WGrf
stuartiana	see *E. bridgesiana*
sturgissiana	WGrf
subcrenulata	CDoC CTsd EUrb WGrf
tetraptera	SPlb WGrf
torquata	SPlb
urnigera	SVen WGrf
vernicosa	WGrf
viminalis	SAth
youmanii	WGrf

Eucharidium see *Clarkia*

Eucharis (*Amaryllidaceae*)

§ **amazonica** ♀H1b	LAma XFar
grandiflora misapplied	see *E. amazonica*

Eucomis ✿ (*Asparagaceae*)

ALOHA	see *E.* 'Leia' (Aloha Lily Series)
autumnalis misapplied	see *E. zambesiaca*
- subsp. **amaryllidifolia**	CBro WCot
- subsp. **autumnalis**	LCro XFar
bicolor ♀H4	Widely available
I 'Black'	WHil
§ **comosa**	CBro CLil CTca EAri EBee GKev LAma MPie NGKo WCot
- 'Amelia'	CBro EBee GKev LAma SPel
- 'Can Can'	LRHS
- 'Cornwood'	CBro CTca EPPr XFar
- dark-stemmed	EPPr
- 'Hula'	GKev LAma
- 'Indian Summer'	CAby ERCP LRHS SPeP
- 'Johannesburg'	CBro WFar
- 'Loumy'	GKev LAma
- 'Millie'	ESwi LAma
- 'Oakhurst'	ESwi WCot WHil
- purple-leaved	CBlu
- 'Sparkling Burgundy'	Widely available
- 'Sparkling Rosy'	LCro NGKo SPoG WFar XFar
'Erundu'	WHil
'Etanga'	EGren
'Freckles'	EPPr SPoG SRms
'Glow Sticks'	CWGN
humilis 'Twinkle Stars'	EWld
'Joy's Purple'	CBro
§ 'Leia'PBR (Aloha Lily Series) ♀H4	ELan LAma LCro SArc
MAUI ('Gsalkele'PBR) (Aloha Lily Series)	EAri LCro
montana	CBlu CBro ERCP EWld LAma WCot
NANI ('Gsalipol'PBR) (Aloha Lily Series)	LCro LRHS
§ **pallidiflora**	CAby CBro CLil CTca EAri EBee EGrl ELan EPPr ERCP EShb EUrb GKev GQue LAma LEdu LRHS SBig SMHy SMad SMrm SPel SPeP WFar WHil WPGP
subsp. **pallidiflora**	
- - 'Goliath'	WCot
I - - 'Purpurea'	SMHy SMrm
- subsp. **pole-evansii** misapplied	see *E. pallidiflora* subsp. *pallidiflora*
'Pink Gin'	CBro SPel SPeP XFar
'Playa Blanca'	EBee EGren
punctata	see *E. comosa*
regia JCA 3.230.709	WCot
'Swazi Pride'	NGKo
vandermerwei ♀H3	CBlu CTca EBee EGrl EPot LAma LEdu SPlb
- 'Octopus'	ELan EUrb MMrt SMad WFar
§ **zambesiaca**	CBro CLil EAri EGren EPot ERCP ESwi GKev NGKo SPlb WCot
- JCA 3.231.010	WCot
- 'White Dwarf'	CBcs ESwi LAma WFar
'Zeal Bronze'	CMHG WCot

Eucommia (*Eucommiaceae*)

ulmoides	CBcs CMCN EBee WJur

Eucrosia (*Amaryllidaceae*)

Harry Hay's hybrid	WMal

Eucryphia ✿ (*Cunoniaceae*)

cordifolia	CBcs CMac MBlu NLar SArc SSta
cordifolia × **lucida**	see *E.* × *penwithensis*
glutinosa ♀H4	GKev WJur
× **hillieri**	WSpi
- 'Winton'	CBct EBee NLar SChF WPGP
× **intermedia**	CDoC CMac CTsd NLar SRms SSta
- 'Rostrevor' ♀H4	CBcs CMac CTsd EBee ELan EPfP GAbr GGGa GKev IArd LMil LSRN MAsh MBlu NCth NLar SArc SSta WPGP
'Leatherwood Cream' (v)	ELon WSpi
lucida	ELon MMuc NLar WJur WSpi
- 'Ballerina' ♀H4	CBcs CBct CJun CMac CMHG EAri EGrl ELan GKin LRHS MAsh SAko SChF SMad SPoG SSta WPGP
- 'Carousel'	LRHS
I - 'Chaplin's Variety'	WPGP
- 'Dumpling'	WPGP
- 'Gilt Edge' (v)	CBcs EAri NLar SPoG
- 'Pink Cloud'	CBcs CDoC CJun CMac CTsd EGrl ELan ELon EPfP EUrb GKin LSRN MBlu MGos NCth NLar SSta WPGP
- 'Spring Glow' (v)	MAsh NLar
- 'Variegata' (v)	LRHS
milliganii	CBcs CDoC CMac EBee EPfP GAbr MBlu SRms SSta WPGP WSpi
moorei	CBcs CMac WPGP
× **nymansensis**	CBct SArc SRms WSpi
- 'George Graham'	WPGP
- 'Nymans Silver' (v)	CBcs CDoC CJun CMac ELan MAsh SPoG SSta

- 'Nymansay' ⚥H4 — CBcs CDoC CLnd CMac CTsd EBee EGren EGrI ELan EPfP LMil LRHS LSRN MAsh MBlu MMuc NCth NLar SAth SDix SPoG SSta WFar WPGP
§ × *penwithensis* — SArc
- 'Penwith' ambig. — GKev NLar

Eudianthe (Caryophyllaceae)
§ *coeli-rosa* — MCtn
- 'Blue Angel' — CSpe SPhx

Eugenia ✿ (Myrtaceae)
pyriformis new — WJur
uniflora — WJur
- ETNA FIRE ('Pf1904') — EGrI
uruguayensis new — WJur

Eulychnia (Cactaceae)
acida — SBig

Euodia (Rutaceae)
daniellii — see *Tetradium daniellii*
hupehensis — see *Tetradium daniellii* Hupehense Group

Euonymus ✿ (Celastraceae)
acanthocarpus — WCru
  Og 07.425 new
aculeatus — WCru
alatus — Widely available
- B&SWJ 8794 — WCru
- 'Blade Runner' — CAco CDoC EPfP ESwi GKin LRHS MBlu MGos NLar SGol
- CHICAGO FIRE — see *E. alatus* 'Timber Creek'
- 'Ciliodentatus' — see *E. alatus* f. *striatus*
- 'Compactus' ⚥H6 — Widely available
- 'Fastigiata' — CJun
§ - 'Fire Ball' ⚥H6 — CJun
- 'Rudy Haag' — CJun EBee
- 'Select' — see *E. alatus* 'Fire Ball'
§ - f. *striatus* B&SWJ 11051 — ESwi WCru
§ - 'Timber Creek' — LCro MBlu
americanus — EPfP MBlu
- var. *angustifolius* — ESwi WCru
  B&SWJ 12905
'Benkomoki' — SAth
bungeanus — see *E. maackii*
§ *carnosus* ⚥H5 — CJun CMCN WJur
- CWJ 12425 — WCru
- NMWJ 14515 — WCru
- 'Belmonte' — CJun EPfP
- 'Red Wine' — CJun EBee EPfP MBlu WCot
- 'Trompenburg Lustre' — CJun
clivicola — CExl ELan EPfP ESwi WCru WPGP
aff. *clivicola* — EPfP
- HIRD 103 — SBrt
cornutus — ELan WJur WPGP
- var. *quinquecornutus* ⚥H6 — CMCN CSpe EPfP ESwi IArd MBlu SPoG WPGP
'Den Haag' — EPfP
europaeus — Widely available
- from Slovakia — WCru
- f. *albus* — EPPr NLar SMad
- 'Atropurpureus' — CMCN EPfP
- 'Aucubifolius' (v) — CMac
- 'Brilliant' — CJun EPfP
- 'Chrysophyllus' — EPfP MBlu
- var. *intermedius* — CJun EPfP MBlu NLar
- 'Miss Pinkie' — CEnd
- 'Red Cascade' ⚥H6 — Widely available
- 'Scarlet Wonder' — CJun EPfP NLar WMat

- 'Thornhayes' ⚥H6 — EPfP
farreri hort. — see *E. nanus*
fimbriatus — CMCN
fortunei BLONDY ('Interbolwi') (v) — CBcs CSBt ELan EPfP LCro LRHS MAsh MGos Midl MMuc SPoG SRms WCot
- 'Canadale Gold' (v) — CMac MAsh
- 'Coloratus' — EPfP MBlu SEND WFar
- 'Country Gold' (v) — WFar
- DAN'S DELIGHT ('Dandel'PBR) (v) — LCro LRHS SGol SPoG
- 'Dart's Blanket' — EBee EHeP ELan EPfP
- 'Dingle Gold' — WCot
- 'Emerald Cushion' — EHeP
- 'Emerald Gaiety' (v) ⚥H5 — Widely available
- 'Emerald 'n' Gold' (v) ⚥H5 — Widely available
- 'Gold Spot' — see *E. fortunei* 'Sunspot'
- 'Gold Tip' — see *E. fortunei* 'Golden Prince'
- GOLDEN HARLEQUIN ('Hoogi'PBR) (v) — CBcs CMac EBee LRHS SPoG
§ - 'Golden Prince' (v) — Midl SRms
- GOLDEN QUINTEN ('Djhen') (v) — IBal LSou
- GOLDY ('Waldbolwi'PBR) — LRHS Midl NLar SPoG
- 'Harlequin' (v) — CBcs CBrac CMac CSBt EGren LBuc LCro LRHS LSRN MAsh MBlu MGos Midl SNig SPoG SRms WFar
- 'Heins Silver'PBR — EBee
- 'Hort's Blaze' — EBee NLar
- 'Kewensis' ⚥H5 — CMac EUrb GEdr LSto LWaG SArc SPoG WCFE WCru
- 'Longwood' — LRHS
- 'Mickaela' — NWbg
- 'Minimus' — CSpe EBee ELan EPPr LWaG WFar WPGP
* - 'Minimus Variegatus' (v) — EPPr SPlb
- 'Prince John' — CSBt
- 'Silver Gem' — see *E. fortunei* 'Variegatus'
- 'Silver Queen' (v) — CBcs CBrac CCoa CEnd CMac EBee EGren ELan EPfP LCro LRHS LSRN MAsh MGos MPri NBir SPoG SRms SSta WFar WSpi
- 'Silverstone'PBR — CMac EPfP SPoG
- 'Sunshine' (v) — EPfP LRHS MAsh SPoG
§ - 'Sunspot' (v) — CBcs CMac EBee LRHS MMuc SRms
§ - 'Variegatus' (v) — SRms WCot
- var. *vegetus* — WFar
- 'Wolong Ghost' ⚥H5 — CBcs CCoa CDoC CExl CMCN EBee EPfP EPPr EUrb EWld GEdr GGro GKev MBlu MMuc NLar SArc SBrt WCot WFar WLov
frigidus KWJ 12275 — WCru
- var. *elongatus* GWJ 9378 — WCru
grandiflorus misapplied — see *E. carnosus*
§ *grandiflorus* Wall. — CJun EPfP IArd NLar WCot
- 'Ruby Wine' — CBcs EBee EPfP LCro MGos MMrt MPkF WMat
- f. *salicifolius* misapplied — see *E. grandiflorus* Wall.
hamiltonianus — CCVT CMCN ELan EPfP
- B&SWJ 14614 — WCru
- NJM 11.006 — WPGP
- 'Fiesta' — CJun
- subsp. *hians* — see *E. hamiltonianus* subsp. *sieboldianus*
- 'Indian Summer' — CBcs CCVT CJun CMac CMCN EPfP LCro LRHS MMrt NLar NPip SPoG WHtc WMat
- 'Koi Boy' — CJun ELan EPfP LRHS LSRN MAsh MPri NLar NPip SGol SPoG WHtc WMat
- 'Miss Pinkie' — CJun EPfP MPri NLar

- 'Pink Delight' ♀H6 — CJun
- 'Poort Bulten' — CJun
- 'Popcorn' — CJun
- 'Red Elf' — CJun
- 'Rising Sun' — CBcs CJun CMac EPfP NLar
§ - subsp. **sieboldianus** — WCru
  B&SWJ 10941
- - 'Calocarpus' — CJun
- - 'Coral Charm' — CBcs CJun EPfP
- - 'Snow' (v) — WCot
- - 'Winter Glory' — CJun
§ **huangii** — CJun CMCN WLov
- B&SWJ 3700 — WCru
japonicus — CBcs CCoa CCVT CDoC CMac EHeP EPfP SArc SAth SEND SEWo
- B&SWJ 11159 — WCru
- 'Albomarginatus' (v) — EHeP EPfP LRHS MPri SEND SRms WCha
- 'Argenteovariegatus' (v) — LRHS
§ - 'Aureomarginatus' (v) — CAco CBrac CCVT LRHS MPri WCha
- 'Aureopictus' — see *E. japonicus* 'Aureus'
- 'Aureovariegatus' — see *E. japonicus* 'Ovatus Aureus'
§ - 'Aureus' (v) — CBcs CCVT CDoC EHeP LRHS MPri SEND SWor
- 'Benkomasaki' — LCro LRHS LSRN SEWo SPoG
- 'Bravo' (v) — CCVT CDoC CoPl CWnw EGren EHeP EPfP LCro LRHS LSto MAsh MGos MPri MSwo SArc SEWo SPoG WCha WCot WFar
- 'Charles'PBR — SPoG
- 'Chedju' (v) — LRHS
- 'Chollipo' (v) ♀H5 — EBee EGren ELan EPfP SEND SPoG
- 'Duc d'Anjou' Carrière (v) — CBcs EBee EHeP ELan EPfP EWes LRHS SEND SPoG
- 'Edward King' — CCVT
- EL DORADO ('Br2012') — LRHS
- 'Elegantissimus Aureus' — see *E. japonicus* 'Aureomarginatus'
- EXSTASE ('Goldbolwi'PBR) (v) — MAsh WCot
- 'Francien' (v) — EBee LRHS
- 'Gold Queen' — EPfP MPri WCha
- 'Gold Rocket'PBR — LSou
- 'Golden Maiden' (v) — ELan EPfP LRHS MAsh SPoG SRms
- 'Green Rocket' — CBrac CCoa CCVT CEnd CSBt EBee EGren ELan EPfP GBin LBom LCro LRHS LSRN LSto MGos MPri NLit SHor SPoG SSta WCha WCot WFar
- 'Green Spider' — SPoG
- 'Green Spire' — CBrac CDoC CEnd CMac CSpe CWnw EGren EHeP EPfP LBom LBuc LRHS LSRN LSto MHed MSwo NHed NLar SEWo SOrN WFar
- 'Green Wonder' — LCro
- 'Happiness'PBR — LRHS
- HIMALAYA ('Lankveld06'PBR) — LCro LRHS MBNS MPri
- 'Jean Hugues' — EGren EHeP LBuc LRHS MHed NHed WCha WReH
- 'Kathy'PBR — CBcs CBrac CWnw EGren ELan ELon EPfP LBom LRHS MAsh NLar SPoG WCha
- 'Latifolius Albomarginatus' (v) — ELan EPfP
- 'Luna' — see *E. japonicus* 'Aureus'
- 'Macrophyllus Albus' — see *E. japonicus* 'Latifolius Albomarginatus'
- 'Maiden's Gold' — CSBt
- 'Marieke' — see *E. japonicus* 'Ovatus Aureus'
- 'Microphyllus' — CMac CSpe EHeP LRHS SArc SGol SRms

§ - 'Microphyllus Albovariegatus' (v) — CBrac CMac CSBt EDAr EHeP ELan ELon EPfP LRHS MGos SRms WCha WFar
§ - 'Microphyllus Aureovariegatus' (v) — CBrac CMac CSBt ELon EPfP LRHS MMuc NLar
- 'Microphyllus Aureus' — see *E. japonicus* 'Microphyllus Pulchellus'
§ - 'Microphyllus Pulchellus' (v) — CBcs CDoC CMac CSBt MGos MMuc SEWo SPoG
- 'Microphyllus Variegatus' — see *E. japonicus* 'Microphyllus Albomarginatus'
- 'Ovatus Albus' (v) — LBom
§ - 'Ovatus Aureus' (v) ♀H5 — CDoC CEnd CMac CoPl CSBt EGren EHeP ELan EPfP LBom LCro LRHS MGos SEND SPlb SPoG SRms WCha WFar
- PALOMA BLANCA ('Lankveld03'PBR) — EGren EPfP LBom LCro LRHS MPro SPoG WCha WFar
- 'Président Gauthier' (v) — CCVT CDoC EBee EGren EHeP ELan
- 'Pulchellus Aureovariegatus' — see *E. japonicus* 'Microphyllus Aureovariegatus'
- 'Robustus' — SSta
- 'Rokujo' — GEdr
- 'Rokujo Variegated' (v) — GEdr WCot
- 'Silver King' — CCVT CMac
- 'Silver Krista' (v) — NLar
- 'Susan' (v) ♀H5 — CMac LRHS MAsh
- 'White Spire'PBR (v) — CSBt EGren ELan LBom LBuc LCro LRHS LSou LSRN MAsh MGos SOrN SPoG WCha WCot WFar
kachinensis B&SWJ 11668 — WCru
kiautschovicus — NLar
  'Berry Hill'
- 'Manhattan' — NLar
latifolius — CJun CMCN LEdu
- B&SWJ 16067 — WCru
- var. **eximius** — WCru
  B&SWJ 16039
§ **laxiflorus** GWJ 9351 — WCru
- HWJ 890 — WCru
lucidus — EBee
§ **maackii** — LSto WJur
- B&SWJ 8782 from — WCru
  South Korea
- 'Dart's Pride' — CJun CMCN NLar
- 'Fireflame' — CJun WCot
- 'Pendulus' — MBlu
- 'Semipersistens' — NLar WCru
macropterus — CJun CMCN IArd
- B&SWJ 12591 — WCru
morrisonensis — see *E. huangii*
myrianthus — CJun CMCN EGrI ELan EPfP LCro LRHS MBlu WCru WJur
- 'Dianmu' — WPGP
§ **nanus** — CMCN NLar WCru WLov
- var. **turkestanicus** — EPfP NLar SBrt SMad SRms
obovatus — SBrt
oxyphyllus — CMCN ELan WCru WJur
- 'Waasland' — EPfP
phellomanus ♀H6 — CBcs ELan EPfP GKin IArd LCro LRHS MBlu MGos NLar NPip SPoG WMat
PIERROLINO ('Heespierrolino'PBR) — LRHS NLar WFar
§ **planipes** — CAco CBcs CCVT CDoC CMCN CSpe EBee EGren EGrI ELan EPfP EWld GKin MBlu MCtn MPri MPro NLar SPoG WJur WMat
- B&SWJ 8660 — WCru
- 'Dart's August Flame' — CJun

Euphorbia 275

- 'Sancho' ♛H6	CJun ELan EPfP NLar WMat
porphyreus	CBcs
- B&SWJ 13914	WCru
- GWJ 9377	WCru
rosmarinifolius	see *E. nanus*
rubescens	see *E. laxiflorus*
sachalinensis misapplied	see *E. planipes*
sachalinensis (F. Schmidt) Maxim.	EPfP
- B&SWJ 10835	WCru
sacrosanctus	MBlu
sanguineus	CJun
schensianus	WCru
B&SWJ 15422 **new**	
sieboldianus	WCru
var. **sanguineus**	
B&SWJ 11140	
- - B&SWJ 11386	WCru
spraguei	EPPr
- CWJ 12446	WCru
tingens	CMCN EBee EGrI MBlu WPGP
tonkinensis FMWJ 13350	WCru
trapococcus	EBee ELan WPGP
vagans Wall.	WCot
verrucosus	CJun EBee MBlu NLar WJur
- NJM 13.024	WPGP
wilsonii	CMCN LMaj MBlu
yedoensis	see *E. hamiltonianus* subsp. *sieboldianus*

Eupatorium ✿ (*Asteraceae*)

from Guatemala	LShi
- B&SWJ 9052	WCru
album misapplied	see *Ageratina altissima*
album L.	NBid
altissimum	SRms
amabile NMWJ 14456	WCru
cannabinum	CBWd CHab CoPl CPud CWat EAri EBee EGren EGrI ELin GJem GJos GQue LCro LShi MAsh MBNS MCtn MHer MMuc MNHC MWts NAts NBir NMir NPer SEND SPhx WHer
- f. *albiflorum*	SPhx
- f. *cannabinum* 'Flore Pleno' (d)	CMac ECha ELan ELon EMor MArl MHer NBir NBro NGdn NLar SDix StAn WCot WFar
capillifolium ♛H3	ESwi EWes SHar SMrm SNoN
- 'Elegant Plume'	EBee LBar LRHS
coelestinum	see *Conoclinium coelestinum*
dubium	see *Eutrochium dubium*
EUPHORIA RUBY	see *Eutrochium* EUPHORIA RUBY
fistulosum	see *Eutrochium fistulosum*
formosanum	LEdu
- from Taiwan	GGro
fortunei FMWJ 13428	WCru
- 'Capri' (v)	LBar MPro WCot
- 'Pink Elegance' (v)	CToG EBee EPfP LRHS LSto MArl MPie NLar SMrm SPoG SRms WCAu WFar WHrl
- 'Pink Frost' (v)	MWts NGdn
ligustrinum	see *Ageratina ligustrina*
lindleyanum	WCru
var. *trisectifolium* B&SWJ 12742	
maculatum	see *Eutrochium maculatum*
makinoi	WCru
var. *oppositifolium* B&SWJ 8449	
'Mask'	LBar MNrw NLar
micranthum	see *Ageratina ligustrina*
perfoliatum	EMor MMuc NLar

purpureum	see *Eutrochium purpureum*
rugosum	see *Ageratina altissima*
* 'Snowball'	NDov NLar SPoG WCAu
weinmannianum	see *Ageratina ligustrina*
yakushimaense	GEdr WCot

Euphorbia ✿ (*Euphorbiaceae*)

'Abbey Dore' ♛H7	ECha GBin MAvo SHar SMHy SPel WCot WMal
amygdaloides	SAth
- 'Athene' **new**	Midl WSpi
- 'Frosted Flame'PBR	LRHS MHol MPro NLar WCot
§ - 'Purpurea'	Widely available
§ - var. **robbiae** ♛H6	Widely available
- - dwarf	EWes
- - 'Redbud'	EWes WCAu
- 'Rubra'	see *E. amygdaloides* 'Purpurea'
- 'Xenia' **new**	Midl WSpi
* × **arendsii**	ECha GBin SDix SMHy
berorohae **new**	SPlb
biglandulosa Desf.	see *E. rigida*
BLACKBIRD ('Nothowlee'PBR)	CBcs CMac CTtf CWGN EGrI LBom LCro MAvo MGos NLar WFar WSpi
'Blue Haze'	ECha WCot WFar WMal WSpi
ceratocarpa ♛H4	CExl CSpe ECha EWes GMaP MBNS SPel WCAu WCot WSpi WTor
- 'Fromefield Gold'	LCro
characias	CBcs CMac LRHS NPer SMrm WBrk WCot
- 'Ascot Moonbeam'	LBuc LRHS MPri SPoG
- 'Black Pearl'	CBcs EGren ELan EPfP EUrb LBar LBom LCro LRHS MAvo MHol MHtn MPro NLar SPel SPoG SRkn WCAu WFar WNPC WSpi
- 'Blue Wonder'	EPfP EWes GMaP LBar NLar WCot WNPC
- 'BQ'	WCot
- subsp. **characias**	CTsd NLar
- - 'Burrow Silver' (v)	EGren EPfP
- - 'Humpty Dumpty'	EBee ELan EPfP GMaP LBuc LRHS MHed NPer WFar
- - 'Joshua'	WCot
- 'Eye-catcher'	WCot
- 'Forescate'	EBee EPfP LRHS
- 'Glacier Blue'PBR (v)	CSpe CWGN EBee ECha ELan EPfP LRHS MAsh MHol SPoG WCot WNPC
- 'Kestrel' (v)	WCot
- 'Portuguese Velvet'	EPfP LRHS MArl MHol NLar SArc WCot
- 'Silver Edge' (v)	ELan EPfP LBar LRHS LSou MHol MPri NLar NSti WFar WNPC
- SILVER SWAN ('Wilcott'PBR) (v)	CBcs CWGN EBee ELan EPfP EUrb EWes GKin LBar LBom LBuc LCro LRHS MGos Midl MPri MPro NLar NWbg SAth SOrN SPoG SRkn WFar WNPC WTor
- 'Tasmanian Tiger'PBR (v) ♛H4	CBcs CTsd CWGN GMaP LBom LCro LRHS LSRN MAvo MGos MHol MHtn Midl MPri MPro NLar SAth SPoG WCot WFar WSpi
- 'Variegata' (v)	CWnw LRHS
- subsp. **wulfenii**	Widely available
- - 'Bosahan'	CExl
- - 'Emmer Green' (v)	EWes WCot
- - 'Golden Balls'	WCot
- - 'Jayne's Golden Giant'	SMad
- - 'Jimmy Platt' ♛H4	WCot
§ - - 'John Tomlinson'	EGrI EWes WSpi
- - Kew form	see *E. characias* subsp. *wulfenii* 'John Tomlinson'

Euphorbia

- - 'Lambrook Gold'	NPer WSpi		NBid NBir NGdn NLar SPoG WBrk
- - - seed-raised	see *E. characias* subsp. *wulfenii*		WCot WCru WFar WSpi WTre
	Margery Fish Group	- 'Fern Cottage'	SMHy WCot
§ - - Margery Fish Group	CCps EPfP LRHS NBir	- 'Fireglow'	Widely available
- - 'Perry's Tangerine'	NPer	- 'King's Caple'	NLar SPoG WCru
§ - - 'Purple and Gold'	LBar	- 'Wickstead'	WCot
- - 'Purpurea'	see *E. characias* subsp. *wulfenii*	'Helena'^PBR (v)	LSRN
	'Purple and Gold'	*henryi*	see *E. sieboldiana*
- - 'Shorty'	CWGN NLar SPoG WNPC	*heptagona*	SEND
- - 'Silver Shadow' (v)	WCot	*horrida* ♀H2	LCro SPlb
- - 'Thelma's Giant'	MAvo	- (m)	NPlm
- - 'Westacre Giant'	EWes	- 'Alba'	NPlm
clavarioides	WCot	*hypericifolia*	CBcs CSpe CTsd LCro LRHS SRkn
var. *truncata*		DIAMOND FROST	WCot
'Cocklebur'	NCft	('Inneuphe'^PBR)	
'Copton Ash'	CBcs ECha	- 'Silverfog'^PBR	LCro
corallioides	ECha EPfP MCtn NPer WHer	*inermis*	NCft
§ *cornigera* ♀H5	EBee ECha EGrI EPfP NBid NGdn	*ingens*	LWaG NHrt NPlm
	SMHy SPel WBrk WCru WFar	I - 'Marmorata' (v)	NPlm
- 'Goldener Turm'	ECha LCro	*jacquemontii*	WCot
corollata	CSpe SBrt	*jolkinii*	CExl GKev
- var. *corollata*	WTre	*lathyris*	NLar NPer SVic WHer
cyparissias	ECha ELan EPot GQue NGdn NLar	*leucocephala*	SPlb
	SArc SHar SRms WBrk WFar	*leuconeura*	LWaG
- 'Betten'	see *E. × gayeri* 'Betten'	*limpopoana*	see *E. schinzii* subsp. *bechuanica*
- 'Clarice Howard'	see *E. cyparissias* 'Fens Ruby'	*longifolia* misapplied	see *E. cornigera*
- clone 2	WCot	*longifolia* D. Don	see *E. donii*
§ - 'Fens Ruby'	Widely available	*longifolia* Lam.	see *E. mellifera*
- 'Orange Man'	CBcs EWes LBar LRHS MArl NGdn	*loricata*	CPic
	NLar SPoG WBrk WFar WKif	*margalidiana* ♀H4	EBee ECha GBin MMrt WCot WMal
- 'Purpurea'	see *E. cyparissias* 'Fens Ruby'	*marginata*	CSpe
- 'Red Devil'	CDor	- 'Snow Top' (v)	MCtn
- 'Tall Boy'	EBee	× *martini*	CBcs CBWd CEnd CSpe CWnw
deflexa	ECha EWes NLar WMal		EGren EHeP ELan EPfP EWes GMaP
§ *donii*	ECha SMHy WSpi		LCro LRHS LShi MGos MPro NBir
- HWJK 2405	WCru		NBro NLar NSti SArc SPoG WCAu
- 'Amjillasa'	CExl ECha SDix SPel WCot		WFar WSpi
dulcis	NBro	- 'Aperitif'	SPoG
- 'Chameleon'	CDor CMiW EGren EGrI GQue LSto	§ - 'Ascot Liliput'**new**	LSou
	MGos NBid NBir NLar NPer NQui	- 'Ascot Petite'	see *E. × martini* 'Ascot Liliput'
	SMHy SPlb WBrk WCAu WCot WFar	- 'Ascot Rainbow'^PBR	Widely available
	WSpi	(v) ♀H5	
enopla	LCro	- 'Baby Charm'	ELan EPfP EUrb LBuc LRHS LSRN
§ *epithymoides*	CAby CBcs CCBP EBee ECha EMor		MGos NGdn NLar WNPC
	GAbr GJos GKev GMaP LCro LRHS	- 'Helen Robinson' ♀H5	WCot WMal
	MArl MAsh MAvo MCtn MHer NClf	- 'Kolibri'	EGren EPfP
	NDov NLar SAko SPlb StAn WCAu	- 'Rudolph'^PBR	EGren ELan LRHS MPri SPoG
	WFar WHil	- TINY TIM ('Waleutiny')	EPfP LBom
- 'Bonfire'^PBR	CBcs ECha EGrI EPfP EUrb MAvo	- WALBERTON'S RUBY GLOW	CBcs EPfP EWes LRHS LSou MHol
	MHer MHol MMrt NLar NSti SPoG	('Waleuphglo')	MPro NCth NLar WCAu WNPC
	WCot	*mauritanica*	EShb
§ - 'Candy'	ECha EGren MHol WFar	§ *mellifera* ♀H3	Widely available
- 'First Blush' (v)	WCot WKif	*milii* var. *milii*	LCro
- 'Golden Fusion'	NClf WMal	- 'Pallas Athene'	LRHS
§ - 'Lacy' (v)	NLar WFar	MINER'S MERLOT	CAbb CSpe CWGN GJos LBar LCro
§ - 'Major' ♀H6	EBee ECha SDix WKif	('Km-mm024')	LRHS LSou Midl MMrt MSwo NLar
- 'Midas'	GBin MNrw NClf SMHy SPel WMal		SMrm SPad WHil WNPC WSpi WTor
- 'Senior'	EBee EPfP EUrb LRHS MNrw WFar		XFar
eritrea	LDro	*myrsinites* ♀H5	Widely available
erythraea	NHrt	*nereidum* ♀H5	EWes WMal
EXCALIBUR ('Froeup'^PBR)	CMac ELan LSRN MBNS MMuc	*nicaeensis*	SPel WCot
	NBir NLar NSti SHor SPel	*obesa* ♀H1c	SBig SPad
fischeriana B&SWJ 8575	WCru	*oblongata*	CSpe EGrI ELan LCro SEND WCot
flanaganii ♀H2	NHrt	*palustris* ♀H7	Widely available
§ × *gayeri* 'Betten'	EBee NLar	- 'Teichlaterne'	NLar SAko SPel
'Golden Foam'	see *E. stricta*	- 'Walenburg's Glorie'	EBee ECha ELon GBin GQue LBar
graminea 'Glamour'	LCro LSou		LCro MMrt MNrw NLar NSti SHar
griffithii	GQue LSto MAsh NBro StAn WFar		SMad
- 'Beauty Orange' **new**	EBee LBar SMad	- 'Woodchippings'	WCot
- 'Dixter'	CSpe EGrI ELan EPfP EUrb GBin	× *pasteurii*	CBcs CDTJ CWnw EPfP EUrb
	GKev GMaP LBar LShi MBlu MMrt		EWes LCro LShi MNrw NBid NBir

- Brown's strain	SIvy SVen WCot WHil WMal WPGP
- Brown's strain	CBct SPel WCot
- 'Honey Pot' ♀H5	CDoC EPfP
- 'John Phillips' ♀H4	CBct CExl EBee EGrI ELan EPfP LRHS MBlu SChF SMad WPGP
- 'Phrampton Phatty' ♀H4	EPfP EUrb MAvo WCot WKif WPGP
- 'Roundway Titan' ♀H6	ELan EPfP LRHS SVen
- 'Skinny Bere'	LEdu LRHS SVen
pentagona	SVen
pilosa 'Major'	see *E. epithymoides* 'Major'
pithyusa	ECha EGrI ELan SPlb
- subsp. *cupanii* 'Ponte Leccia'	WMal
polychroma	see *E. epithymoides*
- 'Purpurea'	see *E. epithymoides* 'Candy'
- 'Variegata'	see *E. epithymoides* 'Lacy'
portlandica	EGrI SVen WHer
§ × *pseudovirgata*	LSto NSti SDix
REDWING ('Charam')	CBcs CMac ELan EPfP LRHS MAvo MHol SPoG WCot
reflexa	see *E. seguieriana* subsp. *niciciana*
resinifera	NPlm WCot
§ *rigida* ♀H6	CBro ECha WCot WPGP WSpi
robbiae	see *E. amygdaloides* var. *robbiae*
sarawschanica	ECha GKev
schillingii ♀H5	CDor EBee ELan EMor EPfP GBin GElm GMaP LRHS LSRN MAvo MMuc NLar NSti SPlb SPoG WCAu WCru WFar WNPC WSpi
§ *schinzii*	SPlb
subsp. *bechuanica* new	
schoenlandii	SPlb
seguieriana	ECha EGrI EWes GMaP LSto SAng SHar SPel SVen
§ - subsp. *niciciana*	EBee GBin LCro LRHS SDix SHor SMHy SPel WCAu WHoo
serrulata Thuill.	see *E. stricta*
sieboldiana	MHol
sikkimensis ♀H5	CCps ECha NLar NPer SPel WFar
- 'Crûg Contrast'	WCru WFar
spinosa	SPlb
§ *stricta*	CBgR MCtn WSpi
stygiana	CBcs CDTJ CExl EGrI ELan EWes MHol NBid SDix SHor SPlb WCot WCru WPGP
- 'Pico'	WPGP
- subsp. *santamariae*	CBct CDTJ CExl EPfP EUrb SMad WPGP WSpi
- subsp. *stygiana*	EBee WPGP
- 'Torridge' ♀H4	WCot
tanquahuete	CExl
tirucalli	EShb NHrt
triangularis	LCro LWaG
trigona	CDoC EGren NHrt NTrD
- f. *rubra*	CAbb CDoC NPlm
umbellata 'Rubra'	EShb
uralensis	see *E.* × *pseudovirgata*
valdevillosocarpa	SPhx WFar
'Velvet Ruby'	LBar LSRN
§ *virgata*	WCot
× *waldsteinii*	see *E. virgata*
wallichii misapplied	see *E. donii*
wallichii Kohli	see *E. cornigera*
wallichii ambig.	GBin GMaP LCro NLar NSti SPoG WTor
wallichii Hook.f.	CExl EPfP LCro LRHS WCAu WCot
'Whistleberry Garnet' ♀H7	CMac ELan EPfP MMuc SPoG

Euptelea (Eupteleaceae)

polyandra	EBee ELan MMuc NLar WJur WPGP

Eurya (Pentaphylacaceae)

japonica 'Moutiers' (v)	CBcs
- 'Variegata' misapplied	see *Cleyera japonica* 'Fortunei'

Euryale (Nymphaeaceae)

ferox	CLil

Eurybia (Asteraceae)

§ *divaricata*	Widely available
- 'Beth Chatto'	CSpe LSou MAvo MPie SHor
§ - 'Eastern Star'	EBlo GBin MNrw MPro NClf WCot WFar WOld WSpi WTre
- Raiche form	see *E. divaricata* 'Eastern Star'
- 'Snow Heron'	EPPr
- 'Tradescant'	GBin MNrw NLar SMad
§ × *herveyi*	CAby CBWd CKno ECha ELan ELon EMor GAbr GBin LBar LCro LEdu NDov NLar NSti SDix SHor SPel SPhx WCAu WCot WFar WOld WTor
§ *macrophylla*	CFis ELan GQue LRHS MCtn MHol NLar SPhx WFar WOld
- 'Albus'	EMor EPPr GBin WFar WHil
- 'Twilight'	see *E.* × *herveyi*
§ *radula*	ECha EPPr EWes MNrw NLar WOld
- 'August Sky'	CKno EBee EPPr LRHS NLar SHor SPhx WCot WFar WHoo
§ *schreberi*	CDor CKno CTtf ECha EPPr EWes LEdu MHol MNrw MPie SPhx WCot WFar WHoo WOld WPGP WTre
§ *sibirica*	MMuc WCAu WOld
§ *spectabilis*	WFar
- 'JS Macho Blue'	MNrw WFar WOld

Euryops (Asteraceae)

abrotanifolius	SVen
§ *acraeus* ♀H4	EPot WAbe
brachypodus	SVen
§ *chrysanthemoides*	CMHG EShb MMuc SEND SVen
evansii Schltr.	see *E. acraeus*
lateriflorus	SPlb
pectinatus ♀H3	CAbb CBcs CCht CCoa CDoC CDTJ CExl CMHG CSBt CSde CTsd CWal ELan EPfP EShb LCro LRHS LShi MMuc SEND SVen
tysonii	ELon ESgI EWes SPlb SVen
virgineus	CTsd EPfP LRHS SPlb SVen

Euscaphis (Staphyleaceae)

japonica	EGrI
- B&SWJ 11359	WCru
- B&SWJ 12739	WCru

Eustachys (Poaceae)

distichophylla	SPel

Eustephia (Amaryllidaceae)

coccinea	WCot
darwinii	WCot

Eustoma (Gentianaceae)

grandiflorum 'Piccolo Green'	MCtn

Eutrema (Brassicaceae)

§ *japonicum*	GGro LEdu MHoo SPre

Eutrochium (Asteraceae)

dubium 'Little Joe'	CTtf GBin LEdu LRHS MSwo WCAu
§ EUPHORIA RUBY ('Floreupre1')	MPro
fistulosum Albidum Group	EWhm
- - 'Bartered Bride'	EBee EMor ESwi EWes LSto NLar WCot
- - 'Ivory Towers'	CDor CKno EBee ECha EMor MCtn NDov WCot
- - 'Massive White' ♀H7	ESwi MNrw NBir NSti
- 'Berggarten'	LEdu
§ *maculatum*	NGdn NLar
- Atropurpureum Group	Widely available
- - 'Ankums August'	CKno EBee
- - 'Gateway'	CDor EBee EBlo ELon EPfP EPPr GQue LEdu LRHS NBid NLar
- - 'Glutball'	EBlo ELon LRHS MNrw SMad
- - 'Orchard Dene' ♀H7	IPot SMHy
- - 'Phantom'PBR	EBee ELon GBin MHol NBid NCth NLar NWbg SAko SPoG WFar
- - 'Prairie Giant'	NDov
- - 'Purple Bush' ♀H7	CDor CKno EBee ELon EPfP ESwi GQue LCro LSto NDov WTre
- - 'Red Dwarf'	ELon EPfP GQue LBar LEdu MPie NCth NLar SBea SHar SPoG WCAu WFar WHoo
- - 'Riesenschirm' ♀H7	CKno EBee ECha ELon EMor EWes GBin GMaP IPot LCro LEdu LRHS LSto MAvo MBel MHol MNrw NLar SAko SDix SHor SMad SPeP SPoG WBrk WCAu WCot WTre
- 'J.S. Humble'	MNrw
- 'Snowball'PBR	LBar XFar
§ *purpureum*	CBcs CHby CMHG ECha ELon GJos GMaP LRHS MHer MHoo MNHC NBro NGdn SMrm SPlb SRms StAn WCAu WCav WHer
- 'Album'	LEdu
- 'Baby Joe'PBR	CBWd CKno CWGN EBee EBlo ECha ELan EPfP GBin LBar LRHS MBel MBNS Midl MNrw MPro NBid NBir NLar SHar SPad SPel SRot WHil XFar

Evolvulus (Convolvulaceae)

BLUE MY MIND ('Usevo1201'PBR)	CSpe

Ewartia (Asteraceae)

nubigena	LRHS
planchonii	SPlb WFar

Exbucklandia (Hamamelidaceae)

populnea	WPGP

Exochorda (Rosaceae)

alberti	see *E. korolkowii*
giraldii var. *wilsonii*	CExl CMac ELan EPfP LRHS MBlu MMuc
§ *korolkowii*	MAsh NLar WJur
× *macrantha* LOTUS MOON ('Bailmoon')	LRHS MPri NCth
§ - 'Niagara'PBR	CAco CBcs CDoC CMac EGren ELan EPfP GKev LCro LSRN MGos NLar SPoG WCha WFar WMat
- SNOW DAY SURPRISE	see *E. × macrantha* 'Niagara'
- 'The Bride' ♀H6	Widely available
racemosa	WJur
- BLUSHING PEARL ('Huibl'PBR)	EBee LRHS WSpi

- MAGICAL SPRINGTIME ('Kolmasprit')	EPfP MMrt NLar WFar
- 'Snow Mountain'PBR	NCth
serratifolia	CBcs ELan EPfP MMuc SPoG WJur
- 'Snow White'	CEnd CWnw EUrb EWes GKin LBom LRHS MBlu NLar

F

Fabiana (Solanaceae)

imbricata	LRHS SPlb
- 'Prostrata'	LRHS
- f. *violacea* hort. ♀H4	CMac CSBt MMuc WKif
- - dark-flowered	CBcs

Fagopyrum (Polygonaceae)

cymosum	see *F. dibotrys*
§ *dibotrys*	CAgr CSpe EBee ECha
I - 'Cally Form'	ESwi
giraldii	see *Pteroxygonum giraldii*

Fagraea (Gentianaceae)

ceilanica FMWJ 13099	WCru

Fagus ✿ (Fagaceae)

from Guangxi, China	WPGP
from Vietnam	WPGP
§ *crenata*	CMen MBlu
- 'Mount Fuji'	CAco
engleriana	CExl
grandifolia	WPGP
subsp. *mexicana* *longipetiolata*	see *F. sinensis*
lucida	CExl MBlu
orientalis 'Iskander'	CNWT EBar MBlu SGol
sieboldii	see *F. crenata*
§ *sinensis*	CBcs CExl CMCN EBee EPfP WPGP
- NJM 11.036	WPGP
sylvatica ♀H6	Widely available
- 'Asterix'	MBlu
§ - Atropurpurea Group	Widely available
- - 'Black Swan'	CAco CBTr CLnd CMCN EBar ELan LRHS MAsh MBlu MGos NOra NPip SMad SPoG WHtc WMat
- - 'Purpurea Latifolia'	CAco
- - 'Purpurea Pendula'	CAco CBcs CBTr CCVT CEnd CMac CMCN ELan EPfP GKin IPap LCro LMaj LRHS MAsh MGos NPip SGol SPoG WFar WMat
- - 'Riversii' ♀H6	CAco CBcs CBTr CEnd CLnd CMCN ELan EPfP GKin MGos MHed NHed NLar SArc SFol WHnu WMat
- - 'Swat Magret'	CAco
- 'Aurea Pendula'	CEnd MBlu
- 'Bicolor Sartini' (v)	MBlu
- 'Bornyensis'	MBlu
- 'Brathay Purple'	MBlu
- 'Cockleshell'	MBlu
- 'Cristata'	MBlu
§ - 'Dawyck' ♀H6	CAco CBcs CCVT CLnd CMac EBar ELan LMaj MGos NLar SHor
- 'Dawyck Gold' ♀H6	CAco CBcs CBTr CEnd CLnd CMac CMCN CSBt EBar ELan GKin IPap LCro LMaj MAsh MBlu MGos NLar NOra NPip SGol WFar WMat
- 'Dawyck Purple' ♀H6	CAco CBcs CBTr CCVT CEnd CLnd CMac CMCN CSBt EBar EGren ELan

Fargesia   279

	EPfP GKin IPap LCro LMaj LSRN MAsh MBlu MGos NLar NOra NPip SGol SPoG WHtc WMat
- 'Fastigiata' misapplied	see *F. sylvatica* 'Dawyck'
- 'Franken' (v)	CAco MBlu
- 'Green Obelisk'	MBlu
- 'Greenwood'	MBlu
- var. ***heterophylla*** 'Aspleniifolia' ♀H6	CEnd CMac CMCN EBar EPfP GKin LMaj MBlu MGos NLar NPip SArc SPoG WMat
- - (Atropurpurea Group) 'Ansorgei'	CMCN MBlu
- - - Midnight Feather ('Verschuurfag 1'PBR)	CBTr ELan NLar
- - 'Incisa'	MBlu
- - f. ***laciniata***	MBlu
- 'Mercedes'	CAco CMCN LRHS MBlu
- 'Horizontalis'	MBlu
- 'Pendula' ♀H6	CAco CBcs CBTr CCVT CEnd CLnd CMac CMCN CSBt EBar ELan LMaj MGos NOra SArc SGol WMat
- 'Purple Fountain' ♀H6	CAco CBTr CEnd CMCN ELan LCro LMaj MAsh MBlu MGos NLar NOra NPip WMat
- Purple-leaved Group	see *F. sylvatica* Atropurpurea Group
§ - 'Purpurea Tricolor' (v)	CAco CMac CMCN IPap MBlu MGos NOra NPip WMat
- 'Red Obelisk'	see *F. sylvatica* 'Rohan Obelisk'
- 'Rohan Gold'	CAco CEnd
§ - 'Rohan Obelisk'	CAco CEnd CMCN LMaj MBlu
I - 'Rohan Pyramidalis'	CEnd CMCN
- 'Rohan Trompenburg'	MBlu
- 'Rohan Weeping'	CAco MBlu NLar
- 'Rohanii'	CAco CBcs CEnd EBar GKin LMaj MGos
- 'Roseomarginata'	see *F. sylvatica* 'Purpurea Tricolor'
- 'Rotundifolia'	LMaj MBlu
- 'Spaethiana'	CAco GKin
- 'Striata'	CAco
- f. ***tortuosa***	MBlu
- - 'Rot Süntel'	CAco
- 'Tricolor' misapplied	see *F. sylvatica* 'Purpurea Tricolor'
- 'Tricolor' (v)	CAco CBcs LMaj NLar NOra
- 'Zlatia'	CAco CLnd CMCN CSBt MBlu

Fallopia (*Polygonaceae*)
aubertii	see *F. baldschuanica*
§ ***baldschuanica***	CBcs CBrac CDoC CMac EBee EGren ELan EPfP LBuc LCro LRHS MAsh MGos SEND SOrN SPlb SPoG WFar WTHo
multiflora	see *Reynoutria multiflora*

Fallugia (*Rosaceae*)
| ***paradoxa*** | MCtn |

Farfugium ✿ (*Asteraceae*)
§ ***japonicum***	CDTJ SBig SHor
- B&SWJ 884	WCru
- B&SWJ 14699	WCru
- from Amami, Japan	CDTJ
- 'Argenteum' (v)	CDTJ LRHS SMad
- 'Aureomaculatum' (v) ♀H3	CAbb CDTJ ESwi SBig SNoN
- 'Crispatum'	CDTJ CLil SBig WFar
- double-flowered (d)	WCru
- var. ***formosanum*** NMWJ 14574	WCru
- var. ***giganteum***	CDTJ EAri LRHS SBig
- - B&SWJ 15122	WCru

- 'Kagami-jishi' (v)	CDTJ
- 'Kaimon Dake' (v)	CDTJ
- 'Kinkan' (v)	CDTJ
- 'Shishi Botan'	CDTJ LRHS WFar
- 'Wavy Gravy'	CBcs CBlu EUrb LBar LRHS NBir SAth SMad WFar
tussilagineum	see *F. japonicum*

Fargesia (*Poaceae*)
from Jiuzhaigou, China	CBdn CDTJ MMuc MWht SBGi SWor WCha WPGP
apicirubens 'White Dragon'	CDTJ
Deep Purple ('Benniel1'PBR)	EGren NCth
demissa 'Gerry'	CWnw NLar
denudata	CDTJ ESwi MAvo NLar SBGi
- L 1575	MWht
- Xian 1	CDTJ
dracocephala	MMuc MWht
Gansu 95-2	NLar
'Green Dragon'	EBee SBGi
'Jiuzaighou 9'	CDoC EGren SBGi
§ ***murielae*** ♀H5	CAgr CBlu CDoC CTsd EGrI GArf LCro LRHS LSto MMuc SArc SBGi SPlb WCha WFar
- 'Bimbo'	CDoC NLar WSpi
- Blue Dragonscale	see *F. murielae* Blue Lizard
§ - Blue Lizard ('Japo 72'PBR)	MWht SPoG WCha
- Deep Forest ('Jan 64')	NLar
- 'Dino'	EPfP LRHS
- 'Grüne Hecke'	MWht
- 'Harewood'	MWht
- 'Joy'	NLar
- 'Jumbo'	CDoC CSBt CWnw EGren NGdn NLar SRms WCha WSpi
- 'Lava'	SBig
- 'Luca'PBR	LRHS NLar
- 'Mae'	CDTJ
- 'Novecento'	SPoG
- 'Panda'PBR	LRHS SBGi
- Red Zebra ('Japo 51'PBR)	MWht NLar SBGi
- 'Simba'	EBee EGren EHeP GMaP LMaj LSRN LSto MBrN MGos NGdn NLar SBGi SPoG WCha WFar
- 'Vampire'	MAsh SPoG
- 'Winter Black'	EGren
§ ***nitida***	CAbb CEnd CWnw ELan GArf MGos MWht SBGi SPoG SRms WCha WPGP
- 'Black Pearl'	CDoC CWnw EGren MAsh MAvo MGos SBig SFol SPoG WCha WPGP
- Gansu 2	MGos
- 'Great Wall'	CDoC CDTJ CSBt LMaj MMuc NLar SPoG WCha
- Jiuzhaigou 1	see *F.* Red Panda
- 'Jiuzhaigou 2'	MWht SBGi
- 'Jiuzhaigou 4'	CDTJ CExl WPGP
- 'Jiuzhaigou Genf'	CDTJ MWht NLar WFar
- 'Pillar'	MAsh SBig WFar
- 'Volcano'	CDoC MAsh MAvo SBGi SBig WFar
'Obelisk'PBR	NLar
Red Dragon	see *F.* Red Panda
§ Red Panda ('Jiu') ♀H5	CBcs LCro MWht NLar SBig SPoG SWor WCha WSpi
§ ***robusta*** ♀H5	CDTJ CSBt ELan LRHS MAvo MBrN MMuc MWht NGdn NLar SBGi SWor WCha WPGP
- 'Asian Wonder'	CBcs CWnw EAri EGren ELan EUrb LCro LRHS MAvo MHtn MSwo NLar SBGi SPeP SWor WCha

- 'Campbell'	CBdn CDoC EBee EGren ELan EPfP EUrb MAvo NLar NPlm SBig SWor WCha
- 'P. King'	MWht
- 'Pingwu'	CDoC CDTJ EAri EGren EPfP LRHS MGos MWht SBGi SWor WCha
- 'Red Sheath'	CDTJ CExl MWht
- 'Wenchuan'	EBee LRHS
- 'Wolong'	CExl EUrb MAvo MWht NLar SWor WPGP
rufa ♀H5	Widely available
scabrida misapplied	see *F. robusta*
similaris KR 4175	MWht
spathacea misapplied	see *F. murielae*
utilis	MMuc MWht SEND
'Winter Joy'	SBGi SBig SPoG WCha WPGP
yulongshanensis	MWht

Fascicularia (Bromeliaceae)
andina	see *F. bicolor*
§ *bicolor*	Widely available
- subsp. *bicolor*	CDoC CMac
- subsp. *canaliculata*	ELon LEdu MNrw SChr SIvy WPGP
kirchhoffiana	see *F. bicolor*
litoralis	see *Ochagavia litoralis*
pitcairniifolia misapplied	see *F. bicolor*
pitcairniifolia (Verlot) Mez	see *Ochagavia litoralis*

× *Fatshedera* ❀ (Araliaceae)
lizei ♀H3	CBcs CMac CSde EBee ELan ELon EPfP EUrb LRHS SArc SDix SEND SPlb SPoG SRms WHtc
- 'Annemieke' (v) ♀H3	CBcs CMac ELan ELon EPfP LRHS MAsh SEND SPoG
- 'Aurea' (v)	EPfP
- compact	CMac EPfP LRHS
- 'Lemon and Lime'	see × *F. lizei* 'Annemieke'
- 'Maculata'	see × *F. lizei* 'Annemieke'
- 'Variegata' (v) ♀H3	CMac CSde EBee ELan ELon EPfP LRHS MAsh SDix SEND
- - compact (v)	CMac SPoG

Fatsia ❀ (Araliaceae)
§ *japonica* ♀H5	Widely available
- 'Camouflage'	see *F. japonica* 'Murakumo-nishiki'
- 'Moseri'	CDTJ ESwi LEdu WCha WCot
§ - 'Murakumo-nishiki' (v)	CBcs CDTJ CWGN ELan LBar LCro LRHS MSCN
- 'Oshima' **new**	WCru
- 'Spider's Web'	see *F. japonica* 'Tsumugi-shibori'
§ - 'Tsumugi-shibori' (v)	Widely available
- 'Variegata' (v) ♀H5	CMac EGren ELan EPfP EUrb LRHS MGos SBig SEND SIvy SPoG WCot
papyrifera	see *Tetrapanax papyrifer*
polycarpa	CDoC CDTJ CExl CWnw MSwo WSpi
- B&SWJ 1776	ESwi WCru
- B&SWJ 3467	WCru
- B&SWJ 7144	WCru
- RWJ 10133	WCru
- from Tregye	EBee
- deeply cut leaf	LEdu SMad WCot WPGP
- giant-leaved	CExl
- GREEN FINGERS	CBcs CCht EBee ELan EPfP EUrb LCro LRHS MPri MSwo NCth NLar SBig WFar

Fatsia × *Hedera* see × *Fatshedera*

Faucaria (Aizoaceae)
tigrina ♀H2	SEND
tuberculosa ♀H2	CPbh CPic ELan LCro

Fauria see *Nephrophyllidium*

Feijoa (Myrtaceae)
§ *sellowiana* (F)	Widely available
- 'Apollo' (F)	EUrb
- 'Gemini' (F)	CAgr SGol
- 'Mammoth' (F)	CBcs
- 'Triumph' (F)	CBcs
- 'Variegata' (F/v)	EBee WFar

Felicia (Asteraceae)
§ *amelloides*	CPbh CWal GBin SPlb
- 'Santa Anita'	SVen
§ - variegated (v)	NPer
capensis	see *F. amelloides*
coelestis	see *F. amelloides*
FELICITARA BLUE ('Wigetablue' PBR)	SPoG
filifolia blue-flowered	SVen
natalensis	see *F. rosulata*
§ *petiolata*	CFis EWes MMuc NSti WCot WFar
§ *rosulata*	CAby EDAr GMaP LShi MAsh MHol NLar SBrt WIce
uliginosa	EWes GEdr SPlb WIce
wrightii	GEdr

Fenestraria (Aizoaceae)
rhopalophylla	SPlb
subsp. *aurantiaca* ♀H2	

fennel see *Foeniculum vulgare*

fenugreek see *Trigonella foenum-graecum*

Ferocactus (Cactaceae)
emoryi	NPlm
glaucescens ♀H2	NPlm
- var. *inermis*	NPlm
gracilis subsp. *coloratus*	NPlm
histrix	CBlu
latispinus ♀H2	NPlm
pilosus	NPlm

Ferraria (Iridaceae)
§ *crispa*	GKev LAma LCro SMrm WCot XFar
- var. *nortieri*	WCot
divaricata	WCot
schaeferi	WCot
undulata	see *F. crispa*
variablis	WCot

Ferula (Apiaceae)
from Central Asia	WPGP
arrigonii	SPhx
assa-foetida	WJek WPGP
chiliantha	see *F. communis* subsp. *glauca*
§ *communis*	CSpe ECha ELan EWes LEdu LWaG MCtn SBeP SDix SEND SPad SPhx SPlb SPoG WCAu WJek
- 'Gigantea'	see *F. communis*
§ - subsp. *glauca*	EBee ECha ELan EWes LEdu SDix SMHy SPhx WCot WPGP
- - B&SWJ 12999	WCru
'Giant Bronze'	see *Foeniculum vulgare* 'Giant Bronze'
glauca	WJek
tingitana B&SWJ 14005	WCru
- 'Cedric Morris'	ECha SBrt SDix SPhx WCot

Ferulago (Apiaceae)

cassia	WCot
nodosa	ECha SPhx
stellata	WCot
sylvatica	CSpe

Festuca (Poaceae)

amethystina	CKno GBin LCro MBel MCtn MMuc MPro NGdn SEND SPhx
arundinacea	CHab MMuc SEND
'Blue Haze'	CKno
filiformis	CHab
§ *gautieri*	EGren EHeP WSpi
- 'Pic Carlit'	NLar
gigantea	CHab MMuc SEND
glauca Vill.	CBcs GMaP GQue MBNS MGos NGdn SAth SPlb SRms WCAu
- AMIGOLD ('Amigol 25')	EGren LRHS
§ - 'Auslese'	NGdn SWor
- 'Azurit'	EWes LRHS LShi NLar SPoG SRms
§ - 'Blaufuchs'	CMHG EHeP ELan EPfP EWes GMaP LRHS MArl MBlu MGos NLar SPlb WFar WSpi
- 'Blauglut'	SRms
- BLUE FOX	see *F. glauca* 'Blaufuchs'
- 'Blue Select'	CWal MCtn
- COMPACTA BLUE ('Amibla'^PBR)	EPfP
- 'Elijah Blue'	Widely available
- 'Golden Toupee'	EBlo ECha EHeP ELan EPfP MAsh MBlu MGos NLar SPlb
- INTENSE BLUE ('Casblue'^PBR) ♀H5	CBrac CKno EBee EGren ELan EPfP EWes LBom LCro LRHS LSRN MAsh MGos Midl MPro SAth SMad SPeP SPoG SRms
- SELECT	see *F. glauca* 'Auslese'
idahoensis 'Tomales Bay'	CKno SHor
mairei	EBee ECha EPPr MMuc NClf
'Miedzianobrody'^PBR	LCro LSou
ovina	CHab NLit SHor
- 'Söhrewald'	EBlo LRHS
paniculata	CKno
pratensis	CHab
punctoria	MMuc
rubra	CHab
scoparia	see *F. gautieri*
tatrae	MMuc SEND
valesiaca 'Buddy Blue'	LRHS Midl MPri
I - var. *glaucantha*	MMuc NGdn
- 'Silbersee'	SRms
vivipara	NBid
* 'Willow Green'	SPlb

Fibigia (Brassicaceae)

clypeata	CSpe

Ficaria (Ranunculaceae)

fascicularis	EPot MNrw NRya WCot
verna Alba Group	LEdu NRya
- anemone-centred	see *F. verna* 'Collarette'
- 'Angele' (d)	WFar
- 'Anita' (v)	WFar
§ - Aurantiaca Group	CDor LEdu NLar NRya WFar
- var. *aurantiacus*	see *F. verna* Aurantiaca Group
- 'Berliner Bronzeblatt'	WFar
- 'Blueberries and Cream'	WFar
- 'Bowles's Double'	see *F. verna* 'Double Bronze', 'Picton's Double'
- 'Brambling'	EBee LEdu WFar
- 'Brazen Hussy'	CDor EBee ECha ELan EMor EPfP EPot GAbr GMaP LEdu LRHS LShi NBir NLar NSti WCav WCot WFar WHil WIce WPnP
- subsp. *bulbilifer*	see *F. verna* subsp. *verna*
§ - subsp. *chrysocephala*	CDor EBee WCot WFar
- - 'Pencarn'	WFar
- 'Claudine' (French Ladies Series) (d)	WFar
- 'Coffee Cream'	WFar
§ - 'Collarette' (d)	CDor EBee ELan LEdu NBir NLar NRya WFar
- 'Coppernob'	CDor LShi WCot WFar
- 'Crimson Damson' (d)	CDor WFar WMal
- 'Cupreus'	see *F. verna* Aurantiaca Group
- 'Damerham' (d)	WFar
- 'Deborah Jope'	WFar
- 'Diane Rowe'	WFar
- double, cream-flowered	see *F. verna* 'Double Mud'
- -white-flowered (d)	EPot
- -yellow-flowered (d)	see *F. verna* Flore Pleno Group
- 'Double Bronze' (d)	LEdu LShi NBir WFar
§ - 'Double Mud' (d)	CDor EPPr LEdu SHar WFar
- 'Dusky Maiden'	NLar NRya WFar
- 'E.A. Bowles'	see *F. verna* 'Collarette'
§ - Flore Pleno Group (d)	CDor CMac GAbr LShi NRya SRms WCot WFar
- 'Florence' (French Ladies Series) (d)	WFar WMal
- 'Fried Egg'	LShi WFar
- 'Graham Joseph' (d)	CDor WFar
- 'Great Queen Rhiannon'	WFar
- 'Green Petal' (d)	CDor CMiW EPPr LShi NBir NRya WFar
- 'Greencourt Gold' (d)	WFar
- 'Hyde Hall'	LShi NLar WCot WFar
- 'Jacqueline' (French Ladies Series) (d)	CDor WFar WMal
- 'Ken Aslet Double' (d)	CDor EPPr WFar
- 'Lambrook Variegated' (v)	WFar
- 'Leo'	WFar
- 'Magnum'	WFar
- subsp. *major*	see *F. verna* subsp. *chrysocephala*
- 'Martin Gibbs'	WFar
- 'Monique' (French Ladies Series) (d)	LEdu WFar WMal
- 'Montacute' (d)	CDor WFar
- 'Nathalie' (French Ladies Series) (d)	CDor WFar
- 'Nicole' (d)	WFar
- 'Old Master'	WCot
- 'Orange Sorbet' (d)	WFar
- 'Orangette' (d)	WFar
§ - 'Picton's Double' (d)	WFar WIce
- 'Primrose'	NRya WFar
- 'Primrose Brassy'	WFar
- 'Pwyll, Prince of Dyfed'	LShi WFar
- 'Quillet' (d)	WFar
- 'Ragamuffin' (d)	WFar
- 'Randall's White'	CDor EMor EPfP WFar
- 'Richard and Val'	WFar
- 'Rita Pirouet'	WCot
- 'Salmon's White'	EPPr LShi NRya WFar
- 'Silver Brambling'	WFar
- 'Silver Collar' (d)	WFar
- 'Single Cream'	WFar
- 'Snow Bunting'	WFar
- 'Sulli' (d)	WFar
- 'Sylvie' (French Ladies Series) (d)	CDor WFar
- 'Tortoiseshell'	EPPr

282 Ficaria

- 'Vanessa' (d)	CDor WFar
§ - subsp. *verna*	WShi
- - 'Chedglow'	WCot
- 'Wisley Double'	see *F. verna* 'Double Bronze', 'Wisley Double White'
§ - 'Wisley Double White' (d)	WFar

Ficinia (Cyperaceae)

§ *nodosa*	SPlb
truncata	WCot
- 'Ice Crystal' (v)	ELan LCro LEdu LRHS SPoG

Ficus (Moraceae)

afghanistanica 'Silver Lyre'	EBee SMad SVen WPGP
altissima	LBom SPre
'Amstel'	NHrt
benghalensis	LBom LWaG NHrt
- 'Audrey'	LBom LDro LWaG NHrt
benjamina ♀H1c	LBom LDro MCtn NHrt
- 'Amstel Gold'	LBom
- 'Audrey'	NHrt
- 'Danielle' PBR	LBom LCro LDro NHrt
- 'Exotica'	LBom LCro LDro
- 'Golden Monique' (v)	LBom
- 'Green Kinky' PBR (v)	LBom LCro
- 'Twilight' (v)	LBom LCro NHrt
I *binnendijkii* 'Alii'	CDoC LBom LCro MPri NHrt NPlm
- 'Amstel King'	LBom LDro NHrt
bussei 'Floris' PBR	LBom
carica (F)	EGren EOli ERom EUrb LWaG SArc SAth SEWo SFol SPad WJur
- 'Adam' (F)	NLar SEND SVen WPGP
§ - 'Aranysárga Óriásfüge' (F)	WJur
- 'Babits' (F)	WJur
I - 'Bauern Feige' (F)	SRms
- 'Black Ischia' (F)	SDix
- 'Bornholm' (F)	LCro SPre
- 'Bourjassotte Grise' (F)	CAgr
- 'Brown Turkey' (F) ♀H4	Widely available
- 'Brunswick' (F)	CAbb CAgr CDoC ELan EPfP EPom LEdu NLar SBmr SDix SEND SPoG SRms SVen WCot WFar WJur WMat
- 'Califfo Blue' (F)	SRms
- 'Celeste' (F)	SRms
- 'Chelsea' (F)	EPom
- 'Dalmatie' (F)	CAgr CDoC EPfP LCro LRHS MPri NOra SEND SRms WMat WPGP
- 'Dauphine' (F)	EPfP EPom LCro SEND WJur
I - 'Digitata' (F)	MBlu
§ - 'Dorée' (F)	CAgr EPfP EPom WJur
- 'Dottato' (F)	WJur
- 'Early Violet' (F)	WJur
- 'Ed's Teacup' (F)	WCot
- 'Goutte d'Or'	see *F. carica* 'Dorée'
- 'Green Sweet'	see *F. carica* Zöld Aszalódó
- 'Ice'	see *F. carica* 'Jégfüge'
- 'Ice Crystal' (F) ♀H5	CBct CBlu CDoC EBee ELan EPfP EUrb LCro LEdu LRHS MBlu NLar NOra NPlm SArc SPoG SRms WCot WFar WMat
§ - 'Jégfüge' (F)	WJur
- 'Jordan' (F)	NOra SPoG
§ - 'Lila Pogácsa' (F)	WJur
- Little Miss Figgy ('Lmf01') (F)	CDoC CSBt ELan EPfP LBuc LCro LRHS SPoG SWor WLov
- 'Longue d'Août' (F)	SPlb WJur
- 'Madeleine des Deux Saisons' (F)	EPom SEND WJur
- 'Maellana Blanca' (F)	EUrb
- 'Merengiana' (F)	WJur
- 'Morena' (F)	SRms
- 'Napolitana' (F)	NPlm
- 'Nero' (F)	EBar
- 'Noire de Caromb' (F)	CAgr EPfP NPlm SRms WJur WMat
- 'Osborn's Prolific' (F)	EPfP LCro SEND WCot
- 'Panachée' (F)	EPom LBom LCro LRHS NLar NOra NPlm SPoG SRms WJur
- 'Pastilière' (F)	EUrb LCro
- 'Piaci Bordó' (F)	WJur
- 'Précoce de Dalmatie' (F)	EUrb NLar SRms WCot
- 'Ronde de Bordeaux' (F)	EPfP EUrb LCro SEND WJur
- 'Rouge de Bordeaux' (F)	CAbb CAgr EPfP EPom LRHS MPri NPlm SPlb SRms SSta WLov
- 'Rovinj' (F)	WJur
- 'San Pedro' (F)	WJur
- 'Scone'	see *F. carica* 'Lila Pogácsa'
- 'Signora' (F)	WJur
- 'Sultane' (F)	CAgr EPom IArd WPGP
- 'Tayip 1' (F)	CAgr
- 'Tayip 2' (F)	CAgr
I - 'Tena' (F)	WJur
- 'Teri néni Ujjas' (F)	WJur
- 'Ujjas Óriás' (F)	WJur
- 'Verdal' (F)	NPlm
- 'Violette de Bordeaux' (F)	EPom
- 'Violette Normande' (F)	SEND
- 'White Adriatic' (F)	CAgr CDoC NLar SRms
- 'White Genoa'	see *F. carica* 'White Marseilles'
§ - 'White Marseilles' (F)	CAgr CMac EPfP EUrb SPoG SRms WMat WPGP
- 'Yellow Giant'	see *F. carica* 'Aranysárga Óriásfüge'
- 'Zamoreica' (F)	SEND
§ - 'Zöld Aszalódó' (F)	WJur
- 'Zöld Hosszúkás' (F)	WJur
carica × *pumila*	EBee WPGP
cyathistipula	LBom LCro LDro NHrt
elastica ♀H1b	LBom LDro MPri NHrt
- 'Abidjan'	LBom LCro LDro LInT LWaG NHrt WFar
- 'Belize' PBR (v)	CDoC LDro NHrt WFar
- 'Melany' PBR	LBom NHrt
- 'Pemela'	LCro
- 'Robusta'	CDoC EGren LBom LCro LDro LInT LWaG NHrt NTrD
- 'Schrijveriana' (v)	LBom
- 'Sofia'	LBom
- 'Tineke' (v)	CDoC LBom LCro LInT LWaG NHrt
'Kinky'	WFar
lyrata ♀H1b	CDoC EGren LBom LCro LDro LInT LWaG NHrt NTrD
- 'Bambino' PBR	LBom LCro LWaG NHrt
microcarpa	CDoC LBom LCro NHrt NTrD WFar
- 'Moclame' PBR	LBom LCro NHrt
aff. *oligodon*	SVen
- NJM 13.084	WPGP
pumila ♀H2	CDoC EShb LWaG MPri
- 'Sonny' (v)	LBom LWaG
- 'Variegata' (v) ♀H2	EShb LBom
- 'White Sunny' (v)	LBom LWaG
religiosa	SPlb
retusa (F)	LBom NGKo
tikoua	IArd SArc SPlb
vaccinioides	WPGP

fig see *Ficus carica*; also AGM Fruit Section

filbert see *Corylus maxima*

Filipendula (Rosaceae)

alnifolia 'Variegata'	see *F. ulmaria* 'Variegata'
auriculata B&SWJ 10828	WCru

camtschatica	EBee EBlo ECha ELan GKev MMuc NBid NLar
- B&SWJ 10987	WCru
- RBS 224	NLar
- 'Rosea'	CTtf
- 'Shiro-sankou-naka-fu' (v)	WFar
digitata 'Nana'	see *F. multijuga*
hexapetala	see *F. vulgaris*
- 'Flore Pleno'	see *F. vulgaris* 'Multiplex'
'Kahome'	CTtf EBee ELon EMor EWhm GAbr GMaP MSCN NBid NBir NGdn NLar NSti WFar
kiraishiensis B&SWJ 1571	WCru
§ *multijuga*	CLil EGrI EWhm MBel NLar WPGP
- B&SWJ 10950	WCru
- 'Hjördis'	EMor LBar MBel MSCN SPeF WHil WHoo
palmata	ECha EGrI LBar WFar
- 'Digitata Nana'	see *F. multijuga*
- 'Elegantissima'	see *F. purpurea* 'Elegans'
- 'Göteborg'	ECha NLar
- 'Nana'	see *F. multijuga*
- 'Rosea'	CMac NBir
- 'Rosenschleier'	LBar
- 'Rubra'	EBee EBlo EPfP LRHS NGdn
purpurea	CLil EBee GQue LCro MMuc SEND SRms WCru WFar
§ - 'Elegans'	EBee EGrI ELon GQue NBid SRms WFar
* - 'Plena' (d)	LShi NLar
'Queen of the Prairies'	see *F. rubra*
§ *rubra*	ELin MCtn
§ - 'Venusta' ♀H5	Widely available
- 'Venusta Magnifica'	see *F. rubra* 'Venusta'
rufinervis B&SWJ 8469	WCru
- B&SWJ 8611	WCru
§ *ulmaria*	Widely available
- 'Aurea'	CDor CMac EBee ECha EGrI EMor EWhm GMaP LBar LEdu LShi MHol MHoo NBid NLar SRms WCot WFar
- 'Corinne Tremaine'	WHer
- 'Flore Pleno' (d)	IPot LBar LShi NBid WCot WFar WHrl
- 'Rosea'	EBlo LEdu MHoo
§ - 'Variegata' (v)	CBen EBee EWhm GQue MHol NBid NGdn NLar SRms WFar WHer
§ *vulgaris*	CDor CGwi CHab CSpe EGren LRHS LShi MMuc MNHC NAts NBro NMir NQui WBrk WHer
- 'Flore Pleno'	see *F. vulgaris* 'Multiplex'
- 'Grandiflora'	EGrI
§ - 'Multiplex' (d)	CDor CMac CSpe CTtf ECha ELan EMor EPfP GKev GMaP LSto MHer MMuc NBid NBir NLar NRya NSti SMHy SRms WFar
- 'Plena'	see *F. vulgaris* 'Multiplex'

Firmiana (Malvaceae)

simplex	EUrb LBom MBlu NLar SIvy WJur WPGP

Fittonia (Acanthaceae)

sp.	EHap
albivenis Argyroneura Group ♀H1a	WFar
- (Verschaffeltii Group) 'Pearcei'	EGren

Fitzroya (Cupressaceae)

cupressoides	CAco IArd
- 'Borde Hill' (f)	CAco

Flueggea (Phyllanthaceae)

suffruticosa	SBrt

Foeniculum (Apiaceae)

vulgare	Widely available
§ - var. *azoricum* 'Fino'	EKin MCtn
- - 'Orion'	EKin
- - 'Rondo' ♀H2	MCtn
- 'Bronze'	see *F. vulgare* 'Purpureum'
- var. *dulce*	ENfk
§ - 'Giant Bronze'	LCro LEdu WCAu WSpi
§ - 'Purpureum'	Widely available
- 'Smoky'	ECha LSto SAth SMHy
- 'Sweet Florence'	LCro MCtn SVic
- subsp. *vulgare*	LWaG
- 'Zefa Fino'	see *F. vulgare* var. *azoricum* 'Fino'

Fokienia (Cupressaceae)

hodginsii	CAco

Fontinalis (Fontinalaceae)

antipyretica	CPud ELin

Forsythia ✿ (Oleaceae)

'Arnold Brilliant'	WCot
'Arnold Dwarf'	SRms
'Beatrix Farrand' ambig.	SEND SRms
'Beatrix Farrand' K. Sax	MMuc
'Fiesta' (v)	EPfP MAsh WCot WFar
giraldiana	SRms
GOLD TIDE	see *F. MARÉE D'OR*
'Golden Nugget'	CMac ELan SPoG WFar
'Golden Times' (v)	CMac EGren MAsh NEoE SPoG WCot WFar
× *intermedia* 'Arnold Giant'	MBlu
- 'Goldrausch'	EBee EGren ELan LCro LRHS MAsh NLar SNig WHtc
- 'Goldzauber'	CBrac
- 'Lynwood Variety' ♀H5	CBcs CBrac CDoC CMac CMCN CoPl CSBt CWnw EGren ELan EPfP LCro LRHS LSto MAsh MMuc MPri MPro NOra NPip SEND SOrN SPoG SRms SSta WFar WHtc WMat
- - variegated (v)	CMac
- MIKADOR ('Minfor6')PBR	LCro LRHS
- MINIGOLD ('Flojor')	CBrac CMac CSBt ELan LRHS NLar SRms
- 'Nimbus'PBR	CWnw EBee EPfP LRHS MAsh MMrt WFar
- SHOW OFF ('Mindor')PBR	LRHS
- 'Spectabilis'	CBrac EBee EGren EHeP EPfP LBuc LCro MPro MSwo SGol SOrN WFar WHtc
- 'Spectabilis Variegated' (v)	NEoE
- 'Spring Glory'	MHer WSpi
- 'Susan Gruninger' (v)	WCot
- 'Variegata' (v)	SRms
- WEEK END ('Courtalyn') ♀H5	CDoC CEnd EGren ELan EPfP LBuc LCro LRHS MAsh MMuc NLar SEND SGol SPlb WFar
'Kanarek'	NLar
§ MARÉE D'OR ('Courtasol') ♀H5	EGren MAsh NLar SPoG WFar
MÉLÉE D'OR ('Courtaneur')	SGol
'Northern Gold'	MBlu
'Paulina'	EDAr MAsh WCot
suspensa	CMac ESwi SPlb SRms WJur WSpi
- f. *atrocaulis*	WSpi
- 'Hewitt's Gold'	LSto
- 'Nymans'	LRHS NSti SEND

Forsythia

§ - 'Taff's Arnold' (v)	WSpi
- 'Variegata'	see *F. suspensa* 'Taff's Arnold'
'Tremonia'	CMac
viridissima	WJur
- 'Bronxensis'	EPot NBir WAbe WCot WMal
- CITRUS SWIZZLE	NLar WCot
('Mckcitrine'^PBR)	
- var. *koreana* 'Kumsom' (v)	NCth
- 'Weber's Bronx'	GKev
'Yatgold'	WCot

Fortunatia see *Oziroë*

Fortunella see *Citrus*

Fothergilla (Hamamelidaceae)

gardenii	CBcs CJun EPfP MBlu NLar
- 'Blue Mist'	CDoC CJun EBee ELan EPfP LRHS MAsh NLar SPoG SSta WFar
- 'Carolina'	NLar
- 'Suzanne'	CJun NCth NLar
- 'Zundert'	NLar
× *intermedia* BEAVER CREEK ('Klmtwo')	NCth NLar
- 'Blue Shadow'	CBcs CJun EPfP LMil MGos NCth NLar
- 'Mount Airy' ♀H5	CBcs CJun EPfP LRHS NLar
- 'Red Licorice'	CBcs CJun NLar
- 'Sea Spray'	CJun NLar
- 'Windy City'	CJun NLar
major ♀H5	CBcs CDoC CJun EBee EGrI LCro LRHS MBlu MGos MMrt MPri NLar WFar WJur
- 'Bulkyard'	CJun
- Monticola Group	CJun MAsh SSta
- - 'Huntsman'	CJun SSta

Fouquieria (Fouquieriaceae)

columnaris	SPlb
splendens	SPlb

Fragaria ✿ (Rosaceae)

alpina	see *F. vesca* 'Semperflorens'
× ***ananassa*** (F)	CoPl EHet MNHC
- 'Albion'^PBR (F)	CAgr IDun LCro LSRN
- 'Alice'^PBR (F) ♀H6	CAgr EHet EPom LCro
- 'Aromel' (F)	MAsh
- bubbleberry (F)	LCro
- 'Buddy'^PBR (F)	EPom
- 'Cambridge Favourite' (F) ♀H6	CAgr CMac CSBt EGren EHet EPfP EPom GQue LBuc LCro MAsh MGos MPri SBmr SEdi SPlb SVic
- 'Cambridge Vigour' (F)	MAsh
- 'Christine' (F)	CAgr CSBt EPom
- 'Cristina'^PBR (F)	MPri
- 'Cupid'^PBR (F)	EPom LCro
- 'Darselect' (F)	EPom
- 'Elan'^PBR (F)	MNHC
- 'Elegance'^PBR (F)	CSBt EPom MPri
- 'Elsanta' (F)	CSBt CWRo EGren EHet EPfP EPom IArd IDun LBuc LCro MBros MPri NBir SBmr SEdi
- 'Eros' (F)	EHet
- 'Fenella'^PBR (F)	CMac EPom LCro MPri
- 'Finesse' (F) ♀H6	CMac
- 'Flamenco'^PBR (F)	CAgr EPom LEdu
- 'Florence'^PBR (F) ♀H6	CAgr EHet EPom LCro MPri SBmr
- 'Florian' (F)	LEdu
- Fraise des Bois	see *F. vesca*
- 'Framberry' (F)	EPom LEdu
- 'Frau Mieze Schindler' (F)	LEdu
- 'Gariguette' (F)	EPom
- 'Hapil' (F) ♀H6	EHet EPom LBuc LCro
- 'Honeoye' (F) ♀H6	CAgr EHet EPfP EPom IDun LBuc LCro MPri
- JUST ADD CREAM ('Tmstr14pnk'^PBR) (F)	EPom LCro
- 'Korona' (F)	CMac EPom MPri
- 'Malling Allure'^PBR (F)	CSBt EPom
- 'Malling Centenary'^PBR (F) ♀H6	EPom IDun
- 'Malling Opal' (F)	EPom
- 'Malwina'^PBR (F)	EPom SVic
- 'Manille' (F)	EPom
- 'Marshmello' (F)	CMac EPom SBmr
- 'Mount Everest' (F)	LCro
- 'Ostara' (F)	EPom LCro MPri
- 'Pegasus' (F) ♀H6	CAgr EHet EPom LCro
- pineberry (F)	EWhm LEdu
- PINK PANDA ('Frel') (F)	CMac EBee ELan GQue LRHS MHer NGdn NLar SIvy SPel SPoG WCAu WCav
- pink-flowered (F)	GAbr
- 'Red Dream' (F)	LCro
- RED RUBY	see *F.* × *ananassa* 'Samba'
- 'Redgauntlet' (F)	EHet
- 'Rhapsody' (F) ♀H6	LSRN
- 'Roman' (F)	NBir
- 'Romina'^PBR (F)	MPri
- 'Royal Sovereign' (F)	CAgr CMac EPom NBir SVic
- 'Ruby' (F)	NBir
§ - 'Samba'^PBR (F)	ELan LRHS MHer NGdn SMrm SVic
- 'Senga Sengana' (F)	SVic
- SNOW WHITE ('Hansawhit'^PBR) (F)	EPom LEdu
- 'Sonata'^PBR (F)	ELan EPom LCro
- 'Sophie' (F)	EHet
- 'Summer Breeze Snow' (F) **new**	MNHC
- 'Sweetheart' (F)	EHet EPfP EPom LCro MPri
- 'Symphony' (F) ♀H6	CAgr CSBt EPom LBuc LCro LSRN SBmr
- 'Temptation' (F)	MCtn SVic
§ - 'Variegata' (v)	MHoo SPoG
- 'Vibrant'^PBR (F) ♀H6	CSBt EPom
- 'White Dream' (F)	LCro
'Bowles's Double'	see *F. vesca* 'Multiplex'
chiloensis (F)	CoPl GQue WKor
- 'Chaval' (F)	ECha EPPr LEdu
- 'Variegata' misapplied	see *F.* × *ananassa* 'Variegata'
indica	see *Duchesnea indica*
LIPSTICK ('Stickbolwi') (F)	MHoo NLar WCAu WSpi
moschata	CAgr LCro MCtn WKor
nilgerrensis from China	GGro
- from India	GGro
nubicola	CAgr
- 'Polka' (F)	IDun
§ **vesca** (F)	Widely available
- 'Alexandria' (F)	ENfk IDun MCtn SHor SVic WKit
- 'Alpina Scarletta' (F)	ENfk
- 'Alpine Yellow' (F)	IDun
- 'Baron Solemacher' (F)	WHer
- 'Capron Royale' (F)	CAgr
- 'Flore Pleno'	see *F. vesca* 'Multiplex'
- 'Fructu Albo' (F)	CAgr LEdu
- 'Golden Alexandra' (F)	ECha EWhm
- 'Mara des Bois' (F)	EPom
- 'Mignonette' (F)	EWhm MCtn
- 'Monophylla' (F)	WHer
§ - 'Multiplex' (d)	EPPr WHer
§ - 'Muricata'	LEdu LShi
- 'Pineapple Crush' (F)	MWlw WHer

- 'Plymouth Strawberry'	see *F. vesca* 'Muricata'
- 'Scarlet Beauty' (F)	EPom
§ - 'Semperflorens' (F)	CoPl
- 'Semperflorens Alba' (F)	CAgr LShi
- 'Variegata' misapplied	see *F.* × *ananassa* 'Variegata'
- 'Yellow Wonder' (F)	CoPl LCro
virginiana	CAgr WKor
viridis	CAgr WKor

Frailea (Cactaceae)
mammifera new	SPlb

Francoa ❁ (Francoaceae)
appendiculata	GKev NBir StAn WHer
'Confetti'	SHar
* dwarf purple	CElw
'Purple Spike'	see *F. sonchifolia* Rogerson's form
ramosa	EBee GKev NBir NBro SDix SMrm
sonchifolia	Widely available
- 'Alba'	GKev
- 'Cally Dwarf Purple'	ESwi
- 'Culm View Lilac'	MMuc
- 'Molly Anderson'	GKev
- 'Petite Bouquet'	EWes LBar MHol SRms WNPC
- 'Pink Bouquet'	CKno CMac LBar LCro LSRN MHol MPro NWbg SRkn WFar WHil
- 'Pink Giant'	CBWd CSpe EPfP EWhm GKev LBar MBNS WFar
§ - Rogerson's form	CElw CMiW MCtn NBir SDix WChS WFar WHil

Frangula (Rhamnaceae)
§ ***alnus***	CBWd CCVT CHab CLnd CMac ELan LBuc LSto MBlu MGos SEWo WFar WJur WMou WRjT
- 'Aspleniifolia'	EPfP LMaj LRHS MBlu MGos MMrt MPri NLar WPGP
- 'Minaret'	MBlu
- 'Ron Williams'	EBee ELan EPfP EUrb LRHS MBlu MGos MMrt MSCN NLar NPip SArc SPoG WFar
californica B&SWJ 14267	WCru

Frankenia (Frankeniaceae)
laevis	SRms
thymifolia	ECha LRHS MAsh MHer SLee SPlb SPoG WHoo

Franklinia (Theaceae)
alatamaha	CBcs LRHS MBlu WPGP

Franklinia × *Gordonia* see × *Gordlinia*

Frasera (Gentianaceae)
speciosa	MPro

Fraxinus ❁ (Oleaceae)
americana	EBar
- 'Autumn Purple'	IPap
angustifolia 'Raywood'	IPap LMaj SEND
bungeana	WJur
chiisanensis B&SWJ 12726	WCru
excelsior	CWRo
- 'Jaspidea'	LMaj
mandshurica	LMaj
mariesii	see *F. sieboldiana*
ornus	EBar ELan SEND
- OBELISK	IPap
pennsylvanica 'Summit'	IPap
§ ***sieboldiana***	WJur
uhdei	GKev

Freesia (Iridaceae)
alba (G.L. Mey.) Gumbl.	CPbh
andersoniae	WCot
'Blue Moon'	LCro
'Delta River'	EPfP SPoG
'Fragrant Sunburst'	EPfP SPoG
fucata	CPbh
'Gold River'	SPoG
§ ***laxa***	CBlu CPbh CSpe CTtf EAri EPot LEdu WFar WSpi XFar
- var. ***alba***	CPbh SChr WFar
- 'Joan Evans'	CTtf WAbe WFar
leichtlinii subsp. ***alba***	SChr WCot
'Red River'	SPoG
refracta	CPbh
Royal Series	MCtn
'White River'	SPoG

Fremontodendron (Malvaceae)
'California Glory' ♀H4	CBcs CDoC CMac EAri EPfP EUrb LCro LRHS LSRN MAsh MBlu MGos MHol MPri SArc SBig SPoG SVen
californicum	EBee ELan NLar SEND SPlb
'Pacific Sunset'	MGos

Freylinia (Scrophulariaceae)
cestroides	see *F. lanceolata*
§ ***lanceolata***	CBcs EUrb SEle SPlb SVen
tropica	SEle
visseri	SVen

Fritillaria ❁ (Liliaceae)
acmopetala ♀H4	CBro CMiW EPot ERCP GArf GKev LAma MCtn MNrw MPie NNys SHar XFar
amana	EPot GKev LAma
arabica	see *F. persica*
assyriaca	EPot
bucharica	GKev LAma
camschatcensis	EPot GArf GEdr GKev GMaP LAma NBir NLar
- 'Alaska'	GArf GEdr GMaP NHar
- 'Aurea'	NHar
- black-flowered	NHar
- double-flowered (d)	GEdr
- f. ***flavescens***	GEdr
davidii	NDry
davisii	EPot GKev LAma NNys
'Early Dream'	GKev LAma
'Early Fantasy'	LCro XFar
'Early Passion'	GKev
'Early Sensation'	GKev LAma
eduardii	GKev
- var. ***eduardii***	GKev LAma
- 'Pollux'	LAma
elwesii	EPot ERCP GKev LAma MNrw NLar XFar
'Helena' ♀H4	EPot ERCP GKev LAma NLar SPhx
imperialis ♀H7	NNys
- 'Argenteovariegata' (v)	GKev LAma LCro
* - 'Aurea'	MArl
- 'Aureomarginata' (v)	GKev LAma XFar
- 'Aurora'	EGren EPot ETay GKev LAma NLar NPer SPhx XFar
- 'Double Gold' (d)	GKev LAma NLar
- 'Garland Star'	GKev LAma NLar
- 'Lutea'	EGren GKev LAma LCro LRHS MArl SPoG XFar
- 'Maxima'	see *F. imperialis* 'Rubra Maxima'

Fritillaria

- 'Maxima Lutea' ♥H7 — CBro EPfP EPot ETay MHtn NLar SPoG
- 'Orange Beauty' — GKev LAma XFar
- 'Prolifera' — GKev LAma
- 'Rubra' ♥H7 — EPfP ETay GKev LAma LCro NLar XFar
§ - 'Rubra Maxima' — EGren EPfP EPot LRHS
- 'Slagzwaard' — GKev LAma
- 'Striped Beauty' — EPot
- 'Sulpherino' — GKev LAma
- 'The Premier' — LAma
- 'William Rex' — EPfP EPot GKev LAma LBuc NLar SPoG

meleagris ♥H5 — Widely available
- 'Eros' — GKev
- var. **unicolor** — CBro ERCP GKev LCro MCtn MHtn
  subvar. **alba** ♥H5 — NNys SDix WShi XFar
- - - 'Aphrodite' — EPot LAma NBir WCot

michailovskyi — ERCP ETay GKev LAma LRHS MNrw SPoG SRms XFar

olivieri — GKev LAma

pallidiflora ♥H5 — CBro CMiW EPot ERCP GKev LAma LCro MCtn MNrw MPie SPhx

'Paradise Beauty' — GKev
§ **persica** — ECha EGren EPfP EPot ERCP ETay GKev LAma LCro LRHS LSto MPro NLar SPeP

- 'Adiyaman' ♥H4 — EGrI
- 'Alba' — SPeP
- 'Bicolor' ♥H4 — CBro GKev LAma
- 'Blues Brothers' — GKev LAma
- 'Green Dreams' ♥H4 — ERCP GKev LAma NLar SPeP XFar
- 'Ivory Bells' ♥H4 — EPot GKev LAma LCro NLar XFar
- 'Magic Bells' — GKev LAma XFar
- 'Minaret' — GKev LAma XFar
- 'Purple Dynamite' ♥H4 — GKev LAma XFar
- 'Purple Favorite' — GKev LAma
* - 'Senkoy' — GKev
- 'Twin Towers Tribute' ♥H4 — GKev LAma XFar

pontica ♥H4 — CBro EPfP EPot LAma MCtn MPie
pyrenaica 'Lutea' — GEdr
raddeana — EAri EPot ERCP GKev LAma LCro NLar SPhx WCot XFar

'Red Beauty' ♥H4 — CBro ERCP GKev LRHS SPhx XFar
reuteri — GKev LAma
- **major** — see *F. imperialis* 'Rubra Maxima'
sewerzowii — EPot GKev LAma LRHS
- 'Green Eyes' — GKev LAma
stenanthera — GKev LAma XFar
'Sunrise' **new** — LAma
'Sunset' ♥H4 — GKev LAma LRHS NLar
thunbergii — LAma SHar
uva-vulpis — CAby EGren EPot ERCP GKev LAma LCro LShi LSto MNrw MPie NBir NNys
verticillata — ECha
'Yellow Beauty' ♥H4 **new** — LAma

Fuchsia ♣ (Onagraceae)

'A.M. Larwick' — SLBF
'Abbé Farges' (d) — SLBF SVic WFar
'Achievement' ♥H4 — SVic
'Adinda' (T) ♥H1c — EPts MHer
'Adrienne' (d) — EPts
'Aisen' — WFar
'Alan Swaby' — EPts
'Alan Titchmarsh' ♥H2 — EPts SLBF
'Alderford' — SLBF
'Alice Hoffman' (d) ♥H4 — CEnd CMac EBee EHeP ELon EPfP EPts LCro LRHS LShi MAsh MGos MPri NLar SLBF SPoG SVic WFar

'Alicia Sellars' — SLBF
'Alison Ewart' — SVic
'Alison Patricia' ♥H2 — SLBF SVic
'All Summer Beauty' (T) — SLBF
'Allen Jackson' — SLBF
alpestris — EPPr SLBF
'Alyssa May Garcia' (d) — EPts SLBF
'Amazing Maisie' (d) — SLBF
'Amelia Rose' — SLBF
'Amy J' — SLBF
'Amy Lye' — SVic
'Angela Leslie' (d) — SVic
'Angel's Kiss' (E) — SLBF
'Anita' — EPts SLBF
'Ann Howard Tripp' — EPts SVic
'Ann Reid' — SLBF
'Anna of York' **new** — SLBF
'Anna Sunshine' (T) — EPts
'Annabel' (d) ♥H4 — EPts LRHS SLBF SMrm SPoG SVic
'Annie Brookfield' (d) — SLBF
'Annie Hall' (E) — SLBF
'Annie M.G. Schmidt' — EPts
'Antigone' — SLBF
aprica misapplied — see *F.* × *bacillaris*
aprica Lundell — see *F. microphylla* subsp. *aprica*
'Apricot Ice' — SVic
'Apryl's Tears' (E) — SLBF
arborea — see *F. arborescens*
§ **arborescens** ♥H1c — CBcs CHll CTsd CWCL EAri ELan EUrb EWld LRHS LShi SIvy SLBF SPad SPel SVic WCot WFar
- B&SWJ 10475 — WCru
'Ariel' (E) — SVic
'Army Nurse' (d) ♥H4 — CEnd ELan ELon EPts LBom LCro MGos NBir NLar SLBF SVic
'Ashley' — SLBF
'Ashtede' — SLBF
'Ashville' — SLBF
'Aurora Superba' — SLBF
'Autumnale' ♥H2 — EPts SLBF SPoG
'Avalanche' ambig. (d) — SLBF
'Awake Sweet Love' (T) — EPts
'Aylisa Rowan' (E) — SLBF
'Azure Sky' (d) — SLBF
'Baby Blue Eyes' ♥H4 — ELan ELon MAsh SLBF SVic
'Baby Chang' — SLBF
§ × **bacillaris** (E) — CAbb EPPr EWes LRHS SEle SIvy SLBF SPoG WHer
§ - 'Cottinghamii' (E) — EWld
§ - 'Reflexa' (E) — NQui
'Ballerina Girl' (E) — SLBF
'Ballet Girl' (d) ♥H2 — LCro SLBF
'Banstead Bell' (d) — SLBF
'Barbara' — EPts SVic
'Bashful' (d) — EPts SVic
'Beacon' — CMac ELon EPts LRHS SLBF SPoG SVic WFar
'Beacon Rosa' ♥H4 — EPts LRHS SLBF SPoG SVic
'Bella Rosella' (California Dreamers Series) (d) ♥H2 — LCro MBros
'Ben de Jong' — SLBF WFar
'Ben Jammin' — CDoC EPts SVic
'Ben-Ben' — SLBF
'Bernie's Big-un' — SLBF
'Bernisser Hardy' ♥H4 — EPts NQui SLBF
'Beverley' — EPts
'Bicentennial' (d) — LCro MBros
'Billy Green' (T) ♥H2 — EPts MHer SVic
'Blacky' (d) — CTsd EUrb LShi SVic WCot WFar
'Bland's New Striped' — EPts SLBF
§ 'Blauer Engel' (d) — LCro

Fuchsia 287

BLUE ANGEL	see *F.* 'Blauer Engel'
'Blue Bush'	EPts SVic
'Blue Gown' (d)	SVic
'Blue Lace' (d)	SVic
'Blue Mirage' (d)	SVic
'Bobby's Girl'	EPts
'Bob's Best' (d)	EPts
boliviana ambig.	MHer
§ *boliviana* Carrière	CHll EAri EGrI EPPr EWld WFar WKif
- B&SWJ 14871	WCru
§ - var. *alba* ♀H2	CHll CSpe EPts SLBF WFar
- var. *boliviana*	CRHN
- var. *luxurians* 'Alba'	see *F. boliviana* Carrière var. *alba*
- f. *puberulenta* Munz	see *F. boliviana* Carrière
'Bon Accorde'	EPts SLBF SVic
'Boogie Nights'	SLBF
I 'Boogie Woogie'	EPts SLBF
'Border Pearl' **new**	SLBF
'Border Queen' ♀H4	EPts SLBF SVic
'Border Regiment'	SLBF
'Bouquet' (d)	SLBF
'Boy Marc' (T) ♀H1c	SLBF
'Breevis Minimus'	SLBF
'Brookwood Belle' (d) ♀H3	EPts SLBF
'Brutus' ♀H4	EPts MAsh SLBF SVic WFar
'Buster' (d)	SLBF
campos-portoi	EBee WPGP
'Cardinal Farges' (d)	SLBF SVic
'Careless Whisper'	SLBF
'Carla Johnston' ♀H2	EPts SVic WFar
'Carmel Blue'	SPoG SVic WFar
'Cecile' (d)	SPoG WFar
'Celia Smedley' ♀H3	EPts LCro SLBF SVic
'Ceri'	WMal
'Chalk 'n' Cheese' (d)	SLBF
'Chang' ♀H2	SLBF
'Chantelle Garcia' (d)	EPts SLBF
'Chapel Rossan' (E)	SLBF
'Charles Welch'	EPts
'Charming'	MAsh SVic
'Checkerboard' ♀H3	EPts MHer SLBF SVic
'Chelsea Louise'	EPts
'Cherry Lee'	SLBF
'Chillerton Beauty' ♀H4	ELan ELon EPts NLar SLBF SVic WFar
'Chilli Red'	LBom LCro LRHS MPro WNPC
'China Lantern'	SVic
'Chris and Kath' (d)	SLBF
cinerea	SLBF
'Citation'	SVic
'Clair de Lune'	SLBF
'Claudia' (d)	MBros SLBF
'Cliff's Hardy'	SVic
'Cliff's Own'	SVic
'Clifton Charm'	EPts SVic
'Cloth of Gold'	SLBF SVic
'Cloverdale Pearl'	MAsh SPoG
'Coachman' ♀H4	EPts SLBF
coccinea	SVic
'Colette Kelly'	SVic
'Colin Dorrington'	SLBF
'Connie' (d)	SVic
'Connor's Cascade'	SLBF
'Conspicua' ♀H4	SLBF SVic
'Constance' (d)	EPts SLBF SVic
'Constance Comer'	SVic
'Coralle' (T) ♀H1c	EBee EPts MNHC SLBF WFar
'Corallina' ♀H4	SVic
* *cordata* B&SWJ 9095	WCru
- B&SWJ 10325	WCru
cordifolia misapplied	see *F. splendens*
corymbiflora misapplied	see *F. boliviana* Carrière
'Cotta Bright Star'	SLBF
'Cotta Christmas Tree' (E)	SLBF WFar
'Cottinghamii'	see *F.* × *bacillaris* 'Cottinghamii'
'Cotton Candy' (d)	SVic
'Countdown Carol' (d)	EPts
'Countess of Aberdeen'	SLBF
cylindracea misapplied	see *F.* × *bacillaris*
'Dana Samantha'	EPts
'Dancing Bloom'	EPts
'Dancing Dawn' (E)	SLBF
'Dancing Flame' (d) ♀H3	EPts MBros MHer SLBF SPoG
'Dark Eyes' (d) ♀H4	LCro MHer SLBF SPoG
'David' ♀H4	ELon EPts LRHS MPro SLBF SPoG WCot WFar
'Dawn Fantasia' (v)	EPts
'DebRon's Black Cherry'	SLBF
'Deep Purple' (d)	WFar
'Delia Smith' (d)	EPts
'Delicate Purple'	EPts LRHS SLBF WFar
'Delphobe'	EPts
'Delta's Bride'	SLBF
'Delta's Groom'	SLBF
'Delta's Paljas'	SLBF
'Delta's Sara'	CBcs ELon EPts EUrb GBin LBom LBuc LCro LRHS MAsh MBros MHer MHtn MPri SPoG SVic WFar
§ *denticulata* ♀H2	EPts MHer SLBF SVic WFar
'Derby Imp'	SLBF
'Devonshire Dumpling' (d) ♀H2	EPts
'Diamond Wedding'	SVic
'Dipton Dainty' (d)	SVic
'Display' ♀H4	EPfP EPts LRHS MGos MPri NPer SLBF SPoG SVic WFar
'Diva'	WCot
'Doc'	EPts SVic
'Doctor Foster' ♀H4	SVic
'Doctor Robert'	EPts
§ 'Dollar Prinzessin' (d) ♀H4	CMac EPfP EPts LBom LCro MBros MGos MHer MPri NPer SLBF SMrm SPlb SVic WFar
'Dopy' (d)	EPts SVic
'Doray'	EPts
'Doreen Redfern'	SVic
'Doris Joan'	SLBF
'Dorothy'	EPts SLBF
'Dorothy Ann'	SLBF
'Dorothy Hanley' (d)	EPts SLBF SVic WFar
'Dotti' (d)	SLBF
'Drame' (d)	SVic
'Duchess of Cornwall' (d)	EPts
'Duke of Wellington' Stokes	SLBF
'Dunrobin Bedder'	SLBF
'Dying Embers' ♀H4	CBcs GBin LBom LRHS LShi LSto MAsh MHer SDix SLBF SVic WCot WFar
'Edith' ambig.	EPts
'Edith' Brown (d)	SLBF
'El Cid'	SVic
'Elfin Glade'	SLBF SVic
'Ellie Jane'	EPts
'Elsa' (d)	SVic
'Emily Eve' (d)	EPts SLBF
'Emma Chapman' (d)	SLBF
'Emma Payne'	SLBF
'Empress of Prussia' ♀H4	EPts LRHS SLBF SVic
§ 'Enfant Prodigue' (d)	SDix SLBF SVic
'Eric' (E) **new**	SLBF
'Ernie' PBR	EPts SLBF

'Ernie Bromley'	SLBF
'Eruption' (T)	CTsd CWCL
'Eternal Flame' (d)	EPts
'Eunice' (E) **new**	SLBF
'Eva Boerg' ♀H4	EPts LCro MBros SPoG WKif
'Evensong'	SVic
'Evita'PBR (Bella Series)	LCro
excorticata ♀H2	CBcs ESwi SIvy SPlb
'Exmoor Woods'	WFar
'Fairy Lights'	LBom LRHS MPri MPro
'Falklands' (d)	EPts SLBF
'Festival Lights' (E)	SLBF
'Ffion'	EPts
'Finn'	EPts
'Fiona'	SVic
'Fiona Pitt' (E)	SLBF
'Flamingo Wings' (d)	EPts
'Flanders Field'	SLBF
'Flash' ♀H4	ELan ELon EPts SLBF SPoG SVic WOld
'Flashlight'	MAsh WFar
'Flat Jack o' Lancashire' (d)	SLBF
'Fleur de Picardie'	SLBF
'Flirtation Waltz' (d)	SVic
'Flocon de Neige'	SLBF
'Flogman'	EWld
'Flying Cloud' (d)	SVic
'Flying Scotsman' (d)	EPts SVic
'Four Farthings' (d)	EPts
'Foxgrove Wood' ♀H4	SLBF SVic
'Frank Saunders'	SLBF
'Frankie Boy'	SLBF
'Frans Boers'	SLBF
'Frau Hilde Rademacher' (d)	EPts SVic
'Fred's First' (d)	SVic
'Frosted Flame'	SLBF
'Frozen Tears'	EPts
'Fuchsiarama '91' (T) ♀H2	SLBF
'Fuji-san'	ELon EPts
fulgens (T) ♀H2	CHll CWal EPpR EWld
* - 'Variegata' (T/v)	EPts
'Fulpila'	SLBF
'Galadriel'	SLBF WFar
'Garden News' (d) ♀H4	EPts LCro LRHS MAsh MBros MHtn NBir NPer SAdn SLBF SVic WFar
'Gartenmeister Bonstedt' (T) ♀H1c	EWld
'Général Monk' (d)	EPts
'Genii' ♀H4	Widely available
'George Evans'	SLBF
'George W. Wilson' (d)	SLBF
'Gina Bowman' (E)	SLBF
'Gladiator' (d)	CMac
'Gladys Lorimer'	EPts
glazioviana ♀H2	EPPr SLBF
§ 'Globosa'	CAgr SBrt
'Golden Dawn'	SVic
'Golden Girl'	SLBF
'Göttingen' (T)	SLBF
gracilis	see *F. magellanica* var. *gracilis*
'Graf Witte'	EPPr SVic
'Grayrigg'	ECha ELon EPPr EPts LSRN LSto MHer SLBF SVic
'Great Ouse' (d)	EPts
'Greenpeace'	SLBF
'Greta's Love' (E) **new**	SLBF
'Grumpy'	SVic
'Hannah Rogers'	SLBF
'Happy'	EPts MHer SVic
'Happy Birthday' (d)	MAsh
'Happy Wedding Day' (d)	LCro MHer SVic
'Harbour Lites'	SLBF
'Harlow Car'	EPts
'Harry Gray' (d) ♀H2	EPts SLBF SPoG
'Harry Taylor' (d)	EPts
'Harry's Sunshine'	SLBF
hartwegii	MHer
hatschbachii ♀H2	CBcs EBee EPPr EWes SBrt SDix SIvy SLBF SPlb SVen WFar WPGP
'Hawaiian Sunset' (d)	SLBF
'Hawkshead' ♀H4	Widely available
'Hayley Jay' (d)	SLBF
'Heidi Ann' (d) ♀H4	EPfP EPts LCro MAsh MBros SLBF SPoG SVic
'Helen Coupland' **new**	SLBF
'Hemsleyana'	see *F. microphylla* subsp. *hemsleyana*
'Herald' ♀H4	MGos SLBF SVic
'Herbé de Jacques'	see *F.* 'Mr West'
'Hermiena'	EPts MHer SLBF SVic
'Herps Serang'	SLBF
'Hi Di'	SLBF
'Hidcote Beauty' ♀H2	SLBF
HILDA ('Bf03')PBR (Bella Series)	SPoG
'Hobson's Choice' (d)	SLBF
'Holly Molly' (d)	SLBF
'Hot Coals'	SVic
'Howlett's Hardy' ♀H4	SVic
'Icecap'	SVic
'Icicles Chandelier'	SLBF
'Icy Pink' (d)	SPoG
'Icy Tears'	SVic
'Imogen Faye' (d)	SLBF
'Insulinde' (T)	EPts MHer SLBF WFar
'Isn't She Lovely'	SLBF
'Jac Damen'	SLBF
'Jack Shahan' ♀H2	EPts
'Jack Stanway' (v)	LRHS
'Jan Everett' (d)	SLBF
'Jane Linda' **new**	SLBF
'Janice Keane'	SLBF
'Janie' (d)	LBuc MAsh SVic
'Jaspers Formidable' (T)	SLBF
'Jaspers Lightning' (T)	SLBF WFar
'Jaspers Unbelievable' (T)	SLBF WFar
'Jean Taylor'	EPts SLBF
'Jean Webb' (v)	WCot
'Jennifer Ann'	SLBF WFar
'Jenny May'	EPts
'Jess'	SLBF
'Jill Holloway' (T)	SLBF
'Jim Dodge' (d)	EPts
'Jim Gordon' **new**	SLBF
'Joan Cooper'	SLBF SVic
'Jo-Anne Fisher' (d)	EPts
'John Galea'	SLBF
'John Maynard Scales' (T) ♀H2	SLBF WFar
'John Ridding'PBR (T/v)	SPoG
'Johnny Boy'	SLBF
I 'Joy'	SLBF
'Joy Patmore'	SLBF
'Judith Coupland'	SLBF
'Just Terry' (d)	SLBF
'Karen Isles' (E)	SLBF
'Karen Louise Tinker'	SLBF
'Kate Taylor' (d)	SLBF
'Kath Barnes' (E)	SLBF
'Katie Rogers'	EPts
'Katjan'	SLBF
'Katrina Thompsen'	EPts SLBF

Fuchsia 289

'Kenny Walkling' ♀H2	SLBF
'Kit Oxtoby' (d)	SPoG
'Kolding Perle'	SLBF
'La Campanella' (d) ♀H2	MBros SPoG WFar
'Lady Boothby' ♀H4	CBcs CCoa CDoC CSde EBee ELan ELon EPts EWld LBom LCro LRHS MHer NLar SAdn SAth SEND SIvy SLBF SMrm SPlb SPoG SVen SVic WFar WJun WOld
'Lady Framlingham' (d)	EPts
'Lady in Black' (d)	ELan ELon LBom LCro MPri SPoG
'Lady Isobel Barnett'	SLBF
'Lady Kindar' **new**	SLBF
'Lady Thumb' (d) ♀H3	CDoC CMac CoPl EBee EHeP ELan EPfP EPts LCro LRHS MAsh MGos NCth NLar SPlb SPoG SVic WFar
'Land van Beveren'	SLBF
'Last Chance' (E)	SLBF
'Laura' ambig.	SVic
I 'Laura' (Dutch)	EPts
'Laura Cross' (E)	SLBF
'Lechlade Gorgon'	LRHS SLBF WJun
'Lechlade Magician'	EPts SEND SLBF
'Lena' (d) ♀H2	CMac EPts SLBF SMrm SPlb SVic
'Leonora'	SVic
'Leslie Bowman' ♀H2	SLBF
'Lett's Delight' (d)	EPts
'Leverhulme'	see *F.* 'Leverkusen'
§ 'Leverkusen' (T)	SLBF
'Liebriez' (d) ♀H4	SVic
'Lilac Lustre' (d)	SVic
'Lillian Annetts' (d) ♀H2	SLBF
'Linda Hinchliffe'	EPts MHer SLBF WFar
'Lionel'	SLBF
'Little Beauty'	SVic
'Little Brook Gem'	SLBF
'Little Catbells' (E)	SLBF
'Little Cracker'	SPoG
'Little Jessica' (E)	SLBF
'Little Tony'	SLBF
'Loeky'	SVic
'Logan Garden'	see *F. magellanica* 'Logan Woods'
'London 2000'	SLBF
'London in Bloom'	SLBF
'Lord Lonsdale'	EPts
'Lord Roberts'	EPts SLBF
'Lorna Swinbank'	SVic
'Lottie Hobby' (E) ♀H3	CMac EGrI ELan EPts LRHS SVic WAbe WCot
'Loveliness'	SVic
loxensis misapplied	see *F.* 'Speciosa'
'Lye's Own'	SLBF
'Lye's Unique' ♀H3	CAby EPts SLBF SVic
'Lyndon'	SLBF
'Lynne Patricia' (d)	EPts
'Machu Picchu'	EPts
'Madame Cornélissen' (d) ♀H4	CMac EHeP ELan LCro LRHS NCth NLar SEND SLBF SVic
magellanica ♀H4	CBcs CoPl CWal GArf MAsh MMuc NPer SVic WFar WOld WSpi
- 'Alba'	see *F. magellanica* var. *molinae* 'Alba'
- 'Alba Variegata' (v)	WFar
- 'Arauco'	CBcs EWld LBom LRHS MBNS MPri MPro NCth SBrt WJun WPGP
- 'Folius Aureus'	WFar
- 'Gold Mountain'	WFar
§ - var. *gracilis* ♀H4	CAgr LRHS NBro
- - 'Aurea' ♀H4	CMac CoPl EHeP ELan ELon EPPr MHer SDix SLBF SRms SVic
- - 'Variegata' (v) ♀H4	LRHS MGos SVic
§ - - 'Versicolor' (v) ♀H4	CBcs CDoC CMac CoPl EBee ECha EHeP ELan ELon EPfP EPPr EPts EWes GKin LRHS MBlu SDix SEND SLBF SPlb SPoG SRms SVic WFar
- 'Lady Bacon'	CBcs EBee ELon EPfP EWes MHer MMrt SEND SLBF SPoG WFar WOld WPGP
§ - 'Logan Woods'	CAby EBee ELon EPfP GKin MBlu SLBF SMrm WFar WPGP
- var. *molinae*	CAby CFis EBee ELan GBin LSto MBlu MHer MNrw NBid NPer SPlb WFar
§ - - 'Alba' ♀H4	CDoC EHeP ESgI EWld GArf LRHS SEND SVic WFar WSpi
I - - 'Alba Aureovariegata' (v)	CBcs CMac LRHS WFar
- - 'Golden Sharpitor' (v)	WFar
- - 'Mr Knight's Blush'	WSpi
§ - - 'Sharpitor' (v) ♀H4	CDoC EBee ECha ELon EPfP NPer SPoG WFar WKif
- 'Pumila'	EPot EWes GArf MHer WAbe WFar
§ - 'Thomsonii' ♀H4	SMHy
- 'Variegata Aurea' (v)	EHeP WFar
'Magic Lanterns'	MPro
'Major Heaphy'	SLBF
'Mancunian' (d)	SLBF
'Mandarin Cream'	WFar
'Maori Maid' (d)	LCro
'Marble Crepe' (T)	SLBF
'Marcus Graham' (d)	SLBF
'Margaret' (d) ♀H4	CoPl ELon EPts LRHS SLBF SVic WFar
'Margaret Aldren'	SLBF
'Margaret Brown' ♀H4	SLBF SVic
'Margaret Viscountess Thurso'	SLBF
'Margarite Dawson' (d)	SVic
'Maria Landy'	SLBF
'Mariana'	EPts
'Marin Glow' ♀H3	SVic
'Marina Kelly'	SLBF
'Marinka' ♀H2	EPts MBros SLBF
MARISKA ('Bfi01'PBR) (Bella Series)	LCro
'Marlies de Keijzer' (E)	EPts SLBF
'Martha Adcock'	SLBF
'Martin's Yellow Surprise' (T)	SLBF
'Mary' (T) ♀H1c	EPts SLBF WCot
'Mauve Beauty' (d)	SLBF
'Mauve Wisp' (d)	SVic
'Mavis Enderby'	SLBF
'Max Cobi'	SLBF
I 'Maxima'	EPts MHer SLBF
'Mersty' (d)	SLBF
'Michael' (d/v)	EPts
'Michael Wallis' (T)	SLBF
michoacanensis misapplied	see *F. microphylla* subsp. *aprica*
michoacanensis Sessé & Moç. B&SWJ 9148 (E)	WCru
'Micky Goult' ♀H2	EPts
microphylla (E) ♀H3	CBcs CElw CFis CTsd CWal EBee GBin GQue SMHy SMrm SPel SRkn SVic WFar
- B&SWJ 10331 (E)	WCru
§ - subsp. *aprica* B&SWJ 9101 (E)	WCru
- - 'Dolly's Dress' (E)	WCru
I - 'David'	WFar
§ - subsp. *hemsleyana* (E)	SVic
- - B&SWJ 10478 (E)	WCru

Fuchsia

– – 'Silver Lining' (E)	CTsd EPPr ESwi LCro SAth SDix WCru WFar WNPC
– 'Variegata' (E/v)	EWes
§ 'Mieke Meursing' ♀H2	SLBF SVic
'Millennium'	EPts
'Millfield Alpha'	EPts
'Millfield Charlie'	EPts
'Millfield Echo'	EPts WFar
'Miniature Jewels' (E)	SLBF
minimiflora misapplied	see *F.* × *bacillaris*
'Minipani'	SLBF
'Minirose'	SLBF
'Miramere'	EPts
'Mischief'	SVic
'Misha Charlotte'	SLBF
'Miss California' (d)	SLBF
'Miss Muffett' (d)	EPts
'Mission Bells'	EPts SLBF SVic
'Mr A. Huggett'	EPts SLBF
§ 'Mr West' (v)	WFar
'Mrs Audrey Berkley' (d)	SLBF
'Mrs Marshall'	EMal SLBF
'Mrs Popple' ♀H4	CDoC CEnd CMac EGren EHeP ELan EPfP EPts GKin LBom LCro LRHS MAsh MGos MNHC MPri NCth NLar SAdn SLBF SPlb SPoG SVic WFar
'Mrs W. Castle'	SVic
'Mrs W. Rundle'	SLBF
'Mrs W.P. Wood' ♀H4	ELon LRHS MSCN SVic
'My Clive' (d) **new**	SLBF
'My Grandchildren'	SLBF
'My Little Angel' (E) **new**	SLBF
'My Mum' Dobson	SLBF
'My Pat'	SLBF
'My Sacha'	SLBF
'Myriad'	SLBF
'Nancy Lou' (d)	SLBF SVic
'Nathan Rhys'	EPts
'Neopolitan' (E)	EPts SVic
'Nephele'	EPts
'New Millennium' (d)	LCro
'Nicki's Findling'	EPts
'Nicola Jane' (d)	EPts SLBF SVic
NIKITA ('Bf05'PBR) (Bella Series)	SPoG
'Northern Jewel'	SLBF
'Northilda'	SVic
'Nottingham Jubilee'	SLBF
'O Sole Mio'	SVic
'Obcylin' (E)	EPts MHer
'Ocean Beach'	EPts
'Olive Smith'	EPts
'Orange Crystal'	SLBF SVic
'Orange Drops'	EPts
'Orange Flare'	SLBF
'Orange Star' (E)	SLBF
'Orangeblossom'	SLBF
'Ornamental Pearl' (v)	SLBF
'Other Fellow'	EPts SLBF
'Oulton Empress' (E)	SLBF
'Oulton Red Imp' (E)	SLBF
'Oulton Travellers Rest' (E)	SLBF
'Our Carol'	SLBF
'Our Debbie'	SLBF
'Our Spencer'	SLBF
'Our Ted' (T)	EPts
'Overbecks'	see *F. magellanica* var. *molinae* 'Sharpitor'
'Overbecks Ruby'	WCot
'P and C'	SLBF
'Pam Plack'	SLBF
'Pan'	SLBF
paniculata (T) ♀H2	CRHN EGrI EPts MHer SLBF
'Papoose' (d)	SVic WFar
parviflora misapplied	see *F.* × *bacillaris*
'Pat Bastiman' **new**	SLBF
'Patio Princess' (d)	EPts MHer SMrm
'Patricia Hodge' (Buds of May Series)	LCro
'Paula Jane' (d) ♀H2	SLBF SPoG SVic
'P.E. King' (d)	SLBF
'Pee Wee Rose'	SVic
'Peppermint Chip' (d)	SLBF
'Perky Pink' (d)	EPts
'Perry Park'	SVic
'Perry's Jumbo'	NPer
perscandens	MWIw
petiolaris B&SWJ 10675	WCru
'Phaenna'	SLBF
'Phileine' (T)	WFar
'Phyllis' (d) ♀H4	EPts SLBF SVic
'Piet van der Sande'	SLBF
'Pink Ballet Girl' (d)	SVic
'Pink Bon Accord'	SVic
'Pink Fantasia' ♀H2	EPts SLBF SVic
PINK FIZZ ('Fngenfu01'PBR)	LRHS
'Pink Galore' (d) ♀H2	MHer SPoG
'Pink Goon' (d)	SVic
'Pink Haze'	SVic
'Pink Ice' (d)	MBros
'Pink Marshmallow' (d) ♀H4	SLBF SPoG
'Pink Spangles'	see *F.* 'Mieke Meursing'
'Pixie'	SLBF SVic
'Playboy' (d)	SVic
'Polar Fairy'	LRHS MPri
'Ponty Boy'	SLBF
'Popsie Girl' (v)	SLBF
'Posset Sparkler'	SLBF
'President Derek Luther'	SLBF
'President George Bartlett' (d) ♀H2	EPts SLBF
'President Joan Morris' (d)	SLBF
'President Moir' (d)	SLBF
'President Peter Holloway'	EPts SLBF
'President Stanley Wilson' (d)	EPts
'President Val Hitchcock'	SLBF
'Preston'	CMac
'Preston Guild' ♀H3	NPer SRms WFar
'Prince of Orange'	SVic
'Princess Dollar'	see *F.* 'Dollar Prinzessin'
procumbens ♀H3	CBcs EArI ELon EPfP EPot EPts ESgI EShb MHer SIvy SLBF WKor
– 'Argentea'	see *F. procumbens* 'Wirral'
– 'Variegata'	see *F. procumbens* 'Wirral'
§ – 'Wirral' (v)	EShb ESwi MHer
'Prodigy'	see *F.* 'Enfant Prodigue'
'Prosperity' (d) ♀H3	EPts MAsh SLBF SPoG
'Pumila'	CMac SDix SVic
'Purple Fountain' (d)	WFar
'Purple Lace'	SVic
'Purple Prince' (d)	SVic
'Purple Rain'	EPts
'Quasar' (d)	SLBF
'Queen of Bath' (d)	SVic
'Query'	SVic
'R.A.F' (d)	EPts
'Ray Wilks' **new**	SLBF
'Raymar'	SLBF
'Reading Five 0' (d) **new**	SLBF
'Reading Show' (d)	SLBF

'Red Spider'	SLBF		'Sister Ann Haley'	EPts
'Red Tyrol'	MPri		'Sister Sister' (d)	SLBF
'Reflexa'	see *F. × bacillaris* 'Reflexa'		'Skyrocket'	CBcs
'Reg Gubler'	SLBF		'Sleepy'	EPts SVic
regia	SLBF		'Sleigh Bells'	SVic
I - 'Cherry'	SBrt		'Small Pipes'	SLBF
- subsp. ***reitzii***	SBig SBrt WFar		'Sneezy'	EPts
- subsp. ***serrae***	EBee		'Snow Burner' (California Dreamers Series) (d)	MBros WFar
aff. ***regia*** grey-leaved	SBrt			
'Remember Carole Anne' (d)	SLBF		'Snowbird' (d)	SLBF
'Remember Eric'	SLBF	§	'Snowcap' (d) ♀H4	ELon GKin LBom LCro LRHS MAsh MGos NPer SLBF SPoG SVic WFar
'Remembering Claire'	EPts MHer SLBF			
'Remembrance' (d)	EPts SLBF		'Snowflake' (E)	EPts
'Rhapsody' ambig.	SVic		'Son of Thumb' ♀H4	EPts SAdn SLBF SVic
'Riccartonii' ♀H6	CAgr CBcs CDoC CEnd CMac EGren EHeP ELan EPfP EPts GAbr LBom LCro LRHS LSRN LSto MAsh MGos MPri NLar NLit NPer SAdn SDix SEND SPoG SVic WFar WSpi		'Sophia'PBR (Bella Series)	LCro
			'Sophie Louise'	EPts
			'South Gate' (d)	EPts MHer SVic
			'Space Shuttle'	SLBF
			'Sparky' (T)	EPts SLBF
'Richard John' (v)	SVic	§	'Speciosa'	EGrI
'Rijs 2001' (E)	SLBF		'Spion Kop' (d)	LCro
'Rivendell'	EPts	§	***splendens*** ♀H2	CWal EWld NPer SLBF
'Rocket Fire' (California Dreamers Series) (d)	SVic		- B&SWJ 10469	WCru
			'Sprigamint'	SLBF
'Roger de Cooker' (T)	EPts SVic		'Squirtie'	SLBF
'Rohees New Millennium' (d)	SLBF		'Star Wars'	EPts LRHS WFar
			'Steirerblut' (T)	SLBF
'Rosalien'	WFar		'Stella Ann' (T)	EPts
'Rose Fantasia' ♀H2	EPts SLBF		'Straat Futami' (E)	EPts MHer
'Rose of Castile'	EPts SLBF SVic		'Straat of Plenty' (E)	SLBF
'Rose of Castile Improved' ♀H4	SLBF		'Strawberry Split'	CDoC
			'String of Pearls'	SLBF SVic
'Rose of Denmark'	SLBF SPoG		'Sue'	SLBF
rosea misapplied	see *F.* 'Globosa'		'Sue Kylymnik'	SLBF
'Rosecroft Beauty' (d/v)	SLBF		'Suffolk Splendour' (d)	EPts
'Royal Academy' (d)	EPts		'Sunray' (v)	CBcs CEnd CMac CTsd ELon LBom LBuc LCro MAsh MGos NCou SLBF SPoG SVen WCot
'Royal Mosaic' (California Dreamers Series) (d)	LCro			
'Royal Velvet' (d) ♀H2	EPts SLBF SVic		'Susan Green'	SLBF
'Rubra Grandiflora'	SIvy WFar		'Susan Hampshire'	SLBF
'Ruby Wedding' (d)	SLBF		'Susan Travis'	SVic
'Rufus' ♀H4	CMac EPts SLBF SVic		'Sweet Sarah' (E)	EPts
'Ruth'	SVic		'Swingtime' (d) ♀H2	EPts LCro MBros SLBF SPoG WFar
'Ryan'	SLBF		'Sylvia Barker' ♀H2	SLBF
SACHA ('Bf07'PBR) (Bella Series)	LCro SPoG		'Syreme' (d)	SLBF
			'Taddle'	SLBF
'Sailor'	EPts		'Tamworth'	SVic
'Salmon Cascade'	EPts SLBF		'Tangerine'	SVic
'Salt 'n' Pepper' (E)	SLBF		'Tennessee Waltz' (d) ♀H2	SLBF SVic
'Santa Cruz' (d)	CMac SLBF SVic		'Tess'	EPts
'Sappho Phaoon' (T)	EPts		***tetradactyla*** misapplied	see *F. × bacillaris*
'Sarah'PBR (Bella Series)	LCro		'Thalia' (T) ♀H1c	CTsd CWCL ELan EPts LCro LSRN MHer SIvy SLBF SPlb SPoG WOld
'Saturnus' ♀H4	SPoG			
'Scarcity'	SVic		'Thamar'	EPts SVic
'Scarlet Jester'	EPts SLBF		'Thank You'	SLBF
'Schneewitcher'	EPts SLBF		'That's It' (d)	SVic
'Sealand Prince'	SVic		'The Tarns'	SVic
serratifolia Ruíz & Pav.	see *F. denticulata*		'Thomas' (d)	EPts
'Seventh Heaven' (d)	LCro		'Thompsonii'	see *F. magellanica* 'Thomsonii'
'Sharpitor'	see *F. magellanica* var. *molinae* 'Sharpitor'		'Thornley's Hardy'	SVic
			'Thumbelina'	LRHS
'Shatzy B'	EPts SLBF		'Thumbelina Gem'	MPro
'Shelford'	EPts SLBF SVic		***thymifolia*** (E)	MHer SEND WCot WKif
'Shell Pink'	SVic		- B&SWJ 10294 (E)	WCru
'Shirley Teece'	EPts		- subsp. ***thymifolia*** (E)	CDoC SEle
'Siberoet' (E)	SLBF		'Tillingbourne' (d)	SLBF
'Sid Garcia'	SLBF		'Time After Time'	MBros SLBF WFar
'Silver Chime'	SLBF		'Timothy Titus' (T) ♀H1c	SLBF
'Silver Surfer'	EPts SLBF		'Tinker Bell' Hodges	SVic
'Siobhan Evans' (d)	SLBF		'Tjinegara'	SLBF
'Sir Matt Busby' (d)	EPts		'Toby Foreman'	SLBF

'Toby S' (d)	SLBF
'Tom Thumb' ♀H4	CMac EGren EHeP ELan EPts GKin LBom LCro LRHS LSto MAsh MGos MHer MNHC MPri NCth NLar SLBF SPlb SPoG SRms SVic WFar
'Tom West' misapplied	see *F.* 'Mr West'
'Tom West' ambig.	MHtn SVic
'Tom West' Meillez (v) ♀H4	CDoC EPts MAsh MBros MHer MSCN SLBF SMrm WFar
'Tomarama' (E)	SLBF
'Tony's Treat' (d)	EPts
'Torchlight'	EPts
'Torvill and Dean' (d)	EPts SLBF
'Tracid' (d)	SVic
'Tranquility' (d)	SLBF
'Trase' (d)	SVic
'Tricolor'	see *F. magellanica* var. *gracilis* 'Versicolor'
'Trientje'	SLBF
triphylla (T)	MHer
'Trudi Davro'	MBros SPoG
'Trudy'	EPts SVic
'Truly Treena' (d)	SLBF
'Trumpeter' Reiter (T)	EPts
'Turkish Delight'	WFar
'Valerie Bradley'	EPts
'Valerie Jane'	SLBF
'Vanessa Jackson'	SVic
'Variegated Procumbens'	see *F. procumbens* 'Wirral'
'Velvet Crush'	EPts SLBF
'Vendeta'	SLBF
venusta B&SWJ 14204	WCru
'Vera Garcia'	EPts
'Versicolor'	see *F. magellanica* var. *gracilis* 'Versicolor'
'Vivien Colville'	SVic
'Voodoo' (d)	EPts LCro MBros SPoG WFar
'Walz Duimelot'	WFar
'Walz Jubelteen' ♀H2	CWCL ELan ELon EPts LCro LRHS SAdn SLBF SVic WCot
'Walz Lucifer'	SLBF
'Walz Polka'	SLBF
'Wapenveld's Bloei'	SLBF
'Water Nymph'	MHer SLBF SVic
'Wattenpost'	SLBF
'Waveney Gem'	SLBF
'Wendy' Catt	see *F.* 'Snowcap'
'Wendy Bendy'	EPts
'Wharfedale' ♀H4	ELon EPts SLBF SVic
'What's-it' (E)	SLBF
'White Academy'	EPts
'White Clove' (E)	SVic
'White Pixie' ♀H4	EPPr EPts SVic
'Whiteknights Amethyst'	SVic
'Whiteknights Blush'	EWes GAbr NBid NLar SMrm
'Whiteknights Cheeky' (T)	EPts SVic
'Whiteknights Pearl' ♀H4	ECha ELon EPts MHer MPro SLBF SMHy SVic
'Whiteknights Ruby' (T)	SLBF
'Wicked Queen' (d)	SVic
'Widnes Wonder'	SLBF
'Wigan Peer' (d)	EPts
'Wilson's Colours'	EPts
'Wilson's Pearls' (d)	SLBF
'Wilson's Sugar Pink'	EPts
'Windhapper'	SLBF
'Windsor Castle'	SLBF
'Winston Churchill' (d) ♀H2	EPts MBros SPoG SVic WFar
'Woodside' (d)	SVic
'Yattendon Lady'	SLBF
'Zifi'	SLBF

Fumana (Cistaceae)

procumbens	EDAr

Fumaria (Papaveraceae)

lutea	see *Corydalis lutea*
officinalis	GJem

Furcraea (Asparagaceae)

bedinghausii	see *F. parmentieri*
foetida	SEND
longaeva misapplied	see *F. parmentieri*
macdougalii	CExl NPlm SBig SPlb
§ **parmentieri**	CBcs CDoC CWnw EShb EUrb LEdu LRHS MCtn NCft SBig SChr SPlb SVen
quicheensis	CExl
selloa	EUrb
- var. **marginata** (v)	NCft NPlm

G

Gahnia (Cyperaceae)

sieberiana	SPlb

Gaillardia (Asteraceae)

Apricot Honey	SMad
aristata misapplied	see *G.* × *grandiflora*
aristata Pursh	SMHy
I - 'Fire Wheels'	EDAr
- 'Maxima Aurea'	LRHS
Goblin	see *G.* × *grandiflora* 'Kobold'
× **grandiflora** 'Amber Wheels'	ELan
- 'Arizona Apricot'	LRHS MCtn
- 'Arizona Red Shades'	LRHS MCtn
- 'Arizona Sun'	LRHS LSRN SVic WCav
- 'Burgunder'	ELan EPfP LCro LRHS LSRN NLar SHar SPoG
- 'Celebration'PBR	LBuc LRHS MPri
- 'Dazzler' ♀H5	ELan LRHS SHar SPoG
§ - 'Fackelschein'	CWal EPfP MCtn
- 'Fanblaze'PBR	LRHS WFar
- 'Fanfare'PBR	EPfP LRHS
- 'Fanfare Amber Glow'	LBar LSou MPro
- 'Fanfare Citronella'PBR	EPfP LBar MPro
- 'Fanfare Coral Glow'	MPro
- Gallo Bright Red ('Florgalbred') (Gallo Series)	EGren
- (Guapa Series) Guapa Flamenco Bicolour ('Flogb0060')	MPri MPro
- - Guapa Red ('Flogb0014')	LRHS MPri MPro
- - Guapa Tango Bicolour ('Floga0001') **new**	MPri
§ - 'Kobold'	CBcs EHeP ELan EPfP GMaP LBuc LRHS SHar SOrN SPlb SPoG
- (Mesa Series) Mesa Bright Bicolour ('Pas888652')	EGren LBar LRHS MPri
- - Mesa Peach ('Pas907056')	EGren LBar LRHS
- - Mesa Red ('Pas953516')	EGren LBar LRHS MPri MPro NLar
- - Mesa Yellow ('Pas888653')	EGren LBar LRHS MPro
- Monarch Group	WFar
- (SpinTop Series) SpinTop Copper Sun	LBar

- - SpinTop Red	LBar
- - SpinTop Red Sunburst	LBar
- - SpinTop Yellow Touch ('Bargaispinyel'PBR)	LBar LRHS
- Sunburst Burgundy (Sunburst Series)	WFar
- (Sunset Dwarf Series) 'Sunset Cutie'	ELan LBuc MPri SPoG
- - 'Sunset Flash'	ELan LBuc MPri SPoG
- - 'Sunset Snappy'	LBuc LRHS MPri SPoG
- - 'Sunset Sunrise'	ELan EPfP LBuc LRHS SPoG
- (Sunset Medium Series) 'Sunset Orange Ruffles' **new**	MPro
- - 'Sunset Spice'	ELan EPfP
- 'Tokajer'	ELan
Torchlight	see *G.* × *grandiflora* 'Fackelschein'

Galactites (Asteraceae)

tomentosus	EGrI

Galanthus ✿ (Amaryllidaceae)

'Acton Pigot No 3'	CElw ENSn
'Ailwyn' (d) ♀H5	ELon GEdr WOld
'Alison Hilary'	CTtf GEdr LEdu MAvo MCor WBrk WOld
'Amy Doncaster's Double' (d)	MCor
'Anne'	WBrk
'Anne of Geierstein'	CElw CTtf
'Ann's Millennium Giant'	CBro GEdr
'Armine'	CElw WCot
'Atkinsii' ♀H5	CBro CElw ECha GEdr GKev LAma LRHS NBir SDix WCot WHoo WShi
'Aul' (Estonian Bird Double Series) (d)	NDry
'Aurelia'	EPot
'Babraham Scented'	GEdr NBir
'Backhouse Spectacles'	GEdr WBrk
'Ballerina' (d)	GEdr MAsh WCot
'Barbara's Double' (d)	EWes GEdr WOld
'Baylham'	ENSn MCor
'Benhall Beauty'	CBro EWes GEdr
'Benton Magnet'	MCor
'Bernhard Röllich' (d)	ENSn
'Bertram Anderson' ♀H5	GEdr WCot WOld
'Bess'	CElw GEdr MAsh WOld
'Betty Hansell' (d)	CTtf MCor
'Big Eyes'	CElw
'Bill Bishop'	CBro CElw CTtf ECha ELon EPot GEdr WCot
'Bitter Lemons'	EGrI ENSn
'Bitton'	see *G. nivalis* 'Bitton'
'Blewbury'	LEdu WOld
'Bloomer'	MCor
'Brenda Troyle'	CBro CElw ECha EPot GEdr LEdu LRHS WCot WOld
'Bright Eyes'	MAsh
'Bungee'	CTtf GEdr
'By Gate'	GEdr
'Byfield Special'	MCor
byzantinus	see *G. plicatus* subsp. *byzantinus*
'Castlegar'	MAsh
caucasicus misapplied	see *G. elwesii* var. *monostictus*
- var. *hiemalis* Stern	see *G. elwesii* Hiemalis Group
'Chantry Taffeta'	LEdu
'Cicely Hall'	CTtf GEdr MAsh
'Cinderella'	MCor
'Claud Biddulph'	LEdu
'Cliff Curtis'	GEdr
corcyrensis spring-flowering	see *G. reginae-olgae* subsp. *vernalis*
'Cordelia' (d)	CElw GEdr MCor
'Corrin'	GEdr
'Cowhouse Green'	CElw GEdr LEdu WOld
'Curly'	CElw CTtf EWes GEdr
'Daglingworth'	CElw GEdr
'David Baker'	CElw GEdr
'Desdemona' (d)	CElw EGrI GEdr GMaP WCot WOld
'Devon Marble'	CElw
'Ding Dong'	CTtf GEdr MAsh MWlw
'Dionysus' (d)	CFis ECha EGrI EPot EWes GEdr GKev LAma LEdu LRHS MAsh NBir
'Dodo Norton'	GEdr MAsh
'Dragonfly'	MAsh WOld
'Dryad Artemis' (Myths and Legends Series)	GEdr NDry
'Dryad Demeter' (Myths and Legends Series)	NDry
'Dryad Echo' (Myths and Legends Series)	NDry
(Dryad Gold Series) 'Dryad Gold Bullion'	GEdr NDry
- 'Dryad Gold Charm'	GEdr MAsh NDry
- 'Dryad Gold Ingot'	NDry
- 'Dryad Gold Medal'	GEdr MAsh NDry
- 'Dryad Gold Ribbon'	MAsh NDry
- 'Dryad Gold Sceptre'	NDry
- 'Dryad Gold Sovereign'	GEdr MAsh NDry
- 'Dryad Gold Standard'	NDry
- 'Dryad Gold Star'	GEdr MAsh NDry
'Dryad Jupiter' (Myths and Legends Series)	NDry
'Dryad Terpsichore' (Myths and Legends Series)	NDry
'Dryad Venus' (Myths and Legends Series)	NDry
'Dryad Zeus' (Myths and Legends Series)	NDry
'Eira'	CBro
'Eliot Hodgkin'	GEdr
§ *elwesii* ♀H5	EGren EGrI EHet ELan EPfP EPot ETay LAma LCro LRHS MAsh NBir SEND SRms WCot WHoo
- 'Athenae'	CBro
- 'Beany'	ENSn LAma MAsh WOld
- 'Beluga'	NBir
- 'Benjamin Britten'	GEdr LAma
- 'Bo Bette'	GEdr
- 'Brian Mathew'	CElw
- 'Cedric's Prolific'	CElw ECha GEdr MCor NRya WBrk WFar
- 'Chantry Green Twins'	GEdr MAsh
- 'Comet' ♀H5	CTtf ELon GEdr GKev MAsh MNrw
- 'Daphne's Scissors'	CElw EGrI GEdr MAsh WBrk
- 'David Shackleton'	CElw GEdr
- 'Deer Slot'	CTtf MAsh
- 'Don Armstrong'	ENSn MAsh
- 'Dryad Blizzard' (Dryad Snow Series) **new**	NDry
- 'Early Twin'	WCot
- (Edward Whittall Group) 'Phil Bryn'	MAsh
- - 'Two Eyes'	GEdr
- 'Elmley Lovett'	CElw MAvo
- var. *elwesii*	GKev
- - 'Big Boy'	CElw GEdr
- - 'Fenstead End'	GEdr MAsh
- - 'Fred's Giant'	CElw GMaP
- - 'Kite'	GEdr MAsh
- - 'Maidwell L'	MAsh

- - 'Mary Ann Gibbs' — CElw
- - 'Paradise Giant' — GEdr
- - 'Pat Mason' — MAsh WOld
- - 'Sibbertoft Magnet' — GEdr WBrk
- - 'Spring Greens' — GEdr MAsh MAvo
- - 'Godfrey Owen' (d) ♀H5 — CElw CFis CTtf EGrI ELon ENSn EPot GEdr LAma LRHS MAsh MCor WBrk
- - 'Green Brush' — CTtf EWes GKev LAma
- - 'Grumpy' — ESgI GEdr MAsh
- - 'Helen Tomlinson' — CElw EPot
- - 'Henley Green Spot' — MAsh
- - 'Hercules' — CElw MAsh
- § - Hiemalis Group — CBro ECha LAma WCot
- - - 'Barnes' ♀H5 — CFis EArI ECha ELon GEdr MCor WCot
- - - 'Donald Sims' Early' — ELon MAsh
- - - 'Earliest of All' — CBro
- - - 'Highdown' — GKev
- - 'Jessica' — GEdr MWIw WOld
- - 'John Tomlinson' — GEdr MAsh
- - 'Jonathan' — MAsh
- - 'Jubilee Green' — CElw MAsh
- - 'Kyre Park' — GEdr
- - 'Ladybird' — GEdr MAsh
- - late-flowering — GEdr
- - Long 'drop' — GEdr WOld
- - 'Louise Ann Bromley' — EPot MAsh MCor
- - 'Maidwell' — EPot GEdr LRHS MAsh
- - 'Mandarin' — CElw EWes
- - 'Margaret Biddulph' — LEdu MAsh
- - 'Margaret Owen' — CElw LEdu MAsh MCor MNrw
- - 'Marielle' — GEdr
- - 'Marjorie Brown' — CElw CFis CTtf ECha EPot GEdr LRHS MAsh MAvo MCor
- - 'Mary Biddulph' — LEdu
- - 'Milkwood' — see *G. elwesii* 'Mrs Macnamara'
- - 'Miss Mowcher' — WCot
- § - var. **monostictus** ♀H5 — CBro ECha
- - - 'A. Vivaldi' **new** — GKev
- - - 'B. Britten' — LRHS MAsh
- - - 'G. Handel' — GKev LAma LRHS MAsh
- - - 'G. Verdi' — LAma LRHS
- - - 'Grayswood' — GEdr
- - - 'H. Purcell' — CElw GEdr GKev LAma LRHS
- - - 'J.S. Bach' **new** — GKev LAma
- - - 'Ludwig van Beethoven' — GKev LAma LRHS MAsh
- - - 'Miller's Late' — EPot
- - - 'Mozart' — GKev LAma MAsh
- - - 'Warwickshire Gemini' — CElw MHCG
- - 'Morgana' — MAsh
- - 'Moses Basket' — CTtf MAsh
- - 'Mount Everest' — EPfP GKev LRHS WFar
- - 'Moya's Green' — LEdu
- - 'Mr Blobby' — LEdu
- § - 'Mrs Macnamara' ♀H5 — CElw CFis ECha GEdr LEdu LRHS MAsh MCor MNrw WBrk WOld
- - November-flowering — WCot
- - 'Penelope Ann' — ECha GEdr NRya
- - 'Peter Gatehouse' — CElw CTtf ELon MAsh
- - poculiform — CTtf
- - 'Polar Bear' — GEdr MAvo NCth
- - 'Pyramid' — CTtf MAsh MCor
- - 'Ransom's Dwarf' — GEdr
- - 'Remember, Remember' — CTtf GEdr
- - 'Rosemary Burnham' — CElw MCor
- - 'Rowan Russell' — CBro
- - 'Ruth Birchall' — EPot
- - 'Sickle' — CFis MAsh
- - 'Sir Edward Elgar' — LAma LRHS
- - 'Spring Pearl' — ENSn
- - 'Three Leaves' — CElw ECha
- - 'Washfield Colesbourne' — see *G.* 'Washfield Colesbourne'
- - 'Wessex Titan' — LEdu
- - 'X Files' — MAvo
- - 'Yvonne Hay' — GEdr
- - 'Zwanenburg' — CElw CTtf MAsh
- 'Ermine House' (d) — GEdr
- 'Ermine Joyce' — LRHS
- 'Erway' — CElw CTtf
- I 'Excelsis' — EPot WOld
- 'Faint Heart' — LEdu
- 'Falkland House' — CElw GEdr MAvo
- 'Fanny' — CElw
- 'Faringdon Double' (d) — CTtf
- 'Fieldgate Prelude' — CFis GEdr MAsh NBir
- 'Fieldgate Tiffany' — WOld
- 'Fly Fishing' — CElw CTtf ECha EGrI GEdr MCor NBir
- 'Forge Double' (d) — GEdr MCor
- ***fosteri*** — GEdr
- 'Franz Josef' — MAsh WOld
- 'G71' (d) — MCor
- 'Gabriel' — EPot GEdr
- 'Galadriel' — ECha GEdr
- 'Galatea' — CElw ECha EGrI EWes NRya
- 'George Elwes' — CTtf GEdr
- 'Gill Gregory' — GEdr MNrw
- 'Ginns' — NBir WBrk
- 'Glenchantress' — ENSn EPot GEdr MAsh MAvo WOld
- § ***gracilis*** — GEdr WCot
- - 'Highdown' — CElw CTtf WOld
- - Kew — CElw
- - 'Vic Horton' — CTtf GEdr
- - 'Yamanlar' — CElw
- ***graecus*** misapplied — see *G. gracilis*
- ***graecus*** Orph. ex Boiss. — see *G. elwesii*
- 'Grayling' — see *G. plicatus* 'Percy Picton'
- 'Gray's Child' **new** — MAvo
- 'Green Arrow' — CElw WOld
- 'Green Comet' — CElw MAsh
- 'Green Eyes' — MAsh
- 'Green Genes' — MAsh
- 'Green Island' — EGrI
- 'Green Man' — GEdr
- 'Green Necklace' — CElw CTtf EWes GEdr WBrk WOld
- 'Green of Hearts' — MAsh
- 'Greenfields' — CElw GEdr WBrk
- 'Greenfinch' — MAsh
- green-tipped double (d) — GEdr
- 'Grüner Nebel' — EPot
- 'Hatpin' (d) — NDry
- 'Headbourne' — ECha LRHS MCor
- 'Heffalump' (d) — CElw GEdr MCor WOld
- 'Hilary's Coquette' **new** — CElw
- 'Hill Poë' (d) — CBro CElw CTtf GEdr MCor
- 'Hippolyta' (d) — CBro CElw CTtf ECha EGrI GEdr GKev LAma LEdu LRHS MCor WCot
- 'Hobson's Choice' — CElw GEdr
- 'Homersfield' — CElw ELon
- 'Hörup' — GEdr
- 'Hoverfly' — MCor
- × ***hybridus*** 'Merlin' ♀H5 — CBro CElw CTtf GEdr WCot WHoo
- - 'Robin Hood' — GEdr MAvo
- 'Icicle' — CElw GEdr WBrk
- ***ikariae*** Bak. — ELan GEdr LCro
- - 'Emerald Isle' — MAsh
- - subsp. ***ikariae*** Butt's form — CElw
- - Latifolius Group — see *G. platyphyllus*
- 'Imbolc' — GEdr WOld
- 'Ivy Cottage Corporal' — GEdr MAsh
- 'Ivy Cottage Green Tip' — EGrI

Galanthus

Name	Suppliers
'Jacquenetta' (d)	CBro CElw CFis EWes GEdr GKev LAma LRHS MAsh
'James Backhouse'	ECha EGrI MCor
'Jennifer Hewitt'	CElw
'Joe Spotted' **new**	CElw
'John Gray' ♀H5	EWes GEdr
'Kath Dryden'	EPot
'Kaur' (Estonian Bird Double Series) (d)	NDry
'Kersen'	WOld
'Ketton'	CElw GEdr LRHS MAsh NRya
'Kildare'	CElw ENSn EPot GEdr LEdu
'Kingston Double' (d)	GEdr MAsh
'Kinn McIntosh'	WCot
'Kiur' (Estonian Bird Double Series) (d)	NDry
krasnovii	EPot
'Lady Beatrix Stanley' (d) ♀H5	CBro CElw EArl ECha ENSn EPfP EPot GEdr LRHS WCot WOld
'Lagle' (Estonian Bird Double Series) (d)	NDry
lagodechianus	CBro GEdr
'Lapwing'	GEdr LEdu MAsh MCor
latifolius Rupr.	see *G. platyphyllus*
'Lavinia' (d)	CElw EWes GEdr SIvy
'Lerinda'	WOld
'Limetree'	CElw EWes GEdr LRHS
'Little Ben'	CElw GEdr GMaP MCor
'Little Dorrit'	GEdr MAsh
'Little John'	GEdr
'Little Poppet'	WCot
'Longnor Hall' (d)	MCor
'Lord Lieutenant'	GEdr
'Lucy'	ENSn WOld
'Luik' (Estonian Bird Double Series) (d)	NDry
lutescens	see *G. nivalis* Sandersii Group
'Lyn'	CBro CElw GEdr NBir
'Magnet' ♀H5	CBro CElw CFis CTtf ECha EGrI GEdr GKev LAma LEdu MAsh MCor MNrw NBir WBrk WCot
aff. 'Magnet'	GMaP
'Megan'	GEdr
'Melanie Broughton'	CElw EWes GEdr MAsh MAvo MCor
'Midas'	LEdu WOld
'Midge'	GEdr
'Midwinter'	CElw
'Mighty Atom'	CBro WBrk
'Miss Muffet'	CElw
'Miss Prissy' (d)	CElw
'Moby Dick'	EWes
'Moccas'	CElw CFis
'Modern Art'	CElw CTtf GEdr MAsh MCor WOld
'Moortown'	CElw GEdr
'Mordred' (d)	WOld
'Mother Goose'	ENSn LAma
'Mrs Backhouse No 12'	MCor
'Mrs Thompson'	CElw CTtf ECha ENSn GEdr MNrw
'Mrs Wrightson's Double' (d)	GEdr
'Muku' (d)	NDry
'Myddelton Giant'	ESgI
'Natalie Garton'	CFis CTtf EGrI GEdr MCor
'Neill Fraser'	EGrI GEdr
'Nerissa' (d)	CFis GEdr
nivalis ♀H5	Widely available
- 'Alan's Treat'	CElw ENSn GEdr WOld
- 'Alburgh Claw'	MAsh
- 'Angelina'	LEdu
- 'Anglesey Abbey'	CElw EWes GEdr MCor
- 'April Fool'	GEdr
- 'Art Nouveau'	CElw CTtf
- 'Ballynahinch'	GEdr
§ - 'Bitton'	GEdr MAsh
- 'Blonde Inge'	CElw CTtf ENSn GEdr MAsh MCor
- 'Chedworth'	CElw GEdr WBrk WOld
- 'Christmas Wish'	GKev
- 'Cornwood'	CElw GEdr WOld
- 'Courteenhall' Wyatt	CTtf
- 'Écusson d'Or'	CElw LEdu
- 'Elfin'	CElw CTtf EWes GEdr WCot
- 'Flight of Fancy'	WOld
- 'Gloucester Old Spot'	GEdr WBrk WOld
- 'Green Diamond'	CElw
- 'Green Tear'	ENSn GEdr
- 'Greenish'	CTtf
- 'Irish Green'	MAsh
- 'Janet Cropley'	MAsh
- 'Lutescens'	see *G. nivalis* Sandersii Group
- 'Margery Fish'	ENSn
- 'Munchkin'	CTtf
- 'Orange Star' **new**	ENSn
- 'Pewsey Vale'	WBrk
- f. *pleniflorus* (d)	EGren GKev MNHC MPri NBir SPoG
- - 'Bagpuize Virginia' (d)	GEdr LEdu
- - 'Bagpuize Walrus' (d)	CTtf LEdu
- - 'Blewbury Tart' (d)	CBro CElw CTtf ECha ELon EWes GEdr LEdu MCor NBir WBrk WCot
- - 'Cockatoo' (d)	CElw
- - 'Doncaster's Double Charmer' (d)	LEdu MAsh
- - 'Elworthy Bumble Bee' (d)	CElw GEdr
- - 'Flore Pleno' (d) ♀H5	CBro CElw EGrI EHet ELan EPfP EPot LAma LCro LRHS MMuc NRya SEND SRms WBrk WCot WShi
- - 'Lady Elphinstone' (d)	CElw ECha ENSn GEdr NBir WCot
- - 'Major Pam' (d)	CElw
- - 'Mrs Tiggywinkle' (d)	LEdu
- - 'Octopussy' (d)	GEdr MAsh
- - 'Pusey Green Tips' (d)	CElw CTtf WCot WOld
- - Scharlockii Group double (d)	CTtf
- - 'Walrus' (d)	GEdr WOld
- Poculiformis Group	CElw
- - 'Angelique'	CTtf
- - 'Crème Anglaise'	CElw
- - 'Henry's White Lady'	GEdr MCor
- - 'Puck'	GEdr
§ - Sandersii Group	GEdr GKev GMaP
- - 'Lowick'	CTtf
- - 'Norfolk Blonde'	CTtf ENSn ESgI GEdr
§ - Scharlockii Group	CElw ECha EGrI MAsh WBrk WOld
- 'Tiny'	GEdr NBir
- 'Tiny Tim'	ENSn GEdr MCor NRya WOld
- 'Tippy Green'	CElw
- 'Tutu' (d)	CElw
- 'Viridapice' ♀H5	CBro CElw CTtf ECha EGrI ESgI GKev GMaP LAma LCro MAsh NBir WCot WFar WOld
- 'Warei'	CElw
- 'White Dream'	CElw GEdr
- 'North Star' (d)	CElw
- 'Nothing Special'	MAsh MWIw NBir WBrk WOld
- 'One Drop or Two'	MAvo
- 'Ophelia' (d)	CBro CElw ECha GEdr GKev MAsh MCor WBrk WHoo WOld
'Orion'	CElw CFis
'Peardrop'	GEdr
'Peg Sharples'	GEdr LRHS
peshmenii	EPot LEdu

Galanthus

'Philippe André Meyer'	MCor
§ **platyphyllus**	LRHS
plicatus ♀H5	CBro CElw EGrI GKev LAma WBrk WCot WShi
- 'Amy Doncaster'	CTtf GEdr LEdu MAsh MCor
- 'Augustus' ♀H5	CBro CElw CTtf ECha EWes GEdr MNrw NBir WCot WHoo
- 'Barbara Buchanan's Late'	CElw
- 'Baxendale's Late'	GEdr GKev WOld
- 'Beth Chatto'	MCor
- 'Blue Trym'	CElw ECha EPot
§ - subsp. **byzantinus**	CBro LAma LRHS
- - 'Conquest'	CBro
- - 'Joe Sharman'	ENSn
- - 'Seraph'	MAsh
- 'Chequers'	GEdr
- 'Clun Green Plicate'	CElw
- 'Colossus'	CBro CElw ECha EPfP EWes MAsh NBir WCot
- 'Cyril Warr'	CElw
- 'Diggory' ♀H5	CTtf GEdr LEdu
- 'Dryad Leto' (Myths and Legends Series) **new**	NDry
- 'Duckie'	CElw GEdr MAvo
- 'E.A. Bowles' ♀H5	GEdr MAsh WOld
- 'Edinburgh Ketton'	CElw
- 'Eric Fisher'	LAma
- 'Florence Baker'	GEdr
- 'Gerard Parker'	GEdr
- 'Gimli'	CElw
- 'Glenorma'	GEdr WOld
- 'Gold Edge'	GEdr
- 'Golden Fleece'	ENSn GEdr LEdu
- 'Green Hayes'	GEdr MCor
- 'Green Lantern'	MAsh
- 'Green Teeth'	CElw GEdr
- 'Greengage' **new**	ENSn
- 'John Long'	GEdr MCor
- 'Josie'	CElw GEdr
- 'Lambrook Greensleeves'	CElw CFis MCor WOld
- 'Madelaine'	CElw CTtf EPot GEdr WOld
§ - 'Percy Picton'	CElw EWes GEdr WOld
- 'Phil Cornish'	CFis GEdr MAsh WOld
- 'Priscilla Bacon'	CElw WOld
- 'Ransom's Late'	CElw
- 'Sally Pasmore'	NBir
- 'Sarah Dumont'	CFis
- 'Sibbertoft Manor'	CElw
- 'Sophie North'	CElw GEdr
- 'The Pearl'	CElw GEdr
- 'Three Ships' ♀H5	CElw GEdr GKev MCor
- 'Trimmer'	ESgI GEdr MAsh
- 'Trinity'	MAsh
- 'Trym'	CElw CTtf EPot GEdr MAsh NBir WFar
- 'Trymlet'	CElw EGrI GEdr MAsh WOld
- 'Trympostor'	CElw GEdr MCor WHoo
- 'Twins'	WCot
- 'Upcher'	ECha
- 'Wandlebury Ring'	CElw EPot
- 'Warham'	CBro CElw MAsh NBir WCot
- 'Wendy's Gold'	CBro CElw CTtf ECha EWes GEdr MAsh MCor NBir WBrk WFar WOld
'Pom-pom'	CElw
'Pride o' the Mill'	CTtf GEdr
'Primrose Warburg' ♀H5	CElw EWes GEdr LRHS MCor WOld
reginae-olgae	GKev MAsh
- 'Blanc de Chine'	NDry
- subsp. **reginae-olgae** 'Cambridge'	EPot
- - 'Tilebarn Jamie'	LEdu WCot
- 'Ruby's Green Dream'	NDry
§ - subsp. **vernalis**	CBro LEdu WCot
- - 'Christine'	CElw
'Reverend Hailstone'	CTtf EWes GEdr MCor NBir
'Richard Ayres' (d)	CElw GEdr LRHS MCor WOld
'Ristpart' (Estonian Bird Double Series) (d)	NDry
rizehensis	CBro GKev
- Baytop 34474	GEdr MAsh WOld
- 'Margaret Billington'	CElw
'Rodmarton' (d)	CElw GEdr MAsh WBrk
'Rodmarton Arcturus'	CElw GEdr MAsh
'Rodmarton Regulus'	GEdr WOld
'Rodmarton Sirius' **new**	WOld
'Ronald Mackenzie'	GEdr
'S. Arnott' ♀H5	CBro CElw EBee EBlo ECha EGrI EPfP GKev GMaP LAma LCro LEdu MAsh MCor NBir NRya SDix WCot WHoo
'Saint Anne's'	CElw GEdr
'Sally Ann'	CElw
'Sally Wickenden'	CTtf
'Sally's Double' (d)	MCor
'Santa Claus'	ELon
'Scharlockii'	see *G. nivalis* Scharlockii Group
'Seagull'	CElw CFis GEdr MAsh MCor WBrk WOld
'Sentinel'	CElw GEdr
'Seren'	CBro
'Shepton Merlin'	CElw
'Shropshire Queen'	GEdr MAsh
'Silverwells'	GEdr
'Sir Henry B-C'	CElw GEdr MAsh
'Sir Herbert Maxwell'	GEdr WOld
'Snow Fox'	GEdr LRHS NBir
'South Hayes' ♀H5	EGrI GEdr NBir
'Spindlestone Surprise' ♀H5	CElw WOld
'Sprite'	CElw GEdr
'St Pancras'	LRHS
'Starling'	CElw
§ 'Straffan' ♀H5	CBro CElw LRHS WBrk WCot WOld
'Sutton Court'	MAsh
'Sutton Courtenay'	GEdr
'The Apothecary'	CElw
'The Linns'	GEdr
'The O'Mahoney'	see *G.* 'Straffan'
'The Pearl' Stern	CElw
'The Wizard'	CElw MAsh WOld
'Titania' (d)	CElw CTtf ELon GEdr MAsh MCor
transcaucasicus	GEdr
'Treasure Island'	ENSn LEdu
'Trojan'	CElw
'Trotter's Merlin'	CElw
'Trumpolute'	MAsh MCor
'Trumps' ♀H5	CElw ECha GEdr MAsh MCor NBir WOld
'Trym Baby'	EGrI GEdr
'Trym Ingram' **new**	CElw
'Trymming'	GEdr
'Tubby Merlin'	CElw WOld
'Tutkas' (Estonian Bird Double Series) (d)	NDry
'Uncle Dick'	CElw
'Under Cherry Plum'	WOld
× **valentinei**	MCor
- 'Celia's Double' (d)	CElw
- 'Compton Court'	CBro GEdr
- 'Northern Lights'	ENSn
- 'Wayside' (d)	CElw

× *Gasteraloe* 297

'Vart' (Estonian Bird Double Series) (d)	NDry
'Walker Canada'	CElw
§ 'Washfield Colesbourne'	CElw ECha
'Washfield Warham'	CElw ECha
'Wasp'	CTtf ESgI EWes GEdr MAsh MCor WCot
'Welshway'	GEdr
'White Dreams'	GEdr
'White Perfection'	MAsh
'White Swan' Ballard (d)	CElw EWes GEdr MCor WBrk
'White Wings'	CElw
'William Thomson'	EWes MAsh WBrk
'Wisley Magnet'	CElw MCor
woronowii ♀H5	CBro CElw CoPl CTtf EGren EGrl EPfP ETay GKev LAma LCro LEdu LRHS MAsh MAvo MCor MNHC NBir WBrk WFar
- 'Cider with Rosie'	LEdu MAsh WOld
- 'Elizabeth Harrison'	ENSn GEdr MAsh
- 'Rodmarton Capella'	MCor

Galatella (Asteraceae)

§ *linosyris*	CKno CSpe EBee EWes MAvo MHol NLar SHar SPhx WFar WOld
- 'Goldilocks'	see *G. linosyris*
§ *sedifolia*	CKno CTtf ECha EPPr LBar LRHS LSou LSto MArl MAvo NSti SEND SNoN SPoG WCot WOld
- subsp. *dracunculoides* RCBAM 5	WCot
- 'Jean Polignier'	LEdu
- 'Nana'	EBee NBir NLar SMHy WCAu WCot WFar WOld

Galax (Diapensiaceae)

aphylla	see *G. urceolata*
§ *urceolata*	MNrw NHar

Galega (Fabaceae)

bicolor	NBir SRms
× *hartlandii*	LShi
- 'Alba' ♀H7	ESgI EWes GBin LShi MArl NWbg SHar WCot
- 'Lady Wilson' ♀H7	ESgI GBin MHol MMrt SRms WCot
'Her Majesty'	see *G. 'His Majesty'*
§ 'His Majesty'	ESgI LEdu NWbg SMrm
officinalis	CAgr CCBP CGHo EBee ELan EMor ENfk EPfP GJos GMaP LBar MCtn MHer MMrt MNHC MNrw NBir NSti SBeP SRms WCAu WFar WHil WSpi WTre
- 'Alba'	CCBP CElw ELan EMor GMaP GQue LEdu LRHS MBrN MHer MMrt NBir SEND SMrm SRms WCAu WFar WSpi WTre
- COCONUT ICE ('Kelgal') (v)	SPoG
orientalis	EBee EWes LEdu MArl MBlu SBrt WCot WPGP
- PAB 6771	WPGP

Galeobdolon see *Lamium*

Galium (Rubiaceae)

glaucum	SPhx
mollugo	CBWd CGwi CHab
- subsp. *erectum*	LShi
§ *odoratum*	Widely available
sylvaticum	MCtn
verum	CBWd CCBP CGwi CHab EBee EHet ENfk EPPr GJem GJos GQue LCro LShi MCtn MHer MMuc MNHC NAts NMir SEND SRms WCav WFar

Galtonia (Asparagaceae)

candicans ♀H4	CAby CBcs CBro CSpe CTtf EBee ECha EGren EGrl ELan EPfP EPot EPPr ERCP GBin GKev LAma LCro MNrw SBeP SPeP WFar WKif
- 'Moonbeam' (d)	GKev LAma
princeps	ECha EPPr WPGP
regalis	WFar WPGP
viridiflora	CBro CTtf ECha EGrl EPPr ERCP GBin GKev LAma MHol MNrw SPeP WFar XFar

Galvezia (Plantaginaceae)

speciosa	CBct CHll EArl EShb SEle

Gamblea ❀ (Araliaceae)

ciliata B&SWJ 13907	WCru
pseudoevodiifolia B&SWJ 11707	WCru

Gardenia (Rubiaceae)

augusta	see *G. jasminoides*
florida L.	see *G. jasminoides*
grandiflora	see *G. jasminoides*
§ *jasminoides* ♀H1c	CBcs EPfP LCro LRHS MPri
- CELESTIAL STAR ('Ps-2013-4') (d)	LCro
- 'Crown Jewel'^{PBR} (d)	CBcs EBee LCro LRHS MAsh SPoG WCot
- DOUBLE DIAMONDS ('Leefour') (d)	LCro
- 'Kleim's Hardy' ♀H3	CDoC CDTJ EBee EGren EGrl ELan ELon EPfP LCro LRHS MAsh MBlu SChF SEle SNig SPlb SPoG WLov
- PINWHEEL ('Piiga-I')	LCro
magnifica	LRHS

garlic see *Allium sativum*; also AGM Vegetables Section

garlic, elephant see *Allium ampeloprasum* 'Elephant'

Garrya ❀ (Garryaceae)

elliptica	CBcs CDoC CMac EHeP EPfP ERom LRHS LSRN LSto MAsh MGos MPri SArc SEWo WHtc WJur
- (f)	WSpi
- (m)	NLar SGol WSpi
- 'James Roof' (m) ♀H4	CBcs CBrac CDoC CMac CSBt CWnw EBee EGren EGrl ELan EPfP LCro LMil LRHS LSRN MAsh MGos MPri NLar SPoG SRms WFar WSpi
× *issaquahensis* 'Glasnevin Wine' (m) ♀H4	ELan SPoG WSpi
× *thuretii*	CBcs ELan EPfP MMuc NLar SGol WFar WSpi

× *Gasteraloe* (Asphodelaceae)

'Apollo'	LCro
'Flow'	NCft
'Green Ice'	NCft
'Grey Ghost'	NCft
'Thais'	NCft
'Wonder'	NCft

× *Gasterhaworthia* (*Asphodelaceae*)
'Royal Highness'   CPic NCft

Gasteria ✿ (*Asphodelaceae*)
acinacifolia   SPlb
batesiana ♀H2   NCft SBrt SEND
- 'Barberton' **new**   SPlb
bicolor   CPic NCft SPlb
  var. *liliputana* ♀H1c
  - - 'Variegata' (v)   SPlb
brachyphylla   SPad
- var. *bayeri*   SPlb
carinata   SPlb
- var. *verrucosa*   EShb SEND SPlb
'D Tiga'   NHrt
disticha   SPlb
- var. *disticha*   SPlb
  f. *monstruosa*
  - - 'Striata' (v)   SPlb
ellaphieae   SPlb
glauca   SPlb
glomerata   SPlb
glomerata × *rawlinsonii*   SPlb
'Little Warty' ♀H2   CoPl CPic NCft NHrt SPad WFar
'Lizard Lips' **new**   SPlb
nitida   NCft
  var. *armstrongii* ♀H2
- var. *nitida* variegated (v) CPic WCot
obliqua 'Variegata' (v)   SPlb
pseudo-nigra   NCft
rawlinsonii   NCft
'Rumpelstiltskin'   NCft
'Salad Cream'   NCft
schweickerdtiana   NCft
'Smokey'   EShb

× *Gaulnettya* see *Gaultheria*

Gaultheria ✿ (*Ericaceae*)
aff. *dumicola* NJM 10.032   WPGP
forrestii BWJ 7809   WCru
itoana   GKev
'Jingle Bells'   LCro
'John Saxton'   WAbe
miqueliana   NLar
mucronata   CDoC EGrI EPfP GKev MAsh WFar
- (m)   CBcs CMac EPfP GKev LCro LRHS WFar
- 'Bell's Seedling' (f/m) ♀H6   CBcs CBrac ELan EPfP LRHS MAsh NBir NLar SPoG WFar
- 'Crimsonia' (f) ♀H6   CBcs CMac EPfP
- 'Lilacina' (f)   CMac MAsh
- 'Lilian' (f)   EPfP LRHS
- MOTHER OF PEARL   see *G. mucronata* 'Parelmoer'
- 'Mulberry Wine' (f) ♀H6   CBcs EPfP
§ - 'Parelmoer' (f)   CBcs
- 'Pink Pearl' (f) ♀H6   LRHS NBir
§ - 'Signaal' (f)   CBcs EPfP LCro LRHS MAsh NLar
- SIGNAL   see *G. mucronata* 'Signaal'
§ - 'Sneeuwwitje' (f)   CBcs ELan EPfP LCro LRHS MAsh WFar
- SNOW WHITE   see *G. mucronata* 'Sneeuwwitje'
§ myrsinoides   GKev
- B&SWJ 14231   WCru
nummularioides   GKev NHar
'Pearls'   EPot GArf WAbe
procumbens ♀H5   CAgr CDoC CDTJ CMac EGren EGrI EHeP ELan EPfP GKev LRHS MAsh MBlu SPlb SPoG WFar
- BIG BERRY ('Gaubi'^PBR)   CDoC LCro LRHS SPoG

- GAULTHIER PEARL ('Specgp11'^PBR) LCro
- VERY BERRY ('Kieverber')   NBir
prostrata   see *G. myrsinoides*
pumila   GAbr GKev
pyroloides   GArf
shallon   CAgr CBrac EHeP MCtn NLar WFar
sinensis   GArf
trichophylla   GArf NHar
× *wisleyensis*   GKev
- 'Ruby'   CMac
- 'Wisley Pearl'   EPfP NLar

Gaura see *Oenothera* (G)
sinuata   see *Oenothera sinuata*

Gazania (*Asteraceae*)
'Christopher Lloyd'   LCro SMrm SPoG
CREMAZU (Sunbathers Series)   EPfP
Daybreak Series   MBros MCtn
- 'Daybreak Bright Orange'   LCro
'Fire and Thunder' **new**   EDAr
Gazoo Series   MPri
'Katua' (Sunbathers Series)   ELan
(Kiss Series) 'Big Kiss White Flame' LBuc
- 'Big Kiss Yellow Flame'   LBuc MPri
krebsiana   LCro
- TANAGER   EDAr
linearis 'Colorado Gold'   EDAr
'Magic'   ELan SPoG
rigens   SHor
Sunburst Series   LCro
Talent Series ♀H3   LCro MCtn SEND
- 'Talent Red Shades'   MCtn
TIGER EYE ('Gazte') (v)   ELan LCro SPoG
TOTONACA ('Suga212') (Sunbathers Series) ELan EPfP SPoG

Gelsemium (*Gelsemiaceae*)
rankinii   LRHS WCot
sempervirens   CBcs CRHN EBee EShb LSRN SNig SPoG WCot

Genista (*Fabaceae*)
aetnensis ♀H5   ECha ELan EPfP EUrb EWes SArc SDix WSpi
decumbens   see *Cytisus decumbens*
hispanica   CBcs CDoC CSBt EHeP ELan LRHS MMuc NLar SRms
horrida   NLar
lydia ♀H5   CBcs CBrac CDoC CMac EHeP EPfP LCro LRHS MAsh MGos MPri NLar SPoG SRms SSta WFar
§ maderensis   MPri
pilosa   EPot
- 'Goldilocks'   LRHS MMuc
- var. *minor*   EPot WAbe
- 'Procumbens' ♀H5   CBrac EDAr GEdr
- 'Vancouver Gold'   CMac SRms
§ - 'Porlock' ♀H3   CBcs CDoC CMac CWnw EPfP LCro LRHS MAsh MPri SEND SNig WAbe
sagittalis   LRHS
§ × *spachiana*   EGren LRHS SPoG
- PHEBUS ('Geni138'^PBR)   EGren MPri
tinctoria   CCBP CHab GQue MCtn MMuc NAts SPhx
- 'Flore Pleno' (d) ♀H6   GEdr
- 'Humifusa'   EPot GEdr
- 'Moesiaca'   WAbe
- 'Royal Gold' ♀H6   NLar SPlb

Gennaria (Orchidaceae)
diphylla   WCot

Gentiana ✿ (Gentianaceae)

§	*acaulis* ♀H5	EDAr EPot EWld GArf GEdr GKev GMaP LRHS MCtn NGdn NLar SPlb SRms WAbe WHoo
	- from Vercors, France **new**	MNrw
	- f. *alba* 'Snowstorm'	GKev
	- 'Arctic Fanfare'	GEdr
	- B.A. selection	EPot
	- 'Belvedere'	GKev
	- 'Krumrey'	EPot GEdr GKev
	- 'Luna'^{PBR}	NLar WIce
I	- 'Maxima Enzian'	GEdr
	- 'Rannoch'	EPot GEdr GKev
	- 'Stumpy'	GEdr
	- 'Trotter's Variety'	EPot GArf GEdr WAbe
	- 'Undulatifolia'	EPot
	- 'Velkokvensis'	EPot GEdr
	'Alex Duguid' ♀H5	GEdr NHar
	'Amethyst'	GEdr WAbe
	angulosa M. Bieb.	see *G. verna* subsp. *pontica*
	angustifolia	GKev NCth
	'Ann's Special'	GEdr
	asclepiadea ♀H5	CBcs CSpe EBee ECha ELan EMor GAbr GEdr GKev GMaP LEdu MCtn MNrw NBid NBir NCth NLar SMHy SRms WCAu WFar WHoo
	- 'Alba'	EBee GEdr GKev LEdu NBid NLar SRms
	- dark blue-flowered	WPGP
	- 'Knightshayes'	EBee GKev LEdu NLar
I	- 'Nana'	EBee GKev
	- pale blue-flowered	WPGP
	- 'Phyllis'	EBee
	- 'Pink Swallow'	GEdr
	- 'Rosea'	GKev
	- 'White Swallow'	GEdr
	- 'Whitethroat'	EBee GKev
	'Balmoral'^{PBR} ♀H5	GMaP NHar
	'Barbara Lyle'	WAbe
	bavarica var. *subacaulis*	SPlb
	'Berrybank Dome'	GMaP LRHS
	'Berrybank Sky'	EWld GEdr GMaP LRHS NHar
	'Berrybank Snowflakes'	GMaP
	'Berrybank Star'	GEdr LRHS
	bisetaea	SRms
	'Blauer Diamant'	GEdr
	'Blauer Kobold'	GEdr
	'Blauer Zwerg'	GEdr
	'Blue Flame'	GEdr
	'Blue Heaven'	GEdr
	'Blue Magic'^{PBR}	IPot NLar
	'Blue Silk' ♀H5	GKev LRHS NHar SPoG WAbe
	brachyphylla	WAbe
	'Braemar'^{PBR} ♀H5	GMaP NHar
*	*burrowthii*	GEdr
	'Cairngorm'	GEdr
	calycosa	GArf
	'Carmen'	GEdr
	× *caroli*	WAbe
	'Compact Gem' ♀H5	GEdr NHar WAbe
§	*cruciata*	ELan GKev GMaP NLar
	'Crystal Ashiro' (Ashiro Series)	LBar
§	*dahurica*	CBcs EBee GKev NGdn NLar
	- var. *dahurica*	GBin
	'Dark Hedgehog'	GEdr
	David Sturrock's dark seedling	NHar
	depressa	WAbe
	'Devonhall'	GEdr NHar WIce
	'Diana'^{PBR}	NLar
	dinarica 'Colonel Stitt'	MWlw
	- 'Frocheneite'	EPot
	'Dumpy'	GEdr
	'Elehn'	LRHS NHar
	'Ettrick'	GEdr
	'Eugen's Allerbester' (d) ♀H5	CAby GEdr GKev GMaP NHar NLar WAbe WIce
	'Eugen's Bester'	NHar
	farreri	WAbe
	- Silken Star Group	WAbe
	'Faszination'	GEdr
	'Gellerhard'	GEdr
	'Gewahn'	GEdr
I	'Glamis Strain'	GEdr NHar
	'Glen Moy'	GEdr
	'Glendevon'	GEdr
§	*gracilipes*	GKev SPlb SRms
	grossheimii	GKev
	'Hamburg'	GEdr
	'Henry'	GEdr
	'Inverleith'	SPlb
	'John Aitken'	GEdr
	'Juwel'	GEdr
	'Kobold'	GEdr
	kochiana	see *G. acaulis*
	kurroo var. *brevidens*	see *G. dahurica*
	lagodechiana	see *G. septemfida* var. *lagodechiana*
	'Lapis Lazuli'	GEdr
	ligustica	EPot WAbe
	'Lipstick Ashiro' (Ashiro Series)	IPot LBar
	'Little Diamond'^{PBR}	NLar
	loderi	GKev
	'Lucerna'	GEdr
	lutea	EBee ECha EMor GAbr GKev MCtn NLar SDix SRms WCAu
	× *macaulayi*	GEdr
	'Blue Bonnets'	
	- 'Elata'	LRHS
	- 'Kidbrooke Seedling'	GEdr GKev WAbe
	- 'Kingfisher'	GEdr WAbe
	makinoi 'Marsha'^{PBR}	SPoG
	'Margaret'	GEdr
	'Maryfield'	GEdr
	'Melanie'	GEdr
	newberryi	GArf
	nipponica	GKev
	'Oban'^{PBR} ♀H5	GMaP NHar
	occidentalis	EPot WAbe
	orbicularis	WAbe
	ornata	GArf GKev WAbe
	pannonica	EDAr GKev
	paradoxa ♀H5	GKev
	- 'Blauer Herold'	EDAr
	phlogifolia	see *G. cruciata*
	pneumonanthe	NLar SPlb
	prolata	GArf
	pumila	WAbe
	subsp. *delphinensis*	
	purdomii	see *G. gracilipes*
	saxosa	NBir WAbe
	scabra 'Little Pinkie'^{PBR}	IPot NCth
	- LUIS EASY BLUE ('Klegh12013'^{PBR}) **new**	LRHS
	- ROCKY DIAMOND BLUE HEART ('Genfire'^{PBR}) **new**	LRHS
	- 'Zuki Rindo' **new**	IPot

septemfida ♀H5	GKev GMaP NBir SPlb SRms WHoo WIce	**anemonifolium**	see *G. palmatum*
* - var. **kuznetzovii**	GKev	'Ann Folkard' ♀H7	Widely available
§ - var. **lagodechiana** ♀H5	GKev	'Anne Thomson' ♀H7	Widely available
- - 'Bella Alpinella'	GEdr GKev SRms WAbe WFar	'Annette'	LBar LSou
'Serenity'	GEdr	× **antipodeum** 'Chocolate Candy'	LBuc LRHS SPoG
'Shot Silk'	CAby GEdr NHar WAbe	- 'Pink Spice'^PBR	CWGN GKin LBuc LRHS SPoG SRms
'Silken Giant'	GEdr LRHS MGos SPoG WAbe		
'Silken Glow'	GEdr WAbe	- 'Purple Passion'^PBR	LBuc LRHS SPoG
'Silken Night'	WAbe	- (*G. sessiliflorum* subsp. *novae-zelandiae* 'Nigricans') × *G. traversii* var. *elegans*)	SRms
'Silken Seas'	GEdr WAbe		
'Silken Skies'	GEdr NHar WAbe		
'Silken Surprise'	GEdr WAbe		
sino-ornata	WAbe		
	CAby GKev GMaP LCro NBir SPoG SRms WAbe WIce	**aristatum**	EBee EPPr LRHS MNrw
- SDR 5127	MGos	**armenum**	see *G. psilostemon*
- 'Angel's Wings'	GEdr	**asphodeloides**	MNrw NBir SHar WBrk WFar
- 'Bellatrix'	GEdr	**atlanticum** Hook. f.	see *G. malviflorum*
- 'Blautopf'	GEdr	'Azure Rush'	CDoC CDor CWGN EBee EBlo EGren ELan EPfP GMaP LBar LHGe LRHS LSou MAvo MHol MPri NCth NSti SPoG SRms WCAu WCra WFar WKif WNPC WPnP WSpi WTor
- 'Brin Form'	SRms		
- 'Downfield'	GKev		
- 'Gorau Glas'	WAbe		
- 'Oha'	GEdr		
- 'Purity'	GEdr GKev LRHS WAbe	'Baby Blue'	see *G. himalayense* 'Baby Blue'
- 'Starlight'	GEdr GKev NHar	'Bertie Crûg'	EAri GKev NBir SRms WSpi
- 'Weisser Traum'	GEdr NLar	BLOOM ME AWAY ('Libluma')	EGren LBar Midl NCth WFar
- 'White Wings'	GEdr	'Bloomtime'	ELan LBar WCra
'Sir Rupert'	GEdr NHar	'Blue Boy'	NLar
'Sternschuppe'	GKev	'Blue Cloud' ♀H7	EPfP EPPr EWoo GMaP LHGe LRHS LSto MBel NBid NBir NDov NLar NSti NWbg SMHy SPoG SRGP WCAu WCra WFar WGwG WHoo WPnP
× **stevenagensis**	WAbe		
dark-flowered			
'Strathmore' ♀H5	GEdr GKev GMaP NBir SPlb WIce		
'Surprise'	GEdr		
ternifolia	GKev	'Blue Pearl'	NBir
- 'Dali'	GEdr	§ BLUE SUNRISE ('Blogold'^PBR) ♀H7	CDor ELan EMor EPfP GMaP LBar LRHS LSRN MAvo MNrw NLar NSti SPoG SRms WCot WCra WFar WSpi WTor
'The Caley' ♀H5	GEdr GMaP NHar		
tibetica	GGro MCtn WCAu WHil		
- PAB 2357	WPGP		
Tough's form	GEdr	'Blue Thunder'	EPPr
triflora	GKev	'Blushing Turtle'^PBR	CWnw EGren ELan EMor EPfP LBar LHGe LRHS LSou MAvo MHol MPri NDov SPoG WCAu WCra WFar WPnP WTor
- (Ashiro Series) 'Meruhen Ashiro'	LBar		
- - 'Shine Blue Ashiro'^PBR	IPot NCth		
'Troon' ♀H5	GMaP NHar	'Bob's Blunder'	EMor LRHS MBNS MHol MNrw NWbg SAko SPoG SRms WCot WCra WFar
'True Blue'	IPot		
veitchiorum	GArf GKev		
verna	CAby EWes LCro MCtn MWlw SPlb SPoG WAbe WHoo	**bohemicum**	WHer
		- 'Orchid Blue'	MCtn
- 'Alba'	GEdr NLar	I **brevicaule** 'Nigricans'	CFis ECha EDAr WFar
§ - subsp. **pontica**	WIce	§ - 'Porters Pass'	EWes SPlb WFar
'Violette'	GEdr	'Brookside' ♀H7	Widely available
waltonii	EWes	'Buckland Beauty'	CExl EWes
zekuensis	WCot	'Buxton's Blue'	see *G. wallichianum* 'Buxton's Variety'

Gentianella (Gentianaceae)
bellidifolia	GKev

		caeruleatum	NLar
		canariense	see *G. reuteri*
		§ × **cantabrigiense**	CMac CSde EPfP MHer MNrw NBir NBro NLar NPer NSti SRms StAn WCru

Geogenanthus (Commelinaceae)
ciliatus	WTra	- 'Andrew Clarke'	EPPr
'Pastaza'	WTra	- 'Berggarten'	EPPr NLar SAko SRGP WBrk WCra
		- 'Biokovo'	Widely available

Geranium ✿ (Geraniaceae)
aconitifolium misapplied	see *G. palmatum*	- 'Cambridge'	CDor EBee ECha EGrI EHeP ELan EMor EPfP EPPr GAbr GJos GKin LBar LBuc LHGe LRHS LWaG SPoG SRms WBrk WCra WFar
aconitifolium L'Hér.	see *G. rivulare*		
'Alan Mayes'	CFis CMac EPPr EWoo GAbr GKin GPSL LBom LHGe LRHS MBel NGdn NWbg WCra WFar WPnP		
		- CRYSTAL ROSE ('Abpp')	EBee ELan EPfP EPPr NLar NSti SRGP WCot WCra WHoo
'Alan's Blue'	EBee	- 'Hanne'	CDor EBee ECha EPPr EWes
albanum	EPPr GPSL	- 'Harz'	CDor EPPr WBrk WCra
albiflorum	EBee	- 'Hilary Rendall'	EPPr WBrk
'Allendale Gem'	EBee		

Geranium

- 'Intense' — CWnw LBar LCro LRHS LSto WNPC WPnP XFar
- 'Karmina' — CDor EBee EBlo ELan EMor EPfP EPPr GJos GPSL LBom LHGe LRHS NLar WBrk WCra WFar WSpi XFar
- 'Rosalina' — EPPr
- 'Show Time' — EPPr
- 'St Ola' — CDor EBee EBlo EGren ELan EMor EPfP EPPr GJos GMaP LRHS MNrw NBid NBro NGdn NLar NSti NWbg WBrk WCAu WCot WCra WCru WHoo WPnP WSpi
- 'Vorjura' — EPPr SPel
- 'Westray'[PBR] — CCBP CDor CMac GJos LCro LRHS MHol MMuc NBir NCou NGdn NRya NSti SEND SRms WCra WIce
- 'Chantilly' — EBee EPPr NBir NLar WCru WGwG
- *christensenianum* B&SWJ 8022 — WCru
- *cinereum* 'Apple Blossom' — see *G.* × *lindavicum* 'Apple Blossom'
- 'Sateene'[PBR] — CAby SRms
- (Cinereum Group) 'Alice'[PBR] — CAby LRHS NLar NSti SRms WFar
- 'Ballerina' ♀[H5] — CSpe EGren EGrI EHeP ELan EPot GJos GMaP LCro LHGe LRHS LSou LSRN MAsh MGos MHer MPnt NLar SLee SPoG SRms WCAu WCra WFar WHoo WKif WSpi
- 'Carol' — CAby CWGN GKin LHGe LSRN WFar WIce
I - 'Heather' — WFar
- JOLLY JEWEL HOT PINK ('Noortjjhpi') — LCro LRHS
- JOLLY JEWEL LILAC ('Noortlil'[PBR]) — CWGN GEdr LHGe LRHS NSti WCra
- JOLLY JEWEL NIGHT ('Noortnight'[PBR]) — CWGN GEdr LRHS MAsh MPnt NLar SMrm WCra
- JOLLY JEWEL PINK — MPnt SMrm
- JOLLY JEWEL PURPLE ('Noortpur'[PBR]) — CWGN GEdr LCro LRHS MAsh MPri SMrm WCra
- JOLLY JEWEL RASPBERRY ('Noortjjrab') — CWGN LBar LHGe LRHS MPnt SMrm WCot WCra
- JOLLY JEWEL RED ('Noortimpred') — CWGN GEdr LHGe LRHS MPnt MPri NLar NSti WCot WCra
- JOLLY JEWEL SALMON ('Noortsal'[PBR]) — CWGN GEdr LCro MHol SMrm
- JOLLY JEWEL SILVER ('Noortjjsil') — CWGN LRHS MPnt MPri NSti WCra
- JOLLY JEWEL VIOLET ('Noortvio') — LBar LHGe MAsh
- 'Lambrook Helen' — CAby CExl
- 'Laurence Flatman' — CAby CExl CSpe EWoo GMaP LHGe LRHS MPnt NBid NDov NQui SPoG SRms WAbe WKif
- 'Lizabeth'[PBR] — WCot
- 'Melody'[PBR] — CAby WIce
- 'Penny Lane'[PBR] — LHGe MHol
- 'Purple Pillow' — CWGN EGrI ELan LShi LSRN SRms WFar WIce
- ROTHBURY GEM ('Gerfos'[PBR]) ♀[H5] — EGrI IBal LHGe LRHS MPri NCth NSti WCra
- 'Signal' — EPot MPnt
- 'Sophie'[PBR] — LRHS WIce
§ - 'Thumbling Hearts' — CWGN EGrI GPSL LCro MPro SAko WCot WFar
- THUMPING HEART — see *G.* (Cinereum Group) 'Thumbling Hearts'
- 'Claridge Druce' — see *G.* × *oxonianum* 'Claridge Druce'
§ *clarkei* 'Kashmir White' — Widely available
- 'Mount Stewart' — CExl
- (Purple-flowered Group) 'Kashmir Purple' — CDor CExl EPfP ESgI GMaP LShi MArl NBid NBir NSti SHar SRms WFar WKif WSpi
- Raina 82.83 — MNrw
- *clarum* B&SWJ 10246 — WCru
- *collinum* — EPPr
- 'Coombland White' — CDor CExl EBee EPfP EWes EWoo GAbr LBar LBom LHGe LRHS MMrt NSti SPoG WCot WCra WFar WNPC WSpi
- 'Copper Tiger' — ESgI LEdu MWlw WPGP
- 'Criss Canning' — EPPr
- 'Curly Girly' — EBee
- 'Cyril's Fancy' — ESgI LRHS
- *dalmaticum* ♀[H5] — EBee ELan EPot EPPr EWld EWoo GQue MArl MHer MMuc SEND SRGP SRms SRot WAbe WCav WChS WCru WFar WGwG WIce WSpi
- 'Album' — EBee SRGP SRms StAn WAbe
- 'Bressingham Pink' — EPPr
- 'Bridal Bouquet' — EPot
- 'Stade's Hellrosa' — EPPr
- *dalmaticum* × *macrorrhizum* — see *G.* × *cantabrigiense*
- 'Danny Boy' ♀[H7] — EBee
- DARK EYES ('Macger001') — CWGN LBar LSou LSRN MNrw MPro NCth NLar WNPC
- 'Deep Purple' — CTtf
- *delavayi* misapplied — see *G. sinense*
- 'Deux Fleurs' — MAvo MNrw WCra
- 'Devon Pride' — CElw
- 'Dilys' ♀[H7] — EBee EPPr LBar LHGe MNrw NBir NClf NDov NGdn NLar NSti SRGP WCra WFar WPnP WSpi
- aff. *donianum*/*stapfianum* W&O 9125 — GGro
- 'Double Jewel' — see *G. pratense* 'Double Jewel'
- DRAGON HEART ('Bremdra'[PBR]) — CSpe EBee EGren ELan EPfP ERCP EWoo LBar LCro LRHS LSRN MAvo MNrw MPnt NLar NSti SRot WCAu WCra WFar WNPC WPnP WSpi
- *drakensbergense* — WFar
- DREAMLAND ('Bremdream'[PBR]) — Widely available
- 'Dusky Crûg' — ELan EMor EPfP GMaP ISha LHGe LSto MAsh SPoG SRot WCot WFar WSpi WTre
- 'Dusky Rose' — CAby CDor CSpe EWoo GJos LShi MPro NLar SHar WFar
- 'Dylis' — WCAu
- 'Elke' — Widely available
- 'Elworthy Eyecatcher' — CDor CElw CFis EBee LBar LHGe LRHS MNrw
- 'Elworthy Tiger' — CElw EBee
- 'Emily' — SRGP
- *endressii* — ECha EGren GMaP LHGe LRHS LShi LWaG MBNS MHer MMuc NBro NPer SEND SPlb SRms WCra WFar
- 'Album' — see *G.* 'Mary Mottram'
- 'Betty Catchpole' — EBee SRGP
- 'Wargrave Pink' — see *G.* × *oxonianum* 'Wargrave Pink'
- *erianthum* — GMaP SMHy WCra
- 'Axeltree' — WCot
- 'Blues in the Night' — EBee
- 'Calm Sea' — WCru
- 'Neptune' — WCru
- *eriostemon* Fischer — see *G. platyanthum*

'Eureka Blue'	EBee EBlo ECha ELan EPfP LBar LBom MHol NLar NSti SPel SPoG WCot WCra		'JS Matu Vu'	CDor CWGN GMaP GPSL LBar LHGe LRHS NCth NSti SPoG WCAu WSpi
'Eva'	LBar SHar WCra WHoo		'Jubilee Pink'	WCru
'Expression'	see *G.* 'Tanya Rendall'	§	'Kanahitobanawa'	CElw ESgI
§ ***farreri***	CExl NBir		'Karen Wouters'	EPPr
'Fay Anna'	CWGN EMor EPfP ESgI MHol SPoG WFar XFar		'Kashmir Blue'	CExl ELan EPfP GMaP LRHS NLar WCAu WCra WFar
'Femme Fatale'	SMHy WCot		'Kashmir Pink'	CExl CMac ECha ELan ESgI EWes GMaP LBom LRHS MGos MMuc MNrw NBid NBir NLar NSti WCAu WFar WSpi
gracile	EPfP GMaP MNrw NBir WCru			
- B&SWJ 16042	WCru			
- 'Blanche'	EPPr			
- 'Blush'	EPPr EWes	§	'Khan'	CElw ECha EPPr EWes EWoo LBar NEoE NLar SMHy SNoN SRGP WCru
- 'Golden Gracile'	see *G.* 'Mrs Judith Bradshaw'			
grandiflorum	see *G. himalayense*			
'Guilty Secret'	WCot		***kishtvariense***	GGro MWlw NSti WCru
gymnocaulon	EBee NLar WCru		***koraiense***	WFar
§ ***hayatanum*** B&SWJ 264	GGro NLar WCru		- B&SWJ 797	WCru
'Hexham Velvet'	LBar MHol MNrw NCth NLar SMHy WCra WPnP WSpi		- B&SWJ 878	CExl WCru
			koreanum misapplied	see *G. hayatanum*
§ ***himalayense***	CBcs ECha EHeP ELan MBNS NBir NBro SPlb SRms WCra WFar		***koreanum*** Kom.	NLar
			- B&SWJ 602	CExl WCru
- CC 1957 from Tibetan border	CExl EPPr		***krameri*** B&SWJ 1142	CExl WCru
- HPA 1347	GGro		'Lakwijk Star'	CCBP CFis EPfP EPPr GPSL LHGe LRHS MBel NClf NLar SPoG SRms WCot WCra WMal
- ***alpinum***	see *G. himalayense* 'Gravetye'			
§ - 'Baby Blue'	EBee EBlo ELon EPPr GKev LBar LHGe LRHS MAvo MBel MNrw MWlw NGdn NLar NSti SRGP WBrk WCAu WCra WCru WPnP		'Larch Cottage Velvet'	MAvo MWlw
			'Lea'	LBar
			libani	EPPr MWlw NBid NSti WBrk WCot
			- RCB RL B-2	EPPr WCot
- 'Birch Double'	see *G. himalayense* 'Plenum'		- 'Kew Gardens'	EPPr
- 'Derrick Cook'	CCBP CDor EBee ECha EMor EPPr ESgI EWoo GElm LHGe MAsh MAvo MBel MNrw MWlw NLar NSti SMHy WBrk WCAu WCra WHoo WPnP WSpi XFar		'Light Dilys'	LCro NDov
			'Lilac Ice'	CDor CWGN EBee GMaP LCro LHGe MAsh MPro NCth NSti WCra WTor
			'Limburg's Bronze Green'	EPPr
- 'Devil's Blue'	EPPr	§	× ***lindavicum*** 'Apple Blossom'	EPot LCro WFar
§ - 'Gravetye'	Widely available			
- 'Irish Blue'	CDor CElw EBee EPPr GElm GMaP NLar NSti SRGP WCra		***linearilobum*** subsp. ***transversale***	CWGN LRHS MPro WCot WSpi
- ***meeboldii***	see *G. himalayense*		'Foundling's Friend'	
- 'Pale Irish Blue'	EPPr	I	- - 'Laciniatum'	WCot
§ - 'Plenum' (d)	CDor CWCL EAri ECha EGrI ELan EPfP LHGe LRHS LSRN MArl NBid NBro NLar NRya NSti SPoG SRms WCAu WCra WFar WKif WPnP XFar		'Little Charmer'	MPro
		§	'Little David'	CFis GPSL LRHS LSou NLar NSti WCra
			'Little Devil'	see *G.* 'Little David'
			'Little Gem'	GMaP GPSL WCra WFar WHoo
'Hola Guapa'	GPSL		'Lydia'	SRGP
ibericum misapplied	see *G.* × ***magnificum***	§	***macrorrhizum***	CGHo CoPl EGren EGrI EHeP EPot GJos GKev GKin IDun LBom LCro LEdu LShi LSto LWaG MCtn MSCN NBro SRms WCAu WFar
ibericum ambig.	NLar SRms WCAu			
ibericum Cav.	StAn			
- 'Bressingham Dazzler'	EBlo		- AL&JS 90179YU	EPPr
- subsp. ***ibericum***	CMac		- 'Album'	CDor CoPl EBlo ECha EHeP EMor EPPr GQue LRHS LShi MBel NBid NBro NLar NQui SAko SRGP WCAu WCot WCra WCru WFar
- subsp. ***jubatum***	LHGe SRms			
- - 'White Zigana'	SRms			
- var. ***platypetalum*** misapplied	see *G.* × ***magnificum***			
- var. ***platypetalum*** Boiss.	see *G. platypetalum* Fisch. & C.A. Mey.		- 'Bevan's Variety'	Widely available
§ - 'Ushguli Grijs'	CElw EBee MWlw NLar WCot		- 'Bulgaria'	EPPr
incanum	CAby CSpe LSto NBir WSpi		- 'Cham Ce'	ECha EPPr
'Ivan' ♀H7	CCBP CElw CFis CMHG EBee ECha LHGe MBel NLar SNoN SPel WCot WCra WCru XFar		- 'Czakor'	CDor CMac EBee EBlo EGren ELan ELon EPfP EPPr ESgI LBar LHGe LRHS NGdn NLar NSti SAko SMrm SRGP SRms WBrk WCot WCra WCru WFar
'Jean Armour'	CFis LHGe LRHS MBNS SPoG WFar WGwG			
× ***johnsonii*** 'Johnson's Blue'	Widely available	I	- 'De Bilt'	EPPr
			- 'Freundorf'	EPPr EWes GQue WBrk
'Jolly Bee'	see *G.* Rozanne		- 'Glacier'	ECha EWes WBrk
'Joy'	CDor CWGN EBee ELan EPfP EWoo LBom LHGe LRHS NBir NSti SRGP SRms WCAu WCra WGwG		- 'Ingwersen's Variety' ♀H7	Widely available
			- 'Lohfelden'	EWes WCra
			- 'Montasch'	NLar

Geranium

Name	Sources
- 'Morris Minor'	EWes SRGP WBrk
- 'Mount Olympus'	see *G. macrorrhizum* 'White-Ness'
- 'Mytikas'	EPPr
§ - 'Olympic Fire'	ELan
- 'Olympos'	EPPr NLar WCra
- 'Pastis'	SPoG
- 'Pindus'	EPPr EWes NLar NSti SRGP WCru WFar
- 'Prionia'	EBee EPPr MWlw
- 'Purpurrot'	EPPr
- 'Ridsko'	EPPr SRGP WCru
- *roseum*	see *G. macrorrhizum*
- 'Rotblut'	EPPr WBrk
- 'Sandwijck'	EPPr ESgl WBrk
- 'Sandy's Smile'	see *G. macrorrhizum* 'Olympic Fire'
- 'Snow Sprite'	EPot EPPr ESgl GKev MHer NEoE NLar WBrk WHrl
- 'Spessart'	CCBP EBee EGren EHeP ELan EPfP EPPr EWoo GMaP GQue LBar LHGe LRHS MAvo MMuc MPro NLar SEND SPoG WChS WFar
- 'Variegatum' (v)	GMaP NBir SRGP SRms WCot WFar
- 'Velebit'	EPPr SRGP WCru
§ - 'White-Ness' ♀H7	Widely available
macrostylum	GKev WCot
- 'Leonidas'	EPPr
- 'Talish'	EPPr
- 'Uln Oag Triag'	EPPr
maculatum	MNrw NLar NSti
- from Kath Dryden	EPPr
- f. *albiflorum*	CElw EBee EBlo ELan ELon EPfP EPPr EWoo LHGe LRHS MBel NLar NSti SRGP WBrk WCAu WCra WCru WFar
- 'Beth Chatto'	CCps CDor CElw CTtf EBee ECha ELan ELon EMor EPfP EPPr GElm GMaP LBar LHGe MBel MCtn MMuc NBid NDov WBrk WCAu WCra WFar WHoo WPnP
- 'Elizabeth Ann' PBR ♀H7	CWGN EWoo LBar MBel MHol MNrw NCth NGdn NLar NSti SDix SPel WCot WCra WFar
- 'Espresso'	Widely available
- 'Putnam County'	EBee EPPr
- 'Schokoprinz'	EPPr SAko
- 'Shameface'	EBee EBlo EPfP EPPr LRHS WCra
- 'Smoky Mountain'	EPPr
- 'Spring Purple'	CElw EPPr MAvo NLar WFar
- STORMY NIGHT ('Macger002')	CKno CWnw EPfP LBar LCro LHGe MHtn WTor
- 'Sweetwater'	EPPr
- 'Vickie Lynn'	CCBP EBee EPPr MBel NLar WCAu WCra
maderense ♀H3	CAbb CAby CBcs CCht CDoC CoPl CPbh CSde CSpe CTsd EArl EBee ELan EShb EUrb LCro LWaG MCtn NBir NPer SArc SPhx SRGP SVen WCru WFar WSpi
- 'Guernsey White'	CPbh CSpe CTsd CWnw MCtn SPhx
- white-flowered	WSpi
§ × *magnificum* ♀H7	Widely available
I - 'Anemoniflorum'	LBar WCAu WCra
- 'Blue Blood'	EGren LBar LHGe NGdn NSti SRms WCot WCra WFar
- 'Ernst Pagels'	CDor
- 'Peter Yeo'	WCra
- 'Rosemoor'	CAby CElw CTsd ELan EPfP GJos LBom LCro LHGe LRHS LSto MAsh MBel NLar WCAu WCra WFar WHoo WSpi
magniflorum	EBee ECha GKev NBid SHar
§ *malviflorum*	CFis ECha NQui NSti SHar WCot
- from Spain	EWes
§ 'Mary Mottram'	CElw ESgl
'Mavis Simpson' ♀H6	Widely available
'Melinda'	WCot
'Memories' PBR	LSRN SRms WIce
'Menna Bach'	MAvo WFar
'Meryl Anne'	MAvo
'Midnight Star'	EBee EWes
× *monacense*	WCru WFar WGwG WMal
- var. *anglicum*	CDor EPPr LHGe NLar
- 'Anne Stevens'	EPPr LHGe
- 'Claudine Dupont'	CDor CElw ECha EPPr ESgl GQue LHGe MWlw WCot
- dark-flowered	WFar
- 'Emma White'	EPPr
- 'Jackie'	EPPr LHGe
- var. *monacense* 'Breckland Fever'	EBee EMor EPPr LHGe MAvo WCra
§ - - 'Muldoon'	NBir SRGP WFar
- 'Spotted in the Pass'	EBee
'Mourning Widow'	see *G. phaeum* 'Lady in Mourning'
'Mrs Jean Moss'	EPPr EWes WCra
§ 'Mrs Judith Bradshaw'	MWlw
napuligerum misapplied	see *G. farreri*
nepalense	SRms
aff. *nepalense* W&O 9124	GGro
'Nicola'	CElw EPPr MWlw SRGP
'Nimbus' ♀H7	Widely available
nodosum	Widely available
- 'Blueberry Ice'	CDor CElw EWld MNrw
- 'Clos de Coudray'	CTtf EBee ELon EPfP EPPr EWld GPSL LHGe LRHS MAvo MNrw NLar NSti SBeP SHar WCAu WCra WFar WPnP
- dark-flowered	see *G. nodosum* 'Swish Purple'
- 'Fielding's Folly'	CElw CSpe CTtf LEdu LSto SHor WPGP
- 'Hexham Big Eye'	CDor EWes MAvo SRGP WBrk WFar
- 'Hexham Face Paint'	WCra
- 'Hexham Feathers'	CDor
- 'Hexham Freckles'	EBee EPPr
- 'Hexham Lace'	CDor EPPr
- 'Hexham Whitethroat'	EBee
- 'Julie's Velvet'	LEdu
- lilac-flowered	EGrl WFar
- 'Marijke'	MNrw
- pale-flowered	see *G. nodosum* 'Svelte Lilac'
- 'Pascal'	EPPr
- pink-flowered	CTtf
- 'Silverwood'	Widely available
- 'Simon'	NLar WCra
§ - 'Svelte Lilac'	EBlo EPfP EPPr EWoo LHGe LRHS NBro NSti SBeP SPoG SRGP WBrk WCAu WChS WCra WCru WFar WPnP
§ - 'Swish Purple'	EPPr NLar SRGP WCru
- 'Tony's Talisman'	EBee EMor LBar LRHS NSti WCra
- 'Whiteleaf'	CDor CElw CMac EPPr SMHy SRGP WCru WFar
- 'Wreighburn House White'	CElw EBee EPPr LHGe MWlw WCra
'Nunwood Purple'	EPPr MAvo
'Old Rose'	LRHS WCru
onaei f. *yezoense*	GGro
§ *orientalitibeticum*	CExl CSpe GKev MMuc NBid NRya SBrt WCot
'Orion' ♀H7	Widely available
'Orkney Blue'	CElw EPPr WCra WCru

MBel NLar WCAu WCra WFar WHoo WSpi

ORKNEY CHERRY ('Bremerry'PBR)	CMac CTsd CWnw EAri EGren GJos GPSL LBom LCro LHGe LRHS MAvo MBel MNrw MPro MSCN SPoG SRkn SRms WCra WNPC WPnP	- 'Spring Fling' (v)	CDor EWes WFar
		- 'Stillingfleet Keira'	EPPr
		- 'Summer Surprise'	EPPr EWes WCru
		- 'Susan'	EWes
		- 'Susie White'	EPPr WCru
'Orkney Dawn'	WTre	- 'Tess'	MHol
'Orkney Flame'	EPPr WCra	§ - f. *thurstonianum*	CMac CSde EPfP EWoo LSto NBir NBro SPoG SRms WBrk WCru WFar WSpi
'Orkney Pink'	EPfP LRHS		
× *oxonianum*	EGrI GQue		
- 'Alice'	SRGP	- - 'Armitageae'	SRGP
- 'Alison Redpath'	WCra	- - 'Breckland Brownie'	EBee EPPr MAvo SRGP
- 'Ankum's White'	EPPr EWes	- - 'Crûg Star'	WCru
- 'A.T. Johnson' ♀H7	CSde EBee ELan EPfP EPPr GKin GMaP LRHS NBir NLar NSti SPoG SRms WCAu WCru WFar WSpi	- - 'David McClintock'	EPPr MArl SRGP WFar
		- - 'Robin's Ginger Nut'	EBee
		- - 'Sherwood'	CSde LShi NSti WFar
		- - 'Southcombe Double'	ELan LHGe SRGP SRms WCra WFar
- 'Barbara' **new**	SRGP		
- 'Beholder's Eye' ♀H7	ESgI GJos MMuc NLar		
- 'Breckland Sunset'	SRGP	§ - - 'Southcombe Star'	EBee EBlo EPPr LHGe NGdn WCru
- 'Bressingham's Delight'	SRGP	- - 'Sue Cox' (d)	EPPr
- 'Chocolate Strawberry'	EBee EPPr	- - 'White Stripes'	EPPr
§ - 'Claridge Druce'	CMac ECha ELan EPfP GKin GMaP LRHS LShi NBir NGdn NLar NQui SRms WFar WKif	- 'Trevor's White'	CDor EBee EMor EPPr NLar SRGP WCAu WCru
		- 'Venus'	EWes
		- 'Wageningen' ♀H7	EBee NGdn NLar SEND WBrk WCot WCru WFar
- 'Coffee Stains'	EPPr ESgI		
- 'Coronet'	GQue		
- 'Cream Chocolate'	EPPr	- 'Walter's Gift'	LRHS MPie NBir NLar NPer NWbg SAko SDix SRGP WChS WCra WFar WHoo WPnP
- 'David Rowlinson'	CDor		
- 'Dawn Time'	CDor		
- 'Ella'	CWGN		
- 'Elworthy Misty'	CCps CElw CFis EPPr SRGP WCra	- - 'Wargrave Pink'	Widely available
- 'Exquisite'	EWes	- - 'Waystrode'	EBee SRGP
- 'Frank Lawley'	NBid WFar	- - 'Westacre White'	ECha EPPr
§ - 'Fran's Star' (d)	WCru	- - 'Whiter Shade of Pale'	EBee
- 'Frilly Gilly'	EBee	- - 'Winscombe'	NLar
- 'Glynis'	SRGP	§ *palmatum* ♀H4	CAbb CBcs CCht CDoC CExl CMac CSpe CTtf EBee ELan EPfP EWoo LCro LWaG MBel MHer MPie NBro NPer SChr SPhx SRGP SRkn WCra WFar WKif WPGP
- 'Hexham White'	EBee EPPr ESgI		
- 'Hollywood'	EPPr NLar NPer NWbg SRms WCra WFar		
- 'Iced Green Tea'	EBee	*palustre*	EBee ELin EPPr LCro MMuc MNrw NLar WCAu WCot WCra
- 'Irene Hatwell'	LShi		
- 'James' **new**	SRGP	- 'Naturtalent' **new**	NCth
- 'Kate Moss'	EBee NSti	'Pastel Clouds'	WFar
- 'Katherine Adele'	CKno CSpe ECha EMor EWes GElm LHGe LRHS LSou MMuc MPnt NLar NSti SEND SOrN SRGP SRms WFar WTre	PATRICIA ('Brempat') ♀H7	Widely available
		peloponnesiacum	EPPr GQue MNrw NLar
		phaeum	Widely available
- 'Königshof'	EPPr	- 'Advendo'	EPPr ESgI LHGe
- 'Kurt's Variegated'	see *G.* × *oxonianum* 'Spring Fling'	- 'Album'	Widely available
- 'Lace Time'	EMor EPPr GKin LRHS LSRN NLar SPoG SRGP SRms WPnP	- 'Alec's Pink'	EBee EMor LBar LHGe MAvo NSti SHar WCAu WCra WPnP
- 'Lady Moore'	LRHS SRGP WPnP	- 'Angelina'	EBee EPPr
- 'Lambrook Gillian'	CCps CFis EPPr SRGP	- 'Anita'	WCra
- 'Laura Skelton'	CElw EBee	- 'Anita Alice'	MNrw WCot
- 'Maurice Moka'	EBee EMor NLar WCra	- 'Ann Logan'	EPPr WCra
- 'Miriam Rundle'	WCru	- 'Aureum'	see *G. phaeum* 'Golden Spring'
- 'Miss Heidi'	ELan EPfP LCro WCAu WHoo	- 'Basket of Lavender'	EBee
- 'Moundmaster' **new**	EPPr	- 'Blauwvoet'	EPPr
- 'Music from Big Pink'	EBee EPPr	- 'Blue Shadow'	EPPr ESgI
- 'Patricia Josephine'	WCAu	- 'Brown Sugar'	EBee
- 'Phantom'	EPPr	- 'Brundall Gold'	EPPr ESgI LHGe
- 'Phoebe Noble'	EPPr LRHS MWlw	- 'Calligrapher'	EPPr
- 'Rebecca Moss'	CFis ECha ELan ESgI GPSL LHGe MWlw NSti SAko WBrk WCra WCru WFar WGwG WHoo WPnP	- 'Chocolate Biscuit'	EPPr LHGe
		- 'Chocolate Chip'	EPPr WCot
		- 'Conny Broe' (v)	CDor
		- 'Dark Dream'	EBee
- 'Red Sceptre'	EBee	- 'David Martin'	EPPr
- 'Rose Clair'	CFis EGren ELan EPfP GJos LCro LHGe LRHS NBir NLar SRGP StAn WCAu WCru	- 'Enid'	EPPr
		- 'Golden Samobor'	EHeP EPPr WCot
		§ - 'Golden Spring'	EMor EPPr NEoE NLar SRGP WCra WFar
- 'Rosenlicht'	EBee GKin LHGe WCAu WCru		
- 'Sandy'	EBee	- 'Green Ghost'	EBee EPPr ESgI
- 'Something Special'	EBee EPPr WMal	- 'Hexham Halo'	EBee

- var. **hungaricum** — EPPr
- 'James Haunch' — CDor EPPr WCra
- 'Jenson's Purple' — EBee
- 'Joseph Green' (d) — CAby EBee ESgl LBar LCro LHGe LRHS MAvo MNrw MWlw NSti SHar WCot WCra WFar WTor XFar
- 'Klepper' — EMor EPPr
- 'Kora' (Censation Series) — XFar
- § 'Lady in Mourning' — CExl EBee ESgl LHGe SBeP SRms WCra WCru WFar
- 'Lavender Pinwheel' — CCps CDor GPSL MWlw WCot
- * 'Lilacina' — CCps ECha LHGe
- 'Lily Lovell' — CCps CDor CElw EBee EGren ELan EMor EPPr EWoo GMaP GQue LCro LHGe LRHS LShi MBel NGdn NLar NSti SDix SRms WBrk WCAu WCot WCra WHer WPnP WRBe
- 'Lisa' (v) — CCps CDor CElw ECha EPPr ESgl MNrw MWlw SMHy SPel WCot WFar WHoo
- 'Little Boy' — EBee NEoE SPel WFar
- var. **lividum** — EMor GMaP SRms WFar
- - 'Joan Baker' — CDor NGdn NSti WFar
- - 'Majus' — EBee EGren ELan EPfP EPPr LHGe WFar
- 'Lustige Witwe' (v) — WCot
- 'Marchants Ghost' — LHGe SMHy
- 'Margaret Wilson' (v) — CDor CElw CWGN ECha EMor EWes GElm MPnt NBir NEoE NGdn NLar NSti WCAu WCot WCra WFar
- 'Mierhausen' — CElw EBee EPPr LHGe WCra
- 'Misty Samobor' — CCps CDor ECha LHGe SHar WCra
- 'Mojito' (v) — ECha WCot
- 'Moorland Dylan' — EPPr WFar
- 'Mottisfont Rose' — CDor CElw
- 'Mourning Widow' — see G. phaeum 'Lady in Mourning'
- 'Mrs Charles Perrin' — ESgl
- 'Night Time' — EBee EPPr
- 'Nightshade' — EBee EPPr LHGe WFar
- 'Our Pat' ♀H7 — EBee EPPr LHGe
- var. **phaeum** Langthorns Blue — ELan EPPr ESgl MNrw
- - 'Samobor' — Widely available
- 'Phantom of the Opera' (v) — EBee EPPr
- 'Purple Moon' — EPPr
- 'Rachel's Rhapsody' — EPPr WCra
- 'Raven' — CCps CDor EMor EPPr EWoo LBar LHGe LRHS MBel NLar WCAu WCra WFar
- 'Ray of Light' — EPPr
- 'Rise Top Lilac' — EBee WCra
- 'Robin's Angel Eyes' — ECha LHGe WCra
- 'Rose Air' — EBee LHGe WFar
- 'Rose Madder' — CCBP CDor CElw EBee MNrw NLar WCru
- 'Rothbury Cherry' — EBee WCra
- 'Rothbury Ruby' — EBee ESgl
- 'Saturn' — EPPr MArl
- 'Séricourt' — WCot WCra
- 'Shadowlight' — EPPr NEoE
- 'Springtime'PBR — CDor EBee EMor GPSL LHGe NGdn NLar NWbg SRms WCAu WCra XFar
- 'Stillingfleet Ghost' — EBee EMor ESgl LBar MWlw NSti
- 'Taff's Jester' (v) — WCot
- 'Tyne Mist' — EBee EPPr LHGe
- § 'Variegatum' (v) — CMac NBir WFar
- 'Walküre' — EPPr EWes EWoo LBar LHGe WCra
- 'Waterer's Blue' — CDor ECha WCra WMal
- 'Wendy's Blush' — EBee EMor ESgl LBar LHGe MAvo NCth NSti WCot WMal
- 'Philippe Vapelle' — Widely available
- 'Pink Delight' — WHoo WMal
- 'Pink Penny' — CDor CWnw EGren LRHS LSou MHol NBir NLar NSti SPoG SRms WCra WFar WHil WNPC WPnP WTor
- 'Pink Petticoats' — MPri
- § **platyanthum** — WCru
- - 'Ankum' — EBee
- **platypetalum** misapplied — see G. × magnificum
- **platypetalum** Franch. — see G. sinense
- § **platypetalum** Fisch. & C.A. Mey. — EBlo EPPr LRHS NBir NSti
- - 'Dark Side of the Moon' — CWal EPPr
- - 'Genyell' — MAvo
- - 'Turco' — EBee EPfP LBar NLar WCra
- § **pogonanthum** — NBir
- - BO 16-049 — GGro
- **polyanthes** — EWes GGro
- **pratense** — CBWd CCBP CGwi CHab CMac CWal EGren EHeP EHet EPPr EWoo GJem GMaP GQue MCtn MHer MNHC NAts NMir SPlb SPoG SRms WCot WCra WFar WOrg WShi
- - 'Akaton' — XFar
- - 'Algera Double' — ELan EPfP LBar WCAu WCra
- - AZURE SKIES ('Tuitsky') (d) — CDor EBee EHeP LBar LCro LSou MPnt WNPC WPnP
- - 'Bittersweet' — EPPr
- - 'Black 'n' White' — CDor EBee ELan LBar LSou NCth WCot
- * - 'Blue Skies' — WFar
- - 'Boom Chocolatta' — LBar LRHS MPri NCth WCAu
- - 'Catforth Cadenza' (v) — MWlw
- - 'Cloud Nine'PBR (d) — CBcs CExl CSde CWCL CWGN GBin GPSL LBar LCro LHGe LRHS MBel MHol Midl MPnt SBeP SHar SMrm WCra WFar WHil WNPC WPnP
- - 'Cluden Sapphire' — EBee EPPr GElm WCru
- - 'Delft Blue' — MSCN NEoE
- - 'Delft Blue Butterfly' — LHGe
- § - 'Double Jewel' (d) — CWGN IPot MHol NBir WFar
- - 'Else Lacey' (d) — CElw EBee EPfP LBar NCou NCth NLar NSti WCot WCra
- - 'Flore Pleno' — see G. pratense 'Plenum Violaceum'
- - 'Hexham Spook' — EBee
- - 'Hocus Pocus' — CWGN EWoo LBar MNrw MPro NBro WCAu WCra WFar
- - 'Hoo House' — WHoo
- - 'Ilja' — EPPr
- - 'Marshmallow' — CDor EBee GPSL LBar MPro NLar NSti SPoG WCot WCra WMal
- - 'Milou' — NLar WCra
- - 'Mrs Kendall Clark' ♀H7 — Widely available
- - 'Pink Coffee' (Censation Series) — XFar
- - 'Pink Splash' — WFar
- - 'Plenum Caeruleum' (d) — CTtf NBid
- § - 'Plenum Violaceum' (d) ♀H7 — CWCL ELan GMaP LBar LHGe NBir SRms WCra WCru WFar WKif
- - 'Pope's Purple' — see G. pratense (Victor Reiter Group) BLACK BEAUTY
- - var. **pratense** f. **albiflorum** — EBee ECha EPPr EWoo GMaP LRHS LSto NBid WFar WSpi
- - - 'Galactic' — GElm GPSL LBar LRHS MArl MMuc NBir NLar SDix SPoG WCot WCru WPnP
- - - 'Laura'PBR (d) — CExl EBee EPfP EWes LBar LCro LHGe LRHS MBel MHol Mrrt MPro

- - - 'Plenum Album' (d)	NLar NSti SPel WCra WFar WPnP WSpi WTre EBee ELan EPfP EWes LBom LSto MNrw NLar NSti SRms WCot WFar WNPC WPnP WSpi	- 'Isparta' - 'Summer Sky' - 'Summer Snow' (Rambling Robin Group) 'Rambling Robin'	SHor SPhx SPoG WCot WFar WPnP WSpi ECha EPPr SPhx WBrk WGoo SRGP CWal CWnw GPSL MCtn WFar WTre
- - - 'Silver Queen'	EPPr GPSL GQue LRHS LSto NBir SPoG WGwG WPnP	*rectum*	NLar
- 'Purple Ghost'	CWGN LRHS MPri MPro NEoE SPoG WFar WSpi	- 'Album'	see *G. clarkei* 'Kashmir White'
- 'Rectum Album'	see *G. clarkei* 'Kashmir White'	'Red Admiral'	CCBP CDor EBee ECha EGren EPfP EPPr ESgl GElm LBar LHGe LRHS
- 'Robin's Grey Beard'	EPPr		LSto MBel MHol NLar NQui NSti
§ - 'Rose Queen'	NBir		SPel SPoG WCAu WCot WCra WFar
- 'Roseum'	see *G. pratense* 'Rose Queen'		WGwG WOld WPnP WSpi
- 'Southease Celestial'	SMHy WGoo	*refractoides*	WCot
- 'Splish-splash'	see *G. pratense* 'Striatum'	*refractum*	CExl
- 'Stanton Mill'	NBid	*regelii*	EBlo
- var. *stewartianum* 'Elizabeth Yeo'	EPPr WCra WCru	*renardii* ♀H6 - 'Tcschelda'	Widely available ECha NBir SRms WCra WFar
- - 'Raina'	EPPr	- 'Zetterlund'	EBee NQui NSti WFar
- 'Storm Cloud' (d)	CTsd CWnw EPfP GJos LBar LCro LRHS LSou Midl MMrt MPri MSCN NCth WHil WPnP	§ *reuteri* 'Richard Nutt' *richardsonii*	WCru EBee EBee EWoo LHGe NBir SPoG WCru
§ - 'Striatum'	Widely available	× *riversleaianum*	Widely available
- variegated, white-flowered (v)	WCot	'Russell Prichard' ♀H4 § *rivulare*	NLar
§ - (Victor Reiter Group) BLACK BEAUTY ('Nodbeauty')	CAby CExl CWGN EBee EGren EWes LBuc LRHS MGos MPnt MPri MPro NLar SPoG SRkn WFar WSpi	*robertianum* § - 'Album' - f. *bernettii*	CoPl EHet ENfk EPPr GQue LWaG MNHC SPhx SRms CoPl EPPr SPhx SRms WHer see *G. robertianum* 'Album'
- - 'Kaya'	EWes IBal LBar NLar WCot WCra XFar	- 'Celtic White' 'Robin's Black Heart'	CSpe EPPr MMuc WFar EBee
- - 'Midnight Blues'	CWGN	*robustum*	NBir SPlb WGoo
- - 'Midnight Clouds'	CWGN EBee WFar	'Rosetta'PBR	EPfP LBar NCth WCAu
- - MIDNIGHT GHOST ('Midnightlyona'PBR)	CCBP EBee WSpi	'Rothbury Red' § ROZANNE ('Gerwat'PBR) ♀H7	WCra Widely available
- - 'Midnight Reiter'	CExl CTsd CWGN EBee EGrl ELan EPfP ERCP GPSL LRHS MCtn MMuc MPro NQui SPoG WCAu WCra WFar	*rubescens* SABANI BLUE ('Bremigo'PBR)	see *G. yeoi* CMac CWGN EBee EWes EWoo LBar LCro LRHS MHol NLar NSti WCot WCra WSpi
- - 'New Dimension'	NLar WSpi	'Salome'	CDor CWGN CWnw EBee ECha
- - 'Purple-haze'	MCtn WFar		LCro NBir NSti SRms WCAu WCot
- - 'Victor Reiter'	CDor LEdu NBir NLar WCot		WCra
- 'Wisley Blue'	EPPr	'Sandrine'PBR	CWGN SPoG SRms WCot
- 'Yorkshire Queen'	NGdn WCru	*sanguineum*	Widely available
'Prelude'	CDor CElw EBee EPPr NBir NEoE SHar SRGP WCAu WMal	- ALAN BLOOM ('Bloger') - 'Album' ♀H7	EBee MArl Widely available
procurrens	CoPl GAbr WBrk WCru	- 'Alpenglow'	ELon EPPr WBrk
- HWJK 2062	WCru	- 'Ankum's Pride' ♀H7	CCps CDor EPfP LHGe MBel NGdn
§ *psilostemon* ♀H7	Widely available		NLar NSti WCra WCru WPnP
- B&SWJ 15324	WCru	- 'Apfelblüte'	ELon GPSL LHGe NLar WCAu WCra
- 'Bressingham Flair'	CDor GAbr LBar NBid NLar SRms WCra WCru WFar	- 'Aviemore' ♀H7 - 'Barnsley'	EPPr NLar NBro
- 'Catherine Deneuve'PBR	CWGN EPfP ERCP EWes GPSL LBar LRHS MPnt MPro NLar NSti SPel WCAu WCra WFar WPnP	- 'Belle of Herterton' - 'Bloody Graham' - 'Canon Miles'	EPPr NEoE WBrk WCru EPPr WBrk EPPr NLar SRms WCra WSpi
- 'Coton Goliath'	EPPr EWes	- 'Catforth Carnival'	EPPr MAvo
- 'French Fancy'	EWes	- 'Cedric Morris'	CElw EBlo ECha ELon EPPr MBel
- 'Harry'	WCot WCra		NLar WBrk WCAu WCra WCru
- 'Madelon'	LHGe NLar	- 'Compactum'	EPPr WCra
- 'Rosefinch'	WCot WCra	- 'Elsbeth'	CCps CDor CElw EBee ECha ELan
- 'Snowfinch'	CDor		ELon EPfP EPPr EWes MArl MBel
punctatum hort.	see *G.* × *monacense* var. *monacense* 'Muldoon'		NGdn NLar NSti SPoG SRGP WCAu WCru WFar WPnP
- 'Variegatum'	see *G. phaeum* 'Variegatum'	- 'Feu d'Automne'	EBee ELon EPPr WBrk
'Purple Rain'	EPPr LBar WCra	- 'Fran's Star'	see *G.* × *oxonianum* 'Fran's Star'
pylzowianum W&O	GGro	- 'Fruit de Fleur'	NCth
pyrenaicum	CBWd NAts NSti WOrg	- 'Glenluce'	CDor CMHG ELon EPfP EPPr LHGe
- f. *albiflorum*	MNrw NBir SRGP WBrk WCot WFar		LRHS LSto MArl NGdn NLar SPoG
- 'Barney Brighteye'	SRGP		SRGP SRms WBrk WCAu WFar
- 'Bill Wallis'	CSpe CWCL CWnw ECha ELan EPfP EPPr GElm LCro LRHS LSto MBrN MMuc NBir NClf NDov NPer		WPnP

	- 'Hampshire Purple'	see *G. sanguineum* 'New Hampshire Purple'
	- 'Hannelore'	WCra
	- 'Holden'	ELon EPPr WBrk
	- 'Inverness'	EBee EPPr NLar WCra
	- 'Joanna'	ELon
	- 'John Elsley'	CCBP CFis EBee EPPr GPSL LBar LSou NBro NEoE NGdn NSti WCra WPnP
	- 'John Innes'	EPPr
	- 'Kristin Jacob'	EPPr
	- var. *lancastrense*	see *G. sanguineum* var. *striatum*
	- 'Leeds Variety'	see *G. sanguineum* 'Rod Leeds'
§	- 'Little Bead' ♀H7	EDAr EPPr
	- 'Max Frei'	Widely available
	- 'Nanum'	see *G. sanguineum* 'Little Bead'
§	- 'New Hampshire Purple'	CElw ELon EPPr NGdn NLar SRGP SRms WCra
	- 'Nyewood'	EPPr NGdn SEND WCra
	- 'Pink Diadem'	LBar
	- 'Pink Pouffe'	CWGN EBee ELon GPSL LRHS Midl NCou SRot WCra
	- 'Pink Summer'	LBar
	- var. *prostratum* (Cav.) Pers.	see *G. sanguineum* var. *striatum*
	- 'Purple Flame'	see *G. sanguineum* 'New Hampshire Purple'
	- 'Red Robin'	EBee EPPr
§	- 'Rod Leeds'	ELon
	- 'Sandra'	SRGP
§	- 'Shepherd's Delight'	EPPr
	- 'Shepherd's Warning' ♀H7	CAby CMiW MMuc NBir NLar SEND WCru WHoo WIce
	- 'Shepherd's Warning' misapplied	see *G. sanguineum* 'Shepherd's Delight'
	- 'Shooting Star'	EPPr NLar WCra
I	- 'Snowflake'	EGren ELon EMor NLar
§	- var. *striatum* ♀H7	Widely available
	- - 'Splendens' ♀H7	LRHS NBid SAko WCru
	- Vision Series	NLar
	- - 'Vision Light Pink'	EGren EPPr LHGe LRHS MHol MPro StAn WCAu WFar
	- - 'Vision Violet'	EGren LRHS SMad SMrm SRms WFar WPnP WTre
	'Sanne'	EWes LRHS LSou WCot WCra WFar
	saxatile 'Snowstar'	EPPr
	'Scapa Flow'	MWlw WCra
	schlechteri	EWes MMuc SEND WBrk WMal
	sessiliflorum	see *G. brevicaule*
	subsp. *novae-zelandiae*	
	- - red-leaved	see *G. brevicaule* 'Porters Pass'
	'Sheilah Hannay'	SHar
	shensianum	GGro
	shikokianum	GGro GKev NLar WCra
	- var. *kaimontanum*	WCru
	- var. *quelpaertense*	EBee
	- - 'Crûg's Cloak'	WCru
	'Shocking Blue'	NLar
	'Shouting Star'	see *G.* 'Kanahitobanawa'
§	*sinense*	CExl GGro
	'Sirak' ♀H7	Widely available
	soboliferum	CFis NBir NLar WCru WFar
	- 'Butterfly Kisses'	LBar
	- var. *kiusianum*	CElw
	- 'Rothbury Star'	WCra
	- 'Starman'	LBar NLar WCra WSpi
	'Solitaire'	WCot
	'Southcombe Star'	see *G.* × *oxonianum* f. *thurstonianum* 'Southcombe Star'
	'Spinners'	CMac EBee EPfP NBid NBir NGdn NLar NQui NSti WCru WFar WPnP
	stapfianum var. *roseum*	see *G. orientalitibeticum*
	'Stephanie'	CElw ESgI EWes MBNS MNrw MWlw NGdn NLar NSti WCAu WCra
	'Storm Chaser'	CBcs CWnw EBee LBar MHol NLar NSti
	subcaulescens ♀H4	CAby ELan LShi LSRN NBid SRms WAbe WFar WIce
	- 'Giuseppii' ♀H5	CExl EGrI EPfP EPot EWoo LHGe LWaG NBir NDov SPoG WCra
	- 'Splendens' ♀H5	CSpe MHer SRms WFar
	'Sue Crûg'	EBee ELan WCru
	'Sue's Sister'	WCru
	'Summer Cloud'	EPPr
	SUMMER SKIES ('Gernic'PBR) (d)	CDor CExl CWCL EBee ELan EPfP ERCP IBal LBar LBom LCro LHGe LRHS MNrw MPri NBro NLar NSti WCAu WCot WCra WSpi
	suzukii B&SWJ 16	CExl
	- NMWJ 14518	GGro WCru
	'Sweet Heidy'PBR	CDor EBee EGren EPfP LBom LRHS MHol MPnt MPri MPro NGdn NLar NSti WCAu WCra WFar
	sylvaticum	NGdn NMir WFar WOrg WShi
	- f. *albiflorum*	NSti
	- - 'Cyril's Superb White'	EBee EPPr
	- 'Album' ♀H7	CDor CSpe ECha ELan EPfP EWoo GMaP LEdu LRHS LSto MArl MBel MMuc NBid NLar SBea SEND SPoG WCAu WCra WFar WHoo WOld WPnP WSpi XFar
	- 'Amanda'	EBee WCra
	- 'Amy Doncaster'	CDor CExl EBee ELan GBin GQue NBir NLar NSti WCot WFar WPnP
	- 'Angulatum'	CElw EPPr
	- 'Arthur'	WCra
	- 'Birch Lilac'	EBee EPPr NLar WCAu WCav WCra
	- 'Bridget Lion'	WCra
	- 'Coquetdale Lilac'	CDor EMor EPPr
	- 'Greek Fire'	NSti
	- 'Ice Blue'	EPPr LBar LRHS LSto NSti WCAu
	- 'Lilac Eyes'	EBee
	- 'Master Charles Wilson'	EBee WCra
	- 'Master Niall Lawson'	EBee WCra WFar
	- 'Mayflower' ♀H7	CDor CMac EBee ECha ELan EPfP EWoo EGlin GJos GMaP GQue LBar LHGe LRHS MArl MMuc NBir NLar NSti SBea SBeP SEND SPoG WCAu WCra WFar WHoo WPnP
	- 'Miss Connie Wilson'	EBee
	- f. *roseum*	NLar
	- - 'Baker's Pink'	EPPr MNrw NBir WCAu WFar WPnP
§	'Tanya Rendall'PBR	LHGe LRHS SRms WCot WCra WFar WPnP
	'Terre Franche'	NSti SNoN WCAu WCra
§	*thunbergii*	GGro GQue WFar
	- 'Jester's Jacket' (v)	EBee LRHS LShi Midl MNrw WFar
	thurstonianum	see *G.* × *oxonianum* f. *thurstonianum*
	'Tinpenny Mauve'	WCra WMal
	'Tiny Monster'	CDor EBee ESgI EWes GElm GKev LBom LHGe LRHS LShi LWaG MAvo MBel MHol MNrw MPri NGdn NLar NQui NSti SPhx SPoG SRms WCAu WCra WHoo WPnP WSpi
	tuberosum	CCBP CDor CElw ECha NBir NGdn NQui WCot WCra WFar
	- 'Richard Hobbs'	EPPr

Geranium

– 'Rosie's Mauve'	MAvo
'Ushguli Grijs'	see *G. ibericum* Cav. 'Ushguli Grijs'
'Vectis'	CElw
'Verguld Saffier'	see *G.* BLUE SUNRISE
versicolor	CBcs CoPl CWal EBee EPfP GAbr GPSL LHGe LRHS MCtn MHer NLar SHar SRms WCAu WCra WFar
§ – 'Snow White'	EPPr WCru
– 'The Bride'	EPPr
– 'White Lady'	see *G. versicolor* 'Snow White'
'Victor Reiter'	see *G. pratense* (Victor Reiter Group) 'Victor Reiter'
wallichianum	EGren NBir NSti
– from RBGE	SMHy
– ALL SUMMER BLUE	see *G. wallichianum* ALL SUMMER JOY
– ALL SUMMER DELIGHT ('Bocoalsdel'PBR)	LBar NCth
§ – ALL SUMMER JOY ('Bocoalsbl'PBR)	LBar
– ALL SUMMER PLEASURE ('Bocoalsple'PBR)	LBar LHGe NCth
§ – 'Buxton's Variety'	CBcs CDor EBee ECha EPfP EPPr GKin GMaP LRHS MCtn MHol MMuc NBir NGdn SDix SPhx SRms SRot WCAu WCru WFar WSpi
– 'Buxton's Variety' × 'Syabru'	LRHS
– 'Crystal Lake'PBR	CWGN EPfP EWoo LCro LHGe MHol MNrw NBir NDov NGdn NSti WCra WFar
– DAILY PURPLE ('Nogeone'PBR)	CWGN LRHS
– 'Happy Buxton'	MHol
– HAVANA BLUES ('Noorthava'PBR)	CDor EBee ECha LCro LHGe LRHS NSti SDix WCot WCra WFar
– 'Kelly Anne'PBR	EHeP LBar LCro LRHS MPri NSti WNPC WPnP WTor
– pink-flowered	WCru
– 'Rise and Shine'PBR	CWGN ELan LCro NSti SRms WCot
– 'Rosetta'	WCAu WCra
– 'Rosie'	SRGP
– 'Syabru'	LRHS
– 'Sylvia's Surprise'PBR	CDor EBee LBar LRHS MPri WCAu WCra
'Wednesday's Child'	WFar
'Westacre Halo'	EBee WCot
'White Doves'	MWlw NDov
wilfordii misapplied	see *G. thunbergii*
Wisley hybrid	see *G.* 'Khan'
wlassovianum	Widely available
– from Crûg Farm	NLar WCra
– 'Blue Star'	NEoE SRGP WCra WFar WHoo
– 'Martyn and Emma'	SRGP
– 'Zeppelin'	LHGe NLar WCra
§ ***yeoi***	NSti
yesoense	GGro NSti WFar
– var. ***nipponicum***	EBee GGro
yoshinoi misapplied	see *G. thunbergii*
yoshinoi Makino	CWnw GGro LBar MCtn
yunnanense misapplied	see *G. pogonanthum*

Gerbera (Asteraceae)

'Classic Femmy' (Garvinea Classic Series)	Midl
(Everlast Series)	ELan
EVERLAST CARMINE ('Amgerbcar')	
– EVERLAST PINK ('Amgerbpink')	ELan
– EVERLAST WHITE ('Amgerbwhi')	ELan
Garvinea Series	EGren Midl
Garvinea Sweet Series	Midl
– GARVINEA SWEET CAROLINE ('Garsweetcaro'PBR)	LRHS
– GARVINEA SWEET GLOW ('Garglow'PBR)	LCro Midl
– GARVINEA SWEET HEART ('Garheart')	ELan
– GARVINEA SWEET LOVE ('Garswlove'PBR)	LRHS
– GARVINEA SWEET MEMORIES ('Garsweetmemo'PBR)	LCro LRHS Midl
– GARVINEA SWEET SMILE ('Garsmile')	LRHS Midl
– GARVINEA SWEET SUNSET	see *G.* 'Sweet Sunset' (Garvinea Sweet Series)
– GARVINEA SWEET SURPRISE ('Garsurprise')	CTsd LRHS
nivea	GEdr
REVOLUTION BICOLOR MIX (Revolution Series)	MBros
§ 'Sweet Sunset' (Garvinea Sweet Series)	LCro Midl

Gethyum (Amaryllidaceae)

atropurpureum	GKev WCot

Geum ✿ (Rosaceae)

'Abendsonne'	MHer NEoE WFar
'Alabama Slammer' (Cocktails Series)	CTtf EBee ELan EMor EPfP GBin GMaP LBar LRHS LSto MPnt MPri MPro NBro NEoE NLar SRms WCAu WFar WNPC
alpinum	see *G. montanum*
'Apricot Delight'	CTtf NEoE
'Apricot Pearl' (Censation Series) (d)	CWGN MHol XFar
'Baked Beans'	GElm NEoE
'Banana Daiquiri' (Cocktails Series)	EBee EGrl ELan EPfP LBar LRHS LSto MPri MPro WCAu WFar WNPC WPnP
'Beech House Apricot'	CDor NBro NEoE NLar
'Beech's Double'	EWes
'Bell Bank' ♥H7	Widely available
'Birkhead's Creamy Lemon'	NBir
'Blazing Sunset' (d)	CSpe CWnw EBee EDAr EGren ELan EPfP LBar LCro LRHS LSou LSto MCtn MHer MHol Midl MNrw MPro NBir NGdn SPoG SRms WCAu WFar WHoo WPnP
'Blood Orange'	EPPr GKev MAvo MBNS NEoE SPoG WFar
'Bohema Pink' (d)	EMor Midl MPro
'Borisii'	Widely available
'Bremner's Nectarine'	CElw EPPr MNrw NEoE SHar WChS WNPC
'Broomrigg Beauty'	NEoE
'Brown Sugar'	NEoE
bulgaricum	EBee NBir NLar NRya WFar
'Café au Lait'	SMHy
'Can-can' (d)	CDor CTtf EBee LBom LRHS LSto MHer MPro MSCN WCAu WHoo WMal
'Cantamos'	NEoE
capense	NLar SPlb
'Centurion'	NEoE
'Citronge' (Cocktails Series)	MNrw
coccineum ambig.	GArf NBir

coccineum Sm. 'Cooky' — EMor EPfP GPSL MNHC NBro NLar SRms WFar
- 'Eos' — CSpe CTtf CWCL LEdu MHol MNrw MPnt NGdn NLar SMrm SPoG SRms WGwG WTor
- 'Koi' — EDAr EGren ELan EPfP LEdu LRHS LSto MBros MHol NEoE SVic WCav WFar
- 'Queen of Orange' — EPfP LRHS MCtn NBir SPoG SRms WCAu WFar
- 'Werner Arends' — MBel WCot WFar
- 'Copper Pennies' — NEoE
'Coppertone' — CElw EGrI ELan NBir
'Cor Limey' **new** — NEoE
'Coral Pearl' (Censation Series) (d) — LCro
CORAL TEMPEST ('Macgeu004') (Tempest Series) — EPfP GPSL LBar LBom LRHS Midl MPro NCth
'Cosmopolitan' (Cocktails Series) — CDor CTtf CWCL CWnw EGrI ELan EMor EPfP GBin LCro LRHS MHol MPnt NEoE NLar WCAu WCot WFar WNPC WPnP
'Cotton Candy' ♀H7 — CMHG NEoE
'Country Rock' — NEoE
'Country Rock Star' — WFar
'Cream Crackers' — NEoE WBrk
'Cumbrian Candy' — NEoE
'Cumbrian Cheddar' — NEoE
'Cumbrian Cherrypie' — NEoE WFar
'Cumbrian Cherrytart' — NEoE
'Cumbrian Cream' — NEoE
'Custard Tart' ♀H7 — NEoE
'Dark and Stormy' (Cocktails Series) — EBee NEoE
'Dawn' — NEoE SMHy
'Dawntreader' (Valley Hi Series) — NEoE
'Deano's Delight' — NEoE
'Diamond White' — EWhm
'Diana' — GElm MNrw NLar
'Dingle Apricot' — GAbr NBir
'Dolly North' (d) — CElw EPPr EWhm MHol NBro NGdn SHar WCAu
'Double Sunrise' (d) — WFar
'East of Eden' — CMHG NEoE
'Eden Apricot' — NEoE
'Eden Rising' — NEoE
'Eden Valley Angel' — MAvo NEoE
'El Wano' — NEoE
elatum — GKev
'Elworthy Coppernob' — CElw
'Emory Quinn' — EPPr ESgI EWes LRHS LSto NEoE NSti
'Etrixia' (Valley Hi Series) — NEoE
'Fancy Frills' — CElw MAvo
'Farmer John Cross' — EBlo EPPr EWld GPSL LRHS LShi MArl MAvo MHol MPro NLar WChS WFar
'Feuermeer' — NLar
§ FIERY RED ('Stocrgeu') (d) — IBal WTor XFar
FIERY TEMPEST ('Macgeu005') (Tempest Series) — EBee EPfP LBar LBom LRHS MAsh MPro NBir SPad SPel WNPC
'Fire Opal' (d) — CElw MNrw NBir
'Fire Storm'PBR — CWGN EPfP LRHS MBel MHol Midl MNrw MPnt MPro NCth NEoE SPoG SRms WFar WMal WNPC
'Fireball' — CWCL MAsh MBNS MPro NLar SOrN
'Firefinch' — NEoE
FIRESTARTER — see *G.* FIERY RED
'Flames of Passion'PBR — Widely available
'Flower of Darkness' — NEoE
'Fluffy Yellow' — NCth
'Georgenberg' — ELan EPfP GMaP MBel MHer MNrw NBir NGdn NLar SReu SRms WCAu WFar
'Gimlet' (Cocktails Series) — CWGN GPSL LEdu MPnt NLar
'Golden Joy' ♀H7 — CDor CElw MAvo MNrw MWlw NEoE WHoo
'Goldfinch' — WFar
I 'Grande Rosso'**new** — Midl
'Hannay's' — GElm LSto MWlw SHar
'Harvest Moon' — NEoE
'Hearts in Amber' — NEoE WFar
'Herterton Primrose' — CElw EPPr MAvo MNrw MWlw NBid NSti WFar
'Hilltop Beacon' (d) ♀H7 — CDor CElw NEoE NLar WFar WGoo WHoo
* ***hybridum luteum*** — NSti
× ***intermedium*** — NGdn NLar
- HELICOPTER — see *G.* × *intermedium* 'Hofrennydd'
§ - 'Hofrennydd' — WCot
'Jolly Roger' — NEoE
'Karlskaer' — CToG CWCL EBlo EWes GQue LRHS MPro MWlw NGdn NLar SHar WCAu WFar
'Lady Clementine' — Midl MPnt MPri NEoE
'Lady Stratheden' (d) — Widely available
'Lemon Delight' — CDor CElw LEdu MAvo WMal
'Lemon Drops' — CBWd CDor CElw CMac EBee ECha EGrI EMor EPfP EPPr GBin GElm GKev GMaP GQue LEdu LSRN LSto MMuc MNrw MWlw NLar NSti SRkn WCAu WCav WFar WPnP WTre
'Lionel Cox' — ELan GMaP LRHS NBir NBro NGdn NLar SReu SRms WCAu WFar
'Lipstick Sunset' — CMHG SPoG
'Lisanne' ♀H7 — CCBP CWCL GMaP LSto MAvo MNrw MPnt NDov NLar SHar SMHy WCAu WFar WMal
'Little Twister' — NEoE
'Maddy Prior' — NEoE
magellanicum — CSpe NLar WMal
'Magic Toybox' — NEoE
'Mai Tai'PBR (Cocktails Series) — Widely available
'Mandarin' (d) — CDor CElw GElm SHar SPel WMal
'Mango Lassi' — NBro NCth NEoE NLar SHar WCAu
'Marmalade' — EWhm GElm MAvo MWlw NLar SHar SMHy WChS WFar WHrl WKif
'McClure's Magic' — NEoE
MISS CLEMENTINE ('Bridclem') (d) — EBee EPfP MAsh MPri
§ ***montanum*** ♀H6 — GKev MMuc NBir SRms
'Moonlight Serenade' — CWCL EBee EPPr MArl NEoE WFar
'Moonrise Melody' (Valley Hi Series) — NEoE
'Moorland Sorbet' — WFar
'Mr Bojangles' **new** — NEoE
'Mr Mojo' — NEoE
'Mrs J. Bradshaw' (d) ♀H7 — Widely available
'Mrs W. Moore' — CWCL GQue MPnt NBir NBro NLar NQui WChS
'Nonna'PBR — EMor LBom LRHS MPri MPro MWlw NCth NLar SHar
'Nordek' — ECha GAbr GQue NGdn SPoG WFar
'Norwell Lemon Lamp' — MAvo MNrw
'Nudge and a Wink' — NEoE
'Orange Pumpkin' (d) — LBar LCro Midl XFar
pentapetalum — see *Sieversia pentapetala*
'Pineapple Crush' — GElm

Geum

'Pink Fluffy' (Censation Series)	MHol MPro NCth SRkn
'Pink Frills'	CElw EPPr EWhm GAbr GBin GQue MAvo MPie NLar SBeP SHar
'Pink Petticoats' ♀H7	CAby CWCL CWnw EGren ELan EMor EPfP GAbr GBin LRHS MBNS MBros Midl MPro NCth SPad SPeP WCAu WHoo WPnP
'Poco'	CMHG CToG CWCL ESgI EWhm LRHS NEoE WFar
'Prairie Dancer'	NEoE
'Present'	EBee
PRETTICOATS PEACH ('Tngeupp') (Pretticoats Series)	EBee EMor LBar LCro MPnt MPri MPro SPad WNPC
'Primrose'	EWhm NBro NGdn NLar
'Primrose Cottage'	GQue WCAu WCav WNPC
'Prince of Orange' (d)	CElw EBlo GAbr LRHS MNrw WFar
'Prinses Juliana' ♀H7	Widely available
'Proud's Pearl'	NEoE WMal
'Rearsby Hybrid'	CElw SHar SPlb
'Red Sky Riders' (Valley Hi Series)	NEoE
'Red Wings' (d)	CWCL GMaP MArl MNrw NBir SHar SPel WGwG
'Rijnstroom'	EPPr MBel SHar WFar
'Rise and Shine'	NEoE
rivale	Widely available
- 'Album'	CCBP EBee ECha EGrI ELan EMor EPfP GMaP GQue LShi MMuc NBid NBir NLar NSti SEND SRms WCAu WChS WFar WGwG WHer
- 'Barbra Lawton'	SHar
- 'Cream Drop'	SHar
- subsp. *islandicum*	SBrt
- 'Leonard's Variety'	CLil CMac CWGN ECha EGrI ELan EMor EPfP EPPr GAbr GMaP GQue LShi MBel MMuc MPro NBid NBir NGdn NLar SIvy WCAu WFar WGwG WPnP WTre XFar
- 'Marika'	EBee
- 'Marmalade'	CElw CWCL SRGP
- pink-flowered	EGrI
- 'Snowflake'	CDor CElw MAvo NLar
'Roger Proud'	NEoE
'Roger's Rebellion'	ESgI NEoE WFar
'Rubin'	NDov NSti WCAu
'Rusty Young'	CBWd CToG CWCL EBee EPfP EPPr ESgI EWes GElm LRHS MBel MWlw NEoE
'Salmon Delight' **new**	EPfP MPro
'Savanna Sunrise'	MNrw
'Savanna Sunset'	CBWd CToG EBee EPPr EWes GElm LBar LRHS LSto LShi MBel MHer NEoE WHrl
SCARLET TEMPEST ('Macgeu001'PBR) (Tempest Series) ♀H7	Widely available
'Sea Breeze' (Cocktails Series)	EPfP
'Shannara' (d)	CElw NEoE
'Sigiswang'	MNrw MWlw WCAu WFar
'Smokey Peach' (d) ♀H7	LBar
'Snowdrop'	NEoE
'Spellbound'	NEoE
'Spider Muffin'	NEoE
'Stacey Proud'	NEoE
'Stacey's Sunrise'	EPPr EWes MBel MNrw NEoE NLar SPoG WFar
'Star of Bethlehem'	NEoE
'Starker's Magnificum'	CElw MWlw WCot
'Stevie Nicks'	NEoE
'Strawberries and Cream'	NEoE
'Sundrud Star'	NEoE
'Sunkissed Lime'PBR	EHeP LBar Midl MPnt NEoE
'Sunrise' (d)	CWnw ECha EDAr EGren GAbr LBar LRHS LSto MHol MPro SAth SVic
'Sweet and Sour'	GElm
'Sweet Angel Dar'	NEoE
'Sweet Stacey'	NEoE
'Tales of Hex' ♀H7	EBee MPnt MPro NLar SDix SHar WCAu XFar
'Tangerine'	Midl
'Tango Dream'	MAvo
TEMPO ORANGE ('Tngeuto') (Tempo Series) (d)	EGren EMor EPfP LRHS Midl
TEMPO ROSE ('Tngeutr') (Tempo Series) (d)	CWnw EBee EGren EHeP EMor EPfP LRHS LSou MBros Midl MPnt MPro NEoE SBeP WNPC WPnP
TEMPO YELLOW ('Tngeuty') (Tempo Series) (d)	EPfP LRHS LSou Midl MPnt WNPC
'Tequila Sunrise' (Cocktails Series)	CBcs CWGN EBee ELan EMor EPfP LBar LRHS LSto MNrw MPnt MPri MPro NEoE NGdn SAth WCAu WNPC
'The Giant Peach'	NEoE
'Tinkerbell'	NEoE
× *tirolense*	EBee
'Toffee Apples'	NEoE
'Tosai'	NEoE NLit NRya
'Totally Tangerine'PBR ♀H7	Widely available
triflorum	CSpe EMor EWes GEdr LEdu MCtn MNrw MPnt NDov SHar SHor SMrm SPhx StAn
- SDR 8121	GKev
- var. *campanulatum*	NEoE
TROPICAL TEMPEST ('Macgeu007') (Tempest Series) (d)	LBom MPro SPad
'Turbango'	NEoE
'Turbango Twister'	NEoE
'Turnover'	WHoo
'Turnpike Tales'	NEoE
'Turnpike Troubadour'	NEoE
'Tutti Frutti'	LBar LRHS MPro
'Two Tone Pearl' (Censation Series) (d)	CWGN NLar
urbanum	CBWd ENfk MNHC NMir WHer
- 'Corinne Tremaine'	WHer
'Wet Kiss' (Cocktails Series)	MPnt
'Wish Song' (Valley Hi Series)	NEoE
'Wyn's Wish'	NEoE

Gevuina (Proteaceae)

avellana	CExl WPGP

Gibasis (Commelinaceae)

'José Puig'	WTra
pellucida	WTra
§ - 'Tahitian Bridal Veil'	WDib
- 'Tricolour' (v)	WTra

Gilia (Polemoniaceae)

achilleifolia	SPhx
capitata	CSpe MCtn
leptantha **new**	MCtn
tricolor	MCtn

Gillenia (Rosaceae)

stipulata	CDor MNrw SHar SPhx WPGP

trifoliata ♀H7   Widely available
- 'Pink Profusion'   CDor CSpe EBee EMor ERCP IPot MHol MMrt MPro NCth NLar WCot WFar

Ginkgo ✿ (*Ginkgoaceae*)

biloba	Widely available
- B&SWJ 8753	WCru
- 'Anny's Dwarf'	MBlu
- 'Autumn Gold' (m) ♀H6	CEnd ELan MBlu MGos MPkF NPip WMat
- 'Barabits' Fastigiata'	MBlu
- 'Barabits' Nana'	CAco MBlu
- 'Beijing Gold'	CAco MBlu NLar
- 'California Sunset' (v)	LRHS MBlu–
- 'Chase Manhattan'	MPkF
- 'Chotek'	MBlu
- 'Conica'	CAco
- 'Denise'	CCVT SMad
- 'Eastern Star' (f)	CAgr
- 'Eiffel'	LRHS
- 'Everton Broom'	CMen MBlu
- 'Fairmount' (m)	MBlu
- 'Fastigiata' (m)	CAco CMCN LMaj MBlu
- 'Fastigiata Blagon'	CAco CCVT ERom LCro LMaj LRHS
- 'Globosa'	CAco MBlu
- 'Goethe'	MBlu
- GOLD SPIRE ('Blagon')	CMCN EBee ELan EPfP LCro NPip SArc SGol WHtc WMat
- 'Golden Dragon'	MBlu
- 'Gresham'	MPkF
- 'Horizontalis'	CAco MBlu
- 'Jade Butterflies' ♀H6	MBlu
- 'Jehosaphat'	MBlu
- 'Jerry Vercade'	MPkF
- 'King of Dongting' (f)	CAco CAgr MBlu
- 'Lakeview' (m)	CAco MPkF
- 'Landliebe'	MBlu
- 'Long March'	CAgr
- 'Magyar'	MBlu
- 'Mariken' (m) ♀H6	CAco CDoC CWGN ELan LMaj MAsh MPkF NLar WCot
- 'Mayfield' (m)	CAco MBlu
- 'McFarland'	CAgr
- 'Menhir'PBR	CAco CBcs CBTr CMCN EBee ELan EPfP LSto MGos WCot WMat
- 'Obelisk'	CAco LMaj
- Ohazuki Group (f)	CAgr
- 'Palo Alto'	CAco
- Pendula Group	CAco CEnd MBlu MPkF NPip WMat
- 'Princeton Sentry' (m) ♀H6	CAco CBcs ELan IPap MBlu WSpi
- 'Pyramidalis'	CAco
- 'Robbie's Twist'	MPkF NLar
- 'San José'	CAco
- 'Santa Cruz'	CAco
- 'Saratoga' (m) ♀H6	CAco CAgr CBcs CEnd CMCN LRHS MBlu MPkF NPip WMat
- 'Shangri-La' (m)	MBlu
- 'Sinclair'	MPkF
- Talon Variegated' (v)	MBlu
- 'Tit'	CAco CEnd LMaj MBlu
- 'Todd'	MBlu
- 'Tremonia'	MBlu MPkF
- 'Troll' ♀H6	CAco MBlu MGos SBig SMad SPoG
- Tubifolia'	MAsh MBlu MPkF WPGP
- 'Ulrich's Gold'	NLar
- (Variegata Group) 'Variegata' (v)	CAco
- 'W.B.'	MPkF
- 'Yellow Mellow'	CAco

Gladiolus ✿ (*Iridaceae*)

(M)	CSpe LCro
'Adi'	WCot
'Adrenalin'PBR (L)	XFar
'Advance' (L) **new**	XFar
'Amanda Mahy' (N)	WCot
'Amber Mystique' (L)	LCro XFar
'Apricot Bubblegum' (L) **new**	XFar
'Atom' (S/P)	GKev LAma XFar
'Aviol' (L) **new**	XFar
'Bibi' (Tub)	GKev LAma XFar
'Bimbo' (L)	LCro
'Black Star'	EPfP ERCP XFar
'Blue Isle' (L)	EGren ERCP
'Blushed Look' **new**	XFar
'Boone' (*dalenii* hybrid)	IPot WCot
'Buggy' (S)	XFar
Butterfly hybrids	XFar
byzantinus	see *G. communis* subsp. *byzantinus*
callianthus	see *G. murielae*
'Cappuccino' **new**	ERCP
cardinalis	CDor CSpe
'Carine' (N)	GKev
carmineus	WCot
carneus	CBro GKev LAma
'Charm' (N/Tub)	GKev LAma XFar
'Charming Beauty' (Tub)	EPot
'Charming Henry' (Tub)	LAma
'Charming Lady' (Tub)	GKev LAma
'Cherry Candy' **new**	XFar
'Circus Color' (L)	XFar
'Claudia' (N)	GKev
× *colvillii* 'Albus'	ERCP
- 'Frozen Sparks'	XFar
- 'Galaxian'	GKev LAma MPro XFar
- 'Irish Gold'	GKev
- 'Red Drizzle'	GKev
communis	WCot
§ - subsp. *byzantinus* ♀H5	Widely available
- 'Côte d'Azur' (G)	XFar
§ *dalenii*	CDor CSpe
§ - subsp. *dalenii*	CBro SChr WCot
- yellow-flowered	CTca
'Dancing Doll'	XFar
'Dark Ruby' (*papilio* hybrid)	LEdu SPel WCot WMal WPGP
'David Hills' (*papilio* hybrid)	CBro CDor CTtf ECha EDAr EPPr EShb ESwi IPot SMHy WCot WHoo WMal
'Deciso' (L)	EGren
ecklonii	CTtf
'Elvira' (N)	GKev LAma
'Emerald Spring' (S)	WCot
'Espresso'PBR (S)	ELan LCro XFar
'Essential'PBR (M)	XFar
'Evergreen'	XFar
'Far West' (L)	XFar
'Fiona'	LAma
'Fiorentina' (L)	XFar
flanaganii	CSpe CTtf GArf GEdr MNrw SBrt WAbe WFar
'Flevo Ocean' (S) **new**	CSpe
floribundus hort.	WCot
'Frizzled Coral Lace' (E)	XFar
'Funny Fiction' (L)	XFar
× *gandavensis* hort.	GBin WCot
garnieri	see *G. dalenii* subsp. *dalenii*
geardii	WCot
'Georgette' (B)	XFar
'Green Star' (L)	LCro
'Halley' (N)	LAma NLar

'Hansnett' — WCot
'Happy Touch' **new** — XFar
'Holland Pearl' (B) — XFar
illyricus — MCtn SPlb
'Impressive' (N) — EPot GKev LAma NLar
'Indian Summer'^PBR (L) — XFar
§ *italicus* — EBee EPfP ETay XFar
'Kio' (L) **new** — XFar
'Las Vegas' (P) — EPot GKev LAma MPro
'Laura Jay' (P) — LAma
'Lemon Drop' (S) — XFar
'Lucky Star' **new** — XFar
'Lumiere' (L) — LCro XFar
'Marina' (P) — WMal
'Match Point' (L) — XFar
'Milka'^PBR (L) — XFar
'Mirella' (N) — CBlu CBro LAma WCot
'Monsieur Piquet' (P) — WCot
'Moonlight Shadow' (L) — XFar
§ *murielae* ♀H3 — CAby CBro CCBP CTtf EGren EGrI EPfP ERCP GKev LAma LCro MHol MPro SPeP SPlb SRms XFar
'Murmansk' (L) — XFar
'My Love' (L) — XFar
natalensis — see *G. dalenii*
'Natan' (L) — WCot
'Nova Lux' (L) — EGren XFar
'Nymph' (N) — EPfP EPot GKev LAma LCro MPro NBir
'Omsk' (L) — XFar
§ *oppositiflorus* — CSpe SPlb
- subsp. *salmoneus* — see *G. oppositiflorus*
'Oscar' (G) — EGren ERCP
palustris — WAbe
papilio — CBlu CDor CElw CMac CRHN CTca CTtf ECha EDAr ELan ERCP EShb EWhm LEdu LSRN MNrw NBid NCth NSti SMHy SPlb WCru WFar WHoo WPGP
- 'Peachy' — CTtf
§ - Purpureoauratus Group — SRms
- yellow-flowered — CTtf SMad WHoo
'Passos'^PBR (S) — XFar
'Peach Blossom' (N) — WCot
'Performer'^PBR (L) **new** — XFar
'Perseus' (P/Min) — XFar
'Pescara' (M) — EPfP
'Peter Pears' (L) — ERCP LCro
'Pink Lightning' (L) **new** — XFar
'Pink Parrot'^PBR (L) — XFar
'Plum Tart' (L) — LCro
primulinus — see *G. dalenii*
'Prince of Orange' (L) — XFar
'Prins Claus' (N) — GKev XFar
'Priscilla' (L) — ERCP
'Purple Art' **new** — ERCP XFar
'Purple Flora' — ERCP XFar
'Purple Heart' **new** — XFar
'Purple Mate' — LCro
purpureoauratus — see *G. papilio* Purpureoauratus Group
'Quepo' (L) **new** — XFar
'Robinetta' (*recurvus* hybrid) ♀H3 — EPot GKev LAma LCro MHtn
'Roma' (L) — XFar
'Rostov' — XFar
'Royal Class'^PBR (L) **new** — XFar
'Ruby' (*papilio* hybrid) — Widely available
'Rusty Chestnut' (L) **new** — XFar
segetum — see *G. italicus*

'Shaka Zulu' (L) — XFar
'Sochi' — XFar
'Sugar Babe'^PBR (L) **new** — XFar
'Sweet Love' **new** — XFar
'Tarantella' (L) **new** — XFar
'Ted's Trump' (L) **new** — XFar
'The Bride' — CBro GKev LAma LCro MHtn MPie NLar
'The Great Queen Elizabeth' (L) **new** — XFar
'Trevor Edwards' — WCot
tristis — CElw EArI GKev MCtn MHer SMHy SPel WAbe
- var. *concolor* — CPbh GKev WCot XFar
'Tula' (L) — XFar
'Vandohia' — XFar
'Velvet Eyes' (L) — ERCP
venustus — CPbh
'Victor Borge' (L) — EGren
'Violet Heart' (L) **new** — XFar
'Vulcano' — ERCP GKev
watermeyeri — CPbh
'White Eyed Miss' (N) — GKev XFar
'White Friendship' (L) — EGren
'White Prosperity' (L) — ELan ERCP LCro XFar
'Wine and Roses' (L) — XFar
'Zizanie' (L) — XFar

Glandora (Boraginaceae)

'Alba' — CTsd EGren MPro SPoG
CRYSTAL BLUE ('Tnlicb') — LRHS
§ *diffusa* (Lag.) D.C.Thomas — SRot
- 'Picos' — WAbe
§ *oleifolia* ♀H4 — GEdr LRHS NBir
prostrata 'Grace Ward' ♀H5 — EBee EGren ELan EPfP GArf LRHS MPri MPro WIce
§ - 'Heavenly Blue' ♀H5 — Widely available
- 'Star' — EGren EPfP GMaP LBar LRHS MPro NLar SPoG WFar WIce WTor
- 'Tidepool Sky Blue' **new** — LRHS MPri WTor
- 'White Star' — WIce
§ *rosmarinifolia* — LRHS

Glandularia (Verbenaceae)

'Abbeville' — WCot
AZTEC SILVER MAGIC ('Balazsilma'^PBR) — MBros
(Aztec Series)
§ 'Claret' ♀H3 — CMac EBee ELan EPfP LCro LRHS SPhx SPoG
corymbosa — CAby ECha EPPr LRHS
'Edith Eddleman' — CMac EPfP LRHS SPoG
elegans — NDov
(Enchantment Series) — MPri
ENCHANTMENT RED
- ENCHANTMENT VIOLET EYE — MPri
(Endurascape Series) — LCro
ENDURASCAPE DARK PURPLE ('Balendakle')
- ENDURASCAPE HOT PINK ('Balendopin') — LCro LRHS
- ENDURASCAPE PINK BICOLOR ('Balendpibi') ♀H3 — LCro LRHS
- ENDURASCAPE PURPLE IMPROVED ('Balendurpi2') — LCro
- ENDURASCAPE WHITE BLUSH ('Balendish') — LCro
'Hammerstein Pink' — EBee EPfP LRHS
'Homestead Purple' — CMac EBee ELan EPfP EUrb LCro LRHS SDix SRkn
'Jennys' Wine' — see *G.* 'Claret'

'La France' ECha EPfP LRHS SMad SMHy SPhx SPoG SRkn
'Lois' Ruby' see *G.* 'Claret'
'Margaret's Memory' ELan LCro LRHS MPro
'Merci' NDov
'Peaches 'n' Cream' MCtn
§ *peruviana* EPot LRHS MPro
'Pink Bouquet' see *G.* 'Silver Ann'
§ Quartz Series ♀H2 MBros MPri
SEABROOK'S LAVENDER ELan EPfP EUrb LCro LRHS SHar
('Sealav'PBR) SRkn
Showboat Series MPri
- 'Showboat Burgundy' LCro
- 'Showboat Dark Violet' LCro
- 'Showboat Mango Orange' MPri
- 'Showboat Midnight' LCro LSou
- 'Showboat White' LCro
§ 'Silver Ann' ♀H3 WMal
§ 'Sissinghurst' ♀H3 ELan LCro SDix SMrm SPoG WMal
'Strawberry Kiss' SPoG
SUPERBENA BURGUNDY MBNS
('Usbenal5'PBR)
(Superbena Series)
'Tenerife' see *G.* 'Sissinghurst'
tenuisecta MCtn
- 'Imagination' MCtn
VANESSA RED (Vanessa Series) WCot
VEPITA BLUE VIOLET MHol
('Invebluvio'PBR)
(Vepita Series)

Glandularia × *Verbena* (Verbenaceae)
METEOR SHOWER LCro
('Invebrutow')

Glaucidium (Ranunculaceae)
palmatum CExl EWld GKev GMaP
- 'Album' see *G. palmatum* var. *leucanthum*
§ - var. *leucanthum* ENun EWld GKev LAma

Glaucium (Papaveraceae)
§ *corniculatum* CSpe ECha EPfP SPhx
flavum ECha MHer NAts SPhx
- *aurantiacum* see *G. flavum* f. *fulvum*
§ - f. *fulvum* EPPr MNrw SDix SMHy
- orange-flowered see *G. flavum* f. *fulvum*
- red-flowered see *G. corniculatum*
phoenicium see *G. corniculatum*

Glaucosciadium (Apiaceae)
cordifolium PAB 9203 LEdu

× *Glebianthemum* (Asteraceae)
§ GRANDAISY YELLOW MBros
('Bonmax 1228')
(Grandaisy Series)

Glebionis (Asteraceae)
coronaria CoPl EHet MNHC
§ *segetum* CHab GJem LCro MCtn MNHC NBir

Glechoma (Lamiaceae)
hederacea CGwi LRIIS NMir WHer
§ - 'Variegata' (v) MPri

Gleditsia (Fabaceae)
caspia NJM 13.019 WPGP
japonica NLar
sinensis WJur
triacanthos CMCN EBar SPlb WJur

- 'Calhoun' CAgr
- 'Elegantissima' (v) EUrb LRHS
- 'Emerald Cascade' CEnd
- f. *inermis* EBar
- - 'Draves'PBR EBar
- - SKYLINE ('Skycole') EBar
- - SPECTRUM ('Speczam') MGos WMat
- - 'Sunburst' Widely available
- 'Millwood' CAgr
- 'Rubylace' CEnd CMac MCMCN EBar EBee LRHS MBlu MGos WMat

Globba ✿ (Zingiberaceae)
marantina CBlu EAri WJun
racemosa EAri
- var. *hookeri* CBlu
- aff. var. *hookeri* WPGP
- - HWJCM 471 ESwi WCot WCru
radicalis WPGP

Globularia (Plantaginaceae)
bellidifolia see *G. meridionalis*
§ *bisnagarica* GKev SMrm SRms WCot WFar WMal
cordifolia ♀H5 EDAr GEdr GKev MMuc NBir SHar SRms WAbe
- RCB UA 30 WCot
- 'Brian Burrow' EPot GEdr
incanescens GEdr
§ *meridionalis* EPot EWes GKev WHoo
- 'Blue Bonnets' GEdr
- 'Hort's Variety' WAbe
nana see *G. repens*
nudicaulis EPot GEdr GKev WMal
punctata see *G. bisnagarica*
pygmaea see *G. meridionalis*
§ *repens* GAbr WAbe
trichosantha GKev SRms
valentina GEdr GKev

Gloriosa (Colchicaceae)
'Lime' XFar
lutea see *G. superba* 'Lutea'
modesta WCot
rothschildiana see *G. superba* 'Rothschildiana'
'Summer Breeze' XFar
superba ♀H1c CSpe
- 'Carsonii' LAma
- 'Greenii' LAma
§ - 'Lutea' LAma
§ - 'Rothschildiana' CBlu CDoC EAri LAma LCro XFar
- 'Sparkling Striped' XFar
- 'Tomas de Bruyne' XFar

Glottiphyllum (Aizoaceae)
grandiflorum CoPl
longum CPic

Gloxinella (Gesneriaceae)
lindeniana WDib

Gloxinia (Gesneriaceae)
gymnostoma see *Seemannia gymnostoma*
sylvatica see *Seemannia sylvatica*

Glumicalyx (Scrophulariaceae)
flanaganii EDAr GArf GBin SPlb
nutans SPlb

Glyceria (Poaceae)
aquatica variegata see *G. maxima* var. *variegata*

Glyceria

maxima	CLil ELin NPer SPlb
§ - var. *variegata* (v)	CBen CLil CPud CToG CWat ECha ELan ELin GMaP LCro LRHS MMuc NBir SRms SVic WMAq
spectabilis 'Variegata'	see *G. maxima* var. *variegata*

Glycine (Fabaceae)
max 'Green Shell'	MCtn SVic

Glycyrrhiza (Fabaceae)
echinata	CAgr
§ *glabra*	CAgr CSpe ENfk MCtn MHer MHoo SPlb SRms WJek WKit
glandulifera	see *G. glabra*
uralensis	CAgr ELan EPPr
yunnanensis	CAgr CSpe ECha EPPr MHer SBig SBrt SDix SMHy WTre XFar

Glyptostrobus (Cupressaceae)
pensilis	CAco CBcs CExl WPGP
- 'Wooly Mammoth'	CAco IArd

Gnaphalium (Asteraceae)
'Fairy Gold'	see *Helichrysum thianschanicum* 'Goldkind'

Godetia see *Clarkia*

Goeppertia (Marantaceae)
'Beautystar'	LBom
burle-marxii	LBom NHrt
concinna	CDoC LBom LCro
§ *crocata* ♀H1a	CDoC EGren
- 'Tassmania'	LBom LCro
elliptica 'Vittata'	LBom
'Flamestar'	LBom NHrt
'Freddie'	CDoC LCro
fucata **new**	NTro
'Fusion Yellow' **new**	NTro
§ *insignis*	CDoC EGren LBom LCro NHrt NTro
kegeljanii	LBom
- NETWORK ('Pp0005'PBR)	LCro NHrt
lietzei 'Fusion White'	LBom LCro NTro
louisae 'Maui Queen' (v)	CDoC
majestica 'Sanderiana'	LBom LInT NHrt
§ *makoyana* ♀H1a	CDoC EGren LBom LCro LInT
orbifolia	LBom LCro NHrt
ornata	LBom LCro
picturata 'Argentea' ♀H1a	NHrt
- 'Roseo-Picta' (v)	LCro
§ *roseopicta* ♀H1a	EGren LBom NHrt
- 'Dottie'PBR	NHrt NTro
- 'Little Princess' (v)	LCro
- 'Surprise Star'	NHrt
rufibarba ♀H1a	LCro NHrt
- 'Blue Grass'	LBom
- 'Wavestar'	CDoC LCro
§ *truncata*	CDoC
veitchiana 'Medaillon'	EGren LCro NHrt NTro
warszewiczii	CDoC LBom
'Whitestar'	LBom LCro NHrt
§ *zebrina* ♀H1a	CDoC LBom LCro NHrt

goji berry see *Lycium barbarum*, *L. chinense*

Gomphocarpus ✿ (Apocynaceae)
§ *fruticosus*	EAri SVen

Gompholobium (Fabaceae)
scabrum	SPlb

Gomphostigma (Scrophulariaceae)
virgatum	CFis CSpe EAri ELan EPPr EWld GMaP MPie SEND SMrm SPhx SPlb WCFE WCot WFar
- 'White Candy'	SVen

Gomphrena (Amaranthaceae)
pulchella TRUFFULA PINK ('Past0517e')	Midl

× *Gonialoaloe* (Asphodelaceae)
'Terrukinae'	NCft

Gonialoe (Asphodelaceae)
§ *variegata* (v) ♀H1c	CBen EShb MPri

Goniolimon (Plumbaginaceae)
collinum 'Sea Spray'	EPPr
incanum 'Blue Diamond'	WCot
speciosum	GJos
§ *tataricum*	EBee EPPr GJos
- var. *angustifolium*	SRms

Goodia (Fabaceae)
lotifolia	WHil

gooseberry see *Ribes uva-crispa*; also AGM Fruit Section

× *Gordlinia* (Theaceae)
grandiflora	LRHS

Gorgonidium (Araceae)
intermedium	WCot WJun

granadilla, purple see *Passiflora edulis*

granadilla, sweet see *Passiflora ligularis*

grape see *Vitis*; also AGM Fruit Section

grapefruit see *Citrus × aurantium* Grapefruit Group

Graptopetalum ✿ (Crassulaceae)
amethystinum	CPic
bellum ♀H2	NCft SPlb
filiferum	SPlb
§ *paraguayense*	CBlu CoPl CPic WFar
- subsp. *bernalense*	SChr
suaveolens	SPlb
superbum	CPic NGKo

Graptopetalum × *Sedum* see × *Graptosedum*

× *Graptosedum* (Crassulaceae)
'Darley Sunshine'	SIvy
'Ghosty'	CPic
'Vera Higgins'	NGKo

× *Graptoveria* (Crassulaceae)
'Bashful'	CPic
'Debbi'	CPic NCft
'Douglas Huth'	CPic
'Fred Ives'	WOld
'Ghostly'	WCot
'Milky Way'	CPic
'Opalina'	CPic
'Pik Ruza'	EAri
'Ron Ginns'	CPic
'Titubans'	MHer

Gratiola (Plantaginaceae)
officinalis — CBen CLil CWat ELin MHer MHoo

Greenovia see *Aeonium*

Grevillea (Proteaceae)
alpina — EGrl WPGP
banksii 'Canberra Hybrid' see *G.* 'Canberra Gem'
 - var. *forsteri* — SPlb
barklyana — SEle
baxteri — SEle
'Bronze Rambler' — LRHS SEle
§ 'Canberra Gem' ♀H4 — CAbb CBcs CCht CCoa CDoC CMac CSBt CSde CWnw EAri EGren EGrl ELan ELon EPfP EUrb LRHS LSRN MAsh SArc SBig SEle SPad SPlb SRkn SWor WFar WKif WLov
'Clearview David' — CCht CCoa CDoC CSde EUrb MMuc SEle SVen WFar
'Coconut Ice' — SEle
crithmifolia — SPlb
diminuta — EUrb
ferruginea — SEle
'Fireworks' — SEle
gracilis — SEle
'Jean O'Neill' — EUrb SEle
juniperina — CBcs CHll CMac EPfP LRHS SArc SEle SVen
 - f. *sulphurea* — CBcs EGrl EUrb MMuc SEle SPlb WFar
 - - prostrate — EUrb SEle
I *lanigera* 'Lutea' — CTsd
 - 'Mount Tamboritha' — CBcs CCht CCoa CDoC CMac CSde CTsd EGrl EPfP EUrb LRHS SEle SPoG WFar
 - prostrate — WAbe
§ - 'Red Salento' — LCro
 - yellow-flowered — SEle
lavandulacea 'Penola' — SEle
leucopteris — SPlb
miqueliana — CBcs CTsd SEle WFar
 subsp. *moroka*
'Murray Valley Queen' — WPGP
'New Blood'PBR — CBcs LRHS SEle
'Olympic Flame' — CAbb CBcs CCht CDoC CEnd CExl CSBt CTsd CWnw EGrl EPfP EUrb LRHS MMuc MPri SEle SPoG SReu WCot WPGP
paniculata — SPlb
'Pink Lady' — CBcs EPfP LRHS MMuc SEle WFar
'Poorinda Constance' — CCht SEle WCot WPGP
rhyolitica — SPlb
robusta ♀H2 — EAri SEle SPlb
 - 'Red Salento' see *G. lanigera* 'Red Salento'
rosmarinifolia ♀H4 — CBcs CMac CSBt CWal GKin SArc SEle SPlb SSta WFar
 - 'Jenkinsii' — CCht CCoa CDoC CMac CSBt CSde CTsd EGrl EPfP LRHS SEle WCot
 - 'Scarlet Sprite' — SEle
§ × *semperflorens* — CCoa CDoC CSde CTsd EUrb SEle SPlb SReu WFar
I *simplex* — WCot
tolminsis see *G.* × *semperflorens*
victoriae — CBcs CCht CCoa CDoC CSde CTsd EAri EPfP GAbr LRHS MBlu MPri SChF SEle SPlb WCot WFar WPGP
 - subsp. *victoriae* — CExl
'White Knight' — SEle
williamsonii — CCht CTsd EUrb SEle

Grewia (Malvaceae)
occidentalis — LRHS WJur

Greyia (Francoaceae)
sutherlandii — EAri SPlb

Griffinia (Amaryllidaceae)
liboniana — WMal

Grindelia (Asteraceae)
§ *camporum* — SPlb
chiloensis — SMad
hirsutula — WHil
integrifolia — GQue MMuc
robusta see *G. camporum*

Griselinia ✿ (Griseliniaceae)
littoralis ♀H5 — Widely available
 - 'Bantry Bay' (v) — CBcs CCoa EBee ELan LBom MSCN NLar SPoG WFar
 - 'Brodick Gold' — GKin
 - 'Dixon's Cream' (v) — CBcs CMac CSBt EBee ELan EPfP LRHS SRms SVen WSpi
 - 'Emerald' — LRHS
 - 'Green Favor' — EBee
 - GREEN HORIZON ('Whenuapai'PBR) — CCoa CGri EGren ELan EPfP EUrb IBal LCro LRHS MSCN MSwo SArc SAth SBig SPoG SWor WHtc
 - 'Green Jewel' (v) — LRHS NLar SArc
 - 'Redge'PBR — CCoa EBee
 - 'Variegata' (v) ♀H4 — Widely available
ruscifolia — CBcs EBee EUrb LEdu
scandens — CBcs SEND WCot

guava, common see *Psidium guajava*

guava, purple or strawberry see *Psidium littorale* var. *longipes*

Guichenotia (Malvaceae)
macrantha — SPlb

Gunnera ✿ (Gunneraceae)
§ × *cryptica* — Prohibited invasive. See Conservation and the Environment, p.42
hamiltonii — ECha LEdu
killipiana B&SWJ 9009 — WCru
macrophylla — CDor
magellanica — CBcs CExl CMac EBee ECha ELan EPfP GAbr GEdr GKev GMaP LCro LEdu LRHS NBir NGdn NGKo SPlb WFar
 - (m) — CToG ELin EPot GBin GQue ISha
 - 'Osorno' — EBee
manicata misapplied see *G.* × *cryptica*, *G. tinctoria*
perpensa — CBcs CBen CToG ESwi SMad SPlb WCot WFar WJun
prorepens — CExl CMac ECha WFar
saint-johnii B&SWJ 14708 — WCru
talamancana B&SWJ 10465 **new** — WCru
tinctoria — Prohibited invasive. See Conservation and the Environment, p.42

Guzmania (Bromeliaceae)
HOPE ('Durahop'PBR) ♀H1b — LCro
'Jazz'PBR **new** — NHrt
lingulata — EGren NHrt WFar
 - 'Francesca' ♀H1a — LCro

'Variada'PBR **new** NHrt
'Voila' LCro

Gymnocalycium (Cactaceae)
albispinum see *G. bruchii*
anisitsii SPlb
  subsp. *anisitsii* **new**
- subsp. *damsii* SPlb
§ bruchii ♀H2 SPlb
gibbosum SPlb
  var. *chubutense*
grandiflorum see *G. monvillei*
§ monvillei SPlb
multiflorum see *G. monvillei*
§ reductum SPlb
  subsp. *reductum*
saglionis ♀H2 SPlb
sibalii see *G. reductum* subsp. *reductum*

Gymnocarpium (Woodsiaceae)
dryopteris ♀H5 CDor CLAP EWld GArf GKev GMaP GQue MPie WAbe WPGP WShi
- PAB 1757 LEdu
- PAB 8351 LEdu
- 'Plumosum' ♀H5 CLAP EBee EMor GEdr ISha LEdu MAsh NAlc NHar WFar
oyamense ♀H5 SPlb WPGP
robertianum CLAP EWld LEdu WAbe

Gymnocladus (Fabaceae)
chinensis EBee WPGP
dioica CBcs CMCN ELan EPfP MBlu WJur WPGP

Gymnocoronis (Asteraceae)
spilanthoides Prohibited invasive. See Conservation and the Environment, p.42

Gymnosphaera (Cyatheaceae)
§ podophylla SBig

Gynandriris see Moraea

Gynerium (Poaceae)
argenteum see *Cortaderia selloana*

Gynostemma (Cucurbitaceae)
pentaphyllum CAgr WCot WJek
- B&SWJ 570 WCru

Gynura (Asteraceae)
aurantiaca LWaG
§ - 'Purple Passion' ♀H1b LWaG
sarmentosa misapplied see *G. aurantiaca* 'Purple Passion'

Gypsophila (Caryophyllaceae)
acutifolia EBee
aretioides LRHS SPlb SRot WAbe
cerastioides see *Acanthophyllum cerastioides*
dubia see *G. repens* 'Dubia'
elegans MCtn SVic
- 'Covent Garden' GJem LRHS LSto MCtn
fastigiata 'Silverstar' EPfP
'Festival Pink Lady' LBar MAsh MPro
  (Festival Series)
gracilescens see *G. tenuifolia*
'Jolien' (v) LBar WIce
'Kermesina' LSto
muralis see *Psammophiliella muralis*
nana EWes
pacifica ECha GJos MCtn

paniculata EPPr LShi MCtn SRms
- 'Bristol Fairy' (d) CDor CSpe ECha ELan GMaP LCro LRHS NLar SMad SPoG WCAu WFar XFar
- 'Compacta Plena' (d) EPfP GMaP LRHS NGdn SRms
- 'Flamingo' (d) CBcs CBWd CDor CSpe ECha LBar LCro NDov NLar SMad SPoG WFar XFar
- 'Pacific Pink' EBee
- 'Perfekta' CBcs
§ - 'Schneeflocke' (d) CSpe EPfP LRHS MCtn MPro SMrm SRms
- SNOWFLAKE see *G. paniculata* 'Schneeflocke'
- WHITE FIRE ('Dangypwhifa') EBee
'Pink Festival' (Festival CDor EPfP LRHS SPoG
  Series) (d)
repens GBin GJos LShi MCtn SPlb StAn WCav WFar
- 'Dorothy Teacher' EPot WAbe WFar WIce
§ - 'Dubia' ECha EPot MHer MWlw SLee SRms SRot WIce
- 'Filou Rose' EDAr ELan EPfP WHil
- 'Filou White' EDAr ELan LBuc
- PINK BEAUTY see *G. repens* 'Rosa Schönheit'
§ - 'Rosa Schönheit' ECha EPot NDov WFar
- 'Rosea' CSpe EBee EGreen ELan GArf GJos GMaP LShi MCtn MMuc NGdn NQui SEND SLee SPoG SRms WFar WHoo WIce
- 'Ruby Gems' WFar
- 'Silver Carpet' (v) ELan LRHS
- white-flowered ECha NGdn WFar
§ 'Rosenschleier' (d) ♀H6 CDor CSpe EBee ECha ELan EPfP GMaP LCro LRHS LShi MPro NDov NGdn SHar SRms WCAu
I 'Rosenschleier Variegata' (v) EBee ELan
'Rosy Veil' see *G. 'Rosenschleier'*
§ tenuifolia EPot EWld GArf GMaP WAbe
§ vaccaria SPhx
VEIL OF ROSES see *G. 'Rosenschleier'*
'White Festival'PBR EPfP LRHS SPoG
  (Festival Series) (d)
'White Flare' (Festival Series) LBar MPro SHar
zhegulensis **new** WMal

H

Haageocereus (Cactaceae)
acranthus LWaG

Haberlea (Gesneriaceae)
ferdinandi-coburgii see *H. rhodopensis*
§ rhodopensis ♀H5 EPot EPPr EWld GArf GEdr NHar SRms WAbe
- 'Connie Davidson' GEdr GKev
- 'Virginalis' GEdr

Haberlea × Ramonda see × Ramberlea

Hablitzia (Amaranthaceae)
tamnoides CAgr MEar NBac

Habranthus (Amaryllidaceae)
andersonii see *H. tubispathus*
brachyandrus SRms WCot
gracilifolius EDAr WAbe
magnoi EDAr
martinezii ♀H2 EDAr

Hamamelis 317

§ **robustus** ♀H2   EShb EWld GKev LAma LCro
§ **tubispathus** ♀H2   EDAr LShi SBrt

Hacquetia see *Sanicula*

Haemanthus (*Amaryllidaceae*)
     albiflos ♀H2   ELan EShb GKev LAma NGKo NSti SRms WFar
- 'Tilbury Toll' × *deformis*   WCot
     amaryllloides   WCot
     barkerae   WCot
     carneus   WCot
     × **clarkei**   WCot
     coccineus ♀H2   LAma WCot
     humilis   WCot
- subsp. *hirsutus*   WCot
     kalbreyeri   see *Scadoxus multiflorus* subsp. *multiflorus*
     katherinae   see *Scadoxus multiflorus* subsp. *katherinae*
     natalensis   see *Scadoxus puniceus*
     nortieri   WCot
     pauculifolius   LAma
     pubescens   WCot
     sanguineus   WCot

Hagenia (*Rosaceae*)
     abyssinica   WPGP

Hakea (*Proteaceae*)
     baxteri   SPlb
     laurina   CPbh CTsd SPlb
§ **lissosperma**   CBcs CTsd EBee EPfP EUrb SEle SMad SPlb WPGP
     microcarpa   IArd
     oleifolia   CPbh
     petiolaris   CPbh
     platysperma   SPlb
§ **salicifolia**   SPlb
     saligna   see *H. salicifolia*
     sericea misapplied   see *H. lissosperma*
     sericea Schrad. & J.C.Wendl. pink-flowered   SPlb
     victoria   CPbh LRHS SPlb

Hakonechloa ✿ (*Poaceae*)
     macra ♀H7   Widely available
§ - 'Alboaurea' (v) ♀H7   CExl CKno CSde EBlo EGren ELan GArf LCro LRHS LSRN MGos MHol MPri SRms
- 'Albovariegata' (v)   CAbb CDoC CKno CSta EBee EMor LCro LEdu LRHS MWlw SBea SMHy SPel WFar
§ - 'All Gold'   Widely available
- 'Aureola' ♀H7   Widely available
- 'Beni-kaze'   CBWd CDor CMiW CSta EBee ELan ELon EMor ISha LCro MAvo MNrw NLar SPel WPnP
- 'Greenhills'   LRHS
- 'Mulled Wine'   EMor EUrb MBNS
- 'Naomi' (v)   CMiW CSta CWnw EBee ELan EMor GArf GKev ISha LRHS SPel WFar
- 'Nicolas'   CCps CDor CExl CMiW CSta EBee ELan ELon EMor EPfP ISha LCro LEdu LRHS LSRN MAvo NLar NSti SBea SPel SPoG WFar WNPC WPnP
- 'Ogon'   see *H. macra* 'All Gold'
- 'Samurai' (v)   CKno LRHS WPGP
- 'Stripe It Rich' (v)   CCht CSta EBee EMor NLar

- SUNFLARE ('Habsfl007')   CBcs CMiW CSta EBee ELon EMor EPfP EUrb LBom LCro LEdu LRHS MBNS MHol Midl MNrw NLar SBea SDix WFar WNPC WPnP
- 'Sunny Delight' (v)   EBee
- 'Variegata'   see *H. macra* 'Alboaurea'

Halesia ✿ (*Styracaceae*)
§ **carolina**   CAco CAgr CBcs CCVT CDoC CEnd CHab CHll CLnd CMac CMCN EBar EBee EGren EGrI EPfP GKev GKin IArd LCro LMaj LRHS MBlu MCtn MGos MMrt SHor WMat WPGP WSpi
- Monticola Group   CBcs CCVT LMaj LSRN
- - 'Arnold Pink'   CCVT
I - - 'Variegata' (v)   LRHS MBlu NLar SSta
- 'Uconn Wedding Bells'   CJun MBlu
- Vestita Group ♀H5   CAco CDoC EPfP MAsh MBlu SSta
- - 'Rosea'   MBlu
     diptera   MBlu
- Magniflora Group   MBlu NLar SSta
     macgregorii   see *Perkinsiodendron macgregorii*
     tetraptera   see *H. carolina*

× Halimiocistus see *Cistus*

Halimium see *Cistus*

Halleria (*Stilbaceae*)
     lucida   CBcs EBee EGrI SEle SPlb SVen WKor

Haloragis (*Haloragaceae*)
     erecta   SPlb SVen
- 'Rubra'   WCot
- 'Wellington Bronze'   CExl CSpe EGrI ESwi LEdu WHer

Hamamelis ✿ (*Hamamelidaceae*)
'Amethyst'   CJun LMaj LRHS MBlu
'Brevipetala'   CEnd CJun
'Danny'   CJun MMuc
'Dishi'   CJun
'Fire Blaze'   CJun MBlu
× *intermedia*   WJur
- 'Advent' ♀H5   CJun
- 'Aimelie' **new**   MPri
- 'Amanda'   CJun NLar
- 'Amanon'   CJun
- 'Andre'   CJun WPGP
- 'Angelly' ♀H5   CJun MBlu NLar
- 'Anne' ♀H5   CJun NCth WPGP
- 'Aphrodite' ♀H5   CBcs CJun EGrI EPfP LMaj LRHS LSRN MAsh MBlu MGos MPri NCth NLar NOra WFar
- 'Arnhem'   CJun WFar
- 'Arnold Promise' ♀H5   Widely available
- 'Athena' **new**   NLar
- 'Aurora' ♀H5   CJun EPfP LRHS MBlu NLar NOra WFar WPGP
- 'Barmstedt Gold' ♀H5   CDoC CJun EGrI ELan LRHS LSRN MAsh MGos NLar NOra SAko SPoG
- 'Basma'   CJun
- 'Bernstein'   CJun
- 'Birgit'   NLar WFar
- 'Brimstone'   CJun
- 'Burning Desire'   CJun NLar
- 'Carmine Red'   CJun CMac LRHS MAsh MPri NLar
- 'Chantal'   CJun
- 'Copper Beauty'   see *H. × intermedia* 'Jelena'
- 'Cyrille'   EGrI

- 'Diane' ♀H5	Widely available	*vernalis*	WJur
- 'Evi'	CJun NLar	- purple-flowered	MBlu
§ - 'Feuerzauber'	CBcs EGren EGrI ELan EPfP LMil	- 'Quasimodo'	MBlu
	LRHS MBlu MPri NLar WFar	- 'Sandra'	LRHS MBlu MGos
- FIRE CRACKER	see *H. × intermedia* 'Feuerzauber'	*virginiana*	CAgr CMCN EGrI LSto MCtn MHtn
- 'Foxy Lady'	MBlu NLar		MMuc WJur
- 'Frederic' ♀H5	CJun EPfP	- 'Mohonk Red'	CJun
- 'Gimborn's Perfume'	EGrI	'Yamina'	CBcs CDoC ELan LMil LRHS MAsh
- 'Gingerbread' ♀H5	CJun		NLar
- 'Glowing Embers'	CJun		
- 'Gold Star'	CJun		
- 'Harry' ♀H5	CBcs CJun LRHS MAsh NLar		
- 'Heinrich Bruns'	CJun		
- 'Hiltingbury'	LRHS MGos NLar		
§ - 'Jelena' ♀H5	Widely available		
- 'John'	CJun		
- 'Limelight'	CJun MBlu		
- 'Livia'	CJun ELan LRHS WPGP		
- 'Luna'	CJun LRHS MPri NLar		
- MAGIC FIRE	see *H. × intermedia* 'Feuerzauber'		
- 'Moonlight'	CJun		
- 'Nina'	CJun EPfP		
- 'Orange Beauty'	CBcs CJun EBee EGren EGrI ELan		
	LCro LRHS MAsh MBlu MGos NLar		
	SAko WFar WPGP		
- 'Orange Peel'	CJun NCth NLar WPGP		
- 'Ostergold'	CJun		
- 'Pallida' ♀H5	Widely available		
- 'Paulina'	CJun		
- 'Primavera'	CJun ELan EPfP LRHS SHor		
- 'Ripe Corn'	CJun MBlu		
- 'Robert' ♀H5	CJun ELan EPfP LRHS		
- 'Rolena'	NLar		
- 'Rubin' ♀H5	CBcs CJun EGren EGrI ELan EPfP		
	LRHS MGos NLar WFar		
- 'Rubinstar'	CJun		
- 'Ruby Glow'	CMac EGren EGrI ELan EPfP LRHS		
	MAsh MGos NLar SPoG WFar		
- 'Sarah'	CJun		
- 'Savill Starlight'	CJun		
- 'Sister Jelena'	CJun		
- 'Spanish Spider'	CJun MBlu		
- 'Strawberries and Cream'	CJun		
- 'Sunburst'	CJun LRHS MBlu MGos NLar SHor		
- 'Swallow Hayes'	LRHS MPri NLar		
- 'Tosca'	CJun		
- 'Twilight'	CJun		
- 'Vesna' ♀H5	CJun CMac EPfP LRHS MAsh MBlu		
- 'Wessel'	CJun		
- 'Westerstede'	CJun CWnw EGrI LCro LMaj LRHS		
	LSRN MBlu MGos NLar WFar		
- 'Wiero'	CJun		
- 'Zitronenjette'	CJun		
japonica	WJur		
- 'Brentry'	CBcs LRHS NLar		
- 'Pendula'	MBlu		
- 'Rubra'	EGrI		
- 'Zuccariniana'	LRHS NLar		
mollis	CBcs CCVT CDoC CEnd CHab		
	CLnd CMac CNWT EGrI ELan		
	EPfP GKin LCro LRHS MAsh		
	MBlu MCtn MGos SHor SPoG		
	SRms WFar WJur		
- 'Coombe Wood'	CJun EGrI		
- 'Imperialis'	CJun		
- 'Iwado'	CJun		
- 'Jermyns Gold' ♀H5	CBcs CJun EPfP LMil LRHS MAsh		
- 'Kort's Yellow'	CJun		
- var. *pallida*	CBrac SEWo		
- 'Wisley Supreme' ♀H5	CJun ELan EPfP MGos		
'Rochester'	CJun		

Haplocarpha (Asteraceae)
rueppellii	SRms

Haplopappus (Asteraceae)
coronopifolius	see *H. glutinosus*
§ *glutinosus*	ECha EPot MMuc SPlb SRms
macrocephalus	EDAr
paucidentatus	SPlb
prunelloides	SPlb

Hardenbergia (Fabaceae)
violacea ♀H3	CHII CRHN CSpe CTsd EAri EShb
	LCro SEle SEND
- f. *alba*	CHII EShb SEND
- 'Regent'	ESwi
- f. *rosea*	CHII SEle

Harrimanella (Ericaceae)
stelleriana	GArf

Harrisia (Cactaceae)
tetracantha	NPlm

Hasteola (Asteraceae)
§ *suaveolens*	LEdu

Hatiora (Cactaceae)
× *graeseri*	CPic
rosea ♀H1b	CoPl
salicornioides ♀H1b	CPic EShb NCft

Haworthia ✿ (Asphodelaceae)
attenuata	see *Haworthiopsis attenuata*
'Black Prince'	EShb
coarctata	see *Haworthiopsis coarctata*
cooperi	CPic NCft
- var. *truncata*	NCft
cymbiformis	LWaG NCft SPlb
- variegated (v)	NCft WOld
fasciata	see *Haworthiopsis fasciata*
glabrata var. *concolor*	see *Haworthiopsis fasciata*
misapplied	'Concolor'
- var. *concolor* (Salm-Dyck) Baker	see *Haworthiopsis attenuata* var. *glabrata*
'Jack Brown'	NCft
limifolia	see *Haworthiopsis limifolia*
margaritifera	see *Tulista pumila* var. *pumila*
marumiana	NCft
- var. *batesiana*	NCft
§ - var. *reddii*	NCft
mirabilis var. *badia*	SPlb
nigra	see *Haworthiopsis nigra*
pumila	see *Tulista pumila*
- subsp. *minima*	see *Tulista minor*
pygmaea 'Ice City'	NCft
- f. *major*	SPlb
reddii	see *H. marumiana* var. *reddii*
retusa ♀H2	CoPl NCft WOld
- 'Grey Ghost'	NCft
- variegated (v)	WOld
× *revendettii*	NCft

starkiana	see *Haworthiopsis scabra* var. *starkiana*		- 'Dentata' ♀H5	EPPr WCha WFar WTHo
tortusa	see *Haworthiopsis* × *tortuosa*		- 'Dentata Aurea'	see *H. colchica* 'Dentata Variegata'
truncata ♀H2	CPic NCft	§	- 'Dentata Variegata' (v) ♀H5	CBcs CDoC CMac ELan EPfP GQue LCro LRHS LSRN MAsh MGos NLar SEND SNig SPoG SRms SWor WFar WTHo
variegata var. *modesta*	NCft			
venosa subsp. *tessellata*	see *Haworthiopsis tessellata* Venosa Group		- - arboreal (v)	WCot
			- 'Paddy's Pride'	see *H. colchica* 'Sulphur Heart'

Haworthiopsis ✿ (Asphodelaceae)

§	*attenuata*	EShb NCft	- 'Sulphur Heart' (v) ♀H5	Widely available
	- var. *attenuata* 'Enon'	NCft	- 'Variegata'	see *H. colchica* 'Dentata Variegata'
§	- var. *glabrata*	EShb	*cristata*	see *H. helix* 'Parsley Crested'
	- 'Super Zebra'	CoPl WCot	*helix*	CMac CoPl CWRo EHeP LCro LRHS LWaG MBros MNHC SFol
	'Big Band'	LCro LWaG NHrt SBig SPad	- 'Adam' (v)	CFis LRHS SEND
§	*coarctata* ♀H2	SEND	- 'Anita'	EHeP GQue
§	*fasciata*	ELan EPfP LBom LCro SEND	- 'Arborescens'	LRHS LWaG NLar
§	- 'Concolor'	CDoC NHrt SPlb	- 'Atropurpurea'	EPPr LRHS LWaG MMuc SEND
§	*limifolia*	CoPl EShb LWaG NCft NHrt SPlb WFar	- 'Bettina' (v)	WCot
			- 'Bird's Foot'	see *H. helix* 'Pedata'
	- SPIDER WHITE ('Lock01'PBR)	LCro MPri	- 'Buttercup' ♀H5	CMac ELan EPfP EPPr GQue LCro LRHS MAsh MGos MMuc NBid SEND SPoG SRms
	- var. *ubomboensis*	NCft		
§	*nigra*	SPlb	- - arborescent	EPPr SDix
	reinwardtii var. *brevicula*	NCft	- 'Caecilia' (v) ♀H5	EPPr
§	*scabra* var. *starkiana*	NCft	- 'Caenwoodiana'	see *H. helix* 'Pedata'
§	*tessellata* Venosa Group ♀H2	LWaG SEND	- 'Carolina Crinkle'	GBin
			- Cavendishii Group (v)	SRms
§	× *tortuosa*	NCft	- 'Ceridwen' (v) ♀H5	SPlb
			- 'Clotted Cream' (v)	CDoC EPfP LCro LSto MAsh SNig WTHo

hazelnut see *Corylus*; also AGM Fruit Section

			- 'Cockle Shell'	EPPr WCot

Hebe see *Veronica* (H)

buxifolia	see *Veronica odora*	§	- 'Congesta' ♀H5	CMac EPPr SRms
cheesemanii	see *Veronica quadrifaria*		- 'Conglomerata'	ELan SRms
divaricata	see *Veronica subfulvida*		- 'Cristata'	see *H. helix* 'Parsley Crested'
fruticeti	see *Veronica subalpina*		- 'Curleylocks'	see *H. helix* 'Manda's Crested'
mackenii	see *Veronica* 'Emerald Gem'		- 'Curly Leaf' **new**	ESwi
recurva	see *Veronica albicans* Recurva Group		- 'Curvaceous' (v)	WCot
			- 'Cyprus'	see *H. pastuchovii* subsp. *cypria*
			- 'Dealbata'	see *H. hibernica* 'Dealbata'

Hebenstretia (Scrophulariaceae)

dura	WFar		- 'Discolor'	see *H. helix* 'Minor Marmorata'
- variegated (v)	ECha WCot WFar	§	- 'Donerailensis'	MBlu
			- 'Duckfoot' ♀H5	EPPr GBin WCot

Hechtia (Bromeliaceae)

lepidophylla	SPlb		- 'Dyinnii'	ELan EPot EPPr EWes GKev LShi NLar SPlb WAbe WCot WFar
			- (Elegantissima Group) 'Marginata Elegantissima' (v)	SArc

Hedera ✿ (Araliaceae)

§	*algeriensis*	SArc	- - 'Tricolor' (v)	CMac SPoG
§	- 'Gloire de Marengo' (v) ♀H5	CBcs CBrac CDoC CMac EBee EGren EHeP ELan EPfP EUrb GKin LCro LRHS LSRN MAsh MGos SDix SEND SNig SPoG SRms SWor WFar WHtc WLov WTHo	- 'Elfenbein' (v)	EPPr WCot
			- 'Emerald Gem'	see *H. hibernica* 'Angularis'
			- 'Erecta'	ELan EPPr LCro LRHS LSto LWaG MBlu NRya SDix SPlb
			- 'Fantasia' (v)	GQue
	- 'Marginomaculata' (v)	MAsh SPoG	- 'Francis'	EPPr
	- 'Montgomery'	LSRN	- 'Glacier' (v) ♀H5	CBcs CMac EBee EGren EHeP ELan EPfP GQue LCro LRHS MAsh MGos SEND SNig SPoG SRms WCot WFar
	- 'Ravensholst' ♀H5	CMac EPPr		
§	*azorica*	EBee WCot		
	- amber-fruited	EBee WCot WMal	- 'Glymii'	EPPr GBin
	- 'Pico'	EPPr EShb	- 'Gold Harald'	see *H. helix* 'Goldchild'
	- 'Saiga'	WCot	- 'Gold Ripple'	see *H. helix* 'Golden Starlight'
	- 'Variegata' (v)	WCot	§	- 'Goldchild' (v) ♀H5	CBcs CMac EBee EGren EHeP EPfP EUrb GQue LCro LRHS MAsh MGos NBir SEND SNig SPoG SWCr SWor WTHo
	canariensis misapplied	see *H. algeriensis*		
	- 'Variegata'	see *H. algeriensis* 'Gloire de Marengo'		
			- 'Golden Ann'	see *H. helix* 'Ceridwen'
	canariensis Willd. var. *azorica*	see *H. azorica*	- 'Golden Curl' (v)	CMac EPfP ESwi WFar
			- 'Golden Ester'	see *H. helix* 'Ceridwen'
	chinensis	see *H. nepalensis*	- 'Golden Gate' (v)	WCot
	- *typica*	see *H. nepalensis*	§	- 'Golden Ingot' (v) ♀H5	LRHS
	colchica	EHeP LCro	- 'Golden Kolibri'	see *H. helix* 'Midas Touch'
*	- 'Arborescens Variegata' (v)	WCot	§	- 'Golden Starlight' (v)	ELan EPPr LCro LWaG SEND

Hedera 319

- 'Goldfinch' — EPPr
- 'Goldheart' — see *H. helix* 'Oro di Bogliasco'
- 'Goldstern' (v) — EPPr
- 'Green Finger' — see *H. helix* 'Très Coupé'
- 'Green Ripple' — CBcs EHeP ELan EPfP EUrb LCro LRHS LWaG MBlu MMuc SEND SNig SPlb SPoG SRms
- 'Halebob' — EPPr
- 'Harald' (v) — LRHS WTHo
- 'Heise' (v) — EPPr
- 'Henriette' (v) — EPPr
- 'Ice Cream' (v) — WCot
- 'Ingrid' (v) — SRms
- 'Ivalace' — EPPr SRms
- 'Jake' — EPPr
- 'Jara' arboreal — WCot
- 'Jasper' — EPPr
- 'Jester's Gold' — EHeP
- 'Jubilee' (v) — WFar
- 'Kaleidoscope' (v) — EPPr
- 'Kolibri' (v) — EHeP SRms
- 'Königer's Auslese' — EPPr
- 'Lightfinger' — EHeP EPPr
- 'Little Diamond' (v) — CMac ELan SRms
- 'Little Luzii' (v) — EPPr
- 'Luzii' (v) — EHeP
- 'Maculata' misapplied — see *H. helix* 'Minor Marmorata'
- § 'Manda's Crested' ♀H5 — ELan EPPr
- 'Melanie' — ECha EPPr WCot
- § 'Midas Touch' (v) ♀H5 — ELan
- 'Midget' — LRHS
- 'Minikin' (v) — WCot
- * 'Minima' misapplied — GEdr GQue
- 'Minima' Hibberd — see *H. helix* 'Donerailensis'
- 'Minima' M.Young — see *H. helix* 'Congesta'
- 'Minor Marmorata' (v) — CFis EPPr
- 'Minty' (v) — EPPr
- 'Misty' (v) — EPPr
- 'Needlepoint' — WTHo
- 'Obovata' — EPPr
- § 'Oro di Bogliasco' (v) — CAco CBrac CDoC CMac EGren EHeP EPfP LCro LRHS LShi LWaG MAsh MMuc SEND SEWo SPlb SRms WFar WTHo
- 'Ovata' — EPPr
- § 'Parsley Crested' ♀H5 — CDoC ELan LRHS
- § 'Pedata' — EPPr SRms
- 'Perkeo' — EPPr WCot
- 'Peter Pan' — EPPr
- 'Pink 'n' Curly' — EPPr WCot
- 'Pink 'n' Very Curly' — WCot
- 'Pittsburgh' — NHrt
- f. *poetarum* — EPPr MBlu WCot
- - 'Poetica Arborea' — SDix
- 'Raleigh Delight' (v) — WCot
- 'Richard John' — see *H. helix* 'Golden Curl'
- 'Ritterkreuz' — EPPr
- 'Romanze' (v) — WCot
- 'Russelliana' — EPPr
- 'Sagittifolia' ambig. — EHeP LRHS MAsh MBlu SPoG
- 'Saint Agnes' — see *H. helix* 'Golden Ingot'
- 'Sally' — EPPr
- 'Salt and Pepper' — see *H. helix* 'Minor Marmorata'
- 'Seabreeze' — EPPr
- 'Shamrock' ♀H5 — EPPr LCro
- 'Silver Ferney' (v) — EPPr
- 'Silver King' (v) — EPPr WCot
- 'Spectre' (v) — EPPr
- 'Spetchley' — see *H. hibernica* 'Spetchley'
- 'Sunrise' — EPPr
- § 'Très Coupé' — MMuc SArc SEND
- 'Triton' — EPPr
- 'Ursula' (v) — EPPr
- 'Very Merry' — EPPr
- 'White Ripple' (v) — ELan EPPr LCro LRHS LWaG SWor WMal
- 'White Wonder' — LCro SPoG
- 'Williamsiana' (v) — EPPr
- 'Wonder' — LCro
- 'Yellow Ripple' — see *H. helix* 'Golden Starlight'
- *hibernica* — CBcs EGren EHeP EPfP LBuc LCro LRHS LWaG SEWo WCha WTHo
- § 'Angularis' — LRHS
- 'Arbori Compact' — ELan EWes
- 'Betty Allen' — EPPr
- § 'Crûg Gold' — WCru
- § 'Dealbata' (v) — CMac EPPr SRms
- 'Deltoidea' ♀H5 — EPPr
- 'Digitata Crûg Gold' — see *H. hibernica* 'Crûg Gold'
- 'Hamilton' — EPPr
- § (Hibernica Group) 'Rona' (v) — EPPr GQue
- 'Lobata Major' — SRms
- 'Palmata' — EPPr
- 'Rona' — see *H. hibernica* (Hibernica Group) 'Rona'
- 'Sagittifolia' — EPfP
- § 'Spetchley' ♀H5 — CMac EPPr GKev NLar NPer SLee WCot
- *iberica* — EPPr
- § *nepalensis* — EPPr
- - KWJ 12345 — WCru
- 'Roy Lancaster' — EPPr
- 'Sino Bart' — EPPr
- 'Suzanne' — EPPr
- *pastuchovii* from Troödos, Cyprus — see *H. pastuchovii* subsp. *cypria*
- 'Ann Ala' ♀H5 — EPPr EUrb LShi MBlu WCot
- § - subsp. *cypria* — EPPr
- *rhombea* — EPPr
- 'Variegata' (v) — EPPr
- × *soroksarensis* 'Woerneri' — SWor

Hedychium ❀ (Zingiberaceae)

- PAB 10111 — WFar
- 'Anne Bishop' — SEND
- *aurantiacum* — CBcs CBlu CDTJ CPbh CTsd EBee ELan LAma LEdu SBig WFar XFar
- *aureum* — EAri LEdu WPGP
- 'Ayo' — CTsd
- *brevicaule* B&SWJ 7171 — WCru
- *chrysoleucum* — SBig
- *coccineum* — CBlu CDTJ CHll CTsd
- - B&SWJ 5238 — WCru
- - from Mizoram, India — WPGP
- - var. *angustifolium* — ESwi
- - - 'Tangerine-Dream' — EAri WCru
- - 'Hungphung Stripe' — EAri ELon LEdu WPGP
- - 'Khangkhui Tall Boy' — LEdu WPGP
- - 'Khonoma Silver' — LEdu WPGP
- - 'Shillong Ghost' — LEdu SNoN WPGP
- *coronarium* ♀H3 — CDTJ CHll CPbh CTsd CWal EAri EBee ELan LAma SAth WFar
- - B&SWJ 3745 — WCru
- - 'Gold Spot' — CBcs CBlu CDTJ CPbh CTsd EPPr LAma WFar WJun
- - var. *maximum* — EAri
- - var. *urophyllum* — see *H. flavum* Roxb.
- 'Coronata Cream' — CDTJ
- 'C.P. Raffill' — see *H.* × *moorei* 'Raffillii'
- *deceptum* — LRHS SChr WPGP

Helenium 321

densiflorum	CBlu CDTJ CHll CPbh CTsd EBee ECha ELan EPPr EUrb LAma LCro LEdu MPie SBig SDix SMad SRms WCot WCru WFar WJun WPGP	- P. Bon. 57188	CExl WPGP
		- PAB 13.0718	LEdu
		- var. *acuminatum*	WPGP
		- broad-leaved	WPGP
- EN 562	CExl	- 'Himalayan Lipstick'	CBlu LAma SPad
- LS&H 17393	CExl	- 'Huani'	ELon LEdu
- 'Assam Orange'	CBcs CBct CBlu CCht CExl CLil CPic CTsd EAri ELon EPPr ESwi EWld LEdu LRHS SDix SMHy SNoN SPlb WCru WJun WPGP	- 'Liberty'	CBcs EAri LEdu WCru WPGP
		- 'Shirui Steps'	EAri ELon EPPr LEdu
		- 'Singalila'	EAri LEdu WCru WPGP
		- 'Tresco'	SBig
		- 'Troglodyte'	LEdu WFar WPGP
- 'Kalimpong Gold'	SBig	*stenopetalum*	EShb MCtn
- 'Kalimpong Yellow'	SBig	- B&SWJ 7155	WCru
- 'Mewa Khola'	EAri WCru	- RF 148	WPGP
- 'Milke Danda'	WCru	- 'Ziyadum'	WFar WPGP
- 'Sorung'	CDTJ CExl ELon LEdu SChr WPGP	'Tahitian Flame' (v)	EAri ELan
		'Tai Pink Princess' (Tai Series)	CTsd WFar
- 'Stephen'	CDTJ CExl EUrb LEdu MNrw SBig SChr SPlb WFar WPGP	'Tara' ♀H4	CBct CBlu CCht CDTJ CExl CLil CPbh CPic EAri EPPr EUrb LEdu SArc SBig SMad SMHy SPad SPel SPlb WCru WFar WMal WPGP
'Devon Cream'	CDTJ CHll CLil CPbh CTsd EAri EUrb SBig SChr WFar WMal WOld WPGP		
		- red	SChr
'Doctor Moy' (v)	CDTJ LRHS WCot	'Telstar 4'	SBig
'Elizabeth'	EUrb LRHS	*tengchongense*	WCru
ellipticum	CBlu CDTJ CTsd EAri ELan LAma SPel WFar WJun XFar	'Trum Trom'	
		thyrsiforme	CBlu CDTJ CPbh CTsd EBee LAma WCru
- PAB 7867	LEdu WPGP		
§ *flavescens*	CBlu CDTJ CTsd EBee ELan LAma LCro SBig	'Vanilla Ice' (v)	EAri
		'Verity' (v)	EAri
flavum misapplied	see *H. flavescens*	*villosum*	SBig
§ *flavum* Roxb.	CBcs EAri	- var. *tenuiflorum*	CDTJ EAri WPGP
- HWJ 604	WCru	- - 'Winter White'	WCru
forrestii misapplied	see *H*. 'Helen Dillon'	*viridibracteatum*	EAri
forrestii Diels	CCht CLil CSpe EAri ESwi EUrb MNrw SPlb WJun	- BWJ 15549	WCru
		wardii	CDTJ CExl CTsd EAri ESwi SBig WCru
- KWJ 12314	WCru		
'Gahili'	SBig	- RF 134	WPGP
gardnerianum ♀H2	Widely available	× *wilkeanum*	CHll
- B&SWJ 12533	WCru	*yunnanense*	CHll LEdu SBig SChr SNoN SPlb WPGP
- 'Tangkhul Naga' new	WPGP		
'Giant Yellow'	CDTJ	- BWJ 7900	ESwi WCru
'Gold Flame'	SBig	- L 633	CExl
'Golden Glow'	SBig	- PAB 7361	WFar
gomezianum	LEdu WPGP	- from Cally Gardens	EAri EPPr
gracile	EAri WCru	- 'Iago'	WCru
greenii	CAby CBcs CBct CBlu CDTJ CHll CPbh CSpe CTsd EAri EBee ESwi EUrb EWld LAma LEdu MNrw SAth SBig SPlb WCru WFar WJun	- 'Y Tŷ'	WCru

Hedysarum (Fabaceae)

boreale	CSpe
coronarium	see *Sulla coronaria*
hedysaroides	GJos
multijugum	see *Corethrodendron multijugum*
tauricum	CSpe GJos

Heimia (Lythraceae)

salicifolia	EBee WPGP

Helenium ✿ (Asteraceae)

'Abbey Dore Bronze'	WHoo
'Adios'	IPot WFar
amarum	MCtn
'Amber'	EBlo LRHS LSto WFar
'Amber Dwarf'	SAko
autumnale	CWal EPfP MNHC WFar
- 'Bandera'	LRHS NLar
§ - Helena Series	MCtn WFar WRBe
- - 'Helena Gold'	CSpe EGren ELan EPfP LRHS LSto
- - 'Helena Rote Töne'	CFis CSpe ELan EPfP LRHS MHol StAn
- - 'Helena Yellow'	EPfP LRHS WCav

(continued)

- NJM 13.086	WPGP
- 'Mhui Fang'	WPGP
griffithianum	CBlu CDTJ CTsd EBee EGren LAma SBig WCru WFar XFar
§ 'Helen Dillon'	EAri ESwi LEdu SBig WCru WPGP
'Keneggy'	SVen
'Lemon Sherbet'	CTsd
'Luna Moth'	WPGP
luteum	CTsd
maximum	CDTJ EAri SChr WPGP
- B&SWJ 8261A	WCru
- HWJ 810	WCru
§ × *moorei* 'Raffillii'	CTsd ELon WCru
nagamiense WWJ 11857 new	WCru
'Orange Glow'	SBig
'Pink Princess'	CBcs CDTJ SBig
'Samsheri'	CHll
spicatum	CBlu CDTJ CExl CTsd EUrb LEdu MNrw SMHy WFar WPGP
- B&SWJ 7231	WCru

- (Mariachi Series) CMac CWGN LCro LRHS LSou MArl MBel MHol MNrw MPro NCth NLar SHar SRms WCAu WHil WNPC
- - 'Ranchera'^{PBR} EUrb LRHS Midl NLar XFar
- - 'Salsa'^{PBR} CMac ELan LCro LRHS LSou MNrw MPro NLar SRms WNPC
- - 'Siesta'^{PBR} CBcs LBom LRHS MNrw NLar SRms WHil XFar
- - 'Sombrero'^{PBR} CBcs LCro LRHS NEoE NLar NSti SPoG XFar
- 'Pumilum' LRHS
- 'Short and Sassy'^{PBR} CBcs CFis EGren ELan EPfP IPot LBar LBom LCro LRHS LSto MAsh MAvo MHer MHtn Midl MNrw MPri MPro NLar NWbg SAth SOrN SPoG SRkn SRms WHil WNPC

'Baudirektor Linne' ♀H7 EBee ESwi SHar WCAu WPGP
'Betty' (UFO Series) CTtf EBlo LRHS LSto MNrw NWbg WCAu
'Biedermeier' LBar MNrw SAko WCAu
'Blütentisch' misapplied see H. 'Riverton Beauty'
'Blütentisch' Foerster ♀H7 GMaP
'Bressingham Gold' EBlo LRHS MNrw WHrl
'Bruno' EBlo MArl SHar SMrm
'Butterpat' ♀H7 CDor EBlo GMaP LRHS MArl MNrw
'Can Can' ELon MHer MNrw NGdn SPel SRms WCAu WFar WGoo
'Carmen' (UFO Series) EBlo LRHS
'Chelsey' EBee EBlo ELan LCro LSRN LSto NSti NWbg SPoG SRms
'Chipperfield Orange' CTtf GMaP MArl NBir NGdn NWbg WOld
'Coppelia' EBlo LRHS NBir NGdn WFar
COPPER SPRAY see H. 'Kupfersprudel'
'Crimson Beauty' EBlo
DARK BEAUTY see H. 'Dunkle Pracht'
'Dauerbrenner' SHar
'Double Trouble'^{PBR} MHol SRms WCot WFar
§ 'Dunkle Pracht' ♀H7 EBee LRHS LSRN LSto NLar SMHy WFar WOld
'El Dorado' CWCL EBee EBlo ELon LBar MBel NDov SHar SRms WCot WFar
'Fata Morgana' LBar MHer WCAu
'Feckenham Ruby' WHoo
'Feuersiegel' ♀H7 EBlo LRHS SAko WOld
'Fiesta' WFar
'Flamenco' WFar
'Flammendes Käthchen' EBee EBlo LRHS SHar
'Flammenrad' SAko
'Flammenspiel' EBlo MNrw
'Fox Cub' SPel
'Gartensonne' ♀H7 SMrm
'Gay-go-round' MAvo
GOLD FOX see H. 'Goldfuchs'
'Gold Intoxication' see H. 'Goldrausch'
GOLDEN YOUTH see H. 'Goldene Jugend'
§ 'Goldene Jugend' ELon WCot
§ 'Goldfuchs' WCot
§ 'Goldrausch' EBlo LRHS MBel MNrw NGdn SAko WCAu WFar WOld
hoopesii see *Hymenoxys hoopesii*
'Hot Button' SPel
'Hot Lava' CWGN LCro LRHS MArl SPoG WHil
'Indianersommer' CDor GMaP LRHS MNrw NLar WCAu WGoo WSpi
'Kanaria' CDor CWnw EBee EBlo GElm LBar MAvo MBel NLar NSti SMrm WFar
'Karneol' ♀H7 EBlo EPfP
'Königstiger' ♀H7 EBlo EUrb LRHS MNrw WFar
'Kugelsonne' WCAu
§ 'Kupfersprudel' SAko WCot

'Kupferzwerg' EBee ELan LSto SPel
'Lemon Queen' SMrm
'Lemon Sundae' (Sundae Series) EPfP LBom LRHS MPri NCth
'Little Orange' NDov WGoo
'Loysder Wieck' CTtf EBee MAvo MBel NGdn SPeP WCAu
'Luc' ♀H7 ECha ELon NDov WCot WMal
§ 'Mahagoni' WCAu
MAHOGANY see H. 'Mahagoni'
MARDI GRAS ('Helbro') CAby CMac ELan EMor EPfP GMaP LBar LBom LRHS LSou MBel MHol MPri NCth NWbg SPel SPoG SRms WCAu WHil WNPC WTor
'Marion Nickig' LSto WFar
'Meranti' MBel NCth NDov WCot WMal
'Mien Ruys' IPot
'Moerheim Beauty' ♀H7 Widely available
'Monique' (UFO Series) LRHS
'Oldenburg' WCot
'Peach Sundae' (Sundae Series) EPfP LBar LRHS MPri MPro
PIPSQUEAK ('Blopip') CCps EBee EBlo LRHS NCth SRms WCAu
'Poncho' SRms
'Potter's Wheel' CCps MAsh NGdn SDix SRms
puberulum LRHS MCtn NBir
'Pumilum Magnificum' ELan EPfP GQue WFar
'Ragamuffin' EBlo LBar WCot
'Rauchtopas' GQue LCro MBel NDov NLar SMHy WGoo WHil WPGP
'Red Army' CCps ECha EMor LRHS SRkn SRms
'Red Jewel' CAby CDor CWnw EBee IPot LRHS MArl MHol Midl NCth NLar SAko SMrm WCAu WCot WHoo WKif WPGP WTor
§ 'Riverton Beauty' ECha LSto MNrw SDix SMHy WCot WHoo
'Riverton Gem' LRHS
'Rotgold' misapplied see *H. autumnale* Helena Series
'Rotgold' Foerster SRms
'Rouge Foncé' LSto WFar
'Rubinzwerg' ♀H7 CBWd CKno CWnw EBee EBlo ELan EMor EPfP GElm GMaP LRHS LSto MBel MPro NBro NDov NGdn NLar NWbg SAko SMHy SMrm SRkn SRms WCAu WFar
'Ruby Charm' EBlo ESgI MArl WCot WFar
§ 'Ruby Thuesday' CBcs CWnw EBlo ELan EPfP GElm GMaP LBom LCro LRHS LSRN LSto MAvo MBNS MMrt MNrw MPro NGdn NLar NSti NWbg SPoG SRms WCAu WFar WSpi
'Ruby Tuesday' see H. 'Ruby Thuesday'
'Sahin's Early Flowerer' ♀H7 Widely available
'Septemberfuchs' EBlo LEdu LRHS SAko SMHy WPGP
'Sonnenwunder' LRHS
'Sophie zur Linden' ECha
'Strawberry Sundae' (Sundae Series) EPfP LBar LRHS Midl MPri
'Sunny Side Up' SPel
'The Bishop' CBWd CCps CMHG EBee EPfP LCro LSto MSwo NWbg WFar
'Tie Dye' LBar NGdn SMHy SPel SPoG WFar
'Tijuana Brass' NLar
'Tip Top' EPfP LRHS MCtn
'Tom' (UFO Series) NDov
'Vicky' SHar
'Vivace' ELon WCot WPGP
'Wagon Wheel' WFar

Helianthemum 323

'Waldhorn'	WPGP	'Henfield Brilliant' ♀H4	CBcs ECha ELan EPfP ESgI EUrb GAbr LRHS MMrt NBir SDix SMad SMHy SPoG SRms WCav WCot WFar WHoo
'Waltraut' ♀H7	CBcs CBWd CCps CElw EBee EBlo ELan ELon EMor EPfP GElm LCro LRHS LSto MBel MNrw NBir NDov NLar SRms WCAu WFar		
		'Highdown'	SRms
		'Highdown Apricot'	SPoG SRms
'Wesergold' ♀H7	CMac EBee EBlo GElm LRHS MArl MBNS MHol MPie NDov NSti SPoG WCAu WFar	'Honeymoon'	ESgI
		'Jubilee' (d) ♀H4	ESgI LRHS LShi MAsh MHol NBir SPoG SRms
'Westerstede'	EBlo	'Karen's Silver'	WAbe
'Wyndley'	CBcs CDor EBlo ELan EPfP GMaP LRHS LSto NBir NGdn NLar SRms WCAu WFar	'Kathleen Mary'	WIce
		'Lawrenson's Pink'	EHeP EPfP GMaP LRHS MPro SRms WCAu WFar WTor
'Zimbelstern'	EBlo ECha LRHS MAvo NLar WCot WFar WPGP	'Lemon Queen'	WCAu
		'Lucy Elizabeth'	ESgI
Helianthella (Asteraceae)		*lunulatum*	SRms WAbe
§ *quinquenervis*	EBlo LRHS MPro NLar WFar	'Marianne'	WIce
		'Mrs Clay'	see *H.* 'Fire Dragon'
Helianthemum (Cistaceae)		'Mrs Croft'	SRms
'Alice Howorth'	WIce	§ 'Mrs C.W. Earle' (d) ♀H4	ELan EPfP ESgI LRHS SRms
'Amabile Plenum' (d)	GBin LShi SPel	'Mrs Lake'	GAbr
'Amy Baring' ♀H5	SRms WHoo	'Mrs Mould'	WIce
'Annabel' (d)	WFar	'Mrs Moules'	SRms
apenninum	ESgI GKev SRms WAbe WSpi	*mutabile*	SPlb SVic WFar
'Apricot Blush'	WAbe	§ *nummularium*	ENfk MCtn MHer MNHC NAts NMir SRms StAn WAbe WIce WOrg
'Baby Buttercup'	LShi		
'Beech Park Red'	EPot WAbe WFar WHoo WIce WKif	§ - subsp. *tomentosum*	GAbr
'Ben Afflick'	MAsh SRms	*oelandicum*	SRms WAbe
'Ben Dearg'	SRms	- subsp. *incanum*	WAbe
'Ben Fhada'	CBcs ELan EPfP GAbr GMaP LRHS LSto MAsh NLar SDix SEND SPoG SRms SRot WAbe WFar WHoo WIce	- subsp. *italicum*	WAbe
		- subsp. *piloselloides*	WAbe
		'Old Gold'	SRms WAbe
'Ben Heckla'	ESgI EUrb GAbr LBar SRms	'Orchard's Nevis'	WIce
'Ben Hope'	EHeP ELan LCro LRHS MMrt SRms WHoo	'Peachy Keen' (d)	ESgI
		'Pershore Orange'	GKev
§ 'Ben Ledi'	CBcs EGren ELan ESgI EUrb GAbr GJos GMaP LRHS LSto MAsh NLar SPoG SRms SRot WAbe WFar WIce	'Pink Angel' (d)	GJos LRHS SRms WAbe WFar
		'Praecox'	SRms
		'Prima Donna'	ELan EPfP
'Ben Lomond'	ESgI GAbr	'Prostrate Orange'	SRms
'Ben More'	CBcs EGren ELan EPfP EPot GAbr GJos GKev GMaP LRHS LShi LSto MAsh NBir SPoG SRms WFar WHoo WIce	'Raspberry Ripple'	ELan EPfP EPot LBar LRHS SPoG SRms
		'Razzle Dazzle' (v)	SRms
		'Red Dragon'	EPot LBar WAbe WIce
'Ben Nevis'	SRms	'Red Orient'	see *H.* 'Supreme'
'Ben Vane'	SRms WIce	'Regenbogen' (d)	SEND
'Boughton Double Primrose' (d)	GMaP WAbe WFar	§ 'Rhodanthe Carneum' ♀H4	CBcs ECha EGren ELan EPfP ESgI EUrb GKev GMaP LRHS LSto MPri NBir SEND SPoG SRms WAbe WCAu WTor
'Bunbury'	GQue LRHS NBir SDix SPoG SRms WFar		
I 'Butter and Eggs'	SRms	§ 'Rosakönigin'	SEND WAbe
I 'Carminium Plenum'	ESgI	'Rose of Leeswood' (d)	ELan LSto MHol SPoG SRms WKif
'Cerise Queen' (d)	ECha EPfP ESgI EUrb LCro LRHS LSto MPro SEND SRms WFar	ROSE QUEEN	see *H.* 'Rosakönigin'
		'Roxburgh Gold'	SRms
chamaecistus	see *H. nummularium*	'Saint John's College Yellow'	SRms
'Cheviot'	ECha ESgI NBir SMHy WHoo	'Salmon Queen'	SEND SRms
'Chocolate Blotch'	SEND SRms	'Shot Silk'	LRHS SRms
'Cornish Cream'	GAbr LBar SRms	'Snow Queen'	see *H.* 'The Bride'
cupreum	GAbr	'Sterntaler'	ESgI GAbr SRms WFar
'David'	ESgI	'Strawberry Fields'	ESgI WIce
'David Ritchie'	WHoo	'Sudbury Gem'	ECha ESgI LRHS MPri SRms
'Diana'	EPot	'Sulphur Moon'	SRms
'Elfenbeinglanz'	LRHS WFar	'Sulphureum Plenum' (d)	LRHS
'Everton Ruby'	see *H.* 'Ben Ledi'	'Sunbeam'	SRms
'Fairy'	ELan EPfP	§ 'Supreme'	ELan EPfP EPot EWes GArf LRHS SRms
§ 'Fire Dragon' ♀H4	ECha ELan EPfP ESgI GMaP LRHS MAsh NBir SRms WAbe		
		§ 'The Bride' ♀H4	CBcs ECha EGren EHeP ELan EPfP ESgI EUrb GAbr GMaP LCro LRHS LShi LSRN LSto MAsh MMrt MPro MSwo NLar SEND SPoG SRms WAbe WCAu WFar WKif WTor
'Fireball'	see *H.* 'Mrs C.W. Earle'		
'Georgeham'	ESgI NBir SRms WHoo WKif		
§ 'Golden Queen'	EHeP EPfP LRHS MAsh MPro SRms WFar WTor		
'Hartswood Ruby'	GMaP LRHS SAko SRms WAbe WFar	'Tigrinum Plenum' (d)	EWes

tomentosum	see *H. nummularium*
	subsp. *tomentosum*
'Welsh Flame'	WAbe
'Wisley Pink'	see *H.* 'Rhodanthe Carneum'
'Wisley Primrose' ♀H4	CBcs ECha EGren ELan EPfP EPot
	GMaP LCro LRHS LSto MAsh MPri
	MSwo NLar SEND SPoG SRms
	WAbe WCAu WFar WHoo
'Wisley White'	ECha ELan SHar
'Yellow Queen'	see *H.* 'Golden Queen'

Helianthus (Asteraceae)

'Anne'	ELon NDov
annuus	SVic
- 'Buttercream' ♀H4	MCtn
- 'Claret' ♀H4	LCro MCtn
- 'Desire Red' **new**	LCro
- 'Earthwalker'	MCtn
- 'Garden Statement'	LCro
- 'Holiday'	MCtn
- 'Little Dorrit'	MCtn
- 'Mongolian Giant'	MCtn
- 'Ms Mars'	LCro MCtn
- Music Box Mixed	MCtn
- 'Red Sun'	MCtn
- 'Ring of Fire'	MCtn
- 'Ronnie Orange' **new**	MCtn
- 'Shock-o-Lat'	MCtn
- 'Sonja'	MCtn
- Sunbelievable Brown Eyed Girl ('Sunbeliv01'PBR) (Sunbelievable Series)	CWGN MBros
- 'Sunsation Yellow' (Sunsation Series) ♀H4	LCro
- 'Teddy Bear' (d) ♀H4	LCro MCtn
- 'Valentine' ♀H4	LCro MCtn
- 'Velvet Queen'	MCtn
argophyllus 'Gold and Silver' **new**	MCtn
atrorubens	MHol NBro
- 'Giganteus'	ELon
'Bitter Chocolate'	LEdu WPGP
'Capenoch Star' ♀H5	CCps GMaP LEdu MNrw NLar SDix WCAu
'Carine'	ECha ELon ESgI GBin MNrw NLar SPel WCot WFar WPGP
'Chocolate'	MCtn
'Cotswold Queen'	WCot
debilis	MCtn
subsp. *cucumerifolius*	
'Italian White'	
- 'Vanilla Ice'	LCro MCtn
decapetalus	WTre
* - 'Kastle Kobena'	CDor
- Morning Sun	see *H.* 'Morgensonne'
'Dorian Roxburgh'	ECha ESgI MHol WCot WHoo
'Double Whammy' (d)	LBar MPro
'Flying Saucers'	MPro
giganteus	ECha LCro SHar
- 'Sheila's Sunshine'	CElw CTtf ECha EPPr ESgI EWes LEdu LRHS LSto MNrw SAko SHar WFar WHrl WOld WTre
'Gullick's Variety' ♀H5	EBlo ESgI LSto MArl NBro NLar WFar
'Happy Days' ♀H5	CTtf EWes MAvo MHol NSti SBea SPeP SRms WCot WFar WHoo WOld XFar
× *kellermanii*	EBee ECha SPhx
§ × *laetiflorus*	ESgI GPSL SEND
§ 'Lemon Queen' ♀H4	Widely available
'Limelight'	see *H.* 'Lemon Queen'
'Loddon Gold' ♀H5	EBlo ELan EMor ESwi LRHS MArl MBel MHer NBir SMrm WCot WFar
§ *maximiliani*	CWRo EBlo ELan ELon LRHS MMuc
microcephalus	EBee ELon NDov
- 'JS Straffe Prairie Gast'	MNrw WFar
'Miss Mellish' ♀H5	EBee LEdu LShi WBrk WCot WFar WHoo
mollis	ESgI WFar
'Monarch' ♀H5	EBee ESgI EWhm MBel MHol NLar SIvy SMad SMrm WCAu WCot WFar WOld
'Morgensonne'	GQue WCot
'O Sole Mio'	WCot WFar
orgyalis	see *H. salicifolius*
quinquenervis	see *Helianthella quinquenervis*
'Razzmatazz'	SAko
rigidus misapplied	see *H.* × *laetiflorus*
'Ruby Eclipse'	MCtn
§ *salicifolius*	Widely available
- 'Table Mountain'PBR	NLar
scaberrimus	see *H.* × *laetiflorus*
'Soleil d'Or'	SRms WFar
strumosus	MHol NBac WCot
Suncatcher Pure Gold ('Bullheli 02'PBR)	LRHS
'Sunshine Daydream'	Midl
'Triomphe de Gand'	MNrw NDov WFar
tuberosus	CoPl NGKo
- 'Bleu Patate'	LEdu
- 'Dwarf'	LEdu NBac
- 'Dwarf Sunray'	NBac
- 'Fuseau'	LCro SVic
- 'Garnet'	LEdu
- 'Sakhalinski'	LEdu
- 'Sugarball'	LEdu

× *Heliaporus* (Cactaceae)

smithii	LRHS

Helichrysum (Asteraceae)

adenocarpum	SPlb
alveolatum	see *H. splendidum*
ambiguum	CFis
amorginum Ruby Cluster ('Blorub'PBR)	LBar SRms
angustifolium from Crete	see *H. microphyllum* (Willd.) Cambess.
§ *arwae*	EDAr WAbe
bellidioides	see *Anaphaloides bellidioides*
bellum	StAn
coralloides	see *Ozothamnus coralloides*
'County Park Silver'	see *Ozothamnus* 'County Park Silver'
'Dargan Hill Monarch'	see *Xerochrysum bracteatum* 'Dargan Hill Monarch'
devium **new**	WMal
'Elmstead'	see *H. stoechas* 'White Barn'
frigidum	EPot WAbe
heldreichii	WMal
hookeri	see *Ozothamnus hookeri*
§ *hypoleucum*	CFis
'Icicles'	ELan GBin LRHS MPri
italicum	CCBP CGHo ECha EGren EGrI EHeP EHet ENfk IDun LCro LRHS LShi MCtn MHer MHoo MNHC SArc SAth SEND SPoG SRms SVen SVic WHer WKit WTre
- 'Dartington'	CAgr ECha ENfk SRms
- subsp. *italicum*	CSBt LCro SEdi
- 'Korma'PBR	EHet ELan EPfP EWhm LRHS MAsh MHol MMrt MPri SRms

Helleborus 325

- subsp. ***microphyllum***	see *H. microphyllum* (Willd.) Cambess.	- - 'Asahi' (d)	EBee MHol XFar
- 'Nanum'	see *Plecostachys serpyllifolia*	- - 'Benzinggold' ♀H6	EBlo
§ - subsp. ***serotinum***	CBcs CCoa LCro SRms	- - 'Bleeding Hearts'	CDor CFis CSpe CTtf EDAr GElm IPot LRHS MMrt MNrw MPro SBea SBeP SPel StAn
ledifolium	see *Ozothamnus ledifolius*		
marginatum misapplied	see *H. milfordiae*	- - 'Burning Hearts'	CTtf CWGN EDAr GElm MAsh MMrt MPro NLar SBea SMad SVic
microphyllum misapplied	see *Plecostachys serpyllifolia*		
microphyllum ambig.	SRms	- - 'Fire Twister'PBR	IPot LCro WTor
§ ***microphyllum*** (Willd.) Cambess.	CCBP EHet ENfk MHoo MNHC SEND WKit	- - 'Funky Spinner'	CWGN LBar LSou Midl MMrt MPri MPro SBea SMad WHil WTor
§ ***milfordiae***	EDAr GArf SPlb SRms WAbe	- - GOLDEN PLUME	see *H. helianthoides* var. *scabra* 'Goldgefieder'
orientale	EPot SArc		
pagophilum	WAbe	§ - - 'Goldgefieder' ♀H6	WFar
petiolare ♀H3	SDix SPoG	- - 'Luna Roja'	IPot LBar LSou MAsh MHtn Midl MPro XFar
- 'Aureum'	see *H. petiolare* 'Limelight'		
- 'Goring Silver' ♀H3	SPoG	- - 'Mars'	WFar
§ - 'Limelight' ♀H3	SPoG	- - 'Prairie Sunset'PBR	MHol
- 'Variegatum' (v) ♀H3	SPoG	- - 'Prima Ballerina'	WHil
populifolium misapplied	see *H. hypoleucum*	§ - - 'Sommersonne'	ELan EMor EPfP IPot LRHS NPer SMrm SRms
'Red Jewel'PBR	LBar MPri		
rosmarinifolium	see *Ozothamnus rosmarinifolius*	- - 'Summer Nights'	CFis EBee ELan GElm IPot LCro MBel MNrw NLar WFar WSpi
§ 'Schwefellicht'	ECha WCAu		
selago	see *Ozothamnus selago*	- - SUMMER SUN	see *H. helianthoides* var. *scabra* 'Sommersonne'
serotinum	see *H. italicum* subsp. *serotinum*		
serpyllifolium	see *Plecostachys serpyllifolia*	- - 'Venus'	LSou MArl SRms WCAu
sessilioides	EPot WAbe	- 'Summer Pink' (v)	CWGN SPoG WCot WFar
§ ***splendidum*** ♀H4	CFis LRHS NBro	- 'Tuscan Sun'PBR	EBee
stoechas 'Silverball'	LRHS	- 'Yellow Spider' (d)	MAsh MSCN
§ - 'White Barn'	CSpe ECha EPPr LShi WCot WMal		

Heliosperma (Caryophyllaceae)

SULPHUR LIGHT	see *H.* 'Schwefellicht'
thianschanicum	SRms
- GOLDEN BABY	see *H. thianschanicum* 'Goldkind'
§ - 'Goldkind'	NBir
- 'White Wonder'	EPfP LRHS
trilineatum misapplied	see *H. splendidum*
witbergense	GKev
woodii	see *H. arwae*

§ ***alpestre***	SHar SRms
- 'Flore Pleno' (d) ♀H7	EDAr EWes MNrw WIce
- 'Starry Dreams'	LRHS SPoG
§ ***pusillum***	EDAr NLar

Heliotropium ✿ (Boraginaceae)

Helicodiceros (Araceae)

§ ***muscivorus***	MCtn WCot

Heliconia ✿ (Heliconiaceae)

psittacorum	NPlm
schiedeana	CHll NPlm

Helictotrichon (Poaceae)

planiculme	EPPr
pratense	CHab
§ ***sempervirens*** ♀H5	CBcs CKno CMac CSde CWnw EBee ECha EGren EHeP ELan ELon EPfP EPPr EUrb GElm GMaP GQue LCro LRHS LSto MAsh MMuc NBro SMHy SPel SPeP SPoG WFar WHoo
- 'Saphirsprudel'	EBee WCot WPGP

Heliophila (Brassicaceae)

coronopifolia	CSpe MCtn

Heliopsis (Asteraceae)

GOLDEN PLUME	see *H. helianthoides* var. *scabra* 'Goldgefieder'
helianthoides	WFar
- 'Helios Fireball'	Midl
- 'Helios Sunset'	Midl
- 'Limelight'	see *Helianthus* 'Lemon Queen'
- LORAINE SUNSHINE ('Helhan'PBR) (v)	CWGN LRHS MHol SBea SIvy SPoG WCot WFar XFar
- 'Midnight Glow' (v)	IPot SMad
- 'Red Shades'	LBar MAsh MSCN
- var. ***scabra***	GAbr MCtn

amplexicaule	SMrm
anchusifolium	see *H. amplexicaule*
§ ***arborescens***	ENfk EShb
- 'Chatsworth' ♀H1c	CAby
- 'Florence Nightingale'	WMal
- 'Gatton Park'	WMal
- 'Lord Roberts'	WMal
- 'Marine'	CSpe LSou MCtn
- 'Nautilus Blue'	MPro
- 'Nautilus White'	MPri
- 'P.K. Lowther'	WMal
- 'President Garfield'	WMal
- 'Princess Marina' ♀H1c	LCro NLar
- SCENTROPIA BLUE ('Heliovi')	MPri
- 'White Lady'	CSpe WMal
- 'White Queen'	WMal
'Butterfly Kisses'	SPoG
'Dwarf Marine'	MCtn
'Midnight Sky'	CTsd
peruvianum	see *H. arborescens*

Helipterum see *Syncarpha*

Helleborus ✿ (Ranunculaceae)

abruzzicus WM 227	MPhe
ANGEL GLOW ('B11-02')	EPfP LBom
§ ***argutifolius*** ♀H5	Widely available
- 'Janet Starnes' (v)	MAsh
- mottled-leaved	see *H. argutifolius* 'Pacific Frost'
- 'Pacific Frost' (v)	CDor MMrt
- 'Silver Lace'	LAma LRHS LWaG NBir SPoG
atrorubens misapplied	see *H. orientalis* subsp. *abchasicus* (A. Braun) B. Mathew Early Purple Group

atrorubens Waldst. & Kit. MPhe
- WM 9028 from Slovenia
- WM 9805 from Croatia MPhe
- spotted MPhe
× *ballardiae* 'Candy Love'^(PBR) EPfP GMaP LCro
- HGC Camelot ('Coseh 940'^(PBR)) EPfP LCro LRHS MAsh MPri NLar WSpi
- HGC Maestro ('Coseh 890'^(PBR)) EPfP LBom MAsh MPri
- HGC Mahogany Snow ('Coseh 930'^(PBR)) MPri
- HGC Merlin ('Coseh 810'^(PBR)) EPfP LRHS MAsh MPri NLar SPoG WSpi
- HGC Snow Dance ('Coseh 800'^(PBR)) EPfP LBom LRHS MPri SPoG
× *belcheri* 'Pink Ice' MAsh
§ *bocconei* GKev MAsh
- WM 1332 from Sicily MPhe
- WM 1334 from Calabria, Italy MPhe
- WM 9905 from Sicily MPhe
- subsp. *bocconei* see *H. bocconei*
corsicus see *H. argutifolius*
croaticus WM 9810 MPhe
'Crystal Love' EPfP
dumetorum GKev
- WM 1306 from Hungary MPhe
- WM 1309 from Slovenia MPhe
- WM 9209 MPhe
* - var. *alba* **new** MSwo
§ × *ericsmithii* LSRN MAsh WSpi
- 'Bob's Best' SRms
- HGC Joker ('Coseh 740'^(PBR)) LRHS SPoG
- HGC Malory ('Coseh 780'^(PBR)) LRHS MPri
- HGC Marlon Cream ('Coseh 980'^(PBR)) LBom LRHS MPri
- HGC Monte Cristo ('Coseh 860'^(PBR)) EPfP LBuc LRHS MPri
- HGC Shooting Star ('Coseh 790'^(PBR)) EPfP LRHS MPri
- 'HGC Silvermoon'^(PBR) NLar
§ - 'Ivory Prince'^(PBR) EPfP LRHS SPoG
- 'Maestro' LRHS
- 'Pink Beauty'^(PBR) LCro NLar SPoG WCot
- 'Pirouette'^(PBR) EBee ELan EPfP LCro LRHS WFar WTor
- 'Snow Love'^(PBR) GMaP NLar
- (ViV Series) ViV Valeria ('Jhe00202'^(PBR)) MPri
- - ViV Viviana ('Jhe00203'^(PBR)) MPri
- 'Winter Moonbeam'^(PBR) ELan EPfP LBuc LCro LRHS LSRN SPoG SRms WCot
- 'Winter Sunshine'^(PBR) EBee EGrI ELan EPfP LBuc LCro LRHS SPoG SRms
foetidus ♀H7 Widely available
- 'Gold Bullion' MAsh SPoG
- 'Miss Jekyll' LRHS MCtn
- 'Red and Yellow' WCot
- 'Ruth' LRHS MAsh
- 'Sopron' LRHS
- Wester Flisk Group CAby LEdu LRHS NPer SEND SPoG StAn WCAu WSpi
- Wilgenbrock selection LRHS
'Harvington Rebekah'^(PBR) ENun
Hello Helleborus Dacaya ('Hiljwlsdaca'^(PBR)) LSou
HGC Cinnamon Snow ('Coseh 700'^(PBR)) LCro MPri NLar
HGC Pink Frost ('Coseh 710'^(PBR)) ELan EPfP MPri NLar SPoG
§ × *hybridus* CBro CMac ECha EGren ELan GKev GMaP LCro LSto MGos Midl MPro NBid SRms WBrk WCAu WCot WPnP
- anemone-centred EGrI MNrw WFar
- - red **new** MSwo
- - yellow LRHS NWbg
- 'Apple Blossom' WFar
- 'Apricot Blush' (Winter Jewels Series) CWGN
- apricot-flowered WFar
- Ashwood Evolution Group anemone yellow-flowered MAsh
- - Daybreak shades MAsh
- - double yellow-flowered (d) MAsh
- - Neon shades MAsh
- - Sunset shades MAsh
- - yellow-flowered MAsh
- Ashwood Garden hybrids ELan MAsh SRms
- - anemone-centred MAsh
- - double-flowered (d) MAsh
- - - green-spotted (d) EGrI
- Ballard's Group WFar
- black-flowered GMaP WFar
- Black Beauty ('Blck1'^(PBR)) WSpi
- 'Blue Lady' (Lady Series) CBcs LRHS NCou NGdn
- 'Blue Metallic Lady' (Lady Series) GAbr GMaP LRHS MHol WSpi
- 'Burgundy' EGrI
- 'Cherry Blossom' (Winter Jewels Series) CWGN
- 'Cinderella'^(PBR) (d) SPoG
- cream-flowered WFar
- Credale strain, double-flowered (d) LRHS
- dark-flowered WFar
- - picotee WFar
- - purple-flowered WFar
- - red-flowered WFar
- 'Decaya Pink' EGren
- deep red-flowered MHol WFar
- double (d) LAma MNrw WFar
- - black-flowered (d) EGren GAbr WFar
- - dark purple-flowered (d) EGrI WFar
- - green-flowered (d) CWnw EGrI WFar
- - picotee (d) WFar
- - pink-flowered (d) WCAu WFar
- - purple-flowered (d) EPfP WFar
- - red-flowered (d) GAbr Midl WFar
- - spotted (Lady Series) (d) EGrI
- - white-flowered (d) MSwo WCAu WFar
- - white picotee (d) EPfP GAbr WSpi
- - yellow-flowered (d) WFar
- - yellow-freckled (d) Midl
- 'Double Ellen Green' (d) Isha LRHS WTor
- 'Double Ellen Picotee' (d) CWGN EGrI LCro LRHS WCAu WTor
- 'Double Ellen Pink' (d) EGrI EHeP LBom LCro LRHS WTor
- 'Double Ellen Pink Spotted' (d) EGrI LCro
- 'Double Ellen Purple' (d) EGren LCro WTor
- 'Double Ellen Red' (d) EGrI EHeP LBom LCro LRHS Midl WTor
- 'Double Ellen Red Splash' (d) EGrI
- 'Double Ellen White' (d) CWGN EGrI LBom LCro SReu WTor

Helleborus

- 'Double Ellen White Spotted' (d) — EGrI LCro LRHS WCAu WTor
- 'Double Ellen Yellow' (d) — EGrI Midl
- 'Double Ellen Yellow Spotted' (d) **new** — WTor
- Farmyard anemone-centred — WFar
- - apple blossom — WFar
- - apricot — WFar
- - black — WFar
- - cream — WFar
- - - spotted — WFar
- - dark pink — WFar
- - double apricot (d) — WFar
- - - black (d) — WFar
- - - cream (d) — WFar
- - - - spotted (d) — WFar
- - - pink (d) — WFar
- - - - spotted (d) — WFar
- - - primrose (d) — WFar
- - - - spotted (d) — WFar
- - - red (d) — WFar
- - - slate-grey (d) — EGrI WFar
- - - waterlily (d) — EGrI WSpi
- - - white (d) — WFar
- - - - spotted (d) — WFar
- - green — WFar
- - - spotted — WFar
- - picotee — WFar
- - pink — WFar
- - - spotted — WFar
- - plum — WFar
- - primrose — WFar
- - - dark-eyed — WFar
- - - spotted — WFar
- - red — WFar
- - slate-grey — WFar
- - - spotted — WFar
- - white — WFar
- - - dark-eyed — WFar
- - - splash — WFar
- - - spotted — WFar
- - woodland — WFar
- 'Gold Red Star' — CWnw WSpi
- 'Golden Lotus' (d) — CWGN
- 'Green Ripple' — WFar
- green-flowered — WFar
- Harvington apricot — ENun LCro NBir NLar
- - double (d) — LRHS
- - - apricot (d) — ENun LCro
- - - blush (d) — ENun LCro
- - - chocolate (d) — ENun LCro LRHS
- - - cream speckled (d) — ENun LRHS SPoG
- - - dark purple (d) — Midl
- - - green speckled (d) — ENun LCro
- - - lilac speckled (d) — ENun LCro LRHS
- - - lime-green (d) — ENun LCro LRHS
- - - pink (d) — ENun LCro LRHS SPoG
- - - - speckled (d) — ENun LCro LRHS
- - - purple (d) — ENun LCro LRHS NBir NLar SPoG
- - - - cascade (d) — ENun
- - - red (d) — ENun LCro LRHS NBir NLar
- - - speckled (d) — SPoG
- - - white (d) — ENun LCro LRHS NBir NLar SPoG
- - - - speckled (d) — ENun LCro LRHS
- - - yellow (d) — ENun LCro LRHS NBir NLar
- - - - speckled (d) — ENun LRHS
- - dusky — ENun LCro LRHS
- - lime — ENun LCro
- - picotee — ENun LCro LRHS NBir NLar SPoG
- - pink — ENun LRHS NLar
- - - speckled — ENun LCro LRHS NLar SPoG
- - red — ENun LCro LRHS NLar SPoG
- - speckled — LRHS
- - white — ENun LCro LRHS NLar SPoG
- - - speckled — ENun LCro
- - yellow — ENun LRHS NLar SPoG
- - - dark eye — LCro LRHS
- - - gold nectaries — ENun
- - - speckled — ENun LCro LRHS NLar SPoG
- - - with dark eye **new** — LCro
- 'Harvington Black' — ENun LCro
- 'Harvington Blush Picotee' — SRms
- 'Harvington Shades of the Night' — ENun LCro LRHS NLar SPoG
- 'Harvington Smokey Blues' — ENun LCro LRHS
- 'Helen Ballard' — MCtn
- Hillier hybrids anemone-centred, pink — EGrI
- - yellow, magenta eye — LRHS
- Lady Series — EUrb LRHS
- maroon-flowered — WFar
- mauve freckled, double (d) — WFar
- 'Mrs Betty Ranicar' (d) — SRms
- nearly black-flowered — WFar
- 'Onyx Odyssey' — CWGN
- pale pink-flowered — WFar
- § Party Dress Group (d) — LSRN NLar WFar
- Picotee Group — LRHS NLar WFar WHoo
- pink freckled, double (d) — WFar
- 'Pink Lady' (Lady Series) — CBcs EGrI GQue LRHS NCou
- 'Pink Lady Spotted' (Lady Series) — EGren EGrI
- pink-flowered — WHoo
- pink-red-flowered — WFar
- plum-flowered — MMuc SEND
- 'Pluto' — WFar
- 'Pretty Ellen Pink' — GKev GMaP LCro LRHS WTor
- 'Pretty Ellen Purple' — EGrI WTor
- 'Pretty Ellen Red' — EGren LCro LRHS WTor
- 'Pretty Ellen White' — GKev GMaP LCro LRHS WTor
- 'Pretty Ellen White Spotted' **new** — WTor
- 'Primrose Picotee' — WFar
- purple-flowered — WFar
- Queen Series, double white-flowered (d) — Midl
- - 'Queen of the Night' — EGrI WSpi
- 'Red Lady' (Lady Series) — CBcs EGrI LSRN MHed MSwo
- 'Red Spotted' — EPfP
- red-flowered — WFar WHoo
- 'Single Black Pearl' — LRHS
- slate-grey — EGrI
- slaty blue-flowered — SEND
- 'Smokey Blue' — ELan
- smokey purple-flowered — LSRN
- § spotted — WCot WFar WHoo
- - cream — NBir WFar
- - double, pink (d) — EGrI WFar
- - - white (d) — WFar
- - - yellow (d) — EGrI GAbr WCAu WFar
- - green — WFar
- - ivory — WFar
- - light purple — WFar
- - pink — NBir SEND WFar WHoo
- - primrose — ELan WFar
- - white — CWnw MMuc NBir SEND WCAu WFar
- - yellow — WFar
- (Spring Promise Series) SP ALICE ('Hlr 270') (d) — LRHS

- - SP Anja Oudolf ('Hlr 200') ELan LRHS
- - SP Conny ('Hlr 160'^PBR) EHeP ELan EPfP
- - SP Elly ('Hlr 190'^PBR) (d) ELan EPfP
- - SP Grace ('Hlr 290') (d) EBee
- - SP John Hopkins ('Hlr 220') EHeP
- - SP Lily ('Hlr 210') (d) EPfP
- - SP Sophie ('Hlr 260') NLar
- 'Tricastin' MHtn
- 'Tutu'^PBR EBee EPfP LCro LRHS SPoG SRms WSpi
- 'Velvet' (Spring Series) ESwi
- (ViV Series) ViV Rosa ('Jhe00137'^PBR) MPri
- - ViV Valentina ('Jhe00113'^PBR) MPri SHar
- - ViV Victoria ('Jhe00091'^PBR) LBom LRHS MPri SHar
- Washfield double-flowered (d) EGrl Midl SRkn
- 'White Lady' (Lady Series) CBcs NCou
- 'White Lady Spotted' (Lady Series) EGren EGrl GKev GQue LRHS
- white-flowered GMaP MHed WFar WHoo
- white-veined WFar
- yellow-flowered SEND WFar WHoo
- - maroon eye ENun LCro
- 'Yellow Lady' (Lady Series) CBcs EGrl GKev MHed SReu
- (Ice N' Roses Series) LBom MPri
- HGC Ice N' Roses Barolo ('Coseh 4600'^PBR)
- HGC Ice N' Roses Bennotta ('Coseh 6600'^PBR) LRHS MPri
- HGC Ice N' Roses Bianco ('Coseh 5500') MPri
- HGC Ice N' Roses Brunello ('Coseh 6000'^PBR) MPri
- HGC Ice N' Roses Carlotta ('Coseh 6500'^PBR) LBom LRHS MPri
- HGC Ice N' Roses Dark Picotee ('Coseh 5100'^PBR) LBom LRHS MPri
- HGC Ice N' Roses Early Red ('Coseh 5300'^PBR) LBom LCro LRHS MPri
- HGC Ice N' Roses Early Rose ('Coseh 4000'^PBR) LBom LCro LRHS MAsh MPri
- HGC Ice N' Roses Frosted Rose ('Coseh 6300'^PBR) MPri
- HGC Ice N' Roses Merlot ('Coseh 4700'^PBR) LRHS MAsh MPri
- HGC Ice N' Roses Nightingale ('Coseh 6100') LRHS MPri
- HGC Ice N' Roses Picotee ('Coseh 5000'^PBR) LBom MPri
- HGC Ice N' Roses Red ('Coseh 4100'^PBR) ELan EPfP ESwi LBom LBuc LCro LRHS MPri
- HGC Ice N' Roses Rosado ('Coseh 5400'^PBR) LBom MPri
- HGC Ice N' Roses Rose ('Coseh 4200'^PBR) ELan LBom LRHS MAsh MPri
- HGC Ice N' Roses Rosetta ('Coseh 6400'^PBR) MPri
- HGC Ice N' Roses White ('Coseh 4500'^PBR) LBom LCro MPri
- × *lemonnierae* HGC Madame Lemonnier ('Lem 100'^PBR) EBee ELan EPfP
- *liguricus* MAsh
- - WM 230 MPhe
- *lividus* EBee LAma LRHS LWaG NBir SBrt SRms
- subsp. *corsicus* see *H. argutifolius*
- - dwarf LBom
- - 'Green Marble' LBom
- - 'Purple Ear' LRHS
- - 'Purple Rose' SRms
- - 'White Marble' LAma LRHS MAsh WFar
- 'Marshmallow' MHol WCot
- 'Moonshine'^PBR NLar
- *multifidus* MCtn NBir
- - WM 1316 MPhe
- subsp. *hercegovinus* GKev
- - WM 622 MPhe
- subsp. *istriacus* CBro
- - WM 9322 MPhe
- - WM 9324 MPhe
- subsp. *multifidus* MPhe
- WM 9833 from Croatia
- *niger* Widely available
- - Ashwood strain MAsh
- - 'Christmas Carol' EGren EHeP ELan EPfP LBom LCro LRHS LWaG SOrN
- - 'Double Fashion' (d) LRHS
- - double-flowered (d) CDor
- - 'Harvington Double Petticoat' (d) ENun
- - Harvington hybrids ENun LRHS MAsh
- - - double-flowered (d) LCro SPoG
- - HGC Diva ('Coseh 1090'^PBR) LRHS MPri
- - HGC Goldmarie ('Coseh 2020'^PBR) LRHS
- - HGC Jacob'^PBR ELan LRHS SRms
- - HGC Jacob Royal ('Coseh 240'^PBR) LRHS
- - HGC Jasper ('Coseh 1010'^PBR) LRHS
- - HGC Jesko ('Coseh 1000'^PBR) LBom LRHS
- - 'HGC Jesse' MPri
- - HGC Joel ('Coseh 210'^PBR) LRHS NLar
- - HGC Jonas ('Coseh 220'^PBR) LRHS
- - 'HGC Josef Lemper'^PBR NLar SRms
- - 'HGC Joshua'^PBR EGren LCro
- - HGC Snow Frills ('Coseh 230'^PBR) NLar
- - HGC Wintergold ('Coseh 2010'^PBR) LBom
- - 'Ivory Prince' see *H.* × *ericsmithii* 'Ivory Prince'
- - Mon Blanc ('Helni 16'^PBR) LBom
- - 'Mont Blanc' EPfP WCot
- - 'Potter's Wheel' EPfP NBir
- - 'Praecox' EPfP MHed
- × *nigercors* EGren LRHS Midl
- - 'Emma'^PBR EGren EPfP GMaP MHol NLar SHar SPoG WCot
- - HGC Ice Breaker Fancy ('Coseh 820'^PBR) EPfP
- - HGC Ice Breaker Max ('Coseh 750'^PBR) ELan EPfP LBuc LRHS MAsh MPri
- - 'Pink Beauty' NLar
- - 'Winter Passion'^PBR EPfP
- × *nigristern* see *H.* × *ericsmithii*
- *odorus* CBro MAsh
- - WM 312 from Bosnia MPhe
- - WM 9018 from Kosovo MPhe
- - WM 9415 MPhe
- - WM 9728 from Hungary MPhe
- subsp. *cyclophyllus* GKev MAsh

Hemerocallis 329

- - WM 1508	MPhe
orientalis misapplied	see *H.* × *hybridus*
orientalis ambig.	EGrI EHeP MPri
orientalis Lam.	CBcs CBro CWnw EHeP EWes GKev GQue LAma LRHS MPhe
- subsp. ***abchasicus*** (A. Braun) B. Mathew	CBro GKev WSpi
§ - - Early Purple Group	SRms
- subsp. ***guttatus*** misapplied	see *H.* × *hybridus* spotted
purpurascens	CBro GKev LCro NBir
- WM 815 from Romania	MPhe
- WM 9211 from Hungary	MPhe
- WM 9412	MPhe
Rodney Davey Marbled Group	MAsh
- (Frostkiss Series) ANNA'S RED ('Abcrd02'^{PBR})	CBcs EGren LBar LBom LBuc LCro LRHS LSou MAsh NWbg SHar SPad SPoG WFar
- - CHARMER ('Epb 21'^{PBR})	LRHS MAsh
- - CHERYL'S SHINE ('Epb 31'^{PBR})	CBcs LRHS NLar SPoG
- - DANA'S DULCET ('Epb 30'^{PBR})	EPfP LBuc LCro LRHS SPoG WCot WFar
- - DOROTHY'S DAWN ('Epb 29'^{PBR})	LRHS SPoG
- - GLENDA'S GLOSS ('Epb 25'^{PBR})	EGren EPfP LRHS WFar
- - ILLUMI LIME ('Epb 24'^{PBR})	LBar
- - MOLLY'S WHITE ('Epbrd01'^{PBR})	CBcs EGren LBom LRHS LSou MAsh WFar
- - MOONDANCE ('Epb 20'^{PBR})	CBcs LRHS MAsh WFar
- - PENNY'S PINK ('Abcrd01')	CBcs LBom LCro LRHS LSRN MAsh MHol SPoG WCot WFar
- - PIPPA'S PURPLE ('Rd09')	LBom LCro LRHS MAsh SPad
- - REANNA'S RUBY ('Epb 32')	LRHS
- - SALLY'S SHELL ('Epb 12'^{PBR})	LRHS SPoG
× *sahinii* 'Winterbells'^{PBR}	CBcs EBee EGren EGrI LCro LRHS SPoG SRms
'Sifra'^{PBR}	LCro
SP TIFFANY (Spring Promise Series)	LRHS
'Star of Passion'	ESwi
× *sternii*	CBcs ENun EPfP LBom LCro LRHS LSto NLar SPoG
- Aberconwy strain	MAsh
- 'Ashwood Silver'	MAsh
- Ashwood strain	LRHS MAsh
- 'Boughton Beauty'	EBee ELan LRHS WSpi
- 'Flame'	WSpi
- pewter-flowered	CSpe WSpi
- 'Silver Dollar'	LAma LBom LRHS LSRN LWaG MAsh SPoG SRms WFar WTor
- 'Tom'	LRHS WSpi
- 'Wilgenbroek'	LRHS
thibetanus	GEdr MAsh
torquatus	MPhe
- WM 609 from Montenegro	MPhe
- WM 617 from Serbia	MPhe
- WM 9820 from Bosnia	MPhe
- 'Dido' (d)	WFar
- double-flowered WM 621 from Montenegro (d)	MPhe
- - hybrids (d)	Midl
- Party Dress Group	see *H.* × *hybridus* Party Dress Group
'Verboom Beauty'	CDoC LBom LCro LRHS
viridis	GKev LEdu SRms
- WM 444 from Italy	MPhe
- WM 1303 from Slovenia	MPhe
- WM 9723 from Italy	MPhe
- subsp. ***occidentalis***	GKev
- - WM 1340 from Germany	MPhe
- - WM 1344 from Spain	MPhe
- - WM 9501 from Wales	MPhe
WALBERTON'S ROSEMARY ('Walhero'^{PBR}) ♀^{H7}	EPfP LCro LRHS MAsh SHar SPoG WSpi
'White Beauty'^{PBR}	LRHS NLar SPoG WCot
(Winter Ballet Series) HGC WINTER BALLET LEONA ('Coseh 7300'^{PBR})	LBom LRHS MPri
- HGC WINTER BALLET LIAH ('Coseh 7100'^{PBR})	LRHS MPri
- HGC WINTER BALLET LIARA ('Coseh 5600'^{PBR})	LRHS MPri
- HGC WINTER BALLET LINDA ('Coseh 6900'^{PBR})	LRHS MPri
- HGC WINTER BALLET LISANN ('Coseh 5900'^{PBR})	LRHS MPri

Heloniopsis (Melanthiaceae)

acutifolia B&SWJ 6817	WCru
- B&SWJ 6836	WCru
japonica	see *H. orientalis*
leucantha B&SWJ 11148	WCru
§ ***orientalis***	CBct CTtf EPot
- var. ***breviscapa***	GEdr LEdu SMad WCru WPGP
- - B&SWJ 5873	WCru
- - 'A-so'	LEdu WCru
- var. ***flavida*** 'Snow White'	GEdr
tubiflora	GEdr
- 'Temple Blue'	CBct EBee EPfP LEdu SMad WCru
umbellata	EBee LEdu
- B&SWJ 1839	WCru
- B&SWJ 3732	EBee

Helosciadium (Apiaceae)

§ ***nodiflorum***	CAgr ELin

Helwingia (Helwingiaceae)

chinensis	CBcs CTsd EGrI ESwi EWld GEdr LRHS MHtn MPie NLar SEND SMad SPoG WLov WPGP
- broad-leaved	EBee NLar SIvy WPGP
- narrow-leaved	EBee ESwi
himalaica	CExl ESwi SBrt
japonica broad-leaved	WPGP
omeiensis	EWld

Hemerocallis ✿ (Asphodelaceae)

'Aabaa'	EWoo
'Aabachee'	CBgR
'Above the Clouds'	EWoo
'Admiral'	WNHG
'Admiral's Braid'	EWoo
'Aerea'	MHol
'African Chant'	ELan
'Ageless Beauty'	ELon LAma
'Ahoya'	CBgR
'Alabama Jubilee'	WNHG
'Alakazam'	EWoo
'Alan'	EBlo LRHS
'Alan Adair'	CSpe
'Alexander the Great'	WHrl
'All American Chief' ♀^{H6}	WNHG
'All American Plum'	WHrl
'All American Windmill'	CBgR EWoo WHrl
'All Fired Up'	ELon
'Allegiance'	WNHG
'Alli Sheldon'	ECha

Hemerocallis

altissima — EAri ECha EWoo GKev MNrw SDix
'Always Afternoon' ♀H6 — CBgR EGrI EWoo MNrw WCAu WHrl WNHG
'Amazon Amethyst' — WCAu
'Ambassador' — CBgR
'Amber Classic' — ELon
'American Revolution' — EGrI ELon ESgI EWoo GBin MHol SBea SMad SPel SPoG WCot WHrl WNHG WSpi
'Anna Warner' — ELon MMuc SEND
'Annabelle's Ghost' — CBgR
'Annie Welch' — ELon
'Antique Lavender' — WCAu
'Anzac' — CBro ECha GArf LShi NGdn
'Apache Bandana' — EWoo
'Apollodorus' — WHrl WNHG
'Apple Court Ruby' — ELon
'Applique' — EUrb
'Après Moi' — NLar
'Apricot Beauty' (d) — WSpi
'Apricot Velvet' — CBgR
'Arachnophobia' — EWoo
'Arctic Snow' ♀H6 — CBgR CBro CMac ECrc ELon EWoo GJos LAma MNrw SReu
'Asian Artistry' — WNHG
'Atlas' — WGwG
'Autumn Prince' — EWoo
'Autumn Red' — CBcs CBgR CFis GKin LRHS MMuc NBir SEND SReu WCot
'Autumn Wood' — ESgI
'Avant Garde' Russell — NCth WCAu
'Avon Crystal Rose' — WNHG
'Awesome Blossom' — MNrw SMrm SReu WHrl
'Baby Blues' — WNHG
'Baby Red Eyes' — WFar
'Baja' — WFar
'Bali Hai' — SRms WHrl WSpi
'Bamboo Blackie' — EWoo
'Banana Cream Beauty' — WSpi
'Barbara Mitchell' — EWoo WCAu WNHG
'Barbaresco' — EWoo
'Baroni' — ECha LShi
'Bat Signal' — EWoo
'Battle Hymn' — WCAu
'Beautiful Edgings' — ESgI
'Bela Lugosi' — ECrc ELon EWoo GQue LRHS LSRN MBNS NBro NQui WHrl WNHG
'Believe It' — WNHG
'Bengal Fire' — WNHG
'Berlin Red' — ECha ELon MNrw WFar
'Berliner Ring' — GBin
'Bertie Ferris' — EWoo NLar
'Best Kept Secret' — EWoo
'Best Seller' — LAma
'Bette Davis Eyes' — CBgR
'Betty's Pick' — EWoo
'Beyond Riches' — NCth
'Big Kiss' (d) — ELon LRHS
'Big Smile' — CWCL MBNS MNrw
'Big Time Happy' — SAth SPoG
'Big World' — CBgR
'Bitsy' — ELon
'Black Ambrosia' — EWoo
'Black Arrowhead' — EPfP WCAu
'Black Emanuelle' — NLar WFar
'Black Eye' — WNHG
'Black Eyed Belle' — EWoo WNHG
'Black Eyed Stella' — WSpi
'Black Eyed Susan' — WNHG
'Black Handlebars' — EWoo
'Black Ice' — ELon EWoo
'Black Knight' — EWoo NLar SRms
'Black Magic' — CBro EPfP ESgI GKin GMaP LSRN MArl MHer NBir NGdn SPoG WHrl WNHG
'Black Plush' — EUrb EWoo SReu WCAu
'Black Prince' — EAri EGren GJos LRHS MBNS
'Black Stockings' — CTtf EBee ELon EWes LAma MHol NLar WCAu
'Blackberry Candy' — GKin MHol WCAu
'Blackberry Sherbert' — WFar
'Blizzard Bay' — WFar
'Blue Sheen' — CMac GMaP MHol WFar WSpi
'Blueberry Breakfast' — WNHG
'Blueberry Candy' — EGren EMor GJos WNHG
'Blushing Belle' — NBro
'Bogeyman' — LBar
'Bold Courtier' — CBgR
'Bonanza' — CBcs CBgR CBro EBlo EGrI EUrb LRHS NBir NBro NGdn NLar SAth SEND WCAu WCot WFar WNHG
'Bone China' — WNHG
'Boney Maroney' — EWoo
'Booroobin Magic' — EWoo
'Border Lord' — EWoo
'Bourbon Kings' — WHrl
'Bowl of Roses' — WCAu
'Breathless Beauty' — WNHG
'Bridget' — ELan
'Bright Side' — CBgR
'Brocaded Gown' — ELan
'Brown Billows' — EWoo
'Brown Exotica' — EWoo
'Brown Witch' — ELon EWoo
'Browns Ferry Royalty' — WFar
'Brutus' — WHrl
'Bud Producer' — CBgR
'Bumble Bee' — WNHG
'Burlesque' — WCot
'Burning Daylight' ♀H6 — CAby CBgR CMHG EBlo EHeP ESgI LRHS MArl MNrw SRms WCAu WCot WFar
'Butterpat' — EBlo
'Butterscotch' — WFar
'Buzz Bomb' — ECrc ELon GKin LRHS LSRN MArl MHol NGdn WCAu WFar WNHG
'Calico Jack' — SPad
'Calypso' — EWoo
'Camelot Green' — WNHG
'Canadian Border Patrol' — LCro LRHS NLar
'Canadian Goose' — SNoN
'Canary Glow' — WFar WNHG
'Canary Wings' — CBgR
'Cape Breton' — MHol
'Capulina' — EWoo
'Cara Mia' — CBgR NBir WFar WNHG
'Caramel Taffy' — WHrl
'Caribbean Jack Dolan' — EWoo
'Caribbean Purple Spires' — WNHG
'Carolicolossal' — ELon
'Carolina Cranberry' — ELan
'Caroline Taylor' — WHrl
'Carrick Wildon' — WFar
'Cartwheels' — EGrI GKin GMaP NBro SRms WCAu WFar
'Catherine Woodberry' — CAby CBcs CBgR CBWd CDoC CMac EBee ECha EHeP ELan ELon EPPr EWoo GQue LRHS MMuc MNrw NBir NGdn NSti SEND SMad WCAu WCot WFar WGwG
'Cathy's Sunset' — EWhm GKin LRHS MBNS NBro NGdn

Hemerocallis 331

Cultivar	Sources
'Cedar Waxwing'	MNrw
'Celebration of Angels'	MHol
'Changing Latitudes'	WHrl
'Charles Johnston'	CBgR EWoo LRHS
'Chartwell'	EWoo
'Cheerful Note'	WNHG
'Cheese and Wine'	EPfP MHol
'Cherry Cheeks'	EBlo ELan ELon MHol MNrw WCAu WCot WFar
'Cherry Eyed Pumpkin' ♀H6	WCAu
'Cherry Valentine'	ELon NWbg
'Chesapeake Crablegs'	EWoo
'Chesières Lunar Moth'	ELon EWoo
'Chicago Apache'	CLil ELon EPfP EWoo NBir WNHG WSpi
'Chicago Aztec'	ELon
'Chicago Blackout'	LRHS WCAu WCot WNHG
'Chicago Cherry'	WNHG
'Chicago Fire'	EUrb
'Chicago Heirloom'	WCAu
'Chicago Jewel'	ELon NSti
'Chicago Knockout'	ELan EWoo
'Chicago Peach'	NBir WCAu
'Chicago Petticoats'	WFar WNHG
'Chicago Picotee Promise'	WNHG
'Chicago Picotee Queen'	WNHG
'Chicago Queen'	WNHG
'Chicago Royal Robe'	CWCL EBlo ELon NBid SRms WCot
'Chicago Silver'	SMrm
'Chicago Star'	WNHG
'Chicago Sunrise'	EBlo ELon EPfP GMaP NGdn WCot WNHG
'Chicago Weathermaster'	ESgI
'Chief Four Fingers'	EWoo
'Children's Festival'	CMac EBlo GMaP NLar WFar
'Chinese Coral'	EWoo
'Chinese Imp'	NLar
'Chiricahua Warrior'	EWoo
'Chokecherry Mountain'	EWoo
'Chorus Line'	WNHG
'Christine Lynn'	WNHG
'Christmas Is'	CBgR CLil CMac ELon GBin GKin WCot WHrl WNHG
'Cimarron Knight'	CBgR
'Cindy's Eye'	WCot
citrina ♀H6	CBgR CMac EBee EWoo GKev MBel WCAu WCot WHoo WHrl
'Classic Caper'	WNHG
'Claudine'	ELon
'Cleo'	EWoo WHrl
'Cleopatra'	ELon EWoo
'Clothed in Glory'	WCot
'Coburg Fright Wig'	EWoo
'Colonel Joe'	WNHG
'Coming Up Roses'	ELon
'Concorde Nelson'	ELon
'Conspicua'	CBgR
'Contessa'	CBro EBlo
'Cool It'	MPie NLar WHrl
'Copper Windmill'	CBgR ELon WNHG
'Coral Crab'	EWoo
'Coral Mist'	ECrc
'Coral Sparkler'	WNHG
'Coral Taco'	EWoo
'Corky'	CAby CBro ECha ELon EPfP ESgI GMaP LEdu LRHS LSRN MBel MNrw NGdn NLar SDix SMHy SPel WCAu WFar WSpi
'Cosmic Hummingbird'	WNHG
'Cosmopolitan'	GBin
'Country Club'	GMaP
'Court Magician'	ESgI EWoo
'Court Troubadour'	ELon
'Cranberry Baby'	MHol WHoo WNHG
'Crazy Pierre'	ELon ESgI EWoo WHrl
'Cream Drop'	EPPr GMaP GQue NBro NGdn NLar NSti StAn WCot WFar WHrl
'Crimson Pirate'	CBgR CLil CMac CWnw ECrc EHeP ELon EUrb EWoo GJos GQue LRHS LSRN NBir NEoE NQui SAth SMHy SPlb SPoG WCAu WFar WHrl
'Croesus'	SRms
'Crystal Pinot'	ELon
'Curls'	CBgR LRHS
'Curly Cinnamon Windmill' ♀H6	ESgI
'Custard Candy' ♀H6	EWoo GKin LCro LRHS WCAu WNHG
'Cynthia Mary'	GKin SRGP
'Daily Dollar'	NGdn
'Dallas Star'	WHrl
'Dances with Giraffes'	EWoo
'Dancing Crab'	CBgR
'Dancing Summerbird'	ELon
'Daring Deception'	EGrI ELon EMor MNrw WCAu
'Darius'	WNHG
'Dark Sprite'	EWoo
'David Holman'	WNHG
'Davidson Update'	WNHG
'Daylight'	WNHG
'Debary Canary'	EWoo
'Decatur Ballerina'	WNHG
'Decatur Captivation'	WNHG
'Decatur Dictator'	WNHG
'Decatur Festival'	WNHG
'Decatur Imp'	WHrl
'Decatur Jewel'	WNHG
'Decatur Rhythm'	WNHG
'Decatur Supreme'	WNHG
'Decatur Treasure Chest'	WNHG
'Desert Dreams'	WCot
'Destined to See'	CBro CLil ELon EWhm NBir NBro SPad WCot WHrl WNHG
'Diabolique'	EWoo
'Diamond Dust'	NLar WSpi
'Dick Kitchingman'	CBgR
'Dipped in Ink'	ESgI
'Distant Galaxy'	WCAu
'Divertissment'	CBgR ELon ESgI EWoo WHrl
'Dominic'	EUrb EWoo WFar WNHG
'Don Stevens'	WHrl
'Don's Wild Heather'	ELon
'Dorethe Louise'	CBgR
'Dorothy McDade'	EWoo MNrw
'Dot Paul'	ELan
'Double Action' (d)	ELon
'Double Cream' (d)	WCot
'Double Cutie' (d)	CCBP NLar SRms WNHG
'Double Dawn Surprise' (d)	ELon
'Double Delicious' (d)	WCot
'Double Dream' (d)	EGrI WHrl
'Double Firecracker' (d)	NBro NLar
'Double Gardenia' (d)	WNHG
'Double Oh Seven' (d)	ELon
'Double Red Royal' (d)	EGrI
'Double River Wye' (d)	CLil GBin GQue MHer NGdn WBrk WCAu WCot WFar WHoo WHrl WNHG
'Dowager Queen'	WNHG
'Dragon's Eye'	ELon EWoo WNHG
'Dream Keeper'	EWoo
'Droopy Drawers'	ELon

'Druid's Chant'	EWoo
'Duke of Durham'	EWoo
'Duke of Earl'	CBgR
dumortieri	CAgr CBro CCBP EBee EBlo ECha EWhm EWoo LRHS MMuc NBid NBir NSti SEND WCot WNHG
- B&SWJ 1283	WCru
'Dune Needlepoint'	WHrl
'Dunkle Prinzessin'	GBin
'Dutch Beauty'	WFar
'Dutch Gold'	MNrw
'Earl of Warwick'	CBgR
'Earlianna'	ELon
'Easy Ned'	ELon EWoo
'Ed Brown'	EWoo
'Ed Murray'	WCAu
'Edgar Brown'	WCot
'Edge Ahead'	CMac CMHG ESgI GKin LRHS WCAu WHrl
'Edge of Darkness'	NLar NSti WFar
'Edna Spalding'	EBlo
'Eenie Allegro'	CBro
'Eenie Fanfare'	NBir
'Eenie Weenie'	CBro ELon NBro SRms
'Eenie Weenie Non-stop'	EGrI EPPr
'Eggplant Electricity'	EWoo
'Eggplant Escapade' ♀H6	CBgR ELon WHrl
'Egyptian Ibis'	EWoo WNHG
'Eight Miles High'	ESgI
'El Desperado'	CLil ELon EWoo GQue LRHS MBNS MHol WCAu WCot WHrl
'Elaine Strutt'	WCot WNHG WSpi
'Elegant Candy' ♀H6	CMac EWoo WCAu
'Eleonor'	WFar
'Elfin Daydream'	EWoo
'Elizabeth Salter'	CWCL ELon NLar
'Eloquent Silence'	WNHG
'Enchanted Forest'	WCAu
'Entrapment'	WFar
esculenta	SMad
'Etched Eyes'	EWoo
'Evelyn Claar'	CMac
(EveryDaylily Series)	LBar
EVERYDAYLILY CERISE ('Ver00157'PBR)	
- EVERYDAYLILY CREAM ('Ver001112'PBR)	LBar LSou
- EVERYDAYLILY GOLD ('Ver00329')	LBar
- EVERYDAYLILY ORANGE ('Ver00326')	LBar
- EVERYDAYLILY PINK CREAM ('Ver00323'PBR)	LRHS
- EVERYDAYLILY PINK WING ('Ver00213'PBR)	LSou
- EVERYDAYLILY PUNCH YELLOW ('Ver00204'PBR)	LRHS
- EVERYDAYLILY RED RIBS ('Ver00322'PBR)	LBar LCro LRHS MNrw
- EVERYDAYLILY ROSE ('Ver00198'PBR)	LBar LRHS
'Exploded Pumpkin'	EBee
'Eye Catching'	EWoo
'Eye on America'	ELon
'Ezekiel'	WHrl
'Fairest Love'	WHrl
'Fall Farewell'	WNHG
'Fantasia'	EWoo
'Fellow'	ELon
'Ferris Wheel'	EWoo
'Final Touch'	CBgR NBro
'Fire Dance'	ELon
'Fire from Heaven'	WHrl
'Fire Tree'	CBgR ELon
'Firestorm'	EWoo
'Flaming Firebird'	WNHG
'Flaming Sword'	WBrk
'Flasher'	EBlo
flava	see *H. lilioasphodelus*
'Flip Flop'	EWoo
'Fluttering Beauty' (d)	EWoo
'Fly Catcher'	CBgR
'Fol de Rol'	EWoo
'Fooled Me' ♀H6	EPfP LRHS NCth WNHG
'For the Good Times'	EWoo
'Forestlake Ragamuffin'	ELon
forrestii	EPot GKev
'Forsooth'	CBgR
'Forty Second Street'	ELon
'Fragrant Reflections'	EPfP LRHS MPro NCth
'Fragrant Returns'	EGrI ESgI LEdu NLit SPoG
'Francis of Assisi'	EWoo
'Frank Smith'	WCAu
'Frans Hals'	CBro CMac CWCL EBlo ECrc EGren EPfP EUrb EWoo GKin GQue LAma LRHS MHol MMuc MNrw MPie NBro NGdn NLar SEND SPoG SRms WCAu WFar WGwG WNHG
'Free Wheelin'	WNHG
'Fresh Air'	MNrw WNHG
'Fritz Schroer'	CBgR
'Frosted Vintage Ruffles'	EPfP MNrw WCAu
'Fuchsia Dream'	ESgI
fulva	CoPl EAri GPSL MMuc NBir SEND SRms WBrk WHrl
- B&SWJ 8647	WCru
- 'Flore Pleno' (d)	CMac GBin NBir NBro NGdn NSti SRms WBrk WCAu WHrl WTre
§ - 'Green Kwanso' (d)	CBgR LRHS WFar
- var. *kwanso*	GMaP
- - B&SWJ 6328	WCru
- var. *littorea*	CMac StAn
- var. *rosea*	EBee EBlo LRHS WCot
§ - 'Variegated Kwanso' (d/v)	ELon EPPr EWoo NBir WCot WFar WHer WHrl
- yellow-variegated (v)	WCot
'Gadsden Goliath'	WNHG
'Gadsden Meshach'	ELon
'Gale Storm'	WNHG
'Garden Portrait'	EWoo
'Gay Octopus'	CBgR WHrl
'Gay Troubadour'	EWoo
'Gemini'	ELon
'Gemini Jack' (d)	ESgI
'Geneva Firetruck'	WHrl
'Gentle Shepherd'	CBcs CBro CSpe ECha EHeP ELon EPfP ESgI EWoo GMaP LCro LRHS MHer NBir NLar NSti SPoG WCAu WCot WGwG
'George Cunningham'	EBlo EGrI ELan NBir WCAu WFar
'George David'	WHrl
'Georgette Belden'	GKin WNHG
'Georgia Cream' (d)	NLar
'Get All Excited'	ELon
'Giant Moon'	CBgR EBlo SRms
'Giddy Go Round'	EWoo
'Give Me Eight'	EWoo
'Glacier Bay'	EWoo
'Gleeman Song'	CBgR
'Going Bananas'PBR	WCot
'Golden Bell'	NGdn
'Golden Chance'	WCAu

'Golden Chimes'	CBgR CBro CPud EBee ECha ECrc EGren EGrl EHeP EPPr ESgI EWoo GMaP LCro LEdu LRHS LSRN MHer MNrw NBir NLar SDix SPoG WCot WFar WHoo	'James Marsh'	CBgR EWoo NSti WCAu WCot WFar WNHG
		'Janice Brown'	EGrl EWoo NLar WHrl
		'Janie Wilson'	ESgI WNHG
'Golden Ginkgo'	WNHG	'Jan's Twister'	MNrw WHrl
'Golden Marvel'	EWoo	'Jenny Wren'	EPPr EWoo NBro
'Golden Prize'	NGdn WCot	'Jersey Jim'	EWoo
Golden Zebra ('Malja'PBR) (v)	NLar NSti SRms WNHG	'Jewel Case'	WNHG
		'Joan Senior'	CBWd ECha EGren ELan EPfP EUrb EWoo GKin LSRN MNrw NGdn NSti SRms WCAu WCot WNHG WSpi
'Graceland'	WHrl		
'Grand Masterpiece'	NGdn WFar		
'Grand Palais'	ELon		
'Granite City Towhead'	ELon EWoo	'Jockey Club' (d)	WHrl
'Grape Arbor'	WNHG	'John Benoot'	WNHG
'Grape Harvest'	WNHG	'Johnny Come Lately'	WNHG
'Grape Magic'	WCot	'Joie de Vivre'	EWoo
'Grape Velvet'	CSpe ESgI EWoo MHer NSti SRms WCAu WNHG	'Jolly Red Giant'	EWoo
		'Jordan'	LSRN
'Green Eyes Wink'	MHol	'Journey to Oz'	EWoo
'Green Flutter'	CTtf GQue LRHS NBir NGdn NSti WSpi	'Judge Roy Bean'	EWoo WHrl
		'Judy Davidson'	WNHG
'Green Widow'	ESgI EWoo	'June Melody'	WNHG
'Grumbly'	ELan	'Jungle Beauty'	CBgR WNHG
'Gypsy Sweetheart'	WNHG	'Justin June'	WHrl
'Hamlet'	WNHG	'Kansas Kitten'	EWoo
'Happy Returns'	EBlo ECha ELan EPfP EWoo LCro LRHS MBel NGdn SRms WCAu	'Karen's Curls' ♀H6	WNHG
		'Kasia'	WHrl
'Harbor Blue'	ELon	'Kathleen Salter'	EWoo
'Hawaiian Nights'	WNHG	'Keene'	EWoo
'Hawk'	ELon	'Kenyan Sun'	EWoo
'Heavenly Angel Ice'	ELon	'Kevin Michael Coyne'	EWoo
'Heavenly Curls'	WNHG	'Kindly Light'	EWoo
'Heavenly Orange Blaze'	EWoo	'King James'	EWoo
'Heidi Eidelweiss'	EWoo	'King's Throne'	WNHG
'Heirloom Lace'	WCAu	'Kwanso Flore Pleno'	see H. fulva 'Green Kwanso'
'Hemlock'	WNHG	'Kwanso Flore Pleno Variegata'	see H. fulva 'Variegated Kwanso'
'Her Majesty's Wizard'	ELon		
'Here Lies Butch'	ELon	'Lacy Doily'	WCAu
'Heron's Cove'	EWoo	'Lacy Marionette'	ELon EWoo
'High Tor'	ELon SHar WHrl WOld	'Lady Betty Fretz'	EBee
'Highland Lord' (d)	WCAu WNHG	'Lady Fingers'	CBgR WHrl
'Holiday Mood'	ELan	'Lady Liz'	WNHG
'Holly Dancer' ♀H6	EWoo	'Lady Neva' ♀H6	CBgR ELon
'Hornby Castle'	CBro EBlo	'Lady Tiger'	WNHG
'Hot Town'	ELan	'Ladykin'	ELon
'Hot Wire'	WNHG	'Lake Norman Spider'	EWoo
'Houdini'	ESgI WCAu WNHG	'Lark Song'	EBlo LRHS WFar WHrl
'House of Bluelights'	WNHG	'Late Summer Rose'	WNHG
'How's the Weather up There?'	EWoo	'Laughing Feather'	EWoo
		'Laughing Giraffe'	WCot
'Hubbles Buddy'	EWoo	'Laughton Tower'	SMHy
'Humdinger'	WCot	'Laurena'	EWoo
'Hyperion'	CMac EBee EBlo ECha ELon EUrb EWoo GKin LRHS MArl MHol NBid NGdn SMrm SPoG WCAu WCot WGwG WNHG	'Lavender Blue Baby'	MHol
		'Lavender Deal'	MNrw WNHG
		'Lavender Light'	EWoo
		'Lavender Memories'	WNHG
'Ice Carnival'	ELon NGdn NLar WSpi	'Lavender Showstopper'	WCAu
'Icecap'	CBgR WNHG	'Lavender Tonic'	WNHG
'Icy Lemon'	WNHG	'Lavender Tutu'	LCro
'In Depth' (d)	EWoo NBro NLar WCot WHrl	'Legs Limmer'	EWoo
'In Strawberry Time'	WNHG	'Lemon Bells'	GKin GMaP LRHS MAvo NBro NCth SHar WCAu WSpi
'Indian Fandango'	EWoo		
'Indian Paintbrush'	ELon NBir WCAu WNHG	'Lemon Dessert'	ELon
'Inner View'	WNHG	'Lemon Fellow'	EWoo
'Invitation to Immortality'	EWoo	'Lemon Meringue Twist'	EWoo
'Irish Elf'	ELon SHar	'Lemon Mint'	ELon
'Iron Gate Glacier'	EPPr MBNS	'Let it Rip'	EWoo
'Irresistible Charm'	LRHS	'Licorice Candy'	ELon
'Islesworth'	EWoo	'Light the Way'	LRHS SPoG WCot WNHG
'Itsy Bitsy Spider'	CBgR EWoo	'Light Years Away'	ELon
'Ivelyn Brown'	EWoo	'Lilac Wine'	ECha

§ *lilioasphodelus* — Widely available
'Lilly Dache' — EWoo
'Lilting Lavender' — ELon WCAu WNHG
'Limited Edition' — EWoo
'Lin Wright' — EWoo
'Lines of Splendor' — EWoo
'Little Anna Rosa' — NWbg
'Little Bugger' — ELon
'Little Deeke' — WHrl
'Little Fantastic' — ELon
'Little Girl' — ELon
'Little Grapette' — ELon NLar NSti SAth SMad WCAu WNHG
'Little Men' — WCAu
'Little Miss Manners' — NLar
'Little Missy' — CBgR WNHG
'Little Red Hen' — ECha GKin NBir NBro NGdn WFar
'Little Show Stopper' — NBro NLar
'Little Sweet Talk' — ELon
'Little Tawny' — ELon
'Little Wart' — WHrl
'Little Wine Cup' — CMac CMHG EBee ECrc ELon ESgI GKin GMaP LRHS NBir NGdn SMrm SPoG SRms WCAu WTre
'Little Women' — WHrl
'Lobo Lucy' — ELon
'Lois Burns' — EWoo
'Lola Branham' — EWoo
'Long John Silver' — ELon
'Long Stocking' — EWoo WCot
'Longfields Anwar' — EGrl EWoo
'Longfields Bandit' — EWoo
'Longfields Beauty' — CWnw EWoo LRHS
'Longfields Maxim' (d) — ELon MHol
'Longfields Pearl' — LRHS
'Longfields Pride' — CLil SRms
'Longfields Purple Eye' — NLar
'Longfields Twins' — WCot WFar
'Longfields Whoopy' — EGrl ELon LAma WCAu
'Longfields X Factor' — LAma
longituba B&SWJ 4576 — WCru
'Look at Me' — ELan
'Lori Goldston' — EWoo
'Lucille Lennington' — WNHG
'Lullaby Baby' — NLar WNHG
'Luscious Honeydew' — WNHG
'Lusty Lealand' — CLil
'Luxury Lace' — CAgr ELan GKin NBir NGdn NLar WCAu WFar WHrl WNHG
'Lynn Hall' — NLar WSpi
'Mabel Fuller' — CBgR WHrl
'Macbeth' — EGrl LAma WNHG
'Mad Max' — ELon EWoo
'Madeline Nettles Eyes' — EBee ELon
'Mahogany Magic' ♀H6 — ELon
'Malaysian Monarch' — WNHG
'Malaysian Spice' — WNHG
'Maleny Mite' — EWoo
'Maleny Think Big' — EWoo
'Mallard' — CBgR EBee EBlo ECha MHer NBir WCot
'Man on Fire' — WNHG
'Margaret Perry' — MNrw NLar
'Margery Fish' — SDix SMHy
'Margo Reed Indeed' — EWoo WNHG
'Marilyn Siwik' — WNHG
'Marion Vaughn' — CBcs EBee ECha EPfP EWoo GKin GMaP NSti SDix SRGP WCAu WCot WFar WHoo
'Mariska' — WNHG
'Marked by Lydia' — ELon
'Martie Everest' — EWoo
'Mary Ethel Anderson' — EWoo
'Mary Todd' — EBee WCAu WNHG
'Masada' — WNHG
'Mask of Time' — ESgI
'Mauna Loa' — ECha ELon GQue MAsh MNrw NLar WCAu WCot WNHG
'May May' — CBgR ELon
'Meadow Mist' — ELon
'Meadow Sprite' — ELon WCot
'Mephistopheles' — EWoo
'Merry Moppet' — EWoo
'Metaphor' — MHol
'Michele Coe' — GKin NBro NGdn WCAu WFar WHrl
'Mico' — ELon
middendorffii — CMac EBee EBlo EWoo GMaP LRHS NSti WSpi
'Midnight Mantis' — WNHG
'Midnight Raider' — EWoo
'Mighty Goliath' — EWoo
'Mikado' — CMac WNHG
'Mike Reed' — WNHG
'Milady Greensleeves' — EWoo WHrl
'Milanese Mango' — EWoo
'Mildred Mitchell' — ELon NLar WCAu WHrl
'Ming Porcelain' — WCAu WNHG
'Mini Pearl' — CPud ELon LRHS MPie
'Mini Stella' — CBro LSou WFar
minor — EBlo EPPr LRHS SRms
– B&SWJ 8841 — WCru
'Miracle Maid' — WNHG
'Miss Jessie' — EWoo
'Missenden' — CBgR MNrw
'Misty Twisty' — EWoo
'Molokai' — NLar
'Moment of Truth' — NCth
'Mont Royal Demitasse' — ELon
'Moonlight Masquerade' — CLil WNHG
'Moonlight Orchid' — WHrl
'Moonlit Caress' — NBro
'Moonlit Masquerade' ♀H6 — ELon MNrw NLar SEND SRms WCAu WHrl
'Moonlit Summerbird' — WNHG
'Moontraveller' — WCot
'Morning Sun' — WCot
'Morocco' — WNHG
'Morocco Red' — CBro ELan
'Moses' Fire' — MHol NLar WFar
'Mossy Glade' — CBgR
'Mount Echo Sunrise' — EWoo
'Mountain Laurel' — GKin WChS WFar WGwG
'Mountain Top Experience' — EWoo
'Moussaka' — CWGN WCAu WFar
'Mrs Hugh Johnson' — WHrl
'Muffet's Little Friend' — WHrl WNHG
'Muscle and Blood' — EWoo
'Mynelle's Starfish' — WHrl
'Nanuq' — ELon
'Naomi Ruth' — WCAu
'Nashville' — CBro ELan WHrl
'Nashville Lights' — CBgR
'Nefertiti' — CBgR ELon NBir WCAu WNHG
'New Wine' — WNHG
'Neyron Rose' — GKin NGdn
'Night Beacon' — CBgR CLil EGrl ELon EWoo GKin MNrw MPie NLar WCAu WHrl WNHG
'Night Embers' — ELon EWoo LAma NGdn NLar SPad WCAu WHrl

'Night Raider'	CBgR WNHG		MNrw NBir NGdn SEND WBrk
'Nigrette'	StAn		WCAu WCot WFar WNHG
'Nile Crane'	CBgR CWnw ELon LRHS MNrw WCAu	'Pink Dazzler'	WNHG
'Nob Hill'	EBlo ELon LRHS WHrl	'Pink Dream'	CBgR NBir
'Nona's Garnet Spider'	ELon	'Pink Lady'	MNrw SRms
'North Wind Dancer' ♀H6	EWoo	'Pink Monday'	WNHG
'Norton Beauté'	WCot	'Pink Puff'	NBir NLar
'Norton Eyed Seedling'	WNHG	'Pink Sundae'	ECha WHrl
'Not Forgotten'	WNHG	'Pink Super Spider'	EWoo
'Nova'	ELon	'Pink Windmill'	ELon EWoo
'Nuclear Meltdown'	EWoo	'Pirate's Patch'	EWoo WCot
'Nutmeg Elf'	EWoo	'Pixie Parasol'	WNHG WSpi
'Oakes Love'	EWoo MNrw	'Plum Beauty'	NLar
'Ocean Rain'	WNHG	'Plumas Lake'	WNHG
× *ochroleuca*	SMHy	'Pony'	ELon WNHG
'Ode to Oz'	EWoo	'Prague Spring'	WCAu WHrl WNHG
'Ojo de Dios'	EWoo	'Prairie Belle'	NLar
'Old Tangiers' ♀H6	WNHG	'Prairie Blue Eyes'	MSwo SPlb WCAu WCot WHrl
'Old-fashioned Maiden'	EWoo	'Prairie Charmer'	SEND WHrl
'Olfactory Evidence'	EWoo	'Prairie Moonlight'	NLar
'Olive Bailey Langdon'	ESgI LCro WCot	'Precious d'Oro'	GQue SAth
'Olive's Odd One'	ELon	'Pretty Miss'	WGwG
'Oloroso'	CBgR	'Preview Party'	WNHG
'Once upon a Time'	EWoo	'Primal Scream' ♀H6	EPfP EWoo LRHS MHol NLar SPoG WCot WNHG
'One Last Straw'	EWoo		
'Oodles'	WHrl	'Prince of Purple'	ELon
'Open Hearth'	WHrl	'Princeton Silky'	ELon
'Open my Eyes'	EGren ELon	'Prize Picotee Elite'	WNHG
'Orange Exotica'	CBgR	'Protocol'	ELon
'Orange Nassau'	WCAu WFar	'Pueblo Dreamer'	EWoo
'Orangeman' misapplied	NGdn	'Puppet Show'	WNHG
'Orchid Candy'	NBir	'Pure and Simple'	ELon
'Orchid Corsage'	ELon	'Purple Bicolor'	WHrl
'Orchid Lady Slipper'	EWoo	'Purple Oddity'	EWoo
'Orion's Band'	EWoo	'Purple Pauper'	WCAu
'Ouachita Beauty'	CBgR ELon EWoo	'Purple Pinwheel'	EWoo
'Outrageous'	CBgR ELon WNHG	'Purple Rain'	MPie
'Outrageous Ramona'	WNHG	'Purpleicious'	LRHS NLar
'Painted Lady'	EGrI WNHG	'Pygmy Plum'	ESgI
'Palace Garden Beauty'	EWoo	'Queen Empress'	WNHG
'Palace Pagoda'	WNHG	'Queen Lily'	WNHG
'Panchen Lama'	WNHG	'Queen of May'	MNrw WCot
'Pandora's Box'	EGrI ELan LRHS MNrw NBir NGdn NLar WCAu WFar WNHG	'Quilt Patch'	WNHG
		'Quirky'	ELon
'Pantherette'	ELon	'Radiant Moonbeam' ♀H6	CBgR
'Paprika Flame'	MHol	'Raging Tiger'	WHrl
'Parade of Peacocks'	CBgR WNHG	'Raining Violets'	EWoo
'Pardon Me'	CBro CBWd EGren EGrI ELan ELon ESgI GJos GKin GMaP LRHS MPie NGdn NLar SPoG WCAu WFar WNHG	'Rajah'	CBgR CMac WHrl
		'Raspberry Candy'	CBro SRms WHrl
		'Raspberry Pixie'	WNHG
		'Red Admiral'	EBlo
		'Red Butterfly'	SMHy
'Parfait'	CBgR EWoo WHrl WNHG	'Red Joy'	WNHG
'Patchwork Puzzle'	EWoo	'Red Precious' ♀H6	MNrw WCot
'Patricia Gentzel Wright'	EWoo	'Red Rain'	EWoo WHrl
'Patsy Bickers'	ELon EWoo	'Red Ribbons'	ELon EWoo
'Patterns'	WNHG	'Red Rum'	EBee LEdu LRHS NBro
'Peach Float'	EWoo	'Red Tallboy'	GBin
'Peacock Curls'	EWoo	'Red Twister'	ELon
'Peacock Maiden'	EWoo WHrl	'Return Trip'	ELon
'Penelope Vestey'	NBir	'Rocket City'	ELan WNHG
'Penny's Worth'	EBlo LEdu LRHS WCot WFar	'Roman Toga'	CBgR
'Perfect Pie'	WCAu	* 'Romantic Rose'	NLar WHrl
'Persian Melon Plus'	WCAu	'Root Beer'	GQue WCAu WHrl
'Persian Ruby'	WNHG	'Rose Corsage'	LAma
'Piano Man'	WNHG	'Rose Fever'	EWoo
'Pink Charm'	CMac CWal ECha EPfP GKin GMaP NBro WCAu	'Roseate Spoonbill'	EWoo
		'Rosy Lights'	EWoo
'Pink Damask' ♀H6	CBcs CMac CPud EAri EBee EBlo ECha EHeP ELan EPfP GBin GMaP LRHS MArl MHer MHol MMuc	'Rosy Returns'	NLar WNHG
		'Royal Braid'	NLar WCot
		'Royal Celebration'	WCot

'Royal Elk'	EWoo	'Smoky Mountain Autumn'	EWoo WHrl
'Ruby Sentinel'	WNHG	'Smuggler's Gold'	GJos
'Ruby Spider' ♀H6	ELon ESgI EWoo	'Snaggle Tooth'	EPfP
'Ruffled Apricot'	WNHG	'Snow Elf'	WNHG
'Ruffled Carousel'	WNHG	'Snowed In'	EWoo
'Rumble Seat Romance'	WNHG	'Snowy Apparition'	ECrc EPfP ESgI GKin SMrm
'Russian Ragtime'	ELon	'Snowy Eyes'	GKin WHrl
'Ruth Love'	WNHG	'So Lovely'	EWoo
'Sabine Baur'	MNrw NLar WCAu WFar	'Somerset Fandango'	CBgR
'Sabra Salina'	WNHG	'Song Sparrow'	CBro
'Saintly'	EWoo	'Soraya Seline'	CBgR
'Sammy'	WHrl	'Sovereign Queen'	WNHG
'Sammy Russell'	CBcs CBgR CMac EHeP EPfP EPPr GKin LRHS LSRN MGos MHol NBir NGdn NSti SPoG SRGP SRms WBrk WCot WNHG	'Spacecoast Scrambled'	NLar
		'Spacecoast Starburst'	WCot
		'Spider Breeder'	CBgR ELon ESgI
		'Spider Man' ♀H6	ELon EWoo WCAu
'Samuel Bell'	EWoo	'Spider Miracle'	EWoo
'Santa's Pants'	EWoo	'Spider Red'	CWGN
'Satin Glass'	EBlo	'Spindazzle'	CBgR
'Scarlet Flame'	ECha	'Spiral Charmer'	EWoo
'Scarlet Orbit'	EWoo	'Spirit of Sapelo'	ESgI EWoo
'Scarlet Prince'	WNHG	'Spooner'	CBgR
'Schnickel Fritz'	WNHG	'Stafford' ♀H6	CAby CBWd CMac EBee EBlo EGrI EHeP ELan EPfP ESgI EWoo GBin GMaP GQue LCro LRHS LSRN MArl MBel MMuc MPro NGdn SDix SEND SMHy WCAu WCot WFar WHoo WSpi
'School Girl'	EBlo		
'Scorpio'	CBgR WHrl		
'Screaming Demon'	WCot WNHG		
'Secretary's Sand'	EWoo		
'Seminole Wind'	EWoo		
'Semiramide'	WNHG		
'Serenity Morgan'	EWoo	'Staghorn Sumac'	GKin WCAu
'Serge Rigaud'	WHrl	'Starling'	EWes EWoo LRHS WSpi
'Shadowed Pink'	WNHG	'Starstruck'	WNHG
'Shady Lady'	WNHG	'Startle'	ELon WCot WHrl
'Sherwood Gladiator'	WNHG	'Statuesque'	EWoo
'Shinto Shrine'	WNHG	'Stella de Oro'	CBcs CBro CMac CWal EBee EBlo EGren EHeP ELan ELon EPfP EPPr GKin GMaP LAma LRHS MAsh MBel MGos NBid NMir SAth SPlb SRms WCAu WChS WCot
* 'Shocker'	EWoo		
'Shuffle the Deck'	EWoo		
'Sigudilla'	WNHG		
'Silent Sentry'	WCAu	'Stellar Masquerade'	WNHG
'Siloam Angel Blush'	MHol	'Stoke Poges'	CBgR CBro ELon EPPr GBin WHrl WNHG
'Siloam Baby Talk'	ELon NBir		
'Siloam Button Box'	SMrm WHrl	'Stoplight'	CBgR ELon WChS WHrl WOld
'Siloam David Kirchhoff'	MBNS	'Strasbourg'	CMac
'Siloam Doodlebug'	CBgR NLar WNHG	'Strawberry Candy' ♀H6	CBgR CMac ELon EWoo LAma LCro MPie NGdn NLar WCAu WHrl WNHG WSpi
'Siloam Dream Baby'	ELon		
'Siloam Fairy Ruffles'	WNHG		
'Siloam French Doll'	NLar	'Strawberry Fields Forever'	EWoo LRHS NLar
'Siloam Helpmate'	WNHG	'Strutter's Ball'	EWoo NGdn WCAu WHrl WNHG
'Siloam June Bug'	WCot	'Stu's Old Pink Spider'	CBgR
'Siloam New Toy'	WHrl	'Sugar Cookie'	EWoo
'Siloam Paul Watts'	EGrI	'Sugar Paint'	WCAu
'Siloam Peewee'	ELon	'Summer Interlude'	WFar
'Siloam Ribbon Candy'	WNHG	'Summer Wine'	CBgR EGrI ELon EMor EPfP ESgI GMaP LRHS NBir NLar NSti WCAu WCot WHoo WHrl WNHG WSpi
'Siloam Show Girl'	EWoo GKin WNHG		
'Siloam Space Age'	WNHG		
'Siloam Sugar Time'	ELon	'Sunday Gloves'	WNHG
'Siloam Tiny Mite'	WHrl	'Sunray Brilliance'	EWoo
'Siloam Ury Winniford'	CBro CMac NLar WHoo WHrl	'Sweet Hot Chocolate'	MNrw
'Siloam Virginia Henson'	WNHG	'Swirling Spider'	CBgR EWoo
'Silver Ice'	WNHG	'Swirling Water'	WNHG
'Silver Lance'	WNHG	'Taj Mahal'	ELon EWoo GQue
'Simmons Overture'	EPfP MNrw	'Tangerine Tango'	EWoo
'Sinbad Sailor'	NLar	'Tarantula'	ELon
'Singing in the Sunshine'	EWoo	'Taruga'	EWoo
'Sink Into Your Eyes'	WHrl	'Tattooed Lady'	ESgI
'Sir Blackstem'	ELon	'Technical Knockout'	EWoo
'Sir Modred' ♀H6	WNHG	'Tejas'	ELon WOld
'Sky over Schuyler'	EWoo	'Tennessee Flycatcher'	EWoo WHrl
'Slapstick'	EWoo	'Tequila and Lime'	EGren EPfP
'Slender Lady'	ELon	'Tet Set'	WNHG
'Smith Brothers'	ELon	'Tetrina's Daughter'	CBgR

Hepatica 337

'Texas Blue Eyes' WNHG
'Texas Sunlight' CLil
'Thelma Perry' LEdu
'Think Pink' EBee
'Thumbelina' ECha EGrI
'Tiger Blood' LAma
'Tigereye Spider' EWoo WCAu
'Tigger' CLil EGrI SPad WCAu
'Tis Midnight' WNHG
'Tone Poem' WNHG
'Too Marvelous' WNHG
'Toothpick' EWoo WHrl
'Topspin' EWoo
'Torpoint' CBgR
'Total Look' MMrt
'Towhead' WCot
'Toyland' NBir NGdn NLar
'Trahlyta' CBgR ELon EWoo WHrl WNHG
'Tropical Depression' EWoo
'Troubled Sleep' ESgI EWoo
'True Gertrude Demarest' WHrl
'True Grit' WNHG
'Turkish Tapestry' CBgR
'Tuscawilla Tigress' CLil GKin WHrl
'Tutankhamun' ESgI
'Tuxedo Junction' ♀H6 ESgI
'Twilight Swan' WNHG
'Twirling Pinata' EWoo
'Twist of Lemon' EWoo
'Two Part Harmony' WHrl
'Valiant' WHrl
'Varsity' NBir
'Veins of Truth' EBee WCAu
'Velvet Shadows' CBgR
'Vendetta' WNHG
'Vernal Tutone' WNHG
'Victoria Aden' CBro
'Victoria Elizabeth Barnes' WNHG
'Victorian Lace' EWoo
'Villa Vanilla' WFar
'Vintage Bordeaux' ELan
'Vintage Burgundy' WNHG
'Vintage Wine' WNHG
'Violet Stained Glass' WNHG
'Viracocha' WNHG
'Volcano Queen' WFar
'Voodoo Dancer' EGrI LCro SPoG WNHG
'Walking on Sunshine' WCot
'Walt Disney' GKin
'Watch Tower' CBgR
'Watermelon Man' EWoo
'Wayne Johnson' WNHG
'Wayside Green Imp' MNrw
'We Love' EWoo
'Wee Willie Winkie' WNHG
'Westward Wind' EWoo
'Whichford' CBgR CBro EBee EBlo ECha EWoo GKin LRHS WGwG
'Whirling Fury' ELon EWoo
'White Coral' NBro
'White Edged Madonna' WHrl
'White Temptation' CWnw EWoo LRHS WNHG
'Whoopie' WHrl
'Wild and Wonderful' EWoo WFar
'Wild Child' ESgI
'Wild Horses' MNrw NLar SMad WCAu WHrl
'Wildest Dreams' EWoo
'Wind Beneath My Sails' EWoo
'Wind Song' ELon
'Windmill Yellow' EWoo
'Window Dressing' EWoo
'Winds of Love' EWoo
'Wineberry Candy' NLar
'Winsome Lady' GKin WHrl
'Wisest of Wizards' WHrl
'Wishing Well' WCot
'Witch Hazel' WCAu
'Witches Brew' CBgR
'Woodside Ruby' WNHG
'Xochimilco' WNHG
'Yazoo Green Octopus' EWoo
'Yellow Angel' ELon WCot
'Yellow Rain' WCot
'Yellow Submarine' MHol
'You Angel You' LAma
'Yuma' WNHG
'Zagora' WCAu
'Zampa' CBgR
'Zuni Mountains' WNHG

Hemiboea (Gesneriaceae)
bicornuta GEdr
- PB 07-1108 GGro WFar
strigosa CBct CExl EAri EBee EWes EWld SBrt WPGP
- PB 374338 GGro WFar
- 'Fen Zhong' LCro
subcapitata CExl EAri EBee ESwi EWld SBrt SPlb WCot WFar WPGP
aff. **subcapitata** BO 15-100 GGro

Hemionitis (Pteridaceae)
arifolia LWaG SPlb
marantae RCB AL B3 WCot

Henckelia (Gesneriaceae)
speciosa 'Crûg Cornetto' WCru

Hepatica ✿ (Ranunculaceae)
acutiloba ♀H6 EPot GEdr GKev LAma MAsh NBir NLar WFar WPnP
- blue-flowered MAsh
- white-flowered MAsh NLar
americana MAsh NBir NLar
- Eco Group seedlings MAsh
- var. **obtusa** 'Ashwood Marble' MAsh
angulosa see *H. transsilvanica*
'Ashwood Charm' **new** MAsh
falconeri MAsh
(Forest Series) 'Forest Purple' LCro
- 'Forest Red' LCro
- 'Forest White' LCro
'Hazelwood Froggie' MAsh
henryi MAsh
aff. **henryi** MAsh
insularis MAsh
maxima EWld GEdr MAsh
× **media** 'Ballardii' GEdr MAsh
- 'Blaue Stunde' GEdr
- Dryad Blush Group NDry
- 'Harvington Beauty' ♀H6 ENun GEdr LRHS NBir
- 'Holzdorfe Silver' GEdr
- 'Kim' GEdr
- 'Millstream Merlin' ♀H6 GEdr MAsh WFar
- 'Silberprinzessin' GEdr
§ **nobilis** ♀H6 EGrI EPot GArf GEdr GKev GMaP GQue LSto MAsh MBel MCtn NBir NHar NLar SAko SRms WAbe WFar WPnP
- 'Acrux' (Star Series) GEdr
- 'Adara' (Star Series) GEdr

Hepatica

- 'Alabaster' seedlings	MAsh	
- 'Alkes' (Star Series)	GEdr	
- 'Ashwood Moonlight'	MAsh	
- 'Baby Rosa'	GEdr	
- 'Bavarian Blue'	MAsh	
- 'Bibo'	MAsh	
- 'Bibo' seedlings, red-flowered	MAsh	
- 'Blue Bicolour'	MAsh	
- 'Blue Cloud'	MAsh	
- blue-flowered	MAsh SPlb WAbe	
- 'Brockman' (d)	GEdr	
- compact evergreen	NDry	
- 'Cremar'	GEdr	
- 'Crenatiloba'	MAsh	
- dark-blue-flowered	NDry	
- 'Elkofener Heidi'	GEdr	
* - var. *glabrata*	MAsh	
- - dwarf white-flowered	NDry	
- - 'Hjalmar' **new**	MAsh	
- - indigo-flowered	MAsh	
- var. *japonica*	EWes GEdr NBir NDry	
- - (7/d)	SAko	
- - 'Aikawa' (5/d)	GEdr	
- - 'Akane' (1)	GEdr	
- - 'Anjyu' (9/d)	GEdr WFar	
- - 'Asahi' (7/d)	GEdr	
- - 'Asahizuru' (6/d)	GEdr	
- - 'Baien' (1)	GEdr	
- - 'Benifusya' (1)	GEdr	
- - 'Benihagure' (9/d)	GEdr	
- - 'Benikanzan' (1)	GEdr	
- - 'Benikujyaku' (7/d)	GEdr	
- - 'Benioiran' (3)	GEdr	
- - 'Benisuzume' (1)	GEdr	
- - 'Benitaiko' (9/d)	GEdr	
- - 'Daishihou' (9/d)	GEdr	
- - 'Dewa' (9/d)	GEdr	
- - 'Ebisu-no-hana' (5A/d)	GEdr	
- - 'Echigobijin' (1)	GEdr NDry	
- - 'Godo'	GEdr	
- - 'Gosho-zakura' (5A/d)	GEdr	
- - 'Gyousei' (1)	GEdr	
- - 'Hakurin' (6/d)	GEdr	
- - 'Hakusetsu' (9/d)	GEdr	
- - 'Hanagoromo' (9/d)	GEdr	
- - 'Haruka' (2)	GEdr	
- - 'Harumo-no-Gatari' (8/d)	GEdr	
- - 'Haruno-awajuki' (9/d)	GEdr WFar	
- - 'Hidamari' (5/d)	GEdr	
- - 'Hohobeni' (9/d)	GEdr	
- - 'Hokutosei' (7/d)	GEdr	
- - 'Hoshizora' (2)	GEdr	
- - 'Isaribi' (1)	GEdr NDry	
- - 'Junissen' (6/d)	GEdr	
- - 'Kagura' (5A/d)	GEdr	
- - 'Kanazawa'	GEdr	
- - 'Kansashi'	NDry	
- - Karako Group (8/d)	WFar	
- - 'Kasumino' (1)	GEdr	
- - 'Kiko' (9/d)	GEdr	
- - 'Kimon' (9/d)	GEdr	
- - 'Konosu'	GEdr	
- - 'Koshi-no-maboroshi' (7/d)	GEdr	
- - 'Kotobuki-hime' (5/d)	GEdr	
- - 'Kouen' (6/d)	GEdr	
- - 'Kougyoku' (9/d)	GEdr	
- - 'Kurotaiyou' (d)	GEdr	
- - 'Kuukai' (8/d)	GEdr	
- - f. *magna*	MAsh	
- - - 'Murasaki-shikibu' (9/d)	GEdr	
- - 'Manazuru' (9/d)	GEdr	
- - 'Minamo' (5/d)	GEdr	
- - 'Miwaku' (1)	GEdr	
- - 'Miyoshino' (1)	GEdr NDry	
- - 'Miyuki' (9/d)	GEdr	
- - 'Momosango'	GEdr	
- - 'Murasaki-sakama' (9/d)	GEdr	
- - 'Nagai'	GEdr	
- - 'Nanakubo' (1)	GEdr	
- - 'Nanto'	GEdr	
- - 'Notaniyama'	GEdr	
- - 'Noumurasaki' (1)	GEdr	
- - 'Oboryo' (1)	GEdr	
- - 'Odoriko' (9/d)	GEdr	
- - 'Okesabayashi'	GEdr	
- - 'Okina' (9/d)	GEdr	
- - 'Ō-murasaki' (1)	GEdr	
- - 'Orihime' (9/d)	GEdr	
- - 'Osaka'	GEdr	
- - 'Reeka' (1)	GEdr	
- - 'Reika' (5/d)	GEdr	
- - 'Rinsen' (9/d)	GEdr	
- - 'Ryokurei' (5A/d)	GEdr	
- - 'Ryokusetsu' (9/d)	GEdr	
- - 'Ryokuun' (9/d)	GEdr NDry	
- - 'Sadobeni' (1)	GEdr	
- - 'Saichou' (7/d)	GEdr	
- - Sandan Group (7/d)	GEdr	
- - 'Satsuma' (5A/d)	GEdr	
- - 'Sayaka' (1)	GEdr	
- - 'Seizan' (9/d)	GEdr	
- - 'Senhime' (9/d)	GEdr	
- - 'Sen-nin' (6/d)	GEdr	
- - 'Sennin-buraku' (8/d)	GEdr	
- - 'Setsudu' (7/d)	GEdr	
- - 'Shikouden' (9/d)	GEdr	
- - 'Shikouryuu' (9/d)	GEdr	
- - 'Shio' (9/d)	GEdr	
- - 'Shirayuki' (9/d)	GEdr	
- - (Shiun Group) 'Shihou' (9/d)	GEdr	
- - 'Shōdo Island' **new**	MAsh	
- - 'Shoujyouno-homare' (9/d)	GEdr	
- - 'Sougetsu' (6/d)	GEdr NDry	
- - 'Souhou' (1)	GEdr	
- - 'Soushyunka' (9/d)	GEdr	
- - 'Subaru' (9/d)	GEdr	
- - 'Suien' (9/d)	GEdr	
- - 'Suzu'	GEdr	
- - 'Suzuka'	GEdr	
- - 'Syouchikubai' (7/d)	GEdr	
- - 'Syunryuu' (9/d)	GEdr	
- - 'Taeka' (9/d)	GEdr	
- - 'Takase' (9/d)	GEdr	
- - 'Takumi' (9/d)	GEdr NDry	
- - 'Tamahime' (8/d)	GEdr	
- - 'Tamakujyaku' (6/d)	GEdr	
- - 'Tamasaburou' (1)	GEdr	
- - 'Tantyoubeni'	GEdr	
- - 'Tantyubai'	GEdr	
- - 'Tenjinbai' (1)	GEdr NDry	
- - 'Tenjin-ume' (1)	GEdr	
- - 'Tennyonomai' (6A/d)	GEdr	
- - 'Toki' (9/d)	GEdr	
- - 'Tonami'	GEdr	
- - 'Touen' (9/d)	GEdr	
- - 'Touhou' (9/d)	GEdr	

- - 'Touryoku' (9/d)	GEdr
- - 'Toyama-chiyo-iwai' (7/d)	GEdr
- - 'Unabara' (9/d)	GEdr
- - 'Wakakusa' (9/d)	GEdr
- - 'Yaegoromo' (6/d)	GEdr
- - 'Yahiko' (5/d)	GEdr
- - 'Yahikomurasaki' (1)	GEdr
- - 'Yamada'	GEdr
- - 'Yamahibiki' (9/d)	GEdr
- - 'Yoro'	GEdr
- - 'Yukishino' (2)	GEdr
- - 'Yumes' (7/d)	GEdr
- - 'Yuunagi' (9/d)	GEdr
- - 'Yuunami' (1)	GEdr
- - 'Yuuzen' (5/d)	GEdr
- - 'Yuzuru' (9/d)	GEdr
- large, pale blue-flowered	WFar
- lavender-flowered	MAsh
- 'Matar' (Star Series)	GEdr
- 'Mira'	EWld
- multipetala	MAsh SAko
- 'Mussel's Plena' (d) **new**	MAsh
- var. *nipponica* 'Golden Picotee Edge' **new**	MAsh
- var. *nobilis* 'Giselle'	EWld MAsh
- 'Oelands Doppelstern'	GEdr
- 'Oeland's Nacht'	GEdr
- Ohleila Group	MAsh
- pale pink-flowered	MAsh
- 'Papillion' seedlings	MAsh
- 'Polens Weisse'	GEdr
- Prickel	MAsh
- var. *pubescens*	MAsh
- Pygmy Group	MAsh WFar
* - var. *pyrenaica*	EWld GKev LEdu MAsh WAbe
* - - 'Apple Blossom'	EWld GEdr MAsh NBir
* - - 'Harold Bawden'	GEdr
- - 'Harold Bawden' seedlings	MAsh
* - - 'Pyrenean Princess'	MAsh
* - - white-flowered	NBir
- 'Pyrenean Marbles'	NBir
- 'Rosa Elite'	GEdr MAsh
- 'Rubra Plena' (d) ♀H6	GEdr MAsh
- 'Selma'	MAsh
- semi-double, blue-flowered **new**	MAsh
- 'Stained Glass' ♀H6	EWld MAsh
- 'Susanne'	GEdr
- 'Tabby'	NDry
- 'Tadeas'	MAsh
- 'Talitha' (Star Series)	GEdr
- 'White Sands'	GEdr
- white-flowered	MAsh
- 'Woodside White'	EWld
- 'Zartila'	MAsh
'Professor Friedrich Hildebrandt'	GEdr
× *schlyteri* ♀H6	MAsh NDry
- Ashwood hybrids	MAsh
- blue-flowered	MAsh NDry
- Silver Shadow Group	MAsh
- 'The Bride' ♀H6	GEdr MAsh
§ *transsilvanica* ♀H5	GEdr MAsh StAn WCot
- 'Ada Scott'	GEdr MAsh
- 'Blue Eyes'	EWld GEdr GKev
- 'Blue Jewel'	GEdr
- blue-flowered	MAsh
- 'Buis'	ECha GEdr NLar
- 'Connie Greenfield'	GEdr
- 'Donner Wolke'	GEdr
- 'Eisvogel'	GEdr NDry
- 'Elison Spence' (d) ♀H5	GEdr MAsh
- 'Fuchs'	GEdr
- 'Grethe' seedlings	GEdr
- 'Hazelwood Grace' **new**	MAsh
- 'Karpati Krönen'	GEdr
- 'Lilacina'	GEdr MAsh NDry
- 'Loddon Blue'	GEdr MAsh
- 'März'	GEdr
- 'Praecox'	GEdr
- 'Supernova'	GEdr MAsh
- white-flowered	GEdr MAsh
triloba	see *H. nobilis*

Heptacodium (Caprifoliaceae)

jasminoides	see *H. miconioides*
§ *miconioides* ♀H7	Widely available
- TEMPLE OF BLOOM ('Smnhmrf')	LRHS NCth NLar
- TIANSHAN ('Minhep'PBR)	NLar NPip SGol WCot

Heptapleurum (Araliaceae)

§ *actinophyllum* ♀H1b	EGren EUrb LBom NPlm SArc
- 'Amate'	LBom LDro LWaG
- 'Nova' **new**	SChF
§ *alpinum*	CBct CExl EBee
- B&SWJ 8247	WCru
- B&SWJ 11827	WCru
- HWJ 936	WCru
- NJM 9.14	WPGP
- NJM 9.157	WPGP
- WWJ 11999 large-leaved	WCru
aff. *alpinum*	CDTJ
§ *arboricola* ♀H1c	CDoC EShb LCro MCtn SArc
- 'Charlotte' (v)	LBom
- 'Compactum'	LDro LInT
- 'Gerda'	LBom
- 'Gold Capella' ♀H1c	LBom LCro LInT NHrt NPlm SEND
- 'Melanie' (v)	LBom LCro
- 'Nora'	LBom LCro
- 'Trinetta'	LCro
- variegated (v)	SEND
§ *bodinieri*	WPGP
§ *brevipedicellatum*	CDTJ
- HWJ 870	WCru
- KWJ 12224	WCru
aff. *brevipedicellatum* NJM 10.102	WPGP
§ *chapanum* B&SWJ 11833	WCru
- B&SWJ 11848	WCru
- HWJ 983	WCru
§ *delavayi*	CBct CDTJ CExl EBee SPlb WCru
	WPGP
§ *enneaphyllum*	CExl
- HWJ 1018	WCru
§ *fantsipanense* B&SWJ 11666	WCru
- B&SWJ 11671	WCru
§ *gracile*	CDTJ
- HWJ 622	WCru
- HWJ 878	WCru
gracile × *taiwanianum*	WCru
hoi B&SWJ 11747	WCru
§ *hypoleucoides* BWJ 15158	WCru
§ *kornasii* B&SWJ 11830	WCru
- HWJ 918	WCru
§ *laxiusculum* B&SWJ 11694 **new**	WCru
'Luseane'PBR	LBom LDro SEND
§ *macrophyllum*	CDTJ
- B&SWJ 11842	WCru

340   *Heptapleurum*

- BWJ 16322	WCru
- WWJ 11681	WCru
§ ***microphyllum***	WCru
B&SWJ 3872	
§ ***multinervium***	WCru
B&SWJ 11727	
§ aff. ***myriocarpum***	WCru
B&SWJ 11828	
§ ***pauciflorum***	ESwi
- WWJ 11986	WCru
§ ***rhododendrifolium***	CDoC CDTJ CExl EBee LRHS WPGP
- GWJ 9375	WCru
§ ***shweliense***	CExl
- NJM 13.13	WPGP
§ ***taiwanianum*** ♀H4	CBcs CBct CCht CDTJ CExl CMHG
	CTsd EBee ELan EPfP ESwi EUrb
	LCro SBig SHor WCot WPGP
- B&SWJ 3575	WCru
- B&SWJ 3788	WCru
- B&SWJ 7096	WCru
- RWJ 10000	WCru
- RWJ 10016	WCru

Heptaptera (Apiaceae)
triquetra	CSpe

Heracleum (Apiaceae)
dissectum	GGro
lehmannianum	WPGP
mantegazzianum	Prohibited invasive. See Conservation and the Environment, p.42
mantegazzianum × *sphondylium*	Prohibited invasive. See Conservation and the Environment, p.42
persicum	Prohibited invasive. See Conservation and the Environment, p.42
sosnowskyi	Prohibited invasive. See Conservation and the Environment, p.42
sphondylium 'Pink Cloud'	ECha MPro
stevenii	WCot WPGP
wallichii B&SWJ 13931	WCru

Herbertia (Iridaceae)
§ *lahue*	SBrt WAbe

Hereroa (Aizoaceae)
glenensis	EAri EDAr LRHS SLee SPlb WAbe

Hermannia (Malvaceae)
flammea	SPlb
stricta	WAbe

Herniaria (Caryophyllaceae)
glabra	CWRo GQue MCtn MHer

Hertia (Asteraceae)
§ *cheirifolia*	CBcs CSde EWes EWld IArd SEND

Hesperaloe (Asparagaceae)
engelmannii	WCot
parviflora	CBlu CSpe ELan EUrb MCtn NPlm
	SBig SPlb WCot
- BRAKELIGHTS	EUrb
('Perpa'^PBR) **new**	
- 'Rubra'	LRHS

Hesperantha ✿ (Iridaceae)
§ *baurii*	GArf
coccinea	CBcs CLil CMac EBee ELin EPfP
	GAbr GKev LAma LCro LRHS MArl
	MCtn MHed NGdn NLar WFar
	WMAq

- f. *alba*	CBro CBWd CExl CMac CoPl CToG
	CWnw EBee ELan ELin EPfP GAbr
	GKev LAma LCro LRHS MArl MHtn
	MPro NBir NGdn NLar SPlb SRms
	WFar WPnP
- 'Anne'	NLar WFar
- 'Autumn's Dawn'	WFar
- 'Ballyrogan Giant'	WFar WHer
- 'Big Moma'	MAvo WFar WHoo WOld
- 'Cardinal'	WFar
- 'Caroline'	CoPl WFar
- 'Cindy Towe'	CCps CKno ELon LBar LRHS LSou
	NSti SPoG WFar
- 'Elburton Glow'	WFar
- 'Eric's Early'	CoPl ELon WFar WOld
- 'Fenland Daybreak'	CCps CDor CKno CMac CoPl EGrl
	ELan LSou MGos NLar SPoG SRms
	WFar
- 'Gigantea'	see *H. coccinea* 'Major'
- 'Good White'	ECha NBir WFar
- 'Grandiflora'	see *H. coccinea* 'Major'
- 'Hilary Gould'	ELon WOld
- 'Ice Maiden'	CAbb CCps CDor CKno CTtf LBar
	LSou MPro NSti NWbg SPeP SPoG
	WNPC
- 'Jack Frost'	EBee WFar
- 'Jennifer' ♀H4	CDor CMac CoPl CTtf EBee ECha
	ELon GArf MMuc NLar SRms WFar
- 'Lipstick'	MArl SPel
- 'Maiden's Blush'	LEdu NLar SRms WFar
§ - 'Major' ♀H4	Widely available
- 'Marchants Seedling'	SMHy
- 'Marietta'	WFar
- 'Mollie Gould'	CCps CDor CoPl EGren EPfP EPot
	LRHS MArl MMrt NCth NLar NWbg
	SPel SRms WFar WHil WHoo WOld
- 'Mrs Hegarty'	CMac CoPl ELin ELon EPfP GMaP
	LCro LRHS MGos MHer NBid NLar
	NLar NQui SAdn SPlb SPoG SRms
	WCAu WFar WPnP
- 'November Cheer'	CMac CMHG NBir NLar
- 'Oregon Sunset'	CBcs CCps CKno CoPl CWnw
	EGren ELin ELon EUrb LRHS LSou
	MHol MPro NLit SPeP WFar WHoo
	WNPC
- 'Pallida'	ELon NBir NCth WFar
- 'Pink Marg'	WFar
- 'Pink Princess'	see *H. coccinea* 'Wilfred H. Bryant'
- pink-flowered	MBel
- 'Professor Barnard'	CCps EBee ELon EPfP LRHS NBir
	NLar NWbg WFar WOld
I - 'Rosea'	EPot LAma MPie WFar
- 'Ruth'	EPfP LBar MPro MSwo SPel WFar
- 'Salmon Charm'	CoPl WFar
- salmon-flowered	CTtf
- 'Salmon's Leap'	CoPl WFar
- 'Salome'	CDor WFar
- 'Scarlet Queen'	CoPl WFar
- 'Simply Pink'	LRHS MPro SEND
- 'Snow Drift'	WFar
- 'Snow Maiden'	CBcs CoPl EBee EGren EUrb LRHS
	MPro NLar WFar WHil
- 'Strawberry'	CoPl ECrc WFar
§ - 'Sunrise' ♀H4	CBcs CBro CCps CExl EBee ECha
	EGren ELan GKev LRHS LSou MArl
	NBir NCth NGdn NLar NLit WCAu
	WFar WKif
- 'Sunset'	see *H. coccinea* 'Sunrise'
- 'Tambara'	CoPl WFar
- 'Vibrant Scarlet'	WFar
- 'Viscountess Byng'	CWCL EBee NBir

Heuchera 341

*	- 'White Admiral'	WFar
§	- 'Wilfred H. Bryant' ♀H4	Widely available
	- 'Zeal Salmon'	CBro CCps CoPl ECha EGrl ELon GAbr NBir WFar
	huttonii	EPPr EWld GEdr NBir WFar
	mossii	see *H. baurii*

Hesperis (Brassicaceae)
	matronalis	CAby CAgr CGHo CSpe CTtf ECha EHet ELan ENfk EPfP EWhm GAbr LCro LEdu LRHS LSto MCtn MHoo MNHC MPri NGdn NLar SPoG SRms WKit WTor
§	- var. *albiflora*	CAby CCBP CSpe CTtf ELan EPfP LCro LEdu LRHS MCtn MHoo MNHC NGdn NLar WBrk WFar WHil WTor
	- - 'Alba Plena' (d)	EBee LRHS WCot
	- double-flowered (d)	CTtf
	nivea	LEdu
	tristis **new**	ESgI

Hesperoyucca (Asparagaceae)
§	*whipplei*	ELan WPGP

Hesperozygis (Lamiaceae)
	'Midnight Mojito' (Supermint Series)	LRHS

Hessea (Amaryllidaceae)
	mathewsii	LAma

Heteromeles (Rosaceae)
	arbutifolia	see *H. salicifolia*
§	*salicifolia*	CMCN LEdu

Heteromorpha (Apiaceae)
	arborescens	SPlb SVen

Heteropanax (Araliaceae)
	chinensis **new**	LDro

Heteropolygonatum (Asparagaceae)
	'Mikinori Ogisu'	GEdr
	roseolum OG 89001	WCru
	urceolatum	WCru

Heteropterys (Malpighiaceae)
	glabra	WCru

Heterotheca (Asteraceae)
	subaxillaris	WCot
	villosa 'Golden Sunshine'	MHer SPhx

Heuchera ✿ (Saxifragaceae)
	'Alan Davidson'	MPnt
	ALFIE ('Gofie') (Fox Series)	EHeP MPnt WNPC
	'Alison'	MPnt
	'Amber Waves'PBR	NBir
§	*americana*	LRHS NBir SHar
	- var. *americana*	MPnt
	- Dale's strain	LSto MPnt SPlb
	- 'Harry Hay'	EPPr LEdu MPnt SMHy WPGP
	- 'Marvelous Marble'	EGren EPfP LRHS LWaG MPnt
	- 'Ring of Fire'	EHeP MPnt SRms
	'Amethyst Myst'	EGren LRHS MPnt
	'Apple Crisp'PBR	EHeP LCro LWaG MPnt WNPC
	'Apple Souffle'	MPnt
	'Apple Twist'PBR (Dolce Series)	EPfP LRHS MHol MPro
	'Apricot'	LRHS MPnt
	'Autumn Glow' (Seasonal Selection Series)	MPnt
	'Autumn Haze'	MPnt
	'Autumn Leaves'PBR	ELan LCro LRHS MPnt SPoG
	'Baby's Breath'	MPnt
	'Bardot'	MPnt
	'Beaujolais'PBR	MPnt
	'Beauty Colour'	ELan GMaP ISha NGdn XFar
	'Bella Notte'PBR	LRHS MPnt MPro NLar WNPC
	'Berry Marmalade'PBR	EBee EPfP MAsh MPnt SPoG
	'Berry Smoothie'PBR	EBee EGren ELan LBom LBuc LRHS LSRN MArl MBNS MGos MHol MHtn MPnt MPro MSwo NBir NLar NPer SPoG WFar WNPC
	'Berry Timeless'PBR	EBee EPfP LBuc LRHS MPnt
	'Big Top Caramel Apple' (Big Top Series) **new**	WNPC
	'Bilberry' (Indian Summer Series)	MPnt
	'Binoche'PBR	EBee ELan LBom LBuc LRHS MPnt MPri
	'Birkin'	MPnt
	'Black Forest Cake'	CWGN EBee EPfP MPnt SPad WNPC WTor
	'Black Pearl'PBR (Primo Series)	CGHo EGren EPfP LBom LBuc LCro LRHS MBel MBros Midl MPnt MPri MPro NLar SRot WFar
	BLACK SEA ('Ds1'PBR)	EPfP MPnt
	'Black Taffeta'PBR	CWGN EBee EGren LBuc MPnt MPro WFar WNPC
	'Blackberry Crisp'	EBee LBuc MPnt
	BLACKBERRY ('Ifhebbr') (Indian Summer Series)	EPfP LBuc MPro
	'Blackberry Jam' ♀H6	CLil EGren ELan GPSL LRHS LSou LSto Midl MPnt NBir WFar WNPC
	'Blackbird'	MPnt WFar WSpi
	'Blackout'	MPnt
	'Blondie'PBR (Little Cutie Series)	CBcs EPfP GJos LCro LRHS Midl MPnt MPri MPro NLar SPoG WNPC
	'Blondie in Lime' (Little Cutie Series) ♀H6	EPfP LBuc LCro LRHS Midl MPnt MPri NLar
	'Blood Vein'	MPnt
	'Bloody Dinosaur'	ISha WNPC
	'Blushing Down'	MPnt
	'Bouquet'	MPnt
	'Boysenberry'PBR (Indian Summer Series)	CBcs EBee EGren ELan EPfP ISha LBuc LRHS MPnt MPri MPro
	bracteata	MPnt
	'Bressingham Glow'	MPnt
	Bressingham hybrids	EPfP MCtn SRms SVic
	'Bressingham Spire'	MPnt
	'Bright and Breezy' (Seasonal Selection Series)	MPnt
	'Bronze Beauty'	GBin MPnt WCot
	'Brown Sugar'	MPnt
	'Brownfinch'	CElw MPnt SBrt SMHy WCot
	'Brownies'	EUrb MPnt WNPC
	BURGUNDY BILL ('Goburg') (Fox Series)	
	'Burgundy Frost'	MPnt
	'Café Olé' ♀H6	MPnt
	'Cajun Fire'PBR	ELan Midl MPnt
	'Can-can' ♀H6	ELan LRHS MPnt NBir WCAu WSpi
	'Canyon Duet'	MPnt
	'Cappuccino'	EBee ELan MPnt SRGP XFar
	'Caramel'PBR	CMac CWGN EBee ELan GMaP LBom LBuc LCro MAsh MHol MNrw SPoG WCAu WNPC
	'Carmen'	MPnt

(Carnival Series)	WNPC	- 'Greenfinch'	EHeP GKev GMaP LRHS LSto MCtn MPnt NBir SHar SPel WTre
CARNIVAL CINNAMON STICK ('Balcarcinn'PBR) **new**		- 'Hyperion'	MPnt
- CARNIVAL LIMEADE ('Balcarmade'PBR)	ELan LRHS	'Da Vinci' (Master Painters Series)	MPnt
- CARNIVAL PLUM CRAZY ('Balcarulm'PBR)	LRHS	'Damask'	MPnt
- CARNIVAL ROSE GRANITA	LRHS WFar	'Dark Beauty'PBR	CBrac CWnw LRHS MHol Midl WFar WNPC
§ - CARNIVAL SILVER STREAK ('Balcarsilk')	LRHS	'Dark Secret'PBR	EBee EPfP LBuc LRHS MPnt MPro
- CARNIVAL WATERMELON ('Balcarmelo'PBR)	MHol	'Dark Storm' (Seasonal Selection Series)	MPnt
		'David'	MPnt
'Cascade Dawn'	EBee EGren LBuc LRHS MPnt NBir	'Delta Dawn'PBR	EBee EGren EHeP MPnt SPoG
'Cassis'	MPnt WCot	'Dennis Davidson'	see *H.* 'Huntsman'
'Celtic Sea'	LRHS	§ 'E and I'	EBee MPnt SRms WSpi
'Cézanne' (Master Painters Series)	MPnt	'Earth Angel'	MPnt
		EBONY AND IVORY	see *H.* 'E and I'
CHAMPAGNE ('Tnheucha'PBR)	EGren LRHS Midl MPnt WNPC	'Eden's Aurora'	MPnt
'Champagne Bubbles'	MPnt	'Electra'PBR	EPfP LCro MPnt NLar
'Changeling' **new**	MPnt WNPC	'Electric Lime'	EGren ELan LBuc MPnt NLar SPoG
CHARLES BLOOM ('Chablo')	MPnt	'Electric Plum' **new**	MPnt WTor
CHARLOTTE ('Gochar') (Fox Series)	MPnt	'Elworthy Rusty'	CElw
'Chatterbox'	MPnt	'Emperor's Cloak'	MCtn
'Checkers'	see *H.* 'Quilter's Joy'	'Encore'PBR	MPnt
'Cherry Cola'PBR ♀H6	CBcs CWnw EBee EGren ELan EPfP GJos LBom LRHS MAsh MHtn Midl MPnt MPri MPro NBir NCth SPoG SRkn WCAu WFar WNPC WTor	'Eternal Flame' **new**	MPnt WTor
		'Evening Gown' (Dressed Up Series)	MPnt
		'Fairy Dance'	MPnt
		'Fire Alarm'PBR	CWGN ELan EPfP LBuc LCro MPnt MPro WNPC
'Cherry Truffles'PBR (Dolce Series)	EBee LBom LCro LRHS MPri WFar	'Fire Chief'PBR	CBcs CWGN CWnw EBee EGrI ELan EPfP GMaP LBom LBuc LRHS LSou LSto MArl MPnt MSwo NBir SPoG SRkn WCAu WFar WNPC
CHERRYBERRY ('Ifhecheb') (Indian Summer Series)	EBee LRHS MPnt		
'Chiqui'	MPnt		
chlorantha	MPnt	'Firebird'	MPnt
CHOCOLATE LIME ('Jonchoc')	MPnt WFar WNPC	FIREFLY	see *H.* 'Leuchtkäfer'
'Chocolate Ruffles'	CBcs EGren EHeP ELan EPfP GMaP LBuc LRHS LSRN MHer MHol NLar SPoG SRkn SRms WCAu WCav WFar WNPC WSpi	'Fireworks'	MPnt NLar
		'Fleur' (Fox Series)	EHeP LBuc MPnt WNPC
		'Florist's Choice'	MPnt
		'Flower Tower' **new**	EBee
'Chocolate Veil'	MPnt	(Forever Series) FOREVER PURPLE ('Tnheufp'PBR)	CWGN EBee EGren EPfP LBuc LCro LRHS LSou LSRN MHol MPnt MPro MSCN NLar WFar WNPC WTor
'Christa'	MPnt		
'Cinnabar Silver'PBR	MPnt NLar		
'Circus'PBR	MPnt WNPC	- FOREVER RED ('Tnheufr'PBR)	CWGN EBee EGren EHeP EPfP LBuc LCro LRHS LSRN MHol MPnt MPro MSCN WFar WNPC WTor
'Citronelle'	CWGN EGrI MPnt MPro WCot WNPC		
'Coco'PBR (Little Cutie Series)	ELan EPfP GJos LRHS Midl MPnt	'French Quarter'	MPnt
'Color Dream'	MPnt	FRILLY ('Alchefril')	EHeP LCro LRHS Midl WNPC
COOL DUDE ('Godud') (Fox Series)	MPnt	'Frilly Lizzie' (Fox Series)	WNPC
		FROST ('Tnheufro'PBR) (Little Cutie Series)	ELan EPfP LRHS MPnt MPro
'Copper Dinosaur'	WNPC	'Frosted Violet'	see *H.* 'Frosted Violet Dream'
coral bells	see *H. sanguinea*	§ 'Frosted Violet Dream'PBR	LBom LSRN MPnt
'Coral Bouquet'	MPnt	'Galaxy'PBR	MPnt
'Coral Cloud'	MPnt	'Gauguin' (Master Painters Series)	LRHS MPnt
'Coral Frost'	LRHS		
'Coral Sea'	WCot	'Georgia Peach'PBR	EBee ELan LBuc LRHS MPnt WFar WNPC
'Coralberry'PBR (Indian Summer Series)	ELan LBuc LRHS MPnt		
'Corallion'	MPnt	'Georgia Plum'	EBee EHeP ELan EPfP LBuc MPnt WNPC
CRANBERRY ('Ifhepr') (Indian Summer Series)	CWGN EGren ELan EPfP LBuc LRHS MHol MPnt MPri WNPC WTor	'Ginger Ale'PBR	CTsd EBee ELan LBom LBuc LRHS MArl MBros MHol MPnt MPro NSti SPoG WFar WNPC WTor
'Crazy Rasta'	LBuc LRHS		
CRÈME BRÛLÉE ('Tnheucb'PBR) (Dolce Series)	EGren ELan MGos Midl NCou NLar SPoG	'Ginger Peach'PBR	EHeP MPnt WNPC
'Crème Caramel'	LBom MPnt	'Ginger Snap' (Little Cutie Series)	LRHS MPnt
'Creole Nights'	MPnt	***glabra***	MPnt
'Crimson Curls'	ELan MPnt SRms	***glauca***	see *H. americana*
'Crispy Curly'	MPnt	'Glitter'PBR ♀H6	EBee EPfP LBuc LRHS LSou MHol MPnt NCth SPoG WNPC
cylindrica	GKev MPnt NAts		
- 'Cream'	MPnt	'Gloire d'Orléans'	MPnt
- 'Francis'	MPnt		

'Gojiberry' (Indian Summer Series)	EBee EPfP LRHS MPnt		'Metallica'	LRHS
			micans	see *H. rubescens*
'Gotham'PBR	LCro MPnt WNPC		*micrantha*	MPnt SRms
'Grape Soda'PBR (Soda Series)	MPnt WNPC		- var. *diversifolia*	see *H. villosa*
'Grape Timeless'PBR	EBee EPfP LRHS MPnt		misapplied	
'Green Ivory'	GMaP MPnt		- 'Martha's Compact'	MPnt
'Green Sashay'	MPnt	§	- 'Ruffles'	ECha EPPr MPnt
'Green Spice' ♀H6	CBcs EBee EGren ELan GMaP LBuc LCro LRHS LSto MPnt MSwo NBir NCth SMHy SOrN SPoG SRkn WHoo WNPC		'Midnight Bayou'	ELan MPnt NLar NPer
			'Midnight Rose'	CDoC CWGN EGren ELan EPfP EWes LBom LBuc LRHS LSou MArl MBel MBNS MGos MHol MPnt MPri MPro NBir SOrN SPoG SRkn WFar WNPC WTor
'Greenberry'	MPnt			
'Guacamole' ♀H6	EPfP MPnt			
'Guardian Angel'	MPnt SRGP		'Midnight Rose Select'	MPnt
'Gypsy Dancer' (Dancer Series)	MPnt		'Midnight Ruffles'	MPnt WFar
			'Milan'PBR	ELan LRHS MPnt MPro
'Hailstorm' (v)	MPnt		'Mini Caramel'	MPnt
hallii	EDAr MPnt SPlb		'Mini Mouse'	MPnt
'Happy Easter'	LRHS		'Mint Frost'	EHeP ELan MPnt
'Happy Flames'	LRHS MHol WNPC		'Miracle'PBR	MPnt
'Happy Moon'	LBuc LRHS WCot		'Mocha'PBR	MNrw MPnt
'Happy Peachy'	LBuc		'Morello'	Midl MPnt WNPC
HARVEST BURGUNDY ('Balheubur')	MPnt		'Mother of Pearl'	MPnt
			MULBERRY ('Ifhemul') (Indian Summer Series)	EPfP LBuc LRHS MPnt WFar
HARVEST SILVER ('Balheusil')	MPnt			
'Havana'	MPnt		'Muscat'	MPnt
'Helen Dillon' (v)	GMaP LRHS MPnt		'Mysteria'PBR	MPnt
'Hercules'PBR	MPnt		'Mystic Angel'	MPnt
'High Hopes'	MPnt		'Neptune'	MPnt MPro
hispida	MPnt		Neueste hybrids	MCtn
'Hollywood'	EBee GJos MBNS MGos Midl MPnt MPro NBir SPoG		(Northern Exposure Series)	EGren MPnt MPro
			NORTHERN EXPOSURE AMBER ('Tnheunea'PBR)	
HUCKLEBERRY ('Ifhehb'PBR) (Indian Summer Series)	LBom LBuc LRHS MPnt MPri			
			- NORTHERN EXPOSURE LIME ('Tnheunel'PBR)	LSou MPnt
§	'Huntsman'	MPnt		
Indian Summer Series	EGren LRHS		- NORTHERN EXPOSURE RED ('Tnheuner'PBR)	MPnt
'Isabella' (Fox Series)	MPnt			
'Jade Gloss'PBR	MPnt WNPC		- NORTHERN EXPOSURE SIENNA ('Tnheunesi')	EGren MPro
'June Bride'	MPnt			
KEY LIME PIE ('Tnheu042') (Dolce Series)	EGren LRHS MGos Midl SRms WFar		- NORTHERN EXPOSURE SILVER ('Tnheunes'PBR)	LRHS
Kira Series	MPnt		'Oakington Jewel'	MPnt
'Lava Lamp'	MPnt		'Obsidian'PBR ♀H6	Widely available
'Lemon Chiffon'	MPnt		'Orange Dream'	MPnt
'Lemon Dinosaur'	WNPC		ORANGEBERRY ('Ifheorr') (Indian Summer Series)	EBee EPfP LBuc LRHS MPnt
'Lemon Love'	EPfP LRHS MPnt MPro			
§	'Leuchtkäfer'	EBee GMaP LRIIS MCtn MHer MPnt MPro NBir SDix SPlb SRms		'Orphée'	MPnt
			'Paprika'PBR	EBee EGren LCro MPnt MPro WFar WNPC
LICORICE ('Tnheu044') (Dolce Series)	MBNS MGos Midl MPnt MPro SPoG WFar			
			'Paris'PBR ♀H6	CBrac CDoC CWGN EGren EPfP LBom LRHS LSRN MAsh MBel MGos Midl MPnt MPri MPro SPoG SRot WCAu WNPC WTor
'Lime Marmalade' ♀H6	Widely available			
'Lime Rickey'PBR	LRHS			
'Lime Ruffles'	LBuc MPnt			
'Lipstick' ♀H6	CWGN EBee LRHS MPnt			
'Little Tinker'	MPnt		*parishii* NNS 93384	MPnt
'Lune Rousse'	MPnt		*parvifolia* var. *nivalis*	MPnt
'Madison Bride' (Fox Series) ♀H6	LCro MMrt MPnt WCot		- var. *utahensis*	MPnt
			'Pauline' (Fox Series)	LBuc Midl MPnt WNPC
'Magnum'	MPnt		'Peach Crisp'	EHeP LRHS MPnt WNPC
'Mahogany'	MPnt WHoo		'Peach Flambé'PBR	CWGN EGrI ELan GJos LRHS MBNS MGos MHol Midl MPnt NBir SPoG WFar
'Malachite'	LRHS MPnt			
'Mango'	MPnt			
'Marmalade'PBR ♀H6	Widely available			
'Mars'	MPnt		'Peach Pie'	MPnt
'Mary Rose'	MPnt		'Peachberry Ice'PBR (Dolce Series)	LRHS MPnt MPro
maxima	MPnt			
'Mega Caramel'	MPnt		'Pear Crisp'	LRHS MPnt
'Mega Citronelle'	MPnt		'Penelope'	MPnt
'Melting Fire'	GPSL LBom LBuc MPnt		PEPPERMINT ('Tnheupp'PBR) (Little Cutie Series)	EHeP ELan EPfP LBuc LRHS Midl MPnt WCot WNPC
'Metallic Shimmer' (Fox Series) ♀H6	LBuc MPnt WNPC			
			'Peppermint Spice'PBR	MPnt
			'Persian Carpet'	MPnt NBir

(Petite Series) 'Petite Marbled Burgundy'	MPnt	- 'Geisha's Fan'	MPnt
- 'Petite Pearl Fairy'	EGrI MPnt	- 'Monet' (v)	MPnt
- 'Petite Pink Bouquet'	MPnt	- 'Ruby Bells'	LRHS MPnt MPro SRms WNPC
'Pewter Moon'	EHeP GMaP MPnt NBir WFar	- 'Snow Storm' (v)	MPnt SRms
'Pewter Veil'	MPnt	- 'Splendens'	EHeP MPnt WCAu
'Phoebe's Blush' (Fox Series)	EPfP LRHS MPnt WNPC	- 'Taff's Joy' (v)	MPnt
		- 'White Cloud' (v)	ECha EPfP GQue LSto MCtn MPnt SRms
'Picasso' (Master Painters Series)	MPnt	'Sashay' ♀H6	GBin MPnt
PINK DANCER ('Godan') (Fox Series)	MPnt	'Saturn'	MPnt
		'Schneewittchen'	MPnt
'Pink Panther'^PBR (Heucheraholics Series)	CWGN EPfP LBuc LRHS MPnt	'Scintillation'	MPnt
		'September Morn' (Seasonal Selection Series)	MPnt
'Pink Pearls'^PBR	MPnt WCot WNPC	'Shanghai'^PBR	EGren EPfP LSRN Midl MPnt MPro WFar
'Pinky Panky'	CWGN LBuc LRHS MPnt WNPC		
'Pinot Bianco'	MPnt	'Shenandoah Mountain'	MPnt
'Pinot Gris'^PBR	MPnt	'Shere Variety'	MPnt
'Pinot Noir'	MPnt	SHIMMER ('Tnheushi') (Little Cuties Series)	MPnt MPro
'Pistache'	MPnt		
§ 'Pluie de Feu'	LCro MPnt	'Silver Blush'	EBee
'Plum Pudding'	CBcs EBee EGren EHeP ELan EPfP EWes LBom LBuc LCro LRHS LSRN LSto MAsh MBNS MGos MPro MBir NGdn SRms StAn WCAu WFar WSpi WTor	'Silver Celebration' (Fox Series) ♀H6	LBuc MPnt WNPC
		'Silver Dollar'	EBee MPnt
		'Silver Gumdrop'^PBR (Dolce Series)	CSpe CTsd CWGN EGren ELan EPfP LBom LBuc LCro LRHS LSou LSto MArl Midl MPnt MPri MPro SRkn WFar WNPC WTor
'Plum Royale'^PBR	ELan MGos MPnt		
'Pretty Perinne'^PBR	MPnt		
'Pretty Polly'	MPnt	'Silver Heart'	EBee MPnt
'Prince'	EBlo ELan MPnt	'Silver Indiana'	MPnt
'Prince of Silver'	MPnt	'Silver Light'	MPnt
'Princess Alice' **new**	EBee	'Silver Lode'^PBR	MPnt
pringlei	see *H. rubescens*	'Silver Scrolls'^PBR	CMac EPfP GMaP LBuc LCro LRHS LSRN MBel MGos MPnt SOrN SPoG WCot
pubescens	MPnt		
- 'Alba'	MPnt		
pulchella	EDAr GKev MHer MPnt SPlb SRms	'Silver Shadows'	MPnt
'Purple Crinkle'	MPnt WNPC	'Silver Streak'	see *H.* (Carnival Series) CARNIVAL SILVER STREAK, × *Heucherella* 'Silver Streak'
'Purple Petticoats' ♀H6	CBcs ELan LRHS MHol MPnt MPro SPoG		
'Quick Silver'	MPnt NBir WCAu	SILVERBERRY ('Ifhesilb') (Indian Summer Series)	LRHS MPnt
§ 'Quilter's Joy'	MPnt		
'Rachel'	GMaP MPnt WCAu	'Sioux Falls'	MPnt
RAIN OF FIRE	see *H.* 'Pluie de Feu'	'Slater's Pink' (Fox Series)	MPnt WNPC
'Raspberry' (Fox Series)	MPnt	'Snow Angel'	MPnt SPoG WCot
'Raspberry Ice'	MPnt	'Snowfire' (v)	MPnt
'Raspberry Regal'	MPnt NBir	'Southern Comfort'^PBR	EGren Midl MPnt NPer SPoG
'Raspberry Sea'	LRHS	'Sparkler'	MPnt
'Rave On'	EBee ELan MPnt	'Sparkling Burgundy'	EGren ELan LRHS MPnt
'Red Dress'	MPnt	'Spearmint'	MPro
'Red Lightning'^PBR	CWGN MPnt	'Spellbound'^PBR	MPnt SPoG
'Red Pearls'	MPnt NCth	SPLASHBERRY ('Ifhesbs') (Indian Summer Series)	EPfP LRHS MPnt MPro
RED SEA ('Ds2'^PBR)	EPfP MPnt WCot		
'Red Spangles'	MPnt	STARRY NIGHT ('Inheustan'^PBR)	MPnt
'Regina' ♀H6	MHol MPnt		
'Renoir' (Master Painters Series)	MPnt	'Steel City'	MPnt
		'Stormy Seas'	EBee EGrI ELan MPnt NBir WCAu
richardsonii	MPnt	'Strawberries and Cream' (v) ♀H6	MPnt
'Rickard'	MPnt		
'Rio'^PBR	EPfP MPnt SRot	'Strawberry Candy'	MPnt NLar
'Robert'	MPnt	'Strawberry Swirl'	CElw MPnt NBir SHar WCAu
'Root Beer'^PBR	LRHS MHol MPnt	'Sugar Beer'^PBR (Little Cutie Series)	LBuc MPnt WCot
§ *rubescens*	NBro		
- var. *versicolor*	GKev	SUGAR FROSTING ('Pwheu0104')	ELan GJos LRHS LSRN MGos MPnt NCou
'Ruby Tuesday'	MPnt		
'Ruffles'	see *H. micrantha* 'Ruffles'	'Sugar Plum'^PBR	EBee EGren ELan EPfP LBuc LRHS LSRN LWaG MPnt WHoo WNPC
'Sanbrot'	MPnt		
§ *sanguinea*	EGren EGrI GKev LRHS MPnt NBir WFar	'Sunrise' (Seasonal Selection Series)	MPnt
		'Sweet Berry'	MPnt
- 'Alba'	MPnt SMHy SPel	'Sweet Caroline' (Fox Series)	MPnt WNPC
- 'Coral Forest'	EGren LWaG WFar WNPC		
- 'Coral Petite'	EDAr		

'Sweet Tart'^PBR (Little Cutie Series)	LCro LRHS MPnt NLar SPoG WNPC		'Brass Lantern'^PBR ♀H6	CSpe EHeP GJos LCro LRHS LSou MAsh MPnt SPoG WNPC
'Swirling Fantasy'	EGrI MPnt WFar		'Burnished Bronze'^PBR	MPnt NLar SPoG
'Tangerine Wave' (Fox Series) ♀H6	EGren EHeP EPfP LBuc LCro MArI MPnt WNPC		'Buttered Rum'^PBR	CWGN EBee LBuc LCro LRHS MPnt WNPC WTor
'Tara'	MPnt		'Butterscotch'	WCot
'Thomas' (Fox Series) ♀H6	GBin LBuc MPnt WNPC		'Catching Fire'	LRHS MPnt
'Timeless Night'	EBee EPfP LBom LRHS MPnt MPri WTor		'Chocolate Lace'	MPnt
			'Cinnamon Bear'	MPnt
'Timeless Treasure'^PBR	EBee EPfP LCro LRHS MPnt		'Citrus Shock'	MPnt SPoG
'Tiramisu'^PBR	LRHS MPnt		'Copper Cascade'^PBR (Cascade Series)	ELan LRHS LSou MPnt
'Tokyo'^PBR (City Series)	CWGN MAvo Midl MPnt NLar SPoG		'Cracked Ice'^PBR	CSpe LBuc LRHS MPnt WNPC
'Topaz Jazz'	MPnt WNPC		'Dayglow Pink'	MPnt
'Twinkle' (Fox Series)	MPnt		'Eye Spy'^PBR (Fun and Games Series)	EBee LRHS MPnt MPro WFar WTor
'Van Gogh' (Master Painters Series)	MPnt			
'Vanilla Spice'	MPnt		'Fan Dancer'	MPnt
'Velvet Night'	EPfP MPnt NBir SPlb		'Fire Frost'^PBR	MPnt
'Venus' ♀H6	MPnt MPro WCot		FIRECRACKER ('Tnherfir')	CLiI EGren MPro
'Vesuvius'	MPnt		'Gold Cascade' (Cascade Series)	ELan EPfP LRHS MPnt WFar
'Victoria' (Fox Series) **new**	MPnt			
'Vienna' (City Series)	MPnt		GOLD STRIKE ('Hertn041')	MPnt
§ ***villosa***	ECha LEdu MPnt WFar		'Golden Zebra'^PBR	LRHS MPnt
- 'Autumn Bride'	CElw LCro LSto MPnt SDix SMHy SPel		'Great Smokies'	MPnt
			'Gunsmoke'	MPnt WFar
- BRESSINGHAM BRONZE ('Absi')	MPnt		HAPPY HOUR LIME ('Tnherhhl')	LBuc LRHS MPnt
- 'Chantilly'	MHol MPnt			
- var. ***macrorhiza***	MBel MPnt		'Heart of Darkness'	MPnt
- 'Palace Purple'	CBcs CDoC ECha EGren EGrI EHeP ELan EPfP GBin GMaP LBom LCro LRHS LShi LSto LWaG MBros MCtn MGos MPro MSwo NBir NGdn SPlb SRms SVic WCAu WTre		'Honey Rose'^PBR	EBee MPnt SPoG
			'Hopscotch' (Fun and Games Series)	EPfP LRHS LSou MHol MPnt MPro WFar WNPC
			'Hot Spot'	MPnt
			'Indigo Frost'	MPnt
- 'Palace Purple Select'	CMac LShi WSpi		'Infinity'^PBR	NCth
'Violet Shimmer' (Fox Series)	MHtn MPnt WNPC		'Kimono'^PBR ♀H6	CBcs CMHG ELan EPfP GBin GMaP ISha LBuc LCro LRHS LSRN LSto MPnt NLar SPel WNPC
'Virginale'	MPnt			
'Walnut' (Fox Series) ♀H6	MPnt WNPC			
'White Marble'	MPnt SHar		'Leapfrog' (Fun and Games Series)	LCro
'White Spires'	MPnt			
'White Swirls'	MPnt		'Mojito'	MPnt
'Wild Rose'^PBR (Primo Series)	CBcs CWnw EBee EGren EPfP LBom LBuc LCro LRHS MPnt MPri MPro NLar WFar WNPC		'Ninja'	see *Tiarella* 'Ninja'
			'Onyx'	CSpe EBee LBuc WNPC
			PEACH TEA ('Tnherpt')	MPnt MPro WFar
'Wildberry' (Dolce Series)	CWGN CWnw EBee EGren EPfP LBuc LCro LRHS MHol MPnt MPri SRkn WFar WNPC		'Pink Fizz'	LRHS MPnt MPri MPro WFar WTor
			PINK REVOLUTION ('Heupire030'^PBR)	NCth
'William How'				
'Winter Joy' (Seasonal Selection Series)	MPnt		PINK WHISPERS ('Hertn042')	MPnt
			'Plum Cascade'^PBR (Cascade Series)	LBuc MPnt WNPC
'Winter Red'	MPnt			
WORLD CAFFÉ AMERICANO ('Jmb 14/11') (World Caffé Series)	EGren		'Quicksilver'	CBcs GMaP LRHS MPnt
			'Red Rover' (Fun and Games Series)	ISha LRHS MPnt MPri
'XXL'	MPnt		'Redstone Falls'^PBR (Falls Series)	CBcs EBee GJos LBuc MPnt MSCN SPoG WNPC
'Zabeliana'	MPnt			
'Zipper'^PBR	MPnt		§ 'Silver Streak'	LRHS MPnt
			'Solar Eclipse'	CBcs EBee EGren EHeP GPSL LCro LRHS MAsh MHol MHtn MPnt MPro NLar NSti SPoG WFar WNPC

Heuchera × *Tiarella* see × *Heucherella*

× *Heucherella* ✿ (Saxifragaceae)

'Alabama Sunrise'^PBR	ELan EWhm ISha LRHS MPnt MPro NBir NLar NPer WFar		'Solar Power'^PBR	EBee ELan EPfP LRHS MPnt MPri WFar WNPC
alba 'Bridget Bloom'	LRHS MPnt SRms WCAu WFar		'Stoplight'^PBR	CWGN ELan EPfP GMaP LRHS MGos MPnt NBir NSti WFar WNPC
§ - 'Rosalie'	MPnt SPlb			
'Art Deco'	ISha MPnt		'Sunrise Falls' (Falls Series)	LRHS MPnt WFar
'Art Nouveau'	ISha LRHS MPnt		'Sweet Tea'^PBR	Widely available
'Autumn Cascade' (Cascade Series)	MPnt		'Tapestry'^PBR ♀H6	EGren ELan EPfP GElm GMaP LRHS MBNS MHol MPnt NSti SPel SPoG SRkn WFar WNPC
'Berry Fizz'	MPnt			
'Birthday Cake'	MPnt		***tiarelloides***	SRms
'Blue Ridge'	ISha MPnt		'Twilight'^PBR	MPnt
			§ 'Viking Ship'	MPnt NBir

'Yellowstone Falls'PBR LBuc MPnt MSCN WNPC
(Falls Series) ♀H6

Hexastylis see *Asarum*

Hibbertia (Dilleniaceae)
aspera	CAbb CBcs CRHN LRHS WFar WKif
pedunculata	WAbe
§ *scandens* ♀H1c	CBcs CHll CRHN EAri EShb SEND
volubilis	see *H. scandens*

Hibiscus (Malvaceae)
acetosella	EShb
calyphyllus	CWal
'Cherry Cheesecake'	EAri LRHS
coccineus	CWal EAri LRHS MCtn SMad SPlb
- white-flowered	EAri
'Cranberry Crush'PBR	CWGN EAri ELan MNrw
'Eruption'	EBee
'Fantasia'PBR	ELan
'Fireball'PBR	EAri ELan SPoG
FULL BLAST	see *H.* 'Resi'
hamabo	CBcs JPap LBom LRHS
'Holy Grail' **new**	EUrb
huegelii	see *Alyogyne huegelii*
'Jazzberry Jam'PBR	SPoG
'Kopper King'PBR	EAri ELan MBNS MNrw SPoG
LITTLE PRINCE ('Lillprinc'PBR)	ELan
'Mahogany Splendor'	WHil
'Midnight Marvel'	CBcs EAri LRHS
militaris	SBrt
moscheutos	EBee SVic
- (Carousel Series) CAROUSEL GEANT RED ('Tahi05'PBR)	EAri EHeP ELan MHtn
- - CAROUSEL JOLLY HEART ('Tahi56'PBR)	EAri ELan LCro
- - CAROUSEL PINK CANDY ('Tahi12'PBR)	CAbb CWGN EAri LRHS
- - CAROUSEL PINK PASSION ('Tahi16'PBR)	EAri ELan LCro LRHS
- - CAROUSEL RED WINE ('Tahi61'PBR)	CAbb LRHS
- 'Galaxy'	MCtn
- 'Old Yella'PBR	EAri ELan EUrb SPoG
- PLANET GRIOTTE ('Tangri'PBR)	CBcs LRHS
- 'Robert Fleming'PBR	EAri
- 'Royal Gems'PBR	ELan
- 'Tansol'PBR	LCro
pedunculatus	MCtn
'Perfect Storm'	EAri
'Plum Crazy'PBR	EAri ELan SPel
§ 'Resi'PBR	EBar
rosa-sinensis	CDoC SPre
sabdariffa	CAgr CSpe MCtn
sinosyriacus 'Lilac Queen'	WPGP
- 'Ruby Glow'	LSRN WPGP
- 'Small Wonders'PBR	ELan
'Starry Starry Night' **new**	EUrb
storckii	CWal
'Summer Storm'PBR	ELan
syriacus	CWal LWaG MCtn WJur
- 'America Irene Scott'PBR (d/v)	LCro LRHS SPoG
- 'Aphrodite'	SSta
- 'Ardens' (d)	CEnd EHeP LBom LRHS SPoG WFar
- AZURRI BLUE SATIN ('Dvpazurri'PBR)	SSta
- BLUE BIRD	see *H. syriacus* 'Oiseau Bleu'
- BLUE CHIFFON ('Notwood3'PBR) (Chiffon Series) (d) ♀H5	EGren ELan LBom LCro LRHS SPoG
- 'Bredon Springs'	SSta
- CHINA CHIFFON ('Bricutts') (Chiffon Series) (d)	LCro LRHS SEND SPoG
- 'Diana' ♀H5	CBcs CCVT CDoC EBee ELan ELon EPfP LSRN MAsh SSta
- 'Dorothy Crane'	LRHS SSta
- 'Duc de Brabant' (d)	CSBt LRHS MBlu
- 'Elegantissimus'	see *H. syriacus* 'Lady Stanley'
- FLOWER TOWER PURPLE	see *H. syriacus* 'Gandini Santiago'
- FLOWER TOWER RUBY	see *H. syriacus* 'Gandini van Aart Ruby'
- 'Freedom' (d)	LRHS
- FRENCH POINT ('Minfren'PBR)	EBee
§ - 'Gandini Santiago'PBR	LCro LSou SGol
§ - 'Gandini van Aart'PBR	LCro LRHS SGol
§ - 'Gandini van Aart Ruby'	LCro
- 'Hamabo' ♀H5	CSBt EGren ELan LRHS LSRN MGos MMuc NPlm SEND SPoG WFar WLov
- 'Helene'	LRHS LSRN MBlu SSta
- 'Honghwarang'	SSta
- 'Jeanne d'Arc' (d)	EBee
§ - 'Lady Stanley' (d)	CCVT CDoC CMac CSBt EBee LRHS
- LAVENDER CHIFFON ('Notwoodone'PBR) (Chiffon Series) (d) ♀H5	CSBt EBee ELan EPfP EUrb EWes LBom LCro LRHS LSou LSRN SEND SPoG
- 'Leopoldii' (d)	WFar
- MAGENTA CHIFFON ('Rwoods5'PBR) (Chiffon Series)	LBom LCro LRHS SPoG
- 'Marina' ♀H5	CDoC ELan LCro LRHS MBlu WFar WLov
- 'Mathilde'	SSta
- 'Mauve Queen'	SSta
- 'Meehanii' misapplied	see *H. syriacus* 'Purpureus Variegatus'
- 'Meehanii' (v) ♀H5	CEnd SPoG SSta
- 'Melrose' ♀H5	SSta
§ - 'Oiseau Bleu' ♀H5	CBcs CBrac CDoC EBee EGren ELan EPfP IPap LCro LRHS LSRN MAsh MMuc NLar NPlm SEND SPlb SPoG SRms SSta WFar
- PINK CHIFFON ('Jwnwood4'PBR) (Chiffon Series) (d)	EBee ELan LCro LRHS
- PINK GIANT ('Flogi')	SSta
- PINKY SPOT ('Minspot'PBR) ♀H5	LRHS
- PURPLE PILLAR	see *H. syriacus* 'Gandini Santiago'
- PURPLE RUFFLES ('Sanchoyo') (d)	CDoC LRHS SPoG
§ - 'Purpureus Variegatus' (v)	CMac
- 'Red Heart' ♀H5	CBrac CCVT CEnd CMac CSBt EGren ELan EPfP LBom LCro LRHS LSou MAsh MGos MMuc NPlm SEND SPoG SRms SSta
- RUSSIAN VIOLET ('Floru')	CEnd EGren
- 'Shintaeyang'	LRHS
- 'Snowdrift'	SSta
I - 'Speciosus' (d)	EHeP LRHS SPoG WFar
- STARBURST CHIFFON ('Rwoods6') (Chiffon Series) ♀H5	LCro LRHS
- 'Totus Albus'	SSta
- ULTRAMARINE ('Minultra'PBR) ♀H5	CDoC LBom LSRN
- 'Variegatus'	see *H. syriacus* 'Purpureus Variegatus'
- 'Violet Clair Double' (d)	CMac

- WHITE CHIFFON   ELan EPfP EWes LBom LCro LRHS
  ('Notwoodtwo'^PBR)   LSRN SPoG
  (Chiffon Series) (d) ♀H5
- WHITE PILLAR   see *H. syriacus* 'Gandini van Aart'
- 'William R. Smith' ♀H5 LCro SSta
- 'Woodbridge' ♀H5   CBcs CBrac CCVT CDoC CEnd
                          CMac CSBt EGren EHeP ELan ELon
                          EPfP EUrb IPap LCro LRHS LSRN
                          MAsh MGos NLar NPlm SEND SPlb
                          SPoG SRms WFar WHtc WLov
tiliaceus   EAri
trionum   CSpe
- 'Sunny Day'   ELan
WALBERTON'S ROSE MOON   LBuc LRHS SPoG
  ('Walhirosmo'^PBR)

hickory, shagbark see *Carya ovata*

Hieracium (Asteraceae)

aurantiacum   see *Pilosella aurantiaca*
brunneocroceum   see *Pilosella aurantiaca*
                         subsp. *carpathicola*
laevigatum subsp. *nivale* MMuc
§ *lanatum*   GJos NBir
maculatum Sm.   see *H. spilophaeum*
pannosum   WCot
pilosella   see *Pilosella officinarum*
scullyi   WFar
§ *spilophaeum*   CGwi GGro MMuc NBid NPer
- 'Blue Leaf'   WCot
- 'Leopard'   GJos
villosum   GJos WHer
welwitschii   see *H. lanatum*

Hierochloe (Poaceae)

odorata   EPPr LEdu MCtn WPGP

Himalayacalamus (Poaceae)

asper   CDTJ
§ *falconeri*   SDix WCot
§ *hookerianus*   LAma
- 'Himalaya Blue'   SBGi

× *Hippeasprekelia* (Amaryllidaceae)

'Durga Pradhan'   CSpe GKev LAma WCot
'Red Beauty'   WCot

Hippeastrum ✿ (Amaryllidaceae)

× *acramannii* ♀H2   WCot
'Amadeus Candy'^PBR (d) **new** LCro
aulicum   WCot
'Black Pearl'   LCro
blossfeldiae   GKev LAma
(Butterfly Group)   XFar
  'Exotic Star'^PBR
- 'Sweet Lilian'   XFar
- 'Wild Amazone' **new** XFar
(Colibri Group)   WCot
  'Balentino'^PBR
- 'Rapido'   LCro
cybister   WCot
(Diamond Group)   ETay
  'Alfresco'^PBR (d)
- 'Charisma' ♀H2   ETay GKev LAma
- 'Christmas Star'   ETay
- 'Fairytale' ♀H2   LCro
- 'Green Magic' ♀H2   LCro
- 'Lemon Star'   GKev
- 'Picotee' ♀H2   GKev LAma LCro XFar
- 'Pyjama Party'   LAma
- 'Tierra'   LCro
- 'Très Chic'   ETay
(Double Galaxy Group)   ETay GKev LAma
  'Aphrodite' (d)
- 'Aquaro' (d)   GKev LAma
- CHERRY NYMPH   LCro XFar
  ('Chernym'^PBR) (d)
- 'Clown' (d) ♀H2   GKev LAma
- 'Dancing Queen' (d)   XFar
- 'Double Dragon'^PBR (d) LAma
- 'Double Dream'^PBR (d) XFar
- 'Flamed Amadeus' (d) **new** XFar
- 'Giant Amadeus'^PBR   LCro
  (d) **new**
- 'Marilyn'^PBR (d)   GKev LAma LCro
- 'Nymph' (d)   LAma XFar
- 'Red Peacock' (d)   XFar
- 'Splash'^PBR (d) **new** LCro
- SWEET NYMPH   XFar
  ('Swenym'^PBR) (d) **new**
(Galaxy Group) 'Ambiance' GKev LAma
- 'Apple Blossom' ♀H2   GKev LAma LCro XFar
- 'Barbados'   GKev LAma
- 'Benfica'   GKev LAma
§ - 'Candy Cream' **new** XFar
- 'Candy Queen'   see *H.* (Galaxy Group) 'Candy Cream'
- 'Cherry Bloss' **new** GKev LAma
- 'Christmas Gift'   GKev LAma LCro
- 'Ferrari'   GKev LCro
- 'Flamenco Queen' ♀H2   LAma
- 'Gervase'   GKev LAma LCro XFar
- 'Grand Diva'   GKev LAma
- 'Hercules'   XFar
- 'Lagoon'^PBR ♀H2   LCro
- 'Limona'^PBR   LCro
- 'Luna'   GKev LAma
- MAGICAL TOUCH ('Nwkmt') GKev LAma
- 'Minerva'   LAma XFar
- 'Mont Blanc'   GKev LAma XFar
- 'Monte Carlo'^PBR ♀H2 LCro
- 'Naranja' ♀H2   GKev LAma
- 'Orange Souvereign'   XFar
- 'Pink Princess'   LAma
- 'Red Lion' ♀H2   GKev LAma LCro XFar
- 'Rilona'   GKev LAma XFar
- 'Royal Velvet' ♀H2   LAma
- 'Samba'   LAma
- 'Spartacus'^PBR   LCro
- 'Susan'   XFar
- 'Temptation'   LAma XFar
- 'Terra Cotta Star'^PBR **new** XFar
× *johnsonii* ♀H2   WCot
'McCann's Double' (d)   GKev LAma
papilio   GKev LAma LCro WCot XFar
psittacinum   WCot
puniceum   GKev LAma WCot
'Royal Red'   LCro
'San Antonio Rose'   WCot
'Snow Queen'   ETay LCro
(Spider Group) 'Bogota' LAma LCro
- 'Carmen'   XFar
- 'Chico' ♀H2   GKev LAma
- 'Emerald'   GKev LAma WCot
- 'Evergreen' ♀H2   LAma LCro XFar
- 'Quito'   GKev LAma
- 'Sumatra'^PBR   LCro XFar
striatum   WCot
stylosum   GKev LAma WCot
'Toughie'   EBee
(Trumpet Group) 'Estella' ETay XFar
- 'Santiago'   LAma XFar
vittatum   WCot

Hippeastrum × *Sprekelia* see × *Hippeasprekelia*
Hippocrepis (Fabaceae)
§	comosa	GJos SPhx WAbe
§	emerus	CBcs CDoC CMac CMHG ELan
		EPfP IArd LCro LRHS MAsh MMuc
		MPri SEND WJur WSpi

Hippophae (Elaeagnaceae)
P	rhamnoides	CBcs CBTr CCVT CHab CLnd CMac
		CMCN EHeP ELan EPfP EPom LBuc
		LEdu LMaj MBlu MMuc SEND SPlb
		WFar WJur WKor
	- (f)	CBWd EGren LWaG SArc SPre
	- (m)	EPom
	- 'Askola' (f/F)	CAgr
	- 'Dorana' (f/F)	CAgr
	- 'Friesdorfer Orange' (f/F)	CAgr LWaG NLar
	- 'Frugna' (f/F)	CAgr
	- 'Hergo' (f/F)	CAgr NLar
	- 'Hikul' (m)	CAgr LRHS NLar
	- 'Juliet' (f/F)	CAgr
	- 'Leikora' (f/F) ♀H7	CAgr LMaj MBlu MGos NLar
	- ORANGE ENERGY ('Habego'PBR) (f/F)	CAgr
	- 'Pollmix' (m) ♀H7	CAgr MBlu NLar
	- 'Pollmix 4' (m)	MGos
	- 'Romeo' (m)	NLar
	- 'Sirola' (f/F)	CAgr
	salicifolia	CAgr WJur WKor
	sinensis LS&E 15724	WPGP

Hippuris (Plantaginaceae)
vulgaris	CBen CLil CPud CWat ELin EWat
	LWaG NPer WMAq

Hirpicium (Asteraceae)
armerioides	SPlb

Histiopteris (Dennstaedtiaceae)
*	dicksonii	SPlb
	incisa	LEdu SPlb WPGP

Hoheria ✿ (Malvaceae)
	'Ace of Spades'	CDoC ELan EPfP NLar SEND WSpi
§	angustifolia	EBee EPfP SChF SVen WJur WPGP
	'Borde Hill'	CBcs CDoC CMac CTsd EBee EGrI
		ELan ELon EPfP LSRN MAsh SChF
		SEND WPGP WSpi
	glabrata	CMac EPfP NBir WPGP
	'Glory of Amlwch'	CBcs CDoC CJun EBee ELan EPfP
		GGGa SChF SMad SPoG WPGP
		WSpi
§	lyallii ♀H4	IDun LRHS SVen WJur WSpi
	microphylla	see *H. angustifolia*
	populnea 'Sunshine' (v)	CDoC SPoG
	× sexangusta	WPGP
	- 'Mother Mary'	WPGP
	sexstylosa	CCVT CWal EBee LEdu LSRN SArc
		SPlb SVen WFar WJur WSpi
	- 'Craetegifolia'	WSpi
	- 'Pendula'	CMac WPGP
	- 'Stardust' ♀H4	CBcs CDoC CEnd CJun CMac
		CMCN CMHG CSBt CTsd
		CWnw EBee ELan ELon EPfP
		LRHS LSRN MAsh MBlu NCth
		NLar SArc SChF SDix SEND
		SNig SPoG WPGP WSpi
	SNOW WHITE ('Hutwhit')	CBcs EUrb LSRN MGos NPip SArc
		SBig SPoG WMat

Holarrhena (Apocynaceae)
pubescens 'Snowflake'	CDoC

Holboellia (Lardizabalaceae)
BWJ 7250 from Thailand	WCru
angustifolia	ESwi WCru
- HWJCM 008	WCru
- subsp. angustifolia	NLar WCru
- - H&M 1504	WPGP
- subsp. linearifolia BWJ 8004	WCru
- - HWJK 2419	WCru
- - WJC 13784	WCru
- - WJC 13811	WCru
- subsp. obtusa DJHC 506	WCru
brachyandra	EBee EWes SChF
- HWJ 1023	WCru WPGP
chapaensis FMWJ 13055	WCru
coriacea	CBcs CRHN EBee EPfP ESwi NQui
	SEND WCru WJur
- BWJ 7487	WCru
coriacea × latifolia **new**	WCru
aff. grandiflora FMWJ 13333	WCru
latifolia	CBcs CHll CMac CRHN CWnw
	EBee EGrI ELan EPfP ESwi LEdu
	NLar SArc SBig SEle SNig SPoG
	WCru WJur WPGP
- B&SWJ 2818	WCru
- DJHC 98442	WCru
- HWJK 2014	WCru
- subsp. chartacea dark-flowered HWJK 2213d	WCru
- - pale-flowered HWJK 2213c	WCru
- lanceolate-leaved	WPGP

Holcus (Poaceae)
mollis 'Albovariegatus' (v)	CWCL EPPr NBid NBro NPer NSti
	SPlb SRms

Holodiscus (Rosaceae)
discolor	CBcs EBee EWes MBlu NQui SPlb

Homalocladium see *Mueblenbeckia*

Homalomena (Araceae)
rubescens 'Maggy'	LCro NHrt SBig
wallisii 'Camouflage'	LCro NTro

Homeria see *Moraea*
breyniana	see *Tulipa breyniana*

Homoglossum see *Gladiolus*

Hoodia (Apocynaceae)
gordonii **new**	NTro

Hordeum (Poaceae)
jubatum ♀H6	CDor CKno CSpe CTtf CWCL EWes
	LCro LEdu LRHS MAsh MCtn MPro
	NClf NGdn NLit SPhx SRot
- 'Early Pink'	NDov
marinum	WCot
secalinum	CHab
vulgare variegated (v)	MNHC WKit

Hormathophylla (Brassicaceae)
spinosa 'Roseum' ♀H5	CSpe ECha ELan EPot GArf WAbe
- 'Rubrum'	EPot

Horminum (Lamiaceae)
pyrenaicum	EDAr GQue LShi MHol MMuc SEND SRms
I - f. *alboviolaceum*	EDAr EWhm
- 'Rubrum'	EDAr
- white-flowered	GKev

Hornungia (Brassicaceae)
alpina	EPfP GEdr WIce

horseradish see *Armoracia rusticana*

Hosta ✿ (Asparagaceae)
'A Dash of Lemon' (v)	SSien
'Abana' (v)	IBal SSien
'Abba Dabba Do' (v)	CDor ELon EMic IBal NRew NSue SSien
'Abby' (v)	CBdn EMic IBal NSue SSien WFar
'Abiqua Ariel'	EMic
'Abiqua Blue Crinkles'	NBir
'Abiqua Blue Edger'	SSien
'Abiqua Blue Madonna'	IBal
'Abiqua Blushing Recluse'	SSien
'Abiqua Delight' (v)	EMic
'Abiqua Drinking Gourd' ♀H7	CBdn CDor ELin EMic EUrb GBin GMaP IBal LRHS MPri MSwo NLar NRew SArc SSien
'Abiqua Moonbeam' (v)	ELon EMic IBal NGdn NRew SSien
'Abiqua Recluse'	EMic
'Abiqua Trumpet'	EMic NGdn NLar SSien
'Academy Flora'	IBal
'Academy Mavrodaphne'	EMic
'Adorable'	IBal LBuc NRew NSue SSien
aequinoctiiantha	IBal SSien
'After Party'	SSien
'Afterglow' (v)	IBal SSien
'Age of Gold' **new**	NRew
'Alabama Gold'	EMic
'Alakazaam' (v) ♀H7	NRew SSien WFar
'Alan Titchmarsh'	NSue SSien
albomarginata	see *H.* 'Paxton's Original'
§ 'Albomarginata' (*fortunei*) (v)	CMac EHeP EMic NBir NGdn SSien WFar
'Alex Summers'	NRew NWbg SSien WFar
'Alice in Wonderland' (v)	NRew
'All Aflutter' (v)	NSue
'All That Jazz' (v)	EMic
'Allan P. McConnell' (v) ♀H7	CBdn EMic LRHS NSue SSien WFar
'Allegan Emperor' (v)	SSien
'Allegan Fog' (v)	CBdn EMic GEdr IBal NRew NSue SSien
'Alligator Alley' (v)	EMic LRHS NRew NSue SSien
'Alligator Shoes' (v)	IBal
'Almost'	IBal SSien
'Alpine Aire'	EMic
'Alternative'	IBal
'Alvatine Taylor' (v)	Isha MPri NGdn SSien
'Amalia'^PBR (v)	CBdn ESwi IBal NRew SSien
'Amanuma'	EMic IBal NSue
'Amazone' (v)	NRew
'Amber Tiara'	NRew NSue SSien
'Ambrosia' (v)	NRew NSue SSien
'American Dream' (v)	EMic NRew SSien
'American Halo'	CBdn ESwi IBal NLar NRew NSti NSue SSien
'American King of the Woods' **new**	CBdn
'American Sweetheart'	NRew SSien
'Americana' (v)	NRew SSien
'Amethyst Gem'	LRHS NRew NSue SSien
§ 'Amime Tachi' (*rectifolia*) (v)	SSien
'Amos'	IBal SSien
'Amy Elizabeth' (v)	EMic
'Andorian'	IBal NSue
'Andrew'	NRew SSien
'Angel Falls' (v)	SSien
'Angel Feathers' (v)	IBal NSue SSien
'Angelique' (v)	CBdn IBal NRew SSien
'Ani Machi' (v) ♀H7	NSue
'Ann Kulpa' (v)	EMic EPfP ESwi LRHS NGdn NRew SSien
'Anne' (v)	NRew NSue SMrm SSien
'Ansly' (v)	IBal
'Antioch' (*fortunei*) (v)	EMic EPfP LRHS NLar NRew SSien WFar
'Aoki' (*fortunei*)	EMic
'Aoki Variegated' (*fortunei*) (v)	EMic
'Aphrodite' (*plantaginea*) (d)	SSien
'Apple Candy' (v)	IBal NSue SSien
'Apple Green'	EMic
'Apple Pie'	CBdn
'Appletini'	IBal NRew NSue
'Arc de Triomphe'	EMic IBal NLar NRew NSue SSien
'Arch Duke'	IBal SSien
'Arctic Blast'	CBdn EMic
'Arctic Circle' (v)	EMic
'Argentea Variegata' (*undulata*)	see *H. undulata* var. *undulata*
'Aristocrat' (Tardiana Group) (v)	EMic LRHS NGdn NRew SSien WFar
'Armani'	SSien
'Arnold Black'	SSien
'Aspen Gold' (*tokudama* hybrid)	EMic
'Athena' (d/v)	SSien
'Atlantis'^PBR (v)	EMic NGdn NRew NSue SSien
'Atom Smasher'	NRew NSue SSien
'Atomic Elvis'	NSue
'August Beauty'	CBdn EMic NRew SSien
'August Moon'	EGren EGrI ELan ELon EMic EMor GMaP ISha LRHS LSto MArl NBir NGdn NLar NRew NWbg SPoG SRms SSien WCAu WFar
'Aureafolia'	see *H.* 'Starker Yellow Leaf'
'Aureoalba' (*fortunei*)	see *H.* 'Spinners'
'Aureomaculata' (*fortunei*)	see *H. fortunei* var. *albopicta*
'Aureomarginata' ambig. (v)	LRHS SSien
'Aureomarginata' (*montana*) (v)	CMac EBlo ELan GMaP MMuc NGdn NLar NRew SSien WFar
§ 'Aureomarginata' (*ventricosa*) (v)	EBlo EMic NBir NGdn WFar
'Aureostriata' (*tardiva*)	see *H.* 'Inaho'
'Austin Dickinson' (v)	EMic ESwi IBal ISha NRew SSien
'Autumn Frost' (Shadowland Series) (v) ♀H7	CBdn EBee EGren EMor EPfP IBal LBom LRHS MHol MPri MPro NGdn NRew NSue SPeP SSien
'Avalanche'	SSien
'Avocado'	ELon EMic IBal NLar NRew NSue NWbg SSien WFar
'Ayesha' (v)	ESwi IBal NRew SSien
'Azuretini'	NSue
'Babbling Brook'	NSue
'Baby Blue' (Tardiana Group)	EMic
'Baby Blue Eyes'	NSue
'Baby Booties' (v)	CBdn ESwi IBal NSue SSien
'Baby Bunting'	NBro NLar NSue SSien
'Baja White'	SSien
'Ballerina'	IBal NRew

'Bam Bam Blue'	IBal
'Banana Kid'	ISha LBar LRHS NRew NSue
'Band of Gold'	LRHS NRew SSien
'Banyai's Dancing Girl'	EMic
'Barbara Ann' (v)	CBdn IBal ISha NGdn NRew NWbg SSien WCAu
'Barbara May'	IBal
'Bashful'	SSien
'Battle Star' (v)	EMic NSue SSien
'Beach Boy' (v)	IBal MNrw NRew NSue SSien
'Beauty Little Blue'	IBal NSue
'Beauty Substance'	SSien
'Beckoning'	NRew NSue SSien
'Bedazzled' (v)	LRHS NRew SSien
'Bedford Blue'	EMic IBal NRew SSien
'Bedford Rise and Shine' (v)	EMic ESwi IBal LRHS NRew SSien
'Bedford Wakey-Wakey'	IBal
'Beet Salad'	SSien
'Behemoth'	IBal NRew NSue SSien
'Bell Bottom Blues'	IBal
bella	see *H. crassifolia*
'Bells of Edinburgh'	SSien
'Ben Vernooij' (v)	EMic EMor ESwi GAbr NRew NSue SSien
'Best of Twenty'	IBal NSue
'Betsy King'	CMac NLar
'Beyond Glory' (v)	CBdn EMic NRew SSien
'Big Beauty' (v)	ESwi IBal
'Big Boy' (*montana*)	IBal NRew SSien
'Big Daddy' (*sieboldiana* hybrid) (v)	Widely available
'Big John' (*sieboldiana*)	NSue
'Big Mama'	CLil IBal MNrw NGdn NRew NSue SSien
'Big Performer' (v)	IBal
'Big Top'	SSien
'Bigga Luigi'	SSien
'Bill Brinka' (v)	EMic SSien
'Bill Dress's Blue'	SSien
§ 'Birchwood Parky's Gold'	EMic GMaP ISha NGdn NLar NRew SSien
'Birchwood Ruffled Queen'	SSien
'Bitsy Green'	NSue
'Black Beauty'	SSien
'Black Hills'	EMic IBal NRew
'Black Light'	IBal SSien
'Blackfoot'	SSien
'Blackjack' (*sieboldiana*)	SSien WFar
'Blarney Stone'	IBal SSien
'Blaue Venus'	IBal
'Blazing Saddles' (v)	EMic NRew SSien
'Blitz' (v)	SSien
'Blonde Elf'	EMic NGdn NWbg
'Blue Angel' misapplied	see *H. sieboldiana* var. *elegans*
'Blue Angel' (*sieboldiana*) ♀H7	CDor EHeP ELan EPfP EUrb GKev GMaP GQue IBal LRHS MHol MMuc MNrw NBid NBir NGdn NLar NSue NWbg SSien WFar WTre
'Blue Arrow' ♀H7	NRew
'Blue Belle' (Tardiana Group)	EMic IBal NEoE NGdn
'Blue Blush' (Tardiana Group)	EMic IBal NGdn NSue NWbg
'Blue Boy'	EMic SSien
'Blue Cadet'	CAby CBcs CMac CPud EBee EGren EMic GBin GKev GQue ISha LRHS LSto MPri NBir NGdn NLar NRew NSue SSien WCAu WFar
'Blue Cascade'	EMic NSue
'Blue Circle' PBR	IBal NRew
'Blue Clown'	NRew

'Blue Cup' (*sieboldiana*)	SRms
'Blue Danube' (Tardiana Group)	ECha IBal
'Blue Diamond' (Tardiana Group)	EMic NSue WFar
'Blue Dimples' (Tardiana Group)	IBal
'Blue Dolphin'	SSien
'Blue Edger'	NBir SSien
'Blue Elf'	NSue
'Blue Eyes'	EMic
'Blue Flame'	EMic IBal SSien
'Blue Hawaii'	IBal LRHS NRew NSue SSien
'Blue Heart' (*sieboldiana*)	ECha EMic
'Blue Ice' (Tardiana Group)	SSien
'Blue Impression'	EMic SSien
'Blue Ivory' (v)	ELon NCou NGdn NRew NSue
'Blue Jay' (Tardiana Group)	IBal NRew
'Blue Lady'	EMic
'Blue Lake'	CBdn
'Blue Lollipop'	GEdr
'Blue Mammoth' (*sieboldiana*) ♀H7	CBdn EPfP EUrb IBal ISha LRHS NLar NRew NSue SMad SSien
'Blue Maui'	IBal
'Blue Monday'	EMic SSien
'Blue Moon' (Tardiana Group)	EMic IBal NGdn SSien
'Blue Mouse Ears' ♀H7	Widely available
'Blue My Mind'	NRew
'Blue Plate Special'	ESwi
'Blue River' (v)	EMic ESwi
'Blue Seer' (*sieboldiana*)	SSien
'Blue Shadows' (*tokudama*) (v)	CBdn ESwi NLar NRew NSue SSien WFar
'Blue Sliver'	NSue SSien
'Blue Umbrellas' (*sieboldiana* hybrid)	CLil ELan GMaP IBal NGdn NLar NRew SSien
'Blue Vision'	EMic EMor EPfP LRHS
'Blue Wedgwood' (Tardiana Group)	GQue NGdn NRew SSien
'Blue Wu'	IBal
'Blueberry à la Mode'	IBal
'Blueberry Muffin'	CBdn EMic NSue
'Blueberry Waffles'	IBal
'Blushing Blue'	ESwi SSien
'Blütenspiel'	IBal
'Bob Deane' (v)	EMic SSien
'Bob Olson' (v)	ESwi IBal SSien WFar
'Bobbie Sue' (v)	SSien
'Bobcat'	IBal ISha LBar NLar NRew NSue SSien
'Bold and Brassy'	ESwi
'Bold Edger' (v)	EMic IBal NRew
'Bold Ribbons' (v)	EMic SSien
'Boondocks' **new**	NRew
'Border Street' (v)	SSien
§ 'Borwick Beauty' (*sieboldiana*) (v)	ELon ISha NGdn NLar NRew SSien
'Bountiful'	IBal NSue
'Bounty' (v)	SSien
'Bouquet'	IBal
'BoyzToy'	CBdn NRew NSue SSien
'Branching Out'	IBal NRew
'Brash and Sassy'	IBal
'Brave Amherst' (v)	SSien
'Brenda's Beauty' (v)	NWbg
'Bressingham Blue'	CLil EBlo ELon GQue LAma LRHS NLar NRew NSue SSien WFar
'Bridal Falls' PBR	CBdn IBal NRew NSue SSien
'Bridal Veil'	EMic
'Bridegroom'	ESwi SSien

'Bridgeville'	IBal	'Challenger'	EMic
'Bright Glow' (Tardiana Group)	IBal	'Champagne Toast' (v)	LRHS NRew SSien
		'Chanticleer'	CBdn NRew SSien
'Bright Lights' (*tokudama*) (v)	CBdn EMic NGdn NRew SSien WFar	'Chantilly Lace' (v)	EMic
		'Chariots of Fire' (v)	SSien
'Bright Star' (v)	IBal NRew NSue SSien	'Cheatin' Heart'	ESwi IBal NSue SSien WFar
'Brim Cup' (v)	CDor EGren EPfP ISha LAma LBom LRHS MPri NBro NGdn NRew NWbg SSien	'Chelsea Babe' (*fortunei*) (v)	IBal SSien
		'Cherish'	NGdn NRew WFar
'Broad Street' (v)	NRew	'Cherokee' (v)	NRew SSien
'Broadband' (v)	IBal MNrw NRew SSien	'Cherry Berry' (v)	CLil CWGN EMic ESwi IBal ISha MBNS MMrt NBro NEoE NRew NWbg SPoG SSien WFar
'Broadway' (v)	EMic IBal NRew SSien		
'Bronx Bomber' (v)	NRew NSue SSien		
'Brooke'	EMic	'Cherry Flip'	SSien
'Brother Ronald' (Tardiana Group)	EMic	'Cherry Tart'	CBdn ESwi NRew NSue SSien
		'Cherub' (v)	EMic IBal NRew SSien
'Brother Stefan' (v)	CBdn EMic IBal NGdn NRew NSue SSien	'Chickadee' (v)	NRew
		'Chief Sitting Bull'	IBal
'Brutus'	IBal SSien	'Childhood Sweetheart' (v)	NSue
'Buckshaw Blue'	EBee EBlo EGren EMic EUrb IBal NBir NEoE NGdn SSien WHrl	'China Girl'	EMic ESwi IBal NRew SSien
		'Chinese Sunrise' (v)	EMic IBal NRew SRms SSien
		§ 'Chōkō-nishiki' (*montana*) (v)	CDor NGdn NRew NSue NWbg
'Buffalo Amber Waves'	NRew		
'Bulletproof'	ISha NGdn NSue	'Choo Choo Train'	EMic SSien
'Bullfrog' (v) **new**	SSien	'Chopsticks'	SSien
'Bumblebee'	SSien	'Chris' China Star'	SSien
'Butter Rim' (*sieboldii*) (v)	IBal	'Chris' Darkest Purple'	SSien
'Buttered Popcorn' (v)	SSien	'Chris' Moving Ruffles'	SSien
'California Gold Rush' (v)	IBal SSien	'Christmas Candy'[PBR]	CBdn IBal ISha LRHS MPri NRew NSue SSien
'California Silver Rush'	IBal		
'Cally Atom'	IBal	'Christmas Charm' (v)	IBal
'Cally Colossus'	IBal	'Christmas Cookies'	SSien
'Cally White' (*nigrescens*)	IBal	'Christmas Island'	NRew NSue
'Calypso' (v)	ESwi NGdn NRew NSue SSien WFar	'Christmas Pageant' (v)	NRew
'Camelot' (Tardiana Group)	IBal NGdn NRew NSue NWbg	'Christmas Tree' (v) ♀[H7]	EMic EMor ESwi IBal NGdn NLar NRew NSue SSien
'Cameo'	GEdr NSue SSien		
'Canadian Blue'	EMic LCro NRew NSue SSien WFar WTre	'Church Mouse'	CBdn IBal NSue SSien
		'Cinderella'	NRew SSien
'Candle Wax'	IBal	'Cinnamon Sticks'	IBal NSue
'Candy Dish'	IBal NRew NSue SSien	'Citric Star'	SSien
'Candy Hearts'	EMic SSien	'City Lights'	EMic ISha NRew
'Cape Cod' (v) **new**	NRew	*clausa*	EMic
capitata B&SWJ 588	WCru	- var. *normalis*	NBir NGdn
'Captain Kirk' (v) ♀[H7]	ESwi IBal LBar NGdn NRew NSue NWbg SSien WFar	'Clear Fork River Valley'	SSien
		'Cleopatra' (v)	SSien
'Captain's Adventure' (v)	EMic EMor LCro LRHS MNrw MPri NRew NSue NWbg SSien WFar XFar	'Clifford's Forest Fire'	IBal NLar NRew NSue SSien WFar
		'Clifford's Stingray' (v)	NRew NSue SSien
		'Climax' (v)	CBdn EMic NRew NWbg SSien
'Carder Blue'	EMic IBal	'Cloudburst'	EMic
'Carin's Wedding' (v)	IBal	'Clown's Collar' (v)	NRew NSue SSien
'Carl'	NRew SSien	'Coal Miner'	IBal SSien
'Carnival' (v)	ESwi LRHS MPro NGdn NRew NSue SPoG SSien	'Coast to Coast' (Shadowland Series)	ISha LBar LRHS NRew NSue SSien
'Carol' (*fortunei*) (v)	EMic IBal NGdn NLar NSue SSien	'Coastal Treasure' (v)	IBal SSien
'Carolina Sunshine' (v)	NRew SSien	'Coconut Custard'	SSien
'Carousel' (v)	EMic IBal SSien	'Cody'	EMic IBal LRHS NSue
'Carry On' (v)	NRew SSien	'Collector's Banner'	NRew
'Cascade Mist' (v)	EMic	'Color à la Mode' (v)	IBal
'Cascades' (v)	NGdn SSien	'Color Festival' (v)	CBdn CDor EBee ELon EMor IBal ISha LBar LRHS NEoE NLar NRew NSue SSien WFar
'Cathedral Windows' (v) ♀[H7]	ESwi IBal ISha LBar NRew NSue SSien		
'Catherine'	CBdn ELon EMor ISha NRew NSue NWbg SSien WFar	'Color Glory'	see *H*. 'Borwick Beauty'
		'Colored Hulk' (v)	EMic EMor ESwi IBal ISha LBar LRHS MHol NRew NWbg SSien
'Cat's Eyes' (*venusta*) (v)	SSien		
'Celebration' (v)	EBlo ELan IBal	'Columbus Circle' (v)	EMic
'Celtic Bouquet'	SSien	'Con Te Partiro' (v)	GEdr NSue SSien WFar
'Celtic Dancer'	IBal SSien	'Cookie Crumbs' (v)	GEdr SSien
'Celtic Uplands'	CBdn EMic ESwi IBal SSien	'Cool as a Cucumber' (v)	NRew SSien
'Center of Attention' (v)	NGdn NRew NSue NWbg SSien	'Cool Mistress' (v)	IBal
'Centerfold'	NRew NSue	'Cool Mouse' (v) **new**	NRew
'Chain Lightning' (v)	CBcs EMic ISha LRHS MHol MPri NRew NSue SSien	'Cooltini'	NRew
		'Corn Muffins'	EMic SSien

Name	Codes	Name	Codes
'Corona' (v)	EMic	'Devon Cloud'	CBdn SSien
'Corryvreckan'	IBal	'Devon Desire' (*montana*)	CBdn NLar SSien
'Cotillion' (v)	EMic GEdr NRew NSue	'Devon Dream' (Tardiana Group)	SSien
'Count Your Blessings' (v)	EMic	'Devon Giant'	EMic SSien
'Country Mouse' (v)	GEdr IBal ISha NSue SPoG SSien WFar	'Devon Gold'	EMic GAbr IBal NRew SSien
'County Park'	IBal	'Devon Green' ♀H7	Widely available
'Cracker Crumbs' (v) ♀H7	CBdn EMic GEdr IBal LRHS MNrw NRew NSue NWbg SSien WAbe WCot WFar	'Devon Mist'	LRHS SSien
		'Devon Tor'	EMic SSien
		'Dew Drop' (v)	EMic
'Cranberry Wine'	IBal NRew NSue SSien	'Dewed Steel'	NRew SSien
§ *crassifolia*	SSien	'Diamond Lake'	CBdn IBal LBar LRHS NRew SSien
'Cream Delight' (*undulata*)	see *H. undulata* var. *undulata*	'Diamond Necklace' (v)	NRew
'Cream Edger' (v)	CBdn SSien	'Diamond Tiara' (v)	EMic LRHS NBir NGdn NRew NSue SSien
'Cream Topping' (v)	NRew		
'Crepe Suzette' (v)	NRew SSien	'Diamonds are Forever' (v)	ESwi IBal NRew NSue SSien
'Crested Reef'	EMic SSien	'Diana Remembered'	CDor EMic EMor IBal NCou NGdn NRew NSue SSien WCAu WFar
'Crested Surf' (v)	EMic IBal		
'Crimson Desire'	CBdn SSien	'Dick Ward'	NRew SSien
'Crinkled Leather'	CBdn SSien	'Dilithium Crystal'	ESwi IBal MWlw NRew NSue WFar
§ *crispula* (v)	CDor EBlo	'Dilys'	EMic MNrw
'Crocodile Socks' (v)	IBal SSien	'Dimple'	EMic
'Crown Prince' (v)	NGdn NRew	'Dinky Donna' (v)	NSue
'Crown Royalty'	EMic IBal	'Dinner Jacket' (v)	EMor IBal LRHS SSien
§ 'Crowned Imperial' (*fortunei*) (v)	EMic IBal	'Dinner Mint' (v)	IBal NRew SSien
		'Dixie Chick' (v)	GEdr NSue SSien
'Crumples' (*sieboldiana*)	IBal	'Dixie Chickadee' (v)	SSien
'Crusader' (v)	CBdn ELon EMic NRew SSien WFar	'Dixie Cups'	IBal
'Crystal Dixie'	EMic NSue SSien WFar	'Dixie Ghost'	SSien
'Cup of Grace'	IBal	'Dixieland Heat'	NRew
'Cup of Joy'	NRew NSue SSien	'Domaine de Courson'	EMic NSue WFar
'Curlew' (Tardiana Group)	EMic	'Don Stevens' (v)	IBal NRew SSien
'Curls'	EMic	'Dorothy'	EMic
'Curly Fries'	IBal NRew NSue SSien	'Dorset Blue' (Tardiana Group)	IBal SSien
'Cutting Edge'	EMic NSue		
'Dahlonega'	SSien	'Dorset Charm' (Tardiana Group)	EMic
'Dance with Me' (v)	EMic NRew NSue SSien		
'Dancefloor Filler'	SSien	'Double D Cup'	SSien
'Dancing Hero' (v) **new**	SSien	'Doubloons'	EMic NWbg SSien
'Dancing in the Rain' (v)	NBro WFar	'Dracula'	SSien
'Dancing Mouse' (v)	GEdr IBal NSue SSien WFar	'Dragon Tails' ♀H7	GEdr LRHS NRew NWbg SSien WAbe WFar
'Dancing Out of Time'	NSue		
'Dancing Queen'	EMic IBal LBar LRHS NRew NSue SSien	'Dragon Warrior' (v)	SSien
		'Dragon's Eye'	SSien
'Danish Mouse'	IBal	'Drake's Tail'	NLar
'Dark Shadows'	EMic IBal NGdn NSti WFar	'Dream Queen' (v)	CDor EMor EPfP ESwi IBal LBuc MSCN NEoE NLar NRew NSue SPad SSien
'Dark Star' (v)	EMic LRHS NGdn NRew NSue SSien		
'Darwin's Standard' (v)	NRew	'Dream Weaver' (v)	ELon IBal MBrN NBro NGdn NRew NSue NWbg SDix SPoG SSien WFar
'Dawn'	EMic IBal NSue SSien		
'Dax'	IBal	'Dress Blues'	CMac EGren EMic IBal ISha NRew NSue
'Daybreak' ♀H7	NBro NRew		
'Day's End' (v)	IBal SSien	'Drip Drop' (v)	SSien
'Deane's Dream' ♀H7	EMic SSien	'Drummer Boy'	EMic IBal
decorata var. *normalis*	EMic	'Dry Ice'	NRew
'Deep Blue Sea'	IBal NSue	'Duchess' (*nakaiana*) (v)	IBal
'Deep Pockets'	IBal	'Duke of Cornwall' (v)	SSien
'Deep Space Nine' (v)	IBal	'DuPage Delight' (*sieboldiana*) (v)	NGdn NLar
'Dee's Golden Jewel'	IBal SSien		
'Déjà Blu' (v) ♀H7	EMic NRew NSue	'Dust Devil' (*fortunei*) (v)	SSien
'Delicious' (v)	IBal SSien	'Dusty Waters'	SSien
'Deliverance'	EMic ESwi NRew	'Dutch Flame' (v)	NSue
'Delta Dawn' (v)	EGren EMic ISha NGdn NRew NSue SSien	'Early Sunrise' (v)	NRew SSien
		'Early Times'	SSien
'Derek Coxs'	EMic IBal	'Earth Angel' PBR (v)	EMic IBal LRHS NGdn NRew NSue SSien
'Desert Mouse' PBR (v)	GEdr IBal NRew NSue SSien		
'Designer Genes'	EMor IBal LBar LRHS NRew SSien WFar	'Eastern Spires'	EMic
		'Ebony Towers'	EMic IBal
'Devil's Advocate'	IBal	'Eclipse' (v)	NRew SSien
'Devon Blue' (Tardiana Group)	CBdn IBal LBom LRHS MPri SSien	'Eclipse of the Heart' (v)	SSien
		'Eco Mirror'	IBal

'Edge of Night'	EMic IBal
'Effervescence'	CBdn NRew SSien
'El Capitan' (v)	NRew
'El Niño'^PBR (Tardiana Group) (v) ♀^H7	CBdn CDor EGren EMic EMor GAbr IBal LBar MNrw NBro NGdn NLar NRew NSue NWbg SPoG SSien WFar
§ 'Elata'	EMic NRew
'Elatior' (*nigrescens*)	EMic IBal SSien
'Eldorado'	see *H.* 'Frances Williams'
'Eleanor Lachman' (v)	EMic NRew SSien
'Electrocution' (v)	ESwi GEdr SSien
'Elegans'	see *H. sieboldiana* var. *elegans*
'Elisabeth'	EMic LRHS MPri
'Elizabeth Campbell' (*fortunei*) (v)	IBal NRew SSien
'Elkheart Lake'	EMic SSien
'Ellen'	EMic
'Ellerbroek' (*fortunei*) (v)	EMic
'Elsley Runner'	LRHS NSue SSien
'Elvis Lives'	EMic NGdn NLar NRew NWbg SSien
'Emerald Charger' (v)	LRHS MPri NRew SSien
'Emerald City Chick'	EMic
'Emerald Crown'	EMic IBal
'Emerald Edger'	EMic
'Emerald Emperor'	IBal SSien
'Emerald Necklace' (v)	EMic
'Emerald Paisley'	IBal
'Emerald Ruff Cut'	IBal NRew SSien
'Emerald Tiara' (v)	EMic LRHS NRew NSue NWbg SSien WFar
'Emeralds and Rubies'	ESwi NRew NSue SSien
'Emily Dickinson' (v)	EMic IBal NRew NSue
'Emma' (v)	SSien
'Empress Wu'^PBR	Widely available
'Enchanted Mist' (v)	CBdn SSien
'Enchiladas' (v)	NRew SSien
'Endearing Endeavor' (v)	CBdn
'Enduring Beacon'	NRew NSue
'English Sunrise' (Tardiana Group)	EMic IBal
'Enterprise' (v)	NGdn NRew NSue SSien
'Envy' (v)	SSien
'Eos'	NLar
'Epiphany' (v)	NRew
'Eric Smith' (Tardiana Group)	EMic SHar WFar
'Eric's Gold'	SSien
'Erie Magic' (v)	EMic IBal SSien
'Eskimo Pie' (v)	NRew WFar
'Essence of Summer'	NRew
'Essence of Sunset' (v)	IBal NSue SSien
'Ester's Dream' (v)	NRew SSien
'Etched Glass' (Shadowland Series) (v)	LBar SSien
'Eternal Flame'	NRew NSue SSien
'Everlasting Love' (v)	EMic NRew NSue
'Excitation'	EMic
'Exotic Presentation' (v)	EMic IBal SSien
'Extasy' (v)	IBal NGdn NRew NSue SSien WFar
'Eye Catcher'	EMic SSien
'Eye Declare' (v)	IBal NRew
'Faith'	EMic NSien
'Faithful Heart' (v)	NRew NSue
'Fall Dazzler' (v)	IBal SSien
'Fall Emerald'	EMic IBal
'Fan Dance' (v)	SSien
'Fantabulous' (v)	ELan SSien
'Fantasy Island' (v)	EMor NRew SSien WFar
'Fashionista' (v)	SSien
'Fat Cat'	SSien
'Fatal Attraction'	SSien
'Feather Boa'	EMic NRew NSue SSien WFar
'Femme Fatal' (*sieboldiana*) (v)	SSien
'Fenman's Fascination'	EMic IBal
'Fiesta' (v)	SSien
'Final Summation' (v)	NSue SSien
'Final Victory' (v)	CBdn IBal NRew SSien
'Fingernails'	NSue
'Fire and Ice' (v)	Widely available
'Fire Dance'	IBal
'Fire Island' ♀^H7	CDor EAri ELan EMor LBar LRHS LSou NRew NSue SMad SSien WCAu WFar
'Firefly' (v)	IBal SSien
'Fireplace' (v)	SSien
'Fireworks' (v) ♀^H7	CDor EAri EMor GEdr ISha LBar LBuc MArl MBel MBNS NBro NRew NSue NWbg SSien WCot
'Firn Line' (v)	CBdn EGren ESwi IBal ISha NEoE NGdn NRew NSue SSien
'First Blush'	CBdn ESwi IBal LBar NRew NSue SSien XFar
'First Dance' (v)	CBdn
'First Frost' (v) ♀^H7	ELan ELin ELon EMic EPfP IBal LCro LRHS LSou MArl MPri MPro NGdn NLar NRew NSue SOrN SPoG SSien
'First Love' (*montana*)	IBal NRew NSue SSien
'First Mate' (v)	SSien
'Fizzle'	NSue
'Flamenco Mouse'	NSue SSien
'Fleet Week'	SSien
'Flemish Angel' (v)	NRew SSien
'Flemish Design'	IBal
'Flemish Master' (v)	EMic IBal SSien
'Flemish Sky'	EMic IBal NGdn NLar NSue
'Flemish Tradition' (v) **new**	CBdn SSien
'Floradora'	EMic NSue
'Floratini'	NSue
'Florence Nightingale'	CBdn IBal SSien
'Fog Light'	IBal NRew SSien
'Fool's Gold' (*fortunei*)	EMic
'Forbidden Fruit'^PBR (v) ♀^H7	CBdn EMic ESwi IBal NGdn NRew NSue SSien XFar
'Forest Fireworks' (v)	SSien
'Forest Shadows'	EMic
'Formal Attire' (*sieboldiana* hybrid) (v)	EMic NRew
'Forncett Frances' (v)	IBal
'Fortis'	see *H. undulata* var. *erromena*
fortunei	EMic GKev NRew SSien WFar
§ - var. *albopicta* (v)	CBcs CPud EBlo ECha EGren EGrI EHeP ELan EMic EPfP GMaP LCro LRHS MArl NLar NRew SRms SSien WBrk WFar
- - f. *aurea*	CMac ECha MMuc NLar SRms SSien WFar
§ - var. *aureomarginata* (v) ♀^H7	CBcs CPud EBlo ECha EGren ELan EMic EPfP EUrb GMaP LRHS MArl MMuc NGdn NLar NRew SEND SPlb SSien SWor WFar
- var. *gigantea*	see *H. montana*
- var. *hyacinthina*	EMic NGdn NLar SSien
- - variegated	see *H.* 'Crowned Imperial'
- var. *stenantha*	EMic
'Fountain of Youth' (*kikutii*)	IBal
'Fourteen Carats'	LRHS
'Fourth of July'	NSue SSien
'Foxfire Night Skye' (v)	IBal SSien

Name	Codes	Name	Codes
'Foxfire Palm Sunday' (v)	IBal	'Giantland Mouse Cheese'	IBal NSue SSien
'Fragrant Blue'	CTsd ELan EPfP GKev IBal ISha LBuc LRHS NBro NGdn NRcw SMrm SPoG	'Giantland Sunny Mouse Ears'	CBdn GEdr IBal NSue SSien
		'Gigantea' (*sieboldiana*)	see *H.* 'Elata'
'Fragrant Blue Ribbons' (v)	IBal NRew SSien	'Gilded Teacup' (v)	NSue
'Fragrant Bouquet' (v) ♀H7	CDor EBee ELan EMic IBal LBar LRHS MPri MPro MSwo NGdn NLar NRew NSue SSien WFar	'Gilt by Association'	EMic NRew SSien
		'Gilt Edge' (*sieboldiana*) (v)	EMic
		'Gingee'	EMic NRew NSue SSien
'Fragrant Dream'	EPfP NLar NRew NSue SSien	'Ginko Craig' (v)	CMac ELan GEdr GMaP IBal NBir NGdn NSue SPoG SSien WFar
'Fragrant Fire'	NRew		
'Fragrant Gold'	EMic	'Ginsu Knife' (v)	EMic
'Fragrant King'	NRew	'Glacial Towers' (v)	IBal SSien
'Fragrant Queen'PBR (v)	NRew NSue SSien	'Glad Rags' (v)	CBdn NRew NSue SSien
'Fragrant Surprise' (v)	NRew SSien	'Glad Tidings'	LRHS MPri NRew
'Fran Godfrey'	EMic SSien	'Glamour'	IBal SSien
'Francee' (*fortunei*) (v) ♀H7	Widely available	'Glass Hearts'	EMic
§ 'Frances Williams' (*sieboldiana*) (v)	Widely available	*glauca*	see *H. sieboldiana* var. *elegans*
		'Glen Triumph'	SSien
'Francheska' (v)	EMic IBal	'Glitter'	EMic SSien
'Frank Lloyd Wright'	IBal	'Glockenspiel'	EMic
'Friar Tuck'	EMic	I 'Gloriosa' (*fortunei*) (v)	NSue
'Fried Bananas' ♀H7	CDor EMic IBal NGdn NRew NSue SSien	'Glory'	IBal SSien
		'Glory Hallelujah'	EMic IBal SSien
		'Gold Bug'	SSien
'Fried Green Tomatoes'	EMic IBal NLar NRew NSue SSien	'Gold Drop' (*venusta* hybrid)	EMic NSue
'Friends' (v)	EMic SSien	'Gold Edger'	CDor CMac EBlo EMic GMaP LRHS NBir NGdn NLar NRew NSti NWbg WFar
'Frilly Fantasy' (v)	CBdn SSien		
'Fringe Benefit' (v)	EMic SSien		
'Frisian Pride'	IBal SSien	'Gold Edger Surprise' (v)	EMic
'Frisian Waving Steel'	EMic IBal NRew	'Gold Flush' (*ventricosa*)	EBlo
'Frost Giant' (v)	CBdn NRew	§ 'Gold Haze' (*fortunei*)	CDor NBir NWbg SSien
'Frosted Dimples'	EMic ESwi NRew NWbg	'Gold Power'	SSien
'Frosted Frolic' (v)	EMic SSien WFar	'Gold Pressed Latinum'	IBal
'Frosted Jade' (v)	EMic MMuc NLar SEND	'Gold Regal'	EMic WFar
'Frosted Lollipop' (v)	IBal SSien	'Gold Rush'	EMic IBal NRew NWbg SSien
'Frosted Mini Hearts'	IBal NSue	'Gold Standard' (*fortunei*) (v)	CAgr CDor CMac CWnw ECha EMic EPfP GMaP ISha LBar LRHS LSto MArl MGos MMuc MPro NBid NBir NGdn NLar NRew NSti NSue SEND SMrm SPoG SRms SSien WFar
'Frosted Mouse Ears'PBR	GEdr IBal NRew NSue SSien		
'Frosted Raspberry' (v)	CBdn NSue SSien		
'Frozen Margarita'	EGren EMic LRHS MPri NLar NRew NSue SSien		
'Fruit Cup'	SSien		
'Fruit Loop' (v) **new**	SSien	'Goldbrook' (v)	EMic
'Fruit Punch'	CBdn NRew SSien	'Goldbrook Gaynor'	IBal
'Fujibotan' (d)	NRew	'Goldbrook Genie'	EMic
'Fukurin-Fu' (*venusta*) (v)	GEdr	'Goldbrook Ghost' (v)	NSue
'Funky Monkey'	EMic ESwi IBal SSien	'Goldbrook Girl'	IBal
'Funny Bones'	CBdn SSien	'Goldbrook Glamour' (v)	SSien
'Funny Frolic' (v)	IBal	'Goldbrook Glimmer' (Tardiana Group) (v)	IBal NRew NSue
'Funny Mouse' (v)	CBdn IBal NGdn NRew NSue SMad SSien WFar		
		'Goldbrook Glory'	IBal NRew SSien
'Futura' (v)	IBal	'Goldbrook Gold'	IBal
'Gabriel's Horn'	IBal	'Goldbrook Good Gracious' (v)	IBal
'Gabriel's Wing' (v)	IBal NSue		
'Gaiety' (v)	EMic	'Goldbrook Grayling'	EMic
'Gaijin' (v)	NSue	'Goldbrook Grebe'	LRHS
'Garden Party' (v)	SSien	'Golden Age'	see *H.* 'Gold Haze'
'Garden Treasure'	SSien	'Golden Empress'	EMic NRew NSue
'Gay Blade' (v)	IBal	'Golden Falls' **new**	CBdn ESwi NRew
'Gay Feather' (v)	SSien	'Golden Fountain'	EMic
'Geisha' (v)	NEoE NGdn NRew NSue NWbg SSien	'Golden Friendship'	SSien
		'Golden Goal'	GAbr
'Gemini Moon' (v)	NRew	'Golden Guernsey' (v)	EMic
'Gemstone'	NRew NSue	'Golden Meadows'PBR (*sieboldiana*)	CBdn CDor ESwi IBal MPri NGdn NRew NSue SSien WFar
'Gene's Joy'	EMic		
'Gentle Giant'	ESwi IBal NRew NSue SSien	'Golden Medallion' (*tokudama*)	EBlo NGdn WFar
'George Smith' (*sieboldiana*)	IBal NRew SSien		
'Georgia Sweetheart' (v)	IBal NRew NSue SSien	'Golden' (*nakaiana*)	see *H.* 'Birchwood Parky's Gold'
'German Yellow Dragon' **new**	NRew SSien	'Golden Needles' (v)	IBal NSue SSien
		'Golden Oriole'	SSien
'Get Nekkid'	ESwi ISha LRHS MPri SSien	'Golden Prayers' (*tokudama*)	ELan NBir NBro NGdn NLar NRew WFar
'Ghost Spirit' (v)	EGren NRew SSien WFar		
'Ghostmaster' (v)	EMic NRew WFar	'Golden Regal'	WFar

'Golden Scepter'	EMic LRHS NRew SRms SSien WFar		GBin ISha LBom LRHS MBrN MPri MPro MSwo NGdn NLar NRew NSue NWbg SPoG SSien WFar WPnP XFar
'Golden Sculpture' (*sieboldiana*)	SSien		
'Golden Spades'	EMic NRew		
'Golden Spider'	EMic SSien	'Guardian Angel' (*sieboldiana*)	IBal NRew NSue SSien
'Golden Sunburst'	ECha NGdn		
'Golden Sweetie'	EMic	'Gum Drop'	EMic
'Golden Tiara' (v) ♀H7	Widely available	'Gun Metal Blue'	LRHS
'Golden Waffles'	ISha SPeP	'Gypsy Rose' ♀H7	EMic IBal LRHS MAvo NGdn NLar NRew NSue NWbg SSien WFar
'Goldene Woge'	SSien		
'Goldsmith'	NRew	'Hacksaw'	NRew NSue SSien
'Gone Fishin' (v)	IBal	'Hadspen Blue' (Tardiana Group) ♀H7	CBdn CDor CWCL ELan EMic EPfP GMaP IBal LRHS MBrN MGos NBir NBro NGdn NRew NWbg SPoG SSien WSpi
'Gone with the Wind' (v)	IBal SSien		
'Good Times'	SSien		
'Goodness Gracious' (v)	IBal NRew NSue SSien	'Hadspen Heron' (Tardiana Group)	EMic
'Gooseberry Sundae'	LAma NGdn NRew NSue		
'Gosan Hildegarde'	SSien	'Hadspen Samphire'	EMic NBir NBro SSien
'Granary Gold' (*fortunei*)	NRew	'Hadspen White' (*fortunei*)	EMic NLar NSue
'Grand Canyon'	SSien	'Haku-chu-han' (*sieboldii*) (v)	LRHS
'Grand Marquee' (v)	CDor IBal NGdn NLar NRew NSue SSien WFar		
		'Hakumuo' (v)	SSien
'Grand Prize' (v)	NRew NSue SSien	§ 'Halcyon' (Tardiana Group) ♀H7	Widely available
'Grand Rapids'	EMic		
'Grand Slam'	NSue	'Half and Half'	IBal NRew SSien
'Grand Tiara' (v)	CDor NGdn NRew NSue SSien	'Hammurabi'	IBal SSien
'Grand Total'	IBal	'Hampshire County' (v)	EMic IBal SSien
'Grape Fizz'	SSien	'Hands Up' PBR (v) ♀H7	CBdn EBee EMic EMor LBar NGdn NRew NSue SPeP SSien XFar
'Gravity Rocks' (v)	CBdn NRew NSue SSien XFar		
'Gray Cole' (*sieboldiana*)	IBal ISha SSien	'Handsome Devil' (v) **new**	ESwi
'Great Arrival'	NRew	'Hanjas Beauty' **new**	IBal
'Great Escape' PBR (v)	GAbr NRew NSue SSien	'Hanjas Big Dane' **new**	IBal
'Great Expectations' (*sieboldiana*) (v)	CDor CMac CWnw EBee EGrI ELan EPfP ISha LBom LRHS LSRN MBNS MHer MNrw NBro NGdn NRew NSti NWbg SPoG SSien WFar WPnP	'Hanjas Blue' **new**	IBal
		'Hanjas Blue Sky' **new**	IBal
		'Hanjas Crazy Mouse' (v)	IBal
		'Hanjas Falls' (v)	IBal
'Green Acres' (*montana*)	IBal LEdu NRew SSien WFar	'Hanjas Grandmother'	IBal
'Green Angel' (*sieboldiana*)	LRHS	'Hanjas Hanging Tree'	IBal
'Green Bag'	ISha NLar	'Hanjas Little Baby'	IBal
'Green Cheese'	IBal	'Hanjas Mojito' (v) **new**	IBal
'Green Dwarf'	NWbg WFar	'Hanjas Oh My Good' **new**	IBal
'Green Eyes' (*sieboldii*) (v)	NSue WFar	'Hanjas Red Edge'	IBal
'Green Fountain' (*kikutii*)	EMic	'Hanjas Red Jet'	IBal
'Green Gold' (*fortunei*) (v)	EMic	'Hanjas Red Spider'	IBal
'Green Guppy'	NSue	'Hanjas Sky' **new**	IBal
'Green Lama'	EMic	'Hanjas Yellow Dream'	IBal
'Green Lava' **new**	NRew	'Hanky Panky' (v)	IBal LBar NGdn NRew NSti NSue SSien WFar
'Green Mouse Ears'	GEdr NSue SSien WFar		
'Green Piecrust'	EMic	'Hans' (v)	IBal NRew SSien
'Green Platter'	EMic	'Happiness' (Tardiana Group)	SSien
'Green Point' **new**	NSue		
'Green Sleeve'	EMic	'Happy Dayz' (v)	CWnw IBal LCro LSou NRew SSien
'Green Summer Fragrance'	NWbg	'Happy Hearts'	EMic
'Green Thumb'	ESwi NSue	'Happy Hour' (v)	SSien
'Green Velveteen'	CDor	'Happy Valley' (v)	NSue SSien
'Green Wings'	SSien	'Harmony' (Tardiana Group)	EMic
'Green with Envy' (v) ♀H7	EMic GEdr MBrN NRew NSue SSien	'Harold Read' (v)	CDor
'Greenie Weenie Bikini'	NSue SSien	'Harry van de Laar'	SSien
'Greenrush'	SSien	'Harry van Trier' ♀H7	EMic NRew SSien WCot
'Grey Ghost'	SSien	'Harvest Delight'	EMic
'Grey Glacier' (v)	IBal NRew SSien	'Harvest Glow'	IBal
'Grey Goose' (Tardiana Group)	EMic	'Hasta Manana' (v)	LRHS SSien
		'Hawaiian Luau' (v)	SSien
'Groo Bloo'	IBal	'Hawkeye' (v)	IBal
'Ground Master' (v)	CMac ELan GMaP NBro NGdn NLar NRew NSti NWbg WFar	'Hazel'	EMic
		'Heart and Soul' (v)	NRew NSue
'Ground Sulphur'	NSue SSien	'Heart Broken'	EMic
'Grunspecht' (Tardiana Group)	IBal	'Heart Throb'	EMic
		'Heartbeat' (v)	SSien
'Guacamole' (v) ♀H7	CBcs CDor CTsd EBee ECha EGren ELon EMic EMor EPfP	'Heartleaf'	EMic
		'Heart's Content' (v)	NSue SSien

'Heartsong' (v)	EMic IBal		'Icy Halo' (v)	SSien
'Heat Wave' PBR (v)	SSien		'Illicit Affair'	CBdn EMic NSue SSien
'Heather Hill' (v)	SSien		'Imp' (v)	IBal
'Heavenly Tiara' (v)	NRew NSue SSien		'Imperial Palace' (v)	IBal
'Heavy Duty'	SSien	§	'Inaho'	NRew NSue
'Helen Doriot' (*sieboldiana*)	EMic IBal		'Inca Gold'	NRew NSue
'Helen Field Fischer' (*fortunei*)	NLar		'Independence' (v)	EMic NBro NRew NSue SPoG SSien WFar
helonioides f. ***albopicta*** misapplied	see *H. rohdeifolia*		'Inniswood' (v)	CDor CWCL EMic IBal NBro NGdn NLar NRew NSti SSien WFar
'Herifu' (v)	EMic		'Invincible'	CDor EMic LRHS NBid NGdn NLar NRew NSue SMad SSien WFar
'Herkules'	EMic		'Invincible Spirit'	CDor SSien
'Hi-Class' (v)	IBal NRew SSien		'Iona' (*fortunei*) (v)	EMic IBal NRew SSien
'Hidden Cove' (v)	IBal NRew SSien		'Irische See' (Tardiana Group)	IBal
'Hideout' (v)	IBal NRew			
'High Noon'	SSien		'Irish Eyes' (v)	EMic IBal NRew SSien
'High Society' (v)	GEdr IBal MNrw NRew SSien		'Irish Luck'	EMic IBal NSue
'High Tide'	IBal		'Iron Gate Glamour' (v)	CDor
'High Voltage' (v)	IBal NSue SSien		'Iron Gate Special' (v)	EMic
'Hi-ho Silver' (v)	SSien		'Island Charm' (v)	EBlo IBal LRHS NLar NRew SSien WFar
'Hillbilly Blues' (v)	EMic NSue			
'Hirao Grande'	NRew		'Itty Gold'	IBal
'Hirao Supreme'	EMic		'Ivory Coast' (v)	EMor IBal MHol NLar NRew NSue SSien
'Hirao Tetra'	SSien			
'His Honor' (v)	EMic SSien		'Ivory Necklace' (v)	SSien
'Holar Arches Park'	IBal SSien		'Ivory Queen' (v)	CBdn IBal NRew SSien
'Holar Black Swan' **new**	CBdn		'Jack Berry'	CBdn IBal SSien
'Holar Early Days'	SSien		'Jack of Diamonds'	SSien
'Holar Garnet Crow'	IBal		'Jade Cascade'	CDor NBir NLar NWbg SSien WFar
'Holar Ice Empress'	CBdn IBal SSien			
'Holar Mystic Purple'	CBdn SSien		'Jade Scepter' (*nakaiana*)	EMic IBal
'Holar Purple Flash'	IBal		'Jadette' (v)	NSue
'Holar Red Spear'	SSien		'Jane Ward' (v)	SSien
'Holar Red Wine'	IBal		'Jane's Blush'	SSien
'Holar Rising Flame'	IBal SSien		'Janet' (*fortunei*) (v)	EMic NGdn NRew SSien
'Holar Sunset Cobra'	IBal		'Janet Day' (v)	EMic
'Holar Sunset Python'	SSien		'Janet's Gold Sox'	EMic
'Holar Wild Side'	IBal SSien		'Janet's Green Sox'	EMic IBal
'Hollywood Lights' (v)	IBal NGdn NSue		'Japan Boy'	see *H.* 'Montreal'
'Holstein' (Tardiana Group)	see *H.* 'Halcyon'		'Jason and Katie' (v)	EMic
'Holy Molé' (v)	SSien		'Java'	SSien
'Holy Mouse Ears' PBR	GEdr IBal NRew NSue SSien		'Jaws'	LRHS NSue SSien
'Honey Bear' (v)	SSien		'Jaz'	SSien
'Honey Moon'	EMic SSien		'Jennifer' (v)	IBal
'Honeybells'	CBcs CDor CMac EBee ECha ELan EMic GBin GQue LEdu NBid NGdn NRew NSti WCAu WFar		'Jennifer Bailey' (v)	SSien
			'Jerry Landwehr'	NRew
			'Jessica Alba'	SSien
'Honeysong' (v)	NWbg SSien		'Jewel of the Nile' (v)	CDor IBal
'Hot Air Balloon'	IBal SSien		'Jiminy Cricket'	NSue
'Hot Kiss' (v)	SSien		'Jimmy Crack Corn'	NGdn NSue
'Hotcakes'	EMic		'Jolly Green Giant' (*sieboldiana* hybrid)	EMic
'Hotshot' **new**	NRew SSien			
'Hudson Bay' (Shadowland Series) (v)	IBal LRHS NRew		'Joseph'	IBal
			'Josephine' (v)	SSien
'Humpback Whale'	CBdn EMic ESwi IBal NRew NSue SSien		'Joshua's Banner' (v)	SSien
			'Journeyman'	EMic
'Hush Puppie'	EMic IBal LRHS MBrN NRew NSue SSien WFar		'Journey's End' (v)	CBdn NRew NSue SSien
			'Joyce Trott' (v)	SSien
'Hyacintha Variegata' (*fortunei*) (v)	CMac NWbg		'Jubilee' (v)	EMic SSien
			'Julia' (v)	EMic IBal NSue SSien
'Hydon Gleam'	NSue		'Julie Morss'	EMic GMaP SSien
'Hydon Sunset'	EBlo ESwi GEdr LRHS NBir NLar NRew NSti NSue SSien WTre		'Jumbo' (*sieboldiana*)	SSien
			'June' (Tardiana Group) (v) ♀H7	Widely available
'Hyuga-urajiro' (v)	GEdr NSue SSien WFar XFar			
'I Dream of Jeanne'	SSien		'June Fever' PBR (Tardiana Group) ♀H7	CBdn CDor EMic ESwi IBal LRHS NBro NGdn NLar NRew NSue NWbg SPoG SSien WFar
'Ice Cream' (*cathayana*) (v)	NGdn NRew NSue SSien			
'Ice Cube' (v)	IBal SSien			
'Ice Follies' (*fortunei*) (v)	NRew			
'Ice Prancer'	EMic IBal SSien		'June Moon' (v)	ESwi SSien
'Iced Lemon' (v) ♀H7	CBdn GEdr IBal LRHS NRew SSien WFar		'June Spirit' (v)	IBal SSien
			'Junonia' **new**	NSue

Name	Sources
'Jurassic Park'	CBdn EAri EBee EMic EMor IBal ISha LRHS MNrw MPri NLar NRew NSue SHor SMad SSien XFar
'Just So' (v)	SSien
'Justine' ᴾᴮᴿ	CBdn IBal NRew NSue SSien
'Kabitan'	see *H. sieboldii* var. *sieboldii* f. *kabitan*
'Kabuki'	NRew NSue
'Kalamazoo' (v)	EMic LRHS SSien
'Kanzi' (v)	NSue SSien
'Karma Chameleon' **new**	SSien
'Katherine Lewis' (Tardiana Group) (v)	EMic NRew SSien
'Katie Q' (v)	EMic NRew SSien
'Katsuragawa-beni' (v)	IBal SSien
'Kayak'	IBal
'Kelsey'	EMic IBal
'Kempen Magenta Blue'	IBal
'Kempen Waving Shadow'	IBal
'Kenzie' (v)	IBal
'Key Lime Pie'	EMic NRew SSien
'Key West'	IBal SSien
'Kifukurin-kiyosumi'	IBal
'Kifukurin-koba' (*sieboldii*) (v)	EMic
'Kifukurin-ko-mame' (*gracillima*) (v)	NSue SSien
'Kifukurin-otome' (*venusta*)	NSue SSien
kikutii	EMic
§ - var. ***yakusimensis***	GArf GEdr SMad
* 'Kimidori Fukurin Otome' (*venusta*)	SSien
'Ki-nakafu-otome' (*venusta*)	SSien
'Kinbotan' (*venusta*) (v)	GEdr SSien
'King Tut'	EMic
'Kingsize'	EGren IBal NRew NSue SArc SSien
'Kinky Boots' (v)	SSien
'Ki-renjyaku' (d)	ESwi NRew NSue SSien
§ 'Kirishima'	NSue
'Kisuji'	see *H.* 'Mediopicta' (*sieboldii*)
'Kitty Cat'	WFar
'Kiwi Black Magic'	IBal
'Kiwi Blue Baby'	CBdn NSue SSien
'Kiwi Full Monty' (v)	CBdn CDor EGren IBal NLar NRew NSue SSien WFar
'Kiwi Gold Rush'	NRew SSien
'Kiwi Jordan'	EMic
'Kiwi Minnie Gold'	EMic
'Kiwi Skyscraper'	IBal
'Kiwi Spearmint'	EMor ISha LBar NRew NSue NWbg SSien WFar
kiyosumiensis	IBal
'Klopping Variegated' (v)	EMic
'Knight's Journey'	SSien
'Knockout' (v)	NBro NGdn NLar NRew
'Knockout Mouse'	SSien
'Komodo Dragon'	EMic ESwi IBal NRew NSue SSien
'Konkubine'	EMic
'Korean Snow'	NSue
'Koriyama' (*sieboldiana*) (v)	EMic
'Krossa Regal' ♀ᴴ⁷	Widely available
'La Donna'	IBal
'Lacy Belle' (v)	CDor EMic NBro NEoE NGdn NRew NSue SSien
'Lady Guineverre'	EGren LAma LRHS MPri NRew NWbg SMrm SSien
'Lady Helen'	EMic
'Lady Luck' (v)	IBal SSien
'Ladybug'	NRew
'Lahn'	EMic
'Lake Hitchcock' (v)	IBal
'Lake Superior'	IBal SSien
'Lake Tekapo' (v)	IBal NRew
'Lakeside Accolade'	IBal
'Lakeside April Snow' (v)	IBal NGdn SSien
'Lakeside Baby Face' (v)	ESwi NRew NSue SSien WFar
'Lakeside Banana Bay' (v)	IBal ISha LRHS MPri NGdn NRew NSue SSien
'Lakeside Beach Bum'	NRew NSue
'Lakeside Beach Captain' (v)	SSien
'Lakeside Black Satin'	WFar
'Lakeside Blue Cherub'	EMic
'Lakeside Breaking News' (v)	SSien
'Lakeside Cha Cha' (v)	NRew SPeP SSien WFar
'Lakeside Circle O' (v)	IBal
'Lakeside Coal Miner'	NGdn NLar NSue SSien
'Lakeside Contender'	SSien
'Lakeside Cupcake' (v)	IBal NGdn NRew NSue SSien
'Lakeside Cupid's Cup' (v)	IBal
'Lakeside Dimpled Darling'	NRew NSue
'Lakeside Doodad' (v)	NRew
'Lakeside Dot Com' (v)	NSue
'Lakeside Down Sized' (v)	MNrw NSue SSien WFar
'Lakeside Dragonfly' (v)	CBdn ELin ELon ISha MNrw NGdn NLar NRew NSue SSien WFar
'Lakeside Elfin Fire'	GEdr NRew
'Lakeside Fancy Pants' (v)	IBal NSue
'Lakeside Fruit Loops' (v)	SSien
'Lakeside Hazy Morn' (v)	SSien
'Lakeside Hoola Hoop' (v)	SSien
'Lakeside Kaleidoscope'	EMic IBal NGdn NSue SSien
'Lakeside Khum Kaw'	IBal
'Lakeside Little Gem'	NSue
'Lakeside Little Tuft' (v) ♀ᴴ⁷	ELin EMor ISha MPri NLar NRew NSue SSien
'Lakeside Lollipop'	ELin SSien
'Lakeside Love Affaire'	NRew WFar
'Lakeside Maestro'	NLar NSue
'Lakeside Maverick'	NRew NSue SSien
'Lakeside Meadow Ice' (v)	SSien
'Lakeside Meter Maid' (v)	CBdn IBal NRew NSue SSien
'Lakeside Miss Muffett' (v)	EMic IBal NSue
'Lakeside Missy Little' (v)	EMic
'Lakeside Neat Petite'	LRHS NSue
'Lakeside Ninita' (v)	LRHS NRew NSue
'Lakeside Old Smokey'	IBal
'Lakeside Paisley Print' (v)	IBal ISha MHol NLar NRew NSue SSien WFar
'Lakeside Premier'	EMic IBal
'Lakeside Prophecy Fulfilled' (v)	IBal SSien
'Lakeside Rhapsody' (v)	SSien
'Lakeside Rocky Top' (v)	IBal SSien WFar
'Lakeside Roy El' (v)	IBal SSien
'Lakeside Sapphire Pleats'	EMic
'Lakeside Scamp' (v) ♀ᴴ⁷	GEdr IBal LRHS NRew NSue SSien
'Lakeside Shockwave' (v)	NRew
'Lakeside Shoremaster' (v)	CBdn NRew
'Lakeside Sparkle Plenty' (v)	NRew
'Lakeside Spellbinder' (v)	IBal LBom LRHS MPri NRew SSien
'Lakeside Spruce Goose' (v)	EMic NRew
'Lakeside Storm Watch'	NLar NRew SSien
'Lakeside Swan Pon' (v)	IBal
'Lakeside Symphony' (v)	EMic
'Lakeside Zinger' (v)	CBdn MBrN NRew NSue SSien
lancifolia	CMac GMaP NGdn NSti SRms SSien WKif WTre

Hosta

'Last Train Home'	SSien	– B&SWJ 10806	WCru
'Laterna Magica'	NRew NSue	– f. *hypoglauca*	SSien
'Laura Lanier'	CBdn EMic IBal SSien	*longissima* var. *brevifolia*	NSue
'Leapin' Lizard'	SSien	'Lost World'	EMic
'Leather Gloss'	IBal	'Louie Louie' (v)	SSien
'Lederhosen'	EMic	'Love of Life' (v)	SSien
'Lemon Candy' (v)	CBdn	'Love of My Life' (v)	IBal
'Lemon Delight'	CBdn EMic ESwi LRHS NRew NSue SSien WFar	'Love Pat' ♀H7	IBal ISha LRHS LSRN MBNS MPro NGdn NLar NRew NSue SSien
'Lemon Frost'	NRew NSue	'Love Song'	IBal SSien
'Lemon Lime'	CDor EMic MBrN MNrw NEoE NRew NSue SSien WAbe WCot	'Loyalist' PBR (v)	CBdn ESwi NGdn NLar NRew NSue SPoG SSien WFar
'Lemon Love Note'	SSien	'Lucky Mouse' PBR (v)	ESwi GEdr IBal NRew NSue SSien
'Lemon Meringue'	EMic SSien	'Lucky Number' (v)	SSien
'Lemon Snap'	LBar NRew SSien XFar	'Lucy Vitols' (v)	CDor ESwi IBal
'Lemon Twist'	CDor	'Lullabye'	EMic
'Lemon Zinger' (v)	CBdn SSien	'Luna Moth'	EMic ESwi IBal NRew NSue SSien
'Lemonade'	NRew	'Lunar Orbit' (v)	EMic NRew SSien
'Lemontini'	NSue SSien	'Mack the Knife'	NLar WFar
'Leola Fraim' (v)	NRew NSue	'Made in Spades' (v)	CBdn NSue SSien
'Let Me Entertain You'	EMic SSien	'Maekawa'	IBal
'Let's Twist Again' (v)	ESwi LBar NRew NSue SSien	'Magic Fire' PBR (v)	NLar NRew NSue SSien
'Leviathan'	EMic	'Magic Island'	EMor LBar LCro MHol NRew NSue NWbg SSien
'Libby'	EMic NRew NSue SSien		
'Liberty' PBR (v) ♀H7	CBcs CBdn CDor CWGN EMic EMor EPfP ESwi IBal LRHS MAvo MHtn MPro NBro NGdn NLar NRew NSue SAko SSien	'Magica'	IBal
		'Magical Mouse Ears'	NSue SSien
		'Majesty'	IBal LRHS NGdn NRew NSue SSien
		'Majordomo'	EMic ESwi
'Light of Day' (v)	CBdn SSien	'Malabar' (v)	SSien
'Light of Zetar'	IBal SSien	'Mama Mia' (v)	EMic IBal LRHS NBro NGdn NRew NWbg SSien WFar
'Li'l Abner' (v)	SSien		
'Lilac Giant'	SSien	'Mango Lettuce'	SSien
* *lilacina*	WFar	'Mango Smoothie'	NRew SSien
'Lily Blue Eyes'	SSien	'Mango Tango' (v)	IBal NRew NSue SSien
'Lime Fizz'	CBdn NSue SSien WFar	'Maple Leaf' (*sieboldiana*) (v)	NRew
'Lime Shag' (*sieboldii* f. *spathulata*)	SSien WFar		
		'Maraschino Cherry'	EMic NGdn NSue
'Limetini'	NRew SSien	'Mardi Gras' (v)	NRew SSien
'Limey Lisa'	NRew NSue	'Marge' (*sieboldiana* hybrid)	EMic
'Lipstick Blonde'	NRew NSue SSien XFar	'Margie's Angel' (v)	NRew NSue
'Lipstick Sunset'	SSien	'Marginata Alba' misapplied	see *H.* 'Albomarginata' (*fortunei*), *H. crispula*
'Little Aurora' (*tokudama* hybrid)	NRew WFar		
		'Marilyn Monroe' ♀H7	EMic GEdr LRHS NRew NSue SSien
'Little Bit'	EMic IBal	'Marmalade on Toast'	EMic MPri NRew
'Little Black Scape'	NGdn NLar NWbg SSien	'Marrakech'	EMic NRew NSue SSien
'Little Bo Beep' (v)	WFar	'Marshmallow Sky' (v)	NRew SSien
'Little Caesar' (v)	IBal LRHS NGdn NRew NSue SSien WFar	'Martini'	SSien
		'Mary Marie Ann' (*fortunei*) (v)	NRew
'Little Devil'	NSue SSien		
'Little Hobber'	NSue	'Masquerade' (v)	NRew SSien WAbe WFar
'Little Ice Mouse' (v)	SSien	'Master of Ceremonies' (v)	SSien
'Little Jay' (v)	NSue SSien	'Mata Hari' (v)	NRew NSue SSien
'Little Maddie'	SSien	'Maui Buttercups'	NRew NSue SSien
'Little Miss Muffett'	ESwi NSue	'Mayan Moon' (v)	NRew
'Little Miss Sunshine'	IBal	§ 'Mediopicta' (*sieboldii*)	NRew NWbg
'Little Prayer'	WFar	'Mediovariegata' (*undulata*)	see *H. undulata* var. *undulata*
'Little Red Joy'	CBdn SSien	'Medusa' (v)	NGdn NRew NSue
'Little Red Rooster'	GEdr NGdn NLar NRew NSue SSien WFar	'Megan's Angel' (v)	SSien
		'Mellow Mood' (v)	CBdn NRew SSien
'Little Sunspot' (v)	NRew NSue	'Memories of Dorothy'	EMic
'Little Treasure' (v)	LBar NRew SSien WFar	'Mesa Fringe' (*montana*)	EMic IBal NLar
'Little White Lines' (v)	GEdr NSue SSien	'Metallica'	SSien
'Little Wonder' (v) ♀H7	CBdn ESwi LRHS NRew NSue SSien	'Midas Touch'	NLar NRew
'Living Water'	EMic SSien	'Middle Ridge'	EMic
'Lizard Lick'	NSue	'Midnight at the Oasis' (v)	NRew NSue SSien
'London Bridge' (v)	SSien	'Midnight Oil'	SSien
'London Fog' (v)	GEdr SSien	'Midnight Ride'	SSien
'Lonesome Dove' (v)	SSien	'Midwest Magic' (v)	EMic IBal NLar NRew
'Long Fellow' (v)	IBal	'Mighty Mite'	IBal
'Long Tail Lights' (v) **new**	CBdn NSue	'Mighty Mouse' (v)	EMor IBal LBar NRew NSue SSien XFar
longipes	SSien		

Name	Codes
'Mike'	SSien
'Mike Shadrack' (v)	SSien
'Mildred Seaver' (v)	EMic LRHS NRew
'Millennium'	IBal
'Ming Jade'	CDor
'Mini Skirt'	CBdn ESwi IBal NRew NSue SSien XFar
'Minke' (v)	NRew SSien
'Minnesota Wild' (v)	IBal SSien
'Minnie Bell' (v)	IBal
'Minnie Klopping'	EMic
§ *minor* Maekawa	LShi NRew WFar
− from Japan	LShi
− − B&SWJ 11103	WCru
− from Korea	IBal
− − B&SWJ 1209	WCru
− − B&SWJ 8775	WCru
'Minor' (*ventricosa*)	see *H. minor* Maekawa
'Mint Candy'	IBal
'Minuteman' (*fortunei*) (v) ♀H7	CBcs CBdn CDor EGren ELon EPfP IBal LBom LRHS MBNS MMuc NGdn NLar NRew NWbg SEND SSien WFar
'Miracle Lemony'	SMrm SSien
'Mirror Lake'	ESwi
'Miss Christa' (v) **new**	IBal SSien
'Miss Ruby'	IBal SSien
'Miss Saigon' (v)	IBal
'Miss Tokyo' (v)	IBal SSien
'Mister Watson'	EMic
'Misweave' (v)	IBal
'Mohrchen'	EMic
'Moi Marleen'	EMic
'Mojito'	EMic
'Monkey Business' (v)	SSien
'Monster Ears'	EMor ESgl IBal LBar NRew SSien
§ *montana*	WFar
− B&SWJ 4796	WCru
− B&SWJ 5585	LEdu WCru
− f. *macrophylla*	NSue
aff. *montana*	SSien WFar
§ 'Montreal'	SSien
'Moody Blues' (Tardiana Group)	NLar
'Moon Dance' (v)	IBal SSien
'Moon Lily'	EMic SSien
'Moon Split' (v)	IBal NGdn NRew NSue SSien
'Moon Waves'	IBal
'Moonbeam'	EMic LRHS
'Moongate Flying Saucer'	EMic
'Moonlight' (*fortunei*) (v)	EMic GMaP LRHS SSien
'Moonlight Sonata'	EMic LRHS MPri NSue SSien
'Moonstruck'^PBR (v)	NRew NSue SSien
'Mopsy' **new**	NSue
'Morning Light'	EMic NBro NGdn NRew SSien WFar
'Morning Star' (v)	EMic IBal LBar LCro NBir NGdn NLar NRew NSue SSien WFar
'Moscow Blue'	NRew
'Moulin Rouge'	IBal NSue SSien
'Mount Everest'	EMic SSien
'Mount Kirishima' (*sieboldii*)	see *H.* 'Kirishima'
'Mount Tom' (v)	IBal SSien
'Mountain Green'	SSien
'Mountain Snow' (*montana*) (v)	SSien
'Mourning Dove' (v) ♀H7	EMic NRew SSien
'Mouse Capades' (v)	CBdn ESwi IBal NSue SSien
'Mouse on the Moon' (v)	SSien
'Mouse Party' (v)	IBal
'Mouse Trap' (v)	NRew
'Mr Big'	NGdn NSue WCot
'Mr Blue'	IBal NRew NSue
'Mrs Minky' ♀H7	EMic SSien
'Muffie' (v)	NRew NSue
'Munchkin Fire'	CBdn NSue SSien
'Munchkin' (*sieboldii*)	SSien WFar
'Muriel Seaver Brown'	ESwi
'My Child Insook' (v)	SSien
'My Claire' (v)	EMic SSien
'My Cup of Tea'	SSien
'My Friend Nancy' (v)	SSien
'My Marianne' (v)	NRew SSien
'My Precious' (v)	IBal NSue
'Mystic Star'	NSue
nakaiana	CDor
'Nakaimo'	NLar
'Nana' (*ventricosa*)	see *H. minor* Maekawa
§ 'Nancy Lindsay' (*fortunei*)	CDor EMic NGdn NLar
'Neat Splash' (v)	CWCL NBir SSien
'Neat Splash Rim' (v)	NRew SSien
'Needlepoint'	IBal SSien
'Neelix'	IBal
'Nemesis' (v)	IBal
'Neptune'	EMic IBal NRew NSue SSien
'Nesmith's Giant'	EMic
'Niagara Falls' ♀H7	IBal NGdn NSue SSien
'Nicola'	EMic IBal NSue
'Nifty Fifty' (v)	SSien
'Night at the Opera' (v)	SSien
'Night before Christmas' (v) ♀H7	EBee EMic EMor LRHS MNrw MPri NBro NCth NGdn NRew NSue NWbg SSien WHoo
'Night Life'	EMic NSue
nigrescens	EMic IBal NRew
'Nippers'	EMic IBal NSue SSien
'None Lovelier' (v)	EMic
'North Hills' (*fortunei*) (v)	EMic NBir NGdn WFar
'Northern Exposure' (*sieboldiana*) (v)	CDor ECha IBal NGdn NLar NRew NSue SPoG SSien WFar
'Northern Halo' (*sieboldiana*) (v)	CDor
'Number Nine'	IBal
'Obi Wan Kenobi' (v)	NSue
'Obscura Marginata' (*fortunei*)	see *H. fortunei* var. *aureomarginata*
'Ocean Isle' (v)	NRew
'October Sky'	EMic NSue SSien
'Oder'	EMic
'Ogon Tsushima'	NRew SSien
'Ogon-amagi-iwa'	NRew
'Ogon-chirifu-hime'	EMic
'Oh Cindy' (v)	NRew
'O'Harra'	NRew NSue SSien
'Old Faithful'	EMic IBal
'Old Glory'^PBR (v)	CBdn EMic EPfP IBal MHol NRew SSien
'Olga's Shiny Leaf'	EMic
'Olive Bailey Langdon' (*sieboldiana*) (v) ♀H7	CDor LAma NRew
'Olive Branch' (v)	SSien
'Olympic Edger'	EMic
'Olympic Glacier' (v)	EMic NRew SSien
'Olympic Gold Medal'	SSien
'Olympic Silver Medal'	EMic SSien
'Olympic Sunrise' (v)	NRew SSien
'Olympic Twilight'	EMic
'On Stage'	see *H.* 'Chōkō-nishiki'
'On the Border' (v)	IBal SSien
'On the Marc'	SSien
'One Iota' (v)	IBal

Hosta

Name	Codes
'One Last Dance' (v)	SSien
'One Man's Treasure'	IBal LRHS NGdn NRew NSue NWbg SSien
'Ooh La La' (v)	EMic
'Ophir'	EMic NRew SSien
'Ops' (v)	EMic GEdr LRHS NRew SSien
'Orange Marmalade' (v) ♀H7	CAbb CBcs CWGN ELan EMic EMor IBal ISha LBom LCro LRHS LSou MBNS MHol MNrw MPnt MPri MPro NGdn NLar NRew NSue NWbg SPoG SSien WFar
'Orange Star'PBR (v)	IBal NRew NSue SSien
'Oriana' (*fortunei*)	EMic SSien
'Orion's Belt' (v)	EMic EMor ESwi ISha LBar NRew NSue
'Osprey' (Tardiana Group)	IBal
'Over the Waves'	CBdn IBal NSue SSien
'Oxheart'	EMic
'Oze' (v)	SSien
pachyscapa	SSien
'Pacific Blue Edger'	EMic MPro NRew WFar
'Paisley Border' (v)	LBar NRew NSue SSien
'Pamela Lee' (v)	EMic NGdn SSien
'Pandora's Box' (v)	GEdr GQue NHar NRew NSue WCot WFar XFar
'Paradigm' (v) ♀H7	EMic EUrb IBal MBrN MPri NGdn NLar NRew SSien
'Paradise Backstage' (v)	SSien
'Paradise Beach'	NRew WFar
'Paradise Expectations' (*sieboldiana*) (v)	EMic NRew SSien
'Paradise Glory' ♀H7	NRew SSien
'Paradise Goldheart'	SSien
'Paradise Island'PBR (*sieboldiana*) (v)	EGrl NGdn NRew NSue SSien WFar
'Paradise Joyce'PBR	EMic EMor IBal NLar NRew SSien
'Paradise Ocean'	EMic IBal SSien
'Paradise on Fire' (v)	NRew SSien
'Paradise Power'PBR	NRew SSien
'Paradise Puppet' (*venusta*) ♀H7	CBdn EMic GEdr GKev IBal NSue SSien
'Paradise Red Delight' (*pycnophylla*)	SSien
'Paradise Sandstorm'	EMic SSien
'Paradise Standard' (d)	CBdn EMic SSien
'Paradise Sunset'	CBdn GEdr NSue SSien WFar
'Paradise Sunshine'	CBdn EMic SSien
'Paradise Surprise' (v)	SSien
'Paradise Tritone' (v)	ESwi IBal
'Parasol' (v)	IBal
'Parky's Prize' (v)	IBal NRew NSue SSien
'Parthenon' (d/v)	SSien
'Party Popper' (v)	CBdn ISha NLar NRew NSue SSien
'Party Streamers' **new**	NRew
'Pastures Green'	EMic
'Pastures New'	EMic NSue
'Pathfinder' (v)	CBdn LRHS MPri NLar NRew NSue SSien WFar
'Patricia'	EMic
'Patriot' (v) ♀H7	Widely available
'Patriot's Fire' (v)	CBdn SSien
'Paul Revere' (v)	NRew NSue
'Paul Vernooij' (v)	SSien
'Paul's Glory' (v) ♀H7	CDor EMic EPfP GMaP IBal NBir NGdn NRew NSue SHor SPoG SSien WCAu WFar XFar
§ 'Paxton's Original' (*sieboldii*) (v)	EGren LBom SSien
'Peacock Strut'	NRew
'Peanut'	NRew NSue SSien
'Pearl Lake'	EMic NBir NGdn NLar
'Peedee Elfin Bells' (*ventricosa*)	CBdn IBal
'Peedee Laughing River' (v)	NRew
'Pelham Blue Tump'	EMic SSien
'Peppermint Ice' (v)	NGdn NRew NSue SSien
'Percy'	SSien
'Peridot' (Tardiana Group)	IBal
'Permafrost' (v)	ISha NRew
'Permanent Wave'	NRew
'Perry's True Blue'	EMic
'Peter Pan'	EMic IBal SSien
'Peter the Rock'	IBal
'Pete's Dark Satellite'	NSue SSien
'Pewter Goblet' **new**	CBdn
'Pewterware'	EMic IBal
'Phoenix'	CDor ECha EMic NLar SSien
'Photo Finish' (v)	IBal SSien
'Phyllis Campbell' (*fortunei*)	see *H*. 'Sharmon'
'Picta' (*fortunei*)	see *H. fortunei* var. *albopicta*
'Pie à la Mode' (v)	SSien
'Piedmont Gold'	NRew SSien
'Pierced Mouse Ears' (v) **new**	NSue
'Pilgrim' (v)	CDor EBee IBal LRHS MHol MMuc MPri NBro NGdn NRew SSien WFar
'Pinani Island Surf' (v)	NSue SSien
'Pinani Splash' (v) **new**	IBal
'Pineapple Poll'	EMic SSien WFar WHoo
'Pineapple Punch' (v)	SSien
'Pineapple Salsa' (v) **new**	NRew SSien
'Pineapple Upside Down Cake' (v)	EMic NRew NSue SSien
'Pin-up' (v)	CBdn LSou NRew NSue SSien
'Pin-up Girl' (v)	SSien
'Piper Cub'	SSien
'Pistache' (v)	IBal
'Pixie Vamp' (v)	SSien
'Pizzazz' (v)	EBee ELin EMic EMor IBal NGdn NLar NRew NSue SSien WFar
plantaginea	EGrl NRew SSien WFar WSpi
- var. *grandiflora*	see *H. plantaginea* var. *japonica*
§ - var. ***japonica***	EBee EMic MNrw NRew WFar WSpi
'Platinum Tiara' (v)	NBir NRew SSien
'Playmate' (v)	IBal SSien
'Plug Nickel'	NSue SSien
'Plum Creek'	SSien
'Plum Nutty'	SSien
'Pocketful of Sunshine' (v)	IBal NRew NSue SSien
'Poker' (v)	LRHS NRew SSien
'Pooh Bear' (v)	SSien
'Popcorn'	NRew NSue SSien
'Popo' ♀H7	IBal NSue SSien
'Porter' (*venusta*)	CBdn NSue
'Potomac Glory' **new**	NSue
'Potomac Pride'	CDor EMic SSien
'Powder Blue' (v)	ELan LRHS NRew
'Prairie Magic' (v)	SSien
'Prairie Moon'	NRew NSue SSien
'Prairie Sky'	IBal NGdn NLar NSue SSien WFar
'Prairie's Edge' (v)	SSien
'Praying Hands' (v) ♀H7	Widely available
'Pretty Flamingo'	EMic NRew
'Prima Donna' (v)	EMic
'Prince of Wales'	LCro LRHS NWbg SMrm SOrN SPoG SSien
'Private Dancer'	IBal
'Prom Queen' (v)	IBal SSien
'Proud Dragon' (v)	ESwi IBal SSien
'Proud Sentry'	EMic IBal NRew SSien
'Proud Treasure' (v)	IBal NRew SSien
'Pull of the Moon' (v)	SSien

Hosta 361

'Punk Rock'	IBal		'Resonance' (v)	NGdn NLar
'Punky' (v)	EMic IBal SSien		'Restless Sea'	EMic NGdn NRew NSue SSien
'Purbeck Mist'	SSien		'Reverend Mac'	IBal
'Purple and Gold'	SSien		'Reversed' (*sieboldiana*) (v)	IBal LSto NBro NGdn NRew WFar
'Purple Boots'	EMic SSien		'Revolution'^PBR (v)	CBdn EGren ELon EMic EMor IBal
'Purple Dwarf'	EMic NLar NSue WCru			ISha LSRN NBro NGdn NLar NRew
'Purple Glory'	LBom SSien			NSue NWbg SSien WFar
'Purple Haze'	NGdn NSue SSien WFar		'Rhapsody' (*fortunei*) (v)	EMic IBal
'Purple Heart'	CBcs CBdn CWnw EBee EMic EPfP		'Rhein' (*tardiana*)	IBal
	EUrb GBin ISha LCro LEdu LRHS		'Rhinestone Cowboy' (v)	SSien
	MPro NEoE NRew NSti NSue SArc		'Rhino Hide' (v)	SSien
	SOrN SSien WCot WNPC WPnP		'Rhythm and Blues'	NSue SSien
'Purple Passion'	EMic LRHS NRew NSue		'Richland Gold' (*fortunei*)	EMic
'Purple Profusion'	EMic		'Richmond' (v)	ESwi
'Purple Sensation'	see *H.* 'Stirfry'		'Rim Rock'	IBal
'Purple Verticulated Elf'	CBdn SSien		'Ringtail'	EMic NSue
'Queen Josephine' (v)	CDor EMic EPfP GAbr LBom LRHS		'Ripped'	CBdn
	MPri NGdn NRew NSue NWbg		'Ripple Effect' (v)	IBal NRew NSue SSien
	SSien WFar		'Rippled Honey'	EMic NEoE NWbg SSien
'Queen of Islip'	SSien		'Rippling Waves'	EMic
(*sieboldiana*) (v)			'Riptide'	NGdn NSue
'Queen of the Seas'	EMic ESwi IBal NSue SSien		'Risa'	IBal
'Quill' ♀^H7	EMic NRew NSue		'Risky Business'^PBR (v) ♀^H7	CBdn EMic EMor EPfP IBal ISha
'Quilting Bee'	EMic IBal NSue			LAma MBel NLar NRew NSue
'Radiance'	SSien			NWbg SSien
'Radiant Edger' (v)	EMic NRew NSue		'Road Rage'	IBal
'Rain Dancer'	EMic SSien		'Robert Frost' (v)	EMic EMor LAma NCth NRew
'Rain Forest'	EMic		'Robusta' (*fortunei*)	see *H. sieboldiana* var. *elegans*
'Rainbow's End' (v)	NLar NRew NSue NWbg SSien		'Robyn's Choice' (v)	NRew
'Rainforest Sunrise' (v)	ELon EMor IBal ISha LBar NGdn		'Rock and Roll'	IBal SSien
	NRew NWbg SMad SSien WFar		'Rock Island Line' (v) ♀^H7	CBdn EMic GAbr LRHS NRew NSue
	XFar			SSien WFar
'Randy Rachel' (v)	LRHS SSien		'Rocket City'	NRew SSien
'Rare Breed' (v)	IBal		'Rocket's Red Glare'	IBal
'Rascal' (v)	CDor EMic IBal SSien		§ *rohdeifolia* B&SWJ 10862	WCru
'Raspberries and Cream' (v)	SSien		(v)	
'Raspberry Sorbet' ♀^H7	NRew NSue SSien		'Roseann Walter' (v)	EMic
'Raspberry Sundae' (v)	CBdn EMor ESwi NRew NSti NSue		'Rosedale Melody of	IBal
	SPoG SSien WNPC		Summer' (v)	
'Rebel Heart' (v)	IBal SSien		'Rosedale Richie Valens'	IBal SSien
rectifolia	IBal		'Rosemoor'	SSien
'Red Alert' (v)	IBal SSien		'Rossing's Pride'	SSien
'Red Bull'	NRew		'Round About Midnight'	CBdn SSien
'Red Cadet'	EMic EPfP ESwi NRew NSue SSien		'Roxsanne'	EMic
	WFar		'Roy Klehm' (v)	EMic
'Red Dog'	NSue		'Royal Charmer' (v)	IBal NRew SSien
'Red Dragon'	IBal SSien		'Royal Crest'	SSien
'Red Hot Flash' (v)	NRew SSien		§ 'Royal Standard'	CMac CWnw EBee EBlo ECha
'Red Hot Poker'	NRew			EGrI EHeP ELan EPfP GBin
'Red Neck Heaven'	GBin NRew SMrm			GMaP GQue LBom LEdu LRHS
(*kikutii* var. *caput-avis*)				MGos MMuc MPri NBid NGdn
'Red October'	EMic GQue LEdu NGdn NRew			NRew SEND SRms SSien WCAu
	NSue NWbg SSien WCAu WFar			WFar WPnP
'Red Salamander'	EMic ESwi NRew SSien		'Royal Wedding' (v)	SSien
'Red Stepper'	EBee EMic ISha NRew SSien WFar		'Royalty'	NRew SSien
'Red Stilts'	IBal SSien		'Rubies and Ruffles' (v)	IBal NRew
'Red Titanium'	SSien		'Ruffed Up'	EMic SSien
'Red Wine Fries'	ESwi IBal SSien		'Ruffled Mouse Ears'	IBal NRew NSue SSien
'Red Zeppelin'	SSien		'Ruffled Pole Mouse' (v)	IBal LRHS NRew NSue SSien
'Reflections' (v)	ESwi SSien		*rupifraga*	SSien
'Regal Rhubarb'	IBal		'Russell's Form' (*ventricosa*)	EMic
'Regal Splendor' (v) ♀^H7	CBdn CDor ELan ELon EMic IBal		'Ryan's Big One'	NRew
	LCro NBro NGdn NRew NSue		§ 'Sagae' (v) ♀^H7	CBdn EBlo EMic EMor EWhm
	SPoG SSien WFar WHoo			GQue IBal LRHS NGdn NRew
'Regal Supreme' (v)	IBal SSien			NWbg SSien WFar
'Regal Tot'	NSue		'Sahara Nights'	SSien
'Reginald Kaye'	EMic		'Sails Ho' (v) **new**	SSien
'Remember Me'^PBR	ELan EMic LBuc LSRN MPnt NLar		'Saint Elmo's Fire' (v)	CDor LRHS SSien
	NRew NSue NWbg SMrm SSien		'Saint Fiacre'	EMic
	WFar		'Saint John'	NSue
'Reptilian'	EMic IBal		'Saint Paul' ♀^H7	CBdn NRew NSue

'Saishu-jima' (*sieboldii* f. *spathulata*)	GEdr
'Saishu-yahato-sito' (v)	IBal NSue
'Saketini'	CBdn
'Salute' (Tardiana Group)	EMic SSien
'Samurai' (*sieboldiana*) (v)	EMor NBir NBro NGdn NLar NRew SSien
'Sandhill Crane' (v)	LRHS SSien WCAu
'Sapphire Pillows'	SSien
'Sara's Gold'	NRew
'Sara's Sensation' (v)	IBal
'Satisfaction' (v) ♀H7	EMic NRew SSien
'Savannah'	IBal NRew
'Sazanami' (*crispula*)	see *H. crispula*
'Scarlet Ribbons' (v)	SSien
'Scheherazade'	SSien
'School Bus'	SSien
'School Mouse' (v)	CBdn NRew NSue SSien
'Sea Angel Wings'	NRew SSien
'Sea Beacon' (v)	ESwi
'Sea Dream' (v)	CDor EMic ESwi NGdn NSue SSien
'Sea Gold Star'	CDor
'Sea Grotto'	ESwi
'Sea Lotus Leaf'	NLar
'Sea Mist' (v)	ESwi
'Sea Thunder' (v)	CDor ESwi IBal NRew SSien
'Sea Yellow Sunrise'	ESwi NRew SSien
'Second Wind' (*fortunei*) (v)	EMic ESwi NRew SSien
'Secret Love'	SSien
'Secret Treasure'^{PBR} (v)	IBal NSue SSien
'Seducer' (v) ♀H7	EMic ESwi NRew SSien
'See No Evil' (v) **new**	NSue
'See Saw' (*undulata*)	EMic
'September Sun' (v)	EMic LRHS NRew SSien
'September Surprise'	SSien
'Serena' (Tardiana Group)	CBdn
'Serendipity'	EMic IBal NRew
'Shade Beauty' (v)	SSien
'Shade Fanfare' (v)	CDor EBlo ELan ELon EPfP GQue MBNS NBir NGdn NLar NRew NSti SSien WFar
'Shade Finale' (v)	IBal
'Shade Master'	EMic
§ 'Sharmon' (*fortunei*) (v)	ELon EMic NLar SSien
'Sharp Dressed Man'	IBal
'Sheila West'	EMic NRew
'Sherborne Profusion' (Tardiana Group)	EMic SSien
'Sherborne Swallow' (Tardiana Group)	EMic SSien
'Sherborne Swift' (Tardiana Group)	EMic ESwi SSien
'Shere Khan' (v)	IBal
'Sherlock'	SSien
'She's got the Moves'	SSien
'Shimmy Shake'	EMic SSien
'Shining Tot'	SSien
'Shiny Penny' (v)	NRew NSue
'Shiny Sonata'	ESwi IBal ISha NRew SSien
'Shirley Levy'	IBal
'Shirley Vaughn' (v)	IBal SSien
'Showboat' (v)	EMic
'Siberian Tiger'	see *H. 'Amime Tachi'*
sieboldiana	CAgr CBcs CMac EGrI GMaP SPlb SRms
§ - var. **elegans** ♀H7	Widely available
§ - var. **sieboldiana**	NGdn SSien
§ **sieboldii** var. **sieboldii** f. **kabitan** (v)	NGdn NRew SSien
- - f. **shiro-kabitan** (v)	NRew
- f. **spathulata**	IBal

'Sienna Susan'	SSien
'Silberpfeil'	NSue
'Silk Road' (v)	IBal ISha MBel NRew NSue
'Silly String' **new**	NSue
'Silver Bay'	SSien
'Silver Crown'	see *H. 'Albomarginata'* (*fortunei*)
'Silver Lance' (v)	EMic
'Silver Light' **new**	NRew
'Silver Lining'	NWbg
'Silver Lode' (v)	NRew
'Silver Moon'	EMic
'Silver Serenity'	IBal SSien
'Silver Shadow' (v)	NBir NGdn NLar NSue SSien
'Silver Spray' (v)	IBal SSien
'Silver Threads and Gold Needles' (v)	LRHS NRew NSue SSien
'Simply Sharon' (v)	IBal
'Singing in the Rain' (v)	NSue
'Sister Act' (v) **new**	CBdn NRew SSien
'Sizzle'	IBal NRew NSue SSien
'Sky Dancer'	EMic NSue
'Skyrocket'	SSien
'Skywriter'	SSien
'Slammin' (v) **new**	IBal
'Sleeping Beauty'	NGdn NSue NWbg SSien
'Sleeping Star'^{PBR} (v)	IBal NRew NSue SSien
'Slick Willie'	EMic
'Slim and Trim' ♀H7	CBdn EMic GEdr IBal LRHS NRew NSue SSien
'Small Parts'	EMic IBal LRHS NSue SSien
'Smash Hit' (v)	IBal NRew NSue SSien
'Smiling Mouse' (v) ♀H7	CBdn IBal NRew SSien
'Smoke Signals'	CBdn
'Smuggler's Cove' **new**	SSien
'Snake Eyes' (v) ♀H7	CBdn ELon IBal ISha LBar LRHS MAvo MPri NGdn NRew NSue SSien
'Snickers' Surprise' (v)	SSien
'Snow Boy' (v)	NRew NSue
'Snow Bunting' (v)	EMic SSien
'Snow Cap' (v)	CDor EMor LRHS NEoE NGdn NLar NRew SPoG WFar
'Snow Crust' (v)	SSien
'Snow Flakes' (*sieboldii*)	CMac NBro NEoE NGdn NLar NRew NSue NWbg WAbe
'Snow Mouse' (v)	IBal NRew SSien WFar
'Snowden' ♀H7	CBdn ECha EMic GMaP NBir NGdn NRew SSien WCru
'Snowy Lake' (v)	IBal SSien
'So Sweet' (v)	ELan EMic GEdr ISha LBom LRHS MPri MPro NBro NGdn NRew NSue NWbg SPoG SSien WCAu WFar
'Something Blue'	EMic IBal
'Something Different' (*fortunei*) (v)	NRew NSue
'Sophisticated Lady' (v)	SSien
'Sorbet' (v)	EMor LBar MPri NRew NSue SSien
'Soul Shine'	SSien
'Southern Gold'	EMic
'Space Odyssey'	IBal NSue SSien
'Sparkle' (v)	IBal
'Sparkling Burgundy'	EMic LRHS NRew
'Spartacus' (v)	CBdn EMic IBal MBel NRew NSue SSien
'Spartan Arrow'	NSue
'Spartan Glory' (v)	IBal SSien
'Special Blend' (v)	IBal
'Special Gift'	EMic IBal SSien
'Spellbound' (v)	SSien
'Spilt Milk' (*tokudama*) (v)	IBal NGdn SSien
§ 'Spinners' (*fortunei*) (v)	ECha EMic IBal

'Splendid Sarah' (v)	SSien	'Sun Mouse'	CBdn EUrb IBal LBar NSue SPeP SSien XFar
'Spock's Ears'	IBal		
'Spring Break' (v)	CBdn EMic SSien	'Sun Power'	ELon NBro NRew SSien
'Spring Fling'	NRew SSien	'Sunlight Child'	NSue WAbe
'Spring Lace' (v)	NRew	'Sunny Disposition'	NRew SSien
'Spring Love'	IBal NRew	'Sunny Halcyon'	IBal LRHS NRew SSien
'Spring Morning'	ELin ISha NRew	'Sunny Smiles' (v)	EMic
'Spritzer' (v)	CDor EMic NRew NSue SSien	'Sunnybrook' (v)	SSien
'Squash Casserole'	NSue	'Sunset'	SSien
'Stag's Leap' (v)	IBal NSue SSien	'Sunset Grooves' (v)	EGren IBal LRHS MPri NBir NRew NSue
'Stained Glass' (v) ♀H7	CBcs CDor EAri EBee ELon EMic EMor EPfP ESwi IBal LAma LBom LRHS MPro NCth NEoE NGdn NRew NSue SSien WFar	'Sunshine Glory' ♀H7	CDor NRew NSue
		'Super Nova' (v)	NRew SSien
		'Super Sagae' (v)	CDor SSien WFar
'Stan the Man'	SSien	'Surfer Girl'	NSue SSien
'Stand by Me' (v)	CBdn EMic GEdr IBal NRew NSue SSien	'Surfing Mouse'	NSue SSien
		'Surprised by Joy' (v)	NRew NSue SSien
'Stand Corrected' (v)	IBal SSien	'Susan' (v)	NSue
'Star Light Star Bright'	EMic IBal	'Sutter's Mill'	EMic
'Stardust'	IBal	'Swamp Thing' (v)	IBal
§ 'Starker Yellow Leaf'	EMic	'Sweet Bo Beep'	EMic
'Starship' (v)	EMic	'Sweet Bouquet'	EMic
'Step Sister'	EMic	'Sweet Home Chicago' (v)	EMic LAma NRew SSien
'Stepping Out' (v)	EMic NRew NSue	'Sweet Innocence' (v)	SSien
'Sterling Medallion'	IBal	'Sweet Sunshine'	SSien
'Stetson' (v)	EMic	'Sweet Susan'	EBlo SSien
'Stiletto' (v)	EGren GAbr GEdr GKev LRHS MBNS MNrw NBro NEoE NGdn NRew NSue NWbg SPoG SSien WFar	'Sweetheart'	EMic
		'Sweetie' (v)	CDor NSue SSien
		'Swirling Hearts'	NSue
'Stimulation'	IBal SSien	'Swirls Design'	ESwi
'Sting' (v)	EPfP ESwi ISha LBar LCro LRHS NEoE NRew NSue	'Swizzle Sticks'	EMic
		'T Dawg' (v)	NLar NRew NSue
'Stir It Up'	SSien	'T. Rex'	CDor CTsd CWnw EAri EBee EGren ELan ELon EMic EMor EPfP ESgI EUrb IBal ISha LAma LRHS NCth NRew NSue NWbg SMad SSien WFar XFar
§ 'Stirfry'	EGren EMic MPri NEoE NGdn NRew NSue SSien		
'Stone's Valentine'	EMic		
'Stormy Seas'	SSien		
'Stranger in the Dark'	CBdn	'Take the Green Path'	SSien
'Strawberry Parfait'	SSien	*takudama*	see *H. sieboldiana* var. *sieboldiana*
'Strawberry Surprise' (v)	EMic NRew SSien	'Tall Boy'	ECha EMic GBin NBir
'Striker' (v)	EMic IBal NSue	'Tambourine' (v)	CBdn EMic LRHS NRew NSue
'Striptease' (*fortunei*) (v)	CDor CMac EMic ESwi LRHS MBNS MNrw NGdn NLar NRew NSue SSien WFar	'Tango'	EMic
		'Tappen Zee' (v)	SSien
		Tardiana Group	NGdn
'Stuck in Time'	IBal SSien	*tardiflora*	CBdn
'Subcrocea'	EBlo SSien	*tardiva*	EBlo NLar
'Sugar and Cream' (v)	EMic IBal LRHS NGdn	'Tattle Tails'	CBdn NSue SSien
'Sugar and Spice' (v)	EGren ELon EMic IBal LRHS MPri NSue SSien	'Tattoo'^PBR (v)	CWGN NLar SSien
		'Tea and Crumpets' (v)	NRew NSue
'Sugar Daddy'	ELin IBal NRew SSien	'Tea at Bettys' ♀H7	EMic NSue SSien
'Sugar Mama' (v)	SSien	'Teacher's Pride'	IBal NRew NSue SSien
'Sugar Plum'	ESwi IBal NRew SSien	'Tears in Heaven' **new**	IBal
'Sugar Snap' (v)	SSien	'Tears of Joy'	WFar
'Sulphur Glory'	SSien	'Teaspoon'	EMic LRHS NRew NSue SSien
'Sultana' (v)	SSien	'Teatime' (v)	SSien
'Sultans of Swing' (v)	SSien	'Teeny-weeny Bikini' (v)	NRew SSien WFar
'Sum and Substance' ♀H7	Widely available	'Templar Gold'	SSien
'Sum of All' (v)	NRew	'Temptation' (v)	IBal NRew SSien
'Sum Zero'	EMic	'Tenryū'	SSien
'Summer Breeze' (v)	EGren EMic EMor LBar NGdn NRew NSue	'Terpsichore'	EMic
		'Thank You'	SSien
'Summer Dress'	NSue	'The British are Coming'	SSien
'Summer Fragrance'	EMic GBin IBal NRew	'The Devil's Edge' (v)	SSien
'Summer Gold'	EMic	'The Fonz'	IBal
'Summer in Georgia'	SSien	'The King' (v)	NRew NSue SSien
'Summer Joy'	CDor	'The Leading Edge' (v)	SSien
"Summer Lovin" (v)	ISha NRew NSue SSien	'The Razor's Edge'	WFar
'Summer Music' (v) ♀H7	CDor IBal NRew SSien	'The Sweetest Thing' (v)	SSien
'Summer Rainbow' (v)	SSien	'Theo's Blue'	EMic LRHS SSien
'Summer Serenade' (v)	NGdn NRew NSue SSien	'Theo's Red'	IBal SSien
'Sumsational' (v)	IBal	'Thomas Hogg'	see *H. undulata* var. *albomarginata*

Name	Sources
'Thumb Nail'	ECha GEdr
'Thumbelina'	EMic IBal NGdn NSue SSien WAbe
'Thunderbolt'^{PBR} (sieboldiana)	CWnw EPfP IBal LBuc LCro MArl MBNS MHol MNrw NGdn NLar NRew NSue SSien WFar
'Tick Tock' (v)	EMic NRew NSue SSien
'Tickle Me Pink'	CBdn IBal WFar
'Tidewater'	SSien
'Tilt-a-Whirl'	IBal
'Timeless Beauty' (v)	CBdn IBal MBNS NRew NSue SSien WFar
'Timothy' (v)	IBal
'Tiny Bubbles'	SSien
'Tiny Star' **new**	NSue
'Tiny Tears'	GAbr SSien
'Titanic'^{PBR}	IBal SSien
'Titanium'	CBdn IBal ISha LRHS NRew NSue SSien
'Toasted Waffles'	WFar
tokudama	EBlo NBir NGdn WFar
§ - f. *aureo-nebulosa* (v)	NGdn NSti SRms SSien
- f. *flavocircinalis* (v)	ELon GMaP ISha LRHS MPri NBro NRew SSien WFar WHoo
'Tokyo Smog' (v)	NSue
'Tom Schmid' (v) ♀H7	EMic IBal LRHS NSue SSien
'Tom Thumb'	IBal NSue SSien
'Tongue of Flame' (v)	LRHS MPri NRew NSue SSien
'Tongue Twister'	EMic IBal SSien
'Tootie Mae'	NRew SSien
'Torchlight' (v)	EMic IBal NRew NSue SSien
tortifrons	GEdr SSien
'Tortilla Chip'	EGren LBom NRew WFar
'Tot Tot'	LRHS NRew NSue SSien
'Totally Twisted'	EMic IBal NSue
'Touch of Class' (v) ♀H7	CBdn CDor EGrI EMor ESwi GBin IBal ISha MBel NBir NCou NGdn NRew NSue NWbg SSien WFar
'Toy Soldier' ♀H7	EMic ESwi GEdr ISha NGdn NRew NSue SSien
'Treasure Hunt' (v)	SSien
'Tremors'	EMic IBal
'Trifecta' (v)	NRew
'Triple Ripple' (v)	SSien
'Trixi' (v)	IBal
'Tropical Dancer'	IBal
'Tropical Storm' (v)	IBal NRew SSien
'Tropicana' (v)	NRew SSien
'True Blue'	EGren
'Tsugaru Komachi'	EMic
'Tsugaru Komachi Kifukurin' (v)	EMic
'Tugaux' (v)	IBal
'Turnabout' (v)	IBal
'Turning Point'	IBal
'Tutu'	SSien
'Twiggie'	EMic
'Twilight' (*fortunei*) (v)	EGrI ELon EMic EMor LBom MBNS MHol NGdn NLar NRew NSue SSien WFar XFar
'Twilight Time'	IBal
'Twin Cities' (v) **new**	CBdn
'Twinkle Little Star' **new**	NSue
'Twinkle Toes'	EMic NRew NSue
'Twist of Lime' (v) ♀H7	CBdn ESwi GKev IBal LRHS NGdn NRew NSue SSien WCot
'Twisted Spearmint' (v)	CBdn NRew NSue SSien
'Twitter'	ESwi
'Tycoon' (v)	SSien
'Tyler's Treasure' (v)	NRew
'UFO'	ESwi LBom NSue SSien WFar
'Ultraviolet Light'	SSien
'Ulysses S. Grant'	IBal
undulata (v)	WFar
§ - var. *albomarginata* (v)	CMac ECha EGren EHeP EMic GMaP ISha LRHS LSRN MPri NBid NBir NGdn NLar NRew SRms WFar
§ - var. *erromena*	EBee EBlo EMic GMaP
§ - var. *undulata* (v) ♀H7	CDor EBlo EGren EMic EUrb GMaP IBal LRHS LSto MPri NGdn NLar NRew NWbg
- var. *univittata* (v)	EMic GKev NBir NEoE NRew SRms WFar
'Unforgettable'	EMic IBal NRew SSien
'Unruly Child'	CBdn ESwi IBal NSue SSien
'Uprising' (v)	SSien
'Urajiro' (*hypoleuca*)	IBal
'Urajiro-hachijo' (*longipes* var. *latifolia*)	IBal
'Urchin' **new**	NSue
'Valentine Lace'	EMic
'Valley's Blue Curaçao'	IBal
'Valley's Chute the Chute'	EMic SSien
'Valley's Glacier' (v)	EMic NRew NSue WFar
'Valley's Lemon Squash'	CBdn IBal NRew
'Valley's Love Birds'	CBdn IBal SSien
'Valley's Paparazzi' (v)	CBdn IBal NSue
'Valley's Pavlova' **new**	SSien
'Valley's Red Scorpion'	IBal SSien
'Valley's Ruffle Shuffle'	SSien
'Valley's Sushi' (v)	IBal SSien
'Valley's Vanilla Sticks'	EMic SSien
'Van Wade' (v)	IBal SSien
'Vanilla Cream' (*cathayana*)	IBal NRew WFar
'Variegata' (*gracillima*)	see *H.* 'Vera Verde'
'Variegata' (*tokudama*) (v)	see *H. tokudama* f. *aureo-nebulosa*
'Variegata' (*undulata*) (v)	see *H. undulata* var. *undulata*
'Variegata' (*ventricosa*) (v)	see *H.* 'Aureomarginata' (*ventricosa*)
'Variegated' (*fluctuans*)	see *H.* 'Sagae'
'Velvet Moon' (v)	EMic EPfP IBal LRHS MBNS MPri NRew NSue SSien
'Venetian Skies' (v)	IBal SSien
ventricosa	CMac EMic MCtn WFar
- BWJ 8160 from Sichuan	WCru
'Venus' (*plantaginea*) (d)	EMic LRHS MBel NRew SSien WFar
'Venus Star'	EMic
venusta	EBee EBlo GEdr IBal NBid NBir NSti NSue SRot SSien WAbe WFar
- B&SWJ 4389	WCru
- dwarf	SSien
- *yakusimensis*	see *H. kikutii* var. *yakusimensis*
§ 'Vera Verde' (v)	NBir
'Verdi Valentine'	EMic
'Verkade's One'	NSue
'Vermont Frost' (v)	IBal
'Verna Jean' (v)	EMic IBal SSien
'Veronica Lake' (v)	EMic GEdr LRHS NRew NSue SSien
'Vibrant Hope'	SSien
'Victory' ♀H7	IBal NRew NSue SSien
'Victory Lap' (v) **new**	NRew
'Viking Ship'	CBdn IBal SSien
'Vim and Vigor'	IBal SSien
'Vina'	IBal
'Virginia Reel' (v)	IBal NRew SSien
'Viridis Marginata'	see *H. sieboldii* var. *sieboldii* f. *kabitan*
'Voices in the Wind' (Shadowland Series) (v) **new**	IBal
'Volcano Island'^{PBR} (v) ♀H7	ESwi IBal NRew SSien
'Vulcan' (v)	EMic NRew NSue SSien
'Wagtail' (Tardiana Group)	SSien
'Waiting in Vein'	IBal
'War Paint' ♀H7	IBal NRew NSue SSien WFar

'Warwick Comet' (v)	EMic GAbr NRew NSue SSien
'Warwick Curtsey' (v)	EMic NRew
'Warwick Delight' (v)	NRew
'Warwick Edge' (v)	EMic SSien
'Warwick Essence'	EMic IBal
'Watermark' (v)	EMic
'Waterslide'	CBdn LBar LRHS NRew NSue SPeP SSien
'Waukon the Moon'	SSien
'Waukon Thin Ice'	EMic
'Waukon Water'	EMic
'Wave Runner' (v)	SSien
'Waving Winds' (v)	IBal
'Waving Wuffles'	EMic
'Wayside Blue'	EMic
'Wayside Perfection'	see H. 'Royal Standard'
'Weihenstephan' (sieboldii)	EMic
'Well Shaked' (v)	IBal
'Weser'	IBal
'Wheaton Blue'	EMic NRew
'Wheaton Thunder' (v)	SSien
'Wheee!' (Shadowland Series)	IBal NSue SSien
'Whirligig' (v)	EMic SSien
'Whirling Dervish' (v)	NRew SSien
'Whirlwind' (fortunei) (v) ♀H7	CBdn CDor ELan EMic EMor ESwi GAbr IBal LRHS MNrw NBro NGdn NLar NRew NSue NWbg SPoG SSien WCAu WFar WHoo
'Whirlwind Tour' (v)	NRew
'Whirly Pop' (v)	NRew
'White Bikini' (v)	CBdn EMor IBal NGdn NRew NSue SSien
'White Ceiling'	IBal
'White Christmas' (fortunei) (v)	NGdn NSue SSien
'White Christmas' (undulata) (v)	NRew SSien
'White Dove' (v)	NEoE NRew NWbg
'White Edger'	EMic NRew
'White Feather' (undulata)	CWGN ELin ISha LCro LSou MHer MNrw NBir NEoE NGdn NLar SMad SPeP SPoG SSien WFar XFar
'White Gold'	EMic SSien
'White Jewel' (v)	NSue SSien
'Wide Brim' (v) ♀H7	Widely available
'Wiggles and Squiggles'	ESwi NRew SSien
'Will of Fortune'	SSien
'William Lachman' (v)	NLar
'Wily Willy'	ESwi SSien
'Wind River Gold'	NRew
'Windfall' (v)	IBal
'Windsor Gold'	see H. 'Nancy Lindsay'
'Winfield Blue'	IBal NBir
'Winfield Gold'	EMic
'Wings of a Prayer' (v)	CBdn NSue
'Winsome' (v)	IBal NSue SSien
'Winter Snow' (v) ♀H7	CBdn CDor EMic ESwi NRew NSue SSien WFar
'Winter Warrior' (v)	NRew SSien
'Wintergreen' (v)	SSien
'Wishing Well'	ESwi SSien
'Wogon' (sieboldii)	GAbr GKev GMaP NSue
'Wogon's Boy'	CDor NRew
'Wolverine' (v)	EMic EMor MBNS NGdn NRew NSue SSien WAbe WFar
'Wonderful Life' (v)	IBal
'Wonderland' (v)	SSien
'Woodland Elf' (v)	IBal NRew SSien
'Woop Woop' (v)	NRew SSien
'World Cup'	IBal NRew SSien
'Worldly Treasure'	EMic
'Wrinkle in Time' (v)	NRew SSien
'Wrinkles and Crinkles' (v)	EMic
'Wu Hoo' **new**	IBal
'Wu-La-La' (v)	CBdn ESwi IBal LRHS NRew NSue NWbg SSien XFar
'Wunderbar' (v)	EMic ESwi IBal SSien
'Wundergold'	CBdn EMic IBal SSien
'Wylde Green Cream'	IBal NGdn NRew SSien
'Xanadu' (v)	NRew
'X-rated' (v)	NRew
'X-ray'	NRew SSien
'Yakushima-mizu' (gracillima)	EMic
'Yankee Blue'	IBal NSue SSien
'Yellow Boa'	EMic ESwi NRew NSue
'Yellow Edge' (fortunei)	see H. fortunei var. aureomarginata
'Yellow Edge' (sieboldiana)	see H. 'Frances Williams'
'Yellow Polka Dot Bikini' (v)	CBdn EMic EMor ESwi IBal NRew NSue SSien
'Yellow River' (v) ♀H7	CBdn EGren EMic ESwi ISha LRHS MPri NCth NGdn NRew NSue SSien WFar
'Yellow Splash' (v)	ECha
'Yellow Splash Rim' (v)	EMic NRew SSien
'Yellow Splashed Edged' (v)	EMic
'Yellow Waves'	SSien
'Yesterday's Memories' (v)	SSien
'Yin' (v)	EMic IBal NRew SSien
yingeri	WPGP
- B&SWJ 546	LEdu WCru
'Yorkshire Life' **new**	NSue
'You're So Vein'	IBal SSien
'Yucca Ducka Do' (v)	EMic SSien
'Zager Blue'	EMic
'Zager Green'	EMic
'Zager White Edge' (fortunei) (v)	EMic SSien
'Zebra Stripes' (v)	LBar NRew SSien XFar
'Zeus' (v)	NSue
'Zion's Hope'	EMic
'Zita'	SSien
'Zitronenfalter'	IBal SSien
'Zora' **new**	NSue
'Zorro'	ESwi IBal SSien
'Zounds'	EBee EBlo EMic NGdn NRew SRms SSien WFar
'Zucchini Fries'	CBdn SSien

Hottonia (Primulaceae)
palustris	CBen CLil CPud ELin EPfk LCro NPer

Houstonia (Rubiaceae)
caerulea L.	SPlb SRot
- var. *alba*	EWes SPlb
- 'Millard's Variety'	LCro WIce
michauxii Fred Mullard	EWes

Houttuynia (Saururaceae)
cordata	CAgr CMac ECha EGren ELin GKev LEdu LShi NSti SDix WCAu WFar WKit
§ - 'Boo-Boo' (v)	CLil CMac CPud CWat ELin EPfk
§ - 'Chameleon' (v)	Widely available
- 'Flame' (v)	EBee ELan EUrb LRHS MBNS MHol MPri MSwo NLit WFar
- 'Flore Pleno' (d)	CBen CLil CMac CPud CToG CWat ECha ELin EWld LCro MSCN NBir NPer SPlb SRms
- 'Joker's Gold'	EPPr

Houttuynia

- 'Pied Piper' (v)	LRHS MPro NBir
- 'Terry Clarke'	see *H. cordata* 'Boo-Boo'
- 'Tricolor'	see *H. cordata* 'Chameleon'
- Variegata Group (v)	NBro

Hovea (Fabaceae)
montana	SPlb

Hovenia (Rhamnaceae)
dulcis	CAgr CBcs CMCN EPfP MBlu MCtn NLar SBrt WJur WKor
- B&SWJ 11024	WCru
- NJM 11.003	WPGP

Howea (Arecaceae)
belmoreana ♀H1b	EHap
§ forsteriana ♀H1a	CDoC EGren EHap LBom LCro LDro NHrt NPlm SArc SPlb

Hoya ✤ (Apocynaceae)
acuta	NTro
§ australis ♀H1b	EShb LCro NTro
- 'Lisa' (v) ♀H1b **new**	NTro
bella	see *H. lanceolata* subsp. *bella*
carnosa ♀H2	CHll CoPl CRHN CTsd CTtf EShb LBom LWaG NHrt NTro
- 'Albomarginata' (v)	LInT LWaG NTro
- 'Compacta'	LBom NCft NTro
§ - 'Compacta Regalis' (v)	NPer
- HINDU ROPE	see *H. carnosa* 'Compacta Regalis'
- 'Krinkle 8' ♀H2	LBom NPer NTro
- 'Tricolor' (v) ♀H2	CDoC EAri LBom LCro LInT NCft NHrt NPer NTro
- 'Variegata' (v)	EShb
curtisii	LBom NTro
darwinii misapplied	see *H. australis*
gracilis ♀H1b	LBom LCro LWaG
kerrii	CDoC EAri LBom LWaG NTro
§ lanceolata	CDoC EShb LBom LCro NTro
subsp. *bella* ♀H1c	
linearis ♀H1b	CDoC CoPl LBom LCro LInT NCft NHrt NTro
puber **new**	NTro
pubicalyx ♀H2	EShb LBom LCro NTro
- 'Splash' (v)	NTro
verticillata **new**	NTro
wayetii	EAri LBom LCro NHrt NTro

Huernia (Apocynaceae)
pendula	NTro
schneideriana	NTro
zebrina subsp. *insigniflora*	NTro

Humata (Davalliaceae)
§ tyermanii ♀H1b	CDoC EShb ESwi ISha LCro LEdu NHrt SPlb WCot
- 'Bunny'	LCro
- 'Sekka'	CMen

Humulus ✤ (Cannabaceae)
lupulus	CBcs CDoC EPfP GQue NLar SRms WSpi
- (f)	MCtn MHoo WJur
- 'Aureus' ♀H6	CBcs CMac EGrl ElAn ENfk EPfP GAbr GQue LCro LRHS MAsh MGos MHer NBir NBro NLar SPlb SPoG SRms WKif WTHo
- 'Aureus' (f)	CRHN CSde MHtn SMrm SPoG WCot
- 'Fuggle'	CAgr SVic

- 'Golden Tassels' (f)	ElAn ELon LRHS MGos MHtn MMuc NLar SEND SPoG SRms WFar
- 'Magnum' (f)	LCro
- 'Northern Brewer' (f)	CAgr CDoC
- 'Prima Donna'	CAgr CMac ElAn LEdu NLar SPoG
- 'Wye Challenger'	CAgr MHer SVic
- 'Wye Northdown'	CAgr
scandens	Prohibited invasive. See Conservation and the Environment, p.42

Hunnemannia (Papaveraceae)
fumariifolia	CSpe

Huodendron (Styracaceae)
biaristatum	CExl
tibeticum	CExl

Hyacinthella (Asparagaceae)
glabrescens	WCot

Hyacinthoides (Asparagaceae)
aristidis	WCot
'Bakkum Blue'	GKev LAma
ciliolata	CBro EPot GKev WAbe WCot
℗ hispanica	CoPl GKev NBir WCot XFar
- 'Alba'	GKev LAma
- subsp. *algeriensis*	WCot
- 'Dainty Maid'	WCot
- 'Excelsior'	LAma XFar
- 'Miss World'	WCot
- 'Queen of the Pinks'	WCot XFar
- 'White City'	WCot XFar
§ italica ♀H6	GKev WCot WShi XFar
lingulata	EDAr WAbe WCot
mauritanica	LAma XFar
§ non-scripta	Widely available
- 'Alba'	EGrl GKev LAma MMuc NBir SEND SRms
- 'Bracteata'	WCot
- long-bracteate, white-flowered	WCot
- 'Mill House Blue' (d)	WCot
- 'Mill House Pink' (d)	WCot
- 'Mill House White' (d)	WCot
- 'Rosea'	EGrl
- 'Wavertree'	WCot
reverchonii	WAbe WCot

Hyacinthus ✤ (Asparagaceae)
amethystinus	see *Brimeura amethystina*
azureus	see *Muscari azureum*
comosus 'Plumosus'	see *Muscari comosum* 'Plumosum'
orientalis	GKev LAma
- 'Aiolos' ♀H4	ETay GKev LAma
- var. *albulus* 'Roman White'	LAma
- 'Anna Liza' ♀H4	GKev LAma
- 'Anna Marie' ♀H4	EGren GKev LAma
- 'Aqua'PBR ♀H4 **new**	XFar
- 'Atlantic'	GKev LAma
- 'Blue Eyes'	XFar
- 'Blue Festival' ♀H4	LCro
- 'Blue Jacket' ♀H4	CBro EGren ETay GKev LAma LRHS SPoG
- 'Blue Pearl'PBR	EGren LCro LRHS
- 'Blue Star'	LCro XFar
- 'Blue Tango'	LAma XFar
- 'Blue Trophy'	ERCP
- 'Carnegie'	CBro EGren EPfP ERCP ETay LCro XFar
- 'Chestnut Flower' (d)	LAma

- 'China Pink' ERCP XFar
- 'City of Haarlem' ⚥H4 CBro EGren ETay LAma LCro LRHS XFar
- 'Crystal Palace' (d) GKev LAma
- 'Dark Dimension' ERCP GKev LAma LCro XFar
- 'Delft Blue' ⚥H4 EGren EPfP ETay GKev LAma LCro LRHS LSto
- 'Eros Double' (d) XFar
- 'Fondant' EGren ETay LCro
- 'General Köhler' (d) ⚥H4 LRHS
- 'Gipsy Princess' GKev LAma LRHS
- 'Gipsy Queen' ⚥H4 EGren ETay GKev LAma LRHS WCot XFar
- 'Hollyhock' (d) ⚥H4 XFar
- 'Jan Bos' ⚥H4 EGren ETay GKev LAma LCro LRHS SPoG XFar
- 'Lili Purple' (d) XFar
- 'L'Innocence' ⚥H4 LSto
- 'Madame Sophie' (d) LAma
- 'Midnight Sky' **new** XFar
- 'Miss Saigon' ⚥H4 CBro LAma XFar
- 'Odysseus' LAma
- 'Peter Stuyvesant' LCro SPoG XFar
- 'Pink Elephant' EPfP ETay GKev LAma
- 'Pink Pearl' EGren EPfP ETay LAma LCro LRHS XFar
- 'Pink Surprise' ERCP
- 'Prince of Love' PBR (d) LAma
- 'Purple Beauty' GKev
- 'Purple Sensation' PBR EGren LCro
- 'Purple Star' LCro
- 'Red Diamond' GKev LRHS
- 'Red Magic' LRHS
- 'Rosette' (d) GKev LAma
- 'Royal Navy' (d) ⚥H4 CBro EPfP ERCP ETay GKev LAma XFar
- 'Sky Jacket' EGren LCro
- 'Snow Crystal' (d) ERCP
- 'Splendid Cornelia' EGren EPfP ERCP
- 'Spring Beauty' **new** ERCP
- 'Spring Field' EGren
- 'White Fleur' (d) LAma
- 'White Pearl' EGren GKev LCro
- 'Woodstock' EGren EPfP ERCP ETay GKev LAma LCro LRHS SPoG XFar
- 'Yellow Queen' ⚥H4 GKev LAma
- 'Yellowstone' ⚥H4 LAma LRHS

Hydrangea ✿ (*Hydrangeaceae*)

B&SWJ 7177 from Thailand WCru
from Guizhou, China EWld SChF WCot WPGP
× *agricola* WCru
- 'Crûg's Elegant' WCru
- 'Crûg's Pink' **new** WCru
alternifolia B&SWJ 6177 WCru
- 'Pink Geisha' WCru
- 'White Haze' **new** WCru
alternifolia × *amamiohsimensis*
§ *ampla* ⚥H5 CBcs CRHN EBee ELan EPfP EUrb GKev MBlu NLar WPGP
- BWJ 8150 WCru
angustipetala see *H. chinensis* f. *angustipetala*
anomala subsp. *anomala* WCru
    BWJ 8052 from China
- - HWJK 2065 from Nepal WCru
- - 'Winter Glow' CMac EBee EPfP LRHS SGol SNig WCru WFar
* - subsp. *glabra* LRHS
* - - B&SWJ 6804 WCru
- - 'Crûg Coral' LCro NLar SGol SPoG WCru WFar

- subsp. *petiolaris* dwarf see *H. petiolaris* var. *cordifolia*
- - var. *tiliifolia* misapplied see *H. petiolaris* var. *megaphylla*
- - var. *tiliifolia* see *H. petiolaris* var. *ovalifolia*
- subsp. *quelpartensis* see *H. petiolaris* var. *ovalifolia*
- 'Winter Surprise' see *H. anomala* subsp. *anomala* 'Winter Glow'
§ *arborescens* WPGP
- 'Annabelle' ⚥H6 Widely available
- BellaRagazza Limetta ('Ncha8' PBR) **new** SGol
- 'Bounty' MAsh MBlu SGol
- Candybelle Bubblegum ('Grhyar1407' PBR) EBee EGren LCro LRHS LSou SGol
- Candybelle Marshmallow ('Grhyar1406' PBR) EBee EGren EPfP LCro SGol
- 'Emerald Lace' CBcs MBlu SGol
§ - 'Grandiflora' CBcs EGren GBin LRHS MMrt NBro NLar
- 'Hayes Starburst' PBR CDoC ELan EPfP LRHS MMrt SGol SPoG
- 'Hills of Snow' see *H. arborescens* 'Grandiflora'
- Incrediball see *H. arborescens* Strong Annabelle
- Invincibelle Ruby see *H. arborescens* Ruby Annabelle
- Invincibelle Spirit see *H. arborescens* Pink Annabelle
- Lime Rickey ('Smnhalr' PBR) LCro LSRN Midl MPri NLar SGol
- Magical Pinkerbell ('Kolpinbel') (Magical Series) SGol
- 'Picadilly' NLar
- Pink Annabelle ('Ncha2') CBcs CDoC EGren EGrI ELan EPfP GBin LBom LCro LRHS LSRN MAsh MBlu Midl MMrt NWbg SGol SMad SPoG WCha WFar WSpi
- 'Pink Pincushion' NBro NLar SGol WFar
- 'Puffed Green' NLar
- subsp. *radiata* SGol WFar WPGP
- - 'Samantha' EPfP SPoG WPGP
§ - Ruby Annabelle ('Ncha3' PBR) LCro LRHS MMrt SGol WFar WSpi
- 'Ryan Gainey' WSpi
- 'Sheep Cloud' MBlu
§ - Strong Annabelle ('Abetwo' PBR) Widely available
- Sweet Annabelle ('Ncha4' PBR) CWnw LCro LRHS WFar
- 'Vasterival' NLar
- 'Visitation' WFar
- White Dome ('Dardom' PBR) NBro
aspera CMac LBom LWaG SSta WCru WPGP
- HWJCM 452 WCru
- from Gongshan, China CExl WPGP
- 'Anthony Bullivant' ⚥H5 CBcs CDoC EPfP EUrb IArd LRHS MAsh NLar SGol WFar
- 'Bellevue' EUrb IArd MBlu NCth SHor WPGP
- 'Dark Chocolate' LRHS
§ - subsp. *discolor* **new** WKif
- Farrell form CExl EBee MBlu WPGP
- Hot Chocolate ('Haopr012' PBR) ⚥H4 CBcs CDoC CSBt CSpe CWnw EBee ELan EUrb GKev LRHS MBlu MGos MPri MPro NCth NLar NWbg SGol SPoG WFar WSpi
- Kawakamii Group CBcs CExl CSpe EBee ESwi LRHS NLar SGol SHyH WCru WPGP
- - B&SWJ 3456 WCru
- - B&SWJ 6702 WCru
- - B&SWJ 6714 WCru
- - B&SWJ 6827 WCru
- - B&SWJ 6996 WCru
- - B&SWJ 7101 WCru
- - 'August Abundance' WCru

Hydrangea

– – 'Formosa'	WCru
– – 'Lishan'	WCru
– – 'Maurice Mason'	CExl
– – 'September Splendour'	WCru
§ – 'Koki'	CExl LRHS WPGP
– 'Macrophylla' ♀H5	EBee EGren ELan GKin LCro LSto MBlu MGos SGol WCru WFar WPGP WSpi
– 'Mauvette'	EPfP EUrb GKin MBlu NBro SGol SHyH SVen WCru
– 'Peter Chappell' ♀H5	CExl CMac EBee LRHS MBlu NLar SVen WPGP
– Purple Passion	see *H. aspera* 'Koki'
§ – subsp. *robusta*	CExl EBee WFar WPGP WSpi
– – B&SWJ 13999	WCru
– – GWJ 9430	WCru
– – KR 10735	EBee WPGP
– – WWJ 11888	WCru
– 'Rocklon'	ESwi NLar SGol
– 'Rosemary Foster' **new**	LRHS MPri
– 'Rosthornii'	see *H. aspera* subsp. *robusta*
– 'Sam MacDonald'	CExl LRHS NLar WPGP WSpi
§ – subsp. *sargentiana*	CCVT CDoC CEnd CExl CWnw EAri EBee EPfP LMil LSRN MBlu MGos NBir NLar SGol WCot WCru WFar WKif WPGP WSpi
– – Gold Rush ('Giel')	EGren LCro MMrt NLar
– – 'La Fosse'	MBlu WPGP
– – large-leaved	CExl WCru
– 'Spinners'	NLar
– subsp. *strigosa*	CExl CSde GKev LRHS SHyH SVen WCru WFar WPGP
– – B&SWJ 8201	WCru
– – KWJ 12151 from northern Vietnam	WCru
– – from Gong Shan, China	CExl
– – 'Elegant Sound Pavilion'	CExl WPGP
– – 'Gongshan'	WPGP
– – 'Sapa'	EBee WPGP
– 'Taiwan Pink'	NLar SGol
– 'The Ditch'	ESwi NLar
– 'Titania'	CExl EBee WPGP
§ – Villosa Group	Widely available
– – 'Trelissick'	CExl EBee WPGP
– – 'Velvet and Lace' ♀H5	EBee LRHS MGos NCth NLar WSpi
asterolasia B&SWJ 10481	WCru
barbara	CMac NLar WCru
– 'Vickie'	NBro NLar
bifida	CExl CMiW EBee EMor EWes EWld GEdr WCru WPGP
– B&SWJ 5436	WCru
– B&SWJ 5551	WCru
– 'Pink-Kii'	WCru
– 'Pink-Shi'	EWld LEdu NLar WCru
'Blue Blush'	WCru
§ 'Blue Deckle' (L)	CMac EWld LRHS MGos NBro NCth SGol
'Boléro'^{PBR}	LCro LRHS WCha
caerulea	CMiW EWes LAma LEdu NLar WCru
– 'Blue Wonder'	CExl CTtf
§ *chinensis*	CBcs
– BWJ 8035	WCru
– BWJ 8000 from Sichuan, China	WCru
– from Taiwan B&SWJ 3410	WCru
– – B&SWJ 3420	WCru
– – B&SWJ 3487	WCru
§ – f. *angustipetala*	EBee WPGP
– – B&SWJ 3454	WCru
– – B&SWJ 3553	WCru

– – B&SWJ 3667	WCru
– – B&SWJ 3733	WCru
– – B&SWJ 3814	WCru
– – B&SWJ 6787	WCru
– – B&SWJ 6802	WCru
– – B&SWJ 7128	WCru
– – 'Monlongshou'	see *H. chinensis* f. *macrosepala* 'Golden Crane'
– 'Big White'	WPGP
– f. *formosana*	WCru
– – B&SWJ 1488	
– – B&SWJ 7097	WCru
– var. *lobbii* B&SWJ 3214	WCru
– f. *macrosepala*	WCru
– – B&SWJ 3476	
– – CWJ 12441	WCru
§ – – 'Golden Crane'	CBcs CMHG EBee WCru WFar WPGP
– – 'Hoop'	ESwi WCru
– f. *obovatifolia*	WCru
– – B&SWJ 3487b	
– – B&SWJ 3683	WCru
– – B&SWJ 7121	WCru
aff. *choufeniana*	WCru
– FMWJ 13217 **new**	
cinerea	see *H. aspera* subsp. *discolor*
§ Cloud Nine ('Tmhy18-1') **new**	CSBt
cordifolia	see *H. petiolaris* var. *cordifolia*
* *crassa* var. *elliptica*	WCru
– FMWJ 13440 **new**	
daimingshanensis	CBct EBee MBlu
– BWJ 15621	WCru
– GUIZ 48	WCru WPGP
Daredevil ('Jpd01'^{PBR}) (L)	CAbb CSpe EBee EGren LRHS NLar SGol SReu
davidii B&SWJ 8307	
– B&SWJ 11692	WCru
– B&SWJ 11717	WCru
– f. *purpurascens*	WCru
– KWJ 12233B	
§ *densifolia*	CExl EWes WPGP
– 'Crûg's Abundant'	WCru
– 'Crûg's Almighty' **new**	WCru
– 'Crûg's Phoenix'	WCru
– 'Hsitou'	WCru
– 'Hsitou Splendour'	WCru
– 'Xitou Survivor' **new**	WCru
'Dharuma'	GKin SGol
Early Sensation ('Bulk'^{PBR})	CCVT CDoC CEnd CMac EBee EPfP GKin LRHS MAsh SGol SHyH SPoG SVen WFar WPGP
fauriei	NLar WPGP
– B&SWJ 1701	WCru
– B&SWJ 6831	WCru
– B&SWJ 7052	WCru
– CWJ 12405	WCru
– CWJ 12433	WCru
– 'Angel Wings'	EAri LCro MBlu NCth NLar
– Windmills ('Plooster')	CWGN LRHS SWCr
febrifuga	CBcs CBct CDoC CHll CMCN EAri EBee SIvy WJek WSpi
– B&SWJ 9734	WCru
– B&SWJ 9753	WCru
– NJM 10.042	WPGP
'First Red'	CEnd
'Garden House Glory'	EBee EPfP LEdu WPGP
glabrifolia	see *H. chinensis*
glandulosa B&SWJ 4031	WCru
§ *glaucescens* DJHS 8071 **new** WCru	
– FMWJ 13014 **new**	WCru
'Glyn Church'	EPfP SChF WPGP

aff. *gracilis* B&SWJ 3869	WCru
- B&SWJ 3942	WCru
§ *heteromalla*	CMCN LEdu NBro SReu WPGP
- B&SWJ 2142 from India	WCru
- BWJ 7657 from China	WCru
- GWJ 9337 from Sikkim	WCru
- HWJ 526 from Vietnam	WCru
- HWJ 938 from Vietnam	WCru
- HWJCM 180	WCru
- HWJK 2127 from Nepal	WCru
- KR 9913 from India	WPGP
- Bretschneideri Group	EBee EUrb GKin LRHS SHyH WCru WFar
- 'Fan Si Pan'	WCru
- 'Gidie'	NLar
- 'Jermyns Lace'	NLar
- 'June Pink'	NLar
- 'Long White'	NLar
- 'Morrey's Form'	WCru
- 'Nepal Beauty'	EBee EPfP ESwi NLar WPGP
- 'Snowcap'	LRHS
- 'Willy'	SGol
- f. *xanthoneura*	WPGP
NJM 11.009	
- - 'Wilsonii'	WCru
- 'Yalung Ridge'	WCru
aff. *heteromalla*	SGol WSpi
'Hidcote Pink'	see *H. macrophylla* 'Juno'
hirsuta B&SWJ 8207 from Vietnam	WCru
- BWJ 16315 from Vietnam	WCru
aff. *hirsuta* B&SWJ 8371 from Laos	WCru
hirta	MBlu
- B&SWJ 5000	WCru
- B&SWJ 11022	WCru
§ *hwangii*	WPGP
- BWJ 15644	WCru
hydrangeoides	CBcs EBee EGrI ELan LCro MBlu MGos SGol SPoG WSpi
- B&SWJ 14622	WCru
- 'Brookside Littleleaf'	see *H. petiolaris* var. *cordifolia* 'Brookside Littleleaf'
- BURST OF LIGHT (v)	SPoG
- f. *concolor* B&SWJ 5954	WCru
- - 'Moonlight' ♀H5	CBcs CDoC CWGN ELan EPfP EUrb LBom LRHS MBlu MGos MPri NLar SBig SGol SMad SPoG SWCr WCot WCru
- var. *hydrangeoides* B&SWJ 5489	WCru
- B&SWJ 5732	WCru
- - 'Iwa Garami'	NLar
- - 'Roseum' ♀H5	CBcs CDoC EAri ELan EWes IArd LCro LSto MBlu MGos SGol SPoG WCot WCru
- 'Rose Sensation'	EBee EGrI LRHS NLar SGol SPoG
- 'Shiro-dai-fukurin' (v)	WCot
- 'Shiro-fuka-fukurin-fu' (v)	SBig
- SNOW SENSATION ('Minsnow3'^PBR)	LBom LRHS NLar
- var. *taquetii* B&SWJ 8771	WCru
- - 'Cheju's Early'	WCru
- var. *ullungdoensis* B&SWJ 8505	WCru
- - B&SWJ 8522	WCru
- var. *yakushimensis* B&SWJ 6119	WCru
indochinensis	WCru
B&SWJ 8307	
- WWJ 11609	WCru
integerrima	see *H. serratifolia*
integrifolia	EBee WPGP
- B&SWJ 22	WCru
- B&SWJ 6967	WCru
involucrata	MMrt SBrt SGol WSpi
- B&SWJ 4790	WCru
- B&SWJ 11578	WCru
- 'Hortensis' (d)	CMac NLar WCru WPGP WSpi WTre
- var. *idzuensis*	WCru
- 'Late Love'	LRHS
- 'Mihara-kokonoe'	SGol WPGP
- 'Multiplex' (d)	ESwi MBlu WCru
- 'Oshima'	MBlu WPGP
- 'Plena' (d)	LRHS NLar SVen WPGP WSpi
- 'Plenissima' (d)	WCru
- 'Sterilis'	WCru WSpi
- 'Viridescens' ♀H4	LRHS NLar WCru WPGP
- 'Yohraku-tama' (d) ♀H4	LRHS NLar SGol WCru WPGP
- 'Yokudanka' (d)	NLar WPGP
'Long March'	EAri EBee LEdu SBrt WPGP
longifolia CWJ 12413	WCru
longipes	CExl WCru
- var. *fulvescens* B&SWJ 8188	WCru
- var. *longipes*	CExl
- - NJM 11.084	WPGP
- 'Trelissick' **new**	EBee
luteovenosa	WCru
- B&SWJ 5647	WCru
- B&SWJ 6220	WCru
macrophylla (H)	CoPl EGren SFol
- 'AB Green Shadow'^PBR (H)	MPri SGol
- 'Adria' (H)	NLar SGol
- AFTER MIDNIGHT ('Jong 02') (L)	LCro
- 'All Summer Beauty' (H)	CSBt ELan ELon
- ALPEN GLOW	see *H. macrophylla* 'Alpenglühen'
§ - 'Alpenglühen' (H)	CBcs CSBt LRHS
- 'Altona' (H) ♀H5	CBcs CBrac CCVT IArd LCro MGos MPri NBir NLar SRms
- 'Ami Pasquier' (H)	CBcs CDoC CMac CSBt EGrI ELan ELon EPfP LRHS LSRN SAko SHyH SPoG SRms WLov
- 'Amor' (H)	MAsh MPri SGol WCha
- 'Amour Toujours' (Rendez-vous Series) (H)	LRHS MPri
- 'Anda'^PBR (H)	LRHS MAsh
- 'Aureovariegata' (L/v)	WCot
§ - 'Ayesha' (H)	CAbb CBcs CBrac CCoa CDoC CEnd CMac CMHG ECha EPfP GBin GKev GKin LSto MBlu MGos MMuc NBir NLar SAdn SChF SDix SGol SHyH SRms WFar WKif WLov WPGP
- 'Bachstelze' (Teller Series) (L)	GEdr WPGP
- 'Bavaria'^PBR (H)	GKin SGol WFar
- 'Beauté Vendômoise' (L)	NCth NLar
- 'Bel Alexandre' (H)	SGol
- 'Bela'^PBR (H)	EGren MAsh
- BELLA PESCHE ('Hore1644') (H)	SGol
- BELLE SEDUCTION ('Bodalan'^PBR) (Seduction Series) (H)	SGol
- 'Benelux' (H)	CBcs
- 'Benxi'^PBR (L)	EGren
- 'Bergfink' (Teller Series) (L)	NLar
- BERLIN ('Rabe'^PBR) (City-line Series) (H)	MAsh SGol

Hydrangea

- -'Bicolor' — see *H. macrophylla* 'Harlequin'
- - Black Steel Series (H) — LRHS
- - - BLACK STEEL BLUE ('Klazu'^PBR) (H) — WCha
- - - BLACK STEEL PINK BALL (H) — WCha
- - -'Black Steel Zambia' (H) — LCro SGol WCot
- -'Black Trombone' (H) — SGol
- - BLACKBERRY PIE ('Makz') (Flair & Flavours Series) (L) — EPfP LRHS SPoG
- § -'Blanc Bleu' (L) — EPfP LSRN WFar
- § -'Blauer Prinz' (H) — NLar SHyH SRms
- § -'Bläuling' (Teller Series) (L) ♀H5 — CCVT CDoC GKin LSRN MPri SGol
- § -'Blaumeise' (Teller Series) (L) ♀H5 — CBrac CDoC CMHG CSBt EGren ELon LCro LRHS MGos MPri SGol SHyH SPoG WFar WPGP WSpi
- - BLOOMSTAR ('Piihmii'^PBR) (Endless Summer Series) (H) — CWnw EGren WCha
- -'Blue Bonnet' (H) — ELon LSRN
- - BLUE BUTTERFLY — see *H. macrophylla* 'Bläuling' (Teller Series)
- § -'Blue Heaven' (Forever & Ever Series) (H) — LCro LRHS
- - BLUE PRINCE — see *H. macrophylla* 'Blauer Prinz'
- - BLUE SKY — see *H. macrophylla* 'Blaumeise' (Teller Series)
- - BLUE TIT — see *H. macrophylla* 'Blaumeise' (Teller Series)
- -'Blue Wave' — see *H. macrophylla* 'Mariesii Perfecta'
- -'Bluebird' misapplied — see *H. serrata* 'Bluebird'
- - BLUEBIRD — see *H. macrophylla* 'Bläuling' (Teller Series)
- § -'Blushing Bride' (H) — CWnw EGren LCro WCha
- -'Bodensee' (H) — CMac EGren LRHS MPri NLar WFar WSpi
- -'Bouquet Rose' (H) — ELon LRHS MMuc NLar
- - BRIGHT WHITE ('Saxbriwhi'^PBR) (Saxon Series) (H) — MAsh
- -'Bristol Red' (H) — SGol
- -'Brügg' (H) ♀H5 — SGol
- - CAIPIRINHA ('H220910'^PBR) (H) — SGol WCha
- -'Cameroun' (H) — SGol
- -'Camilla'^PBR (H) — SGol WFar
- -'Camino' (L) — SGol
- - CARDINAL — see *H. macrophylla* 'Kardinal' (Teller Series)
- § -'Cardinal Red' (H) — ELan EPfP LRHS MPri WFar
- - CHARM ('Hbachar'^PBR) (H) — MPri
- - (Charming Series) — see *H. macrophylla* (Magical Series)
- - CHARMING CLAIRE — MAGICAL CLEOPATRA
- - - CHARMING SOPHIA — see *H. macrophylla* (Magical Series) MAGICAL FLAMENCO
- -'Chique' ('Hbachi'^PBR) (H) — ELan
- -'Choco Chic' (L) — LRHS MAsh MPri SGol
- -'Choco Pur' (Rendez-vous Series) (H) — LRHS
- -'Cocktail' (Rendez-vous Series) (H) — LRHS MPri SGol
- -'Coco Blanc' (Beautensia Series) (H/d) — SGol
- - COLOR FANTASY — see *H. macrophylla* 'Merveille Sanguine'
- -'Cordata' — see *H. arborescens*
- -'Cotton Candy Two' (L) — EPfP LRHS MMrt WCha
- - CURLY SPARKLE ('H213901'^PBR) — LRHS

- -'Dark Angel' (Black Diamonds Series) (L) — CMac EGrI ELan LCro LRHS MPri NLar SGol WCha
- - DEEP PURPLE DANCE ('Schrolla02'^PBR) (Music Series) (H) — LRHS MGos WCha
- - DESIRE ('H213'^PBR) (You & Me Series) (H) — CBcs EGrI
- -'Doctor Jean Varnier' (L) — EPfP SHyH SVen
- - DOLCE CHIC ('Hore0034'^PBR) (Rembrandt Series) (H) — SGol
- - DOLCE FARFALLE ('Dolfarf'^PBR) (H) — WCot
- - DOLCE GIPSY ('Dolgip'^PBR) (L) — NCth SGol
- - DOLCE KISS ('Dolkis'^PBR) (L) — SGol
- -'Domotoi' — see *H. macrophylla* 'Setsuka-yae'
- -'Doppio Bianco' — see *H. macrophylla* 'Wedding Gown' (Double Delights Series)
- - DOPPIO NUVOLA ('Kaho'^PBR) (H/d) — LCro SGol
- -'Doppio Rosa' (L/d) — LCro SGol
- -'Doris' (H) — SGol
- - DOUBLE PINK ('Rie 09') (Forever & Ever Series) (H/d) — SGol
- - DRAGONFLY — see *H. macrophylla* 'Libelle' (Teller Series)
- -'Draps Wonder' — see *H. macrophylla* 'Forever Pink'
- - EARLY BLUE/EARLY PINK ('Hba 202911'^PBR) (H) — CDoC EGren LCro LRHS MAsh MPri SGol SPoG WCha
- - EARLY SEDUCTION (Seduction Series) (H) — SGol
- § -'Early Sensation' (Forever & Ever Series) (H) — CMac EGren GKin LRHS WCha
- § -'Eisvogel' (L) — ELon NCth
- -'Eldorado' (H) — ELon WSpi
- -'Elégance' (Rendez-vous Series) (L) — MAsh MPri SGol
- - ELEGANT ROSA ('Hore0031'^PBR) (Rembrandt Series) (H) — SGol
- -'Elfy' ('H220910') (H) **new** — SGol
- - ENDLESS SUMMER ('Bailmer') (H) — EGren ELan LRHS SEWo WCha
- - ENDLESS SUMMER BLUSHING BRIDE — see *H. macrophylla* 'Blushing Bride'
- § -'Enziandom' (H) — CBcs CSBt LRHS SGol
- -'Étoile Violette' (L/d) ♀H5 — CDoC SGol
- -'Eugen Hahn' (H) — LRHS
- -'Europa' (H) — CBcs CBrac CDoC NLar SHyH
- - EXPRESSION ('Rie 06'^PBR) (Double Delights Series) (H/d) — SGol
- - FABOLO ('H217905') (H) — SGol
- -'Fanfare'^PBR (H) — SGol
- § -'Fasan' (Teller Series) (H) — NBro SGol WFar
- - FAY ('H218914') (L/d) — SGol
- - FEATHER ('H217904') (L/d) — SGol
- - FELINA ('H217901') (H/d) — SGol
- - FINYA ('H218915') (L/d) — SGol
- - FIRELIGHT — see *H. macrophylla* 'Leuchtfeuer'
- - FIREWORKS — see *H. macrophylla* 'Hanabi'
- - FIREWORKS BLUE — see *H. macrophylla* 'Jōgasaki'
- - FIREWORKS PINK — see *H. macrophylla* 'Jōgasaki'
- - FIREWORKS WHITE — see *H. macrophylla* 'Hanabi'
- - FLAME ('H217903') (L/d) — SGol
- - FLEURINE ('H218919') (L/d) — SGol

Hydrangea

- Florencia ('H220912') (H/d) — SGol
- Florentina ('H217902') (H/d) — SGol
- Floria ('H220911') (L/d) — SGol
- Forever ('Rie 01'^{PBR}) (You & Me Series) (H/d) — CAbb CSBt MPri
- (Forever & Ever Series) Forever & Ever — see *H. macrophylla* 'Early Sensation' (Forever & Ever Series)
- - Forever & Ever Blue — see *H. macrophylla* 'Blue Heaven' (Forever & Ever Series)
- - Forever & Ever Red (H) — LCro
- - Forever & Ever White — see *H. macrophylla* 'Rojojo' (Forever & Ever Series)
- § 'Forever Pink' (H) — LCro NLar SGol WCha
- § - 'Frau Mariko' (Lady Series) (H) — SGol
- 'French Cancan' (Rendez-vous Series) (L) — LRHS MAsh MPri SGol WCha
- 'Frillibet' (H) — CMHG NLar
- 'Froufrou' (Rendez-vous Series) (H) — LRHS MAsh MPri
- 'Ganku Bo Chokens' (L) — WCot
- 'Garden Romance' (L) — LCro
- Gemini ('Stramini'^{PBR}) (H) — SGol
- § 'Générale Vicomtesse de Vibraye' (H) ♀H5 — CBcs CCoa CDoC CEnd CMHG CSde EBee ELan ELon EPfP LRHS NBir SHyH SPoG WFar
- Gentian Dome — see *H. macrophylla* 'Enziandom'
- 'Geoffrey Chadbund' — see *H. macrophylla* 'Möwe' (Teller Series)
- § Glam Rock ('Horwack'^{PBR}) (H) — CBcs CDoC EGrI LCro MPri SGol
- 'Glowing Embers' (H) — IArd SGol
- Goldrush ('Nehyosh') (L/v) — EGren SRms WCot
- § 'Grant's Choice' (L) — NBro
- - Great Star — see *H. macrophylla* 'Blanc Bleu'
- - Green Lips ('Hba215910'^{PBR}) — SGol
- 'Grünes Gewölbe' (H) — SGol
- 'Hamburg' (H) — CBcs EHeP SDix WFar
- § 'Hanabi' (L/d) — MBlu NLar SGol WSpi
- § 'Harlequin' (H) — CMac SGol
- 'Hatsu-shime' (L) — NLar
- 'Hercule Poirot' (H) — SGol
- Hi River ('Hiriv'^{PBR}) (H) — EGren
- Hortivoli ('H211905'^{PBR}) (H) — LRHS
- Hot Red ('Agrihydradrie'^{PBR}) (H) — CDoC EPfP LCro LRHS SPoG WCha
- (Hovaria Series) 'Hobella'^{PBR} (L) — CBcs SGol WFar
- - 'Hobergine'^{PBR} (H) — LRHS SGol
- - 'Holibel'^{PBR} (H) — LRHS SGol
- - 'Homigo'^{PBR} (H) — SGol
- - 'Hopaline'^{PBR} (L) — WPGP
- - 'Hopcorn'^{PBR} (H) — SGol
- Ice Girl ('Hba215909'^{PBR}) (H) — LRHS
- 'Immaculata' (H) — CWnw LRHS
- 'Inspire'^{PBR} (H) — MPri SGol
- Intense Seduction ('YYY Mafour') (Seduction Series) (H) — SGol
- 'Izu-no-hana' (L/d) — ELan MBlu MMrt NLar SGol SHyH SPoG WSpi
- 'Izu-no-odoriko' (L) — SGol
- 'James Grant' — see *H. macrophylla* 'Grant's Choice'
- Jip ('H213910') (H) — LRHS SGol
- 'Jofloma' (H) — MMrt NLar
- § 'Jōgasaki' (L/d) — CBcs CCoa CSde MBlu NCth NLar SGol WPGP
- 'Jomari' (Fireworks Series) (L/d) — CBcs SGol
- 'Joseph Banks' (H) — CBcs
- 'Julisa' (H) — CWnw EBee EPfP ESwi LRHS
- § - Juno' (L) — SGol SHyH
- 'Kardinal' (H) — see *H. macrophylla* 'Cardinal Red'
- § - 'Kardinal' (Teller Series) (L) ♀H5 — EPfP LCro LRHS MPri SGol SPoG WCha
- 'Kardinal Lilac' — see *H. macrophylla* 'Kardinal' (Teller Series)
- 'Kardinal Violet' — see *H. macrophylla* 'Kardinal' (Teller Series)
- 'King George' (H) — CBcs CBrac CDoC CSBt EHeP ELon EPfP LSto MGos SAdn SAko SGol SHyH SNig SPoG WFar
- 'King George V' (H) — CCoa
- Kingfisher — see *H. macrophylla* 'Eisvogel'
- § 'Klaveren' (L) ♀H5 — NBro
- 'Koria'^{PBR} (L) ♀H5 — EPfP LRHS SGol SPoG
- § 'Kumico' (H) — SGol
- 'L.A. Dreamin' (H) — SGol
- 'La France' (H) — SHyH SPoG
- 'La Marne' (H) — LRHS
- 'La Vie en Rose' (Rendez-vous Series) (H) — MPri SGol
- 'Lady in Red' (L) — EPfP LRHS MPri SPoG
- 'Lady Mariko' — see *H. macrophylla* 'Frau Mariko' (Lady Series)
- 'Lady Oshie' (Teller Series) (L) — SGol
- 'Lanarth White' (L) ♀H5 — CBcs CCoa CDoC CExl CSBt ELan EPfP LCro LSto MMuc MSwo SEND SGol SHyH SRms WFar WKif WLov WPGP WSpi
- 'Lemon Wave' (L/v) — NLar SGol
- Let's Dance Rhapsody Blue ('Es14') (H) **new** — LRHS
- § 'Leuchtfeuer' (H) — ELon LRHS MPri SGol
- § - 'Libelle' (Teller Series) (L) ♀H5 — CBcs CCVT CEnd CMac CMHG ELan ELon EPfP LCro LRHS MGos MMuc NBir NLar SEND SGol SPoG WSpi
- Light-O-Day ('Bailday') (L/v) — LRHS SBig SGol
- 'Lilacina' — see *H. macrophylla* 'Mariesii Lilacina'
- 'Little Blue' (H) — LCro
- 'Little Pink' (H) — LCro
- 'Little Purple' (H) — LCro
- 'Little White' (H) — EGren LCro
- Love ('Youme H1917'^{PBR}) (H/d) — LCro SGol SPoG
- 'Love You Kiss'^{PBR} (Hovaria Series) (L) — CBcs CDoC CEnd NLar SGol SPoG WCot
- 'Lutin'^{PBR} (L) — CDoC
- § 'Maculata' (L/v) — WGwG
- 'Madame A. Riverain' (H) — EPfP NLar
- 'Madame Emile Mouillère' (H) ♀H5 — CBcs CBrac CCoa CDoC CEnd CMac CSBt EBee EGren ELan ELon EPfP GKev GKin LCro LSto MPri NLar SDix SGol SHyH SNig SPoG SReu SRms SSta WGwG WKif
- 'Madame Plumecocq' (H) — LRHS
- 'Mademoiselle' (Rendez-vous Series) (H) — LRHS MAsh MPri

	– (Magical Series)	NCth		– – Magical Spotlight	SGol
	Magical Allegretto			('Hortmaspoli') (H)	
	('Hortmalegretto'^{PBR})			– – Magical Sunshine	SGol
	(H)			('Hortmasun') (H)	
	– – Magical Amethyst	CBcs CDoC LRHS SGol WCha		– – Magical Wings	MBlu
	('Hokomathyst'^{PBR})			('Hortmawin'^{PBR})	
	(H)			(H) ♀H5	
	– – Magical Amore	SGol		– 'Maréchal Foch' (H)	NLar
	('Hortmamore'^{PBR})			– 'Mariesii' (L)	ELan LSto MSwo NLar SHyH WKif
	(H)		§	– 'Mariesii Grandiflora' (L)	CCoa CMac EPfP MMuc NBro SGol
	– – Magical Anouk	ELan			SRms WFar
	('Kolmagicono'^{PBR})		§	– 'Mariesii Lilacina' (L) ♀H5	MMuc SEND WSpi
	(H)		§	– 'Mariesii Perfecta' (L)	CBcs CBrac CCoa CDoC CMac
	– – Magical Blossom	ELan			CSBt EGren EHeP ELan ELon
	('Hortmablo'^{PBR})				EPfP GKin LCro LRHS LSRN
	(H)				MGos MMuc SGol SHyH SPlb
	– – Magical Bluebells	SGol			WFar WSpi
	('Hortmabluebel'^{PBR})			– 'Marina' (H)	LRHS
	(H)			– 'Masja' (H)	CBcs CCVT EGrl ELon GKin IArd
	– – Magical Bolero	SGol			MGos MMuc NBro NLar SGol
	('Hortmagibo') (H)			– 'Mathilde Gütges' (H)	EBee WFar
	– – Magical Bride	SGol WFar		– 'Max Löbner' (H)	WFar
	('Hortmabrid'^{PBR})			– 'Merveille' (H)	EHeP NBro
	– – Magical Candy Rock	ELan SGol	§	– 'Merveille Sanguine' (H)	CBcs CCoa CDoC CExl CMHG
	('Hortmacaro') (H)				CSpe EAri EGrl ELon EPfP EUrb
§	– – Magical Cleopatra	SGol			EWld GGGa IArd LRHS MBlu MBrN
	('Hortmaclepa') (H)				NLar SAko SGol SPoG SSta SVen
	– – Magical Colourdream	SGol			WCFE WCot WFar WKif WOld
	('Hortmacodre'^{PBR})				WPGP
	(H) ♀H5			– 'Messalina' (L)	LRHS MPri
	– – Magical Coral	CBcs SGol WCha		– 'Mini Penny'^{PBR} (H)	SGol
	('Hokomac'^{PBR}) (H)			– Minty Ice ('Es11'^{PBR})	SGol WCha
	– – Magical Crystal	SGol		(Flair & Flavours Series)	
	('Ankong'^{PBR}) (H)			(H)	
§	– – Magical Flamenco	SGol		– 'Mirai'^{PBR} (H)	CBcs ESwi WCot WPGP
	('Hortmaflam'^{PBR})			– 'Miss Belgium' (H)	CMac GKin
	(H)			– 'Mistral'^{PBR}	WCha
	– – Magical Green Cloud	ELan SGol		– 'Mousmée' (L)	SHyH
	('Hortmagreclo')			– 'Mousseline' (H)	CMHG LRHS
	(H)		§	– 'Möwe' (Teller Series)	CBcs EGrl ELon MMuc NLar SDix
	– – Magical Green Delight	LCro		(L) ♀H5	SGol SRms WLov WSpi
	('Hokomagrede'^{PBR})			– Mrs Kumico	see *H. macrophylla* 'Kumico'
	(H)			– Mrs W.J. Hepburn' (H)	CSBt
	– – Magical Greenfire	SGol	§	– 'Nachtigall' (Teller Series)	WPGP
	('Qufu') (H)			(L) ♀H5	
	– – Magical Harmony	NLar		– 'Nanping'^{PBR} (Sturdy Series)	SPoG
	('Hortmahar'^{PBR})			(L)	
	(H) ♀H5			– Niedersachsen' (H)	WFar
	– – Magical Jade	MBlu NLar WCot		– Nightingale	see *H. macrophylla* 'Nachtigall'
	('Hortmaja'^{PBR}) (H)				(Teller Series)
	– – Magical Jewel	LRHS SGol		– 'Nigra' (H)	CBcs CCoa CMac CWal ELan ELon
	('Hore140103') (H)				EPfP MMuc NBro NLar SAdn SDix
	– – Magical Noblesse	CBcs LCro SGol WCha			SEND WGwG
	('Hokomano'^{PBR})			– 'Nikko Blue' (H)	CBcs GKin SGol SHyH
	(H)			– 'Ningbo'^{PBR} (H)	MAsh
	– – Magical Ocean	NLar		– Nizza ('Ranice'^{PBR})	EGren
	('Hortmoc'^{PBR}) (H)			(City-line Series) (H)	
	– – Magical Red Amethyst	SGol	§	– 'Nymphe' (H)	LRHS
	('Hokomareda') (H)			– 'Oregon Pride' (H)	WFar
	– – Magical Revolution	CBcs CDoC LCro LRHS SGol WCha		– 'Otaksa' (H)	NLar
	('Hokomarevo'^{PBR})			– 'Pax'	see *H. macrophylla* 'Nymphe'
	(H) ♀H5			– Peppermint ('Rie 13'^{PBR})	CSBt SGol
	– – Magical Rhapsody	LSou SGol WFar		(Forever & Ever Series)	
	('Hortmarhso'^{PBR})			(H)	
	(H) ♀H5			– 'Perfection' (Double	SGol
	– – Magical Ruby Red	SGol WFar		Delights Series) (H/d)	
	('Kolmaru'^{PBR}) (H)			– 'Pfau' (Teller Series) (L)	ELon WSpi
	– – Magical Ruby Tuesday	see *H. macrophylla* 'Ruby Tuesday'		– Pheasant	see *H. macrophylla* 'Fasan' (Teller
	– – Magical Sapphire	WCha			Series)
	('Kolmasa') (H)			– 'Pia' (H)	CMac ELon ESwi LRHS NCth SRms
					WAbe WSpi

Hydrangea 373

- Pigeon — see *H. macrophylla* 'Taube' (Teller Series)
- Pink Ever Belles ('Hokomaplico') (H) — SGol
- 'Pink Lollipop' (Flair & Flavours Series) (H) — SGol WCha
- Pink Pop ('Schrolla06'^PBR) (Music Series) (H) — WCha
- 'Pink Sensation'^PBR (H) — MAsh
- 'Pink Sky' (H) — MPri
- 'Pirate's Gold' (L/v) — WFar
- 'Prinses Beatrix' (H) — SHyH
- 'Purple Prince' (H) — EGrI
- 'Quadricolor' (L/v) — CMac SPlb SRms WCot
- 'Queen Elizabeth' (H) — GKin
- 'Radiant' (H) — SRms
- Rathen ('Horath'^PBR) (Saxon Series) (H) — SGol
- 'Red Ace' (H) — MPri
- 'Red Angel' (Black Diamonds Series) (H) — EGren LBom LCro MAsh MPri SGol WCha
- 'Red Baron' — see *H. macrophylla* 'Schöne Bautznerin'
- 'Red Beauty'^PBR (H) — SGol
- 'Red Bull' (L) — EGren
- Red Reggae ('Schrolla03'^PBR) (H) — WCha
- 'Red Riding Hood' (H) — EGrI
- Redbreast — see *H. macrophylla* 'Rotkehlchen' (Teller Series)
- 'Renate Steiniger' (H) — CBrac CSBt IArd LRHS MPri SGol WSpi
- 'R.F. Felton' (H) — CBcs SHyH
- 'Richards Red' (H) — ESwi
- RoCo Black Knight ('Roco131801') (H) — SGol
§ - 'Rojojo'^PBR (Forever & Ever Series) (H) — LCro LRHS
- Romance ('Youmenine'^PBR) (You & Me Series) (H/d) — LRHS MPri SGol SPoG WCot
- 'Romantique' (H) — LRHS
- 'Rosie Blue' (H) — SGol
- 'Rosita' (H) — CBrac LRHS MPri NBir SGol WCha
- Rosso Glory ('Hore0007') (Rembrandt Series) (H) — LRHS SGol
§ - 'Rotkehlchen' (Teller Series) (L) — CEnd GArf LCro LRHS NCth NLar SGol SPlb
- 'Rotschwanz' (Teller Series) (L) ♀H5 — CDoC CMHG CTsd ELon LRHS MBlu MPri NCou NLar SHyH WCot WPGP
- 'Rouge Baiser' (H) — SGol
- Royal Red ('Hbarore'^PBR) (H) — LRHS MAsh MPri SGol
§ - 'Ruby Tuesday'^PBR (H) — LCro LRHS SGol WCha WFar
- 'Sabrina' (Dutch Ladies Series) (H) — CBcs CEnd EGrI EPfP SGol SRkn WFar
- 'Saint Claire' (H) — CBcs
- Salsa ('Sidsalimp'^PBR) (Dutch Ladies Series) (H/d) — CBrac SGol
- 'Sandra' (Dutch Ladies Series) (L) — CBcs EBee ELon EPfP LRHS SGol SNig WFar
- Saskia ('Sidsaskimp'^PBR) (Dutch Ladies Series) (H) — SGol
- 'Schadendorffs Perle' (H) — CMHG
- Schloss Wackerbarth — see *H. macrophylla* Glam Rock
- 'Schneeball' (H) — EGren ELon LCro LRHS MAsh SGol WCha
§ - 'Schöne Bautznerin' (H) ♀H5 — CDoC CEnd EGren EGrI LRHS MPri WFar WSpi
- 'Sea Foam' (L) — NLar

- 'Selina' (Dutch Ladies Series) (L) — CBcs EHeP EPfP LRHS SGol SNig WHtc
- 'Selma'^PBR (Dutch Ladies Series) (L) — CBcs SGol
§ - 'Setsuka-yae' (L/d) — SGol
- 'Shakira' (H) — MBNS SGol
- 'Sheila' (Dutch Ladies Series) (L) — CBcs EPfP LCro
- 'Sibilla' (H) — SGol SPlb WFar
- 'Sidashar' (Dutch Ladies Series) (H) — LRHS
- 'Silver Star' (H) — SGol
- Sister Therese — see *H. macrophylla* 'Soeur Thérèse'
- 'Snow' (L) — LRHS
- So Long Ebony ('Monmar') (H) — SGol
- So Long Sunny ('Tk02') (H) — CWnw LCro SGol
§ - 'Soeur Thérèse' (H) — CBcs CMHG CSBt EGren EPfP MMuc NLar SGol WGwG
- Soft Pink Salsa ('Schrolla07'^PBR) (Music Series) (H) — WCha
- Star Gazer ('Kompeito'^PBR) (Double Delights Series) (L/d) — MAsh MPri SGol
- Strawberries 'N' Cream ('Mak2'^PBR) (L) — EPfP LRHS SPoG
- subsp. *stylosa* — EBee WCru WFar WPGP
- -- MF 942115 — WPGP
* - 'Sunset' (L) — CBcs
- 'Sweet Fantasy' (Hovaria Series) (H) — ELan SGol WCha
- 'Tandem' (H) — LRHS
§ - 'Taube' (Teller Series) (L) — CBcs CMHG ELan EPfP LCro SGol
- Teller Series (L) — CDoC
- 'Teller Pink' — see *H. macrophylla* 'Taube' (Teller Series)
- 'Teller Red' — see *H. macrophylla* 'Rotkehlchen' (Teller Series)
- Teller variegated — see *H. macrophylla* 'Tricolor'
- Teller Weiss — see *H. macrophylla* 'Libelle' (Teller Series)
- Three Sisters (mixed) (H) — WCha
- Three Sisters Blue (mixed) (H)
- 'Tiffany' ('H211902'^PBR) (Flair & Flavours Series) (L) — SGol WCha
- 'Tinkerbell'^PBR (L/d) — SGol
- 'Tivoli'^PBR (H) — LCro LRHS MPri SGol WFar
- Together ('Rie 05') (Forever & Ever Series) (H/d) ♀H5 — CSBt LRHS MAsh SGol SPoG WCha WHtc
- Together ('Youmefive') (You & Me Series) (H/d) — LCro MBNS MPri
- 'Tokyo Delight' (L) ♀H5 — CMac ESwi LRHS SHyH
- 'Tovelit' (H) — SGol
§ - 'Tricolor' (L/v) — CBcs LRHS NLar SGol WFar WKif
- 'Valvert' (H) — SGol
- Vanilla Sky ('Hbavask'^PBR) (H) — SGol
- 'Variegata' — see *H. macrophylla* 'Maculata'
- 'Veitchii' (L) ♀H5 — CBcs CSBt LRHS SDix SHyH
- Vibrant Verde ('Hore0046') (Rembrandt Series) (H) — EGrI NWbg SGol
- 'Vicomte de Vibraye' — see *H. macrophylla* 'Générale Vicomtesse de Vibraye'
- 'Warabe' — see *H. serrata* 'Warabe'

§	- 'Wedding Gown'^{PBR} (Double Delights Series) (L/d) ♀H5	LRHS MAsh MPri SGol		
	- 'Weisse Königin' (H)	SHyH	- GREAT STAR	LCro LRHS LSRN MGos NLar NPer SGol SHyH SSta WFar see *H. paniculata* 'Le Vasterival'
	- 'Westfalen' (H)	CMac SHyH	- 'Greenspire'	LRHS MBlu WFar
	- 'White Caps' (H)	SGol	- 'Harry's Souvenir'	NLar
	- 'White King'^{PBR} (H)	SGol	- HERCULES ('Grhp14'^{PBR})	Midl SGol
	- 'White Mop' (H)	EGrI	§ - 'Jane'^{PBR}	Widely available
	- 'White Spirit' (L)	SGol	- 'Kyushu'	CBcs CMac EBee EHeP ELan EPfP EWhm LSRN LSto MMuc NLar SGol
	- 'White Wave'	see *H. macrophylla* 'Mariesii Grandiflora'		SHyH SRkn SVen WFar WPGP
	- 'Wudu'^{PBR} (H)	LRHS SGol	§ - 'Le Vasterival'^{PBR}	SHyH SVen WSpi
	- 'Xian'^{PBR} (Sturdy Series) (H)	SGol	- 'Levana'^{PBR}	NLar SGol SReu WFar
	- 'Yola' (H)	NBro WFar	- 'Limelight'^{PBR} ♀H5	Widely available
	- 'Zebra'^{PBR} (Black Steel Series) (H)	CBcs ELan ESwi LCro SGol WCot	- 'Little Alf'	Midl SReu
			- LITTLE FRAISE ('Rou 201306'^{PBR})	SGol
	- 'Zhuni Hito' (L)	NLar	- LITTLE LIME	see *H. paniculata* 'Jane'
	- 'Zorro'^{PBR} (L) ♀H5	CBcs CBrac CDoC CEnd CTsd CWnw EGrI ELan EPfP ESwi GGGa LBom LRHS MGos NCou SGol SHyH SPoG WCot WSpi	- LITTLE QUICK FIRE ('Smhplqf'^{PBR})	LCro LRHS SGol SReu
			- LITTLE SPOOKY ('Grhp08'^{PBR})	CSBt CWGN LCro LRHS Midl SGol WLov
			- (Living Creations Series)	SGol
	aff. mangshanensis BWJ 8120	WCru	LIVING COLOURFUL COCKTAIL ('Lc No15'^{PBR})	
	megalocarpa DJH 8114 **new**	WCru	- - LIVING COTTON CREAM ('Lc No7'^{PBR})	SGol
	MISS SAORI ('H2002'^{PBR}) (d)	CAbb CBcs CSBt CWGN EBee EGren EGrI EPfP LBom LCro LRHS MPri SPoG	- - LIVING INFINITY ('Lc No9'^{PBR})	SGol
	moellendorffii	CExl WFar WPGP	- - LIVING LITTLE BLOSSOM ('Lc No8'^{PBR})	LRHS NCth SGol
	- TH 2144	WCru	- - LIVING LITTLE PASSION ('Lc No13')	SGol
§	*obtusifolia*	CRHN EPfP SPoG WCru	- - LIVING LITTLE ROSY ('Lc No16')	SGol
	paniculata	CMCN EAri EGren LMaj		
	- B&SWJ 3556 from Taiwan	WCru WFar	- - LIVING MILK & HONEY ('Lc No17')	SGol
	- B&SWJ 5413 from Japan	WCru		
	- B&SWJ 8894 from Japan	WCru	- - LIVING PINK & ROSE ('Lc No14'^{PBR})	SGol
	- ANGEL'S BLUSH	see *H. paniculata* 'Ruby'		
	- BABY LACE ('Piihpi'^{PBR})	SGol	- - LIVING PINKY PROMISE ('Lc No12'^{PBR})	NCth SGol
	- 'Bee Happy'	EGren		
	- 'Big Ben' ♀H5	EPfP LRHS SGol	- - LIVING RASPBERRY PINK ('Lc No10'^{PBR})	SGol
	- 'Big Dick's White'	ESwi		
	- BOBO ('Ilvobo'^{PBR})	CDoC CTsd CWGN EBee EGren ERom LBom LRHS MGos SBig SGol	- - LIVING RED VELVET ('Lc No19')	SGol
	- 'Bombshell'^{PBR}	EBee EPfP LCro SGol SHyH SVen WSpi	- - LIVING ROYAL FLOWER ('Lc No6'^{PBR})	NCth SGol
	- 'Brussels Lace'	EPfP LSRN NLar SGol SHyH SSta	- - LIVING STRAWBERRY BLOSSOM ('Lc No3')	EGren SGol
	- 'Burgundy Lace'	MBlu		
	- 'Butterfly'	ESwi	- - LIVING SUGAR RUSH ('Lc No11'^{PBR})	NCth SGol
	- CANDLELIGHT ('Hpopr013'^{PBR})	EBee GBin LRHS Midl NLar SGol SReu	- - LIVING SUMMER LOVE ('Lc No2'^{PBR})	EGren SGol
	- 'Chantilly Lace'	EBee EPfP SHyH SVen	- - LIVING SUMMER SNOW ('Lc No5')	EGren SGol
	- CONFETTI ('Vlasveld 02'^{PBR})	EBee EGren LCro LRHS SGol	- - LIVING TOUCH OF PINK ('Lc No4'^{PBR})	SGol
	- DART'S LITTLE DOT ('Darlido'^{PBR})	NLar SGol WFar WPGP	- (Magical Series)	CCVT CDoC ELan LRHS Midl SGol
	- DENTELLE DE GORRON ('Rencri'^{PBR})	SGol	MAGICAL CANDLE ('Bokraflame'^{PBR})	SReu WFar
	- DIAMANT ROUGE ('Rendia'^{PBR})	CCVT CWnw ECul EGrI ELan LBom LCro LRHS MGos MPri SGol	- - MAGICAL FIRE ('Bokraplume'^{PBR})	LRHS NLar SGol WFar WSpi
	- DIAMANTINO ('Ren101'^{PBR})	EBee SGol	- - MAGICAL FLAME ('Bokratorch'^{PBR})	ELan
§	- 'Dolly'	LRHS SGol SPoG		
	- EARLY HARRY ('Hpopr018'^{PBR})	CBcs EBee LRHS NLar SReu WCot	- - MAGICAL HIMALAYA ('Kolmahima'^{PBR})	MGos NLar SGol WFar
	- 'Everest'	CCVT LRHS SPoG	- - MAGICAL MATTERHORN ('Bokomaho'^{PBR})	SGol
	- FIRE LIGHT ('Smhpfl'^{PBR})	LCro LRHS		
	- 'Floribunda'	EPfP LRHS SChF WFar	- - MAGICAL MONT BLANC ('Kolmamon'^{PBR})	EBee LCro LRHS SGol
	- FRAISE MELBA ('Renba'^{PBR})	CWGN LRHS SFol SGol		
	- FRAMBOISINE ('Rensam'^{PBR})	MPri SGol	- - MAGICAL MOONLIGHT ('Kolmagimo'^{PBR})	LRHS NCth SGol
	- GRAFFITI ('Rou201406'^{PBR})	LCro SGol		
	- 'Grandiflora'	CBcs CBrac CCVT CEnd CMac EBee EGren ELan EPfP EWhm GKin		

Hydrangea

- - Magical Starlight	see *H. paniculata* Perle d'Automne	- 'Tender Rose'	NLar
- - Magical Summer	SGol WFar	- 'The Slooten Rocket'	ESwi
('Bokrathirteen')		- 'Unique'	CBcs CCVT EBee EGrI ELan EPfP
- Magical Vesuvio	EBee LRHS MGos SGol		LCro LMaj LRHS LSRN LWaG MAsh
('Kolmavesu'PBR)			MSwo NBro NLar SGol SHyH SSta
- 'Mathilde'	SGol		SVen WFar WPGP
- 'Mega Pearl'	SGol	- Vanille Fraise ('Renhy'PBR)	Widely available
- 'Melody'	NLar	- White Caps	see *H. paniculata* 'Dolly'
- Mojito ('Grhp10'PBR)	LRHS MBros SGol	- 'White Goliath'	NLar SGol
- 'Mount Aso'	NBro SGol	- 'White Lace'	NLar
- 'October Bride'	CEnd NLar WPGP	- 'White Lady'	SGol
- Panama ('Hp221906') **new**	EGren	- 'White Moth'	LEdu LRHS NBro NLar SHyH SVen
- Pancetta	EGren	- Whitelight ('Hylv02'PBR)	LMil LRHS
('Hp221905') **new**		- 'Wim's Red'PBR	CBcs CSBt EAri EBee ECul EGren
- Pandora	EGren		EGrI ELan EPfP ESwi EUrb GAbr
('Hp217902') **new**			LCro LRHS LSto MSwo NCth NLar
- Panflora	EGren		SAth SGol SHyH SReu SSta WFar
('Hp217901') **new**			WLov WPGP WSpi
- 'Papillon'	SGol WPGP	- 'Yuan-Yang'	WCru
- Pastelgreen	ESwi LCro SGol SReu	*peruviana* var. *oerstedii*	WCru
('Renxolor'PBR)		B&SWJ 10750	
- 'Pee Wee'	EGren NLar	- - B&SWJ 10752	WCru
§ - Perle d'Automne	SGol	*peruviana* × *serratifolia*	CRHN
('Degustar')		*petiolaris* ♀H5	Widely available
- (Petite Series) Petite Cherry	SGol	- B&SWJ 6337	WCru
('Couharie') **new**		- from Yakushima, Japan	WCru
- - Petite Flori	SGol WNPC	B&SWJ 5996	
('Coussine') **new**		- - B&SWJ 6038	WCru
- - Petite Star	SGol	- - B&SWJ 6041	WCru
('Coustar02') **new**		- - B&SWJ 6056	WCru
- 'Phantom' ♀H5	Widely available	- - B&SWJ 11487	WCru
- Pink Diamond	CBcs CDoC CEnd CSBt EBee EGrI	§ - var. *cordifolia*	LSto NBro
('Interhydia') ♀H5	ELan EPfP GKin LMil LRHS MGos	§ - - 'Brookside Littleleaf'	MGos NBro WFar WTHo
	MMuc MPri NBro NLar SGol SHyH	- 'Flying Saucer'	LCro LRHS NCth NLar
	SVen WFar WLov WPGP	§ - var. *megaphylla*	WCru
- 'Pink Lady'	Midl MPro NBro	B&SWJ 4400	
- Pinkachu	LRHS	- - B&SWJ 8497	WCru
('Smhppinka'PBR)		* - var. *minor* B&SWJ 5991	WCru
- Pinky-Winky	CDoC CTsd CWGN EGren EPfP	- 'Mirranda' (v)	CBcs CMac CRHN ELan LRHS
('Dvppinky'PBR) ♀H5	ESwi GKin IArd LCro LRHS MBlu		MGos NBro NLar SGol SNig SPoG
	MGos Midl MPri NLar SBig SGol		SRms WFar
	SHyH SPoG SReu SVen WFar	§ - var. *ovalifolia*	CRHN
- 'Polar Bear'PBR	CBcs CWGN CWnw EBee ELan	- - B&SWJ 8799	WCru
	EPfP EUrb LRHS Midl NCth NLar	- - B&SWJ 8846	WCru
	SGol SReu WCha WLov WNPC	- 'Silver Lining'PBR	CBcs CMac CWGN EBee EGren
§ - Polestar ('Breg14'PBR)	CWGN CWnw LCro LRHS LSou		LCro LRHS MBlu MGos NLar SGol
	MBlu MHtn MPri NCth NLar SGol		SMad WCot WFar
	SReu	- 'Summer Snow' (v)	SPoG
- 'Praecox'	WCru	- 'Yakushima'	WCru
- Prim'White ('Dolprim')	EBee LRHS MBlu NLar SGol	'Pink Power'	WCru
- Romantic Ace ('Renvagor')	SGol	§ *platyarguta*	CBcs EBee EGrI EWld SChF WCru
- 'Rosy Morn'	LRHS		WPGP
§ - 'Ruby'	LRHS NLar SGol	- B&SWJ 6266	WCru
- 'Silver Dollar' ♀H5	CDoC EGren ELon EPfP LCro LMil	'Preziosa' ♀H4	Widely available
	LRHS LSRN MAsh MBros MGos	Princess Bride	see *H.* Cloud Nine
	Midl NLar SGol SHor SHyH SNig	*quercifolia*	Widely available
	SVen WCot WFar WHtc WSpi	- 'Alice'	CBcs CDoC CMac CMCN EBee
- Skyfall ('Frenne'PBR)	CBcs CWGN CWnw LCro LRHS		ELan EPfP ESwi LMil LRHS LSRN
	LSRN Midl MPri SArc SGol		MAsh NLar SGol WCot WLov
- 'Slootens Rio Grande'	ESwi		WPGP
- 'Sparkling'	SGol	- 'Alison'	SGol
- 'Starlight Fantasy'	see *H. paniculata* Perle d'Automne	- 'Amethyst' Dirr	NLar SGol
- Sundae Fraise	CCVT CDoC CEnd CWGN EBee	I - 'Applause'	CDoC ELan EPfP LRHS NLar SGol
('Rensun'PBR)	EGren EPfP GGGa LBom LCro		WPGP
	LRHS MAsh MGos MSwo SGol	- 'Back Porch'	NLar SGol
	SOrN	- 'Burgundy'	CBcs ESwi IArd MBlu NLar SGol
- Switch Ophelia	see *H. paniculata* Polestar		WPGP WSpi
- 'Tardiva'	CBcs CCVT EBee EHeP ELan	- 'Flore Pleno'	see *H. quercifolia* Snowflake
	ELon EUrb GKin LCro LRHS LSto	- 'Harmony'	CMac EBee ELan ELon EPfP ESwi
	NBro SDix SGol SHyH SRms		MGos SGol SVen WPGP
	WFar WLov WPGP		

Hydrangea

- ICE CRYSTAL ('Hqopr010'^{PBR}) — CAbb CDoC EAri EBee ELan EPfP ESwi LBom SGol WPGP WSpi
- JETSTREAM ('Piihq-i') — MGos MPri SGol
- 'Lady Anne' — WPGP
- LITTLE HONEY ('Brihon') — CWGN EBee LCro MAsh SGol SMad WPGP
- 'Munchkin' — CDoC CWnw LCro LRHS MBlu MGos SGol
- 'Pee Wee' — CDoC CMac CSpe EBee EGren ELan EPfP SAko SGol SPoG WPGP
- 'Queen of Hearts' — ESwi MGos
- 'Ruby Slippers' — CDoC ESwi IArd LCro LRHS MBlu MGos MPri SGol SMad WSpi
- 'Sike's Dwarf' — ELon NLar SGol
- 'Snow Giant' (d) — SGol
- SNOW QUEEN ('Flemygea') ♀H3 — CBcs CDoC CMCN CSpe EAri EGren ELan EPfP LCro LMaj LMil LRHS LSRN MAsh MGos NLar SGol SPoG SVen WFar WPGP WSpi
- 'Snowcicle' **new** — SMad
- § SNOWFLAKE ('Brido') (d) ♀H5 — CBcs CDoC CEnd CMac CWGN ELan EPfP LCro MAsh MGos NCth NLar SGol SMad SPoG WPGP WSpi
- 'Tennessee Clone' — NLar SGol
- RUNAWAY BRIDE SNOW WHITE ('Ushyd0405'^{PBR}) — CBcs CDoC CWGN CWnw EPfP LCro LRHS MSwo NLar SAth SGol SMad WCha
- *sargentiana* — see *H. aspera* subsp. *sargentiana*
- *scandens* — NBro
  - B&SWJ 5448 — WCru
  - B&SWJ 5481 — WCru
  - B&SWJ 5496 — WCru
  - B&SWJ 5523 — WCru
  - B&SWJ 5602 — WCru
  - B&SWJ 5725 — WCru
  - B&SWJ 5893 — WCru
  - B&SWJ 5929 — WCru
  - B&SWJ 6159 — WCru
  - B&SWJ 6317 — WCru
  - subsp. *chinensis* — see *H. chinensis* f. *macrosepala*
    f. *angustipetala* 'Golden Crane' — 'Golden Crane'
  - subsp. *liukiuensis* — WCru
    - B&SWJ 6022 — WCru
    - B&SWJ 11471 — WCru
  - 'Mine-no-yuki' — SGol
- § *schizomollis* HWJ 1011 — WCru
  - WWJ 11905 — WCru
- *seemannii* — Widely available
  - 'Roger Grounds' (v) — WCot
  - aff. *seemannii* — CEnd GKin LBom WSpi
- SEMIOLA ('Inovalaur'^{PBR}) — CWnw EBee EPfP ESwi LRHS NLar SGol
- *serrata* B&SWJ 6184 — WCru
  - 'Acuminata' — see *H. serrata* 'Bluebird'
  - 'Aigaku' (L) — CExl
  - 'Akabe-yama' (L) — NBro NLar
  - 'Akishino-temari' (L) — WPGP
  - Amacha Group (L) — SGol
  - - 'Amagi-amacha' (L) — NBro NLar
  - - 'Ō-amacha' (L) — WPGP
  - 'Amagyana' (L) — CExl
  - subsp. *angustata* — WCru
  - § 'Annie's Blue' (L) — SGol
  - 'Ao-yama' (L) — WPGP
  - AVELROZ ('Dolmyf'^{PBR}) (L) — SGol
  - 'Belladonna' — NBro
  - 'Belle Deckle' — see *H.* 'Blue Deckle'
  - 'Beni-gaku' (L) — CExl MBlu NBro NLar SGol WTre
  - 'Beni-temari' (L) — NBro
- 'Besshi-temari' (L) — WFar
- 'Blue Billow' (L) — NBro NLar SGol
- BLUEBERRY CHEESECAKE — see *H. serrata* TUFF STUFF
- § 'Bluebird' (L) ♀H4 — CBcs CCoa CEnd CSde EBee EGren EGrI EHeP ELan ELon EPfP GKev LCro LRHS LSRN MBlu MGos MMuc SGol SHyH SNig SPoG WFar WLov
- I 'Boothii' (L) — CMac
- 'Cap Sizun' (L) — SChF SGol SHyH WFar WPGP
- 'Chiba Cherry-lips' (L) — ESwi LSto SDix WCru
- 'Chiri-san Sue' (L/d) — WCru
- COTTON CANDY — see *H. serrata* TUFF STUFF
- 'Crûg Bicolor' (L) — WCru
- 'Crûg Caerulean' (L) — WCru
- 'Crûg Cobalt' (L) — ESwi WCru WFar
- 'Crûg Sō Cool' (L) — ESwi WCru
- 'Diadem' (L) ♀H4 — CAbb CExl CMHG NBro
- 'Forget Me Not' (L) — NBro
- 'Fuji Waterfall' — see *H. serrata* 'Fuji-no-taki'
- 'Fuji-no-taki' (L/d) ♀H4 — EBee EWld GEdr WFar WPGP
- 'Golden Showers' (L) — NBro
- 'Golden Sunlight'^{PBR} (L) — NLar SGol
- 'Gotemba Nishiki' (L/v) **new** — LCro LRHS WFar
- 'Grayswood' (L) ♀H4 — CBcs CCoa CDoC CExl CMac ELan EPfP GBin NBro SDix SGol SHyH WKif WPGP
- 'Hakucho' (L/d) — NBro WPGP
- 'Hallasan' misapplied — see *H. serrata* 'Maiko', 'Spreading Beauty'
- 'Hallasan' R. & J. de Belder (L) — WPGP
- 'Hatsu-shimo' (L/v) **new** — WFar
- 'Hime-benigaku' (L) — MBlu WFar
- 'Hoshi-kuzu' (L) — SGol
- 'Hyuga-shibori' (L) **new** — EWld
- 'Impératrice Eugénie' (L) — NLar
- 'Intermedia' (L) — CExl NBro
- 'Kiyosumi' (L) ♀H4 — CBcs CBrac CExl EBee ELon EPfP GEdr LRHS NBir NLar SBrt SVen WCru WFar WPGP
- 'Klaveren' — see *H. macrophylla* 'Klaveren'
- 'Koreana' (L) — SGol
- 'Kujyuu-no-hanafubuki' (L) **new** — EWld
- 'Kurenai' (L) — EBee EWld NBro NLar WFar WPGP
- 'Kurohime' (L) — NBro WFar WPGP
- 'Macrosepala' (L) — WPGP
- MAGIC PILLOW ('Hsopr015'^{PBR}) (L) — EBee EGren LRHS SGol
- MAGIC SEDUCTION — see *H. serrata* 'Annie's Blue'
- § 'Maiko' (L) — IArd NCth
- 'Midori' (L) — CExl
- 'Mikamba' (L) — see *H. serrata* 'Mikanba-gaku'
- § 'Mikanba-gaku' (L) — SGol
- 'Mikata-yae' (L/d) — WFar WPGP
- 'Miranda' (L) ♀H4 — CExl EPfP NBro NLar SGol WFar
- 'Miyama-yae-murasaki' (L/d) ♀H4 — CExl SGol SRms WPGP
- 'Momo-beni-yama' (L) — NBro
- 'Mont Aso' (L) — IArd NLar
- 'Niji' (L) — WPGP
- 'Odoriko-amacha' (L) — WFar WPGP
- 'Otsu-hime' (L) — NLar
- 'Pretty Maiden' — see *H. serrata* 'Shichidanka'
- 'Professeur Iida' (L) — SHyH
- 'Ramis Pictis' (L) — NBro NCth NLar SHyH
- 'Rosalba' (L) ♀H4 — CExl NBro WFar
- 'Santiago'^{PBR} (L) — SGol WPGP
- 'Sekka' (L) — CExl MBlu WPGP

Hylotelephium

§	- 'Shichidanka' (L/d)	EWld LRHS WFar
	- 'Shichidanka-nishiki' (L/d/v)	CExl
	- 'Shikoubai' (L)	GEdr
	- 'Shinonome' (L/d)	CExl
	- 'Shirahuzi' (L/d)	SGol
	- 'Shirofuji' (L/d) ♀H4	EWld
	- 'Shiro-gaku' (L)	NBro NLar
	- 'Shiro-maiko' (L)	WPGP
	- 'Shirotae' (L/d)	CExl SGol
	- 'Shōjō' (L) ♀H4	MBlu NBro SGol WFar WPGP WTre
*	- subsp. *sinensis*	GKev
§	- 'Spreading Beauty' (L)	WFar WPGP
	- SUMMER GLOW ('Hsopr016'PBR) (L)	LRHS NLar
	- 'Suzukayama-yama' (L)	WPGP
*	- var. *thunbergii* 'Plena' (L/d)	WCru
	- 'Tiara' (L) ♀H4	CAbb CBcs CExl EPfP EWld GGGa LRHS LSRN NBir NBro NCth NLar SGol SHyH SPoG SVen WAbe WFar WPGP WTre
	- TUFF STUFF ('Mak 20'PBR) (L)	CBcs EPfP LRHS SGol SPoG WCha WFar
	- VEERLE ('Opri301') (L)	CAbb CBcs Midl NBro NLar SGol
§	- 'Warabe' (L)	SGol
	- WHITE ON WHITE ('Hsopr014') (L/d)	GBin SGol
	- 'Yae-no-amacha' (L/d)	CBcs CExl NBro NLar
	- subsp. *yezoensis*	EWld NLar SGol WFar
§	*serratifolia*	CExl IArd WPGP
	- HCM 98056	WCru
	sikokiana B&SWJ 5035	WCru
	- B&SWJ 5855	WCru
	- B&SWJ 11381	WCru
	- B&SWJ 11174	WCru
	'Silver Slipper'	see *H. macrophylla* 'Ayesha'
	SO LONG ROSY ('Coumont'PBR) (H)	SGol
	steyermarkii B&SWJ 10501	WCru
	tiliifolia	see *H. petiolaris* var. *ovalifolia*
	tomentella KWJ 12344 **new**	WCru
	× *versicolor*	CAbb CDoC EPfP EWld SBrt SPoG WCru WFar
	viburnoides	CBcs CBct CDoC CMac CRHN CWnw EBee EGren ELan ELon EPfP EUrb LCro LRHS MGos NLar SArc SEND SPoG SSta SWCr WCot WFar WPGP WSpi
	- B&SWJ 3565	WCru
	- B&SWJ 3570 from Taiwan	WCru
	- B&SWJ 7132	SNig WCru
	villosa	see *H. aspera* Villosa Group
§	*wallichii* B&SWJ 2367	WCru
	- NJM 13.104	WPGP
	xanthoneura	see *H. heteromalla*
	× *ytiensis* B&SWJ 11790	WCru
	aff. *zhewanensis* MF 93117	WCru

Hydrastis (Ranunculaceae)

canadensis	EMor LEdu LShi

Hydrocharis (Hydrocharitaceae)

morsus-ranae	CBen CHab CLil CPud ELin EWat MWts NPer

Hydrocotyle (Araliaceae)

asiatica	see *Centella asiatica*
leucocephala	ELin
novae-zeelandiae	CWat ELin
ranunculoides	Prohibited invasive. See Conservation and the Environment, p.42
sibthorpioides	ELin
- 'Crystal Confetti' (v)	CWat ELin
vulgaris	CWat ELin EWat

Hydrophyllum (Boraginaceae)

canadense	EMor SBrt
virginianum	EWld LEdu WPGP

Hygrophila (Acanthaceae)

difformis	ELin
polysperma	ELin
ringens var. *ringens*	ELin

Hylocereus (Cactaceae)

undatus (F)	LWaG WJur

Hylomecon (Papaveraceae)

	hylomeconoides	EAri EWld LShi WCru
§	*japonica*	CMiW EBee ELan EMor GArf GEdr GGro GKev LEdu LRHS LShi NBir NQui NRya StAn WCot WPGP

Hylotelephium (Crassulaceae)

§	'Abbey Dore'	EBee ELan LRHS NBir NLar WCAu
	AMBER ('Florseamb')	WCot
§	*anacampseros*	GQue MMuc NDov NRya
	'Aquarel'	ESuc GBin
	'Autumn Charm'	see *H.* × *mottramianum* 'Lajos'
	'Beach Party' (Party Hardy Series)	ESuc
§	'Bertram Anderson' ♀H7	CAby CDor CMHG EBee ECha EGren ELan EPfP GKev GMaP GQue LRHS LSRN MArl MNrw NBir NLar SHor SMHy SMrm SPlb SRms WCAu WHoo WKif
	'Birthday Party' (Birthday Party Series)	Midl NLar SPoG
	'Blade Runner'	LRHS
	'Bloody Mary' **new**	ESuc
	'Blue Elf'PBR (SunSparkler Series)	ESuc LRHS WSpi
	'Blue Pearl'PBR (SunSparkler Series)	EBee ESuc LBar LCro MPnt SPoG
§	'Carl' ♀H7	CDor CMHG EAri ECha EGren ELan EPfP GElm GMaP GQue LRHS LSRN MArl MAsh MHer NBir NBro NLar NSti SMrm SRms WCAu WCot WFar WHoo
§	*cauticola* ♀H5	EPot MAsh SRms WAbe WIce
	- 'Coca-Cola'	CBWd CMac CPic CWGN CWnw EGren EPPr ESuc GBin GJos GKev LRHS MArl MAsh MSwo NBir NCth NDov SLee SOrN SPoG SRot WCav WFar WHoo WTor
	- 'Lidakense' ♀H5	CAby CoPl CPic CSpe ECha EGrI EPot ESuc LRHS MAsh MHer NLar SHar SPlb SPoG SRot
	- 'Robustum'	see *H.* 'Ruby Glow'
	- 'Rocky' **new**	ESuc
	'Cherry Tart'PBR (SunSparkler Series)	ESuc EUrb LBar LSou MPnt SRot
	'Chocolate Cherry'	ESuc LRHS MBNS MPri MPro WSpi
	'Chocolate Drop'	CWGN LBar MPro NLar SRms
	'Class Act'PBR	EGren LBar LRHS MPri NLar SPoG SRms
	'Cloud Walker'PBR	LBar SPoG WFar
	'Coraljade' (Rock 'n Grow Series) **new**	ESuc
	'Crazy Ruffles'	WCot

Hylotelephium

	cyaneum 'Sakhalin'	LRHS MHer
	'Dark Canyon' **new**	MPri
	'Dark Jack'	ESuc GQue NGdn SMrm WCot
	'Dazzleberry'^{PBR}	EPfP ESuc LBar LCro LRHS LSou
	(SunSparkler Series)	MPnt NEoE
	'Diamond Edge' (v)	ESuc
	'Dream Dazzler'	ESuc LBar SLee
	(SunSparkler Series) (v)	
§	*erythrostictum*	WCru
	B&SWJ 11384	
	- 'Frosty Morn' (v)	CBcs CDor CMac CTtf ESuc GMaP LBar LRHS MArl MGos NBir NGdn SMrm SPoG SRms WCAu WCot WFar
§	- 'Mediovariegatum' (v)	CDor ELan ESuc LRHS WFar
§	*ewersii*	ESuc MAsh NBro SLee SPhx SPlb SRot
	- CC 5288	GKev
	- var. *homophyllum*	ESuc
	- - 'Rosenteppich'	CDoC EPfP EPPr ESuc LBom LCro LRHS MAsh MPri NBir SPoG SRms
	'Firecracker'^{PBR}	EGren ESuc LBar LRHS MBNS MHer MHol MPnt MPri SLee WSpi
	(SunSparkler Series)	
	'Frosted Fire'	GJos LRHS MAsh MPri SRms WFar
	Herbstfreude Group	see *H.* × *mottramianum*
	'Ice Ruffles' (v)	SPoG WFar
	'Jade Tuffet'^{PBR}	ESuc LRHS NEoE
	(SunSparkler Series)	
	'José Aubergine'^{PBR}	CBWd CTtf EBee ECha EGren ESuc LCro LSto MAsh MBel NClf NLar SPoG SRms WCAu WSpi WTre XFar
	'Joyce Henderson'	CDor CElw ELan EPfP LRHS SRGP SRms WBrk WCot
	'Lime Twister'^{PBR}	ESuc LBar LCro LRHS LSou
	(SunSparkler Series) (v)	
	'Lime Zinger'^{PBR}	EGren EPfP ESuc GJos LBar LCro LRHS MBNS Midl MPri WSpi
	(SunSparkler Series)	
§	'Lizzy'	ESuc
	MAGICAL LIZZY	see *H.* 'Lizzy'
I	'Marchants Best Red' ♀H7	ESuc MNrw NCth SMHy WCot WMal
§	'Matrona' ♀H7	Widely available
	(Mojave Jewels Series)	ESuc LBar NEoE
	'Mojave Jewels Diamond'	
	- 'Mojave Jewels Ruby'	ESuc LBar LBom LRHS
	- 'Mojave Jewels Sapphire'	ESuc IPot LBar LBom LRHS
§	× *mottramianum*	GQue LRHS WTre
	- 'Autumn Fire'	EBee MAsh
	- 'Elsie's Gold' (v)	CTtf EBee ESuc MNrw NLar SRms
§	- 'Herbstfreude' ♀H7	Widely available
	- 'Jaws'	CKno NLar WCot WFar
	- 'Lajos' (v)	ESuc MAsh MHer MPro NEoE WCot WFar XFar
	'Mr Goodbud'^{PBR} ♀H7	LRHS MAsh MAvo MHer MNrw MPri NBir NLar SMHy SPoG SRms WCAu WCot WSpi
	'Munstead Purple'	EBee ESuc
§	'Munstead Red'	CDor EBee ECha EGren EGrI EPfP ESuc LRHS MArl MNrw MPri NDov NLar SPoG SRms WCAu WFar
	'Night Embers'	LBar
§	'Oriental Dancer'	LBar LRHS
	PLUM DAZZLED	ESuc LBar LRHS SLee
	('Pldaz2018'^{PBR})	
	(SunSparkler Series)	
§	*pluricaule*	CDor EPot ESuc LRHS NBro SLee SPlb SRms WCav
	'Pool Party' (Party Hardy Series)	NLar SRms
§	*populifolium*	ECha ESuc GQue MHer NLar WMal
	'Red Cauli' ♀H7	CBcs CBWd ECha EGrI ELan ESuc GQue LRHS LSRN MBel MHol MNrw MPnt NBir NCth NLar SMad SPhx SPoG SRkn WCAu WCot WFar WHil WHoo WKif
	'Red Setter'	WMal
	'Red Sparkle'	EPfP ESuc LRHS
	'Ruby Glow' ♀H5	CDor EBee EGrI ELan EPfP ESuc GMaP LCro LRHS LSto MArl MHer NDov NGdn NLar SMrm WSpi
§	*sieboldii*	ESuc LWaG SRms
	- 'Dragon'	LRHS MPri
	- 'Mediovariegatum'	see *H. sieboldii* 'Misebaya-nakafu'
	- 'Misebaya-nakafu' (v) ♀H3	EGren ESuc MHer SPlb
§	*spectabile* ♀H7	ELan GJos LRHS LWaG NBac NGdn SPlb SRms WBrk WFar
	- BLACK BEAUTY ('Florseblab')	ESuc SHar WSpi
	- Brilliant Group	EGrI EHeP LCro LRHS SRms WCAu
	- - 'Abendrot'	ECha ESuc
	- - 'Brilliant' ♀H7	CBcs ECha EGren ELan EPfP LBar LBom LCro MGos MHol NGdn NLar SAth SPoG WFar WSpi
	- - 'Carmen'	NBir
	- - 'Hot Stuff'	EGren ELan GJos LRHS MBNS Midl NCou SPoG SRms WCot
	- - 'Lisa'	ECha NLar
	- - 'Meteor'	NLar
	- - 'Neon'	MAsh
	- - 'Rosenteller'	WBrk
	- - 'Septemberglut'	LRHS WSpi
	- 'Crystal Pink'^{PBR}	LRHS MPri NLar
	- 'Iceberg'	CMHG CTtf EBee ECha EGren EGrI GBin LRHS LShi LSto MAsh MPri NCth NGdn NLar WCAu WFar WSpi
	- 'Pink Chablis' (v)	ESuc WCot
	- SEPTEMBER GLOW	see *H. spectabile* (Brilliant Group) 'Septemberglut'
	- 'Stardust'	CDor CTsd EBee EGren EPfP GKev GMaP LBom LCro MBNS NCth SRms WFar
	- 'Variegatum'	see *H. erythrostictum* 'Mediovariegatum'
	- WALBERTON'S PIZAZZ	EPfP SPoG
	'Steel the Show'	ESuc LBar LSou
§	'Stewed Rhubarb Mountain'	EBee ECha EPfP ESuc LRHS MBNS NLar SMrm WCAu
	'Sunset Cloud'	ESuc
	'Superstar' (Rock 'N Round Series)	LBar LRHS MPro
§	*tatarinowii*	ESuc WCot
	- 'Pure Joy' (Rock 'n Grow Series)	WSpi
*	- 'Summer Ice'	ESuc
§	*telephium*	CWRo NBir SIvy SRms
	- Atropurpureum Group	LRHS NLar
	- - 'African Pearl'	EGrI LRHS
	- - 'Bon Bon'	SPoG
	- - 'Bressingham Purple'	EBee LRHS
	- - 'Chocolate'	GPSL NLar
	- - 'Dark Knight'	GPSL
	- - 'El Cid'	EWes
	- - 'Karfunkelstein' ♀H7	CDor ECha ESuc GQue LCro LRHS NBir NDov NLar SHar SMHy SPhx WCot
	- - 'Lynda Windsor'	GQue NLar
	- - 'Möhrchen'	EGrI LRHS NGdn
	- - 'Picolette'	ESuc LRHS NGdn SHar SPoG SRms WCot
	- - 'Postman's Pride'^{PBR}	CWGN ESuc NGdn
§	- - 'Purple Emperor' ♀H7	Widely available
	- - 'Ringmore Ruby'	ESuc LRHS MNrw WCot

Hypericum 379

- - 'Xenox'^{PBR} ⚥H7	CWGN EBee ESuc LRHS MAsh MAvo MHol MNrw NLar SHar SPoG SRms WCAu WCot WKif XFar
- Black Knight ('Dolseb') **new**	WTor
- 'Cherry Truffle'^{PBR}	EGren NLar
- 'Conga Line'	LBar
- 'Coral Reef'^{PBR}	CoPl EGren ESuc LBar
- 'Dark Magic'^{PBR}	CAby EGren EPfP ESuc EUrb GJos LRHS MAvo MBNS MPri MPro NLar
- Desert Black'^{PBR}	ESuc LSRN MBNS Midl MPro NLar
- Double Martini ('Tnseddm'^{PBR})	EBee WCAu
- Emperor's Waves Group	ELan NGdn
§ - subsp. *fabaria*	ESuc NClf SMrm WCot
- - var. *borderei*	ECha
- Globe Pink ('Olek 6')	LBar
- Globe Purple	LBar
- Globe Yellow	LBar
- 'Jennifer'	EBee ESuc GQue WCot
- 'Marina'^{PBR}	EBee LBar LRHS Midl NLar
- subsp. *maximum*	GJos
- - 'Atropurpureum'	see *H. telephium* Atropurpureum Group
- - 'Gooseberry Fool'	ELan EPfP ESuc GMaP LRHS NEoE SRms WCAu
- 'Moonlight Serenade'^{PBR}	ESuc SRms
- 'Orange Xenox'^{PBR}	EBee NLar XFar
- Peach Pearls ('Tnsedpp')	LBar
- 'Rainbow Xenox'^{PBR}	ESuc NLar
- 'Raspberry Truffle'	LRHS
§ - subsp. *ruprechtii*	CDor ECha EGrI GMaP LRHS SMHy
- - 'Citrus Twist'	LRHS
- - 'Hab Gray'	SMrm SRms
- - 'Pink Dome'	ECha
- Seduction Hot Rose Dark Stems (Seduction Series)	LBar
- 'Strawberries and Cream'	CMac EBee ECha ELan ESuc GMaP LCro LRHS MAsh MBNS MMuc NGdn NLar SMrm
- 'Sunkissed'^{PBR}	NLar SHar WHil XFar
- 'Surrender Red'	LRHS
- subsp. *telephium*	ESuc LRHS
- 'Touchdown Teak'^{PBR} (Touchdown Series)	CFis CTtf EBee ECha ESuc GJos LBar LBom LCro LRHS MAsh WKif WTor
- Yellow Matrona ('Eline'^{PBR})	LCro LRHS MAsh WCAu
- 'Yellow Xenox'^{PBR}	ESuc LRHS NLar WCot XFar
'Thundercloud'^{PBR}	ESuc GJos LBar LBom LRHS MPro SRms
'Thunderhead'^{PBR}	EGren EGrI LBar LRHS NLar WCAu
§ *ussuriense*	EPPr GBin GPSL NBir
- 'Chuwangsan'	WCru
- 'Turkish Delight'	EPfP ESuc
§ 'Vera Jameson' ⚥H5	CAby CMHG ECha EGren ELan EPfP LRHS MMuc MPro NBir SRms WHoo WKif WSpi
§ *verticillatum*	LShi
§ *viviparum* B&SWJ 8662	WCru
Walberton's Pink Whisper	EPfP LRHS SPoG
'Washfield Purple'	see *H. telephium* (Atropurpureum Group) 'Purple Emperor'
'Wildfire'^{PBR} (SunSparkler Series)	EPfP ESuc LBar LCro LRHS MHer Midl MPri SLee SRot

Hymenanthera see *Melicytus*

Hymenocallis (Amaryllidaceae)

× *festalis*	see *Ismene* × *deflexa*
harrisiana	EPfP GKev LAma
longipetala	see *Ismene longipetala*
'Sulphur Queen'	see *Ismene* 'Sulphur Queen'

Hymenolepis (Asteraceae)

parviflora	see *Athanasia parviflora*

Hymenosporum (Pittosporaceae)

flavum	EUrb

Hymenoxys (Asteraceae)

grandiflora	see *Tetraneuris grandiflora*
§ *hoopesii*	CMac CWal EHeP EPfP GMaP LRHS LShi MCtn NBir NLar SRms StAn WFar

Hyophorbe (Arecaceae)

indica	NPlm
lagenicaulis	NPlm
verschaffeltii	NPlm

Hyoscyamus (Solanaceae)

niger	MNHC

Hypericum ✿ (Hypericaceae)

aegypticum	EPot MHer SBrt SPlb WAbe
androsaemum	GJem MMuc NPer WFar
§ - 'Albury Purple'	ESwi
- 'Autumn Blaze'	CBcs
§ - f. *variegatum* 'Mrs Gladis Brabazon' (v)	CMac NBir WCot WFar
aviculariifolium var. *uniflorum*	EDAr
balearicum	MMuc WAbe WIce
§ *beanii*	EPPr
bellum	SBrt
- pale form	EPPr
calycinum	CBrac CMac CWal EGren EHeP ELan EPfP LBuc MCtn MGos NLar SEND SRms WFar
- 'Brigadoon'	SGol
- Carnival	see *H. calycinum* Fiesta
§ - Fiesta ('Crowthyp'^{PBR}) (v)	LRHS
cerastioides	EDAr EWes GJos NGdn SRms WCot
coris	SRms WAbe
× *cyathiflorum* 'Gold Cup'	CMac LRHS
'Daybreak'	MAsh NEoE SPoG
× *dummeri* 'Peter Dummer' ⚥H5	ELan NLar WSpi
'Eastleigh Gold'	CMac
elodes	CWat LCro
empetrifolium	WAbe
'Fancy Pants'	CBcs LEdu WPGP
forrestii ⚥H5	MMuc SEND
fragile misapplied	see *H. olympicum* f. *minus*
grandiflorum	see *H. kouytchense*
henryi L 753	SRms
- subsp. *hancockii* 'September Sun' ⚥H5	WPGP
× *hidcoteense* 'Hidcote' ⚥H5	Widely available
- 'Hidcote Variegated' (v)	SRms
hirsutum	CGwi CHab
× *inodorum* 'Albury Purple'	see *H. androsaemum* 'Albury Purple'
- 'Dream'	NLar
- 'Elstead'	EPfP WSpi
- Golden Beacon ('Willhyp'^{PBR}) ⚥H5	CSpe MMuc NBir SEND WCot
- (Magical Series) Magical Beauty ('Kolmbeau'^{PBR})	CSBt LCro MHtn NBid NEoE SPoG

Hypericum

- - MAGICAL CHERRY ('Kolmcherrip'PBR) ELan
- - MAGICAL INNOCENCE ('Kolmaginno'PBR) CSBt LCro NEoE WCot
- - MAGICAL LIGHTNING ('Kolmligh'PBR) GBin NEoE
- - MAGICAL PUMPKIN ('Kolmapuki'PBR) LEdu NEoE
- - MAGICAL RED ('Kolmred') NEoE NLar SPoG
- - MAGICAL RED FAME ('Kolmaref') GBin LRHS MPri
- - MAGICAL UNIVERSE ('Kolmuni'PBR) LCro MHtn NEoE NLar
- - MAGICAL WHITE ('Kolmawhi') ELan LCro NEoE SPoG
- - 'Rheingold' NLar
- *kalmianum* SBrt
- - 'Gemo' NLar
- - SUNNY BOULEVARD ('Deppe'PBR) CDoC
§ *kouytchense* ♀H5 CMac ELan EPfP EWes LRHS MAsh MMuc SEND SPoG WKif WSpi
lancasteri ♀H5 CBcs EBee ELan EPfP ESwi LRHS SPoG
leschenaultii misapplied see *H.* 'Rowallane'
maclarenii EWes
Miracle Series EGren
- MIRACLE ATTRACTION ('Alldiablo'PBR) CDoC MGos SRms
- MIRACLE BLIZZ ('Allblizz') LSou MGos NLar
- MIRACLE BLOSSOM ('Allblossom'PBR) CMac CSBt
- MIRACLE GRANDEUR ('Allgrandeur'PBR) CMac
- MIRACLE MARVEL ('Allmarvel'PBR) CDoC MGos
- MIRACLE NIGHT ('Allmadne'PBR) CMac LSou
- MIRACLE PISTACHE ('Allpista'PBR) LSou
- MIRACLE SUMMER ('Hymirsum') NEoE NLar
- MIRACLE WONDER ('Hymirwon') NLar
× *moserianum* ♀H5 CMac LCro LRHS MPri NPer SRms WFar
- LITTLE MISSTERY ('Dunnehyp'PBR) (v) CDoC LBar LRHS MBNS NEoE SPoG WLov
- 'Tricolor' (v) CBcs CBrac CMac CSBt EHeP ELan ELon EPfP LCro LRHS MAsh MGos MSwo SPlb SPoG WFar
- 'Variegatum' see *H.* × *moserianum* 'Tricolor'
'Mrs Brabazon' see *H. androsaemum* f. *variegatum* 'Mrs Gladis Brabazon'
olympicum ♀H4 ECha ELan EPot GJos LWaG SEND SRms StAn WIce
- 'Grandiflorum' see *H. olympicum* f. *uniflorum*
§ f. *minus* EPfP NGdn SPlb SRms
§ - - 'Sulphureum' ELon EWes GMaP NBir SRms
- - 'Variegatum' (v) NBir WIce
§ - f. *uniflorum* EPfP GJos MMuc NBro WIce
- - 'Citrinum' ♀H4 CBcs CSpe ECha GKev LBar LRHS LSto MHol MMrt MMuc SEND WAbe WCot WHoo
orientale EWes
patulum var. *henryi* see *H. beanii*
Veitch ex Bean
perfoliatum CAgr WOrg
perforatum CBWd CCBP CGHo CGwi CHab CHby CoPl EGren EHet ENfk EPfP GJem GJos IDun LShi MAsh MCtn MHer MHoo MNHC NMir SEND SRms WHer WJur
polyphyllum misapplied see *H. olympicum* f. *minus*
- 'Citrinum' see *H. olympicum* f. *minus* 'Sulphureum'
- 'Grandiflorum' see *H. olympicum* f. *uniflorum*
prolificum GAbr
quadrangulum L. see *H. tetrapterum*
RADIANCE ('Methyra') (v) **new** CSBt EBee
reptans misapplied see *H. olympicum* f. *minus*
reptans Hook. f. & Thomson EWes
ex Dyer
revolutum PAB 3861 LEdu
§ 'Rowallane' ♀H4 CBcs SDix SPoG
'Sungold' see *H. kouytchense*
'Sweet Lion' CMac
tenuicaule WPGP
§ *tetrapterum* CBWd CGwi CPud CWat
trichocaulon EWes
uralum NLar
- HWJ 520 ESwi WCru

Hypocalyptus (Fabaceae)
sophoroides SPlb

Hypochaeris (Asteraceae)
radicata CGwi CHab GJem NMir WOrg

Hypocyrta see *Nematanthus*

Hypoestes (Acanthaceae)
aristata EShb SVen
- var. *alba* LBom
phyllostachya (v) ♀H1b MCtn

Hypolepis (Dennstaedtiaceae)
ambigua SPlb
dicksonioides CExl LEdu SBig WPGP
glandulifera LEdu
millefolium LEdu LRHS SPlb WCot WPGP
punctata WPGP

Hypoxis (Hypoxidaceae)
longifolia MAsh
§ *parvula* var. *albiflora* CElw EWes GEdr WFar
'Hebron Farm Biscuit'

Hypoxis × *Rhodohypoxis* see × *Rhodoxis*
H. parvula × *R. baurii* see × *Rhodoxis hybrida*

Hypsela (Campanulaceae)
longiflora see *H. reniformis*
§ *reniformis* EDAr EPot GKev MAsh SLee

Hyssopus ✿ (Lamiaceae)
officinalis CCBP CGHo CHby ECha EHet ELan ENfk EPfP GJem GJos GMaP GQue LCro MCtn MHer MHoo MNHC MPri NBir SEdi SPhx SPlb SPoG SRms StAn SVic WCav WKif WKit
- f. *albus* ECha EHet ELan ENfk EPfP EPPr IDun MHer MHoo MNHC SEdi SPhx SRms SVic WFar
- subsp. *aristatus* CTsd ECha ELon ENfk LCro MHer MHoo MNHC SPoG StAn
- 'Caeruleus' EPPr IDun
- 'Roseus' CGHo ECha EHet ELan ENfk EPPr IDun MEar MHer MHoo MNHC SPhx SPoG SVic WKit

Hystrix (Poaceae)
patula EPPr GPSL MNrw SEND SPlb

I

Iberis (Brassicaceae)
ABSOLUTELY AMETHYST ('Ib2401')	EGren GJos GKev LBar LRHS MPro SPoG WFar WIce
commutata	see *I. sempervirens*
DWARF FAIRY MIX (Fairy Series)	LCro MCtn
gibraltarica	GJos MCtn SBeP SRms
- 'Betty Swainson' ♀H4	CElw CSpe SMrm
jordanii	see *I. violacea*
'Masterpiece'PBR	CDoC ELan EPfP LBar LCro LRHS NPer SPoG WFar
MERMAID LAVENDER ('Ibsz0007')	EPfP LRHS WNPC
'Pink Ice'	EGren ELan EPfP GJos LBom LRHS LSRN MPri MPro SPoG WFar WIce WNPC WTor
pruitii	see *I. violacea*
saxatilis	SRms
§ *sempervirens*	EHeP ELan EPfP MAsh MMuc NAts NBro SEND SHar SRms
- 'Appen-Etz'	EPfP GMaP LCro LRHS SRms WFar WTor
- 'Fischbeck'	EPfP LRHS MPro SRms WTor
- 'Golden Candy'	LRHS MHer SPoG SRms WFar WIce
- 'Little Gem'	see *I. sempervirens* 'Weisser Zwerg'
- 'Nevina'	LRHS
- SCHNEEFLOCKE	see *I. sempervirens* 'Snowflake'
- SNOW CONE ('Ibcom'PBR)	SPoG
§ - 'Snowflake' ♀H5	EPot GMaP LCro MHer SMrm SPoG SRms StAn WHoo WIce
- SNOWSURFER FORTE ('Ibsz0002'PBR)	LRHS MPri
- 'Tahoe'	EPfP
§ - 'Weisser Zwerg'	ECha ELan MHer SRms
- 'Whiteout'	EGren LRHS MHol MPro SPoG WFar
- 'Zwergschneeflocke' **new**	LShi
simplex	WAbe
'Snowball'	SRms
spathulata	GJos WIce
§ *violacea*	SPlb

Ichthyoselmis (Papaveraceae)
§ *macrantha* EBee ECha EPfP GKev LEdu NLar WCru

Idesia (Salicaceae)
polycarpa	CBcs EBee EGrI EPfP ESwi SChF WJur WKor WPGP
- CWJ 12837	WCru

Ilex ✿ (Aquifoliaceae)
× *altaclerensis* 'Balearica' (f)	CJun
§ - 'Belgica Aurea' (f/v) ♀H6	CJun EPfP WHtc
- 'Camelliifolia' (f) ♀H6	CJun ELan IDun MBlu SGol WSpi
- 'Camelliifolia Variegata' (f/v)	CMac
- 'Golden King' (f/v) ♀H6	Widely available
- 'Hodginsii' (m)	CBcs CJun LRHS
- 'Howick' (f/v)	CJun
- 'Lady Valerie' (f/v)	IArd
- 'Lawsoniana' (f/v) ♀H6	CBrac CCVT CJun CMac CSBt EBee EGren ELan EPfP LSto MAsh MBlu MMuc SEND SGol SPoG SRms WFar WHtc
- 'Purple Shaft' (f)	CJun CMCN
- 'Ripley Gold' (f/v)	CJun CMac EPfP LRHS MAsh NLar WHtc
- 'Silver Sentinel' (f/v)	see *I.* × *altaclerensis* 'Belgica Aurea'
- 'Wilsonii' (f)	CBcs
- 'W.J. Bean' (f)	CJun
aquifolium ♀H6	Widely available
- 'Alaska' (f)	CBrac CBTr CCVT CLnd CSBt CWnw EGren EHeP ELan EPfP IPap LBuc LCro LRHS LSto MAsh MHed NHed NLar NPip NTrD SEWo SFol WFar WMat WMou
- 'Amber' (f) ♀H6	CJun
- 'Ammerland' (f)	CJun
- 'Angustifolia' (f)	CJun
- - (m or f)	EPfP SPoG
§ - 'Argentea Marginata' (f/v) ♀H6	Widely available
§ - 'Argentea Marginata Pendula' (f/v)	EPfP MAsh SRms WFar
- 'Argentea Pendula' (f/v)	see *I. aquifolium* 'Argentea Marginata Pendula'
- 'Argentea Variegata' (f/v)	see *I. aquifolium* 'Argentea Marginata'
- 'Atlas' (m)	LBuc
- 'Aurea Marginata' (f/v)	CMac EHeP EPfP MGos NPip SEWo WFar WMat
- 'Aureomaculata'	NLar
- 'Aurifodina' (f)	CJun WHtc
- 'Bacciflava' (f)	CBcs CJun CMac ELan ELon EPfP IArd LRHS MBlu MPri NLar SRms
- 'Bowland' (f/v)	LRHS NLar
- 'Calypso' (f/v)	CJun
- 'Chris Whittle'	LRHS NLar
- 'Crassifolia' (f)	EBee
- 'Elegantissima' (m/v)	CBrac CJun
- 'Fastigiata Sartori'	NLar
- 'Ferox' (m)	CJun ELan
- 'Ferox Argentea' (m/v) ♀H6	CBcs CBrac CCVT CDoC CEnd CJun CMac CMCN CSBt EHeP ELan ELon EPfP LBuc LRHS MAsh MBlu MGos MPri MPro NLar SRms WFar WHtc
- 'Ferox Aurea' (m/v)	CDoC CJun LRHS MAsh MPri
§ - 'Flavescens' (f)	MBlu
- 'Frogmore Silver' (m/v)	CJun
- 'Glanzzwerg'	SAko
- 'Gold Flash' (f/v)	CJun
- 'Golden Milkboy' (m/v)	CJun CMac EPfP
- 'Golden Queen' (m/v) ♀H6	SRms
- 'Golden Tears' (f/v)	CJun
- 'Golden van Tol' (f/v)	CJun CSBt CWnw EBee ELan ELon LRHS MAsh MBlu MGos NLar SGol SRms WFar
- 'Handsworth New Silver' (f/v) ♀H6	CBrac CCVT CDoC CJun CMac CSBt EBee ELan EPfP LCro LRHS MAsh MMuc MPri NLar NPip NTrD SEND SPoG SRms WCot WFar WHtc WMat
- HECKENZWERG ('Hachzwerg'PBR)	SAko
- 'Ingramii' (m/v)	LRHS NLar WFar
- 'J.C. van Tol' (f) ♀H6	Widely available
- 'Latispina' (f)	CJun
- 'Lichtenthalii' (f)	CJun

Ilex

- 'Madame Briot' (f/v) ♀H6	CDoC CJun CMac CWnw EBee ELan EPfP LBuc LRHS MAsh SEND SGol SMad SPoG SRms WFar WHtc
- 'Monstrosa' (m)	CJun
- moonlight holly (f)	see *I. aquifolium* 'Flavescens'
- 'Myrtifolia' (m)	CJun CMac ELan EPfP LRHS LSto NLar
- 'Myrtifolia Aurea Maculata' (m/v)	CDoC CJun ELan EPfP MAsh MPri SPoG
- 'Pyramidalis' (f) ♀H6	CBcs CJun CMac EHeP ELan LRHS MAsh MGos NLar SGol SRms WFar
- 'Recurva' (m)	CJun CMac
- RED TIPS ('Spek 02') (m)	NLar
- 'Rubricaulis Aurea' (f/v)	CJun
- 'Scotica' (f)	CJun
- SIBERIA ('Limsi') (f)	LMaj
- 'Silver King' (m/v)	see *I. aquifolium* 'Silver Queen'
- 'Silver Lining' (f/v)	CJun
- 'Silver Milkboy' (f/v)	MBlu WFar
- 'Silver Milkmaid' (f/v)	CJun LRHS MAsh MPri NLar
§ - 'Silver Queen' (m/v) ♀H6	CBcs CCVT CDoC CEnd EGren EPfP LCro MAsh MGos MPro NLar NPip SPoG WHtc WMat
- 'Silver Sentinel' (f/v)	see *I.* × *altaclerensis* 'Belgica Aurea'
- 'Silver van Tol' (f/v)	CDoC EBee ELan LRHS MAsh NLar NPer WFar
* - 'Variegata' (v)	NPlm SArc
§ - 'Watereriana' (m/v)	LRHS
- 'Waterer's Gold' (m/v)	see *I. aquifolium* 'Watereriana'
- 'White Cream' (m/v)	SAko
- 'Zig Zag' (f)	CJun
× *aquipernyi* DRAGON LADY ('Meschick') (f) ♀H6	CCVT IArd LMaj LRHS NLar
- 'San Jose' (f)	CJun
× *attenuata* 'Sunny Foster' (f/v)	CBcs WFar
chapaensis HWJ 946	WCru
'Clusterberry' (f)	CJun
colchica	CMCN
- B&SWJ 15345	WCru
corallina	CBcs
cornuta	CCVT EPfP ESwi SArc
- B&SWJ 8756	WCru
- 'O. Spring' (f/v)	CJun CMac
crenata	CAco CBTr CDoC CMCN CoPl ERom IDun LCro LRHS LWaG MGos SArc WFar
* - 'Akagi'	WFar
- 'Aureovariegata'	see *I. crenata* 'Variegata'
· - 'Blondie'PBR (f)	SArc
- 'Carolina Upright' (m)	CMCN LSRN MPri NHed SEWo SSta WReH
- 'Chato' (f)	CWnw
- 'Convexa' (f) ♀H6	CJun EGren EHeP EPfP LCro MAsh SEWo WCha
- 'Convexed Gold' (f/v)	EPfP LRHS MPri NLar SPoG WFar
- DARK GREEN ('Icoprins11'PBR)	CAco CDoC CLnd EGren ELan ELon EPfP LBuc LCro LRHS LSRN MSwo NHed MArc SFol SHor SVic WCha WFar WReH
- 'Dwarf Pagoda' (f)	SAko
- Fastigiata Group	WFar
- - 'Fastigiata' (f) ♀H6	CAco CNWT EPfP LRHS MAsh NLar SPoG
- - - 'Sky Pencil' (f)	CMCN
- Glorie DwarfPBR	NLar
- 'Glorie Gem' (m)	LRHS
* - 'Glory Gem' (f)	EGren NPlm WFar
- 'Golden Gem' (f/v) ♀H6	CBcs CJun CMac EHeP ELan ELon EPfP GArf LCro LRHS MAsh MGos MPro NLar SPoG WFar WHtc
- 'Green Glory' (f)	MPro
- 'Green Hedger' ♀H6	CLnd CNWT EGren EPfP LMaj LRHS MGos NLar SArc SHor
- 'Hetzii' (f)	LMaj
- 'Kinme' (f)	EGren NPlm SArc SFol
- 'Luteovariegata'	see *I. crenata* 'Variegata'
- LUXUS ('Annys5'PBR) (m)	LCro NLar
- 'Mariesii' (f)	CMac IDun MBlu
I - 'Pyramidalis' (f)	CMac
- 'Samurai'PBR	NLar
§ - 'Shiro-fukurin' (f/v)	CJun ELan EPfP LRHS SPoG
- 'Snowflake' (f/v)	see *I. crenata* 'Shiro-fukurin'
- 'Stokes' (m)	CDoC LRHS NLar
- STRONG CAROLINE ('Annys 99'PBR) (m)	WCha
§ - 'Variegata' (v)	CMac CMCN EPfP LRHS
dimorphophylla	CBcs
- 'Somerset Pixie' (f)	CJun
'Elegance' (f)	MBlu
fargesii	IArd
- subsp. *fargesii* var. *fargesii*	WPGP
aff. *gagnepainiana* FMWJ 13168	WCru
'Good Taste' (f)	CJun
'Hohman' (f)	CJun
'Indian Chief' (m)	CJun IArd
kingiana	EBee
× *koehneana*	CCVT LRHS MMuc SEND WHtc
- 'Chestnut Leaf' (f) ♀H5	CBcs CCVT CDoC CJun CLnd CMCN EBar ELan EPfP LMaj LRHS LSto NSti SArc SMad WFar
latifolia	IArd
'Malcolm S. Whipple' (m)	IArd NLar
'Mary Nell' (f)	CJun NLar
maximowicziana	LRHS
§ × *meserveae* 'Annys Dwarf'PBR (m)	LRHS
- BLUE ANGEL ('Conang') (f)	CCVT CDoC CMac CSBt EBee EHeP ELan EPfP LMaj LRHS LSto MPri MPro NLar SArc SFol SPoG SRms WFar WHtc
- BLUE MAID ('Mesid') (f)	CDoC EGren MGos MSwo NPlm SFol
- BLUE PRINCE ('Conablu') (m) ♀H7	CAco CBcs CBrac CCVT CDoC CMac CMCN EHeP ELan EPfP GQue LBuc LRHS MBlu MPri MPro NHed NLar SArc WFar
- BLUE PRINCESS ('Conapri') (f) ♀H7	CAco CBcs CBrac CCVT CMac CMCN ELan GQue LBuc LCro LRHS MBlu MGos NLar WFar
- 'Casanova'PBR (m/v)	EBee NLar
- CASTLE SPIRE ('Hachfee'PBR) (f)	EPfP LRHS NLar
- CASTLE WALL ('Hecken Star'PBR) (m)	NLar SEWo
- GENTLE	see *I.* × *meserveae* 'Annys Dwarf'
- 'Heckenpracht'PBR (m)	WFar
- LITTLE RASCAL ('Mondo') (m)	CWnw EPfP ESwi LCro LRHS NLar
- 'Little Sensation'	MBlu NLar SPoG
myrtifolia	CDoC MAsh
- (f)	EWld
'Nellie R. Stevens' (f)	CBTr CCVT CDoC CJun CLnd CWnw EBar EBee EGren EHeP ELan EPfP LCro LMaj LRHS LSRN NLar NPip NPlm SArc SAth SEWo SFol WCha WHtc WMat
opaca	CBcs
pedunculosa	MBlu NLar

Impatiens 383

perado subsp. *azorica* B&SWJ 12526	WCru	*apalophylla*	EAri WPGP
- subsp. *platyphylla*	CBcs CMCN EBee EUrb MBlu SArc	aff. *apalophylla* **new**	WPGP
pernyi	CJun IArd	*arguta*	CDTJ CExl EAri EBee EWld GGro SBrt WFar
rotunda	WPGP	- 'Alba'	CExl CSpe EAri EPPr GGro MPie SBeP SBig WFar WJun
- NMWJ 14569	WCru		
'September Gem' (f)	CJun CMCN	- big blue-flowered	EPPr ESwi WJun
serrata	CMac CMen	- dark violet-flowered	GGro
- 'Leucocarpa' (f)	CMac	- tall	GGro WFar
spinigera	CBcs	*auricoma* × *bicaudata*	CAbb EAri EShb MPie SBig SIvy WJun
sugerokii	WCru		
var. *longipedunculata* B&SWJ 10856		*balansae*	CDTJ EAri EBee GGro WPGP
		balfourii	EAri MCtn
triflora var. *kanehirae*	CBcs NLar SArc	*bicaudata*	SPlb
verticillata	CMCN WFar	(Divine Series) DIVINE BLUE PEARL ('Pas842640') (NG) **new**	EGren
- (f)	CBcs EPfP MMrt NLar		
- (m)	EPfP NLar		
- 'Compacta' (f)	see *I. verticillata* 'Nana'	- DIVINE LAVENDER ('Pas425593') (NG)	MBros
- MAGICAL BERRY ('Kolmber') (f)	LRHS NLar		
		ernstii	CExl
- MAGICAL DAYDREAM ('Kolcaroda') (f)	NLar	*flanaganiae*	CDTJ CExl EAri EPPr ESwi SBeP SIvy WFar WPGP
- 'Maryland Beauty' (f)	CJun NLar	*forrestii*	GGro
§ - 'Nana' (f)	CJun	*glandulifera*	Prohibited invasive. See Conservation and the Environment, p.42
- 'Red Sprite' (f)	see *I. verticillata* 'Nana'		
- 'Scarlett O'Hara' (f)	CJun	*gomphophylla*	CDTJ CExl WFar
- 'Southern Gentleman' (m)	CJun MBlu	*grandis*	EAri
- 'Sunset'PBR (f)	CJun	*hawkeri* Divine Series	EGren
- 'Winter Gold' (f)	CJun GKev MBlu	*hochstetteri*	WFar
- 'Winter Red' (f)	CJun MBlu	*insignis*	EBee EPPr ESwi GGro
× *wandoensis*	CJun	*keilii*	WDib
'Washington' (f)	IArd NLar	*kerriae*	WFar
yunnanensis	EBee	*kilimanjari* subsp. *kilimanjari*	CDTJ CSpe MPie
		- subsp. *kilimanjari* × *pseudoviola* pale pink-flowered	CSpe EAri

Iliamna see *Sphaeralcea*

Illicium (Schisandraceae)

anisatum	CBcs CExl CTsd EPfP SSta WPGP
- B&SWJ 8411	WCru
- B&SWJ 11566	WCru
floridanum	CBcs EPfP LRHS NLar SSta WCru WJur
aff. *griffithii* WWJ 11911	WCru
- WWJ 11971	WCru
- WWJ 11974	WCru
henryi	CExl CTsd EBee NLar
aff. *henryi*	CBcs
jiadifengpi	NLar
lanceolatum	CExl
- KWJ 12245	WCru
macranthum B&SWJ 11809	WCru
majus	WPGP
- WWJ 11919	WCru
aff. *majus*	WCru
- WWJ 12017	WCru
merrillianum HWJ 1015	WCru
mexicanum	CExl
oligandrum	CBcs CExl EBee NLar WPGP
philippinense CWJ 12466	WCru
simonsii	CExl MBlu WPGP
- BWJ 8024	WCru
tashiroi CWJ 12468	WCru
'Woodland Ruby'	EPfP WPGP

Ilysanthes see *Lindernia*

Impatiens ✿ (Balsaminaceae)

W&O 8071	GGro
from China, Darrell Probst collection	EWld GGro WFar
from Sikkim	GGro

aff. *langbianensis* HWJ 1054	GGro WCru WFar
macrophylla	EAri
- B&SWJ 10157	WCru WFar
mengtszeana	CDTJ EAri
- PB 02-519	WFar
- trailing	GGro WFar
namchabarwensis	EAri
niamniamensis ♀H1b	CBct CHll CTsd CWal EShb WDib WFar
- 'Congo Cockatoo'	CDTJ NPer SIvy SRms
- 'Golden Cockatoo' (v)	CBct CDTJ CHll EShb
nyimana	ESwi
- CHB 14	GGro
omeiana	CDTJ CSpe CTsd EAri EBee EPPr ESwi EWld GGro LEdu MNrw MSCN NLar SPlb WCru WFar WPGP
- DJHC 98492	GGro WCru WFar
- 'High Voltage'	GGro WFar
- 'Ice Storm'	CDTJ CSpe EAri EBee EPPr ESwi EWld GEdr GGro LEdu NBro NLar SMad WCot WCru WFar WPGP
- long-leaved	WFar
- 'Pink Nerves'	CTsd EAri EBee ELan ESwi EUrb GGro LEdu MPie SBig WFar
- 'Red Leaf'	EPPr ESwi
- 'Sango'	CDTJ CSpe EAri EWld GGro LEdu WFar WPGP
- 'Silver Pink'	GGro
- variegated (v)	GEdr
oxyanthera	GGro WFar
- 'Milo'	GGro SBeP WFar

P1961	EAri EBee EPPr ESwi
parasitica	WDib
pianmaensis CHB 14	GGro
pritzelii	CDTJ
- W&O 9304	EWld GGro
- 'Sichuan Gold'	CDTJ EAri EPPr ESwi LEdu SBeP SBig WFar
puberula	GGro WFar
- HWJK 2063	EBee ESwi SBrt WCru
qingchengshanica 'Emei Dawn'	CExl CSpe EAri EBee EPPr ESwi SBeP SBig WFar
repens ♀H1b	EAri WDib
rhombifolia	GGro
rothii	CExl EBee EPPr ESwi WCot
scabrida	CSpe
§ 'Secret Love'	CDoC
sodenii	CAbb CDTJ EShb SIvy WDib WFar
- 'Flash'	WFar
- 'Ravishing Rhi'	WFar
- white-flowered	WFar
- - red eye	WFar
stenantha	EAri EBee ESwi EWld GGro LEdu WFar WPGP
sultani	see *I. walleriana*
SunPatiens Series (NG)	MPri
- SunPatiens Compact Electric Orange ('Sakimp025'PBR) (NG) ♀H1b	MBros
- SunPatiens Vigorous Blush Pink ('Sakimp023'PBR) (NG)	MBros
- SunPatiens Vigorous Clear White ('Sakimp036'PBR) (NG)	MBros
- SunPatiens Vigorous Lavender ('Sakimp006') (NG)	MBros
- SunPatiens Vigorous Magenta ('Misato Fg3') (NG)	MBros
- SunPatiens Vigorous Orange ('Sakimp056'PBR) (NG)	MBros
- SunPatiens Vigorous White Improved ('Sakimp010'PBR) (NG)	MBros
tinctoria	CAbb CAby CBct CDTJ CExl CHll CSpe EAri EBee EPPr ESwi EWld MNrw SBrt SDix
- from Cherangani, Kenya	EAri EBee EPPr
tuberosa	WDib
uniflora	EBee GGro
usambarensis	EAri
Velvetea	see *I.* 'Secret Love'
§ *walleriana*	EShb MBros
- Beacon Select Mixture (Beacon Series)	EGren LCro MBros
- DeZire Series	MBros MPri
- (Glimmer Series)	LSou
Glimmer Appleblossom ('Balglimapp') (d)	
- - Glimmer Burgundy ('Balglimbur') (d) **new**	LSou
(Wild Romance Series) Wild Romance Blush Pink ('Dongiwiroblupi 20') (NG/d) **new**	LRHS MPri
- Wild Romance Lavender ('Dongiwirola') (NG/d) **new**	LRHS MPri
- Wild Romance Red ('Doimwirored') (NG/d) **new**	LRHS
- Wild Romance White 2022 ('Dongiwirowhi 20') (NG/d) **new**	MPri

Imperata (Poaceae)

cylindrica	CMen EBee
- 'Red Baron'	see *I. cylindrica* 'Rubra'
§ - 'Rubra'	Widely available

Incarvillea (Bignoniaceae)

arguta	GKev
brevipes	see *I. mairei*
compacta	GKev
delavayi	CAby CBcs CTsd ECha EGrI EPfP EPPr GArf GKev LAma LCro LRHS MGos MPri MPro SRms WFar XFar
- 'Alba'	see *I. delavayi* 'Snowtop'
- 'Bees' Pink'	GEdr WHil
§ - 'Snowtop'	CAby CBcs CTsd EBee EDAr EPfP GEdr GKev IPot LAma LRHS StAn WCot WHil
grandiflora	EBee GKev
§ *mairei*	GKev SRms WHil
- var. *mairei* f. *multifoliata*	see *I. zhongdianensis*
olgae	IPot WHil WPGP
sinensis 'Cheron'	MCtn
§ *zhongdianensis*	GArf GEdr WHil
- BWJ 7978	WCru

Indigofera (Fabaceae)

§ *amblyantha*	CBcs LShi MAsh MBlu NLar SPlb WLov WSpi
balfouriana Craib BWJ 7851	WCru
bungeana	MHer SRms
dielsiana	LRHS WSpi
'Dosua'	SEND
gerardiana	see *I. heterantha*
hancockii	SHor
hebepetala	EPfP WJur
§ *heterantha* ♀H5	CBcs CDoC CMCN CSde CSpe CWGN EAri EGren ELan EPfP ESwi LSto MAvo MBlu MMuc SAko SEND SPoG WFar WJur WPGP WSpi WTre
himachalensis	EBee MBlu
- H&M 1818	WPGP
himalayensis 'Silk Road'	CMac CSpe EBee ELan EPfP GKev LCro LRHS MBlu MGos MPri MSCN NLar SPoG WSpi
§ *howellii* 'Reginald Cory' ♀H5	CBcs CExl CSpe EAri EBee ELan EPfP ESwi LRHS MBlu SBrt WCru WPGP
kirilowii	CSpe EAri EPfP MAvo MBlu SBrt SHar WPGP WSpi
- var. *alba*	EBee WPGP
§ *pendula*	CCoa CExl CSde CSpe CWGN EAri EBee ELan EPfP ESwi SPoG WPGP WSpi
- B&SWJ 7741	WCru
potaninii misapplied	see *I. amblyantha*, *I. howellii* 'Reginald Cory', *I. pendula*
potaninii ambig.	CBcs CExl CMac
subverticillata misapplied	see *I. howellii* 'Reginald Cory'
suffruticosa	MCtn
szechuensis	CSde LRHS NLar SChF
tinctoria	MCtn

Indocalamus (Poaceae)
- **latifolius** — MWht
- **solidus** — see *Bonia solida*
- § **tessellatus** ♀H5 — CBcs MWht NGdn NPlm SMad
- - f. **hamadae** — MWht

Inula (Asteraceae)
- **acaulis** — WCot
- **dysenterica** — see *Pulicaria dysenterica*
- **ensifolia** — CBcs ELan EPfP NLar SMrm WCav WHoo
- - 'Compacta' — GJos
- - 'Gold Star' — EBee MHol NBir WCot WFar
- **glandulosa** — see *I. orientalis*
- **helenium** — CCBP CGHo CHby EArl ENfk GJem GJos LCro LEdu LRHS MCtn MEar MHer MHoo MNHC NBid NBir NLar SRms WCot WJek WShi
- **hookeri** — CCBP CElw ECha GBin GKev GMaP LEdu LShi MArl MBel MHer MHol MMuc MPie NBid NLar NPer NSti SAdn SDix SEND WBrk WCAu WCav
- - GWJ 9033 — WCru
- - 'Mude' — EBee
- **macrocephala** misapplied see *I. royleana*
- **magnifica** — Widely available
- - 'Sonnenstrahl' ♀H6 — LEdu NLar SPhx
- **oculus-christi** — EWes LShi WCot
- § **orientalis** — EBee GAbr GJos MCtn MHol MMrt NLar SRms
- - B&SWJ 15379 — WCru
- - 'Grandiflora' — LShi WCAu
- **racemosa** — EPPr EWes GBin GGro GQue MNrw SPeP SPlb SRms
- - 'Sonnenspeer' — GJos NBid NLar
- **rhizocephala** — GGro
- § **royleana** — MNrw
- **salicina** — EBee

Inulanthera (Asteraceae)
- **calva** — WCot WFar

Iochroma (Solanaceae)
- **australe** — see *Eriolarynx australis*
- **cyaneum** ♀H3 — CHll EShb SPlb SVen
- **fuchsioides** — CBcs CHll CSpe EShb
- **gesnerioides** 'Coccineum' — CHll EShb
- **grandiflorum** — see *Trozelia grandiflora*
- **warscewiczii** — see *Trozelia grandiflora*

Ipheion ✿ (Amaryllidaceae)
- 'Alberto Castillo' ♀H5 — CAby CBro CSpe CTtf ECha EGren ELan ELon EPot ERCP ESgI EWes GKev GMaP LAma LCro MNrw MPie NBir SDix SRms WCot WHoo WMal WPGP WTor XFar
- 'Alice' — WCot WMal
- 'Denver Daybreak' — WMal
- 'Diana' — WCot
- 'Dusky Pink' — EPPr WMal
- 'Jessie' — CAby CBro CTtf ECha EGren EPPr ERCP EWes GKev LAma MNrw WBrk WMal WTor
- 'Judy' — WCot
- 'Rolf Fiedler' ♀H4 — CBro ELan EPfP ERCP ETay EWes GKev LAma MNrw NRya SHar SRms
- **sellowianum** — CTtf
- **sessile** — EBee

- 'Tessa'^PBR — ECha ERCP EWes
- § **uniflorum** — CBro EGrI LAma SEND SRms WBrk WCav WCot
- - f. **album** — CBro EBee EGren EWes GArf LRHS WCot WMal
- - 'Charlotte Bishop' — CBro ECha EGren EGrI EPfP ERCP ESgI EWes GKev LAma MMrt MNrw NBir NRya SRms WBrk WCav WCot WHoo WMal
- - 'Froyle Mill' ♀H5 — CBro ERCP SHar SRms WCot WHoo EPPr WHoo WMal
- - 'Hoo House' — EPPr WHoo WMal
- - 'Miss Hannah' — EPPr SPeP WMal
- - 'Rigel' — EPPr WMal
- - subsp. **tandiliense** — EPPr
- - 'Wisley Blue' ♀H5 — CBro CWCL EGren ELan EPot ERCP GKev LAma LCro LRHS NRya SPoG SRms WCot XFar

Ipomoea (Convolvulaceae)
- **acuminata** — see *I. indica*
- **alba** — CSpe EShb MCtn
- **batatas** 'Beauregard' — SVic
- - 'O'Henry' — SVic
- - SOLAR POWER RED ('Balsolared') — MPri
- - SUNTORY BLACK TONE ('Kyuikukan 1'^PBR) — ELan MPri
- - (Sweet Caroline Series) 'Sweet Caroline Light Green'^PBR — ELan MPri
- - - 'Sweet Caroline Purple'^PBR — ELan
- - - SWEET CAROLINE SWEETHEART JET BLACK ('Ncornsp-021shjb') — CSpe MPri
- **cairica** — WCot
- **coccinea** — MCtn
- § **indica** ♀H1c — CRHN EShb
- - 'Betty Mars' — EShb
- - 'Tokiko Kato' — EShb
- **learii** — see *I. indica*
- **leptophylla** — EDAr
- **lindheimeri** — EShb
- § **lobata** ♀H1c — CSpe ESgI LCro MCtn SWor
- **mauritiana** — LBom
- **multifida** — MCtn
- **nil** 'Chocolate' — MCtn
- **ochracea** — EArl MCtn
- **pes-tigridis** — CSpe
- **purpurea** — MCtn
- - 'Dacapo Light Blue' — MCtn
- - 'Grandpa Otts' — LCro MCtn
- - 'Kniola's Black Night' — LCro
- - 'Star of Yelta' — MCtn
- - 'Venice Pink' — MCtn
- **quamoclit** — CSpe
- **tricolor** 'Heavenly Blue' ♀H1c — ELan LCro MCtn
- - 'Kniola's Black' — MCtn
- - 'Pearly Gates' — MCtn
- - 'Scarlett O'Hara' — MCtn
- **versicolor** — see *I. lobata*

Ipomopsis (Polemoniaceae)
- **rubra** — CSpe WHil

Iresine (Amaranthaceae)
- **herbstii** ♀H1c — EShb
- - 'Aureoreticulata' — EShb
- - 'Lime' — EUrb
- - 'Rose' — EUrb

Iris ✿ (Iridaceae)

(J)	NLar SMrm XFar
(La) **new**	CLil
'A Star is Born' (TB) **new**	WCAu
'Abbey Chant' (IB)	WCAu
'Abbondanza' (TB)	WCAu
'Ablaze' (MDB)	EDAr
'About Town' (TB)	WCAu
'Ace' (MTB)	EWoo
'Acropole' (TB)	EWoo
'Action Front' (TB)	CEnd CFis EBee EGren ESgI EWoo GBin LRHS MArl MGos WCAu WGwG
'Action Packed' (TB)	WCAu
'Actress' (TB)	CMHG EPfP ESgI LRHS LSRN MArl MGos WGwG
'Adriatic Noble' (TB)	WCAu
'Afternoon Delight' (TB)	ESgI
'Again and Again' (TB)	EWoo
'Agatha Christie' (IB)	WCAu
'Aggressively Forward' (TB)	WCAu
'Aichi-no-kagayaki' (SpH)	CBen WCot
'Alabaster Unicorn' (TB)	ESgI
'Alaska' (Dut)	LCro XFar
albicans ♀H5	CBro GKev LEdu SBrt
- 'Blue Pygmy'	MPie
'Alcazar' (TB)	EWoo SHor WCAu
'Alene's Other Love' (SDB)	WCAu
'Alice Goodman' (TB)	ESgI
'Alice Harding' (TB)	ESgI
'Alida' (Reticulata)	CBro EGren EPot ERCP ETay GKev LAma LCro LRHS NBir WBrk WCAu
'Alien Mist' (TB)	EIri
'Alizes' (TB) ♀H7	ESgI
'All in Vein' (TB) **new**	WCAu
'All Night Long' (TB)	EWoo
'All Things Considered' (TB) **new**	WCAu
'Ally Oops' (SpH)	CBen CDor WCAu WMal
'Always Lovely' (BB)	WCAu
'Amadora' (TB)	EIri
'Amanda Jane' (AB)	WCAu
'Ama-no-hane' (Sib)	ELon
'Amas' (TB)	EWoo
'Ambassadeur' (TB)	ELan EWoo
'Amber Queen' (SDB)	LRHS NBir WGwG
'Ambroisie' (TB) ♀H7	ESgI
'American Patriot' (IB)	WCAu
'Amethyst Flame' (TB)	ESgI SRms
'Amherst Blue' (IB)	EIri
'Amherst Caper' (SDB)	EIri
'Amherst Glacier' (IB)	WCAu
'Amoena' (TB)	EWoo
'Amphora' (SDB)	CBro
'Ancient Echoes' (TB)	ESgI
'Andalou' (TB) ♀H7	ESgI
'Angela' (Reticulata) **new**	ERCP XFar
anglica	see *I. latifolia*
'Ann Chowning' (La)	CAby CBen CMiW CPud CWat EBee ELin EPfk LCro
'Annabel Jane' (TB)	EnIr WCAu
'Anne Elizabeth' (SDB)	CBro
'Annemarie Troeger' (Sib) ♀H7	ELon
'Antarctique' (IB)	ESgI
aphylla	GKev SBrt WAbe
'Apollo' (Dut)	GKev LAma
'Apricorange' (TB)	SRms WCot
'Apricot Drops' (MTB) ♀H7	ESgI EWoo WCAu
'Apricot Silk' (IB)	NQui
'Apricot Topping' (BB)	WCAu
'Aquamarine' (IB)	MHol
'Arc de Triomphe' (TB)	ESgI
'Archie Owen' (Spuria)	WCAu
'Arctic Chill' (TB) **new**	WCAu
'Arctic Night' (IB)	WCAu
'Arctic Sunrise' (TB)	ESgI
arenaria	see *I. humilis*
'Arpège' (TB)	LCro
'Art Deco' (TB)	ESgI SIri WCAu
'Ascension Crown' (TB)	ESgI
'Ask Alma' (IB)	EWoo
'Attention Please' (TB)	EWoo SBea
attica	CBro EAri EPot GEdr
- blue-flowered	WAbe
- lemon-flowered	EPot EPPr GKev SBrt WAbe WIce
- violet-flowered	GKev
'Attitude' (IB)	WCAu
'Au Sommet' (TB)	LCro LRHS SHar
aucheri	EWoo GKev LAma
'Austrian Sky' (SDB)	CFis CMac EWoo LRHS SPeP WCot
'Autumn Circus' (TB)	WCAu
'Autumn Echo' (TB)	ESgI
'Autumn Encore' (TB)	SRms
'Autumn Leaves' (TB)	WCAu
'Autumn Maple' (SDB)	ESgI
'Autumn Princess' (Dut)	ERCP GKev LAma XFar
'Autumn Riesling' (TB)	WCAu
'Autumn Rose' (TB) **new**	WCAu
'Autumn Tease' (TB) **new**	WCAu
'Autumn Tryst' (TB)	ESgI EWoo WCAu
'Autumn Twilight' (TB)	EWoo
'Avalon Sunset' (TB)	ESgI
'Avanelle' (IB)	GBin
'Awesome Blossom' (TB)	ESgI
'Az Ap' (IB)	WCAu
'Aziyadé' (TB)	EWoo
babadagica	GEdr WAbe
'Babbling Brook' (TB)	EGren ESgI LRHS
'Baby Blessed' (SDB)	CBro WCAu
'Baby Sister' (Sib)	ELon NBro WFar
'Baccarat' (TB)	WCAu
'Badlands' (TB)	WCAu
'Baie Rose' (IB)	SIri
'Bal Masqué' (TB)	ESgI
'Ballet Lesson' (SDB)	ESgI
'Ballistic' (SDB)	WCAu
'Ballyhoo' (TB)	WCAu
'Baltic Star' (TB)	WCAu
'Banbury Beauty' (CH) ♀H4	NLar
'Banbury Gem' (CH)	NLar
'Banbury Ruffles' (SDB)	ESgI NLar WCAu
'Bandera Waltz' (TB)	WCAu
'Bangles' (MTB) ♀H7	EIri WCAu
'Banish Misfortune' (Sib)	EPfP WCAu
'Bar de Nuit' (TB)	ESgI
'Barbara May' (TB)	WCAu
'Barbara My Love' (TB)	WCAu
barbatula BWJ 7663	ESwi WCru
'Batik' (BB)	WCot XFar
'Bayberry Candle' (TB)	WCAu
'Beachgirl' (TB)	WCAu
'Beautician' (TB) **new**	WCAu
'Beauty Becomes Her' (TB)	WCAu
'Bee Wings' (MDB)	EDAr ESgI
'Before the Storm' (TB)	EBee ELan ESgI WCAu
'Being Busy' (SDB)	ESgI
'Bel Avenir' (TB)	ESgI
'Bel Azur' (IB)	ESgI
'Belgian Princess' (TB)	SIri WCAu
'Belise' (Spuria)	WCot

Iris 387

'Belle Aude' (TB)	ESgI
'Belle de Nuit' (TB)	WCAu
'Benton Apollo' (TB)	CEnd EBee ECha EGren ELan EWoo LCro LRHS NCth WCAu
'Benton Argent' (TB)	ECha ESgI EWoo LRHS
'Benton Arundel' (TB)	CEnd ECha EGrI ESgI EWoo
'Benton Bluejohn' (TB)	ECha EWoo
'Benton Caramel' (TB)	ECha ELan EPfP EWoo LCro LRHS LSou NCth SIri
'Benton Cordelia' (TB)	ECha EPfP EWoo LRHS
'Benton Daphne' (TB)	ELan ESgI EWoo NCth
'Benton Dierdre' (TB)	ECha EGren ELan EPfP ESgI EWoo LRHS LSou NCth SMrm SRms WGwG
'Benton Duff' (TB)	ECha ESgI EWoo LRHS
'Benton Evora' (TB)	ECha ESgI EWoo LRHS
'Benton Farewell' (TB)	ECha EPfP EWoo LRHS
'Benton Judith' (TB)	ECha
'Benton Lorna' (TB)	EBee ECha EGren EPfP EWoo LRHS MHol NCth WGwG
'Benton Menace' (TB)	ECha EPfP EWoo LCro LRHS NCth SMHy
'Benton Nigel' (TB)	EBee ECha ELan EPfP EWoo LCro LRHS NCth WCAu
'Benton Nutkin' (TB)	WMal
'Benton Old Madrid' (TB)	ECha EPfP EWoo LRHS
'Benton Olive' (TB)	CCBP ECha EPfP EWoo LCro LRHS NCth
'Benton Opal' (TB)	ECha ESgI EWoo LRHS WCAu WGwG
'Benton Pearl' (TB)	CEnd EBee ECha ELan EPfP ESgI EWoo LRHS NCth WCAu
'Benton Primrose' (TB)	CEnd ESgI EWoo LRHS WGwG
'Benton Sheila' (TB)	ELan EWoo WCot WMal
'Benton Susan' (TB)	CEnd EBee ECha ELan EPfP ESgI EWoo LCro LRHS NCth WGwG
'Beotie' (TB)	EWoo
'Berkeley Gold' (TB)	EWes
'Berlin Bluebird' (Sib)	SMHy
'Berlin Purple Wine' (Sib)	ESgI
'Berlin Ruffles' (Sib) ♀H7	EWes WCAu
'Berlin Tiger' (SpH) ♀H7	CBen EBee EPPr MSCN NLar SDix WCAu
'Best Bet' (TB)	ESgI WCAu
'Bet the Farm' (TB)	WCAu
'Bethany Claire' (TB)	ESgI WCAu
'Better than Butter' (TB)	WCAu
'Better Together' (TB)	WCAu
'Betty Cooper' (Spuria)	WCAu
'Betty Simon' (TB)	EWoo
'Beverly Sills' (TB)	EPfP LCro LRHS WCAu
'Bianco' (TB)	EWoo WCAu WHil
'Bibury' (SDB) ♀H7	WCAu
bicapitata	WAbe
'Big Blue' (Sib)	WFar
'Big Heart' (Sib)	EIri
'Big Squeeze' (TB)	WCAu
biglumis	see *I. lactea*
biliottii	CBro
'Bishop's Robe' (TB)	EWoo LCro
'Black Beauty' (TB)	EPfP
'Black Dragon' (TB)	EGrI LCro LRHS WSpi
'Black Gamecock' (La)	CAby CBen CLil CPud CSpe CTtf CWat EBee EGrI ELin EPfP LCro MHer MSCN MWts NLar SMrm WCAu WFar WMAq
'Black Hope' (TB)	EWoo
'Black is Back' (TB)	WCAu
'Black Joker' (Sib)	ELon ERCP LBar LCro MHol
'Black Knight' (TB)	EGrI EHeP NQui WSpi
'Black Magic' (IB)	EWoo
'Black Stallion' (MDB)	ESgI
'Black Swan' (TB)	CMac ECha EGren ELan EPfP ESgI EWoo LCro LSRN NQui SPeP SPoG SRms WCAu WCot WTor
'Black Taffeta' (TB)	WSpi
'Black Tie Affair' (TB)	CEnd EBee ELan EPfP ESgI EWoo LRHS MAsh MHer MMrt WCAu
'Black Watch' (IB)	LCro
'Blackbeard' (BB) ♀H7	WCAu
'Blackbeard's Ghost' (AB)	WCAu
'Blackberry Tease' (TB)	WCAu
'Blackberry Towers' (TB)	ESgI
'Blackcurrant' (IB)	WCAu
'Blackout' (TB)	ESgI
'Blaeberry Pie' (TB)	EnIr
'Blatant' (TB)	ESgI WCAu
'Blaue Milchstrasse' (Sib)	ESgI MMrt
'Blenheim Royal' (TB)	ESgI WCAu
'Blitzen' (IB)	WCAu
bloudowii	WAbe
'Blowing Kisses' (TB) **new**	WCAu
'Blue Bird' (Sib)	SPoG WFar
'Blue Boy' (IB)	EWoo
'Blue Burgee' (Sib)	ECha
I 'Blue Butterfly' (Sib)	NGdn
'Blue Denim' (SDB)	GMaP MHol NBir NLar WCAu WCot
'Blue Gown' (TB)	EWoo
'Blue Hendred' (SDB)	NBir
'Blue King' (Sib)	CDor CWat ELan EPfP GKev GMaP MSwo NBro NGdn WFar
'Blue King' (Dut)	WCAu
'Blue Luster' (TB)	ESgI
'Blue Mere' (Sib)	MHol
'Blue Moon' (Sib)	ELon WCAu WFar
'Blue my Mind' (TB)	WCAu
'Blue Nile' (TB)	EWoo
'Blue Note' (Reticulata)	EPfP ERCP GKev LAma XFar
'Blue Note Blues' (TB)	WCAu
'Blue Pennant' (Sib)	NLar
'Blue Pigmy' (SDB)	CWat EGren EGrI LRHS NLar WGwG
'Blue Planet' (Reticulata)	ERCP
'Blue Pools' (SDB)	ESgI
'Blue Reverie' (Sib)	ELon
'Blue Rhythm' (TB)	CEnd ECha EGren ELan EPfP EWoo GMaP LRHS SOrN WCAu WTor
'Blue Sapphire' (Dut)	MHol
'Blue Sapphire' (TB)	ESgI
'Blue Shimmer' (TB)	CMac EBee ECha ELan EPfP ESgI EWoo LRHS LSRN SRms WCAu WGwG WHoo
'Blue Splash' (IB)	WCAu
'Blue Staccato' (TB)	ESgI WCAu
'Blue Suede Shoes' (TB)	ESgI EWoo WCAu
'Blue Trill' (TB)	WCAu
'Bluebeard's Ghost' (SDB) ♀H7	WCAu
'Blueberry Fair' (Sib)	CDor
'Blueyed Brunette' (TB)	ESgI WCAu
'Blushing Grapes' (TB) **new**	WCAu
'Bold Encounter' (TB)	WCAu
'Bold Pretender' (La)	EAri EBee EGrI MHol NLar
'Bold Print' (IB)	EWoo GMaP LRHS LSRN MArl MGos NCth SPeP SPoG WCAu WTor
'Bollinger'	see *I.* 'Hornpipe'
'Bonanza' (TB)	EWoo
'Boo' (SDB)	SIri WCAu
'Border Happy' (TB)	WCAu
'Border Town' (Spuria)	WCAu
'Boston Cream' (TB)	WCAu
'Bottled Sunshine' (IB)	LRHS

'Bourgeois' (SDB)	ESgI	'Butterscotch Carpet' (SDB)	WCAu
'Bournemouth Beauty' (Sib) ♀H7	CDor	'Butterscotch Fizz' (Sib) **new**	WCAu
'Bouzy Bouzy' (TB)	ESgI	'Butterscotch Kiss' (TB)	CMac MGos NBir NLar
bracteata	EBee	'Buzzword' (SDB)	WCAu
'Braithwaite' (TB)	EBee EGren ELan EPfP ESgI EWoo LRHS LSou MArl SHar SRms WCAu WGwG WTor	'By Jeeves' (TB)	WCAu
		'Bye Bye Blues' (TB)	ESgI
		'Cabaret Royale' (TB)	WCAu
		'Cable Car' (TB)	ESgI EWoo
'Brannigan' (SDB)	NBir	'Caesar' (Sib)	SRms
'Brasero' (TB)	WCAu	'Caesar's Brother' (Sib)	EWoo LBom LCro LRHS LSto MGos NLar SHar SHor WCAu WFar XFar
'Brasilia' (TB)	NBir		
'Brassie' (SDB)	CBro EHeP		
'Breakers' (TB) ♀H7	ESgI EWoo WCAu	'Caliente' (TB)	EHeP WCAu
'Brenchley' (IB)	SIri	§ Californian hybrids	CElw CMac NBir WCot
brevicaulis	GEdr SBrt	'Calm Stream' (TB)	WCAu
'Bridal Icing' (TB)	WCAu	'Calypso Beat' (TB)	SIri
'Bride's Halo' (TB)	WCAu	'Cambridge' (Sib) ♀H7	WCAu WFar
'Bridesmaid' (TB)	EWoo	'Cameliard' (TB)	EWoo
'Bright Button' (SDB)	ESgI	'Camelot Rose' (TB)	WCAu
'Bright Vision' (SDB)	ESgI	'Cameo Wine' (TB)	ESgI
'Bright White' (MDB)	CBro	'Cameroun' (TB)	ESgI EWoo
'Brighteyes' (IB)	SRms	'Campbellii'	see *I. lutescens* 'Campbellii'
'Brindisi' (TB)	WCAu	***canadensis***	see *I. hookeri*
'Bring it On' (MTB)	EWoo	'Canary Bird' (TB)	ESgI
'Brising' (TB)	EWoo	'Candy Rock' (IB)	EWoo WCAu
'Broad Shoulders' (TB)	WCAu	'Cannington Apricot' (IB)	CWal
'Broadleigh Amanda' (CH)	CBro	'Cannington Bluebird' (TB)	CWal
'Broadleigh Angela' (CH)	CBro	'Cannington Ochre' (SDB)	CBro
'Broadleigh Bright Eyes' (CH) **new**	CBro	'Can't Touch This' (TB)	WCAu
		'Cantab' (Reticulata)	EGren NBir
'Broadleigh Lavinia' (CH)	CBro	'Cape Cod Boys' (Sib)	CDor WCAu
'Broadleigh Midnight' (CH) **new**	CBro	'Captain Indigo' (IB)	ESgI WCAu
		'Captive Sun' (SDB)	EWoo LRHS MAsh SIri WGwG
'Broadleigh Nancy' (CH)	CBro	'Care to Dance' (TB)	WCAu
'Broadleigh Peacock' (CH)	NLar	'Careless Sally' (Sib)	WCAu
'Broadleigh Penny' (CH)	CBro NLar	'Caribbean Dream' (TB)	ESgI NLar
'Broadleigh Rose' (CH)	CBro CElw EGrI MBrN MWlw	'Carmen' (Dut)	ETay
'Broadway Baby' (IB)	ESgI	'Carnaby' (TB)	CEnd EGren EPfP ESgI LRHS MArl SHar WCAu WGwG WHoo WTor
'Bronzaire' (IB)	WCAu		
'Bronze Beauty' van Tubergen (*hoogiana* hybrid)	NBir	'Carnival Time' (TB)	CFis CMac EPfP ESgI LRHS MHer SHar SMrm WHoo
'Brown Chocolate' (TB)	WCAu	'Carolina' (Reticulata)	LAma
'Bruce' (TB)	WCAu	'Carolyn Rose' (MTB) ♀H7	WCAu
'Brummit's Mauve' (TB)	WCAu	'Cascade Sprite' (SDB)	SRms
'Bruno' (TB)	EPfP EWoo NLar	'Cascadian Rhythm' (TB) **new**	WCAu
'Brussels' (TB)	ESgI		
'Bryan's Best Blue' (TB)	EnIr	'Casque d'Or' (TB)	LCro
bucharica ambig.	MNrw	'Casual Attire' (IB) **new**	WCAu
§ ***bucharica*** Foster ♀H5	GKev EWoo	'Caterina' (TB) ♀H7	EWoo
'Buckwheat' (TB)	EWoo SIri	'Catherine Seville' (TB)	EnIr
bulleyana	CBro GKev SRms WCAu	'Cat's Eye' (SDB)	SIri
– BWJ 7912	WCru	***caucasica***	CMac
– black-flowered	GKev	'Cayenne Capers' (TB)	ESgI
aff. ***bulleyana***	WShi	* 'Cedric Morris'	EWes
'Bumblebee Deelite' (MTB) ♀H7	WCAu WMal	'Cee Cee' (TB)	EWoo
		'Celebration Song' (TB)	ESgI WCAu
'Bundle of Joy' (Sib)	LAma WCAu	'Celilo' (SDB)	WCAu
'Bundle of Love' (BB)	WCAu	'Center Line' (TB)	WCAu
'Burgermeister' (TB)	LCro	'Champagne Elegance' (TB)	LCro NBir SIri WCAu
'Burka' (TB)	ESgI	'Chance Beauty' (SpH) ♀H7	CBen WCAu
'Burnt Toffee' (TB)	ESgI EWoo	'Change of Pace' (TB)	ESgI WCAu
'Buto' (TB)	EWoo	'Chanted' (SDB)	WCAu
'Butter and Cream' (Sib)	EGren	'Chantilly' (TB)	EWoo NBir NGdn NLar
'Butter and Sugar' (Sib)	CBcs CDor CTtf CWat EAri EBee EGren EGrI ELan EPfP EWoo GBin GMaP LBom LCro LRHS MHol MNrw NBir NGdn NWbg SHor SMHy SMrm WCAu WCot WFar WHil WMal	'Chapeau' (TB)	ESgI WCAu
		'Charming Billy' (Sib)	EPfP MHol NLar
		'Charnwood Delight' (TB)	EnIr
		'Chartreuse Bounty' (Sib)	CDor EWes GMaP MHol NLar SHor WFar
		'Chasing Rainbows' (TB)	ESgI WCAu
'Buttermere' (TB)	SRms	'Château d'Auvers-sur-Oise' (TB)	SIri WCAu
'Butterpat' (IB)	ESgI		

Iris

'Cheap Frills' (TB)	WCAu	'Colorific' (La)	NLar
'Chelsea Bleu' (TB)	WCAu	'Comme un Sourire' (TB)	LCro LRHS
'Cher and Cher Alike' (TB)	WCAu	'Common Thread' (TB)	WCAu
'Cherished' (TB)	LRHS	'Concertina' (IB)	WCAu
'Cherry Fling' (Sib)	ERCP	'Concord Crush' (Sib)	CAby NGdn WTor
'Cherry Garden' (SDB)	CBro CMHG CWat ECha EGren EGrI ElAn EWes EWoo GMaP NBir NGdn NLar WGwG	'Confection Perfection' (TB) **new**	WCAu
		confusa ♀H4	CBro CWal EArI ESwi EUrb LRHS LWaG SArc SNoN SPlb
'Cherub's Smile' (TB)	ESgI	§ - 'Martyn Rix'	CAbb CBct CMac EArI EGrI EPfP EPPr ESgI ESwi LRHS SEND SRms WGwG WMal
'Chicken Little' (MDB)	CBro EDAr		
'Chilled Wine' (Sib)	ELon		
'Chinook Winds' (Sib)	ESgI WCAu		
'Chivalry' (TB)	ESgI	'Conjuration' (TB)	ELan LRHS WCAu
'Christmas Angel' (TB)	NLar WCAu	'Constant Wattez' (IB)	ESgI LRHS
Chrysofor Group	CAby	'Constantine Bay' (TB)	ESgI
chrysographes ♀H6	CBcs CMHG CToG CTtf EGrI EPfP EWoo GJos GKev LCro LEdu LRHS LSto MArl MHer SPoG StAn WChS WFar WKif WTre	'Contrast in Styles' (Sib)	EPfP MNrw NQui WCAu WFar WHil
		'Cool Change' (TB)	WCAu
		'Copatonic' (TB)	WCAu
		'Copper Capers' (TB)	ESgI
- BWJ 7930	WCru	'Copper Classic' (TB)	EGren ESgI WCAu
I - 'Black Beauty'	EWoo	'Coquet Waters' (Sib)	NBid
I - 'Black Gold'	EPfk ESgI MHol NLar	'Coquetterie' (TB)	EWoo
I - 'Black Knight'	CExl CMHG EGren EPfk EPfP GQue LEdu LRHS SChF SHor SMad	'Coraband' (TB)	NLar
		'Coral Splendor' (TB)	WCAu
I - 'Black Velvet'	GEdr WSpi	'Cordoba' (TB)	WCAu
- black-flowered	CAby EArI EBee EGren ElAn EPPr ERCP GKev GKin LAma LBar LCro LRHS LShi MNrw MPro NGdn WCAu WCru WFar WPGP WSpi WTor	'Coronation Anthem' (Sib)	EWoo
		'Cotillion Gown' (TB) **new**	WCAu
		'Countess' (TB) **new**	WCAu
		'Country Charm' (TB)	WCAu
		'Country Kisses' (TB)	WCAu
- dark-flowered	GKev WFar	'Crackling Caldera' (TB)	MMrt
- hybrid	ESgI WFar	'Cranapple' (BB) ♀H7	ESgI WCAu
- 'Just Around Midnight'	XFar	'Cranberry Swirl' (TB)	CWnw ElAn
- 'Kew Black'	CExl CTtf NBir	'Crathie' (TB)	ECha
- 'Mandarin Purple'	GQue	'Cream Beauty' (Dut)	LCro
- yellow-flowered	WFar	*cretensis*	see *I. unguicularis* subsp. *cretensis*
'Cimarron Rose' (SDB)	ESgI	'Crimson Cloisonné' (Sib)	ELon
'Cimarron Strip' (TB)	LRHS WCot	'Crimson King' (IB)	EWoo
'Cinque Terre' (TB)	WCAu	'Crispette' (TB)	EWoo WCAu
'Circle of Light' (TB)	WCAu	*cristata*	EPot GEdr
'Citronnade' (TB)	ESgI	- 'Abbey's Violet'	SMad
'City Lights' Dunn (TB)	WCAu	- 'Alba'	WAbe
'City of Paradise' (TB)	ESgI	§ - 'Captain Collingwood'	WAbe
'Clairette' (Reticulata)	EGren EPfP EPot GKev LAma LRHS	*cristata* × *lacustris*	EPot
'Clara Garland' (IB)	WCAu	*crocea* ♀H6	WCAu
'Clarence' (TB)	ESgI MHol WCAu	'Croftway Lemon' (TB)	WSpi
clarkei	EWoo WCAu	'Crowned Heads' (TB)	WCAu
- B&SWJ 2122	MHol WCru	'Crushed Velvet' (TB)	WCAu
- CC 2751	CExl	'Crystal Gazer' (TB)	WCAu
- SDR 3819	GKev	'Crystal Glitters' (TB)	ESgI
'Class Ring' (TB)	WCAu	*cuniculiformis*	GKev
'Classic Look' (TB)	ESgI SIri	'Cup Race' (TB)	WCAu
'Classic Navy' (BB)	ESgI	'Cupid's Arrow' (TB)	WCAu
'Cleo' (TB)	NSti	'Curlew' (IB)	WCAu
'Cleo Murrell' (TB)	ESgI EWoo	'Cute or What' (SDB)	ESgI
'Cleve Dodge' (Sib)	EWoo	'Cutie' (IB)	EGren WCAu
'Cliffs of Dover' (TB)	ESgI EWoo LCro LRHS SRms WCAu	'Cyanea' (DB)	EArI EGrI
'Cloud Ballet' (TB)	WCAu	*cycloglossa*	GKev LAma WCAu
'Cloudcap' (TB)	SRms	'Daemon Imp' (MTB)	EIri WCAu
'Clyde Redmond' (La) ♀H5	WMal	'Daffy Duck' (TB)	WCAu
'Coal Face' (TB)	WCAu	'Dance Ballerina Dance' (Sib)	EPfP NLar WCAu WFar WHil
'Coal Seams' (TB)	WCAu		
'Coalignition' (TB)	WCAu	'Dance the Night Away' (TB)	WCAu
'Codicil' (TB)	ESgI WCAu		
'Colette Thuriller' (TB)	WCAu	'Dance til Dawn' (TB)	WCAu
'Collusion' (TB) **new**	WCAu	'Dancer's Veil' (TB)	CMac ESgI WCAu
'Colonel Mustard' (Sib)	EMor MMrt WCAu XFar	'Dancing in the Dark' (TB)	WCAu
'Color Glory' (TB)	SIri	'Dancing in the Moonlight' (IB)	WCAu
'Color Me Blue' (TB)	WCAu		
'Color Splash' (TB)	ESgI	'Dancing Lilacs' (MTB)	ESgI
'Color Strokes' (TB)	WCAu	'Dancing Star' (TB)	WCAu

danfordiae	EGren EWoo GKev LAma LCro	'Domingo' (AB)	WMal
'Dante's Inferno' (TB)	EWoo XFar	'Dominion' (TB)	EWoo
'Daring Deception' (TB)	WCAu	'Don Juan' (TB)	EWoo
'Dark Chocolate' (TB)	EWoo	'Double Lament' (SDB)	CBro EDAr
'Dark Circle' (Sib)	WFar	'Double Standards' (Sib)	NLar WFar
'Dark Crystal' (SDB)	ESgI	*douglasiana*	GKev
'Dark Spark' (SDB)	WCAu	'Dover Beach' (TB)	SIri
'Dark Vader' (SDB)	ESgI	'Dover Castle' (BB) ♀H7	SIri
'Darkness' (IB)	SIri	'Downtown Brown' (TB)	WCAu
'Darkness' (Reticulata)	ESgI	'Draco' (TB)	EBee EPfP ESgI LRHS
'Darley Dale' (TB)	EnIr	'Dracula's Kiss' (TB)	CWnw LCro
'Dashing' (TB)	EWoo	'Drama Queen' (TB)	WCAu
'Dating a Royal' (TB)	WCAu	'Dramatic Style' (TB)	WCAu
'Dauntless' (TB)	CCBP ESgI	'Dream Indigo' (IB)	EWoo WCAu
'Dauphin' (IB)	EWoo	'Dreaming Green' (Sib)	ECha LBar
'Dawn of Fall' (TB)	ESgI	'Dreaming Late' (Sib)	WCAu
'Dawn Waltz' (Sib)	CBro ELon EWoo WCAu WFar	'Dreaming Yellow' (Sib)	CAby CEnd CPud CToG EBee ECha ESgI GKin LRHS MArl WCAu WGwG
'Dawning' (TB) ♀H7	ESgI		
'Dazzling' (TB)	SIri WCAu	'Dresden Candleglow' (IB)	WCAu
'Dazzling Gold' (TB)	ESgI WCAu	'Drink Your Tea' (Sib)	WCAu
'Dear Delight' (Sib)	CBro ELon NLar WCAu WFar	'Dude Ranch' (TB)	WCAu
'Decadence' (TB)	WCAu	'Dunkler Wein' (Sib)	EWes
§ *decora*	WAbe	'Dunlin' (MDB)	CBro NBir
'Deep Black' (TB)	EBee ECha ELan EPfP ESgI EWoo GMaP LCro LRHS LSRN MBNS NLar SOrN SPoG WCAu WTor	'Duplicity' (TB)	WCAu
		'Dusky Challenger' (TB)	EBee EGren EPfP ESgI EWoo LCro LRHS SHor SMrm SRms WCAu
'Deep Currents' (TB) **new**	WCAu		
'Deep Dark Secret' (TB)	ESgI	'Dutch Chocolate' (TB)	ESgI EWes EWoo LCro WCAu
'Deep Pacific' (TB)	EWoo	'Dyonisos' (TB)	SIri
'Deeper Meaning' (TB)	WCAu	'Earl of Essex' (TB)	WCAu
delavayi ♀H6	EWes SBrt	'Early Light' (TB) ♀H7	EIri ESgI WCAu
- SDR 50	CExI GKev	'Eastertime' (TB)	ESgI
- 'Didcot'	LRHS	'Easy' (MTB)	EIri EWoo
'Delirium' (IB)	SIri WCAu	'Eau Vive' (TB)	WCAu
'Delta Butterfly' (La)	WMAq	'Echo de France' (TB)	ESgI EWoo SRms
'Demi-Deuil' (TB)	EWoo	'Eden's Paradise Blue' (Sib)	ELon
'Denys Humphrey' (TB) **new**	WCAu	'Edith Wolford' (TB)	LCro LRHS MMrt
		'Ed's Blue' (DB)	ELan
'Depth of Field' (TB)	EGrI	'Edward' (Reticulata)	EPfP
'Député Nomblot' (TB)	EWoo	'Edward of Windsor' (TB)	EWoo
'Derwentwater' (TB)	SRms WCAu	'Edwardian Era' (TB) **new**	WCAu
'Desert Echo' (TB)	MHer	'Ego' (IB)	ECha ELon GMaP WFar
'Desert Song' (TB)	EGrI WCot	'Egyptian' (TB)	EWoo
'Desert Streams' (TB)	ESgI	'Eldorado' (TB)	EWoo
'Destination Fabulous' (TB)	WCAu	'Eleanor Roosevelt' (IB)	EWoo
'Deuce' (MTB)	EWoo	'Eleanor's Pride' (TB)	SRms WCAu
'Devil May Care' (IB)	ESgI	'Elizabeth Poldark' (TB)	ESgI
'Devil's Dream' (Sib) **new**	WCAu	'Elsa Sass' (TB)	ESgI EWoo
'Devonshire Cream' (TB)	WCAu	'Elsie Petty' (TB)	SIri
'Devoted' (SDB)	WCAu	'Elvinhall' (MTB)	CBro
'Dewful' (Sib)	WFar	'Elysium' (IB)	ESgI
'Dinky Circus' (MDB)	ESgI	'Emperor' (Sib)	CWat NSti
'Dirigo Black Velvet' (Sib)	ELon	'Empress of India' (TB)	EWoo
'Disco Jewel' (MTB)	ESgI	'Endless Love' (TB)	EIri
'Discovered Treasure' (TB)	WCAu	'English Charm' (TB)	ESgI WCAu
'Discovery' PBR (Dut)	XFar	'English Cottage' (TB)	EPfP EWoo GBin LCro LRHS MHer NLar SHor SMrm SRms WCAu WSpi
'Disguise' (TB)	WCAu		
'Ditto' (MDB)	EDAr ESgI	'Ennerdale' (TB)	SRms WCAu
'Ditzy' (SDB)	SIri	§ *ensata*	CBcs CBro CLil EAri EGrI ELan ELin EPfP GArf LCro LRHS MNrw MWts NLar SPlb SRms SVic
'Dividing Line' (MTB)	WCAu		
'Dixie Darling' (TB)	ESgI		
'Dixie Pixie' (SDB)	WCAu	- 'Activity'	ELin WFar
'Dogrose' (TB)	EWoo	- 'Alba'	LCro MMuc
'Dolce' (SpH)	WCAu	- 'Aldridge Snow Maiden'	GBin
dolichosiphon subsp. *orientalis*	GKev	- 'Angel Mountain'	ELin MBNS WFar
		- 'Apollo'	CToG
'Dolly Madison' (TB)	ESgI EWoo	- 'Asian Warrior'	WFar
domestica	EAri EPfP EPPr EUrb EWoo LRHS LShi SPlb SRms	- 'Azure'	WFar
		- 'Carnival Prince'	WFar
- 'Freckle Face'	MHol	- 'Cascade Crest'	WFar
- 'Gone with the Wind'	LBar	- 'Center of Interest'	NBir

	- 'Christina's Gown'	WFar		- 'Rakka-no-utage'	NLar
	- 'Craola Kiss'	ELon		- Rodionenko hybrids	WMal
	- 'Crepe Paper'	WFar	§	- 'Rose Queen' ♀H6	CDor CLil CMac CMHG CToG CTtf
	- 'Crystal Halo' ♀H6	ELin WCAu			ECha ELan EWoo GKin GMaP LCro
	- 'Dace'	GBin			LRHS NBir NGdn NLar SPoG SRms
I	- 'Darling'	ELin WFar			WCAu WFar
	- (Dinner Plate Series)	ELin GAbr LAma		- 'Rowden'	CToG
	'Dinner Plate			- 'Rowden Amir'	CToG
	Blueberry Pie'			- 'Rowden Autocrat'	CToG
	- - 'Dinner Plate	ELin LRHS		- 'Rowden Baronet'	CToG
	Cheesecake'			- 'Rowden Begum'	CToG
	- - 'Dinner Plate Cupcake'	ELin LAma LRHS XFar		- 'Rowden Caesar'	CToG
	- - 'Dinner Plate Ice Cream'	ELin LRHS NLar		- 'Rowden Caliph'	CToG
	- - 'Dinner Plate Jell-O'	ELin LRHS		- 'Rowden Chieftan'	CToG
	- - 'Dinner Plate Tiramisu'	LRHS XFar		- 'Rowden Consul'	CToG
	- - 'Dinner Plate Tub Tim	XFar		- 'Rowden Dictator'	CToG
	Grob' **new**			- 'Rowden Empress'	CToG
	- 'Dramatic Moment'	WFar WSpi		- 'Rowden Gackwar'	CToG
I	- 'Dresden China'	WFar		- 'Rowden King'	CToG
	- 'Eileen's Dream'	ELin LSou		- 'Rowden Knight'	CToG
	- 'Electric Rays'	ELin WFar		- 'Rowden Laird'	CToG
I	- 'Emotion'	CMac ELin WFar		- 'Rowden Marquess'	CToG
	- 'First Act'	ELon		- 'Rowden Mikado'	CToG
I	- 'Fortune'	CLil ELin		- 'Rowden Naib'	CToG
	- 'Freckled Geisha'	CBrac CMac ELin NBir NQui SRms		- 'Rowden Nuncio'	CToG
		WFar		- 'Rowden Queen'	CToG
	- 'Frilled Enchantment' ♀H6	WFar		- 'Rowden Regent'	CToG
	- 'Frosted Intrigue'	LAma NLar		- 'Rowden Sovereign'	CToG
	- 'Frosted Pyramid'	CToG		- 'Rowden Sultan'	CToG
	- 'Galatea Marx'	WFar		- 'Rowden Tetrarch'	CToG
	- 'Geisha Obi'	ELon		- 'Rowden Viceroy'	CToG
	- 'Gipsy'	CBen CMac	I	- 'Royal Banner'	WFar
	- 'Gold Bound'	ELin NLar	I	- 'Ruby King'	ELin
	- 'Gracieuse'	CMiW ELin NLar	I	- 'Sensation'	NLar SRms
	- 'Greywoods Catrina'	ELin EPfP LAma WFar		- 'Sorcerer's Triumph'	WFar
	- 'Gusto'	CMac SRms WFar		- var. **spontanea**	WCru
	- 'Harlequinesque'	ELin EPfP LAma LSou SMad WFar		B&SWJ 1103	
		WHil		- - B&SWJ 8699	WCru
	- 'Hercule'	NBir WFar		- 'Summer Storm' ♀H6	NBir
	- 'Hoshi-akari'	WFar		- 'Tensyukaku'	CMiW
	- 'Imperial Velvet'	WFar		- 'Topas'	WFar
*	- 'Innocence'	NLar SRms WFar		- 'Variegata' (v) ♀H6	CBct CMac CMHG EBee ECha ELin
	- 'Iso-no-nami'	WFar			ELon EPfP GMaP LBar LCro LRHS
	- 'Jocasta'	WFar			MHer MHol MMuc NLar SPoG
	- 'Jodlesong'	WFar			SRms WCAu WFar XFar
	- 'Jupiter'	EGrI		- 'Waka-murasaki-uyeki'	EGrI
	- 'Kalamazoo'	WFar		- 'Wave Action'	ELin
	- 'Katy Mendez' ♀H6	NLar	I	- 'White Ladies'	SPeP WCAu WSpi
	- 'Kogesho'	NLar		- 'Yako-no-tama'	WFar
	- 'Kongo-san'	NLar WFar		- 'Yedo-yeman'	WFar
	- 'Kuma-funjin'	CToG EBee LRHS		'Eramosa Miss' (BB)	WCAu
	- 'Kumo-no-obi'	CAby CFis CMHG CPud ESgI LRHS		'Eric the Red' (Sib)	ELon
		WFar		'Etcetera' (TB)	WCAu
	- 'Lady in Waiting'	WCAu WOld		'Evening Drama' (TB)	SIri
	- 'Landscape at Dawn'	CMiW		'Ever After' (TB)	EWoo
	- 'Laughing Lion'	WCAu WFar		'Ever Again' (Sib)	ELon
	- 'Loyalty'	CLil WFar		'Ewen' (Sib)	GKin GMaP NGdn WCAu
	- 'Michinoku-kogane'	CMiW WMal		'Executive Order' (TB) **new**	WCAu
	- 'Mist Falls'	ESgI		'Exotic Isle' (TB)	ESgI WCAu
	- 'Momogasumi'	MNrw NQui		'Experiment' (SDB)	Elri
§	- 'Moonlight Waves'	CMac CMHG CPud CToG EBee		'Eye Catcher' (Reticulata)	ERCP LAma NBir XFar
		ELan GKin GMaP LShi MHer MHol		'Eye of the Tiger'	see *I.* 'Tigereye'
		NGdn SPoG SRms WCAu WFar		'Eyebright' (SDB) ♀H7	CBro WCAu
		WSpi		'Fabiola' (Reticulata)	EPot ERCP GKev LAma
	- 'Oku-banri'	EPfP WFar		'Fabuleux' (TB)	SIri
	- 'Oriental Eyes'	NGdn		'Face of an Angel' (TB)	WCAu
	- pale mauve-flowered	NBir		'Fall Empire' (TB)	EWoo
	- 'Pin Stripe'	NLar WFar		'Fall Fiesta' (TB)	WCAu
	- 'Pink Frost'	CFis CMHG ESgI WFar		'Fanciful Whimsy' (IB)	WCAu
	- 'Pleasant Earlybird'	WFar		'Fancy Me This' (Sib)	ERCP WCAu
	- 'Prairie Frost'	NLar		'Fancyancy' (TB)	EWoo

'Fanfaron' (TB)	ESgI
'Fantaisie' (TB)	WCAu
'Farleigh Damson' (SDB)	SIri
'Fashion Lady' (MDB)	CBro
'Fashion Week' (TB) **new**	WCAu
'Fathom' (IB)	WCAu
'Feel the Thunder' (TB)	WCAu
'Feu du Ciel' (TB) ♀H7	ESgI WCAu
'Fiddlin' Around' (TB)	WCAu
'Fidget' (SDB)	WCAu
'Film Festival' (TB)	EPfP EWoo SPeP
'Fingertips' (SDB)	ESgI
'Finola' (Reticulata)	LAma
'Fire and Ice' (TB)	WCAu
'First Interstate' (TB)	ESgI
'First Movement' (TB)	ESgI
'Flammenschwert' (TB)	WCAu
'Flash of Light' (TB)	WCAu
flavescens	EWoo WCAu
'Flecks and Specks' (AB)	WCAu
'Fleece of White' (BB)	WCAu
'Flibbertigibbet' (SDB)	SIri
'Flight of Butterflies' (Sib) ♀H7	CAby CBWd CPud CToG EBee EGren ELan EPfP ESgI EWhm GBin GKin GQue LRHS MArl MHer NBid NBro NGdn SHor SPoG WCAu WCot WFar WGwG WKif
'Flirting Again' (SDB) ♀H7	SIri
'Flora Zenor' (TB)	EWoo
§ 'Florentina' (IB/TB) ♀H6	CBro EWoo MHer NBir NLar SEND SRms WCAu
'Florentine Silk' (TB)	WCAu
'Floridor' (TB)	EWoo
'Flumadiddle' (IB)	CBro
foetidissima ♀H6	Widely available
- from Picos de Europa	WMal
- 'Aurea'	WCAu WCot WFar
- *chinensis*	see *I. foetidissima* var. *citrina*
§ - var. *citrina*	EGren EPPr GAbr GKev LEdu NLar WGwG
- 'Fructu Albo'	WCot
- var. *lutescens*	NSti
- 'Variegata' (v) ♀H6	EWes NBir NPer WCAu
'Fogbound' (TB)	EIri WCAu
'Foggy Dew' (TB)	EGren EPfP EWoo LRHS
'Fond Kiss' (Sib)	CDor WCAu
'For Veronica' (TB)	WCAu
'Forecasting Rain' (SDB)	SIri
'Foreign Legion' (TB)	WCAu
'Foreigner' (TB)	WCAu
'Forest Light' (SDB)	CBro ESgI
'Forever Blue' (SDB)	WCAu
* 'Forever Trevor' (CH)	MWlw
'Forge Fire' (TB)	ESgI
formosana B&SWJ 3076	WCru
forrestii ♀H6	CMac EPfk GKev NBir StAn WAbe WCAu
'Fort Apache' (TB)	EWes EWoo WCAu
'Fortunate Son' (TB)	WCAu
'Fountain of Grace' (TB)	ESgI
'Fourfold Blue' (SpH)	GBin
'Fourfold Lavender' (Sib)	NLar
'Fourfold White' (Sib)	ESgI
'Foxy Lady' (TB)	EWoo
'Framboise' (TB)	LCro LRHS
'Frances Iva' (TB)	EWoo
'Francheville' (TB)	EWoo
'Frank Adams' (TB)	EWoo
'Frank Elder' (Reticulata)	EPot
FRAN'S GOLD ('Jf1' PBR)	LCro
'Frans Hals' (Dut)	NBir
'French Can Can' (TB)	SIri WCAu
'Fresno Calypso' (TB)	ESgI
'Frison-roche' (TB)	ESgI WCAu
'Frisounette' (TB)	ESgI
'Frost and Flame' (TB)	CEnd EBee EGren ELan EWoo LCro LRHS MArl MAsh NBir NLar SPoG WCAu WGwG
'Frosted Angel' (SDB)	CBro
'Frosted Velvet' (MTB)	WCAu
'Frosty Elegance' (IB)	ESgI
'Frosty Jewels' (TB)	ESgI
'Frozen Planet' (Reticulata)	EGren EPfP EPot ERCP GKev LAma LCro
'Full Sun' (Spuria)	EWoo
'Full Tide' (TB)	WCAu
'Full Tilt Boogie' (TB)	WCAu
fulva ♀H5	EAri EGrI EPPr ESgI EWat EWhm MMrt NBir NSti SBrt WCAu WCot
× *fulvala* ♀H5	EWoo NBir NSti
'Funambule' (TB)	EWoo
'Furnaceman' (SDB)	CBro EDAr
'Fuzzy' (MDB)	EPot
'Gai Luron' (TB)	LRHS
'Gallant Moment' (TB)	ESgI
'Game Changer' (TB) **new**	WCAu
'Game Plan' (TB)	WCAu
'Gandalf the Grey' (TB)	ESgI
'Garden Spot' (TB) **new**	WCAu
'Gay Head' (TB)	EWoo
'Gelbe Mantel' (Sino-Sib)	NBir WFar
'Gemstone Walls' (TB)	ESgI
'Gentle Manner' (TB) **new**	WCAu
'George' (Reticulata)	LRHS XFar
'Gerald Darby'	see *I.* × *robusta* 'Gerald Darby'
§ *germanica*	ESgI SEND WCAu WCot WGwG
- RCB AL-B-1	WCot
- var. *florentina*	see *I.* 'Florentina'
§ - 'Nepalensis'	WCAu
- 'The King'	see *I. germanica* 'Nepalensis'
'Ghirardelli Square' (TB) **new**	WCAu
'Ghost Train' (TB)	ESgI EWoo SIri
'Gilt-Edged Bond' (TB)	WCAu
'Ginger Twist' (Sib)	CDor ELon WCAu WHil
'Gingerbread Castle' (TB)	EWoo
'Gingerbread Man' (SDB)	CBro EDAr ESgI GEdr SMrm WCAu
'Girl Like You' (TB) **new**	WCAu
'Girly Girl' (TB)	WCAu
'Givendale' (TB)	EnIr
'Glas-y-Dorlan' (Sib)	MWlw
'Gleaming Gold' (SDB)	EPot NLar
'Glowing Embers' (TB)	ESgI EWoo
'Glowing Seraphin' (TB)	WCAu
'Go for Broke' (TB) **new**	WCAu
'Goddess of Green' (IB)	EWoo
'Godfrey Owen' (TB)	WCAu
'Godinton' (TB)	SIri
'Going My Way' (TB)	ESgI EWoo SBea WCAu
'Gold Country' (TB)	ESgI
'Gold Galore' (TB)	SIri
'Gold Imperial' (TB)	WCot
'Golden Alps' (TB)	SRms WCAu
'Golden Beauty' (SpH)	LAma XFar
'Golden Edge' (Sib)	EPfP GQue LRHS NLar WCAu WFar
'Golden Immortal' (TB)	EWoo WOld
'Golden Panther' (TB)	WCAu
'Golden Violet' (SDB)	ESgI
'Golden Zebra' (TB)	LCro MHol
'Good Looking' (TB)	ESgI WCAu
'Good Show' (TB)	ESgI WCAu

Iris 393

'Goodnight My Dear' (TB) **new**	WCAu		'Here Be Dragons' (Sib)	CDor WCAu
'Goring Butterfly' (SpH)	CBro		'Here Comes the Night' (TB)	WCAu
gormanii	see *I. tenax*		'Here Comes the Sun' (TB)	WCAu
'Gossip' (SDB)	CBro		'Hey True Blue' (TB)	WCAu
'Goudhurst' (SDB)	SIri		'Hidden Innocence' (TB) **new**	WCAu
'Gracchus' (TB)	EWoo WCAu		'High Barbaree' (TB)	EWoo
'Grace and Charm' (BB)	WCAu		'High Blue Sky' (TB)	WCAu
gracilipes 'Alba'	EPot GArf		'High Command' (TB)	WCAu
graminea ♀H6	CBro CMac CSpe EGrI GKev NBir SBrt WCAu WCot		'High Desert' (TB)	WCAu
graminifolia	see *I. kerneriana*		'High Octane' (TB)	WCAu
'Granada Gold' (TB)	SRms		'His Royal Highness' (TB)	WCAu
'Grand Illusion' (Spuria)	EWoo		*histrioides* 'Lady Beatrix Stanley' ♀H7	CBro LAma MNrw NBir WCAu
'Grapetizer' (TB)	WCAu		'Hocus Pocus' (SDB)	ESgI EWoo WGwG
'Great Lakes' (TB)	ESgI EWoo		'Hohe Warte' (Sib) ♀H7	EWoo WCAu
'Grecian Skies' (TB)	ESgI		'Höhenflug' (Sib)	GBin
'Green Eyed Lady' (TB)	ESgI		'Holden Clough' (SpH) ♀H7	CMiW EBee ELan EPfP EPPr EWoo LEdu LRHS MMuc MNrw MWlw NBir NGdn NSti WFar WTre
'Green Jungle' (TB)	EWoo			
'Green Pastures' (TB)	EWoo			
'Green Spot' (SDB) ♀H7	CBro ECha EDAr ESgI NBir NLar WCAu		'Holden's Child' (SpH)	CWat WCAu
'Greensand Way' (TB)	SIri		'Holidaze' (IB) ♀H7	EIri
'Grenade' (TB)	EWoo SIri		'Holy Night' (TB)	SRms
grey-flowered (Sib)	ELon		'Honey Mocha Lotta' (Spuria)	EWoo
'Grooving' (BB)	ESgI			
'Gudrun' (TB)	EWoo		'Honeyplic' (IB) ♀H7	SIri
'Guilt Free Sample' (TB) **new**	WCAu		'Honington' (SDB)	WCAu
			'Honky Tonk Blues' (TB)	ESgI
'Gull's Wing' (Sib)	LRHS MHol NLar NWbg SMrm SPoG		*hoogiana* ♀H5	GKev LAma
			- 'Purpurea'	GKev
'Gussied Up' (TB) **new**	WCAu	§	*hookeri*	EPfk EWoo GArf GBin GEdr GKev GMaP MHol SRms WAbe WCAu WIce
'Gypsy' (TB)	EWoo			
'Gypsy Beauty' (Dut)	ELan LCro			
'Gypsy Lord' (TB)	WCAu		'Hope You Dance' (TB)	WCAu
'Gypsy Queen' (TB)	EWoo		'Horizon Bleu' (TB)	EWoo
'Gypsy Romance' (TB) ♀H7	SIri		'Horned Rosyred' (TB)	EWoo
'Gypsy Tart' (SDB)	SIri	§	'Hornpipe' (TB)	EnIr WCAu
'Habit' (TB)	EWoo WCAu		'Hot' (SDB)	ESgI
halophila	see *I. spuria* subsp. *halophila*		'Hot News' (MTB)	WCAu
'Happenstance' (TB)	WCAu		'Hot Spiced Wine' (TB)	EWoo SIri
'Happy Mood' (IB)	WCAu		'Hot to Trot' (TB)	ESgI
'Harbor Blue' (TB)	EWoo NLar WCAu WTre		'House of Cards' (TB)	WCAu
'Harmonium' (IB)	WCAu		'How Audacious' (Sib)	LCro WCAu
'Harmony' (IB)	CBro NNys		'How Wonderful' (TB) **new**	WCAu
'Harmony' (Reticulata) ♀H7	CAby EGren ELan EPfP EPot ERCP EWoo GKev LAma LCro LRHS NBir WBrk		'Howard Weed' (TB)	EGrI
			'Hubbard' (Sib)	ELon SPoG WFar
		§	*humilis*	LShi WAbe
'Harpswell Happiness' (Sib) ♀H7	EBee ELan ELon		'Huntress' (Sib)	CDor
			'I Feel Good' (TB) ♀H7	WCAu
'Harpswell Haze' (Sib)	ECha		'I See Stars' (TB)	LAma XFar
'Harriette Halloway' (TB)	EPfP EWoo LSRN NLar WCot		'Ice and Indigo' (SDB)	WCAu
'Harry's Choice' (TB)	SIri		'Ice Capades' (TB)	WCAu
'Harvest Home' (BB)	SIri		'Ice Etching' (SDB)	WCAu
'Harvest of Memories' (TB)	ESgI EWoo LRHS SPoG		'Ice Pinnacle' (TB)	EnIr
'Haunted Heart' (TB)	WCAu		'Illini Charm' (Sib)	LEdu WFar
'Having Fun' (Sib)	CDor LAma WCAu		*illyrica*	see *I. pallida*
'Headcorn' (MTB) ♀H7	SIri		'I'm Back' (TB)	WCAu
'Headline Banner' (BB)	WCAu		'Immortality' (TB)	EGren ESgI EWoo MHol SRms WCAu
'Heather Carpet' (SDB)	WCAu			
'Heather Stream' (La)	CAby		'Imperative' (IB)	SIri
'Helen Astor' (Sib)	CDor		'Imperator' (TB)	ELan
'Helen Collingwood' (TB)	ESgI EWoo		'Imperial Bronze' (Spuria)	MNrw WCAu
'Helen Proctor' (IB)	ESgI SIri WCot		'Imperial Opal' (Sib)	NGdn WFar
* 'Helga'	EGrI	I	'Imperial Velvet' (Sib)	WFar
'Hello Darkness' (TB) ♀H7	ESgI EWoo WCAu WCot		'In a Flash' (TB)	WCAu
'Hell's Fire' (TB)	WSpi		'In Full Sail' (Sib)	CDor
'Hen Harrier' (TB) **new**	EnIr		'In Town' (TB)	EWoo
'Henry Sidgwick' (TB)	EnIr		'Indeed' (IB)	ESgI
henryi	GKev WAbe		'Indian Chief' (TB)	ELan ESgI EWoo LCro SEND SHor WCAu
'Her Royal Highness' (TB)	EPfk LCro			

'Indian Hills' (TB)	EWoo
'Indigo Princess' (TB)	EWoo
'Indigo Seas' (TB)	EWoo
'Inferno' (TB)	EWoo
'Infrared' (TB)	WCAu
'Initiative' (TB) **new**	WCAu
'Ink Patterns' (TB)	WCAu
'Innocent Pink' (TB)	ESgI
innominata	GArf NBir NBro SRms WAbe
I — 'Clotted Cream'	EGrI
— 'Peacock'	EGrI
— 'Spinners'	MWlw
— yellow-flowered	NRya
'Insaniac' (TB)	WCAu
'Inside Job' (TB)	WCAu
'Inspired' (TB)	WCAu
'Interpol' (TB)	ESgI WCAu
'Invicta Celebration' (BB)	SIri
'Invicta Daybreak' (IB)	SIri
'Invicta Gold' (SDB)	SIri
'Invicta Reprieve' (IB)	SIri
'Invicta Sapphire' (TB)	SIri
'Irisades' (TB)	ELan LCro SIri
'Irish Chant' (SDB)	WCAu
'Irish Harp' (SDB)	ESgI
'Island Sunset' (TB)	SIri
'Italian Ice' (TB)	EIri
'Italian Velvet' (TB)	WCAu
'It's Amazing' (IB)	WCAu
'Jacquesiana' (TB)	EWoo
'Jaguar Blue' (TB)	EWoo
'Jamie Roo' (TB)	SIri
'Jana White' (MTB)	WCAu
'Jane Phillips' (TB) ♀H7	Widely available
japonica ♀H4	CWal NPer SPlb StAn WFar
— B&SWJ 8921	WCru
— 'Bourne Graceful'	CExl
— 'Eco Easter'	ESwi
— 'Ledger'	CAby CExl CMac NCth SIvy
— 'Rudolph Spring'	EPPr
§ — 'Variegata' (v) ♀H4	CBct ESwi NPer SArc WFar
'Jasper Gem' (MDB)	EPot
'Jazz Band' (TB) **new**	WCAu
'Jazz Festival' (TB)	SIri WCAu
'Jean Cayeux' (TB)	ESgI EWoo
'Jean Guymer' (TB)	ESgI
'Jeanne Price' (TB)	ESgI EWoo WCAu
'Jerry Murphy' (Sib)	ERCP WCAu
'Jesse's Song' (TB)	WCAu
'Jewel Baby' (SDB)	CBro
'Jewels' (SDB)	WCAu
'Jiansada' (SDB)	CBro
'Jill Rosalind' (TB)	EnIr
'Jitterbug' (TB)	WCAu
'Jive' (SDB)	WCAu
'Joanna' (TB)	EWoo NLar
'Joyance' (TB)	EWoo
'Joyce' (Reticulata)	WCAu
'Joyce Cole' (Sib)	WCAu
'Joyful Skies' (TB)	WCAu
'J.S. Dijt' (Reticulata)	CBro EGren EPfP EPot ERCP GKev LAma LCro LRHS MGos NNys
'Jubilation' (TB)	EWoo
'Juliet' (TB)	ESgI
'Jump Start' (IB)	WCAu
'June Prom' (IB)	ESgI NCth
'June Rose' (IB)	LRHS
'Jungle Fires' (TB)	WCAu
'Jungle Shadows' (BB)	ESgI EWoo NBir
'Jurassic Park' (TB)	WCAu
'Just Crazy' (TB) **new**	WCAu
'Just Dance' (IB)	ESgI
'Just Jennifer' (BB)	WCAu
'Kabluey' (Sib)	WFar
'Kaboom' (Sib)	ELan MHol WFar
kaempferi	see *I. ensata*
'Kahuna' (IB)	WCAu
'Katharine Hodgkin' (Reticulata) ♀H7	CAby CBro EBee ECha EGren ELan EPfP EPot ERCP EWoo GKev LAma LCro LRHS MNrw MPie NBir NLar WBrk WCAu WCot WFar XFar
'Katharine's Gold' (Reticulata) ♀H7	CBro EPfP EPot ERCP ETay GKev LAma LCro LRHS WBrk XFar
'Kathleen Milne' (TB)	ESgI
'Katy Petts' (SDB)	ESgI
'Keeper's Cottage' (TB)	SIri
kemaonensis PAB 8473	LEdu
'Kenogami' (Sib)	SBeP
'Kent Compote' (IB)	SIri
'Kent Pride' (TB)	CEnd ECha EGren ELan EPfP ESgI EWoo LBom LCro LRHS NBir NLar SPeP SPoG SRms WCAu WHoo WMal WTor XFar
'Kent Skylark' (IB)	SIri
'Kentish Icon' (SDB)	SIri
'Kentish Lad' (IB)	SIri
'Kentucky Derby' (TB)	ESgI
§ ***kerneriana*** ♀H5	CBro GKev NBir
'Kharput' (IB)	EWoo
'Kildonan' (TB)	EnIr WCAu
'Kimboshi' (SpH)	ELin
'King Christian' (IB)	EWoo
'Kirkstone' (TB)	WCAu
'Kiss of Summer' (TB) ♀H7	ESgI
'Kiss the Girl' (Sib)	WCAu
'Kiss the Night' (TB) **new**	WCAu
'Kissed by the Sun' (TB) **new**	WCAu
'Kissing Circle' (TB)	ESgI
'Kita-no-seiza' (Sib/d)	CBro CDor NGdn WFar
'Kiwi Slices' (SDB)	CWat
'Knick Knack' (MDB)	CBro ELan EPot SPoG
'Kuh-e-Abr' (Reticulata)	GKev LAma
'La Senda' (Spuria)	WCot
§ ***lactea***	EPfk SBrt
lacustris	GKev MWlw WAbe WCot
— 'Captain Collingwood'	see *I. cristata* 'Captain Collingwood'
'Lady Belle' (MTB)	ESgI
'Lady Friend' (TB)	WCAu
'Lady in Red' (SDB)	ESgI WCAu
'Lady of the Night' (BB)	WCAu
'Lady Paramount' (TB)	EWoo
'Lady Vanessa' (Sib)	ELon NSti
laevigata	CLil CoPl CToG CWat ELin NBro NPer SRms WCAu WFar WMAq
— var. ***alba***	CToG SRms
— 'Albopurpurea'	CLil
— 'Colchesterensis'	CLil NGdn NPer WCAu WMAq
I — 'Dorothy'	NGdn
* — 'Elgar'	WMAq
— 'Liam Johns'	CToG
— 'Mottled Beauty'	LCro WCAu
— 'Regal'	CLil
— 'Richard Greaney'	CToG
— 'Rose Queen'	see *I. ensata* 'Rose Queen'
— 'Rowden Full Moon'	CToG
— 'Rowden Starlight'	CToG
I — 'Snowdrift'	CLil CToG ELin EPfk NBir NGdn NPer WCAu WFar WMAq
— 'Variegata' (v) ♀H6	CLil CWat ECha EPfk EWat NBro NGdn NPer WBrk WMAq
— 'Weymouth'	see *I. laevigata* 'Weymouth Blue'
§ — 'Weymouth Blue'	CToG EPfk

§ 'Lake Niklas' (Sib)	ELon MHol
'Langport Chapter' (IB)	ESgI
'Langport Claret' (IB)	ESgI EWoo
'Langport Curlew' (IB)	ESgI
'Langport Duchess' (IB)	ESgI
'Langport Fairy' (IB)	ESgI
'Langport Flame' (IB)	ESgI
'Langport Honey' (IB)	WCAu
'Langport Jane' (IB)	EWoo
'Langport Lord' (IB)	ESgI
'Langport Minstrel' (IB)	ESgI
'Langport Star' (IB)	ESgI EWoo
'Langport Storm' (IB)	CFis CWnw ESgI LRHS WTor
'Langport Sun' (IB)	ESgI
'Langport Violet' (IB)	ESgI
'Langport Warrior' (IB)	WCAu
'Langport Wren' (IB) ♀H7	CBro CFis EGren EPfP ESgI EWoo LRHS MBel NBir NGdn WKif WTor WTre
'Lark Ascending' (TB)	WCAu
'Late Hours' (TB)	WCAu
§ *latifolia*	EGrI
- 'Isabella'	ESwi
- 'King of the Blues'	WCAu
- 'Montblanc'	WCAu
'Latin Lark' (TB)	ESgI
'Latino' (IB)	WCAu
'Laura Louise' (La)	CAby EAri
'Lavandulacea' (TB)	EWoo
'Lavender Landscape' (SpH)	WCAu
lazica ♀H5	CBct CBro CMac EBee ELan EPot EPPr EWoo LRHS NBir NCth NSti SBrt SEND SPlb SRms WGwG
- 'Joy Bishop'	EWoo
- 'Primrose Upward'	WCot
* - 'Richard Nutt'	WCot
'Legato' (TB)	ESgI
'Lemon Flare' (SDB)	SRms
'Lemon Ice' (TB)	ECha ESgI EWoo LRHS SPoG WGwG WHoo
'Lemon Pop' (IB)	WCAu
'Lemon Puff' (MDB)	CBro WCAu
'Lemon Tree' (TB)	WCAu
'Lemon Veil' (Sib)	NLar WCAu
'Lena' (SDB)	CBro
'Lent A. Williamson' (TB)	EWoo
'Lenzschnee' (TB)	EWoo
'Leo Hewitt' (Sib)	ELon
leptophylla	GKev
'Let's Elope' (IB)	WCAu
'Light Cavalry' (IB)	ESgI EWoo
'Light Laughter' (IB)	WCAu
'Light of Heart' (Sib) **new**	WCAu
'Light Rebuff' (TB)	EWoo
'Lilac Hymn' (TB)	ESgI
* 'Lilac Times'	EWoo
'Lilli-white' (SDB)	CMHG ESgI GEdr LRHS SPoG WCAu WGwG
'Lime Soda' (TB)	EnIr
'Limeheart' (Sib)	WHoo
'Limelight' (TB)	SRms
'Lion King' (Dut) ♀H6	GKev LAma LCro WCAu XFar
'Little Blackfoot' (SDB)	WCAu WCot
'Little Blue-eyes' (SDB)	ESgI WCAu
'Little Bluets' (SDB)	ESgI
'Little Chestnut' (SDB)	WMal
'Little Episode' (SDB)	CBro EDar
'Little Rosy Wings' (SDB)	CBro EDar
'Little Sapphire' (SDB)	WCAu
'Little Shadow' (IB)	SRms WCAu
'Little Sheba' (AB)	WCAu
'Little Showoff' (SDB)	ESgI
'Little Twinkle Star' (Sib)	WFar
'Living Waters' (TB)	ESgI
'Local Color' (IB)	ESgI SIri WCAu
'Local Hero' (IB)	WCAu
'Lodore' (TB)	SRms
'Lohengrin' (TB)	EWoo
'Lollipop' (SDB)	ESgI
'London Pride' (TB)	EWoo
longipetala	EPPr NBir
'Loop the Loop' (TB)	CMac LCro SPoG SRms WCAu XFar
'Loose Valley' (MTB) ♀H7	SIri
'Loppio' (IB)	EWoo
'Lord Warden' (TB)	CEnd EGren LRHS SHor WCAu WGwG
'Loreley' (TB)	EWoo
'Lorilee' (TB)	ESgI
'Lost in Love' (TB)	WCAu
'Lottie Lou' (TB)	SIri
'Lotus Land' (TB)	WCAu
'Loud Music' (TB)	WCAu
'Louise' (Reticulata) **new**	XFar
'Louvois' (TB)	ESgI EWoo NLar
'Love the Sun' (TB)	ESgI
'Lovely Again' (TB)	EGren WCAu
'Lovely Leilani' (TB)	ESgI
'Lovely Light' (TB)	WCAu
'Lovely Señorita' (TB)	WCAu
'Love's Tune' (TB)	EPfP WTor
'Low Ho Silver' (IB)	WCAu
'Lucky Devil' (Spuria) ♀H7	WCAu
'Lugano' (TB)	EWoo
'Lullingstone Castle' (Kent Castles Series) (IB)	SIri
'Lune et Soleil' (TB)	CTsd ELan LCro LRHS
lutescens ♀H7	EPot GArf GKev WAbe
§ - 'Campbellii'	GArf
- subsp. *lutescens*	GEdr
- subsp. *subbiflora*	WAbe
'Luxuriant' (TB) **new**	WCAu
'Lyrique' (BB)	WCAu
maackii	MCtn
'Mabel Coday' (Sib)	ELon WCAu
'Madame Lynn' (Spuria)	EWoo
'Madeira Belle' (TB)	EGren EPfP ESgI EWoo LRHS LSRN WCAu WTor
'Mady Carriere' (TB)	EWoo
'Magharee' (TB)	ESgI
'Magic Masquerade' (TB)	WCAu
'Magic Ring' (TB) **new**	WCAu
'Magical Encounter' (TB)	EWoo WCAu
'Magneto' (SDB)	WCAu
magnifica ♀H5	GKev LAma
'Mahogany Lord' (Spuria)	WCAu
'Maid of Orange' (BB)	LCro WCAu
'Maisie Lowe' (TB)	ESgI EWoo
'Majestic Ruler' (TB)	WCAu
'Makin' Good Time' (TB)	WCAu
I 'Mandarin' (TB)	ESgI
'Mango Entree' (TB)	WCAu
'Mango Smoothy' (BB)	ESgI
'Marcel Turbat' (TB)	WCAu
'Marcus Perry' (Sib)	CToG
'Margin Call' (TB)	WCAu
'Margot Holmes' (Cal-Sib)	WFar
'Marilyn Holmes' (Sib)	WCot
'Mariposa Autumn' (TB)	EWoo SIri WOld
'Marital Bliss' (TB) **new**	WCAu
'Marjorie' (TB)	SRms
'Marron Chaud' (TB) **new**	WCAu
'Marry the Night' (TB)	WCAu

'Martyn Rix'	see *I. confusa* 'Martyn Rix'	'Mission Bay' (Sib)	LAma NBir WCAu
'Mary Frances' (TB)	WCAu	'Mission Ridge' (TB)	MHol
'Mary Geddes' (TB)	EWoo	'Mission Sunset' (TB)	WCAu
'Mary McIlroy' (SDB) ♀H7	CBro	'Missouri Autumn' (Spuria)	WCAu
'Marybill' (TB)	SIri	***missouriensis***	CMac EPPr
'Material Girl' (TB)	WCAu	'Mme Chéreau' (TB)	EWoo
'Matinata' (TB)	ELan	'Momaguin' (TB)	NLar
'Matt McNames' (TB)	EWoo	'Money in Your Pocket' (TB)	WCAu
'Mattie Gates' (TB)	EWoo		
'Maui Moonlight' (IB) ♀H7	EIri ESgI NLar WCAu	'Monsieur-Monsieur' (TB)	ESgI
'May Allison' (TB)	EWoo	Monspur Group	WCot
'Meadow Court' (SDB)	CBro GEdr WCAu	'Montecito' (Dut)	CBro
'Medallion' (Spuria)	EWoo	'Montmartre' (TB)	WCAu
'Media Luz' (Spuria)	WCAu WCot	'Moon Journey' (TB)	EWoo
'Medici Prince' (TB)	WCAu	'Moon Silk' (Sib)	CBro EGren ELon EWes WFar
'Medway Valley' (MTB) ♀H7	SIri	'Moonlight Waves'	see *I. ensata* 'Moonlight Waves'
'Megglethorp' (IB)	WCAu	'Moonlit Water' (TB)	WCAu
'Melbreak' (TB)	WCAu	'Morning World' (TB)	WCAu
mellita	see *I. suaveolens*	'Morwenna' (TB) ♀H7	ESgI
'Melon Honey' (SDB)	WCAu	'Mother Earth' (TB)	ESgI
'Melted Butter' (TB)	WCAu	'Mount Everest' (TB)	LCro
§ 'Melton Red Flare' (Sib)	CFis EBee EGren ESgI EWoo GAbr LRHS MArl NBir	'Mountain Lake' (Sib)	EBee ESgI LRHS WFar WSpi
		'Mr Moonlight' (TB)	WCAu
'Memphis Memory' (Sib)	ELan ELon MHol NLar WFar	'Mrs Alan Gray' (TB)	EWoo
'Men are from Mars' (TB)	WCAu	'Mrs Horace Darwin' (TB)	EWoo NLar
'Men in Black' (TB)	WCAu	'Mrs Nate Rudolph' (SDB)	WCAu
'Mendacity' (TB) **new**	WCAu	'Mrs Rowe' (Sib)	CToG ELon ESgI WCAu WFar
'Mer du Sud' (TB) ♀H7	CEnd ECha EGren EPfP ESgI LCro LRHS LSRN WCot	'Muggles' (SDB)	SIri
		'Murder Mystery' (TB)	WCAu
'Merchant Marine' (TB)	WCAu	'Music' (SDB)	SIri
* 'Merebrook Blue Lagoon' (La)	WMAq	'Music Maker' (TB)	EGrI
		'Mustard Falls' (SDB)	EDAr
'Merebrook Jemma J' (La)	WMAq	'My Honeycomb' (TB)	WCAu
'Merebrook Purpla' (La)	WMAq	'My Kayla' (SDB)	ESgI
'Merebrook Rum 'n' Raisin' (La)	WMAq	'My Seedling' (MDB)	CBro
		'Mysterieux' (TB)	SIri
* 'Merebrook Rusty Red' (La)	WMAq	'Mystic Art' (TB)	WCAu
'Merebrook Sunata' (La)	WMAq	'Mystic Beauty' (Dut)	GKev LAma LCro
'Merebrook Sunnyside Up' (La)	WMAq	***mzchetica***	EPPr
		'Nada' (SpH)	WCot
'Merebrook Symphony' (La)	WMAq	'Name Game' (TB) **new**	WCAu
		'Nancy Hardy' (MDB)	CBro
'Merlot' (TB)	ESgI	'Naples' (TB)	SIri
'Mesa Pearl' (Sib)	CDor	'Nassak' (TB)	EWoo
'Mescal' (TB)	WCAu	'Natascha' (Reticulata)	EGren EPot GKev LAma
mesopotamica	see *I. germanica*	'Natchez Trace' (TB)	LCro LRHS NLar
'Metolius Blues' (TB)	CWnw ELan LCro	'Navajo Jewel' (TB)	WCAu
'Mexicana' (TB)	EWoo	'Needlepoint' (TB)	ESgI
'Miami Beach' (TB)	WCAu	'Neglecta' (TB)	EWoo
'Michael Paul' (SDB) ♀H7	EAri EGrI	'Negra Modelo' (SDB) **new**	WCAu
'Mickey Gold' (Dut)	GKev LAma	'Neige de Mai' (TB)	ESgI
'Mickey Ocean' (Dut)	GKev LAma	* 'Nel Jupe' (TB)	NLar
'Mickey Sea' (Dut)	LAma	'Nelly Tardivier' (TB) **new**	WCAu
'Midhurst White' (TB)	SIri	***nepalensis***	see *I. decora*
'Midnight Caller' (TB)	ESgI EWoo	'Nestucca Rapids' (TB) **new**	WCAu
'Midnight Majesty' (TB)	EWoo	'New Face' (TB)	WCAu
'Midnight Oil' (TB)	WCAu	'New Idea' (MTB)	CBro ESgI WCAu
'Midnight Treat' (TB)	WCAu	'New Leaf' (TB)	WCAu
'Midsummer Night's Dream' (IB)	ESgI	'Next in Line' (TB)	EWoo
		'Nibelungen' (TB)	CBro ELan EPfP WCAu
'Midsummer Nightsong' (TB)	ESgI	'Nickel' (IB)	WCAu
		'Night Edition' (TB)	ESgI
'Miles Ahead' (TB)	CTsd CWnw ELan	'Night Owl' (TB)	EBee EGrI ESgI LRHS
milesii ♀H3	CExl GKev NBir	'Night Ruler' (TB)	WCAu
'Millennium Falcon' (TB)	SIri	'Night Whispers' (TB)	WCAu
'Millennium Sunrise' (TB)	WCAu	'Nightfall' (TB)	EBee NLar
'Mini-Agnes' (SDB)	CBro EDAr	'Nights of Gladness' (TB)	ESgI
'Minidragon' (SDB)	EPot	'Niklas Sea'	see *I.* 'Lake Niklas'
'Minisa' (TB)	ESgI	'Ninja Turtles' (SDB)	SIri
'Minnie Colquitt' (TB)	WCAu	'No Restraint' (IB)	WCAu
'Miss Apple' (Sib)	GAbr LAma NLar SBeP WCAu	'Noble Gesture' (TB) **new**	WCAu

Iris

'Noctambule' (TB) ♧H7	EWoo SIri WCAu
'Noon Siesta' (TB)	ESgI
'Nora Distin' (Sib)	WCAu
'Nordica' (TB)	WCAu
× *norrisii*	EPfP LRHS MCtn
- KIBA GIANTS (mixed)	EAri
'North Downs' (BB)	SIri
'North Star' (Reticulata)	EPot ERCP XFar
'Not Quite White' (Sib)	LAma
'Nuit Blanche' (TB)	ESgI
'Oblivion' (IB)	WCAu
'Obsidian' (TB)	WCAu
'Ochre Doll' (SDB)	CBro
ochroleuca	see *I. orientalis* Mill.
'October' (TB)	ESgI
'October Sun' (TB)	ELan
'Odin' (TB)	EWoo
'Oh So Cool' (MTB)	ESgI
'Okagami' (SpH)	CBen
'Oklahoma' (TB)	EWoo
'Ola Kalá' (TB)	EBee EHeP ESgI EWoo GMaP LRHS MGos NLar SEND SMrm WCAu
'Old Black Magic' (TB)	ESgI
old Dutch, bearded	SMHy
'Old Hall' (TB)	EnIr
'Old School' (TB) **new**	WCAu
'Old Vienna' (TB)	EWoo
'Olympiad' (TB)	ESgI
'Olympic Challenge' (TB)	ESgI
'Olympic Torch' (TB)	WCAu
'Ombre' (TB)	ESgI
'Ominous Stranger' (TB)	ESgI WCAu
'On Deck' (TB)	WCAu
'On the Move' (TB) **new**	WCAu
'On Thin Ice' (TB)	WCAu
'Once upon a Time' (TB) **new**	WCAu
'One of a Kind' (TB) **new**	WCAu
'Opposing Forces' (TB)	WCAu
'Orageux' (IB)	ESgI WMal
'Orange Caper' (SDB)	CMac ESgI WCot
'Orange Glow' (TB)	GKev
'Orange Glow' (Reticulata)	LAma
'Orange Harvest' (TB)	ESgI
'Orange Jubilee' (TB)	ESgI
'Orange Queen' (MDB)	XFar
'Orchardist' (TB)	WCAu
orchioides misapplied	see *I. bucharica* Foster
'Oregon Skies' (TB)	ESgI WCAu
'Oriental Glory' (TB)	WCAu
orientalis ambig.	ELan EWes MNrw
§ *orientalis* Mill. ♧H6	EPPr MMuc NLar WCot WCru
'Orinoco Flow' (BB) ♧H7	ESgI WCAu
'Orloff' (TB)	ESgI
'Orville Fay' (Sib)	MWlw WCot
'Ottawa' (Sib)	CToG CWat WFar
'Out of the Dark' (TB)	WCAu
'Out Walkin'' (TB)	WCAu
'Out Yonder' (TB)	WCAu
'Outer Edge' (IB)	WCAu
'Outspoken' (SDB)	WCAu
'Overshadowed' (TB) **new**	WCAu
'Owyhee Desert' (TB)	WCAu
'Oxford Countess' (TB)	WCAu
Pacific Coast hybrids	see *I.* Californian hybrids
'Pacific Mist' (TB)	WCAu
'Pacific Panorama' (TB)	ESgI
'Pagan Dance' (TB)	EWoo WCAu
'Pagan Goddess' (TB)	EWoo
I 'Pageant' (Sib)	WCot WFar
'Pageant' (TB)	WFar
'Paint It Black' (TB)	EWoo
'Painted Lady' (Reticulata)	CBro EGren EPot ERCP GKev LAma LCro LRHS XFar
'Painted Woman' (Sib)	CDor EPfP NWbg WHil
§ *pallida*	CBro CFis CMac EWoo GMaP SEND SRms WCAu
§ - 'Argentea Variegata' (TB/v)	CEnd CMac EBee ECha EGren EPfP EWoo GMaP LBar LRHS LSou MAsh MBrN MHol NBir NLar NSti SPoG SRms WCAu WCot WHoo WMal WTor WTre
- 'Aurea'	see *I. pallida* 'Variegata' hort.
- 'Aurea Variegata'	see *I. pallida* 'Variegata' hort.
- subsp. *cengialti*	GKev
- var. *dalmatica*	see *I. pallida* subsp. *pallida*
§ - subsp. *pallida*	CCBP EBee ECha EGren ELan EPfP LRHS SHar
- 'Variegata' misapplied	see *I. pallida* 'Argentea Variegata'
§ - 'Variegata' hort. (v) ♧H7	CBcs CBro CEnd CMac CSde CWat ECha EGren ELan EPfP LRHS MAsh MHol SPlb SPoG SRms WCAu WMal
'Pansy Purple' (Sib)	LEdu MNrw
'Panther' (SDB)	WCAu
'Panther' (Dut)	ERCP
'Papillon' (Sib)	CBWd EBee EGren ELan ELon ESgI EWes EWoo LRHS MArl NBir NGdn NSti SHor WCAu WFar
'Paprikash' (Sib)	EMor ERCP SBeP WCAu XFar
'Parable' (AB) **new**	WCAu
'Paradise' (TB)	NLar
'Paradise Park' (TB)	ESgI
'Parisian Dawn' (TB)	WCAu
'Parisien' (TB)	WCAu
'Park Avenue' (TB)	GKev LAma
'Parting Glances' (IB)	WCAu
'Party Dress' (TB)	CMac EBee EGren ELan ESgI MArl NBir NLar SPoG SRms WTor
'Party's Over' (TB)	WCAu
'Patches' (TB)	ESgI
'Patchwork Puzzle' (TB) **new**	WCAu
'Patina' (TB)	EWoo WCAu
'Patterdale' (TB)	NBir
'Pauline' (Reticulata)	EGren EPot ERCP EWoo GKev LAma LCro LRHS
'Pauline' (TB)	CBro EGrI LCro
'Pause' (SDB)	WCAu
'Peach Eyes' (SDB)	CBro EDAr
'Peach Picotee' (TB)	ESgI
'Pearls of Autumn' (TB)	WCAu
'Peile Hall' (TB)	EnIr
'Penguin Party' (TB)	WCAu
'Penny a Pinch' (TB)	NLar
'Pennywhistle' (Sib)	ELon NLar
'Percheron' (Sib)	SHor
'Perfect Interlude' (TB)	EIri
'Performer' (MTB)	EIri
'Perry's Blue' (Sib)	CBcs CMac CMiW CTsd CWat EHeP EPfP EWoo GKin GMaP LCro LRHS LSto MBel MGos MHol NBir NGdn NPer SHor SRms WFar
I 'Perry's Favourite' (Sib)	CToG
'Perry's Pigmy' (Sib)	ELon
'Persan' (TB)	EWoo
'Persimmon' misapplied	see *I.* 'Tycoon'
'Persimmon' ambig. (Sib)	CAby CDor GKin GQue WFar WGwG
'Peter Hewitt' (Sib) ♧H7	MAvo WCAu WMal
'Petit Tigre' (IB)	SIri WCAu
'Petite Monet' (MTB)	ESgI
'Petite Polka' (SDB)	CWat NLar
'Petticoat Shuffle' (TB)	WCAu

Iris

'Pharaoh's Daughter' (IB) — EWoo
'Philippa Hobart' (TB) **new** — EnIr
'Photo Shoot' (TB) **new** — WCAu
'Picasso' (Dut) — ERCP
'Pinewood Charmer' (CH) — CElw
'Pinewood Sunshine' (CH) — MAvo
'Pink Attraction' (TB) — ESgI
'Pink Bubbles' (BB) — WCAu
'Pink Charm' (TB) — ELan LRHS MHer SPlb SPoG WTor
'Pink Lavender' (TB) — SRms
'Pink Panther' (SDB) — GKev LAma SPeP XFar
'Pink Parfait' (Sib) — MBNS NBir NGdn WFar WTor
'Pink Pele' (IB) — ESgI
'Pink Pinafore' (TB) — EWoo
'Pink Reprise' (BB) — EWoo
'Pinnacle' (TB) — EWoo WCAu
'Pipes of Pan' (TB) — ESgI WCAu
'Pirate Ahoy' (TB) — WCAu
'Pirate Prince' (Sib) — NPer
'Pirate's Quest' (TB) — LRHS MHer NCth
'Pixie' (DB) — GKev LCro NNys WCAu
'Pixie' (Reticulata) ♀H7 — ELan EPot ERCP LAma LRHS
'Play with Fire' (TB) — EWoo
'Pleasures of May' (Sib) — ELon WCAu
§ 'Plicata' (TB) **new** — WCAu
'Poem of Ecstasy' (TB) — WCAu
'Pogo' (SDB) — CMac EWoo MHer NBir NLar SMrm SRms WGwG
'Polar Ice' (Reticulata) — EGren
'Polar Ice' (TB) — EPot ERCP GKev LAma
'Polvere di Stelle' (TB) — ESgI
'Pop Culture' (TB) — WCAu
'Popped White' (TB) — WCAu
'Port of Call' (Spuria) — EWoo
'Power Point' (TB) — WCAu
'Prank' (SDB) — WCAu
'Pretender' (TB) — WCAu
'Pretty Please' (TB) — ESgI
'Pretty Polly' (Sib) — CDor
'Primrose Cream' (Sib) — WCot
'Primrose Drift' (TB) — ESgI
'Prince of Burgundy' (IB) — ESgI LRHS WCAu
'Prince Victor' (TB) — EWoo
'Princess Beatrice' (TB) — WCAu
'Princess Bride' (BB) ♀H7 — WCAu
'Princesse Caroline de Monaco' (TB) — WCAu
prismatica — GArf GKev SBrt
'Private Eye' (TB) — WCAu
'Private Treasure' (TB) — WCAu
'Project Runway' (TB) — WCAu
'Prosper Laugier' (TB) — SEND WCAu
'Proud Tradition' (TB) — SIri WCAu
'Provençal' (TB) — ESgI WCAu
'Prussian Blue' (Sib) ♀H7 — ESgI SPel
pseudacorus — Widely available
- B&SWJ 5018 from Japan — WCru
- 'Alba' — CoPl CPud EPfk NBid NGdn SRms
- var. *bastardii* — CoPl CToG CWat ECha EGrI ELon EPfk GBin LCro NPer WCAu WFar
- cream-flowered — CAby NBir
- 'Crème de la Crème' — ELon EPfk NLar NSti WCAu WFar
- 'Esk' — EPPr
- 'Flore Pleno' (d) — CToG ELin EWat NLar NPer SRms WBrk WCAu WCot WFar
- 'Gigantea' — CToG
- 'Golden Queen' — EWat
- 'Krill' — CDor
- 'Roccapina' — GBin
- 'Rowden Brimstone' — CToG
- 'Roy Davidson' ♀H7 — CLil CToG NLar WCot WFar

- 'Spartacus' — EBee
- 'Sulphur Queen' — NLar WCot
- 'Sun Cascade' — GBin
- 'Turnipseed' — WCot
- 'Variegata' (v) ♀H7 — Widely available
'Puddy Tat' (SDB) — WCAu
pumila — EDAr EGrI
- JJA 199590 — EPot
- f. *atroviolacea* — EWoo WAbe
- 'Nicola' — EDAr
- 'Violacea' (MDB) — SRms
- yellow-flowered — EDAr WAbe
'Pure As Gold' (TB) — ESgI WCot
'Purple Gem' (Reticulata) — EGren EPfP
'Purple Hill' (Reticulata) — CBro ETay
'Purple Pleasure' — see *I.* 'Sibtosa Ruffles'
'Purple Sensation' (Dut) — LCro
'Purple Study' (MTB) — WCAu
I 'Purplelicious' (Sib) **new** — XFar
'Pussycat Pink' (SDB) — ESgI WCAu
'Quaker Lady' (TB) — ESgI EWoo NCth WCAu
'Quark' (SDB) — CBro
'Quartzlight' (SDB) — EIri
'Quechee' (TB) — CEnd EPfP EPPr ESgI EWoo GMaP LBuc LRHS NLar SPoG WGwG WTor
'Queen Flavia' (IB) — EWoo
'Queen in Calico' (TB) — ESgI
'Queen of Angels' (TB) — WCAu
'Queen of May' (TB) — EWoo
'Queen of the Mist' (TB) — WCAu
'Queen's Circle' (TB) ♀H7 — WCAu
'Rabbit's Foot' (SDB) — SIri
'Ragtime' (TB) — WCAu
'Rain Dance' (SDB) ♀H7 — ESgI
'Rainbow Rim' (SDB) — ESgI WCAu
'Raindrops Keep Falling' (TB) **new** — WCAu
'Rajah' (TB) — CEnd EBee EGren ELan ESgI EWoo GBin GMaP LRHS LSRN MArl MHer SBea SEND SPoG WCAu WGwG WHoo WSpi WTor
'Rambunctious' (Sib) — CDor
'Rameses' (TB) — ESgI EWoo
'Ranman' (Sib) — CDor
'Rare Edition' (IB) — LRHS NBir
'Rarer than Rubies' (TB) — WCAu
'Raspberry Acres' (IB) — WCAu
'Raspberry Blush' (IB) ♀H7 — CMHG EBee ECha EGrI EPfP ESgI EWoo LRHS NBir NCth SBea WCAu WGwG WHoo WTor
'Raven Girl' (TB) — WCAu
'Re La Blanche' (TB) — SIri
'Realm' (TB) — EWoo
'Rebecca Perret' (TB) — WCAu
'Rebellion' (TB) — EWoo
'Reckless Abandon' (TB) — WCAu
'Recurring Delight' (TB) — WCAu
'Red Dazzler' (La) — CSde
'Red Ember' (Dut) — EPfP ERCP ETay GKev LAma LCro SPeP XFar
'Red Enigma' (TB) — SIri
'Red Flare' (Sib) — see *I.* 'Melton Red Flare'
'Red Flare' (TB) — WFar
'Red Flash' (TB) — ESgI WCAu
'Red Heart' (SDB) — ESgI
'Red Kite' (TB) — EnIr
'Red Orchid' (IB) — EWoo SRms WCAu
'Red Pike'[PBR] (TB) — EnIr
'Red Revival' (TB) — WCAu
'Red Zinger' (IB) — CMac EWoo XFar

Iris

'Reddy or Not' (Sib) — WOld
'Redeemer's Crimson' (TB) — ESgI
'Redflare' — see *I.* 'Melton Red Flare'
'Reel Cute' (Sib) — ELon WCAu
'Reflections of Love' (TB) — WCAu
'Regal Surprise' (SpH) ♀H7 — CToG EWat SBrt
'Regard Sombre' (TB) — SIri
'Regards' (SDB) — CBro EDAr
'Regency Belle' (Sib) ♀H7 — NLar
'Regency Buck' (Sib) — WFar WOld
§ *reichenbachii* — EDAr GKev LShi WAbe
'Rejoice' (Reticulata) — EPot ERCP GKev
'Remembering Vic' (Spuria) — EWoo
'Renown' (TB) — EWoo
'Respectable' (Spuria) **new** — WCAu
reticulata — EGren ELan ETay GKev LAma LRHS NNys XFar
- var. *bakeriana* — GKev LAma
'Réussite' (TB) — EWoo
'Rhapsody' (Reticulata) — LAma
'Rheinfels' (TB) — EWoo
'Rheingauperle' (TB) — ESgI
'Rhinelander' (TB) — SIri WCAu
'Rigamarole' (Sib) — EGrI WFar
'Right Royal' (TB) — WCAu
'Rikugi-sakura' (Sib) — NLar WCot
'Rimfire' (TB) — MHol
'Ringo' (TB) — EGrI
'Rio' (TB) **new** — WCAu
'Rio Rojo' (TB) — WCAu
'Rip City' (TB) — ESgI EWoo
'Risk Taker' (TB) **new** — WCAu
'Rive Gauche' (TB) — ESgI
'Riveting' (SDB) — WCAu
'Roanoke's Choice' (Sib) — CBro CElw ELon MNrw WFar
'Roaring Jelly' (Sib) — CDor NLar WCAu WCot
§ × *robusta* 'Dark Aura' ♀H7 — EBee EBlo EWoo LBar LCro LRHS MAvo MWlw MWts SNoN SPel WCAu WCot WMal
§ - 'Gerald Darby' — Widely available
- 'Mountain Brook' — CToG
- 'Nutfield Blue' — CToG
'Robusto' (TB) — LRHS
'Rochester Castle' (Kent Castles Series) (IB) — SIri
§ 'Rocket' (TB) — EBee ESgI GMaP LBuc LRHS LSou MArl NBir
'Rococo' (TB) — WCAu
'Roger Perry' (Sib) — CToG
'Roku Oji' (Sib) — CDor
'Romance' (TB) — EWoo
'Romantic Evening' (TB) — EIri WCAu
'Romney Marsh' (IB) — SIri
'Rosace' (Sib) — EWoo
'Rosalie Figge' (TB) — CMac ESgI MHol WCAu WCot
'Rose de Perse' (TB) — CWnw ELan
'Rose Queen' — see *I. ensata* 'Rose Queen'
'Rose Quest' (Sib) — ESgI
'Rose-Marie' (TB) — EWoo
'Rosette Wine' (TB) — ESgI
'Rosselline' (Sib) — MAvo
'Rosy Bows' (Sib) — WCAu WFar
'Rosy Veil' (TB) — ESgI
'Rosy Wings' (TB) — ESgI EWoo
'Rouge Gorge' (TB) — SIri
'Royal' (IB) — EWoo
I 'Royal Blue' (Sib) — ECha
'Royal Contrast' (SDB) — WCAu
'Royal Satin' (TB) — XFar
'Royal Snowcap' (TB) — WCAu
'Roy's Repeater' (SpH) — ELon WCAu
'Ruby Chimes' (IB) — ESgI WCAu
'Ruby Contrast' (SDB) — WCAu
'Ruby Eruption' (SDB) — EIri ESgI WCAu
'Ruby Morn' (TB) — WCAu
'Ruby Wine' (Sib) — NLar
rudskyi — see *I. variegata*
'Ruffled Velvet' (Sib) ♀H7 — CBcs CDor CElw CTsd ELan EPfP GBin GMaP LBom LCro LRHS LSto NLar SPeP WCAu WFar
'Ruffles and Flourishes' (Sib) — WCAu
'Rumor Has It' (TB) — WCAu
'Rustle of Spring' (TB) — WCAu
'Rustler' (TB) — WCAu
'Ruth Rowlands' (TB) — ESgI EWoo
ruthenica — GArf
- var. *nana* — CExl GEdr GKev
'Sable' (TB) — EBee ELan EPfP ESgI EWoo GMaP LRHS LSou LSRN MArl NLar SEND SHar WCAu WGwG
'Sable Night' (TB) — ESgI LCro
'Safari Sunset' (TB) — WCAu
'Sahara' (TB) — EWoo
'Saint Crispin' (TB) — EWoo GMaP SPoG WGwG
'Salamander Crossing' (Sib) ♀H7 — CBro WCAu
'Salonique' (TB) — EWoo NLar
'Saltwood Castle' (Kent Castles Series) (IB) — SIri
'Salvatore' (IB) — LAma
'Salzburg Echo' (TB) — WCAu
'Sam Carne' (TB) — WCAu
'San Francisco' (TB) — ESgI EWoo
'Sanctification' (TB) ♀H7 — ESgI
'Sanderling' (TB) **new** — EnIr
'Sandy Caper' (IB) — WCAu
'Sangone' (IB) — ESgI
'Sangreal' (IB) — EWoo
sanguinea 'Snow Queen' — CBcs CToG CTsd EGren EGrI ELan GQue NQui WCAu WFar
'Sanskrit' (IB) **new** — WCAu
'Sapphire Gem' (SDB) — ESgI WCAu
'Sapphire Hills' (TB) — WCAu
'Sarah Taylor' (SDB) ♀H7 — WCAu
'Sarah Tiffney' (Sib) — WCAu
'Sasha Borisovich' (Sib) — ESgI
'Saturn' (TB) — WCAu
'Saturnus' (AB) — GKev LAma
'Savoir Faire' (Sib) — ECha
'Scent of Chocolate' (AB) — WMal
'Scent Sational' (Reticulata) — EPot ERCP
'Scented Wonder' (TB) — WCAu
schachtii — GArf
- purple-flowered — GArf WAbe
'Schoolboy Heart' (TB) **new** — WCAu
'Scramble' (Sib) — ECha WCAu WCot WFar WOld
'Scribe' (MDB) — NBir
'Sea Breeze' (Reticulata) — EPot ERCP XFar
'Sea Fret' (SDB) — CBro
'Sea Gull' (TB) — EWoo
'Sea of Love' (TB) **new** — WCAu
'Sea Shadows' (Sib) — EGrI NBir
'Seakist' (TB) — WCAu
'Second Wind' (Sib) — EWoo WCAu
'Secret Affair' (TB) — WCAu
'Secret Service' (TB) — WCAu
'Semola' (SDB) — ESgI
'Senlac' (TB) — ELan EWoo NLar
'Séraphita' (TB) — EWoo
serbica — see *I. reichenbachii*
setosa ♀H7 — CMac EGrI EPot EPPr GKev LCro LRHS LShi MWlw WCAu WFar

- var. *arctica*	GKev LEdu	'Snugglebug' (SDB)	WCAu
I - 'Baby Blue'	ELin EPfP LCro LRHS MPri	'So Van Gogh' (Sib)	WCAu
- subsp. *canadensis*	see *I. hookeri*	'Social Event' (TB)	ESgI
- var. *nana*	see *I. hookeri*	'Soft Blue' (Sib) ♀H7	ELon NLar WCAu
'Shadow Cast' (IB)	WCAu	'Solar Fusion' (Spuria)	EWoo
'Shah Jehan' (TB)	EWoo	'Song of Norway' (TB)	ESgI EWoo
'Shaker's Prayer' (Sib) ♀H7	ELon LAma WCAu	*sophenensis*	GKev LAma
'Shall We Dance' (Sib) ♀H7	CDor	'Sopra il Vulcano' (BB)	ESgI
'Shampoo' (IB)	EWoo WCAu	'Sorbonne' (TB)	WCAu
'Share the Spirit' (TB)	WCAu	'Sordid Lives' (TB)	WCAu
'Sharp Dressed Man' (TB)	CTsd CWnw ELan WCAu	'Sostenique' (TB)	ESgI
'Sharp Edge' (TB) **new**	WCAu	'Southcombe White' (Sib)	SMHy
'Sharrie Carrie' (TB)	SIri	'Southland' (IB)	EWoo
'Sheila Ann Germaney' (Reticulata)	CBro EPot ERCP ETay GKev LAma WBrk WCAu	'Souvenir de Madame Gaudichau' (TB)	ESgI EWoo
'Shekinah' (TB)	EWoo	'Sparkling Rose' (Sib)	Widely available
'Sherbert' (TB)	EWoo	'Spartan' (TB)	EWoo
'Sherbet Lemon' (IB) ♀H7	WCAu	I 'Speckles' (Sib)	EPPr
'Sherwood Pink' (TB)	EnIr	'Speeding Star' (Spuria)	WCAu
'Shirley Chandler' (IB) ♀H7	SIri	'Spellbreaker' (TB)	WCAu
'Shirley Pope' (Sib) ♀H7	LRHS NLar NSti SHor WFar WSpi	'Spice Lord' (TB)	WCAu
'Shirley's Choice' (Sib)	ELon	'Spice Trader' (TB)	WCAu
'Shiryukyo' (SpH)	WCAu WMal	'Spiced Custard' (TB)	ESgI WCAu
'Showdown' (Sib)	GMaP LRHS	'Spicy Cajun' (La)	EBee
'Shrawley' (Sib)	WCAu	'Spinning Wheel' (TB)	WCAu
'Shurton Inn' (TB)	SRms WCAu	'Splashacata' (TB)	WCAu
sibirica	CLil CoPl CSpe EPPr GAbr GArf GQue LWaG MBel MCtn MMuc SPlb StAn WBrk WFar WGwG WHer WTre	'Spot On' (Reticulata)	EPot XFar
		'Spreckles' (TB)	ESgI
		'Spree' (SDB)	WCAu
		'Spring Blush' (MTB) ♀H7	EIri
- PAB 6119	LEdu	'Spring Madness' (TB)	WCAu
'Sibirica Alba' (Sib)	ECha EPfP LWaG SRms WFar	*spuria*	CMac EPPr
§ 'Sibtosa Ruffles' (SpH)	WCAu	§ - subsp. *halophila*	ECha
sichuanensis	SPlb	- - WO 8075	GEdr
'Side Effects' (TB)	WCAu	- subsp. *notha* CC 725	WCot
'Sierra Blue' (TB)	EWoo	- subsp. *ochroleuca*	see *I. orientalis* Mill.
'Sign of Leo' (TB)	EWoo	'St Louis Blues' (TB)	ESgI
'Silver Edge' (Sib) ♀H7	Widely available	'Stairway to Heaven' (TB)	ESgI WCAu
'Silverado' (TB)	ESgI EWoo WCAu WSpi	'Stapleford' (SDB)	CBro
'Silvery Beauty' (Dut) ♀H6	CBro ELan GKev LAma LCro NBir	'Staplehurst' (MTB) ♀H7	SIri
'Simply Fabulous' (TB) **new**	WCAu	'Star Cluster' (Sib)	WFar
'Simply Sensational' (TB)	WCAu	'Star in the Night' (TB)	WCAu
sindjarensis	see *I. aucheri*	'Star Shine' (TB)	WCAu
'Sing to Me' (TB)	WCAu	'Starcrest' (TB)	WCAu
'Sinister Desire' (IB)	EWoo SIri	'Starring' (TB)	EIri WCAu
sintenisii ♀H6	GKev MCtn SBrt WAbe	'Starwoman' (IB) ♀H7	WCAu
'Sir Michael' (TB)	ESgI EWoo	'Staten Island' (TB)	ESgI SRms WCAu
'Siva Siva' (TB)	ESgI LRHS	'Stellar Lights' (TB)	EIri EWoo WCAu
'Sixtine C' (TB)	WCAu	'Stephen Wilcox' (Sib)	CDor MAvo
'Skating Party' (TB)	ESgI EWoo	'Stepping Out' (TB) ♀H7	CMac EPfP ESgI EWoo LRHS MHer NCth WCAu
'Skiers' Delight' (TB)	ESgI		
'Skirting the Issue' (TB) **new**	WCAu	'Steve' (Sib)	ESgI EWes NLar
'Sky Wings' (Sib)	CToG MArl WFar	'Steve Varner' (Sib)	NLar
'Skydancer' (SDB)	WCAu	'Steve's Choice' (TB)	SIri
'Skye Blue' (TB)	EnIr	'Stingray' (TB)	ESgI
'Skyfire' (TB)	LRHS XFar	'Stitches' (TB) **new**	WCAu
'Skylark's Song' (TB)	EIri	*stolonifera* 'Augustus'	GKev
'Small Sky' (SDB)	CBro	- 'George Barr'	GKev
'Smart' (SDB)	WCAu	'Stormy Circle' (SDB)	WCAu
'Smart Aleck' (TB)	ESgI	'Storrington' (TB)	CEnd EBee ECha ELan EPfP LRHS NCth SMrm WCAu
'Smart Move' (TB)	ESgI		
'Smiling Faces' (TB)	WCAu	'Strathmore' (TB)	ECha EWoo LRHS
'Snow Fire' (TB)	EGren	'Strawberry Bliss' (TB) **new**	WCAu
'Snow Prince' (Sib)	WCAu	'Strawberry Fair' (Sib) ♀H7	WCAu
'Snow Season' (SDB)	ESgI	'Strictly Jazz' (TB)	WCAu
'Snow Troll' (SDB)	WCAu	'Strike it Rich' (TB)	ESgI
'Snowcrest' (Sib)	CEnd CPud EBee EGren ESgI LRHS MAvo WGwG WHoo	'Strongold' (Dut) ♀H6	GKev LAma
		'Strozzapreti' (TB)	ESgI
'Snowdrift' (TB)	ELin	'Strut your Stuff' (TB)	WCAu
'Snowmound' (TB)	ESgI WCAu	*stylosa*	see *I. unguicularis*
'Snowy Owl' (TB)	WCAu	§ *suaveolens*	EDAr GEdr WIce

– var. *flavescens*	see *I. suaveolens* yellow-flowered	'Telstar' (Dut)	GKev LAma
§ – purple-flowered	EDAr EPot GEdr GKev WAbe	'Temper Tantrum' (Sib)	CBrac CoPl EGrI
– var. *violacea*	see *I. suaveolens* purple-flowered	'Temple Gold' (TB)	NPer
§ – yellow-flowered	GArf WAbe	'Temple Meads' (IB)	ESgI WCAu
'Succès Fou' (TB)	WCAu	'Templecloud' (IB) ♀H7	CWnw
'Sugar' (IB)	NSti WCAu	'Temporal Anomaly' (TB)	WCAu
'Sugar Blues' (TB)	WCAu	'Tempting Fate' (TB)	WCAu
'Sugar Magnolia' (TB)	SIri	§ *tenax*	EDAr
'Sugar Rush' (Sib)	WCAu	'Tennison Ridge' (TB)	WCAu
'Sugarmouse' (BB)	SIri	'Tenterden' (BB)	SIri
'Sultan's Palace' (TB)	CEnd EBee EPfP EWoo LBom LCro LRHS MHer NCth WCAu WSpi	*tenuissima*	GEdr
		'Terra del Fuoco' (TB)	ESgI WCAu
'Summer Revels' (Sib)	EWes NLar	'Teverlae' (Sib)	LRHS
'Summer Sky' (Sib)	CDor ELon LEdu LSto SMHy SPel WCot	'That's All Folks' (TB)	WCAu
		'That's Red' (MTB)	EIri
'Sun Grooves' (Sib)	EBee	'The Black Douglas' (TB)	EWoo
'Sun in Splendour' (SpH)	CToG	'The Red Douglas' (TB)	EWoo
'Sun Shine In' (TB)	WCAu	'The Rocket'	see *I.* 'Rocket'
'Sunny Delight' (TB)	ESgI	'Theodolinda' (TB)	EWoo
'Sunset Sky' (TB)	LRHS	'Third Charm' (SDB)	CBro EDAr
'Sunshine' (Reticulata)	EPot ERCP	'Third World' (SDB)	CBro
'Super Model' (TB)	WCAu	'This and That' (IB)	WCAu
'Superact' (Sib)	ELon	'Thornbird' (TB) ♀H7	EIri ESgI SRms WCAu
'Superstition' (TB) ♀H7	EAri ELan EWes EWoo LCro LRHS WCAu	'Three Part Harmony' (TB)	WCAu
		'Three Quarters' (Sib)	ELon
'Supreme Sultan' (TB)	ESgI EWoo WCAu	'Thriller' (TB)	ESgI WCAu
'Sur la Plage' (TB) **new**	WCAu	'Thundering Ovation' (TB)	WCAu
'Susan Bliss' (TB)	EGren EPfP ESgI EWoo LRHS WCAu WMal	'Tickety Boo' (SDB)	SIri
		§ 'Tigereye' (Dut)	ERCP GKev LAma LCro SPeP XFar
'Swain' (TB)	ESgI	'Time Zone' (TB)	WCAu
'Swan Ballet' (TB)	ESgI	'Timescape' (TB)	EGrI
'Swans in Flight' (Sib)	LAma NLar WCAu	*timofejewii*	WAbe
'Swazi Princess' (TB)	LRHS SHor SRms WSpi	'Tinkerbell' (SDB)	EBee GMaP NBir
'Swedish Lullaby' (TB) **new**	WCAu	'Tipped in Blue' (Sib)	ELan MNrw NEoE WCAu XFar
'Sweet City Woman' (TB) **new**	WCAu	'Tishomingo' (TB)	EWoo
		'Titan's Glory' (TB) ♀H7	CFis CMac EWoo LEdu LRHS NCth SRms WCAu WCot WHoo WSpi
'Sweet Kate' (SDB)	ESgI		
'Sweet Lena' (TB)	ESgI	'Tom Johnson' (TB) ♀H7	WCAu
'Sweet Musette' (TB)	SChr SRms WCAu	'Top Choice' (TB) **new**	WCAu
'Sweeter than Wine' (TB)	WCAu	'Top Flight' (TB)	ELan SRms
'Swerti'	see *I.* 'Plicata'	'Top Gun' (TB)	ESgI WCAu
'Swingtown' (TB)	EWoo WCAu	'Torero' (TB)	SIri
'Swiss Majesty' (TB)	WCAu	'Total Eclipse' (TB)	SRms
'Symphony' (Dut)	ELan NBir	'Touch of Frost' (BB)	ESgI
'Syncopation' (TB)	ESgI WCAu	'Touch of Mahogany' (TB)	WCAu
'Syrian Hills' (TB)	WCAu	'Town Flirt' (TB)	WCAu
'Tabac Blond' (TB)	EWoo	'Tracking' (MTB)	EWoo
'Table for Two' (TB) **new**	WCAu	'Tracy Tyrene' (TB)	WCAu
'Tact' (IB)	SIri	'Trails West' (TB)	EWoo
'Taking Chances' (TB)	WCAu	'Trapel' (TB)	ESgI
'Tall Chief' (TB)	WCAu	'Trenwith' (TB)	ESgI
'Tamberg' (Sib)	ELon LSto NLar	'Triple Whammy' (TB)	ESgI
'Tamerlan' (TB)	EWoo	'Triplicate' (SDB)	SMrm
'Tangerine Sky' (TB)	WCAu	'Tropic Night' (Sib)	CDor CPud EBee EGren EHeP ELan ELon EPfP ERCP EWoo GKin LBom LCro LRHS MAvo MHol NRya NSti SMHy WBrk WCAu WFar WHoo
'Tanzanian Tangerine' (TB)	WCAu		
taochia	WAbe		
'Taremurasaki' (SpH)	CBen		
'Tarn Hows' (TB)	ESgI EWoo SRms	'True Charm' (TB)	EWoo
taurica	WAbe	§ 'Truly' (SDB)	WCAu
'Teal Velvet' (Sib)	CoPl ECha ELon ESgI EWes GAbr LRHS SHor WCAu WChS WFar	'Truth or Dare' (TB) **new**	WCAu
		tuberosa	CBro ECha ERCP ESwi EWoo LAma XFar
'Tealwood' (Sib)	WMal		
'Teapot Tempest' (BB)	EIri	– PB	GKev
'Teasaucer Hill' (MTB) ♀H7	SIri	'Tumble Bug' (Sib)	CDor
tectorum	EAri EWoo WCot WMal	'Tuxedo' (TB)	EGren
– BWJ 8191	WCru	'Twice Is Nice' (TB)	WCAu
– 'Alba'	EPPr	'Twist of Sheree' (TB) **new**	WCAu
– 'Cruella'	EAri EPfP MHol WSpi	§ 'Tycoon' (Sib)	EWoo GAbr LCro LRHS SMrm
– 'Variegata' misapplied	see *I. japonica* 'Variegata'	'Tynedale' (TB) **new**	EnIr
– 'Variegata' (v)	SRms	*typhifolia*	GKev
'Tell Fibs' (SDB)	CBro	'Tyrian Dream' (IB)	WCAu

'Ultimate' (SDB)	ESgI WCAu
'Unbuttoned Zippers' (Sib)	CDor NLar WCAu
'Uncorked' (Sib)	CTtf WCAu
'Under Dog' (TB) **new**	WCAu
'Undercurrent' (TB)	WCAu
'Unfinished Business' (TB)	WCAu
§ *unguicularis*	CBcs CBro CDor CoPl EBee ECha EGrI ELan ELon EPfP ESgI EWoo GEdr GMaP LRHS LSto NLar NQui NSti SMad SPoG SRms WCAu WHoo WOld WSpi WTor
- 'Abington Purple'	MWlw
- 'Alba'	CExl
§ - subsp. *cretensis*	EPot GKev WAbe
- - 'Oxford Dwarf'	CBro
- 'Diana Clare'	MAvo
- 'Maronderra'	CBct
- 'Mary Barnard' ♀H5	CBro EGrI WHoo
- 'Peloponnese Snow'	CBro EPot EPPr GEdr WAbe
- 'Speciosa'	CBro
§ - 'Walter Butt'	CBro ECha
'Vague à l'Âme' (TB)	EWoo
'Valda' (Sib)	ELon EWoo WOld
'Valentine' (Dut)	XFar
'Valerie Joyce' (TB)	WCAu
'Vamp' (IB)	EWoo
'Vanilla Skies' (TB)	WCAu
'Vanity's Child' (TB)	ESgI WCAu
§ *variegata* ♀H7	CDor EBee
- var. *reginae*	LBar
'Velvet Dusk' (TB)	EWoo
'Velvet King' (TB)	ESgI
'Velvet Midnights' (TB)	ESgI
'Venita Faye' (TB)	WCAu
versicolor	CBen CLil CPud CToG CWat EGren ELin EWoo GKev GMaP MMuc MWts SEND SPlb SRms WCAu WFar WMAq WShi
- 'Dottie's Double'	CToG
- 'Kermesina'	CLil CPud CWat ECha ELin EPfk LCro MWlw NPer SRms WFar WMAq
- 'Mysterious Monique'	CLil MWts SPeP
- 'Party Line'	CBen
- purple-flowered	EWat
- 'Rowden Allegro'	CToG
- 'Rowden Anthem'	CToG
- 'Rowden Cadenza'	CToG EWat MWlw
- 'Rowden Calypso'	CToG
- 'Rowden Cantata'	CToG
- 'Rowden Concerto'	CToG
- 'Rowden Jingle'	CToG
- 'Rowden Lullaby'	CToG
- 'Rowden Madrigal'	CToG
- 'Rowden Minuet'	CToG
- 'Rowden Pastorale'	CToG
- 'Rowden Sonata'	CToG
- 'Rowden Symphony'	CToG
'Vi Luihn' (Sib)	ECha ELon WFar
'Vibrant' (TB)	WCAu
'Vibrations' (TB)	ESgI WCAu
'Victoria Falls' (TB)	MHol WCAu
'Victorian Secret' (Sib)	ELon
'Victorine' (TB)	EWoo
'Viel Creme' (Sib)	ESgI
'Viel Schnee' (Sib)	ELon
'Vingolf' (IB)	EWoo
'Violet Harmony' (TB)	ESgI
'Violet Icing' (TB)	CWal
virginica 'De Luxe'	see *I.* × *robusta* 'Dark Aura'
- 'Pond Crown Point'	CToG
'Vishnu' (TB)	EWoo
'Vitafire' (TB)	ESgI
'Vitality' (IB)	ESgI
'Vive la France' (TB)	ESgI
'Voilà' (IB)	ESgI
'Wabash' (TB)	EWoo LRHS WCAu
'Walmer Castle' (Kent Castles Series) (IB)	SIri
'Walter Butt'	see *I. unguicularis* 'Walter Butt'
'War Chief' (TB)	ESgI WCAu
'War Sails' (TB)	WCAu
'Warlsind' (J)	ERCP GKev LAma
'Water Waltz' (TB)	WCAu
'Waterline' (TB) **new**	WCAu
wattii	CExl
- KWJ 12172	WCru
'Wearing Rubies' (TB)	ESgI WCAu
'Webmaster' (SDB)	EPPr
'Wedding Candles' (TB)	NLar
'Wedding Vow' (TB)	EIri
'Weisse Etagen' (Sib)	ELon
'Welcome Return' (Sib)	GAbr
'Welfenprinz' (Sib) ♀H7	GBin
'Well Suited' (SDB)	ESgI
'Wench' (TB)	WCAu
'Wensleydale' (TB)	EnIr
'Westwell' (SDB)	GEdr WCAu
'Wharfedale' (TB)	EnIr
'What It's Worth' (TB)	WCAu
'What's New Pussycat' (BB)	WCAu
'Whee' (SDB)	WCAu
'When Angels Sing' (TB)	WCAu
'Whispering Spirits' (TB)	WCAu
'White Amber' (Sib)	NLar WCAu
'White Caucasus' (Reticulata)	EPot ERCP
'White City' (TB)	EBee EGren EPfP ESgI EWoo GMaP LRHS NPer SRms WCAu
'White Excelsior' (Dut)	CBro SPeP
'White Gem' (SDB)	ESgI
'White Knight' (TB)	EBee EHeP WSpi
'White Swan' (Sib)	WKif
'White Swirl' (Sib)	CBro CBWd CoPl EBee ECha EPfP ESgI GMaP LCro LRHS MArl NBro NLar NSti SHor SRms WCAu WFar WTre
'White Triangles' (Sib)	ELon
'White Wine' (MTB)	WCAu
'Whooper Swan' (TB)	EnIr
'Widow's Veil' (SDB)	ESgI
'Wild' (BB)	WCAu
'Wild Wings' (TB)	WCAu
'William of Orange'^PBR (TB)	EnIr
wilsonii ♀H7	CExl GArf GKev NRya
'Wind Beneath My Wings' (TB) **new**	WCAu
'Wine Wings' (Sib)	WCAu
'Winesap' (TB)	ESgI EWoo
'Wings at Dawn' (TB)	WCAu
'Wink and Smile' (TB)	WCAu
winogradowii ♀H7	ECha
'Winter Olympics' (TB)	ELan EWoo SOrN WGwG WTor
'Winterfest' (TB)	WCAu
'Wintry Sky' (TB)	WCAu
'Wish Upon a Star' (SDB)	WCAu
'Wishful Thinking' (TB)	SIri
'Wizard's Return' (SDB)	SIri
'Wonders Never Cease' (TB)	WCAu
'Wondrous' (TB)	EGren EPfP ESgI EWoo LRHS WGwG
'World Premier' (TB)	CWnw ELan

'Wrangler' (IB)	SIri
xiphioides	see *I. latifolia*
'Yaquina Blue' (TB)	ESgl WCAu
'Yarai' (SpH)	CBen
'Yasha' (SpH)	CBen
'Yellow Flirt' (MTB)	WCAu
'Yellowtail' (Sib)	EMor XFar
'Yes' (TB)	ESgl
'Yippy Skippy' (SDB)	WCAu
'Yosemite Nights' (TB)	EWoo
'Zakopane' (Sib)	EWes
'Zero' (SDB)	ESgl
'Zinger' (BB)	WSpi
'Zweites Hundert' (Sib)	WFar WKif

Isatis (Brassicaceae)

tinctoria	CCBP CGHo CHab CHby CSpe EHet ENfk GJem GQue LShi MCtn MEar MHer MHoo MNHC NAts SRms SVic
- subsp. *athoa*	WCot

Ismene (Amaryllidaceae)

§ × *deflexa* ♀H1c	EGren EPfP LAma LCro MHtn XFar
- 'Zwanenburg'	GKev LAma WHil XFar
§ *longipetala*	LAma
§ 'Sulphur Queen' ♀H1c	EGren EPfP LAma XFar

Isodon (Lamiaceae)

calycinus	see *Coleus calycinus*
effusus	CMHG EBee EWld MHol MNrw WCot WPGP
excisus	EWld SBrt
longitubus	EAri EMor MHol SBrt
- B&SWJ 11027	WCru
rubescens	EMor

Isolatocereus see *Stenocereus*

Isolepis (Cyperaceae)

§ *cernua*	CBen CLil CoPl CPud CWat ELin EPfP EWat LCro LRHS MWts WCot WMAq
'Live Wire'	see *I. cernua*
nodosa (Rottb.) R. Br.	see *Ficinia nodosa*

Isoloma see *Kohleria*

Isomeris see *Cleome*

Isoplexis see *Digitalis*

Isopogon (Proteaceae)

anemonifolius	SPlb
anethifolius	SPlb
dubius	CPbh
formosus	CBcs LRHS
trilobus	SPlb

Isopyrum (Ranunculaceae)

biternatum	LEdu
thalictroides	EPot EPPr LEdu NRya WAbe WCot WPGP

Isotoma (Campanulaceae)

§ *axillaris*	CSpe NPer SPoG
- 'Fairy Carpet'	SLee SRms
- Fizz 'n' Pop Glowing Purple ('Tmlu 1301')	LSou
fluviatilis	NLar

Itea (Iteaceae)

ilicifolia ♀H5	CBcs CDoC CEnd CExl CMac CMCN EBee ELan EPfP EWhm LCro LRHS LSRN LSto MAsh MBlu MGos NLar SDix SMad SPlb SPoG SRms WKif
virginica	CMCN EGrI GKev
§ - 'Henry's Garnet' ♀H5	CBcs CDoC CEnd CMac CMCN EBee EGrI ELan EPfP EWhm GArf LCro LRHS MGos NCth NLar SMad SPad SPoG SRms WFar WPGP
- Little Henry ('Sprich'PBR)	CBcs CMac EBee EPfP LRHS MGos NLar
- 'Long Spire'	NLar
- Love Child ('Bailteaone')	CWnw MMrt
- 'Merlot'	ELon EPfP LRHS MBlu NLar
- 'Sarah Eve'	NLar
- 'Saturnalia'	NLar
- Swarthmore form	see *I. virginica* 'Henry's Garnet'
yunnanensis	CExl MBlu NLar

Ixia (Iridaceae)

'Blue Bird'	SPeP
'Castor'	EGrI SPeP
'Giant'	GKev LAma LShi SPeP
'Hogarth'	GKev LAma MPro SPeP
'Jesse'	LAma
'Mabel'	ECha GKev LAma MPro
'Marquette'	GKev LAma MPro SPeP
mixed	LAma
paniculata 'Eos'	GKev LAma MPro SPeP XFar
'Spotlight'	ECha GKev LAma MPro
'Venus'	EGrI GKev LAma MPro SPeP
viridiflora	LShi
'Yellow Emperor'	ECha GKev LAma

Ixiolirion (Ixioliriaceae)

pallasii	see *I. tataricum*
§ *tataricum*	XFar

J

Jaborosa (Solanaceae)

integrifolia	EBee EWld LEdu MNrw

Jacaranda (Bignoniaceae)

acutifolia misapplied	see *J. mimosifolia*
caucana	SPlb
§ *mimosifolia* ♀H1c	CBcs EAri EShb MCtn SPlb WJur
- Bonsai Blue ('Sakai01'PBR) **new**	LCro

Jacobaea (Asteraceae)

candida	WCot
§ *maritima*	CWRo LWaG SEND
- 'Silver Dust' ♀H4	EGren ELan MCtn
§ *vulgaris*	GJem

Jacobinia see *Justicia*

Jamesia (Hydrangeaceae)

americana	CBcs NLar SBrt WCru

Jancaea × *Ramonda* see × *Jancaemonda*

× *Jancaemonda* (Gesneriaceae)

vandedemii	NHar WAbe

Jasione (Campanulaceae)

§ **heldreichii**	NBir SRms
jankae	see *J. heldreichii*
§ **laevis**	ELan EPfP GAbr GArf SRms
- 'Blaulicht'	ECha EPfP GAbr GJos LRHS MCtn MHol MPri NWbg SPlb WFar
- BLUE LIGHT	see *J. laevis* 'Blaulicht'
montana	EDAr GJos MNHC SRms WOrg
- f. *alba* 'White Delight'	EDAr
perennis	see *J. laevis*

Jasminum ✿ (Oleaceae)

affine	see *J. officinale* f. *affine*
angulare ♀H2	CRHN EShb SEND
azoricum ♀H2	CRHN EShb SEND SPre
beesianum	CBcs CMac CoPl EBee EGren EGrI ELan EPfP LBom LCro LRHS LSto MAsh MBlu MGos MMuc NLar SEND SPad SPoG SRms WFar WJur WTHo
bignoniaceum	WCru WJur
blinii	see *J. polyanthum*
dispermum	CRHN NLar
diversifolium	see *J. subhumile*
duclouxii	WPGP
farreri	see *J. humile* f. *farreri*
fruticans	CHll CMac EBee ELon GAbr MMrt SBrt SEND WCru
- RCB UA 22	WCot
giraldii misapplied	see *J. humile* f. *farreri*
grandiflorum misapplied	see *J. officinale* f. *affine*
grandiflorum L. 'De Grasse'	CRHN EShb WCot
heterophyllum	see *J. subhumile*
humile	CExl NLar SEND WJur WKif
§ - f. *farreri* Farrer 867	WPGP
- var. *glabrum*	see *J. humile* f. *wallichianum*
§ - 'Revolutum' ♀H5	CBcs CMac CRHN CSBt ELan EPfP EShb LCro MGos NLar SEND SPoG SRms WTHo
§ - f. *wallichianum* B&SWJ 2559	WCru
- - PAB 2534	LEdu
- - PAB 9962	LEdu
lanceolaria	LEdu WPGP
laurifolium f. *nitidum* ♀H2	CBcs LRHS
§ **mesnyi** ♀H3	CBcs CHll CMac CRHN EPfP EShb LRHS LSto SEND SVen WCFE WJur
multipartitum ♀H2	CHll EShb
nitidum	see *J. laurifolium* f. *nitidum*
§ **nudiflorum** ♀H5	CBcs CDoC CMac CSBt EBee EGren EHeP ELan EPfP GKin LBom LCro LSRN LSto MAsh MMuc MPri NLar SDix SEND SGol SNig SPlb SPoG SRms WFar WHtc WJur WTHo
- 'Aureum'	CMac ELan MAsh MPri SPoG SRms
* - 'Compactum'	MAsh
officinale	Widely available
§ - f. *affine*	CBcs CRHN ELan EPfP LCro LSto MAsh SDix SRms WTHo
§ - 'Argenteovariegatum' (v) ♀H5	CMac CWGN CWnw ELan ELon EPfP LCro LRHS LSRN MGos MHer SEND SPoG WTHo
- 'Aureovariegatum'	see *J. officinale* 'Aureum'
§ - 'Aureum' (v)	CMac ELan EPfP LRHS LShi MAsh SRms WCFE WTHo
- 'Clotted Cream'	see *J. officinale* 'Devon Cream'
- 'Crûg's Collection'	WCru
§ - 'Devon Cream'	Widely available
- FIONA SUNRISE ('Frojas') ♀H5	CBcs CMac CWGN EBee ELan EPfP LBom LRHS LSRN MAsh MGos MPri NLar SGol SPad SPoG SWCr WFar
- 'Grandiflorum'	see *J. officinale* f. *affine*
- 'Inverleith' ♀H5	EBee ELan ELon EPfP LCro LEdu LRHS MAsh MGos SPad SPoG SWCr WTHo
- SUNBEAM ('Lowbeam')	CDoC EBee ELon LRHS LSou SPoG
- 'Variegatum'	see *J. officinale* 'Argenteovariegatum'
parkeri	CBcs CMac GEdr GMaP LRHS NLar SEND
- 'Bychan'	WAbe
§ **polyanthum** ♀H2	CBcs CBct CRHN CSBt EGren ELan EPfP EShb LBom LCro LRHS SEND SPre SRms WTHo
- dark red-leaved	CExl CSde EPfP
primulinum	see *J. mesnyi*
reevesii hort.	see *J. humile* 'Revolutum'
sambac ♀H2	CHll CRHN SPre SWor
- 'Grand Duke of Tuscany' (d)	CHll
- 'Maid of Orleans' (d)	EShb
sieboldianum	see *J. nudiflorum*
§ **simplicifolium** subsp. *suavissimum*	CHll CRHN
stenalobium	WCot
× **stephanense**	Widely available
- STARRY STARRY SUMMER SCENT ('Ganmin 1701')	CSBt EPfP LCro LRHS MPri SWCr WLov
suavissimum	see *J. simplicifolium* subsp. *suavissimum*
§ **subhumile** NJM 12.044	WPGP

Jatropha (Euphorbiaceae)

cinerea	SPlb
integerrima	EUrb
multifida	CDoC SPlb
podagrica ♀H1b	CDoC LCro MCtn SPad SPlb

Jeffersonia (Berberidaceae)

diphylla	EBee EMor EPot GKev LAma LEdu MBel MNrw NBir WAbe WPnP
dubia	EWes LEdu MCtn MNrw NBir WAbe WCot
- 'Sunago-fu' (v)	GEdr

Jordaaniella (Aizoaceae)

cuprea	EAri

jostaberry see *Ribes* × *nidigrolaria*

Jovellana (Calceolariaceae)

punctata	CBcs CTsd EPfP MCtn SPlb
sinclairii	CBcs CTsd
violacea ♀H3	CAbb CBcs CExl CMac CTsd CTtf EAri EBee EPfP EWld SPad SVen WPGP

Jovibarba ✿ (Crassulaceae)

§ **allionii**	CPic EDAr EPfP EPot ESuc LCro MHer SPlb SRms WAbe WFar WHoo
- 'Oki'	EDAr EPot LRHS SRms
arenaria	NMen
globifera 'Autumn Fires'	NMen SSem
§ **heuffelii**	GArf NCft WFar
- 'Achisia'	NMen
- 'Adagdak'	NMen

- 'Agaffa' NMen
- 'Aldicia' NMen
- 'Alena' NMen
- 'Ambassadeur' NMen
- 'Angel Wings' SRms WHoo
- 'Ardysia' NMen
- 'Arnia' NMen
- 'Askja' NMen
- 'Atoll' NMen
- 'Atria' NMen
- 'Bandana' NMen
- 'Barbel' NMen
- 'Baripper' NMen
- 'Beacon' NMen
- 'Beacon Hill' NMen
- 'Belcore' NMen
- 'Bermuda' NMen
- 'Biapho' NMen
- 'Bibiana' NMen
- 'Big Brother' NMen
- 'Bolero' NMen
- 'Brocade' NMen
- 'Bronze Ingot' NMen
- 'Bulgarien' NMen
- 'Burgharis' NMen
- 'Cauvery' NMen
- 'Centaurus' NMen
- 'Charell' NMen
- 'Cherry Glow' NMen
- 'Chocoleto' NMen
- 'Cimmanon' NMen
- 'Comanchero' NMen
I - 'Compacta' NMen
- 'Copper King' NMen
- 'Corbierie' NMen
- 'Coutanche' NMen
- 'Cover Girl' NMen
- 'Crill' NMen
- 'Deciso' NMen
- 'Dream' NMen
- 'Drechter Gem' NMen
- 'Dynosia' NMen
- 'Elmo's Fire' NMen
* - 'Emerald and Ruby' WFar
- 'Enicia' NMen
- 'Eos Moment' NMen
- 'Ernest' NMen
- 'Etysia' NMen
- 'Fan Joy' NMen
- 'Fandango' NMen
- 'Geronimo' NMen
- 'Ghaysia' NMen
- 'Giuseppi Spiny' NMen
- var. *glabra* WHoo
- - from Treska Gorge, SRms
  Macedonia
- - 'Cameo' NMen
- 'Gladiator' NMen
* - 'Golden Touch' WFar
- 'Grand Slam' NMen
- 'Green Land' NMen
- 'Greenstone' NMen
- 'Henry Correvon' NMen
- var. *heuffelii* NMen
- 'Heulin' NMen
- 'Hot Bikini' NMen
- 'Hot Chocolate' NMen
- 'Hot Lips' NMen
- 'Idylle' NMen
- 'Inferno' NMen
- 'Jackpot' NMen

- 'Jade' NMen
I - 'Jovi King' NMen
- 'June's Choice' NMen
- 'King Sunny' NMen
- 'Konrada' NMen
- var. *kopaonikensis* NMen
- 'Leo' ESuc WHil
- 'Lorelei' NMen
- 'Lucky Bell' NMen
- 'Machon' NMen
- 'Madera' NMen
- 'Major' NMen
- 'Mary Ann' NMen
- 'Miller's Violet' NMen
- 'Mink' NMen
- 'Minuta' NMen
- 'Misty' NMen
- 'Mystique' NMen WHoo
- 'Nannette' NMen
- 'Olivia' NMen
- 'Orion' NMen
- var. *patens* NMen
- 'Penponds' NMen
- 'Pink Skies' NMen
- 'Pink Star' NMen
- 'Prisma' NMen
- 'Pronker' NMen
- 'Purple Heide' NMen
- 'Quennevalis' NMen
- 'Red Rose' NMen
- 'Red Start' NMen
- 'Rhapsody' NMen
- 'Samares' NMen
- 'Sarabande' NMen
- 'Serenade' NMen SRms
- 'Silex' NMen
- 'Springael's Choice' NMen
- 'Summer King' NMen
* - 'Sun and Silver Edge' WFar
- 'Superduper' NMen
- 'Sylvan Memory' NMen
- 'Tancredi' NMen
- 'Torrid Zone' MBrN NMen
- 'Trinity' NMen
- 'Troon' NMen
- 'Try Me' NMen
- 'Tuxedo' NMen
- 'Violet' NMen
- 'Yuppy Alone' NMen
§ *hirta* EDAr GKev LRHS WFar
- from Wintergraben, SPlb SRms
  Austria
- 'Belansky Tatra' NMen SRms
- subsp. *glabrescens* EDAr NMen
  from Smeryouka,
  southern Carpathians
- var. *neilreichii* EDAr LRHS MHer MWIw SRms
§ *sobolifera* EDAr EGrI EPot GArf GKev LSto SPlb
- 'Green Globe' EDAr LRHS MWIw SSem

Jubaea ✿ (Arecaceae)
§ *chilensis* ♡H4 NPlm SArc SBig SPlb
  spectabilis see *J. chilensis*

Juglans ✿ (Juglandaceae)
§ *ailantifolia* B&SWJ 11026 WCru
- var. *cordiformis* 'Brock' CAgr
  (F)
- - 'Campbell Cw3' (F) CAgr
- - 'Fodermaier' seedling (F) CAgr

- - 'Imshu' (F) CAgr
- - 'Rhodes' (F) CAgr
- - 'Simcoe' (F) CAgr
ailantifolia × *cinerea* see *J.* × *bixbyi*
§ × *bixbyi* CAgr
cinerea 'Beckwith' (F) CAgr
- 'Booth' (F) CAgr
- 'Booth' seedling (F) CAgr
- 'Chamberlin' (F) CAgr
- 'Craxezy' (F) CAgr
- 'Kenworthy' seedling (F) CAgr
- 'Myjoy' (F) CAgr
elaeopyren WJur
mandshurica (F) CBcs CMCN WJur
- B&SWJ 12550 from Korea WCru
- BWJ 8097 from China WCru
- RWJ 9905 from Taiwan WCru
microcarpa CMCN
nigra (F) ♀H6 CBcs CBTr CCVT CHab CLnd CMac
    CMCN EBar EPfP IPap LCro LMaj
    MAsh MGos MMuc NOra NPip
    SEND SGol WJur WMat WMou
- 'Beineke 10' 'PBR CAco
- 'Bicentennial' (F) CAgr
- 'Emma Kay' (F) CAgr
- 'Laciniata' EPfP MBlu
- 'Potsdam' (F) CAgr
- 'Thomas' (F) CAgr
- 'Weschke' (F) CAgr
regia (F) Widely available
- 'Apollo' (F) CMac ELan
- 'Axel' (F) CAgr LMaj WMat
- 'Broadview' (F) CAgr CBrac CBTr CEnd CMac ELan
    EPfP EPom LBuc LCro MBlu MGos
    MLod NOra SEWo SPoG SVic WMat
- 'Buccaneer' (F) CAgr CMac ELan EPom LCro LRHS
    MLod MSwo NOra WMat
- 'Chandler' (F) CAgr CMac MLod WMat
- 'Corne du Périgord' (F) CAgr
- 'Europa' (F) EPom LCro
- 'Ferjean' (F) CAgr
- 'Fernette' 'PBR (F) CAgr MLod NOra WMat
- 'Fernor' (F) CAgr WMat
- 'Franquette' (F) ♀H6 CAgr ELan LMaj MLod NOra WMat
- 'Hansen' (F) CAgr
- 'Hartley' (F) CAgr
- 'Jupiter' (F) CAgr CMac ELan LMaj NOra WMat
- 'Laciniata' ♀H6 CMCN
- 'Lara' (F) ♀H6 CAgr ELan LCro NOra WMat
- 'Mars' (F) CAgr LMaj LRHS MLod NOra
    WMat
- 'Mayette' (F) CAgr
- 'Meylannaise' (F) CAgr
- 'Mini Multiflora 14' (F) CAgr
- 'Nr 16' (F) WMat
- 'Parisienne' (F) CAgr LMaj
- 'Plovdivski' (F) WMat
- 'Proslavski' (F) WMat
- 'Purpurea' MBlu
- 'Red Danube' (F) WMat
- 'Rita' (F) LBuc
- 'Ronde de Montignac' (F) CAgr
- 'Saturn' (F) CAgr WMat
- 'Sychrov' (F) CAgr WMat
sieboldiana see *J. ailantifolia*

jujube see *Ziziphus jujuba*

Juncus (Juncaceae)
§ *decipiens* 'Curly-wurly' CDoC CLil CoPl
- 'Spiralis' see *J. decipiens* 'Curly-wurly'

effusus CBen CGwi CHab CLil CoPl CPud
    CWat ELin LCro NPer WMAq
- 'Carman's Japanese' NSti
§ - f. *spiralis* CBen CGwi CLil CPud CSpe CWat
    ELin EWat GQue LCro LRHS MAsh
    NBir NLit SPeP SPlb SVic WFar
    WMAq
ensifolius CBen CMiW CWat ELin EPPr EWat
    GBin GKev MWts NPer NSti
    WMAq
- 'Flying Hedgehogs' CLil ELin MPro
inflexus CPud CWat ELin
- 'Afro' NBro SPlb
pallidus EPPr
patens 'Carman's Gray' CKno
- 'Elk Blue' CKno SPeP

Junellia (Verbenaceae)
azorelloides WAbe
congesta WAbe
§ *micrantha* WAbe
§ *succulentifolia* WAbe
wilczekii WAbe

Juniperus ✿ (Cupressaceae)
ashei CAco
bermudiana CAco
chinensis CAco CMen MAsh
- 'Aurea' ♀H6 SEND
§ - 'Blaauw' ♀H6 CMac CMen
- 'Blue Alps' ♀H6 CAco LRHS MGos MMuc MPri
    SEND SPoG
- 'Bokor' CAco
- 'Expansa Aureospicata' CMac LRHS SPoG SRms
    (v)
§ - 'Expansa Variegata' (v) LRHS
- 'Itoigawa' CAco CMen
- 'Japonica Variegata' (v) LRHS
§ - 'Kaizuka' ♀H6 WCha
- 'Kék' CAco
- 'Keteleeri' CAco
- 'Kuriwao Gold' see *J.* × *pfitzeriana* 'Kuriwao Gold'
- 'Plumosa Albovariegata' LRHS
    (v)
- 'Plumosa Aurea' ♀H6 CAco
- 'Pyramidalis' ♀H6 CBrac EPfP LRHS MAsh
- 'San José' CMen
§ - var. *sargentii* CMen
- 'Shimpaku' CMen
- 'Stricta' CAco CSBt LCro LRHS MPri
    WCha
- 'Sulphur Spray' see *J.* × *pfitzeriana* 'Sulphur Spray'
- 'Torulosa' see *J. chinensis* 'Kaizuka'
communis CAco CHab SPre WKor
- (f) CMac EGren LSto WHtc
- 'Brynhyfryd Gold' GKev
- 'Compressa' ♀H7 CBcs CMac CSBt EPfP EPot LRHS
    MAsh MGos SPoG WAbe
- 'Depressa Aurea' CBrac CSBt
- 'Depressed Star' SPoG
- 'Gold Cone' CBrac ELan LRHS MGos MPri SPoG
- 'Goldschatz' ELan EPfP GKev LRHS MAsh SPoG
- 'Green Carpet' ♀H7 CAco CWnw EGren ELan EPfP
    GKin LBuc LCro LRHS MAsh MGos
    SPoG WCha WFar
- 'Greenmantle' WMat
- 'Hibernica' ♀H7 CBrac CNWT CSBt ELan EPfP LRHS
    MGos SPoG
- 'Hibernica Aurea' CMac
- 'Hornibrookii' SRms
- 'Meyer' CMac

Justicia

- 'Repanda' ⚥H7 — CAco CBcs CBrac CMac CSBt CWnw EHeP EPfP LCro LRHS MGos MPri SPoG WFar
- 'Sentinel' — EBee
- 'Sieben Steinhauser' — NLar
- **conferta** — see *J. rigida* subsp. *conferta*
- - var. **maritima** — see *J. taxifolia*
- **convallium** — CAco
- **davurica** 'Expansa Albopicta' — see *J. chinensis* 'Expansa Variegata'
- **deppeana** var. **zacatecensis** — CAco
- **drupacea** — CAco
- **excelsa** — CAco
- - subsp. **polycarpos** — CAco
- **foetidissima** — CAco
- - 'Karaca Blue' — CAco
- **formosana** — CAco
- × **gracilis** 'Blaauw' — see *J. chinensis* 'Blaauw'
- 'Grey Owl' ⚥H7 — CAco CBrac MMuc SEND SRms
- § **horizontalis** 'Andorra Compact' — EGren
- I - 'Andorra Variegata' (v) — EPfP WFar
- - 'Bar Harbor' — CMac
- § - 'Blue Chip' — CAco ELan EPfP LRHS MAsh MGos SPoG
- - 'Blue Moon' — see *J. horizontalis* 'Blue Chip'
- - 'Glauca' — CBrac
- - 'Golden Carpet' ⚥H7 — CAco EGren ELan LBuc LCro NLar WCha
- - ICEE BLUE ('Monber') ⚥H7 — CWnw ELan NLar SPoG
- § - 'Limeglow' ⚥H7 — CAco CBcs ELan EPfP LRHS MPri NLar SPoG WFar
- - 'Pancake' — LRHS
- - 'Plumosa' — CAco
- - 'Plumosa Compacta' — see *J. horizontalis* 'Andorra Compact'
- - 'Prince of Wales' — EGren MAsh
- - 'Turquoise Spreader' — CSBt
- - 'Villa Marie' — SPoG
- - 'Wiltonii' — EHeP LRHS
- × **media** — see *J.* × *pfitzeriana*
- **navicularis** — CAco
- **occidentalis** — CAco
- § × **pfitzeriana** — CMac WFar
- - 'Blaauw' — see *J. chinensis* 'Blaauw'
- - 'Blue and Gold' (v) — CAco SPoG
- § - 'Carbery Gold' ⚥H6 — CBcs CBrac CMac CSBt EPfP GKin LRHS MAsh MGos SPoG WFar
- - 'Gold Coast' — CBrac CSBt EGren MGos
- - 'Gold Star' — MAsh
- * - 'Golden Joy' — ELan
- - 'Golden Saucer' — LRHS MAsh
- - 'Goldkissen' — MPri
- - 'Hetzii' — CNWT LMaj
- § - 'Kuriwao Gold' — GKin MMuc SEND
- - 'Mint Julep' — CAco CBrac CSBt CWnw EHeP EPfP
- - 'Old Gold' ⚥H6 — CWnw EGren EPfP GKin LCro MGos SEND SPlb WCha WFar
- - 'Old Gold Carbery' — see *J.* × *pfitzeriana* 'Carbery Gold'
- - 'Pfitzeriana Aurea' — CBrac CMac
- - 'Pfitzeriana Glauca' — SFol
- § - 'Sulphur Spray' ⚥H6 — MMuc SEND
- - 'Wilhelm Pfitzer' — LMaj
- **pinchotii** — CAco
- **pingii** 'Hulsdonk Yellow' PBR — LRHS SPoG
- **procumbens** 'Nana' ⚥H7 — CBcs CWnw EPfP LRHS MAsh MGos NLar SPoG WFar
- **pseudosabina** Fisch. & C.A. Mey. — CAco
- **recurva** 'Castlewellan' — NLar WFar
- - var. **coxii** — CAco CMac MBlu SRms
- **rigida** — CAco CMen
- § - subsp. **conferta** — CMac SEND
- - - 'All Gold' ⚥H6 — SPoG
- - - 'Blue Lagoon' — CAco
- - - 'Blue Pacific' — SPoG
- **sabina** 'Tamariscifolia' — EHeP GKin LRHS MAsh MGos MMuc SArc SEND SPoG WFar
- **saltuaria** — CAco
- **sargentii** — see *J. chinensis* var. *sargentii*
- **scopulorum** 'Blue Arrow' ⚥H6 — CAco CBcs CBrac CCVT CSBt CWnw EGren ELan EPfP GKin IPap LCro LRHS MAsh MGos NLar NPip SPoG SRms WCha WFar WHtc WMat
- - 'O'Connor' — CAco
- - 'Skyrocket' — CAco CBcs CCVT CMac CNWT CWal EHeP EPfP IPap LRHS MGos SRms WCha WFar
- - 'Wichita Blue' — CCVT
- **semiglobosa** — CAco
- **squamata** 'Blue Carpet' ⚥H7 — CAco CBcs CMac CSBt CWnw EGren EHeP EPfP LBuc LRHS MAsh MGos MMuc NLar SEND SPoG WCha WFar
- - 'Blue Star' ⚥H7 — CAco CBrac CMac CSBt CWnw EGren EHeP ELan EPfP LCro LRHS MAsh MGos NLar SPoG WCha WFar
- - 'Blue Swede' — see *J. squamata* 'Hunnetorp'
- - 'Chinese Silver' — CAco
- - 'Dream Joy' — NLar
- - 'Floreant' — LRHS SPoG
- - 'Holger' ⚥H7 — CAco CMac EPfP LRHS MAsh MGos MPri NLar SPoG WFar
- § - 'Hunnetorp' — WFar
- - 'Little Joanna' PBR — ELan LRHS NLar
- - 'Tropical Blue' — ELan SPoG
- § **taxifolia** — CSBt
- **tibetica** — CAco
- **virginiana** — CAco CAgr
- - 'Burkii' — SArc
- - 'Pendula' — CAco
- - 'Sulphur Spray' — see *J.* × *pfitzeriana* 'Sulphur Spray'

Jurinea (Asteraceae)

- **mollis** — MCtn

Jussiaea see Ludwigia

Justicia (Acanthaceae)

- **americana** — SBrt
- **aurea** — EAri EShb SPlb
- § **brandegeeana** ⚥H1b — CTsd EShb
- - 'Lutea' — see *J. brandegeeana* 'Yellow Queen'
- - variegated (v) — EShb
- § - 'Yellow Queen' — EShb
- - yellow-flowered — EShb
- § **carnea** — CBct CHll EAri EShb EWld SEle WFar
- - 'Alba' — WFar
- - dark-leaved — CHll EShb
- § **floribunda** ⚥H1b — CAbb CBcs CBrac CHll ELan EMdy SEle WLov
- **guttata** — see *J. brandegeeana*
- **pauciflora** — see *J. floribunda*
- 'Penrhosiensis' — EShb
- **pohliana** — see *J. carnea*
- **radicans** — WFar
- **rizzinii** — see *J. floribunda*
- **spicigera** — EShb
- **suberecta** — see *Dicliptera sericea*

Kadsura (Schisandraceae)

coccinea B&SWJ 11793	WCru
- FMWJ 13489	WCru
heteroclita	WPGP
- FMWJ 13385	WCru
- WWJ 11947	WCru
japonica B&SWJ 1027	WCru
- B&SWJ 4463 from Korea	WCru
- B&SWJ 11109 from Japan	WCru
- B&SWJ 14672	ESwi WCru
- 'Fukurin' (v)	NLar
- 'Variegata' (v)	EPfP
aff. *japonica* NMWJ 14550	WCru

Kaempferia ❀ (Zingiberaceae)

parishii	EAri
roscoeana	EAri
rotunda	EAri LAma
- 'Himalayan Easter'	LAma

Kageneckia (Rosaceae)

oblonga	SPlb

Kalanchoe (Crassulaceae)

beauverdii	EShb
beharensis ♀H1b	CDoC CDTJ EShb EUrb LWaG NCft NPlm WCot
- 'Rusty'	CDTJ EShb
- 'Silver Shadow'	EShb
blossfeldiana ♀H1b	WCor
- 'Don Nando' PBR (d)	LCro
- 'Serenity Bicolour Pink'	LCro
brachyloba	EShb
daigremontiana	CoPl CPic EShb LWaG SEND WCor WFar
§ **delagoensis**	CDoC CoPl EShb LWaG SEND WCor
'Dorothy'	EShb
× **edwardii** 'Fang' ♀H1b	CDTJ EShb WCot
fedtschenkoi	CPic SEND WCor WCot
- 'Variegata' (v)	CPic EShb WCot
hildebrandtii	EShb WCot
humilis	CDoC EShb WCot
laetivirens	CoPl CPic
luciae ♀H1b	CDoC NHrt
manginii ♀H1b	EShb
marmorata ♀H1b	CPic EShb
'Oak Leaf'	EShb
orgyalis	CPic EShb WCot WFar
'Partridge' PBR	LWaG
pinnata	EShb
'Prebella'	CoPl
pumila ♀H1b	CDoC CoPl EShb WCor WFar
rauhii	EShb
rotundifolia new	EShb
scandens 'Kalahari Survivor'	EShb
serrata	EShb
sexangularis	EShb
'Sunny White'	LCro
'Tessa' ♀H1b	EShb WCot
thyrsiflora	CDoC EShb LWaG NHrt
- 'Bronze Sculpture'	CAbb
- RED LIPS ('Ubilips')	LBom LCro
tomentosa ♀H1b	CAbb CDoC CPbh EShb NHrt WCor WCot

- 'Chocolate Soldier'	WCor
tubiflora	see *K. delagoensis*

kale, curly see AGM Vegetables Section

Kalimeris (Asteraceae)

§ **incisa**	EBee GQue MCtn MMuc StAn
- 'Alba'	EBee ECha ELan ELon GMaP MBel SBea SRms WCAu WFar
- 'Blue Star'	EBee ECha ELan ELon GKev GMaP LCro LRHS MNrw NLar WCAu WFar WTor
- 'Charlotte'	EBlo ELon MNrw NDov SMHy SPel SPoG WFar WGoo
- 'Edo Murasaki'	SBrt
- 'Madiva'	EBee ECha ELon NDov SAko SNoN SRms WHoo
- 'Nana Blue'	EBee EGren ELan ELon NDov SPoG SRms
integrifolia	MMuc
- 'Daisy Mae'	NDov
'Mon Jardin'	EBee ECha ELon SHar SPel SRms WCot
§ **mongolica**	EBee ECha LEdu MMuc MWlw NDov SAko SDix SMHy WFar WGoo
- 'Antonia'	ECha MNrw NDov NLar WCot
- variegated (v)	WCot
§ **pinnatifida**	MHol
- 'Hortensis'	MHol MNrw SMHy
§ **yomena** 'Shogun' (v)	CDor CMac CMiW EBee ECha ELon EPfP GKev LEdu MArl MHer MHol MPie NSti SMrm SPoG SRms WFar
- 'Variegata'	see *K. yomena* 'Shogun'

Kalmia ❀ (Ericaceae)

angustifolia ♀H5	GKev WSpi
- f. **rubra** ♀H5	CBcs CDoC EPfP LCro LRHS MAsh NLar WFar WSpi
I - 'Rubra Nana'	CMac
buxifolia subsp. **hugeri**	GKev
latifolia	CBcs EGrI MPri
- 'Alpine Pink'	WSpi
- 'Bandeau'	LRHS
- 'Bay State'	NCth
- BEACON	see *K. latifolia* 'Leuchtfeuer'
- 'Black Label'	LRHS
- 'Bridesmaid'	CBcs
- 'Bullseye'	SPoG
- 'Bumblebee'	LRHS
- 'Carousel'	CBcs
- 'Clementine Churchill'	CMac
- 'Freckles' ♀H6	CMac SPoG
- 'Galaxy'	LMil LRHS
- 'Ginkona'	LRHS
- 'Jans Delight'	EGrI LRHS
- 'Kaleidoscope'	EGrI LCro LMil MAsh
- 'Latchmin'	LRHS
§ - 'Leuchtfeuer'	LRHS
- 'Little Linda' ♀H6	LCro LRHS
- 'Minuet'	CBcs LCro MAsh SPoG
- 'Moyland'	NCth
- f. **myrtifolia** 'Elf'	LCro LRHS
- 'Nancy'	CDoC
- 'Nani'	LMil LRHS
- 'Nipmuck'	CMac
- 'Olympic Fire' ♀H6	CBcs EGrI ELan GGGa LMil WSpi
- 'Olympic Wedding'	LRHS SPoG
- 'Ostbo Red'	CBcs LMil LRHS SPoG
- 'Peppermint'	GGGa NCth
- 'Pink Charm' ♀H6	CMac
- 'Pinkobello'	EGrI

- 'Pinwheel'	MAsh NCth SPoG
- 'Snowdrift'	CBcs LMil
- 'Tad'	EGrI LRHS
- 'Tiddlywinks'	LCro
- 'Tofka'	LRHS
- 'Zebulon'	CBcs LRHS
polifolia	CBcs CDoC LCro LRHS
- var. *compacta* white-flowered	GArf
- 'Newfoundland'	CBcs

Kalmiopsis × *Phyllodoce* see × *Phylliopsis*

Kalmiopsis × *Rhodothamnus* see × *Kalmiothamnus*

× *Kalmiothamnus* (Ericaceae)
'Haytor'	GArf

Kalopanax ✿ (Araliaceae)
pictus	see *K. septemlobus*
§ *septemlobus*	CBcs EBee WJur
- f. *maximowiczii*	EAri LRHS MBlu SBig

Keiskea (Lamiaceae)
japonica	EWld GEdr

Kelseya (Rosaceae)
uniflora	WAbe

Kennedia (Fabaceae)
rubicunda	CTsd EAri SEle

Kentia (Arecaceae)
forsteriana	see *Howea forsteriana*

Kentranthus see *Centranthus*

Kerria (Rosaceae)
japonica 'Albescens'	NLar WCot
- 'Golden Guinea' ♀H5	CBcs CMac EPfP LCro LRHS MAsh MGos MMuc MPri NLar SPoG SRms WLov
§ - 'Picta' (v)	MGos SRms WFar
- 'Pleniflora' (d) ♀H5	CBcs CBrac CMac CSBt EBee EGren EHeP ELan EPfP GAbr LRHS MAsh MGos MMuc MPri NLar SPlb SPoG SRms WFar
- 'Simplex'	CMac SRms
- 'Variegata'	see *K. japonica* 'Picta'

Keteleeria (Pinaceae)
davidiana var. *davidiana*	WPGP
evelyniana	CAco
fortunei	CAco

Kiggelaria (Flacourtiaceae)
africana	SVen

Kirengeshoma (Hydrangeaceae)
palmata	Widely available
- 'Black Style'	EBee IPot NCth
- dwarf	WCot
- Koreana Group ♀H7	CExl CLil EBee ELan GAbr GKev LBar LEdu MBel MHol NBid NLar SPad WCot WCru WFar WPGP

Kitaibela (Malvaceae)
vitifolia	CSpe GElm GKev LShi SPlb WFar

Kitchingia see *Kalanchoe*

kiwi fruit see *Actinidia deliciosa*

Klasea (Asteraceae)
§ *bulgarica*	ECha EPPr ESwi IPot NDov SBeP SBrt SDix SHar SMad WGoo
coronata	IPot
§ - subsp. *insularis* B&SWJ 8698	WCru
- - B&SWJ 12710	WCru
§ *lycopifolia*	CTtf WCot WMal
§ *macra*	EPPr

Kleinia (Asteraceae)
articulata	see *Curio articulatus*
§ *grantii*	CSpe EShb WCot
§ *neriifolia*	NPlm
repens	see *Curio repens*
stapeliiformis	SPlb

Knautia (Caprifoliaceae)
§ *arvensis*	CBWd CCBP CGwi CHab CSpe CTtf EBee EHet ELan EPfP EPPr GJem GJos GQue LCro LShi MAsh MCtn MHer MNHC NAts NLar NMir SPhx SRms WCAu WCot WHer WOrg WShi
- white-flowered	SPhx
dipsacifolia	CElw
'Green Lightning'	SHar
'Jardin d'en Face'	LRHS WTre
§ *macedonica*	Widely available
- 'Crimson Cushion'	CSpe ERCP NLar
- 'Mars Midget'	CSpe EBee EDAr ELan EPfP GJos GMaP LRHS LWaG MCtn MGos MPie MPro NLar SPoG WCAu WFar
- Melton pastels	CDoC CDor EBee EGrI ELan EPfP EPPr ERCP GJos LRHS MCtn MGos MPro MSwo NLar NLit NPer SPoG SRGP SRkn SRms WCAu WCav WFar WTor
- 'Midget Mauves'	EDAr LBar LRHS
- pink-flowered	SRms
- 'Red Knight'	CDor EBee EPfP LRHS LSto MBNS MPro NLar SRms WTor
- 'Thunder and Lightning' PBR (v)	CDoC CSpe CWGN EBee ELan EPfP EWes LBar LRHS LSou MPri NLar SPoG SRms WCot WFar WTor
sarajevensis	MHol

Kniphofia ✿ (Asphodelaceae)
'Ada'	ELon
albescens	SPlb
'Alcazar'	CBcs EGren EHeP ELon EUrb EWhm LCro MAvo MBel MSwo WCAu WFar XFar
'Amazing Fun'	CWGN IBal LRHS NCth NLar
'Ample Dwarf'	WCot
§ *angustifolia*	SPlb
'Apricot'	EBee EBlo WCot
'Apricot Souffle'	WCot WMal
'Atlanta'	WCot
'Backdraft' PBR (Pyromania Series)	LBar LRHS Midl NCth
BANANA POPSICLE ('Tnknibp') (Popsicle Series)	LRHS Midl MPnt SEND
'Barton Fever' ♀H6	WCot
baurii	SPlb
'Bees' Lemon'	CBcs EBee ELan ELon EPfP EPPr ESgI EWhm LBom LCro LRHS LSRN LSto MArl MAvo MHer MNrw NBir

Kniphofia

	NCth NLar NSti SDix SPoG SRkn SRms WCAu WCot WFar WHoo WSpi
§ 'Bees' Sunset' ♀H5	CBWd EBee EBlo ECha EPfP LBar LRHS MBel MMuc SEND SMrm SPoG WCot
'Bob's Choice'	WCot
'Border Ballet'	NBir NGdn
brachystachya	ESgI LEdu SBrt SPlb WPGP
'Bressingham Comet'	EBee ELon NBir SRms WSpi
'Bressingham Gleam'	EBee
BRESSINGHAM SUNBEAM ('Bresun')	EBee NBir
'Brimstone' Bloom ♀H5	CDor LEdu NBid NBir WFar
bruceae	SPlb SVen WCot
'C.M. Prichard' misapplied	see *K. rooperi*
'C.M. Prichard'	WCot
caulescens	CBro CBWd CKno EAri EBee EBlo ECha ELan ELon EPfP GMaP LRHS MNrw NBir NGdn SArc SEND SMrm SPlb WCot WHil WSpi
- 'Coral Breakers'	ELon GMaP MNrw SEND WCot
- early-flowering	WSpi
- 'John May'	WCot
- short	ECha
'Champagne'	WCot
'Chichi'	WCot
'Christmas Cheer'	WMal
citrina	CSpe CTsd EAri GKev MBrN WCot
'Cobra'	CDor EBlo EPPr GMaP SMHy WCot
'Coolknip'	WMal
'Coral Flame' ♀H5	EBee EBlo
'Coral Sceptre'	WCot
'Cotton Candy' (Candy Series)	LBar
'Creamsicle' PBR (Popsicle Series)	LBar Midl MPnt
'David Blake'	EBee EBlo
'Daybreak' **new**	Midl
December-flowering	WCot
'Dingaan'	NBir NLar
'Dorset Sentry'	ELon MBel Midl MNrw NBir NLar WCAu WCot WFar
'Drummore Apricot'	CKno EBee ECha ELon EPfP NBir NLar SMrm SRkn WCot WFar
'Early Buttercup'	WFar
'Echo Mango'	NCth
'Ed's Findling'	WCot
'Elvira' PBR	EBee EBlo MHol SAko SNoN SPoG WCot
EMBER GLOW ('Tneg' PBR) (Glow Series)	EBee LCro NLar
ensifolia	NGdn
'Ernest Mitchell'	WCot
'Fiery Fred' ♀H6	CCBP EBee EBlo ELan ELon EPfP ESgI EWhm GElm LBar LRHS LSto MArl MAsh MMuc MNrw MPie NCth WCot WFar WHoo WMal WSpi
'Fire Brand'	WCot
FIRE GLOW ('Tnfg' PBR) (Glow Series)	CTsd Midl NLar
'First Sunrise' PBR	CWGN NLar
'Flamenco'	EBee EGren ELon EPfP LRHS LSou NGdn SRms SVic WFar
'Florence Bedecked'	WCot
'Frances Victoria'	WCot
galpinii misapplied	see *K. triangularis* subsp. *triangularis*
'Gelbe Flamme'	SAko
'Gilt Bronze'	WCot
'Gladness'	NBir WCot
'Goldelse'	NBir
'Goldfinch'	ESgI WCot
'Grandiflora'	EPfP LRHS LWaG MCtn XFar
'Green Jade'	EBee ECha LEdu LRHS LSto MNrw NBir NLar NSti SEND SRms WCAu WCot WFar WSpi
'Happy Halloween'	CBro LBar LSou MAvo NCth
'H.E. Beale'	WCot
'Hen and Chickens'	SNoN WCot WFar
hirsuta	SRms
- 'Fire Dance'	GEdr GPSL LShi WFar WSpi
- 'Traffic Lights'	LRHS
'Ice Queen'	CBcs CDor CMHG CWnw ECha ELan ELon EMor EPfP EPPr IPot LSou MHer Midl MNrw NCth NLar SAth SEND SMHy SRms WCAu WCot WFar
ichopensis	LEdu WPGP
'Incandesce' ♀H5	CSpe ELan EPPr ESgI EWhm IPot LRHS MNrw SPoG WCot WMal WSpi
'Innocence' ♀H4	EBee EBlo
'Jane Henry'	CDor LEdu
'Jenny Bloom'	EBee EPfP GMaP LEdu LRHS LSto NLar SMrm SRms WCAu WFar WSpi
'Jess's Delight'	WCot
'John Benary'	CBcs EBee GMaP NBir NLar SMrm SRms WCot WSpi
'Jonathan' ♀H5	WCot
laxiflora	WPGP
'Lemon Popsicle' PBR (Popsicle Series)	CAbb CWGN EGren ELan EPfP LBom LRHS MNrw MPro SAth SRms WCav WFar
'Light of the World'	see *K. triangularis* subsp. *triangularis* 'Light of the World'
'Limelight'	EBee ELon
linearifolia	CBlu CExl SPlb WPGP
'Little Elf'	CDor
'Little Maid'	CBcs CDor ECha EGrI EHeP ELan GMaP NBir NCth NLar SRms WCAu WFar WSpi XFar
'Lord Roberts'	WCot WMal
'Luna'	WCot
macowanii	see *K. triangularis* subsp. *triangularis*
'Mango Popsicle' PBR (Popsicle Series) ♀H6	CAbb CMac CSpe CTsd CWnw ELan GMaP LRHS MArl Midl MNrw MPnt MPro NLar NSti NWbg SEND SPoG SRms WCot WFar
'Maurice Blake'	EBlo
'Mermaiden'	SEND
'Minister Verschuur'	CSde EBlo WSpi
'Misty Mars'	WCot
'Moonstone' ♀H5	ELon EMor EPfP EPPr IPot LBar MAvo MNrw NCth NLar NSti SAth SPoG WCot WFar WSpi
'Mount Etna'	WCot
multiflora 'November Glory'	WCot WFar WMal
'Nancy's Red'	CBcs CDor CTsd EBee ECha EGren EPfP EPPr ESgI EUrb GBin GMaP LSRN MHer MHol Midl MSwo NBir NLar SPeP SPoG SRms WCAu WCot WFar WSpi XFar
nelsonii Mast.	see *K. triangularis* subsp. *triangularis*
'New Sensation'	ESgI WCot
'No Rhyme nor Reason'	WCot

§ 'Nobilis' ♀H5	CCht CExl CSde ECha ELan ELon EPfP ESgl EUrb GAbr GBin GMaP LSRN MArl MHol MNrw NGdn SArc SDix SEND SMHy SRms WCAu WCot WMal WSpi	'Samuel's Sensation' Samuel ♀H5	EBee EBlo WCot
		sarmentosa	CExl SPlb WCot
		'Scorched Corn'	LEdu MPro SEND
		'Shining Sceptre' misapplied	see *K.* 'Bees' Sunset'
northiae ♀H4	CBcs CBlu CCht CExl EBee ELan EUrb EWes GKev MHol MNrw NLar SArc SBig SMrm SPad SPlb StAn WCot WPGP WSpi	'Shiny Beast'	WCot
		'Slush Puppy' (Candy Series)	LBar
		'Star of Baden-Baden'	NBir SEND
		'Strawberries and Cream'	EGrl
'Old Court Seedling'	ESgl WCot WFar	'Sunningdale Yellow' ♀H5	ECha EGren EMor ESgl EUrb GMaP MSwo SMHy SRms WCAu WHoo WSpi
'Orange Blaze'PBR (Pyromania Series)	LBar LRHS Midl NCth		
'Orange Flame' **new**	GElm	'Sweet Corn'	LCro SEND
'Orange Fackel'	SAko	'Tawny King' ♀H5	Widely available
'Orange Vanilla Popsicle'PBR (Popsicle Series)	EGren EHeP ELon EMor LCro LEdu MAsh MBros Midl MPnt MPro NWbg SAth SEND SPad SPoG WFar WNPC	'Tetbury Torch'	CExl CWGN MAvo WCAu WSpi
		thomsonii	CExl
		- 'Kichocheo'	EPPr LEdu
		- var. *snowdenii* misapplied	see *K. thomsonii* var. *thomsonii*
§ 'Painted Lady'	CDor CSde GMaP SEND WCot	- var. *snowdenii* ambig.	CExl
'Papaya Popsicle'PBR (Popsicle Series)	CWGN EGren ELan ELon EPfP LBom LCro LRHS Midl MNrw MPnt MPro NLar SAth SPad SPoG SRms WFar WSpi	§ - var. *thomsonii*	LEdu SPel WCot WFar
		- - 'Stern's Trip' ♀H4	WPGP
		'Timothy' ♀H5	CBcs CDor CMac CMHG EBee EBlo EGrl EPfP EPPr EWhm GMaP LBar LEdu LRHS LSou LSRN MBel MNrw MPie NBir NLar SEND SPoG SRms WCAu WMal
parviflora	EBee		
pauciflora	CPbh ESgl WCot WMal		
'Percy's Pride'	CElw CExl CSde EBee EGrl ELon EPfP EPPr GMaP LCro LEdu NBir NSti SMrm SRms WBrk WCAu WCot WFar WSpi		
		'Toffee Nosed' ♀H5	CMac EBee EGren ELon EPfP EPPr ESgl EWhm LBar LRHS LSou LSto MArl MAvo NBir NGdn NLar WCAu WCot WFar WSpi
'Pfitzeri'	SRms		
'Pineapple Popsicle'PBR (Popsicle Series)	CWGN EBee ELon LCro MArl MHtn MPnt NEoE NSti SAth SRms		
		'Torchbearer'	WCot
(Poco Series) POCO CITRON	EGren IPot LCro LSou MPro NCth WFar	*triangularis*	EPfP EUrb GKev WFar
		§ - subsp. *triangularis*	CSde EArl LRHS SRms
- POCO ORANGE ('Tnknipo'PBR)	CBcs EGren LRHS LSou Midl MPro NCth NLar WFar	§ - - - 'Light of the World'	LRHS NBir WFar
		Tuckii Group	GAbr
- POCO RED ('Tnknipr'PBR)	CWGN EGren ELan LCro LRHS LSou Midl MPro WFar	'Tuckii' misapplied	SRms
		'Tyger Tyger'	EBlo
- 'Poco Sunset'	LCro LRHS LSou MBros MMrt NCth WFar	*typhoides*	NBir SPlb WCot
		tysonii	SPlb
- POCO YELLOW ('Tnknipy'PBR)	EGren LCro	*uvaria*	EGren ESgl LBar LBom LCro LRHS NBir SRms WCAu WCot
× *praecox*	WPGP		
'Primrose Upward' ♀H6	WCot	'Vanilla'	MMuc SEND
'Prince Igor' misapplied	see *K.* 'Nobilis'	'Vesta'	EBee EBlo
'Red Rocket'PBR	EGrl	'Victorine'	WCot
		'Vincent Lepage'	LBar LRHS
'Redhot Popsicle'PBR (Popsicle Series)	CWGN EHeP EPfP LCro LRHS MHol MNrw MPnt MPro SPoG WCot	'Wol's Red Seedling'	CBro MNrw SMHy
		'Wrexham Buttercup' ♀H6	CDor EBee ELan EPfP EUrb EWhm GAbr GMaP LRHS MArl MAvo MHol MNrw NLar SRkn WCot WFar WSpi
'Rich Echoes' ♀H5	CDor CWGN ELon EPPr ESgl EWhm LBar LRHS MAvo MHol MNrw NCth NLar WCot WMal		
		'Yellow Cheer'	WCot WMal
ritualis	GEdr	'Yellow Hammer' Slieve Donard	MMuc SEND
'Rocket Junior' **new**	Midl		
'Rocket's Red Glare'PBR (Pyromania Series)	IPot LBar LRHS Midl NCth		

Koeleria (Poaceae)

glauca	EBee ECha EDAr EGren EPfP GMaP LRHS NGdn SPlb WFar
- 'Pygmaea' **new**	WHil
vallesiana 'Mountain Breeze'	CCps EPPr

§ *rooperi* ♀H5	Widely available
'Royal Castle'	CBcs CExl EHeP GMaP LBar LRHS MCtn NBir NGdn SEND SRms WFar
'Royal Standard' ♀H5	CBcs EBlo EGren EHeP ELon GMaP LBom LCro MAsh MAvo SPoG WCAu WFar WSpi

Koelreuteria (Sapindaceae)

bipinnata	WJur
var. *integrifoliola*	
paniculata	CAco CBcs CHll CLnd CMac CMCN CSpe CWal EBar EGrl ELan EUrb GKev IPap LEdu LMaj MCtn MGos MMuc NLar SBrt SEND SHor SPlb WFar WHtc WJun WJur

rufa misapplied	see *K. angustifolia*
rufa Baker	ECha LEdu WMal WPGP
- 'Rasta'	CBcs EUrb GBin LCro LRHS SMrm
aff. *rufa*	ESwi
'Rufus'	MHtn
'Safranvogel' ♀H5	WCot WMal
'Samuel's Sensation' misapplied	see *K.* 'Painted Lady'

- 'Coral Sun' PBR ♀H5 | CDoC CMac CWnw EBee EPfP LCro LRHS MBlu MGos MMrt NPip SHor WHtc WMat
- 'Fastigiata' | EBee ELan MBlu
- 'September' | MBlu

Koenigia (Polygonaceae)
alpina misapplied — see *K.* × *fennica* 'Johanniswolke'
§ *alpina* (All.) T.M. Schust. & Reveal var. *alpina* | SMHy
§ *campanulata* | CElw EAri EBee ECha EGrI EPot GAbr GMaP GQue LShi LSto MAvo MMuc NSti SMad WFar
- Alba Group | CElw
- 'Madame Jigard' | ECha GGro
- 'Rosenrot' | WOld WTre
- 'Southcombe White' | ECha
aff. *campanulata* WJC 13846 | GGro
§ × *fennica* 'Johanniswolke' ♀H6 | CBcs CBct CBWd EBee EBlo ECha ELan EPPr EUrb EWhm GMaP GQue IPot LRHS LWaG NDov NSti SDix SPel SPeP SPlb SPoG WCAu WCot WJun WPnP WSpi
§ *forrestii* | GGro GKev
§ *mollis* BSWJ 7194 | WCru
P *polystachya* | ELan NLar SMrm WCot WTre
§ *weyrichii* | NBir NBro NLar WFar

Kohleria (Gesneriaceae)
'An's Nagging Macaws' | WDib
'Brazil Gem' | WDib
'Bristol's Evil Storm' | WDib
'Cybele' | WDib
'Flashdance' | WDib
'Hcy's Jardin de Monet' | WDib
'Queen Victoria' | WDib
'Silver Feather' | WDib
'Sunrise' ♀H1c | WDib
'Texas Rainbow' | WDib
warszewiczii ♀H1b | WDib
'Yf's Elin' | WDib
'Yf's Emma' | WDib
'Yf's Josse' | WDib
'Yf's Lotta' | WDib
'Yf's Torun' | WDib

kohlrabi see AGM Vegetables Section

Kolkwitzia (Caprifoliaceae)
amabilis | CNWT CSBt ELan SGol SPlb SRms WJur
- DREAM CATCHER ('Maradco') | CMac EBee LRHS NEoE NLar SGol WSpi
- 'Pink Cloud' misapplied | see *K. amabilis* 'Rosea'
- 'Pink Cloud' ambig. | EGren LSto
- 'Pink Cloud' ♀H6 | CBcs CBrac CDoC CMac EBee EHeP ELan EPfP LCro LRHS LSRN MAsh MGos MMuc NLar SGol SPoG SRms WFar WHtc WSpi
§ - 'Rosea' | CBrac

Kumara (Asphodelaceae)
§ *plicatilis* ♀H2 | EShb

kumquat see *Citrus japonica*

Kunzea (Myrtaceae)
ambigua | CBcs CTsd SEle SPlb
- pink-flowered | SEle
'Badja Carpet' | CTsd SEle

baxteri | CPbh
ericifolia | SPlb
§ *ericoides* | CAgr CTsd ELon GKev SArc
parvifolia | SPlb

L

Lablab (Fabaceae)
purpureus 'Ruby Moon' | CSpe LCro MCtn

+ *Laburnocytisus* (Fabaceae)
'Adamii' | EBar ELan EPfP IArd LSRN MGos NLar

Laburnum ❀ (Fabaceae)
alpinum | SPlb WJur
- 'Pendulum' | CAco LCro LSRN MPri SPoG
§ *anagyroides* | IPap MMuc SEND SRms WJur
- 'Erect' | SPoG
- 'Yellow Rocket' | CBcs CBTr EBee ELan EPfP LCro LRHS MPri NLar WMat
'Famous Walk' | see *L.* × *watereri* 'Vossii'
vulgare | see *L. anagyroides*
I × *watereri* 'Fastigiata' | LRHS
- 'Sunspire' | LCro
§ - 'Vossii' ♀H6 | CBcs CBTr CCVT CDoC CHab CLnd CMac EBar EBee EGren EHeP ELan EPfP GKin IPap LBuc LCro LRHS LSRN MGos MPri MSwo NLar SEWo SPoG WFar WHtc WMat

Lachenalia (Asparagaceae)
§ *aloides* | CMiW CPbh
- var. *aurea* | see *L. flava*
- var. *luteola* | see *L. flava*
- var. *quadricolor* | see *L. quadricolor*
bifolia | see *L. bulbifera*
§ *bulbifera* ♀H2 | CBro WCot
contaminata ♀H2 | CPbh
ensifolia | WCot
§ *flava* ♀H2 | WCot
longituba ♀H2 | EDAr
obscura | WCot
I 'Pearsonii' | SPlb
pendula | see *L. bulbifera*
§ *quadricolor* ♀H2 | WCot
'Romelia' (African Beauty Series) | WCot
'Rosabeth' (African Beauty Series) | WCot
'Rupert' (African Beauty Series) ♀H2 | WCot
tricolor | see *L. aloides*

Lactuca (Asteraceae)
alpina | see *Cicerbita alpina*
perennis | GGro WHer
- var. *angustata* | MCtn MNHC

Lagarosiphon (Hydrocharitaceae)
major | Prohibited invasive. See Conservation and the Environment, p.42

Lagarostrobos (Podocarpaceae)
§ *franklinii* | CBcs WPGP

Lagenaria (Cucurbitaceae)
siceraria 'Speckled Swan' | SVic

Lampranthus 413

Lagerstroemia ❀ (Lythraceae)
Enduring Summer Red ('Piilag B5'^{PBR}) **new**	LRHS
Enduring Summer White ('Piilag B1'^{PBR})	CDoC LRHS
fauriei 'Fantasy' **new**	WPGP
- 'Kiowa'	WPGP
- 'Townhouse'	WPGP
'Hopi'	NLar
indica	LMaj NPlm SArc SIvy SPlb SVen WFar
- B&SWJ 12660	WCru
- 'Berlingot Menthe'	CBcs
- Berry Dazzle ('Gamad VI') ♀^{H4}	LCro
- Burgundy Cotton ('Whit VI')	NLar
- 'Cedar Red'	EBee EPfP LEdu SChF WPGP
- 'Cordon Bleu'	CDoC
- Dynamite ('Whit II')	CDoC NLar SEND
- (Indya Charms Series) Braise d'Été ('Indybra'^{PBR})	LRHS
- - Camaïeu d'Été ('Indycam'^{PBR})	LRHS
- - Fuchsia d'Été ('Indyfus'^{PBR})	CBcs LRHS
- - Neige d'Été ('Indynei')	LRHS
- - Violet d'Été ('Indyvio'^{PBR})	LRHS MMrt
- Mimie Fuchsia ('Dablage01'^{PBR})	LRHS
- Petite Pinkie ('Monkie')	EGrI EShb
- Pink Velour ('Whit III')	NLar
- 'Purpurea'	WPGP
- 'Red Imperator'	CBcs EShb LRHS
- Rhapsody in Pink ('Whit VIII')	CBcs CDoC LRHS NLar
- 'Rosea'	CBcs EBar EGren ELan IPap LRHS SEND
- (With Love Series) With Love Babe ('Milaperl'^{PBR})	LRHS SPoG
- - With Love Cherie ('Cov')	SPoG
- - With Love Kiss ('Milarosso'^{PBR})	LRHS
- - With Love Virgin ('Milabla'^{PBR})	LCro
'Natchez'	WPGP
'Sarah's Favorite'	WPGP
subcostata	EPfP LEdu WPGP
'Tuscarora'	WPGP
'Tuskegee'	CBcs CJun LRHS WPGP

Lagotis (Plantaginaceae)
glauca	GEdr
takedana	GEdr

Lagunaria (Malvaceae)
patersonia	WJur

Lagurus (Poaceae)
ovatus	CSpe CTtf LCro LShi MCtn MPro NClf SPhx SRot WChS

Lamiastrum see *Lamium*

Lamium (Lamiaceae)
album	CGwi CHab
- 'Friday' (v)	NBir
§ *galeobdolon*	CoPl IDun LRHS LSto LWaG MHer NAts SRms WCAu WOrg
? - 'Florentinum' (v)	CMac ECha GBin GQue WCAu WFar
- 'Hermann's Pride'	EPfP GKev LShi MAsh MHol NBir NDov NMir SBeP SPoG SRms WFar
- 'Kirkcudbright Dwarf'	EPPr WFar
§ - 'Silberteppich'	ECha
- Silver Carpet	see *L. galeobdolon* 'Silberteppich'
- 'Variegatum'	see *L. galeobdolon* 'Florentinum'
garganicum subsp. *garganicum*	EWes
- subsp. *pictum*	see *L. garganicum* subsp. *striatum*
- subsp. *reniforme*	see *L. garganicum* subsp. *striatum*
§ - subsp. *striatum*	CDor
'Len Speller'	EBlo
luteum	see *L. galeobdolon*
maculatum	LWaG MMuc SRms WCot WHil
- 'Album'	SRms
- 'Anne Greenaway' (v)	WCAu
§ - 'Aureum'	LShi NSti WFar
- 'Beacon Silver'	CBcs CMac EBee ECha EGren EHeP ELan EMor EPfP GBin GQue LBom LCro LRHS LShi LSto MBel MGos MHed MMuc MPie MPnt NBir NSti SPlb SPoG SRms WFar
- 'Brightstone Pearl'	EWld SHar
- 'Chequers Board'	GAbr
- 'Ghost'	EPfP LBuc SRms
- 'Gold Leaf'	see *L. maculatum* 'Aureum'
- Golden Anniversary ('Dellam'^{PBR}) (v)	ELan LRHS MPro
- 'Golden Nuggets'	see *L. maculatum* 'Aureum'
- 'Golden Wedding'	SRms
- Lami Mega Purple (Lami Series)	EBee
- 'Margery Fish'	SRms
- 'Orchid Frost'	GQue
- Pink Chablis ('Checkin'^{PBR})	ELon MPro MSwo NCou NLar
- 'Pink Pearls'	SHar
- 'Pink Pewter'	CDor EBee ECha ELan EMor EPfP GKev GMaP LShi MAsh MBel SHar SPlb SPoG SRms
- 'Purple Dragon'	EMor SPoG
- 'Purple Winter'	EPPr
- 'Red Nancy'	ELan EPfP LRHS LShi WCAu
§ - 'Roseum'	EBee EGren ELan EMor EPfP GMaP LRHS WCAu
- 'Shell Pink'	see *L. maculatum* 'Roseum'
- 'White Nancy'	CCBP CMHG EBee ECha EHeP ELan EMor EPfP GJos GKev GMaP LCro LRHS LShi LSRN LSto MAvo MBel MHol MPro NBir NLar SPoG SRms WCAu WFar
- 'Wootton Pink'	NBir
orvala	Widely available
- 'Album'	CCBP CDor CMiW CTtf EBee ECha EPPr NBir NLar SMad SMrm WCAu WHer
- pink-flowered	LWaG
- 'Silva'	LEdu WCot
purpureum	MCtn
sandrasicum	WAbe

Lampranthus (Aizoaceae)
aberdeenensis	see *Delosperma aberdeenense*
aurantiacus	CBcs
aureus	CoPl
blandus	CBcs
'Blousey Pink'	SVen WCor

414 Lampranthus

brownii	CBcs CoPl EAri ELan EPfP SPlb
coccineus	CoPl
deltoides	see *Oscularia deltoides*
edulis	see *Carpobrotus edulis*
haworthii	CoPl
mauve-flowered	CoPl
multiradiatus	SEND
orange-flowered	CCht CoPl LRHS WCor
oscularis	see *Oscularia deltoides*
'Pink'	CCht CPbh CPic ELan LRHS SAth SRms WCor
purple-flowered	CPic LRHS SAth WCor
roseus	EUrb
'Salmon Pink'	CoPl
'Shanklin'	SVen
spectabilis	CBcs
- double lilac-flowered (d)	CPbh
- orange-flowered	CPbh CPic EUrb LRHS SAth WFar
- peach-flowered	WCor
- purple-flowered	CoPl ELon
- 'Tresco Apricot'	LRHS
- 'Tresco Brilliant'	CCht CPbh CTsd ELon EUrb LRHS SAth SEND SRms WCor
- 'Tresco Fire'	CPbh ELon SRms SVen
- 'Tresco Orange'	CPbh
- 'Tresco Peach'	CPbh WCor
- 'Tresco Purple'	CCht CPbh ELan EUrb
- 'Tresco Red'	CBlu CoPl CPic EUrb SEND WCor
- white-flowered	CoPl EShb SAth SVen WCor WFar
- yellow-flowered	CPbh CPic EShb EUrb SAth SEND SVen WFar
stipulaceus	SPlb
'Sugar Pink'	CoPl

Lamprocapnos (Papaveraceae)

§ *spectabilis* ♀H6	Widely available
- 'Alba' ♀H6	Widely available
- 'Cupid'	EMor IPot LBar NCth SPeP XFar
- 'Gold Heart'^{PBR}	CBcs EBee EMor LBar LRHS MArl MGos MHol NBid NLar NWbg SPeP SPoG SRms WCot WFar WSpi WTor
- 'Ruby Gold'	EGren EMor LBar LSou NWbg SPeP
- VALENTINE ('Hordival'^{PBR}) ♀H6	Widely available
- WHITE GOLD ('Tndicwg'^{PBR})	EMor ESwi LBar LRHS SPeP
- 'Yellow Leaf'	LBar LRHS LSou MAsh NEoE

Lamprothyrsus (Poaceae)

hieronymi	CSde ECha EPPr
- RCB RA K2-2	CCht EBee ELon ESwi MHol SMad WCot WPGP

Lancea (Mazaceae)

tibetica	GEdr

Lantana ✿ (Verbenaceae)

'Calippo Tutti Frutti'	ELan
camara	EShb
- (Bandana Series) BANDANA CHERRY ('Bante Cheria')	EMdy
- - BANDANA ORANGE SUNRISE ('Bante Oransun'^{PBR})	EMdy
- - BANDANA RED 09 ('Bant Reda09'^{PBR})	EMdy
- BLOOMIFY PINK ('Baloomink') **new**	LSou
- (Lucky Series) LUCKY PEACH ('Balucpea')	SPoG
- - LUCKY PURE GOLD ('Balucpure'^{PBR})	SPoG
- - LUCKY RED FLAME ('Balandimfla')	SPoG
- - LUCKY SUNRISE ROSE ('Balandrise'^{PBR})	SPoG
- - LUCKY WHITE ('Balucwite'^{PBR})	SPoG
- orange-flowered	SEND
'Dallas Red'	EAri ELan
'Miss Huff'	EAri EBee ELan EMdy EPfP
§ *montevidensis*	EShb
- f. *albiflora*	EShb
'Radiation'	EAri ELan EPfP
selloviana	see *L. montevidensis*

Lapageria ✿ (Philesiaceae)

rosea ♀H3	CExl CRHN CTsd MCtn SAdn SChF WPGP
- var. *albiflora* ♀H3	CRHN SChF
- - 'Hugletts Blush'	MCtn
- 'Beatrix Anderson'	CRHN
- 'Flesh Pink'	CRHN
- 'Pink Panther'	CRHN

Lapeirousia (Iridaceae)

cruenta	see *Freesia laxa*
laxa	see *Freesia laxa*

Lapiedra (Amaryllidaceae)

martinezii	GKev

Laportea (Urticaceae)

bulbifera	EAri GGro
- 'Hekiga'	EAri GGro
cuspidata **new**	SPlb

Lardizabala (Lardizabalaceae)

biternata	see *L. funaria*
§ *funaria*	CRHN WCru

Larix ✿ (Pinaceae)

decidua	CAco CMen ELan IPap LMaj MGos MMuc SEND SEWo SPlb WHtc WJur
- 'Bükk'	CAco
- 'Corley'	NLar
- 'Globus'	CAco
- 'Horstmann's Recurved'	CAco NLar
- 'Komarek Hexe'	NLar
- 'Kórnik'	MAsh
- 'Krejčí'	NLar
- 'Little Bogle'	CAco MBlu
- 'Oberförster Karsten'	CAco
- 'Pendula'	CAco
- 'Puli' ♀H7	CAco MBlu MPri NLar SPoG
- 'Summer Fog'	NLar
gmelinii var. *olgensis*	CAco
- var. *principis-rupprechtii*	CAco
- 'Tharandt'	CAco
§ *kaempferi*	CAco CMen ELan EPfP IPap LBuc LMaj SArc
- 'Blue Dwarf' ♀H7	CAco MAsh NLar
- 'Blue Rabbit'	CAco
- 'Blue Rabbit Weeping'	CAco
- 'Bohlik'	NLar
- 'Diana'	CAco MAsh NLar
- 'Elizabeth Rehder'	CAco
- 'Grey Pearl'	NLar
- 'Irica'	NLar
- 'Jakobsen'	LRHS NLar
- 'Jakobsen's Pyramid'	MAsh WMat
- 'Kaskade'	CAco

– 'Madurodam'	NLar
– 'Magic Gold'	NLar
I – 'Nana'	CAco
– 'Paper Lanterns'	CAco
– 'Pendula'	CAco EPfP SPoG
– 'Stiff Weeper' ♀H7	CAco NLar
– 'Wehlen'	NLar
– 'Wolterdingen'	CAco NLar
laricina	CAco
– 'Arethusa Bog'	NLar
– 'Deborah Waxman'	NLar
– 'Iron Red'	NLar
– 'Madie G.'	CAco
– 'Michigan Tower'	NLar
– 'Obelisk'	NLar
– 'Porcupine'	NLar
leptolepis	see *L. kaempferi*
× *marschlinsii* 'Orvelte'	CAco
– 'Varied Directions'	CAco
occidentalis 'Nowhere'	CAco

Laser (Apiaceae)

trilobum	CSpe SPhx
– PAB 3382	LEdu WPGP

Laserpitium (Apiaceae)

gallicum	CSpe
latifolium	SPhx
§ *siler*	CSpe ECha SPhx SPlb StAn WPGP WSpi

Lasiagrostis see *Stipa*

Lasiospermum (Asteraceae)

bipinnatum	SPlb

Latania (Arecaceae)

lontaroides	NPlm

Lathraea (Orobanchaceae)

clandestina	MCtn

Lathyrus ✿ (Fabaceae)

§ *aureus*	CAby CDor CSpe EWld GEdr MCtn MHer MNrw NBid NBir SBrt WCAu WFar
chilensis	LShi
chloranthus	MCtn
cyaneus misapplied	see *L. vernus*
davidii	CSpe
gmelinii	SBrt
grandiflorus ♀H6	CCBP CRHN NSti SDix WCot
× *hammettii*	MCtn
'Blue Shift' **new**	
– 'Erewhon'	LCro MCtn
– 'Painted Porcelain' **new**	MCtn
I – 'Primrose' ♀H3	LCro
– 'Turquoise Lagoon'	MCtn
japonicus	CAgr WCot
subsp. *maritimus*	
laevigatus	SBrt
latifolius ♀H7	CAgr CRHN CSde EGren EPPr LRHS MCtn MHol NPer SMrm SRms SVic WBrk WCot WFar
§ – 'Albus' ♀H7	SRms WFar
– deep pink-flowered	WTHo
– pale pink-flowered	SEND WTHo
– Pink Pearl	see *L. latifolius* 'Rosa Perle'
– 'Red Pearl'	CBcs CWGN EBee ELan EPfP GAbr LBuc LCro LSRN MHer MPro NLar SPlb SPoG SRms WFar
§ – 'Rosa Perle' ♀H7	CBcs EBee ELan EPfP LCro LRHS LShi MPro NBir NLar NPer SPoG WFar
– 'White Pearl' misapplied	see *L. latifolius* 'Albus'
– 'White Pearl' ♀H7	CBcs CWGN EBee ECha ELan EPfP GAbr LBuc LCro MHer MPro NBir NLar NPer SPeP SPoG SRms WCAu WFar WKif WTHo
linifolius	NAts
nervosus	CSpe LShi MCtn SRms
niger	EWld LEdu LShi MCtn MHer SHar
odoratus 'Annie B Gilroy'	MCtn
– 'Albutt Blue'	CSpe MCtn
– 'Almost Black'	LCro
– 'America' ♀H3	MCtn
– 'Ballerina Blue' ♀H3	MCtn
– 'Beaujolais'	LCro MCtn
– 'Betty Maiden'	NClf
– 'Black Knight'	MCtn
– 'Black Prince'	MCtn
– 'Blue Velvet'	CSpe
– 'Bobby's Girl' ♀H3	LCro
– 'Bristol' ♀H3	CSpe MCtn
– 'Cathy' ♀H3	MCtn
– 'Charlie's Angel' ♀H3	LCro MCtn
– 'Chatsworth'	LCro
– 'Cupani'	LCro MCtn MNHC
– 'Cupid'	MNHC
– 'Cyril Plater'	MCtn
– 'Daphne'	LCro
– 'Diamond Jubilee' **new**	LCro
– 'Dorothy Eckford' ♀H3	CSpe LCro MCtn
– 'Earl Grey'	MCtn
– 'Eclipse'	LCro
– 'Emily' **new**	MCtn
– 'Fire and Ice' ♀H3 **new**	MCtn
– 'Flagship'	MCtn
– 'Flora Norton'	MCtn
– 'Frolic'	LCro
– Giant Spencer Waved Mixed	MNHC
I – 'Gwendoline' ♀H3	LCro
– 'Happy Birthday'	MCtn
– 'Henry Thomas'	MCtn
– 'High Scent' ♀H2	LCro
– 'Jilly' ♀H3	LCro MCtn
– 'Judith Wilkinson'	MCtn
– 'Juliet'	MCtn
– 'Just Julia' ♀H3	CSpe
– 'Karen Louise'	LCro
– 'King Edward VII' ♀H3	LCro
– 'Kingfisher'	MCtn
– 'Knee High'	LCro
– 'Lady Grisel Hamilton' ♀H3	MCtn
– 'Leamington'	LCro MNHC
– 'Leominster Boy'	MCtn
– 'Linda C'	LCro
– 'Lisa Marie'	LCro
– 'Lord Nelson'	MCtn
– Mammoth Mixed	MCtn
– 'Matucana'	CSpe ELan LCro MCtn MNHC
– 'Memorial Flight'	MCtn
– 'Memories'	MCtn
– 'Midnight'	LCro MCtn
– 'Mollie Rilstone'	LCro
– 'Monarch's Diamond' **new**	MCtn
– 'Mrs Bernard Jones' ♀H3	LCro MCtn
– var. *nanellus* 'Pink Cupid' ♀H3	LCro
– 'Newby Blue' **new**	NClf
– 'Nimbus'	CSpe LCro
– 'Noel Sutton' ♀H3	LCro MCtn

- 'Old Spice'	SVic	
- 'Our Colin' **new**	CSpe	
- 'Our Harry'	MCtn	
- 'Oxford Blue'	LCro	
- 'Painted Lady'	LCro MCtn	
- 'Pandemonium' ♀H3	MCtn	
- 'Pink Panther' **new**	LCro	
- 'Pluto'	LCro	
- 'Prima Donna' ♀H3	MCtn	
- 'Prince Edward of York'	MCtn	
- 'Prince of Orange' Morse	CSpe MCtn	
- 'Princess Elizabeth'	LCro	
- 'Pulsar'	MCtn	
- 'Queen of Hearts' **new**	MCtn	
- 'Restormel'	MCtn	
- 'Rosy Frills'	MCtn	
- 'Route 66'	MCtn	
- 'Royal Wedding'	LCro MCtn	
- 'Senator'	MCtn	
- 'Serenity' **new**	NClf	
- 'Sir Jimmy Shand'	MCtn	
- SPENCER MIXED	LCro MCtn SVic	
- 'Timeless' **new**	NClf	
- 'Together' **new**	NClf	
- 'Top Hat'	LCro	
- 'Watermelon'	MCtn	
- 'White Ensign'	MCtn	
- 'White Frills'	LCro	
- 'Wild Swan' **new**	MCtn	
- 'Windsor'	LCro MCtn	
- 'Winston Churchill'	LCro	
- Winter Elegance Series	MCtn	
- 'Zorija Rose' **new**	MCtn	
palustris	MMuc SPlb	
pannonicus	GKev	
pratensis	CBWd CGwi CHab NAts NMir SPhx WOrg	
roseus	MCtn	
rotundifolius ♀H6	MCtn	
- 'Tillyperone' ♀H7	SPhx	
sativus	CSpe	
- f. albus	WHil	
- f. azureus	MCtn	
subandinus	SPlb	
sylvestris	CGwi GJos LShi MCtn MMuc NAts	
- 'Wagneri'	EBee	
transsylvanicus	MCtn SBrt	
tuberosus	CAgr CRHN EBee EPPr LEdu NBac WCot	
'Tubro'	EBee	
venetus	EBee EWes MNrw	
§ vernus ♀H6	Widely available	
- 'Alboroseus' ♀H6	CDor CTtf EBee ECha EMor EPPr GArf LRHS MNrw NBir NCth NSti SBeP SPoG SRms WCAu WCot WFar WHoo	
- var. albus	EWes GKev GMaP MNrw SRms WCot	
- aurantiacus	see L. aureus	
- 'Caeruleus'	EWes WHoo	
* - 'Cyaneus'	CDor WCot	
- 'Dama Emily'	SHar	
I - 'Filifolius'	CSpe	
- 'Flaccidus'	CAby MNrw WCot	
* - 'Gracilis'	EPPr LEdu SHar	
I - 'Gracilis Alboroseus'	SHar	
- 'Heavenly Blues' **new**	GJos WHil	
- 'Little Elf'	SHar	
- 'Madelaine'	WCot	
- narrow-leaved	CTtf	
I - 'Pendulus'	SHar	

- purple-flowered	LRHS MMuc SEND
- 'Rainbow'	GJos
- 'Rosenelfe'	EMor GEdr GJos LBar LEdu MHer WCot WHil
- 'Spring Melody'	WCot
- 'Subtle Hints'	LBar SHar WCot

Latua (Solanaceae)
pubiflora	WPav WPGP

Laureliopsis (Atherospermataceae)
philippiana	NLar

Laurentia see *Isotoma*

Laurus (Lauraceae)
§ azorica	CBcs	
canariensis	see *L. azorica*	
nobilis ♀H4	Widely available	
- f. angustifolia ♀H4	CDoC CMac MBlu MHoo MMuc NLar SArc SEND SPoG	
- 'Aurea' ♀H4	CBcs CMac ELan ELon LSto NLar SEND SPoG WCot	
- 'Bay Junior' **new**	WCha	
- clipped pyramid	EGren LBom LSRN SArc	
- variegated (v)	CMac SRms	

Lavandula ✿ (Lamiaceae)
'After Midnight'	see *L.* 'Avonview'
'Alba'	see *L. angustifolia* 'Alba', *L. × intermedia* 'Alba'
§ angustifolia	EBee ECul EHet ENfk EPfP GJos GQue LCro LSRN LWaG MCtn MGos MHer MHoo MNHC NGdn NPer SEdi SPlb SPoG SRkn SVic WJur WKit
- 'Alba' misapplied	see *L. angustifolia* 'Blue Mountain White'
§ - 'Alba'	CWnw ELan MHoo SEdi SPlb SVen WJek WSpi
- 'Alba Nana'	see *L. angustifolia* 'Nana Alba'
- 'Anna'	MHed
- 'Arctic Snow'	CBcs CWal ENor EPfP EWhm LCro LRHS LSto MAsh MHer MNHC MPro SFai SOrN SPoG SRms WLav WSpi
- ARDÈCHE BLUE ('Per3225')	EGren
- AROMATICO FORTE BLUE ('Laa20001')	LRHS SPoG
- 'Ashdown Forest'	CBWd EBee ENor EWhm MHol MHoo MPri SAdn SFai SOrN SRGP SRms WLav WSpi
- 'Backhouse Purple'	MHoo
- 'Beechwood Blue' ♀H5	MHer MHoo MNHC WLav
- (BeeZee Series) BEEZEE DARK BLUE ('Kerbeedark'PBR)	EHet ENfk ENor MAsh MPri MPro SMrm SOrN
- - BEEZEE LIGHT BLUE ('Kerbeelight'PBR)	ENfk SMrm SOrN WKit
- - BEEZEE PINK ('Kerbeepink'PBR)	ENfk LRHS MPri SMrm WKit WLov
- - BEEZEE POWER BLUE ('Kerbeepower')	ENfk
- - BEEZEE WHITE ('Kerbeewhite'PBR)	ENfk MAsh MPri SAth SMrm WLov
- BLUE CUSHION ('Schola')	ELan LCro MAsh SPoG SRms WLav
- BLUE ICE ('Dow3')	NLar WLav
§ - 'Blue Mountain White'	EGren MPri WLav
- 'Blue Rider'	WLav
- BLUE SPEAR ('Pas1213794'PBR)	EGren LBar LBuc LRHS LSou MPri MPro WFar

– 'Cedar Blue'	EWhm MHer MHoo SRms WLav	
– 'Coconut Ice'	ELan WLav WSpi	
– 'Compacta'	WLav	
– 'Dursley White'	WLav	
– 'Dwarf Blue'	EHet LRSN MAsh MHed SRms WFar	
– Elizabeth ('Fair 16')	NLar SPoG WLav	
– (Ellagance Series)	SRms	
'Ellagance Ice'		
– – 'Ellagance Purple'	EGren MBros MHol MPro SRms	
– – 'Ellagance Sky'	SRms	
– – 'Ellagance Snow'	EGren MCtn MHtn SVic	
– 'Essence Purple'	EGren ENor MPri MPro SFai	
– 'Felice'PBR	EGren LCro	
– 'Folgate' ♀H5	EPfP EWhm LRHS MHed MHer MHoo NGdn SEdi SRms WHoo WLav WSpi	
– 'Forever Blue'	EBee MHol NLar	
– Granny's Bouquet ('Lavang 38'PBR)	WSpi	
– Havana ('Arbelpaso'PBR)	ELan ENor EPfP LRHS MHol MPri SFai SOrN SPoG WKit WNPC	
§ – 'Hidcote' ♀H5	Widely available	
– 'Hidcote Pink'	EWhm LShi LSto MHer MHoo NGdn SEdi SRms	
– 'Hidcote Superior'	NGdn	
– Ian Lavender	see L. angustifolia 'Purple Treasure'	
– 'Imperial Gem' ♀H5	EBee ELon ENfk ENor EPfP LBom LCro LRHS LSRN MHed MHoo MNHC MPri NLar SEND SPoG SRms WLav WNPC	
– 'Jean Davis'	see L. angustifolia 'Rosea'	
– 'Lady'	NPer WSpi	
– 'Lady Ann'	WLav	
§ – Lavance Deep Purple ('R7890a'PBR)	MPro	
– 'Lavenite Magic Blue Chip'	NLar	
– 'Lavenite Petite'	WLav WSpi	
– Little Lady ('Batlad') ♀H5	EGren ENor EPfP LBom LCro LRHS LSRN LSto MAsh MHed MHoo MPri NLar SFai SOrN SPoG SRms WHoo WKit WLav WSpi	
– Little Lottie ('Clarmo') ♀H5	EWhm MHer MHoo MNHC SEdi WLav	
– 'Loddon Blue'	ENor EPfP EWhm LBom MAsh MHol MHoo SFai SRms WLav WNPC WSpi	
– 'Loddon Pink'	CBcs ELan ENor EPfP EWhm GMaP LBom LRHS MAsh MHed MHoo MPri NGdn SEdi SFai SRms WLav WNPC	
– 'Maillette'	MHoo SRms WLav	
– 'Melissa'	EGren MHol	
– Melissa Lilac ('Dow 4'PBR)	CBcs CSBt ENfk EPfP LBom LCro LRHS LSRN MAsh MGos MHol MHoo MNHC MPri MPro NClf SFai SRms WLav	
– 'Middachten'	LRHS	
– 'Miss Dawnderry'	LBom LRHS	
– 'Miss Katherine' ♀H5	ENor EPfP LBom LRHS MAsh MHed MPri NLar SPoG SRGP WLav	
– Miss Muffet ('Scholmis') ♀H5	MHer SRms WLav	
– 'Munstead'	Widely available	
§ – 'Nana Alba' ♀H5	ELan ELon EWhm GMaP MHer MHoo SEdi SRms WSpi	
– 'Nana Atropurpurea'	MHoo	
– 'Peter Pan'	ELan MHer MHoo NLar WLav	
– 'Princess Blue'	EWhm MHoo SEdi WLav	
– 'Purity'	LRHS MHer MPri	
§ – 'Purple Treasure'	LRHS MPri	
– 'Rosea'	CSBt ECha EGren EHeP EHet ELan ENor EPfP LCro LRHS LSto MCtn MHoo MNHC NBir SFai SPlb SPoG SRms SVic WFar WLav	
– 'Royal Purple'	MHoo NGdn WLav	
– 'Silver Mist'	EPfP LRHS SRms WHer	
– 'SuperBlue'	EGren EHet	
– 'Thumbelina Leigh'PBR	MHoo SRms WSpi	
– 'Twickel Purple'	EBee ELan LBom LRHS LSRN MAsh MHed MHol MHoo MPri SEdi SHor SRms WLav WSpi	
– Valence Deep Violet	see L. angustifolia Lavance Deep Purple	
– 'Vicenza'	MCtn	
– Vienco Early White new	MPri MPro	
– Vintro Blue ('Laaz0006'PBR)	LRHS	
– 'Walberton's Silver Edge'	see L. × intermedia Walberton's Silver Edge	
– White Fragrance ('Florlavwh0')	MPri	
– white-flowered	MBros	
aristibracteata	MHer WLav	
§ – 'Avonview'	MHer WLav	
§ – 'Bee Brilliant'PBR	ENfk EWhm WLav	
§ – 'Bee Cool'	ENfk WLav	
§ – 'Bee Happy'	ENfk EWhm WLav	
§ – 'Bee Pretty'	ENfk EWhm	
– Big Time Blue ('Armtipp01')	ELan LRHS	
– 'Blue Star'	EHet EWhm	
– Bright Luxurious ('Anouk Deluxe 1956'PBR)	LRHS	
buchii var. buchii	WLav	
'Bulls Cross'	WLav	
× cadevallii (Fairy Wings Series) Fairy Wings Blush ('Fw Whimsical')	LRHS MPri SFai	
– – Fairy Wings Pink ('Fw Radiance'PBR)	LCro LRHS SFai	
– – Fairy Wings Purple ('Fw Spellbound')	LCro LRHS MPri SFai	
canariensis	MHer MNHC WLav	
× chaytoriae	MHoo	
'Bridehead Blue'		
– 'Richard Gray' ♀H4	EGren LSRN MHed MHer MHoo SRms WLav	
§ – 'Sawyers' ♀H4	LSRN MHed MHoo NBir NPer SEND SHor SPhx SPoG SRms WKif WMal	
– Silver Sands ('Fair 14'PBR)	ENfk ENor EPfP MNHC SFai SPoG	
× christiana	ENor LRHS MHol MPri SHor WJek WLav WNPC	
'Cornard Blue'	see L. × chaytoriae 'Sawyers'	
dentata	EShb SRms WJek	
§ – var. candicans	MHer SRms WJek WLav	
– var. dentata 'Dusky Maiden'	WLav	
– – 'Royal Crown' ♀H3	WLav	
– silver-leaved	see L. dentata var. candicans	
'Devonshire Compact'	CSBt LRHS MHol MPro SRms	
'Devonshire Compact White'	LRHS	
'Fathead'	CBcs EHet ELan ENor EPfP LRHS LSRN MAsh MGos MHer MHol MPri MPro NGdn NLar SFai SPoG WLav	
'Flaming Purple'	LRHS MPri	
× ginginsii Goodwin Creek Grey' ♀H4	LRHS MHer MPri SRms WJek WLav	
'Hazel'	EPfP LRHS	
'Helmsdale'	CSBt EPfP LSRN NLar	

Lavandula

× *heterophylla* misapplied see *L.* × *heterophylla* Viv. Gaston Allard Group

§ × *heterophylla* WLav
  Viv. Gaston Allard Group
- - 'Meerlo'[PBR] (v) CCht LBar MHer MHol MNHC MPro WCot
- 'Hidcote Blue' see *L. angustifolia* 'Hidcote'
§ × *intermedia* 'Alba' ♀[H5] EHeP MHed MHer MHoo SEdi SEND
 - Anniversary Bouquet ('Dowannibouq') LRHS MPri
 - 'Arabian Night' see *L.* × *intermedia* 'Impress Purple', 'Sussex'
 - 'Arabian Night' ambig. SRms
§ - Dutch Group CBcs CGHo CSBt EGren EHet ENfk ENor EPfP EWhm LBom LCro LRHS MAsh MHoo MNHC MPri SArc SFai SOrN SRms WKit
 - 'Edelweiss' CBcs CGHo CSBt CWnw EHet ENfk ENor EPfP EWhm LBar LShi LSto LWaG MAsh MHed MHoo MNHC NLar SAth SEdi SFai SPoG SRms WLav WSpi
 - 'Fragrant Memories' LRHS MHoo MPri SRms WLav
 - 'Fred Boutin' WSpi
 - 'Grappenhall' misapplied see *L.* × *intermedia* 'Pale Pretender'
 - 'Grappenhall' ambig. CSBt EWhm MHoo WSpi
 - 'Grey Hedge' EWhm MHoo SRms WLav
 - 'Gros Bleu' LWaG WLav
 - 'Grosso' Widely available
 - (Heavenly Series) LRHS
   Heavenly Angel ('Dowphangel')
 - - Heavenly Night ('Dowphnight') LRHS MPri
 - - Heavenly Scent ('Dowphscent') LRHS MHoo MPri
 - 'Hidcote Giant' ♀[H5] NPer WKif WLav WSpi
§ - 'Impress Purple' WLav
 - 'Lullingstone Castle' ENfk EWhm MHoo SIvy SRGP SRms WLav
 - 'Old English' misapplied see *L.* × *intermedia* 'Seal'
 - 'Old English' CBrac ENfk LRHS MHoo MPri SRms
 - Old English Group MMuc SEND WHoo WLav
 - Olympia ('Downoly'[PBR]) LRHS MHol SPoG
§ - 'Pale Pretender' GQue SRms
 - Phenomenal ('Niko'[PBR]) CAby ENor EPfP LCro LRHS LSou MHed MHol MPri NCth NDov SArc SFai SOrN SPad SPoG WCha WLav WLov WNPC
 - Platinum Blonde ('Momparler'[PBR]) CCht LBom LCro LRHS MAsh MHer MPri SPoG
 - 'Provence' CBcs CSBt EHet ENor LRHS MNHC MPri MPro SFai SRms
§ - 'Seal' GMaP SRms
 - Sensational! see *L.* × *intermedia* 'Tesseract' **new**
§ - 'Sussex' ♀[H5] CFis EPfP LRHS MPri WLav
§ - 'Tesseract' CWGN ENor LBar LSou SOrN
 - 'Twickel Purple' ELan EWes MHed NLar
§ - Walberton's Silver Edge ('Walvera') (v) ELan EPfP LBuc LRHS MGos SRms
 'Jamboree' WLav
 'Jean Davis' see *L. angustifolia* 'Rosea'
 lanata ECha SRms WLav
§ *latifolia* IDun MNHC
 'Loddon Pink' see *L. angustifolia* 'Loddon Pink'
 'Madrid Blue' see *L.* 'Bee Happy'
 'Madrid Pink' see *L.* 'Bee Pretty'
 'Madrid Purple' see *L.* 'Bee Brilliant'
 'Madrid White' see *L.* 'Bee Cool'
 multifida CWal MCtn WLav
 officinalis see *L. angustifolia*

 Passionné ('Lavsts 08') ♀[H4] WLav
 pedunculata IDun
 - subsp. *lusitanica* EPfP SPoG
 - - Lusi Pink ('Wijs02'[PBR]) ENor LCro LRHS MPri SFai
 - - Lusi Purple ENor LCro LRHS SFai SPoG
§ - subsp. *pedunculata* CAby ECha EHet ELan EPfP LCro LRHS LSRN MAsh MGos MHoo MPri NGdn SFai SRms WCha WSpi
 - - 'James Compton' ♀[H3] NGdn
 - subsp. *sampaiana* 'Purple Emperor' WLav
 'Pink Panache' MPri
 pinnata CCht EHet ELan ENfk ENor LCro MHol MHoo
 'Pretty Polly' ♀[H4] CBcs ELan EPfP LRHS MAsh NLar SRkn WLav
 'Pukehou' EPfP MAsh WLav
 'Purple Panache' MPri
 'Regal Splendour' CSBt ENor EPfP LCro LSRN MGos MHer SFai SPoG SRms WLav
 Rocky Road ('Fair09') CSBt WLav
 'Rosea' see *L. angustifolia* 'Rosea'
 'Silver Edge' see *L.* × *intermedia* Walberton's Silver Edge
 'Somerset Mist' WLav
 spica see *L. angustifolia*, *L.* × *intermedia*, *L. latifolia*
 - 'Hidcote Purple' see *L. angustifolia* 'Hidcote'
 stoechas CSBt ECha EHeP EHet ELan EPfP LRHS LSRN MCtn MNHC SAth SPlb
 - var. *albiflora* see *L. stoechas* subsp. *stoechas* f. *leucantha*
 - (Anouk Series) 'Anouk'[PBR] ELan EPfP SPoG WCha
 - - Anouk Deep Rose ('Anouk Deluxe 179'[PBR]) LBom
 - - Anouk Supreme ('Anouk Deluxe 901'[PBR]) EGren
 - 'Antibes' (Provençal Series) LRHS MPri SRms
 - 'Bandera' EGren MBros NBir
 - 'Bandera Deep Purple' LBar
 - 'Bandera Pink' EGren LBar LBom LRHS
 - Bella Rose ('Belros') (Bella Series) LRHS
 - 'Blueberry Ruffles'[PBR] (Ruffles Series) ELan EPfP
 - 'Boysenberry Ruffles' (Ruffles Series) ELan
 - Castilliano Violet SVic
 - 'Dark Royalty' ELan
 - deep rose-flowered MHtn
 I - 'Early Summer Improved' (Butterfly Garden Series) **new** MPro
 - Fantasia Early Pink ('Dc000115ls') LCro
 I - 'Giant White Summer Improved' (Butterfly Garden Series) MPro
 - Great Adventure ('Agri811') SWCr
 - Javelin Forte Deep Rose ('Labz0006') (Javelin Forte Series) LRHS
 - Lavender Lace ('Colace') WLav
 - 'Lavita Pink' LBar
 - 'Lavita Purple' LBar
 - (Lavlov Series) Lavlov Pink **new** MPri
 - - Lavlov Purple **new** MPri
 - - Lavlov White **new** MPri

- 'Mulberry Ruffles' (Ruffles Series)	ELan
- 'Night of Passion'	LRHS MPri
- 'Papillon'	see *L. pedunculata* subsp. *pedunculata*
- subsp. ***pedunculata***	see *L. pedunculata* subsp. *pedunculata*
- 'Pink Summer'	MPro
- 'Purley'	SRms
- 'Sancho Panza'	EGrI
§ - subsp. ***stoechas*** f. ***leucantha***	EHeP LRHS
- - - 'Snowman'	CSBt EPfP LRHS MAsh MHer NLar SFai SPoG
- - LILAC WINGS ('Prolil'^{PBR})	ENor EPfP LCro LRHS MAsh SFai SOrN WLav
- - 'Provençal'	LRHS
- - 'Purple Wings'	ELan MAsh MGos
- - f. ***rosea*** 'Kew Red'	ENfk LCro MHer MNHC SFai SRms WKit WLav
- 'Twin Summer' (Butterfly Garden Series)	MPro
- 'Victory'	SPoG
SUPERBLUE ('Balavurlu')	EHet
TIARA ('Fair 10')	CBcs CSBt ENor EPfP LRHS MGos MPri NLar SFai SOrN SPoG SRms WLav
vera misapplied	see *L.* × *intermedia* Dutch Group
vera DC.	see *L. angustifolia*
viridis	EPfP LRHS MHer MHoo NPer SRms WJek WLav
'Willow Vale' ♥^{H3}	EPfP EWhm LRHS MAsh MHer WJek

Lavatera see *Malva*

bicolor	see *Malva subovata*
maritima	see *Malva subovata*

Lecanthus (Urticaceae)

peduncularis	GGro

Ledebouria (Asparagaceae)

adlamii	see *L. cooperi*
concolor misapplied	see *L. socialis*
§ ***cooperi***	ECha EDAr EGrI EShb LEdu SRot WPGP
§ ***socialis***	EShb LEdu MPie SIvy SPlb WFar
violacea	see *L. socialis*

Leea (Vitaceae)

guineensis	MCtn

leek see AGM Vegetables Section

Legousia (Campanulaceae)

speculum-veneris	CSpe

Leibnitzia (Asteraceae)

anandria	GGro

Lemna (Araceae)

gibba	NPer
minor	NPer
trisulca	CWat EWat NPer

lemon see *Citrus* × *limon*

lemon balm see *Melissa officinalis*

lemon grass see *Cymbopogon citratus*

lemon, rough see *Citrus* × *taitensis*

lemon verbena see *Aloysia citrodora*

Leonotis (Lamiaceae)

leonurus	CBcs CDTJ CHll CSpe CWal EAri EMdy ESgI EShb MCtn SAdn SMad SMrm SPlb WJek
- var. ***albiflora***	EAri EShb
nepetifolia	EAri EMdy
- var. ***nepetifolia*** **new**	SEle
ocymifolia	CHll
- var. ***ocymifolia***	SEle

Leontodon (Asteraceae)

hispidus	CBWd CGwi CHab LRHS LShi NMir WOrg
§ ***rigens***	EPPr ESwi GEdr NBid NBir SMrm WFar
- B&SWJ 12527	GGro WCru
- 'Girandole'	see *L. rigens*

Leontopodium (Asteraceae)

alpinum	see *L. nivale* subsp. *alpinum*
- subsp. ***nivale***	see *L. nivale* subsp. *nivale*
discolor	WAbe
franchetii	GKev
himalayanum	GKev
japonicum	GKev
var. ***japonicum***	
nanum	SPlb
§ ***nivale*** subsp. ***alpinum***	CFis EDAr ELan EPfP GAbr GKev LRHS LShi MAsh MCtn SLee SPlb SPoG SRms StAn
- - BLOSSOM OF SNOW ('Berghman')	EGren LBar
- - 'Matterhorn'	GEdr GMaP NLar
- - 'Mignon'	EWes GArf GMaP NLar WAbe
- - 'Watzmann' **new**	MNHC
§ - subsp. ***nivale***	GKev
ochroleucum var. ***campestre***	NLar
pusillum	EDAr SPlb WAbe WIce
souliei	GKev
wilsonii	GKev

Leonurus (Lamiaceae)

cardiaca	CAgr CCBP CGHo CGwi CWRo EGrI GGro MHer MHoo MNHC MPro SRms WTre
- from Cally Gardens	EPPr GGro
- 'Grobbebol'	EPPr MHoo SDix WCot
japonicus	MHoo
sibiricus L.	MCtn
turkestanicus	EBee

Leopoldia see *Muscari*

Lepechinia (Lamiaceae)

hastata	CAbb CAby CSpe EAri ECha EWld SHar SPlb WJek
salviae	SIvy WFar

Lepidium (Brassicaceae)

campestre	CHab
latifolium	CAgr ENfk LEdu
sativum	LCro SVic
- curled-leaved	LCro MCtn

Lepismium (Cactaceae)

cruciforme	NPlm
marnieranum	EShb

Leptinella (Asteraceae)

atrata subsp. *luteola*		ELan
'County Park'		ECha EDAr
dendyi		EWes GEdr MWlw WIce
hispida		see *Cotula hispida* (DC.) Harv.
§	*potentillina*	ECha GQue LRHS MBNS NBro NLar SRms StAn
§	*pusilla*	LRHS
§	*pyrethrifolia*	EPot GEdr GKev
§	*squalida*	ECha ELAr LWaG NSti SLee
*	- 'Minima'	GQue WFar
§	- 'Platt's Black'	CBcs CSde EBee ECha EDAr EPfP EWes GBin GKev GQue ISha LRHS LWaG MHer NLar SIvy SLee SRot WCav WFar WGwG
	traillii	NBro

Leptolepia (Dennstaedtiaceae)

novae-zelandiae	WPGP

Leptopus (Phyllanthaceae)

§	*chinensis*	WCot

Leptosiphon (Polemoniaceae)

§	*grandiflorus* <u>new</u>	CSpe

Leptospermum ✿ (Myrtaceae)

'Copper Sheen'	SEle
'County Park Blush'	ELon SEle
cunninghamii	see *L. myrtifolium*
'Electric Red' (Galaxy Series)	CBcs ELan EPfP LRHS
ericoides	see *Kunzea ericoides*
flavescens misapplied	see *L. glaucescens*
flavescens Sm.	see *L. polygalifolium*
§ *glaucescens*	SPlb
§ *grandiflorum*	CBcs EPfP GAbr SEle SVen
grandifolium	LRHS
'Havering Hardy'	SEle WLov
humifusum	see *L. rupestre*
juniperinum	SPlb
'Karo Pearl Star'	SEle
'Karo Spectrobay'	CDoC SEle
laevigatum	LRHS SVen
§ *lanigerum*	SEle SPlb SVen WJur
- 'Cunninghamii'	see *L. myrtifolium*
liversidgei	SPlb
§ *myrtifolium*	CMac EBee LRHS
nitidum	SPlb
obovatum	LRHS
phylicoides	see *Kunzea ericoides*
'Pink Cascade'	CBcs CMac SEle
§ *polygalifolium*	SEle SPlb
prostratum	see *L. rupestre*
pubescens	see *L. lanigerum*
rodwayanum	see *L. grandiflorum*
rotundifolium	CBcs SPlb
§ *rupestre*	SPlb
scoparium	CTsd EGrl MCtn SPlb SVen WJek WJur WKor
- 'Adrianne'	LRHS SEle
- 'Applebossom' ♀H4	CBcs CDoC ELon EPfP SEle WFar
- 'Autumn Glory'	MMrt SEle
- 'Blossom' (d)	CMac
- 'Burgundy Queen' (d)	CBcs CMac SEle WFar
- 'Cherry Brandy'	SEle
- 'Coral Candy'	CBcs CEnd EGrl ELan LRHS SEle WFar
- 'Crimson Glory' (d)	CTsd EGrl LRHS SEle
- 'Elizabeth Jane'	WFar
- 'Gaiety Girl' (d)	CSBt

- var. *incanum*	ESwi
- - 'Keatleyi' ♀H4	SEle
- 'Jubilee' (d)	CCoa CMac
- 'Martini'	CAbb CBcs CCoa CDoC CMac CSde EGrl ELon EPfP LCro LRHS SEle SPoG
- (Nanum Group) 'Kea'	MHer SEle
- - 'Kiwi' ♀H4	CBcs CBrac CCoa CSBt CSde EBee EGrl ELan EPfP EUrb LRHS MMuc SEle SPoG WFar
- - 'Tui'	CMac CSBt SEle
- 'Nichollsii' ♀H3	CTsd LRHS SEle
- 'Nichollsii Nanum' ♀H4	WAbe
- 'Pink Damask'	SAth
- 'Princess Primanuka'	LCro
- var. *prostratum* misapplied	see *L. rupestre*
- 'Red Damask' (d) ♀H4	CAbb CBcs CBrac CCoa CDoC CMac CSde EGrl ELan ELon EPfP EUrb LCro LRHS LSRN MMrt MMuc SAth SBig SEle SPlb SPoG SVen WFar
- 'Red Ensign'	LBuc LCro SEle SPoG
- 'Red Falls'	LRHS
I - 'Rouge Double Nain'	EGrl SEle
* - 'Ruby Wedding'	ELan LRHS SEle SPoG
- 'Snow Flurry'	CBcs CDoC LRHS SVen WFar
- 'Winter Cheer' (d)	CBcs EGrl
- 'Wiri Donna'	CCoa CSde SEle
- 'Wiri Linda'	CBcs CMac SEle
'Silver Sheen' ♀H3	CAbb CBcs CCoa CDoC CSde CTsd ELan EPfP LRHS MAsh NLar SPoG WPGP
spectabile ♀H3	SEle

Lespedeza (Fabaceae)

bicolor	CAgr CSpe EAri EGrl LRHS WFar
- 'Yakushima'	CBcs NLar
buergeri	NLar
capitata	NLar
cuneata	Prohibited invasive. See Conservation and the Environment, p.42
japonica	SPlb
thunbergii ♀H5	CBcs CDoC CSpe EAri EBee ELan EPfP EUrb LRHS MAsh MBlu NLar SDix SPoG SSta WHil WTor
- subsp. *formosa*	EGrl
- 'Gibraltar'	EAri EBee EPfP NLar WPGP
- 'Summer Beauty'	CBcs
- subsp. *thunbergii* 'Albiflora'	ELan LRHS
- - 'Edo-shibori'	EBee EPfP SChF WPGP
- - 'Little Volcano'	EAri EBee ELan SChF
- - 'White Fountain'	EPfP LRHS MAsh SPoG
tiliifolia	see *Desmodium elegans*

Lessertia (Fabaceae)

frutescens	SPlb
montana	SBrt

lettuce see AGM Vegetables Section

Leucadendron (Proteaceae)

argenteum	CPbh SPlb
'Burgundy Sunset' PBR	CBcs CPbh SEle
conicum	CPbh
coniferum <u>new</u>	CPbh
daphnoides	SPlb
discolor	CPbh SPlb
eucalyptifolium	SPlb
galpinii	CPbh

Leucanthemum 421

gandogeri	CPbh
'Inca Gold' ♀H3	CBcs CPbh
'Jester' (v)	CBcs CPbh SEle
laureolum	CPbh
'Mrs Stanley'	CTsd EUrb SEle
'Safari Sunset' ♀H3	CBcs CPbh EUrb SBig SEle
salicifolium	SPlb
salignum	CPbh SEle
- 'Fireglow'	EUrb
sessile	CPbh
strobilinum	CPbh
tinctum	CPbh

Leucaena (Fabaceae)
leucocephala	CoPl SPlb WJur

Leucanthemella (Asteraceae)
§ *serotina* ♀H7	CElw CKno CMac CTtf EBee ECha ELon EPPr GMaP LEdu LSto MBel MCtn MHer MHol MMuc MNrw NBid NBir NCth NSti SAko SDix SMHy WCAu WCot WFar WMal WOld
- 'Herbststern'	NLar

Leucanthemopsis (Asteraceae)
hosmariensis	see *Rhodanthemum hosmariense*

Leucanthemum ✿ (Asteraceae)
'Angel'	ELon LRHS MBros NCou NLar
catananche	see *Rhodanthemum catananche*
hosmariense	see *Rhodanthemum hosmariense*
maximum misapplied	see *L.* × *superbum*
§ *maximum* (Ramond) DC.	NBro NPer
- *uliginosum*	see *Leucanthemella serotina*
nipponicum	see *Nipponanthemum nipponicum*
'Sante'	CWnw EGren ELan EPfP LRHS Midl MPri MPro MSCN
'Sunshine Peach'	EPfP LRHS SRms
§ × *superbum*	CMac CWal GAbr MMuc SDix SEND SHar StAn WBrk
- 'Adorable'[PBR]	ELan EPfP
- 'Aglaia' (d)	CBcs CDor CMHG EBlo ECha EPfP EWes GAbr GElm GMaP LRHS LSRN LSto MArl MBel MHol MPro NBir NCth NPer SOrN SPoG SRms WCAu WFar WSpi
- 'Alaska'	ELan GQue LRHS MArl NLar SBig SOrN
- 'Amelia'	NLar
- 'Anita Allen' (d)	WCot
- 'Antwerp Star'	EBee NLar
- 'Banana Cream'	CAby CBcs CWGN EGren ELan EPfP LBar LBuc LCro LRHS MAsh MBros MPro MSCN NLar SMrm SPoG WFar
§ - 'Beauté Nivelloise'	CElw EBee GBin NBir SHar SMad SRms WCAu WFar WSpi WTor
- 'Becky'	CMac CoPl EBlo ECha ELan ELon EPfP GBin GMaP LSou MBel NEoE NLar WCAu WCot WSpi
- BELGIAN LACE ('Tnleubl'[PBR])	NLar
- 'Bishopstone'	ELan LEdu SMrm
- 'Brightside'	ELan WFar
- BROADWAY LIGHTS ('Leumayel'[PBR])	EPfP EWes LRHS MAsh MBel MPri SRms WCAu WFar WSpi WTor
- CHRISTINE (Sweet Daisy Series)	LRHS
- 'Christine Hagemann'	CElw SHar WFar
- 'Cloud Cirrus'	EGren
- 'Cloud Cumulus'	EGren LRHS MPri WFar
- 'Cloud Stratus'	EGren
- 'Coconut'[PBR]	ELan Midl WFar
- 'Crazy Daisy'	CWal EGren ELan EMor EPfP LRHS MCtn SPad WFar
- DARLING DAISY ('Kiemar')	WCot
- 'Droitwich Beauty'	WCav
- 'Dwarf Snow Lady'	EDAr
- 'Edgebrook Giant'	WOld
- 'Eisstern'	SHar
- 'Elworthy Sparkler'	CElw MWlw WBrk
- 'Engelina'[PBR]	EBee EPfP LRHS MHol NBir WFar
- 'Esther Read' (d)	ELon GQue LRHS MWlw NBro NLar NWbg SRms WCot WFar
- 'Everest'	SRms
- 'Fiona Coghill' (d)	CMac CWGN EBee GBin MHol NBir NGdn NLar NWbg SHar WCot
- 'Flore Pleno' (d)	MMuc SEND SPlb
- FREAK! ('Leuz0001'[PBR])	CBcs EGren LCro MHol
- 'Goldfinch'[PBR]	CWGN LRHS MHol MPri NBir NGdn SPoG SRkn SRms WCot WFar
- 'Goldrausch'[PBR]	ELan LEdu NBir NGdn SRms WFar
- 'Gruppenstolz'	GBin
- 'H. Seibert'	MArl
- 'Highland White Dream'	LRHS
- 'Horace Read' (d)	CDor EBee NBir
- 'Ice Star'	ELan EPfP NWbg
- 'Jennifer Read'	EBee NLar
§ - 'John Murray' (d)	NBir WFar
- 'King's Crown'	LRHS
- 'LaCrème' (Ooh La Series)	EGren MPro
- 'LaCrosse' (Ooh La Series)	EGren EPfP WFar
- LAGRANDE ('Florleulag'[PBR]) (Ooh La Series)	EGren
- 'LaSpider' (Ooh La Series)	CBcs EGren LRHS MPri
- 'Little Miss Muffet'	CWGN EBee EPfP MArl MBNS SPoG
- 'Little Princess'	see *L.* × *superbum* 'Silberprinzesschen'
- (Lucille Series) 'Lucille Grace'	EGren
- - 'Lucille White'	EGren
- 'Luna'[PBR]	ELan LBar LRHS MHol Midl MPri MSCN NLar WFar
- 'Macaroon'[PBR]	MBros Midl WFar
- 'Madonna'	EGren EPfP LBar LBuc LRHS MHtn MPri
- 'Manhattan'	CDor GBin
- 'Mount Hood' (d)	MBNS WHil
- 'Old Court'	see *L.* × *superbum* 'Beauté Nivelloise'
- 'Paladin'[PBR]	GBin
- 'Phyllis Smith'	EBee MHer MPie MSCN NGdn NWbg SHar SMrm WCAu WCot WFar WKif
- (Realflor Compact Series) 'Real Deal'	EGren LBar LRHS WFar
- - 'Real Dream'[PBR]	ELan LBar WFar WNPC
- - 'Real Neat'	CBcs ELan EPfP LBar MAsh
- (Realflor Medium Series) 'Real Charmer'[PBR]	EGren ELan LRHS MAsh Midl SRms WNPC
- - 'Real Comet'	EGren LRHS
- - 'Real Galaxy'[PBR]	ELan EPfP MHol SPoG
- REAL GLORY ('Reglo'[PBR])	ELan LBar Midl NGdn WFar
- - 'Real Goldcup'	EGren LBar LRHS LSou Midl MSCN WFar
- - 'Real Snowball'	EGren WFar
- 'Shaggy'	see *L.* × *superbum* 'Beauté Nivelloise'
- 'Shapcott Gossamer'	CAby GElm GMaP SPoG SRms WBrk WChS WCot

Leucanthemum

- 'Shapcott Ruffles' — WBrk WCot
- 'Shapcott Summer Clouds' — CDor GMaP SPoG WBrk WCot
- 'Shortstop' — LRHS
§ - 'Silberprinzesschen' — CoPl GMaP LRHS LSto SPlb SRms
- 'Silver Spoon' — EPfP LRHS
- 'Snehurka' — EBee WCot WFar
- 'Snow Lady' — EGren ELan EPfP NLit NPer SRms WFar
- 'Snowbound' — ELan
- 'Snowcap' — LCro MArl WCAu WGwG
- 'Snowdrift' — EBee LRHS NLar WCot WFar
- SOFIE ('Doleuswedaso'[PBR]) (Sweet Daisy Series) — Midl
§ - 'Sonnenschein' — CDor EBee ECha ELan EPfP GMaP GQue LRHS MArl MBel NBir NGdn SMrm SRms WCAu WChs WFar
- 'Spoonful of Sugar' — LRHS
- 'Starburst' (d) — ELan SMrm SRms WFar
- 'Summer Snowball' — see *L.* × *superbum* 'John Murray'
- 'Sunny Side Up'[PBR] — EBee LSou LSto NLar WFar
- SUNSHINE — see *L.* × *superbum* 'Sonnenschein'
- 'T.E. Killin' (d) ♀[H4] — ECha EPfP GElm GMaP LCro LRHS MPri SPoG WCAu WFar
- 'Victorian Secret'[PBR] — ELan EPfP LBuc LRHS MAsh MPri WCot
- WESTERN STAR TAURUS ('Leuz0003'[PBR]) — LBuc MPri
- 'White Breeze' — SHar
- 'White Magic'[PBR] — EGren
- 'Wirral Supreme' (d) ♀[H5] — CBcs CMac CTsd EBee GMaP LCro LRHS MPro NBir NLar SHar SRms WCAu WFar WSpi XFar

'Tizi-n-Test' — see *Rhodanthemum catananche* 'Tizi-n-Test'

§ **vulgare** — Widely available
- 'Filigran' — ELan EPfP WFar
§ - 'Maikönigin' — LRHS NLit SHar
- MAY QUEEN — see *L. vulgare* 'Maikönigin'
'White Knight' — LRHS

Leucocoryne (Amaryllidaceae)

'Andes' ♀[H3] — LAma
'Spotlight' — LAma

Leucogenes (Asteraceae)

grandiceps — WAbe
leontopodium — EPot WAbe

Leucogenes × Raoulia see × Leucoraoulia

Leucojum (Amaryllidaceae)

aestivum — CBcs CCBP CDor EBee EGren GAbr LCro LSto MArl MCtn NBir NLar SEND SRms WCot WFar WShi XFar
- 'Bridesmaid' — EBee EPot GKev
- 'Gravetye Giant' ♀[H7] — Widely available
autumnale — see *Acis autumnalis*
roseum — see *Acis rosea*
tingitanum — see *Acis tingitana*
valentinum — see *Acis valentina*
vernum ♀[H5] — EBee EGren ELan EPfP EPot GKev LAma LCro MNrw NBir NLar NRya SDix SRms WCot WHer WShi XFar
- var. **carpathicum** — MCtn
- var. **vagneri** — CElw ECha EGrI

Leucophyta (Asteraceae)

§ **brownii** — CDoC EGren SPoG

Leucopogon (Ericaceae)

§ **colensoi** — LRHS

× Leucoraoulia (Asteraceae)

§ **loganii** — WAbe

Leucosceptrum (Lamiaceae)

canum — SBrt SPlb
japonicum B&SWJ 10804 — WCru
- B&SWJ 10981 — WCru
- 'Golden Angel' — WFar WHrl
stellipilum — MHol
- var. **formosanum** B&SWJ 1926 — WCru
- - RWJ 9907 — SBrt WCru
- var. **tosaense** B&SWJ 8892 — WCru

Leucospermum (Proteaceae)

'Carnival Copper' (Carnival Series) — CBcs
cordifolium — CPbh
cuneiforme — CPbh
glabrum — SPlb
'Tango' — CPbh

Leucostegia (Davalliaceae)

immersa — LEdu
- PAB 7836 — LEdu
truncata PAB 6859 — WPGP

Leucothoe (Ericaceae)

axillaris — WCha
- CURLY GOLD ('Opstal 55'[PBR]) — WCha WFar
- 'Curly Red'[PBR] — CDoC CMac EBee ELan EPfP LCro LRHS MAsh MGos NLar SOrN SPoG WCha WFar
- TWISTING RED ('Opstal20'[PBR]) — LRHS MBlu
CARINELLA ('Zebekot') — CMac LRHS NLar SPoG
FIRESTAR ('Rant01') (v) — CWnw LCro LRHS WFar
§ **fontanesiana** — CMac WCha
- 'Makijaz'[PBR] (v) — EPfP LRHS LSou NLar SPoG
- 'Rainbow' (v) — CBcs CDoC CMac EGren EGrI LCro LRHS MAsh MGos MPri NLar SGol SPoG SRms WFar
- 'Rollissonii' ♀[H6] — SRms
- WHITEWATER ('Howw'[PBR]) (v) — CBrac CMac LCro LRHS NLar SHor WCha WFar
keiskei — WCha
- BURNING LOVE ('Opstal50'[PBR]) — CMac LCro LRHS LSou NEoE NLar WCha WFar
- 'Royal Ruby' — LRHS MGos NLar SPoG WCha WFar
- 'Little Flames'[PBR] — LRHS LSou MAsh MPkF NCth SOrN WFar
LOVITA ('Zebonard') — LRHS NLar
RED LIPS ('Lipsbolwi'[PBR]) — NLar
SCARLETTA ('Zeblid') ♀[H6] — CBcs CBrac CDoC CMac CSBt EBee EGren EGrI EHeP ELan EPfP LBom LCro LRHS MAsh MGos MHtn NLar SNig SOrN SPoG WCha WFar WSpi
walteri — see *L. fontanesiana*
- 'Hokus Pokus' (v) — NLar WCot

Leuzea (Asteraceae)

centaureoides — see *Rhaponticum centaureoides*

Levisticum (Apiaceae)

officinale — Widely available

Lewisia ✿ (Montiaceae)

'Archangel' — EPot NRya

Ashwood Carousel hybrids   MAsh
- pink shades   NRya
Birch strain   CBcs
brachycalyx ♀H4   MAsh
- pink-flowered   MAsh
Brynhyfryd hybrids   GKev
columbiana   GKev
- 'Alba'   EPot GKev
- subsp. ***rupicola***   WAbe
- subsp. ***wallowensis***   MAsh
congdonii   MAsh
'Constant Comment'   MHol
cotyledon ♀H4   CWal CWCL EDAr EGren EPfP GArf
                             GKev GMaP LCro LRHS LShi MPri
                             SRot
- f. ***alba***   CWCL EDAr
- Ashwood strain   EWes MAsh SRms
- 'Brannan Bar'   MAsh
- ELISE MIXED   EPfP LRHS MHol MPro SRot
- var. ***beckneri***   MAsh
- hybrid   EBee NRya SPoG
- magenta-flowered   CWCL
- orange-flowered   CWCL
§ - REGENBOGEN (mixed)   ESuc GAbr LRHS MCtn MHer
- rose-pink-flowered   CWCL
- (Safira Series) 'Safira Coral' LBar LRHS MArl MPri MPro
- - 'Safira Pink'   LRHS
- - SAFIRA VIOLET   LBar LRHS MPri
    ('Lore3509'PBR)
- - 'Safira White' **new**   MPro
- - 'Safira Yellow'   LBar MPro
- salmon-flowered   CWCL
- Sunset Group ♀H4   GPSL NLar
- 'White Splendour'   MAsh
'George Henley'   EPot EWes WAbe
glandulosa   GKev
(Little Series) 'Little Mango' EDAr ESuc LRHS
- 'Little Peach'   CWCL EDAr EPot LRHS MPro WIce
- 'Little Plum'   EDAr ELan EPfP EPot ESuc GEdr
                             GKev LRHS MAsh NLar NRya WIce
- 'Little Raspberry'   CTsd EDAr GEdr LRHS MAsh MSwo
                             WIce
- 'Little Snowberry'   EDAr ESuc LRHS MAsh
- LITTLE TUTTI FRUTTI (mixed) SVic
MOUNTAIN DREAM (mixed) **new** EPfP ESuc LRHS MSwo
§ ***nevadensis***   MAsh WAbe
I - 'Alba'   GKev
- ***bernardina***   see *L. nevadensis*
'Pinkie'   GArf
pygmaea   GKev MAsh SPlb
Rainbow mixture   see *L. cotyledon* REGENBOGEN
rediviva   WAbe
- pink-flowered   WAbe
- white-flowered   WAbe
tweedyi   see *Lewisiopsis tweedyi*

Lewisiopsis (Montiaceae)
§ ***tweedyi*** ♀H4   EDAr GKev LRHS MAsh SPlb WAbe
- 'Alba'   WAbe
- 'Lovedream'   EDAr
- 'Rosea'   LRHS MAsh WAbe

Leycesteria (Caprifoliaceae)
crocothyrsos   CBcs IArd SPoG WFar
formosa   CAgr CBcs CBrac CDoC CMac
                             CMCN CSBt EBee EGrI EHeP ELan
                             EPfP GJos IDun LRHS MBlu MCtn
                             MGos MMuc MNrw MSwo NBir
                             NLar NLit SEND SPlb SPoG SRms
                             WKor
- 'Gold Leaf'   CMac LShi MEar WFar

- GOLDEN LANTERNS   CBcs CDoC CSBt EBee ELan EPfP
  ('Notbruce'PBR) ♀H4   LBuc LCro LRHS LSRN MAsh MGos
                             MMrt MMuc MPri NLar NLit SDix
                             SEND SMad SPoG SRms WFar WHtc
                             WJur
- LITTLE LANTERNS ('Cdc01') CBcs LRHS LSou
- 'Longstock'   CCps
- 'Lydia'   LRHS
- 'Purple Rain'   CDoC EBee EGren EHeP EPfP EWes
                             LCro MAsh MGos NLar

Leymus (Poaceae)
from the Falkland Islands   ELon EPPr
§ ***arenarius***   CElw CKno EBee ECha EHeP ELan
                             GMaP MMuc NBro SDix SEND SPlb
                             SRms WFar WTre
- 'Blue Dune'   CAby ELan EPfP LRHS NBir SMad
cinereus   WCot
hispidus   see *Elymus hispidus*

Lhotzkya see *Calytrix*

Liatris ❀ (Asteraceae)
aspera   ECha
elegans   SPlb
mucronata   NLar
pycnostachya   CSpe EPPr MCtn NClf NLar SMHy
                             SRms
scariosa 'Alba'   CBcs CSpe EBee EPPr SAko
§ ***spicata***   CBcs CDor CWnw EBee EGren
                             EGrI EHeP ELan EPfP ERCP LAma
                             LRHS LShi LSRN MArl MGos MPri
                             MSCN NBir NCth NGdn NLar NLit
                             NMir SHor SMHy SRms WCAu
                             WCot XFar
- 'Alba'   CMac EBee EGren ELan EPfP LAma
                             LBar LRHS LShi LSRN MArl MAsh
                             MBel MHoo MPri MSCN NLar SPlb
                             WCAu WHoo XFar
- ***callilepis***   see *L. spicata*
- 'Floristan Violett'   CMHG EBee EGren EPfP EPPr
                             GMaP LRHS LSto MCtn MHer MHol
                             MMrt NCth NLar SOrN SPlb SPoG
                             WFar WGwG
- 'Floristan Weiss'   CBWd CMHG EBee EPPr EPPr
                             ERCP GKev GMaP LRHS LSto MCtn
                             MHer MPri NCth NLar NLit SOrN
                             SPoG SRms WFar WGwG
- GOBLIN   see *L. spicata* 'Kobold'
§ - 'Kobold'   CMac EBee ELan LAma LBar LBom
                             LCro LRHS LShi MAsh MBel MHoo
                             MPri NBir NLar SRms WCAu WCot
                             WFar
- pink-flowered   WRBe

Libanotis see *Seseli*
montana   see *Seseli libanotis*

Libertia ❀ (Iridaceae)
breunioides   see *L. cranwelliae*
§ ***chilensis*** ♀H3   CAbb CKno CoPl EArl ECha EGren
                             ELan EPfP EPPr EUrb GAbr LCro
                             LShi LSRN MMuc NBir NGdn SAth
                             SEND SMrm SPel SPlb SRms WChS
- Elegans Group   EBee EPfP WCru
§ - Formosa Group   CBcs CBro EBee EGren ELan EPfP
                             GKev NSti SArc SDix SRms WHer
- Procera Group   CSpe EBee EPfP EWes LEdu MBlu
                             SChF SHor SMad SPlb WPGP
§ ***cranwelliae***   WPGP
formosa   see *L. chilensis* Formosa Group

grandiflora misapplied	see *L. chilensis*		'Gregynog Gold'PBR ♀H6	GMaP NBro NLar
grandiflora ambig.	CCht CDoC CMac CSde CTsd EGrI GKev LRHS MBel MSCN NBir NBro SArc SHor SIvy SPoG WCAu WFar WTre		× *hessei*	GMaP LRHS NLar
			hodgsonii	EPPr
			- B&SWJ 10855	WCru
			japonica	CDor ECha LEdu NLar
			- B&SWJ 2883	WCru
grandiflora (R. Br.) Sweet	CAby GMaP SVen		- 'Rising Sun'	CExl ESwi EUrb NLar WCot WCru
'Grasshopper'	CAby LRHS		'La Duelo Caruso'	EBlo
ixioides	CBcs ECha EGrI LEdu LRHS SDix StAn WKif WPGP		'Laternchen'PBR	SAko
			'Little Rocket'PBR	CExl EPfP LBar MBNS NBro NGdn NLar SPoG WFar
- 'Goldfinger' (v)	EBee ELan EPfP NLar SPoG WFar WHer		'Osiris Café Noir'	EBee MHol NLar WFar
- 'Taupo Blaze'	CMac ELan EPfP SPoG		× *palmatiloba*	see *L.* × *yoshizoeana* 'Palmatiloba'
- 'Taupo Sunset'PBR	EGren EPfP EUrb LRHS NLar WFar WPGP	§	*przewalskii*	Widely available
- 'Tricolor'	CSde GEdr GKev WFar		- SSSE 176	WCot
'Nelson Dwarf'	ESwi EWes		- 'Dragon Wings'	MHol
peregrinans	CSpe ECha EGrI ELan GKev LEdu NBir SRkn WPGP		- 'Dragon's Breath'	MHol
			sibirica	NLar
- 'Gold Leaf'	CTsd EBee EGren ELan EPfP LRHS WFar		- B&SWJ 4383	WCru
			- var. *speciosa*	see *L. fischeri*
- 'Gold Stripe'	NBir WFar		*smithii*	see *Senecio smithii*
sessiliflora	NBir		*speciosa*	see *L. fischeri*
- 'Caerulescens'	CBcs CCht CExl CMac LRHS NBir SChF SMad WFar		*stenocephala*	EAri EBee NBro NLar
'Sunset Strain'	CAbb CSpe CTsd EUrb WFar	I	- 'Globosa'	LRHS
			'Sungold'	CMac EBee EBlo LRHS NGdn
Libocedrus (Cupressaceae)			*tangutica*	see *Sinacalia tangutica*
chilensis	see *Austrocedrus chilensis*		'The Rocket' ♀H6	Widely available
decurrens	see *Calocedrus decurrens*		'Treasure Island'	LBar
			tussilaginea	see *Farfugium japonicum*
Libonia see *Justicia*			*veitchiana*	CToG
			vorobievii	EBee NLar
Licuala (Arecaceae)			*wilsoniana*	MMuc SEND WCAu WFar
grandis	LBom LDro	§	× *yoshizoeana* 'Palmatiloba'	EBlo EWes LRHS MNrw WFar
Ligularia (Asteraceae)			'Zepter' ♀H6	CAby CToG EBlo GAbr GQue LRHS MArl MAsh MMuc WCot WFar
aff. *atkinsonii* WJC 13663	WCru			
'BBQ Banana'	LBar		*Ligusticopsis* (Apiaceae)	
'Bottle Rocket'PBR	LBar LRHS NLar SHar	§	*wallichiana* ♀H6	Widely available
'Britt Marie Crawford'PBR ♀H6	CAby CBcs CDor CExl CLil CMac ELan EMor EPfP ERCP GElm GMaP LRHS LSRN MBNS MHol NBir NBro NCth NLar NSti NWbg SMrm SPoG SRms WCot WFar WKif		- CC 6869	GKev
			- EMAK 886	EBee
			- PAB 3579	LEdu WPGP
			- PAB 8969	LEdu WPGP
			- WJC 13656 from Sikkim	WCru
			- from Bhutan	WPGP
clivorum	see *L. dentata*		- from Manipur	WPGP
§ *dentata*	EBee NBro SRms WTre		- from Nagaland, India	WPGP
- 'Desdemona'	Widely available			
- 'Franz Feldweber'	EBee ECha		*Ligusticum* (Apiaceae)	
- 'Little Golden Ray'	LBar LCro LRHS		*hultenii*	WCot
- 'Midnight Lady'	EAri ELan EPfP LBar LRHS MHol MMrt NLar StAn		*lucidum*	CMCN EPfP LEdu MCtn NSti SHor SPel SPhx WCAu WCot WPGP
- 'Orange Princess'	NPer		- subsp. *lucidum*	CSpe
- 'Orange Queen'	LBar	§	*scoticum*	CAgr CCBP CGwi ELan EWes GBin GElm GJos GMaP GPSL GQue LCro LEdu LRHS MBel MHer MWlw NAts SDix SHor SPhx SRms WFar WJek WPGP WTre
- 'Osiris Fantaisie' (v)	CExl MHol NLar NSti SPoG WFar			
- 'Othello'	CFis EBee EGren EMor EPfP EUrb GJos LRHS MArl MAsh NGdn NLar SMrm SPoG SRms WCAu WChS WFar			
			- variegated (v)	WCot
- 'Pandora'	LBom LRHS MHol MNrw MPri NLar SPad XFar		*Ligustrum* ✿ (Oleaceae)	
- 'Sommergold'	WFar		*confusum*	CBcs WJur
§ *fischeri* B&SWJ 2570	WCru	*	*congestum*	WJur
- B&SWJ 4381	WCru		*delavayanum*	EGren ERom GKev LRHS MPri SArc SAth SFol WCha WJur
- B&SWJ 4478	WCru			
- B&SWJ 5653	WCru		- 'Verstappens Gold'PBR	NLar
- B&SWJ 5841	WCru		*ibota* MUSLI	see *L. ibota* 'Muster'
- B&SWJ 8802	WCru	§	- 'Muster'PBR (v)	EBee EGren LCro NLar SPoG WCot
- CC	GGro		*ionandrum*	see *L. delavayanum*
- var. *megalorhiza* 'Cheju Charmer'	WCru		*japonicum*	CCVT EBar LMaj LSRN SArc SEND SFol SGol
'Gold Torch'	NLar			

	- 'Coriaceum'	see *L. japonicum* 'Rotundifolium'	§	- var. ***platyphyllum*** (IXb/c)	GAbr
	- GREEN CENTURY ('Melgreen'^{PBR})	CNWT WMat		- - B&SWJ 4824 (IXb/c)	WCru
	- 'Korea Dwarf'	NLar		Backhouse hybrids	see *L.* × *dalhansonii* Backhouse Group
§	- 'Rotundifolium'	CBcs CDoC EBee ELan EPfP EUrb IDun NLar SArc SDix SFol SMad SPoG WCot WFar		***bakerianum*** var. ***rubrum*** (IXc/b)	GEdr
				'Bald Eagle' (Ia/b)	LAma
§	- 'Silver Star' (v)	SEND		'Barbara North' (Ic/d)	GEdr
§	- 'Texanum'	CCVT CDoC EGren NLar SArc		'Beijing Moon' (VIb-c/a)	LAma
	- 'Texanum Argenteum'	see *L. japonicum* 'Silver Star'		'Black Beauty' (VIIIb-c/d)	CCBP EGrl GKev LAma LCro
	- 'Variegatum' (v)	SFol SGol		'Bright Diamond' (VIIIa/b)	XFar
	lucidum ♀^{H5}	CBcs CCVT CSBt EGren ELan SArc SEND SGol WFar		'Brindisi'^{PBR} (VIIIa/b)	XFar
				bulbiferum (IXa/b)	GKev
	- Guiz 296	CExl		- var. ***croceum*** (IXa/b)	EDAr
	- 'Excelsum Superbum' (v) ♀^{H5}	CCVT CMac EBar ELan LMaj LRHS LSRN MGos SArc SGol SPoG WCha WCot WFar	§	***canadense*** (IXc/a)	GKev MCtn WCot
				- var. ***flavum***	see *L. canadense*
				candidum (IXb/a)	EGren ELan ERCP GKev LAma LCro WSpi XFar
	- 'Golden Wax'	CJun			
	- 'Tricolor' (v) ♀^{H5}	ELan SFol		'Candy Blossom' (Ia/b)	XFar
	obtusifolium new	LMaj		'Candy Morning' (IIc/d) new	GKev LAma
	- var. ***regelianum***	NLar		'Cannes' (Ia-b/b)	XFar
	ovalifolium	Widely available		***carniolicum***	see *L. pyrenaicum* subsp. *carniolicum*
§	- 'Argenteum' (v)	CBcs CCVT CMac EHeP GArf LRHS LSto MMuc NLar SEND SPoG WFar WHtc			
				'Casa Blanca' (VIIb/b-c) ♀^{H6}	CBro ELan EPfP GKev LAma LCro NBir XFar
	- 'Aureomarginatum'	see *L. ovalifolium* 'Aureum'		'Cavoli' (Ia-b/b)	LCro
§	- 'Aureum' (v) ♀^{H5}	Widely available		'Chill Out' (VIIa/b)	LCro
	- 'Lemon and Lime' (v)	CDoC LCro LSRN MAsh SRms WCot WFar		***ciliatum*** (IXc/d)	MCtn
				'Claude Shride' (IIc/d)	CBcs EBee ERCP GKev LAma LCro MHtn WCot
	- 'Variegatum'	see *L. ovalifolium* 'Argenteum'			
	- 'Vicaryi'	EPfP MGos SDix WFar		'Coldplay' (Colour Carpet Series) (VIIa-b/b-c)	LBuc
	quihoui	EBee ELan EPfP MBlu NLar SDix SEND SPoG WCot			
				columbianum (IXc/d)	MCtn
	sinense	CMCN WPGP		- B&SWJ 9564 (IXc/d)	WCru
	- 'Fragrant Cloud'	LCro		'Conca d'Or'^{PBR} (VIIIb/b) ♀^{H6}	GKev
	- 'Multiflorum'	WFar			
	- 'Sunshine'	EPfP LRHS LSou MAsh MPri SPoG WHtc		'Crimson Pixie' (Ia/b)	LCro
				'Curly Sue' (VIIa-b/b)	LCro MHol
	- 'Wimbei'	WFar		× ***dalhansonii*** (IIc/d)	LRHS
	strongylophyllum	CExl	§	- Backhouse Group (IIc/d)	WFar
	texanum	see *L. japonicum* 'Texanum'		- 'Guinea Gold' (II)	LAma
	tschonoskii	MBlu NLar		- 'Mrs R.O. Backhouse' (IIc/d)	GEdr
	undulatum 'Lemon Lime and Clippers'	CMac NLar SDix SPoG			
				- 'Sutton Court' (IIc/c)	GEdr
	vulgare	CBTr CCVT CGwi CHab CMac CoPl EHeP ELan EPfP LBuc LCro LSto MMuc MSwo NLit SEND SEWo WHnu WHtc WMat WMou WRjT		- Terrace City Group (IIc/d)	EPPr GKev LAma
			§	***dauricum*** (IXa/b)	GKev
				davidii (IXc/d)	GKev WCru
			§	- var. ***willmottiae*** (IXc/d)	WCru
				'Dimension' (Ia/b-c)	LCro
	- 'Black Pearl'	WFar		***distichum*** (IXb-c/d)	WCru
	- 'Lodense'	SArc		'Dizzy' (VIIa-b/b-c)	EGren ELan XFar
				'Double Sensation' (Ia/b d)	XFar
Lilaeopsis (Apiaceae)			***duchartrei*** (IXc/d)	CExl WHil
brasiliensis	CWat ELin		'Eastern Moon' (VIb-c/a)	CAby EBee GKev LAma
				'Easy Samba' (Ia/c)	LCro
Lilium ✿ (*Liliaceae*)			'Easy Vanilla' (Ia/c)	LCro
(IX)	LAma		'Easy Waltz' (Ia/b)	LCro
'Adonis' (Ic/d)	GEdr		'Ellen Willmott' (II)	WMal
African Queen Group (VI-/a) ♀^{H6}	ERCP GKev LAma LCro		'Elodie'^{PBR} (Ia/b)	EGren
			'Elusive' (VIIIb/b-d)	MNrw
- 'African Queen' (VIb-c/a)	LAma XFar		'Eros' (Ic/d)	GEdr
'Alberta Morning' (IIc/d)	EBee GKev LAma		'Fairy Morning' (IIc/c)	GKev LAma WFar
'Albi Morning' (IIc/d)	GKev LAma		'Fangio' (VIIIa/b)	EGrI GKev
'Anastasia' (VIIIb-c/b-d) ♀^{H6}	EGren EGrI GKev LAma LCro		(FantAsiatic Series)	MHol
'Angela North' (Ic/d)	GEdr		FANTASIATIC LIPGLOSS (mixed) (Ia-b/b)	
§	***apertum*** (IX)	GKev		
'Apricot Fudge'^{PBR} (VIIIa/b)	LCro XFar		- FANTASIATIC SPARK (mixed) (Ia/b-c)	MHol
'Apricot Star' (VIIa/b)	XFar			
'Arabian Knight' (IIc/d)	GKev LAma LCro WFar		'Fata Morgana' (Ia/b) ♀^{H6}	XFar
Asiatic hybrids (I)	EGren		'Felino' (VIIIa/b)	GKev
'Aubade' (VIIa/b)	XFar			
auratum 'Gold Band'	see *L. auratum* var. *platyphyllum*		'Forever Marjolein' (Ia/b)	LCro

'Forever Susan' (Ia/b)	EGren		*michiganense* (IXc/d)	GKev
formosanum (IXb/a)	EBee MHol		'Miracle' (Vb/a)	GKev
- short, from high altitude RWJ 10005 (IXb/a)	WCru		'Miss Feya' (VIIIb/c)	CAby EGrI GKev LAma MHol MNrw
- var. *pricei* (IXb/a)	CAby CTtf EAri EBee EDAr ELan EPot GEdr LCro LEdu LShi MCtn MHer Midl MPro WIce	I	'Miss Lily' (VIIIb/b-c)	MNrw XFar
			'Miss Peculiar' (VIIIb-c/a)	LCro
			'Mister Cas' (VIIIb/b)	XFar
			'Mister Pistache' (VIIIb-a/b-c)	LAma
'Friso' (VIIIb/b) ♀H6	EGren GKev			
'Fusion' (IVb-c/b-c) ♀H6	MHol WCot		'Mistery Dream' (Ia/b)	XFar
'Garden Party' (VIIb/b) ♀H6	LAma		'Mona Lisa' (VIIb/b-c)	XFar
'Gizmo'PBR (VIIIb-a/b)	GKev		*monadelphum* (IXc/d)	GKev
Golden Splendor Group (VIb-c/a) ♀H6	GKev LAma LCro XFar		'Montego Bay' (VIIa/b)	XFar
			'Montezuma' (VIIa-b/b)	XFar
'Golden Tycoon'PBR (VIIIa-b/b)	XFar		'Muscadet' (VIIa-b/b)	LCro
			nepalense (IXc/a)	EBee EDAr ERCP GKev LAma LCro MCtn
'Hannah North' (Ic/d)	GEdr			
hansonii B&SWJ 8506 (IXb-c/d)	WCru		'Night Flyer' (Ib-c/b-c)	CAby
			'Nightrider' (VIIIa/b)	LAma XFar
- B&SWJ 8528 (IXb-c/d)	WCru		'On Stage' (VIIIa-b/b)	LCro
henryi (IXc/d) ♀H6	CBro EBee EGren GBin GKev LAma MCtn WCru		'Orange County' (Ia/b)	XFar
			'Orange Electric' (Ia/b)	EGren
'Honeymoon' (VIIIb-c/a-b)	EGrI LCro XFar		'Orange Marmalade' (IIb/c-d)	EAri EBee GKev LAma LCro
'Hotel California' (VIIIb/b)	XFar			
'Hotspot' (VIIb/b)	MHol		'Orange Twins' (Ia-b/b)	XFar
'Josephine' (VIIa/b)	GKev LAma		'Orania' (VIIIb/b)	EGrI
'Karen North' (Ic/d)	GEdr	*	Oriental Superb Group	NGdn
'Kushi Maya' (VIIIc/b-c)	EAri		'Pan' (Ic/d)	GEdr
'Lady Alice' (VI-/d)	GKev LAma MAsh XFar		*pardalinum* (IXc/d) ♀H6	CBro EBee GKev LAma WCot WCru
'Lake Tulare' (IVc/c-d)	GEdr			
§	*lancifolium* (IXc/d)	GBin MCtn StAn		- var. *giganteum* (IXc/d)	MNrw
- B&SWJ 4352 (IXc/d)	WCru	§	- subsp. *vollmeri* (IXc/d)	GKev WPGP
- var. *flaviflorum* (IXc/d)	WFar	§	- subsp. *wigginsii* (IXc/d)	WCru
- 'Flore Pleno' (IXc/d)	EPPr NBir SMrm WCot WCru		'Passion Moon' (VIIb-c/a)	LAma
- var. *fortunei* (IXc/d)	EGrI EPPr SDix		'Patricia's Pride' (Ia-b/b-c)	LAma
- - B&SWJ 539 (IXc/d)	WCru		'Pearl Loraine' (Ib-c/b-c)	LAma
- 'Splendens' (IXc/d)	GKev LAma NBid WCot		'Pearl Melanie' (Ib/c)	LAma
'Landini'PBR (Ia/b)	CAby		'Pearl White' (Ib/b)	LCro
lankongense (IXc/d)	GEdr LCro MHol		'Peggy North' (Ic/d)	GEdr
'Late Morning' (VIIIb/b)	EGren		*pensylvanicum*	see *L. dauricum*
ledebourii (IXc/d)	GKev		'Peppard Gold' (IIc/c)	EBee LAma
leichtlinii (IXc/d)	CAby GEdr		*philippinense* (IXa-b/a)	EBee LAma
leucanthum var. *centifolium* (IXb-c/a)	WCru		'Pink Exposure'	LRHS
			'Pink Flight' (Ic/b-c)	GKev
lijiangense	see *L. tenii*		'Pink Morning' (IIc/c)	ERCP LAma
LOLLYPOP ('Holebibi') (Ia/b)	XFar		Pink Perfection Group (VIb/a) ♀H6	EGrI ELan LAma LCro XFar
longiflorum (IXb/a)	LAma			
- B&SWJ 11376 (IXb/a)	WCru		*poilanei* misapplied	see *L. primulinum*
- 'White Heaven'PBR (Vb/a)	CAby LCro		*poilanei* Gagnep.	see *L. primulinum* var. *poilanei*
'Lotus Beauty' (VIIa/c)	LCro		'Polar Star' (VIIa-b/b)	EGren XFar
'Lotus Breeze' (VIIb/c)	LCro		'Pretty Woman' (VIIIa/b)	CAby LCro MNrw XFar
'Lotus Elegance' (VIIb/c)	LCro	§	*primulinum* WWJ 11679 (IXc/d)	WCru
'Lotus Wonder' (VIIb-c/c)	LCro			
mackliniae (IXc/a) ♀H5	GEdr GKev LAma NBir WPGP		- aff. var. *ochraceum* KWJ 12064 (IXc/a)	WCru
- PAB 9327 (IXc/a)	LEdu WPGP			
- PAB 9668 (IXc/a)	LEdu WPGP	§	- var. *poilanei* BWJ 15633 (IXc/a)	WCru
- 'Naga Pink' (IXc/a)	GKev			
- 'Tantallon' (IXc/a)	GKev	§	*pumilum* (IXc/d)	LAma MHol
'Magic Star'PBR (VIIa-b/b)	EGren XFar		'Purple Dream' (Ia/b)	LAma LCro
'Manitoba Morning' (IIc/c)	GKev LAma		'Purple Marble' (VIIIc/b)	LAma
'Marie North' (Ic/d)	GEdr		'Purple Prince' (VIIIa-b/a-b)	EGrI XFar
'Maroon King' (IIc/b)	WFar		*pyrenaicum* (IXc/d)	GKev MCtn
martagon (IXc/d) ♀H6	CTtf ECha GKev LAma LCro MCtn NBir WShi WSpi XFar	§	- subsp. *carniolicum* (IXc/d)	GKev
			'Red County' (Ia/c-b)	LAma
- var. *albiflorum* (IXc/d)	CTtf LAma		'Red Dutch' (VIIIa-b/c)	XFar
- var. *album* (IXc/d)	CSpe GKev LAma MCtn NBir WShi		'Red Twinkle' (Ib-c/b-c)	MHol
- var. *cattaniae* (IXc/d)	GKev		*regale* (IXb/a) ♀H6	CAby CBro ECha EGren EGrI ELan EPfP ERCP GKev LAma LCro MCtn WHil XFar
*	- var. *rubrum* (IXc/d)	EGrI			
medeoloides B&SWJ 4184 (IXc/d)	WCru			
			- 'Album' (IXb/a)	EBee ERCP GKev LAma LCro
meleagrinum (IX)	GEdr			

'Robert Swanson' (VIIIb-c/b) — CAby
'Robina' (VIIIa-b/b-c) — WCot XFar
ROSELILY ANOUSKA ('DI111067') (VIIa/b) — LCro
ROSELILY CAROLINA ('DI044040') (VIIa-b/b) — LAma LCro
ROSELILY DORIA ('DI111808') (VIIa/b) — GKev LAma
ROSELILY ISABELLA ('DI044033'^{PBR}) (VIIa-b/b) — LAma
ROSELILY LEONA ('DI 112773') (VIIa-b/b) — LAma
ROSELILY LUCIA ('DI170710') (VII) — GKev LAma
ROSELILY NATALIA ('DI04544') (VIIa-b/b) — GKev LAma
ROSELILY THALITA ('DI04992') (VIIa-b/b) — LCro
'Rosemary North' (Ic/d) — GEdr SBrt
rosthornii (IXc/d) — WCru
'Royal Kiss' (VIIIa-b) — LAma
'Royal Sunset' (VIIIa-b/b) — GKev
rubellum (IXb/a) — GEdr
sachalinense RBS 235 (IXa/b) — EPPr
'Salmon Flavour' (Ic/b-c) — LAma
'Saltarello' (VIIIa-b/b) — XFar
'Scheherazade' (VIIIc/d) — GKev LAma
'Serene Angel' (VIIa/c) — WCot
'Silk Road' (VIIIb-c/b) — CAby
'Slate's Morning' (IIc/c) — LAma WCot
'Snowy Morning' (IIc/d) — GKev LAma
'Spark' (Ia-b/b) — MHol
speciosum B&SWJ 4847 (IXb-c/d) — WCru
 - var. *album* (IXb-c/d) — NBir
 - var. *rubrum* (IXb-c/d) — ECha EPfP LCro NBir XFar
§ - - 'Uchida' (IXb-c/d) — GKev LAma
'Spring Pink' (Ia/-) — LAma
'Star Gazer' (VIIa/c) — EGrI EPfP GKev LAma LBuc LCro LRHS XFar
'Strawberry Event' (Ic-d/b) — LAma
'Sunny Morning' (IIc/d) — CBcs EBee GKev LAma
superbum (IXc/d) — GKev MCtn WCru
'Sweet Desire'^{PBR} (VIIIa-b/b) — LAma
'Sweet Rosy' (VIIa-b/b) — EGren XFar
szovitsianum (IXc/d) — GKev
taliense (IXc/d) — WCru
'Tasmania' (Ia/b-c) — XFar
§ *tenii* (IXc/d) — GEdr
tenuifolium — see *L. pumilum*
Tiger Babies Group (VIIIb-c/c-d) — EPfP XFar
'Tigermoon' (VIIIa/b) — XFar
'Tigerwoods' (VIIa/c) — LCro XFar
tigrinum — see *L. lancifolium*
'Tinilco' (Ia/b) — LAma
'Tiny Heroes' (Ia/b-c) — GKev LAma
'Tiny Pearl'^{PBR} (Ia-b/b) — GKev LAma
'Tom Pouce' (VIIa/b) — XFar
'Tribal Dance' (Ia/b-c) — LAma
'Tropical Dragon' (VIIIa/b) — GKev LAma
tsingtauense B&SWJ 4263 (IXa/c) — WCru
'Uchida Kanoka' — see *L. speciosum* var. *rubrum* 'Uchida'
vollmeri — see *L. pardalinum* subsp. *vollmeri*
'White Pixels' (Ia/b) — XFar
'White Proud' (VIIa/b-c) — LAma
'White Twinkle' (Ia-b/b) — LCro

wigginsii — see *L. pardalinum* subsp. *wigginsii*
willmottiae — see *L. davidii* var. *willmottiae*
xanthellum var. *luteum* (IXb-c/d) — WCru
'Yellow Planet' (VIb-a/a) — LCro
'Zelmira' (VIIIa-b/b) — GKev LAma

lime see *Citrus* × *aurantiifolia*

lime, Philippine see *Citrus* × *microcarpa*

limequat see *Citrus* × *floridana*

Limnanthes (Limnanthaceae)
douglasii ♀^{H5} — ELan GJem GQue LCro MCtn NBir
 - subsp. *rosea* — CSpe

Limnobium (Hydrocharitaceae)
laevigatum — CBen ELin

Limnophila (Scrophulariaceae)
aromatica — ELin
sessiliflora — ELin

Limonium (Plumbaginaceae)
bellidifolium — ECha EDAr WHoo
binervosum — NAts
'Blauer Diamant' — EBee
cosyrense — MHer
gmelinii — EPfP SPlb
 - DAZZLE ROCKS ('Ste10'^{PBR}) — CBcs CKno CSde LBar LCro LRHS MHtn XFar
latifolium — see *L. platyphyllum*
minutum — WMal
pastel shades — MCtn
perezii — CBcs EDAr LRHS
§ *platyphyllum* — CBcs CCBP CSpe EPfP GMaP LRHS LShi LSto MCtn MHol MMuc MPie SAng SRms StAn WCAu WCot WHrl
 - 'Blue Cloud' — SRms
 - 'Robert Butler' — SMHy WCot
 - 'Violetta' — EBee ELan EPfP GPSL MHol SPoG WGwG WHoo
sinuatum — SVic
 - QIS APRICOT — LCro
 - QIS WHITE — LCro
 - 'Rose Light' — MCtn
tataricum — see *Goniolimon tataricum*

Linanthus (Polemoniaceae)
grandiflorus — see *Leptosiphon grandiflorus*

Linaria (Plantaginaceae)
aeruginea 'Lindeza Violet' — CSpe
 - 'Neon Lights' — CFis EDAr MCtn MHoo SPoG
alpina — CSpe ECha GJos LShi SRms SRot
 - 'Purpurea' — WAbe
anticaria 'Antique Silver' — ECha LRHS
cymbalaria — see *Cymbalaria muralis*
§ *dalmatica* — CSpe ECha NBid SPel WCot WFar
'Dial Park' — CSpe CWnw ECha ELan GMaP IPot MHol MPro NClf SPel WMal WTor
× *dominii* 'Carnforth' — SHar SPel
'Florence Lily Sophia Brown' — WFar
genistifolia — WCot
 - W&B BG B-6 — WCot WFar
 - subsp. *dalmatica* — see *L. dalmatica*
hepaticifolia — see *Cymbalaria hepaticifolia*
* *lobata alba* — SPlb

maroccana Fairy Bouquet   LCro MCtn
  Group ♀H6
- 'Licilia Peach' (Licilia Series)   MCtn
- 'Licilia Red' (Licilia Series)   LCro MCtn
- NORTHERN LIGHTS (mixed)   CTtf
origanifolia   see *Chaenorhinum origanifolium*
pallida   see *Cymbalaria pallida*
'Peachy'   CDor CSpe ECha GBin GMaP IPot
  LBar LRHS MArl MHol NClf NLar
  SMrm SPel SPoG WCot WFar WTor
pilosa   see *Cymbalaria pilosa*
'Pink Kisses'   ECha LBar MHol SPoG WCot WFar
purpurea   CDor CGHo CGwi CoPl EGrI ELan
  GJem GQue LSto MCtn MHer
  MNHC MPro NBro NPer SEND
  SPhx SRms WCAu WCot WFar
- 'Alba'   see *L. purpurea* 'Springside White'
- 'Brown's White Strain'   WCot
- 'Canon Went'   CBWd CDor CGHo CoPl CSpe
  CWnw EGrI ELan EPfP GJos LCro
  LSto MCtn MHoo NBir NClf SPhx
  SRms WCAu WCot WFar WKif WSpi
  WTor
- pastel shades   CSpe CTtf
- pink-flowered   CSpe IPot LEdu
- 'Poached Egg'   ECha WGoo
- 'Radcliffe Innocence'   see *L. purpurea* 'Springside White'
§ - 'Springside White'   CDor CElw CSpe ECha GJos MCtn
  MPro NBir NGdn SPad SPhx SVic
  WTor
repens   MNrw WCot WHer
× *sepium*   WCot
'Steely Belle'   SMHy
triornithophora   CSpe CTtf ECha SPlb
- 'Pink Budgies'   IPot WFar
- purple-flowered   CTtf
- 'Rosea'   CSpe
tristis   ECha LShi
- var. *lurida*   WAbe
vulgaris   CBWd CGHo CGwi CHab CoPl
  EDAr EHet GJem GQue LCro LSto
  MAsh MCtn MHer MHoo MNHC
  MNrw NAts NMir SRms WHer
  WOrg WShi
- f. *peloria*   WMal
'Whisper'   WFar

Lindelofia (Boraginaceae)
anchusoides misapplied   see *L. longiflora*
anchusoides (Lindl.) Lehm.   NBid SBrt
§ *longiflora*   GGro SMrm

Lindera (Lauraceae)
angustifolia   WJur
- FMWJ 13156   WCru
assamica B&SWJ 13274   WCru
benzoin   MBlu
erythrocarpa B&SWJ 6271   WCru
- B&SWJ 8730   WCru
glauca   WJur
metcalfiana   WCru
  var. *dictyophylla*
  KWJ 12312
neesiana B&SWJ 13984   WCru
obtusiloba ♀H5   MBlu WJur WPGP
- B&SWJ 8723   WCru
- B&SWJ 11054   WCru
- B&SWJ 12555 from Korea   WCru
praecox B&SWJ 10802   WCru
- B&SWJ 10953 from   WCru
  north Japan

- B&SWJ 11125 from   WCru
  south Japan
praetermissa   WPGP
sericea B&SWJ 11123   WCru
- B&SWJ 11141   WCru
- var. *lancea* B&SWJ 11071   WCru
- - B&SWJ 11118   WCru
triloba B&SWJ 5570   WCru
- B&SWJ 11121   WCru
- B&SWJ 11466   WCru

Lindernia (Linderniaceae)
grandiflora   LCro SLee

Linnaea (Caprifoliaceae)
borealis   EPot GEdr WAbe

Linum (Linaceae)
alpinum   MNHC
arboreum ♀H4   GKev
capitatum   EPot
flavum 'Compactum'   EDAr SRms
- 'Gemmell's Hybrid' ♀H4   EWes WAbe
grandiflorum ♀H4   LCro
- 'Bright Eyes'   CSpe
- 'Charmer Salmon'   CSpe
- 'Rubrum'   CSpe GJem MPro
hypericifolium   EDAr
lewisii   EDAr MNHC
monogynum dwarf   WAbe
narbonense   CSpe EDAr SPhx
- 'Heavenly Blue'   SPel
§ *perenne*   CAgr EBee ECha EHet ELan ENfk
  EPfP LCro MCtn MHer MPro SPhx
  SPoG WJek
- 'Album'   ECha EPfP
sibiricum   see *L. perenne*
tenuifolium   EDAr
uninerve   WAbe
usitatissimum   MCtn

Lippia (Verbenaceae)
chamaedrifolia   see *Glandularia peruviana*
citriodora   see *Aloysia citrodora*
dulcis   CAgr ENfk LWaG MCtn SRms WJek
nodiflora   see *Phyla nodiflora*
repens   see *Phyla nodiflora*

Liquidambar ✿ (Hamamelidaceae)
acalycina   CBcs ELan EPfP LRHS SSta WMat
  WPGP
- 'Spinners'   ELan LMil WPGP
chinensis B&SWJ 11756   WCru
formosana   CBcs CMac CMCN SGol SSta
- 'Afterglow'   MBlu
- Monticola Group   SSta
orientalis   CBcs CLnd CMCN EPfP SSta WPGP
styraciflua   Widely available
- 'Andrew Hewson'   CJun CLnd ELan EPfP LMaj LRHS
  MAsh MBlu
- 'Anja'   MBlu SSta
- 'Anneke'   CJun SSta
- 'Aurea'   see *L. styraciflua* 'Variegata'
  Overeynder
- 'Aurea Variegata'   see *L. styraciflua* 'Variegata'
  Overeynder
- 'Aurora'   CJun
- 'Burgundy'   CLnd MBlu SSta
- 'Combi's Upright'   NLar
I - 'Corky'   EPfP SSta WMat
- 'Emerald Sentinel'   SSta

Lithodora 429

- 'Festeri' CEnd SSta
- 'Festival' CLnd MBlu
- 'Globe' see *L. styraciflua* 'Gum Ball'
- 'Golden Sun'^{PBR} CBcs NLar
- 'Golden Treasure' (v) CLnd MGos SSta
- 'Granary Sunset' SSta
§ - 'Gum Ball' CAco CCVT CEnd CMCN EBee
   EHeP ELan EPfP ERom EWes LMaj
   LRHS MGos NLar NPip SPoG SSta
- 'Kia' CEnd
- 'Lane Roberts' ♀^{H6} CAco CBTr CCVT CLnd CMac
   CMCN CSBt EBar EGren EGrI
   ELan EPfP IArd LCro LMaj LMil
   LRHS LSRN MAsh MBlu MGos
   NLar NPip SPoG SSta WMat
   WMou
- 'Lollipop' LRHS
- 'Lynn' SSta
- 'Manon' (v) LRHS
- 'Midwest Sunset' MBlu WPGP
- 'Moonbeam' (v) SSta
- 'Moraine' CAco
- 'Naree' NLar SSta
- 'Oakville Highlight'^{PBR} LMil NLar
- 'Oconee' CEnd LRHS SSta
- 'Paarl' (v) CAco NLar
- 'Palo Alto' ♀^{H6} CAco CBTr CEnd CLnd CMCN
   EBee EPfP LRHS MBlu NPip SMad
   SSta WMat WMou WPGP
- 'Parasol' CEnd CJun CLnd SSta
- 'Pasquali Fastigiata' ELan
- 'Pendula' MBlu SSta
- 'Penwood' ♀^{H6} CJun EPfP SSta
- 'Red Sunset' SSta
- 'Rotundiloba' MBlu
- 'Schock's Gold' SSta
§ - 'Silver King' (v) CAco MGos SFol SGol SSta
- 'Simone' CAco NLar
- 'Slender Silhouette' ♀^{H6} Widely available
- 'Stared' CAco CJun CLnd EBee EPfP LMaj
   LRHS LSto MBlu MGos NLar NOra
   NPip WHtc WMat WMou
- 'Thea' CAco EBee ELan EPfP LCro LMil
   LRHS MAsh MBlu SSta WMat
- 'Variegata' misapplied see *L. styraciflua* 'Silver King'
§ - 'Variegata' Overeynder (v) CMCN LRHS NLar SFol SMad SSta
- 'Wisley King' EPfP LRHS WPGP
- 'Woorby Rose' CJun
- 'Worplesdon' ♀^{H6} Widely available

Liriodendron ✿ (*Magnoliaceae*)
  chinense ♀^{H6} CMCN EBee EPfP EUrb MBlu WPGP
  × sinoamericanum CAco
  - 'Chapel Hill' MBlu
  - 'Doc Deforce's Delight' MBlu NLar
  tulipifera ♀^{H6} Widely available
  - 'Ardis' CMCN
  - 'Aureomarginatum' (v) ♀^{H6} CAco CBcs CEnd CMac EBar ELan
   EPfP EUrb IPap LMaj LRHS LSRN
   MAsh MBlu MGos SAth SGol SPoG
   SSta WCot WMat
  - 'Edward Gursztyn'^{PBR} CAco
  - 'Fastigiatum' CAco CEnd CLnd CMCN CNWT
   EBar ELan EPfP EUrb LCro LMaj
   LRHS MAsh MBlu MGos NLar
  - 'Glen Gold' CEnd MBlu
  - 'Purgatory' MBlu
  - 'Roodhaan' MBlu
  - 'Rotundiloba' MBlu
  - 'Snow Bird' (v) CBTr LRHS MAsh NLar NPip SPoG
   WMat

Liriope ✿ (*Asparagaceae*)
§ exiliflora ELon NLar
  - SILVERY SUNPROOF misapplied see *L. spicata* 'Gin-ryū'
  graminifolia misapplied see *L. muscari*
  'Grassy' ESwi
  hyacinthifolia see *Reineckea carnea*
  'Majestic' EBee WHoo
  minor CMac
  - B&SWJ 8933 WCru
§ muscari ♀^{H5} Widely available
  - B&SWJ 8751 WCru
  - B&SWJ 11412 WCru
  - 'Alba' see *L. muscari* 'Monroe White'
  - AMETHYST ('Liptp') CDor ISha LRHS WNPC
  - 'Big Blue' CAbb CDor CExl CMac CWnw
   EBee EGren ELan ELon EMor
   EPfP GQue LRHS LSRN MBel
   MPie MSwo NLar SArc SBea SPoG
   WFar WNPC WPnP WTre
  - 'Christmas Tree' EBee ELon
  - 'Emerald Cascade' ESwi
  - 'Gold-banded' (v) EBee LCro SBea WFar
  - 'Goldfinger' CExl
  - 'Ingwersen' CDor CExl CKno EBee EGren EHeP
   EPfP EPPr LRHS MAvo
  - 'John Burch' (v) CExl CMac
  - 'Kindi Pink' ELan
  - 'Lilac Wonder' EBee EMor EPfP EPPr
  - 'Majestic' misapplied see *L. exiliflora*
  - 'Moneymaker' CDor EBee EGren ELan ELon EPfP
   LCro LRHS LSou LSRN LWaG MNrw
   NLar SArc SPoG WNPC
§ - 'Monroe White' CBcs CDor CExl CMac CWnw
   EBee EGren ELan EPfP GMaP
   ISha LCro LRHS MAvo MBel
   MMrt NBid NLar SArc SAth SBea
   SPoG WPnP
  - 'Okina' (v) CBro EBee ELon EMor LCro MHol
   MNrw NLar NSti SPoG WCot
  - 'Pee Dee Ingot' SPoG
  - 'Purple Passion' EBee
  - 'Royal Purple' CDor CWnw EBee EGren EPfP
   LCro LRHS MBel MHtn NLar SArc
   SAth WNPC
  - 'Silver Ribbon' CBro MGos
  - 'Super Blue' CDor ESwi NLar
  - 'Variegata' (v) CExl EBee EBlo EGren EPfP EWes
   LCro LRHS LWaG MAvo NBir NLar
   SPoG
  - 'Webster Wideleaf' EBee WCot
  platyphylla see *L. muscari*
  'Samantha' CDor ECha ELan NLar
  spicata EBee
  - B&SWJ 4508 WCru
§ - 'Gin-ryū' (v) CExl LRHS NSti
  - 'Silver Dragon' see *L. spicata* 'Gin-ryū'
§ - 'Spring Gold' ESwi LEdu

Litchi (*Sapindaceae*)
  chinensis WJur

Lithocarpus ✿ (*Fagaceae*)
  densiflorus see *Notholithocarpus densiflorus*
  edulis CBrP SArc
  glaber CBrP
  pachyphyllus CBcs

Lithodora (*Boraginaceae*)
  diffusa see *Glandora diffusa* (Lag.) D.C. Thomas

hispidula SBrt
  subsp. *versicolor*
× *intermedia* see *Moltkia* × *intermedia*
oleifolia see *Glandora oleifolia*
rosmarinifolia see *Glandora rosmarinifolia*
zahnii SVen
- 'Azure-ness' WAbe

Lithophragma (Saxifragaceae)
parviflorum CMiW CTtf EWes

Lithops ✿ (Aizoaceae)
fulviceps MPri
helmutii SPlb
karasmontana ♛H2 LWaG
pseudotruncatella ♛H2 CoPl

Lithospermum (Boraginaceae)
diffusum see *Glandora diffusa* (Lag.)
   D.C.Thomas
doerfleri see *Moltkia doerfleri*
'Heavenly Blue' see *Glandora prostrata* 'Heavenly
   Blue'
officinale CGwi NAts
oleifolium see *Glandora oleifolia*
purpureocaeruleum see *Buglossoides purpurocaerulea*

Litsea (Lauraceae)
NJM 13.047 WPGP
glauca see *Neolitsea sericea*
japonica SVen

Littorella (Plantaginaceae)
uniflora CBen

Livistona ✿ (Arecaceae)
australis NPlm
chinensis ♛H2 NPlm
decora NPlm
mariae NPlm
nitida NPlm
rotundifolia LWaG NHrt

Lobelia (Campanulaceae)
§ *angulata* 'Treadwellii' ECha ELan LRHS NBro SPlb SRms
   WFar
bambuseti SBig
bridgesii CTsd
§ *cardinalis* CFis CLil CMac CPud CWal
   CWat ELin EPfP EWld GMaP
   LCro LRHS MCtn NPer SPlb
   SRms WFar
- f. *alba* EDAr ELan LBar
- 'Bee's Flame' CWGN ESgI LRHS MArl NCth
   NGdn
- 'Black Truffle' see *L. cardinalis* 'Chocolate Truffle'
§ - 'Chocolate Truffle' PBR EBee MPro NCth SRms
§ - 'Elmfeuer' SPlb SPoG
§ - 'Queen Victoria' ♛H3 Widely available
- 'Russian Princess' CBWd CLil CMHG EAri EPfP LRHS
   misapplied MPro NGdn SMad SOrN SPoG SRkn
   WFar
Compliment Series see *L.* × *speciosa* Kompliment
   Series
'Compton Pink' CBcs CMHG CToG ELon EMor
   EWes LBar LBuc LCro LRHS LShi
   MArl MPri NCth NLar NSti WFar
erinus MBros
- 'Cambridge Blue' ♛H2 MBros MCtn
- Cascade Series ♛H2 LCro MCtn
- 'Crystal Palace' ♛H2 EGren LCro MBros MCtn MPri

- (Fountain Series) MBros MCtn MPri
   'Fountain Blue'
- - 'Fountain Rose' MBros
- - 'Fountain White' EGren MBros MPri
- Laura Deep Blue MNHC
   (Laura Series)
- 'Mrs Clibran' ♛H2 LCro MBros
- 'Regatta Marine Blue' MCtn
   (Regatta Series)
- 'Sapphire' EGren LCro MBros MCtn MPri
- 'String of Pearls' ♛H2 LCro MBros
- Waterfall Blue Ice LSou MPri
   (Waterfall Series)
- 'White Lady' EGren MBros
excelsa SEND
'Fairy Footsteps' EDAr
fistulosa CDTJ CTsd EAri WCot
'Flamingo' see *L.* × *speciosa* 'Pink Flamingo'
fulgens see *L. cardinalis*
- Saint Elmo's Fire see *L. cardinalis* 'Elmfeuer'
× *gerardii* see *L.* × *speciosa*
'Infinity Blue' MPri
'Isobel's Blush' MPro
laxiflora ♛H3 CBcs ESwi LRHS SAdn SIvy WFar
- var. *angustifolia* CDTJ CHll CPbh CWCL EAri EWld
   MHer SBrt SMHy SPlb SRms SVen
   WCot WKif
linnaeoides SPlb
Lobelix Blue (Lobelix Midl
   Series) **new**
montana EWld
- B&SWJ 8220 ESwi WCru
oligophylla WIce
pedunculata CSBt EBee ECha EDAr EPfP GQue
   LRHS LShi MAsh SLee SPlb SRms
   SRot WFar WIce
I - 'Alba' ELan EWes SLee SRms SRot WFar
   WIce
- 'County Park' CSpe ECha EDAr ELan EPfP EPot
   LRHS MAsh SLee SPlb SPoG SRms
   SRot WFar WIce
'Queen Victoria' see *L. cardinalis* 'Queen Victoria'
sessilifolia CExl MWlw
- B&SWJ 8875 WCru
siphilitica Widely available
- f. *albiflora* EBee LEdu MBel
- - 'Alba' CPud CToG CWat ELin EMor EPfP
   LRHS LShi MArl SRms WFar
- 'Rosea' MNrw
'Sombre Purple' EBee
§ × *speciosa* EGrI WFar
- Crimson Princess EAri EPfP LRHS SPoG
   ('Gencrim' PBR)
   (Princess Series)
- 'Dark Crusader' EBee EPfP LRHS MArl MHol
- (Fan Series) 'Fan Blau' CLil EGren ELan LRHS MHol MPro
   WFar
- - 'Fan Burgundy' CLil ELan LRHS NGdn
- - 'Fan Lachs' CLil EGren WFar
- - 'Fan Scharlach' EGren ELan SPoG WFar
- - 'Fan Tiefrot' CLil SRms
- - 'Fan Zinnoberrosa' SRms
- 'Hadspen Purple' PBR Widely available
- 'Kimbridge Beet' CMac
§ - Kompliment Series WFar
- - 'Kompliment Blau' WFar
* - - 'Kompliment Pale WFar
   Pink'
- - 'Kompliment LRHS NPer
   Scharlach' ♛H5
- 'Monet Moment' EBee NCth NLar

- 'Pink Elephant' ♀H5	CMHG CPud ELan LBar LRHS MAsh MHol MPie NCth NDov NSti
§ - 'Pink Flamingo'	ELan
- ROSE PRINCESS ('Genross'PBR) (Princess Series)	SPoG
- 'Ruby Slippers'	CMac EBee ELan
I - 'Russian Princess' purple-flowered	CWnw EAri ELan EUrb LBar MArl MBel MHer MHol MPie SMrm SPoG WFar WKif
- SCARLET PRINCESS ('Genlet'PBR) (Princess Series)	EBee
- 'Sparkling Ruby'	EBee EPfP LBar LRHS LShi NDov
- (Starship Series) STARSHIP BLUE ('Pas1302712')	EGren ELan EMor EPfP LBar LRHS MBros MHol MSCN WHil
- - STARSHIP BURGUNDY ('Pas1301790')	EGren ELan EMor LBar LRHS Midl
- - STARSHIP DEEP ROSE ('Pas905518')	EGren ELan EMor EPfP LBar LRHS MBros MHol MSCN WCot WHil
- - STARSHIP SCARLET ('Pas905521')	EGren ELan EMor EPfP LBar LRHS LSou MBros MHol MPro
- - STARSHIP SCARLET BRONZE LEAF ('Pas1302716')	LBar MSCN WHil
- 'Tania'	CBcs CLil CSpe CWGN EAri EBee ELan EMor EPfP GElm IPot LBar LRHS MArl MAsh MBel MHol MPie MPro NGdn NSti SAko SMad SPoG SRms WFar WKif
- 'Tania's Sister'	WCot
§ - 'Vedrariensis'	CMac CSpe CWat ELin LRHS MBel MHer MNrw MPro SRms WCav WFar WHil WHoo WTre
telekii	LShi
treadwellii	see L. angulata 'Treadwellii'
tupa	CBcs CCht CExl CSpe CTsd EAri EBee ECha EGrI ELan EUrb LEdu MNrw NCth SArc SEle SEND SMHy SMrm SPoG WCru WFar WPGP
- Archibald's form	WPGP
vedrariensis	see L. × speciosa 'Vedrariensis'

Lobivia see Echinopsis

Lobularia (Brassicaceae)

maritima 'Carpet of Snow'	MCtn
- 'Easter Bonnet Violet'	MCtn
- EASY BREEZY WHITE ('Balbeezite') new	MPri
- GOLF BRIGHT MIXED (Golf Series)	LCro
- 'Snow Crystals'	MPri
- 'Violet Queen' ♀H3	LCro
SNOW PRINCESS ('Inlbusnopr'PBR)	MHol

loganberry see Rubus × loganobaccus

Lomandra (Asparagaceae)

'Arctic Frost'	CCht EHeP
hystrix	SPlb
longifolia	EPPr LEdu SEND SPlb
§ - PLATINUM BEAUTY ('Roma 13'PBR) (v)	CBcs LBom LCro LRHS SPeP SPoG
- TANIKA ('Lm300'PBR)	CBcs
- WHITE SANDS	see L. longifolia PLATINUM BEAUTY

Lomaria see Blechnum

Lomatia (Proteaceae)

ferruginea	CBcs CDoC CDTJ CExl EPfP EUrb SArc SEle SPoG WJur WPGP
fraseri	CBcs CDoC EPfP SPoG WPGP
longifolia	see L. myricoides
§ myricoides	CBcs CDoC CExl LRHS SArc SEle SPoG
tinctoria	CBcs CExl SPlb

Lomatium (Apiaceae)

columbianum	MCtn
grayi	ECha SHor WHil
nudicaule	SPhx

Lonas (Asteraceae)

inodora	MCtn

Lonicera ✿ (Caprifoliaceae)

§ acuminata	ELan
- B&SWJ 6743	CRHN
- B&SWJ 6815	WCru
albertii	NLar SBrt
alseuosmoides	CBcs CRHN ELan EPfP LRHS NLar SEND SPoG WCru WSpi
× americana misapplied	see L. × italica
× americana ambig.	LCro WTHo
§ × americana (Mill.) K. Koch	CBcs CRHN EPfP LCro LEdu SEND SRms
× amoena 'Rosea'	NCth SEND
§ × brownii 'Dropmore Scarlet'	CBcs CBrac CDoC CMac CRHN CWGN EBee ELan EPfP LBom LCro LRHS LSRN MAsh MGos MPri NBir NLar NPer SEND SNig SPlb SPoG WTHo
- 'Fuchsioides' misapplied	see L. × brownii 'Dropmore Scarlet'
- 'Fuchsioides' K. Koch	LCro LRHS
- GOLDEN TRUMPET ('Mintrump')	CWGN LRHS MGos
caerulea	CDoC EPom MAsh SBmr SEdi SPre SRms SVic WJur WKor
- 'Altaj' (F) new	SPre
- 'Atut'	NLar
- 'Duet'	NLar
- var. edulis	CAgr LBuc LCro LEdu
- var. kamtschatica	CoPl EPom LCro MMuc SBmr
- - 'Balalaika' (F)	CAgr
- - 'Borealis' (F)	CAgr
- - 'Eisbar' (F)	CAgr
- - 'Fialka'PBR (F)	NLar
- - 'Honey Bee' (F)	CAgr
- - 'Indigo Gem' (F)	CAgr
- - 'Indigo Yum' (F)	CAgr
- - 'Kalinka' (F)	CAgr
- - 'Larisa' (F)	LEdu
- - 'Morena'PBR (F)	EPom
- - 'Ruth' (F)	WLov
- - 'Sinoglaska' (F)	NLar
- - 'Vicky' (F)	WFar
- - 'Wojtek' (F)	CAgr NLar SPre
- - 'Zojka' (F)	CAgr NLar
* - var. longifolia	NLar
§ caprifolium	CRHN LCro
- 'Anna Fletcher'	CRHN
- f. pauciflora	see L. × italica
- 'Celestial'PBR	EPfP LCro
chaetocarpa	CEnd SBrt
ciliosa	CRHN WPGP
'Clavey's Dwarf'	EPPr
crassifolia	CBcs CExl EBee EPot EWes EWld GEdr GKev NLar SBrt WPGP

- 'Little Honey'	ELan EPfP GBin GKev LCro MBlu MBNS MMrt NLar SPoG WTor
deflexicalyx	NLar
dioica red-flowered	GGro
'Early Cream'	see *L. caprifolium*
'Elegant'	see *L. ligustrina* 'Elegant'
elisae	CBcs CMac EBee ELan EPfP EWes MMuc NLar SPoG SSta WCot WPGP
etrusca	CRHN
- 'Donald Waterer'	CRHN EPfP WFar
- 'Michael Rosse'	EBee ELan MBNS
- 'Superba' ♧H5	CRHN ELan EPfP NLar SEND WTHo
flexuosa	see *L. japonica* var. *repens*
fragrantissima	CBcs CBrac CDoC CEnd CoPl CSBt EBee EGrI EHeP ELan EPfP GKin LCro LRHS LSRN LSto MHer MNrw NLar NPer SPlb SPoG SRms SSta WFar WHtc WTHo
giraldii misapplied	see *L. acuminata*
giraldii Rehder	CRHN GAbr
glabrata B&SWJ 2150	WCru
- 'Damchin La'	CRHN WPGP
gracilipes	GGro
- JP 5573	SBrt
grata	see *L.* × *americana* (Mill.) K. Koch
harae	WJur
× *heckrottii*	CSBt NLar
§ - 'American Beauty'	LBom LCro LRHS LWaG WTHo
- 'Gold Flame' misapplied	see *L.* × *heckrottii* 'American Beauty'
- 'Gold Flame' ambig.	GKin NLar
- 'Gold Flame' hort.	CBcs CMac EBee EGren ELan EPfP LBom LBuc LCro LRHS MAsh MMuc SEND SNig SPoG SRms WHtc WLov WTHo
§ *henryi*	CBcs CBrac CDoC CMac CRHN CSpe EBee EHeP EPfP GKin LBom LCro LRHS LSto LWaG MAsh MGos MMuc SEND SNig SOrN SPlb SRms SWCr SWor WCFE WFar WTHo
- B&SWJ 8109	WCru
- NJM 11.033	WPGP
- 'Copper Beauty'PBR	CBcs CBrac CDoC CEnd CMac CoPl CTsd EBee EGren EPfP LBom LBuc LCro LRHS LSRN MAsh MGos MPri NLar SBig SEND SPoG SRms SWCr SWor WLov WPGP WTHo
- var. *subcoriacea*	see *L. henryi*
hildebrandiana ♧H2	CExl CRHN EUrb LRHS WPGP
hispidula	SBrt WPGP
'Honey Baby'	CBcs ELon LCro NLar
implexa	CRHN
involucrata	CMCN EBee EWld MBlu MBNS MMuc MNrw SEle SEND
- var. *ledebourii*	EPfP MMrt NLar SPel StAn
- - 'Vian'	NLar
§ × *italica*	
§ - Harlequin ('Sherlite') (v)	CMac SPlb SRms
? *japonica*	CMen WFar
§ - 'Aureoreticulata' (v) ♧H5	CMac EHeP ELan EPfP LCro NPer SRms WFar WTHo
- 'Cream Cascade'	LBom LCro LRHS WTHo
- 'Dart's Acumen'	CRHN
- 'Dart's World'	CSBt LCro LRHS SRms
- 'Halliana'	CBcs CBrac CDoC CEnd CMac EBee EGren EHeP ELan EPfP LBom LCro LRHS LSRN MAsh MGos NBir NLar SNig SPlb SPoG SRGP SRms WFar WHtc WTHo
- 'Hall's Prolific' ♧H5	CBrac CDoC CEnd CSBt EBee EGren ELan EPfP LBom LBuc LCro LRHS LSRN LSto MAsh MBlu MGos MHer SNig SPoG WFar WHtc WTHo
§ - 'Horwood Gem' (v)	CDoC LCro LRHS MGos NLar WTHo
- 'Mint Crisp'PBR (v)	CBrac CDoC CMac CSBt CWGN EBee ELan EPfP LCro LRHS NLar SNig SPoG SRms WHtc WTHo
- 'Peter Adams'	see *L. japonica* 'Horwood Gem'
- 'Princess Kate'	ELan EPfP LRHS SPoG SRms WTHo
- 'Purple Queen'	EBee MMrt
- 'Purpurea'	LCro LRHS WTHo
- 'Red World'	EBee ELan ELon LRHS LSou NCth NLar SNig WTHo
§ - var. *repens* ♧H5	CMac CSBt EHeP ELan EPfP LCro NLar SPoG SRms WFar WTHo
- 'Variegata'	see *L. japonica* 'Aureoreticulata'
korolkowii	CExl LSto MBNS NBir NLar WCot
- 'Blue Velvet'	CAgr NLar
- var. *zabelii* misapplied	see *L. tatarica* 'Zabelii'
lanceolata BWJ 7935	WCru
'Lemon Beauty'	see *L. ligustrina* 'Lemon Beauty'
ligustrina Copper Glow ('Grln03'PBR) (Garden Clouds Series)	LSou WReH
§ - 'Elegant'	LBuc SArc WReH
- Green Breeze ('Grln01'PBR) (Garden Clouds Series) **new**	LSou
§ - 'Lemon Beauty' (v)	CBcs CMac EBee EHeP LRHS LSRN LSto MGos MSwo NLar SRms WFar WHtc
- 'Lime Twist' (v)	LSto
§ - var. *pileata*	CBcs CBrac CEnd CMac CMCN EGren EHeP EPfP GQue LBuc LRHS NLit NPer SAth SRms WFar
- - 'Moss Green'	EBee LRHS
§ - var. *yunnanensis*	CAco CDoC CMac CSBt EGren EHeP GBin LMaj LSto MHed NLar SArc SEND SEWo WHnu WReH
- - 'Baggesen's Gold' ♧H5	CBcs CBrac CDoC CEnd CMac EBee EGren EHeP ELan ELon EPfP GAbr GQue LRHS LSRN LSto MGos MHed NBir NLar SDix SEND SGol SPoG SRms WFar
- - 'Chalons'PBR	LSou NLar
- - Edmée Gold ('Briloni')	WCot
- - 'Ernest Wilson'	EPPr
- - 'Fertilis'	CBrac
- - 'Golden Glow'PBR	LRHS LSRN NEoE NLar
- - 'Lemon Queen'	ELan LSto SEND
§ - - 'Maigrün'	EBee EHeP ELan LRHS LSto NEoE WFar
- - Maygreen	see *L. ligustrina* var. *yunnanensis* 'Maigrün'
- - Purple Storm ('Grln02'PBR) (Garden Clouds Series)	CoPl LSou WReH
- 'Red Tips'	CBcs EBee LRHS NLar SRms
- - Scoop	see *L. ligustrina* var. *yunnanensis* 'Chalons'
- 'Silver Beauty' (v)	CMac EHeP ELan LSto MSwo SPlb SPoG SRms WFar
- 'Silver Lining' (v)	WCFE
- Tidy Tips ('Panmin')	CBcs CDoC CWnw ELan ELon LRHS LSto NEoE
- - 'Twiggy' (v)	CSBt EDAr LRHS Midl MPri NLar NWbg WFar
maackii	CMCN EPfP EPPr NLar WJur
- f. *podocarpa*	MMuc

Loropetalum 433

macrantha B&SWJ 11687	WCru
- WWJ 11606	WCru
'Mandarin' ♀H5	CRHN LCro LRHS MBlu NLar WCot
maximowiczii	WJur
var. *sachalinensis*	
morrowii 'Ullung do'	CMCN
myrtillus	NLar SBrt
nitida	see *L. ligustrina* var. *yunnanensis*
olgae	SBrt
aff. *pamirica*	WPGP
periclymenum	CRHN EGren LWaG MCtn MHer MNHC SPlb WOrg
- 'Assynt Cream'	MBlu
- 'Belgica' misapplied	see *L.* × *italica*
- 'Belgica'	Widely available
- 'Belgica Select'	LRHS SNig SOrN
- CAPRILIA IMPERIAL ('Inov86'PBR)	LCro
- CHIC ET CHOC ('Inov205'PBR)	LCro NLar SPoG
§ - 'Chojnów'PBR	LRHS
* - 'Cream Cascade'	LRHS
- 'Florida'	see *L. periclymenum* 'Serotina'
- FRAGRANT CLOUD	see *L. periclymenum* 'Chojnów'
- 'Graham Thomas' ♀H6	Widely available
- 'Harlequin'	see *L.* × *italica* HARLEQUIN
- 'Heaven Scent'	CDoC LBuc LCro LRHS NLar WFar WTHo
- 'Honeybush'	CWGN MAsh WFar WNPC
- 'Red Gables'	CDoC EBee ELon LRHS MGos NLar SEND WCot WKif
- 'Rhubarb and Custard'	CBcs CDoC EEnd EPfP LCro LRHS MGos SPoG SWCr WNPC
- 'Scentsation'PBR	CEnd CMac CRHN CSBt CWGN EBee ELan EPfP LBom LBuc LCro LRHS MAsh MHtn MPri NLar SOrN SPoG SWCr WNPC WSpi
§ - 'Serotina' ♀H6	CBcs CBrac CDoC CEnd CMac CRHN CSBt EBee EGren EHeP ELan EPfP GKin GQue LCro LRHS LSRN LSto MAsh MGos MHer MPri NLar SPoG SRms WFar WTHo
- 'Strawberries and Cream'	CDoC LCro LRHS MGos NLar WNPC
- 'Sweet Sue'	CDoC CRHN EBee ELan ELon EPfP LCro LRHS MPri NLar SPoG SWCr WFar WTHo
- 'Winchester'	SRms
pileata	see *L. ligustrina* var. *pileata*
- var. *yunnanensis* misapplied	see *L. ligustrina* var. *yunnanensis* 'Fertilis'
- var. *yunnanensis* (Franch.) Rehd.	see *L. ligustrina* var. *yunnanensis*
pilosa Willd. ex Kunth	CRHN
- F&M 207	WPGP
- F&M 256	WPGP
prolifera	CRHN NLar
× *purpusii*	CMac EBee LRHS SRms WFar WJur
- 'Spring Romance'	CMac
- 'Winter Beauty' ♀H6	Widely available
quinquelocularis	WJur
- f. *translucens*	GKev
ramosissima	NLar
reticulata 'Silver'	NLar
sempervirens	CBcs CRHN CSBt LCro LRHS WTHo
- 'Cedar Lane'	EPfP SBrt
- 'Dropmore Scarlet'	see *L.* × *brownii* 'Dropmore Scarlet'
- 'Leo'	CWGN
- f. *sulphurea*	CMCN
- - 'John Clayton'	EPfP LRHS
setifera 'Daphnis'	CExl EBee MBlu SSta WPGP
similis var. *delavayi* ♀H5	CBcs CRHN CWGN EGren ELan EWld LCro LRHS MAsh NLar SDix SEND SPoG SRms SWCr WCot WCru WTHo
- 'Simonet'	EBee
standishii	LRHS WFar
- f. *lancifolia* 'Budapest'	ELan MBlu MMuc NLar SRms WFar
stenantha	SBrt
subaequalis Og 93.329	CExl EWld WPGP
syringantha	CBcs CRHN EBee ELan EPPr EWld LSto MMuc MNrw NLar SEND WCot WFar WLov
tangutica	GGro
tatarica	CMCN
- 'Arnold Red'	MBlu SEND
- 'Hack's Red'	CMCN ELon EPfP NLar SVen WCot
- 'Rosea'	WCot
§ - 'Zabelii'	MNrw
× *tellmanniana* ♀H5	CBcs CBrac CMac CRHN EBee ELan EPfP LBom LCro LRHS MAsh MBlu NLar SNig SPoG SRms SWCr WLov WTHo
thibetica	MBlu
tomentella	WJur
- B&SWJ 2654	WCru
tragophylla ♀H5	EPfP LCro LRHS MBNS
- 'Maurice Foster'	CBcs EBee LEdu LRHS WPGP WSpi
vesicaria	WJur
xylosteum	EPPr LEdu MMuc

Lophomyrtus ✿ (*Myrtaceae*)

§ *bullata*	CDTJ LRHS WJur
- 'Matai Bay'	CBcs
§ *obcordata*	CTsd WJur
× *ralphii*	CoPl
- BLACK PEARL ('Yanearl')	CDoC CMCN WFar
- 'Gloriosa'	LRHS
- 'Kathryn'	CBcs CCoa CDoC EPfP NLar SVen
- 'Krinkly'	CBcs CCoa CSde LCro
- 'Little Star' (v)	LRHS
- Logan's form (v)	CBcs CCoa CDoC CMac CTsd EGrl EUrb LCro LRHS SPoG WFar WSpi
- 'Magic Dragon'PBR (v)	CBcs CCoa CDoC SVen
- 'Multicolor' (v)	CBcs CCoa CDoC LRHS MAsh SPoG SVen
- 'Pixie'	EGrl EUrb
- 'Purpurea'	CBcs CMac EPfP LCro LRHS MAsh MGos StAn WFar
- 'Red Dragon'	LRHS
- 'Wild Cherry'	

Lophophora (*Cactaceae*)

williamsii	SBig

Lophosoria (*Dicksoniaceae*)

quadripinnata	CBrP CDTJ LEdu WPGP

Lophospermum (*Plantaginaceae*)

§ *erubescens* ♀H2	CRHN CSpe EUrb
- white-flowered	CSpe
(Lofos Series) LOFOS COMPACT PINK ('Sunlorose'PBR)	LSou
- LOFOS WINE RED ('Sun-asaro')	EShb
§ 'Magic Dragon'	SEND SPlb
§ 'Red Dragon'	CDoC EShb SPlb

loquat see *Eriobotrya japonica*

Loropetalum (*Hamamelidaceae*)

chinense	SAth SEle WJur

434 *Loropetalum*

– Black Pearl	see *L. chinense* var. *rubrum* 'Pearl'	
– Carolina Moonlight ('Nci 002')	SEle	
– Ever Red	see *L. chinense* var. *rubrum* 'Chang Nian Hong'	
– Hot Spice	EGrI SEle	
– 'Ming Dynasty'	EGrI LRHS MAsh MMuc SEle	
– 'Plum Gorgeous'	CSBt CSpe MBNS	
– var. *rubrum* 'Blush'	CBcs SEle	
§ – – 'Chang Nian Hong'^PBR	CDoC EGrI LCro LRHS SMad	
– – 'Daybreak's Flame'	CCoa CDoC CSde LRHS SEle SIvy	
– – 'Fire Dance'	CBcs CCoa CDoC CSBt CSde CWGN EGren EGrI EUrb LBom LCro LRHS LSRN MAsh MGos MMuc SAng SEle SIvy SOrN SPad SPoG WCha WCot WSpi	
§ – – 'Pearl'^PBR	CBcs CWGN EGren EGrI EHeP LBom LRHS LSRN SAth WCot	
– – 'Pipa's Red'	EGrI	
– Ruby Snow ('Iwai'^PBR)	CBcs EGrI LCro LRHS	
– 'Tang Dynasty'	CBct CDoC LRHS WFar	

Lotononis (Fabaceae)

galpinii	SBrt WCot
aff. *lotononoides*	WCot

Lotus (Fabaceae)

berthelotii	CDTJ CTsd EShb MSCN WKif
– deep red-flowered	ELan
– 'Orange Flash'	MNHC
corniculatus	CAgr CBWd CCBP CGwi CHab EAri EHet GJem GJos LCro LShi MCtn MHer MMuc MNHC MPri NAts NMir SEND SPhx SRms WOrg
– 'Plenus' (d)	EAri EBee EPot
germanicus	MMuc SEND
hirsutus ♀^H4	CCoa EAri ECha EGrI ELan EPfP EPPr GEdr LCro LRHS SAdn SEND SMrm SPlb SPoG
– 'Brimstone' (v)	SIvy SPoG
– Little Boy Blue ('Lisbob'^PBR)	CSBt EPfP LRHS MAsh
– 'Lois'	ESgI LRHS SIvy SPoG
maculatus	EAri
maritimus	EDAr
mearnsii	SPlb
pedunculatus	CAgr CHab NAts NMir WOrg
sessilifolius	CSpe
subsp. *sessilifolius* new	
§ *tetragonolobus*	LCro SVic

lovage see *Levisticum officinale*

Loxostigma (Gesneriaceae)

kurzii	LShi
– GWJ 9342	WCru

Luculia (Rubiaceae)

gratissima	WPGP

Ludwigia (Onagraceae)

arcuata	ELin
glandulosa Walter	ELin
grandiflora	Prohibited invasive. See Conservation and the Environment, p.42
palustris	ELin
peploides	Prohibited invasive. See Conservation and the Environment, p.42

Luetkea (Rosaceae)

pectinata	GArf GEdr WAbe

Luffa (Cucurbitaceae)

aegyptiaca	ELan
cylindrica	LCro MCtn

Luma ✿ (Myrtaceae)

§ *apiculata* ♀^H4	Widely available
§ – 'Glanleam Gold' (v)	CBcs CBct CBrac CCoa CDoC CEnd CMac CTsd EBee ELan EPfP GKev GKin IArd LRHS LSto MAsh MGos NLar SArc SPoG SRms WFar WHtc WJek WPav
– 'Nana'	LEdu WJek WPGP
– 'Penlee'	WJek
– 'Saint Hilary' (v)	WJek
– 'Variegata' (v)	WFar
§ *chequen*	CCoa CTsd EPfP LBom SArc WJek WPav WPGP

Lunaria (Brassicaceae)

§ *annua*	CBWd CoPl EHet ELan GJem GJos LCro LSto MNHC WCot
– var. *albiflora* ♀^H6	LCro LSto MPro NBir SEND WCot
I – – 'Alba Variegata' (v) ♀^H6	CSpe CTtf WBrk
– 'Chedglow'	CSpe ELan EWld LCro LEdu LSto MCtn MHer MPro SDix SHor SPel SPhx WBrk WCot
– 'Corfu Blue' ♀^H6	CDor CSpe ESgI EWes EWld LSto NSti SAng SPhx WCru
– 'Munstead Purple' ♀^H6	CSpe
– f. *pachyrrhiza*	WPGP
– 'Purple Emperor'	CTtf
– 'Variegata' (v)	CSpe CTtf GJos NBir WCot
biennis	see *L. annua*
rediviva ♀^H7	CDor CSpe CTtf EBee ECha EMor EPPr EWld GAbr LCro LEdu MBel MMuc NBid NPer NSti SAng SPel WCAu WCot WFar WPGP WTre
– B&SWJ 15918	WCru
– 'Partway White' (v)	WCot

Lunathyrium (Woodsiaceae)

petersenii	LEdu SPlb WPGP

Lupinus ✿ (Fabaceae)

angustifolius	MCtn
arboreus ♀^H4	CWal CWCL EPfP LShi MNrw NBir SIvy SPlb SPoG SRms SVic WFar
– 'Barton-on-Sea'	CDoC LRHS
– blue and white-flowered	MMrt WFar
– 'Blue Boy'	LRHS Midl
– blue-flowered	CCoa LShi SPlb SPoG SRms WFar
– 'Chelsea Blue'	EPfP
– cream-flowered	SBeP
– 'Lavender Spires'	EPfP LCro LRHS
– 'Snow Queen'	CDoC CWCL SPoG
– white-flowered	CSpe LShi MMrt SPlb
– yellow and blue-flowered	NBir SRkn
– yellow-flowered	CDoC
arcticus	EBee
(Avalune Series) 'Avalune Blue'	LCro
– 'Avalune Lilac-White'	LCro
– 'Avalune Pink'	LCro MCtn
– 'Avalune Red-White'	LCro
– 'Avalune White'	LCro MCtn
Band of Nobles Series	MCtn
'Beefeater'	CWCL ELan EPfP EWes LBom LBuc LCro MHol MPri MPro NCth NLar SPoG
'Bishop's Tipple'	ELan EPfP LCro LRHS MPri MPro

'Blacksmith'	CWCL ELan EPfP MPri MPro
'Blossom'PBR	CWGN ELan EPfP EWes LCro LRHS LSRN MHol MPri MPro SPoG WSpi
caespitosus	see *L. lepidus* var. *utahensis*
'Camelot Yellow' (Camelot Series)	Midl
'Cashmere Cream'	CWCL CWGN EPfP LCro LRHS MPro NCth XFar
'Chandelier' (Band of Nobles Series)	CAby CBcs EGren ELan ELon EPfP GAbr GMaP GQue LCro LShi MAsh MCtn Midl MPri MPro NBir NLar SOrN SPoG WCAu WFar
'Desert Sun'PBR	CBcs CWCL ELan EPfP LCro LRHS MHol MPri MPro NLar SPoG XFar
Dwarf Gallery hybrids	GBin
'Dwarf Lulu'	see L. 'Lulu'
Gallery Series	EGren EPfP MBros SPlb WFar
- 'Gallery Blue'	CTsd EDAr EGren ELan EPfP GBin LBuc LCro LRHS MBros MHol Midl MPri MSCN NLar SPoG WCot WFar WTor
- 'Gallery Pink Bicolor'	EGren GBin Midl
- 'Gallery Pink'	EDAr EGren ELan EPfP GBin LCro LRHS MHol Midl MPri NLar SPoG SRms WFar
- 'Gallery Pink White'	EBee EPfP
- 'Gallery Red'	CTsd EDAr EGren ELan EPfP GBin LCro MBros MHol Midl MPri MSCN NLar SPoG WFar WTor
- 'Gallery Rose'	LRHS SPoG WFar WTor
- 'Gallery White'	EGren ELan EPfP GBin LBuc LCro MBros MHol Midl MPri MSCN NLar SPoG WFar WTor
- 'Gallery Yellow'	EGren ELan EPfP LBuc LCro MBros MHol MPri NLar SPoG WCot WFar WTor
'Gladiator'PBR	CWCL EBee ELan EPfP EWes LCro MHol MPri MPro NLar SOrN SPoG XFar
'King Canute'PBR	CWCL CWGN EBee ELan EPfP LCro MPri MPro XFar
Legendary Series	EGren MPri
- 'Legendary Yellow Shades'	LRHS
lepidus	CPbh WSpi
§ - var. *utahensis*	SPlb
§ 'Lulu'	LRHS SPoG
(Lupinova Series)	WTor
LUPINOVA CUTIE ('Et Lpn 709') **new**	
- LUPINOVA LYANNA ('Et Lpn 813') **new**	WTor
luteus	MCtn SHor SPhx
'Magic Lantern'	CWCL ELan EPfP LCro MHol MPri MPro NCth SPoG
'Manhattan Lights'PBR	CBcs CWCL CWGN EBee ELan EPfP EWes LBom LCro LRHS MHol MPri MPro NLar SOrN SPoG
'Masterpiece'PBR	CBcs CDoC CWCL ELan EPfP EWes LBom LCro LRHS LSRN MHol MPri MPro NLar SOrN SPoG WCAu WNPC
'Melody'	EBee ELan LCro LRHS MPro XFar
'Midnight Majesty'	MPri MPro
Minarette Group	EPfP MNrw SRms
'Mrs Perkins'	SMrm
mutabilis 'Sunrise'	MNHC
'My Castle' (Band of Nobles Series)	CBcs ELan EPfP GAbr GMaP GQue LRHS LSRN MAsh MCtn MGos MNHC MPri MPro NLar NLit SOrN SPoG WCAu WFar
'Noble Maiden' (Band of Nobles Series)	CAby CBcs EGren ELan ELon EPfP GAbr GMaP GQue LBom LCro LShi MCtn MNHC MPri MPro NLar NLit SOrN SPoG WCAu WFar
perennis	MCtn
'Persian Slipper'PBR	CBcs CWCL CWGN EBee ELan EPfP EWes LBuc LCro LSRN MHol MPri MPro NCth NLar SPoG WCAu WNPC
pilosus	SPhx
'Polar Princess'	CBcs CWCL CWGN EBee ELan EPfP EWes LBom LCro MHol MHtn MPri MPro NSti SPoG
polyphyllus	CSpe
- 'Tower Blue-White' **new**	Midl MPro
- 'Tower Purple-Lemon' **new**	Midl
'Purple Emperor'	EPfP LBom LRHS MPri MPro
RACHEL DE THAME ('Wclradeth'PBR)	CWCL CWGN EBee ELan EPfP EWes LBom LCro LRHS MHol MPri MPro SPoG WNPC XFar
'Red Rum'PBR	CWCL CWGN EBee ELan EPfP LBom LBuc LCro LRHS LSRN MPri MPro NLar SPoG
§ × *regalis* Russell Group	EGren EHeP EPfP LRHS MHer SPlb SRms SVic WFar
'Rote Flamme'	ELon
Russell hybrids	see *L.* × *regalis* Russell Group
'Salmon Star'PBR	CWCL CWGN LCro LRHS MPri MPro NLar WSpi XFar
'Salmon Sultan'	LRHS MPro
'Shirley Anne'	CWCL LCro
'Silver Fleece'	MPri WFar
'Tequila Flame'PBR	CWCL ELan EPfP LBuc LCro LRHS MPri MPro SPoG XFar
TERRACOTTA ('Wclterr'PBR)	CWCL ELan EPfP LBom LCro LRHS MPri MPro SPoG WCAu XFar
texensis	CSpe
'The Chatelaine' (Band of Nobles Series)	CAby CBcs EGren ELan ELon EPfP GMaP GQue LCro MAsh MCtn Midl MNHC MPri MPro NBir NLar SOrN SPoG WCAu WFar
'The Governor' (Band of Nobles Series)	CAby CBcs EGren ELan ELon EPfP GAbr GMaP GQue LBom LCro LShi MAsh MCtn Midl MNHC MPri MPro NLar SOrN SPoG SRms WCAu WFar
'The Page' (Band of Nobles Series)	CAby CBcs EGren ELan ELon EPfP GMaP GQue LBom LCro MAsh MCtn Midl MNHC NLar SOrN SPoG WCAu WFar
'Thundercloud'	EBee
'Towering Inferno'	CWCL EBee ELan EPfP LBom LBuc LCro LRHS MPri MPro NLar SPoG XFar

Luronium (Alismataceae)

natans	EWat

Luzula (Juncaceae)

alpinopilosa	EPPr
× *borreri* 'Botany Bay' (v)	WCot
maxima	see *L. sylvatica*
nivalis	GAbr
nivea	Widely available
- 'Lucius'	NLar
pilosa 'Igel'	CKno EPPr LEdu NBid NClf NLar WSpi
purpureosplendens	WCot

	'Snowflake'	CKno
	spicata	SArc
§	***sylvatica***	EBee EGrI EHeP EPfP EPPr LRHS LWaG MMuc NBro NLar NMir SEND WPnP WShi
	- 'A. Rutherford'	see *L. sylvatica* 'Taggart's Cream'
	- from Tatra Mountains, Slovakia	EPPr
	- 'Aurea'	CDoC CKno EBee EBlo ECha EPfP EPPr MMuc NClf NSti SEND SMHy WCot
	- 'Aureomarginata'	see *L. sylvatica* 'Marginata'
I	- 'Auslese'	EPPr
	- 'Bromel'	CKno EPPr
	- 'Hohe Tatra' ♀H7	CSde EPPr EWes GMaP GQue SPoG
§	- 'Marginata' (v) ♀H7	CKno ECha ELan EPPr GMaP MAvo MBNS MMuc MSwo NBid NClf NGdn NSti SArc SEND SMHy SPel WChS WCot WFar WPnP
	- 'Mariusz'	CKno EPPr
*	- f. ***nova***	EPPr
	- 'Solar Flair'	CBWd CKno EBee ELon EMor EUrb GKev LRHS NLar
§	- 'Taggart's Cream' (v)	EBee EPPr
	- 'Tauernpass'	EPPr
	- 'Thierry's Cream' (v)	CAby EBee EPPr MHol MMuc SPoG WCot
	ulophylla	GEdr SPlb WAbe

Luzuriaga (Luzuriagaceae)

	polyphylla HCM 98202	WCru
	radicans	CRHN CTsd GEdr WCru
	- R&H 602	ESwi WCru

Lychnis see *Silene*

alpina	see *Viscaria alpina*
coronata	see *Silene banksia*
× ***haageana***	see *Silene banksia*
preslii minor	see *Silene dioica*
viscaria	see *Viscaria vulgaris*
yunnanensis	see *Silene samojedorum*

Lycianthes (Solanaceae)

	***lycioides* new**	CSpe
§	***rantonnetii***	CBcs CHll EShb SEND SPoG WJur
*	- var. ***stenophylla*** 'Alba'	EShb
	- 'Variegata' (v)	CHll EShb

Lycium (Solanaceae)

afrum	SPlb SVen
barbarum (F)	CAgr CDoC EGren EPom LCro LRHS MAsh MHoo NLar SBmr SEdi SEND SPre SVic WJur WKit WKor
- 'Big Lifeberry' (F)	CAgr
- 'Number 1 Lifeberry' (F)	CAgr
- 'Sweet Lifeberry' (F)	CAgr
chinense	NQui

Lycopsis see *Anchusa*

Lycopus (Lamiaceae)

europaeus	CGwi CHab CPud ELin MMuc NAts NMir

Lycoris (Amaryllidaceae)

aurea	GKev LAma XFar
radiata	GKev LAma LCro XFar

Lygodium (Lygodiaceae)

japonicum	Prohibited invasive. See Conservation and the Environment, p.42

Lyonothamnus (Rosaceae)

floribundus subsp. ***aspleniifolius***	SArc WPGP

Lysichiton (Araceae)

americanus	Prohibited invasive. See Conservation and the Environment, p.42
camtschatcensis ♀H7	CBen CLil CPud CWat ECha ELin GQue LCro LRHS NPer WShi
× ***hortensis***	Prohibited invasive. See Conservation and the Environment, p.42

Lysiloma (Fabaceae)

watsonii	SPlb

Lysimachia (Primulaceae)

§	***atropurpurea***	CSpe EBee ELan LRHS LShi NLar
	- 'Beaujolais'	CWal GElm GJos LBar LCro LShi MCtn MPro SHor SPoG WCAu WTor
	barystachys ♀H6	MArl MBel SHar WCot WFar WHoo
	- PAB 8755	LEdu
	- 'Huntingbrook'	LEdu MArl MAvo NSti WPGP
	CANDELA ('Innlyscand')	Widely available
	candida	CElw WCot
	christinae 'Sunburst'	CoPl EPfP
	- 'Zixin'	CExl EAri EWld LEdu WFar WPGP
	ciliata	CMac GMaP MNrw NBir NGdn NLar
§	- 'Firecracker' ♀H6	Widely available
	- 'Purpurea'	see *L. ciliata* 'Firecracker'
	clethroides ♀H6	Widely available
	- 'Geisha' (v)	ECha WCot
	- 'Lady Jane'	GJos MAvo MCtn MNrw SRms
	- 'Leigong Storm'	WPGP
§	***congestiflora***	NPer
	- 'Midnight Sun' PBR	GBin LRHS MBros
	- 'Persian Chocolate'	CoPl ELon EMor ESgl LBar WFar
	ephemerum ♀H6	Widely available
	fordiana	CExl
	- Og 454	GGro WPGP
	fortunei	GGro LShi LSto WFar
	lichiangensis	EAri GGro GKev NBir
	lyssii	see *L. congestiflora*
	minoricensis	GKev WSpi
	nemorum	CGwi CoPl NAts
	- 'Lola Playle' PBR	WCot
	nummularia	CGwi CLil CoPl CPud CWat ELin LRHS LShi NAts NBir WBrk
§	- 'Aurea' ♀H5	CLil CMac CoPl CPud ECha ELan ELin GAbr GQue LBuc LCro LRHS LSto MBros MHer MMuc MPri NBid NBir NBro NLar SPoG SRms
	- 'Goldilocks'	see *L. nummularia* 'Aurea'
	paridiformis	CExl
	- from Roy Lancaster	ESwi
	- var. ***paridiformis***	CBct EWld LEdu
	- - NJM 11.067	WPGP
	- var. ***stenophylla***	CDTJ CExl CMHG EWld GEdr LEdu SHar WPGP
	- - BO 17-7152	GGro
	punctata misapplied	see *L. verticillaris*
	punctata L.	CoPl ECha EPfP LBar LRHS LSto MHer NBro NMir NPer SRms WBrk WCAu WFar WMAq
§	- 'Alexander' (v)	CDor CMac CoPl CToG ELan ELin ELon EPfP LBar LCro LRHS MArl MMuc MNrw NBid NBir NPer SIvy SMrm SPlb SPoG SRGP SRms WCAu WCot WFar

- 'Gaulthier Brousse'	WCot
- GOLDEN ALEXANDER ('Walgoldalex'PBR) (v)	ELin MMuc NLar WCAu WCot
- 'Golden Glory' (v)	WCot
- 'Hometown Hero'	NLar
- 'Variegata'	see *L. punctata* 'Alexander'
- *verticillata*	see *L. verticillaris*
'Purpurea'	see *L. atropurpurea*
SNOW CANDLES ('L9902')	ELon EWes MNrw SIvy WFar
taliensis	EAri
terrestris	EBee
thyrsiflora	CoPl EBee ELin LWaG NPer WCot WMAq
§ *verticillaris*	MCtn WCot
vulgaris	CGwi CHab CPud GJem GQue MCtn WShi
- subsp. *davurica*	WCot
- - B&SWJ 8632	WCru

Lysionotus (Gesneriaceae)

gamosepalus B&SWJ 7241	WCru
kwangsiensis HWJ 625	WCru
pauciflorus	EShb SMad WAbe
- B&SWJ 303	WCru
- B&SWJ 335	WCru
- HWJ 643 from Vietnam	WCru
- HWJ 811 from Vietnam	WCru
- dwarf B&SWJ 189	WCru
- 'Lady Lavender'	WFar
serratus HWJK 2426	WCru

Lythrum (Lythraceae)

alatum	SHar
anceps	NLar
salicaria	Widely available
- 'Blush' ♀H7	Widely available
§ - 'Feuerkerze' ♀H7	CAby CLiL ELan ELon EPfk EPfP GQue LBar LRHS MArl MBel NBir NSti NWbg SHar SOrN WFar
- FIRECANDLE	see *L. salicaria* 'Feuerkerze'
- HAPPY LIGHTS (mixed)	WHil
- 'Lady Sackville'	CLiL ELon GMaP IPot NLar SMrm
- 'Little Robert'	ELon MPro WFar
- 'Morden Pink'	CLiL ELan ELon LRHS MMuc NLar SEND WFar
- 'Pink Blush'	LSou
- 'Prichard's Variety'	ELon
- 'Robert'	Widely available
- 'Robin'	CLiL EBee EBlo LRHS MHol MPri MPro NLar
- 'Rose'	NBir
- 'Stichflamme'	ELon SBeP
- 'Swirl'	EBee ECha ELan ELon EMor LCro MBel NLar NSti SHar WHoo WTor WTre
- 'The Beacon'	CTtf EBee ELon GQue LRHS NLar SRms
- 'White Swirl'	EMor NCth NSti
- white-flowered	NDov
- - No 10 **new**	SDix
- 'Zigeunerblut'	ELon GQue NLar SMHy
virgatum	SMHy SPel SPhx WCFE
- 'Dropmore Purple'	Widely available
- 'Happyness'	IPot NLar
- 'Hélène'	IPot NDov
- 'Joy'	IPot MBel NLar
- pale-flowered	NDov SMHy
- 'Rosy Gem'	ELan ELin EMor GMaP GQue LRHS LShi LSto NBro NLar NWbg SDix SRms WCav WChS WFar
- 'The Rocket'	EPfP LBar NBro NDov SMrm WFar

M

Maackia (Fabaceae)

amurensis	CAgr CBcs LMaj WJur
hupehensis	MBlu WJur

Macadamia (Proteaceae)

tetraphylla	CAco

mace see *Achillea ageratum*

Macfadyena see *Dolichandra*

Machaeranthera (Asteraceae)

sp.	EBee

Machaerina (Cyperaceae)

rubiginosa 'Variegata' (v)	CLil

Machilus see *Persea*

Mackaya (Acanthaceae)

§ *bella* ♀H1b	EShb WCot

Macleaya (Papaveraceae)

cordata misapplied	see *M.* × *kewensis*
§ *cordata* (Willd.) R. Br. ♀H6	CDor EBee NBir SPlb SRms WCAu
- NJM 11.002	WPGP
§ × *kewensis*	EHeP EPfP SPoG WFar WTre
- 'Flamingo' ♀H6	CMHG EBee ECha MBNS WCot WFar
§ *microcarpa*	CTsd
- 'Kelway's Coral Plume' ♀H6	CBcs CMac CWnw EAri EBee EGrI ELan EPfP GAbr GMaP LCro LSRN MArl MAsh NBid NBro SDix SHor SMad SMrm SPoG
- 'Spetchley Ruby'	EBee ECha SPel WCot

Maclura (Moraceae)

pomifera	CAgr CBcs CMCN ESwi LMaj MBlu MMuc SBrt SPlb WJur
- 'Cannonball'	CDoC
- 'Naughty Boy'	NLar
- 'Pretty Woman'	NLar
tricuspidata	WJur
- B&SWJ 12755	WCru
- 'Parthenos' (F)	CAgr
- seedless (F)	CAgr

Macrodiervilla see *Weigela*

Macropiper see *Piper*

Macrothelypteris (Thelypteridaceae)

torresiana	WPGP

Macrozamia (Zamiaceae)

communis	CBrP NPlm
miquelii	NPlm
moorei	CBrP NPlm

Maddenia (Rosaceae)

hypoleuca	MBlu NLar

Maesa (Primulaceae)

japonica CWJ 12371	WCru

Magnolia ✿ (Magnoliaceae)

acuminata	CAco CMCN LMaj

Name	Codes	Name	Codes
- 'Blue Opal'	CBcs CDoC ELan LMil NLar NPip SWor WCha	*campbellii*	CMCN
- 'Kinju'	CJun	- Alba Group	WPGP
- 'Koban Dori'	CBcs CJun	- - 'Chyverton'	WPGP
- 'Seiju'	CBcs CJun	- - 'Strybing White'	WPGP
- var. *subcordata*	CBcs CJun	I - - 'Trewithen'	CJun
'Miss Honeybee'		- 'Ambrose Congreve'	WPGP
- - 'Mister Yellowjacket'	CJun	- 'Betty Jessel'	CBcs CJun WPGP
'Advance'	CBcs CDoC MBlu	- 'Betty Jessel' × *liliiflora* 'Darkest Purple'	CJun
'A.E. Bold'	CBcs CJun	- 'Darjeeling' ♀H4	CBcs CJun WPGP
'Albatross'	CJun WPGP	- 'Darjeeling' × *denudata* 'Purple Eye'	CJun
'Alex'	CAco CBcs CCVT CJun LMil LRHS NLar	- 'Lionel de Rothschild'	WPGP
'Alixeed'	CJun	- subsp. *mollicomata*	CAco IArd
'Ambrosia'	CJun	- - 'Lanarth'	WPGP
'Angelica'	CJun	- - 'Lanarth' × FELIX JURY ('Jurmag2')	CJun
'Angels Landing'	CJun		
'Anilou'	CJun	- - 'Lanarth Surprise'	CBcs
'Anna'	CJun	- - 'Peter Borlase'	WPGP
'Anne Leitner'	CJun	- - 'Werrington'	CBcs
'Anticipation'	CBcs CEnd CJun WPGP	- 'Queen Caroline'	WPGP
'Antje Zandee'	CBcs CJun	- (Raffillii Group) 'Charles Raffill'	CDoC NPip SPoG
'Aphrodite'	CAco CBcs CJun EBee LRHS NLar NPip WMat	- - 'Kew's Surprise'	WPGP
'Apollo'	CBcs CDoC CJun LMil LSRN WPGP	- 'Sidbury'	CBcs
'Archangel'	CJun	- 'Veitch Clone' × 'Pegasus'	CJun
ashei	see *M. macrophylla* subsp. *ashei*	'Candy Cane'	CJun
'Asian Artistry'	CDoC CJun	'Carlos'	CJun NLar
'Athene' ♀H5	CBcs CDoC CEnd CJun LMil SHor WMat WPGP	*cathcartii*	WPGP
		- B&SWJ 11802	WCru
'Atlas'	CBcs CDoC CEnd CJun WPGP	- HWJ 874	WCru
'Aurora'	CJun	'Cathryn'	WPGP
'Banana Split'	CDoC CMCN LMil NLar	*caveana*	LEdu
'Betty'	CAco CBcs CCVT CDoC CMac EAri EPfP LSRN MBlu MGos MMuc MPri NTrD SFol SSta WCha	- NJM 13.037	WPGP
		- NJM 13.044	WPGP
		'Cecil Nice'	CBcs CJun
'Big Dude'	CBcs CDoC CEnd CJun ELan IArd MGos NOra NPip WMat	'Cedullo' × FELIX JURY ('Jurmag2')	CJun
'Binette'	CJun	CHAMELEON	see *M.* 'Chang Hua'
biondii	MBlu	*champaca*	IArd
'Black Swan'	CBcs WPGP	§ 'Chang Hua'	CJun
BLACK TULIP ('Jurmag1'^{PBR})	Widely available	*chapensis*	CBcs
'Blackberry Rose'	CBcs	'Charisma'	CJun
'Blushing Belle'	CAco CJun	'Charles Coates'	CBcs CJun WPGP
'Brenda'	CJun	'Charming Lady'	CJun
'Brett'	CJun	*chevalieri* B&SWJ 11802	WCru
'Brixton Belle'	CAco CBcs CJun LMaj WPGP	- DJHV 6037	WCru
× *brooklynensis* 'Amber'	CJun	- HWJ 621	WCru
- 'Black Beauty'	CAco CBcs CJun NCth NPip SReu SWor	'Cobhay Pink Spectacular'	CJun
		compressa	EBee LRHS MBlu
- 'Evamaria'	CAco CBcs LRHS	'Coral Lake'	CBcs CJun LMil
- 'Golden Joy'	CJun	'Cornish Chough'	WPGP
- 'Hattie Carthan'	CBcs CJun NLar	*crassifolia* hort.	see *M. fansipanensis*
- 'Woodsman'	CAco CBcs NLar NPip WMat	'Crescendo'	CJun
- 'Yellow Bird'	CAco CBcs CCVT CDoC CEnd CJun CMac CMCN EBar IPap LMaj LRHS LSRN MBlu MGos MPri NLar NPip SPoG WCha WMat	'Crystal Chalice'	CJun
		'Cuckoo'	CJun
		'Cup Cake'	CJun
		'Curlew'	WPGP
'Buksenwhite'	CJun	*cylindrica* misapplied	see *M.* 'Pegasus'
BURGUNDY STAR ('Jurmag4')	CBcs LCro LRHS MGos NPip WMat	*cylindrica* E.H. Wilson	WPGP
'Butterbowl'	CJun	- 'Bjuv'	CJun
'Butterflies'	CAco CBcs CDoC CJun CWnw EBee ELan EPfP LSRN MBlu MGos NCth NOra SHor SRms SSta WCha WFar WMat WSpi	- 'Hohman'	CBcs
		'Daphne' ♀H6	CAco CBcs CCVT CDoC CJun CMCN EAri ELan EPfP IArd LMaj LMil LRHS LSRN LSto MAsh MGos NCth NLar NPip SEWo SPoG WMat WPGP
'Caerhays Belle' ♀H5	CBcs CDoC CJun LMil SPoG WPGP		
'Caerhays Belle' × 'Nelly'	CJun		
'Caerhays Philip'	CBcs	'Darrell Dean'	CJun
'Caerhays Splendour'	CBcs	'David Clulow' ♀H5	CBcs CCVT CJun SSta WPGP
'Caerhays Surprise' ♀H5	CJun WPGP	*dawsoniana*	CAco CMCN WSpi
'Cameo'^{PBR}	CBcs LRHS	- 'Barbara Cook'	CJun

- 'Chyverton Red'	WPGP	- 'Furry Uok'	WPGP
- 'Ruby Rose'	CJun	× *foggii* 'Allspice'	CBcs
- 'Valley Splendour'	CJun	- 'Jack Fogg'	CBcs
'Daybreak' ♀H6	CAco CBcs CJun ELan EPfP LMil MBlu MGos NCth NOra NPip SHor SSta WMat WPGP	*fordiana*	CExl
		'Foster's Late White'	WPGP
		§ *foveolata* B&SWJ 11749	WCru
'Deborah'	CJun	- WWJ 11955	WCru
delavayi	CAco CBcs CMCN EBee EPfP EUrb SArc WPGP	'Frank Gladney'	CJun
		fraseri	CMCN
'Delia Williams'	WPGP	'Galaxy' ♀H6	CAco CBcs CBrac CBTr CDoC CEnd CJun CMac CTsd EBar ELan EPfP IPap LMaj LMil LRHS LSto MAsh MGos MMuc NCth NLar NPip SHor SSta WFar WMat
§ *denudata* ♀H6	CAco CBcs CCVT CMCN MBlu SSta SWor WJur		
- 'Double Diamond' (d)	CAco WCha		
- FESTIROSE ('Minfor')	CWnw EWes		
- FRAGRANT CLOUD ('Dan Xin')	CAco CJun EAri EGren EPfP LMaj NCth SWor	'Genie' PBR	CAco CBcs CCVT CDoC CSBt CWnw EAri EBee EGrI ELan EPfP LCro LMil LRHS LSRN LSto MMrt MMuc NLar NOra NPip SHor SReu WCha WMat WPGP
- 'Gere'	CBcs CJun		
- 'Ghost Ship'	CJun		
- YELLOW RIVER ('Fei Huang')	CAco CBcs CCVT CDoC CEnd CJun EAri EGren IPap LCro LMaj NLar NPip SPoG SWor WFar WMat		
		'George Henry Kern' ♀H6	CAco CBrac EGren ELan IArd LMil LRHS MGos NCth NLar SOrN SReu WCha WFar
doltsopa	CExl IArd LRHS SSta WPGP		
- NJM 12.028	WPGP	'Ghislaine'	CJun WPGP
- NJM 12.047	WPGP	'Gill Day'	CJun
'Early Rose'	CBcs CJun	'Gladys Carlson'	CJun
'Eleanor May'	CBcs	*globosa*	CExl WPGP
'Elegance'	CJun	'Gold Crown'	CJun
'Elisa Odenwald'	CAco CDoC LMil NPip WMat	'Gold Star' ♀H6	CAco CBcs CJun LMil LRHS MGos NOra NPip SPoG SSta WCha WMat WPGP
'Elizabeth' ♀H6	CBcs CBTr CDoC CJun CMCN EPfP LBom LCro LMil MAsh MBlu MGos NCth NLar NOra NPip SPoG SRms WMat		
		'Golden Endeavour'	CJun
		'Golden Gala'	CJun
'Emma Cook'	CJun	'Golden Gift'	CJun LMil WPGP
'Emperor' **new**	CBcs LCro	'Golden Pond'	CJun LMil
§ *ernestii*	IArd WPGP	'Golden Rain'	CJun
'Eskimo'	CJun ELan EPfP LRHS NOra NPip WMat	'Golden Sun'	CBcs CJun
		'Goldfinch'	CBcs CJun
'Eternal Spring' **new**	CJun	I × *gotoburgensis*	WPGP
FAIRY LIME	CBcs	Chollipo clone	
FAIRY MAGNOLIA BLUSH ('Micjur01' PBR)	CAco CBcs CBTr CCVT CDoC CWnw EGren EGrI EPfP LBom LCro LMil LRHS LSRN MBlu MGos MMuc NPip SHor WMat	*grandiflora*	CAco CMCN CWnw EBee EGren EHeP EPfP ESwi EUrb LCro LEdu LMil LSRN LWaG MGos MMuc NCth NLar SArc SAth SEND SEWo SFol SHor SOrN SPlb WCha WJur WMat
FAIRY MAGNOLIA CREAM ('Micjur02' PBR)	CAco CBcs CBTr CCVT CDoC CWnw EGren ELan LBom LCro LMil LRHS LSRN MMuc NLar NPip WMat	- ALTA ('Tmgh' PBR)	CBcs CLnd CMCN LMaj MGos WMat
		- 'Bracken's Brown Beauty'	LRHS NLar
FAIRY MAGNOLIA WHITE ('Micjur05' PBR)	CBcs CBTr CDoC CWnw EGren ELan LBom LCro LMil LRHS LSRN MMuc NLar NPip SPoG WMat	- 'Charles Dickens'	SVen
		- 'D.D. Blanchard'	CJun NLar
		- 'Edith Bogue'	LRHS
		- 'Exmouth'	CBcs CDoC CEnd CLnd CMac CMCN CSBt CWnw ELan EPfP EUrb LCro LRHS LSRN MBlu MGos NLar SHor SPoG SRms SSta WHtc
§ *fansipanensis* FMWJ 13054	WCru		
- FMWJ 13163	WCru		
'Felicity'	CJun		
FELIX JURY ('Jurmag2' PBR)	CAco CBcs CBTr EBee ELan EPfP LCro NCth NOra NPip SEWo WMat	- 'Ferruginea'	CAco CBcs CJun CLnd ELan LRHS LWaG NLar SArc
figo	CBcs CBct CDoC CExl EBee ELan EPfP LRHS MMuc SSta WPGP	- 'Galissonnière'	CAco CBcs CCVT CDoC EBee EGren EOli EPfP ERom LMaj LRHS NPlm SArc SAth SFol SGol SHor WCha
'Fireglow'	CJun NPip		
'F.J. Williams'	CJun WPGP		
'Flaming Heart'	CJun	- 'Gloriosa'	LRHS
'Flamingo'	CBcs CJun NLar	- 'Goliath'	CBcs CCVT ELan EPfP LMaj LRHS SEWo SSta
floribunda FMWJ 13384 from Tonkin, Vietnam	WCru		
		- 'Kay Parris' ♀H5	CAco CBcs CJun EBee ELan EPfP LMil LRHS SPoG WPGP
- NJM 9.179	WPGP		
- WWJ 11874	WCru	- 'Little Gem'	CAco CBcs CCVT CDoC CJun CLnd EAri EBee EGren ELan ELon EPfP EUrb LCro LMil LRHS LSRN NLar SEWo SPoG SSta SVen
- WWJ 11982 from Tonkin, Vietnam	WCru		
- WWJ 11996	WCru		
- WWJ 12003	WCru		
- WWJ 12011	WCru	- 'Mainstreet'	CJun
- 'Fansipan Furry'	WCru	- 'Nannetensis' (d)	ELan EUrb NLar

- 'Praecox' — LRHS
- 'Russet' — CJun
- 'Saint Mary' — CJun
- 'Samuel Sommer' — CJun EBee
- 'Symmes Select' — CJun
- 'Treyvei' — CAco CBcs CCVT CDoC EPfP EUrb LRHS LSRN
- 'Victoria' ♀H5 — CJun ELan EPfP LRHS MBlu SSta
- 'Green Bee' — CBcs CJun
- 'Green Diamond' — CAco
- 'Hannah' **new** — CJun
- 'Hawk' — CJun WPGP
- 'Heaven Scent' ♀H5 — Widely available
- 'Helen Fogg' — CJun
- *heptapeta* — see *M. denudata*
- 'Honey Belle' — CJun
- 'Honey Flower' — CJun
- HONEY TULIP ('Jurmag5') — CBcs EBee ELan LCro LMil LRHS NLar NPip SHor WMat
- § 'Hong Yun' — CJun WCha
- 'Hot Flash' — CBcs CJun
- 'Hot Lips' — CDoC CJun
- *hypoleuca* — see *M. obovata* Thunb.
- 'Ian's Red' — CBcs CDoC CEnd CJun LMil LSRN NPip WMat WPGP
- 'Ian's Red' × *sprengeri* var. *diva* 'Eric Savill' — CJun
- *insignis* — CExl LEdu LRHS WPGP
  - B&SWJ 11810 — WCru
  - NJM 12.04 — WPGP
  - WWJ 11854 — WCru
- 'Iolanthe' — CBcs CBTr CEnd LMil MGos MPri NPip WMat WPGP
- 'Iufer' — CJun
- 'Jane' — CAco CJun CMac LMil LRHS MGos MPri NPip
- 'Janet' — CBcs
- 'J.C. Williams' — CBcs CJun SSta WPGP
- 'Jersey Belle' — CJun
- 'Joe McDaniel' — CAco CBcs
- 'John Bond' — CJun
- 'John Congreve' — CJun WPGP
- 'Joli Pompon' — CBcs CBTr CCVT CJun ELan EPfP LCro LMil LRHS LSto NCth NLar NOra NPip SSta WMat
- 'Jolly Roger' — CJun
- 'Judy Zuk' — CBcs CJun
- 'Katja Landner' — CJun
- × *kewensis* 'Wada's Memory' — see *M. salicifolia* 'Wada's Memory'
- 'Kim Kunso' — SSta
- 'Kittiwake' — CJun
- *kobus* — CBcs CCVT CLnd CMCN CNWT ELan EPfP GKin IPap LMaj MBlu NLar SArc SEWo SReu WJur
  - B&SWJ 12751 — WCru WHtc
  - 'Esveld Select' — CJun
  - 'Janaki Ammal' — CJun
  - 'Maráczy'PBR — CAco
  - 'Morris Fragrant' **new** — CJun
- § 'Norman Gould' — CJun CMCN LMil NPip
  - 'Octopus' — CJun
  - pink-flowered — CBcs CJun
  - 'Rogów' — CJun
  - 'White Elegance' — CJun
  - 'Wisley Star' — CJun
- 'Kronos' — CBcs CJun
- *kwangtungensis* — WPGP
- LA 21 **new** — CJun
- *laevifolia* — CBcs CBct CExl CMCN EBee IArd MBlu WJur WPGP

- arborescent — WPGP
- 'Dali Velvet' — CExl
- 'Gail's Favourite' — CAco EPfP LMil LRHS
- 'Honey Velvet' **new** — CSBt
- 'Kunming' — LRHS
- 'Minnie Mouse' — LMil LRHS
- 'Summer Snowflake' — CBcs
- VANILLA PEARLS ('Gcchu2008') **new** — CSpe
- 'Velvet and Cream' — EBee MBlu WPGP
- 'Laura Saylor' — CJun
- 'Leda' — CBcs CJun LMil MBlu SSta WPGP
- 'Leda' × 'Manchu Fan' — CJun
- 'Legacy' — NCth WPGP
- 'Lemon Star' — CBcs CJun
- 'Lennarth Jonsson' — CJun
- 'Lesa Belle' **new** — CJun
- 'Lesa Burgundy' **new** — CJun
- 'Lesa Purple' — CJun
- 'Lili Diva' — CBcs
- *liliiflora* — CCVT
- 'Darkest Purple' — CJun
- § 'Nigra' ♀H6 — CAco CBcs CBrac CDoC CMac CSBt CTsd EBee EGrI ELan EPfP EUrb GKin LCro LMaj LMil LRHS LSRN MBlu MGos NLar SSta WFar WLov WMou WSpi
- 'Raven' — CBcs WPGP
- 'Limelight' — CAco CJun NOra NPip WMat WPGP
- 'Livingstone' — CBcs CDoC CJun LMil LRHS MGos NCth NPip WMat
- × *loebneri* — LBom
- 'Ballerina' — CAco
- 'Donna' ♀H6 — CDoC CJun LMil NPip SSta
- 'Encore' — CJun
- 'Green Mist' — CJun
- 'Jennifer Robinson' — CJun
- 'Leonard Messel' ♀H6 — Widely available
- 'Lesley Jane' — CJun
- 'Mag's Pirouette' ♀H5 — CBcs CJun LMil NLar NPip SPoG SSta
- 'Merrill' ♀H6 — CAco CBcs CDoC CJun CLnd CMac CMCN CNWT CWnw ELan EPfP LMaj LMil MGos MMuc MPri NLar NPip SFol SSta WJur WPGP
- 'Neil McEacharn' — CJun
- 'Pink Cloud' — CJun
- 'Pink Perfection' — LRHS
- 'Powder Puff' — CBcs CJun
- 'Raspberry Fun' — CAco CBcs CJun IArd NLar
- 'Raspberry Fun' seedling — CAco
- 'Snowdrift' — CAco CJun EPfP
- 'Spring Snow' — CJun
- 'Star Bright' — CJun
- 'Swansong' — WPGP
- 'White Stardust' — CJun
- 'Wildcat' ♀H6 — CAco CBcs CJun LRHS NLar NPip SSta
- 'Willow Wood' — CJun
- 'Lois' ♀H6 — CAco CBcs CJun EGrI EPfP LMil MAsh NPip SSta WPGP
- *lotungensis* — WPGP
- 'Lotus' — CBcs CJun WPGP
- * 'Lu Shan' — LRHS
- 'Lucy Carlson' — CJun
- 'Luscious' — CJun
- *macclurei* — CBcs
- *macrophylla* — CAco CBcs CBrP CMac CMCN MBlu NLar SHor WPGP
- § - subsp. *ashei* — CAco CBcs CBrP WPGP
- - subsp. *ashei* × *sieboldii* — CJun

'Malin'	CJun
'Manchu Fan'	CBcs CDoC CJun EPfP LMil LSRN NPip WMat WPGP
§ 'March til Frost'	CAco CBcs CBTr CDoC EBee ELan LMil NCth NLar NPip WPGP
'Margaret Helen'	CBcs CJun WPGP
'Marguerite'	CJun
'Marillyn'	NPip
'Marj Gossler'	CJun
martinii	CBcs
'Mary Chalice' **new**	CJun
'Mary Nell'	CJun
'Maryland'	CCVT CJun NLar
§ *maudiae*	CExl EBee
'Maxine Merrill'	CAco CBcs CJun LRHS
'May to Frost'	see *M.* 'March til Frost'
'Melon Sky' **new**	CBcs
'Mighty Mouse'	CBcs NLar
'Milky Way' ♀H5	CBcs CJun MGos WPGP
'Mister Yellowjacket'	CJun
'Moondance'	CJun
'Moonspire'	NPip
'Mr Julian'	CBcs
'Nimbus'	CJun WPGP
nitida	CExl
obovata Diels	see *M. officinalis*
§ *obovata* Thunb.	CBcs CMCN LMil NCth WPGP
- B&SWJ 10821	WCru
- B&SWJ 12626	WCru
- pink-flowered	WPGP
§ *officinalis*	CBcs NLar
- var. *biloba*	CMCN LRHS MBlu NLar WPGP
'Old Port'	CBcs NLar
'Olivia'	CBcs CJun NPip WPGP
'Orchid'	CAco
'Ossie's Yellow'	CBcs
'Patty'	CJun
'Paul Cook'	CDoC CEnd
'Peaches 'n' Cream'	CBcs CJun
'Peachy'	CBcs CCVT CJun EBee LMil WMat
§ 'Pegasus' ♀H6	CBcs CEnd CJun LMil NPip SSta WMat
'Peppermint Stick'	NLar NPip WMat
'Peter Dummer'	CBcs
'Peter Smithers'	CJun
'Phelan Bright'	CBcs CJun WPGP
'Phillip Tregunna'	LRHS WPGP
'Phil's Masterpiece'	CJun
'Pickard's Sundew'	see *M.* × *soulangeana* 'Sundew'
'Piet van Veen'	CJun
'Pink Beauty'	CAco WCha
'Pink Butterfly'	CJun WCha
'Pink Delight'	CJun
'Pink Goblet'	CAco
PINK PYRAMID ('Mgpin2010') **new**	CBcs
'Pink Surprise'	CJun
'Pinkie'	CAco CJun
'Porcelain Dove'	CBcs CJun LMil MGos MPri WPGP
'Premier Cru'	CJun LMil NPip WMat WPGP
'Princess Margaret'	CBcs CDoC CJun LMil NOra NPip WMat
'Pristine'	CJun LMil
× *proctoriana*	EBee LMil MBlu WPGP
- 'Robert's Dream'	CJun
- 'Slavin's No 44'	CJun
- 'Slavin's Snowy'	CJun CTsd
'Purple Breeze'	CBTr CJun CMCN MBlu NPip
'Purple Cracker'	CJun
'Purple Globe'	CBcs CEnd CJun
'Purple Sensation'	CBcs CJun WPGP
'Purple Star'	CJun WPGP
'Ramp's Pink'	CJun
'Raspberry Ice'	CCVT CMac SRms
'Raspberry Ripple'	CBcs
'Rebecca's Perfume'	CJun ELan MGos NPip WMat WSpi
'Red as Red'	CAco CBcs CDoC CJun ELan LMil NLar NPip
'Red Baron'	CJun
'Red Lion'	CJun NLar
'Red Lucky'	see *M.* 'Hong Yun'
'Renate'	CJun
'Ricki'	CJun CMac EPfP LMaj MBlu
'Rose Marie'	CBcs CBTr CJun LMil NCth NLar NPip
'Rose Quartz'	CJun
'Roseanne'	CJun
rostrata	CBcs CExl NLar WPGP
'Rouged Alabaster'	CBcs
'Royal Alma'	CJun
'Royal Crown'	LRHS
'Royal Purple'	CBcs CJun
'Royal Splendor'	CAco CBcs
'Ruby'	CJun
I 'Ruth'	CBcs CJun
salicifolia	CBcs CMCN WJur WSpi
- 'Aia'	WPGP
- var. *concolor*	CJun NCth
- 'Jermyns'	CJun
- 'Louisa Fete'	CJun IArd
* - 'Rosea'	CJun
- 'Sandy Carlson'	CJun
- upright	WPGP
- 'Van Veen'	CJun WPGP
§ - 'Wada's Memory' ♀H6	CBTr CExl CJun ELan EPfP LMaj MBlu SSta WMat
- 'Windsor Beauty'	CJun SSta
'Sangreal'	NLar
sapaensis	CBcs
- FMWJ 13315	WCru
- FMWJ 13330	WCru
- HWJ 533	WCru
- NJM 9.168	WPGP
'Sara Koe'	CJun NPip WMat
sargentiana	SSta
- var. *robusta*	CTsd WJur
- - 'Blood Moon'	CBcs CJun LRHS WPGP
- - 'Blood Moon' × 'Star Wars'	CJun
- - 'Marjorie Congreve'	WPGP
- - 'Multipetal'	WPGP
'Sayonara' ♀H6	CDoC CJun EPfP LMil NOra NPip WMat
'Scented Gem'	SSta
'Schmetterling'	see *M.* × *soulangeana* 'Pickard's Schmetterling'
'Sentinel'	CAco CCVT LMaj NCth NLar NPip WMat
'Serene'	CBcs CEnd CJun LMil NLar
SHIRAZZ ('Vulden')	CAco CBcs CDoC CJun CMCN EBee IArd LCro LMil LRHS MBlu NCth NOra NPip SHor SPoG WMat WPGP
'Siddharta'	CJun
sieboldii	CAco CBcs CDoC CJun CMac CMCN EAri EBee EGrl EPfP GKin LMaj LMil LRHS MBlu MGos NCth NLar NPip SHor SPoG WJur WPGP WSpi
- B&SWJ 4127	WCru
- 'Colossus' ♀H6	CJun IArd LMil MBlu NPip WPGP
- 'Genesis' × *tripetala*	CJun

Magnolia

- 'Genesis' × *virginiana* — CJun
- 'Michiko Renge' (d) — CJun
- 'Min Pyong-gal' — CJun
- 'Pride of Norway' — CAco CJun
- subsp. *sieboldii* — WCru
  B&SWJ 12553 from Korea
- subsp. *sinensis* — CAco CJun LCro WPGP
I - - 'Grandiflora' — CJun WPGP
- 'White Flounces' (d) — CJun
'Simple Pleasures' **new** — CJun
sinostellata 'China Town' — CAco CBcs CJun
'Sir Harold Hillier' — CBcs CJun WPGP
'Snow Goose' — CBcs
'Solar Flair' — CAco CBcs CJun LRHS NLar
× *soulangeana* — Widely available
- 'Alba' — see *M.* × *soulangeana* 'Alba Superba'
§ - 'Alba Superba' — CAco CDoC CLnd EPfP LCro LMaj LMil LRHS MBlu MMuc MSwo NLar NPip SHor SPoG WFar WSpi
- 'Alexandrina' — MBlu
- 'André Leroy' — CWnw
- 'Beugnon' — IArd NPip
- 'Big Pink' — CAco
- 'Brozzonii' ♀H6 — CBcs CDoC CMac
- 'Cleopatra' PBR — CAco CBcs CDoC
- 'Deep Purple Dream' — CBcs
- 'Joris' — CJun
- 'Just Jean' — CJun
- 'Lennei' — CAco CBcs CBrac CMac CMCN EPfP IArd IPap LBom LMaj MGos MPri SPoG SRms WFar
- 'Lennei Alba' — CBTr EPfP LRHS MBlu NLar NPip WFar WMat WSpi
- 'Lombardy Rose' — CAco CBcs
- 'Nigra' — see *M. liliiflora* 'Nigra'
- 'Pickard's Ruby' — CBcs
§ - 'Pickard's Schmetterling' ♀H6 — CBcs CTsd LRHS
- 'Pickard's Snow Queen' — CBcs CJun
- 'Pickard's Sundew' — see *M.* × *soulangeana* 'Sundew'
- 'Picture' — CBcs
- RED LUCKY — see *M.* 'Hong Yun'
- 'Rubra' misapplied — see *M.* × *soulangeana* 'Rustica Rubra'
§ - 'Rustica Rubra' — CAco CBcs CMCN CWnw EGrI EHeP LCro LSRN MPri NLar SRms
- 'San José' — CJun LMil
- 'Satisfaction' — CBcs CDoC LBom LCro LRHS NLar WCha
- 'Speciosa' — SSta
§ - 'Sundew' — CBcs
- 'Superba' — CAco EBee NCth WCha
- 'Verbanica' — LMil LRHS
'Spectrum' ♀H6 — CAco CBTr CDoC CJun CMCN EBar ELan EPfP EWes LCro LMaj LMil LRHS MBlu NOra NPip SSta WMat
sprengeri — CAco WJur
- from Guizhou, China — WPGP
- var. *diva* — CBcs CExl WPGP
- - 'Bucklands' — CJun
- - 'Burncoose' ♀H6 — CBcs
- - 'Copeland Court' ♀H6 — CBcs CJun LMil NPip WMat WPGP
- - 'Dark Diva' — CJun
- - 'Diva' — CDoC CMCN WPGP
- - 'Eric Savill' ♀H6 — CBcs CJun WPGP
- - 'Fire' — CJun
- - 'Lanhydrock' — CBcs CDoC CJun NPip WPGP
- - 'Marwood Spring' — CBcs CJun CMHG WPGP
- - 'Thomas Messel' — CJun
- - 'Westonbirt' — CBcs WPGP

'Spring Rite' — CBcs CJun
'Star Wars' ♀H5 — CAco CBcs CCVT CDoC CJun CMac EPfP GGGa LMil MGos NOra NPip SEWo SPoG SSta WMat WPGP
'Stellar Acclaim' — CBcs CJun
stellata — Widely available
- 'Centennial' ♀H6 — CJun LMil
- 'Chrysanthemumiflora' — CJun EPfP
- 'Dawn' — CJun
- 'Jane Platt' ♀H6 — CBcs CJun EBee EGrI EPfP LMil MGos NCth NLar WPGP
- f. *keiskei* — CBcs CJun MGos
- 'Kikuzaki' — CJun
- 'King Rose' — CBcs CJun CTsd EBee ELon EPfP NPip
- 'Lyle's Legacy' — CJun
- 'Massey' — CJun
- 'Norman Gould' — see *M. kobus* 'Norman Gould'
- 'Rosea' — CAco CJun CLnd CMCN CTsd EGren ELan ELon LMaj MGos MMuc MPri NCth NTrD WCha WFar
- 'Royal Star' ♀H6 — CAco CBcs CBrac CCVT CDoC CLnd CMCN CTsd CWnw EGrI EPfP LBom LMil LRHS MBlu MGos MPro NCth NLar NPip SArc SGol SSta WFar
- 'Scented Silver' — CJun
- 'Shi-banchi Rosea' — CJun
- 'Water Lily' — CAco CBcs CBTr CDoC CJun CMac EBee ELan ELon EPfP LMil LRHS LSRN MBlu MGos SPoG SSta CWnw WPGP
'Strawberry Fields' — CBcs NLar
'String of Pearls' — CJun
'Summer Solstice' — CJun NPip WPGP
'Summer Sonnet' — WPGP
'Sun Ray' — CJun
'Sunburst' — CBcs CJun SRms
'Sundance' — CBTr CJun MBlu
'Sunrise' — EGrI LCro LRHS NCth WCha
'Sunsation' — CAco CBcs CDoC CJun EPfP LCro NLar WCha
'Sunset Swirl' — CJun NPip
'Sunspire' — CJun NCth WCha
'Suntown' — CJun
'Susan' ♀H6 — Widely available
'Susanna van Veen' — CBcs CDoC CJun LMil MBlu WPGP
'Sweet Merlot' — CBcs CDoC CJun NPip
'Sweet Sixteen' — CBcs
'Sweet Valentine' — CBcs CJun NPip WPGP
'Sweetheart' ♀H5 — CBcs CJun
'Sybille' — CJun CMCN NPip WPGP
tamaulipana — CBcs EBee WPGP
'Theodora' — CBcs LMil NPip
× *thompsoniana* — CBcs CMCN
- 'Olmenhof' — IArd
'Thousand Butterflies' — CJun
'Tikitere' — CBcs LMil NCth
'Tina Durio' — CBcs CDoC NPip WMat
'Touch of Pink' — CBcs
'Tranquility' — CJun
tripetala — CAco CBcs CExl CMCN EAri LMaj MBlu NLar SSta
'Tropicana' — CBcs
'Ultimate Yellow' — CJun
× *veitchii* — CBcs LMil
- 'Columbus' — CJun WPGP
'Venus' — CBcs CJun NCth NLar NPip
virginiana — CBcs CJun CMCN
§ - 'Jim Wilson' — CJun MBlu NPip

- Moonglow	see *M. virginiana* 'Jim Wilson'	- Sweet Winter	CDoC EBee EGren EPfP LMaj LRHS
'Vulcan'	CAco CBcs CDoC CEnd CJun EGrI ELan EPfP LMil LRHS MPri NCth	('Minganpi'PBR)	LSRN MAsh MPri NLar SArc
'Watermelon'	CBcs LCro LRHS NCth WMat	*eurybracteata* × *nitens*	WPGP
× *watsonii*	see *M.* × *wieseneri*	*eutriphylla* misapplied	see *M. trifolia*
'Wedding Vows'	CJun	*fargesii*	see *M. sheridaniana*
'Westonbirt Hope'	WPGP	*fortunei* 'Curlyque'	WPGP
White Caviar ('Micwc')	CBcs CWnw NCth SReu	*fremontii*	WCot
'White Mystery'	CJun	*gracilipes*	ELan ESwi EWes LRHS MBlu WCru
§ × *wieseneri*	CJun CMCN MBlu SHor WPGP		WPGP
- 'Aashild Kalleberg'	CJun WPGP	*gracilis*	CExl EBee
- 'Charm and Fragrance'	CJun NCth	*haematocarpa*	WPGP
- 'Swede Made'	CJun WPGP	*hartwegii*	CExl WPGP
wilsonii ♥H6	CAco CCVT CDoC CExl CJun EPfP GGro IArd IDun MBlu MGos NCth NPip SPlb SSta WMat WPGP	*huiliensis*	ELan LRHS
		japonica ♥H5	CAco CBcs CDoC CMac EBee EPfP LRHS MAsh MGos MMuc NLar SEND SPoG SRms SSta WCFE
- Eileen Baines ('Richgain') (d)	CBcs EBee ELan LCro LMil LRHS WPGP	- 'Gold Dust'	MBlu
- 'Gwen Baker'	CJun	aff. *japonica*	IDun
- 'Wim Rutten'	CBcs	*lanceolata*	MBlu
'Yaeko'	CAco CBcs CDoC	aff. *lanceolata* F&M 156	CExl
'Yellow Fever'	CBcs CJun WPGP	*leschenaultii* B&SWJ 9535	WCru
'Yellow Garland'	CJun	× *lindsayae* 'Cantab' ♥H4	EBee EPfP WPGP
'Yellow Lantern' ♥H6	CAco CBcs CDoC CEnd CJun EHeP EPfP GGga LMil LSRN MBlu MPri NLar SPoG SSta WCha WPGP	*lomariifolia*	see *M. oiwakensis* subsp. *lomariifolia*
		longibracteata	CExl GKin
'Yellow Sea'	CJun	*mairei*	see *M. duclouxiana*
Yuchelia No 1	CBcs WPGP	× *media* 'Buckland' ♥H5	CMac EPfP LRHS SRms
yunnanensis	CDoC CTsd ELan	- 'Charity'	Widely available
zenii	CAco CBcs CMCN	- 'Lionel Fortescue' ♥H5	CBcs CBrac CMac CSBt CSpe EBee EPfP GKin LRHS MAsh MPri
- 'Pink Parchment'	CJun	- 'Winter Sun' ♥H5	CBcs CBrac CDoC CMac CSBt CWnw EBee EGren EGrI EHeP ELan ELon EPfP LCro LMaj LRHS LSto MAsh MBlu MGos NLar SOrN SPoG SRms WFar WHtc

Magydaris (Apiaceae)
pastinacea	SPhx

× *Mahoberberis* (Berberidaceae)
aquisargentii	CBcs CMac EPfP LRHS MMuc NLar SEND WFar
'Dart's Desire'	NLar
miethkeana	NCth
§ *neubertii*	NLar

Mahonia ✿ (Berberidaceae)
§ *aquifolium*	CAgr CBcs CBrac EHeP LRHS LSto MGos MMuc NLar SAth SEND SPlb	*moranensis*	CExl EBee IArd
- 'Apollo' ♥H5	CBcs CDoC CMac EBee EGren EHeP ELan EPfP LCro LRHS LSRN MAsh MBlu MGos NLar SPoG SRms WFar WSpi	- T 292	WPGP
		napaulensis	NLar
		- 'Maharajah'	CExl IArd
		- 'Tretawn' **new**	CExl
- 'Atropurpurea'	CMac CSBt ELan EPfP	*nervosa*	CMac MBlu WPGP
- 'Fascicularis'	see *M.* × *wagneri* 'Pinnacle'	- B&SWJ 13580	WCru
- 'Magnifica'	WPGP	*neubertii*	see × *Mahoberberis neubertii*
- 'Smaragd'	CMac EHeP ELan LSRN MBlu NLar WSpi	*nitens*	EBee EGrI ELan WCru WPGP
		- 'Cabaret'PBR ♥H4	CBcs CDoC EBee EGren EGrI EPfP EUrb LCro LRHS LSRN MAsh MBlu MGos MMrt NCth NLar SHor SPoG SSta WSpi
- 'Versicolor'	MBlu		
'Arthur Menzies'	EPfP LMil LRHS	*oiwakensis*	EBee ELan LRHS WPGP
§ *bealei*	CBcs CBrac CDoC CExl CSBt CTsd EHeP ELan ELon EPfP LRHS LSto MAsh MGos NLar NPer SGol	- B&SWJ 371	WCru
		- B&SWJ 3660	WCru
		- PBR 371 from Hong Kong	WCru
- 'Cornish Silver'	CExl	§ - subsp. *lomariifolia* ♥H4	CExl EGreen ELan EPfP LRHS SArc
Blackfoot ('Bokrafoot'PBR)	ELan LRHS MAsh	- - var. *tenuifoliola*	EBee EPfP
bodinieri	WPGP	- - - Cox 6509	CExl WPGP
- Og 93.033	WPGP	*pallida*	CExl EBee ELan WJur WPGP
chochoco	CExl	'Pan Demic'	WPGP
§ *duclouxiana*	CExl	'Pan's Peculiar'	EBee WPGP
- KR 7692	WPGP	*pinnata* misapplied	see *M.* × *wagneri* 'Pinnacle'
'Esme'	EUrb WPGP	*pinnata* (Lag.) Fedde 'Ken S. Howard'	WPGP
eurybracteata	CExl LRHS SBrt WCru WJur WPGP	- subsp. *insularis* 'Schnilemoon'	EBee WPGP
- subsp. *ganpinensis*	WPGP	*repens*	WCot WKor WSpi
- - 'Soft Caress'	Widely available	- 'Rotundifolia'	IArd SPlb
- 'Narihira'	LRHS SBig	*russellii*	CExl
		× *savilliana*	WPGP WSpi
		§ *sheridaniana*	NCth
		- Og 93.033	WPGP
		* *sinensis*	ESwi
		Sioux ('Bokrasio'PBR)	LRHS MAsh SPoG

subimbricata BWJ 16211 — WCru
§ *trifolia* — LRHS
 - EKB 4618 — EBee WPGP
volcania B&SWJ 10400 — WCru
VOLCANO ('Myoy') — CBcs LCro
× *wagneri* 'Fireflame' — EBee LRHS MBlu NCth
 - 'Hastings' Elegant' — NLar
§ - 'Pinnacle' ♀H5 — EBee EHeP ELan EPfP LRHS MAsh MBlu NLar SPoG WFar
 - 'Sunset' — MBlu
 - 'Undulata' — MBlu

Maianthemum (Asparagaceae)

bicolor — LEdu
bifolium — ESwi GMaP LEdu MBel NBir NBro SRms WCru WShi
 - from Yakushima, Japan — WFar
§ - subsp. *kamtschaticum* — EMor EPot EPPr GKev IPot LEdu NLar NRya WCot WPGP
 - - B&SWJ 4360 — ESwi WCru
 - - CD&R 2300 — WCru
 - - var. *pumilum* — EAri EBee ESwi LEdu
 - - 'Shunrai' — ESwi
canadense — EBee EPot EPPr ESwi GKev LEdu NBid WCru
chasmanthum — see *M. bifolium* subsp. *kamtschaticum*
dilatatum — see *M. bifolium* subsp. *kamtschaticum*
flexuosum B&SWJ 9069 — WCru
 - B&SWJ 9079 — WCru
 - B&SWJ 9150 — WCru
aff. *flexuosum* — WCru WFar
 B&SWJ 9026
 - B&SWJ 9055 — WCru
formosanum B&SWJ 349 — WFar
fuscum — EBee GKev LAma WCot
 - var. *cordatum* — WCru
 - 'Shirui Giant' — WPGP
 - 'Tangkhul Giant' — LEdu
gigas B&SWJ 10470 — WCru
henryi — LEdu WPGP
 - BWJ 7616 — WFar
japonicum — LEdu
 - B&SWJ 7306 — LEdu
oleraceum — CExl EBee GEdr LAma LEdu WFar
 - B&SWJ 2148 — WCru
paniculatum — LEdu
 - B&SWJ 9137 — WCru
 - B&SWJ 9140 — WCru
 - purple-flowered — WCru
 B&SWJ 9139
 pendent, B&SWJ 10305 — WCru
 from Guatemala
purpureum — LEdu
 - G-W&P 150 — LEdu
racemosum ♀H6 — Widely available
 - subsp. *amplexicaule* — SMHy
 - - B&SWJ 13558 — WCru
 - - 'Emily Moody' — CBct CExl ECha EPPr ESwi WCot WPGP
aff. *salvinii* B&SWJ 9000 — WCru
 - B&SWJ 9030 — ESwi
 - B&SWJ 9088 — WCru
 - B&SWJ 10402 — WCru
scilloideum B&SWJ 10407 — WCru
* - var. *roseum* B&SWJ 10335 — WCru
stellatum — EBee EBlo ECha EMor EPfP EPot EPPr GMaP GQue LEdu LRHS NLar NRya SPel WCru WFar WKor
 - 'San Luis' — ESwi

tatsienense — CDor CExl GEdr LEdu WCot WCru WPGP
 - dark-stemmed — CDor ECha WPGP

Maihuenia (Cactaceae)

poeppigii — SPlb
 - F&W 9670 — WCot
 - JCA 2.575.600 — WCot

Maihueniopsis (Cactaceae)

'Blomiee' **new** — SPlb
cylindriarticulatus — see *Cumulopuntia boliviana* subsp. *dactylifera*
§ *darwinii* — SPlb
fulvicoma — see *Cumulopuntia boliviana* subsp. *boliviana*
pentlandii — see *Cumulopuntia boliviana* subsp. *boliviana*
platyacantha — SPlb
 Werner Rauh **new** — SPlb

Malcolmia (Brassicaceae)

maritima **new** — GJem

Malephora (Aizoaceae)

crocea — CPic

Mallotus (Euphorbiaceae)

japonicus — WJur
 - B&SWJ 14613 — WCru
 - B&SWJ 14679 — WCru

Malope (Malvaceae)

trifida 'Alba' — CSpe MCtn
 - 'Vulcan' — CSpe MCtn

Malotigena (Aizoaceae)

§ *frantiskae-niederlovae* — GEdr WIce
 - 'Album' — see *M. frantiskae-niederlovae* 'White Nugget'
 - 'Gold Nugget' ♀H4 — CPic ESuc LRHS SLee SRms
§ - 'White Nugget' — CPic EDAr ELan EPot ESgI ESuc GEdr LRHS SLee WIce

Malus ✿ (Rosaceae)

§ 'Adirondack' ♀H6 — ELan EPfP LBuc LCro LMaj LRHS MPri NOra NPip SPoG WMat
 'Admiration' — see *M.* 'Adirondack'
 ADMIRATION — see *M.* 'Adirondack'
× *adstringens* 'Hopa' — CAgr CLnd
 - 'Simcoe' — EBee EGren WMou
 'Aldenhamensis' — see *M.* × *purpurea* 'Aldenhamensis'
 'Allow Super' (D) — WMat
 'Amberina' — CLnd
 'Aros' PBR ♀H6 — EBee EGren ELan EPfP EPom LBom LBuc LCro LRHS NLar NOra NPip SBmr WHtc WMat
× *atrosanguinea* — CBTr CCVT CLnd CMac CSBt EBee ELan EPfP EPom EUrb LBuc LCro 'Gorgeous' ♀H6 LRHS LSRN MLod MPri NOra NPip SEdi SEWo SKee SOrN SPoG WMat WMou WWct
baccata — CAda CLnd CMCN GKev LRHS NOra NPip SEND SPlb WJur WMat
 - 'Braendkjaer' — CCVT CLnd
 - var. *mandshurica* — CAda
 - 'Street Parade' — CCVT EBar
 'Barbara' — NOra NPip WMat
§ *bhutanica* — CMCN GKev WJur
 BLADON PIPPIN (D) — CBTr
 BRANDYWINE ('Branzam') — CCVT EBee NOra NPip WMat

brevipes
- 'Wedding Bouquet' ♀H6 — EBee ELan EPfP LCro LRHS LSRN MAsh MLod MPri NLar NOra NPip SOrN WHtc WMat WMou
'Butterball' ♀H6 — CAda CBTr CCVT CLnd CSBt CTsd EBar EBee ELan EPom LCro LMaj LRHS MLod MPri NOra NPip SEdi SGol SPoG SRms SVic WMat WWct
'Candymint' — CLnd EBee LCro LRHS MAsh NOra NPip SGol SPoG WMat
'Cave Hill' — CLnd
'Cheal's Scarlet' — CHab
* 'Cheal's Weeping' — CAco CMac SEdi SRms
CINDERELLA ('Cinzam') — LCro NOra NPip WMat
COCCINELLA ('Courtarou') — SGol
'Comtesse de Paris' ♀H6 — CBcs CLnd EBee EPfP LCro LSto MAsh MBlu MPri NLar NOra NPip WMat
CORALBURST ('Coralcole') ♀H6 — EBee GKev LCro NOra NPip SPoG WMat
coronaria — WJur
- var. ***dasycalyx*** — CCVT
  'Charlottae' (D)
- 'Elk River' — CLnd NOra NPip WMat
'Cowichan' — SSFr
'Crimson Brilliant' — CLnd
'Dartmouth' — CAda CHab
'Directeur Moerlands' — CBTr CCVT CDoC CLnd EBar EHeP EPfP EPom LCro LRHS MSwo NOra WMat
domestica (Cider) — EPom
- 'Acklam Russet' (D) — CHab SKee
- 'Acme' (D) — SKee
- 'Adams's Pearmain' (D) — CAda CBTr CDoC CEnd CHab CLnd LCro LRHS MLod NOra SKee WMat WWct
- 'Admiral'PBR (D) — SKee
- 'Akane' (D) — NOra
- 'Akerö' (D) — SKee
- 'Alexander' (C) — LMaj
- 'Alfriston' (C) — CAgr CHab SKee WMat
§ - 'Alkmene' (D) ♀H6 — CAgr NOra SKee
- 'All Doer' (C/D/Cider) — CAda SEdi
- 'Allen's Everlasting' (C) — SKee
- 'Allington Pippin' (D) — CAda CHab CSBt NOra SKee WMat
- 'Amanda' (Cider) — CAda MLod WMat
- AMBASSY ('Dalili') (D) — SEdi SKee SSFr
- 'American Mother' — see *M. domestica* 'Mother'
- 'Ananas Reinette' (D) — CHab SKee
- 'Angela' (Cider) — EPom
- 'Annie Elizabeth' (C) — CAda CAgr CHab MGos MLod NOra SBmr SKee SSFr SVic WMat WWct
- 'Antonovka' (C) — NOra SKee
- 'Apache' (F) — SSFr
- 'Api' (D) — CMac LMaj LSRN NOra NPip SKee WMat
- 'Api Noir' (D) — SKee
- 'Ard Cairn Russet' (D) — SKee
- 'Arkansas' (D) — NOra SKee
- 'Aromatic Russet' (D) — SKee
- 'Arthur Turner' (C) ♀H6 — CAda CCVT CHab ELan EPom LBuc LCro MLod NOra SBmr SKee SSFr WMat
- 'Arthur W. Barnes' (C) — SKee
- 'Ashmead's Kernel' (D) ♀H6 — CAda CAgr CBTr CEnd CHab CLnd CSBt EPfP EPom LBuc LCro LRHS MLod MPri NOra SBmr SEdi SKee SSFr SVic WMat WWct
- 'Ashton Bitter' (Cider) — CAda CHab
- 'Ashton Brown Jersey' (Cider) — CAda
- 'Autumn Pearmain' (D) — SKee
- 'Baker's Delicious' (D) — CAda NOra SKee SSFr WMat
- 'Baldwin' (D) — NOra
- Ballerina Series (D) — MLod
- - 'Ballerina Bolero' (D) — SKee WMat
- - 'Ballerina Polka' (D) — SKee WMat
- - 'Ballerina Samba' (D) — ELan LCro MLod NLar NOra WMat
- 'Ball's Bittersweet' (Cider) — CAda
- 'Balsam' — see *M. domestica* 'Green Balsam'
- 'Banana Pippin' (F) — CEnd
- 'Banns' (D) — SKee
- 'Bardsey' (D) — CAda CAgr CBTr CEnd CHab EPom LCro MLod NOra SKee WMat
- 'Barnack Beauty' (D) — CAda CHab NOra SKee
- 'Barnack Orange' (D) — SKee
- 'Baron Ward' (C) — CHab
- 'Baron Wood' (C) — SKee
- 'Bascombe's Mystery' (D) — SKee
- 'Baumann's Reinette' (D) — SKee
- 'Baxter's Pearmain' (D) — SKee
- BAYA MARISA (C/D) — CBTr CMac ELan EPom LBuc LCro MGos MLod NOra SKee SSFr WMat
- 'Beauty of Bath' (D) — CAda CAgr CCVT CEnd CHab CLnd CTsd CWnw EGren ELan EPom LBuc LCro MLod NOra SEdi SKee SSFr WMat WWct
- 'Beauty of Bedford' (D) — SKee
- 'Beauty of Hants' (C/D) — SKee
- 'Beauty of Kent' (C) — SKee
- 'Beauty of Moray' (C) — SKee
- 'Beauty of Stoke' (C) — SKee
- 'Bedwyn Beauty' (C) — CAda
- 'Beef Apple' (C) **new** — CAda
- 'Beeley Pippin' (D) — SKee
- 'Bell Apple' (Cider/C) — CAda
- 'Belle de Boskoop' (C/D) ♀H6 — CAda CAgr CCVT CEnd CHab EPom LMaj NOra NPlm SKee
- 'Belle Flavoise' (F) — SKee
- 'Bellefleur Kitika' (D) — SKee
- 'Bembridge Beauty' (F) — CHab
- 'Benenden Early' (D) — SKee
- 'Ben's Red' (D) — CAda CAgr CDoC CEnd CTsd SKee WMat
- 'Bess Pool' (D) — CHab
- 'Betty Geeson' (C) — WWct
- 'Bewley Down Pippin' — see *M. domestica* 'Crimson King'
- 'Bickington Grey' (Cider) — CAda
- 'Bismarck' (C) — SKee
- 'Black Dabinett' (Cider) — CAda CEnd WMat
- 'Blanc Sur' (C/D) — SKee
- 'Blenheim Orange' (C/D) ♀H6 — CAda CAgr CCVT CHab CLnd EGren ELan EPfP EPom LBuc LCro LRHS LSRN MLod NOra SBmr SEdi SEND SEWo SKee SSFr SVic WFar WMat WWct
- 'Bloody Ploughman' (D) — CAda CHab CLnd EPom LBuc LCro MLod NOra SKee WMat WWct
- 'Blue Pearmain' (D) — SKee
- 'Bonum' (D/C) — WMat
- 'Boston Russet' — see *M. domestica* 'Roxbury Russet'
- 'Bountiful' (C) — CAgr CBTr CDoC CLnd CMac CSBt EGren EPom LCro LRHS LSRN MLod MNHC NLar NOra SBmr SKee SSFr WMat WWct
- 'Bow Hill Pippin' (C) — SKee
- 'Box Apple' (D) — SKee
- 'Braddick's Nonpareil' (D) — SKee
- 'Braeburn' (D) — CAgr CBTr CLnd CSBt EGren EPom IPap LBuc LCro LRHS MLod NOra

Name	Codes	Name	Codes
	NTrD SBmr SEdi SEND SEWo SKee SOrN SSFr SVic WMat		NLar NOra SBmr SKee SOrN SPoG SSFr WMat WWct
– 'Braeburn Hillwell' (D)	EPom LCro NOra SKee	– 'Cider Lady's Finger' (Cider)	SKee
– 'Braintree Seedling' (D)	SKee	– 'Cistecké' (D)	SKee
– 'Bramley 20' (C)	CBTr CLnd CSBt EBee ELan EPom LBuc LCro LSRN MLod MNHC NLar NOra SBmr SKee SOrN SPoG WMat WWct	– 'Claygate Pearmain' (D)	CAda CAgr CHab NOra SKee SVic WMat
		– 'Cleeve' (D)	SKee
		– 'Clopton Red' (D)	SKee
– 'Bramley's Seedling' (C) ♀H6	Widely available	– 'Cobra' (F)	CAda CAgr EPom LRHS MLod NOra SKee SPoG SSFr WMat
– 'Bramshott Rectory' (D/C)	SKee SSFr	– 'Cockle Pippin' (D)	CAda CAgr SKee
– 'Bread Fruit' (C/D)	CAda CDoC CEnd	– 'Cockpit' (C)	CHab SKee
– 'Breakwell's Seedling' (Cider)	CAda	– 'Coeur de Boeuf' (C/D)	SKee
– 'Breitling' (D)	SKee	– 'Coleman's Seedling' (Cider)	CAda
– 'Brenchley Pippin' (D)	SKee	– 'Collogett Pippin' (C/Cider)	CAda CDoC CEnd CTsd
– 'Bright Future' (D)	EPom MLod SKee WMat WWct		
– 'Bringewood Pippin' (D)	CHab	– 'Colonel Vaughan' (C/D)	SKee
– 'Brith Mawr' (C)	CHab	– 'Colonel Yate' (D)	SKee
– 'Broad-eyed Pippin' (C)	SKee	– 'Comrade' (D)	SKee
– 'Broadholme Beauty' (C)	EPom LCro NOra WMat	– 'Core Blimey' (D)	CBTr EBee EPom LBuc LCro MLod NOra SKee SPoG WMat
– 'Brookes's' (D)	SKee		
– 'Brown Snout' (Cider)	CAda	– 'Cornish Aromatic' (D)	CAda CAgr CDoC CTsd NOra SBmr SKee WMat
– 'Brownlee's Russet' (D)	CAda CAgr CHab NOra SBmr SKee SSFr WMat		
		– 'Cornish Gilliflower' (D)	CAda CAgr CDoC CEnd CHab CTsd NOra SBmr SKee WMat
– 'Brown's Apple' (Cider)	CAda CAgr CHab EPom NOra WMat WWct		
		– 'Cornish Honeypin' (D)	CAda CDoC CEnd CTsd SKee SSFr
– 'Broxwood Foxwhelp' (Cider)	WWct	– 'Cornish Longstem' (D)	CAda CAgr CDoC CEnd CTsd
– 'Budimka' (D)	SKee	– 'Cornish Mother' (D)	CAda CDoC CEnd CTsd
– 'Burn's Seedling' (D)	SKee	– 'Cornish Pine' (D)	CAda CDoC CEnd CTsd SKee
– 'Burr Knot' (C)	SKee	– 'Cornish Queen' (C/D)	CAda CDoC CTsd
– 'Burrowhill Early' (Cider)	WMat	– 'Coronation' (D)	CHab SKee
– 'Bushey Grove' (C)	SKee	– 'Cortland' (D)	NOra SKee
– 'Buttery Do' (F)	CAda	– 'Costard' (C)	CHab SKee
– 'Byfleet Seedling' (C)	SKee	– 'Cottenham Seedling' (C)	SKee
– 'Calville Blanc d'Hiver' (D)	CAda NOra SKee	– 'Coul Blush' (D)	SKee WMat
		– 'Court of Wick' (D)	CAda CAgr CHab NOra SKee SVic WMat
– 'Cambusnethan Pippin' (D)	SKee	– 'Court Pendu Plat' (D)	CAda CAgr CHab NOra SKee WMat WWct
– 'Camelot' (Cider/C)	CAda CCVT SEdi		
– 'Cap of Liberty' (Cider)	CAda	– 'Court Royal' (Cider/C)	CAda SKee
§ – 'Captain Broad' (Cider/D)	CAda CDoC CEnd CTsd	– 'Cox's Orange Pippin' (D)	Widely available
– 'Captain Kidd' (D)	EPom NOra SKee	– 'Cox's Pomona' (C)	SKee
– 'Captain Tom' (C/D)	WMat	– 'Cox's Rouge de Flandres' (D)	CAda SKee
– 'Carlisle Codlin' (C)	NOra WMat		
– 'Carswell's Honeydew' (D)	SKee	– 'Cox's Selfing' (D)	CBTr CMac CSBt EBee EGren EPfP EPom LBom LBuc LCro MAsh MGos MLod MNHC NLar SKee SPoG WMat WWct
– 'Carswell's Orange' (D)	SKee		
– 'Catherine' (C)	SKee		
– 'Catshead' (C)	CAda CAgr CDoC CHab NOra SKee WMat WWct	– 'Crawley Beauty' (C)	CAda CAgr CHab SKee WMat
		– 'Crawley Reinette' (D)	CHab SKee
– 'Cellini' (C)	NOra SKee	– 'Crimson Beauty' (D)	SKee
– 'Cevaal' (D)	WWct	– 'Crimson Beauty of Bath' (D)	CAgr
– 'Charles Ross' (C/D) ♀H6	CAda CAgr CCVT CEnd CHab CLnd CMac CSBt EPom IArd LBuc LCro LSRN MLod NOra SBmr SKee SSFr WMat WWct	– 'Crimson Bramley' (C)	CAda SKee
		– CRIMSON CRISP ('Coop 39'[PBR]) (D)	SKee
– 'Charlotte' (C)	SKee	§ – 'Crimson King' (Cider/C)	CAda CAgr
– 'Chatley's Kernal' (C/D)	WWct	– 'Crimson King' (D)	CAgr CHab
– 'Cheddar Cross' (D)	CAda CAgr CCVT SKee	– 'Crimson Peasgood' (C)	SKee
– 'Chelmsford Wonder' (C)	SKee	– 'Crimson Queening' (D)	SKee
– 'Cherry Cox' (D)	CAda	– 'Crimson Victoria' (Cider)	CAda
– 'Chips' (F)	SKee	§ – 'Cripps Pink'[PBR] (D)	SSFr
– 'Chisel Jersey' (Cider)	CAda CAgr NOra SKee WWct	– CRISPIN	see *M. domestica* 'Mutsu'
– 'Chivers Delight' (D)	CAda CAgr EBee EPom LBuc LCro LSRN MLod NOra SBmr SKee SSFr WMat	§ – 'Crowngold' (D)	EPom
		– CYBÈLE ('Delrouval') (D)	SKee
		– 'Dabinett' (Cider)	CAda CAgr CHab CLnd EPom LBuc LCro MLod NOra SKee WMat WWct
– 'Christmas Pearmain' (D)	CAda CAgr CLnd SKee SSFr WMat		
– 'Christmas Pippin'[PBR] (D) ♀H6	CBTr CEnd EBee ELan EPfP EPom LBom LBuc LCro LRHS MLod MPri	– 'D'Arcy Spice' (D)	CAda CAgr NOra SBmr SKee WMat WWct

- 'Dawn' (D)	SKee		- 'Empire' (D)	NOra SKee
- 'Decio' (D)	SKee		- 'English Codlin' (C)	CAda
- DELBARD JUBILÉ ('Delgollune') (D)	NPlm		- 'Epicure'	see *M. domestica* 'Laxton's Epicure'
- DELBARESTIVALE ('Delcorf') (red) (D)	LMaj NOra		- 'Esopus Spitzenburg' (D)	NOra SKee
			- 'Excelsior' (C)	SKee
- 'Delprim' (D)	SKee		- 'Exeter Cross' (D)	CAda
- 'Devon Crimson Queen' (D)	CAda CTsd		- 'Exquisite' (D)	CLnd LRHS SKee SRms
			- 'Fair Maid of Devon' (Cider)	CAda CAgr CEnd WMat
- 'Devonshire Buckland' (C)	CAda CEnd CTsd		- 'Fairie Queen' (D)	SKee
- 'Devonshire Quarrenden' (D)	CAda CAgr CHab CTsd NOra SKee SVic WMat		- 'Falstaff' PBR (D)	CAda CAgr EPom LCro LSRN MGos NOra NTrD SBmr SEdi SKee SSFr WFar
- 'Diamond Jubilee' (D)	SKee		- 'Fameuse' (D)	NOra SKee
- 'Dick's Favourite' (C)	WWct		- 'Farmer's Glory' (D)	CAda CAgr SEND WMat
- 'Discovery' (D) ♀H6	Widely available		- 'Fearn's Pippin' (D)	SKee
- 'Discovery NFT' (D)	CEnd WMat		- 'Feuillemorte' (D)	SKee
- 'Doctor Clifford' (C)	SKee		- 'Fiesta' (D) ♀H6	Widely available
- 'Doctor Harvey' (C)	CAda		- 'Fillbarrel' (Cider)	CAda CHab
- 'Doctor Hogg' (C)	CLnd		- 'Fillingham Pippin' (C)	CHab SKee
- 'Doctor Kidd's Orange Red'	see *M. domestica* 'Kidd's Orange Red'		- 'Fiona' (Cider)	CAda WMat
- 'Doddin' (D)	WWct		- 'Firedance' (D)	LRHS
- 'Domino' (C)	SKee		- 'First and Last' (D)	NOra WMat
- 'Don's Delight' (C)	CAda WMat		- 'Flame' (D)	SKee
- 'Dove' (Cider)	CAda		- 'Flamenco'	see *M. domestica* 'Obelisk'
- 'Downton Pippin' (D)	CHab SKee		- 'Florina' (F)	NOra
- 'Dredge's Fame' (D)	SKee	§ - 'Flower of Kent' (C)	CHab EPom LCro MLod NOra SKee SSFr WMat
- 'Duchess of Bedford' (D)	SKee			
- 'Duchess of Oldenburg' (C)	NOra SKee		- 'Flower of the Town' (D)	CHab SKee
			- 'Forfar'	see *M. domestica* 'Dutch Mignonne'
- 'Duchess's Favourite' (D)	SKee		- 'Forge' (D)	CAgr CHab SKee
- 'Duck's Bill' (D)	SKee		- 'Fortune'	see *M. domestica* 'Laxton's Fortune'
- 'Dufflin' (Cider)	CAda		- 'Foster's Seedling' (D)	SKee
- 'Duke of Cornwall' (C)	CAda CDoC CTsd		- 'Foxwhelp' (Cider)	CAda CHab CLnd SKee
- 'Duke of Devonshire' (D)	CAda SKee		- 'Francis' (D)	SKee
- 'Dumeller's Seedling'	see *M. domestica* 'Dummellor's Seedling'		- 'Frederick' (Cider)	CAda CLnd WMat
			- 'Freiherr von Berlepsch' (D)	SKee
§ - 'Dummellor's Seedling' (C) ♀H6	CAda CHab NOra SKee		- 'Freyberg' (D)	NOra SKee
- 'Dunkerton Late Sweet' (Cider)	CAda CCVT CHab NOra SEdi WMat		- 'Frome River' (Cider) **new**	CAda
			- 'Fuji' (D)	LMaj NOra NPlm SKee
- 'Dutch Mignonne' (D)	SKee		- 'Gala' (D)	EBee EGren EPom IPap LCro MSwo NOra SAth SEdi SEWo SKee SSFr SVic WMat
- 'Eady's Magnum' (C)	SKee			
- 'Early Blenheim' (D/C)	CEnd			
- 'Early Bower' (D)	CEnd		- 'Galaxy' (D)	NOra SEdi
- 'Early Julyan' (C)	SKee		- 'Galloway Pippin' (C)	CAda LBuc NLar NOra SKee WMat
- 'Early Victoria'	see *M. domestica* 'Emneth Early'		- 'Garden Fountain' (D)	LRHS
- EARLY WINDSOR	see *M. domestica* 'Alkmene'		- 'Garnet' (D)	SKee
- 'Early Worcester'	see *M. domestica* 'Tydeman's Early Worcester'		- 'Gascoyne's Scarlet' (C/D)	SKee
			- 'Gavin' (D)	CAgr SKee
- 'East Lothian Pippin' (C)	SKee		- 'Genet Moyle' (C/Cider)	WMat
- 'Easter Orange' (D)	SKee		- 'George Carpenter' (D)	SKee
- 'Ecklinville' (C)	SKee		- 'George Cave' (D)	CAda EGren NOra SEdi SEND SKee SSFr
- 'Eden' (D)	CBTr EPom MLod NOra SPoG WMat			
			- 'George Neal' (C)	CAgr SKee
- EDEN ('Sjca38r6a74') (D)	EPom LCro		- 'Gilly' (Cider)	CAda WMat
- 'Edith Hopwood' (D)	SKee		- 'Gin' (Cider)	CAda
- 'Edward VII' (C) ♀H6	CHab NOra SKee WMat WWct		- 'Gladstone' (D)	CAgr NOra SKee WMat WWct
- 'Egremont Russet' (D) ♀H6	Widely available		- 'Glockenapfel' (C)	SKee
			- 'Gloria Mundi' (C)	SKee
- 'Ellis Bitter' (Cider)	CAda CCVT EPom SKee SVic		- 'Gloster '69' (D)	CAda CWnw ELan LMaj SKee
- 'Ellison's Orange' (D) ♀H6	CAda CAgr CEnd CHab CLnd CMac CSBt EPfP EPom LBuc LCro LRHS MLod MMuc MPri NOra SBmr SEdi SEND SKee SRms SSFr SVic WFar WMat WWct		- 'Gloucester Cross' (D)	SKee
			- 'Gloucester Royal' (D)	SKee
			- 'Golden Ball' (Cider)	CAda
			- 'Golden Bittersweet' (D)	CAda CAgr WMat
- 'Elstar' (D) ♀H6	CAda CCVT CLnd CWnw EBar EGren EPom LCro LMaj MSwo NOra SEdi SEWo SKee SSFr WFar		- 'Golden Delicious' (D)	CMac EBar EGren ELan EPom IPap LBuc LCro LMaj LRHS MLod MPri NOra NPlm NTrD SArc SAth SEdi SKee SSFr SVic WMat
- 'Elton Beauty' (D)	SKee		- 'Golden Harvey' (D)	CAgr SKee
§ - 'Emneth Early' (C) ♀H6	CAgr CHab NOra SEdi SKee WMat		- 'Golden Knob' (D)	CAda SKee

Cultivar	Sources
- 'Golden Noble' (C) ♀H6	CAda CAgr NOra SKee
- 'Golden Nugget' (D)	CAgr SKee
- 'Golden Pippin' (C)	CAgr NOra SKee WMat
- 'Golden Reinette' (D)	SKee
- 'Golden Russet' (D)	CAgr NOra SKee
- 'Golden Spire' (C)	CHab NOra SKee
- GOLDRUSH ('Coop 38'PBR) (D)	NOra
- 'Golly Knapp' (Cider) new	CAda
- 'Gooseberry' (C)	SKee
- 'Grandpa Buxton' (C)	CHab
- 'Granny Smith' (D)	CBcs EGren EPom IPap LCro LMaj LSRN MLod NOra SEdi SKee SVic WMat
- 'Grantonian' (C)	SKee
- 'Gravenstein' (D)	CHab LMaj NOra SEdi SKee
§ - 'Green Balsam' (D)	CHab
- 'Green Harvey' (D/C)	SKee
- 'Greenfinch' (D)	LRHS
- 'Greensleeves'PBR (D) ♀H6	CAda CAgr CBTr CMac CWnw ELan EPfP EPom LCro LRHS MMuc NOra SBmr SEdi SEND SKee SSFr WMat WWct
- 'Greenup's Pippin' (D)	CHab
- 'Grenadier' (C) ♀H6	CAda CAgr CHab CLnd EPom LCro MMuc NOra SEdi SEND SKee SSFr WMat WWct
- 'Grimes Golden' (D)	NOra
- 'Guillevic' (Cider)	CHab
- 'Gull' (D)	CAda
- 'Hains' (D/Cider) new	CAda
- 'Halstow Natural' (Cider)	CAgr
- 'Hambledon Deux Ans' (C)	SKee
- 'Hambling's Seedling' (C)	SKee
- 'Hangy Down' (Cider)	CAda WMat
- 'Hanwell Souring' (C)	SKee
- 'Harbert's Reinette' (D)	SKee
§ - 'Harry Master's Jersey' (Cider)	CAda CAgr EPom MLod NOra SKee WMat WWct
- 'Harry Master's Red Streak' (Cider)	SEdi
- 'Harry Pring' (D)	SKee
- 'Harvey' (C)	SKee
- 'Hastings' (Cider)	CAda WMat
- 'Hawkridge' (C/D) new	CAda
- 'Hawthornden' (C)	CHab SKee
- 'Helen's Apple' (Cider)	EPom
- 'Hereford Cross' (D)	SKee
- 'Herefordshire Beefing' (C)	SKee
- 'Herefordshire Redstreak' (Cider)	CAda CAgr EPom LBuc MLod NOra WMat WWct
- 'Herefordshire Russet'PBR (D)	CBTr CDoC EBee ELan EPom LBuc LCro LRHS MLod MPri NLar NOra SBmr SKee SSFr WMat WWct
- 'Herring's Pippin' (C/D)	CAda SKee
- 'Heusgen's Golden Reinette' (D)	SKee
- 'Hibb's Seedling' (C)	SKee
- 'Hibernal' (C)	SKee
- 'Hidden Rose' (D)	LRHS NOra SKee
- 'High View Pippin' (D)	SKee
- 'Histon Favourite' (D/C)	SKee
- 'Hoary Morning' (C)	CAda SKee
- 'Hocking's Green' (C/D)	CAda CAgr CDoC CEnd CTsd
- 'Holland Pippin' (C)	SKee
- 'Hollow Core' (C/Cider/D)	CAgr
- 'Holstein' (D)	CAda IPap NOra SEdi SKee
- 'Honey Pippin' (D)	SKee
- 'Honeycrisp'PBR (D)	LRHS MLod NOra WMat
- 'Hormead Pearmain' (C)	SKee
- 'Horneburger Pfannkuchen' (C)	SKee
- 'Horsford Prolific' (D)	SKee
- 'Horsham Russet' (D)	SKee
- 'Houblon' (D)	SKee
- 'Howgate Wonder' (C) ♀H6	CAda CAgr CCVT CDoC CHab CLnd EGren ELan EPfP EPom LBuc LCro LRHS LSRN MLod MMuc MSwo NOra SBmr SEdi SKee SSFr SVic WMat WWct
- 'Hubbard's Pearmain' (D)	SKee
- 'Hubbardston Nonesuch' (D)	NOra
- 'Hunt's Duke of Gloucester' (D)	SKee
- 'Hunt's Early' (D)	SKee
- 'Idared' (D)	CWnw EGren LCro NOra SEdi SKee SSFr SVic WMat
- 'Improved Keswick Codlin' (C/D)	CEnd
- 'Improved Lambrook Pippin' (Cider)	CAda
- 'Ingall's Pippin' (D)	SKee
- 'Ingall's Red' (D)	SKee
- 'Ingrid Marie' (D)	SKee SSFr
- 'Irish Peach' (D)	CAda CAgr CHab MLod NOra SKee SSFr WMat
- 'Isaac Newton's Tree'	see *M. domestica* 'Flower of Kent'
- 'Isle of Wight Pippin' (D)	SSFr
- 'Jackson's'	see *M. domestica* 'Crimson King'
- 'Jacques Lebel' (C)	SKee
- 'James Grieve' (D) ♀H6	Widely available
- 'James Lawson' (D)	SKee
- JAZZ ('Scifresh'PBR) (D)	SSFr
- 'Jefferies' (D)	SKee
- 'Jersey Black' (D/Cider)	SKee
- 'Jester' (D)	MLod SKee SSFr
- 'Joaneting' (D)	CAgr CHab
- 'John Apple' (C)	SKee
- 'John Broad'	see *M. domestica* 'Captain Broad'
- 'John Standish' (D)	CAgr SKee
- 'John Toucher's'	see *M. domestica* 'Crimson King'
- 'Johnny Andrews' (Cider)	CAgr
- 'Johnny Voun' (D)	CEnd
- 'Jonagold' (D) ♀H6	CAda CLnd EBar EGren ELan EPom IArd IPap LCro LMaj MLod NOra SEdi SKee SSFr
- 'Jonagold Crowngold'	see *M. domestica* 'Crowngold'
§ - 'Jonagored'PBR (D)	EGren NOra SEdi SKee WMat
- 'Jonathan' (D)	NOra SKee
- 'Joybells' (D)	SKee
- 'Jubilee'	see *M. domestica* 'Royal Jubilee'
- 'Jumbo' (C/D)	CAda CBTr CMac NOra SKee WMat
- 'Jupiter'PBR (D) ♀H6	CAgr CBTr CSBt EGren LCro LSRN MLod MPri NLar NOra SEdi SKee SSFr WMat
- 'Kandil Sinap' (D)	SKee
- 'Karmijn de Sonnaville' (D)	NOra SKee
§ - 'Katja' (D)	CAda CAgr CBTr CCVT CDoC CMac CTsd CWnw EBee EGren EPfP EPom IArd LBuc LCro LRHS MGos MLod NOra NTrD SBmr SEdi SEWo SKee SRms SSFr WMat WWct
- KATY	see *M. domestica* 'Katja'
- 'Kent' (D) ♀H6	SKee
- 'Kentish Fillbasket' (C)	SKee
- 'Kentish Pippin' (C/Cider/D)	SKee
- 'Kerry Pippin' (D)	SKee

	– 'Keswick Codlin' (C)	CAda CBTr CHab EBee NLar NOra SKee SSFr WMat	– 'London Pearmain' (D)	SKee
§	– 'Kidd's Orange Red' (D) ♀H6	CAda CAgr CBTr CEnd CMac EBee EPfP EPom LBuc LCro LRHS LSRN MLod NOra SBmr SKee SSFr WMat WWct	– 'London Pippin' (C)	CAgr SKee
			– 'Longkeeper' (D)	CAgr CEnd
			– 'Lord Burghley' (D)	CAda SKee
			– 'Lord Derby' (C)	CAda CAgr CBTr CHab CMac EPom LCro LRHS NLar NOra SBmr SEdi SEND SKee SVic WMat WWct
	– 'Killerton Sharp' (Cider)	CAda		
	– 'King Byerd' (C/D)	CAda CDoC CEnd	– 'Lord Grosvenor' (C)	SKee
	– 'King Charles' Pearmain' (D)	SKee WWct	– 'Lord Hindlip' (D)	CHab MLod NOra SKee WMat WWct
	– 'King Coffee' (D)	WWct	– 'Lord Lambourne' (D) ♀H6	CAda CAgr CBTr CEnd CHab CLnd CMac ELan EPom LCro LSRN MSwo NOra SBmr SEdi SKee SSFr WMat WWct
	– 'King David' (C/D)	NOra		
	– 'King George V' (D)	SKee		
§	– 'King of the Pippins' (D) ♀H6	CAda CHab CLnd EPom LMaj NOra SKee SVic WMat WWct		
			– 'Lord of the Isles' (Cider)	CAgr
	– 'King of Tompkins County' (D)	NOra	– 'Lord Rosebery' (D)	SKee
			– 'Lord Stradbroke' (C)	SKee
	– 'King's Acre Bountiful' (C)	SKee	– 'Lord Suffield' (C)	SKee
	– 'King's Acre Pippin' (D)	CAda NOra SKee WMat	– 'Lucombe's Pine' (D)	CAda CAgr CDoC CEnd SVic
	– 'Kingston Bitter' (Cider)	CAda	– 'Lucombe's Seedling' (D)	SKee
	– 'Kingston Black' (Cider/C)	CAda CAgr CCVT CEnd CHab CLnd EPom LBuc MLod NOra SKee WMat WWct	– 'Lynn's Pippin' (D)	SKee
			– 'Mabbott's Pearmain' (D)	SKee
			– 'Maclean's Favourite' (D)	SKee
	– 'Kirton Fair' (D)	CAda	– 'Macoun' (D)	NOra
	– 'Knobby Russet' (D)	SKee SSFr	– 'Madresfield Court' (D)	SKee WWct
	– 'Knotted Kernal' (Cider)	CAda EPom	– 'Maidstone Favourite' (D)	SKee
	– 'Lady Henniker' (C)	CEnd CHab NOra SKee WMat	– 'Major' (Cider)	CAda CAgr WMat WWct
	– 'Lady Hollendale' (D)	SKee	– 'Maldon Wonder' (D)	SKee
	– 'Lady Isabel' (D)	SKee	– 'Maltster' (D)	SKee
	– 'Lady Lambourne' (C/D)	CHab SKee	– 'Manaccan Primrose' (C/D)	CAda CDoC CEnd CTsd
	– 'Lady of the Wemyss' (C)	SKee		
	– 'Lady Sudeley' (D)	CAda CEnd CHab SKee	– 'Mannington's Pearmain' (D)	SKee WMat
	– 'Lady's Finger' (C/D)	CAda CDoC CEnd		
	– 'Lady's Finger of Lancaster' (C/D)	CHab SKee	– 'Marged Nicolas' (D)	CAda
			– 'Margil' (D)	NOra SKee
	– 'Lakeland' (D)	SKee	– 'Marlpits Late' (Cider) **new**	CAda
	– 'Lamb Abbey Pearmain' (D)	SKee	– 'Marriage-maker' (D)	SKee
			– 'Matravers' (Cider) **new**	CAda
	– 'Lamb's Seedling' (D)	SKee	– 'May Beauty' (D)	SKee
	– 'Landsberger Reinette' (D)	SKee	– 'May Queen' (D)	SKee WWct
	– 'Lane's Prince Albert' (C) ♀H6	CAda CAgr CHab CLnd CSBt EPfP NOra SEdi SKee SSFr SVic WMat	– 'McIntosh' (D)	NOra SKee
			– 'Mead's Broading' (C)	SKee
	– 'Langley Pippin' (D)	SKee	– 'Measday's Favourite' (C)	SKee
§	– 'Langworthy' (Cider)	CAda SKee	– 'Médaille d'Or' (Cider)	SKee WMat
	– 'Lass o' Gowrie' (C)	SKee	– 'Megabite' (C/D)	EPom
§	– 'Laxton's Epicure' (D) ♀H6	CAda CAgr CEnd CHab SKee	– 'Melba' (D)	SKee
	– 'Laxton's Favourite' (D)	SKee	– 'Melrose' (D)	LMaj SKee
§	– 'Laxton's Fortune' (D) ♀H6	CAda CHab CMac CSBt EPom IArd LCro MLod NOra SEdi SKee SSFr WMat WWct	– 'Mère de Ménage' (C)	SKee
			– 'Meridian' PBR (D)	CAgr LCro NOra SEdi SSFr WMat
			– 'Merton Beauty' (D)	SKee
	– 'Laxton's Reargard' (D)	SKee	– 'Merton Charm' (C)	SKee
§	– 'Laxton's Superb' (D)	CAda CBcs CBTr CCVT CHab CLnd CMac EBar EGren EPom GKin LBuc LCro LRHS LSRN MLod MNHC MPri MSwo NOra SEdi SEWo SKee SRms SSFr SVic WMat WWct	– 'Merton Russet' (D)	SKee
			– 'Merton Worcester' (D)	SKee
			– 'Meteor' (F)	SKee
			– 'Michaelmas Red' (D)	CAda SKee
			– 'Michelin' (Cider)	CAda CAgr CCVT NOra SKee WMat WWct
	– 'Laxton's Triumph' (D)	SKee		
	– 'Leatherjacket' (C)	SKee	– 'Miller's Seedling' (D)	NOra SKee
	– 'Lemon Pippin' (C)	NOra SKee	– 'Millicent Barnes' (D)	SKee
	– 'Lewis's Incomparable' (C)	SKee	– 'Minshull Crab' (C)	SKee
	– 'Liberty' (D)	NOra	– 'Mollie's Delicious' (D)	SKee
	– 'Limberland' (C)	CAda	– 'Monarch' (C)	CAda CAgr EPom LCro SKee SSFr
	– 'Limberlimb' (C/D)	CDoC	– 'Montfort' (D)	SKee
	– 'Limelight' (D) ♀H6	CAda CDoC EBee LCro LRHS MLod MPri NLar NOra SKee SSFr WMat	– 'Morgan's Sweet' (C/Cider)	CAda CHab EPom NOra SKee WMat
			§ – 'Mother' (D) ♀H6	CAda CAgr CLnd SKee SSFr
	– 'Linda' (D)	SKee	§ – 'Mutsu' (C/D)	CAda EGren NOra SEdi SEND SKee SSFr WMat
	– 'Link Wonder' (D)	CEnd		
	– 'Little Pax' (D)	CBTr EPom LBuc LCro LRHS MLod NLar NOra SKee WMat	– 'Mylor Pike' (D)	CEnd
			– 'Nancy Jackson' (C)	CHab SKee
	– 'Lodgemore Nonpareil' (D)	SKee	– 'Nanny' (D)	CLnd SKee
			– 'Nasona' (D)	SKee

- 'Nemes Szercsika Alma' (C)	SKee
- 'Newton Wonder' (C)	CAda CAgr CEnd CHab CLnd CSBt EPom LCro MLod MNHC NOra SBmr SEdi SKee SRms SSFr WMat WWct
- 'Newtown Pippin' (D)	NOra
- 'Nigde' (D)	SKee
- 'Nine Square' (D)	CAda
- 'Nolan Pippin' (D)	SKee
- 'Nonpareil' (D)	SKee
- 'Norfolk Beauty' (C)	SKee
- 'Norfolk Beefing' (C)	CAda CHab NOra SKee WMat
- 'Norfolk Royal' (D)	CHab NOra SBmr SKee
- 'Norfolk Royal Russet' (D)	ELan MLod NOra SKee WMat
- 'Norfolk Summer Broadend' (C)	SKee
- 'Norfolk Winter Coleman' (C)	SKee
- 'Northern Greening' (C)	SKee
- 'Northern Spy' (D)	NOra SKee
§ - 'Northwood' (Cider)	CAda SKee WMat
– Nuvar Cheerfull Gold (D)	SKee
– Nuvar Freckles (D)	SKee
– Nuvar Gold (D)	SKee
– Nuvar Golden Elf (D)	SKee
– Nuvar Golden Hills (D)	SKee
– Nuvar Home Farm (D)	SKee
– Nuvar Long Harvest (D)	SKee
– Nuvar Melody (D)	SKee
- 'Oaken Pin' (D)	CAda CEnd
§ - 'Obelisk'^{PBR} (D)	ELan LCro MGos MLod NOra SKee WMat
- 'Old Pearmain' (D)	SKee
- 'Old Somerset Russet' (D)	CAda
- 'Opalescent' (D)	CEnd SKee
- 'Orange Goff' (D)	SKee
- 'Orangenburg' (D)	SKee
- 'Orin' (D)	SKee
- 'Orkney Apple' (F)	SKee
- 'Orleans Reinette' (D)	CAda CAgr CEnd EPom LCro NOra SKee SSFr WMat
- 'Osennee Desertnoe' (D)	SKee
- 'Oslin' (D)	SKee WMat
- 'Otava'^{PBR} (C/D)	SKee
- 'Owen Thomas' (D)	SKee
- 'Oxford Conquest' (D)	SKee
- 'Paignton Marigold' (Cider)	CAda
- 'Palmer's Rosey' (D)	SKee
– Paradice Gold (D)	CBTr EBee EPom MLod SKee SPoG WMat
- 'Park Farm Pippin' (D)	SKee
- 'Paroquet' (D)	SKee
- 'Payhembury' (C/Cider)	CAda CAgr
- 'Peacemaker' (D)	SKee
- 'Pear Apple' (D)	CAgr CEnd
- 'Pearl' (D)	NOra WMat
- 'Peasgood's Nonsuch' (C) ♀H6	CAda CAgr CHab EPom LSRN NOra SBmr SKee WMat
- 'Peck's Pleasant' (D)	SKee
- 'Pendragon' (D)	CAda CDoC CEnd CTsd
- 'Pépin Shafrannyi' (D)	SKee
- 'Peter Lock' (C/D)	CAda CAgr CDoC CEnd SKee
- 'Pethyre' (Cider)	CCVT
- 'Pickering's Seedling' (D)	SKee
- 'Pig Aderyn' (C)	CHab
- 'Pigeon Rouge' (D) new	CLnd
- 'Pigeonette de Rouen' (D)	SKee
- 'Pig's Nose Pippin' (D)	CEnd MLod SKee
- - Type III (D)	CAgr
- 'Pig's Snout' (Cider/C/D)	CAda CDoC CEnd
- 'Pine Apple Russet' (C/D)	CAgr
- 'Pine Apple Russet of Devon' (D)	CEnd
- 'Pine Golden Pippin' (D)	SKee
– Pink Lady	see *M. domestica* 'Cripps Pink'
- 'Pinova'^{PBR} (D)	CAda CAgr EPom LCro NOra SBmr SSFr
- 'Pitmaston Pine Apple' (D)	CAda CHab EPom MLod NOra SKee SSFr WMat WWct
- 'Pitmaston Russet Nonpareil' (D)	SKee WWct
- 'Pixie' (D) ♀H6	CAda CDoC CSBt EPom LCro LRHS MPri NOra SKee WMat WWct
- 'Plum Vite' (Cider/C/D)	CAda CAgr
- 'Plymouth Cross' (D)	SKee
- 'Plympton Pippin' (C)	CAda CDoC CEnd
– Polka ('Trajan') (D)	NOra
- 'Polly' (C/D)	SKee
- 'Polly Prosser' (D)	SKee
- 'Pomeroy of Somerset' (D)	CAda CHab SKee
- 'Ponsford' (C)	CAda CAgr SKee WMat
- 'Port Wine'	see *M. domestica* 'Harry Master's Jersey'
- 'Porter's Perfection' (Cider)	CAda EPom NOra
- 'Pott's Seedling' (C)	SKee
§ - 'Primate' (D) new	CAda
- 'Prince Charles' (D)	SKee
- 'Princesse' (F)	CAda CEnd SKee
- 'Priscilla' (D)	NOra
- 'Purple Haze' (D)	EPom
- 'Purpurroter Cousinot' (D)	SKee
- 'Queen' (C)	CAgr SKee
- 'Queen Alexandra' (C)	WWct
- 'Queen Caroline' (C)	SKee
- 'Queen Cox' (D)	CLnd EGren EPom LCro LSRN NOra NTrD SBmr SEdi SKee SSFr WMat
– Queen of the Realm (D) new	CBTr LRHS MNHC
- 'Rajka'^{PBR} (D)	CAda NOra SKee WWct
- 'Red Alkmene'	see *M. domestica* 'Red Windsor'
- 'Red Belle de Boskoop' (D)	CAgr LMaj
- 'Red Delicious'	see *M. domestica* 'Starking'
- 'Red Devil' (D)	CAgr CBTr CDoC CEnd CLnd CMac CSBt EBee EPom LBom LBuc LCro LRHS MGos MLod MPri NLar NOra SEWo SKee SSFr WMat WWct
- 'Red Ellison' (D)	LCro
- 'Red Falstaff' (D) ♀H6	CAgr CBTr CCVT CDoC CEnd EPfP EPom GKin LBuc LCro LRHS LSRN MLod MPri MSwo NLar NOra SBmr SEND SEWo SKee SPoG WMat WWct
- 'Red Foxwhelp' (Cider)	EPom WMat
- 'Red Gravenstein' (D)	SEdi
- 'Red James Grieve' (D)	SKee
- 'Red Joaneting' (D)	SKee
- 'Red Jonagold'	see *M. domestica* 'Jonagored'
§ - 'Red Jonaprince'^{PBR} (D)	WMat
- 'Red Melba' (C)	CAda
- 'Red Pixie' (D)	WMat
- 'Red Sauce' (C)	SKee
§ - 'Red Windsor' (D) ♀H6	CAda CBTr CEnd CLnd CMac EBee ELan EPfP EPom LBom LBuc LCro LRHS MAsh MLod MPri NLar NOra SKee SPoG SSFr WMat
- 'Red Worthy' (Cider) new	CAda
- 'Redfree' (D)	NOra
- 'Redsleeves' (D)	CAgr CLnd LCro NOra SKee

- 'Reine des Reinettes'	see *M. domestica* 'King of the Pippins'	- 'Severn Bank' (C)	SKee
- 'Reinette d'Obry' (Cider)	CAda	- 'Sharleston Pippin' (D)	SKee
- 'Reinette du Canada' (D)	LMaj SKee	- 'Sheep's Nose' (C)	CHab SKee
- 'Reverend McCormick' (C/D)	CAda	- 'Shenandoah' (C)	SKee
		- 'Sherry Surprise' (D) **new**	CAda
- 'Reverend W. Wilks' (C)	CAda CAgr CEnd CHab EBee EPom LCro MLod NOra SBmr SEdi SKee SSFr WMat WWct	- 'Sidney Strake' (C)	CAgr CEnd
		- 'Sir Isaac Newton's'	see *M. domestica* 'Flower of Kent'
		- 'Sisson's Worksop Newtown' (D)	SKee
- 'Rhode Island Greening' (C/D)	NOra SKee	- 'Slack Ma Girdle' (Cider)	CAda NOra SKee WMat
		- 'Smart's Prince Arthur' (C)	CHab
- 'Ribston Pippin' (D) ♀H6	CAda EPom LBuc LCro MLod NOra SKee SSFr WMat WWct	- 'Somerset Redstreak' (Cider)	CAda CAgr CHab EPom NOra WMat WWct
- 'Rival' (D)	CAgr SKee	- 'Sops in Wine' (Cider/D)	CAda NOra SKee SVic WMat
- 'Rivers' Nonsuch' (D)	CHab	- 'Sour Bay' (Cider)	CAgr
- 'Rosemary Russet' (D) ♀H6	CAda CAgr CHab NOra SBmr SKee SSFr WMat WWct	- 'Sour Natural'	see *M. domestica* 'Langworthy'
- 'Rosette' (D)	CAda CBTr EPfP EPom LCro LRHS MLod NLar NOra SKee WMat	- 'Spartan' (D)	CAda CBTr CCVT CEnd CLnd CMac EBee EGren ELan EPom GKin IPap LCro LRHS MGos MLod MNHC NOra SBmr SEdi SKee SSFr SVic WFar WMat WWct
- 'Ross Nonpareil' (D)	CAgr NOra SKee WMat		
- 'Roter Ananas' (D)	SKee		
- 'Rough and Ready'	see *M. domestica* 'Primate'	- 'Spätblühender Taffetapfel' (D)	SKee
- 'Rough Pippin' (D)	CAda CEnd SKee		
- 'Roundway Magnum Bonum' (C/D)	CAda CAgr	- 'Spencer' (D)	SKee
		- 'Spotted Dick' (Cider)	CAda
- 'Roxbury Russet' (D)	NOra SKee	- 'Stanway Seedling' (C)	SKee
- 'Royal Gala' (D)	CMac EGren EPom LBuc LMaj NTrD SBmr	- 'Star of Devon' (D)	CAda CEnd SKee
		- 'Stark' (D)	CLnd
§ - 'Royal Jubilee' (C)	SKee	§ - 'Starking' (D)	LMaj NOra SKee
- 'Royal Russet' (C)	CAgr CEnd SKee	- 'Starkrimson' (D)	SKee
- 'Royal Snow' (D)	SKee	- 'Stark's Earliest' (D)	SVic
- 'Royal Somerset' (C/Cider)	CAda WMat	- 'Starkspur Golden Delicious' (D)	SKee
- 'Royal Wilding' (Cider) **new**	CAda	- 'Stembridge Cluster' (Cider)	CAda
- 'Rubens' (D)	SKee	- 'Stirling Castle' (C)	CAgr NOra SKee WMat
- 'Rubin' (D) **new**	CAda	- 'Stobo Castle' (C)	SKee
- RUBINETTE ('Rafzubin') (D)	LCro NOra SKee	- 'Stoke Red' (Cider)	CAda NOra SKee WMat WWct
- RUBINETTE ROSSO ('Rafzubex'^PBR) (D)	WMat	- 'Striped Beefing' (C)	CAda SKee
		- 'Stub Nose' (F)	SKee
- 'Rubinola'^PBR (D)	SKee	- 'Sturmer Pippin' (D)	CAda CSBt EBee NOra SKee WWct
- 'Ruby' Seabrook (D)	SKee	- 'Summer Golden Pippin' (D)	SKee
- 'Ruby' Thorrington (D)	SKee		
- 'Saint Ailred' (D)	SKee	- 'Summerred' (D)	EGren
- 'Saint Albans Pippin' (D)	SKee	- 'Sunrise'^PBR (D)	CEnd EGren NOra SKee
- 'Saint Cecilia' (D)	CHab SKee	- 'Sunset' (D) ♀H6	Widely available
§ - 'Saint Edmund's Pippin' (D) ♀H6	CAda CHab NOra SBmr SKee SSFr WMat	- 'Suntan' (D)	CAda NOra SKee
		- 'Superb'	see *M. domestica* 'Laxton's Superb'
- 'Saint Edmund's Russet'	see *M. domestica* 'Saint Edmund's Pippin'	- SURPRIZE (D)	CBTr EPom LBuc LCro NOra WMat
		- 'Sussex Mother' (C/D)	CHab
- 'Saint Everard' (D)	SKee	- 'Swaar' (D)	SKee
- 'Saint Magdalen' (D)	SKee	- 'Sweet Alford' (Cider)	CAda EPom WMat WWct
- 'Saltcote Pippin' (D)	CAda SKee WMat	- 'Sweet Bay' (Cider)	CAgr
- 'Sam Young' (D)	CAgr SKee	- 'Sweet Cleave' (Cider)	CAda
- 'Sandlin Duchess' (D)	NOra WMat WWct	- 'Sweet Coppin' (Cider)	CAda WMat
- 'Sandringham' (C)	CAda SKee	- 'Sweet Lilibet'	see *M. domestica* 'Red Windsor'
- 'Sanspareil' (D)	CAgr SKee	- 'Sweet Pethyre' (C)	CCVT SEdi
- 'Santana'^PBR (D) ♀H6	LCro NOra WMat	- 'Sweet Sixteen' (D)	NOra
- 'Saturn' (D)	CAda CAgr CBTr CCVT LCro MLod NOra SKee SSFr WMat WWct	- 'Sweet Society' (D)	NOra SKee WMat
		- 'Symes Seedling' (Cider) **new**	CAda
- 'Saw Pits' (D)	CAgr CEnd SKee		
- 'Scarlet Nonpareil' (D)	SKee	- 'Tale Sweet' (Cider)	CAda
- 'Scarlet Pimpernel' (D)	SKee	- 'Tamar Beauty' (D)	CEnd
- 'Schöner aus Herrnhut' (D) **new**	CLnd	- 'Taunton Cross' (D)	CAda CAgr WMat
		- 'Taylor's' (Cider)	CAgr
- 'Schoolmaster' (C)	SKee	- 'Teign Harvey' (Cider)	CAda CDoC CEnd
- 'Scotch Bridget' (C)	CAda CHab EBee NBid NOra SKee WMat WWct	- 'Ten Commandments' (Cider/D)	CAda SKee WWct
- 'Scotch Dumpling' (C)	CAda GKin NOra SKee WMat	- 'Tewkesbury Baron' (D)	WWct
- 'Scrumptious'^PBR (D) ♀H6	Widely available	- 'The Rattler' (Cider)	CEnd
- 'Seabrook's Red' (D)	SKee	- 'Thorle Pippin' (D)	SKee

- 'Three Counties'	CAda EPom NOra WMat		- 'Wyken Pippin' (D)	SKee WWct
- 'Tidicombe Seedling' (D)	CAda WMat		- 'Yarlington Mill' (Cider)	CAda CAgr CHab NOra SKee SVic WMat WWct
- 'Tinsley Quince' (D)	WMat		- 'Yellow Ingestrie' (D)	CHab NOra SKee WMat WWct
- 'Tom Legg' (Cider) **new**	CAda		- 'Yorkshire Aromatic' (C)	SKee
- 'Tom Putt' (C)	CAda CAgr CCVT CHab CLnd CSBt LBuc NOra SKee WMat WWct		- 'Yorkshire Greening' (C)	CHab NOra SKee
			- 'Zabergäu Renette' (D)	NOra SKee
- 'Tommy Knight' (D)	CAda CAgr CEnd		'Donald Wyman' ♀H6	CLnd EBar EPfP LMaj MAsh NLar NOra NPip WMat
- 'Topaz'PBR (D) ♀H6	CAda EPom NOra SKee SSFr WWct			
- 'Totnes Apple' (D)	CAda		'Echtermeyer'	LMaj
- 'Tower of Glamis' (C)	CHab SKee		'Elise Rathke'	CLnd
- 'Trecarrell Mill No 1' (Cider)	CAda		'Evelyn'	CBcs CBTr CLnd EBee NOra NPip WMat
- 'Tregonna King' (C/D)	CAda CDoC CEnd CTsd		§ 'Evereste' ♀H6	Widely available
- 'Tremlett's Bitter' (Cider)	CAda CAgr CHab CTsd EPom NOra SKee SVic WMat		*florentina*	LCot NPip WMat
			× *floribunda*	CDoC CEnd CLnd CMac EBee EGren EHeP ELan EPom LCro LMaj MLod MMuc MPri NLar NOra NPip SEdi SEND SGol SPoG SRms WMat WMou
- 'Trinity' (C)	LCro MPri WMat			
- 'Tuscan' (D)	SKee			
- 'Twenty Ounce' (C)	SKee			
§ - 'Tydeman's Early Worcester' (D)	CAda CAgr CHab CLnd EPom LCro SEdi SKee SRms SSFr WWct			
			'Freja'PBR	CWnr
- 'Tydeman's Late Orange' (D)	CAda CHab EPom LCro MLod NOra SBmr SKee WMat		*fusca*	WJur
			'Gardener's Gold' ♀H6	CAda CEnd LCot MLod SRms
- 'Upton Pyne' (C/D)	CAda CEnd		*glaucescens*	WJur
- 'Veitch's Perfection' (C/D)	CAda CDoC WMat		'Golden Gem'	CBTr CLnd LCro LRHS MNHC MPri NLar NOra NPip SEWo SKee WMat
- 'Venus Pippin' (C/D)	CEnd			
- 'Vicky' (Cider)	CAda		'Golden Glory' (Cider/D) **new**	LRHS
- 'Vileberie' (Cider)	EPom			
- 'Violette' (C)	SKee		'Golden Hornet'	see *M.* × *zumi* 'Golden Hornet'
- 'Vista-bella' (D)	SEdi SKee		*halliana*	GKev WJur
- 'Wagener' (D)	SKee		HALLOWEEN	EBee EPfP LBom NLar NOra NPip SWCr
- WALTZ ('Telamon') (D)	SKee			
- 'Wanstall Pippin' (D)	SKee		'Harry Baker' ♀H6	CCVT CDoC CEnd CLnd CMac EGren EPfP EPom LRHS LSRN MBlu NOra NPip SPoG WMat WMou WWct
- 'Warner's King' (C) ♀H6	CAda NOra SKee WMat			
- 'Warrior' (F)	CAda			
- 'Wealthy' (D)	SKee			
- 'Wellington' (Cider)	CAgr		× *hartwigii*	CLnd
- 'Wellington' (C)	see *M. domestica* 'Dummellor's Seedling'		'Hillieri'	see *M.* × *scheideckeri* 'Hillieri'
			hupehensis ♀H6	CCVT CEnd CLnd EGren EHeP ELan EPfP GKev LCot MBlu MGos MPri NLar NOra NPip SDix WJur WMat WMou
- 'Werrington Wonder' (D)	CEnd			
- 'Wheeler's Russet' (D)	SKee			
- 'Whimple Wonder'	CAda CDoC			
- 'White Melrose' (C)	CAda NOra SKee WMat		'Indian Magic' ♀H6	CBTr CLnd CSBt EBee EPfP LCro LRHS NLar NOra NPip WHtc WMat WMou
- 'White Transparent' (C/D)	SKee			
- 'Whitpot Sweet' (Cider)	CEnd			
- 'William Crump' (D)	CAda CEnd CHab NOra SKee WMat WWct		'Indian Summer'	CLnd
			ioensis	WJur
- 'Wilton's Star'PBR (F)	WMat		- 'Fimbriata' (d)	LCro LRHS LSto NLar NOra NPip WMat
- 'Windsor Early' (D)	SSFr			
- 'Winesap' (C/D)	NOra		JELLY KING ('Mattfru') ♀H6	CBcs CBTr EBee ELan EPfP EPom LBuc LCro LRHS LSRN MAsh MNHC MPri NOra NPip SEWo SPoG SWCr WMat WMou WWct
- 'Winston' (D)	CAda CAgr CCVT CMac LRHS SKee SRms SVic WWct			
- 'Winter Banana' (D)	CAda CHab MLod NOra SKee WMat			
- 'Winter Gem' (D)	CAda CAgr CBTr CCVT CEnd CLnd EPom LBuc LCro MLod NOra SBmr SKee SSFr WMat			
			'John Downie' (C)	Widely available
			'Kaido'	see *M.* × *micromalus*
- 'Winter Lemon' (C/D)	SKee		*kansuensis*	CLnd
- 'Winter Peach' (D/C)	CAda CAgr		'Lady Northcliffe'	CLnd
- 'Winter Pearmain' (D)	SKee		'Laura' ♀H6	CLnd EBee ELan EPom LCro LRHS LSRN MPri NOra NPip SKee SPoG WMat
- 'Winter Quarrenden' (D)	SKee			
- 'Winter Queening' (D/C)	CAda			
- 'Winter Stubbard' (C)	CAda		'Louisa'	CMac EBee LSRN NOra NPip WMat
- 'Wolf River' (D/C)	NOra		× *magdeburgensis*	CAco CLnd EHeP
- 'Woodbine'	see *M. domestica* 'Northwood'		'Mariri Red' (D)	WMat
- 'Woolbrook Pippin' (D)	CAda CAgr WMat		'Mary Potter'	CLnd
- 'Worcester Pearmain' (D) ♀H6	CAda CAgr CBcs CBTr CCVT CHab CLnd CMac CSBt CWnw EBee ELan EPfP EPom LBuc LCro MLod MMuc NOra SBmr SEdi SEND SEWo SKee SSFr WFar WMat WWct		'Maypole' (Ballerina Series)	EGren SEdi
			§ × *micromalus*	CLnd
			× *moerlandsii* 'Liset'	CEnd CLnd MPri NOra NPip SEdi
			§ - 'Profusion'	CAda CBcs EBar EGren ELan EPom IPap LCro MGos MPri NOra NPip SGol SKee SRms WHtc WSpi
- 'Wyatt's Seedling'	see *M. domestica* 'Langworthy'			

'Mokum'	CCVT CLnd EBar EHeP LMaj LSRN	'Satin Cloud'	CLnd
MOLTEN LAVA ('Molazam')	CLnd	SCARLET BRANDYWINE ('Scbrazam')	CLnd EBee ELan EPfP LBuc MPri NPip
'Montreal Beauty'	CLnd EPom LCro	'Scarlett' ♀H6	CBTr CCVT CEnd CLnd ELan
niedzwetzkyana	CAda CTsd NPip WMat		EPfP IArd LCro LMaj LSRN
NUVAR CARNIVAL	SKee		NOra NPip SAth SEWo SPoG
NUVAR MARBLE (C)	CMac EBee LRHS NOra NPip SKee WMat		WMat WMou
PERPETU	see *M*. 'Evereste'	× *scheideckeri* 'Hillieri'	CLnd MBlu NOra NPip
'Peter's Red'	CLnd LMaj SHor	§ - 'Red Jade'	CCVT CDoC EGren EHeP ELan
PINK GLOW ('Dolgo')	CAda CAgr CLnd CSBt EPom LCro LRHS MBlu MNHC NLar NOra NPip SKee SPoG WMat	Siberian crab	MGos NPip SLSRN SEND SRms see *M*. × *robusta*
		sieboldii	see *M. toringo*
'Pink Perfection' (d)	CEnd EPfP LCro LRHS NOra NPip SPoG WMat	*sieversii*	NOra
'Prairifire'	CLnd EBee EGrI LCro LRHS MPri NOra NPip SPoG WMat	*sikkimensis* - B&SWJ 2431	WJur WCru
prattii	CLnd WJur	'Simon'	WMat
- 'Pourpre Noir'	CLnd	'Snowcloud'	ELan LCro LRHS NOra NPip WMou
aff. *prattii*	EBee	'Snowdrift'	CLnd
- SICH 775	WPGP	'Street Parade'	CLnd
'Princeton Cardinal' ♀H6	CLnd CMac EBee EPfP LCro LRHS LSto SPoG WMat	× *sublobata* SUGAR TYME ('Sutyzam')	CLnd CLnd EBee SGol
'Professor Sprenger'	see *M.* × *zumi* 'Professor Sprenger'	'Sun Rival' ♀H6	CCVT CDoC CEnd CLnd CMac
'Profusion'	see *M.* × *moerlandsii* 'Profusion'		EGren ELan EPfP EPom LCro
prunifolia	MBlu WJur		LRHS LSRN MAsh MBlu MPri
- var. *rinkii*	CLnd		NOra SEdi SPoG SRms WHtc
§ × *purpurea*	CLnd		WMat
'Aldenhamensis'		*sylvestris*	CBrac CBTr CBWd CCVT CHab
- APPLETINI	see *M.* × *purpurea* 'Gulliver'		CLnd EGren EHeP IPap LBuc
- 'Crimson Cascade'	CBcs CMac ELan LCro LRHS NOra NPip WMat		LCro LMaj MMuc MSwo NTrD SEdi SEND SEWo SPre WHnu
- 'Eleyi'	SEdi		WJur WKor WMou WRjT
§ - 'Gulliver'	LCro	§ *toringo*	CLnd LMaj NOra WJur
- 'Neville Copeman'	CCVT CLnd EPom LCro LRHS SEdi SSFr	I - var. *arborescens* - 'Brouwers Beauty'	CLnd LMaj
'Ralph Shay'	CLnd	- 'Wooster'	CLnd
'Red Barron'	EBee	*toringoides*	see *M. bhutanica*
'Red Glow'	CAco CLnd LCro	*transitoria*	CCVT CEnd CLnd CMac EBee
'Red Jade'	see *M.* × *scheideckeri* 'Red Jade'		EGren ELan EPfP GKin LCot
RED OBELISK ('Dvp Obel')	CBTr CCVT CLnd EBee EPfP LBuc LCro LMaj NOra NPip SPoG WMat		LRHS LSRN LSto MBlu NLar NOra NPip WHtc WJur WMat WMou
'Red Peacock'	CLnd	- 'Roundabarrow Ruby'	EBee LRHS WPGP
'Red Prince'	see *M. domestica* 'Red Jonaprince'	- 'Thornhayes Tansy' ♀H6	CAda LRHS LSto NOra NPip SPoG WMat
R.J. Fulcher'	CAda	*trilobata*	CCVT EBee EHeP ELan MBlu MGos
'Roberts Crab'	LCro NOra NPip WMat		WJur
§ × *robusta*	CLnd LSRN SRms WJur	- 'Guardsman' ♀H6	CMac EPfP LRHS MPri NOra NPip
- 'Red Sentinel' ♀H6	Widely available		WMat WMou
- 'Red Siberian'	EHeP	*tschonoskii*	CAco CDoC CMac CMCN EGren
- 'Yellow Siberian'	CLnd EPfP		EHeP ELan LMaj MBlu MPri SEdi
'Rosehip'	CEnd CLnd LCro LRHS NOra NPip WMat	- 'Belmonte'	SEND SRms WJur WMat EBee MBlu NPip WMat
'Royal Beauty'	CBTr CLnd EBee EPfP EPom EUrb IPap LMaj LRHS MBlu MPri NOra NPip SEdi WHtc WMat WMou	- 'Van Eseltine' 'Veitch's Scarlet'	CAgr CDoC CMac CSBt LMaj LRHS MAsh MPri NPip SEdi WMat CHab
ROYAL RAINDROPS ('Jfskw5' PBR)	CDoC LRHS	WEEPING CANDIED APPLE ('Weepcanzam')	CLnd SGol
'Royalty'	CAco CBcs CDoC CLnd CWnw EBar EBee EHeP ELan EPom IPap LBuc LCro LMaj LRHS MGos MMuc NOra NPip SEdi SEND SGol WMat	'White Angel' 'White Star' 'Winter Gold' 'Wisley Crab' *yunnanensis*	CLnd CCVT CLnd LMaj NOra NPip WMat WMou CNWT LMaj NPip SEdi CLnd SEdi SKee SRms WJur
'Rudolph'	CBTr CCVT CLnd EBar EBee EHeP ELan EPfP EPom IPap LBuc LCot LCro LMaj LRHS LSRN MAsh MGos MPri NOra NPip SEdi SEND SEWo SPoG WFar WHtc WMat	§ × *zumi* 'Golden Hornet' - 'Professor Sprenger'	Widely available CBTr CLnd EPfP EPom LCro LMaj NOra NPip

Malva (Malvaceae)

sargentii	LMaj NOra WJur
- 'Tina' ♀H6	CLnd CWnw NOra NPip SPoG WMat
alcea	CAgr
- var. *fastigiata*	CMac SRms StAn
arborea	CGwi MCtn

Malva

- 'Rosea'	see *M.* × *clementii* 'Rosea'	- MARINA ('Dema'^{PBR})	NLar
- 'Variegata' (v)	ELan NPer SEND WCot	- var. *mauritiana*	LCro MCtn MHoo NLar NPer
bicolor	see *M. subovata*	- - 'Bíbor Felhő'	CSpe
BLUE BIRD ('Renlav')	MNrw	- - 'Primley Blue'	EBee ELan EPfP GMaP LRHS MBNS
cachemiriana	NPer		NLar NPer WFar WSpi
CHAMALLOW ('Inovera'^{PBR})	LSRN	- - 'Zebrina'	CTtf LRHS LShi MCtn MHoo NPer
× *clementii* 'Barnsley'	CBcs CBrac CDoC CMac EBee		WFar WKit
	ECha EGren EHeP ELan ELon EPfP	- 'Perry's Blue'	NPer
	LCro LRHS LSRN LWaG MAsh	- 'Windsor Castle'	LShi
	MGos MPri NGdn NLar SChF SPoG	*thuringiaca* 'Ice Cool'	SChF
	SRms WFar	*trimestris* 'Loveliness'	MCtn
- 'Barnsley Baby'	CBrac CMac EBee EHeP ELan	- 'Mont Blanc'	GJem MCtn
	EPfP LBom LBuc LCro LSou	- 'Silver Cup' ♀^{H3}	LCro MCtn
	MAsh MPri NLar NPer SPoG	'Variegata'	see *M.* × *clementii* 'Wembdon
	SRkn WFar WLov		Variegated'
- 'Blushing Bride'	EGren LRHS MGos NLar	*verticillata*	MEar
- 'Bredon Springs' ♀^{H5}	CBrac CSBt EBee ECha ELon EPfP	'White Angel'	ELon
	LCro LRHS LSto MGos MPri NGdn		
	SEND WLov	## *Malvastrum* (Malvaceae)	
- 'Burgundy Wine' ♀^{H5}	CBcs CBrac CDoC CMac CSBt EBee	× *hypomadarum*	see *Anisodontea* × *hypomadara*
	EGren ELan EPfP EUrb LBom LCro		(Sprague) D.M. Bates
	LRHS MAsh MGos MPri NBir NLar		
	NPer SPoG WFar WLov WMal	## *Malvaviscus* (Malvaceae)	
- 'Candy Floss' ♀^{H5}	CBrac EGren NLar NPer WFar	*arboreus*	CHll
- 'Eye Catcher'	EPPr NLar		
- 'Kew Rose'	NLar NPer SRms	## *Mammillaria* (Cactaceae)	
- 'Lavender Lady'	EPPr NPer SEND	*decipiens*	SPlb
- 'Mary Hope' ♀^{H4}	CDoC EBee EPfP LBom LRHS MAsh	subsp. *camptotricha*	
	MPri	*elongata* ♀^{H2}	LWaG NCft
- 'Pink Frills'	WCot WFar	*erythrosperma*	SPlb
- RED RUM ('Rigrum') ♀^{H5}	CDoC CMac CSBt EBee EPfP LBom	'Ginsa Maru'	NPlm
	LRHS LSRN MAsh MGos MPri NLar	*glassii*	SPlb
	SPoG WFar	*hahniana* ♀^{H2}	NPlm
§ - 'Rosea' ♀^{H5}	CBcs CBrac CDoC CMac EBee	- subsp. *woodsii*	LCro
	EGren EHeP EPfP LCro LRHS LShi	*prolifera*	SPlb
	LSRN MAsh MGos MPie MPri SDix	*rekoi* subsp. *leptacantha*	SPlb
	SPoG	*rhodantha* subsp. *fera-*	SPlb
- RUBY STAR ('Jostar'^{PBR})	EPfP LRHS LSou MAsh MPri NLar	*rubra*	
§ - 'Wembdon Variegated' (v)	NPer	*scheinvariana*	SPlb
'Frederique'	NLar	*sphacelata*	SPlb
'Grey Beauty'	LRHS LShi MHtn MPri SEND	*surculosa* ♀^{H2}	SPlb
'Magenta Magic'^{PBR}	MHol SPoG	*vetula*	SPlb
MARSHMALLOW CHERRY BLUSH	WLov	- subsp. *gracilis*	SPlb
('Jolavwwe') **new**			
moschata	CAgr CBcs CBWd CGHo CGwi	**mandarin** see *Citrus reticulata* Mandarin Group	
	CTtf ECha EGren ELan ENfk EPfP		
	GJem GJos LCro MAsh MCtn	**mandarin, Cleopatra** see *Citrus reticulata*	
	MEar MHer MNHC NAts NBac		
	NLar NMir SPlb SRms WFar WHer	## *Mandevilla* ✿ (Apocynaceae)	
	WOrg WShi	× *amabilis* 'Alice du	EMdy SPre
§ - f. *alba*	CBcs CSpe CTtf ECha EGren ELan	Pont' ♀^{H1c}	
	ELon EPfP GJos GQue LCro LEdu	- SUNDAVILLE APRICOT	EMdy
	LShi MCtn MHer NBir NLar NLit	('Sunpapri'^{PBR})	
	SPoG SRms WBrk WChS WFar	(Sundaville Series)	
	WHer WKif WShi	*boliviensis* ♀^{H1c}	CRHN
- 'Appleblossom'	MCtn	DIAMANTINA OPALE	LCro
- 'Romney Marsh'	see *Althaea officinalis* 'Romney	FUCHSIA FLAMMÉ	
	Marsh'	('Lanmissouri'^{PBR})	
- 'Rosea'	EPfP GMaP MNHC NPer SPoG StAn	(Diamantina Series)	
- 'Snow White'	see *M. moschata* f. *alba*	§ *laxa* ♀^{H2}	CRHN CTsd EAri EMdy EShb LRHS
multiflora	MCtn		SVen WJur
olbia	SPlb SRms WFar	*sanderi*	SPre
- 'Lilac Lady'	ECha ELan ELon LRHS NLar WFar	*suaveolens*	see *M. laxa*
'Princess Pink' (d)	LRHS WLov	(Sundaville Series)	EMdy
§ *subovata* ♀^{H3}	CDoC CMac EGren LBom LRHS	SUNDAVILLE COSMOS	
	MPri SEND SRkn SRms WCot WFar	CARMINE RED	
- 'Princesse de Lignes'	LRHS	('Sunpararekin'^{PBR})	
sylvestris	CAgr CGwi GJem GJos IDun MCtn	- SUNDAVILLE CREAM PINK	EMdy
	NBac SRms	('Sunparapibra'^{PBR})	
- 'Blue Fountain'^{PBR}	NLar SRms	- SUNDAVILLE EARLY SCARLET	EMdy
- 'Brave Heart'	CTtf	('Sunparaclare'^{PBR})	

- Sundaville Gold ('Sunpa 0931')	EMdy
- Sundaville Pearl ('Patmandewi')	EMdy
- Sundaville Pink ('Sunmandecripi'PBR)	EMdy LCro
- Sundaville Red ('Sunmandecrim'PBR)	EMdy LCro
- Sundaville White ('Sunparacoho')	LCro
(Vogue Series) 'Audrey'PBR	CWGN SPoG
- 'Ginger'	CWGN SPoG
- 'Ruby'	CWGN

Mandragora ✿ (Solanaceae)
autumnalis	GEdr
caulescens	GEdr
§ officinarum	ESwi GEdr

Manettia (Rubiaceae)
cordifolia	EAri

Manfreda see Agave

× Mangave see Agave

Mangifera (Anacardiaceae)
indica (F)	NPlm SPre

Manglietia see Magnolia

mango see Mangifera indica

Manihot (Euphorbiaceae)
carthaginensis	SPlb
grahamii	SPlb

Mantisia (Zingiberaceae)
saltatoria PAB 4208	LEdu WPGP

Maranta (Marantaceae)
arundinacea 'Variegata' (v)	EAri
leuconeura	LBom LCro NHrt WFar
- var. erythroneura ♀H1a	LBom NHrt WFar
- - 'Lemon Lime'	LCro LInT NHrt
- var. kerchoveana ♀H1a	LWaG NHrt
- var. leuconeura 'Fascinator'	LBom LCro LInT LWaG
- 'Silver Band' (v) new	LInT

Marcetella (Rosaceae)
moquiniana	EAri SPlb

Margyricarpus (Rosaceae)
§ pinnatus	EWld WPav
setosus	see M. pinnatus

Mariscus see Cyperus

marjoram, pot see Origanum onites

marjoram, sweet see Origanum majorana

marjoram, wild, or oregano see Origanum vulgare

Marlothistella (Aizoaceae)
uniondalensis new	SPlb

marrow see AGM Vegetables Section

Marrubium (Lamiaceae)
§ bourgaei var. bourgaei 'All Hallows Green'	ECha SRms
candidissimum	see M. incanum
* cylleneum 'Velvetissimum'	WCot
§ incanum	EPPr SPhx
libanoticum	ECha
supinum	SPhx
vulgare	CCBP CGHo CGwi ENfk GQue MHer MHoo MNHC SRms WJek

Marsdenia (Apocynaceae)
oreophila	CBcs CExl CRHN EBee ELan LRHS SEND SPoG WPGP

Marsilea (Marsileaceae)
mutica	EWat
quadrifolia	CBen CWat ELin

Mascarena see Hyophorbe

Massonia (Asparagaceae)
amoena new	LAma
'Bedford' new	LAma
* bredasdorpensis new	LAma
citrina ♀H2 new	LAma
depressa ♀H2	LAma SChF WCot
- 'Kammies Kroon' new	LAma
§ dregei new	LAma
echinata	LAma WCot
hirsuta new	LAma
inaequalis new	LAma
jasminiflora	LAma
latebrosa new	LAma
longipes	LAma WAbe WCot
mimetica new	LAma
obermeyerae new	LAma
'Outeniqua' new	LAma
pseudoechinata	LAma WCot
pustulata ♀H2	LAma MCtn WCot
- purple-leaved	WCot
pygmaea subsp. kamiesbergensis	LAma
roggeveldensis new	LAma
thunbergiana	LAma WCot
visserae	see M. dregei

Mathiasella (Apiaceae)
bupleuroides 'Green Dream'	CBcs CCBP CMHG CSpe EAri EBee EGrl ELan EPfP GBin GMaP LBar LCro MArl MHol Midl MPie MPnt SHor SPel SPoG WCot

Matricaria (Asteraceae)
chamomilla	see M. recutita
parthenium	see Tanacetum parthenium
§ recutita	EHet MCtn MNHC WJek

Matteuccia (Onocleaceae)
orientalis ♀H5	CAby CDTJ CLAP CSta ECha ELan EMor EUrb GArf GMaP ISha LEdu NAlc NBro NLar SPlb SRot WPGP WPnP
pensylvanica	LSto
struthiopteris ♀H5	Widely available
- 'Bedraggled Feathers'	LEdu
- 'Jumbo'	MAsh WPGP
- 'The King'	EBee ISha LRHS WCot

Matthiola (Brassicaceae)

'Apricot' (Excelsior Mammoth Column Series)	LCro MCtn
fruticulosa 'Alba'	EPfP
- subsp. *perennis*	WHil
incana	CBgR LCro SVic WKif
- 'Alba'	EBee ECha ELan EUrb MHol SMHy SPhx
- ANYTIME RED ('Antred') (Anytime Series)	LCro
- ANYTIME YELLOW ('Antyel') (Anytime Series)	MCtn
- 'Appleblossom'	LCro MCtn
- 'Avalanche'	LCro
- Cinderella Series, mixed ♀H4	LCro
- 'Low'	WCot
- 'Pillow Talk'	ECha LShi MCtn WMal
- purple-flowered	LCro
- 'Vintage Brown'	CSpe
- VINTAGE MIXED	MCtn
longipetala	MCtn
- subsp. *bicornis* new	CSpe GJem
scapifera	WAbe
white-flowered, perennial	CSpe NPer

Matucana ✿ (Cactaceae)

aurantiaca subsp. *currundayensis* new	SPlb

Maurandya (Plantaginaceae)

§ *barclayana* ♀H2	EShb
erubescens	see *Lophospermum erubescens*
'Magic Dragon'	see *Lophospermum* 'Magic Dragon'
'Red Dragon'	see *Lophospermum* 'Red Dragon'

Maytenus (Celastraceae)

boaria	CBcs LEdu SArc SEND
magellanica	WPGP

Mazus (Mazaceae)

radicans	EPot StAn
reptans	CBen CPud CWat EBee ELin EPfk GEdr LRHS LShi NLar NPer WFar
- B&SWJ	CExl
- 'Albus'	CPud CWat EBee EGren ELin EPfk GKev LShi NLar SLee SPlb WFar
- 'Blue'	ELin LCro

Meconopsis ✿ (Papaveraceae)

'Andrew Houston'	GEdr
'Arley Hall'	GEdr
'Ascreavie White'	GEdr
§ *baileyi* ♀H5	CBcs EBee GKev LCro Midl NBir
* - var. *alba*	GKev LBar MHol MPro
- 'Hensol Violet'	EWes MCtn WHil
- hybrids	EWld NLit
- mixed	LRHS StAn
'Ballyrogan'	GEdr GKev
betonicifolia misapplied	see *M. baileyi*
'Biggar Park'	GEdr
cambrica	see *Papaver cambricum*
chelidoniifolia	see *Cathcartia chelidoniifolia*
'Cluny White'	GEdr
'Clydeside Early Treasure'	GEdr GKev
× *cookei* 'Old Rose'	GKev GMaP
'Dippoolbank'	GKev
'Edrom'	GEdr
'Edrom White'	GEdr
'Evelyn'	GEdr
(Fertile Blue Group)	see *M.* (Fertile Blue Group)
'Blue Ice'	'Lingholm'
- 'Harry Bush'	GEdr
§ - 'Lingholm' ♀H5	CAby CMiW CTsd EBee EDAr ELan GAbr GEdr GKev GMaP LCro MGos MHol Midl MPro NBid NGdn NLar SPoG
- 'Louise'	GEdr GKev GMaP
- 'Mop-head' ♀H5	GEdr GKev GMaP
gakyidiana	GKev
George Sherriff Group	MCtn
- 'Ascreavie'	GEdr GKev GMaP
- 'Barney's Blue'	GEdr GKev GMaP
- 'Branklyn' ambig	CExl GEdr WPGP
- 'Dalemain' ♀H5	GEdr GKev GMaP
- 'Dorothy Renton' ♀H5	GEdr
- 'Huntfield'	GEdr GKev GMaP
- 'Jimmy Bayne'	GEdr GKev GMaP
§ - 'Susan's Reward' ♀H5	GEdr GKev GMaP
grandis misapplied	see *M.* George Sherriff Group
grandis Prain 'Himal Sky'	GEdr GKev
'Great Glen'	GEdr GKev
aff. *horridula*	MCtn
(Infertile Blue Group)	GEdr GKev GMaP
'Bobby Masterton' ♀H5	
- 'Bryan Conway'	GEdr
- 'Crarae' ♀H5	GEdr GKev GMaP
- 'Crewdson Hybrid'	GEdr GKev GMaP
- 'Cruickshank'	GKev
- 'Dawyck'	see *M.* (Infertile Blue Group) 'Slieve Donard'
- 'Maggie Sharp'	GEdr
- 'Mrs Jebb' ♀H5	GArf GEdr GKev
- 'P.C. Abildgaard' ♀H5	GEdr GKev GMaP
§ - 'Slieve Donard' ♀H5	ENun GArf GEdr GKev GMaP LRHS WPGP
integrifolia subsp. *souliei*	GKev
'Inverewe' ♀H5	GEdr GKev GMaP
'James Aitken'	GKev
'Keillour' ♀H5	GEdr GKev GMaP
'Keillour Violet'	GKev
'Kilbryde Castle White'	GEdr GMaP
'Lunanhead'	GEdr
'Marit' ♀H5	GEdr GKev GMaP
'Mervyn Kessell'	GEdr GKev
'Mildred' ♀H5	GEdr GKev GMaP
'Moonglow'	GEdr
nudicaulis	see *Oreomecon nudicaulis*
'Pride of Angus'	GEdr
punicea	GKev
quintuplinervia ♀H5	GKev
robusta	GKev
× *sheldonii* ambig.	NPer
simplicifolia	GKev
'Stewart Annand'	GEdr GKev GMaP
'Strathspey'	GEdr GKev GMaP
sulphurea	GKev
'Willie Duncan'	GEdr GKev GMaP
wilsonii subsp. *australis*	GKev
zhongdianensis new	GKev

Medeola (Asparagaceae)

virginiana	LAma

Medicago (Fabaceae)

arborea	CAgr SEND SPlb
lupulina	CBWd CHab WOrg
sativa	SVic

Medinilla (Melastomataceae)

magnifica	CDoC LBom LCro

- 'Flamenco'PBR   LBom
- 'Lambada'PBR   LCro

Mediolobivia see *Rebutia*

medlar see *Mespilus germanica*; also AGM Fruit Section

Meehania (*Lamiaceae*)
urticifolia   EBee EMor GEdr WCot WPnP
- B&SWJ 1210   ESwi WCru

Melaleuca (*Myrtaceae*)
acuminata   SPlb
alternifolia   CAgr MHer MHoo SEle SPlb SVen
armillaris   CBcs ELan SEND SPlb
cuticularis   SPlb
decussata   CDoC CTsd SPlb
ericifolia   CTsd SEND SPlb
fulgens   SEle SPlb
gibbosa   CBcs SEle SEND SVen
hypericifolia   SPlb SVen
linariifolia   SPlb
nesophila   SPlb
pungens   SPlb
pustulata   SEle SVen
squamea   SPlb
squarrosa   CBcs ELan SEle SPlb SVen
thymifolia   CAgr SPlb
trichophylla   SPlb

Melampodium (*Asteraceae*)
§ **montanum** AZTEC GOLD   MBNS MPri
  ('Starbini'PBR)
- 'Safari'   LSou
- SANTIAGO BRIGHT YELLOW **new**   MPri
- 'Sunbini'PBR   LSou
- 'Sunlight'   MPri

Melandrium see *Silene*

Melanoselinum (*Apiaceae*)
§ decipiens   CSpe EAri ELan EPfP ESwi MNrw
                SDix WPGP

Melanoseris (*Asteraceae*)
atropurpurea   EBee
- BWJ 7891   GGro
- W&O 8108   GGro
cyanea W&O 9171   GGro
aff. cyanea   EBee

Melanthium (*Melanthiaceae*)
virginicum   MNrw

Melia (*Meliaceae*)
§ azedarach   CBcs SPlb WJur
- var. japonica   see *M. azedarach*

Melianthus (*Francoaceae*)
comosus   CDTJ ESwi EUrb SPlb
major ♀H3   Widely available
villosus   SPlb WPGP

Melica (*Poaceae*)
altissima 'Alba'   CWnw EGren GBin GKev LCro
                    LSto MBel
- 'Atropurpurea'   CWal EBee ECha EMor EPPr GQue
                    LRHS LSto MCtn MWlw SEND SPlb
                    SPoG
ciliata   CBWd CWal EBee ECha EMor EPPr
           GQue LCro LRHS LSto MCtn

cupani   EPPr
nutans   CKno EPPr GMaP MAsh MBel WCot
persica   EPPr
transsilvanica 'Red Spire'   LShi
uniflora   SPhx
- f. albida ♀H7   CKno CSpe ECha EGrl EPPr GKev
                   GMaP LSto MBel NClf SBeP SDix
                   SHor SMHy SPel SPhx WCot WTre
- 'Variegata' (v)   EPPr WCot

Melicytus (*Violaceae*)
alpinus   WJur
angustifolius   WJur
crassifolius   CBcs EBee ELon
obovatus   NLar

Melilotus (*Fabaceae*)
albus   SPhx
officinalis   CHab WHer
- subsp. albus   SPhx

Meliosma (*Sabiaceae*)
dilleniifolia   WJur
- WJC 13819   WCru
- subsp. cuneifolia   CExl
- subsp. dilleniifolia   WPGP
- subsp. tenuis   CExl
myriantha var. discolor   WCru
  MF 97132
pinnata   WJur
- var. oldhamii   CExl
veitchiorum   CExl

Melissa ✿ (*Lamiaceae*)
officinalis   Widely available
- 'All Gold'   ECha EHet ENfk GQue MHoo
                MNHC NBid SPoG SRms SVic WFar
                WJek
- subsp. altissima   CAgr MNHC
§ - 'Aurea' (v)   CCBP CGHo CTsd EHet ELan LSto
                   MEar MHer MHoo MMuc MNHC
                   NBid NBir NBro SPoG SRms WFar
* - 'Compacta'   LEdu
- 'Gold Leaf'   IDun WKit
- 'Lemona'   CAgr EHet IDun SPhx
- 'Lime Balm'   LEdu MHer MHoo MNHC
- 'Mandarina'   CAgr MCtn MHer
- 'Variegata' misapplied   see *M. officinalis* 'Aurea'

Melittis (*Lamiaceae*)
melissophyllum   CAby CSpe CTtf LEdu MAsh MHol
                   MNrw MPnt SHar WCAu WCot
                   WTre
- subsp. albida   EBee LEdu WCot WTor
- 'Cyclamenroze'   SHar
- pink-flowered   LEdu WCot
- 'Royal Velvet   EBee ELan ELon EMor EPfP LBar
  Distinction'PBR   MHer MHol MMrt MPro SHar SPoG
                      WCot WFar WHil WPnP WTor WTre
- white-flowered   LBar SHar WCAu WFar
- 'Wit Laag'   SHar

Melliodendron (*Styracaceae*)
xylocarpum   CExl EPfP WPGP
- pink-flowered   WPGP

Melocactus (*Cactaceae*)
bahiensis   EGren EHap NPlm
broadwayi   LCro
matanzanus   LCro SBig
salvadorensis   SPlb

violaceus SPlb
- subsp. *margaritaceus* SPlb

melon see AGM Vegetables Section

Melothria (Cucurbitaceae)
scabra EAri LCro MCtn SVic
- 'Green Marble' MNHC

Menispermum (Menispermaceae)
dauricum NLar
- B&SWJ 16094 WCru

Mentha ✿ (Lamiaceae)
from Vietnam MMen
angustifolia Corb. see *M.* × *villosa*
angustifolia Host see *M. arvensis*
aquatica CBen CGwi CHab CPud CWal
 CWat ELin EPfk IDun LCro LWaG
 MCtn MHer MMen MWts NAts
 NMir NPer SPlb SRms SVic WHer
 WKit WMAq
- var. *crispa* 'Lothar' MMen
- 'Mandeliensis' CLil CoPl ELin
§ **arvensis** EHet LWaG MHer MMen WKit
 WOrg
- 'Banana' EHet ENfk GQue IDun LCro LShi
 MHer MHoo MMen MNHC SEdi
 SRms SVic WFar WJek WKit
- 'Lemon' LEdu MHer MMen SVic
- var. *piperascens* IDun LEdu MHer MMen SRms WJek
 WKit WPGP
- 'Thai' ENfk IDun LCro MHer MMen SRms
 WJek WKit
'Berries and Cream' EHet ELan ENfk EWhm IDun LCro
 MHer MHoo MMen SRms WJek
'Blackcurrant' ENfk IDun LCro MHer MHoo
 MMen MNHC WKit
Bowles's mint see *M.* × *villosa* var. *alopecuroides*
 Bowles's mint
'Camphor' MMen
× *carinthiaca* MMen
cervina CBen CLil CPud CWat ELin LCro
 LEdu MHer MHoo MMen MWts
 SRms WJek
* - *alba* CLil CPud ENfk MMen MWts WJek
I 'Chocolate Peppermint' CCBP ENfk EWhm IDun LEdu
 MHoo NBir NLar SPhx
citrata see *M.* × *piperita* f. *citrata*
cordifolia see *M.* × *villosa*
corsica see *M. requienii*
crispa L.(1753) see *M. spicata* var. *crispa*
cucumber mint MMen
cunninghamii MMen
'Dionysus' MMen
× *dumetorum* MMen
* **dutomasum** MMen
'Eau de Cologne' see *M.* × *piperita* f. *citrata*
eucalyptus mint MHer MMen
× *gentilis* see *M.* × *gracilis*
§ × *gracilis* EHet ELan ENfk EWhm LWaG
 MBros MEar MMen MPri NLar NSti
 SEdi SRms SVic WFar WKit
- 'Aurea' see *M.* × *gracilis* 'Variegata'
§ - 'Variegata' (v) CCBP CGHo GQue IDun LCro LEdu
 MHer MHoo MMen MNHC MPri
 SPlb WHer WJek WKif
'Grannie's Gloucester' MMen
graveolens MHoo
haplocalyx MMen
* 'Hillary's Sweet Lemon' ECul ENfk LCro MHer MMen SRms

'Jessica's Sweet Pear' EHet ELan ENfk EWhm IDun LCro
 MMen MNHC WKit
'Julia's Sweet Citrus' MHer MMen
lavender mint LEdu MEar MHer MMen MNHC
 SRms
§ **longifolia** ENfk GQue LEdu MCtn MHoo
 MMen MMuc MNHC SPlb SRms
 WKit
- from Crete MMen
- from Lahij, Azerbaijan MMen
- from Vaik, Armenia MMen
- var. *asiatica* MHer MMen
- Buddleia Mint Group CCBP ENfk EWhm LEdu MHer
 MMen NSti WFar WJek
- - variegated (v) MMen WJek
- 'Habek' MMen
- 'Lake Van' MMen
- subsp. *schimperi* MHer MMen SRms WJek WKit
- silver-leaved CTsd LEdu MHer MHoo MMen
 MNHC NBir SEND SRms SVic WFar
 WJek
- 'Tajik Silver' MMen
- var. *teydea* MMen
* - 'Variegata' (v) MHoo SRms
Nile Valley mint SRms
× *piperita* CHby CoPl EGren EHet GJos GQue
 LCro LWaG MHer MHoo MMen
 MNHC MPri SPlb SVic WFar WKit
- 'After Eight' CGHo ECul EHet ELan ENfk IDun
 LCro LShi MHer MMen MNHC
 WFar
- 'Black Mitcham' CCBP MMen SPhx WFar WJek
- black peppermint CAgr CGHo CHby EHet ELan ENfk
 EPfP IDun MEar MHoo MMen
 MMuc MNHC NBir NLar SRms SVic
 WFar WKit
§ - f. *citrata* Widely available
- - 'Basil' CoPl CWal ECul EHet ELan LCro
 LEdu LShi MHer MHoo MMen
 MNHC SEdi SRms SVic WFar WJek
 WKit
- - 'Bergamot' SRms
- - 'Chartreuse' MMen
- - 'Chocolate' CTsd ECul EHet ELan ENfk EPfP
 EWhm GJos GQue LCro LEdu LShi
 LWaG MEar MHer MHoo MMen
 MNHC NPer SEdi SPlb SRms SVic
 WFar WJek WKit
- - 'Freiburger Münsterplatz' MMen
- - 'Granada Orange' MMen
- - 'Grapefruit' CoPl EHet EWhm IDun LCro LShi
 MHer MHoo MMen MNHC SRms
 SVic WKit
- - 'Johannisdorf' MMen
- - 'Lime' CTsd EHet ENfk EWhm LCro LShi
 MHer MHoo MMen MNHC NBir
 SEdi SPlb SRms SVic WFar WJek
 WJun WKit
- - 'Mandarin' MMen
- - 'Nevis' MMen
- - 'Orange' EHet ENfk EWhm GJos LCro LEdu
 MHer MMen MMuc MNHC NPer
 SEdi SRms WJek WKit
- - 'Swiss Ricola' MHer MMen WJek
- 'Logee's' (v) MHoo MMen WFar
- 'Lydia' MMen
- 'Maine-et-Loire' MMen
§ - 'Multimentha' MMen SRms
- f. *officinalis* MNHC
- - 'Aurea' MMen
- 'Pfälzer Kölleda' MMen

- f. *piperita*	MCtn	- 'Thai Bai Saranae'	MMen
- - 'Agnes'	MMen	- subsp. *tomentosa*	MMen
- - 'Eichenau'	MMen	- YAKIMA	MMen
- 'Reine Rouge'	MMen	I 'Strawberry Mint'	CCBP ECul EHet EWhm IDun LEdu
- 'Ricqlès'	MMen		MHer MNHC NBir SEdi SRms WFar
- 'Strawberry'	CCBP CoPl EHet ENfk GJos LCro		WJek WKit
	LWaG MEar MHoo SVic WFar	§ *suaveolens*	CAgr CCBP CGHo CHby EHet ELan
- 'Swiss'	ENfk GJos LCro LWaG MHoo MMen		ENfk GJos GMaP GQue LCro LSto
	NLar SRms WHer WKit		LWaG MBros MEar MHer MHoo
* - var. *vulgaris*	CWal		MMen MNHC SPlb SRms SVic WFar
* - white-flowered	MHoo		WKit
pulegium	CBen CBWd CGHo CPud CWat	- 'Calixte' (v)	MMen
	EHet ELin ENfk EWhm GJos GQue	* - var. *crispa* 'Mojito'	CGHo EHet ELan EWhm MHer
	IDun MCtn MHer MHoo MMen		MMen MNHC
	MNHC SPlb SRms SVic WHer WOrg	* - 'Grapefruit'	CAgr ECul GJos LEdu WFar
- 'Cunningham Mint'	MMen WJek	- 'Jokka'	MMen
- 'Upright'	ENfk MHer MHoo MMen SRms	- 'Le Boues'	MMen
	WJek WKit	* - 'Pineapple'	CGHo CoPl ECul EHet ENfk
- upright, from Portugal	MMen		EWhm IDun LWaG MHoo SVic
§ *requienii*	CCBP CGHo CoPl CTsd ENfk GAbr		WFar WJek
	GJos IDun LCro LEdu LRHS LWaG	- subsp. *timija*	IDun LEdu MHer MHoo MMen
	MCtn MHer MHoo MMen MNHC		SRms WJek WKit
	NBir SDix SPlb SRms SVic WJek	- 'Variegata' (v)	CCBP CGHo CoPl ELan GJos
	WKit WNPC		GMaP GQue LCro LEdu LShi
rotundifolia misapplied	see *M. suaveolens*		LSto MHer MMen MNHC MPri
rotundifolia (L.) Huds.	see *M.* × *villosa*		NSti SPlb SRms WHer WKit
rubra var. *raripila*	see *M.* × *smithiana*	'Sweet Pear'	MHer SRms WJek
'Russian' curled leaf	MHoo MMen	*sylvestris* L.	see *M. longifolia*
- plain leaf	MMen	I 'Tangerine Mint'	LEdu MMen
sachalinensis	MMen SVic	Thüringer minze	see *M.* × *piperita* 'Multimentha'
§ × *smithiana*	GQue LCro MHer MHoo MMen	'Turkish Green'	MMen
	MNHC NBir SRms SVic WFar WJek	§ × *villosa*	CoPl ENfk LCro MMen MMuc
	WKit		SEND
§ *spicata*	Widely available	- var. *alopecuroides*	GQue
- from Cyprus	MMen	§ - - Bowles's mint	CCBP CoPl EWhm LCro LEdu MEar
- from the Berbers, Morocco	MMen		MHer MHoo MMen MNHC NBir
- 'Abura'	MMen		NLar NSti SRms WFar WHer WJek
- Algerian fruity	MMen	- - 'Hollandia'	MMen
- ALMIRA	MMen	- subsp. *villosa*	EHet
- 'Canaries'	MMen	*viridis*	see *M. spicata*
- 'Carmagnola'	MMen		
- 'Cretan'	MMen	## *Mentzelia* (Loasaceae)	
* - var. *crispa*	EHet ENfk IDun MHer MMen	*decapetala*	CSpe
	MNHC SPlb SRms SVic WFar WJek		
- - from Tunisia	MMen	## *Menyanthes* (Menyanthaceae)	
- - 'Moroccan'	CCBP CGHo ECul EHet ENfk	*trifoliata*	CBen CLil CPud CToG CTtf CWat
	EWhm GAbr GBin GJos IDun LCro		ELin EPfk EWat LCro NPer WMAq
	LEdu LWaG MEar MHer MHoo		
	MMen MMuc MNHC MPri NBir	## *Menziesia* see *Rhododendron*	
	NLar SEdi SRms SVic WBrk WKit		
	WTre	## *Mercurialis* (Euphorbiaceae)	
- - 'Regarica'	MMen	*perennis*	WHer WShi
- 'Erdbeere'	WFar		
- subsp. *glabrata*	MMen	## *Merendera* see *Colchicum*	
'Deli Mona'		*pyrenaica*	see *Colchicum montanum* L.
- 'Guernsey'	MMen SRms		
- 'Hugo'	MMen	## *Merremia* (Convolvulaceae)	
- 'Kentucky Colonel'	LCro LEdu MMen	*tuberosa*	EAri MCtn
- 'Mexican'	MMen		
- 'Newbourne'	MMen SRms	## *Merrilliopanax* ✿ (Araliaceae)	
- 'Nile Valley'	MMen WJek	*alpinus* B&SWJ 13906	WCru
- 'Russian'	CAgr SVic WFar	- B&SWJ 13939	WCru
- 'Spanish'	ECul EHet MMen NLar SRms WFar	*membranifolius*	WPGP
	WKit		
- 'Spanish Furry'	MHer	## *Mertensia* (Boraginaceae)	
- 'Spanish Pointed'	CGHo WKit	*lanceolata*	GEdr
- 'Stavordale'	MMen	§ *maritima*	CEls CSpe EBee EWes GKev MCtn
- 'Tashkent'	CCBP CGHo CHby EHet ENfk		SPlb SRms WHoo
	EWhm LCro LEdu LSto MHer	- subsp. *asiatica*	see *M. maritima*
	MHoo MMen MNHC SRms WFar	*pterocarpa*	see *M. sibirica*
	WHer WJek	*pulmonarioides*	see *M. virginica*

§	*sibirica*	GKev SPlb
§	*virginica* ♀H4	CMiW CSpe EBee EBlo EGrI EPot
		GKev ISha LAma LBar LCro LEdu
		LRHS MNrw NLar NSti SRms WFar
		WTre
	viridis	SPlb

Merwilla (Asparagaceae)
§ *dracomontana* — WCot
§ *plumbea* — WCot

Merxmuellera (Poaceae)
cincta — see *Capeochloa cincta*
macowanii — WPGP

Mesembryanthemum (Aizoaceae)
sp. — MAsh
brownii — see *Lampranthus brownii*
criniflorum — see *Cleretum bellidiforme*
crystallinum — MCtn MPri

Mespilus ✿ (Rosaceae)
germanica (F) — CHab CLnd CMCN CNWT IPap LMaj MSwo NLar WJur
- 'Bredase Reus' (F) — ELan LCro SKee
- 'Dutch' (F) — SKee
- 'Flanders Giant' (F) — CAgr WMat
- 'Iranian' (F) ♀H6 — CAgr SKee
- 'Large Russian' (F) — CAgr
- 'Macrocarpa' (F) — SKee
- 'Nottingham' (F) ♀H6 — CAda CAgr CBcs CBTr CCVT CDoC CEnd CHab CSBt EBee EGren ELan EPfP EPom LBuc LCro MAsh MGos MMuc NOra SBmr SEdi SEND SEWo SKee SPoG SSFr SVic WFar WMat
- 'Royal' (F) — CAgr LCro NLar NOra SKee WMat
- SIBLEY'S PATIO MEDLAR (F) — EPom
- 'Westerveld' (F) — CAgr CLnd EPom LCro LMaj SKee

Metapanax ✿ (Araliaceae)
davidii — CBct CExl EBee SPlb WJur WPGP
delavayi — CBct CExl EBee WPGP

Metaplexis (Apocynaceae)
japonica — SBrt

Metasequoia ✿ (Cupressaceae)
glyptostroboides — Widely available
- 'All Bronze' — CAco NLar
- AMBER GLOW ('Wah-08ag'PBR) — EUrb NLar
- 'Blue-isch' — NLar
- 'Chubby'PBR — CAco EPfP
- 'Daweswood Tawny Fleece' — CAco NLar
- 'Fastigiata' — see *M. glyptostroboides* 'National'
- GOLD RUSH — see *M. glyptostroboides* 'Golden Oji'
- 'Golden Dawn' — NLar
- GOLDEN MANTLE — see *M. glyptostroboides* 'Golden Oji'
§ - 'Golden Oji' ♀H7 — CAco CBcs CMac ELan EPfP EUrb LRHS MAsh MBlu MGos MMrt MPri NCth NLar NOra NPip SMad SPoG WFar WHtc WMat
- 'Hamlet's Broom' — NLar
- 'Little Creamy' (v) — CAco NLar
- 'Little Giant' — MBlu
- 'Matthaei' — CAco MAsh MBlu
- 'McCracken's White' — see *M. glyptostroboides* 'Snow Flurry'
- 'Miss Grace' — CAco NLar
§ - 'National' — MBlu
- 'Schirrmann's Nordlicht' — MAsh NLar
- 'Sheridan Spire' — CEnd MBlu
§ - 'Snow Flurry' (v) — NLar
- 'Waasland' — MBlu
- 'White Spot' (v) — MBlu

Metrosideros (Myrtaceae)
carminea — CTsd SEle
§ *excelsa* — CHll SEle
- 'Parnell' — CBcs
- 'Variegata' (v) — CHll
kermadecensis — SEle
- 'Sunninghill' (v) **new** — EAri
- 'Twisty' (v) — SEle
- 'Variegata' (v) — SEle
lucida — see *M. umbellata*
robusta — SPlb
- *aureovariegata* (v) — EShb
× *subtomentosa* 'Mistral' — WPGP
tomentosa — see *M. excelsa*
§ *umbellata* — CBcs EBee
- 'Gold Nugget' — SSta
- MOONLIGHT ('Lowmoo') — SEle SIvy

Meum (Apiaceae)
athamanticum — CSpe ELan EPfP EPPr LEdu MHol SPhx StAn WJek

Michauxia (Campanulaceae)
campanuloides — CSpe EDAr
tchihatcheffii — CDTJ

Michelia see Magnolia
chingii — see *Magnolia maudiae*
fulgens — see *Magnolia foveolata*
wilsonii — see *Magnolia ernestii*

Micranthemum (Scrophulariaceae)
micranthemoides — ELin

Micranthes (Saxifragaceae)
§ *manchuriensis* — GKev
§ *mertensiana* — EAri NBir

Microbiota (Cupressaceae)
decussata ♀H7 — CAco CBcs CSBt LRHS WFar
- CELTIC PRIDE — see *M. decussata* 'Prides'
- 'Gold Spot' (v) — CAco MBlu WFar
- 'Lucas'PBR — CAco
§ - 'Prides' — CAco
- 'Sibirteppe' — CAco

Microglossa (Asteraceae)
albescens — see *Aster albescens*

Microlepia (Dennstaedtiaceae)
strigosa — CLAP ISha LEdu WPGP
- 'MacFaddeniae' ♀H4 — LEdu WPGP

Micromeria (Lamiaceae)
sp. — SRms
fruticosa — WJek
rupestris — see *M. thymifolia*
thymifolia — CAgr SPlb

Micromyrtus (Myrtaceae)
navicularis — WJur

Microseris (Asteraceae)
ringens hort. — see *Leontodon rigens*

Microsorum (*Polypodiaceae*)
§ *diversifolium* — CDoC EShb LBom LCro LEdu LRHS SPlb WPGP
musifolium — CDoC NHrt
'Crocodyllus'^PBR
pteropus — ELin
- 'Windeløv' — ELin
pustulatum — WCot

Microstegium (*Poaceae*)
vimineum — Prohibited invasive. See Conservation and the Environment, p.42

Microtropis (*Celastraceae*)
petelotii HWJ 719 — WCru

Milium (*Poaceae*)
effusum 'Aureum' ♀H7 — Widely available
- 'Yaffle' (v) — CKno EBee EPPr

Millettia (*Fabaceae*)
reticulata — see *Wisteriopsis reticulata*

Mimetes (*Proteaceae*)
chrysanthus — SPlb
cucullatus — CPbh

Mimosa (*Fabaceae*)
sp. — NTrD
acanthocarpa — WJur
aculeaticarpa **new** — WJur
pudica — CDoC CDTJ LCro LWaG MCtn

Mimulus (*Phrymaceae*)
'Andean Nymph' — see *M. naiandinus*
§ *aurantiacus* ♀H2 — CMac CSpe EShb NGKo NPer SPlb SPoG SRms WFar WMal
- (Mai Tai Series) MAI TAI ORANGE **new** — LSou
- - MAI TAI RED ('Dmimmitird') **new** — LSou
'Bonfire' — LCro
cardinalis ♀H4 — CLil CWat ELan ELin EPfP EWes EWld GEdr GKev MCtn WCot
- 'Red Dragon' — MHol
- yellow-flowered — CoPl
cupreus 'Rote Kaiser' — ELin LCro
- 'Whitecroft Scarlet' ♀H4 — LShi
'Eleanor' — EShb WMal
glutinosus — see *M. aurantiacus*
- *atrosanguineus* — see *M. puniceus*
- *luteus* — see *M. aurantiacus*
§ *guttatus* — ELin LCro NPer WMAq
'Highland Orange' — MAsh SPoG
'Highland Pink' — MAsh SPoG
'Highland Red' ♀H4 — MAsh SPoG
'Highland Yellow' — SPoG
hose-in-hose (d) — NPer
langsdorffii — see *M. guttatus*
lewisii ♀H3 — MNrw SRms
luteus — CLil CWat LCro LShi NPer WBrk WFar
- 'Queen's Prize' — GQue
- 'Variegatus' ambig. (v) — NPer
Magic Series — SVic
§ *naiandinus* ♀H4 — GKev LShi SPlb
'Orange Glow' — LShi
'Popacatapetl' — CSpe WMal
primuloides — EDAr EWes SPlb
§ *puniceus* — SChF WFar WMal

ringens — CBen CLil CPud CWat EBee ELin EPfk LShi NBir NPer SPlb SRms WMAq
'Tigrinus' — ELin

Mina see *Ipomoea*

mint, apple see *Mentha suaveolens*

mint, basil see *Mentha × gracilis*

mint, Bowles's see *Mentha × villosa* var. *alopecuroides* Bowles's mint

mint, curly see *Mentha spicata* var. *crispa*

mint, eau-de-Cologne see *Mentha × piperita* f. *citrata*

mint, emperor's see *Micromeria*

mint, ginger see *Mentha × gracilis*

mint, horse or long-leaved see *Mentha longifolia*

mint, round-leaved see *Mentha suaveolens*

Minuartia (*Caryophyllaceae*)
parnassica — see *M. stellata*
§ *stellata* — EPot GArf GKev
verna subsp. *caespitosa* — see *Sagina subulata* var. *glabrata* 'Aurea'
'Aurea'

Miqueliopuntia (*Cactaceae*)
miquelii — SPlb

Mirabilis (*Nyctaginaceae*)
dichotoma — EShb
jalapa — EBee EGren LAma MCtn SAth SEND SRms XFar
- 'Broken Colours' — CoPl
longiflora — EShb LCro SBrt
multiflora — WHil

Miscanthus ✿ (*Poaceae*)
capensis — SPlb
chejuensis B&SWJ 8803 — WCru
flavidus — ESwi SRms
- B&SWJ 6749 — EPPr
floridulus misapplied — see *M. × giganteus*
floridulus ambig. — EHeP EUrb MMuc MNrw SPlb
§ × *giganteus* — CKno ELon EPPr EUrb GBin GElm LBom LRHS MAsh MNrw MWht SVic WCot
- ALLIGATOR ('Lottum'^PBR) (v) — EUrb LCro WFar
- 'Gilt Edge' (v) — ELon EPPr WCot
- 'Gotemba' (v) — ELon EPPr
- 'Jubilar' (v) — MWht
- 'Meidl' — SAko
lutarioriparius — SBig WPGP
nepalensis — CAby CElw CExl CKno CMiW CSde CSpe CTsd EBee ECha ELan EMor EPfP EPPr EWes GBin LCro LEdu LRHS MAvo MNrw NCIf NDov SDix SHor SMad SMHy SPlb SRms WPGP
- 'Shikola' — WCru
nudipes — EPPr ESwi
§ *oligostachyus* 'Afrika' — EPPr MNrw WPGP

I	- 'Nanus'	WCot
	'Purpurascens'	CKno ECha ELan EPfP GPSL LRHS LSRN SPel
§	'Rosi'	CKno EPPr SMHy SNoN SPel WPGP
	sacchariflorus misapplied	see *M.* × *giganteus*
	sacchariflorus ambig.	CBcs CKno EBee ECha ELan EPfP MBrN SPeP
	sacchariflorus (Maxim.) Hack.	LEdu WPGP WSpi
	sinensis	CWal MCtn SAth StAn WFar
	- CL 1325	EPPr
	- 'Abundance'	CKno EPfP EPPr
	- 'Adagio' ♀H6	CBWd CDor CKno CSde EGren ELan ELon EPfP EPPr EWhm GKev LRHS MWlw SPoG SRms WCot
	- 'Afrika'	see *M. oligostachyus* 'Afrika'
	- 'Aldebaran'	EPPr
	- 'Andante'	CKno
	- 'Arabesque'	EPPr SMHy
	- 'Augustfeder'	EPPr
	- 'Autumn Light'	EPPr
	- 'Beth Chatto'	ECha EPPr LEdu SMHy SPel WPGP
	- 'Blütenwunder'	EBee EPPr
	- 'Bogenlampe'	EBee EPPr
	- 'Boucle'	MBNS SPeP XFar
	- 'Brazil' PBR	EBee LCro LRHS MPro WFar
	- 'China' ♀H6	CKno ELon EPfP EPPr EWes GKev LEdu LRHS MAsh MNrw MWlw NCth SMHy SPel SRms WHoo
	- 'Cindy'	CKno EPfP EPPr LRHS
	- var. *condensatus*	CBcs CKno EBee ELan EPfP EPPr EUrb GMaP LEdu LSRN NLar NSti SPoG WCot WFar WSpi
	'Cabaret' (v)	
	- - 'Central Park'	see *M. sinensis* var. *condensatus* 'Cosmo Revert'
§	- - 'Cosmo Revert'	EPPr
	- - 'Cosmopolitan' (v) ♀H6	CDoC CKno CSde EAri ELan ELon EMor EPPr EWes GMaP LBom LCro LEdu LRHS LSRN MMuc MNrw SDix SEND WCot
	- - 'Emerald Giant'	see *M. sinensis* var. *condensatus* 'Cosmo Revert'
	- 'Cute One'	ELan LEdu LRHS MBNS Midl SBea WFar
	- 'David'	ELon EPPr
	- 'Dixieland' (v)	CKno ELan ELon EPPr EWes NLar SMHy
	- 'Dreadlocks'	EBee EMor EPPr LEdu MNrw
	- 'Dronning Ingrid'	CKno ECha EPPr MNrw WHil
	- 'Elfin'	CKno EPPr
	- 'Emmanuel Lepage'	CKno EPPr MAvo NClf
	- 'Etincelle'	ELon EWes
	- 'Ferner Osten' ♀H6	Widely available
	- 'Fire Dragon' **new**	LRHS
	- 'Flamingo' ♀H6	CExl CKno CMac CMiW EBee EGren ELan ELon EPfP EPPr GElm GMaP LRHS MAsh MBel MNrw MSwo MWlw NDov NGdn NLar SArc SBea SDix SMHy SRms WCau WFar WHoo WSpi
	- 'Flammenmeer'	EPPr LRHS
*	- 'Foehn' **new**	EBlo
	- 'Gearmella'	EPPr
	- 'Gewitterwolke' ♀H6	EWes
	- 'Ghana' ♀H6	CSpe ECha ELon EPfP EPPr EUrb LEdu Midl MNrw SMHy SPoG SRms WFar WPGP
	- 'Giraffe'	CDTJ ELon LRHS MWlw
	- 'Gnome'	CKno ELon EPfP EPPr LRHS MAsh SRms WFar
	- 'Gold Bar' PBR (v)	CWGN ECha ELan ELon EPfP EUrb LCro LRHS LSRN MAsh MBNS NGdn NLar SPoG WFar
	- 'Gold Breeze' PBR	CDoC LRHS
	- 'Golden Fleece'	EWes
	- 'Goldfeder' (v)	EWes
	- 'Goliath'	ELon EPPr GElm NLar
	- 'Gracillimus'	CBcs CKno CMac CSde EBee ECha EGren EHeP ELan ELon EPPr EUrb EWes LCro LRHS LSto LWaG MSwo NBro NClf NGdn NLar SArc SAth SRms WCha WCot WFar WSpi XFar
	- 'Gracillimus Nanus'	LWaG
	- 'Graziella'	CEnd CKno EPPr LRHS MAsh SArc SRms WFar
	- 'Grosse Fontäne' ♀H6	ELon EPPr EUrb LEdu LSRN NLar WCot
	- 'Haiku'	EPPr LEdu
	- 'Hercules'	EPPr
	- 'Hermann Müssel'	EPPr EWes
§	- 'Hinjo' (v)	ECha ELon EPfP EPPr GKev LRHS MAsh NGdn WCot
I	- 'Jubilaris' (v)	ELon EPPr
	- 'Juli'	EPPr WSpi
	- 'Kaskade' ♀H6	CKno EBlo EGren EPPr LEdu MBel NDov NLar
	- 'Kleine Fontäne' ♀H6	CKno EBee ELan ELon EPfP EPPr EUrb IArd LBom LCro LEdu LRHS LSRN LSto MAsh MMuc MNrw NLar NSti SMHy WCAu WCot WFar WPGP WSpi
	- 'Kleine Silberspinne' ♀H6	CKno CSde EBee EGren EHeP ELon EPfP EPPr GKev GMaP LBom LCro LRHS LSRN LSto MBel MGos MMuc MPri MWlw NGdn SBig SDix SEND SRms WHoo WOld WSpi WTre
	- 'Korea'	EPPr
	- 'Krater'	ECha ELon EPPr MBrN NClf
	- 'Kupferberg'	NLar
	- 'Kupferzwerg'	EBee EPPr
§	- 'Little Kitten'	ELon EPPr LEdu SRms
	- LITTLE NICKY	see *M. sinensis* 'Hinjo'
	- 'Little Zebra' PBR (v)	CDoC EPPr EUrb GMaP LRHS MGos SRms WCha
	- 'Malepartus'	Widely available
	- 'Memory'	CKno EPPr NClf
	- 'Moonlight'	LRHS
	- 'Morning Light' (v) ♀H6	Widely available
	- 'Mysterious Maiden' PBR (v)	EWes
	- 'Navajo' PBR	CSpe EAri ECha ELan EPfP EUrb IPot LRHS MBNS SBea SDix WPGP
	- NEIL LUCAS ('Nica 20') **new**	ELan EWes
	- 'Nippon'	EPfP EPPr GBin LRHS MAsh NGdn NLar WCAu WSpi
	- 'Nishidake'	CKno ELon EPPr
	- 'November Sunset'	ECha EPPr
	- 'Overdam'	NGdn
	- PINK CLOUD ('Empmis02' PBR)	EGren WFar XFar
	- 'Poseidon'	ECha EPPr SNoN
	- 'Positano'	ELon EPPr
	- 'Professor Richard Hansen'	CKno ELon EPPr EWes
	- 'Pünktchen' (v)	ELon EPPr SRms
	- 'Purple Fall'	CBWd CDor CSpe EBee ECha GMaP IPot LEdu LRHS MNrw SPeP WFar WPGP
	- 'Red Bere'	WPGP
	- 'Red Chief'	CKno CMiW EAri ECha EGren ELon EPfP EPPr EUrb EWes GElm

	LRHS MAvo MNrw MSwo MWlw NLar SBig WCha WCot WTor
- Red Cloud ('Emppis01'^PBR)	CBcs EGren LCro LRHS NDov SMad WFar XFar
- 'Red Meister'	EPfP EPPr
- 'Red Spear'	CKno
- 'Red Tower'	ELan
- Red Zenith ('Robnith')	CAbb EHeP EWes LCro WPGP
- 'Roland'	ELon EPPr
- 'Rosi'	see *M.* 'Rosi'
- 'Roterpfeil'	EPPr EUrb NLar
- 'Rotfeder'	EPPr
- 'Rotfuchs'	CMac SMHy
- 'Rotsilber'	CKno ECha EPfP EPPr GMaP IArd LEdu MAsh MMuc NLar SRms WHoo WOld WPGP
- Ruby Cute ('Rica 20')	ESwi WTor
- 'Samurai'	EPPr
- 'Sarabande' ♀H6	EPPr NLar WSpi
- 'Septemberrot' ♀H6	EPPr MMuc SEND
- 'Serim'	EPPr
§ - 'Silberfeder' ♀H6	CEnd CKno EBee ECha EGrI EHeP ELan ELon EPfP EPPr GMaP LRHS LSRN MAsh MBrN MGos MMuc MNrw NSti SDix SPlb SPoG WCAu WCot WFar
- 'Silberspinne'	CWnw EBee ELon EPPr SPlb
- 'Silberturm'	EPPr
- 'Silver Charm' **new**	XFar
- Silver Cloud ('Emppis03'^PBR)	EGren WFar
- Silver Feather	see *M. sinensis* 'Silberfeder'
- 'Silver Sceptre'	MAvo MWlw
- 'Silver Stripe'	EPPr
- 'Sioux'	EPfP EPPr WCAu
- 'Sirene'	EPPr MMuc NBir
- 'Spätgrün'	EPPr
- 'Starlight'	CKno EPPr LRHS
- 'Strictus' (v) ♀H6	Widely available
- Sunlit Satin ('Robtin')	CAbb LCro LSou WFar WPGP
- 'Super Stripe' (v)	EPPr
- 'Taiwan'	EBee EPPr
- 'Tiger Cub' (v)	EPPr
- 'Undine' ♀H6	EPfP EPPr MBel MBrN MMuc
- 'Vanilla Sky'	EWes
- 'Variegatus' (v)	ECha EGren ELan ELon EPfP EPPr GMaP LSRN MMuc NGdn NLar NSti SDix SPoG SRms WCot WSpi
- 'Vorläufer'	EPPr
- 'Westacre Wine'	EPPr EWes
- 'Wetterfahne'	EPPr
- 'Yaka Dance'^PBR	NLar NLit
§ - 'Yaku-jima'	ECha ELan EPPr GBin MGos MWht SMad WFar
- 'Yakushima Dwarf'	CEnd CExl EGren ELan ELon EMor EPfP EPPr EUrb GKev LRHS NClf NSti SBea SMHy SPel SRms WCot WHoo WOld
- 'Zebrinus' (v) ♀H6	Widely available
- 'Zwergelefant'	CKno
'Smokey Embers'	MNrw
transmorrisonensis	EBee EPPr LEdu LRHS MWlw NDov SPel WCot WOld WPGP
- 'Sunset'	CKno
- 'Taoshan'	LEdu
yakushimensis	see *M. sinensis* 'Little Kitten', 'Yaku-jima'

Mitchella (Rubiaceae)

repens	CBcs EBee EPot GEdr LWaG

Mitella (Saxifragaceae)

acerina B&SWJ 11029	EWld GGro WCru
breweri	CDor CMac EBee ECha EWld MPnt NSti WFar
caulescens	NBro
formosana B&SWJ 125	WCru
furusei var. *subramosa* B&SWJ 11097	GGro WCru
× *inami* B&SWJ 11122	GGro WCru
japonica B&SWJ 4971	WCru
- 'Variegata' (v)	GGro
kiusiana	WFar
- B&SWJ 5401	GGro WFar
- B&SWJ 5888	WCru
makinoi	ECha EWld
- B&SWJ 4992	CExl GGro WCru
ovalis	ECha GGro WCot
pauciflora B&SWJ 6361	WCru
- B&SWJ 11067	GGro
stylosa B&SWJ 5669	WCru
- PB 04-301	EWld GGro
yoshinagae	WFar
- B&SWJ 4893	CExl EPPr WCru

Mitraria (Gesneriaceae)

coccinea	CDoC CExl CMac CRHN CTsd GEdr GKev MBlu NLar SPlb
- Clark's form	NLar SIvy
- 'Lago Puyehue'	CBcs CDoC CExl EBee EPfP EUrb SPlb SVen WFar
- 'Lake Caburgua'	ELon EWld NLar WAbe WPav

Modiolastrum (Malvaceae)

lateritium	CRHN CSpe CTtf EBee EGrI EPPr LCro MMrt MNrw NBir NLar SIvy SPhx SPoG SRms

Moehringia (Caryophyllaceae)

muscosa	WCot

Molinia ✿ (Poaceae)

altissima	see *M. caerulea* subsp. *arundinacea*
caerulea	CCps CKno EGrI EPPr LRHS MBlu MCtn
§ - subsp. *arundinacea*	CCps CFis CKno CSpe EPPr WChS
- - 'Bergfreund'	CKno EPPr ESwi GBin LSto NLar SMHy
- - 'Black Arrows'	EBee ECha GBin NClf NDov SMHy
- - 'Breeze'	CKno ELon EPPr
- - 'Cordoba'	EBee ECha EPPr GQue MWlw WFar
- - 'Crystal Veil'	NDov
- - 'Fontäne'	ECha EPPr GQue MAvo MWlw
- - 'Golden Chimes'	EPPr
- - 'JS Mostenveld' (v)	CKno ECha ELon EPPr WFar
- - 'JS Witches Broom'	EPPr
- - 'JS Yellow Pipe'	ECha
- - 'Karl Foerster'	CBWd CCps CDor CKno CWnw EBee ELon EMor EPfP EPPr EUrb EWhm GBin GElm GMaP GQue LRHS LSRN MAsh MNrw NBid NLar SBea SMHy WCAu WCot WPnP
- - 'Les Ponts de Cé'	ECha EPPr
- - 'Liebreiz'	CKno EPPr
- - 'Skyracer' ♀H7	CKno CSde ELan ELon EMor EPPr EUrb GBin GMaP GQue LRHS MBel MNrw NCth NLar SPoG WCot WPGP
- - 'Sunbeam'	EPPr
- - 'Tears of Joy'	EBee ECha ELon EPPr

Molinia

- - 'Transparent' ♀H7 — Widely available
- - 'Windsaule' — CKno ECha ELon EPPr MAvo NDov
- - 'Windspiel' ♀H7 — CAby CSde CWCL EGrI ELon EPfP EPPr GBin GQue MAsh MAvo MNrw SPoG WCAu WCot WFar
- - 'Zuneigung' — ECha ELon EPPr MAvo
- subsp. *caerulea* — EPfP EPPr StAn
- - 'Carmarthen' (v) — ELon
- - 'Claerwen' (v) — ECha ELon
- - 'Coneyhill Gold' (v) — EPPr
- - 'Dark Defender' — ECha LEdu NDov SMHy SPel
- - 'Dauerstrahl' — CBWd CKno EPPr GMaP GQue LEdu LRHS MAsh MBel MNrw NBid NCth NDov SMHy
- - 'Edith Dudszus' ♀H7 — CBWd CCps CKno ECha EGren ELan ELon EMor EPPr GQue LRHS MAvo MBel MBrN MWlw NClf NDov WCAu WFar WPnP WTor WTre
- - 'Heidebraut' — CBWd CCps ECha ELon EPfP EPPr GMaP GQue LCro LRHS MAvo MBel NLar SMHy WCot WFar
- - 'Heidezwerg' — ECha ELon EPPr GQue LRHS
- - 'Heinrichs Dauerstrahl' — EPPr
- - 'Moorflamme' — ELon LCro MAvo
- - 'Moorhexe' ♀H7 — CBWd CCps CDor CWnw EBee ECha EGren ELon EMor EPfP GBin GKev GMaP GQue MWlw NBid NGdn NLar NSti SPel WCAu WCot WFar WHoo
- - 'Overdam' — CKno EMor MNrw NDov
- - 'Poul Petersen' ♀H7 — CKno ELan MBel NClf NDov WHoo
- - 'Rotschopf' — NLar
- - 'Strahlenquelle' — CFis EPPr GQue LSto MArl WCAu WFar
- - 'Variegata' (v) ♀H7 — CCps CMac EBee ECha EGren EHeP ELan ELon EPfP GBin GMaP GQue LRHS MBrN MGos NBro NSti SPlb SRms WCAu WFar WHoo
- 'Torch'PBR — CKno WFar
- 'Winterfreude' — EPPr
- *litoralis* — see *M. caerulea* subsp. *arundinacea*

Molopospermum (Apiaceae)
- *peloponnesiacum* — CSpe EBee ELan EPPr IPot LEdu LRHS MCtn SBrt SDix SHor SMHy SPhx SPlb WCru WPGP

Moltkia (Boraginaceae)
- § *doerfleri* — NBir SBeP WPGP
- § × *intermedia* ♀H4 — SMrm WAbe
- *petraea* — EDAr

Moluccella (Lamiaceae)
- *laevis* — CSpe LCro MCtn SVic

Monadenium see *Euphorbia*

Monanthes ❀ (Crassulaceae)
- *laxiflora* — WCot

Monarda ❀ (Lamiaceae)
- 'Adam' — NLar
- 'André Eve' — WMon
- 'Aquarius' — GQue LSto MHol NLar WCAu WFar WMon
- 'Baby Spice' — WFar
- § 'Balance' — EBee LRHS NGdn WCAu
- 'Beauty of Cobham' ♀H4 — CBWd CDor EBee ECha EGrI ELan EPfP EWhm GMaP LCro MAvo MGos MHer MHol MPro NDov NLar SBea SRms WCAu WChS WFar WMon
- 'Bergamo' — CSpe LCro MCtn MPro
- 'Berry Taffy' (Sugar Buzz Series) **new** — MPro
- § 'Blaustrumpf' — EGrI EPfP EWes LRHS WFar WMon
- 'Blue Moon' (Sugar Buzz Series) — EBlo EPfP IPot LBar LRHS LSou MHoo MPro NCth WMon
- BLUE STOCKING — see *M.* 'Blaustrumpf'
- BOWMAN — see *M.* 'Sagittarius'
- *bradburyana* — CAgr EBee
- - 'Indian's Footprint' **new** — IPot
- - 'Maramek' — EBee NLar
- 'Cambridge Scarlet' — Widely available
- 'Camilla' — WGoo WMon
- 'Capricorn' — WMon
- 'Cherokee' — WFar WMon
- *citriodora* — EHet IDun LCro MCtn MHoo NSti SRms
- 'Comanche' — WFar WMon
- 'Croftway Pink' — CAby CBcs CMac ECha EGren EGrI EHeP ELan EPfP GMaP GQue LCro LShi LSto MArl MHoo Midl MNHC WCAu WCav WFar WMon
- 'Danish Dark' — IPot
- I 'Dark Ponticum' — WMon
- 'Deep Purple' — NDov
- *didyma* — ENfk MCtn MHoo MNHC NBro SRms StAn WFar
- - 'Alba' — WMon
- - (Balmy Series) BALMY LILAC ('Balbalmac'PBR) — EGren ELan LRHS MHol MPro SMrm SPoG WHil WMon
- - BALMY PINK ('Balbalmink'PBR) — EGren LRHS MHoo MPri MPro SPoG WHil WMon
- - BALMY PURPLE ('Balbalmurp'PBR) — EGren LRHS MHol MHoo MPro SPoG WFar WHil WMon
- - BALMY ROSE ('Balbalmose'PBR) — EGren EPfP LRHS MPro WHil WMon
- - (Bee-You Series) BEE-BRIGHT ('Monbebr') — ELin GPSL MAsh NEoE WMon
- - BEE-FREE ('Mon0012bfr'PBR) — CWGN MAsh SRkn WMon
- - BEE-HAPPY ('Mon0001bha'PBR) — CWGN ELin MAsh Midl MNrw MPie NCth NEoE NLar SPeP SRkn WHil WMon WPGP
- - BEE-LIEVE ('Mon0004bli'PBR) — ELin MMrt MNrw NLar NSti WHil WMon
- - BEE-MERRY IMPROVED — NCth WHil WMon
- - BEE-PRETTY ('Monard0044'PBR) — WHil WMon
- - BEE-PURE ('Monard0039'PBR) — GMaP LRHS Midl WHil WMon
- - BEE-TRUE ('Mon0005btr'PBR) — CWGN ELin Midl MNrw NLar SPeP SRkn WHil WMon
- 'Bubblegum Blast' (Sugar Buzz Series) — EBlo ELan LBar LCro LRHS MPro NCth WMon
- 'Cherry Pops' (Sugar Buzz Series) — WMon
- 'Coral Reef' — WFar WMon
- 'Cranberry Lace'PBR — ELan EPfP MHol MPro NLar SPoG WCAu WMon
- DANCING BIRD ('Allmobird'PBR) — EPfP LRHS MPro NSti WMon
- 'Grape Gumball'PBR (Sugar Buzz Series) — EBee LBar MPro NCth WMon
- 'Lilac Lollipop' (Sugar Buzz Series) — WMon
- 'Melua Appleblossom' — LBar WMon
- 'Melua Burgundy' — LBar MPro WMon
- 'Melua Pink' — MPro WMon

- 'Melua Violet'	LBar MBel MPro WMon		§	'Oneida' ♀H4	CMHG EAri EBee ECha ELan EpfP EWhm GMaP LCro MBel MHer MHol MPie NBro NDov NGdn NLar SRkn WFar WMon
- (Pardon My Series)	WFar				
'Pardon My Cerise'					
- - 'Pardon My Lavender'	WMon				
- - 'Pardon My Pink'	EBee WMon			'Othello'	EPfP NDov WGoo WMon
- - 'Pardon My Purple'	NLar SPoG WMon			'Ou Charm'	EWes MBel NLar WCAu WFar WMon
- 'Pink Lace' PBR	EGren ELan EPfP MHol MPro NLar NSti SPoG WCAu WFar WMon			Panorama Series	MCtn SPlb WMon
- 'Purple Lace' PBR	EPfP LCro MPro NSti WFar WMon			- 'Panorama Red Shades'	EPfP LRHS SMrm WFar WMon
- 'Sugar Lace' PBR	LRHS WMon			'Pawnee'	GBin WGoo WMon
'Earl Grey'	SEdi WFar			PETITE DELIGHT ('Acpetdel')	EBee WMon
'Electric Neon Pink'	LRHS			'Petite Wonder'	WFar
(Electric Neon Series)				'Pink Frosting' (Sugar Buzz Series)	LBar LRHS LSou MHoo MPro NCth WMon
'Elegant Magenta' new	WMon				
'Elegant Rose' new	WMon			'Pink Supreme' PBR	ELan MPro NLar SMrm WFar WHil WMon XFar
'Elsie's Lavender'	EPfP GMaP NDov NLar WFar WMon				
'Elworthy'	CElw			PISCES	see M. 'Fishes'
'Eugens Kirschrot'	WMon			'Poyntzfield Pink'	LEdu WMon
'Feckenham Foundling'	WHoo WMon			PRAIRIE NIGHT	see M. 'Prärienacht'
§	'Feuerschopf'	WMon	§	'Prärienacht'	CBcs CDor CMac EBee ECha EGrI EHeP ELan EPfP GMaP MBel MHer MHtn NGdn NLar SPlb SRms WCAu WFar WMon WNPC XFar
'Fireball' PBR	CBcs EGren LCro LRHS LSRN MHol MPro NCou NLar SPoG WCAu WFar WHil WMon XFar				
FIRECROWN	see M. 'Feuerschopf'				
§	'Fishes'	CMac EBee GQue LEdu LShi NDov NGdn WFar WMon		punctata	CAgr MCtn MNHC WMon
				- 'Bee Bop'	LCro
fistulosa	CAgr CGHo CHby CMac GPSL IDun LEdu MCtn MHoo MNHC SRms SVic WMon WPGP			'Purple Tower'	EWes
				'Raspberry Wine'	CDor EBee EBlo EPPr ESgI EWes LEdu LRHS NLar WFar WMon WPGP
- 'Feckenham Danielle'	WHoo WMal WMon				
- 'Feckenham Fanfare'	WMon			'Rebecca'	NDov WMon
- 'Feckenham Frills'	WMon			'Remie'	WMon
- 'Feckenham Nicki'	WHoo WMon			'Rockin' Raspberry' new	WMon
- var. menthifolia	NDov WGoo WMon			'Ruby Glow'	WMon
'Mohikaner'			§	'Sagittarius'	NGdn SPoG WFar
- - 'Pummel'	WMon			'Saxon Purple'	MBel
- tetraploid	EBee		§	'Schneewittchen'	CBcs EBee ECha ELan EPfP LCro MArl MBel MHol MPoG SRms WCAu WFar WMon WNPC XFar
- 'Wahpe Washtemna'	WMon WCot WMon				
'Gardenview Scarlet' ♀H4	Widely available			'Scorpion'	CBWd EBee EGren ELan ELin EPfP GAbr GQue LCro NBir NGdn NSti SPoG WCAu WMon
GEMINI	see M. 'Twins'				
'Gewitterwolke'	EGrI NDov WFar WMon				
'Hartswood Wine'	EWes LEdu WFar WMon			'Shelley'	WFar WMon
'Häuptling'	NDov			'Snow Maiden'	see M. 'Schneewittchen'
'Heidelerche'	WFar			'Snow Queen'	EBee EWhm MHoo WMon
'Huckleberry'	GBin NDov WMon			SNOW WHITE	see M. 'Schneewittchen'
'Jacob Cline'	CDor EBlo ESgI EWes EWhm GBin IPot LRHS MAsh MBel MPie NCth NLar SRms WCAu WFar WHoo WMon WPGP			'Squaw'	see M. 'Oneida'
				'Sugar'	WMon
				'Talud' ♀H4	IPot NDov WMon
'Judith's Fancy Fuchsia'	WMon		§	'Twins'	NLar WFar
'Kardinal'	GBin NLar WMon			'Vintage Wine'	CElw NDov WMon
'Knight Purple'	EBee MPro WMon			'Violacea'	WFar WMon
'Knight Rose'	WFar WMon			'Violet Queen'	CMHG EBee ELan ERCP EUrb EWes GQue LEdu LRHS MPie NEoE WCot WFar WMon WPGP
'Knight Violet'	WMon				
'Lambada'	MCtn				
'Leading Lady Plum' PBR	WMon			'Violette'	WFar WMon
'Lederstrumpf'	IPot WFar WMon			'Westacre Purple'	ECha EGrI EPPr ESgI EWes LShi LSto WMon
LIBRA	see M. 'Balance'				
'Loddon Crown'	CAby MHoo Midl NLar SHar WCAu WFar WMon WNPC				

Monardella (Lamiaceae)

'Mahogany'	EBee ELan EPfP LRHS LSto MHol SPoG WFar WMon
odoratissima	MHer

Monochoria (Pontederiaceae)

'Marshall's Delight' ♀H4	CDor ESgI EWes GPSL GQue MAvo MNrw WCAu WFar WMon XFar
§ *hastata*	CLil CWat EWat

Monocostus (Zingiberaceae)

'Melissa'	NLar
menthifolia	MCtn SRms
'Mohawk'	EPfP GQue MHol NGdn NLar WCAu WFar WMon
uniflorus	SBrt

Monstera (Araceae)

'Neon'	LRHS NDov NLar WMon
'On Parade'	GPSL LEdu MMrt NDov NGdn WFar WMon
acacoyaguensis new	NTro
acuminata new	NTro

adansonii — CDoC LBom LCro LWaG NHrt NTro WFar
— Monkey Leaf ('Ppimon001') — NTro
deliciosa (F) ♀H1b — CDoC EGren EUrb LBom LCro LDro LInT LWaG MCtn NHrt NPlm NTrD NTro SBig SPlb WFar
— 'Tauerii' — LCro
— 'Thai Constellation' (v) — LCro LInT NTro WFar
— 'Variegata' (v) ♀H1b — LBom LCro LDro LInT NTro WFar
dissecta new — NTro
dubia new — NTro
'Monkey Mask' — LBom LCro LWaG NHrt NPlm NTro
obliqua — NHrt NTro
pinnatipartita — LCro NTro
siltepecana new — NTro
standleyana new — NTro
subpinnata new — NTro

Montanoa (Asteraceae)
aff. *hibiscifolia* — EAri

Montbretia see *Crocosmia*, *Tritonia*

Montia (Montiaceae)
perfoliata — see *Claytonia perfoliata*
sibirica — see *Claytonia sibirica*

Moraea (Iridaceae)
alticola — EPPr GAbr SPlb
bipartita — WCot
huttonii — CElw CFis CPbh CSpe ESgI EWoo GAbr GEdr GKev LShi SBrt WFar
iridioides — see *Dietes iridioides*
monticola — GKev
polystachya — CSpe
sisyrinchium — GKev
spathacea — see *M. spathulata*
§ *spathulata* — CExl GKev WCot
vegeta — SBrt

Morella (Myricaceae)
californica — CAgr
pensylvanica — CAgr WJur

Morina (Caprifoliaceae)
bulleyana — see *M. nepalensis* subsp. *delavayi*
longifolia — CDor CSpe EBee ECha EDAr ELan EPfP GKev MCtn MHol MNrw MPro NBir NGdn NGKo SDix SPlb SPoG StAn WCAu WCot WKif
nepalensis — GKev
§ — subsp. *delavayi* — GKev
persica — GKev

Morinda (Rubiaceae)
citrifolia — MCtn

Moringa (Moringaceae)
oleifera — MCtn SPlb

Morisia (Brassicaceae)
hypogaea — see *M. monanthos*
§ *monanthos* — GEdr SRot WIce
— 'Fred Hemingway' — ELan GArf WAbe

Morus ✿ (Moraceae)
§ *alba* — CBcs CHab CMCN ELan IPap LBuc LMaj LRHS SPre SVic WFar
— 'Agate' (F) — CAgr
— 'Laciniata' — EBee

— 'Macrophylla' — MBlu
— 'Pakistan' (F) — CAgr LCro LRHS NLar NOra SPoG WMat
— 'Paradise' (F) — CAgr
— 'Pendula' — CAco CBTr CEnd CMac ELan LCro MBlu MPri NOra NPip SBmr SPoG WMat
— 'Platanifolia' — see *M. alba* 'Macrophylla'
— var. *tatarica* — CAgr NLar
'Black Tabor' (F) — CAgr
'Capsrum' (F) — CAgr
'Carman' (F) — CAgr ELan LRHS NLar NOra NPip
Charlotte Russe — see *M.* 'Matsunaga'
'Illinois Everbearing' (F) — CAgr WPGP
'Italian' (F) — CAgr
'Ivory' (F) — CAgr
kagayamae — see *M. alba*
latifolia 'Spirata' — NLar
macroura — EPfP LCro MLod SBmr
§ 'Matsunaga' (F) — CBcs CBTr CWnw LCro LRHS NLar NOra SBmr SPre WCot
Mojo Berry — see *M.* 'Matsunaga'
nigra (F) — Widely available
— 'Charlton House' (F) new — LRHS
§ — 'Chelsea' (F) ♀H6 — CBcs CBTr CEnd CMac CSBt EBee EPfP EPom LCro LRHS MGos MLod NLar NOra NPip SEWo SKee SPoG WMat
— dwarf (F) — SPre
— 'Izvor' (F) — CAgr
— 'Jerusalem' (F) ♀H6 — NOra WMat
— 'King James' — see *M. nigra* 'Chelsea'
— 'Large Black' (F) — EPom
— 'Mulle' (F) new — EGren
— 'Repsime' (F) — CAgr LCro
— 'Sham Dudu' (F) — CAgr
'Waisei-kirishima-shikinari' — see *M.* 'Matsunaga'
'Wellington' (F) — CCVT CEnd CMac EBee ELan EUrb LCro LSRN MPri NLar NOra WMat

Mosla (Lamiaceae)
dianthera — WCot

Muehlenbeckia (Polygonaceae)
astonii — EBee ELan EShb EUrb LWaG SArc SIvy WJur WPGP
axillaris misapplied — see *M. complexa*
§ *axillaris* (Hook. f.) Endl. — CBcs ELan EShb GBin LEdu MSwo SSta WPGP
§ *complexa* — CBcs CMac EBee ELan EPfP EShb LCro LRHS LWaG MBlu NQui SAdn SArc SBig SEND SIvy SPoG WCFE WCot WPGP
— (f) — CDoC CSde EGren EUrb GKev LBom LWaG SNig
— 'Golden Girl'PBR — GKev LSou
— Maori — see *M. complexa* 'Top Secret'
— 'Nana' — see *M. axillaris* (Hook. f.) Endl.
— 'Spotlight'PBR (v) — EShb
— 'Texture Big Leaf' — EBee EPfP SChF WPGP
§ — 'Top Secret' — ESwi LRHS
— var. *trilobata* — EShb ESwi SSta
— 'Variegata' (v) — LBom LWaG
platyclada — EShb ESwi
'Sealand Compact' — ESwi
volcanica B&SWJ 14921 — WCru

Muhlenbergia (Poaceae)
capillaris — CBcs CSpe CWnw EBee EDAr EGren EUrb GMaP LCro LRHS LSRN MBel SDix SEND WSpi

dumosa	CKno SMad WCot WPGP	§ *sikkimensis* ♀H2	CDTJ CTsd EAri SPlb SWor
lindheimeri	CKno EBee WCot	- 'Bengal Tiger'	CAbb CAby CCht CTsd EAri ELan LAma MSwo NLar
mexicana	SRms	- 'Red Tiger'	CBlu CDTJ LRHS NPlm SAth SBig SWor
reverchonii UNDAUNTED ('Pund01s')	EDAr	*thomsonii*	LAma
rigens	CKno EPPr WSpi	*velutina* ♀H1b	CCht LAma MCtn NPlm SBig

Mukdenia (Saxifragaceae)

acanthifolia	GEdr LEdu WPGP
rossii	EBee EUrb LEdu LShi MBel MNrw NBid NCth NLar StAn WCAu WFar WOld WPGP
- 'Crimson Fans'	see *M. rossii* 'Karasuba'
§ - 'Karasuba'	Widely available
- 'Shishiba'	GEdr LEdu

× *Mukgenia* (Saxifragaceae)

§ 'Flame'	CBcs EBee ELan EUrb GBin GMaP IPot LRHS LSou MHol Midl MNrw MPnt MPro SPoG
NOVA	see × *M.* 'Flame'

mulberry see *Morus*

Muraltia (Polygalaceae)

spinosa	SPlb

Murdannia (Commelinaceae)

I *acutifolia* 'Variegata' (v)	WTra
loriformis BRIGHT STAR ('Ppimur004') (v)	LBom LCro WTra

Murraya (Rutaceae)

koenigii	see *Bergera koenigii*

Musa ✿ (Musaceae)

§ *acuminata*	LCro LWaG NHrt
- Cavendish Group (AAA Group) (F)	NHrt
§ - 'Dwarf Cavendish' (AAA Group) (F) ♀H1b	CAbb CBlu CDoC CTsd EGren ELan LCro LDro LWaG NHrt NLar SBig SMrm SPlb
- 'Dwarf Red' (AAA Group) (F)	EGren
- 'Siam Ruby' (AA Group) (F)	EUrb
balbisiana	EAri LAma NPlm
basjoo ♀H2	Widely available
- 'Sakhalin'	LRHS
'Cavendish Super Dwarf'	LWaG NPlm
cavendishii	see *M. acuminata* 'Dwarf Cavendish' (AAA Group)
'Dajiao'	CCht NPlm
ensete	see *Ensete ventricosum*
'Hazaray'	LAma
'Helen'	EAri
hookeri	see *M. sikkimensis*
'Jamesonii'	CTsd EAri
lasiocarpa ♀H2	CBct CBlu CCht CDTJ CLil CTsd ELan EUrb LCro LRHS LWaG MGos MSwo NPlm SArc SAth SBig SMrm SPlb SWor
laterita	LAma
nana misapplied	see *M. acuminata* 'Dwarf Cavendish' (AAA Group)
nana Lour.	see *M. acuminata*
× *paradisiaca*	LAma
- 'Malbhog' (AAB Group) (F)	LAma
- 'Ney Poovan' (AB Group) (F)	LAma

Musanga (Urticaceae)

cecropioides	EAri

Muscari ✿ (Asparagaceae)

adilii	GKev
ambrosiacum	see *M. racemosum* Mill.
anatolicum	WCot
armeniacum ♀H6	CBro CoPl EGren ETay GAbr GKev LAma LCro LRHS SRms WCot WShi XFar
- PAB 6748	LEdu
- 'Album'	GKev
- 'Alida'	SDix
- 'Big Smile'	EGren
- 'Blue Spike' (d)	CBro GKev LAma NBir
- 'Cupido'	LAma
- 'Dark Eyes'	ELan GQue LRHS
- 'Fantasy Creation'	GKev LAma XFar
- 'Gül'	WCot
- 'Helena'	LAma
- 'Manon'	GKev LAma
- 'Night Eyes'	EGren XFar
- 'Saffier' ♀H6	EWld WCot
- 'Siberian Tiger' ♀H6	CDoC EPfP EPot ERCP ETay GKev LAma LRHS SPhx WTor
- 'Touch of Snow'	ELan ETay GKev LAma LCro LRHS SPhx
- 'Valerie Finnis'	CBro EGren EPfP EPot GKev LAma LSto NLar WCot XFar
'Arthur Henry'	WCot
aucheri ♀H6	NRya
* - var. *bicolor*	WCot
- 'Blue Magic'	EGren EPot GKev LAma LRHS
- 'Ocean Magic'	CBro GKev LAma LCro NLar
- 'White Magic'	CBro EGren EPfP LAma LCro WCot WFar XFar
§ *azureum* ♀H6	CBro EGren EPfP ERCP GKev LAma LCro NBir WCot WFar
- 'Album'	WCot
- 'Bling Bling'	LRHS XFar
'Baby's Breath'	see *M.* 'Jenny Robinson'
'Big Smile'	EPfP LRHS
'Blue Eyes'	WCot
botryoides	GKev WCot
- 'Album'	EGren GKev LAma LCro SRms WCot WShi
bourgaei	GKev
'Carola'	GKev
caucasicum	GKev WCot
chalusicum	see *M. pseudomuscari*
coeleste	GKev WCot
coeruleum	GKev
commutatum	GKev
white-flowered	
comosum	EDAr ERCP GKev LAma LCro MCtn WCot WFar XFar
- 'Monstrosum'	see *M. comosum* 'Plumosum'
- 'Pinard'	GKev
§ - 'Plumosum'	EGren ELan ETay GKev LAma LCro XFar
cycladicum subsp. *subsessile*	GKev
dionysicum	WCot

468 Muscari

'Double Beauty' (d)	XFar		*nobile*	see *M. hortensia*
'Esther'	XFar			
grandifolium JCA 689 450	WCot		***Myosotis*** (Boraginaceae)	
'Imogen'	WCot		***alpestris*** 'Alba'	LSto MCtn
'Ivor's Pink'	WCot		***arvensis***	EHet MCtn
§ 'Jenny Robinson' ♀H5	CBro EGren EPfP EPot ERCP		***australis***	WCot
	LAma LRHS SDix WCot WHoo		'Compindi'	MCtn
	XFar		***glabrescens***	EPot
'Joyce Spirit'	ELan ERCP GKev		MY OH MY ('Myomark'PBR)	CSpe LRHS MPro
'Julia' **new**	XFar		***palustris***	see *M. scorpioides*
latifolium ♀H6	CAby CBro CDoC EGren ELan EPfP		***petiolata***	SPlb
	ERCP GKev LAma LCro LRHS LSto		***pulvinaris***	EDAr GArf SPlb
	NLar WCot WFar XFar		***rakiura***	EWes
* - 'Blue Angels'	NBir	§	***scorpioides***	CHab CLil CoPl CPud CWat
- 'Grape Ice'	CBro EGren ELan EPfP ERCP GKev			ELin LCro MCtn MMuc MWts
	LAma LCro LRHS MNrw SDix WFar			NAts SPlb SRms WBrk WMAq
	XFar			WOrg
'Lindsay'	GKev SPhx		- 'Alba'	CLil CPud MWts
macrocarpum	ECha WAbe		- 'Ice Pearl'	ECha
- 'Golden Fragrance'PBR	EGren LAma LCro MNrw XFar		- MAYTIME ('Blaqua') (v)	NBir
'Maxabel'	LAma		- 'Mermaid'	CBen ECha SRms
'Memory of Gary Fisher'	WCot		- 'Snowflakes'	CWat
moschatum	see *M. racemosum* Mill.		- variegated (v)	CLil
'Mount Hood'	XFar		***sylvatica***	LCro MMuc
'Mountain Lady'	EGren ERCP GKev LAma LRHS		- 'Indigo'	ELan
muscarimi	see *M. racemosum* Mill.		- 'Mon Amie Blue'	LCro
'Nature's Beauty' (d) **new**	ERCP LAma		- 'Ultramarine' ♀H6	LCro
§ ***neglectum***	GKev LAma LCro NLar SEND WCot		- Sylva Series ♀H6	EGren
	WShi		- - 'Bluesylva' ♀H6	EGren MCtn
pallens	GKev		- - 'Rosylva' ♀H6	MCtn
paradoxum	see *Bellevalia paradoxa*		- - 'Snowsylva'	MCtn
parviflorum	GKev WCot		'Sylvia Blue'	LCro
'Peppermint'	EGren EPfP ETay GKev LAma LCro			
	LRHS WCot		***Myrceugenia*** (Myrtaceae)	
'Pink Sunrise'	CBro EGren EPot ERCP ETay GKev		***chrysocarpa***	WJur
	LAma LRHS WCot XFar		***lanceolata*** **new**	WJur
'Pink Surprise'	LAma		***ovata*** var. ***nannophylla***	WPGP
§ ***pseudomuscari*** ♀H5	WCot			
pulchellum	GKev		***Myrica*** (Myricaceae)	
subsp. ***pulchellum***			***gale***	CAgr NLar WSpi
racemosum (L.) Medik.	see *M. neglectum*			
§ ***racemosum*** Mill.	WCot XFar		***Myricaria*** (Tamaricaceae)	
'Rosy Sunrise'	WCot		***germanica***	NLar
'Ruth'	WCot			
'Soulmate' **new**	XFar		***Myriophyllum*** (Haloragaceae)	
spreitzenhoferi	GKev		***aquaticum***	Prohibited invasive. See Conservation and
'Superstar'	GKev LAma WCot			the Environment, p.42
'Venus'	LAma WCot		***heterophyllum***	Prohibited invasive. See Conservation and
weissii	GKev			the Environment, p.42
'White Beauty'	WCot		***hippuroides***	ELin
'White Pearl'	GKev LAma		***spicatum***	CLil CWat ELin EWat LWaG MWts
'Winter Amethyst'	WCot			WMAq

Muscarimia see *Muscari*

ambrosiacum	see *Muscari racemosum* Mill.

Musella see *Musa*

Musschia (Campanulaceae)

wollastonii	CTsd EAri WCot
- red-flowered	CTsd EAri

Mutisia (Asteraceae)

oligodon	GKev

Myoporum (Scrophulariaceae)

laetum	SPlb SVen

Myosotidium (Boraginaceae)

§ *hortensia*	CMiW CTsd EAri ELan EPfP GKev
	LRHS MAsh MCtn StAn

Myrrhidendron (Apiaceae)

donnellsmithii	SBig

Myrrhis (Apiaceae)

odorata	Widely available
- 'Forncett Chevron'	LEdu WPGP

Myrsine (Primulaceae)

africana	EShb MHer SEND
australis	SArc SVen
divaricata	SVen WJur

Myrteola (Myrtaceae)

§ *nummularia*	EPot GArf WAbe WPav
- from Falkland Islands	GAbr

Myrtillocactus (Cactaceae)

geometrizans	LWaG NPlm

Myrtus ✿ (Myrtaceae)

apiculata misapplied	see *Luma apiculata*
bullata	see *Lophomyrtus bullata*
chequen	see *Luma chequen*
communis ♀H4	Widely available
- 'Baetica'	WJur
- fastigiate	WJur
- 'Jekka's All Gold'	WJek
- 'Jenny Reitenbach'	see *M. communis* subsp. *tarentina*
- 'Merion'	WJek
- 'Microphylla'	see *M. communis* subsp. *tarentina*
- 'Nana'	see *M. communis* subsp. *tarentina*
- 'Pyewood Park'	SRms WJek
§ - subsp. *tarentina* ♀H4	Widely available
- - 'Compacta'	LRHS
- - 'Microphylla Variegata' (v)	MNHC SRms WJek
I - - 'Variegata' (v)	CGHo MHoo
- Tricolor'	see *M. communis* 'Variegata'
§ - 'Variegata' (v)	CCoa CGHo CMac CSBt CTsd EBee ELan ELon ENfk EPfP EUrb LRHS MHer MHoo MSwo NLar SEND SPoG WCFE WFar WJek
'Glanleam Gold'	see *Luma apiculata* 'Glanleam Gold'
lechleriana	see *Amomyrtus luma*
luma	see *Luma apiculata*
nummularia	see *Myrteola nummularia*
obcordata	see *Lophomyrtus obcordata*
* **paraguayensis**	EBee LRHS
ugni	see *Ugni molinae*

N

Nandina (Berberidaceae)

domestica	Widely available
- B&SWJ 11113	WCru
- BLUSH PINK ('Aka'PBR)	CDoC CMac EGren ELan LCro LRHS LSou LSRN MAsh MHtn MPkF SOrN SPoG WCha WFar
- BRIGHTLIGHT ('Selten004'PBR)	EBee EGrI LRHS SGol
- CURLY OBSESSED ('Pb01') new	LRHS
- 'Filamentosa'	LRHS NLar SGol WCot
- Fire Power'	Widely available
- FLIRT ('Murasaki'PBR)	EBee EGren ELan EUrb LRHS LSou MPkF SGol WFar
- 'Gulf Stream'	EGren EGrI ELan ELon EPfP ERom LRHS LSRN MAsh MGos MHtn MPkF SAth SBig SFol SOrN WCha WFar
- 'Harbour Dwarf'	LRHS WFar
- MAGICAL LEMON AND LIME ('Lemlim'PBR)	CBcs EBee ELan LCro LRHS LSou MPri NLar SGol SOrN SPoG WCha
- 'Moon Bay'	LRHS
- 'Nana'	see *N. domestica* 'Pygmaea'
- OBSESSED	see *N. domestica* 'Seika'
- PLUM PASSION ('Monum')	EGrI EUrb MGos
§ - 'Pygmaea'	EGren ELon
- 'Red Dragon'	MPkF
- RED LIGHT ('Nrl2015')	EGren LSou MBNS
- 'Richmond' ♀H5	CBcs CDoC EBee EHeP ELan ELon EPfP LRHS MAsh MGos NLar SPoG WFar
§ - 'Seika'PBR	Widely available
- SIENNA SUNRISE ('Monfar')	LSou MPkF SGol WCha

- 'Sunset'PBR	CBcs EBee GKev LRHS LSRN Midl NLar WFar
- 'Twilight'PBR (v)	CDoC CMac CSBt CWGN EBee ELan EPfP EUrb LCro LRHS LSou MAsh MPkF SMad SPoG WFar
- 'Wood's Dwarf'	CBcs EGrI WFar

Nannorrhops (Arecaceae)

arabica	see *N. ritchieana*
§ **ritchieana**	NPlm SPlb

Napaea (Malvaceae)

dioica	EAri LEdu SPhx SPlb WCot WPGP

Narcissus ✿ (Amaryllidaceae)

'Accent' (2)	ETay
'Acropolis' (4)	ETay LAma WFar XFar
'Actaea' (9) ♀H6	CBro EGren LAma LCro NNys WFar
'Albus Plenus Odoratus'	see *N. poeticus* 'Plenus' ambig.
'Alexis Beauty' (2)	ETay
alpestris (13)	NDry
'Altun Ha' (2)	ETay
'Amadeus' (2) **new**	XFar
'Ambergate' (2)	ETay LAma
'Amico' (2)	ETay
'Androcles' (4)	ETay
'Andy Blanchard' (5)	NDry
'Angelina' (6)	NDry
'Angel's Breath' (5) ♀H6	CBro EPot GKev LAma
'Angel's Flight' (6)	NDry
'Angel's Whisper' (5) ♀H6	CBro EPfP GKev LAma LRHS SPhx
'Apotheose' (4)	EGren
'Apple Pie' (11a)	ERCP GKev LAma
'Apricot Whirl' (11a)	GKev LAma LCro XFar
'Arctic Gold' (1) ♀H6	GKev LAma
'Arkle' (1) ♀H6	ETay
'Art Design' (4)	LAma
'Art Perfume' (4) **new**	GKev LAma XFar
'Articol' (11a)	LAma
'Ascot' (4)	XFar
§ **assoanus** (13)	EPot LAma WCot WShi
§ **asturiensis** (13)	EPot GKev NDry WShi
- giant	see *N. asturiensis* 'Wavertree'
§ - 'Wavertree' (1)	LAma MCor
'Aureolin' (7)	NDry
'Avalanche' (8) ♀H4	ELan ETay GKev LAma LCro XFar
'Avalon' (2)	ETay GKev LAma LCro XFar
'Baby Boomer' (7)	ERCP GKev LAma LCro LRHS
'Baby Moon' (7)	EGren EPot GKev LAma LRHS
'Bantam' (2) ♀H6	ETay
'Barrett Browning' (3)	EGren LAma XFar
'Beauvallon' (4)	ETay
'Bebop' (7)	CBro
'Beige Beauty' (3)	ETay
'Bell Song' (7)	CBro EGren GKev LAma LCro NNys
'Bella Estrella' (11a)	ERCP
'Best Seller' (1)	WFar
bicolor (13) **new**	WFar
'Bilbo' (6)	CBro
'Binkie' (2)	EPfP ETay WFar
'Biondina' (1)	NDry
'Birma' (3)	ETay
'Blarney' (3)	ETay
'Blessing' (2)	ETay
'Blushing Lady' (7)	NBir
'Bobbysoxer' (7)	CBro
'Bowles's Early Sulphur' (1)	CTtf
'Bowles's Early Sulphur' × *cyclamineus*	GEdr
'Brackenhurst' (2)	ETay

'Bravoure' (1) ♀H6 — GKev LAma
'Bridal Crown' (4) ♀H6 — CDoC EGren EPfP ETay GKev LAma LCro LRHS SPoG XFar
'British Gamble' (1) — GKev LAma
broussonetii from Morocco WPGP (13)
bulbocodium (13) ♀H4 — CBro LCro NNys SMrm SRms WCot
- 'Arctic Bells' (10) — EPfP EPot ERCP ETay GEdr GKev MNrw NNys
§ - subsp. *bulbocodium* (13) — CBro
§ - - var. *citrinus* (13) — ENun LRHS SPlb
§ - - var. *conspicuus* (13) — CBro EGrI ERCP GKev LAma WCot WShi
* - - var. *filifolius* (13) — CBro
- - var. *nivalis* (13) — NDry
§ - Golden Bells Group (10) — CAby EPfP EPot ETay GKev LAma LCro XFar
- subsp. *obesus* (13) — GKev NDry
§ - - 'Diamond Ring' (10) — LAma
- - 'Lee Martin' (10) — GEdr NDry
- subsp. *praecox* var. *paucinervis* Rrw84.18 (13) — NDry
- subsp. *tananicus* — see *N. cantabricus* subsp. *tananicus*
- subsp. *vulgaris* — see *N. bulbocodium* subsp. *bulbocodium*
'Bundle' (7) — NDry
'Busbie' (12) — NDry
'Butter and Eggs' (4) — GKev
'Buttertubs' (12) **new** — NDry
calcicola (13) — NDry
'Calgary' (4) — ETay WCot
'Callisto' (10) — NDry
'Camelot' (2) ♀H6 — EPfP ETay WFar
'Campernelli Plenus' — see *N.* 'Double Campernelle'
'Can Can Girl' (2) — XFar
'Canaliculatus' (8) — EGren EPfP ERCP LAma LCro
canaliculatus Gussone — see *N. tazetta* subsp. *lacticolor*
'Candlepower' (1) — NDry
cantabricus (13) — LCro NDry
- subsp. *cantabricus* var. *eu-albidus* (13) — NDry
- - var. *foliosus* (13) ♀H4 — GKev
- - var. *petunioides* (13) — NDry
* - subsp. *monophyllus* var. *laciniatus* (13) — NDry
§ - subsp. *tananicus* (13) — LAma
'Carlton' (2) ♀H6 — EGren EPfP GKev LAma LCro XFar
'Carrara' (3) — ETay
'Cassata' (11a) — GKev LAma LCro NBir
'Casual Elegance' (10) — ECha GKev LAma LRHS
× *cazorlanus* (13) — NDry
'Cedric Morris' (1) — CExl ECha ENsn WCot
'Cha-cha' (6) — CBro XFar
'Changing Colors' (11a) — ETay
'Charlotte Vreeburg' (11b) — LAma
'Cheeky Chappie' (6) — NDry
'Cheerfulness' (4) ♀H6 — EGren ELan ETay GKev LAma LCro MBros NNys NPer
'Chirp' (1) — NDry
'Chit Chat' (7) ♀H6 — SPlb
'Chitter' (2) — NDry
'Chromacolor' (2) ♀H6 — ETay GKev LAma XFar
citrinus — see *N. bulbocodium* subsp. *bulbocodium* var. *citrinus*
'Citron Baby' (2) — NDry
'Cloud Nine' (2) — CBro
'Color Run' (2) — GKev LAma
'Columba' (10) — NDry

'Compressus' — see *N.* × *intermedius* 'Compressus'
'Congress' (11a) — ETay
'Conspicuus' ambig. (3) — LAma
'Conspicuus' Barr (3) — GKev
'Coo' (12) — NDry
'Cool Crystal' (3) — ETay
'Cool Flame' (2) — ETay
'Cornish Gold' (1) — EPfP LCro
'Cosette' (6) — NDry
'Cosmopolitan' (7) — XFar
'Cotinga' (6) — CBro ETay
'Cragford' (8) — ETay SPoG
'Craigton Chorister' (13) — NDry
'Craigton Clumper' (13) — WMal
'Cream Satin' (2) — NDry
'Creation' (1) — ETay
Crème Fraîche Group (3) — NDry
cuatrecasasii (13) — GKev NDry
'Curlew' (7) ♀H6 — ETay LCro
cyclamineus (13) ♀H6 — CBro CExl CTtf ECha ENun EPot GEdr GKev LCro LEdu LRHS SRms
'Cyllene' (10) **new** — NDry
'Dainty Miss' (7) — GKev
'Daphnis' (10) — NDry
'Daydream' (2) — ETay
'Dear Lotte' (3) — XFar
'Dear Love' (11a) — SPoG
'Delnashaugh' (4) — EPfP GKev LAma WFar
'Deryn' (6) — NDry
'Diamond Ring' — see *N. bulbocodium* subsp. *obesus* 'Diamond Ring'
'Dick Wilden' (4) — XFar
'Dinnerplate' (2) ♀H6 — XFar
'Doctor B' (2) **new** — NDry
'Doll Baby' (7) — WFar
'Dormouse' (1) — NDry
§ 'Double Campernelle' (4) — WShi
'Double Fashion' (4) — WFar
double pheasant eye — see *N. poeticus* 'Plenus' ambig.
'Double Smiles' (4) — EPfP LAma
'Dream Castle' (3) — WFar
'Dutch Master' (1) ♀H6 — EGren EPfP GKev LAma LCro XFar
'Early Flame' (2) — EGren
'Eaton Song' (12) ♀H6 — LCro
'Edinburgh' (11a) — GKev
'Edna Earl' (2) — ETay
'Elara' (10) — NDry
'Elka' (1) ♀H6 — CAby CBro ECha EPot ERCP GKev LAma LRHS MCor SPhx WBrk WShi
'Elvin's Voice' (5) — GKev LAma
'Emerald Green' (2) — GKev
'Eminent' (3) — ETay WFar
'Empress of Ireland' (1) — ETay
'Englander' (6) ♀H6 — EPot GEdr
'Erlicheer' (4) — LCro WCot XFar
§ *eugeniae* (13) — WCot
'Every Day' (2) — GKev
'Exemplar' (1) — ETay
'Exotic Beauty' (4) — ETay
'Exotic Mystery' (11a) — XFar
'Extravaganza' (4) — GKev LAma
'Fairy Chimes' (5) — EPot
'Fairy Gold' (6) — NDry
'Falconet' (8) ♀H6 — ETay
'Fat Rascal' (12) — NDry
'February Gold' (6) ♀H6 — CBro ECha EGren ELan EPfP EPot ERCP ETay GKev LAma LCro NBir NNys SRms WFar WShi XFar
'February Silver' (1) — CBro LAma NNys
'Feeling Lucky' (2) — ETay
'Felindre' (9) — ETay

fernandesii (13)	EPot WCot	'Ice Follies' (2) ♀H6	EGren EPfP ETay GKev LAma LCro LRHS NBir NNys WFar XFar
- var. *cordubensis* (13)	CBro CTtf ERCP GKev LAma NDry XFar	'Ice King' (4)	EPfP LCro NBir XFar
'Filly' (2)	ETay	'Ice Wings' (5) ♀H6	ETay XFar
'Finland' (2)	LAma	'Inbal'PBR (8)	XFar
'Fling' (6)	NDry	§ × *incurvicervicus* (13)	NDry
'Flower Drift' (4)	WFar	'Innovator' (4)	GKev LAma
'Flurry' (1)	NDry	× *intermedius* (13)	CBro
'Fly Half' (2)	ETay	§ - 'Compressus' (8)	CBro
'Fortissimo' (2)	ETay	'Intrigue' (7) ♀H6	ETay
'Fortune' (2)	EGren GKev LAma	'Iolana' (5) **new**	NDry
× *fosteri* (13)	NDry	*italicus* (13)	GKev
'Fragrant Breeze' (2)	ETay	'Itzim' (6) ♀H6	CBro LAma
'Fragrant Rose' (2)	ETay	'Iwona' (6)	GKev LAma
'Fragrant Spring' (4) **new**	XFar	'Jack Snipe' (6) ♀H6	CAby CBro EGren ELan ERCP ETay GKev LAma LCro LRHS WCot XFar
'Fresh Breeze' (6)	NDry		
'Frileuse' (11a)	LAma	'Jack the Lad' (4)	ETay
Fringella Group (6)	NDry	'Jean Blanchard' (1) **new**	NDry
'Frisk' (12) **new**	NDry	'Jedna' (2)	ERCP
'Frostkist' (6)	CBro	'Jenny' (6) ♀H6	ECha ETay GKev LAma LCro NBir
'Frosty Snow' (2)	GKev LAma	'Jetfire' (6) ♀H6	EGren EPfP EPot ERCP ETay GKev LAma LCro LRHS LSto NNys SPoG WFar XFar
gaditanus (13)	CBro		
Galantoquilla Group (12)	NDry		
'Gale Force' (6)	NDry	'Jim Lad' (2)	NDry
'Galilee' (3)	LCro	'Johann Strauss' (2)	ETay
'Gay Kybo' (4) ♀H6	ETay	'Johanna' (5)	CBro
'Gentleman at Arms' (2)	EPfP ETay	*jonquilla* (13)	CBro EPot LAma WShi
'Georgie Boy' (2)	ETay WFar	- subsp. *cerrolazae* (13)	GKev
'Geranium' (8) ♀H6	CBro ECha EGren ERCP ETay GKev LAma LCro LRHS WFar XFar	§ - var. *henriquesii* (13)	EPot
		'Joy Bishop'	see *N. romieuxii* 'Joy Bishop'
'Gianna' (6)	NDry	'Juanita' (2)	LCro NPer
'Gipsy Queen' (1)	CBro ECha EPot MCor WCot	'Julia Jane'	see *N. romieuxii* 'Julia Jane'
'Giselle' (10)	NDry	'Jumblie' (12) ♀H6	CBro EPfP SPoG
'Goblet' (1)	GKev LAma	*juncifolius* Req. ex Lag.	see *N. assoanus*
'Gold Medal' (1) ♀H6	ETay	'Kalyke' (10)	NDry
'Golden Aura' (2) ♀H6	ETay	'Kari' (10)	NDry
'Golden Bells'	see *N. bulbocodium* Golden Bells Group	'Katie Heath' (5)	GKev LAma WBrk
		'Kaydee' (6) ♀H6	GKev LAma
'Golden Dawn' (8) ♀H4	GKev LAma WFar	'Kedron' (7)	ERCP WFar
'Golden Ducat' (4)	GKev LAma LRHS NBir	'Kimmeridge' (3)	EPfP
'Golden Echo' (7)	ETay XFar	'King Alfred' (1)	LCro LRHS WFar
'Golden Harvest' (1)	GKev LAma NPer	'Kokopelli' (7) ♀H6	CBro GKev LCro
'Golden Joy' (2)	ETay	'La Delicatesse' (2) **new**	GKev LAma
'Golden Spur' (1)	LAma	'Lady Madonna' (6) **new**	XFar
'Gossamer' (3)	ETay	'Lancaster' (3)	ETay
'Gracie' (1) **new**	NDry	'Las Vegas' (1)	XFar
'Grand Primo' (8)	ETay LCro	'Lemnos' (2)	ETay
'Grand Soleil d'Or' (8)	EGren GKev LAma LCro XFar	'Lemon Beauty' (11b)	ETay GKev LAma
'Great Leap'	WFar	'Lemon Breeze' (6)	NDry
'Green Island' (2)	ETay	'Lemon Drops' (5)	LAma LCro XFar
'Hammoon' (3)	ETay	'Lemon Silk' (6)	CBro ELan ETay
'Harpsicord' (11a)	ETay	'Lieke' (7)	CBro EPot ERCP LCro
'Hawera' (5) ♀H6	CBro EGren EPfP ERCP ETay GKev LAma LCro WFar WShi XFar	'Limbo' (2)	ETay
		'Lingerie' (4) ♀H6	ETay
'Heamoor' (4) ♀H6	ETay	'Little Dryad' (6)	NDry
hedraeanthus (13)	NDry	'Little Emma' (12)	EPot ERCP GKev LAma MNrw MPie SPhx
- subsp. *luteolentus* (13)	NDry		
'Helene' (10)	NDry	'Little Finn' (6)	NDry
hellenicus	see *N. poeticus* var. *hellenicus*	'Little Jen' (5)	NDry
henriquesii	see *N. jonquilla* var. *henriquesii*	'Little Lemon' (2) **new**	NDry
'High Note' (7)	ETay	'Little Oliver' (7)	EPfP
'High Society' (2) ♀H6	EPfP ETay LCro	'Little Racer' (6)	NDry
'Highfield Beauty' (8) ♀H6	ETay	'Little Rusky' (7)	CBro
'Hillstar' (7) ♀H6	EPfP GKev LAma	'Little Sentry' (7)	CBro EPot
hispanicus	GKev	'Little Witch' (6)	LAma
subsp. *hispanicus* (13)		*lobularis* (Haw.) Schult. & Schult. f. (13)	CAby CBWd CHab EPfP ETay LCro WFar XFar
'Hollands Chase' (4)	EGren		
'Hors d'Oeuvre' (1)	CBro	'Lorikeet' (1)	GKev
'Iapetus' (10) **new**	NDry	'Lothario' (2)	EPfP WFar
'Ice Baby'PBR (1)	CBro EPfP ERCP GKev LAma LRHS SPoG WBrk WFar WShi	'Louise de Coligny' (2)	ERCP
		'Love Call' (11a)	XFar

'Love You More' (2) **new**	GKev LAma
'Lucky Number' (1) **new**	XFar
'Ma Belle' (1)	ETay LAma
'Malinky' (2)	NDry
'Malvern City' (1)	ETay
'Manly' (4) ♀H6	XFar
'Marie Curie Diamond' (7) ♀H6	EGren LCro WFar
'Martinette' (8)	EGren ETay GKev LAma LCro LRHS WFar
marvieri	see *N. rupicola* subsp. *marvieri*
'Mary Poppins' (10)	LAma MNrw WShi
× *medioluteus* (13)	CBro
'Midas Touch' (1)	ETay
Minicycla Group (6)	NDry
minimus misapplied	see *N. asturiensis*
'Minionette' (6)	NDry
'Minnow' (8) ♀H6	CAby CBro EGren ELan EPfP ERCP ETay GKev LAma LCro LRHS MPie NBir XFar
minor (13) ♀H5	ECha MCor
- 'Little Gem' (1) ♀H6	CBro LAma
- var. *pumilus* 'Plenus'	see *N.* 'Rip van Winkle'
'Mint Julep' (3) ♀H6	ETay
'Mirar' (2)	ETay
'Miss Poppy' (1) **new**	NDry
'Misty' (6) **new**	NDry
'Misty Glen' (2) ♀H6	ETay GKev LAma LCro
'Mite' (6) ♀H6	CBro EPot
'Mitimoto' (10)	NDry
'Modern Art' (2)	ETay
'Mona Lisa' (2)	ETay
'Mondragon' (11a)	ETay WFar XFar
'Moonlight Sensation' (5) ♀H6	ERCP GKev LAma SPhx
'More and More' (7) ♀H6	CTtf EPot ERCP GKev LAma
moschatus (13) ♀H6	CBro EPot GKev LAma WShi
'Mother Duck' (6)	EPot GKev LAma XFar
'Mount Hood' (1) ♀H6	EGren EPfP ETay GKev LAma LRHS NBir WFar XFar
'Mrs Langtry' (2)	ERCP
'My Story' (4) ♀H6	ETay LAma
'Navarre' ambig. (2)	CTtf
× *neocarpetanus* var. *romanensis* (13)	NDry
'New World' (2)	ETay
'New-Baby' (7)	XFar
'Nightcap' (1)	XFar
'Nir'PBR (8)	LCro
§ *nobilis* (13)	GKev
- var. *nobilis* (13)	EPot
'Oakwood' (3)	ETay
'Obdam' (4)	LCro XFar
obsoletus (13)	WCot
obvallaris (13) ♀H6	CBWd EGren ERCP ETay LAma LCro WFar WShi
× *odorus* (13)	WShi
- 'Plenus' (4)	ERCP WShi
old pheasant's eye	see *N. poeticus* var. *recurvus*
'Omri' (8)	GKev LAma
'Orangery' (11a)	GKev LAma
'Ornatus' (9)	GKev
'Oxford Gold' (10) ♀H6	CTtf EPot GKev LAma MNrw
'Pacific Coast' (8) ♀H6	LCro
'Pacific Rim' (2)	ETay
'Pageboy' (12)	NDry
'Palila' (2) **new**	NDry
'Pallene' (10)	NDry
pallidiflorus (13)	ECha
'Palmares' (11a)	GKev
'Palomina' (6) **new**	NDry
'Pandia' (10) **new**	NDry
Panna Cotta Group (2)	NDry
'Paper White'	see *N. papyraceus*
'Paper White Grandiflorus' (8)	EPfP
'Papillon Blanc' (11b)	GKev LAma LCro
§ *papyraceus* (13)	EGren ETay
- 'Ziva' (8)	GKev LAma LCro XFar
'Paricutin' (2)	ETay
'Parterre' (2)	ETay
'Passionale' (2) ♀H6	NBir
'Pastorale' (2)	ETay WFar
'Patois' (9)	CBro
'Peach Cobbler' (4)	XFar
'Peach Prince' (4)	XFar
'Peach Twist' (1) **new**	NDry
'Peeping Jenny' (6)	LAma
'Peeping Tom' (6) ♀H6	CBro ETay LAma SRms
'Pencrebar' (4)	EPot
'Petit Four' (4)	GKev LAma
'Petrel' (5)	ERCP GKev LAma LCro MNrw XFar
'Pink Charm' (2)	ETay NBir XFar
'Pink Pride' (2)	EGren
'Pink Silk' (1)	ETay
'Pink Smiles' (2)	LAma
'Pipe Major' (2)	ETay GKev LAma
'Pipit' (7)	CBro EGren ELan ERCP ETay GKev LAma LRHS NBir WFar WShi XFar
'Pistachio' (1) ♀H6	ETay
poeticus (13)	XFar
§ - var. *hellenicus* (13)	CBro ETay
- old pheasant's eye	see *N. poeticus* var. *recurvus*
- var. *physaloides* (13)	GKev
§ - 'Plenus' ambig. (4)	ERCP LAma WShi XFar
§ - var. *recurvus* (13) ♀H6	CBro ELan EPfP EPot ERCP ETay GKev LAma LCro MBros NBir NNys SPoG WShi XFar
'Polar Ice' (3)	GKev LAma XFar
'Popeye' (4)	ETay
'Praecox' (9)	CBro
I 'Precocious' (2) ♀H6	ETay LAma XFar
'Primrose Beauty' (4)	EGren
'Princess Zaide' (3)	ETay LAma
'Professor Einstein' (2)	ETay GKev LAma XFar
'Prom Dance' (11a) ♀H6	ETay GKev LAma WFar
Propeller Group (12)	NDry
'Prototype' (6)	LAma
pseudonarcissus (13)	CHab LCro MMuc WShi
- subsp. *eugeniae*	see *N. eugeniae*
- subsp. *nobilis*	see *N. nobilis*
'Pueblo' (7)	EGren ETay GKev LAma LCro NNys
'Pupina' (2)	NDry
'Quail' (7) ♀H6	CBro EPfP ETay GKev LAma
'Rainbow' (2) ♀H6	ETay WFar
'Rainbow of Colors' (11a)	LCro
'Rapture' (6) ♀H6	CAby CBro ERCP ETay LAma LCro MNrw SDix WBrk
'Rataplan' (12)	WBrk
'Red Devon' (2)	EGren GKev LAma LCro
'Redstart' (3)	EPfP ETay
'Reggae' (6) ♀H6	CBro LAma
'Replete' (4)	EGren XFar
requienii	see *N. assoanus*
rifanus	see *N. romieuxii* subsp. *romieuxii* var. *rifanus*
'Rijnveld's Early Sensation' (1) ♀H6	CBro ECha ERCP ETay GKev LAma LCro NNys WBrk
'Rikki' (7)	CBro GKev
§ 'Rip van Winkle' (4)	CAby EGren ELan EPfP ERCP ETay GKev LAma LCro NBir WBrk WFar WShi XFar

'Rogue' (2)	CBro	'Sun Disc' (7) ♀H6	CBro ECha EGren ETay GKev LAma LCro
'Romance' (2) ♀H6	GKev LAma	'Sunlight Sensation' (5)	CBro GKev LAma LCro LRHS SPhx
romieuxii (13) ♀H4	EPot GArf WCot	'Sunlover' (2)	XFar
- SF 370 (13)	WCot	'Sunny Girlfriend' (11a)	WFar
- subsp. *albidus* (13)	LAma	'Susan Cox' (6)	NDry
- - SF 110 (13)	NDry WCot	'Sweet Petite' (6)	NDry
- - var. *zaianicus* (13)	EPot	'Sweet Pomponette' (4)	ETay
- - - SB&L 82 from Morocco (13)	WCot	'Sweetness' (7) ♀H6	ETay GKev LAma LCro WShi XFar
- - - M168 (13)	NDry	'Swiftlet' (6) **new**	NDry
§ - 'Joy Bishop' (10)	NDry WCot WMal	'Tahiti' (4) ♀H6	ELan ETay LAma LCro WFar
§ - 'Julia Jane' (10)	CAby ERCP GKev LAma LCro LRHS MNrw SDix WCot XFar	× *taitii* (13)	GKev
		'Tamara' (2)	WFar
- 'Mrs McGee' (10)	NDry	*tazetta* (13)	LRHS
* - subsp. *pallidus* SB&L 237 (13)	WCot	§ - subsp. *lacticolor* (13)	ERCP GKev LAma
		- subsp. *tazetta* (13)	GKev
§ - subsp. *romieuxii* var. *rifanus* B 8929 (13)	WCot	§ 'Telamonius Plenus' (4)	SEND
		'Tête Bouclé' PBR (4) ♀H6	CBro ERCP GKev LAma LCro WFar XFar
'Rosemoor Gold' (7) ♀H6	ETay		
'Roulette' (2)	ETay	'Tête Deluxe' (4)	ETay WBrk
'Roundita' (1)	EPot GKev	'Tête Rosette'	GKev LAma LCro
rupicola (13)	LAma NDry	'Tête-à-tête' (12) ♀H6	CAby CBro EGren EGrI EPfP EPot ERCP ETay GAbr GKev LAma LCro LRHS LSto LWaG MBros MNHC NNys WFar XFar
§ - subsp. *marvieri* (13)	NDry		
§ - subsp. *watieri* (13)	GKev NDry		
'Sabatini' (1)	XFar		
'Sabine Hay' (3)	ETay XFar	'Tethys' (10)	NDry
'Sabrosa' (7) ♀H6	CBro LCro	I 'Thalia' (5)	CBro ECha EGren ELan EPfP ERCP ETay GKev LAma LCro LRHS LSto NBir NNys SDix SPhx WFar WShi XFar
'Sacajawea' (2)	WFar		
'Sailboat' (7) ♀H6	CBro EGren EPfP ERCP ETay GKev LAma LCro MPie NNys		
		'Themisto' (10)	NDry
'Saint David's Day' (2)	ETay	'Tickled Pinkeen' (2)	ETay XFar
'Saint Keverne' (2) ♀H6	EGren ETay	'Tiny Bubbles' (12) ♀H6	CBro ETay GKev LAma
'Saint Patrick's Day' (2)	NBir	'Toddler' (1) **new**	NDry
'Salome' (2) ♀H6	EGren ETay GKev LAma LCro NBir NPer WFar	'Topolino' (1) ♀H6	CBro EGren EPfP EPot ERCP GKev LAma LCro LRHS SPoG XFar
'Salou' (4)	LCro	'Toto' (12) ♀H6	CBro ERCP GKev LAma LCro SPhx XFar
scaberulus (13)	NDry		
'Seagull' (3)	GKev LAma	'Toyama' (4)	XFar
'Sealing Wax' (2)	EPfP ETay WFar	'Tracey' (6)	GKev LAma
'Sedna' (10)	NDry	'Tranquil Morn' (3)	ETay
'Segovia' (3) ♀H6	CBro ELan ETay LAma XFar	'Trena' (2) ♀H6	LAma
'Sempre Avanti' (2)	EGren GKev LAma	'Trepolo' (11b)	LAma XFar
'Shiraume' (10)	NDry	'Tresamble' (5)	CBro EGren EPfP ETay GKev LAma LCro LRHS NBir NNys
'Shrike' (11a) ♀H6	ETay GKev LAma		
'Sidora' (1)	NDry	*triandrus* subsp. *triandrus* (13)	NDry
'Silver Chimes' (8)	CBro EPfP ETay GKev LAma LCro NBir NNys		
		- - var. *loiseleurii* (13) **new**	NDry
'Silver Smiles' (7)	LAma		
'Sinopel' (3)	ETay GKev LAma	'Tricollet' (11a)	ETay
'Sir Winston Churchill' (4) ♀H6	ETay GKev LAma LCro LRHS NNys WFar	'Tripartite' (11a) ♀H6	ETay
		'Trumpet Voluntary' (1)	NDry
'Sleek' (6)	NDry	'Tullybeg' (3)	ETay
'Snipe' (6) ♀H6	EPfP EPot GKev LRHS SDix WShi	'Turncoat' (6)	ETay
'Snowboard' (2)	ETay	'Twin Cam' (12)	NDry
'Snowtip' (2)	XFar	'Twinkling Yellow' (7) ♀H6	CBro GKev LRHS
'Soldier Brave' (2)	ETay		
'Soleil d'Or' (8)	ETay	× *ubriquensis* hort.	see *N.* × *incurvicervicus*
'Solveig's Song' (12)	WCot	'Unique' (4) ♀H6	ETay
'Sophie's Choice' (4)	ERCP	'Unsurpassable' (1)	LAma
'Speedie' (6)	NDry	'Van Sion'	see *N.* 'Telamonius Plenus'
'Spoirot' (10) ♀H6	CBro EGrI EPot ERCP GEdr GKev LAma MNrw MPie WTor XFar	'Vanilla Peach' (11a)	LAma
		'Velocity' (6)	ETay LAma
'Spring Dawn' (2)	EPfP ETay LCro WFar	'Verger' (3)	EPfP LAma
'Spring Paradijs' (4) **new**	XFar	'Vernal Prince' (3) ♀H6	ETay
'Spring Sunshine' (12)	XFar	'Victory' (6)	ETay
'Stainless' (2)	GKev LAma XFar	'Virginia Sunrise' (2)	ETay
'Star War' (2)	ETay	'Vitrina' (5)	NDry
'Starlight Sensation' (5)	CBro ERCP GKev LAma LCro SPhx	'Waltz' (11a)	LAma
'Starlit' (1)	NDry	'Warbler' (6) ♀H6	ETay
'Stint' (5) ♀H6	CBro GKev LAma SPhx	'Waterperry' (7)	XFar
'Suave' (3)	ETay		

watieri	see *N. rupicola* subsp. *watieri*
'Wave' (4)	ETay
'Wavertree'	see *N. asturiensis* 'Wavertree'
'Wee Dote' (1)	NDry
'Wee Nod' (6)	NDry
'Whippet' (6)	NDry
'White Lady' (3)	ERCP GKev LAma
'White Lion' (4) ♀H6	GKev LAma NBir
'White Marvel' (4)	EPfP XFar
'White Petticoat' (10)	EPot ERCP GEdr SDix
'Widgeon' (2)	WFar
willkommii (13)	CBro EPot
'Winter Waltz' (6) ♀H6	CBro ERCP GKev LAma MNrw
'Wisley' (6) ♀H6	LCro
'Woodstar' (5)	EPot
'Worcester' (2)	ETay
'W.P. Milner' (1)	EPfP ERCP GKev LAma LCro WBrk WShi
'Xit' (3)	CBro GKev LAma SPlb
'Yellow Cheerfulness' (4) ♀H6	ELan ETay GKev LAma LCro
'Yellow Ocean' (5) **new**	XFar
'Yellow Sailboat' (7) ♀H6	CBro EPfP NClf

Nassauvia (Asteraceae)

digitata	SPlb
gaudichaudii	GArf SPlb WAbe

Nassella (Poaceae)

cernua	EPPr
tenuissima	see *Stipa tenuissima*
trichotoma 'Palomino'	EPPr

Nastanthus (Calyceraceae)

caespitosus	SPlb

Nasturtium (Brassicaceae)

officinale	CPud CWat EHet GJem LCro LWaG MCtn MHoo MWts SVic WKit WMAq

Natal plum see *Carissa macrocarpa*

nectarine see *Prunus persica* var. *nectarina*

Nectaroscordum see *Allium*

Neillia (Rosaceae)

affinis	CExl EBee EPfP LRHS NBid NLar SPoG
incisa	CExl EHeP
§ - 'Crispa'	CBcs CDoC CMac EBee EGrI EHeP EPfP GArf GKin MBlu SRms StAn WFar
- 'Prostrata'	see *N. incisa* 'Crispa'
longiracemosa	see *N. thibetica*
ribesioides	WJur
sinensis	NLar
tanakae	CBcs CExl CMac ELan EPfP GQue LCro MBlu SRms WFar
§ *thibetica*	CBcs CDoC CExl CMac CMCN EGrI ELan EPfP GKin LEdu MBlu MMuc NLar SRms SSta WFar
thyrsiflora	EBee
- PAB 3267	LEdu
- var. *tunkinensis* HWJ 957	WCru
uekii	MBlu NLar

Nelumbo (Nelumbonaceae)

'Baby Doll'	CLil
§ 'Boli Furen'	CLil EWat
'Charles Thomas'	CBen CLil
'Debbie Gibson'	CLil
'First Lady'	CBen
'Louise Slocum'	CBen
'Maggie Belle Slocum'	CBen
'Momo Botan'	CLil
'Mrs Perry D. Slocum'	see *N.* 'Boli Furen'
nucifera 'Chawan Basu'	CLil
- 'Shiroman' (d)	CLil
'Perry's Giant Sunburst'	EWat
'Perry's Super Star' (d)	EWat
'Pink 'n' Yellow'	EWat
'Yu Ta Jiugui'	CBen

Nematanthus (Gesneriaceae)

'Apres'	WDib
'Black Magic' ♀H1b	WDib
'Christmas Holly'	WDib
'Freckles'	WDib
gregarius ♀H1b	WDib
- 'Golden West' (v) ♀H1b	WDib
'Tropicana' ♀H1b	WDib

Nemesia (Scrophulariaceae)

§ AMELIE ('Fleurame'PBR)	LBuc SPoG
(Aroma Series) AROMA BANANA SPLIT	EMdy
- AROMA PLUMS AND CUSTARD	EMdy MPri
- AROMA RHUBARB AND CUSTARD	EMdy LCro LSou MBros MPri SPoG WFar
BERRIES AND CREAM ('Fleurbac'PBR)	LBuc LCro SPoG WFar
BLUE CLOUD ('Penblu')	EGren
'Blueberry Ice' (Sundae Series)	MPnt
BLUEBIRD ('Hubbird'PBR)	CHll
'Bordeaux'	SPoG
BOYSENBERRY (Fairy Kisses Series) **new**	MSwo
'Candy Floss'	LRHS MPri
CASSIS (Fairy Kisses Series) **new**	LSou
§ *denticulata* ♀H3	LRHS MHer
- 'Celebration'PBR ♀H3	LRHS
- 'Confetti'	see *N. denticulata*
'Easter Bonnet'PBR (French Connection Series)	LCro MPri SPoG
'Fleurie Blue'	LBuc SPoG
'Forest Fruits' (Sundae Series)	MPnt
FRAMBOISE ('Fleurfram'PBR)	LBuc LCro MPri WFar
(Honey Series) HONEY BICOLOUR ORANGE FLAME	EMdy LCro
- HONEY BICOLOUR WINE **new**	LCro
- HONEY WHITE **new**	LCro
'Innocence'	EGren
(Karoo Series) KAROO DARK BLUE ('Innemkadab'PBR)	LSou MSwo
- KAROO WHITE ('Innkarwhi'PBR)	MSwo
(Lady Series) 'Lady Anne'	LCro
- 'Lady Kate'	LSou
- 'Lady Lisa'	LSou MBros
'Lavender Sherbet' (Sundae Series)	MPnt
'Mirabelle'	LBuc SPoG
MYRTILLE ('Fleurmyr'PBR)	LBuc LCro MPri SPoG
(Nesia Series) NESIA BANANA SWIRL	MPri
- NESIA BURGUNDY	LCro MPri
- NESIA SNOW ANGEL	LRHS

– NESIA TROPICAL	LCro		*laetus* ♀H3	CBcs CBct CTsd EBee LRHS SArc
(Nuvo Series) 'Nuvo Blue Bicolour'	LSou			SBig WCot WJur WPGP

– 'Nesia Tropical' LCro
(Nuvo Series) 'Nuvo Blue LSou
  Bicolour'
– 'Nuvo Burgundy Bicolour' LRHS
– 'Nuvo Pink Bicolor' LSou
OPAL INNOCENCE see *N.* AMELIE
PINK LEMONADE LSou
  ('Innempinle'PBR)
  (Fairy Kisses Series)
RASPBERRIES AND CREAM LBuc SPoG
  ('Fleurras'PBR)
'Raspberry Cream' MPnt
  (Sundae Series)
SUNDROPS MIXED MBros MPri
(Sunpeddle Series) MPri
  SUNPEDDLE PAINTED ROSE
  ('Sunjon 008'PBR) **new**
– SUNPEDDLE PLUM WHITE EMdy MPri
  BICOLOUR
– SUNPEDDLE RASPBERRY RED MPri
  BICOLOUR **new**
– SUNPEDDLE RED MPri
  ('Sunjon 1138'PBR) **new**
– SUNPEDDLE WHITE PERFUME EMdy MPri
  ('Sunjon 2562'PBR)
– SUNPEDDLE YELLOW WHITE EMdy MPri
(Sunsatia Series) SUNSATIA SPoG
  BANANA ('Intraibana')
(Sunsatia Plus Series) LRHS SPoG
  SUNSATIA PLUS CHERRY
  ON ICE ('Innemcheoi'PBR)
– SUNSATIA PLUS LITTLE MSwo
  CHERRY **new**
VANILLA BERRY LSou
  ('Innemvanbe'PBR)
  (Fairy Kisses Series)
'Vanilla Ice' (Sundae Series) MPnt
'Wisley Vanilla' EMdy LBuc LCro LRHS LSou MBros
  MPri SPoG

Nemophila (Boraginaceae)
menziesii MCtn
– 'Penny Black' CSpe

Neobuxbaumia (Cactaceae)
polylopha NPlm

Neocardenasia see *Neoraimondia*

Neodypsis see *Chrysalidocarpus*

Neohenricia (Aizoaceae)
sibbettii ♀H2 WAbe

Neohymenopogon (Rubiaceae)
parasiticus WPGP

Neolitsea (Lauraceae)
glauca see *N. sericea*
aff. *polycarpa* from WPGP
  northern Vietnam
§ *sericea* EBee WPGP
– B&SWJ 12738 WCru
– CWJ 12800 WCru
– yellow-fruited CWJ 12830 WCru

Neomarica (Iridaceae)
caerulea EAri WCot

Neopanax (Araliaceae)
§ *arboreus* CDTJ EBee ESwi LEdu SArc SEND

laetus ♀H3 CBcs CBct CTsd EBee LRHS SArc
  SBig WCot WJur WPGP

Neoporteria see *Eriosyce*

Neoraimondia (Cactaceae)
herzogiana NPlm

Neoregelia ✿ (Bromeliaceae)
'Adonis' NCft
'Anteia' NCft
'Atlantis' NCft
'Bonkers' NCft
carolinae (Meyendorffii NCft
  Group) 'Meyendorffii'
chlorosticta NCft
'Chrissy' NCft
'Cougar' NCft
'Dad's Special' NCft
'Fireball' ♀H1b NCft
'Grace' NCft
'Hannibal Lecter' CDTJ
'Iphigenie' (v) NCft
'Kahala Dawn' NCft
'Klingon' NCft
'Lillipet' NCft
lilliputiana NCft
'Magali' NCft
marmorata NCft
'Martin'PBR NCft
'Mephisto' NCft
'Midas' NCft
'Narciss' NCft
'Palmares' NCft
pauciflora NCft
I 'Paulinae' NCft
'Pink Sensation' NCft
'Red Waif' (v) NCft
'Rio Grande' NCft
I 'Rosea Striata' NCft
'Royal Burgundy' NCft
schultesiana hort. NCft
– 'Fireball Striped' ♀H1b CDTJ
I – 'Variegata' (v) NCft
'Shamrock' NCft
'Spring Song' NCft
'Tabby' NCft
'Tibbit' NCft

Neoshirakia (Euphorbiaceae)
japonica MBlu WJur WPGP

Neotinea (Orchidaceae)
ustulata LAma

Nepenthes ✿ (Nepenthaceae)
sp. SRms
'Bloody Mary'PBR CDoC LCro
ventricosa LBom LCro

Nepeta ✿ (Lamiaceae)
'Blue Beauty' see *N. sibirica* 'Souvenir d'André
  Chaudron'
'Blue Dragon' ♀H6 CBWd CCBP CDor CKno CSde
  ECha ERCP GQue IPot LBar LRHS
  LSou MHol MPie NLar SBeP SPoG
  SRkn SRms WCot WFar WHil WKif
  WOld
bucharica GBin WMal
* *buddlejifolium* NLar
* – 'Gold Splash' NLar

Nepeta

camphorata	WSpi
cataria	CGHo CoPl EHet ELan ENfk GJos IDun LCro MCtn MHer MHoo MNHC NBro NLar SRms SVic WKit WSpi
§ - 'Citriodora'	CTsd ENfk IDun MHoo SRms SVic
- 'Lemony'	SVic
- 'Cat's Pajamas'^{PBR}	LBar LBom LBuc LCro LRHS LSou MHol MHtn NCth WFar WHoo
- 'Chettle Blue'^{♀H7}	CDor CKno ECha GBin MAvo SPel
citriodora Dum.	see *N. cataria* 'Citriodora'
clarkei	GMaP WSpi
curviflora	ELan SHor SPhx
§ *cyanea* ^{♀H7}	CDor CSpe EBee ELan GBin MBel NLar NSti SDix SHor WCAu WCot WTre
- 'Dropmore'	EBee NLar WSpi
- 'Early Bird'	MAvo
§ × *faassenii*	CBcs CDor CSpe EBee EGren ELan ELon EPfP GKev GMaP GQue LCro LRHS MGos NLar NPer SAng SAth SPlb SPoG SRms WCAu WKit
- 'Alba'	EBee ELan EWhm MHoo NLar SRms WSpi
- 'Blue Wonder' ^{♀H7}	EBee EBlo ELan EPfP LRHS MHol NCth NLar SPhx WCAu WFar WSpi
- 'Crystal Cloud'	EPfP LRHS MHol NLar SHar
- 'Gletschereis'	GBin NDov NLar
- JUNIOR WALKER ('Novanepjun'^{PBR}) ^{♀H7}	CBcs CBWd EBee EBlo EGren EPfP EUrb GMaP LBar LBom LCro LRHS LSRN MPri MPro NLar SPhx WCAu WCot WNPC WTor XFar
- 'Kit Cat' ^{♀H7}	CBcs CBWd EBee EBlo GBin LRHS MAsh LBel MHer MHoo WCAu WChS WSpi
- 'Kitten Around'	LBuc LRHS LSou
- 'Purrsian Blue'^{PBR ♀H7}	Widely available
- (Whispurr Series) WHISPURR BLUE ('Balpurrlu'^{PBR})	EGren LSou
- - WHISPURR PINK ('Balpurrink'^{PBR})	EGren EPfP LBar
'Florina'	CBWd LRHS SMHy
glechoma 'Variegata'	see *Glechoma hederacea* 'Variegata'
govaniana ^{♀H6}	CDor EBee ECha ELan EMor EPfP GBin GElm GJos GMaP GQue LBar LEdu LShi MCtn MHol NBid NBir NDov NSti SHor SMrm SPoG SRms WCAu WChS WFar WPGP WTre
grandiflora	CDor SMHy
- 'Blue Danube'	EBee ECha GBin
- 'Blue Elf'	MHoo NDov
- 'Bramdean' ^{♀H6}	CBWd CCBP CDor CMac CWal EBee EPfP EWes GBin LBar LRHS LSto MHol NLar SPel SPhx SRms WCAu WCot WHoo WKif
- 'Dawn to Dusk'	CBcs CDor CMac CMHG CWnw EBee ECha ELan EPfP EPPr ESgI GBin GMaP GQue LRHS LSto NBir NLar NSti SAth SMrm SNoN SPhx SPoG SRms WCAu WFar WTor
- 'Pool Bank'	EBee NLar SMrm
- 'Summer Magic'^{PBR ♀H6}	CKno EBee EBlo ECha EPfP GBin LBar LCro LRHS LSou MBel MHol MPro NClf NCth NLar SBea SHar SOrN SPel SPhx SPoG SRkn WCAu WFar WNPC WTor
- 'Wild Cat' ^{♀H6}	CWnw NLar WCAu
- 'Zinser's Giant' ^{♀H6}	EBee LBar
hederacea 'Variegata'	see *Glechoma hederacea* 'Variegata'
'Hill Grounds'	CKno EBee ECha GBin LSto MAvo MHol NLar SPel SPhx SRkn WCot
italica	EBee LRHS SHar
'Joanna Reed'	IPot NLar WSpi
kubanica	see *N. cyanea*
§ 'Leeds Castle'	CCBP EBee EPfP LRHS MHol NGdn NSti SHar SMrm SPoG WCAu WCav WFar
LITTLE TRUDY ('Psfike')	ELan EPfP
longipes hort.	see *N.* 'Leeds Castle'
macrantha	see *N. sibirica*
manchuriensis 'Manchu Blue'	LBar
mussinii misapplied	see *N.* × *faassenii*
mussinii Spreng.	see *N. racemosa*
nepetella	ECha SDix
subsp. *aragonensis*	
NEPTUNE ('Bokratune')	CKno EGren LBar LBom LCro LRHS LSou LSRN MHol MHtn MNHC MPri NCth SAth WNPC XFar
nervosa	CDor CSpe ECha ELan GJos MCtn NBro NLar NSti SHar
- 'Blue Carpet'	CSpe
- 'Blue Moon'	CCBP CMHG EBee EGren EPfP EWes GBin LShi MBNS MHol MPie MPnt NGdn NLar SRms WFar WSpi
- 'Pink Cat'	CDor EGren EPfP LBom WFar
- 'Schneehäschen'	SAko WSpi
§ *nuda*	ECha GBin GQue LShi MMrt SHar SPel WGoo
- 'Alba'	LEdu
- subsp. *albiflora*	ECha
- 'Anne's Choice'	GBin IPot SPel
- 'Lake Sevan'	LEdu
- 'Purple Cat' ^{♀H7}	EBee GBin IPot
- 'Romany Dusk' ^{♀H7}	CSpe ECha IPot LEdu NClf SMHy SMrm SPhx WPGP WSpi
- 'Snow Cat'	SHar
pannonica	see *N. nuda*
parnassica	EPPr GQue MHol MMuc SHar SMrm
'Pink Candy'	SRms
'Poseidon'	CKno MHol SPel
'Purple Haze'^{PBR}	ELan EPfP LBar MHol
§ *racemosa*	CHby CMac EHet EPfP EWhm GJos LRHS MHoo MNHC StAn WRBe WCot
- RCB AM 3	CDor ECha MHoo
- 'Alba'	CBWd CCBP CElw CKno EBlo ECha EPfP LRHS LSto MHer NDov SDix SNoN WFar WGoo WMal WTor
- 'Amelia' ^{♀H7}	NLar
- 'Blauknirps'	ELan EPfP WFar WHil
- 'Felix'	EBee LRHS NLar SPel SPoG WSpi
- 'Grog'	ECha EPfP GKev LBar LRHS LShi LSto MMrt NGdn NLar WHoo
- 'Little Titch'	CBcs CBWd CCBP CWnw EBee ELan ELon EPfP EPPr EUrb GMaP LRHS LSto MAsh MPnt MWlw NBir NCth NLar NSti SAth SMrm SPoG WCAu WSpi XFar
- 'Snowflake'	NDov SMHy
- 'Toria'	Widely available
- 'Walker's Low' ^{♀H7}	EWes
'Rae Crug'	see *N. racemosa*
reichenbachiana	SPhx
'Rotherbridge Blue'	CGHo ECha EPfP LBar LRHS MHol NBid NBro SRkn WCAu WCot
§ *sibirica*	CDor EBee EPfP GElm GMaP LSto MHol NLar SPoG WCAu WSpi
- 'Souvenir d'André Chaudron'	Widely available
'Six Hills Giant' ^{♀H7}	

'Six Hills Gold' (v)	CDor CGHo EBee EGren LBuc LRHS LShi WCot WSpi		'Berlioz' × 'Mars'	WCot
			'Bettina'	WCot
stenantha	WCot		'Betty Hudson'	WCot
stewartiana	ECha EPfP MPro		'Bishops Sutton'	WCot
- W&O 7173	GGro		'Blanche'	WCot
subsessilis	CBcs CBWd ELan EPfP LSRN NBid NBir NGdn NSti SPoG SRms WCAu		'Blanchefleur'	WCot
			'Blenheim'	WCot
- 'Blue Dreams'	MHol NLar SBea SHar SPhx WSpi		'Blushing Bride'	WCot
- BLUE PRELUDE ('Balneplud'PBR)	EGren LBar LSou MHol NCth WHil		'Borde Hill'	WCot
			'Borde Hill White'	WCot
- 'Candy Cat'	NLar		'Boscastle'	WCot
- 'Cool Cat'	EBee		'Botley'	WCot
- 'Pink Dreams'	ECha ELan EMor MCtn MPro SHar		*bowdenii* ♀H5	Widely available
- PURPLE PRELUDE ('Balprelurp'PBR)	LBar MPro		- 'Alba' misapplied	see *N. bowdenii* 'Pallida'
			- 'Alba' ambig.	CBlu CBro CTsd EBee EGren ERCP GKev LAma MNrw WCot WFar XFar
- 'Sweet Dreams' ♀H6	GBin NLar NSti			
- 'Washfield' ♀H7	EBee EMor NLar SAko			
transcaucasica	SDix		- 'Albivetta'	CBlu GKev LAma MNrw WHil
- 'Blue Infinity'	GMaP WFar		- 'Amandi'PBR	ERCP GKev LAma WHil
tuberosa	CTsd ECha LShi WFar		- 'Bianca Perla' ♀H5	ELan GKev LAma WHil
'Veluws Blauwtje'	ECha IPot NLar WSpi		- 'Bicolor'	SMad
'Weinheim Big Blue' ♀H6	CKno IPot MAvo MHol MWlw NCth NLar		- 'Bionce'	EGren GKev LAma
			- 'Codora'	see *N.* 'Codora'
'Weinheim Summer Blues' ♀H7	ECha GBin		- 'Edelweiss'	WHil
			- 'Ella K'	EPfP LCro WFar
* *yunnanensis*	EPPr GGro NBid SMrm WFar		- 'Emma'	WCot
			- 'Flügel'	XFar
Nephrolepis (*Lomariopsidaceae*)			- 'Gletsjer'	WCot
'Boston'	LWaG NHrt		- Irish clone	WCot
cordifolia	CDTJ SBig		- 'Isabel' ♀H5	CAby CBlu CBro CMac CTsd ECha EGren ELan ERCP EShb EWes GKev LAma LCro WCot WHoo XFar
duffii	EShb LWaG			
exaltata ♀H1b	LBom LCro LWaG SEND			
- 'Bostoniensis' ♀H1b	EGren EShb NHrt		- 'John Crisp' ♀H5	WCot
- 'Green Lady'	LBom LCro LInt LRHS LWaG NHrt		- 'Like a Virgin'	EGren GKev LAma
- 'Marisa'	EShb		- 'Lipstick'	CBro EBee EGren GKev LAma LRHS MNrw WCot WMal XFar
- 'Smithii'	EShb			
- 'Tiger Fern' (v)	LCro		- 'Manina'	WMal
- 'Verona'	WCot		- 'Marjorie' ♀H5	EMal EPfP
obliterata 'Emerald Queen'	LRHS		- 'Mark Fenwick'	CBro WCot
			- 'Marney Rogerson'	CBro WCot
		§	- 'Mollie Cowie' (v)	WCot WCru
Nephrophyllidium (*Menyanthaceae*)			- 'Mount Stewart' ♀H5	EPPr WCot
crista-galli	GGro		- 'Nikita'	WCot
			- 'Ostara'	CAby EBee EGren ELan EPfP GKev LAma LCro LRHS WCot WFar
Nerine ✿ (*Amaryllidaceae*)				
'Ada Bryson'	WCot	§	- 'Pallida'	WCot
'Administrator'	WCot		- 'Patricia'	EGrI MNrw
'Afterglow'	WCot		- 'Pink Surprise' ♀H5	WCot WMal
'Alexandra'	WCot		- 'Praecox'	WMal
'Alresford'	WCot	§	- 'Quinton Wells' ♀H6	WCot
'Amalfi'	WCot		- - pale yellow-leaved	WCot
'Amschel'	WCot		- 'Richard Blakeway-Phillips'	WCot
'Ancilla'	WCot			
'Andromeda'	WCot		- 'Robert Smith'	WCot
'Angelico'	WCot		- 'Sheila Owen'	WCot
angustifolia	WAbe		- 'Sofie'	EBee WCot
'Anne Baring'	WCot		- 'Stam 63' ♀H5	CAby EGren ERCP GKev LRHS WCot WHil WHoo
'Anne Rolls'	WCot			
'Aquila'	WCot		- 'Stefanie' ♀H5	EAri EBee EShb
'Aries'	WCot		- 'Stewart Gilkison'	SHar
'Ashmore'	WCot		- 'Tess Allen'	WCot
'Atlanta'	WCot		- 'Variegata'	see *N. bowdenii* 'Mollie Cowie'
'Audrey'	WCot		- 'Vesta K'	CTsd EGren GKev LAma XFar
'Audrey Clarke'	WCot		- 'Welland Pale' ♀H5	SHar WCot
'Audrey Holland-Hibbert'	WCot		- 'Wellsii'	see *N. bowdenii* 'Quinton Wells'
'Aurora'	WCot		- subsp. *wellsii*	WCot
'Bach'	WCot		'Brahms'	WCot
'Baghdad'	SChr WCot		'Bredon'	WCot
'Belladonna'	WCot		'Brickfielder'	WCot
'Bennett-Poë'	WCot		'Brightest Orange Flame'	WCot
'Berlioz'	WCot		'Brocade'	WCot

'Bulawayo-koo'	WCot		'Dorabella'	WCot
'Cadnam'	WCot		'Doris Vos'	WCot
'Caelum'	WCot		'Dorothea'	WCot
'Californian Hybrid'	WCot		'Dorothy Palmer'	WCot
'Caliph'	WCot		'Dorothy Trotter'	WCot
'Canasta'	WCot		'Dover'	WCot
'Candy'	WCot		'Dover' × 'Emmaline Smith'	WCot
'Captain Dunne Cooke'	WCot		'Drucilla'	WCot
'Cardinal'	EAri WCot		'Druid'	WCot
'Carisbrooke'	WCot		'Druid' × 'Inchmery Kate'	WCot
'Carlos'	WCot		'Dunkirk'	WCot
'Carnival' × 'Joyous'	WCot		'Early Snow'	EAri
'Caroline'	WCot		'Early Snow' × 'Ken Hall White'	WCot
'Caryatid'	WCot WFar			
'Casanova'	WCot		'Eddy'	WCot
'Cassius'	WCot		'Edith Amy'	WCot
'Catherine'	WCot		'Eleanor'	WCot
'Catkin'	WCot		Elegance Series	WCot
'Cavalcade'	WCot		- 'Elegance Red'	CBro
CDE 5A1	WCot		'Elspeth'	WCot
CDE 5AC	WCot		'Empire Day'	WCot
CDE 5AG	WCot		'Enchantress'	WCot
CDE 5AQ	WCot		'Enigma'	WCot
CDE 5AR	WCot		'Erubescens'	WCot
CDE 5AS	WCot		'Esteem'	WCot
CDE 5BA	WCot		'Eve'	WCot
CDE 5X	WCot		'Exbury Leo'	WCot
CDE 51	WCot		'Exbury Red'	WCot
CDE 58B	WCot		'Exbury White'	WCot
CDE 58C	WCot		'Fairhaven'	WCot
'Celestial'	WCot		'Fairylight'	WCot
'Celum'	WCot		'Falaise'	WCot
'Celum' × 'Phoenix'	WCot		'Fatima'	WCot
'Cephus'	WCot		'Ffiske'	WCot
'CGF'	WCot		'Fiesta'	WCot
'Chanticleer'	WCot		*filamentosa* misapplied	see *N. filifolia* Baker
'Cherry'	WCot	§	*filifolia* Baker	EAri EPot WAbe
'Cherubino'	WCot		'Firelight'	WCot
'Chocolate Flavour'	WCot		'Flamenco'	WCot
'Chorister'	WCot		'Fortune'	WCot
'Christmas'	WCot		'Foudroyant Wavebush'	WCot
'Christmas Dreams'	WCot		'Fred Wynniatt'	WCot
'Clarabel'	WCot		'Frosted Orange'	WCot
'Clarissa'	WCot		'Frou Frou'	WCot
'Clent Charm'	WCot		'Funchal'	WCot
'Cleopatra'	WCot		*gaberonensis*	WAbe
§ 'Codora'	EPfP LCro MHtn WCot WFar		'Gaby Deslys'	WCot
'Corallina'	WCot		'Gaiety'	WCot
'Corlette'	WCot		'George'	WCot
'Countdown'	WCot		'Ghost Dancer'	WCot
'Countess Maria Plater'	WCot		'Gipsy Queen'	WCot
'Countess of Mulgrave'	WCot		'Giraffe'	WCot
'Coverack'	WCot		'Glacier'	CBro
'Cradley'	WCot		'Glamour'	WCot
'Cranfield'	WCot		'Glenbourne'	WCot
crispa	see *N. undulata* Crispa Group		'Glencoe'	WCot
'Curiosity'	WCot		'Glensavage Gem'	CBro WCot
'Cynthia Brooke'	WCot		Glensavage No 37	WCot
'Cynthia Chance'	WCot		'Gloaming'	WCot
'Dame Alice Godman'	WCot		'Godiva'	WCot
'Danks Seedling'	WCot		'Gorgeous'	WCot
'Daphne'	WCot		'Gossamer'	WCot
'Darling'	WCot		'Grace'	WCot
'Dawn'	WCot		'Grandeur'	WCot
'Defford'	WCot		'Grania'	WCot
'Delius'	WCot		'Grogarry Loch'	WCot
'Delius' × 'Inchmery Kate'	WCot		'Guy Fawkes'	WCot
'Desdemona'	WCot		'Gweek'	WCot
'Diana Clare'	WCot		'Hailstorm'	WCot
'Diana Oliver'	WCot		'Halcyon'	WCot
'Dingaan'	WCot		'Hambledon'	WCot

'Hamilton'	WCot		'Judith' Barr	WCot
'Hamlet'	WCot		'Julie'	WCot
'Hanley Castle'	WCot		'Juliet Berkeley'	WCot
'Happiness'	WCot		'Julietta'	WCot
'Harlequin'	WCot		'Kalahari Lawn'	WCot
'Harry Adams No 25'	WCot		'Kashmir'	EPot GKev WCot
'Harry Dalton'	WCot		'Kate Cicely'	WCot
'Hawaii'	WCot		'Kedive'	WCot
'Heather'	WCot		'Kemp'	WCot
'Helen Smith'	WCot		'Kempsey'	WCot
'Helena'	WCot		'Kenilworth'	EAri WCot
'Helford'	WCot		'Killarney'	WCot
'Henrietta'	WCot	*	'Killi'	WCot
'Henry Elwes'	WCot		'Kim'	WCot
'Hera'	CBro		'King Leopold'	WCot WFar
'Herga'	WCot		'King of the Belgians'	WCot
'Hermione'	WCot		'Kings Somborne'	WCot
'Hertha Berg'	WCot		'Kingship'	WCot
'Hesta'	WCot		'Kinn McIntosh'	WCot
'Highdown Scarlet'	WCot		'Kipling'	WCot
'Highlight'	WCot		'Kirsty'	WCot
'Hirao No 1'	WCot		'Kit'	WCot
'Hirao No 3'	WCot		'Kleeve'	WCot
* *hirsuta*	WCot		'Knight Templar'	WCot
'Hitomi'	WCot		'Kobi'	WCot
'Hon. Miss Gibbs'	WCot		'Koja'	WCot
'Hon. Mrs Kingscote'	WCot		'Koko'	WCot
'Honorable Mrs Wyne'	WCot		'Konak'	WCot
'Hotspur'	WCot		'Koppie'	WCot
humilis ♀H2	CBro WAbe		'Koriba'	WCot
– from Bredasdorp, South Africa	WCot		*krigei*	WCot
			'Krishna'	WCot
– Breachiae Group	SAng WCot		'Kronborg'	WCot
– Peersii Group	WCot		'Kyle'	WCot
humilis × 'Mars'	WCot		'Kynance'	WCot
'Ibsen'	WCot		'Kyoto'	WCot
'Ibsen' × *sarniensis*	WCot		'Kyrie'	WCot
'Ice Cap'	WCot		'La Reine'	WCot
'Idaho'	WCot		'Lady Corder'	WCot
'Ides'	WCot		'Lady Cynthia Colville'	WCot
'Iman'	WCot		'Lady de Walden'	WCot
'Imp'	WCot		'Lady Downe'	WCot
'Impact'	WCot		'Lady Eleanor Keane'	WCot
'Incarol'	WCot		'Lady Havelock-Allen'	WCot
'Inchmery Elizabeth'	WCot		'Lady Llewellyn'	EAri WCot
'Inchmery Kate'	WCot		'Lady Lucy Hicks Beech'	WCot
'Iona'	WCot		'Lady Mary Shelley'	WCot
'Iowa'	WCot		'Lady Redesdale'	WCot
'Isa'	WCot		'Lady St Aldwyn'	WCot
'Island Prince'	WCot		'Lady Stanley'	WCot
'Isobel'	EGrI LEdu MPro WFar		'Lady Stirling Maxwell'	WCot
'Isolation'	WCot		'Laguna'	WCot
'Itchen Stoke'	WCot		'Lambourne'	WCot
'Ixianthia'	WCot		'Lamousmee'	WCot
'Jackie'	WCot		*laticoma*	WCot
'Jacqueline'	WCot		'Latu'	WCot
'Janet'	WCot		'Lavant'	WCot
'Jaunty'	WCot		'Lavendu'	WCot
'Jennifer'	WCot		'Lawlord'	WCot
'Jenny Wren'	WCot		'Laysan'	WCot
'Jerry'	WCot		'Leila Hughes'	WCot
'Jezebel' × 'Peter Barber'	WCot		'Lenin'	WCot
'Jho Oho Sama'	WCot		'Leo'	WCot
'Jill'	WCot		'Libby'	WCot
'Joan'	WCot		'Lilywhite'	WCot
'Joan' × 'June Rolls'	WCot		'Lionel'	WCot
'Joan' × *platypetala*	WCot		'Loch Bhanain'	WCot
'Joan Mary'	WCot		'Loch Bornish'	WCot
'Joy'	WCot		'Loch Caslub'	WCot
'Joyous'	WCot		'Loch Hermidale'	WCot
'Judith' ambig.	SChr		'Loch Naid'	WCot

'Loch Roag'	WCot	'Osborne'	WCot
'Loch Spotal'	WCot	'Othello'	WCot
'Lochart'	WCot	'Ovington'	WCot
'Long Island Beauty'	WCot	'Owslebury'	WCot
'Louis I'	WCot	'Pamela'	EPot GKev LAma WCot
'Lovely Lady'	WCot	'Pamela Norris'	WCot
'Lucia'	WCot	'Pandora'	WCot
'Lucinda'	WCot	'Pantaloon'	WCot
'Lucy Loo'	WCot	'Paragon'	WCot
'Lumen'	WCot	'Patricia Clarke'	WCot
'Lymington'	WCot	'Pauliniana'	WCot
'Lyndhurst Salmon'	WCot	'Pearls of Cherry'	ERCP GKev LAma XFar
'Madua'	WCot	(Elegance Series)	
'Maggie'	WCot	'Peeress'	WCot
'Malvern'	WCot	'Peking'	WCot
'Mandarin' × *sarniensis*	WCot	'Penelope'	WCot
'Maria'	WCot	'Perhaps'	WCot
'Marie-Louise Agius'	WCot	'Pershore'	WCot
'Mariloo'	WCot	'Peter Barber'	WCot
'Martyrworthy'	WCot	'Phillips'	WCot
masoniorum ♀H2	WAbe	'Phoenix'	WCot
'Meadowbankii'		'Phyllis Norris'	WCot
'Mevagissey'	WCot	'Pink Delight'	WCot
'Miss Baring'	WCot	'Pink Distinction'	WCot
'Miss Carrington'	WCot	'Pink Fairy'	WCot
'Miss E. Cator'	WCot	'Pink Galore'	WCot
'Miss Edith Godman'		'Pink Hex'	WCot
'Miss Florence Brown'	WCot	'Pink Triumph'	CBcs CMac CTsd ELan GKev WCot
'Miss Frances Clarke'	WCot	'Plymouth'	EAri SChr WCot
'Miss Moore'	WCot	'Prince of Orange'	EPot GKev LAma
'Miss Rosamund Elwes'	WCot	'Priscella'	WCot
'Miss Willmott'	WCot	*pudica* pink-flowered	WCot
'Monet'	WCot	'Purple Prince'	EAri WCot
'Morning Star'	WCot	'Purple Robes'	WCot
'Mother of Pearl'	WCot	'Quarr'	WCot
'Mottistone'	WCot	'Queen Mother'	WCot
'Mr John'	CBlu CBro EAri EGrI LAma WCot XFar	'Queen Salote'	WCot
		'Quest'	WCot
'Mrs Berkeley'	WCot	'Quivotina'	WCot
'Mrs Bromley'	WCot	'Radnor'	WCot
'Mrs C. Goldsmith'	WCot	'Rainbow'	WCot
'Mrs Cooper'	WCot	'Ramsdown'	WCot
'Mrs Dent Brocklehurst'	WCot	'Random'	WCot
'Mrs Harrison'	WCot	'Random Knot'	WCot
'Mrs Hooker'	WCot	'Red Admiral'	WCot
'Murilla'	WCot	'Red Deer'	WCot
'Myfanwi'	WCot	'Red Emperor'	WCot
'Nabob'	WCot	'Red Letter Day'	WCot
'Nancy Perth'	WCot	'Red Maple'	WCot
'Natasha'	WCot	'Red Pimpernel'	EPot GKev LAma WHil
'Natron'	WCot	'Regina' ♀H5	WCot
'Navita'	WCot	'Regulus'	WCot
'Neige'	WCot	'Rembrandt'	WCot
'Nena'	WCot	'Revlon'	WCot
'Nero'	WCot	'Rhododendron'	WCot
'New Zealand 95'	WCot	'Rhodora'	EAri WCot
'Nidia'	WCot	'Riches'	WCot
'Night Glow'	WCot	'Rochelle'	WCot
'Noel'	WCot	'Rock'	WCot
'Nora Hamilton'	WCot	'Romsey'	WCot
'Norris's White'	WCot	'Rosa Stevenson'	WCot
'Novelty'	WCot	'Rose Godman'	WCot
'November Cheer'	EPot GKev LAma	'Rose Princess'	WCot
'Oberon'	WCot	'Rosy Veil'	WCot
'October David'	WCot	'Rotherside'	WCot
'Oldnall'	WCot	'Rotunda'	WCot
'Ophelia'	WCot	'Royalty'	WCot
'Orange Flame'	WCot	'Rushmere Star'	SChr WCot
'Orange Queen'	WCot	'Rushmere Victor'	WCot
'Orangeade'	WCot	'Ruth'	WCot WFar
'Orion'	WCot	'Saint Mary Bourne'	WCot

Nicotiana 481

	'Salmon Décor'	WCot		'Yealm King'	WCot
	'Salmon Flame'	WCot		'Yealm Queen'	WCot WMal
	'Salmon Supreme'	WCot		'Yiggit'	WCot
	'Salmonia'	WCot		'Zanya'	WCot
	'Sappho'	WCot		'Zeal Giant' ♀H3	CBlu CBro EGren GKev WCot WFar
	'Sarah'	WCot		'Zeal Grilse'	WCot
	sarniensis	CBlu CBro ECha GKev LAma WCot WFar XFar		'Zeal Purple Stripe'	WMal
				'Zeal Silver Stripe'	WCot
*	- (Alba Group) 'Alba'	WCot		'Zennor'	WCot
	- 'Corusca Major'	CAby CBro EGrI LAma WCot		'Zulu Warrior'	WCot
	- 'Fothergillii'	WCot			
	- 'Queen Mary'	WCot			
	'Scarlet Admiral'	WCot			
	'Scarletta'	WCot			
	'Seabather'	WCot			
	'Seaview'	WCot			
	'Serendipity'	WCot			
	'Shan'	WCot			
	'Shardlow Beauty'	WCot			
	'Sheelagh Mulholland'	WCot			
	'Sheila'	WCot			
	'Smokey'	WCot			
	'Smokey Special'	WCot			
	'Snowflake'	WCot			
	'Sol Pud'	WCot			
	'Solent Swan'	WCot			
	'Speke'	WCot			
	'Spetchley Park Pink'	WCot			
	'Spitfire'	WCot			
	'Springbank Alice'	WCot			
	'Springbank Jo'	WCot			
	'Springbank Sophie'	WCot			
	'Stephanie'	CTsd EAri LEdu MNrw WCot WHoo			
	'Stockbridge'	WCot			
	'Stoke Charity'	WCot			
	'Sugar Stick'	WCot			
	'Sunset Frills'	WCot			
	'Surprising Dreams'	WCot			
	'Susan Norris'	WCot			
	'Sveva Pio'	WCot			
	'Tamilla'	WCot			
	'Tancred'	WCot			
	'The Choir'	WCot			
	'Thestral'	WCot			
	'Treasure'	WCot			
	'Tugela'	WCot			
	'Tweedledee'	WCot			
	'Tweedledum'	WCot			
	'Twyford'	WCot			
	'Uncle A'	WCot			
	undulata	EGrI GKev LAma MPie WMal			
§	- Crispa Group	CBlu EPfP WFar WHil XFar			
	- 'Engcobo'	WMal			
	- (Flexuosa Group)	CBro WCot			
	'Alba' ♀H3				
	- 'Seaton' ♀H5	CBro WCot WMal			
	'Uriel'	WCot			
	× *versicolor* 'Mansellii'	CBro WCot			
	'Vestal'	WCot			
	'Vicky'	WCot			
	'Victor'	WCot			
	'Victor' × 'Wolsey'	WCot			
	'Westmead Giant'	WCot			
	'White Star'	WCot			
	'White Supreme'	LAma			
	'Winter Sun'	SRms			
	'Wisley Bridesmaid'	WCot			
	'Wolsey'	WCot			
	'Wombe'	WCot			
	'Xanthia'	WCot			
	'Yaverland'	WCot			

Nerium (Apocynaceae)

§	*odoratum* 'Miss Agnes Campbell'	SEND
	oleander L. ♀H3	CAbb CTsd EShb EUrb SArc SAth SPlb SPoG
	- from Morocco	WPGP
	- 'Agnes Campbell'	see *N. odoratum* 'Miss Agnes Campbell'
	- 'Album'	SEND
	- 'Album Plenum' (d)	EAri
	- 'Alsace'	SEND
	- 'Angiolo Pucci'	EAri EShb
I	- 'Barcelona'	SEND
I	- 'Claudia'	SEND
	- double apricot-flowered (d)	SEND
	- dwarf	WJur
	- 'Flavescens Plenum' (d)	EAri
	- 'Madame Allen' (d)	EShb
	- 'Magaly'	SEND
	- 'Margaritha'	SEND
	- 'Minouche'	SEND
	- 'Oasis' (d)	EAri
	- subsp. *oleander*	NPlm
	- pink-flowered	EUrb NPlm SPad
	- 'Professeur Granel' (d)	EShb
	- 'Provence' (d)	EAri
	- red-flowered	EAri EUrb NPlm SPad
	- 'Roseum Plenum' (d)	CRHN SEND
I	- 'Rubis' (d)	EAri
	- 'Splendens Giganteum' (d)	EAri EShb
	- 'Tito Poggi'	EAri
	- 'Variegatum' (v)	EAri EShb
	- white-flowered	EUrb NPlm SPad

Neviusia (Rosaceae)

alabamensis	NLar

Nicandra (Solanaceae)

physalodes	ELan ENfk MCtn NBir WFar
- 'Violacea'	CSpe SRms

Nicotiana ✿ (Solanaceae)

alata	CSpe LCro MCtn MNHC SPhx WFar
- 'Grandiflora'	LCro
'Babybella'	MCtn
'Black Knight'	CSpe
excelsior	MCtn
glauca	CDTJ SPlb WJun
glutinosa	CSpe EAri MCtn
- 'Peach Screamer' new	CSpe
knightiana	CDTJ CSpe
langsdorffii ♀H2	CSpe EAri LCro LSto SPhx WFar
- 'Bronze Queen'	CSpe LCro
'Lime Green' ♀H2	CSpe LCro MCtn SPhx
mutabilis	CSpe LCro MCtn SPhx
quadrivalvis	SPhx
rustica	CSpe MCtn
× *sanderae* Avalon Series	MBros

– Cuba Series	MPri
– (Perfume Series) 'Perfume Deep Purple'	CSpe MCtn SPhx
– – 'Perfume Lime'	MCtn
solanifolia	SPlb
suaveolens	CSpe SPhx
sylvestris ♀H2	CDTJ CSpe ELan EPfP LCro LWaG MCtn MPri SPhx SPoG
tabacum 'Tobaco Rosa'	MCtn MNHC
'Tinkerbell'	MCtn
WHISPER MIXED	LCro MCtn

Nidularium (Bromeliaceae)
'Fireball'	LWaG

Nierembergia (Solanaceae)
§ *repens*	NLar WCot
rivularis	see *N. repens*

Nigella (Ranunculaceae)
bucharica 'Blue Stars'	CSpe MCtn
damascena 'Albion Black Pod'	MCtn
– 'Albion Green Pod'	LCro MCtn
– 'Miss Jekyll' ♀H3	LCro LSto MCtn MNHC MPro
– 'Miss Jekyll Alba' ♀H3	CSpe LCro MCtn
– 'Mulberry Rose'	LSto MPro
– 'Oxford Blue'	LCro
– Persian Jewels Group	GJem MCtn MNHC SVic
– – indigo-flowered	MCtn
hispanica L.	LCro MCtn MNHC
orientalis 'Transformer'	MCtn
papillosa 'African Bride'	CSpe LCro MCtn MPro
– 'Delft Blue'	LCro MCtn
– 'Midnight'	CSpe MCtn
sativa	MCtn

Niphidium (Polypodiaceae)
crassifolium	EShb LEdu WCot

Nipponanthemum (Asteraceae)
§ *nipponicum*	EBee ESgI GGro MMuc NLar NSti SAko SPoG SRms

Nolina (Asparagaceae)
excelsa	CExl
greenei **new**	CExl
§ *hibernica*	CExl EUrb NPlm WPGP
'La Siberica'	see *N. hibernica*
lindheimeriana	WCot
longifolia	NPlm SArc SBig
nelsonii	CDoC EUrb LRHS NPlm SArc SBig SPlb WPGP
texana	WCot

Nomocharis see *Lilium*
forrestii	see *Lilium apertum*

Nonea (Boraginaceae)
lutea	EPPr NAts NSti

Nothaphoebe (Lauraceae)
cavaleriei	CExl WPGP

Nothofagus ✿ (Nothofagaceae)
§ *alpina*	LCot WJur
antarctica	CAco CMCN CNWT EBee ELan EPfP GKin MAsh MBlu MMuc NLar NOra NPip SAko WJur WMat
betuloides	SPlb
cunninghamii	IArd SAko
dombeyi ♀H5	CBrP EPfP IArd LEdu MBlu SArc SPlb WGrf WPGP WSpi
fusca	WPGP
gunnii	CBrP
menziesii	MBlu WPGP
moorei	MBlu WPGP
nervosa	see *N. alpina*
obliqua	GAbr IPap
procera Oerst.	see *N. alpina*

Notholaena see *Cheilanthes*

Notholirion (Liliaceae)
campanulatum	MNrw
macrophyllum	GArf
thomsonianum	GKev

Notholithocarpus (Fagaceae)
§ *densiflorus*	CMCN
– var. *echinoides*	WPGP

Nothopanax see *Polyscias*

Nothoscordum (Amaryllidaceae)
dialystemon	EDAr EPot WAbe
montevidense	GKev WCot
neriniflorum	see *Allium neriniflorum*
ostenii	WCot

Notocactus see *Parodia*

Nototriche (Malvaceae)
macleanii	WAbe

Nuphar (Nymphaeaceae)
japonica	CLil CToG
lutea	CBen CHab ELin EPfk LCro
pumila	CLil CToG

Nuytsia (Loranthaceae)
floribunda	SPlb

Nylandtia see *Muraltia*

Nymphaea ✿ (Nymphaeaceae)
'Afterglow' (T/D)	CLil
alba (H)	CBen CHab CPud CWat ELin EPfk LCro MWts NBir WMAq
'Alba Plenissima' (H)	CBen
'Albatros' misapplied	see *N.* 'Hermine'
§ 'Albatros' Latour-Marliac (H)	ELin NPer WMAq
'Albatross'	see *N.* 'Albatros' Latour-Marliac, *N.* 'Hermine'
* 'Albida'	CWat WMAq
'Almost Black' (H)	CBen CLil CPud CWat ELin EWat LCro
'Amabilis' (H)	CBen CLil ELin EWat WMAq
'Andreana' (H)	CBen CLil ELin EWat
'Arc-en-ciel' (H)	CBen CLil ELin WMAq
'Arctic Maiden' **new**	CLil
'Atropurpurea' (H)	CBen CLil EWat NPer WMAq
'Attraction' (H)	CBen CLil CPud ELin EPfk LCro MWts NPer WMAq
'Aurora' (H) ♀H5	CBen CLil EPfk LCro MWts WMAq
'Barbara Dobbins' (H)	CBen CLil CPud ELin EWat LCro
'Bateau' (H)	CBen
'Berit Strawn' (H)	CBen
'Black Cherry' (H)	CBen
'Black Princess' (H) ♀H5	CBen CLil CPud CWat EPfk EWat LCro MWts
'Bory de Saint-Vincent' (H)	CBen

Nymphaea

'Burgundy Princess' (H) — CBen ELin EWat NPer
caerulea (T/D) — CBen
candida (H) — CBen CPud NPer WMAq
'Candidissima' (H) — CBen CLil CPud MWts
capensis (T/D) — LCro
'Carolina Sunset' (H) — CBen
'Caroliniana Nivea' (H) — CBen CLil ELin
'Caroliniana Perfecta' (H) — CBen
'Charlene Strawn' (H) — ELin EWat WMAq
'Charles de Meurville' (H) — CBen CLil CPud CWat LCro NPer WMAq
'Château le Rouge' (H) — CBen
'Cliff Tiffany' (H) — CBen
'Clyde Ikins' (H) — ELin EWat
'Colonel A.J. Welch' (H) — CBen NPer WMAq
'Colorado' (H) ♀H5 — CBen CLil CPud CWat ELin NPer
'Colossea' (H) — CBen NPer
'Comanche' (H) — CBen CLil ELin NPer WMAq
'Conqueror' (H) — CBen CWat NPer
'Crème de la Crème' **new** — CLil
§ 'Darwin' (H) — CBen CoPl CPud CWat MWts NPer WMAq
'David' (H) — CBen EWat
'Denver' (H) — EWat
'Doctor Anthonia Capelleti' (H) — CBen
'Doll House' (H) — ELin
'Dorset Blue' (T) **new** — CLil
'Electra' (TD) **new** — CLil
'Ellisiana' (H) — CLil CPud CWat ELin NPer
'Escarboucle' (H) ♀H5 — CBen CLil CWat ELin EPfk LCro NPer WMAq
'Eucharis' (H) — CBen
'Eugénia de Land' (H) — CBen
'Excalibur' (T/D) — CLil
§ 'Fabiola' (H) — CLil ELin NPer WMAq
'Fiesta' (H) — CBen
'Fire Crest' (H) — CBen CLil CPud ELin NPer WMAq
'Formosa' (H) — ELin
'France' (H) — CBen
'Fritz Junge' (H) — CBen
'Froebelii' (H) ♀H5 — CBen CLil CPud CWat EWat NPer WMAq
'Galatée' (H) — CBen CLil
'Geisha Girl' (H) — CBen CLil
'Georgia Peach' (H) — CLil CWat
'Gladstoniana' (H) ♀H5 — CBen CLil CPud CWat ELin MWts NPer WMAq
'Gloire du Temple-sur-Lot' (H) — CBen CLil NPer WMAq
'Gloriosa' (H) — CBen EWat MWts NPer
'Gold Medal' (H) — CBen
'Goliath' (H) — CBen
'Gonnère' (H) ♀H5 — CBen CLil CPud CWat EWat LCro NPer WMAq
'Granat' (H) — CBen
'Hawaiian Gold' (H) — CBen
'H.C. Haarstick' (T/N) — CLil
'Helen Fowler' (H) — CLil WMAq
× *helvola* — see *N.* 'Pygmaea Helvola'
§ 'Hermine' (H) ♀H5 — CBen CLil CPud CWat ELin NPer WMAq
'Hollandia' misapplied — see *N.* 'Darwin'
'Hollandia' ambig. — CLil ELin
'Honeymoon' (H) — CBen
'Indiana' (H) — CBen CLil NPer WMAq
'Inner Light' (H) — EWat
'Irene Heritage' (H) — CBen
'Jakkaphong' (H) — CBen
'James Brydon' (H) ♀H5 — CBen CLil CPud CWat ELin EWat NPer WMAq
'James Hudson' (H) — CBen
'J.C.N. Forestier' (H) — CBen
§ 'Joanne Pring' (H) — CBen
'Joey Tomocik' (H) ♀H5 — CBen CLil CPud CWat ELin EWat MWts WMAq
'King of Siam' (T/D) — CLil
'La Vésuve' (H) — CLil CWat ELin
'Lactea' (H) — CBen CLil
'Laydekeri Alba' (H) — CLil
'Laydekeri Fulgens' (H) ♀H5 — CBen CLil CPud CWat ELin EWat WMAq
'Laydekeri Lilacea' (H) — CBen CLil CPud ELin WMAq
'Laydekeri Purpurata' (H) — CLil CPud WMAq
'Laydekeri Rosea' misapplied — see *N.* 'Laydekeri Rosea Prolifera'
§ 'Laydekeri Rosea Prolifera' (H) — CBen EWat
'Lemon Chiffon' (H) — CBen CLil
'Lemon Mist' (H) — CWat
'Lily Pons' (H) — CBen
'Liou' (H) — CBen ELin
'Little Champion' (H) — CBen
'Little Sue' (H) — CBen CLil CPud
'Livingstone' (H) — CBen
'Luciana' — see *N.* 'Odorata Luciana'
'Lucida' (H) — CBen CLil ELin WMAq
'Madame Bory Latour-Marliac' (H) — CBen
'Madame de Bonseigneur' (H) — CLil
'Madame Wilfon Gonnère' (H) — CBen CPud CWat ELin EPfk EWat LCro NPer WMAq
'Marliacea Albida' (H) — CBen CLil CPud CWat EWat LCro LWaG MWts NPer WMAq
'Marliacea Carnea' (H) — CBen CLil CPud ELin LCro MWts NPer WMAq
§ 'Marliacea Chromatella' (H) ♀H5 — CBen CLil CPud CWat ELin EWat LCro WMAq
'Marliacea Flammea' (H) — CBen
'Marliacea Rosea' (H) — CBen ELin WMAq
'Marliacea Rubra Punctata' — ELin
'Martha' (H) — EWat
'Mary Patricia' (H) — ELin
'Masaniello' (H) — CBen CLil ELin WMAq
'Maurice Laydeker' (H) — CBen CLil
'Maxima' — see *N.* 'Odorata Maxima'
'Mayla' (H) ♀H5 — CBen CWat ELin EPfk NPer
§ 'Météor' (H) — CBen CLil EWat WMAq
mexicana (H) — CBen
'Midnight' (T/D) — CLil
'Millennium Pink' (H) — CBen CLil
'Moorei' (H) — CBen CLil ELin MWts WMAq
'Mrs C.W. Thomas' (H) — ELin
'Mrs Richmond' misapplied — see *N.* 'Fabiola'
'Mrs Richmond' Latour-Marliac (H) ♀H5 — CBen CPud MWts
'Neptune' (H) — CLil
'Newchapel Beauty' — CBen WMAq
'Newton' (H) — CLil CPud WMAq
'Norma Gedye' (H) — CBen WMAq
odorata (H) — CBen WMAq
§ - var. *minor* (H) ♀H5 — CBen WMAq
- 'Pumila' — see *N. odorata* var. *minor*
- subsp. *tuberosa* (H) — CBen
'Odorata Alba' — see *N. odorata*
'Odorata Juliana' (H) — CBen
§ 'Odorata Luciana' (H) — CBen
§ 'Odorata Maxima' (H) — WMAq
'Odorata Sulphurea' (H) — CLil
'Odorata William B. Shaw' — see *N.* 'W.B. Shaw'

'Pam Bennett' (H)	CBen
'Paranee' (H)	CBen
'Parc de la Tête d'Or' (H) **new**	CBen
'Patio Joe' (H)	CBen CLil
'Paul Hariot' (H)	CBen CLil CPud ELin EWat MWts NPer WMAq
'Peach Glow' (H)	EWat
'Peaches and Cream' (H)	ELin
'Pearl of the Pool' (H)	EWat
'Perry's Baby Red' (H) ♀H5	CBen CLil CPud EWat MWts NPer WMAq
'Perry's Crinkled Pink' (H)	CBen
'Perry's Double White' (H)	ELin NPer
'Perry's Fire Opal' (H)	CBen CLil CPud CWat EWat NPer
'Perry's Orange Sunset' (H)	CBen CWat
'Perry's Pink' (H)	WMAq
'Perry's Pink Bicolor' (H)	CBen
'Perry's Red Bicolor' (H)	CBen
'Perry's Red Wonder' (H)	CBen
'Perry's Super Rose' (H)	CBen
'Perry's Viviparous Pink' (H)	CBen
'Perry's Yellow Sensation'	see *N.* 'Yellow Sensation'
'Peter Slocum' (H)	CBen CLil
'Phoebus' (H)	CBen CLil ELin
'Pink Opal' (H)	CBen
'Pink Panache' (H)	CLil
'Pink Sensation' (H) ♀H5	CBen CLil CWat EWat NPer WMAq
'Pinwaree' (H)	CBen
'Prakaisad' (H)	CBen
'Princess Elizabeth' (H)	ELin
'Purple Fantasy' (H)	CBen CWat
'Pygmaea Alba'	see *N. tetragona*
§ 'Pygmaea Helvola' (H) ♀H5	CBen CLil CPud ELin EWat LCro LRHS MWts NPer WMAq
'Pygmaea Rubis' (H)	WMAq
'Pygmaea Rubra' (H)	CLil CPud CWat ELin EPfk EWat LCro LRHS NPer WMAq
'Queen of the Whites' (H)	CBen
'Rattana Ubol' (H)	CBen
'Ray Davies' (H)	CBen ELin
'Red Queen' (H)	CWat
'Red Spider' (H)	NPer
'Rembrandt' misapplied	see *N.* 'Météor'
'Rembrandt' Koster (H)	CPud CWat ELin
'René Gérard' (H)	CBen CPud CWat NPer WMAq
'Rose Arey' (H)	CBen CLil CPud ELin LCro NPer WMAq
'Rose Magnolia' (H)	CLil
'Rosennymphe' (H)	CBen ELin NPer WMAq
'Rosy Morn' (H)	CBen
'Seignoureti' (H)	CLil
'Siam Jasmine' (H)	CBen
'Siam Purple 2' (H)	CBen
'Sioux' (H)	CBen CLil ELin NPer WMAq
'Sirius' (H)	CBen CLil CPud
'Snow Princess' (H)	CBen CWat EWat
'Solfatare' (H)	EWat
'Splendida' (H)	WMAq
'Steven Strawn' (H)	CBen
'Sunny Pink' (H)	CBen CLil
'Sunrise' (H)	CLil LCro
'Superba' (H)	CBen
'Sylphida' (H)	CBen
§ *tetragona* (H)	CLil CPud CWat ELin EWat LCro LWaG MWts NPer WMAq
- 'Alba'	see *N. tetragona*
- 'Johann Pring'	see *N.* 'Joanne Pring'
'Texas Dawn' (H) ♀H5	CBen CLil CPud CWat ELin WMAq
'Tina' (T/D)	CLil
'Tuberosa Flavescens'	see *N.* 'Marliacea Chromatella'
'Tuberosa Richardsonii' (H)	CBen NPer
'Venusta' (H)	EWat
'Virginalis' (H)	CBen CPud CWat EPfk NPer WMAq
'Walter Pagels' (H)	CLil EWat WMAq
'Wanvisa' (H)	CBen CWat ELin EWat LCro
'W.B. Shaw' (H)	CBen ELin NPer
'Weymouth Red' (H) ♀H5	CBen
'White Sensation' (H)	CBen
'White Sultan' (H)	CWat LCro
'William Falconer' (H)	CBen CLil CPud NPer
'Wow' (H)	CLil
'Xiafei' (H)	CPud CWat ELin MWts
'Yellow Dazzler' (T/D)	CLil
'Yellow Princess' (H)	CLil CWat
'Yellow Queen' (H)	CLil
§ 'Yellow Sensation' (H)	CBen CWat ELin LCro
'Yul Ling' (H)	CBen EWat
'Zeus' (H)	CLil CPud

Nymphoides (Menyanthaceae)

aquatica	ELin
? *peltata*	CBen CHab CPud CWat ELin EWat LCro NPer WMAq

Nyssa ❀ (Nyssaceae)

aquatica	MBlu
leptophylla	CJun
shweliensis	see *N. sinensis*
§ *sinensis*	CJun CMCN EGrl MAsh MBlu MPkF WJur WPGP
- 'Inferno'	SPoG WMat
- 'Jim Russell' ♀H5	WPGP
- 'Volcano'	CJun
sylvatica	CBcs CCVT CDoC CJun CLnd CMac CMCN CTsd EBee EGrl ELan ELon EPfP IArd IPap LCro LMaj LRHS MAsh MBlu MMuc NLar SEWo SGol SHor SSta WHtc WJur WMat
- 'Autumn Cascades'	ELan MAsh MBlu
- var. *biflora*	SSta
- 'Haymen's Red'	see *N. sylvatica* RED RAGE
- 'Jermyns Flame' ♀H6	CJun LRHS MAsh
- JOLLY ('Yiping') (v)	MPkF
- Lakeside Weeper'	ELan MAsh
- 'Miss Scarlet' (f)	NLar WPGP
§ - RED RAGE ('Haymanred')	MAsh MBlu MPkF NCth
- 'Valley Scorcher'	LRHS
- 'Wildfire'	CCVT CJun NLar
- 'Windsor'	see *N. sylvatica* 'Valley Scorcher'
- 'Wisley Bonfire' (m) ♀H6	CBcs CJun CMCN ELan EPfP MAsh SChF SMad SPoG WMat WPGP
- 'Zydeco Twist'	NLar

O

Oakesiella see *Uvularia*

Ochagavia (Bromeliaceae)

carnea	WPGP
elegans	WCot
§ *litoralis*	SArc
* *rosea*	SPlb

Ochroma (Malvaceae)
pyramidale	EAri SPlb

Ocimum (Lamiaceae)
'African Blue'	CSpe EHet ENfk EWhm LCro MHer MHol MNHC SPoG SRms
§ × *africanum*	EHet ENfk IDun MCtn MHoo MNHC SPoG WKit
- 'Lesbos'	MHer
- 'Lime'	IDun MHoo MNHC
- 'Perpetuo'[PBR] (v)	ENfk
- 'Siam Queen'	MHer MHoo SRms
americanum	MCtn
basilicum	EHet EWhm LCro LWaG MCtn MHoo MNHC MPri SPoG SRms WKit
- 'Anise'	see *O. basilicum* 'Horapha'
- 'Ararat'	SRms
- 'Aristotle'	MHer SRms
- 'Aroma 2' ♀[H1c]	LCro MCtn
- 'Blue Spice'	SEdi
I - 'British Basil'	MCtn MHer SRms
- *camphorata*	see *O. kilimandscharicum*
- 'Christmas'	SEdi SRms
- 'Cinnamon'	CGHo IDun MCtn MNHC SEdi SRms WJek
- 'Coldasil'	ENfk LCro
- 'Crimson King'[PBR]	SRms
- 'Dark Opal'	SEdi SRms
- D-FENCESIL	LCro
- 'Fine Verde'	MCtn
- 'Genovese'	CGHo LCro MCtn MEar MNHC SEdi WKit
- 'Glycyrrhiza'	see *O. basilicum* 'Horapha'
- 'Green Globe'	SRms
- 'Green Ruffles'	SPoG SRms
- 'Holy'	see *O. tenuiflorum*
- 'Holy Tulsi'	see *O. tenuiflorum*
§ - 'Horapha'	EHet ENfk LCro LWaG MCtn MNHC SEdi SPoG SVic WJek WKit
* - 'Horapha Nanum'	ENfk SRms
- 'Lemonade' ♀[H1c]	SRms
- lettuce leaf	LCro LWaG SEdi
- 'Magic Mountain'	LCro SPoG
- 'Magic White'	EHet MNHC SPoG
- 'Mrs Burns' Lemon' ♀[H1c]	EKin LCro MCtn SRms
- 'Napoletano'	LCro MCtn SRms
- 'Pluto' ♀[H1c]	LCro
- 'Puck'	SRms
- 'Purple Delight'	EHet
- var. *purpurascens*	CGHo MHoo
- - 'Purple Ruffles'	LCro MCtn SRms
- - 'Red Rubin'	MCtn MEar MHer SRms WJek
- - 'Red Shiraz'	IDun MNHC
- 'Sweet Genovese'	IDun MNHC SVic WKit
- 'Thai'	see *O. basilicum* 'Horapha'
- 'Wild Magic'[PBR]	ENfk
× *citriodorum*	see *O.* × *africanum*
gratissimum	SEdi
§ *kilimandscharicum*	MHoo
minimum	CGHo EHet ENfk LCro MCtn MEar MHoo MNHC SRms WKit
sanctum	see *O. tenuiflorum*
'Spice'	ENfk
§ *tenuiflorum*	LCro MCtn MHoo MNHC SPre SVic WJek

Oemleria (Rosaceae)
cerasiformis	CBcs EBee EGrI EPfP EWes LEdu MMuc WCot WGwG

Oenanthe (Apiaceae)
javanica 'Flamingo' (v)	CBen CGwi CoPl CWat EBee ELan ELin LEdu MWts SRms WFar
pimpinelloides	CBWd CGwi CHab ECha SPhx WFar WHil

Oenothera ✿ (Onagraceae)
§ *acaulis*	CSpe MNrw WCot
'Apricot Delight'	MCtn
§ *biennis*	CBWd CGHo CoPl ELan ENfk GAbr LCro MCtn MHer MHoo MNHC NBro SPhx SRms WBrk WHer WOrg
'Blood Orange'	GEdr
cinaeus	see *O. fruticosa* subsp. *glauca*
'Cold Crick'	EBee
'Crown Imperial'	MArl MPro NBir
§ *elata* subsp. *hookeri*	EWes
erythrosepala	see *O. glazioviana*
§ *fruticosa*	NLar SPlb
- 'African Sun'	LBar MPro
- FIREWORKS	see *O. fruticosa* 'Fyrverkeri'
§ - 'Fyrverkeri'	CBcs GMaP SMad WCAu WFar
§ - subsp. *glauca*	CElw EPfP NLar SRms
- - 'Erica Robin' (v)	CDor GBin MNrw NGdn SMad WCav WHoo
- - 'Longest Day'	EHeP MBrN
- - SOLSTICE	see *O. fruticosa* subsp. *glauca* 'Sonnenwende'
§ - - 'Sonnenwende'	CElw EBee NEoE NLar
- HIGHLIGHT	see *O. fruticosa* 'Hoheslicht'
- 'Hoheslicht'	EBee
- 'W. Cuthbertson'	EBee
- 'Yellow River'	CElw EBee
glabra Miller	see *O. biennis*
glabra misapplied	ECha
§ *glazioviana*	CGwi EHet NBir
hookeri	see *O. elata* subsp. *hookeri*
ICE COOL ROSY ('Harcool') (G)	EBee SHar
kunthiana	ECha GJos MCtn
- 'Glowing Magenta'	LBar SPoG
lamarckiana	see *O. glazioviana*
'Lemon Sunset'	ECha EGrI
LILLIPOP PINK ('Redgapi')[PBR] (G)	CAby CTsd LBar LRHS Midl SPoG
* 'Lime Green' (G)	LRHS
lindheimeri (G) ♀[H4]	CBcs CSpe EAri EBee EBlo ECha EGren ELan EPfP LCro LRHS MGos SAth SDix SHar SMHy SPoG SRot WCAu WHoo WRBe XFar
- BABY BUTTERFLY DARK PINK ('Uriblbp'[PBR]) (G)	LBar MNrw MPro NLar
- Belleza Series (G)	CWCL EPfP LRHS MPri
- - BELLEZA DARK PINK ('Kleau04263') (G)	MPri
- - BELLEZA WHITE ('Kleau04264') (G)	EGren LRHS
- 'Blaze'[PBR] (G)	LRHS NLar
- CHERRY BRANDY ('Gauchebra'[PBR]) (G)	EBee ELan EPfP LCro LRHS MNrw
- 'Chiffon' (G)	LSto SHar
- compact, pink-flowered (G)	SRot
- 'Cool Breeze' (G)	CDor EAri EBee ECha EPfP MCtn MNrw SDix SPel SPhx WHoo
- 'Corrie's Gold' (G/v)	EBee ECha ELan EPfP LBar LRHS Midl
- 'Crimson Butterflies'[PBR] (G)	CWGN ELan EPfP LRHS SAdn
- 'Dwarf White' (G)	LRHS

- 'Elurra' (G) — EGren LRHS LSou Midl NBir
- 'Emmeline Pink Bouquet' (G) **new** — WHil
- 'Flamingo Pink' (G) — ELan Midl MSwo
- 'Flamingo White' (G) — ELan LRHS Midl WHil
- FREEFOLK ROSY ('Harrfolk') (G/v) — CAby ELan LBar LBom LCro LRHS Midl MPri SHar SHor SIvy WNPC
- 'Gambit Compact White' (G) — LBar
- 'Gambit Rose' (G) — EGren LBar LRHS Midl MPri SAdn
- 'Gambit Variegata Rose' (G/v) — LBar MPri
- 'Gambit White' (G) — LBar NLit
- § GAUDI PINK ('Florgaucompi'^PBR) (G) — EPfP EUrb LRHS Midl MPri
- GAUDI RED ('Florgaured') (G) — EPfP EUrb LBar LRHS Midl
- GAUDI ROSE ('Florgaucomro'^PBR) (G) — EBee EPfP LRHS Midl NLit
- GAUDI WHITE ('Florgauwh2') (G) — EBee LBar Midl
- (Geyser Series) GEYSER PINK ('Gaudros'^PBR) (G) — EBee EGren EPfP LRHS WTor
- - GEYSER WHITE ('Gaudwwhi'^PBR) (G) — EBee EGren EPfP LRHS
- GOLD FOUNTAIN ('Walgolfou') (G/v) — LRHS
- 'Jo Adela' (G/v) — ECha
- KARALEE WHITE ('Nugauwhite'^PBR) (G) — CAby CTsd CWnw ELan LRHS MBel Midl SIvy SPoG WTor
- 'Little Janie' (G) — EGren MBros
- PAPILLON ('Nugaupapil'^PBR) (G) — CWnw ELan LBar LRHS LSto Midl MPri MSwo SPoG
- - 'Passionate Blush'^PBR (G) — CBcs CBWd LBar LRHS MAsh MGos MHtn Midl SOrN SPoG SRms SRot WHil
- 'Passionate Pink' (G) — LRHS
- 'Passionate Rainbow'^PBR (G/v) — EPfP LRHS SRms
- 'Pink Dwarf' (G) — EBee LRHS
- PINK FOUNTAIN ('Walgaupf') (G) — EPfP LBom LRHS
- 'Pink Gin' (G) — SPoG
- ROSYJANE ('Harrosy'^PBR) (G) — Widely available
- RUBY RUBY ('Harruby'^PBR) (G) — SHar
- short (G) — EGren
- 'Siskiyou Pink' (G) — CBcs CMHG CSpe CWnw EBee ECha EGren ELan EPfP LBom LCro LRHS LWaG MHer MNrw SAdn SAth SOrN WKif XFar
- SNOW FOUNTAIN ('Walsnofou') (G) — EPfP LRHS MNrw WNPC
- SNOWBIRD ('Flogausnb'^PBR) (G) — MNrw
- 'Snowstorm' (G) — LWaG
- 'Sparkle White' (G) — EBee EGren ELan ELon EPfP LRHS MCtn MNrw NLar WFar WHil
- STRATOSPHERE PINK PICOTEE — see *O. lindheimeri* GAUDI PINK
- 'Summer Breeze' (G) — CDor CWal EBee EDAr ELan EPfP EPPr LRHS MCtn NDov SBeP SPel WChS
- 'Summer Emotions' (G) — EGren LRHS LSou WCot WFar
- 'Sunset Dreams' (G) — LBar SAdn
- 'The Bride' (G) — Widely available
- 'Tutti Frutti' (G) — LRHS
- I 'Variegata' (G/v) — SRms
- 'Whirling Butterflies' (G) — Widely available
- 'Whiskers Deep Rose' (G) — EGren LCro MPro WFar
- 'White Dove' (G) — CWnw Midl WFar
- 'White Heron' (G) — MNrw
- *linearis* — see *O. fruticosa*
- § *macrocarpa* ♀^H5 — CAby CBWd CHab EBee ECha EHeP ELan EPfP LBar MArl MHer MNrw SPlb SPoG SRms SRot SVic WCAu
- subsp. *fremontii* 'Silver Wings' — ELan
- subsp. *incana* 'Silver Blade' — GEdr
- *missouriensis* — see *O. macrocarpa*
- *odorata* misapplied — see *O. stricta*
- *odorata* Hook. & Arn. — see *O. biennis*
- *odorata* Jacquin cream-flowered — CSpe
- *organensis* — EBee MNrw
- *pallida* 'Innocence' — LCro
- *perennis* — SRms
- *pilosella* 'Mella Yella' — EBee
- - 'Yella Fella' — ELan
- 'Rose Fan' (G) **new** — SHar
- ROSY SHIMMERS ('Harshim') (G) — SHar
- § *sinuosa* (G) — CAby ECha SHar SPel WMal
- *speciosa* — SRms
- * - 'Alba' — EBee
- - 'Pink Petticoats' — ECha NPer
- - 'Rosea' — SPlb
- - 'Siskiyou' — CAbb CAby CBcs EBee ECha EGren ELan EPfP LBar LCro MArl MMrt MNrw SPoG WMal
- - TWILIGHT ('Turner01'^PBR) (v) — EBee ELan MPri NLar SHar
- - 'Woodside White' — SMrm
- § *stricta* — EPPr MNrw
- - 'Sulphurea' — CBWd CDor ELan EPfP EPPr LCro NClf NPer SMrm SPhx
- 'Summer Sun' — CBcs CBWd LBar LSou MAsh MPie NLar WCAu
- 'Sunny Delight' — EGren
- *taraxacifolia* — see *O. acaulis*
- *tetragona* — see *O. fruticosa* subsp. *glauca*
- var. *fraseri* — see *O. fruticosa* subsp. *glauca*
- *versicolor* 'Sunset Boulevard' — CSpe EPfP GEdr MCtn

Olea (Oleaceae)

- *europaea* (F) — Widely available
- - 'Aglandau' (F) — CAgr
- - 'Arbequina' (F) — EOli NPlm
- - 'Cipressino' (F) — CAgr EOli
- - 'El Greco' (F) — CAgr
- - 'Frantoio' (F) — EOli
- - 'Hojiblanca' (F) — EUrb NPlm
- - 'Leccino' (F) — CAgr EOli SFol
- - 'Maurino' (F) — EOli
- - 'Picual' (F) — EOli EUrb NPlm
- - 'Salonenque' (F) **new** — CAgr

Olearia ✿ (Asteraceae)

- *avicenniifolia* — CMac GAbr
- × *capillaris* — LRHS
- § *cheesemanii* — SVen
- - compact — LRHS
- *erubescens* — LRHS
- *gunniana* — see *O. phlogopappa*
- × *haastii* — CBcs CBrac CDoC CMac CMCN CSBt EBee EHeP ELan EPfP GArf GKin LCro LRHS NLar SRms WFar
- - 'McKenzie' — ELon
- § 'Henry Travers' — EPfP WPGP

ilicifolia	WPGP
insignis	see *Pachystegia insignis*
lepidophylla	NLar
macrodonta ♀H4	CBcs CBrac CCht CCoa CDoC CMac CMCN CSBt CTsd EHeP ELan EPfP GArf GKin LCro LRHS SArc SEND SPlb SRms WFar WSpi
- 'Major'	GAbr LSto NLar
- 'Minor'	CDoC CMac ELan EPfP SPlb SRms WPGP WSpi
§ × *matthewsii*	LRHS WKif
× *mollis* misapplied	see *O.* × *matthewsii*
× *mollis* (Kirk) Cockayne	CMac
- 'Zennorensis' ♀H4	CMCN GAbr SPlb
nummularifolia	CBcs CDoC CWal ELan EPfP GAbr LRHS NLar SEND SVen
× *oleifolia* 'Waikariensis'	LRHS SEND
paniculata	CBcs CCoa CDoC EPfP SEND SRms SVen
§ *phlogopappa*	SVen
- 'Comber's Blue'	EPfP
§ - 'Comber's Pink'	CTsd EPfP EWld NPer SPoG
- 'Rosea'	see *O. phlogopappa* 'Comber's Pink'
- 'Spring Bling'	CBcs LCro NLar
ramulosa 'Blue Stars'	LRHS SRms
rani misapplied	see *O. cheesemanii*
× *scilloniensis* misapplied	see *O. stellulata* DC.
× *scilloniensis* ambig.	CBcs CCoa CDoC CTsd EWld SPoG WKif
× *scilloniensis* Dorrien-Smith 'Master Michael' ♀H4	ELon EWld SPoG
semidentata misapplied	see *O.* 'Henry Travers'
solandri	CCoa CMac NLar SDix SEND
- 'Aurea'	CBcs NLar
'Stardust'	SVen
stellulata misapplied	see *O. phlogopappa*
§ *stellulata* DC.	CMac CSBt
- 'Michael's Pride'	CExl
traversii	see *O. traversiorum*
§ *traversiorum*	CBcs CCoa CDoC CSBt ELon EPfP NLar SArc SEND SRms WLov
- 'Compacta'	CCoa ELan
- 'Tweedledee' (v)	SEND
- 'Tweedledum' (v)	CBcs CCoa ELan
virgata	NLar
- var. *lineata*	CCoa CTsd
- - 'Dartonii'	CBcs LRHS NLar SEND SPlb SSta SVen

Oligoneuron see *Solidago*

Oligostachyum (Poaceae)
lubricum	see *Semiarundinaria lubrica*

olive see *Olea europaea*

Olsynium (Iridaceae)
biflorum	GEdr
§ *douglasii* ♀H5	EBee EPot GArf GEdr NHar NRya
- 'Album'	CTtf EPot EWes GKev NHar WAbe WFar
- FRF 7880 white with purple stripes	NHar
- FRF 7882 large purple, long petals	NHar
- FRF 7883 striped	NHar
- FRF 7885 tall purple	NHar
- FRF 8590 white with pink base	NHar
§ *junceum*	EDAr SPlb

Omphalodes ❀ (Boraginaceae)
cappadocica ♀H5	CDor CMac EPot EWld LEdu NBro NPer SRms StAn WPGP
- 'Alba'	SPoG
- 'All Summer Blues'	EBee NLar
- 'Blue Eyes'	WCot WMal
- 'Cherry Ingram' ♀H5	Widely available
- 'Lilac Mist' ♀H5	EBee GEdr SRms
- 'Starry Eyes' ♀H5	CDor CMac CMiW EBee EMor LCro LSRN LSto NBid NBir NCth NLar SMrm SRms WFar WSpi
§ *linifolia* ♀H3	CSpe LCro MCtn SPhx
- *alba*	see *O. linifolia*
nitida	CSpe ECha EWes GAbr GEdr MMuc MNrw NQui
verna	CDor CMiW CSpe EBee ECha EGrl ELan EPPr EUrb GEdr GKev MArl MHtn NGdn NLar SPlb SPoG WCAu WFar
- 'Alba'	CDor CMac CWnw EBee ECha EGrl ELan EPfP EPPr GAbr GKev GMaP LBar NBid NGdn NLar SRms WBrk WCAu WMal
- 'Elfenauge'	EBee ECha EMor EPPr ISha NBir NLar WCot
I - 'Grandiflora'	WCot

Oncostema see *Scilla*

onion see *Allium cepa*; also AGM Vegetables Section

Onixotis (Colchicaceae)
stricta	see *Wurmbea stricta*

Onobrychis (Fabaceae)
viciifolia	CGwi LShi MCtn SPhx

Onoclea (Onocleaceae)
sensibilis ♀H6	Widely available
- copper-leaved	EBee WPGP
- var. *interrupta*	LEdu WPGP
* - var. *minima*	LEdu WPGP
- 'Rotstiel'	EBee

Ononis (Fabaceae)
repens	NAts WOrg
spinosa	CDor GEdr WSpi

Onopordum (Asteraceae)
acanthium	CDor CTtf ECha ELan ENfk MCtn NSti SEND SHar WFar WSpi
arabicum	see *O. nervosum*
§ *nervosum* ♀H7	CSpe

Onosma (Boraginaceae)
alborosea ♀H5	ECha SEND
nana	EDAr EPot GKev WAbe
polyphylla	EDAr
taurica ♀H4	EDAr

Onosmodium (Boraginaceae)
molle	GKev

Onychium (Pteridaceae)
contiguum	LEdu WCot
japonicum	CExl CLAP LEdu SPlb WAbe WCot

Operculicarya (Anacardiaceae)
decaryi	SPlb

Ophiopogon ✿ (*Asparagaceae*)

NJM 11.018	WPGP
alatus B&SWJ 11673	WCru
'Black Dragon'	see *O. planiscapus* 'Kokuryū'
bockianus CB CH347	GGro
bodinieri	CKno EWes ISha LEdu SEND WAbe
– B&L 12505	EBee EPPr
caulescens B&SWJ 8230	WCru
– B&SWJ 11813	WCru
aff. *caulescens* B&SWJ 11287	WCru
– HWJ 590	WCru
chingii	CKno EBee EPPr EWes GBin ISha LEdu WCot
* – 'Crispum'	EBee ESwi
clarkei	StAn
– WJC 13794	WCru
clavatus KWJ 12267	WCru
aff. *cordylinoides*	WPGP
formosanus B&SWJ 3659	ESwi WCru
'Gin-ryu'	see *Liriope spicata* 'Gin-ryū'
graminifolius	see *Liriope muscari*
grandis KWJ 12031	WCru
'Hosoba Kokuryū'	LCro LRHS
intermedius	EPPr ESwi MWlw WCot
– B&SWJ 1842	ESwi WCru
– B&SWJ 3655	EPPr WCru
– BWJ 8244 from Vietnam	WCru
§ *jaburan*	CMac EBee LEdu
– 'Variegatus'	see *O. jaburan* 'Vittatus'
§ – 'Vittatus' (v)	EWes LEdu MWlw WCot
japonicus	CMac EBee ELin LEdu SWor
– B&SWJ 1871	ESwi WCru
– 'Compactus'	EBee EWes WPGP
– 'Kigimafukiduma'	CMac EBee LRHS NGdn
– 'Kyoto'	ESwi
– 'Lengteng Giant'	LEdu
– 'Minor'	CKno CTsd EBee EDAr ELon EPPr GBin GMaP ISha NLar SBig WAbe WPGP
– 'Nanus'	ELan
– 'Nanus Variegatus' (v)	ELon ESwi
– 'Nippon'	EPPr NGdn
– 'Silver Dragon' (v)	EPPr
– 'Tama-ryū'	WAbe
– 'Tama-ryū Number Two'	ESwi
* – 'Variegatus' (v)	CDTJ CMac ISha LRHS SRms WCAu
longifolius FMWJ 13278	WCru
malcolmsonii B&SWJ 7271	WCru
megalanthus FMWJ 13118	WCru
parviflorus GWJ 9387	WCru
– HWJK 2093	WCru
planiscapus	CCps CKno CSpe EGrl EPPr EUrb GArf GMaP LWaG NBro
* – 'Albovariegatus' (v)	CKno SArc WFar
– Black Beard ('Yapard'PBR)	CKno EUrb GQue LRHS MAsh MBlu Midl NBir SPoG WFar
– 'Chocolate Mint'	WCot
– 'Kansu'	ESwi
§ – 'Kokuryū' ♀H5	Widely available
– f. *leucanthus*	CDor EPPr WCot WPGP
– 'Little Tabby' (v)	CBen EBlo ESwi WCot WHoo
– 'Nigrescens'	see *O. planiscapus* 'Kokuryū'
'Sparkler'	ESwi
'Spring Gold'	see *Liriope* 'Spring Gold'
umbraticola	WPGP

Ophrys (*Orchidaceae*)

apifera	CHab

Oplopanax (*Araliaceae*)

horridus	WPGP

Opopanax (*Apiaceae*)

chironium	SDix WTre
– PAB 845	LEdu WPGP
– PAB 872	WPGP
hispidus	SPhx WCot

Opuntia (*Cactaceae*)

sp.	EUrb
aciculata	NPlm
angustata	see *O. phaeacantha*
articulata	see *Tephrocactus articulatus*
atrispina	SBig
basilaris	SPlb WJur
bergeriana	NPlm SChr
camanchica	see *O. phaeacantha*
* *camptotricha*	NPlm
cantabrigiensis	SChr
compressa	see *O. humifusa*
cylindrarticulata	see *Cumulopuntia boliviana* subsp. *dactylifera*
cylindrica	see *Austrocylindropuntia cylindrica*
darwinii	see *Maihueniopsis darwinii*
erinacea var. *utahensis*	see *O. polyacantha* var. *erinacea*
§ *ficus-indica*	CBlu SArc SPlb WKor
fragilis	NCft SPlb
fulgida	see *Cylindropuntia fulgida*
galapageia	SPlb
gosseliniana	CBlu EUrb SBig
grandiflora	see *O. humifusa* 'Grandiflora'
§ *humifusa*	CBlu CDTJ LWaG NPlm SBig WKor
– 'Grandiflora'	SChr
* – subsp. *littoica*	SPlb
inermis	see *O. stricta*
invicta	see *Corynopuntia invicta*
joconostle	see *O. ficus-indica*
leptocarpa	SChr
leucotricha	NPlm
littoralis	SEND WCot
macrocentra	CBlu NPlm
– 'Alba'	MPri
microdasys ♀H2	LCro LWaG NHrt
§ – 'Albata' ♀H2	EShb SPlb
– 'Albispina'	NPlm SPad
– 'Angel's Wings'	see *O. microdasys* 'Albata'
– 'La Vila'	NPlm
– 'Malena'	NPlm
– var. *pallida*	NPlm
molinensis	see *Tephrocactus molinensis*
monacantha	CoPl SPlb
§ *phaeacantha*	SChr WJur
– NNS 99-264	WCot
– var. *major* NNS 95-285	WCot
– 'Sunrise'	CBlu
pollardii	see *O. humifusa*
polyacantha	EUrb SEND SPlb WJur
§ – var. *erinacea*	WCot
§ – var. *hystricina*	NPlm
quimilo new	EUrb
rhodantha	see *O. polyacantha* var. *hystricina*
robusta	NPlm SChr SEND
robusta × *scheeri*	SChr
salmiana	SEND
scheeri	SBrt SChr
'Semi Inermis'	NPlm
sphaerica	see *Cumulopuntia sphaerica*
§ *stricta*	NPlm

syringacantha	see *Tephrocactus articulatus*	*dactylifolius*	WCot
'Titania'	NPlm	echinops B&SWJ 10302	WCru
verschaffeltii	see *Austrocylindropuntia verschaffeltii*	ellsworthii B&SWJ 14898 **new**	WCru
vestita	see *Austrocylindropuntia vestita*	I *flabellatus* B&SWJ 14449	WCru
		floribundus	see *O. incisus*
		glabrifolius B&SWJ 14728	WCru
		hypargyreus B&SWJ 14870	WCru
		impolitus B&SWJ 14766	WCru
		§ *incisus* B&SWJ 10669	WCru
		langlassei	see *O. xalapensis*
		lehmannii	WCru
		mutisianus B&SWJ 14912	WCru
		aff. *nymphaeifolius* B&SWJ 14940	WCru
		I *ocanensis* B&SWJ 14344 **new**	WCru
		sectifolius B&SWJ 14355	WCru
		- B&SWJ 14805	WCru
		- B&SWJ 14833	WCru
		§ *xalapensis* B&SWJ 10444	WCru
		- B&SWJ 10449	WCru

orange, sour or Seville see *Citrus × aurantium* Sour Orange Group

orange, sweet see *Citrus × aurantium* Sweet Orange Group

Orbea (Apocynaceae)
§ *variegata* ♀H2   NTro WCor

Orchis (Orchidaceae)
foliosa	see *Dactylorhiza foliosa*
fuchsii	see *Dactylorhiza fuchsii*
maculata	see *Dactylorhiza maculata*
maderensis	see *Dactylorhiza foliosa*
§ mascula	WHer

oregano see *Origanum vulgare*

Oreocereus (Cactaceae)
leucotrichus	NPlm
trollii ♀H2	NPlm

Oreocharis (Gesneriaceae)
aurea B&SWJ 11718	WCru
billburttii × speciosa	WAbe
× calliantha	WAbe
convexa B&SWJ 6624	WCru
- B&SWJ 7182	WCru

Oreomecon (Papaveraceae)
§ alpina	MAsh SRot
§ miyabeana	CSpe
§ 'Moondance'	LBom LRHS SPoG
§ nudicaulis	EHeP LBom LCro
- Champagne Bubbles Group	EGren LBom MCtn SPoG WFar
- - 'Champagne Bubbles Pink'	MCtn
- - 'Champagne Bubbles White'	MCtn
- Deluxe Mixed	CSpe
- Garden Gnome Group	see *O. nudicaulis* Gartenzwerg Group
§ - Gartenzwerg Group ♀H7	EGren EPfP LBom LRHS MPri SPoG SRot
- 'Kelmscott Giant'	SVic
- 'Pacino'	EPfP
- 'Spring Fever Red' (Spring Fever Series)	MPri

Oreomyrrhis (Apiaceae)
argentea	SPhx

Oreopanax (Araliaceae)
sp.	SBig
bogotensis B&SWJ 14900	WCru
brachystachyus B&SWJ 14773	WCru
capitatus	CExl
- B&SWJ 14765	WCru
aff. *catalpifolius* B&SWJ 14764	WCru
cecropifolius B&SWJ 14761	WCru
- B&SWJ 14762	WCru

Oreostemma (Asteraceae)
alpigenum	GEdr

Oresitrophe (Saxifragaceae)
rupifraga	CTtf GEdr LEdu WCot

Origanum ✿ (Lamiaceae)
from Kalamata, Greece	SEND
amanum ♀H4	EWes NBir WAbe
'Amethyst Falls'	IPot LBar LCro MPro NCth
'Barbara Tingey'	ELan EWes SRms WIce
BELLISSIMO	see *O.* 'Solferino'
'Bristol Cross' ♀H4	ECha EPot SMHy SPel WCAu WFar WGoo WHoo WMal
caespitosum	see *O. vulgare* 'Nanum'
§ calcaratum	ELan WMal
creticum	see *O. vulgare* subsp. *hirtum*
dictamnus	MHoo SPlb WAbe WIce WJek
'Dingle Fairy'	ECha EMor EWes LBar MHer NBir SPoG WIce WSpi WTor
'Emma Stanley'	WAbe WMal
'Frank Tingey'	ELan
'French' ♀H5	EHet IDun SRms WJek
'Gold Splash' (v)	MHoo
heracleoticum L.	see *O. vulgare* subsp. *hirtum*
'Hot and Spicy' ♀H5	CGHo EHet ELan ENfk EWhm GJos LCro MHoo MNHC NBir SRms WFar WJek WKit
'Jekka's Beauty'	WJek
'Jekka's Spice'	WJek
'Kent Beauty' ♀H4	Widely available
laevigatum	EWhm NBro NPer WCot WKif WTre
* - aureum	CoPl
- 'Dingle'	NLar
- 'Herrenhausen' ♀H6	Widely available
- 'Hopleys' ♀H6	CDor CElw EBee ECha EPfP LEdu MHer MHol MHoo NBir NLar SEND SPhx SPoG
- 'Purple Charm'	SRms
libanoticum	LRHS
majorana ♀H2	CAgr CGHo CHab EHet ENfk GQue MCtn MHer MHoo MNHC SRms SVic WJek
- Italian	SEdi
- var. *tenuifolium*	WJek
× *majoricum*	WJek
'Marchants Seedling'	SMHy

Origanum 489

490 *Origanum*

'Norton Gold'	NPer
onites	CHby ENfk GQue MHer MHoo MNHC SPlb SRms
'Pilgrim'	WCAu
'Rosenkuppel'	CAby CCBP CDor CElw EBee ECha ELan EPfP EWhm GBin GQue LCro MBel MHol MHoo MPro NDov SPhx SPlb SRms WCAu WChS WTor
rotundifolium ♀H4	MHoo NBir
- 'Jan's Pink' ♀H4	ECha
'Soledad'	WMal
§ 'Solferino' PBR	IPot LBar LCro
syriacum	LWaG MNHC WJek WKit
'Teddy'	EBee
tournefortii	see *O. calcaratum*
virens	CAgr
vulgare	Widely available
- 'Acorn Bank'	ENfk EWhm MHer MHoo SPoG SRms WFar WJek
- var. ***album***	MNHC
- 'Aureum' ♀H6	CCBP CGHo CWal ELan EMor ENfk EPfP EWhm GJos GMaP GQue LCro LShi LSto MHol MHoo MMuc MNHC MPri NGdn SEND SPlb SPoG SRms WFar WKif WKit
- 'Aureum Crispum'	ECha ENfk GQue IDun MHoo NBid SRms WFar
- 'Compactum' ♀H5	CCBP CGHo EBee ECha EHet ENfk EWhm GBin MHer MHoo MNHC NBir SPlb SRms WChS WHoo WJek WKit
- 'Corinne Tremaine' (v)	WHer
- 'Country Cream' (v)	CCBP CElw CGHo CTsd ECul EHet ENfk EPfP EWes EWhm GAbr GQue LCro LShi LWaG MBel MHer MHoo MNHC MPri NBir NGdn SEdi SPoG SRms SVic WFar
- 'Curly Gold'	GAbr
- GENTLE BREEZE ('All120506')PBR	MHoo SPel
- 'Gold Nugget' ♀H5 **new**	IDun
§ - 'Gold Tip' (v)	ENfk EWhm IDun LCro MHer MHoo MNHC SPlb SRms WFar WHer
- 'Golden Shine'	CTsd EWes EWhm MHoo SEdi
- 'Greensleeves'	WFar
§ - subsp. ***hirtum***	CAgr CHby CTsd LCro MHoo SPlb
- - 'Greek'	CAgr CCBP CGHo ECul EHet ENfk EWhm IDun MHer MNHC SEdi SRms SVic WJek
- 'Nanum'	SRms WJek
- 'Pink Mist' ♀H4	MNrw SRms WHoo
- 'Pink Thumbles'	ECha
- 'Polyphant' (v)	MHoo SRms
- 'Supreme'	MNHC
- 'Thumble's Variety'	EBee EBlo ECha ELan EPfP EPot LRHS LSto MHer SDix SRms WFar
- 'Variegatum'	see *O. vulgare* 'Gold Tip'
- 'White Charm'	MHoo SEdi
- yellow, long-leaved	CGHo

Orixa (Rutaceae)

japonica	CBcs NLar WPGP
- 'Variegata' (v)	NLar

Orlaya (Apiaceae)

grandiflora ♀H7	CMiW CSpe CTtf EDAr ELan LCro LEdu LRHS LSto MAvo MCtn MPro NClf SHor SPhx WTor

Ornithogalum (Asparagaceae)

arabicum	CBro GKev LAma SRms
arcuatum	WCot
balansae	see *O. oligophyllum*
caudatum	see *O. longibracteatum*
I ***dictaeum***	GKev
dubium ♀H2	EGren GKev
lanceolatum	WCot
§ ***longibracteatum***	CPic SChr WHer WJun
magnum	CBro WCot
'Mount Fuji'	LAma
narbonense	GKev WCot
nutans ♀H5	CAby ECha EGren EPfP EPot GKev LAma LShi MNrw MPie NBir SEND
§ ***oligophyllum***	EGren EPot GKev LAma LRHS MNrw NBir XFar
ponticum	WCot
- 'Sochi'	CCBP ERCP GKev XFar
pyramidale	GKev LAma
- short	SMHy
pyrenaicum	CSpe CTtf ECha EPPr WCot WShi
reverchonii	ERCP LAma SBrt
saundersiae	LAma XFar
sintenisii	GKev
thyrsoides ♀H2	CSpe GKev LAma LCro
umbellatum	CBWd CHab EGren EGrI EHet GKev LAma LCro MNrw SEND SRms WShi XFar

Orobanche (Orobanchaceae)

hederae	MCtn

Orontium (Araceae)

aquaticum	CBen CLil CPud CToG CWat ELin EPfk EWat LCro NPer WMAq

Orostachys (Crassulaceae)

furusei	WFar
iwarenge	ESuc LCro SPlb
- 'Fuji' (v) **new**	ESuc
japonica **new**	ESuc
minuta **new**	ESuc
§ ***spinosa***	EDAr ESuc EWes SPlb WAbe WFar

Oroxylum (Bignoniaceae)

indicum	MCtn

Oroya (Cactaceae)

peruviana	SPlb

Orthophytum (Bromeliaceae)

gurkenii	WCot

Orthrosanthus (Iridaceae)

chimboracensis JCA 13743	EBee
laxus	CAbb CWCL EGrI ELan GKev LRHS NBir SIvy SMad
multiflorus	CPbh CSde LShi
polystachyus	CTsd MCtn SMHy WCot

Orychophragmus (Brassicaceae)

violaceus	MCtn

Oryzopsis (Poaceae)

lessoniana	see *Anemanthele lessoniana*
miliacea	CSpe ELan EPPr NSti SEND SPhx WCot WPGP
paradoxa	EPPr

Osbeckia (Melastomataceae)
stellata var. *crinita* — WPGP

Oscularia (Aizoaceae)
caulescens — WAbe
§ *deltoides* ♥H2 — CoPl EShb WCor WFar

Osmanthus (Oleaceae)
armatus — CBcs CJun CMac EBee EPfP LMaj LSRN NLar
× *burkwoodii* ♥H5 — Widely available
§ *decorus* — CBcs CBrac CJun CMac CTsd EBee EPfP NLar SArc SEND SReu
- 'Angustifolius' — NLar
delavayi ♥H5 — Widely available
- 'Frank Knight' — CJun EPfP MAsh
- 'George Gardner' — CJun CMac SRms
- 'Heaven Scent' — SPoG
- 'Latifolius' — CExl CJun ELon EPfP LRHS MAsh
forrestii — see *O. yunnanensis*
× *fortunei* — CBcs CCVT EBee EPfP LMaj
fragrans — CBcs CCVT LMaj SFol WJur
§ *heterophyllus* — CBcs CDoC CMac EBee EHeP ELan ERom LMaj MGos NLar SArc SFol SRms WFar
§ - 'Allgold' — CBcs CMac EBee ELan EPfP SPoG
- 'Argenteomarginatus' — see *O. heterophyllus* 'Variegatus'
§ - 'Aureomarginatus' (v) — CBcs CMac ELon SRms
- 'Aureus' misapplied — see *O. heterophyllus* 'Allgold'
- 'Aureus' Rehder (v) — see *O. heterophyllus* 'Aureomarginatus'
§ - 'Goshiki' (v) ♥H5 — Widely available
- 'Gulftide' — EGrI EHeP EPfP LRHS MAsh NLar
- 'Kembu' (v) — NLar
- 'Myrtifolius' — CMac
- 'Ōgon' — NLar
- PARTY LIGHTS — see *O. heterophyllus* 'Shien'
- 'Purple Shaft' ♥H5 — ELan
- 'Purpureus' — CBcs CCVT CMac EBee EGrI ELon EPfP EShb LMaj LRHS LSto NLar SArc SEND SGol WLov
- 'Rotundifolius' — CMac
- 'Sasaba' — CBcs
§ - 'Shien' (v) — SNig WFar WLov
- TRICOLOR — see *O. heterophyllus* 'Goshiki'
§ - 'Variegatus' (v) ♥H5 — CBcs CBrac CDoC CMac CSBt CTsd EHeP ELan ELon EPfP LCro LRHS LSRN LSto MAsh NLar SEND SGol SHor SPoG SRms SVen WCha WFar WHtc WLov
ilicifolius — see *O. heterophyllus*
'Perfume of Nature' — ELan LCro LRHS
serrulatus — NLar WJur WPGP
suavis — CJun LRHS NLar
§ *yunnanensis* ♥H5 — CBcs CMCN EBee ELon EPfP EUrb MBlu SArc SEND WPGP

× *Osmarea* see *Osmanthus*

Osmaronia see *Oemleria*

Osmunda ❀ (Osmundaceae)
asiatica — WCru
cinnamomea ♥H6 — CLAP ELan EMor EPfP EWes ISha LEdu LRHS NAlc NBid NBro SPlb SRot
claytoniana — CLAP EBee ISha LEdu NBid NBro WCot
japonica — CDor CLAP CLil EArl EBee EGren EGrI ELon EMor EUrb GBin ISha LBom LSto NBir NBro SBig SHor WBrk WCAu XFar
regalis ♥H6 — Widely available
- from southern USA — CLAP
- 'Cristata' ♥H6 — LRHS
- 'Purpurascens' — CSpe CSta CTsd EArl EBee ECha EGren ELan ELon EMor EWld ISha LEdu LRHS LSto MAvo MGos NAlc NBid NBir NBro NCth NLar SPeP WFar WTre
- var. *spectabilis* — CLAP LRHS MAsh

Osteomeles (Rosaceae)
subrotunda — EBee WPGP

Osteospermum (Asteraceae)
3D Series (d) — SPoG
- 3D BERRY WHITE ('Kleoe11185') (d) — LCro
- 3D BLUEBERRY SHAKE ('Kleoe18048'^PBR) (d) — LCro
- 3D PURPLE ('Kleoe12198') (d) — MBros
- 3D STEEL BLUE ('Kleoe23764') (d) **new** — LSou
- 3D VIOLET ICE ('Kleoe14223') (d) — EUrb MBros
- 'African Queen' — see *O.* 'Nairobi Purple'
(Akila Series) AKILA SUNSET SHADES ('Pas1260426') (mixed) — MCtn
- AKILA WHITE PURPLE EYE ('Pas857288') — LCro WKif
(Astra Series) ASTRA LAVENDER — MPri
- ASTRA ORANGE BRIQUE ('Balostor') — MPri
- ASTRA PURPLE ('Florospur1'^PBR) — MPri
- ASTRA ROSE WHITE ('Floroswhipi'^PBR) — MPri
- ASTRA WHITE ('Florosteo White') — MPri
barberae misapplied — see *O. jucundum*
barberae (Harv.) Norl. 'Compactum' — GArf WFar
'Blue Streak' — CMac
'Buttermilk' ♥H3 — ELan
'Cannington John' — CWal LShi
'Cannington Kira' — CWal
'Cannington Roy' — CBcs CEnd CMac CWnw EBee ELan ELon EUrb LCro SEND WFar WMal
caulescens misapplied — see *O.* 'White Pim'
Dalina Series **new** — MPri
ecklonis — CDTJ MBros NBro
- var. *prostratum* — see *O.* 'White Pim'
(FlowerPower Series) FLOWERPOWER ICE WHITE ('Kleo06123') — LCro
- FLOWERPOWER LAVENDER PINK ('Kleoe14235') — LCro
'Hopleys' ♥H3 — SEND
'In the Pink' — ELan LBar LCro MHol MPro MSwo MWlw WHil
'Irish' — CTtf EPot ESgI MHer WIce
§ *jucundum* ♥H3 — CCht ECha EPfP EPPr GAbr LCro LShi LSRN MNrw NBir NPer SRms
- 'Blackthorn Seedling' ♥H3 — CWGN ECha
- var. *compactum* — CMac CTsd EGren ELan ELon EUrb LSRN MPri NPer SIvy SPoG StAn WFar WTor

492 Osteospermum

- 'Elliott's Form'	WHoo WMal	§ 'White Pim' ♀H3	CDTJ NPer SEND
- 'Langtrees' ♀H3	ELon GAbr	'Wine Purple'	see O. 'Nairobi Purple'
- 'Nanum'	EDAr		
§ 'Lady Leitrim' ♀H3	CTsd CWGN CWnw EBee ECha	## *Ostrowskia* (Campanulaceae)	
	ELan EPPr ESgI GMaP LBar LShi	*magnifica*	EPot
	LSRN MHol MPri MPro NPer SDix		
	SEND SPoG WTor	## *Ostrya* (Betulaceae)	
§ 'Nairobi Purple'	CBcs CDoC EBee EDAr EGren ELan	*carpinifolia*	CBcs CHll CMCN EBee EHeP ELan
	EPfP EShb EUrb LBar LBom LCro		IPap LMaj LRHS LSto MBlu MMuc
	LRHS MHol MPri SEND WFar WHil		NOra NPip SEND WJur WMat
Orange Symphony	SEND	*virginiana*	WJur
('Seimora'PBR)			
(Symphony Series)		## *Otacanthus* (Plantaginaceae)	
'Pale Face'	see O. 'Lady Leitrim'	*caeruleus* 'Atlantis'	CDoC
'Peggyi'	see O. 'Nairobi Purple'		
'Pink Gem'	MHer WFar	## *Otatea* (Poaceae)	
'Port Wine'	see O. 'Nairobi Purple'	*acuminata*	WCot
Purple Sun ('Kleoe19396')	LCro MPri		
(FlowerPower Series)		## *Otholobium* (Fabaceae)	
'Sennen Sunrise'	CBcs CCht CTsd ELan LBar LRHS	*glandulosum*	EBee
	MPri WTor		
(Serenity Series) Serenity	LCro LSou MBros MPri	## *Othonna* (Asteraceae)	
Blue Eyed Beauty		*capensis*	see *Crassothonna capensis*
('Balostlueye'PBR)		*cheirifolia*	see *Hertia cheirifolia*
- Serenity Blushing Beauty	MBros MPri		
('Balostush')		## *Ourisia* (Plantaginaceae)	
- Serenity Deep Yellow	MPri	× *bitternensis*	WAbe
('Balserdelo')		'Cliftonville Damask'	
- Serenity Pink Eyed Beauty	LCro	- 'Cliftonville Pink'	WAbe
('Balostroseye')		- 'Cliftonville Roset'	WAbe
- Serenity Red ('Balsered')	MBros	*caespitosa*	GArf
- Serenity Sunshine Beauty	see O. 'Sunshine Beauty' (Serenity	- var. *gracilis*	GKev
	Series)	*coccinea*	EBee GArf GKev
'Shire Pink'	LShi	'Loch Ewe'	CExl GKev
'Silver Sparkler' (v) ♀H3	CDTJ MHer SVen	*macrophylla*	GKev
'Snow Pixie'	CBcs CWGN CWnw EArI ELan ESgI	*microphylla*	WAbe
	LBar LCro LRHS MPri SPoG WFar	- f. *alba*	WAbe
	WHil WIce	*polyantha* 'Cliftonville	WAbe
'Stardust'	EUrb NPer	Scarlet'	
§ SummerHero Pure Orange	LSou	'Snowflake' ♀H4	GAbr GArf
('Kleoe19400')			
(SummerHero Series)		## *Oxalis* (Oxalidaceae)	
(Summersmile Series)	EUrb	*acetosella*	GQue MHer NAts NQui WHer WShi
Summersmile Orange		- var. *subpurpurascens*	WCot
('Inostorang'PBR) **new**		*adenophylla* ♀H4	CMiW CoPl EGren ELan EPfP EPot
- Summersmile Sunrise **new**	EUrb LRHS MSwo		GKev LAma SPoG SRms XFar
- Summersmile Yellow	EUrb	'Anne Christie'	NRya
('Inostyellow'PBR) **new**		*arenaria* F&W 10584	WCot
(Sunny Series) 'Sunny Bronze'	CSpe WKif	§ *articulata*	ELan GElm NPer SEND WCav
- 'Sunny Carlos'PBR	SPoG	- 'Alba'	ELan WCot
- 'Sunny Cherry'	SPoG	- f. *crassipes* 'Alba'	WCot
- 'Sunny Mary'PBR	LCro SPoG	'Autumn Pink'	XFar
- 'Sunny Nathalie'	LRHS	'Black Velvet' (Xalis Series)	ELan
- 'Sunny Sonja'PBR	SPoG	*bowiei*	WCot
- 'Sunny Victoria'PBR	SPoG	*brasiliensis*	EPPr ESwi LShi
- 'Sunny Xena'PBR	SPoG	*conorrhiza*	NBir
§ 'Sunshine Beauty'	LSou	'Dark Eye'	MNrw
(Serenity Series)		*debilis* 'Aureoreticulata'	EShb
I 'Superbum'	WFar	- var. *corymbosa*	ELin
'Tauranga'	see O. 'Whirlygig'	*deppei*	see O. *tetraphylla*
'Tresco Peggy'	see O. 'Nairobi Purple'	§ *depressa*	EWes LShi NBir NRya
'Tresco Purple'	see O. 'Nairobi Purple'	*enneaphylla* ♀H4	CElw GEdr MNrw NRya SPlb WAbe
'Upright Purple'	CDoC	- 'Alba'	CElw CMiW GArf GKev NRya
(Voltage Series) Voltage Gold	see O. SummerHero Pure Orange	- subsp. *ibari*	EPot EPPr GEdr NRya
	(SummerHero Series)	- 'Minutifolia'	GEdr GQue NRya
- Voltage Yellow	EUrb	- 'Rosea'	LAma NRya
('Balvoyelo')		- 'Sheffield Swan'	GEdr GKev
'Weetwood' ♀H3	ELan EPot EPPr LShi MHer SPoG	*fabifolia*	ECha
	WFar WMal	'Fanny'	GKev
'Westwood White'	EDAr	*flava* white-flowered	EPot
§ 'Whirlygig' ♀H3	CWal	*floribunda* misapplied	see O. *articulata*

Pachypodium 493

griffithii double-flowered (d)	CMiW GGro WFar
- 'Snowflake'	CMiW
'Gwen McBride'	GArf GEdr
hirta 'Gothenburg'	EPPr EShb GKev LAma
incarnata	CoPl
inops	see *O. depressa*
'Ione Hecker' ♀H4	CMiW GArf GMaP NRya
* *karroica*	WCot
laciniata ♀H3	GKev
- hybrid	GEdr
lactea double-flowered	see *O. magellanica* 'Nelson'
magellanica	CMiW GAbr SPlb WCot
- 'Flore Pleno'	see *O. magellanica* 'Nelson'
§ - 'Nelson' (d)	CMiW EPPr GBin NBir NPer SMad
massoniana ♀H2	ECha WAbe WCot XFar
megalorrhiza misapplied	see *O. mirbelii*
melanosticta	WCot
§ - 'Ken Aslet' ♀H5	GKev LAma NBir
§ *mirbelii*	CoPl EAri SChr
obtusa	ECha
oregana	CMac ECha EPPr EWld GBin MNrw WCot WCru
- 'Bob Haszeldine'	GEdr GKev
- 'Klamath Ruby'	EWld
- f. *smalliana*	CMiW EPPr EWld GEdr MNrw NBro NLar WCot WCru
- white-flowered	GBin WCot
peduncularis	CoPl
perdicaria	EPot WAbe WIce
- 'Citrino'	CTtf WAbe WCot
'Pink Spider' **new**	XFar
polyphylla	GEdr
var. *heptaphylla*	
'Pom Pom' (d)	XFar
§ *purpurea*	CoPl
- 'Ken Aslet'	see *O. melanosticta* 'Ken Aslet'
regnellii	see *O. triangularis* subsp. *papillonacea*
semiloba	EPPr LShi
speciosa	see *O. purpurea*
spiralis	see *O. vulcanicola*
subsp. *vulcanicola*	
§ *tetraphylla*	CoPl GKev NPer
- 'Iron Cross'	CoPl EGren ELan EPPr GKev LAma LCro LRHS MPie SBeP SPlb WFar XFar
- purple-leaved	EPPr
triangularis	EGren ELan EWld LAma LBom LCro LShi MHer NPer WBrk WFar XFar
- 'Birgit'	GKev
- BURGUNDY WINE ('JR Oxburwi') (Xalis Series)	CWGN NPer
- 'Mijke'	GKev LAma
§ - subsp. *papillonacea* ♀H3	GKev LAma WCot XFar
- - 'Atropurpurea'	CSpe LBom
- subsp. *triangularis*	GKev LAma MPie
tuberosa	CoPl EAri LEdu MEar NBac SPoG WKor
'Ute' ♀H3	CElw EPot EPPr EWld GEdr GKev GMaP NRya
versicolor ♀H3	EPot ETay GEdr GKev LAma NBir XFar
- 'Golden Cape'	EPot XFar
§ *vulcanicola*	WJun
- 'Burgundy'	CoPl
- 'Plum Crazy' (v)	WFar WJun
- 'Sunset Velvet'	CoPl WCot WJun
- 'Zinfandel'	WJun
I 'Waverley Hybrid'	GKev GMaP
'White Spider' **new**	XFar

Oxycoccus see *Vaccinium*

Oxydendrum ❀ (Ericaceae)

arboreum	CBcs CMCN EBee EGrl ELan LRHS MBlu MCtn SPoG SSta

Oxypetalum (Apocynaceae)

caeruleum	see *Tweedia caerulea*

Oxyria (Polygonaceae)

digyna	CAgr GGro GKev MEar NBac WKor
- CC 3755	WCot

Oziroë (Asparagaceae)

biflora	NNys

Ozothamnus (Asteraceae)

§ *coralloides*	SPlb WAbe
§ 'County Park Silver'	EPot GEdr LShi
§ *hookeri*	CDoC LRHS MBlu SEle SVen WJek WPGP
§ *ledifolius*	CBcs CCoa CDoC ELon
§ *rosmarinifolius*	CBcs CDoC ELan EPfP LRHS MAsh SVen
- 'Silver Jubilee'	CBcs CCoa CSBt CSde CWnw ELan ELon LRHS MAsh SPlb WFar
§ *selago*	WCot
- 'Major'	EDAr SPlb
'Sussex Silver'	CBcs
'Threave Seedling'	CDoC ELan EPfP LRHS MAsh

Pachira (Malvaceae)

aquatica	CDoC EGren LBom LCro LDro LWaG NHrt NPlm SPre

Pachycereus (Cactaceae)

§ *marginatus*	NPlm
pecten-aboriginum	NPlm
pringlei	LCro NPlm

Pachyphragma (Brassicaceae)

§ *macrophyllum*	CBcs CCBP CDor CSpe EBee ECha ELan EMor EWld GMaP LBar LEdu LRHS MBel MMuc MPri NLar NSti SDix WCAu WCot WCru WHil WPGP WPnP WTor

Pachyphytum ❀ (Crassulaceae)

bracteosum	CDoC CPic CSBt LCro SIvy SPoG
'Chiseled Stones'	WCor
compactum	CPic WCor
dark red-leaved	SPoG
hookeri	CPic EUrb
oviferum ♀H2	CPic
werdermannii	CPic

Pachypleurum (Apiaceae)

mutellinoides	MNrw
- pink-flowered **new**	WHil

Pachypodium (Apocynaceae)

geayi ♀H1a	NPlm SPlb
lamerei ♀H1a	NPlm SPad SPlb
lealii subsp. *saundersii*	SPlb
mikea	SPlb

Pachyrhizus (Fabaceae)
erosus — MCtn

Pachysandra (Buxaceae)
axillaris — CMac GKev WCot WPGP
- BWJ 8032 — WCru
- 'Crûg's Cover' — EBee ESwi EWld SMad WCru WFar
procumbens — EBee GKev MNrw NLar WCot
- 'Angola' (v) — WCot
terminalis — CBcs CDoC CMac EBee ECha EGren EGrI EHeP ELan EMor EPfP GBin LBuc LCro LRHS LShi LSto MGos MHtn MPri NLar NLit SArc SBig SGol SPlb StAn WFar WPnP
- 'Green Carpet' — CBcs CBWd CDoC CSBt CWnw EBee EGren ELan EPfP EUrb GMaP LBom LRHS LSRN LSto MArl MAsh MAvo MGos MMuc MPri NLar SHor SNig SPoG WCAu WFar
- 'Green Sheen' ♀H5 — ECha ELan EUrb GQue LRHS LWaG MAvo WCAu
- 'Variegata' (v) ♀H5 — CBcs CDoC CMac CoPl ECha EGren EHeP ELan EMor EPPr EUrb LCro LRHS LShi LSto MAsh MAvo MGos MMuc NBir NLar SGol SPlb SPoG SRms WFar

× *Pachysedum* (Crassulaceae)
'Ganzhou' — CPic

Pachystegia (Asteraceae)
§ **insignis** — CBcs LRHS
- DAIZEA ('Hardec') — SMad

× *Pachyveria* (Crassulaceae)
sp. — CPic NCft SIvy
'Clavifolia' **new** — CSBt LCro SMrm
'Ice Crystal' — CPic
'Orpet' — NCft
'Powder Puff' — CPic
scheideckeri — CDoC EAri NCft
- 'Albocarinata' — WCor

Paederota (Plantaginaceae)
§ **bonarota** — GEdr GKev WAbe
lutea — GEdr GKev WCot

Paeonia ❀ (Paeoniaceae)
'All That Jazz' — GBin LPmr LRHS WCAu XFar
'America' — GBin LPmr NLar WCAu
'Amy Jo' — LPmr NLar
'Anderson's Kaleidoscope' — GBin
'Angelet' (S) — WCAu
'Anna Marie' (S) — ELan GBin WCAu
anomala — GBin GKev WCAu
§ - subsp. **anomala** — LPmr MPhe
§ - subsp. **veitchii** ♀H6 — CExl CMiW EWld GBin GKev GMaP LPmr LRHS StAn WCAu WCot WSpi
'Apricot Queen' — GBin LPmr
'Archangel' — GBin LPmr WCAu
arietina — GKev
- W&B BG A-4 — WCot
- 'Northern Glory' — GBin
I 'Artemis' Daphnis (S) — WCAu
'Athena' ♀H6 — GBin LPmr WCAu
'Auten's Red' — WCAu
'Avant Garde' — GBin
'Bai Xue Ta' (S) — NTPC
'Ballarena de Saval' — GBin LPmr

banatica — see *P. officinalis* subsp. *banatica*
§ 'Bartzella' ♀H6 — CHll ELan EPfP GBin GMaP IArd LCro LPmr LRHS MNrw NLar SHar SMad SPeP SPoG WCAu WCot XFar
BELLE TOULOUSAINE ('Rtpiv78906') **new** — WCAu
beresowskii — see *P. anomala* subsp. *veitchii*
'Berry Berry Fine' — LPmr WCAu
'Berry Garcia' — GBin
'Black Panther' (S) — WCAu
'Black Pirate' (S) ♀H5 — WCAu
'Black Star' — LPmr
'Blaze' ♀H6 — EPfP GMaP LPmr LRHS NLar WCAu WCot
'Blushing Princess' — GBin LPmr WCAu
'Border Charm' — GBin GEdr LPmr
'Boreas' (S) — WCAu
'Bride's Dream' — GBin
broteri — GKev
'Buckeye Belle' — EBee EGren EGrI ELan ERCP GBin GMaP LBom LCro LPmr LRHS LSRN MBel NLar SHor SPoG WCAu WCot WTor XFar
'Burma Joy' — WCAu
'Burma Midnight' — GBin WCAu
'Callie's Memory' — EGrI EPfP GBin LPmr LRHS MPro NCth NLar WCAu WKif XFar
cambessedesii ♀H3 — CSpe EPot ESwi GBin GEdr GKev GMaP MCtn NBir WAbe WCot
- dwarf — GKev
'Canary Brilliant'PBR — ESwi GBin LPmr LRHS WCAu XFar
'Carina' — GBin WCAu
* 'Carl G.Klehm' — LPmr
'Carol' — LPmr LRHS LSRN WCAu
CAROLINE CONSTABLE ('Rtpiv79138') **new** — WCAu
caucasica — see *P. daurica* subsp. *coriifolia*
'Center Stage' (S) **new** — ELan
× **chamaeleon** — WCAu
'Cherry Panna Cotta' — SBrt
'Cherry Ruffles' — WCAu
'Chief Black Hawk' — GBin LPmr WCAu
'Chinese Dragon' (S) — WCAu
'Chocolate Soldier' — GBin WCAu
'Christmas Velvet' — GBin LPmr WCAu
'Claire de Lune' ♀H6 — GBin GMaP LPmr LRHS NLar SHor WCAu WCot
'Claudia' — GBin WCAu
'Clouds of Colour' — GBin LPmr
'Color Magnet' — GBin WCAu
'Command Performance' — GBin LPmr LRHS NLar WCAu
'Convoy' — WCAu
'Cora Louise' ♀H6 — ELan ESwi GBin LPmr LRHS MAsh MHol MPro NCth NLar SPeP WCAu WKif XFar
'Coral Beach' — LRHS MPri
'Coral Charm' ♀H6 — CWnw EAri EGrI EPfP GBin GMaP LAma LCro LPmr LSRN MHol MMrt MPri NBir NCth NLar SAth WCAu WCot WHoo WTor XFar
'Coral Fay' — GBin LRHS MPri WCAu
'Coral 'n' Gold' — GBin MPri WCAu
'Coral Sunset' ♀H6 — CWnw EAri EBlo EGren EGrI GBin LAma LCro LPmr LRHS MHol MPri MPro NLar SAth SMad WCAu WCot WTor
'Coral Supreme' — GBin LPmr LRHS MPri
corallina — see *P. mascula* subsp. *mascula*
coriacea — GKev
'Court Jester' — ELan GBin LPmr WCAu

'Cuckoo's Nest'	WCAu
'Cutie'	WCAu
'Cytherea'	GBin LPmr WCAu
'Daedalus' (S)	GBin
'Dancing Butterflies'	see *P. lactiflora* 'Zi Yu Nu'
'Dao Jin' (S)	LCro
'Dark Eyes'	GBin LPmr WCAu
§ ***daurica***	GKev WCot
§ - subsp. ***coriifolia***	CBro
- - RCB UA 12	WCot
§ - subsp. ***macrophylla***	WCru
B&SWJ 15391	
§ - subsp. ***mlokosewitschii*** ♀H6	CExl CJun ECha ELan ENun EWld GBin GEdr GKev GMaP LCro LEdu LPmr LRHS MAsh MCtn NBid NBir SDix WAbe WCAu WCot WKif WSpi
- - hybrids	GKev
§ - subsp. ***wittmanniana***	ECha WCAu
- - 'Rosea'	GBin WCAu
'Dearest'	GBin
decomposita	NTPC
decora	see *P. peregrina*
delavayi (S)	CMCN EPfP GEdr GGro GMaP LCro LSto MGos NBir NTPC SDix SPoG SRms WCAu WCot WJur WTre
- BWJ 7775 (S)	WCru
- from China (S)	MPhe
- var. ***angustiloba*** (S)	GKev
- - f. ***alba*** (S)	CExl
§ - - f. ***angustiloba*** (S)	GKev NTPC WPGP
§ - - f. ***trollioides*** (S)	CExl
- - - BO 15-142	GGro
- var. ***delavayi*** f. ***lutea*** (S)	CDoC ELan EPfP GKev MGos NBir SArc SIvy SPoG SRms StAn WCAu WJur WTre
- var. ***lutea***	see *P. delavayi* var. *delavayi* f. *lutea*
- Mrs Sarson strain (S)	EWes
- Potaninii Group	see *P. delavayi* var. *angustiloba* f. *angustiloba*
- 'Tapestry' (S)	CSpe
- Trollioides Group	see *P. delavayi* var. *angustiloba* f. *trollioides*
- 'Xia Ye' (S) **new**	NTPC
'Diana Parks'	GBin LPmr NLar WCAu
'Don Richardson'	WCAu
'Dreamtime'	WCAu
'Dynasty'	**LPmr**
'Early Glow'	**GBin WCAu**
'Early Scout'	**GBin NLar WCAu**
'Early Windflower'	**ELan GBin GMaP LPmr LRHS NLar WCAu**
'Eden's Perfume'	LPmr NCth
'Eliza Lundy' ♀H6	GBin LPmr WCAu
'Elizabeth Foster'	WCAu
'Ellen Cowley'	GBin LPmr WCAu
emodi ♀H6	CSpe GKev LPmr WCAu WCot WMal XFar
'Enduring Rainbow'	LPmr
'Erda' **new**	WCAu
'Etched Salmon'	GBin LPmr WCAu XFar
'Eventide'	WCAu
'Ezra Pound' (S)	ELan WCAu
'Fairy Princess'	GBin WCAu
§ × ***festiva*** 'Alba Plena'	EGren LPmr NLar WFar
§ - 'Mutabilis Plena'	LPmr
§ - 'Rosea Plena' ♀H6	EGren EPfP GBin LBom LPmr LRHS WCAu WCot WFar
- 'Rosea Superba Plena'	LPmr
§ - 'Rubra Plena' ♀H6	CWal EGren EGrI GBin GMaP LPmr LRHS MBel NGdn NLar SRms WCAu WCot
'Firelight'	GBin WCAu
'First Arrival' ♀H6	GBin LPmr LRHS MHol MPro WCAu
'First Dutch Yellow'	see *P.* 'Garden Treasure'
'Flame'	CWnw EAri EPfP GBin LPmr LSto MBel MNrw NCth NSti WCAu WCot WTor XFar
§ Gansu Group (S)	GKev MPhe NTPC
- 'Bai Bi Lan Xia' (S)	MPhe
- 'Bei Ji Guang' (S)	NTPC
- 'Dan Ding He' (S)	NTPC
- 'Dan Feng Ling Kong' (S)	NTPC
- 'Er Long Xi Zhu' (S)	NTPC
- 'Fen Guan Yu Zhu' (S)	NTPC
- 'Fen He' (S)	MPhe NTPC
- 'Gan Lan Yu' (S)	NTPC
- 'Gui Fu Ren' (S)	NTPC
- 'He Ping Er Qiao' (S)	NTPC
- 'Hei Fa Nü Lang' (S)	NTPC
- 'Hei Feng Die' (S)	MPhe
- 'Hei Tian E' (S)	NTPC
- 'Hei Xuan Feng' (S)	MPhe
§ - 'Highdown' (S)	MCtn
- 'Hong Lian' (S)	NTPC
- 'Hui He' (S)	MPhe
- 'Jiao Rong' (S)	MPhe
- 'Lan He' (S)	MPhe
- 'Lan He Qi Ming' (S)	NTPC
- 'Lan Yu San Cai' (S)	NTPC
- 'Long Yu Er Qiao' (S)	NTPC
- 'Long Yuan Hong' (S)	MPhe
- 'Pan Deng' (S)	NTPC
- 'Pin Hong' (S)	NTPC
- 'Qing Hua Yan' (S)	NTPC
- 'Qing Si Wan Lü' (S)	NTPC
- 'Ri Yue Tong Hui' (S)	MPhe
- 'San Hua Nu' (S)	MPhe
- 'Shi Ji Ju Xing' (S) **new**	NTPC
- 'Shu Sheng Peng Mo' (S)	MPhe NTPC
- 'Tie Mian Wu Si' (S)	MPhe
- 'Wu Kong Xiu Xing' (S)	NTPC
- 'Xiong Mao' (S)	MPhe
- 'Xue Hai Bing Xin' (S)	MPhe NTPC
- 'Xue Lian' (S)	NTPC
- 'Yan Wei Bai' (S)	NTPC
- 'Ye Guang Bei' (S)	MPhe NTPC
- 'Zi Ban Bai' (S)	NTPC
- 'Zi Die Ying Feng' (S)	MPhe NTPC
- 'Zi Ju Ban Yue' (S)	NTPC
- 'Zi Lian Deng' (S)	NTPC
- 'Zi Yan' (S)	NTPC
- 'Zong Ban Bai' (S)	NTPC
Gansu Mudan Group	see *P.* Gansu Group
'Garden Peace'	GBin LPmr WCAu
§ 'Garden Treasure'	EPfP GBin LPmr LRHS MHol NLar SPoG WCAu
'Gauguin' (S)	WCAu
'Going Bananas'	LPmr LRHS NLar
'Gold Sovereign' (S) **new**	WCAu
'Golden Dream'	see *P.* 'Bartzella'
'Golden Fairy'	LPmr
'Gordon E. Simonson' **new**	WCAu
'Halcyon'	WCAu
'Hei Hua Kui'	see *P.* × *suffruticosa* 'Hei Hua Kui'
'Hélène Martin' (S)	GBin LPmr NLar
'Henry Bockstoce'	GBin LPmr LRHS NCth NLar WCAu
'Hillary'	ESwi GBin GMaP LPmr LRHS NLar SPeB WCAu XFar
'Ho-gioku'	NCth
'Honor'	GBin WCAu
humilis	see *P. officinalis* subsp. *microcarpa*
'Huo Lian Jin Dan' (S)	NTPC

'Icarus' (S)	GBin	- 'Candy Heart'	GBin WCAu
'Illini Belle'	EBlo WCAu	- 'Candy Stripe'	GBin LPmr LRHS MAsh SMad
'Illini Warrior'	GBin GMaP WCAu	- 'Catharina Fontijn'	CWnw EPfP GBin LPmr LRHS WCAu
'Impossible Dream'	LPmr WCAu		
intermedia	WCot	- 'Celebrity'	LBuc LPmr LRHS MHol
japonica ambig.	GEdr	- 'Charles Burgess'	GBin LPmr WCAu
japonica (Makino) Miyabe & Takeda	see *P. obovata*	- 'Charlie's White'	GBin LPmr LRHS MPri NLar WCAu
		- 'Charm'	EGrI WCAu
'Jin Ge' (S)	LCro NTPC	- 'Cheddar Charm'	WCAu
'Joanna Marlene'	GBin LPmr WCAu	- 'Cheddar Cheese'	LPmr WCAu
'John Harvard'	WCAu	- 'Cheddar Gold'	GBin WCAu
'Joker'	GBin LBuc LPmr MAsh WCAu	- 'Cherry Hill'	GBin WCAu
'Joseph Rock' not Klehm	see *P.* (Gansu Group) 'Highdown'	- 'Chiffon Clouds'	WCAu
'Joyce Ellen'	LPmr NCth WCAu	- 'Chiffon Parfait'	LPmr WCAu
'Julia Rose'	ELan EPfP GBin LPmr LRHS MPro NLar SPoG WCAu XFar	- 'Chinook'	GBin
		- 'Chippewa'	GBin
'Juliska'	GBin	- 'Class Act'	GBin LPmr WCAu
kavachensis	EGrI ESwi GEdr	- 'Cora Stubbs'	GBin NLar WCAu
'King's Day' **new**	XFar	- 'Cornelia Shaylor'	WCAu
'Kopper Kettle'	ELan GBin LPmr WCAu	- 'Cotton Candy' **new**	WCAu
'La Donna'	GBin WCAu	- 'Couronne d'Or'	GBin LPmr LRHS WCAu
lactiflora 'Abalone Pearl'	GBin WCAu	- 'Cream Puff'	WCAu
- 'Adolphe Rousseau'	LCro LPmr WCAu	- 'Cringley White'	SRms
- 'Agida'	EBee EBlo LRHS LSto	- 'Crystal Beauty'	LPmr
- 'Albert Crousse'	CBcs LPmr NBir WCAu	- 'Dawn Pink'	WCAu
- 'Alertie'	EPfP GBin LPmr LRHS	- 'Dayton'	WCAu
- 'Alexander Fleming'	EGren EGrI EPfP GBin LBom LCro LPmr LRHS MHtn MPri NBir SOrN WCAu WFar WTor	- 'Dinner Plate'	GBin LPmr LRHS NLar SHar WCAu
		- 'Do Tell'	GBin LBuc LPmr LRHS NLar WCAu XFar
- 'Alice Harding'	GBin LPmr NLar WCAu	- 'Doreen' ♀H6	EPfP GBin LPmr LRHS SHar WCAu WTor
- 'Allan Rogers'	WCAu		
- 'Amabilis'	LPmr WCAu WTor	- 'Doris Cooper'	WCAu
- 'Amalia Olson'	GBin WCAu	- 'Dresden'	WCAu
- 'Angel Cheeks'	GBin LCro LPmr LRHS NLar SMad WCAu WKif	- 'Dresden Pink'	GBin
		- 'Dublin' (Patio Peony Series)	LPmr LRHS
- 'Ann Cousins'	LPmr WCAu	- 'Duchesse de Nemours' ♀H6	Widely available
- 'Aphrodite's Kiss'	LPmr		
- 'Armistice'	WCAu	- 'Easy Lavender'	GBin
- 'Auguste Dessert'	WCAu	- 'Edulis Superba'	CFis EBee ELan GBin LEdu LPmr LRHS MPri NPer SMrm WCAu
§ - 'Augustin d'Hour' ♀H6	LPmr WCAu WTor		
- 'Avalanche'	EPfP GBin LPmr LRHS NLar WCAu	- 'Elsa Sass'	GBin LPmr LRHS WCAu
- 'Balliol'	GBin	- 'Emma Klehm' ♀H6	GBin WCAu WCot
- 'Barbara' ♀H6	LPmr WCAu	- 'Evelyn Tibbets'	GBin
- 'Baroness Schröder'	EBee GBin LPmr LSto WCAu	- 'Evening World'	ECha
- 'Barrington Belle' ♀H6	GBin LPmr WCAu WFar	- 'Fairy's Petticoat'	GBin LPmr WCAu
- 'Bella Donna'	LPmr	- 'Félix Crousse'	CBcs EBee EGrI EPfP GBin GMaP LCro LPmr LRHS LSRN MPri NBir WCAu WFar
- 'Belle Center'	WCAu		
- 'Belleville'	GBin		
- 'Bess Bockstoce'	WCAu	- 'Felix Supreme'	GBin LBom
- 'Best Man'	LPmr LRHS MPri WCAu	- 'Festiva Maxima' ♀H6	CWnw EAri EBee EGren EPfP GBin LCro LPmr LRHS LSto MHol MPri NBir NLar SHor SOrN SPoG SRms WCAu WFar WHoo WKif WTor XFar
- 'Better Times'	WCAu		
- 'Bev'	GBin		
- 'Big Ben'	EPfP LPmr NLar WSpi WTor		
- 'Black Beauty'	EPfP ERCP LPmr	- 'Festivity'	GBin LPmr
- 'Blush Queen'	GBin LPmr WCAu	- 'Fiona'	WCAu
- 'Border Gem'	EBee LRHS WCAu	- 'Fire Works'	LPmr
- 'Bouchela'	LPmr NSti	- 'Florence Nicholls' ♀H6	ELan GBin LPmr WCAu
- 'Boule de Neige'	LPmr LRHS	- 'Foxtrot'	GBin
- 'Bouquet Perfect' ♀H6	EGren GBin WCAu	- 'François Ortegat'	EPfP
- 'Bowl of Beauty'	Widely available	- 'Garden Lace'	LPmr WCAu
- 'Bowl of Cream'	ELan GBin LCro LPmr WCAu	- 'Gardenia'	EPfP GBin LPmr LRHS NLar SHor WCAu WCot
- 'Bridal Gown'	GBin LPmr WCAu		
- 'Bridal Icing'	GBin LPmr MArl WCAu	- 'Gay Paree' ♀H6	GBin LPmr LRHS MArl MHol NCth NLar SHar WCAu
- 'Bridal Shower'	GBin LPmr NLar XFar		
- 'Bright Knight'	WCAu	- 'Gayborder June'	LRHS WCAu
- 'Brother Chuck'	LPmr	- 'Général MacMahon'	see *P. lactiflora* 'Augustin d'Hour'
- 'Bunker Hill'	GBin LPmr LRHS LSto WCAu	- 'Germaine Bigot'	WCAu
- 'Burnished Bronze'	LPmr	- 'Gertrude Allen'	LPmr
- 'Butch'	WCAu	- 'Gilbert Barthelot'	WCAu
- 'Bu-te'	LAma	- 'Glory Hallelujah'	GBin WCAu
- 'Butter Bowl'	GBin WCAu	- 'Golden Fleece'	WCAu

- 'Golden Frolic'	GBin WCAu	- 'Lord Cavin'	GBin
- 'Goldilocks'	GBin LPmr WCAu	- 'Lord Kitchener'	EPfP GBin LPmr LRHS WCAu
- 'Goldmine'	GBin SMrm SPeP	- 'Lotus Queen'	LSto WCAu
- 'Green Halo'	GBin LPmr WCAu WCot	- 'Louis van Houtte'	EGrI
- 'Green Lotus'	LPmr NLar XFar	- 'Love's Touch'	GBin
- 'Guidon'	WCAu	- 'Lowell Thomas'	GBin LPmr
- 'Hansina Brand'	GBin	- 'Ma Petite Cherie' ♀H6	GBin WCAu
- 'Helen Hayes'	WCAu	- 'Madame Calot'	LPmr LRHS MPri NCth NLar WCAu
- 'Henri Potin'	NCth	- 'Madame Claude Tain'	GBin LPmr LRHS WCAu WCot
- 'Henry Sass'	LPmr WCAu	- 'Madame de Verneville'	GBin
- 'Hermione'	GBin LPmr WCAu	- 'Madame Edouard Doriat'	WCAu
- 'Highlight'	LPmr	- 'Madame Emile Débatène'	EGren EGrI LPmr LRHS MHol MPri WCAu WFar XFar
- 'Hit Parade'	WCAu		
- 'Honey Gold'	ELan GBin LPmr LRHS SPoG WCAu WSpi	- 'Madame Gaudichau'	WCot
		- 'Madame Jules Dessert'	LPmr
- 'Hot Chocolate'	GBin WCAu	- 'Madrid' (Patio Peony Series)	LCro LPmr
- 'Immaculée' ♀H6	CWnw EPfP GBin LCro LPmr LRHS NCth NLar SHar SHor SPoG WTor XFar		
		- 'Maestro'	GBin
		- 'Mammoth Rose'	GBin
- 'Inspecteur Lavergne'	EBee EPfP GBin LBom LPmr LRHS NGdn SMrm WCAu WCot WTor	- 'Margaret Clark'	WCAu
		- 'Margaret Truman'	LPmr LRHS WCAu
- 'Instituteur Doriat'	WCAu	- 'Marie Lemoine'	CWnw GBin LBuc LPmr LRHS MArl MPri WCAu WCot
- 'Jacorma'	GBin LPmr		
- 'Jan van Leeuwen' ♀H6	CWnw EPfP GBin GMaP LCro LPmr LRHS NCth SHor WCAu WCot WKif WTor	- 'Martha Reed'	WCAu
		- 'Mary E. Nicholls'	GBin LPmr WCAu
		- 'Mary Elizabeth'	GBin
- 'Jubilee'	LPmr	- 'Matilda Lewis'	GBin
- 'Judith Eileen'	GBin WCAu	- 'May Treat'	GBin
- 'June Rose'	WCAu	- 'Midnight Sun' ♀H6	GBin WCAu
- 'Kakoden'	GBin	- 'Minnie Shaylor' ♀H6	WCAu
- 'Kansas' ♀H6	CWnw EAri EBee EGren ELan EPfP ERCP GBin LCro LPmr LRHS MArl MPri NBir NCth NGdn SAth SOrN SPoG WCAu WCot WFar	- 'Mischief'	WCAu
		- 'Miss America'	GBin LBuc LCro LPmr LRHS NCth WCAu
		- 'Miss Eckhart'	EBee GBin WCAu
- 'Karen Gray'	GBin WCAu	- 'Miss Mary'	LPmr NLar
- 'Karl Rosenfield'	CBcs CWnw EAri EBee EGren EHeP EPfP GBin LAma LBom LCro LPmr LRHS LSRN MHol MHtn MNrw MPri NLar SAth SPoG SRms WCAu WFar WTor WTre	- 'Missie's Blush'	GBin
		- 'Mister Ed'	ELan GBin WCAu
		- 'Monsieur Jules Elie' ♀H6	ELan EPfP GBin LCro LPmr LRHS MHol NGdn NLar WCAu WTor WTre
- 'Kelway's Glorious' ♀H6	GBin GPSL LPmr LRHS LSto MHol NLar SHor WCAu WHoo	- 'Monsieur Martin Cahuzac'	GBin LRHS MPri WCAu
		- 'Moon of Nippon' ♀H4	LPmr LRHS NCth NLar WCAu WCot
- 'Kiev' (Patio Peony Series)	LPmr	- 'Moon Over Barrington' **new**	WCAu
§ - 'Koningin Wilhelmina'	GBin		
- 'Krekler's Red'	WCAu	- 'Moon River'	GBin LPmr NLar WCAu
- 'Krinkled White'	EBee EGren EPfP GBin GMaP LCro LPmr LRHS MPri NLar SHor SPeP SPoG WCAu WTor	- 'Moonstone'	GBin
		- 'Morning Kiss'	LBuc LPmr
		- 'Moscow' (Patio Peony Series)	LPmr
- 'Lady Alexandra Duff'	GBin GMaP LPmr LRHS MPri NBir NGdn WCAu WKif WTor	- 'Mother's Choice'	GBin LCro LPmr NGdn NLar SHar WCAu WCot
- 'Lady Anna'	LPmr	- 'Mr G.F. Hemerik'	EGrI GBin WCAu WCot
- 'Lady in Red'	MHol	- 'Mrs Franklin D. Roosevelt'	GBin
- 'Lady Kate'	LPmr	- 'Mrs J.V. Edlund'	GBin
- 'Lady Liberty'	LPmr NCth	- 'Mrs Livingston Farrand'	GBin
- 'Lady Orchid'	GBin WCAu	- 'My Pal Rudy'	GBin WCAu
- 'Lancaster Imp'	GBin LBom LRHS MPri WCAu	- 'Myrtle Gentry' ♀H6	ELan GBin LPmr WCAu
- 'Largo'	WCAu	- 'Nancy Nicholls'	GBin WCAu
- 'Laura Dessert'	ELan GBin LCro LPmr WCAu	- 'Nancy Nora' ♀H6	WCAu
- 'Laura Shaylor'	WCAu	- 'Nellie Saylor' ♀H6	GBin WCAu
- 'Lavender Whisper'	GBin WCAu	- 'Neon'	GBin LPmr LRHS NLar WCAu
- 'Le Cygne'	WCAu	- 'Nice Gal'	GBin LPmr WCAu
- 'Lemon Queen'	GBin	- 'Nick Shaylor'	GBin WCAu
- 'Leslie Peck'	WCAu	- 'Nippon Beauty'	EGrI GBin LBom LPmr LRHS MPri NLar SHar WCAu WCot WFar WTor
- 'Liebchen'	WCAu		
- 'Lilac Times'	WCAu	- 'Noémie Demay' ♀H6	LPmr LRHS
- 'Lillian Wild'	LPmr WCAu	- 'Norma Volz'	GBin WCAu
- 'Linda's Dream' **new**	WCAu	- 'Nymphe' ♀H6	EAri EGren EPfP LPmr LRHS NLar WCAu
- 'Little Medicineman'	WCAu		
- 'Little Pink Lullaby'	GBin	- 'Omeo Snow'	GBin WCAu
- 'London' (Patio Peony Series)	LCro LPmr	- 'Oslo' (Patio Peony Series)	LPmr LRHS

Name	Sources
- 'Paul M. Wild'	ELan GBin LPmr LRHS MPri NLar WCAu
I - 'Peaches and Cream'	LPmr LRHS
* - 'Pecher'	EAri EGren EPfP GBin LRHS NPer
- 'Peter Brand'	ELan ERCP GBin LBom LPmr LRHS NLar
- 'Petite Elegance'	GBin WCAu
- 'Petite Porcelain'	WCAu
- 'Petticoat Flounce'	LPmr
- 'Philippe Rivoire'	GBin LPmr NLar WCAu
- 'Philomèle'	GBin WCAu
- 'Pietertje Vriend Wagenaar'	GBin MArl
- 'Pillow Talk'	ELan GBin LPmr LRHS SPoG WCAu
- 'Pink Cameo'	WCAu WCot WFar
- 'Pink Delight'	GBin
- 'Pink Giant'	GBin LPmr WCAu
I - 'Pink Panther'	EGren
- 'Pink Parfait'	ELan GBin LPmr LRHS WCAu
- 'Pink Princess'	GBin WCAu
- 'Pink Spritzer'	GBin
- 'Plink Platters'	GBin
- 'Polly Sharp' **new**	WCAu
- 'President Franklin D. Roosevelt'	LRHS
- 'President Taft'	see *P. lactiflora* 'Reine Hortense'
- 'Primevère'	EAri EGren GBin LPmr LRHS NBir NLar WCAu WFar
- 'Princess Bride'	GBin MArl
- 'Princess Margaret'	WCAu
- 'Puffed Cotton'	GBin LPmr
§ - 'Purple Spider'	EGrI LPmr LRHS NLar XFar
- 'Queen of Hearts'	GBin LPmr
- 'Queen of Sheba'	WCAu
- 'Queen Wilhelmina'	see *P. lactiflora* 'Koningin Wilhelmina'
- 'Raoul Dessert'	WCAu
- 'Raspberry Sundae'	ELan EPfP LAma LCro LPmr LRHS NLar SPoG WCAu WCot
- 'Red Emperor'	WCAu
- 'Red Queen'	GBin GMaP WCAu
- RED SARAH BERNHARDT	EPfP GBin LBom LCro LPmr MPro XFar
- 'Red Satin'	WCAu
- 'Red Spider'	see *P. lactiflora* 'Purple Spider'
§ - 'Reine Hortense'	GBin LPmr WCAu
- 'Renato'	GBin MHol WCAu WTor
- 'Riches and Fame'	LPmr LRHS
- 'Roland'	WCAu
- 'Rome' (Patio Peony Series)	LCro LPmr
- 'Rozella' **new**	WCAu
- 'Ruth Cobb'	GBin WCAu
- 'Santa Fe'	LBuc NLar WCAu
- 'Sarah Bernhardt' ♀H6	Widely available
- 'Seashell'	GBin GMaP LRHS MPri WCAu
- 'Sebastiaan Maas'	LPmr
- 'Serene Pastel'	GBin WCAu
- 'Shawnee Chief'	GBin
- 'Shirley Temple' ♀H6	CWnw EBee EGren EGrI EPfP GBin LAma LBom LCro LPmr LRHS MArl MGos MPri NBir NGdn SPoG WCAu WCot WFar WTor XFar
- 'Silver Rose'	GBin
- 'Snow Mountain'	LPmr
- 'Soft Salmon Joy'	EGrI GBin
- 'Solange'	LPmr LRHS WCAu
- 'Sorbet'	EGren LBuc LCro LPmr LRHS MHol MHtn NBir NLar NPer SMad WCAu WFar XFar
- 'Soshi'	GBin
- 'Steve's Choice' **new**	WCAu
- 'Super Gal'	WCAu
- 'Surugu'	WCAu
- 'Susie Q'	WCAu
- 'Sweet Marjorie' **new**	WCAu
- 'Sweet Sixteen'	GBin LPmr WCAu
- 'Sword Dance' ♀H6	EGrI EPfP GBin LCro LPmr WCAu WSpi
- 'The Fawn' ♀H6	GBin LPmr LRHS WCAu
- 'The Nymph'	NBir
- 'Tom Cat' **new**	LBuc
- 'Tom Eckhardt'	GBin LPmr WCAu
- 'Top Brass'	GBin LPmr LRHS WCAu
- 'Topeka Garnet'	WCAu
- 'Touch of Class' **new**	WCAu
- 'Tourangelle'	GBin
- 'Unique'	WCAu
- 'Ursa Minor'	WCAu
- 'Victoire de la Marne'	LPmr WTor
- 'Victoria Blush'	WCAu
- 'Vivid Rose'	GBin WCAu
- 'Vogue'	ELan LPmr SPeP WCAu
- 'West Elkton'	GBin
- 'Westerner'	GBin WCAu
- 'White Angel'	LPmr
- 'White Cap' ♀H6	GBin GMaP LPmr LRHS MAsh NCth NLar WCAu XFar
- 'White Grace'	GBin WCAu
- 'White Sands'	GBin
- WHITE SARAH BERNHARDT	WCot
- 'White Wings'	CBcs CWnw EGren ELan GBin GMaP LPmr LRHS MAsh MBel MMrt NCth NLar NSti SMrm WCAu WCot WTor
- 'Whitleyi Major' ♀H6	WCot
- 'Wiesbaden'	WCAu
- 'Wilbur Wright'	WCAu
- 'Wine Red'	GBin
- 'Władysława' ♀H4	ELan GBin LBom LPmr LRHS MAsh MPri NCth SOrN WCot WTor
§ - 'Zi Yu Nu'	LPmr LRHS NBir
- 'Zuzu'	GBin
'Lafayette Escadrille' (S)	GBin LPmr
× *lagodechiana*	see *P. daurica* subsp. *mlokosewitschii*
'Late Windflower'	GBin GKev LPmr NLar WCAu WMal
'Lavender Baby'	GBin
'Le Printemps'	GBin LPmr WCAu
× *lemoinei* 'Alice Harding' (S)	GBin WCAu
- 'High Noon' (S) ♀H5	EAri LPmr LRHS MPhe WCAu
- 'Marchioness' (S)	GBin
- 'Souvenir de Maxime Cornu' (S)	LRHS
'Lemon Chiffon' ♀H6	GBin LPmr MAsh NCth NLar WCAu WCot XFar
'Lemon Dream' PBR	ELan GBin LPmr WCAu
'Ling Hua Zhan Lu' (S)	LRHS
'Little Darlin''	GBin
lobata 'Fire King'	see *P. peregrina*
'Lois' Choice'	GBin
'Lollipop'	EGren ELan GBin GMaP LPmr LRHS WCAu XFar
'Lorelei'	GBin WCAu
'Love Affair'	ELan LPmr WCAu
'Lovebirds'	GBin WCAu
'Lovely Rose'	GBin LPmr WCAu
ludlowii (S)	CBcs CMCN CTsd CWal EGrI EPfP LRHS MArl MMuc MPhe NBid NBir NLar NPer SBeP SEND SMrm SPlb SPoG WCot WJur WSpi
lutea	see *P. delavayi* var. *delavayi* f. *lutea*

'Luxuriant' GBin
'Magenta Gem' GBin
'Magical Mystery Tour' GBin LPmr LRHS WCAu XFar
'Mahogany' GBin
'Mai Fleuri' GBin WCAu
mairei CExl GGro StAn
— WO 9175 GEdr
'Many Happy Returns' EPfP GBin LAma LPmr LRHS WCAu
'Martha Bulloch' LPmr
mascula CBro ECha EGrI EPot GKev NBir WCot
§ — subsp. *mascula* GKev NLar
§ — subsp. *russoi* GKev WCot
— — 'Reverchoni' EPot WAbe
— subsp. *triternata* see *P. daurica*
'May Lilac' WCAu
'Merry Mayshine' GBin GKev
mlokosewitschii see *P. daurica* subsp. *mlokosewitschii*
'Mock Orange Yellow' GBin WCAu
mollis see *P. officinalis* subsp. *officinalis*
'Momo Taro' **new** WCAu
'Montezuma' WCAu
'Moonrise' GBin LPmr MBel NLar WCAu
'Morning Lilac' ♀H6 GBin LPmr LRHS SPeP WCAu
'Mother's Best' MPri
'Muramatsu-no-yuki' LPmr
'My Love' GBin LPmr MPro WCAu
'Nike' WCAu
'Normie' WCAu
'Norwegian Blush' GBin LPmr WCAu
'Nosegay' GBin WCAu
'Nova' GBin
§ *obovata* CExl GKev WPGP
— subsp. *obovata* 'Alba' ♀H5 CExl GKev WAbe WSpi
— subsp. *willmottiae* CExl GGro GKev WCot
officinalis GKev WCot
— WM 9821 from Slovenia MPhe
— from NW Croatia LEdu
— 'Alba Plena' see *P. × festiva* 'Alba Plena'
— 'Anemoniflora Rosea' ♀H6 EGrI LPmr LRHS WCAu XFar
§ — subsp. *banatica* MPhe WCAu
§ — subsp. *humilis* see *P. officinalis* subsp. *microcarpa*
§ — subsp. *huthii* LPmr LRHS SEND
— 'James Crawford Weguelin' WCot
§ — subsp. *microcarpa* LPmr WCot
— 'Mutabilis Plena' see *P. × festiva* 'Mutabilis Plena'
§ — subsp. *officinalis* LPmr NLar WCAu
— 'Rosea Plena' see *P. × festiva* 'Rosea Plena'
— 'Rubra Plena' see *P. × festiva* 'Rubra Plena'
— subsp. *villosa* see *P. officinalis* subsp. *huthii*
'Old Faithful' GBin LPmr SHar WCAu
'Old Rose Dandy' ELan GBin LPmr LRHS NLar WCAu
'Oriental Gold' WCAu
ostii (S) CExl
— 'Feng Dan Bai' (S) GEdr
'Paladin' GBin
papaveracea see *P. × suffruticosa*
paradoxa see *P. officinalis* subsp. *microcarpa*
'Pastel Splendor' ELan GBin LPmr LRHS NCth NLar SMad WCAu
'Pastelegance' LPmr WCAu
'Paula Fay' EHeP GBin GMaP LPmr LRHS MAsh MPri NBir NCth NLar WCAu WCot
'Pehrson's Violet Frisbee' GBin
§ *peregrina* CBro ECha GEdr GKev LEdu MPhe WAbe WCAu
— 'Fire King' LPmr WCAu
§ — 'Otto Froebel' GBin LPmr LRHS WCAu WCot
— 'Rosabella' LRHS
— 'Sunshine' see *P. peregrina* 'Otto Froebel'

'Picotee' GBin WCAu
'Pink Ardour' GBin LPmr
'Pink Double Dandy' GBin LPmr
'Pink Hawaiian Coral' ELan EPfP GBin LCro LPmr LRHS MPri NLar WCAu WCot WTor
'Pink Pom Pom' WCAu
'Pink Vanguard' GBin LPmr WCAu
'Pluto' (S) WCAu
'Postilion' GBin
potaninii see *P. delavayi* var. *angustiloba* f. *angustiloba*
'Prairie Charm' EPfP GBin LPmr LRHS WCAu
'Prairie Moon' GBin WCAu
'Promenade' **new** WCAu
'Purple Sensation' GBin
'Quitzin' GBin
'Raggedy Ann' ELan GBin LPmr
'Raspberry Charm' LPmr WCAu
'Red Charm' ♀H6 EPfP GBin LAma LPmr LRHS MHol NCth WCAu WCot WFar WSpi
'Red Glory' WCAu
'Red Grace' GBin LPmr WCAu
'Red Magic' LRHS WFar WSpi
'Red Red Rose' GBin WCAu
'Renown' (S) WCAu
'Requiem' GBin LPmr WCAu
§ *rockii* (S) CBcs GKev MCtn MPhe WJur WSpi
— from Tai Bai Shan, China MPhe
§ — subsp. *atava* (S) GKev
— hybrid see *P.* (Gansu Group) 'Highdown'
— subsp. *linyanshanii* (S) CJun
— subsp. *taibaishanica* see *P. rockii* subsp. *atava*
romanica see *P. peregrina*
'Rose Flame' (S) WCAu
'Rose Garland' GBin
'Rosedale' GBin WCAu
'Roselette' GBin WCAu
'Roselette's Child' GBin
'Rosy Prospects' **new** WCAu
'Roy Pehrson's Best Yellow' GBin
'Royal Blush' GBin
russoi see *P. mascula* subsp. *russoi*
'Salmon Beauty' WCAu
'Salmon Chiffon' GBin LPmr NLar WTor
'Salmon Dream' GBin LPmr WCAu
'Sanctus' GBin LPmr WCAu
'Scarlet Heaven' EGren GBin LPmr MNrw NLar SMad WCAu
'Scarlet O'Hara' ♀H6 LPmr LRHS MAsh NLar WCAu WCot
'Scrumdidleumptious' GBin LPmr LRHS WCAu XFar
'Sebastian Maas' LCro LPmr LRHS
'Sequestered Sunshine' GBin LPmr WCAu
'Seraphim' GBin
'Serebrenyi Velvet' GBin
'Serenade' WCAu
'Shining Light' LPmr
'Show Girl' GBin LPmr WCAu
'Silver Dawn' GBin
'Simply Red' EGren GBin
'Singing in the Rain' GBin LPmr LRHS WCAu
sinjianensis see *P. anomala* subsp. *anomala*
'Smith Family Yellow' LPmr WCAu
× *smouthii* GEdr
'Soft Salmon Saucer' GBin LPmr NLar WCAu
'Sonoma Amethyst' GBin LPmr WCAu
'Sonoma Apricot' GBin LPmr WCAu
'Sonoma Blessing' GBin LPmr
'Sonoma by the Bay' GBin LPmr
'Sonoma Floozy' ELan GBin LPmr
'Sonoma Halo' GBin LPmr WCAu XFar

Paeonia

'Sonoma Kaleidoscope'	ELan GBin LPmr
'Sonoma Opal'	GBin LPmr
'Sonoma Rosy Future'	GBin LPmr WCAu
'Sonoma Sun'	GBin LPmr WCAu
'Sonoma Velvet Ruby'	GBin LPmr WCAu
'Sonoma Welcome'	GBin LPmr
'Sonoma YeDo'	GBin LPmr
'Spetchley'	WCot
'Stardust'	WCAu
'Starlight'	GBin LCro LPmr LRHS SHar WCAu WCot
'Strawberry Crème Brûlée' **new**	ELan WCAu
§ × *suffruticosa* (S)	CDoC MGos
- 'Bai Yuan Hong Xia' (S)	LCro
- Bird of Rimpo	see *P.* × *suffruticosa* 'Rimpo'
- Black Dragon Brocade	see *P.* × *suffruticosa* 'Kokuryū-nishiki'
- Black Flower Chief	see *P.* × *suffruticosa* 'Hei Hua Kui'
- 'Chu Wu' (S)	LCro
- 'Dou Lu' (S)	NTPC
- Eternal Camellias	see *P.* × *suffruticosa* 'Yachiyo-tsubaki'
- 'Feng Dan Bai' (S)	LCro
- Flight of Cranes	see *P.* × *suffruticosa* 'Renkaku'
- Floral Rivalry	see *P.* × *suffruticosa* 'Hana-kisoi'
- 'Gekkyu-den' (S)	LPmr LRHS
- 'Hai Huang' (S)	NTPC
- 'Hakushin' (S)	LPmr
§ - 'Hana-kisoi' (S)	LPmr LRHS
§ - 'Hei Hua Kui' (S)	NTPC
- 'Jitsugetsu-nishiki' (S)	LPmr
- 'Joseph Rock'	see *P.* (Gansu Group) 'Highdown'
§ - 'Kamada-fuji' (S)	LPmr
§ - 'Kaow' (S)	LPmr
- King of Flowers	see *P.* × *suffruticosa* 'Kaow'
§ - 'Kokuryū-nishiki' (S)	LPmr LRHS
- 'Koshi-no-maihime' (S)	LPmr
- 'Kuro-ageha' (S)	LPmr LRHS
- 'Lan Bao Shi' (S)	NTPC
- 'Lu He Hong' (S)	GBin LCro
- 'Mo Run Jue Lun' (S)	LCro
- 'Nigata Akashigata' (S)	LPmr
§ - 'Okan' (S)	LPmr LRHS
§ - 'Renkaku' (S)	LPmr
§ - 'Rimpo' (S)	WSpi
- subsp. *rockii*	see *P. rockii*
- 'Rou Fu Rong' (S)	GBin LRHS WSpi
- 'Shichi-fukujin' (S)	LPmr
- 'Shimadaijin' (S)	LPmr
- 'Shimane-chōjuraku' (S)	LPmr
- 'Shimane-seidai' (S)	LPmr
- 'Shimanishiki' (S)	LPmr
- 'Shimazu-kurenai' (S)	LPmr
- 'Shunkoju' (S)	LPmr
§ - 'Taiyo' (S)	LPmr WCAu
- 'Teikan' (S)	LPmr LRHS
- The Sun	see *P.* × *suffruticosa* 'Taiyo'
- Wisteria at Kamada	see *P.* × *suffruticosa* 'Kamada-fuji'
- 'Wu Long Peng Sheng' (S)	LRHS WSpi
- 'Xue Ta' (S)	GBin LCro LRHS
- 'Xue Ying Tao Hua' (S)	LCro
§ - 'Yachiyo-tsubaki' (S)	LPmr
- 'Yin Hong Qiao Dui' (S)	GBin NTPC
- 'Yu Ban Bai' (S)	EGrI
- 'Zhao Fen' (S)	NPer SRms
'Sugar 'n' Spice'	GBin
'Summer Glow'	LPmr WCAu
'Sunny Girl'	GBin WCAu
'Sunshine'	see *P. peregrina* 'Otto Froebel'
* *szowitsianum*	GKev
'Tango'	MBel WCAu
tenuifolia	CBro CJun CSpe ELan EWes GBin GEdr GKev LPmr LRHS NCth NLar NSti SMad WCAu WSpi
- 'Plena'	GBin LBom WCAu
- 'Rosea'	GBin WCAu
'Terrific Gal'	GBin
'The Mackinac Grand' ♀H6	GBin WCAu WCot
'Thunderbolt' (S)	WCAu
'Tolomeo No 59'	GBin LPmr
'Tranquil Dove'	LPmr WCAu
'Tria' (S)	WCAu
'Unique' ♀H6	ELan GBin LPmr WCAu
'Vanilla Schnapps'	GBin LPmr WCAu
veitchii	see *P. anomala* subsp. *veitchii*
- var. *woodwardii*	see *P. anomala* subsp. *veitchii*
'Velvet Candy'	LBuc LPmr LRHS
'Vesuvian'	GBin WCAu
'Viking Full Moon'	GBin LPmr NLar WCAu
'Vision of Sugar Plums'	GBin WCAu
'Walter Mains'	WCAu
'Watermelon Wine' ♀H6	ELan GBin LPmr WCAu
'Waucedah Princess' (S) **new**	WCAu
wendelboi	GKev
'White Charm'	GBin
'White Emperor'	GBin LPmr WCAu
'White Imperial'	WCAu
'White Innocence'	GBin LPmr WCAu
'White Towers'	NLar WFar
'Whopper'	GBin
'Wine Angel'	GBin
wittmanniana	see *P. daurica* subsp. *wittmanniana*
'Yankee Doodle Dandy'	GBin LPmr LRHS WCAu
'Yellow Crown'	GBin LAma LPmr LRHS MHol NCth NLar WCAu XFar
'Yellow Dream'	LPmr LRHS
'Yellow Gem'	LPmr
'Yellow Heaven'	LPmr
'Yellow Waterlily'	GBin LPmr LRHS

Paesia (Dennstaedtiaceae)

scaberula	LEdu NBir SMHy WCot WPGP

pak choi see AGM Vegetables Section

Paliurus (Rhamnaceae)

spina-christi	WJur

Pallenis (Asteraceae)

maritima 'Golden Dollar'	LRHS

Pamianthe (Amaryllidaceae)

peruviana	MCtn

Panax (Araliaceae)

japonicus	WCru
- BWJ 7932	WCru
quinquefolius	MCtn

Pancratium (Amaryllidaceae)

maritimum	LAma XFar

Pandanus (Pandanaceae)

utilis	NPlm

Pandorea (Bignoniaceae)

jasminoides ♀H1c	CDoC CHll CRHN EShb MCtn SEle WJur
- 'Alba'	CHll CRHN EShb
§ - 'Charisma' (v)	CBcs CHll EArI ELan EPfP EShb LSRN SEND

- 'Rosea' — SMrm
- 'Rosea Superba' ♀H1c — CBcs CRHN
- 'Variegata' — see *P. jasminoides* 'Charisma'
- **lindleyana** — see *Clytostoma calystegioides*
- **pandorana** — CHll CRHN
- 'Golden Showers' — CBcs CRHN SEND WCot

Panicum (Poaceae)
- **amarum** — EPPr LRHS
- 'Dewey Blue' — ECha EWes NLar
- 'Sea Mist' — CKno
- **bulbosum** — EBee EPPr
- **capillare** 'Frosted Explosion' — CSpe MPro
- 'Sparkling Fountain' — LCro
- **clandestinum** — EWes
- **miliaceum** 'Violaceum' — MCtn
- 'Sprinkles' — MCtn
- **virgatum** — CAby CWal EPPr MCtn SPeP
- 'Black and Blue' — MNrw SMHy
- 'Black and Light' — MNrw
- 'Blue Fountain' **new** — EWes
- 'Blue Giants' — EPPr LEdu SDix WFar WPGP
- 'Blue Tower' — CKno ELon EPPr
- 'Buffalo Green'^PBR — LCro
- 'Cardinal' — ECha EPPr LEdu WFar WHoo
- 'Carthage' — EPPr
- 'Cave-in-Rock' — EPPr
- 'Cheyenne Sky' — EPPr LRHS MPro WHoo
- 'Cloud Nine' ♀H5 — CBWd CKno EBee EPPr SMHy
- 'Dallas Blues' ♀H5 — CKno CSpe EBee EBlo ECha ELan ELon EPfP EPPr EUrb EWes LRHS MAvo MBNS NLar SNoN SPeP SPoG WFar
- 'Diwali' — EPPr
- 'Emerald Chief' — EPPr WFar
- 'Fontaine' **new** — MPro
- 'Forestburg' — EPPr
- 'Hänse Herms' ♀H5 — EBlo ELon LRHS MPri NLar
- 'Heavy Metal' ♀H5 — Widely available
- 'Heavy Metal Mk II' — SMHy
- 'Heiliger Hain' — CBWd EBee ECha ELon LEdu NLar WCot WFar WHoo WPGP XFar
- HOT ROD 'Ecgphr019' — EBee ELan LRHS LSRN MBNS NCth XFar
- 'JS Blue Darkness'^PBR — LRHS SPoG
- 'JS Dark Night'^PBR — LRHS NCth
- 'Külsenmoor' — EBee WCot
- 'Kupferhirse' — ECha ELon EPPr MWlw
- 'Kurt Bluemel' — EBee ECha EPPr
- 'Merlot' — CKno
- 'Nican' — EPPr MWlw
- 'Northwind' ♀H5 — CBWd CKno CMHG CSde EBee EBlo EGren ELon EMor EPfP EPPr LBom LRHS LSou MAsh MAvo MBel Midl MWlw NLar SAth SMad SMHy SPoG SRms WCha WChS WFar
- 'Oxblood Autumn'^PBR — CBWd EBee ELan EPfP LRHS LSRN Midl SPeP WFar
- 'Prairie Sky' — CBWd CKno CMHG CWnw EBee EBlo EGren ELon EPfP EPPr EWhm GKev GMaP LBom LCro LEdu LRHS MAsh NLar SRms WCha WCot WFar
- PURPLE BREEZE ('Joz276'^PBR) — LCro LRHS LSou
- 'Purple Haze' — EBlo ECha LRHS SNoN
- 'Red Cloud' — CKno ELon LBom
- 'Rehbraun' — CSde EGren ELan EPPr LCro LSRN SRms WCau
- 'Rotstrahlbusch' — EBee EGren EHeP EPfP EPPr GMaP LCro MWlw SHar SRms WCot
- 'Rubrum' — EBee EBlo MAvo SRms

- 'Sangria'^PBR — CBWd CSpe ELan LEdu LRHS SPeP SPoG
- 'Shenandoah' ♀H5 — Widely available
- 'Straight Cloud' — EPPr LRHS
- 'Strictum' — EBlo EPPr EWes SMHy
- 'Sunburst' — EPPr
- 'Thundercloud' — CKno LCro LRHS NCth SBig SPeP XFar
- 'Warrior' — CBWd CKno ELon EMor EPfP EPPr EWhm LCro LRHS MAsh MAvo NLar SMHy SPeP SPoG WCAu WFar WHoo WTor WTre
- 'Wood's Variegated' (v) — WCot

Papaver (Papaveraceae)
- **alpinum** — see *Oreomecon alpina*
- **atlanticum** — GQue SMrm SPlb
- 'Flore Pleno' (d) — CSpe
- **burseri** — see *Oreomecon alpina*
- § **cambricum** — CDor CMac CTtf EBee ECha ELan EMor EPfP GJem GQue LEdu MCtn MNHC NAts WBrk WCAu WCot WFar WHer WTre
- var. **aurantiacum** — CDor CTtf MCtn WCot
- § 'Frances Perry' — CSpe EPPr
- 'Rubrum' — see *P. cambricum* 'Frances Perry'
- **commutatum** ♀H5 — CSpe LCro MCtn NClf SPhx
- 'Ladybird' ♀H5 — MNHC MPro NClf SPoG
- **dubium** subsp. **lecoqii** 'Albiflorum' — CSpe ECha LCro SHor SPhx
- **glaucum** — CSpe
- **guerlekense** W&B BG-K-5 — WCot
- 'Heartbeat' (Super Poppy Series) — MHol WFar
- **heldreichii** — see *P. pilosum* subsp. *spicatum*
- **heterophyllum** — CSpe
- **lateritium** — SRms
- 'Medallion' (Super Poppy Series) — MPie
- **miyabeanum** — see *Oreomecon miyabeana*
- 'Moondance' — see *Oreomecon* 'Moondance'
- **nanum** 'Flore Pleno' — see *P.* (Oriental Group) 'Fire Ball'
- **nudicaule** — see *Oreomecon nudicaulis*
- Oriental Group — EHeP
- 'Aglaja' — CDor IPot NLar WCot WSpi XFar
- 'Allegro' — CBcs LBom LRHS MPri NGdn SPlb SPoG SVic WFar
- 'Baby Kiss'^PBR — WFar
- 'Beauty of Livermere' — CDor EGren ELan LBom LCro LRHS MAvo MPri MPro NGdn NLar SPoG SRms WCAu WFar
- § - - clonal — WCot
- 'Beauty Queen' — CDor
- 'Bill's Red' **new** — SDix
- 'Bolero' — IPot MHol
- 'Brilliant' — CWal LBom LRHS MCtn MPri MPro NLar WFar
- 'Brooklyn' (New York Series) — EGrl
- 'Burning Heart' — CWGN
- 'Carneum' — SPoG SRms
- 'Cedric Morris' ♀H7 — ECha
- 'Central Park' (New York Series) — NLar WFar
- 'Coral Reef' — GQue MCtn
- 'Curlilocks' — SRms WFar
- 'Double Red Shades' (d) — NGdn
- 'Doubloon' (d) — WFar
- 'Dwarf Allegro' — LRHS MPri
- 'Fancy Feathers'^PBR — NLar
- § 'Fire Ball' (d) — WCot
- 'Flamenco' — WFar

- 'Forncett Summer' — EPfP LCro NLar SPoG WCot
- 'Fruit Punch' — EPfP
- 'Goliath' — SRms WFar
- 'Guardsman' — see *P.* (Oriental Group) 'Beauty of Livermere' clonal
- HAREMSTRAUM (mixed) — WFar
- 'Harlem' (New York Series) — CBcs IPot MAsh NLar
- 'Harvest Moon' (d) — EPfP NPer
- 'Indian Chief' — NPer WFar
- 'Karine' ♀H7 — EGren ERCP LCro
- 'King Kong' — NLar WFar
- 'Kleine Tänzerin' — SEND WFar
- 'Ladybird' — LRHS
- 'Little Patty Plum'PBR — MHol
- 'Louvre' (Parisienne Series) — WFar
- 'Manhattan' (New York Series) — EPfP LCro NSti WFar
- 'Marlene' — ERCP XFar
- 'May Queen' (d) — WCot WFar
- 'Miss Piggy'PBR — LCro NLar WFar
- 'Mrs Marrow's Plum' — see *P.* (Oriental Group) 'Patty's Plum'
- 'Mrs Perry' — NPer SRms WFar
- 'Nanum Flore Pleno' — see *P.* (Oriental Group) 'Fire Ball'
- 'Paradiso'PBR — NLar
§ - 'Patty's Plum' — CBcs CDor EGrI ELan ERCP GMaP LBom LCro MArl MAvo MHer MHol MPri NBir NLar NQui NSti SPoG WBrk WCAu WCot WFar WSpi XFar
- 'Perry's White' — EHeP NLar SRkn WSpi XFar
- 'Picotée' — WFar
- 'Pink Perfection' — LBar LCro LRHS MidI WTor XFar
- 'Pink Ruffles'PBR — WFar XFar
- 'Pinnacle' — WFar
- 'Pizzicato' — EGren GQue MArl MCtn MPro NPer WFar
- 'Plum Pudding' — ELan EPfP LBom
- 'Prinz Eugen' — WFar
- 'Prinzessin Victoria Louise' — CDor ELan EPfP LBom LCro LRHS MPri MPro NGdn SEND SPoG SRms
- 'Queen Alexandra' — CDor EPfP
- 'Raspberry Queen' — CDor IPot MSwo
- RED RUMBLE ('Hg01') **new** — MidI WTor
- 'Rembrandt' — LRHS WCot
- 'Royal Chocolate Distinction' — ELan ERCP MHol WFar
- 'Royal Wedding' — CBcs CDor EBlo ECha EGren ELan EPfP LBom LCro LRHS LShi MArl MCtn MGos MPri NLar SEND SRms WCot WFar WSpi
- 'Ruffled Patty'PBR — ELan NLar WCot
- 'Salmon Glow' (d) — WFar
- 'Scarlett O'Hara'PBR (d) — WFar
- 'Snow Goose' — CDor CWGN EPfP EPPr NLar SPoG WCot
- 'Sweet Sensation' — MHol
- 'Türkenlouis' — NQui SPoG WBrk WFar
- 'Turkish Delight' — NBir
- 'Waltzing Mathilda'PBR **new** — LBar
- 'Watermelon' — SPoG
- 'White Ruffles'PBR — CoPl XFar
orientale — CBcs EGren EGrI SRms
pilosum — MCtn
§ - subsp. *spicatum* — CSpe ECha NBir WCot
rhoeas — CHab EHet GJem LCro MCtn MHoo MNHC SPhx SVic WKit
- 'Amazing Grey' — CSpe LCro MCtn MPro
- 'Angel's Choir Mixed' — MCtn
- 'Bridal Silk' — CSpe LCro MCtn
- 'Bridal White' — SPhx
- 'Falling in Love' — MCtn
- Mother of Pearl Group — CSpe LCro MCtn SPhx
- 'Pandora' — CSpe LCro MCtn MPro SPhx
- 'Paradise' — CSpe
rupifragum — ECha LShi WCot
- 'Double Tangerine Gem' — see *P. rupifragum* 'Flore Pleno'
§ - 'Flore Pleno' (d) — CDor CSpe EPPr MCtn MPri MPro SVic WBrk
'Shasta' (Super Poppy Series) — WFar
somniferum — ENfk MNHC SVic
- 'Blackcurrant Fizz' (d) — LCro
- 'Boudoir Babe' (d) — CSpe
- 'Hen and Chickens' — MCtn
- 'Hungarian Blue' — LCro MPro
- (Laciniatum Group) — LCro MCtn
  'Black Swan'
- - 'Danebrog' — MCtn
- 'Lauren's Grape' — CSpe LCro LRHS MCtn SHor SPhx
- 'Lilac Pompom' (d) — LCro MCtn
I - 'Maanzaad' — LCro MNHC
- (Paeoniiflorum Group) — CSpe
  'Black Beauty' (d)
- - 'Black Paeony' (d) — LCro MCtn
- - 'Flemish Antique' (d) — MCtn
- - 'Frosted Salmon' (d) — MCtn
- - 'Scarlet Paeony' (d) — WCot
- single black-flowered — CSpe SPhx
- - white-flowered — CSpe
- 'Sissinghurst White' — SPhx
- 'White Cloud' (d) — CSpe
triniifolium — ECha SPhx WCot

papaya (pawpaw) see *Carica papaya*

Parabenzoin see *Lindera*

Paradisea (Asparagaceae)
liliastrum misapplied — see *P. lusitanica*
liliastrum (L.) Bertol. ♀H5 — EBee EPfP GKev NBid
§ *lusitanica* — CMHG CSpe CTtf EBee EGrI ELan GKev LEdu MCtn MHol SDix WCot

Parahebe see *Veronica* (P)
olsenii — see *Veronica bookeriana*

Parajubaea (Arecaceae)
torallyi — NPlm

Paramongaia (Amaryllidaceae)
weberbaueri — WMal

Paranomus (Proteaceae)
reflexus — SPlb

Paraquilegia (Ranunculaceae)
adoxoides — see *Semiaquilegia adoxoides*
§ *anemonoides* — CExl EDAr GKev
grandiflora — see *P. anemonoides*

Pararchidendron (Fabaceae)
pruinosum — WJur

Parasenecio (Asteraceae)
delphiniifolius — WCru
  B&SWJ 11415
farfarifolius — WCru
- var. *bulbifer* — WCru
tebakoensis B&SWJ 11536 — WCru

Paraserianthes (Fabaceae)
distachya — see *P. lophantha*
§ *lophantha* ♀H2 — CExl CTsd EAri EShb SPlb WJur

Parastyrax (Styracaceae)
   BWJ 15185 from   WCru
      Northern Vietnam

Parathelypteris (Thelypteridaceae)
   beddomei   LEdu SMHy WCot WPGP
   - crested   LEdu

× *Pardancanda* see *Iris*

Parietaria (Urticaceae)
   judaica   WHer

Paris (Melanthiaceae)
   incompleta   CTtf EPPr GEdr LEdu WCru
   japonica   ENun GEdr
   lancifolia B&SWJ 3044   WCru
      from Taiwan
   polyphylla   CTtf ECha EGrI EWld GKev LAma NBid WCru
   - B&SWJ 2125   WCru
   - HWJCM 475   WCru
   - var. **stenophylla**   WCru
   * - var. **yunnanensis** f. **alba**   WCot
   quadrifolia   CSpe CTtf EBee GEdr GKev LEdu NClf WCru WHer
   thibetica   CTtf EBee GKev LAma

Parkinsonia (Fabaceae)
   aculeata   CSpe SPlb WJur

Parnassia (Celastraceae)
   cabulica   GKev
   gansuensis SDR 5128   GKev
   glauca new   GKev
   grandifolia   GKev
   nubicola   GKev
   palustris   GKev

Parochetus (Fabaceae)
   communis ambig.   CExl EWld MSCN NPer WFar

Parodia (Cactaceae)
   leninghausii ♀H2   NPlm
   magnifica ♀H2   SBrt
   mammulosa   SPlb
   scopa subsp. **scopa** ♀H2   SPlb
   warasii   SPlb

Parolinia (Brassicaceae)
   ornata   WCot

Paronychia (Caryophyllaceae)
   argentea   EDAr
   § **capitata**   SRms
   kapela   GKev SPlb
   nivea   see *P. capitata*

Parrotia ✿ (Hamamelidaceae)
   persica   Widely available
   - NJM 13.005   WPGP
   - 'Bella'   CJun CLnd EBee EPfP ESwi LMaj LRHS LSto MBlu NLar WHtc WMat
   - 'Biltmore'   CJun SSta
   - 'Burgundy'   CJun
   - 'Cobhay Upright'   CJun
   - fastigiate   CJun SSta
   - 'Felicie'   CJun IArd NLar
   - 'Horizontalis'   CJun
   - 'Jodrell Bank'   CJun ELan MBlu NLar SSta WMat

   - 'Pendula'   CJun MBlu SSta
   - 'Persian Lace' (v)   SEle
   - PERSIAN SPIRE ('Jlpn01'PBR)   CBcs CCVT CWnw EBee ELan EPfP LCro LMil LRHS MGos MSCN NLar SGol WMat
   - 'Summer Bronze'   CJun ELan LRHS MAsh
   - 'Vanessa' ♀H6   CBcs CJun CLnd CMCN CWnw EBee EGren EGrI ELan EPfP EWes IArd IPap LMaj LRHS LSRN LSto MAsh MBlu NCth NLar SGol SSta WMat WMou
   subaequalis   CJun MBlu NLar SGol WPGP

Parrotia × *Sycopsis* see × *Sycoparrotia*

Parrotiopsis (Hamamelidaceae)
   jacquemontiana   CBcs IArd LMaj MBlu NLar WJur

parsley see *Petroselinum crispum*

parsnip see AGM Vegetables Section

Parsonsia (Apocynaceae)
   heterophylla   WCot

Parthenium (Asteraceae)
   hysterophorus   Prohibited invasive. See Conservation and the Environment, p.42
   integrifolium   CAgr SMHy SPhx

Parthenocissus ✿ (Vitaceae)
   § **henryana** ♀H4   Widely available
   himalayana   MCtn WJur
   - 'Purpurea'   see *P. himalayana* var. *rubrifolia*
   § - var. **rubrifolia**   CMac CRHN ELan LRHS MAsh WCru
   inserta misapplied   see *P. quinquefolia*
   ? **inserta** ambig.   CMac NLar
   ? **quinquefolia**   Widely available
   - var. **engelmannii**   CBcs CWnw EBee EShb LBuc LRHS LWaG NLar SEND
   - 'Guy's Garnet'   WCru
   - 'Kirigami'   CWnw EBee LRHS
   - RED WALL ('Troki')   EBee EPfP WTHo
   - STAR SHOWERS ('Monham')   NLar
      (v)
   semicordata B&SWJ 6551   WCru
   striata   see *Clematicissus striata*
   thomsonii   see *Yua thomsonii*
   § **tricuspidata**   EPfP LWaG MAsh MCtn MGos SArc WCha
   - 'Beverley Brook'   CRHN LCro LRHS LSRN NLar SRms WTHo
   - 'Crûg Compact'   WCru
   - 'Green Spring'   CBcs ELan IArd LRHS MGos NLar WFar
   - 'Lowii'   CDoC CMac ELan LRHS MBlu NLar SPoG
   - 'Robusta'   LRHS
   § - 'Veitchii' ♀H5   CBcs CBrac CDoC CMac CRHN CSBt EGren EHeP ELan EPfP ERom LCro LRHS LSto MAsh MBlu MGos MMuc MPri NCth NLar NPer SEND SPoG SRms WFar WTHo

Pasithea (Asphodelaceae)
   caerulea   CSpe MCtn MHol WCot WPGP

Paspalum (Poaceae)
   glaucifolium   MNrw
   quadrifarium RCB RA S-5   WCot

Passiflora ✤ (Passifloraceae)
actinia	SPlb
alata (F) ♕H1c	LCro WJur
× **alatocaerulea**	see *P.* × *belotii*
§ 'Amethyst' ♕H3	CBcs CDoC CHll CRHN EAri LCro LRHS LSRN MAsh SPoG
amethystina misapplied	see *P.* 'Amethyst'
antioquiensis misapplied	see *P.* × *exoniensis*
antioquiensis ambig.	CHll SEND
§ × **belotii**	NPlm
- 'Impératrice Eugénie'	see *P.* × *belotii*
'Betty Myles Young'	CBcs CRHN CSde EAri ELan EPfP LRHS
bogatensis B&SWJ 14951	WCru
§ **caerulea** ♕H4	Widely available
- 'Avalanche'	WFar
- 'Clear Sky'PBR	ELan LRHS SRms
- 'Constance Eliott' ♕H4	CAgr CBcs CBrac CHll CMac CRHN EAri EGren ELan EPfP LBom LCro LRHS MGos MPri NLar SPoG SWCr SWor WLov WTHo
I - 'Rubra'	CBcs CDoC LCro LRHS WTHo
- WHITE LIGHTNING ('Yanpas'PBR)	ELan LRHS SPoG WTHo
× **caeruleoracemosa**	see *P.* × *violacea*
× **caponii**	CHll
chinensis	see *P. caerulea*
cuatrecasasii B&SWJ 14834	WCru
§ 'Damsel's Delight'	CWGN EBee ELan EUrb LBom LCro LRHS SPoG SWCr WLov
edulis (F)	CBcs CHll EAri LCro MCtn SPre WJur
- 'Lilikoi' (F)	CAgr
'Empress Eugenie'	see *P.* × *belotii*
§ × **exoniensis** ♕H2	CHll CRHN EAri
incarnata (F)	CAgr SPlb WJur
'Incense' (F)	WFar
'Justine Lyons'	LRHS
'Lavender Lady'	see *P.* 'Amethyst'
§ **ligularis** (F)	WJur
lowei	see *P. ligularis*
manicata (F)	CSpe
- B&SWJ 14284 (F)	WCru
- B&SWJ 14868 (F)	WCru
mayana	see *P. caerulea*
mixta (F)	SEND
- B&SWJ 14832 (F)	WCru
aff. **mixta** B&SWJ 14302	WCru
mollissima misapplied	see *P. tarminiana*
mollissima ambig. (F)	CBlu EShb SPlb
mollissima (Kunth) L.H. Bailey (F) ♕H2	CAgr CRHN WJur
- B&SWJ 14876 (F)	WCru
'Purple Haze'	CDoC EGren LBom LCro LRHS SWCr WFar WTHo
quadrangularis (F) ♕H1a	CHll
racemosa ♕H1a	LCro MCtn
semiciliosa B&SWJ 14824	WCru
'Silly Cow'	see *P.* 'Damsel's Delight'
'Snow Queen'PBR	CBcs CHll CSde CWGN EAri EBee ELan EPfP EUrb LBom LCro LRHS MBros NLit NWbg SNig SWCr WHil WLov WTHo
'Star of Surbiton'	ELan
§ **tarminiana** (F)	CRHN
- B&SWJ 14960 (F)	WCru
tetrandra	CExl
tripartita B&SWJ 14768	WCru
- B&SWJ 14807	WCru
§ × **violacea** ♕H2	CBcs CRHN LCro
- 'Victoria'	CSde WFar
vitifolia (F)	MCtn

passion fruit see *Passiflora*

passion fruit, banana see *Passiflora mollissima* (Kunth) L.H. Bailey

Pastinaca (Apiaceae)
lucida	CExl
sativa	CHab MCtn SVic WCot
- 'Gladiator' ♕H5	EKin LCro MCtn
- 'Hollow Crown'	SVic
- 'Javelin'	MCtn
- 'Palace'PBR	EKin LCro
- 'Tender and True'	LCro MCtn SVic
- 'White Gem'	SVic

Patersonia (Iridaceae)
occidentalis	SPlb

Patrinia (Caprifoliaceae)
gibbosa	CElw CSpe CTtf EBee EMor GKev LShi MMrt NLar SHar WFar
- B&SWJ 874	ESwi WCru
heterophylla	GGro GKev
intermedia	GKev
monandra	GKev
cf. **monandra**	EBee ESwi
punctiflora	CAby CElw CSpe GGro SDix WPGP
aff. **punctiflora**	ECha NAts NDov SHar SMHy WGoo
rupestris	CSpe
- B&SWJ 12654	WCru
scabiosifolia	CAby CElw CKno CMiW CSpe CTtf ECha EMor ESwi GGro GQue LEdu LSto MCtn MHer MHol NBir NLar SBea SDix SMrm SPhx StAn WFar WHoo
- B&SWJ 8740	WCru
- 'Nagoya'	MNrw
triloba	CMiW CSpe EMor GEdr MMrt NLar SHar WFar
- var. **palmata**	EBee GKev NBro SBeP WFar
villosa	CExl EMor GGro GKev MNrw SHar

Paulownia ✤ (Paulowniaceae)
catalpifolia	NLar
elongata	EGrI
fargesii ambig.	WCot
fortunei	MBlu SPlb
- NMWJ 14533	WCru
- BLUE BALL ('Minpaul')	CWnw
- FAST BLUE ('Minfast') ♕H5	CCVT CExl CWnw EPfP LCro LRHS LSRN NLar SBig
kawakamii	EBee ELan EPfP ESwi MBlu WJur WPGP
- NMWJ 14552	WCru
- RWJ 9909	WCru
- 'Purple Spendour'	EPfP
taiwaniana NMWJ 14529	WCru
tomentosa ♕H5	Widely available
- 'Coreana'	WCru
- 'Wilson's Giant'	WPGP

Pavonia (Malvaceae)
praemorsa	MCtn

pawpaw (false banana) see *Asimina triloba*

pawpaw (papaya) see *Carica papaya*

Paxistima (Celastraceae)
   myrsinites   SBrt

pea see AGM Vegetables Section

peach see *Prunus persica*

pear see *Pyrus communis*; also AGM Fruit Section

pear, Asian see *Pyrus pyrifolia*

Pedilanthus see *Euphorbia*

Pelargonium ✿ (Geraniaceae)

abrotanifolium (Sc)	ENfk EPPr EShb EWoo MHer SMHy SVen
acetosum	CCBP EPPr EWoo MHer SMrm
acraeum	EWoo
alchemilloides	EWoo
alpinum	EWoo MHer
ANGELEYES ORANGE ('Paccrio'^{PBR}) (Angeleyes Series) (A)	EWoo
'Ansbrook Beauty' (Sc/v)	MHer
(Antik Series) ANTIK ORANGE ('Tikorg'^{PBR}) (Z)	SPoG
- ANTIK PINK ('Tikpink'^{PBR}) (Z)	SPoG
- ANTIK SCARLET ('Tikscarl'^{PBR}) (Z)	SPoG
- ANTIK VIOLET ('Tikvio'^{PBR}) (Z)	SPoG
appendiculatum	EWoo MHer
'Apple Betty' (Sc)	EWoo
'Apple Blossom Rosebud' (Z/d) ♀H1c	CGHo ELan EShb EWoo MHer SMrm
APPLEBLOSSOM (Z)	SBeP WFar
'Apricot Glace' (U/Sc)	EWoo MHer
'April Hamilton' (I)	LCro
AQUARELLO ('Fisaqua') (Z)	MPri
'Arctic Star' (Z/St) ♀H1c	CSpe WBrk WFar
'Arcturus' (Min)	MHer
'Ardens' ♀H1c	CPbh CSpe CTsd ELan EPts EWoo LCro MHer SMrm WCot
'Ardwick Cinnamon' (Sc) ♀H1c	ENfk EWoo MHer SDix SPel SRms
aridum	EWoo
'Arnside Fringed Aztec' (R)	MHer
'Ashby' (Dec/Sc) ♀H1c	ENfk EPPr EPts ESgl EWoo MHer
asperum Ehr. ex Willd.	see *P.* 'Graveolens'
§ 'Atomic Snowflake' (Sc/v)	CGHo ENfk EPts EWoo MHoo MNHC SRms
'Atrium' (U)	MHer
'Attar of Roses' (Sc) ♀H1c	CCBP CCht CGHo CSpe ENfk EPPr EPts EWoo LCro MHer MHoo MNHC NCou SAng SEdi SHor SMHy SMrm SPoG SRms WTre
australe	CTsd EPts EWoo MHer SPhx
- from Tasmania, Australia	WTre
- pink-flowered	EWoo
'Australian Mystery' (Dec) ♀H1c	CSpe EPts
'Aztec' (R) ♀H1c	EPts
'Barbe Bleu' (I/d) ♀H1c	LCro
'Bath Beauty' (Dw)	CSpe WFar
'Beauty of Eastbourne' misapplied	see *P.* 'Lachskönigin'
'Berkswell Carnival' (A)	ELan
'Berkswell Golden Anniversary' (A)	MHer
'Berkswell Lace' (A)	MHer
'Beromünster' (Dec) ♀H1c	EPts EWoo MHer
'Betty Catchpole' (Z)	EWoo
betulinum	CPbh EWoo
'Big Apple' (Sc)	EWoo SRms
'Bird Dancer' (Z/C/Dw/St) ♀H1c	CSpe EPPr EWoo MHer MNHC SDix SIvy WBrk WFar
(Birdbush Series) 'Birdbush Bobby' (Sc)	SRms
- 'Birdbush Bold and Beautiful' (Sc)	SRms
- 'Birdbush Nutty' (Sc)	SRms
'Bitter Lemon' (A/Sc)	EWoo
'Black Butterfly'	see *P.* 'Brown's Butterfly'
'Black Knight' (A)	EWoo
'Black Knight' (R)	MHer
'Black Prince' (R/Dec)	CSpe EWoo
'Black Velvet' (R)	EWoo
'Blackman Beauty'	EWoo
BLANCHE ROCHE ('Guitoblanc') (I/d)	MHer
§ 'Blandfordianum' (Sc)	EWoo MHer
'Blandfordianum Roseum' (Sc)	EWoo MHer
BLIZZARD DARK RED ('Fisblizdark') (Blizzard Series) (I)	EWoo
'Bolero' (U) ♀H1c	CGHo EPts
'Bontrosai'^{PBR} (Sc)	EWoo MHer WCot
'Both's Snowflake' (Sc/v)	EWoo
'Bourbon Rose' (Sc)	MHer
'Brackenwood' (Dw/d) ♀H1c	EPts
'Brenda' (Min/d)	EPts
'Brian Pope' (R)	EPts
'Brilliant' (Dec)	ENfk
'Brilliantine' (Sc)	ENfk EWoo MHer SRms
(Brocade Series) BROCADE CHERRY NIGHT (Z/C/d)	MPri
- BROCADE FIRE (Z/C/d)	MPri
- BROCADE SALMON NIGHT (Z/C/d)	MPri
§ 'Brown's Butterfly' (R)	EWoo
'Brunswick' (Sc)	ESgl EWoo MHer SMrm
BullsEye Series (Z) **new**	EGren
'Bushfire' (R) ♀H1c	EWoo
'Butterfly' (Min/v)	EPts
caespitosum	MHer
'California Brilliant' (U)	MHer
'Camphor Rose' (Sc) ♀H1c	CGHo EPts SRms
candicans	EWoo
(Candy Flowers Series) CANDY FLOWERS BRIGHT RED ('Camred'^{PBR}) (R)	EWoo
- CANDY FLOWERS VIOLET ('Camvio'^{PBR}) (R)	EWoo
- CANDY FLOWERS WHITE ('Camwh') (R)	EWoo
canescens	see *P.* 'Blandfordianum'
capitatum	ENfk EWoo
'Capri' (Sc)	SPel
'Capricorn' (Min/d)	SPel
'Captain Starlight' (A) ♀H1c	EShb EWoo MHer
'Cardington' (St/Dw)	WCot
'Carefree' (U) ♀H1c	EPts
carnosum	EWoo MHer
'Caroline' (Dec)	EPts
'Catford Belle' (A)	MHer
caucalifolium	EWoo MHer
subsp. *caucalifolium*	
caylae	EWoo

Pelargonium

'Charity' (Sc/v) ♀H1c	ENfk EPts EShb EWoo MHer MHoo SDix SRms
'Charmay Hampshire' (Z/d)	MHer
'Charmay Marjorie' (A)	MHer
'Charmay Snowflake' (Sc/v)	SRms
CHOCOLATE ('Gencho'PBR) (Z/C/St)	CGHo
§ 'Chocolate Peppermint' (Sc/C)	CCBP CGHo ELan ENfk ESgI EWoo MHer SRms WOld
'Chocolate Tomentosum'	see P. 'Chocolate Peppermint'
'Chocolate Twist' (St/C)	EPts
'Choun Cho' (I)	LCro
'Citriodorum' (Sc) ♀H1c	ELan EWoo MHer
'Citronella' (Sc)	ESgI EWoo SRms
'Claret Rock Unique' (U)	EWoo
CLASSIC CALYPSO IMPROVED ('Pecz0007') (Z)	MPri
'Clorinda' (U/Sc)	CGHo ENfk EPts ESgI EShb EWoo MHer SDix SRms
'Cola Bottles' (Sc)	CCht CGHo CSpe CTsd ELan EPts EWoo LCro MHer MNHC MPri NPer SMrm SPoG
'Concolor Lace'	see P. 'Shottesham Pet'
'Contrast' (Z/C/v)	SPoG
'Copthorne' (U/Sc) ♀H1c	CGHo ESgI EShb EWoo MHer SRms
cordifolium	EPPr EWoo
- var. *rubrocinctum*	EShb EWoo MHer
coriandrifolium	see P. *myrrhifolium* var. *coriandrifolium*
cortusifolium	EWoo MHer
'Cottenham Glamour' (A) ♀H1c	MHer
'Cottenham Harmony' (A)	ELan
'Cottenham Jubilee' (A)	MHer
'Cottenham Surprise' (A) ♀H1c	EPts
'Cottenham Wonder' (A) ♀H1c	MHer
cotyledonis	EWoo
'Countess of Scarborough'	see P. 'Lady Scarborough'
'Creamy Nutmeg' (Sc/v)	ENfk EShb EWoo MHer SEND SRms
'Crimson Unique' (U) ♀H1c	CSpe EAri ELan ENfk ESgI EWoo MHer
§ *crispum* (Sc)	WOld
- 'Cy's Sunburst' (Sc/v) ♀H1c	EPts MHer
- 'Peach Cream' (Sc/v)	ENfk
- 'Variegatum' (Sc/v) ♀H1c	ENfk EWoo MHer SRms WCot WOld
crithmifolium	EWoo MHer
'Crocketta' (I/d/v) ♀H1c	EPts
'Crocodile' (I/C/d) ♀H1c	EAri ELan EPts EShb EWoo MHer MNHC WBrk WCot WFar WOld
cucullatum 'Flore Pleno' (d)	EWoo
- subsp. *strigifolium*	EWoo
'Cynthia'PBR (R)	LCro
'Dainty Maid' (Sc)	ENfk
'Dark Secret' (R)	CSpe SMrm
'Dark Venus' (R)	EWoo
dasyphyllum	EWoo
'Dean's Delight' (Sc)	EWoo
'Decora Pink'	see P. 'Decora Rouge'
'Decora Red'	see P. 'Decora Rouge'
§ 'Decora Rouge' (I)	SEND
'Deerwood Angel Wings' (A)	EWoo
'Deerwood Lavender Lad' (Sc)	ENfk EPts EWoo MHer MHoo
'Deerwood Lavender Lass' (Sc)	ESgI EWoo MHer SPel SRms
'Delli' (R) ♀H1c	EPts MHer NPer SMrm

denticulatum	EWoo MHer
§ - 'Filicifolium' (Sc)	CGHo ELan ENfk EPts EWoo MHer SDix WFar
DIABOLO ('Fiscrid') (Z/d)	MPri
'Diana' Fibrex Nurseries	EWoo MHer WOld
dichondrifolium (Sc)	EWoo MHer
'Distinction' (Z/C)	CSpe EWoo SPoG WBrk WMal
'Dodd's Super Double' (Z/d)	SMrm
× *domesticum* new	MSwo
'Don Franco'PBR (R)	LCro
'Don Mila' (R)	LCro
'Don Palido'PBR (R)	LCro
'Don Valentino'PBR (R)	LCro
'Dresden Pink' (Dw)	MHer
'Dresden White' (Dw)	MHer
'Duke of Edinburgh'	see P. 'Hederinum Variegatum'
echinatum	MHer WFar
- 'Album'	EWoo SIvy
ELBE SILVER ('Pensil') (I) ♀H1c	EPts
(Elegance Series) ELEGANCE IMPERIAL (R)	LCro
- ELEGANCE JEANETTE ('Rg8036'PBR) (R)	LCro
elongatum	SChr
'Els' (Dw/St)	WBrk
'Els' 1870	WFar
endlicherianum	EDAr EPot EWoo WAbe WCot
exhibens	EWoo
exstipulatum	EPPr EWoo MHer
'Fair Ellen' (Sc)	EWoo MHer
'Fairfields' (d/St)	EPts
'Fandango' (Z/St)	SMrm
'Fanny Eden' (R)	EWoo
'Fern Mint' (Sc)	EWoo MHer SRms
'Fieldings Unique' (U)	EWoo
'Fiesta' (I/d)	EWoo
'Filicifolium'	see P. *denticulatum* 'Filicifolium'
'Fir Trees Catkins' (A)	MHer
'Fir Trees Echoes of Pink' (A)	EWoo
'Fir Trees Eileen' (St)	SMrm
'Fir Trees Flamingo' (Dw)	EWoo
'Fir Trees Hayley' (R)	EPts
'Fir Trees Muffin' (Dec/Sc) ♀H1c	EPts
'First Blush' (R)	ELan
'Floria Moore' (Dec)	EWoo
fragrans	CoPl ENfk EPts EWoo LCro MNHC SRms WTre
Fragrans Group (Sc)	CGHo MHer
§ - 'Fragrans Variegatum' (Sc/v) ♀H1c	CGHo EPts EWoo LCro MHoo SPoG
- 'Snowy Nutmeg'	see P. (Fragrans Group) 'Fragrans Variegatum'
'Fragrant Frosty' (Sc/v)	EWoo
'Frank Headley' (Z/v) ♀H1c	EPts EShb EWoo NPer SEND SPoG WFar
'Freak of Nature' (Z/v)	MHer
'Frensham' (Sc)	ENfk EWoo MHer
'Friesdorf' (Fr/Dw)	EAri MHer WMal
'Fringed Aztec' (R) ♀H1c	MHer
'Fruity' (Sc)	SRms
fruticosum	EWoo SDix
fulgidum	EWoo MHer
'Gabriel' (A)	EWoo
'Galway Star' (Sc/v) ♀H1c	MHer
'Garland' (R)	EPts
'Gartendirektor Herman' (Dec) ♀H1c	EWoo MHer
'Gemma' (R)	EPts

'Gemstone' (Sc) ♀H1c	CGHo ENfk MHer
'Giant Oak' (Sc)	EWoo
'Gibbosina Bicolor' **new**	CSpe
gibbosum	CSpe ESgI EWoo MHer
I − 'Maroon'	CSpe
'Giroflée' (I/d)	MHer
glaucum	see *P. lanceolatum*
§ *glutinosum*	EWoo
'Goblin' (Min/d)	MHer
'Golden Ears' (Dw/St/C) ♀H1c	NPer
'Golden Staphs' (Z/C/St)	MHer
'Golden Warwick'	MHer
'Gooseberry Leaf'	see *P. grossularioides*
'Grace Thomas' (Sc) ♀H1c	EWoo MHer
'Grandad Mac' (Dw/St) ♀H1c	EPts MHer
GRANDEUR CLASSIC PINK (Z) **new**	MNHC
GRANDEUR CLASSIC WHITE (Z) **new**	MNHC
GRANDEUR DECO CHOCO SCARLET (Z/C) **new**	MPri
GRANDEUR RED PEPPER (Z) **new**	MNHC
grandiflorum	EShb EWoo MHer
− white-flowered	SPel
graveolens L'Hér.	see *P.* 'Graveolens'
graveolens ambig.	SEND
§ 'Graveolens' (Sc)	CMHG CoPl ENfk LWaG MHer
'Graveolens Minor' (Sc)	EWoo
'Great Glemham Lemon' (Sc)	EWoo
'Green Eyes' (I/d)	MHer
'Grey Lady Plymouth' (Sc)	CGHo CPbh EWoo LCro MHer MHoo
§ *grossularioides*	EWoo MHer
'Gustav Emich' (Z/d)	WMal
'Hadleigh' (Min)	MHer
'Harlequin Liverbird' (I)	MHer
havlasae	WAbe
§ 'Hederinum Variegatum' (I/v)	EPts
'Helen Christine' (Z/Dw/St) ♀H1c	EAri MHer
'Henry Weller' (A) ♀H1c	EPts
'Hills of Snow' (Z/v)	MHer
'Hindoo' (Dec) ♀H1c	EWoo
hirtum	EWoo
hispidum	EWoo MHer
Horizon Series (Z)	MBros
− 'Horizon Deep Salmon Improved' (Z)	MBros
− 'Horizon Deep Scarlet' (Z)	MBros
'Hula' (R × U)	EWoo
'Ignescens'	EWoo
'Imperial Butterfly' (A/Sc) ♀H1c	ENfk EPts MHer SRms
ionidiflorum	CSpe EShb EWoo MHer SRms WAbe
'Islington Peppermint' (Sc)	EPts EWoo SRms
§ 'Jackie' (I/d) ♀H1c	EWoo MHer
'Jackie Davies' (R)	EWoo
'Jackie Gall'	see *P.* 'Jackie'
'Jean Bart' (I)	MHer
§ 'Jeanne d'Arc' (I/d)	MHer
'Jer' Rey' (A)	EWoo
'Jip's Joan the Wad' (St)	EPts
'Jip's Sandra Ann' (Z/C/d/v) **new**	MHer
'Joan Morf' (R) ♀H1c	EWoo
'Joan of Arc'	see *P.* 'Jeanne d'Arc'
'Joy' (R) ♀H1c	CSpe
I 'Joy' (Z/d)	EPts
'Joy Lucille' (Sc)	CGHo EWoo
karooicum	EWoo
'Karrooense'	see *P. quercifolium*
'Katie' (R)	EWoo
'Kewensis' (Z)	EShb EWoo
'Key's Unique' (U)	SEND
'La France' (I/d) ♀H1c	LCro MHer
'Lady Mary' (Sc)	EWoo MHer SRms
'Lady Plymouth' (Sc/v) ♀H1c	CGHo CPbh ELan ENfk EPPr EPts EWoo MHer MHoo SEND SMrm SRms
§ 'Lady Scarborough' (Sc)	ENfk EWoo MHer SRms
laevigatum	MHer
§ *lanceolatum*	EWoo MHer
'Land of Song' (A)	ENfk
'Lara Ballerina' (Sc/d) ♀H1c	SRms
'Lara Beacon'	CSpe EWoo
'Lara Candy Dancer' (Sc) ♀H1c	CGHo CSpe ELan EPts EWoo MAsh
'Lara Jester' (Sc)	ENfk EWoo
'Lara Rajah' (R)	EWoo
'Lara Starshine' (Sc) ♀H1c	ENfk EPPr EPts EWoo MHer SRms
'Lara Viking'	EWoo
'Laurel Heyward' (R)	EPts
'Lavender Lindy' (Sc)	CGHo CSpe ENfk EWoo MHer SMHy
'Lawrenceanum'	EWoo LCro MHer.
laxum	EWoo
'L'Élégante' (I/v) ♀H1c	EWoo MHer SIvy SMrm
'Lemon Crisp'	see *P. crispum*
'Lemon Fancy' (Sc) ♀H1c	CGHo ENfk ESgI EWoo MHer SRms
'Lemon Fizz'	CGHo LCro MHoo
'Lemon Kiss' (Sc)	CSpe EWoo MHoo
'Leslie William Burrow' (Dec)	EPts EWoo
'Letitia' (A)	ENfk MHer
'Lilac Gem' (I/Min/d)	ENfk
'Lilian Pottinger' (Sc) ♀H1c	ENfk EWoo MHer
'Limoneum' (Sc)	ENfk EWoo MHer
'Little Gem' (Dw/Sc)	ENfk EWoo MHer
'Little Spikey' (Z/Min/St/d)	MHer
lobatum	EWoo
longicaule	EWoo
'Lord Bute' (R) ♀H1c	CAbb CGHo CMHG CSpe ELan ENfk EPts EWoo LCro MHer NPer SMrm WOld
'Lord de Ramsey'	see *P.* 'Tip Top Duet'
'Lotusland' (Dw/St/C) ♀H1c	SPoG
'Louise' (Min)	EPts
'Mabel Grey' (Sc) ♀H1c	CGHo CSpe ENfk EPts EShb EWoo MHer MNHC NPer
madagascariense	EWoo
§ 'Madame Auguste Nonin' (U/Sc)	ENfk EWoo MHer
'Madame Crousse' (I/d) ♀H1c	EWoo
'Madame Margot'	see *P.* 'Hederinum Variegatum'
magenteum	MHer
'Maple Leaf' (Sc)	EWoo
(Marcada Series)	LSou
MARCADA MAGENTA ('Kleip13348'PBR) (I × Z)	
− MARCADA PINK ('Kleip13347'PBR) (I × Z)	LSou
− MARCADA PINK PURPLE ('Kleip18162'PBR) (I × Z)	LSou

508 *Pelargonium*

– Marcada Violet ('Kleip23785') (I × Z) **new**	LSou
– Marcada White ('Kleip19284'PBR) (I × Z)	LSou
'Maréchal MacMahon' (Z/C)	ENfk
'Marmalade' (Min/d)	WFar
I 'Maureen' Hoddinott (Z/d)	MHer
'Meadowside Dark and Dainty' (St)	WBrk
'Melanie Day' (St) ♀H1c	EPts
'Michael' (A) ♀H1c	ELan EPts EWoo MHer
'Mike West' (St)	EPts
'Millfield Gem' (I/d)	WKif
'Millfield Rose' (I/d)	EWoo
'Milly' (Sc)	ENfk
'Minnie' (Z/St/d)	WBrk
'Minstrel Boy' (R)	EWoo
'Miss Burdett Coutts' (Z/Dw/C/v)	MHer
§ 'Miss Stapleton'	EWoo LCro MHer
'Misterioso' (R)	EWoo
'Misty Morning' (R)	EWoo
mollicomum	EWoo
'Molly' (A)	ENfk
'Monica Bennett' (Dw)	WFar
'Monsieur Ninon' misapplied	see *P.* 'Madame Auguste Nonin'
'Morwenna' (R)	EWoo MHer WCot
(Mosquitaway Series) Mosquitaway Eva (A)	LCro
– Mosquitaway Lizzy ('Floang01'PBR) (A)	LCro
'Mr Henry Cox' (Z/C/v) ♀H1c	MHer
'Mr Wren' (Z)	EAri EShb SIvy WFar
'Mrs Pollock' (Z/C/v)	ELan EPts EShb MBros MNHC SMrm
'Mrs Quilter' (Z/C) ♀H1c	SMrm WBrk WFar
'Mrs Taylor' (Sc)	SDix
multicaule	EWoo
myrrhifolium	EWoo
§ – var. *coriandrifolium*	EWoo MHer
'Mystery' (U) ♀H1c	LCro
'Needham Market' (A)	ENfk
'Nellie' (R)	EPts
'Nervosum' (Sc)	ENfk
'Nervous Mabel' (Sc) ♀H1c	EWoo MHer
'New Gypsy' (Dec)	ELan MHer
'Nicola Buck' (R) ♀H1c	EPts
'Night' (I)	EWoo
'Noblesse' (Z)	MPri
'Noche' (R)	SMrm
oblongatum	EWoo
'Occold Shield' (Dw/C/d) ♀H1c	SMrm
ochroleucum	EWoo
odoratissimum (Sc) ♀H1c	ENfk EPts EWoo MHer SRms
'Old Spice' (Sc)	CGHo ENfk MHer
'Oldbury Duet' (A/v) ♀H1c	MHer
'Orange Fizz' (Sc) ♀H1c	CCht EWoo MHer SRms
'Orange Fizz' (Z/d)	CSpe ENfk EPts LCro
'Orion' (Z/d)	MHer
'Orsett' (Sc) ♀H1c	CGHo EWoo MHer
'Our Flynn' (Z/St)	MHer
'Our Gynette' (Dec)	EWoo
ovale	EWoo
'Pagoda' (Z/St/d)	MHer WBrk
Palladium Series	MBros
'Pam Tutcher' (St)	EPts
panduriforme	EWoo
papilionaceum ♀H1c	ELan EPPr EShb EWoo MHer SPlb WFar
'Parisienne' (R) ♀H1c	EWoo
'Pat Hannam' (St)	WBrk
'Paton's Unique' (U/Sc) ♀H1c	CGHo ELan ENfk EWoo MHer WCot
* 'Patricia' (I)	LCro
'Patricia Andrea' (Z/T) ♀H1c	NPer
'Paul Crampel' (Z) ♀H1c	EShb EWoo MHer
'Peaches and Cream' (R)	EWoo
peltatum	EWoo
'Peppermint Lace' (Sc)	EPts EWoo
'Pershore Princess'	WBrk
'Petals' (Z/v)	SPoG WBrk
'Phyllis Variegated' (U/v)	ENfk EPts EWoo MHer WCot
'Pink Capitatum'	see *P.* 'Pink Capricorn'
§ 'Pink Capricorn' (Sc)	CGHo CTsd ENfk EPPr EPts EShb EWoo LCro MHer MHoo SAng SPel SRms
'Pink Champagne' (Sc)	EWoo MHer
'Pink Gay Baby'	see *P.* 'Sugar Baby'
'Pink Happy Thought' (Z/C/v)	MHer
'Pink Hindoo' (Dec)	EWoo
'Pink Needles' (Z/Min/St)	MHer
'Plum Rambler' (Z/d)	EShb EWoo
'Polka' (U) ♀H1c	EPts EWoo
polycephalum	EWoo
'Poquita' (Sc)	SRms
Precision Bright Lilac (Precision Series) (I)	LCro
'Pride of Exmouth'	CWCL
'Prince of Orange' (Sc) ♀H1c	CGHo CSpe CTsd ELan ENfk EPts EWoo LCro MHer MHoo SEND SRms
'Priory Salmon' (St/d)	EShb
pseudoglutinosum	EWoo MHer
'Pungent Peppermint' (Sc)	SRms
'Purple Unique' (U/Sc)	ENfk EShb EWoo MHer
'Quantock Candy' (A) ♀H1c	ELan EPts EWoo
'Quantock Double Dymond' (A/d) ♀H1c	MHer
'Quantock Kirsty' (A) ♀H1c	EWoo
'Quantock Matty' (A) ♀H1c	EPts
'Quantock Perfection' (A) ♀H1c	EPts MHer
'Quantock Sally' (A/d)	ENfk
'Queen of the Lemons' (Sc)	EWoo
§ *quercifolium* (Sc)	CGHo EPts EWoo LCro
quinquelobatum	CSpe EWoo
radens (Sc)	ENfk EWoo
'Radula' (Sc) ♀H1c	CSpe ELan MHer SDix SRms
'Radula Roseum' (Sc)	EWoo
'Rager's Star' (Dw)	MHer
'Red Capri' (Sc)	EWoo
'Red Gables'	WCot WMal
'Red Rambler' (Z/d)	CGHo
'Red Robin' (R)	ENfk EPPr WCot
'Red Spider' (Dw/Ca)	EAri MHer
'Red Witch' (Dw/St/d)	ESgI EWoo MHer
'Redondo' (Dw/d)	EWoo WFar
'Rembrandt' (R)	MHer
'Renate Parsley' ♀H1c	EPts EWoo LCro MHer
reniforme	EWoo MHer SMHy
'Retah's Crystal' (Z/v)	MHer
'Richard Gibbs' (Sc)	ENfk EWoo MHer
'Rietje van der Lee' (A)	ENfk
'Rimfire' (R) ♀H1c	EWoo LCro MHer
'Rio Grande' (I/d)	MHer

'Rober's Lemon Rose' (Sc)	CSpe ENfk EWoo MHer SRms
'Robin's Unique' (U)	MHer
'Roller's Pioneer' (I/v)	ENfk EShb EWoo
'Roller's Satinique' (U)	EWoo MHer
'Rollison's Unique' (U)	MHer
'Romeo' (R)	EWoo
'Rose Bengal' (A)	ENfk
'Rose Silver Cascade' (I)	MHer
'Rosmaroy' (R)	EPts
'Royal Ascot' (Dec) ♀H1c	EPts EWoo SMrm
'Royal Oak' (Sc/C) ♀H1c	CGHo CPbh ENfk EPPr EShb EWoo MHer MHoo MNHC SEND SPoG SRms
'Royal Surprise' (R)	EWoo
'Ruffled Velvet' (R)	EWoo
'Rushmoor Bondi Blue' (Z/C/Min/St/d)	MHer
'Rushmoor Golden Ruffles' (Z/C/St/Min/d)	MHer
'Saint Elmo's Fire' (St/Dw/d)	MHer WFar
'Salmon Angel'	CSpe
'Sancho Panza' (A)	CSpe
'Sanguineum'	CSpe
'Scarlet Gem' (Z/St)	WBrk
'Scarlet Pet' (U) ♀H1c	ENfk SMrm
'Scarlet Pimpernel' (Z/C/d)	MHer
'Scarlet Rambler' (Z/d)	EShb SMrm
'Scarlet Unique' (U)	CSpe EShb EWoo
schizopetalum	EWoo MHer
'Schottii' ♀H1c	CPbh EWoo MHer
'Secret Love' (Sc)	SRms
'Seeley's Pansy' (A)	EWoo MHer
'Shannon' (Z)	EWoo
'Shelley' (Dw)	WFar
§ 'Shottesham Pet' (Sc)	ENfk EWoo LCro MHer SRms
'Shrubland Rose' (Sc)	EShb
sidoides ♀H1c	CGHo CPbh CSpe CTtf CWCL EArI EBee EGrI ELan ENfk EPts EWoo LCro MHer SBeP SChr SDix SHor SMHy SMrm SPel SPhx SPlb SVen WAbe WFar WKif WOld WTre
– black-flowered	EWoo
– magenta-flowered **new**	ELan
– 'Sloe Gin Fizz'	CPbh
'Silver Dawn' (Z/Min/St/v)	MHer
'Silver Snow' (Z/v/Min/St/d)	MHer
'Snowbright' (St/d)	WBrk
'Snowflake'	see *P.* 'Atomic Snowflake'
'Solferino' (A)	ENfk
'Sophie Emma' (Z/d) ♀H1c	EPts
'Southern Sundae' (Dw/d)	MHer
'Souvenir de Prue' (Sc)	EWoo
'Spanish Angel' (A) ♀H1c	MHer
§ *'Splendide'* ♀H1c	CPbh CSpe CTtf EWoo MHer
'Spot-on-bonanza' (R) ♀H1c	EPts
'Springfield Black' (R)	EPts
'Stadt Bern' (Z/C) ♀H1c	CSpe
× *stapletoniae*	see *P.* 'Miss Stapleton'
'Star Flecks' (St) ♀H1c	EPts
'Startel Salmon' (Z/St)	MHer
'Stella Ballerina'	SMrm
'Stuts Dream'^PBR (Z) **new**	ELan
'Suffolk Garnet' (Dec)	EPts
§ 'Sugar Baby' (I/Dw)	MHer
SUMMER TWIST RED/WHITE ('Gentwiststar') (Summer Twist Series) (Z/St)	MBros
'Supreme Lilac' (I)	EPts
'Supreme Red' (I)	EPts
'Supreme White' (I)	EPts
'Susan Payne' (Dw/d)	MHer
'Sweet Mimosa' (Sc) ♀H1c	CPbh ELan ENfk EPts EWoo LCro MHer SEND SRms WTre
'Tamie' (Dw/d)	EPts
tetragonum	EShb EWoo MHer SBrt SIvy
'The Boar' (Z/C/Fr) ♀H1c	EShb EWoo
'The Culm' (A)	MHer
'The Kenn-Lad' (A)	EWoo
'The Marchioness of Bute' (R)	ELan ESgI MHer
'The Tamar' (A)	EWoo MHer
'Thessaloniki' (St)	EPts
§ 'Tip Top Duet' (A)	ELan LCro MHer SMrm
tomentosum (Sc) ♀H1c	CGHo CMHG CPbh CSpe ENfk EPPr EPts EShb EWoo LCro LWaG MHer MHoo SDix SEND SMrm
– 'Chocolate'	see *P.* 'Chocolate Peppermint'
TOMMY ('Pactommy') (I)	ELan
tongaense	EWoo
'Tornado' (R) ♀H1c	LCro
'Torrento' (Sc)	ESgI EWoo LCro MHer SEND SRms
transvaalense	CPbh EWoo
tricolor misapplied	see *P.* 'Splendide'
tricolor Curt.	CPbh
tricuspidatum	CCBP EShb EWoo MHer
trifidum	EWoo
triste	EWoo MHer
'Trudie' (Fr/Dw)	MHer
'Turkish Coffee' (R)	EPts ESgI
'Tyabb Princess' (R)	EWoo
'Unique Aurore' (U)	CGHo MHer
urbanum	EWoo
'Vancouver Centennial' (Dw/St/C) ♀H1c	EPts MHer SPoG WOld
'Vandersea' (Sc)	EWoo MHer
'Variegated Fragrans'	see *P.* (Fragrans Group) 'Fragrans Variegatum'
'Variegated Petit Pierre' (Min/v)	MHer
'Vectis Blaze' (I)	EWoo
'Vectis Cascade' (I)	EWoo
'Vectis Glitter' (Z/St) ♀H1c	EPts SMrm WBrk WCot
'Vicki' (R)	EWoo MHer
'Vicky Claire' (R)	EWoo SMrm
VILLE DE DRESDEN ('Pendresd') (I)	EWoo
violareum misapplied	see *P.* 'Splendide'
'Viscossisimum' (Sc)	EWoo MHer
viscosum	see *P. glutinosum*
vitifolium	EWoo
'Vivienne' (St)	EPts
'Voodoo' (U) ♀H1c	CGHo CMHG CPbh CSpe EArI ENfk EPts EWoo MHer WCot
'Wantirna' (Z/v) ♀H1c	EPts
'Warrenorth Emerald' (Z)	MHer
'Wayward Angel' (A)	ENfk
'Welling' (Sc)	ENfk
'Westdale Appleblossom' (Z/C/d)	ELan MHer
'Westside' (Z/d)	MHer
'Whisper' (R)	EWoo
'White Boar' (Z/C/Fr)	EShb EWoo WFar
'White Feather' (Z/St)	MHer
'Wilhelm Langath' (Z/v)	EArI EShb WBrk
'Woottens Unique' (U)	EWoo
worcesterae	EWoo
'Wychwood' (A/Sc)	EWoo
'Yhu' (R)	EWoo SMrm
'Zofia Pope' (R)	EPts
zonale	EWoo

Peliosanthes (Asparagaceae)
caesia B&SWJ 5183 — WCru
macrostegia B&SWJ 3639 — ESwi WCru
teta subsp. **humilis** — WCru
   RWJ 10044

Pellaea (Pteridaceae)
falcata ♀H4 — ISha
ovata — SPlb
paradoxa 'Glowstar' — ISha
rotundifolia ♀H2 — CBrP CLAP CTsd ISha LCro LEdu MAsh MPri NBro SArc SEND WCot
viridis — CBrP EShb WCot WPGP

Peltandra (Araceae)
undulata — see *P. virginica* (L.) Schott
§ **virginica** (L.) Schott — NPer

Peltaria (Brassicaceae)
alliacea — CCBP CSpe LEdu NBac WCot WTre

Peltiphyllum see *Darmera*

Peltoboykinia (Saxifragaceae)
§ **tellimoides** — ESwi LEdu LShi NBir WFar WPGP
watanabei — CElw EBee ELan EMor GEdr GPSL LEdu LRHS LShi NLar WCru WFar WPnP WTre

Pennisetum ✿ (Poaceae)
advena 'Chelsea'^PBR — LRHS LSou
- 'Fireworks'^PBR (v) — CAbb CBcs EAri LBom LCro LRHS LSou MAsh Midl WFar
§ - 'Rubrum' ♀H3 — CBcs CExl CKno CSBt EAri EBee EGren LBom LCro LRHS MAsh MBros Midl MPri SMad
§ **alopecuroides** — CBcs CBWd CWal EGren EHeP EUrb EWhm LBom MCtn NBir NGdn SPlb WCot
- AUTUMN WIZARD — see *P. alopecuroides* 'Herbstzauber'
- 'Black Arrow' — CKno LRHS
- 'Black Beauty' — EBee EBlo ECha ELon LRHS MBNS NLar SMad SMHy SPel WHoo ELon NLar
- 'Burgundy Bunny' —
- 'Cassian's Choice' ♀H3 — CKno EWes LRHS NLar SHar SHor WHoo WPGP
- 'Dark Desire' — CKno CSde ELon EPfP LEdu LRHS WPGP
- 'Foxtrot' — EPPr
- 'Gelbstiel' — ELon Midl
- 'Goldstrich' — ELon
- 'Hameln' ♀H3 — Widely available
- 'Hameln Gold'^PBR — CKno ELon EPfP EWes LBom LCro LRHS NLar WFar
§ - 'Herbstzauber' — ELon MWlw SMHy
- 'JS Jommenik'^PBR — ELon
- 'Lady U' — Midl
- 'Little Bunny' — CBWd CMac CSde EBee EGren EHeP ELan ELon EPfP EUrb LBuc LCro LSRN MHol NGdn NLar WFar WSpi
- 'Little Honey' (v) — ELan ELon
- 'Magic' — ELon NLar
- 'Moudry' — CDor CExl CSde EBee EGren ELon Midl NLar NLit SBig
- 'National Arboretum' — Midl
- 'Piglet'^PBR — CKno NLar
- 'Red Head' ♀H3 — Widely available
- f. **viridescens** — EDAr EGren EPPr LCro LEdu MPro SMad SMrm WFar

- 'Weserbergland' — CKno EBlo ELon LRHS
- 'Woodside' — CKno
clandestinum — EShb
compressum — see *P. alopecuroides*
'Fairy Tails' ♀H3 — CBWd CKno CMac ECha ELon EPfP EPPr LCro LRHS MAsh MAvo MSwo SHor SMHy SPel SPoG WPGP WSpi XFar
flaccidum — EPPr
glaucum 'Purple Baron' — LRHS MPro
- 'Purple Majesty' — CSpe MPri
longistylum misapplied — see *P. villosum*
macrourum ♀H3 — CElw CKno CSde CSpe ECha ELan EMor EPfP EPPr EUrb LEdu LRHS MAsh MNrw NClf NDov SEND SHor SMad SMHy SPel SPlb WHoo WPGP
- blue-leaved — WCot
- 'Short Stuff' — CKno ECha MAsh WPGP
- 'Tail Feathers' — NLit
massaicum 'Red Bunny Tails' — CBWd EAri LRHS SRms
- 'Red Buttons' — see *P. thunbergii* 'Red Buttons'
orientale ♀H3 — CSde CSpe EBee ECha EDAr EGren EGrI EPfP MCtn NBir NClf NDov SEND SMHy SPel
- 'Flamingo' — EBee EBlo XFar
- 'JS Dance with Me'^PBR — LSou Midl XFar
- 'Karley Rose'^PBR — CKno CSpe EGren EWes LRHS MAsh MBNS NDov NSti SMad WFar WPGP
I - 'Robustum' — EPPr WPGP
- 'Shogun' — CKno ECha EPPr LRHS MAsh SPel
- 'Tall Tails' — CSde EBee EPPr EWes
PRINCESS CAROLINE ('Tift-17') — LRHS
purpureum — SRms
setaceum — Prohibited invasive. See Conservation and the Environment, p.42
- 'Rubrum' — see *P. advena* 'Rubrum'
thunbergii — CAby EDAr
§ - 'Red Buttons' — CKno CSde EBee ECha ELon EPfP EPPr LEdu LRHS MAsh MAvo MCtn MNrw SMHy SPel SPoG WHoo WKif WPGP
VERTIGO ('Tift-8'^PBR) — WCot
§ **villosum** ♀H3 — CAby CDoC CExl CKno CSde CSpe EBee ECha EGren EGrI ELan EPfP EPPr LBom LCro LEdu LRHS LSRN MCtn SEND SMad SMHy SMrm SPel SRms WChS

pennyroyal see *Mentha pulegium*

Penstemon ✿ (Plantaginaceae)
'Abbotsmerry' — EGrI ELon
§ 'Alice Hindley' — CMac CSpe ELan EPfP LShi LSRN NBir SEND SHar SRms WCAu WCot WFar WHoo WKif WMal
alpinus — CSpe
§ 'Andenken an Friedrich Hahn' ♀H5 — Widely available
§ **angustifolius** — CSpe EDAr MPro
'Apple Blossom' misapplied — see *P.* 'Thorn'
'Apple Blossom' — CMac EBee EGrI EHeP EPfP LCro LShi LSRN MBel MGos SPlb SPoG SRms WCAu WFar
'Arabesque Appleblossom' — EGren LBar LCro LSou MSCN WFar WTor
'Arabesque Orchid' — EGren LBar LSou WFar
'Arabesque Pink' — EGren MHol WFar

'Arabesque Red'	EGren LBar WFar WTor	*davidsonii*	EPot GEdr
'Arabesque Violet'	EGren LBar LSou MHol WFar	- var. *menziesii*	GEdr
arizonicus	see *P. whippleanus*	'Microphyllus'	
attenuatus	SPlb	- var. *praeteritus*	GEdr
subsp. *militaris*		- 'Silverwells'	EPot GEdr
'Audrey Cooper'	CMac	'Delfts Blue Riding Hood'^{PBR}	LCro
azureus	LShi	(Riding Hood Series)	
- subsp. *angustissimus*	GKev	*digitalis*	CBWd CWal EGrI SRms StAn
'Barbara Barker'	see *P.* 'Beech Park'	- 'Blackbeard' **new**	LBar
§ *barbatus*	GElm SRms	- (Dakota Series)	CAbb EGren EMor LBar LCro LRHS
- 'Cambridge Mixed'	LRHS	DAKOTA BURGUNDY	MPro SPad WFar WTor
- 'Coccineus'	CSde CSpe GBin LEdu SMHy	('Tnpendb'^{PBR})	
- 'Jingle Bells'	EDAr EPfP GArf SPeP	- - DAKOTA VERDE	LRHS
- orange-flowered	SPlb	('Tnpendv'^{PBR})	
- (Pinacolada Series)	CSpe	- 'Gold Foil'	LShi
'Pinacolada Violet'		- 'Goldfinger'	EMor EPfP LRHS
- - 'Pinacolada White'	SRms	- 'Husker Red'	Widely available
- 'Roseus'	SHar	- 'Isa'	WCot
'Beckford'	MBNS	- 'Mystica'	SRms
§ 'Beech Park' ♀^{H4}	ELan SRms	- 'Purpureus'	see *P. digitalis* 'Husker Red'
'Bisham Seedling'	see *P.* 'White Bedder'	§ 'Drinkstone Red'	SRms
'Blackbird' (Bird Series)	CBcs CElw CWnw EBee EGren	'Drinkwater Red'	see *P.* 'Drinkstone Red'
	EGrI ELan EPfP EUrb EWes LShi	*eatonii*	GKev
	LSRN LSto MBNS MHer Midl MPri	(Elgar Series) 'Elgar Crown	WCot
	MSwo NLar SAth SBeP SOrN SRms	of India'	
	WFar WHoo WKif WMal	- 'Elgar Firefly'	WCot
'Blue Riding Hood'^{PBR}	LRHS SPoG	- 'Elgar Light of Life'	WCot
(Riding Hood Series)		- 'Elgar Nimrod'	WCot
'Blue Spring' misapplied	see *P. heterophyllus* 'Blue Spring'	- 'Ellenbank Cardinal'	WKif
'Bodnant' ♀^{H4}	WMal	- 'Elmley'	MBNS
'Boysenberry Taffy'^{PBR}	IPot	§ *erianthereus*	SPlb
'Burford Purple'	see *P.* 'Burgundy'	ETNA ('Yatna') (Volcano	EPfP LRHS SRms
'Burford Seedling'	see *P.* 'Burgundy'	Series)	
'Burford White'	see *P.* 'White Bedder'	*euglaucus*	GKev MMuc
§ 'Burgundy'	CMac CWnw EGren GMaP MSCN	§ 'Evelyn' ♀^{H4}	CMac MBNS MHer NCth SPoG
	NBir NPer SAth SEND SRms		SRms WKif
caeruleus	see *P. angustifolius*	'Firebird'	see *P.* 'Schoenholzeri'
§ *campanulatus*	SRms	'Flame'	EGren
cardinalis	GKev	'Flamingo'	EBee EGren EWes IPot MBNS MPro
'Castle Forbes'	EBee GMaP SRms		MSwo NLar SAth SHar SMrm SRms
'Cathedral Rose'	EBee ELan EPfP	*fruticosus*	GEdr
'Catherine de la Mare'	see *P. heterophyllus* 'Catherine de la	§ - var. *scouleri* ♀^{H4}	EDAr GKev
	Mare'	- - 'Amethyst'	EPot WAbe
'Cha Cha Cherry'^{PBR}	ELan	FUJIYAMA ('Yayama')	EPfP LRHS MPro SRms
'Cha Cha Hot Pink'^{PBR}	ELan EPfP	'Garden Red'	see *P.* 'Windsor Red'
'Cha Cha Lavender'^{PBR}	ELan EPfP IPot LRHS	'Garnet'	see *P.* 'Andenken an Friedrich Hahn'
'Cha Cha Pink'^{PBR} **new**	LRHS	*gentianoides* B&SWJ 10271	WCru
'Cha Cha Purple'^{PBR}	ELan EPfP LRHS	'Geoff Hamilton'	LRHS MBNS SPoG WCot
'Charles Rudd'	ELan ELon LRHS LSRN MBNS MHer	§ 'George Home' ♀^{H3}	GBin MBNS SMrm SRms
	MPro SRms	'George Moon'	SPad
§ 'Cherry'	SHar	*glaber*	EBee GQue LShi SPlb WKif
'Cherry Ripe' misapplied	see *P.* 'Cherry'	- 'Roundway Snowflake'	SHar SRms
'Cherry Sparks'^{PBR}	LRHS	*hallii*	EPot SPlb
§ 'Chester Scarlet'	EGrI WKif	(Harlequin Series)	LBar LRHS MPro
'Choirboy'	EWes	HARLEQUIN LILAC	
cobaea	CSpe MCtn	('Tnpenhl')	
'Comberton'	SRms	- HARLEQUIN MAGENTA	LBar MPro NWbg
confertus	EBee ECha EPot LShi	('Tnpenhm')	
- RCB/MO A-7	WCot	- HARLEQUIN PINK	LBar MPro
'Connie's Pink' ♀^{H4}	SRms	('Tnpenhpi')	
'Coral Sea'	WFar	- HARLEQUIN VIOLET	LBar MPro
'Cottage Garden Red'	see *P.* 'Windsor Red'	('Tnpenhv')	
§ 'Countess of Dalkeith'	EPfP GBin SHar SRms WKif	*hartwegii* 'Albus'	SHar SRms
cristatus	see *P. erianthereus*	§ *heterophyllus*	LRHS SRms
* *cyananthus* var. *utahensis*	WCot	- 'Blue Gem'	CElw EPot
'Dark Towers'^{PBR}	CAbb CWGN EBee ELan EMor	§ - 'Blue Spring'	CSpe WAbe
	GBin LBar LRHS LSRN MArl	§ - 'Catherine de la Mare'	CBWd EBee EGrI ELan EPfP GBin
	MAsh MHol MHtn Midl MMuc		LBar LRHS MHtn MPro SHar SOrN
	MNrw MPie NEoE SAth SMad		SPel WSpi
	SPad SPhx SPoG SRkn WCot	- 'Electric Blue'	EGren LBar LBom LRHS MHol WFar
	WFar		WHil

– 'Heavenly Blue'	CAby CBcs CBlu CBWd CDor CEnd CMac CWnw EBee EGrl ELan EPfP GMaP LRHS LShi LSto MSwo NLar SMrm SPoG SRkn SRms WSpi WTor		'Osprey' (Bird Series) ♀H3	CWGN EBee EPfP EWes MPro NBir SHar SRms
– 'Jeanette'	GMaP		*ovatus*	CMac SRms
– 'Margarita Bop'	CWnw MNHC MPro		'Overbury'	SRms
– 'True Blue'	see *P. heterophyllus*		'Papal Purple'	MBNS SHar SRms
– 'Züriblau'	ELan SPla		'Partybells Red'	LBar
'Hewell Pink Bedder' ♀H4	CAby CBcs CWnw EGren ELon EPfP LRHS LSto MBNS MPro NCou NCth SHar SMrm SRms		'Partybells Violet'	LBar
			'Patio Wine'	LRHS
			'Peace'	GBin WMal
			'Pennington Gem' (Pensham Series) 'Pensham Amelia Jane'	MHer NBir SHar SRms CAby CWGN CWnw EGrl ELan ELon EPfP LRHS MPro NLar SRms
hidalgensis	SDix SPla			
'Hidcote Pink' ♀H3	CBcs CDor ELan EPot GMaP LCro LRHS LShi MHer MPri MPro NBir SEND SOrN SPlb SRms WFar WHoo WKif WMal		– 'Pensham Arctic Fox'	CSpe EPfP LRHS LSto SPoG WSpi
			– 'Pensham Avonbelle' ♀H4	SRms
'Hidcote Purple'	SHar		– 'Pensham Bilberry Ice'	EGrl
'Hidcote White'	MHer WMal		– 'Pensham Blackberry Ice'	CWnw LRHS SRms
hirsutus	EBee		– 'Pensham Charlotte Louise'	SRms
– 'Blue Foam'	MNrw		– 'Pensham Czar'	CAby CDor CWnw ELan ELon EPfP LRHS MBNS MGos MHed MPro NCth NLar SAth SMrm SPoG SRkn SRms WFar
– var. *pygmaeus*	EDAr EPfP EPot LBar NRya SPlb SRms WHoo WIce			
– – f. *albus*	EBee GArf LBar			
'Hot Pink Riding Hood' PBR (Riding Hood Series)	LCro LRHS		– 'Pensham Dorothy Wilson'	EGrl
			– 'Pensham Eleanor Young'	CWnw ELan EPfP LRHS
'John Nash' misapplied	see *P.* 'Alice Hindley'		– 'Pensham Freshwater Pearl'	SRms
'John Nash'	CDor SRms		– 'Pensham Jessica Mai'	SRms
'Juicy Grape' (Ice Cream Series)	WCot		– 'Pensham Just Jayne' ♀H4	CWnw EGrl MPri SPoG SRms WSpi
'June'	see *P.* 'Pennington Gem'		– 'Pensham Laura'	CAby CDor CWGN CWnw EGrl ELan EPfP LCro LRHS MBNS MPro NLar SRms WCav WFar WTor
KILIMANJARO ('Yajaro') (Volcano Series)	EPfP LRHS MHol SRms WFar			
'King George V'	CAby CBlu CDor CMac CWCL CWnw EBee EGren EGrl ELan ELon EPfP EPot EUrb GMaP LRHS MBNS MHer NCth NLar NPer SEND SOrN SPoG SRms		– 'Pensham Miss Wilson'	SRms
			– 'Pensham Plum Jerkum'	CDor CWGN CWnw EGrl ELan EPfP GMaP LCro LRHS LSou MBNS MHer MPie NDov NLar SRms WFar
laetus subsp. *roezlii*	EPot MAsh		– 'Pensham Skies'	SRms
'Lilac and Burgundy'	SHar SRms		– 'Pensham Son of Raven'	WCot
'Lord Home'	see *P.* 'George Home'		– 'Pensham Tayberry Ice'	SRms
lyallii	SRms		– 'Pensham Victoria Plum' ♀H4	SHar SRms
'Macpenny's Pink'	CMac MBNS		– 'Pensham Wedding Bells'	SRms
'Marchants Cherry Red'	SMHy		– 'Pensham Wedding Day'	CTsd EGren EPfP LRHS LSRN MSwo NLar SAth SEND SMrm SPoG WFar
'Margery Fish' ♀H3	CFis EWes			
'Maurice Gibbs' ♀H3	CMac EGrl ELon EWes LRHS LSRN MBNS SRms		– 'Pensham Westminster Belle'	SRms
'Melting Candy' (Ice Cream Series)	WCot		(Pentastic Series) PENTASTIC PINK ('Yapmine' PBR)	LCro MHol
mensarum	EPfP		– PENTASTIC RED ('Yapruby' PBR)	CWGN LCro MHol WFar
Mexicali hybrids 'Carillo Purple' (Carillo Series)	LRHS		– PENTASTIC ROSE ('Yaprose' PBR)	CWGN LCro LRHS MHol
– PIKE'S PEAK PURPLE ('P007s')	GArf		'Pershore Carnival'	SRms
			'Pershore Pink Necklace'	SRms
× *mexicanus* 'Sunburst Amethyst'	EDAr ELan SRms		(Phoenix Series) PHOENIX APPLEBLOSSOM 09 ('Peni Ablos09')	LRHS
– 'Sunburst Ruby'	EDAr ELan			
'Midnight'	EGrl ELan MPro MSwo SEND SHar		– PHOENIX APPLEBLOSSOM ('Pheni Ablos')	ELan EPfP
'Midnight Masquerade'	CWnw EMor			
'Miniature Bells'	EPfP		– PHOENIX MAGENTA 09 ('Peni Mag09')	LRHS
'Modesty'	SRms			
'Mother of Pearl'	EMor EPfP GMaP MPro MSwo SHar SRms WKif		– PHOENIX MAGENTA ('Pheni Magna')	ELan EPfP
'Mrs Morse'	see *P.* 'Chester Scarlet'		– PHOENIX PINK ('Pheni Pinka')	EGren ELan EPfP LRHS
multiflorus	EBee			
'Myddelton Gem'	SRms		– PHOENIX RED ('Pheni Reeda' PBR)	EGren ELan EPfP LRHS SRms
newberryi ♀H5	EDAr GKev			
– f. *humilior*	EPot LShi		– PHOENIX VIOLET 09 ('Peni Vio09' PBR)	EPfP LRHS
– subsp. *sonomensis*	SRms WAbe			
'Newbury Gem'	SHar		– PHOENIX VIOLET ('Pheni Vio')	EGren ELan SRms
'Onyx and Pearls'	EGren EMor LBar MHol NWbg			

'Phyllis'	see P. 'Evelyn'	'Royal White'	see P. 'White Bedder'
pinifolius ♀H4	EDAr ELan EPot GArf GBin GKev GQue LShi MMuc MNrw SRms SRot WFar WIce	'Rubicundus' ♀H4	EBlo EGren ELan ELon LRHS MPro NCth SRms
- 'Compactum'	GKev	'Ruby' misapplied	see P. 'Schoenholzeri'
- 'Mersea Yellow'	CAby EBee EDAr ELan EPot GKev LShi SPlb SRms WHoo WIce	*rupicola* ♀H5	GArf
		- 'Albus'	WAbe
- 'Wisley Flame' ♀H4	CAby EPfP EPot EWes GEdr GKev MHer WHoo WMal	- 'Conwy Lilac'	WAbe
		- 'Conwy Rose'	WAbe
'Pink Bedder'	see P. 'Hewell Pink Bedder'	*rydbergii*	SPlb
'Pocahontas'	LBar NLar WTor	'Schoenholzeri' ♀H4	CBcs CDor CMac CTsd EGren ELan ELon EPfP EUrb GMaP LRHS MBel MHer MPro MSwo NBir NCth NGdn SEND SMrm SOrN SPlb SPoG SRms WFar WHoo
(Polaris Series) POLARIS PURPLE ('Florpenpu')	LBuc LRHS MPri		
- POLARIS RED ('Florpenred')	LBuc LRHS MPri		
- POLARIS ROSE ('Florpenrose')	LBuc LRHS	*scouleri*	see P. *fruticosus* var. *scouleri*
		'Sissinghurst Pink'	see P. 'Evelyn'
'Port Wine' ♀H3	ELon GMaP NBir SEND SPoG WKif	'Six Hills'	EDAr EPot WAbe
'Precious Gem'	LBar	*smallii*	EBee EMor EPfP ESgI GKev LRHS MHer SMrm
(Pristine Series) PRISTINE LILA PURPLE ('Dopensprislipur'PBR)	EGren LRHS		
		'Snow Storm'	see P. 'White Bedder'
		'Snowflake'	see P. 'White Bedder'
- PRISTINE SCARLET ('Dopenspriscarl')	LBuc	*sonomensis*	see P. *newberryi* subsp. *sonomensis*
		'Sour Grapes' misapplied	see P. 'Stapleford Gem'
procerus	GEdr	'Sour Grapes' ambig.	CAby CBcs CDor EGren EHeP ELon LShi NGdn SMrm SPoG WCAu
var. *brachyanthus*			
- - 'Alba'	GEdr		
§ - var. *formosus*	GKev SRms WAbe	§ 'Sour Grapes' M. Fish ♀H4	CMac CWnw EBee ECha ELan EPfP EUrb GBin GMaP LCro LRHS LShi LSRN MHer MNHC MPro MSwo NLar SAth SHar SPel SRms WHoo WKif
§ - 'Roy Davidson' ♀H5	EPot MHol MMrt WAbe		
- var. *tolmiei*	EPot GEdr GKev		
pubescens	see P. *hirsutus*		
pulchellus Greene	see P. *procerus* var. *formosus*		
pulchellus Lindl.	see P. *campanulatus*	'Southgate Gem'	SRms
'Purple and White'	see P. 'Countess of Dalkeith'	'Souvenir d'André Torres' misapplied	see P. 'Chester Scarlet'
'Purple Bedder'	CMac EGren EGrI ELan EPfP LRHS LSRN SAth SPoG SRkn SRms	*spatulatus*	EPot
		'Species RLB'	EGrI
'Purple Passion'	EBee EBlo EGren ELan EPfP ERCP IPot LRHS MPro	*spectabilis*	CSpe
		§ 'Stapleford Gem' ♀H4	CElw CFis CMac CWnw EUrb LBom LShi LSto NCth SHar SRms WCAu WFar WHoo
PURPLE PERFECTION ('Pmoore14'PBR)	LRHS		
'Purple Riding Hood'PBR (Riding Hood Series)	LCro LRHS	'Strawberries and Cream' (Ice Cream Series)	CWnw LRHS MPro NLar SPoG WCot
'Purple Sea'	WFar	'Strawberry Fancy'	SRms
'Purpureus Albus'	see P. 'Countess of Dalkeith'	'Strawberry Fizz'	SRms
QUARTZ RED ('Balquared'PBR) (Quartz Series) **new**	LBar	*strictus*	EBee ECha EMor EPfP
		STROMBOLI ('Yaboli') (Volcano Series)	WHoo
'Raven' (Bird Series) ♀H3	CMac CTsd CWal CWGN CWnw EBee EHeP EPfP ERCP GMaP LBom LCro LShi MHed MNHC MPro NBir NCth NLar SEND SPel SRms WCAu WCot WFar WTre		
		'Summertime Pink'	LBar
		superbus	CAby EDAr GElm MPro WCot
		'Sweet Cherry' (Ice Cream Series)	WCot
'Razzle Dazzle'	SPlb SRms WCot	§ 'Thorn'	CWnw EGren MPro SMrm SRms
'Red Riding Hood'PBR (Riding Hood Series)	EPfP LCro SPoG	'Threave Pink'	SHar SMrm SRms WHoo
		'True Sour Grapes'	see P. 'Sour Grapes' M. Fish
RED ROCKS ('P008s')	GBin GQue WCot WHoo	*tubaeflorus*	EBee
'Red Sea'	WFar	'Vanilla Plum' (Ice Cream Series)	EGrI
'Rich Purple'	MBNS SPlb		
'Rich Ruby' ♀H3	CAby CFis CWnw EBlo EGren ELan EPfP EWes GBin LRHS MPro NBir SBeP SHar SPlb WCAu	VESUVIUS ('Yasius') (Volcano Series)	EPfP LRHS SRms WFar
		virgatus 'Blue Buckle'	EPfP SPlb WFar
(Rock Candy Series) ROCK CANDY BLUE ('Novapenblu'PBR)	ELan EPfP LRHS	§ *whippleanus*	EBee GJos MPro SPlb WFar
		- 'Chocolate Drop'	CWal MCtn
- ROCK CANDY LIGHT PINK ('Novapenlig')	ELan LRHS	§ 'White Bedder'	Widely available
		'Whitethroat' Sidwell	MBNS WMal
- ROCK CANDY PINK ('Novapenpin')	ELan LRHS	'Willy's Purple'	CDor MNrw
		'Windsor Red'	ELon EPfP LRHS MNHC SRms WCot WKif
- ROCK CANDY RUBY ('Novapenrub'PBR)	EBee LRHS		
		'Woodpecker'	CWGN ELon MPro SRms
roezlii Regel	see P. *laetus* subsp. *roezlii*		
'Rosy Blush'	SPlb		
'Roy Davidson'	see P. *procerus* 'Roy Davidson'		

Pentaglottis (Boraginaceae)

§ *sempervirens*	EPfP MNHC SRms

Pentapanax see *Aralia*

Pentapterygium see *Agapetes*

Pentas (Rubiaceae)
    lanceolata   ELan EShb

Penthorum (Saxifragaceae)
    sedoides   SBrt

Peperomia ✿ (Piperaceae)
    albovittata 'Piccolo Banda'^{PBR}   CDoC NHrt
§   **argyreia** ♀H1b   CDoC LBom LCro LWaG NHrt
    arifolia   CDoC
    caperata   CWal LBom NHrt
    - 'Luna Red' ♀H1b   NHrt
    - 'Quito'^{PBR}   LBom
    - 'Schumi Red Sienna'   LBom
    clusiifolia   NHrt
    - 'Jellie'   NHrt
    'Eden Rosso'^{PBR}   NHrt
    ferreyrae   CDoC EShb LBom LCro NHrt
    graveolens   NHrt
    'Hope'^{PBR}   LBom
    incana ♀H1a   CDoC
    nitida 'Variegata' (v)   CDoC NHrt
    obtusifolia ♀H1b   LInT NHrt
    - (Magnoliifolia Group) 'Golden Gate' (v)   NHrt
    - 'Obtipan'^{PBR}   NHrt
    - 'Variegata' (v)   LCro NHrt
    'Pepperspot'   LCro NHrt
    polybotrya   ELan
    - 'Raindrop'   CDoC LCro LWaG
    prostrata hort.   CDoC LBom LCro LWaG NHrt
    pulchella   see *P. verticillata*
    quadrangularis   CDoC LCro LWaG NHrt
    rotundifolia   LCro NHrt
    sandersii   see *P. argyreia*
§   **verticillata**   EShb NHrt

pepino see *Solanum muricatum*

peppermint see *Mentha* × *piperita*

Perezia (Asteraceae)
    lanigera   WAbe

Pericallis (Asteraceae)
    × **hybrida**   EShb
    - Senetti Series   MPri NPer SPoG
    - - Senetti Blue ('Sunsenebu')   SPoG
    - - Senetti Blue Bicolor ('Sunseneribuba'^{PBR})   MGos SPoG
    - - Senetti Magenta ('Sunsenere'^{PBR})   SPoG
    - - Senetti Magenta Bicolor ('Sunsenereba'^{PBR})   MGos SPoG
    'Spring Glory'   MCtn

Perilla (Lamiaceae)
    frutescens   CSpe EAri LCro MNHC WJek WKit
    - var. **purpurascens**   MNHC WJek
    - 'Shizo Green'   MNHC

Periploca (Apocynaceae)
    graeca   CBcs EAri EWld SEND WHil WJur
    sepium   CExl GEdr WJur

Perkinsiodendron (Styracaceae)
§   **macgregorii**   MBlu

Pernettya see *Gaultheria*

Perovskia see *Salvia* (Pe)
    atriplicifolia   see *Salvia yangii*

Persea (Lauraceae)
    americana   LWaG NPlm
    bracteata   CExl WPGP
    ichangensis   CExl
    indica B&SWJ 12535   WCru
    japonica   CBcs
    - B&SWJ 12789   WCru
    thunbergii   EBee WPGP
    - B&SWJ 12747   WCru

Persicaria ✿ (Polygonaceae)
    affinis   see *Bistorta affinis*
    alata   see *P. nepalensis*
    Alba Junior   see *Bistorta* Alba Junior
    alpina   see *Koenigia alpina*
    amphibia   CPud ELin EWat
    amplexicaulis   see *Bistorta amplexicaulis*
    bistorta   see *Bistorta officinalis*
    campanulata   see *Koenigia campanulata*
    capitata from Afghanistan   MCtn WJun
    - 'Pink Bubbles'   CExl
    chinensis 'Crûg Charisma' **new**   WCru
    - aff. var. **hispida** MCW 29   EPPr GGro
§   - var. **ovalifolia** 'Indian Summer' ♀H4   CExl EPPr EWld GGro SBrt WCot WFar WMal
    dshawachischwilii   see *Koenigia alpina* (All.) T.M. Schust. & Reveal var. *alpina*
    'Ellie's Pink'   see *Bistorta* 'Ellie's Pink'
    filiformis f. **albiflora**   WHil
    - 'Ballet'   SNoN WCot
    - 'Batwings' ♀H6   LWaG WJun
    - 'Brushstrokes' ♀H6   LSto SDix SNoN WCot WJun
    - 'Compton's Red' ♀H6   CExl EBee EPPr EUrb LBar SNoN SPel WCot WFar WPGP
    - 'Guizhou Bronze' ♀H6   CExl EBee GGro SBrt SNoN SPel
    - 'Lance Corporal'   CMac EMor EPPr EUrb GBin GElm GPSL LCro MAvo MHol NLar WHoo WJun
✻   **hydropiper** var. **rubra**   WJek
    'Indian Summer'   see *P. chinensis* var. *ovalifolia* 'Indian Summer'
    macrophylla   see *Bistorta macrophylla*
    microcephala   LWaG
    - 'Dragon's Eye'   EBee LBar
    - 'Night Dragon'   EMor LBar
    - 'Red Dragon'^{PBR} ♀H4   Widely available
    - 'Silver Brown'   LBar
    milletii   see *Bistorta milletii*
    mollis   see *Koenigia mollis*
    nakaii   LBar WCot
§   **nepalensis**   CExl EPPr GGro
§   **odorata**   CGHo EHet ENfk LCro LWaG MHer MHoo MNHC SEdi SPre SRms WHer WJek WJun WKit
    orientalis   CSpe SMrm SPel
§   **perfoliata**   Prohibited invasive. See Conservation and the Environment, p. 42
    'Pink Elephant'   see *Bistorta* 'Pink Elephant'
    polystachya   see *Koenigia polystachya*
    'Purple Fantasy'   Widely available

Petunia 515

regeliana	see *Bistorta officinalis* subsp. *pacifica*
§ *runcinata*	EBee LSto WFar
scoparia	see *Polygonum scoparium*
'Silver Dragon' ♀H4	CBct EAri EBee EMor MHol MPie NSti SHor SPel SPoG WCot
sinuata EN	CExl GGro
sphaerostachya Meisn.	see *Bistorta macrophylla*
tenuicaulis	see *Bistorta tenuicaulis*
vacciniifolia	see *Bistorta vacciniifolia*
virginiana 'Alba'	EPPr SNoN
- var. *filiformis*	CAby CSpe EMor LEdu LSto MBel MPie SBrt SDix SMhy SNoN SPoG SRkn WCot
- Variegated Group (v)	ECha MBNS SNoN WCot
- - 'Painter's Palette' (v)	CDTJ CMac EBee EMor EUrb EWld GKev LBar LShi MHol MPie SDix SRms WCot WHil WOld
wallichii	see *Koenigia polystachya*
weyrichii	see *Koenigia weyrichii*

persimmon see *Diospyros virginiana*

persimmon, Japanese see *Diospyros kaki*

Petagnia (Apiaceae)
saniculifolia	SBrt

Petalostemon see *Dalea*

Petamenes see *Gladiolus*

Petasites (Asteraceae)
albus	NSti
fragrans	ELan SRms WHer
§ *frigidus* var. *palmatus*	EAri LShi NLar WCot
- - 'Golden Palms'	EUrb WFar
hybridus	LRHS
japonicus	CAgr CBcs
- var. *giganteus*	EAri ECha ELan ESwi EUrb GGro LEdu WCru WJun
§ - - 'Nishiki-buki' (v)	CMac EAri ECha GGro GQue LEdu LShi NBir NSti SMad SRms WFar WJun
- - 'Variegatus'	see *P. japonicus* var. *giganteus* 'Nishiki-buki'
palmatus	see *P. frigidus* var. *palmatus*
paradoxus	EWld LEdu WCot WFar

× *Petchoa* (Solanaceae)
(BeautiCal Series) BEAUTICAL CARAMEL YELLOW ('Sakpxc024'PBR)	MPri
- BEAUTICAL CINNAMON ('Sakpxc021'PBR)	MPri

Petrea (Verbenaceae)
volubilis	CSpe MCtn

Petrocallis (Brassicaceae)
lagascae	see *P. pyrenaica*
§ *pyrenaica*	WAbe
- white-flowered	WAbe

Petrocoptis (Caryophyllaceae)
pyrenaica	EWes GKev SRms

Petrocosmea ✿ (Gesneriaceae)
barbata 'Marion King'	WDib
begoniifolia misapplied	see *P. chrysotricha*
§ *chrysotricha*	SPlb WDib
§ *cryptica*	WAbe WDib
- 'Yumebutai'	WDib
flaccida	WDib
'Fluffer Nutter'	WDib
§ *formosa* 'Crûg's Capricious'	WAbe
forrestii	WAbe WDib
grandiflora misapplied	see *P. thermopuncta*
'Ht-2'	WDib
iodioides ♀H2	WDib
kerrii	WAbe
- 'Crème de Crûg'	WCru
- var. *crinita*	WDib
'Keystone's Angora'	WDib
'Keystone's Bantam'	WDib
'Keystone's Barnswallow'	WDib
'Keystone's Belmont'	WDib
'Keystone's Blue Jay'	WDib
'Keystone's Lafayette'	WDib
'Keystone's Magic'	WDib
aff. *martini* 'Crûgs Capricious'	see *P. formosa* 'Crûg's Capricious'
minor misapplied	see *P. rotundifolia*
parryorum	WDib
'Paul Kroll'	WDib
rosettifolia misapplied	see *P. cryptica*
§ *rotundifolia*	WDib
sericea	WDib
§ *thermopuncta*	WAbe WDib
'Yuki-no-sei'	WDib

Petrophytum (Rosaceae)
caespitosum	GKev MWlw WAbe
cinerascens	WFar
§ *hendersonii*	GArf GKev

Petrorhagia (Caryophyllaceae)
illyrica	SHar
saxifraga ♀H4	CSpe EPfP EPPr SRms

Petroselinum (Apiaceae)
§ *crispum*	CGHo EGren EHet ELan ENfk LCro MHoo MNHC MPri SPoG SRms WKit
- 'Bravour' ♀H6	MHer
- 'Champion Moss Curled'	MBros MCtn SVic WKit
- 'Curlina' ♀H4	LCro
- 'Extra Moss Curled'	LCro
- 'Extra Triple Curled 2' **new**	MNHC
- French	CCBP CGHo EHet ELan ENfk LCro MBros MHer MHoo MNHC MPri SPoG SRms
- 'Italian'	see *P. crispum* var. *neapolitanum*
- 'Laura'PBR	MNHC
- 'Lisette'PBR	LCro MNHC
- 'Moss Curled' ♀H6	CCBP CHby EKin MHoo SRms WKit
§ - var. *neapolitanum*	EGren EHet ELan ENfk LCro MCtn MHoo SPoG SRms SVic WKit
§ - var. *tuberosum*	EHet MCtn SRms SVic
hortense	see *P. crispum*
tuberosum	see *P. crispum* var. *tuberosum*

Petunia (Solanaceae)
AMAZONAS PLUM COCKATOO ('Dpetampluc') (Amazonas Series) **new**	MPri
AMORE QUEEN OF HEARTS ('Damorqueen'PBR) (Amore Series)	MBros MPri MPro

× *atkinsiana* MPro
  (Fortado Series)
    Fortado Burgundy
    Vanilla **new**
- (Fortado Special Series) MPro
    Fortado Special
    Banoffee Pie **new**
- - Fortado Special Purple MPro
    Green Edge **new**
- Pegasus Queen of Hearts LSou
  (Pegasus Series)
- (StarTunia Series) StarTunia MPro
    Blue **new**
- - StarTunia Pink **new** MPro
- 'Storm Lavender' ♀H2 LCro
- Tidal Wave Series LCro
- - Tidal Wave Red Velour LCro MCtn
  ('Pas1085269')
- - 'Tidal Wave Silver' LCro MCtn
axillaris MCtn
- 'Hualco' CSpe
'Back to Black' MPro
Balcony Mix LCro
Bedding Striped Mix LCro
Belinda (Tumbelina Series) MBros
  (d)
Bella (Tumbelina Series) (d) MBros
Black Velvet LCro MBros
  ('Balpevac'^PBR)
Black Velvet Improved MPri
Burgundy Gem (Sweetunia MPri
  Series) **new**
Candyfloss ('Kercan'^PBR) MBros
  (Tumbelina Series) (d)
(Capella Series) Capella MPri
    Hello Yellow
    ('Dpethloylw') **new**
- Capella Rose **new** MPri
Cascadias Rim Magenta MPri
  ('Dcas298'^PBR)
  (Cascadias Series) ♀H2
Crazy Ripple (Tumbelina MBros
  Series)
(Crazytunia Series) MPri
    Crazytunia Cosmic Pink
    ('Wespecracopi') **new**
- Crazytunia Mandeville MPri
  ('Wespecramand')
- Crazytunia Pink Flamingo MPri
  ('Wespecrapifl') **new**
(Designer Series) Designer MPri
    Bridal Blush **new**
- Designer Buzz Purple LSou MBros MPri
  ('Kerbuzzby'^PBR) ♀H2
- Designer Cappuccino **new** LCro
Double Pirouette Series (d) LCro
- 'Double Pirouette Rose' LCro
  (d)
Duo Series MBros
(Easy Wave Series) MBros
    Easy Wave Berry Velour
    ('Pas982903')
- Easy Wave Red Velour LCro
  ('Pas933560')
- Easy Wave Silver LCro
  ('Pas1016992')
exserta CSpe MCtn SPlb
Fanfare Appleblossom MBros
  ('Kerappfan'^PBR)
  (Fanfare Series)
Fantasia Mix LCro
Fiona Flash MPri
  ('Dopetsweefiflas'^PBR)
  (Sweetunia Series)
Frenzy Series MBros
- Frenzy Reflection Mix EGren LCro
GlacierSky MPri
  ('Kleph18370'^PBR)
  (SkyFamily Series)
Inga (Tumbelina Series) (d) MBros
LightningSky MPri
  ('Kleph18389'^PBR)
  (SkyFamily Series)
Margarita ('Kermar') MBros
  (Tumbelina Series)
Maria (Tumbelina Series) (d) MBros
Miss Marvelous MPri
  ('Duepetmimar'^PBR)
  (Sweetunia Series)
MysterySky ('Kleph19440') MPri
  (SkyFamily Series)
NightSky ('Kleph15313') LSou MBros MPri SPoG
  (SkyFamily Series) ♀H2
Ovation Dark Heart MPri
  (Ovation Series)
patagonica EDAr GKev SPlb WAbe
Phantom ('Balpephan'^PBR) MBros
Pinstripe ('Balpepin'^PBR) MBros
Priscilla ('Kerpril'^PBR) LSou MBros MPri MPro
  (Tumbelina Series)
  (d) ♀H2
'Prism Sunshine' MBros
  (Prism Series)
RoyalSky ('Kleph20512') MPri
  (SkyFamily Series)
Shock Wave Deep Purple LCro
  ('Pas933531')
(Sophistica Series) MCtn
    Sophistica Blackberry
    ('Pas933539')
- Sophistica Lime Green MCtn
  ('Pas933349')
(Supertunia Series) MSwo
    Supertunia Vista
    Jazzberry
    ('Wnpesvjaz') **new**
- Supertunia Vista Paradise MSwo
  ('Bbtun98901') **new**
(Surfinia Series) Surfinia Blue LSou MPri
  ('Sunblu')
- Surfinia Blue Topaz MBros
  ('Sunsurfbupa')
- Surfinia Blue Vein LCro MBros
  ('Sunsolos'^PBR)
- Surfinia Burgundy LSou MBros
  ('Keiburtel'^PBR)
- Surfinia Deep Red ('Sunsurf LCro
  Akatora'^PBR) ♀H2
- Surfinia Giant Purple MBros
  ('Sunlapur'^PBR)
- Surfinia Heavenly Blue LSou
  ('Sunsurf Skytatsu'^PBR)
- Surfinia Hot Pink LSou MBros MPri
  ('Sunrovein'^PBR) ♀H2
- Surfinia Hot Red LSou MBros
  ('Sunhore'^PBR)
- Surfinia Impulz Snow LSou MBros MPri
  ('Sunsurfkuri'^PBR) ♀H2
- Surfinia Lagoon Blue Star LSou
  ('Keiperurihem')
- Surfinia Lime LCro MBros
  ('Keiyeul'^PBR)

Philadelphus 517

- SURFINIA PINK VEIN   MBros
  ('Suntosol') ♀H2
- SURFINIA PURPLE   LSou MPri
  ('Sunpurple'PBR) ♀H2
- SURFINIA ROSE VEIN   MBros
  ('Sunrove'PBR)
- SURFINIA SWEET PINK   MBros
  ('Sunsurfmomo'PBR)
- SURFINIA TRAILING BURGUNDY   MPri
  YELLOW PICOTEE
  ('Surf M21062') **new**
- SURFINIA VARIEGATED PURPLE   LSou
  MINI ('Sunpapuhu'PBR)
  (v)
- SURFINIA WHITE ('Kesupite')   LCro
- SURFINIA YELLOW DREAM   MBros
- SUZIE STORM ('Dueswesustor') MPri
  (Sweetunia Series)
- VERANDA AZUR (Veranda   MSwo
  Series) **new**

Peucedanum (Apiaceae)
- *cervaria* 'Purple   CSpe
  Flush' **new**
- *japonicum*   GGro
- *officinale*   CSpe SDix SHor SPlb
- *ostruthium* 'Daphnis' (v)   EAri EBee ECha EWhm LEdu LShi
                                MNrw NLar SBeP WCot WFar
- *rablense*   CSpe ECha EPPr GBin SMHy SPhx
- *verticillare*   CSpe EBee ELan GBin LEdu MBel
                                MCtn MNrw NDov SBeP SDix
                                SMHy SPhx StAn WCot

Pfeiffera (Cactaceae)
- *boliviana*   LCro

Phacelia (Boraginaceae)
- *bolanderi*   GEdr
- *campanularia*   MCtn
- *sericea*   EDAr LShi
- *tanacetifolia*   GJem LCro MCtn

Phaedranassa (Amaryllidaceae)
* *haurii*   WCot
- *viridiflora*   WCot

Phaenocoma (Asteraceae)
- *prolifera*   SPlb

Phaenosperma (Poaceae)
- *globosa*   CSpe ECha GElm SPlb WCot
                                WPGP

Phagnalon (Asteraceae)
- *saxatile*   WHil

Phaiophleps see *Olsynium*
- *nigricans*   see *Sisyrinchium striatum*

Phalaris (Poaceae)
- *arundinacea*   CPud ELin SPlb SVic
- - 'Elegantissima'   see *P. arundinacea* var. *picta* 'Picta'
- - var. *picta*   CBen EHeP ELin MHol NBir NPer
                                SMrm WCAu WFar
- - - 'Arctic Sun' (v)   LBuc LRHS MAsh MHol MMuc
                                SMrm SPoG
- - - 'Aureovariegata' (v)   NPer
- - - 'Feesey' (v)   CMac ECha EPPr EWes LBuc LRHS
                                MAsh MMuc NBid NBro SDix SEND
                                SIvy SMad SPoG SRms
- - - 'Luteopicta' (v)   EPPr MMuc

§ - - 'Picta' (v)   CLil CoPl EBee ELan ELin EPfP
                                LRHS MMuc
- - 'Streamlined' (v)   EPPr
- *canariensis*   MCtn

Phanerophlebia (Dryopteridaceae)
- *caryotidea*   see *Cyrtomium caryotideum*
- *falcata*   see *Cyrtomium falcatum*
- *fortunei*   see *Cyrtomium fortunei*

Pharbitis see *Ipomoea*

Phegopteris (Thelypteridaceae)
§ *connectilis*   CLAP LEdu NHar WAbe
- *decursive-pinnata*   LEdu LRHS MMuc MWlw NLar
                                SEND
- *hexagonoptera*   LEdu SPlb WPGP
- *levingei*   LEdu

Phellodendron (Rutaceae)
- *amurense*   CBcs CMCN IPap LMaj MBlu SEND
                                WJur
- - B&SWJ 11000   WCru
- *japonicum*   WJur
- - B&SWJ 11175   WCru

Phemeranthus (Montiaceae)
- *calycinus*   SBrt
- *sediformis* 'Zoe'   GKev

Pherosphaera (Podocarpaceae)
- *fitzgeraldii*   WPav

Philadelphus ✿ (Hydrangeaceae)
- 'Atlas' (v)   NLar
- 'Avalanche'   CExl MMuc SRms WFar
- 'Beauclerk' ♀H6   CBrac CDoC EPfP SRms WLov WSpi
- 'Belle Étoile' ♀H6   Widely available
- 'Bicolore'   NLar WSpi
- 'Bouquet Blanc'   SGol SRms
- 'Burfordensis'   MMuc SEND WSpi
- *californicus*   see *P. lewisii* subsp. *californicus*
- 'Casa Azul'   EBee SChF WPGP
- *coronarius*   CBcs EPfP LBuc LMaj WFar WSpi
- - 'Aureus' ♀H6   Widely available
- - 'Bowles's Variety'   see *P. coronarius* 'Variegatus'
- - ILLUMINATI TOWER   CBcs
  ('Smnpvg') **new**
§ - - 'Variegatus' (v) ♀H6   CMac EGren ELan EPfP LRHS MAsh
                                NLar SDix SPoG SRms WFar WKif
                                WSpi
- *coulteri*   EBee WPGP
- 'Dainty Lady'PBR   CCps LCro
- 'Dame Blanche' (d)   EGren EGrI ELan EPfP LCro NLar
                                WFar
- *delavayi*   EPfP EPPr NLar WPGP WSpi
- - aff. var. *calvescens*   WCru
  BWJ 8005
- - f. *melanocalyx*   WPGP
- - B&L 12168   EBee WPGP
- - - 'Nyman's Variety' ♀H5   CExl EPfP WKif
- 'Enchantement' (d)   SDix
- 'Erectus'   CSBt EBee ELan ELon EPfP NLar
                                SPoG WHtc WLov WSpi
- 'Fragrant Falls' **new**   LCro SHor
- 'Frosty Morn' (d)   CBcs EBee LRHS LSou MBlu SPoG
- *incanus* B&SWJ 8616   WCru
- 'Innocence' (v) ♀H6   CAgr CExl CMac CTsd CWGN
                                ELan EPfP LRHS MAsh MMuc
                                MPro MSwo NEoE SPad SPoG
                                SRms WFar WLov

'Innocence Variegatus'	see *P.* 'Innocence'
§ **insignis**	CBcs NLar
'Kalina'	NLar
'Karolinka'	NLar
karwinskianus	EBee
- F&M 152	WPGP
'Lemoinei'	CBcs EGren EHeP LRHS SAdn SOrn WFar WHtc WSpi
lewisii	SPhx
§ - subsp. **californicus** B&SWJ 14069 **new**	WCru
- 'Waterton'	ELon WSpi
'Little White Love'	LRHS SGol
maculatus 'Mexican Jewel'	CExl EBee ELan ELon EPfP LEdu SChF SPad WLov WPGP
- 'Sweet Clare' ♀H5	CBcs CSpe EPfP LBom LCro LRHS LSou MMrt MPri SPoG WLov WSpi
madrensis	EBee SChF
- F&M 326	WPGP
- 'Rosemary Brown'	SChF WPGP
'Manteau d'Hermine' (d) ♀H6	Widely available
'Marjorie'	NLar
mexicanus	SPlb
- B&SWJ 10253	WCru
- 'Rose Syringa'	CExl CMHG EBee SBrt WPGP
microphyllus	CBrac CMCN EBee ELan ELon EPfP NLar SPoG WFar WKif
'Minnesota Snowflake' (d)	CBcs EBee EHeP ELan EPfP LCro LRHS LSRN NLar WFar
'Mont Blanc'	CBcs GKin NLar
'Mrs E.L. Robinson' (d)	CMac EPfP LBom LRHS MGos MPri NLar WHtc WLov
myrtoides B&SWJ 10436	WCru
'Natchez' (d)	CMac MBNS MMrt NLar SChF
palmeri	WPGP
'Patricia'	WHtc
PEARLS OF PERFUME ('G15097'PBR) **new**	CBcs LCro
pekinensis	CExl NLar
'Polar Star'	NCth NLar
purpurascens	CExl EBee EPfP EPPr EWes MBlu NLar WCFE WJur WPGP
- BWJ 7540	ESwi WCru
'Purpureomaculatus'	WPGP
'Pyramidal' (d)	CBrac
'Rachel'	CMac
satsumi	NLar
- B&SWJ 10811	WCru
- B&SWJ 11004	WCru
schrenkii B&SWJ 8465	ESwi WCru
sericanthus	NLar
§ 'Silberregen' ♀H6	CMac EHeP ELan ELon EPfP MGos MMuc NLar SHor SPoG SRms WFar
SILVER SHOWERS	see *P.* 'Silberregen'
'Snowbelle' (d)	CBcs CDoC EBee EHeP ELan EPfP LBom LCro LRHS MAsh MPri MPro NLar SPoG SRms WHtc WLov WSpi
'Souvenir de Billiard'	see *P. insignis*
'Starbright'PBR	CBcs EBee EGren ELan EPfP MMrt NLar SAth SMad SPoG
subcanus L 524	CExl
'Sybille' ♀H5	CMac EPfP MSwo SRms WKif WSpi
tomentosus	WPGP
- B&SWJ 2707	WCru
- GWJ 9215	WCru
'Virginal' (d)	Widely available
'Voie Lactée'	NLar WSpi
WHITE ROCK ('Pekphil') ♀H6	CMac NLar
'Yellow Cab'	MAsh
'Yellow Hill'	CMac EPfP NLar

Philesia (Philesiaceae)

buxifolia	see *P. magellanica*
§ **magellanica**	CExl CRHN WAbe WCru

Philibertia (Apocynaceae)

§ **stipitata**	EAri

Phillyrea (Oleaceae)

angustifolia	CBcs CMCN CSpe CTsd CWnw EBee ELan EPfP ERom LMaj LRHS LTop MGos NLar SArc SEND SHor WPGP WReH
- f. **rosmarinifolia**	CCoa EPfP
- - 'French Fries'	EBee ELan WPGP
decora	see *Osmanthus decorus*
§ **latifolia**	CBcs CCoa CDoC EBee ELan EPfP EUrb LMaj LTop SArc SEND SHor SWor WJur WPGP
media	see *P. latifolia*

Philodendron (Araceae)

'Atom'	EHap LBom LCro NTro
billietiae new	NTro
bipennifolium	NPlm SPlb
bipinnatifidum ♀H2	CDoC EHap LBom LWaG MCtn NHrt SEND
- 'Cum Laude'	EHap LBom
- GOLDEN XANADU ('Twyph0007'PBR)	LCro
- 'Little Hope'PBR	EHap LBom
- 'Xanadu-II' **new**	EHap
§ 'Birkin' (v)	LBom LCro NTro
'Black Cardinal'	LCro NTro
brandtianum new	EHap NTro
burle-marxii new	EHap NTro
* 'Cobra' (v)	EHap LBom LCro NTro
corcovadense	NTro
elegans new	EHap NTro
erubescens 'Red Emerald'	EHap LCro NHrt
'Florida Beauty' **new**	LInT
'Florida Ghost' (v) **new**	LInT
'Fun Bun'	LBom LCro
gloriosum	EHap LBom NTro
'Green Princess'	LCro NHrt
hastatum	CDoC EHap LBom LCro NHrt
hederaceum	EHap NTro
§ - 'Brasil' (v)	CDoC EGren LBom LCro LWaG MPri NHrt NTro
- var. **hederaceum** ♀H1b	CDoC EHap LBom LCro LInT LWaG MPri NHrt
- - 'Green Emerald'	EHap
- - 'Lime'	LCro NTro
- - 'Micans Lime'	EHap LCro
'Imperial Green'	LCro LWaG NHrt
'Imperial Red'	LBom LCro LWaG NHrt
'Lemon Lime'	EHap LCro
mamei new	NTro
martianum new	NTro
mayoi new	NTro
melanochrysum	LBom LCro
mexicanum new	NTro
'Mini Santiago' **new**	NTro
'Moonlight'	LCro
'Narrow Escape' **new**	EHap
'Painted Lady'	LBom LCro
'Paraiso Verde' (v) **new**	LInT
pedatum	EHap
'Pink Princess' (v)	EHap LBom LCro LInT NHrt NTro SPre

Phlox 519

plowmanii **new**	EHap
'Prince of Orange'	EHap LCro NHrt NTro
scandens 'Brasil'	see *P. hederaceum* 'Brasil'
'Silver Queen'	EHap LCro
squamiferum	EHap LBom
tortum	EHap LBom LCro LInT NTro
verrucosum	LBom
- INCENSI	EHap
('Ppipve007'^{PBR}) **new**	
- 'Mini' **new**	NTro
'White Knight' (v) **new**	LInT
WHITE MEASURE	see *P.* 'Birkin'
'White Princess' (v)	LCro NTro
'Winterbourn' **new**	EHap
xanadu	LBom LCro LWaG NHrt SAth SPlb

Philotheca (Rutaceae)

§ *myoporoides*	CBcs EGrI
- 'Flower Girl Pink'	LCro
- 'Flower Girl White'	LCro LRHS

Phlebodium (Polypodiaceae)

§ *aureum* ♀H1b	CDoC CSpe LCro SBig SPlb WCot
- var. *areolatum*	EShb WCot
- 'Blue Star'	ISha LBom LCro LWaG NHrt
- DAVANA ('Raadphle01'^{PBR})	EShb LCro NHrt
- 'Glaucum'	CSpe WCot
pseudoaureum ♀H3	LEdu SEND WCot
- 'Virginia Blue'	LEdu

Phlebodium × *Pyrrosia* see × *Phlebosia*

× *Phlebosia* (Polypodiaceae)

'Nicolas Diamond'^{PBR}	WCot

Phleum (Poaceae)

hirsutum	WCot
phleoides	LRHS

Phlomis (Lamiaceae)

alpina	see *Phlomoides alpina*
* *anatolica*	ELan LRHS
atropurpurea	see *Phlomoides atropurpurea*
bourgaei	CWnw EBee LRHS
- NJM 12.008	WPGP
bovei subsp. *maroccana*	ESgI SEND SNoN
cashmeriana	CDor EBee EPfP MHoo NQui WCFE WSpi
chrysophylla ♀H5	ECha ELan EPfP LRHS MAsh WCFE WMal WSpi
cretica	SVen WMal
'Edward Bowles'	ECha EPfP NBid NLar SEND SNoN WCru WSpi
* 'Elliot's Variety'	CExl
fruticosa ♀H5	Widely available
aff. *fruticosa*	WSpi
grandiflora	EBee MCtn MNrw SEND
- NJM 10.014	WPGP
- 'Lloyd's Silver' ♀H5	CCoa ELan LRHS MAsh SHar
italica	CBcs CCoa CMac CSde CWnw EBee ECha EGren ELan EPfP ESgI GMaP LCro LRHS LSRN MAsh MMrt MNrw MPri NBir SDix SEND SPoG SRkn SRms WCFE WCot WFar WKif WTre
lanata	CCoa CSde EPfP WCFE
'Le Chat'	WMal
'Le Sud'	WCot
leucophracta	SVen
longifolia	CDoC CMac EPfP MNrw SDix SEND WCot WFar WPGP

- var. *bailanica* ♀H4	ELan EPfP LRHS SMrm
- var. *longifolia*	WSpi
'Marina'	WMal
'Orangette'	ESgI WMal
purpurea	CWal CWnw ELan EPfP MAsh NBir SEND SHor WCot
I - 'Alba'	EAri WCot
§ *russeliana* ♀H6	Widely available
- PAB 7444	LEdu
- 'Dappled Shade' (v)	WCot
samia Boiss.	see *P. russeliana*
samia L.	CMac ESgI LBar MNrw NBir NGdn NLar SBrt SNoN WMal
- JMT	EPPr
- 'Green Glory'	WCot
taurica	SEND
'Toob'	SBrt WPGP
tuberosa	see *Phlomoides tuberosa*
viscosa misapplied	see *P. russeliana*

Phlomoides (Lamiaceae)

§ *alpina*	SPlb
§ *atropurpurea* BWJ 7922	GGro WCru
maximowiczii	EBee
§ *tuberosa*	CBcs EAri EGren ELan EPfP EPPr ESgI GJos LEdu LSRN LSto MCtn MNrw MPnt NLar SDix StAn WCAu WTre
- 'Amazone' ♀H5	Widely available
- 'Bronze Flamingo'	CMac EPfP ESgI LBar LRHS MBNS MHol MNrw MPnt MPro NLar SMad SPoG SRms WSpi

Phlox ✿ (Polemoniaceae)

adsurgens 'Alba'	WFar
- 'Wagon Wheel'	SRms WFar
amplifolia	WCot
- 'Apanatschi'	WCot
- 'Augenstern'	NCth WFar
- GOLIATH ('Versgolia')	NCth XFar
- 'Hercules'	XFar
× *arendsii* 'Andrew'	WCot
- 'Autumn's Pink Explosion'	WCot
- 'Babyface'	LRHS NGdn NLar
- 'Casablanca'	NDov
- 'Dylan'	WCot
- 'Gary'	WCot
- 'Hesperis'	CMiW CSpe ELon ERCP LEdu LRHS MNrw NBir NDov NLar SHar SMHy SPel WCAu WTor
- 'Lilac Star'	SHar
- 'Luc's Lilac' ♀H7	CMHG EPPr MHol NDov NSti WCAu WCot
§ - 'Miss Jill' (Spring Pearl Series)	EBee ELan EPfP WCot
§ - 'Miss Karen' (Spring Pearl Series)	EBee
§ - 'Miss Margie' (Spring Pearl Series)	EGrI
§ - 'Miss Mary' (Spring Pearl Series) ♀H7	EBee ELan ELon EPfP LRHS NLar
§ - 'Miss Wilma' (Spring Pearl Series)	EBee ELan EPfP
- 'Paul'	MNrw WCot
- 'Utopia' ♀H7	CSpe ELon GBin NDov WCot
austromontana	EPot GKev
'Bedazzled Lavender'	LRHS
bifida	EDAr
- 'Alba'	ELan EPot
- 'Ralph Haywood'	EPot MNrw
'Bořanovice'	EPot WAbe

borealis	see *P. sibirica* subsp. *borealis*	'Fashionably Early Princess'	LBar LCro LSou NCth
caespitosa	EDAr EWes	'Fashionably Lavender Ice'	LBar LCro LRHS LSou NCth SMad
- subsp. *pulvinata*	see *P. pulvinata*	'Flare'	see *P. paniculata* 'Neon Flare' (Neon Series)
- 'Zigeunerblut'	ECha EDAr EPot MNrw MWlw WAbe	'Forncett Twilight'	SMHy
canadensis	see *P. divaricata*	§ *glaberrima* 'Bill Baker' ♀H6	ECha EGrI EMor EPPr GElm GMaP LRHS MAsh NBir NSti SBeP SPel WCAu WFar WKif
carolina 'Bill Baker'	see *P. glaberrima* 'Bill Baker'	
- 'Magnificence'	EWes SMad SPlb WCot	
- 'Miss Lingard' ♀H6	CDor LSto NBir NGdn NLar NSti NWbg WCot	- 'Morris Berd'	WFar
'Chattahoochee'	see *P. divaricata* subsp. *laphamii* 'Chattahoochee'	- 'Griff Blink'	NLar
		- 'Jeff's Pink'	NCth NLar
'Daniel's Cushion'	see *P. subulata* 'McDaniel's Cushion'	- 'Kelly's Eye' ♀H5	LRHS LShi NBir SPoG
		kelseyi 'Lemhi Purple'	WAbe
§ *divaricata* ♀H5	LRHS SPlb	- 'Rosette'	LRHS
- 'Blue Dreams'	MNrw WFar	Light Pink Flame ('Bareleven' PBR)	SPoG WCot
- 'Blue Moon'	CWCL ELon EWes LSou NBro NLar WFar	*maculata*	EGrI
- 'Blue Perfume'	EBee LCro	- 'Alba'	CMHG EGrI SAko
- 'Clouds of Perfume'	Widely available	- 'Alpha' ♀H6	EBee ECha EMor ERCP GMaP LEdu LRHS MArl MPro NLar SPoG WCAu WFar
- 'Dirigo Ice'	MPnt NLar	
- 'Fuller's White'	CWCL	
- subsp. *laphamii*	EBee EWes NLar WFar	- Avalanche	see *P. maculata* 'Schneelawine'
§ - - 'Chattahoochee' ♀H5	CBcs CSpe EGren ELan EMor EPot EWes GKev LBar LCro MMrt MNrw MPro NDov NLar SPoG WCAu WSpi	- 'Delta'	EMor LRHS MPro NLar SAko SHar SRkn
- - - 'Chattahoochee Variegated' (v)	MPro	- 'Natascha' ♀H7	CMac EBee ELon EMor EWes GMaP LRHS LSRN MArl MPro NCth NGdn NLar SMad SRkn WCAu WFar WHil
- 'May Breeze'	CBWd CWCL ELon GElm GKev GMaP LBar MBel MNrw MPnt MPro SHar SPoG WFar	
		- 'Omega' ♀H6	CMac ECha EGren EMor LEdu LRHS LShi NCth NGdn NLar WCAu WFar WSpi
- 'White Perfume'	CTsd CWCL EBee ELan EPfP EWes GPSL LRHS LSto MArl MBel MMrt NDov NLar SHar SPoG WFar	
		- 'Princess Sturdza' ♀H6	NDov SDix
douglasii	SRms	- 'Reine du Jour'	MHol NDov SPeP
- 'Boothman's Variety' ♀H6	ECha SRms	- 'Rosalinde'	GBin LRHS NLar SAko SPoG WCAu
- 'Crackerjack' ♀H6	EPot ESgI GMaP LCro LRHS NBir SLee SPoG SRot WIce	§ - 'Schneelawine'	EMor MPro SPlb WCAu WSpi
		'Minnie Pearl'	EWes NDov WCot
- 'Eva'	EDAr EPot GArf GMaP GQue LCro LRHS LSRN NBir NLar SLee WFar	*nana*	GKev
		nivalis 'Nivea'	EPot WAbe
- 'Georg Arends'	WFar	(Opening Act Series)	WHil
- 'Ice Mountain'	EDAr EGren ELan EPot LRHS MWlw SPoG SRot WFar	'Opening Act Blush' **new**	
		- 'Opening Act Pink-a-Dot'	LBar
- 'J.A. Hibberson'	EPot EWes	- 'Opening Act Ultrapink'	LBar WHil
- 'Lilac Cloud'	MPro	*paniculata*	CFis CWal ELon EPPr LEdu MCtn NBid WCot WPGP WTre
- 'Napoleon'	GArf	
- 'Ochsenblut'	EPot GArf LRHS NLar SRms WIce	- (Adessa Series) Adessa Orange	MPro NLar
- 'Red Admiral' ♀H6	EGren ELan EPot GEdr GMaP LRHS WFar	- - Adessa Pink Star	LRHS MidI NLar
		- - Adessa Red	NLar
- 'Rosea'	EGrI ELan LCro MMuc SLee SRot WIce	- - Adessa Rose Eye	NLar
		- - Adessa Special Fire	MPro NLar
- 'Sprite'	SRms	- - Adessa Special Lilac Twist	MidI
- 'Tycoon'	see *P. subulata* 'Tamaongalei'	
- 'Violet Queen'	GArf	- - Adessa Special Purple Star	MidI MPro NLar
- 'Waterloo'	EPot LRHS	
I - 'White Admiral'	ELan LRHS LSRN	- - Adessa White	MidI MPro NLar
I *drummondii* 'Brilliant'	MCtn	- Adinda ('Geeradinda')	NCth
- 'Cherry Caramel'	LCro MCtn	- var. *alba*	ECha SMHy WCot
- 'Crème Brûlée'	LCro	- 'Alba Grandiflora' ♀H7	MNrw WCAu WCot WHoo
- *grandiflora alba*	MCtn	- 'Alexandra' PBR	LCro NCth
I - 'Phlox of Sheep'	MCtn	- 'All in One'	NLar
- Popstars (mixed)	LSou MBros	- 'Amethyst' misapplied	see *P. paniculata* 'Lilac Time'
- Tapestry Mixed **new**	MCtn	- 'Amethyst' ambig.	EGrI
- 'Twinkling Beauty'	MCtn	- 'Amethyst' Foerster	ELon NBir NLar WCAu
'Fancy Feelings' (Feelings Series)	NLar	- 'Anastasia' PBR	NCth
		- 'Balmoral'	CMac
(Fashionably Early Series)		- (Bambini Series)	CWGN LRHS
'Fashionably Early Crystal'	EGren LBar LCro	Bambini Candy Crush ('Verscan' PBR)	
- 'Fashionably Early Flamingo'	EGren LBar LSou MPri NCth	- - Bambini Desire ('Versde' PBR)	CWGN WHil

- - Bambini Lucky Lilac ('Versluck')	WHil	
- - Bambini Primadonna ('Verpri'^{PBR})	WHil	
- - Bambini Sweet Tart ('Versweta')	NCth	
- 'Becky Towe'^{PBR} (v) ♀^{H7}	MHol MNrw SPoG WCot	
- 'Blind Lion'^{PBR}	XFar	
- 'Blue Boy'	CBWd EBee EGren ELan EPfP GMaP NBir WCAu WFar	
- 'Blue Evening'	EBee LCro NLar	
- Blue Flame	MNrw	
- 'Blue Paradise'	Widely available	
- 'Blushing Bride'	MCtn SRms	
- 'Border Gem'	CBcs CMac ELon MHol NLar SDix WCAu WCot	
- 'Bosvigo Pink'	ELon SHar	
- 'Brigadier'	MHol MNrw SRms	
- 'Bright Eyes'	CBcs EGren EGrI ELon EPfP GBin LCro LEdu LSou LSRN LSto MArl MAvo MBel MHer MHol MMuc MPro MSwo NBir NGdn NLar SDix SRkn WCAu WFar WSpi	
- 'Burgi'	SDix SMHy	
- 'Butonik'	ELon GBin LEdu	
- 'Cardinal'	NCth NDov	
- 'Caroline van den Berg'	SRms	
- 'Charlotte'	WGoo	
- 'Cherry Cream'^{PBR}	EGren MPri	
- 'Chintz'	SRms	
- 'Cleopatra'^{PBR}	NLar XFar	
- Compact Lilac	see *P. paniculata* (Sweet Summer Series) Sweet Summer Favourite	
- Compact Rose White	see *P. paniculata* (Sweet Summer Series) Sweet Summer Candy	
- 'Cool Best'	NDov	
- 'Cool Water'	NLar	
- Coral Flame ('Barsixtytwo'^{PBR}) (Flame Series)	CMac EUrb LRHS NLar SMrm SPoG WHil	
- 'Coral Queen'	SRms	
- 'Cosmopolitan'^{PBR}	EGren EPfP MHol MNrw	
- Count Zeppelin	see *P. paniculata* 'Graf Zeppelin'	
- 'Cover Girl' (Garden Girls Series)	LBar	
- 'Danielle' ♀^{H7}	SHar	
- 'Darwin's Choice'	see *P. paniculata* 'Norah Leigh'	
- 'David' ♀^{H7}	Widely available	
- 'David's Lavender' ♀^{H7}	ELon LRHS WSpi	
- 'Delilah'^{PBR}	CWGN NLar	
- 'Discovery'	EWes LCro SHar WCAu	
- 'Dodo Hanbury-Forbes'	MNrw	
- 'Doghouse Pink'	SDix	
- 'Dresden China'	SHar	
§ - 'Düsterlohe'	CCps ELon EPfP ERCP GBin LRHS MHer MSwo NBir NDov NGdn NLar NSti SPel SRkn SRms WCAu WCot WSpi	
- 'Eclaireur' misapplied	see *P. paniculata* 'Düsterlohe'	
- 'Eden's Flash'	CElw	
- 'Elizabeth Arden'	ELon NLar	
- 'Elizabeth Campbell'	EPPr	
- 'Europa'	EBee ELan EPfP NBir NGdn NLar WCAu	
- 'Eva Cullum' ♀^{H7}	EBee ELan ELon EPfP GBin GMaP LRHS MAsh MHol WCAu WCot WFar	
- 'Eventide'	CMac EBee LSto MHol MNrw WFar	
- (Famous Series) Famous Cerise ('Appofamcer'^{PBR})	ELan EPfP LRHS MPri MPro	
- - Famous Light Purple ('Appofalp'^{PBR})	EPfP LRHS MPri MPro	
- - Famous Pink **new**	MPro	
- - Famous Pink Dark Eye ('Appofapide')	ELan LRHS Midl MPri	
- - Famous Pink Eye Improved	LRHS MPro	
- - Famous Purple ('Appotwpu'^{PBR})	ELan LRHS MPri MPro	
- - Famous White ('Appotwwh'^{PBR})	ELan LRHS Midl MPri MPro	
- - Famous White Eye ('Appofamwe'^{PBR})	ELan LRHS Midl MPri MPro	
- 'Feniks'	MNrw	
- (Flame Series) Flame Light Blue	LRHS NLar WHil	
- - Flame Watermelon **new**	WHil	
- 'Franz Schubert' ♀^{H7}	CDor ELan ELon EPfP ERCP GBin LCro LRHS LSto MArl MAvo MSwo NBir NGdn NSti WCAu WCot WFar WTor	
§ - 'Frau Alfred von Mauthner'	EBee ELon	
- 'Fujiyama'	see *P. paniculata* 'Mount Fuji'	
- 'Geisha's Blush'	SMHy	
- 'Glamour Girl'^{PBR} (Garden Girls Series)	LBar	
- 'Goldmine'^{PBR} (v)	NSti SPoG SRms WCot	
§ - 'Graf Zeppelin'	EBee MMuc NLar SRms	
- 'Green Lion'^{PBR}	XFar	
- 'Grenadine Dream'^{PBR}	CWGN EGrI LRHS	
- 'Grey Lady' ♀^{H7}	MNrw SHar WGoo	
- 'Harlequin' (v)	CWGN ECha WCot	
- 'Herbstwalzer'	ELon SDix WCot WTre	
- 'Ice Cream'	CWGN ESgI NCth	
- 'Imogen's Blush'	WCot	
- 'Iris'	MNrw SRms WCot	
- 'Jade' (Neon Series)	GQue LEdu MNrw NLar WCot	
- 'Jeana'	LBar MNrw	
- 'Jeff's Blue'	WCot	
- 'Julia'	NCth	
§ - 'Juliglut'	LRHS WCot	
- July Glow	see *P. paniculata* 'Juliglut'	
- Ka-Pow Series	EGren LBuc MSCN	
- - Ka-Pow Lavender ('Balkapolav'^{PBR})	EGren MPro	
- - Ka-Pow Pink ('Balkapopink'^{PBR})	EGren LBar MPro	
- - Ka-Pow Purple ('Balkapopur'^{PBR})	EGren LBar MPro WHil	
- - Ka-Pow Soft Pink ('Balkaposin')	LBar WHil	
- 'Katherine'	NLar	
- 'Katie'	MAvo	
- 'Katja'	EGrI NLar	
- 'Kirchenfürst'	CElw GElm LCro NBir SMHy WCAu WFar	
- 'Königin der Nacht' (Zauberflöte Series) ♀^{H7}	EBlo	
- 'Lady Clare'	SRms	
- 'Landhochzeit'	WFar	
- 'Larissa'^{PBR}	LCro LRHS MNrw	
- 'Laura'	see *P. paniculata* 'Uspekh'	
§ - 'Lavendelwolke'	EPPr NBir WCot	
- Lavender Cloud	see *P. paniculata* 'Lavendelwolke'	
- 'Lavender Lady'	WCot	
- 'Le Mahdi' ♀^{H7}	NLar SRms	
- 'Lichtspel'	NDov	
- 'Light Brigade'	WCot	
§ - 'Lilac Time'	EGren GMaP LRHS NLar WSpi	
- 'Little Boy'	CElw ELon MNrw NLar	
- 'Little Laura'	CFis LSRN MAsh MHol MNrw NGdn NLar NWbg WCot WHoo	

- 'Little Princess'	ELon
- 'Little Sara'	NDov
- 'Logan Black'	SDix SHar WOld
- 'Long Border Mauve'	SDix
- MAGICAL	see *P. paniculata* Sweet Summer Series
- 'Manoir d'Hézèques'	WCot
- 'Marchant's Darkest'	SMHy
- 'Mardi Gras'	ELan EPfP
- 'Margery Fish'	SDix SPel
- 'Mary Christine' (v)	NBid
- 'Maude Stella Dagley'	WCot
- 'Mies Copijn'	NLar
- 'Mike's Favourite'	EBee EGren ESgI
- 'Milly van Hoboken'	WKif
- 'Miss Elie' ♀H7	ELon
- 'Miss Holland'	ELon
- 'Miss Jill'	see *P. × arendsii* 'Miss Jill' (Spring Pearl Series)
- 'Miss Karen'	see *P. × arendsii* 'Miss Karen' (Spring Pearl Series)
- 'Miss Kelly'	NLar
- 'Miss Margie'	see *P. × arendsii* 'Miss Margie' (Spring Pearl Series)
- 'Miss Mary'	see *P. × arendsii* 'Miss Mary' (Spring Pearl Series)
- 'Miss Pepper' ♀H7	ELon MMuc NCth NGdn NLar WCAu
- 'Miss Universe'	ELon
- 'Miss Wilma'	see *P. × arendsii* 'Miss Wilma' (Spring Pearl Series)
- 'Modern Art'	MNrw
- 'Monica Lynden-Bell' ♀H7	CBcs CCBP CDor CWGN EBee ECha EGren ELon ERCP GBin GMaP GQue LSto MArl MBel Midl MMuc MNrw NBid NSti WCot
- 'Mother of Pearl' ♀H7	WSpi
§ - 'Mount Fuji'	CDor CElw CMac ECha EPfP ESgI GBin GQue LCro LRHS LShi LSRN LSto MArl MAsh MHol MMuc NBir NDov NLar NSti SRms WCAu WCot WKif WSpi
- 'Mount Fujiyama'	see *P. paniculata* 'Mount Fuji'
- 'Mrs A.E. Jeans'	SRms
§ - 'Neon Flare' (Neon Series)	CWGN MHol NCth
- 'Newbird'	SRms
- 'Nicky'	see *P. paniculata* 'Düsterlohe'
- 'Nirvana'	NCth
§ - 'Norah Leigh' (v) ♀H7	CBcs CMac CMHG CWGN EBee ECha ELan ELon EPfP EWes GKev LRHS MArl MBel MHer MPie NLar NPer NSti NWbg SDix SPoG SRms WCAu WCot WFar WOld
- 'Oljenka'	ELon NCth
- 'Olympus' (v)	NEoE XFar
- 'Orange Perfection'	see *P. paniculata* 'Prince of Orange'
- 'Orchid Green' **new**	XFar
- 'Othello'	MArl MAsh MHol NGdn NSti WHoo
- 'Otley Choice'	EGrI NSti
- 'Otley Purple'	MHer
- 'Party Girl' (Garden Girls Series)	LBar
- 'Pastorale'	WCot
- 'P.D. Williams'	WCot
- (Peacock Series)	LRHS
PEACOCK LILAC ♀H7	
- - PEACOCK NEON PURPLE ♀H7	LRHS
- - PEACOCK PURPLE BICOLOR	SPoG
- 'Peppermint Twist'	CWGN GKev MNrw NCth SOrN WFar
- 'Picasso'	CWGN NLar
- 'Pina Colada'PBR	CWGN EGren LRHS MPri NCth WFar
- PINK EYE FLAME ('Barthirtyfive'PBR) ♀H7	SPoG SRms WHil
- PINK FLAME ('Bartwelve'PBR) (Flame Series)	EGren EPfP LRHS NLar SRms WHil
- 'Pink Lady'PBR	WFar
- 'Pink Posie' (v)	WCot
- PINK RED EYE FLAME ('Barthirtyfour') (Flame Series)	SPoG
- 'Pinky Hill'	NLar
- 'Popeye'	LRHS NCth NLar WCot
§ - 'Prince of Orange' ♀H7	CBcs EBee EGren LRHS MArl MAsh MAvo MHol SRms WCAu WCot
- 'Prospero' ♀H7	CElw CSpe NBid
- PURPLE EYE FLAME ('Barthirtythree'PBR) (Flame Series) ♀H7	NLar WCot WFar
- 'Purple Kiss'PBR	CWGN EGren LRHS MHol Midl MPri NCth WFar
- 'Rainbow'	NLar
- 'Rainbow Dancer'	NCth
- 'Raving Beauty'	ERCP NCth
- 'Red Caribbean'	EGren LRHS MPri NLar
- 'Red Feelings' (Feelings Series)	ESgI LSto MArl
- 'Red Flame'	CWGN MNrw WFar
- 'Red Riding Hood'	see *P. × arendsii* 'Miss Mary' (Spring Pearl Series)
- 'Rembrandt'	ELon EPfP LCro WCAu XFar
- 'Rijnstroom'	CBcs EBee ECha ELon LRHS NLar WBrk WCAu
- 'Robert Poore'	ERCP
- 'Roberta'	LCro NLar
- 'Rosa Pastell' ♀H7	CDor CSpe ELon GBin GKev GMaP LRHS SHar SHor SMrm WCot
- 'Rosanne'	MNrw
- 'Rowie'	NBid NLar
- 'Roze Casablanca'	NDov
- 'Rumyanyi'	MNrw
- 'Russkaya Krasavitsa'	MNrw
- 'Sandringham'	NBir
- 'Shockwave' (v)	WCot
- 'Skylight'	SDix
- 'Speed Limit 45'	WCot
- 'Spitfire'	see *P. paniculata* 'Frau Alfred von Mauthner'
- 'Starfire' ♀H7	CBcs CMac EBee EGren ELan ELon EPfP GMaP LCro LRHS MArl MAvo MPie NSti SDix SPel SPoG SRms WCAu WCot
I - 'Stars and Stripes'	NCth
- 'Sterling Brocade' (v)	WCot
- 'Strawberry Daiquiri'PBR	EGren WFar
- (Super Ka-Pow Series) SUPER KA-POW CORAL ('Balsukaco')	LBar LSou
- - SUPER KA-POW FUCHSIA ('Balsukafus'PBR) **new**	LBar
- - SUPER KA-POW LAVENDER ('Balsukalav'PBR)	LBar
- - SUPER KA-POW PINK ('Balsukapin'PBR)	LBar LSou
- - SUPER KA-POW WHITE ('Balsukawi'PBR)	LBar MPro
- SWEET MELODY	see *P. paniculata* (Sweet Summer Series) SWEET SUMMER MELODY
§ - (Sweet Summer Series) SWEET SUMMER CANDY ('Ditosdre'PBR)	LRHS XFar

- - Sweet Summer Dream ('Ditomdre'PBR)	MPri NLar WCAu XFar	- - Younique White ('Verswhite')	LEdu WFar
- - Sweet Summer Fantasy ('Ditopur'PBR)	LRHS MPri NCth WCAu XFar	- Zenobia ('Geerzenobia')	NCth
§ - - Sweet Summer Favourite ('Ditomfav'PBR) ⚥H7	LRHS NLar WCAu	- 'Zhukovskii'	MNrw
- - Sweet Summer Festival ('Ditoros'PBR)	WCAu	'Peppermint Candy'	WFar
- - Sweet Summer Fireball	LRHS MPri	'Petticoat'	EPot
§ - - Sweet Summer Melody ('Ditosmel'PBR)	WCAu	× *procumbens* 'Variegata' (v)	SLee
- - Sweet Summer Ocean ('Ditoocean'PBR)	CWGN NCth XFar	§ *pulvinata*	SPlb WAbe
- - Sweet Summer Purple White	see *P. paniculata* (Sweet Summer Series) Sweet Summer Temptation	Purple Flame ('Barfourteen'PBR) (Flame Series)	EPfP LRHS SRms WCAu WFar WHil
- - Sweet Summer Queen ('Ditoran'PBR)	MPri NLar	'Rose Bouquet' (Earlibeauty Series)	CMiW MPri
- - Sweet Summer Rose	LRHS	'Sherbet Cocktail'PBR	CWGN
- - Sweet Summer Sensation ('Ditosse'PBR)	EGren LRHS MPri	§ *sibirica* subsp. *borealis*	EPot WAbe
- - Sweet Summer Snow ('Ditosnow'PBR)	WCAu XFar	'Sileniflora'	EPot WAbe
- - Sweet Summer Surprise ('Ditomsur'PBR)	LRHS MPri NCth WCAu	'Smokey'	NCth
§ - - Sweet Summer Temptation ('Ditostem'PBR)	EGren LRHS NCth	*stolonifera*	MNrw
- - Sweet Summer Wine ('Ditowine'PBR)	NLar	I - 'Alba'	EPfP LBar NLar WFar
- 'Swizzle'	CWGN WFar	- 'Ariane'	MNrw
- 'Tenor'	EBee EPfP GBin LSto MArl MAsh NLar SRms WCAu	- 'Blue Ridge' ⚥H6	CExl EBee ECha ELan EPfP EWld LBar NLar SRms WFar
- 'Tequila Sunrise'PBR	MNrw	- 'Fran's Purple'	MNrw WBrk WFar WKif WMal
- 'The King' ⚥H7	EGrl NLar WSpi	- 'Home Fires'	ELan LBar LRHS NLar SPlb
- 'Tiara'PBR (d)	NGdn WCot	- 'Pink Ridge'	WFar
- 'Twister'	MAsh MNrw WFar	- 'Purpurea'	ELan EPfP
- 'Uptown Girl' (Garden Girls Series)	LBar	*subulata* 'Alexander's Surprise'	EPot NBir
§ - 'Uspekh' ⚥H7	CDor CMac EBee EBlo EPfP EPPr ESgI EWes GQue LRHS MArl MHer MNrw NCth NGdn NLar NSti SRms WCAu WSpi	- 'Amazing Grace'	EPfP EPot EWes LCro LRHS LSto MPro NBir SPoG SRms WCav WFar
- 'Vintage Wine'	MNrw	- 'Apple Blossom'	SPoG SRms
- 'Violetta Gloriosa'	WFar	- 'Atropurpurea'	EPfP LRHS MPro SPoG WTor
- 'Volcano Betty'	MNrw	- 'Bavaria'	EGren EPfP EPot LBar LCro LRHS MHol MPro SRms WFar WTor
- 'Watermelon Punch'	WFar	- 'Blue Eyes'	see *P. subulata* 'Oakington Blue Eyes'
- 'Wendy House'	LEdu	- 'Blue Saucer'	EPot
- 'White Admiral' ⚥H7	CBcs CElw EBee ELan EPfP ESgI GArf GKev GMaP LRHS MAsh MNrw NLar SRms WCAu WFar WTor	- 'Bonita'	EPot LRHS
- White Flame ('Bartwentynine'PBR) (Flame Series) ⚥H7	CDor CWGN EGren LBuc WCot	- 'Bressingham Blue Eyes'	see *P. subulata* 'Oakington Blue Eyes'
- 'Willow Lodge'	SHar	- 'Candy Stripe'	see *P. subulata* 'Tamaongalei'
- 'Windsor'	EBee EMor EPfP MArl MAsh NLar SRms WCAu	- 'Coral Eye'	EGren ELan LBar MHol
- (Younique Series) Younique Bicolor ('Versbicolor')	WFar	- 'Drumm'	see *P. subulata* 'Tamaongalei'
- - Younique Mauve ('Versmauve')	LCro	- 'Drummons Pink'	EGren LBar MPro
- - Younique Old Blue ('Versoldblue')	CDor CWGN ELon NCth WFar	- (Early Spring Series) Early Spring Purple ('Barseventyfour'PBR)	EPfP
- - Younique Old Cerise ('Verscerise')	CDor NLar WFar	- - Early Spring White ('Barseventythree'PBR)	GKev
- - Younique Old Pink ('Versoldpink')	WFar	- 'Emerald Cushion'	EGrl ELan EPfP LRHS LSto NQui WCav WTor
- - Younique Old Purple ('Versorange')	WFar	- 'Emerald Cushion Blue'	EGren ELan EPfP LBar LRHS MHol MMrt MPro NBir SPlb SPoG SRot WFar
- - Younique Orange ('Versorange')	LRHS	- 'Eye Candy'	ELan EPfP SLee
- - Younique Trendy ('Verstrendy')	NCth	- (Fabulous Series) Fabulous Blue Violet ('Florphfabv')	MPro
		- - Fabulous Dark Rose Eye ('Flophfadr')	LRHS
		- - Fabulous Rose ('Florphfaro')	EPfP LRHS MPro
		- - Fabulous White ('Florphfawh')	EPfP LRHS MPro
		- 'Fort Hill'	ELan LRHS
		- 'G.F.Wilson'	see *P. subulata* 'Lilacina'
		- 'Holly'	EPot
		- 'Kimono'	see *P. subulata* 'Tamaongalei'
		§ - 'Lilacina'	ECha EPfP MBel
		§ - 'Maischnee'	SPlb

- 'Marjorie'	EGrI GArf GKev MHer NBir SPoG		- subsp. *hookeri*	CBcs CCht CDoC CSBt EBee EGren
- May Snow	see *P. subulata* 'Maischnee'		'Cream Delight' (v) ♀H4	EGrI EHeP EPfP LRHS LSRN MAsh MGos NLar SPeP WFar
§ - 'McDaniel's Cushion' ♀H6	ECha EGren ELan EPfP EPot GKev GMaP LRHS LShi LSto MAsh MHol MMuc MPro SLee SPlb SPoG StAn WCAu WCav WFar WIce WTor		- - 'Tricolor' (v) ♀H4	CBcs CBrac CDoC CDTJ CKit CMac CSBt CWal CWnw EBee EGren ELan EUrb LCro LRHS MGos SArc SPoG SRms WCha WFar
- 'Mikado'	see *P. subulata* 'Tamaongalei'		'Dark Delight'	CBcs LRHS
- 'Millstream Daphne'	ELan		'Dazzler' (v)	MAsh
- 'Nettleton Variation' (v)	EPot EWes MMuc SPoG SRms WFar		'Duet' (v) ♀H3	EGren ELan NLar SEND
§ - 'Oakington Blue Eyes'	SRms		'Dusky Chief'	CSBt CWal
- 'Purple Beauty'	EGren ELan EPfP GKev GMaP LRHS MPro SPoG WFar		'Evening Glow' (v)	CBcs CDoC CKit EGren EHeP EPfP LRHS LSRN MAsh MGos SPoG SRms WCha WFar
- 'Red Wings' ♀H6	EPfP LRHS SRms			
- 'Samson'	EPot LRHS MPro SRot		'Firebird'	LSRN
- 'Scarlet Flame'	EGren EGrI ELan EPot LBar LCro MPro NWbg SLee StAn		'Flamingo' (v)	CBcs CDoC CDTJ CKit EGren EHeP EPfP LBom LRHS MHol NPlm SFol SPoG WFar
- 'Snow Queen'	see *P. subulata* 'Maischnee'			
- 'Snowflake'	LCro LShi		'Gold Ray' (v)	CKit CTsd CWnw EGren EPfP LBom LRHS MAsh MHed SFol SPoG WCha WFar
§ - 'Tamaongalei'	EDAr EGren ELan EPot ESgI EWes GKev GMaP LRHS MHol MMuc MNrw MPro NBir SLee SPoG SRot WFar WIce WTor			
			'Gold Sword' (v)	CBcs CMac CSBt EUrb
- 'Temiskaming'	EWes MBel SRms		'Golden Alison'	see *P.* 'Alison Blackman'
- 'White Delight'	EGren ELan EPfP LRHS LSto MPro NWbg SPoG WCAu		'Green Sword'	EHeP WCha
			'Jack Spratt' (v)	EGren
'Swirly Burly'	NLar		'Jester' (v)	CBcs CBrac CCht CDoC CMac CSBt CTsd CWnw EGren ELan EPfP EUrb LBom LCro LRHS LSto MAsh MGos MHed SAth SFol SPoG SRkn SRms WCha WFar
Violet Flame ('Barsixtyone'PBR) (Flame Series)	CDor EUrb LRHS MHol NBir NLar SPoG SRkn WCot			
'Violet Pinwheels'	WFar			
White Eye Flame ('Barsixty'PBR) (Flame Series)	CDor CWGN LRHS NLar SPoG SRkn WHil		'Licorice and Lime'PBR	CBcs CKit SArc WFar
			'Limelight'	SEND
'Zwergenteppich'	EPfP LRHS SPoG WFar WTor	§	'Maori Chief' (v)	CSBt MAsh WFar
		§	'Maori Maiden' (v)	CBcs CDoC CKit CWnw EGren EHeP EPfP LRHS MHed SRms WCha WFar
Phoenix ✿ (*Arecaceae*)				
andamanensis S.Barrow	NPlm	§	'Maori Queen' (v)	CBcs CDoC CDTJ CKit CMac EGren EHeP EPfP LBom LCro LRHS MAsh MGos MHed SAth SEND WCha WFar
canariensis ♀H2	CDoC EOli EPfP ERom EUrb LCro LRHS MPri NHrt NPlm SArc SAth SBig SChr SEND SMad SPlb SPoG			
dactylifera (F)	NPlm	§	'Maori Sunrise' (v)	CBcs CBrac CDoC CMac EGrI EHeP EPfP IArd LCro LRHS LSRN MGos SPoG SRms
loureiroi	NPlm			
roebelenii ♀H1b	LCro LDro NPlm SBig SPlb		'Margaret Jones'PBR	CWnw LRHS
rupicola	NPlm		'Pink Panther' (v)	CBcs CWnw EGren EHeP EPfP LRHS LSRN SPoG SRms WFar
theophrasti	NPlm SArc			
			'Pink Stripe' (v)	CBcs CSBt CWal CWnw EGren EGrI EPfP LCro LRHS MAsh MGos NPlm SPeP SPoG WCha WFar
Phormium (*Asphodelaceae*)				
§ 'Alison Blackman'PBR	CBcs EBee LRHS LSRN MAsh MGos SBig SEND SFol SPoG WFar		'Platt's Black'	CBcs CKit CWnw EBee EPfP LBom LCro LRHS MAsh MGos NBir NPlm SArc SBig SPeP SPoG WCha WFar
'Amazing Red'	NBir SPoG			
'Apricot Queen' (v)	CBcs CDoC CSBt EBee EGren EHeP EPfP LCro LRHS LSRN MGos Midl NLar SBig SEND SPoG WCha WFar			
			'Rainbow Chief'	see *P.* 'Maori Chief'
			'Rainbow Maiden'	see *P.* 'Maori Maiden'
Back in Black ('Seilack'PBR)	CBcs CBrac CCht EHeP EUrb LBom NLar WFar		'Rainbow Queen'	see *P.* 'Maori Queen'
			'Rainbow Sunrise'	see *P.* 'Maori Sunrise'
'Black Adder'PBR	EGren EPfP MAsh NWbg SPoG		'Red Sensation'	CBrac CDoC EGren EPfP LSRN WCha
'Black Rage'	CBcs			
Black Velvet ('Seivel'PBR)	CBcs CCht CSpe CTsd EPfP EUrb LBom LRHS SEND WCot WFar		'Sundowner' (v) ♀H3	CBcs CMac CSBt CWnw EBee EGren EGrI EPfP LCro LRHS MAsh MGos MHed MHtn Midl NBir SEND SFol SPoG WCha
'Blondie'PBR (v)	EUrb LBom LCro Midl WFar			
'Bronze Baby'	CBcs CDoC CKit CSBt EBee EGren EHeP ELan EPfP LBom LSRN MAsh MGos MHol NLar NPlm SBig SPoG WCha WFar			
			'Sunset' (v)	CSBt
			'Surfer' (v)	CDoC LRHS
			'Surfer Bronze'	WCha
Brown Sugar ('Rogph1'PBR)	LRHS MPri SEND		***tenax***	CAgr CBcs CBrac CKit CMac EHeP EUrb GArf LCro LSto LWaG MCtn MGos MPri NGdn SArc SAth SEND SFol SPlb SPoG StAn WFar
'Buckland Ruby'	EBee			
'Chocomint'PBR	CDoC CWnw LCro LRHS SBig SPoG			
			- 'All Black'	MGos
colensoi	see *P. cookianum*		- 'Croce di Malta'	SArc
§ ***cookianum***	SArc WPGP			

Phygelius 525

– 'Joker' (v)	CBcs CDoC EHeP LRHS NLar SPoG	*prionophylla*	EUrb
– Purpureum Group ♀H5	CBrac CDoC CKit CMac EBee EGren EGrI EHeP ELan EPfP ERom IDun LRHS LSto MPri NLar SBig SEND SFol SPlb WCha WFar	'Redstart'	CMac ELan LRHS MMuc NLar SEND WFar
		§ *serratifolia*	NLar SArc SEND WFar WPGP
		– var. *ardisiifolia* NMWJ 14513	WCru
– 'Tiny Tiger' (v)	EPfP	I – 'Compacta'	MPri
– 'Tom Thumb'	NLar	– Crunchy ('Rev100'PBR)	ELan EPfP LBuc LRHS MAsh NLar SPoG
– 'Variegatum' (v) ♀H5	CDoC CDTJ CWnw EGren EPfP IDun LRHS MGos MPri NPlm SArc SAth SBig SEND SFol SRms WCha	– Curly Fantasy ('Kolcurl'PBR)	NLar
		– 'Jenny'	NLarWFar
– 'Veneer'PBR (v)	CBcs	– Pink Crispy ('Oploo5'PBR)	CAco CWnw ELan LCro LRHS LSRN MAsh SPoG WCha WFar
– 'Yellow Queen' (v)	WFar		
'Wings of Gold'	LRHS	*serrulata*	see *P. serratifolia*
'Yellow Wave' (v) ♀H4	Widely available	Super Hedge ('Branpara'PBR)	WFar
		Super Red ('Parsur')	CSBt LRHS MHed NLar

Photinia ❀ (*Rosaceae*)

amphidoxa new	WJur	*villosa*	WJur
arbutifolia	see *Heteromeles salicifolia*	– B&SWJ 8665	WCru
beauverdiana	WJurWPGP	– var. *coreana*	CBcs EBee WPGP
– var. *notabilis*	CBcs	– – B&SWJ 8789	WCru
davidiana	CMac CMCN EBee ELan SRms SVen	– var. *laevis*	WPGP
– 'Dwarf Ness'	GKev	– – B&SWJ 8877	WCru
– 'Palette' (v)	CBrac CMac LRHS MMrt NLar NPip SGol SPoG SRms WFar WMat	– f. *maximowicziana*	CDoC NLar
		* – var. *zollingeri* B&SWJ 8903	WCru
– 'Thunder's Dwarf'	WPGP		
– var. *undulata* 'Fructu Luteo'	CMac SEND		

Phragmites (*Poaceae*)

– – 'Prostrata'	CMac NLar	from Sichuan, China	EPPr
'Diamond Red'	CDoC	§ *australis*	CBen CHab CLil CPud CWat ELin MCtn NMir SVic WMAq
× *fraseri*	CBTr LBom		
I – 'Atropurpurea Nana'	CBcs CDoC EPfP MPri	– subsp. *australis* var. *striatopictus*	EPPr
– 'Birmingham'	CMac SRms		
– 'Canivily' ♀H5	CEnd CWnw LCro LSto MGos NLar	– – 'Variegatus' (v)	CBen CLil CWat EPPr MMuc NBir SEND
– 'Carré Rouge'	CBrac CBTr CWnw EGren ELan LMaj LRHS MAsh MHed MPri MPro SArc SAth SEWo SNig SOrn SPoG WReH	– subsp. *humilis*	CHab
		– subsp. *pseudodonax*	EPPr
		communis	see *P. australis*
– Chico ('Br2011')	LCro LRHS LSou NLar WFar	*karka* 'Candy Stripe' (v)	CLil
– 'Dicker Tony'	NLar		

Phuopsis (*Rubiaceae*)

– 'Little Fenna'PBR	LSou NLar	§ *stylosa*	CCBP EBee ECha EGrI ELan GBin GMaP GPSL GQue LCro LSto MHer MHol MMuc NBid NBir NBro NSti SEND SRms WCAu
– 'Little Red Robin'	Widely available		
– Louise ('Mclarlou'PBR) (v)	CBcs CBTr CSBt EBee ELan EPfP EUrb LBuc LCro LRHS LSou MGos MPri NLar SAth WFar WHtc		
		– 'Purpurea'	ECha MNrw MWIw WCAu WFar
– Magical Volcano ('Kolmvoca'PBR)	EBee ELan LRHS MAsh MPri MSCN NCth NLar SArc SGol SPoG WFar		

Phycella (*Amaryllidaceae*)

– Pink Marble ('Cassini') (v) ♀H5	CBcs CBrac CBTr CDoC CEnd EBee EGren ELan EPfP LCro LRHS LSRN MAsh MGos NLar SPoG SRms WCha WCot WFar WHtc WSpi	*cyrtanthoides*	WCot

Phygelius (*Scrophulariaceae*)

– 'Red Devil'	LBom	*aequalis* 'Aureus'	see *P. aequalis* 'Yellow Trumpet'
– 'Red Robin' ♀H5	Widely available	– 'Cream Trumpet'	see *P. aequalis* 'Yellow Trumpet'
– 'Red Robin Variegated' (v)	ERom	– 'Indian Chief'	see *P.* × *rectus* 'African Queen'
– 'Red Select'	EBee EGren MAsh MHed WFar	– 'Sani Pass'	CMac ELon SIvy SPlb
– 'Robusta'	CMac EGren EPfP SRms	– 'Trewidden Pink' ♀H5	EAri ELan LRHS NLar
I – 'Robusta Compacta'	CCVT LSRN WCha	§ – 'Yellow Trumpet' ♀H5	CMac EHeP GKev LSRN MAsh SEND
– 'Scarlet Blaze'	LBom LRHS MPri		
glabra	SArc	Candy Drops Salmon Orange ('Kerphysalm'PBR) (Candy Drops Series)	SRms
§ – 'Parfait' (v)	CMac		
– 'Pink Lady'	see *P. glabra* 'Parfait'	*capensis*	SRms
– 'Rubens'	EPfP LRHS MAsh	– 'Coccineus'	EHeP
– 'Variegata'	see *P. glabra* 'Parfait'	Cherry Ripe ('Blacher'PBR)	EUrb GBin
glomerata Rehder & E.H.Wilson	SBrt WPGP	– 'Golden Gate'	see *P. aequalis* 'Yellow Trumpet'
		'Midas Touch'	ELon
lasiogyna	CMCN	'Passionate'PBR	NLar
lucida	WCru	§ × *rectus* 'African Queen' ♀H5	CMHG ELan EPfP MMrt MPie NBir NGdn SEND SPlb WKif
microphylla	CBcs		
– B&SWJ 11837	WCru	– (Colorburst Series) Colorburst Deep Red ('Tnphycdr')	EGren LBar LRHS MMrt MPro
– HWJ 564	WCru		
niitakayamensis	SEND WJur		NWbg
– CWJ 12245	WCru		

Phygelius

– – Colorburst Orange ('Tnphyco')	EGren LBar MPro NWbg WFar	
– – Colorburst Rose ('Tnphycro')	EGren LBar LSou MPro WFar	
– – Colorburst White ('Tnphycw')	CoPl EGren LBar MMrt MPro NWbg	
– – Colorburst Yellow ('Tnphycy')	EGren LBar MPro NWbg	
– 'Devil's Tears' ♀H5	CBcs NLar SEND WPnP	
– 'Ivory Twist'	NLar	
– 'Jodie Southon'	ELon EsgI LSou WCot	
– 'Moonraker'	CAby CBcs ELan ELon EPfP LRHS MAsh NGdn SEND SPlb SRms	
– New Sensation ('Blaphy'PBR)	SRms	
– 'Raspberry Swirl'	ELon	
– 'Rory'PBR	SRms	
– 'Salmon Leap' ♀H5	CBcs EArl ELan ELon EPfP EUrb LSRN MGos NLar SPlb SRms	
– (Somerford Funfair Series) Somerford Funfair Coral ('Yapcor')	CMac CoPl EGrI MAsh NLar SRkn	
– – Somerford Funfair Cream ('Yapcre')	MBros MPro SPoG	
– – Somerford Funfair Orange ('Yapor')	CoPl EUrb LRHS MAsh MPri MPro SRms	
– – Somerford Funfair Wine ('Yapwin')	CAby EGrI ELan MAsh MPri MPro NBir SPoG	
– – Somerford Funfair Yellow ('Yapyel')	CoPl MAsh	
§ – 'Winchester Fanfare'	MGos NLar	
– 'Winton Fanfare'	see *P.* × *rectus* 'Winchester Fanfare'	

Phyla (Verbenaceae)

§ *nodiflora*	ECha ELin SRms WJek
– 'Alba'	SEND

× *Phylliopsis* (Ericaceae)

'Coppelia' ♀H5	GArf GKev
hillieri	GArf
– 'Askival'	GArf
'Hobgoblin'	GArf
'Mermaid'	GArf
'Puck'	GArf

Phyllitis see *Asplenium*

Phyllocladus (Podocarpaceae)

trichomanoides	LRHS
var. *alpinus* 'Blue Blades'	
– – 'Highland Lass'	LRHS MGos

Phyllodoce (Ericaceae)

aleutica	GKev
breweri	GArf
caerulea ♀H7	GArf
– *japonica*	see *P. nipponica*
– 'Murray Lyon'	GArf
× *intermedia* 'Drummondii'	GArf
– 'Fred Stoker'	GArf
§ *nipponica*	GKev

× *Phyllosasa* (Poaceae)

tranquillans	MMuc SEND
– 'Shiroshima'	CDoC CDTJ EUrb MAvo MBrN MMuc MWht SEND SWor

Phyllostachys ❀ (Poaceae)

sp.	WCha
angusta	MWht
arcana 'Luteosulcata'	MMuc MWht
§ *atrovaginata*	MWht
– 'Green Perfume'	WCha
aurea ♀H5	Widely available
– 'Albovariegata' (v)	MWht SPoG
– 'Holochrysa'	CDTJ CJun MWht NLar
– 'Koi'	CDTJ MWht SAth SBGi SBig
aureocaulis	see *P. aureosulcata* f. *aureocaulis*, *P. vivax* f. *aureocaulis*
aureosulcata	CAco NLar
§ – f. *aureocaulis*	CBcs CBdn CJun EArl EGren EPfP EUrb LCro LRHS LSRN MAvo MGos MWht NLar SArc SAth SBGi SBig SEWo SPoG SWor WCha
– 'Lama Tempel'	CDTJ CJun
– f. *spectabilis* ♀H5	CBcs CBdn CDoC CWnw EGren ELan ERom EUrb LCro LRHS LSRN MBrN MGos MPri MWht NLar NPlm SArc SAth SBGi SBig SPoG SWor WCha WCot WFar WPGP
bambusoides 'Allgold'	see *P. bambusoides* 'Holochrysa'
– 'Castillonii Inversa'	MWht WPGP
§ – 'Holochrysa' ♀H5	CDTJ EGren MMuc MWht NPlm SBig SEND SWor
– f. *lacrima-deae*	CDTJ
– 'Tanakae'	CDTJ
bissetii ♀H4	CAgr CBcs CCVT CDoC EArl EGren EPfP EUrb LCro LRHS MAsh MAvo MBrN MGos MMuc MPri MWht NLar NPlm SArc SAth SBGi SBig SEND SPlb SWor WCha WFar
congesta misapplied	see *P. atrovaginata*
decora	MMuc MWht
dulcis	MWht SBGi SBig
§ *edulis*	CAgr SArc SBGi SPlb
– f. *pubescens*	see *P. edulis*
flexuosa	CBcs MWht SBGi
glauca	EPfP MWht SWor
– f. *yunzhu*	MWht
heteroclada	WCot
– 'Solid Stem' misapplied	see *P. purpurata* 'Straight Stem'
– var. *pubescens*	see *P. edulis*
humilis	EUrb MWht SAth
iridescens ♀H5	MWht
kwangsiensis	MWht
mannii	MWht
nigra ♀H5	Widely available
– 'Boryana'	CEnd MMuc MWht NLar SBGi SEND
– 'Hale'	MWht
– f. *henonis* ♀H5	MMuc MWht NLar SEND
– 'Megurochiku'	MWht
– f. *nigra*	SBGi SWor
– f. *punctata*	MAvo MMuc SEND SWor
nuda	MWht
– f. *localis*	MWht
parvifolia	MWht NLar
praecox	MWht SBGi
propinqua	MWht
§ *purpurata* 'Straight Stem'	MWht
rubromarginata	MWht
stimulosa	MWht
sulphurea 'Houzeau'	MMuc SEND
– 'Sulphurea'	see *P. sulphurea* f. *sulphurea*
– f. *sulphurea*	NPlm
violascens	CAgr MWht
viridiglaucescens	CAgr CDTJ MMuc MWht NPlm SBGi SEND WCot

vivax
§ - f. *aureocaulis* ♀H5   MWht NLar SAth SBGi SBig WCha
                            CAgr CCVT CDoC CEnd EPfP
                            EUrb LEdu LRHS LSRN MGos
                            MMuc MWht NLar NPlm SBig
                            SEND SWor WPGP
- - 'Huangwenzhu'   CDTJ MWht SWor
* - 'Katrin'   LEdu

Phymatosorus (Polypodiaceae)
diversifolius   see *Microsorum diversifolium*

Phymosia (Malvaceae)
§ *umbellata*   EAri EBee SEle WOld
- 'Blood of Pan'   EBee MBlu SChF WPGP

Phyodina see *Callisia*

Physalis (Solanaceae)
alkekengi ♀H7   EPfP NBir StAn WJur
- var. *franchetii*   CBcs CMac CWal EBee EGren
                             ELan EPfP LCro LRHS LShi NBir
                             NBro SPoG SRms WFar WOld
- - dwarf   MCtn NLar
- - 'Gigantea'   CAby ECha EUrb IDun MCtn Midl
                             NLar SPlb WFar
- - 'Gnome'   see *P. alkekengi* var. *franchetii*
                             'Zwerg'
- - monstrous form   LEdu SMad WCot WPGP
- - 'Variegata' (v)   EPPr EWes LEdu MMuc WPGP
§ - - 'Zwerg'   CDor EDAr SEdi
- 'Halloween King'   EBee NLar
- 'Halloween Queen'   NLar
edulis   see *P. peruviana*
§ *peruviana* (F)   NGKo SPlb SPre SVic
philadelphica 'Purple   MCtn
  de Milpa'
'Verdelino'   MCtn

Physaria (Brassicaceae)
alpina   GEdr SPlb

Physocarpus ✿ (Rosaceae)
capitatus 'Tilden Park'   EBee EGren
LITTLE DEVIL   see *P. opulifolius* 'Donna May'
opulifolius   EGrI
- ALL BLACK ('Minall2'^PBR) CBcs CWGN EBee LRHS MAsh
                             NCth WCha WCot
- ALL RED ('Minalco')   GJos NEoE NLar WLov WNPC
- AMBER JUBILEE   CBcs CDoC CSpe LCro LRHS MBNS
  ('Jefam'^PBR) ♀H7   MPri NEoE SRms WLov
- ANGEL GOLD   CDoC EPfP LRHS MPri SPoG
  ('Minange'^PBR) ♀H7
- 'Anny's Gold'^PBR   SRms WFar
- 'Brown Sugar'   WNPC
- 'Burning Embers' ♀H7   CDoC EGrI EPfP LRHS SRms
- 'Chameleon'   NEoE
- COPPERTINA   see *P. opulifolius* DIABLE D'OR
- 'Dart's Gold' ♀H7   CBcs CDoC CEnd CMac EGren
                             EGrI EHeP ELan EPfP ERom GArf
                             LCro LRHS LSto MAsh MGos MSwo
                             SGol SNig SPoG SRms WCot WFar
                             WSpi
§ - DIABLE D'OR ('Mindia'^PBR) CDoC CEnd CMCN CoPl EBee EPfP
                             LCro LSRN MAsh MBlu MGos NOra
                             SGol WCha WLov
- 'Diabolo'   Widely available
§ - 'Donna May'^PBR   EPfP LRHS MAsh NEoE SArc WFar
                             WHtc
- FIREBRAND ('Hyfbrand')   NEoE
§ - LADY IN RED   Widely available
  ('Tuilad'^PBR) ♀H7

- LITTLE ANGEL   CSBt CWGN EGren LCro LRHS
  ('Hoogi016'^PBR)   LSou MSCN SPoG WCha
- LITTLE DEVIL   see *P. opulifolius* 'Donna May'
- LITTLE JOKER   LSou MBlu NLar
  ('Hoogi041'^PBR)
§ - 'Luteus'   CoPl EHeP
- MAGIC BALL ('Lp1'^PBR)   NCth NLar NWbg WNPC
- MIDNIGHT   CBcs EGren EPfP LRHS NLar WFar
  ('Jonight'^PBR) ♀H7
- 'Nugget'   NLit
- PANTHER ('N5'^PBR)   CWGN ELan WNPC
- PURPLE HORIZON   CSBt
  ('Kapdar 2') **new**
- RASPBERRY LEMONADE   ELan LSou NCth WNPC
  ('Zleye12')
- 'Red Baron'   EGren MPro NCth NLar WFar
- RUBY SPICE   see *P. opulifolius* LADY IN RED
- SUMMER MOON ('Tuimon')   NEoE NLar WFar
- SUMMER WINE   CDoC EBee EGren ELan EPfP LRHS
  ('Seward'^PBR)   NLar WSpi
- SWEET CHERRY TEA   ELan LSou WNPC
  ('Zlebic5') **new**
- SWEET DREAMS   WNPC
  ('Kapdar 1') **new**
- TINY WINE ('Smpotw'^PBR)   EPfP MMrt NLar SPoG
- TINY WINE GOLD   LRHS SPoG
  ('Smnpotwg'^PBR)
ribesifolius 'Aureus'   see *P. opulifolius* 'Luteus'

Physochlaina (Solanaceae)
orientalis   CSpe GEdr WCot

Physoplexis (Campanulaceae)
§ *comosa* ♀H6   EWld

Physostegia (Lamiaceae)
§ *virginiana*   CBen CWal CWat ELin GMaP LShi
                             MBel SRms WKif
- 'Alba'   CMac CWnw EBee ELon EMor EPfP
                             GMaP LEdu LRHS LSto MBel NBir
                             SHar SPlb StAn
- 'Autumn Carnival'^PBR   NLar
§ - 'Crown of Snow'   CLil EPfP LShi MCtn SBea WTre
- 'Crystal Peak White'   EGren LBar LCro LRHS Midl MPri
                             MPro NLar WFar
- 'Grandiflora'   WTre
- 'Miss Manners'   CBcs EBee EPfP MArl MPie NCth
                             NGdn NLar
- 'Pink Manners'   NLar
- 'Red Beauty'   LBar NLar
- 'Rose Crown'   MCtn
- 'Rose Queen'   EMor WFar
- 'Rosea'   EPfP GJos NCou NGdn SPoG WFar
                             WHrl
- SCHNEEKRONE   see *P. virginiana* 'Crown of Snow'
- 'Snow Queen'   see *P. virginiana* 'Summer Snow'
§ - var. *speciosa* 'Bouquet CFis CLil CMac CMHG EBee ECha
  Rose'   EPfP LBar LEdu LRHS LSto MArl MHol
                             NBir NLar SRms StAn WCAu WFar
- - ROSE BOUQUET   see *P. virginiana* var. *speciosa*
                             'Bouquet Rose'
- - 'Variegata' (v)   CLil CMac ELan LBar NBir NGdn
                             NLar SBea SMrm SPeP SPoG SRms
                             WCAu WCot WFar
§ - 'Summer Snow' ♀H7   CBcs ELan LBar MHol NLar SRms
                             WCAu WCot
- 'Vivid' ♀H7   CCBP CMac EBee ECha ELan EPfP
                             LSto MArl MHer MNrw MPie MPro
                             NLar NWbg SMrm SPlb SRms
                             WCAu WCav WCot
- 'Wassenhove'   SMrm

Phyteuma (Campanulaceae)
comosum	see *Physoplexis comosa*
halleri	see *P. ovatum*
nigrum	GEdr NBid SBrt
§ **ovatum**	SPlb
scheuchzeri	CAby ECha EDAr ELan EPfP MMrt SPad SRms WIce
spicatum	NBro

Phytolacca (Phytolaccaceae)
acinosa	CCBP CExI EAri EWld WHil WJun
- HWJ 647	WCru
§ **americana**	EAri EGrI ESwi EWld LShi MCtn MHer MPie SEND SPlb SRms WHil WJun
- B&SWJ 8817A	WCru
- B&SWJ 12743	ESwi
- gold-leaved **new**	WJun
- 'Silberstein' (v)	EAri WFar WJun
bogotensis	WCru
B&SWJ 14221	
clavigera	see *P. polyandra*
decandra	see *P. americana*
dioica	SPlb WJur
esculenta	LEdu
icosandra 'Laca Boom'	EUrb
- Purpurascens Group	SPel WFar
- - B&SWJ 11251	WCru WFar
japonica	EAri WHil
- B&SWJ 3005	GGro WCru
- B&SWJ 3522	WCru
'Laka Boom'	EWld
§ **polyandra**	EGrI EUrb GGro NBid NBro SRms

Picea ✿ (Pinaceae)
§ **abies**	CAco CBTr CCVT CLnd CMac EHeP IPap LBuc MCtn MMuc MNHC SPoG WHtc WMou WRjT
- 'Aarburgh'	CAco
- 'Acrocona' ♀H7	CAco MAsh NLar
- 'Argentospica' (v)	CAco
- 'Aurea'	CAco
- 'Aurea Magnifica'	CAco
- 'Chub'	CAco
- 'Cincinnata'	CAco
- 'Cobra'	CAco
- Compacta Group	CAco
- 'Cranstonii'	CAco
I - 'Cruenta'	CAco
- 'Cupressina'	CAco MAsh
- 'Dáblice'	CAco
- 'Diedorfiana'	CAco
- 'Dundaga'	CAco
- 'Echiniformis'	CAco
- 'Elegantissima'	CAco
- 'Excelsa'	see *P. abies*
- 'Finedonensis'	CAco
- 'Formánek'	CAco MBlu
- 'Frohburg'	CAco CWnw LRHS NLar
- 'Glimra'	CAco
- 'Globosa'	CAco
- 'Gold Drift'	CAco NLar
- 'Hystrix'	MGos
- 'Inversa' ♀H7	CAco CWnw MBlu NLar
- 'J.W. Daisy's White'	see *P. glauca* var. *albertiana* 'J.W. Daisy's White'
- 'Kámon'	CAco
- 'Lithuanian Snake'	CAco
- 'Little Gem' ♀H7	ELan LCro MAsh MGos NLar
- LITTLE SANTA ('Dougart12'PBR)	NLar
- 'Loreley'	CAco
- 'Lubecensis'	CAco
- 'Lucky Strike'	CAco CWnw NLar
- 'Maxwellii'	CAco
- 'Nana Compacta'	MAsh
- 'Nidiformis' ♀H7	CAco CMac CMen MGos SRms
- 'Ohlendorffii'	CAco MAsh
- 'Pachyphylla'	CAco
- 'Parviformis'	CAco
- 'Pasmas' **new**	NLar
- 'Pendula'	CAco
- 'Pumila'	WCFE
- 'Pumila Nigra'	CAco
- 'Pusch'	CAco
- 'Razzle' (v)	NLar
- 'Reflexa'	CAco
- 'Remontii'	NLar
- 'Repens'	CAco
- 'Roseospicata'	CAco
- 'Rothenhausii'	CAco
- 'Rubra Spicata'	CAco
- 'Rydal' ♀H7	CAco MAsh SArc
- 'Tompa'	CAco
- 'Tuka Puka'	CAco
- 'Vermont Gold'	NLar
- 'Virgata'	CAco
I - 'Virgata Aurea'	CAco
I - 'Virgata Glauca'	CAco
- 'Weeping Blue'	CAco
- 'Wild Strawberry'PBR **new**	NLar
- WILL'S DWARF	see *P. abies* 'Wills Zwerg'
§ - 'Wills Zwerg'	CAco ELan NLar
- 'Ylivska Snake'	CAco
alcoquiana	CAco
§ - var. **alcoquiana**	CAco
asperata	CAco
- glaucous-leaved	CAco
bicolor	see *P. alcoquiana* var. *alcoquiana*
brachytyla	CAco
- var. **brachytyla**	CAco
breweriana ♀H6	CAco GKin IPap MBlu MGos NLar SSta
- 'Emerald Midget'	CAco
chihuahuana	CAco
crassifolia	CAco
engelmannii	CAco
- 'Blue Magoo'	CAco EUrb NLar
- 'Bush's Lace'	CAco
- Glauca Group	CAco
- 'Jasper'	CAco NLar
- 'Lace'	NLar
- 'Lobo'	CAco
- subsp. **mexicana**	CAco
- - 'Pervana'	CAco
- 'Snake'	NLar
- 'Tomschke'	CAco
farreri	CAco WPGP
glauca	CAco
- var. **albertiana**	CAco
- - ALBERTA BLUE ('Haal')	CAco
- - 'Alberta Globe' ♀H7	CAco CBrac ELan EPfP GKev GKin LCro LRHS MAsh MGos SPoG
- - 'Conica' ♀H7	CAco CBcs CBrac CMac CSBt EGren ELan EPfP EUrb LCro LRHS MAsh MGos MMuc MPri MPro SArc SPoG SRms
§ - - 'J.W. Daisy's White' ♀H7	CBcs ELan EPfP GKin LCro LRHS MGos NLar SPoG
- - 'Laurin' ♀H7	CAco

	- - 'Lilliput'	EPfP LRHS SPoG		- 'Białobok'	CAco
	- - 'Piccolo'	NLar		- 'Blue Diamond'^PBR	CAco LMaj SPoG
	- - 'Sander's Blue'	CAco GKin MAsh SPoG		- 'Blue Pearl'	CAco
	- 'Arneson's Blue Variegated' (v)	MGos		- 'Corbet'	NLar
	- 'Biesenthaler Frühling'	LRHS		- 'Edith' ♀H7	CAco LRHS NLar NPip WMat
	- 'Cecilia'	CAco		- 'Erich Frahm'	CAco LCro MAsh NLar NPip SPoG WCha WMat
	- 'December'^PBR	CAco		- 'Fat Albert' ♀H7	CAco EGren EPfP LMaj LRHS SPoG WCha
	- 'Eagle Rock'	NLar			
	- 'Echiniformis' ♀H7	CAco		- Glauca Group	CAco CBrac CCVT EHeP IPap MPro SPoG
	- 'Goldilocks'	CAco			
	- 'Jalako Gold'	CAco ELan		- - 'Barabits' Blue'	CAco
I	- 'Julian Potts Monstrosa'	NLar		- - 'Bizon Blue'	CAco
	- 'Pardubicky WB' **new**	NLar		- - 'Blue Totem'	CAco
	- 'Pendula'	CAco EUrb		- - 'Glauca Pendula'	CAco
	- PERFECTA ('Hb07')^PBR	CAco EGren LRHS	I	- - 'Globosa' ♀H7	CAco CBcs LRHS MAsh NLar SPoG WCha
	- 'Rainbow's End' (v)	CAco LRHS MGos MPri NLar			
	- 'Speedy'	CAco		- - 'Hoopsii' ♀H7	CAco CCVT EPfP EUrb GKin LCro LMaj LRHS MGos NLar NPip SPoG WCha WMat
	- 'Sun on the Sky'^PBR	CAco EPfP LRHS			
	- 'Super Green'	CAco			
	- 'Zuckerhut'	CAco		- - 'Iseli Fastigiate'	CAco GKin LRHS SPoG WMat
	glehnii	CAco		- - 'Khaibab'	CAco
	jezoensis	CAco CMen	§	- - 'Koster'	CAco EPfP LRHS SPoG
	- subsp. *hondoensis*	CMen		- - 'Misty Blue'	CAco
	- 'Landis'	CAco		- - 'Oldenburg'	CAco WCha
	- 'Mariánské Làznĕ'	NLar		- - 'Thomsen'	CAco
	- 'Yatsabusa'	CMen		- - 'Virgata'	CAco
	koraiensis	CAco		- 'Globe'	CMen MGos
	kosteri 'Glauca'	see *P. pungens* (Glauca Group) 'Koster'		- 'Horizontalis Glauca'	CAco
				- 'Iseli Foxtail'	CAco NLar
	koyamae	CAco NLar		- 'Karaten'	LCro
	- 'Bedgebury Blue'	CAco		- 'Maigold' (v)	CAco MAsh NLar
	- 'Bedgebury Cascade'	CAco		- 'Mecki'	NLar
	likiangensis	CAco		- 'Novák'	CAco
	- var. *balfouriana*	see *P. likiangensis* var. *rubescens*		- 'Ökrös'	CAco
§	- var. *rubescens*	CAco NLar		- 'Omega'	CAco
	mariana	CAco MAsh		- 'Pali'	CAco
	- 'Nana' ♀H7	CAco CMac CMen EPfP MGos MMuc SPoG		- 'Prostrate Blue Mist'	CAco MAsh
				- 'Royal Blue'	CAco
	× *mariorika* 'Machala'	CAco		- 'Silvanus Conica'	CAco
	meyeri	CAco		- 'Super Blue Seedling'	CAco EGren ELan
	obovata	CAco		- 'The Blues'	CAco NLar
I	- 'Glauca'	CAco		- 'Waldbrunn'	CAco
	omorika ♀H7	CAco CBcs CCVT CMCN EGren EHeP ELan EWhm IPap LBuc LSto MCtn MMuc NLar SSta WFar		- 'Waterfall'	CAco
				purpurea	CAco
				retroflexa	CAco
	- 'Cinderella'	NLar		× *saaghii*	CAco
	- 'De Ruyter'	LRHS NLar		*schrenkiana*	CAco
	- 'Golden Rain'	see *P. omorika* 'Wolski Gold'		*sitchensis*	CAco IPap MAsh
	- 'Karel'	CAco CWnw MGos		- 'Foxtail'	CAco
	- 'Linda'	NLar		- 'Foxy Lady'	CAco
	- 'Nana' ♀H7	CAco		- 'Glenmasson'	NLar
	- 'Pendula' ♀H7	CAco MBlu SSta		- 'Nana'	CAco
	- 'Pendula Bruns'	CAco CWnw MBlu SAko		- 'Papoose'	CAco ELan EPfP LRHS
	- 'Treblitsch'	NLar		- 'Silberzwerg'	CAco
	- 'Virgata'	CAco		- 'Tenas'	CAco LRHS SPoG
§	- 'Wolski Gold'	NLar		*smithiana*	CAco
	orientalis ♀H7	CAco ELan	I	- 'Aurea'	CAco WMat
	- 'Aurea' (v) ♀H7	CAco LRHS		- 'Sunray'	NLar
	- 'Aureospicata'	CAco EUrb MAsh MBlu		*torano*	CAco
	- 'Early Gold' (v)	CAco		*wilsonii*	CAco
	- 'Golden Start'	CAco LRHS		'Wodan'	NLar
	- 'Gracilis'	CAco			
	- 'Horstmann'	CAco			

Picrasma (Simaroubaceae)

	- 'Juwel'	LRHS NLar
	- 'Mount Vernon'	CAco
	- Nana Group	CAco GKin
	- 'Shadow's Broom'	CMen
	- 'Skylands' ♀H7	CAco EUrb MAsh
	pungens	CAco CCVT EWhm LMaj
	- 'Baby Blueeyes'	CCVT NLar

	ailanthoides	see *P. quassioides*
§	*quassioides*	EBee SChF WJur WPGP

Pieris (Ericaceae)

'Balls of Fire'	CMac
'Bert Chandler'	CMac WSpi
'Brouwer's Beauty'	NLar SPoG

'Flaming Silver' (v) ♀H5	CBcs CDoC CEnd CMac CSBt CWnw EGren ELan EPfP EUrb LBom LCro LMil LRHS LSRN MAsh MGos Midl MPri SArc SPoG SRms SSta WCha WFar WSpi
'Forest Flame' ♀H5	Widely available
formosa B&SWJ 2257	WCru
- var. *forrestii*	CDoC
- - 'Charles Michael'	CExl
- - 'Jermyns'	CMac
- - 'Wakehurst' ♀H5	CDoC CExl CMac ELon EPfP GKin LMil MAsh SAko WSpi
HAVILA ('Mouwsvila') (v)	CMac LRHS MAsh SReu
japonica	CMac EGren WCha
- 'Bisbee Dwarf'	GKev
- 'Blush' ♀H5	LRHS
- 'Bonfire' ♀H5	CBcs EUrb LCro LWaG MAsh MGos MPro NLar SPoG WFar
- 'Carnaval' (v) ♀H5	CDoC CMac CSBt CWnw ELan EPfP LBuc LMil LRHS LSto MAsh MGos MPri SPoG WFar
§ - 'Christmas Cheer'	CMac
- 'Cupido'	EGren LRHS MAsh NBir WFar
- 'Debutante' ♀H5	CDoC EGren GKin LBom LBuc LRHS LSto MAsh Mgos NLar WCha WFar
- 'Don'	see *P. japonica* 'Pygmaea'
- 'Dorothy Wyckoff'	NLar SSta
- 'Erik'	GKev
- 'Flamingo'	CMac
- 'Katsura' PBR	CDoC CMac ELan EPfP EUrb GKin LBom LBuc LCro LMil LRHS LSRN MAsh MBlu MGos NLar SPoG WFar
- 'Little Heath' (v)	Widely available
- 'Little Heath Green'	CBrac CMac EGren GKin MGos SArc SPoG WFar
- 'Minor'	GKev WFar
- 'Mountain Fire' ♀H5	CBcs CDoC CEnd CWnw EGren EGrI EHeP EPfP EUrb GKin LBom LCro LMil LRHS LSRN MAsh MGos Midl MPri MPro NBir NCth SArc SPlb SPoG SRms WCha WFar
- 'Passion' PBR	CDoC CEnd CSBt EBee EGrI EPfP EUrb LCro LMil LRHS LSou LSRN MAsh MBros MMrt NLar WCha WFar
- 'Pink Delight' ♀H5	CDoC LMil LSRN MGos SRms
- PINK PASSION ('Opstal 69' PBR)	LSou NCth
- POLAR PASSION ('Ppobas' PBR) (v)	EBee LCro LSou MHtn
- 'Prelude' ♀H5	EPfP LMil LRHS MAsh NCth WAbe
- 'Purity' ♀H5	CEnd CMac LCro MGos SArc WFar
§ - 'Pygmaea'	EGrI GKev
- 'Ralto' PBR	LBom LCro MAsh MGos SPoG
- RED MILL ('Zebris')	CEnd MPro
- 'Sarabande' ♀H5	MAsh
- Taiwanensis Group	CMac GKin LRHS SRms WFar
- - NMWJ 14537	WCru
- 'Temple Bells'	MPro
- 'Valley Rose'	EGren GKin MAsh NLar
- 'Valley Valentine' ♀H5	CBcs CDoC CMac EGrI LCro MAsh MGos NLar SPoG SRkn WFar
- 'Variegata' misapplied	see *P. japonica* 'White Rim'
- 'Variegata' ambig.	EHeP LMil LRHS LSto Midl SArc SReu WCha
- 'Variegata' (Carrière) Bean (v)	MAsh
- VIKING ('Jww6' PBR)	GKev NLar
- 'Wada's Pink'	see *P. japonica* 'Christmas Cheer'
- 'White Cascade'	MPro
§ - 'White Rim' (v) 'Tilford'	CMac MPro SPlb CMac

Pilea (Urticaceae)

sp.	EHap
CBTW1516	GGro
DS 834	GGro
angulata	GGro LEdu
subsp. *petiolaris*	
- - PB 16-1074	EWld WPGP
- - PB 96-1074	GGro
cadierei ♀H1c	EShb LBom LCro LWaG
depressa	LBom
glauca 'Greyze'	LBom NHrt
glaucophylla	LBom NHrt
insolens	GGro SIvy SPhx WPGP
involucrata ♀H1a	WFar
- 'Moon Valley'	LBom
kiotensis	SPlb
- PB 08-880	GGro
libanensis	EShb
matsudae 'Taiwan Silver'	CBct EArI EBee EPPr GGro SHor SPlb WFar WPGP
mollis	LWaG
- 'Moon Valley'	LWaG
peperomioides ♀H1c	CCBP CDoC CWal ELan LBom LCro LInT LWaG NHrt WFar
- MOJITO ('Mospilmoj') (v)	LCro
plataniflora CMBTW 1485	GGro
- 'Glossy'	GGro
- 'Pelling'	GGro
scripta	SPhx
- PB 02-520	GGro
umbrosa	SIvy SPhx
- PB 2522	GGro

Pileostegia see *Hydrangea*

Pilgerodendron (Cupressaceae)

uviferum	CAco

Pilosella (Asteraceae)

§ *aurantiaca*	CBWd CGwi CoPl ECha EHet ELan EPfP EPPr GAbr GJem GQue LCro LEdu LShi MCtn MHer MNHC NBid NBir SDix SPhx SRms WCot WHer WShi
§ - subsp. *carpathicola*	MMuc
§ *officinarum*	NRya
tardans	GJos

Pilosocereus (Cactaceae)

gounellei	NHrt

Pilularia (Marsileaceae)

globulifera	CPud CWat

Pimelea (Thymelaeaceae)

coarctata	see *P. prostrata*
ferruginea	SVen
oreophila	GArf
§ *prostrata*	EPot EWes GEdr

Pimpinella (Apiaceae)

anisum	MCtn MNHC SVic
major	LEdu
- 'Rosea'	Widely available
saxifraga	CHab NAts SPhx WOrg
- 'Rosea'	NAts
tripartita	ECha SPhx WPGP
- PAB 6112	LEdu

pineapple see *Ananas comosus*

pineapple guava see *Feijoa sellowiana*

Pinellia (Araceae)

cordata	ESwi LEdu SBig SMad WCot WCru
- green-leaved	ESwi
pedatisecta	GKev ISha LAma WCot
pinnatisecta	see *P. tripartita*
ternata	EBee NLar
§ **tripartita**	CExl EPPr GKev LAma

Pinguicula (Lentibulariaceae)

'Cherry Blossom'	WFar
grandiflora ♀H6	EWld NRya WAbe
'Tina'	WFar
vulgaris	GKev

pinkcurrant see *Ribes rubrum* (P)

Pinus ✿ (Pinaceae)

albicaulis	CAco
- 'Falling Rock'	CAco
- 'Lake Sabrina'	CAco
- 'Nana'	see *P. albicaulis* 'Noble's Dwarf'
§ - 'Noble's Dwarf'	CAco
aristata misapplied	see *P. longaeva*
aristata ambig.	CAco
aristata Engelm. 'Bashful'	CAco
- 'Blue Cover'	CAco
- 'Doc'	CAco
- 'Elko'	CAco
- 'Elko Run'	CAco
- 'Green Cover'	CAco
- 'Lemon Frost'	CAco
I - 'Schneverdingen'	CAco
- 'Sherwood Compact'	CAco
- 'Silver Day'	CAco
- 'Silver Doll'	CAco
- 'Timberline'	CAco
arizonica var. **ornelasii**	CAco
armandi	CAco SArc
- 'Vanc Gold'	CAco
attenuata	CAco
austriaca	see *P. nigra* subsp. *nigra*
ayacahuite	CAco SPlb
- 'Maya'	CAco
- var. *veitchii*	CAco
balfouriana	CAco
'Bambino'	see *P.* 'Gaëlle Brégeon'
banksiana	CAco
- 'Arctis'	CAco
- 'Manomet'	CAco NLar
- 'Schneverdingen'	CAco
- 'Uncle Fogy'	CAco
- 'Velda'	CAco
'Bayo'	CAco
bhutanica	CAco
BREPO	see *P.* 'Pierrick Bregéon'
brutia	CAco
- var. **brutia**	CAco
- var. **eldarica**	CAco
- var. **pityusa**	CAco
bungeana	CAco MBlu
- 'Silver Ghost'	CAco
- white bark	CAco
canariensis	CAco CExl
cembra	CAgr IPap
- 'Aurea'	see *P. cembra* 'Aureovariegata'
§ - 'Aureovariegata' (v)	CAco
- 'Compacta Glauca'	CAco
- Glauca Group	CAco LRHS MPri
- 'Stricta'	CAco
cembroides	CAco
- 'Fancy Nancy'	CAco
- subsp. **orizabensis**	CAco
clausa	CAco
contorta	CAco IPap SPlb WCha
- 'Anna'	CAco
- 'Asher'	CAco
- 'Chief Joseph' ♀H6	CAco ELan NLar
- var. **contorta**	CAco
- 'Frisian Gold'	CAco
- 'Krňák' **new**	NLar
- var. **latifolia**	CAco
- var. **murrayana**	CAco
- 'Spaan's Dwarf'	CAco NLar
- 'Taylor's Sunburst'	CAco NLar
coulteri	CAco CBrP CMCN EPfP WPGP
densata	CAco
densiflora	CAco CBrP EUrb
- 'Alice Verkade' ♀H7	CAco ELan LRHS MAsh SArc WFar
- 'Aurea'	CAco NLar
- 'Burke's Red Variegated' (v)	CAco
- erect	CAco
- 'Glitzer's Weeping'	CAco
- 'Golden Ghost'	CAco NLar
- 'Haybud'	CAco
- 'Heavy Bud'	CAco
- 'Kim'	CAco NLar
- 'Low Glow'	CAco LRHS NLar SPoG
- 'Meylan Compact'	CAco
- 'Oculus-draconis' (v)	CAco
- 'Pendula'	CAco MBlu
- 'Rainbow' (v)	CAco
- 'Rata'	CAco
- 'Umbraculifera'	CAco CNWT CWnw MAsh
- 'Vibrant'	CAco
× **densithunbergii** 'Beni-kujaku'	CAco
- 'Edsal Wood'	CAco
- 'Jane Kluis' ♀H7	CAco ELan LRHS SPoG
§ **devoniana**	CAco
durangensis	CAco WPGP
echinata	CAco
edulis	CAco
elliottii	CAco
engelmannii	CAco CBrP WPGP
fenzeliana	CAco
flexilis	CAco
- 'Blackfoot'	CAco
- 'Cesarini Blue'	CAco CWnw NLar
- 'Damfino'	CAco
- 'Extra Blue'	CAco
- 'Firmament'	CCVT NPip WMat
- 'Lil Wolf'	NLar
- 'Navajo'	CAco
I - 'Pygmaea'	CAco
- var. **reflexa**	CAco
- 'Tiny Temple'	CAco
- 'Vanderwolf's Pyramid'	CAco CCVT CWnw LCro MGos NLar WMat
'Fulda'	CAco
§ 'Gaëlle Brégeon'	CAco
gerardiana	CAco
- from Kohistan, Pakistan	CAco
- from Waziristan, Pakistan	CAco
glabra	CAco
greggii	CAco WPGP
griffithii McClell.	see *P. wallichiana*

× *hakkodensis*	CAco		*monophylla*	CAco
halepensis	CAco IPap NLar SEND		- 'Hot Summer'	CAco
hartwegii	CAco		- 'Oregon'	CAco
§ *heldreichii*	CAco NPip WMat		*montezumae* ambig.	CAco
- 'Atze Saule'	CAco NLar		*montezumae* Lamb.	CAco SArc
- 'Aureospicata'	CAco		- 'Forde Abbey'	CAco
- 'Barabits' Compact'	CAco		- glaucous-leaved, from Mexico	CAco
- 'Beran Conical'	CAco			
§ - 'Biała Chmura'	CAco NLar		- 'Grahame Oakey Pendula'	CAco
- 'Compact Gem' ♀H6	CAco IArd LRHS SBig		- var. *montezumae*	CAco
- 'Den Ouden'	CAco		- 'Nymans'	CAco
- 'Dolce Dorme'	CAco		- 'Sheffield Park'	CAco
- 'Emerald Arrow'	CAco		*monticola*	CAco
- 'Green Bun'	CAco		- 'Ammerland'	CAco
- 'Green Giant'	CAco NLar		- 'Ondulata'	CAco
- 'Green Pyramid'	CCVT		- 'Pendula'	CAco
- 'Grüne Lagune'	CAco NLar		- 'Snow White'	CAco
- 'Honorio Fastigiata'	CAco		- 'Strobicola'	CAco MPri
- 'Indigo Eyes'	CAco		*mugo*	CAco CNWT EGren EHeP LMaj MAsh MGos WJur
- 'Irish Bell'	CAco			
- var. *leucodermis*	see *P. heldreichii*		- 'Agnieszka'	CAco
- 'Lindenhof'	CAco		- 'Allgäu'	CAco SBig
- 'Little Dracula'	CAco LRHS NLar		- 'Benjamin'	CAco CWnw LRHS NLar
- 'Malink'	CAco CWnw EUrb IArd NLar		- 'Big Tuna'	CAco
- 'Mint Truffle'	CAco		- 'Boži Dar'	CAco NLar
I - 'Nana'	CAco		- 'Carstens' ♀H7	CAco CBcs EGren ELan EPfP IArd LSRN MAsh MGos NLar SArc SBig SPoG WFar
- 'Pirin No 3'	CAco SAko			
- 'Pirin No 4'	NLar			
- 'Satellit' ♀H6	CAco CWnw IArd MAsh SBig		- 'Columbo'	CAco CWnw LRHS WFar
- 'Schmidtii'	see *P. heldreichii* 'Šmidtii'		- 'Corley's Mat'	CAco LRHS NLar
§ - 'Šmidtii' ♀H6	CAco CMen EUrb MAsh NLar SPoG		- 'Cristata Contorta'	CAco
- 'Vichren Banderica'	NLar		- 'Echiniformis'	WFar
- WHITE CLOUD	see *P. heldreichii* 'Biała Chmura'		- 'Elemér'	CAco
× *holfordiana*	CAco EPfP WPGP		- 'Filigran'	CAco
hwangshanensis	WPGP		- 'Fischleinboden'	CAco
jeffreyi	CAco CBrP EPfP		- 'Frohlings Gold'	CAco
- 'Joppi'	CAco NLar		- 'Fructata'	CAco
- 'Misty Lemon'	CAco		- 'Gnom'	CAco EPfP GKin LRHS MAsh MGos
- 'Paula'	CAco		- 'Gold Star'	CAco
kesiya	CAco		- 'Golden Glow'	CAco LRHS NLar SPoG
koraiensis	CAco		- 'Grüne Kugel'	CAco LSRN
- 'Anna'	CAco NLar		- 'Heinis Triumph'	CAco
- 'Blue Ball'	CAco		- 'Humpy' ♀H7	CAco LRHS MAsh
- 'China Boy'	NLar		- 'Jakobsen'	CAvo
- 'Compacta Glauca'	CAco		- 'Jalubi'	MAsh
- 'Dragon Eye'	CAco		- 'Kissen' ♀H7	CAco EPfP NLar
- 'Jack Corbit'	CAco WFar		- KLOSTERGRUN	see *P. mugo* 'Klosterkötter'
- 'Morris Blue'	CAco		§ - 'Klosterkötter'	CAco
- 'Shibamichi' (v)	CAco		- 'Kobold'	CAco
- 'Silver Lining'	CAco		- 'Krauskopf'	CAco
- 'Silveray'	CAco CWnw NLar		- 'Laarheide'	CAco ELan LRHS SPoG
- 'Spring Grove'	NLar		- 'Laurin'	CAco
- 'Tsingtao'	NLar		- 'Lemon'	CAco
- 'Variegata' (v)	CAco		- 'Little Gold Star'	ELan LRHS
- 'Verkade's Select'	CAco		- 'Little Lady'	CAco LRHS
- 'Winton'	CAco		- 'March'	CAco
lambertiana	CAco		- 'Mini Mini'	NLar
- 'Mount Baden-Powell'	CAco NLar		- 'Minikin'	MAsh
latteri	CAco		- 'Minima Kalous'	CAco
lawsonii	CAco		- 'Misty Lemon'	CAco
leiophylla	CAco		- 'Mops' ♀H7	CMen CWnw ELan EPfP IPap LCro LRHS MAsh MBlu MGos SBig SPoG WCha
leucodermis	see *P. heldreichii*			
§ *longaeva*	CAco			
- 'Schulman Grove'	CAco		- 'Mops Gold'	CAco
I - 'Sherwoods Compact'	CAco		- 'Mops Midget'	CAco ELan MAsh
luchuensis	CAco		- var. *mughus*	see *P. mugo* subsp. *mugo*
magnifica	see *P. devoniana*		§ - subsp. *mugo*	CBcs CWnw EGren EHeP EPfP LCro LRHS LSRN
'Marie Bregéon'PBR	CAco LRHS SArc			
massoniana	CAco		- - 'Milky Way'	CAco
maxmartinezii	CAco		- 'Mumpitz'	CAco SBig
maximinoi	CAco		- 'Northern Lights'	LRHS

	- 'Ophir' ♀H7	CAco ELan LRHS MGos SPoG		- 'Pirin'	CAco
	- 'Pal Maleter' (v)	CAco SPoG		- 'Richard'	CAco EUrb NLar
	- 'Pici'	CAco		- 'Rondello'	CAco NLar
	- 'Picobello'	CAco MAsh NLar SArc SPoG WCot	§	- subsp. *salzmannii*	CAco
	- Pumilio Group	CAco EGren ELan EPfP EUrb IPap LRHS LWaG MGos MMuc MPri SArc SEND WCha WSpi		- 'Smaragd'	CAco NLar
				- 'Spielberg'	CAco NLar
				- SUMMER BREEZE	see *P. nigra* 'Aron'
	- 'Rigi'	CAco NLar		- 'Wabito'	CAco
	- var. *rostrata*	see *P. mugo* subsp. *uncinata*		*oocarpa*	CAco
	- subsp. *rotundata* 'Ježek'	MAsh		*palustris*	CAco
	- 'Schwartzenburg'	NLar		*parviflora*	CAco SPlb
	- 'Sherwood Compact'	CAco LRHS MAsh NLar		- 'Adcock's Dwarf' ♀H7	CAco NLar
	- 'Starkl'	CAco		- 'Al Fordham'	CAco
	- 'Sunshine' (v)	CAco		- 'Ama-no-gawa'	CAco
	- 'Tuffet'	CAco		- 'Aoi'	CAco
§	- subsp. *uncinata*	CAco LRHS SArc		- 'Ara-kawa'	CAco CMen
	- - 'Boris'	CAco MAsh		- Azuma-goyo Group	CAco
	- - 'Grüne Welle'	CAco	I	- 'Baasch's Form'	CAco
	- - 'Heideperle'	CAco		- 'Bergman'	CAco MAsh NLar
	- - 'Kostelnicek'	CAco NLar		- 'Blue Angel'	CAco MBlu NLar
	- - 'Paradekissen'	CAco		- 'Blue Giant'	CAco MBlu
	- 'Varella'	CAco NLar		- 'Blue Lou'	CAco NLar
	- 'Winter Gold' ♀H7	CWnw LCro LRHS MGos NLar SArc		- 'Bonnie Bergman' ♀H7	CAco EUrb NLar
	- 'Winter Sun'	CAco CWnw LRHS NLar WMat		- 'Brevifolia'	CAco EGren
	- 'Yellow Marble'	CAco		- 'Bunty'	NLar
	- 'Yellow Tip' (v)	CAco NLar		- 'Catherine Elizabeth'	NLar
	- 'Zundert'	LRHS SPoG		- 'Chikusa Goten'	CAco
	- 'Zwergkugel'	SAko		- 'Fatsumo'	CAco
	muricata	CAco		- 'Filip's Blue Diamond'	NLar
	× *murraybanksiana*	CAco		- 'Floppy Joe'	NLar
	nigra	CAco CBcs CLnd CMac CWnw EHeP EPfP EUrb MGos NLar SArc SFol WCha WHtc		- 'Frankenhof'	CAco
				- 'Frick Estate'	NLar
				- 'Fukai' (v)	CAco NLar SArc
§	- 'Aron' PBR	WMat		- 'Fuku-zu-mi'	CAco
	- var. *austriaca*	see *P. nigra* subsp. *nigra*		- 'Fu-shiro'	CAco
	- 'Black Prince' ♀H7	CAco NPip WMat		- Glauca Group	CAco CWnw LRHS MAsh MBlu
	- 'Bobo'	CAco		- - 'Glauca' ♀H7	CAco
	- 'Buda'	CAco		- 'Goykuri'	CAco
	- var. *calabrica*	see *P. nigra* subsp. *laricio*		- 'Green Monkey'	CAco
	- 'Caperci's Golden Cream'	CAco		- 'Gyok-kasen'	CAco
	- var. *caramanica*	see *P. nigra* subsp. *pallasiana*		- 'Hagaromo Seedling'	CAco CMen
	- var. *cebennensis*	see *P. nigra* subsp. *salzmannii*		- 'Hakko'	NLar
	- 'Cobra'	CAco		- 'Ha-tzumari'	CAco NLar
	- var. *corsicana*	see *P. nigra* subsp. *laricio*		- 'Himburgii'	CAco
	- subsp. *dalmatica*	CAco		- 'Hobbit'	NLar
*	- 'Fastigiata'	CAco CNWT		- 'Ichi-no-se'	CAco
	- 'Felek'	NLar		- 'Iona'	NLar
	- 'Globosa'	CAco		- 'Iri-fune'	CAco EUrb
	- 'Globosa Viridis'	EUrb NLar		- 'Jyu-roko-ra-kan'	CAco
	- 'Green Tower'	CAco CWnw LRHS NLar		- 'Kenwith'	CAco
	- 'Helga'	CAco LCro NLar		- 'Kin-po'	CAco
	- 'Hornibrookiana'	CAco NLar		- 'Kiyomatsu'	CAco LRHS
	- 'Hubert'	CAco		- 'Kobe'	CAco NLar
	- 'Karaca Ball'	CAco		- 'Kokonoe'	CAco CMen
	- 'Komet'	CAco NLar SAko		- 'Kokuho'	CAco
§	- subsp. *laricio*	CAco CCVT CMac EHeP EPfP EUrb MMuc SArc SEND WPGP		- 'Mai-tsuzumi'	CAco
				- 'Mano-jama'	CAco
	- - 'Aurea'	CAco MBlu		- 'Myo-jo'	NLar
	- - 'Goldfinger'	NLar		- 'Negishi' ♀H7	CAco CMen CWnw EUrb IArd LRHS MAsh SArc WMat
	- - 'Wurstle'	CAco			
	- subsp. *maritima*	see *P. nigra* subsp. *laricio*		- 'Nellie D.'	CAco
	- 'Molette'	CAco		- 'Ōgon-goyo'	CAco NLar
	- 'Moseri'	CAco NLar		- 'Ōgon-janome'	CAco MAsh NLar
	- 'Nana'	CAco CWnw LRHS		- 'Ooh La La'	CAvo NLar
§	- subsp. *nigra*	CAco CBrac CCVT CLnd CMac CNWT IPap LMaj MMuc SEND	I	- var. *pentaphylla* 'Glauca'	NLar
				- 'Ryu-ju'	CAco NLar
	- - 'Bright Eyes'	MAsh WMat		- 'Sage Tiers'	CAco
	- 'Obelisk'	NLar WMat		- 'San-bo'	CAco NLar
	- 'Oregon Green'	CAco NLar SBig	§	- 'Saphir'	CAco EUrb
§	- subsp. *pallasiana*	CAco		- 'Schoon's Bonsai'	CAco CWnw MGos NLar
	- - 'Pyramidalis'	CAco CWnw		- 'Shika-shima'	CAco LRHS NLar

- 'Shikoku-goyo Group'	CAco NLar	*serotina*	CAco
- 'Shinbacu'	CAco	*strobiformis*	CAco WJur
- 'Shin-sen'	CAco	- 'Coronado'	CAco
- 'Shirobana'	CAco	- 'Densata'	CAco
- 'Shizukagoten'	CAco	- 'Foxtail'	CAco
- 'Shu-re'	CAco	- 'Loma Linda'	CAco NLar
- 'Tanima-no-yuki'	CAco NLar	- 'White Winter'	NLar
- 'Tayo-nishiki'	CAco	*strobus*	CAco CBcs CCVT IPap LMaj LRHS
- 'Tempelhof'	CAco LRHS NLar		MGos MMuc MPri WMat
- 'Tenysu-kazu'	CAco LRHS NLar	- 'Angel Falls'	CAco
- 'Tokyo Dwarf'	CAco NLar	- 'Anna Fiele'	CAco
- 'Zelkova'	CMen	- 'Aurea'	CAco
- 'Zui-sho'	CAco	- 'Bennett Fastigiate'	NLar
patula ♀H4	CAco CTsd EPfP NPip SArc SPlb	- 'Bergman's Mini'	CAco LRHS NLar
	SPoG WMat WPGP	- 'Blue Clovers'	NLar
peuce	CAco LRHS	- 'Blue Shag' ♀H7	CAco LRHS NLar
- 'Arnold Dwarf'	CAco LRHS	- 'Bob's Wishes'	CAco
- 'Cesarini'	NLar	- 'Brevifolia'	CAco SArc
- 'Pacific Blue'	CAco	- 'Cesarini'	CAco
- 'Wageningen'	CAco CWnw	- var. *chiapensis*	CAco
'Pichounet'	CAco	- 'Connecticut Slate'	CAco NLar
§ 'Pierrick Bregéon'	CAco LRHS NLar SArc	- 'Contorta'	CAco
pinaster	CAco CBcs IPap MMuc SEND	- 'Elf'	NLar
pinea ♀H4	CAco CAgr CBlu CCVT EPfP EUrb	- 'Elkins Dwarf'	NLar
	IPap LRHS MCtn MGos MMuc SArc	- 'E.R.'	MGos NLar
	SEND SPlb WJur WPGP	- 'Fastigiata'	CAco CWnw MBlu
- 'Gold Crest'	CAco	- 'Golden Candles'	CAco
- 'Silver Crest'	ELan LRHS	- 'Green Curls'	LRHS
ponderosa	CAco CMCN IPap MMuc SArc	- 'Green Twist'	CAco
- 'Heike'	NLar	- 'Ground Hugger'	CAco NLar
- 'Mary Ann Heacock'	CAco	- 'Hillside Gem'	NLar
- 'Penaz'	CAco	- 'Krügers Lilliput'	CAco SArc
- 'Pendula'	CAco	- 'Louie' ♀H7	CAco LRHS MAsh NLar
- var. *ponderosa*	CAco	- 'Macopin'	CAco LMaj WFar
- 'Trumbell'	CAco	- 'Merrimack'	CAco
pseudostrobus	CAco	- 'Minima' ♀H7	CAco EUrb LSRN MAsh MBlu NLar
- var. *apulcensis*	CAco		SPoG
pumila	CAco	- 'Minuta'	CAco
- 'Blue Note'	CAco	- 'Niagara Falls'	CAco LRHS NLar
- 'Chlorocarpa'	CAco	- 'Oliver Dwarf'	NLar
- 'Draijer's Dwarf'	CAco NLar	- 'Ontario'	MGos
- 'Dwarf Blue'	CAco	- 'Pacific Sunrise'	NLar
- 'Glauca' ♀H7	CAco	- 'Pendula'	CAco MBlu
- 'Globe'	CAco	- 'Prostrata'	NLar
- 'Jeddeloh'	CAco	- 'Radiata'	CAco EUrb
- 'Säntis'	CAco NLar	- 'Reinshaus'	CAco
- 'Saphir'	see *P. parviflora* 'Saphir'	- 'Sea Urchin'	CAco MAsh
pungens	CAco	- 'Secrest'	CAco LRHS
- 'Custer's Locks'	CAco	- 'Custer's Locks'	CAco NLar
- 'Johnny's Goldstrike'	CAco	- 'Stowe Pillar'	CAco NLar
- 'Mountain Gold' **new**	NLar	- 'Tiny Kurls'	CAco CWnw LCro LRHS MAsh
radiata	CAco CBcs CBrac CCoa CCVT		MGos NLar SArc WMat
	CDoC CMac CNWT CSde ELan	- 'Torulosa'	CAco MBlu MGos
	EPfP EUrb IPap LMaj MMuc NPip	- 'White Mountain'	CAco MBlu
	SArc WHtc WMat	*sylvestris*	Widely available
- Aurea Group	SPoG WMat	- from the Casadéen Massif,	CAco
- - 'Aurea' ♀H5	CAco MAsh NPip SArc	Auvergne	
resinosa	CAco	- 'Anny's Wintersun'	NLar
- 'Don Smith'	CAco	- Aurea Group	MBlu NLar NPip SArc WMat
- 'Nana'	CAco	- - 'Aurea' ♀H7	CAco ELan
- 'Pillnitz'	CAco LRHS	- 'Beuvronensis' ♀H7	CAco CMen LRHS
- 'State Trooper'	CAco	- 'Bialogon'	CAco
rigida	CAco	- 'Blue Sky'	CAco NLar
roxburghii	CAco	- 'Brentmoor Blonde'	CAco
sabineana	CAco	- 'Candlelight'	CAco
- 'Isabella'	NLar	- 'Chantry Blue'	CAco CCVT EPfP LRHS MAsh MGos
× *schwerinii*	CAco LRHS		NLar NPip SPoG WMat WPGP
- 'Wiel's Champion'	NLar	- 'Doone Valley'	CAco
- 'Wiel's Discovery' **new**	NLar	- 'Edwin Hillier'	CAco NPip WMat
- 'Wiethorst' ♀H7	CAco CWnw LRHS LWaG NPip	- 'Fastigiata Group'	CAco CNWT ESwi EUrb LRHS NLar
	SBig WMat		WHtc

	- 'Filip's Silver Surprise'	CAco
	- 'Frensham' 🏆H7	CAco LRHS MAsh
I	- 'Glauca'	CAco
	- 'Globosa'	CAco
	- 'Gold Coin' 🏆H7	CAco CCVT EPfP SPoG
	- 'Gold Medal'	CAco MAsh WMat
	- 'Green Penguin'	CAco LRHS NLar
	- 'Greg's Variegated' (v)	CAco
	- var. ***hamata***	CAco
	- 'Hillside Creeper'	CAco MAsh SArc
	- 'Isaszeg'	CAco
	- 'Janssen Witch'	CAco
	- 'Kelpie'	CAco
	- 'Lodge Hill'	CMen MAsh SArc
	- 'Martulka'	CAco
	- 'Meffen Gold' 🏆H7	CAco NLar
	- var. ***mongolica***	CAco
	- 'Mosaic'	CAco
	- 'Nana' misapplied	see *P. sylvestris* 'Watereri'
	- Nana Group	CAco
I	- - 'Nana Arguta'	CAco
	- - 'Nana Compacta'	CMen
§	- 'Nisbet's Gem'	CAco
	- 'Norska'	CAco
	- 'Ødegård'	CAco
	- 'Pévé Miba'	NLar
	- 'Reedham'	NLar
I	- 'Repandens'	CAco
	- 'Repens'	CAco
	- 'Rita'	CAco
	- 'Sandringham'	CAco NLar
	- 'Saxatilis'	CAco CMen
	- subsp. ***scotica***	CAco NTrD
	- 'Scott's Dwarf'	see *P. sylvestris* 'Nisbet's Gem'
	- 'Sé'	CAco
	- 'Tabuliformis'	CAco
	- 'Treasure'	MAsh
	- 'Trollguld'	CAco CCVT NLar
	- 'Vinney Ridge'	CAco
§	- 'Watereri'	CAco CCVT CNWT CWnw EGren IArd LCro LMaj SArc SBig WCha
	- 'Westonbirt'	CMen MAsh NLar WMat
	- 'Wintergold'	CAco
	- 'Xavery'	CAco NLar
	tabuliformis	CAco IPap SPlb
	- 'Jiuzhaigou Valley'	CAco NLar
	- var. ***mukdensis***	CAco
	- 'Shenyang'	CAco MAsh
	taeda	CAco
	taiwanensis	CAco
	- var. ***taiwanensis***	CAco
	tecunumanii	CAco
	teocote	CAco
	thunbergii	CAco CMen
	- 'Akame'	CMen
	- 'Banshosho'	CAco CMen EUrb NLar WMat
	- 'Compacta'	CMen
	- var. ***corticosa***	CAco
	- 'Emery's Dwarf'	NLar
	- 'Frosty Patches' (v)	CAco
	- 'Hayabusa'	CMen
	- 'Ichiyo'	CAco
	- 'Janome' (v)	NLar
	- 'Kotobuki'	CAco CCVT NLar
	- 'Kyushu'	CAco
	- 'Maijima'	CAco
	- 'Mikawa'	CAco CMen MBlu
	- 'Ogi-matsu'	CAco
	- 'Ōgon'	CAco CMen NLar SArc
§	- 'Sayonara' 🏆H7	CAco CMen MAsh NLar
	- 'Senryu'	CMen
	- 'Shio-guro'	CAco NLar
	- 'Suchiro'	CAco
	- 'Sunsho'	CMen
	- 'Taihei'	CMen
I	- 'Thunderhead' 🏆H7	CAco EUrb MAsh NLar
	- 'Torafu'	CAco
	- 'Yatsubusa'	see *P. thunbergii* 'Sayonara'
	- 'Ye-i-kan'	CAco
	- 'Yumaki'	CAco
	torreyana	CAco
	uncinata	see *P. mugo* subsp. *uncinata*
	virginiana 'Topknot'	CAco
	- 'Wate's Golden'	CAco
§	***wallichiana*** 🏆H6	CAco CBrP CCVT CLnd CMCN CNWT CTsd EHeP EPfP IDun IPap LMaj LRHS LWaG MAsh MBlu MGos NLar NPip SArc SGol WJur WMat
	- 'Densa Hill'	CAco LRHS
	- 'Frosty'	CAco
	- 'Glauca'	CAco
	- 'Nana' 🏆H6	CAco MBlu NLar
	- 'Umbraculifera'	CWnw
	- 'Winter Light'	CAco NLar
	- 'Zebrina' (v)	CAco MBlu NLar
	yunnanensis	CAco SPlb
	- var. ***pygmaea***	CAco

Piper (*Piperaceae*)

	heydei B&SWJ 10445	WCru
	kadsura	SBrt
	nigrum	WJur

Piptanthus (*Fabaceae*)

	forrestii	see *P. nepalensis*
	laburnifolius	see *P. nepalensis*
§	***nepalensis***	CSpe EBee EWld GKev NBid NLar SRms WJur

Pistacia (*Anacardiaceae*)

	chinensis	CMCN LMaj WJur
	lentiscus	CBcs EBee SEND SVen WJur WPGP
	terebinthus	WJur
	- NJM 11.004	WPGP

Pistia (*Araceae*)

Ϸ	***stratiotes***	ELin

Pitcairnia (*Bromeliaceae*)

	bergii	CHII
	heterophylla	WCot
	pungens	WCot
	punicea	WCot
	ringens	WCot

Pittosporum (*Pittosporaceae*)

	adaphniphylloides	CBcs
	anomalum	SEle
	- (m)	SEle
	'Arundel Green' (f) 🏆H4	CDoC ELon EPfP LRHS MAsh
	bicolor	CTsd EBee
	brevicalyx	WPGP
	buchananii	SVen
	'Collaig Silver'	CCVT EPfP LRHS MAsh MHed MSwo WFar
	crassifolium	CBcs CCoa CSde CTsd SPlb
	- 'Variegatum' (v)	CBcs CCoa LRHS
	'Crinkles' (f)	SVen
	crispulum VdL 80626 **new**	WPGP
	dallii	SPlb
	daphniphylloides	EBee LRHS SArc WPGP

Pittosporum

- B&SWJ 6789	WCru			SHor SOrN SPoG WCha WFar
- CWJ 12404	WCru			WHtc WReH WSpi
- RWJ 9913	WCru	- 'Green Elf'	EHeP WSpi
eugenioides	CCht CCoa CMCN CSde EBee ELon LRHS SEND	- 'Green Thumb'	CMac EBee EPfP LRHS
		- 'Irene Paterson' (m/v) ♀H4	Widely available
- 'Variegatum' (v) ♀H3	CBcs CCoa CDoC CMac CWnw EPfP EUrb LBom LRHS LSRN MGos MPri NLar SEND SVen WSpi	- IRISH LUCK ('Ptg18'PBR)	SArc
		- 'John Flanagan'	see *P. tenuifolium* 'Margaret Turnbull'
'Garnettii' (v) ♀H3	Widely available	- 'Limelight' (v)	CSBt EBee EPfP LSRN SPoG
glabratum	EBee WPGP	- 'Loxhill Gold'	CCoa EPfP LRHS MPri NLar
- var. *neriifolium*	WCru	§ - 'Margaret Turnbull' (v)	LRHS MPri NLar
B&SWJ 11685		- 'Marjory Channon' (v)	EPfP MSwo
heterophyllum	CBcs EGrI EPfP EUrb EWes LRHS MHtn SEND WJur	- 'Midget'	ECul ESwi LRHS
		- 'Mountain Green'	CMac
- variegated (v)	EPfP	* - 'Nanum'	SFol
illicioides	EBee	- 'Nutty's Leprechaun'	SSta
var. *angustifolium*		- 'Oliver Twist'	EPfP LBom LRHS MAsh SSta
- - B&SWJ 14560	WCru	- 'Petite Plum'	NLar WCot
- - RWJ 9846	WCru	- 'Pink Select' (v)	SArc
- var. *illicioides* B&SWJ 6712	WCru	- 'Pompom'	EGren ELan LRHS LSou LSRN MGos MHed SArc WSpi
- - PAB 9004	LEdu	- 'Purpureum' (m)	CBrac CDoC CMac CSBt EGren ELon EPfP LBom LSRN SEND SFol SPoG SRms WCot WFar
× *intermedium* 'Craxten' (f)	EBee EUrb LRHS		
'Nanum Variegatum'	see *P. tobira* 'Variegatum'	§ - 'Rotundifolium' (v)	CWal
oblongilimbum DJHV 6137	WCru	- 'Silver Ball' (v)	CBcs CDoC CSBt CWnw EGren ELan EPfP ESwi LBom LRHS LSou LSRN MAsh MHtn MSwo SAth SHor SOrN WCha
omeiense	EBee EWes		
parvilimbum	WPGP		
ralphii 'Variegatum' (v)	EBee LRHS WPGP		
rhombifolium	see *Auranticarpa rhombifolia*	- 'Silver Magic' (v)	EGren LRHS
'Saundersii' (v)	ELon	- 'Silver Queen' (f/v) ♀H4	Widely available
tenuifolium	CBcs CBrac CCoa CCVT CDoC CExl CMac CSBt CWnw EGren EGrI EHeP ELan IDun LCro LRHS LWaG MAsh MHed SArc SFol SPlb SReu SRms WCFE WFar WJur WReH	- 'Silver Sheen' (m)	CMac CWnw EBee LRHS SArc
		- 'Stevens Island'	CCoa CDoC SArc
		- 'Tandara Gold' (v)	CBcs CCoa CDoC CMac CSBt ELan ELon EPfP EUrb LCro LRHS LSRN MAsh MGos SArc SRms WHtc
- 'Abbotsbury Gold' (f/v)	CBcs CBrac CCoa CDoC CMac CSde ELan EUrb EWes LRHS LSRN MGos MSwo SArc SEND WHtc	- 'Tom Thumb' ♀H4	Widely available
		- 'Variegatum' (m/v)	CBcs CCVT CSBt CWnw EBee EGren ELon EPfP EUrb LCro LRHS LSRN MGos MHed SArc SBig SEND WCha WFar
- 'Atropurpureum'	CBcs EGrI ELan LBom		
- BANNOW BAY ('Breebay')	CWnw ECul EGren EUrb LBom LCro LRHS LSou LSRN MBros MHed NLar SArc WFar		
		- 'Victoria' (v)	CBcs CTsd EBee EGren LRHS WFar
- BEACH BALL ('PittIb2')	EUrb LRHS SNig	- 'Warnham Gold' (m) ♀H4	CBcs CDoC CMac EBee ELan EPfP LRHS MAsh MGos NLar SPoG SRms
- 'Brockhill Compact'	LRHS		
- 'Cap Sizun'	LRHS	- 'Wendle Channon' (m/v)	CMac LRHS
- 'County Park'	CBrac EUrb LRHS SRms	- 'Wrinkled Blue'	CBcs CDoC CTsd EBee ELan EPfP EUrb LBom LRHS MPri MSwo SBig SPoG WFar
- 'County Park Dwarf'	LRHS SFol		
- 'County Park Green'	ELon EUrb		
- 'Cratus'	CWnw EBee EGren ELan EUrb LRHS LSRN MMrt SArc SBig SWor WCha	*tobira* ♀H3	CBcs CCoa CDoC CMac CSde EGren EGrI EPfP EUrb LBom LRHS LSRN MGos MPri MSwo SArc SBig SDix SEND SFol SPoG SRms SVen SWor WFar WJur WKif WLov
- 'Elizabeth' (m/v)	Widely available		
- EMERALD DOME ('Minpitto'PBR)	EGren EPfP LRHS SOrN	* - 'Nanum'	CBcs CCoa CDoC CMac CSde CWnw EGren EGrI ELan EPfP EUrb LBom LCro LRHS LSRN LWaG MGos MSwo SArc SAth SBig SHor SPoG WFar WLov
- 'French Lace'	CCoa CDoC CSde ELan LRHS MPri NLar WFar WHtc		
- 'Gloria Robinson'	see *P. tenuifolium* 'Rotundifolium'		
- 'Godsmark Green'	LCro NLar	- 'Tall 'n' Tough'	EBee WPGP
- 'Gold Star'	CCoa CSde ELan ELon EUrb LCro LRHS LSRN MGos SFol SNig SPoG SRms WFar	§ - 'Variegatum' (v) ♀H2	CBcs CCoa CMac CSde ELan EPfP EUrb LSRN MGos MMrt SArc SEND SPoG SWor
- 'Golden Ball'	CDoC EBee ECul ELan EPfP EUrb LRHS LSou MAsh MPri SOrN WLov	- 'West Acre Gold'	ELan
		- 'Trim's Hedger'	ELan SSta
		truncatum	CExl WJur
- 'Golden King'	CBrac CCVT CMac CSBt LRHS MPri SRms WHtc	*undulatum*	WJur
		viridiflorum	WJur
- 'Golf Ball'PBR	CBcs CBrac CDoC CSBt CWnw EGren EHeP ELan EPfP LCro LRHS LSou LSRN LWaG MGos MHed MSwo SArc SBig SEWo		

Plagianthus (Malvaceae)

lyallii	see *Hoheria lyallii*
regius	CBcs SArc

Plagiorhegma see *Jeffersonia*

Plantago (Plantaginaceae)
coronopus	CAgr MEar NBac SHor WFar WKor
holosteum	GKev
lanceolata	CAgr CBWd CHab CoPl NMir
major 'Atropurpurea'	see *P. major* 'Rubrifolia'
- 'Bowles's Variety'	see *P. major* 'Rosularis'
- 'Purple Perversion'	EPPr GGro IDun
- 'Rosenstolz'	CTtf
§ - 'Rosularis'	CTtf GGro IDun NBro SRms WFar WHer
§ - 'Rubrifolia'	GGro MEar SRms WFar WTre
- 'Variegata' (v)	GGro IDun WFar
media	CHab MHer NMir
nivalis	GEdr
rosea	see *P. major* 'Rosularis'
sempervirens	StAn

Platanus ✿ (Platanaceae)
× **acerifolia**	see *P.* × *hispanica*
§ × **hispanica** ♀H6	CAco CCVT CDoC CLnd CMCN EHeP ELan EPfP IPap LMaj LRHS NPip SArc SAth SEND SEWo WCha WHtc WMat WMou
- 'Pyramidalis'	IPap
occidentalis	WJur
orientalis	CAco CCVT ESwi IPap WJur WPGP
- PAB 346	LEdu
§ - f. **digitata** ♀H6	CCVT CMCN EHeP LMaj
- var. **insularis**	WPGP
- 'Laciniata'	see *P. orientalis* f. *digitata*
- 'Minaret'	LMaj
- 'Mirkovec'	IArd

Platycarya (Juglandaceae)
strobilacea	CBcs WJur

Platycerium (Polypodiaceae)
alcicorne misapplied	see *P. bifurcatum*
§ **bifurcatum** ♀H1b	CDoC EShb LBom LCro LWaG MPri NCft NHrt SPlb
grande hort.	see *P. superbum*
§ **superbum**	WCot

Platycladus (Cupressaceae)
§ **orientalis**	CAco LEdu MAsh
§ - 'Aurea Nana' ♀H7	CBrac CMac CSBt EPfP EPot LCro LRHS MAsh MGos SPoG WCha
- 'Franky Boy' ♀H7	SPoG
- 'Golden Pygmy'	MAsh
- 'Miller's Gold'	see *P. orientalis* 'Aurea Nana'
- 'Morgan'	NLar
- 'Rosedalis'	CSBt MAsh
- 'Shirley Chilcott'	MAsh

Platycodon (Campanulaceae)
grandiflorus ♀H5	ECha ELan EPfP EPPr LRHS MHoo SRms
- 'Albus'	EPfP
- Apoyama Group ♀H5	GKev
- (Astra Series) 'Astra Blue'	EPfP GKev LRHS LShi SPoG
- - 'Astra Double Blue' (d)	NBir
- - 'Astra Pink'	LRHS SPoG
- - 'Astra White'	EPfP GKev LShi SPoG
- 'Florist Blue'	MCtn
- 'Fuji Blue'	EBee
- 'Fuji Pink'	EBee EPPr GKev
- 'Hakone Double Blue' (d)	SRms
- 'Hakone White'	ELan
- 'Mariesii' ♀H5	EBee NBir SRms
- 'Zwerg'	CSpe

Platycrater see *Hydrangea*
arguta	see *Hydrangea platyarguta*

Plecostachys (Asteraceae)
§ **serpyllifolia**	LCro

Plectranthus ✿ (Lamiaceae)
ambiguus 'Nico'	CBct SDix
amboinicus	see *Coleus amboinicus*
argentatus	see *Coleus argentatus*
australis misapplied	see *P. verticillatus*
'Brusendorf'	SNoN WOld
calycinus	see *Coleus calycinus*
caninus	see *Coleus caninus* (B. Heyne ex Roth) Vatke
ciliatus	CWal EAri EShb SPhx SRkn WFar
- 'Easy Gold' (v) ♀H1c	MPie WDib
- 'Nico'	EShb SNoN
- 'Sasha' (v)	CHll
- 'Troy's Gold' (v)	EShb
coleoides 'Variegatus'	see *Coleus madagascariensis* 'Variegated Mintleaf'
ecklonii	EShb
ernstii	EShb WCot WFar
- blue-flowered	WCot
'Franklin's Limelight'	SNoN
'Franklin's Olive'	CBct SNoN
fruticosus	SNoN
- 'James'	CWCL EShb WKif
hadiensis	see *Coleus hadiensis*
MONA LAVENDER ('Plepalila'PBR) ♀H1b	MHol WKif
neochilus	see *Coleus neochilus*
oertendahlii ♀H1c	CBct EAri EShb WDib
'Santana' (v)	CoPl EAri
Swedish ivy	see *P. verticillatus*
'Velvet Elvis'PBR	CBct ELan EUrb
venteri	see *Coleus venteri*
§ **verticillatus**	EShb WFar
- 'Barberton'	SNoN
zuluensis ♀H2	EUrb SDix SPel SRkn WOld

Pleioblastus (Poaceae)
§ **argenteostriatus** f. **pumilus**	GMaP LCro NLar SPlb
auricomus	see *P. viridistriatus*
- 'Vagans'	see *Sasaella ramosa*
chino f. **elegantissimus**	MMuc SEND
fortunei	see *P. variegatus* 'Fortunei'
'Gauntlettii'	see *P. argenteostriatus* f. *pumilus*
glaber 'Albostriatus'	see *Sasaella masamuneana* 'Albostriata'
humilis var. **pumilus**	see *P. argenteostriatus* f. *pumilus*
kongosanensis 'Aureostriatus' (v)	MWht
linearis	MWht
§ **pygmaeus**	ELan GMaP MBrN NLar SRms
- 'Distichus'	NLar
* - var. **pygmaeus** 'Mini'	MMuc WCot
§ **simonii**	CAgr MMuc MWht SEND SPoG
- 'Variegatus' (v)	CBcs LRHS SPoG
variegatus (v) ♀H5	CBcs GMaP LCro MBrN MWht SPlb SRms SWor WFar
§ - 'Fortunei' (v)	MMuc SEND SWor
- 'Tsuboii' (v)	CDTJ MBrN MWht NLar NPlm SWor WFar

§ *viridistriatus* ♀H5   CMHG ELon GMaP MMuc MWht SBig SDix SEND SRms WFar
– f. *variegatus* (v)   SBig SWor

Pleione ✿ (Orchidaceae)
aurita   GKev
– hybrid   LAma
Berapi gx 'Purple Sandpiper'   WPGP
Brigadoon gx 'Stonechat'   LEdu WPGP
Britannia gx 'Doreen'   WPGP
formosana ♀H3   CTsd LCro LEdu WFar WPGP
– Alba Group   WFar
– – 'Snow Bunting'   LEdu WPGP
– – 'Clare'   LEdu WPGP
– 'Snow White'   WPGP
Glacier Peak gx × *humilis*   LAma
§ *grandiflora*   GKev LAma
Haven Oliver gx   LAma
pinkepankii   see *P. grandiflora*
Rakata gx 'Skylark'   LEdu WPGP
Stromboli gx 'Fireball'   LEdu WPGP
Sunisa gx   LAma
Tolima gx 'Moorhen'   LEdu WPGP
Tongariro gx   CBlu LCro LEdu MNrw WPGP
Versailles gx 'Bucklebury'   WPGP
yunnanensis   GKev

Pleiospilos (Aizoaceae)
nelii ♀H2   WFar

Pleomele see *Dracaena*

Plerandra (Araliaceae)
§ *elegantissima* ♀H1b   MCtn MPri

Pleroma (Melastomataceae)
'Edwardsii' ♀H2   CRHN WCot
foveolatum   CHll EGrl EPfP SEle SIvy SPoG
§ *heteromallum*   CHll CRHN
§ *urvilleanum* ♀H2   CAbb CBcs CBct CEnd CSBt CTsd EAri EGrl ELan EMdy SChF SEle SIvy SRkn
– variegated (v)   WCot

Pleuropetalum (Amaranthaceae)
darwinii   MCtn

Pleurospermum (Apiaceae)
sp.   GGro
benthamii B&SWJ 2988   WCru

plum see *Prunus domestica*

Plumbago (Plumbaginaceae)
§ *auriculata* ♀H2   CBcs CHll CSBt CSpe CWCL EShb LCro LWaG SEND SMad SPoG SRms WJun
– f. *alba* ♀H2   CHll CRHN ELan EShb SEND
– 'Crystal Waters'   CHll ELan EShb
– dark blue-flowered   CRHN
– (Escapade Series) 'Escapade Blue'   CWGN EShb SPre
– – 'Escapade White'   EShb
capensis   see *P. auriculata*
larpentiae   see *Ceratostigma plumbaginoides*

Plumeria (Apocynaceae)
sp.   EAri SPre
'Divine'   XFar
'Jubilee'   XFar

'Mini White'   XFar
rubra ♀H1b   NPlm
– Hawaiian Opal Pink ('Php2016'PBR)   LCro
'Symphony'   XFar

Poa (Poaceae)
alpina   EBee
chaixii   EBee
cita   EBee MMuc SHor SPlb
glauca   LRHS
labillardierei   CKno EBee ECha ELan EPfP EPPr LCro LRHS MMuc SEND SHor SNoN
– 'Marchants Needle'   SMHy
pratensis   CHab

Podalyria (Fabaceae)
calyptrata   SPlb
leipoldtii   SPlb
sericea   SPlb

Podanthus (Asteraceae)
ovatifolius   SVen

Podocarpus ✿ (Podocarpaceae)
acutifolius   CBcs
– 'Golden Lady' (f)   CBcs
andinus   see *Prummopitys andina*
'Blaze' (f)   GKev LEdu MHtn MMuc
chilinus   see *P. salignus*
'Chocolate Box' (f)   ELan LRHS MAsh MPri NLar WFar
'County Park Fire'PBR (f) ♀H5   CBcs LRHS MAsh MGos NLar SRms WFar
elatus   WJur
elongatus 'Blue Chip'   CBcs
'Flame' (m)   GKev LRHS MAsh MPri
lawrencei 'Blue Gem' (f)   CAco GKev LRHS MAsh MMuc MPri NLar WFar
– 'Purple King'   NLar
– 'Red Kiss'   CAco
– 'Red Tip'   CAco GKev LRHS MGos
macrophyllus   CAco SArc WJur WPGP
– 'Aureus'   CBcs
matudae   WPGP
neriifolius   WJur
nivalis   GKev NGKo SRms
– 'Kilworth Cream' (m/v) ♀H6   CBcs GKev LCro LRHS WCot WFar
– 'Otari' (m)   MAsh
'Red Embers' (f)   CBcs EPfP GKev LCro LRHS MPri WFar
§ *salignus* ♀H4   CBcs CExl SArc WPav WPGP
– (f)   EPfP WCru
'Spring Sunshine' (f)   NLar
totara 'Aureus'   CBcs MAsh MMuc
– 'Pendulus'   WFar
'Young Rusty' (f)   CBcs MAsh WFar

Podophyllum (Berberidaceae)
aurantiocaule   CExl ESwi GGGa GKev
§ *delavayi*   CExl WCot
difforme   LEdu
emodi var. *chinense*   see *Sinopodophyllum hexandrum* var. *chinense*
hexandrum   see *Sinopodophyllum hexandrum*
'Kaleidoscope' (v)   CDTJ CMiW EBee LEdu NLar WCot WPGP
peltatum   CBct CMiW CTtf EBee EBlo EGrl EMor EWld GKev ISha LAma LEdu LRHS MBel NLar

Polygala 539

	NSti SBig SMad WCru WFar WPGP WPnP
pleianthum ♀H4	CBct CMiW GEdr LEdu WCot WCru WPGP
- B&SWJ 282 from Taiwan	WCru
- var. *album*	GEdr
- short	WCru
veitchii	see *P. delavayi*
versipelle	CDTJ GKev LEdu WCru
- subsp. *boreale*	LEdu
- 'Spotty Dotty'PBR (v) ♀H4	Widely available
- subsp. *versipelle*	CBct

Podranea (Bignoniaceae)

brycei	SPlb
§ *ricasoliana* ♀H1c	EShb SPoG

Pogonia (Orchidaceae)

ophioglossoides	GArf

Polaskia (Cactaceae)

chichipe	NPlm

Polemonium ✿ (Polemoniaceae)

ambervicsii	see *P. pauciflorum* subsp. *hinckleyi*
'Apricot Beauty'	see *P. carneum* 'Apricot Delight'
§ *archibaldiae* ♀H5	NBir SRms
'Blue Pearl'	GJos LBar LRHS MCtn NBro NGdn NLar SHar WFar WSpi WTre
§ *boreale*	LRHS MPri
- 'Heavenly Habit'	GJos LRHS
brandegeei misapplied	see *P. pauciflorum*
§ *caeruleum*	CBWd CGHo CWal ECha EHet ELan ENfk EPfP GKev GMaP GQue LCro LRHS LWaG MCtn MHer MMuc MNHC NAts NBro NLar SPlb SPoG SRms WBrk WCAu WOrg WShi WSpi
- subsp. *amygdalinum* 'Album'	see *P. caeruleum* subsp. *caeruleum* f. *album*
- 'Bambino Blue'	EPfP LRHS MPri SIvy SRms
- Brise d'Anjou ('Blanjou'PBR) (v)	CMac ELan EPfP EWes GKev LBom LRHS LShi MArl MHol MHoo MPri MPro NBir NLar SPeP SPoG XFar
- subsp. *caeruleum*	GKev
§ - - f. *album*	CBcs EBee ECha ELan EPfP GQue LBuc LRHS MArl MBel MHer MHoo MMuc NBro SPoG SRms WCAu WSpi WTre
- - - 'White Pearl'	LShi MCtn
- - 'Filigree Skies'	NGdn
§ - subsp. *himalayanum*	EAri
- - CC 7325	GGro
- 'Humile'	see *P.* 'Northern Lights'
- 'Snow and Sapphires' (v)	CWGN MPnt NPer
- white-flowered	GJos
carneum	ECha
§ - 'Apricot Delight'	CFis CTtf EMor GJos LRHS LShi MNrw NGdn NQui SBeP SIvy SRms WSpi
cashmerianum	see *P. caeruleum* subsp. *himalayanum*
'Elworthy Amethyst'	CElw
foliosissimum misapplied	see *P. archibaldiae*
foliosissimum A. Gray 'Bressingham'	LBom
- 'Cottage Cream'	WFar
- var. *foliosissimum*	WSpi
'Glebe Cottage Lilac'	CDor NBir
'Golden Feathers'PBR (v)	EMor LBar LBom LRHS LSou MHtn MPri MPro WFar XFar
'Hannah Billcliffe'	MBrN WFar
'Heaven Scent'PBR	EBee EHeP ELan EMor EPfP LBar LCro LRHS LSou MArl MBel MBNS MPnt MPri MPro MSwo NDov NLar SPad WCAu WCav XFar
§ 'Hopleys'	MNrw NDov
× *jacobaea*	ECha EPPr WCot
'Katie Daley'	see *P.* 'Hopleys'
kiushianum	GGro
'Lambrook Mauve'	CDor CMiW EBee ECha EMor EPfP EPPr GBin GMaP LBom LCro LSto Midl MNrw MPie NBir NLar NQui NSti WCAu WCav WChS WCot WFar WHoo WKif
§ 'Northern Lights' ♀H6	CBcs CMHG CSpe EBee ELon EWes GBin GElm GMaP GQue LBar LBom LShi LSto MAvo MBel MNrw MPie NLar SPoG SRms WCAu WCot WFar WKif
'Norwell Mauve'	MNrw MWlw WFar
§ *pauciflorum*	CTtf GJos MCtn NBir
§ - subsp. *hinckleyi*	GKev
- 'Sulphur Trumpets'	EPfP GJos SMrm
'Pink Beauty'	EBee ELan EPfP LBar LRHS NGdn
pulchellum Salisb.	see *P. reptans*
pulchellum Turcz.	see *P. caeruleum*
pulcherrimum misapplied	see *P. boreale*
- 'Tricolor'	see *P. boreale*
pulcherrimum Hook.	GJos
- subsp. *delicatum*	GKev StAn
§ *reptans*	EPfP GJos MHer NBro SRms
- 'Album'	see *P. reptans* 'Virginia White'
- 'Jacob's Gold' (v)	EBee ELan EPfP
* - 'Sky Blue'	NBro
- 'Stairway to Heaven'PBR (v)	Widely available
- 'Touch of Class'PBR (v)	CWGN EBee EMor MHoo MPri NLar SPoG
§ - 'Virginia White'	ECha EWes NQui WCAu
richardsonii misapplied	see *P.* 'Northern Lights'
richardsonii Graham	see *P. boreale*
'Sonia's Bluebell'	EPPr EWes GBin MWlw NDov NLar NSti WFar
'Triffids' Lilac'	CTtf
viscosum	GKev SPlb
yezoense	WFar
- var. *hidakanum* Bressingham Purple ('Polbress')	CAby CSpe CTtf EBee EBlo ELan EMor EPfP EWes GMaP LBar LCro LRHS LSto MArl MBel MBNS MHol Midl MPri NBir NLar NSti SOrN SPoG SRms WCAu WHoo
- - 'Halfway to Paradise'	EPfP
- - 'Purple Rain'	CDor CMac CSpe EBee ELan ELon EMor EPfP GAbr GJos GMaP GQue LRHS LSto MCtn MHoo MPro NLar SRkn SRms WCot WFar WTre
- 'Kaleidoscope' (v)	LRHS MPnt MPri MPro WNPC XFar

Polianthes see Agave

Poliomintha (Lamiaceae)

bustamanta	NBir

Poliothyrsis (Salicaceae)

sinensis	CBcs EBee WJur WPGP

Pollia (Commelinaceae)

hasskarlii	WTra
japonica	ESwi LEdu WCot

Polygala (Polygalaceae)

'Africana'PBR	CPbh

540 *Polygala*

africana 'Nana'	LRHS SEle		*hookeri*	CBct CExl CTtf EBee EDAr EPot GBin GEdr GKev GMaP GQue LSto NBid NLar WCru WFar
calcarea ♀H7	WAbe			
- Bulley's form	EPot			
- 'Lillet' ♀H7	EPot GEdr WAbe	§	*humile*	CBct EBee EBlo ELan EMor EPfP EPPr EWld GAbr GKev LRHS MAvo NGdn NLar NWbg WBrk WCru WHil WPGP
chamaebuxus	see *Polygaloides chamaebuxus*			
§ × *dalmaisiana* ♀H1c	CAbb CCoa CDoC CSde CSpe CTsd EGrI ELan EShb LRHS SEle SEND SIvy			
			- 'Shiro-shima-fu' (v)	ESwi WFar
'Dolomite'	EPot GEdr	I	- 'Variegatum' (v)	CMac WCot
myrtifolia ♀H2	LRHS SAdn SPlb	§	× *hybridum* ♀H7	Widely available
- 'Grandiflora'	see *P.* × *dalmaisiana*		- 'Bere'	LEdu WPGP
'Purple Passion'	SRms WFar		- 'Betberg'	CTtf ECha ELon EPPr LEdu NBir NLar WCot WFar WHoo
tenuifolia	CSpe			
			- 'Flore Pleno' (d)	CTtf

Polygaloides (Polygalaceae)

			- 'Nanum'	WCot
§ *chamaebuxus* ♀H7	MGos SRms		- 'Purple Katie'	EPPr ESwi MAvo
I - *alba*	WAbe	§	- 'Striatum' (v)	Widely available
§ - 'Grandiflora' ♀H7	EPot GAbr GEdr GKev MGos NBir SPlb SPoG WAbe WIce		- 'Variegatum'	see *P.* × *hybridum* 'Striatum'
			- 'Wakehurst'	LEdu
- 'Purpurea'	see *P. chamaebuxus* 'Grandiflora'		- 'Weihenstephan'	EBee EMor EPPr GKev LBar LEdu WPGP
- 'Rhodoptera'	see *P. chamaebuxus* 'Grandiflora'			
			- 'Welsh Gold' (v)	EBee ESwi

Polygonatum (Asparagaceae)

			inflatum	WCru
altelobatum B&SWJ 286	WCru		- B&SWJ 922	WCru
annamense HWJ 9752	WCru		*involucratum*	WCru
arisanense B&SWJ 271	WCru LEdu MAvo		- B&SWJ 4285	WCru
- B&SWJ 3839	WCru		*japonicum*	see *P. odoratum*
§ *biflorum*	CAgr CPud EBee EBlo ELan ELon EPfP GElm GMaP LAma LSto MArl NLar SMHy SPoG WCAu WCru WFar WPnP		*kingianum*	CDor GGro LEdu
			- red-flowered	GEdr
			- yellow-flowered B&SWJ 6545	WCru
- dwarf	EBlo LRHS		- - B&SWJ 6562	WCru
blue-fruited BO 16-113 from Jiajinshan, China	GGro		'Langthorn's Variegated' (v)	ELan
			lasianthum	WCru
brevistylum B&SWJ 2421	WCru		- B&SWJ 671	WCru
canaliculatum	see *P. biflorum*	§	*latifolium*	EBlo ECha EMor EPPr WCru
cathcartii B&SWJ 2429	WCru		- W&B BG C-2	WCot
- yellow-flowered B&SWJ 2412	WCru		- 'Robustum'	WCru
			macranthum B&SWJ 5727	WCru
cirrhifolium	EBee EPot GEdr GKev LAma LEdu MAvo MNrw WCru		- B&SWJ 11425	LEdu WCru
			maximowiczii	EPPr WCru
- from China	WCru	§	*mengtzense* HWJ 861	GGro LEdu WCru
- red-flowered	NLar		- f. *mengtzense* HWJ 588	WCru
commutatum	see *P. biflorum*		- f. *tonkinense* B&SWJ 8246	LEdu WCru
costatum B&SWJ 6599	WCru			
cryptanthum	WCru		- - HWJ 551	WCru
curvistylum	CDor EAri ECha EPPr ESwi EWld GEdr LEdu LSto MAvo NLar SMHy WCru WFar		- - HWJ 567	WCru
			- - HWJ 573	WCru
			'Multifide'	EBee
cyrtonema misapplied	see *Disporopsis pernyi*		*multiflorum* misapplied	see *P.* × *hybridum*
cyrtonema Hua	ESwi WCru		*multiflorum* ambig.	SPeP
* *desoulavyi* var. *yezoense* B&SWJ 764	WCru		*multiflorum* (L.) All.	CAgr CBcs CDoC CHab CMac CTsd EBee EBlo ECha EGrI EHeP EPfP GAbr LBar MArl MBel MHol NGdn NLar SPlb SRms WCAu WCru WFar WHer WShi
falcatum misapplied	see *P. humile*			
falcatum A. Gray	EPot GEdr			
- B&SWJ 1077	WCru			
- B&SWJ 5054	WCru		- CC 4572	WCot
- NJM 11.012	WPGP		- 'Flore Pleno' (d)	WFar
- 'Shikoku Silver'	CTtf EPPr ESwi LEdu WCru		- *giganteum* hort.	see *P. biflorum*
- 'Silver Mist'	LEdu		- 'Ramosissima'	LEdu WCru
- 'Variegatum'	see *P. odoratum* var. *pluriflorum* 'Variegatum'		- var. *ramosum*	LEdu
			nodosum	WCru
'Falcon'	see *P. humile*	§	*odoratum*	CBro EBee ECha GMaP LAma LEdu MPnt NBid NLar NRya StAn WCru
filipes	EBee EPPr LEdu WCru			
fuscum	WCru		- 'Amanogawa' (v)	LAma
geminiflorum	LEdu WCru WFar		- 'Byakko' (v)	NWbg WFar
giganteum	see *P. biflorum*		- 'Dai Koga' (v)	GEdr WFar
glaberrimum	EBee WCot WPGP		- 'Dusky Bere'	ESwi WPGP
'Golden Gift'	WCot	§	- dwarf	LEdu
§ *graminifolium*	EBee EBlo ESwi GEdr LRHS WCru		- 'Echigo-nishiki' (v)	LAma
hirtum	see *P. latifolium*		- 'Flatmate'	ESwi LEdu WCru

Polypodium 541

- 'Flore Pleno' (d)	CDor GKev LEdu MHer WCot WHoo		- Og 94047	WCru
- 'Goldilocks' (v)	WCot		*zanlanscianense*	EPPr ESwi LEdu WCru
- 'Grace Barker'	see *P.* × *hybridum* 'Striatum'		aff. *zanlanscianense*	SPlb
- Kew form	EPot			
- 'Kouda-nishiki' (v)	LAma			

Polygonum (Polygonaceae)

affine	see *Bistorta affinis*
amplexicaule	see *Bistorta amplexicaulis*
aubertii	see *Fallopia baldschuanica*
baldschuanicum	see *Fallopia baldschuanica*
bistorta	see *Bistorta officinalis*
equisetiforme misapplied	see *P. scoparium*
forrestii	see *Koenigia forrestii*
multiflorum	see *Reynoutria multiflora*
odoratum	see *Persicaria odorata*
perfoliatum	see *Persicaria perfoliata*
polystachyum	see *Koenigia polystachya*
runciforme	see *Persicaria runcinata*
§ *scoparium*	CSpe EPPr LRHS SVen WFar WOld
vaccinifolium	see *Bistorta vaccinifolia*
weyrichii	see *Koenigia weyrichii*

- 'Kouga' (v) — LAma
- var. *odoratum* — GKev
- 'Pangolin' — WPGP
- § var. *pluriflorum* 'Variegatum' (v) — Widely available
- 'Pruhonice' — EBee ECha
- 'Red Legs' — GEdr
- 'Red Stem' — EBlo ECha LEdu LRHS LSto MAvo WCru WFar
- 'Shiro-kujaku' (v) — LAma
- 'Silver Wings' (v) — ECha LEdu LSto NBir NLar NWbg WFar
- 'Taiga' (v) — ESwi
- var. *thunbergii* — WCru
- 'Tora-fu' (v) — LAma
- 'Triglav' — MAvo
- 'Ussuriland' — EPPr LEdu MAvo
- 'Ussuriland Roundleaf' — ESwi LEdu MAvo

officinale — see *P. odoratum*
oppositifolium — EBee LAma
- B&SWJ 2537 — WCru
§ *orientale* — EBee EBlo EPfP ESwi GKev LRHS NLar
- S&F 364 — EPPr WCot
pluriflorum — see *P. graminifolium*
polyanthemum — see *P. orientale*
praecox new — WCru
prattii — EBee GKev LAma WCru
- CLD 325 — GEdr LEdu
pubescens — WCru
pumilum — see *P. odoratum* dwarf
punctatum misapplied — see *P. mengtzense*
punctatum ambig. — NBid WPGP
punctatum Royle ex Kunth — GKev WCot
- B&SWJ 2395 — WCru
- B&SWJ 13993 — WCru
- WJC 13880 — WCru
roseum — EBee EPPr ESwi GKev MAvo MMrt WCru
sewerzowii — EMor EPPr
sibiricum — ESwi WCru WFar
- DJHC 600 — LEdu MAvo
singalilense — LEdu WCru
stenophyllum — WCru
stewartianum — EBee EPPr ESwi MAvo NRya
tessellatum PAB 8336 — LEdu WPGP
- PAB 13.471 — WCot
verticillatum — CBct CBro EBee EBlo ECha EMor EPfP EPPr ESwi EWld GEdr GKev LEdu LRHS LSto MMuc MNrw SMad WCru WFar WShi
- B&SWJ 2147 — WCru
- CLD 1308 — EPPr
- PAB 2455 — LEdu
- 'Giant One' — LCro
- 'Himalayan Giant' — CSpe EBlo EMor EPPr LRHS WCAu
- 'Krynica' — LEdu WPGP
* - 'Roseum' — EBee EBlo
- 'Rubrum' — CBct CSpe EMor EPPr GEdr GGro IPot LEdu NBid NLar NWbg SMad WCot WCru WFar WHoo
- 'Serbian Dwarf' — CBct ESwi GKev
aff. *verticillatum* — CTtf
vietnamicum — CExl
yunnanense — CBct ESwi LEdu WPGP

Polylepis (Rosaceae)

australis	IArd
- tall	WPGP
quadrijuga B&SWJ 14375	WCru

Polymnia (Asteraceae)

sonchifolia 'Red China'	WPGP

Polypodiodes (Polypodiaceae)

formosana ♀H3	WCot

Polypodium ✿ (Polypodiaceae)

aureum	see *Phlebodium aureum*
australe	see *P. cambricum*
- 'Pulcherrimum'	EWld
azoricum	WCot
californicum	LEdu WPGP
calirhiza 'Sarah Lyman'	CLAP LEdu MWlw WOld WPGP
§ *cambricum*	CLAP ELon NAlc SMrm SPlb WCot
- 'Barrowii'	CLAP LEdu WAbe WGwG
- 'Bychan'	MWlw
- 'Cambricum' ♀H7	WAbe
- 'Conwy'	WAbe
- 'Cristatum'	LEdu NAlc WCot
- (Cristatum Group) 'Grandiceps Fox' ♀H7	CLAP
- 'Herbert Whitley'	LEdu SPel
- old form	WCot
- 'Hornet'	CLAP SMHy WCot
- 'Macrostachyon'	LEdu NBid SPel
- 'Oakleyae'	CDor LEdu MWlw NAlc NCth SMHy WCot
- 'Omnilacerum Oxford'	LEdu SPel WCot
- 'Prestonii'	CDor CLAP MWlw WCot
- Pulcherrimum Group	WAbe WCot
- - bifid	EBee
- - 'Pulcherrimum Addison'	LEdu WCot
- - 'Pulchritudine'	MWlw WCot
- - 'Trippitt'	MWlw
- 'Richard Kayse' ♀H7	CLAP EWes MPie MWlw SMHy SPel SPlb WAbe WBrk WCot WMal
- Semilacerum Group	WCot
- - 'Carew Lane'	LEdu SPel
- - 'Falcatum O'Kelly'	WCot WOld
- 'Wavy Lines'	WCot
- 'Whilharris' ♀H7	CDor SPel WCot
'Dancing Girls'	WCot
glycyrrhiza	LEdu NBro SMHy
- 'Lawrence Crocker'	CLAP LEdu MWlw WCot
- 'Longicaudatum' ♀H7	CLAP LEdu SMHy WAbe WBrk WCot

Polypodium

- 'Malahatense' — CLAP SMIly SPel
- - (sterile) — SPel WAbe WCot
- **glycyrrhiza × scouleri** — CLAP WPGP
- **guttatum** — SPlb
- **interjectum** — EMor WCot
- **macaronesicum** — LEdu WCot
- **× mantoniae** — CLAP LEdu
- - 'Bifidograndiceps' — CLAP GQue NBid SPel
- - 'Cornubiense' ♀H7 — CDor CLAP EWld LEdu NBid NBir NHar SMHy WCot WOld
- **scouleri** — CLAP EMor ESwi ISha LEdu MAsh NBro WCot WPGP
- 'Shorty' — WCot
- **vulgare** — Widely available
- - 'Bifidocristatum' — CDor CLAP CTsd ELon GEdr ISha LEdu LRHS MAsh MGos NLar WBrk
- - 'Bifidomulticeps' — WCot
- * - 'Congestum Cristatum' — SRms
- - 'Cornubiense Grandiceps' — SRms
- * - 'Cornubiense Multifidum' — WCot
- - 'Elegantissimum' — LEdu MWlw NBid SPel
- - 'Parsley' — LEdu MWlw WCot
- - 'Ramosum Hillman' — WCot
- - 'Trichomanoides Backhouse' — CLAP WAbe
- 'Whitley Giant' — CBcs CDor EBee ELon EMor ESwi GEdr ISha LEdu LRHS MHol MPie NBid NLar SBig SPel WCot

Polypompholyx see *Utricularia*

Polyscias (Araliaceae)
- **balfouriana** — LCro
- 'Fabian' — LCro NHrt
- **fruticosa** — LBom LCro NHrt
- 'Roble' — NHrt
- **scutellaria** 'Marginata' (v) ♀H1c — LCro

Polyspora (Theaceae)
- **longicarpa** — CBcs EBee WPGP
- - B&SWJ 11704 — WCru
- - WWJ 11604 — WCru
- - WWJ 11894 — WCru
- **speciosa** — CBcs WPGP

Polystichum ❀ (Dryopteridaceae)
- **acrostichoides** — CDTJ CLAP EGren EMor ISha LEdu NAlc NBro NLar SBig SPlb WCot WPGP
- **aculeatum** ♀H7 — CBWd CLAP ECha EGren ELan EMor GBin GMaP ISha LBom LCro LRHS MAsh MGos MMuc NBid NLar SPoG SRms WCAu
- - 'Cristatum' — LBom
- I - Densum Group — LBom
- - 'Divisilobum' — EGren LBom
- **andersonii** — CLAP LSto NBro
- **biaristatum** — EBee GBin LRHS WPGP
- **bissectum** — CExl
- **braunii** — CBcs CDoC CDor CLAP EBee ELan EMor GMaP ISha LRHS MAsh NBid NBro NLar SPoG WCot WPnP
- **caryotideum** — see *Cyrtomium caryotideum*
- **× dycei** ♀H5 — CDor CLAP MAsh WCot WPGP
- **falcatum** — see *Cyrtomium falcatum*
- **fortunei** — see *Cyrtomium fortunei*
- **makinoi** — CDor CElw CLAP EBee ELan EMor LEdu MAsh NBid NBro NCth NLar SPlb WCot
- **mayebarae** — CLAP

- **munitum** ♀H7 — Widely available
- **neolobatum** — CLAP EBee EMor ISha LCro LEdu NAlc NBro NLar SBig WCot WPGP
- - BWJ 8182 — WCru
- **ovatopaleaceum** — LEdu
- **polyblepharum** ♀H7 — Widely available
- - 'Jade' — EGren LRHS
- **proliferum** misapplied — see *P. setiferum* Acutilobum Group
- **proliferum** (R. Br.) C. Presl — CLAP EWld LBuc SAth WAbe WCot WPGP
- * - **plumosum** — SBig
- **retrorsopaleaceum** — ISha
- **rigens** — CAbb CAby CBlu CLAP CSde CSta CTsd LCro LRHS MAsh MAvo NBro NLar SDix SPoG SRms SRot WHoo
- **setiferum** ♀H7 — Widely available
- § - Acutilobum Group — ECha GMaP ISha LBom LEdu LRHS MAsh NHar SDix SPad SRms WCAu WPGP
- - 'Barfod's Dwarf **new** — WAbe
- - Congestum Group — CDor CLAP ELon NBro NLar SRms SRot WBrk WFar
- - - 'Congestum' — CBWd CSta ELan EPfP EWld ISha LEdu LRHS MAsh MHtn MSwo NAlc NBir NGdn SPel SPoG
- - - 'Congestum Cristatum' — CLAP WAbe
- - 'Cristatopinnulum' — CExl EBee LEdu NHar WPGP
- - Cristatum Group — CLAP SRms
- - - 'Cristatum' — LBom
- - (Decompositum Group) 'Proliferum' — ISha
- - Divisilobum Group ♀H7 — CLAP EBee ELan EWld MGos SRms WAbe WFar WHoo WPGP
- - - 'Caernarfon' — CExl
- - - 'Dahlem' — CSta EBee ECha EGren ELan ELon EMor GMaP LRHS LSRN MAsh NAlc NBid NLar
- - - 'Divisilobum Densum' ♀H7 — NBir
- - - 'Divisilobum Grandiceps' — CLAP
- - - 'Divisilobum Iveryanum' ♀H7 — CLAP SRms
- - - 'Divisilobum Laxum' — EBee
- § - - 'Divisilobum Wollaston' — CDTJ CExl CLAP CSta EBee ELan ISha LBom LCro LRHS MGos NBid NLar SHor WCot
- - - 'Herrenhausen' — Widely available
- - - 'Mrs Goffey' — CExl
- - - 'Proliferum' — EGren EMor EUrb LEdu NAlc NLar WFar
- - 'Gracile' — NBir
- § - 'Gracillimum' — CLAP
- - 'Grandiceps' — CExl
- - GREEN LACE — see *P. setiferum* 'Gracillimum'
- - 'Hirondelle' — SRms
- - Multilobum Group — SRms
- - Perserratum Group — NBid
- - 'Plumo-Densum' — see *P. setiferum* Plumosomultilobum Group
- - 'Plumosodensum' — see *P. setiferum* Plumosomultilobum Group
- - Plumosodivisilobum Group — EBee ECha MPnt NBid NBro WAbe
- § - Plumosomultilobum Group — CDor CFis EPfP GBin GQue LBom LCro LSto MGos NBir NLar SPel SPoG WCot WFar WHoo WPnP XFar
- I - - 'Plumosomultilobum Densum' — CLAP CSta EMor EUrb LRHS MAvo MBel MHer MPie NAlc NCth SMad SPel WBrk WCot WFar

Potentilla 543

- Plumosum Group	CSpe ELon LRHS MAsh MSwo NHar SArc
* - - 'Plumosum Grande Moly'	SRms
- - 'Washfield form'	SMHy
- Proliferum Group	see *P. setiferum* Acutilobum Group
- 'Proliferum Wollaston'	see *P. setiferum* (Divisilobum Group) 'Divisilobum Wollaston'
- 'Pulcherrimum Bevis' ♀H6	CLAP CSpe LEdu MAsh SArc SMHy WPGP
- (Rotundatum Group) 'Cristatum'	CLAP
- 'Smith's Cruciate'	WOld WPGP
- 'Wakeleyanum'	EWld SRms
'Spiny Holly'	CLAP EBee NCth SBig
tsussimense ♀H6	CBdn CLAP CMac CSta EBee EGren ELan EMor EPfP EUrb LBom LCro LEdu LRHS LWaG MAvo NAlc NBir NBro SPlb SPoG SRms SRot WBrk WFar WPnP
wawranum	WPGP
xiphophyllum	CLAP LEdu NBro SPlb WPGP
yunnanense	CCht CWnw EBee LEdu LRHS NLar WPGP

pomegranate see *Punica granatum*

Poncirus see *Citrus*

Pontechium (Boraginaceae)

§ *maculatum*	CBcs CSpe EPfP EUrb LRHS LWaG MCtn MHoo SMHy SMrm SPhx SPlb

Pontederia (Pontederiaceae)

cordata ♀H5	CBen CLil CPud CToG CTtf CWat ECha ELan ELin EPfP EWat LCro LWaG MWts NPer SPlb WMAq
- f. *albiflora*	CLil CPud CToG CWat ELin EPfP EWat MWts
- 'Blue Spires'	CLil ELin
- dark blue-flowered	ELin
§ - var. *lancifolia*	CBen CToG CWat ECha ELin EPfP MNrw MWts NPer
- pink-flowered	ELin
dilatata	see *Monochoria hastata*
lanceolata	see *P. cordata* var. *lancifolia*

Populus ✿ (Salicaceae)

× *acuminata*	WMou
alba	CBcs CBTr CCVT CLnd CMac EHeP IPap LBuc SEWo WMou
- 'Bolleana'	see *P. alba* 'Pyramidalis'
- 'Nivea'	LMaj
§ - 'Pyramidalis'	EHeP WMou
- 'Richardii'	SDix WCot WMou
§ - 'Balsam Spire' (f)	CMac WMou
§ *balsamifera*	CCVT CLnd EHeP WCot WFar
- 'Vita Sackville West'	MBlu
× *canadensis*	CBTr
§ - 'Aurea' ♀H7	WMat WMou
- 'Columbia'	WMou
- 'Eugenei' (m)	WMou
- 'Gaver'	CBTr
- 'Ghoy' (m)	CBTr
- 'Robusta' (m)	CCVT CLnd EHeP WMou WRjT
- 'Serotina' (m)	WMou
× *canescens*	CLnd WMou
- 'Tower'	WMat
ciliata	WPGP
deltoides 'Fuego'	SGol
- 'Purple Tower' PBR	CBTr CLnd EBee MBlu MMuc NOra NPip SDix WMat
× *generosa* 'Beaupré'	CBTr WMou
glauca	WPGP
× *jackii* 'Aurora' (f/v)	CBcs CMac IPap NPip WFar WMou
lasiocarpa	ELan MBlu WMou WPGP
- (m/f)	WPGP
nigra	CHab
- (f)	CHab CLnd MMuc
- (m)	MMuc
- subsp. *betulifolia*	CBTr CCVT CHab CLnd EHeP WMou WRjT
- - (f)	WMou
- - (m)	WMou
- 'Hanging Tree'	CBTr EBee WMat
§ - 'Italica' (m) ♀H7	CBTr CCVT CLnd CMac EHeP ELan IPap LBuc LMaj MMuc SArc WHtc WMou
- 'Pyramidalis' (m)	see *P. nigra* 'Italica'
purdomii	CBcs IArd WPGP
'Serotina Aurea'	see *P.* × *canadensis* 'Aurea'
simonii 'Fastigiata'	WMou
§ *szechuanica* var. *tibetica*	WPGP
tacamahaca	see *P. balsamifera*
'Tacatricho 32' (f)	see *P.* 'Balsam Spire'
tomentosa	WMou
tremula	CBTr CCVT CHab CLnd CMac EGren EHeP ELan IPap LBuc MMuc SEWo WHtc WMou WRjT
§ - 'Erecta' ♀H7	CEnd LMaj MBlu MMuc NPip WMat
- 'Fastigiata'	see *P. tremula* 'Erecta'
- 'Pendula' (m)	CEnd
trichocarpa	CBTr EHeP
- 'Columbia River' (m)	CBTr
- 'Fritzi Pauley' (f)	CBTr
- 'Scott Pauley' (m)	CBTr
- 'Trichobel'	CBTr
violascens	see *P. szechuanica* var. *tibetica*
× *wilsocarpa* 'Beloni'	WPGP
wilsonii	WPGP
- KR 3993	WPGP
- MF 20088	WPGP
yunnanensis	WMou

Portulaca (Portulacaceae)

sp.	MBros
gilliesii	CoPl
grandiflora	MCtn
oleracea	ENfk MCtn SVic
- var. *aurea*	MNHC

Portulacaria (Didiereaceae)

afra	CDoC CPic EShb EUrb LWaG NCft
- 'Mediopicta' (v)	CPic NCft
- 'Variegata' (v)	CDoC EShb EUrb LBom LWaG NCft

Potamogeton (Potamogetonaceae)

crispus	CBen CLil CWat WMAq

potato see AGM Vegetables Section

Potentilla ✿ (Rosaceae)

alba	ECha LShi SHar WCAu
alchemilloides	CMac
alpina (Willk.) Zimmeter	see *P. aurea*
ambigua	see *P. cuneata*
ancistrifolia var. *dickinsii*	GEdr
anserina	CAgr MHer SPhx
- 'Golden Treasure' (v)	NSti
arbuscula misapplied	see *P. fruticosa* (Sulphurascens Group) 'Elizabeth'
'Arc-en-ciel'	EBee GElm LBar MArl MBel MBNS MNrw MPnt MPro NEoE NQui

Potentilla

Name	Nurseries
	NWbg SBeP SMrm SRkn SRms WCAu WFar XFar
argentea	SPlb WFar
argyrophylla	see *P. atrosanguinea* var. *argyrophylla*
* - *insignis rubra*	StAn
atrosanguinea	CMac EBee ECha EGren EPfP GJos GKev GMaP LCro LRHS LShi MBel MMuc NGdn NSti SPlb SPoG SRms WFar WKif
- CC 7167	GGro
§ - var. *argyrophylla*	CDor EBee ECha ELan GKev GPSL NBir NBro NLar SMHy SRms
- - CC 7185	EPPr
- - 'Golden Starlit'	ELan SVic
§ - - 'Scarlet Starlit'	CAby CDor EDAr EGren ELan GElm GJos LRHS MBNS NEoE SVic
- 'Chadwell's Tibetan Velvet'	GGro
- 'Fireball' (d)	ELan
- var. *leucochroa*	see *P. atrosanguinea* var. *argyrophylla*
§ *aurea*	GArf MNHC
- 'Plena' (d)	NRya
'Blazeaway'	EBee LSto MArl NGdn SRms
calabra	ECha EWes MMuc
'Congo'	LRHS
crantzii	SRms
§ *cuneata* ♀H7	ELan
davurica 'Abbotswood'	see *P. fruticosa* 'Abbotswood'
delphinensis	GQue
'Emilie' (d)	MNrw NLar NWbg WFar
§ *erecta*	CGwi GQue MNHC SRms
eriocarpa	GArf WAbe
'Esta Ann'	CMac EBee GAbr LRHS LShi MArl MBel NLar NSti WCAu
'Etna'	LShi MArl MNrw NBir NLar WCAu WFar WHrl
'Everest'	see *P. fruticosa* 'Mount Everest'
'Fireflame'	NLar
fissa	MNrw NBir NLar
'Flambeau' (d)	CAby ESgI MArl NGdn NSti SMHy WCAu WCot
'Flamboyant' (d)	LBar MMrt
'Flamenco'	NBir WFar
fragariiformis	see *P. megalantha*
fruticosa	CoPl LBuc
§ - 'Abbotswood' ♀H7	CBcs CBrac CDoC CEnd EBee EGren EHeP ELan EPfP IArd LCro LRHS LSRN LSto MAsh MGos NLar SAth SGol SPlb SPoG SRms WFar WHtc
- var. *arbuscula* misapplied	see *P. fruticosa* (Sulphurascens Group) 'Elizabeth'
- BELLA APPLE ('Hachapp'^{PBR})	LSou NEoE NLar
- BELLA BIANCA ('Hachbianca'^{PBR})	EHeP LCro NLar WLov
- BELLA HENDRIKSEN	NLar
- BELLA LINDSEY ('Hendlin'^{PBR})	EBee EHeP ELan LCro LSou NLar
- BELLA ROSA ('Hachrosa') **new**	WLov
- BELLA SOL ('Hachdon'^{PBR})	CWGN EHeP ELan EUrb LCro NCth NLar WLov
- BELLISSIMA ('Hachliss'^{PBR})	CBcs CBrac CWGN ELan LCro LRHS MAsh MPri NLar WLov
- 'Bewerley Surprise'	WFar
- 'Bo-Peep'	CEnd WFar
- 'Chelsea Star' ♀H7	CDoC CMac ELan EPfP LRHS MAsh SPoG SRGP
- CREAM'ISSIMA ('Minjau06'^{PBR})	LRHS
- 'Dakota Sunrise'	WFar
- DANNY BOY ('Lissdan'^{PBR})	ELan EPfP LCro LRHS MAsh NEoE NLar SPoG
- 'Daydawn'	CBrac CMac EHeP ELan EPfP MAsh MMuc NLar SAth SRms WFar
- DOUBLE PUNCH CREAM ('Mincrero01'^{PBR}) (d)	EBee ELan MAsh MMrt
- DOUBLE PUNCH PASTEL ('Mincrero04'^{PBR}) (d) **new**	LRHS
- DOUBLE PUNCH PEACH ('Minjaro01'^{PBR}) (d) **new**	CBcs LRHS
- DOUBLE PUNCH TANGO ('Minora07'^{PBR}) (d)	MAsh
- 'Farreri'	see *P. fruticosa* 'Gold Drop'
§ - 'Gold Drop'	CMac
- 'Goldfinger'	CAgr CBrac CDoC CSBt EBee EHeP EPfP LRHS MAsh MGos MMuc SAth SPlb SPoG WFar
- GOLDKUGEL	see *P. fruticosa* 'Gold Drop'
- 'Goldstar'	IArd LRHS MMuc SEND SRms WFar
- 'Goldteppich'	LBuc NLar
- 'Grace Darling'	NLar SRGP
- 'Groneland' ♀H7	EPfP SPoG
- 'Hopleys Orange' ♀H7	CBrac CDoC EBee ELan EPfP LRHS NLar SRms WFar
- 'Jackman's Variety' ♀H7	EPfP SRms
- 'Katherine Dykes'	EBee EHeP ELan EPfP GKin LRHS SRms WFar WHtc
§ - 'Klondike'	CBrac EGren
- 'Kobold'	CDoC EHeP ELan NLar
- 'Lemon and Lime'	see *P. fruticosa* 'Limelight'
§ - 'Limelight' ♀H7	CSBt ELan EPfP GKin LRHS MAsh MMuc MSwo NCth NEoE SRms WFar
- 'Lovely Pink'	see *P. fruticosa* 'Pink Beauty'
§ - 'Maanelys'	NLar
- 'Macpenny's Cream'	CMac SRms
- 'Manchu'	CMac GKev SRms
- MANGO TANGO ('Uman'^{PBR})	CSBt ELan EPfP LRHS LSRN MAsh MPri NEoE SAth SPoG WFar
§ - MARIAN RED ROBIN ('Marrob'^{PBR}) ♀H7	CDoC EHeP ELan EPfP GKin LCro MAsh NCth NRms WFar
- 'McKay's White'	ELan NCth NLar
- 'Medicine Wheel Mountain' ♀H7	ELan EPfP IArd MAsh MMrt NEoE SPoG WFar
- MOONLIGHT	see *P. fruticosa* 'Maanelys'
§ - 'Mount Everest'	CMac MMuc
- 'New Dawn'	GKin
- 'Orangeade'	EPfP MAsh SPoG
§ - 'Pink Beauty'^{PBR} ♀H7	CBrac CDoC CSBt EBee ELan EPfP GKin LCro LRHS LSRN LSto MAsh NCth SPoG SRkn SRms WFar WLov
- PINK PARADISE ('Kupinpa'^{PBR})	CMac MAsh
- 'Pink Pearl'	WFar
- 'Pink Queen'	EGren
- 'Pink Whisper'	SRms
- 'Pretty Polly'	EHeP NLar WFar
- 'Primrose Beauty' ♀H7	CDoC CMac EBee EHeP ELan EPfP LCro LRHS LSRN MAsh MMuc NLar SEND SPlb WFar
§ - PRINCESS ('Blink')	CBcs CDoC EBee ELan EPfP LSto MAsh NLar SRms WFar
- 'Red Ace'	CAgr CBcs CBrac CDoC CMac CSBt CSpe EGren EHeP ELan EPfP EUrb LRHS LSto MAsh MGos NLar SGol SRms WFar WHtc

- 'Red Joker'	NLar	- 'Rubra'	GEdr GKev NBir WAbe
- 'Red Lady'PBR	EBee MAsh NEoE SNig SPoG	*palustris*	CPud CWat ELin EWat MWts NAts NLar SHar SPhx
- RED ROBIN	see *P. fruticosa* MARIAN RED ROBIN		
- 'Red Surprise'	WFar	*parvifolia* 'Klondike'	see *P. fruticosa* 'Klondike'
- SILVER 'N' GOLD ('Lisstreas')	ELan LRHS	'Pink Panther'	see *P. fruticosa* PRINCESS
- 'Snowbird'	WFar	*pulvinaris*	EPot GKev
- 'Sommerflor' ♀H7	ELan EPfP MAsh	*recta*	CFis MMuc NCth SRms
§ - (Sulphurascens Group) 'Elizabeth'	CBcs CMac EGren EHeP LRHS LSto MGos MMuc NLar SGol SRms WFar WHtc	- 'Alba'	GMaP
		- 'Citrina'	see *P. recta* var. *sulphurea*
		- 'Macrantha'	see *P. recta* 'Warrenii'
- - 'Longacre Variety'	CMac IArd	§ - var. *sulphurea*	ECha EGrI EPPr GElm GKev MNrw NBir NLar NSti SHar SMHy SPhx SRkn WBrk WCAu WHrl
- 'Summer Sorbet'	LRHS		
- 'Sunset'	CBrac CMac GKin LRHS LSRN NEoE NLar SRms WFar		
		§ - 'Warrenii'	EGren GMaP NBir SHar SRms WCAu WHrl
- 'Tangerine'	CBcs CBrac CDoC CMac EBee EGren EHeP ELan EPfP EUrb LRHS LSto MAsh MGos MMuc NLar SPlb SRms WFar WHtc		
		'Red Giant'	NCth XFar
		reptans 'Pleniflora' (d)	WCot
		- 'Roxanne' (d)	MHer
- 'Tilford Cream'	CBcs CDoC EGren EHeP EPfP GKin LSRN LSto SRms WFar	*rupestris*	ECha GJos GQue NSti WCAu WFar WTre
- 'Tom Conway'	CMac SRms	*salesoviana*	GKev
- 'Vilmoriniana'	CMac ELan EPfP MAsh SPoG WSpi	SCARLET DREAMS	NCth
- 'Whirligig'	CMac	'Scarlet Starlet'	see *P. atrosanguinea* var. *argyrophylla* 'Scarlet Starlit'
- 'White Lady'PBR	NEoE		
- 'Wickwar Trailer'	EPot	*speciosa*	EWes
- 'Yellow Bird' ♀H7	MAsh	'Star of the North'	LRHS
gelida	EWes	*sterilis*	WHer
'Gibson's Scarlet' ♀H7	CBcs CMac EBee ECha EHeP GKev GMaP GQue LCro LRHS MBel MNrw NBir NLar SPoG SRms WCAu WFar WHoo WPnP	* *sundermanii*	WHrl
		tabernaemontani	see *P. neumanniana*
		thurberi	GKev NLar SPhx
		- 'Monarch's Velvet'	Widely available
§ *glandulosa* subsp. *nevadensis*	MAsh	× *tonguei* ♀H5	EAri ECha EGrI ELan EPfP ESgI GBin GKev GMaP LCro LShi MArl MHol MMuc MNrw MPnt NBir NCou NLar SRkn SRms WFar WIce
'Gloire de Nancy' (d)	LRHS NBir NLar		
'Herzblut'	NLar		
× *hopwoodiana*	CSpe CTtf ECha GMaP LEdu MArl MNrw MPnt MPro NBir NDov SHar WCAu WFar		
		tormentilla	see *P. erecta*
		tridentata	see *Sibbaldiopsis tridentata*
× *hybrida* 'Jean Jabber'	MWlw NEoE NLar WFar	'Twinkling Star'	MHol NCth NEoE
'Light My Fire'	MHol	*verna* misapplied	see *P. neumanniana*
'Mandshurica'	see *P. fruticosa* 'Manchu'	'Versicolor Plena' (d)	NLar
§ *megalantha*	CBcs CBro ECha ELan EPfP GGro GQue LRHS MBNS NBir NSti SHar SRms StAn	'Volcan'	EWes LBar LRHS LSto MWlw WCAu WFar
		'White Queen'	GElm SHar SRms
'Melton Fire'	GKin GPSL LRHS MWlw NBir NWbg	'William Rollisson' ♀H7	CBcs CMac CMHG EBee ELan ESgI GKin GMaP LCro LRHS MBNS MNrw NBir NLar NSti SRms WCAu WFar
micrantha 'Purple Haze'	LEdu		
- 'Purple Heart'	WPGP		
- 'Monarch's Velvet'	see *P. thurberi* 'Monarch's Velvet'	*willmottiae*	see *P. nepalensis* 'Miss Willmott'
'Monsieur Rouillard' (d)	CMac EBee GElm GPSL MArl MNrw NGdn NLar	'Yellow Queen'	CMac GKin GMaP GPSL NLar SRms

Poterium see *Sanguisorba*

'Mont d'Or'	EBee GKev LBar NLar
montenegrina	GJos
nepalensis	NBro
- 'Helen Jane'	CCBP CDor EPfP EPPr GJos NBir NLar WFar WHrl

sanguisorba	see *Sanguisorba minor*

Pothos (Araceae)

scandens	NHrt

§ - 'Miss Willmott'	Widely available
- 'Ron McBeath'	CDor ELan GMaP LRHS MAvo MPro NLar NSti SDix SHar SRkn SRms WPnP

Prangos (Apiaceae)

ferulacea	SDix

Pratia see *Lobelia*

- 'Roxana'	EAri EBee ELan NBro
- 'Shogran'	EBee EDAr EPfP GJos GQue MNHC MPro NLar

Primula ✿ (Primulaceae)

acaulis	see *P. vulgaris*
§ *neumanniana*	EPfP MAsh NBir
- 'Nana' ♀H7	EPot GArf LRHS MAsh NRya SLee SPlb SRms WFar WHoo WIce
- orange-flowered	MNrw
- 'Pygmaea'	see *P. neumanniana* 'Nana'
nevadensis	see *P. glandulosa* subsp. *nevadensis*
nitida	GKev MAsh WAbe
- 'Alba'	GArf GEdr

'Alexina' (*allionii* hybrid) (Au)	NHar
algida (Al)	GKev
§ *allionii* (Au)	WAbe
- 'Aire Waves'	see *P. × loiseleurii* 'Aire Waves'
- 'Allen Moonbeam' (Au)	NHar
- 'Anna Griffith' (Au)	WAbe
- 'Cherry' (Au)	WAbe

Primula

- 'Chivalry' (Au) — WAbe
- 'Eureka' (Au) — WAbe
- 'Eveline Burrow' (Au) — WAbe
- 'Fanfare' (Au) — NHar
- 'Gilderdale Glow' (Au) — NHar
- 'Grandiflora-alp' (Au) — GKev
- 'Henry Burrow' (Au) — WAbe
- 'Hocker Edge' (Au) — GKev
- 'Lee Mayers' (Au) — WFar
- 'Lepus' (Au) — WAbe
- 'Lindum Frosty Morn' (Au) — WIce
- 'Lucy' (Au) — NHar
- 'Neptune's Wave' (Au) — NHar
- 'Peggy Wilson' (Au) — EWld
- 'Pennine Pink' (Au) — GArf
- 'Pinkie' (Au) — WAbe
- 'Tranquility' (Au) — WMal
- **alpicola** (Si) ♀H6 — CTsd GEdr GKev GQue LShi MCtn NBid NGdn
- - var. *alba* (Si) — NBid
§ - var. ***alpicola*** (Si) — CFis GKev LShi
- - 'Kevock Sky' (Si) — GKev
- - 'La Luna' (Si) — WHil
- - var. *luna* — see *P. alpicola* var. *alpicola*
- - mixed (Si) — GEdr
- - var. *violacea* (Si) — GAbr GGro MNrw NBid WHil
- **anisodora** — see *P. wilsonii* var. *anisodora*
- 'Annemijne' (Pr/Poly) — WCot
- 'Antique Silver Shadow' (Pr/Prim) (Antique Series) **new** — EGren
I 'Appleblossom' (Pr/Prim/d) — NCth
- × ***arctotis*** — see *P. × pubescens*
- ***aurantiaca*** (Pf) — CLil GKev WHil
- - 'Harperley Pink' (Pf) — MArl
- ***auricula*** L. (Au) ♀H5 — GKev MAsh SPlb SPoG
- - subsp. ***bauhinii*** (Au) — GKev
- ***auricula*** hort (Au) — CWal CWCL GMaP LSto MCtn
I - '1-2-3' (Au) **new** — WHil
- - A74 (Au) — MMuc
- - 'Abdor' (Au/St) — EWoo
- - 'Abigail' (Au/A) — WHil
- - 'Abundance' (Au/A) — EWoo
- - 'A.C. Hadfield' (Au) — WHil
- - 'Achates' (Au/A) — EWoo WHil
- - 'Admiral' (Au/A) — WHil
- - 'Adrian's Cross' (Au/A) — EWoo
- - 'Adrienne' (Au/A) — EWoo GKev WHil
- - 'Adrienne Ruan' (Au/A) — WHil
- - 'Agamemnon' (Au/A) — EWoo
- - 'Alamo' (Au/A) — WHil
- - 'Albert Bailey' (Au/d) — WFar WHil
- - 'Alexandra Georgina' (Au/A) — WHil
- - 'Alf' (Au/A) — WHil
- - 'Alice Haysom' (Au/S) — EDAr ELan EWoo WHil
- - 'Alicia' (Au/A) — WHil
- - 'Alison' (Au/S) — EWoo
- - 'Alison Jane' (Au/A) — WHil
- - 'Alison Telford' (Au/A) — WHil
- - 'All Gold' (Au/d) — WHil
- - 'Allard' (Au/A) — WHil
- - 'Amethyst' (Au/A) — WHil
- - 'Amy Nuttall' (Au/A) — WHil
- - 'Ancient Society' (Au/A) — EWoo WFar
- - 'Andrea Julie' (Au/A) — WFar WHil
- - 'Andrew Hunter' (Au/A) — WFar WHil
- - 'Andy Cole' (Au/A) — WFar WHil
- - 'Angel Eyes' (Au/St) — EWoo
- - 'Angel Islington' (Au/S) — EWoo
- - 'Angela Gould' (Au/B) — EWoo WHil
- - 'Angostura' (Au/d) — EWoo WHil
- - 'Anne Hyatt' (Au/d) — WHil
- - 'Antoc' (Au/S) — EWoo
- - 'Anwar Sadat' (Au/A) — EWoo WFar WHil
- - 'Apple Blossom' (Au/B) — WHil
- - 'Applecross' (Au/A) — WHil
- - 'April Moon' (Au/S) — EWoo
- - 'Argus' (Au/A) — WFar WHil
- - 'Arras' (Au/d) — WHil
- - 'Artwork' (Au/S) — WHil
- - 'Arundell' (Au/S/St) — WFar
- - 'Arwen' (Au/A) — WFar WHil
- - Ashwood strain (Au) — MAsh
- - 'Asner' (Au/A) **new** — WHil
- - 'Astolat' (Au/S) — WHil
- - 'Atlantic' (Au/S) — EWoo
- - 'Autumn Fire' (Au/A) — EWoo WHil
- - 'Autumn Jewels' (Au/d) — WHil
- - 'Avon Citronella' (Au/d) — WHil
- - 'Avon Twist' (Au/d) — EWoo
- - 'Avril' (Au/A) — WFar
- - 'Avril Hunter' (Au/A) — EWoo WFar
- - 'Bacchus' (Au/A) — WHil
- - 'Balbithan' (Au/B) — WHil
- - 'Baltic Amber' (Au/d) — WHil
- - 'Bank Error' (Au/S) — EWoo
- - 'Barbarella' (Au/S) — EWoo WHil
- - 'Barr Beacon' (Au/A) — WFar
- - 'Bartl' (Au/A) — ELan
- - 'Basuto' (Au/A) — EWoo WFar WHil
- - 'Beatrice' (Au/A) — EWoo WFar WHil
- - 'Beeches Variegated' (Au/A/v) — GEdr WFar
- - 'Beervelde' (Au/B) — WHil
- - 'Belgravia Gold' (Au/B) — WHil
- - 'Bellamy Pride' (Au/B) — WHil
- - 'Bendigo' (Au/S) — EWoo
- - 'Beppi' (Au/B) — WHil
- - 'Big Thrill' (Au) — WFar
- - 'Bilbo Baggins' (Au/A) — MPnt
- - 'Bill Bailey' (Au/d) — EWoo WHil
- - 'Bitterne Primrose' (Au/d) — EWoo
- - 'Black Jack'[PBR] (Au/d) — ELan LCro MHol WCAu
- - 'Blackhill' (Au/A) — EWoo
- - 'Blackpool Rock' (Au/St) — WHil
- - 'Blairside Yellow' (Au/B) — WAbe
- - 'Blossom' (Au/A) — EWoo WHil
- - 'Blue Bonnet' (Au/A/d) — EWoo WHil
- - 'Blue Chip' (Au/S) — WFar WHil
- - 'Blue Cliff' (Au/S) — EWoo
- - 'Blue Heaven' (Au/A) — EWoo WHil
- - 'Blue Jay' (Au/A) — WHil
- - 'Blue Nile' (Au/S) — WHil
- - 'Blue Velvet' (Au/B) — EWoo GQue
- - 'Blue Yodeler' (Au/A) — WFar WHil
- - 'Blush Baby' (Au/St) — EWoo WFar WHil
- - 'Bob Dingley' (Au/A) — WHil
- - 'Bonafide' (Au/d) — EWoo
- - 'Bonnie the Cat' (Au/A) — WFar WHil
- - 'Bookham Firefly' (Au/A) — WFar WHil
- - 'Border Bandit' (Au/B) — EWoo WHil
- - 'Boromir' (Au/A) — EWoo
- - 'Bowen's Blue' (Au/B) — EWoo
- - 'Bradford City' (Au/A) — LCro WFar
- - 'Brasso' (Au/S) — EWoo
- - 'Brazil' (Au/S) — EWoo WFar WHil
- - 'Breckland Joy' (Au/A) — WHil
- - 'Brenda's Choice' (Au/A) — EWoo WHil
- - 'Brian Paige' (Au/B) — WHil
- - 'Brick Lane' (Au/S) — EWoo
- - 'Bright Ginger' (Au/S) — EWoo WHil

- 'Brixton' (Au/S)	WHil
- 'Broad Gold' (Au/A)	WHil
- 'Broadwell Gold' (Au/B)	WHil
- 'Brown Ben' (Au/A)	EWoo WFar WHil
- 'Brown Bess' (Au/A)	WHil
- 'Brownie' (Au/B)	EWoo NBir WHil
- 'Buoyance' (Au/A)	WHil
- 'Buttered Lemon' (Au/B)	MPnt
- 'Butterscotch' (Au/d)	MPnt
- 'Butterwick' (Au/A)	WHil
- 'Cadiz Bay' (Au/d)	EWoo
- 'Calypso' (Au/d)	EWoo
- 'Cambodunum' (Au/A)	WFar WHil
- 'Cambrai' (Au/d)	WHil
- 'Camelot' (Au/d)	EWoo WFar
- 'Carmel' (Au/d)	EWoo
- 'Carnaval' (Au/B)	WFar WHil
- 'Carnival' (Au/A)	WHil
- 'Carousel' (Au/B)	EWoo WHil
- 'Carzon' (Au/A)	WHil
- 'Chaffinch' (Au/S)	EWoo GQue
- 'Chamois' (Au/B)	WFar WHil
- 'Charles Rennie' (Au/B)	EWoo WFar WHil
- 'Charlie's Aunt' (Au/A)	WHil
- 'Checkmate' (Au/d)	EWoo
- 'Cheeky' (Au/d)	EWoo
- 'Chelsea Bridge' (Au/A)	EWoo WFar WHil
- 'Cheops' (Au/A)	WHil
- 'Cheyenne' (Au/S)	EWoo
- 'Chiffon' (Au/S)	EWoo
- 'Chiquita' (Au/d)	EWoo WFar
- 'Choir Boy' (Au/A)	WHil
- 'Chorister' (Au/S)	EWoo WFar WHil
- 'Cinnamon' (Au/d)	WFar WHil
- 'Clara' (Au/d)	WFar
- 'Clatter-Ha' (Au/d)	WHil
- 'Claudia Taylor' (Au)	WHil
- 'Clemmy the Cat' (Au/B)	WHil
- 'Clotted Cream' (Au/B)	LRHS
- 'Clouded Yellow' (Au/S)	WHil
- 'Cloudy Bay' (Au/B)	WCot
- 'Clyde the Cat' (Au/B)	WHil
- 'Coffee' (Au/S)	WFar
- 'Colbury' (Au/S)	WFar
- 'Coleman' (Au/d)	WHil
- 'Connaught Court' (Au/A)	EWoo WHil
- 'Conquistador' (Au/A)	WHil
- 'Conservative' (Au/S)	WHil
- 'Consett' (Au/S)	EWoo WHil
- 'Coppi' (Au/A)	EWoo
- 'Corntime' (Au/S)	EWoo
- 'Cortina' (Au/S)	EWoo WFar WHil
- 'Coventry Street' (Au/S)	EWoo WHil
- 'Cranborne' (Au/A)	WHil
- 'Crimple' (Au/S)	WFar
- 'Crimson Glow' (Au/d)	LCro WHil
- 'Crinoline' (Au/S)	WHil
- 'Cuckoo Fair' (Au/S)	EWoo WFar
- 'Cuddles' (Au/A)	EWoo
- 'Curry Blend' (Au/B)	EDAr EWoo WHil
- 'Dagmar' (Au/d) **new**	WHil
- 'Dakota' (Au/S)	EWoo
- 'Dales Red' (Au/B)	EWoo WFar WHil
- 'Dan Tiger' (Au/St)	EWoo WHil
I - 'Daniel' (Au/d)	WHil
- 'Daniel T. Taylor' (Au/A)	WHil
- 'Dark Eyes' (Au/B)	EWoo WFar WHil
- 'Dedham' (Au/d)	WHil
- 'Del Boy' (Au/A)	WHil
- 'Delilah' (Au/d)	WFar WHil
- 'Denna Snuffer' (Au/d)	EWoo
- 'Derwent Water' (Au/S)	EWoo
- 'Dick Rogers' (Au/B)	MPnt
- 'Dido' (Au/B)	WFar
- 'Dilemma' (Au/A)	WHil
- 'Dill' (Au/A)	WFar WHil
- 'Dilly Dilly' (Au/A)	WHil
- 'Divint Dunch' (Au/A)	WFar WHil
- 'Doctor Lennon's White' (Au/A)	EWoo WHil
- 'Dolly' (Au/B)	WHil
I - 'Dolly Mixture' (Au/B)	WHil
- 'Donhead' (Au/A)	WHil
- 'Dorothy' (Au/S)	WHil
- 'Doublet' (Au/d)	WHil
- 'Doublure' (Au/d)	EWoo WHil
- 'Douglas Bader' (Au/A)	WFar WHil
- 'Douglas Black' (Au/S)	EWoo
- 'Doyen' (Au/d)	EWoo WHil
- 'Dragon's Hoard' (Au/A)	WHil
- 'Drax' (Au/A)	WHil
- 'Dubarii' (Au/A)	WHil
- 'Dusky Maiden' (Au/A)	EWoo WFar WHil
- 'E. G. Linton' (Au/A)	WHil
- 'Eastern Promise' (Au/A)	EWoo WFar WHil
- 'Eaton Dawn' (Au/S)	EWoo
- 'Eden Alexander' (Au/B)	EWoo WFar WHil
- 'Eden Blue Star' (Au/B)	EWoo WFar WHil
- 'Eden Bramley' (Au/B)	WFar
- 'Eden Carmine' (Au/B)	EWoo
- 'Eden David' (Au/B)	WFar
- 'Eden Elegance' (Au/B)	WFar WHil
- 'Eden Ensign' (Au/B)	WFar WHil
- 'Eden Fanfare' (Au/B)	WFar
- 'Eden Goldfinch' (Au/B)	EWoo WFar WHil
- 'Eden Greenfinch' (Au/B)	EWoo WFar WHil
- 'Eden Lilactime' (Au/B)	WFar WHil
- 'Eden Moonlight' (Au/B)	WFar WHil
- 'Eden Rhiann' (Au/B)	WHil
- 'Eden Royalty' (Au/B)	WFar WHil
- 'Eden Sunrise' (Au/B)	WFar WHil
- 'Elegance' (Au/S)	WFar
- 'Eli Jenkins' (Au/A)	WHil
- 'Ellen Thompson' (Au/A)	WFar WHil
- 'Elsie May' (Au/A)	EWoo WFar WHil
- 'Eric the Red' (Au/St)	WHil
- 'Erica' (Au/A)	EWoo WHil
- 'Erjon' (Au/S)	EWoo
- 'Eschman Starflower' (Au/S)	WHil
- 'Everest Blue' (Au/S)	EWoo WFar WHil
- 'Excalibur' (Au/d)	WHil
- 'Exhibition Blau' (Exhibition Series) (Au/B)	WHil
- 'Eyeopener' (Au/A)	WHil
- 'Fabuloso' (Au/St)	EWoo
- 'Faliraki Fanciful' (Au/A)	WHil
- 'Fanciful' (Au/S)	WHil
- 'Fancy Free' (Au)	EWoo
- 'Fandango' (Au/St)	WFar WHil
- 'Fanfare' (Au/S)	WFar
- 'Fanny Meerbeck' (Au/S)	EPfP EWoo WHil
- 'Farmyard Firefly' (Au)	WFar
- 'Faro' (Au/S)	EWoo
- 'Favourite' (Au/S)	EWoo WFar WHil
- 'Fenby' (Au/S)	EWoo
- 'Fennay' (Au/S)	EWoo WHil
- 'Ferrybridge' (Au/A)	WHil
- 'Ferryden' (Au/B) **new**	WHil
- 'Festubert' (Au/d)	WHil
- 'Fiddler's Green' (Au/d)	WCot WFar

- 'Finchfield' (Au/A) EWoo WHil
- 'Firsby' (Au/d) WFar
- 'First Lady' (Au/A) WFar
- 'First Light' (Au/B) WHil
- 'Fleet Street' (Au/S) WFar WHil
- 'Forest Almost There' WHil
  (Au/St/d)
- 'Forest Autumn Glow' WHil
  (Au/d)
- 'Forest Beech' (Au/d) WHil
- 'Forest Big Smile' (Au/A) WHil
- 'Forest Blue Ice' (Au/d) WHil
- 'Forest Blush' (Au/d) WHil
- 'Forest Bordeaux' (Au/d) WHil
- 'Forest Bracken' (Au/d) EWoo WFar WHil
- 'Forest Bronze' (Au/d) WHil
- 'Forest Brown Sugar' WHil
  (Au/d)
- 'Forest Burgundy' (Au/d) WFar WHil
- 'Forest Burnt Gold' (Au/d) WHil
- 'Forest Buttercup' (Au/d) WHil
- 'Forest Canary' (Au/d) WHil
- 'Forest Cappuccino' EWoo WHil
  (Au/d)
- 'Forest Clown' (Au/St/d) WHil
- 'Forest Clown 2' (Au/St/d) WHil
- 'Forest Coffee' (Au/d) WFar WHil
- 'Forest Dark Angel' (Au/S) WHil
- 'Forest Dawn' (Au/d) WHil
- 'Forest Dazzler' (Au/St/d) WHil
- 'Forest Delight' (Au/d) WHil
- 'Forest Devon Cream' WHil
  (Au/d)
- 'Forest Devon Dream' WHil
  (Au/d)
- 'Forest Diamond' (Au/d) WHil
- 'Forest Disco Dancer' WHil
  (Au/d)
- 'Forest Dream' (Au/d) WHil
- 'Forest Duet' (Au/d) EWoo WFar WHil
- 'Forest Dusk' (Au/d) WHil
- 'Forest Dusky Pink' (Au/d) WHil
- 'Forest Emperor' (Au/d) WHil
- 'Forest Evermore' (Au/d) WHil
- 'Forest Fall' (Au/d) WHil
- 'Forest Fancy That' (Au/d) WHil
- 'Forest Fire' (Au/d) EWoo WHil
- 'Forest Flame' (Au/d) WHil
- 'Forest Fooled Me' (Au/d) WHil
- 'Forest Forever' (Au/d) WHil
- 'Forest Foxy Girl' (Au/d) WHil
- 'Forest Fred' (Au/S) WHil
- 'Forest Frost' (Au/d) WHil
- 'Forest Frosted Star' WHil
  (Au/St)
- 'Forest Garnet' (Au/d) WHil
- 'Forest Gingernut' (Au/d) WHil
- 'Forest Glade' (Au/d) WHil
- 'Forest Gold' (Au/d) WHil
- 'Forest Golden Crown' WHil
  (Au/d)
- 'Forest Golden Harvest' WHil
  (Au/d)
- 'Forest Goldfinch' (Au/d) WHil
- 'Forest Gorge' (Au/d) WHil
- 'Forest Greenfinch' (Au/d) WHil
- 'Forest Happy' (Au/d) WHil
- 'Forest Harvest' WHil
  (Au/d) **new**
- 'Forest Heartbreaker' WHil
  (Au/d)
- 'Forest High Hopes' WHil
  (Au/d)
- 'Forest Hint of Pink' WHil
  (Au/d)
- 'Forest Hot Stuff' (Au/d) WHil
- 'Forest Kingcup' (Au/d) WHil
- 'Forest Lemon' (Au/d) EWoo WFar WHil
- 'Forest Lemon Sorbet' WHil
  (Au/d)
- 'Forest Lime' (Au/d) WHil
- 'Forest Love' (Au/d) WHil
- 'Forest Marmalade' (Au/d) WHil
- 'Forest Mayday' (Au/d) WHil
- 'Forest Old Gold' (Au/d) WHil
- 'Forest Old Thumper' WHil
  (Au/d)
- 'Forest Peach' (Au/d) WHil
- 'Forest Pecan' (Au/d) WHil
- 'Forest Plum' (Au/d) WFar WHil
- 'Forest Pocket Rocket' WHil
  (Au/d)
- 'Forest Pretty Woman' WHil
  (Au/d)
- 'Forest Prince' (Au/d) WHil
- 'Forest Purple Penny' WHil
  (Au/d)
- 'Forest Raspberry' (Au/d) WHil
- 'Forest Red Beret' (Au/d) WHil
- 'Forest Red Mist' (Au/d) WHil
- 'Forest Red 'n' Fred' WFar WHil
  (Au/d)
- 'Forest Red Ruby' (Au/d) WHil
- 'Forest Red Velvet' (Au/d) WHil
- 'Forest Redstart' (Au/St) WHil
- 'Forest Rocket' (Au/d) WHil
- 'Forest Rose' (Au/d) EWoo
- 'Forest Sage' (Au/d) WHil
- 'Forest Sahara' (Au/d) WHil
- 'Forest Scarlet Woman' WHil
  (Au/d)
- 'Forest Sensation' (Au/d) WHil
- 'Forest Shade' (Au/d) WHil
- 'Forest Sherbet' (Au/d) WHil
- 'Forest Sherbet Fizz' WHil
  (Au/d)
- 'Forest Shy Girl' (Au/d) WHil
- 'Forest Sleepy' (Au/d) WHil
- 'Forest Smokey' (Au/d) WHil
- 'Forest Snow' (Au/d) WHil
- 'Forest Splendid' (Au/d) WHil
- 'Forest Spring' (Au/d) WHil
- 'Forest Springtime' (Au/d) WHil
- 'Forest Starlight' (Au/d) WHil
- 'Forest Storm' (Au/d) WHil
- 'Forest Stormcloud' (Au) WHil
- 'Forest Sunbeam' (Au/d) WHil
- 'Forest Sunburst' (Au/d) WFar WHil
- 'Forest Sunfire' (Au/d) WHil
- 'Forest Sunlight' (Au/d) WHil
- 'Forest Sunshade' (Au/d) WHil
- 'Forest Sunshine' (Au/d) WHil
- 'Forest Thatch' (Au/d) WHil
- 'Forest Tiger' (Au/St/d) WHil
- 'Forest Tiger Toes' WHil
  (Au/St/d)
- 'Forest Treasure' (Au/A) WHil
- 'Forest Twilight' (Au/d) EWoo WHil
- 'Forest Zest' (Au/d) WHil
- 'Foxfire' (Au/A) WHil
- 'Fradley' (Au/A) WFar WHil
- 'Frank Bailey' (Au/d) EWoo

- 'Frank Crosland' (Au/A) WHil
- 'Frank Faulkner' (Au/A) WHil
- 'Frank Jennings' (Au/A) WHil
- 'Fred Booley' (Au/d) EWoo WFar WHil
- 'Fred Livesley' (Au/A) WHil
- 'Freya' (Au/S) WHil
- 'Fridl' (Au) ELan
- 'Friskney' (Au/d) EWoo
- 'Fromelles' (Au/d) WHil
- 'Funny Valentine' (Au/d) EWoo
- 'Gail Atkinson' (Au/A) WHil
- 'Gala' (Au/d) WHil
- 'Gary Pallister' (Au/A) WHil
- 'Gary Thomson' (Au/A) WHil
- 'Gas Lane' (Au/A) WHil
- 'Gay Crusader' (Au/A) WFar
- 'Generosity' (Au/A) WHil
- 'Geordie' (Au/A) WHil
- 'George Jennings' (Au/A) WHil
- 'George Swinford's Leathercoat' (Au/B) WHil
- 'Geronimo' (Au/S) EWoo
- 'Gimli' (Au/A) WHil
- 'Ginger Spice' (Au/B) WHil
- 'Girl Guide' (Au/S) WFar WHil
- 'Gizabroon' (Au/S) EWoo GQue WFar WHil
- 'G.L.Taylor' (Au/A) WHil
- 'Gladiator' (Au/A) WHil
- 'Gleam' (Au/S) EDAr EWoo WFar WHil
- 'Gleneagles' (Au/S) WHil
- 'Glenelg' (Au/S) WHil
- 'Glenluce' (Au/S) EWoo
- 'Gnome' (Au/B) GArf WHil
- 'Goeblii' (Au/B) EWoo WHil
- 'Golden Boy' (Au/A) WFar WHil
- 'Golden Chartreuse' (Au/d) EWoo
- 'Golden Fleece' (Au/S) EWoo
- 'Golden Glory' (Au/A) WHil
- 'Golden Hind' (Au/d) EWoo WHil
- 'Golden Splendour' (Au/d) EWoo WFar WHil
- 'Golden Wedding' (Au/A) WHil
- 'Goldie' (Au/S) EWoo
- 'Gollum' (Au/A) WFar WHil
- 'Good Day' (Au/d) WHil
- 'Good Report' (Au/A) WFar WHil
- 'Googie' (Au/d) WHil
- 'Gorey' (Au/A) EWoo WFar
- 'Grandad's Favourite' (Au/B) EWoo
- 'Green Abundance' (Au/B) EWoo WHil
- 'Green Finger' (Au/S) EWoo
- 'Green Goddess' (Au/St) EWoo
- 'Green Parrot' (Au/S) WHil
- 'Green Shank' (Au/S) WFar WHil
- 'Greenpeace' (Au/S) WFar
- 'Greswolde' (Au/d) EWoo
- 'Greta' (Au/S) WHil
- 'Grey Lag' (Au/S) WFar WHil
- 'Grey Monarch' (Au/S) EWoo
- 'Guinea' (Au/S) EWoo
- 'Gwai Loh' (Au/B) WHil
- 'Gwen Baker' (Au/d) WFar
- 'Gwenda' (Au/A) WHil
- 'Gypsy' (Au/A) WHil
- 'H Old Gold' (Au/S) EWoo
- 'Habanera' (Au/A) WFar WHil
- 'Haffner' (Au/S) WHil
- 'Handsome Lass' (Au/St) EWoo WFar
- 'Hannah' (Au/A) WHil
- 'Harmony' (Au/B) EWoo WHil
- 'Harry' (Au/A) WHil
- 'Harry Hotspur' (Au/A) WFar WHil
- 'Harry 'O' (Au/S) EWoo
- 'Harvest Glow' (Au/S) WFar WHil
- 'Harvest Gold' (Au/S) EWoo
- 'Hawkwood' (Au/S) WHil
- 'Hazel' (Au/A) WHil
- 'Headdress' (Au/S) EWoo
- 'Heady' (Au/A) EWoo WHil
- 'Hebers' (Au/A) WHil
- 'Helen' (Au/S) EWoo WHil
- 'Helen Barter' (Au/S) WHil
- 'Helen Ruane' (Au/B) GKev GQue WFar WHil
- 'Henry's Bane' (Au/St) WHil
- 'High Wood' (Au/d) WHil
- 'Highland Park' (Au/A) WFar WHil
- 'Hillhook' (Au/A) WHil
- 'Hinton Fields' (Au/S) LCro WFar WHil
- 'Hit Parade' (Au)
- 'Honey' (Au/d) EWoo WHil
- 'Hopleys Coffee' (Au/d) EWoo
- 'Hot Lips' (Au/S) WHil
- 'Hurstwood Midnight' (Au) WFar
- 'Ice Cap' (Au/d) WHil
- 'Ice Maiden' (Au/A) WFar WHil
- 'Idgy' (Au/d) WHil
- 'Idmiston' (Au/S) WFar WHil
- 'Imari Stripe' (Au/St) WHil
- 'Indian Love Call' (Au/A) WFar WHil
- 'Jack' (Au/A) WHil
- 'Jack Dean' (Au/A) WFar
- 'Jane Myers' (Au/d) WHil
- 'Janet Watts' (Au/B) EWoo
- 'Janie Hill' (Au/A) WHil
- 'Jeanne' (Au/A) EWoo
- 'Jenny' (Au/A) EWoo WFar WHil
- 'Jersey Bounce' (Au/A) EWoo WHil
- 'Jessie Lightfoot' (Au/A) WHil
- 'Jessy' (Au/A) WHil
- 'Jim Lister' (Au/St) WFar
- 'Joanne' (Au/d) MPnt
- 'Joanne' (Au/A) EWoo
- 'Joannie' (Au/d) **new** WHil
- 'Joe Perks' (Au/A) EWoo WFar WHil
- 'Joel' (Au/S) EWoo WHil
- 'Johann Bach' (Au/B) EWoo
- 'John Hart' (Au/A) WFar WHil
- 'John Radford' (Au/A) WHil
- 'John Wayne' (Au/A) EWoo
- 'Joy' (Au/A) EWoo GQue WHil
- 'Joyce' (Au/A) WFar
- 'Judith Borman' (Au/d) GKev WFar
- 'Julie Nuttall' (Au/B) EWoo WHil
- 'Jungfrau' (Au/d) EWoo
- 'K S' (Au/S) EWoo
- KALEIDOSCOPE (mixed) (Au) EDAr ELan EPfP
- 'Karen Cordrey' (Au/S) EWoo WFar WHil
- 'Kate Haywood' (Au/B) WHil
- 'Ken Chilton' (Au/A) EWoo WHil
- 'Kentucky Blues' (Au/d) EWoo
- 'Kercup' (Au/A) EWoo
- 'Khachaturian' (Au/A) WHil
- 'Khaki' (Au/d) WHil
- 'Kidderminster' (Au/A) WHil
- 'Kilby' (Au/A) WFar
- 'Kingfisher' (Au/A) EWoo WHil
- 'Kirklands' (Au/d) WHil
- 'Kohinoor' (Au/A) WFar WHil
- 'Krithia' (Au/d) WHil

- 'Lady Daresbury' (Au/A)   WHil
- 'Lady Day' (Au/d)   EWoo WFar
- 'Lady Diana' (Au/S)   EWoo
- 'Lady of the Vale' (Au/A)   WHil
- 'Lady Zoë' (Au/S)   EWoo
- 'Lambert's Gold' (Au/B)   EWoo WHil
- 'Lamplugh' (Au/d)   EWoo WHil
- 'Lancelot' (Au/d)   EWoo
- 'Lancing' (Au/St) **new**   WHil
- 'Langley Park' (Au/A)   WHil
- 'Laredo' (Au/A)   EWoo
- 'Larry' (Au/A)   EWoo WFar WHil
- 'Late Romantic' (Au/d)   MHol WHil
- 'Lavender Lady' (Au/B)   EWoo
- 'Laverock' (Au/S)   NBir WHil
- 'Lazy River' (Au/A)   EWoo WHil
- 'Le Cateau' (Au/d)   WHil
- 'Leathercoat' (Au/B)   EWoo
- 'Lechistan' (Au/S)   EWoo WHil
- 'Lee Daniel' (Au/A)   WHil
- 'Lee Paul' (Au/A)   EWoo WFar WHil
- 'Lee Sharpe' (Au/A)   EWoo WHil
- 'Legolas' (Au/A)   WHil
- 'Leicester Square' (Au/S)   EWoo
- 'Lemon and Lime' (Au/d)   WHil
- 'Lemon Drop' (Au/S)   EWoo GQue
- 'Lemon Sherbet' (Au/B)   EWoo GQue WFar WHil
- 'Lester' (Au/d)   WHil
- 'Leverton' (Au/d)   WHil
- 'Light Hearted' (Au/A)   WHil
- 'Likely Lad' (Au/St)   EWoo
- 'Lila' (Au/A)   WHil
- 'Lilac Domino' (Au/S)   EWoo WFar
- 'Lilac Ladywood' (Au/d)   EWoo WFar
- 'Lilian Hill' (Au/A)   EWoo
- 'Limelight' (Au/S)   EWoo
- 'Lincoln Bullion' (Au/d)   EWoo WFar WHil
- 'Lincoln Chestnut' (Au/d)   EWoo
- 'Lincoln Imperial' (Au/d)   WHil
- 'Linda' (Au/A)   WFar WHil
- 'Lindley' (Au/S)   EWoo
- 'Lintz' (Au/B)   EWoo WHil
- 'Lisa' (Au/A)   EWoo WFar
- 'Lisa Clara' (Au/S)   EWoo WFar
- 'Lisa's Smile' (Au/S)   EWoo WHil
- 'Little Rosetta' (Au/d)   WHil
- 'Lockey's Red' (Au) **new**   WHil
- 'Lockyer's Green' (Au/B)   EWoo WHil
- 'Lolita' (Au/St)   EWoo WFar WHil
- 'Lord Saye and Sele' (Au/St)   EWoo
- 'Lottie Files' (Au/A)   WHil
- 'Louis' (Au/d)   ELan
- 'Lovebird' (Au/S)   EWoo
- 'Luca' (Au/d)   WHil
- 'Lucy Locket' (Au/B)   LCro MPnt WFar
- 'Lunar Eclipse' (Au/d)   MHol MWlw WHil
- 'Lupy Minstrel' (Au/S)   EWoo
- 'Luthien' (Au/S) **new**   WHil
- 'Lynn Cooper' (Au/S)   EWoo
- 'MacWatt's Blue' (Au/B)   EWoo GArf WHil
- 'Macy the Cat' (Au/S)   WHil
- 'Maggie' (Au/A)   WHil
- 'Mamba' (Au/S)   WHil
- 'Mametz' (Au/d)   WHil
- 'Mandarin' (Au/A)   WFar WHil
- 'Mandy' (Au/S)   EWoo
- 'Margot Fonteyn' (Au/A)   EWoo WHil
- 'Mariandl' (Au/A)   ELan
- 'Marie Crousse' (Au/d)   WCot WFar WHil
- 'Marmion' (Au/S)   WHil
- 'Martin Luther King' (Au/S)   EWoo
- 'Mary Zach' (Au/S)   EWoo WHil
- 'Matthew' (Au)   GKev
- 'Matthew Yates' (Au/d)   WCot WHil
- 'May' (Au/A)   EWoo
- 'Mazetta Stripe' (Au/S/St)   WHil
- 'Meadowlark' (Au/A)   EWoo WFar WHil
- 'Mehta' (Au/A)   WHil
- 'Mellifluous' (Au/A)   WHil
- 'Melody' (Au/S)   EWoo
- 'Merlin' (Au/S)   WFar WHil
- 'Merlin Stripe' (Au/St)   WHil
- 'Mermaid' (Au/d)   WFar
- 'Merridale' (Au/A)   WHil
- 'Mersey Tiger' (Au/S)   WHil
- 'Mick' (Au/A)   WHil
- 'Mikado' (Au/S)   WHil
- 'Millicent' (Au/A)   WHil
- 'Minley' (Au/S)   NBir
- 'Mipsie Miranda' (Au/S)   EWoo
- 'Mirandinha' (Au/A)   WHil
- 'Mish Mish' (Au/d)   WFar WHil
- 'Miss Bluey' (Au/d)   EWoo
- 'Miss Newman' (Au/S)   WFar
- 'Miss Pinky' (Au/d)   EWoo
- 'Mojave' (Au/S)   GArf GEdr GQue WFar WHil
- 'Mollie Langford' (Au/A)   WFar WHil
- 'Moneymoon' (Au/S)   EWoo WHil
- 'Monica' (Au/A)   WHil
- 'Moon Fairy' (Au/S)   WHil
- 'Moonlight' (Au/S)   EWoo GEdr
- 'Moonrise' (Au/S)   EWoo
- 'Moonriver' (Au/A)   EWoo
- 'Moonstone' (Au/d)   EGren WHil
- 'Mr A' (Au/S)   EWoo
- 'Mrs L. Hearn' (Au/A)   EWoo WFar WHil
- 'Murray Lakes' (Au/A)   EWoo WHil
- 'Mystery' (Au)   WFar
- 'Neat and Tidy' (Au/S)   EWoo WFar
- 'Nefertiti' (Au/A)   EWoo
- 'Nessun Dorma' (Au/S)   EWoo
- 'Neville Telford' (Au/S)   EWoo WFar
- 'Nickity' (Au/A)   EWoo WFar
- 'Nicola Jane' (Au/A)   EWoo
- 'Nina Ann' (Au/S)   WHil
- 'Nocturne' (Au/S)   WFar
- 'Noelle' (Au/S)   WFar
- 'Nona' (Au/d)   EWoo
- 'Nonchalance' (Au/A)   WHil
- 'Norma' (Au/A)   EWoo WHil
- 'Northern Blue' (Au/S)   EWoo
- 'Nymph' (Au/d)   EWoo WHil
- 'Odette' (Au/d)   WHil
- 'Old Black Isle Dusty Miller' (Au/B)   WHil
- 'Old Buffer' (Au/St)   WHil
- 'Old Clove Red' (Au/S)   EWoo WHil
- 'Old Cottage Blue' (Au/B)   EWoo WFar WHil
- 'Old Gold' (Au/S)   WFar
- 'Old Gold Double' (Au/d)   EWoo
- 'Old Irish Blue' (Au/S)   WCot
- 'Old Irish Green' (Au/S)   WFar WHil
- 'Old Irish Scented' (Au/B)   EWoo WHil
- 'Old Mustard' (Au/B)   WFar
- 'Old Pink Dusty Miller' (Au/B)   EWoo WHil
- 'Old Red' (Au)   GArf
- 'Old Red Dusty Miller' (Au/B)   EWoo WFar WHil
- 'Old Red Elvet' (Au/S)   WFar

- 'Old Smokey' (Au/A) EWoo WFar WHil
- 'Old Suffolk Bronze' (Au/B) EWoo WHil
- 'Old Tall Purple Dusty Miller' (Au/B) EWoo WFar
- 'Old Yellow Dusty Miller' (Au/B) EWoo NLar WFar WHil
- 'Olton' (Au/A) WFar
- 'Optimist' (Au/St) EWoo
- 'Opus One' (Au/A) EWoo
- 'Orange Peel' (Au/B) WHil
- 'Orb' (Au/S) WFar WHil
- 'Orwell Tiger' (Au/St) EWoo WFar WHil
- 'Osborne Green' (Au/B) EWoo GArf GQue WHil
- 'Ossett Sapphire' (Au/A) WFar
- 'Otto Dix' (Au/A) WHil
- 'Ovillers' (Au/d) WHil
- 'Paddlin' Madeleine' (Au/A) EWoo
- 'Pale Blue' (Au/B) WHil
- 'Paleface' (Au/A) WHil
- 'Pang Tiger' (Au/St) EWoo
- 'Paradise Yellow' (Au/B) EWoo GEdr
- 'Paragon' (Au/A) WHil
- 'Parakeet' (Au/S) EWoo
- 'Party Animal' (Au/St) WHil
- 'Passchendaele' (Au/d) EWoo WHil
- 'Pastures New' (Au) WHil
- 'Patience' (Au/S) EWoo WHil
- 'Paula' (Au/A) WHil
- 'Pauline' (Au/A) WHil
- 'Pavarotti' (Au/A) WHil
- 'Paxton's Blue Eden' (Au/B) WFar
- 'Pearl the Cat' (Au/B) WHil
- 'Pegasus' (Au/d) EWoo WHil
- 'Peggy's Lad' (Au/A) WHil
- 'Pen Pink Stripe' (Au/St) WHil
- 'Pendle Pearl' (Au/A) WHil
- 'Pendle Promise' (Au/B) WHil
- 'Pequod' (Au/B) WFar
- 'Phantom' (Au/d) WHil
- 'Pharaoh' (Au/A) EWoo WFar
- 'Phyllis Douglas' (Au/A) WHil
- 'Piccadilly' (Au/S) EWoo
- 'Pierot' (Au/A) WFar WHil
- 'Piers Telford' (Au/A) LCro MPnt WFar WHil
- 'Piglet' (Au/d) EWoo WHil
- 'Pink Floyd' (Au/A) WHil
- 'Pink Fondant' (Au/d) WFar
- 'Pink Hint' (Au/B) EWoo
- 'Pink Lady' (Au/A) WFar WHil
- 'Pink Lilac' (Au/A/S) EWoo
- 'Pink Panther' (Au/S) EWoo
- 'Pink Triumph' (Au/B) WHil
- 'Pinkerton' (Au/d) EWoo
- 'Pinkie Dawn' (Au/B) EWoo
- 'Pinstripe' (Au/St) WHil
- 'Pioneer Stripe' (Au/S) EWoo
- 'Pippin' (Au/A) EWoo WFar WHil
- 'Pixie' (Au/A) EWoo WHil
- 'Playboy' (Au/A) WHil
- 'Plum Pudding' (Au/d) EWoo WHil
- 'Poacher's Starlight' (Au/d) WFar
- 'Polestar' (Au/A) WHil
- 'Polly' (Au/B) WFar WHil
- 'Pop's Blue' (Au/S/d) EWoo
- 'Pot o' Gold' (Au/S) EWoo WFar WHil
- 'Powder Puff' (Au/B) EWoo WHil
- 'Prague' (Au/S) NBir
- 'Pretender' (Au/A) WHil
- 'Pride of Poland' (Au/S) EWoo
- 'Prince Bishops' (Au/S) EWoo
- 'Prince John' (Au/A) EWoo WHil
- 'Proctor's Yellow' (Au/S) WHil
- 'Prometheus' (Au/d) EWoo WHil
- 'Provence' (Au/d) WHil
- 'Psyche' (Au/S) WHil
- 'Purple Dragon' (Au/S) WHil
- 'Purple Emperor' (Au/A) WHil
- 'Purple Patch' (Au/d) WHil
- 'Purple Pip' (Au/d) ELan
- 'Purple Rosebud' (Au/d) WHil
- 'Purple Sage' (Au/S) WHil
- 'Purple Velvet' (Au/S) WHil
- 'Pye Powder' (Au/S) WHil
- 'Pyrites' (Au/d) WHil
- 'Quality Chase' (Au/A) WHil
- 'Quarry Lane' (Au/A) WFar WHil
- 'Quatro' (Au/d) EWoo
- 'Queen Alexandra' (Au/B) EWoo
- 'Queen Bee' (Au/S) EWoo
- 'Quintessence' (Au/A) EWoo WHil
- 'Rabley Heath' (Au/S) WHil
- 'Rachel' (Au/A) WHil
- 'Rajah' (Au/S) EWoo WHil
- 'Raleigh Stripe' (Au/St) EWoo WFar
- 'Rameses' (Au/A) WFar
- 'Real Purple Dragon' (Au/A) WHil
- 'Rebecca Baker' (Au/d) WHil
- 'Red Admiral' (Au/S) EWoo
- 'Red Baron' (Au/S) WHil
- 'Red Bordeaux' (Au/S) EWoo
- 'Red Fire' (Au/B) WHil
- 'Red Gauntlet' (Au/S) EWoo WHil
- 'Red Rays' (Au/A) WHil
- 'Red Sonata' (Au/S) EWoo
- 'Red Wire' (Au/St) WHil
- 'Redcar' (Au/A) WHil
- 'Reddown First Swallow' (Au/B) WHil
- 'Redstart' (Au/S) EWoo
- 'Regency' (Au/A) WHil
- 'Regency Carousel' (Au/St) WHil
- 'Regency Emperor' (Au/St) EWoo WFar WHil
- 'Regency Saint Clements' (Au/St) WFar
- 'Remus' (Au/A) WFar
- 'Rene' (Au/A) WHil
- 'Renishaw Hall' (Au/S) WHil
- 'Resi' (Au/A) WHil
- 'Rhubarb Rock' (Au/B) WHil
- 'Riatty' (Au/d) EWoo
- 'Richard Shaw' (Au/A) EWoo
- 'Ring of Bells' (Au/S) EWoo
- 'R.L. Bowes' (Au/A) WHil
- 'Robbo' (Au/B) EWoo WHil
- 'Robin Hood' (Au/A) WHil
- 'Robin Hood Stripe' (Au/St) EWoo
- 'Robinette' (Au/d) EWoo WFar
- 'Rock Sand' (Au/S) EWoo
- 'Rockbourne' (Au/A) WHil
- 'Rodeo' (Au/A) EWoo
- 'Rolts' (Au/S) WFar
- 'Rondy' (Au/S) EWoo
- 'Rose Conjou' (Au/d) EWoo WFar WHil
- 'Rosebud' (Au/S) EWoo
- 'Rosemary' (Au/S) EWoo

Primula

- 'Rosewood' (Au/d) — EWoo
- 'Rosie' (Au/S) — EWoo
- 'Rowena' (Au/A) — WHil
- 'Roxborough' (Au/A) — EWoo
- 'Roxie' (Au/d) — WHil
- 'Roy Keane' (Au/A) — WHil
- 'Roy Le Sauvage' (Au/B) — WHil
- 'Royal Mail' (Au/S) — EWoo
- 'Royal Velvet' (Au/S) — WFar WHil
- 'Ruby Hyde' (Au/B) — EWoo WHil
- 'Ruby Tuesday' (Au/B) — WHil
- 'Ruddy Duck' (Au/S) — EWoo
- 'Ruffled Red' (Au) **new** — WHil
- 'Rumbled' (Au/St) — WHil
- 'Runwell' (Au/B) — WHil
- 'Rusty Dusty' (Au) — EWoo
- 'Saginaw' (Au/A) — WHil
- 'Sailor Boy' (Au/S) — EWoo
- 'Sale Green' (Au/S) — EWoo
- 'Sam Gamgee' (Au/A) — WHil
- 'Samantha' (Au/d) — WFar
- 'Sanctuary Wood' (Au/d) — WHil
- 'Sandhills' (Au/A) — WHil
- 'Sandpiper' (Au/d) — MWlw
- 'Sandra' (Au/A) — WFar WHil
- 'Sandra's Lass' (Au/A) — EWoo
- 'Sandwood Bay' (Au/A) — EWoo WHil
- 'Sarah Lodge' (Au/d) — WFar WHil
- 'Sarah Millington' (Au/d) — WHil
- 'Saruman' (Au/A) — WHil
- 'Sasha Files' (Au/A) — WHil
- 'Satsuma' (Au/d) — WHil
- 'Scorcher' (Au/S) — EWoo WFar WHil
- 'Shadow Boxer' (Au/St) — WFar
- 'Shalford' (Au/d) — WCot WFar WHil
- 'Sharon Louise' (Au/S) — EWoo
- 'Sheila' (Au/S) — EWoo WHil
- 'Shere' (Au/S) — EWoo WHil
- 'Sibsey' (Au/d) — EWoo WFar
- I 'Silas' (Au/A) **new** — WHil
- 'Silas' (Au/B) — WHil
- 'Simply Red' (Au/S) — EWoo WFar WHil
- 'Sir John' (Au/A) — WHil
- 'Sir John Hall' (Au/A) — WHil
- 'Sirbol' (Au/A) — EWoo WFar WHil
- 'Sirius' (Au/A) — EWoo WFar WHil
- 'Skylark' (Au/A) — WHil
- 'Slim Whitman' (Au/A) — WHil
- 'Slioch' (Au/S) — EWoo WFar
- 'Snowline' (Au/S) — WHil
- 'Soliloquy' (Au/B) — WHil
- 'Somme' (Au/d) — WHil
- 'Soncy Face' (Au/A) — WHil
- 'Sonja' (Au/S) — EWoo
- 'Sooty' (Au/d) — EWoo WHil
- 'South Barrow' (Au/d) — WHil
- 'Southport' (Au/B) — EWoo WHil
- 'Stant's Blue' (Au/S) — EWoo
- 'Star Wars' (Au/S) — WHil
- 'Starburst' (Au/S) — WHil
- 'Starling' (Au/B) — EWoo WHil
- 'Stella South' (Au/A) — WFar
- 'Stonnal' (Au/A) — WHil
- 'Stormin' Norman' (Au/A) — WFar
- 'Strawberry Fields' (Au/S) — WHil
- 'Stripe Tease' (Au/St) — EWoo
- 'Striped Ace' (Au/St) — EWoo
- 'Stromboli' (Au/d) — EWoo WCot WHil
- 'Sue Ritchie' (Au/d) — WHil
- 'Suede Shoes' (Au/S) — EWoo
- 'Sugar Plum Fairy' (Au/S) — EWoo

- 'Summer Wine' (Au/A) — EWoo WHil
- 'Sumo' (Au/A) — EWoo WFar
- 'Sunflower' (Au/A/S) — EWoo WHil
- 'Sunlit Tiger' (Au/S) — EWoo WFar WHil
- 'Sunstar' (Au/S) — EWoo
- 'Super Para' (Au/S) — WFar WHil
- 'Susan' (Au/A) — WHil
- 'Susannah' (Au/d) — EWoo WFar WHil
- 'Sweet Caramel' (Au/d) — WHil
- 'Sweet Pastures' (Au/S) — WFar
- 'Sword' (Au/d) — EWoo WFar
- 'Symphony' (Au/A) — WHil
- 'T.A. Hadfield' (Au/A) — EWoo WHil
- 'Taffeta' (Au/S) — EWoo LCro WFar
- 'Tay Tiger' (Au/St) — EWoo WHil
- 'Teawell Pride' (Au/d) — EWoo WHil
- 'Ted Gibbs' (Au/A) — WHil
- 'Ted Roberts' (Au/A) — WHil
- 'Teem' (Au/S) — WFar
- 'Temeraire' (Au/A) — WHil
- 'Terpo' (Au/A) — WHil
- 'That's It' (Au/A) — WHil
- 'The Baron' (Au/S) — EWoo WFar WHil
- 'The Bishop' (Au/S) — WHil
- 'The Blues' (Au/B) — WHil
- 'The Cardinal' (Au/d) — EWoo
- 'The Czar' (Au/A) — WFar
- 'The Egyptian' (Au/A) — EWoo WHil
- 'The Lady Galadriel' (Au/A) — WHil
- 'The Raven' (Au/S) — EWoo WHil
- 'The Sneep' (Au/A) — EWoo WFar WHil
- 'The Snods' (Au/S) — EWoo
- 'Thetis' (Au/A) — WHil
- 'Thor' (Au/S) — WHil
- 'Threapwood' (Au) **new** — WHil
- 'Three Way Stripe' (Au/St) — EWoo WFar WHil
- 'Tim' (Au/d) — WHil
- 'Tim's Fancy' (Au/S) — WHil
- 'Tiptoe' (Au/St) — EWoo WHil
- 'Toffee Crisp' (Au/A) — EWoo WFar WHil
- 'Tomboy' (Au/S) — EWoo
- 'Toolyn' (Au/S) — EWoo
- 'Tosca' (Au/S) — WHil
- 'Trafalgar Square' (Au/S) — EWoo WHil
- 'Tregor Orange' (Au/d) — WCot
- 'Tromen' (Au/d) — WHil
- 'Trones Wood' (Au/d) **new** — WHil
- 'Trouble' (Au/d) — EWoo GQue WHil
- 'Troy Aikman' (Au/A) — WHil
- 'Trudy' (Au/S) — EWoo
- 'Trumpet Blue' (Au/S) — EWoo
- 'Tumbledown' (Au/S) — EWoo WHil
- 'Tummel' (Au/A) — EWoo WFar WHil
- 'Twiggy' (Au/S) — EWoo MPnt WFar
- 'Two Steeples' (Au/S) — WHil
- 'Typhoon' (Au/A) — EWoo WHil
- 'Uncle Arthur' (Au/S) — WHil
- 'Upton Belle' (Au/S) — EWoo
- 'Vee Too' (Au/A) — WFar WHil
- 'Venetian' (Au/S) — EWoo WHil
- 'Vera Hill' (Au/A) — WHil
- 'Vesuvius' (Au/d) — EWoo WHil
- 'Victoria de Wemyss' (Au/A) — WFar WHil
- 'Victoria Park' (Au/A) — WFar
- 'Vimy Ridge' (Au/d) — WHil
- 'Violet Surprise' (Au/St) — EWoo WHil
- 'Vroni' (Au/A) — ELan
- 'Vulcan' (Au/A) — WHil
- 'Walton' (Au/A) — EWoo WFar

Primula 553

- 'Walton Heath' (Au/d) EWoo WCot WFar WHil
- 'Warpaint' (Au/St) EWoo WHil
- 'Watchett' (Au/S) EWoo
- 'Wedding Day' (Au/S) EWoo
- 'Westbourne Park' (Au/S) WHil
- 'Westminster' (Au/S) WHil
- 'Whistlejacket' (Au/S) EWoo
- 'White Pyne' (Au/B) WHil
- 'White Water' (Au/A) EWoo WHil
- 'Whoopee' (Au/A) EWoo
- 'Wide Awake' (Au/A) WHil
- 'William Gunn' (Au/d) EWoo MWlw WHil
- 'Wincha' (Au/S) EWoo
- 'Windways Mystery' (Au/B) WFar
- 'Winifred' see *P.* × *pubescens* 'Winnifred'
- 'Wong Il' (Au/A) WHil
- 'Woodmill' (Au/A) EWoo WFar WHil
- 'Wookey Hole' (Au/A) WFar
- 'Woottens Advent' (Au/B) EWoo
- 'Woottens Bloody Warrior' (Au/S) EWoo
- 'Woottens Cranberry' (Au/B) EWoo
- 'Woottens Crimson Border' (Au/B) EWoo WHil
- 'Woottens Easter Chick' (Au/B) EWoo
- 'Woottens Egg Custard' (Au/B) EWoo
- 'Woottens Glory' (Au/S) EWoo
- 'Woottens Rich Cherry' (Au/B) EWoo
- 'Woottens Shepherd's Delight' (Au/B) EWoo
- 'Woottens Straw Boater' (Au/B) EWoo
- 'Wycliffe Midnight' (Au/B) EWoo WFar WHil
- 'Yellow Ace' (Au) WFar
- 'Yellow Border' (Au/B) WHil
- 'Yellow Ribbon' (Au/A) WHil
- 'Yitzhak Rabin' (Au/A) WFar
- 'Young Vic' (Au/A) WHil
- 'Ypres' (Au/d) WHil
- 'Zambia' (Au/d) GAbr WHil
- 'Zus' (Au/A) WHil
auriculata (Or) CTsd SVic
'Barbara Barker' (Au) GEdr
'Barbara Midwinter' (Pr) EBee GAbr MNrw MWlw SHar WAbe WCot
Barnhaven Gold-laced Group see *P.* Gold-laced Group Barnhaven
'Beamish Foam' (Pr/Poly) GAbr
'Beatrice Wooster' (Au) GArf WFar
'Beeches' Pink' GAbr LShi
beesiana (Pf) ♀H6 Widely available
(Belarina Series) WHil
  BELARINA BALTIC BLUE ('Kerbelbal') (Pr/Prim/d)
  - BELARINA BEAUJOLAIS see *P.* (Belarina Series) BELARINA CHAMPAGNE RUBY
  - BELARINA CHAMPAGNE RUBY WHil ('Kerbeljolais') (Pr/Prim/d) **new**
  - BELARINA COBALT BLUE LSou NLar ('Kerbelcob'PBR) (Pr/Prim/d)
  - BELARINA CREAM CDor LCro WHil ('Kerbelcrem'PBR) (Pr/Prim/d)

  - BELARINA LIVELY LILAC ELan MHol ('Kerbelil'PBR) (Pr/Prim/d)
  - BELARINA PINK CHAMPAGNE ELan LBar LSou NLar WFar WHil ('Kerbelchamp'PBR) (Pr/Prim/d)
  - BELARINA PINK ICE CDor LRHS LSou WHil ('Kerbelpice'PBR) (Pr/Prim/d)
  (Belarina Rosette Series) CDor LSou MHol WHil
  BELARINA AMETHYST ICE ('Kerbelpicotee'PBR) (Pr/Prim/d)
  - BELARINA BUTTERCUP CDor ELan LSou WHil ('Kerbelbut'PBR) (Pr/Prim/d)
  - BELARINA BUTTERMILK LRHS LSou ('Kerbelmilk'PBR) (Pr/Prim/d)
  - BELARINA LEMON CHIFFON LBar WHil ('Kerbelchiffon') (Pr/Prim/d)
  - BELARINA NECTARINE CDor ELan LBar LRHS SPoG ('Kerbelnec'PBR) (Pr/Prim/d)
  - BELARINA ROSETTE VALENTINE CDor LSou NLar WHil ('Kerbelred'PBR) (Pr/Prim/d)
beluensis see *P.* × *pubescens* 'Freedom'
× *berninae* (Au) GArf
'Berries and Cream Shades' LRHS (Pr/Prim/d)
'Bewerley White' see *P.* × *pubescens* 'Bewerley White'
× *biflora* (Au) GArf
bileckii see *P.* × *forsteri* 'Bileckii'
'Blake's Winter Cheer' (Pr) WCot
'Blindsee' (Au) NHar NRya
'Blue Gem' (Alaska Series) NBir (Pr/Prim)
'Blue Riband' (Pr/Prim) WFar
'Blue Sapphire' (Pr/Prim/d) SBeP
'Bon Accord Cerise' GAbr LShi (Pr/Prim/d)
Bonneli Series (Pr/Prim) **new** EGren
boothii (Pe) CSpe
'Boothman's Ruby' see *P.* × *pubescens* 'Boothman's Variety'
brachystoma (Pf) GKev
bracteata (Bu) GKev WAbe WHil
'Broadwell Chameleon' (Au) MWlw NHar NRya
'Broadwell Milkmaid' (Au) ♀H5 WAbe WIce WMal
'Broadwell Ruby' (Au) WAbe
'Buckland Wine' (Pr/Prim) EBee
bullata (Bu) GKev
- var. *delavayi* GKev WHil
× *bulleesiana* (Pf) CAby CDor EPfP GAbr GKev GMaP MCtn NGdn SAko SHar SMrm WFar
bulleyana (Pf) ♀H7 Widely available
burmanica (Pf) GKev WHil WHoo
'Buttercream' (Alaska Series) MPri (Pr/Prim) **new**
Candelabra hybrids (Pf) EDAr EGrI GAbr NBir NGdn SMrm WHil
CANDY MIX (Pr/Prim) LRHS MPri
capitata (Ca) CBcs CLil CWat GArf GKev LRHS SRot WCAu WFar WHil
- CC 3843 (Ca) SRms
- subsp. *mooreana* (Ca) CAby CExl CSpe CTsd EDAr EMor GKev MHol NGdn NLar SPlb

Primula

- 'Noverna Deep Blue' (Ca)	MPro SRms
- 'Salvana' (Ca)	MPro
'Cassis' (Alaska Series) (Pr/Prim)	LRHS MPri
§ *chionantha* (Cy) ♀H6	GArf GKev MCtn NBir NGdn WFar WHil
- subsp. *chionantha* (Cy)	GKev
§ - subsp. *sinopurpurea* (Cy)	GKev NBir WHil
chungensis (Pf)	CDor EAri ELan GAbr GArf GKev GQue LRHS LShi MArl MPri NBir NGdn NLar WFar
'Cisca' (Pr)	WCot
'Clarence Elliott' (Au) ♀H5	GArf MPnt WFar WIce
clusiana (Au)	WAbe
- 'Murray-Lyon' (Au)	NHar
cockburniana (Pf) ♀H6	CSpe CTsd WHil
- SDR 1967 (Pf)	GKev
- 'Kevock Sunshine' (Pf)	GKev
- orange-flowered (Pf)	GKev
concholoba (Mu)	GKev
'Corporal Baxter' (Pr/Prim/d)	LShi
cortusoides (Co)	EPfP
'Cottage Cream' (Pr)	EGren LCro LSou
'Craven Gem' (Pr/Poly)	LEdu WMal
'Crescendo Orange' (Crescendo Series) (Pr/Poly)	MCtn
'Crimson Velvet' (Au)	WFar
'Dark Rosaleen' (Pr/Poly)	CExl EMor LShi MBNS MMuc MNrw NCth SPoG WFar
'David Valentine' (Pr/Poly)	EPPr WCot
'Dawn Ansell' (Pr/Prim/d)	CDor NBir WHer
deflexa (Mu)	GKev
'Dentelle' (Pr/Prim/d)	XFar
denticulata (De) ♀H6	Widely available
- var. *alba* (De)	CAby CBcs CBWd CMHG CPud CToG CTsd EBee ECha ELan EPfP GArf GMaP GQue LBar LRHS LShi MBel MMuc MPri NGdn NLar NRya SPoG WCAu WFar
- blue-flowered (De)	EPfP MPri NLar
- 'Bressingham Beauty' (De)	EBee
- var. *cachemiriana* hort. (De)	EBee LBar
- hybrids (De)	EGrI WFar
- lavender-flowered (De)	CAby
- lilac-flowered (De)	CBWd ELan EPfP LBar LRHS SMrm WTor
- (Prom Series) 'Prom Deep Rose' (De)	MPro
- - 'Prom Lilac' (De)	MPro
- - red-flowered (De)	CAby EPfP NBir
- 'Ronsdorf' (De)	GEdr MCtn
- 'Rubin' (De)	CTsd EBee ELan EPfP GAbr GKev GMaP LBar LRHS MBel NLar SPoG SRms WFar WTor
- 'Snowball' (De)	MCtn
dickieana (Am)	GKev
'Don Keefe' (Pr/Poly)	NLar WFar
'Double Lilac'	see *P. vulgaris* 'Lilacina Plena'
'Duchess of York' (Pr/Poly)	GAbr LShi NLar
'Easter Bonnet' (Pr/Prim)	MMuc
'Eclipse Blue' (Pr/Prim) new	LCro
edgeworthii	see *P. nana*
§ *elatior* (Pr) ♀H6	CDor CTsd CTtf EHet ELin EMor EPfP EWoo GEdr GJos GKev GMaP LCro LShi MBel MHer MNHC MNrw NAts NLar SDix SPoG SRms WBrk WHil

- hybrids (Pr)	SPlb
- subsp. *pallasii* (Pr)	GKev SPhx
- subsp. *pseudoelatior* (Pr)	GKev SBrt
- subsp. *ruprechtii* (Pr)	GKev
'Elizabeth Browning' (Pr/Poly)	GAbr WCot
'Elizabeth Killelay'PBR (Pr/Poly/d)	CExl GElm NBir WFar WTor
euprepes	see *P. melanantha*
fangii (Pu)	GKev
farinosa (Al)	GArf MCtn NGdn SPlb
fasciculata (Ar)	SPlb
I 'Firecracker' (Pr/Poly)	LRHS
Firefly Group (Pr/Poly)	LShi
§ *firmipes* (Si)	GArf
§ *flaccida* (Mu)	GKev MCtn
florindae (Si) ♀H7	Widely available
- bronze-flowered (Si)	NBir
- copper-flowered (Si)	GKev
- 'Dave's Red' (Si)	LEdu
- hybrids (Si)	CMac LBar WFar WHil
- Keillour hybrids (Si)	NGdn
- orange-flowered (Si)	GArf GPSL SRms
- peach-flowered (Si)	CSpe
- 'Ray's Ruby' (Si)	MNrw NBir
- red-flowered (Si)	CSpe GKev GPSL NBid WFar
- terracotta-flowered (Si)	NGdn
forbesii (Mo)	WHil
- CC 4084 (Mo)	CExl
forrestii (Bu)	GKev WHil
- SDR 4304 (Bu)	CExl
§ × *forsteri* (Au)	NLar
§ - 'Bileckii' (Au)	GMaP NBir NHar WIce
- 'Dianne' (Au)	WAbe
'Francisca' (Pr/Poly) ♀H7	CExl EPfP LSto MBNS NLar SPad WCAu WFar WTor
frondosa (Al) ♀H5	WAbe
'Garryarde Guinevere'	see *P.* 'Guinevere'
'Gigha' (Pr/Prim)	GKev GQue WFar
'Gilded Garnet' (Pr/Poly/d)	LRHS
glaucescens (Au)	GKev
'Glowing Embers' (Pf)	NBir
glutinosa All.	see *P. allionii*
Gold-laced Group (Pr/Poly)	CDor EDAr ELan EPfP LCro LShi MMuc NClf NGdn SPlb SPoG WCAu WFar WHil
§ - Barnhaven (Pr/Poly)	NBir
- - 'Gold-laced Jack in the Green' (Pr/Poly)	LShi
- red-flowered (Pr/Poly)	ELan
gracilipes (Pe)	NHar WFar
- 'Minor'	see *P. petiolaris* Wall.
graminifolia	see *P. chionantha*
grandis (Sr)	GKev
'Groenekan's Glorie' (Pr/Prim)	EBee NBir WAbe WCot WFar
'Guernsey Cream' (Pr/Prim/d)	XFar
§ 'Guinevere' (Pr/Poly) ♀H6	CExl CSpe EBee GArf GKev GMaP LShi LSto MMuc MNrw NBid NBir NClf NLar SBeP SDix SPlb WCot WFar WMal
'Hall Barn Blue' (Pr/Prim)	CSpe EBee ELan EWhm GArf GMaP LSto MMuc WCot
§ *halleri* (Al)	GKev
- 'Longiflora'	see *P. halleri*
Harlow Car hybrids (Pf)	GQue NCth WHil
helodoxa	see *P. prolifera*
'Hemswell Blush' (Au)	GKev WFar
heucherifolia (Co)	WHil

Primula 555

– SDR 3224 (Co)	GKev		*limbata* (Cy)	GKev
hirsuta (Au)	MMuc WAbe		'Lindum Angelic' (Au)	NHar
– white-flowered (Au)	NRya		'Lindum Arctic Fire' (Au)	NHar
hirsuta × *minima*	see *P.* × *forsteri*		'Lindum Aria' (Au)	NHar
hoffmanniana	NHar SPlb		'Lindum Celebration' (Au)	NHar
hose-in-hose (Pr/Poly/d)	EWes		'Lindum Countess' (Au)	NHar
Husky Series (Pr/Prim) ♥H5	EGren		'Lindum Crepes Suzette' (Au)	NHar
– HUSKY RASPBERRY PUNCH (Pr/Prim)	LCro MPri		'Lindum Dove' (Au)	NHar
ianthina	see *P. prolifera*		'Lindum Finale' (Au)	NHar
'Ice Cap' (Au) **new**	WAbe		'Lindum Flirtatious' (Au)	NHar
incana (Al)	GKev		'Lindum Gecko' (Au)	NHar
'Ingram's Blue' (Pr/Poly)	EBee		'Lindum Golden Orb' (Au)	NHar
'Innisfree' (Kennedy Irish)	LRHS		'Lindum Ibis' (Au)	NHar
Inshriach hybrids (Pf)	CMHG		'Lindum Lyric' (Au)	NHar
§ 'Inverewe' (Pf)	EBee GEdr NBir		'Lindum Memories' (Au)	NHar
'Iris Mainwaring' (Pr/Prim)	EBee ELan WMal		'Lindum Morning Flight' (Au)	NHar
irregularis hybrid (Pe)	NHar		'Lindum Saffron' (Au)	NHar
'Jackie Richards' (Au)	GKev		'Lindum Storm Cloud' (Au)	NHar
Jack-in-the-Green Group red-flowered (Pr/Poly)	MMuc		'Lindum Wedgwood' (Au)	GEdr NHar
– yellow-flowered (Pr/Poly) **new**	WHil		'Lingwood Beauty' (Pr/Prim)	CElw GAbr
'Jack-the-Lad' (Pr/Prim/d)	XFar		*littoniana*	see *P. vialii*
japonica (Pf)	CPud ECha ELin GAbr GQue MWts NBro NGdn		'Lizzie Green' (Pr/Prim)	NLar
			× *loiseleurii* 'Aire Mist' (Au) ♥H5	NRya WFar
– 'Alba' (Pf)	EMor EPfP EWoo LBar LRHS LSto MHol MPri NGdn NLar SHar WCAu WFar WHil		§ – 'Aire Waves' (Au)	EDAr NHar NRya
			longiflora	see *P. halleri*
– 'Apple Blossom' (Pf)	CAby CBcs CDor CMHG CToG CTsd CTtf EBee ECha EDAr EGrI ELan EMor EPfP GKev LBar LRHS LSto MHol NBid NGdn NLar WFar WHil WPnP		'Lopen Red' (Pr/Prim)	GKev
			luteola (Or)	GEdr NGdn
			macrocalyx	see *P. veris*
			'MacWatt's Cream' (Pr/Poly)	CTtf EDAr GAbr LEdu NLar
			magellanica (Al)	GKev SPlb WAbe
* – 'Carminea' (Pf)	CDor EBee LBar LShi NBro NGdn WFar		*malacoides*	MCtn
			marginata (Au) ♥H5	EWld EWoo GAbr GEdr LShi MMuc WAbe
– 'Fuji' (Pf)	NBro			
– hybrids (Pf)	CMac WCav WFar		– 'Adrian Evans' (Au)	GEdr GMaP WIce
– 'Miller's Crimson' (Pf) ♥H6	Widely available		– 'Alba' (Au)	EPot GEdr GKev NBro NRya
– 'Postford White' (Pf) ♥H6	CBcs CDor CLil CMac CPud CToG CTsd EBee ECha ELan GAbr GKev GMaP LShi NBir NCth SPoG SRms WCAu WHil		– 'Baldock's Purple' (Au)	NRya
			– 'Barbara Clough' (Au)	GEdr NRya
			– 'Beamish' (Au) ♥H5	GEdr NBro NRya
			– 'Beatrice Lascaris' (Au)	GEdr NRya WAbe
– Redfield strain (Pf)	MCtn		– 'Bill Crow' (Au)	GEdr NRya
– red-flowered (Pf)	CMHG		– 'Caerulea' (Au)	GArf GEdr GKev NRya WFar
'Jenny' ambig.	GArf		– 'Casterino' (Au)	NRya WAbe
jesoana (Co)	GKev		– 'Crookes Variety' (Au)	NRya
'Joan Hughes' (*allionii* hybrid) (Au)	WAbe		– 'Doctor Jenkins' (Au)	NRya
'Joanna' (Pr/Poly)	WPGP		– 'Drake's Form' (Au)	GEdr GKev NRya
'Johanna' (Pu)	GArf GKev LEdu NGdn WAbe		– dwarf (Au)	NRya
'John Fielding' (Pr)	CBro		– 'Earl L. Bolton'	see *P. marginata* 'El Bolton'
juliae (Pr)	GKev NBid SPlb WAbe		§ – 'El Bolton' (Au)	NRya
– white-flowered (Pr)	GKev		– 'Elizabeth Fry' (Au)	GEdr
'Ken Dearman' (Pr/Prim/d)	NBir		– 'Herb Dickson' (Au)	GEdr NRya
× *kewensis* (Sp) ♥H3	GKev		– 'Hilary' (Au)	GEdr
'Kinlough Beauty' (Pr/Poly)	EBee GKev SRot		– 'Holden Variety' (Au)	NRya
§ *kisoana* (Co)	CExl		– 'Holly Leaf' (Au)	GEdr
– var. *shikokiana*	see *P. kisoana*		– 'Ivy Agee' (Au)	NRya
komarovii (Pr)	SPlb		– 'Janet' (Au)	GEdr
'Kusum Krishna' (Au)	GEdr GQue MHol MPie NLar NRya WFar		– 'Jenkins Variety' (Au)	GEdr
			– 'Johannes Holler' (Au)	NRya
'Lady Greer' (Pr/Poly) ♥H5	CMac EBee ELan EPfP EPPr GAbr GKev LShi NClf NGdn NHar NLar SBrt WCAu WChS WFar		– 'Kesselring's Variety' (Au)	GEdr WFar WIce
			– 'Laciniata' (Au)	GKev
			– 'Lemon Sorbet' (Au)	GEdr
§ *latifolia* (Au)	GArf		– 'Linda Pope' (Au) ♥H5	GArf GEdr GQue NBir
laurentiana (Al)	GKev		– 'Manfield' (Au)	NRya
'Lee Myers' (*allionii* hybrid) (Au)	WFar		– maritime form (Au)	GArf
			– 'Mrs Carter Walmsley' (Au)	NRya
leucophylla	see *P. elatior*		– 'Mylene' (Au)	GEdr NRya
'Lilian Foster' (Pr/Prim)	WCot		– 'Napoleon' (Au)	GEdr NRya

- 'Peggy Fell' (Au)	GEdr WHil		- Pretty Polly! Buttercream	MPri
- 'Pixie' (Au)	GEdr		('Kerpolicrem')	
- 'Prichard's Variety'	EPot GEdr GMaP NRya WAbe		(Pr/Poly/d) **new**	
(Au) ♀H5			- Pretty Polly! Deep Lilac	MPri
- 'Sheila Denby' (Au)	NRya		('Kerpolila')	
- 'Susan Tindall' (Au)	GEdr		(Pr/Poly/d) **new**	
- 'Viv' (Au)	GEdr		- Pretty Polly! Soft Pink	MPri
- 'Waithman's Variety' (Au)	GMaP NRya		('Kerpolisopin')	
- wild-collected (Au)	GArf		(Pr/Poly/d) **new**	
Marli Rose Shades	LRHS		(Prima Belarina Series) Prima	WHil
(Marli Series)			Belarina Mandarin	
(Pr/Prim/d)			('Kerbelman')	
'Marven' (Au)	EPot GEdr		(Pr/Prim/d) **new**	
'Mary Anne' (Pr)	LShi		- Prima Belarina Ocean Blue	WHil
matthioli	see *Cortusa matthioli*		('Kerbelocean')	
maximowiczii (Cy)	EDAr GEdr		(Pr/Prim/d) **new**	
- var. *maximowiczii* (Cy)	GKev		Primlet Series (Pr/Prim)	MPri
megaseifolia (Pr)	WAbe		- 'Primlet Lavender Shades'	MPri
§ *melanantha* (Cy)	GKev		(Pr/Prim)	
'Milkshake' (Pr)	LRHS		- 'Primlet Lemon' (Pr/Prim)	MPri
'Millstream Cream' (Au)	NLar		- 'Primlet Pink' (Pr/Prim)	MPri
'Millwood Blush' (Pr/Prim)	WMal		- 'Primlet Purple' (Pr/Prim)	MPri
minima (Au)	NBro WAbe		- 'Primlet Red' (Pr/Prim)	MPri
- var. *alba* (Au)	NLar		- 'Primlet Rose Edge'	MPri
'Miss Indigo' (Pr/Prim/d)	CDor		(Pr/Prim)	
mistassinica (Al)	GKev		- 'Primlet Rose' (Pr/Prim)	MPri
miyabeana (Pf)	GKev		- 'Primlet Sunrise'	MPri
'Moerheimii' (Pr/Prim)	GEdr GKev MNrw		(Pr/Prim)	
moupinensis (Pe)	CExl		- 'Primlet Yellow' (Pr/Prim)	MPri
'Mrs Frank Neave'	WFar	§	*prolifera* (Pf) ♀H4	CMHG CToG GKev LRHS NGdn
(Pr/Prim)		§	× *pubescens* (Au) ♀H5	CDor CTsd ECha EPfP GKev MHer
'Mrs Marjorie Banks' (Pr)	GKev			NGdn SPoG WTor
§ *munroi*	GArf GKev	§	- Beverley White' (Au)	EBee WHil
subsp. *yargongensis* (Ar)		§	- 'Boothman's Variety' (Au)	GMaP NLar
muscarioides (Mu)	GKev		- 'Carmen'	see *P.* × *pubescens* 'Boothman's
§ *nana* (Pe)	NHar			Variety'
'Netta Dennis' (Pe)	WAbe		- 'Christine' (Au)	NBir WBrk WCot
nivalis Pallas	see *P. chionantha*		- 'Cream Viscosa' (Au)	SPlb WFar
nutans Delavay ex Franch.	see *P. flaccida*		- 'Faldonside' (Au)	GEdr GMaP
'Oak Leaf Magenta' (Pr)	LRHS	§	- 'Freedom' (Au)	GKev GPSL NBir
obconica subsp.	GKev		- 'George Harrison' (Au)	GArf
werringtonensis (Ob)			- 'Harlow Car' (Au)	GEdr MPnt
× *obristii* (Au) **new**	GKev		- 'Hazel's White' (Au)	GEdr WFar
odontocalyx 'Snow Flurry'	GKev		- 'Lilac Fairy' (Au)	GKev
(Da)			- 'Rufus' (Au) ♀H5	GEdr NHar
'Old Port' (Pr/Poly)	GKev GQue LShi MNrw		- 'Rumbling Bridge' (Au)	WCot
(Ooh La La Series) 'Ooh La La	LRHS		- 'Sid Skelton' (Au)	NRya
Orange' (Pi × Sp)			- 'The General' (Au)	GEdr
- 'Ooh La La Pastel Pink'	LCro LRHS MPri	§	- 'Wedgwood' (Au)	WHil
(Pi × Sp)		§	- 'Winnifred' (Au)	EGrI
- 'Ooh La La Rose' (Pi × Sp)	LRHS		*pulverulenta* (Pf) ♀H6	CAby CBcs CDor CToG CTsd CWat
ovalifolia (Da)	GKev			ECha ELan EPfP GAbr GEdr GElm
palinuri (Au)	GKev WMal			GKev GMaP LCro LSto MBNS MCtn
palmata (Co)	GEdr			MPri MSCN NGdn NLar StAn WCAu
parryi (Pa)	GEdr GKev WHil			WPnP
pedemontana 'Alba' (Au)	GEdr		- Bartley hybrids (Pf) ♀H6	MArl
'Perle von Bottrop'	WCot		- 'Purple Storm' (Pr/Prim/d)	WFar
(Pr/Prim)			- 'Purpurkissen' (Pr/Prim)	NCIf
'Peter Klein' (Or)	GKev		- 'Quaker's Bonnet'	see *P. vulgaris* 'Lilacina Plena'
petiolaris misapplied	see *P.* 'Redpoll'		- 'Rachel Kinnen' (Au)	EDAr GAbr WFar
§ *petiolaris* Wall. (Pe)	NHar		- 'Ravenglass Vermilion'	see *P.* 'Inverewe'
- Sherriff's form	see *P.* 'Redpoll'	§	- 'Redpoll' (Pe)	GArf NHar
'Petticoat' (Pr/Prim/d)	WCot		*reidii* (So)	GKev
'Pink Aire' (Au)	WIce		- var. *williamsii* (So)	GKev
poissonii (Pf)	CDoC CDor CLil GKev NGdn WHil		*renifolia*	WAbe
polyneura (Co)	EGrI GArf GKev MHol NGdn WCot		'Rheniana' (Au)	NRya
'Porcelain Blue' (Pr/Prim)	LCro		'Ringo Starr' (Pr)	LRHS
(Pretty Polly! Series)	MPri		'Romance' (Pr/Prim/d)	LRHS
Pretty Polly! Blushing			'Rose Madder' (Pr/Prim)	WCot
Peach ('Kerpoliblush')			*rosea* (Or) ♀H5	CAby ELan GKev LRHS MMuc NBid
(Pr/Poly/d) **new**				NBir NRya SPlb WPnP

	- 'Gigas' (Or)	GKev WHil
	- 'Grandiflora' (Or)	CMac EPfP SPoG SRms WCav
	'Rosemary Cottage' (Pr/Poly)	WCot
I	'Rowena' (Pr/Prim)	WCot
	Rubens Series (Pr/Prim/d)	MPri WHil
	rubra	see *P. firmipes*
	rusbyi (Pa)	GEdr
	scandinavica (Al)	GKev WHil
	scapigera (Pe)	WFar
§	'Schneekissen' (Pr/Prim)	EBee NBro SRot WCAu WFar
	scotica (Al)	GKev WAbe
	secundiflora (Pf)	CTsd ELan EWes GArf GKev NBir SPlb
	serratifolia (Pf)	GKev
	'Sheryl Louise' (Pr/Prim)	NHar
	'Showstopper Cream' (Pr/Poly) **new**	MPri
	'Showstopper Purple' (Pr/Poly) **new**	LCro
	'Showstopper White' (Pr/Poly) **new**	LCro
	sibthorpii	see *P. vulgaris* subsp. *sibthorpii*
	sieboldii (Co) ♀H5	EMor GKev LRHS MAsh MNrw SMrm SRms
I	- '10' (Co)	WFar
	- 'Aiaigasa' (Co)	CSta
	- 'Aka-tonbo' (Co)	CSta WFar
	- 'Akedori' (Co)	CSta
	- 'Akenotama' (Co)	WFar
	- 'Aketamagari' (Co)	WFar
	- 'Aki-no-yosooi' (Co)	CSta
	- 'Alba' (Co)	CSta EBlo LRHS WFar
	- 'Amaenbou' (Co)	CSta
	- 'Andromeda' (Co)	EBee
	- 'Ankoan' (Co)	WFar
	- 'Aoba-no-fue' (Co)	CSta WFar
	- 'Aoi-no-ue' (Co)	CSta
	- 'Aoyagi-zome' (Co)	CSta
	- 'Appare' (Co)	CSta
	- 'Ariake' (Co)	CSta WFar
	- 'Arimayama' (Co)	CSta WFar
	- 'Asahi' (Co)	CSta WFar
	- 'Asahigata' (Co)	CSta WFar
	- 'Ayanami' (Co)	WFar
	- 'Ayasegawa' (Co)	CSta WFar
	- 'Banshun' (Co)	WFar
	- 'Beeches Star' (Co)	EBee
	- 'Benjamin' (Co)	CSta EBee EBlo WFar
	- 'Bide-a-Wee Blue' (Co)	NBid
	- 'Bide-a-Wee Lace' (Co)	NBid
	- 'Bijyonomai' (Co)	WFar
I	- 'Blue Lagoon' (Co)	CSta EBee EPfP NLar WFar
	- blue-flowered (Co)	CSta
	- 'Blush' (Co)	CSta WFar
	- 'Bonbori' (Co)	CSta WFar
	- 'Bureikou' (Co)	CSta WFar
	- 'Carefree' (Co)	CSta NLar WFar
	- 'Cherubim' (Co)	CSta EBee WFar
	- 'Chidoriasobi' (Co)	CSta
	- 'Chononemuri' (Co)	WFar
	- 'Daikoshi' (Co)	CSta WFar
	- 'Daiminnishiki' (Co)	CSta WFar
	- 'Dairiki-muso' (Co)	WFar
	- 'Dancing Ladies' (Co)	WFar
I	- 'Dark Lady' (Co)	WFar
	- 'Dart Rapids' (Co)	CSta WFar
	- 'Doushi-bai' (Co)	WFar
	- 'Duane's Choice' (Co)	CSta
	- 'Edasango' (Co)	WFar
	- 'Edomurasaki' (Co)	CSta WFar
	- 'Ekiji-no-suzu' (Co)	CSta
	- 'Ekiro-no-suzu' (Co)	CSta WFar
	- 'Elegance' (Co)	CSta WFar
I	- 'Elsie' (Co)	WFar
	- 'Emerald Sun' (Co)	WFar
	- 'Essie' (Co)	CSta WFar
	- 'Flamenco' (Co/d)	WFar
	- 'Frilly Blue' (Co)	CSta EBee WFar
	- 'Frilly White' (Co)	WFar
	- 'Fuji Shishi' (Co/d)	WFar
	- 'Fuji-no-mai' (Co)	CSta
	- 'Fuji-no-sato' (Co)	WFar
	- 'Fukiagezakura' (Co)	CSta
	- 'Fukuju' (Co)	CSta
	- 'Futami-gauri' (Co)	WFar
	- 'Galactic' (Co)	CSta WFar
	- 'Geisha Girl' (Co)	CDor CSpe CSta EBee NLar WFar
	- 'Genyo-rakis' (Co)	WFar
	- 'George' (Co)	CSta
	- 'Ginfukurin' (Co)	CSta WFar
	- 'Gin-kaji-oku' (Co)	WFar
	- 'Gin-pukurin' (Co)	CSta WFar
	- 'Ginsekai' (Co)	WFar
	- 'Girl of the Limberlost' (Co)	CSta WFar
	- 'Gloaming' (Co)	WFar
	- 'Gunma' (Co)	WFar
	- 'Gunma Niizatia' (Co)	CSta
	- 'Gyokk-bai' (Co)	CSta
	- 'Hakutaka' (Co)	CSta
	- 'Hamana-no-kasane' (Co)	WFar
	- 'Hana-angya' (Co/d)	CSta WFar
	- 'Hanachirusato' (Co)	WFar
	- 'Hana-fubuki' (Co)	WFar
	- 'Hanaguruma' (Co)	CSta WFar
	- 'Hana-kamachi' (Co)	CSta
	- 'Hanako' (Co)	WFar
	- 'Hana-monyo' (Co)	CSta
	- 'Hana-nishiki' (Co)	CSta WFar
	- 'Haru-no-aretonbo' (Co)	WFar
	- 'Haru-no-yoi' (Co)	CSta WFar
	- 'Harutugedoric' (Co)	WFar
	- 'Hashi-benkei' (Co)	WFar
	- 'Hatu-garasu' (Co)	CSta WFar
	- 'Hatu-goromo' (Co)	CSta WFar
	- 'Hazel' (Co)	CSta
	- 'Heart's Desire' (Co)	EBee WFar
	- 'Hidamari' (Co)	CSta
	- 'Higurasi' (Co)	WFar
	- 'Hi-no-hakama' (Co)	CSta
	- 'Hinomaru' (Co)	CSta
	- 'Hitome' (Co)	WFar
	- 'Hokutosei' (Co)	CSta
	- 'Hutaezuru' (Co)	WFar
	- 'Ikoko-no-e-beni' (Co)	WFar
	- 'Inukima Mincura' (Co)	CSta WFar
	- 'Inukine White' (Co)	CSta
	- 'Irino-no-miyako' (Co)	CSta
	- 'Isamijishi' (Co)	CSta
	- 'Iso-botan' (Co)	CSta WFar
	- 'Izutu' (Co)	CSta WFar
	- 'Janomegasa' (Co)	CSta
	- 'Jessica' (Co)	CSta WFar
	- 'Jintsūriki' (Co)	WFar
	- 'Jisshū-no-sora' (Co)	WFar
	- 'Jyuuyuunoutage' (Co)	WFar
	- 'Kafajin' (Co)	CSta
	- 'Kakako-asobi' (Co)	WFar
	- 'Kakuremino' (Co)	CSta
	- 'Kamiyo-no-kanmuri' (Co)	CSta
	- 'Kansenden' (Co)	WFar

- 'Kara-chirimen' (Co)	CSta	- 'Okinosabi' (Co)	WFar
- 'Karafune' (Co)	CSta WFar	- 'Old Vienna' (Co)	WFar
- 'Karakoromo' (Co)	CSta WFar	- 'Oni-gokko' (Co)	CSta WFar
- 'Kashima' (Co)	CSta WFar	- 'Oriental Beauty' (Co)	EBee
- 'Kassai' (Co)	WFar	- 'Oshibori' (Co)	CSta GKev MNrw NLar WFar
- 'Keepsake' (Co)	CSta	- 'Otomenosode' (Co)	WFar
- 'Kenkou' (Co)	CSta WFar	- 'Ouchikazri' (Co)	WFar
- 'Kiaryodai' (Co)	WFar	- 'Our White' (Co)	WFar
- 'Kicchou' (Co)	CSta	- 'Pago-Pago' (Co)	CSta WFar
- 'Kihi-no-yume' (Co)	CSta WFar	- 'Pale Moon' (Co)	WFar
- 'Kiraboshi' (Co)	WFar	- 'Pink Laced' (Co)	WFar
- 'Koenji' (Co)	CSta	- pink-flowered (Co)	NBir NRya
- 'Kohara-biyori' (Co)	CSta	- 'Purity' (Co)	WFar
- 'Kokonoe-beni' (Co/d)	CSta WFar	- 'Purple Dusk' (Co)	WFar
- 'Kokoroiki' (Co)	CSta WFar	- 'Raspberry Buttons' (Co)	WFar
- 'Komodo-ne' (Co)	WFar	- 'Rasyoumon' (Co)	WFar
- 'Ko-odori' (Co)	WFar	- 'Rock Candy' (Co)	CSta WFar
- 'Kotobuki' (Co)	CSta WFar	- 'Saiun' (Co)	CSta WFar
- 'Kotonoshirabe' (Co)	CSta WFar	- 'Sakuragawa' (Co)	CSta WFar
- 'Kotyou-no-mail' (Co)	CSta WFar	- 'Sakura-no-miya' (Co)	WFar
- 'Kourohou' (Co)	WFar	- 'Sangoguko' (Co)	GKev MNrw
- 'Kozakura-genji' (Co)	CSta	- 'Sasanake' (Co)	WFar
- 'Kumoizuru' (Co)	CSta	- 'Sato-zakura' (Co)	CSta WFar
- 'Kuni-no-hikari' (Co)	WFar	- 'Sekidaiko' (Co)	CSta
- 'Kurama' (Co)	WFar	- 'Sened Star' (Co)	WFar
- 'Kyoho' (Co)	WFar	- 'Senshō' (Co)	CSta WFar
- 'Kyô-kanoko' (Co)	CSta WFar	- 'Sen-yū' (Co)	CSta
- 'Laced Lady' (Co)	WFar	- 'Seraphim' (Co)	CSta EBee NLar WFar
- 'Lacewing' (Co)	CSta	- 'Seto-no-ume' (Co)	WFar
- f. *lactiflora* (Co)	CSta	- 'Shibori Gasane' (Co/d)	WFar
- 'Lacy Lady' (Co)	WFar	- 'Shibori-tatuta' (Co)	CSta
- 'Lilac Blue' (Co)	CSta WFar	- 'Shikishima' (Co)	WFar
- 'Lilac Crinoline' (Co)	WFar	- 'Shiokemuri' (Co)	CSta
- 'Lilac Sunbonnet' (Co)	WFar	- 'Shira-saba-sishi' (Co)	WFar
- 'Mai-momiji' (Co/d)	CSta WFar	- 'Shirasagi' (Co)	WFar
- 'Mai-ōgi' (Co)	CSta WFar	- 'Shiratama' (Co)	WFar
- 'Makazebeni' (Co)	WFar	- 'Shira-tonbo' (Co)	CSta WFar
- 'Maki-no-o' (Co)	CSta	- 'Shira-washi' (Co)	CSta WFar
- 'Managuruma' (Co)	WFar	- 'Shirousagi' (Co)	WFar
- 'Manakoora' (Co)	EGrl WFar	- 'Shishi-funjin' (Co)	CSta EBlo WFar
- 'Mangeto' (Co)	WFar	- 'Shunputaitou' (Co)	WFar
- 'Martin Nest Blue' (Co)	CSta WFar	- 'Sikoubai' (Co)	WFar
- 'Martin Nest Pink' (Co)	WFar	- 'Sinakatonba' (Co)	WFar
- 'Masquerado' (Co)	WFar	- 'Sinipukurn' (Co)	CSta WFar
- 'Matu-no-yuki' (Co)	CSta WFar	- 'Sinnkirou' (Co)	WFar
- 'Mejirodai' (Co)	CSta	- 'Sinseto' (Co)	CSta WFar
- 'Miho-no-koji' (Co)	CSta WFar	- 'Siritonbo' (Co)	WFar
- 'Mikado' (Co)	CSta EBee LRHS WFar	- 'Sitikenjin' (Co)	WFar
- 'Mikini-no-mare' (Co)	CSta WFar	- 'Smudge' (Co)	CSta
- 'Mikuni-beni' (Co)	CSta	- 'Snooch' (Co)	WFar
- 'Mitajiman' (Co)	CSta WFar	- 'Snow Flakes' (Co)	CSta
- 'Mitanohikari' (Co)	WFar	- 'Snowbird' (Co)	CSta
- 'Miyako-sakura' (Co)	WFar	- 'Snowdrop' (Co)	CDor CSta GKev MBel WCot WFar
- 'Miyakowakare' (Co)	WFar	- 'Snowflake' (Co)	CSta EBee EBlo GKev LRHS NLar WFar WTre
- 'Miyuki' (Co)	WFar		
- 'Molly' (Co)	CSta WFar	- 'Sorcha's Pink' (Co)	CSta WFar
- 'Momijbashi' (Co)	CSta WFar	- 'Soshiari' (Co)	CSta WFar
- 'Momo-kagari' (Co)	WFar	- 'Sotodorihime' (Co)	WFar
- 'Momozono' (Co)	WFar	- 'Spring Blush' (Co)	CSta WFar
- 'Mukashi-no-ume' (Co)	WFar	- 'Spring Song' (Co)	CSta WFar
- 'Murasaki-koume' (Co)	WFar	- 'Suibijin' (Co)	WFar
- 'Musashino' (Co)	CSta EBee EBlo LRHS WFar	- 'Sumida-no-hatu' (Co)	WFar
- 'Naka-fu' (Co)	WFar	- 'Sumisonegawa' (Co)	CSta WFar
- 'Nami-no-ue' (Co)	CSta	- 'Sumizomegenji' (Co)	CSta WFar
- 'Nankin-kozakura' (Co)	CSta WFar	- 'Swasasi' (Co)	WFar
- 'Nirvana' (Co)	WFar	- 'Sweetie' (Co)	CSta WFar
- 'Noboruko' (Co)	CSta WFar	- 'Syosin' (Co)	CSta WFar
- 'Nuretubame' (Co)	CSta WFar	- 'Syutyuka' (Co)	CSta WFar
- 'Ochibagoromo' (Co)	CSta	- 'Tagonoura' (Co)	CSta WFar
- 'Ohseki' (Co)	WFar	- 'Tairou-no-tsuki' (Co)	CSta
- 'Okinanotomo' (Co)	WFar	- 'Takane-no-yuki' (Co)	CSta

- 'Taki-mei' (Co) — CSta WFar
- 'Tamagawa-zome' (Co) — CSta WFar
- 'Tama-sango' (Co) — CSta
- 'Tamashiki-no-miya' (Co) — CSta WFar
- 'Tanuki-bayashi' (Co) — CSta
- 'Taoyami' (Co) — CSta WFar
- 'Tatuta-no-yūbe' (Co) — CSta WFar
- 'Tobitake' (Co) — CSta
- 'Tochirimen' (Co) — WFar
- 'Tokasamesi' (Co) — WFar
- 'Tokiji-gata' (Co) — WFar
- 'Tokimeki' (Co/d) — CSta WFar
- 'Toyonoharu' (Co) — WFar
- 'Trade Winds' (Co) — CSta WFar
- 'Tsuki-no-miyake' (Co) — CSta
- 'Tsukumo-jishi' (Co) — CSta
- 'Tukasamesi' (Co) — CSta WFar
- 'Turu-no-kegoromo' (Co) — CSta
- 'Ue-no-ume' (Co) — CSta
- 'Ukima Aka' (Co) — CSta WFar
- 'Ukimashiro' (Co) — CSta WFar
- 'Usujanome' (Co) — CSta WFar
- 'Utyū' (Co) — CSta
- 'Vivid Pink' (Co) — CSta WFar
- 'White Buttons' (Co) — WFar
- 'Winter Dreams' (Co) — GKev MBel NBid NBro WFar
- 'Yodai-no-yume' (Co) — WFar
- 'Yousei' (Co) — CSta
- 'Yugeshiki' (Co) — CSta WFar
- 'Yūhi-beni' (Co) — CSta WFar
- 'Yukiguruma' (Co) — WFar
- 'Yuki-meimaki' (Co) — WFar
- 'Yukizakura' (Co) — CSta

sikkimensis (Si) ♀H6 — GEdr GKev MBel NGdn SPoG WCAu
- var. *pseudosikkimensis* (Si) — GKev
- var. *pudibunda* (Si) — GArf GKev
- red-flowered (Si) — GKev
- aff. *sikkimensis* (Si) — NGdn
- Silver-laced Group (Pr/Poly) — EPfP LShi SPoG WFar
- black-flowered (Pr/Poly) — LShi

simensis (Sp) — GKev
sinopurpurea — see *P. chionantha* subsp. *sinopurpurea*
smithiana — see *P. prolifera*
'Snow Carpet' — see *P.* 'Schneekissen'
'Snow White' (Pr/Poly) — GMaP
SNOWCUSHION — see *P.* 'Schneekissen'
sorachiana — see *P. yuparensis*
spectabilis (Au) — GKev
STAR FEVER WHITE (Pr/Prim) — MPri
× *steinii* — see *P.* × *forsteri*
Stella Series (Pr/Poly) — EGren LCro MPri
- 'Stella Pink Champagne' (Pr/Poly) **new** — MPri
- 'Stella Scarlet Pimpernel' (Pr/Poly) — MPri
stenodonta (Pf) — GKev
'Stradbrook Charm' (Au) — NRya
'Stradbrook Dainty' (Au) — WFar
'Stradbrook Dream' (Au) — WFar
'Stradbrook Lucy' (Au) — GEdr
'Strong Beer' (Pr/Prim) — EBee GElm SBeP WCot WFar WTor
'Sue Jervis' (Pr/Prim/d) — LShi NBir
suffrutescens (Su) — WAbe
SUNRISE RUBY ('Kerpriruby') (Pr/Prim/d) — WHil
'Sunshine Susie' (Pr/Prim/d) — GArf

§ SWEETHEART (mixed) (Pr/Prim) — LCro
szechuanica (Cy) — GKev
'Tantallon' (Pe) — NHar
'Tawny Port' (Pr/Poly) — CElw
'Theodora' (Pr) — EBee ELan WFar
'Tie Dye' (Pr/Prim) — NLar SAko WCot WFar
'Tomato Red' (Pr/Prim) — WFar
§ *veris* (Pr) ♀H5 — Widely available
- Coronation Cowslips Group (Pr) — EGren
- hose-in-hose (Pr/d) — EWes WHil WMal
- 'Katy McSparron' (Pr/d) — CDor CExl LRHS NLar WFar
- 'Lime with Orange' (Pr) — LBar MPri
- subsp. *macrocalyx* (Pr) — EPPr
- orange-flowered (Pr) — MPri NLar
- red-flowered (Pr) — NBid NGdn
- 'Sunset Shades' (Pr) — CDor CSpe ELan EPfP LBar LShi MCtn NGdn NLar WCAu
- subsp. *veris* (Pr) — LSou
'Veristar Lemon' (Pr/Poly) — MPri
'Veristar Marmalade' (Pr/Poly) — MPri
'Veristar Yellow' (Pr/Poly) — MPri
vernalis — see *P. vulgaris*
verticillata (Sp) — GKev
§ *vialii* (So) ♀H5 — Widely available
- ALISON HOLLAND ('Aliholl'PBR) (So) — LBar LCro MBel MPro SPad SRot WTor
villosa var. *commutata* (Au) — GKev
'Vintage' (Pr/Prim/d) — LRHS
violacea (Mu) — GKev
viscosa All. — see *P. latifolia*
× *vochinensis* (Au) — GEdr
§ *vulgaris* (Pr/Prim) ♀H7 — Widely available
- var. *alba* (Pr/Prim) — WBrk
- 'Alba Plena' (Pr/Prim/d) — LShi
- 'Avoca' (Pr/Prim) — WFar
- 'Avondale' (Kennedy Irish Series) (Pr/Prim) — CDor CElw EBee LRHS MNrw MWlw SPoG WCot WHil
- 'Blarney Castle Blush' (Pr/Prim) — WFar
- 'Blarney Castle Red' (Pr/Prim) — GAbr
- 'Carrigdale' (Pr/Prim) — CDor GAbr WChS WCot WFar
- 'Catherine Thompson' (Pr/Prim) — NBir
- 'Claddagh' (Pr/Prim) — WCot
- Cornish pink (Pr/Prim) — GKev
- DRUMCLIFFE ('K74'PBR) (Pr/Prim) — EBee LRHS WCot WFar
- 'Dunbeg' (Kennedy Irish Series) (Pr/Prim) — CDor LRHS
- 'Glengarriff' (Kennedy Irish Series) (Pr/Prim) — EBee LRHS
- 'Golden Gem' (Pr/Prim/d) — WCot
- green-flowered — see *P. vulgaris* 'Viridis'
- hybrids (Pr/Prim) — CTsd
- INNISFREE ('K72'PBR) (Pr/Prim) — CDor MMuc WCot WFar
§ - 'Lilacina Plena' (Pr/Prim/d) — GArf LShi SBeP WFar
- 'Moneygall' (Kennedy Irish Series) (Pr/Prim) — LRHS WFar
- OAKLEAF YELLOW PICOTEE ('Ifproy') (Pr/Poly) — MPri SBea
- 'Raspberry Rose' (Pr/Prim) — LCro MPri
§ - subsp. *sibthorpii* (Pr/Prim) ♀H5 — CAby CDor CMac EBee ELan GKev MHer MNrw NBro NClf SRms WFar WHil WMal

- 'Taigetos' (Pr/Prim) ♀H7 CBro CExl
- 'Tarragem Sparkling Ruby' LRHS
  (Pr/Prim/d)
- 'Vanilla Cream' (Pr/Prim) WCot
§ - 'Viridis' (Pr/Prim/d) MNrw
- subsp. *vulgaris* CPud WCav
  (Pr/Prim) ♀H7
waltonii (Si) GEdr MCtn MNrw WHil
'Wanda' (Pr/Prim) ♀H7 CBcs CPud EBee ELan EPfP
  GAbr GKev GQue LShi LSto
  MArl MBel MHer MMuc NBid
  SMrm SRms WCAu WCot
  WFar WGwG
Wanda Group (Pr/Prim) NBro
- 'Wanda Hose-in-hose' NBid NBir
  (Pr/Prim/d)
- 'Wanda Jack-in-the-Green' WCot
  (Pr/Prim)
- 'Wanda Tomato Red' LShi NCth
  (Pr/Prim)
warshenewskiana (Or) EWes GKev WAbe WGwG
watsonii (Mu) GKev
'Wedgwood' see *P. × pubescens* 'Wedgwood'
'Wharfedale Bluebell' (Au) NBir NHar WHil
'Wharfedale Gem' WIce
  (*allionii* hybrid) (Au)
'Wharfedale Sunshine' (Au) GKev WFar
'Wharfedale Village' (Au) MPnt NHar
'White Linda Pope' (Au) GArf GEdr MPnt
wilsonii (Pf) NBir NGdn StAn WHil
- SDR 7824 (Pf) GKev
§ - var. *anisodora* (Pf) GKev MPro NGdn
- var. *wilsonii* (Pf) GKev
'Woodland Dell' (Pr/Prim) EGren LCro
'Woodland Walk' (Pr/Prim) EPfP SRms
yargongensis see *P. munroi* subsp. *yargongensis*
§ *yuparensis* (Al) GArf
zambalensis (Ar) GKev
'Zebra Blue' (Pr/Prim) EMor EPfP MPri WHil

Primulina (Gesneriaceae)
'Aiko' WDib
'Candy' WDib
'Chastity' WDib
'Diane Marie' WDib
dryas 'Hisako' WDib
'Erika' WDib
flavimaculata WDib
heterotricha WDib
'Keiko' WDib
'Periwinkle' WDib
'Stardust' WDib
'Sweet Dreams' WDib
tabacum 'Deco' WDib

Prinsepia (Rosaceae)
sinensis MBlu NLar

Pritchardia (Arecaceae)
pacifica NPlm

Pritzelago see *Hornungia*

Prosartes ✿ (Liliaceae)
§ *hookeri* CMiW EBee MNrw
§ - var. *oregana* EBee EBlo WCru
§ *lanuginosa* EPPr ESwi LEdu WCru WFar WPGP
§ *maculata* LEdu MNrw WCru
§ *smithii* EBlo ESwi EWld IDun LEdu LRHS
  MNrw NHar NLar SPeP WCru
  WPGP

Proserpinaca (Haloragaceae)
palustris ELin

Prosopis (Fabaceae)
juliflora Prohibited invasive. See Conservation and the Environment, p.42

Prostanthera ✿ (Lamiaceae)
aspalathoides CTsd SEle
'Badja Peak' GKev
baxteri SEle
calycina CTsd
cuneata ♀H4 CBcs CCht CCoa CDoC CMac
  CSde CSpe EAri EBee EGrI
  ELan EPfP EUrb GArf LCro
  LRHS MGos MMuc MPro NBir
  NLar SPad SPlb SPoG SRms
  WFar WPGP
denticulata CTsd
* *digitiformis* CTsd
incana CTsd
incisa EGrI
lasianthos ♀H3 CBcs CTsd ELan LRHS SPlb
- 'Kallista Pink' CTsd
melissifolia CTsd
'Mint-Ice' LRHS
ovalifolia ♀H3 SEle
I - 'Variegata' (v) CBcs CCoa CKit CMac CSde CTsd
  EHeP ELan LCro LRHS MAsh MHoo
  SEle
phylicifolia CBcs CTsd
rotundifolia ♀H2 CAbb CCoa CSde CTsd EBee EGrI
  ELan EPfP LRHS MHoo SVen
- 'Chelsea Girl' see *P. rotundifolia* 'Rosea'
§ - 'Rosea' ♀H2 CTsd LRHS
sieberi Benth. CTsd
I - 'Variegata' (v) CTsd
spinosa CTsd
'Starlight' (v) CTsd
staurophylla CTsd
walteri EGrI LRHS

Protea (Proteaceae)
aurea SPlb
- subsp. *aurea* CPbh
burchellii CPbh SPlb
compacta CPbh
coronata CPbh SPlb
cryophila SPlb
cynaroides CPbh LRHS SEle SPlb
effusa SPlb
eximia CPbh SPlb
grandiceps CPbh SPlb
lacticolor SPlb
laurifolia SPlb
longifolia CPbh
magnifica CPbh MCtn
mundii CPbh
nana CPbh SPlb
neriifolia CPbh SPlb
- 'Snowcrest' CPbh
obtusifolia CPbh SPlb
repens CPbh SPlb
scolymocephala SPlb
subvestita SPlb
susannae CPbh SPlb

Prumnopitys (Podocarpaceae)
§ *andina* LRHS WPav
elegans see *P. andina*

Prunella (Lamiaceae)
- 'Blue Pearl' — MHol MHoo
- § **grandiflora** — ECha SRms StAn
  - 'Alba' — EBee ELan GMaP NBid NLar SRms WCAu
  - 'Altenberg Rosa' — SNoN WCAu
  - 'Bella Deep Rose' — SPoG
  - 'Blue Loveliness' — EBee
  - 'Carminea' — EBee
  - light blue-flowered — NLar WFar
  - 'Loveliness' — CMac ECha ELan GMaP NBro NGdn NSti SPlb WCAu WFar
  - 'Pagoda' — NBro NLar
  - 'Pink Loveliness' — EBee SRms WCAu WFar
  - 'Rubra' — ECha NLar
  - violet-flowered — EPfP LRHS NSti
  - 'White Loveliness' — CMac SRms
- **incisa** — see *P. vulgaris*
- **laciniata** white-flowered — MHoo
- 'Rose Pearl' — EPfP MHol MHoo SPoG SRms
- SUMMER DAZE — LBar
  ('Binsumdaz'PBR)
- § **vulgaris** — CBWd CGHo CHab CoPl EHet ENfk EPfP GJem GQue LCro MAsh MCtn MHoo MNHC NMir SRms SVic WHer WOrg
  - f. **leucantha** — WHer
  - × **webbiana** — see *P. grandiflora*

Prunus ✿ (Rosaceae)
- 'Accolade' (d) ♀H6 — Widely available
- § 'Amanogawa' ♀H6 — Widely available
- **amygdalus** — see *P. dulcis*
- APRIKYRA (Cherrycot Series) (F) — LCro MLod
- 'Aprimira' (Miracot Series) (F) — CAgr EBee LCro
- APRISALI (Aprium Series) (F) — EBee ELan NOra NPip
- **armeniaca** — MPri NPlm SAth
  - 'Alfred' (F) — EPom LCro SKee
  - 'Bergecot' (F) — SKee
  - 'Bergeron' (F) — CBTr CMac EPom NOra SKee SSFr WMat
  - 'Bergeval' (F) — CAgr CBTr CMac ELan
  - 'Breda' (F) — WFar
  - 'Bredase' (F) — MSwo
  - COMPACTA (F) — CMac LCro MLod NOra SBmr WMat
  - 'Delicot'PBR (F) — SSFr
  - 'Early Moorpark' (F) — CAgr LCro NOra SBmr SEND SSFr WMat
  - FLAVORCOT ('Bayoto'PBR) (F) — CAgr EPom LCro NOra SBmr SKee SSFr WMat
  - 'Garden Aprigold' (F) — EPom LCro SSFr WMat
  - 'Goldcot' (F) — CAgr LRHS NOra SKee SPoG SSFr WMat
  - 'Golden Glow' (F) — CAgr EPfP EPom LCro LRHS NOra SKee WMat
  - 'Goldrich' (F) — CAgr
  - 'Hargrand' (F) — CAgr SVic
  - 'Harogem' (F) — CAgr
  - 'Helena de Roussilon' (F) — CAgr NOra
  - 'Hemskirke' (F) — SKee
  - 'Hungarian Best' (F) — SVic
  - 'Kioto'PBR (F) — CAgr CBTr EBee LCro NOra WMat
  - 'Moorpark' (F) — CHab CWnw EGren ELan LBuc LRHS MPri SEdi SKee
  - 'New Large Early' (F) — EGren LCro SEdi SEND
  - ORANGE SUMMER ('Zaitorde'PBR) (F) — EPom
  - 'Petit Muscat' (F) — EPom SBmr SKee
  - 'Pink Marry' (F) — CBTr EBee LCro NOra WMat
  - 'Robada'PBR (F) — CAgr CBTr LCro NOra
  - 'Tomcot' (F) — CAgr ELan EPfP EPom LBuc LCro LRHS LSRN MLod NOra SBmr SKee SPoG SSFr WMat
  - 'Tross Orange' (F) — EGren
  - 'Vigama' (F) — NOra WMat
  - 'Asano' (F) — CMac LCro LRHS
  - 'Athos' (F) — LCro MGos WMat
- **avium** — Widely available
  - 'Amber Heart' (F) — NOra SKee WMat
  - 'Bigarreau Burlat' (D) — LCro LMaj NPlm
  - 'Bigarreau de Schrecken' (F) — SKee
  - 'Bigarreau Gaucher' (F) — SKee WMat
  - § 'Bigarreau Napoléon' (F) — EBee EPom LCro LMaj NOra SBmr SEdi SKee SSFr SVic WMat
  - 'Birchenhayes' — see *P. avium* 'Early Birchenhayes'
  - 'Black Elton' (F) — SKee
  - 'Black Oliver' (F) — NOra WMat
  - 'Black Tartarian' (F) — SKee
  - 'Black Varik' (F) — MSwo
  - 'Bradbourne Black' (F) — SKee
  - 'Bullion' (F) — CAda CEnd
  - 'Burcombe' (F) — CAda CAgr CEnd MLod WMat
  - CELESTE ('Sumpaca'PBR) (D) — CAgr CMac LCro NOra SBmr SPoG WMat
  - 'Cherokee' — see *P. avium* 'Lapins'
  - 'Colney' (F) — EPom LCro NOra SBmr SKee SSFr WMat
  - 'Coroon' (F) — SKee
  - 'Danelia' (D) — WMat
  - 'Dönissens Gelbe Knorpelkirsche' (D) — WFar
  - 'Dun' (F) — CAda CHab WMat
  - § 'Early Birchenhayes' (F) — CAda CEnd
  - 'Early Rivers' (F) — CAda EGren IArd NOra SEdi SKee SSFr SVic WMat
  - 'Emperor Francis' (F) — SKee
  - 'Fice' (F) — CAda CEnd CTsd
  - 'Florence' (F) — SKee
  - 'Garden Bing' (F) — EPom
  - 'Giorgia' (D) — WMat
  - 'Goodnestone Black' (D) — SKee
  - 'Governor Wood' (F) — SKee
  - 'Grandiflora' — see *P. avium* 'Plena'
  - 'Greenstem Black' (F) — CAda
  - 'Hannaford' (D/C) — CHab
  - 'Hertford' (F) — NOra SBmr SEdi SKee SSFr WMat
  - 'Inga' (F) — SKee
  - 'Karina' (D) — LCro WMat
  - 'Kassins Frühe Herz' (F) — WFar
  - 'Kentish Red' (F) — SKee
  - 'Knight's Early Black' (D) — NOra WMat
  - 'Kordia' (D) ♀H5 — CAda CCVT EPom LCro LMaj LSRN NOra SBmr SKee SSFr WFar WMat
  - 'Kozerska' (F) — WMat
  - 'Landscape Bloom' **new** — MSwo
  - § 'Lapins' (F) ♀H6 — CAda CAgr CBTr CWnw EGren ELan EPfP EPom LCro LMaj NLar NOra NPlm SBmr SEdi SKee SPoG SSFr WFar WMat
  - 'Mansfield Black' (F) — SKee
  - 'Maraly'PBR (F) — NOra
  - 'May Duke' — see *P. × gondouinii* 'May Duke'
  - 'Merchant' (F) ♀H6 — ELan LCro NOra SEdi SKee SSFr WMat
  - 'Merton Bigarreau' (F) — NOra SBmr SKee SSFr WMat
  - 'Merton Crane' (F) — SKee
  - 'Merton Favourite' (F) — SKee

562 *Prunus*

- 'Merton Glory' (F)	CAda CAgr EGren ELan EPfP LBom LCro MLod NOra SBmr SEdi SKee SPoG SSFr WMat
- 'Merton Premier' (F)	SVic
- 'Merton Reward'	see *P.* × *gondouinii* 'Merton Reward'
- 'Mizia' (D)	WMat
- 'Nabella' (F)	LCro
- 'Napoléon'	see *P. avium* 'Bigarreau Napoléon'
- 'Nimba'^{PBR} (F)	NOra
- 'Noble' (F)	SKee
- 'Noir de Guben' (F)	SKee WMat
- 'Noir de Meched' (D)	SKee
- 'Octavia' (D)	WMat
- 'Old Black Heart' (F)	SKee
- 'Pacific Red'^{PBR} (F)	NOra
- 'Penny' (F) ♀^{H5}	CAgr EPom LBom LCro MNHC NOra SKee WMat
- 'Petit Noir' (F)	NOra WMat
§ - 'Plena' (d) ♀^{H6}	Widely available
- 'Polstead Black' (F)	SKee
- 'Regina' (F)	EGren EPom LCro NOra SKee WMat
- 'Ronald's Heart' (F)	SKee
- 'Roundel Heart' (F)	SKee WMat
- 'Sasha' (F)	LCro
- 'Skeena'^{PBR} (F)	NOra WMat
- 'Small Black' (F)	CAda CHab
- Starblush ('Spc207'^{PBR}) (F)	NOra WMat
- Stardust ('13n-7-70') (F)	ELan LCro MNHC NOra WMat
- 'Stella' (F) ♀^{H5}	Widely available
- 'Stella Compact' (F)	EGren LSRN SEdi
- 'Summer Sun' (D) ♀^{H6}	CAgr CBTr CLnd CMac EPom LBuc LCro LRHS MGos MLod MPri NLar NOra SBmr SKee SPoG SSFr WFar WMat
- 'Summit' (F)	SEdi SKee SSFr WMat
- 'Sunburst' (D)	Widely available
- 'Sweetheart' (F) ♀^{H5}	CAgr CBTr CLnd ELan EPfP EPom LCro LMaj LRHS LSRN MLod NOra SEWo SKee SPoG WMat
- 'Sylvia' (F)	CAgr NOra WMat
- 'Tamara' (F)	NOra
- 'Van' (F)	CAgr EPom LCro LMaj NLar NOra SEdi SKee WMat
- 'Vanda'^{PBR} (F)	NOra WMat
- 'Vega' (F)	CAgr NOra SEdi SKee SSFr WMat
- 'Walter' (F)	ELan
- 'Waterloo' (F)	NOra SKee WMat
- 'Weisse Spanische' (D)	WFar
- 'White Heart' (F)	CHab LCro SKee
§ 'Beni-tamanishiki'^{H6}	LCro NOra NPip WMat
'Beni-yutaka' ♀^{H6}	CBcs CBTr CCVT CTsd EGren EHeP EPfP EPom LCro LRHS LSRN MAsh NOra NPip WFar WMat WMou
besseyi	WKor
'Blaze'	see *P. cerasifera* 'Nigra'
× *blireana* (d) ♀^{H5}	CAco CEnd CLnd EHeP EPfP LCro LMaj SPoG
Blushing Bride	see *P.* 'Shōgetsu'
campanulata 'Felix Jury'	CBcs EBee LRHS LSRN NOra NPip WMat WPGP
Candy Floss	see *P.* 'Matsumae-beni-murasaki'
'Carmine Jewel' (F)	CAgr
caroliniana	SArc
'Catherine'	MGos NPip
cerasifera (F)	CAco CAgr CBrac CHab EPom LBuc LRHS MSwo SKee WHnu WHtc WJur WKor WRjT
- 'Countess' (F)	EBee EPom NOra NPip
- Crimson Pointe ('Cripoizam')	EBee ELan LCro LRHS MGos NOra NPip SPoG
- 'Golden Sphere' (F)	CAgr CBTr EPom LCro MLod NOra SKee SSFr WMat WWct
- 'Gypsy' (F) ♀^{H2}	CAda CAgr CBTr EBee EPom LCro MLod NOra SKee SSFr WMat WWct
§ - Myrobalan Group (F)	SPre SVic WMat
§ - 'Nigra' (F) ♀^{H6}	Widely available
§ - 'Pissardii'	CDoC EGren ERom LCro LSRN WCha WFar WHtc
- 'Ruby' (F)	CAgr EPom SKee
cerasus 'Maynard' (F)	SSFr
- 'Meteor Korai' (F)	CAgr NOra WMat
- 'Montmorency' (F)	NOra SKee
- 'Morello' (C) ♀^{H6}	Widely available
- 'Nabella' (F)	SKee
- 'Semperflorens'	CLnd
- 'Cheal's Weeping'	CWnw EBar NTrD
Chocolate Ice	see *P.* 'Matsumae-fuki'
§ × *cistena* ♀^{H6}	CBcs CDoC EBee EHeP ELan EPfP MAsh MGos SPoG WFar
- 'Crimson Dwarf'	see *P.* × *cistena*
- 'Collingwood Ingram' ♀^{H6}	ELan EPfP LCro LRHS MBlu MGos NCth NOra NPip WMat
'Cot-N-Candy' (Aprium Series) (F)	CAgr EPom
'Daikoku'	CBcs EBee LRHS NOra NPip WMat
davidiana	SPlb
'Delma'^{PBR} (F)	NOra WMat
domestica (D/C)	SPre
- 'Angelina Burdett' (D)	CHab SKee
- 'Anna Späth' (C/D)	SKee
- 'Ariel' (C/D)	SKee
- 'Avalon' (D)	CAgr CBTr CCVT CLnd LBuc MLod NLar NOra SBmr SEdi SKee SSFr WMat
- 'Beauty' (D)	LCro
- 'Belgian Greengage' (F)	CHab SKee
- 'Belle de Louvain' (C)	CAda CHab CLnd EGren NOra SEdi SKee SVic WMat
- 'Birchenhayes' (F)	CEnd
- 'Blaisdon Red' (C)	CCVT NOra SKee WMat WWct
- 'Blue Rock' (C/D)	SKee
- 'Blue Tit' (C/D) (F) ♀^{H5}	CAgr EPom LCro MMuc NOra SEND SKee SSFr WMat WWct
- 'Bohemian' (C)	SKee
- 'Bonne de Bry' (D)	SKee
- 'Bountiful' (C)	SEdi
- 'Brandy Gage' (C/D)	SKee
- 'Bryanston Gage' (D)	SKee WMat
- 'Burbank's Giant'	see *P. domestica* 'Giant Prune'
- 'Burbank's Tangerine' (D)	EPom LCro
- 'Burcombe' (F)	CEnd CTsd
- 'Cambridge Gage' (D) ♀^{H5}	CAgr CBTr CCVT CEnd CHab CMac EBee EGren EPfP EPom LCro LRHS LSRN MAsh MLod NOra SBmr SEdi SEND SEWo SKee SSFr WMat WWct
- 'Chrislin' (F)	CAda
- 'Coe's Golden Drop' (D)	CAgr CHab CLnd EPom LCro MLod NOra SEdi SKee WMat WWct
- 'Conwy Castle' (F)	WMat
- 'Cropper'	see *P. domestica* 'Laxton's Cropper'
- 'Czar' (C) ♀^{H6}	Widely available
- 'Delicious'	see *P. domestica* 'Laxton's Delicious'
- 'Denbigh' (C)	CHab WWct
- 'Denniston's Superb'	see *P. domestica* 'Imperial Gage'
- 'Des Béjonnières' (D)	SKee
- 'Dittisham Black' (F)	CAda

Prunus 563

- 'Dittisham Ploughman' (C) — CAda SKee WMat
- 'Dunster Plum' (F) — CAda WMat
- 'Early Laxton' (C/D) — CHab SEdi SEND SKee
- 'Early Prolific' — see *P. domestica* 'Early Rivers'
§ - 'Early Rivers' (C) ♀H5 — CAgr CBTr CHab EBee EPom LBom LCro LSRN MLod NOra SEdi SKee SSFr SVic WMat WWct
- 'Early Transparent Gage' (C/D) — CAgr CBTr CEnd CMac LBuc LCro MLod NOra SKee SSFr WMat
- 'Edda' (D) — NOra WMat
- 'Edwards' (C/D) — EGren LCro SEdi SKee SSFr
- 'Excalibur' (D) — CAgr EPom LBuc LSRN NOra SBmr SEdi SKee WMat WWct
- 'Finger Plum' (F) — WMat
- 'Frampton Magnum' (C/D) — WWct
§ - German Prune Group (C) — LRHS MLod NOra SKee WMat WWct
§ - 'Giant Prune' (C) — MMuc SEdi SEND SKee SSFr
- 'Gold Dust' (F) — WMat
- 'Golden Transparent' (D) — SKee
- 'Goldfinch' (D) — SEND SKee
- 'Gordon Castle' (D) — CAgr NOra SKee SSFr WMat
- Green Gage Group — see *P. domestica* Reine-Claude Group
- 'Grey Plum' (F) — CAda
- 'Grove's Late Victoria' (D) — WWct
- 'Guinevere' (C) — CAgr CBTr CEnd EPom LBom LCro LRHS MAsh NLar NOra SKee WMat
- 'Guthrie's Late Green' (D) — SKee
- 'Haganta'PBR (F) ♀H5 — CAgr CBTr LCro MLod NOra SKee WMat
- 'Hauszwetsche' (C/D) — CAda LCro LMaj
- 'Herman' (D) — CAgr CBTr CEnd CMac EPom LCro MAsh MLod NOra SBmr SKee WMat WWct
- 'Heron' (C) — NOra SKee WMat WWct
§ - 'Imperial Gage' (D) ♀H5 — CAda CAgr CBTr CCVT CLnd CMac EPom LCro MLod MMuc NOra SEND SKee SSFr WMat
- subsp. *italica* (D) — WFar
- 'Jan James' (F) — CEnd
- 'Jefferson' (D) — CAgr CHab CLnd NOra SKee SSFr SVic WMat WWct
- JOGANTA (D) — WFar
- 'JoJo'PBR (F) — WFar
* - 'Jubilaeum' (D) — CAda CAgr CLnd CMac EPom LBuc LCro NOra SBmr SEWo SKee SSFr WMat
- 'Katinka'PBR — CBTr LCro WMat
- 'Kea' (C) — CAda CTsd NOra SKee WMat
- 'Kirke's' (D) — CHab ELan LCro NOra SKee SSFr WMat WWct
§ - 'Kulinaria' (D) — CAgr CBTr LCro NLar NOra SPoG WMat
- 'Landkey Yellow' (F) — CAda WMat
- 'Langley Gage' (D) — CAgr
- 'Late Muscatelle' (D) — SKee
- 'Late Transparent Gage' (D) — SKee
§ - 'Laxton's Cropper' (C) — CHab SEdi SKee
§ - 'Laxton's Delicious' (D) — CHab
- 'Laxton's Jubilee' (C/D) — SPoG SSFr WMat
- 'Mallard' (D) ♀H6 — NOra SKee WMat
- 'Malling Elizabeth' (D) **new** — EBee
- 'Manaccan' (C) — CAda CTsd WMat
- 'Manns No 1' (C/D) — CAgr SKee WMat WWct
- 'Marjorie's Seedling' (C) ♀H5 — Widely available
- 'Meritare' (F) — CAgr NOra WMat
- 'Merton Gage' (D) — SKee
- 'Merton Gem' (D) — SKee
- 'Miraclaude' (F) — EPom
- 'Monarch' (C) — SKee
- Old English gage (F) — CLnd EBee EPom SEdi
- 'Ontario' (D) — CWnw EGren
- 'Opal' (D) ♀H6 — Widely available
- 'Oullins Gage' (C/D) ♀H5 — Widely available
- 'Pershore' (C) — CAgr CBTr CHab EGren LCro MLod NOra SEdi SKee SPoG WMat WWct
- 'Pershore Emblem' (F) — WWct
- 'Pozegaca' (C/D) — SKee
- 'President' (C) — CHab LCro MMuc NOra NPlm SEND SSFr
- 'Purple Pershore' (C) ♀H5 — CAda CAgr CHab MLod NOra SKee SSFr WMat WWct
- 'Queen's Crown' (C/D) — WMat
- 'Quetsche d'Alsace' — see *P. domestica* German Prune Group
- 'Reeves' (C) — CAgr NOra SKee WMat
- 'Regina Claudia' (D) — LMaj
§ - Reine-Claude Group (D) — CAgr CWnw ELan MPri NOra SEND SKee WMat
- - 'Count Althann's Gage' (D) — CHab LCro NOra SSFr WWct
- - 'Ingall's Grimoldby (D) Green Gage' — SKee
- - 'Lindsey Gage' (F) — CBTr LCro MLod NOra SKee WMat
- - 'Old Green Gage' — see *P. domestica* (Reine-Claude Group) 'Reine-Claude Vraie'
- - 'Reine-Claude de Bavais' (D) — CLnd NOra SSFr WMat
- - 'Reine-Claude de Vars' (D) — SVic
- - 'Reine-Claude Dorée' — see *P. domestica* Reine-Claude Group
- - 'Reine-Claude Violette' (D) — CAgr LCro NOra SKee SSFr WMat
§ - - 'Reine-Claude Vraie' (C/D) — CAgr CBTr CCVT CDoC EGren ELan EPfP EPom LBuc LCro LRHS MLod MNHC MPri NOra SSFr WMat
§ - - 'Willingham Gage' (C/D) — CAgr CBTr EBee LSRN MLod NOra SKee WMat
- 'Sanctus Hubertus' (D) — SKee WWct
- 'Seneca' (D) — EPom LCro NOra SBmr SKee SSFr WMat
- 'Severn Cross' (D) — SSFr
- 'Stanley' (C/D) — CCVT LMaj SVic
- 'Stella' (F) — CCVT LRHS LSRN MLod MPri
- 'Stella's Star' (D) — CAgr CBTr EGren LCro MLod NOra WMat
- 'Swan' (C) — NOra SKee WMat WWct
- 'Syston White' (F) — MGos
- 'Thames Cross' (D) — NOra
- 'Tommy's Island Gage' (D) — EPom
- TOPTASTE — see *P. domestica* 'Kulinaria'
- 'Transparent Gage' (D) — SKee
- 'Valor' (D) ♀H5 — LCro NOra SKee
- 'Verity' (C/D) ♀H5 — SKee WMat
- 'Victoria' (D) ♀H5 — Widely available
- 'Victory' (D) — EBee NOra
- 'Violet' (F) — MLod
- 'Violetta'PBR (D) — CAgr
- 'Voyageur' (F) — LCro
- 'Warwickshire Drooper' (C) ♀H5 — CAda CAgr CHab MLod MNHC NOra SKee SSFr WMat WWct
- 'Willingham' — see *P. domestica* (Reine-Claude Group) 'Willingham Gage'
§ *dulcis* — CAco CHab EPfP EPom LRHS SEND WJur
- 'Ai' (F) — CAgr

Prunus

- 'Ardéchoise' (F)	CAgr
- 'Ferraduel' (F)	CAgr
- 'Ferragnès' (F)	CAgr
* - 'Phoebe' (F)	CAgr
- 'Princesse' (F)	EPom LCro SKee
- SIBLEY'S PATIO ALMOND	EPom
- 'Sultane' (F)	LCro SKee
'Flavor King' (Pluot Series) (D)	CAgr EBee LCro SPoG WMat
'Flavour Supreme' (F)	EPom
FRAGRANT CLOUD	see *P.* 'Shizuka'
FRILLY FROCK ('Fpmspl') (v)	CBTr EBee ELan EPfP LCro LRHS MGos MPri NLar NOra NPip SPoG WHtc WMat
fruticosa	WFar
'Fugenzō' misapplied	see *P.* 'Kofugen'
§ 'Fugenzō' ♀H6	CBcs CCVT CLnd CMac CWnw EBar EGren EHeP EPfP EPom GKin IPap LCro LMaj LRHS LSRN MMuc MSwo NOra NPip SGol SOrN WMat
glandulosa 'Alba Plena' (d)	CEnd CMac LRHS SDix SPlb SRms
- Rosea Plena'	see *P. glandulosa* 'Sinensis'
§ - 'Sinensis' (D)	CEnd SRms
§ × *gondouinii* 'May Duke' (F)	LCro SKee
§ - 'Merton Reward' (F)	EGren SEdi SKee
GORIS GOLD ('Goris11'^PBR)	WFar
grayana B&SWJ 10903	WCru
'Gyoikō'	CBcs CEnd EBee LRHS NOra NPip WMat
'Hally Jolivette'	CEnd EBee LRHS MAsh MPri NOra NPip SPoG WMat
§ 'Hanagasa' ♀H6	CBcs CEnd EBee EPfP LBom LCro LRHS MLod NOra NPip WMat
'Hillieri Spire'	see *P.* 'Spire'
'Hilling's Weeping'	EGren LCro
himalaica	EBee NOra NPip WMat WPGP
'Hokusai' ♀H6	CBcs CBrac EBee EPfP LCro LRHS NLar NOra NPip SGol WHtc WMat
HOLLYWOOD	see *P.* 'Trailblazer'
'Horinji' (d)	CBcs LRHS NLar NPip WHtc WMat
'Howard No 3'	WMat
§ 'Ichiyo' (d) ♀H6	CBcs EPfP LCro LRHS MLod MNHC NLar NPip WMat
ilicifolia subsp. *lyonii*	EBee WPGP
× *incam* 'Dream Catcher'	LRHS MPri
- 'First Lady'	LRHS
- 'Okamé' ♀H6	CDoC CLnd CMac CWnw EGrI EHeP EPfP EUrb IPap LBom LCro LMaj LRHS LSRN LSto MGos MMuc NLar NPip SEND SEWo SPoG WCha WFar WMat
- 'Shosar'	see *P.* 'Shosar'
incisa	WJur
- 'Compacta' **new**	CBTr
- 'February Pink'	NLar
- 'Fujimae' ♀H6	NLar
- 'Kojo-no-mai' ♀H6	Widely available
- 'Lotte'	NLar WFar
- 'Mikinori'	CBcs CEnd CMac CSBt ELan ELon LRHS MBlu NLar NOra NPip WMat
- 'Oshidori' (D) ♀H6	CMac CSBt ELon EPfP NCth NLar NPip NQui SRms WFar WMat WSpi
- 'Paean'	ELon NLar WFar
- 'Pendula' ♀H6	CBcs ELan LRHS NPip WMat
- 'Praecox'	CSBt EPfP LRHS NPip WMat
§ - f. *yamadei* ♀H6	ELan LCro LRHS MPri NLar NOra NPip WSpi
insititia (F)	MLod MSwo MWht NPlm
- 'Abergwyngregin' (C)	WMat
- 'Aylesbury Prune' (C)	CAgr NOra SKee WMat
- 'Blue Violet Damson' (C)	CAgr CCVT NOra SKee SSFr WMat
§ - 'Bradley's King Damson' (C)	CLnd EBee NOra SKee WMat
- bullace (C)	LEdu SEdi
- 'Dittisham Damson' (C)	WMat
- 'Farleigh Damson' (C) ♀H6	CAda CAgr CBTr CDoC CHab EBee EGren EPfP EPom LBuc LCro MPri NLar NOra SEdi SKee SVic WMat WWct
- 'King of Damsons'	see *P. insititia* 'Bradley's King Damson'
- 'Langley Bullace' (C)	CAgr NOra SKee SSFr WMat
- 'Lisna' (C)	WMat
- 'Merryweather Damson' (C) ♀H6	Widely available
- 'Michaelmas Damson' (C)	WWct
- 'Mirabelle Countess' (C)	CBTr EPom LCro MLod WMat
- 'Mirabelle de Metz' (C)	SKee
- 'Mirabelle de Nancy' (C)	CAda CAgr CBTr CTsd EPom LCro LMaj NOra SBmr SEWo SKee WMat WWct
- 'Mirabelle Ruby' (C)	CBTr LCro LRHS MLod NOra SBmr SPoG WMat
§ - 'Prune Damson' (C) ♀H6	CAda CAgr CBTr CHab CMac EBee EPfP EPom LBom LBuc LCro LRHS MLod MMuc MPri NLar NOra SBmr SEND SEWo SKee SSFr WMat WWct
- 'Shepherd's Bullace' (C)	CAda EBee MLod NLar SKee WMat
- 'Shropshire Damson'	see *P. insititia* 'Prune Damson'
- 'Small Bullace' (C)	SKee
- 'Westmorland Prune' (C)	CHab NLar
- 'Yellow Apricot' (C)	SKee
'Jacqueline' ♀H6	CBTr EBee EPfP LCro MPri NLar NPip WHtc
'Jō-nioi'	CEnd
'Kanzan' (D) ♀H6	Widely available
'Kiku-shidare-zakura'	Widely available
'Kobuku-zakura'	NPip WMat
'Kofugen'	LCro LSRN WMat
Korean hill cherry	see *P. verecunda*
'Kursar'	CBcs CBTr CDoC CLnd CMac EPfP GKin LCro LRHS LSRN NLar NPip SSFr WHtc WMat WSpi
laurocerasus	CAco CBcs CBrac CBTr CCVT CDoC CGri CMac EBee ELan EPfP GKin LMaj LRHS MGos MHed MPri MPro SArc SFol SGol WCha WFar WHnu WHtc WMat WMou WRjT
- 'Angustifolia'	CDoC
- BONAPARTE ('Flippi01'^PBR)	CSBt EUrb LSou
- 'Camelliifolia'	CMac MBlu
§ - 'Castlewellan' (v)	CBrac CDoC CMac CMCN ELon EPfP LRHS MGos NLar SDix SPoG WFar
- 'Caucasica'	CEnd LMaj NLar SGol
- 'Cherry Brandy'	WCot
- ETNA ('Anbri'^PBR) ♀H5	CCVT
- ELLY ('Verstra'^PBR)	CCVT CMac EGren EHeP LBuc LCro SArc WCha
- GENOLIA ('Mariblon'^PBR)	CCVT LMaj MHed SArc SGol
- 'Herbergii'	WCot
- 'Latifolia'	LRHS
- 'Magnoliifolia'	see *P. laurocerasus* 'Latifolia'
- 'Marbled White'	see *P. laurocerasus* 'Castlewellan'
- 'Mount Vernon'	LBuc MBlu WCot
- 'Novita'	CCVT CDoC EGren LMaj LRHS LSRN MPri NHed NLar SAth WCha WReH
- 'Obelisk'^PBR	LCro

Prunus 565

- 'Otto Luyken' ♀H5	CBrac CMCN EBee EGren EHeP ELan EPfP LBuc LRHS LSto MGos NBir SArc SPlb WCot WFar			LSRN MGos MMuc MSwo NPip SEND SEWo SFol SPoG SSFr WFar WMat WMou
- 'Piranha'PBR	NEoE	§	*pendula* f. *ascendens* 'Rosea' ♀H6	LRHS NPip WMat
- RENAULT ACE ('Renlau')	SArc		- 'Pendula Plena Rosea' (d)	MGos NPip WMat
- 'Reynvaanii'	SArc	§	- 'Pendula Rosea'	CAco EHeP LCro WCha
- 'Rotundifolia' ♀H5	Widely available	§	- 'Pendula Rubra' ♀H6	CLnd CMac EGren EHeP ELan EPom LCro LRHS NPip SPoG WMat
- 'Schipkaensis'	SArc			
- 'Variegata' misapplied	see *P. laurocerasus* 'Castlewellan'	§	- 'Stellata' ♀H6	EPfP LRHS NPip WMat
- 'Variegata' ambig. (v)	SRms		*persica*	SPre
- 'Zabeliana'	CMac EBee EPfP SRms		- 'Amsden June' (F)	NOra SEdi SKee WMat
- 'Zsófi'PBR	CWnw		- 'Avalon Pride' (F)	CAgr EPom LCro MLod NOra SBmr SKee SPoG SSFr WMat
litigiosa	EBee LRHS MLod NPip WMat			
'Little Pink Perfection'	CBTr CNWT ELan EPom LCro LRHS MPri NLar NPip NTrD SPoG WMat		- 'Bellegarde' (F)	NOra SKee WMat
* *longipedunculata*	LRHS		- 'Bonanza' (F)	EPom LSRN SSFr
lusitanica ♀H5	Widely available		- 'Carman' (F)	WMat
- 'Angustifolia'	see *P. lusitanica* 'Myrtifolia'		- 'Crimson Bonfire' (F)	EPom
- subsp. *azorica*	EBee LRHS		- 'Darling' (F)	SVic
- - TICO ('Ybrazo01'PBR)	LCro LMaj LRHS NLar WFar		- 'Diamond' (F)	EPom
- 'Brenelia'PBR	CCVT CWnw LMaj LSRN SArc SBig WReH		- 'Dixi Red' (F)	CAgr
			- 'Duke of York' (F)	EPom LCro SBmr SKee SSFr
§ - 'Myrtifolia' ♀H5	CCVT CDoC CNWT EGren EPfP ERom LMaj LRHS LSRN LSto MHed MPro MSwo NHed NLar NPip SArc SAth SFol SGol SHor SPoG WCha WHtc WMat WReH		- 'Francis' (F)	SKee
			- 'Frost' (F)	WMat
			- 'Garden Lady' (F)	EPom NOra WMat
			- 'Gorgeous' (F)	EBee MLod NOra SKee WMat
- 'Variegata' (v)	CBrac CMac EGren ELan EUrb LMaj MGos NLar SGol SPoG WFar		- 'Hale's Early' (F)	CAgr LRHS NOra SEdi SKee WMat
			- 'Jalousia' (F)	EPom SVic
maackii	LMaj		- 'Kestrel' (F)	SKee
- 'Amber Beauty'	EPfP IPap LMaj LRHS MGos MMuc NPip SEND WMat		- 'Lacrima' (F)	EPom
			- 'Melred' (F)	EGrI LRHS
mahaleb	CAgr CNWT		- 'Mesembrine'PBR (F)	EPom NOra WMat
maritima	WKor		- var. *nectarina* 'Armking'	NPlm
§ 'Matsumae-beni-murasaki'	CBcs ELan LRHS MLod NLar NPip WMat WMou		- - 'Earliglo' (F)	WMat
			- - 'Early Rivers' (F)	LSRN WMat
'Matsumae-beni-tamaniшiki'	see *P.* 'Beni-tamanishiki'		- - 'Fantasia' (F)	EPom LCro SSFr
§ 'Matsumae-fuki' ♀H6	CBcs CBTr EBee ELan EPfP LBom LCro LRHS LSRN MPri NLar NPip SEND WHtc WMat		- - 'Flavortop' (F)	SSFr
			- - 'Garden Beauty' (F/d)	EBee NOra SBmr WMat
			- - 'Honey Kist'PBR (F)	EPom
'Matsumae-hanagasa'	see *P.* 'Hanagasa'		- - 'Humboldt' (F)	CAgr SEdi SKee WMat
maximowiczii B&SWJ 10967	WCru		- - 'Lord Napier' (F)	CAgr CMac CSBt EGren EPfP EPom IPap LCro MGos MLod NOra SBmr SEdi SKee SSFr SVic WMat
'Mikuruma-gaeshi'	LCro WMat			
'Mount Fuji'	see *P.* 'Shirotae'		- - 'Madame Blanchet' (F)	CWnw SVic
mume	CMen WJur		- - 'Nectared' (F)	EGren
- 'Beni-chidori' ♀H5	CBTr CEnd CMac CSBt EGren LCro MBlu MPri NLar NPip SPoG WCot WMat		- - 'Nectarella' (F)	EPom LCro LSRN NOra WMat
			- - 'Pineapple' (F)	CAgr EBee NOra SKee WMat
			- - RUBIS ('Necta Zee'PBR) (F)	EPom
§ - - 'Omoi-no-mama' (d)	CEnd CMen LRHS NLar			
- 'Omoi-no-wac'	see *P. mume* 'Omoi-no-mama'		- - 'Sauzee Bel' (F)	EPom
myrobalana	see *P. cerasifera* Myrobalan Group		- - 'Sauzee King' (F)	EPom
nigra	WMat		- - 'Snow Baby' (F)	EPom
nipponica var. *kurilensis* 'Brillant'	CBcs CDoC EPfP LRHS MMrt MPri NLar SPoG		- - 'Snow Queen' (F)	SSFr
			- - 'Terrace Ruby' (F)	WMat
- - 'Ruby'	LCro LSRN		- 'Peregrine' (F)	CAgr CLnd CMac CWnw EGren ELan EPfP EPom IPap LCro LRHS LSRN MAsh MGos MLod NOra SBmr SEdi SEND SKee SSFr WMat
'Okame Harlequin' (v)	MLod WCha			
'Oku-miyako' misapplied	see *P.* 'Shōgetsu'			
padus	CBTr CBWd CCVT CHab CLnd CMac EGren EHeP ELan LBuc LCot LMaj LSto MGos NLar SEND SEWo WHnu WHtc WKor WMou WRjT		- 'Redhaven' (F)	CAgr EPom LCro NOra SAth SKee SVic WMat
			- 'Redlate Necta'PBR (F)	SEdi
- 'Albertii'	CCVT MMuc NPip WMat		- 'Redwing' (F)	CAgr
- 'Colorata' ♀H6	CCVT EHeP ELan IPap LRHS MMrt NLar SGol WMou		- 'Robin Redbreast' (F)	CAgr MLod
			- 'Rochester' (F)	CAgr CMac ELan EPom LCro LRHS LSRN MLod NLar NOra SBmr SEdi SKee SSFr WMat
- 'Grandiflora'	see *P. padus* 'Watereri'			
- 'Le Thoureil'	MMrt NPip WHtc			
§ - 'Watereri' ♀H6	CCVT CLnd CMac EGren EHeP SEWo SGol WMat		- ROYAL GLORY ('Zaifer') (F) **new**	NPlm
'Pandora' ♀H6	CBrac CCVT CLnd EBee EHeP EPfP EPom LCro LMaj LRHS		- 'Sanguine de Savoie' (F)	EPom WMat

- 'Sanguinole' (F)	LCro			§	- 'Shizuka' ♀H6	CAco CBcs EGren ELan IPap LBuc LCro LRHS MLod MPri MSwo NLar NPip WMat WMou

- 'Sanguinole' (F)	LCro	
- 'Saturne' (F)	CAgr CMac EGren EPom LCro MAsh MLod NOra SKee SSFr WMat	
§ - 'Spring Snow'^PBR (F)	EGren	
- STARK SATURN ('N.J.F-2') (F) **new**	LRHS	
- 'Terrace Amber' (F)	SSFr WMat	
- 'Terrace Diamond' (F)	WMat	
- 'Terrace Garnet' (F)	WMat	
× *persicoides*	EHeP	
- 'Ingrid' (F)	CAgr CBTr CEnd ELan MGos NOra SKee SSFr WMat	
- 'Robijn' (F)	CAgr ELan EPom LCro NOra SKee SVic	
- 'Spring Glow'	CEnd EGren EPfP EUrb LCro LRHS MLod NOra NPip WFar WMat	
phaeosticta NJM 10.072	WPGP	
'Pink Ballerina'	EBee LRHS	
'Pink Candy' (F)	EPom	
PINK CHAMPAGNE	see *P.* 'Ichiyo'	
PINK PARASOL	see *P.* 'Hanagasa'	
'Pink Perfection' ♀H6	CAco CBcs CBrac CBTr CLnd CNWT EBee EGren EHeP ELan EPfP EPom LCro LMaj LRHS MGos NPip NTrD SAth SBmr SSFr WHtc WMat WMou	
'Pink Shell'	CLnd EGren EPfP EPom LCro NPip SFol SSFr WMat	
PINK SNOW SHOWERS ('Pisnshzam')	EPom LBom	
pissardii	see *P. cerasifera* 'Pissardii'	
'Pissardii Nigra'	see *P. cerasifera* 'Nigra'	
prostrata	WCot	
'Royal Burgundy' (d) ♀H6	Widely available	
ROYAL FLAME ('Mieke')	EBee EPfP MLod NPip	
rufa	CBcs CBTr EBee LRHS MLod NPip WMat	
- 'Len Beer' ♀H6 **new**	LRHS	
salicina 'Beauty' (F)	EPom	
- 'Blackamber' (D) **new**	NPlm	
- 'Golden Japan' (F)	NPlm	
- 'Lizzie' (F)	EPom LCro	
- 'Methley' (D)	CAgr NOra WMat	
sargentii	CBcs CCVT CLnd CMac EGren ELan EPfP EPom IPap LBuc LCro LMaj MBlu MGos NLar NPip SEWo SGol SSta WFar WMat WMou	
- 'Charles Sargent' ♀H6	CMCN ELan LCro LMaj LSRN MBlu	
- 'Columnaris'	EBee NPip WMat	
- 'Rancho'	CLnd LMaj LRHS MPri SPoG WMat	
× *schmittii*	EHeP NOra NPip SFol WMat	
'Sekiyama'	see *P.* 'Kanzan'	
serotina	CAgr	
§ *serrula*	Widely available	
- AMBER SCOTS ('Minscots')	CWnw LRHS	
- 'Branklyn' ♀H6	CNWT EBee EPfP IArd LCro LRHS MGos NPip	
- 'Dorothy Clive' ♀H6	EBee	
- 'Princesse Sturdza'	MBlu NCth	
- var. *tibetica*	see *P. serrula*	
serrula × *serrulata*	EBee WPGP	
serrulata 'Erecta'	see *P.* 'Amanogawa'	
- 'Grandiflora'	see *P.* 'Ukon'	
- 'Longipes'	see *P.* 'Shōgetsu'	
- 'Miyako' misapplied	see *P.* 'Shōgetsu'	
- var. *pubescens*	see *P. verecunda*	
- 'Rosea'	see *P.* 'Kiku-shidare-zakura'	
'Shidare-zakura'	see *P.* 'Kiku-shidare-zakura'	
'Shimizu-zakura'	see *P.* 'Shōgetsu'	
'Shirofugen'	see *P.* 'Fugenzō'	
§ 'Shirotae' ♀H6	Widely available	

§ - 'Shizuka' ♀H6	CAco CBcs EGren ELan IPap LBuc LCro LRHS MLod MPri MSwo NLar NPip WMat WMou
§ - 'Shōgetsu' ♀H6	CAco CBcs CDoC CEnd CLnd CMac CMCN CTsd CWnw EHeP ELan EPfP EPom LCro LMaj LRHS LSRN MAsh MMuc NLar NPip NTrD SEWo SOrN WMat WMou
§ - 'Shosar' ♀H6	CBcs CEnd LCro LRHS MPri NPip
simonii	SPre
'Snow Goose'	CBTr CMac EBee EGren ELan EPfP EPom LCot LCro LSto MBlu MMuc MPri NLar NPip SAth SPoG WMat
'Snow Showers'	CBTr CCVT CDoC CEnd CMac EBee EGren ELan EPfP EPom LBom LCro LRHS LSRN MGos MPri NLar NPip SEND SPoG WMat
spinosa	Widely available
- 'Plena' (d)	MBlu
- 'Purpurea'	MBlu WMou
§ - 'Spire' ♀H6	CBcs CCVT CDoC CLnd CMac CMCN EBee EHeP ELan IPap LBuc LCot LCro LRHS LSRN MBlu MGos MMuc MPri NOra NPip SEND SGol WFar WMat
SPRING SNOW	see *P.* 'Beni-tamanishiki'
'Spring Snow'	see *P. persica* 'Spring Snow'
'Stefania'	WMat
× *subhirtella* 'Autumnalis'	Widely available
- 'Autumnalis Rosea'	Widely available
- 'Falling Stars'	LRHS
- 'Fukubana'	CLnd CMac NLar WMat WMou
- 'Pendula' misapplied	see *P. pendula* 'Pendula Rosea'
- 'Pendula Rosea'	see *P. pendula* 'Pendula Rosea'
- 'Pendula Rubra'	see *P. pendula* 'Pendula Rubra'
- 'Rosea'	see *P. pendula* f. *ascendens* 'Rosea'
- 'Stellata'	see *P. pendula* 'Stellata'
'Sunset Boulevard' ♀H6	CCVT CLnd EBee EHeP ELan LCro LMaj LRHS LSRN MGos MLod NOra NPip WMat WMou
- 'Tai-haku' ♀H6	Widely available
'Taoyame' ♀H6	EPfP
§ *tenella*	ECha WCot WJur
- 'Alba'	WFar
- 'Fire Hill'	CBcs ECha ELan EPfP LCro LRHS MGos WCot WSpi
'The Bride' ♀H6	CAco CBcs CBrac CBTr CDoC CEnd CLnd CMHG EBee EPfP EPom LCot LCro LRHS MAsh NOra NPip SChF SEWo WMat
tibetica	see *P. serrula*
'Tiltstone Hellfire'	CCVT EBee LCro LRHS MLod NLar NOra NPip WMat
tomentosa	CAgr WFar WJur WKor
§ 'Trailblazer' (C/D)	CEnd CLnd CMac EHeP LRHS NPip SKee
triloba	LCro MBlu WCha
- 'Multiplex' (d)	SRms
- ROSEMUND ('Korros')	CBcs WFar
§ - 'Ukon' ♀H6	CBcs CCVT CLnd CMac CMCN CWnw EHeP ELan EPfP LCro LRHS MAsh MGos NLar NOra NPip SGol WFar WHtc WMat
'Umineko'	CCVT CLnd CMCN EGren EHeP LCro LMaj MGos MMuc SEND SEWo WFar
§ *verecunda*	CLnd
'Victoria Willis'	WMat
virginiana	WKor
- 'Canada Red'	CCVT ELan WMou
- 'Schubert'	CMac EHeP ELan

Pseudowintera 567

'White Cloud'	CAco		*laetus*	see *Neopanax laetus*
'Woodfield Cluster'	IArd		*lessonii*	SArc
'Yae-murasaki'	LRHS		- 'Gold Splash' (v) ♀H3	CBcs CDTJ EBee LRHS SBig SEND SHor SVen
yamadae	see *P. incisa* f. *yamadei*		- 'Goldfinger'	LRHS
× *yedoensis*	CCVT CLnd CMac CWnw EBar EGren EHeP ELan EPfP LCot LCro LMaj LRHS LSRN NOra WCha WHtc WMat WMou		- 'Rangitira'	CBcs LRHS SBig
			'Linearifolius'	CBcs CDTJ ELan LEdu
			'Moa's Toes'	CBcs CCht CSde CTsd EArI ELon LRHS MBlu MHtn SArc SBig SDix SEND SIvy SMrm SPad WCot
- 'Ivensii'	CAco CWnw EPom LCro LMaj			
- 'Pendula'	see *P.* × *yedoensis* 'Shidare-Yoshino'		'Purpureus' ♀H3	CBcs CDTJ ELan EPfP SVen WCot WFar
- 'Perpendens'	see *P.* × *yedoensis* 'Shidare-Yoshino'			
§ - 'Shidare-Yoshino'	CAco CMac EPom EUrb IPap LBuc LCro MGos NLar NPip WMat		'Sabre'	CBcs CDTJ EBee ELon LCro LRHS SEND WFar
§ - 'Somei-Yoshino' ♀H6	LRHS NPip SSFr		'Trident' ♀H3	LCro LRHS SEND SVen
'Yoshino'	see *P.* × *yedoensis* 'Somei-Yoshino'		'Tuatara'	CDTJ LRHS MHtn SArc
'Yoshino Pendula'	see *P.* × *yedoensis* 'Shidare-Yoshino'			

Psammophiliella (Caryophyllaceae)
muralis 'Gypsy Deep Rose' LRHS SPoG

Pseudocodon (Campanulaceae)
§ *convolvulaceus*	WCru
subsp. *forrestii*	
BWJ 7847	
§ *grey-wilsonii* ♀H4	GEdr
- B&SWJ 7532	WCru
- 'Alba'	see *P. grey-wilsonii* 'Himal Snow'
§ - 'Himal Snow'	GEdr WCru

Pseudocydonia (Rosaceae)
§ *sinensis* CBcs CHab CMen WJur WKor

Pseudodictamnus (Lamiaceae)
§ *acetabulosus*	ECha EGren WCot
§ *mediterraneus* ♀H4	CBcs CCBP CMac CTtf EBee ECha ELan EPfP GMaP LCro LSRN LSto NPer SDix SEND SMrm WCAu WFar WGwG WTor WTre
- B&M 8119	WCot WPGP
- from Crete	ECha
- 'Candia'	LShi SHar
- compact	CExl

Pseudofumaria see *Corydalis*
alba see *Corydalis ochroleuca*

Pseudogynoxys (Asteraceae)
§ *chenopodioides* CSpe EShb

Pseudolarix (Pinaceae)
amabilis ♀H7 CAco CMen ELan MBlu MMuc WJur
kaempferi (Lamb.) Gordon see *Larix kaempferi*

Pseudomuscari see *Muscari*

Pseudopanax ✿ (Araliaceae)
(Adiantifolius Group) 'Adiantifolius'	CBcs CDTJ CTsd EBee ELan SVen WCot
- 'Cyril Watson' ♀H3	CBcs CDTJ EBee ELan EPfP LCro LRHS SEND SVen WFar WPGP
arboreus	see *Neopanax arboreus*
'Bronze Eagle'	LRHS
'Chainsaw'	CBct CDTJ EBee WPGP
chathamicus	CExl SArc SPlb
crassifolius	CBrP CDTJ CTsd SArc SBig WPGP
- var. *trifoliolatus*	CBct CDTJ EBee ELan EPfP SBig WPGP
'Dark Star'	CBcs LRHS
ferox	CBcs CBrP CDTJ EUrb LCro SArc SBig SPlb SVen
'Gecko Gold' (v)	CBcs

Pseudophegopteris see *Phegopteris*

Pseudophoenix (Arecaceae)
sargentii NPlm

Pseudopodospermum (Asteraceae)
§ *hispanicum* CAgr MCtn NBac
- 'Long Black Maximum' SVic

Pseudorhipsalis (Cactaceae)
ramulosa LCro
- 'Red Coral' LCro

Pseudosasa (Poaceae)
sp.	CAco
§ *japonica* ♀H5	CAco CAgr CBcs CBdn CWRo ERom GArf LCro MMuc MWht NLar NPlm SArc SAth SBGi SBig SEND SPoG SWor WCha WFar
I - var. *pleioblastoides*	MWht
- 'Tsutsumiana'	ELon MWht
viridula	MWht

Pseudostellaria (Caryophyllaceae)
heterophylla GEdr
- W&O 9215 GGro

Pseudotsuga (Pinaceae)
§ *menziesii*	CAco CBcs CBTr CLnd ELan LMaj MBlu MMuc SSta WHtc WRjT
- 'Bhiela Lhota'	CAco
- 'Blue Wonder'	CAco NLar
- 'Fastigiata'	CAco
- 'Fletcheri'	CAco
- var. *glauca*	CAco
- 'Glauca Pendula'	CAco MBlu
- 'Holata'	CAco
- 'Holmstrup'	CAco
- 'Little Jon'	CAco
- 'Maruška'	CAco
- 'Misty First'	CAco
- 'Moerheimii'	CAco
- 'Pannonia'	CAco
- 'Serpentine'	CAco MBlu
- 'Skryje'	CAco
- 'Tidal Wave'	CAco
taxifolia	see *P. menziesii*

Pseudowintera (Winteraceae)
§ *colorata*	CBcs CDoC CMac EBee GAbr GKin LRHS NLar
- 'Marjorie Congreve'	CBcs CDoC GKin IArd
- 'Moulin Rouge'	CBcs SEle
- 'Red Leopard'	LRHS NLar SEle

Psidium (Myrtaceae)
acutangulum	WJur
cattleyanum	see *P. littorale* var. *longipes*
guajava (F)	SPlb
littorale var. **littorale** (F)	WKor
§ - var. **longipes** (F)	WJur WKor

Psophocarpus (Fabaceae)
tetragonolobus misapplied	see *Lotus tetragonolobus*
tetragonolobus (L.) DC.	MNHC

Psoralea (Fabaceae)
aphylla	SPlb SVen
* fleta	SEle SPlb
glabra	SPlb
glandulosa	SPlb
oligophylla	SPlb
pinnata	IArd WCot

Psylliostachys (Plumbaginaceae)
suworowii	CSpe GJos MCtn

Ptelea (Rutaceae)
trifoliata	CBcs CMCN ELan EPfP LMaj MBlu SRms WJur WPGP
- 'Aurea' ♀H6	CBcs ELan MBlu MMuc

Pteridium (Dennstaedtiaceae)
aquilinum	WFar

Pteridophyllum (Papaveraceae)
racemosum	CMiW EWld GEdr WFar

Pteris (Pteridaceae)
cretica var. **albolineata**	see *P. nipponica*
- 'Mayi' (v)	LCro MAsh WCot
- 'Ouvradii'	SPlb
- 'Parkeri'	LRHS
- 'Rivertoniana'	ISha
- 'Wimsettii' ♀H4	LRHS MAsh SArc WCot
§ nipponica ♀H1c	CAbb CBcs CCht EShb ISha LCro LRHS MAsh MMuc SEND WCot
- 'Cristata'	SArc
quadriaurita	CTsd
tremula	EShb ISha NBro WCot
tricolor	LBom LCro LWaG
umbrosa	CAbb CCht CDTJ CLAP CTsd EBee EShb EUrb ISha MAsh MBlu MHol MMuc NAlc NBro SEND SPlb WCot WPGP
wallichiana	CDTJ WCot WPGP

Pterocactus (Cactaceae)
fischeri	SPlb
hickenii F&W 10240	WCot
kuntzei	see *P. tuberosus*
reticulatus	SPlb
§ tuberosus ♀H2	SPlb

Pterocarya ✿ (Juglandaceae)
fraxinifolia	CBcs CMCN EHeP IPap LRHS MBlu
- NJM 13.007	WPGP
- PAB 13.052	LEdu
- 'Abbotsbury Giant'	WPGP
- var. **dumosa** B&SWJ 16349	WCru
macroptera var. **insignis**	CExl EUrb WPGP
× **rehderiana**	CMCN MBlu
rhoifolia	CMCN

stenoptera	CDTJ NLar WJur
- 'Fern Leaf' ♀H6	CExl EBee MBlu WPGP
tonkinensis	WPGP

Pterocephalus (Caprifoliaceae)
depressus	EDAr
hookeri	GKev
parnassi	see *P. perennis*
§ perennis	MHer SRms WAbe

Pterostylis (Orchidaceae)
curta ♀H2	CBro

Pterostyrax ✿ (Styracaceae)
corymbosus	CBcs CMCN EUrb MBlu WJur
- CWJ 12838	WCru
hispidus ♀H5	CBcs CMCN EBee EPfP ESwi MBlu NLar WFar WJur
psilophyllus	MBlu
- var. **leveillei**	CBcs CExl EBee MBlu SChF WPGP
- trilobed	WPGP

Pteroxygonum (Polygonaceae)
§ giraldii	GGro

Ptilotrichum see *Alyssum*

Pueraria (Fabaceae)
montana var. **lobata**	Prohibited invasive. See Conservation and the Environment, p.42

Pulicaria (Asteraceae)
§ dysenterica	CBWd CGwi CHab GJem MAsh MNHC NMir WHer

Pulmonaria ✿ (Boraginaceae)
angustifolia	GKev GMaP SRms
- 'Azurea'	CElw EBee EGrI ELan EMor GAbr GMaP ISha MMuc NBro SRms WCAu WSpi
- 'Blaues Meer'	EBee EPfP NSti WSpi
- 'Munstead Blue'	NRya SRms
'Ann Waygood'	WCot
'Anne Wood'	MNrw
'Ballyrogan Blue' ♀H6	LRHS WBrk
'Barfield Regalia'	NSti
'Benediction'	LShi MNrw MWlw NSti WBrk WCot
'Beth's Pink'	LShi
'Blake's Silver'	CDor GElm MHol SMrm WCAu WCot
'Blauer Hügel'	NSti
'Blue Ensign' ♀H6	Widely available
'Blue Moon'	see *P. officinalis* 'Blue Mist'
'Bubble Gum'PBR	NLar NSti
Cally hybrid	EPPr MNrw
'Cleeton Red'	MNrw
'Cotton Cool' ♀H6	CBWd CMHG EBee ECha GQue LRHS MArl MBel MBNS NLar NSti SMrm WFar WGwG WOld
'Dark Vader'	NCth SPoG
'Darkling Thrush'	MNrw
'Diana Clare' ♀H6	Widely available
'Elworthy Rubies'	MNrw
'Elworthy Sentinel'	MNrw WBrk
'Excalibur'	NLar SRms
'Gavin Compton' (v)	MNrw
'Glacier'	WCot
'High Contrast'	EBee
'Highdown'	see *P.* 'Lewis Palmer'
'Ice Ballet' (Classic Series)	EBee EPfP LSto NCth WCAu
'Joan Curtis'	EWld MNrw

§	'Lewis Palmer' ♀H6	CBro CDor GMaP MNrw NBir SRms WHoo
	'Little Star' ♀H6	EBee NSti WFar
	longifolia	ELan EPfP LSto NBir SRms
§	- 'Ankum'	NBir WCot
	- 'Bertram Anderson'	EBee EMor GMaP ISha LRHS NBir SRms WCAu WFar WHil
	- subsp. *cevennensis*	NLar WBrk WFar WSpi
	- 'Coen Jansen'	see *P. longifolia* 'Ankum'
	- 'Dordogne'	NBir NLar
	- 'Howard Eggins'	WBrk
	'Mado'	ECha
	'Majesté'	CDor CMiW EBee ECha ELan EMor EPfP GMaP LRHS MPri NBir NLar NSti SPoG SRms WCAu WCot WFar
	'Margery Fish'	WBrk
	'Mary Mottram'	NBir NSti WCot
	'Mawson's Blue'	NBir
	Milky Way'	SPoG
	'Miss Elly'	NCth NSti WCAu WTor
	mollis	EPPr MNrw NSti WCAu
	'Moonshine' PBR	EBee EPfP MAsh MPro NSti WCAu WFar
	'Mrs Kittle'	NBir NLar NSti WCAu
	obscura	MNHC
	officinalis	CGHo CWRo EGren MHer MHoo MNHC StAn WBrk
	- 'Alba'	WBrk
§	- 'Blue Mist'	NBir WCot
	- 'Bowles's Blue'	see *P. officinalis* 'Blue Mist'
	- Cambridge Blue Group	LRHS NBir WBrk WCot WFar
	- 'White Wings'	NLar
	OPAL ('Ocupol') ♀H6	Widely available
	'Open Skies' (v)	MNrw MWlw WCot
	'Patric's Early Dawn'	ECha
	'Pierre's Pure Pink'	EBee
	'Pink Haze' PBR	WCAu
	'Pretty in Pink'	EBee ELan EMor LBar LRHS SHar WTor
	'Raspberry Coulis'	WCot
	'Raspberry Splash' PBR	CBcs CMiW CoPl ECul EGren EMor EPfP LBar LCro LRHS MNrw MPro NBir NLar NSti SDix WCAu WCot WFar WPnP
	'Richard Nutt'	WBrk WCot
	'Roy Davidson'	CDor GKev LRHS NBir SRms
	rubra	CBcs CCps CElw ECha GAbr LCro LShi MNrw NBid NLar NSti SRms WCAu
	- var. *alba*	see *P. rubra* var. *albocorollata*
§	- var. *albocorollata*	EBee ECha
	- 'Ann'	GQue
	- 'Barfield Pink'	NBir NLar WBrk
	- 'Bowles's Red'	CCps LRHS NBir WCAu WFar
	- 'David Ward' (v)	CCps ECha ELan MAvo NBir NLar SPoG SRms WCAu
	- 'Rachel Vernie' (v)	EWld MNrw NQui NSti WCot
	- 'Redstart'	CDor EMor EWld GKev LRHS MNrw NBir NCth NLar SRms WBrk WCAu WFar
§	*saccharata*	ECha EHeP GMaP MMuc SRms
	- 'Alba'	SRms
	- Argentea Group ♀H6	GMaP NGdn
	- 'Dora Bielefeld'	ECha EGrI EWes GMaP ISha LRHS LSto MArI NBir NSti WCAu WFar WOld
	- 'Frühlingshimmel'	ECha
	- 'Leopard'	CDor EMor MArI MAvo NBir NGdn WCAu WCot WHoo WSpi
	- 'Mrs Moon'	CTsd EBee EHeP GMaP ISha LCro LRHS NLar WBrk WCAu
	- 'Old Rectory Silver'	NBir
	- 'Picta'	see *P. saccharata*
	- 'Pink Dawn'	EBee WCAu
	- 'Reginald Kaye'	ECha
	- 'Silverado' PBR	LRHS NGdn
	'Saint Ann's'	EBee MNrw NSti
	'Samurai' ♀H6	MNrw NLar WFar
	'Shrimps on the Barbie'	CDor EBee EGren ELan EMor EUrb ISha LBar LRHS LSou MPro NCou NCth SPad WFar WHil WPnP
	'Silver Bouquet' PBR	CTsd ECul EGren EMor EPfP EUrb GKev LCro LShi MPro NLar NSti WCAu WFar
	'Sissinghurst White' ♀H6	Widely available
	'Smoky Blue'	ISha LBar LRHS NCth
	'Spot On'	LBar
	'Spring Awakening'	WCAu
	'Stillingfleet Meg'	CBWd CDor MBNS NSti WCAu WOld
	'Trevi Fountain' ♀H6	Widely available
	'Twinkle Toes'	EBee EPfP LBar LRHS
	'Vera May' ♀H6	EWld MNrw WBrk
	'Victorian Brooch' PBR	CWCL GKev MBel MHol MNrw MPro NSti SPoG WCAu WSpi
	'Wan One'	WCot
	'Weetwood Blue'	EBee EPfP MNrw WBrk

Pulsatilla (Ranunculaceae)

	albana var. *flavescens*	GEdr
	alpina	SPlb SRms
	ambigua	GEdr
	campanella	GArf GEdr GKev
	halleri subsp. *taurica*	GEdr
	montana	GEdr SPlb StAn
	occidentalis	GEdr GKev
§	*patens*	GEdr GJos NGdn WIce
	- subsp. *flavescens*	GEdr
	pratensis	SRms
	- subsp. *nigricans*	EDAr GEdr GJos WAbe
	rubra	EGrI ELan EMor EPfP GMaP LRHS LShi MHer NBir NGdn NLar SMHy SPoG SRms SRot WAbe WHoo WIce
	subslavica	WAbe
	tatewakii	EDAr GEdr GKev
	turczaninovii	EDAr GEdr WFar
§	*vernalis*	EBee EDAr GEdr WAbe
	violacea	CBcs
§	*vulgaris* ♀H5	Widely available
	- 'Alba'	CAby CBWd CMHG CTsd EBee ECha EDAr EGrI ELan EPfP GJos GKev MArI MBel MHer NBir NGdn SPoG WFar WHoo WIce WKif
	- 'Blaue Glocke'	CAby EDAr GBin GEdr GJos MBel SHar StAn
	- double, fringed (d)	EDAr
	- subsp. *grandis*	GEdr MCtn NLar
	- - 'Alba'	CAby
	- - 'Budapest Seedling'	GKev
	- - 'Papageno'	CAby CDor CSpe EBee ELon EMor EPfP GEdr LRHS MHol MNrw NLar
	- Heiler hybrids	MArl MBel MCtn MPie NDov NGdn SVic
	- 'Perlen Glocke'	GEdr LShi MPro NLar WHil
	- pink-flowered	WFar
	- (Pinwheel Series) PINWHEEL BLUE VIOLET SHADES	EGren LCro LRHS MHol SMrm
	- - PINWHEEL DARK RED SHADES	EGren LCro LRHS MHol
	- - PINWHEEL WHITE	EGren LCro LRHS MHol SMrm WFar

Pulsatilla

- 'Pulsar Red Shades'	MPro
- 'Pulsar Violet Shades'	LBar
- RED CLOCK	see *P. vulgaris* 'Röde Klokke'
- red-flowered	EBee EDAr GAbr LRHS WFar
§ - 'Röde Klokke'	CAby CTsd EPot GBin GEdr GJos GKev MPro SHar SLee SPoG
- ROTE GLOCKE	see *P. vulgaris* 'Röde Klokke'
- 'Violet Bells'	GBin GKev
- violet-blue-flowered	EBee SPoG
§ - 'Weisse Schwan'	GEdr GMaP
- 'White Bells'	WFar
- WHITE SWAN	see *P. vulgaris* 'Weisse Schwan'

Pultenaea (Fabaceae)

juniperina	SPlb

Punica (Lythraceae)

granatum	CBcs CMCN CMen EBee EGren EPfP SEND SPre WJur
- 'Acco' (F)	WJur
- 'Chico' (d)	CBcs ELan EPfP SEND WJur
- 'Dente di Cavallo' (F)	LCro
- 'Forbidden City' (F)	ESwi
- 'Legrelleae' (F/d)	WMal
- 'Maxima Rubra' (d)	CBcs WMal
- 'Mollar de Elche' (F)	CAgr WJur
- var. *nana* ♀H3	CMen CMHG EPfP EShb LEdu MCtn SFol SMrm SPre SRms SVen SWor WJur WKor WPGP
I - 'Nana Gracilissima' (F) **new**	EPom
- 'Nana Plena' (d)	SWor
- 'Nana Racemosa'	LRHS
- 'Parfianka' (F)	WJur
- f. *plena* (d)	CBcs EPfP WCFE
- - 'Albescens Flore Pleno' (d)	WJur
- 'Provence' (F)	EPom LCro
- 'Wonderful' (F)	CAgr WJur

Puschkinia (Asparagaceae)

scilloides	NBir
- var. *libanotica* ♀H6	ECha EGren EPfP EPot ERCP GKev LAma LCro LRHS MPie NBir SEND WShi XFar
- - 'Alba'	EGren EPot GKev LAma LRHS

Puya ✿ (Bromeliaceae)

RH 1809	WCot
alpestris	EUrb MCtn SArc SBig SPlb
§ - subsp. *zoellneri*	CDTJ SPlb SVen WCot
assurgens	NPlm
× berteroniana misapplied	see *P. alpestris* subsp. *zoellneri*
× berteroniana Mez	CBcs CTsd SBig
bicolor B&SWJ 14869	WCru
castellanosii	NPlm SPlb
chilensis	CAbb CDTJ SPlb SVen WCot
coerulea	CDTJ CTsd SPlb
§ - var. *violacea*	NPlm SBig
dyckioides	WCot
ferruginea	SPlb
hromadnikii	SPlb
killipii B&SWJ 14801	WCru
laxa	SPlb WCot
mirabilis	CAbb CDTJ CSpe SBig SPlb
- B&SWJ 14827	WCru
aff. *nitida* B&SWJ 14396	WCru
- B&SWJ 14887	WCru
raimondii	SBig
santosii B&SWJ 14783	WCru
venusta	CDTJ NPlm SPlb SVen WCot WJun
violacea	see *P. coerulea* var. *violacea*
weberbaueri	SBig

Pycnanthemum (Lamiaceae)

albescens	ECha
curvipes	EBee
flexuosum	EBee
incanum	CAgr
muticum	CAgr CSpe EBee EPPr LEdu MHol SBrt SDix SPhx StAn WPGP
pilosum	CAgr EBee IDun MCtn MHer MNHC SDix SPhx WJek
tenuifolium	SPhx
virginianum	EBee

Pycnostachys see *Coleus*

Pygmea see *Veronica*

Pyracantha (Rosaceae)

ALEXANDER PENDULA ('Renolex')	SRms
angustifolia KR 2481	WPGP
§ atalantioides	SPlb
- 'Aurea'	EHeP
coccinea	SArc
- 'Lalandei'	CMac
- 'Red Column'	Widely available
- 'Red Cushion'	EHeP ELan SArc SRms
- 'Red Star'PBR	LCro LRHS
DART'S RED ('Interrada')	CSBt LRHS
'Fiery Cascade'	EHeP SPoG
gibbsii	see *P. atalantioides*
'Golden Charmer'	CDoC CMac EGren EHeP EPfP LBuc LRHS LSto MGos MSwo SNig SPoG SRms WCha WFar
'Golden Glow'	SGol
'Golden Paradise'PBR	LRHS NEoE SNig
'Golden Sun'	see *P.* 'Soleil d'Or'
'Harlequin' (v)	CMac SGol
'Knap Hill Lemon'	MBlu
'Mohave'	ELan LBom LRHS MAsh SArc SNig SRms WFar
'Mohave Silver' (v)	CMac
'Navaho'	EGren LMaj
'Orange Charmer'	CBrac CMac EHeP ELan LRHS MGos SPlb WFar
'Orange Glow' ♀H6	CBrac CSBt EGren EHeP EPfP LBuc LRHS LSto MAsh MGos MSwo NBir NLar SArc SEND SEWo SGol SRms WCha WFar WHtc
'Red Charmer'	LBom
rogersiana	EHeP
- 'Flava' ♀H5	CSBt EHeP LRHS SPoG WHtc
SAPHYR JAUNE ('Cadaune')	CBcs CBrac CDoC CEnd EBee EPfP LCro LRHS MAsh MGos NLar WFar
SAPHYR ORANGE ('Cadange') ♀H6	CBcs CBrac CDoC CEnd CMac CSBt EBee ELan EPfP LBom LCro LRHS MAsh MGos MPri NLar
SAPHYR ROUGE ('Cadrou') ♀H6	CBcs CBrac CDoC CEnd CMac CSBt EBee ELan EPfP LBom LCro LRHS MAsh MGos MHed NHed NLar NLit SEND SRms WFar
'Shawnee'	CMac MSwo
§ 'Soleil d'Or'	CBrac EBee EGren EHeP ELan EPfP EUrb LRHS LSto MAsh MSwo NLar SEND SEWo SGol SPlb SRGP SRms WFar
'Sparkler' (v)	CMac EBee EGren ELan SPoG

Pyrus 571

'Teton' ♀H6	CMac EHeP ELan EPfP LRHS LSto MAsh MGos MSwo SPoG SRms WFar	- 'Beurré Précoce Morettini' (D)	WWct
'Waterei'	EHeP WSpi	- 'Beurré Rance' (C/D)	SKee
'Yellow Sun'	see *P.* 'Soleil d'Or'	- 'Beurré Superfin' (D) ♀H6	SKee SSFr WMat WWct
		- 'Bishop's Thumb' (D)	SKee
		- 'Black Worcester' (C)	CHab LRHS MLod NOra SKee WMat WWct

Pyrethropsis see *Rhodanthemum*

Pyrethrum see *Tanacetum*

Pyrgophyllum (Zingiberaceae)
    yunnanense   SBrt

Pyrrosia (Polypodiaceae)

drakeana	LEdu SPlb WAbe	- 'Blakeney Red' (Perry)	CAda CHab NOra SKee WMat WWct
hastata	CMen WAbe WCot	- 'Blickling' (D)	SKee
- 'Harima Jishi'	CMen	- 'Brandy' (Perry)	CAda CAgr CHab NOra SKee WMat WWct
- 'Ryujin'	CMen	- 'Bristol Cross' (D)	CAgr CHab
- 'Sekaiichi'	CMen	- 'Bunte Julibirne' (D)	WFar
- 'Shikoku Jishi'	CMen	- 'Butt' (Perry)	CAda CHab WWct
- 'World Champion'	CMen	- 'Calebasse Bosc' (D)	SKee
heteractis	WAbe	- 'Cannock' (F)	WMat
linearifolia 'Urakoryu Jishi'	CMen	- 'Catillac' (C)	CAda CAgr CBTr CHab NOra SKee WMat WWct
lingua	CMen ISha LEdu SPlb	- 'Charneaux' (F)	LMaj
- 'Hiryu'	CMen	- 'Chaumontel' (D)	SKee
- 'Ôgon Nishiki' (v)	LEdu WCot	- 'Christie' (F)	CBTr WMat
- 'Tachiba Koryu'	CMen	- 'Citron des Carmes' (C)	SKee
- 'Variegata' (v)	CDTJ	- 'Clapp's Favourite' (D)	CAda CHab LMaj NOra SEdi SKee SVic WMat
- 'Yabane Fu' (v)	CSta ISha	- 'Concorde' (D) ♀H6	Widely available
polydactyla	CMen WCot	- 'Conference' (D) ♀H6	Widely available
porosa	WAbe	- 'Conference Moors' (D)	LCro MLod
sheareri	CDTJ ISha LEdu SPlb WAbe WCot	- 'Docteur Jules Guyot' (D)	CAgr
		- 'Doyenné Boussoch' (D)	SKee
		- 'Doyenné d'Été' (D)	SKee
		- 'Doyenné du Comice' (D) ♀H6	Widely available

Pyrus ✿ (Rosaceae)

amygdaliformis	WJur	- 'Durondeau' (D)	NOra SKee WMat
- W&B B-10	WCot	- 'Emile d'Heyst' (D)	SKee WMat WWct
boissieriana	WJur	- 'Fertility' (D)	CLnd SBmr
calleryana	WJur	- 'Fertility Improved'	see *P. communis* 'Improved Fertility'
- 'Bradford'	CLnd		
- 'Chanticleer'	Widely available	- 'Flemish Beauty' (F)	NOra
- 'Redspire'	CCVT CLnd EHeP	- 'Fondante d'Automne' (D)	CAda CAgr NOra SKee WMat
caucasica	WJur WMat		
communis (F)	CCVT CLnd LBuc SPlb SPre	- 'Forelle' (D)	SKee
- 'Bambinella' (D)	SKee	- 'Gansel's Bergamot' (D)	SKee
- 'Barland' (Perry)	CHab SKee	- 'Garden Gem' (F)	WMat
- 'Barnet' (Perry)	CAda CHab WWct	- 'Garden Pearl' (F)	LRHS
- 'Baronne de Mello' (D)	NOra SKee WMat	- 'Gieser Wildeman' (F)	CWnw
- 'Beech Hill' (F)	CLnd EBee EHeP	- 'Gin' (Perry)	CAda CHab WMat WWct
- 'Belle Guérandaise' (D)	SKee	- 'Glou Morceau' (D)	CAgr NOra SKee SSFr WMat WWct
- 'Belle Julie' (D)	SKee	- 'Gorham' (D) ♀H6	CAda CAgr NOra SKee SSFr WMat
- BENITA ('Rafzas') (F)	LCro WMat	- 'Green Horse' (Perry)	CHab WMat
- 'Bergamotte d'Automne' (D)	WFar	- 'Green Pear of Yair' (D)	SKee
- 'Bergamotte Esperen' (D)	SKee	- 'Hacon's Incomparable' (D)	SKee
- 'Beth' (D) ♀H6	CAda CAgr CBTr CDoC CHab CMac CWnw EBee EGren ELan EPfP EPom IArd LBuc LCro MAsh MLod MPri NLar NOra SBmr SEdi SKee SSFr WMat WWct	- 'Harvest Queen' (D/C)	CAgr
		- 'Hellen's Early' (Perry)	CHab SKee WMat
		- 'Hendre Huffcap' (Perry)	CAda CAgr CHab EPom MLod NOra SKee WMat WWct
		- 'Hessle' (D)	CAgr CHab SEdi SKee
- 'Beurré Alexandre Lucas' (D)	CWnw LCro SKee	- HUMBUG ('Pysanka') (D)	CBTr EPom MLod NOra SKee WMat
	§	- 'Improved Fertility' (D)	CAgr SBmr SKee
- 'Beurré Bedford' (D)	SKee	- INVINCIBLE ('Delwinor') (D/C)	CAgr CBTr EPom LBuc LCro LRHS MGos MLod NOra SPoG SSFr WMat
- 'Beurré Clairgeau' (C)	SKee		
- 'Beurré d'Amanlis' (D)	SKee		
- 'Beurré d'Avalon' (D)	SKee	- 'Jargonelle' (D)	CAda CAgr CHab NOra SKee WMat
- 'Beurré de Beugny' (D)	SKee		
- 'Beurré Dumont' (D)	CAgr	- 'Joséphine de Malines' (D) ♀H6	CAda CAgr CBTr MLod NOra SKee WMat
- 'Beurré Giffard' (D)	CAgr		
- 'Beurré Hardy' (D) ♀H6	CAda CAgr CCVT CMac EGren ELan EPfP EPom IArd IPap LCro LMaj MLod NOra SBmr SEdi SEND SKee SSFr WMat WWct	- 'Judge Amphlett' (Perry)	EPom MLod NOra WMat WWct
		- 'Laxton's Foremost' (D)	CAgr
		- 'Le Lectier' (D)	SKee
		- 'Légipont' (D)	CAgr

Pyrus

- 'Louise Bonne of Jersey' (D) — CAda CAgr CBTr CLnd CMac EGren EPfP EPom LCro MLod NOra SBmr SEdi SKee SSFr WMat WWct
- 'Magyar Kobak' (C) — SKee
- 'Marie-Louise' (D) — SKee
- 'Martin Sec' (C/D) — SKee
- 'Merrylegs' (Perry) — CHab
- 'Merton Pride' (D) — CAda CAgr CLnd EPom LCro NOra SKee SSFr WMat WWct
- 'Merton Star' (D) — SKee
- 'Monsieur le Curé' — see *P. communis* 'Vicar of Winkfield'
- 'Moonglow' (F) — CAgr MLod NOra SKee WMat
- 'Moorcroft' (Perry) — SKee WWct
- 'Nouveau Poiteau' (C/D) — CAgr SKee
- NUVAR ANNIVERSARY (D) — SKee
- NUVAR CELEBRATION (F) — SKee WMat
- 'Nye Russet Bartlett' (F) — CAgr
- 'Obelisk' (D) — CBTr EBee ELan EPom LCro MLod NOra SPoG WMat
- 'Old Home' (Perry) — WMat
- 'Oldfield' (Perry) — CHab
- 'Onward' (D) — CAda CAgr CBTr CHab EBee ELan EPom IArd LCro LRHS MLod NOra SKee SSFr WMat WWct
- 'Ovid' (D) — CAgr
§ - 'Packham's Triumph' (D) — CAgr EPom LCro NOra SEdi SKee SSFr WMat
- 'Parsonage' (Perry) — CHab
- 'Passe Crassane' (D) — SKee
- 'Pear Apple' (D) — CHab
- 'Penrhyn' (F) — WMat
I - 'Petite Poire' (D) — EPom LCro
- 'Pierre Corneille' (D) — WWct
- 'Pitmaston Duchess' (C/D) — SKee WMat WWct
- 'Précoce de Trévoux' (D) — SKee
- 'Red Beurre Hardy' (C) — CBTr LRHS
- 'Red Comice' (D/C) — SKee
- 'Red Pear' (Perry) — CBTr CHab WMat
- 'Red Sensation Bartlett' (D/C) — CAgr CBTr EPom LCro LRHS MLod NOra SKee SSFr WMat
- 'Redbald' (D) — SKee
- 'Robin' (C/D) — EGren SEdi SKee WMat
- 'Santa Claus' (D) — CBTr MLod SKee WMat
- 'Seckel' (D) — NOra SKee
- 'Shipova' — see × *Sorbopyrus auricularis* 'Shipova'
- 'Sierra' (D) — CAgr
- 'Snowdon Queen' (D) — CHab
- 'Swan's Egg' (D) — CAda SKee
- 'Taynton Squash' (Perry) — NOra WMat
- 'Terrace Pearl' (D) — WMat
- 'Thorn' (Perry) — CAgr CHab EPom MLod SKee WMat WWct
- 'Triumph' — see *P. communis* 'Packham's Triumph'
- 'Uvedale's St Germain' (C) — SKee
- 'Verbelu' (C) — SKee
- 'Verdi' (F) — EPom
§ - 'Vicar of Winkfield' (C) — SKee
- 'Williams' Bon Chrétien' (D/C) — Widely available
- 'Williams' Red' (D/C) — EGren LCro SEdi SKee
- 'Williams' Rouge Delbard' (F) — EPom
- 'Windsor' (D) — SKee
- 'Winnal's Longdon' (Perry) — CAda EPom WMat
- 'Winter Nelis' (D) — CAgr CHab NLar NOra SKee WMat WWct
- 'Woodhall' (F) — WMat
cossonii — WJur
elaeagrifolia — LMaj WJur
- subsp. *kotschyana* — LRHS
- 'Silver Sails' — CBcs CLnd EBee NOra NPip WHtc WMat WPGP
× *michauxii* — SVen
nivalis — CLnd EHeP
- 'Catalia' — CLnd WMat
pashia — LEdu NLar WMat
phaeocarpa — WJur
pyraster — CHab WJur
pyrifolia — WJur
- '20th Century' — see *P. pyrifolia* 'Nijisseiki'
- 'Chojuro' (F) — CAgr
- 'Hosui' (F) — CAgr SVic
- 'Kosui' (F) — SVic
- 'Kumoi' (F) — CAgr EPom LCro MAsh MGos MLod MNHC NOra SKee SSFr WMat
§ - 'Nijisseiki' (F) — LCro SKee SVic
- 'Shinko' (F) — CAgr SVic
- 'Shinseiki' (F) — CAgr MGos MLod MNHC NOra SBmr SKee SVic WMat
- 'Shinsui' (F) — SKee
- 'Tama' (D) — SVic
salicifolia 'Pendula' ♀H6 — Widely available
ussuriensis — WJur

Q

Quercus ✿ (Fagaceae)
§ *acuta* — CBrP CMCN
acutissima — CAco CMCN IPap
aegilops — see *Q. ithaburensis* subsp. *macrolepis*
affinis ♀H5 — CMCN
agrifolia — CMCN
ajudaghiensis — see *Q. hartwissiana*
alba — CAco CMCN IPap
alnifolia — CAco CBrP CMCN
'Bear Creek Ranch' — MBlu
benthamii — CMCN
berberidifolia — CMCN
bicolor — CAco CMCN IArd IPap MBlu
§ × *bimundorum* 'Crimschmidt' — CAco CCVT MBlu SGol
borealis — see *Q. rubra*
brantii — CMCN
breweri — see *Q. garryana* var. *breweri*
buckleyi — CBcs CMCN EPfP IPap
- 'Dazzling Red' — MBlu
× *bushii* — CMCN
- 'Seattle Trident' — MBlu
calophylla — CMCN
canariensis ♀H5 — EPfP IPap WJur
canbyi — CMCN
castaneifolia 'Green Spire' ♀H7 — CAco CMCN EBee MBlu MMuc
cerris — CAco CBcs CCVT CMCN EHeP IPap LMaj MGos SEND
- 'Afyon Lace' — MBlu
§ - 'Argenteovariegata' (v) — CAco CMCN ELan EPfP MBlu
- 'Athena' — MBlu
- 'Bolte's Obelisk' — MBlu
- 'Curly Head' PBR — CAco
- 'Variegata' — see *Q. cerris* 'Argenteovariegata'
- 'Wodan' — MBlu
chenii — CMCN

Quercus 573

chrysolepis	CBrP CMCN WPGP
coccifera	CExl CMCN EPfP SVen WJur WPGP
coccinea	CAco CBcs CLnd CMCN IArd IPap MBlu SEWo WJur
- 'Splendens' ♀H6	CAco CEnd CMCN ELan MBlu SPoG
× *crenata* 'Ambrozyana'	CMCN
- 'Bloemendaal'	IArd
- 'Diversifolia'	CAco CMCN MBlu SEND
- 'Fulhamensis'	CAco CMCN MBlu MMuc
§ - 'Lucombeana' ♀H6	CAco CMCN MBlu MMuc
- 'Waasland Select'	MMuc NLar SEND
- 'Wageningen'	IPap MMuc
CRIMSON SPIRE	see *Q.* × *bimundorum* 'Crimschmidt'
dentata	CAco CMCN WJur
- 'Carl Ferris Miller'	CAco CMCN LMaj MBlu
- 'Pinnatifida'	MBlu
- 'Sir Harold Hillier'	CAco CMCN MBlu
- subsp. *yunnanensis*	MBlu
durata	CMCN
ellipsoidalis	CMCN
- 'Hemelrijk' ♀H6	CMCN MBlu
faginea	WJur WPGP
- aff. subsp. *broteroi*	CMCN
falcata var. *pagodifolia*	see *Q. pagoda*
'Fire Water'	MBlu
frainetto	CAco CMCN ELan EPfP IPap
- 'Hungarian Crown' ♀H6	MBlu MMuc
- 'Trump'	CAco
gambelii	CMCN
garryana	CAco CMCN
- var. *breweri*	CMCN WPGP
- var. *fruticosa*	see *Q. garryana* var. *breweri*
gilva	CBrP CMCN
glabrescens	CMCN
glandulifera	see *Q. serrata* Murray
glauca	CAco CBrP CMCN IPap LEdu NLar WJur WPGP
grisea	CMCN
§ *hartwissiana*	CMCN
hemisphaerica	CMCN
× *hickelii*	CMCN
hintoniorum	CMCN
aff. × *hispanica*	CBTr
hypoleucoides	CMCN
ilex	Widely available
ilicifolia	CMCN
imbricaria	CAco CMCN IPap
incana Roxb.	see *Q. leucotrichophora*
infectoria	WPGP
§ *ithaburensis*	CMCN LEdu
subsp. *macrolepis*	
- - 'Hemelrijk Silver'	EPfP MBlu
kelloggii	CAco CMCN
× *kewensis* ♀H6	CMCN
laevigata	see *Q. acuta*
laevis	CMCN
§ *laurifolia*	CMCN
§ *leucotrichophora*	LEdu
× *libanerris*	CAco IPap
- 'Rotterdam'	CMCN
libani	CAco WJur
lobata	CAco CMCN WPGP
× *lucombeana*	see *Q.* × *crenata* 'Lucombeana'
- 'William Lucombe'	see *Q.* × *crenata* 'Lucombeana'
lyrata	CMCN
- 'Arnold'	MBlu
macranthera	CMCN
- PAB 13.002	LEdu
macrocarpa	CAco CBcs CMCN IPap
macrolepis	see *Q. ithaburensis* subsp. *macrolepis*
marilandica	MBlu
'Mauri'	CAco MBlu
'Maya' ♀H4	CAco CBcs CMCN WMat
§ *michauxii*	CMCN MBlu
mongolica	EPfP MBlu
- subsp. *crispula*	CBrP
§ *montana*	CBrP CMCN
'Monument'	WCot
muehlenbergii	MBlu
myrsinifolia	CBcs CBrP CMCN ELan IPap SArc
aff. *myrsinifolia*	CAco
nigra	CAco CMCN IPap
- 'Beethoven'	MBlu
- 'Thierry'	MBlu
nuttallii	see *Q. texana*
obtusa	see *Q. laurifolia*
oglethorpensis	CMCN
§ *pagoda*	CMCN IPap MBlu WPGP
palustris ♀H6	CAco CBcs CCVT CLnd CMCN EHeP ELan IArd IPap LMaj MBlu NLar NPip SArc SEWo SGol WJur
- 'Flaming Suzy'	MBlu
- 'Green Dwarf'	CAco CMCN LCro LMaj MBlu
- GREEN PILLAR ('Pringreen')	CAco CBTr CNWT EBee EPfP LCro LMaj MAsh MBlu NLar NOra NPip SArc SGol WMat
- 'Isabel'	CAco EPfP LSRN WCha WMat
- 'Pendula'	CEnd
- 'Swamp Pygmy'	CAco CMCN MBlu
- 'Windischleuba'	MBlu
pedunculata	see *Q. robur*
§ *petraea*	CBcs CBTr CCVT CDoC CHab CLnd EHeP ELan GAbr IPap LSto MBlu MMuc NLar WFar WHtc WRjT
- 'Laciniata'	see *Q. petraea* 'Laciniata Crispa'
§ - 'Laciniata Crispa'	CEnd MBlu
- 'Purpurea'	CMCN MBlu
- 'Rubicunda'	see *Q. petraea* 'Purpurea'
phellos	CAco CMCN IPap MBlu NLar
phillyreoides	CBcs CMCN IPap
Pondaim Group	CAco CMCN NOra NPip
pontica	CAco CMCN LMaj MBlu
prinus misapplied	see *Q. michauxii*, *Q. montana*
prinus L.	CMCN
pubescens	CMCN IPap MMuc SEND
- subsp. *pubescens*	WPGP
pumila Michx.	see *Q. montana*
pyrenaica	IPap WJur
rhysophylla	see *Q. rysophylla*
§ *robur*	Widely available
- 'Argenteomarginata' (v)	CMCN MBlu
- 'Atropurpurea'	WJur
- 'Compacta'	MBlu
- 'Concordia'	CAco CBcs CMCN ELan EPfP MBlu
- Cristata Group	CMCN
- 'Dissecta'	CMCN
- Fastigiata Group	CCVT CLnd EBee IArd MGos SGol
- - 'Koster' ♀H6	CAco CMac CMCN CNWT IPap LMaj MBlu NPip SArc WMat
§ - - 'Salfast'	MBlu
- 'Filicifolia' misapplied	see *Q. robur* 'Pectinata'
- 'Filicifolia' Hort. ex Loud.	CEnd
- var. *haas*	CAco
- 'Irtha'	MBlu
- 'Menhir'	MBlu
§ - 'Pectinata'	CAco MBlu
- 'Pendula'	CEnd MBlu
- 'Purpurascens'	CAco CEnd

Quercus

	- 'Purpurea'	MBlu
	- 'Salicifolia Fastigiata'	see *Q. robur* (Fastigiata Group) 'Salfast'
	- 'Timuki'	CAco MBlu
	- 'Tromp Dwarf'	MBlu
	- (Variegata Group) 'Fürst Schwarzenburg' (v)	MBlu
	× *rosacea* 'Columna'	CAco
	rotundifolia	CAgr CMCN
§	*rubra*	Widely available
	- 'Aurea'	CEnd CMCN MBlu
	- 'Bolte's Gold'	CAco CMCN ELan MBlu NOra NPip WMat
	- 'Magic Fire' ♀H6	CMCN MBlu
	- 'Red Queen'	EPfP MBlu
*	- 'Sunshine'	WCot
§	*rysophylla*	MBlu
	salicina	CBrP LEdu WPGP
	× *sargentii* 'Thomas'	CAco MBlu
	sartorii	CMCN
	× *schochiana*	MBlu
	semecarpifolia	MBlu WPGP
§	*serrata* Murray	CAco CMCN LEdu
	- 'Herkenrode'	MBlu
	sessiliflora	see *Q. petraea*
	shumardii	CAco CMCN IPap LMaj MBlu
	stellata	CMCN EPfP
	suber	CAgr CBrP CMCN CTsd ELan IArd IPap LEdu LMaj MBlu SArc SEND SPlb WCot WJur WPGP
	- 'Sopron'	CAco MBlu
§	*texana*	CAco CMCN IPap NOra
	- 'New Madrid'	CAco ELan EPfP MAsh MBlu NPip WCha WMat WPGP
	trojana	CAco CMCN SEND
	× *turneri*	CMCN WSpi
	- 'Pseudoturneri' ♀H5	CAco ELan MBlu
	variabilis	CMCN WPGP
	velutina	CAco CMCN IPap
	- 'Albertsii'	MBlu
	- 'Golden Dragon'	MBlu
	- 'Oakridge Walker'	MBlu
	- 'Rubrifolia'	CMCN
	virginiana	CMCN
	vulcanica	MBlu
	× *warei*	CMCN
	- 'Chimney Fire'	MBlu
§	- 'Long'	CAco CNWT EBee ELan EPfP LRHS MBlu NOra NPip WMat
	- REGAL PRINCE	see *Q.* × *warei* 'Long'
	- 'Windcandle'	CAco MBlu
	wislizeni	CMCN NLar

Quesnelia (Bromeliaceae)
sp. — EAri

Quillaja (Quillajaceae)
lancifolia **new** — WJur
saponaria — CBcs EBee ELan EPfP SPlb

quince see *Cydonia oblonga*

R

Racosperma see Acacia

Radermachera (Bignoniaceae)
sinica ♀H1b — EShb LCro MCtn

radish see AGM Vegetables Section

Raffenaldia (Brassicaceae)
primuloides — GKev

× Ramberlea (Gesneriaceae)
'Inchgarth' — NHar WAbe

Ramonda (Gesneriaceae)
§ *myconi* ♀H5 — GEdr GKev MCtn SRms WAbe
 - 'Jim's Shadow' — WAbe
 - 'Rosea' — WAbe
pyrenaica — see *R. myconi*

Ranunculus (Ranunculaceae)

abnormis	WAbe
aconitifolius	CTtf EBee ECha GKev GMaP NLar SHar WFar
- Cally form	MNrw
- 'Flore Pleno' (d) ♀H7	CMac CMiW CTtf EBee ECha ELan EPfP GAbr GMaP LEdu LRHS MBel NBir NDov NLar NRya NSti SRms WCAu WFar
acris	CBWd CGwi CHab ELin MNHC NBir NMir NPer SPhx SRms SVic WOrg
- subsp. *acris* 'Stevenii'	SDix
- 'Citrinus'	CElw CMiW CTtf ECha GKev GQue MPro SRot WCot WFar
- 'Flore Pleno' (d) ♀H7	CDor ECha ELin EPfP GMaP LEdu NBid NBro NGdn NRya NSti SBeP SPoG SRms WCAu WFar
- 'Sulphureus'	EBee WCAu
alpestris	GEdr GKev SBrt WAbe
- 'Flore Pleno' (d)	GEdr
amplexicaulis	EBee GEdr GKev GMaP
aquatilis	CHab CLil CPud CWat ELin EWat MWts WMAq
asiaticus	ERCP
- var. *albus*	XFar
- Aviv Series	LAma
- - 'Aviv Orange'	ERCP LAma
- - 'Aviv Picotee Café'	ERCP LAma MHtn XFar
- - 'Aviv Picotee Orange'	ERCP LAma XFar
- - 'Aviv Picotee Roze'	ERCP LAma XFar
- - 'Aviv Purple'	ERCP XFar
- - 'Aviv Red'	LAma LCro
- - 'Aviv Rose'	ERCP LAma LCro
- - 'Aviv White'	ERCP LAma LCro
- - 'Aviv Yellow'	ERCP LAma
- (Bloomingdale Series) 'Bloomingdale Rose Shades'	MCtn
- - 'Bloomingdale White Shades'	MCtn
- (Elegance Series) ELEGANCE BIANCO SFUMATO (d)	XFar
- - ELEGANCE BIANCO STRIATO (d)	XFar
- - ELEGANCE CIOCCOLATO (d)	XFar
- - ELEGANCE CLEMENTINE (d)	XFar
- - ELEGANCE CREMA (d)	XFar
- - ELEGANCE GIALLO STRIATO (d)	XFar
- - ELEGANCE MALVA (d)	XFar
- - ELEGANCE PASTELLO (d)	XFar
- - ELEGANCE ROSA (d)	XFar
- - ELEGANCE ROSA STRIATO (d) **new**	XFar
- - ELEGANCE ROSSO (d)	XFar

Rehderodendron

- - Elegance Viola (d) — XFar
- var. *flavus* — XFar
- (Riviera Series) 'Riviera Golden Yellow' (d) **new** — MPro
- - 'Riviera Hot Pink' (d) **new** — MPro
- - 'Riviera Lemonade' (d) **new** — MPro
- - Riviera Mix (d) **new** — MPro
- - 'Riviera Orange' (d) **new** — MPro
- - 'Riviera Orange-apricot' (d) **new** — MPro
- - 'Riviera Orange Pink' (d) **new** — MPro
- - 'Riviera Red' (d) **new** — MPro
- - 'Riviera White' (d) **new** — MPro
- Vortex Series — see *R. asiaticus* Riviera Series
- var. *sanguineus* — XFar
- *bilobus* — GArf GEdr WAbe
- *bulbosus* — WOrg
- *farreri* — see *R. bulbosus* 'F.M. Burton'
- § - 'F.M. Burton' — WCot
- - 'Speciosus Plenus' — see *R. constantinopolitanus* 'Plenus'
- *calandrinioides* ♀H5 — NBir SBrt WCot
- § *constantinopolitanus* — CMiW ECha GMaP LShi MNrw
  - 'Plenus' (d) — NBid NBro NLar WCot WMal
- *cortusifolius* — StAn
- *crenatus* — GEdr
- *ficaria* — see *Ficaria verna*
- × *flahaultii* — GArf
- *flammula* — CBen CHab CLil CPud CToG CTtf CWat ELin MWts
- *gouanii* — GKev NRya
- 'Gowrie' — GEdr
- *gramineus* ♀H7 — EBee EDAr GMaP NRya SBrt SDix SHar SRms WFar
- - 'Pardal' — SMHy
- *hederaceus* — CWat
- *illyricus* — ECha
- *insignis* — GKev
- *japonicus* — GKev
- *lanuginosus* — EPPr
- *lingua* — CPud ELin NMir SPlb
- - 'Grandiflorus' — CLil EGren NPer WMAq
- *lyallii* — GKev
- *malessanus* **new** — SBrt
- *millefoliatus* — WAbe
- *montanus* double-flowered (d) — ECha SHar WAbe WCot
- - 'Miss Austria' (d) — GEdr
- - 'Molten Gold' ♀H5 — GEdr GMaP LBar WAbe WFar
- *nivicola* — WCot
- *parnassiifolius* — GEdr GKev WAbe WCot
- *platanifolius* — SBrt
- × *prietoi* 'Moonlight' — GEdr LEdu
- 'Purple Heart' (d) — EPfP LCro
- *repens* 'Buttered Popcorn' (v) — EBee
- (Rococo Series) — LRHS
  - Rococo Orange ('Rocorange'PBR)
- - Rococo Peach ('Rocpeach'PBR) **new** — LBar
- - Rococo Pink ('Rocpink'PBR) — LBar LRHS
- - Rococo Yellow ('Rocyellow'PBR) — LBar LRHS
- *seguieri* — GEdr WAbe
- *speciosus* 'Flore Pleno' — see *R. constantinopolitanus* 'Plenus'
- *thora* — GKev

Ranzania (Berberidaceae)
- *japonica* — EWld GEdr GKev

Raoulia (Asteraceae)
- *australis* misapplied — see *R. hookeri*
- *australis* ambig. — EDAr EPot GKev GMaP SEle SRot StAn WTor
- *australis* Hook.f. ex Raoul — MAsh
- § - Lutescens Group — ECha EPot SPlb WIce
- *glabra* — EPot
- § *hookeri* — ECha EDAr EPot EWes MAsh MWlw SPlb SRms
- × *loganii* — see × *Leucoraoulia loganii*
- *lutescens* — see *R. australis* Lutescens Group
- *petriensis* — WAbe
- × *petrimia* 'Margaret Pringle' — WAbe
- *subsericea* — ECha EWes
- *tenuicaulis* — ECha EPot GArf SPlb

Raphanus (Brassicaceae)
- *sativus* — SVic

raspberry see *Rubus idaeus*; also AGM Fruit Section

Ratibida (Asteraceae)
- *columnifera* — LShi MCtn
- - f. *pulcherrima* — CBcs
- - - 'Red Midget' — CSpe MCtn
- *mexicana* — EBee EPfP
- *pinnata* — CBcs CDor CSpe MNrw NBir SPhx SPlb StAn WCot

Raukaua (Araliaceae)
- *laetevirens* — WPGP

Ravenala (Strelitziaceae)
- *madagascariensis* — MCtn NPlm SPlb
- - 'Ambanja' — NPlm

Ravenea (Arecaceae)
- *rivularis* — NPlm

Rebutia ✿ (Cactaceae)
- 'Burnt Orange' — SPlb
- § *canigueralii* ♀H2 — SPlb
- - 'Violacidermis' — LCro
- - 'Coffee Cream' — SPlb
- *fabrisii* var. *aureiflora* — SPlb
- 'Flame' — SPlb
- *krugerae* — SPlb
- 'Parma Violet' — SPlb
- *pulchra* — see *R. canigueralii*
- § *pygmaea* ♀H2 — SPlb

Rechsteineria see *Sinningia*

redcurrant see *Ribes rubrum* (R); also AGM Fruit Section

Regelia (Myrtaceae)
- *velutina* — CPbh SPlb

Rehderodendron (Styracaceae)
- *indochinense* B&SWJ 12115 — WCru
- - NJM 9.116 — WPGP
- - WWJ 11869 — WCru
- *kwangtungense* WWJ 11940 — WCru

Rehderodendron

kweichowense		WCru
WWJ 12019		
macrocarpum		CBcs EBee LEdu MBlu WPGP
- B&SWJ 11841		WCru
- KWJ 12310		WCru
- WWJ 11952		WCru

Rehmannia (Orobanchaceae)

angulata misapplied		see *R. elata*
§ *elata* ♀H3		CAbb CBcs CSpe CTsd CWal EAri EBee ELan LShi MArl MHol SRms
henryi		LRHS
piasezkii		MCtn
'Schneetiger'		CSpe
WALBERTON'S MAGIC DRAGON ('Walremadra'PBR)		EPfP LBuc LCro LRHS LSRN SHar SPoG SRms

Reineckea (Asparagaceae)

§ *carnea*		CDor CExl EAri EBee ECha EMor EPPr ESwi EWld GEdr GKev LEdu NSti SEND SPlb StAn WCot WJun WPGP
- B&SWJ 4808		WCru
- 'Baoxing Booty'		WCru
- 'Crûg's Broadleaf'		ESwi WCru
- 'Crûg's Linearleaf'		LEdu
- 'Jinfo Jewel'		ESwi GGro WCru
- RBGE form		GGro
- 'Sapa Surprise'		WCru
- 'Variegata' (v)		WCot
aff. *carnea* from Sichuan		WCot
incurva RKN 3605		EBee
- 'Crûg's Linearleaf'		EBee ESwi WCru WPGP
yunnanensis		see *R. carnea*

Reinwardtia (Linaceae)

indica		CExl CHll
trigyna		see *R. indica*

Remusatia (Araceae)

hookeriana		EAri GKev LAma
- B&SWJ 2529		WCru
pumila		CBct EAri GKev LAma MPie
vivipara		GKev LAma SBig SPlb

Renealmia (Zingiberaceae)

sp.		SBig

Reseda (Resedaceae)

alba		MCtn
lutea		SRms
luteola		CGwi CHab CHby MCtn MEar MHer MNHC SPhx
odorata 'Ameliorata'		MCtn
- 'Grandiflora'		MCtn

Restio (Restionaceae)

paniculatus		CDTJ
subverticillatus ♀H2		CPbh
tetraphyllus		see *Baloskion tetraphyllum*

Reynoutria (Polygonaceae)

§ *multiflora*		LEdu
- var. *hypoleuca*		SPoG
- - B&SWJ 120		WCru

Rhagodia see Chenopodium

Rhamnus (Rhamnaceae)

§ *alaternus*		CBcs CDoC CMac CWal EBee ELan
'Argenteovariegata' (v) ♀H5		EPfP EUrb LRHS MAsh MBlu MGos NLar SEND SPoG SSta WCot WHtc
- 'Variegata'		see *R. alaternus* 'Argenteovariegata'
cathartica		CBWd CCVT CHab CLnd CMac ELan LBuc LMaj SEWo WHnu WJur WMou WRjT
frangula		see *Frangula alnus*
imeretina		SArc SBrt WCot WPGP
ludovici-salvatoris		SBrt
schneideri		WJur
var. *manshurica*		

Rhaphidophora (Araceae)

decursiva		LBom
tetrasperma		LBom LCro NHrt

× Rhaphiobotrya (Rosaceae)

§ 'Coppertone'		CDoC ELan IPap LMaj LRHS NPlm SArc SEND WPGP

Rhaphiolepis (Rosaceae)

× *delacourii*		EPfP SEND WSpi
- 'Coates' Crimson'		CBcs CDoC ELan EPfP LCro
- ENCHANTRESS ('Moness')		EPfP LRHS MAsh
indica		SEND
- B&SWJ 8405		WCru
- 'Coppertone'		see × *Rhaphiobotrya* 'Coppertone'
- SPRINGTIME ('Monme')		CBcs EGrI LCro LRHS
- 'White Cloud'PBR		ELan LRHS MAsh SMad
integerrima		CMCN
minor B&SWJ 14669		WCru
umbellata		CBcs CTsd EGrI ELan GKev LEdu LRHS LSto MAsh MHtn SEND SVen WLov WPGP WSpi
- f. *ovata* B&SWJ 4706		WCru

Rhaphithamnus (Verbenaceae)

cyanocarpus		see *R. spinosus*
§ *spinosus*		CBcs CMCN EBee EPfP LEdu SPoG WJur WPav WPGP

Rhapidophyllum (Arecaceae)

hystrix		NPlm

Rhapis (Arecaceae)

§ *excelsa* ♀H1b		EGren LCro LDro LWaG NHrt NPlm SEND SPlb
humilis		LDro

Rhaponticum (Asteraceae)

§ *centaureoides*		ECha LRHS NBid NSti WCAu WCot WSpi

Rhazya (Apocynaceae)

orientalis		see *Amsonia orientalis*

Rheum ✿ (Polygonaceae)

GWJ 9329 from Sikkim		WCru
§ 'Ace of Hearts' ♀H6		CDor CLil ECha ELan EWhm GMaP MGos NBid NGdn NLar NSti SPoG SRms WCot WFar
'Ace of Spades'		see *R.* 'Ace of Hearts'
acuminatum		WPGP
- HWJCM 252		WCru
- HWJK 2354		WCru
- PAB 2487		LEdu
alexandrae		CBct ECha EWes GEdr GKev NCth NLar SPlb WFar WPGP
- SDR 2924		EBee
- W&O 8143		GGro
§ *australe*		EBlo GEdr LRHS NLar WCot WFar
- 'Pink Marble' (v)		WCot
'Cally Giant'		EWes LRHS

Rhodiola 577

× *cultorum*	see *R.* × *hybridum*
delavayi	GKev NLar
emodi	see *R. australe*
'Great Bere'	LEdu WPGP
§ × *hybridum*	MEar SBmr WKit
- 'Apple Delight'	EBee EPfP LCro
- 'Champagne'	CAgr CDoC EHet EPom LCro LEdu LRHS MCtn MHer NLar SBmr SPoG SRms SVic SWCr WKit WMat
- 'Early Victoria'	SRms
- 'Fulton's Strawberry Surprise' ♀H5	CDoC CMac EPfP EPom LRHS SWCr
- 'Glaskin's Perpetual'	CAgr EHet LBuc LRHS MPro SPoG SRms SVic SWCr
- 'Goliath'	CMac EBee LCro MPri SBmr SPoG SWCr
- 'Grandad's Favorite'	EBee EBlo EPfP LRHS
- 'Hawke's Champagne'	WCot
- 'Holsteiner Blut'	EBee NLar SPoG
- 'Livingstone'PBR	CDoC EGren EPom LCro LRHS SPoG
- 'Pink Champagne'	EBee EPfP
- 'Prince Albert'	EPfP
- 'Raspberry Red' ♀H5	CDoC EGren EHet EPfP EPom LCro LRHS SPoG
- 'Red Champagne'	ELan LBuc LCro MAsh SBmr WSpi
- 'Stockbridge Arrow'	CDoC LBuc LCro LRHS NLar
- 'Strawberry'	LCro NBir
- 'Sutton's Seedless 29'	NLar
- 'Thompson's Terrifically Tasty'	EPom
- 'Timperley Early' ♀H5	CDoC CMac CSBt EBee EHet EKin ELan EPfP EPom LBuc LCro LRHS LSRN MGos MPri NLar SEdi SPoG SWCr WMat
- 'Timperley Early 1'	SBmr SRms
- 'Valentine'	LCro
- 'Victoria'	CAgr CMac CSBt EGren EHet ELan EPfP EPom LBuc LCro LEdu LRHS LSRN MAsh MCtn MGos MHer MNHC MPro NLar SBmr SEdi SPoG SVic SWCr WKit WMat
- 'Vroege Engelse'	LEdu
kialense	EBee NBid NSti
moorcroftianum	GEdr
nobile	EDAr
officinale	CBct
palmatum	CBcs CLil CPud EBee ECha ELan EPfP IDun LRHS MGos NGdn SRms
- 'Atropurpureum'	see *R. palmatum* 'Atrosanguineum'
§ - 'Atrosanguineum'	CBct CDor CLil CPud CToG ECha ELan EPfP LEdu LRHS MArl MBel NBro NSti SPlb SPoG WCru WFar WSpi
- 'Bowles's Crimson' ♀H6	WCot
- 'Ferguson's Red'	WCot
- 'Hadspen Crimson' ♀H6	WCot
- 'Red Herald'	WCot
- 'Rubrum'	CToG LRHS NBir
§ - var. *tanguticum*	CAgr CBct CDoC CDor CLil CSpe EArl EBee ECha EGren EHeP ELan ELon EUrb GKev GMaP LRHS MCtn MPie NBid SDix SHor SPoG SRms WFar WPnP
rhabarbarum	CWal
rhaponticum	NLar
ribes	WCot WCru
spiciforme	GKev
tanguticum	see *R. palmatum* var. *tanguticum*

Rhexia (Melastomataceae)

virginica	MCtn

Rhinanthus (Orobanchaceae)

minor	CGwi CHab GJem LCro MCtn SVic

Rhipsalis (Cactaceae)

agudoensis	EShb
baccifera	LCro LWaG
- subsp. *horrida*	EShb LCro
- subsp. *shaferi*	NPlm
cereuscula	WCor
elliptica	EShb NTro
grandiflora	EShb
occidentalis	EShb
paradoxa	LBom LCro
pilocarpa ♀H1b	CPic EShb
pulchra	LCro
teres	NPlm
- f. *capilliformis* red	NPlm
- f. *heteroclada*	NPlm

Rhodanthe (Asteraceae)

chlorocephala subsp. *rosea* 'Pierrot'	CSpe MCtn
humboldtiana	MCtn

Rhodanthemum (Asteraceae)

'African Eyes'	ELan MBrN MGos SVen
'African Rose'	LCro MHol
'African Spring'	CDoC EPfP LBar LRHS
'Casablanca'PBR (Atlas Daisy Series)	CDoC EPfP LCro LRHS MPri SPoG WTor
§ *catananche*	EWes
§ - 'Tizi-n-Test'	WAbe
- 'Tizi-n-Tichka'	EDAr EWes WAbe WIce
gayanum 'Pretty in Pink'	LBar MHol SPoG
§ *hosmariense* ♀H4	ECha EDAr ELan EPfP EPot GMaP LRHS MHol SEND SRms WIce
- 'Zagora Orange'	EPfP LBar LRHS MPri WTor
- 'Zagora Pink'	LBar LRHS MPri
- 'Zagora Yellow'	LBar LRHS MPri
'Marrakech' (Atlas Daisy Series)	CDoC EPfP LBar LCro LRHS MPri SPoG SRms WTor
'Tangier' (Atlas Daisy Series)	LBar MPri

Rhodiola (Crassulaceae)

bupleuroides HWJK 2326	WCru
chrysanthemifolia WJC 13669	WCru
crassipes	see *R. wallichiana*
cretinii	NRya
- HWJK 2283	WCru
§ *fastigiata* BWJ 7544	WCru
§ *heterodonta*	ECha WCot
himalensis (D. Don) Fu	ESuc
- WJC 13723	WCru
§ *integrifolia*	SPlb
- subsp. *integrifolia*	GKev
kirilowii var. *rubra*	EBee EGrI
macrocarpa	SBrt
§ *pachyclados*	CPic EGrI EPot EPPr ESuc GJos GKev GMaP LRHS LShi MHer MMuc MSwo NBir NRya SEND SLee SPlb SPoG SRot WAbe WCot WFar
rhodantha	NLar
§ *rosea*	EBee ECha EGrI ESuc GKev GQue MCtn MHer MMuc MNBid NBir NGdn SBrt SPoG SRms WCAu WCot WFar

§ saxifragoides	EDAr EPot ESuc LRHS SPlb SRms WAbe	'Anneke' (A)	CDoC EGren EGrI ELan LMil LRHS MGos MSwo NLar SPoG SSta WFar
semenovii	GKev		
sinuata HWJK 2318	WCru	'Anouk' (EA)	CDoC CEnd LMil LRHS MPro SPoG
trollii	see *R. saxifragoides*	**anthopogon**	LMil
§ wallichiana	NBid	- 'Betty Graham'	LMil
- GWJ 9263	WCru	- subsp. ***hypenanthum***	LMil LRHS
- HWJK 2352	WCru	'Annapurna'	
§ yunnanensis BWJ 7941	WCru	'Antilope' (Vs) ♀H6	LMil SSta
		§ 'Anuschka'	LMil MAsh

Rhodochiton (Plantaginaceae)

		anwheiense	GGGa LMil
§ ***atrosanguineus*** ♀H2	CSpe EPfP LCro MCtn SPoG	***apodectum***	see *R. dichroanthum* subsp. *apodectum*
volubilis	see *R. atrosanguineus*		
		'Apollonia'	SSta

Rhodocoma (Restionaceae)

		'Apple Blossom' ambig.	CMac GKin
capensis ♀H4	CPbh SArc	'Appleblossom'	see *R.* 'Ho-o' (Kurume)
gigantea	LRHS SPlb	'Apricot Blaze' (A)	SSta
		'Apricot Fantasy'	LMil

Rhododendron ✿ (Ericaceae)

		'Apricot Surprise'	EGrI MAsh
aberconwayi	LMil	'April Chimes'	WFar
- 'His Lordship'	GGGa LMil	'April Showers' (A)	LMil
'Actress'	LMil	'Arabesk' (EA)	CDoC EGren GKin LMil LRHS MAsh MGos MPro WFar
'Addy Wery' (EA)	ELon		
adenogynum	GKev LMil	***arborescens*** (A) ♀H6	GGGa LMil
adenosum	GGGa LMil	***arboreum***	CTsd GGGa LMil NLar SLdr WPGP
'Admiral Piet Hein'	SSta	- B&SWJ 2244	WCru
'Adonis' (EA/d) ♀H5	CBcs CMac WFar	- subsp. ***albotomentosum***	LMil
'Advance' (EA)	SLdr	KW 21976	
aeruginosum	see *R. campanulatum* subsp. *aeruginosum*	- subsp. ***cinnamomeum*** ♀H4	GGGa LMil WPGP
		- - Sch 2049	LMil
'Agayon'	CBcs LMil	- - WJC 13821	WCru
AIKO PINK ('Ilvoaiko01'PBR) (EA)	LCro	- - var. ***album***	GKev
		- - 'Everest Reunion'	LMil LRHS
AIKO ROSE ('Ilvoaiko04'PBR) (EA)	LCro	- - var. ***roseum***	GGGa
		- - - 'Tony Schilling'	GKin SSta
'Airy Fairy'	LMil	- subsp. ***delavayi***	GGGa LMil
'Aksel Olsen'	EGrI	- 'Rubaiyat'	GKin LMil
'Aladdin' (*auriculatum* hybrid)	SLdr SSta	- 'Rubrum'	LRHS
		I - 'Stonefield Best'	LMil
(Aladdin Group) 'Aladdin'	CBcs SLdr	'Arctic Fox' (EA)	LMil
'Alan Leslie' (Vs)	LMil	'Arctic Tern' ♀H5	CAco CDoC LCro LMil MGos NLar SReu WFar
(Albatross Group) 'Albatross'	SSta		
		'Ardeur' (EA)	WFar
- 'Albatross Townhill Pink'	LMil	§ ***argipeplum***	GGGa LMil
'Albert Schweitzer' ♀H5	CAco CDoC EGren EGrI LMil LSRN NLar SReu	- 'Fleurie'	LMil
		(Argosy Group) 'Argosy'	LMil
albrechtii (A)	GGGa LMil	***argyrophyllum*** subsp. ***nankingense***	GGGa
- Whitney form (A)	LMil		
'Album'	SReu	- - 'Chinese Silver' ♀H5	LMil
'Album Grandiflorum' (G)	SReu	***arizelum***	GGGa LMil
'Alexander' (EA) ♀H4	CBcs LMil LRHS LSRN SReu	'Arneson Gem' (A) ♀H6	CBcs CDoC GGGa GKin LMil SPoG
'Alfred'	CAco LRHS WFar	§ (Aronense Group) 'Fumiko' (EA)	CBcs CDoC EGren ELon LCro LMil LRHS MPro NLar SLdr WFar
'Alice' ♀H5	LMil		
Alison Johnstone Group	SLdr	§ - 'Hanako' (EA)	LMil WFar
- 'Alison Johnstone'	CAco	§ - 'Hisako' (EA)	LCro
'All Gold'	GGGa	§ - 'Kazuko' (EA/d)	CDoC LCro LMil LRHS NLar SReu WFar
ambiguum	LMil		
- 'Jane Banks'	LMil	§ - 'Momoko' (EA)	EGren EGrI LCro LRHS WFar
'Amilcar'	SSta	§ - 'Satschiko' (EA) ♀H6	CBcs CDoC GGGa LMil LRHS NLar SOrN SReu WFar
'Amity'	LMil		
'Anah Kruschke'	CAco EGren LCro LMil MAsh SPoG SReu	'Arpège' (Vs)	LMil
		'Arthur Bedford'	SLdr
'Analin'	see *R.* 'Anuschka'	'Arthur J. Ivens'	SLdr
Angelo Group	GGGa LMil	'Arthur Osborn'	SLdr
- 'Angelo'	CBcs LMil SLdr SSta	'Arthur Stevens'	SLdr
'Anna Baldsiefen'	CAco LRHS SPoG	***asterochnoum***	GKev
'Anna Rose Whitney'	CAco CBcs EPfP LMil LSRN SReu WFar	'Astrid'	LMil
		atlanticum (A)	GGGa LMil LRHS SReu WFar
annae	LMil	- 'Seaboard' (A)	LMil
'Anne Frank' (EA)	CDoC LMil LRHS NLar WFar	***augustinii***	CBcs CTsd GGGa LMil SLdr SSta
'Anne Teese'	LMil	- 'Bowood Blue'	LMil LRHS NLar

Rhododendron 579

- 'Carolles'	LRHS	
- Electra Group	LMil	
§ - - 'Electra' ♀H4	GGGa	
- Exbury form	GGGa LMil	
* - 'Trewithen'	LMil	
I - 'Werrington'	SSta	
aureum	GKev	
auriculatum	GGGa LMil SSta WPGP	
I *auritum* 'Leo'	SReu	
austrinum (A)	LMil	
AUTUMN EMPRESS ('Conles')	EGrI	
(Encore Azalea Series) (EA/d)		
AUTUMN FIRE ('Roblez'PBR)	LCro LSou SReu	
(Encore Azalea Series) (EA/d)		
'Autumn Gold'	SLdr	
AUTUMN MOONSTRUCK ('Roblezf') (Encore Azalea Series) (EA)	LSou	
AUTUMN STARBURST ('Robleze') (Encore Azalea Series) (EA)	LSou WFar	
AUTUMN SUNBURST ('Roblet') (Encore Azalea Series) (EA)	LCro LSou SReu	
AUTUMN SUNSET ('Roblen') (Encore Azalea Series) (EA)	EGrI	
(Avalanche Group) 'Avalanche'	LMil	
Avocet Group	LMil	
'Award'	LMil	
(Azor Group) 'Azor'	SLdr	
§ 'Azuma-kagami' (Kurume) (EA)	CAco LMil	
'Azurika'	CAco EGren MPro NLar SReu WFar	
'Azurro'	CAco CBcs EGren LMil MSwo	
BABUSCHKA ('Hachbabu') (EA/d)	LMil LRHS	
'Baden-Baden' ♀H6	CMac EGrI GKin LCro LMil MAsh WFar	
'Bagshot Ruby'	SLdr	
balangense	LMil	
'Ballkönigin'	SSta	
'Baltic Amber' (A)	CDoC	
'Balzac' (K)	GKin	
'Barbara Reuthe'	SSta	
'Barbarella'	LMil	
barbatum	GGGa GKev LMil	
- WJC 13686	WCru	
'Barbecue' (K)	EGrI LMil	
'Barnaby Sunset'	LMil LRHS MAsh	
'Bashful' ♀H5	LRHS	
§ *basilicum*	LMil	
bauhiniiflorum	see *R. triflorum* var. *bauhiniiflorum*	
beanianum compact	see *R. piercei*	
'Beatrice Keir'	SSta	
(Beau Brummell Group) 'Beau Brummell'	LMil	
'Beethoven' (Vuykiana) (EA)	SLdr	
BELAMI ('Hachbela')	CAco LMil LRHS NLar	
'Belkanto'	CAco GKin LMil MPri NLar	
'Bellini'	CAco LMil	
'Ben Cruachan' (K)	GGGa	
'Ben Lawers' (K)	GGGa	
'Ben Morrison' (EA)	LMil LRHS	
'Bengal'	CDoC EGrI LRHS MAsh NLar WFar	
'Bengal Fire' (EA)	CMac SLdr	
benhallii 'Honshu Blue'	GGGa	
- 'Plum Drops'	GGGa	
- 'Slieve Donard'	CMac	
'Beni-giri' (Kurume) (EA)	CMac	
'Beni-kirin' (A) **new**	SReu	
'Benny Gery' (EA)	LRHS NLar	
'Bergensiana'	SSta	
'Berg's Queen Bee'	LMil LRHS	
'Bernard Shaw'	SSta	
'Bernstein'	CAco CBcs NLar	
'Berryrose' (K) ♀H6	CBcs CDoC CMac EGrI EPfP GKin LMil MAsh SReu WFar	
'Bert's Own'	CBcs	
'Betty' (Kaempferi) (EA)	SLdr	
'Betty Anne Voss' (EA)	CEnd LMil LRHS MAsh MPri SLdr SReu	
'Betty Wormald'	CMac LMil SLdr	
bhutanense	WPGP	
Bibiani Group	LMil	
'Big Point' (EA)	LMil	
'Bijou de Ledeberg' (Indian) (EA/v)	CMac	
'Birthday Girl'	LMil	
(Biskra Group) 'Biskra'	GGGa LMil	
'Blaauw's Pink' (Kurume) (EA) ♀H4	CMac EGrI ELon GKin LCro LMil LRHS SPlb SPoG WFar	
'Black Knight' (EA)	SLdr	
'Black Magic'	CAco GKin LMil MAsh	
'Black Pearl'	LMil	
'Black Widow'	LMil SSta	
'Blattgold' (v)	CAco	
BLAUE DONAU	see *R.* 'Blue Danube'	
'Blaue Jungs'	LMil	
'Blewbury' ♀H5	LMil LRHS	
BLOOMBUX ('Microhirs3'PBR) (Inkarho)	LCro LMil LRHS	
BLOOMBUX MAGENTA ('Microhirs9'PBR)	LCro LMil LRHS	
BLOOMCHAMPION PINK ('Rlh1-8p1') (EA)	LCro	
BLOOMCHAMPION PURPLE ('Rlh1 11p1'PBR) (EA)	LCro	
BLOOMCHAMPION RED ('Rlh1 9p7'PBR) (EA)	LCro	
'Blue Boy'	LMil	
§ 'Blue Danube' (EA) ♀H3	CBcs CDoC CMac CTsd EGren EGrI ELon EPfP GKin LCro LMil LRHS MAsh MGos MPri NLar SLdr SPoG SReu SSta WFar	
Blue Diamond Group	EPfP	
- 'Blue Diamond'	CAco EGren EGrI ELon LRHS LSRN MAsh SLdr	
'Blue Hawaii'	LMil	
'Blue Jay'	CAco LCro	
'Blue Monday' (EA)	SLdr	
'Blue Peter' ♀H6	CAco CBcs LCro SSta	
'Blue Pool'	LMil LRHS	
'Blue Print'	LMil	
'Blue Silver'	CAco LMil LRHS MAsh WFar	
'Blue Star'	EGrI	
'Blue Steel'	see *R. fastigiatum* 'Blue Steel'	
Blue Tit Group	CBcs CDoC CMac EPfP LRHS MAsh MGos NLar WFar	
Bluebird Group	SReu	
'Blurettia'	WFar	
'Blutopia'	LMil NLar	
'Boddaertianum'	LMil SLdr	
BOHLKEN'S LUPINENBERG LAGUNA	LMil NLar	
BOHLKEN'S SNOW FIRE	LMil	
BOLLYWOOD	see *R.* 'Farrow'	
Bo-peep Group	CBcs	
- 'Bo-peep'	SLdr	

Rhododendron

(Bow Bells Group)	EGrI EPfP LMil LRHS MAsh SReu
'Bow Bells' ♀H4	
brachycarpum	GKev
§ - subsp. *fauriei*	GKev
- - B&SWJ 4326	WCru
brachysiphon	see *R. maddenii* subsp. *maddenii*
'Bremen'	LMil LRHS
Bric-à-brac Group	CBcs
'Brigitte'	CAco LMil
'Brilliant'	LRHS
'Brilliant Crimson' (EA)	SLdr
'Brisanz'	LRHS
'Britannia'	SSta
'Bronze Fire' (A)	SSta
'Brown Eyes'	CAco
Bruce Brechtbill'	GKin NLar
§ 'Bruns Gloria'	LMil LRHS NLar
'Bruns Schneewitchen'	LRHS MGos
'Buccaneer' (Glenn Dale) (EA)	SReu
'Buffalo' **new**	LMil
bullatum	see *R. edgeworthii*
'Bungo-nishiki' (Wada) (EA/d)	CMac
bureavii ♀H6	GGGa GKev LMil SSta
- 'Corrour'	LMil
'Burletta'	LRHS
burmanicum	CBcs
Bustard Group	LMil
BUSUKI ('Hachbusk')	LMil LRHS NLar
calendulaceum (A)	GGGa LMil
- orange-red-flowered (A)	LMil
callimorphum	GKev
calophytum ♀H5	GGGa LMil
calostrotum 'Gigha' ♀H6	GGGa LMil
§ - subsp. *keleticum* ♀H6	EPfP LCro LRHS MPri MPro
- - R 58	GGGa LMil
§ - - Radicans Group	GGGa WAbe
'Calsap'	LMil LRHS
Calstocker Group	LMil
campanulatum	LMil
- B&SWJ 13934	WCru
- HWJCM 409	WCru
§ - subsp. *aeruginosum*	LMil
'Campfire' J.B. Gable (EA)	SLdr
campylocarpum	LMil
campylogynum	LCro LMil
- SBEC 519	GGGa
- (Charopoeum Group) 'Patricia'	EGrI
- (Cremastum Group) 'Bodnant Red'	LMil
- Myrtilloides Group ♀H5	CBcs GGGa LMil LRHS WAbe
camtschaticum	GGGa GKev LMil
- var. *albiflorum*	GKev
- red-flowered	GGGa
canadense (A)	WPGP
- f. *albiflorum* (A)	LMil
- dark-flowered (A)	LMil
'Canary'	EGren
CANDY LIGHTS ('UMinn's Candy Lights') (A)	CBcs
§ *canescens* (A)	EGren LMil
'Cannon's Double' (K/d) ♀H6	CBcs CDoC GKin LMil MGos NLar SPoG
'Canzonetta' (EA/d) ♀H5	CEnd EPfP GGGa LMil LRHS MAsh MGos MPri NLar SAko
'Captain Jack'	GGGa
cardiobasis	see *R. orbiculare* subsp. *cardiobasis*
(Carmen Group) 'Carmen' ♀H6	EGrI GGGa GKin LMil

'Caroline Allbrook'	EPfP LRHS MAsh MSCN NLar WFar
I 'Caroline de Rothschild' (A)	LMil
carolinianum	see *R. minus* var. *minus* Carolinianum Group
CARUSO ('Hachcaru')	LMil
'Cary Ann'	CAco EPfP LMil LRHS MAsh SReu
'Cassata'	CAco
catawbiense	EGren WFar
'Catawbiense Album'	CAco EGren LMil MAsh
'Catawbiense Boursault'	CAco LMil SReu
'Catawbiense Grandiflorum'	CAco LCro LMil LRHS MAsh
'Caucasicum Pictum' (1853)	LMil SLdr
'Cecile' (K)	CBcs CMac EGrI GKin LSRN
'Celestial' (EA)	CMac
'Centennial'	see *R.* 'Washington State Centennial'
'Centennial Gold' PBR	LMil LRHS
cephalanthum	LMil
- subsp. *cephalanthum* Crebreflorum Group	LMil WAbe
cerasinum	LMil
- CHERRY BRANDY	LMil
- COALS OF FIRE	GGGa
'Chanel' (Vs)	LMil NLar SSta
changii	LMil
chapaense	see *R. maddenii* subsp. *crassum*
'Chariots of Fire' (A)	LMil
charitopes	LMil
- F 25570	LMil
* 'Charlotte de Rothschild' (EA)	SLdr
'Charlotte Megan' (A)	LMil
'Cheer'	CAco EGren MAsh
'Chelsea Reach' (K/d) ♀H6	LMil
'Chelsea Seventy'	CMac
'Cherry Drops' (EA)	SPoG
CHERRY KISS ('Hachcher' PBR)	CAco GGGa LMil
'Chetco' (A)	LMil
'Chevalier Félix de Sauvage'	SReu WFar
'Chikor'	CDoC EGrI GKin MGos
'Chionoides'	CMac
'Chipmunk' (EA/d)	LRHS MAsh
'Chippewa' (Indian) (EA)	LMil LRHS SAko
'Chocolate Dane'	LMil
(Choremia Group) 'Choremia' ♀H5	LMil
'Christina' (Vuykiana) (EA/d)	EGrI
'Christine Belli' (EA)	LRHS
'Christine Magic' (EA)	LRHS
'Christine Siena' (EA)	LRHS
'Christmas Cheer'	see *R.* 'Ima-shojo' (Kurume)
'Christmas Cheer' (*caucasicum* hybrid) ♀H5	CAco CBcs CDoC EPfP GGGa GKin LCro LMil MAsh MGos NLar SLdr
ciliatum deep rose-flowered	SLdr
Cilpinense Group	CBcs
- 'Cilpinense' ♀H5	EPfP LMil MAsh MPri
cinnabarinum	LMil SLdr
- subsp. *cinnabarinum* BL&M 234	LMil
- - 'Nepal'	LMil
- Roylei Group	GGGa LMil
- - B&SWJ 13972	WCru
- - 'Vin Rosé'	LMil
- Cinzan Group	LMil
§ - subsp. *xanthocodon*	GGGa GKev LMil WPGP
- - 'Apricot Belle'	LMil
§ - - Concatenans Group	GGGa LMil
- - - KW 5874	LMil
citriniflorum var. *citriniflorum*	LMil

Rhododendron 581

- var. *horaeum* F21850	LMil	*decorum* ♀H6	GGGa LMil SLdr WPGP
'Claudine'	LMil	- subsp. *cordatum*	GGGa
clementinae F 25705	LMil	C&H 7132	
'Cliff Garland'	LMil LRHS	- subsp. *diaprepes*	LRHS
'Coccineum Speciosum' (G) ♀H6	CBcs CMac LMil	I - 'Greeneye'	LMil
		- pink-flowered	GGGa
'Cockatoo' (K)	LMil	§ *degronianum*	LMil
coeloneurum	LMil	subsp. *degronianum*	
- EGM 334	LMil	- subsp. *heptamerum*	LMil
'Colyer' (EA)	SLdr SReu	'Ho Emma'	
concatenans	see *R. cinnabarinum* subsp. *xanthocodon* Concatenans Group	- - 'Oki Koki'	LMil LRHS
		- 'Rae's Delight'	LMil
		'Delicatissimum' (O) ♀H5	CBcs GGGa GKin
concinnum	GGGa	'Delta'	CDoC EGren LRHS LSRN MGos NLar SPoG WFar
Pseudoyanthinum Group ♀H5		*dendrocharis*	LMil
'Concorde'	CMac	- GLENDOICK GEM ('Gle002')	GGGa
'Connie' (Kaempferi) (EA)	SSta WFar	* 'Denny's Rose' (A)	SSta
'Contina'	LMil	'Denny's Scarlet'	SSta
'Conversation Piece' (EA)	CEnd	'Denny's White' (A)	LMil SSta
'Cora Grant' (EA)	SReu	*denudatum*	LMil
'Corany' (EA)	CDoC LMil LRHS NLar SLdr	- EGM 294	LMil
coriaceum	LMil	Diamant Group lilac-flowered (EA)	LMil
'Corneille' (G/d)	CBcs LMil		
Cornish Early Red Group	see *R.* Smithii Group	- pink-flowered (EA)	LRHS
'Cornish Red'	see *R.* Smithii Group	§ - red-flowered (EA)	EGrI
'Cosmopolitan'	CDoC EGren LCro LRHS MGos SOrN SPoG SReu WCha WFar	'Diamant Rot'	see *R.* Diamant Group red-flowered
		dichroanthum	LMil
'Cotton Candy'	LMil	§ - subsp. *apodectum*	LMil
'Countess of Athlone'	CMac	§ - subsp. *scyphocalyx*	EHeP LMil LRHS
'Countess of Haddington'	CBcs LMil	*didymum*	see *R. sanguineum* subsp. *didymum*
Cowslip Group	LMil MAsh MGos MPri		
- 'Cowslip' ♀H4	CDoC EGrI EPfP	'Diorama' (Vs)	SSta
'Crane' ♀H5	EPfP GGGa LMil LRHS MAsh MPri	*discolor*	see *R. fortunei* subsp. *discolor*
crassum	see *R. maddenii* subsp. *crassum*	'Doc'	CBcs LMil WFar
'Cream Crest'	CDoC GKin LMil NLar	'Doctor A. Blok'	SLdr
'Creamy Chiffon'	CAco	'Doctor H.C. Dresselhuys'	CWnw LMil
crinigerum	LMil	'Doctor M. Oosthoek' (M)	GKin
'Crinoline' (K)	SLdr	'Doctor Reiger'	CDoC NLar
Crossbill Group	CBcs SLdr	'Doloroso' (A)	NLar
'Crosswater Belle'	LMil	'Dopey' ♀H5	CAco CBcs CDoC ELan EPfP LMil LRHS MAsh MGos MPri NLar SReu SSta WFar
'Crosswater Red' (A) ♀H6	EGrI LMil		
cumberlandense (A)	LMil		
- 'Sunlight'	LMil	'Dora Amateis' ♀H6	CBcs EGren ELan GGGa GKev LMil LRHS MAsh MGos MPri WFar
'Cunningham's White'	CAco CBcs CDoC CMac EGren EHeP ELan EPfP GGGa LCro LMil LRHS MAsh MGos MSwo NLar SArc SOrN SPoG SSta WCha WFar		
		Dormouse Group	LMil
		'Dorothy Hayden' (EA)	EGren SArc
		'Dotella'	SSta
'Curlew' ♀H5	CMac EGren EHeP ELan GKin WFar	DRAMATIC DARK ('Hachdram'PBR)	LMil LRHS
cyanocarpum	GKev		
'Cynthia' ♀H6	CMac GGGa LMil SLdr SSta	'Dreamland' ♀H5	CBcs CDoC EGren ELan EPfP LCro LMil LRHS MAsh MGos MPri NLar SPoG SReu SSta WFar
'Daimio' (Kaempferi) (EA)	LMil		
Damozel Group	LRHS		
- 'Damozel'	LMil	'Duftecke'	see *R.* WHITE DUFTHECKE (Inkarho)
dauricum 'Album'	see *R. dauricum* 'Hokkaido'	DUFTHECKE ROSA ('Rhodunter 151'PBR) (Inkarho)	LMil
§ - 'Hokkaido'	LMil		
- 'Mid-winter' ♀H6	GGGa LMil		
davidii	LMil	'Dusty Miller'	EPfP LMil LRHS MAsh MPri WFar
davidsonianum ♀H5	CMac LMil	'Earl of Donoughmore'	SSta
- Bodnant form	LMil	'Easter Parade' (EA)	SReu
- 'Caerhays Blotched'	GGGa	*eclecteum*	GGGa
- 'Ruth Lyons'	LMil	§ *edgeworthii* ♀H3	CBcs GGGa LMil WPGP
'Daviesii' (G) ♀H6	CBcs CDoC CEnd ELan EPfP GKin LCro LMil LRHS MAsh MPri NLar SLdr SPoG SSta WFar	'Edith Bosley'	CDoC
		'Edna Bee' (EA)	LMil LRHS
		'Egret' ♀H4	GGGa LMil LRHS NLar
'Daybreak'	see *R.* 'Kirin' (Kurume)	'Ehrengold'	CAco
'Dear Grandad' (EA)	LMil	(Eleanore Group) 'Eleanore'	SLdr
'Dear Grandma' (EA)	LMil	'Electra'	see *R. augustinii* (Electra Group) 'Electra'
'Dearest' (EA)	LMil MAsh MPri		
'Debbie Dane'	LMil	(Elisabeth Hobbie Group) 'Elisabeth Hobbie' ♀H5	CDoC LMil LRHS NLar
'Debutante'	SSta		

Rhododendron

'Elizabeth' (EA)	CMac SLdr WFar	'First Light' (V)	LRHS
Elizabeth Group	LMil MAsh SLdr	'Flaming Gold'	LSRN SLdr
§ - 'Creeping Jenny'	GGGa	§ *flammeum* (A)	LMil
- 'Elizabeth'	CBcs LRHS LSRN	'Flanagan's Daughter'	LMil LRHS MPri
'Elizabeth Jenny'	see *R.* (Elizabeth Group) 'Creeping Jenny'	Flava Group	see *R.* Volker Group
		floccigerum	LMil
'Elizabeth Red Foliage'	LMil MAsh	*floribundum*	LMil
'Elsie Lee' (EA/d) ♀H5	CEnd CSBt ELon EPfP LMil MAsh MPri SLdr WFar	'Florida' (EA/d) ♀H4	CDoC CMac LMil LRHS WFar
		'Flower Arranger' (EA)	EPfP LMil LRHS MAsh
'Emasculum'	SLdr	*formosum*	CBcs
'Endsleigh Pink'	LMil	§ - var. *formosum*	GGGa
'English Roseum'	LMil	Iteaphyllum Group	
eriocarpum 'Gumpō' (EA)	CBcs CMac SLdr SReu	*forrestii*	GKev
eriogynum	see *R.* facetum	- subsp. *forrestii*	LMil
'Ernie Dee' **new**	SReu	- - Repens Group	LMil
erosum	SReu WPGP	- - - 'Seinghku'	GGGa
'Esmeralda'	CMac	*fortunei* ♀H5	GGGa LMil
'Etoile de Sleidinge'	LMil	§ - subsp. *discolor* ♀H5	CBcs LMil
'Etta Burrows'	GGGa	- - (Houlstonii Group)	LMil
'Eucharitis'	EHeP LCro SSta	'John R. Elcock'	
euchroum	LMil	I - 'Hachmann's Best'	LMil
'Eunice Ann' (A)	SSta	- 'Mrs Butler'	see *R.* 'Sir Charles Butler'
'Europa'	LMil SSta	'Fragrant Memories'	LMil
EVERRED ('851C'^PBR)	GGGa LMil	'Fragrant Star' (A)	CBcs
exasperatum KW 6855	LMil	'Fragrantissimum' ♀H3	CBcs CDoC CEnd GGGa LMil NLar
'Exbury Calstocker'	LMil	'Frank Galsworthy'	SLdr
excellens	LMil WPGP	(Fraseri Group) 'Fraseri' (M)	LMil
I 'Excelsior'	LRHS MGos	'Fred Peste' ♀H4	MGos
'Excelsior' (EA)	MPro	(Fred Wynniatt Group)	LMil
eximium	see *R.* falconeri subsp. *eximium*	'Fred Wynniatt'	
'Exquisitum' (O) ♀H5	EGrl GGGa GKin LMil	'Fred Wynniatt Stanway'	see *R.* 'Stanway'
'Extraordinaire'	CBcs SSta	'Freya' (R/d)	LMil LSRN
(Fabia Group) 'Fabia' ♀H5	CMac GGGa GKin LMil SLdr	'Frilly Lemon' (Ad)	EPfP
§ - 'Fabia Tangerine'	CMac	'Frosted Orange' (EA)	LMil LRHS SReu
- 'Fabia Waterer'	LMil LRHS NLar	'Frosthexe'	LRHS WFar
facetum	GGGa LMil	'Frühlingszauber'	CMac
- 'Robert Clarke'	LMil	'Fulbrook'	LMil
'Faggetter's Favourite' ♀H5	LMil SSta	*fulgens*	LMil
Fairy Light Group	LMil	*fulvum* ♀H5	GGGa LMil SSta
faithiae CGG 14142	GGGa	'Furious Fujiori' (EA)	LRHS
falconeri ♀H4	GGGa GKev IDun LMil	'Furnivall's Daughter' ♀H5	CAco CBcs CMac LMil SLdr SReu SSta
- WJC 13825	WCru		
§ - subsp. *eximium*	GGGa LMil	*fuyuanense*	GGGa
Fandango Group	SReu	'Gabrielle Hill' (EA)	SReu
'Fantasia'	EGren	'Gaiety' (Glenn Dale) (EA)	LMil LRHS
'Fantastica' ♀H6	CAco CDoC EHeP ELan EPfP GGGa LMil LRHS MAsh MGos MPri MSCN MSwo NLar SPoG SReu WFar	*galactinum*	GGGa LMil
		- 'Galacticus'	LMil
		'Gandy Dancer'	CAco
§ 'Farrow' (EA)	LCro LRHS	'Gartendirektor Glocker'	CDoC EGrl LMil MGos NLar
fargesii	see *R.* oreodoxa var. *fargesii*	'Gartendirektor Rieger' ♀H5	CBcs GGGa LMil LRHS WFar
farinosum	LMil	'Geisha Lilac'	see *R.* (Aronense Group) 'Hanako'
fastigiatum	EGrl GKev LMil WAbe	'Geisha Orange'	see *R.* (Aronense Group) 'Satschiko'
§ - 'Blue Steel' ♀H6	GKin LMil LRHS MAsh SPlb SReu WAbe	'Geisha Pink'	see *R.* (Aronense Group) 'Momoko'
		'Geisha Purple'	see *R.* (Aronense Group) 'Fumiko'
- 'Indigo Steel'	GGGa	'Geisha Red'	see *R.* (Aronense Group) 'Kazuko'
'Fastuosum Flore Pleno' (d) ♀H6	CMac GGGa LMil LRHS SSta	'Geisha White'	see *R.* (Aronense Group) 'Hisako'
		GELB DUFTHECKE ('Rhodunter 150'^PBR) (Inkarho)	LMil NLar
faucium	LMil		
fauriei	see *R.* brachycarpum subsp. *fauriei*	'General Wavell' (EA)	CMac LMil SLdr SReu
ferrugineum	LMil	'Gene's Favourite'	SSta
'Feuerwerk' (K)	CBcs LMil NLar	'Geoffroy Millais'	LMil
fictolacteum	see *R.* rex subsp. *fictolacteum*	'Georg Arends' (A)	CDoC EPfP LMil LRHS MAsh SPoG
'Filigran'	LMil	'George Hyde' (EA)	EPfP LSRN MAsh MPri
Fine Feathers Group	CMac	'Germania'	CBcs CDoC CWnw EGren EHeP LCro LMil LRHS MAsh MGos SPoG SReu SSta WFar
'Fire Rim'	LMil MAsh		
'Fireball' (K) ♀H6	CBcs CDoC EGrl EPfP GGGa GKin LMil LRHS MAsh MGos SPoG		
		Gertrud Schäle Group	CDoC EGrl LRHS NLar SPoG
'Firecracker' (A)	LRHS MAsh	'Gibraltar' (K) ♀H6	CBcs CDoC CWnw EGren EGrl EPfP GGGa GKin LMil LRHS MAsh MGos MPri NLar SSta WFar
'Fireglow' (EA)	GKin		
'Firelight' (EA)	CDoC		
'Firelight' (hybrid)	GKin LMil NLar		

Rhododendron 583

Gibraltar Group	LMil WFar
'Gilbert Mullie' (EA)	CDoC LMil LRHS SPoG WFar
'Ginger' (K)	LMil
'Ginny Gee' ♀H5	CAco CBcs CDoC EGrI EPfP GGGa GKin LMil LRHS MAsh MGos MPri SPoG SSta WFar
'Girard Yellow Pom Pom' (A)	LMil
§ 'Girard's Hot Shot' (EA)	LRHS MPri
§ 'Girard's Variegated Hot Shot' (EA/v) ♀H4	ELon GGGa MAsh SPoG WFar
'Glacier' (EA)	SLdr
glanduliferum	GGGa
- 'Peter the Great'	LMil
§ *glaucophyllum*	GGGa LMil
- 'Deer Dell'	LMil
GLENDOICK AUTUMN DAWN ('Gle059')	GGGa
GLENDOICK CANDYFLOSS ('Gle033') (EA/d)	GGGa
GLENDOICK CHIFFON ('Gle034') (EA/d)	GGGa
GLENDOICK FLAMINGO ('Gle026')	GGGa
GLENDOICK FRANGIPANI ('Gle035') (EA/d)	GGGa
GLENDOICK GARDENIA ('Gle036') (EA/d)	GGGa
GLENDOICK GEORGETTE ('Gle037') (EA/d)	GGGa
GLENDOICK GLACIER ('Gle009') (EA)	GGGa
GLENDOICK GLAMOUR ('Gle039') (EA)	GGGa
GLENDOICK GOBLIN ('Gle010') (EA)	GGGa
GLENDOICK GOLD ('Gle011')	GGGa
GLENDOICK MYSTIQUE ('Gle014')	GGGa
GLENDOICK PETTICOATS ('Gle015')	GGGa
GLENDOICK PRINCESS ('Gle040') (EA/d)	GGGa
GLENDOICK ROSEBUD ('Gle022') (EA)	GGGa
GLENDOICK SHERBET ('Gle029')	GGGa
GLENDOICK VANILLA ('Gle017')	GGGa
glischrum	CTsd
- subsp. *glischroides*	LMil
'Gloria'	see *R.* 'Bruns Gloria'
'Glory of Littleworth' (Ad)	LMil
'Glowing Embers' (K)	CDoC EGrI GKin LCro LMil LRHS MAsh MGos NLar SReu SSta
'Goldbukett'	WFar
'Golden Coach'	CAco
'Golden Eagle' (K) ♀H6	CBcs CDoC EGrI GKin LMil MGos NLar SPoG WFar
GOLDEN EVEREST ('Hachgold'PBR)	GGGa LMil
'Golden Flame' (A)	EGrI
'Golden Flare' (A)	CBcs EGrI GKin SLdr SReu
'Golden Fleece'	LMil
'Golden Gate'	CDoC LMil LRHS MGos NLar SPoG SReu
'Golden Lights' (A)	EGrI GKin LRHS NLar
'Golden Nectarine' (A)	LMil
'Golden Princess'	LMil LRHS
'Golden Splendour'	LMil
'Golden Sunset' (K) ♀H6	EPfP LMil LRHS MAsh WFar
'Golden Torch' ♀H5	CBcs CDoC EGren EHeP ELan EPfP LCro LMil LRHS MAsh MGos NLar SPoG SReu WFar
'Golden Wedding'	LMil MAsh
'Golden Wonder'	LRHS MAsh NLar
'Goldflimmer' (V)	CDoC EGren EPfP LCro LMil LRHS MAsh MGos NLar SPoG SReu WFar
'Goldika'	LMil
GOLDINETTA ('Hachinetta')	LMil
'Goldkrone' ♀H5	LMil MAsh NLar SPoG
GOLDSCHATZ ('Goldprinz')	LMil
'Goldsworth Orange'	CAco CMac
'Goldtopas' (K)	EPfP GGGa GKin LMil LRHS MPri
'Gomer Waterer' ♀H6	CBcs CWnw EGren ELan EPfP GGGa LCro LMil LRHS MAsh MGos MPri NLar SLdr SPoG SReu SSta WFar
'Gorbella' (EA)	CDoC
Gowenianum Group (Ad)	LMil MGos
'Grace Seabrook' ♀H5	GGGa
GRAFFITO ('Hachgraf')	CBcs GGGa LMil NLar
grande	LMil
- WJC 13804	WCru
gratum	see *R. basilicum*
'Graziella'	CAco CBcs CWnw EGren GGGa LCro LRHS MGos NLar SArc SPoG SSta WFar
'Great Dane'	LMil
'Greenway' (Kurume) (EA)	CBcs SLdr
'Greeting' (EA)	SReu
'Greta' (EA)	SReu
griersonianum	CTsd GGGa LMil SLdr
- F 30392	LMil
griffithianum	LMil
- B&SWJ 2425	WCru
'Gristede' ♀H5	CDoC LMil LRHS NLar SSta
groenlandicum	LMil NLar
- 'Compactum'	NLar
- 'Helma'	LMil NLar SReu
(Grosclaude Group) 'Grosclaude'	LMil
'Grumpy'	EGren EPfP LMil MAsh MPri SReu
'Gwenda' (EA)	SLdr
habrotrichum	LMil
'Hachlady' (EA)	LMil SAko
'Hachmai' (EA)	GGGa
'Hachmann's Brasilia'	LMil SSta
'Hachmann's Charmant'	CBcs GGGa LSRN
'Hachmann's Constanze'	LMil
'Hachmann's Eskimo'	CAco LMil LRHS NLar
'Hachmann's Finesse'	CBcs
'Hachmann's Juanita' (K)	LMil NLar SLdr SReu WFar
'Hachmann's Junifeuer'	NLar SSta
HACHMANN'S KABARETT ('Hachkaba')	CDoC LMil NLar
'Hachmann's Marlis' ♀H6	LMil LRHS
§ 'Hachmann's Metallica'	CBcs LMil LRHS
§ 'Hachmann's Orakel'	LMil LRHS NLar SSta
HACHMANN'S PICOBELLO ('Hachpico'PBR)	LMil LSRN
'Hachmann's Pinguin'	CBcs LMil SSta
§ 'Hachmann's Polaris' ♀H7	CBcs CDoC EGren LCro LMil LSRN MPri MSwo SReu WFar
'Hachmann's Porzellan' ♀H6	EPfP LMil LRHS MPri
§ 'Hachmann's Rokoko' (EA)	CEnd LMil SSta
'Hachmann's Sunny Boy' (A)	LMil
'Hachpepp' (EA)	LMil
'Hachpfau'	GGGa
haematodes	GGGa LMil
'Halfdan Lem' ♀H5	CBcs CDoC GKin LMil MGos NLar SLdr SPoG SSta

'Hallelujah'	CBcs
'Halopeanum'	CBcs GGGa LMil
'Hamlet' (M)	LMil
'Hammondii'	LMil
'Hampshire Belle'	LMil SSta
'Hanger's Flame' (A)	LMil
HANS HACHMANN ('Hachhaus')	LMil
HAPPYDENDRON PUSHY PURPLE ('Hachmagic')[PBR]	LMil
'Hardy Gardenia' (EA/d)	SSta
'Harkwood Red' (EA)	SLdr
'Harry Tagg'	CBcs SLdr
'Harvest Moon' (K)	LCro NLar WFar
'Hatsu-giri' (EA)	CMac LCro LMil MPro SSta
'(Hawk Group) Crest' ♀[H5]	LMil SSta
'Heidi'[PBR] (EA)	LRHS
'Helen Close' (Glenn Dale) (EA)	SLdr
'Helena Evelyn' (A)	LMil
'Helene Schiffner'	SSta
hemsleyanum	LMil
'Hendrik's Kers' (V)	LRHS
'Herbert' (EA)	CDoC CMac LMil LRHS MGos NLar
'Herbstfreude'	LMil
§ 'Hexe de Saffelaere' (EA)	LRHS
'H.H. Hume' (EA)	SLdr
'High Summer'	LMil
'Hilda Margaret'	SSta
'Hinamayo'	see *R.* (Obtusum Group) 'Hinomayo'
'Hino-crimson' (Kurume) (EA) ♀[H5]	CBcs CDoC CMac EGren EGrI GKin LMil MAsh SPoG SSta WFar
'Hinode-giri' (EA)	CBcs CMac
'Hino-scarlet' (EA)	CBcs
hippophaeoides	CBcs GKev LMil WFar
- 'Bei-ma-shan'	see *R. hippophaeoides* 'Haba Shan'
§ - 'Haba Shan' ♀[H6]	LMil
hirsutum	LMil
hirtipes	GGGa
hodgsonii	LMil
- B&SWJ 2195A	WCru
'Holden'	MAsh
'Homebush' (K/d) ♀[H6]	CBcs CDoC CMac CWnw EGrI EPfP LCro LMil LRHS MAsh MGos NLar SPoG SSta WFar
'Honeysuckle' (K)	SSta
§ 'Ho-o' (Kurume) (EA)	EGrI SLdr
hookeri	WPGP
'Hoppy'	CBcs CDoC LMil LRHS MAsh MGos NLar
'Horizon Lakeside'	GGGa
'Horizon Monarch' ♀[H4]	CAco CBcs CDoC EGren EGrI ELan GKin LMil LRHS MGos NLar SSta WCha WFar
'Hortulanus H. Witte' (M)	SSta
'Hot Shot'	see *R.* 'Girard's Hot Shot'
'Hot Shot Variegated'	see *R.* 'Girard's Variegated Hot Shot'
'Hotei'	CAco EGrI GKin LMil SSta
(Hotspur Group) 'Hotspur Red' (K) ♀[H6]	EGren EGrI ELan GKin MSwo WFar
huanum	LMil
- EGM 316	LMil
'Hugh Koster'	SLdr
'Huisman's Sun Star' (A/d)	EPfP LMil
Humming Bird Group	EGrI
'Hussar'	LMil
'Hydon Dawn' ♀[H5]	LMil SReu SSta
'Hydon Hunter' ♀[H5]	CSBt LMil SSta
'Hydon Velvet'	CBcs LMil NLar
hyperythrum	GGGa LMil
'Iceberg'	see *R.* (Lodauric Group) 'Lodauric Iceberg'
§ 'Ilam Melford Lemon' (A)	LMil
§ 'Ilam Ming' (A)	LMil
'Ilam Violet'	CMac LMil
'Imago' (K/d)	LMil
§ 'Ima-shojo' (Kurume) (EA/d)	CMac EGrI LRHS MPri WFar
impeditum	EAri EGren EGrI ELan GKev LCro LMil LRHS MGos SReu SSta
- 'Blue Steel'	see *R. fastigiatum* 'Blue Steel'
- 'Indigo'	GKin
- 'Pygmaeum'	WAbe
- white-flowered	CAco MPro
(Impi Group) 'Impi'	LMil
§ *indicum* 'Macranthum' (EA)	SLdr SRms
insigne ♀[H6]	GGGa LMil
Intrifasi Group	GGGa
'Invitation'	CBcs
'Irene Koster' (O) ♀[H5]	CBcs CDoC EGrI GGGa GKin LMil MGos
'Irohayama' (Kurume) (EA) ♀[H5]	CBcs CEnd CMac EPfP LMil MAsh
irroratum	CTsd LMil
- 'Polka Dot'	GGGa LMil
- subsp. *yiliangense* EGM 339	LMil
Isabella Group	WFar
iteaphyllum	see *R. formosum* var. *formosum* Iteaphyllum Group
'Ivette' (Kaempferi) (EA)	CMac
'Izumi-no-mai' (EA)	ELon
'Jacksonii'	CMac
'James Barto'	LMil
'James Burchett' ♀[H6]	LMil
'James Gable' (EA)	SLdr
Janet Group	LMil
'Janet Rhea' (EA)	SLdr
'Janet Ward'	LMil
japonicum (A. Gray) Valck.Sur.	see *R. molle* subsp. *japonicum*
- var. *pentamerum*	see *R. degronianum* subsp. *degronianum*
'J.C. Williams'	CBcs SReu
'Jean Marie Montague'	see *R.* 'The Honourable Jean Marie de Montague'
'Jeanne Church'	LMil
'Jenny'	see *R.* (Elizabeth Group) 'Creeping Jenny'
'Jens Jörgen Sörensen'	NLar
'Jessica de Rothschild'	LMil
'Jessica Rose' (A)	LMil
'Jingle Bells'	WFar
'J.M. de Montague'	see *R.* 'The Honourable Jean Marie de Montague'
'Jock Brydon' (O) ♀[H6]	GGGa LMil
'Johann Sebastian Bach' (EA)	SLdr
'Johanna' (EA) ♀[H5]	CBcs CDoC CEnd EGrI EPfP LMil LRHS MAsh MGos MPri NLar SLdr WFar
'John Cairns' (Kaempferi) (EA)	CMac
Johnnie Johnston Group	LMil
johnstoneanum	CBcs GGGa SLdr
- NJM 12.068	WPGP
- 'Double Diamond' (d)	
'Jolie Madame' (Vs) ♀[H6]	CBcs CDoC EGrI EGrI ELan EPfP GKin LMil LRHS MAsh MGos MPri NLar WFar
'Joseph Hill' (EA)	SReu
'June Fire' (A)	SSta
'Juniduft' (A)	GGGa

Rhododendron 585

'Junigold' **new** | LMil
kaempferi (EA) | CBcs LMil
  – orange-flowered (EA) | CMac
'Kalinka' | CDoC EGren EPfP LMil LRHS MAsh MGos SPoG WFar
'Karen Triplett' | LMil
'Karl Naue' | GGGa LMil
'Karminduft' (A) | LMil
KARMINKISSEN ('Hachkarmin') | LMil
'Katy Watson' | SSta
keiskei var. **ozawae** | LMil
  'Yaku Fairy' ♀H5
keleticum | see *R. calostrotum* subsp. *keleticum*
'Kermesinum' (EA) | CDoC EGren LMil LRHS MAsh MGos MPro
I 'Kermesinum Album' (EA) | LMil
I 'Kermesinum Rosé' (EA) ♀H6 | CDoC LMil LRHS NLar
kesangiae | GGGa LMil
  – var. **album** | GGGa
  (Kewdec Group) 'Kewdec White Lady' **new** | LRHS
Kewense Group | LMil
keysii | GKev LMil WPGP
(Kilimanjaro Group) | LMil
  'Kilimanjaro'
'King George' Loder | see *R.* (Loderi Group) 'Loderi King George'
'Kings Ride' | LMil
§ 'Kirin' (Kurume) (EA/d) | CBcs LMil SReu SRms
kiusianum (EA) | LMil WAbe
I – 'Album' (EA) | LMil WAbe
  – 'Hillier's Pink' (EA) | LMil
'Klondyke' (K) ♀H6 | CBcs CDoC CWnw EGrI EPfP GGGa GKin LCro LMil LRHS MAsh MGos MPri NLar SPoG WFar
'Kluis Sensation' ♀H5 | CAco CMac LMil SLdr SSta
'Kluis Triumph' | SSta
'Knap Hill Apricot' (K) | LMil
'Knap Hill Pink' (K) | SOrN
'Knap Hill Red' (K) | LMil
'Knap Hill Salmon' (K) | EGrI
'Kobold' (EA) | ELon
'Koichiro Wada' | see *R. yakushimanum* 'Koichiro Wada'
'Kokardia' | LMil WFar
'Königstein' (EA) | LMil
§ 'Koningin Emma' (M) | LMil WFar
§ 'Koningin Wilhelmina' (M) | LMil
'Koran-yuki' (EA) | SRms
'Koster's Brilliant Red' (M) | LCro SSta
§ 'Kure-no-yuki' (Kurume) (EA/d) | LMil
kyawii | LMil
lacteum | LMil
'Lady Alice Fitzwilliam' ♀H3 | CBcs GKin IArd LMil SReu
(Lady Chamberlain Group) 'Salmon Trout' | LMil LSRN
'Lady Clementine Mitford' ♀H6 | CMac LMil
'Lady Louise' (EA) | SReu
lanatum | LMil
lanigerum | LMil
lapponicum Parviflorum Group | GGGa
'Laramie' | LMil
'Lavender Girl' ♀H6 | LMil LRHS SSta
'Lavendula' | LMil
'Le Progrès' | LMil
'Lee's Dark Purple' | CAco
'Lemon Dream' | CDoC EPfP MAsh MGos

'Lemonora' (M) | GKin
'Lem's Cameo' ♀H5 | GGGa LMil SSta
'Lem's Monarch' ♀H4 | CBcs GGGa LMil SSta
'Lem's Tangerine' | LMil
'Lemur' (EA) | EGrI GGGa LMil
'L'Engin' | LMil
'Leni' | LMil MAsh
'Leo' (EA) | WFar
'Leonore' | LMil
lepidostylum | CMac GGGa LMil WFar
'Libretto' | LMil LRHS NLar
LILAC DUFTHECKE ('Rhodunter 149'PBR) (Inkarho) | LMil
'Lilac Time' (EA) | SLdr
'Liliatum' (EA) | LMil
'Linda' ♀H5 | CMac EPfP GGGa LMil LRHS LSRN
lindleyi | LRHS
  – 'Dame Edith Sitwell' | LMil
  – 'Linearifolium' | see *R. stenopetalum* 'Linearifolium'
Lionel's Triumph Group | LMil
'Little Ben' | EGrI
'Little Favourite' (EA) | EGrI
'Loch Awe' | GGGa LMil
'Loch Earn' | GGGa
'Loch Faskally' | GGGa
§ (Lodauric Group) 'Lodauric Iceberg' | LMil
'Lodbrit' | LMil
Loderi Group | SLdr
  – 'Loderi Game Chick' | LMil
  – 'Loderi Helen' | LMil
§ – 'Loderi King George' ♀H5 | CAco CBcs GGGa GKin LMil SLdr SSta
  – 'Loderi Pink Coral' | LMil
  – 'Loderi Pink Diamond' ♀H5 | CBcs LMil SLdr
  – 'Loderi Pink Topaz' | LMil
  – 'Loderi Sir Edmund' | LMil
  – 'Loderi Titan' | SSta
  – 'Loderi Venus' ♀H5 | LMil SSta
'Loder's White' ♀H5 | CMac LMil SReu SSta
longipes | LMil
  – EGM 336 | LMil
  – var. **chienianum** | LMil
'Lord Roberts' ♀H6 | CAco CBcs CDoC CMac EGrI ELan LCro LMil MAsh MGos NLar SLdr SReu SSta WFar
'Louisa' (EA) | SReu
'Louise' (EA) | SLdr
'Louise Dowdle' (Glenn Dale) (EA) | LMil SLdr
'Lovely William' | CMac LMil
'Lucy Lou' | GGGa
ludlowii | GGGa
'Lugano' | LRHS NLar
'Lumina' | NLar
lutescens | CBcs CMac CTsd LMil SLdr
  – 'Bagshot Sands' ♀H4 | GGGa LMil
  – 'Exbury' | LMil
P **luteum** (A) | CAco CDoC CMac CWnw EGren EGrI EPfP GGGa GKin IArd LCro LMil LRHS LSRN MAsh MGos MMrt MPri NCth SArc SOrN SPoG SReu SRms SSta
* 'Mac Ovata' | CMac
macabeanum ♀H4 | GGGa GKin LMil SArc SSta
macranthum | see *R. indicum* 'Macranthum'
macrosmithii | see *R. argipeplum*
'Madame Ad. van Hecke' (EA) | ELon GKin MAsh

'Madame Albert van Hecke' (EA)	CDoC EGren LCro LMil LRHS NLar SLdr WFar	
'Madame Cyrille van Gele' (EA)	CDoC EGren LRHS NLar	
'Madame Masson' ♀H6	CAco CDoC EGren ELan EPfP LCro LMil LRHS LSRN MAsh MGos MPri NLar SReu SSta WFar	
maddenii	LMil	
§ - subsp. *crassum*	CBcs GGGa LMil LRHS	
§ - subsp. *maddenii*	WPGP	
- - Polyandrum Group	CBcs	
'Madras'	EGren MGos	
'Magic Flute' (EA)	LRHS MAsh MPri	
I 'Magic Flute' (V)	LMil MPri	
MAGISNOW WINTER BEAUTY (EA)	LCro	
'Maja' (G)	SSta	
§ *makinoi* ♀H5	LMil SSta WPGP	
- 'Fuju-kaku-no-matsu'	NLar	
mallotum	LMil	
'Manda Sue'	NLar	
'Mandarin Lights' (A)	EGrl NLar	
'Maraschino' (EA)	SAko	
'Mardi Gras'	LMil MGos SReu	
'Maria Elena' (EA/d)	CDoC LRHS MGos NLar	
'Maricee'	LMil	
'Marie Curie'	LMil	
'Marie Fortie'	CDoC CWnw EHeP LMil MGos NLar WFar	
'Marie Hoffman'	LMil	
'Marilee' (EA)	EPfP MAsh SLdr	
'Marina' (K)	LMil	
'Marinja' (EA)	LMil	
'Markeeta's Prize' ♀H4	CAco CDoC EHeP ELan EPfP GGGa LMil LRHS MAsh MGos NLar SLdr SReu	
'Maroon Sappho'	LMil	
'Marsalla'	SAko	
'Martha Hitchcock' (Glenn Dale) (EA)	LMil LRHS	
'Martha Isaacson' (Ad)	LMil SLdr SReu	
'Martha Wright'	CDoC GGGa	
'Maruschka' (EA) ♀H5	CDoC EPfP GGGa LMil LRHS MAsh MPri	
'Mary Desby' (EA)	CEnd	
'Mary Fleming'	SLdr SReu	
'Mary Helen' (Glenn Dale) (EA)	CDoC LMil LRHS MAsh MGos NLar SLdr	
'Mary Poppins' (A)	CBcs EGrl GKin LSRN Midl SLdr SReu	
'Masai Mara'	LMil	
(Matador Group) 'Matador'	SLdr SReu	
'Mathie' (A)	SSta	
§ 'Maxwellii' (EA)	CMac SLdr	
May Day Group	CBcs ELon	
- 'May Day' ♀H5	CMac SLdr	
'Mayor Johnstone'	EPfP LRHS MAsh	
meddianum	LMil	
var. *atrokermesinum* F 2649		
'Megan' (EA)	SLdr	
megaphyllum	see *R. basilicum*	
megeratum 'Bodnant'	WAbe	
'Melford Lemon'	see *R.* 'Ilam Melford Lemon'	
'Merganser' ♀H4	GGGa	
'Merlin' (Glenn Dale) (EA)	LMil	
METALLICA	see *R.* 'Hachmann's Metallica'	
metternichii	see *R. degronianum*	
var. *pentamerum*	subsp. *degronianum*	
'Mi Amor'	LMil	
'Michael Hill' (EA)	SReu	
'Michael's Pride'	CBcs	
micranthum	LMil SArc	
microgynum	GGGa	
'Midnight Beauty'	EPfP LMil MAsh	
'Midnight Mystique'	SSta	
'Midori' (EA)	SReu	
'Midsummer'	SLdr	
'Midsummer Coral' (A)	LMil	
'Midsummer Girl' (A)	LMil	
'Midsummer Mermaid' (A)	LMil MAsh	
'Midsummer Moon' (A)	LMil	
'Midsummer Rose' (A)	LMil	
'Midsummer Star' (A)	LMil	
'Midsummer Wedding' (A)	LMil LRHS	
'Mikado' (Kaempferi) (EA)	SLdr WFar	
'Millennium' (A)	LRHS	
'Millennium Gold'PBR	LMil	
'Milton' (R)	LMil	
'Mimi' (Kaempferi) (EA)	CMac	
'Ming'	see *R.* 'Ilam Ming'	
'Minnetonka'	CDoC	
minus	GKev	
'Miss Millie'	LMil	
'Moerheim' ♀H5	CBcs EGren MAsh MPri MPro WFar	
'Mogambo'	LMil	
'Moidart' (Vs)	LMil	
'Moira Salmon' (EA)	SLdr	
molle (M)	LRHS	
- 'Arctic Flush'PBR (M)	EGrl Midl	
- Exbury hybrid (M)	LRHS	
§ - subsp. *japonicum* (M)	CBrac LMil	
- orange-flowered (M)	GKin SRms	
- pink-flowered (M)	GKin SRms	
- red-flowered (M)	GKin	
- yellow-flowered (M)	GKin SRms	
'Molly Ann'	EGrl	
'Molten Gold' (v)	EPfP GGGa LMil LRHS MAsh MGos MPri	
'Monkey Jane'	LMil	
'Monsieur Marcel Ménard' ♀H6	CDoC EGren EPfP LCro LMil LRHS LSRN MAsh MGos MSwo NLar SReu SSta WCha WFar	
montroseanum	GGGa LMil	
'Moon Fire'	LMil	
Moonstone Group	CMac LMil	
'Moonwood Ivory' (V)	LRHS	
§ 'Morgenrot'	CDoC LRHS WFar	
morii	GGGa	
'Morning Cloud'	CDoC EPfP LMil LRHS MAsh MGos	
MORNING RED	see *R.* 'Morgenrot'	
'Moser's Maroon'	CBcs CDoC CMac GGGa LMil LSRN MSwo SLdr WFar	
'Mother of Pearl'	SLdr	
'Mother's Day' (Kurume) (EA) ♀H4	CBcs CDoC CMac CSBt EGrl ELon EPfP GKin LCro LMil LSRN MAsh MGos MPri NLar SPoG SRms SSta WFar	
'Mount Everest'	LMil SSta	
'Mount Saint Helens' (A)	CDoC	
'Mount Seven Star'	see *R. nakaharae* 'Mount Seven Star'	
moupinense	CBcs GGGa	
'Mrs A.C. Kenrick'	SLdr	
'Mrs A.T. de la Mare' ♀H6	LMil SSta	
'Mrs Betty Robertson'	CMac	
'Mrs Charles E. Pearson' ♀H6	CBcs LMil	
'Mrs Davies Evans'	SSta	
'Mrs James Horlick'	CAco	
'Mrs J.G. Millais'	LMil	
'Mrs T.H. Lowinsky' ♀H6	CBcs CDoC CMac GGGa GKin LMil LRHS MGos NLar WFar	
'Mrs W.C. Slocock'	SLdr	

Rhododendron 587

× *mucronatum* (EA) — CBcs MPro
mucronulatum — GKev LRHS WPGP
- var. *albiflorum* — LMil
'Muffet' (EA) — SLdr
'Nabucco' (A) — CBcs EGren EGrI EHeP ELan LRHS NLar WFar
nakaharae (EA) ♀H5 — SLdr
§ - 'Mount Seven Star' (EA) ♀H5 — LMil WAbe
§ - orange-flowered (EA) — LMil LRHS MAsh
'Nakahari Orange' — see *R. nakaharae* orange-flowered
'Nancor' — CBcs
'Nancy Evans' ♀H5 — CBcs CDoC EGren EPfP GGGa GKin LCro LMil LRHS LSRN MAsh MGos MPri NLar SSta WFar
'Nancy of Robinhill' (EA) — WFar
'Nani-wagata' (EA) — CTsd EGrI
'Nanki-Poo' (EA) — SLdr
(Naomi Group) 'Exbury Naomi' — LMil
- 'Naomi Nautilus' — LMil
- 'Naomi Stella Maris' — LMil
'Narcissiflorum' (G/d) ♀H6 — CBcs EGrI GKin LMil
'Naselle' — CBcs LMil
neriiflorum — LMil
- CN&W 906 — LMil
- subsp. *neriiflorum* Euchaites Group — SLdr
§ - subsp. *phaedropum* — LMil
- - KR 9308 — LMil
'Netty Koster' — SLdr
'Newcomb's Sweetheart' — LMil
'Niagara' (Glenn Dale) (EA) ♀H5 — CMac LMil LRHS
'Niamh' (A) — LMil
'Nicholas de Rothschild' (A/d) — LMil
'Nico' (EA) — CMac LMil LRHS MAsh
'Night Sky' ♀H5 — CDoC EPfP GGGa LMil MAsh MGos MPri SReu
'Nimrod' — SLdr
'Nishiki' (EA) — CMac SReu
niveum ♀H5 — GGGa GKev LMil
- B&SWJ 2659 — WCru
- B&SWJ 2675 — WCru
Nobleanum Group — GGGa LMil SSta
- 'Nobleanum Coccineum' — CMac LMil
- 'Nobleanum Venustum' — LMil SSta
Nobleanum Album Group — CMac GGGa LMil SReu
'Nofretete' — LMil LRHS
'Norman's Choice' (A) — LMil
'Northern Hi-Lights' (A) — CBcs CDoC GKin LMil MGos NLar WFar
'Nova Zembla' — CAco CBcs CDoC CTsd EGren EGrI EHeP EPfP LCro LMil LRHS MAsh MGos SReu SSta WCha WFar
'Nuccio's Blue Moon' (EA) — CBcs LMil LRHS
nudiflorum — see *R. periclymenoides*
nuttallii — LMil
Obtusum Group (EA) — SLdr
- 'Amoenum' (EA/d) — CBcs CMac EGrI LMil SDix SLdr SReu WFar
- 'Amoenum Coccineum' (EA/d) — SSta
§ - 'Hinomayo' (EA) ♀H5 — CBcs CMac GKin LMil
occidentale (A) — GKin LMil SLdr
- SIN 1830 (A) — GGGa
ochraceum ♀H5 — GGGa LMil
- C&H 7042 — LMil
'Odee Wright' — CAco
'Oh! Kitty' — SReu

'Oi-no-mezame' (Kurume) (EA) — SLdr
'Old Port' — LMil
oldhamii (EA) — CBcs
- B&SWJ 3742 (EA) — WCru
'Olga' ♀H5 — LMil SSta
'Olga Niblett' (EA) — WFar
'Olive' — SLdr
'Olivia' — LMil
'Onkel Dines' — LMil WFar
I 'Ophelia' — SLdr
'Opossum' (EA) — GGGa
ORAKEL — see R. 'Hachmann's Orakel'
'Orange Beauty' (Kaempferi) (EA) — CBcs EGrI SLdr SRms WFar
'Orange Flirt' — LMil SArc
'Orange King' (Kaempferi) (EA) ♀H5 — CDoC EPfP LMil LRHS MGos MPri NLar SLdr SPoG
orbiculare ♀H5 — CTsd LMil
§ - subsp. *cardiobasis* — LMil
'Oregon' (EA) — SLdr
Oregonia Group — LMil
oreodoxa — LMil
§ - var. *fargesii* ♀H5 — GGGa LMil
- var. *oreodoxa* — LMil
oreotrephes ♀H5 — CTsd LMil SLdr WPGP
- 'Pentland' — GGGa LMil LRHS
'Osaraku Seedling' (EA) — LMil LRHS MPri SReu
'Osmar' ♀H5 — GGGa
'Osterschnee' — LMil
pachysanthum ♀H5 — GGGa GKin LMil
- 'Crosswater' — LMil
- 'Little White Dane' — LMil
pachytrichum — GGGa
- var. *pachytrichum* 'Sesame' — LMil
'Palestrina' (Vuykiana) (EA) — CBcs CMac EPfP GKin LMil SLdr SSta
'Pamela Mary' — LMil
'Pancake' — CMac LRHS
'Panda' (EA) ♀H5 — EPfP GGGa SSta
'Paola' — LMil
'Parkfeuer' (A) ♀H6 — GGGa
parmulatum — LMil
- KW 5876 — LMil
- 'Ocelot' — GGGa LMil
'Patty Bee' ♀H5 — CBcs CDoC EGrI EPfP GGGa LMil LRHS MAsh MGos MPri SSta
'Pavlova' (A) — LMil
'Pearce's American Beauty' — CAco LMil LRHS
'Peeping Tom' — SSta
'Peggy' — LMil
pemakoense — GKev
'Penheale Blue' ♀H5 — GKev GKin LMil LRHS
'Penjerrick' — GGGa
pennivenium — see *R. tanastylum* var. *pennivenium*
'Pennsylvania' (Vs) — LRHS
'Penny Tomlin' — SSta
'Percy Wiseman' ♀H5 — CBcs CDoC EGren EHeP ELan EPfP GGGa GKin LCro LMil LRHS MAsh MGos MPri NLar SReu SSta WCha WFar
'Perfectly Pauline' (A) — LMil
§ *periclymenoides* (A) — LMil
'Perla del Lago' (A) — SArc
'Persil' (K) ♀H6 — CBcs CWnw EGrI ELan EPfP GGGa GKin LCro LMil LRHS MAsh MPri MSwo NLar SSta WFar
'Peter Alan' — LMil LRHS
'Peter Bee' — LMil
'Peter John Mezitt' — see *R.* (PJM Group) 'Peter John Mezitt'

'Peter Koster' (hybrid)	GKin
petrocharis	GGGa
PETTICOAT ('Hachpett') (EA)	LMil
phaedropum	see *R. neriiflorum* subsp. *phaedropum*
phaeochrysum 'Glossy Dane'	LMil
'Phalarope'	EGrl LRHS
'Phyllis Korn'	LMil NLar SLdr
§ **piercei**	GGGa LMil LRHS
pingianum	GGGa
- EGM 304	LMil
'Pink Cameo'	CAco
'Pink Cascade' (EA) **new**	SReu
'Pink Cherub' ♀H6	LMil LRHS MAsh
I 'Pink Delight' (K)	GKin
'Pink Drift'	LMil LRHS
'Pink Gin'	LMil
'Pink Lady' ambig. (A)	WFar
'Pink Pancake' (EA) ♀H4	CBcs EPfP LMil MAsh MPri
'Pink Pearl' (EA)	see *R.* 'Azuma-kagami' (Kurume)
'Pink Pearl' (hybrid) ♀H4	GGGa LMil SLdr SSta
'Pink Pebble' ♀H5	CExl
'Pink Perfection'	CMac
'Pink Polar Bear'	LMil
'Pink Purple Dream'	LRHS MPri
'Pink Spider' PBR ♀H4	EPfP LCro LMil LRHS MPri
'Pintail'	LMil MAsh WFar
'Pippa' (EA)	CMac
§ (PJM Group) 'Peter John Mezitt'	NLar
- 'PJM Regal'	EGren
planetum	GKev
platypodum	LMil
- CGG 14005	GGGa
'Pleasant White' (EA)	CDoC EGren LCro LMil LRHS NLar
'Polar Bear' (EA)	CAco CBcs LRHS SLdr
Polar Bear Group	LMil
- 'Polar Bear'	GKin LMil
'Polaris'	see *R.* 'Hachmann's Polaris'
'Polarnacht'	CBcs EGren LCro LMil LRHS NLar WFar
polylepis	SReu
'Polyroy'	GGGa
P **ponticum**	CAco CMac WFar
§ - 'Variegatum' (v)	CAco CMac EHeP EPfP LMil LRHS MAsh NLar SPoG SReu SRms WFar
'Pook'	LMil
'Port Wine' (EA)	SReu
Praecox Group	WCFE
'Praecox' ♀H6	CBcs CDoC GGGa GKin LCro LMil LRHS MAsh MGos NBir NLar SPoG
praestans	GKin LMil
praevernum	WPGP
prattii	GGGa
'President Roosevelt' (v)	CMac GKin LMil SPoG SSta
'Pridenjoy'	LMil
primuliflorum 'Doker-La'	GGGa LMil WAbe
- white-flowered	WAbe
'Princess Anne' ♀H6	CBcs CDoC CMac EGren LCro LMil LRHS MGos MSwo NLar SPoG SReu SSta WFar
'Princess Margaret of Windsor' (K)	LMil
principis	LMil
- (Vellereum Group) 'Lost Horizon'	LMil
prinophyllum (A)	GGGa LMil
- 'Philip Holmes'	LMil
'Prins Bernhardt' (EA/d)	SReu
'Prinses Juliana' (Vuykiana) (EA)	SLdr
'Prinses Máxima'	LMil LRHS
pronum R.B. Cooke form	GGGa
proteoides	GGGa LMil
protistum	GKev
prunifolium (A)	LMil
- 'August Fire' (A)	LMil
- 'Ted's Red' (A)	LMil
pseudochrysanthum ♀H6	CTsd GGGa LMil
- RWJ 9807 dwarf	WCru
'Psyche' (EA)	SLdr
'Ptarmigan' ♀H6	GGGa LMil LRHS
pubicostatum	LMil
'Pulchrum Maxwellii'	see *R.* 'Maxwellii'
pumilum	WAbe
PURE WHITE JULIA ('Homlea') (Encore Azalea Series) (EA)	LCro LSou WFar
'Purple Cushion' (EA)	EPfP LRHS MAsh
'Purple Gem'	CDoC LMil LRHS MGos NLar
'Purple Passion' PBR	CDoC LMil LSRN
'Purple Splendor' (Gable) (EA)	CMac SReu
'Purple Splendour'	LMil LRHS MGos SSta WFar
'Purple Triumph' (Vuykiana) (EA) ♀H5	LMil
'Purpureum Grandiflorum'	LMil
'Purpurkissen' (EA)	LMil
'Purpurtraum' (EA) ♀H5	LMil
qiaojiaense	GKev
- NN 903	LMil
'Quail'	GGGa
'Queen Alice'	CDoC
'Queen Elizabeth II'	LMil
QUEEN EMMA	see *R.* 'Koningin Emma'
'Queen Mary'	SSta
QUEEN WILHELMINA	see *R.* 'Koningin Wilhelmina'
'Queenswood Centenary'	LMil
'Quiet Thoughts'	LRHS
quinquefolium (A)	LMil
RABATZ ('Hachraba')	GGGa LMil
racemosum ♀H6	CBcs CTsd GKev LMil WAbe
- 'Rock Rose' ♀H5	LMil SLdr
'Racoon' (EA)	GGGa LMil LRHS
radicans	see *R. calostrotum* subsp. *keleticum* Radicans Group
'Ramapo' ♀H6	CDoC EGren GGGa LMil LRHS MAsh MGos MPri SReu WFar
'Rani'	LMil LRHS NLar
'Rasputin'	LRHS NLar
'Razorbill' ♀H5	CDoC GGGa GKin LMil LRHS NLar SPoG
recurvoides	LMil
Red Admiral Group	LMil
'Red and Gold' (v)	EPfP GGGa LMil
'Red Dawn'	SReu
'Red Delicious'	LMil
RED DEVIL ('Hort18' PBR)	LCro LRHS
'Red Diamond'	see *R.* Diamant Group red-flowered
'Red Fountain' (EA)	SReu
'Red Heart'	LMil
'Red Jack'	CWnw EGren LCro LMil LRHS SOrN SPoG SSta WFar
'Red Wing'	see *R.* 'Hexe de Saffelaere'
'Red Wood'	GGGa
'Redwing'	see *R.* 'Hexe de Saffelaere', *R.* 'Redwings'
§ 'Redwings' (EA) **new**	SReu
Remo Group	CMac
'Renoir' ♀H5	CSBt LMil SReu

Rhododendron 589

reticulatum (A) — LMil
'Rêve d'Amour' (Vs) — SSta
rex ♀H5 — GGGa GKin LMil
- EGM 295 — LMil
§ - subsp. *fictolacteum* ♀H5 — GGGa GKin LMil
'Rexima' — LMil LRHS
'Ria Hardijzer' (Ad) — LMil
rigidum — GGGa
- 'Album' — LMil
'Ring of Fire' — LMil
riparioides — LMil
ririei — GGGa LMil
'Robert Seleger' — EPfP GKin LCro LMil LRHS MAsh
'Robin Hill Gillie' (EA) — SLdr
I 'Rocket' (A) — LMil SLdr SReu WFar
'Rocket' (hybrid) — CAco CDoC LRHS MAsh MGos NLar SPoG
'Roehr's Peggy Ann' (EA) — MPro
'Rokoko' — see *R.* 'Hachmann's Rokoko'
'Rosa' (EA) — CDoC LRHS WFar
'Rosa Perle' — LMil
Rosalind Group — CMac
- 'Rosalind' — LMil WFar
'Rosata' (Vs) ♀H5 — LMil SSta
'Rose Bud' — CBcs
'Rose Glow' (A) — SSta
'Rose Gown' — SReu
'Rose Greely' (Gable) (EA) ♀H5 — NLar SLdr WFar
'Rose Haze' (Vs) — SSta
'Rosebud' (EA/d) — CMac SLdr SSta
roseum — see *R. canescens*
'Roseum Elegans' — CAco CDoC LCro LMil LRHS MAsh NLar SReu WFar
'Rosevallon' — LMil
Rosinetta ('Hachrosi') (EA) — LMil LRHS
'Rosy Fire' (A) — LMil
rothschildii — GGGa LMil
roxieanum — GGGa LMil
- var. *oreonastes* ♀H5 — GGGa LMil
'Royal Command' (K) — CBcs EPfP GKin LMil LRHS
Royal Flush Group — CBcs
'Rubicon' — LMil
rubiginosum ♀H6 — CBcs GGGa LMil
'Rumba' (K) — LMil
russatum ♀H6 — LMil
- blue-black-flowered — LMil
Russautinii Group — LMil
'Rusty Dane' — LMil
'Sabina' (EA) — EGren
'Sacko' — CDoC LMil LRHS NLar SPoG
'Saffrano' — SReu WFar
'Saffron Queen' — CBcs CTsd LMil
'Saint Breward' — SLdr
'Saint Merryn' ♀H5 — EGrI
'Saint Tudy' — SLdr
'Salmon's Leap' (EA/v) — CMac LMil MAsh MPri SSta
saluenense — LMil
'Samuel Taylor Coleridge' (M) — GKin
sanguineum — LMil
§ - subsp. *didymum* — GGGa
- subsp. *sanguineum* — LMil
  var. *cloiophorum*
-- R 10922 — LMil
-- var. *didymoides* — LMil
--- R 10903 — LMil
--- R 15638 — LMil
-- var. *haemaleum* — GGGa LMil
-- var. *sanguineum* — LMil
  F 25521

'Santa Maria' (EA) ♀H5 — CDoC ELon LMil LRHS NLar SPoG SSta WFar
'Sappho' — CAco CMac GGGa GKin LMil SSta
sargentianum — WAbe
(Sarled Group) 'Sarled' ♀H5 — LMil LRHS
'Sasonade' — LMil LRHS
'Satan' (K) ♀H6 — LMil NLar SSta WFar
'Satsop Sunrise' — SLdr
Satsuki Group (EA) — SReu SRms
- 'Gumpo Pink' (EA) — SLdr
- 'Gumpo Pink and White' (EA) — SLdr
- 'Gumpo White' (EA) — SPoG
'Saturnus' (M) — EGrI GKin
saxifragoides (V) — LRHS
'Saxon Blush' (V) — LRHS
§ *scabrifolium* — CMac
  var. *spiciferum*
'Scarlet Wonder' ♀H6 — CBcs CDoC EGren EGrI ELan EPfP GKin LCro LMil LRHS MAsh MGos MPri NLar SReu WFar
Scarlett O'Hara Group — LMil
schistocalyx — LMil
- F 17637 — LMil
schlippenbachii (A) ♀H6 — GGGa LMil
'Schneekrone' ♀H6 — LMil LRHS NLar SReu
§ Schneeperle ('Hachschnee') (EA) ♀H6 — EPfP LMil LRHS MAsh MPri NLar
'Scintillation' ♀H6 — CDoC EHeP ELan LMil MGos NLar WFar
scopulorum — SLdr
'Scout' (EA) — LMil
scyphocalyx — see *R. dichroanthum* subsp. *scyphocalyx*
searsiae — WPGP
'Seaview Sunset' — GGGa
seinghkuense — LMil
- CCH&H 8106 — LMil
semnoides — LMil
'Sennocke' — LMil
'September Red' — LMil
'September Song' ♀H4 — GGGa LMil
serotinum — GGGa LMil
serpyllifolium (A) — LMil
- var. *albiflorum* (A) — LMil
'(Seta Group) 'Seta' — LMil SLdr SReu
'Shamrock' ♀H6 — CDoC EGrI EPfP LCro LRHS MAsh MGos MPri NLar SPoG SReu WFar
'Sheila' (EA) — MPri
'Shelley' (EA) — LMil
'Shiko Lavender' (A) — LMil LRHS SPoG
Shilsonii Group — LMil
sikangense — GKev
'Silbervelours' — LMil
§ 'Silberwolke' ♀H6 — EGren LMil LRHS MAsh WFar
Silver Cloud — see *R.* 'Silberwolke'
'Silver Copper' — LMil
'Silver Dane' — LMil
'Silver Edge' — see *R. ponticum* 'Variegatum'
'Silver Glow' (EA) — CMac SReu
'Silver Jubilee' ♀H4 — LMil LRHS
'Silver Queen' (EA) — ELon SPoG
'Silver Sixpence' — EPfP LRHS LSRN MPri
'Silver Skies' — LMil SReu
'Silver Slipper' (K) ♀H5 — GKin LCro LMil LRHS NLar SSta WFar
'Silver Sword' (EA/v) — ELon LRHS SPoG SReu
'Silvester' (Kurume) (EA) — LMil LRHS MAsh SLdr
simsii (EA) — CMac
sinofalconeri — GGGa LMil SReu WPGP
- KR 7342 — LMil

– SEH 229	LMil
sinogrande ♀H4	GGGa GKev GKin LMil
– KR 4027	LMil
§ 'Sir Charles Butler'	LMil
'Sir Charles Lemon' ♀H4	GGGa LMil MAsh
'Sir Robert' (EA)	EPfP LMil LRHS MAsh
'Sleeping Beauty'	WAbe
'Sleepy'	MAsh
smirnowii	LMil
smithii	see *R. argipeplum*
§ Smithii Group	CBcs
'Sneezy' ♀H5	CBcs EGren EPfP LMil LRHS MAsh MGos SLdr SReu SSta WFar
'Snipe'	CDoC LMil LRHS MAsh MGos MPro NLar
'Snow Crown' (*lindleyi* hybrid)	LRHS MAsh SReu
'Snow Hill' (EA) ♀H5	CEnd LMil LRHS
'Snow Lady'	CDoC EGrI EPfP GKin LMil LRHS MAsh MPri SLdr
'Snow Pearl'	see *R.* SCHNEEPERLE
Snow Queen Group	LMil
– 'Snow Queen'	LMil
Snow White Group	NLar
'Snowbird' (A)	CBcs ELan
'Snowflake'	see *R.* 'Kure-no-yuki' (Kurume)
'Snowwhite' (EA)	CDoC LMil LRHS MGos
'Snowy River'	LMil
'Soft Lights' (A/d)	LMil
'Soir de Paris' (Vs) ♀H6	GGGa GKin LMil LRHS SSta WFar
'Solidarity'	CAco SSta
'Sonata'	GGGa
'Sonatine'	LMil
'Songbird'	CMac LMil LRHS
'Sonnenköpfchen'	LMil
sororium (V)	LMil
souliei	LMil
'Souvenir de D.A. Koster'	SLdr
'Souvenir of Anthony Waterer'	SSta
'Sparkler' (A)	LRHS
'Special Dane'	LMil
speciosum	see *R. flammeum*
'Spek's Orange' (M)	GKin
sphaeranthum	see *R. trichostomum*
sphaeroblastum	LMil
'Super Dane'	
spiciferum	see *R. scabrifolium* var. *spiciferum*
'Spinner's Glory'	SReu
'Spitfire'	SSta
'Spring Sunshine'	LMil
'Squirrel' (EA) ♀H5	CDoC GGGa GKin LMil LRHS MAsh SLdr SPoG
'Stadt Essen'	LMil LRHS
§ 'Stanway'	LMil
'Starbright Champagne'	LMil LRHS MPri SSta
STARSTYLE LILAC ('Azaare02') (EA)	ELan LMil WFar
STARSTYLE PINK ('Azaare01') (EA)	ELan LMil WFar
STARSTYLE WHITE ('Azaare03') (EA)	ELan LMil WFar
§ *stenopetalum* 'Linearifolium' (EA)	CMac LMil LRHS SLdr SMad
stenophyllum	see *R. makinoi*
'Sternzauber'	LRHS MGos
stewartianum	LMil
'Stewartstonian' (EA)	CMac ELon LCro
'Stopham Girl' (A)	LMil
'Stopham Joy' (A)	LMil
'Stopham Lad' (A)	LMil

'Strawberry Cream'	CMac EPfP LMil LRHS
'Strawberry Ice' (K) ♀H6	CBcs EGrI GGGa GKin LMil
strigillosum	GGGa
Subsection *Grandia* from Arunachal Pradesh	WPGP
'Suga-no-ito' (Kurume) (EA)	SLdr
'Summer Dawn'	LMil
'Summer Flame'	LMil
'Summer Fragrance' (A) ♀H6	LMil SSta
'Summer Sorbet'	LMil
'Summer Sunshine' (A)	LMil
'Sun Fire'	EGrI LMil MHtn MPri
'Sun Star' (EA)	LMil LRHS MPri
'Sunte Nectarine' (K) ♀H6	CBcs GKin
suoilenhense	GGGa LMil
'Surprise' ambig (EA)	EGrI SLdr WFar
'Surrey Heath'	CBcs CDoC EPfP LMil LRHS MGos MPri NLar
'Susan' (EA)	CMac SLdr SSta
'Susan' J.C. Williams	LMil
'Susannah Hill' (EA)	SReu
sutchuenense	GGGa GKev LMil
'Swansong' (EA)	CMac
'Sweet Simplicity'	CMac
'Swift' ♀H4	EPfP GGGa LMil LRHS MAsh MPri
'Talavera'	LMil
taliense	LMil
– SBEC 350	GGGa
– 'Honigduft'	LMil
– 'Woolly Dane'	LMil
'Tama-no-utena' (EA)	SLdr
§ *tanastylum* var. *pennivenium*	LMil
'Tangerine'	see *R.* (Fabia Group) 'Fabia Tangerine'
'Taragona'	LMil LRHS MGos
'Taurus' ♀H5	CBcs EPfP GKin LMil MAsh MPri SAko SLdr
'Ted Millais'	LMil
'Teddy Bear'	SSta
Temple Belle Group	CBcs EGrI
'Terracotta'	LMil
'Terry' (EA) **new**	EGren
'Thai Gold' (V)	LRHS
§ 'The Honourable Jean Marie de Montague' ♀H4	CDoC GGGa GKin LMil MGos SLdr SSta
'The Marquis of Lansdowne'	LRHS
'The Master'	LMil
'Thomas David' (A)	LMil LRHS
thomsonii	GGGa GKev LMil
– WJC 13737	WCru
– subsp. *lopsangianum*	WPGP
'Thor'	GGGa
'Tibet'	LMil
'Tidbit' ♀H3	LMil
'Tinkerbird'	CBcs CDoC EPfP GGGa LMil LRHS MAsh MGos MPri NLar
'Tinner's Blush'	CBcs
titapuriense	GGGa
'Titian Beauty'	CDoC EPfP GGGa LRHS MAsh MGos SPoG SReu WFar
'Tit-Willow' (EA)	EPfP LMil MAsh
'Too Bee'	EGrI
'Torchlight' (EA) ♀H5	CDoC LMil MGos NLar SPoG
'Toreador' (EA)	EGren SLdr
'Tornado'	EGrI
'Toro Toro' **new**	LMil
(Tortoiseshell Group) 'Champagne' ♀H3	CDoC LMil MAsh SLdr
– 'Tortoiseshell Orange' ♀H3	CBcs CSBt EGren ELan LMil MGos MSwo NLar SOrN SReu SSta

Rhododendron 591

-'Tortoiseshell Wonder' ♀H3	EPfP LMil MAsh SLdr
'Toucan' (K)	LMil
'Tower Dragon' (A)	LMil
traillianum	LMil SReu
- var. *dictyotum* 'Kathmandu'	LMil
'Tree Creeper'	GGGa GKev LMil
trichanthum 'Honey Wood'	LMil SLdr
trichocladum	GKev
§ *trichostomum*	GGGa WAbe
- (Ledoides Group) 'Collingwood Ingram' ♀H4	SLdr
triflorum	LMil
§ - var. *bauhiniiflorum*	CMac
'Tromba'	LMil
'True Blue'	EGren LMil LRHS SSta
tsariense	LMil LRHS
- var. *trimoense*	LMil
- - KW 8288	LMil
- var. *tsariense*	WPGP
'Tsuta-momiji' (EA)	SLdr
tubiforme	see *R. glaucophyllum*
'Tuffet' (EA)	LMil
'Tunis' (K)	EGrI
ungernii 'Rachel Foster'	LMil
uvariifolium 'Reginald Childs'	LMil
'Valencia'	LMil
'Valentine Surprise' (EA)	LMil LRHS
'Van'	CDoC LMil LRHS MGos NLar
'Van Nes Sensation'	LMil
Vanessa Group	LMil
- 'Vanessa Pastel' ♀H4	CMac GGGa LMil SSta
vaseyi (A) ♀H5	GGGa LMil
- white-flowered (A)	LMil
'Vayo' (EA)	SLdr
veitchianum Cubittii Group	CBcs
venator	GGGa
'Venetia' (K)	SSta
vernicosum Euanthum Group	WPGP
'Veryan Bay'	LMil
'Vida Brown' (Kurume) (EA/d)	CMac
'Vinecourt Dream' (M)	GKin
'Vinecourt Duke' (A/d)	GKin
'Vineland Dream' (K/d)	GKin
'Vintage Rosé' ♀H5	LMil LRHS SSta
'Violetta' (Glenn Dale) (EA)	SLdr
'Virginia Richards'	EGren EHeP LRHS MAsh WFar
viridescens	CBcs
- 'Doshong La'	LMil LRHS NLar
viscosum (Vs) ♀H6	CBcs CDoC CMac GGGa LCro LMil NLar SLdr WFar
- 'Framingham' (Vs)	LRHS
- 'Grey Leaf' (Vs)	LMil
- 'Queen's Choice' (Vs)	LMil
- f. *rhodanthum* (Vs)	LMil
- 'Sea of Stars' (Vs)	LMil
- 'Weston's Lemon Drop' (Vs)	LMil
- 'White Ness' (Vs)	LMil
'Viscy' ♀H5	CBcs GKin LMil
'Vladimir Bukovsky' (V)	LRHS
§ Volker Group	LMil LRHS WFar
'Vulcan' ♀H4	EPfP LMil MAsh MPri
'Vulcan's Flame'	ELan
'Vuyk's Rosyred' (Vuykiana) (EA) ♀H6	CBcs CMac EGrI ELon GKin MAsh SPoG SRms WFar
'Vuyk's Scarlet' (Vuykiana) (EA) ♀H6	CBcs CMac CSBt EGrI GKin LRHS MAsh MPri SPlb SReu SSta
wadanum	LMil
WALKÜRE ('Hachwalk')	LMil
wallichii	WPGP
'Wallowa Red' (A)	CBcs EGrI
'Wanna Bee'	LMil
wardii	LMil
'Ward's Ruby' (EA)	SLdr
§ 'Washington State Centennial' (A)	LMil
wasonii	LMil
- f. *rhodoactylum*	LMil
'Water Baby' (A)	LMil
'Water Girl' (A)	LMil
'Water Pixie'	LMil
'Waterfall'	SLdr
'Wee Bee' ♀H5	CBcs CDoC EGren EGrI ELan GKin LMil LRHS MAsh MGos NLar SPoG SReu SSta WFar
'Weinlese'	SAko
'Westminster' (O)	LMil
W.F.H. Group ♀H5	LMil SLdr
'What a Dane'	GGGa
'Whidbey Island'	LMil
'Whisperingrose'	EGrI
'White Brocade'	SSta
'White Dane'	LMil
§ WHITE DUFTHECKE ('Rhodunter 48' PBR) (Inkarho)	LMil NLar
'White Gold'	GGGa SLdr
'White Jade' (EA)	SLdr
'White Lady' (Kaempferi) (EA)	SLdr
'White Moon' (EA)	CBcs
'White Pearl' (EA)	SLdr
'White Perfume' (A)	SSta
'White Swan' (hybrid)	LMil
'Whitethroat' (K/d) ♀H6	CBcs CTsd LMil SReu SSta
'Whitney's Orange'	SLdr
'Wigeon'	LMil LRHS
'Wilgen's Ruby'	CDoC EGren LMil MGos SLdr WFar
'Wilgen's Surprise'	SLdr
'Willbrit'	CBcs MAsh
williamsianum ♀H5	EGrI GGGa LMil
'Willy' (Kaempferi) (EA)	LMil LRHS
wiltonii ♀H5	GGGa LMil
'Wine and Roses' PBR	CBcs EGren ELan GGGa LCro LMil LRHS MSwo SReu WFar
Winsome Group	CMac MAsh
- 'Winsome' ♀H5	CBcs CDoC EPfP GKin LCro MGos SLdr SSta
'Wintergreen' (EA)	SReu
'Witchery'	GGGa
'Wombat' (EA) ♀H5	CDoC EPfP GGGa LMil MAsh MGos MPri SLdr SPoG
'Wonderland'	LMil
wongii	CMac SLdr
'Wren' ♀H5	EGrI GGGa LMil LRHS NLar SPoG WFar
xanthocodon	see *R. cinnabarinum* subsp. *xanthocodon*
XXL ('Hort02' PBR) (EA)	LCro LMil MAsh MGos MPri SSta
'Yaku Angel'	LMil
'Yaku Incense'	LMil
yakushimanum ♀H5	GKin LMil SSta
- from Exbury	CMac
- 'Edelweiss'	LMil
- FCC form	see *R. yakushimanum* 'Koichiro Wada'

Rhododendron

§	- 'Koichiro Wada' ♀H6	CMac GGGa LMil NLar	
	- 'Mist Maiden'	LMil	
	- 'Snow Mountain'	LMil	
	Yellow Hammer Group	SSta	
	- 'Yellow Hammer' ♀H5	CAco CBcs GGGa GKin LMil SLdr SReu	
	'Yellow Rolls Royce'	LMil	
	'Youthful Sin'	CMac	
	yuefengense	GGGa	
	yunnanense	CTsd GGGa GKev LMil	
	- 'Openwood' ♀H4	LMil	
	- red-blotched	LMil	
	- 'Snow Shower' **new**	LMil	
	zaleucum	LMil	

Rhodohypoxis ✿ (*Hypoxidaceae*)

'1000 Cranes'	WPGP
'Alice'	WFar
'Andromeda'	EWes
'Annelies'	GEdr
baurii ♀H3	ECha SPoG WAbe WCav WIce
- 'Alba'	EPfP EWes GMaP WFar
- 'Albrighton'	EWes GEdr WAbe
- 'Apple Blossom'	EWes WFar WPGP
- 'Badger'	WAbe
- var. *baurii*	EWes
- 'Bridal Bouquet' (d)	EWes GEdr WFar
- 'Caro'	EWes
- 'Charlotte'	EWes
- 'Coconut Ice'	EPot EWes LEdu WPGP
- var. *confecta*	CElw EWes GEdr WFar
- 'Daphne Mary'	EWes
- 'David Scott'	EWes
- 'Dawn'	EWes GEdr
- 'Douglas'	EWes GEdr LEdu WPGP
- 'Dulcie'	EWes GEdr
- 'Emily Peel'	EWes GEdr
- 'Eva-Kate'	EWes GEdr
- 'Fred Broome'	EWes GEdr LEdu WAbe WFar
- 'Goliath'	EWes GEdr WIce
- 'Harlequin'	EWes GEdr
§ - 'Helen'	EWes GEdr LEdu WAbe WPGP
- 'Jacqueline Potterton'	EPot
- 'Jeanette'	EWes
- 'Kitty'	EWes WFar
- 'Lily Jean' (d)	EAri EWes GEdr WFar WIce
- 'Luna'	EWes
- 'Margaret Rose'	EWes
- 'Mars'	EWes GEdr GMaP LEdu WFar WPGP
- 'Monique'	EWes
- 'Perle'	EWes GEdr WAbe
- 'Picta' (v)	EWes LEdu
- 'Pink Pearl'	EWes WAbe
- var. *platypetala*	EWes GEdr
- 'Rebecca'	EWes
- 'Red King'	EWes
- red-flowered	SPlb
- 'Ruth'	EWes GEdr WFar
- 'Snow Flurry'	WIce
- 'Susan Garnett-Botfield'	EWes GEdr
- 'Tetra Pink'	EWes GEdr LRHS
- 'Tetra Red'	EGrI EWes GEdr WFar
- 'The Bride'	EWes GEdr
'Bernadette'	GEdr
'Betsy Carmine'	GEdr WFar
'Beverly' PBR	LCro
'Bright Eyes' (d)	EWes
'Candy Stripe'	EWes GEdr
'Carina'	EWes
'Caroline'	EWes WFar
'Cathy'	EWes
'Confusion'	EWes LEdu
'Dainty Dee' (d)	EWes
deflexa	EWes GEdr LEdu MNrw WFar WPGP
'Donald Mann'	EShb EWes GEdr WAbe
'Dusky'	EWes GEdr
'E.A. Bowles'	EWes WAbe WFar
'Fire Wings'	GEdr
'Flashing Ruby'	GEdr WFar
'Forge Robies'	EWes
'Garnett'	EWes WFar
'Gemma'	EWes
'Great Scot'	EWes GEdr WAbe
'Hebron Farm Biscuit'	see *Hypoxis parvula* var. *albiflora* 'Hebron Farm Biscuit'
'Hebron Farm Cerise'	see × *Rhodoxis* 'Hebron Farm Cerise'
'Hebron Farm Pink'	see × *Rhodoxis hybrida* 'Hebron Farm Pink'
'Hinky Pinky'	GEdr
'Holden Rose' (d)	WFar
'Hope' (d)	GEdr
'Janey'	GEdr
'Jeffrey'	GEdr
'Jehane'	GEdr
'Jupiter'	GEdr WFar
'Kiwi Joy' (d)	EAri EGrI EWes GEdr
'Knockdolian Red'	GEdr WFar
'Lisette'	EWes
'Midori'	EPfP EWes GEdr WFar
milloides	CAby EPot EWes GEdr LEdu LRHS WFar WIce WPGP
- 'Claret'	CElw ELon EWes GEdr LRHS SIvy WAbe WFar
- 'Claudia'	EPfP GMaP WFar
- 'Damask'	EWes LRHS
- 'Drakensberg Snow'	EWes GEdr
- giant	WFar
- 'Susan'	EWes
'Monty'	EWes GEdr WAbe WFar
'Mystery'	EWes WAbe
'Naomi'	EWes
'New Look'	EWes GEdr
'Ori Zuru'	GEdr
'Origami'	LEdu
'Pat Lacey'	EWes GEdr
'Paula'	GMaP
'Pink Glow'	GEdr
'Pink Ice'	GEdr
'Pinkeen'	EWes WAbe WFar
'Pinkie'	WFar
'Pintado'	EAri EWes GEdr GMaP LEdu WAbe WFar WIce WPGP
'Raspberry Ice'	WFar
'Rosie Lee'	EWes
'Ruby Giant'	GEdr WFar
'Sarniensis'	GEdr
'Shell Pink'	EWes
'Snow'	EWes
'Snow White'	EWes
'Starlett'	EWes
'Starry Eyes' (d)	EWes WFar
'Stella'	EWes GEdr WFar
'Summer Pink'	GEdr
'Sunburst'	GEdr
'Tetra Rose'	GEdr
'Tetra White'	see *R. baurii* 'Helen'
thodiana	EWes GEdr WFar
'Two Tone'	EWes GEdr
'Venetian'	WAbe WFar
'Westacre Picotee'	EWes GEdr

'White Prince'	WFar	*punjabensis*	WJur
'Wild Cherry Blossom'	EWes	*succedanea*	see *Toxicodendron succedaneum*
		trilobata	EBee

Rhodoleia (Hamamelidaceae)

championii	WPGP	§ *typhina*	CAgr CBcs CBrac CDoC CMac EAri
– B&SWJ 11603	WCru		EBee EGren EHeP ELan EPfP ERom
– FMWJ 13155	WCru		GKin IPap LCro LRHS MAsh MGos
– WWJ 11858	WCru		SAth SEND SGol SSta WFar WJur
henryi	EBee WPGP		WSpi
aff. *henryi* B&SWJ 11782	WCru	§ – 'Dissecta' ♀H6	CBcs CDoC CMac CWnw EBee
– DJHV 640	WCru		EGren EHeP ELan EPfP LCro LRHS
parvipetala FMWJ 13422	WCru		MGos MPri SArc SEND SGol WFar
– WWJ 11866	WCru	– 'Laciniata' hort.	see *R. typhina* 'Dissecta'
– WWJ 11943	WCru	– RADIANCE ('Sinrus') ♀H6	LRHS MBlu SPoG
		– TIGER EYES	CBcs CDoC CWal CWnw EBee
		('Bailtiger'PBR) ♀H6	ELan EPfP EUrb IArd LCro LRHS

Rhodophiala (Amaryllidaceae)

bifida	MCtn		LSRN MAsh MGos MPri NCth SGol
rosea	GKev LAma WCot		SMad WSpi
		vernicifluo	see *Toxicodendron vernicifluum*

Rhodotypos (Rosaceae)

Rhynchospora (Cyperaceae)

kerrioides	see *R. scandens*	*colorata*	CWat LCro NPer
§ *scandens*	CBcs CExl EBee EPfP ESwi GKev	*latifolia*	SMad
	LEdu NLar NQui SPoG WCru WJur		

× Rhodoxis ✿ (Hypoxidaceae)

Ribes ✿ (Grossulariaceae)

'Abigail'	EWes GEdr WFar	*alpinum*	NAts SRms WKor WSpi
'Aurora'	EWes LRHS WFar	*americanum* 'Variegatum'	NLar
'Betsy'	EWes	(v)	
'Bloodstone'	EWes	*aureum* misapplied	see *R. odoratum*
FAIRYTALE ('Hil200802'PBR)	EAri IBal	*aureum* ambig.	CAgr WKor
'Hebron Farm Biscuit'	see *Hypoxis parvula* var. *albiflora*	*aureum* Pursh	EGrI
	'Hebron Farm Biscuit'	– subsp. *gracillimum*	SBrt
§ 'Hebron Farm Cerise'	CElw EWes GEdr LEdu LRHS WFar	§ × *beatonii*	CMac EBee EGrI EPfP EWld LEdu
§ *hybrida*	EWes		LSto MMuc NCth NLar SBeP SGol
– 'Aya San'	EWes LRHS WFar		SPoG SRms WCot WMal WSpi
§ – 'Hebron Farm Pink'	CElw EWes GEdr LRHS WFar WIce	'Ben Hope' (B)	CAgr CDoC CSBt EBee EPom GQue
– 'Hebron Farm Red Eye'	EWes GEdr LRHS WAbe WFar WIce		LRHS MPri SPoG
– 'Ruby Giant'	EWes GEdr	'Black Velvet' (D)	CAgr
– 'White Stars'	EWes	*bracteosum* B&SWJ 14159	WCru
'Little Pink Pet'	EWes WFar	*cereum*	SBrt
'Otterlo Ruby'	WFar	× *culverwellii* (F)	CAgr EPom LBuc LCro LEdu NLar
'Sandy'	EWes		SBmr SVic
'Sue'	EWes WFar	*divaricatum*	CAgr LEdu WKor
(Summer Stars Series)	WFar	*gayanum*	LEdu NLar WKor
'Summer Stars Peppermint'		*glaciale* PAB 3004	LEdu
– 'Summer Stars Pink Blush'	WFar	× *gordonianum*	see *R.* × *beatonii*
– 'Summer Stars Pinky'	CDoC WFar	*griffithii*	WCot
		– GWJ 9331	WCru
		– PAB 4871	LEdu

Rhoicissus (Vitaceae)

digitata	EShb	jostaberry	see *R.* × *nidigrolaria*
		laurifolium	CBcs CEnd EBee ELan EWes LRHS

Rhopalostylis ✿ (Arecaceae)

sapida	CTsd		LSto MAsh NLar WSpi
		– (f)	EPfP SBrt SRms
		– (m)	CBct CMac LCro WFar WMal

rhubarb see *Rheum* × *hybridum*; also AGM Vegetables Section

– 'Mrs Amy Doncaster'   CBcs CMac EBee EPfP LEdu LRHS
LSto MAsh NLar SBrt SMad SPoG
SRms WCot WLov WMal WSpi

Rhus ✿ (Anacardiaceae)

ambigua	see *Toxicodendron orientale*	– Rosemoor form	CDoC EBee EPfP NLar SPoG WCot
aromatica	CAgr NLar WKor		WMal
chinensis	CBcs	*malvaceum*	SBrt
cotinus	see *Cotinus coggygria*	*menziesii*	EWes NQui WCot
glabra	CBcs CWnw	*nevadense*	SBrt
– 'Laciniata' ambig.	CWnw EGrI MPri WFar	§ × *nidigrolaria* (F)	CDoC CMac EGren LWaG MAsh
hirta	see *R. typhina*		MEar SEdi SPoG
incisa	see *Searsia incisa*	– black-fruited (F)	EGren
potaninii	ELan NLar WJur WPGP	– red-fruited (F)	LWaG
× *pulvinata* (Autumn Lace Group) 'Red Autumn Lace' ♀H6	MBlu	*nigrum* (B)	SAth
		– 'Baldwin' (B)	LCro NLar SEdi SSFr WMat
		– 'Barchatnaja' (B)	CAgr
		– 'Ben Alder' (B)	CAgr EPom LRHS SRms WFar
		– 'Ben Connan' (B) ♀H6	CAgr CBTr CMac CSBt EPfP EPom
			LBuc LCro LRHS LSRN MAsh MGos

- 'Ben Gairn' (B)	MNHC NLar SBmr SEND SPoG SRms SSFr WMat CAgr MMuc
- 'Ben Lomond' PBR (B)	CAgr CBTr CDoC CSBt EGren EPom LBuc LRHS LSRN MAsh MGos NLar SBmr SEdi SPoG SRms SSFr SVic WFar WMat
- 'Ben More' (B)	CAgr CBTr MPri NLar SOrN
- 'Ben Nevis' (B)	CAgr EBee EGren MEar SEdi WFar
- 'Ben Sarek' (B)	CAgr CBTr CDoC CMac EBee EGren EPfP EPom LBuc LCro LRHS LSRN MAsh MGos NLar SBmr SEdi SOrN SRms SSFr WFar WMat
- 'Ben Tirran' (B)	CAgr CDoC CSBt EPom LBuc LRHS LSRN MAsh MGos NLar SRms WFar WMat
- 'Big Ben' PBR (B) ♀H6	CDoC EPom LBuc LCro LRHS LSRN MEar SBmr SPoG WMat
- 'Black Reward' (B)	CAgr
- BLACK'N'RED PREMIERE (B)	CBTr MNHC SPoG
- 'Boskoop Giant' (B)	CAgr ELan
- 'Byelorussian Sweet' (B)	CAgr
- 'Cassis Blanc' (B)	CAgr
- 'Ebony' (B)	CMac EPom SVic
- 'Goliath' (B)	MPri
- 'Hystawneznaya' (B)	CAgr
- 'Jet' (B)	CAgr
- 'Kosmicheskaya' (B)	CAgr
- 'Pilot Alexander Mamkin' (B)	CAgr
- 'Polar' (B)	CAgr
- 'Seabrook's' (B)	CAgr
- 'Titania' (B)	CBTr CoPl EGren LRHS NLar SBmr SEdi SPoG WFar WJur WMat
- 'Vertti' (B)	CAgr
- 'Wellington XXX' (B)	CAgr EGren SEdi SSFr
§ *odoratum*	CBcs CMac EBee EHeP ELan ELon EPfP EWld LSto MGos MMrt MMuc MNrw NLar SPoG SRms WCot WSpi
- 'Crandall' (F)	CAgr LEdu MEar
- 'Dorotheas Early' (F)	LEdu WPGP
orientale PAB 7066	LEdu
praecox	MMuc SEND
rubrum 'Blanka' (W) ♀H6	CAgr CMac EPfP LRHS SVic
- 'Cascade' (R)	CAgr
- 'Cherry' (R)	CAgr
- 'Gloire de Sablons' (P)	EPom LCro MAsh SPoG SRms
- 'Jonkheer van Tets' (R) ♀H6	CAgr CDoC CSBt EGren EHet ELan EPfP EPom IArd LCro LRHS MPri NLar SBmr SEdi SEND SRms SSFr WFar WMat
- 'Junifer' (R)	CAgr CMac EPom NLar
- 'Laxton's Number One' (R)	CAgr CDoC EPom LCro LSRN LWaG NLar SPoG SRms SSFr WMat
- 'Red Lake' (R) ♀H6	CAgr EGren ELan EPfP EPom LBuc MGos MPri NLar SEdi SPoG SRms SSFr WFar WMat
- 'Redstart' (R)	CAgr LBuc MMuc WMat
- 'Rolan' (R)	CAgr
- 'Rondom' (R)	CAgr SVic
- 'Rosetta' (R)	CAgr CDoC LCro LRHS SRms
- 'Rovada' (R) ♀H6	CAgr CMac CoPl CSBt EHet ELan EPfP EPom LBuc LRHS LSRN MAsh MNHC NLar SEdi SPoG SRms SVic WFar WMat
- 'Stanza' (R) ♀H6	CAgr MEar SEND
- 'Versailles' (R)	MAsh SBmr
§ - 'Versailles Blanche' (W/C)	CAgr CSBt EGren EHet EPfP EPom GQue LBuc LCro LSRN MMuc MPri SBmr SEdi SRms SSFr
- 'Weisse Langtraubige' (W)	CAgr
- 'White Grape' (W) ♀H6	LEdu
- 'White Pearl' (W)	CoPl ELan SEdi SVic
- WHITE VERSAILLES	see *R. rubrum* 'Versailles Blanche'
sanguineum	EHeP
- 'Alan Grey'	WCot
- AMORE ('Annys2003') PBR	LCro
- 'Barbie Pink'	WCot
- 'Brianjou'	SRms
- 'Brocklebankii'	CMac SRms
- 'Elkington's White'	ECul EPfP LCro LSRN LSto MAsh MGos SRms WCot WSpi
- 'King Edward VII'	CBcs CBrac CDoC CMac EBee EGrI EHeP ELan EPfP LBuc LCro LRHS LSto MGos MHer NLar SEWo SGol SRms WFar
- 'Koja' ♀H6	EPfP LSRN MGos MMuc SGol SPoG SRms WCot WFar WSpi
- 'Lombartsii' ♀H6	EPfP WCot
- 'Poky's Pink' ♀H6	EBee EPfP LRHS MAsh SPoG SRms
- 'Pulborough Scarlet'	CBcs CBrac CDoC CMac EBee EGrI EGren ELan EPfP GAbr LCro LRHS MArl MAsh MGos MHtn NBir NLar SGol SPlb SPoG SRms WFar WSpi
- 'Red Bross'	EPfP LRHS MAsh MPri
- 'Red Pimpernel'	MAsh SRms WFar
- 'Somerset White'	CWnw EPfP MAsh
- 'Tydeman's White'	WSpi
- var. *variegata*	CMac
- WHITE ICICLE ('Ubric') ♀H6	CBcs CDoC EBee ELan EPfP LSto MArl MAsh MBlu MHer NBir SPoG SRms WFar
speciosum ♀H4	CBcs CBct CDoC CEnd CMac CWal EBee EGrI EPfP EWes LCro LRHS MGos MMuc MNrw NLar SEND SPoG SRms WFar WMal
uva-crispa 'Annelii' (F)	CAgr
- 'Captivator' (C)	CBTr CDoC CMac EPom LBuc LCro LRHS MAsh NLar SPoG SRms SVic WMat
- 'Careless' (C/D) ♀H6	EGren EPom LSRN MAsh MGos SEdi WFar
- 'Early Sulphur' (D)	ELan
- 'Greenfinch' (C) ♀H6	CAgr
- 'Hinnonmäki' (D)	CAgr
- 'Hinnonmäki Grön' (D)	CAgr CBTr CDoC CMac CSBt EBee EGren EPom LCro LRHS LSRN MAsh SBmr SEdi SPoG SRms WFar
- 'Hinnonmäki Gul' (D)	CAgr CBTr CDoC CMac CSBt EBee EGren EHet EPfP EPom LCro LRHS MAsh MGos SBmr SEdi SPoG SRms SSFr SVic WFar WMat
- 'Hinnonmäki Röd' (C/D)	CAgr CBTr CDoC CMac CoPl CSBt EBee EGren EPfP EPom LBuc LCro LEdu LRHS LSRN MAsh MPri NLar SBmr SEdi SPoG SPre SRms SSFr SVic WFar WJur WMat
- 'Invicta' (C/D) ♀H6	CAgr CBTr CDoC CMac CSBt EGren EPfP EPom LBuc LCro LRHS LSRN MAsh MGos MNHC MPri NLar SBmr SEdi SEND SPoG SRms SSFr SVic WFar WMat
- 'Jubilee' (C/D)	LBuc
- 'Jubilee Careless' (C/D)	EPom
- 'Larell' (C/D)	CAgr
- 'Leveller' (D) ♀H6	EGren SEdi
- 'Mucurines' (D)	CAgr
- 'Pax' (D)	CAgr MMuc SSFr SVic
- REDEVA PBR (D)	CAgr
- 'Rokula' (C/D)	ELan WMat
- 'Spinefree' (C)	CAgr

Rodgersia 595

- 'Whinham's Industry' (C/D) ⚥H6	EGren ELan LBuc MGos SEdi SEND SRms	- - 'Cherry Blush'	NLar
- XENIA ('Rafzuera'PBR) (D)	EPom LCro SPoG SVic WMat	- - hybrid	NLar
valdivianum	WCot WFar	- large-leaved	EBee EBlo
viburnifolium	NLar SEND	- 'Red Leaf'	GQue
'Worcesterberry' (C)	CHab	'Badenweiler'	EBlo ECha
		'Blickfang' ⚥H6	EBlo
		'Bloody Mary'	WFar

Ricinus (Euphorbiaceae)

communis	CDTJ CSpe LWaG SPlb	'Bronze Peacock'	CBWd CCht CMiW CPud CTsd CWnw EAri EBee ELan EUrb GAbr GElm GKev LCro LRHS LSto MArl MHol NCth NEoE NLar SArc SDix SHor SMrm SPeP SPoG SRkn WNPC
- 'Bolivian Red'	EAri ELan		
- 'Carmencita' ⚥H2	MCtn		
- 'Carmencita Bright Red'	EAri		
- 'Carmencita Pink'	CDTJ EAri LWaG	'Dark Pokers'	MHol NCth NLar SRms
- 'Carmencita Red'	CDTJ SBig	'Die Anmutige'	SMHy
- 'Dominican Republic'	CDTJ	'Die Schöne'	NLar
- 'Gibsonii'	CDTJ MCtn	'Die Stolze'	LEdu
- 'Impala'	CDTJ MCtn	'Grande Blanche'	EBlo LRHS
- 'New Zealand Black'	CDTJ CSpe EShb MCtn	'Herkules'	ECha ELon GMaP LEdu MBNS MMuc NLar NQui WCot
- 'Zanzi Palm'	MCtn		
- 'Zanzibariensis' ⚥H2	CDTJ EAri MCtn	'Irish Bronze' ⚥H6	EBlo EMor EPfP GBin GPSL LEdu LRHS LSRN LSto MArl MHer NSti WCAu WChS WCot WFar WPnP

Ridolfia (Apiaceae)

segetum	LCro SPhx	'Kupfermond'	EBlo LRHS NBir
		'La Blanche'	ELon LEdu LRHS MHol NLar

Rigidella see *Tigridia*

nepalensis — LEdu WPGP

Riocreuxia (Apocynaceae)

		- HWJK 2140	WCru
		- 'High Flier'	WCru
torulosa	SPlb	'Parasol'	CBro CDor CMac NBir
		pinnata	CPud CSpe EGren EHeP GMaP GQue LEdu LRHS LSRN MGos SArc SPeP SRms WCot WPnP

Robinia (Fabaceae)

hispida	CBcs CEnd EUrb MBlu WJur		
- var. *kelseyi*	WSpi	- B&SWJ 7741A	CBcs WCru
- 'Macrophylla'	CEnd	- L 1670	CExl ELan
- var. *rosea*	LSRN	- 'Alba'	EMor LShi
× *margaretta* CASQUE ROUGE	see *R.* × *margaretta* 'Pink Cascade'	- 'Buckland Beauty' ⚥H6	CDor EBlo LRHS WFar
		- 'Cally Salmon'	EWes GQue
§ - 'Pink Cascade'	CEnd EBee EGren EHeP ELan EPfP IPap LCro LRHS MAsh MGos NPip SGol WMat	- 'Candy Clouds' (d)	NLar
		- 'Chocolate Wing'	Widely available
		- 'Crûg Cardinal'	EBlo ELon GBin NLar WCru
pseudoacacia	CAgr EHeP ELan IPap LBuc MMuc SEND SGol SPlb WJur	- 'Elegans' ⚥H6	CDor CPud EBee EBlo EMor EPfP GKev GMaP LEdu LRHS MArl MAvo MSwo SDix SPoG SRms WCAu WPnP
- 'Bessoniana'	EHeP ELan		
- 'Frisia'	CBcs CBrac CBTr EBee EGren EHeP ELan IPap LCro LRHS LSRN MGos MSwo NLar NPip SEND SGol WFar WHtc WMat	- 'Fireworks'PBR	EBee NLar
		- 'Jade Dragon Mountain'	LEdu
		- 'Maurice Mason' ⚥H6	CExl EBlo GKev LRHS NLar
		- 'Pink Beauty'	EBee
- 'Inermis' hort.	see *R. pseudoacacia* 'Umbraculifera'	- pink-flowered	WCru
§ - 'Lace Lady'PBR	CBTr CDoC CSbt EBee ELan EPfP EUrb LBuc LCro LRHS MAsh MGos MPri NLar SArc SMad SPoG WHtc WMat	- 'Rubra' **new**	EBlo
		- 'Shangri-La'	WCru
		- 'Snow Clouds'	EBee NCth
		- 'Superba' ⚥H6	CLil CMac EBee EBlo ECha EGren GAbr GKev GMaP LCro LRHS MBel NBir NPer SMad WFar WPnP
- var. *rectissima*	WJur		
- 'Tortuosa'	CEnd		
- 'Twisty Baby'	see *R. pseudoacacia* 'Lace Lady'	- white-flowered	WCru
§ - 'Umbraculifera'	LSRN SArc	*podophylla*	CAby CExl CMac EBlo ECha ELon EPPr GAbr GKev GMaP GQue LCro LEdu LRHS MMuc NBid NBir NCth NLar NRya NSti SDix SMHy WChS WCru WFar WHoo
× *slavinii* 'Hillieri' ⚥H6	CEnd ELan LSRN MAsh MBlu WSpi		

Rochea see *Crassula*

Rodgersia (Saxifragaceae)

CLD 1432	CExl	- B&SWJ 10818	WCru
from Castlewellan	EBlo LRHS	- B&SWJ 10823	WCru
from Tibet	EBee EBlo LRHS	- 'Braunlaub'	LCro NBro SMad
aesculifolia ⚥H6	CBcs CDoC CDor CExl CLil CMac CPud EBee EGren EHeP ELan ELon EMor EPfP GKev GMaP GQue LCro LRHS MHer MSwo NLar SMrm SPeP SPlb SRms WCAu WPnP WTre	- 'Crûg's Colossus'	WCru
		- 'Flowering Fountain'	WCru
		- 'Rotlaub' ⚥H6	EBee EBlo GBin
		- 'Smaragd'	CToG EBee EBlo LRHS NBir NLar
		purdomii hort.	CMac EBlo LRHS WCot WPGP
- SSSE 36	SMHy	*sambucifolia*	CBcs CLil CMac EBlo GKev LEdu LRHS MMuc NBir NLar SEND WCAu WFar WPnP
- var. *henrici*	CLil EBlo EGren GElm NBro WCAu		
- - KW 21015	WCru		

- B&SWJ 7899 — WCru
- large, red-stemmed — NBir
- 'Mountain Select' — EBee
- 'Stoke Gabriel' — WKif
- *tabularis* — see *Astilboides tabularis*

Rohdea (Asparagaceae)
delavayi — WCot
japonica — CMac WCot WPGP
- B&SWJ 4853 — WCru
- B&SWJ 5091 — WCru
- 'Godaishu' (v) — WCot
- 'Gunjaku' (v) — EPPr WCot
- 'Lance Leaf' — WPGP
- long-leaved — WCot
- 'Miyakonojo' (v) — WCot
- 'Talbot Manor' (v) — CBct WCot WPGP
- 'Tama-jishi' (v) — WCot
- 'Tuneshige Rokujo' (v) — WCot
pachynema — WCot
§ *tonkinensis* HWJ 562 — WCru
watanabei B&SWJ 1911 — WCru
wattii — WCot

Roldana (Asteraceae)
§ *cristobalensis* — CSpe WCot
§ *petasitis* — CAbb CBct CHll EAri WCot WCru
- purple-leaved — CoPl

Romanzoffia (Boraginaceae)
unalaschcensis — SRms

Romneya (Papaveraceae)
coulteri ♀H5 — Widely available
§ - 'White Cloud' ♀H5 — CExl EBee SChF WPGP WSpi
× *hybrida* hort. — see *R. coulteri* 'White Cloud'

Romulea (Iridaceae)
bulbocodium — MCtn
- var. *crocea* — GKev
macowanii var. *alticola* — GArf
pratensis — GKev
ramiflora — CExl
requienii — EDAr

Rosa ✿ (Rosaceae)
W&O 9219 (CI) — GGro
'A Faithful Friend' (F) — ESty NTrD
A MILLION DREAMS ('Foramill') (HT) — ESty
A SHROPSHIRE LAD ('Ausled') (S) ♀H6 — SPoG
A WHITER SHADE OF PALE ('Peafanfare'^PBR) (HT) ♀H6 — CBcs CDoC CSBt EBls EGren ELan EPfP ESty LBuc LCro LRHS LSRN MAsh MGos MPro SPoG SSea
ABRACADABRA ('Korhocsel') (HT) — ESty
ABRAHAM DARBY ('Auscot') (S) — ETWh LSRN
ABSENT FRIENDS ('Dicemblem'^PBR) (F) — ESty
ABSOLUTELY CRACKERS ('Raw1252') (F) — ESty
ABSOLUTELY FABULOUS ('Wekvossutono'^PBR) (F) ♀H6 — CDoC EBls EGren ELan EPfP ESty LBuc LRHS LSRN MAsh MGos MPri MPro NLar SEas SPad SPoG SSea SWCr
abyssinica — LEdu
ACAPELLA — see *R.* CHARLIE'S ROSE
acicularis — EBls
var. *nipponensis*
'Adam' (CIT) — EBls
'Adam Messerich' (Bb) — EBls ETWh NLar
'Adélaïde d'Orléans' (Ra) ♀H6 — CRHN EBls EPfP ETWh LRHS SEND
ADMIRAL ('Tan08996'^PBR) — CDoC LCro SEas SSea
'Agatha' (G) — EBls
AGATHA CHRISTIE ('Kormeita') (CIF) — EBls EPfP LBuc LRHS LSRN
'Aglaia' (Ra) — ETWh
'Agnes' (Ru) — CDoC EBls ETWh IArd MGos NLar
'Aimée Vibert' (N) — EBee EBls ETWh NLar
ALABASTER ('Tan02226'^PBR) **new** — SReu
'Alain Blanchard' (G) — EBls ETWh
ALAN TITCHMARSH ('Ausjive'^PBR) (S) — LCro
ALAN'S PRIDE ('Smiheap3') (F) **new** — ESty
ALASKA ('Korjoslio'^PBR) (ClHT) — ESty SSea
§ × *alba* 'Alba Maxima' (A) ♀H6 — EBls ETWh GAbr LRHS MAsh MPri NLar SEND
§ - 'Alba Semiplena' (A) ♀H6 — EBls ETWh NLar
- CELESTIAL — see *R.* 'Céleste'
'Albéric Barbier' (Ra) ♀H5 — CBcs CDoC CEnd CRHN EBee EBls EPfP ETWh LBom LCro LRHS NLar SEas SEND SHor SWCr WHer
'Albertine' (Ra) ♀H6 — CBcs CDoC CEnd CSBt EBls EGren ELan EPfP ESty ETWh LCro LRHS MAsh MGos MNHC MPri NLar SEas SPoG SSea SWCr
'Alchymist' (ClS) — CRHN EBls ESty ETWh SWCr
ALEC'S RED ('Cored') (HT) — CBcs EBls EGren LSRN MGos SPoG SWCr
ALEXANDER ('Harlex') (HT) ♀H6 — EBls EGren LSRN
'Alexander Hill Gray' (T) — EBls
'Alexandre Girault' (Ra) ♀H6 — CRHN EBee EBls ETWh LRHS WHer
'Alfred Colomb' (HP) — EBls
'Alfred de Dalmas' misapplied — see *R.* 'Mousseline'
ALFRED SISLEY ('Delstrijor'^PBR) (S) — ESty
'Alfresco'^PBR (ClHT) — MGos SEas
§ 'Alibaba'^PBR (ClHT) ♀H6 — CDoC CSBt ELan EPfP ESty LSRN MPri SEas SPoG SWCr
ALICE ('Guestrive') (CI) **new** — ESty
'Alida Lovett' (Ra) — CRHN
ALISON ('Coclibee') (F) — LSRN
ALISSAR, PRINCESS OF PHOENICIA ('Harsidon'^PBR) (S) — LRHS NLar
'Alister Stella Gray' (N) ♀H5 — EBls EHeP ESty ETWh MMuc NLar
ALL AMERICAN MAGIC ('Meiroylear'^PBR) (HT) — ESty
ALL MY LOVING ('Fryrisky') (HT) — EBls LRHS MAsh SPoG SWCr
ALL THAT'S JAZZ ('Twoadvance') **new** — LBom
ALL THE BEST ('Raw2540') (HT) — ESty
'Allen Chandler' (ClHT) — EBls
ALNWICK CASTLE — see *R.* THE ALNWICK ROSE
'Aloha' (ClHT) ♀H6 — EBee EBls EGren EPfP ESty ETWh MGos NLar SPoG SRGP SWCr
alpina — see *R. pendulina*
'Alpine Sunset' (HT) — EGren MGos SPoG
altaica misapplied — see *R. spinosissima* 'Grandiflora'
altaica Willd. — see *R. spinosissima*
ALTISSIMO ('Delmur') (Cl) — CEnd EBls EGren ETWh SSea
ALWAYS REMEMBER ME ('Macpadspo') (HT) — LSRN

ALWAYS REMEMBERED ('Raw1114') (HT) — ESty
ALWAYS YOU ('Webalways') (HT) — ESty
AMADEUS ('Korlabriax') (CI) — EHeP
'Amadis' (Bs) — ETWh
AMANDA ('Beesian') (F) — EBls ESty
'Amanda Paternotte' (D) — ETWh
AMAZING DAY ('Raw1113') (S) — ESty
'Amazing Grace' (HT) — EGren
'Ambassador Nogami' (S) — EBls
AMBER QUEEN ('Harroony') (F) ♀H6 — EGren EHeP ELan IArd LBuc LCro SWCr
AMBER SWEET DREAM ('Fryritz') (Patio) — CDoC CSBt MGos
'Amélia' — see *R.* 'Celsiana'
AMELIA ('Poulen011'^PBR) (Renaissance Series) (S) — ETWh
AMÉLIE NOTHOMB ('Delathom') (HT) — EBls
'American Pillar' (Ra) — CDoC CEnd EBls EGren EGrI EHeP ELan EPfP ETWh LCro LRHS MAsh MGos NLar SPoG SWCr
AMETHYST QUEEN ('Raw1074') (F) — ESty
AMNESTY INTERNATIONAL ('Delcreja') (CI) — EBls ESty SEas SSea
'Amy Robsart' (RH) — EBls
'Anemone' (CI) — EBls ETWh
anemonoides — see *R.* 'Anemone'
ANGEL EYES ('Albravo') (HT) — EBls LRHS MAsh MPri SEas SWCr
'Angel Wings' (HT) — MCtn
ANGELA ('Grifgela') (S) — LSRN NLar
ANGELA RIPPON ('Ocaru') (Min) — CSBt
ANN ('Ausfete') (S) — LSRN
ANN ('Raw2717') (F) **new** — ESty
'Anna Pavlova' (HT) — EBls
ANNE BOLEYN ('Ausecret'^PBR) (S) — LBom
'Anne of Geierstein' (RH) — EBls
ANNE'S ROSE ('Frynippy'^PBR) (F) — EBls LRHS LSRN MAsh SWCr
ANNIVERSARY WALTZ ('Raw237') (HT) — ESty
ANNIVERSARY WISHES ('Noa140721') (F) — EBls LBuc LCro LRHS MAsh SWCr
'Anthony' (S) — EBls
ANTIQUE '89 ('Kordalen') (CIF) — EBls ETWh NLar
APHRODITE ('Tan00847'^PBR) (S) ♀H6 — EBee ESty ETWh LSRN
APHRODITE ('Tanetidor') (HT) — ELan LCro LRHS NLar SSea
apothecary's rose — see *R. gallica* var. *officinalis*
'Apple Blossom' (Ra) — EBls SHar
'Archiduc Joseph' misapplied — see *R.* 'Général Schablikine'
'Ards Rover' (CIHP) — EBls
'Arethusa' (Ch) — ETWh
§ *arkansana* var. *suffulta* — EBls ETWh
ARMADA ('Haruseful') (S) — EBls
'Arthur Bell' (F) ♀H6 — Widely available
'Arthur de Sansal' (DPo) — ETWh
arvensis — CBWd CCVT CHab CLnd EBls ETWh LDrf
AS GOOD AS IT GETS ('Basgoodas') (F) — EBls LBuc
§ 'Aschermittwoch' (CIHR) — EBls
ASCOT ('Tan01757'^PBR) (HT) — SEas
ASH WEDNESDAY — see *R.* 'Aschermittwoch'
'Astra Desmond' (Ra) — EBls ETWh MNrw
I 'At Peace Rose' (HT) — LSRN NTrD

ATTLEBOROUGH ('Beaat') (ClHT) — EBls
AUDIENZ — see *R.* TIMELESS CREAM
AUDREY (Fragrant Bella Series) — see *R.* JELENA (Frayla Series)
AUDREY WILCOX ('Frywilrey') (HT) — ELon
Austrian copper rose — see *R. foetida* 'Bicolor'
'Autumn Delight' (HM) — ETWh
AUTUMN FIRE — see *R.* 'Herbstfeuer'
AUTUMN SONG — see *R.* PURE POETRY
'Autumn Sunset' (ClS) — EBls
AVA (Fragrant Bella Series) — see *R.* MILEVA (Frayla Series)
AVEC AMOUR ('Tan04341'^PBR) (HT) — SEas
'Aviateur Blériot' (Ra) — CRHN
AVON ('Poulmulti'^PBR) (GC) — EBls ETWh
AWAKENING ('Probuzeni') (ClHT) — CEnd EBee EBls EGren EPfP ETWh NLar SWCr
AYA ('Poulren021'^PBR) (Renaissance Series) (S) — ETWh
'Ayrshire Splendens' — see *R.* 'Splendens'
'Baby Faurax' (Poly) — EBls ETWh
BABY MASQUERADE ('Tanba') (Min) — EGren EHeP MGos
BABYFACE ('Rawril'^PBR) (Min) — ESty
'Ballerina' (HM/Poly) ♀H6 — CDoC CEnd CSBt CWal EBee EBls ELan EPfP ESty ETWh LCro LRHS LSRN MAsh MGos MPri NLar SDix SEas SMad SOrN SPoG SSea SWCr WKif
BALMORAL ('Poulcas027'^PBR) (Palace Series) (Patio) — EBls LRHS SWCr
BALOU — see *R.* FLOWER CARPET CHERRY
'Baltimore Belle' (Ra) — CRHN EBee EBls
banksiae (Ra) — SRms
- *alba* — see *R. banksiae* var. *banksiae*
§ - var. *banksiae* (Ra/d) — CBcs CExl CRHN CSBt EBls ELan EPfP ETWh LCro LRHS SMad WCot WLov
- 'Lutea' (Ra/d) ♀H5 — CBcs CSBt EBls EGren ELan EPfP ETWh LCro LRHS LSRN MGos SChF SEND SMad SMrm SNig SPoG SRkn SSea WCot WFar WHer WLov
- 'Lutescens' (Ra) — CExl EBee EBls ETWh WPGP
- var. *normalis* (Ra) — CExl CSBt EBee EBls SChF WCot WPGP
I - 'Rosea' (Ra) — CExl EPfP
'Bantry Bay' (ClHT) — EBls ELan LSRN SOrN
BARAKURA ('Beajap') (GC/S) — EBls
BARBARA ANN — see *R.* SCENT FROM HEAVEN
BARKAROLE ('Tanelorak') (HT) — SEas
'Baron Girod de l'Ain' (HP) — EBee EBls ETWh
'Baroness Rothschild' ambig. — see *R.* 'Baronne Adolph de Rothschild', *R.* BARONNE EDMOND DE ROTHSCHILD
§ 'Baronne Adolph de Rothschild' (HP) — EBls ETWh
§ BARONNE EDMOND DE ROTHSCHILD ('Meigriso') (HT) — EGren
'Baronne Prévost' (HP) — EBls EGren
BATHSHEBA ('Auschimbley'^PBR) (Cl) — EGren EPfP ESty IArd LBom LRHS MAsh NLar SWCr
× *beanii* (Ra) — SMad
BEATRIX POTTER ('Beafolly') (S) — EBls
BEAUTIFUL BRITAIN ('Dicfire') (F) — SWCr
BEAUTIFUL SUNRISE ('Bostimebide'^PBR) (ClPatio) — EGren SWCr

'Belinda' (HM)	EBls
BELLA CHRISTINA ('Mandella') (F)	LSRN
BELLA DIANA ('Mandiana') (F)	LSRN
BELLA ROSA ('Chewnicebell') (F)	LRHS
'Bellard' (G)	ETWh
'Belle Amour' (A × D)	ETWh NLar
'Belle de Crécy' (G)	CBcs EBls EPfP ETWh LCro LRHS MAsh MNrw MPri NLar SWCr
BELLE DE JOUR ('Delijaupar') (F)	CBcs CDoC CWal EBee EBls EPfP ESty ETWh LBuc LCro LRHS LSRN MAsh MGos MPro NLar SEas SHor SMad SSea SWCr
'Belle des Jardins' misapplied	see R. × centifolia 'Unique Panachée'
BELLE EPOQUE ('Adasilthe') (HT)	SWCr
BELLE EPOQUE ('Fryyaboo'PBR) (HT)	ESty LRHS
'Belle Isis' (G)	EBls ETWh NLar
BELLES RIVES ('Meizolnil') (HT)	EBls LRHS MAsh MPri
'Belvedere' (Ra) ♀H6	ETWh NLar
BENJAMIN BRITTEN ('Ausencart'PBR) (S)	SWCr
'Bennett's Seedling' (Ra)	ETWh
BERKSHIRE ('Korpinka') (GC) ♀H6	SWCr
BERRY DELIGHTFUL ('Chewdelight'PBR) (S)	EBls
BEST IMPRESSION ('Tan04247'PBR) (HT)	SEas
BEST OF FRIENDS ('Raw2330') (F)	ESty
BETTY HARKNESS ('Harette'PBR) (F)	LBuc
'Betty Sherriff' (Ra)	ETWh
BETTY'S SMILE ('Websmile') (HT)	LSRN
BIANCO ('Cocblanco') (Patio/Min)	CSBt
BIENVENUE ('Delrochipar') (Cl)	EBls
'Big Ben'	see R. 'Jack Hume'
BIRTHDAY BOY ('Tan97607'PBR) (HT)	CDoC CSBt ESty LSRN MGos MPro SEas SPoG SWCr
BIRTHDAY GIRL ('Meilasso') (F)	CDoC CSBt EBls EGren EPfP ESty LBuc LRHS LSRN MAsh MPri MSwo SEas SPoG SSea SWCr
BIRTHDAY SURPRISE ('Guesyoga') (F)	ESty
BIRTHDAY WISHES (Patio)	see R. SHRIMP HIT
BIRTHDAY WISHES ('Guesdelay') (HT)	EPfP LSRN SOrN SSea SWCr
BIRTHE KJÆR ('Poulren033') (Renaissance Series) (S)	ETWh
BLACK BACCARA ('Meidebenne'PBR) (HT)	EGren ETWh LCro SBmr
'Black Prince' (HP)	EBls
BLACKBERRY NIP ('Somnip'PBR) (HT)	ELon
'Blairii Number Two' (ClBb)	EBls ETWh NLar
Blanche Double de Coubert' (Ru) ♀H7	CBcs CDoC EBee EBls EGren EPfP ETWh GQue LBuc LCro LSRN NLar SWCr
'Blanche Moreau' (CeMo)	ETWh
'Blanchefleur' (Ce × G)	EBls ETWh
'Blessings' (HT)	EBls EGren LRHS LSRN MGos MSwo NTrD SWCr
'Bleu Magenta' (Ra) ♀H6	CRHN EBls ETWh IArd NLar
BLISS ('Kormarzau'PBR) (F)	EBls SEas
BLOOM OF RUTH ('Harmedley'PBR) (HT)	ESty
'Bloomfield Abundance' (Poly)	EBls ETWh
'Bloomfield Courage' (Ra)	ETWh
BLOOMING MARVELLOUS (Patio)	MNHC
BLUE DIAMOND ('Athysumo'PBR) (HT)	ESty
BLUE FOR YOU ('Pejamblu'PBR) (F) ♀H6	CDoC CEnd EBls EGren ELan ELon EPfP ESty LBuc LCro LRHS MAsh MGos MPri MPro SEas SMad SPoG SSea SWCr
BLUE MOON ('Tannacht') (HT)	CDoC EBls EGren ELan LRHS MGos MPro SEas SPoG SRGP SWCr
'Blush Boursault' (Bs)	MMuc
'Blush Damask' (D)	EBls
'Blush Excelsa' (Ra)	SWCr
'Blush Noisette'	see R. 'Noisette Carnée'
'Blush Rambler' (Ra)	CRHN EBls ETWh MMuc NLar
BLUSHING BRIDE ('Harfling') (F)	EGren
'Blushing Lucy' (Ra) ♀H6	CRHN ETWh MNrw NLar SMrm
'Bobbie James' (Ra) ♀H6	CRHN EBee EBls ETWh LRHS MGos MNrw NLar SEas SHor SWCr WFar
'Bobby Charlton' (HT)	LSRN
BOBBY DAZZLER ('Smi 13302'PBR) (F)	CDoC ESty MGos
'Bobolink' (Min)	EGren
'Bon Silène' (T)	EBls
BONICA ('Meidomonac') (GC) ♀H6	CDoC CSBt EBee EBls EGren ELan EPfP ESty ETWh LCro LRHS MAsh MNrw NLar SDix SEND SPoG SSea SWCr WCot WFar
BORDURE ABRICOT ('Delbora') (F)	EBls
BORDURE CAMAIEU ('Delcapo') (S)	EBls
BORN AGAIN	see R. RENAISSANCE
BOSCOBEL ('Auscousin'PBR) (S)	EGren ELan EPfP LBom LCro LRHS MBNS NLar SPoG SWCr
'Botzaris' (D)	ETWh NLar
'Boule de Neige' (Bb)	CBcs CSBt EBls ETWh LCro LRHS NLar
'Bouquet de Marie' (HP/N)	ETWh NLar
'Bouquet d'Or' (N)	EBls
BOUQUET PARFAIT ('Lenbofa') (HM)	EBls
'Bouquet Tout Fait' (N)	EBee ETWh
BOWLED OVER ('Tandolgnil'PBR) (F) ♀H6	SEas
§ bracteata (S)	EBls ETWh EWes SSea
BREATH OF LIFE ('Harquanne'PBR) (ClHT)	CDoC EBls EGren MGos NLar SWCr
'Brenda Colvin' (Ra)	EBls
BRENDA'S BEAUTY ('Guesjoyful') (S) new	ESty
BRIAN'S MAGIC ('Gueskiln') (F) new	ESty
BRIDE ('Fryyearn') (HT)	LSRN
'Bride and Groom'PBR (HT)	CDoC ESty LSRN SPoG SWCr
BRIDGE OF SIGHS ('Harglowing'PBR) (Cl)	CDoC EHeP EPfP ESty LBuc MGos MNHC NLar SEas SPoG SWCr
BRIGHT AS A BUTTON ('Chewsumsigns'PBR) (S) ♀H5	EBls ETWh LRHS MAsh MPri NLar SEas SWCr

Bright Fire ('Peaxi'^PBR) (CIHT)	LRHS
Bright Future ('Kirora'^PBR) (CI)	CDoC ELan ELon ESty SRGP
Bright Ideas ('Horcoffdrop'^PBR) (CIHT)	EBls EPfP MPri SEas SWCr
Brilliant Pink Iceberg ('Probril') (F)	EGren
Bring Me Sunshine ('Ausernie'^PBR) (S)	LBom LRHS MAsh SPoG SWCr
Brother Cadfael ('Ausglobe'^PBR) (S)	ETWh SWCr
Brownie	see *R.* Chocolate Ripples
§ *brunonii* (Ra)	EBls EWes WFar
– HPA 1386 (Ra)	GGro
Brush-Strokes ('Guescolour') (F)	ESty SEas
'Buff Beauty' (HM) ♀^H6	CBcs CDoC CEnd CSBt EBee EBls EGren EPfP ETWh LCro LRHS NLar WFar
'Bullata'	see *R.* × *centifolia* 'Bullata'
§ 'Burgundiaca' (G)	EBls ETWh
§ Burgundy Ice ('Prose'^PBR) (F)	CWal EBee EBls EGren ELan EPfP LBuc LCro LRHS MGos MNHC MSwo NLar SEas SMad SPoG SSea SWCr WKif
'Burgundy Iceberg'^PBR	see *R.* Burgundy Ice
'Burgundy Rose'	see *R.* 'Burgundiaca'
burnet, double white	see *R. spinosissima* double, white-flowered
Burning Desire ('Frysizzle') (F)	EBls MAsh
Burning Desire ('Jacladin') (HT)	EBls LRHS MAsh SWCr
Buxom Beauty ('Korbilant'^PBR) (HT) ♀^H6	EBls LSRN MGos SSea
§ *caesia* subsp. *vosagiaca*	LRHS
Café au Lait ('Simgrey') (F)	ESty
californica 'Plena'	see *R. nutkana* 'Plena'
'Callisto' (HM)	ETWh NLar
Calypso ('Poulclimb') (CIHT)	ETWh NLar
'Camayeux' (G)	EBls ETWh
Cambridgeshire ('Korhaugen'^PBR) (County Series) (GC)	EBls ETWh SWCr
Camelot ('Tan05372'^PBR) (CIF)	ESty SSea
Camille Pissarro ('Delstricol') (F)	EBls ESty
'Canary Bird'	see *R. xanthina* 'Canary Bird'
Candy Land ('Wekrosopela') (CIHT)	ESty SSea
canina (S)	CBTr CBWd CCVT CHab CLnd CoPl EGren EHeP ELan EPfP EPom LBuc LCro LSto LWaG MCtn MSwo NLar SEWo WHnu WKor WMat WMou WRjT
'Cantabrigiensis' (S) ♀^H6	ETWh LRHS
§ Canzonetta ('Noa84497d') (F)	LRHS MAsh MPri SWCr
Capel Manor House ('Beajammie') (CIS)	EBls
'Capitaine John Ingram' (CeMo)	EBls ETWh NLar
Capri ('Tan08344'^PBR) (HT) **new**	SEas
Caprice de Meilland ('Meisionver'^PBR) (HT) **new**	EGren
'Captain Christy' (HT)	EPfP
'Cardinal de Richelieu' (G)	CBcs EBls EPfP ETWh LCro LRHS NLar SPoG SWCr
Carefree Days ('Meirivoui') (Patio) ♀^H6	CDoC EBls LBuc LRHS MPri MPro SPoG SSea SWCr
Cariad ('Auspanier'^PBR) (HM)	LRHS
Carimbo ('Poulcy032'^PBR)	LRHS
Carol ('Gueshope') (F)	ESty
Carol Ann ('Peapost') (F)	LSRN
'Caroline Testout'	see *R.* 'Madame Caroline Testout'
Caroline Victoria ('Harprior'^PBR) (HT)	LSRN
'Caroline's Heart' (S)	EBls
Carolyn Knight ('Austurner'^PBR) (S)	LCro SWCr
Carris ('Harmanna'^PBR) (HT)	LRHS NTrD
§ Casino ('Macca') (CIHT)	EBls ETWh LRHS
'Castle Shrimp Pink'	see *R.* Fascination
'Castle Yellow'	see *R.* Summer Gold
Catherine ('Guesgala') (*persica* hybrid) (F)	ESty
§ 'Cécile Brünner' (Poly) ♀^H5	EBee EBls ELan ETWh LRHS LSRN NLar SEas
Celebration Time ('Wekcobeju'^PBR) (F) ♀^H6	SEas
§ 'Céleste' (A) ♀^H6	EBls ETWh NLar SEND
'Célina' (CeMo)	LSRN
'Céline Forestier' (N)	EBee EBls ETWh
§ 'Celsiana' (D) ♀^H7	EBls ETWh LSRN NLar
Centenaire de Lourdes ('Delge') (F)	EBls
§ × *centifolia* (Ce)	EBls ETWh
§ – 'Bullata' (Ce)	EBls
§ – 'Cristata' (Ce) ♀^H6	EBls EGren ETWh LCro
§ – De Meaux' (Ce)	EBls ETWh NLar
§ – 'Muscosa' (CeMo)	EBls ETWh
– 'Parvifolia'	see *R.* 'Burgundiaca'
§ – 'Shailer's White Moss' (CeMo)	EBls ETWh
– 'Spong' (Ce)	ETWh
§ – 'Unique' (Ce)	EBls ETWh NLar
§ – 'Unique Panachée' (Ce)	EBls ETWh
'Centifolia Variegata'	see *R.* × *centifolia* 'Unique Panachée'
Centre Stage ('Chewcreepy'^PBR) (S/GC) ♀^H6	EPfP SWCr
'Cerise Bouquet' (S) ♀^H6	EBls ETWh WSpi
'C.F. Meyer'	see *R.* 'Conrad Ferdinand Meyer'
Champagne Celebration ('Frylimbo') (HT)	EBls EPfP MAsh
Champagne Celebration ('Simluck') (F)	SWCr
Champagne Cocktail ('Horflash') (F)	EGren
§ Champagne Moment ('Korvanaber'^PBR) (F) ♀^H6	CBcs CDoC CEnd CSBt EBls EGren ELan EPfP ESty LBuc LCro LRHS LSRN MAsh MGos MPri SEas SMad SPoG SSea SWCr
Chandos Beauty ('Harmisty'^PBR) (HT) ♀^H6	CDoC EGren EHeP EPfP ESty ETWh LBuc LRHS LSRN MGos MPro NLar SEas SHor SPoG SSea SWCr
'Chanelle' (F)	EBls EGren SDix
Chapeau de Napoléon	see *R.* × *centifolia* 'Cristata'
Chardonnay ('Simtely') (F)	ESty
Charisma ('Jelroganor') (F)	MPri
Charisma ('Noa16071'^PBR) (HT)	EBls EPfP LBuc LCro LRHS SPoG SWCr

Rosa

CHARLES AUSTIN ('Ausles') (S) — ETWh MGos NLar SEas
CHARLES DARWIN ('Auspeet'^PBR) (S) — EGren ELan EPfP ESty LRHS MAsh MBNS NLar SWCr
'Charles de Mills' (G) ♀H6 — CDoC EBls EGren ELan ETWh LCro LRHS MGos MSwo NLar WHer WKif
CHARLES DICKENS ('Raw1064') (HT) — ESty
§ CHARLIE'S ROSE ('Tanallepa') (HT) ♀H6 — ELan ESty MPro SEas
CHARLOTTE ('Auspoly'^PBR) (S) ♀H6 — EGren LCro MBNS SWCr
CHARTREUSE DE PARME ('Delviola') (S) — EBls ESty ETWh NLar
CHAWTON COTTAGE ('Harxcel') (S) — EHeP NLar
CHECKMATE ('Diclanky') (CIF) — CDoC
§ CHEEK TO CHEEK ('Poulslas'^PBR) (Courtyard Series) (CIMin) — EBls
CHERISHED PET ('Gues11-50') (F) — ESty
CHERRY BONICA ('Meipeporia'^PBR) (S) — CDoC SEas SWCr
CHERRY GIRL ('Korkosieb'^PBR) (F) — EBls EPfP LRHS MAsh SWCr
'Cheshire Life' (HT) — EGren
'Chevy Chase' (Ra) — EBls SEas
'Chewton Rose' (S) — EBls
CHIANTI ('Auswine') (S) — ETWh NLar
CHICAGO PEACE ('Johnago') (HT) — EBls EGren
CHILD OF MY HEART ('Beapeace') (HT) — EBls
CHILTERNS ('Kortemma') (GC) — CBcs SWCr
'Chinatown' (CIF) ♀H6 — EGren LRHS MAsh MGos MPri SWCr
chinensis Jacq. (S) — EBls
- 'Minima' *sensu stricto* hort. — see *R.* 'Rouletii'
- 'Mutabilis' — see *R.* × *odorata* 'Mutabilis'
- 'Old Blush' — see *R.* × *odorata* 'Pallida'
- 'Semperflorens' (Ch) — SMad WCot
- var. *spontanea* (S) — WMal
- 'White Beauty' (Ch) — WCot
CHLOE ('Poulen003'^PBR) (Renaissance Series) (S) — ELon ETWh NLar
'Chloris' (A) — EBee ETWh NLar
CHOCOHOLIC ('Kenmahogany') (CI) **new** — SHor
§ CHOCOLATE RIPPLES ('Simstripe') (CI) — ESty
CHRIS ('Kirsan') (ClHT) — ESty ETWh NLar
CHRISTINA ('Poulren044') (Renaissance Series) (S) — ETWh
'Cinderella' ambig. — SWCr
'Cinderella' (Min) — CSBt
'Cinderella' (Ra) — EBee
CINDERELLA ('Korfobalt') (CIS) — ETWh SSea SWCr
CITY LIVERY ('Harhero 2000') (F) — EHeP
CITY OF CARLSBAD — see *R.* HANKY PANKY
'City of Leeds' (F) — EGren MGos
CITY OF YORK — see *R.* 'Direktör Benschop'
CLAIR MATIN ('Meimont') (CIS) — ETWh
CLAIRE AUSTIN ('Ausprior'^PBR) (CI) — EGren ELan EPfP ESty LBom LCro LRHS MAsh NLar SPoG SWCr
'Claire Jacquier' (N) — ETWh MMuc

CLAIRE MARSHALL ('Harunite'^PBR) (F) — SSea
CLAIRE ROSE ('Auslight'^PBR) (S) — LSRN
'Clarence House' (CI) — EBee EBls EPfP LCro LRHS MAsh SWCr
CLAUDE MONET ('Delstrirocrem'^PBR) (CI) — SEas
CLAUDE MONET ('Jacdesa') (HT) — EBls ESty
CLEAR COVER ('Poultc013') (Towne & Country Series) (GC/S) — ETWh
'Clementina Carbonieri' (T) — EBls ETWh
'Cliff Richard' (F) — ESty LSRN MPro
'Climbing Allgold' (CIF) — EGren
'Climbing Arthur Bell' (CIF) — EBls EGren EHeP ELon ESty ETWh LCro MAsh MPri SPoG SRGP SSea SWCr
CLIMBING BETTINA ('Mepalsar') (ClHT) — EBls
'Climbing Blue Moon' (ClHT) — EGren ELan ESty SRGP
'Climbing Captain Christy' (ClHT) — SWCr
'Climbing Cécile Brünner' (ClPoly) ♀H5 — CEnd EBls ETWh LCro LSRN SEND SHor SSea SWCr
§ 'Climbing Columbia' (ClHT) — EBls EShb ETWh
'Climbing Crimson Glory' (ClHT) — EBls EGren ETWh
'Climbing Devoniensis' (ClT) — EBls ETWh
'Climbing Ena Harkness' (ClHT) — EBls EGren SPoG SRGP SWCr
'Climbing Étoile de Hollande' (ClHT) ♀H5 — CSBt EBee EBls EGren EPfP ETWh LCro MPri SEas SPoG SSea SWCr
'Climbing General MacArthur' (ClHT) — EBls
§ 'Climbing Golden Dawn' (ClHT) — EBls
'Climbing Iceberg' (CIF) ♀H5 — CDoC CSBt EBee EBls EGren EHeP ELan EPfP ESty ETWh IArd LBom LCro LSRN MAsh MGos MNHC MPri NLar SPoG SSea SWCr
'Climbing Jazz' — see *R.* THAT'S JAZZ (Courtyard Series)
'Climbing Josephine Bruce' (ClHT) — EBls ETWh
§ 'Climbing Lady Hillingdon' (ClT) ♀H4 — EBls EGren ELan EPfP ETWh LSRN MGos NLar SHor SWCr
'Climbing Lady Sylvia' (ClHT) — EBls ETWh LSRN
'Climbing Little White Pet' — see *R.* 'Félicité-Perpétue'
'Climbing Lovers Meeting'^PBR (ClHT) — EGren
'Climbing Madame Butterfly' (ClHT) ♀H6 — EBls
'Climbing Madame Caroline Testout' (ClHT) — EBls ETWh
'Climbing Masquerade' (CIF) — EBls ETWh SEas SSea SWCr
'Climbing Mrs Herbert Stevens' (ClHT) — EBls ETWh
'Climbing Mrs Sam McGredy' (ClHT) — EBls ETWh
'Climbing Ophelia' (ClHT) — EBls ETWh
§ 'Climbing Paul Lédé' (CIT) — CEnd EBls ETWh
'Climbing Peace' (ClHT) — ETWh
§ 'Climbing Pompon de Paris' (ClMinCh) — EBls MNrw SEND
'Climbing Roundelay' (CI) — EBls

'Climbing Ruby Wedding' (ClHT)	LSRN	CREAM ABUNDANCE ('Harflax') (Abundance Series) (F)	LRHS
'Climbing Shot Silk' (ClHT) ♀H6	ETWh	CREAM DREAM ('Koromtar') (HT)	NTrD
§ 'Climbing Souvenir de la Malmaison' (ClBb)	EBls ETWh LRHS NLar	'Creme' (S)	EGren
'Climbing White Cloud'	see *R.* WHITE CLOUD	CRÈME DE LA CRÈME ('Gancre'PBR) (ClHT)	CDoC CSBt EBee EBls EGren ELan ESty ETWh MPro NLar SEas SHor SPoG
CLODAGH MCGREDY ('Macswanle'PBR) (F)	SEas	'Crépuscule' (N)	EBee ETWh
'Coconut Ice' (HT)	EBee SWCr	crested moss	see *R.* × *centifolia* 'Cristata'
COLONEL MUSTARD ('Forwhisdri') (F)	ESty	CRIMSON CASCADE ('Fryclimbdown') (ClHT) ♀H6	CDoC EBls EGren ELan EPfP ESty LBuc LRHS MGos MPri MPro SHor SPoG SWCr
colonial white	see *R.* 'Sombreuil'	crimson damask	see *R. gallica* var. *officinalis*
'Columbian'	see *R.* 'Climbing Columbia'	'Crimson Glory' (HT)	EBls NLar
COMEBACK	see *R.* TIMELESS PINK	'Crimson Shower' (Ra)	EGren ELan ETWh LBom LRHS MMuc NLar SHor WHer
'Commandant Beaurepaire' (Bb)	ETWh	CRIMSON SILUETTA ('Korsilu 06') (Ra)	EBls LRHS
common moss	see *R.* × *centifolia* 'Muscosa'	CRIMSON SWEET DREAM ('Frynogo') (Patio)	ESty MGos SWCr
'Compassion' (ClHT) ♀H6	Widely available	'Cristata'	see *R.* × *centifolia* 'Cristata'
'Complicata' (G)	EBls ETWh LRHS NLar SEND	CROCUS ROSE ('Ausquest'PBR) (S) ♀H6	ETWh LCro
'Comte de Chambord' misapplied	see *R.* 'Madame Boll'	CROWN PRINCESS MARGARETA ('Auswinter'PBR) (Cl) ♀H6	EGren ELan LCro LSRN SPoG SWCr
COMTESSE ANDRÉ D'OULTREMONT ('Vel15mkama') (HM)	EBls	CRYSTAL FAIRY ('Spekren'PBR)	EGren NLar
'Comtesse Cécile de Chabrillant' (HP)	ETWh NLar	cuisse de nymphe	see *R.* 'Great Maiden's Blush'
'Comtesse de Lacépède' misapplied	see *R.* 'Du Maître d'École'	CUMBERLAND ('Harnext'PBR) (CIF)	EHeP MNHC NLar SWCr
'Comtesse du Caÿla' (Ch)	SDix	'Cupid' (ClHT)	EBls ETWh
'Conditorum' (G)	ETWh	I 'Cutie' (Patio)	ESty SEas
CONGRATULATIONS ('Korlift') (HT)	EGren IArd LCro MGos MPro SWCr	CUTIE PIE ('Rop007'PBR) (Min)	CSBt LCro LRHS LSou WLov XFar
§ 'Conrad Ferdinand Meyer' (Ru)	EBee EBls	*cymosa*	EBee EBls
CONSERVATION ('Cocdimple') (Min/Patio)	SWCr	- 'Rebecca Rushforth' (Cl)	EBee WPGP
CONSTANCE FINN ('Hareden') (F)	SEas	'Dad's Delight' (F)	ESty
'Constance Spry' (ClS) ♀H6	EBee EBls EGren EPfP ETWh LBom LCro LRHS MGos MMuc NLar SEas SWCr WKif	'D'Aguesseau' (G)	ETWh
		'Dainty Bess' (HT)	EBls ETWh
'Cooperi' (Ra)	CRHN EBls ETWh SSea WPGP	× *damascena* var. *bifera*	see *R.* × *damascena* var. *semperflorens*
COPPER LIGHTS ('Simhigh') (HT)	ESty	- 'Kazanlik' (D)	EBls ETWh
'Coral Dawn' (ClHT)	EBls	§ - 'Professeur Émile Perrot' (D)	NLar
CORAL DRIFT ('Meidrifora'PBR) (GC)	MPro	§ - var. *semperflorens* (D) ♀H6	EBls ETWh LRHS
CORAL GEM ('Simplan') (HT)	ESty	- 'Trigintipetala' misapplied	see *R.* × *damascena* 'Professeur Émile Perrot'
CORAL SWEET DREAM ('Fryrader') (Patio)	SWCr	§ - 'Versicolor' (D)	EBls SSea
'Coralie' (D)	EBls	'Dame de Coeur' (HT)	EPfP
'Cornelia' (HM) ♀H6	CBcs CWal EBee EBls EPfP ETWh IArd LCro LRHS LSRN NLar SMad SWCr	DAME DEBORAH JAMES ('Hardelicate') (F) **new**	LRHS NLar
		DAME JUDI DENCH ('Ausquaker'PBR) (HM)	EGren ELan EPfP ESty LBom LCro LRHS MBNS NLar SWCr
'Coryana' (S)	ETWh NLar	'Danaë' (HM)	EBls ETWh
corymbifera (S)	EBls	DANCING QUEEN ('Fryfestoon') (ClHT) ♀H6	CDoC EBls EPfP LBuc LRHS MAsh SSea SWCr
cottage maid	see *R.* × *centifolia* 'Unique Panachée'	DANCING QUEEN ('Tan99303') **new**	SEas
COTTAGE MAID ('Poulspan') (S)	ELon	DANCING SUNSET ('Guesunusal') (ClHT)	ESty
COUNTESS OF WESSEX ('Beacream') (S)	EBls EPfP LCro LRHS MPri SWCr	DANIEL ('Webwhite') (HT)	ESty
COUNTY OF YORKSHIRE ('Korstarnow'PBR) (GC) ♀H6	EBls ESty SEas	DANNAHUE ('Ausa6b15') (S) **new**	LBom LRHS
'Cramoisi Supérieur' (Ch)	ETWh	§ 'Danse du Feu' (ClF)	CBcs EBls EGren ELan ETWh MGos SWCr
CRAZY FOR YOU ('Wekroalt') (F) ♀H6	EBls ESty MPro SEas SRGP	'Daphné' Vibert, 1819 (G)	EBls
CRAZY IN LOVE ('Raw1127') (S)	ESty	DARCEY BUSSELL ('Ausdecorum'PBR) (S) ♀H6	CAco EGren ELan LCro LSRN SPoG SWCr

Darling Daughter ('Raw2332') (F)	ESty	'Direktör Benschop' (CIF)	EBls EPfP ETWh LBuc LRHS NLar SWCr
David Hockney ('Meibritty') (CI) **new**	ETWh	Dixieland Linda ('Beadix') (ClHT)	EBls EPfP LSRN SWCr
davidii (S)	EBls ETWh	Dizzy Heights ('Fryblissful'^PBR) (CIHT) ♀H6	EPfP LRHS NLar SEas
David's Rose ('Raw2792') (F) **new**	ESty	Dolce Vita ('Delcentoran') (F)	ESty SEas
Dawn Chorus ('Dicquasar') (HT) ♀H6	CBcs CDoC CSBt EBls EGren SPoG SSea	Dolly ('Poulvision') (F)	LSRN
'Daybreak' (HM)	ETWh	Domaine de Chantilly ('Delagak') (HT)	ESty
'De Meaux'	see *R.* × *centifolia* 'De Meaux'	'Don Juan' (ClHT)	ETWh
§ 'De Resht' (DPo) ♀H7	CDoC EBls EPfP ETWh MAsh MGos MPri NLar SHor	'Doncasteri' (*moyesii* hybrid) (S)	EBls
Dear Barbara ('Rawbar') (HT)	LSRN	'Doreen' (HT)	LSRN
Dear Dad ('Smi87-02') (HT)	ESty	Doreen's Dream ('For2020-006') (F) **new**	ESty
'Dear Daughter' (F)	ESty	'Doris Tysterman' (HT)	EBls EGren
Dear Granny ('Forkalia') (F)	ESty	Dorothy ('Cocrocket'^PBR) (F)	LRHS LSRN
Dear Joan ('Rawjo') (F)	LSRN	'Dorothy Perkins' (Ra)	CRHN EBls EGren ETWh NPer
Dear Margaret ('Raw293') (HT)	LSRN	'Dortmund' (S) ♀H7	EBls ETWh WMal
Dear Michael ('Raw1065') (F)	LSRN	Double Delight ('Andeli') (HT)	EBls EGren EHeP ELan LSRN SEas SSea
Dear Sister	see *R.* Heart's Desire	Douglas ('Cocfresco') (F)	LSRN
'Dearest' (F)	EGren SWCr	§ Draga ('Bozdragfra'^PBR) (Frayla Series) (S)	ETWh
Deb's Delight ('Legsweet'^PBR) (CIMin)	LSRN	Drama Queen ('Horstarstruck') (F)	EGren
'Debutante' (Ra) ♀H7	CRHN EBls ETWh	Dream Lover ('Peayetti') (Patio)	ESty
Deep Love (CIS) **new**	EBee SMad	'Dreaming Spires' (CIHT)	EGren
'Deep Secret' (HT)	CSBt EBls EGren ELan ELon EPfP MGos MPri MPro SRGP SWCr	§ 'Du Maître d'École' (G)	EBls WHer
Del Boy ('Raw2767') (F) **new**	ESty	Dublin Bay ('Macdub') (CIF) ♀H6	CDoC CEnd CSBt EBls ELan EPfP ETWh IArd LBuc LRHS MAsh MGos MPri MPro NLar SEas SPoG SRGP SSea SWCr WTre
Delightful ('Curspoglo') (CIMin)	ESty LRHS	'Duc de Guiche' (G) ♀H7	ETWh NLar WHer
Delightful Dorothy ('Raw2794') (F) **new**	ESty	'Ducher' (Ch/T)	ETWh
Delightful Parfuma ('Korbevmahe'^PBR) (F) **new**	SEas	Duchess of Cornwall ('Tan97159'^PBR) (HT) ♀H6	CDoC CSBt EBee EBls ELon ESty ETWh LCro MGos NLar SEas SSea SWCr
Della Balfour ('Harblend'^PBR) (CIHT)	EBls	'Duchess of Portland'	see *R.* 'Portlandica'
Desdemona ('Auskindling'^PBR) (HM)	EGren ELan EPfP ESty LBom LRHS MAsh MBNS NLar SWCr	Duchess of York	see *R.* Sunseeker
Designer Sunset ambig.	EPfP LRHS MAsh MNHC SWCr	'Duchesse d'Angoulême' (Ce × G) ♀H7	EBls ETWh NLar
'Designer Sunset' (Patio)	EBls	'Duchesse d'Auerstädt' (N)	EBls
Desiree ('Tan10898') (HT)	SEas	'Duchesse de Buccleugh' (G)	EBls ETWh
§ 'Desprez à Fleur Jaune' (N)	EBls ETWh IArd NLar SEND	§ 'Duchesse de Montebello' (G) ♀H7	EBls ETWh NLar
'Devoniensis'	see *R.* 'Climbing Devoniensis'	'Duke of Edinburgh' (HP)	LRHS MNHC
Diamond ('Korgazell'^PBR) (Patio) ♀H6	LSRN	'Duke of Wellington' (HP)	EBls ETWh
'Diamond 60th Anniversary' (F)	NTrD	Dunham Massey ('Beajelly') (S)	EBee EBls EPfP LCro LRHS SWCr
Diamond Anniversary ('Morsixty') (Min)	LSRN	'Dunwich Rose' (SpH)	EBls ETWh NLar WCot
'Diamond Celebration' (HT)	LSRN	'Dupontii' (S) ♀H6	EBls ETWh
Diamond Dad	see *R.* White Meidiland	'Dusky Maiden' (F)	EBls ETWh MPro WKif
Diamond Days ('Hartribe'^PBR) (HT)	CDoC EHeP ESty LSRN SPoG	'Dutch Gold' (HT)	EGren MGos
Diamond Days Forever ('Fryjess'^PBR) (F)	EBls EPfP LRHS LSRN MAsh	'Earl of Eldon' (N)	ETWh
Diamond Eyes ('Wekwibypur') (Min)	CDoC ESty	'Easlea's Golden Rambler' (Ra) ♀H5	EBls ETWh NLar
'Diamond Jubilee' (HT)	CEnd EBls EGren LBom	§ Easy Does It ('Harpageant'^PBR) (F) ♀H6	CDoC ELan ELon NLar SEas
Diamond Jubilee ('Tan022260') (F)	ELan	Easy Going ('Harflow') (F) ♀H6	IArd NLar SWCr
Diamond Wedding ('Raw1150') (F)	ESty	§ Ebb Tide ('Weksmopur'^PBR) (F)	CSBt EBls EPfP ESty LCro LRHS MAsh MGos MPro SHor SPoG SSea SWCr
'Diamond Wishes'	see *R.* Misty Hit (PatioHit Series)		
Dinky ('Velheav') (HM)	EBls		
Dioressence ('Deldiore') (F)	ESty		

ecae (S)	ETWh	'Everest Double Fragrance' (F)	EBls
'Éclair' (HP)	EBls	EVERGLOW RUBY ('Geus1713') (S)	CWGN LCro XFar
'Eddie's Jewel' (*moyesii* hybrid) (S)	EBls	EXCELLENT COVER ('Poultc017'^PBR) (Towne & Country Series) (GC)	ELan
'Eden Rose' (HT)	NLar		
EDEN ROSE '88 ('Meiviolin') (CIHT)	EBls ETWh SWCr	'Excelsa' (Ra)	CoPl EBls EGrI IArd LRHS SPoG SWCr
EDITH HOLDEN ('Chewlegacy') (F)	WMal	EYE OF THE STORM ('Wekeots') (F)	CDoC ETWh NLar
EDWARD'S ROSE ('Smi73/7/97') (F)	ELan ESty MPro	EYE OF THE TIGER ('Chewbullseye'^PBR) (*persica* hybrid) (S)	CDoC CWal EBls ELan EPfP ESty ETWh LBom LRHS MAsh MPri MPro NLar SEas SMad SPoG SSea SWCr
eglanteria	see *R. rubiginosa*		
EGLANTYNE ('Ausmak') (S)	EGren LCro SWCr		
EIRENE ('Tan10696') (F)	SSea	EYES FOR YOU ('Pejbigeye') (F) ♀H6	CEnd EBee EBls EPfP ESty ETWh LBuc LCro LRHS MAsh MGos MPri NLar SEas SPoG SSea SWCr WKif
'Eleanor' (Patio)	LSRN NLar		
ELEANOR ('Poulberin') (S)	ETWh		
elegantula (S)	WPGP		
§ – 'Persetosa' (S)	EBls ETWh	FAB AT 50 ('Woraunt') (F)	LSRN NTrD
§ ELINA ('Dicjana') (HT) ♀H6	EBls EGren ETWh LSRN	FABULOUS AT 40 ('Webcountry') (F)	LSRN
ELIZABETH ('Ausmajesty'^PBR) (S)	NLar		
ELIZABETH ('Coctail') (F)	LRHS MAsh	FABULOUS AT 50 ('Rawfabsal') (F)	LSRN SWCr
'Elizabeth Harkness' (HT)	EGren MSwo		
'Elizabeth Harwood' (Cl)	EBls	FABULOUS AT 60 ('Rawfabor') (F)	NTrD SWCr
ELIZABETH OF GLAMIS ('Macel') (F)	EGren	FABULOUS AT 65 ('Raw1041') (F)	LSRN
'Ellen Willmott' (HT)	EBls ETWh	FABULOUS AT 70 (F)	LSRN NTrD SWCr
ELVIS ('Adablarop'^PBR) (HT)	LSRN	FABULOUS AT 80 ('Rawcox') (F)	LSRN NTrD
ELY CATHEDRAL ('Beajolly') (S)	EBls EPfP LRHS SWCr		
EMILIA MARIA	see *R.* LA ROSE DE MOLINARD	FAIR EVA ('Seaeva') (Ra/GC)	ESty
EMILY BRONTË ('Ausearnshaw'^PBR) (S)	EGren ELan EPfP ESty LBom LCro LRHS MBNS NLar SWCr	'Fairy Rose'	see *R.* 'The Fairy'
		FAITHFUL FRIEND ('Beachallenge') (S)	EBls
'Emily Gray' (Ra)	CRHN EBee EBls EGren ETWh LSRN MPri	FALSTAFF ('Ausverse'^PBR) (S)	CSBt ETWh LCro LSRN SWCr
EMMA ('Raw1217') (HT)	ESty	'Fantin-Latour' (Ce) ♀H6	CDoC EBls EGren ELan ETWh LCro MMuc NLar SHor SWCr WKif
EMPEREUR CHARLES IV ('Vel15mscwi') (F)	EBls		
'Ena Harkness' (HT)	CDoC EGren LRHS MGos	*fargesii* hort.	see *R. moyesii* var. *fargesii*
ENCHANTRESS ('Tan97281'^PBR) (HT)	EBee EBls MGos	*farreri* f. *persetosa*	see *R. elegantula* 'Persetosa'
'Enfant de France' (HP)	LSRN	§ FASCINATION ('Poulmax'^PBR) (F) ♀H6	LRHS SWCr
ENGLISH GARDEN ('Ausbuff') (S)	EGren ETWh LSRN	FAVOURITE FRIEND ('Forform') (HT)	ESty
'English Miss' (F)	CDoC EBls EGren LRHS MAsh MGos MPri MPro SEas SPoG SWCr	'F.E. Lester'	see *R.* 'Francis E. Lester'
		fedtschenkoana Regel	EBls
'Erfurt' (HM)	EBee ETWh NLar	aff. *fedtschenkoana*	ETWh
'Ernest H. Morse' (HT)	EGren	cf. *fedtschenkoana* from Tajikistan	GGro
'Esme' (HT)	ETWh		
ESPECIALLY FOR YOU ('Fryworthy') (HT) ♀H6	EGren ESty SWCr	FÉE DES NEIGES	see *R.* ICEBERG
		'Felicia' (HM) ♀H6	CBcs CSBt EBee EBls ETWh LCro LRHS LSto MAsh MPri NLar SEND SHor WKif WLov
§ 'Étendard' (ClHT)	CDoC CSBt EBls ETWh MGos SPoG SWCr		
ETERNAL FLAME ('Korassenet'^PBR) (F)	SEas	'Félicité Parmentier' (A × D) ♀H6	EBls ETWh NLar
ETERNITY ('Noa150097') (F)	MAsh SWCr	§ 'Félicité-Perpétue' (Ra) ♀H6	CBcs CRHN EBee EBls EPfP ETWh LCro LRHS MSwo NLar SEND SHor SWCr WKif
ETERNITY ('Ricity') (Min)	EPfP LRHS		
'Ethel' (Ra)	EBls ETWh		
'Étoile de Hollande' (HT)	CDoC EBee EBls LSRN MGos NLar	'Fellemberg' (ClCh)	ETWh
EUREKA ('Meizambaizt'^PBR) (HT)	EBls LRHS	FELLOWSHIP ('Harwelcome') (F) ♀H6	EGren LCro SSea SWCr
EUSTACIA VYE ('Ausegdon'^PBR) (S)	EGren EPfP ESty LBom LRHS MAsh NLar SPoG SWCr	'Ferdinand Pichard' (Bb) ♀H6	CBcs CSBt EBls EGren ELon EPfP ESty ETWh LCro LRHS MAsh MPri NLar SEas SMad SSea SWCr WKif
'Eva' (HM)	MGos		
'Evangeline' (Ra)	EBls		
EVE RUGGIERI ('Adarylop') (HT)	LSRN	I 'Fern's Rose' (F)	EGren
EVELINE WILD (Taste of Love Series)	see *R.* NATALIJA (Frayla Series)	*ferruginea*	see *R. glauca* Pourr.
		FESTIVE JEWEL ('Beacost') (S)	EBls EPfP LRHS MAsh SWCr
EVELYN ('Aussaucer') (S)	ETWh LSRN	FETZER SYRAH ROSÉ ('Harextra') (S)	EHeP LRHS MNHC
§ EVELYN FISON ('Macev') (F)	EBls EGren		
'Evelyn May' (HT)	EBls EPfP LCro LRHS MAsh SWCr	FIGHTING TEMERAIRE ('Austrava'^PBR) (S)	SWCr

§ *filipes* 'Kiftsgate' (Ra) ♥H6 — CBcs CDoC CSBt EBee EBls ETWh GKin LRHS MCtn NLar SEas SEND SHor SSea SWCr WKif
'Fimbriata' (Ru) — ETWh
FIONA ('Meibeluxen') (S/GC) — EBls
FIRESTAR — see *R.* EASY DOES IT
FIRST GREAT WESTERN ('Oracharpam'^PBR) (HT) — ELon ESty
§ 'F.J. Grootendorst' (Ru) — EBls ETWh WHer
FLAMING STAR ('Kortaltal') (HT) — EBls
FLANDERS ROSE ('Beaknight') (F) — EBls
FLIRT ('Korkopapp'^PBR) (F) — LRHS MAsh
FLIRT ('Korvondra') (F) — LRHS
'Flora' (Ra) — EBls ETWh
'Flora McIvor' (RH) — EBls
'Florence Mary Morse' (S) — SDix
FLORENCE NIGHTINGALE ('Ganflor') (F) — SEas
FLORENTINA ('Kortrameilo'^PBR) (CI) — EBls LBom SEas
FLOWER CARPET AMBER ('Noa97400a'^PBR) (GC) ♥H6 — CDoC CSBt EBls EPfP LBuc LCro LRHS LSRN MAsh MPri SPoG SSea
§ FLOWER CARPET CHERRY ('Noa20054'^PBR) — EBls LRHS
'Flower Carpet Coral'^PBR (GC) ♥H6 — EBls EPfP LBuc LCro LRHS LSRN MAsh MPri SWCr
FLOWER CARPET GOLD (GC) ('Noalesa'^PBR) — CDoC EBls LBuc LRHS MAsh MPri SPoG SSea
FLOWER CARPET PINK — see *R.* PINK FLOWER CARPET
FLOWER CARPET PINK SUPREME ('Noa168098f') (GC) — EBls EPfP LRHS MAsh
FLOWER CARPET RED VELVET ('Noare'^PBR) (GC/S) ♥H6 — EBls ELan EPfP LBuc LCro LRHS MPri
FLOWER CARPET RUBY (GC) — CDoC EBee EBls LBuc LRHS LSRN MAsh MPri SPoG SSea SWCr
FLOWER CARPET SCARLET ('Noa83100b'^PBR) (GC) ♥H6 — EBee EBls LCro LRHS SSea SWCr
FLOWER CARPET SUNSET ('Deseo') (S) — CDoC LCro LRHS MAsh MPri
§ FLOWER CARPET SUNSHINE ('Noason') (GC) ♥H6 — EBls ELan LCro LRHS MPri
FLOWER CARPET WHITE ('Noaschnee') (GC) ♥H6 — CDoC EBee EBls ELan EPfP LBuc LCro LRHS LSRN MAsh MPri SPoG SSea SWCr
FLOWER POWER ('Frycassia'^PBR) (Patio) ♥H6 — CDoC CSBt EBls EPfP ESty LCro LRHS MAsh MGos MPri SOrN SPoG SWCr
FLOWER POWER GOLD ('Fryneon') (Patio) — CDoC EBls EPfP ESty LRHS MAsh MPri SOrN SPoG SWCr
foetida (S) — ETWh
§ - 'Bicolor' (S) — EBls ETWh
§ - 'Persiana' (S) — EBls
foliolosa — EBls WJur
FOND MEMORIES ('Kirfelix'^PBR) (Patio) — EBls ESty SPoG SWCr
FOR YOU WITH LOVE ('Fryjangle') (Patio) — CDoC EBls EPfP LBuc LRHS LSRN MAsh SWCr
FOR YOUR EYES ONLY ('Cheweyesup'^PBR) (S) — CDoC CSBt CWal EBee EBls EGren EHeP ELan ELon EPfP ESty ETWh LBom LBuc LCro LRHS LSRN MAsh MGos MNrw MPri NLar SEas SPoG SSea SWCr WKif
FORGET ME NOT ('Coccharm'^PBR) (HT) — ESty
forrestiana (S) — EBls ETWh
× *fortuneana* (Ra) — CoPl

Fortune's double yellow — see *R.* × *odorata* 'Pseudindica'
FOUR-LEGGED FRIEND ('Gueslink') (F) **new** — ESty
FRAGONARD ('Delparviro'^PBR) (HT) — EBls SEas
FRAGRANT CELEBRATION ('Beamerry') (CI) — EBls EPfP LBuc LRHS SWCr
FRAGRANT CLOUD ('Tanellis') (HT) — CBcs CEnd EBls EGren ELan EPfP ETWh LBuc LRHS LSRN MGos MPri SEas SPoG SWCr
'Fragrant Delight' (F) ♥H6 — CDoC CSBt EBls EGren ELan MGos MSwo SRGP
'Francesca' (HM) — EBls ETWh
'Francis Copple' (S) — EBls
'Francis Dubreuil' (T) — EBls
§ 'Francis E. Lester' (HM/Ra) ♥H6 — CEnd EBee EBls ELan ETWh LBom LCro NLar SHor SMrm
× *francofurtana* misapplied — see *R.* 'Impératrice Joséphine'
× *francofurtana* 'Empress Josephine' — see *R.* 'Impératrice Joséphine'
'François Juranville' (Ra) ♥H6 — CRHN EBee EBls ETWh LCro LRHS MMuc NLar SHor SWCr WFar
'Frau Karl Druschki' (HP) — ETWh
FREDDIE MERCURY ('Batmercury') (HT) — LSRN
FREEDOM ('Dicjem') (HT) ♥H6 — CBcs CDoC EBls EGren ELon SSea SWCr
'Frensham' (F) — EBls SSea
FRIEND FOR LIFE ('Cocnanne'^PBR) (F) ♥H6 — ELan MPro
FRIENDS FOREVER ('Korapriber') (F) ♥H6 — CDoC EBls
'Friendship' (Patio) — ESty NTrD
FRIENDSHIP OF STRANGERS ('633D9') (CI) — EBls
FRILLY CUFF ('Beajingle') (S) — EBls EGren EPfP LRHS MAsh
FRILLY KNICKERS ('Raw2289') (F) — ESty
'Fritz Nobis' (S) ♥H6 — ETWh
'Fru Dagmar Hastrup' (Ru) ♥H7 — CBcs CDoC EBee EBls EPfP ETWh LBuc LCro NLar SEND
'Frühlingsduft' (SpH) — ETWh
'Frühlingsgold' (SpH) ♥H7 — EBls ELan ETWh MSwo NLar
'Frühlingsmorgen' (SpH) ♥H7 — EBls ETWh NLar
GABRIEL OAK ('Auscrowd'^PBR) (S) — EGren ELan EPfP ESty LBom LRHS MAsh MBNS NLar SPoG SWCr
§ *gallica* (G) — EBls ETWh
§ - var. *officinalis* (G) ♥H7 — EBls EPfP ETWh LCro LRHS MHer NLar SRms SSea SWCr WFar WHer
- 'Velutiniflora' (G) — EBls
§ - 'Versicolor' (G) ♥H7 — CBcs CDoC CEnd EBee EBls EGren EPfP ETWh LCro LRHS LSRN MAsh MHer NLar NSti SSea SWCr WKif
GALWAY BAY ('Macba') (CIHT) — EPfP ETWh LRHS MAsh NLar SWCr
GARDEN OF ROSES — see *R.* JOIE DE VIVRE
'Gardeners' Glory'^PBR (CIHT) ♥H6 — CDoC ELan ESty LBuc LRHS MGos MPri SEas SPoG SSea SWCr
GARDENERS' GOLD ('Harzoltan') (CIS) — EHeP NLar
GARDENERS' JOY ('Beadrum') (S) — EBls
'Gardenia' (Ra) — EBls
'Garland's Gold' (F) — EGren
GARTENPRINZESSIN MARIE-JOSÉ ('Korgehaque'^PBR) (F) — LCro SSea
GARTENSPASS ('Korgohowa'^PBR) (F) — ETWh
'Gaujard' — see *R.* ROSE GAUJARD

'Gelbe Dagmar Hastrup'	see *R.* YELLOW DAGMAR HASTRUP		'Golden 50th Anniversary' (F)	MPri NTrD SWCr
'Général Kléber' (CeMo) ♀H7	EBls		GOLDEN ANGEL ('Poulpa1056'PBR) (Patio)	EBls LRHS
§ 'Général Schablikine' (T)	ETWh WMal		'Golden Anniversary' (Patio)	MGos SSea
gentiliana misapplied	see *R.* 'Polyantha Grandiflora'		GOLDEN BEAUTY ('Clebeau') (Min)	LRHS NLar
gentiliana H. Lév. & Variot	see *R. multiflora* var. *cathayensis*		GOLDEN BEAUTY ('Korberbeni'PBR) (F)	CEnd EBee EBls ETWh LBuc MAsh SWCr
GENTLE HERMIONE ('Ausrumba'PBR) (S)	EGren EPfP LBom LCro LRHS SPoG SWCr		GOLDEN CELEBRATION ('Ausgold') (S) ♀H6	EGren EPfP ESty LBom LCro LRHS LSRN NLar SPoG SWCr
GENTLE TOUCH ('Diclulu') (Min/Patio)	CSBt SWCr		'Golden Dawn'	see *R.* 'Climbing Golden Dawn'
GEOFF HAMILTON ('Ausham'PBR) (S)	ETWh LSRN MBNS		GOLDEN DELICIOUS ('Wekgobafa') (HT)	ESty SEas
GEORGE ('Simetna') (F)	ESty		GOLDEN EYE ('Baieye') (GC/S) **new**	LBom
GEORGE BEST ('Dichimanher'PBR) (Patio) ♀H6	LSRN		GOLDEN GATE ('Korgolgat'PBR) (ClHT) ♀H6	EBls EHeP EPfP LBuc LRHS SEas SWCr
'Georges Vibert' (G)	ETWh NLar		GOLDEN GATE ('Korrogilo') (HT)	SSea
'Geranium' (*moyesii* hybrid) (S) ♀H5	CBcs CDoC EBls ElAn EPfP ETWh IArd LCro LRHS NLar		GOLDEN JEWEL ('Tanledolg') (F/Patio)	ESty
GERBE D'OR	see *R.* CASINO		GOLDEN JUBILEE ('Cocagold') (HT)	EGren
GERTRUDE JEKYLL ('Ausbord'PBR) (S) ♀H6	EGren ElAn EPfP ESty IArd LBom LCro LRHS LSRN MAsh MBNS NLar SPoG SWCr		GOLDEN MEMORIES ('Korholesea'PBR) (F) ♀H6	CSBt EBls EGren LBuc MGos MPri MSwo SWCr
GETTYSBURG ('Poulen001'PBR) (F)	ETWh		'Golden Moment'PBR (HT)	CSBt MGos
'Ghislaine de Féligonde' (HM) ♀H5	EBee EBls EGrI ElAn EPfP ESty ETWh LBom LBuc LCro LRHS MAsh MNrw MPri NLar SEND SHor SWCr WMal		'Golden Rambler'	see *R.* 'Alister Stella Gray'
			'Golden Showers' (Cl)	CBcs CDoC CEnd CSBt EBee EBls EGren ElAn EPfP ETWh LBom LBuc LCro LRHS LSRN MAsh MGos MMuc MNHC NLar NTrD SPoG SWCr
GHITA	see *R.* MILLIE (Renaissance Series)			
§ GIARDINA ('Tan08576'PBR) (HT)	SEas SSea		GOLDEN SMILES ('Frykeyno'PBR) (F) ♀H6	CDoC EBls ElAn ESty LRHS MPri MPro SWCr
§ GIARDINA ('Tan97289'PBR) (Cl)	ESty		GOLDEN TRIBUTE ('Horannfree') (F)	EGren
'Gift of Life' (Cl)	EGren SEas		GOLDEN TRUST ('Hardish') (Patio)	SWCr
gigantea × *longicuspis*, from Yunnan	WPGP		GOLDEN WEDDING ('Arokris') (F)	CBcs CDoC CSBt EBls EGren ElAn EPfP ETWh IArd LCro LRHS LSRN MAsh MGos MPro SEas SOrN SPoG SSea
GILL'S WISH ('Raw2784') (HT) **new**	ESty			
GINGER SYLLABUB ('Harjolina'PBR) (ClHT)	EHeP ESty LRHS MGos NLar SPoG SSea		GOLDEN WEDDING ANNIVERSARY (F)	LSRN NTrD SWCr
GINGERNUT ('Coccrazy') (Patio)	EGren		'Golden Wedding Celebration' (F)	CEnd LSRN
GIPSY BOY	see *R.* 'Zigeunerknabe'		'Golden Wings' (S)	EBls EGren ETWh NLar
GISELA'S DELIGHT ('Horpink') (S)	EBls		'Goldfinch' (Ra)	EBls ETWh LCro MMrt NLar SEND SWCr WFar
GLAD TIDINGS ('Tantide') (F)	EBls MPro		GOOD AS GOLD ('Chewsunbeam'PBR) (ClMin)	EGren SWCr
glauca Vill. ex Lois.	see *R. caesia* subsp. *vosagiaca*			
glauca ambig.	EGrI LSto MHer WTre		GORDON'S COLLEGE ('Cocjabby'PBR) (F) ♀H6	MGos MPro
§ *glauca* Pourr. (S) ♀H7	CSBt EBee EBls ECha EGren ElAn EPfP ETWh LCro LRHS MMuc NLar SDix SEND SMad SPoG SSea WCot WJur		GORGEOUS ('Poulpmt009'PBR) (HT)	CDoC CEnd EBls ElAn EPfP LBuc LRHS MPri
			GORGEOUS GIRL ('Forshow') (HT)	ESty
GLOBAL BEAUTY ('Tan 94448') (HT)	CDoC EBee ETWh LCro NLar SEas SSea SWCr		GRACE ('Auskeppy'PBR) (S) ♀H6	EPfP ESty LBom LRHS NLar SWCr
'Gloire de Dijon' (ClT)	CEnd EBee EBls EGren ElAn ETWh LRHS LSRN NLar		'Graciously Pink' (Min)	EBls EHeP EPfP SWCr
'Gloire de France' (G) ♀H7	ETWh NLar WHer		GRAHAM THOMAS ('Ausmas') (S) ♀H6	EBee ETWh LCro LSRN SPoG SWCr
'Gloire de Guilan' (D)	ETWh			
'Gloire des Mousseuses' (CeMo)	ETWh		GRAND AWARD ('Poulcy014'PBR) (Courtyard Series) (ClF)	EBls ElAn ETWh NLar
'Gloire Lyonnaise' (HP)	EBls ETWh NLar			
'Gloria Mundi' (Poly)	ETWh			
GLORIANA ('Chewpope') (ClMin)	CDoC EPfP LBuc LRHS MAsh SEas SMad SOrN SPoG SSea SWCr			
GLORIOUS PARFUMA	see *R.* MADAME ANISETTE			
'Glory of Seale' (S)	SSea			
GLYNDEBOURNE ('Harpulse'PBR) (S)	EHeP SWCr			
GOLD CHARM ('Chewalbygold') (Cl)	LRHS			
'Goldbusch' (RH)	EBls			

Grande Duchesse Louise ('Korbrocaze') (HT) **new**	SEas	Happy Couple ('Raw2766') (F)	ESty
'Grandma' (F)	LRHS	Happy Days ('Harquad'^{PBR}) (S)	CDoC CSBt
Grandma's Rose ('Meiancyid') (F)	LRHS MAsh MPri	Happy Gardening	see *R.* Wonderful Friend
Grand-mère Jenny ('Grem') (HT)	EBls	Happy Golden Wedding	see *R.* Golden Smiles
		'Happy Memories' (F)	EBls
'Grandpa Dickson' (HT)	EGren MGos	Happy Pearl Wedding (HT)	EBls LRHS MAsh
Grandpa's Rose	see *R.* Canzonetta	Happy Retirement ('Tantoras'^{PBR}) (F) ♀H6	CBcs EBls ELan ESty LBuc LCro LRHS LSRN MAsh MPri NLar SEas SPoG SSea SWCr
Great Expectations ambig.	EGren		
Great Expectations ('Mackalves') (F)	CDoC CSBt IArd MGos NLar	Happy Ruby Wedding ('Frynoble'^{PBR}) (HT)	CBcs CDoC ELan LRHS MAsh MPri SSea SWCr
§ 'Great Maiden's Blush' (A) ♀H7	EBls EPfP ETWh NLar SWCr	Happy Silver Wedding ('Frysilva') (F)	CDoC LRHS LSRN MAsh MPri SWCr
'Great Ormond Street' (F)	EBls	Happy Times ('Bedone'^{PBR}) (Patio/Min)	NTrD
'Great Western' (Bb)	EBls	× *harisonii* (SpH)	EBls
Greetings ('Jacdreco') (F)	LRHS	§ - 'Williams' Double Yellow' (SpH)	EBls ETWh NLar
'Grimpant Cramoisi Supérieur' (ClCh)	EBls		
'Grootendorst'	see *R.* 'F.J. Grootendorst'	Harlow Carr ambig	LRHS
Grosvenor House (HT)	EPfP LCro LRHS SWCr	Harlow Carr ('Aushouse') (S)	EPfP LSRN
Grouse ('Korimro') (S/GC)	EBls ETWh NLar SEND		
Gruss an Aachen (Poly) ♀H6	EBls ETWh	Harlow Carr ('Kirlyl') (F)	EGren ELan LBom NLar SWCr
		'Harry Edland' (F)	EGren EHeP LCro
'Gruss an Teplitz' (China hybrid)	EBls ETWh NLar	'Harry Wheatcroft' (HT)	EGren
		Havana Hit ('Poulpah032'^{PBR}) (Patio)	EBls EPfP LRHS MPri
Guardian Angel ('Harpresto') (F)	EBls LRHS MAsh MPri		
'Guinée' (ClHT)	EBls EGren ELan ETWh LCro LRHS NLar SEas WCot WMal	'Hazel Le Rougetel' (Ru)	EBls WFar
		'Heart of Gold' (Ra)	CSBt MGos
Guirlande d'Amour ('Lenalbi') (HM)	EBls	Heart of Gold ('Coctarlotte'^{PBR}) (HT) ♀H6	EGren ESty
Guirlande Rose ('Velwichba') (Ra)	EBls	§ Heart's Desire ('Raw1063') (F)	ESty
Guy Savoy ('Delstrimen'^{PBR}) (F)	EBls EGren ETWh SEas	Heavenly Pink ('Lennedi') (HM)	EBls
Guy's Gold ('Harmatch'^{PBR}) (HT)	LRHS MPri SEas SPoG SWCr	'Hebe's Lip' (D × H)	ETWh NLar
Gwent ('Poulurt') (GC)	CBcs CSBt SEND	Helen ('Guesgem') (F)	ESty
gymnocarpa	EBls	'Helen Knight' (*ecae* hybrid) (S)	SEas
Gypsy Boy	see *R.* 'Zigeunerknabe'	Helena ('Poulna'^{PBR}) (Renaissance Series) (S)	ETWh
Hallie (Fragrant Bella Series)	see *R.* Draga (Frayla Series)		
Hamilton Princess ('Harzinc') (HT)	CDoC MNHC	*helenae*	EBee EBls ETWh WPGP
Hampshire ('Korhamp') (GC)	CBcs SWCr	- hybrid	ETWh
		hemisphaerica (S)	EBls
Händel ('Macha') (ClHT)	CDoC CSBt EBls EGren ELan EPfP ETWh LRHS MAsh MGos MPri SPlb SRGP SWCr	Henri Delbard ('Delclaudibi') (HT)	EBls ELan ESty SEas
		§ 'Henri Martin' (CeMo) ♀H7	EBls ETWh NLar
§ Hanky Panky ('Wektorcent'^{PBR}) (F)	CDoC EBls ESty SEas	Henri Matisse ('Delstrobla') (F)	ESty ETWh LRHS NLar SPoG SReu
Hannah Gordon ('Korweiso') (F)	EBls	Henrietta Barnett ('Harmaxim'^{PBR}) (F)	NLar
'Hansa' (Ru)	EBls ETWh LBuc	'Herbstfeuer' (RH)	EBls
Hansestadt Rostock ('Tan04603'^{PBR}) (F)	CDoC LBom LRHS SWCr	Heritage ('Ausblush') (S)	ETWh
		'Hermosa' (Ch)	ETWh NLar
Happy 60th Birthday	LSRN	Hertfordshire ('Kortenay') (GC) ♀H6	SEas SEND SWCr
Happy 70th Birthday ('Rawday') (F)	LSRN		
Happy 80th Birthday	LSRN	Herzogin Christiana ('Korgeowim'^{PBR}) (F)	EBls ETWh
Happy Anniversary ambig.	CSBt NLar	× *hibernica* (SpH)	EBls
Happy Anniversary ('Bedfranc') (F)	LSRN MPri SWCr	High Flier ('Fryfandango'^{PBR}) (ClHT)	EBls
Happy Anniversary ('Delpre') (F)	CDoC EPfP LCro LRHS MAsh MGos SPoG	High Hopes ('Haryup'^{PBR}) (ClHT)	EPfP SSea
Happy Birthday (HT)	EPfP ESty LCro LRHS MAsh SSea	'Highdownensis' (*moyesii* hybrid) (S)	EBls ELan
'Happy Birthday' (Min/Patio)	ESty LCro LRHS LSRN MGos SSea SWCr	Highgrove ('Hornightshade') (Cl)	EBls EPfP ESty LRHS MPri
Happy Birthday to You ('Gues1231') (F)	ESty		

'Highworth' (Ra)	ESty
'Hippolyte' (G)	NLar
hirtula (S)	EBls
holodonta	see *R. moyesii* f. *rosea*
holy rose	see *R.* × *richardii*
HOME SWEET HOME ('Sim2008/10') (HT)	ESty
HOMMAGE À BARBARA ('Delchifrou'[PBR]) (HT)	EBls ELan ESty ETWh NLar WKif
HONEY BUNCH ('Cocglen') (F)	EGren MGos
HONEY DIJON ('Weksproulses'[PBR]) (F)	ESty
HONEYBUN ('Tan98264'[PBR]) (Patio)	ESty
'Honorine de Brabant' (Bb) ♀H6	EBls ETWh
HOPES AND DREAMS ('Tan14833') (HT)	EBls LBuc LRHS
HORATIO NELSON ('Beahor') (S)	EBls
horrida	EBls
HOT CHOCOLATE ('Wekpaltlez') (F) ♀H6	CDoC CSBt CWal EBls EGren ELan ELon EPfP ETWh LBuc LCro LRHS MAsh MGos MPro NLar SEas SHor SMad SPad SPoG SSea SWCr
'Hugh Dickson' (HP)	ETWh NLar
hugonis	see *R. xanthina* f. *hugonis*
- 'Plenissima'	see *R. xanthina* f. *hugonis*
Hume's blush	see *R.* × *odorata* 'Odorata'
'Hunter' (Ru)	EBls
ICE CREAM ('Korzuri') (HT) ♀H6	CDoC SHor SPoG SWCr
§ ICEBERG ('Korbin') (F) ♀H6	Widely available
'Ilse Krohn Superior' (ClHT)	EBls
IMOGEN ('Austritch'[PBR]) (S)	SWCr
§ 'Impératrice Joséphine' (Gn) ♀H7	EBls ETWh NLar
IN MEMORY OF	LSRN
IN MEMORY OF MY CAT ('Webyum') (HT)	LSRN
IN MEMORY OF MY DOG ('Rawbark') (F)	LSRN
INDIAN SUMMER ('Peaperfume') (HT) ♀H6	CSBt MGos
INDIANNA MAE ('Beacrunch') (S)	EBls
'Indica Major' misapplied	see *R.* 'Clotilde'
'Indigo' (DPo)	EBls ETWh
INGRID BERGMAN ('Poulman'[PBR]) (HT) ♀H6	CBcs EBls EHeP EPfP ETWh LBom LSRN MGos MPro SSea
'Inspiration' (ClHT)	LBuc LRHS MAsh
INSPIRATION ('Nor19597') (HT)	EBls LRHS
INSPIRE ('Frytempo') (HT)	SEas
INTRIGUE ('Jacum') (F)	EGren
'Ipsilanté' (G)	EBls
IRENE R ('Beakiwi') (S)	EBls
'Irène Watts' (Ch)	EBls NLar
'Irene's Delight' (HT)	LSRN
IRISH EYES ('Dicwitness') (F) ♀H6	ESty IArd LRHS MGos SEas SWCr
IRISH WONDER	see *R.* EVELYN FISON
ISABELLA ('Poulisab') (Renaissance Series) (S)	ETWh MPro
§ ISIDORA ('Bozisidfra') (Frayla Series) (S)	ETWh
ISIS	see *R.* SILVER ANNIVERSARY
ISN'T SHE LOVELY ('Diciluvit'[PBR]) (HT) ♀H6	EBls ELan MPro
'Ispahan' (D) ♀H6	EBls ETWh NLar SHor
IT'S A WONDERFUL LIFE ('Dictwix'[PBR]) (F)	CSBt EBee EBls EGren EPfP LBuc LCro LRHS MAsh MPri MPro SSea
IVOR'S ROSE ('Beadonald') (S)	EBee EBls LRHS MAsh SWCr
IVORY CASTLE ('Guesoverlay') (HT)	CDoC
IVORY DRIFT ('Meijeunom'[PBR]) (GC) **new**	EHeP
§ 'Jack Hume' (ClHT)	ESty
JACK'S WISH ('Kirsil') (HT)	LSRN
§ × *jacksonii* 'Max Graf' (GC/Ru)	NLar
- RED MAX GRAF	see *R.* ROTE MAX GRAF
Jacobite rose	see *R.* × *alba* 'Alba Maxima'
JACQUELINE DU PRÉ ('Harwanna') (S) ♀H6	CDoC ESty ETWh LCro NLar SEas
'Jacques Cartier' misapplied	see *R.* 'Marchesa Boccella'
JAM AND JERUSALEM ('Frymojo'[PBR]) (F)	CDoC EPfP MGos SWCr
JAM-A-LICIOUS ('Spekjam') (Ru)	CSBt LCro MHtn
JAMES GALWAY ('Auscrystal'[PBR]) (Cl)	EGren EPfP ESty LBom LRHS LSRN MAsh MBNS SWCr
JAMES L. AUSTIN ('Auspike'[PBR]) (S)	EGren EPfP IArd LBom LCro LRHS SWCr
'James Mason' (G)	EBls NLar
'James Veitch' (DPoMo)	CoPl
JANE ('Raw1268') (F)	ESty
JANE AUSTEN ('Harzircon') (F)	LRHS
'Japonica' (CeMo)	ETWh NLar
§ JARDINS DE BAGATELLE ('Meimafris') (HT)	LSRN MGos
JASMINA ('Korcentex'[PBR]) (ClHT)	CDoC EBls ESty ETWh NLar SEas SSea
'Jaune Desprez'	see *R.* 'Desprez à Fleur Jaune'
JAZZ	see *R.* THAT'S JAZZ (Courtyard Series)
JEAN ('Cocupland'[PBR]) (Patio)	LSRN
JEAN STEPHENNE ('Velgrav') (HM)	EBls
'Jeanne de Montfort' (CeMo)	ETWh
JEEPERS CREEPERS ('Scrivpinkedge') (GC)	CDoC
§ JELENA ('Bozjelefra') (Frayla Series) (S)	ETWh
'Jenny Duval' misapplied	see *R.* 'Président de Sèze'
'Jenny Wren' (F)	EBls
'Jens Munk' (Ru)	ETWh
JILL'S ROSE ('Ganjil') (F)	LSRN
JILLY JEWEL ('Benmfig') (Min)	LSRN
JOANNE ('Forjon') (S)	ESty
JOHANN WOLFGANG VON GOETHE ROSE	see *R.* PURE POETRY
JOHN ('Simbro') (HT)	ESty
'John Gwilliam'	MAvo MHCG WMal
'John Hopper' (HP)	ETWh
§ JOIE DE VIVRE ('Korflocí 01'[PBR]) (Patio/S) ♀H6	CDoC CEnd EBls EGren ELan EPfP ESty ETWh LCro LRHS MPri NLar SEas SMad SPoG SSea SWCr
JOLEEN ('Poulren032'[PBR]) (S)	ETWh
'Josephine Bruce' (HT)	EBls
'Joseph's Coat' (ClS)	EBls ETWh IArd LRHS SEas SRGP SWCr
JUBILÉ PAPA MEILLAND ('Meiceazar'[PBR]) (HT)	SEas SSea

'Jubilee Celebration' (F)	EGren		La Rose de Molinard ('Delgrarose'PBR) (S) ♀H6	ELon ETWh LSRN NLar
Jubilee Celebration ('Aushunter'PBR) (S)	EGren SPoG SWCr	§	La Rose de Petit Prince ('Delgramau') (F)	EBls ETWh
Jude the Obscure ('Ausjo'PBR) (S)	SWCr		'La Rubanée'	see R. × centifolia 'Unique Panachée'
Judi Dench ('Peahunder') (F)	IArd		La Sévillana ('Meigekanu') (F/GC)	EBls WCot
'Julia's Rose' (HT)	EGren LSRN MPro		La Villa Cotta ('Korbamflu'PBR) (L)	EBls
Julie ('Raw2541') (HT)	ESty		'La Ville de Bruxelles' (D) ♀H6	ETWh
Julio Iglesias ('Meistemon'PBR) (F)	SEas		'Lady Elgin'	see R. Thaïs
'Juno' (Ce)	EBls NLar		Lady Emma Hamilton ('Ausbrother'PBR) (S) ♀H6	LCro WSpi
Just Alex ('Fortigg') (CI)	ESty		'Lady Gay' (Ra)	ETWh
Just for You ('Gues 15-94') (F)	ESty		'Lady Godiva' (Ra)	ETWh
Just Jane ('Raw1046') (F)	LSRN		'Lady Hillingdon' (CIT)	see R. 'Climbing Lady Hillingdon'
'Just Jenny' (Min)	LSRN		'Lady Hillingdon' (T)	EBls NLar
'Just Joey' (HT) ♀H6	CWal EBls EGren ELan ELon ETWh IArd LCro LSRN MGos MPro SPoG SRGP SSea SWCr		Lady Marmalade ('Hartiger'PBR) (F)	CDoC MGos MNHC MPri NLar SPoG SWCr WSpi
Just Robert ('Raw1075') (F)	LSRN		'Lady Mary Fitzwilliam' (HT)	EBls ETWh
Just Steve ('Raw890') (F)	LSRN		Lady of Shalott ('Ausnyson'PBR) (S) ♀H6	EGren ELan EPfP ESty IArd LBom LCro LRHS MAsh NLar SPoG SWCr
Karen ('Gueshead') (S)	ESty		Lady Penelope ('Chewdor') (CIHT)	LRHS SEas
'Kasteel Hex' (S)	EBls	§	'Lady Penzance' (RH)	EBls
Katarina (Frayla Series)	see R. Theo Clevers (Taste of Love Series)		Lady Rose ('Korlady') (HT)	EPfP MAsh MPri SWCr
'Katharina Zeimet' (Poly)	ETWh NLar		Lady Salisbury ('Auscezed'PBR) (S)	SWCr
'Kathleen' (HM)	EBls ETWh LSRN		'Lady Sylvia' (HT)	EBls LSRN
'Kathleen Harrop' (Bb)	EBee EBls EGren ETWh LCro MMuc NLar SWCr		'Lady Waterlow' (CIHT)	EBls ETWh NLar WSpi
Kathryn ('Rawkat') (F)	LSRN		laevigata (Ra)	EBls MMuc
'Katie' (CIF)	LSRN		- 'Anemonoides'	see R. 'Anemone'
Katie's Rose ('Horrapture') (F)	ETWh LSRN		Laguna ('Koradigel'PBR) (CIHT)	SEas
'Kazanlik' misapplied	see R. × damascena 'Professeur Émile Perrot'		L'Aimant ('Harzola'PBR) (F) ♀H5	EBls EPfP SWCr
Keep Smiling ('Fryflorida') (HT) ♀H6	CDoC EBls LRHS SPoG SSea		Lalande de Pomarol ('Delcherot') (S)	SEas
'Keith Maughan' (CI)	EBls EPfP LCro LRHS		L'Alhambra	see R. Giardina
§	Kent ('Poulcov') (Towne & Country Series) (S/GC) ♀H6	CBcs CDoC CSBt EBls EGren ELan ESty ETWh LCro LSRN MMuc NLar SEND SHor SPoG SSea SWCr	'Lamarque' (N)	ETWh
			Lambada ('Korapfhecki'PBR) (S)	EBls
§	Kesse Lippe ('Noa241101'PBR) (S)	EBls LRHS	Lancashire ('Korstesgli') (GC) ♀H6	ESty ETWh LSRN NLar SSea SWCr
	Kew Gardens ('Ausfence'PBR) (S) ♀H6	ELan EPfP LCro LRHS MBNS	Lancelot ('Tan03542'PBR) (CI)	ESty SEas
	'Kew Rambler' (Ra)	CRHN EBls ETWh LRHS NLar	§	'Lanei' (CeMo)	ETWh NLar
	'Kiftsgate'	see R. filipes 'Kiftsgate'	latibracteata	EBls
	'Kiftsgate Superior' (S)	EBls	Laudatio	see R. Timeless Purple
	'Kim' (Patio/F)	LSRN	Laura ('Raw2722') (F)	ESty
	'King's Ransom' (HT)	EBls SWCr	Laura Ford ('Chewarvel') (CIMin) ♀H5	ELan LRHS MAsh MGos SPoG SWCr
	Kiss Me Kate ('Kornagelio') (CIS)	EBls SEas SSea	'Laura Louisa' (CI)	EBls ETWh NLar
	Kisses of Fire ('Chewmultiseek') (CIMin)	CDoC NLar	'Laure Davoust' (Ra)	EBls ETWh MMuc NLar
	Kitty ('Beaarty') (S)	EBls	Lavender Cover ('Poulrust'PBR) (GC) **new**	LBom
	× kochiana	EBls		
	Koko Loco ('Wekbijou') (F)	EBls ESty SEas	Lavender Ice ('Tan04249'PBR) (F)	EBee LCro SPoG
§	'Königin von Dänemark' (A) ♀H7	CBcs EBls ETWh LCro LRHS LSRN MGos NLar	'Lavender Lassie' (HM)	EBls EGren ETWh NLar
	'Korresia' (F) ♀H7	CDoC CSBt EBee EBls EGren EPfP LBuc MAsh SPoG SWCr	Lavender Siluetta ('Korsilu 08') (Ra)	EBls LBuc
	Kronprinsesse Mary ('Poulcas018') (F)	ETWh LBom	Lavender Symphonie ('Meiptima') (Patio)	EBls SWCr
	'Kronprinzessin Viktoria von Preussen' (Bb)	ETWh	laxa	EBls
	'La Belle Distinguée' (RH)	ETWh	Layla (Fragrant Bella Series)	see R. Isidora (Frayla Series)
	'La France' (HT)	ETWh		
	'La Perle' (Ra)	CRHN		
	'La Reine Victoria'	see R. 'Reine Victoria'		

L.D. Braithwaite ('Auscrim') (S)	EGren ETWh	Lord Byron ('Meitosier') (CIHT)	ESty SWCr
Le Rouge et le Noir ('Delcart') (HT)	ELon	'Lord Penzance' (RH)	EBls ETWh
'Le Vésuve' (Ch)	EBls ETWh	Lots Of Kisses	see R. Kesse Lippe
Leah Tutu ('Hornavel') (S)	EBee EBls EPfP ESty LCro LRHS MAsh SEas SWCr	Lots of Love ('Forchriso') (F)	ESty
		'L'Ouche' misapplied	see R. 'Louise Odier'
Leaping Salmon ('Peamight'^{PBR}) (CIHT) ♀^{H6}	CSBt EGren ETWh LRHS MGos SEas SWCr	'Louis XIV' (Ch)	EBls ETWh
		Louise ('Raw2796') (F) **new**	ESty
'Leda' (D)	EBls ETWh NLar	'Louise Bugnet' (Ru)	ETWh
Lemon Couture ('Peacasino') (Patio)	EHeP MNHC	Louise Clements ('Clelou') (S)	EBls EPfP LRHS
'Lemon Pillar'	see R. 'Paul's Lemon Pillar'	§ 'Louise Odier' (Bb)	EBls EGren EPfP ETWh IArd LCro LRHS LSRN NLar SEas SRGP
'Léontine Gervais' (Ra)	CRHN EBls	Love & Peace ('Baipeace'^{PBR}) (HT) ♀^{H7}	ELan ESty LBom
'Leo's Eye' (Ra)	ETWh NLar WFar		
Let There Be Love ('Frysoda') (F)	EBls EPfP LBuc LRHS MAsh	Love Knot ('Chewglorious'^{PBR}) (ClMin) ♀^{H6}	CDoC CSBt EGren ELan EPfP LBuc LRHS MAsh MGos NLar SWCr
Let's Celebrate ('Fryraffles'^{PBR}) (F) ♀^{H5}	CDoC EBls EPfP LBuc LRHS MAsh MPri SEas SPoG		
'Leverkusen' (ClF) ♀^{H6}	EBls ETWh NLar SWCr	'Love Never Dies' (Patio)	NTrD
'Ley's Perpetual' (ClT)	EBls	Love of My Life ('Raw2325') (HT)	ESty
Libertas ('Tan99134'^{PBR}) (Ra) **new**	SEas	Lovely Boy ('Simjas') (HT)	ESty
Lichfield Angel ('Ausrelate'^{PBR}) (S) ♀^{H6}	EGren EPfP LRHS NLar SWCr	§ Lovely Bride ('Meiratcan'^{PBR}) (Patio)	EBls EPfP LBuc LRHS MAsh SPoG SWCr
Lichtkönigin Lucia ('Korlillub') (S)	EBls	Lovely Lady ('Dicjubell'^{PBR}) (HT) ♀^{H6}	CDoC CSBt EBls ELan SEas SSea
Life Begins at 40! ('Horhohoho') (F)	NTrD	Lovely Lynn ('Sty04-04') (F) **new**	ESty
Lilac Bouquet ('Chewlilacdays') (Cl)	EBls ELon EPfP ESty LBuc LRHS MPri SEas SSea SWCr	Lovely Meidiland	see R. Lovely Bride
		Lovely Parfuma (F)	CDoC EBls ELon SSea
'Lilac Domino' (Ra)	ETWh	'Lovers' Meeting' (HT)	EGren
Lilac Wine ('Dicmulti') (F) ♀^{H5}	CDoC EGren LSRN NLar	Lovestruck ('Dicommatac') (F)	CDoC CSBt EBls EGren ELan LBuc LCro LRHS MAsh MSwo NLar SWCr
Liliana ('Poulsyng'^{PBR}) (S)	EBee ETWh LSRN MPro	Loving Memory ('Korgund81') (HT)	CSBt EBls EGren IArd LCro LSRN MGos MPri NTrD SEas SPoG SWCr
Lilli Marlene ('Korlima') (F)	EBee EGren MPro SSea SWCr		
Lily (Fragrant Bella Series)	see R. Theo Clevers (Taste of Love Series)	§ 'Loving Mum'^{PBR} (HT)	CSBt ESty
'Lincolnshire Yellow Belly' (F)	ELan ESty	Loving Son ('Fornate') (HT)	ESty
Lion's Fairy Tale	see R. Champagne Moment	Loyal Companion ('Beaqueen') (Patio)	EBls MPri
Little Amy ('Battamy') (Min)	LSRN	§ *lucieae*	EBee NLar SDix WPGP
Little Angel ('Poulpal038'^{PBR}) (S)	EBls EPfP LRHS SWCr	- var. *onoei*	WPGP
Little Duet ('Guesbliss') (F)	ESty	Lucky! ('Frylucy') (F) ♀^{H6}	CBcs CDoC EBls EPfP MGos MPri SEas SPoG SSea SWCr
'Little Emily' (Patio)	LSRN	Lucy ('Kirlis') (F)	LSRN
'Little Fin' (Min)	LSRN	Luke ('Weblib') (ClF) **new**	ESty
'Little Gem' (DPMo)	EBls ETWh	Lyda Rose ('Letlyda') (S)	EBls
Little Jackie ('Savor') (Min)	LSRN	'Lykkefund' (Ra)	EBls ETWh
Little Lucy ('Guesjury') (F) **new**	ESty	Macartney rose	see R. bracteata, R. The McCartney Rose
Little Rambler ('Chewramb') (MinRa) ♀^{H6}	CDoC CSBt EBls ELan ESty LCro MGos SEas SSea SWCr	Macmillan Nurse ('Beamac') (S)	CDoC EBls EPfP ESty ETWh LCro LRHS MAsh MPro NLar SPoG SWCr WKif
'Little White Pet'	see R. 'White Pet'	'Macrantha' (Gallica hybrid)	EBls
Liverpool Hope ('Beapike') (S)	EBls EPfP LRHS MAsh SWCr	*macrophylla* (S)	LEdu
		- B&SWJ 2603 (S)	WCru
Liwa ('Poulcy035'^{PBR}) (S) **new**	LRHS	- GWJ 9306 (S)	WCru
Lizzy ('Tan10553'^{PBR}) (ClMin)	SEas	'Madame Alfred Carrière' (N) ♀^{H5}	CBcs CDoC CRHN CSBt EBee EBls EGren ELan EPfP ESty ETWh IArd LBom LCro LRHS MGos MPro MSwo NLar SEas SEND SHor SMad SPoG SRGP SSea SWCr WKif WTre
'Lolabelle' (S)	ETWh		
Lolita Lempicka ('Meizincaro'^{PBR}) (HT)	EGren		
'Long John Silver' (Cl)	EBls		
longicuspis misapplied	see R. 'Mulliganii'	'Madame Alice Garnier' (Ra)	CRHN ETWh
longicuspis Bertol. var. *sinowilsonii* (Ra)	ETWh	§ Madame Anisette ('Korberonem'^{PBR}) (HT) **new**	SEas
Loraine ('Poulren046') (Renaissance Series) (S)	ETWh	'Madame Antoine Mari' (T)	ETWh
		'Madame Berkeley' (T)	WMal
		§ 'Madame Boll' (DPo)	EBls EGren ETWh LCro LRHS LSRN NLar SEas SHor SWCr

§ 'Madame Caroline Testout' (HT) — LRHS
'Madame d'Arblay' (Ra) — ETWh
'Madame de la Roche-Lambert' (DPMo) — EBls ETWh NLar
'Madame de Sancy de Parabère' (Bs) — EBls ETWh
'Madame Ernest Calvat' (Bb) — ETWh
§ 'Madame Grégoire Staechelin' (ClHT) ♀H6 — EBls EGren ELan EPfP ETWh LCro SPlb SWCr WKif
'Madame Hardy' (D) ♀H6 — CDoC EBls ETWh LCro LRHS LSRN NLar SWCr
'Madame Isaac Péreire' (ClBb) — CBcs CDoC CSBt EBls ELan ETWh LCro LRHS NLar SEas SRGP
'Madame Jules Gravereaux' (CIT) — EBls
'Madame Knorr' misapplied — see R. 'Madame Boll'
'Madame Knorr' (DPo) ♀H7 — EPfP
'Madame Laurette Messimy' (Ch) — ETWh
'Madame Legras de Saint Germain' (A × N) — EBls ETWh
'Madame Louis Lévêque' (DPMo) — EBls ETWh
'Madame Pierre Oger' (Bb) — EBls EGren ELan ETWh LCro
'Madame Zoëtmans' (D) — ETWh
'Madeleine Seltzer' (Ra) — ETWh
'Madge' (HM) — LSto SDix
MAGIC CARPET ('Jaclover'^PBR) (S/GC) ♀H6 — CDoC EBls EGren NLar
MAGIC HARLEQUIN — see R. 'Saloon'
MAGIC MOMENT ('Forrusty') (HT) — ESty
'Maid of Kent' (Cl) — LSRN SWCr
'Maiden's Blush' (A) — ELan LEdu LRHS MAsh MMuc WHer
'Maiden's Blush, Great' — see R. 'Great Maiden's Blush'
'Maigold' (ClSpH) ♀H6 — EBls EGren ELan ETWh LBom LBuc LCro LRHS MGos NLar SWCr
MAISIE (Fragrant Bella Series) — see R. MARIJA (Frayla Series)
Maltese rose — see R. 'Cécile Brünner'
MALVERN HILLS ('Auscanary'^PBR) (Ra) ♀H5 — EGren EPfP ESty LBom LRHS NLar
MAMMA MIA! ('Fryjolly'^PBR) (HT) ♀H6 — CDoC CSBt EBls EPfP LRHS MAsh MGos SEas SPoG SWCr
MANDARIN ('Korcelin') (Min) — CDoC EBls ESty SWCr
'Maning' (Patio) — LSRN
'Manning's Blush' (RH) — EBls
'Mannington Cascade' (Ra) — EBls
'Mannington Mauve Rambler' (Ra) — EBls
MANY HAPPY RETURNS ('Harwanted') (F) ♀H6 — CDoC CSBt EBls EPfP LBuc LRHS LSRN MAsh MGos MPri MSwo SWCr
MARC CHAGALL ('Delstrirojacre') (F) new — SEas
§ 'Marchesa Boccella' (DPo) ♀H7 — CBcs EPfP ETWh LCro LRHS MPri MPro NLar SPoG SWCr WHer
'Maréchal Niel' (N) — EBls ETWh SSea
MARGARET GREVILLE ('Beajoker') (S) — EBls
MARGARET MERRIL ('Harkuly') (F) — CBcs CDoC CSBt EBee EBls EGren ELan EPfP ESty ETWh IArd LCro LRHS LSRN MAsh MGos MPri NTrD SEas SHor SPoG SRGP SSea SWCr
'Marguerite Hilling' (S) — ETWh
MARIA ('Poulen010'^PBR) (Renaissance Series) (S) — ETWh

MARIE ANTOINETTE ('Tan96201') (F) new — SEas
'Marie Louise' (D) — EBls ETWh
'Marie Pavič' (Poly) — ETWh
'Marie-Jeanne' (Poly) — EBls
'Marigold' (HT) — CDoC
§ MARIJA ('Bozpiflam') (Frayla Series) (S) — ETWh
MARJORIE FAIR ('Harhero') (Poly/S) ♀H6 — EBls ELan SEas SRGP SWCr
'Martha' (Bb) — EBls LSRN
MARTIN ('Guesjudo') (F) new — ESty
'Martin Frobisher' (Ru) — EBls
MARY BERRY ('Harupon') (HT) — LRHS SWCr
§ MARY DELANY ('Ausorts'^PBR) (S) ♀H6 — EPfP LBom LRHS MAsh NLar SWCr
MARY ROSE ('Ausmary') (S) — SPoG
'Masquerade' (F) — CDoC EBls EGren ELan NLar
MATADOR ('Tanrodat'^PBR) (HT) — CDoC
MATAWHERO MAGIC — see R. SIMPLY THE BEST
MATHILDE ('Poulren026') (Renaissance Series) (S) — ETWh
MATTHEW ('Simanders') (HT) — ESty
'Maurice Bernardin' (HP) — EBls
MAURICE UTRILLO ('Delstavo') (HT) — ESty
'Max Graf' — see R. × jacksonii 'Max Graf'
'Maxima' — see R. × alba 'Alba Maxima'
MAXIMA ROMANTICA ('Meikerira'^PBR) (HT) — EBls LRHS MPro SWCr
'Maxime Corbon' (Ra) — ETWh
'May Queen' (Ra) — CRHN ETWh NLar SEND
'McCartney Rose' — see R. THE MCCARTNEY ROSE
MEDLEY RUBY — see R. RUBY ROMANCE
'Meg' (ClHT) — EBls ETWh
'Meg Merrilies' (RH) — EBls
MEGAN ('Foreyes') (F) — ESty
'Mermaid' (Cl) ♀H5 — CSBt EBls ETWh LCro SEND SSea
METEOR ('Korzeigar'^PBR) (F) new — EBls LBuc
§ 'Mevrouw Nathalie Nypels' (Poly) — EBls ETWh WKif
MIA (Fragrant Bella Series) — see R. NATALIJA (Frayla Series)
MICHAEL ('Forson') (F) — ESty
× micrugosa — EBls
- 'Alba' — EBls SBrt
'Midnight' ambig. — SReu
MIDNIGHT BLUE ('Wekfabpur') (S) — CDoC EBls ESty MGos
MIDSUMMER ('Tan02280'^PBR) (F) — SEas
MIDSUMMER NIGHT'S DREAM ('Rawroyal') (F) — ESty
§ MILEVA ('Bozmilefra'^PBR) (Frayla Series) (S) — ELan ETWh
§ MILLIE ('Poulren013'^PBR) (Renaissance Series) (S) ♀H4 — CBcs CDoC EBls EGren ELan ELon ESty ETWh LBuc LCro LRHS LSRN MGos MPri MPro NLar SEas SHor SPoG SRGP SWCr
MIND GAMES ('Dickylie') (F) — MPro
MINERVA ('Visancar') (F) — EBls ESty LRHS MPri SEas SSea
'Minnehaha' (Ra) — EBls SSea
MIRANDA ('Ausimmon'^PBR) (S) — ETWh
MISCHIEF ('Macmi') (HT) — EGren LSRN
'Miss Edith Cavell' (Poly) — EBls ETWh NLar
MISSING YOU ('Raw1107') (S) — EGren ESty
§ 'Mister Lincoln' (HT) — EBls EGren
§ MISTY HIT ('Poulhi011'^PBR) (PatioHit Series) (Patio) — CDoC EBls LRHS SWCr

Mokarosa ('Frywitty'PBR) (F)	EBls ESty LCro LRHS MPri		Nadia ('Poulen007'PBR) (Renaissance Series) (S)	ETWh LBom
Molineux ('Ausmol'PBR) (S) ♀H6	EGren EPfP LSRN		Nahéma ('Deléri') (CIHT)	EBls SHor SSea
Moment in Time ('Korcastrav'PBR) (F) ♀H6	CDoC CSBt EBee EBls LBuc LRHS MAsh MPri MPro SPoG SWCr		Nancy ('Poulninga') (Renaissance Series) (S)	ETWh NLar
Moody Blue ('Fryniche') (HT)	CDoC EPfP LBuc LCro LRHS MAsh MGos SEas		Naomi ('Poulren022'PBR) (Renaissance Series) (S)	ETWh LBuc LRHS SEas SWCr
Moon Dancer ('Fordan') (Cl)	ESty		'Narrow Water' (Ra) ♀H6	EBls ETWh NLar SHor
'Moonlight' (HM)	EBls ETWh MGos MSwo SWCr		'Nastarana' (N)	ETWh
'Morletii' (Bs)	ETWh MMuc		Natalie ('Poulren014'PBR) (Renaissance Series) (S)	ETWh MPro
'Morning Jewel' (ClF) ♀H7	EGren LRHS		Natalija ('Boznatafra'PBR) (Frayla Series) (S)	ELan ETWh
§ 'Morsdag' (Poly/F)	ELan LSRN MSwo		Natasha Richardson ('Harpacket'PBR) (F)	SEas
Mortimer Sackler	see R. Mary Delany		'Nathalie Nypels'	see R. 'Mevrouw Nathalie Nypels'
moschata (Ra)	EBls ETWh MCtn WMal		'National Trust' (HT)	EGren IArd SWCr
- var. nepalensis	see R. brunonii		Nelly ('Poulren038') (Renaissance Series) (F)	ETWh
Mother's Day	see R. 'Morsdag'		Nelson's Journey ('Beaflirt') (S)	EBls
Mount Aorangi ('Sanaran') (HT)	ESty		'Nelson's Pride' (F)	EBls
Mountbatten ('Harmantelle') (F) ♀H6	EGren EHeP SPoG SWCr		'Ness' (S)	ETWh NLar
'Mousseline' (DPoMo)	EBls ETWh		'Nestor' (G)	ETWh NLar
§ moyesii (S)	EBls ELan ETWh GGro GKev		'Nevada' (S)	CBcs EBls ETWh IArd
§ - var. fargesii (S)	EBls ETWh		New Beginnings ('Korprofko'PBR) (F) ♀H5	EBls LBuc
- holodonta	see R. moyesii f. rosea		§ 'New Dawn' (Cl) ♀H7	CDoC CEnd CRHN CSBt EBee EBls EGren ELan EPfP ETWh GKin LCro LRHS LSRN MAsh MGos MPri NLar SEas SHor SMad SPlb SPoG SSea SWCr WCot
§ - f. rosea (S)	EBls			
'Mr Lincoln'	see R. 'Mister Lincoln'			
'Mrs John Laing' (HP)	EBls ETWh NLar SRGP			
'Mrs Oakley Fisher' (HT)	EBls ETWh NLar SDix			
'Mrs Paul' (Bb)	ETWh			
'Mrs Reynolds Hole' (T)	ETWh		§ Newly Wed ('Dicwhynot'PBR) (Patio) ♀H6	EGren SSea SWCr
'Mrs Sam McGredy' (HT)	EBls		Newsflash ('Kenduch'PBR) (F) ♀H5	ESty ETWh
'Mrs Yamada' (Bb)	EBls		Nice Day ('Chewsea'PBR) (ClMin)	EPfP ESty LRHS MGos SPoG SWCr
mulliganii	see R. 'Mulliganii'		Night Owl ('Wekpurosot') (Cl)	CDoC CEnd ESty ETWh LRHS LSRN MGos NLar SPoG SSea
'Mulliganii' (Ra)	ETWh GKin MMuc			
multibracteata (S)	EBls ETWh			
multiflora (Ra)	EBls ETWh LBuc NLar		Nina ('Mehnina'PBR) (S)	LSRN
- 'Carnea' (Ra)	EBls		Nina ('Poulren018'PBR) (Renaissance Series) (S)	ETWh
§ - var. cathayensis (Ra)	EBls			
§ - 'Grevillei' (Ra)	ETWh MMuc		Nipper ('Hareco') (GC)	LRHS
- 'Platyphylla'	see R. multiflora 'Grevillei'		nitida	EBls
- var. watsoniana	see R. watsoniana		Noble Antony ('Ausway'PBR) (S)	EGren
Mum and Dad ('Raw2687') (F)	ESty		§ 'Noisette Carnée' (N) ♀H7	EBls EGren EPfP ETWh LBom LCro LRHS LSRN MBNS MGos NLar SEas SHor SRGP SSea SWCr WKif
Mum in a Million	see R. Millie (Renaissance Series)			
Mummy	see R. Newly Wed			
mundi	see R. gallica 'Versicolor'		Norfolk ('Poulfolk') (GC)	ETWh SWCr
Munstead Wood ('Ausbernard'PBR) (S) ♀H6	LCro SPoG SWCr WSpi		'Norwell' (Ra)	MNrw WFar
murielae	EBls		'Norwich Castle' (F)	EBls
'Muscosa Alba'	see R. × centifolia 'Shailer's White Moss'		Norwich Cathedral ('Beacath') (HT)	EBls
'Mutabilis'	see R. × odorata 'Mutabilis'		'Norwich Union' (F)	EBls
My Angel ('Poulty023'PBR) (Min)	EBls EPfP LRHS MAsh		Nostalgia ('Savarita') (Min)	EPfP
My Brother ('Raw1056') (F)	ESty		§ Nostalgia ('Taneiglat') (HT) ♀H6	CEnd CSBt CWal EBls EGren EHeP ESty ETWh LBom LBuc LRHS MAsh MGos MPri SEas SMad SPoG SSea SWCr
My Dad ('Boseltay'PBR) (F)	CBcs CDoC EBls LSRN MPro MSwo SEas SWCr			
'My Darling Husband' (F)	LSRN			
'My Darling Wife' (F)	LSRN			
My Girl ('Tan00798'PBR) (HT)	CDoC EBee SWCr		Nostalgie	see R. Nostalgia
'My Joy' (HT)	LSRN		'Notre-Dame de Calais' (Cl)	EBls
'My Lovely Mum' (F)	EPfP LBuc LCro MPri SWCr		Novalis ('Korfriedhar'PBR) (F)	EBls LBom
My Mum ('Webmorrow'PBR) (F)	CBcs EBls ESty LSRN MPro SEas SPoG SWCr		'Nozomi' (ClMin/GC)	EBls ELan ESty ETWh NLar SWCr
My Nan ('Fornan') (HT)	ESty		'Nuits de Young' (CeMo) ♀H7	EBls ETWh NLar
My Valentine ('Korcoluma'PBR) (HT)	EBls		'Nur Mahal' (HM)	ETWh
My Valentine ('Mormyval') (Min)	LSRN			

Nurse Tracey Davies ('Frykookie'PBR) (F) ♡H6 — MAsh SWCr
nutkana (S) — EBls
§ - var. *hispida* (S) — EBls
§ - 'Plena' (S/D) ♡H7 — EBls ETWh GKin LRHS WHer
Nye Bevan ('Auspital'PBR) (S) — LBom LRHS NLar
'Nymphenburg' (HM) — ETWh
'Nyveldt's White' (Ru) — EBls
Octavia Hill ('Harzeal'PBR) (F) — ETWh NLar
× *odorata* 'Diana Clare' (Ch) — WCot
- 'Florence Brown' (Ch) — WCot
- 'Fortune's Double Yellow' — see *R.* × *odorata* 'Pseudindica'
- 'Hume's Blush Tea-scented China' (ClCh) — ETWh
§ - 'Mutabilis' (Ch) ♡H5 — CDoC CRHN EBls ELan EPfP ETWh LCro LRHS LSRN MNrw SDix SEND SHor SPoG SSea WCot WMal
- 'Ochroleuca' (Ch) — ETWh
§ - 'Odorata' (Ch) — EBls
- old crimson China (Ch) — EBls
§ - 'Pallida' (Ch) — EBls ETWh LRHS NLar SHor WCot
§ - 'Pseudindica' (ClCh) — EBls IArd
§ - Sanguinea Group (Ch) — LRHS SEND
- - 'Bengal Crimson' (Ch) ♡H5 — CRHN EPfP ETWh LRHS LSto SDix SEND SHor SMad SPoG WCot
- - 'Bob's Beauty' (Ch) — WCot
§ - - 'Viridiflora' (Ch) — EBls ETWh SSea WCot
Odyssey ('Franski'PBR) (F) — ESty
officinalis — see *R. gallica* var. *officinalis*
Oh Wow! ('Wekspitrib'PBR) (ClHT) — CDoC ESty
'Oklahoma' (HT) — EGren
Ol' Blue Eyes ('Wekyolovefoy') (F) — CSBt
old blush China — see *R.* × *odorata* 'Pallida'
old cabbage — see *R.* × *centifolia*
Old John ('Dicwillynilly') (F) — LSRN
old pink moss rose — see *R.* × *centifolia* 'Muscosa'
Old Port ('Mackati') (F) — ELon IArd SEas
old red moss — see *R.* 'Henri Martin', 'Lanei'
old velvet moss — see *R.* 'William Lobb'
old yellow Scotch — see *R.* × *harisonii* 'Williams' Double Yellow'
§ Olivera ('Bozolivfra') (Frayla Series) (S) — ETWh
Olivia ('Wekquahofa') (HT) — ETWh
Olivia Rose Austin ('Ausmixture'PBR) (S) — EGren ELan EPfP ESty LBom LCro LRHS MAsh NLar SPoG SWCr
'Olympic Flame' (F) — LRHS MAsh
'Omar Khayyám' (D) — EBls ETWh LRHS NLar
omeiensis — see *R. sericea* subsp. *omeiensis*
Ondella ('Meirokad') (HT) new — SReu
One in a Million ('Poulren024'PBR) (S) — ELan ESty ETWh MGos MPro NLar SEas SHor SPoG
One Love ('Fryyulo') (F) — EBls LRHS MAsh
Ooh La La ('Gues05-64') (F) — ESty
Oops A Daisy ('Gues11-25') (F) — ESty
Open Arms ('Chewpixcel'PBR) (ClMin) ♡H6 — EBls LBom LCro LRHS SEas SMad SSea SWCr
'Ophelia' (HT) — ETWh
Orange Blossom Special ('Smi 5202'PBR) (ClMin) — ESty
'Orange Sensation' (F) — EGren
Orange Sunblaze ('Meijikatar'PBR) (Min) — LRHS SWCr

Oranges and Lemons ('Macoranlem') (F) — CDoC EBls ESty MGos SEas SSea SWCr
Othello ('Auslo'PBR) (S) — EGren SRGP
Our Beth ('Beacarol') (S) — EBls EPfP LCro LRHS MAsh SWCr
'Our Dream' (Patio) — EBls LRHS MAsh SWCr
Our Hilda ('Lancoro') (F) — LSRN
Our Jane ('Horengland') (F) — LSRN
Our Liz ('Raw2707') (F) new — ESty
'Our Millie' (HT) — LSRN
Our Molly ('Dicreason') (GC/S) — LSRN
Oxford Physic Rose ('Beaquality') (S) — EBls LRHS MAsh
Oxfordshire ('Korfullwind'PBR) (GC) ♡H6 — SWCr
Ozeana ('Tan11616'PBR) (Cl) — EBls LRHS MAsh MPri
'Pablito' (Min) — MMuc
Pacific Blue ('Tan98485') (HT) — SEas SHor SSea
Paisley Abbey ('Harrestore'PBR) (S) — NLar
Panache ('Poultop'PBR) (Patio/Min) — EBls LCro LRHS MPri SWCr
Paper Anniversary (Patio) — LSRN
Papi Delbard ('Delaby') (ClHT) — EBee EBls ETWh LSRN NLar
'Papillon' (Ch) — EBls
Papworth's Pride ('Beamelon') (S) — EPfP SHor
I 'Parade' (Cl) ♡H6 — EBls ETWh LSRN SWCr
Parfum d'Armor ('Adanuaman'PBR) (HT) new — EHeP
Parfum d'Orléans ('Saunalid'PBR) (F) new — LSRN
'Parkdirektor Riggers' (Cl) — EBls ETWh LCro NLar
Parky ('Harpresto'PBR) (S) — EHeP
Parson's pink China — see *R.* × *odorata* 'Pallida'
Partridge ('Korweirim') (GC) — EBls
parvifolia — see *R.* 'Burgundiaca'
Pascali ('Lenip') (HT) — CBcs EGren SWCr
Pasillo ('Poulcy034'PBR) (Cl) new — LRHS
Pastella ('Tan98130') (S) — SEas
Pat Austin ('Ausmum') (S) — ETWh LSRN
Paul ('Smi158-4-04') (F) — ESty
'Paul Dauvesse' (Ra) — ETWh
'Paul Lédé' — see *R.* 'Climbing Paul Lédé'
'Paul Neyron' (HP) — ETWh
'Paul Noël' (Ra) — ETWh LSRN
'Paul Ricault' (Ce × HP) — EBls ETWh NLar
'Paul Transon' (Ra) ♡H6 — CRHN EBls ETWh LRHS MMuc
'Paula's Rose' (Patio) — LSRN
§ 'Paulii' (Ru/GC) — WSpi
'Paulii Alba' — see *R.* 'Paulii'
'Paul's Himalayan Musk' (Ra) ♡H6 — CBcs CDoC CEnd CRHN CSBt EBee EBls EGren EGrI EPfP ETWh GKin IArd LBom LCro LRHS MMuc NLar SEas SHor SPoG SSea SWCr WFar
§ 'Paul's Lemon Pillar' (ClHT) — ETWh NLar
'Paul's Scarlet Climber' (Cl/Ra) — CDoC EBls EGren LBom LCro MPri SWCr
'Paul's Single White Perpetual' (Ra) — ETWh
Paws ('Beapaw') (S) — EBls
'Pax' (HM) — EBls ETWh

PEACE ('Madame A. Meilland') (HT) ♀H6 — CBcs CEnd CSBt EBls EGren EHeP ELan EPfP LCro LRHS LSRN MAsh MPri MPro SEas SPoG SSea SWCr
PEACH DRIFT ('Meiggilli') (GC) — LSou MPro
'Peach Grootendorst' (Ru) — ETWh
PEACH MELBA ('Kormelpea'^PBR) (ClHT) — CDoC CSBt EBee EBls ELan ETWh LBuc LCro LRHS MAsh MPri NLar
PEACH VAZA ('Bozvaz019') (Art Vaza Series) (S) — ETWh
PEACHY ('Macrelea') (HT) — EBls EPfP LRHS MAsh SPoG SWCr
PEAR ('Bozedib023') (Taste of Love Series) (S) — ETWh
PEARL ('Korterschi'^PBR) (F) ♀H6 — EBls LRHS
PEARL ('Wekpearl') (HT) — CSBt EPfP
PEARL ABUNDANCE ('Harfrisky'^PBR) (F) — EHeP NTrD
PEARL ANNIVERSARY ('Whitston'^PBR) (Min/Patio) — CDoC CSBt EBls ESty LCro LSRN MPro NLar SSea
PEARL DRIFT ('Leggab') (S) — CEnd EBls ETWh NLar SWCr WKif
PEARL OF ST LUKE'S ('Beaoscar') (S) — EBls
PEARL VAZA ('Bozlenfra') (Art Vaza Series) (S) — ETWh LBom
PEAUDOUCE — see R. ELINA
PEGASUS ('Ausmoon') (S) — ETWh
§ *pendulina* — EBls ETWh
'Penelope' (HM) ♀H5 — CDoC EBee EBls EGren ELan ETWh LCro LRHS LSRN MAsh MNrw MSwo SSea SWCr WKif
'Penelope Hobhouse' (HM) — EBls
PENNI OUR SPECIAL GIRL ('Raw1130') (F) — ESty
PENNY LANE ('Hardwell') (ClHT) ♀H6 — EBee EGren EHeP ELan EPfP LBuc LCro LRHS MGos NLar SEas SHor SOrN SPoG SSea SWCr
× *penzanceana* — see R. 'Lady Penzance'
PEPPERMINT SPLASH — see R. RACHEL LOUISE MORAN
PERENNIAL BLUE ('Mehv9601') (Ra) ♀H6 — CDoC EBls EGrI ESty MGos NLar SEas SSea SWCr
PERENNIAL BLUSH ('Mehbarbie'^PBR) (Ra) ♀H6 — CDoC ELan ESty LRSN MGos SEas
PERFECT GENTLEMAN ('Raw1059') (F) — ESty
PERFECT HARMONY ('Tangustedv') (HT) — CDoC EBls ESty LCro SEas SSea
PERFECT MATCH ('Hartie') (F) — NTrD
PERFECT PET ('Smi122-2-04'^PBR) (F) — ESty
§ 'Perle d'Or' (Poly) ♀H6 — EBls ETWh NLar SDix
PERPETUALLY YOURS ('Harfable'^PBR) (Cl) — EBls MGos NLar
PERSIAN MYSTERY ('Hartroy') (*persica* hybrid) — EHeP
Persian yellow — see R. *foetida* 'Persiana'
PETER ('Raw2555') (HT) — ESty
PETER BEALES ('Cleexpert') (S) — EBls MAsh
PETER PAN ('Chewpan') (Min) ♀H6 — LRHS
PETER PAN ('Sunpete') (Patio) — SWCr
PETER'S PERSICA ('Chewgoldeneye') (*persica* hybrid) (CIS) — ETWh
'Petite de Hollande' (Ce) — EBls ETWh NLar
PHEASANT ('Kordapt') (GC) — EBls
PHILLIPA ('Poulheart'^PBR) (S) — ETWh

PHIL'S FAVOURITE ('Raw2788') (F) **new** — ESty
PHOENIX ('Harvee') (Min) — SEas
'Phyllis Bide' (Ra) ♀H6 — EBee EBls EGren ELan EPfP ETWh IArd LCro LRHS NLar SHor SSea SWCr WKif
PICCADILLY ('Macar') (HT) — EGren
PIGALLE '84 ('Meicloux') (F) — EBee SMad SWCr
'Pilgrim' — see R. THE PILGRIM
pimpinellifolia — see R. *spinosissima*
- 'Altaica' — see R. *spinosissima* 'Grandiflora'
- double yellow-flowered — see R. × *harisonii* 'Williams' Double Yellow'
PINK BELLS ('Poulbells') (GC) — EBls
'Pink Bouquet' (Ra) — CRHN
PINK CHAMPAGNE ('Forchamp') (Cl) — ESty
'Pink Cloud' (ClHT) — EGren LCro
PINK FLOWER CARPET ('Noatraum') (GC) ♀H6 — CDoC CSBt EBee EBls LBuc LCro LRHS LSRN MAsh MPri SEND SPoG SSea SWCr
'Pink Grootendorst' (Ru) — EBls ETWh
'Pink Gruss an Aachen' (F) — EBls ETWh
§ PINK HIT ('Poultipe'^PBR) (Min/Patio) — EBls LRHS LSRN
'Pink Leda' (D) — ETWh NLar
PINK MARTINI ('Tan04608'^PBR) (HT) — CDoC EBee EBls MGos SSea SWCr
pink moss — see R. × *centifolia* 'Muscosa'
PINK PARADISE ('Delfluoros'^PBR) (HT) — EBls EGren ETWh LRSN SEas
PINK PEACE ('Meibil') (HT) — EGren MSwo
PINK PERFECTION ('Korpauvio'^PBR) (HT) ♀H5 — CDoC CEnd EBls LRHS MAsh SSea
'Pink Perpétué' (Cl) — CSBt EBls EGren EPfP ETWh SPoG SRGP SWCr
'Pink Prosperity' (HM) — ETWh NLar
'Pink Showers' (ClHT) — EGren
PINK SWANY ('Meifafiot') **new** — EGren
PIPPIN ('Beajaffa') (S) — EBls EPfP LCro LRHS MAsh SSea SWCr
PIROUETTE ('Poulyc003'^PBR) (CIS) — EBls LRHS MAsh SWCr
'Plaisanterie' (HM) — SSea WMal
PLEINE DE GRÂCE ('Lengra') (S) — ETWh
POETICAL LIZ ('Beanatasha') (Cl) — EBls
POETRY IN MOTION ('Harelan') (HT) — EBls
POLAR STAR ('Tanlarpost') (HT) — EGren SWCr
'Polly' (HT) — LSRN
§ 'Polyantha Grandiflora' (Ra) — ETWh SVic
pomifera — see R. *villosa* L.
'Pompon Blanc Parfait' (A) — EBls
'Pompon de Bourgogne' — see R. 'Burgundiaca'
'Pompon de Paris' (CIMinCh) — see R. 'Climbing Pompon de Paris'
'Pompon de Paris' (MinCh) — SHor WAbe
POPCORN DRIFT ('Novarospop'^PBR) (Min) — LSou MPro
POPPY ROSE (HM) — EBls
PORT SUNLIGHT ('Auslofty'^PBR) (HM) ♀H6 — EGren ELan EPfP LRHS NLar SWCr
Portland rose — see R. 'Portlandica'
§ 'Portlandica' (DPo) — EPfP ETWh LRHS NLar SWCr
prairie rose — see R. *setigera*
prattii — EBls
'Precious Amber' (F) — EBls EPfP LBuc LCro LRHS MAsh SWCr

PRECIOUS GOLD ('Noa55504'PBR) (F) — EBls LCro LRHS MAsh SWCr
PRECIOUS GRANDDAUGHTER ('Raw1193') (F) — ESty
PRECIOUS GRANDSON ('Raw1088') (F) — ESty
PRECIOUS LOVE ('Kirlowo'PBR) (F) — EBls EPfP LBuc LCro LRHS MAsh SWCr
'Precious Memories' (Min) — LSRN
PRECIOUS MEMORIES ('Dichello'PBR) (F) — EGren ESty
PRECIOUS RUBY ('Noa16131') (F) — LCro LRHS
PRECIOUS TIME ('Oramarpa'PBR) (HT) — MPro
§ 'Président de Sèze' (G) ♀H6 — ETWh
PRETTY IN PINK ('Dicumpteen'PBR) (GC) ♀H6 — ELan
PRETTY JESSICA ('Ausjess') (S) — ETWh MGos NLar SEas
PRETTY POLLY ('Meitonje') (Min) ♀H6 — EGren EPfP ESty LCro LRHS MAsh MPro SEas SPoG SWCr
PRIDE AND JOY ('Raw2688') (S) — ESty
PRIDE OF ENGLAND ('Harencore') (HT) — LRHS MNHC NTrD
'Pride of Seale' (Cl) — SSea
'Prima Ballerina' (HT) — EGren LRHS SWCr
primula — ETWh
'Prince Charles' (Bb) — ETWh NLar
PRINCE JARDINIER ('Meitroni'PBR) (HT) ♀H6 — EGren ELon ESty
PRINCESS ALEXANDRA ('Pouldra') (Renaissance Series) (S) ♀H6 — ETWh NLar
PRINCESS ALEXANDRA OF KENT ('Ausmerchant'PBR) (S) — EGren ELan EPfP ESty LBom LRHS SWCr
PRINCESS ANNE ('Auskitchen'PBR) (S) ♀H6 — EGren EPfP LBom LRHS SWCr
'Princess Louise' (Ra) — EBls
PRINCESS OF MONACO ('Meimagarmic') (S) — LCro
PRINCESS OF WALES ('Hardinkum') (F) ♀H6 — EGren EHeP SWCr
'Princesse de Nassau' (Ra) — ETWh WMal
'Princesse Louise' (Ra) — EBls
'Princesse Marie' Jacques (Ra) — EBls
'Prolifera de Redouté' misapplied — see *R.* 'Duchesse de Montebello'
PROPER JOB ('Tan02733'PBR) (HT) — CDoC EBee EBls ETWh NLar SEas SHor SWCr
PROSECCO FIZZ ('Raw2287') (F) — ESty
'Prosperity' (HM) ♀H6 — EBls ELan ETWh LRHS NLar
PROSPERO ('Auspero') (S) — ETWh
§ PURE POETRY ('Jacment') (F) — EGren SWCr
§ PURE POETRY ('Tan04179') (HT) — EBee EBls ELon NLar SEas
'Purezza' (Ra) — EBls ETWh
PURPLE EDEN — see *R.* EBB TIDE
PURPLE SKYLINER ('Franwekpurp'PBR) (ClS) — EBls ELan EPfP LCro LRHS MPri SEas SPoG SWCr
PURPLE TIGER ('Jacpurr'PBR) (F) — EGren ESty
quatre saisons — see *R.* × *damascena* var. *semperflorens*
'Quatre Saisons Blanche Mousseuse' (DMo) — ETWh

QUEEN ANNE ('Austruck'PBR) (S) — LSRN
QUEEN ELIZABETH — see *R.* 'The Queen Elizabeth'
QUEEN MOTHER ('Korquemu') (Patio) ♀H6 — ELan SWCr
QUEEN OF DENMARK — see *R.* 'Königin von Dänemark'
QUEEN OF HEARTS — see *R.* 'Dame de Coeur'
QUEEN OF SWEDEN ('Austiger'PBR) (S) — EGren ELan EPfP LRHS MAsh NLar SWCr
'Queen of the Musks' (HM) — ETWh
RACHAEL'S ROSE ('Raw2551') (F) — ESty
'Rachel' ambig. — EGren
'Rachel' (HT) — CDoC LBuc LSRN MAsh MPri SWCr
I 'Rachel' (S) — MGos SMad SRGP
RACHEL ('Booyol') (S) — EBee
RACHEL ('Tangust') (HT) ♀H6 — CSBt EBls EPfP ESty ETWh LBuc LCro NLar SEas SPoG SSea
§ RACHEL LOUISE MORAN ('Jacdrama'PBR) (HT) — ESty SEas
RACHEL'S JOY ('Beaquick') (S) — EBls
RACQUEL ('Poulren023'PBR) (S) — ETWh
'Rambling Rector' (Ra) ♀H6 — CBcs CDoC CEnd CRHN CSBt EBee EBls EGren ELan EPfP ESty ETWh LBom LBuc LCro LRHS LSRN MAsh MBNS MGos MPri NLar SEas SHor SMad SPoG SSea SWCr WFar
RAMBLING ROSIE ('Horjasper'PBR) (Ra) ♀H6 — CDoC EBee EBls EGren EPfP ESty ETWh LBom LRHS LSRN MPro NLar SEas SSea SWCr WCot
'Ramona' (Ra) — EBls ETWh
RASPBERRY CREAM TWIRL ('Meiteratol'PBR) (ClHT) — EBls EPfP LBuc LRHS MAsh
'Raspberry Royale' (F/Patio) ♀H6 — CDoC EBls EPfP LRHS MAsh SPoG
'Raubritter' ('Macrantha' hybrid) — EBls ELan ETWh NLar
RAYMOND BLANC ('Delnado') (HT) — ETWh NLar
'Raymond Carver' (S) — EBls LRHS MAsh SWCr
REBECCA (Patio) — ESty
REBECCA MARY ('Dicjury'PBR) (F) — LSRN
REBEKAH HIT ('Poulpah046') (Patio) — LCro
RED DEVIL ('Dicam') (HT) — CDoC EGren
RED EDEN ROSE ('Meidrason'PBR) (Cl) — ESty SEas
RED FINESSE ('Korvillade'PBR) (F) ♀H6 — ETWh
RED FLAME ('Adabaring'PBR) (ClHT) — EPfP LBuc LRHS
'Red Grootendorst' — see *R.* 'F.J. Grootendorst'
RED LEONARDO DA VINCI ('Meiangele'PBR) (Poly) **new** — LSRN
RED LETTER DAY ('Beajackdaw') (S) — EBls EPfP SWCr
'Red Max Graf' — see *R.* ROTE MAX GRAF
red moss — see *R.* 'Henri Martin'
RED NEW DAWN — see *R.* 'Étendard'
RED PARFUM DE PROVENCE ('Meiafone'PBR) (HT) — EGren SEas
'Red Patio' (F/Patio) — LSRN NTrD SWCr
RED PERFUMELLA ('Meikeneza'PBR) (HT) — ELan ELon
RED QUEEN ('Liebestraum') (HT) — EHeP

red rose of Lancaster — see *R. gallica* var. *officinalis*
REDOVA ('Poulcy030'^{PBR}) — EBls LBuc LRHS MAsh SWCr
  (Courtyard Series) (Cl)
'Reine des Violettes' — EBls EGren ELon ETWh IArd LCro
  (HP) ♀^{H6} — LSRN MPri NLar SEas SHor
§ 'Reine Victoria' (Bb) — CDoC EBls ETWh LCro NLar
§ REMEMBER ('Poulht001'^{PBR}) — EBls EPfP LBuc SPoG
  (HT) ♀^{H6}
REMEMBER ME ('Cocdestin') — CDoC CSBt EBls EGren ELan ESty
  (HT) ♀^{H6} — IArd LCro LRHS LSRN MAsh MGos
  MPro SEas SPoG SWCr
REMEMBRANCE — EGren EHeP LBuc LSRN MNHC
  ('Harxampton') (F) — MPri NTrD SEas SPoG SWCr
§ RENAISSANCE ('Harzart'^{PBR}) — EGren
  (HT)
'René André' (Ra) — CRHN ETWh NLar
RÉPUBLIQUE DE MONTMARTRE — EGren
  ('Delparfrou') (F)
'Rescht' — see *R*. 'De Resht'
'Rêve d'Or' (N) — EBls ETWh
RHAPSODY IN BLUE — CBcs CSBt CWal EBee EBls EGren
  ('Frantasia'^{PBR}) (S) ♀^{H6} — EHeP ELan ELon EPfP ESty ETWh
  LBuc LCro LRHS LSRN MAsh MGos
  MNHC MPri MPro NLar SEas SMad
  SPoG SRGP SSea SWCr WKif
RHUBARB AND CUSTARD — ESty
  ('Raw1138') (F)
§ × *richardii* — EBls ETWh
RICK STEIN ('Tan96205'^{PBR}) — LSRN
  (HT)
RISING SUN ('Forsunny') (F) — ESty
'Rita' ambig. — WKif
'River Gardens' — NPer
'Rivers's George IV' (Ch) — ETWh
RNLI ('Beasaved') (S) **new** — EBls
ROALD DAHL ('Ausowlish'^{PBR}) — EGren ELan EPfP ESty IArd LBom
  (S) — LCro LRHS MBNS NLar SPoG SWCr
'Robin Hood' (HM) — EBls ETWh
ROCK & ROLL ('Wekgobnez') — ELan ESty
  (HT)
'Rock and Roll'^{PBR} — EGren
ROMANCE ('Tanezamor'^{PBR}) — LSRN
  (S)
ROMANTIC SILUETTA — EBls LRHS
  ('Korsilu 09') (Ra)
'Rosa Mundi' — see *R. gallica* 'Versicolor'
ROSALITA ('Lentrihel') (HM) — EBls
ROSARIUM UETERSEN — EBls
  ('Kortersen') (ClHT)
'Rose Ball' (S) — LRHS
§ 'Rose d'Amour' (S) ♀^{H6} — EBls
'Rose de Meaux' — see *R.* × *centifolia* 'De Meaux'
'Rose de Rescht' — see *R*. 'De Resht'
ROSE DES CISTERCIENS — ESty ETWh NLar
  ('Delarle') (HT)
'Rose du Maître d'Ecole' — see *R*. 'Du Maître d'École'
'Rose du Roi' (HP/DPo) — ETWh
ROSE FOR ELAINE — LSRN
  ('Rawdenqueen') (HT)
§ ROSE GAUJARD ('Gaumo') — EGren EPfP LRHS SWCr
  (HT)
ROSE SYNACTIF BY SHISEIDO — see *R*. LA ROSE DE PETIT PRINCE
'Rose-Marie Viaud' (Ra) — ETWh MMuc
ROSEMARY HARKNESS — MNHC SRGP
  ('Harrowbond') (HT)
ROSEMOOR ('Austough'^{PBR}) — SWCr
  (S) ♀^{H6}
'Roseraie de l'Haÿ' (Ru) ♀^{H7} — CBcs CDoC CSBt EBee EBls EGren
  EPfP ETWh LBuc LCro LRHS LSRN
  MPri NLar SEas SEND SPoG SSea
  SWCr

ROSIE ('Benros') (Min) — LSRN
'Rosy Cheeks' (HT) — EPfP LRHS MAsh SWCr
ROSY CUSHION ('Interall') — EBls ETWh LRHS NLar
  (S/GC)
§ ROTARY SUNRISE ('Fryglitzy') — LRHS
  (HT)
§ ROTE MAX GRAF ('Kormax') — EBls
  (GC/Ru)
'Rouletii' (Min) — WFar
'Roundelay' (HT) — EBls ETWh
roxburghii — ETWh GKev MCtn
  - PAB 7331 — WPGP
  - W&O 9218 — GGro
  - f. *normalis* — EBls
'Royal Air Force' (HT) — EGren ELan
§ ROYAL BROMPTON ROSE — ESty MPro
  ('Meivildo') (HT)
ROYAL COPENHAGEN — see *R*. REMEMBER
ROYAL JUBILEE — LCro SWCr
  ('Auspaddle'^{PBR}) (S)
ROYAL PARFUMA — EBls LBom LCro SSea
  ('Kordiagraf'^{PBR}) (HT)
ROYAL WILLIAM — CDoC CSBt EGren ELan LBuc LCro
  ('Korzaun') (HT) ♀^{H6} — LSRN MGos MNHC MPri
§ *rubiginosa* (S) — CBWd CCVT CLnd EBls ETWh
  LBuc WKor WOrg
rubra — see *R. gallica*
rubrifolia — see *R. glauca* Pourr.
RUBY ANNIVERSARY — CDoC EBls EGren ELan ELon EPfP
  ('Harbonny'^{PBR}) (Patio) — LBuc LCro LRHS LSRN MAsh MGos
  SEas SPoG SSea SWCr
RUBY CELEBRATION — CSBt EBls ELan MPro
  ('Peawinner'^{PBR})
  (F) ♀^{H6}
§ RUBY ROMANCE — EBls LRHS SPoG SWCr
  ('Noa140715'^{PBR}) (Min)
RUBY RUBY — see *R*. RUBY SLIPPERS
§ RUBY SLIPPERS — LRHS SPoG
  ('Weksactrumi') (Min)
'Ruby Wedding' (HT) — CBcs CDoC CEnd CSBt EBee EGren
  ELan IArd LSRN MAsh MGos MPro
  SWCr
'Ruby Wedding — LSRN NTrD
  Anniversary' (F)
RUBY WEDDING ANNIVERSARY — ESty
  ('Raw2768') (F) **new**
? *rugosa* (Ru) — CAgr CCoa CLnd EGren EPom
  GAbr LBuc LSto SPlb WFar WMat
  - 'Alba' (Ru) — CBcs CBTr CCVT CLnd CSBt EBee
  EBls EGren ELan EPfP EPom ETWh
  LBuc LCro LShi LSto MPri NLar SEdi
  SSea SVic SWCr WFar WHnu WMat
  WRjT
  - 'Rubra' (Ru) — CBcs CBTr CCVT CSBt EBee
  EGren ELan EPom LBuc LCro
  NLar SEdi SPoG SSea SVic SWCr
  WHnu WRjT
  - var. *ventenatiana* (Ru) — EBls
  - *Rugosa Atropurpurea*' (Ru) — EPom
'Rural England' (Ra) — EBls EPfP LCro MNrw SWCr
'Russelliana' (Ra) — ETWh NLar
'Sadler's Wells' (S) — EBls
SAINT ETHELBURGA — EBls LCro LRHS SWCr
  ('Beabimbo') (S)
Saint John's rose — see *R.* × *richardii*
Saint Mark's rose — see *R*. 'Rose d'Amour'
'Saint Nicholas' (D) — EBls
SAINT SWITHUN ('Auswith') (S) — EGren LBom SWCr
'Salet' (DPMo) — EBls ETWh
'Sally Holmes' (S) ♀^{H6} — CDoC EBls EGren ETWh LSRN
  NLar SEas SEND

SALLY'S ROSE ('Canrem') (HT)	EBls LSRN
§ 'Saloon' (HT) **new**	EBls
SALSA	see *R.* CHEEK TO CHEEK (Courtyard Series)
SAMARITAN ('Harverag') (HT)	EHeP MNHC SEas SWCr
sancta	see *R.* × *richardii*
'Sander's White Rambler' (Ra) ♀H6	CEnd CRHN EBee EBls ETWh NLar WFar
SANDRA ('Koreinek') (HT)	LSRN MPro
SANDRA ('Poulen005'PBR) (Renaissance Series) (S)	ETWh LSRN
SANDRA'S SENSATION ('Raw2781') (F) **new**	ESty
SANDRINGHAM ('Beamolly') (S)	EBls EPfP LCro LRHS MAsh SWCr
'Sanguinea'	see *R.* × *odorata* Sanguinea Group
SAPHIR ('Tanrikas') (HT)	CBcs EBls
SARAH	see *R.* JARDINS DE BAGATELLE
SARAH, DUCHESS OF YORK	see *R.* SUNSEEKER
'Sarah van Fleet' (Ru)	CDoC EBls ETWh IArd
SAVOY HOTEL ('Harvintage') (HT)	EBls EGren MPro SWCr
'Scabrosa' (Ru) ♀H7	EBls EPfP ETWh LBuc SWCr
SCARLET FIRE	see *R.* 'Scharlachglut'
SCARLET GLOW	see *R.* 'Scharlachglut'
SCARLET HIT ('Poulmo'PBR) (PatioHit Series) (Min/Patio)	EBls EPfP LCro LRHS LSRN
SCARLET PATIO ('Kortingle') (Patio)	EPfP LRHS MAsh SPoG
§ SCENT FROM HEAVEN ('Chewbabaluv') (ClHT)	CDoC CEnd EBls EGren ELan EPfP ESty ETWh LBom LBuc LCro LRHS LSRN MAsh MGos MPri MPro MSwo NLar SEas SPoG SSea SWCr
SCENTED CARPET ('Chewground'PBR) (GC) ♀H6	CDoC ETWh NLar SEas
SCENTED GARDEN ('Chewscentity') (S)	CDoC ESty
SCENTIMENTAL ('Wekplapep'PBR) (F)	EBls ELan ESty MGos MPro NTrD SEas SMad SWCr
SCENT-SATION ('Fryromeo'PBR) (HT)	CDoC MSwo SPoG
'Scentsation' (Min)	MGos SWCr
SCEPTER'D ISLE ('Ausland') (S)	EGren ELan EPfP LBom LRHS MAsh
§ 'Scharlachglut' (ClS)	EBls ETWh
SCHLOSS BAD HOMBURG	see *R.* 'Alibaba'
SCHNEEWITTCHEN	see *R.* ICEBERG
§ 'Schneezwerg' (Ru) ♀H7	EBls ETWh
SCHÖNE VOM SEE ('Korbylosang'PBR) (F) **new**	SReu
'Schoolgirl' (ClHT)	CDoC EBls EGren ELan EPfP LCro MGos MPri MSwo SWCr
Scotch rose	see *R. spinosissima*
Scotch yellow	see *R.* × *harisonii* 'Williams' Double Yellow'
'Seagull' (Ra) ♀H6	EBls EPfP ETWh LCro LSRN MAsh SHor SMrm SWCr
'Seale Pink Diamond' (S)	SSea
SEALED WITH A KISS ('Simwhart') (HT)	ESty
'Sealing Wax' (*moyesii* hybrid) (S)	ETWh
SECRET SMILE ('Dicswifty') (F)	EGren
'Semiplena'	see *R.* × *alba* 'Alba Semiplena'
sempervirens (Ra)	EBls
SERENITY ('Poulht009'PBR) (HT)	EPfP ESty LRHS
sericea var. *morrisonensis*	WCru
B&SWJ 7139	
§ - subsp. *omeiensis*	GKev LEdu WPGP
- - BWJ 7550	WCru
- - PAB 2883	LEdu
- - f. *pteracantha* (S)	CBcs EBls ELan ETWh GKev SSea
- subsp. *sericea*	LEdu
§ *setigera*	EBls
setipoda	EBls
seven sisters rose	see *R. multiflora* 'Grevillei'
SEXY REXY ('Macrexy') (F)	EBls LRHS MGos SPoG SWCr
'Shailer's White Moss'	see *R.* × *centifolia* 'Shailer's White Moss'
SHARIFA ASMA ('Ausreef') (S)	ETWh
SHARON ('Raw2702') (HT)	ESty
SHEILA'S PERFUME ('Harsherry') (F) ♀H6	CDoC CEnd EBls EGren EHeP ELan LRHS LSRN MAsh MGos SEas SPoG SWCr
SHOWMEE MUSIC ('Chewdaybell') (GC)	CDoC
SHOWMEE SUNSHINE ('Kenveron') (GC)	CDoC
SHOWSTAR	see *R.* 'Loving Mum'
'Showtime' Lindquist (HT)	EBls LRHS MAsh SWCr
SHOWTIME ('Baitime') (ClS)	LRHS SPoG
§ SHRIMP HIT ('Poulshrimp'PBR) (Patio)	EBls EGren LRHS SPoG SWCr
SHROPSHIRE STAR ('Chewsummit') (ClS)	ESty SEas
SILAS MARNER ('Ausraveloe'PBR) (S)	EGren EPfP LRHS MBNS NLar SWCr
SILKY SMOOTH ('Forfree') (HT)	ESty
'Silver 25th Anniversary' (F)	EHeP
SILVER ANNIVERSARY ambig.	EGren LSRN NLar
SILVER ANNIVERSARY ('Meiborfil') (HT)	ELon
§ SILVER ANNIVERSARY ('Poulari') (HT) ♀H6	CBcs CDoC CEnd CSBt EBls ELan ETWh LRHS LSRN MAsh MGos MPri MPro SEas SPoG SSea SWCr
SILVER CELEBRATION ('Guescloud') (F)	ESty
'Silver Jubilee' (HT)	CBcs EBls EGren IArd SWCr
'Silver Lining' (HT)	EGren
SILVER SHADOW ('Frystereo'PBR) (HT)	ESty
'Silver Wedding' (HT)	CDoC EGren IArd MGos NTrD SWCr
'Silver Wedding Celebration' (F)	ELan ESty LSRN
SILVER WISHES	see *R.* PINK HIT
SIMON ('Raw2693') (F)	ESty
'Simone' (A)	ETWh
SIMPLY STUNNING ('Poulpal065'PBR) (F)	MAsh
§ SIMPLY THE BEST ('Macmaster'PBR) (HT) ♀H6	CDoC CEnd CSBt EBls EGren ELan EPfP ESty LRHS MAsh MGos MPri SEas SPoG SRGP SWCr
'Sir Cedric Morris' (Ra)	ETWh NLar
SIR GALAHAD ('Hareasy') (F)	MNHC
SIR JOHN BETJEMAN ('Ausvivid'PBR) (S)	EGren
SIR JOHN MILLS ('Beadaffy') (Cl)	EBls
'Sir Joseph Paxton' (Bb)	ETWh
SIR PAUL SMITH ('Beapaul') (ClHT)	EBls
SIR WALTER RALEIGH ('Ausspry') (S)	MGos NLar SEas

SIRIUS ('Tan05415'PBR) (F) **new**	SEas	*spaldingii*	see *R. nutkana* var. *hispida*
SMARTY ('Intersmart') (S/GC)	EBls	'Spanish Beauty'	see *R.* 'Madame Grégoire Staechelin'
SMILING EYES ('Chewrocko'PBR) (S/GC)	EBls EPfP ETWh LRHS NLar	SPARKLE ('Frymerlin'PBR) (HT)	EBls EPfP ESty LBuc LRHS MAsh SWCr
SMILING SUN ('Vel20dabje') (S) **new**	EBls	SPARKLER	see *R.* KENT (Towne & Country Series)
SNAZZEE ('Wekzazette'PBR) (F)	ESty SEas	SPARKLING BURGUNDY ('Raw1007') (F)	ESty
SNOW BUNNY ('Korsnokinu'PBR) (Min)	EBls	SPARKLING SCARLET ('Meihati') (ClF)	LBuc LRHS MAsh SWCr
'Snow Dwarf'	see *R.* 'Schneezwerg'	SPECIAL ANNIVERSARY ('Whastiluc'PBR) (HT) ♀H6	CBcs CDoC CSBt EBls EGren ELan ELon EPfP ETWh LCro LRHS LSRN MAsh MGos MPri NLar SEas SPoG SSea SWCr
SNOW GOOSE ('Auspom'PBR) (ClS)	SWCr	SPECIAL BIRTHDAY ('Forrome') (HT)	ESty
SNOWBALL ('Macangeli') (Min/GC)	LSRN	SPECIAL CHILD ('Taniripsa'PBR) (F/Patio) ♀H6	CDoC ELan SEas SSea SWCr
SNOWCAP ('Harfleet') (Patio)	ESty	'Special Dad' (HT)	LCro NTrD SWCr
'Snowdon' (Ru)	EBls MMuc	'Special Daughter' (F)	NTrD
SOEUR EMMANUELLE ('Delamo'PBR) (S)	ETWh	SPECIAL DAY ('Gues19-114') (F)	EBls ESty LRHS
'Soldier Boy' (Cl)	ETWh NLar	SPECIAL EVENT ('Meibrelon') (HT)	ESty
SOLEIL VERTICAL ('Delsov') (Cl)	EBls ELan SEas	SPECIAL FRIEND ('Kirspec') (Patio)	EBls ESty SEas SWCr
SOLO MIO	see *R.* SOPHIA (Renaissance Series)	'Special Grandad' (Patio)	LSRN NTrD SWCr
§ 'Sombreuil' (ClT)	EBls ETWh IArd LRHS NLar	SPECIAL GRANDCHILD ('Flimika') (F)	ESty
SOMEONE SPECIAL ('Raw1231') (F)	ESty	SPECIAL GRANDMA (F)	ESty LSRN NTrD SWCr
SOMETHING SPECIAL ('Macwyo'PBR) (HT)	ESty	SPECIAL GRANDPA (F)	ESty
SOMMERGOLD ('Noa51071'PBR) (Cl)	EPfP LBuc LRHS SWCr	SPECIAL LADY ('Raw2321') (F)	ESty
§ SOPHIA ('Poulen002'PBR) (Renaissance Series) (S)	ESty ETWh	'Special Mum' (F)	EHeP LCro LSRN NTrD SWCr
SOPHIE ('Guesjewel') (S) **new**	ESty	SPECIAL OCCASION ('Fryyoung') (HT)	MGos SWCr
SOPHIE LUISE ('Tan12662') (HT) **new**	SEas	SPECIAL SON (F)	ESty
'Sophie's Perpetual' (ClCh)	EBls ETWh NLar	'Spectabilis' (Ra)	EBls ETWh
SOPHY'S ROSE ('Auslot'PBR) (S)	LRHS	SPECTACULAR	see *R.* 'Danse du Feu'
SORBET FRUITÉ ('Meihestries'PBR) (ClF)	SEas SSea	§ *spinosissima*	EBls EGren ELan ETWh EWld GQue LBuc WKor
SOUL ('Tan09505'PBR) (S)	LCro LSRN SEas	- 'Cedric Morris'	WCot WMal
soulieana (Ra/S)	ETWh	§ - double, white-flowered ♀H7	EBls ECha ETWh LEdu
'Southampton' (F) ♀H6	EBls SRGP SSea SWCr	- 'Falkland'	ECha
SOUVENIR DE BADEN-BADEN ('Korsouba'PBR) (HT)	EBls	- 'Firth of Forth'	ETWh
'Souvenir de Claudius Denoyel' (ClHT)	ETWh	§ - 'Grandiflora'	EBls ETWh
'Souvenir de Jeanne Balandreau' (HP)	EBls	- 'Marbled Pink'	ETWh
'Souvenir de la Malmaison' (Bb)	EBls ETWh	- 'Mary, Queen of Scots'	EBls ETWh SRms
'Souvenir de la Malmaison' (ClBb)	see *R.* 'Climbing Souvenir de la Malmaison'	- 'Merthyr Mawr'	ECha WCot
SOUVENIR DE LOUIS AMADE ('Delilac') (S)	EBls	- 'Mrs Colville'	EBls
'Souvenir de Madame Auguste Charles' (Bb)	ETWh	- 'Single Cherry'	EBls
'Souvenir de Madame Léonie Viennot' (ClT)	ETWh	- 'William III'	EBls WCot WMal
'Souvenir de Pierre Vibert' (DPMo)	ETWh	SPIRIT OF FREEDOM ('Ausbite'PBR) (S)	SWCr
'Souvenir de Saint Anne's' (Bb)	EBls ETWh	§ 'Splendens' (Ra)	EBls ETWh
'Souvenir d'Elise Vardon' (T)	EBls	STAMFORD'S SANCTUARY ('Beajealous') (Cl)	EBls
'Souvenir du Docteur Jamain' (ClHP)	CBcs CSBt EBee EBls EGren ELan ETWh LCro LRHS LSRN NLar SEas SMad SPoG SRGP WKif	'Stanwell Perpetual' (SpH) ♀H7	EBls ETWh NLar SEas SHor
		'Star Appeal' (GC)	CDoC
		'Star of Waltham' (HP)	ETWh NLar
		'Star Performer'PBR (ClPatio)	CDoC EPfP ESty LBuc LRHS MAsh SEas SPoG SWCr
		STARLIGHT EXPRESS ('Trobstar') (Cl)	CDoC EGren ELon EPfP LBuc LRHS MAsh MGos MPri SWCr
		STARLIGHT SYMPHONY ('Harwisdom') (ClS)	CDoC CEnd EBls EHeP ELon EPfP LBuc LCro LSRN MGos MNHC NLar SSea SWCr
		STARRY EYED ('Horcoexist') (Patio)	CDoC MMrt
		STELLA (HT)	LSRN

stellata var. *mirifica*   ETWh
STEP BY STEP   ESty
  ('Sim2008-108') (F) **new**
STÉPHANIE D'URSEL   EBls
  ('Vel15fchpo') (HM)
'Stephen'   LSRN
§ 'Stephen Fry' (F)   EGren
STEPHEN'S ROSE   see *R.* 'Stephen Fry'
STEVE ('Smi36-2-02')   ESty
STORYTELLER ('Diccayman')   EGren
  (F)
STRAWBERRIES AND CREAM   ESty
  ('Geestraw') (Min/Patio)
STRAWBERRY FAYRE   ESty MGos SPoG
  ('Arowillip')
  (Min/Patio)
STRAWBERRY HILL   EGren EPfP ESty LBom LCro LRHS
  ('Ausrimini'^PBR)   MAsh NLar SWCr
  (Cl) ♀H6
STRIKE IT RICH   CDoC CSBt MGos
  ('Wekbepmey'^PBR)
  (HT) ♀H6
'Stromboli' (F)   EGren
'Suffolk' (HT)   SWCr
SUFFOLK ('Kormixal')   CSBt EBls
  (S/GC) ♀H6
suffulta   see *R. arkansana* var. *suffulta*
SUGAR AND SPICE ('Peaallure')   MGos SPoG
  (Patio)
SUGAR MOON   ESty ETWh SEas SSea
  ('Wekmemolo') (HT)
SUGAR 'N' SPICE ('Tinspice')   CDoC
  (Min)
SUMA ('Harsuma') (GC)   ESty
SUMMER BEAUTY   EBls EPfP LRHS MPro SWCr
  ('Kororbe'^PBR) (F) ♀H6
§ SUMMER GOLD ('Poulreb'^PBR)   LRHS MAsh SWCr
  (F)
SUMMER LOVING ('Raw1152')   ESty
  (Cl)
SUMMER MEMORIES   EBls ETWh NLar
  ('Koruteli'^PBR)
  (Palace Series) (F)
SUMMER ROMANCE   LCro
  ('Kortekcho'^PBR) (F)
SUMMER SONG   EGren LBom LRHS LSRN MAsh
  ('Austango'^PBR) (S)   NLar
SUMMER SWEETHEART   EHeP MNHC NLar
  ('Harquasar'^PBR)
  (ClMin)
SUMMER WINE ('Korizont'^PBR)   CDoC EBls EPfP ESty ETWh MAsh
  (ClHT) ♀H6   SPoG SWCr
SUMMERTIME   CDoC EBls ELan LRHS MGos MPri
  ('Chewlarmoll'^PBR)   SPoG
  (ClPatio) ♀H6
SUMMERTIME   LRHS SWCr
  ('Meipiokou'^PBR) (HT)
SUN HIT ('Poulsun'^PBR)   EBls LCro LRHS SPoG
  (PatioHit Series)
  (Min/Patio)
SUNBLEST ('Landora') (HT)   EGren EHeP
SUNNY DAY ('Savasun') (S)   NLar
SUNNY SILUETTA ('Korsilu 05')   EBls LRHS
  (Ra)
SUNNY SKY ('Koraruli'^PBR)   CDoC CSBt EPfP LBuc LRHS MAsh
  (HT)   MGos MPri MPro SPoG SWCr
SUNRISE ('Kormarter') (S)   EGren ESty LRHS SEas SPoG
§ SUNSEEKER ('Dicracer')   LRHS MAsh SPoG SWCr
  (F/Patio) ♀H6
SUNSET BOULEVARD   SWCr
  ('Harbabble') (F)

SUNSET CELEBRATION   see *R.* WARM WISHES
SUNSET GLOW   see *R.* 'Alibaba'
SUPER DOROTHY ('Heldoro')   LSRN SSea
  (Ra) ♀H6
SUPER ELFIN ('Helkleger'^PBR)   CDoC LCro NLar SEas SWCr
  (Ra)
SUPER EXCELSA ('Helexa')   EBls ELan SWCr
  (Ra) ♀H6
SUPER FAIRY ('Helsufair'^PBR)   CDoC EBee EBls ETWh LRHS LSRN
  (Ra) ♀H6   MGos NLar SSea
§ SUPER STAR ('Tanorstar')   EBls EGren MGos
  (HT)
SUPER TROUPER   CDoC CSBt EBls EGren ELan EPfP
  ('Fryleyeca'^PBR) (F) ♀H6   ESty LRHS LSRN MAsh MGos SEas
   SPad SSea SWCr WCot
'Surpasse Tout' (G)   EBls ETWh
SURREY ('Korlanum')   CDoC CSBt EBls EGren ESty ETWh
  (GC) ♀H6   LCro LSRN NLar SSea SWCr
SUSAN ('Korkilt') (HT) **new**   NLar
SUSAN HAMPSHIRE ('Meinatac')   EBls
  (HT)
SUSAN WILLIAMS-ELLIS   EGren ELan EPfP IArd LBom LRHS
  ('Ausquirk'^PBR) (S)   NLar SPoG SWCr
SUSIE ('Harwhistle')   EHeP ESty LSRN NLar SEas SSea
  (ClPatio)
SUSSEX ('Poulave') (GC)   CBcs SMad SWCr
SWAN LAKE ('Macmed') (Cl)   CEnd EBls ELan ETWh
SWAN LAKE ('Schwanensee')   EGren LRHS MPro NLar SWCr
  (Patio)
SWANY ('Meiburenac')   EBls EGren ESty
  (Min/GC)
SWEET CAROLINE   LSRN
  ('Micaroline') (Min)
SWEET CHILD OF MINE (HT)   ESty LCro LRHS SEas SSea SWCr
SWEET DREAM ('Fryminicot')   CDoC CSBt EBls EGren EPfP LCro
  (Patio) ♀H6   LSRN MAsh MGos MPro SPoG SSea
   SWCr
'Sweet Fairy' (Min)   SSea
SWEET HAZE ('Tan97274'^PBR)   SEas
  (F) ♀H6
SWEET HONEY ('Korkularis')   CWal
  (HT)
SWEET HONEY   CDoC CSBt EBls EPfP ETWh LBuc
  ('Kormecaso'^PBR) (F)   LCro LRHS MAsh MGos MPri MPro
   NLar SEas SSea SWCr
SWEET JESSICA   ESty
  ('Wekneflocjuc') (F)
SWEET JULIET ('Ausleap') (S)   EGren
SWEET LEMON DREAM   SWCr
  ('Fryrich') (Patio)
SWEET MAGIC ('Dicmagic'^PBR)   MGos SPoG SWCr
  (Min/Patio) ♀H6
SWEET MEMORIES   CDoC CSBt EBls EHeP ELan EPfP
  ('Whamemo') (Patio)   ESty LRHS MPri SOrN SPoG SSea
   SWCr
§ SWEET PARFUM DE PROVENCE   CDoC EBls ELan LRHS LSRN SEas
  ('Meiclusif'^PBR)   SSea
  (HT) ♀H6
SWEET PAULINE ('Raw2783')   ESty
  (F) **new**
SWEET REMEMBRANCE   SWCr
  ('Kirrans') (HT)
SWEET SILUETTA ('Korsilu 07')   EBls LRHS
  (Ra)
SWEET SISTER ('Guesgrade')   ESty
  (HT)
SWEET SUE ('Raw1192')   ESty
  (HT) **new**
SWEET SYRIE ('Harwilling')   CDoC EHeP MNHC SSea
  (Cl)
'Sweet Wonder' (Patio)   EPfP LRHS MNHC SWCr

sweginzowii	EPPr EWld
'Sydonie' (HP)	ETWh NLar
'Sympathie' (ClHT)	EBls EHeP
'Taben Syorin Siro' (Ra) **new**	WMal
Tall Story ('Dickooky') (F) ♀H6	EBee EBls
Tallulah	see *R.* Wellenspiel
Tangerine Tango ('Cheworangemane') (Cl)	SEas SSea
Tango Showground ('Chewpatterns'PBR) (GC)	ESty
Tatton ('Fryentice'PBR) (F)	CSBt EBls
§ Tausendschön' (Ra)	EBls
Taxandria ('Viscampina') (S)	NLar
Tea Clipper ('Ausrover'PBR) (S)	EGren
Teasing Georgia ('Ausbaker'PBR) (Cl) ♀H6	SWCr
Temptress ('Korramal') (ClS) ♀H6	ELan LSRN
Ten out of Ten ('Forout') (HT)	ESty
Tenacious ('Macblackpo'PBR) (F)	ESty SEas
Tequila Sunrise ('Dicobey') (HT) ♀H6	EBls EGren ELan ESty MGos MPro SEas SSea SWCr
Tess of the d'Urbervilles ('Ausmove'PBR) (S)	EGren
§ Thaïs ('Memaj') (HT)	EBls
Thank You ('Chesdeep'PBR) (Patio)	EBls ESty LBuc LCro LSRN SWCr
Thanks a Million ('Raw2550') (F)	ESty
§ That's Jazz ('Poulnorm'PBR) (Courtyard Series) (ClF)	LRHS
The Albrighton Rambler ('Ausmobile'PBR) (Ra)	EGren EPfP ESty LBom LRHS NLar
The Alexandra Rose ('Ausday') (S)	ETWh
§ The Alnwick Rose ('Ausgrab'PBR) (S)	EGren SWCr
The Ancient Mariner ('Ausoutcry') (S)	EGren ELan EPfP LCro LRHS NLar SWCr
The Anniversary Rose	see *R.* Sweet Parfum de Provence
The Bee's Knees ('Guesbehold') (F)	ESty
The Bosworth Rose ('Raw1014') (F)	ESty
The Brownie Rose ('Harlassie'PBR) (F)	MNHC
The Cheshire Regiment ('Fryzebedee') (HT)	SEas
The Churchill Rose ('Horoften') (S)	EBee EBls EPfP LRHS MAsh SWCr
The Compassionate Friends ('Harzodiac'PBR) (F)	MGos
The Coventry Cathedral Rose ('Smi72-02') (F)	ESty
The Debbie Phillips Rose ('Harverve') (HT)	EHeP
The Diamond Wedding Rose ('Meidiaphaz') (HT)	EBls ELan ESty LSRN MPro SEas SHor SWCr
'The Doctor' (HT)	EBls
§ 'The Fairy' (Poly) ♀H6	CDoC CSBt EBee EBls ELan EPfP ETWh LCro LRHS LSto MGos MPro MSwo NLar SDix SEas SRGP SSea SWCr WCot WHer WMal
'The Garland' (Ra) ♀H6	EBls ETWh NLar
The Generous Gardener ('Ausdrawn'PBR) (Cl) ♀H6	CDoC EGren ELan EPfP ESty IArd LCro LRHS LSRN MAsh SWCr
The Hilda Ogden Rose ('Korchakon') (Patio)	SWCr
The Jack Duckworth Rose ('Korlutmag'PBR) (Patio)	EBls LRHS SWCr
The Lady Gardener ('Ausbrass'PBR) (S)	EGren EPfP LBom LRHS MBNS NLar SWCr
The Lady of the Lake ('Ausherbert'PBR) (Ra)	EGren EPfP LBom LRHS WSpi
The Lakeland Rose ('Harspiral') (Cl)	NLar
The Lark Ascending ('Ausursula'PBR) (S)	EGren EPfP LBom LCro LRHS NLar
The Mayflower ('Austilly'PBR) (S) ♀H6	EPfP LBom LRHS SWCr
§ The McCartney Rose ('Meizeli') (HT)	LSRN SDix
The Mill on the Floss ('Austulliver'PBR) (S)	LCro SWCr
'The New Dawn'	see *R.* 'New Dawn'
The Perse Rose ('Beajargon') (S)	EBls
§ The Pilgrim ('Auswalker') (S) ♀H6	EGren ELan EPfP ESty LBom LCro LRHS LSRN SPoG SWCr
The Poet's Wife ('Auswhirl'PBR) (S)	EGren ELan EPfP ESty LBom LRHS NLar SPoG
The Prince's Trust ('Harholding'PBR) (Cl)	EGren LRHS SWCr
§ 'The Queen Elizabeth' (F)	EBls EGren LCro LRHS LSRN MAsh MGos MNHC MPri MSwo NTrD SReu SSea SWCr
The Queen's Jubilee Rose ('Beajubilee') (S)	CEnd EBls EPfP LCro LRHS SWCr
The Reformation Rose ('Poulcas053'PBR) (Castle Series) (F)	MPro
§ The Rita Sullivan Rose ('Korzweenu'PBR) (Min)	LRHS SWCr
The Rotarian	see *R.* Rotary Sunrise
'The Royal Brompton Rose'	see *R.* Royal Brompton Rose
The Shepherdess ('Austwist'PBR) (S)	EGren IArd
The Simple Life ('Hartrifle'PBR) (Cl)	SEas SSea
The Wren ('Kormamtiza'PBR) (F/Patio)	EBls EPfP LRHS SWCr
§ Theo Clevers ('Bozkatafra') (Taste of Love Series) (S)	ETWh
'Thérèse Bugnet' (Ru) ♀H7	EBls ETWh
Thinking of You ('Frydandy'PBR) (HT) ♀H6	CBcs CDoC EBls EGren ELon EPfP ESty LBuc LSRN MPri MPro SSea SWCr
'Thisbe' (HM)	EBls ETWh
Thomas à Becket ('Auswinston'PBR) (S)	EGren EPfP ESty LBom LCro LRHS MBNS NLar SWCr
Thousand Beauties	see *R.* 'Tausendschön'
threepenny bit rose	see *R. elegantula* 'Persetosa'
Tickled Pink ('Fryhunky'PBR) (F) ♀H6	EPfP LCro LRHS MAsh MPri SPoG SSea SWCr
§ Timeless Cream ('Noa1112130'PBR) (HT)	EBls EPfP LBuc LCro LRHS MAsh SWCr
§ Timeless Pink ('Noa1811108'PBR) (HT)	EBls EPfP LBuc LCro LRHS MAsh
§ Timeless Purple ('Noa38121'PBR) (HT)	EBls EPfP LBuc LCro LRHS MAsh SWCr
Times Past ('Harhilt'PBR) (ClHT)	LRHS MGos NLar SEas SPoG

'Tina Turner' (HT)	LSRN		VICTORIA ('Simlast') (HT)	ESty
'Tipo Ideale'	see *R*. × *odorata* 'Mutabilis'		VICTORIA PENDLETON	LRHS
TITANIC ('Macdako')[PBR] (F)	ESty		('Harpace')[PBR] (F)	
'Toby Tristam' (Ra)	CRHN		'Village Maid'	see *R*. × *centifolia* 'Unique
TOGETHER FOREVER	EBls SWCr			Panachée'
('Dicecho')[PBR] (F)		§	*villosa* L.	CAgr EBls ETWh WKor
TOGMEISTER ('Beahappy') (F)	EBee EBls EPfP LRHS MAsh SWCr		'Violacea' (G)	ETWh
'Tom Marshall' (Ra)	ETWh		VIOLET CLOUD ('Harquick')[PBR]	CDoC
'Tom Wood' (HP)	ETWh		(Min)	
TOM'S TRIUMPH ('Sty04-02')	ESty		'Violette' (Ra)	ESty ETWh
(F) **new**			*virginiana* ♀[H7]	EBls SDix WTre
TOP MARKS ('Fryministar')	SWCr		- 'Plena'	see *R*. 'Rose d'Amour'
(Min/Patio)			'Viridiflora'	see *R*. × *odorata* 'Viridiflora'
TOPAZ JEWEL	see *R*. YELLOW DAGMAR HASTRUP		VIVACIOUS ('Guescharm')	ESty
TOTTERING-BY-GENTLY	ELan EPfP LBom LRHS MAsh MBNS		(HT)	
('Auscartoon')[PBR] (S)	NLar SWCr		VOLCANO ('Korcolipas')	EBls LRHS
'Tour de Malakoff' (Ce)	NLar		(HT) **new**	
TOYNBEE HALL ('Korwonder')	EBls		*vosagiaca*	see *R*. *caesia* subsp. *vosagiaca*
(F)			VULCANO KORDANA	MAsh
TRANQUILITY ('Barout') (HT)	ELan EPfP LRHS MBNS NLar SWCr		('Korpot007')[PBR] (Min)	
TRANQUILLITY ('Ausnoble')[PBR]	EGren ESty LBom		WALFERDANGE ('Lenwal')	EBls
(S)			(HM)	
'Treasure Trove' (Ra)	CRHN EBls		WALTZ ('Poulkrid')[PBR]	NLar
TRENCIN ('Poulcas066')	ETWh		(Courtyard Series)	
(Castle Series) (F)			(ClPatio)	
'Tricolore de Flandre' (G)	ETWh		'Waltz Time' (HT)	EGren
'Trier' (Ra)	ETWh NLar WMal		*wardii* var. *culta* (S)	ETWh
'Trigintipetala' misapplied	see *R*. × *damascena* 'Professeur		WARM WELCOME ('Chewizz')	CDoC CEnd EBls EGren ELan EPfP
	Émile Perrot'		(ClMin) ♀[H6]	ESty ETWh LCro LRHS LSRN
'Triomphe des Noisettes'	ETWh NLar			MGos MPro SEas SMad SPoG
ambig. (N)				SSea SWCr
TROIKA ('Poultroi') (HT)	EGren LRHS SWCr	§	WARM WISHES ('Fryxotic')[PBR]	CBcs CEnd CSBt EBls EGren ELan
'Tropicana'	see *R*. SUPER STAR		(HT) ♀[H6]	EPfP LBuc LRHS LSRN MAsh MGos
TROPICANA ('Tan02060')	SSea			MPri MSwo SSea SWCr WCot
(HT) **new**			WARWICKSHIRE ('Korkandel')	EBls
TRUE FRIEND ('Smi35-2-02')	ESty		(GC)	
(F)			WATERLOO ('Lencena') (HM)	EBls
TRULY LOVED ('Poulpal044')	EBls LBuc LRHS MAsh SWCr	§	*watsoniana* (Ra)	EBls
(F/Patio)			WB YEATS ('Dicoodles') (F)	MPro
'Truly Scrumptious'[PBR] (HT)	MGos		*webbiana*	ETWh
TRUMPETER ('Mactru')	EBee EGren ELan IArd LBuc LRHS		WEDDING BELLS	ELan LSRN MPro
(F) ♀[H6]	MAsh SPoG WKif		('Korsteflali')[PBR] (HT)	
'Tuscany Superb' (G) ♀[H7]	CBcs CDoC EBee EBls EGren ELan		WEDDING CELEBRATION	EBls
	ETWh LCro LSRN MGos NLar SHor		('Poulht006')[PBR] (HT)	
	SSea WHer		'Wedding Day' (Ra)	CBcs CDoC CEnd CSBt EBee EBls
TWICE IN A BLUE MOON	CDoC CSBt EBls EGren ELan ELon			EGren ELan EPfP ETWh LCro LRHS
('Tan96138')[PBR]	ESty MGos MPro SEas SPoG SSea			LSRN MAsh MGos MPri NLar SHor
(HT) ♀[H6]	SWCr WKif			SPoG SSea SWCr WFar
TWILIGHT ZONE	CDoC SEas SSea		WEDDING PIANO	SEas
('Wekebtidere') (HT)			('Tan09469')[PBR]	
UNCLE WALTER ('Macon') (HT)	EBls EGren		(HT) **new**	
UNFORGETTABLE TIMES	ESty		'Weetwood' (Ra)	CRHN
('Forhart') (HT)			WEISSE WOLCKE	see *R*. WHITE CLOUD
'Unique Blanche'	see *R*. × *centifolia* 'Unique'		WELL-BEING ('Harjangle')[PBR]	EHeP SEas
VALENTINE ('Forbrit') (HT)	ESty		(S)	
VALENTINE HEART ('Dicogle')	CSBt ELan IArd MPro SPoG SRGP	§	WELLENSPIEL	SEas
(F) ♀[H6]			('Korwimcres')[PBR]	
VANESSA BELL ('Auseasel')[PBR]	EGren EPfP ESty IArd LBom LRHS		(S) **new**	
(S)	NLar SWCr		WELWYN GARDEN GLORY	EHeP NLar
'Vanity' (HM)	ETWh		('Harzumber')[PBR] (HT)	
'Variegata di Bologna' (Bb)	EBls ETWh		'Wendy Cussons' (HT)	EBls EGren
'Vatertag' (Min)	LSRN		WESTERLAND ('Korwest')	CDoC EBls ETWh LRHS MAsh NLar
'Veilchenblau' (Ra) ♀[H7]	CDoC CRHN CSBt EBee EBls EGren		(S) ♀[H6]	SHor SSea
	ELan EPfP ESty ETWh LBom LCro		WHERE THE HEART IS	ESty
	LRHS MNHC MPri NLar SEND		('Cocoplan')[PBR] (HT)	
	SMrm SPoG SSea SWCr WMal		WHISKY MAC ('Tanky') (HT)	CBcs CDoC EBee EBls EGren ELan
VELVET FRAGRANCE	CSBt EBls MSwo SPoG			LSRN MGos SEas SRGP
('Fryperdee') (HT)			WHISKY SOUR ('Forwhisky')	ESty
'Verschuren' (HT/v)	SSea		(HT)	
versicolor	see *R*. *gallica* 'Versicolor'		'White Bath'	see *R*. × *centifolia* 'Shailer's White
'Vick's Caprice' (HP)	EBls ETWh NLar			Moss'

§	WHITE CLOUD ('Korstacha'^PBR) (CIHT)	CDoC ESty SEas		WONDERFUL MEMORIES ('Raw2293') (F)	ESty
	'White Cockade' (CIHT)	ETWh		WONDERFUL NEWS ('Jonone'^PBR) (Patio)	ESty SEas
	WHITE COVER	see R. KENT (Towne & Country Series)		WONDERFUL WIFE ('Raw1025') (HT)	ESty
	WHITE DIAMOND ('Interamon') (F)	EGren		WONDERFUL WORLD ('Harbeguile') (CIF)	EBls EHeP LRHS
	'White Grootendorst' (Ru)	EBls ETWh		WONDERFUL YOU ('Smi 170-2-4') (HT)	ESty
§	WHITE MEIDILAND ('Meicoublan') (S/GC)	EBls LBuc LRHS LSRN MAsh MPri SWCr		*woodsii* (S)	EBls
	white moss	see R. × centifolia 'Shailer's White Moss'		- var. *fendleri*	EBls ETWh
	'White Patio' (Min/Patio)	EBls EPfP LCro LRHS MAsh SPoG SWCr		- var. *ultramontana*	EBls
	WHITE PERFUMELLA ('Meicalanq'^PBR) (HT)	ELan MPro SEas		WORCESTERSHIRE ('Korlalon'^PBR) (GC) ♀^H6	SWCr
§	'White Pet' (Poly) ♀^H6	EBee EBls ELan ETWh LCro LRHS LSRN MPro NLar SEND SHor SWCr WKif		WYMONDHAM ABBEY ('Beadevil') (CIHT)	EBls EPfP LRHS SWCr
	white Provence	see R. × centifolia 'Unique'	§	*xanthina* 'Canary Bird' (S) ♀^H6	CBcs CDoC EBee EBls EGren ELan EPfP ESty ETWh LCro MGos MMrt MPro NLar SPoG SSea SWCr
	white rose of York	see R. × alba 'Alba Semiplena'			
	WHITE SKYLINER ('Franwekwhit'^PBR) (CIS)	SSea	§	- f. *hugonis*	ELan ETWh
	WHITE STAR ('Harquill') (CIHT) ♀^H6	EBls SEas SWCr		'Yellow Cécile Brünner'	see R. 'Perle d'Or'
	'White Symphonie' (HT)	EGren	§	YELLOW DAGMAR HASTRUP ('Moryelrug') (Ru)	ETWh
	WHITE WEDDING ('Tan02360')	NTrD	*	'Yellow Dream' (Patio)	EGren
	'White Wings' (HT)	ETWh		YELLOW FLOWER CARPET	see R. FLOWER CARPET SUNSHINE
	wichurana	see R. *luciae*		'Yellow Mutabilis' (Ch)	EBls LRHS
	'Wickwar' (Ra) ♀^H6	EBls ETWh		'Yellow Patio' (Min/Patio)	EPfP LRHS MAsh SPoG SWCr
	WILD EDRIC ('Aushedge'^PBR) (Ru) ♀^H6	LRHS MMuc		yellow Scotch	see R. × harisonii 'Williams' Double Yellow'
	WILD ROVER ('Dichirap') (F) ♀^H6	CDoC EBls SMad		'Yesterday' (Poly/FCl) ♀^H6	EBls ETWh NLar
	WILDEVE ('Ausbonny'^PBR) (S) ♀^H6	EGren EPfP LBom LRHS SWCr		'Yolande d'Aragon' (HP)	ETWh
	WILDFIRE ('Fryessex'^PBR) (Patio)	CDoC EBls ESty LCro LRHS MAsh MGos MPro SEas SPoG SWCr		York and Lancaster	see R. × damascena 'Versicolor'
				YORK MINSTER ('Harquest') (F)	CSBt
	WILLIAM AND CATHERINE ('Ausrapper'^PBR) (S)	LBom LCro LRHS NLar		YORKSHIRE ('Korbarkeit') (GC)	EBls ELan
	'William Cobbett' (F)	SSea		'Yorkshire Lady' (HT)	LSRN
§	'William Lobb' (CeMo) ♀^H7	CDoC EBls ETWh LCro MNrw NLar SWCr WHer WKif		YOU ARE MY SUNSHINE ('Frykwango'^PBR) (HT) ♀^H6	NTrD
	'William Tyndale' (Ra)	ETWh		'You Only Live Once' (F)	LSRN
	'Williams' Double Yellow'	see R. × harisonii 'Williams' Double Yellow'		YOUNG AT HEART ('Raw922') (F)	ESty
	willmottiae	ETWh		YOUNG LYCIDAS ('Ausvibrant'^PBR) (S)	EPfP LBom LRHS LSRN SWCr
	WILTSHIRE ('Kormuse') (S/GC) ♀^H6	CSBt ETWh NLar SEND SSea SWCr		'Your Wedding Day' (F)	LBuc NTrD
	WINCHESTER CATHEDRAL ('Auscat') (S)	EGren ETWh LCro LSRN SPoG		YOU'RE BEAUTIFUL ('Fryracy'^PBR) (F) ♀^H6	CDoC CSBt EBee EBls EGren ELan LBuc LCro LRHS MAsh MGos SHor SPoG SWCr
	WINDRUSH ('Ausrush') (S)	ETWh			
	WINTER SUN ('Korbatam'^PBR) (HT)	EBls		YOU'RE THE ONE ('Wektaclagoma') (Min)	ELan MPro
	WISLEY ('Ausintense'^PBR) (S)	ELan		YVES PIAGET	see R. ROYAL BROMPTON ROSE
	WISLEY 2008 ('Ausbreeze'^PBR) (S)	EGren EPfP IArd LBom LRHS SWCr		YVONNE ('Raw2771') (F) **new**	ESty
	WITH THANKS ('Fransmoov'^PBR) (HT)	MSwo		'Yvonne Rabier' (Poly) ♀^H6	EBls ETWh
	WOLLERTON OLD HALL ('Ausblanket'^PBR) (CI)	EGren EPfP ESty LBom LCro LRHS MAsh MBNS NLar SWCr		ZARA (Fragrant Bella Series)	see R. OLIVERA (Frayla Series)
				ZEPETI ('Meibenbino'^PBR) (Min)	LRHS
	WONDERFUL CHILD ('Raw2691') (F)	ESty		'Zéphirine Drouhin' (Bb)	CBcs CDoC CEnd CSBt EBls EGren ELan EPfP ETWh LCro LRHS MGos MPri NLar SEas SHor SPoG SRGP SSea SWCr
	WONDERFUL DAD ('Raw2715') (HT)	ESty			
§	WONDERFUL FRIEND ('Smi89-2-04') (HT)	ESty	§	'Zigeunerknabe' (S)	EBls ETWh NLar
	WONDERFUL GRANDPARENTS ('Gueskind') (F) **new**	ESty		ZWERGENFEE 09	see R. THE RITA SULLIVAN ROSE
	WONDERFUL HUSBAND ('Raw982') (F)	ESty			

Roscoea ✿ (Zingiberaceae)

	alpina	CBlu CBro CExl CMiW EAri GEdr NHar SBig WCru WFar
	- CC 3667	EPPr
	- f. *pallida*	GEdr

§ *auriculata* ♀H5 — CBlu CBro CLAP CSpe EAri EBee EMor GEdr GKev LAma LEdu MAsh WCru
- B&SWJ 2594 — WCru
- B&SWJ 2687 — WCru
- GWJ 9230 — WCru
- early-flowering — WCru WFar
- 'Floriade' — CJun EBee LAma WFar WPGP
- 'India' — CBlu EAri EBee GKev LAma
- late-flowering — WCru
- 'White Cap' — CJun EBee
auriculata × *cangshanensis* — WCru
auriculata × *purpurea*, pale-flowered — WCru
australis — CBlu EBee GEdr MNrw WCru WFar
'Ballyrogan White' — NHar
× *beesiana* ♀H5 — CBlu CDTJ EBee EBlo EMor EPfP GKev LRHS MAsh MMuc NHar WChS WCru WFar
- 'Ballyrogan Purple' — CJun
- Cream Group — CJun EBee ELan ELon LAma NBir WCru
- Gestreept Group — CBro CLAP ECha LAma MHol MPie NWbg WCru
- 'Lemon and Lavender' — CJun
- 'Monique' — CDTJ CJun EAri EBee NHar WFar
- 'Moonlight' — CJun
bhutanica PAB 3826 — LEdu WFar
Blackthorn strain — WCru
cangshanensis — CMiW WFar
- BWJ 7848 — WCru
cautleyoides — CBro CMiW ECha EGrI ENun EWld GKev LAma LSto MAsh MNrw NGdn NHar WCru WFar XFar
- blue-leaved — NHar
- 'Crûg's Late Lemon' — WCru WFar
- 'Early Purple' — CJun
- early-flowering — MAsh
- 'Ice Age' — CDor CMiW ELon
- 'Jeffrey Thomas' ♀H5 — CBro CJun EAri ENun LRHS WCru
- 'Lemon Giraffe' — CJun
- 'Nguluko Village' — WFar
- 'Pennine Purple' — NHar
- var. *pubescens* — CJun
- 'Purple Giant' — CJun
- 'Purple Queen' ♀H5 — WFar
- purple-flowered — CMiW
- 'Reinier' — CJun WCru
- f. *sinopurpurea* — GKev
- 'Vanilla' — CJun
- 'Yeti' — CJun
aff. *cautleyoides* — SPlb
'Crûg's Early Fruity' — WCru
forrestii ♀H5 — CBlu
- f. *forrestii* — NHar
- f. *purpurea* — CBlu
'Harvington Evening Star' — CJun CLAP ECha ENun LCro NHar WFar
Harvington hybrids — NHar
'Harvington Raw Silk' ♀H5 — CBro CJun CLAP ECha ENun LCro LEdu NHar WFar
'Harvington Royale' — CJun ENun LRHS NHar WFar
'Harvington Summer Deep Purple' — ENun WFar
humeana — CBlu CBro CMiW EAri EPot GEdr NHar WAbe WCru WFar
- f. *alba* — CJun MAsh NHar WAbe
- 'Broadleigh Moonlight' — CBro
- cream-flowered — MAsh
- 'Long Acre Sunrise' — CJun
- f. *lutea* ♀H5 — CJun GEdr NHar WFar
- pink-flowered — MAsh
- 'Purple Streaker' — CJun EAri
- purple-flowered — ECha ENun MAsh
- 'Rosemoor Plum' — CJun CMiW
- 'Snowy Owl' — CJun GEdr WFar
- 'Stephanie Bloom' ♀H5 — EBlo NHar
- 'Two Tone' — CJun
- f. *tyria* ♀H5 — CJun
- yellow-flowered — MAsh
'Ice Maiden' — CJun
'Kew Beauty' ♀H5 — CBlu CBro CExl CJun CLAP CMiW EAri EBee EBlo ECha EPfP MPie NCth NHar SPoG WFar
'McBeath's Pink' — ENun LRHS MAsh NHar WFar
nepalensis — CJun
Paul Bygrave's hybrids **new** — IPot
praecox — GEdr
procera misapplied — see *R. auriculata*
procera Wall. — see *R. purpurea*
'Purple King' — CJun
§ *purpurea* — CBro CDTJ ECha EGrI ELan ELon EMor EPfP LAma LRHS MAsh NBir NGdn SPlb SPoG WCru WFar WHer WMal XFar
- CC 3628 — CExl
- HWJK 2175 — WCru
- HWJK 2400 — WCru WFar
- HWJK 2407 — WCru
- MECC 2 — CJun
- MECC 10 — CJun
- 'Ant Marian' — EAri LAma
- Blackthorn hybrids — CLAP NHar
- bronze-leaved — CMiW
- 'Brown Peacock' — CJun EAri EBee GKev IPot LAma MBNS NHar WCru WFar
- 'Butterfly' — WFar
- 'Chichina Chace' — WCru
- 'Cinnamon Stick' — CBlu CJun CLAP CSpe CWGN EAri EBee GKev LAma MAsh NHar SPad
- Emperor Group — NHar
- 'Green Giant' **new** — WCru
- 'Harvington Bethany' — ENun NHar
- 'Harvington Imperial' — CBro ENun LRHS NHar
- 'Harvington Polly' — ENun NHar
- 'Julie's Glory' — WFar
- 'Nico' — CJun EAri ELan
- pale-flowered — WFar
- 'Peacock' — CJun
- 'Peacock Eye' — CJun EBee GEdr GKev LAma WFar
- var. *procera* — see *R. purpurea*
- 'Red Foot' — WFar
- 'Red Gurkha' — see *R. purpurea* f. *rubra*
- 'Red Riding Hood' — WFar
- red-stemmed — NHar
- Royal Purple Group — CJun IPot MAsh NHar WPGP
- f. *rubra* ♀H5 — CBlu CBro CDor CDTJ CJun CMiW CSpe EAri ECha ENun GEdr MAsh MBNS MNrw NHar NWbg SPel WCot WFar WPGP
- - 'Gurkha Redstem' — CJun CLAP SPoG WCru WFar
- 'Salt 'n' Pepper' — GKev LAma
- 'Snow Goose' — CLAP WCru
- 'Spice Island' — CBlu CJun CLAP CSpe CWGN ELon GEdr IPot MAsh SPoG WCot WFar WPGP
- Sultan Group — NHar WHoo
- 'Summer Snow' — WFar
- tall — WCru

Rubus 623

- 'Twin Towers'	EMor GKev IPot LAma
- 'Vannin'	CJun CLAP ELon LEdu WCru WFar
- 'Vincent'	CBlu CJun EMor GKev IPot LAma WFar
- 'Wisley Amethyst'	CBro CJun ENun LRHS MAsh MNrw NHar WFar
schneideriana	CJun WFar
scillifolia	CBro GEdr MAsh NBir SPlb
- f. *atropurpurea*	CMiW WCru
- black-flowered	EAri
- f. *scillifolia*	NWbg WCru WFar
aff. *scillifolia* purple-flowered	GEdr
'Snow Queen'	NHar
'Summer Deep Purple' ♀H5	CJun LRHS NHar WFar
tibetica	EAri GArf GEdr GKev MAsh SPlb WCru WFar
- ACE 2538	WCru
- BWJ 7878	WCru
- f. *atropurpurea* BWJ 7640	WCru
'Two Tone'	CJun
wardii ♀H5	CExl GKev

rosemary see *Salvia rosmarinus* (Ro)

Rosmarinus see *Salvia* (Ro)

corsicus 'Prostratus'	see *Salvia rosmarinus* Prostrata Group
officinalis	see *Salvia rosmarinus*
repens	see *Salvia rosmarinus* Prostrata Group

Rostrinucula (Lamiaceae)

dependens	CBcs CMCN EAri EBee ELan EPfP EShb ESwi EWes LCro NLar SBrt SMrm SPad
sinensis	CExl

Rosularia (Crassulaceae)

§ *aizoon*	EDAr ESuc LRHS SRms WFar
alba	see *Sedum sedoides* var. *album*
alpestris	ESuc
§ *chrysantha*	EDAr EPot ESuc MWlw SPlb SRms WAbe WFar
crassipes	see *Rhodiola wallichiana*
libanotica RCB RL 20	WCot
§ *muratdaghensis*	MWlw SPlb
pallida A. Berger	see *R. chrysantha*
pallida Stapf	see *R. aizoon*
pallida ambig.	EPot
platyphylla misapplied	see *R. muratdaghensis*
rechingeri	GArf SRms
sempervivum	EWes
§ - subsp. *glaucophylla*	SPlb SRms WFar
serpentinica	EPot ESuc MWlw WAbe
spatulata hort.	see *R. sempervivum* subsp. *glaucophylla*

Rotala (Lythraceae)

indica	ELin
macrandra	ELin
rotundifolia	ELin
wallichii	ELin

Rotheca (Lamiaceae)

myricoides	SEle
§ - 'Ugandense' ♀H1b	CHll EShb SEle WCot

Roystonea (Arecaceae)

regia	NPlm

Rubia (Rubiaceae)

tinctorum	CHab CHby MEar MHer MNHC SRms

Rubus ✿ (Rosaceae)

RCB/Eq C-1	WCot
acuminatus	ESwi LEdu SBrt WCot
alceifolius Poir. B&SWJ 1833	WCru
amabilis DS 70	GGro
arcticus	LEdu NHar SHar WKor WPGP
- subsp. *stellarcticus* 'Beata' (F)	LEdu
- - 'Tarja' (F)	LEdu
bambusarum	EBee GGro NLar WCru
'Benenden' ♀H5	CBcs CExl CMac EBee ELan EPfP GKin GQue LSRN MMuc NBid NLar WSpi
'Betty Ashburner'	CAgr CBcs CDoC EHeP EPPr LRHS MGos NLar SPoG
biflorus ♀H6	LEdu MBlu MMuc SEND WKor
bifrons	WJur
'Boysenberry' (F)	CMac LCro WJur
boysenberry, thornless (F)	CDoC EPom LBuc
buergeri B&SWJ 5555	WCru
caesius	WCot WKor
calophyllus	CBcs CDTJ EPfP ESwi MBlu WPGP
- PAB 13.171	WPGP
calycinoides Hayata ex Koidz.	see *R. rolfei*
calycinoides ambig.	CoPl EHeP
calycinoides Kuntze	GKev
chingii var. *chingii*	SPre
choachiensis B&SWJ 14914	WCru
cockburnianus (F)	CBcs EGren EHeP ELan EPfP LBuc LCro LShi LSto MMuc NLar NSti SPlb SRms WSpi
- 'Goldenvale' ♀H6	CBcs CDoC EPfP LSto MBlu MMuc NBir NLar NSti SDix SEND SPoG SRms WFar
flagelliflorus	NLar
fockeanus misapplied	see *R. rolfei*
formosensis	LRHS SBrt WFar
- B&SWJ 1798	EBee ESwi
formosensis × *reflexus* var. *lanceolobus*	WPGP
fruticosus agg.	CWRo WOrg
- 'Adrienne' (B)	CAgr CDoC CHab LBuc LCro MAsh SRms SSFr
- 'Arapaho' (B) **new**	CBTr
- 'Apache' (B)	CHab LCro SPoG
- 'Ashton Cross' (B)	SBmr SSFr
- 'Asterina' (B)	CMac
- 'Bedford Giant' (B)	CHab LCro MAsh SBmr SSFr
- 'Black Butte' (B)	CHab EPom SVic
- 'Black Cascade'	see *R. fruticosus* agg. 'Dart's Black Cascade'
- 'Black Satin' (B)	CAgr MBlu NLar SEdi SVic
- 'Chester' (B)	CMac EBee EPom MMuc
- 'Coolaris Late' (B)	WCot
§ - 'Dart's Black Cascade' (B)	EPom LCro
§ - 'Dima' (B)	EHet EPom
- 'Helen' (B)	CAgr SBmr SSFr
- 'Himalayan Giant' (B)	CHab NLar
- 'Karaka Black'^PBR (B)	CHab EPom LBuc MAsh SBmr SPoG SSFr SVic
- 'Loch Maree'^PBR (B/d)	CHab EPom
- 'Loch Ness' (B) ♀H6	CAgr CHab CMac EHet EPfP EPom IArd LCro LSRN SBmr SSFr SVic

Rubus

- 'Loch Tay'^PBR (B) ♀H6 — CHab CMac EPom SPoG
- LOWBERRY LITTLE BLACK PRINCE (B) — EHet
- 'Merton Thornless' (B) — CDoC CSBt EPfP LBuc LCro LEdu LSRN MAsh MGos SRms
- 'Navaho' (B) — CBTr CHab EBee EGren ELan EPfP MNHC SPoG
- 'Oregon Thornless' (B) — CAgr CBTr EPfP LCro MAsh MNHC NLar SBmr SEdi SPoG SRms SSFr WMat
- 'Ouachita'^PBR (B) — CMac LCro SPoG
- 'Purple Opal' (B) — LCro
- 'Reuben'^PBR (B) — CHab EPom LCro SPoG SRms WMat
- 'Thornfree' (B) — CAgr EBee EHet LCro NLar SBmr WMat
- TINYBLACK — see *R. fruticosus* agg. 'Dima'
- 'Triple Crown' (B) — CHab CMac
- 'Variegatus' (B) — CMac MBlu WCot
- 'Waldo' (B) — CAgr CDoC EPom LBuc LCro LSRN MAsh SBmr SRms SSFr
- 'Glen Carron'^PBR (F) — EBee
- 'Glencoe' (B) — EPom SVic
- *henryi* — CBcs ELan NLar SPoG WFar
- — var. *henryi* — WCru
- *ichangensis* — CBcs ESwi MBlu NLar WCru WJur
- - 'Precious Metal' — EAri WPGP
- *idaeus* — CWRo
- - 'All Gold' (F) ♀H6 — CAgr CDoC CMac CSBt EGren ELan EPfP EPom LCro LRHS NLar SRms SVic WFar WMat
- - 'Alpengold'^PBR (F) — CAgr EBee SPoG
- - 'Aureus' (F) — ECha LShi NBid WCot
- - 'Autumn Amber' (F) — LRHS
- - 'Autumn Bliss' (F) — Widely available
- - 'Autumn Treasure'^PBR (F) — EPom SBmr SVic
- - 'Black Jewel' (F) — SBmr
- - BONBONBERRY YUMMY ('Jdeboer19'^PBR) (F) — EHet EPom LCro LRHS
- - 'Cascade Delight' (F) — EBee EGren EPom LCro LRHS MAsh SBmr SPoG SWCr WFar
- - 'Chemainus' (F) — EPom
- - 'Driscoll Carmelina' (F) — SFol
- - 'Driscoll Maravilla'^PBR (F) — SFol
- - 'Erika'^PBR (F) — EBee EPom LCro NLar SRms WMat LWaG MMuc
- - 'Fallgold' (F) — LWaG MMuc
- - 'Glen Ample'^PBR (F) ♀H6 — CAgr CBTr CMac EBee EGren ELan EPfP EPom LBuc LCro LRHS MAsh MNHC NLar SBmr SEdi SPoG SRms SSFr SVic SWCr WFar WMat
- - 'Glen Clova' (F) — CAgr CDoC EBee EGren MAsh NLar SEdi SPoG SRms WFar WMat
- - 'Glen Dee' (F) — LRHS SRms
- - 'Glen Doll'^PBR (F) — CAgr CSBt LRHS LSRN MAsh NLar SRms SWCr WMat
- - 'Glen Ericht'^PBR (F) — LRHS SPoG SWCr
- - 'Glen Fyne'^PBR (F) — CAgr
- - 'Glen Lyon' (F) — CSBt EPfP LBuc LRHS LSRN MAsh SEdi SWCr
- - 'Glen Magna'^PBR (F) ♀H6 — CAgr EGren LRHS MAsh SEdi SRms WFar
- - 'Glen Moy'^PBR (F) — CAgr EPfP MAsh MGos
- - 'Glen Prosen'^PBR (F) — CAgr CDoC EGren MAsh MGos MPri SEdi SPlb SPoG SRms SSFr WFar WMat
- - 'Golden Everest' (F) — MNHC
- - GROOVY ('Jdeboer005') (F) — LCro LRHS
- - 'Heritage' (F) — LBuc LRHS MAsh SRms SWCr WFar
- - 'Joan J'^PBR (F) ♀H6 — CAgr CBTr CMac CSBt EBee ELan EPom LRHS LSRN SBmr SPoG SRms SSFr SWCr

- 'Leo'^PBR (F) — EPom LCro LRHS MAsh SRms SSFr SWCr
- LOWBERRY LITTLE SWEET SISTER (F) — CBTr LRHS MNHC MPri
- 'Malling Admiral' (F) ♀H6 — CSBt EGren EPfP EPom LRHS MAsh SWCr
- 'Malling Delight' (F) — SEdi SPlb
- 'Malling Jewel' (F) ♀H6 — CAgr CDoC CSBt EGren EPfP EPom LBuc LCro LRHS LSRN MAsh MPri SEdi SPoG SRms SWCr WFar
- 'Malling Juno'^PBR (F) — CAgr CBTr CMac EBee ELan EPom SVic WFar
- 'Malling Minerva' (F) ♀H6 — CAgr CMac EPom SRms SVic
- 'Malling Promise' (F) — CSBt LCro LRHS LWaG SWCr WFar
- 'Octavia'^PBR (F) ♀H6 — CAgr CDoC CMac EGren ELan EPfP EPom LBuc LRHS MAsh NLar SEdi SWCr WFar WMat
- 'Paris'^PBR (F) — EPom
- 'Polka'^PBR (F) ♀H6 — CDoC CSBt EGren EPfP EPom LBuc LCro LRHS LSRN MAsh MMuc SBmr SRms SSFr SWCr WMat
- RUBY BEAUTY ('Nr7'^PBR) (F) — CDoC EPom LCro LSRN MPri SPoG SRms
- 'Sanibelle' (F) — LRHS
- 'Sugana'^PBR (F) — LCro LRHS
- 'Tadmor'^PBR (F) — CBTr EPom LCro SRms WMat
- 'Tulameen' (F) ♀H6 — CAgr CBTr CDoC CSBt EBee EGren ELan EPfP EPom LCro LRHS LSRN MAsh NLar SEdi SPoG SRms SSFr WFar WMat
- 'Tulameen Pearl' (F) — SVic
- TWOTIMER SUGANA YELLOW (F) — SRms
- 'Zeva' (F) — SRms SWCr
- *illecebrosus* (F) — GGro WKor
- *irenaeus* — LEdu LRHS NLar SBrt SEND
- Japanese wineberry — see *R. phoenicolasius*
- 'Kenneth Ashburner' — NLar
- *laciniatus* 'Thornless Evergreen' — EGren LWaG
- *lambertianus* PAB 8931 — LEdu
- — var. *glandulosus* B&SWJ 14507 — WCru
- *leucodermis* — WKor
- *lineatus* — CBcs CDTJ CMCN EPfP EWes GGro IArd LEdu MMuc WCru WJur WPGP
- - PAB 13.163 — LEdu
- - HWJK 2045 from Nepal — WCru
- - B&SWJ 11261 from Sumatra — WCru
- - from Vietnam — WFar WPGP
- - - HWJ 892 — WCru
- *liui* B&SWJ 1735 — WCru
- × *loganobaccus* (F) — CMac
- - 'Ly 59' (F) — EPfP SRms
- - 'Ly 654' (F) ♀H5 — CMac EGren EPom LBuc SBmr SSFr SVic
- - thornless (F) — CAgr CDoC EPfP EPom MNHC SEdi SPoG WMat
- *malvaceus* FMWJ 13324 — WCru
- NAVAHO BIGANDEARLY ('Lub Mb223'^PBR) (B) — SBmr
- NAVAHO SUMMERLONG ('Lub Mb333'^PBR) (B) — CBTr EPfP
- § *nepalensis* — CAgr GKev LEdu WKor WPGP
- - CC 7626 — GGro
- *niveus* — MCtn WKor
- *nutans* — see *R. nepalensis*
- *occidentalis* — WKor
- *odoratus* — CAgr ELan LEdu MBlu NBid NLar WKor
- *palmatus* — MMuc
- var. *coptophyllus*

paniculatus CC 7525	GGro		- 'City Garden'	EBlo Midl SRms WFar
parkeri PAB 6891	LEdu	§	- var. *deamii* ♀H6	Widely available
parviflorus	WKor		- 'Early Bird Gold'	CWGN EPfP GMaP LBar LCro MHol
- 'Bill Baker'	LEdu			Midl WCav WFar
- double-flowered (d)	EPPr		- Forever Gold ('Joteve')	CKno Midl NCth NEoE
parvifolius 'Ogon'	GGro		- var. *fulgida*	EAri EBee EPfP EPPr LEdu SPoG
pectinellus CB JP1204	GGro		- 'GoldBlitz'	LBar LRHS MPro
- var. *trilobus*	WFar		- 'Little Goldstar'PBR	CAby CBcs CKno EGren ELan EPfP
- - B&SWJ 1669B	WCru			LBar LCro LRHS MAsh MAvo MHol
- - B&SWJ 3639	GGro			Midl MPri MPro NLar SAth SPoG
peltatus	NLar			SRms WFar WHil WNPC WTor
pentalobus	see *R. rolfei*	§	- var. *speciosa* ♀H6	EAri EBee ECha ELan ELon EPfP
§ *phoenicolasius*	CAgr CBcs CMac ELan EPom EPPr			EPPr GAbr GBin LRHS MMuc SDix
	GGro LCro LEdu MAsh MBlu MCtn			SEND SHar SPlb SRms WFar WOld
	SBmr SPoG SPre SVic WFar WJur		- var. *sullivantii*	CDoC
	WKor WPGP		- - 'Goldsturm' ♀H6	Widely available
§ *rolfei*	GGro GQue WPGP		- Sun Ka-Ching ('Rudbddg')	LBar MPri
- B&SWJ 3546 from Taiwan	WCru		- Viette's Little Suzy ('Blovi')	EBlo EPfP LRHS LSou MSwo NLar
- B&SWJ 3878 from the	WCru			SRms WFar
Philippines			*gloriosa*	see *R. hirta*
- 'Emerald Carpet' ♀H5	CAgr NLar	§	*hirta*	MCtn SIvy
- 'Taroko Loco'	WPGP		- 'Amarillo Gold' **new**	LRHS
rosifolius 'Coronarius' (d)	EBee MHol NLar WCot		- August Series	see *R. hirta* Enchanted Series
rubrisetulosus PAB 9532	LEdu		- Autumn Colors (mixed) ♀H3	CWnw ELan EPfP LCro LRHS SPhx
'Rushbrook Redleaf'	SBrt		- 'Autumn Forest'	MCtn
saxatilis	WKor		- (Big Smileyz Series)	Midl
setchuenensis	CMCN EPPr GGro NLar WJur		'Big Kiss Smileyz'	
- W&O 0093	GGro		- - 'Big Love Smileyz'	Midl
? *spectabilis*	EPPr LEdu WKor	§	- Big Luck Smileyz	MPro
- 'Flore Pleno'	see *R. spectabilis* 'Olympic Double'		('Rudlu203'PBR) ♀H3	
§ - 'Olympic Double' (d)	CBcs CExl CMac CMCN ECha EGrI		- 'Big Smile Smileyz'	Midl
	ELon EPfP EWhm EWld GAbr LCro		- 'Blushing Smileyz'	LRHS Midl
	MBlu MMuc NBid NLar NSti SMrm		(Smileyz Series)	
	WBrk WFar WHer WSpi		- 'Cappuccino' ♀H3	EBee ELan EPfP LRHS MCtn Midl
- 'Olympic Gold' (d)	NBid			MPro SPhx
splendidissimus	WCru		- Cherokee Sunset (mixed)	CSpe EUrb MCtn
B&SWJ 2361			(d)	
squarrosus	CBcs ELan ELon WFar		- 'Cherry Brandy'	CSpe EGren EUrb LCro LRHS MCtn
'Sunberry' (F)	SBmr			NLar SHor SPhx
swinhoei CBTW1518	GGro		- 'Cheyenne Gold' ♀H3	MCtn
taiwanicola	GEdr		- Chim Chiminee (mixed)	MCtn SPhx
- B&SWJ 317	ESwi GGro		- 'Chocolate Smileyz'	LRHS WSpi
Tayberry Group (F)	CSBt LSRN MGos NLar SBmr SPre		(Smileyz Series)	
	SRms SVic		- 'Denver Daisy'	MCtn
- 'Buckingham' (F)	CMac EPom LBuc LCro MNHC		- (Enchanted Series)	LCro LRHS
	NLar NPer SBmr SEdi SPoG SVic		Enchanted Cosmic Eye	
	WMat		- - Enchanted Embers	LCro LRHS
- 'Medana Tayberry' (F)	CAgr EPom LCro LEdu MAsh NLar		- - Enchanted Romance	LBar LCro
	SEdi SPoG WMat		- - Enchanted Ruby Crush	LBar LCro LRHS
- 'Tayberry' (F) ♀H7	CDoC LWaG WJur		- - Enchanted Sun	LCro
- thornless	EGren		('Vpru 17/49')	
§ *thibetanus* ♀H6	CBcs CDoC CMac CWal EBee EHeP		- Enchanted Velvet Flame	LBar LCro LRHS
	ELan EPfP LRHS MMuc NLar SEND		- (Flamenco Series)	LBar
	SPoG WSpi		Flamenco Apricot	
- 'Silver Fern'	see *R. thibetanus*		- Flamenco Vanilla	LBar
treutleri B&SWJ 2139	WCru		- 'Giggling Smileyz'PBR	LRHS Midl MPri
tricolor	CAgr CBcs CDoC CMac EHeP ELan		(Smileyz Series)	
	GGro GKev LRHS MBlu MMuc NLar		- 'Gloriosa Double Golden	LRHS
	SDix		Daisy' (d)	
trilobus B&SWJ 9096	WCru		- 'Goldilocks' (d)	MCtn Midl SVic
ulmifolius 'Bellidiflorus'	EHeP EPPr NLar		- 'Happy Smileyz'PBR	LRHS Midl MPro
(d)			(Smileyz Series)	
ursinus	SVic WKor		- 'Indian Summer'	EBee EPfP Midl SPhx
xanthocarpus	GGro LEdu NLar		- 'Irish Eyes'	MCtn SPhx SVic
			- 'Kissing Smileyz'PBR	LRHS Midl MPri
			(Smileyz Series) ♀H3	

Rudbeckia (Asteraceae)

Autumn Sun	see *R. laciniata* 'Herbstsonne'
californica B&SWJ 14105	WCru
deamii	see *R. fulgida* var. *deamii*
fulgida	WFar
- 'American Gold Rush'PBR	LRHS SHar

- 'Laughing Smileyz'PBR	LRHS Midl MPro
(Smileyz Series)	
- Lemon Smileyz	Midl
('Rudle169'PBR)	
(Smileyz Series)	

Rudbeckia

- Loving Smileyz ('Rudlo175'PBR) (Smileyz Series)	Midl MPro	
- Lucky Smileyz	see *R. hirta* (Big Smileyz Series) Big Luck Smileyz	
- 'Marmalade'	SPhx SVic	
- 'Party Smileyz' (Smileyz Series)	Midl	
- 'Prairie Sun'	EBee ELan EPfP EUrb LRHS MBros MCtn Midl MPro SPhx	
- Sahara (mixed) (d)	CWnw MCtn WSpi	
- Star of Life Smileyz ('Rubsol') (Star Smileyz Series)	LBom Midl	
- 'Tiger Smileyz' (Smileyz Series)	LRHS Midl MPri MPro	
- Toto Series	MCtn	
- - 'Toto'	LCro LRHS	
- - 'Toto Rustic'	LRHS	
July Gold	see *R. laciniata* 'Juligold'	
laciniata	CAgr CKno CMac CSpe EBee ELan EPPr GElm GQue LEdu LSto MCtn MNrw NBac NLar SPhx SRms WCot WTre	
- 'Golden Glow'	see *R. laciniata* 'Hortensia'	
- 'Goldquelle' (d)	EBee ECha EGren ELan ELon EMor EPfP GMaP LBar MAsh NLar NWbg SPoG SRms WCAu WFar	
§ - 'Herbstsonne' ♀H6	Widely available	
§ - 'Hortensia' (d)	EBlo EPPr ESgI LRHS WBrk WCot WFar WOld	
§ - 'Juligold'	CMHG EBee EBlo ELon LBar LRHS MAsh MBNS MPie NGdn NLar SMrm SPoG WSpi	
- 'Starcadia Razzle Dazzle' ♀H6	ECha SMHy WCot WFar	
maxima	CAby CKno CSpe CTsd EAri EBee ECha GElm GMaP LEdu MBel MCtn MHol NSti SAng SMad SPeP SPlb WCAu WCot WFar	
missouriensis	CSpe EPfP LRHS MNrw NDov	
newmannii	see *R. fulgida* var. *speciosa*	
nitida	WSpi	
occidentalis 'Black Beauty'PBR	WSpi XFar	
- 'Green Wizard'	CMac EBee ELan EPfP ESgI EUrb GQue LRHS LShi MAsh MCtn MPro NSti SRms WSpi	
* *paniculata*	CDor ECha WCot	
'Peking'PBR	MHol	
purpurea	see *Echinacea purpurea*	
(Rudy Mini Series) Rudy Mini Brown Orange **new**	MPro	
- Rudy Mini Yellow Black **new**	LBar MPro	
'Russet Glow'	MPro	
speciosa	see *R. fulgida* var. *speciosa*	
subtomentosa	EBlo EWes LEdu LRHS NDov NSti WCot WOld WSpi	
- 'Henry Eilers'	CCBP CKno CMiW CSde CTtf EBee ECha EGren ELan ELon EPPr ERCP ESgI GElm GMaP GQue LCro LEdu LSto MGos MHol MNrw NLar NSti SDix SRms WChS WFar WOld	
- 'Little Henry'PBR	CBcs CBWd CKno CMHG EBee EUrb LRHS LSou MAsh MAvo MHol SPoG WCot WFar	
- 'Loofahsa Wheaten Gold' ♀H6	ECha NDov SHar SNoN WCot WGoo	
- 'Poligny'	MNrw	
Summerdaisy's Bronze Bicolor	MPro	
Summerdaisy's Choco Sun	MPro	
Summerdaisy's Double Choco **new**	MPro	
Summerdaisy's Orange Bicolor **new**	MPro	
Summerdaisy's Red Bicolor	MPro	
Summerdaisy's Yellow	MPro	
Summerina Series	CDoC Midl
- Summerina Brown ('Et Rdb 03'PBR)	Midl SPoG
- Summerina Butterscotch Biscuit ('Et Rdb 410'PBR)	EBee EPfP LRHS MPro
- Summerina Electra Shock ('Et Rdb 404'PBR)	EPfP LRHS
- Summerina Fringle Fudge	LRHS MPri MPro
- Summerina Orange ('Et Rdb 01'PBR)	EPfP LRHS MPri SPoG
- Summerina Pecan Pie ('Et Rdb 401'PBR)	EBee EPfP LRHS
- Summerina Pumpernickel ('Et Rdb 402'PBR)	EBee EPfP
- Summerina Sizzling Sunset ('Et Rdb 621')	EPfP LRHS MPro SPad
- Summerina Yellow ('Et Rdb 02'PBR)	EBee EPfP LRHS Midl MPri SPoG
(Sunbeckia Series) Sunbeckia Alicia	LRHS MPri
- Sunbeckia Carla	EGren LBar LRHS
- Sunbeckia Carolina	Midl
- Sunbeckia Emelia ('Bullrudi 05'PBR)	LRHS
- Sunbeckia Laura	LRHS
- Sunbeckia Lucia	LBar
- Sunbeckia Luna	MPro
- Sunbeckia Maya	EGren LBar LRHS Midl
- Sunbeckia Mia	LBar LRHS MPri MPro
- Sunbeckia Ophelia ('Bullrudi 09'PBR) ♀H3	LBar LRHS Midl MPri MPro
- Sunbeckia Sarah	EGren LBar LRHS MBros
(Sunburst Series) 'Sunburst Flame'	Midl
- 'Sunburst Glow'	Midl
- 'Sunburst Radiant'	MBros Midl
- 'Sunburst Solar'	Midl
- 'Sunburst Sunset'	EGren Midl
Tiger Eye Gold ('Syntigeygol')	SPoG
triloba ♀H6	CSpe CTtf CWal ECha ELan EPfP GJos LCro MCtn MNrw SHar SPhx WCAu WSpi
- 'Blackjack Gold'	CFis EDAr LBar LRHS LSou MHol Midl MPro NCth SPhx
- 'Prairie Glow'	Widely available

rue see *Ruta graveolens*

Ruellia (Acanthaceae)

amoena	see *R. brevifolia*
§ *brevifolia*	EShb SBrt
humilis	ECha MNrw StAn
macrantha	EAri EShb
strepens	EBee SBrt
tuberosa	CSpe
tweediana	EAri EShb
- pink-flowered	EShb

Rulingia see *Commersonia*

Rumex (Polygonaceae)

acetosa	CAgr CBWd CCBP CGHo CGwi CHab CHby CTsd CWRo EHet ENfk MCtn MHer MHoo MNHC

Sagittaria 627

	NBir SRms WCot WHer WJek WKit WOrg
- 'Abundance'	LEdu
- subsp. **acetosa** 'Saucy' (v)	MHol WCot
- broad-leaved	SVic
- 'De Belleville'	MEar
- 'Profusion'	MEar NBac
- red-veined	IDun LCro MCtn WKit
acetosella	CAgr CGwi CHab SRms
alpinus	LEdu WCot WPGP
hydrolapathum	CGwi CHab MMuc SEND SPlb WCot
patientia	CAgr CGwi CHab MEar NBac
sanguineus	CGHo CWat EGrl EHet ENfk LCro LEdu LShi LWaG MEar MHoo NBac NLar NQui SRms
- var. **sanguineus**	CAgr ElAn GQue LCro MHer MNHC NBro WFar WHer WKit
scutatus	CCBP CGHo CHby ENfk LRHS MHoo MNHC SPlb SRms WJek
- subsp. **induratus**	SEND
- 'Silver Shield'	MHer SPhx SRms
thyrsoides new	CAgr

Rumohra (Dryopteridaceae)

adiantiformis ♀H3	LEdu LWaG MAsh
- RCB RA-D-2	WCot
aristata 'Variegata'	see *Arachniodes simplicior*

Rungia (Acanthaceae)

klossii	EHet ENfk WJek WKit

Ruschia (Aizoaceae)

putterillii	EAri SPlb
spinosa	SPlb
tumidula	SPlb
uncinata	EAri

Ruscus ✿ (Asparagaceae)

aculeatus	CBcs CBWd CMac ElAn ESwi LEdu NLar SPlb SRms WCru WSpi
- B&SWJ 15020 from Sicily	WCru
- B&SWJ 15260 from Slovenia	WCru
- hermaphrodite	ElAn EPfP ESwi MNrw SEND SMad WCru
- - B&SWJ 15988	WCru
- var. **aculeatus** 'Lanceolatus' (f)	WCru
- var. **angustifolius**	WCot
- - (f)	WCru
- - B&SWJ 16017	WCru
- - PAB 254	LEdu
- - andromonoecious	WCru
- 'John Redmond'^{PBR} (f/m) ♀H5	WCot WSpi
- var. **platyphyllus** B&SWJ 15015	WCru
colchicus	CBct EBee WPGP
- PAB 1753	LEdu
- B&SWJ 16367 from Abkhazia	WCru
- B&SWJ 16006 from Russia	WCru
- B&SWH 16065 from Sochi	WCru
- B&SWJ 16065 from Russia	WCru
- 'Trabzon'	WCru
hypoglossum	LEdu SEND WCot WSpi
- from Italy B&SWJ 15267	WCru
- - B&SWJ 15930	WCru
hypophyllum B&SWJ 14000 from Spain	WCru
- B&SWJ 14035 from Italy	WCru

- B&SWJ 15009	WCru
- B&SWJ 15021 from Sicily	WCru
- f. **crispatus** B&SWJ 15099	WCru
- **latifolius** B&SWJ 15023	WCru
× **microglossus** (f)	LEdu
- B&SWJ 14041 (f)	WCru
× **murtae** B&SWJ 15081	WCru
racemosus	see *Danae racemosa*
streptophyllus B&SWJ 15117	WCru

Russelia (Plantaginaceae)

equisetiformis ♀H1c	CBcs WJun
- 'Lemon Falls' ♀H1c	EShb
- yellow-flowered	CBcs

Ruta (Rutaceae)

corsica	MHoo
graveolens	CCBP CGHo CHab CWal ENfk GQue IDun LShi LWaG MCtn MHoo MNHC SVic WJek WKit WTre
- 'Jackman's Blue'	EGrl ElAn MHoo MNHC SRms WFar WSpi
- 'Variegata' (v)	LShi MHoo NPer SRms

S

Sabal ✿ (Arecaceae)

§ **bermudana**	NPlm
causiarum	NPlm
etonia	NPlm
maritima	NPlm
§ **mexicana**	NPlm
minor	NPlm SArc SPlb
palmetto	EOli NPlm
princeps	see *S. bermudana*
texana	see *S. mexicana*
uresana	NPlm
yapa	NPlm

Sabatia (Gentianaceae)

angularis	CSpe

Saccharum (Poaceae)

officinarum	EAri SPlb
- purple-stemmed	SPlb WCot
- var. **violaceum**	SDix SIvy
ravennae	SMad SPlb

sage see *Salvia officinalis*

sage, annual clary see *Salvia viridis*

sage, biennial clary see *Salvia sclarea*

sage, pineapple see *Salvia elegans*

Sagina (Caryophyllaceae)

subulata	LRHS LShi LWaG MCtn SPoG SVic
- var. **glabrata**	MAsh SRot
§ - - 'Aurea'	ECha EDAr ElAn GMaP MAsh MHer SRms SRot WIce
- 'Lime Moss'	ElAn EPfP LRHS SPoG

Sagittaria (Alismataceae)

australis	ELin
- Silk Stockings ('Benni')	ELin
graminea	CToG LCro SBrt

japonica see *S. sagittifolia*
P *latifolia* CAgr CToG ELin NPer
montevidensis CLil
§ *sagittifolia* CBen CLil CPud CToG CWat ELin
EPfk EWat MWts WMAq
- var. *leucopetala* CLil CWat EWat NPer
 'Flore Pleno' (d)
subulata ELin

Saintpaulia see *Streptocarpus* (AV)

Salicornia (Amaranthaceae)
europaea CSpe EHet LCro MNHC WKit
maritima MCtn

Salix ❀ (Salicaceae)
acutifolia WeWi
- 'Blue Streak' (m) ♀H6 CEnd EBee EWes MBlu NBir NLar
WMou
'Aegma Brno' (f) WMou
aegyptiaca MBlu WMou
alba CBTr CCVT CHab CLnd CNWT
EAri LBuc LSto SEWo WeWi WHtc
WMou WRjT
- f. *argentea* see *S. alba* var. *sericea*
- 'Aurea' WCot WMou
- var. *caerulea* CAco EHeP WMou
- 'Cardinalis' (f) WeWi
- 'Chermesina' hort. see *S. alba* var. *vitellina* 'Britzensis'
- 'Flame' EHeP
- 'Golden Ness' ♀H6 EBee ELan EPfP GQue MAsh MBlu
NLar NOra NPip WeWi WFar WMat
- 'Hutchinson's Yellow Bark' ELan NLar WeWi
- 'Liempde' (m) EHeP
- 'Raesfeld' (m) WeWi
§ - var. *sericea* ♀H6 CLnd LShi MBlu NLar WCot WMou
- 'Splendens' see *S. alba* var. *sericea*
- 'Tristis' misapplied see *S. × sepulcralis* var. *chrysocoma*
§ - 'Tristis' ambig. CBrac CBTr CLnd EGren ELan IPap
LCro MGos NOra NPip SEWo
- 'Tristis' Gaudin. NLar
- var. *vitellina* EGren EHeP LRHS LSto MBNS NLar
SRms
§ - - 'Britzensis' (m) Widely available
- - 'Nova' ELan
§ - - 'Yelverton' ♀H6 EBee EPfP LRHS LSto MAsh NLar
NOra NPip SPoG WeWi WFar WMat
- 'Vitellina Tristis' see *S. alba* 'Tristis' ambig.
§ *alpina* EDAr NHar WAbe
'Americana' (m) WeWi
apennina WeWi
apoda (m) EBee
appendiculata WeWi
§ *arbuscula* ELan
arenaria see *S. repens* var. *argentea*
babylonica CAco CEnd CMCN CWRo SArc
SAth SFol WMou
- 'Annularis' see *S. babylonica* 'Crispa'
- 'Bijdorp' NLar
§ - 'Crispa' ELan LRHS MMrt NLar NQui SMad
SPoG WFar
- 'Pan Chih-kang' NLar
- var. *pekinensis* 'Pendula' IArd
§ - - 'Tortuosa' (f) CAco CBcs CSBt EHeP ELan IPap
LMaj LRHS LSto MPri NLar NPer
SArc SAth SPlb SRms WFar WHtc
bebbiana CBTr WeWi
bockii EPfP ESwi LSto SBrt SPlb
§ 'Bowles's Hybrid' EHeP WMou
'Boydii' (f) ♀H7 EPot GEdr GKev NBir NHar WAbe
WFar

burjatica 'Korso' WeWi
caesia WeWi
× *calliantha* 'William WeWi
Rogers'
candida LSto WeWi
caprea CBcs CBTr CBWd CCVT CHab
CLnd CNWT CoPl EHeP LBuc LRHS
SEWo WMou WRjT
- 'Curly Locks' LRHS
§ - 'Kilmarnock' (m) CBcs CBTr CCVT CDoC CMac
EGren EHeP ELan EPfP IPap LCro
LRHS MAsh MGos MMuc MSwo
NLar NPip NTrD SPoG WCha WFar
WHtc
- var. *pendula* (f) see *S. caprea* 'Weeping Sally'
- - (m) see *S. caprea* 'Kilmarnock'
- 'Silberglanz' WeWi
§ - 'Weeping Sally' (f) WMat
capusii LEdu WPGP
cashmiriana GEdr
'Chocolate' SArc
'Chrysocoma' see *S. × sepulcralis* var. *chrysocoma*
cinerea CBcs CBTr CBWd CLnd LSto MSwo
NTrD WeWi WMou WRjT
'Coire Kander' GKev
daphnoides CBcs CBTr CCVT CLnd CMac
EGren LRHS NLar SRms WMou
- 'Continental Purple' LSto WeWi
- 'Oxford Violet' (m) WeWi
- 'Sinker' WeWi
§ × *doniana* 'Kumeti' WeWi
'E.A. Bowles' see *S.* 'Bowles's Hybrid'
§ *eleagnos* CCVT EHeP LShi SAth SMHy WMou
WSpi
§ - subsp. *angustifolia* ♀H6 ELan LShi LSto MMuc NLar SEND
SRms WeWi
'Elegantissima' see *S. × pendulina*
var. *elegantissima*
exigua ♀H6 CBcs CLnd ELan EPfP EWes LEdu
MBlu MBrN NLar SChF SMad WeWi
WMou WPGP WSpi
fargesii ♀H6 CBcs CBrac CDoC CEnd CExl
CMac EBee ELan EPfP MBlu MMuc
NBid NOra
formosa see *S. arbuscula*
§ × *fragilis* CCVT CHab CLnd EHeP LRHS LSto
WMou
- 'Basfordiana' (m) CLnd MBNS NLar WMou
- 'Bouton Aigu' WeWi
- 'Flanders Red' (f) WeWi
§ - var. *furcata* EDAr EPot GEdr GKev GMaP LShi
WAbe
- 'Golden Willow' WeWi
- 'Jaune de Falaise' WeWi
- 'Jaune Hâtive' WeWi
- 'Laurina' WeWi
- 'Parsons' WeWi
- var. *russelliana* WeWi
- 'Sanguinea' WeWi
fruticulosa see *S. × fragilis* var. *furcata*
'Fuiri-koriyanagi' see *S. integra* 'Hakuro-nishiki'
furcata see *S. × fragilis* var. *furcata*
glabra WeWi
'Golden Curls' (m) see *S. × sepulcralis*
'Erythroflexuosa'
gracilistyla SDix WMou
§ - 'Melanostachys' (m) ♀H5 ELan EPfP GQue MBlu MMuc NBir
NLar SBrt SRms WeWi WFar
- 'Mount Aso' (m) Widely available
hastata 'Wehrhahnii' CBcs EHeP MBlu MMrt NBir
(m) ♀H6

Salix 629

helvetica ♀H7	CBcs CMac EBee EHeP MBlu NBir NLar WeWi WFar	- 'Green Dicks'	LSto WeWi
herbacea	GEdr WAbe	- 'Helix'	see *S. purpurea*
hibernica	see *S. phylicifolia*	- 'Howki' (m)	WMou
himalayas	WeWi	- 'Irette' (m)	WeWi
hookeriana	CExl MBlu WCFE WeWi WMou	- var. *japonica*	see *S. koriyanagi*
humilis	WeWi	- 'Lancashire Dicks' (m)	WeWi
incana	see *S. eleagnos*	- 'Light Dicks'	WeWi
integra	WeWi	- 'Nancy Saunders' (f) ♀H6	CBcs EWld GBin LEdu LSto MBlu MBNS MBrN NBir NClf NLar NSti SDix WCot
- 'Albomaculata'	see *S. integra* 'Hakuro-nishiki'		
- 'Flamingo' PBR	EGren ELan LCro LRHS NLar SPoG	- 'Nicholsonii Purpurascens'	WeWi
§ - 'Hakuro-nishiki' (v) ♀H5	CCVT CDoC CEnd CMac CWnw EBee EGren EHeP ELan ELon EPfP IPap LCro LRHS LSRN MAsh MGos MPri MSwo NLar SAth SMad SNig SPoG SRms SSta WCha WFar WHtc	- 'Norbury'	WeWi
		- 'Pendula' ♀H6	CCVT CEnd CMac LRHS
		- 'Procumbens'	WeWi
		- 'Whipcord'	WeWi
		pyrenaica	EWes
- 'Pendula' (f)	CEnd MAsh WHtc	*pyrifolia*	LSto WeWi
irrorata ♀H5	CLnd EPfP LRHS LSto MBlu NOra NPip WeWi WMat	*radinostachya* KR 7622	WPGP
		repens	SRms
'Jacquinii'	see *S. alpina*	§ - var. *argentea*	LRHS MMuc WFar
§ *koriyanagi*	NLar WeWi	*reticulata* ♀H7	GKev NBir NHar WAbe
'Kumeti'	see *S. × doniana* 'Kumeti'	*retusa*	EWes NBir
'Kuro-me' (m)	see *S. gracilistyla* 'Melanostachys'	*rosmarinifolia* misapplied	see *S. eleagnos* subsp. *angustifolia*
lanata ♀H7	CMac EHeP GKev GQue LShi MGos NBir NLar	*rosmarinifolia* L.	WeWi
		'Roth Cheviot' PBR	WeWi
lapponum	NLar SRms	'Roth Hambleton' PBR	WeWi
- (m)	WAbe	'Roth Mourne' PBR	WeWi
- from Glen Lochay, Scotland	GKev	× *rubens*	see *S. × fragilis*
magnifica	CBcs CExl EBee EPfP MMuc SBrt WCot WeWi WFar WMou WPGP WSpi	× *rubra* 'Eugenei' (m)	MBlu
		- 'Harrison's' (f)	LSto
		sachalinensis 'Kioryo'	WeWi
'Mark Postill' (f)	LRHS	SCARLET CURLS ('Scarcuzam')	MPri WLov
matsudana 'Tortuosa' (f)	see *S. babylonica* var. *pekinensis* 'Tortuosa'	*schraderiana*	WeWi
		schwerinii	WeWi
- 'Tortuosa Aureopendula' (m)	see *S. × sepulcralis* 'Erythroflexuosa'	× *sepulcralis* 'Caradoc'	WeWi
		§ - var. *chrysocoma* ♀H5	Widely available
'Melanostachys' (m)	see *S. gracilistyla* 'Melanostachys'	- 'Dart's Snake' (m)	ELan LShi NLar WCot WFar
miyabeana	WeWi	§ - 'Erythroflexuosa' (m) ♀H5	CBcs CEnd EBee ELan EPfP LCro LRHS MGos MMuc MPri NOra NPip NTrD SPoG WeWi WMat
× *mollissima* var. *hippophaifolia*	WeWi		
moupinensis	CBcs EBee EPfP	× *sericans*	WeWi
aff. *moupinensis* from Vietnam	EBee	*serpyllifolia*	EBee GKev
		serpyllum	see *S. × fragilis* var. *furcata*
§ *myrsinifolia*	ELan LSto MBlu NLar WeWi	*sessilifolia*	WeWi
myrsinites	see *S. alpina*	'Setsuka' (m)	see *S. udensis* 'Sekka'
var. *jacquiniana*		*silesiaca*	WeWi
myrtilloides 'Pink Tassels' (m)	MMrt NHar	*sitchensis*	WeWi
		subopposita	SBrt
nakamurana	GKev	*triandra*	WeWi WMou
- var. *yezoalpina*	CDoC ELan GAbr GBin GEdr LShi MBlu MMrt NHar NLar WeWi WFar WLov	- 'Belge'	WeWi
		- 'Black Hollander' (m)	NLar
		- 'Black Maul'	WeWi
nigricans	see *S. myrsinifolia*	- 'Faux Plant de Tourraine'	WeWi
nivalis	LShi	- 'Grisette Noire'	WeWi
§ × *pendulina*	WeWi	- 'Long Bud'	WeWi
var. *elegantissima*		- 'Noir de Challans'	WeWi
pentandra	CLnd NAts NLar WeWi WMou	- 'Noir de Villaines' (m)	WeWi
phlebophylla	GKev	- 'Whissander'	WeWi
§ *phylicifolia*	WeWi WMou	*udensis* 'Golden Sunshine' PBR	CBcs CMac EPfP LCro LRHS MAsh MMrt NEoE NLar SDix
pseudopentandra	WeWi		
§ *purpurea*	CBTr CCVT LRHS WeWi WMou	§ - 'Sekka' (m)	CBcs MBlu NBir WMou
- 'Brittany Blue'	WeWi	'Ulbrichtweide'	WeWi
- 'Brittany Green' (f)	WeWi	*viminalis*	CBTr CCVT CDoC CLnd EHeP LBuc LMaj LSto WMou WRjT
- 'Carl Jensen'	WeWi		
- 'Dark Dicks' (f)	NLar WeWi	- 'Black Satin'	WeWi
- 'Dicky Meadows' (m)	LSto WeWi	- cane osier	WeWi
* - 'Elegantissima'	WeWi	- 'Mulattin'	WeWi
- 'Goldstones'	NLar WeWi	- 'Reader's Red' (m)	WeWi
- 'Gracilis'	LSou LWaG MMuc NLar WCot WeWi	- 'Riefenweide'	WeWi
		- 'Stone Osier'	WeWi
		- 'Suffolk Osier'	WeWi

630 *Salix*

vitellina 'Pendula' — see *S. alba* 'Tristis' ambig.
'Yelverton' — see *S. alba* var. *vitellina* 'Yelverton'

Salpiglossis (Solanaceae)
sinuata 'Black Trumpets' **new** — CSpe
- 'Kew Blue' — CSpe MCtn
- Royale Series ♀H2 — LCro

Salsola (Amaranthaceae)
komarovii — MCtn
soda — LCro MCtn

Salvia ✿ (Lamiaceae)
acetabulosa — see *S. multicaulis*
adenophora — EWld
'African Sky' — CAby CCBP CGHo CMac CMHG CWGN ELan ENfk EPfP EPPr EWld EWoo LBom LRHS MAvo MHer Midl MPie MPro SAng SEle SIvy SMrm SPel SPhx WKif
africana-lutea — see *S. aurea*
agnes — SAng
'Allen Chickering' — CSpe ECha
'Amante' — CBcs CGHo CWGN EBee EGrI ENfk EPfP ERCP EWld IPot LBom LCro LRHS LSou LWaG Midl MNrw MPri SIvy SPeP SPhx WFar WHil WNPC
'Amber' — WFar
ambigens — see *S. guaranitica*
'Amena' — CAby CSpe
AMETHYST LIPS ('Dyspurp') — Widely available
'Amigo' — CWGN ENfk LCro Midl MPro SIvy
'Amistad'^PBR ♀H3 — Widely available
§ *amplexicaulis* — MMuc NLar SRms
'Angel Wings' — ENfk EPfP ESgl EWld LRHS MHoo Midl MPnt MPri MPro MSCN SIvy SPeP SRkn
angustifolia Cav. — see *S. reptans*
angustifolia Mich. — see *S. azurea*
'Animo' — CWGN ENfk LBom LCro LRHS Midl MPro NDov
'Annabel' — MHoo
apiana — MCtn SAng SPhx SPlb SRms SVen
(Arctic Blaze Series) — EWld
  ARCTIC BLAZE FUCHSIA ('Novasalfuc')
- ARCTIC BLAZE PURPLE ('Novasalpur') — IPot NCth
argentea ♀H5 — CBcs CDor CSpe CTsd EArI ECha ELan LRHS LShi MCtn MHoo MPro SMad WCAu WKif
- 'Artemis' — MPri
arizonica — EWld SIvy
atrocyanea — CAby CSpe EWes EWld NClf SIvy SMHy SPel WKif
atropatana — WCot
§ *aurea* — CSpe EArI EUrb SPlb
- 'Kirstenbosch' — CTtf ESgl EWld SAng SPhx WCot
aurita — EWld
'Azure Snow' (Color Spires Series) — LCro LRHS MPri
§ *azurea* — SEND SPhx SPlb
- var. *grandiflora* — WCot
bacheriana — see *S. buchananii*
'Back to the Fuchsia' — LRHS
'Ballerina Pink' (Fashionista Series) — LBar
§ *barrelieri* — ESwi
'Belhaven' — EBee EPPr SRms

'Betty's Scarlet Gem' (Gem Series) **new** — ENfk
bicolor — see *S. barrelieri*
BIG BLUE ('Pas1246577') ♀H3 **new** — MPro
'Black Knight' — MAsh
blancoana — see *S. lavandulifolia* subsp. *blancoana*
blepharophylla — EArI MHoo
- 'Painted Lady' — MAsh
'Bleu Armor'^PBR — LRHS SPhx
'Blue Butterflies' — ENfk EWld Midl MPro SAng SBeP
'Blue Haze' (Pe) — EGren SMHy
'Blue Merced' — CTtf CWGN ENfk LRHS Midl MPro SPeP
'Blue Moon' — SPhx
§ 'Blue Note'^PBR — Widely available
'Blue Sky' — EWld Midl MPri WFar
'Blue Spire' (Pe) ♀H5 — Widely available
brandegeei — SAng
§ *buchananii* — EBee EWld MAsh MHoo SRkn WKif
bulleyana misapplied — see *S. flava* var. *megalantha*
bulleyana Diels — CExl MHoo NQui
- 'Blue Lips' — Midl SBea WHil
bullulata — CAby EWld SBeP
- pale blue-flowered — EBee EWld SIvy
cacaliifolia — CExl CSde CWCL EBee EGrI ESgl EWld MAsh MHer Midl SAng SEND SRkn WKif
caerulea misapplied — see *S. guaranitica*
campanulata B&SWJ 9232 — WCru
- CC — GGro
- CC 7473 — GGro
- GWJ 9232 — GGro
- GWJ 9294 — WCru
- aff. var. *hirtella* GWJ 9397 — GGro WCru
canariensis — CSpe CWal EWld WCot WFar WSpi
candelabrum ♀H3 — CSpe ESgl MHer WKif
'Candy Dream' **new** — ENfk Midl
cardinalis — see *S. fulgens*
'Carine's Amazing Blue'^PBR — ENfk IPot
carnea — MAsh
'Cavalieri d'Alto' — MAvo SPhx
'Cavaliero Celeste' — SPhx
cedrosensis — SAng
§ *chamaedryoides* — EBee MAsh MHoo SAng SBrt SIvy
- var. *isochroma* — EWld MAsh WPGP
- 'Marine Blue' — MAsh
- silver-leaved — CSpe WHrl WPGP
chamelaeagnea — EArI EPPr EWoo SAng SMHy
CHERRY LIPS ('Dysceri') — Widely available
'Cherry Pie' — ENfk EPfP IDun MHer Midl MPie MPro
'Cherry Queen' — MAsh
chiapensis — MAsh
'Christine Yeo' — EBee EGrI ENfk EPPr MAsh Midl MNrw MPie MPro SEND SPhx
cleistogama misapplied — see *S. glutinosa*
clevelandii — SAng
clinopodioides — EBee EWld
'Clotted Cream' — CBcs CDoC CWGN EBee ENfk EWld IDun LBom LRHS LWaG MAsh MHoo Midl MNHC MPri MPro SBeP SIvy WFar WHoo WMal
coahuilensis ambig. — MAsh SIvy SRkn
coccinea — CWal
- 'Brenthurst' — Midl SBeP
concolor misapplied — see *S. guaranitica*

concolor Lamb. ex Benth. — CAby EPPr EWld
confertiflora ♀H2 — CAby CBcs CExl CHll CMHG CSpe CWCL EAri EBee EGrI EPPr ESgI EUrb EWld IPot LWaG MAsh MHer MHol MPie SDix SIvy SPlb SRkn SVen WFar WJun WOld
'Cool Cream' — CWGN LCro LRHS MHer Midl MMrt MPro SHor SMrm SPhx
corrugata ♀H3 — CMHG CTsd CWal EAri EBee EPfP EWld LRHS MAsh MHer SEND SIvy WFar
'Courson Pink' — WHoo
'Crazy Dolls' — CGHo
'Crème Caramel' — MAsh MAvo Midl
(Cuello Series) CUELLO CREAM — MPnt WNPC ('Dysecc') **new**
- CUELLO PINK ('Dysecp') — EHeP LBom Midl MPnt SMrm WNPC
- CUELLO WHITE ('Dysecw') — LBom Midl MPnt WNPC
curviflora — CElw EAri EBee ENfk EPPr ESgI EWld LRHS MAsh MPie NClf SDix SIvy SRkn
- 'Tubular Bells' — MHoo WFar
cyanescens — CSpe EPot
cyclostegia — CExl
'Dad's Brown Trousers' — SIvy
daghestanica — CSpe
'Dancing Dolls' — CAby CMiW EWoo Midl
I *dangitalis* SDR 4332 — CExl
darcyi misapplied — see *S. roemeriana*
darcyi J. Compton — CAby CExl ESgI EWes EWld SDix
- peach-flowered — CSpe ESgI
'Day Glow' — EArl EPfP IDun LRHS Midl MPro SAdn
'Delice Feline' — Midl
deserta — GGro SBrt SDix
§ × *digenea* — EBee ECha ELan EPfP LRHS LShi LSRN SRms WCAu WHoo
- 'Adora Blue' — MCtn
- 'Adrian' — EPfP LSRN SAng SPoG WCot
- (Bordeau Series) BORDEAU ROSE — LBuc LRHS
- - BORDEAU STEEL BLUE ('Sagz0002') — EPfP LRHS SRms
- 'Lyon Rose' — EBee
§ - 'Merleau' — LRHS
- 'Merleau Pink' — LRHS
- 'Merleau Rose' — EBee EPfP SRms
- 'Merleau White' — ELan LRHS
* - 'Rosea' — EBee
I - 'Superba' — CAby
discolor — CHll CSpe CWal EBee EPPr ESgI EWld EWoo MAsh MHer Midl SAng
disermas — SPlb
disjuncta — SBrt
dombeyi — CAby EBee EWld SIvy WCot WJun WPGP
dorisiana — MAsh MHer
'Dyson's Crimson' — CSde EPPr ESgI LSto SPhx WCot WTre
'Dyson's Gem' — EPPr MAvo
'Dyson's Joy' ♀H3 — CBcs CDoC CSpe CWnw EBee EPfP LBom LCro LRHS LSto MAsh MHer Midl MPri MPro SAth SPhx SRkn WCav WNPC WTor
§ *elegans* — CGHo CHll CWal EBee EHet EWes EWhm IDun LCro LWaG SEdi SEND WFar WJun WKit
- 'Golden Delicious' — EBee EUrb EWes EWld IDun SMrm SRms WFar WJun
- 'Honey Melon' — ENfk EWhm IDun MAsh SRms
- 'Scarlet Pineapple' — CExl CGHo EHet ELan ENfk ESgI MHer MHoo MNHC SAng SIvy SMrm SPoG SRms SVen WJek WKit
- 'Sonoran Red' — GBin
- 'Tangerine' — CGHo EHet ENfk EWhm IDun LCro MHer MHoo NQui SAng SRms WJek WKit
EMBER'S WISH ('Sal 0101'[PBR]) — CAby CBcs CGHo EBee EGrI ELan ENfk EPfP LCro LRHS MAsh MHoo Midl MPro SMrm SPel SPoG SRkn WFar
'Endless Love' — EBee LRHS Midl SRms
'Eveline' — CMac Midl NCth SHar SRms XFar
'Evening Attire'[PBR] (Fashionista Series) — LBar MPri
farinacea — MPri
- 'Blue Victory' — MCtn
- 'Evolution' — MCtn
- 'Fairy Queen' — MCtn
- (Farina Series) 'Farina Bicolor Blue' — MPri
- - 'Farina Silver Blue' — MPri
- 'Rhea' — SPoG
- SALLYFUN DEEP OCEAN ('Dsaldpocn'[PBR]) — MPri
- 'Strata' — MBros SPoG
- VELOCITY BLUE ('Salv Bule') — LRHS (Velocity Series)
- 'Victoria' — LCro
- 'White Victory' — MCtn
FEATHERS FLAMINGO ('Bocoffla') — LBar LCro MHol MHtn SMad SOrN WNPC XFar
FEATHERS PEACOCK ('Bocofpea') — LBar LCro XFar
'Filigran' (Pe) — GPSL LRHS LSto NLar SBrt SPel SPoG WSpi
'Fire Dancer' (Suncrest Series) — LRHS Midl
'Flamenco Rose' (Suncrest Series) — ELan LRHS Midl
§ *flava* var. *megalantha* — EPfP ESwi GGro LSRN
'Flower Child' — CSpe ESgI SPhx WFar
forreri — EBee ESgI SIvy
§ *forskaehlei* — CCBP CElw CExl EMor GAbr GGro GQue MCtn MNrw NSti SAko SEND WCAu WCot WFar WTre
- B&SWJ 15317 from Turkey — WCru
§ *fruticosa* — LRHS SRms
§ *fulgens* ♀H3 — EWld MAsh SIvy SRkn WFar WJun
gesneriiflora — EWld
'Gigi' — ESgI EWld WFar
glabrescens B&SWJ 11152 — GGro WCru
* - var. *robusta* B&SWJ 11147 — WCru
- white-flowered — GGro
glechomifolia — EWld
§ *glutinosa* — CMac CSpe EBee GGro MMuc NAts NBro NLar NSti SHar SIvy SMHy WCAu WFar
'Golden Rosiene' **new** — WNPC
grahamii — see *S. microphylla* var. *microphylla*
greggii — CWal SPlb SRms
- 'Alba' — MHoo Midl WCAu
- 'Blue Note' — see *S.* 'Blue Note'
- 'Blush Pink' — see *S. microphylla* 'Blush Pink'
- 'Caramba' (v) — EArl LRHS
- 'Cream' — LRHS
§ - 'Desert Blaze' (v) — CGHo ESgI LRHS Midl SPoG
- 'Devon Cream' — see *S. greggii* 'Sungold'
- 'Diane' — MAsh
- 'Emperor' — see *S.* × *jamensis* 'Emperor'
- 'Flame' — ELan EPfP Midl

Salvia

Name	Suppliers
- 'Icing Sugar'^{PBR}	CDoC CGHo CMHG CWGN CWnw EBee ELan ENfk EWoo IDun LCro LSto MAsh MHer MHol MHoo Midl MPnt MPro SIvy WNPC WTor
- 'Lara'	LEdu LRHS Midl MPro
- 'Lipstick'	CExl EBee EPfP LCro LSou LSto MAsh Midl MPro
- 'Magenta'	WKif
- (Mirage Series) MIRAGE BLUE ('Balmirleu'^{PBR})	CWGN EGren WTor
- - MIRAGE BURGUNDY ('Balmirbur'^{PBR})	EAri ELan LRHS WTor
- - MIRAGE CHERRY RED ('Balmircher'^{PBR}) ♀^{H4}	CWGN EAri EPfP LCro LRHS MPri WFar
- - MIRAGE CREAM 2019 ('Balmircemi')	EGren LRHS WFar
- - MIRAGE DEEP PURPLE ('Balmirdepur'^{PBR})	CWGN EGren EPfP LCro LRHS WFar
- - MIRAGE HOT PINK ('Balmirhopi')	EGren LCro LRHS
- - MIRAGE NEON ROSE ('Balmirnose')	CWGN EGren LRHS
- - MIRAGE ROSE BICOLOUR ('Balmirrobi'^{PBR}) ♀^{H4}	EGren ENfk EPfP NWbg
- - MIRAGE SALMON ('Balmirsal')	EGren LRHS
- - MIRAGE SOFT PINK ('Balmirsopin')	CWGN EGren ELan EPfP LRHS MPri WFar
- - MIRAGE VIOLET ('Balmirvio'^{PBR})	EAri EGren EPfP IPot LRHS
- - MIRAGE WHITE ('Balmirwite') ♀^{H4}	EGren NWbg WTor
- 'Peach'	MAsh
- 'Pink Preference'	MAsh
- 'Purple Pastel'	Midl
- 'Rose Pink'	MHoo
- salmon-flowered	Midl
- 'Salvito Scarlet' **new**	Midl
- 'Salvito Violet' **new**	Midl
- 'Sierra San Antonio'	see S. × jamensis 'Sierra San Antonio'
- 'Sparkler'	see S. greggii 'Desert Blaze'
- 'Stormy Pink'	CSpe MAsh Midl MNrw MPie WFar WTre
- 'Strawberries and Cream'	CSpe ENfk LRHS Midl MNrw SPel
§ - 'Sungold'	MAsh MHoo WFar
§ *guaranitica*	CGHo CHll EAri MHer Midl WPGP WTre
- 'Argentina Skies'	CAby EGrI SIvy SMrm
- 'Black and Bloom'	CDoC CSpe CWGN EBee LBuc LRHS MPro WFar
- 'Black and Blue'	Widely available
- 'Blue Enigma' ♀^{H3}	CAby CCBP CExl CWGN EBee ECha ELan EPfP ESgI MAsh MBel Midl MPie SDix SIvy SMHy WSpi
- 'Costa Rica Blue'	SIvy WKif
- 'Indigo Blue'	MAsh
- 'Midnight'	CSpe
- purple-flowered	EPPr
- 'Super Trouper'	EWld LRHS MArl Midl SPhx
haematodes	see S. pratensis Haematodes Group
haenkei	EWld
- 'Prawn Chorus'	MAsh
'Harvest Sunset'	CWGN ENfk ESgI Midl MPro
hians	ESgI ESwi LShi MCtn SPhx SRms
- CC 1787	CExl
hierosolymitana	EWes SBeP
hispanica misapplied	see S. lavandulifolia
hispanica L.	CSpe MCtn
'Hooksgreen'	MHoo
horminum	see S. viridis var. comata
§ - 'Hot Lips' ♀^{H5}	Widely available
- 'Hybrida' (Pe)	WMal
'I Cavalieri del Tau'	Midl MPnt MPro WFar
indica	SPhx
- 'Indigo Spires'	CExl CSpe ECha MAsh Midl NDov SDix SHar SMrm SPhx WFar WKif WOld
interrupta	EWld
involucrata ♀^{H3}	CAby CHll CWal EGrI EWld NBro SVen
- 'Bethellii' ♀^{H3}	CMHG CSde CTsd CWCL EBee ELan EPfP ESgI EWes EWld EWoo MAsh MHer MMrt MNrw MPie SDix SEND SPhx SRkn WFar WJun WKif WSpi
- 'Boutin' ♀^{H3}	EPPr MAsh MHol
§ - 'Hadspen'	CSpe EBee EPPr ESgI EWes SIvy WHer WTre
- 'Mrs Pope'	see S. involucrata 'Hadspen'
'Jackson's Cassis'	MHoo
'Jackson's Kir Royale'	MHoo
'Jackson's Pink Gin'	MHoo
'Jackson's Purple'	MHoo
× *jamensis*	MAsh
- BELLE DE LOIRE ('Barsabel')	ENfk Midl SIvy WTor
- 'Blackberry Ripple' **new**	ENfk Midl WNPC
- 'Blue Amor'	CGHo CWnw LRHS
- 'California Sunset'	ENfk ESgI MAsh Midl MPro SPeP
- 'Dark Dancer'	MAsh
- 'Delice Roselilac'	Midl
§ - 'Emperor'	CCBP CWal CWGN ENfk ESgI EWes LSto MAvo MBrN Midl SIvy SPeP WFar
- 'Flammenn'^{PBR}	EPfP Midl SIvy SPel
- 'Golden Girl'	CSpe LRHS Midl MPie
- (Heatwave Series) 'Heatwave Blast'^{PBR}	Midl
- - HEATWAVE BLAZE ('Eggben005')	Midl
- - 'Heatwave Glimmer'^{PBR}	CSpe EAri EPfP LRHS Midl SPel SPhx
- - 'Heatwave Glitter'^{PBR}	Midl
- - HEATWAVE SPARKLE ('Eggben004')	Midl
- 'Ignition Purple' (Vibe Series)	CTsd EWld MAsh Midl WKif
- 'Javier' ♀^{H4}	CSpe CWGN EBee ECha EPPr EWld LSto MAsh MHoo Midl SIvy SPhx
- 'La Luna'	ELan EPPr MAsh Midl
- 'La Siesta'	EBee MAsh
- 'La Tarde'	MAsh
- 'Lemon Light'	CCBP CSpe EAri ELan ENfk EPfP LBom LRHS MAvo Midl MNrw MPro WKif
- 'Los Lirios'	CSpe
- 'Maraschino'	MAsh Midl SIvy SRms
- 'Melen'^{PBR}	EBee ECul EPfP SMrm SRms
- 'Moonlight Over Ashwood' (v)	MAsh
- 'Moonlight Serenade'	CWGN MAsh Midl MPro
- 'Pat Vlasto'	WMal
- 'Peter Vidgeon' ♀^{H4}	CMiW ECha ENfk EPPr ESgI EWld MAsh Midl MPri MPro SIvy SPhx WMal WPGP
- 'Pleasant Pink'	MAsh
- 'Pluenn'^{PBR}	ENfk EPfP LRHS LSRN Midl
- 'Raspberry Royale'	ESgI EWhm MAsh MHoo SMrm WHrl
- 'Red Velvet'	MAsh MNrw SPhx WHrl
- RÊVE ROUGE ('Fauresal02'^{PBR})	EPfP EWoo LRHS MAsh
- 'Señorita Leah'	CWGN ENfk MAsh MPro SIvy WFar

	- 'Shell Dancer'PBR	LRHS Midl MPie	
§	- 'Sierra San Antonio'	MAsh Midl SMrm	
§	- 'Trebah'	CWnw MAsh MHoo Midl MPie	
	- 'Trenance'	CGHo	
	- VIOLETTE DE LOIRE	CBlu CGHo CWnw ECul EWld	
	('Barsal'PBR)	LRHS SPhx SRms	
	japonica var. *formosana*	WCru	
	NMWJ 14469		
	'Jean's Purple Passion'	MAsh	
	JEMIMA'S GEM ('Jemco')	CWGN EBee EGren ENfk EWld	
	(Gem Series)	LRHS MHol Midl MPie MPro NDov WNPC	
§	'Jeremy'	ENfk LBom LRHS Midl MNrw MPri SRms	
	'Jezebel' ♀H3	CWGN GBin Midl MPro	
	'Joan'	CWGN EPPr ESgl EWld MAsh MAvo MHol SPhx SRGP WJun	
	'Josh'	CWGN LCro Midl MPro SPeP	
	jurisicii	CSpe MCtn Midl	
	- pink-flowered	Midl	
	karwinskyi	EAri EBee ESgl EWld Slvy	
	'Kisses and Wishes'PBR	EBee EGren ELan EMdy ENfk LCro LRHS MAsh MHoo Midl MPri MPro NLar SMrm SRot WNPC	
	koyamae	EWld	
	- B&SWJ 10919	WCru	
	'Krystle Pink'	ESgl Midl MPro	
	'La Mancha'	ENfk MHoo MPro WCot WFar	
	LACEY BLUE ('Lisslitt'PBR) (Pe)	CWGN EBee EGren EPfP LBar LCro LRHS LWaG SPel WHil	
	'Lady Camilla'	MHoo	
	'Lady Jane'	MHoo	
	LAKE LADOGA ('Tl965')	Midl	
	(Salgoon Series)		
	LAKE MCKENZIE ('Tl835')	Midl	
	(Salgoon Series)		
	LAKE TAHOE ('Tl831')	EWld Midl	
	(Salgoon Series)		
	'Lalarsha'	ENfk LCro LSou MAsh Midl MPro	
	lanceolata	CSpe EWld	
	× *lavandulacea* misapplied	see *S. rosmarinus* Prostrata Group	
§	*lavandulifolia*	CSpe EPfP LWaG MAsh MCtn MHer MHoo MNHC SAng SMHy SRms WJek WKif WKit	
§	- subsp. *blancoana*	ECha	
	'Lavender Dilly Dilly'	ENfk LBom LRHS MAvo MHoo MPro Slvy	
	lemmonii	see *S. microphylla* var. *wislizeni*	
	'Lemon Pie'	CTtf ESgl LSto MHoo Midl MPro	
	leptophylla	see *S. reptans*	
	leucantha ♀H2	CAbb CCoa CGHo CMCN EAri ENfk EPPr ESgl EWld MAsh MNrw SPlb SRkn SVen WFar WKif	
	- 'Eder' (v)	MAsh	
	- 'Midnight'	CMHG	
	- 'Northcourt'	SVen	
	- 'Purple Velvet' ♀H2	CSpe EBee ESgl EWld MAsh MHer NClf SDix Slvy WFar	
	- 'Santa Barbara'	ELan MAsh WFar	
	- 'White Mischief'	SDix Slvy WCot	
	leucophylla	SAng	
	'Lilac Lipstick' (Fashionista Series)	ELan EPfP LBar MPro	
	'Little Azur'	EPPr	
	LITTLE LACE ('Novaperlac') (Pe)	LRHS	
	'Little Spire'PBR (Pe)	Widely available	
	'Longin' (Pe)	LRHS	
	longistyla	SVen	
	LOVE AND WISHES ('Serendip6'PBR)	CBcs CDoC EGren EGrl ELan EMdy ENfk EPfP LBom LCro LRHS MArl	

		MAsh MAvo MHoo MHtn Midl MPri MPro MSwo NCou NLar SHor SMrm SPoG SRkn SRot WCot WTor	
	lyrata 'Burgundy Bliss'	see *S. lyrata* 'Purple Knockout'	
§	- 'Purple Knockout'	EPfP	
	- 'Purple Volcano'	see *S. lyrata* 'Purple Knockout'	
	- 'Purple Vulcano'	see *S. lyrata* 'Purple Knockout'	
	macellaria misapplied	see *S. microphylla*	
	macrophylla ♀H4	WPGP	
	- purple-leaved	EBee EWld WPGP	
	'Madeline'PBR	LBar LCro LRHS MHol Midl MNrw XFar	
	'Magenta Magic'	EWld IPot	
	'Magic Potion'	CWGN	
	'Mauve Lips'	EPfP	
	'Mauve Midget'	MPro	
	mellifera	SAng WHil	
	'Merlin's Magenta'	ENfk	
	mexicana 'Limelight'	ESgl	
	- var. *minor*	EWld Slvy	
§	*microphylla*	CMac EGrl EWhm MHoo SVen	
	- 'Albert'	LCro	
	- 'Anduus'	Midl	
	- 'Aphrodite'	Midl WTor	
	- 'Baby Doll'	Midl	
	- 'Belize'	MArl MAsh	
	- 'Blind Faith'	CSpe ESgl SPhx	
	- 'Blue Monrovia'	CCBP ENfk GBin LRHS Midl MPro SPeP WKif	
§	- 'Blush Pink'	CAby CTtf MAvo	
	- 'Bordeaux'	CAbb CAby CSpe GBin LBuc Midl Slvy SPel SPhx	
	- 'Carolus'	Midl	
	- 'Cerro Potosí' ♀H4	Widely available	
	- 'Delice Aquamarine'	IPot Midl MSCN WTor	
	- 'Delice Fiona'	Midl	
	- 'Delice Gold and Wine'	Midl	
	- 'Delice Hesperides'	Midl	
	- 'Delice Ondine'	Midl	
	- GLACIER	see *S. microphylla* 'Gletsjer'	
§	- 'Gletsjer'	ENfk EWld Midl MPro	
	- 'Hot Lips'	see *S.* 'Hot Lips'	
	- 'Kew Red'	CMHG MHoo MNrw	
	- 'Little Kiss'	CWGN LSou Midl	
	- 'Lucia'	Midl	
I	- 'Lutea'	ENfk IDun MAsh	
	- 'Makris'	EUrb Midl	
	- 'Marchants Chalk White'	CSpe ESgl GBin SDix SMHy SPel SPhx	
	- 'Maroon'	CCBP MAvo MPro SPeP WCot WHoo	
§	- var. *microphylla*	ENfk EPPr LCro LSRN MHer MHoo MNHC SAng SEND SRms SVic	
I	- - 'Blackcurrant'	EHet WKit	
	- - 'La Foux'	SMrm SPhx	
	- - 'Newby Hall'	CAby CSde EPfP EWes EWld MAvo SPhx	
	- var. *neurepia*	see *S. microphylla* var. *microphylla*	
	- 'Oxford'	EGrl Midl	
	- 'Papajan'	IPot Midl	
	- 'Pink Blush'	ELan ENfk MAsh MHer MHoo MNHC SEND SMrm SNig SRkn WKif	
	- 'Ruby Star'	WNPC	
	- 'San Carlos Festival'	MAsh Midl	
	- 'Suzanne'	Midl	
	- 'Trelawny Rose Pink'	see *S.* 'Trelawney'	
	- 'Trelissick Creamy Yellow'	see *S.* 'Trelissick'	
	- 'Trewithen Cerise'	see *S.* 'Trewithen'	
	- 'Triffids Tall Pink'	CTtf	

- 'Wendy's Surprise' EWld SRkn
- 'Westacre White' **new** EWes
- 'Wild Watermelon' CMHG CWGN EBee ESgI EWes
 EWld GPSL MAsh MAvo MHer Midl
 NQui SIvy
- 'Wine and Roses' EBee ESgI LCro LRHS LSou MHoo
 Midl MPro MSwo WNPC
§ — var. *wislizeni* CElw
 'Midnight Model' ELan LBar LRHS Midl MPri
 (Fashionista Series)
miltiorrhiza CSpe GGro MHoo WPGP
miniata EBee EWld SIvy
muelleri ambig. CSpe
'Mulberry Jam' CAby CGHo EBee ENfk ESgI IPot
 MAsh Midl MNrw MPro SDix SIvy
 SMHy SPhx SRkn WFar
§ *multicaulis* ♀H3 MAsh
Mystic Spires Blue CSpe CWGN EGren EPfP EWld
 ('Balsalmisp') ♀H3 LRHS MBros SPoG
Mystic Spires Sky Blue WTor
 ('Balsaluchl') ♀H3 **new**
'Nachtvlinder' ♀H5 Widely available
namaensis EWld WKif
nana SAng
- 'Curling Waves' PBR EPfP LRHS MHoo
'Naomy Tree' ENfk GBin LRHS Midl MPri MPro
 SMrm SPel WCot
napifolia EWes MNrw NLar
- 'Baby Blue' MHoo
- 'Nel' EBee WMal
nemorosa LSRN MCtn SMrm SPhx SRms
- 'Amethyst' ♀H7 CDor CWGN CWnw EBee EBlo
 ECha EGren ELon EPfP LCro LRHS
 MBel NClf NDov NLar SBeP SHor
 SMHy SPhx SRms WCAu WCot
 WHoo WKif WTor XFar
- Blue Bouquetta ('Alklf') CWGN LBar LRHS MHol Midl NLar
 WNPC
- Blue Mound see *S. × sylvestris* 'Blauhügel'
- (Bumble Series) EPfP GPSL LBar
 'Bumbleberry'
- - 'Bumbleblue' LRHS MPro
- - 'Bumblesnow' LRHS
- 'Caradonna' ♀H7 Widely available
- 'Caradonna Compact' LSou
- Caradonna Pink Inspiration Widely available
 ('Tucarink')
- Dark Matter Midl
 ('Dsaldrkmtr') **new**
- East Friesland see *S. nemorosa* 'Ostfriesland'
- 'Flores' **new** Midl
- 'Giovanni' Midl
- 'Ibiza' **new** Midl
- 'Jersey' **new** Midl
- 'Kate Glenn' Midl MPro WSpi
- 'Katsjing' Midl
- 'Little Friesland' LRHS
- 'Lubecca' ♀H7 EGren EPfP LBar LRHS MArl Midl
 NDov NGdn NLar SPel SPhx WCAu
 WFar
- Lyrical Silvertone WFar
 ('Balyricsil' PBR)
- Lyrical White see *S. nemorosa* (Sensation Series)
 Sensation White
- 'Malta' **new** Midl
- Marcus ('Haeumanarc' PBR) EBee ELan EPfP LBom LRHS MBNS
 Midl SPel SPoG WFar
- Midnight Purple EUrb LBar
 ('Dosalmipu' PBR)
- Midnight Rose LBar LRHS
 ('Dosalmiro' PBR)
- (New Dimension Series) EGren LRHS Midl WFar
 New Dimension Blue
 ('Pas889972')
- - New Dimension Rose LRHS Midl
 ('Pas1302721')
§ - 'Ostfriesland' ♀H7 Widely available
- 'Pink Beauty' CBcs EPfP LSto MAvo WHoo XFar
- 'Pink Friesland' PBR CCht CDor GJos GMaP LSou NGdn
 SDix WCAu WSpi
- 'Plumosa' see *S. nemorosa* 'Pusztaflamme'
§ - 'Pusztaflamme' ♀H7 EBee EPfP LBar
- 'Rose Queen' EWld GMaP LWaG MAvo MCtn
 NBir WCot WFar
- 'Rosenwein' CDor
- 'Royal Distinction' NLar
- (Salute Series) 'Salute ELan EPfP LBar LRHS Midl
 Deep Blue'
- - 'Salute Ice Blue' EPfP LBar Midl
- - 'Salute Light Pink' LRHS Midl
- - 'Salute White' ELan EPfP LBar LRHS Midl
- 'Salvatore Blue' EGren EPfP LBar LRHS WNPC
- 'Schwellenburg' EWes GBin LCro LRHS LSRN MMrt
 SBeP
- (Sensation Series) LRHS MPro
 Sensation Blue
 ('Florsalvioblu' PBR)
- - Sensation Blue Improved Midl
- - Sensation Compact Bright EPfP LRHS Midl
 Rose ('Florsalbro' PBR)
- - Sensation Compact Deep LRHS Midl NLar WHil
 Blue ('Florsaldblue')
- - Sensation Compact White LRHS WHil
 ('Florsalcwh')
- - Sensation Deep Rose LRHS
 ('Flor Sal Roz')
- - Sensation Deep Rose LRHS Midl SPoG
 Improved
- - Sensation Medium Midl
 Violet **new**
- - Sensation Medium White Midl
 ('Florsalmwh')
- - Sensation Pink LRHS Midl
- - Sensation Rose EGren EGrI LCro LRHS LSou LSRN
 MBel MHol MMrt SRms
- - Sensation Sky Blue NLar
 ('Flor Sal Sky')
§ - - Sensation White CWGN CWnw EGren EPfP GBin
 ('Florsalwhite') LBar LRHS Midl NWbg
- 'Smash White' LBar
§ - subsp. *tesquicola* WFar
§ - 'Violet Queen' EUrb
- 'West Friesland' see *S. nemorosa* 'Violet Queen'
- 'Wesuwe' ECha Midl NDov
'Neon' EBee MAsh Midl MPro WNPC
neurepia see *S. microphylla* var. *microphylla*
nipponica EBee
- B&SWJ 5829 WCru
nubicola CExl ESwi GKev
- CC 6306 GGro
aff. *nubicola* HPA 1735 GGro
'Nuchi' ENfk Midl MPro SPoG SRms
nutans CSpe EBee ESgI EWes GElm LBar
 MCtn MHoo SAng SPhx
officinalis Widely available
- 'Albiflora' CBcs ECha MHoo MNHC WJek
- 'Aurea' ambig. MHoo
- 'Berggarten' ♀H5 CCBP ECha EWhm MHer SPhx
 WHer
- 'Berggarten Variegated' (v) EHet EWhm MNHC
- 'Blackcurrant' CGHo WFar
§ - broad-leaved MHer SEdi WJek

- 'Evita Strong' **new**	MNHC		NDov SAng SDix SIvy SPlb SRms
- 'Extrakta'	MNHC		WFar WJun WKif
- 'Grete Stölzle'	SEND	Pink Amistad ('Arggr17011')	CBWd EBee EGrI EMdy ENfk EPfP
- 'Grower's Friend'	MNHC		EUrb IPot LBar LCro LRHS LSou
- 'Herb Centre's Traditional'	MNHC		MPri SBeP
- hybrid No 4	MNHC	Pink Lips	see *S.* 'Jeremy'
§ - 'Icterina' (v) ♀H5	CBcs CGHo CTsd EBee ECha EHeP	'Pink Mulberry'	ENfk GBin Midl MPro SIvy
	EHet ELan ENfk EWhm GJos LCro	'Pink Neck'	Midl
	LRHS LShi LSto LWaG MGos MHer	'Pink Pong'	CWGN ENfk ESgI LBom LCro LRHS
	MHoo MNHC SEND SPoG SRms		LSto Midl MPri MPro SDix SIvy
	SVic WFar WJek		SMHy
- *latifolia*	see *S. officinalis* broad-leaved	*pratensis*	CCBP CWal EHet EPfP GJos LCro
- 'Maxima'	MNHC		MCtn MNHC SPhx SRms WCot
- narrow-leaved	see *S. lavandulifolia*	- W&B BGH-3	WCot
- 'Nazareth'	LCro MNHC WKit	- (Ballet Series) 'Meadow	MCtn
- *prostrata*	see *S. lavandulifolia*	Ballet Blend'	
- 'Purpurascens' ♀H5	Widely available	- - 'Rose Rhapsody'	CDor ELan EPPr LBar NLar
- 'Salina'	MNHC	- - 'Sky Dance'	CDor Midl
- Tomentosa Group	SPhx	- - 'Swan Lake'	CDor ELan LRHS MCtn NLar SPlb
- 'Tricolor' (v)	CGHo CTsd EBee EHet ELan ENfk	- - 'Sweet Esmeralda'	CDor EGrI ELan EPfP Midl NGdn
	EWhm LShi LWaG MAsh MHoo	- - 'Twilight Serenade'	CDor ELan EPfP EPPr LBar Midl
	MNHC SEdi SPoG SRms WFar WJek		MPro NLar SPhx
	WKit	- 'Dear Anja'	see *S. × sylvestris* 'Dear Anja'
- 'Variegata'	see *S. officinalis* 'Icterina'	§ - Haematodes Group ♀H7	ECha EGren MNrw SRms
omeiana BWJ 8026	WCru	- 'Indigo' ♀H7	LCro LRHS MAsh NLar SPhx SPoG
- 'Crûg Thundercloud'	GEdr WCru		WCot WPGP
oppositiflora misapplied	see *S. tubiflora*	- 'Lapis Lazuli'	LCro MPri
'Orchid Glow' (Suncrest	EAri ELan LRHS Midl	- 'Pink Delight'PBR	Midl NLar SRms
Series)		'Pretty in Pink' (Fashionista	GBin LRHS Midl MNrw MPri MPro
Oriental Dove ('Dysmau')	CWGN EHeP ENfk EUrb IPot MHoo	Series)	
	Midl MPnt MPro SHar SIvy SMrm	*procurrens*	EBee EGrI ESgI EWld GEdr LShi
	WNPC	*przewalskii*	CExl EWld
oxyphora	EBee EWld Midl MPie SAng SIvy	- ACE 1157	WCru
	WFar WOld	- BWJ 7920	GGro WCru
'Pam's Purple'	MAsh	- W&O 9222	GGro
'Pasadena'	EWld	- var. *przewalskii*	MHoo
§ *patens* ♀H3	CAby CSpe EBee ECha EGren	'Purple and Bloom'	EGren LRHS LSou
	LCro LRHS MAsh MBel MHoo	'Purple Majesty'	SMrm WSpi
	Midl NGdn SChF SDix SRms	'Purple Queen'	EBee ENfk WCot WFar
	WFar WKif WSpi	*purpurea*	LSRN
- 'Alba' misapplied	see *S. patens* 'White Trophy'	'Radio Red'	CSpe CWGN EGren LBom LSou
- 'Beyond Blue'	LCro Midl MPri MPro SBeP		Midl MPnt MPro WFar
- 'Blue Angel'	CCht CWal CWGN EPfP EWes	*recognita*	CSpe MHoo
	MCtn Midl	'Red Swing'PBR	CGHo EAri EBee EPfP LRHS LShi
* - 'Blue Trophy'	Midl		Midl
- 'Cambridge Blue' ♀H3	CAby CExl CSpe CWGN EBee ECha	*regla*	CHll MAsh
	ELan EWoo MAsh MHoo Midl NLar	§ *reptans*	ECha SBrt SDix
	NPer SDix WFar	- from western Texas, USA	GBin WCot WFar
- 'Chilcombe'	CAby CSpe	- 'Summer Skies'	Midl
- 'Dot's Delight'	CExl CSpe SHar	'Rhubarb and Custard'	ENfk
- 'Guanajuato'	CExl CTsd CWnw EWld MHoo	'Ribambelle' ♀H3	CSpe MAsh SPhx WHoo WHrl
	Midl NLar SBeP SHar SMrm WKif	'Rocketman' (Pe)	CSBt EBee LBar LRHS LSou MAsh
- large-flowered	CSpe ESgI		MPri
- Oceana Blue ('Salsyll')	EBee Midl	Rockin' Blue Suede Shoes	LRHS LSou MAsh Midl SRkn
- 'Oxford Blue'	see *S. patens*	('Bbsal01301')	
- 'Panama Blue'	MPro	Rockin' Deep Purple	ENfk LRHS LSou MAsh Midl
- (Patio Series) 'Patio Deep	CWGN EGren LRHS MHer Midl	('Bbsal09001')	
Blue'	SPoG WHil WTor	Rockin' Fuchsia	CAby LRHS LSou MAsh Midl MSwo
- - 'Patio Sky Blue'	LRHS MHer Midl WSpi	('Bbsal00301')	
- 'Pink Ice'	EWld Midl	Rockin' Lavender	LSou MAsh MSCN
- 'Royal Blue'	see *S. patens*	§ *roemeriana*	CSpe
- 'White Trophy'	CExl EWes MHoo Midl SBeP SMrm	- 'Arriba'	CFis EDAr
'Peach Cobbler'	CTtf CWGN ENfk Midl MPro	- 'Hot Trumpets'	EGren MHoo
'Peach Parfait'	CSpe CWGN MAvo Midl MPro	- 'Rose Queen' ambig.	LRHS MHoo
	NDov	§ *rosmarinus* (Ro)	Widely available
'Peaches and Cream'	Midl	- 'Abraxas' (Ro)	EHet MHer MNHC WFar
'Penny's Smile'	CAby CElw ELon EWld MAsh Midl	- Albiflora Group (Ro)	CBcs ENfk EWhm LRHS MHoo
	MSCN SIvy SPhx WFar WTre		SEND SPlb MSCN SRms WJek
'Phyllis' Fancy'	CAby CGHo CMHG CSpe CWGN	- - 'Lady in White' (Ro)	CSBt ELan EPfP LRHS SPoG SRms
	EAri ECha ELan ENfk EPfP EWes		WGwG WJek
	EWld MAsh MHer Midl MPro NClf	- 'Alderney' (Ro)	WGwG WJek

Salvia

§	- (Angustifolia Group) 'Benenden Blue' (Ro)	CSBt ECha ELan LRHS MHoo SDix SPlb SPoG SRms WGwG WJek WSpi	- 'Pointe du Raz' (Ro)	CDoC CWnw EWhm LRHS SRms WGwG WSpi
	- - 'Corsican Blue' (Ro) ♀H4	LRHS MHer SRms WGwG	§ - 'Primley Blue' (Ro)	CTsd EWhm MHoo MNHC SRms SVic WGwG WJek
	- 'Arp' (Ro)	ENfk MHoo SEdi SRms WGwG	- Prostrata Group (Ro)	Widely available
§	- 'Aurea' (Ro/v)	MHoo SRms WHer WJek	- - 'Capri' (Ro)	ELan EPfP LSto SRms WFar WJek
	- 'Aureovariegatus' (Ro/v)	see *S. rosmarinus* 'Aurea'	§ - - 'Lockwood de Forest' (Ro)	WGwG WHer
	- 'Barbecue'^PBR (Ro)	ECul EHet ELan ENfk EWhm LCro LRHS MHoo MNHC MPri SRms WKit	- - 'Rampant Boule' (Ro)	EWhm GQue MHoo MNHC SMad SRms WGwG WJek
	- BLUE CASCADE ('Lowros3') (Ro)	LCro WSpi	- - 'Sea Level' (Ro)	MHer WGwG
	- 'Blue Lagoon' (Ro)	CCBP CDoC CTsd ECul EHet ELan ENfk EUrb EWhm LBom LCro LRHS MHer MHoo MNHC MPri SRms WGwG WHer WJek	- - 'Sheila Dore' (Ro)	SVen
			- - white-flowered (Ro)	LRHS
			- - 'Whitewater Silver' (Ro)	CCoa ELan EPfP EWhm LBom LRHS MHer MHoo MPri SArc SHor WJek SRms WGwG
	- 'Blue Rain' (Ro)	CTsd EWhm MHer NQui WFar WGwG WHer	- 'Rex' (Ro)	SRms WGwG
	- 'Blue Spears' (Ro) ♀H4	WMal	- 'Roman Beauty'^PBR (Ro) ♀H4	CBcs CSBt EBee ELan EPfP EWhm LBom LCro LRHS LSRN MHol MMrt MNHC MPri SRms WFar WSpi
	- 'Blue Winter' (Ro)	MNHC		
	- 'Bolham Blue' (Ro)	LRHS	- 'Rosea' (Ro) ♀H4	CCBP CCoa CMac EHet ELan ENfk EPfP EWhm LRHS MHer MHoo MNHC SEND SPoG SRms SVen WGwG WJek
	- 'Capercaillie' (Ro)	MHoo WGwG		
	- 'Cascade' (Ro)	LRHS		
	- 'Collingwood Ingram'	see *S. rosmarinus* (Angustifolia Group) 'Benenden Blue'	- 'Salem' (Ro)	MHer
			- 'Santa Barbara' (Ro)	MHoo
	- 'Farinole' (Ro)	MNHC SRms WGwG	- 'Severn Sea' (Ro)	CBcs CCoa CSBt CSde ELan EWhm LRHS MGos MHoo MNHC SEdi SRms SVen SVic WGwG WJek WSpi
	- 'Fota Blue' (Ro)	CGHo EWhm MHer MHoo MNHC SMHy SRms SVen WGwG WJek		
	- 'Foxtail' (Ro) ♀H4	CDoC CGHo EHet ENfk EPfP EWhm LCro LRHS LSto MHer MHoo MNHC SRms WJek WKit WMal	- 'Shimmering Stars' (Ro)	WGwG
			- 'Silver Sparkler' (Ro)	WFar WHer
			- 'Sissinghurst Blue' (Ro)	CCoa CDoC CSde EBee ELan EPfP LRHS MHer MNHC SPlb SRms WGwG WKif
	- 'Frimley Blue'	see *S. rosmarinus* 'Primley Blue'		
	- 'Gorizia' (Ro)	LRHS SArc SRms	- 'Sorcerer's Apprentice' (Ro)	MHoo MPri WMal
	- 'Golden Rain'	see *S. rosmarinus* 'Joyce DeBaggio'		
	- 'Green Ginger' (Ro)	CDoC CGHo CSBt EBee ECha EHet ELan EPfP EWhm LBom LRHS LSto MEar MGos MHer MHoo MNHC MPri NPer SPoG SRms SVen WGwG WJek	- 'Speedy' (Ro)	MNHC WKit
			- 'Sudbury Blue' (Ro)	CTsd EHet ELan EWhm MHoo SRms SVic WGwG
			- 'Sunkissed'^PBR (Ro)	LCro LRHS SRms
			- 'Tuscan Blue' (Ro)	CBcs CWal CWnw ECha EPfP EUrb EWhm LCro LRHS MHer MHoo MHtn MNHC MPri SRms WGwG WKit
	- 'Guilded'	see *S. rosmarinus* 'Aurea'		
	- 'Haifa' (Ro)	CCBP CCoa CSde ENfk EWhm MHoo MNHC SEdi SRms WGwG WKit		
			- 'Variegatus'	see *S. rosmarinus* 'Aurea'
	- 'Heavenly Blue' (Ro)	WGwG WHer	- 'Vatican Blue' (Ro)	WJek
	- 'Herb Centre 16' (Ro)	MNHC	'Royal Bumble' ♀H4	Widely available
	- 'Huntington Carpet' (Ro)	MHoo	'Royal Crimson Distinction'^PBR	SHar SHor
	- 'Iden Blue Boy' (Ro)	SRms		
	- 'Ingauno' (Ro)	EWhm MNHC	'Royal Velours'	WJun
	- 'Jekka's Blue' (Ro)	WJek WTre	*rutilans*	see *S. elegans*
	- 'Jekka's Green Dragon' (Ro)	WJek	*sagittata*	EBee ESgI EWld LShi MHer SDix SEle SPlb
§	- 'Joyce DeBaggio' (Ro/v)	MHer WGwG WHer	'Saint Jean de Beauregard'	ESgI WFar
	- 'King Hussein' (Ro)	MHoo	'Sally Light Blue'	MidI
	- 'Lilies Blue' (Ro)	WGwG	SALLYFUN BLUE ('Dansalfun1')	LRHS MPri
	- 'Lockwood Variety'	see *S. rosmarinus* (Prostrata Group) 'Lockwood de Forest'	SALLYFUN SNOW WHITE	LRHS
			SALMIA DARK PURPLE ('Hybsv16016')	WFar
	- 'Majorca Pink' (Ro)	CBcs CBrac CSBt CSpe ELan ENfk EPfP EWhm LCro LRHS MHer MNHC MPri SRms WGwG WHer WJek WMal	SALMIA ORANGE ('Hybsv18020')	LCro
			SALMIA PINK ('Hybsv16017')	EWld LCro WFar
	- 'Marenca' (Ro)	MNHC SRms WGwG	'Salmon Dance'	CGHo CWGN EAri ELan EPfP ESgI EWld LCro LRHS MAvo MPro WNPC
	- 'Margaret Sarah' (Ro)	EMal		
	- 'McConnell's Blue' (Ro)	EHeP EPfP EWhm LRHS MGos MHoo MNHC SRms WGwG WHer WJek	'Savannah Purple' (Savannah Series)	WKif
*	- 'Miss Jessopp's Prostrate' (Ro)	LBom SEdi	*scabra*	EBee EWld GKev SPhx
			- 'Good Hope'	MidI
	- 'Miss Jessopp's Upright' (Ro) ♀H4	Widely available	*sclarea*	CCBP CGHo CHby EHet ENfk GJem LCro LWaG MCtn MHoo MidI MNHC NLar SEdi SRms SVic WKit
	- 'Périgord' (Ro) **new**	MHed		

Salvia

– var. *sclarea*	EPfP
– var. *turkestanica* hort.	see *S. sclarea* var. *turkestaniana* 'Vatican Pink'
– var. *turkestaniana* (Bruant) Mottet	CBcs CDor
– – 'Piemont'	MCtn
§ – – 'Vatican Pink'	CDor CHll CSpe CTtf ECha EPfP EUrb LBar LSRN MCtn SHar WKif
§ – – 'Vatican White'	CDor CSpe ECha MCtn SHar SHor WFar
– white-bracted	see *S. sclarea* var. *turkestaniana* 'Vatican White'
'Sebastian'	CSpe ESgI LRHS MHoo Midl
semiatrata misapplied	see *S. chamaedryoides*
semiatrata ambig.	EWld SPhx
semiatrata Zucc.	EPPr
serboana	EBee EWld WPGP
– B&SWJ 10236	ESwi WCru
'Shame'	CSpe MAvo
'Shangri La'	EWld
'Silas Dyson'	CMHG CTtf EBee ELon ENfk EWld LRHS MAsh MAvo SEND SPhx SPoG WFar WKif
'Silke's Dream'	EBee MAsh SHar WMal
'Silke's Red'	WFar
'Snow Kiss' (Color Spires Series)	LBar LRHS
'Snowball' **new**	ENfk Midl
'So Cool Pink'	CWGN ENfk LBom LCro LRHS Midl MPro
'SoCool Pale Blue'^{PBR}	CSpe CWGN ELan ENfk LRHS MAsh Midl NDov SHor SIvy
'SoCool Purple'^{PBR}	CWGN ELan EPfP Midl
'SoCool Violet'	ENfk LBom LRHS Midl MPri MPro WFar
somalensis	EBee
spathacea ♀^{H4}	SAng
Spencer Lake ('Tl832') (Salgoon Series) **new**	LRHS
splendens	LRHS
– 'Flamingo'	Midl MPro
– 'Lighthouse Purple'	CSpe
– 'Vanguard' ♀^{H3}	MPri
– Vista Red ('Pas3285') (Vista Series) **new**	EGren
stachydifolia	SIvy WPGP
– CDPR 3071	EBee WPGP
staminea	MCtn
stolonifera	EPPr EWes EWld EWoo MAsh MAvo MHer SIvy SMHy SPhx WPGP
styphelus	Midl
'Sunset Strip'	LRHS
'Sunshine Dream' **new**	ENfk Midl
× *superba*	see *S.* × *digenea*
– Merleau Blue	see *S.* × *digenea* 'Merleau'
× *sylvestris* April Night ('Dsalrs203')	LBar LRHS MNHC
– Bazuin Dark Night ('Sabadate')	XFar
§ – 'Blauhügel' ♀^{H7}	CBWd CDoC ECha EGren ELan EPfP LCro LRHS LSto MArl MAvo MHed MPri NDov SPhx SRms WCAu WHoo
– 'Blaukönigin'	EPfP GMaP LRHS LSto MCtn Midl SHar SPlb SPoG SRms WCav WCot WFar WHil
– 'Blue by You'	EGren EPfP LBom LRHS LSou
– Blue Marvel ('Balsalvr'^{PBR})	CWGN CWnw EGren EPfP IPot LBar LBom LBuc LCro LRHS LSRN MHol Midl MPri SPoG SRms WFar WHil
– Blue Queen	see *S.* × *sylvestris* 'Blaukönigin'
– 'Bumblesky' (Bumble Series)	EGren EPfP LBar LBuc LRHS MHol MMrt MPri WTor
– 'Crystal Blue'^{PBR} (Color Spires Series)	CBcs CWGN CWnw EPfP LBar LCro LRHS Midl MPie SHar
§ – 'Dear Anja'	CDor EBee LCro LRHS Midl NDov WCAu WCot
– 'Lye End'	WCot
– Lyrical Rose ('Balyricose'^{PBR}) (Lyrical Series)	SPoG
§ – 'Mainacht' ♀^{H7}	Widely available
– May Night	see *S.* × *sylvestris* 'Mainacht'
– 'Negrito'	NCth NLar
– 'Night Field'^{PBR}	SPhx
– 'Perfect Profusion'	Midl
– Purple Spring ('Sally2014'^{PBR})	IPot LBar LCro
– 'Rhapsody in Blue'^{PBR}	LBar MHol Midl NLar WCot
– 'Rianne'^{PBR}	LBar Midl SRot
– Rose Marvel^{PBR}	CWGN EGren EPfP IPot LBom LBuc LRHS LSou MHol Midl MPri WCot WHil
– 'Rose Queen'	CMac EGren ELan EPfP GJos LCro LRHS LSto MArl MCtn MHoo NSti SHar SHor SPoG SRms WCav
– 'Rügen'	EBlo ELon GQue LRHS
– 'Schneehügel'	CBcs CBWd CMac EBee ECha EGren ELan ELon EPfP EPPr GMaP LCro LRHS LSto MArl MBel MBNS Midl NLar SAng WCAu XFar
– 'Serenade'	GBin MArl MBel Midl NDov WCot WMal WTre
– Sky Blue Marvel ('Balsalskarv'^{PBR})	EPfP LRHS MHol
– 'Tänzerin' ♀^{H7}	Midl NDov NLar
– 'Viola Klose' ♀^{H7}	CBWd EBee EBlo ECha ELan EPfP GElm GPSL LCro LRHS LSRN MArl MAvo Midl MNrw NCth NDov NGdn NLar SRms
– 'Violet Riot' **new**	LBar
tachiei hort.	see *S. forskaehlei*
taraxacifolia	SAng
tesquicola	see *S. nemorosa* subsp. *tesquicola*
'Theresia'	EGrI
tiliifolia	SRms
transsylvanica	GJos MHoo NSti SRms
– 'Blue Spire'	SPhx SRkn
– 'Trebah Lilac White'	see *S.* × *jamensis* 'Trebah'
§ – 'Trelawney'	CBlu EPPr EWld MHer MHol MHoo Midl MPie
§ – 'Trelissick'	CBlu CGHo EGren ENfk ESgI GBin LRHS LSto MAsh MHer MHoo Midl MPnt SAth SDix SEND SMHy SRkn
– 'Trewithen'	ELan LRHS MHoo Midl
trijuga	EWld GGro WHil
triloba	see *S. fruticosa*
tubiflora ♀^{H2}	MAsh
'Tutti Frutti'	Midl MMrt SMHy WHoo
uliginosa ♀^{H4}	Widely available
– 'Ballon Azul'	CCBP CCps CSde CSpe CWnw EBee ECha ELan ELon EMor EPPr EWes GMaP LSou MAsh Midl NLar SAng SMad SMrm SPoG
'Ultra Violet'	EPfP
'Vanity Fair' (Fashionista Series)	LBar MPro
'Vatican City'	see *S. sclarea* var. *turkestaniana* 'Vatican White'
'Velvet Gem' (Gem Series)	ENfk
verbenaca	CGwi MCtn MHer NMir

verticillata — CCBP GQue NLar SPhx SRms WFar
§ - 'Alba' — CDor EBee EMor EPfP EPPr GQue Midl NGdn NLar WCAu
- 'Hannay's Blue' — CDor ECha EPPr GMaP Midl SBeP SMHy WCAu WFar WHrl
- 'Hannay's Purple' — EPPr EWld Midl
- 'Purple Fairy Tale' — LSto MCtn WTre
- 'Purple Rain' — CBcs CDor CKno CMac CSpe EBee ECha EGrI ELan EMor EPfP GMaP LCro LRHS LSRN MArl Midl NClf NGdn NLar SAng SAth SEND SPel SPeP SPhx SRms WCAu WTor
- 'Smouldering Torches' — EPPr
- 'White Rain' — see *S. verticillata* 'Alba'
- 'Vevina' — Midl
villicaulis — see *S. amplexicaulis*
'Viola's Darling' **new** — Midl
'Violin Music'^{PBR} — CGHo CWnw EBee ENfk LRHS MHer Midl MPro WHrl
viridis — CGHo CHby MHoo MNHC NLar
- 'Blue Denim' — MCtn
- 'Blue Monday' — LCro
- blue-flowered — LCro
- Claryssa Series — SRms
§ - var. *comata* — WJek
- (Marble Arch Series) — CSpe LRHS
   'Marble Arch Blue'
- - 'Marble Arch Rose' — LRHS
- - 'Marble Arch White' — WFar
viscosa ambig. — ESwi EWld
viscosa Jacq. — ESgl
vitifolia — SAng SDix WKif
'Walsingham White' — SPeP
'Waverly' — ECha EGrI EPPr ESgl EShb EWld MAsh MHer NSti SPhx
'Wendy's Wish'^{PBR} — CDoC CGHo EBee EGren EGrI ELan EPfP EUrb LCro LRHS MAsh MHol MHoo Midl MPri MPro NLar SMrm SPoG SRms WNPC WTor
× *westerae* 'Petra' — ESgl
'White Full Moon' **new** — Midl
§ *yangii* (Pe) — EWld LShi MHer StAn WChS WKif
- 'Blue Jean Baby'^{PBR} (Pe) — LCro
- 'Blue Shadow' (Pe) — LRHS
- BLUE SPRITZER — LRHS
  ('Balperobritz') (Pe)
- 'Blue Steel' (Pe) — EGren GJos LRHS MBros MCtn Midl MPro StAn
- 'Bluesette' (Pe) — LBar
- CRAZYBLUE — CCoa EBee
  ('Balpercruz'^{PBR}) (Pe)
- 'Prime Time' (Pe) **new** — Midl
- SILVERY BLUE — CMac EPfP LBar LCro LRHS NBir
  ('Lissvery'^{PBR}) (Pe) SPoG WNPC
aff. *yunnanensis* BWJ 7874 — ESwi

Salvinia (Salviniaceae)

molesta — Prohibited invasive. See Conservation and the Environment, p.42
natans — CBen ELin

Sambucus ✿ (Viburnaceae)

'14th December' — WCot
adnata — LShi
- BWJ 7937 from Yunnan, China — WCru
'Black Cherry' — WCot
caerulea — see *S. nigra* subsp. *caerulea*
'Cappuccino' — WCot
cerulea — EPfP

'Chocolate Marzipan' — CTsd Midl WCot
coraensis — see *S. williamsii* subsp. *coreana*
ebulus — EBee EPPr LEdu LShi NSti SEND WCot
- B&SWJ 15307 — WCru
- B&SWJ 15339 from Turkey — WCru
- var. *deborensis* — LEdu SMad WPGP
'Ed's Brown' — WCot
'Esme Gold' — WCot
'Florence' — WCot
formosana — WCot
'Gate into Field' — WCot
* *himalayensis* — WCot
§ *javanica* — WCot
mexicana B&SWJ 10349 — WCot WCru
'Milk Chocolate' — CTsd EUrb WCot
'Milk Chocolate Orange' — WCot
miquelii — MCtn WCot
nigra — CBcs CBTr CCVT CoPl CWRo EGren EHeP EPom LBuc LCot LRHS MSwo NTrD SEWo SVic WHnu WKor WMat WMou WRjT
- 'Albomarginata' — see *S. nigra* 'Marginata'
- 'Ardwall' — CAgr EPPr WCot
- 'Aurea' — CBcs EHeP EPom WCot
- 'Aureomarginata' (v) — EPPr MMuc SEND WCot WFar
- 'Beaujolais' — NLar
- BLACK BEAUTY — see *S. nigra* f. *porphyrophylla* 'Gerda'
- BLACK LACE — see *S. nigra* f. *porphyrophylla* 'Eva'
- 'Bont Oosterwoldë' — WCot
- 'Bradet' (F) — CAgr WCot
- 'Broadway' (v) — WCot
- 'Cae Rhos Lligwy' (F) — CAgr WCot WHer
- subsp. *caerulea* — WCot WKor WPGP
- subsp. *canadensis* — WKor
- - 'Adams' (F) — WCot
- - 'Aurea' — WCot
- - 'Johns' (F) — CAgr WCot
- - 'Maxima' — SMrm WCot
- - 'Rubra' — WCot
- - 'York' (F) — CAgr WCot
- 'Castledean' — WCot
- 'Dart's Greenlace' — WCot
- 'Dolomite' (v) — WCot
- 'Donau' (F) — CAgr WCot
- 'Frances' (v) — WCot
- 'Franzi' (F) — CAgr WCot
- 'Fructuluteo' — WCot
- 'Godshill' (F) — CAgr WCot
- GOLD SPARK ('Alcsam') (v) — NEoE NLar
- GOLDEN TOWER — CCht CDoC CWnw ELan EPfP EUrb
  ('Jdeboer001'^{PBR}) LCro LRHS MBros SMrm SPoG WLov
- 'Haidegg 17' (F) — CAgr MEar
- 'Haschberg' (F) — CAgr MEar SVic WCot WMat
- 'Heterophylla' — see *S. nigra* 'Linearis'
- 'Hillier's Dwarf' — WCot
- 'Ina' (F) — CAgr WCot
- INSTANT KARMA — LRHS
  ('Sanivalk'^{PBR}) (v)
- 'Kiora' — WCot
- 'Körsör' (F) — WCot
- f. *laciniata* ♀^{H6} — CBcs EBee EHeP ELan EPfP MBlu MMuc SDix SPoG WCot WFar
§ - 'Linearis' — NLar WCot
- 'Long Tooth' — WCot
- 'Lutea Punctata' — WCot
- 'Madonna' (v) — EPfP LRHS MBlu NLar NQui SMad SPoG WCot WJur
§ - 'Marginata' (v) — CMac EHeP MHer WCot WFar

	- 'Marion Bull' (v)	WCot
I	- 'Marmorata'	WCot
	- 'Mint Julep'	WCot
I	- 'Monstrosa'	WCot
	- 'Nana'	WCot
	- 'Naomi'	WCot
	- 'Norfolk Speckled' (v)	WCot
	- 'Pingo Trail'	WCot
	- 'Plena' (d)	WCot
	- f. *porphyrophylla*	CCht CCVT CDoC EBee ELan EPfP
	BLACK TOWER	EUrb LCro LMaj LRHS NEoE NLar
	('Eiffel 1'PBR)	NOra NPip SBig SGol SPoG WCot WFar WHtc WMat
	- - BLUE SHEEN ('Hyfsheen')	MGos Midl NLar WCot
	- - CHERRY LACE ('Hyfjolais')	MHtn WNPC
§	- - 'Eva'PBR ♀H6	Widely available
§	- - 'Gerda'PBR ♀H6	Widely available
§	- - 'Guincho Purple'	CBcs EGrI EHeP NLar SPlb WCot WFar
§	- - LACED UP ('Snr1292')	EHeP MBros NLar SPad
	- - 'Purple Pete'	WCot
	- - 'Thundercloud' ♀H6	ELon MAsh MMrt MNrw NEoE NLar WCot
	- *Pulverulenta*' (v)	NQui SRms WCot WFar
	- 'Purpurea'	see *S. nigra* f. *porphyrophylla* 'Guincho Purple'
	- 'Pyramidalis'	WCot
	- 'Riese aus Vossloch'	WCot
	- 'Robert Piggin' (v)	WCot
	- var. *rotundifolia*	WCot
	- 'Sambu' (F)	CAgr WCot
	- 'Samdal' (F)	CAgr WCot
	- 'Samidan' (F)	CAgr WCot
	- 'Samnor' (F)	CAgr WCot
	- 'Sampo' (F)	CAgr WCot
	- 'Samyl' (F)	CAgr WCot
	- STRAIT LACED	see *S. nigra* f. *porphyrophylla* LACED UP
	- 'Urban Lace'	CAgr WCot
	- 'Variegata'	see *S. nigra* 'Marginata'
	- f. *viridis*	CAgr WCot
	'Ocean Depths'	NEoE WCot
	palmensis	WCot
	racemosa	WCot WKor
	- 'Altamont'	WCot
	- 'Aurea'	WFar
	- var. *callicarpa*	WCot
	- subsp. *kamtschatica*	WCot
	- var. *melanocarpa*	WCot
	- 'Plumosa Aurea'	CMac EHeP LRHS MGos NLar SMad SRms WCot
	- var. *pubens*	WCot
§	- var. *sieboldiana*	WCot
	- 'Sutherland Gold' ♀H7	CBcs CBrac CCVT CDoC CMac CSBt EBee EGren EGrI EHeP ELan ELon EPfP EUrb GKin LRHS LSRN LSto MAsh MGos MHoo MPro NLar SGol SPoG WCot WFar WLov
	- 'Tenuifolia'	WCot
	'Rainbow'	WCot
	sieboldiana	see *S. racemosa* var. *sieboldiana*
	× *strumpfii* SERENADE ('Jonade')	EBee EPfP LCro LRHS NEoE NLar SAth SMrm WCot WFar
	SUNNY DAYS ('Jonsun')	CSBt
I	'The Sweet One'	WCot
	tigranii	WCot
	'Vermilion Summers'	WCot
	WELSH GOLD ('Walfinb'PBR)	MAsh SPoG
	wightiana	see *S. javanica*
§	*williamsii* subsp. *coreana*	WCot

Sandersonia (Colchicaceae)

aurantiaca	LAma

Sanguinaria (Papaveraceae)

canadensis	CTtf EAri EGrI EMor EPot EPPr GKev LAma LEdu MHoo MMuc
- f. *multiplex* (d)	EPot NBir WAbe
- - 'Plena' (d) ♀H5	CTtf EAri ENun EWld GEdr GKev GQue LAma LRHS MCor NHar NQui NRya NWbg WHil
- pink-flowered	GBin
- 'Rosea'	GKev

Sanguisorba ❀ (Rosaceae)

from Japan	GGro MAvo MPie
§ *albiflora*	CDoC CKno EBlo ECha ELan EMor EPfP EWhm LEdu LRHS LShi Midl MMuc MNrw MPro NDov NGdn NLar SMrm SRkn WCAu
'All Time High' ♀H7	CCBP LEdu LRHS NDov NLar SDix SPel WFar
alpina	MMuc SMrm
'Ankum's Thums'	MAvo MHol
applanata	EBlo GGro LRHS SBrt WCot WFar WPGP
§ *armena*	LEdu MNrw SPel WFar
'Autumn Bliss'	GMaP
'Autumn Red'	EBee MAvo
'Beetlewings' ♀H7	LRHS NClf NDov SBeP WPGP
'Blackthorn'	CElw CKno CTtf EMor EPfP GMaP GQue LRHS LSto MBel MPro NDov NLar SBeP SMad SMHy WCAu WCot WFar WHoo WOld WTor XFar
'Burr Blanc' ♀H7	CKno GMaP MBel MMrt SMHy WHoo
'Bury Court'	NDov
canadensis	CBcs CCBP CKno CMac ECha ELan EPfP EPPr EWhm GMaP GQue LBar LCro MAvo MHol MNrw NBir NDov NLar NSti SBeP SRms WChS WCot WGwG WOld
- hybrid	CKno SMHy
'Candy Floss'	MAvo WHoo
'Cangshan Cranberry' ♀H7	EBee ECha GMaP LCro LRHS MBel NLar SDix SMad SMHy SPel WCAu WCot WTor
'Ccc'	MAvo
'Chinese Winter' ♀H7	SPel WPGP
'Chocolate Tip'	CDor EBee EGren EPPr ESgI GMaP MBel Midl SBeP WFar
'Foxtail'	MAvo
'Frilly Green'	see *S. armena*
hakusanensis	CKno CTtf EBee EBlo ECha ELan EMor ESgI EWhm GBin GKev GMaP LEdu LRHS LShi MNrw NBir NBro NLar WCAu WCot WFar
- 'Alster Luft'	LBar SPel
- 'Chirisan Chignon' ♀H7	SPel WCru
- 'Lilac Squirrel'	CAby CKno CTtf EMor ERCP EWhm GBin GMaP IPot LBar LCro LEdu LRHS MBel MNrw MPro NCth NGdn NLar SBeP SDix SMad SMHy SPad SPel SRms WCAu WFar WTor
'Hendrickx'	LEdu
'Ice Cap'	MAvo
'Ivory Towers' ♀H6	MAvo SPhx WFar
'John Coke'	NLar
'Joni'	CKno IPot MWlw NDov WFar WPGP
'Just Joe'	MAvo

Sanguisorba

'Little Angel' ♀H4	Widely available	'Raspberry Coulis' ♀H7	MAvo NDov WMal
'Maartjes Merlot' ♀H7	LRHS NDov	'Raspberry Mivvi'	WMal
magnifica	EWes LEdu	'Red Busby'	MAvo SMHy
- *alba*	see *S. albiflora*	'Red Sentinel' **new**	WPGP
menziesii	Widely available	'Rock and Roll'	CKno EBee EPPr LBar NLar
- 'Dali Marble' (v)	GQue NLar	'Ruby Velvet'	IPot MNrw
- 'Wake Up'	ELan LBar MMrt NDov NLar WFar	'Sangria'	MAvo MHol
- 'Midnight's Child'	CElw	'Sanguine Dwarf'	MAvo SMHy
§ ***minor***	CAgr CCBP CGHo CGwi CHby EGren EHet GJem GQue MCtn MHer MHoo NAts NBac SPlb SRms WHer WKit	'Scapino'	MAvo SMHy
		sitchensis	see *S. stipulata*
		'Skinny Fingers'	MAvo
		§ ***stipulata***	CMac EBlo EPfP LEdu LRHS MNrw SMHy
- subsp. *minor*	CHab	- var. *riishirensis*	EPPr WFar
- subsp. *muricata*	CGwi	'Swan Song'	MAvo
'Miss Elly' ♀H7	NDov	'Swarm'	MAvo
'Noet'	WPGP	'Tanna'	Widely available
obtusa	CDoC CMac CSde EBee ECha EGrI EPPr EWhm GMaP LCro LEdu LShi MBel MHer Midl MMuc NEoE NLar NSti SMrm SPoG SRms WCAu WCot WOld	***tenuifolia***	ECha LShi NLar WCot
		- var. *alba*	Widely available
		- - 'John Coke'	CKno
		- - 'Korean Snow'	EPPr GMaP LEdu LRHS NDov
		- 'Big Pink'	MAvo Midl WFar
- 'Chatto'	GMaP MAvo NLar WMal WPGP	- 'Bordeaux'	CDor EBee ESgI
- silver-leaved	EPPr MNrw WFar	- 'Henk Gerritsen'	MAvo NLar WCAu WFar
- white-flowered	EBee MBel	§ - var. *parviflora*	EMor ESgI LEdu LShi NLar WHoo WPGP
officinalis	CBWd CGwi CHab CSpe ECha EGrI GQue LShi LSto MAsh MCtn MHer MHoo NMir SPhx SRms StAn WCAu WFar	- 'Pink Elephant'	CKno EBee ECha EMor EPPr EWhm GKev GMaP GQue LRHS MAvo MBel Midl NLar WCAu WFar
- CDC 262	EPPr LEdu SMHy	- 'Purpurea'	CKno EBee EGren EPPr GPSL GQue MBel WCAu WCot WPGP
- CDC 282	CSpe		
- CDC 292	WCot	- 'Rosea' **new**	SMHy
- DJHC 535	LEdu	- 'Stand Up Comedian' ♀H7	GQue MAvo MNrw NLar WPGP
- 'Arnhem'	CAby CDor CKno EBee EPPr GPSL NDov NLar SMHy WCAu WCot WTor	- 'Strawberry Frost'	CFis EMor LBar MAvo MHol
		- 'Strawberry Fruli'	LEdu WPGP
		- 'Sturdy Guard' ♀H7	EPPr LEdu NLar WPGP
- 'Crimson Queen'	CDor CKno EBee GMaP GQue MBel Midl MPro NLar	- 'The Invisible' ♀H7	MAvo SPel WCAu
		- 'White Tanna' ♀H7	EPPr LEdu
- dark-flowered	WMal	'White Brushes'	CKno LBar Midl WTor
- early-flowering	GMaP		
- 'False Tanna'	WFar	## *Sanicula* (Apiaceae)	
- 'Jam Session' PBR **new**	EBee LBar XFar	***epipactis*** ♀H7	CCBP CDor ECha EGrI ENun EWld GAbr GEdr GKev GMaP GQue LCro LRHS MNrw NBir NBro WCot WKif
- 'Janet's Jewel'	CKno		
- 'Japan'	CSpe		
- 'Lemon Splash' (v)	EBee LShi WCot WFar	- 'Harry Foley' (v)	GEdr
- 'Lum' ♀H7	MAvo NClf NDov SPel	- 'Thor' (v)	ECha EWld GEdr GQue MNrw NBir WAbe
- 'Martin's Mulberry'	ERCP EWes LCro LEdu MNrw NClf SHar WTor		
		europaea	CEls CTtf GEdr NAts NMir
- 'Morning Select'	EBee EPPr GMaP NLar	## *Sansevieria* (Asparagaceae)	
- 'Red Buttons'	MAvo NDov WMal	***bacularis***	NHrt
- 'Red Thunder'	CDor CElw CSpe EBee EGren EPPr ESgI EWhm GMaP GPSL LBar LCro LEdu MAvo MBel MHol MPro NClf WCAu WCot WGwG WHoo WPGP WTor	- 'Mikado'	LCro NHrt
		'Black Coral'	LBom LCro NHrt
		'Black Dragon'	NHrt
		cylindrica	CDoC EShb NGKo NHrt SPlb
- 'Shiro-fukurin' (v)	CDor EBee EWes EWhm GMaP MHol MNrw NLar WCot WFar	- 'Motum Kenya'	LCro
		- 'Straight'	LCro NHrt
- 'Tsetseguun'	LEdu WPGP	- 'Fernwood Mikado'	NHrt
parviflora	see *S. tenuifolia* var. *parviflora*	***kirkii***	NHrt
pimpinella	see *S. minor*	- 'Farah' PBR	LCro
'Pink Brushes'	CBWd CKno CTtf ELan EMor EPPr GMaP IPot LBar LRHS LSou MAvo MBel MHtn MNrw MPro NCth NDov NLar SPad SRkn WCAu WFar WNPC WPGP WTor	- 'Silver Blue' (v)	LCro
		masoniana **new**	NHrt
		- 'Victoria'	LCro
		metallica	LCro
		trifasciata	CWal LBom LWaG NGKo NHrt
'Pink September' ♀H7	MAvo MHol	- 'Diamond Flame' PBR	NHrt
'Pink Tanna'	Widely available	- 'Futura'	EGren LWaG
'Plum Drops' **new**	CKno LBar MPro	- 'Golden Flame'	LCro
'Prim and Proper'	CKno MAvo MHol MWlw SDix	- 'Golden Hahnii' (v) ♀H1b	NHrt
'Proud Mary'	CSpe CWnw EPfP LBar LCro MBel NLar XFar	- 'Hahnii' ♀H1b	EShb LCro NGKo NHrt
'Purple Tails'	CKno EMor	- var. *laurentii* (v) ♀H1b	CDoC LBom LCro LWaG NHrt

- 'Moonshine' ♀H1b CDoC EShb LCro LWaG NHrt
- 'Variegata' (v) LBom
zeylanica LCro NHrt
- 'Silver Flame'ᴾᴮᴿ (v) LCro NHrt

Santolina ✿ (Asteraceae)
'Apple Court' LRHS
§ chamaecyparissus Widely available
  - var. corsica misapplied see S. chamaecyparissus 'Nana'
  - 'Lambrook Silver' CFis EBee ENfk EPfP LRHS MHoo NLar
  - 'Lemon Queen' EGrI ENfk EPfP EWhm LRHS MAsh NBir NLar SRms
§ - 'Nana' ♀H5 EPfP LRHS MAsh MHer MHoo SRGP SRms
  - 'Pretty Carroll' ♀H5 CDoC EBee ELan EPfP LRHS SPoG WFar
  - 'Small-Ness' MHer NLar SRms WAbe
etrusca ECha IDun LShi MHoo
incana see S. chamaecyparissus
pectinata see S. rosmarinifolia subsp. canescens
pinnata MSwo
§ - subsp. neapolitana ♀H5 ECha ELan ENfk EPfP SEND
  - - cream-flowered see S. pinnata subsp. neapolitana 'Edward Bowles'
§ - - 'Edward Bowles' CCBP EBee ECha EGrI EWhm GMaP LShi LSRN MHer MHoo NBir NPer SHar SPoG SRms SVen WFar WHer
  - - 'Sulphurea' CDoC CFis EGrI EPfP LRHS SPhx WKif
rosmarinifolia CCBP EHeP GQue MHoo NLar SPlb SRms WKit
§ - subsp. canescens EGrI
  - 'Green Fizz' WFar
  - 'Lemon Fizz' ♀H5 CBcs CDoC CMac CSpe EBee ELan ELon ENfk EPfP GMaP LCro LRHS LShi MAsh MHer MHoo MPri MPro MSwo NBir NLar SPoG SRms WFar WHil WLov WTor
§ - subsp. rosmarinifolia EGren EGrI ELan ENfk LShi LSto MHer MHoo MNHC SAng SDix SEND SRms WFar WKit
  - - 'Olivia' MNHC
  - - 'Primrose Gem' ♀H5 CBcs CDoC ECha EGrI EPfP MPri SEND SHar SRms
  - - white-flowered WHer
SHADES OF JADE ('Sant101') SRms
tomentosa misapplied see S. pinnata subsp. neapolitana
virens see S. rosmarinifolia subsp. rosmarinifolia
viridis see S. rosmarinifolia subsp. rosmarinifolia

Sanvitalia (Asteraceae)
AZTEKENGOLD see Melampodium montanum AZTEC GOLD
procumbens SPoG

Sapindus (Sapindaceae)
mukorossi WJur
- B&SWJ 14689 WCru

Saponaria (Caryophyllaceae)
'Bressingham' ♀H5 EDAr EGren GJos LCro LRHS WAbe WFar WIce
Bressingham hybrid MAsh
caespitosa EWes
§ intermedia NDov WCot
× lempergii 'Fritz Lemperg' NDov SEND WCot WMal

- 'Max Frei' CCBP EBee ECha EPPr LCro NDov SHar SPeP SPhx WCot WMal
ocymoides ♀H5 EBee ECha ELan EPfP GJos LRHS LShi MAsh MCtn MHol SPlb SPoG SRms StAn
- 'Alba' ECha EGren LCro LShi WFar
- 'Snow Tip' LBar NGdn
officinalis CCBP CGHo ENfk EWhm GQue LShi MCtn MHer MHoo MNHC SMrm SPlb SRms WCAu WHer
- 'Alba Plena' (d) CTsd EBee NLar SEND WCAu WFar
- 'Betty Arnold' (d) EPPr EWes LShi WCot
- 'Flore Pleno' (d) LShi WFar
- 'Red Splash' WFar
- 'Rosea Plena' (d) CMac EBee ELan EPfP GMaP LEdu MHol MMuc NBid NBir NGdn NLar SEND SMrm WFar WGwG
- 'Rubra Plena' (d) CCBP EPPr EWes MMuc SEND
× olivana ♀H5 EPot GArf LRHS MAsh NLar
pumilio Boiss. GKev
sicula subsp. intermedia see S. intermedia
zawadskii see Silene zawadskii

Saracha (Solanaceae)
punctata B&SWJ 14882 WCru
quitensis B&SWJ 14748 WCru

Sarcandra (Chloranthaceae)
§ glabra B&SWJ 11102 WCru

Sarcococca ✿ (Buxaceae)
bleddynii KWJ 12222 WCru
confusa ♀H5 Widely available
hookeriana ELon GKin LSRN MBlu NLar SFol SNig WFar WPGP WSpi
- HWJK 2393 WCru
- HWJK 2428 WCru
- 'Crûg's Purple Tips' WCru
- var. digyna CBcs CBrac CEnd CMac CMCN CSBt EGrI ELon EPfP LCro LEdu LRHS LSRN MAsh MMuc SEND SGol SHor SPoG SRms SSta WJur WPGP
- - SDR 7816 GKev
- - 'Purple Stem' ♀H5 CBcs CDoC CExl EBee EGren ELan GKin LBom LCro LEdu LRHS LSto MAsh MGos SBig SHor SOrN SPoG SWor WCru WFar WSpi
- - 'Tony Schilling' CExl
- var. hookeriana LSRN WJur
- - GWJ 9222 WCru
- - GWJ 9344 WCru
- - GWJ 9369 WCru
- - HWJK 2102 WCru
- - HWJK 2366 WCru
- - HWJK 2393 WCru
- - 'Daman' CExl
- - 'Ghorepani' ♀H5 LCro LRHS MPri WHtc WJur
- var. humilis CBcs CDoC CSBt EBee EGren EGrI ELan ELon EPfP GKin IArd LBuc LCro LRHS LSRN MAsh MGos MNrw MPri NLar SPoG WCha WCru WFar WJur WLov WPGP WSpi
- - FRAGRANT MOUNTAIN ('Sarsid2') LCro
- - FRAGRANT VALLEY ('Sarsid1') LCro NLar
- PURPLE GEM ('Purplerij1'ᴾᴮᴿ) **new** LBuc MPri
- WINTER GEM ('Pmoore03'ᴾᴮᴿ) CBcs CDoC CMac CSBt EBee ECha EGren ELan EPfP LBom LCro LRHS

	LSou LSRN MAsh MGos SHor SPoG	
	SRkn WFar WLov WSpi	
orientalis	CBct CExl CMCN EBee ELon EPfP	
	ESwi LRHS LSto MAsh MPri NLar	
	SChF SPoG WJur WLov WPGP WSpi	
'Roy Lancaster'	see *S. ruscifolia* var. *chinensis*	
	'Dragon Gate'	
'Rudolph'	CDoC EPfP	
ruscifolia	CBcs CBrac CExl CHab CMCN CSBt	
	EBee EGren EHeP ELon EPfP LBom	
	LRHS LSto MAsh MGos MHed	
	MMuc SEND SEWo SHor SRms	
	WCru WFar WJur	
- var. *chinensis*	WCru WPGP	
§ - - 'Dragon Gate' ♀H5	CBcs CDoC CExl CMHG EBee	
	EGren EGrI ELan EPfP EUrb	
	LBom MAsh MGos SChF SMad	
	SOrN SPoG WCru WFar WPGP	
	WSpi	
saligna	CBcs CExl SOrN WCru WFar WJur	
- HWJK 2428	WCru	
- MF P2056	WCru	
- NJM 12.043	WPGP	
I *taiwaniana* RWJ 9999	ESwi WCru	
trinervia B&SWJ 9500	WCru	
vagans B&SWJ 7285	WCru	
- B&SWJ 9760 from Vietnam	WCru	
- B&SWJ 9766 from Vietnam	WCru	
aff. *vagans* B&SWJ 7265	WCru	
from north Thailand		
wallichii	CBcs CExl CMCN EPfP LEdu LRHS	
	MBlu SPoG WCot WJur WLov WPGP	
- B&SWJ 2291	WCru	
- GWJ 9427	WCru	
- HWJK 2425	WCru	
- HWJK 2428	WCru	
- PAB 13.077	LEdu	
aff. *wallichii*	EBee	
- NJM 12.043	WPGP	
zeylanica B&SWJ 10199	WCru	
- var. *brevifolia* GWJ 9480	WCru	
- - GWJ 9483	WCru	

Sarcopoterium (*Rosaceae*)
spinosum	SVen

Sarcostemma see *Cynanchum*
marapirmail 'Coimbrata'	EAri
stipitatum	see *Philibertia stipitata*

Sarmienta (*Gesneriaceae*)
repens	see *S. scandens*
§ *scandens* ♀H1c	CExl WAbe WPGP

Sarracenia ❁ (*Sarraceniaceae*)
'Ace of Spades'	WFar
× *ahlesii*	WFar
alata	WFar WSSs
- from Deer Park, Alabama, pubescent	WFar
- from George County, Mississippi	WFar
- from Nicholson County, Mississippi	WFar
- from Robertson County, Texas	WFar
- 'Black Tube' ♀H4	WFar WSSs
- 'Citronelle'	WFar
- heavily veined	WSSs
- - from East Texas	WFar
- large lid, robust, from Texas	WFar
- var. *nigropurpurea*	WSSs
- var. *ornata*	WSSs
- pubescent	SPlb WSSs
- 'Red Lid'	WSSs
- red lid from Nicholson County, Mississippi, USA	WFar
- - from W Louisiana, USA	WFar
- var. *rubrioperculata*	WSSs
- veined from Angelina County, Texas	WFar
- wavy lid	WSSs
- white-flowered	WSSs
alata × *flava*	see *S.* × *soperi*
× *areolata*	WFar WSSs
'Asbo'	WFar
'Barbapapa'	WFar
'Bella' ♀H3	WFar WSSs
'Bloodwulf'	WFar
'Broken Resolution'	WFar
'Camisole'	WFar
× *catesbaei*	WFar WSSs
- 'Heterophylla'	WFar
- Melanorhoda Group	WFar
- red	WFar
- snakeskin-veined	WFar
× *chelsonii*	WFar
'Complexion'	WFar
× *courtii*	WFar
'Dainty Maid'	WFar
'Dana's Delight'	WFar
'Daniel Rudd'	WFar
'Dappled Orange'	WFar
'Dawn Prince'	WFar
'Decora'	WFar
'Devil's Stick'	WFar
'Diane Whittaker'	WFar WSSs
'Dixie Lace' ♀H5	WFar
'Dutch Stevens' ♀H3	WFar
'Eva' ♀H3	WFar WSSs
'Evendine'	WFar
× *excellens*	WSSs
- 'Judy'	WFar
- 'Loch Ness'	WFar
× *excellens* × *leucophylla*	WFar
× *rubra* subsp. *gulfensis*	
× *exornata*	SPlb SRms WFar
- 'Peaches'	WFar WSSs
'Fiona'	WFar
flava	LCro WSSs
- all green giant	see *S. flava* var. *maxima*
- 'Ann Mundy'	WFar
- var. *atropurpurea*	WFar WSSs
- - from Blackwater, Florida	WFar
- - from North Carolina	WFar
- - from Wewahitchka, Florida	WFar
- 'Claret'	WSSs
- var. *cuprea*	WSSs
- - from North Carolina	SPlb WSSs
- var. *flava*	WSSs
- - from Prince George County, Virginia	WFar
- - 'Bronze Blush'	WFar
- 'Marston Dwarf'	WFar
- 'Goldie'	WFar
§ - var. *maxima*	WFar WSSs
- var. *ornata*	WFar WSSs
- - from Apalachicola, Florida	WFar
- - from Bay County, Florida	WFar
- var. *rubricorpora*	SPlb WSSs WFar

Sarracenia

- - from Apalachicola, Florida	WFar
- - 'Burgundy'	WSSs
- - 'Claret'	WFar
- - 'Claret' × *oreophila* × *purpurea*	WFar
- var. *rugelii*	SPlb WSSs
- - from Milton County, Florida	WFar
- - from N. Florida	WFar
- - from Prince George County, Virginia	WFar
- - from Telogia, Florida	WFar
- - giant and robust	WFar
- - wavy lid	WFar
× *formosa*	WFar
'Freckles'	WFar
'Frogita'	WFar
'Gelber Schnee'	WFar
'Ghost'	WFar
'Giraffe'	WFar
'God's Gift'	WFar
'Gorgo'	WFar
'Green Goddess'	WFar
× *harperi*	WFar
'Hugh Jampton'	WFar
'Hummer's Hammerhead'	WFar
'Imhotep'	WFar
'Jagger'	WFar
'Jedi'	WFar
'Joanna'	WFar
'Judith Hindle' ♀H3	ISha WFar WSSs
'Juthatip Soper' ♀H3	LCro WFar WSSs
'Kaspar Hauser'	WFar
'Labyrinth' ♀H3	WFar
'Ladies in Waiting' ♀H3	WFar
'Langford Williams'	WFar
'Laughing Wizard'	WFar
leucophylla	CDoC LCro SPlb SRms WSSs
- from gas station site, Perdido, Alabama	WFar
- from Perdido, Alabama	WFar
- var. *alba*	ISha WSSs
- anthocyanin-free	WFar
- 'Cronus'	WFar
- 'Deer Park Alabama'	WSSs
- green	WSSs
- green from Milton, Florida	WFar
- green and white	WSSs
- 'Helmut's Delight'	WFar
- pubescent	WFar WSSs
- red and white	WFar
- 'Schnell's Ghost' ♀H3	WFar WSSs
- Slack clone	WFar
- 'Tarnok'	WFar WSSs
- f. *viridescens*	WSSs
- white-topped	WFar
'Leviathan'	WFar
'Lovebug'	WFar
'Lynda Butt' ♀H3	WSSs
'Manky'	WFar
'Mardi Gras'	WFar
'Maria Marten'	WFar
'Maroon'	ISha LCro
'Max Rawlings'	WFar
'Mercury'	WFar
'Mieke'	WFar
× *miniata*	WSSs
minor	WSSs
- from Pine Mountain, Georgia	WFar
- from Waycross, Georgia	WFar
- anthocyanin-free	WFar
- 'Okee Giant'	WSSs
- var. *okefenokeensis*	WSSs
- - from Deeland County, Florida	WFar
- - from Waycross, Georgia	WFar
× *mitchelliana*	WFar WSSs
- 'Mary Cheek' ♀H3	WFar
- 'Mr Purplehaze' ♀H3	WFar WSSs
- pale	WFar
× *moorei*	WFar WSSs
- 'Adrian Slack'	WFar WSSs
- 'Brooks's Hybrid' ♀H4	SPlb WFar WSSs
- 'Elizabeth'	WFar
- 'Esme Cowlard'	WFar
- 'Leah Wilkerson'	WFar WSSs
- 'Marston Clone'	WFar
- 'Marston Mill'	WFar
- 'Paleface'	WFar
- 'Peaches'	WFar
- 'Welsh Dragon'	WFar
'Mr Pink Rim'	WFar
'Nicely Inconspicuous'	WFar
'Night Sky'	WFar
oreophila	SPlb WSSs
- from Boaz, Alabama	WFar
- from Cherokee, Alabama	WFar
- from DeKalb, Illinois	WFar
- from Sand Mountain, Georgia	WFar
- heavily veined	WFar
× *popei*	WFar WSSs
'Pout'	WFar
'Praetorian Guard'	WFar
'Pretty 'n' Pink'	WFar
psittacina	SRms WSSs
purpurea	MCtn WCot
- 'Dracula'	LCro
- subsp. *purpurea* ♀H6	SPlb WFar WSSs
- - f. *heterophylla* ♀H5	WSSs
- - 'Lake Hiron'	WFar
- subsp. *venosa*	ISha SPlb WSSs
- - var. *burkii* ♀H3	WFar WSSs
- - var. *montana*	ISha
'Raspberry Ice'	WFar
× *readei*	ISha LCro WSSs
'Red Sentinel'	WFar
'Redneck'	WFar
× *rehderi*	WFar WSSs
rubra	WSSs
- subsp. *alabamensis*	WSSs
- subsp. *gulfensis*	WSSs
- - f. *luteoviridis*	WSSs
- subsp. *jonesii*	WSSs
- - from McClures Bog, North Carolina	WFar
* - - f. *heterophylla*	WFar
- - f. *viridescens*	WSSs
- subsp. *rubra*	WSSs
- - long lid	WFar
- subsp. *wherryi*	WSSs
- - 'Chatom Giant'	WFar
- - giant	WSSs
- - yellow-flowered	WSSs
'Scarlet Belle'	WFar
'Scarlet Empress'	WFar
'Skywatcher'	WFar
'Snake's Skin'	WFar
× *soperi* 'Roy Cheek'	WFar
- (*S. alata* × *S. flava* var. *maxima*)	WFar WSSs

Sarracenia

× *swaniana*	SRms WFar
'Tara'	WFar
'Tiger's Eye'	WFar
'True Blood'	WFar
'Tygo'^{PBR}	WFar
'Up Periscope'	WFar
'Vampire'	WFar
'Vampire's Blood'	WFar
'Vampire's Lust'	WFar
'Vampire's Scream'	WFar
'Vogel' ♀H3	WFar WSSs
'White Zombie'	WFar
× *willisii*	WFar
× *wrigleyana*	SRms WFar

Saruma (Aristolochiaceae)

henryi	EAri EMor ESwi EWld GEdr GGro GKev LCro SBrt SMad SPel WCot WCru WFar

Sasa (Poaceae)

glabra f. *albostriata*	see *Sasaella masamuneana* 'Albostriata'
kurilensis	MWht
nipponica 'Aureostriata'	SWor
§ *palmata*	LCro MMuc SArc SWor
- f. *nebulosa*	CBcs LCro NLar SArc SWor
- var. *niijimae*	MWht
tessellata	see *Indocalamus tessellatus*
tsuboiana	CBcs MWht NLar
§ *veitchii*	CBcs ECha LCro LRHS MMuc MWht NLar SBig WFar

Sasaella (Poaceae)

glabra	see *S. masamuneana*
§ *masamuneana*	SBig
§ - 'Albostriata' (v)	MMuc MWht
§ *ramosa*	CBcs NLar

Sassafras (Lauraceae)

albidum	CBcs CMCN EPfP LMaj LRHS MPkF SPoG WPGP

satsuma see *Citrus reticulata*

Satureja ✿ (Lamiaceae)

biflora	WJek
douglasii	WJek
- 'Indian Mint'^{PBR}	EHet ENfk MHer MNHC SRms
hortensis	ENfk LCro MCtn MHer MHoo MNHC SRms SVic WJek
montana	CCBP CGHo CHby CWRo EHet ELan ENfk EWhm GQue IDun LCro LWaG MCtn MHer MHoo MMuc MNHC SEND SPhx SRms SVic WJek WKit WTre
* - *citriodora*	MHoo
§ - subsp. *illyrica*	MHoo WJek
- 'Purple Mountain'	MHer
- *subspicata*	see *S. montana* subsp. *illyrica*
repanda	see *S. spicigera*
§ *spicigera*	CGHo ENfk EPot EWhm IDun LEdu MHer MHoo MMuc SRms WJek
thymbra	SPhx SRms

Sauromatum (Araceae)

gaoligongense	WCot
§ *giganteum*	EAri EBee GKev LAma SBig WJun
guttatum	see *S. venosum*
horsfieldii	WPGP
§ aff. *horsfieldii*	EWld

§ *venosum*	CExl CSpe EAri EBee EGrl ELan EUrb EWld GKev LAma LEdu NGKo SPlb WCot WJun XFar
- 'Indian Giant' **new**	WPGP

Saururus (Saururaceae)

cernuus	CBen CLil CPud CTtf CWat EAri ELan ELin WMAq
- 'Hertford Streaker' (v)	WCot
chinensis	ELin SBrt
- PB 95-85	GGro WFar

Saussurea (Asteraceae)

centiloba aff. subsp. *pachyneura* W&O 7247	GGro
costus	GGro
nepalensis	GKev MCtn
stella	GKev

savory, summer see *Satureja hortensis*

savory, winter see *Satureja montana*

Saxegothaea (Podocarpaceae)

conspicua	CBcs IArd
- 'Ray Wood'	WPGP

Saxifraga ✿ (Saxifragaceae)

(4)	see *Micranthes*
acerifolia (5)	GEdr GKev
'Ada' (× *petraschii*) (7)	WHoo
§ 'Afrodite' (*sempervivum*) (7)	EPot WAbe
'Ailsa Ruth' (8)	GKev
aizoides (9)	GKev
'Akibare' (*fortunei*) (5)	GEdr
'Alan Hayhurst' (8)	WAbe
'Alan Martin' (× *boydilacina*) (7)	EWes
'Alba' (× *apiculata*) (7) ♀H5	EPot MAsh SHor SPlb SRms
'Alba' (*oppositifolia*) (7)	ELan EWes WAbe
'Albert Einstein' (× *apiculata*) (7) ♀H5	MWlw
'Albertii' (*callosa*)	see *S.* 'Albida' (*callosa*)
§ 'Albida' (*callosa*) (8)	WAbe
'Allendale Bamby' (× *lismorensis*) (7)	WAbe
'Allendale Beauty' (7)	WAbe
'Allendale Bonny' (7)	WAbe
'Allendale Bravo' (× *lismorensis*) (7)	WHoo
'Allendale Charm' (Swing Group) (7)	GKev MWlw WAbe WHoo WIce
'Allendale Comet' (7)	GMaP
'Allendale Desire' (7)	WAbe
'Allendale Divine' (7)	WAbe
'Allendale Elegance' (7)	WAbe
'Allendale Elf' (7)	WAbe WHoo
'Allendale Elite' (7)	WAbe
'Allendale Epic' (7)	WAbe
'Allendale Grace' (7)	EPot MWlw WAbe WIce
'Allendale Harvest' (7)	WAbe WIce
'Allendale Snow' (× *rayei*) (7)	EWes
alpigena (7)	WAbe
ALPINO EARLY CARNIVAL ('Saxz0015'^{PBR}) (× *arendsii*) (15) **new**	EPfP LRHS
ALPINO EARLY LIME ('Saxz0007') (× *arendsii*) (15)	EPfP LCro LRHS WFar

Saxifraga 645

ALPINO EARLY PICOTEE ('Saxz0010') (× *arendsii*) (15) — EPfP LCro LRHS
ALPINO EARLY PINK ('Saxz0009') (× *arendsii*) (15) — LCro
ALPINO EARLY WHITE ('Saxz0003') (× *arendsii*) (15) — EPfP LRHS
ALPINO RED ('Saxz0014') (× *arendsii*) (15) — LCro
'Amberine' (× *anglica*) (7) — WAbe WHoo
angustifolia Haw. — see *S. hypnoides*
'Anneka Hope' (8) — GKev
'Aphrodite' (*sempervivum*) — see S. 'Afrodite' (*sempervivum*)
× *apiculata* sensu stricto hort. — see S. 'Gregor Mendel' (× *apiculata*)
× *apiculata* (7) — GMaP MAsh NBro
'Apple Blossom' (Mossy Group) (15) — LRHS NEoE
'April Showers' (*paniculata*) (8) — GKev
'Archdale' (*paniculata*) (8) — LRHS
'Arco' (× *arco-valleyi*) (7) — EPot
× *arendsii* (15) — CWal LWaG MCtn
- purple-flowered (15) — MMuc SPlb
'Arleta' (Southside Seedling Group) (8) — WIce
'Assimilis' (× *petraschii*) (7) — EPot
'Atropurpurea' (*paniculata* subsp. *cartilaginea*) (8) — EDAr GMaP WFar WHoo WIce
'Audrey Lowe' (*oppositifolia*) (7) — WAbe
'Auguste Renoir' (Decora Group) (7) — EPot
'Aurea' (*umbrosa*) — see S. 'Aureopunctata' (× *urbium*)
'Aurea Maculata' (*cuneifolia*) — see S. 'Aureopunctata' (× *urbium*)
§ 'Aureopunctata' (× *urbium*) (11/v) — CMac ECha ELan EPfP GAbr LEdu LRHS MHer MPnt SMad SPlb SPoG SRms SRot WFar
'Autumn Grace Hikari' (*fortunei*) (5) **new** — LBar SHar
'Autumn Tribute' (*fortunei*) (5) — GEdr WAbe WFar
'Ayako' (*fortunei*) (5) — GEdr WFar
'Baldensis' — see *S. paniculata* var. *minutifolia*
§ 'Beatrix Stanley' (× *anglica*) (7) — LRHS
'Beautiful Girl' (*fortunei*) (5) — WFar
'Ben Loyal' (× *concinna*) (7) — WAbe
'Beni-guruma' (*fortunei*) (5) — GEdr
'Beni-karen' (*fortunei*) (5) — GEdr WFar
'Beni-kirin' (*fortunei*) (5) — GEdr WFar
'Benimine' (*fortunei*) (5) — GEdr WFar
'Beni-tsukaji' (*fortunei*) (5) — NBro
'Beni-tsukasa' (*fortunei*) (5) — GEdr GMaP NLar WFar
'Beni-zakura' (*fortunei*) (5) — GEdr WFar
'Benny' (8) — EPot
BLACK RUBY (*fortunei*) (5) — CExl CSpe EBee ECha ELan EPfP GKev GMaP LEdu LRHS MNrw NBro NLar SMad SPlb SPoG WFar WPnP WSpi
'Blackberry and Apple Pie' (*fortunei*) (5) ♀H4 — CExl LRHS SMad WFar
'Bohemia' (7) — WAbe
'Bohemian Karst' (Prominent Group) (7) — WAbe
'Boston Spa' (× *elisabethae*) (7) — MAsh MWlw NLar SPlb
bronchialis (10) — GKev

'Bryn Llwyd' (Vanessa Group) (7) — WAbe
× *burnatii* (8) — WFar
burseriana (7) — WAbe
'Bychan' (*fortunei*) (5) — WAbe
caesia L. (8) — SRms
§ *callosa* (8) ♀H5 — GKev LRHS WAbe
§ - subsp. *catalaunica* (8) — WAbe
- *lingulata* — see *S. callosa*
canaliculata (15) — StAn
× *canis-dalmatica* — see S. 'Canis-dalmatica' (× *gaudinii*)
§ 'Canis-dalmatica' (× *gaudinii*) (8) — CTtf EPot GAbr GArf GKev GQue WFar
'Carmen' (× *elisabethae*) (7) — EPot GMaP
§ 'Carniolica' (*paniculata*) (8) — EDAr NBro
carolinica — see S. 'Carniolica' (*paniculata*)
cartilaginea — see *S. paniculata* subsp. *cartilaginea*
catalaunica — see *S. callosa* subsp. *catalaunica*
cebennensis dwarf (15) — WAbe
cespitosa (15) — WAbe
'Chambers' Pink Pride' — see S. 'Miss Chambers' (London Pride Group)
CHEAP CONFECTIONS (*fortunei*) (5) — GEdr SMad SPoG
CHERRY PIE (*fortunei*) (5) — GEdr NBir
'Chodov' (Holenka's Miracle Group) (× *megaseiflora*) (7) — EPot
'Clare Island' (*rosacea*) (15) — SLee
§ 'Clarence Elliott' (London Pride Group) (*umbrosa*) (11) ♀H5 — EPPr EWes GJos GKev GMaP MHer NDov NRya WFar WIce
'Cloth of Gold' (*exarata* subsp. *moschata*) (15) — CAby ECha EGren ELan EPfP MAsh NEoE SPlb SPoG SRms SRot WIce
cochlearis (8) — EPot NBro WAbe
- hybrid (8) — MAsh
'Cockscomb' (*paniculata*) (8) — MWlw
conifera (15) — WAbe
'Conwy Snow' (*fortunei*) (5) ♀H4 — WAbe WFar
'Conwy Star' (*fortunei*) (5) — GEdr WAbe WFar
'Coolock Gem' (7) — WAbe WHoo
'Coolock Kate' (7) ♀H5 — WAbe WFar WHoo
'Correvoniana' misapplied — see S. 'Lagraveana' (*paniculata*)
'Correvoniana' Farrer (*paniculata*) (8) — MHer MMuc SEND
cortusifolia — CBct
var. *stolonifera* (5) —
COTTON CROCHET (*fortunei*) (5/d) — NBro
cotyledon (8) — GMaP LEdu WAbe
'Cream Seedling' (× *elisabethae*) (7) — WIce
'Crimson Rose' (*paniculata*) — see S. 'Rosea' (*paniculata*)
'Crinoline' (7) — WAbe
§ *crustata* (8) — EPot GKev
- var. *vochinensis* — see *S. crustata*
CRYSTAL PINK (*fortunei*) (5/v) — CExl EBee
'Cultrata' (*paniculata*) (8) — NBro
'Cumulus' (7) ♀H5 — SPlb WHoo
§ *cuneifolia* (11) — MHer
- from Italy (11) — MMuc
'Cuscutiformis' (*stolonifera*) (5) — CAby CCBP CExl EWld GEdr SRms WFar
dahurica — see *S. cuneifolia*
'Dai Uchu' (*fortunei*) (5) — GEdr
'Dana' (Prichard's Monument Group) (× *megaseiflora*) (7) — EPot

Saxifraga

(Dancing Pixies Series)
- DANCING PIXIES TAJA LBar MPro
  ('Sh 1933'^{PBR})
  (*cortusifolia*) (5)
- DANCING PIXIES TALLY LBar MPro
  ('Sh 1934')
  (*cortusifolia*) (5)
- DANCING PIXIES THEA LBar MPro
  ('Sh 1931')
  (*cortusifolia*) (5) **new**
- DANCING PIXIES TILDA LBar MPro
  ('Sh 1919')
  (*cortusifolia*) (5)
- DANCING PIXIES TINI LBar MPro
  ('Sh 1914')
  (*cortusifolia*) (5)
- DANCING PIXIES TONI LBar MPro
  ('Sh 1925'^{PBR})
  (*cortusifolia*) (5)
- DANCING PIXIES TWINKIE LBar LRHS MPro
  ('Sh 1923')
  (*cortusifolia*) (5)
'Darcies Cross' EDAr
'Darius' NHar
'Dawn Frost' (7) EPot WIce
'Deirdre' GKev
'Dentata' (× *geum*) see *S*. 'Dentata' (London Pride Group) (× *polita*)
'Dentata' (× *urbium*) (11) see *S*. 'Dentata' (London Pride Group) (× *polita*)
§ 'Dentata' (London Pride Group) (× *polita*) (11) CMiW ECha LEdu MPnt
I 'Diana' (× *lincolni-fosteri*) (7) WIce
diapensioides (7) WAbe
dinnikii (7) WAbe
× *dinninaris* (7) WAbe
'Doctor Clay' (*paniculata*) (8) EPot GKev NHar NRya SPlb
'Doctor Ramsey' (8) EWes GArf LRHS
'Doctor Watson' (7) EPot
'Dotty Darcy' (8) EDAr
'Earl Grey' (8) WAbe
'Eiga' (*fortunei*) (5) GEdr
'Elegance' WFar
'Elf' (7) see *S*. 'Beatrix Stanley' (× *anglica*)
'Elf' (*exarata* subsp. *moschata*) (15) MAsh SRms
'Elf Rose' (15) NEoE SPoG
× *elisabethae* sensu stricto hort. see *S*. 'Carmen' (× *elisabethae*)
'Elliott's Variety' see *S*. 'Clarence Elliott' (London Pride Group) (*umbrosa*)
'Emily Rose' (8) GKev
epiphylla BWJ 8177 (5) WCru
erioblasta (15) WAbe
'Esther' (× *burnatii*) (8) GKev GMaP LRHS SLee WHoo
fair maids of France see *S*. 'Flore Pleno' (*granulata*)
'Fairy' (*exarata* subsp. *moschata*) (15) NBir NEoE
'Falstaff' (*burseriana*) (7) EPot
× *farreri* (15) WFar WIce
§ *federici-augusti* (7) WFar
§ - subsp. *grisebachii* (7) ♀^{H5} WAbe WFar
ferdinandi-coburgi (7) WAbe
'Findling' (Mossy Group) (15) LRHS SPoG WAbe WIce
'Firebrand' (× *kochii*) (7) WAbe
'Flavescens' misapplied see *S*. 'Lutea' (*paniculata*)
§ 'Flore Pleno' (*granulata*) (15/d) CElw CMiW GEdr LBar LEdu NBir XFar

'Flowers of Sulphur' see *S*. 'Schwefelblüte'
fortunei (5) ♀^{H4} CMac NBir SRms WAbe WFar
- f. *alpina* (5) NBro
- var. *obtusocuneata* (5) GEdr WAbe
- pink-flowered (5) WAbe
'Foster's Gold' (× *elisabethae*) (7) EPot
'Four Winds' (Mossy Group) (15) EWes SPoG
'Francis Cade' (8) GAbr WAbe
'Franz Liszt' (7) EPot
frederici-augusti see *S. federici-augusti*
'Frederik Chopin' (7) EPot
'Fumiko' (*fortunei*) (5) SPlb WAbe
'Fuzzypeg' (London Pride Group) (× *geum*) (11) **new** SMHy
'Gaia' (*fortunei*) (5) LEdu
'Gaiety' (15) NEoE SPoG
'Ganymede' (*burseriana*) (7) EPot
'Gelber Findling' (7) EPot
'Gelbes Monster' (*fortunei*) (5) EBee ELan GEdr NLar WCot WSpi
§ × *geum* (11) ECha EPPr SDix WFar
- Dixter form (11) EWes LEdu
'Ginkgo 98' (*stolonifera*) (5) GGro WFar
'Glauca' (*paniculata* var. *brevifolia*) see *S*. 'Labradorica' (*paniculata*)
'Gleborg' (Mossy Group) (15) SPoG
'Gloria' (*burseriana*) (7) EDAr MAsh
'Golden Falls' (Mossy Group) (15/v) SPlb SPoG
GOLDEN PRAGUE (× *pragensis*) see *S*. 'Zlatá Praha' (× *pragensis*)
'Gosho-guruma' (*stolonifera*) (5) GGro
'Grace Farwell' (× *anglica*) (7) NLar WHoo
§ 'Gregor Mendel' (× *apiculata*) (7) ♀^{H5} CAby EPot NLar SRms WHoo
grisebachii see *S. federici-augusti* subsp. *grisebachii*
- subsp. *montenegrina* see *S. federici-augusti*
'Hakubai' (*fortunei*) (5) GEdr
'Hare Knoll Beauty' (8) EDAr GAbr GKev LRHS WAbe WFar WIce
'Harlow Car' (× *anglica*) (7) EPot WIce
'Harvest Moon' (*stolonifera*) (5) WFar
'Herbert Cuerden' (× *elisabethae*) (7) EPot MWlw
'Hi-Ace' (Mossy Group) (15/v) SPlb
'Highlander Red' (Mossy Group) (15) LCro
'Highlander Rose Shades' (Mossy Group) (15) LRHS
'Highlander White' (Mossy Group) (15) EGren LRHS
'Highlander White and Red' (Mossy Group) (× *arendsii*) (15) EGren
'Hi Ho Silver' (8) GKev
'Hime' (*stolonifera*) (5) GGro SRms
'Hindhead Seedling' (× *boydii*) (7) WAbe
'Hi-no-mai' (*fortunei*) (5) GKev
'Hiogi' (*fortunei*) (5) GEdr
hirsuta (11) CMac ESwi EWld LEdu MMuc MNrw SBrt WCot WCru
'Hirsuta' (× *geum*) see *S*. × *geum*

Saxifraga 647

'Hirsuta' (*paniculata*) (8)	WFar	*Ilonakhensis* (1)	WAbe
'Hirtella' misapplied	see *S.* 'Hirsuta' (*paniculata*)	'Lohengrin'	EPot
'Hirtella' Ingwersen (*paniculata*) (8)	EPot	(× *boerhammeri*) (7)	
'His Majesty' (× *irvingii*) (7)	EPot	LOVE ME	see *S.* 'Miluj Mne' (× *poluanglica*)
'Hiten' (*fortunei*) (5)	EBee	'Luschtinetz' (Mossy Group) (15)	LRHS
hostii (8)	GArf	'Lutea' (*aizoon*)	see *S.* 'Lutea' (*paniculata*)
- subsp. *rhaetica* (8)	NBro	§ 'Lutea' (*paniculata*) (8)	EPot GMaP LRHS NBro NRya SHar
'Hsitou Silver' (*stolonifera*) (5)	WCot	'Lydia' (× *hornibrookii*) (7)	WAbe
'Hyoseki' (*fortunei*) (5)	GEdr	*macedonica*	see *S. juniperifolia*
§ *hypnoides* (15)	WAbe	'Maigrün' (*fortunei*) (5)	EBee GKev
- var. *cantabrica* (15)	EPot	'Mai-hime' (*fortunei*) (5)	GEdr
ICE COLOURS PEARL WHITE ('Florsaxpwh'^{PBR}) (× *arendsii*) (Ice Colours Series) (15) **new**	MPri	'Maiko' (*fortunei*) (5)	GEdr
		manchuriensis	see *Micranthes manchuriensis*
		marginata (7) ♥^{H5}	MWIw WAbe
		- subsp. *marginata* var. *coriophylla* (7)	EPot WAbe
		- - var. *rocheliana* (7)	EPot
'Iceland' (*oppositifolia*) (7)	EWes	'Maria Callas' (× *poluanglica*) (7)	WAbe
'Ingeborg' (Mossy Group) (15)	CElw SLee	'Maria Luisa' (× *salmonica*) (7)	WAbe
× *irvingii* sensu stricto hort.	see *S.* 'Walter Irving' (× *irvingii*)	'Maroon Beauty' (*stolonifera*) (5)	EBee EPPr NBid WCot WFar
'Iyo Haksui' (*fortunei*) (5)	GEdr	'Martin Luther' (Wittenberg Group) (7)	EPot
'Jaromir' (8)	MWIw NHar WAbe		
'Jenkinsiae' (× *irvingii*) (7)	CAby MMuc MWIw NLar WAbe WIce	(Marto Series) MARTO HOT ROSE ('Florsaxhro') (× *arendsii*) (15)	LRHS
'Joachim Barrande' (× *siluris*) (7)	EPot	- MARTO ROSE ('Florsaxrose1'^{PBR}) (× *arendsii*) **new**	LRHS
'John Byam-Grounds' (Honor Group) (7)	WAbe	- MARTO WHITE ('Florsaxwh1') (× *arendsii*) (15)	EGren LRHS
'Jorg' (× *biasolettoi*) (7)	EPot		
§ *juniperifolia* (7)	EDAr SRms StAn	'Mary Golds' (Swing Group) (7)	NLar
'Karlštejn' (× *borisii*) (7)	EPot		
'Kath's Delight' (8)	GKev	'Masami' (*fortunei*) (5)	GEdr
'Kawazu-beni' (*fortunei*) (5)	GEdr	'Matthew Ruane' (8)	GKev
'King Lear' (× *bursiculata*) (7)	LRHS	× *megaseiflora* sensu stricto hort.	see *S.* 'Robin Hood' (× *megaseiflora*)
'Kinki Purple' (*stolonifera*) (5)	CDoC CDTJ CSpe CTsd EPPr EWld ISha LRHS MWIw SMHy WCru WFar WPnP	*mertensiana*	see *Micranthes mertensiana*
		'Mikawa-beni' (*fortunei*) (5)	GEdr
		§ 'Miluj Mne' (× *poluanglica*) (7)	CAby WAbe WHoo WIce
'Klondike' (× *boydii*) (7)	WAbe	'Minor' (*cochlearis*) (8) ♥^{H5}	EPot
'Knapton Pink' (Mossy Group) (15)	NEoE SPoG WIce	'Minor' (*paniculata*)	see *S. paniculata* var. *brevifolia*
'Kokoryu-nishiki' (*fortunei*) (5)	GEdr	'Minor Glauca' (*paniculata*)	see *S.* 'Labradorica' (*paniculata*)
'Komochi-daimonji' (*fortunei*) (5)	EDAr GEdr WFar	§ 'Miss Chambers' (London Pride Group) (11)	CMac EWes WCot WFar
'Kon Tiki' (7)	EPot	'Moe' (*fortunei*) (5) ♥^{H4}	GEdr
'Labe' (× *arco-valleyi*) (7)	EPot	'Mollie Broom' (7)	WAbe
§ 'Labradorica' (*paniculata*) (8)	NRya	'Momo Tarou' (*fortunei*) (5)	GEdr
'Lady Beatrix Stanley'	see *S.* 'Beatrix Stanley' (× *anglica*)	'Mona Lisa' (× *borisii*) (7)	EPot WAbe
§ 'Lagraveana' (*paniculata*) (8) ♥^{H5}	GKev LRHS SLee WFar	'Monarch' (8) ♥^{H5}	EDAr EPot EWes GAbr GKev LRHS MNrw SHar WAbe WFar WIce
'Laka' (7)	EPot	'Moondance' (*cochlearis*)	GKev
'Lantoscana' (*callosa*) subsp. *callosa* var. *australis* (8)	GKev	Mossy Group (15)	MBros MHol
		- pink-flowered (15)	MMuc SPoG
'Lemon Puff' (8)	WFar	- red-flowered (15)	SPoG
'Lenka' (× *byam-groundsii*) (7)	EPot	- white-flowered (15)	MMuc
'Leonardo da Vinci' (7)	WAbe	'Mossy Triumph'	see *S.* 'Triumph' (× *arendsii*)
'Letchworth Gem' (London Pride Group) (× *urbium*) (11)	EPPr GAbr WFar	'Mount Nachi' (*fortunei*) (5) ♥^{H4}	EWes GEdr GMaP NBro NHar SPlb WAbe WSpi
'Lilliput' (*stolonifera*) (5)	GGro WFar	'Mrs Helen Terry' (× *salmonica*) (7) ♥^{H5}	GArf
'Lincoln Foster' (8)	EDAr		
lingulata	see *S. callosa*	'Mugen' (*fortunei*) (5)	GEdr
'Lissadell' (*callosa*) (8)	GKev	'Namiyama' (*fortunei*) (5)	EDAr GEdr
* 'Little Piggy' (*epiphylla*) (5)	ESwi WCru	'Nezu-jinja' (*stolonifera*) (5)	GGro
'Lizzy' (7)	EPot	'Nicholas' (8)	GKev
		nigroglandulifera (1)	GKev

Saxifraga

'Nouhime' (*fortunei*) (5)	GEdr
§ ***obtusa*** (7)	MHer
'Odysseus' (*sancta*) (7)	MWlw
'Ogon-no-mai' (*fortunei*) (5)	GEdr
'Omar Khayyám' (7)	EPot
oppositifolia (7)	SPlb SRms WAbe
- subsp. ***oppositifolia***	ELan GArf WIce
- var. ***latina*** (7)	
paniculata (8)	GMaP LRHS SPlb SRms
§ - var. ***brevifolia*** (8)	LRHS
§ - subsp. ***cartilaginea*** (8)	GKev
- 'Foster's Red' (8)	NHar
- subsp. ***kolenatiana***	see *S. paniculata* subsp. *cartilaginea*
§ - var. ***minutifolia*** (8)	EDAr GQue LRHS NBro NRya SLee SPlb WAbe WHoo WIce
paradoxa (15)	LRHS NHar
'Parcevalis' (× *finnisiae*) (7 × 9)	WAbe
'Peach Blossom' (7)	LRHS
'Peach Melba' (7) ♀H5	CAby EPot NLar WHoo WIce
'Pearly King' (Mossy Group) (15)	EGren WAbe WCav
'Penelope' (× *boydilacina*) (7)	NLar
'Peter Pan' (Mossy Group) (15)	EGren EPfP GAbr GMaP LRHS MHer MPro NLar SPoG WCav WFar WIce WTor
'Pink Cloud' (*fortunei*) (5)	GEdr GKev NBro NHar WAbe
'Pink Froth' (× *geum*) (11)	SMHy
'Pink Haze' (*fortunei*) (5) ♀H4	GEdr GKev WAbe WFar
'Pink Melba' (7)	LRHS NLar
'Pink Mist' (*fortunei*) (5)	GEdr GKev WAbe WFar
'Pink Pagoda' (*nipponica*) (5)	EBee WCot WCru WFar
'Pink Star' (× *boydilacina*) (7)	GMaP NLar
Pixi Pan Appleblossom ('Florsaxapple'PBR) (× *arendsii*) (15)	LRHS
'Pixi Pan Red' (Mossy Group) (15)	EGren
'Pixie' (15)	EPfP LRHS MAsh NRya SLee SPoG SRms SRot WFar WIce
'Pixie Alba'	see *S.* 'White Pixie'
'Pixie Pearls' (Mossy Group) (15)	EDAr
'Plena' (*granulata*)	see *S.* 'Flore Pleno' (*granulata*)
'Poils Hirsutes' (*stolonifera*) (5)	GGro
'Polar Drift'	EPot LRHS WFar WHoo WIce
poluniniana (7)	WAbe
'Pompadour' (15)	NEoE
porophylla (7)	GBin
'Precious Piggy' (*epiphylla*) (5)	GGro WCru
'Primrose Dame' (× *elisabethae*) (7)	EPot
'Primulaize Salmon' (9 × 11)	NHar
'Primuloides' (*umbrosa*) (11)	MMuc SRms SRot
'Primuloides' variegated (*umbrosa*) (11/v)	SRms
'Princess' (*burseriana*) (7)	EPot
'Probynii' (*cochlearis*) (8)	EPot WAbe WFar
'Pseudo-valdensis' (*cochlearis*) (8)	WAbe
pubescens (15)	WAbe
- subsp. ***iratiana*** (15)	EDAr WAbe
'Pungens' (× *apiculata*) (7)	EPot
'Purple Piggy' (*epiphylla*) (5)	WCru
'Purple Robe' (× *arendsii*) (15)	LBar
'Purpurea' (*fortunei*)	see *S.* 'Rubrifolia' (*fortunei*)
'Pyramidalis' (*cotyledon*) (8)	GKev LBar
'Rachel' (8)	GKev
'Rainsley Seedling' (8)	EDAr GKev NBro
'Ray Woodliffe' (× *dinninaris*) (7)	WAbe
'Red Poll' (× *poluanglica*) (7)	WAbe
retusa (7)	WAbe
'Rex' (*paniculata*) (8)	CMac
§ 'Robin Hood' (× *megaseiflora*) (7)	WHoo
'Rocco Red' (× *arendsii*) (15)	EGren EPfP
'Rockies White' (× *arendsii*) (Rockies Series) (15)	LRHS
'Rockrose' (× *arendsii*) (15)	SPoG
§ 'Rockwhite' (× *arendsii*) (15)	LRHS WIce
'Rokujō' (*fortunei*) (5) ♀H4	NBro NLar
'Rosa Tubbs' (8)	EWes
'Rosaleen' (× *salmonica*) (7)	EPot
'Rosalind' (7)	GKev
§ 'Rosea' (*paniculata*) (8) ♀H5	EGren GMaP MMuc NBro NRya SRms WFar
rotundifolia (12)	ECha GKev MPnt
'Rubra' (*aizoon*)	see *S.* 'Rosea' (*paniculata*)
§ 'Rubrifolia' (*fortunei*) (5) ♀H4	CMac ECha LEdu NBro SMad WCot WCru WFar WPnP
* 'Ruby Red' (Mossy Group) (15)	EDAr
* 'Ruby Wedding' (*cortusifolia*) (5)	WFar
'Rumba' (7)	EPot
'Ruth Draper' (*oppositifolia*) (7) ♀H5	WAbe
'Salomonii' (× *salmonica*) (7)	SRms
sancta (7)	SRms
- subsp. ***pseudosancta***	see *S. juniperifolia*
- - var. ***macedonica***	see *S. juniperifolia*
'Saotome' (*fortunei*) (5)	GEdr
sarmentosa	see *S. stolonifera*
'Satchmo' (Blues Group) (7)	WIce
'Saturn' (× *megaseiflora*) (7)	EPot
'Saxony Red' (× *arendsii*) (Saxony Series) (15)	EPfP GPSL
§ ***scardica*** (7)	GArf NBro
- var. ***dalmatica***	see *S. obtusa*
(Scenic Series) 'Scenic Red' (× *arendsii*) (15)	EPfP
- 'Scenic White' (× *arendsii*) (15)	EPfP
§ 'Schelleri' (× *petraschii*) (7)	SPoG
'Schneeteppich' (15)	LBar
§ 'Schwefelblüte' (15)	GMaP
sempervivum (7)	NGdn WFar
'Seren y Gwanwyn' (*oppositifolia*) (7)	WAbe
'Setomidori' (*fortunei*) (5)	GEdr
'Setsu-gekka' (*stolonifera*) (5/v)	GGro
'Shaggy Hair' (*stolonifera*) (5)	WFar
'Shanghai' (*stolonifera*) (5)	GGro
'Sherlock Holmes' (7)	WAbe
'Shiomoe' (*fortunei*) (5)	GEdr

Saxifraga

'Shiranami' (*fortunei*) (5) ♀H4 — CBcs ELan EWes GEdr GGro GKev SMad SPlb WCot WFar WSpi
'Sibyll Trelawney JP' (*fortunei*) (5) — EBee EDAr ELan EPfP GPSL LRHS NHar
§ 'Silver Cushion' (15/v) — ELan SPlb SPoG SRms SRot WIce
'Silver Mound' — see *S.* 'Silver Cushion'
'Sissi' (7) — ECha GMaP WAbe
'Slack's Ruby Southside' (Southside Seedling Group) (8) ♀H5 — MWlw WFar WIce
'Slack's Supreme' (8) — WFar
'Slack's Vesuvius' (8) — MNrw WFar
'Snowcap' (*pubescens*) (15) — WAbe
'Snowdon' (*burseriana*) (7) — EPot MWlw
'Snowflake' (Silver Farreri Group) (8) ♀H5 — WAbe
Southside Seedling Group (8) — EDAr EPfP EPot GAbr GArf GEdr GKev GMaP MAsh MMuc MNrw NBro NHar SEND SMad SPoG SRms SRot WAbe WFar WHoo WIce
— red-flowered (8) — EPot
'Southside Star' (Southside Seedling Group) (8) ♀H5 — LEdu WAbe
spathularis (11) — WCot
'Splendens' (*oppositifolia*) (7) ♀H5 — GAbr GKev SRms
'Spotted Dog' — see *S.* 'Canis-dalmatica' (× *gaudinii*)
'Sprite' (15) — SPoG
'Stansfieldii' (*rosacea*) (15) — SPlb SPoG
'Starfire' (8) — NHar
startorii — see *S. scardica*
'Stellar Cloud' (*fortunei*) (5) — GEdr
'Stellar Moon' (*fortunei*) (5) — GEdr
'Stellar Starburst' (*fortunei*) (5) — GEdr
§ ***stolonifera*** (5) ♀H2 — CoPl CSpe EAri ECha GGro ISha LBom LCro LWaG NBro NLar SDix WCot WFar
— large-flowered (5) — WCot
'Strawberry Melba' (7) — CAby WIce
stribrnyi (7) — WHoo
'Sturmiana' (*paniculata*) (8) — SRms
'Sue Tubbs' (8) — GKev
'Tamayura' (*fortunei*) (5) — GEdr
'Tenerife' (Swirly Group) (7) — EWes WIce
'Theoden' (*oppositifolia*) (7) — EWes GArf WAbe
TOURAN DEEP RED ('Rockred') (Mossy Group) (15) — ELan EPfP LBuc LRHS MHer
TOURAN LARGE WHITE ('Rocklarwhi'PBR) (Mossy Group) (15) — EPfP LRHS
TOURAN LIMEGREEN ('Rocklime') (× *arendsii*) (15) — LRHS MPri
TOURAN PINK ('Saxz0011'PBR) (× *arendsii*) (15) — EPfP LRHS MPri
TOURAN RED ('Saxz0006') (× *arendsii*) (15) — MPri SPoG WIce
TOURAN WHITE — see *S.* 'Rockwhite' (× *arendsii*)
TOURAN WHITE IMPROVED ('Saxz0004') (× *arendsii*) (15) — LCro SPoG WIce
'Tricolor' (*stolonifera*) (5) ♀H2 — CDoC WCot WFar
§ 'Triumph' (× *arendsii*) (15) — EGren GMaP MAsh SPoG
'Tumbling Waters' (8) ♀H5 — GKev WAbe
§ 'Tvůj Přítel' (× *poluanglica*) (7) — GArf
§ 'Tvůj Úsměv' (× *poluanglica*) (7) ♀H5 — NLar

§ 'Tvůj Úspěch' (× *poluanglica*) (7) — CAby
'Two Kings' (*fortunei*) (5) — WFar
'Tysoe' (7) — EPot
'Tysoe Blush' (Blues Group) (7) — WFar
'Tysoe Burgundy' (Blues Group) (7) — WFar
'Tysoe Dream' (7) — EPot
'Uchiwa' (*stolonifera*) (5) — GGro
umbrosa (11) — CMac EDAr EHeP EPfP GAbr LEdu LRHS MMuc SHar SPlb SPoG SRms SRot WFar
* — ***subinteger*** — MMuc
× ***urbium*** (11) ♀H5 — CAby CCBP CoPl EGrI ELan EMor GKev GMaP GQue LBar LCro LEdu LRHS LSto LWaG MBel NSti SHor SRms WCAu WHoo WSpi WTor WTre
'Vaccariana' (*oppositifolia*) (7) — SHar
'Variegata' (*umbrosa*) — see *S.* 'Aureopunctata' (× *urbium*)
I 'Variegata' (*cuneifolia*) (11/v) — ESuc LRHS MMuc NRya SLee SPlb SPoG WBrk WIce
I 'Variegata' (*exarata* subsp. *moschata*) (15/v) — GMaP
I 'Variegata' (× *urbium*) (11/v) — CAby EBee EMor EPfP GPSL LBar LRHS LSto NLar SHor SRms WFar WHoo WTor
vayredana (15) — WAbe
'Večerní Hvězda' (7) — WAbe
veitchiana (5) — GGro NBro NHar WFar
'Verona' (× *caroli-langii*) (7) — WAbe
'Vikos Gold' (7) — WAbe
'Vladana' (× *megaseiflora*) (7) — GArf
'Vreny' (8) — GKev
'Wada' (*fortunei*) (5) — CMac CSpe GArf GKev GMaP MNrw NBir NBro NHar SRms WCot WFar WOld WPnP
'Walter Ingwersen' (*umbrosa*) (11) — SRms
§ 'Walter Irving' (× *irvingii*) (7) ♀H5 — WAbe
'Welsh Dragon' (15) — WAbe WFar
'Welsh Rose' (15) — WAbe
§ 'White Pixie' (15) — EPfP GAbr LRHS MHer MPro NEoE NRya SLee SPlb SPoG SRms SRot WCAu WFar WIce WTor
'White Star' (*fortunei*) (5) — EPfP LRHS
'White Star' (× *petraschii*) (7) — see *S.* 'Schelleri' (× *petraschii*)
'Whitehill' (8) ♀H5 — EDAr ELan GAbr GEdr GMaP LRHS NRya SLee WHoo
'Winifred' (× *anglica*) (7) — WAbe
'Winifred Bevington' (8 × 11) — CAby ECha EDAr EPot GBin GEdr GMaP MBel NBro NLar NRya SHar SLee SRms WFar WHoo WIce
'Winston Churchill' (15) — NEoE
I 'Winston Churchill Variegata' (15/v) — WIce
'Winton' (× *paulinae*) (7) — EPot
'Wisley' (*federici-augusti* subsp. *grisebachii*) (7) ♀H5 — GKev
YOUR FRIEND — see *S.* 'Tvůj Přítel' (× *poluanglica*)
YOUR GOOD FORTUNE — see *S.* 'Tvůj Úspěch' (× *poluanglica*)
YOUR SMILE — see *S.* 'Tvůj Úsměv' (× *poluanglica*)
YOUR SUCCESS — see *S.* 'Tvůj Úspěch' (× *poluanglica*)
'Zlatá Praha' (× *pragensis*) (7) — WAbe

Scabiosa (Caprifoliaceae)

alpina L.	see *Cephalaria alpina*
argentea	CSpe WPGP
atropurpurea	LCro MCtn
- 'Ace of Spades'	LRHS
- 'Beaujolais Bonnets'	CWal EPfP LRHS MCtn MPro SMrm
- 'Black Knight'	CSpe CWal LCro MCtn MPro SPhx
- 'Blue Beau'	MCtn
§ - 'Chile Black'	CBcs ELan EPfP LRHS LShi NLar SPoG
- 'Fata Morgana'	CSpe LCro MCtn
- 'Oxford Blue'	LRHS MCtn
- 'Salmon Queen'	MCtn
- 'Snowmaiden'	MCtn
- 'Summer Berries'	MCtn
- 'Summer Sundae'	LRHS
- tall double mixed (d)	MCtn
banatica	see *S. columbaria*
'Barocca'	EBee ELan ELon EPfP LBar MPro NLar SRms
BLUE DIAMONDS ('Kiescalibu')	GJos WFar
'Blue Eyes'	LBar
'Blue Mound'	SEND
§ 'Butterfly Blue'	Widely available
caucasica	CMac CWal EPfP
- var. *alba*	CBcs EPfP LShi
- 'Clive Greaves' ♀H4	EBee EPfP GMaP LRHS MHol NCth NLar SPad SRms WCAu WFar
- 'Fama'	CSpe EPfP MPro NBir NLar SPlb SRms WFar
- 'Fama Deep Blue'	CDor EPfP LBar LRHS MHol Midl NCth SHar WFar
- 'Fama White'	EPfP LBar LRHS Midl MPro NCth SHar
- 'Goldingensis'	EPfP
- House's hybrids	MCtn NGdn SRms
- 'Isaac House'	WFar
- 'Kompliment'	WFar
- 'Miss Willmott' ♀H4	EBee MArl MAsh MHol NLar SPad WCAu
- Perfecta Series	LRHS NGdn NLar SPoG
- - 'Perfecta Alba'	CCBP CDor EPfP GMaP LBar LCro LRHS MBel MCtn MHer MHol Midl NLar SPoG WCAu WTor
- - 'Perfecta Blue'	CDor EGren EPfP ERCP GMaP LBar LRHS LSto MArl MHol MPie NLar WTor WTre
- - 'Perfecta Mid Blue'	LCro MCtn
- 'Stäfa'	EBee MBel MHol NLar
'Chile Black'	see *S. atropurpurea* 'Chile Black'
colchica B&SWJ 15320	WCru
§ *columbaria*	CCBP CFis CGwi CHab CWal EBee EHet GQue LCro LRHS MCtn NMir SPhx StAn WRBe
- 'Big Blue'	EPfP LRHS
- 'Blue Note'^PBR	LBar LRHS MCtn MPri
- (Flutter Series) FLUTTER DEEP BLUE ('Balfluttdelu'^PBR)	EGren LBar LBom LCro LRHS LSou MAsh MHol MPro NDov WHil
- - FLUTTER PURE WHITE ('Balflutturite'^PBR)	EGren LBar LBom LCro LRHS LSou MPri MPro NDov NWbg WHil
- - FLUTTER ROSE PINK ('Balfluttropi'^PBR)	EGren EPfP LBar LBom LCro LRHS LSou MHol MPri MPro WHil
- 'Mariposa Blue'^PBR	EGren LBar LRHS LSou MHol MPri NBir NWbg WHil
- 'Misty Butterflies'	CAby EGren GJos MBNS NGdn NLar SAth SRms WFar
- 'Nana'	EPfP GArf GQue NBir NGdn WAbe
§ - subsp. *ochroleuca*	CCBP CDor CElw CKno CSpe CWal ECha EPfP EPPr GKev LBar MCtn NBir NDov SBeP SHar SHor
	SMHy SPhx SPoG SRms WCAu WTre
- - B&SWJ 16346 from Russia	WCru
- - 'Moon Dance'	CBcs CDor EBee EDAr MHol SAth SPoG WCot WHil WHoo
- 'Pincushion Blue'	EDAr LRHS LWaG
- 'Pincushion Pink'	EDAr GJos NGdn WHil
drakensbergensis	WCAu
GELATO BLUEBERRY (Gelato Series)	LRHS
gigantea	see *Cephalaria gigantea*
graminifolia	EBee NBir SRms StAn
'Irish Perpetual Flowering'	see *S.* 'Butterfly Blue'
japonica var. *alpina*	EBee GGro GKev NGdn WFar WHoo
- - 'Blue Star'	EBee
- - pink-flowered	NBir
- - 'Ritz Blue'	EDAr EHeP MHer WCav WHil
- - 'Ritz Rose'	EDAr
Kudo Series	CKit CWGN ELan LBar LRHS MHol Midl NLar NSti SAth SPoG WHil WNPC
- KUDO PINK ('Ichpin'^PBR)	CBWd CSpe LCro LRHS MMrt MPri NBir SHar SOrN WHil
- KUDO WHITE ('Ichwhit')	CKit CWGN ELan EPfP LCro LRHS MBros MHol Midl MPnt NSti SAth SHar WNPC
lachnophylla	ESwi GQue
- 'Blue Horizon'	CDor
- 'Little Cracker'	LSto
- 'Little Emily'	ELon
lucida	EPfP GKev MMuc NLar SEND WCAu WIce
§ MAGIC ('Pmoore02')	CCps LBar
'Misty Pink'	EBee EPfP
montana Mill.	see *Knautia arvensis*
ochroleuca	see *S. columbaria* subsp. *ochroleuca*
parnassi	see *Pterocephalus perennis*
'Perpetual Flowering'	see *S.* 'Butterfly Blue'
PINK BUTTONS ('Walminipink')	MArl
'Pink Diamonds'	ELan EPfP LRHS MCtn NLar WFar
'Pink Mist'	CBcs CBWd EBee EGren ELan EPfP LBar LCro LRHS LSto MArl MPro NBir NLar SPoG SRms WCAu
pterocephala	see *Pterocephalus perennis*
RASPBERRY KISSES	see *S.* MAGIC
RED VELVET SCOOP ('Drevelscop') (Scoop Series)	EBee
rumelica	see *Knautia macedonica*
'Satchmo'	see *S. atropurpurea* 'Chile Black'
stellata	LCro LSto
- 'Sternkugel'	MCtn
succisa	see *Succisa pratensis*
tatarica	see *Cephalaria gigantea*
tschiliensis W&O 0127	GGro
'Vivid Vi'^PBR	CAby CDor EBee EGren ELan EPfP LSRN MHol MMuc MPro NLar

Scadoxus ✿ (Amaryllidaceae)

membranaceus	WCot WMal
multiflorus	EGren GKev LAma XFar
§ - subsp. *katherinae* ♀H1b	CSpe LAma WCot
§ - subsp. *multiflorus*	WCot
natalensis	see *S. puniceus*
§ *puniceus*	WCot

Scaevola (Goodeniaceae)

aemula 'Blue Fan'	see *S. aemula* 'Blue Wonder'

- Blue Print ('Kingscablin') LSou
§ - 'Blue Wonder' NPer SPoG
- (Fancy Series) Fancy LSou
  Blue new
- - Fancy Pink Improved new LSou
- - Fancy White new LSou
- (Surdiva Series) LSou
  Surdiva Deep Violet Blue
  ('Bonsca 1430'^{PBR})
- - Surdiva Fashion Pink LSou
  ('Bonsca 1433'^{PBR})
- - Surdiva Snow Blanket LSou
  ('Bonsc 14206'^{PBR})
- - Surdiva White 2011 MBros
  ('Bonsca7288')

Sceletium (Aizoaceae)
tortuosum ESuc SPlb

Schefflera (Araliaceae)
actinophylla see *Heptapleurum actinophyllum*
alpina see *Heptapleurum alpinum*
arboricola see *Heptapleurum arboricola*
bodinieri see *Heptapleurum bodinieri*
brevipedicellata see *Heptapleurum brevipedicellatum*
chapana see *Heptapleurum chapanum*
delavayi see *Heptapleurum delavayi*
elegantissima see *Plerandra elegantissima*
enneaphylla see *Heptapleurum enneaphyllum*
fantsipanensis see *Heptapleurum fantsipanense*
fasciculifoliolata see *Heptapleurum laxiusculum*
gracilis see *Heptapleurum gracile*
kornasii see *Heptapleurum kornasii*
macrophylla see *Heptapleurum macrophyllum*
microphylla see *Heptapleurum microphyllum*
multinervia see *Heptapleurum multinervium*
myriocarpa see *Heptapleurum* aff. *myriocarpum*
pauciflora see *Heptapleurum pauciflorum*
rhododendrifolia see *Heptapleurum rhododendrifolium*
shweliensis see *Heptapleurum shweliense*
taiwaniana see *Heptapleurum taiwanianum*
trevesioides see *Heptapleurum hypoleucoides*
trianae see *Sciodaphyllum trianae*
vietnamensis see *Heptapleurum chapanum*

Schima (Theaceae)
argentea CBcs CExl EBee WCru WPGP
aff. *argentea* NJM 13.042 WPGP
khasiana CExl WPGP
wallichii CExl WCru

Schinus (Anacardiaceae)
lentiscifolius SArc SPlb SVen
molle CAgr SPlb
polygama SPlb

Schisandra (Schisandraceae)
arisanensis CRHN EBee MBlu
- B&SWJ 3050 WCru
chinensis CAgr CRHN GKev LEdu LRHS MBlu NLar WPGP
- B&SWJ 4204 WCru
- B&SWJ 4611A WCru
- B&SWJ 4611B WCru
- 'Bere' LEdu WPGP
- 'Sadova No 1' CAgr
grandiflora ♀^{H4} ELan MBlu WPGP
- PAB 3673 LEdu
- WJC 13666 WCru
- var. *cathayensis* see *S. sphaerandra*
- 'Jamu' (m) WCru
- 'Lahlu' (f/F) CRHN WCru
aff. *grandiflora* CRHN
- WJC 13817 WCru
grandiflora × *rubriflora* WPGP
henryi subsp. *yunnanensis* WCru
  B&SWJ 6546
incarnata BWJ 7898 WCru
lancifolia MBlu
nigra see *S. repanda*
perulata FMWJ 13100 WCru
plena HWJ 664 WCru
propinqua CMac CRHN LEdu NLar
  subsp. *sinensis*
- - BWJ 8148 WCru
§ *repanda* B&SWJ 11455 WCru
rubriflora ♀^{H5} EPfP MBlu MGos WPGP
- BWJ 7557 WCru
- (f) WSpi
- 'Bodnant Redberry' (f) WCru
§ *sphaerandra* MBlu
- BWJ 7739 WCru
- BWJ 8082 WCru
sphenanthera EBee MBlu NLar
- BWJ 8151 WCru

Schismatoglottis (Araceae)
wallichii new LInT NTro

Schizachyrium (Poaceae)
§ *scoparium* CKno CWal MCtn
- Blue Heaven ('MinnblueA') ELon LEdu NDov SMHy SPoG WPGP WSpi
- 'Cairo' EBee
- 'Chameleon'^{PBR} (v) SPad WTor
- 'Prairie Blues' CSpe GQue MCtn NClf SPoG WCot WHil WHoo
- 'Smoke Signal'^{PBR} SPeP
- 'Standing Ovation'^{PBR} CSpe ELan LCro LSou MHtn MMrt NClf WSpi
- 'Twilight Zone'^{PBR} IPot MArl SPeP

Schizanthus (Solanaceae)
wisetonensis Angel Wings MCtn Group

Schizocarpus (Asparagaceae)
nervosus WCot

Schizophragma see *Hydrangea*
hypoglaucum see *Hydrangea glaucescens*
integrifolium see *Hydrangea ampla*
- var. *minus* see *Hydrangea glaucescens*
molle see *Hydrangea schizomollis*

Schizostylis see *Hesperantha*

Schlumbergera (Cactaceae)
× *buckleyi* ♀^{H1b} CPic
'Caribbean Dancer' LCro
'Exotic Dancer' LCro
'Malissa' LCro
'Purple Dancer' LCro
'Thor Wild Cactus Orange' LCro
truncata CoPl

Schoenoplectus (Cyperaceae)
§ *lacustris* CLil CPud CWat ELin
§ - subsp. *tabernaemontani* CSpe

- - 'Albescens' (v)	CBen CLil CWat EPfk MMuc MNrw		§ *litardierei* ♀H6	CBro EGrl EPot EPPr GKev LAma XFar
- - 'Zebrinus' (v)	CBen CLil CPud CToG CWat ELin MNrw SPlb WMAq		*luciliae* misapplied *luciliae* ambig.	see *S. forbesii* LCro

Schoenus (*Cyperaceae*)
pauciflorus WCot

Sciadopitys (*Sciadopityaceae*)

verticillata ♀H6	CAco CBcs CMac CMCN EAri ELan GKin LRHS LSRN MAsh MBlu MGos SPoG WCha
- 'Carstens'	CAco NLar
- 'Eiffel Tower'	CAco
- 'Firework'	NLar
- 'Gold Star'	CAco
- 'Goldammer'	CAco
- Green Diamond ('Dierks1') **new**	CAco
- 'Grüne Kugel'	CAco NLar
- 'Henks Garden' **new**	NLar
- 'Kobito' **new**	LRHS NLar
- 'Koja Maki'	NLar
- 'Koningstuin'	NLar
- 'Kugelblitz'	NLar
- 'Marylin Monroe'	NLar
- 'Megaschirm'	CAco
- 'Mireille'	CAco
- 'Nettie' **new**	NLar
- 'Ossorio Gold'	CAco
- 'Perlenglanz'	CAco
- 'Picola'	CAco NLar
- 'Queen's Parasol'	NLar
- 'Richie's Cushion'	CAco
- 'Shine a Light' (v)	CAco NLar
- 'Sternschnuppe'	CAco ELan LRHS NLar
- 'Tsai Cheng'	CAco
- variegated (v)	CAco
- 'Wiels Beauty'	NLar

Scilla ✿ (*Asparagaceae*)

adlamii	see *Ledebouria cooperi*
amethystina	see *S. litardierei*
amoena	WCot
autumnalis	EPot GKev LAma SChr WShi
bifolia ♀H6	EPot GKev LAma SDix WCot WShi
- 'Alba'	LAma
- 'Chris's Favourite' **new**	EPot
- 'Rosea'	EGrl ERCP GKev LAma MPie XFar
bithynica ♀H6	CFis GKev WCot WShi
'Blue Giant'	ELan EPfP EPot ERCP LAma LCro LRHS WCot
campanulata	see *Hyacinthoides hispanica*
chinensis	see *S. scilloides*
cilicica	GKev WCot
dracomontana	see *Merwilla dracomontana*
§ *forbesii*	CBro EGren EPfP EPot ETay GKev LAma LCro NBir SRms
- 'Violet Beauty'	EGren EPot ERCP GKev LAma LCro XFar
greilhuberi	EPot EPPr WAbe WCot
hohenackeri	GKev WAbe WCot
- BSBE 811	WCot
§ *hughii*	CBro
hyacinthoides	CMiW CSpe ERCP GKev WCot
- 'Blue Arrow'	EPfP GKev LAma WFar
ingridiae	WCot
italica	see *Hyacinthoides italica*
japonica	see *S. scilloides*
libanotica	CoPl MPie
liliohyacinthus	CBro CToG GKev WCot WShi
luciliae (Boiss.) Speta ♀H6	CBro EGren ELan LAma LCro XFar
- 'Alba'	EGren ETay LAma LRHS XFar
§ - Gigantea Group	GKev LAma
- - 'Alba'	EPot GKev LCro
- 'Rosy Queen'	EPot GKev LAma MPie
lutea hort.	see *Ledebouria socialis*
madeirensis	CHll WCot XFar
melaina	WCot
mesopotamica	GKev
messeniaca	GKev
- MS 38 from Greece	WCot
mischtschenkoana ♀H6	CAby EPot LCro WShi
- 'Tubergeniana' ♀H6	ECha GKev LAma WCot XFar
- 'Zwanenburg'	WCot
monophyllos	GKev WCot
morrisii	GKev
natalensis	see *Merwilla plumbea*
non-scripta	see *Hyacinthoides non-scripta*
nutans	see *Hyacinthoides non-scripta*
obtusifolia subsp. *intermedia*	WCot
persica ♀H4	GKev WCot
peruviana	Widely available
- SB&L 43850	WCot
- 'Alba'	CBro CWCL ECha WCot
- 'Blue Moon'	CDoC EPfP
- Caribbean Jewels Series	LRHS MHol
- - 'Sapphire Blue'	LBuc LCro LRHS MHtn WFar
- 'Hughii'	see *S. hughii*
- var. *venusta* S&L 311/2	WCot
- 'White Moon'	CoPl EBee ERCP GKev LAma XFar
'Pink Giant'	CBro ECha EGren ELan EPfP EPot ERCP ETay LAma LCro LRHS NBir XFar
pratensis	see *S. litardierei*
rosenii 'Cloudy Sky'	WCot
sardensis ♀H6	CAby ECha EGren EPot ERCP LAma SRms WCot WShi
§ *scilloides*	EPot
siberica ♀H6	CAby EGren EPfP ETay GKev LAma LCro LRHS WShi XFar
- 'Alba'	EGren EPfP EPot GKev LAma WShi XFar
- 'Spring Beauty'	ECha EPot ERCP GKev LAma SRms LAma
siehei 'Rosea'	LAma
'Tubergeniana'	see *S. mischtschenkoana* 'Tubergeniana'
'Valentine Day'	EPot
verna	GKev WAbe WCot WShi
violacea	see *Ledebouria socialis*

Scindapsus (*Araceae*)

aureus	see *Epipremnum aureum*
pictus (v)	LBom NHrt
- 'Argyraeus' ♀H1c	EHap LBom LCro LWaG NHrt
- 'Trebie'	EHap LBom LCro LWaG NHrt

Sciodaphyllum (*Araliaceae*)
§ *trianae* B&SWJ 14313 WCru

Scirpus (*Cyperaceae*)

cernuus	see *Isolepis cernua*
'Green Mist'	WCot
lacustris	see *Schoenoplectus lacustris*
- 'Spiralis'	see *Juncus effusus* f. *spiralis*
tabernaemontani	see *Schoenoplectus lacustris* subsp. *tabernaemontani*

Scleranthus (Caryophyllaceae)
- **biflorus** — EDAr EPot ESgI EWes GQue LCro SPlb WFar
- **uniflorus** — ELan EPot EUrb GArf LEdu SPlb SRot
- - 'Selected Bronze' — ELan ELon

Sclerochiton (Acanthaceae)
- **harveyanus** — EShb

Scoliopus (Liliaceae)
- **hallii** — GKev NHar

Scopolia (Solanaceae)
- **anomala** — EAri
- - HWJK 2252 — WCru
- - PAB 4925 — LEdu
- **carniolica** — CTtf EAri ECha EPPr EWld LEdu LShi NLar NSti SBrt SPlb WCru WFar
- - from Poland — LEdu
- § - var. **brevifolia** — CTtf EAri EBee EBlo EPfP EPPr LEdu LRHS WCot WPGP
- - 'Zwanenburg' — EAri EPPr LEdu NLar WFar
- **hladnikiana** — see *S. carniolica* var. *brevifolia*
- **lurida** — see *Anisodus luridus*
- **stramoniifolia** — WPav

Scorzonera (Asteraceae)
- **hispanica** — see *Pseudopodospermum hispanicum*

Scorzoneroides (Asteraceae)
- **autumnalis** — CGwi CHab NMir WOrg

Scrophularia (Scrophulariaceae)
- **aquatica** misapplied — see *S. auriculata*
- § **auriculata** — CGwi CHab CPud ELin NPer WHer
- § - 'Variegata' (v) — EBee ECha EPfP MArl
- **buergeriana** 'Lemon and Lime' misapplied — see *Teucrium viscidum* 'Lemon and Lime'
- **calliantha** — WMal
- **macrantha** — WMal
- **nodosa** — CGwi CoPl GKev NMir WHer
- - **variegata** — see *S. auriculata* 'Variegata'
- **umbrosa** subsp. **umbrosa** — CWat
- **vernalis** — CBgR

Scutellaria (Lamiaceae)
- § **alpina** — GKev SPlb SRms
- - 'Arcobaleno' — GKev
- **altissima** — ELan GPSL NBro SPlb WFar
- - pink-flowered — WFar
- **baicalensis** — CSpe MHoo MNHC
- **canescens** — see *S. incana*
- **galericulata** — CGHo CGwi CHab CPud ENfk MHer MHoo MNHC NAts WOrg
- § **incana** — CSpe ECha ELan SHor SMrm SPhx WCot WTre
- - 'White Sky' — LBar
- - white-flowered — SPhx
- **indica** — GEdr
- - var. **japonica** — see *S. indica* var. *parvifolia*
- § - var. **parvifolia** — EBee GEdr NBir SLee WFar
- **lateriflora** — SRms
- - PAB 3921 — LEdu
- **maekawae** — EBee
- **orientalis** — EDAr
- **resinosa** 'Smokey Hills' — WHil
- **scordiifolia** — CSpe EBee EGren NRya SHar SRms WCav WFar

- 'Seoul Sapphire' — GBin LEdu
- **SHERBERT LEMON** ('Yascut') — EGren GKev
- **suffrutescens** — ESgI MHoo WHil
- - 'Texas Rose' — CSpe EGren LBar LCro LRHS MMrt SLee SRot WAbe WFar WHoo WIce WTor
- **supina** — see *S. alpina*
- **tournefortii** — SHar
- * **zhongdianensis** — EPPr

seakale see *Crambe maritima*

Searsia (Anacardiaceae)
- § **incisa** — SPlb

Sebaea (Gentianaceae)
- **thomasii** — GEdr WAbe
- - 'Bychan' — WAbe

Securigera (Fabaceae)
- § **varia** — EWes EWld LEdu MMrt MMuc SEND SRms WHil

Sedastrum see *Hylotelephium*

× *Sedeveria* (Crassulaceae)
- 'Blue Lotus' — NCft
- 'Harry Butterfield' — EShb WCot
- **hummellii** — EAri
- 'Letizia' — SChr WCor
- I 'Lutea' — WCor

Sedum ✿ (Crassulaceae)
- 'Abbey Dore' — see *Hylotelephium* 'Abbey Dore'
- **acre** — GJos GQue LRHS LWaG MAsh MCtn MNHC NAts NMir SPlb
- - 'Aureum' — CoPl CPic EDAr ELan ESuc EUrb LRHS MAsh NLar NRya SLee SPoG SRms WCot WIce
- - 'Elegans' — ESuc
- - 'Golden Queen' — SPlb SPoG SRms
- - 'Minus' — ESuc LRHS MWlw SRms
- § - subsp. **neglectum** var. **majus** — NLar
- - 'Oktoberfest' — ESuc GJos
- **aizoon** — ESuc SPlb WFar
- - 'Aurantiacum' — see *S. aizoon* 'Euphorbioides'
- § - 'Euphorbioides' — ECha ESuc LShi MHer NLar SEND SHar SPlb
- - subsp. **maximowiczii** — ESuc
- **alatum** — WFar
- **albescens** — see *S. forsterianum* f. *purpureum*
- **alboroseum** — see *Hylotelephium erythrostictum*
- § **album** — CoPl CPic ESuc GJos GQue LRHS LShi NBro SEND SRms WCor
- - subsp. **album** var. **balticum** — ESuc
- - 'Bella d'Inverno' — ESuc WIce
- - 'Coral Carpet' — CPic ELan EPfP EPot EPPr ESuc EUrb LRHS LWaG MAsh NLar NRya SLee SPoG WFar
- I - 'Farö Form' — ESuc
- I - 'Green Ice' **new** — ESuc
- - 'Hildebrandtii' **new** — ESuc
- I - 'Laconicum' **new** — ESuc
- - subsp. **teretifolium** var. **micranthum** — CPic ESuc LRHS
- - - 'Chloroticum' — CoPl
- § - - var. **murale** — LRHS WFar
- - - 'Cristatum' — LRHS
- - 'Twickel Purple' **new** — ESuc

Sedum

altissimum	see *S. sediforme*
anacampseros	see *Hylotelephium anacampseros*
anglicum	CoPl ESuc
athoum	see *S. album*
AUTUMN JOY	see *Hylotelephium* × *mottramianum* 'Herbstfreude'
beauverdii	ESuc
subsp. *vietnamense*	
- - HWJ 824	WCru
'Bertram Anderson'	see *Hylotelephium* 'Bertram Anderson'
beyrichianum misapplied	see *S. glaucophyllum*
borissovae	ESuc
borschii	ESuc
§ *brevifolium*	ESuc WIce
var. *quinquefarium*	
burrito	CDoC EShb LBom LRHS LWaG NHrt SIvy WCor
'Carl'	see *Hylotelephium* 'Carl'
cauticola	see *Hylotelephium cauticola*
cepaea	ESuc
clavatum	CPic WCor
commixtum	ESuc
compressum	see *S. palmeri* subsp. *palmeri* tetraploid
confusum Hemsl.	CPic SChr SEND SIvy WMal
crassipes	see *Rhodiola wallichiana*
crassularia	see *Crassula setulosa* 'Milfordiae'
cryptomerioides B&SWJ 54	WCru
dasyphyllum	CoPl NBir NRya SPlb SRms WCor WCot
- subsp. *dasyphyllum* var. *macrophyllum*	CoPl ESuc
dendroideum subsp. *praealtum*	SEND WJun
divergens	ESuc GKev
douglasii	see *S. stenopetalum* 'Douglasii'
ebracteatum	ESuc
'Eleanor Fisher'	see *Hylotelephium telephium* subsp. *ruprechtii*
ellacombeanum	see *S. kamtschaticum* var. *ellacombeanum*
'Elworthy Rose'	CElw
emarginatum **new**	ESuc
erythrostictum	see *Hylotelephium erythrostictum*
ewersii	see *Hylotelephium ewersii*
fabaria	see *Hylotelephium telephium* subsp. *fabaria*
farinosum	SEND
fastigiatum	see *Rhodiola fastigiata*
'Fire Cracker'	ESuc
floriferum	see *S. kamtschaticum* var. *floriferum*
forsterianum	ESuc GQue LWaG
- subsp. *elegans*	ESuc LRHS SEND SPlb
- - 'Silver Stone'	ESuc MMuc
§ - f. *purpureum*	ESuc NRya
furfuraceum	ESuc SPlb WAbe
§ *glaucophyllum*	EDAr GJos
- 'Silver Frost'	LRHS
'Gold Mound'	EPfP ESuc EUrb GJos SPoG
gracile	ESuc
grisebachii subsp. *kostovii*	ESuc
'Harvest Moon'	ESuc
Herbstfreude Group	see *Hylotelephium* × *mottramianum*
hernandezii	CPic
heterodontum	see *Rhodiola heterodonta*
hidakanum	see *Hylotelephium pluricaule*
hispanicum	ESuc GJos SPlb WIce
'Blue Carpet'	EPPr ESuc WFar
- *glaucum*	see *S. hispanicum* var. *minus*
§ - var. *minus*	MMuc SEND SPlb WCot
- - 'Aureum'	ESuc
'Honey Gold'	ESuc NLar WMal
humifusum	ESuc SPlb WAbe WFar
hybridum 'Czar's Gold'	ESuc GJos NGdn
- 'Immergrünchen'	ESuc
'Indian Chief'	see *Hylotelephium* × *mottramianum* 'Herbstfreude'
indicum var. *yunnanense*	see *Sinocrassula yunnanensis*
integrifolium	see *Rhodiola integrifolia*
'Joyce Henderson'	see *Hylotelephium* 'Joyce Henderson'
kamtschaticum ♀H5	CPic GJos
- B&SWJ 10870	WCru
§ - var. *ellacombeanum* ♀H5	ESuc LRHS MAsh MMuc SEND SRms WCot
- - B&SWJ 8853	WCru
- 'Cutting Edge' (v)	ESuc
§ - var. *floriferum*	GJos LRHS
§ - - 'Weihenstephaner Gold'	ELan ESuc GKev GMaP LRHS MHer MMuc NBir SLee SPlb SPoG SRms SRot WCav WFar WIce
- var. *kamtschaticum*	CPic ELan ESuc LRHS MHer MMuc
- 'Variegatum' (v) ♀H7	NRya SLee SPoG SRms SRot WIce
'Katharine's Gold'	MNrw
kimnachii	CoPl ESuc
'Lemon Ball'	ESuc LBar LCro LRHS
lineare	CDoC CoPl ESuc
litorale	ESuc
'Little Miss Sunshine'	EGren ESuc LRHS SLee
lucidum 'Obesum'	CPic
§ *lydium*	EGrI ESuc LRHS SPlb
- 'Bronze Queen'	see *S. lydium*
- 'Majestic Kiss' **new**	ESuc
makinoi	CWal ESuc LRHS
- 'Ōgon'	ESuc
- 'Tornado'PBR	ESuc LRHS
'Manoir de Gaudon'	ESuc WCot
'Matrona'	see *Hylotelephium* 'Matrona'
maweanum	see *S. acre* subsp. *neglectum* var. *majus*
mendozae	EAri
middendorffianum	MBrN MHer SRms SRot WAbe WHoo
- 'Striatum'	EDAr ESuc MMrt
monregalense	ESuc
§ *montanum*	ESuc MMuc
- 'Bronze' **new**	ESuc
moranense	ESuc MMuc SEND
morganianum ♀H1c	CSBt EShb LBom LCro LRHS LWaG NCft NMen SIvy
- 'Magnum'	CPic
morrisonense B&SWJ 7078	WCru
'Mr Goodbud'	see *Hylotelephium* 'Mr Goodbud'
multiceps	ESuc WAbe
'Munstead Red'	see *Hylotelephium* 'Munstead Red'
murale	see *S. album* subsp. *teretifolium* var. *murale*
muscoideum	ESuc
nevii misapplied	see *S. glaucophyllum*
nevii ambig.	SPlb
nicaeense	see *S. sediforme*
niveum	ESuc
nussbaumerianum ♀H2	CoPl GJos LCro SIvy WCot
oaxacanum	WAbe
obcordatum	ESuc
obtusatum misapplied	see *S. oreganum*
§ *obtusatum* A. Gray	NBro

obtusifolium	GKev WAbe
- var. *listoniae*	EDAr ESuc GEdr MHer
ochroleucum	ESuc GJos WCot WFar
- subsp. *montanum*	see *S. montanum*
- subsp. *ochroleucum* glaucum	ESuc
- 'Red Wiggle' **new**	ESuc
oppositifolium	see *S. spurium* 'Album'
§ *oreganum*	CoPl CPic ECha ESuc GAbr GJos GKev GMaP LRHS LShi MHer NBir SLee SPlb SRms SRot
- 'Procumbens'	see *S. oreganum* subsp. *tenue*
§ - subsp. *tenue*	ESuc NRya
§ *oregonense*	ESuc MHer WFar
'Oriental Dancer'	see *Hylotelephium* 'Oriental Dancer'
pachyclados	see *Rhodiola pachyclados*
pachyphyllum	CPic WJun
pallidum	ESuc
- var. *bithynicum*	ESuc
palmeri	CPic EDAr ESuc NBir SChr
§ - subsp. *palmeri* tetraploid	ESuc SChr SEND SIvy
pluricaule	see *Hylotelephium pluricaule*
polytrichoides 'Chocolate Ball'	CoPl CPic EGren LBar MHer SLee
populifolium	see *Hylotelephium populifolium*
pulchellum	CPic GKev LBar LRHS NBir WFar
quinquefarium	see *S. brevifolium* var. *quinquefarium*
'Red Canyon'	ESuc LBar
'Red Cauli'	see *Hylotelephium* 'Red Cauli'
reflexum L.	see *S. rupestre* L.
rhodiola	see *Rhodiola rosea*
rosea	see *Rhodiola rosea*
rubens	ESuc
rubroglaucum misapplied	see *S. oregonense*
rubroglaucum Praeger	see *S. obtusatum* A. Gray
× *rubrotinctum* ♀H3	CoPl CPic EPot ESuc GJos LCro NCft SEND SIvy WCor WJun
- 'Aurora' ♀H3	CDoC CPic ESuc NCft SIvy WJun
'Ruby Glow'	see *Hylotelephium* 'Ruby Glow'
§ *rupestre* L.	EGrI ELan GJos GQue LRHS LWaG MMuc MNHC SEND SPlb SRms SRot WFar
- 'Angelina'	CPic EGren ELan EPPr ESuc EWes GKev LBar LRHS LWaG MHer NBir NDov NLar SLee SPoG SRGP WCor WCot WFar WIce
- 'Angelina's Teacup' (SunSparkler Series)	ESuc LBar Midl
- 'Aureum'	CoPl ESuc LShi WCav WFar
- 'Blue Cushion'	ELan ESuc GJos LCro LShi MSwo
- 'Blue Spruce'	CPic ESuc LBar
- 'Chameleon'	ESuc
- 'Cosmic Comet' (SunSparkler Series)	ESuc LBar
- 'Cristatum'	CPic ESuc MHtn
- 'Green Cushion'	ESuc
- 'Monstrosum Cristatum'	ESuc NBir WCot WFar
- red-leaved	ESuc
- 'Sandy's Silver Crest' **new**	ESuc
- 'Yellow Cushion'	ESuc
ruprechtii	see *Hylotelephium telephium* subsp. *ruprechtii*
'Sandra Mottram'	WCor
sarcocaule hort.	see *Crassula sarcocaulis*
sarmentosum	ESuc NBac
§ *sediforme*	ESuc GJos LRHS MMuc SEND SRms
- 'Gold'	ESuc LRHS
- *nicaeense*	see *S. sediforme*
§ *sedoides* var. *album*	EDAr ESuc SPoG SRms
selskianum	NLar
- 'Goldilocks'	ESuc
sexangulare	CoPl EPfP ESuc GJos LRHS MHer MMuc NRya SPlb SRms WCor WIce
- f. *elatum*	WFar
- subsp. *montenegrinum* **new**	ESuc
- 'Weisse Tatra'	WFar
sieboldii	see *Hylotelephium sieboldii*
'Silvermoon'	ESuc
spathulifolium	ECha LCro
- Atropurpureum Group	GQue SRot
- 'Cape Blanco' ♀H6	Widely available
- 'Carneum' **new**	ESuc
- var. *majus*	ESuc
- 'Purpureum' ♀H5	CPic EDAr ELan EPfP EUrb GAbr GArf GJos GKev GMaP LRHS MHer MPro NAts NRya SPlb SPoG WAbe
- subsp. *yosemitense* 'Red Raver'	ESuc
I - 'Waight Hybrid' **new**	ESuc
- 'William Pascoe'	ESuc MWIw
spectabile	see *Hylotelephium spectabile*
spinosum	see *Orostachys spinosa*
'Spiral Staircase'	ESuc
spurium	CoPl CPic GJos GKev MMuc SEND SRms StAn WFar
§ - 'Album'	NRya
- 'Atropurpureum'	LRHS
- 'Coccineum'	EPfP ESuc GJos GQue LRHS LShi MCtn MMuc SEND
- DRAGON'S BLOOD	see *S. spurium* 'Schorbuser Blut'
- 'Elizabeth' **new**	ESuc
- 'Fool's Gold' (v)	ESuc
- 'Fuldaglut'	EGrI EPPr ESuc LRHS MNrw NRya SMrm SRms
- 'Green Mantle'	ECha ESuc
- 'John Creech'	ESuc
- LITTLE GECKO ('Tat1801' PBR) (v) **new**	ESuc
- 'Mahogany Red'	MPro
- PURPLE CARPET	see *S. spurium* 'Purpurteppich'
- 'Purpureum'	SLee SRms
§ - 'Purpurteppich'	ESuc NBro NLar SRms
- 'Raspberry Red' **new**	ESuc
- 'Red Rock' **new**	ESuc
- 'Roseum'	SRms
- 'Ruby Mantle'	ESuc GKev NBro NEoE SPoG SRms
§ - 'Schorbuser Blut' ♀H7	CPic CSBt ECha EGren ELan EPfP EPPr ESuc GKev LBar LRHS LSto NBir SHor SLee SPlb SRGP SRms SRot WFar WHoo WIce
- SPOT ON DEEP ROSE ('Setz0001' PBR) **new**	ESuc LBar LRHS
- 'Summer Glory'	ESuc
- 'Summer Snow'	ESuc GJos
§ - 'Tricolor' (v)	CPic ECha EDAr EGren ESuc GEdr GKev LRHS LShi MHer NRya SIvy SLee SPlb SPoG SRot
- 'Variegatum'	see *S. spurium* 'Tricolor'
- 'Voodoo'	EDAr EGren EWes LRHS LShi MCtn MHer NBro NGdn
stahlii	CPic ESuc SIvy
stenopetalum	ESuc GJos SPlb
§ - 'Douglasii'	ESuc MHer SRms
'Stewed Rhubarb Mountain'	see *Hylotelephium* 'Stewed Rhubarb Mountain'
stoloniferum	ESuc GJos
subtile	ESuc
- PB 08-639	GGro
takesimense	GJos NBir

Sedum

– B&SWJ 8518	WCru
– ATLANTIS ('Nonsitnal'^{PBR}) (v)	CPic EGren EHeP ELan EPfP ESuc GJos LBar LCro LRHS MBel Midl NBir NCth SLee WCot WNPC WTor
tatarinowii	see *Hylotelephium tatarinowii*
telephium	see *Hylotelephium telephium*
ternatum	EDAr ESuc GJos
tetractinum 'Coral Reef'	CPic LBar LRHS NBir SRms
trollii	see *Rhodiola saxifragoides*
urvillei	ESuc
– Stribrnyi Group	ESuc
ussuriense	see *Hylotelephium ussuriense*
'Vera Jameson'	see *Hylotelephium* 'Vera Jameson'
verticillatum	see *Hylotelephium verticillatum*
viviparum	see *Hylotelephium viviparum*
'Washfield Purple'	see *Hylotelephium telephium* (Atropurpureum Group) 'Purple Emperor'
'Weihenstephaner Gold'	see *S. kamtschaticum* var. *floriferum* 'Weihenstephaner Gold'
weinbergii	see *Graptopetalum paraguayense*
'Winter Sun' **new**	ESuc
yezoense	see *Hylotelephium pluricaule*
yunnanense	see *Rhodiola yunnanensis*
zentaro-tashiroi	WAbe

Seemannia (Gesneriaceae)

§ *gymnostoma*	WFar
nematanthodes	SDix
– 'Evita'	CSpe EShb ESwi WCot WFar
§ *sylvatica*	CSpe WFar
– 'Bolivian Sunset'	WDib

Selaginella (Selaginellaceae)

apoda	LWaG
helvetica	EBee ISha
kraussiana ♀^{H2}	CTsd GArf ISha WCot
– 'Aurea'	ISha MAsh
– 'Gold Tips' ♀^{H3}	GGro MAsh WPGP
lepidophylla	GKev LAma SVic
martensii 'Jori' (v)	WCot
uncinata ♀^{H1b}	LRHS

Selenicereus (Cactaceae)

anthonyanus	EShb
chrysocardium	EShb LWaG
grandiflorus	EShb
nelsonii	EShb
validus	NPlm

Selinum (Apiaceae)

KWJ 12281 from northern Vietnam	WCru
candollei HWJK 2329	WCru
carvifolium	CCBP CExl CMac GElm LEdu MHol MNrw NLar WCot WSpi
– HWJK 2347	ESwi WCru
– PAB 2676	LEdu
cryptotaenium FMWJ 13250	WCru
– PAB 8948	LEdu
filicifolium	EBee GGro MHol WCot
tenuifolium	see *Ligusticopsis wallichiana*
wallichianum	see *Ligusticopsis wallichiana*

Selliera (Goodeniaceae)

radicans	GAbr LShi

Semele (Asparagaceae)

androgyna	CRHN EShb WCot

Semiaquilegia (Ranunculaceae)

§ *adoxoides*	GGro GKev GQue
– double-flowered (d)	EDAr GKev
§ *ecalcarata* ♀^{H5}	CDor CSpe EBee EDAr GArf MCtn NGdn SBeP SHar SRms
'Moody Blues'	WFar
simulatrix	see *S. ecalcarata*
'Sugar Plum Fairy'	LSto SPoG WFar
'Tinkerbell'	WFar

Semiarundinaria (Poaceae)

§ *fastuosa* ♀^{H6}	CBcs CJun MAsh MMuc MWht SArc SBGi SBig SEND SPlb WCha
– var. *viridis*	MWht WCru
kagamiana	MMuc MWht
§ *lubrica*	MWht
makinoi	EUrb MWht
nitida	see *Fargesia nitida*
§ *okuboi*	MWht
villosa	see *S. okuboi*
yamadorii	MWht
yashadake	MWht
– f. *kimmei*	MAsh MMuc MWht NLar SPoG SWor

Semnanthe see Erepsia

Sempervivella see Rosularia

Sempervivum ✿ (Crassulaceae)

'Aaroundina'	NMen
'Abba'	NMen
'Abbe'	NMen
'Achalm'	NMen
'Adelaar'	NMen
'Adelmoed'	NMen
'Ageet'	NMen
§ 'Aglow'	ESuc LCro
'Agnetta'	NMen
'Agua'	MWlw NMen
'Aladdin'	MWlw NMen SRms
'Albertine'	NMen
'Alchimist'	NMen
'Aldo Moro'	NMen WIce
'Alenco'	NMen
'Alfons-Roelands'	NMen
'Aline'	NMen
allionii	see *Jovibarba allionii*
'Alluring'	NMen
'Almaros'	NMen
'Alpha'	NMen SRms
altum	LRHS SPlb SRms
'Amanda'	MBrN NMen SRms
'Ambergreen'	NMen
'Ambroise'	NMen
'Americanos'	NMen
'Amtmann Fischer'	NMen
'Andinn Banker07'	NMen
'Andinn Emma'	NMen
'Andinn Lambo'	NMen
'Andinn Tunrida'	NMen
andreanum	see *S. tectorum* var. *alpinum*
'Andrenor'	NMen
'Andrenor' sport	NMen
'Antiquity'	WFar
'Apache' Haberer	NMen
'Apanatschi'	NMen
'Apollo's Frog'	NMen
'Apple Blossom'	NMen
APPLETINI (Chick Charms Series)	see *S.* 'Reinhard'

Sempervivum

'Aqua' NMen
arachnoideum ♀H7 CPic EArI EDAr ELan EpfP ESgI GArf GKev GMaP GQue LCro LRHS MAsh MBros MSwo SPlb SPoG SRms SRot SSem WAbe WFar WHoo WIce
- Arctic White ('Belsemcob2') (Colorockz Series) MPri SPoG
- var. ***bryoides*** LRHS MWlw SRms SSem WFar
- 'Calypso' NMen
- 'Clärchen' EDAr NMen WAbe
- Coconut Crystal ('Belsemmag1') (Colorockz Series) ESuc
- Coral Red ('Belsemred1' 'PBR') (Colorockz Series) EPfP ESuc LCro LRHS MPri SPoG
* - ***densum*** EPPr SSem WAbe
- Emerald Swirl ('Belsemgre1' 'PBR') (Colorockz Series) **new** ESuc
§ - 'Emily' LCro
- giant WFar
- 'Gorges d'Héric' EPot
- 'Happy Birthday' MWlw
- 'Laggeri' see *S. arachnoideum* subsp. *tomentosum* (C.B. Lehm. & Schnittsp.) Schinz & Thell.
- Lemon Flare ('Belsemyel2') ESuc LRHS
- 'Opitz' SRms
- 'Piletina' WFar
- 'Red Papaver' EPot LRHS
- 'Red Wings' NMen
- 'Rubin' CPic LRHS MSwo WFar
- 'Rubrum' CDoC ESuc GMaP SPlb SSem WFar
- Ruby Lime ('Belsemcha1' 'PBR') (Colorockz Series) **new** ESuc
- 'Shampoo' MWlw NMen
- 'Spider's Nest' WFar
- 'Spider's Web' WFar
- subsp. ***tomentosum*** misapplied see *S.* × *barbulatum* 'Hookeri'
- subsp. ***tomentosum*** ambig. LRHS
§ - subsp. ***tomentosum*** (C.B. Lehm. & Schnittsp.) Schinz & Thell. ♀H7 EDAr EPot GKev LRHS NPer SPlb SRms SSem WAbe
§ - - 'Minor' EDAr WFar
§ - - 'Stansfieldii' EPPr LRHS SRms WFar
- 'Web Cluster' WFar
- 'Whisper' EDAr
§ - 'White Christmas' MHer NMen
'Argus Eye' NMen
'Arondina' NMen
'Arrowheads Red' NMen
'Artist' NMen
'Ashes of Roses' EGrI NMen WAbe
'Athen' NMen
'Atlantic' SRms
atlanticum GAbr MMuc MWlw SSem
- from Oukaïmeden, Morocco SRms
- 'Edward Balls' NMen SRms WFar
'Atlantis' ambig. NMen SRms
'Atropurpureum' ambig. EGrI EPot GAbr MBrN NMen WFar
'Attraction' NMen
'Aureum' see *Aeonium aureum*
Autumn Apple (Chick Charms Series) see *S.* 'Dakota'

'Babette' NMen
'Baby Skrocki' NMen
balcanicum SRms
ballsii SRms
'Banderi' NMen
'Bandi' NMen
'Banjo' NMen
'Banyan' SRms
§ × ***barbulatum*** 'Hookeri' EDAr NMen WAbe WHoo
'Baronesse' NMen
'Bascour Zilver' SRms
I 'Beate' G. Dillmann NMen
'Beatles Memory' NMen
'Beaute' NMen
'Bedazzled' NMen
'Bedivere' NMen SRms
* 'Bedley Hi' NMen
'Begbroke' EDAr
'Bella Donna' NMen
'Bella Meade' SRms
'Bellissima' NMen
'Benala' NMen
'Bennerbroek' NMen
'Berello' EDAr
'Bernstein' EDAr EPPr GKev MHer NMen WIce
Berry Blues (Chick Charms Series) see *S.* 'Pacific Blue Ice'
'Beta' NMen WAbe
'Bianca' NMen
'Big Daddy' **new** ESuc
'Bijou' NMen
Bing Cherry (Chick Charms Series) see *S.* 'Aglow'
'Birchmaier' NMen
'Björn' NMen
I 'Black' **new** ESuc
'Black Beauty' MHer NMen WFar
'Black Cap' NMen
'Black Knight' MHer SPlb SRms
'Black Mini' NBir NMen SRms
'Black Mountain' GKev NMen
'Black Velvet' NMen
'Black Widow' NMen
§ 'Blade of Steel' ESuc NMen
'Blauer Ritter' NMen
'Blood Tip' LRHS MHer NMen NRya SPlb SPoG SRms SSem WFar
'Bloody Goose' NMen
'Bloody Mary' NMen
'Blue Angel' NMen
'Blue Bird' NMen
'Blue Boy' EPPr GAbr LRHS MHer NMen SPlb SPoG SRms SSem WFar
'Blue Lady' NMen
'Blue Moon' NMen SSem
'Blue Time' WFar WHoo
'Blushes' SSem
Blushing Garnet ('Belsemmag2') **new** ESuc
'Bokkenrijders' NMen
'Bold Chick' NMen
'Booth's Red' NMen
borisii see *S. ciliosum* var. *borisii*
borissovae EPot
'Boromir' NMen
'Boule de Neige' EPot NMen NRya WFar
'Bowles's Variety' NMen
'Braunella' NMen
'Bright Spark' SSem
'Brilland Red Brun' NMen
'Britta' NMen

'Brock'	NMen SRms SSem
'Bronco' ♀H5	EGrI EPfP ESuc GAbr LRHS LWaG MWlw NMen NRya SPoG SRms SRot SSem WBrk WCot WFar WPGP
'Bronze Pastel'	NMen SRms SSem
'Brown Owl'	EDAr NMen SRms SSem
'Brownii'	NMen
'Brunhilde'	NMen
'Burgundy'	NMen
'Burning Bush'	NMen WFar
'Burning Desire'	NMen
'Burnished Bronze'	NMen
'Burnt Embers'	NMen
'Butterbur'	NMen
'Butterfly'	NMen
'Butterpat'	NMen
BUTTERSCOTCH BABY (Chick Charms Series)	see S. 'Hordubal'
'Café'	NMen SRms
calcareum	CPic EPfP EPot GKev MMuc MPnt NBro SArc SPlb SPoG SRms SSem WFar
- GDJ 92.16 from Petite Ceüse, France	SRms
- from Cleizé, France	see *S. calcareum* 'Limelight'
- from Colle St Michel, France	SRms
- 'Button'	WFar
- 'Extra' ♀H5	EWes GAbr LRHS MHer NMen SRms SSem WFar
- 'Greenii'	NMen SPlb SRms
§ - 'Grigg's Surprise'	NMen SPlb WAbe
- 'Guillaumes' ♀H5	LRHS SRms SSem WHoo
§ - 'Limelight'	LRHS NMen SSem WHoo
- 'Monstrosum'	see *S. calcareum* 'Grigg's Surprise'
§ - 'Mrs Giuseppi'	CSpe EGrI ESuc GAbr LCro NMen NWbg SRms SSem WAbe WFar WIce
- 'Pink Pearl'	NMen SPlb
- 'Sir William Lawrence' ♀H5	EBee EDAr EGrI EPfP EPot GMaP LRHS NMen SRms SRot SSem WAbe
'Caliph's Hat'	NMen
'Campagha'	NMen
'Canada Kate'	NMen
'Candy Floss'	NMen
cantabricum	MMuc WFar
- subsp. *cantabricum* from Leitariegos, Spain	GAbr
- subsp. *guadarramense* from Pico del Lobo, Spain, No 1	SRms
- subsp. *urbionense*	SRms
'Cantal'	NMen
'Caramel'	NMen
'Carlo's II'	NMen
'Carmen'	NMen
'Carnival'	NMen
'Casablanca'	NMen SSem
'Caspara'	NMen
caucasicum	LRHS SRms
'Cavo Doro'	NMen
'Celon'	NMen
'Centennial'	NMen SSem
CHERRY BERRY (Chick Charms Series)	see *S.* 'Rocknoll Rosette'
'Cherry Dream'	EDAr NMen SSem
'Cherry Frost'	NMen
'Cherry Tart'	NMen SPlb
'Chivalry'	NMen
'Cho'	NMen
'Chocolate'	WAbe WFar
CHOCOLATE KISS (Chick Charms Series)	see *S.* 'Pacific Devils Food'
'Choctaw'	NMen
'Cholie'	NMen
'Chrome Green' (BigSam Series)	ESuc
chrysanthum	CPic
ciliosum ♀H7	EDAr EPot NRya SPlb SRms WIce
§ - var. *borisii*	EPPr NRya SSem WAbe WFar
- subsp. *octopodes*	GAbr NBir NMen NRya SSem
- - 'Apetalum'	EPPr GAbr NMen WHoo
'Cindy'	SRms
CINNAMON STARBURST (Chick Charms Series)	see *S.* 'Jeanne d'Arc'
'Clara Noyes'	NMen
'Clare'	MHer NMen
'Classic Rock'	NMen
'Climax' ambig.	EPfP WFar
'Climax' Ford	NMen
'Cobweb Capers'	NMen
'Cobweb Centres'	EWes NMen
'Colchicum'	SRms
'Commander Hay'	EWes GKev GMaP NMen NPer NRya SRms
'Compte de Congae'	ESuc NMen
'Cono'	NMen
'Corona'	NMen
'Corsair'	EPPr GKev MBrN NMen SRms SSem WFar
COSMIC CANDY (Chick Charms Series)	see *S.* 'Urmina'
COTTON CANDY (Chick Charms Series)	see *S. arachnoideum* 'Emily'
CRANBERRY COCKTAIL (Chick Charms Series)	see *S.* 'Killer'
'Cream Tea'	NMen
'Crimson Velvet'	NMen
'Crimson Webb'	WFar
§ 'Crispyn' ♀H5	EPot LRHS NMen SRms SSem WFar
'Crows'	NMen
'Crucify'	NMen
'Crystal Ball' **new**	ESuc
'Cupream'	SRms
§ 'Dakota'	ESuc NMen
'Dallas'	NMen SRms
'Damask'	NMen
'Dancer's Veil'	NMen
'Danji'	NMen
'Darjeeling'	NMen
'Dark Beauty'	MBel SRms WAbe WCAu WCot
'Dark Cloud'	GAbr NMen WHoo
'Dark Point'	NMen
'De Kardijk'	NMen
'Deep Fire'	MWlw NMen SRms SSem
× *degenianum*	NMen
'Delta' ♀H5	NMen
densum	see *S. tectorum*
'Desert Dream'	NMen WFar
'Devil's Touch'	SSem
'Dippy Dame'	NMen
'Dipsy'	NMen
'Director Jacobs'	NMen
'Disney Festival'	WFar
'Doeskin'	SSem
'Dolle Dina's'	NMen
dolomiticum	NMen
'Donarrose'	NMen
'Donnerlüttchen'	NMen SSem
'Dornröschen'	NMen
'Downland Queen'	NMen
'Dr Fritz Köhlein'	ESuc NMen SSem

'Draco'	ESuc LRHS
'Dragoness'	NMen SSem
'Dream Catcher'	NMen
'Duke of Windsor'	NMen
'Dune'	NMen
'Dusty'	EDAr ESgI
'Dyke'	GAbr
dzhavachischvilii	NMen
'Edge of Night'	SRms
'Eefje'	NMen
'Eisbär'	SSem
'El Misti'	NMen
'El Toro'	SSem
'Electra'	SSem
'Elene'	MPnt
'Elva'	NMen
'Emerald Empress'	NMen
'Emerald Giant'	SRms
'Emerald Haze'	WFar
'Emerald Lustre'	WFar
'Emerson's Giant'	NMen SRms
'Emmchen'	NMen
'Engle's'	GKev LRHS MMuc NMen SPlb SRms SSem WFar
'Engle's 13-2'	NMen
'Engle's Rubrum'	NMen NRya
'Erdbeermond'	NMen
erythraeum	SPlb SRms SSem
'Essence of Lime'	NMen
'Euphemia'	NMen
'Evening Glow'	NMen
'Excalibur'	NMen
'Exhibita'	SRms
'Exorna'	NMen SSem
'Eyjafjalla'	SSem
'Fair Lady'	NMen
'Fairy'	NMen
'Fame'	NMen SPlb
'Faramir'	NMen
'Farida'	NMen
§ 'Fashion Diva'	ESuc LCro
'Fat Jack'	NMen
× *fauconnetii* 'Rubellum'	EDAr
– 'Thompsonii'	SRms
'Feldmaier'	NMen WFar
'Fernanda'	NMen
'Fernwood'	NMen
'Fernzünder'	SSem
'Festival'	NMen
'Fiery Furness'	NMen
'Fiesta' ambig.	NMen
'Fifty One Shades'	WFar
× *fimbriatum* 'Joy of Life'	SSem
'Finerpointe'	NMen
'Fire Glint'	NMen SRms WFar
'Firgrove Early Riser'	NMen
'Firlefanz'	SSem
'First Try'	NMen
'Flaming Heart'	MBrN NMen
'Flaming Sword'	NMen
'Flaming Web'	WFar
'Flanders Passion'	EWes NMen SRms SSem
'Flasher'	NMen SSem
'Forden'	NMen
'Ford's Spring'	EDAr NMen SRms SSem
'Foxy Lady'	NMen WFar
'Freckles'	NMen
'Fresh Fine Orange'	NMen
'Fromika'	GAbr NMen SRms
'Frosty'	SRms
'Fuego' ♀H5	NMen SRms SSem
× *funckii*	EGrI MBrN NMen
'Galahad'	NMen
'Galaxis'	NMen
'Gallivarda' ♀H5	NMen
'Gamma'	NMen SRms
'Gargamel'	SSem
'Garnet'	NMen
'Gay Jester'	NMen WHoo
'Georgia Rowan'	NMen
'Ginger Nut'	ESuc NMen
'Ginnie's Delight'	NMen
'Gipsy'	NMen
giuseppii ♀H7	LRHS SRms
– from Peña Espigüete, Spain	SRms
'Glaucum Minor'	NMen
'Gloriosum' ambig.	NMen
'Glowing Embers'	NMen
'Glückskinder'	NMen
'Godaert'	MMuc
'Gog'	NMen
'Gold Nugget' (Chick Charms Series)	ESuc LCro MHtn NMen WFar
'Golden Valley'	NMen
'Goldie'	NMen
'Goldmarie'	NMen SSem
'Goovy'	NMen
'Granada'	NMen
'Granat'	MHer NMen SRms
'Grand Mère'	NMen
'Grannie's Favourite'	NMen
GRAPE GALAXY (Chick Charms Series)	see *S.* 'Blade of Steel'
'Grapetone'	NMen
'Gratiana'	NMen
'Green Apple'	NMen
'Green Caro'	NMen
'Green Disk'	SRms
'Green Dragon'	EGrI LRHS NMen SRms
'Green Ice'	MWlw NMen SSem
'Green Wheel'	NMen
'Greenwich Time'	NMen
* *greigii*	EPot
'Grey Dawn'	SRms
'Grey Ghost'	CPic NMen SSem
'Grey Lady'	NMen
'Grey Owl'	NMen SRms WFar
'Grey Velvet'	NMen
'Greyfriars'	EPot LRHS NMen SRms SSem
'Greyolla'	NMen
'Grunspur'	NMen
'Gulle Dame'	NMen SRms
'Gummibärchen'	NMen
'Gwendolyn'	NMen
'Gwiazda'	MHtn WFar
'Halemaumau'	NMen
'Halley'	NMen
I 'Hall's Hybrid'	NBro SRms
'Happy'	LRHS NMen SRms SSem
'Hart'	MWlw NMen SSem
'Havana'	NMen
'Havendijker Splitt'	NMen
'Havendijker Teufel'	MWlw NMen SSem
'Havendijks Black'	NMen
'Havendijks Millenium'	NMen
'Havendijks Perfection'	NMen
'Havendijks Pride'	NMen
'Hayling'	EDAr EWes NMen SRms SSem WFar
'Haynaldii'	NMen
'Heigham Red'	EPot GKev LRHS NMen SRms SSem WFar WIce
'Helen'	LRHS NMen WFar

'Heliotroop'	NMen		'King Lear'	NMen
'Hermann Näpfel'	NMen		'Kohala'	SSem
'Hester'	MBrN NBro NMen		'Koko Flanel'	NMen SRms SSem
'Hey-hey'	EGrI EPot MBrN NMen SPlb SSem WCot		'Korspel Beauty'	NMen
			'Korspel Cherry'	NMen
'Hidde'	EGrI SPlb		'Korspelsegietje'	GAbr NMen SRms
'Highland Mist'	NMen		*kosaninii* from Koprivnik, Slovenia	WAbe
HIPPIE CHICKS (mixed)	EGren			
'Hirsutum'	see *Jovibarba allionii*		- 'Hepworth'	EDAr SPlb
hirtum	see *Jovibarba hirta*		'Kramer's Spinrad'	EPPr GKev NMen SPlb SRms WFar WHoo
'Honigmond'	MWlw NMen SSem			
'Honymoon'	NMen		'Krater'	NMen
'Hookeri'	see *S.* × *barbulatum* 'Hookeri'		'Lady Di'	NMen
'Hopi'	NMen		'Lamia'	NMen
§ 'Hordubal'	CSpe ESuc LRHS		'Landemine'	NMen SSem
'Hot Boyz'	NMen		'Latex'	SSem
§ 'Hot Summer'	ESuc NWbg		'Laura Lee'	MMuc
'Hualālai'	NMen		'Lavender and Old Lace'	EPot LRHS NMen SPlb SRms SSem WFar WIce
'Hula Girl'	NMen			
'Hullabaloo'	NMen		'Lavenderspross'	NMen
'Hurricane'	NMen		'Le Congai'	NMen
'Icicle'	LRHS NBro NMen SRms		'Legolas'	NMen
'Impact'	NMen		'Lemon Babies'	ESuc NMen
'Imperial'	SPlb		'Lemon Ball' **new**	ESuc
'Ingemarie'	NMen		'Leneca'	NMen
'Intensity'	MWlw NMen		'Lennik's Glory'	see *S.* 'Crispyn'
'Irazu'	EDAr EPot LRHS NMen SRms SSem WHoo		'Lentezon'	NMen
			'Leocadia's Nephew'	NMen
'Isaac Dyson'	SRot SSem		'Leopold'	SSem
'Isabelle'	NMen		'Lilac Queen'	NMen
'Iwo'	NMen		'Lilac Time' ♀H5	EPPr MBrN MHer NMen SPlb SRms SSem WFar
'Jack Frost'	NBro			
'Jacquette'	NMen		'Lilehammer'	NMen
'Jade' ambig.	NMen		'Lion King'	NMen
'Jadestern'	NMen		'Lioness'	NMen
§ 'Jeanne d'Arc'	ESuc LCro		'Lipari'	NMen SRms WCot
'Jelly Bean'	NMen		'Little Flirt'	NMen
'Jet Stream' ♀H5	NMen SPlb SRms SSem WFar		'Lively Bug'	EPot EPPr LRHS NMen SRms SSem
'Jewel Case'	SRms		'Lonzo'	NMen SRms
'Jim Knopf'	NMen		'Lord Alan'	NMen
I 'John Hobbs seedling No 2'	NMen		'Lord Morton'	NMen
'Joke'	ESuc		'Lovely Roset'	NMen
'Jolly Green Giant'	NMen		'Lucy Liu'	NMen SSem
'Jubilee'	ELan LRHS MAsh MHer MWlw NMen SRms		'Ludmila'	NMen
			'Lumeseen'	NMen
'Jubilee Tricolor'	NMen SPlb WAbe WFar		'Luminosity'	NMen
'Jungle Fires'	NMen SRms WHoo		'Lynn's Choice'	NMen
'Jungle Shadows'	MWlw NMen		'Lyra'	NMen
'Jupiter'	GKev		*macedonicum*	SPlb SRms
'Just Peachy'	NMen		'Magic Morning'	SSem
'Justine's Choice'	NMen SRms		'Magic Spell'	NMen
'Kai'	NMen		'Magical'	LRHS NMen
'Kalinda'	EGren ESuc MSwo SMrm		'Mahogany'	EGrI GKev MHer NMen NRya SRms
'Kappa'	EDAr NBro NMen		'Mai Appel'	NMen
'Karin'	NMen SSem		'Maia'	MWlw
'Kautangel'	NMen		'Maigret'	NMen SSem
'Keder'	NMen		'Majanka'	NMen
'Keiko'	NMen		'Majestic'	NMen
'Kermit'	NMen		'Malby's Hybrid'	see *S.* 'Reginald Malby'
KEY LIME KISS (Chick Charm Series)	see *Jovibarba allionii*		'Manhattan'	NMen
			'Maria Laach'	NMen
'Khaleesi'	WFar		'Marijntje'	NMen
'Kibo'	NMen		'Mariska'	NMen
'Kidlington'	NMen		'Marland Ruby'	NMen WCot
'Kildare'	NMen		'Marmalade'	NMen
§ 'Killer'	ESuc LCro NMen NWbg WFar		§ *marmoreum*	EPot LRHS SRms
'Kim'	NMen		- from Okol, Albania	NMen
'Kimba'	NMen		- 'Brunneifolium'	GAbr LRHS
kindingeri	SRms		- subsp. *marmoreum* var. *dinaricum*	MHer
'King Alfred'	NMen			
'King George'	EDAr MMuc NMen SRms		'Marsupilami'	NMen

'Mary-Beth'	NMen
'Matthew's Day Dream'	GKev NMen
'May Red'	NMen
'Mayfair'	NMen
'Maytime'	NMen
'Meadow Blaze'	WFar
'Melanie'	MBrN NMen SSem
'Mercury'	NBro NMen SRms
'Michael'	NMen SSem
'Mickey Mouse'	NMen
'Midas'	LRHS SRms
'Mike'	NMen WFar
'Mini Frost'	NMen
MINT MARVEL (Chick Charms Series)	see *S. calcareum* 'Mrs Giuseppi'
'Minuet'	NMen
'Mira'	MHol
'Moerkerk's Merit'	LRHS NMen
'Mona Lisa'	NMen
'Mondstein'	NMen SRms
montanum	WAbe WFar
subsp. *carpaticum*	
'Cmiral's Yellow'	
- 'Rubrum'	see *S.* 'Red Mountain'
- subsp. *stiriacum*	SRms
- - 'Lloyd Praeger'	NMen
'Moondrops'	NMen
'More Honey'	NMen
'Morning Glow'	NMen
'Mount Hood'	NMen SRms
'Mount Skippet'	NMen
'Mount Usher'	ESuc NMen
'Mulberry Wine'	EDAr SRms SSem WHoo
'Mystic'	MBrN NMen SSem
'Naemi'	NMen
'Nellie'	NMen
'Neon'	NMen
§ 'Neptune'	ESuc LCro WFar
nevadense	GArf NRya SRms
- 'Hirtellum'	SRms
'New Rose'	LRHS WFar
'Nico'	NMen SRms
'Night Detector'	NMen
'Nigrum'	see *S. tectorum* 'Nigrum'
'Niobe'	NMen
'Nocturno'	NMen
'Noellie'	NMen
'Noir'	NBro NMen SSem WFar
'Norbert'	NMen SRms
'Nörtofts Beauty'	NMen
'Nouveau Pastel'	NMen
'Nova'	NMen
'Novalis'	NMen
'Obaldina'	MWlw NMen
'Oberon'	NMen
'Obsession'	WFar
'Ockerwurz'	NMen WFar
'Octet'	NMen
'Oddity'	MBrN MHer NMen WFar
'Oh My'	NMen
'Ohio Burgundy'	NMen SRms WAbe WFar
'Ohu ôm Ohu'	NMen
'Olcina'	NMen
'Old Man Sage'	NMen SPlb
'Olivia'	NMen
'Omega'	NMen
'One Hundred'	NMen
'Onyx' (SuperSemps Series)	EPfP ESuc
'Orange Glow'	SSem
'Orestes'	NMen
'Ornatum'	EPot MHer WAbe
ossetiense	GAbr
'Othello' ♀H5	GAbr NBir NMen SRms SSem WCot WPGP
'Ottelein'	NMen
'Pachamama'	NMen
'Pacific Blazing Star'	NMen SSem
§ 'Pacific Blue Ice'	ESuc LCro SSem
'Pacific Dawn'	NMen
§ 'Pacific Devils Food'	ESuc LCro MHer NMen
'Pacific Purple Shadows'	NMen WFar
'Pacific Red Tide' **new**	ESuc
'Pacific Second Try'	NMen
'Pacific Sexy'	NMen SSem
'Pacific Tart'	NMen
'Packardian'	NMen
'Palissander'	GAbr NMen
'Pandaros'	SSem
'Papucchini'	NMen
'Passionata'	NMen SSem
'Pastel'	MHer NMen
patens	see *Jovibarba heuffelii*
'Patrician'	NMen SRms
'Peggy'	ESuc NMen
'Pekinese'	LRHS MBrN NBro NMen SRms
'Peridot'	MWlw NMen
'Persephone'	NMen
'Petsy'	NMen SRms
'Phoebe'	NMen
'Picasso'	NMen SSem
'Pilatus'	LRHS SRms WFar
'Pine Cone'	NMen
PINEAPPLE PARADISE (Chick Charms Series)	see *S.* 'Hot Summer'
'Pink Astrid'	NMen
'Pink Cloud'	NMen SSem
'Pink Flamingoes'	NMen SSem
'Pink Grapefruit'	MWlw NMen
'Pink Lemonade'	ESuc NMen SSem
'Pink Mist'	SRms
'Pink Pomelo' (BigSam Series)	ESuc LRHS
'Pink Puff'	NMen
'Pinkerton'	SSem
'Pinochio'	NMen
'Pip'	NMen
'Pippin'	NMen SRms SSem
pittonii ♀H5	WAbe
'Pixie'	NMen
'Plum Frosting'	MWlw NMen WFar
PLUM PARFAIT (Chick Charms Series)	see *S.* 'Prairie Sunset'
'Plumb Rose'	NMen
'Pluto'	NMen
'Polaris'	GMaP NMen SSem
'Poldark'	NMen
'Pompeja'	NMen
'Poollicht'	MWlw NMen SSem
'Popocatepetl'	SSem
§ 'Prairie Sunset'	ESuc LCro NMen
'Princess Little'	NMen
'Proud Zelda'	NMen SSem
'Pseudo-ornatum'	SRms
'Pulmosa' **new**	ESuc
pumilum	LRHS SRms
- from Techensis, Caucasus Mountains	SRms
'Purdy'	EDAr ESgI GAbr WAbe
'Purdy's 50-6'	NMen
'Purdy's Big Red'	NMen
'Purple Beauty'	NMen
'Purple Dazzler'	NMen SSem

'Purple Haze'	NMen WFar		'Ruby Heart'	CPic EGren GJos LCro LRHS MBNS WCav
'Purple King'	NMen			
'Purple Quartz' (BigSam Series)	ESuc		'Ruby Meadows'	WFar
			'Russian River'	WHoo
'Purple Queen'	EPPr GAbr LRHS MWlw NMen NRya SRms SSem WFar		*ruthenicum*	EPPr LRHS NMen NRya SRms
			'Ruth's Choice'	WFar
'Purpurkranz'	NMen		'Saffron'	NMen
'Pygmalion'	NMen		'Saga'	NMen
'Queen Amalia'	see *S. reginae-amaliae*		'Samwise'	NMen
'Queen Elizabeth'	SSem		'Sanford's Hybrid'	NMen
'Quintessence'	NMen SRms		'Sanne'	NMen
'Raspberry Ice'	NBro NMen		'Santis'	NMen
'Rauer Kulm'	NMen		'Sarah'	NMen
'Red Ace'	NBro NEoE WFar		'Sardonyx'	NMen
'Red Beam'	EDAr		'Sarotte'	NMen
'Red Beauty'	EGren ESuc		'Sassy Frass'	NMen
'Red Chief'	SPoG		'Saturn'	NMen SRms WFar
'Red Cross'	GAbr NMen		*schlehanii*	see *S. marmoreum*
'Red Delta'	NBir NMen WCot WPGP		'Schwarze Rose'	NMen SSem
'Red Devil'	EGrI NMen SPlb SRms SSem WHoo		'Scooby'	WFar
			'Sea Coral'	NMen
'Red Lion'	NMen		'Seminole'	NMen WIce
§ 'Red Mountain'	NMen NRya SRms		'Seneca'	NMen
'Red Pink'	NMen		'Sephora'	NMen
'Red Planet'	NMen		'Sha'uri'	NMen
'Red Shine'	NMen		'Sheila'	GAbr
'Red Spider'	EDAr ESgI MWlw NBro NMen		'Shepherd's Warning'	WFar
'Red West'	NMen		'Show Baby'	NMen
'Regal'	EBee NMen		'Sideshow'	NMen
'Regenbogen'	SSem		'Silberkarneol' misapplied	see *S.* 'Silver Jubilee'
'Regensburger Knirps'	NMen		'Silberkarneol' ambig.	EGrI
'Regensburger Kokon'	NMen		'Silberspitz'	EPPr LRHS MHer NBro NMen SPlb SRms
reginae	see *S. reginae-amaliae*			
§ *reginae-amaliae*	GKev LRHS SRms		'Silver Andre'	NMen
§ 'Reginald Malby'	NMen SRms		§ 'Silver Jubilee'	EPPr NBro NMen SPlb SRms WFar WHoo
§ 'Reinhard' ♀H5	EDAr ESuc GMaP LCro LRHS MAsh MBrN MHer NMen SMrm SPlb SPoG SRms SRot SSem WFar WHoo WIce		'Silver Queen'	ESuc
			'Silver Spitz'	LRHS
			SILVER SUEDE (Chick Charms Series)	see *S.* 'Neptune'
'Remus'	ELan NMen SRms		'Silver Thaw'	GMaP LSto
'Rex'	NMen		'Silverine'	EGren NMen
'Rhône'	NMen		'Silvertone'	NMen
'Rhubarb Crumble'	NMen		'Simonkaianum'	see *Jovibarba hirta*
'Rhubarb Splash' (BigSam Series)	ESuc		'Sioux'	MBrN NMen SSem
			'Sirius'	EBee EPfP LRHS MBNS MHol MSwo NMen
'Rio de Janeiro'	NMen			
'Rita Jane'	NMen SSem		'Skrocki's Beauty'	GAbr LRHS NMen SRms WFar
'Robin'	NBro NMen SRms		'Smaragd'	LRHS NMen
§ 'Rocknoll Rosette'	ESuc LCro		'Smit's Seedling'	NMen
'Rococo'	NMen		'Smokey Jet'	NMen
'Romantic Knights'	NMen		'Smokey Quartz'	ESuc
'Romantik Ritter'	NMen		'Snow Baby'	NMen
I 'Ronsdorfer Hybride'	NMen		'Snowberger'	NMen SRms
'Roosemaryn'	EDAr GMaP		*soboliferum*	see *Jovibarba sobolifera*
'Rosa Mädchen'	ESuc MWlw NMen		§ 'Soft Line'	ESuc NWbg
'Rosenherz'	SSem		'Solar Meadows'	WFar
'Rosenhügel'	MWlw SSem		'Sombrero'	NMen
'Rosie'	CPic GMaP MAsh MMuc NMen SRms WFar WIce		'Sonnenkuss'	SSem
			'Soothsayer'	NMen
'Rosy Glow'	EDAr		'Soul'	NMen
'Rotes Meer'	NMen		'Space Dog'	NMen
'Rotkopf' ♀H5	NMen SSem		'Spangle' sport	NMen
'Rotmantel'	NMen		'Spanish Dancer'	NMen
'Royal Opera'	EPot		'Spartan's Sunrise'	WFar
'Royal Ruby'	EGren ESuc MWlw NMen SMrm		'Spherette'	MBrN MWlw NMen WAbe
'Royal Twist'	EDAr		'Spider's Lair' ♀H5	EPot SRms
'Rubin'	CPic CTsd EPfP GQue LRHS LSto MAsh MBNS MHol NBir NMen SPoG SRms SSem WAbe WIce		'Spiver's Velvet'	NMen
			'Spring Beauty'	NMen
			'Spring Mist'	EPot LRHS SRms SSem
I 'Rubra Ash'	NMen		'Sprite'	LRHS MWlw NMen SRms SSem
I 'Rubra Ray'	NMen			

Sempervivum

'Squib'	EDAr NMen SSem
'Standard Green'	CPic LRHS LSto
stansfieldii	see *S. arachnoideum*
	subsp. *tomentosum* 'Stansfieldii'
'Starburst'	NMen
'State Fair'	NMen SSem
'Steerosentern'	NMen
STRAWBERRY KIWI (Chick Charms Series)	see *S.* 'Fashion Diva'
'Strawberry Vale'	EDAr ESgI
'Strider'	NMen
'Stuffed Olive'	NMen SRms
SUGAR SHIMMER (Chick Charms Series)	see *S.* 'Soft Line'
'Sugary'	NMen
'Suite Minuet'	MWlw SSem
'Sun Kiss'	NMen
'Sunray Desire'	NMen
'Sunray Magic'	SSem
'Sunrise'	NMen
'Super Dome'	NMen
'Superama'	NMen
'Supernova'	NMen
'Svava'	NMen
'Sweet Brown Sugar'	NMen
'Syston Flame'	NMen
'Tamberlane'	EDAr
'Tarita'	NMen
'Taurus'	ESuc
'T'Boz'	NMen
§ ***tectorum*** ♀H7	CGHo CPic ELan MCtn MHoo MNHC MWlw NMen SPlb SSem
§ - var. ***alpinum***	LRHS NBro SRms
- 'Atropurpureum'	ELan SRms
- 'Atroviolaceum'	SPlb
- var. ***boutignyanum***	SRms
GDJ 94.04 from Route de Tuixén, Spain	
- monstrose	SPlb SRms
§ - 'Nigrum'	EGrI MHer NBro
- 'Red Flush'	MBrN NMen
- 'Royanum' ♀H7	NMen SRms
- 'Sunset'	EGren ESuc EWes NMen
- subsp. ***tectorum*** 'Triste'	NMen
- 'Violaceum'	SPlb SRms
'Teddy Bear'	NMen
'Tederheid'	NMen
'Teide'	SSem
'Telfan'	NMen
'Terlamen'	NMen
'Terracotta Baby'	LRHS NMen WFar
'Tesoro'	NMen SSem
'Thayne'	NMen
'The Flintstones'	CPic NMen
'The Red Carpet'	NMen
'Thistle Hill'	NMen
'Thunder'	NMen
'Timmy'	NMen
'Tinner Bell'	NMen
'Tintenblut'	NMen SSem
'Tintinabulum'	NMen
'Tip Top'	EPot NMen WFar
'Titania'	NMen
'Tjabine'	NMen
'Tohuwabohu'	NMen
'Topaz'	NMen SRms
'Tordeur's Memory'	NMen SRms
'Tormulin'	SPoG
I 'Tourmalyi'	NMen
'T'Pol'	NMen
'Traffic Lights'	SSem
'Trail Walker'	NMen SRms
'Tree Beard'	NMen
'Trine'	NMen
'Tristan' **new**	ESuc
'Tristesse' ♀H5	LRHS NMen SSem
'Truva'	NMen
'Tutti Fruity'	MWlw SSem
'Twilight Blues'	SRms
'U4'	NMen
'Udine'	NMen
'Uralturmalin'	NMen
'Urmel'	NMen
§ 'Urmina'	ESuc LCro NMen
'Utopian'	EGrI LRHS
'Van der Steen'	NMen
'Vanbaelen'	NMen
'Vasi Petru'	NMen
'Vega'	MHol
'Veronique'	NMen
'Veughelen'	EDAr NMen SSem
vicentei	WFar
- from Gatón, Spain	LRHS
'Video'	NMen
'Viking'	NMen
'Virgil'	LRHS MBrN NMen SPlb SSem WAbe WCot WFar WIce
'Vossa Nova'	NMen
'Vulcano'	NMen
'Walnut Tree'	NMen
'Wasti'	NMen
'Watermelon Rind'	NMen
'Web of Intrege'	NMen
webbianum	see *S. arachnoideum* subsp. *tomentosum* (C.B. Lehm. & Schnittsp.) Schinz & Thell.
'Webbyola'	NMen
'Webster'	NMen
'Weitblick'	SSem
'Wendy'	NMen
'Westerlin'	NMen
'Wheel of Fire'	NMen
'Whirlpool'	NMen
'White Christmas'	see *S. arachnoideum* 'White Christmas'
'White Ladies'	NMen
'White Star'	WHoo
'Whitening'	GAbr WFar
× ***widderi***	NMen
'Wilhelm Tell'	NMen
'Wine Queen'	NMen
'Wok'	NMen
I 'Woolcott's Variety'	NBir NMen SRms
'Yanisha'	NMen
'Yolanda'	NMen
'Yvette'	NMen
'Zaccour'	NMen
'Zackenkrone'	NMen
'Zannalee'	NMen
'Zeeuwse Winner'	NMen
'Zelca'	NMen
zeleborii	NMen
'Zenith'	NMen SRms
'Zepherin'	NMen
'Zilver Moon'	NMen
'Zilver Snowflake'	NMen
'Zilver Suzanna'	NMen
'Zilverprinsesje'	NMen
'Zircon'	NMen
'Zone'	NMen
'Zorba'	NMen
'Zulu'	NMen

Sempervivum

'Zwergengnom'	NMen

× *Semponium* (Crassulaceae)

'Destiny' **new**	CAbb LCro
'Diamond' **new**	CAbb EAri
'Sienna' **new**	CAbb EAri LRHS

Senecio (Asteraceae)

angulatus	CPic EShb
articulatus	see *Curio articulatus*
§ *barbertonicus*	EShb NHrt
bidwillii	see *Brachyglottis bidwillii*
candicans misapplied	see *Jacobaea maritima*, *S. candidans*
candidans ANGEL WINGS ('Senaw'^{PBR})	CBcs CSBt CTsd CWGN CWnw EGren ELan EPfP LBar LBom LCro LRHS LSou MArl MBros Midl MPri MPro NLar NWbg SAth SIvy SMad WCot
chrysanthemoides misapplied	see *Euryops chrysanthemoides*
cineraria	see *Jacobaea maritima*
cinerascens	SVen
coccinilifera hort.	see *Kleinia grantii*
compactus	see *Brachyglottis compacta*
confusus	see *Pseudogynoxys chenopodioides*
crassissimus	CSBt EShb LWaG NCft WCot
cristobalensis	see *Roldana cristobalensis*
'Donkey's Ears'	LBar
doria	EPfP EShb SAko
elegans	SVen
ficoides	see *Curio ficoides*
gerberifolius B&SWJ 10357	WCru
- B&SWJ 10361	MHol WCru
'Gregynog Gold'	see *Ligularia* 'Gregynog Gold'
greyi misapplied	see *Brachyglottis* (Dunedin Group) 'Sunshine'
greyi Hook.f.	see *Brachyglottis greyi* (Hook.f.) B. Nord.
haworthii	see *Caputia tomentosa*
herreianus	CoPl LCro LWaG MPri NHrt SIvy
hoffmannii	EShb
jacobaea	see *Jacobaea vulgaris*
jacobsenii	EShb
kleinia	see *Kleinia neriifolia*
kleiniiformis	CoPl CPic EShb WCor
laxifolius hort.	see *Brachyglottis* (Dunedin Group) 'Sunshine'
macroglossus	EShb
- 'Variegatus' (v) ♀^{H1c}	CPic EShb
mandraliscae	see *Curio talinoides* subsp. *mandraliscae*
maritimus	see *Jacobaea maritima*
mikanioides	see *Delairea odorata* Lem.
monroi	see *Brachyglottis monroi*
niveoaureus	CTsd MHol
- 'Silver Feathers'	LRHS MHtn MPro
peregrinus	CoPl CPic LBom LCro LWaG NCft WOld
petasitis	see *Roldana petasitis*
polyodon	CFis GElm GQue LBar SPhx SRms
- var. *polyodon*	EPfP GBin LRHS WCAu
- 'Sandra' (v)	CCps
- var. *subglaber*	CSpe EWes MHol MNrw
przewalskii	see *Ligularia przewalskii*
pulcher	CDTJ MHol SHar SMrm
reinoldii	see *Brachyglottis rotundifolia*
rowleyanus	see *Curio rowleyanus*
scandens	see *Delairea odorata* Lem.
scaposus	see *Caputia scaposa*
seminiveus	EBee
serpens	see *Curio repens*
§ *smithii*	NBid
'Sunshine'	see *Brachyglottis* (Dunedin Group) 'Sunshine'
talinoides 'Himalaya' misapplied (green-leaved)	see *S. barbertonicus*
tamoides	EShb SPlb
tanguticus	see *Sinacalia tangutica*

Senna (Fabaceae)

alexandrina	EShb
artemisioides ♀^{H1b}	WCot
§ *corymbosa*	CCoa CHll CRHN SEND WJur
hebecarpa	SBrt
§ *marilandica*	WCot

Sequoia (Cupressaceae)

sempervirens ♀^{H6}	CAco CBcs CCVT CLnd CMCN CMen CTsd IPap LMaj MBlu MCtn MMuc NOra NPip SArc SEND SGol SSta WMat WMou
- 'Adpressa'	CAco MGos MMuc
- 'Cantab'	WMou
- 'Filoli'	CAco
- 'Lightning'	CAco
- 'Loma Prieta Spike'	CAco
- 'Martin'	CAco
- 'Prostrata'	CAco EWhm

Sequoiadendron (Cupressaceae)

giganteum ♀^{H6}	Widely available
- 'Barabits Requiem'	CAco MBlu
- 'Bultinck Yellow'	MBlu
- 'Cannibal'	NLar
- 'French Beauty'	CAco NLar
- 'Glaucum'	CAco EPfP EUrb LMaj MAsh MBlu NLar
* - 'Glaucum Compactum'	MBlu
- 'Greenpeace'	CAco MBlu NLar SArc
- 'Kyoxonera'	NLar
- 'Lighting Green'	CAco NLar
- 'Little Stan'	NLar
- 'Pendulum'	CAco CCVT ELan MBlu
- 'Philip Curtis'	CAco NLar
- 'Pierie'	CAco
- 'Powdered Blue'	NLar
- 'Vida Magical'	NLar

Serenoa (Arecaceae)

repens	NPlm
- silver-leaved	NPlm

Sericocarpus (Asteraceae)

asteroides	GArf GKev

Seriphidium see *Artemisia*

Serratula (Asteraceae)

bulgarica	see *Klasea bulgarica*
coronata subsp. *insularis*	see *Klasea coronata* subsp. *insularis*
gmelinii	see *Klasea macra*
lycopifolia	see *Klasea lycopifolia*
shawii	see *S. tinctoria* var. *seoanei*
tinctoria	CSpe NLar
§ - var. *seoanei*	CKno CMiW CTtf ECha EGrI ELan ESgI GKev LEdu LRHS MHer MHol MNrw NBid NBir NDov SAko SHar SLee SMHy SNoN SPhx SRms WCot WMal WPGP

Serruria (Proteaceae)
florida	SPlb
phylicoides	SPlb

Sesbania (Fabaceae)
punicea	WJur

Seseli (Apiaceae)
elatum subsp. *osseum*	CSpe LEdu SHor SPhx WHil
globiferum	SPhx
gracile	CSpe ECha LEdu SHor SPhx WHil
gummiferum	CSpe EBee ELan MCtn MPro SHor SMHy SPhx StAn WHil
hippomarathrum	CSpe MMrt MNrw SBrt SMHy SPhx WCot WFar
lehmannii	WCot
§ *libanotis*	EBee ELan EPPr LCro LEdu NLar SPhx WFar
- W&B BGB 10	ESwi
montanum	CMiW CSpe EBee NDov SHar WCot
petraeum	CSpe
rigidum	CSpe WMal WPGP
transcaucasicum	LEdu
- B&SWJ 15352	WCru

Sesleria (Poaceae)
§ *argentea*	CBWd CKno SPoG
autumnalis ♀H7	CBWd CElw CKno CSde CWnw EBee EGren ELan EPPr EWes GBin GKev GMaP LCro LSto NClf SHar SMHy WCAu WChS WSpi WTor WTre
caerulea	CKno CSde ECha EGrI ELan GMaP GQue LCro LEdu LRHS SPoG WCAu
- 'Malvern Mop'	EBee WHrl
cylindrica	see *S. argentea*
'Greenlee'	CKno SMHy
heufleriana	GBin LCro LRHS NRya SPhx SPlb WCot WSpi
nitida	CBWd CKno GMaP GQue LEdu WChS WSpi
sadleriana	EBee NClf
'Spring Dream'	CKno
'Summer Skies'	CKno EPfP LRHS

Sesuvium (Aizoaceae)
portulacastrum	CoPl

Setaria (Poaceae)
italica 'Lowlander'	MCtn
- 'Red Jewel'	CSpe MCtn
macrostachya	ELon SPhx
palmifolia ♀H2	EShb EUrb SBig SBrt SDix SIvy SPel SPlb
viridis	WCot

Sharon fruit see *Diospyros kaki*

Shepherdia (Elaeagnaceae)
argentea	WKor

Shibataea (Poaceae)
kumasaca ♀H6	CBcs EAri LCro LEdu MWht

Shortia (Diapensiaceae)
galacifolia	EPot
soldanelloides	GEdr
- var. *magna*	EPot
uniflora	EPot

Sibbaldia (Rosaceae)
procumbens	GKev

Sibbaldiopsis (Rosaceae)
§ *tridentata*	GArf
- 'Nuuk'	GJos MPro

Sibthorpia (Plantaginaceae)
europaea	CExl

Sida (Malvaceae)
hermaphrodita	EAri EPPr

Sidalcea ✿ (Malvaceae)
'Brilliant'	CBcs EGren LRHS NBir WCAu WFar
candida	ELan GMaP GQue LBar LRHS MArl MBNS MHol MMuc NGdn NLar NSti SPel WCAu WCot
- 'Bianca'	CFis CSpe ELan EPfP LRHS NDov NLar StAn WFar
'Candy Girl'	LBar NCth NLar WCot WFar XFar
'Crimson King'	WFar
'Croftway Red'	CMHG EBee NBro NGdn NLar WFar
'Elsie Heugh' ♀H7	CBWd CDor EBee ELan EPfP GBin GMaP LCro LRHS MArl MMuc MPro NBir NBro NCth NGdn NLar NSti SEND SPoG SRkn SRms WCAu WFar WTor
LILAC CANDICE ('Midawioha')	WFar
'Little Princess'PBR	EBee EWes GKev LBar LRHS NGdn NLar SPoG WCot WFar XFar
'Loveliness'	CMHG EBee MArl NBro SPoG WFar WKif
malviflora	SRms
- 'Alba'	CoPl
'Monarch'	WFar
'Moorland Rose Coronet'	WFar
'Mrs Borrodaile'	NBro NEoE NGdn NLar WFar
'My Love'	ECha
'Nimmerdor'	EBlo LRHS
'Oberon' ♀H7	EBee EBlo LRHS
oregana subsp. *spicata*	WFar
'Party Girl'	EBee ELan EPfP LRHS MArl MAsh MCtn MNrw NBro NGdn NLar SPlb SPoG WFar
'Purpetta'	LRHS NEoE NLar
'Reverend Page Roberts'	WCot
'Rosaly'	CoPl CSpe ELan ERCP GAbr LRHS MNrw NLar StAn WFar
'Rose Bud'	WFar
'Rose Queen'	EBee GKev MArl NBro SHar SRms WFar
Stark's hybrids	SRms
'Sussex Beauty'	LRHS LSto MAsh MBel MHol NCth NDov NGdn SMrm SPoG WCot WFar
'Wensleydale'	MWIw WFar
'William Smith' ♀H7	CMHG EBee LRHS MArl MMuc NBir NGdn NLar SEND WFar
'Wine Red'	CoPl EBee GPSL LRHS MArl MAsh NGdn NLar SPoG

Sideritis (Lamiaceae)
syriaca	IDun MCtn MHer
- RCB UA 2	WCot

Sieversia (Rosaceae)
§ *pentapetala*	GEdr GKev
- 'Flore Pleno' (d)	EDAr

Silaum (Apiaceae)
silaus   SPhx

Silene (Caryophyllaceae)
acaulis	EDAr EPot GKev SLee SRms WAbe WIce
§ - subsp. *acaulis*	SPlb SRms WIce
- 'Alba'	EPot WAbe
- 'Blush'	EDAr
- 'Correvoniana'	NLar
- subsp. *elongata*	see *S. acaulis* subsp. *acaulis*
- 'Frances'	EDAr EPot NLar SLee SRot WAbe
- 'Helen's Double' (d)	GArf
- 'Mount Snowdon'	ELan EWes GArf LRHS NLar SLee SPlb SPoG SRms WFar WHoo
- 'Pedunculata'	see *S. acaulis* subsp. *acaulis*
alba	see *S. latifolia* subsp. *alba*
alpestris	see *Heliosperma alpestre*
(Arkwrightii Group) 'Lipstick'	LBar
- 'Orange Zwerg'	EDAr
- 'Vesuvius'	CBcs CFis EBee GJos MBNS MCtn SRms WCot
armeria	see *Atocion armeria*
asterias	see *Viscaria asterias*
atropurpurea	see *Viscaria vulgaris* dark purple-red-flowered
baccifera	GGro MCtn NLar
§ *banksia*	SRms
- 'Hill Grounds'	CElw EBee ECha LBar Midl MPro WCot WGoo
- 'Molten Lava'	EDAr GEdr LRHS MHol SRms WFar
I - 'Plena' (d)	WFar
bolanthoides	EDAr WAbe
chalcedonica ♀H7	Widely available
- 'Alba'	CSpe EPfP EPPr WCAu WHrl
- 'Carnea'	CBWd CSpe CWal EBee ELan EPPr ERCP ESgI GJos LBar LRHS MBel MCtn NGdn SBeP WCAu
- 'Dusky Salmon'	WHrl
- 'Flore Pleno' (d)	WCot
- 'Pinkie'	MMuc NLar WFar
- 'Rauhreif'	EBee NLar WFar WHer WHil
- 'Rosea'	EGrI LBar NBir WHrl
- 'Salmonea'	CTtf EAri EPPr GPSL NBir SRms
coeli-rosa	see *Eudianthe coeli-rosa*
cognata B&SWJ 4234	ESwi WCru
- W&O 7151	GGro
compacta	see *Atocion compactum*
'Confetti'	CSpe ECha SHar
§ *coronaria* ♀H7	Widely available
- 'Alba' ♀H7	Widely available
- Atrosanguinea Group	CDoC CMHg EPfP GMaP LBar LRHS MBel MHol MMuc NGdn NSti SMrm WHoo WTor
- 'Blood Red'	CSpe LEdu SBeP SMrm WBrk
- 'Cerise'	MArl NBir
- GARDNERS' WORLD ('Blych') (d)	CTtf EBee ECha ELan EPfP EWes LBar MArl MAsh MBNS MHol NSti SAko SMad SMrm SPel SRkn WCot
- MESE 356	ECha SPhx
- Oculata Group	CSpe CTtf EBee ELan EMor EPfP EPPr MMuc SPlb WFar WKif WTor
- - 'Angel's Blush'	CFis EBee EPfP LRHS LShi MCtn MHol MPro NBir SMrm SRkn
§ *davidii*	GKev WAbe
delavayi	WHil
§ *dioica*	CBWd CCBP CGwi CHab CoPl CTtf EBee GJem GJos GQue LCro LRHS LSto MAsh MCtn MHer MNHC MPri NAts NLar NMir SPhx SPoG SRms WCav WOrg WShi
- 'Clifford Moor' (v)	EPfP MHer
- 'Compacta'	see *S. dioica* 'Minikin'
- 'Firefly'PBR (d)	CDor NSti
§ - 'Flore Pleno' (d)	EGrI MHol NBid NBro NGdn WHoo
- golden-leaved	LShi
- 'Minikin'	NGdn
- 'Purple Prince'	MMuc SEND
- 'Rollie's Favorite'PBR	EBee EGren EMor EPfP LBar LRHS MHol Midl MNrw MPri MPro NSti SHar SPoG WCAu
- 'Rosea Plena' (d)	MHer
- 'Rubra Plena'	see *S. dioica* 'Flore Pleno'
- 'Thelma Kay' (d/v)	NGdn
- 'Valley High' (v)	LBar LSou WCot
§ *fimbriata*	CAby CCBP CSpe CTtf EBee ECha ELan EPPr ERCP MMrt MNrw NLar NSti SBeP SDix SMrm WCAu WCot WFar WKif WTre
flos-cuculi	Widely available
- 'Albiflora'	CoPl WHer WTre
- JENNY ('Lychjen') (d)	EBee EGrI EMor EPfP LCro LEdu LRHS LSRN MBNS Midl MNrw SRkn WCAu WCot
- 'Nana'	NGdn NLar
- PETIT HENRI ('Iflyph')	LEdu LRHS MAsh MBNS MHol Midl MPri MPro NLar NSti NWbg SOrN WCot WNPC WPnP WTor
- 'Petite Jenny' (d)	EBee ELan EPfP LRHS MBNS MHol Midl MPri MPro NLar NWbg SOrN SPoG SRms WCot WNPC WTor
- 'White Robin'	Widely available
flos-jovis ♀H6	MWlw NBir SRms WFar WHil
- 'Hort's Variety'	EBee NBir
- 'Peggy'	ECha GEdr NGdn NLar
frivaldskyana	SDix
'Frivola Rose'	EWes LRHS MHol
hookeri	SPlb
- Ingramii Group	WAbe
'Jiggy Pink'	MPro
kantzeensis	see *S. davidii*
keiskei var. *minor*	WAbe
laciniata 'Starburst'	CSpe SPhx
latifolia	CGwi CHab EHet GJos LCro MAsh MCtn MHer MNHC NMir SMHy GJem SPhx
§ - subsp. *alba*	GJem SPhx
maritima	see *S. uniflora*
multifida	see *S. fimbriata*
multiflora	EPPr
nigrescens	EDAr GGro
noctiflora	CHab CoPl MNHC
nutans	GAbr MCtn NAts SRms
pusilla	see *Heliosperma pusillum*
quadridentata	see *Heliosperma alpestre*
regia	CSpe CTtf SBrt SPhx WHil
rubra	see *S. dioica*
rupestris	see *Atocion rupestre*
§ *samojedorum*	GKev MWlw NClf NSti SPhx
schafta ♀H5	EBee EGrI EPfP GJos LRHS MAsh MPie NBid SRms
- 'Shell Pink'	ECha EPfP EPot EWes GJos LRHS MMuc NBid SEND WAbe WHoo
SPARKLING ROSE	see *S. noctiflora* × *Viscaria asterias*, SPARKLING ROSE ('Insilsparo')
suksdorfii	EPot
tatarica	EBee GGro GJos GKev
§ *uniflora*	CHab EPfP GJos LCro LRHS LShi MMuc MNHC NAts NBro SHar SPlb SRms StAn WOrg

Sisyrinchium

- 'Alba Plena'	see *S. uniflora* 'Robin Whitebreast'
§ - 'Druett's Variegated' (v)	ECha ELan EPot EWes GMaP MAsh SPlb SPoG SRms SRot WIce
- 'Flore Pleno'	see *S. uniflora* 'Robin Whitebreast'
§ - 'Robin Whitebreast' (d)	ECha GMaP NBid NBro SRms
- Rosea'	GJos LRHS MHol MMuc NBir SPlb SRot
- 'Variegata'	see *S. uniflora* 'Druett's Variegated'
- WEISSKEHLCHEN	see *S. uniflora* 'Robin Whitebreast'
- 'White Bells'	WKif
viscaria	see *Viscaria vulgaris*
§ *vulgaris*	CAgr CBWd CCBP CGwi CHab GJos LShi MCtn MMuc MNHC NBac NMir SPhx SRms WHer
- subsp. *maritima*	see *S. uniflora*
- subsp. *vulgaris*	MCtn
wallichiana	see *S. vulgaris*
wilfordii	GKev WHil
- 'Karafuto'	EDAr
yunnanensis	GAbr GGro SPhx
zawadskii	EPfP GGro GJos GKev SBrt SDix

Silene × Viscaria (Caryophyllaceae)

§ *S. noctiflora × V. asterias*, LRHS MHol Midl SPARKLING ROSE ('Insilsparo')

Siler (Apiaceae)

montanum	see *Laserpitium siler*

Silphium (Asteraceae)

integrifolium	SPhx WCot
laciniatum	CAgr CMac CSpe EBee LEdu LShi SBrt SMad SPhx
mohrii	CSpe ECha EDAr MCtn MPro NCth NDov SDix SHar SMHy SPhx
perfoliatum ♀H7	EBee GQue LEdu MMuc NDov NLar SDix SMrm SPhx WCot WHrl
- var. *connatum*	SPhx
- JS MAYA ('Maya')	EBee ECha LBar SHar WCot
simpsonii	SBrt
terebinthinaceum	CSpe SBrt SPhx WCot
trifoliatum	EPPr SPhx WCot
wasiotense	CSpe ECha WCot

Silybum (Asteraceae)

marianum	CCBP EHet ELan MCtn MHoo MNHC NBir SRms

Sinacalia (Asteraceae)

§ *tangutica*	ECha GQue NBid NLar NSti SDix WCot

Sinapis (Brassicaceae)

alba	MCtn

Sinarundinaria (Poaceae)

anceps	see *Yushania anceps*
jaunsarensis	see *Yushania anceps*
murielae	see *Fargesia murielae*
nitida	see *Fargesia nitida*

Sinningia (Gesneriaceae)

bullata	WDib
calcaria	WDib
canescens ♀H1a	WDib
cardinalis	WDib
conspicua	WDib
iarae	WDib
leucotricha	CSpe
nivalis	WDib

speciosa 'Corina'	LCro
- 'Hollywood'	LCro
- 'Kaiser Friedrich'	XFar
- 'Kaiser Wilhelm'	XFar
- 'Mont Blanc'	XFar
- 'Violacea'	LCro
tubiflora	CBct CBro ESgI EShb ESwi SBrt WCot WFar

Sinocalycanthus see Calycanthus

Sinocrassula (Crassulaceae)

§ *yunnanensis*	CDoC EUrb LWaG SPlb

Sinofranchetia (Lardizabalaceae)

chinensis	WJur WPGP

Sinojackia ✿ (Styracaceae)

xylocarpa	CBcs CMCN LCro WJur WSpi

Sinopodophyllum (Berberidaceae)

§ *hexandrum*	EBee ELan ENun EPot EWld GGro GKev GMaP LAma MNrw NBid NBir NLar SMrm SPlb WFar WKor WPnP
- from Kangding, Mugecuo Lake, Sichuan, China	SBrt
§ - var. *chinense*	GEdr LEdu
- - BO 16109	GEdr
- - BWJ 7908	WCru
- - SDR 4409	CExl
- 'Chinese White'	CExl
- var. *emodi* 'Majus'	CMiW

Sinowilsonia (Hamamelidaceae)

henryi	WJur

Siphocranion (Lamiaceae)

§ *macranthum*	EBee EWes WPGP

Sisyrinchium (Iridaceae)

× *anceps*	see *S. angustifolium*
§ *angustifolium*	EGren EGrI ESgI GKev NBir SPlb SRms WCav
- f. *album*	ECha MPro NLar
- 'Lucerne'	LBar
§ *arenarium*	CWCL EDAr GArf
bellum hort.	see *S. idahoense* var. *bellum*
bermudiana	see *S. angustifolium*
'Biscutella'	CKno CoPl EPfP ESgI GKev GMaP LBar LEdu SPlb SRot WCav WChS WFar WHoo
'Blue Eyed Boy' **new**	EDAr
'Blue Ice'	NLar WAbe
'Blue Skies'	WCav
boreale	see *S. californicum*
brachypus	see *S. californicum* Brachypus Group
'Californian Skies'	CElw CExl CKno CLil CoPl EBee ECha GMaP LRHS NBir NDov SMrm SRms WIce
§ *californicum*	CBen CDoC CLil CWat EBee ESgI GQue
§ - Brachypus Group	EAri EPfP NBir SLee SPlb
* - 'Variegatum' (v)	CoPl
- 'Yellowstone'	LBar SRms
* *capsicum*	CExl
convolutum	NDov
- B&SWJ 9117	WCru
cuspidatum	see *S. arenarium*
'Deep Seas'	EDAr

Sisyrinchium

depauperatum	EDAr
'Devon Skies'	ESgI GArf LBar MHer MNrw NLar SRms WAbe
douglasii	see *Olsynium douglasii*
'Dragon's Eye'	CAby CoPl EDAr EPot ESgI GKev MBrN MHer MNrw SRot WAbe WFar WIce
'E.K. Balls'	CoPl EBee EDAr EPot ESgI GAbr GMaP LCro LRHS LShi MAsh SLee SPoG SRms SRot WAbe WChS WIce
grandiflorum	see *Olsynium douglasii*
'Iceberg'	ECha EWes LBar MMrt
'Icicle' **new**	EDAr
idahoense	GKev NDov SPlb SRms
§ - var. *bellum*	EPfP SRms
- - pale-flowered	SMHy
- - 'Rocky Point'	CoPl EPfP EWes SPoG WFar
- var. *macounii*	ELan GPSL SPlb
§ - - 'Album' ♀H4	CElw EWes MBel WAbe WFar WIce
- - 'Moody Blues'	ECha EPot ESgI MPro SLee SMrm StAn
'Janet Denman' (v)	ECha EDAr ESgI EWes LSto SBeP SRot WFar
junceum	see *Olsynium junceum*
littorale	CExl
'Louis'	EDAr MNrw
macrocarpon misapplied	see *S. macrocarpum*
§ *macrocarpum*	EDAr EWld
'Marchants Seedling'	SMHy
'Marion'	MBrN SRot
'May Snow'	see *S. idahoense* var. *macounii* 'Album'
narcissiflorum	GArf
'North Star'	see *S.* 'Pole Star'
nudicaule	GAbr
palmifolium	CSpe EAri EPPr LEdu MHer MNrw SBeP SMad WFar
patagonicum	CExl GKev
§ 'Pole Star'	GKev NLar
'Purple Dream' **new**	EDAr
'Quaint and Queer'	CExl ECha ESgI MBrN MNrw NBir SAng SHor
'Raspberry'	ECha ESgI WFar
'Rufus' **new**	EDAr
'Sapphire'	CAby CKno EDAr ELan LBar MHol MNrw MPro NLar SPoG
§ *striatum*	Widely available
§ - 'Aunt May' (v)	CLil CMac ECha EPfP EWoo GMaP MArl SMrm SPoG SRms WCAu WCot
- 'Variegatum'	see *S. striatum* 'Aunt May'
aff. *unispathaceum* B&SWJ 10683	WCru

Sium (Apiaceae)

sisarum	CGwi ECha LEdu MCtn MEar NBac SDix SHor SPhx WKor

Skimmia ✿ (Rutaceae)

anquetilia	CMac
- (f)	WCru
- (m)	WCru
arborescens B&SWJ 11799	WCru
- B&SWJ 13902	WCru
- PAB 8774	LEdu
- subsp. *nitida* B&SWJ 8239	WCru
arisanensis B&SWJ 7114	WCru
- CWJ 12187	WCru
black-fruited B&SWJ 8259 from northern Vietnam (f/m)	WCru
× *confusa* 'Kew Green' (m) ♀H5	Widely available
'Daddy's Dream'	SOrN
japonica	CDoC CMac CoPl EGrI EHeP MGos SSta WFar WJur
- (f)	CMac SRms
- B&SWJ 5053 (f)	WCru
- B&SWJ 5053 (m)	WCru
- 'Alba' (f)	see *S. japonica* 'Wakehurst White'
- 'Attraction' (m)	MGos
- 'Bowles's Dwarf Female' (f)	CEnd
- 'Bowles's Dwarf Male' (m)	MPri
- 'Bronze Knight' (m)	CMac LRHS MPri NLar SRms
- 'Carberry' (f)	CMac
- 'Chameleon' (f)	EHeP
- 'Dad's Red Dragon' (f)	CDoC CMac LRHS MPri SRms
- DELIGHT ('Delibolwi' PBR) (Gold Series) (m)	CDoC
- 'Emerald King' (m)	LRHS MPri
- 'Finchy' PBR (m)	EPfP LBom LRHS MAsh NLar
- 'Foremanii' (f)	see *S. japonica* 'Veitchii'
§ - 'Fragrans' (m) ♀H5	CDoC CMac CSBt EGren EPfP LBom LCro LRHS LSRN MAsh MPri NLar SOrN SPoG SRms WCha WFar
- 'Fragrant Cloud' (m)	see *S. japonica* 'Fragrans'
- 'Fructu-albo' (f)	IDun LRHS MPri
- 'Godrie's Dwarf' (m)	MAsh MPri NLar WFar
- 'Humpty Dumpty' (f)	WFar
- var. *intermedia*	see *S. japonica* subsp. *japonica* var. *intermedia*
- - var. *intermedia* f. *repens* B&SWJ 5560	WCru
- - - B&SWJ 11165	WCru
- 'Kew White' (f)	CBcs CBrac CDoC CoPl ELan ELon EPfP IArd LCro LRHS MAsh MPri SSta WMal
- LUWIAN ('Wanto') (m)	LRHS
- 'Macpenny Dwarf' (m)	CMac SRms
- 'Magic Marlot' PBR (m/v)	ELan LCro LRHS MAsh MGos SPoG
- 'Marlot' (m)	CDoC ELan EPfP LRHS MAsh NLar SPoG
- 'Mystic Marlot' PBR (m)	ELan EPfP LRHS MAsh WCha
- 'Nymans' (f) ♀H5	CDoC CEnd EBee ELan EPfP LCro LRHS MAsh MGos MPri SEND SPoG SRms
- OBSESSION ('Obsbolwi' PBR) (m/f)	LCro LRHS LSRN MAsh
- 'Olympic Flame' (f)	CDoC IArd MAsh MBlu SPoG
- 'Pabella' PBR (f)	CDoC ELan LBom MAsh MPri SOrN SPoG WFar
- 'Perosa' PBR (m)	EPfP LCro LRHS
- 'Pigmy' (f)	CExl
- PINK DWARF ('Moerings 47' PBR) (f)	CDoC LCro LRHS
- RED DWARF ('Moerings 2' PBR) (m)	LCro LRHS
- 'Red Princess' (f)	CDoC LRHS MAsh
- 'Red Riding Hood' (f)	LCro MAsh NCth NLar WCot
- 'Redruth' (f)	CBcs CMac CSBt LCro LRHS MAsh SEND
§ - subsp. *reevesiana*	CBrac CMac CSBt EGrI ELan EPfP LBom LCro LRHS MGos SEND SOrN SPoG SRms WJur
- - B&SWJ 3763	MAsh WCru
- - 'Chilan Choice' (m/f)	WPGP
- - var. *reevesiana* B&SWJ 3544	WCru
- Rogersii Group	CMac
§ - - 'George Gardner' (m)	LRHS
- - 'Rogersii' (f)	CMac

- - 'Snow Dwarf' (m)	LRHS MPri
- 'Rubella' (m) ♀H5	Widely available
- Rubesta ('Moerings 3'PBR) (m)	CDoC LRHS NLar WCha
- Rubesta Jos ('Moerings 45'PBR)	EGren
- Rubesta Optima ('Moeropti'PBR) (m)	NLar
- 'Rubinetta' (m)	IArd LRHS MAsh
- 'Ruby Dome' (m)	CDoC LRHS MPri
- 'Ruby King' (m)	LSRN NLar
- 'Scarlet Dwarf' (f)	LRHS MPri
- 'Silvretta'	EGren
- 'Tansley Gem' (f)	MAsh SPoG
- 'Temptation'PBR (m/f)	CDoC EPfP LCro WCha
§ - 'Veitchii' (f)	CBcs CBrac CDoC CMac CSBt EHeP EPfP IDun LRHS LSRN MPri SEND SPoG SRms
§ - 'Wakehurst White' (f)	CMac CSBt SPoG SRms
- 'White Bella' (m)	LRHS
- White Dwarf ('Moerings 1'PBR) (m)	LCro
- White Globe ('Fm1'PBR) (m)	EGren EPfP LRHS
- 'Winifred Crook' (f)	LRHS
- 'Winnie's Dwarf' (f)	LRHS MAsh
laureola	SRms WJur
- GWJ 9364	WCru
- 'Kew Green'	EGrI
- subsp. laureola HWJK 2095	WCru
- subsp. multinervia GWJ 9374	WCru
reevesiana	see S. japonica subsp. reevesiana
rogersii	see S. japonica Rogersii Group

Smallanthus (Asteraceae)

sonchifolius	CWRo EAri LWaG MEar WKor
- 'Morado'	WPGP
uvedalius	SBrt

Smilacina see Maianthemum

Smilax (Smilacaceae)

B&SWJ 6628 from Thailand	WCru
aspera	CMac EShb ESwi LEdu WCru WJur WPGP
china B&SWJ 4427	WCru
discotis	SEND
glaucophylla B&SWJ 2971	WCru
nipponica B&SWJ 4331	WCru
rotundifolia	LEdu
sieboldii	LEdu
- B&SWJ 744	WCru
- B&SWJ 12814	ESwi

Smithiantha (Gesneriaceae)

'Extra Sassy'	EShb

Smyrnium (Apiaceae)

olusatrum	CCBP CGwi CHab CSpe CWRo LEdu MEar SRms WHer WKit WKor
- Cretan giant	LEdu WPGP
P perfoliatum	CDor CSpe CTtf EBee ECha ELan EPfP EWes LCro LEdu MCtn NAts NBir SDix SMrm SPhx WCot
rotundifolium	WCot
- PAB 6174	LEdu WPGP

Solandra (Solanaceae)

grandiflora misapplied	see S. maxima
hartwegii	see S. maxima
§ maxima	EAri

Solanum (Solanaceae)

abutiloides	CAgr
aerial-rooting climbing species B&SWJ 14398	WCru
atropurpureum	CDTJ EAri SPlb WCot
betaceum (F) ♀H1b	CCht CDTJ CWal MCtn SPlb SVic WJur
- 'Oratia Red' (F)	WCot
- yellow-fruited (F)	SPlb
burchellii	SPlb
capsicastrum	see S. pseudocapsicum
chrysotrichum new	EAri
conchifolium hort.	see S. linearifolium
corymbiflora	EAri EBee
crispum 'Autumnale'	see S. crispum 'Glasnevin'
§ - 'Glasnevin' ♀H4	Widely available
dulcamara	MNHC
- 'Variegatum' (v)	EBee MAsh
jasminoides	see S. laxum
laciniatum	CDTJ CExl EShb NSti SArc SBeP SBig SEND SPlb SVen WJur
§ laxum	CMac EBee LBom LCro LRHS SEND SNig SRms
- 'Album' ♀H4	CBcs CDoC CMac CRHN CSBt CSpe CWnw EBee ELan EPfP LBom LCro LRHS LSRN MAsh MGos MPri SDix SEND SHor SNig SPlb SPoG SRms WFar WHtc WTHo
- 'Album Variegatum' (v)	WTHo
* - 'Aureovariegatum' (v)	CMac EBee SPlb
- 'Coldham'	EPPr MNrw SDix SMad
- 'Crèche du Pape'	ECha SHor SRms
§ linearifolium	CSpe WPGP
lycopersicum	LWaG MBros SVic WKit
* - var. grandifolium	EAri
marginatum	SPlb
muricatum (F)	CoPl SPlb
- 'Pepino Gold' (F)	EShb
pimpinellifolium	MNHC
- 'Gold Rush Currant'	SVic
- 'Sweet Pea Currant'	SVic
§ pseudocapsicum ♀H2	MPri SPlb
- 'Thurino'	LSou SPoG
- variegated (v)	WCot
pyracanthon ♀H2	CDTJ CTtf EAri ESwi MCtn SArc SPlb WCot
quitoense (F) ♀H1c	CDTJ SPlb
rantonnetii	see Lycianthes rantonnetii
sisymbriifolium	MCtn SPlb
aff. stenophyllum B&SWJ 10744	WCru
tuberosum	SVic
villosum	SVen
wendlandii	CHll

Soldanella (Primulaceae)

alpina	CTsd GKev NLar SRms WAbe
I - 'Alba'	WAbe
carpatica	CTtf EDAr EPot GEdr GKev LEdu SPlb WAbe WPGP
- 'Alba'	LEdu
cyanaster	CTtf LEdu NQui
dimoniei	CTtf GArf GKev LEdu WFar
minima	GEdr GJos GKev LEdu
montana	CTtf EDAr EWes GJos LEdu NLar
pindicola	GEdr LEdu
'Spring Symphony'	GArf GEdr GKev GMaP MNrw NBro NHar SPoG WAbe WFar WPnP

'Sudden Spring'	WAbe
villosa ♀H6	CTtf GAbr GEdr GKev GPSL LEdu NHar WCot

Soleirolia (Urticaceae)
soleirolii	CDoC CoPl CWal EBee EGren ELan EPot EUrb GQue LCro LSto LWaG MPri SEND SVic WFar WJun
- 'Argentea'	see *S. soleirolii* 'Variegata'
§ - 'Aurea'	CoPl ELan EPot LWaG NBid SIvy SVic
- 'Golden Queen'	see *S. soleirolii* 'Aurea'
- 'Minty'	LWaG
- 'Silver Queen'	see *S. soleirolii* 'Variegata'
§ - 'Variegata' (v)	CoPl ELan SVic

Solenopsis (Campanulaceae)
axillaris	see *Isotoma axillaris*

Solenostemon see *Coleus*

Solidago (Asteraceae)
'Autumn Blaze'	WFar
BABYGOLD	see *S.* 'Goldkind'
'Ballardii'	SRms
brachystachys	see *S. cutleri*
caesia	CTtf EBee NBir SAko WFar WOld
- 'Maryland'	SHar
canadensis	SPlb WFar WHer WOld
- var. ***scabra***	MMuc
'Citronella'	GQue
'Cloth of Gold'	CMac EHeP EPfP SPoG WOld
§ 'Crown of Rays'	EBlo ELan GBin LRHS SAko WFar
§ ***cutleri***	EDAr NLar SPlb SRms WFar
I ***nana***	SLee
'Dennis Strange'	MAvo MHol MWlw NDov WCot
'Ducky'	LBar
'Early Bird'	WFar
'Featherbush'	EBlo LRHS
flabelliformis	WCot
§ ***flexicaulis***	GMaP SAko WCot
- 'Variegata' (v)	EBee GMaP NLar NSti NWbg WFar
'Foxbrook Fountain'	EPPr MAvo
'Foxbrook Gold'	ECha MAvo MHol MWlw WFar
'Gardone' ♀H7	WFar
gigantea	WFar
glomerata	MMuc NLar SMrm
GOLDEN BABY	see *S.* 'Goldkind'
§ 'Golden Dwarf'	LRHS NLar SPoG SRms
'Golden Fleece'	see *S. sphacelata* 'Golden Fleece'
'Golden Thumb'	see *S.* 'Queenie'
'Goldenmosa' ♀H7	CMac GMaP LBar NLar WCAu WFar
'Goldilocks'	SRms
§ 'Goldkind'	CAgr CWal EBee EGren ELan GAbr LCro LRHS MAsh MCtn MMuc SRms WFar
GOLDZWERG	see *S.* 'Golden Dwarf'
'Hiddigeigei' (v)	WCot WFar WMal
hybrida	see *S.* × *luteus*
latifolia	see *S. flexicaulis*
'Laurin'	EGren NLar
'Ledsham'	GBin MArl SPhx SPoG
'Lena'	SRms
'Linner Gold'	SAko
'Little Lemon'PBR	CMHG EBee NEoE
§ × ***luteus***	EBee SRms WFar
- 'Lemore' ♀H7	CDor CMiW CTtf EBee EPPr GMaP LSou NSti SAko SBeP SPhx SPoG SRms WCot WFar WOld
ohioensis	NLar
§ 'Queenie'	MHer

rigida	SMrm
- subsp. ***humilis***	EPPr
- - 'Golden Rockets'	LRHS SPhx
rugosa	ECha MMuc MWlw WBrk WCot
- 'Fireworks' ♀H7	Widely available
- 'Loydser Crown'	CSpe ECha ELon ESwi MAvo NClf NDov NSti SAko SMHy SPhx WCot
sempervirens	WFar WHrl WOld
- 'Goldene Wellen'	SAko
shortii 'Solar Cascade'	LBar SAko
speciosa	GQue SPhx WCot
spectabilis var. ***confinis***	EBee
§ ***sphacelata*** 'Golden Fleece'	CBcs ELan EPfP LBar LRHS SRms
STRAHLENKRONE	see *S.* 'Crown of Rays'
'Super'	WCot
SWEETY ('Barseven'PBR)	LRHS
'Tom Thumb'	NBir SRms
uliginosa	NLar
ulmifolia	EBee
virgaurea	CGHo MHer MNHC NAts NLar SRms WHer
- var. ***cambrica***	see *S. virgaurea* subsp. *minuta*
- subsp. ***leiocarpa***	WFar
- subsp. ***minuta***	GArf GEdr
'Yellow Stone'	EBee ELan

× *Solidaster* see *Solidago*
hybridus	see *Solidago* × *luteus*

Sollya see *Billardiera*

Sonchus (Asteraceae)
acaulis	CTsd SPlb
arboreus	CTsd SIvy SPlb
§ ***brassicifolius***	CTsd EAri EUrb SPlb
canariensis	EAri
congestus	CTsd
fruticosus	EAri SIvy SPlb
gomerensis	SPlb

Sophora (Fabaceae)
cassioides	EUrb WJur
- NJM 8.008	WPGP
§ ***davidii***	CBcs CExl ELan ELon EPfP ESwi LEdu MBlu SPoG WCot WJur
howinsula	WCot
japonica	see *Styphnolobium japonicum*
§ 'Little Baby'	CDoC ELan EPfP EUrb LRHS MGos SArc SDix SIvy SPoG
longicarinata	WPGP
macrocarpa	CTsd EPfP
microphylla	WJur
molloyi 'Dragon's Gold'	CBcs ELan ELon EPfP EUrb LRHS SEND SPoG WCot
prostrata misapplied	see *S.* 'Little Baby'
prostrata Buchanan	WJur
SUN KING ('Hilsop') ♀H4	CBcs CDoC CWGN EAri ELan EPfP EUrb EWes LCro LMaj LRHS LSRN MGos MPri NCth SArc SMad SPoG WCot
tetraptera	CBcs SEND WCot WJur WPGP
viciifolia	see *S. davidii*

Sorbaria (Rosaceae)
aitchisonii	see *S. tomentosa* var. *angustifolia*
arborea	see *S. kirilowii*
CRIMSON FEATHERS **new**	WNPC
§ ***kirilowii***	CExl CMac NLar SMad
sorbifolia	CBcs CMCN EHeP MMuc NLit SEND SPlb WFar
- PINK HOPI ('Cousorb05'PBR)	MPri SGol

Sorbus

- 'Sem' PBR ♀H5 — Widely available
§ *tomentosa* — MMuc NBid SEND
  var. *angustifolia* ♀H5

× *Sorbaronia* (Rosaceae)
fallax 'Likjornaja' (F) — LRHS NLar WHtc

× *Sorbopyrus* (Rosaceae)
§ *auricularis* 'Shipova' (F) — CAgr MAsh NOra WMat

Sorbus ✿ (Rosaceae)
alnifolia — CLnd CMCN MBlu WJur
- B&SWJ 8461 — WCru
- B&SWJ 10948 — WCru
- 'Red Bird' — EBee EPfP MBlu NPip
- 'Amber Light' — EBee NLar NPip SOrN WMat
americana — CLnd
- 'Belmonte' — LMaj
amoena — EGrI
'Apricot' — CEnd
'Apricot Lady' — EGren
'Apricot Queen' — CLnd EBee EPom LCro SGol WFar
aria — CBTr CCVT CHab CLnd EHeP IPap LBuc LCot MGos MMuc SEND SGol WKor WMou WRjT
- 'Aurea' — CLnd EHeP
- 'Decaisneana' — see *S. aria* 'Majestica'
- 'Lutescens' ♀H6 — Widely available
- 'Magnifica' — CLnd EBar ELan SEWo
§ - 'Majestica' ♀H6 — CCVT CLnd CMac EBar EBee EHeP LMaj NPip WFar WHtc
- 'Mitchellii' — see *S.* 'John Mitchell'
aria × *pseudovilmorinii* — EBee
arnoldiana 'Golden Wonder' — see *S.* 'Lombarts Golden Wonder'
aronioides misapplied — see *S. caloneura*
§ *aucuparia* — CBcs CBrac CBTr CCVT CHab CLnd CMac CNWT EHeP ELan EPfP EPom IPap LBuc LCro LMaj LRHS MAsh MGos MPri MSwo NLar NTrD SEWo SPoG WFar WKor WMat WMou
- 'Aspleniifolia' — CCVT CMac CMCN EBar EBee EHeP EPom IPap LCro LMaj LRHS MGos MPri NLar NPip WFar WHtc WMat WMou
- subsp. *aucuparia* — CDoC EGren LCot LSto MLod MMuc MNHC NPip WHtc WRjT
§ - 'Beissneri' — CAgr EHeP LCro NLar NPip WHtc
- CARDINAL ROYAL ('Michred') — CCVT CDoC CLnd EBar EGren EHeP IPap LCro LRHS MMuc MPri SEWo WFar WHtc
- 'Dirkenii' — WMat
§ - var. *edulis* (F) — CWnw EBar EHeP LBuc
- - 'Rossica' misapplied — see *S. aucuparia* var. *edulis* 'Rossica Major'
§ - - 'Rossica Major' — CCVT EBar EHeP MMuc SEWo
§ - 'Fastigiata' — CEnd GKin
- 'Fingerprint' PBR — CBTr EBee NLar NOra NPip
- subsp. *maderensis* — MBlu
- *pluripinnata* — see *S. scalaris* Koehne
- var. *rossica* Koehne — see *S. aucuparia* var. *edulis*
- 'Sheerwater Seedling' ♀H6 — CBcs CCVT CDoC CMCN CWnw EBar EBee EGren EHeP ELan EPfP EPom GKin IPap LCro LMaj MGos MPri NPip SGol WFar WHtc
- AUTUMN SPIRE ('Flanrock') ♀H6 — CBcs CDoC CEnd CWnw EBee EGren ELan EPfP EUrb GKin IPap LBom LCro LRHS LSRN MAsh MGos SAth SEWo SGol SOrN SPoG WHtc WMat WMou

§ *bissetii* — CBTr EBee LCro NOra NPip
- Yu 14299 — WCru
- PEARLS — see *S. bissetii*
brevipetiolata B&SWJ 11771 — WCru
bristoliensis — CCVT
bulleyana — WJur
- KR 2809 — WCru
- MF 96170 — GKev
§ *caloneura* — CBcs EBee MBlu WJur WPGP
- Guiz 80 — WCru
§ *carmesina* — CBTr LCro LSto NLar NOra NPip WJur WMat
- B&L 12545 — GKev WCru
- 'Emberglow' — see *S. carmesina*
cashmiriana misapplied pink-fruited — see *S. rosea*
cashmiriana Hedl. ♀H6 — CBcs CLnd CMac EGren ELan EPfP EPom GKev IPap LCro LRHS MBlu NLar NPip SGol SPoG WMat
aff. *cashmiriana* ambig. — EGren EHeP EUrb LCro MAsh MPri NOra WFar
chamaemespilus — GKev
'Chinese Lace' — CBcs CBTr CMac CMCN EBee EGren EHeP ELan EPom EUrb GKin LCro LRHS LSRN MBlu MGos MPri NPip SGol WFar WHtc WMat
§ *commixta* — CEnd CLnd CMCN CWnw EGren EHeP LCro LMaj LRHS MBlu MGos SAth SGol WJur
- B&SWJ 11043 — WCru
- 'Carmencita' — CMCN MBlu
- 'Embley' ♀H6 — CBcs CLnd CMCN EHeP LCot LCro LRHS MBlu MGos MMuc MPri NLar NPip SAth SEND WFar
- OLYMPIC FLAME — see *S. ulleungensis* 'Olympic Flame'
- 'Ravensbill' — EBee EPfP MAsh NLar NOra NPip SGol WMat
- var. *rufoferruginea* B&SWJ 11486 — WCru
- - prostrate — WCru
conradinae Koehne — see *S. esserteauana*
'Copper Kettle' ♀H6 — CBcs EBee ELan EPfP EPom LCro LRHS MBlu MPri NLar NPip SGol WMat WMou
'Coral Beauty' — CLnd
corymbifera WWJ 11860 — WCru
'Covert Gold' — CEnd
'Croft Coral' — EBee LCro MAsh NLar NPip WHtc
cuspidata — see *S. vestita*
decora var. *nana* — see *S. aucuparia* 'Fastigiata'
devoniensis — CAda WJur
- 'Devon Beauty' — CAgr
discolor misapplied — see *S. commixta*
discolor (Maxim.) Maxim. — CBTr EBee EGren EPom GKev IPap LCro MBlu NPip
- MF 96172 — MAsh
- MF 97103 — WCru
domestica — CLnd ELan MMuc WJur WPGP
- 'Maliformis' — see *S. domestica* f. *pomifera*
§ - f. *pomifera* — LEdu WPGP
- 'Rosie' — CAgr
dumosa — LRHS
dunnii — EBee WPGP
'Eastern Promise' ♀H6 — CBTr CCVT CTsd EBee EGren EPfP EPom LCro LRHS MAsh MBlu MLod MPri NLar NPip WHtc WMat WMou
§ *eburnea* — GKev
- Harry Smit 12799 — NHar WPGP
eleonorae — EBee MBlu WPGP
§ *esserteauana* — CLnd

Sorbus

'Ethel's Gold' — MBlu
'Fastigiata' — see *S. aucuparia* 'Fastigiata', *S.* × *thuringiaca* 'Fastigiata'
folgneri — CMCN WJur
- 'Emiel' ♀H6 — CBcs CBTr EPfP IArd LRHS MBlu NOra NPip WMat
- 'Lemon Drop' — CEnd CLnd MBlu NOra WMat
foliolosa — CLnd
forrestii ♀H6 — EBee ELan GKev MMuc
§ *frutescens* ♀H5 — ELan GKev
fruticosa 'Koehneana' — see *S. koehneana* C.K. Schneid.
'Ghose' — CBTr LCot NPip WMat
§ *glabriuscula* — GKev WJur
'Glendoick Spire' — EBee ELan LCro LRHS NPip WMat
'Glendoick White Baby' — ELan NPip WMat
globosa HWJ 537 — WCru
'Golden Wonder' — see *S.* 'Lombarts Golden Wonder'
gonggashanica — EPfP WPGP
§ *graeca* — GKev WCot
'Granatnaja' — see × *Crataegosorbus* 'Granatnaja'
granulosa HWJ 1041 — WCru
harrowiana — CBcs EBee WMat WPGP
- KW 21009 — WPGP
- from Burma — WPGP
- from Yunnan — WPGP
- pink-berried — WPGP
Harry Smith — LRHS
hedlundii — CExl EBee EPfP NLar NOra NPip WMat WPGP
- GWJ 9363 — WCru WPGP
- KR 1687 — WPGP
- KR 1810 — WPGP
- WJC 13806 — WCru
helenae — EBee NOra NPip WPGP
- EN 3088 — GKev WPGP
hemsleyi — CExl CLnd EBee WPGP
- 'John Bond' ♀H6 — LRHS NLar NOra NPip WMat
henryi — WFar
× *hostii* — CLnd
hugh-mcallisteri CLD 310 — GKev
hupehensis misapplied — see *S. pseudohupehensis*
- 'Rosea' — see *S. pseudohupehensis*
- 'November Pink' — see *S. pseudohupehensis*
- white-berried — see *S. glabriuscula*
aff. *hupehensis* — EGren EHeP NOra NPip SGol WFar
hybrida L. 'Gibbsii' ♀H6 — LRHS MNHC NOra NPip WMat
incana — LMaj
insignis NPT 148 — WPGP
- from Arunachal Pradesh, India — WPGP
- from Nepal — WPGP
intermedia — CAco CBcs CBTr CCVT CLnd CNWT EHeP IPap LMaj MMuc SEND SGol WRjT
- 'Brouwers' — CLnd EBar EHeP LMaj WMou
japonica — NOra NPip WMat
- B&SWJ 10813 — WCru
§ 'John Mitchell' ♀H6 — CAgr CEnd CLnd CMCN EBee EHeP EPfP LRHS MBlu MGos NLar NPip SPoG WMat
'Joseph Rock' — Widely available
aff. *karchungii* — EBee
- AGS/ES 347 — WPGP
I *keenanii* NJM 13.05 — WPGP
keissleri — EBee
- PAB 7916 — LEdu
'Keith Rushforth' — WCru
§ × *kewensis* — CLnd SPlb
khumbuensis — GKev
'Kirsten Pink' — CLnd EHeP
koehneana misapplied — see *S. frutescens*

§ *koehneana* C.K. Schneid. — CLnd GKev MMrt WCru
aff. *koehneana* C.K. Schneid. — see *S. eburnea*, *S. tenuis*
lanata misapplied — see *S. vestita*
latifolia 'Henk Vink' — EBar
'Leonard Messel' ♀H6 — CBTr CMac LRHS MAsh NPip WMat
§ 'Lombarts Golden Wonder' — CLnd EBar EHeP LMaj NLar
* *maculata* KR 5334 — GKev
* 'Maiden's Blush' — LRHS
matsumurana misapplied — see *S. commixta*
matsumurana (Makino) Koehne — WPGP
'Matthew Ridley' — CBTr EBee ELan LRHS NLar NPip
megalocarpa — CMCN EBee WJur WPGP
- var. *cuneata* — EBee WJur WPGP
meliosmifolia — WJur
microphylla agg. — GKev
- GWJ 9252 — WCru
monbeigii (Cardot.) N.P. Balakr. — CLnd
moravica 'Laciniata' — see *S. aucuparia* 'Beissneri'
muliensis F 22177 — GKev
munda — MMuc
needhamii NJM 11.005 — EBee WPGP
'Nevezhinskaja' — MBlu
olivacea — ELan GKev
pallescens 'White House Farm' — WPGP
paniculata NJM 13.092 — WPGP
parvifructa — WPGP
'Peaches and Cream' — LCro LRHS
'Pearly King' — MAsh
§ 'Pink Pearl' — CBTr EBee EPfP NLar NPip
'Pink-Ness' — CMac EBee EPfP MBlu MLod NLar NPip WMat
pohuashanensis misapplied — see *S.* × *kewensis*
poteriifolia ♀H5 — GEdr GKev NHar
prattii misapplied — see *S. munda*
§ *pseudohupehensis* — Widely available
- 'Pink Pagoda' — see *S. pseudohupehensis*
pseudovilmorinii — CBTr EBee GKev NOra NPip WCru WMat
- SBEC 974 — WPGP
randaiensis — SPlb
- B&SWJ 3202 — WCru
reducta ♀H5 — GAbr GEdr GKev NHar NLar
aff. *reducta* — SRms
reflexipetala misapplied — see *S. commixta*
rehderiana misapplied — see *S. aucuparia*
rehderiana Koehne — GKev
rhamnoides — WJur
'Rose Queen' — MBlu NPip
§ *rosea* ♀H6 — ELan GKev NOra NPip WJur WMat
- SEP 492 — WCru WPGP
- 'Rosiness' — see *S. rosea*
'Rowancroft Coral Pink' — EBee
rubescens — GKev
rushforthii KR 5789 — GKev
rutilans — GKev
'Salmon Queen' — CLnd EHeP
sargentiana ♀H6 — CBcs CBTr CCVT CEnd CLnd CMac CMCN EBee EHeP ELan EPfP LRHS MBlu MPri NLar NOra NPip SPoG WHtc WMat WMou
scalaris ambig. — CBcs CMCN EGren ELan GKev MAsh NOra SPoG
§ *scalaris* Koehne — CBTr CEnd EGren MBlu MPri WJur WMat
'Schouten' — CMCN EHeP
scopulina misapplied — see *S. aucuparia* 'Fastigiata'

Sphaeralcea

section *Discolores* KR 5585 — WCru
- KR 6308 — WCru
setschwanensis — CMCN
'Showa' — CExl EBee WCru WPGP
§ *splendens* — CBTr EBee LCro MNHC WJur
- CH 7122 — CExl WPGP
subulata FMWJ 13252 — WCru
- HWJ 925 — WCru
'Sunshine' — CBTr CCVT CLnd EGren EHeP LMaj MAsh MMuc NPip SGol WFar WHtc
§ *tenuis* — GKev
thibetica — WJur
aff. *thibetica* BWJ 7757a — WCru
thomsonii GWJ 9363 — WCru
- WWJ 12004 — WCru
§ × *thuringiaca* 'Fastigiata' — CLnd EBar EHeP LCro NPip WMat
tianschanica — WCru
'Titan' — MBlu
torminalis — CAgr CBcs CBrac CBTr CCVT CHab CLnd CMac CWRo EBee EHeP ELan EPfP LBuc LCot LMaj LRHS MCtn MGos MMuc SEND SEWo SPoG WJur WKor WMou WSpi
ulleungensis — WPGP
- B&SWJ 8515 — WCru
- B&SWJ 12640 — WCru
- 'Dodong' — CLnd SMad
§ - 'Olympic Flame' ♀H6 — CBTr CCVT CEnd EBee ELan EPfP IArd IPap LBuc LCot LCro LRHS LSRN MAsh MBlu MGos MPri NLar NOra NPip SEWo SPoG WFar WHtc WMat WMou WPGP
umbellata var. *cretica* — see *S. graeca*
§ *vestita* — WCru
vexans — GBin
vilmorinii ♀H6 — CBcs CBTr CDoC CEnd CLnd CMac CMCN EBee ELan EPfP EPom GKev IPap LBuc LCot LCro LRHS LSRN LSto MAsh MBlu MGos MMuc NLar NOra NPip SGol WMat WSpi
- 'Pink Charm' — CBTr EPfP LCro LRHS LSto MAsh NPip SGol WMat
- 'Robusta' — see *S.* 'Pink Pearl'
aff. *vilmorinii* — CWnw EGren EHeP GKin
- KR 6453 — WCru WPGP
wallichii NJM 13.127 — WPGP
wardii — CBcs CBTr EPfP LCro MBlu NPip
- KR 21127 — EBee WPGP
'White Wax' — CMCN EGren EHeP MGos
'White-Ness' — GKev
'Wilfrid Fox' — EHeP
wilsoniana misapplied — see *S. splendens*
wilsoniana C.K. Schneid. — CLnd CMHG EBee NLar WJur
- PW 47 — WPGP
'Wisley Gold' ♀H6 — CBTr EBee LCro LRHS MPri NPip WMat WMou
yuana — WPGP
zahlbruckneri C.K. Schneid. — WPGP

Sorghastrum (Poaceae)
nutans — SMHy
- 'Indian Steel' — ECha

Sorghum (Poaceae)
nigrum — MCtn

sorrel, common see *Rumex acetosa*

sorrel, French see *Rumex scutatus*

soursop see *Annona muricata*

Sparaxis (Iridaceae)
elegans — SPlb
grandiflora — CPbh
  subsp. *acutiloba*
- subsp. *grandiflora* — CPbh
mixed — EGren
tricolor — LAma

Sparganium (Typhaceae)
§ *erectum* — CPud CWat ELin EPfh NMir NPer WMAq
ramosum — see *S. erectum*

Sparrmannia (Malvaceae)
africana ♀H1c — CHll CTsd EArl ELan EShb LWaG SEND SPlb SVen WCot
- 'Flore Pleno' (d) — CBcs

Spartina (Poaceae)
? *pectinata* 'Aureomarginata' — ELan GMaP

Spartium (Fabaceae)
junceum ♀H5 — CBcs CDoC CMac EHeP ELan ELon EPfP LRHS MMrt NSti SArc SEND SRms WJur
- 'Brockhill Compact' — CDoC EPfP LRHS

Spathantheum (Araceae)
orbignyanum — WCot

Spathipappus see *Tanacetum*

Spathiphyllum (Araceae)
Bingo Cupido ('Spapril'PBR) — LBom LCro LWaG MPri
'Chopin' new — LInT
'Cupido' — LBom
Diamond ('Sp7018') (v) — LCro
Largo Cupido ('Spagrodo'PBR) — EGren
'Lima'PBR — NHrt
Sensation ('Gorgusis 1') new — LDro
'Sweet Lauretta' — LCro NHrt NTrD
wallisii — LWaG NHrt SPre
- 'Bellini' — LCro NHrt

Spathodea (Bignoniaceae)
campanulata — SPlb

spearmint see *Mentha spicata*

Speirantha (Asparagaceae)
convallarioides — see *S. gardenii*
§ *gardenii* — CBct CDTJ CExl CMHG CTtf EBee EPfP EPot EPPr ESwi LEdu MHol MMrt WCru WPGP

Spergularia (Caryophyllaceae)
rubra new — GKev

Sphacele see *Lepechinia*

Sphaeralcea (Malvaceae)
ambigua — CSpe SPlb
'Childerley' — CDor CSpe CTtf LBar MHol MPie SBeP SEle SPoG WCot WFar WMal
coccinea — CSpe ESgI SPlb
fendleri — CCoa CSde
incana — CCoa CSde CSpe CTtf LBar WMal
- 'Sourup' — SMHy SPel WCot

Sphaeralcea

munroana	SRkn
'Newleaze Coral'	CCoa CSpe ELon LBar MNrw MPie SBeP SDix SEle SIvy SMad SMHy SPoG SRkn WCot WFar WMal
'Newleaze Pink'	SRkn
remota	CExl SPlb
umbellata	see *Phymosia umbellata*

Sphaeropteris (Cyatheaceae)

§ *cooperi* ♀H3	CAbb CBrP CCht CDTJ CTsd EUrb LRHS LWaG NAlc NPlm SBig
- 'Brentwood'	ELan ISha NAlc
§ *felina*	SBig
§ *medullaris* ♀H3	LWaG MCtn SBig
§ *tomentosissima*	CDTJ ISha NPlm

Sphenomeris (Dennstaedtiaceae)

chinensis B&SWJ 6108	WCru

Spigelia (Loganiaceae)

'Little Redhead'	MMrt XFar
marilandica	WCot

Spilanthes (Asteraceae)

acmella misapplied	see *Acmella oleracea*
oleracea	see *Acmella oleracea*

spinach see AGM Vegetables Section

Spiraea (Rosaceae)

alba var. *latifolia*	MMuc
arborea	see *Sorbaria kirilowii*
§ 'Arguta' ♀H6	CBcs CBrac CCVT CDoC CMac CWnw EBee EGren EHeP ELan EPfP GKin GQue LCro LRHS LSto MAsh MGos MPri MPro NLar SPoG SRms WFar
aff. 'Arguta'	WHtc
× *arguta* 'Bridal Wreath'	see *S.* 'Arguta'
betulifolia	WFar
- var. *aemiliana*	MMuc
- 'Tor'	EPPr GKev NLar
- 'Tor Gold'PBR ♀H6	CBcs ELan EPfP LBuc LRHS MMrt SPoG
blumei CWJ 12829	WCru
× *bumalda* 'Wulfenii'	see *S. japonica* 'Walluf'
canescens	CExl GKin
× *cinerea* 'Grefsheim' ♀H6	CBcs CCVT CSBt EGren EHeP ELan LBuc NLar SAth SPlb
crispifolia misapplied	see *S. japonica* 'Bullata'
decumbens	EPPr
densiflora var. *splendens*	SBrt
DOUBLE PLAY BIG BANG	see *S.* 'Tracy' (Double Play Series)
douglasii	CMac
formosana B&SWJ 1597	CExl WCru
fritschiana	CMac
hayatana	SBrt
- RWJ 10014	WCru
hendersonii	see *Petrophytum hendersonii*
japonica 'Alpina'	see *S. japonica* 'Nana'
- 'Alpine Gold'	NEoE
- 'Anthony Waterer' (v)	CBcs CBrac CBWd CDoC CMac EBee EGren EHeP ELan EPfP GKev LCro LRHS LSto MAsh MGos MSwo NLar SDix SFol SGol SPoG SRGP SRms WFar WHtc
- 'Barkby Gold'	EHeP
§ - 'Bullata'	CMac EBee NLar WAbe
- 'Candlelight'	CSBt ELan GKin LRHS LSou MAsh SGol SPoG
- 'Crispa'	EPfP NEoE WFar
- 'Dart's Red' ♀H6	EHeP GKin
- (Double Play Series) DOUBLE PLAY ARTISAN ('Galen')	LRHS SPoG
- - DOUBLE PLAY GOLD ('Yan')	LRHS SPoG
- - DOUBLE PLAY RED ('Smnsjmfr')	LRHS
- 'Firelight'	CDoC CSBt EBee EGren ELan ELon EPfP GKin LRHS LSou MAsh MGos NCth NLar SGol SNig SOrN SRms
- 'Froebelii'	EBee NLar
§ - 'Genpei'	CMac EGren LCro MMuc NLar SGol SPoG SRms
- 'Gold Mound'	CBrac CMac EBee EGren EHeP ELan EPfP LRHS MAsh MGos NLar SDix SGol SPlb SRms WFar WHtc
- GOLDEN PRINCESS ('Lisp')	CDoC CMac ELan EPfP LBuc LRHS MAsh MGos SGol SOrN SRms WFar
- 'Goldflame'	CBcs CBrac CDoC CMac EGren EHeP ELan EPfP LCro LRHS LSto MGos MHer MMuc MPro MSwo NLar SPlb SPoG SRGP SRms WFar WHtc
- 'Little Princess'	CBcs CDoC CMac EBee EGren EHeP ELan LRHS MAsh MSwo SGol SOrN SRGP SRms WFar WHtc
- MAGIC CARPET ('Walbuma'PBR) (v)	CBcs EGren EPfP LBuc LRHS MAsh MMuc NLar SPoG SRms
- MERLO GREEN ('Davrou01'PBR)	LRHS
§ - 'Nana' ♀H6	MAsh SRms
- 'Nyewoods'	see *S. japonica* 'Nana'
- 'Nyewoods Gold'	CMac
- 'Odensala'	NLar
- 'Odessa'PBR	GKev
- 'Shiburi'	see *S. japonica* 'Shirobana'
- 'Shirobana' misapplied	see *S. japonica* 'Genpei'
§ - 'Shirobana'	CBrac CMac CSBt EHeP ELan EPfP LRHS NLar SRms WFar
- WALBERTON'S PLUMTASTIC ('Walplum'PBR) ♀H6	EPfP LBuc LRHS WNPC
§ - 'Walluf'	CMac GBin
- 'White Cloud'	CDoC
- 'White Gold'PBR	CMac CSBt ELan EPfP LRHS NEoE SPoG SRms WFar
media DOUBLE PLAY BLUE KAZOO ('Smsmbk') (Double Play Series)	LRHS
micrantha	CExl
nipponica 'Halward's Silver'	NEoE NLar
- 'June Bride'	LCro
§ - 'Snowmound' ♀H6	CBcs CBrac CCVT CDoC CMac CSBt EBee EGren EHeP ELan EPfP LCro LRHS MAsh MGos MMuc MPri MPro MSwo NLar SEND SGol SPlb SPoG SRms WFar WHtc
- var. *tosaensis* misapplied	see *S. nipponica* 'Snowmound'
palmata 'Elegans'	see *Filipendula purpurea* 'Elegans'
prunifolia (d)	CMac EPfP LRHS NLar WCFE WFar
- 'Golden Bar' **new**	LRHS
× *pseudosalicifolia* 'Triumphans'	EHeP MMuc
salicifolia	WFar
SPARKLING CHAMPAGNE ('Lonspi'PBR)	CCps CSBt LCro LRHS LSou LSRN MPri NEoE NLar
tarokoensis	CMCN
§ *thunbergii* ♀H6	CBcs CBrac CMac EHeP EPfP MMuc SBrt SDix SRms
- 'Fujino Pink'	EPfP
- 'Golden Times'	SPoG

- 'Mellow Yellow'	see *S. thunbergii* 'Ōgon'		*discolor*	see *Betonica nivea*
- 'Mount Fuji'	CMac WFar		*germanica*	GQue NAts
§ - 'Ōgon'	NLar WFar		*grandiflora*	see *Betonica macrantha*
* - 'Variegata' (v)	SRms		'Hidalgo'	SRms
§ 'Tracy'^{PBR} (Double Play Series) ⚘H6	LRHS MMrt NEoE SMad WCot		*lanata* Jacq.	see *S. byzantina*
			lavandulifolia	StAn WAbe WIce
ulmaria	see *Filipendula ulmaria*		*macrantha*	see *Betonica macrantha*
× *vanhouttei*	CMac EBee ELan EPfP MMuc SEND SReu SRms WFar		- 'Hummelo'	see *Betonica officinalis* 'Hummelo'
- 'Gold Fountain'	CMac ELan GKev LSou LSRN MMuc NLar SEND WCot WFar WHtc		*mexicana* misapplied	see *S. thunbergii*
- 'Pink Ice' (v)	CMac EPfP LRHS MAsh NLar SPlb SPoG WFar		*monieri* misapplied	see *Betonica officinalis*
			monieri ambig.	EPfP NLar NSti
venusta 'Magnifica'	see *Filipendula rubra* 'Venusta'		- white-flowered	EBee
			§ *monieri* (Gouan) P.W. Ball	LEdu
			* - 'Rosea'	EBee LEdu NDov NLar SHor SRms

Spiranthes (Orchidaceae)

× *bightensis* 'Chadds Ford' ⚘H4	CExl CTsd EBee EGrI LRHS MMrt NCth SPoG WHil WTor

nivea see *Betonica nivea*
officinalis see *Betonica officinalis*
olympica see *S. byzantina*
palustris CGwi CHab CPud CWat ELin LWaG MMuc NBac NLar SEND SRms
- from Islay, Hebrides MMuc SEND

Spodiopogon (Poaceae)

sibiricus	SPel StAn
- 'West Lake'	ESwi NDov

recta EPPr StAn WCAu
setifera MHol
spicata see *Betonica macrantha*
sylvatica CGwi CHab LRHS LWaG WHer
'The Bride' NDov
thirkei SAng WCot WMal

Sporobolus (Poaceae)

airoides	CKno EPPr SHor
heterolepis	CAby CBWd CKno CSde CSpe EBee ECha ELan EWes GMaP LEdu MBel MCtn MPie NClf NDov SBig SMHy WCot WPGP WTre
- 'Cloud'	NDov
I - 'Wisconsin Strain'	CSpe EBee
'JS Delicatesse'	LRHS
wrightii	EPPr SHor StAn

§ *thunbergii* GBin MBrN
§ - 'Danielle' EGrI EPfP NLar SRkn SRms
tuberifera see *S. affinis*
'White Lightning' CKno LBar MArl

Stachyurus (Stachyuraceae)

chinensis	CBcs CJun CMCN EGrI EWes NLar
- 'Celina' ⚘H5	CJun EPfP GKin LCro LRHS MGos NLar SPoG
- 'Joy Forever' (v) ⚘H5	CBcs CDoC CEnd CMac EPfP ESwi LRHS MGos MMrt NLar SPoG SSta
himalaicus	CMCN
- HWJK 2035	WCru
- pink-flowered	see *S. himalaicus* subsp. *purpureus*
§ - subsp. *purpureus* HWJK 2052	WCru WPGP
aff. *macrocarpus* B&SWJ 14678	WCru
praecox ⚘H5	CBcs CDoC CEnd CHll CJun CMac EGrI EPfP LEdu LRHS MBlu MGos MMrt NLar NQui SPlb SPoG SSta WCot WFar WJur
- B&SWJ 8898	WCru
- B&SWJ 10899	LCro WCru
- var. *leucotrichus*	CJun
- var. *matsuzakii*	CJun NLar
- - B&SWJ 11229	WCru
- 'Petra'	CJun
retusus	CExl
'Rubriflorus'	CJun EPfP
salicifolius	CBcs CExl CJun EPfP LRHS NLar SPoG SSta WPGP
sigeyosii	CExl EBee ESwi SSta WPGP
- B&SWJ 6915	WCru
- CWJ 12420	WCru
aff. *szechuanensis*	CExl
- BWJ 8153	WCru
yunnanensis	NLar WJur

Sprekelia (Amaryllidaceae)

formosissima	GKev LAma LCro LEdu XFar

squashes see AGM Vegetables Section

Stachys (Lamiaceae)

aethiopica 'Danielle'	see *S. thunbergii* 'Danielle'
§ *affinis*	LEdu MEar NBac NGKo SPlb SVic WKor
betonica	see *Betonica officinalis*
§ *byzantina*	CCBP CDor EBee ECha EGren EHeP ELan EPfP LRHS LShi LSto LWaG MArl MGos MHol NBir NBro NGdn NPer SAth SMrm SPlb SPoG SRms StAn WCAu WHil WKif WRBe WTre
§ - 'Big Ears'	CDoC EBee ECha EGren EHeP ELan EPfP GMaP GQue LBar LBom LCro LRHS LSRN MGos MMuc NLar SMrm SPhx SPoG SRms WCAu WCot WFar WHoo WMal
§ - 'Cotton Boll'	ECha EGrI SRms WFar
- 'Countess Helen von Stein'	see *S. byzantina* 'Big Ears'
- gold-leaved	see *S. byzantina* 'Primrose Heron'
- large-leaved	see *S. byzantina* 'Big Ears'
- 'Limelight'	SAng WCot
§ - 'Primrose Heron'	EBee ECha EGrI GMaP GQue LBar LRHS MAsh NLar SMrm WCAu WFar WMal
- 'Sheila McQueen'	see *S. byzantina* 'Cotton Boll'
- 'Silky Fleece'	CTsd ECha ELan EPfP LShi NLar SRms
- 'Silver Carpet'	Widely available
- 'Tiny Ears'	WCAu
chamissonis var. *cooleyae*	GBin
citrina	ECha SLee
densiflora	see *S. monieri* (Gouan) P.W. Ball

Stapelia (Apocynaceae)

marmoratum	see *Orbea variegata*
variegata	see *Orbea variegata*

Staphylea ✿ (Staphyleaceae)

'Black Tower' **new**	NLar

Staphylea

bumalda	CJun LEdu NLar WJur
– B&SWJ 11053	WCru
– B&SWJ 12744 from Korea	WCru
colchica	CBcs CJun CMCN ELan EWes LEdu MGos WJur
– B&SWJ 16009	WCru
– 'Black Beauty' **new**	CJun EBee
– 'Black Jack'	NLar
holocarpa	CJun
– 'Innocence'	CJun NLar WPGP
– var. *rosea*	CBcs CJun CMCN EBee EWes MBlu SChF WPGP
pinnata	CAgr CBcs CJun LRHS MCtn NLar SEND WJur
– B&SWJ 15319	WCru
– PAB 8427	LEdu
trifolia	CAgr WJur

Statice see *Limonium*

Stauntonia (Lardizabalaceae)

from northern Vietnam	WCru
aff. *chinensis* DJHV 6175	WCru
hexaphylla	CBcs CBrac CRHN CWGN EBee EGrI EPfP ESwi LRHS NLar SPoG SSta WJur
– B&SWJ 4858	WCru
– B&SWJ 14655	ESwi WCru
libera FMWJ 13177	WCru
– KWJ 12218	WCru
obovata B&SWJ 3670	WCru
– CWJ 12353	WCru
obovatifoliola B&SWJ 3685	WCru
purpurea	WPGP
– B&SWJ 1697	WCru
– B&SWJ 3690	WCru
yaoshanensis B&SWJ 8223	WCru
– FMWJ 13171	WCru
– HWJ 1024	WCru

Stellaria (Caryophyllaceae)

graminea	CHab
holostea	CBWd CHab CTtf NBir WOrg WShi

Stemmacantha see *Rhaponticum*

Stemodia (Scrophulariaceae)

durantifolia **new**	EWat

Stenanthium (Melanthiaceae)

gramineum	EWes

Stenocactus (Cactaceae)

phyllacanthus **new**	SPlb

Stenocereus (Cactaceae)

dumortieri	NPlm
marginatus	see *Pachycereus marginatus*
thurberi	NPlm

Stenotaphrum (Poaceae)

secundatum	EShb
– 'Variegatum' (v)	EShb

Stephanandra see *Neillia*

Stephania (Menispermaceae)

aff. *hernandiifolia* B&SWJ 14950	WCru
japonica CWJ 12823	WCru

pierrei	LBom
aff. *tetrandra* WWJ 11896	WCru

Stephanotis (Apocynaceae)

floribunda ♀H1b	CBcs CDoC LCro MCtn NPlm SPre

Sterculia (Malvaceae)

rupestris	see *Brachychiton rupestris*

Sternbergia (Amaryllidaceae)

candida	CBro
lutea ♀H4	CBro ECha EPot EWes GKev LAma LCro MNrw WHoo
– Angustifolia Group	CBro
sicula	CBro GKev
– 'John Marr'	WCot

Stetsonia (Cactaceae)

coryne	LCro LWaG NPlm

Stevia (Asteraceae)

rebaudiana	CCBP EHet ENfk LCro LShi MCtn MHoo SPre SRms SVic WCot WJek WKit
– 'Sugar Love'	LCro

Stewartia ✿ (Theaceae)

gemmata	see *S. sinensis*
× *henryae* 'Skyrocket'	CJun
'Korean Splendor'	see *S. pseudocamellia* Koreana Group
koreana	see *S. pseudocamellia* Koreana Group
monadelpha	CJun EBee MBlu SArc WJur
ovata	CJun WJur
pseudocamellia ♀H5	CBcs CDoC CHll CJun CWnw EBee EGrI ELon EPfP GKin IPap LMaj LMil LRHS MAsh MBlu MGos NCth NLar SGol SHor SPoG SReu SSta WJur WMat WPGP
– B&SWJ 11044 from North Japan	WCru
§ – Koreana Group ♀H5	CBct CEnd CJun CMCN GKin SChF
pteropetiolata	CBcs
– WWJ 11939	WCru
rostrata	CBcs CExl CJun CMCN EBee EGrI LMaj LRHS MBlu NCth NLar
– 'Hulsdonk Pink'	CJun
serrata	CJun EGrI WCru
§ *sinensis* ♀H5	CDoC CJun EGrI LMaj MBlu WJur

Stipa (Poaceae)

ambigua	EPPr
arundinacea	see *Anemanthele lessoniana*
barbata	CSpe ECha EPPr ESwi MNrw SHor StAn
– 'Silver Feather'	MCtn MPro
brachytricha	see *Calamagrostis brachytricha*
§ *calamagrostis* ♀H4	CBcs CBWd CCps CElw EBee ECha EGren EPPr GMaP LCro MBel MCtn NBro SEND SRms StAn WCAu
– 'Algäu' ♀H4	CBWd CKno ECha EMor EPfP LEdu MidI WCot WTor
– 'Lemperg' ♀H4	NDov SNoN
capillata	CSpe EBee EPPr EWhm SHor
* – 'Lace Veil'	MCtn
charruana ♀H4	EPPr
elegantissima	CDoC
extremiorientalis	CCps EPPr NCth SHor
gigantea ♀H4	Widely available

Streptocarpus 677

- 'Alberich'	CExl ECha EPPr IPot NCth
- 'Gold Fontaene' ♀H4	CKno EPfP EPPr EWes LEdu MNrw NClf NDov SMad SMHy SPel WChS WCot WPGP
- 'Goldilocks'	CKno ECha LEdu MAsh SPel WPGP
- 'Pixie'	EBee EBlo EPfP LRHS
ichu ♀H4	CElw CKno CSpe ECha EDAr GAbr GElm IPot LRHS LSto MAsh MAvo NDov SDix SHor SPhx
lasiagrostis	see *S. calamagrostis*
lessingiana ♀H5	CExl EPPr SEND SMHy
pennata	MPro SMad
pseudoichu ♀H5	CCht CElw ECha ELan EPPr MAvo NClf SHor SMHy WCot WHoo WPGP
- RCB/Arg Y-1	EBee ELon
pulcherrima	EPPr StAn
robusta	EPPr
splendens misapplied	see *S. calamagrostis*
splendens Trin.	ECha EPPr SAko
tenacissima	CKit LRHS
tenuifolia misapplied	see *S. tenuissima*
tenuifolia Steud.	NBir NBro WCAu
§ *tenuissima* ♀H4	Widely available
- 'Wind Whispers'	CExl LEdu MBel SMHy WSpi

Stoebe (Asteraceae)
alopecuroides	SPlb
plumosa	SPlb

Stokesia (Asteraceae)
cyanea	see *S. laevis*
§ *laevis*	ECha EGrI LRHS MCtn NLar SPlb SRms WCAu
- 'Alba'	EGrI ELan GPSL NLar WCAu
- 'Amethyst'	LBar Midl
- Blue Frills ('Synstokhar')	EPfP
- 'Blue Star'	CAby CBcs CDor CWGN EBee ELan ELon EPfP LRHS LShi LSou MAsh MHer MHol MPie MPro SPoG SRkn WCAu
- 'Divinity'	LBar LRHS Midl MPri MPro
- 'Elf'	NLar
- 'Klaus Jelitto'	CAby CDor LBar Midl MPie MPro SHar SPoG
- 'Mary Gregory'	CAby CMac EBee EBlo EPfP GKev LBar LRHS MArl MBel MPie NLar
- 'Mega Mel's' PBR	LBar LCro
§ - 'Mel's' PBR	LBar LBom LRHS Midl MPri MPro SHar
- Mel's Blue	see *S. laevis* 'Mel's'
- 'Mini Mel's' PBR	MPro
- 'Omega Skyrocket'	SRms
- 'Peachie's Pick'	LRHS NLar SPad
- 'Purple Parasols'	CDor CMac CWGN EBee EPfP GKev LRHS MArl MAsh MBel MHer MPie NLar SPoG
- 'Silver Moon'	CDor EPfP LRHS MArl NLar
§ - 'Träumerei'	CFis CWGN EBee EPfP MAsh MPie SPoG
- 'White Star'	see *S. laevis* 'Träumerei'

Stranvaesia see *Photinia*

× *Stranvinia* see *Photinia*

Stratiotes (Hydrocharitaceae)
⚲ *aloides*	CBen CLil CPud CWat ELin EPfk EWat LCro MWts NPer WMAq

strawberry see *Fragaria*; also AGM Fruit Section

Strelitzia (Strelitziaceae)
alba	CoPl LDro NPlm SBig SFol
juncea	MCtn
nicolai	CDoC EUrb LBom LCro LDro LInT MCtn NHrt NPer NPlm SArc SBig SPlb
reginae ♀H1b	CDoC CTsd ELan EUrb LBom LCro LDro MCtn NHrt NPer NPlm SArc SBig SFol SPlb

Streptanthus (Brassicaceae)
farnsworthianus	CSpe

Streptocarpella see *Streptocarpus*

Streptocarpus ✿ (Gesneriaceae)
'8e-Ajisai' (AV)	WDib
'Abigail'	LCro WDib
'Adele'	WDib
'Ae-Amur Elit' (AV)	WDib
'Ae-Lucifer' (AV)	WDib
'Ajohn's Fruit Cocktail' (AV)	WDib
'Ajohn's Yellow Submarine' (AV)	WDib
'Alana'	LCro WDib
'Alan's Fallen Angel' (AV/d/v)	WDib
'Alan's White Feather' (AV)	WDib
'Albatross'	CTsd LCro WDib
'Alchemy Yellow Star' (AV)	WDib
'Alexis' Kisses' (AV)	LCro
'Alissa'	CTsd WDib
'Allegro Appalachian Trail' (AV)	WDib
'Always Pink' (AV)	WDib
'Amazing Grace' (AV)	WDib
'Ambiente' ♀H1c	WDib
'Amethyst' (AV)	WDib
'Amoeba' (AV/d)	WDib
'Amy'	WDib
'Ancient Lace' (AV/d)	WDib
'Anne' (d)	LCro WDib
'Anouk' (AV)	WDib
'An-Rio Rita' (AV)	WDib
'Anthoflores Edith' (AV)	WDib
'Anwen'	WDib
'Apache Magic' (AV)	WDib
'Apache Maiden' (AV/v)	WDib
'Apache Thunderbolt' (AV)	WDib
'Aussie Magic' (AV)	WDib
'Austin's Smile' (AV)	WDib
'Awena'	WDib
baudertii	WDib
'Beacon Trail' (AV)	WDib
'Beatrice Trail' (AV)	WDib
'Bella'	WDib
'Berry Splash' (AV/v)	WDib
'Bethan' ♀H1c	LCro WDib
'Betty Stoehr' (AV)	WDib
'Bianca'	WDib
'Black Panther'	WDib
'Black Rain' (AV/d)	WDib
'Bliznecy' (AV)	WDib
'Bloomlover's Cat' (AV/d)	WDib
'Blue Dragon' (AV/d)	WDib
'Blue Frills' ♀H1c	WDib
'Blue Gem'	WDib
'Blue Leyla'	see *S.* 'Leyla'
'Blue Moon'	EAri WDib
'Blue Nymph'	WDib

Streptocarpus

'Blue Tail Fly' (AV)	WDib
'Blushing Ivory' (AV)	WDib
'Bob Serbin' (AV/d)	WDib
'Bob's Omega' (AV)	WDib
'Bourane' (AV/v)	WDib
'Boysenberry Delight'	WDib
'Br-Afina' (AV/d)	WDib
'Branwen'	WDib
brevipilosus (AV)	WDib
'Bristol's Black Bird'	LCro WDib
'Bristol's Very Best'	WDib
'Buckeye Dress Parade' (AV/d/v)	WDib
'Buckeye Irish Lace' (AV)	WDib
'Buffalo Hunt' (AV/d)	WDib
caeruleus	WDib
'Caitlin'	LCro WDib
candidus	WDib
'Candy Fountain' (AV)	WDib
'Candy Swirls' (AV)	WDib
'Cappuccino'	WDib
'Cariad'	WDib
'Carnival'	WDib
'Carol'	WDib
'Carys' ♀H1c	WDib
'Cathedral' (AV)	WDib
caulescens	WDib
'Cedar Creek Trail of Hope' (AV)	WDib
'Celebration' (AV/d/v)	CTsd LCro
'Celebration'	WDib
'Chantaspring' (AV)	WDib
'Chanticleer' (AV/d)	WDib
'Charlotte' ♀H1c	WDib
'Cherokee Trail' (AV/v)	WDib
'Cherries 'n' Cream' (AV)	WDib
'Chiffon Fiesta' (AV)	WDib
'Chiffon Pageant' (AV)	WDib
'Chiffon Vesper' (AV)	WDib
'Chloe'	WDib
'Cirelda' (AV)	WDib
'Colorado Sky' (AV/d/v)	WDib
'Constant Nymph'	WDib
'Country Romance' (AV/d/v)	WDib
'Crimson Ice' (AV)	WDib
'Crystal Beauty'	WDib
'Crystal Blush'	WDib
'Crystal Charm'	WDib
'Crystal Dawn'	WDib
'Crystal Ice'PBR ♀H1c	LCro WDib
'Crystal Snow'	WDib
'Crystal Wonder'	WDib
'Cupid's Jewel' (AV)	WDib
'Cupie Doll' (AV)	WDib
cyaneus	WDib
- subsp. *polackii*	WDib
'Cynthia'	WDib
'Daphne'	WDib
'Dawn Michelle' (AV)	WDib
'Dee'	WDib
'Deep Sky' (AV)	WDib
'Delft' (AV/d)	WDib
'Delia'	WDib
'Denim'	CTsd LCro WDib
denticulatus	WDib
'Diana'	WDib
'Dibley's Beate' (AV)	WDib
DIBLEY'S DRAGONS (mixed)	MCtn
'Dibleys Kaarina' (AV)	WDib
'Dibley's Leopold' (AV)	WDib
'Dibleys Marion' (AV)	WDib
'Dibley's Pat' (AV)	WDib
'Dibley's Sasha' (AV)	WDib
'Dinas'	WDib
'Dolly Dimples' (AV)	WDib
'Ds-Horus'	WDib
dunnii	WDib
'Dwynwen'	WDib
'East Wind' (AV/d)	WDib
'Edee's Rosebud Trail' (AV)	WDib
'Ek-Gost'ya iz Budushchego' (AV)	WDib
'Ek-Sady Semiramidi' (AV)	WDib
'Ek-Shedevr Khudozhnika' (AV)	WDib
'Ek-Snezhnyi Bars' (AV)	WDib
'Ek-Vrata Raia' (AV)	WDib
'Elin'	WDib
'Elsi'	WDib
'Emerald Love' (AV)	WDib
'Emily'	WDib
'Ethel's Wild Side' (AV)	WDib
'Eve'	WDib
'Faith'	WDib
'Falling Stars' ♀H1c	LCro WDib
'Favorite Child' (AV)	WDib
'Festival Wales'	WDib
'Fiesta'	WDib
'Fiona'	WDib
'Fire Mountain' (AV)	WDib
'Flashy Angel' (AV/v)	WDib
'Flashy Trail' (AV)	WDib
floribundus	WDib
formosus	WDib
'Franken Skye'	WDib
'Freya'	WDib
'Frosty Diamond' ♀H1c	WDib
gardenii	WDib
'Gecko's Vespa Vino' (AV)	WDib
glandulosissimus ♀H1c	WDib
'Gloria' ♀H1c	WDib
'Gold Dust'	CTsd WDib
'Gold Rose'	WDib
'Goluboi Tuman' (AV)	WDib
'Grandmother's Halo' (AV)	WDib
'Green Dragon' (AV)	WDib
'Green Lace' (AV/d)	WDib
'Gwen'	WDib
'Halo's Aglitter' (AV)	WDib
'Hand-picked' (AV/v)	WDib
'Hannah' ♀H1c	CSpe LCro WDib
'Harlequin'	LCro
'Harlequin Blue'PBR ♀H1c	LCro WDib
'Harlequin Damsel'	WDib
'Harlequin Dawn'	WDib
'Harlequin Delft'	WDib
'Harlequin Lace'PBR ♀H1c	LCro WDib
'Harlequin Purple'	LCro WDib
'Harlequin Rose'	WDib
'Harriet'	WDib
'Hayley'	WDib
'Heart's Delight' (AV)	WDib
'Heaven's A-calling' (AV)	WDib
'Heidi'	WDib
'Helen'	WDib
'Hope'	LCro WDib
'Hot Summer Day' (AV)	WDib
'Ian-Minuet' (AV/d)	WDib
'Imp's Pretty Deadly' (AV)	WDib
'Indian Trail' (AV)	WDib
'Indigo Ruffles' (AV)	WDib

'Iona'	WDib
ionanthus subsp. *grotei* (AV)	WDib
- subsp. *ionanthus* (AV)	WDib
- subsp. *rupicola* (AV)	WDib
- subsp. *velutinus* (AV)	WDib
'Isabella'	WDib
'Isla'	WDib
'Island Breezes' (AV)	WDib
'Jacquie'	WDib
'Jennifer'♀H1c	WDib
'Jenny Lilac' (AV/d)	WDib
'Jessica'♀H1c	WDib
'Joanna'	WDib
johannis	WDib
'Joli Concerto' (AV)	WDib
'Jolly Champ' (AV)	WDib
'Jolly Gala' (AV)	WDib
'Jolly Gold' (AV)	WDib
'Jolly Orchid' (AV/d)	WDib
'Jolly Prize' (AV/d)	WDib
'Jolly Sun Chaser' (AV/d)	WDib
'Jolly Texan' (AV/d)	WDib
'Joy'	WDib
'Karen'	WDib
'Katie'PBR ♀H1c	CTsd LCro WDib
kentaniensis	WDib
'Kentucky Strawberries' (AV/d)	WDib
'Kim'♀H1c	WDib
kirkii	WDib
'Kosmicheskaia Legenda 2' (AV)	WDib
'Kostina Fantaziia' (AV)	WDib
'Kz-Danochka' (AV/d)	WDib
'Laura'♀H1c	WDib
'Leah'♀H1c	WDib
'Le-Aisedora' (AV/d)	WDib
'Le-Eseniia' (AV/d)	WDib
'Le-Karusel' (AV/v)	WDib
'Le-Kolca Saturna' (AV)	WDib
'Le-Macho' (AV)	WDib
'Le-Małachitovaia Roza' (AV/d)	WDib
'Le-Master Yoda' (AV/d)	WDib
'Le-Rozhdenyi Galaktiki' (AV)	WDib
'Le-Sashen'ka' (AV/d)	WDib
'Lela Marie' (AV/d/v)	WDib
'Lemon Sorbet'	LCro WDib
'Letnaya Noch' (AV)	WDib
'Letnie Sumerki' (AV)	WDib
§'Leyla'PBR	CTsd WDib
'Lil Bit O'Irish' (AV)	WDib
'Lilla Blaklockan' (AV)	WDib
'Little Axel' (AV)	WDib
'Little Bo Peep' (AV)	WDib
'Little Chatterbox' (AV)	WDib
'Little Seagull' (AV)	WDib
'Lollipop' (AV)	WDib
'Looking Glass' (AV)	WDib
'Louise'	CSpe WDib
'Louise Croteau' (AV/d)	WDib
'Louisiana Lullaby' (AV/d)	WDib
'Love Spots' (AV)	WDib
'Lowri'	WDib
'Lucky Ladybug' (AV)	WDib
'Lucy'	CTsd WDib
'Luminescence' (AV)	WDib
'Lunar Lily White' (AV/d)	WDib
'Lyndee'	WDib
'Lynne'	WDib
'Lyon's Minnie-Haha' (AV)	WDib
'Lyon's Plum Pudding' (AV)	WDib
'Maassen's White'	WDib
'Mabel'	LCro WDib
'Mac's Black Jack' (AV)	WDib
'Mac's Blowing Bubbles' (AV)	WDib
'Mac's Carnival Clown' (AV)	WDib
'Mac's Glacial Grape' (AV)	WDib
'Mac's Just Jeff' (AV)	WDib
'Mac's Nocturne' (AV/d)	WDib
'Mac's Pizza Pizzicato' (AV/d)	WDib
'Mac's Rouge Rogue' (AV)	WDib
'Mac's Southern Springtime' (AV/d)	WDib
'Madison Red' (AV)	LCro
'Manon'	WDib
'Margaret' Gavin Brown	WDib
'Marie'	WDib
'Marion'	WDib
'Ma's Ching Dynasty' (AV/d)	WDib
'Ma's Easter Parade' (AV)	WDib
'Matilda'	WDib
'Megan'	WDib
'Melanie' Dibley	WDib
'Menai'	WDib
meyeri	WDib
'Midget Silver Fox' (AV/v)	WDib
'Midnight Flame' (AV/d)	WDib
'Mikinda Girl' (AV/v)	WDib
'Minnie'	WDib
modestus	WDib
'Myfanwy'	WDib
'MyJoy' (MyViolet Series) (AV)	WDib
'Nadine'	WDib
'Nancy Reagan' (AV/d/v)	WDib
'Natalie'	WDib
'N-Ditya Eloiz' (AV)	WDib
'N-Duimovochka' (AV)	WDib
'Nerys'	WDib
'Ness'Antique Red' (AV)	WDib
'Ness' Cherry Smoke' (AV)	WDib
'Ness' Crinkle Blue' (AV/d)	WDib
'Ness' Fantasy Gold' (AV/d)	WDib
'Ness' Midnight Fantasy' (AV)	WDib
'Ness' Orange Pekoe' (AV)	WDib
'Ness' Satin Rose' (AV)	WDib
'Ness' Sheer Peach' (AV)	WDib
'Neverfloris' (AV)	WDib
'Newtown Ohio' (AV)	WDib
'Nia'	WDib
'Nicola'	WDib
'Norseman' (AV)	WDib
'Number 32' (AV)	WDib
'Ode to Grace' (AV)	WDib
'Okie Easter Bunny' (AV)	WDib
'Oksana' (AV)	WDib
'Olivia'	WDib
'Optimara Little Moonstone' (AV)	WDib
'Otoe' (AV/d)	WDib
'Padarn'	WDib
'Painted Silk' (AV/v)	WDib
pallidiflorus	WDib
'Parnikovyi Effekt' (AV)	WDib
'Pat Champagne' (AV/v)	WDib
'Pat Tracey' (AV)	WDib
'Paula'	WDib

'Pearl' ♀H1c	WDib
pentherianus	WDib
'Phobos' (AV)	WDib
'Picasso' (AV/v)	WDib
'Pink Leyla' ♀H1c	WDib
'Pink Mint' (AV/d)	WDib
'Pink Souffle'	WDib
'Pixie Blue' (AV)	WDib
'Pixie Pink' (AV)	WDib
'Playful Dreamer' (AV/d)	WDib
'Podvenechnaia' (AV/d)	WDib
'Polka-Dot Purple' ♀H1c	CTsd LCro WDib
'Polka-Dot Red'	WDib
polyanthus	WDib
subsp. *dracomontanus*	
'Powder Keg' (AV/d)	WDib
'Powwow' (AV/d/v)	WDib
'Prancing Pony' (AV)	WDib
primulifolius	WDib
prolixus	WDib
'Pt-Anzhelika' (AV/d)	WDib
'Purple Passion' (AV)	WDib
'Purple Velvet'	WDib
'Rachael'	WDib
'Rainbow's Limelight' (AV/d)	WDib
'Rainbow's Quiet Riot' (AV)	WDib
'Ramblin' Amethyst' (AV)	WDib
'Ramblin' Lassie' (AV)	WDib
'Ramblin' Spots' (AV/v)	WDib
'Ramblin' Sunshine' (AV)	WDib
'Raspberry Crisp' (AV)	WDib
'Rebel's Amy' (AV)	WDib
'Rebel's Splatter Kake' (AV)	WDib
'Rebel's Strawberry Bites' (AV)	WDib
'Red Lantern' (AV/d)	WDib
'Reflections of Spring' (AV/d)	WDib
'Reka Enisej' (AV/v)	WDib
rexii	WDib
'Rhapsodie Clementine' (AV)	WDib
'Rhiannon'	WDib
'Rob's Antique Rose' (AV/d)	WDib
'Rob's Argyle Socks' (AV/d)	WDib
'Rob's Bed Bug' (AV/v)	WDib
'Rob's Chilly Willy' (AV/d/v)	WDib
'Rob's Dust Storm' (AV/d)	WDib
'Rob's Flim Flam' (AV)	WDib
'Rob's Heat Wave' (AV/d)	WDib
'Rob's Hot Tamale' (AV)	WDib
'Rob's Ice Ripples' (AV/d)	WDib
'Rob's Jitterbug' (AV)	WDib
'Rob's Lilli Pilli' (AV)	WDib
'Rob's Love Bite' (AV/d)	WDib
'Rob's Mad Cat' (AV/d)	WDib
'Rob's Melon Wedges' (AV)	WDib
'Rob's Peedletuck' (AV)	WDib
'Rob's Pewter Bells' (AV)	WDib
'Rob's Sarsparilla' (AV/d)	WDib
'Rob's Scrumptious' (AV)	WDib
'Rob's Shadow Magic' (AV/d/v)	WDib
'Rob's Slap Happy' (AV/v)	WDib
'Rob's Smarty Pants' (AV/d)	WDib
'Rob's Vanilla Trail' (AV/d)	WDib
'Rob's Wooloomooloo' (AV/d)	WDib
'Rose Halo'	WDib
'Rosebud'	WDib
(Roulette Series) 'Roulette Azur'PBR ♀H1c	WDib
– 'Roulette Cherry'	LCro WDib
'Rs-Annabel' (AV)	WDib
'Rs-Barbie' (AV)	WDib
'Rs-Bog Solntsa' (AV/d)	WDib
'Rs-Boyarinya' (AV)	WDib
'Rs-Gertsoginya' (AV)	WDib
'Rs-Iolanta' (AV/v)	WDib
'Rs-Kabaret' (AV)	WDib
'Rs-Korrida' (AV)	WDib
'Rs-Romantika' (AV)	WDib
'Rs-Strast' (AV)	WDib
'Rs-Utonchennyy-vkus' (AV)	WDib
'Rs-Vodevil' (AV/v)	WDib
'Rs-Zhabo' (AV/d)	WDib
'Rubina'PBR	CTsd WDib
'Rubina Pink' ♀H1c	WDib
'Ruby'	WDib
'Ruffled Skies' (AV)	WDib
'Ruth'	WDib
'Sadie'	WDib
'Sally'	WDib
'Sandra'	WDib
'Santa Anita' (AV)	WDib
'Sapphire Halo' (AV)	WDib
'Sarah'	WDib
saxorum	EAri EShb MPri WDib
– compact ♀H1c	WDib
'Scarlett'	WDib
'Senk's Arctic Fox' (AV)	WDib
'Senk's Big Bells' (AV)	WDib
'Senk's Longlegs' (AV/d)	WDib
'Senk's Say What' (AV/v)	WDib
'Senk's Vespa Verde' (AV)	WDib
'Seren'	CTsd WDib
'Sharon's Way' (AV)	WDib
shumensis (AV)	WDib
'Shy Blue' (AV)	WDib
'Sian'	WDib
silvaticus	WDib
'Sioned' ♀H1c	WDib
'Sky Bells' (AV/v)	WDib
'Sm-Olesya' (AV/d)	WDib
'Snow Leopard' (AV)	WDib
'Snow White' ♀H1c	WDib
'Sparkleberry' (AV)	WDib
'Special Treat' (AV)	WDib
'Sphinx'	LCro
§ 'Stella' Fleischle (Marleen Series) ♀H1c	CTsd LCro WDib
'Stephanie'	WDib
stomandrus	WDib
'Summer Carnival' (AV/d)	WDib
'Sun Sizzle' (AV)	WDib
'Sunkissed Rose' (AV)	WDib
'Susan' ♀H1c	WDib
'Susan Brooks' (AV)	WDib
'Sweet Melys'	WDib
'Sweet Rosy'	WDib
'Sweet Sam' (AV)	WDib
'Taboo' (AV/d)	WDib
'Taffeta Blue' (AV/d)	WDib
'Tanga'	see *S.* 'Stella' Fleischle (Marleen Series)
'Tanya'	WDib
'Teleri'	WDib
'Texas Hot Chili'	WDib
'The King' (AV)	WDib
'The Madam' (AV)	WDib
thompsonii	WDib

THREE SISTERS (mixed)	WDib
'Tiger' (AV/v)	WDib
'Tina' ♀H1c	LCro WDib
'Tina's April Fantasy' (AV)	WDib
'Titania'	WDib
'Tomorrow's Pink Ice' (AV/d)	WDib
'Top Dark Blue' (AV)	LCro
'Toy Castle' (AV)	WDib
'Tracey'	WDib
'Tula' (AV)	WDib
'Two-w Miss Sophie' (AV/d)	WDib
'Vallartas Campanas Moradas' (AV)	WDib
vandeleurii	WDib
variabilis	WDib
'Vat-Kaleidoscope' (AV/v)	WDib
'Victorian Velvet' (AV/d)	WDib
wendlandii	WDib
'Wendy'	WDib
'Whirligig Star' (AV)	WDib
'White Butterfly' ♀H1c	CTsd WDib
'White Madonna' (AV/d)	WDib
'Wiesmoor Red'	WDib
'Wild Irish Rose' (AV)	WDib
'Winifred'	WDib
'Wisteria' (AV/d)	WDib
'Wrangler's Jealous Heart' (AV)	WDib
'Wrangler's Snowfield's' (AV/v)	WDib
'Yesterday's Child' (AV)	WDib
'Zivai' (AV/d)	WDib
'Zoe'	LCro WDib

Streptopus (Liliaceae)
amplexifolius	EBee ESwi EWld MNrw WCru
- var. *papillatus*	GEdr
streptopoides	EBee EPPr LEdu

Streptosolen (Solanaceae)
jamesonii ♀H1c	CHll EShb WCot

Strobilanthes (Acanthaceae)
CB CH862	GGro
angustifrons	SBrt
anisophylla	CMCN EShb SHor WSpi
- 'Assam'	LCro
- BRUNETTHY ('Lankveld15'^{PBR})	LCro
atropurpurea misapplied	see *S. attenuata*
atropurpurea Nees	see *S. wallichii*
§ *attenuata*	CoPl EBee EGrl EWld LEdu MNrw MPie SDix SPoG SVen WCot WCru WPGP WSpi
- 'Blue and White'	EBee SHar
- 'Blue Carpet'	ESwi
- 'Latham's Form'	ESwi
dyeriana ♀H1b	EAri EShb EWld SPlb WCot WJun
flexicaulis	CBcs SDix
- B&SWJ 354	EPPr ESwi GGro WCru
aff. *flexicaulis* CMBTW1531	GGro
formosana CMBTW	GGro
glutinosa	SVen WJun
heyneana	ESwi
aff. *inflata* B&SWJ 7754	WCru
* *lactea*	EShb ESwi EWld
nutans	EAri EBee ESwi EWld GGro NSti SBrt
'Orizaba'	EShb ESwi EWld

pentastemonoides	EPPr GGro SDix
rankanensis	CBcs EPPr EWld SHar SMHy SPel
- B&SWJ 1771	WCru
- CMBTW 1484 marbled-flowered	GGro
violacea misapplied	EShb
wakasana CB JP2008	GGro
§ *wallichii*	CBcs CMac CSpe EBee EPPr ESwi EWes EWld MMuc NSti WCAu WCru WHil WJun WMal WTre
- from Picton	WFar

Stromanthe (Marantaceae)
amabilis	see *Ctenanthe amabilis*
sanguinea ♀H1b	LBom NHrt
- 'Triostar'^{PBR} (v)	LBom LCro NHrt

Strongylodon (Fabaceae)
macrobotrys	CHll

Strophanthus (Apocynaceae)
speciosus	CHll

Strumaria (Amaryllidaceae)
discifera subsp. *bulbifera*	WCot
gemmata	LAma
karoopoortensis new	LAma
truncata white-flowered new	LAma

Struthiopteris (Blechnaceae)
niponica	see *Blechnum niponicum*

Strychnos (Loganiaceae)
spinosa	SPlb

Stuartia see Stewartia

Stylidium (Stylidiaceae)
debile new	ISha
graminifolium	CTsd SPlb

Stylomecon see Papaver

Stylophorum (Papaveraceae)
diphyllum	EWld LEdu NQui WCru WPGP
lasiocarpum	CExl CSpe EAri EPPr EWld NBid NSti SMHy WCru

Styphelia (Ericaceae)
colensoi	see *Leucopogon colensoi*

Styphnolobium (Fabaceae)
§ *japonicum*	CAco CAgr CBcs CHab CMac CMCN IPap LMaj SPlb WJur
- 'China Gold'	SPoG
- 'Gold Standard'	ELan
- 'Pendulum'	CCVT ELan LRHS MPri SAth WCha

Styrax ❀ (Styracaceae)
from Guizhou, China NJM 11.013	WPGP
- NJM 11.085	WPGP
americanus Kankakee form	CJun EBee WPGP
confusus	CExl
dasyanthus	CExl
faberi	CExl
formosanus	WJur
- var. *formosanus*	CBcs CExl CJun EBee ELan EPfP LEdu MBlu SChF WPGP

Styrax

	- - B&SWJ 3803	WCru
	- - B&SWJ 6786	WCru
	grandiflorus	CExl WPGP
§	*hemsleyanus* ♀H5	CExl EGrI LEdu MBlu WJur
	hookeri	CExl WPGP
	huanus	see *S. hemsleyanus*
	japonicus	CBcs CDoC CExl CMCN CNWT EGrI EPfP GKin IPap LEdu LMaj LSRN MAsh MBlu MGos NLar SArc SGol SPoG WCha WJur WPGP
	- B&SWJ 4405	WCru
	- B&SWJ 8770	WCru
	- B&SWJ 11078	WCru
	- Guiz 216	CExl WPGP
	- (Benibana Group) 'Pink Chimes'	CBcs CJun CMCN EBee GKin LCro MBlu NCth NLar NPip SMad WCha WMat
	- 'Evening Light'PBR	CBcs LRHS NCth NLar SHor
	- 'Fargesii' ♀H5	CBcs CDoC CExl CJun SHor
	- 'Fragrant Fountain'	MBlu NLar WCha
	- 'June Snow'PBR	CBcs LMaj
	- 'Pendulus'	CBcs CMHG EBee ELan EPfP LMaj LSRN SMad WPGP
	- 'Pink Bells Compacta'	NLar
I	- 'Pink Snowbell'	CBcs ELan LRHS
	- 'Purple Dress' ♀H5	CJun EPfP MBlu
	- SNOWCONE ('Jfs-D')	CBcs CHll LMaj LSRN NCth NLar
	- 'Snowfall'	CJun CMCN
	- 'Sohuksan' ♀H5	CExl CJun EBee MBlu SMad WPGP
	aff. *japonicus* B&SWJ 14182 from Heuksando, South Korea	WCru
	limprichtii	CExl
	obassia	CLnd CMCN EBee EPfP LMaj MBlu NLar WJur WPGP
	- B&SWJ 6023	WCru
	- B&SWJ 10890	WCru
	odoratissimus	CExl EBee WPGP
	officinalis	CJun WJur
	- NJM 12.007	WPGP
	serrulatus	CExl
	shiraianus	CExl EBee MBlu WPGP
	suberifolius var. *hayataianus*	WPGP
	- - B&SWJ 6823	WCru
	tonkinensis FMWJ 13134	WCru
	'Wespelaar'	CJun EBee EPfP WPGP
	wilsonii	CExl WPGP
	wuyuanensis	CMCN EBee WPGP

Succisa (*Caprifoliaceae*)

§	*pratensis*	Widely available
	- 'Buttermilk'	CDor EWes LEdu WHoo
	- 'Cassop'	GEdr GKev
	- 'Derby Purple'	CSpe WHoo
	- early-flowering	LEdu
	- 'Nana'	EBee
	- 'Peddar's Pink'	SPhx

Succisella (*Caprifoliaceae*)

	inflexa	ECha ESwi LSto SPhx WCAu WTre
	- 'Frosted Pearls'	CDor CElw CFis EBee ECha EMor EPPr GBin LBar LSto MCtn NLar SHar StAn

Sulcorebutia see *Rebutia*

Sulla (*Fabaceae*)

§	*coronaria*	CSpe LShi SMHy SPoG

sunberry see *Rubus* 'Sunberry'

Sutera (*Scrophulariaceae*)

cordata	see *Chaenostoma cordatum*

Sutherlandia see *Lessertia*

Swainsona (*Fabaceae*)

galegifolia	CSpe
- 'Albiflora'	CHll

sweet cicely see *Myrrhis odorata*

sweet corn see AGM Vegetables Section

sweet pepper see *Capsicum*; also AGM Vegetables Section

Swertia (*Gentianaceae*)

bimaculata	CSpe ECha
- PAB 8845	LEdu
perennis	GEdr

Syagrus (*Arecaceae*)

§	*romanzoffiana*	NPlm

× *Sycoparrotia* (*Hamamelidaceae*)

semidecidua	CBcs CJun EBee EPfP LMaj MBlu NLar SSta WFar WJur
- 'Purple Haze'	CBcs CJun IArd LRHS NLar SArc

Sycopsis (*Hamamelidaceae*)

sinensis	CBcs CExl CJun EBee EPfP ESwi LMaj LRHS NLar SSta WJur WPGP

Symphoricarpos (*Caprifoliaceae*)

	albus	CAco CMac EHeP ELan
	- 'Constance Spry'	SRms
§	- var. *laevigatus*	LBuc
	× *chenaultii*	EHeP SRms
	- 'Hancock'	CMac EGren EHeP ELan EPfP LRHS
	× *doorenbosii*	EGren
	- 'Magic Berry'	CBrac EGren EHeP LCro
	- 'Mother of Pearl'	EGren EHeP EPfP LCro SRms WHtc
	- 'White Hedge'	EHeP EPfP LBuc SPlb
	guatemalensis B&SWJ 1016	WCru
	(Magical Series) MAGICAL CANDY ('Kolmcan'PBR)	CSBt LCro LSou LSRN MPri NEoE SPoG
	- MAGICAL GALAXY ('Kolmgala'PBR)	CBrac LCro MPri SPoG
	- MAGICAL SWEET ('Kolmaswet'PBR)	LCro SPoG
	orbiculatus 'Bowles's Golden Variegated'	see *S. orbiculatus* 'Foliis Variegatis'
§	- 'Foliis Variegatis' (v)	CMac
	- 'George Gardiner'	CMac
	- MAGICAL WINTER BERRY ('Kolmaberc') (Magical Series) new	LSou
	- 'Variegatus'	see *S. orbiculatus* 'Foliis Variegatis'
	rivularis	see *S. albus* var. *laevigatus*

Symphyandra see *Campanula*

Symphyotrichum ✿ (*Asteraceae*)

§	× *amethystinum*	MNrw WCot
	- 'Freiburg'	EPPr LShi MNrw WCAu WOld
	'Anja's Choice'	EPPr MNrw WCAu WTor
	'Ann Leys'PBR	LBar MNrw WCot

'Aqua Compact' (Autumn Jewels Series)	EUrb LRHS MSwo WHil	- var. *parryi*	ECha
		GRANAT ('Kiastgranat') (Autumn Jewels Series)	EGren EUrb LRHS NLar
'Beauté du Nord'	WCot	§ *greatae*	EBee
'Bee Lee Elliott'	SPhx	- KM.K. 186.02	EPPr
'Blue Butterfly'	WOld	'Herfstweelde'	LEdu MNrw SMad
'Blütenregen'	ESgI MNrw WCot WFar	'Hill Close Blue'	MAvo
'Bressingham Blue Cushion'	EBlo	'Hon. Vicary Gibbs' (*ericoides* hybrid)	WOld
chilense 'Purple Haze'	EPPr	'Jessica Jones'	EPPr NClf SHar SMHy WOld
§ *ciliolatum*	LRHS	'Johan'	LEdu
'Claudia'	WOld	§ *laeve*	CDor LEdu NLar
§ 'Climax' Vicary Gibbs	MNrw WFar WOld	- 'Anneke Van der Jeugd'	MNrw WFar
'Coombe Fishacre' ♀H7	CCBP CDor EBee ELan ELon EPPr ESgI GQue LCro LRHS LSto MNrw NDov NLar SDix SMrm SPeP SRms WCAu WCot WHil WHoo WOld WSpi WTor	§ - 'Arcturus'	CDor CElw LEdu MBel MNrw NBir SDix WCot WFar WOld
		- 'Black Ice'	ECha MAvo
		- 'Blauhügel'	SPeP
cordifolium	MNrw	- 'Blauschleier'	NLar
- from Piney Fork, Ohio, USA	EPPr	- 'Blue Bird'	WOld
- 'Aldebaran'	WOld	§ - 'Calliope'	CElw CKno EBee ECha GBin GElm GMaP GQue LEdu MHol MMuc MNrw NBid NLar SEND SMHy SMrm WFar WHoo WKif WOld WPGP WSpi
- 'Blue Heaven'	EPPr MNrw SAko		
- 'Chieftain' ♀H7	WOld		
- 'Elegans'	EBee EPPr SDix WOld		
- 'Ideal'	CCBP NLar SBea		
- 'Silver Spray'	CKno ELon GMaP MBel		
- 'Sweet Lavender' ♀H7	WOld	- 'Cally Compact'	GQue MHol NLar WFar
- 'White Chief'	WOld WTre	§ - 'Climax'	EBee ELan MMuc NBid NSti SDix SEND SMrm
'Diamond Jubilee'	EAri MAvo MWIw WOld		
divaricatus pale green-leaved	GElm	- 'Glow in the Dark'	CCBP CSpe EAri ECha EPPr ESgI LBar LEdu LRHS MNrw MWIw NCth NLar SMad SPeP WCAu WCot WHoo WMal WOld WPGP
dumosum 'Azurit'	LRHS		
- 'Beryll'	WFar		
- 'Biteliness'	NLar		
- 'Blue Lapis'	LRHS WFar	- 'Jane Ward'	MNrw
- SAPPHIRE ('Kiesapphire'PBR) (Autumn Jewels Series)	EGren LBar LRHS LSRN MPro MSwo NCou SRkn	- 'Les Moutiers'	CDor CTtf EPPr LEdu LSto MAvo MNrw SDix WBrk WCot WFar WOld
		- 'Nightshade'	EPPr ESgI MAvo MNrw WFar WOld
§ *ericoides*	WOld	- 'Novemberblau'	EPPr MNrw
- 'Blue Star' ♀H7	CDor EBlo ELon LRHS NLar SMHy WCAu WOld	- 'Orpheus'	ECha ESgI GBin LEdu MNrw SPel WBrk WFar WOld
- 'Blue Wonder'	ELon LRHS WCAu	- 'Tall, Dark and Handsome'	EWes
- 'Brimstone' ♀H7	WOld	- 'Vesta'	WOld
- 'Cinderella'	EBee ELon NSti WOld	§ - 'White Climax'	CDor MNrw WCot
- 'Cirylle'	LEdu SPhx	- white-flowered	WBrk WOld
- 'Constance'	EPPr WOld	*lanceolatum* 'Edwin Beckett'	MNrw NSti WFar WOld
- 'Deep Danziger'	SAko SPhx		
- 'Erlkönig'	EBee ELon GQue LEdu NGdn NLar WCAu WCot WFar	§ *lateriflorum*	WOld
		- 'Bleke Bet'	LEdu WCot WFar
- 'Esther'	ECha LRHS MNrw WOld	- 'Buck's Fizz'	WOld
- 'First Snow'	WCot WFar	- 'Chloe'	CDor LSto MNrw NCth NLar SDix SPel WCot WFar WOld
- 'Foxbrook Fairy'	MAvo MWIw		
- 'Golden Spray' ♀H7	EBee ELan ELon EPfP EPPr GMaP GQue NLar WOld	- var. *horizontale* ♀H7	CAby CMHG EBee ECha ELan ELon EPfP EPPr GKev GQue LBar LShi LSto NBro NGdn SDix SMHy SPel SPlb SRms WCAu WOld WSpi
- 'Monte Cassino'	see *S. pilosum* var. *pringlei* 'Monte Cassino'		
- 'Pink Cloud' ♀H7	CBWd ELan ELon EPfP EPPr GKev GQue LBar LEdu LRHS LSto MArl NCth SAko SDix SHar WCAu WOld WTre	- 'Lady in Black'	CBcs CBWd CDor CMac CSpe ELan ELon EPfP GMaP GQue LBar LRHS MNrw MPie NBir NLar NSti SMHy SMrm SRms WCAu WFar WOld WTre
- var. *prostratum*	EPot GKev SAko WCAu		
§ - - 'Snow Flurry' ♀H7	CSpe ECha ELon EPPr ESgI GBin GKev GQue LEdu MAvo MNrw NLar SAko SMHy SMrm SPel WCAu WCot WHoo WOld WPGP WTre	- 'Lovely'	WCot
		- 'Prince'	CDor CMac ECha ELan ELon ESgI EWes GMaP MHer MNrw NBir NGdn SPeP SPoG SRms WCAu WFar WOld WSpi
- 'Rosy Veil'	EPPr ESgI NBir NGdn SPel WOld		
- 'Vimmer's Delight'	WCot WFar WMal		
- 'White Heather'	NLar WOld	'Little Carlow' (*cordifolium* hybrid) ♀H7	Widely available
- 'Yvette Richardson'	WOld		
'Faith's Fancy' **new**	WOld	'Maggie May'	WOld
§ *falcatum*	WCot	'Newstars Glory' (Newstars Series)	EBlo LRHS WFar
- var. *commutatum*	WCot	'Nicholas'	WCot WFar WOld
'Florence'	WCot	'Nineteen'	WOld
foliaceum from Montana	EPPr	'Noreen'	ECha MAvo WOld

Symphyotrichum

§ **novae-angliae**

- 'Abendsonne'	SAko
- 'Alex Deamon'	ELon WBrk WOld
- 'Anabelle de Chazal'	ELon NLar WBrk WFar WOld
- 'Andenken an Alma Pötschke'	Widely available
- 'Andenken an Paul Gerber' ♀H7	ELon EPfP MAvo NLar SAko SRGP WBrk WCAu WOld
- 'Augusta'	ELon NGdn NLar SAko SBea SPeP WBrk WOld
- AUTUMN SNOW	see *S. novae-angliae* 'Herbstschnee'
- 'Badsey Pink' ♀H7	GQue WBrk WCot WOld
- 'Barr's Blue'	CMac EBee ELan ELon EPfP IPot MAvo MMuc NLar SBea SEND SRms WBrk WCAu WOld
- 'Barr's Pink'	CMac EBee ELan ELon EPfP GBin IPot MAvo SRms WBrk WFar WOld
- 'Barr's Purple' ♀H7	EPfP LSou LSto SRGP WBrk WOld
- 'Barr's Violet'	MAvo NSti SRms WBrk WCot WFar WOld
- 'Betel Nut'	EPPr WOld
- 'Beth Picton'	WOld
- 'Bishop Colenso'	EPPr LShi WBrk
- 'Blackheart'	ELon
- 'Bob's Purple'	WCot
I - 'Brightness'	WBrk WCot
- 'Brockamin'	EPPr WBrk
- 'Brockamin Regal'	WBrk
- 'Brunswick' ♀H7	WBrk WFar WOld
- 'Christopher Harbutt'	LEdu
- 'Colwall Century' ♀H7	WBrk WOld
- 'Colwall Constellation'	ELon WBrk WOld
- 'Colwall Galaxy'	WBrk WOld
- 'Colwall Orbit'	ELon WBrk WOld
- 'Constanze'	EBee ELon WBrk WOld
- 'Crimson Beauty'	ELon MHer MNrw SAko WBrk WFar WOld
- 'Dapper Tapper'	ELon MAvo WCot WOld
- 'Dark Desire'	MNrw
- 'Denise'	WBrk
- 'Dwarf Alma Pötschke'	SMrm
- 'Early Bird'	ELon
- 'Evensong'	WBrk WOld
- 'Festival'	WBrk
- 'Foxy Emily'	WBrk WOld
- 'Grape Crush'	LBar
- 'Guido en Gezelle'	ELon MAvo MNrw MWlw SPel WBrk WOld
- 'Harrington's Pink'	CDor CMac EBee ELan ELon EMor GMaP LRHS LSto MArl MAvo MHer MNrw NGdn NSti SBea SDix SPeP SPoG SRGP SRkn SRms WBrk WCAu WCot WFar WOld WSpi
- 'Harrington's Red'	WBrk WOld
- 'Helen Picton' ♀H7	CDor ELon EPPr IPot LEdu LRHS LSto MBrN MHer NClf NLar SMHy SPel SRms WBrk WCAu WFar WHoo WMal WOld
§ - 'Herbstschnee'	Widely available
- 'Hoo House'	WHoo
- 'Ivy Patterson'	MAvo WBrk WOld
- 'James' ♀H7	EPPr MAvo WBrk WOld
- 'James Ritchie' ♀H7	CFis CTtf GPSL IPot LRHS MMuc MPro MAvo SEND WCAu WHoo WMal WOld
- 'John Davis' ♀H7	MNrw WBrk WOld
- 'John Dickinson'	WBrk WOld
- 'Jon Baker'	WBrk
- 'Kate Deamon'	WBrk WOld
- 'Kylie'	EPPr LBar MNrw MPie MWlw NLar WBrk WCAu WCot WFar WOld
- 'Lachsglut' ♀H7	EAri ELon EPPr ESgI NLar SAko SMrm WCot WOld
- 'Ladies Day'	WOld
- 'Little Bella'	WBrk WOld
- 'Lou Williams'	ELon MNrw NLar SMHy WFar WOld
I - 'Lucida'	SRms WOld
- 'Lye End Beauty'	CDor ELon MAvo MHer MNrw MPie WBrk WCot WFar WOld
- 'Mabelle'	WBrk WOld
- 'Mandie's Choice'	WBrk WCot
- 'Marina Wolkonsky'	CMiW ELon ESgI EWes GBin IPot LEdu LRHS MNrw NGdn NLar SAko SBeP SDix SPel SPhx SRms WBrk WCot WFar WKif WMal WOld
- 'Millennium Star'	ELon SAko WOld
- 'Miss K.E. Mash'	NLar SRGP WBrk WCAu WFar WOld
- 'Mrs S.T. Wright'	EWes LCro LEdu MBrN WBrk WCAu WFar WOld
- 'Mrs S.W. Stern'	WBrk WOld
- 'Nachtauge'	SAko
- 'Naomi'	WBrk WOld
- 'Patricia'	MAvo WBrk
- 'Percy Picton'	LEdu
- 'Pink Parfait'	ESgI LShi MAvo NGdn SRms WCot WFar WOld
- 'Pink Victor'	CTtf EPPr SRms WFar
- 'Pontis Supreme'	WBrk
- 'Pride of Rougham'	EWes SAko WBrk
- 'Primrose Upward'	MNrw SAko SPel SPhx WChS WCot WOld
- 'Purple Cloud'	ELon ESgI MHer NGdn WBrk WOld
I - 'Purple Dome'	Widely available
- 'Purple Paradise'	WOld
- 'Quinton Menzies' ♀H7	ELon NLar SMHy WOld
- 'Red Cloud'	ELon ESgI LEdu MAvo MHer SMrm WBrk WOld
- 'Rosa Sieger' ♀H7	ELon EPPr GMaP MAvo MNrw MWlw NGdn SPel WBrk WFar WHoo WMal WOld
- 'Rose Williams'	MAvo
- 'Röter Stern'	MPie WBrk
- 'Röter Turm'	SAko
- 'Rougham Pink'	WBrk
- 'Rougham Purple'	EWes
- 'Rougham Violet'	WBrk
- 'Rubinschatz'	ELon MAvo NLar SAko SRms WOld
- 'Rudelsburg'	ELon MAvo NLar SHar WOld
- 'Rudolph'	EWes
- 'Saint Michael's'	EPPr ESgI WBrk WFar WOld
- 'Sayer's Croft'	ELon SRms WBrk WCot WFar WOld
- SEPTEMBER RUBY	see *S. novae-angliae* 'Septemberrubin'
§ - 'Septemberrubin'	ELan ELon EPfP EPPr GQue LEdu MBel NSti SPel SPeP SRms WCAu WFar WOld WSpi
- 'Treasure'	ELon EPPr EWes SMrm SRGP WBrk WOld
- 'Vibrant Dome'	ELon NLar
- 'Violet Dusk'	ELon WBrk
- 'Violet Haze'	ELon WBrk
- 'Violetta' H. Klose	EBlo ECha ESgI GMaP LCro MNrw MPie SMHy SPel WBrk WCAu WFar WOld
- 'W. Bowman'	NLar WBrk WOld
- 'Warm Throng'	WCot
- 'Wow'	CDor ELon SMrm WBrk
§ **novi-belgii**	EGren WHer WRBe
- 'Ada Ballard'	CFis CMac EBee LSRN WFar WOld
- 'Albanian'	SRms WOld
- 'Alderman Vokes'	WOld
- 'Algar's Pride'	SHar WFar WOld

Symphyotrichum 685

- 'Alice Haslam' — CMac ELan EPfP LBar LRHS NBir NLar SRms WCAu WFar WOld
- 'Anita Ballard' — WOld
- 'Anita Webb' — CDor NBir WOld
- 'Anneke' — EGrI MPro NLar WHil WOld
- 'Apollo' — LBar NLar WFar WOld
- 'Apple Blossom' — LSto WFar WOld
- 'Audrey' — CDor CMac EHeP EPfP GMaP LRHS NGdn SRms WFar WOld
- 'Autumn Beauty' — WOld
- 'Autumn Days' — WOld
- 'Autumn Glory' — WOld
- 'Autumn Rose' — WOld
- 'Baby Climax' — WOld
- BAHAMAS ('Dasone') (Island Series) — EAri EPfP LBar LRHS MPro SPoG SRms WCot
- BARBADOS ('Dastwo') (Island Series) — EPfP NBir NLar SPoG WCot WFar
- 'Beauty of Colwall' — WOld
- 'Beechwood Beacon' — WFar
- 'Beechwood Challenger' — MNrw MPie WOld
- 'Beechwood Charm' — WFar WOld
- 'Beechwood Rival' — CDor
- 'Benary's Composition' — MCtn
- 'Blandie' — WOld
- 'Blauglut' — LShi WFar WOld
- 'Blue Baby' — CMac
- 'Blue Bouquet' — SRms WFar WOld
- 'Blue Boy' — WOld
- 'Blue Danube' — WOld
- 'Blue Eyes' — SMHy WOld
- 'Blue Gown' — GQue WOld
- 'Blue Lagoon' — CDor LSRN WBrk WCAu WOld
- I 'Blue Moon' — CDor WFar WOld
- 'Blue Radiance' — WOld
- 'Blue Spire' — WOld
- 'Blue Whirl' — WOld
- 'Boningale Blue' — WOld
- 'Boningale White' — MArl SAko WFar WHil WOld
- 'Bonnie' — WOld
- 'Bright Eyes' — WOld
- 'Brightest and Best' — WOld
- 'Brigitte' — CDor GBin NLar
- 'Brockamin Bright' — WMal
- 'Cameo' — WOld
- 'Cantab' — WOld
- 'Carlingcott' — WOld
- 'Carnival' — CMac
- 'Cecily' — WOld
- 'Charles Wilson' — WOld
- 'Chatterbox' — CDor ELan EPfP ESgI LRHS SPeP SRms WFar WOld
- 'Chelwood' — WFar WOld
- 'Chequers' — SRms WFar WOld
- 'Christina' — see *S. novi-belgii* 'Kristina'
- 'Christine Soanes' — WOld
- 'Cliff Lewis' — WFar WOld
- 'Climax Albus' — see *S. laeve* 'White Climax'
- 'Cloudy Blue' — WOld
- 'Colonel F.R. Durham' — WOld
- 'Coombe Gladys' — WOld
- 'Coombe Margaret' — WOld
- 'Coombe Radiance' — SDix WOld
- 'Coombe Rosemary' — NLar WOld
- 'Coombe Violet' — WOld
- 'Countess of Dudley' — CFis WFar WOld
- 'Crimson Brocade' — CBWd CDor ELan EPfP GBin GPSL LBar LCro LRHS MPro NGdn NLar SAko SPoG SRms WFar
- 'Dandy' — CFis CMac EBlo ESgI GPSL LRHS NBir NGdn NWbg SRms WFar WOld
- 'Daniela' — SRms WBrk WFar WOld
- 'Dauerblau' — WOld
- 'Davey's True Blue' — ESgI SHar WFar WOld
- 'David Murray' — WOld
- 'Dazzler' — CDor WFar WOld
- DEBBIE ('Dasdebi'^PBR) (Mystery Lady Series) (d) — NBir
- 'Destiny' — WOld
- 'Diana Watts' — WOld
- 'Dietgard' — WFar WOld
- 'Dolly' — NBir SRms WOld
- 'Dora Chiswell' — WOld
- 'Dusky Maid' — ELon WFar WOld
- 'Elizabeth Hutton' — SRGP WFar WOld
- 'Elsie Dale' — WOld
- 'Elta' — WOld
- 'Erica' — MWlw WOld
- 'Ernest Ballard' — WOld
- 'Eva' — ELon SRms WOld
- 'Eventide' — LRHS LSRN WFar WOld
- 'Fair Lady' — WOld
- 'Faith' — WFar WOld
- 'Farncombe Lilac' — EBlo LRHS MAvo SRms
- 'Feckenham Rival' — WMal WOld
- 'Fellowship' (d) ♀^H6 — CAby CDor CTtf EBee ECha ELon EPfP LEdu LRHS LSou MMuc MNrw MPro NLar SAko SBea SEND SHar SRms WCAu WCot WFar WOld
- 'Flamingo' — SRms WOld
- 'Fran' — WOld
- 'Freda Ballard' — GMaP LSto WFar WOld
- 'Freya' — SRms WOld
- 'Fuldatal' — WFar WOld
- 'Gayborder Blue' — WFar WOld
- 'Gayborder Royal' — WFar WOld
- 'Goliath' — WOld
- 'Grey Lady' — WFar WOld
- 'Guardsman' — WOld
- 'Gulliver' — SRms WFar WOld
- 'Gurney Slade' — CDor WFar WOld
- 'Guy Ballard' — WOld
- 'Harrison's Blue' — CDor WOld
- 'Heinz Richard' — ECha MHer NBir NGdn SRms WOld
- 'Helen' — ELon ESgI WOld
- 'Helen Ballard' — ESgI NBid SRms WFar WOld
- 'Herbstgruss vom Bresserhof' — LRHS NLar SAko WFar WOld
- 'Hilda Ballard' — WOld
- 'Ilse Brensell' — WOld
- 'Irene' — WOld
- 'Janet McMullen' — WOld
- 'Janet Watts' — WOld
- 'Jean' — ELon SRms WFar WOld
- 'Jean Gyte' — ESgI WOld
- 'Jeanette' — SRms WFar WOld
- 'Jenny' — ELan EPfP EPPr ESgI GMaP GQue LRHS LShi LSRN MSwo NBid NBir NGdn SBea SPeP SRms WCAu WFar WHil WOld
- 'Julia' — WOld
- 'Kassel' — SRms WFar WOld
- 'King of the Belgians' — WFar WOld
- 'King's College' — WOld
- 'Kristina' — CMHG EBlo ECha ESgI LRHS MMuc NBir NWbg SDix WFar WOld
- 'Lady Frances' — SRms WOld
- 'Lady in Blue' — EGren ELan EPfP ESgI LEdu LRHS LShi MArl MBNS MGos MHol NBir NGdn NWbg SPoG SRms WCAu WFar WOld
- 'Lassie' — SRms WFar WOld

- 'Lavender Dream'	WOld		- 'Remembrance'	CDor SRms WFar WOld
- 'Lawrence Chiswell'	WFar WOld		- 'Reverend Vincent Dale'	WOld
- 'Leuchtfeuer'	SAko		- 'Richness'	WOld
- 'Lisa Dawn'	WFar WOld		- 'Rose Bonnet'	SPlb WFar WOld
- 'Lisette'	WOld		- 'Rosebud' Ballard (d)	CDor WOld
- 'Little Blue Baby'	WFar		- 'Rosenquartz'	EGren NLar WFar
- 'Little Boy Blue'	CDor CMac LRHS SRms WFar WOld		- 'Rosenwichtel'	CDor LRHS NLar SRms WOld
- 'Little Man in Blue'	CDor WOld		- 'Royal Blue'	WOld
- 'Little Ness'	ESwi GKev MNrw WFar WMal		- 'Royal Ruby'	CFis EBlo LRHS MArl NLar SRms
- 'Little Pink Beauty'	CCBP CMHG EGrl EHeP ELan EPfP LRHS MBNS NGdn SRGP SRms WCAu WFar WOld		- 'Royal Velvet'	WOld SHar WOld
- 'Little Pink Lady'	SRms WFar WOld		- 'Rufus'	WFar WOld
- 'Little Pink Pyramid'	SRms WOld		- 'Saint Egwyn'	WOld
- 'Little Red Boy'	WOld		- 'Sam Banham'	MNrw WFar WOld
- 'Madge Cato'	SRms WOld		- Samoa ('Dasthree') (Island Series)	EGren EPfP EUrb LBar LRHS MPro NLar SPoG SRms WCot
- 'Mammoth'	WOld		- 'Sandford White Swan'	WFar WOld
- 'Margery Bennett'	WOld		- 'Sarah Ballard'	EPfP LCro MPro NLar WFar WOld
- 'Marie Ann Neil'	SRms WOld	§	- 'Schneekissen'	ELan EPfP GKev GMaP LRHS LShi MHer MPro SRms WFar WOld
- 'Marie Ballard'	CAby CDor CMac ESgl GMaP LEdu LRHS LSto MArl MHer NGdn NLar NPer SBea SRms WCAu WFar WOld		- 'Schöne von Dietlikon'	CKno NLar SAko SHar WFar WOld
			- 'Schoolgirl'	ESgl WOld
			- 'Sheena'	WFar WOld
- 'Marie's Pretty Please'	WOld		- 'Silberblaukissen'	WOld
- 'Marie-Theres'	SAko		- Snow Cushion	see *S. novi-belgii* 'Schneekissen'
- 'Marjorie'	LRHS WOld		- 'Snowsprite'	EBlo ELan ESgl MArl NLar SRms WOld
- 'Mary Spiller'	LSto		- 'Sonata'	GMaP WOld
- 'Mauve Magic'	SRms WFar WOld		- 'Sophia'	SHar WOld
- 'Melbourne Magnet'	WOld		- Starletta Blue ('Asflo Blue')	NBir
- 'Merry'	WOld		- 'Starlight'	CDor ESgl LRHS NLar WCAu WFar
- 'Midget'	WOld		- 'Steinebrück'	WOld
- 'Mistress Quickly'	ESgl WFar WOld		- 'Sunset'	WOld
- 'Mittelmeer'	WOld		- 'Sweet Briar'	WOld
- 'Mount Everest'	CDor WOld		- 'Terry's Pride'	SRms WFar WOld
- 'Mrs Leo Hunter'	WOld		- 'The Archbishop'	WOld
- 'Nachtlicht'	SAko		- 'The Bishop'	WOld
- 'Neron'	MNrw MPie MPro MWlw NDov SHar WCAu WFar WMal WOld		- 'The Cardinal'	WOld
			- 'The Dean'	WOld
- 'Nesthäkchen'	WOld		- 'The Sexton'	WOld
- 'Niobe'	WOld		- 'Thundercloud'	CDor WOld
- 'Norman's Jubilee'	EPfP NBir WFar WOld		- 'Timsbury'	CDor SRms WOld
- 'Nursteed Charm'	WOld		- Tonga ('Dasfour') (Island Series)	EAri EPfP EUrb LBar LRHS MPro NBir NLar NWbg SPoG SRms
- 'Pamela'	WOld			
- 'Patricia Ballard' (d)	CBcs CDor CMac EBee EGren ELan EPfP GMaP LCro MArl NBir NLar NPer WCAu WFar WOld		- 'Tovarich'	WOld
			- 'Tropical Night'	WCAu
			- 'Trudi Ann'	NBir WOld
- 'Peace'	WOld		- 'Twinkle'	WOld
- 'Percy Thrower'	CDor WOld		- 'Victor'	WOld
- 'Peter Chiswell'	SRms WOld		- Victoria Series	EGren
- 'Peter Harrison'	GMaP LRHS NBir WOld		- 'Vignem'	NSti
- 'Pink Buttons'	MAvo		- 'Violet Lady'	WOld
- 'Pink Lace'	WOld		- 'Violetta' VEG Bornimer Staudenkulturen	LRHS
- 'Pink Topas'	EGren			
- 'Plenty'	WOld		- 'Waterperry'	WOld
- 'Porzellan'	MAvo MNrw NGdn NLar WCot WFar WMal WOld WPGP		- 'White Ladies'	CBcs CMHG EGren EPfP ESgl GMaP GPSL LCro LRHS MMuc MNrw MPro NLar SBea WCAu
- 'Pride of Colwall'	SRms WOld			
- 'Priory Blush'	CDor SHar SRms WOld		- 'White Wings'	LSto WOld
- 'Professor Anton Kippenberg'	EGren ELan EPfP GMaP GQue LRHS MSwo NLar SAko SRms WFar WOld		- 'Winston S. Churchill'	CAby CDor EAri ELan EPfP GMaP LBar LEdu LRHS LSto MBel MPro NLar SPlb SPoG WCAu WOld
- 'Prosperity'	WOld			
- 'Purple Dome'	ECha EGrl ELan LEdu LSRN MHer NBir SHar SMrm SRkn WChS WFar WOld		- 'Zwerghimmel'	SAko
			oblongifolium	MCtn SPel
			- 'October Skies'	EBee EBlo LBar LCro LRHS MNrw SHar SPhx
- 'Purple Dream'	WFar			
- 'Ralph Picton'	WFar WOld		'Ochtendgloren' (*pilosum* var *pringlei* hybrid) ♀H4	CDor CTtf EBee EPPr EWes MAsh MHol MMuc MNrw NCth NLar WMal WOld
- 'Red Robin'	LShi			
- 'Red Star'	WMal			
- 'Red Sunset'	SRms	§	'Oktoberlicht'	EPPr NCth SHar SMrm WHoo WOld
- 'Rembrandt'	MArl NGdn		'Orchidee'	EWes WOld

'Photograph' ♀H7	CTtf EWes GBin LEdu MPie NLar SDix SMrm WOld WPGP
§ *pilosum*	WCot WFar WOld
§ - var. *pringlei* ♀H7	ECha EWes
§ - - double-flowered (d)	WOld
§ - - 'Monte Cassino'	EPPr GQue LBar LEdu LRHS MBNS MPro SPel SPhx SRms WCAu WMal WSpi
- - 'October Glory'	WFar
- - 'Phoebe'	WOld
'Pink Star'	EBlo ELon EPPr GMaP MNrw NSti SPel WCAu WFar
'Pinwheel'	LEdu WCot
'Pixie Dark Eye' (*ericoides* hybrid)	EBee SRms WCot WOld
'Pixie Red Eye' (*ericoides* hybrid)	EBee ELon LBar LEdu NCth WCot WFar
'Prairie Perse'	WCot
'Prairie Pink'	WOld
'Prairie Purple'	CDor CKno ECha ELon EPPr NClf SBea SMHy SPel SPhx WCot WFar WHoo WMal WOld WTre
'Prairie Sky'	ECha GBin
'Primrose Path'	CDor CKno EAri ECha EPPr LEdu MNrw MWlw WBrk WCot WFar WOld
§ *puniceum*	EPPr LRHS MMuc SEND
'Purple Diamond' (Autumn Jewels Series)	EGren LBar LRHS WFar WHil
'Ringdove' (*ericoides* hybrid) ♀H7	LSto MAvo NCth NSti SMHy SPel WCot WOld
'Rose Crystal' (Autumn Jewels Series)	EGren LBar LRHS Midl MSwo
'Rose Glow'	EPPr
'Rose Quartz' (Autumn Jewels Series)	NLar
'Rose Queen'	MNrw SRms WOld
× *salignum* Scottish form	WOld
'Sea Spray'	WCot
'Small-Ness'	EBlo GBin LRHS MAvo
'Soft Lass'	WCot
'Star of Chesters'	MAvo
'Sunhelene'	EBee ELon MWlw WCot
SUNPLUM ('Danasplum'PBR)	CTtf
'Superstar'	MNrw SHor SPeP SPhx WFar WHoo WMal WOld
§ *tradescantii*	MBNS NSti SMad WCot
'Treffpunkt'	MAvo MNrw NLar
§ *turbinellum* ambig.	EMor WPGP
turbinellum misapplied ♀H7	EWes LSto NGdn SPhx
turbinellum Lindl.	EBee EMor EPfP GKev LEdu NQui SDix WCot WOld WPGP
- 'El Fin'	MNrw
- hybrid	CSpe CTtf EDAr SMHy WOld WSpi
- 'Leaflet'	LEdu SPel WOld
'Vasterival'	CKno EAri EPPr LEdu MPie NCth NDov SBeP SHar SHor WCAu WPGP
'Wood's Blue'	EBlo
'Wood's Pink'	WCAu
'Wood's Purple'	MPro

Symphytum (Boraginaceae)

'Angela Whinfield'	CTtf LShi MWlw WMal
asperum	CCBP ECha EPPr LShi NLar
* *azureum*	EBee EGren WCAu
'Belsay Gold'	NBid NBir
'Bocking'	see *S.* × *uplandicum* 'Bocking 4', 'Bocking 14'
bulbosum PAB 4886	LEdu
caucasicum	CFis ECha LEdu MHoo NLar SRms WTre
cordatum	EPPr LEdu MNrw WPGP
§ 'Goldsmith' (v)	EBee ECha ELan EPfP GKev MHol MHtn NBid NBir NLar NPer NWbg SPoG WCAu WFar
grandiflorum	CMac GKev LEdu LWaG MEar MHer NLar
'Hidcote Blue'	ECha ELan EPfP EPPr LShi LSto MHoo MMuc MSwo NBro SEND SPoG SRms WCAu WChS WPnP
§ 'Hidcote Pink'	CTsd ECha ELan EPfP EPPr LShi LSto MHoo MMuc MNrw NBir NLar NSti SEND SRms WCAu WChS WFar WPnP
'Hidcote Variegated' (v)	CMac SRms
ibericum	CAgr CCBP ECha EGrI ELan GKev LShi MHoo MMuc NBac NSti SEND SMrm SRms WChS
- 'All Gold'	ECha LShi MNrw WFar
- 'Blaueglocken'	ECha
- 'Gold in Spring'	WFar
- 'Jubilee'	see *S.* 'Goldsmith'
- 'Lilacinum'	CFis WHer
- variegated (v)	MHoo
- 'Variegatum'	see *S.* 'Goldsmith'
- 'Wisley Blue'	CAgr CBcs CTsd LRHS NLar WCAu WFar
'Lambrook Sunrise'	CFis NBro SRms WCot
'Langthorns Pink'	EBee NLar
officinale	CAgr CGHo CGwi CHab EBee ENfk GJem GQue IDun LCro LWaG MCtn MHer MHoo MNHC NPer SPoG SRms WCAu WHer
- blue-flowered	MHoo
- var. *ochroleucum*	WHer
orientale	CCBP EPPr GQue MNrw NSti
peregrinum	see *S.* × *uplandicum*
'Romanian Red'	ECha
'Roseum'	see *S.* 'Hidcote Pink'
'Rubrum'	ELan MHoo NBro NLar WCAu
tuberosum	EPPr LEdu LShi MMuc WCot WFar WHer
§ × *uplandicum*	MMuc SVic
- 'Axminster Gold' (v)	WCot
§ - 'Bocking 4'	CAgr
§ - 'Bocking 14'	CAgr CHby GAbr LCro LEdu MEar MHoo MNHC NBac SRms
- 'Droitwich' (v)	WCot
- 'Moorland Heather'	CDor CSpe CTtf ECha EPPr LEdu LShi LSto MHer MHoo MNrw WCot WMal
- 'Padworth Purple'	LEdu
- purple-flowered	MMuc
- 'Variegatum' (v)	CTtf NBir NGdn WSpi

Symplocos (Symplocaceae)

paniculata	WJur

Synadenium see *Euphorbia*

grantii	see *Euphorbia umbellata*

Syncarpha (Asteraceae)

vestita	SPlb

Syncolostemon (Lamiaceae)

'Candy Kisses' (v)	WCot

Syneilesis (Asteraceae)

aconitifolia	ESwi WCot
- B&SWJ 879	WCru

subglabrata B&SWJ 298 — ESwi
- NMWJ 14528 — WCru
aff. *tagawae* B&SWJ 11191 — WCot

Syngonium (Araceae)

'Arrow' (v) — LBom LCro NHrt
chiapense **new** — NTro
erythrophyllum — NTro
 'Red Arrow' **new**
podophyllum ♀H1a — CDoC
- 'Albovariegatum' (v) **new** — LInT
- 'Neon Robusta' — LBom LCro
- 'Pink Allusion' — LBom NTro
- 'Pixie' — CDoC LBom
- 'Variegatum' (v) — LCro NTro SBig
rayi **new** — NTro
'Red Heart' **new** — LInT
wendlandii — LBom NTro
 'White Butterfly' — LBom LCro LInT LWaG

Synnotia see *Sparaxis*

Synthyris see *Veronica*

Syringa ❀ (Oleaceae)

afghanica misapplied — see *S. protolaciniata*
BLOOMERANG DARK PURPLE — CWGN ELan EPfP LCro LRHS LSRN
 ('Smsjbp7'^{PBR}) MAsh MGos SGol SPoG WCha WSpi
BLOOMERANG PINK PERFUME — see *S.* 'Pink Perfume'
× *chinensis* — EPfP
- 'Saugeana' — MBlu
× *diversifolia* — MBlu NLar
emodi 'Aureovariegata' — see *S. emodi* 'Variegata'
- 'Elegantissima' (v) — CEnd CMac SPoG
§ - 'Variegata' (v) — EPfP LRHS
× *hyacinthiflora* — ELan
 'Angel White'
- 'Clarke's Giant' — SGol
- 'Esther Staley' ♀H6 — EPfP
- 'Maiden's Blush' ♀H6 — LRHS SGol
- 'Sweetheart' (d) — NPip WMat
JOSÉE ('Morjos 060f') — CLnd ELan ELon EPfP LCro MAsh
  MPri NLar SGol SNig WFar WHtc
  WLov
× *josiflexa* 'Agnes Smith' — CMac NLar WSpi
- 'Bellicent' ♀H6 — CEnd CMac ELan EPfP LRHS MAsh
  MHtn MMrt MMuc NLar SMad
  SPoG SRms WFar WLov WSpi
- 'James MacFarlane' — NLar
- 'Redwine' — LRHS NLar
josikaea — CAco CMCN CSBt LMaj NLar WMat
- 'Oden' — WMat
komarowii — ESwi GGGa
§ - subsp. *reflexa* — EPfP MBlu WPGP
§ × *laciniata* Mill. — CMCN EBee EGren ELan ELon EPfP
  SIvy WCFE WLov WPGP
meyeri — SVen
- (Flowerfesta Series) — LCro LSou
 FLOWERFESTA PINK
  ('Anny200817'^{PBR})
- - FLOWERFESTA PURPLE — LCro LSou
  ('Anny200809'^{PBR})
- - FLOWERFESTA WHITE — LCro LSou NCth
  ('Anny200810'^{PBR})
§ - 'Palibin' ♀H5 — CBcs CBrac CDoC CSBt CSpe
  CWnw EBee EGren EHeP EPfP
  GKin LBom LBuc LCro LRHS LSRN
  LSto MAsh MGos NBir NLar NPip
  SGol SPoG SRms SVen WFar WHtc
  WSpi
microphylla — see *S. pubescens* subsp. *microphylla*

'Minuet' — CBcs LBuc SGol
oblata — CMCN
palibiniana misapplied — see *S. meyeri* 'Palibin'
patula misapplied — see *S. meyeri* 'Palibin'
patula (Palib.) Nakai — see *S. pubescens* subsp. *patula*
pekinensis BEIJING GOLD — see *S. reticulata* subsp. *pekinensis*
 'Zhang Zhiiming'
× *persica* ♀H5 — EPfP MGos WFar
- 'Alba' ♀H5 — SDix WFar
- var. *laciniata* — see *S.* × *laciniata* Mill.
§ 'Pink Perfume'^{PBR} — CLnd CMac ELan EPfP LCro LRHS
  LSRN MAsh MGos NPip SGol SPoG
  WCha WSpi
pinnatifolia — CBcs EBee ELan EPfP WPGP
× *prestoniae* 'Desdemona' — LRHS MMuc
- 'Elinor' ♀H6 — EPfP
- 'Nocturne' — WFar
§ - *protolaciniata* — CBcs
pubescens subsp. *julianae* — MGos MPri
 'George Eastman'
- - 'Roy Lancaster' — WCru
§ - subsp. *microphylla* — LSto
- - 'Superba' ♀H6 — CBcs CCVT CDoC CMac EBee
  EHeP ELan EPfP IArd LCro MAsh
  MGos MMuc MSwo NLar SPoG SSta
  WFar WSpi
§ - subsp. *patula* — CMac LRHS MMuc SVen
- - 'Miss Kim' ♀H6 — CCVT CMac CSBt ELan EPfP LRHS
  LSRN MAsh MGos MPri NLar SNig
  SPoG SRkn SSta WFar WHtc
'Red Pixie' — CDoC EBee ELan EPfP LCro LRHS
  MGos MMrt NCth NLar SRkn WLov
'Red Prince' — LRHS
reflexa — see *S. komarowii* subsp. *reflexa*
reticulata — CMCN MBlu WJur
- 'Ivory Silk' — WMat
- subsp. *pekinensis* — EBee MGos
 CHINA SNOW
  ('Morton') ♀H6
- 'Yellow Fragrance' — MBlu NLar
- - 'Zhang Zhiiming' — NCth
tomentella — CBcs EBee LEdu SRms WPGP
- subsp. *sweginzowii* — EPPr GKin NLar WSpi
- subsp. *yunnanensis* — CExl EBee GKev SBrt
velutina Kom. — see *S. pubescens* subsp. *patula*
villosa — SPlb WJur
vulgaris — CAco EGren EHeP LRHS LSto
- 'Amethyst' — EPfP
§ - 'Andenken an Ludwig — Widely available
  Späth' ♀H6
- 'Aucubifolia' (d/v) — WCot
- 'Aurea' — WFar
- BEAUTY OF MOSCOW — see *S. vulgaris* 'Krasavitsa Moskvy'
- 'Belle de Nancy' (d) — CDoC EGren ELan ELon IPap LMaj
  LRHS MAsh MMuc MPri SEND SGol
  WFar
- CARPE DIEM — see *S. vulgaris* 'Evert de Gier'
- 'Charles Joly' (d) ♀H6 — Widely available
- 'Dappled Dawn' (v) — MMrt
- DENTELLE D'ANJOU — CDoC
  ('Mindent')
- 'Edward J. Gardner' (d) ♀H6 — SEND
§ - 'Evert de Gier'^{PBR} — CBcs CBTr NCth NLar WSpi
- 'Firmament' ♀H6 — SEND WFar WSpi
- 'Général Pershing' Lemoine, — WSpi
  1924(d)
- 'Hope' — see *S. vulgaris* 'Nadezhda'
- 'Kardynał' (d) — LRHS
- 'Katherine Havemeyer' — Widely available
  (d) ♀H6
- KINDY ROSE ('Gaby'^{PBR}) — EBee

§ - 'Krasavitsa Moskvy' (d) ♀H6	CBTr CCVT CDoC CNWT ELan EPfP EWes IArd LRHS I.Sto MPri NCth NLar NPip SEND SGol SOrN WCha WFar WMat WSpi	- erecta	CoPl
		- CRACKERJACK (mixed)	MCtn
		- 'Discovery' ♀H2	MCtn
		- INCA I ORANGE (Inca I Series) ♀H2	LCro
- 'Krasnaya Moskva'	LRHS	- (Taishan Series) TAISHAN GOLD ('Pas1060547') **new**	EGren
- 'Lila Wonder'PBR	Midl SPoG		
- 'Madame Antoine Buchner' (d) ♀H6	CBcs WFar WSpi		
- 'Madame Florent Stepman'	CMac ELan EPfP WFar WSpi	- - TAISHAN ORANGE ('Pas1060545') **new**	EGren
- 'Madame Lemoine' (d) ♀H6	Widely available		
- 'Maréchal Foch'	CCVT	- - TAISHAN YELLOW ('Pas1060543') **new**	EGren
- 'Michel Buchner' (d)	CBcs CDoC CLnd EGren LMaj LRHS MBlu MGos MPri MSwo NLar SGol WCha WFar WHtc WMat		
		- 'Vanilla'	MBros
		filifolia	CSpe
		- 'Dropshot'	CSpe
- 'Miss Ellen Willmott' (d)	WCha	*lemmonii*	GBin SDix SNoN
- 'Mrs Edward Harding' (d) ♀H6	CBTr EGren EPfP LRHS NLar WFar	- 'Martin's Mutant'	SDix SNoN
		'Lemon Gem'	MCtn
§ - 'Nadezhda' (d)	EBee ELan	*lucida*	CSpe ENfk LCro LEdu MHer MNHC SRms SVic WFar WJek WKit
- 'Ogni Moskvy' **new**	MPri		
- 'Paul Thirion' (d)	SGol	*minuta*	MCtn
- 'Président Grévy' (d)	CMac SGol SPoG	*patula*	CoPl
- 'Primrose' ♀H6	CBcs CBTr CMac EBee EGren ELan EPfP IPap LCro LRHS MAsh MGos MPri NPip SEND SGol SPoG WFar WMat WSpi	- 'Alumia Vanilla Cream' (Alumia Series)	CSpe
		- Bonanza Series (d) ♀H2	LCro MBros
		- BONITA (mixed)	MCtn
- 'Prince Wolkonsky' (d)	CBTr ELan EPfP LSRN MAsh MGos NPip WFar	- 'Bonita Carmen' **new**	MCtn
		- 'Burning Embers'	CSpe LCro MCtn
- 'Princesse Sturdza'	CCVT LMaj LRHS	- 'Dainty Marietta' ♀H2	LCro
- ROSE DE MOSCOU ('Minkarl'PBR)	MMrt	- Durango Series	EGren
		- DWARF DOUBLE MIXED (d)	LCro
- 'Ruhm von Horstenstein'	WFar	- 'Fireball' (d) ♀H2	CSpe
- 'Sensation' ♀H6	Widely available	- FRENCH FANCY (mixed) (d)	LCro
- 'Souvenir d'Alice Harding' (d) ♀H6	LMaj	- Hero Series	MBros
		- 'Honeycomb' ♀H2	MCtn
- 'Souvenir de Louis Spaeth'	see *S. vulgaris* 'Andenken an Ludwig Späth'	- 'Konstance'	MCtn
		- 'Naughty Marietta'	LCro
- variegated (v)	EWes	- 'Red Cherry'	MCtn
- 'Victor Lemoine' (d)	WCha	- 'Strawberry Blonde' (d)	LCro MCtn
- 'Viviand-Morel' (d)	CMac LRHS	- 'Tiger Eyes' (King; Marshall) ♀H2	MCtn
- 'Zhemchuzhina' (d)	CCVT		
- 'Znamya Lenina'	WSpi	*tenuifolia* 'Golden Gem'	LCro
wolfii	GKev	- 'Starfire'	MCtn MNHC
		- 'Tangerine Gem'	MCtn MNHC
		zypaquirensis B&SWJ 14840	WCru

Syzygium ✿ (Myrtaceae)

paniculatum	CExl WJur
- 'Newport'	CBcs
smithii	CBcs EShb WCot WJur
- variegated (v)	EShb
zeylanicum	EShb

T

Tacca (Taccaceae)

chantrieri	LAma MCtn XFar
- 'Green Isle'	LAma
- 'Nivea'	XFar
integrifolia	LAma

Taccarum (Araceae)

weddellianum	WCot

Tacitus see *Graptopetalum*

Taenidia (Apiaceae)

integerrima	CSpe SPhx

Tagetes (Asteraceae)

'Cinnabar'	CSpe MCtn

Taiwania (Cupressaceae)

cryptomerioides	CAco

Talbotia (Velloziaceae)

elegans blue-flowered	WCru

Talinum (Talinaceae)

paniculatum	CAgr

tamarillo see *Solanum betaceum*

tamarind see *Tamarindus indica*

Tamarindus (Fabaceae)

indica (F)	SPlb WJur

Tamarix (Tamaricaceae)

gallica	SArc
hampeana	SEND
'Hulsdonk White'PBR	CBcs SEle
§ *parviflora* ♀H5	CMac LRHS
pentandra	see *T. ramosissima*, *T. ramosissima* 'Rosea'
§ *ramosissima*	EBee MAsh SRms

690 *Tamarix*

- 'Pink Cascade' ♀H5	CBcs CCoa EBee EGren ELan EPfP LCro LRHS MBlu MGos SAth SMHy SPoG	
§ - 'Rosea'	CBcs	
§ - 'Rubra'	EGren EPfP MGos SEND	
- 'Summer Glow'	see *T. ramosissima* 'Rubra'	
tetrandra ♀H5	CBcs CCoa CDoC EBee EGren EHeP ELan EPfP LRHS MAsh MBlu MGos MPri NPer SEND SPad SPlb SRms WFar	
- var. *purpurea*	see *T. parviflora*	

Tanacetum (Asteraceae)

argenteum subsp. *canum*	EDAr
aureum	IDun
§ *balsamita*	CCBP CGHo CGwi EBee ENfk EPPr GJos IDun MHer MHoo MNHC SEND SRms WCot WHer WJek
§ - subsp. *balsamita*	GQue SRms WJek
§ - subsp. *balsamitoides*	MHer SRms
- var. *tanacetoides*	see *T. balsamita* subsp. *balsamita*
- *tomentosum*	see *T. balsamita* subsp. *balsamitoides*
camphoratum	SRms
§ *cinerariifolium*	IDun MNHC
§ *coccineum*	WFar
- 'Alfred'	MNrw
- 'H.M. Pike'	EBee
- 'James Kelway'	EPfP
- 'Laurin'	EBlo LRHS MHol
- Robinson's, mixed	LRHS
- - crimson-flowered	LRHS
- - giant-flowered	GJos LRHS SRms
- - pink-flowered	EBee ELan EPfP GMaP LRHS MHol SMrm
- - red-flowered	CBcs EBee ELan EPfP GMaP LRHS LShi MHol MPro NLar SPlb
- - rose-flowered	LRHS NLar
- 'Vanessa'	MNrw
§ *corymbosum*	WCot
- 'Bukke'	LEdu
- 'Festtafel'	LEdu
densum subsp. *amani*	ECha GKev SEND
§ *haradjanii*	WKif
karelinianum	GKev
macrophyllum misapplied	see *Achillea grandifolia* Friv.
§ *macrophyllum* (Waldst. & Kit.) Sch.Bip.	EPPr MCtn
- 'Cream Klenza'	WCot
niveum	WCot
- 'Jackpot'	ECha ELan SHar
§ *parthenium*	CBWd CCBP CGHo CGwi CHab CHby CoPl EHet ENfk GQue LCro MCtn MEar MHer MHoo MNHC NPer SRms SVic WFar WHer WKit WOrg
- 'Aureum'	CGHo CTtf EHet ELan ENfk EWhm MHer MHoo MNHC SPlb SRms WCot WFar WHer
- double white-flowered (d)	CTtf MHoo NPer SRms
- 'Golden Ball'	WFar
- 'Magic Lime Green'	WFar
- 'Malmesbury'	MHoo WHer
- 'Plenum' (d)	MNrw
- 'Rowallane' (d)	MMuc SEND
- 'Selma Star' (d)	MNrw WFar WHer WMal
- 'Sissinghurst White'	see *T. parthenium* 'Rowallane'
- 'White Bonnet' (d)	WHer WMal
ptarmiciflorum	SRms SVen
'Silver Feather'	

Radiant Deep Pink ('Tntadp')	LRHS MHol
Radiant Light Pink ('Tntalp')	LRHS
vulgare	CBWd CCBP CGHo CGwi CHab CHby CWal ECha EGren ENfk GJem GQue IDun LCro MCtn MHer MHoo MNHC NMir SRms SVic WFar WKit
- 'All Gold'	SMad SRms
- var. *crispum*	EBee ENfk SMad SRms WFar
- 'Golden Fleece'	WCot
- 'Isla Gold' (v)	CDor EWes LEdu MHer MMuc NBid NSti SEND SMrm WCot WFar
- 'Silver Lace' (v)	EBee WFar

Tanakaea (Saxifragaceae)

radicans	EWld

Tara (Fabaceae)

§ *spinosa*	SPlb WJur

Taraxacum (Asteraceae)

albidum	GGro LShi
ceratophorum	GGro
faeroense	GGro WCot
leucanthum	GGro
luridum W&O 9253	GGro
officinale agg.	CHab CoPl MNHC SVic
- white-flowered	WFar
pseudoroseum	GGro LShi WFar
rubrifolium	MCtn WFar

tarragon see *Artemisia dracunculus*

Tasmannia (Winteraceae)

§ *lanceolata*	Widely available
- (m)	GAbr IDun
- 'Red Spice'	ELan EPfP LCro LRHS LSRN NCth SEle WFar
- 'Suzette' (v)	MBlu SRms

Taxodium ✿ (Cupressaceae)

ascendens 'Nutans'	see *T. distichum* var. *imbricarium* 'Nutans'
distichum	CAco CCVT CLnd CMac CMCN CMen EBee EGren EHeP ELan EPfP IPap LMaj MBlu MCtn MGos MMuc SArc SEND SEWo SPlb SPoG WFar WHtc WJur WMou
- 'Cascade Falls'	CAco MBlu MPri NPip
I - 'Contorta' **new**	NLar
- var. *imbricarium*	CAco
§ - - 'Nutans'	CAco EPfP MBlu NLar NPip WMat
- 'Minaret'	MBlu
- 'Pendens'	NLar
- 'Péve Minaret'	CMen ELan LMaj NLar SArc
- 'Péve Yellow'	MBlu NLar
- 'Secrest'	MBlu
- Shawnee Brave ('Mickelson')	LRHS MBlu
- 'Twisted Logic'	CAco
mucronatum	CAco CExl
- NJM 9.037	WPGP

Taxus ✿ (Taxaceae)

baccata ♀H7	Widely available
- 'Amersfoort'	CAco NLar
- 'Anna' PBR	LRHS
- Aurea Group	ELan SFol SRms
I - 'Aureomarginata' (v)	CBcs LRHS MAsh
- 'Barabits' Express'	CAco
- 'Bence'	CAco

Teloxys 691

- 'Black Tower'	CAco CBcs LRHS WFar
- 'Corleys Coppertip'	ELan MMuc
- 'Cristata' (m)	MBlu NLar
- 'David' (m)	CAco CCVT EPfP IArd LCro LRHS MGos NLar SPoG
- 'Dovastoniana' (m or f)	CAco LMaj NBir NLar
- 'Dovastonii Aurea' (m or f/v)	CAco CBcs GKin LRHS MBlu NLar SGol SRms
- 'Elegantissima' (f/v)	EPfP LMaj LRHS SPoG
§ - 'Fastigiata' (f) ♀H7	CAco CBcs CCVT CMac CNWT CSBt CWnw EBar EHeP ELan EPfP LRHS LWaG MGos MMuc NPip SGol SPoG SRms WMat WSpi
- Fastigiata Aurea Group	CAco CCVT CWnw EBar EGren EHeP IArd LCro LMaj LRHS MAsh MGos MSwo NLar SArc SGol SRms WFar
- 'Fastigiata Aureomarginata' (m/v) ♀H7	CMac CSBt EPfP LRHS MGos SPoG
- 'Fastigiata Robusta' (f)	CAco CSBt CWnw EGren ELan EPfP LCro LMaj LRHS LSto LWaG MAsh MGos MSwo NLar NPip SPoG WFar WMat
- 'Globus'	CAco
- 'Golden Carol'PBR **new**	LRHS
- 'Goldener Zwerg' (m)	MBlu
- 'Graciosa'	NLar
- 'Grayswood Hill'	WFar
- 'Great Column' (f)	MBlu
- 'Green Column' (f)	NLar
- 'Green Diamond'	MBlu NLar
- 'Hibernica' (f)	see *T. baccata* 'Fastigiata'
- 'Icicle' ♀H7	CAco MAsh NLar
- 'Ivory Tower'	CAco NLar
- 'Klitzeklein'	NLar
- 'Lakatos'	CAco
- 'Luca'PBR	CAco NLar
- 'Lutea' (f)	CAco
- 'Micro'	NLar
- 'Overeynderi' (m)	CAco LRHS
- 'Pendula' (m)	CAco
- 'Pyramidalis' (m)	EGren
- 'Renke's Kleiner Grüner'	ELan LRHS
- 'Repandens' (f) ♀H7	CAco IArd LCro WFar WSpi
I - 'Repens Aurea' (v) ♀H7	CBcs CMac EPfP MPri SRms WFar WSpi
- 'Semperaurea' (m) ♀H7	CBcs CMac LBuc MAsh SGol SPoG WFar WSpi
- SNOW LADY ('Her2009t03') (v)	CAco
- 'Standishii' (f) ♀H7	CBcs CBrac CMac CSBt CWnw ELan EPfP GKin IArd LRHS MAsh MGos MPri NLar NOra NPip SPoG WHtc WMat
- 'Summergold' (v)	CBrac ELan LCro LMaj LRHS MPri NBir WSpi
- 'Zöld'	CAco
cuspidata	CAco CMen
- var. *nana* hort. ex Rehder	CAco
- 'Silver Queen'	CAco
× *media* 'Brownii' (m)	CAco
- 'Densiformis' (m)	CAco
- 'Green Mountain'	CAco
- 'Groenland'	CWnw
- 'Hicksii' (f)	CAco LBuc LRHS
- 'Hillii' (m)	CAco CCVT LBuc
- 'Kazio'PBR	CCVT LRHS
§ - 'Oene'PBR	CAco
- RISING STAR	see *T.* × *media* 'Oene'
- 'Stefania'PBR (f)	CAco LRHS

- 'Tymon'PBR	MGos
- 'Viridis' (m)	CAco
wallichiana	CAco

tayberry see *Rubus* Tayberry Group; also AGM Fruit Section

Tecoma (Bignoniaceae)

× *alata*	WJur
capensis ♀H1c	CHll CRHN EUrb SVen
- 'Aurea'	EShb
- 'Coccinea'	EShb SEle
- 'Lutea'	CCoa EShb SEle
- yellow-flowered	CHll SEle
garrocha	EShb
ricasoliana	see *Podranea ricasoliana*
stans ♀H1c	EShb WJur

Tecomanthe (Bignoniaceae)

speciosa	CRHN

Tecomaria see *Tecoma*

Tecophilaea (Tecophilaeaceae)

cyanocrocus ♀H3	EPot GKev LAma NDry
- 'Leichtlinii' ♀H3	GKev LAma NDry
- 'Purpurea'	see *T. cyanocrocus* 'Violacea'
- Storm Cloud Group	GKev LAma
§ - 'Violacea'	GKev LAma NDry

Tectona (Verbenaceae)

grandis	EAri

Telanthophora (Asteraceae)

grandifolia	EAri

Telekia (Asteraceae)

§ *speciosa* ♀H7	CMac CSpe EBee GJos GQue LBar LEdu MCtn MMuc NBro NLar SDix SPlb SRms WBrk

Telesonix see *Boykinia*

Teline see *Genista*

Tellima (Saxifragaceae)

grandiflora	Widely available
- 'Delphine' (v)	EPPr WCot
- 'Forest Frost'	CMac EBee ELan EMor EPfP EPPr GElm LRHS LSto MArl MBel MBNS MPie MPnt NLar WCAu WChS WCot WHrl
- Odorata Group	ECha WCot
- 'Purpurea'	see *T. grandiflora* Rubra Group
- 'Purpurteppich'	EPPr GPSL MPnt WCot
§ - Rubra Group	CMac CTtf ECha EGren EHeP ELan EMor EPfP GKev GMaP GQue LRHS MCtn NLar NPer SPlb SRms WCAu WChS WCot WFar WHoo
- 'Silver Select'	EPPr

Telopea (Proteaceae)

oreades	SPlb
SHADY LADY CRIMSON ('T90101'PBR)	LRHS
speciosissima	SEle SPlb
truncata	SPlb

Teloxys (Amaranthaceae)

aristata	MCtn

Templetonia (Fabaceae)
retusa — WHil

Temu (Myrtaceae)
§ *cruckshanksii* — CBcs CCoa CExl CMHG CSde CTsd MMuc WJur WPGP

Tephrocactus (Cactaceae)
§ *articulatus* — SPlb
§ *molinensis* — SPlb

Tephroseris (Asteraceae)
integrifolia — GEdr SPlb
  subsp. *capitata*

Terminalia (Combretaceae)
buceras **new** — LDro

Ternstroemia (Pentaphylacaceae)
chapaensis WWJ 11918 — WCru
gymnanthera — WCru
kwangtungensis FMWJ 13402 — WCru
luteoflora FMWJ 13360 — WCru

Tetracentron (Trochodendraceae)
§ *sinense* — CBcs CMCN EPfP MBlu WPGP
  - WJC 13818 from the Himalaya — WCru
  - var. *himalense* — see *T. sinense*

Tetradium (Rutaceae)
§ *daniellii* — CBcs CDoC CHab CMCN CSpe EBee ELan EPfP ESwi IArd LMaj LRHS NPip SAko WJur WMat WPGP WSpi
  - from Korea — WPGP
§ - Hupehense Group — CMCN
fraxinifolium PAB 9101 — LEdu
  - WJC 13750 — WCru
aff. *fraxinifolium* WWJ 11615 — WCru
glabrifolium B&SWJ 6882 — WCru
  - CWJ 12364 — WCru
ruticarpum — MBlu WPGP
  - B&SWJ 3541 — WCru

Tetragonia (Aizoaceae)
tetragonoides — LCro

Tetragonolobus see *Lotus*

Tetraneuris (Asteraceae)
§ *grandiflora* — SPlb
scaposa — EPot
torreyana — GEdr

Tetrapanax (Araliaceae)
§ *papyrifer* ⚥H3 — CDoC CDTJ EAri ELan ESwi LRHS MCtn NCft SDix SHor SIvy SPlb SVen WLov
  - 'Di-Sue-Shan' — CDTJ SPlb
  - 'Empress' — WCru
  - 'Meifeng' — WCru
  - 'Rex' — Widely available
  - 'Steroidal Giant' — CDTJ SBig

Tetrapathaea see *Passiflora*

Tetrastigma (Vitaceae)
obtectum — CRHN EShb WJun

Teucrium (Lamiaceae)
* *ackermannii* hort. ⚥H5 — CBcs CMCN ECha ELan GKev LCro MHer MHol SHar SPhx WAbe WCot WHoo WIce WPGP
aroanium — ECha EPot GEdr MWlw NBir WAbe
asiaticum — ECha
aureum — CHll CSpe
botrys — MHer
chamaedrys misapplied — see *T.* × *lucidrys*
chamaedrys L. — CCBP ECha EGrI ELan ENfk GJos GMaP GQue LEdu LRHS LSRN MHoo MNHC SEND SLee SPhx SPlb SRms SRot SVen WBrk
  - f. *albiflora* — CCBP ECha ELan WFar WSpi WTor
  - 'Rose' — SRms
  - 'Summer Sunshine' — MHoo
aff. *chamaedrys* — ESgI MCtn NRya WKif
creticum — SPhx
flavum — CSde EBee EPPr SEND SPhx
fruticans — CBcs CBct CBrac CDoC CExl CHll CMac CMCN EBee EGren EGrI EHeP ELan EPfP LRHS LSRN LSto MSwo NPer NSti SEND SHor SNig SPlb SPoG SSta SVen WKif
  - 'Azureum' ⚥H3 — CCBP CCoa CDoC CRHN CSde CTsd EBee ECha ELan ELon EPfP EUrb LRHS LSRN SEND SPoG SRkn SRms WKif
  - 'Compactum' — CDoC EBee ELan ELon LRHS SPoG WCot WPGP WSpi
  - CURAÇAO ('Ventecu'PBR) **new** — LSou
  - 'Drysdale' — CCoa CDoC CSBt EPfP
hircanicum — CAby CBcs CCBP CElw EBee ECha EGrI GJos GKev MNrw NBir SDix SEND SMHy SPhx WRBe
  - PAB 13.341 — LEdu
  - 'Paradise Delight' — NLar
  - 'Purple Tails' — CSpe EBee ELan LShi MHol MHoo MPro NBir SRms WFar
laciniatum — GKev
§ × *lucidrys* — Widely available
  - 'Lucky Gold'PBR — CBcs LRHS SPoG SRms
luteum — WMal
marum — CBcs ECha LRHS MHoo SRms WJek WMal
massiliense misapplied — see *T.* × *lucidrys*
montanum — ECha SPhx
orientale — SPhx
polium — SPhx
pyrenaicum ⚥H7 — ECha EDAr EPot EWes GEdr MWlw WAbe
scorodonia — CBWd CCBP CGHo CGwi CHab EMor MAsh MHer MNHC NLar NMir SRms WHer WJek
  - 'Binsted Gold' — EMor LBar LRHS NSti
  - 'Crispum' — CCBP EUrb LEdu LRHS LWaG MHer MHoo NBro NLar SRms WJek WKif
  - 'Crispum Marginatum' (v) — EBee ECha EMor EPPr LEdu MMrt WFar
§ *viscidum* 'Lemon and Lime' (v) — NSti

Thalia (Marantaceae)
dealbata — CBen CLil EAri ELin SArc SBig SDix SPlb WMAq
geniculata — CLil ELin SPlb
  - f. *rheumoides* — ELin

Thalictrum ❀ (*Ranunculaceae*)

CC 4576	CExl
MCW 109	EPPr
W&O 0107	GGro
from Afghanistan	see *T. isopyroides*
actaeifolium	MTha
- B&SWJ 4664	WCru
- B&SWJ 6310	WCru
- var. *brevistylum*	MTha WCot
- - B&SWJ 8819	LEdu WCru
- compact B&SWJ 4946	WCru
- 'Perfume Star'	LEdu MTha NCth WSpi
adiantifolium	see *T. minus* 'Adiantifolium'
alpinum	EDAr EPPr LSht MTha SHor WFar
angustifolium	see *T. lucidum*
'Anne'PBR	CDor CWCL EBee LBar LRHS MHol MHtn MTha NLar SPoG WCot WPnP WSpi XFar
aquilegiifolium	Widely available
- 'Album'	CWnw EBee ECha EPPr GMaP MBel Midl MPro MTha NBid NBir SHor StAn WCAu WFar WSpi
* - 'Hybridum'	WFar
- var. *intermedium*	MTha
- - B&SWJ 10965	WCru
- 'My Little Favourite'	LRHS MAsh MAvo MPro MTha NEoE NLar XFar
- 'Purpureum'	LSto MTha NBir NLar NQui
- var. *sibiricum*	MTha
- - B&SWJ 11207	WCru
- 'Small Thundercloud'	SMHy
- The Cloud **new**	EBee LBar MTha
- 'Thundercloud'	CDor CExl EBee EPfP GMaP GQue LRHS LSou LSto MAsh Midl MPri MSwo MTha NLar NQui WCAu WCot WFar XFar
- 'White Cloud'	LBar MTha NCth
'Black Stockings' ♀H7	Widely available
calabricum	MTha NLar
CHANTILLY LACE ('Mactha002')	MTha SHar
chelidonii HWJK 2216	WCru
coreanum	see *T. ichangense*
coriaceum	MTha
cultratum	EBee
dasycarpum	EPPr MTha SPhx WCot
§ *delavayi*	Widely available
- BWJ 7800	WCru
- BWJ 7903	WCru
- var. *acuminatum*	ELan LRHS MTha
- - BWJ 7535	WCru
- - BWJ 7971	WCru
- lilac-white-flowered **new**	MTha
- 'Album'	Widely available
- 'Ankum' ♀H7	EBee LRHS MNrw MTha NBid NLar
- var. *decorum*	CAby CElw CSpe LBar MPro MTha WCot WCru WPGP WTor
- - BWJ 7770	WCru
- CD&R 2135	ESwi
- aff. var. *decorum*	CExl
- 'Gold Laced'	MTha NLar
- 'Hewitt's Double' (d)	Widely available
- Hinkley'	CMiW IPot MNrw MTha NLar WSpi
- var. *mucronatum*	MTha WCru
- - DJHC 473	ESwi WCru
- purple-stemmed BWJ 7748	WCru
diffusiflorum	MTha WCru
dioicum	MTha
dipterocarpum misapplied	see *T. delavayi*
dipterocarpum Franch.	CMac

'Elin' ♀H7	Widely available
'Fairy Wings'	LCro LRHS MBcl MPro MTha SPeP
filamentosum	MTha WCot
- B&SWJ 777	WCru
- B&SWJ 4145	WCru
- B&SWJ 14145	ESwi
aff. *filamentosum*	CMiW
finetii misapplied	ECha MTha
aff. *finetii*	LRHS
flavum	CHab CMac EBee EWld GBin GQue MTha NBro NMir SBea SMrm WFar WShi WTre
- 'Chollerton'	see *T. isopyroides*
§ - subsp. *glaucum*	Widely available
- - 'Ruth Lynden-Bell' ♀H7	EBee LBar MAvo MHol MTha NCou SPoG WCot WHoo
- - 'Silver Sparkler' (v)	MTha WCot
- 'Illuminator'	CDor CElw EBlo MArl MTha SMrm WCot WFar Wtre
flexuosum	see *T. minus* subsp. *minus*
fortunei W&O 0108	GGro
'Freefolk Purple'	MTha
honanense BWJ 7962	WCru
§ *ichangense*	CExl CSpe EBee GEdr LEdu MBel MTha WCot
- B&SWJ 8203	WCru
- 'Evening Star' (v)	MTha NCth
- var. *minus* 'Chinese Chintz'	WCru
- 'Purple Marble'	CWGN ESwi MTha WCot WSpi
§ *isopyroides*	EBee EBlo EPPr ESwi GKev GKin LEdu LRHS MHol MTha NBir SHar WCot
javanicum	MTha
- B&SWJ 9506	WCru
- NJM 11.051	WPGP
- PAB 9431	LEdu WPGP
- var. *puberulum*	MTha
- - B&SWJ 6770	WCru
kiusianum	CMiW EBee ECha ESgI EWes GEdr GMaP MTha NBir SHar WAbe WCot WFar WTor
koreanum	see *T. ichangense*
'Little Pinkie' (Censation Series)	CSpe CWGN GEdr LCro LRHS MHol MPri MPro MTha NLar WHil WPnP
§ *lucidum*	CElw CExl CSpe EBee EPPr GMaP GQue LEdu MCtn MHol MPie MTha NLar NQui NSti SHar SHor SPhx WCot WPnP
minus	GQue LEdu MMuc SEND
§ - 'Adiantifolium'	ECha ESwi MTha NGdn SHar SHor SRms StAn WSpi
- var. *hypoleucum*	MTha NCth
- - B&SWJ 8634	WCru
§ - subsp. *minus*	MTha
- var. *sipellatum* B&SWJ 5051	WCru
'Monica Lynden-Bell' **new**	MTha
morisonii	MTha
- subsp. *mediterraneum*	MTha
(Nimbus Series) NIMBUS PINK ('Tntnp')	CDor CMHG ELan LBar LRHS MArl MAsh MAvo MBel MHer Midl MNrw MPri MTha NCth NDov WNPC WPnP
- NIMBUS WHITE ('Tntnw')	CDor ELan LBar LCro LRHS MAsh MBel Midl MNrw MPri MPro MTha NCth NSti WNPC WPnP WTor
'Nishiki'	GEdr MTha WFar
omeiense BWJ 8049	WCru
osmundifolium	MTha WCru

Thalictrum

petaloideum	EDAr GGro MBel MTha NLar
- 'Ghent Ebony'	CWGN MTha NCth SPeP WTor
platycarpum B&SWJ 2261	WCru
podocarpum B&SWJ 14297	WCru
polygamum	see *T. pubescens* Pursh
przewalskii	MTha WCru
§ *pubescens* Pursh	EPPr MTha NDov NLar SHar SPel
punctatum	MTha
- B&SWJ 1272	ESwi WCru
PURPLE WINGS ('Macthapuwi') **new**	MidI MPro MTha WTor
'Purplelicious'	LBar MTha NLar
ramosum	MTha
- BWJ 8126	WCru
reniforme	LEdu MTha
- B&SWJ 13969	WCru
- GWJ 9311	WCru
- HWJK 2403	WCru
- WJC 13761	WCru
rochebruneanum ♀H7	Widely available
- 'Lavender Mist'	MPro MTha StAn
rubescens B&SWJ 10006	WCru
sachalinense	MTha
- RBS 279	EPPr NLar
simplex	ECha EPPr MTha
- var. *brevipes* B&SWJ 4794	WCru
speciosissimum	see *T. flavum* subsp. *glaucum*
sphaerostachyum	see *T. flavum* subsp. *glaucum*
'Splendide'	Widely available
SPLENDIDE WHITE ('Fr21034'PBR) ♀H7	Widely available
squarrosum	EBee MTha
tenuisubulatum BWJ 7929	WCru
tuberiferum	MTha
- B&SWJ 10999	WCru
- var. *yakusimense*	WAbe
- - B&SWJ 6094	WCru
tuberosum	CElw CMiW CSpe GKev MMrt MTha NDov SHar WAbe WCot
- 'Rosy Hardy'	MTha WCot
'Tukker Princess' ♀H7	EMor EWhm MAvo MPro MTha NDov NLar WCot WKif
uchiyamae	CExl ESwi GKev MCtn MTha WCot WPGP
'Ulrike'	MTha
urbainii	MTha
- B&SWJ 7085	WCru
'Wray Castle' **new**	MTha
'Yulia'	MHol
yunnanense	WCru

Thamnocalamus (Poaceae)

crassinodus 'Gosainkund'	CDTJ MWht
- 'Kew Beauty' ♀H3	CDTJ MAvo MBrN MWht WCot WPav WPGP
- 'Langtang'	CDTJ WPGP
- 'Merlyn'	CDTJ MWht
falconeri	see *Himalayacalamus falconeri*
spathaceus misapplied	see *Fargesia murielae*
spathiflorus subsp. *nepalensis*	MMuc MWht
tessellatus	see *Bergbambos tessellata*

Thamnochortus (Restionaceae)

insignis ♀H3	SPlb
lucens	SPlb

Thapsia (Apiaceae)

decipiens	see *Melanoselinum decipiens*
villosa B&SWJ 14014	WCru

Thea see *Camellia*

Thelesperma (Asteraceae)

burridgeanum	MCtn

Thelocactus ✿ (Cactaceae)

hexaedrophorus	SPlb
subsp. *lloydii*	

Thelypteris (Thelypteridaceae)

kunthii	CCht CLAP EBee ISha WCot
palustris	EBee NBir NBro NLar SRms
phegopteris	see *Phegopteris connectilis*

Themeda (Poaceae)

japonica	EPPr
triandra	SPlb

Theobroma (Malvaceae)

cacao	WJur

Thermopsis (Fabaceae)

caroliniana	see *T. villosa*
chinensis	EAri EBee ECha ELan LRHS MHer MNrw WHil
fabacea	see *T. lupinoides*
lanceolata	CAby LSto NQui SHar WCAu WCot WFar
§ *lupinoides*	CDor CSpe ECha SRms
macrophylla	WPGP
mollis	CExl
montana	CFis LBar MPie
- var. *montana*	EPfP GMaP MBel MMuc NBir NLar NSti SEND
- - NNS 99-480	WCot
§ *villosa*	NGdn NLar StAn

Therorhodion see *Rhododendron*

Thevetia (Apocynaceae)

peruviana	EAri

Thladiantha (Cucurbitaceae)

aff. *davidii* BO 16037	GGro
dubia	EAri EBee ESwi SDix WCot

Thlaspi (Brassicaceae)

alpinum	EPot
arvense	MCtn
biebersteinii	see *Pachyphragma macrophyllum*

Thrinax (Arecaceae)

parviflora	NPlm
radiata	NPlm

Thuja ✿ (Cupressaceae)

'Extra Gold'	see *T. plicata* 'Irish Gold'
occidentalis	SArc
- 'Amber Glow'	CAco CSBt MAsh SPoG SRms
- 'Anniek'PBR	ELan EPfP MAsh SPoG
- Aurea Group	CBrac
- 'Brabant' ♀H7	LMaj NHed NLar SFol WMou
- 'Brobeck's Tower' ♀H6	LRHS NLar SPoG
- 'Danica' ♀H7	CBrac CMac EGren ELan GKin LCro MAsh MPri SPoG SRms
- 'Danica Gold'	LRHS SPoG
- 'Degroot's Spire'	MGos
- 'Elegantissima'	WCha
- EMERALD	see *T. occidentalis* 'Smaragd'
- 'Ericoides'	SRms

Thymus   695

- 'Filips Magic Moment' SPoG
- FIRE CHIEF ('Congabe'PBR) ELan LRHS MAsh MPri SPoG
- 'Golden Anne'PBR SPoG
- 'Golden Brabant'PBR MPri WFar
- 'Golden Globe' CWnw EGren LSRN
- GOLDEN SMARAGD ('Janed Gold'PBR) CCVT CWnw EPfP LRHS LSRN SFol SPoG
- 'Golden Tuffet' ♀H7 CWnw EGren ELan GKin LRHS MAsh MPri SPoG WCha
- 'Hetz Midget' ♀H7 GKin SPlb WFar
- 'Holmstrup' ♀H7 CBrac CMac LRHS MAsh MPri SRms
- 'Jantar'PBR LRHS MPri SPoG
- 'Konfettii' (v) SPoG
- 'Little Gem' SRms
- 'Mirjam'PBR (v) CWnw LRHS MPri SPoG
- 'Perk Vlaanderen' (v) LRHS
- 'Rheingold' ♀H7 CAco CBcs CBrac CMac CSBt ELan GKin LCro LRHS MAsh MGos SPlb SPoG SRms WFar
§ - 'Smaragd' ♀H7 CBrac CCVT CWnw EGren ELan EPfP LBuc LCro LRHS MAsh MGos MPri NHed SEWo SFol SPoG WCha WHtc
- 'Starstruck' SPoG
§ - 'Stolwijk' (v) LRHS
- 'Sunkist' ♀H7 CBrac CMac ELan LRHS MAsh MPri SRms WFar
- SUNNY SMARAGD ('Hoogi023'PBR) LCro MAsh
- 'Teddy' EGren EPfP LRHS MAsh MPri NLar SPoG
- 'Tiny Tim' CMac EGren MAsh
- TOTEM SMARAGD ('Thucavlo') LCro
- 'Wansdyke Silver' (v) CMac
- 'Wareana' CMac
- 'White Smaragd' (v) EPfP LRHS
- 'Woodwardii' LRHS
- 'Yellow Ribbon' CSBt SRms
orientalis see *Platycladus orientalis*
plicata CBcs CBrac CBTr CCVT CMac CWal EGren ELan IPap LSto MMuc
- 'Atrovirens' ♀H6 CBrac EGren ELan LBuc LCro LMaj MAsh MGos MHed SEWo SGol SHor SRms WHtc WMat
- 'Aurea' ♀H6 MAsh SRms
- 'Can-can' (v) CBrac
I - 'Cole's Variety' EHeP
- 'Collyer's Gold' LSto SRms
- 'Copper Kettle' GKin
- 'Excelsa' LMaj WMou
- 'Gelderland' ♀H6 ELan EPfP LRHS SPoG
- GOLDY ('4ever'PBR) CWnw EGren ELan LCro LRHS MPri SPoG
§ - 'Irish Gold' (v) CMac
- 'Little Boy'PBR MGos NLar
- 'Martin' CBrac EHeP MAsh MPri SFol SRms
- 'Rogersii' ♀H6 CBrac CMac LRHS MAsh MPri SPoG SRms
- 'Semperaurescens' (v) CMac
- 'Stolwijk's Gold' see *T. occidentalis* 'Stolwijk'
- 'Stoneham Gold' ♀H6 CBrac CMac GKin MAsh MGos SRms
- VERIGOLD ('Courtapli') MMuc SEND
- 'Whipcord' ♀H6 CAco CBcs EGren ELan EPfP LRHS NLar SMad SPoG
- 'Zebrina' (v) ♀H6 CAco CBcs CBrac CMac ELan EPfP LMaj MAsh MGos MMuc MPri SEND SPoG

Thujopsis (Cupressaceae)

dolabrata ♀H6 CAco CBrac CCVT LRHS MMuc NLar WFar
- 'Laetevirens' see *T. dolabrata* 'Nana'
§ - 'Nana' CAco CMac LCro NLar SPoG SRms
- 'Solar Flare' NLar
- 'Variegata' (v) CBcs CCVT CMac ELan GKin NLar SRms

Thunbergia ✿ (Acanthaceae)

alata EGren LRHS MCtn SPoG
- AFRICAN SUNSET (mixed) CCht LCro MCtn
- ARIZONA DARK RED (Arizona Series) LCro
- - ARIZONA ROSE SENSATION ('Volthu7898'PBR) EBee
- 'Lemon' CHll
- (Sunny Susy Series) SUNNY SUSY BROWNIE ('Sumthun 04'PBR) LCro
- - SUNNY SUSY NEW ORANGE ('Sumthun 03'PBR) LCro
- - SUNNY SUSY ROSE SENSATION LCro
- - SUNNY SUSY YELLOW DARK EYE LCro
- (Sunrise Series) 'Sunrise White With Eye' MCtn
- - 'Susie Orange Black Eye' LCro
- - 'Susie White Black Eye' CSpe LCro
coccinea B&SWJ 7166 WCru
fragrans GWJ 9441 ESwi WCru
grandiflora 'Alba' CHll
gregorii ♀H1b CHll CSpe EAri EShb
laurifolia B&SWJ 7166 WCru

Thymbra (Lamiaceae)

spicata SPhx

thyme, caraway see *Thymus herba-barona*

thyme, garden see *Thymus vulgaris*

thyme, lemon see *Thymus citriodorus*

thyme, wild see *Thymus serpyllum*

Thymus ✿ (Lamiaceae)

from Turkey EWes LEdu SPhx
§ 'Alan Bloom' LRHS
'Albus' ENfk
'Anderson's Gold' see *T. pulegioides* 'Bertram Anderson'
'Aureus' ambig. LRHS
azoricus see *T. caespititius*
'Bressingham' EDAr ELan EWhm GMaP GQue LCro LRHS MHer MHoo MNHC SPlb SRms WIce
'Caborn Wine and Roses' CCBP CGHo EHet ELan ENfk EPPr LCro MNHC SRms WFar WJek WKit
§ *caespititius* MHer MNHC NRya SPlb SRms WAbe WJek
caespitosus see *T. praecox* subsp. *praecox*
camphoratus ENfk EWes GArf LShi MHoo NBir SEdi WAbe WJek
- 'Derry' CSpe
'Carol Ann' (v) ENfk EWes MNHC SRms
CASCATA LEMONADE ENfk LCro
cilicicus misapplied see *T. caespititius*
cilicicus ambig. SRms

cilicicus Boiss. & Bail.	WAbe	'Lime'	LEdu WFar
citriodorus misapplied	see *T.* 'Culinary Lemon'	*longicaulis*	ECha LRHS SAng SRms
citriodorus ambig.	GQue SRms WTre	*longiflorus*	EDAr IDun MHoo
citriodorus (Pers.) Schreb.	LEdu LWaG	'Magic Carpet'	MCtn WJek
- 'Archer's Gold'	see *T. pulegioides* 'Archer's Gold'	*marschallianus*	see *T. pannonicus*
- 'Aureus'	see *T. pulegioides* 'Aureus'	*mastichina*	IDun MCtn
- 'Bertram Anderson'	see *T. pulegioides* 'Bertram Anderson'	- 'Didi'	MHer
'Coccineus'	see *T.* Coccineus Group	- 'PomPom' **new**	MNHC
§ Coccineus Group ♀H5	CGHo ECul EDAr ELan ENfk GMaP LCro LRHS LWaG MHer MHoo MNHC MPri NRya SPoG SRms SRot WAbe WCav WFar WHoo WIce WJek WKit WTor WTre	*micans*	see *T. caespititius*
		minus	see *Calamintha nepeta*
		neiceffii	ECha
		'Orange'	EHet SEdi SRms WFar WKit
		orange-scented	SEND SVic
		§ *pannonicus*	MHer
- 'Atropurpureus' Schleipfer	see *T.* (Coccineus Group) 'Purple Beauty'	'Peace'	ENfk
		'Peter Davis'	ENfk GBin LCro MHoo NBir SPoG SRms WAbe WFar WIce WJek
§ - 'Purple Beauty'	ECha EPot LRHS MHer SRms WHoo		
'Coccineus Major'	SRms	§ 'Pinewood'	MHer WFar WJek
'Creeping Lemon' misapplied	see *T. pulegioides* 'Kurt'	'Pink Ripple'	CGHo EHet ENfk EWes EWhm MHer MNHC SRms WHoo WJek WKit
§ - 'Culinary Lemon'	CGHo EHet ENfk GJos IDun LCro MBrN MHer MHoo MNHC MPri SEdi SVic WFar WJek	*polytrichus* misapplied	see *T. praecox*
		§ *polytrichus* A. Kern. ex Borbás subsp. ***britannicus***	CGHo ECha EHet EWhm GBin GJos GMaP LCro LRHS LSto MHer MHoo MNHC NBir NBro NClf SPlb SRms WJek WKit
'Culinary Lime'	MHoo		
'Dartmoor'	WJek		
'Desboro'	see *T. serpyllum* 'Desborough'	- - 'Thomas's White' ♀H5	LRHS
'Dillington'	ENfk WJek	'Porlock'	EPfP MHer SRms WJek
'Doone Valley' (v)	CCBP CGHo ECha ECul EHet ELan ENfk EPfP EPot EWhm GKev LCro LRHS LShi LSto MAsh MHer MHoo MMuc MNHC MPri NBir SPlb SPoG SRms SRot WFar WIce WKit	§ *praecox*	EHet EWhm LRHS MHer
		- 'Albiflorus'	WTor
		- subsp. ***arcticus***	see *T. polytrichus* A. Kern. ex Borbás subsp. *britannicus*
		- - 'Albus'	see *T. polytrichus* subsp. *britannicus* 'Thomas's White'
drucei	see *T. polytrichus* A. Kern. ex Borbás subsp. *britannicus*		
'E.B. Anderson'	see *T. pulegioides* 'Bertram Anderson'	§ - subsp. ***praecox***	GAbr
× *faustinoi*	EHet MNHC WHoo WKit	prostrate	MHoo
'Fragrantissimus'	CGHo EHet ELan ENfk EWhm GQue IDun LCro MHer MHoo MNHC SPlb WJek WKit WTre	'Provence'	GQue
		pulegioides	CCBP CGHo CHby ENfk GQue IDun LShi LSto MHer MHoo SRms SRot WFar WJek WKit
'Golden King' (v)	ELan ENfk LSRN MAsh MHer SRms		
'Golden Lemon' misapplied	see *T. pulegioides* 'Aureus'	§ - 'Archer's Gold'	EHet ENfk EPfP EPot LCro LSRN MAsh MHer MHoo MNHC MPri NBir SRms WFar WKit
'Golden Lemon' (v)	WJek		
'Golden Queen' (v)	CGHo SRms WFar	§ - 'Aureus' ♀H5	EHet ENfk GMaP LCro LRHS MAsh MNHC SPlb SRms
'Goldie'	IDun		
§ 'Hartington Silver' (v)	ECha EDAr ENfk EPot EWes EWhm LRHS MHer MHoo SPlb SPoG SRms WTor	§ - 'Bertram Anderson' ♀H5	CAby CGHo ECha ENfk EPfP LRHS LShi LWaG MAsh MHer MHoo MPri NBir NRya SPoG SRms
herba-barona	CCBP CGHo ECha EHet GQue MHer MHoo MNHC SRms WJek WKit	- 'Foxley' (v)	CCBP CGHo CTsd ECul EHet ENfk EPfP EWhm GMaP LRHS LSto MHer MHoo MNHC MPri SPlb SPoG SRms WFar WJek WKit WTor
- *citrata*	see *T. herba-barona* 'Lemon-scented'		
§ - 'Lemon-scented'	ECha LEdu MHer MWlw SRms WJek	- 'Golden Dwarf'	WFar
'Highland Cream'	see *T.* 'Hartington Silver'	§ - 'Kurt'	ELan ENfk LEdu MHer MHoo SRms WJek
§ 'Iden'	MHoo WJek		
'Jekka'	EHet ELan EWhm LCro LSto MEar MHer MNHC SRms WHoo WJek WKit WTre	- 'Tabor'	EHet ENfk EWhm MHoo MNHC SRms WKit
		'Rainbow Falls' (v)	CTsd EPfP MHoo SEdi SRms WFar
'Jekka's Autumn Pink'	WJek	'Rasta' (v)	EPot MHer
'Jekka's Bee Haven'	WJek	'Redstart'	ECha ENfk EPot MHer SRms WJek
'Jekka's Rosy Carpet'	WJek WTre	rose-scented	LCro MNHC
'Kurt'	see *T. pulegioides* 'Kurt'	'Ruby Glow'	CGHo EHet ENfk EWes EWhm LCro LShi MHer MNHC NBir
'Lavender Sea'	EWes		
'Lemon Caraway'	see *T. herba-barona* 'Lemon-scented'	*serpyllum* ambig.	SPhx SVic WFar
		serpyllum L.	EGren GJos IDun LBuc LRHS MCtn MHoo SPlb SRms
'Lemon Curd'	EHet ELan ENfk LRHS MHoo MNHC SPlb SPoG SRms WJek WKit	- var. *albus*	CGHo ECha GAbr GMaP GQue MHoo MNHC SRms SRot WCav WFar WHoo WTre
* 'Lemon Variegated' (v)	ELan ENfk EPfP EWhm LCro MHoo MNHC SPoG		
'Lilac Time'	ENfk EWes MHer SPlb SRms WJek	- 'Albus Variegatus'	see *T.* 'Hartington Silver'

Tiarella 697

- 'Annie Hall'	ELan EPfP EPot MAsh MHer MNHC SRms WAbe WJek	
- 'Atropurpureus'	see *T.* (Coccineus Group) 'Purple Beauty'	
- *coccineus* 'Minor' misapplied	see *T.* Coccineus Group	
- *coccineus* 'Minor' Bloom	see *T.* 'Alan Bloom'	
- 'Conwy Rose'	ECha WAbe	
§ - 'Desborough'	MHer	
- 'East Lodge'	MHer MNHC SRms	
- 'Elfin'	EWes LRHS SPhx SPlb SRms SRot WAbe WTor	
- 'Goldstream' (v)	ENfk IDun SPlb SRms WCav	
- 'Iden'	see *T.* 'Iden'	
- 'Minimalist'	see *T. serpyllum* 'Minor'	
- 'Minimus'	see *T. serpyllum* 'Minor'	
§ - 'Minor'	ECha EDAr ENfk LCro LRHS MHer MHoo MNHC SLee SPlb SRms SRot WAbe WFar WHoo	
- 'Minus'	see *T. serpyllum* 'Minor'	
- 'Pink Chintz' ♀H4	CCBP CGHo ECha ECul EHet ELan ENfk EPfP EPot EWhm GMaP LCro LRHS MHer MHoo MNHC NRya SPhx SPlb SPoG SRms WFar WIce WJek WKit WTor	
- Pink Magic ('Tuthpim') **new**	MNHC	
- 'Purple Beauty'	see *T.* (Coccineus Group) 'Purple Beauty'	
- 'Red Carpet'	EHet LRHS SPhx SRms WFar	
- 'Russetings'	CGHo ENfk EPfP EUrb GJos LCro MHer MHoo MNHC SDix SPoG SRms WCav WFar	
- 'September'	MHer	
- 'Snowdrift'	CCBP ECul EDAr EHet ELan EPfP EPot LCro LRHS LSto MHer MNHC SPlb SRms WFar WIce WKit WTre	
- 'Variegatus'	see *T.* 'Hartington Silver'	
- 'Vey'	MHer SRms	
'Silver King' (v)	ENfk WKit	
'Silver Posie'	CAby CGHo CTsd ECul EDAr EGren EHet ELan ENfk EPfP EWhm LCro MAsh MHer MHoo MNHC MPri SDix SPoG SRms SRot WFar WKit	
'Silver Queen' (v) ♀H5	CBcs ECha EGren EHet ELan ENfk EPfP EWhm GKev GMaP LRHS LShi LWaG MHoo MNHC MPri SPlb SRms SVic WJek WTre	
'Sparkling Bright' (v)	EHet ELan ENfk EWhm LCro MNHC WKit	
§ *vulgaris*	Widely available	
* - 'Compactus'	EHet ELan ENfk GMaP MHer MHoo MNHC SRms WFar WJek WKit	
- 'Deutsche Auslese'	see *T. vulgaris*	
- English, winter	GQue IDun MCtn SRms WKit	
- French	see *T. vulgaris*	
- French, summer	MCtn	
- gold-leaved	MNHC	
- 'Lucy'	MHer	
- 'Pinewood'	see *T.* 'Pinewood'	
zygis	IDun	

Thyrsopteris (Thyrsopteridaceae)
elegans   SBig

Thysanolaena (Poaceae)
latifolia   WCot

Tiarella ✿ (Saxifragaceae)

Angel Wings ('Gowing')^PBR (Fox Series) ♀H5	CWnw EHeP LBar LRHS Midl MPnt WNPC
'Appalachian Trail' (American Trails Series)	ISha MPnt
'Black Snowflake'	MPnt
'Black Velvet'	MPnt
'Braveheart'	MPnt
'Butter and Sugar'	MPnt
'Butterfly Wings'	MPnt
'Candy Striper'	ISha LRHS MPnt MPro NLar
'Cascade Creeper'^PBR	MPnt
collina	see *T. wherryi*
cordifolia ♀H5	CBcs CMac EBee ECha EGren EHeP ELan EPfP GAbr GMaP ISha LSto LWaG MGos MPnt NBir SRms WCAu
- 'Glossy'	MPnt
- 'Milk Chocolate'	MPnt
- 'Oakleaf'	MPnt NBro WCAu
- 'Rosalie'	see × *Heucherella alba* 'Rosalie'
- 'Running Tapestry'	MPnt
'Crow Feather'^PBR	MPnt
'Cutting Edge'	MPnt
'Cygnet'	CDor MPnt
'Dunvegan'	MPnt
'Elizabeth Oliver'	MPnt
'Emerald Ellie' (Fox Series)	EHeP LBar MPnt NSti SHar WNPC
'Finger Paint'	MPnt
'Happy Trails' (American Trails Series)	ISha MPnt WNPC WPnP
'Inkblot'	MPnt
'Iron Butterfly'^PBR (v)	CDor EAri EBee GJos GMaP LSRN MPnt MSwo NLar SPoG SRms StAn WHoo
'Iron Cross'	SPlb
'Jeepers Creepers'^PBR	ISha MPnt
'Martha Oliver'	MPnt
'Mint Chocolate'	MPnt NBir NGdn NLar
'Moorgrün'	EBee EPPr
Morning Star ('Tntia042')	GQue MPnt SRkn
'Mystic Mist'^PBR (v)	CDor CWGN EGren MHol MPnt MPro SPoG
'Neon Lights'^PBR	MPnt NBir
§ 'Ninja'	MPnt NBir
'Oregon Trail' (American Trails Series)	MNrw MPnt
'Pacific Crest' (American Trails Series)	MPnt
'Pink Bouquet'	CSpe ECha LSto MPnt WFar WPnP
'Pink Brushes'^PBR	MPnt
'Pink Skyrocket'^PBR ♀H6	Widely available
'Pinwheel'	MPnt
'Pirate's Patch'^PBR	MPnt
polyphylla	GElm MPnt WCru
- W&O 9029	GGro
- 'Baoxing Pink'	MPnt WCru
- 'Filigran'	GElm GQue MPnt
Raspberry Sundae ('Gosund') (Fox Series) ♀H6	EHeP LRHS MPnt WNPC
'Running Tiger'	MPnt
'Sea Foam'	MPnt
'Simsalabim'	MPnt
'Skeleton Key'	MPnt
'Skid's Variegated' (v)	MPnt SPoG
'Skyrocket'	CLil
'Spanish Cross'	MPnt
'Spring Symphony'^PBR ♀H7	CBcs CDor CLil ECha EGren ELan EMor EPfP GAbr GMaP ISha LBom LCro LRHS MAsh MBel MPnt MPri MPro NBir NLar NPer SHar SHor SPoG WCav WNPC
Starburst ('Tntia041'^PBR)	MPnt
'Sugar and Spice'^PBR	CDor CMHG CSpe CWGN ECha EGren EHeP EPfP LCro LRHS LSto

	MPnt MPri MPro NLar SAth WCAu WNPC
'Sunset Ridge'^{PBR} (American Trails Series)	ISha LRHS MPnt
SYLVAN LACE ('Tntiasl') (Sylvan Series)	MPnt
'Tiger Stripe'	EBee MPnt
'Timbuktu'	MPnt
trifoliata	MPnt
- var. *unifoliata*	MPnt
'Viking Ship'	see × *Heucherella* 'Viking Ship'
§ *wherryi* ♀H5	CBcs EBee ECha EGren ELan EMor EPfP LRHS LShi MCtn MPnt NBir NBro SPlb StAn WCAu
- 'Bronze Beauty'	MPnt
- 'Green Velvet'	MPnt

Tibouchina (Melastomataceae)

grandifolia	see *Pleroma foveolatum, P. heteromallum*
grossa	see *Chaetogastra grossa*
heteromalla	see *Pleroma heteromallum*
organensis	see *Pleroma foveolatum*
paratropica	see *Chaetogastra paratropica*
semidecandra misapplied	see *Pleroma urvilleanum*
urvilleana	see *Pleroma urvilleanum*

Tigridia (Iridaceae)

immaculata B&SWJ 10345	WCru
orthantha 'Red-Hot Tiger'	EBee MNrw WCot WCru
pavonia	CAby CExl EGren LAma
- 'Alba Grandiflora'	LAma
- 'Aurea'	LAma
- 'Canariensis'	LAma
- 'Lilacea'	LAma
- 'Speciosa'	LAma

Tilia ✿ (Malvaceae)

americana	CLnd CMCN WJur
- AMERICAN SENTRY ('McKSentry')	IPap
- 'Redmond'	MBlu
amurensis	CMCN
- from Korea	WPGP
argentea	see *T. tomentosa*
begoniifolia	see *T. dasystyla* subsp. *caucasica*
callidonta	WPGP
§ *caroliniana*	CMCN IArd MBlu WPGP
subsp. *heterophylla*	
chinensis	CMCN WPGP
- F 30558	WPGP
chingiana	WPGP
concinna	WPGP
cordata	CAco CAgr CBcs CBrac CBTr CCVT CDoC CHab CLnd CMac CMCN EGren EHeP ELan EPfP IPap LBuc LCot LRHS MCtn MMuc NPip SArc SEND SEWo SFol WHtc WMat WMou WRjT
- 'Greenspire' ♀H6	CBTr CCVT CLnd CMCN EBar EHeP EPfP IPap LCro LMaj LRHS NPip SEWo WMat WMou
- 'Len Parvin'	WPGP
- 'Rancho'	EBar
- 'Roelvo'	EHeP
- 'Streetwise'	SArc
- 'Winter Orange' ♀H6	CBcs CBTr CCVT CEnd CMac CMCN CNWT EBee EGren ELan EPfP MBlu MSwo NPip SEWo WMat
§ *dasystyla*	WPGP
subsp. *caucasica*	

- - A&L 16	WPGP
- - NJM 13.029	WPGP
endochrysea	EPfP WPGP
× *euchlora*	CCVT CLnd EBar EBee EHeP IPap LMaj NPip SArc SEWo WMat
§ × *europaea*	CLnd SFol
- GOLDEN SUNSET ('Wiltil')	LCro WReH
- 'Pallida'	CLnd EBar EHeP IPap LMaj MBlu WSpi
- 'Wratislaviensis' ♀H6	MBlu
§ 'Harold Hillier'	CMCN MBlu WPGP
henryana	CBcs CCVT CEnd CLnd CMCN CWnw EBar ELan EPfP IPap MBlu NPip WHtc WMat WPGP
- 'Arnold Select'	CBcs WMou WPGP
- 'Bluebell'	MBlu
- 'Kerdalo'	WPGP
'Hillieri'	see *T.* 'Harold Hillier'
insularis misapplied	see *T. japonica, T. japonica* 'Ernest Wilson'
§ *japonica*	CMCN EBee WPGP
§ - 'Ernest Wilson' ♀H6	MBlu
- large-leaved, from China	WPGP
kiusiana	CBcs CMCN MBlu WPGP
mandshurica	CMCN WPGP
maximowicziana	EPfP MBlu WPGP
mexicana	EBee WPGP
- CD&R 1318	WPGP
miqueliana	CMCN MBlu
× *moltkei*	WPGP
mongolica	CMCN EBar EPfP MBlu WPGP
- 'Buda'	ELan WPGP
- 'Harvest Gold'	CLnd EBar MBlu
monticola	see *T. caroliniana* subsp. *heterophylla*
nobilis	EPfP MBlu
- KR 226	WPGP
oliveri	MBlu WPGP
aff. *oliveri* HRS 2808	WPGP
paucicostata	IArd
platyphyllos	CAgr CBcs CCVT CHab CLnd CMCN EBar EHeP EPfP IPap LBuc LCro NPip SEND WHtc WMat WMou
- 'Aurea'	MBlu NPip WMat
- 'Corallina'	see *T. platyphyllos* 'Rubra'
- 'Fastigiata'	CCVT EHeP
- 'Laciniata'	MBlu
§ - 'Rubra' ♀H6	CCVT CLnd EBar EHeP SEWo
- 'Tiltstone Filigree'	WMou
- 'Tortuosa'	MBlu
× *stellata*	WPGP
§ *tomentosa*	CAco CLnd LCro MMuc SEND
- 'Brabant' ♀H6	CCVT EBar EHeP LMaj WFar
- 'Petiolaris' ♀H6	CCVT CEnd CLnd EHeP ELan IArd MBlu WMou
tuan	WPGP
- var. *chenmoui*	CMCN MBlu WPGP
× *vulgaris*	see *T.* × *europaea*
'Westonbirt Dainty Leaf'	CAco WPGP

Tillaea see *Crassula*

Tillandsia (Bromeliaceae)

sp.	NCft
abdita	LCro
aeranthos	NCft
- var. *alba*	NCft
* - 'Albo Flora'	NCft
- 'Bronze'	NCft
- 'Miniata'	NCft

Tillandsia

- 'Minime'	NCft		caulescens × dura	NCft	
- 'Minuette'	NCft		duratii	NCft	
- purple-flowered	NCft		dyeriana ♀H1c	LWaG	
- var. rosea	NCft		edithae	NCft	
aeranthos × bergeri	NCft		ehlersiana	NCft	
aeranthos × juncea	NCft		elongata	NCft	
aeranthos × stricta	NCft		'Eric Knobloch'	NCft	
aeranthos × stricta 'Petropolis'	NCft		exserta	NCft	
			exserta × juncea	NCft	
aeranthos × tenuifolia	NCft		extensa	NCft	
aizoides	NCft		fasciculata	NCft	
albertiana	NCft		festucoides	NCft	
albertiana × argentina	NCft		flavobracteata	NCft	
albida	NCft SPlb		flavoviolacea	NCft	
- dwarf	NCft		flexuosa	NCft	
andicola	NCft		- viviparous	NCft	
araujei	NCft		floribunda	NCft	
arequitae	NCft		× floridana	NCft	
argentea ♀H1c	LCro NCft		fresnilloensis	NCft	
argentina	NCft		fuchsii f. gracilis	NCft	
baileyi	NCft		funebris	NCft	
- 'Halley's Comet'	NCft		gardneri	NCft	
* - var. vivipara	NCft		geminiflora	NCft	
balbisiana	NCft		geminiflora × stricta	NCft	
balsasensis	NCft		glabrior	NCft	
bandensis	NCft		globosa × sucrei	NCft	
barthlottii	NCft		'Gordon C'	NCft	
bartramii	NCft		grao-mogolensis	NCft	
bella × stricta	NCft		hammeri	NCft	
bergeri	NCft SChr SPlb		harrisii	NCft	
bergeri × tenuifolia	NCft		heteromorpha	NCft	
bryoides	NCft		hondurensis	NCft	
bulbosa	SPlb		'Houston'	NCft	
- 'Gigante'	NCft		'Houston Enano'	NCft	
'Buttercup'	NCft		incarnata	NCft	
butzii	NCft		intermedia	NCft	
- var. roseiflora	NCft		ionantha	CDoC LCro NCft	
cacticola	NCft		* - 'Fuego'	NCft	
cacticola × purpurea	NCft		- var. ionantha	LCro	
caerulea	NCft		- - 'Druid'	NCft	
* - var. major	NCft		- var. maxima 'Huamelula'	see T. ionantha var. stricta	
* - var. minor	NCft		- 'Peach'	NCft	
'Califano'	NCft		I - 'Rubra'	NCft	
caliginosa	NCft		- var. scaposa	see T. kolbii	
capillaris	NCft		§ - var. stricta	NCft	
- f. incana	NCft		ixioides	NCft	
- f. virescens	NCft		jonesii	NCft	
capitata	NCft		jucunda	NCft	
- 'Domingensis'	NCft		juncea	NCft	
- var. guzmanoides	see T. lautneri		karwinskyana	NCft	
- mauve	NCft		'Kashkin'	NCft	
- 'Peach'	LCro NCft		'Kimberly'	NCft	
- red-leaved	NCft		§ kolbii	NCft	
- 'Yellow Star'	NCft		kuntzeana	NCft	
cardenasii	NCft		latifolia	NCft	
caulescens	NCft		- var. divaricata	NCft	
cauligera	NCft		- 'Enano Latifolia'	NCft	
chartacea	NCft		- var. latifolia	NCft	
chiapensis	NCft		§ lautneri	NCft	
chusgonensis	NCft		leiboldiana	NCft	
cocoensis	NCft		§ leonamiana	NCft	
concolor	NCft		lepidosepela	NCft	
'Cotton Candy'	NCft		loliacea	NCft	
crocata	NCft		lorentziana	NCft	
- 'Brandywine'	NCft		magnusiana	NCft	
- 'Copper Penny'	NCft		mallemontii	NCft	
crocata × caliginosa	NCft		marconae	NCft	
crocata × loliacea	NCft		§ matudae	NCft	
cyanea	LCro		mereliana	NCft	
- 'Anita' ♀H1c	MPri		mima var. chiletensis	NCft	
diaguitensis	NCft		minutiflora	NCft	

mitlaensis	NCft
- var. *tulensis*	NCft
montana	NCft
muhrii	see *T. zecheri* var. *cafayatensis*
multiflora	LCro
myosura	NCft
'Mystic Burgundy'	NCft
'Mystic Flame'	NCft
'Mystic Haze'	NCft
'Mystic Rainbow'	NCft
'Mystic Trumpet'	NCft
nana	NCft
neglecta	NCft
'Nezley'	NCft
nolleriana	NCft
novakii	NCft
'Old Man's Gold'	NCft
paleacea	NCft
- var. *apurimacensis*	NCft
- 'Enano Paleacea'	NCft
paleacea × *tectorum*	NCft
pardoi	NCft
pedicellata	NCft
peiranoi	NCft
plagiotropica	NCft
pohliana	NCft
polystachia	NCft
pringlei	NCft
pruinosa	NCft
pueblensis	NCft
punctulata	NCft
purpurea	NCft
- 'Shooting Star'	NCft
queroensis	NCft
× *rectifolia*	NCft
recurvata	NCft
recurvifolia	NCft
- var. *subsecundifolia*	see *T. leonamiana*
'Redy'	NCft
reichenbachii	NCft
retorta	NCft
schatzlii	NCft
schiedeana	NCft
- 'Major'	NCft
I - 'Minor'	NCft
schreiteri	NCft
schusteri	NCft
seideliana	NCft
setiformis	NCft
simulata	NCft
sphaerocephala	NCft
stellifera	NCft
straminea	NCft
streptocarpa	NCft
stricta	NCft
- var. *albifolia*	NCft
I - 'Amethyst'	NCft
- compact	NCft
- 'Grey'	NCft
- 'Hard Leaf'	NCft
- 'Petropolis'	NCft
- var. *stricta*	NCft
tectorum	NCft
- caulescent	NCft
tenuifolia	NCft
- 'Amethyst'	NCft
- blue-flowered	NCft
- bronze-leaved	NCft
I - 'Minima'	NCft
- var. *tenuifolia*	NCft
- var. *vaginata*	NCft
toropiensis	NCft
tricholepis	NCft
tricolor	NCft
- var. *melanocrater*	NCft
'Twisted Tim'	NCft
usneoides	CDoC CoPl LBom LInT LWaG NCft SPlb
- 'Capellini'	NCft
- fine-leaved	NCft
- thick-leaved	NCft
velickiana	see *T. matudae*
vernicosa	NCft
vicentina	NCft
werdermannii	NCft
'Wonga'	NCft
xerographica	CDoC LBom LCro
xiphioides	NCft
§ *zecheri* var. *cafayatensis*	NCft

Tinantia (Commelinaceae)

erecta	MCtn
pringlei	GEdr MPie SBeP SBrt SNoN WPGP WTra
- AIM 77	EBee ESwi WCot
- pale-leaved	WTra
- variegated (v)	WFar WTra

Tipuana (Fabaceae)

tipu	WJur

Titanopsis (Aizoaceae)

calcarea ♀H1c	CPic

Titanotrichum (Gesneriaceae)

oldhamii	CBcs ESwi GEdr IPot LRHS SBrt SPlb

Tithonia (Asteraceae)

diversifolia	EAri
rotundifolia	CBlu LWaG
- 'Fiesta del Sol'	MCtn
- 'Torch'	CSpe LCro LWaG MCtn MPro SMrm
'Torchlight'	SPhx

Todea (Osmundaceae)

barbara	CBrP CDTJ CTsd WPGP

Tofieldia (Tofieldiaceae)

coccinea	GArf GEdr WCot WCru

Tolmiea (Saxifragaceae)

menziesii	CMac MCtn NBro SPlb
- 'Cool Gold'PBR	ESwi GMaP

Tolpis (Asteraceae)

barbata	MCtn

tomatoes see AGM Vegetables Section

Toona (Meliaceae)

hexandra **new**	EUrb
§ *sinensis*	CAgr CBcs CWRo ELan EPfP LSRN SMrm WJur WPGP
- 'Flamingo' (v)	ELan EPfP EUrb LCro LMil LRHS LSRN MAsh NCth NLar NPip SAth SGol SHor SMad SPoG WMat
- 'Lise'	CMCN

Torenia (Linderniaceae)

fournieri **new**	CSpe

Torilis (Apiaceae)
- japonica — SPhx

Torreya (Taxaceae)
- californica — CAco WPGP
- nucifera — CAco WJur
- taxifolia — WPGP

Tovara see Persicaria

Townsendia (Asteraceae)
- incana — GEdr
- scapigera — GEdr
- spathulata — SPlb

Toxicodendron ✿ (Anacardiaceae)
- § orientale B&SWJ 3656 — WCru
  - B&SWJ 10884 large-leaved — WCru
- § succedaneum — CDTJ EBee
- § vernicifluum — NLar

Trachelium (Campanulaceae)
- asperuloides — SPlb WAbe
- caeruleum 'Black Knight' — CSpe WCot

Trachelospermum ✿ (Apocynaceae)
- § asiaticum ⚘H4 — CBcs CDoC CExl CMac CMen CRHN CSBt CSde CWnw EBee EGrI ELon EPfP LCro LEdu LRHS LSRN LWaG NLar SArc SEle SEND SNig SPad SPoG SRms SSta WFar WLov WTHo
  - 'Bella'
  - CHILI & VANILLA ('Livano') — LRHS MPri WCot
  - 'Golden Memories' — CBcs CExl CMac CRHN CWGN EBee ELan ELon EPfP LRHS LSRN SEND SNig SPoG SRms WCot
  - 'Goshiki' (v) — SEle
  - 'Kulu Chirimen' — WCot
  - Ōgon-nishiki' (v) — CWGN EBee SEle SNig SPoG WFar
  - 'Pink Showers' — Widely available
  - STAR OF MILANO ('Trsuz01') (v) — CAbb EPfP ESwi LRHS SNig SWCr WLov
  - 'Summer Sunset' — CBcs ELan ELon EUrb SGol SRms WCot
  - 'Theta' — ELon LRHS WCot WFar WPGP
  - 'Chameleon' — ELan LRHS SMad
  - 'Christabel Bielenberg' — EBee LRHS WSpi
- jasminoides ⚘H4 — Widely available
  - 'Major' — CMac ELan MAsh SRms WNPC
- § var. pubescens — CRHN LRHS SPoG
  - 'Japonicum'
  - 'Rose d'Inde' — CCVT
  - STAR OF TOSCANA ('Selbra'PBR) — CBcs CWGN ELan ELon EPfP ESwi LBom LCro LRHS LSRN LWaG MAsh SEND SPoG WCha WFar WLov WTHo
  - 'Tricolor' (v) — EUrb SEle SGol SNig SWor WFar
  - 'Variegatum' (v) ⚘H4 — CBcs CBrac CDoC CMac CRHN CSBt CWGN EBee ELan ELon EPfP EUrb LCro LRHS LSRN MGos SNig SPoG SRms SSta SWor WLov WTHo
  - 'Waterwheel' — CBcs CDoC CMac CSde EBee ELan ELon LBom LRHS NLar SAdn
  - 'Wilsonii' — CExl CMac ELon EPfP LSRN NLar SEND SPoG WCot WNPC
  - WINTER RUBY ('Trared'PBR) — CBcs CDoC CWnw LCro MPri
- majus misapplied — see T. jasminoides var. pubescens 'Japonicum'
- majus Nakai — see T. asiaticum

Trachycarpus (Arecaceae)
- from Manipur — NPlm
- § fortunei ⚘H5 — Widely available
- latisectus — NPlm
- 'Nainital' — SArc
- princeps — CBlu SArc SChr
- takil Becc. — EUrb
- ukhrulensis NJM 13.085 — WPGP
- wagnerianus ⚘H5 — CBlu CBrP CDoC CDTJ CExl CTsd EOli LRHS NPlm SArc SBig SChr WPGP

Trachymene (Apiaceae)
- coerulea — CSpe GJos MCtn MPro SPhx

Trachystemon (Boraginaceae)
- orientalis — CCBP CDor CExl CMac CToG ECha EGrI EPPr EUrb GQue LEdu LShi MHol MMuc MNrw NBid NLar SBig WBrk WCot WCru WFar WHer WHil WPGP
  - 'Bamian' — WFar
  - 'Sundew' — WFar

Tradescantia ✿ (Commelinaceae)
- albiflora — see T. fluminensis
- × andersoniana W. Ludwig & Rohw. — see T. Andersoniana Group
- § Andersoniana Group — EGrI ESwi LShi
  - 'Baby Doll' — GElm
  - 'Bilberry Ice' — CDor CMac EDAr GElm GMaP MAsh NBir NBro NGdn NLar SMrm SVen WGwG
  - 'Blue and Gold' — ELan EPfP EWhm NSti WCot WHil
  - 'Blue Stone' — CDor ECha EGrI SRkn SRms SVen WHoo
  - 'Bridal Veil' — see Gibasis pellucida 'Tahitian Bridal Veil'
  - 'Caerulea Plena' — see T. virginiana 'Caerulea Plena'
  - CARMINE GLOW — see T. (Andersoniana Group) 'Karminglut'
  - 'Charlotte' — CDor ECha LRHS NBro NGdn NLar
  - 'Concord Grape'⚘H6 — CMac ECha EGrI ELan EPfP GElm GMaP LRHS MArl MAsh MGos NBro NGdn NSti SPeP WCAu WCot WFar WGwG WHoo WKif
  - 'Good Luck'PBR — WHil
  - 'In the Navy' — NLar
  - 'Innocence' — CAby CDor CWnw ECha GElm GMaP LBar LRHS MArl MBel NBir NGdn NSti SPoG WGwG
  - 'Iris Prichard' — GMaP LRHS NLar
  - 'Isis' — CAby GMaP LRHS MMuc NBir NGdn WGwG WKif
  - 'J.C.Weguelin' — EGrI NBir SRms WCAu
  - 'JS Brainstorm' — LBar LRHS MPri WNPC XFar
- § 'Karminglut' — GMaP LShi NBir NGdn NLar
  - 'Leonora' — NLar
  - 'Little Doll' — CDor ESwi NBro NLar WHil
  - 'Little White Doll' — LRHS
  - 'Mrs Loewer' — ECha
  - 'Osprey' — CBcs CDor CWnw EBlo ECha EGrI GElm LRHS LShi MArl MBel NGdn NLar NSti SMrm SRms WCAu WGwG
  - 'Pauline' — NBir NLar
  - 'Perinne's Pink' — EPfP NSti WCAu
  - 'Pink Chablis' — NBro NLar SPeP
  - 'Purewell Giant' — CMac LRHS NBro NLar WKif

- 'Purple Dome'	CAby CFis ELan GMaP LRHS MArl MMuc NBir NBro NGdn SMrm SPeP SPoG WCAu WGwG		- 'Cream' (v)	WTra
			- 'Dwarf'	WTra
			- 'Rainbow' (v) ♀H1c	LCro SPre WTra
- 'Red Grape'	CDor EPfP MBel NSti SPel		- Sitara Gold	WTra
- 'Rubra'	EGrI EPfP LRHS SRms		('Hansoti02'PBR) (v)	
- 'Sunshine Charm'PBR (Charm Series)	NLar		- 'Vittata'	WTra
			'Sweet Tabby' (v)	WTra
- 'Sweet Kate'	CMac NBro NLar SMad SPoG SRms		Sweetness ('Ec-trade-2011') (v)	WTra
- 'Valour'	LRHS			
- 'Zwanenburg Blue'	ECha NLar SPlb SPoG		'Tenderness' (v)	WTra
'Angel Eyes'	EBee WHil		tricolor	see *T. zebrina*
'Angel Wings'	WTra		'Unicorn' (v)	WTra
'Blushing Bride' (v)	ELon EUrb LCro SBig		*virginiana* 'Alba'	CMac SRms
brevifolia 'Scout'	WTra	I	- 'Brevicaulis'	ECha NBro
'Brightness' (v) **new**	MPri	§	- 'Caerulea Plena' (d)	GElm
'Brown Hill'	LBom WTra		- 'Rubra'	SPlb
canaliculata	see *T. ohiensis*		'White Giant'	WTra
cerinthoides 'Green Nanouk'	WTra		*zanonia* 'Mexican Flag' (v)	WTra
		§	*zebrina*	CDoC CPic EGren EShb EUrb LCro LInT LWaG MPri NHrt
- 'Limelight'	WTra			
- 'Nanouk'PBR (v) ♀H1c	CPic LBom LCro LWaG MPri SPre WFar		- 'Burgundy' (v)	WTra
			- 'Deep Purple' (v)	WTra
- 'Pink Furry' (v)	WTra		- 'Discolor' (v)	WTra
- 'Red Hill'	WTra		- 'Discolor Multicolor' (v)	WTra
chrysophylla 'Baby Bunny Bellies'	WFar WTra		- 'Evanesce' (v)	WTra
			- 'Flame Dance' ♀H1b	WTra
- variegated (v) **new**	WTra		- 'HappiLee' (v)	WTra
crassifolia F&M 258	WPGP		- 'Leprechaun' (v)	WTra
§	*fluminensis*	CoPl LInT LWaG MPri NHrt SChr WDib WFar	- 'Little Hill' (v)	WTra
			- 'Minima' (v)	WTra
- 'Aurea'	CoPl CPic GQue WTra		- *pendula*	see *T. zebrina*
- 'Bicolor'	WTra		- 'Pink Paradise' (v) **new**	WTra
- 'Laekenensis'	see *T. fluminensis* 'Lavender'		- 'Purple Plush'	WTra
- 'Lavender' (v)	WTra		- 'Purpusii'	LBom WDib WTra
- 'Quicksilver' (v) ♀H1c	EShb		- 'Quadricolor' (v) ♀H1c	CDoC LBom LInT MPri WTra
- 'Variegata' (v)	WTra		- 'Silver Smudge' (v)	WTra
- 'Viridis'	WTra		- 'Superba' (v)	WTra
- 'Yellow Hill' (v)	LBom WFar WTra		- 'Tikal' (v)	WTra
'Gelfling' (v)	WTra		- 'Violet Hill' (v) ♀H1c	WTra
hirta 'Swifttale'	WTra			
'Ivory Hill' (v)	WTra		**Tragopogon** (Asteraceae)	
'Maiden's Blush' (v) ♀H1c	CoPl CSpe EShb SMrm SPlb SVen WTra		*crocifolius*	CSpe
			porrifolius	GQue SVic WCot
I	'Mini Pink'	WTra	- 'Mammoth'	MCtn
multiflora	see *Tripogandra multiflora*		*pratensis*	CAgr GQue NMir
mundula 'Fairy Wings' (v)	WTra		- subsp. *orientalis*	LRHS
- 'Green Hill'	LBom LCro WTra		- subsp. *pratensis*	CGwi
- 'Lisa' (v)	WTra			
navicularis	see *Callisia navicularis*		**Trapa** (Lythraceae)	
§	*ohiensis*	SBrt	℗	*natans*	ELin LWaG
'Pale Puma'	EShb WTra			
pallida	CPic EShb		**Trautvetteria** (Ranunculaceae)	
- 'Blue Sue'	WTra		*carolinensis*	EWes WCot
- 'Green Moon' **new**	WTra		- var. *japonica*	GEdr GKev LRHS WCot WCru
- 'Jade King' **new**	WTra		- - B&SWJ 10861	WCru
- 'Kartuz Giant'	MPie WCot WTra		- var. *occidentalis*	EBee LEdu WCru WFar WPGP
- 'Ocampo White'	WTra			
- 'Pink Stripe' (v)	EShb WTra		**Triadica** (Euphorbiaceae)	
- 'Purple Pixie'	WTra		*sebifera*	Prohibited invasive. See Conservation and the Environment, p.42
§	- 'Purpurea' ♀H3	CoPl EShb LWaG SBig SMrm SPlb WTra		
- 'Shadow Hill'	WTra		**Trichocereus** see *Echinopsis*	
pendula	see *T. zebrina*		*macrogonus*	NPIm
'Pink Dragon' (v) **new**	WTra			
'Pink Hill'	WTra		**Trichodiadema** (Aizoaceae)	
'Pink Lilac' (v)	WTra		*densum* ♀H1c	CPic EAri
'Purple Sabre'	see *T. pallida* 'Purpurea'		*intonsum*	SPlb
purpurea	see *T. pallida* 'Purpurea'		*mirabile*	CoPl
sillamontana ♀H1c	CPic EShb LWaG SChr WTra			
- 'Gold Stripes' (v)	EShb WTra		**Trichopetalum** (Asparagaceae)	
spathacea	LBom WTra	§	*plumosum*	CBro
- 'Concolor'	WTra			

Trichosanthes (Cucurbitaceae)
W&O 0109   GGro

Trichostema (Lamiaceae)
'Blue Bonnets'   MMuc

Tricuspidaria see *Crinodendron*

Tricyrtis (Liliaceae)
'Adbane'   CLAP EWes MPro WFar WGwG
affinis B&SWJ 11442   WCru
- 'Early Bird'   WCru
'Amanagowa'   CLAP
bakeri   see *T. latifolia*
'Blue Wonder'   EUrb LBuc WFar WHil XFar
dilatata   see *T. macropoda*
'Empress'   CAby CBct CDor CLAP CSpe EGren ELan EWes LBar LSou MBNS MPro NLar SDix SRkn WHil
formosana   ECha EGren GMaP MMuc MNrw SRms StAn WKif
- B&SWJ 306   LEdu
- B&SWJ 355   WCru
- B&SWJ 3073   WCru
- B&SWJ 3712   WCru
- B&SWJ 6970   WCru
- RWJ 10109   WCru
- 'Autumn Glow' (v)   EAri LBar LRHS LSou MPri WTor
- 'Blushing Toad'   ESwi WCru WFar
- 'Dark Beauty'   CCBP CDor CLAP CMiW EBee EGrI ELan EMor LBar LCro LRHS MHol WCAu WFar
- dark-flowered   IPot
- 'Emperor' (v)   ESwi
- 'Gilt Edge' (v)   CBct ELon EMor MNrw WFar WTre
- var. *grandiflora*   ESwi WFar
  'Long-Jen Violet'
- 'Ink Spot'   WFar
- 'Kestrel' (v)   CBct ESwi WFar
- 'Purple Beauty'   CTsd IPot LRHS
- 'Samurai' (v)   EBee LBar WFar
- 'Seiryu'   EBee
- 'Shelley's'   CLAP
- 'Small Wonder'   WCru
- 'Spotted Toad'   CDor LEdu
§ - Stolonifera Group   CBcs CDor CMac CMHG EPfP GAbr LRHS MArl SHar
- - B&SWJ 7046   WCru
- 'Taroko Toad'   WCru WFar
- 'Variegata' (v)   LEdu NBir SRms
- 'Velvet Toad'   WCru WFar
§ *hirta*   CBcs CDor CMac CMiW CSpe EBee EGren EGrI EUrb LCro LSto MCtn NBro SDix SPlb XFar
- B&SWJ 5971   WCru
- B&SWJ 11227   WCru
- 'Akachan'   LCro MPri
- 'Alba'   CMac EMor GArf GKev
- 'Albomarginata' (v)   CMac CToG EBee EWhm LBar LSto MArl MHtn MPie NSti SPoG WFar WGwG
- 'Golden Gleam'   WCot
- 'Matsukaze'   EWes WFar
- 'Miyazaki'   CMac EBee GElm GKev LSto MHer NSti SPeP SPoG WCAu
- 'Taiwan Atrianne'   CDor CLAP CSpe CToG EBee EMor ESwi GElm MBNS MNrw NCth SPoG WCAu
- 'Variegata' (v)   EBee EWes LRHS WCot

Hototogisu   CToG EBee ESwi LBar LEdu MArl MAvo MHer NLar SPoG WFar WKif
ishiiana var. *surugensis* LEdu WCru WFar
japonica   see *T. hirta*
lasiocarpa   ESwi
- B&SWJ 6861   ESwi WCru
- 'Alba'   ESwi
- 'Royal Toad'   WCru
§ *latifolia*   EMor WCru WFar
- 'Saffron'   WCru
'Lightning Strike' (v)   CDor WCot
macrantha   EMor GKev WCru
macranthopsis   CBct CDor EWld MNrw WCot
- 'Juro' (d)   WCru
§ *macropoda* B&SWJ 5013   WCru
- B&SWJ 5847 from Japan   WCru
- B&SWJ 8700   WCru
- B&SWJ 8829 from Korea   WCru
'Moonlight Treasure'PBR   WCot
ohsumiensis   CMiW ECha WFar
- 'Fukurin-fu' (v)   WCot WFar
- tall   WFar
perfoliata   LEdu
- 'Spring Shine' (v)   WCru
PINK FRECKLES ('Innotripf'PBR) CBct CDoC CDor CLAP EGren ELan ELon ESwi LSou MAvo MPro NCou SPad WHil
'Raspberry Mousse'   ELon ESwi
ravenii   WFar
- B&SWJ 3229   WCru
setouchiensis   WCru
'Shimone'   WFar
'Sinonome'   EBee MNrw
stolonifera   see *T. formosana* Stolonifera Group
suzukii RWJ 10111   WCru
'Taipei Silk'PBR   CLAP
'Tojen'   CLAP EBee EPfP ESwi EWes LBar MNrw NLar WCAu WFar XFar
'White Towers'   CLAP ESwi LBar MAvo NCth NSti SRms WCAu WFar

Trifolium (Fabaceae)
'Beauty' (Angel Clover Series) GAbr
'Chocolate' (Angel Clover Series) WHil
dubium   SPre
fragiferum   NAts
incarnatum   CSpe MCtn SPhx
macrocephalum   EBee
montanum   SPhx
ochroleucon   CDor CGwi CTtf EBee EPPr GMaP LBar LEdu MCtn MHol MMrt MPie MPro SBeP SHar WCAu WFar WPGP
pannonicum   MNrw SMHy SPhx
- 'White Tiara'   ESwi
pratense   CBWd CGwi CHab EHet GJem GJos MCtn MHer MNHC NMir SPhx SRms SVic
- 'Dolly North'   see *T. pratense* 'Susan Smith'
- 'Ice Cool'   see *T. repens* 'Green Ice'
§ - 'Susan Smith' (v)   EBee EPfP
purpureum   SPhx
repens   CBWd CGwi GJem LCro MCtn MHer SVic
- DARK DEBBIE   LEdu
  ('Trifpot001'PBR)
- 'Dragon's Blood'   EPPr LEdu MMuc
- 'Estelle'PBR   LEdu
- 'Gold Net'   see *T. pratense* 'Susan Smith'
§ - 'Green Ice'   NSti WFar
- 'Harlequin' (v)   WCot

704 *Trifolium*

– 'Isabella'^PBR	LEdu WFar WPGP
– 'Purpurascens'	GQue MAsh MHer SPoG WFar
§ – 'Purpurascens' Quadrifolium'	CAby ECha GAbr LEdu LRHS LShi NMir NPer SAdn SBeP SPlb WFar WHil WTor
– 'Tetraphyllum Purpureum' see *T. repens* 'Purpurascens Quadrifolium'	
– 'Wheatfen'	NPer
– 'William'	MMuc WCot WFar
rubens	CAby CBWd CCBP CDor CTtf EAri EBee EGrI EPfP EPPr ERCP LBar LCro MCtn MHer MMuc MNHC MNrw MPie MPnt NLit NSti SBeP SMHy SPhx SPlb WCAu WFar
– 'Drama'	ELon LEdu MNrw WPGP
– 'Frosty Feathers'	CDor CFis CSpe MNHC MPnt MPro SHar
– 'Peach Pink'	CDor ELon EPPr LBar MMrt MPro SBeP SHar WCAu WCot
– 'Red Feathers'	CSpe EGren ELon EPPr GQue MBel MHoł MPro SHar
– white-flowered	EAri WCAu
trichocephalum	EBee EPPr MNrw

Trigonella (Fabaceae)

foenum-graecum	EHet MCtn SVic

Trillidium see *Trillium*

Trillium ✿ (Melanthiaceae)

albidum ♀^H5	ENun GEdr GKev MNrw
albidum × ***kurabayashii***	WCot
amabile	GEdr
angustipetalum	GEdr
apetalon	GEdr
camschatcense	CExl GEdr LAma
– from Japan	EWld
§ ***catesbaei***	CExl GKev LAma MNrw
chloropetalum	CBro CElw ENun EPot EPPr GEdr GKev
§ – var. ***giganteum*** ♀^H5	CExl EGrI GArf GKev LEdu NHar WAbe
– var. ***rubrum***	see *T. chloropetalum* var. *giganteum*
– white-flowered	GKev
cuneatum	CBcs CExl CMiW EBee ENun EPot EWld GEdr ISha LAma MHtn NBir SPeP WFar WPGP
erectum ♀^H5	CBcs CElw CExl CMiW EAri EBee EGrI EPot GArf GEdr GKev ISha LAma LCro MHtn MNrw NBid NBir NHar SPlb WFar
– f. ***albiflorum***	ECha GKev MNrw
– – Harvington clone	ENun LRHS
– Harvington dark form	ENun
– red-flowered	GKev
flexipes	EBee GEdr GKev ISha LAma MNrw
– 'Harvington Dusky Pink'	ENun
– 'Harvington Select'	ENun LRHS
govanianum	EBee GKev LAma
grandiflorum ♀^H5	CBcs CBro CElw CMiW CTsd CTtf EAri EBee ECha EGrI ENun EPot GEdr GKev GMaP ISha LAma LCro LEdu MBel MHtn MNrw NBid NBir NHar WFar WPGP WSpi
– Harvington pale pink	ENun
– f. ***polymerum*** 'Flore Pleno' (d)	CBro ENun GArf GEdr NHar
– – 'Snowbunting' (d)	EWes GKev LAma LEdu
– f. ***roseum***	ENun GEdr GKev
– white-flowered	EGrI

Harvington hybrids (*flexipes* × *simile*)	ENun LRHS
kurabayashii	CExl EGrI ENun GEdr GKev MNrw SChF WPGP
ludovicianum	SBrt
luteum ♀^H5	CBcs CExl CMiW EBee EGrI ENun EPot EWld GArf GEdr GKev ISha LAma LCro
ovatum f. ***hibbersonii***	EPot GEdr
– 'Roy Elliott'	CExl
parviflorum	GEdr
pusillum	CExl EBee EGrI EPot GEdr GKev LAma MNrw
recurvatum	CBcs EBee EGrI GAbr GEdr GKev ISha LAma LEdu
rivale ♀^H4	CExl EGren EPot GEdr GKev WAbe
– Purple Heart Group	GEdr
rugelii	GEdr MNrw
– Askival hybrids	MNrw
sessile	CExl EAri EGrI GEdr GKev ISha LAma NBir WKif
– 'Rubrum'	see *T. chloropetalum* var. *giganteum*
simile	ENun LEdu WPGP
smallii	GEdr LAma
stylosum	see *T. catesbaei*
sulcatum	CExl ENun EPot GEdr GKev LEdu
tschonoskii	GEdr LAma
vaseyi	EWes GEdr GKev ISha
viridescens	EBee EPPr GEdr LAma

Trinia (Apiaceae)

glauca	CSpe SPhx

Triosteum (Caprifoliaceae)

erythrocarpum	LEdu
himalayanum	GKev NBid
– BWJ 7907	ESwi WCru
pinnatifidum	EWld GGro GKev MMrt WCAu

Tripleurospermum (Asteraceae)

maritimum 'Flaggy Shore'	GElm

Tripogandra (Commelinaceae)

§ ***multiflora***	LBom
serrulata 'Purple Scimitars'	WTra

Tripolium (Asteraceae)

§ ***pannonicum***	CEls WHer

Tripora (Lamiaceae)

§ ***divaricata***	CMCN NQui SBrt WFar
– 'Blue Butterflies'	CBcs CBct EBee WPGP
– 'Electrum'	WCot WFar
– pink-flowered	WFar

Tripsacum (Poaceae)

dactyloides	EPPr

Tripterospermum (Gentianaceae)

HEHEHE 220	GEdr

Tripterygium (Celastraceae)

doianum B&SWJ 11467	WCru
aff. ***doianum*** CWJ 12852	WCru
regelii B&SWJ 5453	WCru
– B&SWJ 8666 from Korea	WCru
– B&SWJ 10921	WCru
wilfordii	EBee LEdu
– BWJ 7852 from China	WCru
– NJM 11.029 from China	WPGP
– NMWJ 14466 from Taiwan	WCru

Triteleia (Asparagaceae)

– WWJ 12009	WCru
'Aquarius' (d)	CBro EGrI ERCP
californica	see *Brodiaea californica*
§ 'Corrina' ♀H4	EPot ERCP GKev LAma XFar
'Double Touch' (d)	WCot
'Foxy'	CBro CTtf GKev LAma MNrw
grandiflora	WCot
hendersonii	GKev
hyacinthina	MNrw WCot
– NNS 06-560	WCot
§ *laxa*	ECha EGrI
§ – 'Koningin Fabiola'	CBro CSpe CTtf EGren EGrI EPfP GKev LAma MNrw NBir WCot
– QUEEN FABIOLA	see *T. laxa* 'Koningin Fabiola'
§ *peduncularis*	WCot
'Rudy' ♀H4	CBro CTtf CWCL EPot ERCP GKev LAma MNrw WCot
'Silver Queen' ♀H4	CBro EGren EPot ERCP GKev LAma WCot
uniflora	see *Ipheion uniflorum*

Trithrinax (Arecaceae)

brasiliensis	NPlm
campestris	CBrP NPlm SBig SPlb

Tritoma see *Kniphofia*

Tritonia (Iridaceae)

crocata 'Prince of Orange'	WMal
deusta	CPbh
disticha	EDAr EGrI GKev SPlb
§ – subsp. *rubrolucens*	CBlu CBro CCBP CExl CTca CTtf CWCL EArI ECha EGrI EPPr GAbr GMaP LEdu MMuc NBir SIvy SRkn WFar WKif WOld WPGP
drakensbergensis	CSpe MCtn
gladiolaris 'Parvifolia'	CBlu
laxifolia	CBlu EGrI LAma XFar
rosea	see *T. disticha* subsp. *rubrolucens*
securigera	GKev WMal

Trochocarpa (Ericaceae)

clarkei	NHar

Trochodendron (Trochodendraceae)

aralioides	CBcs CBct CMac EBee EPfP EUrb GKin LShi MBlu MMuc SArc SBig SDix SMad SSta
– B&SWJ 6080 from Japan	WCru
– from Taiwan	CDTJ WPGP
– – B&SWJ 1651	WCru
– – CWJ 12357	WCru
– – RWJ 9845	WCru

Trollius (Ranunculaceae)

ACE 1187	CExl
acaulis	EWes WAbe
altaicus	ELan
buddae	LBar NLar
§ *chinensis*	ELin GKev
– 'Golden Queen' ♀H7	Widely available
– 'Morning Sun'	ELan
× *cultorum* 'Alabaster'	CExl CMiW EBee ECha ELon EMor EPfP GKev GMaP LBar LCro LSto MArl MAsh MHol Midl MNrw MPro NBir NGdn NLar SPoG WCot WFar WSpi WTre
– 'Baudirektor Linne'	NGdn
– 'Bressingham Sunshine'	EBlo
– 'Canary Bird'	NGdn SRms WSpi
– 'Cheddar'	see *T.* × *cultorum* 'Taleggio'
– 'Earliest of All'	LBar NGdn NLar WSpi
– 'Etna'	CLil LBar MPro NLar SHar
§ – 'Feuertroll'	ECha NGdn NLar WSpi
– FIREGLOBE	see *T.* × *cultorum* 'Feuertroll'
– FULL MOON ('Mactro010')	LBar Midl MPro
– 'Golden Cup'	NBir NGdn
– 'Goldquelle' ♀H7	EBee
– 'Goliath'	NLar
– 'Helios'	ECha
– 'Lemon Queen'	CLil CMiW CWat EMor EPfP GBin GMaP LBar LRHS MBel MPro NCth NLar NQui SHar SRms WHil
– 'New Moon'	CAby CBcs CBWd CDor CLil CSpe CToG EBlo EMor EPfP GElm GQue LBar LRHS LSto MArl MBel MBNS MHer MPie NCth NLar NQui SMrm SPoG WHoo WNPC
– 'Orange Crest'	ELon NLar
– 'Orange Globe'	GMaP LBar XFar
– 'Orange Princess' ♀H7	CDor CWat LBar LCro NBro SRms
– 'Prichard's Giant'	ELon NBro WSpi
§ – 'Superbus' ♀H7	ELin ELon GMaP LBar MHol NGdn WFar XFar
– 'T. Smith'	NBro
§ – 'Taleggio'	CTtf EBlo ELan EMor GMaP LBar LRHS MArl MAsh Midl MPro NBro NLar NWbg SHar SPad SPoG SRms WNPC WPnP WSpi
'Dancing Flame'	CMac LCro LRHS NLar SHar SPoG SRms
europaeus	CAby CBWd CTtf EBee ECha EHeP ELan EMor EPfP LEdu LRHS LShi MCtn MHol MPro NGdn NMir NSti SRms StAn WShi WTre
– subsp. *europaeus*	WFar
– 'Lemon Supreme'	CDor EArI ELan EMor EPfP GKev MMrt MPro
– 'Superbus'	see *T.* × *cultorum* 'Superbus'
farreri var. *farreri*	GKev WAbe
hondoensis	NLar
ircuticus	ECha GKev
laxus 'Albiflorus'	CExl EBee
ledebourii misapplied	see *T. chinensis*
'Orange Triumph'	LBar
pumilus	ECha EPfP LBar WIce
– ACE 1818	CExl MHer
– 'Wargrave'	EBlo
– 'Super Bowl'	EMor
yunnanensis ♀H6	EBlo GBin GQue
– orange-flowered	CExl

Tropaeolum (Tropaeolaceae)

'Baby Rose'	LCro WKit
brachyceras	LAma
ciliatum	StAn WCot WCru WPGP
lepidum	GKev
majus	CGHo ENfk MHoo SVic
– Alaska Series (v) ♀H3	EHet ENfk GJem LCro MCtn MHoo MNHC WKit
– – 'Alaska Salmon Orange'	LCro
– 'Black Velvet' (Tom Thumb Series)	LCro MCtn
– 'Blue Pepe'	LCro MCtn MNHC
– 'Cherry Rose Jewel' (Jewel Series)	MCtn MHoo MNHC
– 'Empress of India'	LCro MCtn MNHC WKit
– Gleam Series	MCtn
– 'Hermine Grashoff' (d)	CSpe
* – 'Indian Chief'	MCtn

Tropaeolum

- Jewel Series	ENfk
- 'Jewel of Africa'	MCtn
- 'Ladybird' (Ladybird Series)	MCtn
- 'Margaret Long' (d)	CSpe
- 'Milkmaid'	MCtn
- 'Pepperspark'	MNHC
- 'Salmon Baby'	MCtn
- 'Salmon Gleam' (Gleam Series)	MCtn
- 'Tip Top Apricot' (Tip Top Series)	MCtn
- 'Tip Top Mahogany' (Tip Top Series)	MCtn
- Tom Thumb Series	MCtn
- Whirlybird Series ♀H3	LCro MCtn MHoo
- - 'Whirlybird Cream' **new**	MCtn
minus 'Bloody Mary'	LCro
- 'Ladybird Rose'	LCro MCtn
pentaphyllum	CRHN CSpe
peregrinum	MCtn
polyphyllum ♀H3	CSpe EAri EWld LAma NBir SBrt SMHy
smithii	EPPr WPGP
speciosum ♀H5	CBcs CExl CSpe CWGN EBee ELan EPfP GAbr GKev GKin LCro MArl MCtn NBid NBir NLar NPer StAn WCru WPGP WSpi
tricolor ♀H2	CRHN CWCL GKev LAma SBrt WCot
tuberosum	CAgr CEnd EAri LAma MEar NBac SPoG WKor
- var. *lineomaculatum*	CAbb CSpe EBee ELan EPfP EPot GAbr LAma NLar WFar
'Ken Aslet' ♀H3	

Trozelia (Solanaceae)

§ *grandiflora*	SEND

Tsuga ✿ (Pinaceae)

canadensis	CAco CCVT LMaj MMuc
- 'Ashfield Weeper' **new**	NLar
§ - 'Branklyn'	WCFE
- 'Cole's Prostrate' ♀H7	CAco MAsh NLar
- 'Everitt Golden'	NLar
- 'Gentsch White' (v)	MAsh NLar
- 'Golden Splendor'	MAsh
- 'Greenwood Lake'	NLar
- 'Jacqueline Verkade'	NLar
- 'Jeddeloh' ♀H7	CAco MAsh
- 'Minuta' ♀H7	WAbe
- 'Nana'	CWnw
- 'Prostrata'	see *T. canadensis* 'Branklyn'
heterophylla ♀H6	CAco CBcs CCVT CLnd GJos IPap MMuc SMad WFar
- 'Thorsens Weeping'	CAco NLar
menziesii	see *Pseudotsuga menziesii*
mertensiana 'Blue Star'	CAco
- 'Glauca'	CAco
sieboldii 'Green Ball'	NLar

Tuberaria (Cistaceae)

lignosa	WAbe

Tulbaghia ✿ (Amaryllidaceae)

acutiloba	LEdu
alliacea	LEdu WCot
* *allioides*	CBro
'Ashanti'	ENfk
capensis	LEdu NBir
'Cariad'	EPPr LEdu MWlw SMHy SPel
cernua CD&R 199	EBee LEdu
§ *coddii*	MHer
cominsii	LEdu
cominsii × *violacea*	EPPr WHoo
'Cornish Beauty'	CTca
'Cosmic'	CTtf EBee ENfk EPPr LEdu MWlw SBeP SMHy WMal
'Fairy Snow'	LEdu WCot
'Fairy Star'	CCBP CCht CWGN ELan EShb EUrb LEdu MWlw SAth WCot
'Fairy Star Mk II'	SMHy
fragrans	see *T. simmleri*
'Hazel'	CFis LEdu MHer WMal
'John May's Special'	EShb LEdu SMHy WCot WHoo
'Kilimanjaro'	ENfk LRHS
leucantha ♀H2	CTtf EAri ENfk EPPr LEdu MWlw
- H&B 11996	LEdu
ludwigiana	MHer
maritima	CMHG LEdu MHer
Marwood seedling	MHer
montana	EBee LEdu MWlw SPlb
'Moshoeshoe'	LEdu MWlw WPGP
'Moya'	EPPr
natalensis ♀H2	CBro CTtf SBeP
poetica	see *T. coddii*
'Purple Eye' ♀H2	CAbb CBro CCht CDoC ECha ELan EPfP EPPr LCro LEdu LRHS LSou MHol MHtn MPri MWlw SPoG WCot WMal WNPC
§ *simmleri* ♀H3	LEdu
- 'Cheryl Renshaw'	WCot
'Snow White'	LEdu MWlw SMHy WCot WMal
verdoorniae	LEdu
violacea ♀H3	Widely available
* - 'Alba'	CWnw EBee ECha EGrI EShb GKev LAma LBar MHer
- 'Harry Hay'	SMHy
- 'John Rider'	EPPr
- large-flowered	SMHy
- 'Pallida'	CBro EBee
- 'Pearl'	ENfk
- var. *robustior*	ECha
- 'Silver Lace' (v) ♀H3	Widely available
- 'Variegata'	see *T. violacea* 'Silver Lace'

Tulipa ✿ (Liliaceae)

'Abba' (2)	EGren GKev LAma LRHS
'Absalon' (9)	GKev LAma
acuminata misapplied	see *T.* 'Cornuta'
'Addis' (14)	LAma
'Aesculapius' (5) **new**	LAma
'Affaire' (3)	ERCP GKev LAma
'Agrass White' (3)	EGren
aitchisonii	see *T. clusiana*
'Aladdin' (6)	EGren LCro
'Alba Regalis' (1)	LAma
'Albert Heijn' (13) ♀H4	CBro
'Alexander Pushkin' PBR (3)	XFar
'Alexandrine' (7)	GKev LAma
'Alfred Cortot' (12) ♀H6	LAma
'Alibi' (3)	ERCP XFar
'Alison Bradley' (2)	GKev LAma
'Amazing Grace' (2)	EGren ERCP XFar
'Amazing Parrot' (10)	EPfP ERCP LCro XFar
'Amber Glow' (3)	ERCP
'American Dream' (4)	GKev LAma XFar
'Ancilla' (12) ♀H6	CBro LAma
'André Rieu' (5)	LCro
'Angélique' (11) ♀H6	CBro EGren EPfP ERCP ETay LAma LCro LSto NBir XFar
'Angels Wish' (5) ♀H6	EPfP ETay GKev LAma
'Annie Schilder' (3)	ERCP LCro LRHS
'Annie Smulders' (2)	GKev LAma

Tulipa

'Annika' (15) — XFar
'Antarctica'PBR (3) — EGren EPfP GKev LAma
'Antoinette'PBR (5) — GKev LAma LCro
'Antraciet' (11) — CBro EPfP ERCP GKev LAma LCro
'Apeldoorn' (4) — EGren ETay GKev LCro
'Apeldoorn's Elite' (4) ♀H6 — GKev LAma XFar
'Aphrodite' (3) — XFar
'Apricona' (3) — GKev LAma XFar
'Apricot Beauty' (1) ♀H6 — EGren ERCP LCro NBir NNys XFar
'Apricot Copex' (3) — ERCP
'Apricot Delight' (4) — GKev LAma
'Apricot Foxx' (3) — EGren ERCP LCro LRHS
'Apricot Impression'PBR (4) — ERCP GKev LAma LCro
'Apricot Jewel' — see *T. linifolia* (Batalinii Group) 'Apricot Jewel'
'Apricot Parrot' (10) ♀H6 — EGren ERCP GKev LAma XFar
'Apricot Pride' (4) — XFar
'Aquilla' (11) — LAma
'Arabian Beauty' (3) — ETay LCro
'Arabian Mystery' (3) — GKev
'Archeron' (5) **new** — LAma
'Arlette Hanson' (2) — LAma
'Artist' (8) ♀H6 — ERCP GKev LAma XFar
'Asahi' (3) — LCro
'Atlantis' (5) — LCro
'Attila' (3) — EGren LAma LCro
aucheriana (15) ♀H5 — GKev LAma
australis (15) — GKev
'Aveyron' (11) — LAma
'Avignon' (5) — ERCP GKev LCro
aximensis (15) — XFar
'Backpacker' (11) — ERCP LCro
'Ballade' (6) ♀H6 — CBro EGren ERCP GKev LAma LCro XFar
BALLADE DREAM — see *T.* 'Sonnet'
'Ballade Gold' (6) — LAma
'Ballerina' (6) ♀H6 — CAby CBro EGren EPfP ERCP ETay GKev LAma LCro NNys XFar
'Banja Luka' (4) — EGren LRHS XFar
'Barbados' (7) — LAma XFar
'Barcelona' (3) ♀H6 — ERCP ETay GKev LAma LCro
'Bastia' (7) — LAma
batalinii — see *T. linifolia* Batalinii Group
'Beauty of Apeldoorn' (4) — LAma
'Beauty of Spring' (4) — ETay LAma XFar
'Beautytrend' (3) **new** — LRHS
'Belicia' (2) — XFar
'Berlioz' (12) — ETay
§ *biflora* (15) — CBro ERCP LAma XFar
bifloriformis (15) — CBro
- 'Starlight' (15) ♀H6 — GKev
'Big Brother' (5) **new** — GKev LAma
'Big Chief' (4) ♀H6 — XFar
'Big Smile' (5) — EGren GKev LAma
'Black and White' (9) — GKev LAma
'Black Bean' (5) — EGren GKev LAma
'Black Hero' (11) — CAby EGren ERCP GKev LAma LCro NNys XFar
'Black Parrot' (10) ♀H6 — CAby CBro EGren EPfP ERCP ETay GKev LAma LCro LRHS NNys XFar
'Bleu Aimable' (5) — EGren ERCP GKev LAma XFar
'Blue Beauty' (3) — EGren GKev LAma LCro
'Blue Diamond' (11) — CBro EGren ERCP GKev LAma LCro LRHS
'Blue Heaven' **new** — XFar
BLUE HEAVEN (mixed) — ERCP
'Blue Heron' (7) ♀H6 — ERCP LCro
'Blue Parrot' (10) — EGren ERCP GKev LAma LCro XFar
'Blue Ribbon' (3) — LCro
'Blue Spectacle' (11) — LCro
'Blue Wow' (11) — LCro XFar
BLUEBERRY RIPPLE — see *T.* 'Zurel'
'Blumex Favourite'PBR (10) — LCro
'Blushing Apeldoorn' (4) — GKev LAma
'Blushing Girl' (5) — EGren LAma XFar
'Blushing Impression' (4) — GKev LAma
'Blushing Lady' (5) — EPfP GKev LAma NBir
'Boston' (3) — LAma
'Boutade' (14) — NPer
§ *breyniana* (15) — XFar
'Bridesmaid' (5) — LAma
'Brisbane' (7) — ERCP XFar
'Brooklyn' (11) — NPer
'Brown Sugar' (3) — ERCP ETay LAma LCro LRHS
'Brownie' (2) — EGren XFar
'Bruine Wimpel' (5) — LCro
'Budlight' (6) — LAma
'Burgundy' (6) — ETay LAma LCro
'Burgundy Lace' (7) — EGren ETay LAma LCro LRHS
'Burning Fire' (7) — GKev LAma
'Burning Flame' (7) — GKev LAma
'Buttercup' (14) — EGren
'Cabanna' (10) **new** — GKev LAma XFar
'Cacharel' (7) — ERCP
'Café Noir' (5) — LAma LCro
'Cairo' (3) — ERCP XFar
'Calgary' (3) ♀H6 — ETay LAma LCro
'Calgary Flames' (3) ♀H6 — CAby XFar
'Calgary Red' (3) **new** — XFar
'Calypso' (14) ♀H6 — EPfP
'Camargue' (5) — LAma
'Candy Apple Delight' (4) — GKev LAma
'Candy Club' (5) — ERCP ETay LAma LCro XFar
'Candy Corner' (3) — EGren
'Candy Prince'PBR (1) ♀H6 — EGren ERCP GKev LAma LCro
'Cape Cod' (14) — EGren ETay GKev LAma
'Cape Town' (1) ♀H6 — GKev LAma
'Caravaggio' (2) — GKev LAma
'Caravelle' (5) — ERCP
'Cardinal Mindszenty' (2) — LAma
'Caribbean Parrot' (10) — GKev LAma
'Carlton' (2) — EGren
'Carnaval de Nice' (11/v) ♀H6 — EPfP ERCP ETay GKev LAma LCro XFar
'Carnaval de Rio' (3) — LCro XFar
'Carola' (3) — LCro
'Carre' (3) — GKev LAma
'Carrousel' (7) — XFar
'Casa Grande' (14) ♀H6 — LCro
'Cassini' (3) — EGren GKev LAma LSto
'Catherina' (5) — LCro XFar
'Chansonnette' (3) — EPfP ERCP
'Charade'PBR (3) — XFar
'Charmeuse' (14) — GKev LAma
'Charming Beauty' (11) — LCro
'Charming Lady' (11) — ERCP LRHS XFar
'Cheers' (3) — ETay
'Cherry Delight' (4) — GKev LAma XFar
'China Pink' (6) ♀H6 — LAma LCro
'China Town' (8) ♀H6 — ERCP GKev LAma LCro XFar
'Chopin' (12) — LAma
'Christmas Dream' (1) — GKev LAma
chrysantha — see *T. montana*
'Cistula' (6) — ETay
'City of Vancouver' (5) — EGren
'Claudia' (6) — ETay GKev LAma
§ *clusiana* (15) — ERCP GKev LAma MNrw
- var. *chrysantha* (15) ♀H6 — GKev LAma XFar
- - 'Tubergen's Gem' (15) — EPot GKev LAma
- 'Cynthia' (15) ♀H6 — CAby EPot GKev LAma MNrw MPie
- 'Sheila' (15) — GKev LAma
§ - var. *stellata* (15) ♀H6 — CBro

Tulipa

'Coldplay' (7) **new**	XFar
'Colour Fusion' (7) **new**	GKev LAma XFar
'Columbine' (5)	GKev LAma
'Concerto' (13) ♀H6	CBro EGren LRHS NPer
'Conqueror'PBR (4)	GKev LAma
'Continental' (3)	ERCP GKev LAma
'Cool Crystal' (7)	XFar
'Copper Image' (11)	EGren EPfP ERCP ETay GKev LAma LCro LRHS XFar
'Corinna' (5)	LAma
§ 'Cornuta' (15)	ERCP GKev LAma LCro XFar
'Cosmopolitan' (4)	LAma
'Couleur Cardinal' (3) ♀H6	CBro GKev LAma LCro XFar
'Cranberry Thistle' (7/d) **new**	XFar
'Cream Flag' (3)	LSto
'Crème Upstar' (11)	EGren ERCP LAma LCro
cretica 'Hilde' (15)	XFar
'Crown of Dynasty' (16) **new**	EGren LAma
'Crown of Negrita' (16)	ERCP LAma XFar
'Crunchy Cummins' (7)	XFar
'Crystal Star' (7)	EGren GKev LAma
'Cuban Night' (7)	LAma
'Cum Laude' (5)	LAma
'Cummins' (7)	LCro XFar
'Curly Sue' (7)	ERCP ETay
'Czaar Peter' (14) ♀H6	NPer
'Danceline' (11)	GKev LAma LCro XFar
'Dancing Show' (8)	GKev LAma
'Danique' (15)	XFar
dasystemon (15)	GKev LAma
'Davenport' (7)	ERCP
'Daydream' (4) ♀H6	EGren
'Daytona' (7)	LCro
'Dee Jay Parrott' (10) **new**	XFar
'Delta White' (3)	GKev LAma
'Design Impression' (4)	ERCP LCro
'Diamond Jubilee' (3) ♀H6	ETay
'Dior' (2)	ERCP
'Doll's Minuet' (6)	EGren ERCP GKev LAma LCro LRHS
'Dom Pedro' (5)	GKev LAma
'Don Quichotte' (3) ♀H6	EGren ERCP LCro LRHS
'Dordogne' (5) ♀H6	EGren ERCP LAma LCro LRHS
'Double Blizz' (11)	XFar
'Double Flag' (2)	LRHS
'Double Flaming Parrot'PBR (10)	LAma
'Double Red Riding Hood' (14/v)	LAma LRHS
'Double Shake' (11)	XFar
'Double Sugar' (11)	GKev LAma XFar
'Double Surprise' (11) **new**	XFar
'Double Touch' (11)	ERCP
'Dow Jones'PBR (3)	XFar
'Drakensteyn' (7) **new**	XFar
'Dream Club' (5)	GKev LAma
'Dream Touch' (11)	EPfP ETay LAma LCro XFar
'Dreamer'PBR (2)	CAby ERCP
'Duc van Tol' (1)	LAma
'Duc van Tol Aurora' (1)	LAma
'Duc van Tol Cochineal' (1)	LAma
'Duc van Tol Double' (2)	LAma
'Duc van Tol Max Cramoisie' (1)	LAma
'Duc van Tol Primrose' (1)	LAma
'Duc van Tol Red and White' (1)	LAma
'Duc van Tol Red and Yellow' (1)	LAma
'Duc van Tol Rose' (1)	LAma
'Duc van Tol Salmon' (1)	LAma
'Duc van Tol Scarlet' (1)	LAma
'Duc van Tol Violet' (1)	LAma
'Duc van Tol White' (1)	LAma
'Dutch Dancer' (6)	GKev LAma
'Dynasty' (3)	EGren
'Eagle Wings' (10)	EGren
'Early Glory' (3)	LCro
'Early Harvest' (12) ♀H6	GKev LAma
'Easter Surprise' (14) ♀H6	GKev LAma
'Ego Parrot' (10)	LCro
eichleri	see *T. undulatifolia*
'El Niño' (5)	LAma
'Elegans Alba' (6)	LAma
'Elegant Crown' (16) **new**	EGren LAma
'Elegant Lady' (6)	EGren LAma LCro
'Esperanto' (8/v) ♀H6	GKev LAma NPer
'Esprit' (7)	LCro
'Estella Rijnveld' (10)	CBro EPfP ERCP ETay GKev LAma LCro XFar
'Eternal Flame' (2)	LCro
'Evergreen' (3)	LCro XFar
'Exotic Emperor' (13) ♀H6	CBro EGren ERCP GKev LAma LCro LRHS NNys XFar
'Exquisit' (11)	LAma LCro
'Eyelash' (7)	LRHS XFar
'Fabio' (7)	GKev LAma XFar
'Fancy Frills' (7) ♀H6	EGren ERCP GKev LAma LRHS XFar
'Fantasy Lady' (2)	GKev LAma
'Fashion' (12)	EGren LRHS
ferganica (15)	WCot
'Fiery Club' (5)	XFar
'Fiery Dream' (7)	XFar
'Finola' (11)	EGren ERCP LCro NNys XFar
'Fire Wings' (6)	CAby CBro GKev LAma
'Firework' (6)	GKev LAma LRHS XFar
'First Proud' (5)	LAma
'Flair' (1)	GKev LAma LRHS
'Flames Mystery' (13) ♀H4 **new**	GKev LAma
'Flaming Baltic' (7) ♀H6	XFar
'Flaming Club' (5)	LAma
'Flaming Flag' (3)	EGren EPfP ETay GKev LAma LCro LRHS XFar
'Flaming Parrot' (10)	CAby ETay GKev LAma LCro XFar
I 'Flaming Purissima' (13) ♀H6	EGren GKev LAma
'Flaming Springgreen' (8)	ETay LAma LCro
'Flashback' (10)	LAma XFar
'Flig Flag' (3)	ERCP
'Florosa' (8)	LCro XFar
'Flower Power' (10)	GKev LAma
'Fly Away' (6)	CBro XFar
'Flying Dragon' (3)	GKev LAma
'Fontainebleau' (3)	ERCP GKev LAma LCro
'Foxtrot'PBR (2) ♀H6	EGren ERCP GKev LAma
'Foxy Foxtrot' (2) ♀H6	GKev LAma
'Françoise' (3)	LCro
'Friendship'	see *T.* 'World Friendship'
'Fringed Elegance' (7) ♀H6	LCro
'Fringed Solstice' (7)	EGren
'Fritz Kreisler' (12) ♀H4	GKev LAma
'Frozen Night' (10)	GKev LAma
'Fusarino' (3)	EGren
'Gander's Rhapsody' (3)	EGren
'Gavota' (3) ♀H6	CBro EGren ETay GKev LAma LCro XFar
'Generaal de Wet' (1)	LCro
'Georgette' (5)	LAma
'Gerard Dou' (2)	GKev LAma
× *gesneriana* (15)	WCot

Tulipa

'Giuseppe Verdi' (12)	EGren LAma
§ 'Go Go Red' (6) **new**	GKev LAma
'Golddust' (7)	XFar
'Golden Apeldoorn' (4)	EGren EPfP ETay GKev LAma LCro LSto
'Golden Artist' (8)	GKev LAma LCro XFar
'Golden Emperor' (13)	LAma
'Golden Oxford' (4)	GKev LAma
'Golden Parade' (4)	XFar
'Gorilla' (7)	GKev LAma LCro
'Goudstuk' (12) ♀H4	GKev LAma
'Graceland' (3)	XFar
'Grand Perfection' PBR (3) ♀H6	CAby EGren LCro
'Granny Award' (11)	EGren GKev LAma LRHS
'Great Barrier Reef' (7/d)	ERCP
'Green Mile' PBR (6)	XFar
'Green Power' (3) **new**	CAby
'Green Spirit' (8)	EGren ERCP GKev LAma
'Green Wave' (10)	ERCP GKev LAma LCro LRHS XFar
'Greenstar' (6)	CBro EPfP ERCP LAma LCro
'Greuze' (5)	LCro
'Groenland' (8)	EGren GKev LAma LCro XFar
'Gudoshnik' (4)	LRHS
'Gudoshnik Double' (11) **new**	XFar
hageri (15)	GKev LAma SPhx
'Hakuun' (4)	CAby GKev LAma
'Hamilton' (7)	LAma
'Hans Brinker' (4) **new**	EGren
'Happy Feet' (3) **new**	GKev LAma
'Happy Generation' (3)	GKev LAma LCro
'Happy People' (3)	LCro
'Harvest Moon' (3)	LRHS
'Havran' (3)	ERCP GKev LAma LCro XFar
'Heart's Delight' (12)	GKev LAma
'Helmar' (3) ♀H6	CAby LCro LRHS XFar
'Hemisphere' (3)	EGren GKev LAma XFar
'Hermitage' (3)	CAby ERCP GKev LAma
heweri (15)	GKev LAma
'High Five' (3)	GKev LAma
'Hocus Pocus' (5)	LAma
'Holland Beauty' PBR (3)	EGren
'Holland Chic' (6)	GKev LAma XFar
'Holland Queen' PBR (3)	XFar
'Hollywood' (8)	GKev LAma
'Honeymoon' (7)	EGren EPfP ETay GKev LAma LCro
'Honky Tonk' (15) ♀H6	CBro EPfP LAma LCro
'Hot Chocolate' (3)	LRHS
'Hotpants' (3)	EGren GKev LAma
'Hugs and Kisses' (3) **new**	CAby
§ *humilis* (15)	LRHS
- 'Eastern Star' (15)	GKev LAma XFar
- 'Helene' (15)	LCro XFar
§ - 'Lilliput' (15)	LAma
- 'Odalisque' (15)	EPot ERCP GKev LAma
- 'Persian Pearl' (15)	EPfP ERCP GKev LAma LCro XFar
- var. *pulchella*	EPot ERCP GKev LAma LCro XFar
Albocaerulea Oculata Group (15)	
- 'Samantha' (15)	XFar
§ - Violacea Group (15)	XFar
- - black base (15)	EPot ERCP GKev LAma LCro MNrw
- - yellow base (15)	EPot GKev LAma
hungarica	GKev
'Ice Age' (11)	ETay
'Ice Cream' (11)	GKev LAma LCro XFar
'Ice Cream Banana' (11)	GKev LAma XFar
'Ice Cream Strawberry' (11)	XFar
'Ice Stick' (12) ♀H6	CBro
'Ice Wonder' (11)	EPfP
'Icoon' PBR (11)	LCro
'Île de France' (5)	EGren ERCP GKev LAma LCro
iliensis (15)	EPot
'Indeland' (3)	ERCP
'Indian Velvet' (5)	LCro
'Infinity' (3)	ETay GKev LAma
'Inner Wheel' (5)	LAma
'Innuendo' (3)	EGren
'Insulinde' (9)	GKev LAma
'Inzell' (3)	EGren LSto
'Irene Parrot' (10)	EGren GKev LAma
'Isaak Chic' (6)	LRHS
'Ivo'	see *T.* 'Go Go Red'
'Ivory Floradale' (4) ♀H6	EGren GKev LAma
'Jackpot' (3)	EPfP
'Jacqueline' (6)	LCro
'Jacuzzi' (3)	ERCP LCro
'James Last' (10)	EGren ERCP
'Jan Reus' (3)	CBro EGren LCro
'Je t'Aime' (6)	XFar
'Jennie Butchart' (6)	GKev LAma
'Jimmy' (3)	EGren
'Johann Strauss' (12)	EGren EPfP GKev LAma LCro
'Kansas Proud' (3)	EGren ERCP GKev LAma XFar
'Karate' (3) **new**	GKev LAma
'Katinka' (11) **new**	XFar
* *kaufmanniana*	GKev
'Aurora' **new**	
'Keizerskroon' (1)	LAma
'Kickstart' (2)	LCro
'Kikomachi' (3)	LRHS
'Kingsblood' (5) ♀H6	EGren ERCP GKev LAma LCro
'Kleurenpracht'	see *T.* 'Princess Margaret Rose'
'Koh-i-Noor' (1)	LAma
kolpakowskiana (15) ♀H6	EPot ERCP GKev LAma
'La Belle Époque' (2)	ERCP GKev LAma LCro NNys XFar
'La Joyeuse' (5) **new**	LAma
'La Paz' (5) **new**	ERCP
'La Perla' (6)	ERCP GKev LAma
'Labrador' (7)	EGren ERCP
'Lac van Rijn' (1)	LAma
'Lady Jane' (15) ♀H6	EPfP ERCP ETay GKev LAma XFar
'Lady Smile' (7) **new**	XFar
'Lady van Eijk' (4)	ERCP GKev
'Lalibela' (4)	ETay LCro
'Lambada' (7) ♀H6	LCro
lanata (15)	GKev WCot
'Laptop' PBR (3)	LCro
'Lasting Love' (3)	EGren ERCP GKev LAma LCro
'Le Lavandou' (11) **new**	XFar
'Lemon Beauty' (7) **new**	XFar
'Libretto Parrot' (10)	LCro
'Light and Dreamy' (4)	ERCP GKev LAma LCro LRHS XFar
'Light Pink Prince' (3)	EGren
'Lilac Crystal' (7)	LCro
'Lilac Love' (3)	LAma
'Lilac Perfection' (11)	XFar
'Lilac Time' (6)	LAma
'Lilac Wonder'	see *T. saxatilis* (Bakeri Group) 'Lilac Wonder'
'Lilliput'	see *T. humilis* 'Lilliput'
'Lilyrosa' (6)	ETay
'Limelight' (3)	LAma
linifolia (15) ♀H5	CBro EPot GKev LAma MNrw SPhx XFar
§ - Batalinii Group (15) ♀H5	GKev MCtn
§ - - 'Apricot Jewel' (15)	CBro
- - 'Bright Gem' (15) ♀H5	CAby CBro EPot GKev LAma NPer SPhx WHoo XFar
- - 'Bronze Charm' (15)	EGrI GKev LAma SPhx
- - 'Red Gem' (15)	WCot

Tulipa

Name	Sources
- - 'Red Hunter' (15) ♀H5	ERCP LAma LCro XFar
- - 'Salmon Gem' (15)	ETay LAma
- - 'Salmon Jewel' (15)	GKev
'Little Beauty' (15) ♀H6	CAby CBro EGrl EPfP EPot GKev LAma LCro MNrw SPhx WCot WHoo
'Little Girl' (14)	LAma
'Little Princess' (15) ♀H6	CBro EPot GKev LAma MNrw XFar
'Long Lady' (5)	GKev LAma
'Louvre Orange' (7)	ERCP
'Love Song' (12)	CBro
'Mabel' (9)	GKev LAma
§ 'Madame Lefeber' (13)	EGren GKev LAma LCro XFar
'Madonna' (10)	EPfP ETay
'Madras' (5)	LAma
'Mango Charm' (3)	GKev LAma LCro
'Margarita' (2)	EGren ERCP LCro
'Mariage' (2) ♀H6	XFar
'Marianne' (6)	XFar
'Marie Jo'PBR (2)	GKev LAma
'Mariette' (6)	CAby CBro ERCP GKev LAma LCro XFar
'Marilyn' (6)	ERCP XFar
'Mariss Jansons' (12) ♀H4	GKev LAma
'Marquis de la Coquette' (14)	ETay
'Mary Ann' (14) ♀H6	LAma LCro
'Mascara' (3)	ERCP
'Mascotte' (7)	XFar
'Match' (3)	LCro
'Maureen' (5) ♀H6	ERCP LAma LCro
'Maytime' (6)	LAma LCro
'Menton' (5) ♀H6	EGren ERCP GKev LAma LCro LRHS NNys
'Menton Exotic' (11)	LCro
'Mercure' (7) **new**	GKev LAma
'Merlot' (6)	EGren ERCP ETay GKev LAma LCro XFar
'Miranda' (11)	EGren
'Mistress' (3)	ERCP ETay LAma LCro LSto
'Mistress Mystic' (3)	ERCP LRHS
'Mondial'PBR (2) ♀H6	EGren LCro XFar
'Monsella' (2)	GKev LAma
§ montana (15)	WCot
'Monte Carlo' (2) ♀H6	EGren GKev LAma LRHS
'Montreux' (2)	EGren LAma
'Moonblush' (6)	GKev LAma
'Mount Tacoma' (11)	EGren ERCP GKev LAma LCro NNys
'Muscadet' (5)	EGren LCro
'Mystery Valley' (13/d) **new**	XFar
'Mystic van Eijk'PBR (4)	ERCP GKev LAma
'Nachtwacht' (2)	GKev LAma XFar
'National Velvet' (3)	EGren EGrl EPfP ERCP ETay GKev LAma LCro
'Negrita' (3)	EGren ERCP GKev LAma LCro LRHS
'Negrita Double' (11)	EGren EPfP ERCP GKev LAma LCro XFar
'Negrita Parrot' (10)	EGren ERCP GKev LAma
'New Design' (3/v)	GKev LAma LCro
'New Santa' (7)	EPfP LRHS
'Nicholas Heyek' (3)	LCro
'Night Club' (5)	ERCP LAma LCro XFar
'Night Vision' (3)	GKev LAma
'Nightrider' (8)	ETay LCro XFar
'Norah' (15)	MNrw XFar
'Novi Sun'PBR (4) **new**	EGren
'Ollioules' (4) ♀H6	XFar
'Olympic Flame' (4) ♀H6	LCro
'Orange Angélique' (11)	LAma
'Orange Balloon'PBR (4)	ERCP
'Orange Brilliant' (13)	EGren GKev LAma LCro
'Orange Cassini' (3)	EGren LCro
'Orange Emperor' (13) ♀H6	EGren ERCP ETay GKev LAma XFar
'Orange Favourite' (10)	EGren
'Orange Pride' (4)	GKev
'Orange Princess' (11) ♀H6	ERCP GKev LAma LCro XFar
'Orange Princess Design' (2)	XFar
'Orange Toronto' (14)	EGren
'Orange van Eijk' (4)	EGren GKev LAma
'Orca' (2)	EPfP ETay GKev LAma
orphanidea 'Flava' (15)	ERCP ETay GKev LAma LCro
- Whittallii Group (15) ♀H6	LAma
'Oscar' (3)	GKev LAma XFar
ostrowskiana (15)	GKev
'Pallada' (3)	EGren LCro LRHS
'Palmyra'PBR (2)	ERCP
'Parade' (4) ♀H6	GKev LAma
'Parrot King' (10)	EGren
'Parrot Prince' (10)	GKev
'Parrot Sweet' (10)	LAma
'Passionale' (3) ♀H6	EGren EPfP GKev LAma LCro LRHS
'Paul Rubens' (2)	GKev LAma
'Paul Scherer' (3) ♀H6	EPfP ERCP ETay LCro
'Peach Blossom' (2)	EGren ETay LCro
* 'Peaches and Cream' (11)	ETay
Peacock Group	ETay
'Peppermintstick' (15) ♀H6	CBro ERCP ETay GKev LAma LCro MNrw XFar
'Peptalk' (11)	GKev LAma XFar
'Perestroyka' (5)	LAma
'Picture' (16)	ERCP
'Pieter de Leur' (6)	EGren ERCP GKev LAma LCro
'Pim Fortuyn' (3)	LCro
'Pimpernel' (8/v)	GKev LAma
'Pink Ardour' (3) **new**	EGren
'Pink Diamond' (5)	EGren ERCP LAma LCro
'Pink Impression' (4) ♀H6	EGren ERCP GKev LAma LCro
'Pink Pride' (4)	GKev LAma
'Pink Star' (11)	ERCP LCro XFar
'Pinksize' (11)	XFar
'Pinocchio' (14) ♀H6	CBro EGren LCro
'Pittsburg' (3)	LAma LCro
'Plaisir' (14) ♀H6	GKev LAma
polychroma	see *T. biflora*
'Power Parrot' (10) **new**	XFar
praestans (15)	ETay
- 'Fusilier' (15) ♀H6	CBro EGren GKev LAma XFar
- 'Paradox' (15/v)	EGren
- 'Shogun' (15)	CAby EGrl ERCP GKev LAma LCro WCot
- 'Unicum' (15/v)	XFar
- 'Van Tubergen's Variety' (15)	GKev LAma NPer
- 'Zwanenburg Variety' (15)	LCro
'Pretty Lady' (6)	LCro
'Pretty Love' (6) **new**	EGren
'Pretty Princess' (3) ♀H6	EPfP ERCP GKev LAma LCro XFar
'Pretty Woman' (6)	ETay
'Prince Albert' (5)	LAma
'Princeps' (13)	GKev LAma
'Princess Angélique' (11)	XFar
§ 'Princess Margaret Rose' (5)	GKev
'Princesse Charmante' (14) ♀H6	LCro
'Prinses Irene' (3) ♀H6	CBro EGren ERCP GKev LAma LCro NBir NNys XFar
'Prinses Irene Parkiet'PBR (10)	ERCP XFar

'Prinses Margriet' (3)	ERCP LAma	'Sanne' (3) ♥H6	ERCP LCro
'Professor Röntgen' (10)	ERCP LAma LCro	'Sapporo' (6)	EGren LCro
pulchella humilis	see *T. humilis*	'Sarah Raven' (6)	ERCP
§ 'Purissima' (13) ♥H6	CBro EGren EPfP GKev LAma LCro XFar	'Saskia' (9)	LAma
		saxatilis (15)	CBro GKev LAma LCro
'Purissima Design' (13) ♥H6	ERCP GKev LAma	§ - (Bakeri Group) 'Lilac Wonder' (15) ♥H6	CAby CBro EPot ERCP GKev LAma LCro NPer XFar
'Purple Bouquet' (3)	LAma	'Scarlet Baby' (12)	EPfP
'Purple Circus' (7)	GKev XFar	'Seadov' (3) ♥H6	EGren LCro
'Purple Crystal' (7)	ERCP GKev	'Secret Perfume' (2)	LRHS
'Purple Dance' (8) **new**	GKev	'Sensual Touch' (7) ♥H6	GKev LAma XFar
'Purple Doll' (6)	EGren ERCP ETay GKev LAma LCro	'Shining Parrot' (10)	GKev LAma
PURPLE DREAM	see *T.* 'Yume no Murasaki'	'Shirley' (3)	EGren LAma LCro XFar
'Purple Flag' (3)	EGren LCro	'Shirley Double' (11)	EGren EPfP ERCP GKev LAma XFar
'Purple Heart' (6)	CAby ERCP LRHS	'Showcase' (2)	EPfP ERCP LCro
'Purple Lady'PBR (3)	LCro XFar	'Showwinner' (12) ♥H6	LAma LCro XFar
PURPLE PRIDE ('Zantapur') (4) **new**	GKev LAma	'Silk Road' (2)	EGren
		'Silver Cloud' (3)	ERCP
'Purple Prince' (1) ♥H6	EGren GKev LAma LCro	'Silver Parrot' (10)	EGren GKev LAma XFar
'Purple Purissima' (13)	GKev LAma	'Silverstream' (4)	ETay
'Purple Rain' (3)	LCro	'Slawa'PBR (3)	EPfP ERCP GKev LAma LCro LRHS XFar
'Purple Tower' (7)	XFar	'Snow Crystal' (11)	XFar
'Quebec' (14)	CBro EGren GKev LAma	'Sonnet' (6)	GKev LAma
'Queen of Marvel' (2)	ERCP	'Sorbet' (5) ♥H6	CAby
'Queen of Night' (5)	CAby CBro EGren EPfP ERCP ETay GKev LAma LCro LRHS LSto MBros NBir NNys XFar	'Spitsbergen' (3)	ERCP
		sprengeri (15) ♥H6	CBro CSpe ECha ENun ERCP GKev MCtn MNrw SDix XFar
'Queensday' (11)	EGren	- Trotter's form (15)	GKev WCot
'Queensland' (7)	EPfP GKev LAma XFar	'Spring Green' (8) ♥H6	CBro EGren EPfP ERCP ETay GKev LAma LCro NNys XFar
'Rasta Parrot' (10)	GKev LCro XFar		
'Ravana' (3)	XFar	'Spryng Break' (3)	GKev LAma LRHS
'Red Baby Doll' (2)	ETay LAma	'Spryng Tide' (3)	LRHS
'Red Dress' (16)	EGren ERCP LAma XFar	***stellata***	see *T. clusiana* var. *stellata*
'Red Emperor'	see *T.* 'Madame Lefeber'	'Stresa' (12) ♥H6	CBro EGren LCro XFar
'Red Georgette' (5) ♥H6	GKev LAma NBir	'Striking Match' (6)	GKev LAma
'Red Hat' (7) ♥H6	LCro	'Striped Crown' (16) **new**	XFar
'Red Impression'PBR (4) ♥H6	CAby EGren EPfP ETay GKev LAma LCro XFar	'Striped Sail' (3)	GKev LAma
		'Strong Gold' (3) ♥H6	EGren
'Red Madonna' (10) **new**	GKev LAma	'Stunning Apricot' (5)	LCro
'Red Princess' (11) ♥H6	ERCP GKev LAma	'Sun Lover' (11)	EPfP
'Red Proud' (4)	GKev LAma LCro	'Suncatcher' (3)	GKev LAma
'Red Riding Hood' (14) ♥H6	CBro EGren EPfP ETay GKev LAma LCro LRHS NBir XFar	'Sunny Prince'PBR (1)	CBro EGren LCro
		'Sunset Miami' (7)	ERCP LAma LCro XFar
'Red Rover' (3)	LCro	'Sunshine Club' (5)	LAma
'Red Shine' (6) ♥H6	LCro	'Super Parrot' (10)	EGren ERCP GKev LAma XFar
'Red Springgreen' (8)	GKev LAma LCro	'Swan Wings' (7)	LAma LCro XFar
'Rembrandt' (2)	LAma	'Sweet Flag' (3)	EGren
'Rems Favourite' (3)	ERCP LCro XFar	'Sweetheart' (13)	LCro
'Renegade' (3)	LCro	***sylvestris*** (15)	CAby CBro EHet EPfP EPot ERCP GKev LAma LCro NBir SBeP SDix SPhx WCot WShi XFar
'Request' (3)	ERCP LCro XFar		
'Ridgedale' (11)	ERCP LCro		
'Rob Verlinden' (14)	EPfP		
'Rococo' (10)	CBro EGren ERCP GKev LAma LCro	'Synaeda Amor' (3)	ETay GKev LAma LCro
		'Synaeda Blue' (3)	EGren LCro
'Rococo Double' (10)	LCro	'Synaeda King' (6) ♥H6	LCro
'Ronaldo' (3)	EGren ERCP GKev LAma LCro	'Tabledance' (11)	ERCP LRHS
'Rosalie' (3)	LCro	***tarda*** (15) ♥H6	CBro EPfP ERCP GKev LAma LCro MCtn MNrw SPhx XFar
'Rosy Delight' (4)	GKev LAma XFar		
'Royal Acres' (2)	LRHS	'Temple of Beauty' (5) ♥H6	EGren ERCP GKev LAma
'Royal Celebration' (6)	ETay		
'Royal Pretender' (6)	LCro	'Tender Whisper' (3)	GKev
'Royal Tower' (11) **new**	XFar	'Texas Flame' (10)	GKev LAma
'Royal Virgin' (3)	ERCP GKev LAma	'Texas Gold' (10)	LAma
'Saint Petersburg' (1)	XFar	'The Edge' (2)	LRHS
'Salmon Dynasty' (3)	EPfP	'The First' (12) ♥H6	CBro EGren EPfP GKev LAma
'Salmon Impression' (4)	CAby ERCP LAma LCro	'Timeless' (3) ♥H6 **new**	GKev
'Salmon Jewel' (3)	EPot	'Tinka' (15) ♥H6	CBro EPfP LAma
'Salmon Parrot' (10)	ETay	'Tiny Timo' (15)	CBro LCro
'Salmon Prince' (1)	EGren ERCP LCro LSto	'Tom Pouce' (3)	EGren LCro
'Salmon van Eijk' (4)	GKev LAma LCro	'Toplips' (11)	GKev LAma
'San Clemente' (7) **new**	GKev LAma	'Toronto' (14) ♥H6	EGren GKev LAma

'Toucan' (3)	LAma	
'Très Chic' (6)	EPfP ETay GKev LAma LCro	
TRÈS CHIC FESTIVAL (mixed) (6) **new**	GKev LAma	
tschimganica 'Elodie' (15)	GKev	
turkestanica (15) ♀H5	CAby EPot ERCP GKev LAma LCro MCtn MNrw NPer SDix SPhx WHoo XFar	
'Turkish Delight' (14)	NPer	
'Uncle Tom' (11)	EGren ERCP LAma LCro XFar	
§ *undulatifolia* (15)	WCot	
'United States' (14) ♀H6	GKev LAma NPer	
urumiensis (15) ♀H5	ERCP LAma	
'Valdivia' (2)	XFar	
'Van Eijk'PBR (4)	EGren LCro	
'Vanille Coupe' (11)	XFar	
'Vaya con Dios' (7)	GKev LAma	
'Verandi' (3)	EPfP	
'Verona' (2)	ERCP LRHS	
'Verona Sunrise' (2)	ERCP	
'Véronique Sanson' (3)	ERCP LCro	
'Victoria's Secret' (3)	ETay GKev LAma LCro XFar	
'Victoria's Secret Pink' (10)	XFar	
'Vincent van Gogh' (7) ♀H6	GKev LAma XFar	
violacea	see *T. humilis* Violacea Group	
'Violet Beauty' (5)	EGren LCro XFar	
'Violet Bird' (8)	GKev LAma LCro	
'Violet Pranaa' (11)	ERCP	
'Virichic' (8)	ERCP GKev LCro	
'Vogue' (11)	ERCP GKev LAma LCro	
'Voicemail' (2) **new**	LRHS	
'Vovos' (10)	LCro XFar	
vvedenskyi 'Tangerine Beauty' (15) ♀H6	GKev	
'Wallflower' (5)	GKev LAma	
'Washington' (3)	LCro	
'Weber's Parrot' (10)	LCro	
'Wedding Gift' (11)	XFar	
'Weisse Berliner' (3)	GKev LAma LCro	
'West Point' (6)	EGren LCro	
'Whispering Dream' (3)	ETay LAma	
'White Bridge' (11)	GKev LAma LRHS	
'White Dream' (3)	EGren ETay LCro XFar	
'White Elegance' (6)	XFar	
'White Emperor'	see *T.* 'Purissima'	
'White Heart' (11)	LCro	
'White Liberstar' (16)	EGren XFar	
'White Lizzard' (10)	XFar	
'White Mountain' (11)	LCro	
'White Parrot' (10)	EGren GKev LAma LCro XFar	
'White Prince' (1)	EGren GKev LAma LCro	
'White Proud' (3)	GKev LAma	
'White Triumphator' (6) ♀H6	CBro EGren EPfP ERCP GKev LAma LCro NBir NNys	
whittallii	see *T. orphanidea* Whittallii Group	
§ 'Willem van Oranje' (2)	LRHS	
'Willemsoord' (2)	GKev LAma	
WILLIAM OF ORANGE	see *T.* 'Willem van Oranje'	
wilsoniana	see *T. montana*	
'Wisley' (5) ♀H6	LCro	
'World Bowl' (2) **new**	EGren	
§ 'World Friendship' (3)	GKev LAma LRHS	
'World Peace'PBR (4)	LCro	
'Wyndham' (11)	ERCP XFar	
'Yellow Baby' (2) ♀H6 **new**	LRHS	
'Yellow Crown' (16)	XFar	
'Yellow Emperor' (5)	XFar	
'Yellow Flight' (3)	GKev	
'Yellow Madonna' (10)	GKev	
'Yellow Pompenette'PBR (11)	ERCP	
I 'Yellow Purissima' (13) ♀H6	GKev LAma	
'Yellow Springgreen' (8)	ERCP LAma	
'Yellow Valery' (7)	XFar	
'Yokohama' (3)	GKev LAma XFar	
'Yonina' (6)	LCro	
§ 'Yume no Murasaki' (6)	CBro EGren ERCP GKev LAma LCro XFar	
'Zomerschoon' (5)	LAma	
§ 'Zurel' (3)	ERCP LAma	

Tulista (Asphodelaceae)

§ *minor*	SPlb
§ *pumila* ♀H2	SEND
§ - var. *pumila*	NCft

Tunica see *Petrorhagia*

Tunilla (Cactaceae)

soehrensii	WJur

Tupistra (Asparagaceae)

aurantiaca	GEdr LEdu WPGP
- B&SWJ 2267	WCot WCru
- B&SWJ 2401	WCru
chinensis 'Eco China Ruffles'	WCot
grandistigma	WCot
- B&SWJ 11773	WCru
jinshanensis	WCot
tonkinensis	see *Rohdea tonkinensis*
wattii B&SWJ 8297	WCru

Turbinicarpus ✿ (Cactaceae)

swobodae	SPlb

Turpinia (Staphyleaceae)

ternata CWJ 12360	WCru

Tussilago (Asteraceae)

farfara	MHer MNHC WHer

Tweedia (Apocynaceae)

§ *coerulea*	CBcs CDTJ CSpe EAri SChF SIvy SPad
- 'Heavenborn'	EShb MCtn

Tylecodon (Crassulaceae)

decipiens **new**	SPlb
paniculatus	SPlb

Typha (Typhaceae)

angustifolia	CBen CPud CWat ELin EPfk LCro MMuc NPer SPlb WMAq
latifolia	CBen CPud CWat ELin MCtn NBir NPer SVic WMAq
- 'Variegata' (v)	ELin EPfk WMAq
§ *laxmannii*	CBen CLil CPud ELin EPfk
lugdunensis	MWts
minima	CBen CLil CPud CToG CTtf CWat ELan ELin EPfk EWat LCro MWts NPer WMAq
shuttleworthii	CBen
stenophylla	see *T. laxmannii*

Typhonium (Araceae)

giganteum	see *Sauromatum giganteum*
aff. *horsefieldii*	see *Sauromatum* aff. *horsfieldii*
roxburghii	EBee WFar
venosum	see *Sauromatum venosum*

U

Ugni ✿ (Myrtaceae)
candollei	EBee SVen WJur WPGP
§ **molinae**	CBcs CCht CCoa CDoC CExl CMac
	CoPl CSde CSpe EAri EBee ELan
	ELon EPfP LEdu LRHS MHoo MMuc
	SAdn SChF SEle SEND SPlb WJek
	WJur WKor WLov WPav WPGP
- PAB 1347	SBrt
- 'Butterball'	CBcs CDoC CMac EBee EHeP EPfP
	LEdu LRHS MHoo SEle SPoG
- 'Elite'	LEdu
- 'Flambeau' (v)	CAgr CBcs CCoa CDoC CExl CMac
	CSde EBee ELan ELon EPfP LCro
	LEdu MAsh MBlu NLar SEle SEND
	SPoG SRms WPav
- 'Frampton Feast'	WPGP
- KA'POW ('Yanpow')	CBcs CCBP CCoa CDoC EBee LCro
	MHtn WFar WPGP
- 'Miss Green'	WPGP
- orange-leaved	WJek
- 'Red Devil'	LEdu
- 'Variegata' (v)	LEdu WJek
- 'Villarica Strawberry'	EBee LEdu WPGP
montana	WJur

Ulex (Fabaceae)
europaeus	CBcs CHab CMac CoPl EHeP ELan
	ELon LBuc LRHS MCtn SEWo WKor
§ - 'Flore Pleno' (d) ♀H6	CBcs CCoa CDoC CSBt CSde ECha
	EHeP ELan ELon GEdr IArd MBlu
	MMuc SDix WFar WHer
- 'Irish Double' (d)	GAbr NLar
- 'Plenus'	see *U. europaeus* 'Flore Pleno'

Ulmus ✿ (Ulmaceae)
'Columella'	CCVT ELan WPGP
'Dodoens'	EBar MBlu
'Fiorente'PBR (Resista Series)	SEWo
'Frontier'	ELan SGol
§ **glabra**	CAco CAgr IPap MGos
- 'Camperdownii'	CMac
- 'Crispa'	NLar
- 'Lutescens'	NOra NPip WMat
× **hollandica** 'Belgica'	EHeP
§ - 'Dampieri Aurea' ♀H7	CCVT ELon LBuc MAsh MBlu MPri
	NLar NPip SPoG WFar
- 'Jacqueline Hillier'	CSpe EUrb LMaj MMuc NLar NRya
	SArc SEND SGol WAbe WCFE WFar
	WOld
- 'Wredei'	see *U.* × *hollandica* 'Dampieri
	Aurea'
laevis	CLnd EBee WPGP
lamellosa	WPGP
'Lobel'	EBar EHeP
LUTÈCE ('Nanguen'PBR)	NOra NPip
minor	MGos
- 'Dampieri Aurea'	see *U.* × *hollandica* 'Dampieri
	Aurea'
- var. **suberosa**	CAco
montana	see *U. glabra*
'New Horizon'PBR **new**	CCVT
parvifolia	CAco CMen WJur
- 'Geisha' (v)	NLar
§ - 'Hokkaido'	EPot EWes GKev NLar WAbe
- 'Pygmaea'	see *U. parvifolia* 'Hokkaido'
- 'Sagei'	NLar

- 'Yatsubusa'	EPot
'Pioneer'	ELan
procera	MGos
pumila 'Beijing Gold'	ELan
'Sapporo Autumn Gold'	EHeP
VADA ('Wanoux'PBR)	EBar ELan SEWo
× ***viminalis*** 'Aurea' **new**	IArd
- 'Marginata' (v)	NLar
wallichiana	NLar
'Wingham'	ELan LBuc LCro LRHS NPip SEWo

Umbellularia (Lauraceae)
californica	NLar
- dwarf, from SW Oregon	WPGP

Umbilicus (Crassulaceae)
§ **oppositifolius** ♀H5	CAby CoPl ECha ELan EMor EUrb
	EWld GKev LRHS LShi MPro NBid
	SLee SPlb SRms SRot WFar WKif
	WTor
- 'Frosted Jade'	see *U. oppositifolius* 'Jim's Pride'
- 'Jane's Reverse' (v)	WCot
§ - 'Jim's Pride' (v)	EWes GKev GPSL MHer NBir NPer
	NRya SRms WFar
rupestris	MMuc SChr WHer WShi

Uncarina (Pedaliaceae)
decaryi	SPlb

Uncinia (Cyperaceae)
from Chile	EPPr
* **cyparissias** from Chile	NBir
egmontiana	LRHS LShi
rubra	CEnd CoPl EBee ECha EGren EHeP
	ELan EMor EPfP EPPr GMaP LRHS
	MGos NSti SPad SPlb SPoG WFar
§ - 'Belinda's Find'PBR	EBee EGren LBom LCro LRHS LSou
	MBNS MPri MPro NBir SDix SPoG
	SRms
- EVERFLAME	see *U. rubra* 'Belinda's Find'
uncinata	CBcs ECha EGrI
* - **rubra**	CDoC CSde MAsh SRms

Uniola (Poaceae)
latifolia	see *Chasmanthium latifolium*

Urginea (Asparagaceae)
maritima	see *Charybdis maritima*

Urospermum (Asteraceae)
dalechampii	EAri EPPr

Ursinia (Asteraceae)
speciosa	MCtn

Urtica (Urticaceae)
galeopsifolia	NBac

Utricularia (Lentibulariaceae)
sp.	CLil
vulgaris	CLil

Uvularia ✿ (Colchicaceae)
sp.	ENun
grandiflora ♀H7	Widely available
- gold-leaved	CMiW
- 'Lynda Windsor'	CDor LEdu
- var. **pallida**	CMiW CTtf EAri EBee EBlo ECha
	EMor EPfP EPPr GEdr GKev ISha
	LEdu LRHS LSto NCth NLar SPel
	WCru WFar

Uvularia

- 'Susie Lewis'	WCru
perfoliata	CExl EBee ECha EDAr EPot EPPr ESwi GKev LAma LEdu MHtn NBir SPeP SPlb WCot WCru WFar
- tall	EPPr
sessilifolia	CExl CMiW EAri EBlo ISha LEdu LRHS WCru
- 'Cobblewood Gold' (v)	EPPr LEdu WCru WFar

V

Vaccaria see *Gypsophila*
- hispanica — see *Gypsophila vaccaria*
- segetalis — see *Gypsophila vaccaria*

Vaccinium ❀ (Ericaceae)

'Berkeley' (F)	CAgr CEnd EGren GKin MBlu SEdi SPre
BERRYBUX ('Zf08095'PBR) (BrazelBerry Series) (F)	LCro
'Bluejay' (F)	EGren ELan EPfP NLar SEdi SPoG WCha
'Blueray' (F)	GKin NLar
'Brigitta' (F)	CEnd CTrh EPom LRHS LSRN MAsh NLar SPoG SPre WFar
chaetothrix	WAbe
'Chandler' (F)	CAgr CBTr CDoC CEnd CMac CTrh CTsd EGren EPom GKin LCro SEdi SSFr WCha WFar
'Chippewa' (F)	LRHS
consanguineum B&SWJ 10486	WCru
corymbosum (F)	EGrI SSta
- 'Ama' (F)	NLar
- 'Aurora'PBR (F)	EPom
- 'Blauweiss-Goldtraube' (F)	CAgr EGren EHet ELan GKin LCro LRHS NLar SPoG SVic WFar
- 'Blue Duke' (F)	EHet LSRN
- 'Blue Sapphire' (F)	LCro
- BLUE SUEDE ('Th682'PBR) (F)	CDoC CMac LCro NLar
- 'Bluecrop' (F)	Widely available
- 'Bluegold' (F)	CMac EGren EPfP LCro LRHS SPoG WCha WFar
- 'Bluetta' (F)	CAgr ELan MPri SPoG
- CABERNET SPLASH ('Vacbri1') (F)	LCro NLar WPGP
- 'Calypso'PBR (F)	EBee
- 'Coville' (F)	WFar
- 'Darrow' (F)	CAgr LCro LRHS WFar WMat
- 'Dixie' (F)	CAgr NLar SPoG WFar
- 'Draper'PBR (F)	EHet EPom
- 'Duke' (F) ♀H6	CDoC CMac CTsd EHet ELan EPfP EPom LCro LRHS MAsh SBmr SPoG SPre SSFr WCha
- 'Elizabeth' (F)	LRHS
- 'Elliott' (F)	CDoC CMac WFar WJur
- FLAMINGO ('Hoogi045') (F)	LCro
- 'Grover' (F)	EGren SEdi
- 'Hardyblue' (F)	CAgr
- 'Heerma' (F)	WFar
- 'Hortblue Petite'PBR (F)	EPom LRHS SVic WFar
- 'Jersey' (F)	CAgr CEnd EGren EPfP LCro LRHS LSRN MAsh MGos NLar SEdi SPoG SVic WCha
- 'Legacy' (F)	CTrh
- 'Liberty'PBR (F)	CBTr CTrh EPfP EPom LRHS
- 'Nui' (F)	CEnd EPom LSRN
- 'Patriot' (F)	CAgr CBcs CBTr CEnd CTrh CWnw EGren ELan EPom GKin LBom LBuc LCro LRHS MPri NBir NLar NTrD SBmr SPre SSFr WFar WMat
- 'Pioneer' (F)	SPoG WFar
- 'Polaris' (F)	CEnd
- 'Reka' (F)	CAgr NPer WFar
- 'Sierra' (F)	LRHS
- 'Spartan' (F) ♀H6	CAgr CDoC CMac EGren EPom LCro LSRN WCha WFar
- 'Stanley' (F)	EPfP SPoG
- 'Toro' (F)	SPre
- YELLOBERRY BLUE ('Andval1601') (F)	LCro
crassifolium	LRHS
subsp. *sempervirens* 'Well's Delight' (F)	
cylindraceum ♀H4	CEnd LSto NLar SSta WFar WJur
delavayi	GArf NLar SSta
dunalianum var. *caudatifolium* B&SWJ 1716	WCru
- - NMWJ 14558	WCru
- var. *megaphyllum* HWJ 515	WCru
'Earliblue' (F)	CAgr GKin LBuc LRHS MPri SPoG WMat
floribundum	GArf
glaucoalbum ♀H5	CMac EGrI MBlu SPoG
'Goldtraube 71' (F)	MAsh SEdi WCha
'Herbert' (F)	CAgr EGren EPom LBuc SEdi
macrocarpon (F)	SPre SRms WJur WKor
- 'Early Black' (F)	EPom GKin SVic
- 'Hamilton'	GArf
- 'Langlois' (F)	NLar
- 'Olson's Honkers' (F)	CAgr
- 'Pilgrim' (F)	CAgr CMac LCro LEdu MAsh SBmr SPoG WMat
- 'Stevens' (F)	CAgr
myrtillus	CAgr EPom NLar SPlb SVic
'Northland' (F)	CBTr EPom LRHS LSRN MNHC NLar SPoG WCha WMat
'Northsky' (F)	WFar
nummularia	GKev LRHS NLar WAbe
ovatum (F)	CMac GKev GKin NLar
- 'Thundercloud' (F)	SSta
§ *oxycoccos* (F)	CAgr
'Ozarkblue' (F)	EPom LCro NLar SEdi SPoG WFar
palustre	see *V. oxycoccos*
PINK BONBONS ('Minpink1')	LEdu NLar
§ 'Pink Lemonade' (F)	CBTr EBee EHet ELan EPfP EPom LBom LCro LRHS MAsh MHtn MNHC MPri NLar NTrD SBmr SEdi SPoG SPre SSFr WCha WFar
'Pink Sapphire'	see *V.* 'Pink Lemonade'
praestans	GArf
randaiense B&SWJ 14601	WCru
sikkimense	GArf
'Spring Surprise'	EPot WAbe
'Sunshine Blue' (F)	CAgr CBTr CEnd CMac ELan EPom LBuc LRHS NLar SBmr SPoG SSFr
'Tophat' (F)	EHet LRHS
vitis-idaea	EPfP EWes MHoo SVic WKit WKor
- FIREBALLS ('Lirome'PBR) (F)	CDoC LCro LSRN SBmr SPre
- 'Ida' (F)	LBuc
- Koralle Group ♀H5	CAgr EPot GArf GKin NLar
- subsp. *minus*	NLar
- 'Red Candy'PBR (F)	LCro SPoG
- 'Red Pearl' (F)	EPom SBmr

Vachellia (Fabaceae)
§ *farnesiana*   WJur
§ *karroo*   SPlb WJur
  nilotica new   WJur

Vagaria (Amaryllidaceae)
parviflora   GKev

Valeriana (Caprifoliaceae)
'Alba'   see *Centranthus ruber* 'Albus'
alliariifolia   GQue NBro SPhx
 - PAB 3001   LEdu WPGP
 - var. *tiliifolia*   LEdu WPGP
'Coccinea'   see *Centranthus ruber*
dioica   SHor
jatamansi   GKev SRms
 - PAB 6846   LEdu WPGP
montana   CTtf EBee ECha EPPr GGro LEdu
     MMuc NBro NRya SHar SRms
officinalis   Widely available
 - 'Chiri Fu' (v)   WCot
 - subsp. *sambucifolia*   EPPr MNrw SHar
phu   EGrI
 - 'Aurea'   CCBP CDor CHby EBee ECha EGrI
     GKin GPSL GQue LBar MArl MPie
     NBid NBir NBro NLar NSti SPoG
     SRms StAn WCAu
pyrenaica   CAby CTtf EBee ECha EPPr GBin
     GGro LEdu MMuc MNrw SEND
     SHar SPhx WCot WPGP
wallrothii   MWlw WCot

Valerianella (Caprifoliaceae)
§ *locusta*   MNHC SVic
 - 'Medaillon'   LCro
 - 'Vit'   MCtn
 olitoria   see *V. locusta*

Vallea (Elaeocarpaceae)
stipularis   CBct IArd
 - B&SWJ 14366   WCru

Vallisneria (Hydrocharitaceae)
americana   ELin
spiralis   ELin
 - 'Tortifolia'   ELin

Vallota see Cyrtanthus

Vancouveria (Berberidaceae)
chrysantha   CExl ECha EPPr GEdr GKev WFar
     WPGP
hexandra   CExl ECha EGrI EMor EPPr GBin
     GEdr GKev LEdu NBir NSti SPlb
     SRot WAbe WCru WPGP
planipetala   GEdr WCru

Vasconcellea (Caricaceae)
§ *pubescens*   CCht CDTJ EAri SPlb WCot

Vatricania (Cactaceae)
§ *guentheri*   NPlm

Veltheimia ✿ (Asparagaceae)
§ *bracteata* ♀H2   SRms
§ *capensis* ♀H2   ESwi WCot
  viridifolia misapplied   see *V. capensis*
  viridifolia Jacq.   see *V. bracteata*

× **Venidioarctotis** see Arctotis

Venidium see Arctotis

Veratrum (Melanthiaceae)
album ♀H7   ECha GEdr GKev MNrw NBid WCot
 - PAB 537   LEdu
 - var. *flavum*   MNrw WCot WCru
 - - 'Primrose Warburg'   GEdr
 - subsp. *lobelianum*   EAri LEdu WCot
 - 'Lorna's Green' ♀H7
californicum ♀H3   CBct ECha ESwi LEdu MNrw NBid
formosanum   GEdr MNrw WCot WPGP
 - RWJ 9806   WCru
grandiflorum B&SWJ 4416   WCru
maackii   ECha GArf MNrw
 - green-flowered   MNrw
 - var. *japonicum*   MNrw
 - var. *maackii*   MNrw
nigrum ♀H6   CBro EAri ECha EMor GEdr GMaP
     LEdu MMrt MNrw NBid NBir SMad
     SPlb WCAu WCot WMal WPGP
schindleri   EPfP GEdr MNrw WPGP
 - B&SWJ 4068   ESwi WCru
viride   EAri LEdu NBid WCot WCru

Verbascum (Scrophulariaceae)
adzharicum   WCot
'Arctic Summer'   see *V. bombyciferum* 'Polarsommer'
arcturus   SVen
blattaria   CBgR CBWd CGwi NBir NDov
     WHer
 - f. *albiflorum*   CSpe LEdu LRHS MCtn NClf NDov
     SHar SHor SMHy SPhx SPlb WHer
     WRBe
'Blue Lagoon'   see *V. luridiflorum* 'Blue Lagoon'
§ *bombyciferum*   CWRo ECha ELan LWaG SHor SRms
I - 'Arctic Snow'   SPoG
§ - 'Polarsommer'   CSpe LRHS MCtn NBir SHar WTre
 - 'Silver Lining'   NPer
'Broussa'   see *V. bombyciferum*
(Caribbean Crush Group)   ELan LBar MBNS Midl MPro SMrm
  'Caribbean Crush'   SPoG WSpi
 - 'Mango'   NLar
chaixii   GAbr MBel NBir NBro SDix StAn
     WCAu WFar
 - 'Album'   CBcs CDor CSpe CWal ECha ERCP
     GBin GJos GMaP GQue LCro LRHS
     LSto LWaG MArl MCtn NBir NBro
     NDov NGdn NLar SAth SDix SHor
     SRms WCAu WFar WHoo WSpi
     WTre
 - 'Sixteen Candles'   WFar
 - 'Wedding Candles'   CFis ELan EPfP GElm MPro NGdn
     WFar
'Chantilly'   LCro
'Cherry Helen' PBR   LCro
'Christo's Yellow   ECha LBar SPoG WCot
  Lightning' ♀H6
'Clementine'   EPPr LBar LCro LWaG MSwo WFar
     WSpi
'Coneyhill Yellow'   EPPr
(Cotswold Group)   CBcs CFis EPfP LBar LSou LSto
  'Cotswold Beauty'   NGdn SHar SPel
 - 'Cotswold Queen'   CBcs EPfP EPPr GMaP LBar LCro
     MArl MAsh MMrt WCAu WHoo
     WSpi
 - 'Gainsborough' ♀H6   CDor ELan GMaP LCro NLar SPoG
     WCAu WSpi
 - 'Pink Domino' ♀H6   CBcs EPfP EWhm GMaP LCro LSto
     MArl MHol SMrm SPel WSpi
 - 'Royal Highland'   CFis LBar MArl MBNS SPoG

Verbascum

- 'White Domino'	WSpi		- 'Little One'	ECha MAsh
'Cotswold King'	see *V. creticum*		- 'Little Tommie'	MVer
§ *creticum*	CSpe WCot		- 'Lollipop'^{PBR}	Widely available
'Dark Eyes'^{PBR}	CWGN LRHS MPro NWbg		- 'Royal Dreams'	Midl MVer
dumulosum ♀^{H4}	WAbe		- 'Violetta'	Midl MPro MVer
faurei	WCot		*bonariensis* × *incompta*	WMal
'Firedance'	CBcs EPfP MBNS MHol		*brasiliensis* misapplied	see *V. bonariensis*
'Golden Wings' ♀^{H4}	WAbe		*chamaedrifolia*	see *Glandularia peruviana*
'Helen Johnson'	CBcs CWCL CWnw EGren LRHS LShi WSpi		*hastata*	CAby CSpe EBee ECha EGrI EHeP ELan EPfP GKev LBom LCro LEdu LSto LWaG MBel MNHC MNrw MVer NSti SMrm SPhx SPlb SRms StAn WCav WFar WTre
'Honey Dijon'	Midl			
× *hybridum* 'Banana Custard'	EAri EPfP LRHS WSpi			
- 'Snow Maiden'	EPfP LShi		* - 'Alba'	CAby CSpe ELan EPfP GPSL MBel MVer NSti WCAu WFar
- 'Wega'	NLar			
'Jester'	SPoG WSpi		- 'Blue Spires'	CTtf EPfP EPPr GKev IPot LBar MCtn MVer
'June Johnson'	CBcs CMHG CWnw MArl			
'Kynaston'	CBcs EPfP MArl WHoo		- f. *rosea*	CAby CElw CSpe CTtf ECha EGrI ELan EPfP EPPr GKev GMaP LCro LEdu MBel MNrw MVer NDov NSti SPhx WCAu WFar WMal
'Lavender Lass'	EPfP LBar LRHS Midl MPri NLar WSpi			
'Letitia' ♀^{H4}	EDAr WAbe WKif			
longifolium var. *pannosum*	see *V. olympicum*		- - 'Pink Spires'	ESgI GQue IPot LBar LRHS LSto MCtn MVer
§ *luridiflorum*	CWGN		- 'White Spires'	ECha EPfP LBar LRHS LSto MCtn MVer
'Blue Lagoon'^{PBR}				
lychnitis	CSpe SPhx		*lasiostachys*	EBee MVer
'Megan's Mauve'	WSpi		- 'Lilac Spires'	NDov
'Merlin'^{PBR}	CBcs EPfP LBar MArl		*litoralis*	MVer
nigrum	CGwi CHab CLiI GJos LShi MCtn NGdn NMir WOrg WRBe		*macdougalii*	StAn
			- 'Lavender Spires'	CSpe ECha EPPr GBin LBar LRHS LSto MPro MVer NDov SHar SHor SPel SPhx SRms WNPC WTor
- var. *album*	LWaG NGdn WSpi			
§ *olympicum*	CBcs ELan EPfP GJos MCtn SDix SMrm SRms WCAu WCot		*officinalis*	CCBP CGHo CGwi EBee EHet ENfk MAsh MCtn MHer MNHC MVer NAts SRms WHer
'Petra'	LBar LRHS			
phlomoides	SPel			
phoeniceum	CBcs ELan EPPr GAbr MCtn SPlb SPoG WFar WSpi WTre		- 'Bampton' Purple Haze' ambig.	Widely available NClf
			Quartz Series	see *Glandularia* Quartz Series
* - 'Album'	CSpe WTre		§ *rigida* ♀^{H3}	Widely available
§ - 'Flush of White'	CDor EDAr GElm LRHS MCtn Midl MPro NGdn WFar WHil		- f. *lilacina*	LCro
- hybrids	MCtn		- - 'Lilac Haze'	CMac MVer
- 'Rosetta'	EDAr EPfP LRHS LSto MCtn MPro WFar		- - 'Polaris'	EBee ELon EPfP MVer NDov SMHy WMal
- 'Violetta'	CSpe ECha EDAr EPfP EPPr ERCP GElm GQue LCro LShi LSto LWaG MCtn MHol MPro NGdn NSti SMHy WCAu WFar		- 'Santos'	EGren GPSL LBar LCro LRHS MVer NBir
			scabridoglandulosa	see *Junellia succulentifolia*
			serpyllifolia	see *Junellia micrantha*
- 'White Bride'	see *V. phoeniceum* 'Flush of White'		*stricta*	EBee ECha EPPr MVer
'Pink Kisses'	SPoG		- pink-flowered	NDov
'Pink Petticoats'	LBar LRHS MBNS Midl MPro WHil		- white-flowered	EPPr LRHS MVer
'Plum Smokey'^{PBR}	EGren MPri NEoE NWbg		'Triffids Purple Haze'	CSpe CTtf MVer
'Primrose Path'	EGren LRHS MBNS Midl MPro NLar		*venosa*	see *V. rigida*
pyramidatum	EBee EPPr SPhx			
roripifolium	CSpe ESgI NClf		***Verbesina*** (*Asteraceae*)	
'Rosie'	Midl		*alternifolia*	EBee EMor MCtn StAn
'Royalty'	LRHS SPad		- 'Goldstrahl'	EPPr LShi WFar
'Southern Charm'	EGren MCtn MPro NQui WHil		***Vernicia*** (*Euphorbiaceae*)	
'Spica'	MCtn		*cordata*	WPGP
'Sugar Plum'^{PBR}	LCro LRHS		*fordii*	SPlb WPGP
thapsus	CCBP CGHo CGwi CHab EGrI ENfk GJem GJos GQue LRHS MArl MCtn MHoo MNHC NBir NMir SRms		***Vernonia*** (*Asteraceae*)	
			§ *arkansana*	EBee ECha EGrI ESwi LSto SDix SHar SHor SMHy WFar
'Ventnor Giant'	SVen			
			- 'Alba'	EBee ESwi
Verbena (*Verbenaceae*)			- 'Betty Blindeman'	MNrw
(G)	see *Glandularia*		- 'Mammuth' ♀^{H7}	CKno EBee ECha ELon EMor EWes LBar LEdu MHol MNrw SHor SMad SPoG WCot
× *baileyana* 'Purple Haze' **new**	SDix WHoo			
- purple-leaved	LRHS MNrw SPhx WMal			
§ *bonariensis* ♀^{H4}	Widely available		*baldwinii*	EBee ESwi LRHS SPhx
- 'Bonnie Blue' **new**	LSou		*crinita*	see *V. arkansana*

Veronica 717

fasciculata	EWes LRHS MHol MPro NLar SMrm SPel SPhx WCot	'Baby Doll'^PBR	LRHS SPoG
gigantea	MHer MMuc MNrw NLar WTre	'Baby Marie' (H)	CDoC CSBt EGren EHeP ELan EPfP GJos GKin LBom LBuc LCro LRHS NLar NPer SHeb SPoG SRms WSpi
glauca	WCot	§ *baylyi* (H)	SHeb
lettermannii	CFis CSpe EBee LSto MHer MPro SDix SHar SPhx	'Beatrice' (H)	SHeb
- 'Iron Butterfly'	EBee WPGP	*beccabunga*	CBen CGwi CHab CLil CPud CWat ELin EWat MMuc MWts NPer WMAq WSpi
missurica	ESwi		
noveboracensis	EBee EWhm GElm SHar SHor SMad WCAu	'Bergen's Blue'	NLar SHar
- 'Albiflora'	EPPr EWes	§ *besseya* (H)	GEdr
- 'White Lightning'	CDor EBee EMor SHar	'Beverley Hills' (H)	CSBt EBee
		'Bicolor Wand' (H)	LRHS SHeb

Veronica ✿ (*Plantaginaceae*)

albicans (H) ♀^H4	CBcs CBrac CCoa CDoC CMac CWnw EGren EHeP ELan EPfP GJos GKin LCro LRHS LSRN MAsh MGos MHed SHeb SRms WSpi	*bidwillii* (P)	EDAr SRms
		- 'Kea' (P)	SRot
		bishopiana (H)	EPfP
		'Black Beauty' (H)	LRHS MAsh
		'Black Panther' (H)	ELon
- prostrate	see *V. albicans* 'Snow Cover'	BLUE BOUQUET	see *V. longifolia* 'Blaubündel'
§ - Recurva Group (H)	CCoa CoPl SHeb SRms	'Blue Clouds' (H)	WMal
§ - - 'Aoira' (H)	SHeb SPlb	BLUE ELEGANCE ('Lowgeko') (Garden Elegance Series) (H)	ELan LCro LRHS
- - 'Boughton Silver' (H) ♀^H4	LSRN MMuc SHeb		
- - 'Fiona' (H)	SHeb	'Blue Gem' (H)	CCoa CDoC CMac
- - green-leaved (H)	SHeb	BLUE HAZE ('Lowchi'^PBR) (Garden Beauty Series) (H)	LRHS
§ - 'Snow Cover' (H)	EWes SHeb		
- 'Snow Drift'	see *V. albicans* 'Snow Cover'	BLUE ICE ('Lowapb') (Garden Beauty Series) (H)	LRHS
- 'Snow Mound' (H)	SHeb		
'Alicia Amherst' (H)	SHeb	'Blue Indigo'	NGdn
allionii	EBee GKev	'Blue Spire'	WSpi
'Amanda Cook' (H/v)	NPer	BLUE STAR ('Vergeer 1'^PBR) (H) ♀^H4	CDoC EPfP GJos LBom LBuc LCro LRHS MAsh SHeb SPoG SRms
'Amethyst' (H)	SHeb		
'Amethyst Mist' (H)	SHeb	'Bluebell' (H)	SHeb
amplexicaulis clone 4 (H)	SHeb	BLUSH ELEGANCE ('Lowele') (Garden Elegance Series) (H)	ELan LCro LRHS
§ 'Amy' (H)	ELon NPer SHeb WCot WKif		
× *andersonii* (H)	CDoC EGren NBir SHeb	'Blush Wand' (H)	SHeb
- 'Andersonii Variegata' (H/v)	EGren SHeb SRms	*bombycina*	WAbe
'Anna'^PBR van den Hoogen	NDov	- subsp. *bolkardaghensis*	WAbe
'Anne Pimm' (H/v)	SHeb	*bonarota*	see *Paederota bonarota*
'Annie's Winter Wonder' (H/v)	LRHS MPri	'Boscawenii' (H)	SHeb
		'Bouquet'^PBR (H)	LSou
'Aoira'	see *V. albicans* (Recurva Group) 'Aoira'	§ 'Bowles's Hybrid' (H)	MSwo SEND SHeb SRms
aphylla	GKev	*brachysiphon* (H)	MMuc SEND SHeb SRms
armena	EBee EWes MHer WAbe	'Bracken Hill' (H)	SHeb
§ *armstrongii* (H)	MMuc WKif	*breviracemosa* (H)	SHeb
ASPIRE ('Tnvera'^PBR)	LBar NLar	BRONZE GLOW ('Lowglo') (Garden Beauty Series) (H)	CDoC EGren LBuc LRHS
(Atomic Ray Series) 'Atomic Hot Pink Ray'	WFar		
- 'Atomic Silvery Pink Ray'	NLar	'Bronzy Baby'^PBR (H/v)	EGren MAsh SPoG
austriaca var. *dubia*	see *V. prostrata*	*buchananii* (H)	MHer NPer SHeb
- 'Ionian Skies'	GBin LEdu SBeP SRot WAbe WIce WKif	§ - 'Fenwickii' (H)	WHoo
		- 'Minor' ambig. (H)	GKev SHeb WAbe
§ - subsp. *teucrium*	EBee MHol SRms	'Burgundy Blush' (H)	LBuc LRHS SPoG
- - 'Crater Lake Blue' ♀^H6	CCps CDor EBee ECha ELan EPfP EWld GElm LBar MArl MBel MHol SBeP SMrm SPlb SRms StAn WCAu WChS WCot WFar WKif	'Burning Heart' (H/v)	LBuc LCro LRHS
		buxifolia	see *V. odora*
		§ 'Caledonia' (H)	CBcs CDoC CoPl EGren EGrI ELan EPfP LCro LRHS MAsh MGos NPer SHeb SPoG SRms WSpi
- - 'Fresh'	WCot		
- - 'Kapitän'	MMrt MNrw NGdn SEND WFar	*candida*	see *V. spicata* subsp. *incana*
- - 'Knallblau'	LRHS MNrw NLar WFar	'Candy' (H)	SHeb
- - 'Lapis Lazuli'	WCAu	× *cantiana* 'Kentish Pink'	EBee WFar
- - 'Royal Blue' ♀^H6	CAby CFis EBee EPfP GMaP MHol MPro NSti SRms WFar WKif	'Carey Pink' (H)	SHeb
		'Carl Teschner'	see *V.* 'Youngii'
'Autumn Beauty' (H)	SHeb	'Carnea' (H)	SHeb
'Autumn Glory' (H)	CBrac CDoC EGren ELan EPfP LCro MAsh NBir SHeb SPlb SPoG SRGP WSpi	'Carnea Variegata' (H/v)	SHeb SRms
		carnosula	see *V. baylyi*
'Avalon' (H)	SHeb	*catarractae* (P)	ECha ELan EPfP EWld NBir SHar SRms WKif
'Baby Boo' (H/v)	CDoC ELan		

- 'Avalanche' PBR (P)	CAbb CMac CWGN EBee ELan GMaP LCro LRHS MAsh MMrt MSCN SAth SPoG WNPC
§ - 'Delight' (P) ♀H4	GMaP MHer MMrt NPer
- subsp. *diffusa*	see *V. lanceolata*
- 'Miss Willmott' (P)	SPlb
- 'Pink Avalanche' (P)	CSpe CWnw EHeP LCro LSou MAsh MHtn WFar WNPC
- 'Porlock' (P)	CDoC CTsd CWnw EPfP GKev LRHS SDix SRms SRot WCav WHoo
- 'Rosea' (P)	GKev SRms
- white-flowered (P)	EGrI EWld GAbr SRms
- 'Whittallii' (P)	GBin
'Celebration' PBR (H/v)	EGren LBuc LRHS LSou Midl
'Celine' (H)	CCoa EHeP EPfP LBuc LCro LRHS
chamaedrys	NMir
'Champagne' (H)	CBrac CDoC EGren ELan LCro LRHS MBlu NLar NLit SHeb SRms
'Champagne Ice' (H)	LBuc
CHAMPION ('Champseiont') (H) ♀H4	GJos MMrt NLar SHeb
'Charming White' (H)	CoPl
'Christensenii' (H)	SHeb
'Claret Crush' PBR (H)	LBuc LRHS SPoG
'Clear Skies' (H)	SRms
'Cobb Valley' (H)	LRHS
'Combe Royal' (H)	SHeb
'Conwy Knight' (H)	SRms
corriganii (H)	SHeb
'County Park' (H)	GAbr SHeb
'C.P. Raffill' (H)	SHeb
'Cranleighensis' (H)	LRHS SHeb
cupressoides (H)	WFar
- 'Boughton Dome' (H)	ELan EPot GAbr MHer WAbe WHoo
'Dark Angel' (H)	EBee LBuc LRHS SHeb SPoG
DARK BLUE MOODY BLUES ('Novaverblu')	EGren ELan EPfP LRHS Midl WHil
'Dark Martje'	NLar
'Darwin's Blue'	NLar
decumbens (H)	EWes GArf GBin
densifolia (P)	GArf
'Diamond' (H)	SRms
'Diana' (H)	SHeb
dieffenbachii (H)	SAng SHeb SVen
diosmifolia (H)	CDoC CTsd SHeb
- 'Celina' (H)	EPfP
- 'Wairua Beauty' (H)	CDoC
× *divergens* (H)	SHeb SPlb
'E.A. Bowles' (H)	SHeb
'E.B. Anderson'	see *V.* 'Caledonia'
'Edington' (H)	WCFE
'Ellen Mae'	EGrI EPPr EWes MNrw WCAu WCot
elliptica (H)	CDoC SHeb
- 'Anatoki' (H)	SAng SHeb
- 'Charleston' (H)	SHeb
- 'Variegata'	see *V.* 'Silver Queen'
'Emerald Dome'	see *V.* 'Emerald Gem'
§ 'Emerald Gem' (H)	CAby EGren EGrI EHeP ELan EPfP EUrb LCro LRHS LSRN LSto MGos MHer MMuc SHeb SPlb SPoG SRot
'Emerald Green'	see *V.* 'Emerald Gem'
'Eveline' PBR Oudshoorn	EGren NLar
§ 'Eveline' pre-1960	SHeb WKif
evenosa (H)	SHeb
'Eversley Seedling'	see *V.* 'Bowles's Hybrid'
exaltata (d)	SMrm WSpi
'Eyecatcher' PBR (H/v)	CSBt Midl SHeb
'Fairfieldii' (H)	MHer
'Fairytale' PBR	LRHS NGdn
'First Light' (H)	CDoC EHeP NLar SRms
formosa (P)	SPlb
'Fragrant Jewel' (H)	SEND SHeb
× *franciscana* (H)	CoPl SHeb
- 'Blue Gem' misapplied	see *V.* × *franciscana* 'Lobelioides'
- 'Blue Gem' ambig. (H)	CBrac EHeP ELan LRHS NBir NPer SEND SPlb SPoG SRms WSpi
- 'Foreness Pink' (H)	SEND
- 'Lavender Queen' (H)	SHeb
- lime variegated (H/v)	SEND
§ - 'Lobelioides' (H)	EGren EPfP
- 'Variegata'	see *V.* 'Silver Queen'
- yellow-variegated (H/v)	SHeb
I - 'White Gem' (H)	EGren SRms
'Frozen Flame' (H/v)	EGren ELan LBuc LRHS MAsh SPoG WMal
(Garden Beauty Series) GARDEN BEAUTY BLUE ('Cliv' PBR) (H)	CDoC CSBt LBuc LCro MAsh SRms WSpi
- GARDEN BEAUTY PINK ('Lowpito' PBR) (H)	CDoC SRms
- GARDEN BEAUTY PURPLE ('Nold' PBR) (H)	CSBt EPfP LBuc LCro LRHS MAsh WSpi
- GARDEN BEAUTY WHITE ('Lowhi' PBR) (H)	EBee
'Gauntlettii'	see *V.* 'Eveline' pre-1960
gentianoides	Widely available
- 'Alba'	EBlo EPfP LEdu LRHS
- 'Barbara Sherwood' ♀H7	EBee EBlo EPfP LRHS NGdn WFar
- 'Blue Bittersweet'	NLar
- 'Little Blues'	ECha GKev MPro WHil
- 'Mountain Breeze'	EBee EPfP ESgI LBuc LRHS SHar SPoG WFar
- 'Nana'	NBro NLar
- 'Pallida'	GKev MMuc SPlb WCAu
- 'Robusta'	CMHG EBee GMaP LBar NClf NGdn WFar
- 'Tissington White'	CBWd CTtf EBee EGren ELan EPfP ESgI GMaP LBar LCro LRHS MHol MPie MPri MPro NBir NBro NClf NGdn NLar NWbg SHar SMrm SPoG SRms WCAu WFar
- 'Variegata' (v)	EBee ECha ELan EPfP GMaP NBir WCAu
gigantea	GKev
I *glaucophylla* (H/v)	LRHS SHeb
- 'Clarence' (H)	SHeb
- 'Joan Hunwick' (H)	SHeb
'Gloriosa' (H)	SHeb
'Gold Beauty' (H/v)	SRms
'Golden Pixie' (H)	LBuc LCro LRHS
'Goldrush' PBR (H/v)	SPoG
gracillima	see *V. leiophylla*
grandis	EBee LShi MMuc SBeP SEND WFar
'Gran's Favourite' (H)	SHeb
'Great Orme' (H)	CBrac EGren EHeP ELan LRHS LSRN MHtn NPer SEND SHeb SPlb SPoG SRms WCFE
'Green Globe'	see *V.* 'Emerald Gem'
'Greencourt'	see *V. catarractae* 'Delight'
'Grethe' (H)	EGren SEND SHeb
'Hadspen Pink' (H)	CDoC
'Hanne' (H)	CoPl
'Headfortii' (H)	EGrI SHeb
'Heartbreaker' PBR (H/v)	CDoC CoPl EGren ELan EPfP LBuc LCro LRHS MAsh MGos MPri MPro SPoG WSpi
HEBEDONNA ALEXA ('Zander' PBR) (H) **new**	EGren
HEBEDONNA ANNA ('Zebora' PBR) (H)	LRHS
HEBEDONNA EMMA ('Zassa' PBR) (H)	LCro LRHS

Veronica

HebeDonna Eva ('Hop102'PBR) (H) **new**	EGren LRHS		§ - 'Blaubündel'	ELan NGdn
			- 'Blauer Sommer'	EPfP MArl NGdn
HebeDonna Jenna ('Zilk'PBR) (H) **new**	EGren LRHS		§ - 'Blauriesin'	ECha ELan EPfP GMaP LSto NLar SRms WSpi
HebeDonna Kamilla ('Zindy'PBR) (H)	LCro		- Blue Giantess	see *V. longifolia* 'Blauriesin'
			- 'Blue John'	MPie NDov NLar
HebeDonna Nikka	see *V.* 'Zita'		- 'Blue Shades' **new**	StAn
HebeDonna Sofia ('Zerina') (H) **new**	LBom		- 'Candied Candle'	EBee
			- 'Charlotte'PBR (v)	CDor CWGN EBee ECha EGren EMor GElm GMaP LBar LCro LRHS MBel MHol MPro NLar NSti SHar SPoG WCAu WCot
hectorii var. *demissa* (H)	GKev			
'Helena' (Addenda Series) (H)	CDoC EGren			
'Hielan Lassie' (H)	SHeb		- 'Charming Pink'	CDor SAko
'High Voltage' (H)	EBee EHeP GJos LSou MHtn NEoE WSpi		- 'Christa'PBR	LBar LRHS
			- dark blue-flowered	WHoo
'Highdown Pink' (H)	SHeb		- 'Fascination'	MPro NEoE NGdn
'Highdownensis' (H)	LRHS SHeb		- First Glory ('Alllord'PBR)	CCBP EBee ELan LRHS MPri MPro NCth WHil
'Hinderwell' (H)	NPer			
'Hobby' (H)	EGren		- First Lady ('Alllady'PBR)	ELan EPfP LRHS MPri MPro NCth NDov NEoE NLar WHil
§ *hookeriana* (P)	GKev			
hulkeana (H)	GBin MHer MMrt NLar WAbe WKif		- 'Foerster's Blue'	see *V. longifolia* 'Blauriesin'
'Imposter' (H)	SHeb SRms		- 'Lila Karina'	GBin NLar SHor WHoo
incana	see *V. spicata* subsp. *incana*		- 'Marietta'PBR	CDor CSpe ERCP LCro MArl MHol MPro NDov NLar NSti SHar SPoG SRms WCot WTre
'Inspiration' (H)	SHeb SRms			
Inspire Blue ('Yabblu'PBR)	LBuc LRHS MPnt MPro			
Inspire Pink ('Yabpin'PBR)	LBuc LRHS MPnt MPro NBir		- 'Melanie White'	EGren MBel MPro NSti
'Jack's Surprise' (H)	SHeb		- 'Pink Eveline'PBR	EBee ELan EPfP LRHS MHol NDov NGdn WTre
'Jane Holden' (H)	SHeb			
'Jasper' (H)	SHeb		- 'Schneeriesin'	EBee ECha GMaP GPSL NBir WCAu
'Jewel of the Nile'PBR (H/v)	EBee ELan EUrb LBom LCro LRHS MMrt MPri NLar SAth SPoG WFar		- Vernique White (Vernique Series)	MPro
			lyallii (P)	EBee ELan EPfP GMaP MHer MMuc NQui SPlb SRms WIce WKif
Joan Mac ('Tull304'PBR) (H)	EGren ELan LBuc LRHS			
'John Collier' (H)	SEND		- 'Snowcap' (P)	EBee LCro LRHS SPlb SRms
'Johny Day' (H)	CoPl		*lycopodioides* (H)	LRHS
'Karo Golden Esk' (H)	LRHS		- 'Aurea'	see *V. armstrongii*
'Katrina' (H/v)	CDoC LCro SHeb		*macrantha* (H)	GArf GJos SHeb
kellereri	see *V. spicata*		*macrocarpa* (H)	CDoC EUrb SHeb
'Kenty Pink' (P)	CWnw LRHS MMuc		- var. *latisepala* (H)	CDoC SHeb
'Killiney Variety' (H)	SHeb		- var. *macrocarpa* (H)	SHeb
'Kirkii' (H)	EHeP ELan MSwo NLar		*macroura*	see *V. stricta* var. *macroura*
kiusiana	EBee NLar		'Magic Summer'PBR (H)	LBuc LRHS MAsh SPoG
'Knightshayes'	see *V.* 'Caledonia'		'Maori Gem' (H)	LRHS SHeb
'La Favorite'	SHeb		'Margret' (H)	CDoC CSBt CWnw EBee EGren EPfP GArf GJos LBom LBuc LCro LRHS MAsh MGos MHtn SPoG SRms WSpi
'Lady Ann'PBR (H/v)	EGren EPfP LBuc SAth SPoG WSpi			
'Lady Ardilaun'	see *V.* 'Amy'			
§ *lanceolata* (P)	NPer SRot			
lavaudiana (H)	SHeb		'Maria' (H)	LBom SHeb
'Lavender Queen' (H)	SHeb		'Marie Antoinette' (H)	LSRN
§ *leiophylla* (H)	SEle SHeb		'Marilyn Monroe'PBR (H)	ELan LBuc LCro LRHS SPoG
Leopard ('Lowand') (Garden Beauty Series) (H/v)	ELan LRHS MPri NPer SHeb SPoG SRms WFar		'Marjorie' (H)	CMac EGren EHeP ELan EPfP LSRN NPer SHeb SPoG SRms WFar
			'Marshmallow' (H)	LBuc LRHS
'Leopard Spot' (H/v)	LCro Midl		'Martje'	SMrn
Light Blue Moody Blues ('Novaverlig') (Moody Blues Series)	EGren Midl		*matthewsii* Turkish Delight' (H)	CWnw NEoE
			Matty Brown ('Tull 303'PBR) (H)	CSBt CWnw LBom LRHS LSou MHtn MPri SPoG
'Lilac Wand' (H)	SHeb			
'Linda' (H)	SEND		Mauve Moody Blues ('Novavermau') (Moody Blues Series)	EGren ELan EPfP LRHS
'Lindleyana' (H)	SHeb			
'Lindsayi' (H)	SHeb			
linifolia 'Blue Skies' (P)	EPot		'Mauvena' (H)	SHeb
liwanensis	EPot MNrw		'McKean'	see *V.* 'Emerald Gem'
'Liz' (H)	LBuc LCro SPoG		× *media* First Choice ('Allchoice'PBR)	NLar WHil
'Longacre Variety' (H)	SHeb			
longifolia	CElw CFis CMac CSpe CWal EGrI GQue SMHy WCAu		- First Kiss ('Allkiss'PBR)	EBee ELan LRHS NLar
			- First Love ('Alllove'PBR)	ELan EPfP LRHS MArl MHer MMrt MPri MPro NCth NGdn NLar SPel SRms WHil
- 'Alba'	ELan MArl MMuc WCot			
- 'Antarctica'	EBee			
- 'Berenice Blue'	LBar		- First Match ('Allvglove'PBR)	EPfP LRHS MPro NLar WCot WHil
- 'Berenice Pink'	LBar			

- First Memory ('Allv1461'PBR)	EBee ELan EPfP LRHS
'Menzies Bay' (H)	SHeb
'Merlot Memories'PBR (H)	LBuc LRHS SPoG
'Mette' (H)	CBrac EGren ELan MAsh
Midnight Sky ('Lowten'PBR) (Garden Beauty Series) (H) ♀H4	CDoC EGren EUrb LCro LRHS MPri SPoG WCot
'Midsummer Beauty' (H)	EGren EPfP LCro LSRN NBir SEND SHeb SPlb SPoG SRms
'Milmont Emerald'	see V. 'Emerald Gem'
'Mint Chocolate' (H) ♀H4	LBuc LCro LRHS LSou SPoG
'Miss Fittall' (H)	SHeb
missurica	GKev
- 'Major'	see V. *missurica* subsp. *missurica*
§ - subsp. *missurica*	EBee GKev WFar
- subsp. *stellata*	CMiW EBee EPfP GAbr GElm GKev GMaP GQue LEdu LSto MHol MMrt MPie NBir NCth NSti
'Mist Maiden' (H)	SHeb
§ 'Mohawk' (H)	EHeP LBuc LCro LRHS SPoG WSpi
montana 'Corinne Tremaine' (v)	SRms
(Moody Blues Series) Moody Blues Dark Pink ('Balmoodink')	EGren
- Moody Blues Mauve Improved ('Balmoomaui'PBR)	EGren
'Mrs E.Tennant' (H)	SHeb
§ 'Mrs Winder' (H) ♀H4	CBrac CMac EGren EHeP ELan EPfP LBom LCro LRHS MAsh MGos NPer SHeb SPoG SRGP WSpi
'Nantyderry' (H)	CDoC SHeb
§ 'Neil's Choice' (H)	ELon
'New Pink Explosion' (Explosion Series)	LBar
'New Zealand' (H)	CWnw GBin LCro LRHS
'Nicola's Blush' (H)	CDoC EBee EGren EHeP ELon EPfP LBom LCro LSRN MHed MSwo NLar SEND SHeb SPoG SRGP SRms WMal
ochracea 'James Stirling' (H) ♀H4	CAby CMac EHeP ELan GArf GKev LCro LSRN LSto MAsh MGos NLar SPlb SPoG WSpi
§ *odora* (H)	CCoa ELan GAbr GKev LSto WSpi
I - 'Nana' (H)	LCro MMuc SHeb
- 'New Zealand Gold' (H)	EHeP EPfP LCro LRHS MMuc SHeb
- prostrate (H)	NLar SHeb SRms
- 'Summer Frost' (H)	CCoa CDoC CSde CTsd
- 'Wintergreen' (H)	SHeb
officinalis	GQue MCtn
oltensis	EPot SPlb WAbe
'Oratia Beauty' (H)	CCoa CDoC EHeP EPfP LSRN LSto SEND SHeb
'Orphan Annie' (H/v)	CDoC
orsiniana 'Sappheiros'	WAbe
'Pacific Ocean'	NLar
'Pacific Paradise' (H)	SPoG
parviflora misapplied	see V. 'Bowles's Hybrid'
parviflora Vahl 'Holdsworth' (H)	SHeb
- 'Palmerston' (H)	SHeb
'Pascal' (H)	CoPl ELan EPfP LBuc LCro LRHS MGos SPoG SRms WFar
'Pastel Blue' (H)	EHeP
pauciramosa (H)	SRms
'Paula' (H)	SHeb
'Pearl of Paradise'PBR (H)	LBuc LRHS SPoG
peduncularis 'Oxford Blue'	see V. *umbrosa* 'Georgia Blue'
perfoliata (P)	CCoa CDor CSde CSpe CTtf ECha EGrI EWld GMaP LEdu MMrt MMuc MNrw SPlb SRms WOld
'Perry's Rubyleaf' (H)	NPer
'Peter Chapple' (H)	SHeb
petraea 'Madame Mercier'	CSpe LBar SRot
'Pewter Dome' (H) ♀H5	CCoa CMac LRHS SDix SHeb SRms
pimeleoides (H)	SAth
- 'Glauca' (H)	NPer SHeb
- 'Quicksilver' (H) ♀H4	CAby CoPl CSBt ELan EPfP GArf LCro LRHS MGos NPer SLee SRms WSpi
pinguifolia (H)	NLar SHeb SPlb StAn
- 'Pagei' (H) ♀H4	CAgr CBcs CBrac CDoC CMac CSBt CWal CWnw EGren EHeP ELan EPfP GJos LBom LRHS LSRN MAsh MGos MHer NBir NLar SHeb SPoG WFar
- 'Sutherlandii' (H)	CBcs CBrac CDoC EGren EHeP EPfP GJos LBom LRHS LSto MAsh MGos NLit SArc SHeb WFar WSpi
Pink Candy ('Tulpink'PBR) (H) ♀H4	EBee
'Pink Damask'	ELan ELon GMaP NDov NGdn NLar SRms WHoo
'Pink Elephant' (H/v)	CDoC EPfP LBuc SPoG
'Pink Fizz' (H)	LBuc LRHS
'Pink Goddess' (H)	EPfP SEND
'Pink Lady'PBR (H)	ELan SPoG
Pink Moody Blues ('Novaverpin') (Moody Blues Series)	EGren ELan EPfP LRHS Midl MPri
'Pink Paradise' (H)	ELan SPoG SRms
'Pink Payne'	see V. 'Eveline' pre-1960
'Pink Pixie' (H)	LBuc LCro LRHS MAsh SPoG SRms
'Pink Princess' (H)	LSou MHtn
'Pink Wand' (H)	SHeb
(Plumosa Series) Plumosa Amethyst Plume	WFar
- Plumosa Blue Plume	MHol
- Plumosa Lavender Plume	CWGN
'Porlock Purple'	see V. *catarractae* 'Delight'
I 'Prostrata' (H)	CSBt EBee LRHS SHeb
§ *prostrata* ♀H5	CSpe EPfP EUrb GBin GKev LSto MSwo NLit SLee SRms WHoo WIce
- 'Aztec Gold'PBR	CMac SPoG
§ - 'Blauspiegel'	EBee LRHS SRot
- Blue Mirror	see V. *prostrata* 'Blauspiegel'
- 'Blue Sheen'	NBir
- Goldwell ('Verbrig') (v)	EBee LRHS WFar
- 'Lilac Time'	ECha GJos GKev NBir SLee SRms WAbe WFar
- 'Loddon Blue'	SRms WCot
- 'Mrs Holt'	MHer NBir NLar SRms
- 'Nana'	EWes WIce
- 'Nestor'	SRms
- 'Rhapsody in Blue'	SRms
- Rosea'	SRot
- 'Spode Blue' ♀H5	CMac GKev GQue MHer SLee SPoG SRms
- 'Trehane'	CBcs ELan GJos LRHS LShi MHer NRya SPlb SPoG SRms SRot WFar WIce
pulvinaris (H)	WAbe
'Purple Emperor'	see V. 'Neil's Choice'
'Purple Explosion' (Explosion Series)	LBar
'Purple Paradise' (H)	NLar SPoG
'Purple Pillow' (H)	LSou
Purple Pixie	see V. 'Mohawk'

'Purple Princess' (H)	EPfP	'Spender's Seedling' hort. (H)	SEND SHeb SPoG SRms
PURPLE SHAMROCK ('Neprock'^PBR) (H/v)	CDoC EPfP LBom LBuc LRHS MAsh NLar SPoG SRms	§ *spicata*	CBWd EBee EGrI ELan GAbr LBuc SRms StAn WCAu WFar WHil WShi
'Purple Tips' misapplied	see *V. speciosa* 'Variegata'	- 'Alba'	CBcs EPfP LSto NLar StAn WFar
'Purpleicious Harmony'^PBR	CDor EBee EGren ELon LRHS MBel NLar NWbg	- ANNIVERSARY BLUE ('Florvsbl1'^PBR)	LRHS LSou
§ *quadrifaria* (H)	WAbe	- ANNIVERSARY ROSE ('Florvsro1'^PBR)	LRHS LSou Midl
RAINBOW ('Markbow') (H)	LRHS LSou	- BUBBLEGUM CANDLES ('Verspi'^PBR)	LBar LRHS LSou NEoE NLar
§ *rakaiensis* (H) ♀^H4	CBcs CBrac CDoC CMac EGren EHeP ELan EPfP GAbr LCro MAsh MGos MHed MMuc MSwo NBir SArc SHeb SPoG WCFE WCha WFar WSpi	- 'Erika'	ECha NBir NGdn
		§ - 'Glory'^PBR	CBcs CDor CWGN ELan EPfP LBar LCro LRHS MPri SPoG WPnP XFar
- 'Golden Dome'	see *V. rakaiensis*	- 'Heidekind'	EBee ECha ELan GMaP LCro LRHS NBir NGdn SRms SRot WCAu WCav WHoo WIce
raoulii (H)	GKev WAbe		
'Raven' (H)	CDoC		
'Red Edge' (H) ♀^H4	Widely available		
'Red Ruth'	see *V.* 'Eveline' pre-1960		
'Reine des Blanches' (H)	SHeb	I - subsp. *hybrida* 'Elaine's Form'	WCot
repens	EBee EPfP LRHS NEoE SPlb		
RHUBARB AND CUSTARD ('Tull 302'^PBR) (H)	LBuc LCro LRHS MAsh Midl SPoG WCot	§ - 'Icicle'	WCAu
rigidula (H)	SHeb	- subsp. *incana* ♀^H5	MMuc SPlb SRms
'Ronda' (H)	EBee	- - 'Mrs Underwood'	ECha
'Rosalinde'	NGdn	- - 'Nana'	NBir SRms
ROSE ELEGANCE ('Lowtop') (Garden Elegance Series) (H)	LCro	- - 'Silver Carpet'	CBWd CCBP EPfP MArl SMrm WSpi
		- 'Nana Blauteppich'	CSpe LRHS SPoG
		- subsp. *orchidea*	SRms
'Rosie' (H)	LBuc LCro LRHS	- 'Pink Goblin'	EDAr ELan LRHS
'Royal Pink'	NLar	- 'Pink Marshmallow'	NLar
'Ruby Port'^PBR (H)	LBuc LRHS	- 'Pink Panther'^PBR	WCot
rupestris	see *V. prostrata*	- 'Pink Passion'^PBR	MAsh
salicifolia (H)	CMac ELan EPfP GAbr LRHS NLit SEND SHeb SPlb WFar WSpi	- PURPLEGUM CANDLES ('Verpurg')	LBar MHtn
- pale blue-flowered (H)	SEND	- RED FOX	see *V. spicata* 'Rotfuchs'
'Sandra Joy' (H)	LSRN	- 'Romiley Purple'	EBee WSpi
'Sangria Sensation'^PBR (H)	LBuc LRHS	- 'Ronica Fuchsia' (Ronica Series)	GQue MPri
'Santa Monica' (H)	NLar SHeb WCot	- 'Rosalind'	NLar
'Sapphire' (H)	EGren EPfP LCro MAsh SHeb SRms WKif	- *rosea*	see *V. spicata* 'Erika'
		§ - 'Rotfuchs'	CBcs CSde EBee EGren ELan ELon EPfP GBin GJos LCro LSto MHer NBir NGdn NWbg SPoG SRms WCAu WHoo XFar
'Sarana' (H)	SHeb		
saturejoides	SRms		
schmidtiana 'Nana'	EDAr GKev		
serpyllifolia	CGwi WOrg	- 'Royal Candles'	see *V. spicata* 'Glory'
'Shirley Blue' ♀^H6	EGren EGrI ELan EUrb LBar LCro LSto MHer MHol MMuc SHar SRGP SRms WCAu WSpi	- 'Sightseeing'	NBir SRms
		- SNOW CANDLES ('Joca128'^PBR)	LBar LRHS MPri WPnP
'Silver Anniversary' (H)	EPfP SHeb	- 'Total Eclipse'^PBR	ELan EPfP
'Silver Dollar' (H/v)	CBcs CoPl ELan EPfP GArf LBuc LCro LRHS SPoG SRms	- 'Ulster Blue Dwarf'	CMHG CWnw EBee EPfP GElm GMaP LRHS LSou NGdn SMrm SPoG WCAu XFar
'Silver Queen' (H/v) ♀^H3	CBcs CCoa CDoC CoPl CSBt EGren EHeP ELan EPfP LCro LRHS MAsh MPri NLar NPer SEND SPoG SRms		
		- YOUNIQUE BABY BLUE	MSCN
		'Spring Glory' (H)	EPfP LRHS
'Simon Délaux' (H)	EPfP SEND SHeb WCot	*spuria* L.	MMuc
SKY BLUE MOODY BLUES ('Novaversky') (Moody Blues Series)	EGren EPfP LRHS MPri	STARLIGHT ('Marklight') (H/v)	EHeP LBuc LCro LRHS LSou
		stelleri	see *V. wormskjoldii*
		§ *stenophylla* (H)	EUrb GBin LSRN MHed NLar SArc SDix SHeb SPlb
'Snow Clouds' (P)	CElw CSpe CTsd CWnw ELan GKev LRHS MPri NEoE SDix SPad SRot WFar WHoo WTor	*stricta* (H)	CDoC SEND SHeb SPlb
		- var. *egmontiana* (H)	SHeb
'Sparkling Sapphires' (H)	SPoG	- var. *macroura* (H)	SHeb
speciosa (H)	SHeb	§ *subalpina* (H)	CSBt LRHS SHeb
- 'La Séduisante' (H)	SEND SHeb WSpi	§ *subfulvida* (H)	SHeb
- 'Patti Dossett' (H)	CDoC LRHS	'Summer Blue' (H)	EPfP MBlu
- 'Purple Queen'	see *V.* 'Amy'	'Summer Breeze'	NBro
- 'Red Hugh' (H)	SEND WSpi	'Sunny Border Blue'	EBee EGren NLar WCot
§ - 'Variegata' (H/v)	EGren LRHS NPer	'Sunrise' (H)	LCro LRHS
'Spender's Seedling' misapplied	see *V. stenophylla*	'Sunset Boulevard' (H)	MSCN
		'Super Red' (H)	CSBt EHeP LRHS
'Spender's Seedling' ambig. (H)	MMuc WSpi	'Sweet Dreams' (H/v)	EGren ELan MAsh NLar
		'Sweet Kim' (H/v)	LBuc SPoG

Veronica

tetrasticha (H)	WAbe
teucrium	see *V. austriaca* subsp. *teucrium*
thymoides	ECha
subsp. *thymoides*	
'Tidal Pool'	SPoG
'Tiptop' (H/v)	LRHS Midl
topiaria (H) ♀H4	CAby CAgr CBrac CDoC CMac CoPl CSBt CWnw EGren LRHS MMuc NBir SEND SHeb SPoG StAn WAbe WSpi
- 'Doctor Favier' (H)	SRms
traversii 'Mason River' (H)	SHeb
- 'Woodside' (H)	SHeb
'Tricolor'	see *V. speciosa* 'Variegata'
'Trixie' (H)	EHeP WSpi
'True Love' (H) **new**	EGren
umbrosa	EBee
I - 'Alba'	CSpe
§ - 'Georgia Blue' ♀H5	CMac CSpe EBee ECha EGrI EPPr GBin GMaP LBar LRHS LShi MNrw NBir NClf SAko SMad SPlb SPoG SRms SRot WCav WChS WCot WFar WGwG WHoo WIce
urvilleana (H)	SHeb
'Valentino' (H)	SHeb
venustula (H)	SHeb
- 'Patricia Davies' (H)	SHeb
- 'Sky Blue' (H)	LRHS
vernicosa (H)	CCoa CDoC CWnw EGren EHeP LRHS MGos MHer SArc SHeb SPlb SPoG WAbe WSpi
'Very Van Gogh'	LBar
'Violet Wand' (H)	SHeb
virginica	see *Veronicastrum virginicum*
'Waikiki'	see *V.* 'Mrs Winder'
§ 'Warley' (H)	CDoC EPfP WSpi
'Warleyensis'	see *V.* 'Warley'
'Watson's Pink' (H)	SHeb WKif
'White Gem' (*brachysiphon* hybrid) (H)	NPer SHeb
'White Heather' (H)	EPfP SHeb
'White Icicle'	see *V. spicata* 'Icicle'
'White Jolanda'	EGren NLar
WHITE MOODY BLUES ('Novaverwhi') (Moody Blues Series)	EGren EPfP LRHS WHil
'White Paradise' (H)	SPoG
'White Quartz' (Gemstone Series) (H)	NEoE NLar
'White Spritzer'PBR (H)	LBuc LRHS SPoG
'White Wand' (H)	SHeb
whitleyi	MMuc
'Wild Romance' (H)	CDoC ELan LBuc LRHS MAsh SPoG
'Willcoxii'	see *V. buchananii* 'Fenwickii'
'Wingletye' (H)	EPfP LRHS WAbe WMal
'Winter Glow' (H)	EBee
'Wiri Charm' (H) ♀H4	CBcs CCoa CDoC CMac CSBt EGrI ELan ELon EPfP LCro LRHS SEND SHeb
'Wiri Cloud' (H) ♀H4	CBcs CDoC CMac EGrI ELan EPfP LRHS MMuc SEND SRms
'Wiri Dawn' (H)	EGrI ELan EPfP SRms
'Wiri Icing Sugar' (H)	SHeb
'Wiri Image' (H)	CBcs CCoa CSBt SEND SHeb SReu
'Wiri Joy' (H)	CBcs LRHS SEND
'Wiri Mist' (H) ♀H4	CBcs CoPl EGren ELan EPfP LCro LRHS
'Wiri Prince' (H)	ELan
'Wiri Splash' (H)	SHeb
'Wiri Vision' (H)	CSBt SEND
§ *wormskjoldii*	GKev MBrN MMuc SRms
§ 'Youngii' (H)	CDoC CSBt EGren ELan EPfP GBin GJos LCro LRHS MHer SEND SHeb SPlb SPoG SRms WHoo WSpi
§ 'Zita'PBR (H)	LRHS

Veronicastrum ❀ (*Plantaginaceae*)

japonicum var. *australe* B&SWJ 11009	WCru
- 'White Apollo'	IPot
latifolium	WCot
- BWJ 8158	EPPr ESwi GGro WCot WCru
'Red Arrows'	CDor CKno EBee EPPr EWhm GBin GElm LRHS LSou MArl MBel MHol MNrw MPro NBir NCth NDov NLar NSti SHar SPel SPeP SPoG WCAu WCot WFar WOld WSpi
sibiricum	EBee ECha EPfP LShi MHoo MMuc SEND SHar SRms StAn WSpi WTre
- BWJ 6352	WCru WFar
- 'Kobaltkaars'	ECha NDov SMHy SPel
- var. *yezoense*	ECha WFar
- - RBS 290	EPPr WFar
- - 'Manhattan Skyline' **new**	IPot
villosulum	NBro
§ *virginicum*	EBee EPfP LSto MHoo NBir NLar SRms StAn WFar WSpi
- 'Adoration'	CBWd CSpe EBee ELon EPPr EWhm GAbr LCro LRHS MArl MHoo NDov NLar SHor SPel SPhx SRkn WCAu WCot WFar WSpi
- 'Album' ♀H7	Widely available
- 'Amethyst'	LBar
- 'Apollo'	CBWd CDor EBee ELon EPPr GAbr GBin GMaP GQue LBar LEdu LRHS LSou MHol NBir NBro NLar NSti SPel WCAu WFar WHil WHoo WPGP WSpi
- f. *caeruleum*	MCtn
- 'Challenger'PBR	CKno EBee IPot LBar LSou MPro NCth NDov NLar WNPC WSpi WTor XFar
- 'Cupid'	CDor CKno EBee ELon EWes GMaP GPSL LBar LEdu MHtn MNrw NGdn NLar SHar WFar WSpi WTor XFar
- 'Diane'	CBWd CCBP CDor CKno CMHG EBee ECha ELan ELon EPfP EPPr EWhm GMaP IPot LBar LRHS LSou MArl MAvo MBNS NDov NLar SHar SMHy SPeP SPhx WCAu WSpi
- 'Du Jardin'	LEdu
- 'Erica'	Widely available
- 'Fascination'	Widely available
- var. *incarnatum*	see *V. virginicum* f. *roseum*
- 'Klein Erica'	CWnw ELon GBin LBar
- 'Lavendelturm' ♀H7	Widely available
- 'Miss World'	IPot
- 'Pointed Finger'	GMaP GQue LEdu NLar SMHy SMrm
§ - f. *roseum*	CWnw EBee ECha ELan ELon EPPr GMaP GQue LRHS LShi MHoo NBro NDov SMHy SPel SPhx WChS WHrl WSpi
- - 'Pink Glow'	Widely available
- 'Spring Dew'	EBee LBar MNrw NBid NEoE NLar WCAu WSpi XFar
- 'Temptation'	CBWd EPPr GMaP LEdu MAvo MHol MPro NBro NEoE NLar SHor WPGP

Vesalea (*Caprifoliaceae*)
§ *floribunda* ♀H4   CCoa CExl CMac CSde EBee EGrI
                      ELan EPfP LCro LRHS MAsh NLar
                      SPoG SRms WCot WSpi

Vestia (*Solanaceae*)
§ *foetida*   CBcs CExl SEle SEND WPav
  lycioides   see *V. foetida*

Viburnum ❀ (*Viburnaceae*)
  NJM 11.008   WPGP
  alnifolium   see *V. lantanoides*
  atrocyaneum   CExl EBee SBrt WFar
  - B&SWJ 7272   WCru
  - HIRD 113   WPGP
  aureum   see *V. lantana* 'Aureum'
  betulifolium   CBcs CExl EBee EGrI EPfP EWes
                      GKev GKin MCtn WJur WPGP
  - 'Hohuanshan'   NLar SSta WCru
  × *bodnantense*   EBee SReu WFar
  - 'Charles Lamont' ♀H6 CBcs CCVT CDoC CWnw EBee
                      EGrI EHeP ELan ELon EPfP LCro
                      LRHS LSRN LSto MAsh MGos MMrt
                      MMuc MPri NCth NLar SGol SRms
                      WFar WSpi
  - 'Dawn' ♀H6   Widely available
  - 'Deben' ♀H6   EGrI
  brachyandrum   WCru
    B&SWJ 5784
  buddlejifolium   CMac MMuc WCru
  × *burkwoodii*   Widely available
  - 'Anne Russell'   CBcs CEnd CExl ELan EPfP EWes
                      IArd LSRN MAsh MGos NLar SAth
                      SHor SPoG SRms SSta WFar
  - 'Compact Beauty' WSpi
  - 'Conoy'   ELon WHtc
  - 'Fulbrook'   MAsh SSta
  - 'Mohawk' ♀H6   CBcs CDoC CEnd CWnw EPfP LRHS
                      MAsh MGos MMrt WCFE WSpi
  - 'Park Farm Hybrid' ♀H6 CDoC CMac EGrI ELan EPfP LRHS
                      LSto MAsh MGos SPoG SRms SSta
                      WHtc WKif WSpi
  calvum   CBcs CExl
  aff. *calvum* WWJ 12012 EBee WCru
  × *carlcephalum* ♀H6 CBcs CDoC CEnd CMac CNWT
                      EGren EGrI ELan EPfP GKin LCro
                      LRHS MAsh MBlu MGos MPri SGol
                      SPoG
  - 'Cayuga' ♀H5   WLov WSpi
  carlesii   CBcs CBrac CCVT CDoC CMac
                      EGren EGrI GKin LRHS LSRN MBlu
                      MGos SGol SRms WFar WJur WKif
  - B&SWJ 8838   WCru
  - 'Aurora' ♀H6   CBcs CBrac CDoC CEnd CMac
                      CMCN EBee EGren ELan EPfP LEdu
                      LSRN MAsh MBlu MGos MPri SGol
                      SPoG SSta WPGP
  - 'Charis'   EBee WPGP
  - 'Compactum'   MAsh MBlu MPri SSta
  - 'Diana' ♀H6   CCVT CEnd CMac EBee LSRN
                      MAsh MBlu SPoG SSta WPGP WSpi
  cassinoides   EBee EPfP LRHS
  'Chesapeake'   EWes SEND
  chingii   WCru
  cinnamomifolium ♀H5 CBcs EPfP LMaj LRHS NLar SArc
                      SPoG WCot WSpi
  cotinifolium   CExl
  - CC 4541   CExl
  cylindricum   CBcs EPfP LEdu LRHS NLar SBrt
                      WCru

  - B&SWJ 6479 from Thailand WCru
  - B&SWJ 7239   WCru
  - B&SWJ 9719 from Vietnam WCru
  - HWJCM 434 from Nepal WCru
  - 'Chino-Crûg'   WCru
  dasyanthum   WJur
  davidii ♀H5   CBcs CBrac CDoC CEnd EBee EGrI
                      EHeP ELan GKin LCro LRHS LSRN
                      MGos MPri SGol SPoG WFar WHtc
                      WLov WSpi
  - (f)   CMac CSBt EGren EPfP EUrb LBom
                      LRHS LSto LWaG MAsh Midl NLit
                      SArc SAth SBig SFol SOrN SPoG
                      SRms
  - (m)   CMac EPfP SPoG SRms
  - 'Angustifolium'   CEnd EBee NLar
  dentatum   WJur
  - AUTUMN JAZZ   see *V. dentatum* 'Ralph Senior'
  - BLUE MUFFIN ('Christom') CBcs CDoC EBee LRHS MGos SGol
                      WFar
  - 'Moonglow'   NLar
  - 'Morton'   SSta
  - PATHFINDER ('Patzam') SSta
  - var. *pubescens* SSta
    'Longifolium'
§ - 'Ralph Senior'   NLar
  - 'White and Blue' NLar
  dilatatum   WJur
  - B&SWJ 5844   WCru
  - B&SWJ 8734   WCru
  - B&SWJ 10830   WCru
  - PAB 6831   LEdu
  - 'Asian Beauty'   SSta
  - CARDINAL CANDY   see *V. dilatatum* 'Henneke'
§ - 'Henneke'   NCth NLar
  - 'Iroquois'   SSta
  - 'Michael Dodge'   MBlu NLar
  - 'Sealing Wax'   NLar
  erosum B&SWJ 8735 WCru
  - B&SWJ 8893   WCru
  - B&SWJ 11083   WCru
  erubescens   NLar WJur
  - HWJK 2163   WCru
  - VdL 4122   WPGP
  - var. *gracilipes* NLar
  - 'Milke Danda'   EBee WPGP
  - 'Ward van Teylingen' NLar
  'Eskimo' ♀H5   CBcs CEnd CMac EBee ELan EPfP
                      LRHS MAsh MBlu MGos SPoG SRms
                      SSta
  fansipanense B&SWJ 8302 WCru
  - KWJ 12239   WCru
§ *farreri* ♀H6   CBcs CBrac CMCN CSBt EBee EGrI
                      ELan LBuc LEdu LSRN LSto MGos
                      SGol
  - 'Album'   see *V. farreri* 'Candidissimum'
§ - 'Candidissimum'   CExl CMac ELan ELon EPfP LRHS
                      MMuc NCth NLar SGol SPoG SRms
  - 'December Dwarf' CTsd EPfP LCro LRHS
  - 'Farrer's Pink'   CExl NLar
  - 'Nanum'   CMac EGrI LRHS MAsh MBrN MHtn
                      WLov
  foetidum   LEdu
  - var. *rectangulatum* WPGP
  - - B&SWJ 1888   WCru
  - - B&SWJ 3451   WCru
  formosanum CWJ 12460 WCru
  fragrans Bunge   see *V. farreri*
  furcatum ♀H6   CMCN GKin NLar WJur
  - B&SWJ 5939   WCru
  - B&SWJ 10880   WCru

Viburnum

aff. *furcatum* — GKin
× *globosum* 'Jermyns Globe' — CMac SPoG WFar
grandiflorum — NLar StAn
- 'De Oirsprong' — NLar
- f. *grandiflorum* — LMaj
harryanum — CSBt CTsd EBee GEdr NLar WCru WPGP
× *hillieri* 'Winton' ♀H6 — CBcs CMac EBee EPfP LRHS LSRN MGos MPri NCth NLar SGol SPoG WFar WSpi
hoanglienense — CBcs WFar
- B&SWJ 8281 — EBee WCru
- HWJ 934 — WCru
- KWJ 12283 — WCru
- PAB 7833 — LEdu
hupehense MF 93087 — SSta
'Huron' — NLar
ichangense — NLar
integrifolium CWJ 12424 — WCru
§ *japonicum* — EBee WPGP
- B&SWJ 5968 — WCru
× *juddii* — CBcs CBrac CMac EBee ELan EPfP GKin LCro MAsh MBlu MGos WHtc WSpi
koreanum B&SWJ 4231 — WCru
lantana — CBrac CBTr CBWd CCVT CHab CLnd CMac CNWT EHeP ELan LBuc LSto MSwo SEWo SVic WHtc WJur WMat WRjT
- 'Aureum' — MBlu NLar
- var. *discolor* — NLar
- 'Mohican' — NLar
- 'Variegatum' (v) — ELan
§ *lantanoides* — SSta
aff. *lautum* B&SWJ 10290 — WCru
'Le Bois Marquis'PBR — CCVT CDoC EGrI EPfP ESwi LCro LRHS LSRN MAsh MMrt NLar SPoG
lentago — CMac WJur
luzonicum B&SWJ 3637 — WCru
- var. *formosanum* — WCru
  B&SWJ 3585
- var. *oblongum* — EBee WCru
  B&SWJ 3549
- var. *sinuatum* — WCru
  B&SWJ 4009
macrocephalum — EPfP LRHS LSRN
- 'Sterile' — SSta
mariesii — see *V. plicatum* f. *tomentosum* 'Mariesii'
mullaha B&SWJ 2251A — WCru
- GWJ 9227 — WCru
aff. *mullaha* GWJ 9388 — WCru
nervosum HWJK 2373 — WCru
nudum BRANDYWINE ('Bulk') — CCVT LRHS MGos SSta
- 'Pink Beauty' — EBee EGrI EPfP LCro LSRN MPri SChF SPoG SSta WFar WSpi
- 'Winterthur' — SSta
obovatum — SBrt
odoratissimum misapplied — see *V. japonicum*, *V. odoratissimum* var. *arboricola*, *V. odoratissimum* var. *awabuki*
odoratissimum Ker Gawl. RWJ 10046 — WCru
§ - var. *arboricola* — CBcs EBee
- - B&SWJ 3052 — WCru
- - B&SWJ 3397 — WCru
- - B&SWJ 6913 — WCru
§ - var. *awabuki* — CExl EGrI EPfP MAsh MBlu WCot
- - B&SWJ 8404 — ESwi WCru

- - B&SWJ 11374 from Wabuka, Japan — WCru
- - 'Emerald Lustre' — SEND WFar
- COPPERTOP ('Brant01'PBR) — CBcs CSBt CWnw EGren ELan EPfP LRHS LSou Midl MPri
aff. *odoratissimum* B&SWJ 3913 from the Philippines — WCru
oliganthum 'Kyo Kanzashi' — EBee WPGP
opulus — Widely available
§ - var. *americanum* — LRHS NLar WJur WKor
- - 'Bailey's Compact' — EPfP MGos
- - 'Phillips' — CAgr
- - 'Wentworth' — CAgr MGos
- 'Apricot' — NLar
- 'Aureum' — CMac ELan LRHS MGos MMuc MPri NLar SPoG
- var. *calvescens* — WJur
- - B&SWJ 10544 — WCru
- 'Compactum' ♀H6 — CBcs CBrac CDoC CEnd CMac EBee EGren EHeP ELan EPfP LRHS LSRN MAsh MGos NLar NPer SDix SGol SPoG WFar WHtc WSpi
- 'Fructuluteo' — CMCN SGol
* - 'Harvest Gold' — SGol
- 'Lady Marmalade' — NLar
- 'Nanum' — EPot NLar
- 'Notcutt's Variety' ♀H6 — WLov
- 'Park Harvest' — EPfP NLar
§ - 'Roseum' ♀H6 — Widely available
- 'Sterile' — see *V. opulus* 'Roseum'
- 'Sylvie' — NLar
- 'Xanthocarpum' ♀H6 — CExl CMac EBee EHeP ELan MMuc NLar SGol SPoG SRms WFar WSpi
orientale B&SWJ 15305 — WCru
parviflorum — GEdr
parvifolium — NLar
- B&SWJ 3375 — WCru
- B&SWJ 6768 — WCru
phlebotrichum B&SWJ 11470 — WCru
plicatum — EGren
- 'Nanum' — see *V. plicatum* f. *tomentosum* 'Nanum Semperflorens'
- OPENING DAY ('Piivib-II') — LRHS
- f. *plicatum* 'Grandiflorum' — CMac EPfP LRHS NLar SPoG
- - 'Mary Milton' ♀H5 — IArd
- NEWPORT ('Newzam') — LRHS MAsh
- - 'Popcorn' ♀H6 — CDoC CMac ELan EPfP LBom LRHS MAsh SGol SPoG SSta WSpi
- - 'Rosace' — EPfP MAsh MBlu NLar
- - 'Rotundifolium' — IArd MGos WFar
§ - f. *tomentosum* — SGol SPoG
- - 'Cascade' ♀H6 — ELan WSpi
- - 'Dart's Red Robin' ♀H6 — NLar
- - 'Elizabeth Bullivant' — LRHS
- - 'Fireworks' — NCth
- - KILIMANJARO ('Jww1'PBR) — CDoC EBee EGren ELan EPfP LCro LRHS LSRN MAsh MBlu MGos MPri NLar SPoG WCot WSpi
- - KILIMANJARO SUNRISE ('Jww5'PBR) ♀H5 — CBcs CWnw EBee EPfP EUrb LCro LRHS MAsh MGos NCth
- - 'Lanarth' — CBcs CBrac CDoC CExl CMac EBee ELan EPfP LRHS LSRN MAsh MBlu MGos MPri SGol WFar WHtc WSpi
§ - - 'Mariesii' — Widely available
- - 'Molly Schroeder' ♀H5 — NLar SSta
§ - - 'Nanum Semperflorens' — CBcs CBTr CMac CMCN ERom LRHS NLar SPoG WFar
- - 'Pink Beauty' ♀H6 — CBcs CDoC CMac EBee EGrI ELan EPfP LCro LMaj LRHS MAsh MBlu

		MGos MMrt MPri NCth NLar SMad SPoG WFar WHtc WSpi	
- - 'Saint Keverne'	GKin	- SPIRIT ('Anvi'PBR)	CEnd CSBt CWnw EGren ELan EPfP LRHS MAsh MBros NCth NEoE SBig SPoG
- - 'Shasta'	CMCN EPfP EUrb WFar WSpi	- 'Spring Bouquet'	LRHS MAsh
- - 'Shoshoni'	WSpi	- subsp. *subcordatum*	see *V. treleasei*
- - 'Summer Snowflake' ♀H6	CEnd CWGN ELan EPfP LCro LRHS MAsh MPri NCth NLar SGol SPoG WFar	- 'Variegatum' (v)	CCoa CMac EBee ELan EPfP LRHS MAsh NLar SGol SPoG SRms WFar WJun
- - 'Tennessee'	CBTr	*tomentosum*	see *V. plicatum* f. *tomentosum*
- 'Watanabe'	see *V. plicatum* f. *tomentosum* 'Nanum Semperflorens'	§ *treleasei*	EUrb
'Pragense' ♀H6	CBcs CMCN EGrl NLar	- B&SWJ 12544	WCru
propinquum	SArc WFar	*trilobum*	see *V. opulus* var. *americanum*
- CWJ 12395	WCru	*triphyllum* B&SWJ 10757	WCru
- CWJ 12426	WCru	*utile*	LRHS MPri NLar
- var. *propinquum*	EBee SChF	*wilsonii*	WJur
- - Guiz 222	WPGP	*wrightii*	WJur
prunifolium	WCru	- B&SWJ 5871	WCru
- 'Mrs Henry's Large'	NLar	- var. *stipellatum* B&SWJ 8780A	WCru
× *rhytidophylloides*	CEnd		
- 'Willowwood'	ELan LRHS MAsh MGos MPri NLar WHtc	**Vicia** (Fabaceae)	
		benghalensis	SPhx
rhytidophyllum	CBcs CMac CNWT EHeP MCtn MGos MMuc NLar NLit SAdn SArc SEND SGol SRms WJur	*cracca*	CGwi CHab GJem NMir SPhx WOrg
		faba	LCro
sambucinum	EBee WFar	*pisiformis*	MCtn
- HWJ 838	WCru	*sativa*	CHab
- var. *tomentosum* HWJ 733	WCru	*sylvatica*	NAts
sargentii B&SWJ 8695	WCru		
- 'Onondaga' ♀H6	CBcs CDoC CEnd CMac FGrl ELan ELon EPfP LRHS LSRN MAsh MGos MMuc NLar SEND SGol SPoG SRms WFar WKif WSpi	**Vigna** (Fabaceae)	
		radiata	SVic
semperflorens	see *V. plicatum* f. *tomentosum* 'Nanum Semperflorens'	**Villaresia** see *Citronella*	
§ *setigerum*	EBee NLar WFar	**Vinca** (Apocynaceae)	
- BWJ 8409	WCru	*difformis*	CCps CDor CFis CWal ECha LRHS NBir SDix SHor SReu SRms WHer
- 'Aurantiacum'	SChF	- 'Alba'	CSpe
SHINY DANCER ('Ncvx1')	EBee LCro LRHS MAsh NCth	- Greystone form	EPPr SEND
sieboldii B&SWJ 2837	WCru	- 'Jenny Pym'	CBcs CCps CDor CExl CFis CMac CoPl EBee ELan EPfP EWes EWld LSto MBNS NLar SEND SIvy SPoG SRms WBrk WHoo WTor
- CWJ 12808	WCru		
subalpinum	NLar		
sympodiale	CExl		
taitoense	CBcs WPGP	- 'Ruby Baker'	CDoC EPfP EPPr EWes LShi SPoG WFar WMal
- CWJ 12406	WCru	- subsp. *sardoa*	CCps CoPl CSpe ECha EPfP EPPr ESwi EWes LRHS WCot WFar
taiwanianum B&SWJ 3009	WCru		
- CWJ 12467	WCru	- 'Snowmound'	CCps CSBt NLar SPoG WTre
theiferum	see *V. setigerum*	*herbacea* RCB UA 21	WCot
tinus	Widely available	'Hidcote Purple'	see *V. major* var. *oxyloba*
- B&SWJ 15054	WCru	*major*	CBcs CBrac CoPl CSBt EHeP ELan LBuc LCro LRHS LSto MGos SAth SGol SRms WFar
- 'Eve Price' ♀H4	Widely available		
- 'French White' ♀H4	CBrac CCoa CDoC CMac EBee EGren ELan EPfP LBom LCro MAsh SRms	- 'Alba'	CMac CoPl
		- 'Elegantissima'	see *V. major* 'Variegata'
- 'Gwenllian' ♀H4	CBrac CDoC CEnd CMac EBee EGrl ELan EPfP LRHS LSRN LSto MAsh MGos MPri MPro NLar SGol SPoG SRms WFar WGwG WLov	- var. *hirsuta* misapplied	see *V. major* var. *oxyloba*
		§ - subsp. *hirsuta* (Boiss.) Stearn	CMac WCot
- 'Israel'	LRHS	- 'Jason Hill'	CCps
- 'Ladybird'	CDoC CWnw LRHS NLar	§ - 'Maculata' (v)	CBcs CCps CSBt EHeP LBom LRHS SEND SGol SPoG WFar
- 'Lisarose'PBR	CBcs CDoC EBee EGren ELan EPfP LBom LCro LRHS LSou LSRN LSto MAsh MGos NLar SOrn SPoG WCha WLov WSpi	- var. *oxyloba*	CCBP CExl CFis CoPl ECha ELan EPfP EPPr LRHS LShi SRms WHer WTre
- 'Little Bognor'	NLar	- var. *pubescens*	see *V. major* subsp. *hirsuta* (Boiss.) Stearn
- 'Lucidum'	CCoa CCVT LMaj SFol		
- 'Lucidum Variegatum' (v)	CMac MAsh	- 'Surrey Marble'	see *V. major* 'Maculata'
* - 'Macrophyllum'	LRHS NLar	§ - 'Variegata' (v) ♀H6	CBcs CBrac CDoC CMac CSBt ECha EGren EHeP ELan LBuc LCro LRHS MAsh MGos NLar SGol SPoG SReu SRms WFar
- 'Peter's Purple'	SPoG		
- 'Purpureum'	CBcs CBrac CSBt EBee EPfP LRHS MAsh MGos NLar WFar		

Vinca

- 'Wojo's Jem' (v) — CMac ELan GJos MGos MPro SWor WCot
- *minor* — CBcs CDoC CoPl CTsd EGren EHeP ELan GAbr GKin GQue LCro LRHS MAsh MGos MPro SAth SVic WFar WTor
  - f. *alba* — CBcs CDoC CMac CoPl ECha EGren ELon EPfP EPPr GJos LCro LRHS LShi LSRN LSto MAsh MPro SAth SHor WCot WFar WTor
  - - 'Alba Aureovariegata' — see *V. minor* f. *alba* 'Alba Variegata'
  § - - 'Alba Variegata' (v) — CBrac CExl EHeP LSRN NEoE SRms WCot WFar WHoo
  - - 'Elisa' — NLar
  - - 'Gertrude Jekyll' — Widely available
  § - 'Argenteovariegata' (v) ♀H6 — CBcs CBrac CDoC CDor CMac CWal ECha EGren ELan ELon GArf GQue LBom LRHS MGos MMuc SRms WFar
  § - 'Atropurpurea' ♀H6 — Widely available
  § - 'Aureovariegata' (v) — CBcs CMac EBee EHeP ELan ELon EPfP EPPr GAbr MGos SPlb
  § - 'Azurea Flore Pleno' (d) ♀H6 — CDoC CMac ECha EHeP ELon EPfP EPPr GAbr GQue LCro LRHS LShi LSto SBeP SPoG SRms SWor WFar WHoo WMal
  - 'Blue and Gold' (v) — EPPr LRHS
  - 'Bowles's Blue' — see *V. minor* 'Bowles's Variety'
  - 'Bowles's Purple' — GMaP LShi NCou
  § - 'Bowles's Variety' ♀H6 — CBcs CBrac CDoC CDor CExl CSBt ECha ELan ELon EPfP LBom LBuc LCro LRHS LSRN MAsh NLar SOrN SPoG SRms WFar WSpi
  - 'Burgundy' — SRms
  - 'Caerulea Plena' — see *V. minor* 'Azurea Flore Pleno'
  - 'Colada' — EWes
  - 'Dartington Star' — see *V. major* var. *oxyloba*
  - 'Double Burgundy' — see *V. minor* 'Multiplex'
  - 'Evelyne'^{PBR} (v) — CDor WFar
  - 'Flower Power' — EPPr
  - GREEN CARPET — see *V. minor* 'Grüner Teppich'
  § - 'Grüner Teppich' — EHeP WFar
  - 'Illumination' (v) — CBcs CDoC CMac CoPl CSBt EBee ELan ELon EPfP EPPr EPPr GAbr GJos GKin LCro LRHS LSRN MAsh MGos MHtn MMuc MPro NBro NLar SAth SPoG SRms WFar WHoo
  - 'Josefine' — NLar
  - 'La Grave' — see *V. minor* 'Bowles's Variety'
  - 'Marie' — ELon EPPr NLar
  - MOONLIT ('Parvin') (v) — LRHS
  - 'Mrs Betty James' (d) — EPPr WCot
  § - 'Multiplex' (d) — EPPr LBom LBuc LRHS SRms
  - 'Panta' — LRHS MPri
  - 'Purpurea' — see *V. minor* 'Atropurpurea'
  - 'Ralph Shugert' (v) ♀H6 — CDoC CDor CExl CMac ELan ELon EPfP EPPr EWes GJos IBal LBom LCro LRHS LSRN LSto MAsh MGos MPri NLar SNig SPoG SRms WFar WLov WTor
  - 'Rubra' — see *V. minor* 'Atropurpurea'
  - 'Silver Service' (d/v) — EPPr WFar
  - 'Snowdrift' — EPPr
  - 'Variegata' — see *V. minor* 'Argenteovariegata'
  - 'Variegata Aurea' — see *V. minor* 'Aureovariegata'
  - 'White Power' — NLar

Vincetoxicum (Apocynaceae)

- *amplexicaule* — GGro
- *forrestii* — CExl
- *fuscatum* — EBee
- *hirundinaria* — EAri EBee EPPr SPhx WCot WHil
  - HPA 1358 — GGro
- *nigrum* — EBee EPPr ESwi WCot
- *scandens* — EPPr

Viola ✿ (Violaceae)

- 'Abigail' (Vtta) — LEdu WFar
- 'Admiral Avellan' — see *V.* 'Amiral Avellan'
- 'Alethia' (Va) — GAbr WGoo
- 'Alice Kate' (Va) — WGoo
- 'Alice Witter' (Vt) — GBin SHar
I 'Alison' (Va) — WGoo
- *altaica* — SPlb
- 'Amelia' (Va) — WGoo
§ 'Amiral Avellan' (Vt) — CDor LShi WFar
- 'Annalesia' (Vt) — LShi
- 'Annette Ross' (Va) — WGoo
- 'Ardross Gem' (Va) — GArf LShi WGoo
- 'Arkwright's Ruby' (Va) — LShi MCtn
- *arvensis* — CHab MCtn
- 'Aspasia' (Va) ♀H5 — MAsh WGoo
- 'Avril Lawson' (Va) — GKev SHar WGoo
- 'Baroness de Rothschild' ambig. (Va) — LShi WHer
- 'Baronne Alice de Rothschild' (Vt) — CDor NLar SHar
- 'Beatrice' (Vtta) — WGoo
- 'Beetroot' (Vt) — LShi
- 'Bel Viso Pineapple Crush' (Bel Viso Series) **new** — EGren
§ 'Belmont Blue' (C) — EWes GBin GKev GMaP LCro LRHS LSto MHol NBir NSti SHar WCAu WFar WGoo WSpi WTor
- 'Beshlie' (Va) ♀H5 — WGoo
- *biflora* — EWld LShi MNrw
- 'Blue Butterfly' (C) — MHol
- 'Blue Ice' (Va) — WFar
- 'Blue Moon' (C) — LShi MAsh WGoo
- BLUE MOON ('Smev1') (Celestial Series) (Va) — ELan
- 'Blue Moonlight' (C) — MHer
- BONNIE LASSIES SARAH (Bonnie Lassies Series) (Va) — LRHS MHer
- 'Boughton Blue' — see *V.* 'Belmont Blue'
- 'Bournemouth Gem' (Vt) — CDor LShi
§ 'Bowles's Black' (T) — CFis CSpe NBro SRms
- *brevistipulata* — GEdr GKev WFar
  var. *hidakana*
  - var. *laciniata* — GEdr
- 'Bruneau' (dVt) — WFar
- *bubanii* — GKev
- 'Buttercup' (Vtta) — MHol SPoG WGoo
- 'Butterpat' (C) — GQue MAsh WFar WGoo
- 'Candy' (Vt) — WFar
- *canina* — NBro
- 'Carol' (Vt) — WFar
- *chaerophylloides* 'Beni-zuru' — EDAr GGro GKev
§ - var. *sieboldiana* — GGro
- 'Chantreyland' (Va) — MCtn
- 'Charles W. Groves' — see *V.* 'Charles William Groves', 'Charles Winston Groves'
§ 'Charles William Groves' (Vt) — WFar
§ 'Charles Winston Groves' (Vt) — WFar
- 'Chicky Chicks' — MCtn
- 'Christie's Wedding' (Vt) — WFar
- 'Christmas' (Vt) — LShi WFar
- 'Clementina' (Va) ♀H5 — WGoo

'Clive Groves' (Vt)	CDor		'Etain' (Va)	CAby EGren ELan EPfP GAbr LBar LCro LShi MHol MPro NLar SPoG WFar
'Coeur d'Alsace' (Vt)	CLAP EBee GBin GMaP LShi NLar SRms WFar			
'Colombine' (Vt)	CAby LShi MAsh WKif		'Exmoor Cream'	WMal
'Columbine' (Va)	CDor EGren EPfP LBar LShi MHer MHol MPro NDov SPoG WFar WGoo		'Fabiola' (Vtta)	GAbr
		I	'Fantasy'	WGoo
			'Ferndale' (dPVt)	LShi
§ 'Conte di Brazza' (dPVt)	LShi NLar WHer		'Fiona' (Va)	GAbr WGoo
'Cordelia' (Vt)	CDor LShi		'Fiona Lawrenson' (Va)	WGoo
cornuta ♀H5	CAgr CDor CElw EPot MNrw NBir NBro SRms StAn WFar WHoo		'Florence' (Va)	WGoo
			'Flower Girl' (Va)	LShi
- Alba Group (C) ♀H5	CBro CDor CElw CSpe ECha ELan GMaP GQue LCro MAsh MHol NBir NBro SMHy SRms WChS WGoo WHoo		'Foxbrook Cream' (C)	MAsh WGoo
			'Francesca' (Va)	WGoo
			'Freckles'	see *V. sororia* 'Freckles'
			'Fred Morey' (Vt)	CDor WFar
- 'Alba Minor' (C)	EWes LShi NBro NDov WFar WHoo		*glabella*	GGro
- blue-flowered (C)	MHer		'Glanmore'	WFar
- 'Brimstone' (C)	LShi MHol	I	'Glenda'	WGoo
- 'Cleopatra' (C)	MHol MNrw		'Glenholme'	LShi MWIw WOld
- 'Clouded Yellow' (C)	MHol MNrw WFar		'Governor Herrick' (Vt)	WFar
- 'Cream Gem' (C)	MHol WFar		*gracilis* 'Lutea'	CElw
- 'Gypsy Moth' (C)	GAbr LShi MHol SMHy		*grisebachiana*	GKev
- 'Halo Golden Yellow' (Halo Series) (C)	MPro		'Gustav Wermig' (C)	MHol WGoo
			'Heartthrob' (v)	GEdr LBar MPro SPoG WCAu
- 'Hobbit Sam' (C)	WFar	*	'Heaselands'	SMHy
- 'Icy But Spicy' (C)	MAsh MHol NDov WFar WGoo	§	*hederacea*	CExl CoPl EAri EMor EPfP GJos GQue LCro LShi MBel SDix SRms WFar
- Lilacina Group (C)	ECha			
- 'Maiden's Blush' (C)	MHol WFar			
- 'Marchants Purple' (C)	CSpe SMHy		'Helen Mount' (T)	MCtn
- 'Minor' (C)	LShi MAsh NBro		'Hudsons Blues'	CElw MNrw
- 'Netta Statham' (C)	MHol WGoo		'Huntercombe Purple' (Va) ♀H5	NBir WFar
- 'Pale Apollo' (C)	MHol WFar			
- 'Spider' (C)	MAsh MHol WFar WGoo		'Iden Gem' (Va)	WGoo
- 'Swallowtail' (C)	GAbr MHol		'Inverurie Beauty' (Va) ♀H5	GAbr GBin GMaP SMHy WGoo WOld
- 'Ulla' (C)	WHer			
- 'Victoria's Blush' (C)	CDor CElw GMaP MAsh MHol NBir NDov WGoo WTor		'Irish Elegance'	see *V.* 'Sulfurea'
			'Irish Molly' (Va)	ELan EPfP EPot LShi MAsh SPoG WFar WGoo
corsica	CSpe EBee LShi SPhx WHoo			
'Covent Garden' (Vt)	LShi WFar		'Isabel'	MAsh SRms WGoo
'Crepuscle' (Vt)	WFar		'Isabella' (Va)	LRHS WFar
cucullata ♀H5	SRms		'Ivory Queen' (Va)	GAbr WFar WGoo
§ - 'Alba' (Vt)	NBir SRms		'Jackanapes' (Va) ♀H5	EBee ELan LCro LShi MAsh MPro NLar SPoG
* - 'Striata Alba' (Vt)	NBro			
'Czar'	see *V.* 'The Czar'		'Janet' (Va)	LRHS SPoG
'Dawn' (Vtta)	CAby LRHS NLar SPoG WFar WGoo WTor		'Janette' (Va)	WGoo
			'Jean Arnot' (Vt)	LShi
'Delicia' (Vtta)	WGoo		'Jean Jeannie' (Va)	NDov WFar WGoo
'Deltini Honey Bee' (Deltini Series) (C)	MBros SPoG		'Jeannie Bellew' (Va)	WGoo
			'Jennifer Andrews' (Va)	LShi WGoo
'Des Charentes' (Vt)	LShi		*jooi*	WAbe
'Desdemona' (Va)	GKev		'Josie' (Va)	WGoo WOld
'Devon Cream' (Va)	WGoo		'Judy Goring' (Va)	NDov
'Diana Groves' (Vt)	WFar		'Juno' (Va)	GAbr
'Dick o' the Hills' (Vt)	LShi WFar		*kamtschadalorum*	WFar
dissecta var. *sieboldiana*	see *V. chaerophylloides* var. *sieboldiana*		'Kerry Girl' (Vt)	WFar
			'Kim' (Vt)	LShi
'Donau' (Vt)	LShi WFar		'Kitten'	LShi MHol WFar WGoo
'Doreen' (Vt)	WFar		'Kitty White' (Va)	GAbr
'Double White' (dVt)	WHer	§	'Königin Charlotte' (Vt)	CTsd EBee GAbr GBin GMaP GQue LShi MCtn MHer SRms SVic WCAu WCav WCot
'Duchesse de Parme' (dPVt)	NLar SRms WHer			
'D'Udine' (dPVt)	LShi SRms WFar WHer			
'E.A. Bowles'	see *V.* 'Bowles's Black'		*labradorica* misapplied	see *V. riviniana* Purpurea Group
'Eastgrove Blue Scented' (C)	WFar WGoo WMal		- *purpurea*	see *V. riviniana* Purpurea Group
'Eastgrove Ice Blue' (C)	WGoo		*labradorica* ambig.	GAbr GKev LCro WCAu WHer
eizanensis	GGro		'Lady Hume Campbell' (dPVt)	WHer
'Elaine Quin' (Va)	LRHS SPoG WGoo			
§ *elatior*	CSpe EMor EPPr MNrw		'Laura' (C)	LRHS MCtn
'Elizabeth Bailes' (Vt)	LShi		'Lavender Lights' (Vt)	CDor WFar
'Elworthy Velvet'	CElw		'Lees Blue' (Vt)	WFar
'Emperor Magenta Red'	SVic		'Letitia' (Va)	MAsh WTor
erecta	see *V. elatior*		'Lianne' (Vt)	LShi SRms

Viola

'Lindsay'	WGoo		'Pat Kavanagh' (C)	WGoo
'Lisa Tanner' (Va)	WGoo		pedata	EPot GKev LAma WAbe
'Little David' (Vtta) ♀H5	LShi WGoo		- 'Bicolor' (Vt)	WAbe
§ 'Lord Primrose' (Celestial Series) (Va)	EGren MPro		pedatifida	CSpe EDAr
'Lorna Cawthorne' (C)	WGoo		- white-flowered	GEdr
'Louisa' (Va)	GAbr MWlw		'Petra' (Vtta)	WGoo
'Lucy' (Va)	MAsh		pinnata	EAri SBrt
§ lutea	LShi WAbe WGoo		'Prince Henry' (T)	MCtn
- subsp. elegans	see V. lutea		'Prunella' (Va)	LShi WFar
'Lydia Groves' (Vt)	CAby CDor SRms WFar		pubescens var. eriocarpa	SRms
'Maggie Mott' (Va) ♀H5	GArf MAsh WFar WGoo		pumila	GEdr
mandshurica	GKev		QUEEN CHARLOTTE	see V. 'Königin Charlotte'
- 'Fuji Dawn' (v)	GGro LShi WCot		'Raven' (Va)	WGoo
'Marie Rose' (Vt)	WFar		'Rebecca' (Vtta)	CAby CDor EGren ELan EPfP GKev LRHS LSou LSRN MAsh MBel MHol MPro NBir NDov NLar SPoG WFar WGoo WTor
I 'Mars'	WSpi			
'Martin' (Va) ♀H5	CAby ECha GMaP LSRN MAsh NDov SHor SPoG WFar WGoo WOld			
			'Rebecca Cawthorne' (C)	MHol
'Marylyn' (Va)	WFar		'Red Charm' (Vt)	WCav
'Mauve Radiance' (Va)	GAbr WGoo		reichenbachiana	EBee
microphylla	SPlb		'Reine des Blanches' (dVt)	SRms
(Miracle Series) 'Miracle Barley Pink' (Vt)	CSpe		'Reine des Neiges' (Vt)	CDor LShi MCtn NLar WFar
			reniforme	see V. hederacea
- 'Miracle Bride White' (Vt)	SHar WFar		riviniana	CBWd CoPl GJos GQue MNHC NAts WHer WShi
- 'Miracle Classy Blue' (Vt)	WFar			
- 'Miracle Classy Pink' (Vt)	MHol WFar		§ - Purpurea Group	CAby CBcs CDor CMac CoPl EBee ECha EGren EMor EPfP EWes GMaP LShi LSto MMuc MPie NBir NRya SPlb SRms WFar
- 'Miracle Ice White' (Vt)	NLar WFar			
- 'Miracle Intense Blue' (Vt)	GAbr WFar			
'Misty Guy' (Vtta)	MAsh			
'Molly Sanderson' (Va) ♀H5	CAby CSpe ECha ELan EPot GKev LShi MAsh MBel MHer NLar SPlb SPoG SRms SRot WFar WTor		- 'Rosea'	MMuc
			- white-flowered	EWes MMuc
			'Roscastle Black' (Va)	MAsh NDov WGoo WSpi
'Moonlight' (Va) ♀H5	ELan		'Rose Marie' (Va)	WFar
'Morwenna' (Va)	MAsh WGoo		rosulata **new**	ESuc
'Mrs Lancaster' (Va)	ELan EPfP LRHS LShi LSRN MPri NLar SPoG WFar		'Rosy Rayne' (Va)	LShi WFar
			'Royal Wedding' (Vt)	CFis MHer StAn SVic
'Mrs Pinehurst' (Vt)	SRms		'Rubra' (Vt)	EMor EPfP EPPr SBea SVic
'Mrs R. Barton' (Vt)	CDor SRms		* rupestris rosea	GGro WHer
'Myfawnny' (Va)	WFar WGoo		sacchalinensis var. alpina	GGro
'Neptune' (Va)	WFar		'Sea Horse'	LShi
'Netta Statham'	see V. 'Belmont Blue'		selkirkii 'Variegata' (v)	GGro
'Nora' (Va)	NDov WFar WGoo		septentrionalis	see V. sororia
NORTHERN LIGHTS ('Smev4') (Celestial Series) (Va)	EGren ELan EPfP LBar MPro		'Showgirl' (Va)	WFar
			'Silver Samurai' (Vt)	WCot
odorata (Vt)	CBcs CDor CHab CoPl EBee GQue LCro LShi MCtn NMir SHor SRms WCAu WJek		'Skylark' (Va)	WFar
			'Smugglers' Moon' (Va)	LShi WGoo
			Sorbet Series (Va)	LCro MBros MPri
- 'Alba' (Vt)	CDor CLAP EBee ELan EMor EPPr GQue LShi MCtn SEND SRms WCAu WFar		- SORBET BLACK DELIGHT IMPROVED ('Pas211779') (Va)	MBros
- 'Amethyst Witch' (Vt)	WFar		- SORBET YELLOW FROST (Va)	LCro
- apricot-flowered	see V. 'Sulfurea'		(Sorbet XP Series) SORBET XP T&M Mix (Va)	EGren MBros
- 'Carol Lockton' (Vt)	WFar			
- 'Ellie' (Vt)	WFar		§ sororia	CAgr NBir NBro
- 'Empress Augusta' (Vt)	LShi		* - 'Albiflora' (Vt) ♀H6	CTtf EMor EPfP EPPr GKev GPSL LEdu SBea
- 'Hungarian Beauty' (Vt)	LCro			
- 'Katy' (Vt)	CLAP		- 'Dark Freckles' (Vt)	CFis EBee ELan EMor NLar NRya WFar WTre
- 'Melanie' (Vt)	CAby CDor CLAP			
- 'Miracle White'	EBee WFar		§ - 'Freckles' (Vt)	CBro CMac CTtf EAri EBee ECha ELan EMor EPfP EWld GKev LEdu MAsh MBel NBir NLar NRya SBea SDix SMrm SPlb WCAu WCav WFar
- 'Mrs R.O. Barlow' (Vt)	CLAP			
- pink-flowered	see V. odorata Rosea Group			
- var. praecox (Vt)	SEND		- 'Hungarian Beauty' (Vt)	EBee GBin
§ - Rosea Group (Vt)	CDor SEND SRms		- 'Priceana' (Vt)	ECha LEdu LRHS NBir SPlb WCot
- rosea	see V. odorata Rosea Group		- SORORITY SISTERS (mixed) (Vt)	CFis GAbr SVic
- 'Sulphurea'	see V. 'Sulfurea'			
'Olive Edwards' (Va)	WGoo		- 'Speckles' (Vt/v)	WCot
palustris	NLar WShi		spathulata	WAbe
papilionacea	see V. sororia		STARRY NIGHT (Celestial Series)	see V. 'Lord Primrose' (Celestial Series)
'Parme de Toulouse' (dPVt)	NLar		'Steyning' (Va)	WFar
'Pat Creasy' (Va)	NDov WGoo		stojanowii	WIce

§	'Sulfurea' (Vt)	CDor CLAP EPfP LShi MCtn NRya WCot WFar
	'Sulfurea' lemon-flowered (Vt)	WFar
	'Sultan' (Vt)	CDor
	'Sunshine' (Va)	WFar
	'Susie' (Va)	EGren MHol WFar
	'Suzie' (Va)	MPro
	'Swanley White'	see *V.* 'Conte di Brazza'
	'Sybil' (SP)	WGoo
	TEARDROPS MIXED (P)	EGren LCro
	'Teardrops Yesterday, Today, Tomorrow' (P)	LCro
§	'The Czar' (Vt)	CAby CTtf SRms
	'Tiger Eye Red' (C)	LCro
	'Tiger Eyes' (Va)	LCro SPoG StAn
	'Tony Venison' (C/v)	LShi NLar WFar
	tricolor	CGHo CGwi CHab EHet ENfk EPfP EWhm GJem GJos GQue LCro LShi MCtn MHer MHoo MNHC MPri SRms WKit
	- 'Sawyer's Black' (T)	ENfk WJek
	TWILIGHT ('Smev3') (Celestial Series) (Va)	EGren ELan MPro
	verecunda	GGro WOld
	- B&SWJ 604a	WCru
	'Victoria Cawthorne' (C)	LShi MAsh MHol NDov WFar WGoo
	'Vita' (Va)	SRms WFar WGoo
	walteri 'Silver Gem'	EBee EMor
	'White Ladies'	see *V. cucullata* 'Alba'
	'White Pearl' (Va)	LShi WGoo
	'White Swan' (Va)	MAsh WFar
	'Winifred Jones' (Va)	GKev WGoo
	'Winnie' (Va)	WFar
	'Winona Cawthorne' (C)	MHol
	'Wisley White'	MHol SHor WTor
	× *wittrockiana* COASTAL SUNRISE MIXED (P)	LCro
	- Cool Wave Series (P)	LCro
	- Delta Series (P)	EGren
	- Frizzle Sizzle Series (P)	LCro
	- - 'Frizzle Sizzle Blue' (P)	LCro
	- - 'Frizzle Sizzle Burgundy' (P)	LCro
	- - FRIZZLE SIZZLE MIX (P)	EGren
	- - 'Frizzle Sizzle Orange' (P)	LCro
	- - 'Frizzle Sizzle Yellow' (P)	LCro
	- - 'Frizzle Sizzle Yellow-blue Swirl' (P)	LCro
	- (Frizzle Sizzle Mini Series) 'Frizzle Sizzle Mini Purple Shades' (P)	LCro
	- Joker Series (P) ♕H5	MCtn
	- - 'Joker Light Blue' (P)	LCro
	- Matrix Series (P)	EGren MBros MPri
	- - MATRIX CASSIS (P)	MBros
	- - MATRIX MORPHEUS (P)	MBros
	- - MATRIX RED BLOTCH (P)	MBros
	- - MATRIX SUNRISE (P)	MBros
	- - MATRIX YELLOW BLOTCH (P)	MBros
	'Yellowtail' (Va)	GAbr
	yezoensis	GKev
	'Zoe' (Vtta)	EGren EPfP LRHS MAsh MPro SPoG WFar

Viscaria (Caryophyllaceae)

	W&O 8096	GGro
§	*alpina*	EDAr EPfP NGdn WFar
	- 'Rosea'	NBir
	- 'Snow Flurry'	GKev

§	*asterias*	CCBP EDAr GGro MNrw SBrt SHar SHor
	- 'Darcies Pink' **new**	EDAr
	'Cherry Bubbles' **new**	LBar MPri
§	*vulgaris*	CSpe ECha EPPr GJos GPSL GQue
	- 'Alba'	ECha EGrl
§	- dark purple-red-flowered	CSpe ELan EWes GJos MPie SRms WCAu
	- 'Feuer'	EWes MHol
	- 'Firebird'	EWes
	- 'Plena' (d)	NBir SRkn WHil
	- 'Schnee'	NLar
	- SNOW CLOUD ('Yatnis')	EGren LBom WCAu
	- 'Splendens'	CSpe EGrl WCav WFar
	- 'Splendens Plena' (d) ♕H5	EBee EGren

Visnaga (Apiaceae)

§	*daucoides*	CHby CSpe EPfP LCro LRHS NClf SPhx SRms WTor
	- 'Green Mist'	CSpe LCro LSto MCtn MPro WSpi

Vitaliana (Primulaceae)

§	*primuliflora*	GArf GBin GKev NRya
	- subsp. *assoana*	EPot WAbe
	- subsp. *cinerea*	EPot GKev
	- subsp. *praetutiana*	SPlb

Vitex (Lamiaceae)

	agnus-castus	CAgr CBcs CBWd CCBP CCht CCoa CMCN CSde CSpe EBee EGren EPfP EUrb LRHS MCtn MHoo NLar SPlb WJek WJur
	- f. *alba*	EPfP LRHS MBlu SPoG
	- - PAB 9281	LEdu
	- - 'Silver Spire'	EBee ELan EPfP LRHS SRms WPGP
	- BLUE DIDDLEY ('Smvacbd'PBR)	ELan
	- DELTA BLUES ('Piivac-I')	ELan LCro WCot
	- f. *latifolia* ♕H4	CCBP EGren EGrl ELan EPfP EUrb LEdu LRHS LSRN MHer NLar SEND SPoG WPGP
	- PINK PINNACLE ('V07-sc-op-4')	ELan LRHS MPri SEND
	- 'Santamaria'	ELan
	chinensis	see *V. negundo* var. *heterophylla*
	incisa	see *V. negundo* var. *heterophylla*
	negundo	LEdu WJur
§	- var. *heterophylla*	EWes
	trifolia 'Purpurea'	EUrb WJur

Vitis ✿ (Vitaceae)

	'Alden' (O/B)	WSuV
	× *alexanderi* 'Concord' (O/B)	WJur
	- 'Isabella' (O/B)	SVic WJur
	amurensis	CDoC WSpi
	- B&SWJ 4138	WCru
	- B&SWJ 4299	WCru
§	'Aurore' (W)	CAgr
	'Baco Noir' (O/B)	CAgr WSuV
	'Bianca' (O/W)	EGren SBmr SSFr SVic
	BLACK HAMBURGH	see *V. vinifera* 'Schiava Grossa'
*	'Black Strawberry' (B)	CAgr WSuV
	'Brant' (O/B)	CAgr CBcs CDoC CMac EBee EHeP ELan MAsh MGos NLar NPer NTrD SEWo SPlb SPoG SRms SSFr WMat WSuV
	'Brilliant' (B)	WSuV
	'Buffalo' (B)	WSuV
	'Cabernet Blanc'PBR (W) **new**	WSuV

Vitis

'Cabernet Cortis' (B)	WSuV
californica (F)	NLar
'Canadice' (O/R/S)	WSuV
'Cascade'	see *V.* SEIBEL 13053
'Castel 19637' (B)	WSuV
'Chambourcin' (B)	WSuV
CLARET CLOAK ('Frovit') ♀H5	ELan LRHS LSRN MBlu SChF WSpi
coignetiae ♀H5	CBcs CDoC CMac CRHN ECha EGrI EHeP ELan EPfP GKin LCro LRHS LSRN LSto MAsh MBlu MGos NCth NLar SArc SDix SEND SPoG WJur WSpi
- B&SWJ 4550 from Korea	WCru
- B&SWJ 4744	WCru
- from Japan B&SWJ 10882	WCru
- - B&SWJ 10908	WCru
- var. *glabrescens* B&SWJ 8537	WCru
'Edwards No 1' (O/W)	WSuV
'Einset' (B/S)	LCro WSuV
flexuosa B&SWJ 5568	WCru
- B&SWJ 6304	WCru
- var. *choii* B&SWJ 4101	WCru
§ 'Fragola' (O/R)	CAgr CMac ECha ELan EPfP EPom LCro MAsh NLar SPoG SRms SVic WMat WSpi WSuV
'Gagarin Blue' (O/B)	CAgr EPom SVen WSuV
'Glenora' (F/B/S)	CAgr WSuV
henryana	see *Parthenocissus henryana*
'Himrod' (O/W/S)	EGren ELan WSuV
'Horizon' (O/W)	WSuV
inconstans	see *Parthenocissus tricuspidata*
'Interlaken' (O/W/S)	CAgr WSuV
'Johanniter' (W)	SPre WSuV
'Kempsey Black' (O/B)	CAgr WSuV
'Kyoho' (B)	WSuV
labrusca	WJur
'Léon Millot' (O/G/B)	CAgr LSRN WSuV
'Lucy Kuhlman' (B)	WSuV
'Maréchal Foch' (O/B)	EGren WSuV
'Maréchal Joffre' (O/R)	CAgr WSuV
'Mars' (O/B/S)	WSuV
'Munson R.W.' (O/R)	WSuV
'Muscat Bleu' (O/B)	EGren EPom LCro NLar SPoG SSFr WMat WSuV
'Nero'[PBR] (O/B)	CAgr EOli
'New York Muscat' (O/B)	WSuV
'New York Seedless' (O/W/S)	WSuV
'Niederother Monschrebe' (O/R)	WSuV
'Orion' (O/W)	WSuV
'Paletina' (O/W)	SEdi
parsley-leaved	see *V. vinifera* 'Apiifolia'
'Philipp'[PBR] (O/B)	EPfP
'Phönix' (O/W)	CAgr EPom LBuc LCro LSRN MAsh MGos SBmr SEND SPoG SPre SSFr SVic WMat WSuV
piasezkii var. *pagnuccii*	WCru
* 'Pink Strawberry' (O)	WSuV
'Pirovano 14' (O/B)	WSuV
'Poloske Muscat' (W)	EPom NLar SPoG WMat
pulchra	WCru
purpurea 'Spetchley Park' (O/B)	CAgr WSuV
quinquefolia	see *Parthenocissus quinquefolia*
RAVAT 51 (O/W)	WSuV
'Regent'[PBR] (O/B)	CAgr EPom LCro MGos MPri NLar SPoG SPre SVic WMat WSuV
'Reliance' (O/R/S) ♀H5	CAgr WSuV
'Rembrant' (R)	CAgr WSuV
riparia	NLar
'Romulus' (O/G/W/S)	WSuV
'Rondo' (O/B)	CAgr SPre SVic WMat WSuV
'Saturn' (O/R/S)	CAgr WSuV
§ 'Schuyler' (O/B) ♀H5	CAgr CMac EGren ELan EPom LBuc LCro LWaG MGos WSuV
SEIBEL 5279	see *V.* 'Aurore'
§ SEIBEL 13053 (O/B)	CMac MAsh SEND SRms WSuV
'Seyval Blanc' (O/W)	CAgr MAsh SEND SVic WSuV
SEYVE VILLARD ambig.	NPer
SEYVE VILLARD 5276	see *V.* 'Seyval Blanc'
SEYVE VILLARD 20.473 (F)	NPer
'Solaris' (O/W)	WMat WSuV
'Sovereign Coronation' (B/S) ♀H5	WSuV
'Suffolk Seedless' (B/S)	EPom
SUPERIOR SEEDLESS ('Sugraone') (G/S)	NPlm
'Tereshkova' (O/B)	CAgr WSuV
'Thornton' (O/S)	WSuV
thunbergii 'Lobata'	WPGP
'Triomphe d'Alsace' (O/B)	CAgr NPer WSuV
'Trollhaugen' (O/B/S)	WSuV
'Trollinger'	see *V. vinifera* 'Schiava Grossa'
'Vanessa' (O/R/S)	EGren EPom SVic WSuV
'Venus' (O/B/S)	SVic
vinifera	EOli LMaj MPri SAth SFol WCha
- 'Abouriou' (O/B)	WSuV
- 'Acolon' (O/B)	WSuV
§ - 'Alicante' (G/B)	CBcs WSuV
§ - 'Apiifolia'	EBee WPGP
- 'Autumn Royal Seedless' (B/S)	EPom NPlm
- 'Bacchus' (O/W)	CAgr LBuc NLar SPoG SVic WMat WSuV
- 'Baresana' (G/W)	EGren LWaG SRms WFar
- 'Beauty' (B/S)	CAgr
- 'Black Alicante'	see *V. vinifera* 'Alicante'
- 'Black Frontignan' (G/O/B)	WSuV
- BLACK HAMBURGH	see *V. vinifera* 'Schiava Grossa'
- 'Black Prince' (G/B)	CAgr WSuV
- 'Blue Portuguese'	see *V. vinifera* 'Portugieser'
- 'Cabernet Cantor' (B) **new**	WSuV
- 'Cabernet Sauvignon' (O/B)	EBee EPfP MAsh MGos NPer SBmr SVic WMat WSuV
- 'Cardinal' (O/R)	MGos
- 'Carla' (O/R)	WSuV
- 'Centennial' (O/N/S)	MPri
- 'Centennial Seedless' (W/S)	LCro
- 'Chardonnay' (O/W)	CAgr CDoC LCro LSRN MAsh NLar NPer SBmr SPre SVic
§ - 'Chasselas' (G/O/B)	LCro
- 'Chasselas Blanc' (O/W)	LCro
- 'Chasselas de Fontainebleau' (G/O/B)	CWnw SVic
- 'Chasselas d'Or'	see *V. vinifera* 'Chasselas'
- 'Chasselas Rosé' (G/R)	CAgr MGos SPre
- 'Chasselas Rosé Royal' (O/R)	SVic
- 'Chenin Blanc' (O/W)	SVic
- 'Crimson Seedless' (R/S)	EBee EPom LCro LRHS MGos NLar NPlm
- 'Dattier Saint Vallier' (O/W)	SVic
- 'Divico' (O/G/B)	SVic WSuV
- 'Dolcetto' (O/B)	WSuV
- 'Dornfelder' (O/R)	CMac SPoG SVic WMat
- EARLY RED GLOBE ('Sheegene 5'[PBR]) (R)	NPlm
- 'Exalta' (G/W/S)	LCro NLar

- 'Excelsior' (W)   WSuV
- 'Faber' (O/W)   WSuV
- 'Fiesta' (W/S)   WSuV
- 'Findling' (W)   WSuV
- 'Flame' (R/S)   CAgr LRHS WMat
- 'Flame Red' (O/D)   EPom
- 'Flame Seedless' (G/O/R/S)   CMac EPom NPlm SPre SSFr
- 'Gamay Noir' (O/B)   SVic
- § 'Garnacha Tinta' (B)   SVic
- 'Gewürztraminer' (O/R)   MAsh SVic
- 'Glory of Boskoop'   see V. 'Schuyler'
- 'Golden Chasselas'   see V. vinifera 'Chasselas'
- 'Grenache'   see V. vinifera 'Garnacha Tinta'
- 'Huxelrebe' (O/W)   SVic
- 'Incana' (O/B)   EBee EPfP SVen WCot WPGP
- 'Lakemont' (O/W/S) ♀H5   CAgr CDoC CMac CRHN ELan EPfP EPom LBuc LCro LEdu MGos NLar NTrD SBmr SEdi SPoG SPre SSFr SVic WMat WSuV
- 'Lival' (O/B)   WSuV
- 'Macabeo'   see V. vinifera 'Viura'
- 'Madeleine Angevine' (O/W)   CAgr LSRN MAsh NPer SPoG SVen SVic WSuV
- 'Madeleine Sylvaner' (O/W)   MAsh NPer SPoG
- 'Madresfield Court' (G/B)   WSuV
- 'Merlot' (G/B)   MGos SVic WSuV
- § 'Müller-Thurgau' (O/W)   LCro LRHS LSRN MAsh SPoG SVic
- 'Muscaris' (W) **new**   WSuV
- 'Muscat Hamburg' (G/B)   CWnw LRHS LSRN MAsh
- 'Muscat of Alexandria' (G/W)   CBcs CRHN EGren SRms SVic WMat
- 'Optima' (O/W)   WSuV
- 'Parellada' (W)   SVic
- 'Perlette' (O/W/S)   EPom LRHS
- 'Petit Rouge' (R)   WSuV
- 'Picurka' (O/W/S)   SVic
- 'Pinot Blanc' (O/W)   EBee EPfP LCro LRHS MAsh SPoG SVic
- 'Pinot Gris' (O/B)   SVic
- § 'Pinot Meunier' (B)   SVic WSuV
- 'Pinot Noir' (O/B)   CDoC LCro SVic WSuV
- § 'Portugieser' (O/W)   WSuV
- 'Précoce de Bousquet' (O/W)   WSuV
- 'Précoce de Malingre' (O/W)   CAgr
- 'Prima' (O/B)   WSuV
- 'Purpurea' (O/B) ♀H5   CBcs CDoC CMac CRHN CSde EBee EGren EGrI EHeP ELan EPfP LSRN MAsh MGos MNrw NBid NBir NPer SPoG SRms SSta WCot WHtc
- 'Queen of Esther' (B)   WSuV
- 'Reichensteiner' (O/G/W)   CAgr SVic
- 'Rhea' (G/O/R)   SVic
- 'Riesling' (O/W)   EGren LCro LRHS MAsh SVic WSuV
- RIESLING-SILVANER   see V. vinifera 'Müller-Thurgau'
- 'Rotberger' (O/G/B)   WSuV
- 'Royal Muscadine' (G/O/W)   WMat WSuV
- 'Saint Laurent' (G/O/W)   SVic WSuV
- 'Sauvignon Blanc' (O/W)   CTsd EBee EPfP SVic
- § 'Schiava Grossa' (G/B/D)   CBcs CDoC CMac EGren EHeP EPfP EPom LCro LSRN MAsh NPer SPre SVic WFar WMat
- 'Schönburger' (O/W)   SVic
- 'Schwarzriesling'   see V. vinifera 'Pinot Meunier'
- 'Sémillon' (G/O/W)   LRHS LSRN MAsh SVic
- 'Siegerrebe' (O/W/D)   CAgr MAsh NPer SPoG SVic

- 'Souvignier Gris' (R) **new**   WSuV
- 'Spetchley Red' (O/B) ♀H5   CRHN ECha LRHS MNrw WCot WCru WHtc WLov WSpi
- strawberry grape   see V. 'Fragola'
- 'Suffolk Red' (G/R/S)   EPfP EPom MSwo NLar SPoG SVic
- § 'Sultana' (W/S)   CAgr
- 'Syrah' (G/B)   SVic
- 'Tempranillo' (O/B)   NPlm SVic
- 'Thompson Seedless'   see V. vinifera 'Sultana'
- * 'Triomphe' (O/B)   SVic WSuV
- 'Uva di Troia' (B) **new**   EOli
- 'Verdejo' (O/W)   SVic
- 'Victoria' (O/W)   NPlm
- § 'Viura' (G/W)   SVic
- 'Vroege van der Laan' (O/W)   EGren NLar SNig SRms WFar WHtc
- 'Zalagyöngye' (W)   CAgr

Volutaria (Asteraceae)
muricata   CSpe WSpi

Vriesea (Bromeliaceae)
'Astrid' ♀H1a   LBom LCro NCft
bleheri   NCft
correia-arauji   NCft
'Era'^{PBR}   LCro LWaG
'Eros P'   MPri
fenestralis   NCft
fosteriana 'Red Chestnut'   NCft
gigantea 'Nova'   NCft
hieroglyphica   NCft
'Porto'^{PBR}   LCro
saundersii   NCft
splendens ♀H1a   MPri
sucrei   NCft

W

Wachendorfia (Haemodoraceae)
multiflora   CPbh
thyrsiflora   CBct CDoC CExl CTsd EBee ESwi EUrb LEdu SPlb SVen WCot WPGP
- 'Pan's Persistent'   WPGP

Wahlenbergia (Campanulaceae)
albomarginata   EDAr
gloriosa   EDAr EPot MNrw WAbe
hederacea   GArf
pumilio   see Edraianthus pumilio
undulata   CSpe

Waldsteinia (Rosaceae)
fragarioides   GKev
geoides   CFis EMor EPPr GKev MAvo MHtn MMuc NEoE NLar
ternata   Widely available
§ - 'Mozaick' (v)   EBee EHeP NBir
- 'Variegata'   see W. ternata 'Mozaick'

Wallichia (Arecaceae)
disticha   NPlm

walnut, black see Juglans nigra

walnut, common see Juglans regia

Wasabia (Brassicaceae)
wasabi   see Eutrema japonicum

Washingtonia ❀ (Arecaceae)
× *filibusta* SEND
filifera ♀H1c NPlm SArc SBig SPlb
robusta CBlu EGren ERom EUrb LBom
 LWaG NHrt NPlm SAth SBig SFol
 SPlb

Watsonia (Iridaceae)
aletroides CPbh EPPr SVen
angusta CExl EBee SPlb
ardernei see *W. borbonica* subsp. *ardernei*
 (Sander) Goldblatt 'Arderne's White'
beatricis see *W. pillansii*
§ *borbonica* EShb
 -subsp. *ardernei* see *W. borbonica* subsp. *ardernei*
  misapplied (Sander) Goldblatt 'Arderne's White'
§ - subsp. *ardenei* (Sander) CExl
  Goldblatt 'Arderne's
  White'
borbonica 'Peach Glow' CBlu EBee EGrI EPPr EShb XFar
coccinea dwarf CPbh
'Curly Blooms' CPbh
'Dart Sea Trout' EBee EGrI
fourcadei EGrI
galpinii WCot
hybrid, burnt-orange- CPbh
 flowered
- dark pink-flowered CPbh
- orange-flowered CPbh
- peach-flowered CPbh
laccata CPbh
lepida SPlb
× *longifolia* EBee
marginata CPbh
marlothii CExl EBee MNrw WCot WMal
 WPGP
meriana EBee EGrI GKev LAma MHtn
- var. *bulbillifera* CPbh EBee EShb ESwi GAbr SMrm
'Peachy Pink Orphan' EBee
§ *pillansii* CExl CPbh EPfP EShb GBin LEdu
 SVen
- apricot-flowered CTsd
- hybrid WMal
- peach-flowered CExl
- pink-flowered CExl
- red-flowered CExl
- salmon-flowered CSpe
pink-flowered EBee
pyramidata see *W. borbonica*
'Special Red' CPbh
'Stanford Scarlet' CExl
tabularis CPbh
transvaalensis EBee
'Tresco Dwarf Pink' CExl EBee EGrI LEdu LRHS WPGP
Tresco hybrids CAbb CExl CPbh EPfP EShb SRkn
vanderspuyae CBcs CExl EAri EGrI
wilmaniae CExl WFar
zeyheri CPbh

Wattakaka see *Dregea*

Weigela ❀ (Caprifoliaceae)
'Abel Carrière' SRms WFar WSpi
(All Summer Series) CSpe EGren EPfP LCro LRHS MAsh
 ALL SUMMER PEACH MMrt MPri NLar
 ('Slingpink'PBR)
§ - ALL SUMMER RED CEnd CWGN EBee EGren EPfP
 ('Slingco 1'PBR) LCro LRHS MAsh MMrt MPri NLar
 SPoG WSpi
'Avalanche' misapplied see *W.* 'Candida'

BLACK AND WHITE CBcs CDoC CSBt CWGN CWnw
 ('Courtacad 1'PBR) EBee ELan EPfP LRHS LSRN NEoE
 NLar SGol SNig SPoG
§ BRIANT RUBIDOR CEnd CMac MGos MMrt MSwo NLar
 ('Olympiade') (v) NQui SGol SPlb SPoG WFar WSpi
'Bristol Ruby' CBcs CBrac CBWd CMac CSBt EBee
 EGren EHeP ELan EPfP GKin LCro
 LRHS LSto MGos MHer MMuc
 MSwo NLar SAdn SEND SGol SPlb
 SRms WFar WKif WSpi
'Bristol Snowflake' CMac EHeP EPfP MBlu NLar SRms
CAMOUFLAGE ('Tmwg15-01') LSto WLov
 (v)
§ 'Candida' CBrac EGren ELan SAdn SGol WSpi
CAPPUCCINO ('Verweig2'PBR) MBlu NLar SGol
CARNAVAL ('Courtalor') ♀H6 CBcs EGren MSwo
'Chameleon' NEoE SGol
CHERRY LOVE CSBt
 ('Slingco 2') **new**
coraeensis ♀H6 CBcs CHll EPfP MBlu MMrt MNrw
 NLar SBrt
CRIMSON KISSES see *W.* (All Summer Series) ALL SUMMER
 RED
decora B&SWJ 10834 WCru
EBONY AND IVORY ('Velda'PBR) EPfP LCro LRHS NLar SGol
'Eva Rathke' EHeP NLar
'Evita' MBlu
floribunda B&SWJ 10831 WCru
florida CMac EHeP SAdn SAth
- B&SWJ 8439 WCru
§ - 'Alexandra' ♀H6 CBcs CDoC CSBt EGrI GKev LRHS
 LSRN MAsh MGos NBro SAdn SAth
 SNig SRGP SRkn
- ALL SUMMER MONET CSBt LCro LSou SNig
 ('Verweig 8'PBR)
 (All Summer Series)
- 'Bicolor' CMac ELan
- 'Foliis Purpureis' CBcs CBrac CMac EGren EHeP
 ELan LRHS LSto MGos NLar SPlb
 SRms WHtc
- 'Gustave Malet' CMCN
- MAGICAL RAINBOW EBee EPfP LCro LRHS MAsh NEoE
 ('Kolmagira'PBR) SAth SGol SPoG
- MINOR BLACK EGren EPfP MGos MHtn NBro
 ('Verweig 3'PBR) NEoE SGol SPoG
- MONET ('Verweig'PBR) (v) CDoC CMac CWnw EBee EGren
 EPfP LBuc LCro LRHS LSRN MAsh
 MGos MMrt NBro NLar SAdn SGol
 SPoG SRms
- MOULIN ROUGE ELan EPfP MAsh MGos
 ('Brigela'PBR)
- 'Pink Princess' EPfP MSwo NLar
- 'Princess Ayla' MHtn NLar
- RUBIGOLD see *W.* BRIANT RUBIDOR
- STRAWBERRIES AND CREAM see *W. florida* 'Versicolor'
- (Towers of Flowers Series) WLov
 TOWERS OF FLOWERS APPLE
 BLOSSOM ('Tmwg16-02')
- - TOWERS OF FLOWERS CHERRY CSBt
 ('Tmwg16-04')
§ - 'Versicolor' CMHG LShi MPro SRGP SRms
- VINTAGE LOVE ('Tvp1'PBR) MBNS
 (Love Series) **new**
- WINE AND ROSES see *W. florida* 'Alexandra'
- 'Wings of Fire'PBR EBee EGrI ELan EPfP LCro NLar
'Florida Variegata' (v) ♀H6 CBcs CBrac CMac CWal EBee
 EGren EHeP ELan EPfP LCro LSto
 MAsh MBNS MGos MHer MMuc
 MSwo NBid SDix SEND SGol SPlb
 SPoG SRGP SRms WFar WHtc
'Gold Rush' NLar

'Golden Candy'	NEoE		- 'Morning Light' (v)	SEle
hortensis	CExl		- 'Variegata' (v)	CCoa CPbh CSde SRms SVen
- B&SWJ 10808	WCru		*longifolia*	SEle
'Hulsdonk'	NLar		*rosmariniformis*	see *W. fruticosa*
japonica 'Dart's Colourdream'	EWes GPSL MMuc SAdn SEND SGol		'Wynyabbie Gem'	MMuc SEle SEND SPoG SVen
'Jean's Gold'	MBlu			

whitecurrant see *Ribes rubrum* (W); also AGM Fruit Section

'Kosteriana Variegata' (v)	CDoC CSBt EBee EGren ELan EPfP LRHS MSwo SRms SVen
'Little Red Robin'	NEoE WFar
'Looymansii Aurea'	CBrac EPfP SGol SRms WFar
LUCIFER ('Courtared')	WSpi
'Marjorie'	EGren NLar
§ *middendorffiana*	CBcs CEnd CExl CMac CMCN EBee EGrI ELan EPfP LRHS MAsh MBlu MMuc NLar SBrt SNig SPoG SVen WCru WFar WPGP
- 'Mango'	LCro
'Minuet'	MSwo NEoE SGol
'Mont-Blanc'	MAsh MMrt
NAIN ROUGE ('Courtanin')	NLar
'Nana Variegata' (v)	EGren ELon LCro LSto NLar SOrN WFar
NAOMI CAMPBELL ('Bokrashine'^PBR)	EGrI MMuc SGol
'Newport Red'	see *W.* 'Vanicek'
PICOBELLA ROSA ('Tvp2'^PBR)	CWGN EBee LCro LRHS MBros NLar WSpi
PICOBELLA ROSSO ('Tvp3'^PBR)	LSou NLar WHtc
PINK POPPET ('Plangen'^PBR)	CEnd CSBt ELan EPfP LRHS LSRN MAsh MGos SPoG SRkn SVen WLov
praecox	WPGP
- B&SWJ 8705	WCru
'Praecox Variegata' (v) ♀H6	CMac EPfP LRHS MAsh NBir SDix SPoG SRms WKif
'Red Prince' ♀H6	CBcs CDoC CoPl EBee EGren EPfP LRHS MAsh MNrw MSwo NLar SGol
RUBIDOR	see *W.* BRIANT RUBIDOR
RUBIGOLD	see *W.* BRIANT RUBIDOR
'Ruby Anniversary'	NLar
'Ruby Queen'^PBR	CMac
'Rumba'	CMac
sessilifolia	see *Diervilla sessilifolia*
'Snowflake'	EPfP SRms
'Stelzneri'	EGren
subsessilis B&SWJ 1056	WCru
- B&SWJ 4206	WCru
'Suzanne' (v)	NLar
'Tango'	ELan NEoE WFar
§ 'Vanicek'	CBrac
'Victoria'	CMac EGren LRHS MGos MPro MSwo NBir SAdn
WHITE LIGHTNING ('Wf-2009') (v)	NEoE

Weingartia see *Rebutia*

Weinmannia (Cunoniaceae)
trichosperma	CBcs

Weldenia (Commelinaceae)
candida	GEdr NHar SChF WCot

Wendtia (Francoaceae)
gracilis **new**	SBrt

Westringia (Lamiaceae)
brevifolia	CCoa CSde SVen
eremicola 'Blue'	CAbb
§ *fruticosa* ♀H2	CBcs CCoa CMCN CSde LRHS SEle SRms SVen

Whiteheadia (Asparagaceae)
bifolia	LAma

Wikstroemia (Thymelaeaceae)
gemmata	see *Daphne gemmata*

wineberry see *Rubus phoenicolasius*

Wisteria ✿ (Fabaceae)
§ *brachybotrys*	MPri WSpi
§ - f. *albiflora* 'Shiro-kapitan' ♀H6	CBcs CEnd CWGN CWnw EBee ELan EPfP LCro LRHS LSRN MGos MPri NLar SArc SPoG WHtc WPGP WSpi WTHo
- (Grande Diva Series) BARBARA ('Minwikb25')	CWGN
- - NATHALIE ('Minwijd04')	CWGN CWnw
- 'Howick'	NCth NLar
- 'Okayama' ♀H6	CCVT CDoC CWnw EGren EPfP EUrb LBom LCro LRHS MGos SVen WMat WTHo
- 'Showa-beni' ♀H6	CAco CEnd CWGN CWnw ELon EPfP LBom LCro LMaj LRHS MBlu MGos MPri NCth NLar SPoG SVen WPGP WSpi
'Burford'	see *W.* × *valderi* 'Burford'
floribunda	CBcs CBrac CRHN EGren LCro NPlm SEWo
- B&SWJ 12748 from South Korea	WCru
§ - f. *alba* 'Shiro-noda' ♀H6	Widely available
- BLACK DRAGON	see *W. floribunda* 'Kokuryū'
- CECILIA ('Minwica05') (Grande Diva Series)	CWnw LRHS
§ - 'Domino' ♀H6	CBcs CDoC CMac CWGN CWnw EBee ELon EPfP LBom LCro LRHS LSRN MAsh MGos MPri MSwo NCth NLar SSta WCha WSpi
- 'Ed's Blue Dragon' (d)	CWGN EBee EPfP LRHS
- 'Eranthema'	see *W.* × *valderi* 'Eranthema'
- 'Fragrantissima'	see *W. sinensis* var. *sinensis* f. *alba* 'Jako'
- 'Geisha'	CBcs CEnd EPfP LRHS NCth NLar SRms SVen WPGP
- 'Golden Dragon'	see *W.* × *valderi* 'Murasaki-kapitan'
- 'Harlequin'	CBcs EBee ELon EPfP LCro LRHS
- 'Honey Bee Pink'	see *W. floribunda* f. *rosea* 'Hon-beni'
- 'Issai Perfect'	LRHS LSRN NLar
- 'Issai-naga'	EBee NLar
- 'Jakohn-fuji'	see *W. sinensis* var. *sinensis* f. *alba* 'Jako'
- 'Kimono' ♀H6	LCro LRHS MBlu NLar
§ - 'Kokuryū' ♀H6	CBcs CCVT CDoC CEnd CMac EGren EGrI ELan IPot LCro LRHS MAsh MPri NLar SPoG WHtc WPGP WSpi WTHo
- 'Lawrence' ♀H6	CCVT CMac CWGN LCro LRHS NLar SPoG WPGP
- 'Lipstick'	see *W. floribunda* f. *rosea* 'Kuchi-beni'
- 'Longissima'	see *W. floribunda* f. *multijuga* 'Kyushaku'

- 'Longissima Alba'	see *W. floribunda* f. *alba* 'Shiro-noda'		- 'Amethyst' ♀H6	CBcs CCVT CDoC CEnd EGrI EPfP LCro LRHS LSRN MAsh MGos WCha WLov WPGP WSpi
- 'Macrobotrys'	see *W. floribunda* f. *multijuga* 'Kyushaku'		- 'Consequa'	see *W. sinensis* 'Prolific'
- f. *microphylla* 'Hime'	WPGP		- 'Cooke's Special'	see *W. sinensis* 'Prolific'
- f. *multijuga*	CCVT CEnd CMac CWGN EBee ELan ELon EPfP LCro LRHS MBlu MGos NLar SArc SPoG SRms SSta WHtc WPGP WSpi WTHo	I	- 'Oosthoek's Variety' - 'Pink Ice' - 'Prematura' - 'Prematura Alba'	see *W. sinensis* 'Prolific' MAsh SRms see *W. floribunda* 'Domino' see *W. brachybotrys* f. *albiflora* 'Shiro-kapitan'
- - 'Cascade'	CBcs LRHS NLar WSpi			
§ - - 'Kyushaku'	LBom LRHS MAsh MBlu MPri SVen WPGP	§	- 'Prolific' ♀H6 - 'Rosea'	Widely available LSRN MPri
- MURASAKI-NAGA	see *W. floribunda* 'Purple Patches'		- 'Shiro-capital'	see *W. brachybotrys* f. *albiflora* 'Shiro-kapitan'
- 'Nana Richin's Purple'	CEnd			
- 'Peaches and Cream'	see *W. floribunda* f. *rosea* 'Kuchi-beni'		- var. *sinensis* f. *alba*	CBcs CDoC EHeP ELan EPfP ERom LCro LRHS LSRN LSto MAsh MGos MPri MSwo SPoG SRms WFar
- 'Pink Ice'	see *W. floribunda* f. *rosea* 'Hon-beni'			
§ - 'Purple Patches'	LRHS WSpi	§	- - - 'Jako' ♀H6	CEnd LCro LRHS SArc
- REINDEER	see *W. sinensis* var. *sinensis* f. *alba* 'Jako'		- 'Texas Purple' - 'Tiverton'	LRHS LRHS
			× *valderi*	CDoC
§ - f. *rosea* 'Hon-beni' ♀H6	CBcs CDoC CEnd CMac CWGN EBee EGrI ELan ELon EPfP IArd LCro LRHS LSRN MBlu MGos MPri MSwo NLar SPoG SRms SWor WCha WHtc WMat	§	- 'Burford' ♀H6 - 'Eranthema' - 'Lavender Lace'	CEnd CMac CWGN EPfP LCro LRHS LSRN MAsh MGos MPri MSwo SRms WMat WPGP WSpi NCth NLar CBcs EPfP LCro LRHS MAsh NLar
§ - - 'Kuchi-beni'	CBcs CCVT CEnd ELan EPfP IPot LCro LRHS LSRN MGos NLar SPoG SRms	§	- 'Murasaki-kapitan' *venusta*	CEnd CMac CWGN EPfP LMaj LRHS see *W. brachybotrys* f. *albiflora* 'Shiro-kapitan'
- 'Royal Purple'	see *W. floribunda* 'Kokuryū'		- 'Alba'	see *W. brachybotrys* f. *albiflora* 'Shiro-kapitan'
- 'Russelliana'	see *W. floribunda* 'Kokuryū'			
- 'Shiro-naga'	see *W. floribunda* f. *alba* 'Shiro-noda'		- var. *violacea*	see *W. × valderi* 'Murasaki-kapitan'
- 'Snow Showers'	see *W. floribunda* f. *alba* 'Shiro-noda'			
- 'Strella'	NLar		***Wisteriopsis*** (Fabaceae)	
- 'Variegata' (v)	CWGN	§	*reticulata*	LCro LMaj
- 'Violacea Plena'	see *W. floribunda* 'Yae-kokuryū'		- 'Satsuma'	see *W. reticulata*
§ - 'Yae-kokuryū' (d) ♀H6	CBcs CCVT CEnd CMac CWGN EBee ELan EPfP LCro LMaj LRHS LSRN NLar SPoG SRms SSta WCha WMat		***Withania*** (Solanaceae)	
			sinensis BWJ 8093	WCru
			somnifera	MHoo
× *formosa*	CCVT CEnd LCro		***Wittsteinia*** (Alseuosmiaceae)	
- BLACK DRAGON	see *W. floribunda* 'Kokuryū'		*vacciniacea*	GEdr WCru
- 'Caroline'	CBcs CDoC CMac CWGN CWnw EPfP LCro LRHS LSRN MAsh MGos MPri NCth NLar SPoG SRms WMat WPGP WSpi WTHo		***Wodyetia*** (Arecaceae)	
			bifurcata	NPlm
			Wollemia (Araucariaceae)	
- 'Domino'	see *W. floribunda* 'Domino'		*nobilis*	CAco CDTJ EGren ELan MGos NPlm NTrD SArc SPoG
- 'Enchantment'	MBlu NCth NLar			
- 'Issai' Wada *pro parte*	see *W. floribunda* 'Domino'		***Woodsia*** (Woodsiaceae)	
- 'Ivy Hatch'	WPGP		*obtusa*	CLAP EBee EMor ISha LRHS NBro SPoG SRms SRot WCot
- 'Kokuryū'	see *W. floribunda* 'Kokuryū'			
- 'Yae-kokuryū'	see *W. floribunda* 'Yae-kokuryū'		*polystichoides*	SRms
frutescens	CDoC LCro LRHS MPri			
- 'Alba'	see *W. frutescens* 'Nivea'		***Woodwardia*** (Blechnaceae)	
- 'Amethyst Falls'PBR	CBcs CEnd CMac CSpe CWGN EGren ELan EPfP EUrb IArd LBuc LCro LRHS LSRN MGos Midl MMuc MPri SPoG WLov		from Emei Shan, China	CLAP
			areolata	WPGP
			fimbriata ♀H3	Widely available
			orientalis	CLAP ESwi LEdu MAsh
- 'Longwood Purple'	CDoC LCro MGos		- var. *formosana*	LEdu SPlb
- var. *macrostachya* 'Aunt Dee'	CWGN CWnw LRHS NLar		- - B&SWJ 6865 *prolifera* ♀H3	ESwi WCru ECha EPfP EUrb LEdu SHor SPlb WPGP
- - 'Blue Moon'	LCro LRHS MBlu WSpi			
- - 'Clara Mack'	CWGN LCro LRHS WSpi		*radicans* ♀H3	CAbb CDTJ EUrb EWld NBir SMad
- - 'Magnifica'	LRHS		*unigemmata* ♀H4	CLAP CTsd EWes EWld LEdu LRHS SPlb WAbe WCot WPGP
§ - 'Nivea'	CCVT EPfP LRHS			
Kapitan-fuji	see *W. brachybotrys*			
multijuga 'Alba'	see *W. floribunda* f. *alba* 'Shiro-noda'		**Worcesterberry** see *Ribes* 'Worcesterberry'	
sinensis	CBcs CCVT CWnw EGrI EHeP EPfP LCro LRHS LSRN LSto MCtn MGos MPri SArc SAth SEWo SRms SSta SWor WFar WJur WLov WTHo			

Wulfenia (Plantaginaceae)
- amherstiana — GEdr
- baldaccii — EBee GKev SBrt
- carinthiaca — EBee EMor GArf GEdr GKev LEdu MCtn NBir NLar WCot
- - 'Alba' — GEdr GKev
- × schwarzii — CDor CMiW LEdu

Wurmbea (Colchicaceae)
§ stricta — WCot

Wyethia (Asteraceae)
- angustifolia — SBrt
- mollis B&SWJ 14067 — WCru

X

Xanthisma (Asteraceae)
- coloradoense — GEdr
  - pink-flowered
- - white-flowered — GEdr

Xanthoceras (Sapindaceae)
- sorbifolium ♀H7 — CAgr CBcs CMCN EBee MBlu MCtn NLar SPoG WPGP WSpi

Xanthocyparis (Cupressaceae)
§ nootkatensis — CAco MAsh
- - 'Aurea' — CAco
- - 'Boyko's Sundown' — CAco
- - 'Flaming Arrow' — CAco
- - 'Glauca' — CAco
- - 'Gloria Polonica'PBR (v) — CAco NLar
- - 'Golden Waterfall' — CAco NLar
- - 'Gracilis' — CAco
- - 'Green Arrow' ♀H7 — CAco NLar NPip
- - 'Jubilee' — NPip
- - 'Moon Shot' — CAco NLar
- - 'Nordkroken' — CAco
- - 'Pendula' ♀H7 — CAco CCVT ELan EPfP ESwi MAsh MBlu MPri
I - 'Pendula Aurea' — CAco
- - 'Sparkling Arrow' — CAco
- - 'Strict Weeper' — CAco NLar
- - 'Variegata' (v) — CAco
- vietnamensis — WPGP

Xanthogalum see Angelica

Xanthorhiza (Ranunculaceae)
- simplicissima — CBcs CToG EPfP LEdu NBir NLar SEle WCot WPGP

Xanthorrhoea (Asphodelaceae)
- australis — SPlb
- fulva — SPlb
- johnsonii — NPlm SPlb
- preissii — CTsd NPlm SBig SPlb

Xanthosoma (Araceae)
- lindenii — see Caladium lindenii
- sagittifolium — EAri LAma
- violaceum — CLil CTsd EAri LAma SBig

Xeranthemum (Asteraceae)
- annuum — MCtn
- cylindraceum — MCtn

Xerochrysum (Asteraceae)
- bracteatum 'Coco' — CSpe WMal
§ - 'Dargan Hill Monarch' — SRms
- - 'King Fireball' — CSpe
- - 'Nevada Gold' — LRHS
- - 'Nevada Orange' — LRHS
- - 'Nevada Red' — LRHS
- - 'Salmon Rose' — CSpe MCtn
- - 'Scarlet' — MCtn
- - 'Silvery Rose' — CSpe MCtn

Xeronema (Xeronemataceae)
- callistemon — CTsd

Xerophyllum (Melanthiaceae)
- tenax — LRHS MCtn

Xerophyta (Velloziaceae)
- retinervis — SPlb

Y

Ypsilandra (Melanthiaceae)
- cavaleriei — CExl GEdr WCot WFar
- thibetica — CBct CExl CSpe CTtf EBee ELan EPfP EPPr ESwi GEdr GKev LEdu MBlu MNrw SMad WCAu WCot WCru

Yua (Vitaceae)
§ thomsonii BWJ 8123 — EPPr

Yucca ✿ (Asparagaceae)
- aloifolia — CBcs CBlu CDTJ SArc SPlb
§ - f. marginata (v) — NPlm
- - 'Purpurea' — NPlm
- - 'Variegata' — see Y. aloifolia f. marginata
- angustifolia — see Y. glauca
- arizonica — CDTJ
- baccata — CAgr CDoC EUrb NPlm SPlb
- campestris — CDTJ
- carnerosana — CBlu CDTJ EUrb
- constricta — CDTJ
§ elata — NPlm
* elegans — NPlm
§ elephantipes ♀H2 — CDTJ LCro LInT LWaG MPri NHrt NPlm NTrD SAth SEND
- - 'Elmila' (v) — NPlm
- - 'Jewel' (v) — EPfP EUrb MPri NPlm SBig SEND SWor
- - 'Puck' (v) — SEND
- - variegated (v) — EBee SEND
- faxoniana — CDTJ EUrb NPlm SPlb
- filamentosa — CAgr CBcs CLil CMac CWal EBee EHeP ELan EPfP EUrb LCro LRHS MGos MSwo SAth SEND SIvy SPlb SRms WHtc XFar
- - 'Bright Edge' (v) ♀H4 — CBcs EHeP ELan EUrb LCro LRHS SGol WCha XFar
- - 'Color Guard' (v) ♀H5 — CBcs CTsd ELan EPfP EUrb LRHS MGos NPlm SBig SIvy SMad SPeP SPoG WCha WMal
- - 'Garland's Gold' (v) — CBcs
- - 'Gold Heart' (v) — LRHS NPlm SHor WCot
- - 'Variegata' (v) — SArc SRms
- filifera — EOli EUrb NPlm SPlb
- - 'Australis' — NPlm

Yucca

flaccida 'Golden Sword' (v) ♀H4	CBcs EBee EGren EHeP ELan GMaP MGos NLar SRms WCha WFar XFar
- 'Ivory' ♀H5	CTsd GMaP LRHS NLar SRms
× *floribunda*	SArc
§ *glauca*	CExl EUrb SPlb WCot
gloriosa ♀H5	CBcs CMac CWnw ERom GBin SArc SBig SEND SPlb WCha WFar
- 'Aureovariegata'	see *Y. gloriosa* 'Variegata'
- Bright Star ('Walbristar'^PBR) (v) ♀H5	CCht EUrb LCro LRHS LSou
- 'Lone Star'	EUrb NPlm
§ - 'Variegata' (v) ♀H5	CBcs CDoC CMac CSBt EGrl EHeP ELan ELon EPfP GMaP LRHS MAsh NPlm SArc SAth SBig SEND SFol SIvy SPlb SPoG SRms WCha WHtc
guatemalensis	see *Y. elephantipes*
harrimaniae	SPlb WCot
linearifolia	NPlm
linearis	see *Y. thompsoniana*
mexicana	CDTJ
pallida	NPlm SPlb
potosina	NPlm
radiosa	see *Y. elata*
recurvifolia ♀H5	SArc SBig
- Banana Split ('Monca') (v)	WCot
- 'Gold Stream' (v)	WCot
rigida	CDTJ NPlm
- 'Blue Sentry' **new**	LRHS
rostrata	CBcs CBlu CCht CDoC CDTJ CSpe EOli EUrb LRHS NPlm SArc SAth SBig SFol SPlb
- 'Blue Swan'	NLar NPlm
- 'Hidra'	NPlm
- 'Sapphire Skies'	CMac CSpe LRHS
§ *thompsoniana*	CDTJ EUrb NPlm
torreyi	CDTJ
treculeana	CBlu NPlm
'Vittorio Emanuele II'	SMad
whipplei	see *Hesperoyucca whipplei*

Yushania (Poaceae)

KR 7698	MWht
§ *anceps*	CAgr CBcs MMuc MWht SEND
- 'Pitt White'	CAgr MWht
brevipaniculata	MWht
maculata	CAgr CExl ELon MWht
Yunnan 5	CExl MWht

Z

Zabelia (Caprifoliaceae)

§ *triflora*	CExl MBlu NLar SChF SEND WPGP
§ *tyaihyonii*	CBcs CMCN ELan EPfP LRHS MBlu NLar NQui
- Bridal Bouquet ('Monia')	ELan LRHS MPri SChF
§ *umbellata*	SBrt

Zaluzianskya (Scrophulariaceae)

capensis 'Midnight Candy'	MCtn
elongata	SPlb
microsiphon	SPlb
ovata	CBcs CPbh CTtf EPfP EPot GElm GKev LCro LShi MHer SPlb SPoG WFar WIce
- 'Orange Eye'	CPbh EDAr ELan GKev LCro WIce
- 'Star Balsam'	CAby CTsd LRHS Midl
pulvinata	SPlb

Zamia (Zamiaceae)

floridana	NPlm
furfuracea	NPlm
pumila	SPlb

Zamioculcas (Araceae)

zamiifolia ♀H1b	CDoC EHap LBom LCro LWaG NHrt SPre
- Raven ('Dowon'^PBR)	LBom LCro LInT NHrt
- Zenzi ('Hansoti 13'^PBR)	NHrt

Zantedeschia (Araceae)

§ *aethiopica*	CBcs CBen CDoC CDor CExl CLil CoPl CTsd EAri EGren EGrl ELin EUrb EWat EWes GKev LAma LCro LRHS LShi LWaG NBir NPer SAth SBig SDix SRms WFar XFar
- 'Apple Court Babe'	ELon
- 'Childsiana'	EBee EPfP
- 'Crowborough' ♀H4	CBcs CLil CMac CSde CToG CWat EBee ECha EGren ELan ELin ELon EPfP GMaP LCro SArc SEND SHor SMrm SPlb SPoG SRms WCot WCru WFar WSpi
- 'Flamingo'^PBR	CDoC CDor LBar LRHS
- 'Glencoe'	CBct EBee ESwi GAbr MAvo MHol MNrw SMad SPad WCot WFar WHoo WMal WPGP
- 'Glow'	CExl CMac
- 'Green Goddess' ♀H4	CBcs CCps CDor CExl CLil CMac CSde CToG EBee ECha ELan EPfP EUrb LBar LEdu LRHS MAsh NPlm NWbg SBig SRms WCot WFar
- 'Little Gem'	SMad
- 'Luzon Lovely'	ESwi WCru
- 'Marshmallow'	CCps CToG EPfP LBar MMrt WFar
- 'Mr Martin'	ELon WCot WFar
- 'Pershore Fantasia' (v)	CCps CDTJ CExl EAri WCot WFar
- 'Snow White'^PBR	LBar
- 'Spotted Giant'	CDTJ
- 'White Gnome'	CCps WCot WFar
'Airbrush'^PBR	LRHS
'Akela'	XFar
albomaculata	SPlb WMal WPGP XFar
- subsp. *albomaculata*	CCps SPlb WCot
'Auckland'^PBR	XFar
'Best Gold'	see *Z.* 'Florex Gold'
'Black Magic'	CMac
'Calgary'^PBR	LRHS
Callafornia Red ('Gscccare'^PBR)	MAsh WFar
'Cancun'^PBR	LCro
'Cantor'^PBR	LRHS XFar
(Captain Series) 'Captain Brunello'^PBR	LRHS
- 'Captain Kelso'^PBR	LCro
- 'Captain Murano'^PBR	SPoG XFar
- 'Captain Prado'^PBR	SPoG XFar
- 'Captain Promise'^PBR	XFar
- 'Captain Romance'^PBR	LCro XFar
- 'Captain Rosette'^PBR	XFar
- 'Captain Safari'^PBR	XFar
- 'Captain Samba'^PBR	LRHS
- 'Captain Tulsa'	LCro
- 'Captain Ventura'^PBR	XFar
'Cherry Kiss'^PBR	LCro
'Crystal Blush'	LRHS
'Crystal Clear'	MAsh
Dubai Nights ('Dozanduni'^PBR)	LRHS

elliottiana ♀H1c	WMal
'Festival'PBR	SRms
§ 'Florex Gold'	XFar
'French Kiss'	LCro
'Garnet Glow'	LCro
'Gold Crown'	MAsh
'Goliath'	WPGP
'Havana'PBR **new**	LRHS
'Helen O'Connor'	CExl
'Hercules'	CCps EAri ESwi NPlm
'Hot Shot'	WMal XFar
'Kiwi Blush'	CCps CDoC CDor CExl CLil CSpe CToG EAri ELan ELon EPfP LBar WCot WFar
'Lime Lady'	ECha
Macau ('Dozanmaca'PBR)	LRHS
'Mango'	SRms XFar
'Memories'PBR	EAri LRHS
'Morning Sun'PBR	LCro LRHS MAsh
'Night Club' **new**	MAsh
'Nightlife'PBR	SRms
'Odessa'PBR	LCro
odorata	WCot
'Paco'PBR	LCro
'Picasso'PBR	CCps XFar
'Pink Jewel'PBR	XFar
'Purple Haze'	XFar
'Red Alert'PBR	LRHS
'Red Charm'PBR	LRHS
'Red Sox'PBR	XFar
rehmannii ♀H1c	SRms
Ruby Sensation ('Gsccrute'PBR)	WFar
'Sapporo'PBR	LRHS
'Schwarzwalder'PBR	XFar
'Sunclub'PBR	LRHS
'White Giant'	CCps CDor EUrb EWat MAvo MPie WCot

Zanthorhiza see *Xanthorhiza*

Zanthoxylum (Rutaceae)

sp.	WPGP
acanthopodium	WJur WPGP
- GWJ 9287	WCru
- PAB 8760	LEdu
- WJC 13653	WCru
ailanthoides	CDTJ LEdu
- from Japan	WPGP
- - B&SWJ 11115	WCru
americanum	ELan ESwi WJur
armatum	CAgr WJur
- B&SWJ 12753	WCru
- CWJ 12824	WCru
- FMWJ 13091	WCru
- NJM 11.08	WPGP
- PAB 8902	LEdu
bungeanum	NLar WJur
- BWJ 8040	ESwi WCru
coreanum	NLar
fauriei B&SWJ 11080	WCru
aff. *fauriei* B&SWJ 11371	WCru
- B&SWJ 11523	WCru
* *giraldii*	EBee LEdu WJur
laetum FMWJ 13175	WCru
oxyphyllum	WPGP
- GWJ 9428	WCru
- HWJK 2131	WCru
piperitum	CAgr ELan EPfP LEdu LRHS MEar WFar WJek WJur WPGP WTre
- B&SWJ 11377	WCru
- B&SWJ 14677	WCru
- var. *inerme*	WPGP
- - B&SWJ 10934	WCru
§ - 'Kuro-fune'	CBcs CDTJ CExl EPfP EUrb SBig WPGP
- purple-leaved	see *Z. piperitum* 'Kuro-fune'
schinifolium	CAgr WJur
- B&SWJ 11080	WCru
simulans	CAgr CBcs CExl ESwi LCro LEdu MBlu MCtn MHoo NLar WJek WJur WPGP
tomentellum B&SWJ 13903	WCru

Zauschneria see *Epilobium* (Z)

californica	see *Epilobium canum*
- subsp. *angustifolia*	see *Epilobium canum*
- subsp. *mexicana*	see *Epilobium canum*
villosa	see *Epilobium canum*

Zebrina see *Tradescantia*

Zelkova ✿ (Ulmaceae)

abelicea	CBcs CMCN MBlu WPGP
carpinifolia	MBlu WPGP
- PAB 13.047	LEdu
- NJM 13.016 from Azerbaijan	WPGP
serrata ♀H6	CAco CBcs CCVT CLnd CMCN CMen EBar EGrI EHeP ELan IPap LMaj MGos MMuc SEND SHor SPlb StAn WHtc WJur
- 'Burgundy Fall'	MBlu
- 'Goblin'	MBlu
- Green Vase ('Flekova')	LMaj MBlu NLar
- 'Kiwi Sunset'PBR	LRHS MGos SPoG
- 'Ogon'	MBlu
- 'Variegata' (v)	CJun EBee MBlu SGol
sicula	WPGP
× *verschaffeltii*	MBlu

Zenobia (Ericaceae)

pulverulenta	CBcs CDoC CMac ELan MAsh MBlu MGos SPad WFar
- 'Blue Sky'	CBcs CDoC EAri EPfP LRHS MAsh MBlu MMrt NLar SPoG WPGP
- 'Misty Blue'	ELan
- f. *nitida*	CMac
- 'Raspberry Ripple'	CBcs EAri ELan LRHS MAsh NLar SPoG

Zephyranthes (Amaryllidaceae)

candida	CBro EBee ELin EWld GKev LAma SMrm XFar
carinata	CTsd
citrina	GKev LAma
'Krakatau'	WCot
La Bufa Rosa Group	WCot
minuta ♀H2	ELin
robusta	see *Habranthus robustus*
rosea	GKev LAma

Zigadenus (Melanthiaceae)

elegans	see *Anticlea elegans*

Zingiber ✿ (Zingiberaceae)

chrysanthum	EAri SBig
clarkei	CTsd
malaysianum	EAri
mioga ♀H2	CAgr CExl CSpe CTsd EAri ELan LEdu LRHS MHoo NBid NCft SBig SNoN SPlb SRms WPGP

- 'Crûg's Zing'	EAri EPPr EWld LEdu SBrt WCru WFar WJun WPGP
- 'Dancing Crane' (v)	CExl CMac EAri EPPr EShb ESwi LEdu SBig SMad SRms WPGP
- 'Silver Arrow' (v)	EAri LEdu WPGP
- 'White Arrow'	EAri
- 'White Feather'	CExl EAri LEdu MAvo SHor WFar WPGP
officinale	SAth SPlb SPre
zerumbet	SBig

Zinnia (Asteraceae)

DAHLIA-FLOWERED MIXED	LCro MCtn
elegans	SVic
- (Benary's Giant Series) 'Benary's Giant Coral'	MCtn
- - 'Benary's Giant Golden Yellow' ♀H2	MCtn
- - 'Benary's Giant Lime'	CSpe MCtn
- BENARY'S GIANT MIXED	MCtn
- - 'Benary's Giant Salmon Rose' ♀H2	CSpe MCtn
- - 'Benary's Giant Scarlet' ♀H2	CSpe MCtn
- - 'Benary's Giant White'	MCtn
- - 'Benary's Giant Wine'	CSpe MCtn
- 'Envy' (d) ♀H2	LCro MCtn
- 'Inca' (d)	CSpe
- LILLIPUT MIXED	MCtn
- 'Luminosa'	MCtn
- 'Mazurkia' (d)	MCtn
- 'Purple Prince' (d) ♀H2	LCro MCtn
- (Queen Series) 'Queen Lime' (d)	MCtn
- - 'Queen Lime Orange' (d)	CSpe MCtn
- - 'Queen Lime Red' (d) ♀H2	CSpe LCro MCtn
- - 'Queen Lime with Blotch' (d)	MCtn
- SCABIOUS-FLOWERED MIXED (d)	MCtn
- 'Senora'	CSpe
- 'Super Yoga Rose' (Super Yoga Series)	MCtn
- WHIRLIGIG MIXED (d)	MCtn
- 'Zinderella Lilac' (d)	LCro MCtn
- 'Zinderella Peach' (d) ♀H2	MCtn
- 'Zinderella Purple' (d)	MCtn
GIANT CACTUS FLOWERED MIXED	MCtn
haageana JAZZY MIXED (d)	MCtn
marylandica ZAHARA FIRE ('Pas719124') (Zahara Series)	CSpe
Oklahoma Series ♀H2	LCro MCtn
- 'Oklahoma Pink'	MCtn
- 'Oklahoma Salmon'	MCtn
'Polar Bear'	MCtn
PROFUSION MIX (Profusion Series)	LWaG MBros
'Red Spider'	CSpe MCtn
'Super Yoga Dark Red'	MCtn
Zahara Series	MCtn

Zizia (Apiaceae)

aptera	SPhx
aurea	CAgr CSpe MNrw SDix SHor SMHy SPhx

Ziziphus (Rhamnaceae)

§ *jujuba* (F)	MBlu WJur
- 'Dongzao' (F)	WJur
- 'Lang' (F)	CAgr WJur
- 'Li' (F)	CAgr
sativa	see *Z. jujuba*

III
RHS AWARD OF GARDEN MERIT
FRUIT

Award of Garden Merit Fruit

This is a directory of RHS Award of Garden Merit (AGM) fruit offered by nurseries participating in the current edition of the *RHS Plant Finder*. It does not represent a complete list of AGM fruit.

Entries are accompanied by a short description and the relevant **hardiness rating** for the UK (see p.39 for an explanation of these). The figures to the left of the rating indicate the year of the award. Cultivars particularly suitable for culinary use are flagged **(C)**, while **(D)** denotes dessert fruit. **PG** indicates the pollination or flowering group (see Pollination).

Cultivation

All fruits are best grown in sheltered sites, with protection from spring frosts and cold winds. Brief guidance is given below on suitability for different locations, rootstocks, pollination and storage.

Location

Most of the **apple** cultivars listed here succeed all over the country, including the north of England. Those which have been found to be particularly successful in higher-rainfall and colder areas are **marked with an asterisk**; this is also used to highlight other fruits that have been found to be successful in northern regions. **Pears** crop best in sheltered warm situations; in the more exposed areas and northern counties, some pears will benefit from the protection of walls. **Plums** are susceptible to spring frosts and also need warm summers to ripen fully. Only early ripening plums can be relied upon in the shorter season of northern counties.

Currants, **gooseberries**, **raspberries** and **berry fruits** are generally satisfactory in most parts of the country, but cold winds at flowering time can be a problem. **Strawberries** can be grown all over the country, but will need some protection in exposed sites and from spring frosts. **Blueberries** are hardy plants but require light, well-drained, moisture-retentive, acid soil (pH 4.0–5.5).

Figs can crop satisfactorily in sheltered, warm situations in southern England. In northerly areas they will need protection such as a south-facing wall, or to be grown under glass or in polytunnels.

Pollination

Most tree fruits need to be pollinated by another tree of the same kind growing reasonably close by, which flowers at approximately the same time. Flowering groups are given in descriptions; for good pollination, choose cultivars from the same group, though those from adjacent groups will also serve as pollinators. **Apples** and **pears** listed as triploid are poor pollinators and require a normal (i.e. diploid) pollinator to set fruit. Gardeners should be aware that this diploid pollinator will not itself set fruit unless pollinated by another diploid tree. Many *Malus* species and crab apples, such as 'Golden Hornet' and 'Evereste', are also a good source of pollen for dessert and culinary apples. A number of the **plums** listed are self-fertile or partly self-fertile and will produce crops without a pollinator, but a pollinator is needed for all other plums. **Cherries** listed as self-fertile will crop without a pollinator, but otherwise cherries need a pollinator. Soft fruits are self-fertile, except that **blueberries** may need a pollinator.

Rootstocks

All tree fruits are grafted onto rootstocks of varying vigour. Choice of rootstock will determine the ultimate size of the tree and hence needs to be borne in mind when selecting new trees for the garden. For example, **apple trees** on 'M9' rootstock will be suitable for small gardens, while those on 'M25' will produce large, standard trees. The size of the tree will also be determined by the vigour of the cultivar. It is often advisable to obtain a very vigorous cultivar, for example 'Bramley's Seedling', on a more dwarfing stock. **Apples** are available on 'M27' (very dwarfing), 'M9' (dwarfing), 'M26' (semi-dwarfing), 'MM 106' (semi-vigorous), and 'M25' (vigorous) rootstocks. **Pears** are available on 'Quince C' (dwarfing), 'Quince A' (semi-vigorous), 'BA 29' (semi-vigorous) and seedling pear (vigorous) rootstocks. Some pear cultivars are incompatible with a quince rootstock and these are sold with a pear interstock (usually 'Beurré Hardy'). **Plums** are available on 'Pixy' (semi-dwarfing) and 'Saint Julien A' (semi-vigorous) rootstocks; cherries on 'Tabel' (very dwarfing), 'Gisela 5' (dwarfing), and 'Colt' (semi-vigorous).

Storage

Early **apples** and **pears** will not store, but many more of the apple and pear cultivars listed will store to Christmas and some to the spring. This calls for good storage conditions, i.e. a cool, dark, frost-free place that is not subject to fluctuating temperatures. Often this can be achieved in sheds and garages, but in general centrally heated houses are not suitable for long-term storage.

APPLE (*Malus domestica*)

98 H6 **'Alkmene'** (D)
PG 2. Aromatic, Cox-like flavour. Good, regular crops; some resistance to scab and mildew. Season: late Sept.–late Oct.
CAgr NOra SKee
'American Mother' *see* 'Mother'

93 H6 **'Arthur Turner'** (C)
PG 3. Flavoursome cooker. Large, golden exhibition fruit. Good, regular crops; prone to mildew; some resistance to scab. Striking deep pink blossom, for which an Award of Merit was given in 1945. Season: Sept.–Nov.
CAda CCVT CHab ELan EPom LBuc LCro MLod MLod NOra SBmr SKee SSFr WMat

93 H6 **'Ashmead's Kernel'** (D)
PG 4. Intense fruit-drop flavour. Cropping erratic; prone to bitter pit. Season: Dec.–Feb.
CAda CAgr CBTr CEnd CHab CLnd CSBt EPfP EPom LBuc LCro LRHS MLod MLod MPri NOra SBmr SBmr SEdi SKee SSFr SVic WMat WWct

93 H6 **'Belle de Boskoop'** (C/D)
Triploid. PG 3. Needs little or no extra sugar when cooked; mellows to brisk eating apple. Good, regular crops; very vigorous tree. Season: Oct.–Apr.; keeps well.*
CAda CAgr CEnd CHab EPom LMaj LMaj NOra NPlm SKee

93 H6 **'Blenheim Orange'** (C/D)
Triploid. PG 3. Characteristic nutty flavour. Use early for cooking. Some resistance to mildew; very vigorous tree; partial tip-bearer; light crops. Season (C): from late Sept. (D): Oct.–Dec./Jan.*
CAda CAgr CCVT CHab CLnd EGren ELan EPfP EPom LBuc LCro LCro LRHS LSRN MLod NOra SBmr SEdi SEND SEWo SKee SSFr SVic WFar WMat WWct

93 H6 **'Bramley's Seedling'** (C)
Triploid. PG 3. Cooks to very sharp, savoury purée; retains acidity to spring. Heavy crops; prone to bitter pit and scab; partial tip-bearer; can bear fruit parthenocarpically; can be biennial if over-cropped; blossom susceptible to frost. Very vigorous tree. Season: Nov.–Mar.; stores well.*
CAda CAgr CBcs CBTr CCVT CEnd CLnd CMac CWnw EBar EBee EGren ELan EPfP EPom GKin IPap LBom LBuc LCro LMaj LRHS LSRN MGos MLod MMuc MPri MSwo NLar NOra NTrD SBmr SEdi SEND SEWo SKee SOrN SRms SSFr SVic WFar WMat WWct

93 H6 **'Charles Ross'** (C/D)
PG 3. Quite rich flavour; needs no sugar when cooked. Handsome exhibition fruit. Good, regular crops; hardy tree; some resistance to scab. Season: Oct.–Dec.*
CAda CAgr CCVT CEnd CHab CLnd CMac CSBt EPom IArd LBuc LCro LCro LSRN MLod MLod NOra SBmr SKee SSFr WMat WWct

14 H6 **'Christmas Pippin'** (D)
PG 3. Medium vigour; upright spreading habit; good, regular crops. Medium-sized, attractive; red flushed over a yellow background; crisp, juicy, sweet-sharp flesh; mellows with keeping. Well-flavoured, good quality apple.
CBTr CEnd EBee ELan EPfP EPom LBom LBuc LCro LCro LCro LRHS MLod MLod MPri NLar NOra SBmr SKee SOrN SPoG SSFr WMat WWct

93 H6 **'Discovery'** (D)
PG 3. Bright red, crisp, juicy; keeps longer than most earlies. Ornamental tree. Good, regular crops; partial tip-bearer; good resistance to scab and mildew. Season: mid Aug.–Sept.*
CAda CAgr CBcs CBTr CCVT CDoC CLnd CMac CSBt CWnw EBar EBee EGren EPfP EPom GKin IPap LBom LBuc LCro LRHS MGos MLod MPri NLar NOra SBmr SEdi SKee SOrN SSFr SVic WFar WMat WWct

93 H6 **'Dummellor's Seedling'** (C)
PG 4. Also sold as 'Dumelow's Seedling'. Cooks to well-flavoured, juicy purée; retains acidity to spring. Good, regular crops, but fruit can be small for a cooker. Season: Nov.–Apr.*
CAda CHab NOra SKee

93 H6 **'Edward VII'** (C)
PG 6. Cooks to well-flavoured purée, not as acidic as 'Bramley's Seedling'. Large, regular, exhibition fruit. Deep pink blossom; flowers very late so escapes frosts; needs late-flowering pollinator. Good, regular crops; resistant to scab; some resistance to mildew. Season: Dec.–Apr.*
CHab NOra SKee WMat WWct

93 H6 **'Egremont Russet'** (D)
PG 2. Characteristic nutty flavour. Good, regular crops; fruit resistant to scab, but prone to leaf scab; very prone to bitter pit and woolly aphids. Season: Oct.–Dec.*
CAda CAgr CBTr CCVT CEnd CHab CLnd

CMac CSBt CWnw EBee EGren ELan
EPfP EPom LBuc LCro LRHS LSRN MGos
MLod MMuc MNHC MPri MSwo NLar
NOra SBmr SEdi SEND SEWo SKee SRms
SSFr SVic WMat WWct

93 H6 **'Ellison's Orange'** (D)
PG 4. Rich, aniseed flavour. Good, regular
crops; some resistance to scab, but susceptible to
canker. Season: late Sept.–late Oct.
CAda CAgr CEnd CHab CLnd CMac CSBt
EPfP EPom LBuc LCro LCro LRHS LRHS
MLod MLod MMuc MPri NOra SBmr SEdi
SEND SKee SRms SSFr SVic WFar WMat
WWct

93 H6 **'Elstar'** (D)
PG 3. Intense flavour, honeyed, crisp. Heavy
regular crops. Season: late Oct.–Dec.
CAda CCVT CLnd CWnw EBar EGren
EPom LCro LCro LMaj MSwo NOra SEdi
SEWo SKee SSFr WFar

93 H6 **'Emneth Early'** (C)
PG 3. Codlin type, cooking to fluffy purée;
needs hardly any sugar. Heavy but biennial
crops; needs thinning for size. Some resistance
to scab and mildew. Season: Aug.–Sept.*
CAgr CHab NOra SEdi SKee WMat

'Epicure' *see* 'Laxton's Epicure'

93 H6 **'Fiesta'** (D)
PG 3. Aromatic, Cox-like flavour. Heavy,
regular crops; frost-resistant blossom; less prone
to disease than Cox, but can be susceptible to
scab and develop canker on some sites. Season:
Oct.–Dec./Jan.*
CAda CAgr CBTr CCVT CDoC CLnd
CMac EBee EGren EPfP EPom LBuc LCro
LRHS MGos MLod MMuc MPri NLar
NOra SBmr SEdi SEND SKee SPoG SRms
SSFr WMat WWct

'Fortune' *see* 'Laxton's Fortune'

93 H6 **'Golden Noble'** (C)
PG 4. Cooks to a well-flavoured purée, not as
acidic as 'Bramley's Seedling'. Attractive
blossom. Good, regular crops; partial tip-bearer;
some scab and mildew resistance. Season:
Oct.–Dec. and longer.
CAda CAgr NOra SKee

93 H6 **'Greensleeves'** (D)
PG 3. Crisp, brisk, becoming sweeter. Very
precocious and heavy, regular crops; needs
thinning for good fruit size. Blossom has some
frost resistance. Can be susceptible to scab.
Season: late Sept.–Oct.
CAda CAgr CBTr CMac CWnw ELan EPfP
EPom LCro LCro LRHS MMuc NOra SBmr
SEdi SEND SKee SSFr WMat WWct

93 H6 **'Grenadier'** (C)
PG 3. Cooks to sharp purée. Heavy, regular crops;
good disease resistance. Season: Aug.–Sept.*

CAda CAgr CHab CLnd EPom LCro MMuc
NOra SEdi SEND SKee SSFr WMat WWct

14 H6 **'Howgate Wonder'** (C)
PG 3. Very large, late-season, heavy-cropping
apple with a very mild flavour. Vigorous; fruit
yellow-green flushed with red. Partially
self-fertile.
CAda CAgr CCVT CDoC CHab CLnd
EGren ELan ELan EPfP EPom LBuc LCro
LCro LRHS LSRN MLod MLod MMuc
MSwo NOra SBmr SEdi SKee SSFr SVic
WMat WWct

93 H6 **'James Grieve'** (D)
PG 3. Savoury, crisp to melting flesh; when
cooked keeps shape, with juicy, delicate flavour.
Good, regular crops; fruit bruises easily. Prone
to scab, canker; resistant to mildew; requires
well-drained soil. Season: Sept.–Oct. and
longer.*
CAda CAgr CBcs CBTr CCVT CDoC CEnd
CHab CLnd CMac CSBt CWnw EBar EBee
EGren EPfP EPom LBuc LCro LMaj LRHS
LSRN MAsh MGos MLod MMuc MPri
MSwo NLar NOra SBmr SEdi SEND SEWo
SKee SRms SSFr SVic WFar WMat WWct

93 H6 **'Jonagold'** (D)
Triploid. PG 3. Attractive, crisp, honeyed taste;
large fruit. Heavy, regular crops; prone to
canker. Fruit can be poorly coloured, but many
more colourful sports exist. Vigorous. Season:
Nov.–Jan./Feb.; stores well.
CAda CLnd EBar EGren ELan EPom IArd
IPap LCro LMaj MLod NOra SEdi SKee SSFr

93 H6 **'Jupiter'** (D)
Triploid. PG 3. Cox-like flavour, but sharper.
Heavy crops, but biennial if allowed to
over-crop; fruit can be irregular shape and
heavily russetted. Vigorous. Season: late Oct.–
Jan.*
CAgr CBTr CSBt EGren LCro LSRN MLod
MPri NLar NOra SEdi SKee SSFr WMat

14 H6 **'Kent'** (D)
PG 3. Good flavour; good reliable crops; keeps
well.
SKee

93 H6 **'Kidd's Orange Red'** (D)
PG 3. Very attractive; rich aromatic, perfumed
taste. Good, regular crops; fruit prone to coarse
russet. Season: Nov.–Jan.
CAda CAgr CBTr CEnd CMac EBee EPfP
EPom LBuc LCro LCro LRHS LSRN MLod
MLod NOra SBmr SKee SSFr WMat WWct

93 H6 **'King of the Pippins'** (D)
PG 5. Well ripened, good flavour. Cooked,
keeps shape, flavoursome; suited to open tarts,
etc. Heavy, regular crops; upright habit; good
resistance to disease; keeps well. Season:
Oct.–Dec.; can store to Feb.*

CAda CHab CLnd EPom EPom LMaj NOra SKee SVic WMat WWct

93 H6 **'Lane's Prince Albert'** (C)
PG 3. Cooks to brisk purée, not as acidic as 'Bramley's Seedling'. Large fruit. Good, regular crops; fruit easily bruised. Hardy; makes neat small tree. Resistant to scab; very prone to mildew; prone to canker on all but very well-drained soils. Season: Nov.–Mar.; stores well.*
CAda CAgr CHab CLnd CSBt EPfP NOra SEdi SKee SSFr SVic WMat

93 H6 **'Laxton's Epicure'** (D)
PG 3. Delicate, aromatic, Cox-like flavour. Heavy, regular crops; needs thinning for size; prone to bitter pit, canker. Season: late Aug.–Sept. Awarded as 'Epicure'.*
CAda CAgr CEnd CHab SKee

93 H6 **'Laxton's Fortune'** (D)
PG 3. Sweet, lightly aromatic flavour; needs to colour well for good quality. Good crops, but tendency to be biennial. Fruit bruises easily, can be poorly coloured. Prone to canker, good resistance to scab. Season: Sept.–Oct.
CAda CHab CMac CSBt EPom IArd LCro MLod NOra SEdi SKee SSFr WMat WWct

14 H6 **'Limelight'** (D)
PG 3. Crisp and refreshing; heavy-cropping.
CAda CDoC EBee LCro LRHS MLod MLod MPri NLar NOra SKee WMat

93 H6 **'Lord Lambourne'** (D)
PG 2. Sweet, juicy, attractive flavour. Skin can become greasy when stored. Good, regular crops. Partial tip-bearer; resistant to mildew. Season: late Sept.–Nov.*
CAda CAgr CBTr CEnd CHab CLnd CMac ELan EPom LCro LCro LSRN MSwo NOra SBmr SEdi SKee SSFr WMat WWct

93 H6 **'Mother'** (D)
PG 5. Sweet, perfumed, distinctive flavour. Crops can be erratic, light; good resistance to scab and mildew. Season: Oct.–Dec.*
CAda CAgr CLnd SKee SSFr

93 H6 **'Peasgood's Nonsuch'** (C)
PG 3. Cooks to sweet, delicately flavoured purée; needs no or little extra sugar. Exhibition apple with large, handsome regular shape. Good, regular crops; resistance to mildew and red spider; moderate resistance to scab. Season: late Sept.–Dec.
CAda CAgr CHab EPom LSRN NOra SBmr SKee WMat

93 H6 **'Pixie'** (D)
PG 4. Intensely aromatic, Cox-like flavour, but sharper and firmer-fleshed. Good to heavy crops, but small fruit unless thinned. Season: Dec.–Mar.*
CAda CDoC CSBt EPom LCro LRHS MPri NOra SKee WMat WWct

14 H6 **'Red Falstaff'** (D)
PG 3. Late-season, heavy-cropping sport of 'Falstaff' with a fruity flavour and crisp, juicy flesh. Self-fertile and moderately vigorous. Skin flushed with orange-red when ripe. Season: Nov.–Jan.
CAgr CBTr CCVT CDoC CEnd EPfP EPom GKin LBuc LCro LCro LRHS LSRN LSRN MLod MLod MLod MPri MSwo NLar NOra SBmr SEND SEWo SKee SPoG WMat WWct

19 H6 **'Red Windsor'** (D)
PG 2; partially self-fertile. Perfect for smaller gardens; deep red fruits, ready to eat in September. Happy grown in a large pot; good resistance to many of the common diseases.
CAda CBTr CBTr CEnd CLnd CMac EBee ELan EPfP EPom LBom LBuc LCro LCro LRHS MAsh MLod MLod MPri NLar NOra SKee SPoG SSFr WMat

93 H6 **'Ribston Pippin'** (D)
Triploid. PG 2. Intense, rich, aromatic flavour; more acidity and more robust than Cox. Good, regular crops; resistant to scab; prone to mildew and canker. Season: Oct.–Jan.
CAda EPom LBuc LCro MLod NOra SKee SSFr WMat WWct

93 H6 **'Rosemary Russet'** (D)
PG 3. Sweet-sharp acid drop taste, resembling 'Ashmead's Kernel'. Crops good, regular; vigorous tree with upright habit. Season: Nov./Dec.–Mar.
CAda CAgr CHab NOra SBmr SKee SSFr WMat WWct

93 H6 **'Saint Edmund's Pippin'** (D)
PG 2. Very attractive; richly flavoured when fully ripe. Good, regular crops; fruit bruises easily. Prone to mildew. Season: late Sept.–Oct. AGM reconfirmed 2017.*
CAda CHab NOra SBmr SKee SSFr WMat

14 H6 **'Santana'** (D)
PG 4. Medium to quite vigorous tree, with upright spreading habit. Good to heavy crop, with low susceptibility to scab. Midseason apple; picking early September and keeping well. Bright red flushed; sweet, crisp, juicy flesh; good flavour.
LCro NOra WMat

09 H6 **'Scrumptious'** (D)
PG 3. Regular cropper, good fruit size, attractive ornamental fruit. Good tree habit; easily managed. A good dessert apple: sweet, good flavour, crisp, juicy.
CAda CAgr CBTr CCVT CDoC CMac CSBt EBee EGren ELan EPfP EPom LBom LBuc LCro LRHS LSRN MGos MLod MPri NLar NOra SBmr SEWo SKee SOrN SPoG SSFr WMat

93 H6 **'Sunset'** (D)
PG 3. Aromatic, like small early Cox, but sharper. Heavy, regular crops, but small fruit. Resistant to scab; prone to mildew and canker. Season: Oct.–Dec.
CAda CAgr CBTr CCVT CDoC CEnd CHab CLnd CMac CSBt EBee EGren EPfP EPom GKin LBom LBuc LCro LRHS LSRN MLod NOra SBmr SEdi SEND SKee SSFr SVic WMat WWct

14 H6 **'Topaz'** (D)
PG 4. Medium vigour, with upright spreading habit. Good crop, with resistance to scab; late season, picking in early/mid October. Medium size; attractive; red flushed over a yellow background; crisp, juicy flesh, sweet-sharp taste; mellows with keeping.
CAda EPom NOra SKee SSFr WWct

93 H6 **'Warner's King'** (C)
Triploid. PG 2. Cooks to well-flavoured purée; not as acidic as 'Bramley's Seedling'. Attractive, deep pink blossom. Heavy, regular crops; fruit can be very large. Prone to bitter pit. Vigorous. Season: late Sept.–Dec.
CAda NOra SKee WMat

93 H6 **'Worcester Pearmain'** (D)
PG 3. Intense strawberry flavour when well-ripened and scarlet. Tip-bearer; heavy, regular crops. Resistant to mildew; some susceptibility to canker. Season: late Sept.–Oct.
CAda CAgr CBcs CBTr CCVT CHab CLnd CMac CSBt CWnw EBee ELan EPfP EPom LBuc LCro LCro LCro MLod MMuc NOra SBmr SEdi SEND SEWo SKee SSFr WFar WMat WWct

BLACKBERRY (*Rubus fruticosus*)

Season extends from late July to early September.

93 H6 **'Loch Ness'** (B)
Large, well-flavoured berries. Thornless; heavy-cropping; moderate vigour; hardy. Good resistance to purple blotch and botrytis, but prone to downy mildew. Reconfirmed after trial 2015.
CAgr CHab CMac EHet EPfP EPom IArd LCro LCro LSRN SBmr SSFr SVic

15 H6 **'Loch Tay'** (B)
No spines; has a good blackberry flavour and shiny fruit. Healthy but not too vigorous, producing good replacement canes. Early.
CHab CMac EPom SPoG

BLACKCURRANT (*Ribes nigrum*)

Season extends from early July to mid August.

95 H6 **'Ben Connan'**
Large fruit; medium long strigs. Heavy crops; compact habit. Good resistance to mildew, leaf-curling midge. Season: early.
CAgr CBTr CMac CSBt EPfP EPom LBuc LCro LCro LRHS LSRN MAsh MGos MNHC NLar SBmr SEND SPoG SRms SSFr WMat

12 H6 **'Big Ben'**
Fairly vigorous medium-sized bush, flowering early to midseason. Fruit large and easy to pick. Good yields, showing resistance to mildew and leaf spot. Fresh fruit flavour pleasant to quite sweet; rich when cooked.
CDoC EPom LBuc LCro LRHS LSRN MEar SBmr SPoG WMat

BLUEBERRY (*Vaccinium corymbosum*)

Blueberries begin to ripen mid July and continue to late August.

03 H6 **'Duke'**
Good flavour, medium to large fruit. Crops well; easy to grow. Flowers late; good for frost-prone sites; partly self-fertile. Season: early.
CDoC CMac CTsd EHet ELan EPfP EPom LCro LRHS MAsh SBmr SPoG SPre SSFr WCha WCha WCha

03 H6 **'Spartan'**
Excellent flavour; medium-sized fruit. Quite good crops; not self-fertile. Vigorous; upright habit. Good autumn colour. Season: early–mid.
CAgr CDoC CMac EGren EPom LCro LSRN WCha WCha WFar

CHERRY (MORELLO) (*Prunus cerasus*)

93 H6 **'Morello'** (C)
Dark red, acid cherry; excellent for preserves, tarts, etc. Regular, good crops; very attractive in blossom; self-fertile. Crops on north-facing site. Season: late July–early Aug.
CAda CAgr CBTr CCVT CDoC CLnd CMac CSBt CTsd CWnw ELan EPfP EPom IPap LBuc LCro LRHS LSRN MGos MLod MMuc MNHC MPri MSwo NLar NOra SAth SBmr SEdi SEND SEWo SKee SSFr SVic WFar WMat

CHERRY (SWEET) (*Prunus avium*)

14 H5 **'Kordia'** (D)
PG 5. Mid to late season; large to very large, true black cherry; bold appearance; excellent rich flavour. Spreading habit; can show some bare wood; medium vigour. Heavy, reliable crops; easy to grow. Not self-fertile; usually pollinated by 'Regina' or 'Sylvia' in commercial orchards; can also be pollinated by 'Summer Sun', 'Stella' (early bloom only). Blossom can be a little frost-sensitive. Good garden cherry.
CAda CCVT EPom LCro LCro LMaj LSRN NOra SBmr SKee SSFr WFar WMat

14 H6 **'Lapins'**
PG 4. Mid to late season; large, dark red cherry; very good flavour. Upright habit; medium vigour. Heavy, reliable crops. All-round excellent cherry; self-fertile.
CAda CAgr CBTr CWnw EGren ELan EPfP EPom LCro LMaj NLar NOra NPlm SBmr SEdi SKee SPoG SSFr WFar WMat

95 H6 **'Merchant'**
PG 3. Early black cherry; well-flavoured. Regular crops. Pollination: a universal donor, but not self-fertile. Season: early July. Reconfirmed 2014.
ELan LCro NOra SEdi SKee SSFr WMat

14 H5 **'Penny'**
PG 4. Mid to late season; dark red, very large, meaty cherry; excellent flavour. Upright spreading habit; medium vigour; prone to some bare wood. Crops well and regularly on 'Gisela 5'; bred for UK conditions. Not self-fertile; pollinated by late to midseason cultivars, e.g. 'Summer Sun', 'Skeena', 'Regina'; needs sufficient pollination to ensure heavy crops.
CAgr EPom LBom LCro LCro MNHC NOra SKee WMat

93 H6 **'Stella'**
PG 4. Black cherry; large, rich, high quality. Heavy, regular crops; self-fertile. Prone to splitting in wet weather. Season: late July. Reconfirmed 2014.
CAda CAgr CBTr CDoC CEnd CHab CLnd CMac CWnw EGren ELan EPfP EPom IPap LBom LBuc LCro LMaj LRHS MAsh MGos MLod MMuc MSwo NLar NOra NTrD SAth SBmr SEdi SEND SEWo SKee SPoG SSFr SVic WMat

04 H6 **'Summer Sun'** (D)
PG 4. Late (July). Produces firm, well-flavoured, red to black fruit. Very good crops. Some resistance to bacterial canker. Attractive, upright, spreading habit; moderate vigour. Not self-fertile. Reconfirmed 2014.
CAgr CBTr CLnd CMac EPom LBuc LCro LCro LCro LRHS MGos MLod MPri NLar NOra SBmr SKee SPoG SSFr WFar WMat

14 H5 **'Sweetheart'**
PG 4. Dark red cherry; latest of the season. Good flavour; very firm fruit. Medium vigour, upright spreading habit. Heavy, regular crops; fruits moderate size. Slightly prone to canker and brown rot. Only late-season self-fertile cultivar available. Prolific blossom, making a tree exceptionally pretty in the spring. Sets dense clusters of fruits, which can be prone to botrytis/brown rot.
CAgr CBTr CLnd ELan EPfP EPom LCro LCro LMaj LRHS LRHS LSRN MLod MLod NOra SEWo SKee SPoG WMat

DAMSON (*Prunus insititia*)

00 H6 **'Farleigh Damson'** (C)
PG 4. Excellent flavour. Regular, heavy crops. Blossom shows some resistance to frost. Season: late Aug.
CAda CAgr CBTr CBTr CDoC CHab EBee EGren EGren EPfP EPom LBuc LCro LCro MPri NLar NOra SEdi SKee SVic WMat WWct

22 H6 **'Merryweather Damson'** (C)
Has damson flavour, but is a plum. Colour dark blue with light bloom often with lighter dots; round, oval in shape. Large fruit, which makes excellent jam. A wonderful cooked flavour and always reliable. Season: mid to late September.
CAda CAgr CBTr CCVT CDoC CHab CLnd CMac CSBt EGren EPfP EPom LBom LBuc LCro LRHS MAsh MGos MLod MMuc MPri NLar NOra NTrD SBmr SEdi SEND SEWo SKee SPoG SSFr WFar WHtc WMat WWct

98 H6 **'Prune Damson'** (C)
PG 4. Larger fruits than 'Farleigh Damson', but typical damson flavour. Regular, good crops. Season: late Aug. Reconfirmed 2022.
CAda CAgr CBTr CBTr CHab CMac EBee EPfP EPom LBom LBuc LCro LRHS MLod MLod MMuc MPri NLar NOra SBmr SEND SEWo SKee SSFr WMat WWct

FIG (*Ficus carica*)

93 H4 **'Brown Turkey'**
Fruits regularly in the open in southern England and in many parts of the Midlands and East Anglia in a warm position. For good crop, root restriction advisable. Season: mid Aug.–mid Sept., depending on site.
CAda CAgr CBcs CBlu CBrac CCVT CDoC CLnd CMac CRHN CSBt CTsd CWal CWnw EBee EGren ELan ELon EPfP EPom EUrb GQue IPap LBuc LCro LEdu LMaj LRHS LSRN LWaG MAsh MBlu MGos MHer MHol MHtn Midl MLod MMuc MNHC MPri MSwo NLar NOra NPer NPlm NTrD SAth SBmr SEND SEWo SGol SKee SMad SNig SOrN SPlb SPoG SPre SRms SSta SVen SVic SWor WFar WJur WLov WMat WMou WPGP WTre

GOOSEBERRY (*Ribes uva-crispa*)

Season extends from early June to mid August. For culinary use, pick from early June. For ripe fruit pick from early July.

93 H6 **'Careless'** (C/D)
Green fruit. Reliable, good crops. Good for tarts, jam, etc. Prone to mildew. Season: mid.
EGren EPom LSRN MAsh MGos SEdi WFar

94 H6 **'Greenfinch'** (C)
Green fruit; compact bush. Some resistance to mildew and leaf spot. Season: mid; similar to 'Careless'.
CAgr

93 H6 **'Invicta'** (C/D)
Green fruit; quite good flavour. Heavy crops; very vigorous; spreading habit; large thorns. Some resistance to mildew. Young shoots can be damaged on exposed site. Season: mid; slightly earlier than 'Careless'. Main use culinary.
CAgr CBTr CDoC CMac CSBt EGren EPfP EPom LBuc LCro LRHS LSRN MAsh MGos MNHC MPri NLar SBmr SEdi SEND SPoG SRms SSFr SVic WFar WMat

93 H6 **'Leveller'** (D)
Large, yellow fruit; good dessert quality. Season: mid to late.
EGren EGren SEdi

93 H6 **'Whinham's Industry'** (C/D)
Red fruit; quite good dessert quality. Heavy, reliable crops. Very susceptible to mildew. Season: mid.
EGren ELan LBuc MGos SEdi SEND SRms

GRAPE (*Vitis* species)

21 H5 **'Lakemont'** (O/W/S)
Raised from a cross between 'Thompson's Seedless' and 'Ontario'. The oval yellow grapes are large for an outdoor grape, with a good neutral flavour. It has good disease resistance. Probably the best of the outdoor white seedless grapes.
CAgr CDoC CMac CRHN ELan EPfP EPom LBuc LCro LEdu MGos NLar NTrD SBmr SEdi SPoG SPre SSFr SVic WMat WSuV WSuV

21 H5 **'Reliance'** (O/R/S)
A cross with *Vitis lambrusca*: hardy and vigorous. Reliable, seedless, with good-sized fruits; strawberry flavour develops as it ripens. In less sunny years, can be white with a very pale pink blush.
CAgr WSuV WSuV

04 H5 **'Schuyler'** (O/B)
Black grape. Good outdoor vine for the amateur, both dessert and wine; crops reliably; disease-resistant. Moderately good flavour, but better than many shop-bought grapes. Awarded as 'Gloire de Boskoop'.
CAgr CMac EGren ELan EPom LBuc LCro LWaG MGos WSuV WSuV WSuV

21 H5 **'Sovereign Coronation'** (B/S)
Raised in Canada, from a cross between 'Patricia' and 'Himrod'. Good flavour, ripening early in the season. Good-sized fruits for an outdoor grape. Large leaves, and reputed to be very hardy.
WSuV

HAZELNUT (*Corylus maxima*)

14 H6 **'Gunslebert'**
Good-sized nut; kernel fills the shell; very few blanks. Excellent flavour; very tasty. Midseason. Regular, good crops; nuts held as large clusters of four nuts. Medium vigour tree; moderate amount of suckering. Pollinated by 'Kentish Cob', 'Cosford'. Good tree habit, with a natural goblet shape and exceptionally attractive with prolific catkins making it also an ornamental tree. A mainstay of Kent nut production. Reliable, hardy hazel nut, easy to grow in a garden situation; productive and ornamental; requires a pollinator.
CCVT CMac NOra SPoG SRms SSFr WMat

14 H6 **'Kentish Cob'**
Good-sized nut; kernel fills the shell; very few blanks. Excellent flavour; rich and meaty. Early season, cropping before the squirrels become active. Regular, good crops. Medium vigour tree; moderate amount of suckering. Pollinated by 'Gunslebert', 'Cosford', 'Hall's Giant' ('Merveille de Bollwiller'). The main cultivar of commercial nut plantations in Kent. Reliable hazel nut, easy to grow in a garden situation; needs a pollinator.
CAda CAgr EBee EGren ELan EPfP EPom IArd LBuc LCro MSwo NLar SBmr SEdi SEWo SPoG SRms SSFr SVic WMat WMou

LOGANBERRY (*Rubus* × *loganobaccus*)

93 H6 **'Ly 654'** (C)
Large, dark fruit; distinctive flavour; good crops. Thornless. Season: July.
CMac EGren EPom LBuc SBmr SSFr SVic

MEDLAR (*Mespilus germanica*)

17 H6 **'Iranian'**
Compact bushy tree with small leaves and bunches of fruit. Fruit ripens early, so can be picked before they fall off. Fruit can be eaten off the tree. Has a pleasant taste with a good balance of sweetness and acidity.
CAgr SKee

PEAR (*Pyrus communis*)

93 H6 **'Beth'** (D)
PG 4. Attractive; good quality and flavour. Small fruit. Heavy, regular crops. Season: mid/late Aug.–early Sept.; short season once picked.
CAda CAgr CBTr CDoC CHab CMac CWnw EBee EGren ELan EPfP EPom IArd LBuc LCro LCro MAsh MLod MLod MPri

NLar NOra SBmr SEdi SKee SSFr WMat WWct WWct

93 H6 **'Beurré Hardy'** (D)
PG 3. Very melting and fragrant with rose-water perfume. Good, regular crops. Very hardy, vigorous tree; slow to bear; resistant to scab. Season: Nov.–Dec.*
CAda CAgr CCVT CMac EGren ELan EPfP EPom IArd IPap LCro LMaj MLod NOra SBmr SEdi SEND SKee SSFr WMat WWct

06 H6 **'Beurré Superfin'** (D)
PG 3. An excellent September-cropping cultivar for the amateur gardener, with a lovely cinnamon-russet colour and an exquisite flavour. Gives a good, consistent yield and is not over-vigorous. Midseason.
SKee SSFr WMat WWct

93 H6 **'Concorde'** (D)
PG 4. Sweet, buttery, fragrant flavour, similar to 'Conference', but superior. Heavy, regular crops; frost-tolerant blossom. Young trees very precocious. Season: late Oct./Nov.–Dec.
CAda CAgr CBTr CCVT CDoC CMac CWnw EBee EGren ELan EPfP EPom IArd LBuc LCro LRHS LSRN MAsh MGos MLod MNHC MPri MSwo NLar NOra NTrD SBmr SEdi SEWo SKee SOrN SPoG SPre SSFr SVic WMat WWct

93 H6 **'Conference'** (D)
PG 3. Sweet, buttery, quite rich taste. Heavy, regular crops. Can produce fruits without pollinators, but resulting fruits often misshapen. Season: Oct.–Nov./Dec.*
CAgr CBcs CBTr CCVT CDoC CLnd CMac CTsd CWnw EBee EGren ELan EPfP EPom IPap LBom LBuc LCro LMaj LRHS LSRN MAsh MGos MLod MMuc MPri MSwo NLar NOra NPlm NTrD SAth SBmr SEdi SEND SEWo SKee SOrN SPoG SSFr SVic WFar WMat WWct

93 H6 **'Doyenné du Comice'** (D)
PG 4. Very rich flavour; very juicy, buttery, perfumed. Excellent quality, but moderate crops, although older trees more regular. Vigorous tree; prone to scab. Season: Nov.–Dec. Not compatible with 'Onward'.
CAda CAgr CBcs CBTr CCVT CHab CLnd CMac CTsd CWnw EBee EGren ELan EPfP EPom IArd LBuc LCro LMaj LRHS MLod MMuc MPri MSwo NLar NOra SBmr SEdi SEND SEWo SKee SOrN SSFr SVic WMat WWct

06 H6 **'Gorham'** (D)
PG 4. A beautiful green pear with a good covering of russet, with fine, cream, sweet, juicy, aromatic flesh. Has an excellent flavour; a good reliable cropper and is readily available. Late.
CAda CAgr NOra SKee SSFr WMat

93 H6 **'Joséphine de Malines'** (D)
PG 3. Very rich, buttery and perfumed. Crops good, reliable, but needs warm site. Fruit easily bruised. Tip-bearer; resistant to scab. Season: Nov.–Dec./Jan.
CAda CAgr CBTr MLod NOra SKee WMat

PLUM (*Prunus domestica*)

95 H5 **'Blue Tit'** (C/D)
PG 5. Pleasant flavour; blue plum. Regular, good crops. Self-fertile. Season: mid Aug. Reconfirmed 2022.
CAgr EPom LCro MMuc NOra SEND SKee SSFr WMat WWct

98 H5 **'Cambridge Gage'** (D)
PG 4. Honeysweet excellent greengage quality, but more reliable than most greengages. Reasonably regular crops in favourable situations. Partly self-fertile. Season: mid Aug. Reconfirmed 2022.
CAgr CBTr CCVT CEnd CHab CMac EBee EGren EPfP EPom LCro LCro LCro LCro LRHS LSRN MAsh MLod MLod MMuc NOra SBmr SEdi SEND SEWo SKee SSFr WMat WWct

93 H6 **'Czar'** (C)
PG 3. Well-flavoured; early blue plum; used for jam but also moderate eating quality. Heavy, regular crops. Self-fertile. Season: mid Aug. Reconfirmed 2022.
CAda CAgr CBTr CCVT CDoC CEnd CHab CLnd CMac CSBt CWnw EGren ELan EPfP EPom IPap LBuc LCro LRHS MAsh MGos MLod MMuc MPri MSwo NOra SBmr SEdi SEND SFol SKee SPoG SSFr SVic WFar WMat WWct

22 H5 **'Early Rivers'** (C)
PG 3. Season mid to late July. Dark blue with heavy bloom; surface of skin slightly hammered. Round oval shape. Best for jam making; mildly sharp, but mild flavour when cooked. Reliable performer and early. An all-round cooker and dessert plum. When really ripe, also good for eating fresh.
CAgr CAgr CBTr CHab EBee EPom LBom LCro LCro LCro LSRN MLod MLod NOra SEdi SKee SSFr SVic WMat WWct

22 H6 **'Gypsy'**
A very attractive rounded bright red fruit of good size with orange flesh; flavour sugary and rich. Partially self-fertile. One of the best dessert myrobalan plums. Early flowering. A very reliable cropper; very early, the first plum. Excellent for bottling and other culinary uses.
CAda CAgr CBTr CBTr EBee EPom EPom EPom LCro MLod MLod NOra SKee SSFr WMat WWct

14 H5 **'Haganta'**
PG 3. Large dark blue plum, late-ripening, with good consistent crop; juicy; sweet; sugary; and stone almost free; good flavour; potential for cold storage to extend the eating season to the end of October. Reconfirmed 2022.
CAgr CBTr LCro MLod NOra WMat

93 H5 **'Imperial Gage'** (D)
PG 2. Gage quality but not as rich as 'Cambridge Gage'. Regular crops. Partly self-fertile. Season: mid Aug. Reconfirmed 2022.
CAda CAgr CBTr CCVT CLnd CMac EPom LCro LCro LCro LCro LCro MLod MMuc NOra SEND SKee SSFr WMat

00 H6 **'Mallard'** (D)
PG 1. Medium-sized red plum; quite good flavour. Good, regular crops. Moderate vigour; not self-fertile. Season: mid–late Aug.
NOra SKee WMat

93 H5 **'Marjorie's Seedling'** (C)
PG 5. Late blue plum. Good for jam. Reliable good crops; vigorous, upright habit. Self-fertile. Season: late Sept.–early Oct. Reconfirmed 2022.
CAda CAgr CCVT CDoC CEnd CHab CLnd CMac EGren EPfP EPom LBom LBuc LCro LRHS LSRN MAsh MGos MLod MMuc MPri NOra SAth SBmr SEdi SEND SKee SSFr WMat WWct

95 H6 **'Opal'** (D)
PG 3. Small purple plum; good flavour. Reliable, heavy crops; needs thinning. Partly self-fertile. Blossom buds very prone to bird damage. Season: early–mid Aug. Reconfirmed 2022.
CAda CAgr CBTr CCVT CMac CWnw EBee EGren ELan EPfP EPom LBom LBuc LCro LRHS LSRN MAsh MGos MLod MMuc MPri NLar NOra SAth SBmr SEdi SEND SKee SSFr WMat WWct

93 H5 **'Oullins Gage'** (C/D)
PG 4. Large, yellow flushed with pink. Not typical gage quality, but quite rich. Heavy, regular crops. Partly self-fertile. Season: mid Aug.
CAda CAgr CBTr CCVT CLnd CMac CTsd CWnw EGren ELan EPfP EPom LBom LBuc LCro LRHS MLod MMuc MPri NOra SAth SEdi SEND SEWo SKee SPoG SSFr SVic WMat WWct

14 H5 **'Purple Pershore'** (C)
PG 3. Good flavour; reliable good crops. Reconfirmed 2022.
CAda CAgr CHab MLod NOra SKee SSFr WMat WWct

95 H5 **'Valor'** (D)
PG 2. Blue, medium-sized plum with sweet greenish yellow flesh. Good quality. Moderately good, regular crops. Not self-fertile. Season: late Aug.
LCro NOra SKee

22 H5 **'Verity'** (C/D)
PG 5. Blue skin, orange flesh; ripens in September. A good fresh eating plum, cropping late with good flavour; reliable. A pretty tree with red stalks; a good late season variety.
SKee WMat

93 H5 **'Victoria'** (D)
PG 3. Red plum; reasonable to good eating quality; excellent for bottling, jam and tarts. Heavy, regular crops. Self-fertile. Season: mid to late Aug. Reconfirmed 2022.
CAda CAgr CBTr CCVT CDoC CHab CLnd CMac CTsd CWnw EBee EGren ELan EPfP EPom GKin IArd IPap LBom LBuc LCro LMaj LSRN MAsh MGos MLod MMuc MNHC MPri MSwo NLar NOra NTrD SAth SBmr SEdi SEND SEWo SHor SKee SOrN SPoG SSFr SVic WFar WMat WWct

22 H5 **'Warwickshire Drooper'** (C)
PG 2. Season early to mid September. A reliable late dual purpose plum, cropping heavily and regularly. Large and attractive; bright yellow with some green streaks. Covered in thin white bloom. Good for culinary and dessert. Rarely frosted. A large tree.
CAda CAgr CHab MLod MLod MNHC NOra SKee SSFr WMat WWct

QUINCE (*Cydonia oblonga*)

17 H5 **'Serbian Gold'**
Good resistance to leaf blight, and said to be fireblight-resistant. A compact tree for modern gardens, with a small leaf and pretty flowers. Consistently good cropper, with roundish fruit; quite acidic when eaten raw. Good jelly-making quince.
CAda CBTr CCVT CEnd CMac EGren ELan EPom LCro LCro MLod MNHC NLar NOra SKee WMat

RASPBERRY (*Rubus idaeus*)

Raspberries crop from late June to early August. Autumn primocanes from late July to early October.

09 H6 **'All Gold'**
Autumn-cropping. Yellow-/golden-fruited; needs to be left to ripen well before the flavour is fully tasted. Yield generally peaking at the end of August and early September. An upright habit with easy-to-manage cane.
CAgr CDoC CDoC CMac CSBt EGren ELan EPfP EPom LCro LRHS NLar SRms SVic WFar WMat

00 H6 **'Glen Ample'**
Summer-cropping. Large fruit, excellent flavour. Recommended for freezing. Heavy crops; spine-free canes. Resistant to main aphid vector of virus disease; some tolerance to phytophthora root rot; some susceptibility to leaf and bud mite. Season: mid. Reconfirmed after trial 2009.
CAgr CBTr CMac EBee EGren ELan EPfP EPom LBuc LCro LRHS MAsh MNHC NLar SBmr SEdi SPoG SRms SSFr SVic SWCr WFar WMat

09 H6 **'Glen Magna'**
Summer-cropping. A very vigorous cultivar with long, strong fruiting laterals. It has large fruit with a good flavour. Yields high with a long cropping season.
CAgr EGren LRHS MAsh SEdi SRms WFar

09 H6 **'Joan J'**
Autumn-cropping. Easy to grow and pick; upright habit; good berry size.
CAgr CBTr CMac CSBt EBee ELan EPom LRHS LSRN SBmr SPoG SRms SSFr SWCr

93 H6 **'Malling Admiral'**
Summer-cropping. Good quality; medium to large, attractive fruit. Consistent, moderate to good crops; tall canes; withstands wet conditions, but laterals easily damaged in exposed sites. Good disease resistance. Season: mid to late. Reconfirmed after trial 2009.
CSBt EGren EPfP EPom LRHS MAsh SWCr

93 H6 **'Malling Jewel'**
Summer-cropping. Good flavour and crops. Season: early to mid. Reconfirmed after trial 2009.
CAgr CDoC CSBt EGren EPfP EPom LBuc LCro LRHS LSRN MAsh MPri SEdi SPoG SRms SWCr WFar

22 H6 **'Malling Minerva'**
Summer-fruiting, early main season. Attractive mid red, glossy, medium-sized fruit, conic in shape, cohesive, with moderate/good flavour. Reliable. Awarded for container use, but in a previous RHS trial this variety was also found to be suitable for in soil planting.
CAgr CMac EPom SRms SVic

22 H6 **'Octavia'**
Summer-fruiting, late season cropping. Large to very large fruit, round/conic in shape; drupe large but set can be uneven at times and cause some lack of cohesiveness. High yields of well-flavoured fruits. Awarded for container use.
CAgr CDoC CMac EGren ELan EPfP EPom LBuc LRHS MAsh NLar SEdi SWCr WFar WMat

09 H6 **'Polka'**
Autumn-cropping. Early flush of fruit with good berry size and appearance; good upright habit with medium vigorous cane growth.
CDoC CSBt EGren EPfP EPom LBuc LCro LRHS LSRN MAsh MMuc SBmr SRms SSFr SWCr WMat

09 H6 **'Tulameen'**
Summer-cropping. Outstanding cultivar, with strong cane growth and upright habit. Spine-free and easily handled, with exceptional fruit quality and high yield. Less prone to pest and disease than other varieties.
CAgr CBTr CDoC CSBt EBee EGren ELan EPfP EPom LCro LRHS LSRN MAsh NLar SEdi SPoG SRms SSFr WFar WMat

REDCURRANT (*Ribes rubrum*)

Redcurrants crop from mid July to early September.

93 H6 **'Jonkheer van Tets'**
Heavy crops of large sweet fruits on long strigs; one of the earliest varieties to ripen. Self-pollinating. Season: early.
CAgr CDoC CSBt EGren EHet ELan EPfP EPom IArd LCro LRHS MPri NLar SBmr SEdi SEND SRms SSFr WFar WMat

93 H6 **'Red Lake'**
Good quality medium to large fruit; cropping on long trusses. Prone to wind damage in exposed sites; in summer prune early. Season: mid to late.
CAgr EGren ELan EPfP EPom LBuc MGos MPri NLar SEdi SPoG SRms SSFr WFar WMat

19 H6 **'Rovada'**
Heavy-cropping, late summer-ripening cultivar, producing long strigs of larger fruit, making it easy to harvest.
CAgr CMac CoPl CSBt EHet ELan EPfP EPom LBuc LRHS LSRN MAsh MNHC NLar SEdi SPoG SRms SVic WFar WMat

93 H6 **'Stanza'**
Medium-sized fruit; good quality. Compact habit; heavy crops. Season: mid to late.
CAgr MEar SEND

STRAWBERRY (*Fragaria* × *ananassa*)

In an early season, strawberries begin to crop mid June; in a late season, mid to late June.

06 H6 **'Alice'**
A good consistent cropper, with a high percentage of mid to large, bright orange-red, sweet, juicy fruit. Scored well in taste tests and performed well at different geographical locations (Stafford, Kent, Dundee) in HDC trials. Has good resistance to verticillium wilt; very useful to home gardener. Mid to late season.
CAgr EHet EPom LCro

93 H6 **'Cambridge Favourite'**
Good flavour; medium size, but rather soft berries. Moderate crops; excellent resistance to disease. Good runner production. Season: mid.
CAgr CMac CSBt EGren EHet EPfP EPom GQue LBuc LCro MAsh MGos MPri SBmr SEdi SPlb SVic

18 H6 **'Finesse'**
An everbearer, producing good yields of goodsized, well-flavoured berries in long trusses from early summer to early autumn. It has very good disease resistance, but produces few runners.
CMac

18 H6 **'Florence'**
Bright dark red berries of good size; late main season fruit with consistent good flavour.
CAgr EHet EPom LCro MPri SBmr

94 H6 **'Hapil'**
Large glossy berries; good flavour. Heavy crops; vigorous. Susceptible to verticillium wilt. Season: early/mid. Reconfirmed after trial 2004.
EHet EHet EPom LBuc LCro

93 H6 **'Honeoye'**
Excellent flavour. Heavy crops; susceptible to verticillium wilt. Season: early. Reconfirmed after trial 2004.
CAgr EHet EPfP EPom IDun LBuc LCro LCro MPri

18 H6 **'Malling Centenary'**
Large bright red berries with consistently good flavour.
EPom IDun

94 H6 **'Pegasus'**
Good flavour; quite soft flesh. Good disease resistance; tolerance to verticillium wilt. Season: mid. Reconfirmed after trial 2004 and 2006.
CAgr EHet EHet EPom LCro

94 H6 **'Rhapsody'**
Good flavour; medium to large berries. Resistant red core; some resistance to verticillium wilt and mildew. Season: late. Reconfirmed after trial 2006.
LSRN

95 H6 **'Symphony'**
Good flavour; bright, firm berries. Vigorous; good resistance to red core; susceptible to mildew. Good runner production. Season: mid to late. Reconfirmed after trial 2006.
CAgr CSBt EPom LBuc LCro LSRN SBmr

18 H6 **'Vibrant'**
Early fruit; best June bearer; attractive dark berry with good flavour.
CSBt EPom

TAYBERRY (*Rubus*)

93 H7 **'Tayberry'**
Distinctive flavour. Larger fruit; heavier crops than loganberry. Excellent for cooking, freezing, jam, etc. Season: July. Reconfirmed after trial 2015.
CDoC LWaG WJur

WALNUT (*Juglans regia*)

15 H6 **'Franquette'**
Old French variety, known since 19th century; received the designation *appellation d'origine contrôlée* in 1938 as 'Noix de Grenoble' and in 2002 as 'Noix du Perigord'; remains a main market walnut of France; long recommended for planting in UK. Tree upright with rounded crown; moderate vigour; late-leafing; tolerates disease. Good, regular crops; reliable and productive. Nuts easily husked; quite soft shell, and can be cracked with fingers; well-sealed and well-filled nut; medium size, long, oval shape. Flavour excellent. Season: quite late/late. Pollinated by 'Meylanaise', 'Ronde de Montignac', 'Fernette'; reported partially self-fertile.
CAgr ELan LMaj MLod MLod NOra WMat

15 H6 **'Lara'**
French cultivar; seedling of American cultivar 'Payne'. One of the main cultivars of modern walnut plantations. Good habit, making broad spreading tree, but not very vigorous; quite early leafing out; lateral bearing; good disease resistance. Good, regular crops; reliable and productive. Nuts easily husked; medium to quite large, globose; well-sealed, well-filled; well-flavoured as fresh nut and as dried nut. Season: early. Pollinated by 'Franquette', 'Meylanaise' and 'Ronde de Montignac'.
CAgr ELan LCro NOra WMat

WHITECURRANT (*Ribes rubrum*)

19 H6 **'Blanka'**
Consistent long trusses of pearly white, large, evenly sized berries, with good flavour; easy growing; late cultivar, which extends the season well.
CAgr CMac EPfP LRHS SVic

93 H6 **'White Grape'**
Attractive, translucent berries; good flavour. Season: mid July.
LEdu

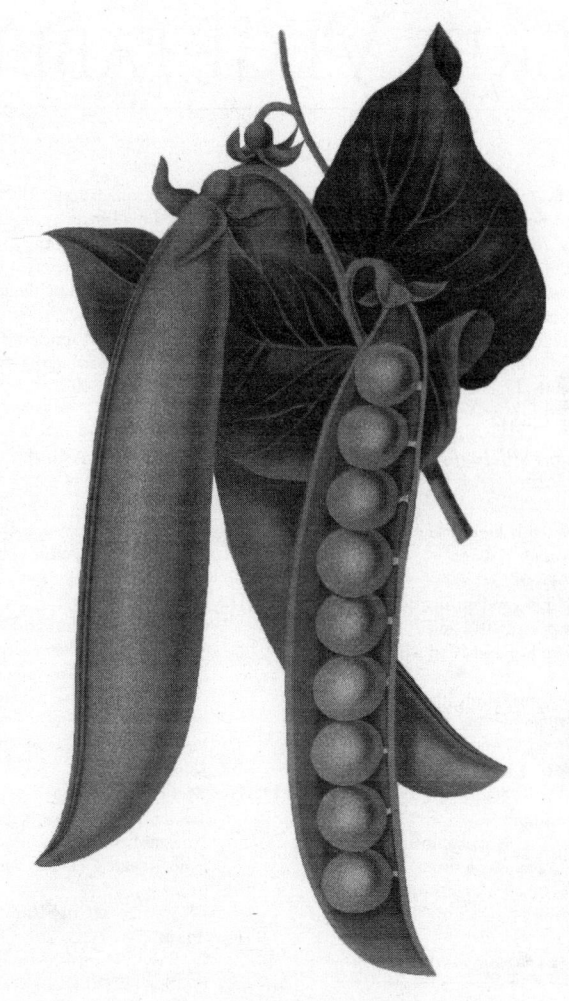

IV
RHS AWARD OF GARDEN MERIT
VEGETABLES

Award of Garden Merit Vegetables

This is a directory of RHS Award of Garden Merit (AGM) vegetables offered by nurseries participating in the current edition of the *RHS Plant Finder*. It does not represent a complete list of AGM vegetables.

Entries are accompanied by a short description and the relevant hardiness rating for the UK. **Hardiness ratings** are explained on p.39. The figures to the left of the rating indicate the year the Award of Garden Merit was given.

Vegetables present some nomenclatural peculiarities that may require explanation. Cultivars that are repeatedly raised by different growers, while retaining their essential characteristics, can become recognisably different. These strains are referred to as maintenances and are often distinguished by the use of **maintenance names** which exist separately from the cultivar name. Here maintenance names appear after the cultivar name separated by a dash following the Vegetable Seed (England) Regulations 2002.

Asparagus (*Asparagus officinalis*)

01 H4 **'Backlim'**
F$_1$ hybrid; consistently high yield of large spears.
EPom LCro SBmr

93 H4 **'Connover's Colossal'**
Early; heavy yield of good quality spears. Reconfirmed after trial 2001 and 2012.
EKin ELan LCro LSRN MCtn MNHC SVic

01 H4 **'Gijnlim'**
F$_1$ hybrid; early. Consistently high yield of mid green spears with purple tips. Reconfirmed after trial 2012.
EDel EGren EHet EKin ELan EPom LCro SBmr WFar

12 H5 **'Guelph Millennium'**
Bred in Canada. Excellent cold tolerance. Lateness helps to avoid frost damage. Sound yield of slender stems with pleasing flavour.
EHet ELan EPom LCro

Aubergine (*Solanum melongena*)

95 H1c **'Bonica'**
F$_1$ hybrid. Early-cropping, good quality, attractive glossy black fruits are a good size. Plants are tall, but also strong and vigorous. Reconfirmed after trial 2008, 2018.
MCtn

18 H1c **'Clara'**
Best of the whites, with good yield of very good oval-shaped fruits, sometimes with a slightly ribbed shape. Whites tend to be more tender than the usual dark purple fruits.
MCtn

Basil (*Ocimum basilicum*)

12 H1c **'Aroma 2'**
Standard Genovese type. Lovely aroma, good disease resistance, quite tall.
LCro MCtn

12 H1c **'Lemonade'**
Compact, even plant growing to c.30cm. Aromatic with a sherbet-lemon scent and taste. Fine leaves: keeled as young foliage. Flowers are white, and attractive to bees. Plants hold well and show good disease- and weather-resistance. Previously listed as basil × *africanum*.
SRms

12 H1c **'Mrs Burns' Lemon'**
Tall, upright, neat habit, growing to c.60cm. Fine, mid green leaves, aromatic and intensely lemon-scented. Flowers white, and attractive to bees.
EKin LCro MCtn SRms

12 H1c **'Pluto'**
Bush type, of small, even, dome-shaped habit, growing to c.20cm. Leaves are fine, mid green and aromatic. Holds form well and slow to flower.
LCro

Beans

Broad beans (*Vicia faba*)

95 H5 **'Aguadulce'**
November sown. Dark green foliage, showing some variability. Long pods; the highest yielding in the trial. May also be sold as 'Aquadulce'.
CHby LCro

93 H5 **'Aqaudulce Claudia'**
Spring sown. Not too tall; a good compact plant. An early crop when spring-sown, but can also be sown in November. One of the most reliable cultivars for overwintering. Reconfirmed after trial 1999, 2011.
EGren EKin LCro MCtn

11 H4 **'De Monica'**
Short pods; well filled. Good ratio of seed to pod; excellent cropping.
EKin MCtn SVic

93 H4 **'Express'**
Spring sown. Quick to mature, with well-filled pods.
EKin

11 H4 **'Giant Exhibition Longpod'**
Smooth, slender pods of good length; long cropping period.
EKin MCtn

93 H3 **'Imperial Green Longpod'**
Spring sown. Green-seeded, with long smooth pods; good green colour and flavour; particularly good for freezing. Reconfirmed after trial 1999, 2011.
EKin LCro

99 H3 **'Masterpiece Green Longpod'**
Spring sown. Slender, well-filled pods; stands well; good green colour and flavour; suitable for freezing; reconfirmed after trial 2011.
EDel EGren EKin LCro MCtn

11 H4 **'Suprifin'**
Pale green pods of mid size; pleasant taste. Early-cropping.
LCro

93 H3 **'The Sutton'**
Spring sown. Dwarf compact plants, with nice flavour; ideal for smaller gardens or containers and windy situations. Reconfirmed after trial 1999, 2011.
EKin LCro MCtn SVic

99 H4 **'Witkiem' - Manita**
Spring sown. Traditional 'Witkiem' type; sets well. Good early yield, with uniform pods; reconfirmed after trial 2011.
CHby EKin

CLIMBING FRENCH BEANS (*Phaseolus vulgaris*)
00 H2 **'Cobra'**
Very high early yield, with a long season, of long, smooth, round, sweetly flavoured stringless pods with exceptional flavour. The pale violet flowers in summer are also worthy of the ornamental garden. Reconfirmed after trial 2008.
CHby EKin LCro MCtn

93 H2 **'Eva'**
Very early. Long straight fleshy pods, wider-podded than other round varieties. Reconfirmed after trial 2000, 2008 and 2023.
CHby

08 H2 **'Golden Gate'**
Good crop of golden, fleshy, flat pods with a sweet, fresh flavour.
CHby LCro

93 H2 **'Hunter'**
Attractive long flat stringless pods. Slow to show seed development. Reconfirmed after trial 2000 and 2008.
EKin MCtn

08 H2 **'Limka'**
Consistently high yields of good quality, flat, light green pods with a good flavour.
CHby

DWARF FRENCH BEANS (*Phaseolus vulgaris*)
93 H2 **'Annabel'**
Dark green colour, compact habit, fine foliage, tender fleshy tasting pods. Reconfirmed after trial 1996, 2010 and 2019.
EKin

19 H2 **'Elba'**
Good yield and colour, producing a heavy crop of long, slender beans; healthy plants.
MCtn

93 H2 **'Sprite'**
Heavy yield, with long, dark green pods. Reconfirmed after trial 2019.
EKin LCro

10 H2 **'Stanley'**
Mid to dark green colour; tender and sweet. Taller plant. Uniform and picks over long period.
EKin MCtn

RUNNER BEANS (*Phaseolus coccineus*)
06 H2 **'Benchmaster'**
Long, fairly straight beans, good yield; reconfirmed after trial 2013.
EKin LCro

06 H2 **'Celebration'**
High yield of attractive, straight, smooth, good quality, fleshy pods with good colour and flavour. Flowers are a decorative pink. Reconfirmed after trial 2013, 2017.
EKin MCtn

13 H2 **'Firestorm'**
Hybrid of runner and French bean parentage. Excellent yield, slender, straight, smooth-skinned, fleshy pods. Self-setting. Reconfirmed after trial 2017.
EDel EKin LCro MCtn

13 H2 **'Moonlight'**
Hybrid of runner and French bean parentage; grown commercially. Very high yielding. Easy to pick; leaves pedicel behind on picking. Smooth, straight, fleshy pods, with good length and nice

colour. Self-setting. Reconfirmed after trial 2017.
EGren EKin LCro LCro MCtn

06 H2 **'St George'**
Bicolour variety; prized for ornamental value. Some French bean parentage. Popular commercial variety; easy to pick, leaving pedicel behind. Slender beans, straight, pale green. Reconfirmed after trial 2013, 2017.
CHby

99 H2 **'White Lady'**
Late; very fleshy pods. Reconfirmed after trial 2006, 2013.
CHby EGren EKin LCro LCro MCtn

BEETROOT (*Beta vulgaris*)

05 H3 **'Alto'**
Long red root. F_1 hybrid; early. Cylindrical, uniform, smooth roots with very good internal colour and good long shape. Potential to bulk up well. Reconfirmed after trial 2016.
EKin EKin

93 H3 **'Boltardy'**
Round red root. Open-pollinated; good bolting resistance.
EKin LCro MCtn SVic

16 H3 **'Bona'**
Round red root. Open-pollinated; even size with very smooth skin.
MCtn

93 H3 **'Pablo'**
Round red root. F_1 hybrid; very early. Uniform roots with very smooth skins; very good internal colour and freedom from internal rings. Uniform roots with very smooth skins and very good internal colour. Appears to have good bolting resistance. Widely used as a show cultivar. Reconfirmed after trial 2001, 2005 and 2016.
EKin MCtn

01 H3 **'Red Ace'**
Round red root. F_1 hybrid; uniform roots with good flesh colour and no rings. Reconfirmed after trial 2016.
EKin EKin

05 H3 **'Solo'**
Round red root. F_1 hybrid. Round to slightly flattened shape. Bulks up well; smooth roots of good internal colour. Reconfirmed after trial 2016.
LCro

BORECOLE OR CURLY KALE (*Brassica oleracea* Acephala Group)

15 H5 **'Black Magic'**
A British-bred Cavolo Nero variety with distinctively tall, narrow dark grey-green leaves which have a savoyed appearance. The leaves have a rich flavour and delicate texture, and can be harvested as baby leaf or left to mature. Shows some resistance to bolting. Good yield.
MCtn

99 H5 **'Redbor'**
F_1 hybrid. Tall, uniform plants with open habit; strongly curled purple-green leaves. Good salad leaf, with ornamental value too. Winters well. Reconfirmed after trial 2015.
EDel EKin EKin LCro

93 H5 **'Winterbor'**
F_1 hybrid. Tall plants with finely curled blue-green leaves; winters well. Developed from (but superior to) 'Westland Winter'. Reconfirmed after trial 1999, 2015.
EGren EKin MCtn

BROCCOLI (*Brassica oleracea* Italica Group)

SEE UNDER CALABRESE FOR CALABRESE BROCCOLI

PURPLE SPROUTING

13 H5 **'Cardinal'**
Tidy upright plants, some variability in height, as expected for open-pollinated cultivars. Dense spears of deep purple. Good for late crop.
EKin

95 H4 **'Claret'**
F_1 hybrid. Very tall; heavy yield of dark purple spears from March through April. Reconfirmed after trial 2013.
EDel EKin EKin LCro LCro

13 H5 **'Mendocino'**
Sturdy vigorous plants, with large, attractive deep purple spears of good quality.
EDel

BRUSSELS SPROUTS (*Brassica oleracea* Gemmifera Group)

15 H5 **'Brodie'**
Clean buttons, developing unevenly; the customer favourite for flavour in supermarket trials because of its exceptional sweet mild taste. It has a good holding ability and can be harvested between September and December. Ideal for Christmas.
LCro

99 H5 **'Cascade'**
F_1 hybrid; late. Smooth, clean, well-spaced, fairly round sprouts. Uniform plants which stand and yield well.
EKin LCro

15 H4 **'Crispus'**
Early to midseason. Clubroot-resistant; nice colour, with mild, slightly nutty taste when cooked.
EKin

15 H5 **'Doric'**
Tall plants, with sparse large buttons. Slightly bitter, with slight aftertaste when cooked.
EDel

15 H4 **'Marte'**
Tall plants with sprouts well spaced. Buttons quite round; good size; nice and dense. Not bitter, even uncooked.
EKin

06 H4 **'Maximus'**
F_1 hybrid; early to mid season. Leading commercial variety; uniform plants, producing a good crop of mid to dark green, smooth, solid sprouts, slightly sweet and crunchy after cooking. Reconfirmed after trial 2015.
EKin LCro LCro MCtn

CABBAGE (*Brassica oleracea* Capitata Group)

16 H2 **'Cabbice'**
Summer. Hybrid; Japanese flat cabbage. Sweet, heavy and dense, with good flavour.
EKin

16 H2 **'Caraflex'**
Summer. Hybrid; early sweetheart type. Quite big for the garden, but capable of making smaller heads.
EDel EKin LCro

08 H5 **'Deadon'**
Uniform, attractive 'January King' type with a flattened round head. Reconfirmed after trial 2019.
EDel EKin EKin

93 H5 **'Duncan'**
Spring heading, pointed. F_1 hybrid. Mid to dark green uniform heads with well-closed bases. A good early yield; compact neat habit; plants heart slowly to produce small, solid, well-filled heads. Reconfirmed after trial 2001, 2011, 2022 as spring greens and hearted cabbage.
EDel EGren

98 H2 **'Elisa'**
Summer, June to August. F_1 hybrid; early. Compact round heads with bright green glossy leaves. Reconfirmed after trial 2016.
EDel

93 H5 **'Marabel'**
F_1 hybrid; 'January King' type. Mid green leaves with good, deep red colour; round well-filled heads with good standing ability. Reconfirmed after trial 2000, 2007 and 2019.
MCtn

16 H2 **'Regency'**
Summer. Hybrid; pointed type, producing very uniform and compact hearts with a strong base and good standing ability. It has dark green outer leaves and a tight, light green pointed heart that can be harvested between June and September. Commercially successful; earlier than 'Dutchman'.
EGren

93 H2 **'Stonehead'**
Summer, June to August. F_1 hybrid; late. Uniform, round, mid green heads. Stands well. Also useful for cropping into the autumn from later planting. Reconfirmed after trial 2016.
EGren EKin MBros

01 H5 **'Tundra'**
Winter hybrid. F_1 hybrid; dark green, slightly blistered leaf; heads solid and attractive. Sweet-tasting; overwinters well. Reconfirmed after trial 2007 and 2019, and as spring cabbage after trial 2022.
EGren EKin MCtn

CALABRESE BROCCOLI (*Brassica oleracea* Italica Group)

03 H3 **'Belstar'**
F_1 hybrid; May-sown. Mid to late season; uniform medium-sized plants, with attractive heads and medium to small buds.
EKin

07 H3 **'Green Magic'**
Autumn-cropping; very good yield of slightly domed, good-sized heads with small beads. Known to make good side-shoots. Reconfirmed after trial 2013.
EKin LCro MCtn

13 H2 **'Ironman'**
A top-performing calabrese, popular with commercial growers because of its long cropping period (May to October), producing uniform domed heads of tight blue-green buds. Crops quickly – ready to harvest 75 days from transplanting. It shows good tolerance to hollow stem and resistance to bolting.
EDel EKin

03 H3 **'Kabuki'**
F_1 hybrid; May-sown; early. Short, compact plants, producing a good crop of medium green, deep, well-rounded heads with uniform buds. Average yield of medium-sized secondaries, produced 3 to 5 weeks after the primary heads. Could be closely spaced to produce baby heads. Reconfirmed after trial 2007, 2013.
MCtn

13 H2 **'Marathon'**
Exceptionally reliable and long-harvesting summer calabrese, producing dense, medium-sized, dome-shaped heads with a great flavour. It will grow in most soils and shows some resistance to disease.
EKin

CARROT (*Daucus carota*)

99 H3 **'Adelaide'**
F_1 hybrid; very early. Good weight and colour; sweet-flavoured; quickly forms very smooth, stump-ended roots; almost coreless; fine tops. Ideal for successional sowings and early sowing in frames. Reconfirmed after trial 2006 and 2010 as early, suitable for containers.
EKin LCro

06 H4 **'Amsterdam Forcing 3'**
Open-pollinated. Relatively smooth with good flesh and core colour; bulks up well. Strong foliage that does not grow too tall.
EKin MCtn

14 H7 **'Deep Purple'**
Maincrop. Purple skin and flesh, with tapered roots and pleasant flavour; reasonable uniformity of crop.
MCtn

05 H4 **'Eskimo'**
F_1 hybrid; medium-length, smooth roots with good colour. Useful size, well-filled. Grows with crowns at or below ground level, so very little crown discoloration. Good overwintering cultivar. Reconfirmed after trial 2014.
EKin LCro MCtn

99 H3 **'Flyaway'**
F_1 hybrid. Maincrop; medium-length, well-filled, stump-ended roots with good flesh and core colour. Good strong tops. Partial resistance (i.e. lack of attraction) to carrot flies. Reconfirmed after trial 2006.
EKin LCro LCro MCtn

99 H4 **'Maestro'**
F_1 hybrid. Best lifted before Christmas. Blunt, smooth-skinned, medium to slim, fairly well-filled roots, uniform in size and shape. Mid to pale internal colour with some green shoulders. Widely grown by organic carrot growers. Reconfirmed after trial 2005, 2014.
LCro

10 H3 **'Marion'**
Early to mature; uniform crop of slightly tapered roots with good weight. Smooth skin, deep orange flesh and good core colour. Suitable for containers.
EKin

99 H4 **'Nairobi'**
F_1 hybrid; second early/early maincrop. Strong tops, with uniform, broader-shouldered, cylindrical, stump-ended roots. Heavy yields. Reconfirmed after trial 2006, 2014.
EKin

05 H4 **'Sugarsnax 54'**
F_1 hybrid. Very long, smooth, 'Imperator' type with roots of good internal colour. Suited to deep, light soils. Commercially used, cut into short lengths and sold as pre-packed baton carrots.
EKin MCtn

05 H4 **'Sweet Candle'**
F_1 hybrid; short, blunt, quite smooth, well-filled, uniform roots. Good internal colour. Reconfirmed after trial 2014.
EKin LCro LCro

14 H4 **'Tozresis'**
A 'Nantes' type. Bred for intermediate carrot fly resistance. Smooth skin, good uniformity, well-stumped root, good colour, nice flavour.
EGren MCtn SVic

CAULIFLOWER (*Brassica oleracea* Botrytis Group)

05 H5 **'Aalsmeer'**
Spring heading, maturing from March to May. Open-pollinated cultivar, producing medium to small, cream-coloured, slightly lumpy, well-protected curds that have a good depth. Under trial, this cultivar produced several multiple heads and sideshoots, many of usable quality.
EKin

06 H3 **'Aviron'**
Hybrid; late. High quality, well-protected, large to medium-sized solid, white heads. Reconfirmed after trial for autumn heading 2015 and for summer heading 2018.
EKin

15 H3 **'Boris'**
Autumn or summer heading. Good, deep, round curd. Reconfirmed for summer heading after trial 2018.
EKin

15 H3 **'Clapton'**
Autumn heading, September to November. Neat, well-covered variety, with lovely curds and good upright habit.
EDel EKin

05 H3 **'Graffiti'**
F_1 hybrid. Small to medium, high quality, solid curds of a very attractive amethyst colour. The colour fades a little if boiled, and is retained better if steamed. The raw curds have a good flavour and would be a colourful addition to a salad or dish of crudités. Midseason. Reconfirmed after trial 2006.
EKin EKin

97 H5 **'Jerome'**
spring heading, maturing from March to May F_1 hybrid; early midseason. Vigorous plant, producing good quality, well-covered curds. Curds well-rounded, medium to small and cream-coloured. Reconfirmed after trial 2005.
EDel

02 H3 **'Skywalker'**
Autumn heading, September to November.

F₁ hybrid; early with a short cropping period; very good white colour, size and depth. Reconfirmed after trial 2015.
EKin

15 H3 **'Tirza'**
Autumn heading, September to November. Produces a compact head of pure white curds; perfect for small spaces or containers. Heavy cropping, it is the earliest cauliflower of the season, and shows some disease resistance.
EKin

05 H3 **'Veronica'**
F₁ hybrid; appetising light green Romanesco type. Uniform good-sized, solid, well-shaped heads.
EDel EKin

CELERIAC (*Apium graveolens* var. *rapaceum*)

00 H4 **'Prinz'**
Smooth, deep, white-skinned; small to medium, flattened and round; compact plant with healthy foliage. Reconfirmed after trial 2011, 2022.
CHby EDel EKin LCro MCtn SVic

CELERY (*Apium graveolens* var. *dulce*)

93 H2 **'Celebrity'**
Self-blanching, fairly short plants, with ribbed petioles and good flavour. Reconfirmed after trial 2001.
MCtn

01 H2 **'Tango'**
Open-pollinated; slower-maturing, long, mid green, fleshy petioles. Reconfirmed after trial 2005, 2022.
EKin

94 H2 **'Victoria'**
F₁ hybrid. Tall, well-filled plants with medium-green, smooth, fleshy petioles. Widely used for commercial crops. Reconfirmed after trial 2005, 2022.
EDel EGren EKin

CHARD (*Beta vulgaris* subsp. *cicla* var. *flavescens*)

00 H3 BRIGHT LIGHTS
Good colourful mix, including reds, yellows and whites; very ornamental and decorative. Often grown as an annual, but may overwinter in areas where the soil is not too wet.
CHby EGren MNHC SVic

00 H3 **'Bright Yellow'**
Bright golden-yellow petioles and mid green puckered leaf; uniform; sweet taste; reconfirmed after trial 2011.
LCro MCtn

00 H3 **'Fordhook Giant'**
Attractive shiny light green, puckered leaf with white stem and long succulent broad white petioles; old blister-leaf chard type.
EKin MCtn

00 H3 **'Rhubarb Chard'**
Dark green leaves and red stem; uniform; blister-type leaf; reconfirmed after trial 2011.
EKin LCro LCro MBros MCtn SVic

CHICORY (*Cichorium intybus*)

02 H5 **'Palla Rossa'**
Leafy – radicchio. Medium to large heads; well-filled red hearts; fairly uniform. No bolting.
CHby MCtn SRms

02 H5 **'Pan di Zucchero'**
Leafy – sugar loaf. Uniform plants with medium to large frames and dark green outer leaves. Hearts blanch well.
CHby

CHILLI (*Capsicum* SPECIES)

06 H1c **'Apache'**
Decorative, growing to 45cm; does well in both large and small pots. Produces large crop of small, juicy, hot peppers that ripen from bright green to red and are held outwards from the stems. Reconfirmed after trial trial 2013, 2023.
EHet EKin MBros MPri SPre

13 H1c **'Basket of Fire'**
Multi-branched, open habit, height to c.25cm. Numerous upright fruits, maturing through cream, lemon, yellow and orange to red.
EDel EHet EKin LCro SPre SVic WKit

13 H1c **'Bolivian Rainbow'**
Compact plant, height c.32 cm, with mid green foliage. Stumpy, broad-based fruit held erect. Fruit ripening cream through orange to red.
SVic

06 H1c **'Caribbean Antillais'**
Quite small, blocky, bright red fruits; aromatic and very hot, of a type widely used in South American and Caribbean cooking. Later-cropping, best sown in January and given a higher temperature to germinate.
SVic

06 H1c **'Demon Red'**
A small, ornamental plant, starred with white flowers, producing an abundant crop of tiny upward-pointing fruits that mature to dark, bright red. Fruits are hot and used in Thai cooking. Reconfirmed after trial 2013.
EHet EKin MCtn SPre SVic

13 H1c **'Hot Thai'**
Bushy yet compact habit, height to 25cm. Dainty dark green foliage. Small, hot fruits

(1.5cm in length, and 1cm wide), held erect. Ideal for a windowsill. Reconfirmed after trial 2023.
EKin

06 H1c **'Hungarian Hot Wax'**
Conical fruits ripening from pale yellow to bright red; medium hot; very good for frying, stuffing and using in salads. One of the easiest to grow. Suitable for growing in pots. Reconfirmed after trial 2023.
CHby EKin LCro MCtn SVic

14 H1c **'Pot Black'**
Upright plant with branching habit; height c.36cm. Stem, foliage, fruit very dark purple. Fruit blocky in shape, held erect above the foliage. Interesting and unusual variety.
EDel SVic WKit

06 H1c **'Prairie Fire'**
Very attractive, short (20cm high), spreading plants covered in a mass of very small, very hot, upright peppers that ripen from white, through yellow and orange, to red. Ideal for pots or a windowsill. Reconfirmed after trial 2013.
LCro SVic

23 H1c **'Spangles'**
Novel, attractive and interesting plant with open bushy habit. Many round, thick-fleshed, purple fruit, finally turning red.
LCro

06 H1c **'Super Chili'**
Ornamental plants; well suited to growing in pots. Produces a high yield of very hot, thin-walled fruits that are held upright and ripen from light green to orange-red.
SPre SVic

CHINESE CABBAGE (*Brassica rapa* Pekinensis Group)

03 H3 **'Yuki'**
Barrel-shaped. Medium green, slightly savoyed outer leaves; very short internal stem; medium-sized heavy head; well-blanched. Reconfirmed after trial 2018.
EKin MCtn

CORIANDER (*Coriandrum sativum*)

14 H2 **'Calypso'**
Vigorous, bushy strong growth; holds well; good leaf yield. Ideal size for the home gardener.
EKin MCtn WKit

14 H5 **'Confetti'**
Neat and clean, with distinct fern-like look; uniform. Ideal for smaller gardens.
EKin LCro MCtn MHoo MNHC

14 H2 **'Cruiser'**
A compact plant, with big leaves and good germination.
EDel MCtn MNHC WKit

COURGETTE (*Cucurbita pepo*)

93 H2 **'Defender'**
F_1 hybrid. A high yield of medium-sized, slender, very lightly flecked fruits. Reconfirmed after trial 2021.
EGren EKin LCro MCtn

93 H2 **'Early Gem'**
F_1 hybrid; a high yield of slender, lightly speckled fruits. Easy to see on the plant.
EKin MCtn

98 H2 **'El Greco'**
F_1 hybrid. Bush type; plant of open habit with mid green fruits.
LCro

98 H2 **'Jemmer'**
As courgette, awarded 1998: also awarded as a summer squash, 2006. F_1 hybrid. Bush type; good yield of bright, light yellow, cylindrical fruits. Vigorous, healthy, upright plants with fruits that are easy to see and pick.
LCro LCro

13 H2 **'Orelia'**
Upright plant, producing a good yield of yellow fruits. Vigorous plants, showing good mildew resistance. Reconfirmed after trial 2021.
EKin

06 H2 **'Parador'**
Hybrid; crops early and gives a high yield. Nicely shaped fruits are cylindrical, straight and an attractive bright yellow. Flowers are held on the fruits until completely faded. Plants are healthy and compact. Also grown as squash. Reconfirmed after trial 2013 as bush courgette.
EGren

13 H2 **'Patio Star'**
Compact plant, ideal for small space or container. No mildew. Glossy, dark green fruits.
EDel

CUCUMBER (*Cucumis sativus*)

02 H1c **'Carmen'**
F_1 hybrid; standard length, dark green, slightly ribbed fruits. Reconfirmed after trial 2009, 2021.
EKin MCtn

09 H1c **'Cucino'**
Smooth, small, dark green, uniform fruits with good flavour and texture. Highly productive plants.
SVic

09 H1c **'Emilie'**
Useful mid length fruits with attractive dark green colour and good flavour. Previously listed as 'Emile'. Reconfirmed after trial 2021.
LCro

95 H1c **'Marketmore'**
Ridge cucumber. Good yield of short, attractive, dark green fruits. Grown in the open garden. Reconfirmed after trial 2001, 2019.
CHby EDel EKin LCro MCtn

09 H1c **'Mini Munch'**
Highly productive plants producing abundant small, crunchy, shiny-skinned fruits with good flavour. Reconfirmed after trial 2021.
EKin MCtn

DILL (*Anethum graveolens*)

14 H2 **'Domino'**
A compact dill variety producing full, heavy foliage with a deep blue-green colour. It has an excellent aroma, perfect for cooking, and is suitable for open ground or container growing. It has a good standing ability and is slow to bolt so can be harvested between May and September.
MNHC

ENDIVE (*Cichorium endivia*)

96 H3 **'Pancalieri'**
Curled. Very strong cut-leaf type. Does not blanch well.
CHby EKin MCtn

FLORENCE FENNEL (*Foeniculum vulgare* var. *azoricum*)

19 H2 **'Rondo'**
Even bulbs; no bolting during the RHS trial. Harvested in its first year; if allowed to grow on, small, yellow flowers carried in flat, delicate umbels are produced in the second year.
MCtn

GARLIC (*Allium sativum*)

04 H4 **'Cristo'**
Soft neck. Uniform crop of attractive, white-skinned bulbs; high yield. Also performed well at Harlow Carr.
EGren LCro

04 H4 **'Germidour'**
Late-maturing, virus-free selection. Soft necks; well-packed, purple-skinned cloves.
LCro

04 H4 **'Solent White'**
Late. Soft neck; many purple-skinned, very attractive cloves, with appealing bouquet; high yield; keeps beyond Christmas (up to March). Also performed well at Harlow Carr.
EGren EKin LCro LCro

LEEK (*Allium porrum*)

09 H5 **'Blauwgroene Winter' - Bandit**
Winter hardy. Good open-pollinated cultivar. Dark blue-green flags; reasonable length of blanch.
EDel EKin

00 H4 **'Jolant'**
Autumn and early winter. High yield; medium to dark green flags; long, solid shafts with little bulbing and very few bolters. Low levels of rust infection. Has a long season and peels nicely. Reconfirmed after trial 2002, 2015.
EKin MCtn

15 H5 **'Lancaster'**
Winter hardy. Hybrid; lovely leek, dark green and upright; really uniform.
MCtn

00 H4 **'Mammoth Blanch'**
Autumn and early winter. A show variety suitable for December sowing. Early-maturing, with high yields of well-shaped leeks with pale green flags, long, heavy shafts and no bolters.
EKin

02 H5 **'Mammoth Pot Leek'**
Winter hardy. Uniform, with whole stem blanched and light green flag. High December yield. A good short garden plant.
EKin

02 H5 **'Oarsman'**
Winter hardy. F$_1$ hybrid; erect plant, with very straight shank, uniform, smooth; flag leaf clean. Good yield. Reconfirmed after trial 2015.
EGren EKin

LETTUCE (*Lactuca sativa*)

12 H2 **'Amaze'**
Cos. A 'Red Gem' type; good colour; green heart, red outer leaves. Compact, uniform crop, sweet taste.
EKin MCtn

95 H2 **'Black-seeded Simpson Improved'**
Leafy. Yellow-green leaves with frilled edges. Cos-like in growth.
MCtn

95 H2 **'Catalogna'**
Leafy. Strong-growing oak-leaved type. Light green slightly blistered leaves.
MCtn SVic

07 H2 **'Chatsworth'**
Cos. Medium-sized with rugose leaves; dense

hearts make a good weight and have a good blanch. Very good flavour.
LCro

97 H2 **'Clarion'**
Butterhead, for autumn cropping under protection or summer cropping in the open garden. Open heads, with pale to mid green leaves. Reconfirmed after trial 2002.
LCro

95 H2 **'Cocarde'**
Leafy. Large oak-leaved type, with bronze green-tinged leaves. Has a very good flavour and doesn't bolt.
EDel

99 H2 **'Crisp Mint'**
Cos; very fast growing. A heritage variety with a pale-coloured heart and crisp, bright green, wrinkly leaves which form an upright cluster.
EKin MCtn

93 H2 **'Little Gem'**
Cos. Small solid heads with mid green, medium-blistered leaves. Reconfirmed after trial 1999, 2007, 2012.
CHby EGren EKin LCro MBros MCtn WFar

93 H2 **'Lobjoit's Green Cos'**
Cos. Large, rather open heads, with relatively smooth mid green leaves. Reconfirmed after trial 1999.
EKin SVic

12 H2 **'Maureen'**
Cos. Uniform crop, with mid green leaves. One of the most popular commercial 'Gem' varieties.
EDel EKin

95 H3 **'New Red Fire'**
Leafy. Large, with puckered light bronze outer leaves.
EKin MCtn

99 H3 **'Parris Island Cos'**
Vigorous with pale green uniform heads; reconfirmed after trial 2007.
EKin

95 H3 **'Salad Bowl'**
Leafy. Large open-hearted plants with light green frilled leaves.
CHby EKin LCro MCtn

03 H2 **'Sioux'**
Crisphead. Smooth leaves, large frame, with a green heart and outer leaves tipped red. Slow to bolt.
LCro

00 H2 **'Winter Density'**
Semi-Cos with leafy, erect habit; dark green, very uniform. Reconfirmed after trial 2007, 2012.
EDel EKin LCro MCtn

SEE UNDER PEAS FOR MANGETOUT

MARROW (*Cucurbita pepo*)

97 H2 **'Tiger Cross'**
F_1 hybrid with high yields. A high-quality bush marrow variety, bred in the UK, which is quick to grow and early to crop. It produces a uniform crop of green and cream striped fruits that can be harvested as courgettes or left to mature to full-sized marrows. Shows good resistance to cucumber mosaic virus. Harvest June to October.
EGren EKin LCro MCtn SVic

MELON (*Cucumis melo*)

09 H1c **'Alvaro'**
Big crop; attractive pale green skins with dark green stripes and salmon-orange flesh. Good flavour. Reconfirmed after trial 2022.
EDel MCtn

09 H1c **'Emir'**
Good crop of netted Charentais-type fruits with orange flesh; H2 for outdoor use.
EKin LCro MCtn

ONION (*Allium* SPECIES)

93 H3 **'Centurion'**
From sets. F_1 hybrid. Flattened globe-shaped bulbs with straw-coloured skins of good thickness. Reconfirmed after trial 2002, 2013.
EGren LCro

20 H4 **'Fasto'**
Spring sown. Good skin colour and quality. Uniform sample. Stored well in trial.
EKin

02 H3 **'Hercules'**
From sets. F_1 hybrid; slightly elongated bulbs with good skin. No bolters. Reconfirmed after trial 2013.
LCro

20 H3 **'Hybound'**
Attractive brown bulbs with an excellent skin quality and long storage life. Early maturing variety with a great flavour.
EKin

05 H3 **'Red Baron'**
Red, globe, from seed and sets. High yield of attractive, dark-skinned, globe-shaped bulbs with good internal colour. Plants in the trial grown from seed produced a higher yield and bolder bulbs than those grown from sets. Reconfirmed after trial 2013, 2020.
CHby EGren EKin LCro MCtn

05 H3 **'Redspark'**
Red, globe, from seed and sets. Attractive

globe-shaped, uniform, medium-sized bulbs with tight, dark skins and good internal colour. Reconfirmed after trial 2020.
EDel

13 H3 **'Rumba'**
From sets. Uniform crop; large bulb size, globe-shaped, with brown skin. Stores well.
EGren EKin

02 H3 **'Sturon'**
From sets. Very good yield of globe-shaped, slightly high-shouldered bulbs, with good yellow-brown skins. Reconfirmed after trial 2002, 2013.
CHby EGren EKin LCro

02 H3 **'Stuttgarter'**
From sets. High yield, well shaped, deep bulb, good skin.
EGren EKin LCro

SALAD ONION

04 H3 **'Apache'**
Traditional. Vigorous plants with bright, medium-green leaves; of good shape. Attractive deep red-purple colour to base. Also sold as 'Deep Purple'.
MCtn

04 H3 **'Guardsman'**
Non-bulbing. F_1 hybrid: cross between *A. fistulosum* and *A. cepa*. Medium to dark green leaves. Very vigorous; well-blanched with some bulbing. Also performed well at Harlow Carr.
MCtn

96 H5 **'Ishikura'**
Non-bulbing; strong-growing and long-stemmed. Exceptionally long harvest period from summer to autumn without the need for successive sowings.
MCtn

17 H4 **'Matrix'**
Very even, with very thick roots and good flavour; has a kick.
EDel

04 H3 **'Parade'**
Non-bulbing. Very straight, strong-growing, uniform plants with good length of blanch; slow to bolt. Also performed well at Harlow Carr.
EDel

93 H4 **'White Lisbon'**
Traditional. Medium-green leaves with good length of blanch. Good for early and successional sowing. Reconfirmed after trial 2004.
CHby EKin LCro MCtn SVic

93 H4 **'Winter White Bunching'**
Traditional. Strong-growing with dark green leaves. Overwinters well.
EKin

SHALLOT

01 H3 **'Longor'**
From sets; good yield and shape; also suitable for exhibition. Reconfirmed after trial 2018.
EGren LCro

01 H3 **'Matador'**
From seed; F_1 hybrid; thick skins, and good yield. Reconfirmed after trial 2018.
EDel EKin MCtn SVic

18 H3 **'Meloine'**
From sets. Attractive, with high uniform yield. Stores well. Downy mildew resistant.
LCro

18 H3 **'Zebrune'**
From seed. A heritage variety of torpedo-shaped, brownish pink-skinned bulbs with a superb flavour, popular for gourmet cooking. Late but good yield, suitable for storing; good resistance to bolting.
MCtn

OREGANO (*Origanum* species)

23 H5 **'Compactum'**
Bushy, forming a low mound to 15cm tall, with small aromatic leaves and loose sprays of tiny pale pink flowers opening from summer to early autumn. Popular with bees, and a pleasant smell.
CCBP CGHo EBee ECha EHet ENfk EWhm GBin MHer MHoo MNHC NBir SPlb SRms WChS WHoo WJek WKit

23 H5 **'French'**
Vigorous habit, consistent, reliable, with pretty white flowers. Gentle, mild flavour.
EHet IDun SRms WJek

23 H5 **'Hot and Spicy'**
Very hardy, and highly recommended for culinary use. Flavour true to name. Popular with pollinators.
CGHo EHet EHet ELan ENfk EWhm GJos LCro MHoo MNHC NBir SRms WFar WJek WKit

23 H2 **sweet marjoram**
O. majorana. Superb flavour, dries well, widely recommended in culinary circles. Perennial, frost tender. White, pale pink or mauve flowers are popular with bees and other pollinators.
CAgr CGHo CHab EHet ENfk GQue MCtn MHer MHoo MNHC SRms SVic WJek

PAK CHOI (*Brassica rapa* Chinensis Group)

10 H3 **'Red Choi'**
Good germination rate. Very little bolting. Stands well. Attractive purple leaves and tender green stem. Good hearting, uniform clean,

healthy crop. Ideal size for cooking.
EDel EKin MCtn

PARSLEY (*Petroselinum crispum*)

97 H6 **'Bravour'**
An attractive curled variety that grows to around 30cm but with a compact habit. The masses of tightly curled dark green leaves have a great flavour; could also be planted as an ornamental, and in containers. Reliable cropper.
MHer

97 H4 **'Curlina'**
Compact and uniform variety with attractive, tightly curled leaves. Ideal for windowsill pots or mixed patio planters in a sunny or partially shaded position.
LCro

93 H6 **'Moss Curled'**
Aromatic, deeply cut, tightly curled leaves and small umbels of yellow-green flowers in summer.
CCBP CHby EKin MHoo SRms WKit

PARSNIP (*Pastinaca sativa*)

01 H5 **'Gladiator'**
F_1 hybrid; very smooth skin, good potential yield, uniform shape, shallow lenticels. Reconfirmed after trial 2009.
EKin LCro MCtn

PEAS (*Pisum sativum*)

93 H2 **'Hurst Green Shaft'**
Maincrop; heavy yield of dark green, medium-length, pointed pods. Excellent taste, with good number of peas per pod. Nicely progressive yield. Reconfirmed after trial 1998, 2005, 2017.
EKin LCro MCtn

97 H2 **'Kelvedon Wonder'**
Early maincrop. Long, dark green pods, with an average of 7 to 8 peas per pod. Reconfirmed after trial 2004, 2005.
EDel EKin LCro MCtn

05 H2 **'Serge'**
Maincrop; semi-leafless plants produce a heavy crop of easy-to-pick pods. Medium-length pods have an average of ten peas per pod, with good flavour.
EKin LCro

MANGETOUT

00 H2 **'Delikata'**
Tall, with similar pods to 'Oregon Sugar Pod'. A shade earlier and carries a heavy crop. Pods soon form strings if not picked regularly. Mildew- and fusarium-resistant.
LCro

SUGARSNAP PEAS

00 H2 SUGAR DWARF SWEET GREEN (**'Norli'**)
Medium height; good for garden use. About the earliest to mature and a heavy cropper, but over a short period and so requires successional sowing. Reconfirmed after trial 2009.
CHby MCtn

00 H2 **'Cascadia'**
Dwarf habit, producing very fleshy, crisp, sweet pods, which remain tender and sweet over a longer period than many snaps. Heavy crops over a long picking season. Reconfirmed after trial 2009.
EGren LCro

00 H2 **'Delikett'**
Dwarf habit. Young, dark green pods stringless but soon form strings; become fleshier and sweeter with age. Very well cropped and a long season of picking. Reconfirmed after trial 2009.
EKin MCtn MNHC

00 H2 **'Sugar Ann'**
Medium height. Early to crop and gives a good yield of juicy, sweet pods. Good flavour. Reconfirmed after trial 2009.
CHby EKin

POTATO (*Solanum tuberosum*)

98 H2 **'British Queen'**
Second early. Heavy and uniform crop of white-skinned and floury-textured tubers of delicious flavour for all cooking purposes.
GPoH LCro

14 H2 **'Carolus'**
Maincrop. Particoloured skin, yellow flesh, oval tubers, good blight tolerance; an excellent cultivar which bakes, roasts, chips and mashes well.
GPoH LCro

13 H2 **'Casablanca'**
Early in containers. A new, multi-purpose first early potato with a smooth white skin, shallow eyes and creamy flesh. An attractive potato, which is rapidly becoming an exhibitor's favourite; ideal for chipping, baking or boiling. Trials show good resistance to potato blackleg.
EDel EGren EKin GPoH LCro

98 H2 **'Charlotte'**
Second early or salad. Long oval variety producing yellow-skinned and waxy tubers with creamy yellow flesh of first-class flavour either hot or cold. Reconfirmed after trial 2013 as early for container use.
EDel EGren EKin GPoH LCro

14 H2 **'Desiree'**
Maincrop. Red skin, light yellow flesh, oval tubers; reliable, and still the world's most popular red.
EGren GPoH LCro

98 H2 **'Foremost'**
First early. Originally 'Suttons Foremost'. Ever popular new potato with slightly waxy, firm, white, good-flavoured flesh that does not discolour or disintegrate on cooking.
EGren EKin LCro LCro

13 H2 **'Jazzy'**
Early in containers. Attractive, oval, uniform crop. Yellow skin and flesh, waxy tubers with sweet taste.
EKin

98 H3 **'Lady Christl'**
Bulks up very quickly and is almost a first early. Long oval, shallow-eyed, pale yellow-skinned and creamy flesh which remains firm on cooking. Eelworm-resistant. Reconfirmed after trial 2007; also in 2013 after trial as early for container use.
EKin LCro

13 H2 **'Maris Bard'**
Early in containers. White flesh, thin skin, good flavour and texture; fairly uniform crop.
EDel EGren EKin GPoH LCro

14 H2 **'Maris Piper'**
Maincrop. Cream skin, cream flesh, oval tubers; a massive favourite with gardeners.
EGren GPoH LCro

98 H2 **'Nadine'**
Second early. Exceptionally smooth skin and shallow eyes. Cream flesh with a moist, waxy texture that does not discolour and remains firm on cooking. Heavy uniform yields; scab-free. Reconfirmed after trial 2017.
EGren EKin

07 H2 **'Orla'**
First early. Can also be used as a second early and maincrop. Good yield of round to oval creamy white tubers; flesh slightly waxy with good flavour. Popular with organic gardeners.
EDel EGren GPoH LCro

93 H2 **'Picasso'**
Early maincrop. One of the heaviest croppers with creamy skin and striking bright red eyes. Waxy fine-flavoured flesh, particularly when boiled. Eelworm-resistant and good resistance to common scab. Reconfirmed after trial 1998, 2014.
EGren LCro

03 H2 **'Pink Fir Apple'**
Salad. Late main crop (22 weeks from planting). Very vigorous plants; elongated, knobbly tubers; good flavour.
EGren EKin GPoH LCro SVic

03 H2 **'Ratte'**
Salad; early main crop. Moderate yields; long oval tubers; waxy yellow flesh with distinctive chestnut flavour. Worth the smaller number of tubers for the excellent taste.
GPoH

98 H2 **'Red Duke of York'**
First early. Oval red sport of 'Duke of York' with moist pale yellow flesh of superb flavour. Excellent roasted, but a good all-rounder as tubers bulk up quickly if left to mature as a late second early.
EGren EKin GPoH LCro

14 H2 **'Rooster'**
Maincrop. Very popular red-skinned variety, with medium yellow flesh and oval tubers; superb for roasting with flavour and good yield.
GPoH

14 H2 **'Sarpo Mira'**
Maincrop. Red skin, white flesh, oval tubers; still the leading blight benchmark.
EDel EGren GPoH LCro

17 H2 **'Saxon'**
Second early. Good tuber count, with good shape and white flesh with good flavour; cooked well during trial and did not disintegrate, with attractive skin even when cooked.
LCro

13 H2 **'Sharpe's Express'**
Early in containers. Heritage variety; white skin, uniform crop size. Slightly waxy, good flavour.
GPoH LCro

07 H2 **'Vivaldi'**
First early. Can be left to bulk up as summer baker. Good yield of oval, pale yellow, smooth-skinned tubers with creamy flesh.
EKin LCro

98 H2 **'Winston'**
First early. Bulks up quickly to produce large, even-shaped tubers. Creamy moist flesh of excellent flavour which does not discolour on cooking.
EKin LCro

RADISH (*Raphanus sativus*)

08 H2 **'Amethyst'**
Decorative purple roots; very uniform flattened-round shape with a fine tap root. Tops are short and leaves are distinctively entire. No pithiness. Strong flavour. Reconfirmed after trial 2013.
MCtn

13 H2 **'Escala'**
Hybrid. Globe-shaped, bright cherry-red, with thin tap root; not pithy. Very uniform crop.
LCro

08 H2 **'Pink Beauty'**
Attractive, shiny pink roots. Crunchy texture and good, sweet flavour. No pithiness.
LCro

96 H2 **'Scarlet Globe'**
Round roots with red skin and crisp white flesh; mild flavour.
EKin

96 H2 **'Sparkler'**
Slightly flattened round roots. Unique colour split: red upper with white lower skin. Reconfirmed after trial 2013.
CHby EKin MCtn

RHUBARB (*Rheum* × *hybridum*)

03 H5 **'Fulton's Strawberry Surprise'**
Maincrop. Very attractive bright red colour. Strong plant, but not too vigorous for the garden.
CDoC CDoC CMac EPfP EPom LRHS SWCr

12 H5 **'Raspberry Red'**
First early. High quality rich red stalks. Crops heavily and reliably.
CDoC CDoC EGren EHet EPfP EPom LCro LRHS SPoG

03 H5 **'Timperley Early'**
First early. Thick stems, early, high yield. Bred for forcing; performs very well outside, but even better colour when forced.
CDoC CMac CSBt EBee EHet EKin ELan EPfP EPom LBuc LCro LRHS LSRN MGos MPri NLar SEdi SPoG SWCr WMat

SHALLOT: SEE UNDER ONION

SPINACH (*Spinacia oleracea*)

08 H2 **'Amazon'**
F_1 hybrid; resistant to mildew races 1–10. Vigorous plants that bulk well; leaves are large, round and a good glossy dark green.
MCtn SVic

00 H2 **'Matador'**
A leafy prolific spinach that has thick, dark green, upright leaves all summer through in to autumn. Plants show some resistance to bolting under dry conditions.
EKin LCro LCro

00 H2 **'Medania'**
Open-pollinated; resistant to mildew races 1 and 3. Good yield from slower-growing plants that are slow to bolt. Slightly blistered, large round leaves. Reconfirmed after trial 2008, 2023.
EKin MCtn

08 H2 **'Missouri'**
F_1 hybrid; resistant to mildew races 1–10. Heavy yield of bright, medium green leaves with an upright habit. Reconfirmed after trial 2023.
EKin LCro

SPINACH OR LEAF BEET (*Beta vulgaris* subsp. *cicla* var. *cicla*)

00 H4 **'Perpetual Spinach'**
Mid to pale green with fairly soft texture, medium vigour; uniform; stable and clean; flat leaf with good green petiole; reconfirmed after trial 2011.
CHby EDel EKin LCro MCtn SVic

SQUASH (*Cucurbita* species)

06 H2 **'Bush Baby'**
Summer. A compact marrow variety producing attractive, edible yellow flowers in summer followed by striped, and slightly ribbed, baby marrows. The fruits are tender and have an excellent flavour. Harvest between June and October.
MCtn

11 H2 **'Crown Prince'**
Winter. Large fruits, with blue-grey skin and excellent storage quality. Popular, reliable variety. Fruits have high flesh content, of deep orange colour and excellent flavour.
EGren EKin MCtn SVic

11 H2 **'Harlequin'**
Winter. High sugar cultivar. Decorative ridged fruits, striped yellow, gold and green; mid sized with a typical diameter 10–13cm. Good yield per plant and excellent storage quality. Plant has a semi-bush habit. Firm flesh of smooth texture and sweet flavour.
EDel SVic

08 H2 **'Harrier'**
An outstanding British-bred butternut squash, producing an early crop of sweet-tasting, small to medium-sized, pear-shaped fruits with a small seed cavity. Ideally suited to the short growing season and is ready to harvest just over 3 months from sowing. Noted for its reliability and good performance; stores well.
EDel LCro

11 H2 **'Honey Bear'**
Winter. High sugar variety. Dark green, mini-acorn-shaped fruits of uniform size, typically 8–10cm in diameter. Sweet flavour; ideal size for baking whole. Compact, bushy habit, giving a reasonable yield of fruits, with excellent storage qualities. Plant demonstrates good resistance to powdery mildew.
MCtn SVic

08 H2 **'Hunter'**
Butternut. A very high yield of uniformly small to medium, long pear-shaped fruits with a small seed cavity. Early ripening with orange-gold flesh.
EGren EKin MCtn SVic

06 H2 **'Jemmer'**
See under Courgette.

06 H2 **'Parador'**
See under Courgette.

06 H2 **'Sunburst'**
Summer. Hybrid; attractive yellow, scallop-shaped fruits. Used for baby veg; best harvested when small (5–6cm diameter).
EDel

11 H2 **'Sweet Dumpling'**
Winter. Original sweet dumpling type. Uniform crop of small fruit, approximately 9 to 10cm in diameter; ridged, cream-coloured with green stripes and mottling; sweetly flavoured orange flesh. Trailing habit, producing a good yield of fruits with excellent storage quality.
CHby EKin MCtn

SUGARSNAP: SEE UNDER PEAS

SWEETCORN (*Zea mays*)

03 H2 **'Earlibird'**
F_1 hybrid; 2nd early supersweet. Uniform cobs; good vigour. Reconfirmed after trial 2009, 2016.
EGren EGren EKin MCtn

16 H2 **'Goldcrest'**
Supersweet. Well filled and uniform. Even-sized cobs; quite tall plant.
EDel LCro

03 H2 **'Lark'**
F_1 hybrid; 2nd early extra tender sweet. High yield of well-filled cobs with very sweet, clean flavour. Reconfirmed after trial 2009, 2016.
LCro MCtn

09 H2 **'Mirai 003'**
Early; uniform, small, exceptionally sweet cobs.
LCro

16 H2 MIRAI PICNIC (**'Mirai 003Y'**)
Yellow augmented supersweet. Most widely listed Mirai cultivar. Small cobs. Tall plants. Good cob fill.
EKin MCtn

03 H2 **'Swift'**
F_1 hybrid; early extra tender sweet. High yield of cobs with excellent eating quality. Good sweet flavour and tender kernels. Very popular variety. Thin pericarp is prone to damage. Reconfirmed after trial 2009, 2016.
EKin LCro MCtn SVic

SWEET PEPPER (*Capsicum* species)

05 H1c **'Corno di Toro Rosso'**
Open-pollinated; later-cropping. Long, horn-shaped, very fleshy fruits that have a good flavour. Maturing from pale green to bright red. Big fruits, huge yield. Reconfirmed after trial 2016.
CHby LCro MCtn

05 H1c **'Friggitello'**
Open-pollinated; productive plants with small, long, slim, pointed fruits. Ripening from mid green to red; the versatile sweet-flavoured fruits have the appearance of a hot pepper and are also suitable for stirfry and pickling.
MCtn

05 H1c **'Mohawk'**
F_1 hybrid. Medium-sized, blocky, bell-shaped fruits that ripen from dark green to bright yellow; good flavour. Dwarf-growing plants are well suited to growing in pots. Reconfirmed after trial 2016.
EKin

05 H1c **'Redskin'**
F_1 hybrid; small to medium, blocky, bell-shaped fruits that ripen from dark green to a glossy, dark red. Compact plants give a high yield and are well suited to growing in pots. Original windowsill pepper. Reconfirmed after trial 2016.
EKin LCro

05 H1c **'Topepo Rosso'**
Open-pollinated; productive, early-cropping plants. Medium-sized, beef tomato shape that is good for stuffing. Attractive fruits mature from dark green to bright red and have a good flavour.
MCtn

TOMATO (*Solanum lycopersicum*)

07 H1c **'Apero'**
Cherry tomato. Good yield of oval fruits on compact trusses; good flavour.
MCtn

14 H1c **'Beefmaster'**
Beefsteak tomato. Multilocular; large fruit; deeply ribbed; light, smooth taste, good yield.
EKin LCro MCtn

17 H1c **'Bite Size'**
Cherry tomato. Quite sweet. Good size, with good balanced flavour.
EKin LCro

14 H1c **'Bountiful'**
Beefsteak tomato. Good yield of heavy fruit; classic appearance; 'Marmande' type; light taste, good yield.
MCtn

07 H1c **'Cherrola'**
Cherry tomato. High yield, with attractive fruit well spaced on long trusses. Good flavour; not too fleshy inside. Reconfirmed after trial 2017.
LCro

03 H1c **'Costoluto Fiorentino'**
Beefsteak tomato. High yield; medium-sized, attractive bright red, highly ribbed, succulent fruit with good flavour.
LCro MCtn

14 H1c **'Gigantomo'**
Beefsteak tomato. Irregular-shaped heavy fruit; light but pleasant flavour; good yield.
EKin LCro MBros MCtn MNHC

04 H1c **'Ildi'**
Plum tomato. Vigorous, indeterminate plants; heavy crop of small, attractive, yellow, plum-shaped fruit.
LCro

03 H1c **'Marmande'**
Beefsteak tomato. High yield; large, bright red, attractive fruits, with solid flesh and good flavour.
CHby LCro MCtn

14 H1c **'Orange Wellington'**
Beefsteak tomato. Pleasing flavour; orange-golden fruit; smooth skin; cat-faced but not too deep; good yield.
EKin

17 H1c **'Rosella'**
Cherry tomato. Very high yield, with nice size and good taste.
LCro MCtn MNHC

07 H1c **'Sakura'**
Cherry tomato. High yield; very bright fruits carried on long trusses; very sweet flavour.
EDel

93 H1c **'Shirley'**
F_1 hybrid; fairly early. Uniform trusses; nice round red fruit of medium size and average flavour. Reconfirmed after trial 1997.
EDel EKin LCro LCro MBros SVic

07 H1c **'Sungold'**
Cherry tomato. Good yield of attractive round golden-orange fruits. Good flavour.
EDel EKin LCro MCtn MNHC SVic

17 H1c **'Sweet Aperitif'**
Cherry tomato. Decent yield, with good flavour. Juicy. Borderline between cherry and currant.
LCro

98 H1c **'Sweet Million'**
Cherry tomato. F_1 hybrid. Long open trusses of sweet, round, bright red fruits; good yield. Reconfirmed after trial 2017.
EDel MBros MCtn

04 H1c **'Sweet Olive'**
Plum tomato. F_1 hybrid; very early. Very high yield from vigorous, healthy, determinate plants. Small, red, round to plum-shaped fruits, a little difficult to pick, but of good flavour.
MCtn

93 H1c **'Tigerella'**
Interesting attractive striped fruit with quite good flavour; reconfirmed after trial 1997. H2 for outdoor use.
EDel LCro MCtn SVic

14 H1c **'Tomande'**
Beefsteak tomato. Multilocular; smooth skin; good-sized fruit; light taste, good yield.
LCro

V
PLANTS FOR POLLINATORS

RHS Plants for Pollinators

Subspecies and cultivars of plants listed here are also **Plants for Pollinators**, except for those that provide significantly reduced floral resources (i.e. pollen and nectar). This includes most doubles.

Key to codes: T tree S shrub C climber B bulb / corm A annual Bi biennial H herbaceous perennial † denotes an archaeophyte (a naturalised plant introduced before 1500)

Wildflowers

Short Grass (up to 15cm)

Ajuga reptans bugle	H
Bellis perennis daisy	H
Campanula rotundifolia common harebell	H
Hippocrepis comosa horseshoe vetch	H
Lotus corniculatus bird's foot trefoil	H
Potentilla anserina silverweed	H
Potentilla erecta tormentil	H
Potentilla reptans creeping cinquefoil	H
Primula veris common cowslip	H
Prunella vulgaris selfheal	H
Ranunculus repens creeping buttercup	H
Sanguisorba minor salad burnet	H
Taraxacum officinale dandelion	H
Thymus polytrichus wild thyme	H
Thymus pulegioides large thyme	H
Trifolium pratense red clover	H
Trifolium repens white clover	H
Veronica chamaedrys germander speedwell	H

Hedges, Shrub Borders and Woodland Edges

Acer campestre field maple	S or T
Alliaria petiolata garlic mustard	Bi
Allium ursinum ramsons	B
Aquilegia vulgaris columbine	H
Ballota nigra black horehound	H
Berberis vulgaris barberry †	S
Betonica officinalis betony	H
Bryonia dioica white bryony	C/H
Buxus sempervirens common box	S
Campanula trachelium nettle-leaved bellflower	H
Clematis vitalba old man's beard, traveller's joy	C
Clinopodium vulgare wild basil	H
Cornus sanguinea common dogwood	S
Crataegus monogyna common hawthorn	S or T
Cytisus scoparius common broom	S
Digitalis purpurea common foxglove	Bi
Euonymus europaeus spindle	S
Ficaria verna subsp. *verna* lesser celandine	H
Fragaria vesca wild strawberry	H
Frangula alnus alder buckthorn	S
Galium mollugo hedge bedstraw	H
Galium odoratum sweet woodruff	H
Galium verum lady's bedstraw	H
Geranium robertianum herb robert	A/Bi
Geum urbanum wood avens	H
Hedera helix common ivy	C
Helleborus foetidus stinking hellebore	H
Hyacinthoides non-scripta bluebell	B
Hylotelephium telephium orpine	H
Ilex aquifolium common holly	T
Lamium album white deadnettle	H
Lamium galeobdolon yellow archangel	H
Ligustrum vulgare wild privet	S
Lonicera periclymenum common honeysuckle	C
Malus sylvestris crab apple	T
Malva sylvestris common mallow	H
Myosotis sylvatica wood forget-me-not	H
Primula vulgaris primrose	H
Prunus avium wild cherry, gean	T
Prunus padus bird cherry	T
Prunus spinosa blackthorn, sloe	S
Rhamnus cathartica purging buckthorn	S
Rosa species rose	S
Rubus fruticosus blackberry	S
Salix caprea goat willow (male form only)	S or T
Salix cinerea subsp. *oleifolia* grey willow (male form only)	S
Sanicula europaea sanicle	H
Silene dioica red campion	H
Silene latifolia subsp. *alba* white campion	H
Smyrnium olusatrum alexanders †	Bi
Sorbus aria common whitebeam	T

Sorbus aucuparia rowan, mountain ash — T
Sorbus torminalis wild service tree — T
Stellaria holostea greater stitchwort — H
Symphytum officinale common comfrey — H
Teucrium scorodonia wood sage — H
Tilia cordata small-leaved lime — T
Viburnum lantana common wayfaring tree — S
Viburnum opulus guelder rose — S
Vicia cracca common tufted vetch — H
Vicia sativa common vetch — H

Disturbed Ground

Agrostemma githago corncockle † — A
Anchusa arvensis bugloss † — A
Anthemis arvensis corn chamomile † — A
Anthemis cotula stinking chamomile † — A
Centaurea cyanus cornflower † — A
Cichorium intybus chicory † — H
Dipsacus fullonum common teasel — Bi
Echium vulgare viper's bugloss — Bi
Glebionis segetum corn marigold † — A
Iberis amara wild candytuft — A
Lamium amplexicaule henbit deadnettle † — A
Matricaria recutita scented mayweed † — A
Mentha arvensis corn mint — H
Myosotis arvensis field forget-me-not † — A/H
Onopordum acanthium cotton thistle † — Bi
Papaver dubium long-headed poppy † — A
Papaver rhoeas common poppy † — A
Sinapis arvensis charlock † — A
Sonchus arvensis perennial sowthistle — H
Tussilago farfara coltsfoot — H
Verbascum thapsus great mullein — Bi

Flower Beds

Calluna vulgaris heather, ling excl. bud-blooming cultivars — S
Erica ciliaris Dorset heath — S
Erica cinerea bell heather — S
Erica tetralix cross-leaved heath — S

Long Grass (above 50cm)

Arctium minus lesser burdock — Bi
Carduus crispus welted thistle — Bi
Carduus nutans musk thistle — Bi
Chamaenerion angustifolium rosebay willowherb — H
Cirsium arvense creeping thistle — H
Cirsium vulgare spear thistle — Bi
Conopodium majus pignut — H
Cynoglossum officinale hound's tongue — H
Daucus carota wild carrot — Bi
Geranium pratense meadow cranesbill — H
Heracleum sphondylium hogweed — Bi
Hypericum perforatum perforate St John's wort — H
Knautia arvensis field scabious — H
Lathyrus pratensis meadow vetchling — H
Pastinaca sativa wild parsnip — Bi
Succisa pratensis devil's bit scabious — H
Tanacetum vulgare tansy † — H
Thalictrum flavum meadow rue — H
Tragopogon pratensis goat's beard — Bi
Verbascum nigrum dark mullein — Bi/H

Medium Height Grass (up to 50cm)

Achillea millefolium common yarrow — H
Achillea ptarmica sneezewort — H
Agrimonia eupatoria agrimony — H
Anthyllis vulneraria kidney vetch — H
Armeria maritima thrift, sea pink — H
Campanula glomerata clustered bellflower — H
Centaurea nigra common knapweed, hardheads — H
Centaurea scabiosa greater knapweed — H
Centaurium erythraea common centaury — Bi
Echium vulgare viper's bugloss — Bi
Erigeron acris blue fleabane — A/H
Filipendula vulgaris dropwort — H
Helianthemum nummularium common rockrose — H
Hypochaeris radicata cat's ear — H
Inula conyzae ploughman's spikenard — H
Leontodon hispidus rough hawkbit — H
Leucanthemum vulgare ox-eye daisy — H
Linaria vulgaris common toadflax — H
Malva moschata musk mallow — H
Ononis repens common restharrow — H
Origanum vulgare wild marjoram — H
Pilosella officinarum mouse-ear hawkweed — H
Ranunculus acris meadow buttercup — H
Ranunculus bulbosus bulbous buttercup — H
Reseda lutea wild mignonette — Bi/H
Rhinanthus minor yellow rattle — A
Scabiosa species — A/H
Scorzoneroides autumnalis autumn hawkbit — H
Silene vulgaris bladder campion — H
Solidago virgaurea goldenrod — H

Ponds, Pond Margins & Wet Soils

Alisma plantago-aquatica water plantain — H
Angelica sylvestris wild angelica — Bi
Bistorta officinalis common bistort — H
Butomus umbellatus flowering rush — H
Caltha palustris marsh marigold — H
Cardamine pratensis cuckoo flower, lady's smock — H
Cirsium dissectum meadow thistle — H
Epilobium hirsutum great willowherb — H
Eupatorium cannabinum hemp agrimony — H
Filipendula ulmaria meadowsweet — H
Galium palustre marsh bedstraw — H
Geum rivale water avens — H
Hypericum tetrapterum square-stalked St John's wort — H
Iris pseudacorus yellow iris — H

Lotus pedunculatus greater bird's-foot trefoil	H	*Ranunculus sceleratus* celery-leaved buttercup	A
Lycopus europaeus gypsywort	H	*Sagittaria sagittifolia* arrowhead	H
Lysimachia nummularia creeping Jenny	H	*Sanguisorba officinalis* great burnet	H
Lysimachia vulgaris yellow loosestrife	H	*Scrophularia auriculata* water figwort	H
Lythrum salicaria purple loosestrife	H	*Scutellaria galericulata* common skullcap	H
Mentha aquatica water mint	H	*Silene flos-cuculi* ragged robin	H
Menyanthes trifoliata bogbean	H	*Stachys palustris* marsh woundwort	H
Myosotis scorpioides water forget-me-not	H	*Valeriana officinalis* common valerian	H
Nasturtium officinale common watercress	H	*Veronica beccabunga* brooklime	H
Nuphar lutea yellow waterlily	H		
Nymphaea alba white waterlily	H	**Shingle – Gravel Garden**	
Oenanthe aquatica fine-leaved water dropwort	A/Bi		
Oenanthe crocata hemlock water dropwort	H	*Cakile maritima* sea rocket	A
Persicaria amphibia amphibious bistort	H	*Crambe maritima* sea kale	H
Polemonium caeruleum Jacob's ladder	H	*Crithmum maritimum* rock samphire	H
Pulicaria dysenterica common fleabane	H	*Eryngium maritimum* sea holly	H
Ranunculus aquatilis common water crowfoot	A/H	*Glaucium flavum* yellow horned poppy	Bi/H
Ranunculus flammula lesser spearwort	H	*Sedum acre* biting stonecrop	H
Ranunculus fluitans river water crowfoot	H	*Sedum album* white stonecrop †	H
Ranunculus lingua greater spearwort	H	*Silene uniflora* sea campion	H

Garden Plants

Winter (nov – feb)

		Buxus sempervirens Native plant; common box	S
		Caltha palustris Native plant; marsh marigold	H
Clematis cirrhosa Spanish traveller's joy	C	*Campanula* species bellflower	H
Crocus species crocus (winter-flowering)	B	*Ceanothus* species California lilac	S
Eranthis hyemalis winter aconite	B	*Centaurea* species knapweed, cornflower	A or H
× *Fatshedera lizei* tree ivy	S	*Cercis siliquastrum* Judas tree	T
Erica species heath – hardy types	S	*Chaenomeles* species Japanese quince	S
Galanthus nivalis common snowdrop	B	*Cornus mas* Cornelian cherry	S
Helleborus species and hybrids hellebore (winter-flowering)	H	*Cotoneaster conspicuus* Tibetan cotoneaster	S
		Crataegus monogyna Native plant; common hawthorn	S or T
Lonicera caprifolium perfoliate honeysuckle	S	*Crocus* species crocus (spring-flowering)	B
Lonicera fragrantissima winter-flowering honeysuckle	S	*Doronicum* species leopard's bane	H
		Erica species heath – hardy types	S
Lonicera × *purpusii* Purpus honeysuckle	S	*Erysimum* species wallflower	Bi or H
Mahonia species Oregon grape	S	*Euphorbia* species spurge – hardy types	H or S
Salix species willow	S or T	*Geranium* species cranesbill	H
Sarcococca species sweet box	S	*Geum rivale* Native plant; water avens	H
Viburnum tinus laurustinus	S	*Helleborus* species & hybrids hellebore (spring-flowering)	H

Spring (mar – may)

		Iberis sempervirens perennial candytuft	H
Acer campestre Native plant; field maple	S or T	*Ilex aquifolium* Native plant; common holly	T
Acer platanoides Norway maple	T	*Lamium maculatum* spotted dead nettle	H
Acer pseudoplatanus sycamore	T	*Lunaria annua* honesty	Bi
Acer saccharum sugar maple	T	*Mahonia* species Oregon grape (spring-flowering)	S
Aesculus hippocastanum horse chestnut	T		
Ajuga reptans Native plant; bugle	H	*Malus* species apple, crabapple	T
Arabis alpina subsp. *caucasica* alpine rock cress	H	*Mespilus germanica* common medlar	T
Armeria caespitosa juniper-leaved thrift	H	*Muscari armeniacum* Armenian grape hyacinth	B
Aubrieta species aubretia	H	*Nectaroscordum* species honey garlic	B
Aurinia saxatilis gold dust	H	*Ornithogalum umbellatum* common star of Bethlehem	B
Berberis darwinii Darwin's barberry	S		
Berberis thunbergii Japanese barberry	S	*Pieris* species lily-of-the-valley bush	S
Bergenia species elephant ear	H	*Primula veris* Native plant; common cowslip	H

RHS Plants for Pollinators 771

Primula vulgaris Native plant; primrose — H
Prunus species (cherry, laurel) — S or T
Pulmonaria species lungwort — H
Pyrus communis pear — T
Ribes nigrum blackcurrant — S
Ribes rubrum Native plant; common redcurrant — S
Ribes sanguineum flowering currant — S
Salix species willow — S or T
Skimmia japonica skimmia — S
Smyrnium olusatrum Native plant; alexanders † — Bi
Stachyurus chinensis stachyurus — S
Stachyurus praecox stachyurus — S
Vaccinium corymbosum blueberry — S
Veronica (shrubby species previously called *Hebe*) hebe — S

Summer (June – Aug)

Achillea species yarrow — H
Actaea japonica baneberry — H
Aesculus indica Indian horse chestnut (resistant to leaf-mining moth) — T
Aesculus parviflora bottlebrush buckeye — S
Agastache species giant hyssop — H
Ageratum houstonianum flossflower — A
Alcea rosea hollyhock — Bi
Allium species ornamental and edibles (when allowed to flower) — B
Alstroemeria species Peruvian lily — H
Anchusa species alkanet — A
Angelica archangelica angelica — Bi
Angelica gigas purple angelica — Bi
Angelica sylvestris Native plant; wild angelica — Bi
Antirrhinum majus snapdragon — A or H
Aquilegia species columbine — H
Argemone platyceras crested poppy — A or H
Armeria maritima Native plant; thrift — H
Aruncus dioicus goat's beard (male form only) — H
Asparagus officinalis common asparagus — H
Astrantia major greater masterwort — H
Betonica macrantha big sage — H
Bistorta amplexicaulis red bistort — H
Bistorta officinalis Native plant; common bistort — H
Borago officinalis borage — A
Brachyglottis (Dunedin Group) 'Sunshine' brachyglottis 'Sunshine' — S
Brachyglottis monroi Monro's ragwort — S
Buddleja davidii butterfly bush — S
Buddleja globosa orange ball tree — S
Buphthalmum salicifolium yellow ox-eye — H
Bupleurum fruticosum shrubby hare's ear — S
Calamintha nepeta Native plant; lesser calamint — H
Calendula officinalis common marigold — A
Callicarpa bodinieri var. *giraldii* beautyberry — S
Callistephus chinensis China aster — A
Calluna vulgaris Native plant; heather — S
Campanula species bellflower — H
Campsis radicans trumpet honeysuckle — C

Caryopteris × *clandonensis* caryopteris — S
Catalpa bignonioides Indian bean tree — T
Centaurea species knapweed, cornflower — A or H
Centranthus ruber red valerian — H
Cerinthe major 'Purpurascens' honeywort 'Purpurascens' — A
Cirsium rivulare 'Atropurpureum' purple plume thistle — H
Clarkia unguiculata butterfly flower — A
Clematis vitalba Native plant; old man's beard, traveller's joy — C
Consolida ajacis giant larkspur — A
Convolvulus tricolor dwarf morning glory — A/C
Coreopsis species tickseed — H or A
Cornus alba red-barked dogwood — S
Cosmos species cosmos — A
Cota tinctoria dyer's chamomile — H
Crambe cordifolia greater sea kale — H
Crataegus monogyna Native plant; common hawthorn — S or T
Cucurbita pepo marrow, courgette — A
Cynara cardunculus including Scolymus Group globe artichoke and cardoon — H
Cynoglossum amabile Chinese forget-me-not — H
Dahlia species dahlia — H
Delphinium elatum candle larkspur — H
Dianthus barbatus sweet william — Bi
Dictamnus albus dittany — H
Digitalis species foxglove — Bi
Dipsacus fullonum Native plant; common teasel — Bi
Doronicum species leopard's bane — H
Echinacea purpurea purple coneflower — H
Echinops species globe thistle — H
Echium vulgare Native plant; viper's bugloss — A
Elaeagnus species silverberry, oleaster — S
Epilobium canum Californian fuchsia — S
Erica species heath – hardy types — S
Erigeron species fleabane — H
Eriophyllum lanatum golden yarrow — H
Eryngium species eryngo, sea holly — H
Erysimum species wallflower — H or S
Escallonia species escallonia — S
Eschscholzia californica California poppy — A
Eupatorium cannabinum Native plant; hemp agrimony — H
Euphorbia species spurge – hardy types — H or S
Eutrochium maculatum Joe Pye weed — H
Ferula communis giant fennel — H
Foeniculum vulgare common fennel † — H
Fragaria × *ananassa* garden strawberry — H
Fuchsia species fuchsia – hardy types — S
Gaillardia × *grandiflora* blanket flower — H
Geranium species cranesbill (summer-flowering) — H
Geranium pratense Native plant; meadow cranesbill — H
Geum species avens (summer-flowering) — H
Gilia capitata blue thimble flower — A
Glebionis segetum corn marigold † — A
Gypsophila species baby's breath — A

Helenium species Helen's flower	H	*Paeonia* species peony	H
Helianthus species sunflower	A or H	*Papaver orientale* oriental poppy	H
Heliopsis helianthoides smooth ox-eye	H	*Papaver rhoeas* Native plant; common poppy †	A
Heliotropium arborescens common heliotrope	A	*Parthenocissus tricuspidata* Boston ivy	C
Heracleum sphondylium Native plant; hogweed	Bi	*Penstemon* species beard-tongue	T
Hesperis matronalis dame's violet	H	*Phacelia campanularia* Californian bluebell	A
Hydrangea paniculata paniculate hydrangea (only cultivars with many fertile flowers, e.g. 'Kyushu', 'Big Ben', 'Floribunda', 'Brussels Lace')	S	*Phacelia tanacetifolia* fiddleneck	A
		Phaseolus coccineus scarlet runner bean	A
		Phlomis species sage	S
		Phlox paniculata perennial phlox	H
Hydrangea petiolaris climbing hydrangea	C	*Phuopsis stylosa* Caucasian crosswort	H
Hydrangea viburnoides climbing hydrangea	C	*Polemonium caeruleum* Native plant; Jacob's ladder	H
Hylotelephium spectabile & hybrids ice plant	H	*Potentilla* species cinquefoil	H or S
Hylotelephium telephium Native plant; orpine	H	*Prostanthera cuneata* alpine mint bush	S
Hyssopus officinalis hyssop	S	*Prunus* species (cherry, laurel)	S or T
Iberis amara Native plant; wild candytuft	A	*Ptelea trifoliata* hop tree	S
Ilex aquifolium Native plant; common holly	T	*Pyracantha* species firethorn	S
Inula species harvest daisy	H	*Reseda odorata* garden mignonette	A
Jasminum officinale common jasmine	C	*Ridolfia segetum* false fennel	A
Kalmia latifolia mountain laurel	S	*Robinia pseudoacacia* false acacia	T
Knautia arvensis Native plant; field scabious	H	*Rosa* species rose	S
Knautia macedonica Macedonian scabious	H	*Rubus fruticosus* agg. Native plant; blackberry	S
Koelreuteria paniculata pride of India	T	*Rubus idaeus* Native plant; common raspberry	S
Lathyrus latifolius broad-leaved everlasting pea	H	*Rudbeckia* species coneflower	A or H
Laurus nobilis bay tree	S	*Salvia* species sage	A or H
Lavandula species lavender	S	*Salvia rosmarinus* rosemary	S
Leucanthemum × *superbum* Shasta daisy	H	*Salvia yangii* Russian sage	S
Leucanthemum vulgare Native plant; ox-eye daisy	H	*Sanvitalia procumbens* creeping zinnia	A
Liatris spicata button snakewort	H	*Scabiosa* species	A/H
Ligustrum ovalifolium garden privet	S	*Sidalcea malviflora* checkerbloom	H
Ligustrum sinense Chinese privet	S	*Silene flos-cuculi* Native plant; ragged robin	H
Limnanthes douglasii poached egg flower	A	*Solidago* species goldenrod	H
Limonium platyphyllum broad-leaved statice	H	*Sorbus aria* Native plant; common whitebeam	T
Linaria purpurea purple toadflax	H	*Sorbus aucuparia* Native plant; mountain ash, rowan	T
Lobularia maritima sweet alyssum	A		
Lonicera periclymenum Native plant; common honeysuckle	C	*Spiraea japonica* Japanese spiraea	S
		Stachys byzantina lamb's ear	H
Lysimachia vulgaris Native plant; yellow loosestrife	H	*Stokesia laevis* Stokes' aster	H
Lythrum salicaria Native plant; purple loosestrife	H	*Symphoricarpos albus* snowberry	S
Lythrum virgatum wand loosestrife	H	*Tagetes patula* French marigold	A
Malope trifida large-flowered mallow wort	A	*Tamarix ramosissima* tamarisk	S
Malva species mallow	H	*Tanacetum coccineum* pyrethrum	H
Matthiola incana hoary stock	Bi	*Tanacetum vulgare* Native plant; tansy †	H
Mentha aquatica Native plant; water mint	H	*Telekia speciosa* yellow ox-eye	H
Mentha spicata spearmint	H	*Tetradium daniellii* bee-bee tree	T
Monarda didyma bergamot	H	*Teucrium chamaedrys* Native plant; wall germander	H
Myosotis species forget-me-not	Bi		
Nemophila menziesii baby blue eyes	A	*Thymus* species thyme	S
Nepeta species catmint	H	*Tilia* × *europaea* common lime	T
Nicotiana alata flowering tobacco	A	*Tilia maximowicziana* lime	T
Nicotiana langsdorffii Langsdorff's tobacco	A	*Tilia oliveri* lime	T
Nicotiana sylvestris flowering tobacco	Bi	*Tilia platyphyllos* Native plant; broad-leaved lime	T
Nigella damascena love-in-a-mist	A	*Tithonia rotundifolia* Mexican sunflower	A
Oenothera species evening primrose	Bi	*Trachymene coerulea* blue lace flower	A
Oenothera lindheimeri white gaura	H	*Trollius* species globeflower	H
Olearia species daisy bush	S	*Tropaeolum majus* garden nasturtium	A
Onopordum acanthium cotton thistle	Bi	*Verbascum* species mullein	Bi
Origanum species marjoram, oregano	H or S	*Verbena bonariensis* purple top	H

Verbena rigida slender vervain	A
Veronica (shrubby species previously called *Hebe*) hebe	S
Veronica longifolia garden speedwell	H
Veronica spicata Native plant; spiked speedwell	H
Veronicastrum virginicum Culver's root	H
Viburnum lantana Native plant; common wayfaring tree	S
Viburnum opulus Native plant; guelder rose	S
Vicia faba broad bean	A
Weigela florida weigelia	S
Zinnia elegans youth and old age	A

Autumn (sept – oct)

Aconitum carmichaelii Carmichael's monk's hood	H
Actaea simplex simple-stemmed bugbane	H
Anchusa species alkanet	A
Anemone hupehensis Chinese anemone	H
Anemone × hybrida Japanese anemone	H
Arbutus unedo strawberry tree	S or T
Campanula species bellflower	H
Centaurea species knapweed, cornflower	A or H
Ceratostigma plumbaginoides hardy blue-flowered leadwort	H
Chrysanthemum species & hybrids chrysanthemum	H
Clematis heracleifolia tube clematis	C
Colchicum species autumn crocus	B
Crocus species crocus (autumn-flowering types)	B
Dahlia species & hybrids dahlia	H
Elaeagnus species silverberry, oleaster	S
Erica species heath – hardy types	S
Eryngium species eryngo, sea holly	H
Fatsia japonica Japanese aralia	S
Hedera species ivy	C
Helianthus species sunflower	A or H
Leucanthemella serotina autumn ox-eye	H
Machaeranthera tanacetifolia tansy-leaf aster	A
Malva species mallow	H
Origanum species marjoram, oregano	H or S
Salvia species sage (autumn-flowering types)	H
Symphyotrichum species and hybrids Michaelmas daisy	H
Tilia henryana Henry's lime (one of the last to flower)	T

HPS
HARDY PLANT SOCIETY
Gardening with hardy perennials
www.hardy-plant.org.uk

The Hardy Plant Society is a national charity dedicated to promoting plant knowledge, fostering communities, and enhancing well-being. We are dedicated to championing the environment and facilitating plant focused research and partnerships.

Our members come from across the UK and abroad and find relaxation, happiness, and joy in gardening. They range from experienced nursery owners and horticulturalists to new gardeners and everything in between.

Everyone is welcome to join and contribute to The Hardy Plant Society, we believe in the joy of plants and the goal of sharing that joy as widely as possible.

- Meet with like-minded gardeners. We have local groups around the country and special interest groups, which focus on one type or group of plants. They hold talks, events, and plant sales to bring members together.
- Support the Conservation Scheme which works to conserve those older and less-well known garden cultivars in danger of being lost to cultivation.
- Enjoy the advantages of the Seed Distribution Scheme which offers the opportunity to grow something unusual from over 2000 varieties of seed donated by members.
- Receive HPS Publications – Our journal, 'The Hardy Plant' is published twice a year and the Newsletter goes out 3 times a year keeping you informed of what is happening in the HPS. There is also an option to subscribe to Cornucopia which is published twice a year and is a digest of articles from local and special interest groups newsletters.
- The Hardy Plant Society offers small bursaries, for students and for people who are employed in horticulture.

For more information about these activities and how to join the Hardy Plant Society visit www.hardy-plant.org.uk

Or contact us at:
Hardy Plant Society, 3 Basepoint Business Centre, Crab Apple Way, Evesham WR11 1GP
Tel: 01386 710317 or e-mail clare@hardy-plant.org.uk

The Hardy Plant Society is a registered charity No 208080

VI
NURSERIES

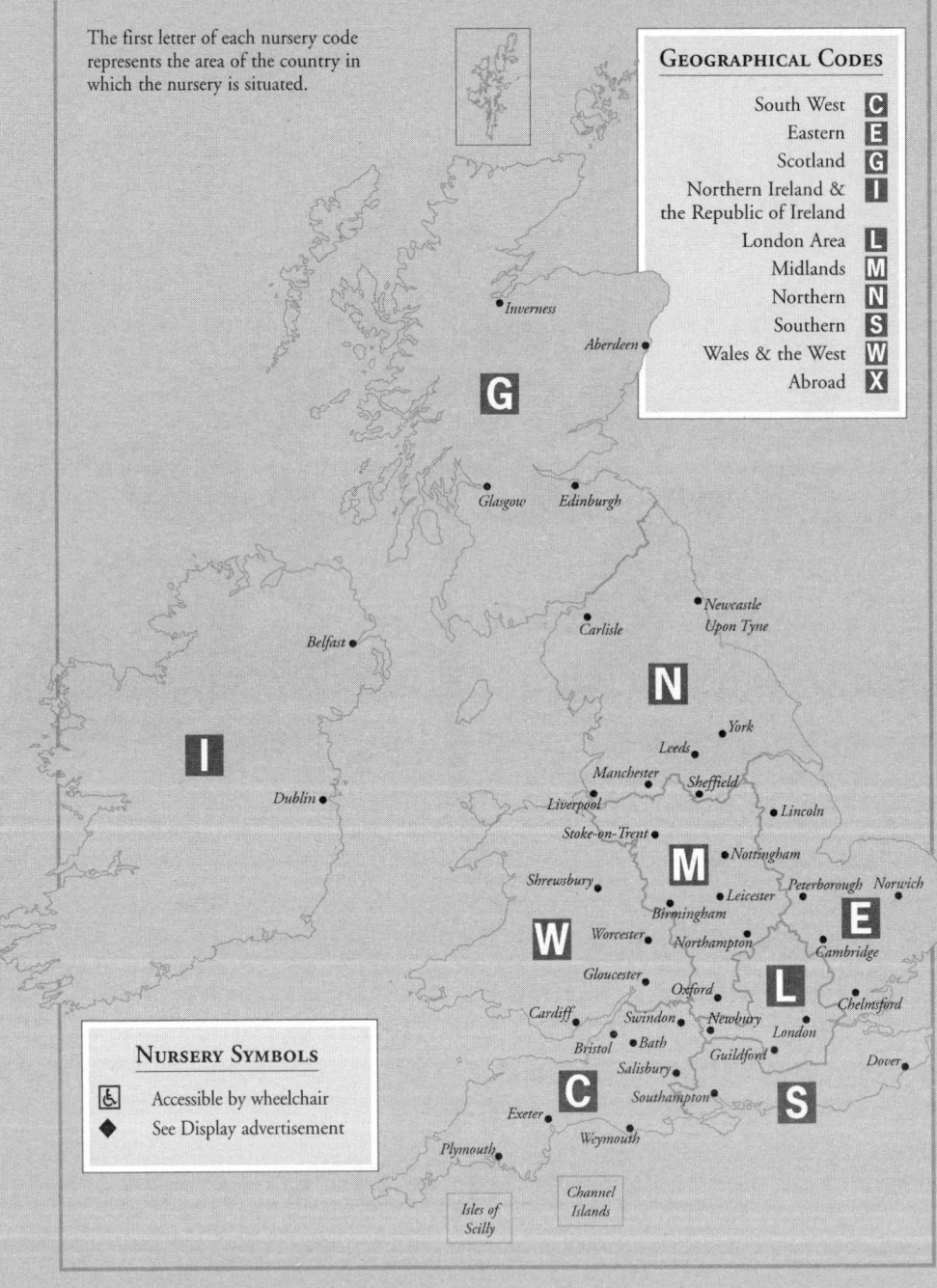

Using the Nursery Listings

Your main reference from the Plant Directory is the Nursery Details by Code listing, which includes all relevant information for each nursery in order of nursery code. The Nursery Index by Name is an alphabetical list for those who know a nursery's name but not its code and wish to check its details in the main list.

1 Nursery Details by Code

Once you have found your plant in the Plant Directory, turn to this list to find out the name, address, opening times and other details of the nurseries whose codes accompany the plant.

KEY
    Accessible by wheelchair   ♦ See Display advertisement

A geographical code is followed by three or four letters reflecting the nursery's name → **ESwi**

SWINES MEADOW FARM NURSERY ♦
47 Towngate East, Market Deeping,
Peterborough, Lincolnshire, PE6 8LQ
(T) 07432 627766/07432 627766
(E) rareplants@me.com
(W) www.swinesmeadowfarmnursery.co.uk
Contact: Colin Ward
Opening Times: 0900–1600 Mon–Sat,
1000–1600 Sun. Closed Jan–Feb except by appt. only.
Min Mail Order UK: £10
Min Mail Order EU: £10
Specialities: Hardy exotics, tree ferns, bamboos & *Hostas*. Wollemi pine stockist. Many specialities available in small quantities only.
Notes: Delivers to shows. Wheelchair accessible.

A brief summary of the plants available

Other information about the nursery

2 Nursery Index by Name

If you are looking for a particular nursery, use this alphabetical index to find it, note its code and then turn to the Nursery Details by Code listing for full information.

Sue Proctor Plants	NSue
Sunnybank Vine Nursery (National Vine Collection)	WSuV
Swallows Nursery & Plant Centre	MSwo
Swines Meadow Farm Nursery	ESwi
Taylors Clematis Nursery	NTay
The Backyard Larder	**NBac**
The Crocosmia Gardens	ECrc
The English Iris Company	EnIr
The Hardy Geranium Nursery	LHGe
The Hawthornes Nursery	NHaw

How to Use the Nursery Listings

The details given for each nursery have been compiled from information supplied to us in answer to a questionnaire. In some case, because of space constraints, the entries have been abbreviated.
Nurseries are not charged for their entries and inclusion in no way implies a value judgement.

Nursery Details by Code (p.780)

Each nursery is allocated a code, for example GDaD. The first letter of each code indicates the region of the British Isles in which the nursery is situated. In this example G = Scotland. The remaining three or four letters reflect the nursery's name, in this case Dachshund Dahlia Plant Nursery.
In this listing, nurseries are given in alphabetical order of code for quick referral from the Plant Directory. All of the nurseries' details, such as addresses, opening times, etc. will be found in this index.

Opening Times

These are published as submitted. It is always advisable, especially if travelling a long distance, to double-check with the nursery before setting out.

Mail Order

Many nurseries offer a mail order service. This is often restricted to certain times of the year or to particular genera. Please check the **Notes** section of the nursery entry for restrictions or special conditions.
Due to changes in plant import/export regulations since BREXIT, many nurseries are no longer offering a mail order service outside of the UK or, in the case of the Republic of Ireland, to the UK. Where nurseries are still offering this service, the minimum charge to the EU will be noted. Some nurseries may not be prepared to send tender or bulky plants.
Where a nursery offers a mail order only service, this will be noted under **Opening Times** in the nursery entry. Many nurseries offer a mail order online service with some only operating in this way.

Export

This refers to mail order beyond the EU and indicates nurseries that are prepared to consider this. There is usually a substantial minimum charge and, in addition, all the costs of phytosanitary certificates and Customs have to be met by the purchaser.

Catalogue Cost

Only a small number of nurseries now offer a printed catalogue. Some may not charge or may ask for stamps to bear the cost of postage. If plant lists are available in an electronic format, some nurseries have indicated that they will email them to enquirers.
The majority of nurseries now publish their catalogues only on the internet as this is more cost-effective than producing a printed copy and enables them to reflect stock changes throughout the year.

Specialities

This is where nurseries list the plants or genera in which they specialise and any National Collections that they hold. Please note that some nurseries may charge an entry fee to visit a National Collection. Charges may also be levied to visit any garden to which the nursery is attached.
Nurseries also indicate here if they only have small quantities of individual plants available for sale or if they will propagate to order.

Notes

This section contains: information on restrictions to mail order or export; whether payment in euros is accepted; whether nurseries deliver to shows; details of partial wheelchair access; the nursery site address if this differs from the office address; and any other non-horticultural or general information.

Wheelchair Access ♿

Nurseries are asked to indicate if their premises are suitable for wheelchair users.

We use the wheelchair symbol for those nurseries that tell us their site is fully accessible. Where only partial or restricted access is offered, this is stated in the **Notes** section of the nursery's details and the nursery is not marked with the symbol.

Please note that wheelchair access does not necessarily relate to any gardens to which the nursery may be attached.

The assessment of ease of access is entirely the responsibility of the individual nursery.

Delivers to Shows

Many nurseries will deliver pre-ordered plants to flower shows for collection by customers. Contact the nursery for details of shows that they will be attending.

Payment in Euros

A number of UK nurseries will accept payment in euros. You should check with the nursery concerned before making such a payment, as some will only accept cash and some only cheques, whilst others will expect the purchaser to pay bank charges.

Nursery Index by Name

An alphabetical index of nurseries is included (p.841). Nurseries new to the book and those making a re-entry are shown in embolden type.

Deleted Nurseries

Every year some nurseries ask to be removed from the book. This may be a temporary measure because, for example, they are relocating or because their plant stocks are low due to adverse growing conditions, or it may be permanent following closure, sale, retirement or a change in the way they trade.

Some nurseries miss the deadline for submissions and may ask to re-enter the book in the following edition. Other nurseries do not respond at all and, as we have no current information on their trading status, they are not included in the book.

We recommend that you use the latest edition of the *RHS Plant Finder*

Nursery Details by Code

Please note that all these nurseries are listed in alphabetical order by their code. All nurseries are listed in alphabetical order by their name in the **Nursery Index by Name** on page 841.

South West

CAbb **Abbotsbury Sub-Tropical Gardens** &
Bullers Way, Abbotsbury, Weymouth, Dorset, DT3 4LA
Ⓣ (01305) 871344
Ⓔ info@abbotsburygardens.co.uk
Ⓦ www.abbotsbury-tourism.co.uk/gardens/
Contact: David Sutton
Opening Times: 1000–1800 daily, mid-Mar–1st Nov. 1000–1500, Nov–mid-Mar.
Specialities: Less common & tender shrubs incl. palms, tree ferns, bamboos & plants from Australia, New Zealand & S. Africa.
Notes: Wheelchair accessible.

CAby **Forde Abbey Nursery** &
Forde Abbey, Chard, Somerset, TA20 4LU
Ⓔ info@fordeabbey.co.uk
Ⓦ www.fordeabbey.co.uk
Contact: Paul Bygrave
Opening Times: 1030–1630 7 days, 1st Mar–31st Oct.
Cat. Cost: None issued.
Specialities: Hardy herbaceous perennials.
Notes: Wheelchair accessible.

CAco **Acorn Trees and Shrubs**
Hilltown Farm, Rackenford, Tiverton, Devon, EX16 8DX
Ⓣ (01884) 881633
Ⓔ goakey101@gmail.com
Ⓦ www.acorntreesandshrubs.co.uk
Contact: Grahame Oakey
Opening Times: By appt. only, but generally 7 days.
Min Mail Order UK: £200
Min Mail Order EU: £1000
Cat. Cost: Free via website.
Specialities: Conifer specialist including pendulous and long needle types, e.g. *Pinus montezumae*, *palustris*, *schwerinii*, *holfordiana* and shorter needle types too. Stock subject to availability. Many items in the web shop are the exact item offered with photo of the actual tree you are buying. Also specialises in procurement from a massive availability list of tens of thousands of items, not all of which can be listed in the directory.
Notes: Seedling to specimen sizes 5m/up to 45yrs old. Enviable collection of short-needled *Pinus parviflora* cvs. Also sells choice broadleaves and rhododendrons. The conifer collection is probably the most diverse for sale within the UK, with more than 1500 species/cvs. Partial wheelchair access (except toilet).

CAda **Adam's Apple Trees**
Ⓜ 07521 648502
Ⓔ sales@adamsappletrees.co.uk
Ⓦ https://www.adamsappletrees.co.uk/
Opening Times: By appt. only. You can contact the nursery via email, or telephone Mon–Fri 0900–1630.
Specialities: Apple, Pear, Plum, Quince, Cherry and Nut trees, as well as native broadleaf trees.
Notes: A fruit tree nursery offering over 260 varieties of apples, 35 pear, 25 plum and damson and 15 cherry. Also medlar, nuts and soft fruit. Use green manures and no artificial fertilisers or chemicals in their growing methods. Working to become plastic-free. Partial wheelchair access.

CAgr **Agroforestry Research Trust**
46 Hunters Moon, Dartington, Totnes, Devon, TQ9 6JT
Ⓣ (01803) 840776
Ⓔ mail@agroforestry.co.uk
Ⓦ www.agroforestry.co.uk
Contact: Martin Crawford

Opening Times: Not open. Mail order only.
Cat. Cost: 4 × 1st class.
Specialities: Top & soft fruit, nut trees including *Castanea, Corylus, Juglans, Pinus*. Also seeds. Some plants available in small quantities only.
Notes: Euro accepted.

CBcs **BURNCOOSE NURSERIES** &
Gwennap, Redruth, Cornwall, TR16 6BJ
ⓉT (01209) 860316
Ⓔ info@burncoose.co.uk
Ⓦ www.burncoose.co.uk
Contact: C. H. Williams
Opening Times: 0830–1630 Mon–Sat & 1100–1600 Sun.
Cat. Cost: Free.
Specialities: Extensive range of over 3500 ornamental trees & shrubs and herbaceous. Rare & unusual *Magnolia, Rhododendron*. Conservatory plants. 30-acre garden.
Notes: 30-acre garden with free entry. Click and collect available. Many care articles and videos to be found on website. Also sells wholesale. Delivers to shows. Wheelchair accessible.

CBct **BARRACOTT PLANTS**
Old Orchard, Calstock Road, Gunnislake, Cornwall, PL18 9AA
Ⓣ (01822) 832234
Ⓜ 07811 207186
Ⓔ gandt@barracottplants.co.uk
Ⓦ www.barracottplants.co.uk
Contact: Geoff & Thelma Turner
Opening Times: By appt. only.
Min Mail Order UK: £20
Specialities: Herbaceous plants: shade-loving, foliage & form. *Aspidistra, Begonia, Bergenia, Convallaria, Disporum, Liriope, Maianthemum, Plectranthus, Polygonatum, Schefflera* & ferns.

CBdn **BOWDEN HOSTAS**
Sales Office, Bowdens Nursery Ltd, Bowden Place, Sticklepath, Devon, EX20 2NL
Ⓣ (01837) 849267
Ⓔ sales@bowdenhostas.com
Ⓦ www.bowdenhostas.com
Contact: Tim Penrose
Opening Times: 1000–1600 Mon–Sat, Apr–Sep. Oct–Mar, please ring before travelling.
Cat. Cost: Online catalogue.
Specialities: *Hosta*, ferns, bamboos, *Agapanthus*. National Plant Collection of *Hosta* (Halcyon and sports) and *Agapanthus* (Pine Cottage hybrids).
Notes: Also sells wholesale. Exports beyond EU.

CBen **BENNETTS WATER GARDENS** &
Putton Lane, Chickerell, Weymouth, Dorset, DT3 4AF
Ⓜ 07812 175688
Ⓔ orders@waterlily.co.uk
Ⓦ www.waterlily.co.uk
Contact: James Bennett
Opening Times: Please see website for opening hrs.
Cat. Cost: 2 × 1st class.
Specialities: National Plant Collection of *Nymphaea* (hardy water lilies).
Notes: Bare-root plants available by mail order. Potted plants available in store. Wheelchair accessible.

CBgR **BEGGAR'S ROOST PLANTS**
Lilstock, Bridgwater, Somerset, TA5 1SU
Ⓣ (01278) 741519
Ⓔ ro@lilstock.eclipse.co.uk
Contact: Lady Rosemary FitzGerald
Opening Times: Not open. Mail order only.
Min Mail Order UK: £10
Min Mail Order EU: £15
Cat. Cost: 3 × large 2nd class.
Specialities: *Hemerocallis* (incl. heritage) grown in British conditions.
Notes: Mail order for speciality *Hemerocallis*. Ask for list. Euro accepted.

CBlu **BLUE NURSERIES LTD**
(Office) Brook Cottage, 2 Bleet, Steeple Ashton, Wiltshire, BA14 6EA
Ⓜ 07813 894026
Ⓔ office@bluenurseries.com
Ⓦ www.bluenurseries.com
Contact: Richard Hill
Opening Times: Not open. Mail order only.
Min Mail Order UK: £6.95
Cat. Cost: Online only.
Specialities: South African plants & hardy palms with slowly expanding range of plants but main focus is on architectural & rare.
Notes: Online based but displays at plant and horticultural shows. Also sells wholesale. Euro accepted via PayPal only.

CBrac **BRACKENDALE NURSERIES** &
Horton Road, Three Legged Cross, Wimborne, Dorset, BH21 6SD

C

ⓉT (01202) 822349
Ⓔ sales@brackendalenurseries.co.uk
Ⓦ www.brackendalenurseries.co.uk
Contact: Nicola Stainer
Opening Times: Subject to seasonal change. See website.
Specialities: Wide range of plants, especially shrubs, conifers and hedging. Established specimen-sized shrubs and native, ornamental and fruit trees available. Acid loving *Azalea*, *Camellia* & *Rhododendron* together with coastal favourites.
Notes: Wheelchair accessible.

CBro BROADLEIGH GARDENS ♿
Bishops Hull, Taunton, Somerset, TA4 1AE
Ⓣ (01823) 286231
Ⓔ info@broadleighbulbs.co.uk
Ⓦ www.broadleighbulbs.co.uk
Contact: Christine Skelmesdale
Opening Times: 0900–1600 Mon–Fri for viewing only (charity donation). Orders may be collected if notice given.
Cat. Cost: 2 × 1st class.
Specialities: Jan catalogue for bulbs in growth & herbaceous woodland plants. Extensive list of *Agapanthus* and other South African bulbs. June: dwarf & unusual bulbs. National Plant Collection of Alec Grey hybrid daffodils.
Notes: Display garden and nursery open. Euro accepted as cash payment only. Wheelchair accessible.

CBrP BROOKLANDS PLANTS
25 Treves Road, Dorchester, Dorset, DT1 2HE
Ⓣ (01305) 265846
Ⓔ cycads@btinternet.com
Ⓦ www.brooklandsplants.weebly.com/
Contact: Ian Watt
Opening Times: By appt. only for collection of plants.
Min Mail Order UK: £50 + p&p
Cat. Cost: Online only.
Specialities: Rare and unusual trees grown from seed.
Notes: Fern nursery that also specialises in unusual conifers, plants from New Zealand, cycads, palms, pines and oaks. Generally only small/young specimens available. Some species available in small quantities only. Mail order available on small plants only. Euro accepted.

CBTr BOWHAYES TREES
Bowhayes Farm, Venn Ottery, Ottery St Mary, Devon, EX11 1RY

Ⓣ (01404) 812229
Ⓔ contact@bowhayestrees.co.uk
Ⓦ www.bowhayestrees.co.uk
Contact: Fiona Hughes
Opening Times: 0900–1700 Mon–Fri, 0930–1230 Sat Mar–Oct. By appt. only Nov–Feb. Closed Sun.
Min Mail Order UK: £2.95
Specialities: Screening, woodland, ornamental and fruit trees. Hedging plants. Bare-root and container plants available.
Notes: Established in 1992, Bowhayes Trees is a retail and mail order plant nursery. We specialise in hedging, trees, fruit, garden shrubs and accessories for delivery across mainland UK.

CBWd BLOOMING WILD NURSERY
Cabbage Ln, Horsington, Templecombe, Somerset, BA8 0DA
Ⓣ (01963) 371060
Ⓜ 07730 302826/07595 116108
Ⓔ info@bloomingwild.co.uk
Ⓦ www.bloomingwild.co.uk
Contact: Steven & Lindsay Lister
Opening Times: 0930–1630 Wed–Fri, 1000–1600 Sat, closed Sun–Tue 1st Mar–31st Oct.
Min Mail Order UK: £20
Specialities: We grow herbaceous perennials, ornamental grasses and wildflowers. Ideal for naturalistic planting schemes and to attract wildlife to any outdoor space.
Notes: Peat-free nursery. We are situated about half a mile up Cabbage Lane. We are on the right hand side as the road turns to the left.

CCBP CB PLANTS
Lower Severalls Nursery, Crewkerne, Somerset, TA18 7NX
Ⓜ 07851 468430
Ⓔ cbplantsinfo@gmail.com
Ⓦ www.cbplants.co.uk
Contact: Catherine Bond
Opening Times: 1000–1700 Wed–Sat, early Mar–end Sep.
Specialities: Nectar-rich hardy perennials herbs and wild flowers all grown peat-free. Available in small quantities only.
Notes: Small nursery situated just off the A30, half a mile east of Crewkerne.

CCht CHESTNUT NURSERY (SHELTERED WORK OPPORTUNITIES PROJECT) ♿
75 Kingland Road, Poole, Dorset, BH15 1TN

T (01202) 685999
E info@chestnutnursery.org.uk
W www.chestnutnursery.org.uk
Contact: Andrew Verreck
Opening Times: Please check website for opening times.
Specialities: Wide selection of herbaceous perennials, evergreen shrubs, ornamental grasses, annual bedding and southern hemisphere exotics.
Notes: A registered charity providing work for adults with severe and enduring mental illness. Wheelchair accessible.

CCoa COASTAL HEDGING
Marsh Lane Nursery, West Charleton, Kingsbridge, Devon,
TQ7 2AQ
T (01548) 531734
M 07775 201595
E info@coastalhedging.co.uk
W www.coastalhedging.co.uk
Contact: William Hornby
Opening Times: By appt. only.
Min Mail Order UK: £6.75
Cat. Cost: Online only.
Specialities: *Griselina, Elaeagnus, Olearia*.
Notes: Euro accepted.

CCps CHAMPION PLANTS
North Perrott Nursery, Church Lane,
North Perrott, Somerset,
TA18 7SJ
T (01460) 75732
M 07891 661763
E championgardenplants@gmail.com
W www.championplants.co.uk
Contact: Jason Champion
Opening Times: By appt. only. Collection via the website by appt.
Specialities: *Buddleja* (over 60 varieties listed) bred by Peter Moore Plants, *Zantedeschia*, grasses, shrubs & a wide range of perennials, including unusual and difficult to source varieties, exotics in season.
Notes: We are a family run business with a history of commercial horticulture spanning more than 50 years, we pride ourselves in growing unusual varieties of plants as well as more well-known varieties, We propagate over 90% of our plants here on site which gives us confidence in the plants being true to name, healthy and available. Plants are available mail order via our website with quick dispatch and secure transit.

CCVT CHEW VALLEY TREES LTD
Chew Road, Winford, Bristol, BS40 8HJ
T (01275) 333752
E info@chewvalleytrees.co.uk
W www.chewvalleytrees.co.uk
Contact: Wendy Downer
Opening Times: 0800–1700 Mon–Fri all year. 0800–1630 Sat. Closed Sun. Closed B/hols & Sat Jul & Aug.
Cat. Cost: Free.
Specialities: Native British & ornamental trees, shrubs, fruit trees & hedging.
Notes: Also sells wholesale. Wheelchair accessible.

CDoC DUCHY OF CORNWALL
Cott Road, Lostwithiel, Cornwall, PL22 0HW
T (01208) 872668
E plants@duchyofcornwallnursery.co.uk
W www.duchyofcornwallnursery.co.uk
Contact: Nicky Hill
Opening Times: 0900–1700 Mon–Sat, 1000–1600 Sun.
Cat. Cost: None issued.
Specialities: Large range of garden plants including trees, shrubs, roses, perennials, fruit and conservatory plants.
Notes: Partial wheelchair access.

CDor DORSET PERENNIALS
Berkeley Perennials, Holnest, Sherborne, Dorset, DT9 5PR
T (01963) 210643
E sales@dorsetperennials.co.uk
W www.dorsetperennials.co.uk
Contact: Dawn & Martin Preston
Opening Times: Open for collections only. Please check with nursery first.
Cat. Cost: Online only.
Specialities: An eclectic mix of hardy perennials, many that have fallen out of the general trade. Plants for herbaceous borders & cottage gardens with a good mix of oddities to tempt the discerning. Particularly good collections of *Ficaria, Iris sibirica, Epimedium* & *Hosta*.
Notes: All plants available via website. Delivers to shows.

CDTJ DESERT TO JUNGLE
Henlade Garden Nursery, Lower Henlade, Taunton, Somerset, TA3 5NB
T (01823) 443701
M 07969 652547
E plants@deserttojungle.com

784 Nursery Details by Code

C

Ⓦ www.deserttojungle.com
Contact: Rob Gudge
Opening Times: 1000–1700 Mon, Tue & Thu–Sun (closed Wed), 1st Mar–31st Oct. Thu, Fri & Sat only Nov–Feb. Opening times may vary during RHS shows, please phone to check.
Cat. Cost: Online only.
Specialities: Exotic-looking plants giving a desert or jungle effect in the garden. Incl. *Agave*, *Canna*, aroids, succulents, ferns, tree ferns & bamboos.
Notes: Nursery shares drive with Mount Somerset Hotel. Also sells wholesale. Delivers to shows. Wheelchair accessible. No mail order to EU.

CEls Elsworth Herbs
Farthingwood, Broadway, Sidmouth, Devon, EX10 8HS
Ⓣ (01395) 578689
Ⓔ john.twibell@btinternet.com
Contact: Drs J. D. & J. M. Twibell
Opening Times: By appt. only.
Min Mail Order UK: £10
Cat. Cost: By email only.
Specialities: National Plant Collection (Scientific & Reference) of *Artemisia*. Stock available in small quantities only. Orders may require propagation from Collection material, for which we are the primary reference source. Native coastal plants.
Notes: Mail order only on small scale in exceptional circumstances. Partial wheelchair access.

CElw Elworthy Cottage Plants &
Elworthy Cottage, Elworthy, Nr Lydeard St Lawrence, Taunton, Somerset, TA4 3PX
Ⓣ (01984) 656427
Ⓔ mike@elworthy-cottage.co.uk
Ⓦ www.elworthy-cottage.co.uk
Contact: Mrs J. M. Spiller
Opening Times: By appt. only Apr–Sep & Feb for *Galanthus*. Open for NGS days.
Specialities: Unusual herbaceous plants esp. *Galanthus*, hardy *Geranium*, *Geum*, *Crocosmia*, *Epimedium*, *Monarda*, *Pulmonaria* & *Viola*. Some varieties only available in small quantities. *Galanthus* available by mail order in Feb.
Notes: Nursery on B3188, 5 miles north of Wiveliscombe, in centre of Elworthy village. Mail order for *Galanthus* only. Delivers to shows. Wheelchair accessible.

CEnd Endsleigh Gardens Nursery &
Milton Abbot, Tavistock, Devon, PL19 0PG
Ⓣ (01822) 870235
Ⓔ info@endsleigh-gardens.com
Ⓦ www.endsleighgardens.co.uk
Contact: Adrian Steele
Opening Times: 0800–1700 Mon–Sat. 1000–1600 Sun.
Specialities: Choice & unusual trees & shrubs incl. *Acer*, alpines, bamboos, climbers, conifers, *Cornus*, heathers, old apple & cherry varieties, *Rosa*, *Wisteria*. Grafting service. Modern fruit trees, soft fruit and good selection of perennials.
Notes: Wheelchair accessible (but no disabled toilets).

CExl Exclusive Plants Nursery
Tretawn, High Cross, Constantine, Falmouth, Cornwall, TR11 5RE
Ⓣ (01326) 341496
Ⓜ 07775 811385
Ⓔ pbonavia3@aol.com
Ⓦ www.exclusiveplants.com
Contact: Paul Bonavia
Opening Times: W/ends or by appt. only.
Min Mail Order EU: £25
Cat. Cost: 2 × 1st class.
Specialities: A plantsperson's nursery, offering rare & unusual plants from around the world. Also new introductions & the best forms of our better known plants.
Notes: Euro accepted.

CFis Margery Fish Plant Nursery
East Lambrook Manor Gardens, Silver Street, East Lambrook, South Petherton, Somerset, TA13 5HH
Ⓣ (01460) 240328
Ⓜ 07710 484745
Ⓔ enquiries@eastlambrook.com
Ⓦ www.eastlambrook.com
Contact: Ellie Hanscomb
Opening Times: 1000–1700 Tue–Sat, Feb–Oct, plus Sun in Feb. Nov–Jan by appt.
Cat. Cost: None issued.
Specialities: Cottage garden plants and interesting perennials including hardy *Geranium*, snowdrops and plants propagated from East Lambrook Manor Gardens. Stock available in small quantities only. Major collection of hardy geraniums in garden.
Notes: Partial wheelchair access.

CFst   Forest Edge Nurseries (The Heather Garden)
Verwood Road, Woodlands, Wimborne, Dorset, BH21 8LJ
Ⓣ (01202) 824387
Ⓔ info@theheathergarden.co.uk
Ⓦ www.theheathergarden.co.uk
Contact: David Edge
Opening Times: 0900–1630 Mon. Collection available by arrangement on other days.
Min Mail Order UK: £8.95
Specialities: Heathers incl. *Calluna, Erica, Daboecia*.
Notes: Also sells wholesale. Euro accepted.

CGHo   Glenholme Herb Nursery
Ⓜ 07814 461385
Ⓔ glenholmeherbnursery@gmail.com
Contact: Maxine Kellaway
Opening Times: Please check our website for up-to-date opening hours. Mail order available spring to autumn.
Specialities: Culinary and medicinal herbs. Pelargoniums and Salvias.
Notes: We are a small family nursery selling direct to the public. We can also grow to order for larger projects. We grow using peat reduced, and where possible peat-free media. Plants can be bought at the nursery, by post, and at a selection of markets and shows (please see website). We are able to host groups for tours and talks. Partial wheelchair access. Most of the site and gardens are wheelchair accessible. Please do contact us with any questions regards accessibility.

CGri   Griselinia R Us ♿
Griselinia Fields, Old Portreath Road, Sparnon Gate, Redruth, Cornwall, TR16 4JA
Ⓜ 07517 098118/07528 546622
Ⓔ tsyass@hotmail.co.uk/tsyass@sky.com
Ⓦ www.griseliniarus.co.uk/
Contact: Teresa & Paul Symons/Tim Syass
Specialities: *Griselinia littoralis*, Green Horizons and variegated strains of the New Zealand indigenous hedging. Cherry laurel variety of the prunus evergreen hedging.
Notes: Large-scale nursery. All materials and products are organic, all fertilisers, composts are organic & peat-free. Sustainable farming in Cornwall and ALL plants grown from cuttings & home-grown seed within a 5-mile radius. Range of plant sizes from fresh cuttings to 21ltr pots. Free delivery throughout the South West of England, and will consider free deliveries anywhere in UK, dependant on a minimum order value with 100% emission free vehicles. Mail order considered. Licenced growers and sellers of the Dark Green Horizons variety in the UK and DEFRA registered. Wheelchair accessible.

CGwi   Grow Wilder ♿
181 Frenchay Park Road, Bristol, BS16 1HB
Ⓣ 0117 965 7086
Ⓜ 07421 226089
Ⓔ growwilder@avonwildlifetrust.org.uk
Ⓦ www.growwilder.co.uk
Contact: Shaun Waycott
Opening Times: 0900–1700 Mon–Fri all year round 1000–1600 w/ends Mar–Nov.
Specialities: UK native wildflowers, herbs & unusual edibles.
Notes: Part of Avon Wildlife Trust, Grow Wilder operates as a wildflower nursery and living seed bank, offering face to face and online sales to retail, community & wildlife groups, local councils. Please enquire with the nursery regarding deliveries to shows. Wheelchair accessible.

CHab   Habitat Aid Ltd.
Hookgate Cottage, South Brewham, Somerset, BA10 0LQ
Ⓣ (01749) 812355
Ⓔ info@habitataid.co.uk
Ⓦ www.habitataid.co.uk
Contact: Nick Mann
Opening Times: Not open. Mail order only.
Min Mail Order UK: £50 incl. p&p
Cat. Cost: None issued.
Specialities: British trees, wildflowers and seeds. Local provenance seed mixes. Native aquatic plants. Ornamental trees for bees. Heritage fruit trees.
Notes: Also sells wholesale.

CHby   The Herbary
161 Chapel Street, Horningsham, Warminster, Wiltshire, BA12 7LU
Ⓣ (01985) 844442
Ⓔ info@beansandherbs.co.uk
Ⓦ www.beansandherbs.co.uk
Contact: Pippa Rosen
Opening Times: Nursery not open to the public. Mail order for seed only.
Cat. Cost: Online only.
Specialities: Culinary, medicinal & aromatic herb seeds.
Notes: Culinary, medicinal, aromatic and dye

herb seed organically grown. Mail order all year for organic vegetable, flower, bean and herb seed.

CHll   HILL HOUSE NURSERY LTD
Landscove, Nr Ashburton, Newton Abbot, Devon, TQ13 7LY
Ⓣ (01803) 762273
Ⓔ bluebird@hillhousenursery.com
Ⓦ www.hillhousenursery.com
Contact: Mathew Hubbard
Opening Times: 1100–1700 (or dusk, if earlier).
Cat. Cost: None issued.
Specialities: 3000+ varieties of plants, most propagated on premises, many rare or unusual. The garden, open to the public with free entry, was laid out by Edward Hyams. Pioneers of glasshouse pest control by beneficial insects.
Notes: Partial wheelchair access to nursery & garden. Seasonal tea room.

CJun   JUNKER'S NURSERY
Higher Cobhay, Milverton, Somerset, TA4 1NJ
Ⓔ karan@junker.co.uk
Ⓦ www.junker.co.uk
Contact: Karan or Torsten Junker
Opening Times: Strictly by appt. only. Email nursery for directions (do not rely on Sat Nav).
Cat. Cost: Free list available by email.
Specialities: Unusual shrubs & trees incl. *Acer palmatum*, *Betula*, *Cornus*, *Daphne*, *Magnolia*, *Parrotia*, *Stewartia* and *Styrax* cvs. Mature plants available. A wide range of cultivars available in limited numbers of each.
Notes: Extensive display planting to showcase plants growing in natural conditions. We propagate & grow all our own plants on site. An increasing number are grown naturally in open ground, incl. larger sizes plus younger plants in pots. No mail order to EU.

CKit   KITS NURSERY
Kits Cottage, Lanhainsworth, Cornwall, TR9 6DW
Ⓜ 07967 795602/07956 560649
Ⓔ kitsnursery@outlook.com
Contact: Lucy and Stephen
Opening Times: Open seasonally and by appt. only.
Specialities: *Phormium*, ornamental grasses, *Cordyline*, hardy plants, some peat-free and using compostable pots.
Notes: Small local Cornish business supporting landscapers and build projects. Also sells wholesale. Propagate to order. Also offer a planning and design service and has a sister landscaping business.

CKno   KNOLL GARDENS 🦽
Hampreston, Wimborne, Dorset, BH21 7ND
Ⓣ (01202) 873931
Ⓔ enquiries@knollgardens.co.uk
Ⓦ www.knollgardens.co.uk
Contact: N. R. Lucas
Opening Times: 1000–1700 Wed–Sat, Feb–Dec. See website for further details.
Cat. Cost: None.
Specialities: Grasses (main specialism). Flowering perennials. National Plant Collection of *Pennisetum*.
Notes: Also sells wholesale. Wheelchair accessible.

CLAP   LONG ACRE PLANTS 🦽
South Marsh, Charlton Musgrove, Wincanton, Somerset, BA9 8EX
Ⓣ (01963) 32802
Ⓔ info@longacreplants.co.uk
Ⓦ www.plantsforshade.co.uk
Contact: Nigel Rowland
Opening Times: By appt. only.
Min Mail Order UK: £20 + p&p
Cat. Cost: Catalogue available online.
Specialities: Ferns, woodland bulbs & perennials. Marginal/bog plants. Specialise in plants for shade, carrying a wide range of unusual and tough shade tolerant perennials and ferns.
Notes: Mail order online. Delivers to shows. Wheelchair accessible.

CLil   DORSET WATER LILY CO
Yeovil Road, Halstock, Yeovil, Somerset, BA22 9RR
Ⓣ (01935) 891668
Ⓔ dorsetwaterlily@outlook.com
Ⓦ www.dorsetwaterlily.co.uk
Contact: Richard Gallehawk
Opening Times: 1000–1600 Mon–Fri.
Specialities: Aquatics & pond plants. Specialist in moisture-loving plants & tropicals.
Notes: Also sells wholesale. Retail and grow-to-show services, design and planting services. Peat-free and propagate to order. Instagram: @dorsetwaterlily.

CLnd LANDFORD TREES
Landford Lodge, Landford, Salisbury,
Wiltshire, SP5 2EH
⓪ (01794) 390808
Ⓔ trees@landfordtrees.co.uk
Ⓦ www.landfordtrees.co.uk
Contact: Ed
Opening Times: 0800–1630 Mon–Thu,
0800–1530 Fri May–Sep, 0800–1700 Mon–
Thu 0800–1530 Fri Oct–Apr.
Cat. Cost: Free.
Specialities: Deciduous ornamental trees.
Notes: Also sells wholesale.

CMac MAC PENNYS NURSERIES
154 Burley Road, Bransgore, Christchurch,
Dorset, BH23 8DB
⓪ (01425) 672348
Ⓔ office@macpennys.co.uk
Ⓦ www.macpennys.co.uk
Contact: T. & V. Lowndes & S. Lowndes
Opening Times: 0900–1700 Mon–Sat,
1000–1700 Sun & B/hols. Closed Xmas to
New Year.
Cat. Cost: A4 sae with 4 × 1st class.
Specialities: Wide range of plants – available
in small quantities only.
Notes: Mail order available Oct–Feb incl. UK
only. Also sells wholesale. Partial wheelchair
access.

CMCN MALLET COURT NURSERY ♿
Marshway, Curry Mallet, Taunton, Somerset,
TA3 6SZ
⓪ (01823) 481493
Ⓜ 07713 091521
Ⓔ malletcourtnursery@btinternet.com
Ⓦ www.malletcourt.co.uk
Contact: J. G. S. & P. M. E. Harris F.L.S.
Opening Times: 0930–1700 Mon–Fri
summer, 0930–1600 winter. Sat & Sun by
appt.
Cat. Cost: £1.50.
Specialities: Maples, oaks, *Magnolia*, hollies
& other rare and unusual plants including
those from China & South Korea.
Notes: Mail order throughout the year. Also
sells wholesale. Exports beyond EU. Euro
accepted. Wheelchair accessible.

CMen MENDIP BONSAI STUDIO
Byways, Back Lane, Downside,
Shepton Mallet, Somerset, BA4 4JR
⓪ (01749) 344274
Ⓜ 07711 205806

Ⓔ john@mendipbonsai.co.uk
Ⓦ www.mendipbonsai.co.uk
Contact: John Trott
Opening Times: By appt. only.
Cat. Cost: None issued. Workshop lists
available.
Specialities: *Bonsai, potensai*. Many plants
available in small numbers only. Young trees
for garden or bonsai culture. Many rare &
unusual ferns from Japan for 'accent' use and
gardens (very limited numbers).
Notes: Talks & lectures on bonsai. Stockist of
most bonsai pots, related bonsai sundries &
large range of bronze figurines. Please note:
We do not stock large trees/shrubs for the
garden.

CMHG MARWOOD HILL GARDENS ♿
Marwood, Barnstaple, Devon, EX31 4EB
⓪ (01271) 342528
Ⓔ info@marwoodhillgarden.co.uk
Ⓦ www.marwoodhillgarden.co.uk
Contact: Mrs P. Stout
Opening Times: 1100–1630, 7 days. Closed
Nov–Mar.
Min Mail Order UK: £15 + p&p
Cat. Cost: Please see website.
Specialities: National Plant Collection of
Astilbe. Large range always in stock.
Notes: Mail order for all plants. Wheelchair
accessible.

CMiW MILLWOOD PLANTS
Millwoods, Colleton Mills, Umberleigh,
Devon, EX37 9ET
Ⓜ 07756 515084
Ⓔ millwoodplants@mail.com
Ⓦ www.millwoodplants.com
Contact: Gary Buckingham
Opening Times: 1000–1700 Mon–Wed &
Fri (closed Thu) Apr–Sep.
Specialities: Hardy herbaceous perennials for
woodland gardens and shade. Old fashioned
roses.
Notes: Hardy, unusual & authentic plants.
Traditional propagation methods retain colour,
size & hardiness. Exhibits at shows all year.
See website for details. Nursery postcode for
Sat Nav is EX37 9ES. Delivers to shows.

CNWT NEW WOOD TREES
The Barn, Broadley Lane, Stoke Gabriel,
Totnes, Devon, TQ9 6RR
⓪ (01803) 782666
Ⓔ hello@newwoodtrees.co.uk

W www.newwoodtrees.co.uk
Contact: Caleb Wales
Opening Times: 0800–1600 Mon–Fri.
Specialities: Multi-stem trees and shrubs, all fields grown.
Notes: Established in 2008 to supply the UK market with British field grown, multi-stem trees, our 35-acre site is situated in the rolling hills of South Devon and is home to over 90 different tree varieties. Also sells wholesale.

CoPl CORNWALL PLANTS
Wheal Bull, St Austell, Cornwall, PL26 7UA
M 07982 996713
E mail@cornwallplants.com
W www.cornwallplants.com
Contact: Rebecca Mole
Opening Times: Not open, online only.
Specialities: Whilst we stock a cross section of plants in sizes suitable for mail ordering, we specialise in wildlife friendly & native species, hardy perennials, shrubs & ground cover, and the more unusual & rarer houseplants, orchids & succulents.
Notes: We are a small yet passionate family run nursery that grows a diverse range of plants offering you; potted plants, seeds & accessories delivered direct to your door. Our team consists of dedicated professional horticulturalists with extensive experience who believe in the use of organic & sustainable practices & the importance of the personal touch. Online mail order only. Orders accepted all year round. Contract ordering available (please contact nursery for details).

CPbh PENBERTH PLANTS
St Buryan, Penzance, Cornwall, TR19 6HJ
M 07470 909775
E info@penberthplants.co.uk
W www.penberthplants.co.uk
Contact: Jeff Rowe
Opening Times: Not open. Mail order.
Cat. Cost: Online only.
Specialities: *Protea*, *Restio*, succulents and other unusual plants.
Notes: Sells at RHS shows. Open days throughout the year, check website or contact nursery for dates. Card payment accepted at shows. Mail order through website only. Delivers to shows.

CPic PICCOLO PLANTS NURSERY
Berry Hill, Branscombe, Devon, EX12 3BD
M 07722 486750
E piccoloplants.nursery@gmail.com
W www.piccoloplantsnursery.co.uk
Contact: Tom Adkin
Opening Times: 0900–1700 Mon–Sat (spring/summer) 0900–1600 Mon–Fri (autumn/winter).
Specialities: Succulents.
Notes: Piccolo Plants Nursery is a plant nursery located in the village of Branscombe, in South East Devon (UK). The nursery offers a wide variety of beautiful succulents for sale online, but also seasonal plants, shrubs, flowers and indoor plants at the nursery. We grow everything we sell at the nursery on site. Partial wheelchair access but nursery becomes very muddy in winter. Please contact us if you require any assistance. Delivers to shows. Mobile coverage is poor so best to email.

CPud PUDDLEPLANTS
The Barn, Cwmceiliog Fawr, Taliaris, Llandeilo, Carmarthenshire, SA19 7NL
T (01558) 615056
E sonia@puddleplants.co.uk
W www.puddleplants.co.uk
Contact: David Thomas
Opening Times: Not open, online only.
Cat. Cost: Online only.
Specialities: Marginal, bog garden, oxygenating and pond plants. A range of native aquatic plants to the UK available.
Notes: An on-line nursery retailing to the public and trade, specialising in British native pond and bog garden plants. Also have a very good selection of ornamentals, including irises (both pond and bog), and water lilies. Deliver anywhere in the UK all year around via 24 hour courier. Euro accepted.

CRHN ROSELAND HOUSE NURSERY
Chacewater, Truro, Cornwall, TR4 8QB
T (01872) 560451
E clematis@roselandhouse.co.uk
W www.roselandhouse.co.uk
Contact: Charlie Pridham
Opening Times: 1300–1700 Tue & Wed, Apr–Jul. Other times by appt.
Cat. Cost: Online only.
Specialities: Climbing & conservatory plants. National Plant Collections of *Clematis viticella* & *Lapageria rosea*. Named *Lapageria* in short supply but occasionally available.
Notes: Delivery to England, Scotland and Wales only. Garden open to the public. Delivers to shows.

CSBt   St Bridget Nurseries Ltd ⚅
Clyst St. Mary, Exeter, Devon, EX5 1AE
☏ (01392) 876281
✉ gardening@stbridgetnurseries.co.uk
🌐 stbridget.uk/
Contact: Sales Dept.
Opening Times: 0900–1700 Mon–Sat, 1000–1600 Sun. Closed Xmas Day, Boxing Day, New Year's Day & Easter Sun.
Specialities: General nursery propagating a range of top quality plants, with a retail garden centre near Exeter. Founded 1925.
Notes: No mail order, collection only. Wheelchair accessible.

CSde   Seaside Plants
Marsh Lane Nursery, West Charleton, Kingsbridge, Devon, TQ7 2AQ
📱 07775 201595
✉ info@seasideplants.co.uk
🌐 www.seasideplants.co.uk
Contact: Michael Hornby
Opening Times: Not open. By appt. only.
Cat. Cost: Online only.
Specialities: Wide range, esp. coastal plants, *Callistemon*, *Corokia*, *Elaeagnus*, *Euonymus*, grasses, *Griselinia*, *Hydrangea*, *Olearia*, *Pittosporum* & ferns.
Notes: Euro accepted.

CSgt   Strete Gate Camellias
17 Seymour Drive, Torquay, Devon, TQ2 8PY
☏ (01803) 770710
📱 07964 824673
✉ plants@stretegatecamellias.co.uk
🌐 www.stretegatecamellias.co.uk
Contact: Jeremy Wilson
Opening Times: Nursery not open to public, but collection can be arranged.
Specialities: Growing around 500 varieties of *Camellia*, some in small numbers.
Notes: Nursery is not open to the public and is at a different address, but orders can be collected. Plants can be collected from Kingsbridge Farmers Market. Facebook page @stretgatecamellias. Delivers to shows. Also sells wholesale.

CSpe   Special Plants
Hill Farm Barn, Greenways Lane, Cold Ashton, Chippenham, Wiltshire, SN14 8LA
☏ (01225) 891686
✉ derry@specialplants.net

🌐 www.specialplants.net
Contact: Derry Watkins
Opening Times: 1000–1700 7 days, Mar–Oct. Other times please ring first.
Min Mail Order UK: £10 + p&p
Cat. Cost: Free.
Specialities: Tender perennials, *Pelargonium*, *Salvia*, hardy geraniums, *Anemone*, *Papaver*, umbels & grasses. Many varieties propagated in small numbers only. Seeds.
Notes: Mail order Sep–Mar only. Delivers to shows.

CSta   Staddon Farm Nurseries ⚅
Staddon Road, Holsworthy, Devon, EX22 6NH
📱 07547 711189
✉ penny@pennysprimulas.co.uk
🌐 www.pennysprimulas.co.uk
Contact: Penny Jones
Opening Times: By appt. only.
Cat. Cost: Online only.
Specialities: *Primula*. National Plant Collection of *Primula sieboldii* Japanese cvs. Modest collection of *Epimedium* & ferns.
Notes: Delivers to shows. Wheelchair accessible.

CSto   Stone Lane Gardens
Stone Farm, Chagford, Devon, TQ13 8JU
☏ (01647) 231311
✉ admin@stonelanegardens.com
🌐 www.stonelanegardens.com
Contact: Paul Bartlett
Opening Times: By appt. only Mon–Fri. Orders can be made via website, email or phone.
Min Mail Order UK: £9.95
Cat. Cost: Online.
Specialities: National Plant Collections (scientific status) of *Betula* & *Alnus*.
Notes: Charity devoted to public education through the conservation, research and distribution of birch and alder. Arboretum open all year round with National Plant Collections of birch and alder. See mature specimens of the trees available in our nursery. Admission charge applies.

CTca   Trecanna Nursery
The Old Barn, Chilsworthy, Cornwall, PL18 9PB
☏ (01822) 834680
📱 07785 242148

Ⓔ trecannanursery@gmail.com
Ⓦ www.trecanna.com
Contact: Mark Wash
Opening Times: Not open. Mail order only.
Min Mail Order UK: £22
Cat. Cost: Online only.
Specialities: Hardier South African plants, specialising in *Crocosmia* & *Eucomis*.
Notes: Talks given to garden societies. Mail order to UK only.

CToG   TOR GARDEN PLANTS
Tor Gardens, Brentor, Tavistock, Devon, PL19 0NG
Ⓜ 07718 224641
Ⓔ sales@torgardenplants.co.uk
Ⓦ www.torgardenplants.co.uk
Contact: Emma Robertson
Opening Times: By appointment only.
Specialities: Water *Iris*, aquatic, marginal and moisture loving plants.
Notes: National Plant Collection of the Rowden Nursery Plant Collection. Featured on Gardeners' World.

CTrh   TREHANE NURSERY ♿
Stapehill Road, Hampreston, Wimborne, Dorset, BH21 7ND
Ⓣ (01202) 873490
Ⓔ office@trehanenursery.co.uk
Ⓦ www.trehanenursery.co.uk
Contact: Lorraine Summers
Opening Times: 0830–1630 Mon–Fri all year (excl. Xmas & New Year).
Specialities: Extensive range of *Camellia* species, cultivars & hybrids. Many new introductions. Blueberries.
Notes: Wheelchair accessible.

CTsd   TRESEDERS NURSERY ♿
Wallcottage Nursery, Lockengate, St. Austell, Cornwall, PL26 8RU
Ⓣ (01208) 832234
Ⓔ Treseders@btconnect.com
Ⓦ www.treseders.co.uk
Contact: James Treseder
Opening Times: 0900–1700 Mon–Sat. Closed Wed. 1000–1600 Sun.
Cat. Cost: Online or by email only.
Specialities: A wide range of choice & unusual plants grown in peat-free compost. National Plant Collection of *Prostanthera*.
Notes: Plants sometimes only available in small quantities. Enquiries welcome. Wheelchair accessible.

CTtf   TRIFFIDS
The Nursery, Withy Lane, Oakhill, Radstock, Somerset, BA3 5SE
Ⓣ (01749) 840561
Ⓜ 07779 868133
Ⓔ jackietriffids@hotmail.co.uk
Contact: Jackie Williams
Opening Times: By appt. only. Please phone for details.
Cat. Cost: None issued.
Specialities: Traditional & unusual perennials, plants for shade, potted bulbs, *Galanthus*, *Geum*, *Gladiolus* species, *Epimedium* and wildflowers.
Notes: Mail order for *Galanthus* only. Please email nursery for list. Plants available at plant fairs and shows. Delivers to shows.

CWal   THE WALLED GARDENS OF CANNINGTON ♿
Church Street, Cannington, Somerset, TA5 2HA
Ⓣ (01278) 655042
Ⓔ uglowb@btc.ac.uk
Ⓦ www.canningtonwalledgardens.co.uk
Contact: Bryony Uglow
Specialities: Summer flowering herbaceous perennials from our 70m-long 'Herbaceous Border'. Blue flowering plants from our Blue Garden. Mediterranean plants from our Dry Garden. Sub-tropical plants from our sub-tropical walk and glasshouse. Houseplants, cacti, succulents and tropical plants.
Notes: RHS Partner Garden and part of Bridgewater and Taunton College. The majority of our plants are propagated on-site by staff, students and volunteers from the vast array of plants in our Gardens and Botanical Glasshouse. We also propagate to order. All profits go to the college. Wheelchair accessible.

CWat   THE WATER GARDEN ♿
Hinton Parva, Swindon, Wiltshire, SN4 0DH
Ⓣ (01793) 790558
Ⓔ ben@thewatergarden.co.uk
Ⓦ www.thewatergarden.co.uk
Contact: Ben Newman
Opening Times: 1000–1700 Wed–Sat. 1000–1600 Sun.
Min Mail Order UK: £10 + p&p
Cat. Cost: 4 × 1st class.
Specialities: Waterlilies, marginal & moisture plants, oxygenators & alpines.
Notes: Also sells wholesale. Wheelchair accessible.

CWCL **WESTCOUNTRY NURSERIES (NORTH DEVON) LTD**
Donkey Meadow, Woolsery, Devon,
EX39 5QH
Ⓣ (01237) 431111
Ⓔ info@westcountrylupins.co.uk
Ⓦ www.westcountry-nurseries.co.uk
Contact: Sarah Conibear
Opening Times: Mon–Fri, open for collection of plant orders by appt. only. Please ring beforehand 1000–1530 weekdays only, closed w/ends.
Cat. Cost: 2 × 1st class + A5 sae for full colour cat.
Specialities: *Lupinus, Lewisia, Helleborus, Clematis, Cyclamen*, select perennials, grasses, ferns & climbers. National Plant Collection of *Lupinus*.
Notes: Delivers to shows.

CWGN **WALLED GARDEN NURSERY** ♿
Brinkworth House, Brinkworth,
Nr Malmesbury, Wiltshire,
SN15 5DF
Ⓜ 07921 436283
Ⓔ sales@clematis-nursery.co.uk
Ⓦ www.clematis-nursery.co.uk
Contact: Fraser Wescott
Opening Times: 1000–1700 Mon–Sat, 1000–1600 Sun Mar–Oct. 1030–dusk Mon–Fri, Nov & Feb. Closed Dec & Jan.
Specialities: *Clematis* & climbers, with a selection of unusual perennials & shrubs.
Notes: Wheelchair accessible.

CWnw **WINROW NURSERIES**
Lewis Drove, Panborough, Wells, Somerset,
BA5 1PT
Ⓣ (01934) 712571
Ⓔ plants@winrownurseries.com
Ⓦ www.winrownurseries.com
Contact: Lucy Watson
Opening Times: 0800–1600 Mon–Fri.

CWRo **WILD BUT ROOTED**
Ⓜ 07455 218990
Ⓔ wildbutrooted@gmail.com
Contact: Stacey Thomas
Opening Times: Not open. Online/mail order only.
Specialities: Native and perennial edibles.
Notes: Small nursery in South West UK specialising in Food Forests: native edible perennial plants and trees. Online to public and wholesale. All of our plants are grown without pesticides and herbicides and delivered in biodegradable packaging. Partial wheelchair access.

EASTERN

EAri **RB PLANTS**
Nayland Road, West Bergholt, Colchester,
Essex, CO6 3DH
Ⓜ 07973 630359
Ⓔ rbplants22@gmail.com
Ⓦ www.ebay.co.uk/str/aridplants
Contact: Richard Bookham
Opening Times: Mail order only.
Specialities: Exotics and other plants.
Notes: Plants sometimes only available in small quantities. Wholesale enquiries welcome. Mail order for retail customers only.

EBar **BARCHAM TREES PLC**
Eye Hill Drove, Ely, Cambridgeshire,
CB7 5XF
Ⓣ (01353) 720950
Ⓔ info@barchamtrees.co.uk
Ⓦ www.barcham.co.uk
Opening Times: Office hours 0900–1730 Mon–Fri. Nursery visits by appt. only.
Cat. Cost: £15–£25.
Specialities: Containerised tree nursery stocking over 450 varieties from 3 metres tall and up.
Notes: As trees range from 3–8 metres, all are despatched on lorries rather than through the mailing service. Also sells wholesale. Delivers to shows. Euro accepted.

EBee **BEECHES NURSERY** ♿
Crown Hill, Ashdon, Saffron Walden, Essex,
CB10 2HB
Ⓣ (01799) 584362
Ⓔ sales@beechesnursery.co.uk
Ⓦ www.beechesnursery.co.uk
Contact: Alan Bidwell/Philip Seymour
Opening Times: 0830–1700 Mon–Sat, 0930–1630 Sun & B/hols.
Min Mail Order UK: £15
Min Mail Order EU: £20
Cat. Cost: Online.
Specialities: Herbaceous specialists & extensive range of other garden worthy plants. Rarities available in limited numbers only.
Notes: Orders accepted throughout the year. No trees or very large shrubs by mail order – selected trees can be dispatched direct from our grower. Wheelchair accessible.

Nursery Details by Code

EBlo   **Bressingham Gardens Nursery**
Low Road, Bressingham, Diss, Norfolk,
IP22 2AB
Ⓣ (01379) 688282
Ⓔ info@bressinghamgardens.com
Ⓦ www.thebressinghamgardens.com/shop/
Contact: Jason Bloom
Opening Times: (Office) 0830–1630 Mon–Fri. Mail order only.
Min Mail Order UK: £6.95 + p&p
Cat. Cost: Free.
Specialities: Perennials and grasses, many from The Bressingham Gardens' extensive collection raised by Alan Bloom, and more recently Adrian Bloom and garden curator Jaime Blake. All plants grown at Bressingham Gardens Nursery. The 17-acre Bressingham Gardens are open from the end of March to end of October – visit for inspiration. See our website for details.
Notes: Mail order only. Also sells wholesale.

EBls   **Peter Beales Roses** ♿ ◆
London Road, Attleborough, Norfolk,
NR17 1AY
Ⓣ (01953) 454707
Ⓔ info@peterbealesroses.com
Ⓦ www.classicroses.co.uk
Contact: Mrs Tina Limmer
Opening Times: 0900–1700 Mon–Sat 1000–1600 Sun & B/hols.
Specialities: Old and modern roses, companion climbers, herbaceous shrubs.
Notes: Show garden and wildlife garden. Licenced restaurant. Workshops. Exports beyond EU. Wheelchair access.

ECha   **Beth Chatto's Plants and Gardens** ♿
Clacton Road, Elmstead Market, Colchester,
Essex, CO7 7DB
Ⓣ (01206) 822007
Ⓔ nursery@bethchatto.co.uk
Ⓦ www.bethchatto.co.uk
Contact: David Ward
Opening Times: Please see website for opening times.
Min Mail Order UK: See website
Cat. Cost: Online only.
Specialities: Predominantly herbaceous perennials, grasses & ferns. Many unusual for special situations.
Notes: Border design service. Peat-free potting compost used onsite. Delivers to shows. Wheelchair accessible.

ECrc   **The Crocosmia Gardens**
9 North Street, Caistor, Lincolnshire,
LN7 6QU
Ⓣ (01472) 859269
Ⓜ 07834 725392
Ⓔ thecrocosmiagardens@live.co.uk
Ⓦ www.facebook.com/crocosmiaplants
Contact: Mark Fox
Opening Times: 1000–1700 Mon, Wed–Sun. Closed Tue.
Min Mail Order UK: £5
Min Mail Order EU: £5
Cat. Cost: None issued.
Specialities: *Crocosmia*. National Plant Collection of *Crocosmia*. Available in small quantities only.
Notes: Sent bare-root only, Oct–Apr. Exports beyond EU. Euro accepted.

ECul   **John Cullen Gardens Ltd**
Eagle Lodge, Archers Lane, Algarkirk,
Lincolnshire, PE20 2AG
Ⓜ 07931 634933
Ⓔ design@johncullengardens.com
Ⓦ www.johncullengardens.com
Contact: John Cullen
Opening Times: By appt. only. Open days throughout the year – please check website for details.
Specialities: Scented plants, plants for pollinators, herbs, shrubs & bulbs.
Notes: A wide selection of plants from shrubs to perennials, bulbs & herbs. Delivers to shows.

EDAr   **D'Arcy & Everest**
Meadowsweet Nursery, Pidley Sheep Lane (B1040), Pidley, Cambridgeshire, PE28 3FL
Ⓣ (01480) 497672
Ⓔ info@darcyeverest.co.uk
Ⓦ www.darcyeverest.co.uk
Contact: Luke Whiting
Opening Times: Open on selected days, please see website/contact nursery for dates. Also for nursery tour dates (bookable in advance only). Coach parties welcome by appt. Closed Oct–Feb.
Cat. Cost: None available.
Specialities: Alpines, perennials & sempervivums.
Notes: Delivers to shows.

EDel   **Delfland Nurseries Ltd**
Benwick Road, Doddington, March,
Cambridgeshire, PE15 0TU

① (01354) 742022
Ⓔ info@delfland.co.uk
Ⓦ www.delfland.co.uk
Contact: John Overvoorde
Opening Times: Mon–Sat 0900–1600 Sun 1000–1600 (summer) Mon–Fri 0900–1600 Sat 0900–1300 Closed Sun (winter).
Min Mail Order UK: 1 tray – £31.50 incl. delivery
Specialities: Plants for bedding and containers (retail sales); organic vegetable, salad and glasshouse plants.
Notes: Also sells wholesale (propagate to order), nursery shop and online plants by the tray – 136 plants per tray of the same variety. Minimum order of 1 tray £31.50 incl. delivery (www.delfland.co.uk). Plants in the shop which we grow ourselves are peat-free. Bought-in plants may not be. Also sells wholesale. Partial wheelchair access.

EGren GRENVILLE NURSERIES ♿
Cow Watering Lane, Writtle,
Chelmsford, Essex,
CM1 3SB
① (01245) 420400
Ⓔ info@grenvillenurseries.co.uk
Ⓦ www.grenvillenurseries.co.uk
Contact: Charlie Lauman
Opening Times: 0830–1730 Mon–Thu. 0830–1900 Fri. 0900–1700 Sat. 1000–1700 Sun.
Cat. Cost: Online only.
Specialities: Trees, shrubs, herbaceous ferns, climbers, grasses and bamboo. Seasonal bare-root and rootball hedging and trees. Bulbs available in large quantities.
Notes: Leading plant nursery open to both the public and trade. Growers of seasonal bedding and herbaceous plants. Also stock seasonal bare-root and rootball hedging and trees and bulbs. Also sells wholesale. Wheelchair accessible.

EGrl GREEN ISLAND GARDENS
Park Road, Ardleigh, Colchester, Essex,
CO7 7SP
① (01206) 230455
Ⓔ info@greenislandgardens.co.uk
Ⓦ www.greenislandgardens.co.uk
Contact: Fiona Edmond
Opening Times: 10th Jan–30th Nov.
Cat. Cost: None issued.
Specialities: Acers, camellias and autumn-flowering camellias, cornus, hydrangeas, hamamelis, dwarf rhododendrons.
Notes: Large selection of acers & camellias (incl. autumn-flowering camellias). Unusual trees & shrubs, all seen growing in the gardens.

EHap HAPPY HOUSEPLANTS
Ⓜ 07732 702881
Ⓔ sales@happyhouseplants.co.uk
Ⓦ www.happyhouseplants.co.uk
Opening Times: Not open to the public. Online mail order only.
Specialities: *Alocasia, Aloe, Agave, Aglaonema, Aspidistra, Asplenium, Beaucarnea, Calathea, Chamaedorea, Chlorophytum, Chrysalidocarpus, Crassula, Dracaena, Epipremnum, Euphorbia, Ficus, Howea, Monstera, Maranta, Nephrolepis, Pachira, Peperomia, Philodendron, Sansevieria, Spathiphyllum, Strelitzia, Yucca.*
Notes: Happy Houseplants is a prominent Houseplant brand in the UK, and is celebrated for its remarkable achievements, including winning a prestigious RHS Chelsea gold medal. Happy Houseplants offers a huge selection of beautiful houseplants online including rare indoor plants, indoor plant pots, and planters. Our unwavering passion revolves around recognising the profound impact of plants, both in creating happiness and as essential elements in the field of commercial biophilic design.

EHeP HEDGING PLANTS DIRECT ♿
Long Road West, Dedham,
Colchester, Essex,
CO7 6ER
① (01206) 804732
Ⓔ info@hedgingplantsdirect.co.uk
Ⓦ www.hedgingplantsdirect.co.uk
Contact: Will Bodsworth
Opening Times: 0730–1630 Mon–Fri, 1000–1400 Sat–Sun.
Min Mail Order EU: £75
Specialities: Based in Essex on a 14-acre nursery we specialise in hedging, large shrubs and semi-mature trees.
Notes: Hedging Plants Direct is part of Plants Group and is a family run specialist plant centre open to both general public and professional landscapes alike. Based at Dedham which is set in the Constable Country in the beautiful Stour valley on the Suffolk-Essex border. Euro accepted. Delivers to shows. Wheelchair accessible.

EHet **HETTY'S HERBS AND PLANTS**
Tall Trees, Beach Lane, Gosberton Risegate,
Spalding, Lincolnshire, PE11 4JH
Ⓣ (01775) 663790
Ⓔ info@hettysherbs.co.uk
Ⓦ www.hettysherbs.co.uk
Contact: Liz Nieburg
Opening Times: 0900–1700 Mon–Fri.
Specialities: Herbs, wildflowers, chillis, soft fruits & asparagus.
Notes: Over 200 varieties of both popular and unusual herbs, lavenders, wildflowers, chillis and more. Eco-friendly packaging used. Also offers wholesale.

EIri **IRISESONLINE**
Slade Cottage, Petts Lane, Little Walden, Essex, CB10 1XH
Ⓣ (01799) 526294
Ⓔ Clare@irisesonline.co.uk
Contact: Clare Kneen
Opening Times: By appt. only.
Cat. Cost: Online only.
Specialities: *Iris*. Some varieties available in small quantities only.
Notes: Small family-run nursery. Delivers to shows.

EKin **E W KING & CO. LTD. (KINGS SEEDS)**
Monks Farm, Pantling Lane, Coggeshall Road, Kelvedon, Essex, CO5 9PG
Ⓣ (01376) 570000
Ⓔ info@kingsseeds.com
Ⓦ www.kingsseeds.com
Contact: Andrew Tokely
Opening Times: 0830–1230 1330–1700 Mon–Fri.
Cat. Cost: Free.
Specialities: Vegetable, flower, grass, sweet pea and pea & bean seeds, incl. many hybrid & unusual items.
Notes: Incorporating Suffolk Herbs. Also sells wholesale.

ELan **LANGTHORNS PLANTERY** ♿
High Cross Lane West, Little Canfield, Dunmow, Essex, CM6 1TD
Ⓣ (01371) 872611
Ⓔ info@langthorns.com
Ⓦ www.langthorns.com
Contact: E. Cannon
Opening Times: 0900–1700 6 days. Closed Mon & Xmas fortnight.
Min Mail Order UK: £20
Cat. Cost: Online only.
Specialities: Wide general range with many unusual plants.
Notes: Mail order any plant under 4ft tall. Wheelchair accessible.

ELin **LINCOLNSHIRE POND PLANTS LTD**
139e Brookenby Business Park, Brookenby, Market Rasen, Lincolnshire, LN8 6HF
Ⓣ (01472) 566970
Ⓔ sales@lincspplants.co.uk
Ⓦ www.lincspplants.co.uk
Contact: Dawn Fisher
Opening Times: 1000–1600 Mon–Sat but mostly offer plants online.
Specialities: Pond plants.
Notes: A family run nursery with a wide range of aquatic plants for ponds and tropical fish tanks. Our main goal is to provide quality plants for ponds that are grown within Lincolnshire.

ELon **LONG HOUSE PLANTS** ♿
The Long House, Church Road, Noak Hill, Romford, Essex, RM4 1LD
Ⓣ (01708) 371719
Ⓔ tim@thelonghouse.net
Ⓦ www.longhouse-plants.co.uk
Contact: Tim Carter
Opening Times: 1000–1700 Fri, Sat & B/hols, 1000–1600 Sun, beginning Mar–end June Sat 1000–1700 beginning July–end Sep or by appt.
Specialities: Choice trees, shrubs, herbaceous perennials grassed & ferns. Many unusual varieties incl. *Agapanthus*, *Aster*, *Camellia*, *Hemerocallis*, *Iris sibirica*, *Kniphofia*, *Phlox* & *Symphyotrichum*. Some only available in small quantities.
Notes: See website for garden open days. Wheelchair accessible. Disabled toilet.

EMac **FIRECREST TREES & SHRUBS NURSERY** ♿
Hall Road, Little Bealings, Woodbridge, Suffolk, IP13 6LG
Ⓣ (01473) 625937
Ⓔ firecrest98@tiscali.co.uk
Ⓦ www.firecrest.org.uk
Opening Times: By appt. only.
Specialities: Trees & Japanese maples 10–90ltr pots and bare-root hedging Nov–Mar time frame.
Notes: Please call or email for an appointment. Also sells wholesale. Bare-root mail order only. Euro accepted. Wheelchair accessible.

EMal MARSHALL'S MALMAISONS
Hullwood Barn, Shelley, Ipswich, Suffolk,
IP7 5RE
(T) (01473) 822400
(M) 07768 454875
(E) jimmalmaisons@gmail.com
Contact: J. M. Marshall/Sarah Cook
Opening Times: By appt. only.
Min Mail Order UK: £33 incl. p&p
Min Mail Order EU: £36 incl. p&p
Cat. Cost: 1st class sae.
Specialities: National Plant Collection of Malmaison carnations, perpetual flowering carnations (pre 1970) & Cedric Morris Irises. *Iris* stock only available in small quantities.
Notes: Also sells wholesale. Wheelchair accessible.

EMdy MANDY PLANTS
(office) 4 Stevens Road, Little Snoring, Norfolk, NR21 0GZ
(T) (01328) 878144
(M) 07432 112245
(E) enquiries@mandyplants.com
(W) www.mandyplants.com
Contact: Liz Spanton
Opening Times: By appt. only.
Min Mail Order EU: £25
Specialities: *Mandevilla, Dipladenia, Lantana* & other tender perennials.
Notes: Visitors are welcome but by appointment only. Nursery is at Little Snoring, Norfolk. Also sells wholesale. Delivers to shows. Wheelchair accessible.

EMic MICKFIELD HOSTAS
The Poplars, Wetheringsett Road, Mickfield, Stowmarket, Suffolk,
IP14 5LH
(T) (01449) 711576
(E) mickfieldhostas@btconnect.com
(W) www.mickfieldhostas.co.uk
Contact: Melanie Collins
Opening Times: Please check website for opening times.
Cat. Cost: Online only.
Specialities: National Plant Collection of *Hosta* containing over 2000 varieties. Waiting list for rarities & some limited quantity plants only available at nursery. Will divide parent plants for collectors if feasible. Expect to pay more for root divisions of mature plants.
Notes: See website for details of cvs held & latest availability. Gardens under development. Delivers to shows. Wheelchair accessible.

EMor MOORE AND MOORE PLANTS
London Road, Billericay, Essex,
CM12 9HR
(M) 07799 865946
(E) contact@mooreandmooreplants.co.uk
(W) www.mooreandmooreplants.co.uk
Contact: Lynne Moore
Opening Times: By appt. only, please email. For nursery open days please see website.
Cat. Cost: Online only.
Specialities: Specialists in shade tolerant and woodland plants. Great selection of plants that attract pollinating insects and plants tolerant of clay soils. Most plants available in small quantities only.
Notes: See website or contact nursery for appointment. Appointments available for garden groups/societies to visit nursery also. Delivers to shows. Wheelchair accessible.

ENfk NORFOLK HERBS ♦
Blackberry Farm, Dillington, Dereham, Norfolk, NR19 2QD
(T) (01362) 860812
(E) info@norfolkherbs.co.uk
(W) www.norfolkherbs.co.uk
Contact: Rosemary or Oliver Clifton-Sprigg
Opening Times: 0900–1700 Mon–Sat Mar 1st–Sep 30th. 1000–1600 Fri & Sat Oct 1st–Feb 28th. Closed Sun & Dec 24th–Jan 31st. At all other times please contact nursery.
Specialities: Growers & suppliers of naturally raised culinary, medicinal & aromatic herb plants, salvias, bay trees & scented pelargoniums.

EnIr THE ENGLISH IRIS COMPANY
Marshgate House, 24 Marshgate, North Walsham, Norfolk, NR28 9EF
(M) 07789 670299
(E) info@englishiriscompany.com
(W) www.englishiriscompany.com
Contact: Simon Dodsworth
Opening Times: By appt. only.
Cat. Cost: online.
Specialities: Tall bearded Irises.
Notes: Specialist Iris nursery supplying an exclusive collection of award-winning British Irises hybridised by the late Bryan Dodsworth; he is the most celebrated twentieth century British Iris Hybridiser and winner of twelve Dykes Medals for Iris hybridising. These are top quality irises with perfect flower shape, clear, clean colours and highly distinctive branching.

ENor — Norfolk Lavender
Caley Mill, Heacham, King's Lynn, Norfolk, PE31 7JE
T (01485) 570384
M 07787 550286
E info@norfolk-lavender.co.uk
W www.norfolk-lavender.co.uk
Contact: Shelley Eagle
Opening Times: 1000–1700 7 days, Mar–Oct. 1000–1600 7 days, Dec–Feb.
Cat. Cost: Free.
Specialities: National Plant Collection of *Lavandula*, sect. *L. dentata* & *L. pterostoechas*.
Notes: Wheelchair accessible.

ENSn — Norfolk Snowdrops
Stackyard Barn, Topcroft, Bungay, Norfolk, NR35 2BB
M 07867 690155
E drew@norfolksnowdrops.co.uk
Opening Times: By appointment only.
Specialities: *Galanthus* & rare bulbs.
Notes: We are a small, family run plant nursery specialising in Snowdrops and rare bulbs. We are open most weekdays after 5pm and Sundays after 1pm by appointment only during January and February. Please contact us in advance of your visit to arrange an appointment.

ENun — Twelve Nunns
16 Carisbrook Grove, Stamford, Lincolnshire, PE9 2GF
T (01778) 590455
E penny@twelvenunns.co.uk
W www.twelvenunns.co.uk
Contact: Penny Dawson
Opening Times: Not open. Mail order only.
Cat. Cost: Free.
Specialities: *Helleborus* (incl. plants with Harvington prefix.), *Roscoea*, *Erythronium* & *Trillium*. Plants bred, propagated & grown on nursery.
Notes: Also sells wholesale.

EOli — The Norfolk Olive Tree Company
Bixley Farm, Bixley, Norfolk, NR14 8RX
M 07766 730893
E thenorfolkolivetreecompany@gmail.com
W www.thenorfolkolivetreecompany.co.uk
Contact: Antonia Smith
Opening Times: By appt. only. Online only.
Min Mail Order UK: £2.95
Min Mail Order EU: £50
Specialities: We specialise in the *Arbequina*, *Picual* and *Gordal* olive tree. Large selection of UK hardy palms.
Notes: Award-winning suppliers of olive trees, specialising in hardy exotics and Mediterranean plants. Delivery UK-wide (extra charges may apply). All of our olive trees have plant passports and phytosanitary certificates. Wheelchair accessible.

EPfk — Pondfolk
Stackyard Barn, Barford Road, Topcroft, Norfolk, NR35 2BB
M 07867 690155
E drew@pondfolk.co.uk
W www.pondfolk.co.uk
Contact: Drew Wiley
Opening Times: 0900–1700 Mar–Sep.
Specialities: Pond and wetland plants.

EPfP — The Place for Plants
East Bergholt Place, East Bergholt, Suffolk, CO7 6UP
T (01206) 299224
E sales@placeforplants.co.uk
W www.placeforplants.co.uk
Contact: Sara Eley
Opening Times: 1000–1700 (or dusk if earlier) 7 days. Closed Easter Sun & Xmas B/hol. Mail order (winter only).
Cat. Cost: Online only.
Specialities: Wide range of specialist & popular plants. National Plant Collection of deciduous *Euonymus*. 20-acre mature garden with free access to RHS members Apr–Sep, excluding Sun. Mail order Oct–Mar.
Notes: Delivers to shows. Wheelchair accessible.

EPom — Pomona Fruits Ltd
The Barn, Brook Farm, Stones Green Road, Great Oakley, Harwich, Essex, CO12 5BN
T (01255) 440410
E Info@PomonaFruits.co.uk
W www.PomonaFruits.co.uk
Contact: Ming Yang/Claire Higgins
Opening Times: Not open. Mail order only.
Cat. Cost: Free.
Specialities: Fruit stock.

EPot — Pottertons Nursery
Moortown Road, Nettleton, Caistor, Lincolnshire, LN7 6HX
M 07507 770728

Ⓔ sales@pottertons.co.uk
Ⓦ www.pottertons.co.uk
Contact: Robert Potterton
Opening Times: 1000–1500 Tue–Fri, Mar–Oct.
Cat. Cost: £2 in stamps.
Specialities: Alpines, dwarf bulbs & woodland plants.
Notes: Talks given nationally & internationally to garden clubs & societies. Group nursery tours by arrangement. Delivers to shows. Euro accepted. Wheelchair accessible.

EPPr THE PLANTSMAN'S PREFERENCE ♿
Church Road, South Lopham, Diss, Norfolk, IP22 2LW
Ⓣ (01379) 710810
Ⓜ 07799 855559
Ⓔ office@plantpref.co.uk
Ⓦ www.plantpref.co.uk
Contact: Tim Fuller
Opening Times: 0930–1700 Thu, Fri, Sat Mar–Oct. Other times by appt.
Min Mail Order UK: £25 + p&p
Cat. Cost: Online only.
Specialities: Ornamental grasses, hardy Geraniums and unusual & interesting perennials incl. lots for shade/woodland. Ivies (*Hedera*) and some choice shrubs. National Plant Collection of *Molinia*.
Notes: Mail order all year except Xmas–New Year. Now using peat-free compost. Delivers to shows. Wheelchair accessible.

EPts POTASH NURSERY LTD ♿
Cow Green, Bacton, Stowmarket, Suffolk, IP14 4HJ
Ⓣ (01449) 781671
Ⓔ enquiries@potashnursery.co.uk
Ⓦ www.potashnursery.co.uk
Contact: M. W. Clare
Opening Times: Not open except for collection of pre-ordered plants by appt. only.
Min Mail Order UK: £27
Cat. Cost: 1 × 1st class.
Specialities: *Pelargonium, Fuchsia.*
Notes: Peat-free. Delivers to shows. Wheelchair accessible.

ERCP ROSE COTTAGE PLANTS
Bay Tree Farm, Epping Green, Essex, CM16 6PU
Ⓣ (01992) 573775
Ⓔ anne@rosecottageplants.co.uk
Ⓦ www.rosecottageplants.co.uk
Contact: Anne & Jack Barnard
Opening Times: Most Fri Mar–Oct. Also by appt. & for special events. See website for details.
Min Mail Order EU: £20
Cat. Cost: Online only.
Specialities: Hardy bulbs, dahlias and a select range of hardy perennials.
Notes: Mail order for *Dahlia* tubers and hardy bulbs. Delivers to shows.

ERom THE ROMANTIC GARDEN ♿
The Street, Swannington, Norwich, Norfolk, NR9 5NW
Ⓣ (01603) 261488
Ⓜ 07802 722072
Ⓔ enquiries@romantic-garden-nursery.co.uk
Ⓦ www.romantic-garden-nursery.co.uk
Contact: John Powles
Opening Times: 1000–1700 Mon–Sat incl. B/hol Mons.
Min Mail Order UK: £18
Specialities: Conservatory. *Buxus* topiary, ornamental standards, large specimens. Hedging. Topiary.
Notes: Wheelchair accessible. Also sells wholesale.

ESgI SEAGATE NURSERIES ♿
A17 Long Sutton By-Pass, Long Sutton, Lincolnshire, PE12 9RX
Ⓣ (01406) 364028
Ⓜ 07766 862603
Ⓔ sales@irises.co.uk
Ⓦ www.irises.co.uk
Contact: Chris Davey
Opening Times: 1000–1700 Mon–Sat, 1000–1600 Sun Mar–Oct. Other times by appt.
Min Mail Order UK: £20 + p&p
Specialities: Different types of *Iris*, bearded, beardless & species hybrids with about 800+ varieties, both historic & modern. Plants available in pots & bare-root in lifting season. Some only available in small quantities. A growing selection of choice perennials.
Notes: Delivers to shows. Wheelchair accessible.

EShb SHRUBLAND NURSERIES
Maltings Farm, Whatfield Road, Elmsett, Ipswich, Suffolk, IP7 6LZ
Ⓜ 07890 527744
Ⓔ gill@shrublands.co.uk
Ⓦ www.shrublands.co.uk
Contact: Gill & Catherine Stitt

Opening Times: Variable. Please see website or contact nursery directly.
Specialities: Conservatory plants, exotic plants, succulents, half-hardy perennials and shrubs. Some more unusual plants may be in short supply.
Notes: Please check before visiting that nursery is open & that any plants you require are in stock. Nearby building work could cause access to the nursery to be temporarily repositioned.

ESMi   STRAIGHT MILE NURSERY GARDENS ♿
Ongar Road, Pilgrims Hatch, Brentwood, Essex, CM15 9SA
(T) (01277) 374439
(E) info@straightmile.net
(W) www.straightmile.net
Contact: David Sisley
Opening Times: Seasonal variation, check website for details.
Cat. Cost: Epimedium catalogue only.
Specialities: General nursery stock. Japanese maples, *Epimedium*. Some in small quantities only. Mail order *Epimedium* only.
Notes: Delivers to shows. Wheelchair accessible.

ESty   STYLE ROSES ♿
Cackle Hill Farm, Boston Road North, Holbeach, Lincolnshire, PE12 8AG
(T) (01406) 424089
(M) 07760 626750
(E) mail@styleroses.co.uk
(W) www.styleroses.co.uk
Contact: Margaret Styles
Opening Times: 0900–1700 Mon–Fri at nursery address only, other times by appt. Rose field Jun–Oct.
Cat. Cost: Free in UK.
Specialities: Standard & bush garden roses sold bare-root, order from July and available for dispatch from November to March only. Potted roses available all year round. Mail order and collection service.
Notes: Nursery at Cackle Hill Farm, Boston Road North, Holbeach, Spalding, Lincolnshire, PE12 8AG. Bush roses available by mail order mainland UK all year. Std roses as bare-root Nov–Mar. Potted roses by collection/shows all year. We no longer sell roses at wholesale prices and regrettably, we are no longer able to sell or send our roses to the EU. Delivers to shows. Wheelchair accessible.

ESuc   SOUTHWOLD SUCCULENT CO.
(M) 07368 431650
(E) info@southwoldsucculentco.co.uk
(W) southwoldsucculentco.co.uk/
Contact: Niamh Mullally
Opening Times: Mail order only.
Specialities: Hardy succulents.
Notes: Suffolk grown hardy succulents. Check website for stockists and events. Individual plants by mail order only.

ESwi   SWINES MEADOW FARM NURSERY ♿ ◆
47 Towngate East, Market Deeping, Peterborough, Lincolnshire, PE6 8LQ
(M) 07432 627766/07432 627766
(E) rareplants@me.com
(W) www.swinesmeadowfarmnursery.co.uk
Contact: Colin Ward
Opening Times: 0900–1600 Mon–Sat, 1000–1600 Sun. Closed Jan–Feb except by appt. only.
Min Mail Order UK: £10
Min Mail Order EU: £10
Specialities: Hardy exotics, tree ferns, bamboos & *Hostas*. Wollemi pine stockist. Many specialities available in small quantities only.
Notes: Delivers to shows. Wheelchair accessible.

ETay   BULBS.CO.UK @ TAYLORS BULBS
Washway House Farm, Washway Road, Holbeach, Lincolnshire, PE12 7PP
(T) (01406) 426216
(E) info@bulbs.co.uk
(W) www.bulbs.co.uk
Contact: Charlotte Daubney
Opening Times: Mail order only.
Min Mail Order UK: £5.50
Cat. Cost: Free.
Specialities: Daffodils and other fine bulbs.
Notes: We specialise in daffodils growing over 400 varieties.

ETWh   TREVOR WHITE OLD FASHIONED ROSES
Bennetts Brier, 59, The Street, Felthorpe, Norwich, Norfolk, NR10 4AB
(T) (01603) 755135
(E) sales@trevorwhiteroses.co.uk
(W) www.trevorwhiteroses.co.uk
Contact: Trevor White
Opening Times: 0900–1630 Mon–Fri (office).
Min Mail Order UK: One plant + p&p
Min Mail Order EU: One plant + p&p

Specialities: Old, shrub, climbing and rambling roses.
Notes: Specialist grower of roses for over 40 years. All plants grown by us and available via the website. Unique collection of ancient and modern varieties for all types of garden. Bare-root plants are top quality and lifted to order (not stored). Some varieties available potted (all in peat-free compost).

EUrb URBAN JUNGLE
Ringland Lane, Old Costessey, Norwich, Norfolk, NR8 5BG
T (01603) 744997
E Please use 'Contact Us' button on website
W www.urbanjungle.uk.com
Contact: Christopher Brett
Opening Times: Second nursery site at London Road, Beccles, Suffolk, NR34 8TT 1000–1700 7 days Mar–Oct. 1000–1600 7 days Nov–Feb (or dusk, if earlier).
Specialities: An extensive range of high performing plants carefully chosen from a global palette, including palms, bamboo, hardy, Mediterranean and sub-tropical trees, shrubs, perennials, and architectural evergreens.
Notes: Two Nurseries, one just outside Norwich and the other near Beccles, Suffolk. Both nurseries have display gardens where plants can be seen growing in situ, an extensive range of houseplants, shop and coffee shop. Most plants grown by us. Mail order available. Partial wheelchair access. Dogs on short leads welcome.

EWat WATER GARDEN PLANTS
Beck View, Chequers Road, Gresham, Norwich, Norfolk, NR11 8RQ
T (01263) 577627
E sales@watergardenplants.co.uk
W www.watergardenplants.co.uk
Contact: Anna Robinson
Opening Times: Mail order only.
Cat. Cost: Online.
Specialities: Range of water garden plants: water lilies, floating plants, oxygenating plants, marginals, marsh plants. Some stock in small quantities.

EWes WEST ACRE GARDENS
Tumbleyhill Road, West Acre, King's Lynn, Norfolk, PE32 2BW
T (01760) 755562
E info@westacregardens.co.uk
W www.westacregardens.co.uk

Contact: J. J. Tuite
Opening Times: 0930–1700 7 days 1st Feb–30th Nov. Other times by appt. PLEASE NOTE: WE ARE SORRY, BUT WE ARE UNABLE TO OFFER MAIL ORDER UNDER ANY CIRCUMSTANCES.
Cat. Cost: None issued.
Specialities: Very wide selection of herbaceous & other garden plants incl. *Rhodohypoxis*, *Primula auricula* & *Galanthus*.
Notes: Wheelchair accessible. WE ARE SORRY BUT MAIL ORDER NOT AVAILABLE UNDER ANY CIRCUMSTANCES.

EWhm WALTHAM HERBS
Willow Vale Nursery, North Kelsey Road, Caistor, Lincolnshire, LN7 6SF
T (01472) 859481
M 07949 883091
E angelasach2@aol.com
W www.walthamherbs.co.uk
Contact: Steve Penney
Opening Times: By appt. only.
Min Mail Order UK: £3.75
Specialities: Herbs, lavenders and perennials, also some shrubs. Peat-free and pesticide-free.
Notes: For open days, see website or contact nursery. Delivers to shows.

EWld WOODLANDS
Peppin Lane, Fotherby, Louth, Lincolnshire, LN11 0UW
T (01507) 603586
M 07422 331566
E annbobarmstrong@btinternet.com
W www.woodlandsplants.co.uk
Contact: Ann Armstrong
Opening Times: Very flexible, all year by appt.
Cat. Cost: None issued.
Specialities: Small but interesting range of unusual plants, esp. woodland, *Codonopsis* and *Salvia*, all grown on the nursery in limited quantity. National Plant Collection of *Codonopsis*.
Notes: Mature garden, art gallery & refreshments. Credit cards now accepted.

EWoo WOOTTENS OF WENHASTON
The Iris Field, Hall Road, Wenhaston, Suffolk, IP19 9HF
T (01502) 478258
E info@woottensplants.co.uk
W www.woottensplants.com

Contact: Gillian Morris
Opening Times: Nursery open seasonally to visitors 1000–1600 Wed–Sat, Mar–Oct. 0900–1700 Mon–Fri for mail order/enquiries. Please see our website for full details.
Min Mail Order UK: £7.50
Cat. Cost: Online only.
Specialities: *Pelargonium*, *Hemerocallis*, *Auricula*, *Iris* and hardy *Geranium*.
Notes: Suffolk based plant nursery specialising in *Iris*, *Auricula*, *Pelargonium* and *Hemerocallis* as well as many other herbaceous perennials. Our mail order service runs throughout the year and the nursery is open to the public every Saturday from Mar–Oct and select events. Specialist event days throughout the year. Delivers to shows. Wheelchair accessible.

SCOTLAND

GAbr   ABRIACHAN NURSERIES
Loch Ness Side, Inverness, Inverness-shire, IV3 8LA
(T) (01463) 861232
(E) info@lochnessgarden.com
(W) www.lochnessgarden.com
Contact: Mr & Mrs D. Davidson
Opening Times: 0900–1900 daily (dusk if earlier) Feb–Nov.
Cat. Cost: 4 × 1st class.
Specialities: Herbaceous perennials, old-fashioned *Primula*, *Helianthemum*, hardy geraniums, *Sempervivum* & *Primula auricula*.
Notes: Delivers to shows. Partial wheelchair access (to nursery only).

GArf   ARDFEARN NURSERY
Bunchrew, Inverness, Highland, IV3 8RH
(T) (01463) 243250
(E) ardfearn@gmail.com
(W) www.ardfearn-nursery.co.uk
Contact: Alasdair Sutherland
Opening Times: Please check website for updates. Visits by appt, welcome throughout the year.
Cat. Cost: Online.
Specialities: Extensive selection of alpines & woodland plants, including *Ericaceae*, *Primulaceae*, trilliums & celmisias. Many Asiatic and Southern Hemisphere varieties available.
Notes: Specialist grower of alpines and hardy plants in the Scottish Highlands. Many rare and unusual varieties. Friendly, expert advice. Attend Scottish Rock Garden Club shows. Mail order available. Wheelchair accessible. Delivers to shows.

GBin   BINNY PLANTS
Binny Estate, Ecclesmachan Road, Near Broxburn, West Lothian, EH52 6NL
(T) (01506) 858931
(M) 07753 626117
(E) contact@binnyplants.com
(W) www.binnyplants.com
Contact: Billy Carruthers
Opening Times: 1000–1700, 7 days. Closed over Xmas & New Year.
Cat. Cost: 4 × 1st class.
Specialities: Over 250 varieties of *Paeonia*, plus a good range of herbaceous perennials, grasses & ferns incl. *Astilbe*, *Bergenia*, *Geranium*, *Molinia*, *Persicaria* & *Iris*.
Notes: Also sells wholesale. Exports beyond the EU. Delivers to shows. Wheelchair accessible.

GEdr   EDROM NURSERIES
Coldingham, Eyemouth, Berwickshire, TD14 5TZ
(T) (01890) 771386
(E) mail@edrom-nurseries.co.uk
(W) www.edrom-nurseries.co.uk
Contact: Mr Terry Hunt
Opening Times: Not open. Mail order & plant fairs only.
Cat. Cost: Free.
Specialities: *Epimedium*, *Gentiana*, *Primula*, *Meconopsis*, *Rhodohypoxis*, *Trillium*, *Hepatica*, Japanese *Saxifraga* & Japanese *Hepatica*.
Notes: Delivers to shows.

GElm   ELMLEA PLANTS
Elmlea, Old Minnigaff, Newton Stewart, Dumfries & Galloway, DG8 6PX
(T) (01671) 402514
(M) 07876 822431
(E) moiradavies@yahoo.co.uk
(W) www.elmleaplants.co.uk
Contact: Giles Davies
Opening Times: 1000–1700 Thu–Sun Mar–Oct. Closed Mon–Wed.
Min Mail Order UK: £10.50
Specialities: There is always a good selection of *Geum*, *Achillea* and *Geranium*, a wide choice of late flowers such as *Helenium* and many of the taller perennials which we love. Our range of grasses includes many larger and

unusual cultivars as well as choice smaller varieties.
Notes: We are a small, family-run nursery specialising in herbaceous perennials and grasses. We sell here at the nursery, at shows in Scotland, Ireland, Cumbria and by mail order. We grow a wide range of plants but not in huge quantities so please check for availability.

GGGa   GLENDOICK GARDENS LTD
Glendoick, Perth, Perthshire, PH2 7NS
Ⓔ orders@glendoick.com
Ⓦ www.glendoick.com
Contact: Kenneth Cox
Opening Times: Nursery not open. Garden centre open 0900–1700 7 days. Gardens open Apr & May, details on website or contact nursery for details.
Min Mail Order UK: £125
Min Mail Order EU: Not able to export to EU. Norway £500
Cat. Cost: Online only.
Specialities: Rhododendrons, azaleas, woodland plants. Plants from wild seed. Most but not all plants available at garden centre. Three National Plant Collections.
Notes: Wheelchair access to garden centre.

GGro   GROWILD NURSERY
Loganhill Farm, Cumnock, East Ayrshire, KA18 3BX
Ⓔ info@growildnursery.co.uk
Ⓦ www.growildnursery.co.uk
Contact: Lisa Wesley & Andrew Blackwood
Opening Times: Not open, mail order only.
Cat. Cost: Online only.
Specialities: Grow rare and unusual species plants, in particular, hardy perennials from Japan, China and the Himalayas. Sell the largest selection of Asian *Impatiens, Begonia* & members of the *Urticaceae* family in the UK, as well as woodland plants and rarely grown UK wildflowers that attract pollinating insects.
Notes: No peat-based products are used in the nursery. No chemicals or animal-derived products are used on our plants and only seaweed fertiliser is used. We also sell a wide range of seeds collected from our plants all year round. As well as payment by all major credit and debit cards and PayPal, we also accept payment by Google Pay and Apple Pay.

GJem   JEMIMA'S GARDEN
Ⓜ 07340 501492
Ⓔ jane@jemimasgarden.co.uk
Ⓦ https://jemimasgarden.co.uk
Contact: Jane Cureton
Opening Times: Mail order only.
Specialities: Flower seeds to benefit pollinators and other wildlife, including UK native wildflowers, cottage garden plants and herbs.
Notes: Seeds grown without pesticides, UK grown, many from our own garden in Dumfries and Galloway, Scotland. Only plastic-free recyclable packaging used.

GJos   JO'S GARDEN ENTERPRISE ♿
Easter Balmungle Farm, Eathie Road, by Rosemarkie, Ross-shire, IV10 8SL
Ⓣ (01381) 621006
Ⓔ jos*garden*enterprise@hotmail.co.uk
Contact: Joanna Chance
Opening Times: 1000 until dusk, 7 days.
Cat. Cost: None.
Specialities: Alpines & herbaceous perennials. Selection of native wild flowers.
Notes: Wheelchair accessible.

GKev   KEVOCK GARDEN PLANTS
Kevock Road, Lasswade, Midlothian, EH18 1HX
Ⓣ (0131) 454 0660
Ⓔ info@kevockgarden.co.uk
Ⓦ www.kevockgarden.co.uk
Contact: Elea Strang
Opening Times: Mail order only.
Min Mail Order UK: £30
Cat. Cost: 2 × 2nd class.
Specialities: Chinese and Himalayan plants. *Trillium, Daphne, Paeonia, Primula, Meconopsis, Iris,* woodland plants, alpine plants, rock plants, marginal and bog plants, bulbs, Chinese and Himalayan trees and shrubs, *Sorbus, Rhododendron.*
Notes: We only sell by mail order as we are a nursery and so we are not open to the public. Please purchase plants by mail order or from plant stalls at the shows we attend. Delivers to shows. Also sells wholesale.

GKin   KINLOCHLAICH GARDEN PLANT CENTRE
c/o Blarchasgaig, Appin, Argyll, PA38 4BB
Ⓜ 07881 525754
Ⓔ fiona@kinlochlaich.plus.com
Ⓦ www.kinlochlaichgardencentre.co.uk
Contact: Fiona Hutchison
Opening Times: 1000–1600 Mar–mid-Oct, 1000–1500 or by appt. mid-Oct–Feb.
Cat. Cost: None issued.

Specialities: Hardy shrubs, trees, azaleas, perennials. Also Gulf Stream plants such as *Tropaeolum, Embothrium, Eucryphia, Drimys* & more. Good selection of hardy seaside plants.
Notes: Does not offer mail order but will post where possible. Limited wheelchair access (gravel paths).

GMaP   MACPLANTS
Berrybank Nursery, 5 Boggs Holdings, Pencaitland, East Lothian, EH34 5BA
T (01875) 341179
E sales@macplants.co.uk
W www.macplants.co.uk
Contact: Gavin McNaughton
Opening Times: 1030–1700 7 days, Mar–end Sep. 1030–1600 Mon–Fri, Oct. Closed Nov–end Feb except by appt.
Cat. Cost: 4 × 2nd class.
Specialities: Herbaceous perennials, alpines, hardy ferns & grasses. *Meconopsis*. National Plant Collection of *Sanguisorba*.
Notes: Also sells wholesale. Delivers to shows. Wheelchair accessible.

GPoH   POTATO HOUSE
East Mains Farm, Auchterhouse, Dundee, DD3 0QN
T (01382) 320454
E amy@potatohouse.co.uk
W potatohouse.co.uk
Contact: Amy Skea
Opening Times: 24 hour on-line sales. Office manned from 0900–1700 Mon–Fri.
Specialities: Seed potatoes. Over 70 varieties of seed Potatoes, including speciality, organic, heritage, coloured and traditional favourites for spring and summer planting. Delivery within UK mainland only.
Notes: Home of quality seed potatoes. Certified seed producers. Supply potatoes for 'Potato Day' events across the UK. Wheelchair accessible.

GPSL   PLANTS, SHOOTS AND LEAVES
The Garden House, Hartrigge, Jedburgh, TD8 6TF
M 07885 444241
E karen.leys@btinternet.com
W www.plantsshootsandleaves.co.uk
Contact: Karen Leys
Opening Times: 1000–1700 1st Apr–1st Oct. Closed Mon. Please phone first. Nursery may be closed when we are attending shows.

Min Mail Order UK: £3.50
Min Mail Order EU: £6.60
Cat. Cost: Online only.
Specialities: *Epimedium*. Hardy geraniums. Perennials and some shrubs. Some available in small quantities only.
Notes: Delivers to shows. Euro accepted. Partial wheelchair access.

GQue   QUERCUS GARDEN PLANTS LTD
Whitmuir Farm, Lamancha, West Linton, Scottish Borders, EH46 7BB
T (01968) 660708
E quercusgardenplants@gmail.com
W www.quercusgardenplants.co.uk
Contact: Rona Dodds
Opening Times: 1000–1700 Wed–Sun.
Cat. Cost: Online only.
Specialities: Tough plants for Scottish gardens. Wide range of plants, including old favourites and many unusual varieties of herbaceous perennials, grasses, trees, shrubs & plants for shade, wet ground and other challenging garden area suited to growing in exposed gardens.
Notes: Our plants are grown at 850ft above sea level, making them tough and well acclimatised to Scottish growing conditions. Virtually all plants propagated on site. Display gardens show customers what can be grown in these challenging conditions.

N. IRELAND & REPUBLIC

IArd   ARDCARNE GARDEN CENTRE
Ardcarne, Boyle, Co. Roscommon, F52 RY61
T +353 7196 67091
E info@ardcarne.ie
W www.ardcarne.ie
Contact: James Wickham, Mary Frances Dwyer, Kirsty Ainge
Opening Times: 0900–1800 Mon–Sat, 1200–1800 Sun & B/hols.
Specialities: Native & unusual trees, choice perennials, roses, plants for coastal areas, fruit trees, incl. heritage Irish apple trees, vegetable plants, specimen plants & semi-mature trees. Wide general range.
Notes: Plants can only be posted within the Republic of Ireland. Café. Groups & tours welcome. Ample free parking. Garden design & landscape service available. Euro accepted. Wheelchair accessible. Please note that due to changes to import/export regulations since Brexit, there may be restrictions in place

exporting plants to the UK. See www.rhs.org.uk/prevention-protection/importing-and-exporting-plants for further details. Please check directly with the nursery for details.

Bal   BALI-HAI MAIL ORDER NURSERY
42 Largy Road, Carnlough, Ballymena, Co. Antrim, N. Ireland, BT44 0EZ
(T) (028) 2888 5289
(M) 07708 257164
(E) balihainursery@btinternet.com
(W) www.mailorderplants4me.com
Contact: Mrs M. E. Scroggy
Opening Times: Mon–Sat by appt. only.
Cat. Cost: Online only.
Specialities: National Plant Collection of *Hosta* and *Agapanthus*, part planted in 1.5 acres, open to the public by appt. *Crocosmia*, *Rhodohypoxis*, tree ferns & other perennials. Hostas grown to order.
Notes: Also sells wholesale. Export beyond EU restricted to bare-root perennials, no grasses. Euro accepted. Please note that due to Brexit, we currently have restrictions in place exporting to the UK. See www.rhs.org.uk/prevention-protection/importing-and-exporting-plants.

Dun   DUNLADY PLANTS AND HERBS
34, Dunlady Road, Dundonald, Belfast, BT16 1TT
(M) 07832 769099
(E) dunladyherbs@gmail.com
Contact: Simon Burrowes
Opening Times: By appt. only. No set opening times. Public invited to drop in 9–5 Tue–Sat, but best to make an appt.
Specialities: Herbs, shrubs and trees.
Notes: A family run nursery in the hills (200m above sea level) of County Down specialising in growing herbs (no pesticides/herbicides!) for retail and wholesale. We are also creating a herb garden to showcase examples of mature herb plants. In addition we grow a range of trees, shrubs and hedging. Mail order not provided but local delivery may be possible. Partial wheelchair access.

Pap   PAPERVALE TREES
48 Old Newry Road, Rathfriland, Newry, County Down, BT34 5BQ
(T) (02830) 850059
(M) 07753 117287
(E) info@papervaletrees.com
(W) www.papervaletrees.com
Contact: Jonathan Jackson
Opening Times: Mon–Fri by appt. only, 0800–1800 Sat.
Cat. Cost: Available online.
Specialities: Almost 300 varieties of home-grown containerised trees grown in peat-free compost.
Notes: Based at the foothills of the Mourne mountains, Papervale Trees produces almost 300 species and cultivars of 'Home Grown' trees. Our range includes many hard to find varieties as well as traditional garden favourites, all grown in peat-free compost. Also sells wholesale. Delivers to shows.

Pot   THE POTTING SHED ◧
Bolinaspick, Camolin, Enniscorthy, Co. Wexford, Y21 TD93
(M) +353 8660 45715
(E) susan@camolinpottingshed.com
(W) www.camolinpottingshed.com
Contact: Susan Carrick
Opening Times: 1300–1700 Thu–Fri 24th Mar–2nd Sep, other times by prior arrangement.
Cat. Cost: 3 × 1st class.
Specialities: Grow a wide range of unusual, hard to find & new introductions of herbaceous perennials, ornamental grasses *Clematis* and *Wisteria*.
Notes: Member of the Irish Specialist Nursery Assoc. (ISNA). Only orders to EU countries will be despatched but please contact us re: charges to your individual country. Due to Brexit we can no longer send plants to UK. Delivers to shows. Euro accepted. Wheelchair accessible. Please note that due to changes to import/export regulations since Brexit, there may be restrictions in place exporting plants to the UK. See www.rhs.org.uk/prevention-protection/importing-and-exporting-plants for further details. Please check directly with the nursery for details.

Sha   SHADY PLANTS ◧
Coolbooa, Clashmore, Waterford, P36 EY19
(T) +353 (24) 86998
(M) +353 8605 42171
(E) mike@shadyplants.ie
(W) www.shadyplants.net
Contact: Mike Keep
Opening Times: Not open, mail order only.
Cat. Cost: Online only.
Specialities: Ferns, *Arisaema*, trilliums & erythroniums.

Notes: We specialise in hardy ground ferns and also have a wide range of other shade-loving plants such as aroids, trilliums, erythroniums and others. We do not use chemical pesticides or herbicides in our production, preferring organic methods such as nematodes & predator attraction. Delivers to shows. Euro accepted. Wheelchair accessible. Please note that due to changes to import/export regulations since Brexit, there may be restrictions in place exporting plants to the UK. See www.rhs.org.uk/prevention-protection/importing-and-exporting-plants for further details. Please check directly with the nursery for details.

LONDON AREA

LAma   JACQUES AMAND INTERNATIONAL LTD &
The Nurseries, 145 Clamp Hill, Stanmore, Middlesex, HA7 3JS
Ⓣ (0208) 4207110
Ⓔ bulbs@jacquesamand.co.uk
Ⓦ www.jacquesamandintl.com
Contact: John Amand
Opening Times: 0900–1700 Mon–Fri, 1000–1600 Sat.
Cat. Cost: 1 × 1st class.
Specialities: Rare and unusual species bulbs esp. *Arisaema*, *Trillium*, *Fritillaria*, tulips.
Notes: Also sells wholesale. Exports beyond EU. Delivers to shows. Euro accepted. Wheelchair accessible.

LAyl   AYLETT NURSERIES LTD &
North Orbital Road, St Albans, Hertfordshire, AL2 1DH
Ⓣ (01727) 822255
Ⓔ info@aylettnurseries.co.uk
Ⓦ www.aylettnurseries.co.uk
Contact: Julie Aylett
Opening Times: 0900–1630 Mon–Sat, 1030–1630 Sun.
Cat. Cost: Free.
Specialities: *Dahlia*. 2-acre trial ground and garden adjacent to garden centre.
Notes: Wheelchair accessible.

LBar   BARNES NURSERIES
46 Woodmansterne Lane, Wallington, Surrey, SM6 0SW
Ⓣ (0208) 6478213
Ⓔ barnes_nurseries@hotmail.com
Ⓦ www.barnesnurseries.co.uk
Contact: Jan Phillips

Specialities: Perennials.
Notes: Perennial garden nursery.

LBom   BOMA GARDEN CENTRE
51–53 Islip Street, London, NW5 2DL
Ⓣ 020 7284 4999
Ⓔ boma@bomagardencentre.co.uk
Ⓦ bomagardencentre.co.uk/
Contact: Sean Dunn
Opening Times: 0900–1800 Mon–Sat 1100–1700 Sun Mar–Oct 0900–1700 Mon–Sat 1000–1600 Sun Nov–Feb.
Specialities: Indoor & outdoor plants including fruit, herbs and specimens, containers & compost.
Notes: Based in the heart of Kentish Town London NW5, this urban paradise is an independent family-owned garden centre offering quality plants, knowledgeable horticulturists and a friendly atmosphere.

LBuc   BUCKINGHAM NURSERIES &
14 Tingewick Road, Buckingham, Buckinghamshire, MK18 4AE
Ⓣ (01280) 822133
Ⓔ web-enquiries@hedging.co.uk
Ⓦ www.hedging.co.uk
Contact: R. J. & P. L. Brown
Opening Times: 0900–1730 Mon–Sat, 1000–1600 Sun.
Cat. Cost: Free.
Specialities: Bare-rooted and container grown hedging. Fruit trees, soft fruit, trees, shrubs, herbaceous perennials, alpines, grasses & ferns.
Notes: Garden centre with a large range of container grown plants, many unusual. Well stocked shop and restaurant. Wheelchair accessible.

LCot   COTSWOLD TREES LTD
Ⓣ (01451) 700022
Ⓔ james@cotswoldtrees.com
Contact: James Murnaghan
Opening Times: Not open to the public. Mail order only.
Specialities: Native garden trees and a small range of non-native garden trees for home delivery.
Notes: Native tree specialist. Supplying peat-free ornamental garden trees from our woodland nursery in Oxfordshire. Many of our native trees are grown from our own seed orchard. We deliver small trees nationwide and large trees within a wide radius of Oxfordshire.

LCro CROCUS
Nursery Court, London Road, Windlesham,
Surrey, GU20 6LQ
T (01344) 578000
E customerservices@crocus.co.uk
W www.crocus.co.uk
Opening Times: Online and mail order only. Order lines open 24 hours, 7 days.
Min Mail Order UK: Delivery charges apply
Cat. Cost: Free.
Specialities: Large nursery selling perennials, shrubs, climbers, roses, bubs, ferns, grasses, herbs and house plants.
Notes: Online and mail order nursery. See website for details of open days. Also sells wholesale.

LDro PLANT DROP
Not open to the public
T (0203) 887 2139
E hello@plantdrop.co.uk
Contact: Linda Wadley, Nursery Manager
Opening Times: Not open to the public.
Specialities: Large houseplants and specimen outdoor plants.

LEdu EDULIS
(office) 1 Flowers Piece, Ashampstead, Reading, Berkshire, RG8 8SG
T (01635) 578113
M 07802 812781
E edulisnursery@gmail.com
W www.edulis.co.uk
Contact: Paul Barney
Opening Times: Tue–Sat by appt. only. Please phone or email nursery.
Min Mail Order UK: £20 + p&p
Min Mail Order EU: £30 + p&p
Cat. Cost: Online only.
Specialities: Unusual edibles, ferns, shade lovers, permaculture plants & many of our own collections.
Notes: Nursery is at The Walled Garden, Tidmarsh Lane, Pangbourne, RG8 8HT. Also sells wholesale. Delivers to shows. Euro accepted. Wheelchair accessible.

LHGe THE HARDY GERANIUM NURSERY
Church Farm, nr The Walled Garden,
The Street, Betchworth, Surrey,
RH3 7DH
E info@hardygeraniumnursery.co.uk
W hardygeraniumnursery.co.uk
Contact: Suzie Dewey
Opening Times: Open to the public on selected open days throughout the year. Please check the website for open days before visiting.
Specialities: A small independent nursery specialising in Hardy Geraniums, holding over 150 different cultivars in stock at the height of the growing season.
Notes: The Nursery is on agricultural land and there is a limit to how many days per year the nursery can open to the public. Please visit the FAQ section on the website for Open Day dates and directions on how to find the nursery. Purchases can be made online and collected from the nursery. The nursery is closed from November 1st to late February. What3Words: cities.head.timing.

LHom HOME FARM PLANTS
Home Farm, Shantock Lane, Bovingdon, Hertfordshire, HP3 0NG
M 07773 798068
E homefarmplants@gmail.com
W www.homefarmplants.co.uk
Contact: Graham Austin
Opening Times: 0900–1730 Fri & Sat, 1000–1600 Sun, viewing by appt. only Mon–Thu, 1st Apr–end Oct (subject to weather conditions).
Cat. Cost: 1st class sae for list.
Specialities: *Delphinium elatum* (over 100 cultivars). Hardy perennials. Show area of 200+ delphiniums (contact nursery for flowering times). Some varieties only available in small quantities.
Notes: If travelling, please contact nursery to confirm plant availability. Delivers to shows. Limited wheelchair access.

LInT IN THE GARDEN LTD
High Street Plant Shop, In the Garden Ltd, 92 Mill Lane, West Hampstead, London, NW6 1NL
T (0208) 616 9360
E holly@inthegardenuk.com
W www.inthegarden.com
Contact: Holly Barsby
Opening Times: Urban plant shop open to the public 0830–1630 Tue–Thu, 0900–1700 Fri–Sat, 1000–1600 Sat. Closed Mon London markets; Golborne Road market W10 every Sat, Chiswick Flower and Plant market first Sun of the month.
Specialities: Houseplants and container gardening.
Notes: In the Garden is an urban plant shop

retailing an ever changing display of indoor and outdoor plants. We champion small space gardening in towns and cities. We plant indoor and outdoor container arrangements and window boxes which are ready to take-away or made to order. Peat-free products included and peat-free potting medium sold. Plants available to order and local delivery and collection available.

L

LMaj MAJESTIC TREES
Chequers Meadow, Chequers Hill (Junc 9, M1), Flamstead, St Albans, Hertfordshire, AL3 8ET
T (01582) 843881
E steve.mccurdy@majestictrees.co.uk
W www.majestictrees.co.uk
Contact: Steve McCurdy
Opening Times: 0830–1700 Mon–Fri. 1000–1600 Sat, Nov–Feb. 1000–1700 Sat, Mar–Oct. Closed Sun, B/hols, Xmas through New Year.
Specialities: Semi-mature & mature containerised trees primarily grown in AirPots from 50ltr to 5000ltr.
Notes: Also sells wholesale. Supplies for private & public planting needs, including flower shows. Comprehensive delivery & planting services available. All stock using the planting service carries a one year establishment warranty (subject to conditions). Delivers to shows. Euro accepted. Disabled access by golf buggy can be arranged by appt. Partial wheelchair access to building.

LMil MILLAIS NURSERIES
Crosswater Farm, Crosswater Lane, Churt, Farnham, Surrey, GU10 2JN
T (01252) 792698
E sales@rhododendrons.co.uk
W www.rhododendrons.co.uk
Contact: Daniel Turner/Vanessa Young
Opening Times: 0900–1630 Mon–Fri all year. Please phone or see website for additional w/end opening in spring.
Cat. Cost: Full catalogue online.
Specialities: Rhododendrons, azaleas, magnolias, camellias & acers. Garden open in spring.
Notes: Mail order all year. Wheelchair accessible. No sales to EU.

LPmr PRIMROSE HALL PEONIES
Toddington Road, Westoning, Bedford, Bedfordshire, MK45 5AH
E hello@primrosehallpeonies.co.uk
W www.primrosehallpeonies.co.uk
Opening Times: 09.30–12.30 Mon–Fri. Please contact us via the contact us page on our website or by emailing hello@primrosehallpeonies.co.uk.
Specialities: National Plant Collection Holder *Itoh* hybrids. Rare varieties.
Notes: Also sells wholesale. Delivers to shows. Euro accepted.

LRHS WISLEY PLANT CENTRE (RHS)
RHS Garden Wisley, Woking, Surrey, GU23 6QB
T (01483) 211113
E wisleyplantcentre@rhs.org.uk
W www.rhs.org.uk/wisleyplantcentre
Contact: Wisley Plant Centre
Opening Times: 0900–1700 Mon–Sat, Oct–Feb. 0900–1800 Mon–Sat, Mar–Sep. 1100–1700 Sun all year, browsing from 1030.
Specialities: Over 10,000 plants, many rare or unusual, reflecting the plantings in the RHS flagship garden at Wisley. Range of heathers to reflect the replanted National Heather Collection. Also houseplants, bedding plants, bulbs & seed potatoes, plus a range of garden sundries and gifts.
Notes: Plants subject to seasonal availability. A further range of plants is available online via www.rhsplants.co.uk. Wheelchair accessible.

LShi SHIRE PLANTS
The Paddock, Buckingham Road, Gawcott, Buckinghamshire, MK18 1TN
T (01280) 817800
E enquiries@shireplants.co.uk
W shireplants.co.uk
Contact: Matt Killick
Opening Times: Please see website for opening times. Collection of orders welcome by arrangement.
Cat. Cost: Online only.
Specialities: Unusual, heritage and rare plants. Specialities include old fashioned Pinks (*Dianthus*), perennial tufted violas, sweet violets, perennial wallflowers (*Erysimum*) and hardy *Chrysanthemums*.
Notes: Traditional plant nursery offering an expanding range of plants, many of which are not widely available. A mix of heritage varieties, new discoveries and familiar favourites. Everything sold is grown on site and we are happy to offer advice about the plants we grow and sell.

LSou SOUTHON PLANTS ♿
Mutton Hill, Dormansland, Lingfield, Surrey, RH7 6NP
Ⓣ (01342) 870150
Ⓔ lyn@southon-plants.co.uk
Ⓦ www.southon-plants.co.uk
Contact: Lyn Southon
Opening Times: See website or telephone for up-to-date opening hours.
Cat. Cost: Online only.
Specialities: New & unusual hardy & tender perennials, specialising in *Agapanthus* (over 30 varieties), & *Heuchera* (over 30 varieties). Many new varieties for tender perennials/patio plants.
Notes: Wheelchair accessible.

LSRN SPRING REACH NURSERY ♿
Long Reach, Ockham, Guildford, Surrey, GU23 6PG
Ⓣ (01483) 284789
Ⓜ 07884 432666
Ⓔ info@springreachnursery.co.uk
Ⓦ www.springreachnursery.co.uk
Contact: Nursery Manager
Opening Times: 1000–1700 Mon–Sat, 1030–1630 Sun, 7 days. Open B/hols. Closed 23rd Dec–2nd Jan.
Specialities: Shrubs, evergreen climbers, *Clematis*, perennials, roses, grasses, ferns, bamboos, trees, hedging, soft fruit & top fruit trees and specimen plants. Plants for chalk & clay. Deer & rabbit proof plants. Specimen & acid-loving plants.
Notes: Please ring for mail order details. Also sells wholesale. Delivers to shows. Wheelchair accessible.

LSto STOTTS NURSERY ♿
Ibstone Road, Stokenchurch, High Wycombe, Buckinghamshire, HP14 3XS
Ⓜ 07542 718307
Ⓔ billystott@stottsnursery.co.uk
Ⓦ www.stottsnursery.co.uk
Contact: Billy Stott
Opening Times: 1000–1700 Tue–Sat British summertime. 1000–1600 Tue–Sat Winter – Greenwich Mean Time. Check website.
Specialities: Hardy plants.
Notes: Hardy plant specialists. Peat-free and UK grown. We offer a wide range of common and unusual hardy annuals, perennials, shrubs, climbers and a wide range of hedging plants, pot grown and bare-rooted. Wheelchair accessible.

LTop TOPIARY ARTS
(office) Red Roofs, Higher Street, East Quantoxhead, Bridgwater, Somerset, TA5 1EL
Ⓣ (01278) 741799 (office)
Ⓜ 07775 602704
Ⓔ jcb@topiaryarts.com
Ⓦ www.topiaryarts.com
Contact: James Crebbin-Bailey
Opening Times: By appt. only.
Min Mail Order UK: £30
Cat. Cost: Free.
Specialities: Topiary. Many individual sculptural pieces.
Notes: Nursery is at Walled Garden, Copped Hall, Upshire, Epping, Essex CM16 5HS. Field stock area. English grown plants. Also sells wholesale. Delivers to shows. Additional nursery in Hermitage, Berkshire. Please contact office for appointment to view.

LWaG WALWORTH GARDEN ♿
206 Manor Place, London, SE17 3BN
Ⓣ (0207) 5822652
Ⓔ info@walworthgarden.org.uk
Ⓦ walworthgarden.org.uk
Contact: Oliver Haden
Opening Times: 0800–1700 Mon–Fri 1000–1700 Sat & Sun (1000–1600 in winter).
Specialities: Community and student-led, gardening for wildlife and using repurposed materials.
Notes: We specialise in plants for the city garden, growing plants that thrive in dry and shady conditions, promote biodiversity, pollinators and give a luscious jungle feel. The Garden is a popular place for respite and escape in ever-bustling South London. As well as an award-winning demonstration garden, horticultural training centre, and therapy provider, a true centre of learning and growth for the local area. Wheelchair accessible.

MIDLANDS

MArl ARLEY HALL NURSERY ♿
Estate Office: Arley Hall & Gardens, Northwich, Cheshire, CW9 6NA
Ⓣ (01565) 777479
Ⓔ arleyhallplantnursery@gmail.com
Ⓦ www.arleyhallandgardens.com
Contact: Nathan Morris
Opening Times: 1000–1730 Mon–Sun 1st Mar–31st Oct.

Specialities: Wide range of herbaceous incl. many unusual varieties, some in small quantities. Wide range of unusual pelargoniums.
Notes: Nursery is beside car park at Arley Hall Gardens. Wheelchair accessible.

MAsh **ASHWOOD NURSERIES LTD** ♿
Ashwood Lower Lane, Ashwood, Kingswinford, West Midlands, DY6 0AE
℡ (01384) 401996
✉ mailorder@ashwoodnurseries.com
🌐 www.ashwoodnurseries.com
Contact: Rachel Maiden & Steve Lampit
Opening Times: 0830–1700 Mon–Sat, (winter) 0900–1700 Sun, (summer) 0830–1730 Mon–Sat, 0900–1730 Sun.
Cat. Cost: £2.50.
Specialities: Large range of hardy plants, shrubs & dwarf conifers. Roses, alpines & herbaceous plants. Also specialises in auriculas, *Cyclamen, Galanthus*, hellebores, *Hepatica, Hydrangea* & *Salvia*. National Plant Collection of *Lewisia*.
Notes: Tea room overlooking display garden. Ample parking. Regular events. Groups by appt. to visit private garden. Wheelchair accessible.

MAvo **AVONDALE NURSERY** ♿
Rear of Russell's Nursery, Mill Hill, Baginton, Coventry, CV8 3AG
📱 07367 590620
✉ enquiries@avondalenursery.co.uk
🌐 www.avondalenursery.co.uk
Contact: Gary Leaver
Opening Times: 1000–1600 Mar–Sep 7 days. Limited opening times outside these times – please see website for details.
Specialities: Rare & unusual perennials esp. asters, *Eryngium, Geranium, Geum, Crocosmia, Sanguisorba* & grasses. National Plant Collections of *Symphyotrichum novae-angliae, Anemone nemorosa* & *Sanguisorba*.
Notes: Please see website for plant availability. Limited mail order for some plants. Display garden open. Groups welcome. Wheelchair accessible.

MBel **BLUEBELL COTTAGE NURSERY** ♿
Lodge Lane, Dutton, Cheshire, WA4 4HP
℡ (01928) 713718
✉ info@bluebellcottage.co.uk ADMIN sue@bluebellcottage.co.uk
🌐 www.bluebellcottage.co.uk
Contact: Sue Beesley
Opening Times: 1000–1700 Tue–Sat 1st Apr–30 Sep. 1000–1600 Wed–Fri 31st Mar & all of Oct.
Min Mail Order UK: £4.95 (based on weight)
Cat. Cost: Online only.
Specialities: *Achillea, Anthemis, Brunnera, Centaurea, Echinacea, Geranium, Geum, Lychnis, Persicaria, Potentilla, Sanguisorba, Thalictrum* & ornamental grasses. Some items stocked in small quantities.
Notes: Mail order available all year round. Peat-free. No neonicotinoid pesticides used. Plants are fully established, ready to plant out in 9cm (3 pots). RHS Partner Garden open Apr–Sep. Refreshments available. Delivers to shows. Wheelchair accessible.

MBlu **BLUEBELL ARBORETUM & NURSERY** ♿
Annwell Lane, Smisby, Nr Ashby de la Zouch, Derbyshire, LE65 2TA
℡ (01530) 413700
✉ sales@bluebellnursery.com
🌐 www.bluebellnursery.com
Contact: Robert & Suzette Vernon
Opening Times: 0900–1700 Mon–Fri & 1000–160 Sun, Mar–Oct. 0900–1600 Mon–Sat (not Sun) Nov–Feb. Closed 24th Dec–1st Jan incl. & Easter Sun.
Min Mail Order UK: £8.95
Cat. Cost: £1.50 + 3 × 1st class.
Specialities: Specialists in rare & unusual plants. Uncommon trees & shrubs. Rare *Acer, Betula, Cornus, Fagus, Magnolia, Liquidambar, Quercus* & *Tilia*. Woody climbers.
Notes: 9-acre woodland garden & arboretum surrounds nursery. RHS partner garden. Guide dogs only. Working nursery, so wear appropriate clothing & sturdy footwear if visiting. Delivers to shows. Wheelchair accessible but please call first if weather wet.

MBNS **BARNSDALE GARDENS** ♿
Exton Avenue, Exton, Oakham, Rutland, LE15 8AH
℡ (01572) 813200
✉ info@barnsdalegardens.co.uk
🌐 www.barnsdalegardens.co.uk
Contact: Charlotte Darch
Opening Times: 0900–1700 Mar–Oct & 1000–1600 Nov–Feb, 7 days. Closed 24th & 25th Dec.

Cat. Cost: Online only.
Specialities: Wide range of choice & unusual garden plants but specialising in perennials.
Notes: Mail order from website or by telephone ordering only. Delivers to Gardeners' World Live flower show. Wheelchair accessible.

MBrN **BRIDGE NURSERY** ♿
Nursery Barn, Tomlow Road, Napton, Warwickshire, CV47 8HX
T (01926) 812737
E chris.dakin25@yahoo.com
W www.Bridge-Nursery.co.uk
Contact: Christine Dakin & Philip Martino
Opening Times: 1000–1600 Sat, Sun & B/hols Mar–Oct. Other times by appt.
Min Mail Order UK: £10
Cat. Cost: Online only.
Specialities: Ornamental grasses, sedges & bamboos. Also range of shrubs & perennials. Display garden.
Notes: Limited range available by mail order, please check with nursery. Also sells wholesale. Euro accepted. Wheelchair accessible.

MBros **BROOKSIDE NURSERY** ♿
School Lane, Hints, Tamworth, Staffordshire, B78 3DW
T (0333) 335 6789
E care@brooksidenursery.co.uk
W www.brooksidenursery.co.uk
Contact: James Thomas
Opening Times: Office/Customer Services 0930–1630 Mon–Fri all year round. Please see website for up-to-date retail nursery opening times.
Cat. Cost: Free – Postal and Online.
Specialities: *Begonia*, *Lobelia*, *Petunia*, *Geranium*.
Notes: Producer of bedding and hanging basket plants. Veg & perennials sold as young plug plants and bare-root plants for mail order and as finished plants for collection from the nursery. Also sells wholesale. Wheelchair accessible.

MCms **CHRYSANTHEMUMS DIRECT**
Holmes Chapel Road, Over Peover, Knutsford, Cheshire, WA16 9RA
T (0800) 046 7243
M 07977 312593
E sales@chrysanthemumsdirect.co.uk
W www.chrysanthemumsdirect.co.uk
Contact: Martyn Flint

Opening Times: Not open. Mail order only.
Cat. Cost: 4 × 1st class.
Specialities: *Chrysanthemum*. Young plants grown to order. Delivery within 28 days.
Notes: Delivers to shows.

MCor **MORLAS PLANTS**
Woodlands, Nant Lane, Selattyn, Oswestry, Shropshire, SY10 7HA
T (01691) 655244
M 07930 221062
E jane@morlasplants.co.uk
W www.morlasplants.co.uk
Contact: Jane Rowlinson
Opening Times: Not open. Mail order only.
Cat. Cost: Online only.
Specialities: We grow and breed *Galanthus* species and cultivars, *Erythronium*, *Narcissus* and other bulbs. Some of our rare named plants are available in limited numbers only. All our plants are grown in peat-free compost.
Notes: Unfortunately, due to a number circumstances beyond our control there will be no in the green sales for our UK customers during the 2024 season. Normal service will resume in 2025. We export dormant bulbs to the EU and internationally, please contact us for more information. Please see our website for more details. Exports beyond EU.

MCtn **CHILTERN SEEDS LTD**
Crowmarsh Battle Barns, 114 Preston Crowmarsh, Wallingford, Oxfordshire, OX10 6SL
T (01491) 824675
E info@chilternseeds.co.uk
Contact: Nina Marshall/Kate Neighbour
Opening Times: Mail order only.
Specialities: Unusual seed varieties, not always available elsewhere. Also offer a large range of heritage and heirloom vegetable seeds and seeds for growing cut flowers.
Notes: We are a small family run seed company, which has been run by the same family for almost 50 years. We currently stock 2600+ varieties, including the weird and wonderful!

MEar **EARTHED UP!**
Belper Lane End, Belper, Derbyshire, DE56 2DL
T 01773 856226
E hello@earthedup.com

Ⓦ https://earthedup.com
Contact: Ryan Sandford-Blackburn
Opening Times: By appt. only. See website for spring opening.
Specialities: Hardy, proven perennial vegetables, culinary herbs, and dye plants. Some soft fruit.
Notes: We grow all our own edible and useful plants peat-free without harmful chemicals. As a not-for-profit co-operative, income pays workers and grows gardens. Plants are available by mail order via our website or for collection.

M

MEch ECHIUM WORLD
Ⓜ 07957 602073
Ⓔ echiumworld@gmail.com
Ⓦ www.echiumworld.co.uk
Contact: Linda Heywood
Opening Times: By appt. only. Please telephone or email.
Min Mail Order UK: See website for details
Specialities: Growers of 35 varieties of *Echium* including the giant tree *Echium*, *Echium pinanana*. Rare & endangered species available.
Notes: Holders of the National Plant Collection of *Echium* species & cvs from the Macaronesian Islands.

MGos GOSCOTE NURSERIES LTD ♿
Syston Road, Cossington, Leicestershire, LE7 4UZ
Ⓣ (01509) 812121
Ⓔ sales@goscote.co.uk
Ⓦ www.goscote.co.uk
Contact: James Toone
Opening Times: 7 days, all year excl. Xmas to New Year.
Cat. Cost: Online only.
Specialities: Japanese maples, rhododendrons & azaleas, *Magnolia*, *Camellia*, *Pieris* & other *Ericaceae*. Ornamental trees & shrubs, conifers, fruit, heathers, alpines, roses, *Clematis* & unusual climbers.
Notes: Design & landscaping service available. Café & show garden. Also sells wholesale. Wheelchair accessible.

MHCG HILL CLOSE GARDENS ♿
Bread and Meat Close, Warwick, Warwickshire, CV34 6HF
Ⓣ (01926) 493339
Ⓜ 07434 810555
Ⓔ headgardener@hcgt.org.uk

Ⓦ www.hillclosegardens.com
Contact: Neil Munro
Opening Times: 1100–1700, 7 days, Apr–Oct. 1100–1600 Mon–Fri only, Nov–Mar.
Cat. Cost: 2 × 1st class or online.
Specialities: Hold dispersed National Plant Collection of hardy *Chrysanthemum*. Also specialise in *Symphyotrichum* (asters) & *Galanthus*.
Notes: Small retail nursery attached to heritage garden which is open to the public. Wheelchair accessible.

MHed HEDGEXPRESS ♿
Buckland Road, Bampton, Oxfordshire, OX18 2AA
Ⓣ (01993) 850979
Ⓔ sales@hedgexpress.co.uk
Ⓦ www.hedgexpress.co.uk
Contact: Gavin Stevens
Opening Times: 0900–1600, Mon–Fri.
Min Mail Order UK: £120
Cat. Cost: Online only.
Specialities: Hedging, lavenders & lawn edging.
Notes: Also sells wholesale. Wheelchair accessible.

MHer THE HERB NURSERY ♿
Thistleton, Oakham, Rutland, LE15 7RE
Ⓣ (01572) 767658
Ⓔ info@herbnursery.co.uk
Ⓦ www.herbnursery.co.uk
Contact: Peter & Christine Bench
Opening Times: 0900–1700 Mon–Sat, incl. B/hols 1000–1600 Sun. Closed Xmas until 1st Feb.
Cat. Cost: Free with A5 sae.
Specialities: Herbs, wild flowers, cottage garden plants and a range of alpines. Large collections of *Pelargonium*, *Thymus*, *Mentha*, *Lavandula* and *Salvia*.
Notes: Open garden weekend 22nd and 23rd June 2024 (see website for details). Five acres of nursery, gardens and woodland not normally open to the public. Refreshments available. Proceeds to village church repairs and maintenance. Delivers to shows. Wheelchair accessible.

MHol HOLLIES FARM PLANT CENTRE
Uppertown, Bonsall, Nr Matlock, Derbyshire, DE4 2AW
Ⓣ (01629) 822734
Ⓔ rbrt.wells@googlemail.com

Ⓦ www.holliesfarmplantcentre.co.uk
Contact: Robert or Linda Wells
Opening Times: 0900–1700 every day excl. Wed.
Specialities: Range of rare & unusual herbaceous perennials.
Notes: Garden designers welcome.

MHoo HOOKSGREEN HERBS LTD
1, The Yard, Hooksgreen Road, Oulton Heath, Stone, Staffordshire, ST15 8SR
Ⓜ 07977 883810
Ⓔ sales@hooksgreenherbs.com
Ⓦ www.hooksgreenherbs.com
Contact: Malcolm Dickson
Opening Times: Visit by telephone appointment only. Some open days held in the summer – please see website for details.
Min Mail Order UK: £10
Min Mail Order EU: £10
Specialities: Herbs including *Agastache*, *Allium*, *Artemisia*, basil, comfrey, *Echinacea*, lavender, mint, oregano, parsley, *Pelargonium*, rosemary, sage (including a large collection of flowering salvias), savory, thyme.
Notes: An award-winning, family-run herb nursery, supplying high-quality, culinary, medicinal, scented, and flowering herbs. Partial wheelchair access.

MHtn HINTONS NURSERY ♿
Coventry Road, Guy's Cliffe, Warwick, Warwickshire, CV34 5FJ
Ⓣ (01926) 492273
Ⓔ info@hintonsnursery.co.uk
Ⓦ www.hintonsnursery.co.uk
Contact: Sarah Ridgeway
Opening Times: Open all year round, except Christmas Day through to New Year's Day 1000–1630 Mon–Sat 1030–1600 Sun (1st Nov–28th Feb) 1000–1700 Mon–Fri 1000–1730 Sat 1030–1600 Sun (1st Mar–30th Oct).
Specialities: Specialise in fruit (soft fruit & trees) and veg. Nearly 200 varieties of veg plants ready to plant out. Also offer more unusual fruit such as Chilean guava, honeyberries, worcesterberries, *Aronia* and pluots.
Notes: Grow & sell all types of plant from alpines, herbs, aquatics, herbaceous, shrubs and climbers to trees, ferns, bamboos & roses in a range of sizes. Plug plants for summer bedding available in spring. Also sells wholesale. Wheelchair accessible.

MIdl MIDDLETON NURSERIES
Coppice Lane, Middleton, Tamworth, Staffordshire, B78 2BT
Ⓣ (0121) 2957185
Ⓔ sales@middletonnurseries.co.uk
Ⓦ www.middletonnurseries.co.uk
Contact: John Zako
Opening Times: By appt. only. Online store.
Min Mail Order UK: £5
Cat. Cost: Online.
Specialities: We specialise in growing *Salvia* which are all available to purchase at our online store. Our collections can also be purchased at all the RHS shows.
Notes: Middleton Nurseries are located in the village of Middleton in Staffordshire and have been growing plants since 1975. We are dedicated to growing new & unusual perennials, specialising in the *Salvia* species. We attend the RHS shows up and down the country. We also have our own online store. Delivers to shows. Also sells wholesale.

MLod LODGE FARM PLANTS & WILDFLOWERS ♿
Lodge Farm, Case Lane, Fiveways, Hatton, Warwick, Warwickshire, CV35 7JD
Ⓜ 07962 222276
Ⓔ lodgefarmplants@btinternet.com
Ⓦ www.lodgefarm-plants.com
Contact: Nik Cook
Opening Times: 1000–1630 winter. 1000–1730 summer.
Cat. Cost: No catalogue. See website.
Specialities: Fruit trees, trained fruit trees, ornamental trees, native trees, hedging, wildflowers, herbs and soft fruit.
Notes: Trees sell out very quickly, please contact us with your requirements. We will be happy to reserve them for you. Euro accepted. Wheelchair accessible.

MMen MINTOPIA
Fullersmoor Cottage, Smithy Lane, Brown Knowl, Cheshire, CH3 9JY
Ⓜ 07782 378697
Ⓔ intmintmint@gmail.com
Ⓦ www.mintopia.org
Contact: Simon Poole
Opening Times: Online only.
Min Mail Order UK: £1.50
Specialities: *Mentha* collection of just less than 150 varieties. As our stock grows, we intend to seek National Plant Collection

812   Nursery Details by Code

Holder status. Very rare sub-species, hybrid and varieties available. Option to buy small collections for those with specific interests.
Notes: Mintopia is a plastic-free, organic cottage industry that collects and specialises in *Mentha* (Mint). We offer bare-root, plug, pot and specimen-sized plants, often propagated to order. Please note that we are not open to the public, but offer an online mail order service. Please contact us if you wish to order plants larger than bare-root to arrange correct payment. Larger plants may take longer to be delivered.

MMrt   Morton Nurseries Ltd
Mansfield Road, Morton, Retford, Nottinghamshire, DN22 8HE
T (01777) 702530
M 07940 434298
E enquiries@morton-nurseries.com
W www.morton-nurseries.co.uk
Contact: Gill McMaster
Opening Times: 1000–1600 Tue–Sun. Closed Mon.
Min Mail Order UK: £5 + p&p
Cat. Cost: None issued.
Specialities: Shrubs & perennials.
Notes: Delivers to shows. Wheelchair accessible.

MMuc   Mucklestone Nurseries
Rock Lane, Mucklestone, Nr Market Drayton, Shropshire, TF9 4FA
T (01630) 674284
M 07714 241668/241667
E info@botanyplants.co.uk
W http://botanyplants.co.uk/mucklestone-nursery/
Contact: William & Louise Friend
Opening Times: 0930–1700 (or dusk) Wed, Fri, Sat. Please check website for details.
Cat. Cost: Online.
Specialities: A range of trees and plants for acid & damp soils. Also grow complementary range for dry, chalk & coast at our Kent nursery. Extensive grounds showing plants in situ. Small numbers only of each variety available.
Notes: Please send plant requests by email or contact Louise Friend on 07714 241667 to discuss orders & availability. Plants listed under nursery code SEND (in Kent) can be ordered for collection from Mucklestone or sent/delivered direct. Talks by arrangement in Shropshire/Staffs/Cheshire area.

MNHC   The National Herb Centre
Banbury Road, Warmington, Nr Banbury, Oxfordshire, OX17 1DF
T (01295) 690999
E info@herbcentre.co.uk
W www.herbcentre.co.uk
Contact: Plant Centre Staff
Opening Times: 0900–1730 Mon–Sat, 1030–1700 Sun.
Specialities: Herbs, culinary & medicinal. Extensive selection of rosemary, thyme & lavender in particular.
Notes: Wheelchair accessible.

MNrw   Norwell Nurseries & Gardens
Woodhouse Road, Norwell, Near Newark, Nottinghamshire, NG23 6JX
T (01636) 636337
E wardha@aol.com
W www.norwellnurseries.co.uk
Contact: Dr Andrew Ward
Opening Times: 1000–1700 Mon, Wed–Fri & Sun (Wed–Mon May & Jun). By appt. Aug & 18th Oct–1st Mar.
Min Mail Order UK: £25 + p&p
Cat. Cost: Online only.
Specialities: Large collection of 2500+ unusual herbaceous perennials esp., asters, *Geum*, hardy geraniums, bog plants, cottage garden plants, woodland plants and alpines. National Plant Collection of hardy *Chrysanthemum* & *Astrantia*.
Notes: One-acre garden & tea room. Talks given and garden tours. Hardy Plant Society names us within top perennial gardens. Also sells wholesale. Delivers to shows. Wheelchair accessible.

MPhe   Phedar Nursery
42 Bunkers Hill, Romiley, Stockport, Cheshire, SK6 3DS
T (0161) 430 3772
E mclewin@phedar.com
W www.phedar.com
Contact: Will McLewin
Opening Times: Frequent but irregular. Please phone to arrange appt.
Cat. Cost: Online or write for printed version.
Specialities: Species *Helleborus*, *Paeonia*. Limited stock of some rare items.
Notes: Also sells wholesale. Exports beyond EU subject to destination & on an ad hoc basis only. Please contact nursery for details. Euro accepted.

MPie PIECEMEAL PLANTS
Lantern Lane, East Leake, Loughborough,
Leicestershire, LE12 6QN
(T) (01509) 672056
(M) 07950 757444
(E) nursery@piecemealplants.co.uk
(W) www.piecemealplants.co.uk
Contact: Mary Thomas
Opening Times: Currently only open by arrangement between March and September. Please check website for latest details.
Cat. Cost: Online only.
Specialities: Wide range of quality, hardy herbaceous perennials. Unusual varieties & cottage garden favourites. Most in small quantities. Selection of flowering bulbs, half hardy & tender plants.
Notes: Nursery relocated from Whatton House Gardens to south Nottinghamshire. As usual, we will be attending various Midlands plant fairs and shows between March and September where pre-ordered plants may be collected. Please see website or Facebook page (Piecemeal Plants) for details of all events.

MPkF PACKHORSE FARM NURSERY &
Sandyford House, Lant Lane, Tansley, Matlock, Derbyshire, DE4 5FW
(T) (01629) 57206
(M) 07974 095752
(W) www.packhorsefarmnursery.co.uk
Contact: Hilton W. Haynes
Opening Times: 1000–1500 Tue & Wed, 1st Apr–30th Sep. Other times by appt. only.
Cat. Cost: 2 × 1st class for plant list.
Specialities: *Acer*, rare stock is limited in supply. Other more unusual hardy shrubs, trees & conifers.
Notes: Delivers to shows. Wheelchair accessible.

MPnt PLANTAGOGO.COM
Jubilee Cottage Nursery, Snape Lane, Englesea Brook, Crewe, Cheshire, CW2 5QN
(T) (01270) 820335
(M) 07713 518271
(E) info@plantagogo.com
(W) www.plantagogo.com
Contact: Vicky & Richard Fox
Opening Times: By appt. only. See description for open days.
Min Mail Order UK: £6.95 (mainland only)
Cat. Cost: Online only.
Specialities: Specialist nursery of *Heuchera, Heucherella* & *Tiarella*. Large selection of perennials. Plants listed in the book available

in good quantities, others not listed available on request. National Plant Collections of *Heuchera, Heucherella* & *Tiarella*.
Notes: Visits by appointment only which can be booked via the website. Please also see website for nursery open days and workshops.

MPri PRIMROSE COTTAGE NURSERY &
Altrincham Road, Styal, Wilmslow, Cheshire, SK9 4JE
(M) 07798 754457
(E) info@primrosecottagenursery.co.uk
(W) www.primrosecottagenursery.co.uk
Contact: Caroline Dumville
Opening Times: 0930–1630 Mon–Sat, 1000–1630 Sun (summer). 0930–1600 Mon–Sat, 1000–1600 Sun (winter).
Specialities: Perennials, herbs, patio & hanging basket plants, always lots of new & unusual varieties. Shrubs, roses, ornamental trees, fruit trees, soft fruit bushes, bedding & vegetable plants.
Notes: In Styal Village, close to National Trust Quarry Bank Mill and estate. Village café next door to nursery. Wheelchair accessible.

MPro PROCTORS NURSERY
99, High Lane, Brown Edge, Stoke-on-Trent, Staffordshire, ST6 8RT
(T) 01782 504739
(E) info@proctorsnursery.co.uk
(W) proctorsnursery.co.uk
Contact: Barry Proctor
Opening Times: 0930–1630 7 days. Closed for 2 wks over Christmas holidays.
Specialities: Herbaceous perennials, shrubs, hedging, new and unusual perennials.
Notes: A family run business based in the North Staffordshire countryside. Established in 1999, the business has grown to its present size of 18 acres of production at Endon and at Brown Edge which has been in the Proctor family since the 1870s. Proctors includes a sales area to the nursery at Brown Edge which is open to the public & trade customers 7 days a week. We sell all kinds of perennial plants and shrubs as well as seasonal items such as wreaths during the festive season. From November to March we offer a selection of hedging plants. We grow the majority of the plants we supply from cuttings or seeds raised on the nursery. Proctors Nursery has had a long-standing policy of being environmentally friendly by using (IPM) Integrated Pest Management, Using Organic Materials and

re-using plastic pots wherever possible. Delivers to shows.

MSCN STONYFORD COTTAGE NURSERY 🅖
Stonyford Lane, Cuddington, Northwich, Cheshire, CW8 2TF
Ⓣ (01606) 888970/888128 (answerphone)
Ⓔ info@stonyfordcottagegardens.co.uk
Ⓦ www.stonyfordcottagenursery.co.uk
Contact: Andrew Overland
Opening Times: 1000–1700 Tue–Fri Mar–Oct.
Cat. Cost: None.
Specialities: Wide range of herbaceous perennials, *Iris*, hardy *Geranium*, moisture-loving & bog plants. *Sempervivum*, *Paeonia*, candelabra *Primula*.
Notes: Mail order available all year round. Wheelchair accessible.

MSwo SWALLOWS NURSERY & PLANT CENTRE
Mixbury, Brackley, Oxfordshire, NN13 5RR
Ⓣ (01280) 811093
Ⓔ enq@swallowsnursery.co.uk
Ⓦ www.swallowsnursery.co.uk
Opening Times: Mon–Fri 0900–1700 Sat & Sun 1000–1600. Check website for winter opening times.
Min Mail Order UK: £15
Specialities: Growing a wide range of shrubs, climbers and herbaceous perennials for the general public and trade customers.
Cat. Cost: Please contact nursery for details.
Notes: Plants grown to order. Garden packages available. Trade discounts. Show gardens now open. Currently limited mail order.

MTha NATIONAL PLANT COLLECTION OF THALICTRUM
Not open to the public
Ⓜ 07792 202254
Ⓔ n.d.g.hook@gmail.com
Contact: Nicholas Guntrip-Hook
Opening Times: Not open to the public.
Specialities: *Thalictrum* species, varieties and cultivars, as well as *Anemonella* spp., var and cv. National Plant Collection of *Thalictrum*. National Plant Collection of *Anemonella* (ongoing application).
Notes: Please note this is not a nursery, but a home garden hosting the National Plant Collection of Thalictrum. Open for viewings by appointment only. Propagate to order under special request only, in order to preserve the National Collection. Advice given on how to plant, look after and propagate Thalictrum.

MVer MANOR FARM BOTANICS
9 Chalfield Close, Crewe, Cheshire, CW2 6TJ
Ⓜ 07533 013968
Ⓔ mfbotanics@gmail.com
Ⓦ www.manorfarmbotanics.com
Contact: Tracy Jones
Opening Times: By appt. only. Please contact Tracy Jones for details.
Specialities: Herbalist garden selling medicinal herbs. Also holds the National Plant Collection of *Verbena*.
Notes: Holds herbalism workshops using herbs from the garden and opens for the NGS. Will open for groups by appt. All plants are propagated on site and many are only available in small quantities and grown using peat-free compost and no pesticides. Talks given to gardening clubs, WI's, U3A & other groups, follow the link: https://manorfarmbotanics.com/talks.

MWht WHITELEA NURSERY 🅖
Whitelea Lane, Tansley, Matlock, Derbyshire, DE4 5FL
Ⓣ (01629) 55010
Ⓔ sales@uk-bamboos.co.uk
Ⓦ www.uk-bamboos.co.uk
Contact: David Wilson
Opening Times: By appt. only.
Cat. Cost: Online only. Price list available 2 × 1st class.
Specialities: Bamboos. Substantial quantities of 45 species/cvs of bamboo, remainder stocked in small numbers only. Limited stocks of grasses, trees & shrubs.
Notes: Mail order limited by carrier restrictions, Palletised deliveries to retail customers subject to a minimum order size of £400 inclusive of VAT but excluding delivery costs. Please contact nursery or see website for details. Also sells wholesale. Wheelchair accessible.

MWlw WILDWOOD PLANTS 🅖
Wildwood, Southam Road, Farnborough, Banbury, Oxfordshire, OX17 1EL
Ⓣ (01295) 690282
Ⓜ 07767 078882
Ⓔ wildwoodplants@hotmail.com
Contact: Kathryn Hart
Opening Times: 1000–1500 Wed–Sat, Apr–Oct, please email or phone first.
Specialities: Unusual perennials, especially hardy chrysanthemums.
Notes: A small nursery with an interesting

range of perennials, all home grown. Delivers to shows. Wheelchair accessible.

MWts WATERSIDE NURSERY
Not open to the public
Ⓜ 07931 557082
Ⓔ info@watersidenursery.co.uk
Ⓦ www.watersidenursery.co.uk
Contact: Linda Smith
Opening Times: Mail order only.
Cat. Cost: Online only.
Specialities: Aquatic pond plants, marginal shelf pond plants, miniature waterlilies, water lilies, submerged oxygenating plants, bog garden & moisture-loving plants.

NORTHERN

NAlc ALCHEMY FERNS
Oak Tree Nursery, Boroughbridge, Upper Poppleton, York, Yorkshire, YO26 6QB
Ⓜ 07976 983190
Ⓔ info@alchemyferns.co.uk
Ⓦ www.alchemyferns.co.uk
Contact: Mark Taylor
Opening Times: By appt. only.
Specialities: Hardy ferns and tree ferns.
Notes: A small family-run retail nursery established in 1997 situated on the outskirts of York that specialise in hardy ferns and tree ferns. We attend a large number of horticultural shows and events up and down the country throughout the season and although the public are always welcome on the nursery, with us being away for much of the season visits can sadly only be by appointment. Delivers to shows.

NAts NATURAL SURROUNDINGS
Bayfield, Nr Glandford, Holt, Norfolk, NR25 7JN
Ⓣ (01263) 711091
Ⓔ wildlife@naturalsurroundings.info
Ⓦ www.naturalsurroundings.info
Contact: Anne Harrap
Opening Times: 1000–1700, 7 days May–Sep. 1000–1600 Tue–Sun Oct–Mar. Open B/hol Mon.
Specialities: British wild flowers, native trees, shrubs and cottage garden plants, plus a selection of unusual hardy perennials. Also seed.
Notes: Propagate & grow in peat-free compost. Plants available in limited quantities.

Wildlife-friendly demonstration gardens and semi-natural meadows open to the public (small charge). Group visits by arrangement; talks to clubs and societies in Norfolk. Limited wheelchair access.

NBac THE BACKYARD LARDER
Not open to the public
Ⓔ plants@backyardlarder.co.uk
Contact: Alison Tindale
Opening Times: Not open to the public – mail order only.
Specialities: Perennial vegetable plants, roots, tubers and bulbs.
Notes: Very small peat-free nursery growing a constantly varying selection of plants over the year. E-newsletter available to give notice of plants about to appear in the online shop each week. No plant reservations or growing to order.

NBid BIDE-A-WEE COTTAGE GARDENS ♿
Stanton, Netherwitton, Morpeth, Northumberland, NE65 8PR
Ⓣ (01670) 772004
Ⓔ Bideaweec@gmail.com
Ⓦ www.bideawee.co.uk
Contact: Mark Robson
Opening Times: 1200–1630 Thu–Sat 11th Apr–7th Sep. Group visits at other times, except Sun.
Min Mail Order UK: £28
Specialities: Unusual herbaceous perennials, *Agapanthus*, *Primula*, ferns, grasses. National Plant Collection of *Centaurea*.
Notes: Wheelchair accessible.

NBir BIRKHEADS SECRET GARDENS & NURSERY
Birkheads Lane, Sunniside, Gateshead, Newcastle, Tyne & Wear, NE16 5EL
Ⓣ (01207) 232262
Ⓜ 07778 447920
Ⓔ birkheadsnursery@gmail.com
Ⓦ www.birkheadssecretgardens.co.uk
Contact: Christine Liddle
Opening Times: 1100–1500 Fri–Sun, Apr–Sep incl. Additional summer opening and Oct–March dates to be confirmed. Please check website before visiting.
Cat. Cost: None issued.
Specialities: Hardy herbaceous perennials, grasses, hardy bulbs. Herbs. *Allium*, *Euphorbia*, *Galanthus*, *Geranium*, *Iris*, *Primula*, *Sedum* & *Rodgersia*.

NBro **BROWNTHWAITE HARDY PLANTS** 🌿
Fell Yeat, Casterton, Kirkby Lonsdale, Lancashire, LA6 2JW
Ⓣ (01524) 271340 (after 1800 hrs).
Ⓔ oswald5@btconnect.com
Ⓦ www.hardyplantsofcumbria.com
Contact: Chris Benson
Opening Times: 1000–1700, 1st Apr–20th Sep.
Cat. Cost: 3 × 1st for fern list.
Specialities: Herbaceous perennials and hardy ferns incl. *Athyrium, Dryopteris, Polystichum, Hosta, Primula, Hydrangea paniculata* & *Hydrangea serrata* varieties.
Notes: Follow brown signs from A65 between Kirkby Lonsdale & Cowan Bridge. Mail order for ferns. Delivers to shows. Wheelchair accessible.

NCft **CRAFTYPLANTS**
(office) 64 Dunkirk Lane, Leyland, Lancashire, PR25 1TX
Ⓣ (01772) 657564
Ⓔ sales@craftyplants.co.uk
Ⓦ www.craftyplants.co.uk
Contact: Graham Sigsworth/Alex Donaldson
Opening Times: Mail order only. Not open except for nursery open days (see website or phone for details).
Cat. Cost: Online. Printed list available on request.
Specialities: *Tillandsia*. Interesting cacti, succulents, bromeliads and other unusual plants.
Notes: Nursery at Eezitill, Startley Nook, Preston PR4 4XW. Attends some flower shows & plant fairs (see events page on website or call for dates). Also sells wholesale. Delivers to shows.

NClf **CLIFF BANK NURSERY**
Harrogate Road, North Rigton, North Yorkshire, LS17 0BZ
Ⓜ 07762 943320
Ⓔ ben@cliffbanknursery.co.uk
Ⓦ www.cliffbanknursery.co.uk
Contact: Ben Preston
Opening Times: 0900–16.30 Apr–Oct (Closed Aug).
Specialities: Collections of woodland anemones, rare and unusual *Miscanthus*. More generally; unusual herbaceous perennials, ornamental grasses and hardy annuals. We also have a growing collection of tender *Salvia*.
Notes: We are a small independent nursery in Yorkshire growing nearly everything ourselves from seeds, cuttings and division. We accept group visits and will travel to give talks. Display garden at the nursery.

NCou **COURTYARD PLANTERS** 🌿
9 Westgate, Otley, West Yorkshire, LS21 3AT
Ⓣ (01943) 462390
Ⓔ katie@courtyardplanters.co.uk
Ⓦ www.courtyardplanters.co.uk
Contact: Katie Burnett
Opening Times: 0930–1700 Tue, Fri & Sat. Closed Jan.
Cat. Cost: Online only.
Specialities: Perennials. Plants for heavy clay soils. Peat-free.
Notes: Gardening classes & workshops. Also sells wholesale. Wheelchair accessible.

NCth **CATHS GARDEN PLANTS** 🌿
The Walled Garden, Heaves Hotel, Heaves, Levens, Cumbria, LA8 8EF
Ⓣ (01539) 561126
Ⓔ cathsgardenplants61126@gmail.com
Ⓦ www.cathsgardenplants.co.uk
Contact: Rachel James
Opening Times: Mail order available Mar–May & Sep–Nov.
Min Mail Order UK: £25 + p&p
Specialities: Perennials.
Notes: We have a wide range of traditional and unusual herbaceous perennials, and a large selection of herbaceous *Paeonia* all grown outside, naturally. Please note that not all items are available to mail order. Delivers to shows. Wheelchair accessible.

NDov **DOVE COTTAGE NURSERY & GARDEN** 🌿
Shibden Hall Road, Halifax, West Yorkshire, HX3 9XA
Ⓣ (01422) 203553
Ⓔ info@dovecottagenursery.co.uk
Ⓦ www.dovecottagenursery.co.uk
Contact: Stephen & Kim Rogers

Notes: RHS Partner Garden. Gardens are on a sloping site so wheelchair access is limited to the nursery & coffee shop, please ring for special access directions. Coffee shop closes 30 mins before the gardens. Mon–Wed pre-booked special events & pre-arranged groups only. Also open B/hol Mon 1100–1500. Feb, Mar & autumn opening hours to be arranged. Please check our website.

Opening Times: 1000–1700 Wed–Sat 6th Apr–17th Sep. Please check website or phone before travelling.
Cat. Cost: Online.
Specialities: Grasses and perennials and nursery display stock beds.
Notes: Wheelchair accessible.

NDry DRYAD NURSERY
130 Prince Rupert Drive, Tockwith, York, North Yorkshire, YO26 7PU
Ⓣ (01423) 358791
Ⓔ dryadnursery@gmail.com
Ⓦ www.dryad-home.co.uk
Contact: Anne Wright
Opening Times: Not open, mail order only.
Min Mail Order UK: £5.50
Min Mail Order EU: £8.70
Cat. Cost: Online only.
Specialities: Miniature and species *Narcissus*, *Galanthus*, wood anemones, *Hepatica* and other small bulbs.
Notes: Grower and breeder of miniature daffodils, snowdrops and hepaticas. Holder of large collection of wood anemones. All plants available in limited numbers and from seasonal lists only. All our plants are propagated at the nursery, or by Brian Duncan in Ireland. UK mainland delivery only.

NEoE EAST OF EDEN NURSERY ♿
Ainstable, Carlisle, Cumbria, CA4 9QN
Ⓣ (01768) 896604
Ⓜ 07788 142969
Ⓔ roger@east-of-eden-nursery.co.uk
Ⓦ www.east-of-eden-nursery.co.uk
Contact: Roger Proud
Opening Times: Mar–Nov. Days & times variable, so please phone or email before calling.
Min Mail Order UK: £10
Cat. Cost: None issued.
Specialities: Interesting & unusual shrubs, perennials & alpines, esp. astilbes & geums with over 60 new *Geum* cvs, bred & raised on nursery.
Notes: Delivers to shows. Wheelchair accessible.

NGdn GARDEN HOUSE NURSERY ♿
The Square, Dalston, Carlisle, Cumbria, CA5 7LL
Ⓣ (01228) 710297
Ⓜ 07595 219082
Ⓔ stephickso@hotmail.co.uk

Ⓦ www.gardenhousenursery.co.uk
Contact: Stephen Hickson
Opening Times: 0930–1700 Mon–Fri, 1000–1630 Sat–Sun, mid–Mar to Oct. Oct please call if visiting at w/ends. PLEASE NOTE: This nursery will be closing down during 2025 but will remain trading until it closes its doors. Please contact the nursery for further details.
Cat. Cost: Plant list online only.
Specialities: *Geranium*, *Hosta*, *Hemerocallis*, *Iris*, grasses, *Brunnera*, *Pulmonaria* & *Aconitum*.
Notes: Also sells wholesale. Wheelchair accessible. PLEASE NOTE: This nursery will be closing down during 2025 but will remain trading until it closes its doors. Please contact the nursery for further details.

NGKo GREENKOOS
16 Elm Grove, Droylsdon, Greater Manchester, M43 6LP
Ⓣ (0161) 612 5705
Ⓜ 07806 893816
Ⓔ keeflong@hotmail.com
Ⓦ www.greenkoos.co.uk
Contact: Keith Long
Opening Times: By appt. only.
Min Mail Order UK: £20
Cat. Cost: Online only.
Specialities: Exotic and architectural plants including *Brugmansia*, *Lochroma*, *Canna*, Aroids and *Eucomis*. Also grow and sell a wide range of trees, shrubs, perennials, ferns, bonsai and medicinal plants.
Notes: Plant nursery based in Manchester, best known for their *Brugmansia*. No online shop available yet. Please phone or email nursery for orders or details of plant fairs attended. Delivers to shows.

NHal HALLS OF HEDDON
West Heddon Nurseries, Heddon-on-the-Wall, Northumberland, NE15 0JS
Ⓣ (01661) 852445
Ⓔ enquiry@hallsofheddon.co.uk
Ⓦ www.hallsofheddon.co.uk
Contact: David Hall
Opening Times: 0900–1700 Mon–Sat 1000–1700 Sun.
Min Mail Order UK: £10
Min Mail Order EU: £35
Cat. Cost: 3 × 2nd class.
Specialities: *Chrysanthemum* & *Dahlia*.
Notes: Also sells wholesale.

N

NHar HARTSIDE NURSERY GARDEN
Penrith Road, Alston, Cumbria, CA9 3BL
(T) (01434) 381372
(E) enquiries@plantswithaltitude.co.uk
(W) www.plantswithaltitude.co.uk
Contact: Mr Neil Huntley
Opening Times: Please check our website for current opening hours or contact us by phone or email to make an appointment.
Cat. Cost: 4 × 1st class.
Specialities: *Primula*, including asiatic, petiolaris, European species and forms of *P. allionii*, saxifrages, autumn flowering gentians, erythoniums, roscoeas, trilliums.
Notes: If visiting our nursery we strongly advise checking our opening hours, especially during busy periods and in adverse weather conditions. Please check website for latest news. Delivers to shows.

NHaw THE HAWTHORNES NURSERY &
Marsh Road, Hesketh Bank, Nr Preston, Lancashire, PR4 6XT
(T) (01772) 812319
(E) richardhaw@talktalk.net
(W) www.hawthornes-nursery.co.uk
Contact: Irene & Richard Hodson
Opening Times: By appointment only.
Min Mail Order UK: £10
Cat. Cost: None issued.
Specialities: *Clematis*. National Plant Collection of *Clematis viticella*, *viorna* & *texensis* groups.
Notes: Wheelchair accessible.

NHed HEDGING UK (NURSERIES) LIMITED
Boundary House Farm, Holmeswood Road, Holmeswood, Lancashire, L40 1UA
(T) (01704) 827224
(E) sales@hedginguk.com
(W) https://hedginguk.com/
Contact: Russell Birchall
Opening Times: Not open to the public unless by prior appointment. Mail order open 0800–1600 Mon–Fri.
Specialities: Hedging plants and instant hedges.
Notes: Specialist growers of quality hedging plants and instant hedges. Wholesale to the trade and mail order through our website. Buy direct from the grower.

NHrt HORTOLOGY LTD
Unit 1D, Marconi Road, Burgh Road Industrial Estate, Carlisle, Cumbria, CA2 7NA
(T) 0330 390 4505
(E) info@hortology.co.uk
(W) hortology.co.uk
Contact: Mark McCance
Opening Times: Online only.
Specialities: *Alocasia*, *Aloe*, *Agave*, *Aglaeonema*, *Aspidistra*, *Asplenium*, *Beaucarnea*, *Calathea*, *Chamaedorea*, *Chlorophytum*, *Chrysalidocarpus*, *Crassula*, *Dracaena*, *Epipremnum*, *Euphorbia*, *Ficus*, *Howea*, *Monstera*, *Maranta*, *Maranta*, *Nephrolepsis*, *Pachira*, *Peperomia*, *Philodendron*, *Sansevieria*, *Spathiphyllum*, *Strelitzia*, *Yucca*.
Notes: Inspirational, quality assured houseplants, indoor plant pots & planters for lush living. Wellbeing style, delivered directly to your home or office. Create your urban jungle, mix & match sleek designer plants or retro rustic pots with exotic rainforest foliage, woodland ferns or desert cacti.

NLar LARCH COTTAGE NURSERIES &
Melkinthorpe, Penrith, Cumbria, CA10 2DR
(T) (01931) 712404
(E) plants@larchcottage.co.uk
(W) www.larchcottage.co.uk
Contact: Peter & Joanne Stott
Opening Times: Daily from 0900–1700 (or dusk in winter), all year excl. Xmas, Boxing Day & New Year's Day.
Min Mail Order UK: £20 + p&p
Specialities: Comprehensive plant collection in unique garden setting. Rare & unusual plants, particularly shrubs, trees, perennials, dwarf conifers & Japanese maples. *Acer*, *Hamamelis*, *Magnolia* & *Cornus kousa* cvs. Old-fashioned roses, bamboo & alpines.
Notes: Terraced restaurant, art gallery and shop open every day. RHS partner gardens open Wed and Sun 1pm–4pm throughout the summer. Please check website for details. Wheelchair accessible.

NLit THE LITTLE GREEN PLANT FACTORY
Not open to the public
(T) (01482) 860474 (please leave message… rarely in the office)
(M) 07769 750435
(E) claire@thelittlegreenplantfactory.co.uk
Contact: Claire Brodie
Opening Times: 24hrs, online only. Nursery NOT open to the public.
Specialities: Young trees, shrubs and perennials.
Notes: Online only nursery. Small independent

nursery wanting to make a difference to the way we grow. Delivery is by courier at a flat rate (see website). Local free delivery. Propagation to order, depending on the plant and if bio-secure material available (contact nursery for details). Bio-secure nursery with all propagation done on site. Peat-free throughout the whole process from propagation to sale (Dalefoot Compost). No chemicals used throughout the nursery or plant production. No single use plastics used throughout the process, finished plants come in bio-degradable coir pots that are to be planted straight into the ground. Water is all rainwater harvested on site. No heating, electricity etc. on site. The only help we get is from the sun.

NMen Mendle Nursery
Holme, Scunthorpe, North Lincolnshire, DN16 3RF
(T) (01724) 850864
(E) ann.earnshaw@tiscali.co.uk
(W) www.mendlenursery.co.uk
Contact: Mrs A. Earnshaw
Opening Times: Not open to the public. Mail order only.
Specialities: *Jovibarba, Sempervivum*.

NMir Mires Beck Nursery
Low Mill Lane, North Cave, Brough, East Riding, Yorkshire, HU15 2NR
(T) (01430) 421543
(E) sales@miresbeck.co.uk
(W) www.miresbeck.co.uk
Contact: Sue Hewitt
Opening Times: 1000–1600 7 days, 1st Mar–30th Sep. 1000–1600 Mon–Fri, 1st Oct–30th Apr.
Specialities: Wildflower plants of Yorkshire provenance.
Notes: Mail order for wildflower plants & plugs only. Also sells wholesale. Wheelchair accessible.

NNys Peter Nyssen Ltd
Not open to the public
(T) (0161) 7474000
(E) info@peternyssen.com
Contact: Stephen
Opening Times: Not open to the public. Mail order only.
Specialities: Flower bulbs.
Notes: A flower bulb specialist, supplying dry bulbs online and to the trade. Autumn flowering bulbs, summer flowering bulbs and perennials.

NOra Orange Pippin Ltd
(office) 33 Algarth Rise, Pocklington, York, Yorkshire, YO42 2HX
(T) (01759) 392007
(E) trees@orangepippin.com
(W) www.orangepippintrees.co.uk
Contact: Maureen Borrie
Opening Times: Not open. Mail order online only.
Cat. Cost: Online only.
Specialities: Specialist online retailer of fruit and ornamental trees.
Notes: We list over 280 fruit varieties, traditional and modern. Wide choice of rootstocks & tree forms. Fruit tree expert available most days. Order online all year round. Deliveries from Aug–Apr. Exports beyond EU (to USA).

NPer Perry's Plants
The River Garden, Sleights, Whitby, North Yorkshire, YO21 1RR
(M) 07879 498623
(E) richardperry008@hotmail.co.uk
(W) www.perrysplants.co.uk
Contact: Sharon & Richard Perry
Opening Times: 1000–1700 mid-Mar–Oct.
Cat. Cost: None published.
Specialities: *Lavatera, Malva, Erysimum, Euphorbia, Anthemis, Osteospermum & Hebe*. Uncommon hardy & container plants & aquatic plants.
Notes: Euro accepted. Wheelchair accessible.

NPip Pippin Trees
(Office) 33 Algarth Rise, Pocklington, York, Yorkshire, YO42 2HX
(T) (01759) 392007
(E) info@pippintrees.co.uk
(W) www.pippintrees.co.uk
Contact: Maureen Borrie
Opening Times: Not open, mail order only.
Specialities: Specialist online retailer of ornamental trees.
Notes: We offer over 300 ornamental tree varieties, including a wide range of flowering cherries, crab apples, rowan trees, magnolia, lilac and many more. Order online all year round. Deliveries from Aug–Apr.

NPlm The Palm Tree Company
Meadcroft, Clitheroe Road, Whalley, Lancashire, BB7 9AD
(T) (01254) 447964

Nursery Details by Code

(M) 07970 772743
(E) sales@thepalmtreecompany.com
(W) www.thepalmtreecompany.com
Contact: Christopher Day
Opening Times: Online only 24hrs 7 days.
Specialities: Palm trees, olive trees, tree ferns, yuccas, large cacti, grapevines, large agaves, bamboo, topiary trees, citrus trees, cycads, dasylirions, unusual collector palms.

NQui QUIET CORNER PLANTS
(M) 07932 159204
(E) hal@uwclub.net
(W) www.quietcornerplants.co.uk
Contact: Howard Leslie
Opening Times: By appt. only. Please contact the nursery for further information.
Cat. Cost: Online only.
Specialities: Hardy herbaceous & shrubby perennials, incl. small quantities of lesser known and harder to find plants.
Notes: Also sells wholesale. Delivers to shows.

NRew REWELA HOSTAS ♿
Rewela Cottage, Skewsby, York, North Yorkshire, YO61 4SG
(M) John 07711 555665/Daphne 07539 428892
(E) rewelacottage@gmail.com
(W) www.rewelahostas.com
Contact: John Plant/Daphne Ellis
Opening Times: Mail order and by appointment only.
Specialities: *Hosta*.
Notes: Orders sent 1st class Royal Mail all year round. We aim to send out orders placed before 11pm Mon–Thu on the same day. Orders placed Fri–Sun will be sent on Mon. Wheelchair accessible.

NRya RYAL NURSERY ♿
East Farm Cottage, Ryal, Northumberland, NE20 0SA
(T) (01661) 886562
(E) ruthhadden@btinternet.com
Contact: R. Hadden
Opening Times: Mar–Jul by appt. please telephone in advance.
Cat. Cost: Sae.
Specialities: Alpine & woodland plants, mainly available in small quantities only. National Plant Collection of *Primula marginata*.
Notes: Also sells wholesale. Delivers to shows. Wheelchair accessible.

NSti STILLINGFLEET LODGE NURSERIES ♿
Stewart Lane, Stillingfleet, York, YO19 6HP
(T) (01904) 728506
(E) info@stillingfleetlodgenurseries.co.uk
(W) www.stillingfleetlodgenurseries.co.uk
Contact: Vanessa Cook
Opening Times: 1300–1700 Wed & Fri, 1st Apr–30th Sep. 1300–1700, 1st & 3rd Sat & Sun in each month.
Cat. Cost: Online only.
Specialities: Foliage & unusual perennials. Hardy geraniums, *Pulmonaria*, variegated plants & grasses.
Notes: Wheelchair accessible.

NSue SUE PROCTOR PLANTS ♿
69 Ings Mill Avenue, Clayton West, Huddersfield, West Yorkshire, HD8 9QG
(T) (01484) 866189
(M) 07917 006636
(E) hostas@sueproctorplants.co.uk
(W) www.sueproctorplants.com
Contact: Sue Proctor
Opening Times: By appt. only. Please telephone first.
Cat. Cost: 1st class sae.
Specialities: *Hosta*, miniature *Hosta*.
Notes: Wheelchair accessible.

NTay TAYLORS CLEMATIS NURSERY
Sutton Road, Sutton, Nr. Askern, Doncaster, South Yorkshire, DN6 9JZ
(E) info@taylorsclematis.co.uk
(W) www.taylorsclematis.co.uk
Contact: Chris Cocks
Opening Times: Not open to the public.
Cat. Cost: £2.
Specialities: *Clematis* (over 250 varieties).
Notes: Largest selection of *Clematis* in the UK. Nursery is open for the collection of pre-ordered *Clematis* by appointment only.

NTPC TREE PEONY COMPANY
Willow Cottage, Rillington, Malton, North Yorkshire, YO17 8JU
(T) (01944) 758280
(E) info@treepeony.co.uk
(W) www.treepeony.co.uk
Contact: Thelma Scruton, Roger Scruton
Min Mail Order UK: £15
Cat. Cost: None.
Specialities: Tree peonies. *Paeonia suffruticosa*, *P.* Gansu Group, *P. rockii*.
Notes: Also sells wholesale. Euro accepted. Delivers to shows.

NTrD TREE2MYDOOR LTD
(T) (0161) 870 6590
(E) hello@tree2mydoor.com
(W) https://tree2mydoor.com/
Opening Times: Not open to the public. Lines open 0900–1600 Mon–Fri.
Specialities: Native trees, citrus trees, roses, fruit and ornamental trees.
Notes: We are a specialist tree and plant gifting business, offering gift-wrapped trees and plants for delivery to recipients all over Great Britain. We also offer larger trees for personal growing and also bulk orders for large-scale gifting with a big focus on promoting sustainability.

NTro GROWTROPICALS
Not open to the public
(E) hello@growtropicals.com
Opening Times: Not open to the public. Mail order only.
Specialities: Rare and unusual houseplants, aroids and succulents.
Notes: Since the start of GrowTropicals, our core mission has been to provide the widest range of quality plants, with the best service, in a sustainable and ethical way. We offer over 2000 varieties of rare plants on our website from rare tropicals to unusual cacti, succulents and orchids.

NWbg WILLOWBRIDGE PLANTS LTD
Root Lane, Catforth, Preston, Lancashire, PR4 0JB
(M) 07393 904348
(E) sales@willowbridgeplants.co.uk
Contact: Karl and Angela Shorrock
Opening Times: Please check on nursery website or social media for seasonal opening times.
Specialities: *Acer* (grafted), *Hosta* and perennials. Wildlife friendly plants.
Notes: We are a small family nursery who are now open to the public and sell online also. Karl is always here to give advice. We grow peat-free. We graft Acers and propagate a large amount of out other plants, but do source plants to expand our range.

SOUTHERN

SAko AKORN AND OAKE
18 Twyford Avenue, Southampton, Hampshire, SO15 5NP
(T) (023) 8034 4040

(M) 07973 149404
(E) stefan.rau@hotmail.co.uk
Contact: Stefan Rau
Opening Times: Open by appt. only.
Specialities: *Saxifraga*.
Notes: Delivers to shows.

SAng ANGHARAD PIKE GARDENER AND PLANTS ♿
Old Workshop, St Peters Road, Hayling Island, Hampshire, PO11 0RX
(T) (02392) 468036
(E) angharad.pike@gmail.com
(W) www.angharadpike.com
Contact: Angharad Pike
Opening Times: By appointment only. Please see website for details. No mail order available.
Notes: All plants listed are available to view in the gardens at The Old Workshop. Plants can be pre-ordered for collection at any of the open gardens we are attending. Plants are sold in 1ltr pots, grown in peat-free compost. All our plants are British grown. Wheelchair accessible.

SArc ARCHITECTURAL PLANTS ♿
Stane Street, Pulborough, West Sussex, RH20 1DJ
(T) (01798) 879213
(E) enquiries@architecturalplants.com
(W) www.architecturalplants.com
Contact: Sophie Pett Gallacher
Opening Times: 0900–1700 Mon–Sat incl. Easter, May, Aug B/hol.
Specialities: Evergreens and deciduous large trees and shrubs. Hardy exotics and topiary. Rare and home-grown plants.
Notes: Architectural Plants is a specialist horticultural nursery in Pulborough, West Sussex, set within 32 acres of open fields surrounded by farmland overlooking the South Downs. Experts in plants that are both shapely and exotic – Japanese Niwaki and European topiary, hardy palms, bananas and other unusual tropical specimens. Mail order for tools and ladders currently, with online plant shop coming soon. Delivers to shows. Wheelchair accessible.

SAth ATHELAS PLANTS
Straight Lane, Hooe, TN33 9HU
(T) (01424) 893593
(E) enquiries@athelasplants.co.uk
(W) athelasplants.co.uk/

Nursery Details by Code

SAdn   Babylon – The Nursery 🦽
Duddleswell, Ashdown Forest, East Sussex, TN22 3JP
Ⓣ (01825) 712300
Ⓔ thenursery@babylon.eco
Ⓦ www.babylon.eco
Contact: Rob Laughton
Opening Times: 0900–1700 winter, 0900–1700 summer. Greenfingers Café open 0930–1700.
Specialities: *Lapageria*, *Fuchsia*, conservatory climbers, unusual shrubs. Available in small quantities only.
Notes: Wheelchair accessible.

SBea   Bean Place Nursery
Watersfield, Bletchenden Road, Headcorn, Kent, TN27 9JB
Ⓜ 07779 728378
Ⓔ info@beanplace.co.uk
Ⓦ www.beanplace.co.uk
Contact: Anita Waters
Opening Times: 1000–1600 Fri–Sun Apr–Aug & Sep–Oct.
Min Mail Order UK: £5.95
Cat. Cost: Online.
Specialities: Ornamental grasses, herbaceous perennials & cottage garden plants.
Notes: Growers of hardy herbaceous perennials, bearded iris, ornamental grasses and hardy garden ferns. Delivers to shows.

SBeP   Beechbridge Plants
1 Beechbridge Cottages, Goudhurst Road, Marden, Kent, TN12 9NN
Ⓜ 07432 130112
Ⓔ info@beechbridgeplants.co.uk
Ⓦ www.beechbridgeplants.co.uk
Contact: Victoria Mummery
Opening Times: By appointment only. Mail order available.
Specialities: Herbaceous perennials.
Notes: A small nursery selling mostly herbaceous perennials, the majority of which are propagated by us on site and grown in peat-free compost. Selling on site by appointment, by mail order and at plant fairs in the southeast. Happy to take orders to fairs or to propagate to order.

Contact: Matt Barfoot
Notes: An independent, family-run nursery offering a diverse range of traditional, architectural and tropical plants. Sister nursery to Bamboo Giant.

SBGi   Bamboo Giant 🦽
Athelas Plants, Hooe Road, Ninfield, Sussex, TN33 9EL
Ⓣ (01424) 563045
Ⓜ 07703 325321
Ⓔ matt@bamboogiant.co.uk
Ⓦ www.bamboogiant.co.uk
Contact: Matt
Opening Times: 0900–1700 Mon–Sat, 1000–1600 Sun. 1000–1600 B/hols.
Specialities: *Phyllostachys*.
Notes: We are a family run specialist bamboo nursery selling online and retail. We stock a range of clumping and non-clumping bamboo perfect for any environment for screening and adding privacy to your garden. Also sells wholesale. Wheelchair accessible.

SBig   Big Plant Nursery ◆
Hole Street, Ashington, West Sussex, RH20 3DE
Ⓣ (01903) 891466
Ⓔ enquiries@bigplantnursery.co.uk
Ⓦ www.bigplantnursery.co.uk
Opening Times: 0900–1700 Mon–Sat 1000–1600 Sun.
Specialities: Hardy exotic plants, palms, bamboos, cacti & succulents, shrubs and trees, olives.

SBmr   Blackmoor Nurseries
Blackmoor Estate, Blackmoor, Nr Liss, Hampshire, GU33 6BS
Ⓣ (01420) 477978
Ⓔ jon@blackmoor.co.uk
Ⓦ www.blackmoor.co.uk
Contact: Jon Munday
Opening Times: Not open. Mail order online only. Orders taken 0730–1600 Mon–Thu or 0730–1500 Fri.
Cat. Cost: None issued.
Specialities: Fruit trees, soft fruit & ornamental trees.
Notes: Blackmoor is one of the very few nurseries in the UK offering gardeners the opportunity to buy fruit plants directly from our nursery. It is part of the Blackmoor Estate in Hampshire, which has been maintained by the Selborne family for several generations. Please note nursery is not open to the public. Orders via website only. Collection available during opening times above.

SBrt   Brighton Plants 🦽
Small Dole, Sussex, BN5 9YJ
Ⓜ 07955 744802

Ⓔ brighton.plants@gmail.com
Ⓦ www.brightonplants.blogspot.com
Contact: Steve Law
Opening Times: Open by appt. only. Please email/phone before visiting.
Cat. Cost: 4 × 1st class.
Specialities: Hardy herbaceous and woody plants. Drought-tolerant plants.
Notes: Delivers to shows. Euro accepted. Wheelchair accessible.

SCam CAMELLIA GROVE NURSERY ♿
Market Garden, Lower Beeding, Horsham, West Sussex, RH13 6PP
Ⓣ (01403) 891412
Ⓔ lp@hortic.com
Ⓦ www.camellia-grove.com
Contact: Chris Loder
Opening Times: 1000–1600 Mon–Sat, please phone first so we can give you our undivided attention.
Cat. Cost: Please enquire.
Specialities: *Camellia japonica, C. williamsii, C. sasanqua* & *C. reticulata*, from the purest white to richest red flowers.
Notes: Also sells wholesale. Exports beyond EU. Delivers to shows. Euro accepted. Wheelchair accessible.

SChF CHARLESHURST FARM NURSERY
Loxwood Road, Plaistow, Billingshurst, West Sussex, RH14 0NY
Ⓣ (01403) 752273
Ⓜ 07736 522788
Ⓔ info@charleshurstplants.co.uk
Ⓦ www.charleshurstplants.co.uk
Contact: Clive Mellor
Opening Times: Normally 0900–1730 Fri, Sat, Sun, Feb–Oct, but please ring before travelling.
Cat. Cost: Online only.
Specialities: Shrubs including some more unusual species. Good range of Daphnes & Japanese maples.
Notes: Delivers to shows. Euro accepted.

SChr JOHN CHURCHER
47 Grove Avenue, Portchester, Fareham, Hampshire, PO16 9EZ
Ⓣ (023) 9232 6740
Ⓜ 07717 495861
Ⓔ johnchurcher47@btinternet.com
Contact: John Churcher
Opening Times: By appt. only. Please phone or email.

Cat. Cost: None issued.
Specialities: Architectural & hardy exotics: bromeliads, bulbs, palms, perennials & succulents incl. *Aeonium, Agave, Aloe, Chamaerops, Crinum, Hedychium, Nerine* and *Trachycarpus*. Stock available in small quantities only.

SDix GREAT DIXTER NURSERIES ♿
Dixter Road, Northiam, Rye, East Sussex, TN31 6PH
Ⓣ (01797) 254044
Ⓔ nursery@greatdixter.co.uk
Ⓦ www.greatdixter.co.uk
Contact: Michael Morphy
Opening Times: 0900–1700 Mon–Sat, 1000–1700 Sun Apr–end Oct. 0900–1230 & 1330–1630 Mon–Fri, 0900–1230 Sat. Sun closed Nov–end Mar.
Specialities: *Clematis*, shrubs and plants. Gardens open.
Notes: Usual and unusual shrubs and perennials. Mail order Oct to end of Mar. Wheelchair accessible.

SEas EASTCROFT ROSES
Eastcroft Farm, Town Road, Cliffe, Rochester, Kent, ME3 7RL
Ⓜ 07710 028737
Ⓔ info@eastcroftroses.co.uk/sales@eastcroftroses.co.uk/ customerservices@eastcroftroses.co.uk
Ⓦ https://www.eastcroftroses.co.uk
Contact: Peter Cox
Opening Times: Please contact nursery for details.
Specialities: Roses.
Notes: We sell containerised garden roses all year round and bare-root roses between November and March. Roses are selected for their ease of cultivation and freedom of flowering. Online sales available.

SEdi EDIBLECULTURE ♿
The Horticultural Unit, The Abbey School, London Road, Faversham, Kent, ME13 8RZ
Ⓣ (01795) 537662
Ⓜ 07926 961056
Ⓔ info@edibleculture.co.uk
Ⓦ www.edibleculture.co.uk
Contact: Chris or David
Opening Times: 0900–1700 Mon–Sat 1000–1600 Sun, Mar–Jan. Jan–Feb by appt. only but telephone/email orders taken.
Cat. Cost: online only.

Specialities: Herbs, vegetables, fruit trees and soft fruit, herbaceous perennials, hedgerow plants.
Notes: UK's first plastic free nursery and garden centre. Focus on interesting plants grown sustainably. Specialists in establishing and maintaining orchards. Wheechair accessible.

SEle ELEPLANTS NURSERY
32 Framfield Road, Uckfield, East Sussex, TN22 5AH
Ⓜ 07810 660109
Ⓔ eleplantsnursery@talk21.com
Ⓦ www.eleplantsnursery.com
Contact: Martin Batchelor
Opening Times: Not open. By appt. only.
Specialities: Shrubs.
Notes: Exports beyond EU. Delivers to shows.

SEND EAST NORTHDOWN NURSERY 🚹
George Hill Road (B2052), Margate, Kent, CT10 3BN
Ⓣ (01843) 862060
Ⓜ 07714 241667/07714 241668
Ⓔ info@botanyplants.co.uk
Ⓦ http://botanyplants.co.uk/east-northdown-nursery/
Contact: Louise & William Friend
Opening Times: 0900–1700/dusk 7 days, all year except Sun & Mon in winter. Closed Xmas week. See website for details.
Cat. Cost: Online only.
Specialities: Chalk & coast-loving plants. Specimen shrubs & bamboos available. Complementary range of plants for damp/acid conditions available to order from our Mucklestone Nursery (MMuc). Collection of rare Mediterranean plants.
Notes: Tea room, gardens, grounds and business centre. Close to Botany Bay. Lectures given to gardening groups in Kent. Garden tours by appt. See website for full list & details. Please include your address when emailing us. Wheelchair accessible.

SEWo ENGLISH WOODLANDS 🚹
Burrow Nursery, Herrings Lane, Cross-in-Hand, Heathfield, East Sussex, TN21 0UG
Ⓣ (01435) 862992
Ⓔ sales@englishwoodlands.com
Ⓦ www.englishwoodlands.com
Opening Times: 0800–1700 Mon–Fri. 0800–1600 Sat. Closed Sun & B/hols.
Min Mail Order UK: £35

Cat. Cost: Free.
Specialities: Trees, shrubs, hedging. Please telephone to check plant availability before visiting.
Notes: Also sells wholesale. Wheelchair accessible.

SFai FAIRWEATHER'S GARDEN CENTRE 🚹
High Street, Beaulieu, Hampshire, SO42 7YB
Ⓣ (01590) 612307
Ⓔ info@fairweathers.co.uk
Ⓦ www.fairweathers.co.uk
Contact: Tamarin Glinkowski
Opening Times: 0900–1700 7 days.
Cat. Cost: None issued.
Specialities: *Agapanthus* & *Lavandula*.
Notes: Wheelchair accessible.

SFol FOLIUM AND FLOS PLANTS LTD
Meadow Farm, Sway Road, Hampshire, SO41 6FR
Ⓣ (01590) 619066
Ⓔ enquiries@foliumandflos.co.uk
Ⓦ https://foliumandflos.co.uk/
Contact: Jack Warman
Opening Times: By appt. only 0800–1600 Mon–Fri. Closed Sat & Sun.
Notes: Folium and Flos is a family run plant nursery based in the New Forest stocking a wide range of trees, hedging, shrubs, topiary, olives and much more. With new stock arriving weekly, Jack and his team work closely with garden designers, landscapers, and developers across the UK providing competitive pricing, expert knowledge, and high-quality plants. Partially wheelchair accessible.

SGol GOLDEN HILL NURSERIES 🚹
Lordsfield, Goudhurst Road, Marden, Kent, TN12 9LT
Ⓣ (01622) 833218
Ⓜ 07826 523655
Ⓔ enquiries@goldenhillplants.com
Ⓦ www.goldenhillplants.com
Contact: Roger Butler
Opening Times: 0900–1700 Mon–Sat, 1st Mar–31st Oct. 0900–1600 Mon–Sat, 1st Nov–28th Feb. 1100–1600 Sun from 3rd Sun in Feb–end Oct.
Cat. Cost: Online only.
Specialities: *Hydrangea, Chaenomeles, Camellia* & *Viburnum*. Specimen trees & shrubs, ground cover and hedging.
Notes: Also sells wholesale. Euro accepted. Delivers to shows. Wheelchair accessible.

SHaC Hart Canna ⓵
Lincluden Nursery, Shaftesbury Road, Bisley, Woking, Surrey, GU24 9EN
Ⓣ (01252) 514421
Ⓜ 07762 950000
Ⓔ sales@hartcanna.com
Ⓦ www.hartcanna.co.uk
Contact: Keith Hayward
Opening Times: By appt. only.
Cat. Cost: Online only.
Specialities: *Canna*. National Plant Collection of *Canna*.
Notes: Wheelchair accessible.

SHar Hardy's Cottage Garden Plants
Priory Lane Nursery, Freefolk Priors, Whitchurch, Hampshire, RG28 7FA
Ⓣ (01256) 896533
Ⓔ info@hardysplants.co.uk
Ⓦ www.hardysplants.co.uk
Contact: Rosemary Hardy
Opening Times: Nursery opening times vary. Please see website for details.
Cat. Cost: Online only.
Specialities: Wide range of herbaceous perennials incl. *Achillea, Gaura, Geum, Geranium, Hemerocallis, Heuchera, Lathryus vernus, Paeonia, Penstemon* & *Salvia*.
Notes: Accepts HTA Gift Tokens. Offers trade discount. Delivers to shows.

SHeb The Hebe Society
Ⓣ (01634) 786878
Ⓜ 07743 939490
Ⓔ hebeplants@gmail.com
Contact: Stephen Harding
Opening Times: Not open. Mail order only.
Specialities: Hebes, Parahebes.
Notes: Retail only, propagate to order, all plants peat-free.

SHor The Plant Centre at Hortus Loci
Hound Green, Hook, Hampshire, RG27 8LQ
Ⓣ (01189) 326487
Ⓔ enquiries@hlplantcentre.co.uk
Ⓦ hortusloci.co.uk/retail-plant-centre/
Contact: Robin Wallis/John Winterson
Opening Times: 0930–1630 Oct–Mar 0930–1730 Apr–Sep.
Specialities: Wide range of plants including own-grown peat-free perennials, including many large pot sizes. Also specialists in supplying & planting very large and mature trees. We pride ourselves in our ranges of specially selected Iris, peonies and roses. Hedging plants in autumn–winter.
Notes: While most good garden centres boast a few hundred different varieties, here at The Plant Centre we have access to well over 4000 including the rare and unusual! This means that our customers not only have much more choice, but will be able to get hold of the latest plant introductions much sooner than elsewhere. Lovely coffee shop on site making it the perfect place to meet your friends and browse with a coffee. Come and shop where the garden designers come to buy their plants! We hope to see you soon. Also sells wholesale.

SHyH Hydrangea Haven ⓵
Market Garden, Lower Beeding, West Sussex, RH13 6PP
Ⓣ (01403) 891412
Ⓔ lp@hortic.com
Ⓦ www.hydrangea-haven.com
Contact: Chris Loder
Opening Times: 1000–1600 Mon–Sat, please phone first.
Cat. Cost: Please enquire.
Specialities: *Hydrangea*: mophead, lacecap & panicle. *Agapanthus*.
Notes: Also sells wholesale. Exports beyond EU. Delivers to shows. Euro accepted. Wheelchair accessible.

SIri Iris of Sissinghurst
Roughlands Farm, Goudhurst Road, Marden, Kent, TN12 9NH
Ⓣ (01622) 831511
Ⓔ orders@irisofsissinghurst.com
Ⓦ www.irisofsissinghurst.com
Contact: Sue Marshall
Opening Times: Contact nursery or see website for opening times.
Cat. Cost: Online only.
Specialities: *Iris*, short, intermediate & tall bearded, *ensata, sibirica* & many species.
Notes: Delivers to shows (pre-ordered plants). Delivery to UK mainland only.

SIvy Ivy Hatch Plant Supplies
Coach Road, Ivy Hatch, Kent, TN15 0PE
Ⓔ debs.ednieivyhatchplantsupplies@gmail.com
Ⓦ www.ivyhatchplantsupplies.weebly.com
Contact: Debs Ednie
Opening Times: By appointment only.
Min Mail Order UK: £5
Cat. Cost: None.
Specialities: Hardy salvias and succulents including *Echeveria*. Good variety of *Aeonium*

and a range of tropical plants.
Notes: Sole supplier for The World Garden Nursery, Lullingstone Castle. Unusual varieties. Limited stock, can source/grow to order. Also sells wholesale. Full range available by mail order or at The World Garden Nursery, Lullingstone, Kent. Unable to accept mail as no post box at nursery site.

SKee   KEEPERS NURSERY
Gallants Court, Gallants Lane, East Farleigh, Maidstone, Kent, ME15 0LE
Ⓣ (01622) 326465
Ⓔ nurserymanager@keepers-nursery.co.uk
Ⓦ www.keepers-nursery.co.uk
Contact: Karim Habibi
Opening Times: By appt. only.
Min Mail Order UK: £14.50
Cat. Cost: Online only.
Specialities: A very large range of old & rare as well as modern fruit tree varieties on a variety of rootstocks & in different trained forms. Custom grafting, plants to order from National Plant Collection. Soft fruit plants & nut trees.
Notes: A family-run fruit tree nursery producing and selling the widest range of bare-root fruit trees in the country. Orders taken from May onwards for distribution throughout the following winter period. Limited number of open days. Open for collection of orders by arrangement through winter months only.

SLBF   LITTLE BROOK FUCHSIAS 🈯
Ash Green Lane West, Ash Green, Nr Aldershot, Hampshire, GU12 6HL
Ⓣ (01252) 329731
Ⓜ 07817 272361
Ⓔ carol.gubler@outlook.com
Ⓦ www.littlebrookfuchsias.co.uk
Contact: Carol Gubler
Opening Times: 1000–1700 Wed–Sun, 1st Jan–28th Jun.
Cat. Cost: 70p + sae.
Specialities: Fuchsias, old & new.
Notes: Nursery located off White Lane in Ash Green. Wheelchair accessible.

SLdr   LODER PLANTS 🈯
Market Garden, Long Hill, Lower Beeding, West Sussex, RH13 6PP
Ⓣ (01403) 891412
Ⓔ sales@rhododendrons.com
Ⓦ www.rhododendrons.com
Contact: Chris Loder

Opening Times: 1000–1600 Mon–Sat, please telephone first.
Cat. Cost: Please enquire.
Specialities: Rhododendrons & azaleas in all sizes. Some in very limited quantities only. *Agapanthus.*
Notes: Also sells wholesale. Exports beyond EU. Delivers to shows. Euro accepted. Wheelchair accessible.

SLee   LEESA'S NOT JUST ALPINES
'Rhode Acres', Woodrow, Fifehead Neville, Sturminster Newton, Dorset, DT10 2AQ
Ⓜ 07900 815636
Ⓔ leesasalpines20@gmail.com
Ⓦ www.leesasalpines.co.uk
Contact: Leesa Barrett
Opening Times: Nursery open by appt. only. Please call for details.
Specialities: Alpines and perennials.
Notes: Small nursery growing a good selection of garden worthy alpine and rock garden plants. A range of cottage garden perennials also available. Collections available from plant fairs. Also sells wholesale. Delivers to shows.

SMad   MADRONA NURSERY 🈯
Pluckley Road, Bethersden, Kent, TN26 3EG
Ⓔ madrona@hotmail.co.uk
Ⓦ www.madrona.co.uk
Contact: Liam Mackenzie
Opening Times: 1000–1700 Sat, Mon & Tue, 1300–1700 Sun. 14th Mar–1st Nov. Other times by appt.
Cat. Cost: Free.
Specialities: Unusual shrubs, conifers & perennials. *Eryngium.*
Notes: Delivers to shows. Euro accepted. Wheelchair accessible.

SMHy   MARCHANTS HARDY PLANTS
2 Marchants Cottages, Mill Lane, Laughton, Lewes, East Sussex, BN8 6AJ
Ⓜ 07942 385673
Ⓔ marchantshardyplants@gmail.com
Ⓦ www.marchantshardyplants.co.uk
Contact: Hannah Fox
Opening Times: 1000–1700 Thu–Sat mid-Mar–mid-Oct.
Cat. Cost: Website download or collect from nursery.
Specialities: Uncommon hardy perennials and choice range of grasses including many varieties of *Agapanthus, Aster, Epimedium, Galanthus, Molinia, Polypodium, Salvia,*

Sangiusorba. Please refer to website for catalogue, and email or call before travelling as many unusual plants may be limited in number.
Notes: Unique specialist nursery with reputable display garden. All stock propagated on site by knowledgeable staff. Please check opening hours before travelling. Pre booked tours of garden/nursery welcomed. Please note that garden opens mid-May. Check website for dates/greater detail.

SMil MILES JAPANESE MAPLES
Cherries, Fox Court, Storrington, West Sussex, RH20 4JL
Ⓣ (01444) 390306
Ⓔ miles@milesjapanesemaples.co.uk
Ⓦ milesjapanesemaples.co.uk
Contact: Miles Hayward
Opening Times: By appt. only.
Cat. Cost: Online only.
Specialities: *Acer palmatum*.
Notes: *Acer palmatum* specialists. Delivers to shows.

SMor MOREHAVENS
Meadow House, Larkfield Road, Farnham, Surrey, GU9 7DB
Ⓣ (01252) 214074
Ⓔ morehavens@camomilelawns.co.uk
Ⓦ www.camomilelawns.co.uk
Contact: J. Draper
Opening Times: Mail order direct to you only. Open for pre-arranged collection.
Min Mail Order UK: £21
Min Mail Order EU: £21 + p&p
Cat. Cost: Free.
Specialities: *Chamaemelum nobile* 'Treneague' & *Chamaemelum nobile* dwarf.
Notes: Also sells wholesale.

SMrm MERRIMENTS GARDENS ♿
Hawkhurst Road, Hurst Green, East Sussex, TN19 7RA
Ⓣ (01580) 860666
Ⓔ stephen@merriments.co.uk
Ⓦ www.merriments.co.uk
Contact: Imogen Stephens
Opening Times: 0900–1700 Mon–Sat, 1000–1630 Sun.
Cat. Cost: Online only.
Specialities: Specialist in perennials. Extensive range of unusual perennials, tender perennials, grasses & annuals. Also large selection of roses & seasonal shrubs. 4-acre show garden.
Notes: Wheelchair accessible.

SNig NIGHTINGALE NURSERY LTD ♿
Gardeners Lane, East Wellow, Romsey, Hampshire, SO51 6AD
Ⓣ (023) 80814350
Ⓔ gfnightingale4@gmail.com
Ⓦ www.nightingalenursery.co.uk
Contact: Graham Farmiloe
Opening Times: 0800–1700 Mon–Fri & open 7 days from mid–Mar to mid–Jun. 0800–1630 winter.
Cat. Cost: Free via email for wholesale only.
Specialities: Specialists in *Clematis*. We also grow climbers & wall shrubs, herbaceous (for retail only), seasonal bedding & hanging baskets.
Notes: Also sells wholesale. Wheelchair accessible.

SNoN THE NO NAME NURSERY
Sandwich, Kent
Ⓜ 07809 646237
Ⓔ steven.edney@live.com
Ⓦ https://www.thenonamenursery.co.uk/
Opening Times: Not open to the public. Trade, group visits and guided tours by arrangement. Contact nursery for details.

SOrN ORCHARD NURSERY PLANT CENTRE LTD
Holtye Road, East Grinstead, West Sussex, RH19 3PP
Ⓣ (01342) 311657
Ⓔ enquiries@orchardnursery.co.uk
Ⓦ www.orchardnursery.co.uk
Contact: Clare Bradford
Opening Times: 0900–1730 Mon–Sat, Apr–Nov (0900–1700 during winter) 1000–1600 Sun all year.
Specialities: Perennials are our passion. We also grow the majority of our own seasonal bedding stock.
Notes: As a retail nursery, we pride ourselves on the quality of the plants that we grow and source from our trusted suppliers. Set within an old walled garden, the aspect of the nursery is perfect for growing, and we try to provide our customers with a natural setting and superb quality plants and service.

SPad PADDOCK PLANTS
The Paddock, Upper Toothill Road, Rownhams, Southampton, Hampshire, SO16 8AL
Ⓣ (023) 8073 9912
Ⓜ 07763 386717
Ⓔ rob@paddockplants.co.uk
Ⓦ paddockplants.co.uk

Contact: Rob & Joanna Courtney
Opening Times: See website for details.
Cat. Cost: Online only.
Specialities: *Abutilon* hybrids. Some varieties are currently only available in limited quantities.
Notes: A family-run nursery offering an interesting range of perennials, grasses, ferns & shrubs, incl. some more unusual varieties or plants new to the UK market. All plants are grown in a peat-free medium. Courier delivery (plastic free) throughout the UK.

SPel PELHAM PLANTS
Rose Cottage, Top of Spence's Farm Lane, off Common Lane, Laughton, East Sussex, BN8 6BZ
Ⓜ 07377 145970
Ⓔ pelhamplants@gmail.com
Ⓦ pelhamplants.co.uk/nursery/
Contact: Paul Seaborne
Opening Times: By appt. only. See website for details.
Specialities: Hardy herbaceous perennials and grasses, especially *Aster* and *Salvia*.
Notes: Independent nursery set in the Sussex countryside propagating most plants on site. Group bookings taken for tours of our private garden. Also attend many plant fairs in the South East. Delivers to shows.

SPeP PEAKE PERENNIALS
Hookswood Lane, Farnham, Dorset, DT11 8DQ
Ⓜ 07708 872918
Ⓔ helen@peakeperennials.co.uk
Ⓦ www.peakeperennials.co.uk
Contact: Helen Hunt
Opening Times: By appt. only. Please contact nursery.
Specialities: Specialising in tall & unusual herbaceous perennials & grasses. Also increasing stock range of popular perennials with a twist. Reservation service for out of stock plants. Local delivery. Range of landscaping perennials.
Notes: For details of special events we attend please telephone or check website for details. Register on the website for regular news on events and plants. Delivers to shows.

SPhx PHOENIX PERENNIAL PLANTS
Paice Lane, Medstead, Alton, Hampshire, GU34 5PR
Ⓣ (01420) 560695
Ⓜ 07909 528191
Ⓔ marina@phoenixperennialplants.co.uk
Ⓦ www.phoenixperennialplants.co.uk
Contact: Marina Christopher
Opening Times: By appt. only.
Specialities: Perennials, many uncommon & hardy, selected for beneficial insects particularly pollinators. *Agastache, Centaurea, Salvia, Sanguisorba, Sedum, Thalictrum, Verbascum*, bulbs, prairie plants, umbellifers & late-flowering perennials.
Notes: Also sells wholesale. Delivers to shows.

SPlb PLANTBASE ♿
Sleepers Stile Road, Cousley Wood, Wadhurst, East Sussex, TN5 6QX
Ⓣ (01892) 785599
Ⓜ 07967 601064
Ⓔ plantbaseuk@gmail.com
Ⓦ www.plantbase.co.uk
Contact: Graham Blunt
Opening Times: 1000–1600, 7 days all year (appt. advisable).
Cat. Cost: Online only.
Specialities: Wide range of alpines, perennials, shrubs, climbers, waterside plants, herbs, Australasian, South African & South American plants in particular. Some available in small quantities only.
Notes: Mail order by request only. Delivers to shows. Wheelchair accessible.

SPoG THE POTTED GARDEN NURSERY ♿
Ashford Road, Bearsted, Maidstone, Kent, ME14 4NH
Ⓣ (01622) 737801
Ⓔ markreeve@coolings.co.uk
Ⓦ www.coolings.co.uk/shop
Contact: Mark Reeve
Opening Times: 0900–1700 Mon–Sat & 0900–1630 Sun. Extended opening hours Apr–Jul 0900–1730 Mon–Sat. Xmas/New Year period opening times on website or answerphone.
Notes: Mail order not available. Wheelchair accessible.

SPre PLANTS4PRESENTS ◆
The Glasshouses, Fletching Common, Newick, Lewes, East Sussex, BN8 4JJ
Ⓣ (01825) 721162
Ⓔ plants@4presents.co.uk
Ⓦ www.plants4presents.co.uk
Contact: Emily Rae
Opening Times: Not open. Mail order only.

Cat. Cost: Online only.
Specialities: Well-established nursery offering a range of unusual flowering and fruiting plants, incl. citrus trees.
Notes: Delivers to shows.

SReu REUTHE'S – THE LOST GARDENS OF SEVENOAKS
Sevenoaks Road, Sevenoaks, Kent, TN15 0HB
(T) (01732) 806202
(E) hello@reuthesevenoaks.com
(W) https://reuthes.com/
Contact: Claire Price
Opening Times: 0830–1630 summer 0830–1530 winter all year round, except Christmas Day. Café open every day from 0830 for breakfast, lunch & afternoon tea.
Specialities: Woodland ericaceous plants, roses and perennials.
Notes: We are specialists in woodland ericaceous plants, with a wide range of species on offer including rare rhododendrons, camellias, magnolias, acers, liquid amber, cornus, and hydrangea. We also stock roses & perennials.

SRGP ROSIE'S GARDEN PLANTS
Fieldview Cottage, Pratling Street, Aylesford, Kent, ME20 7DG
(T) (01622) 715777
(M) 07740 696277
(E) jcaviolet@aol.com
(W) www.rosiesgardenplants.com
Contact: Jacqueline Aviolet
Opening Times: Not open. Mail order only.
Cat. Cost: Online only.
Specialities: Hardy *Geranium*, *Symphyotrichum* & *Aster*, herbs & roses.
Notes: Some species & varieties available in small quantities. Exports beyond EU.

SRiv RIVER GARDEN NURSERIES
Troutbeck, Otford, Sevenoaks, Kent, TN14 5PH
(M) 07717 277175
(E) box@river-garden.co.uk
(W) www.river-garden.co.uk
Contact: Jenny Alban Davies
Opening Times: By appt. only.
Min Mail Order UK: £10 + p&p
Min Mail Order EU: £50 + p&p
Cat. Cost: Online only.
Specialities: *Buxus* species & cultivars. *Buxus* topiary.
Notes: Also sells wholesale. Delivers to shows.

SRkn RAPKYNS NURSERY
Street End Lane, Broad Oak, Heathfield, East Sussex, TN21 8UB
(M) 07718 972819
(E) rapkynsnursery@hotmail.com
(W) www.rapkynsnursery.co.uk
Contact: Morag Hockin
Opening Times: 1030–1700 Tues & Thu–Sat.
Cat. Cost: Online only.
Specialities: Unusual shrubs, perennials & climbers including Asters, geraniums, penstemons & grasses. New collections of *Crocosmia, Anemone, Heuchera, Heucherella, Phlox, Coreopsis* & *Helleborus*. Extensive range of *Salvia* & *Monarda*.
Notes: Nursery next door to Scotsford Farm, TN21 8UB. Mail order Sep–Apr incl. Also sells wholesale. Partial wheelchair access. Delivers to shows.

SRms RUMSEY GARDENS &
117 Drift Road, Clanfield, Waterlooville, Hampshire, PO8 0PD
(T) (023) 9259 3367
(E) info@rumsey-gardens.co.uk
(W) www.rumsey-gardens.co.uk
Contact: Mrs M. A. Giles
Opening Times: 0900–1700 Mon–Sat & 1000–1600 Sun & B/hols. Closed Xmas to New Year B/hol.
Min Mail Order UK: £15
Cat. Cost: Online only.
Specialities: Wide general range. Herbaceous, alpines, heathers & ferns. National & International Plant Collection of *Cotoneaster*.
Notes: Wheelchair accessible.

SRot ROTHERVIEW NURSERY &
Ivyhouse Lane, Three Oaks, Hastings, East Sussex, TN35 4NP
(T) (01424) 756228
(E) rotherview@btinternet.com
(W) www.rotherview.com
Contact: Wendy Bates
Opening Times: 0930–1700 7 days (summer)1000–1600 Tue–Sun (autumn/winter).
Min Mail Order UK: £10
Cat. Cost: 6 × 1st class.
Specialities: *Camellia*, alpines and ferns.
Notes: Rotherview Nursery and Coghurst Camellias are on the same site. Delivers to shows. Euro accepted. Wheelchair accessible.

SSea **SEALE ROSE GARDEN**
Seale Nurseries, Seale Lane, Seale, Farnham, Surrey, GU10 1LD
(T) (01252) 782410
(E) catherinemay@sealenurseries.co.uk
(W) www.sealenurseries.co.uk
Contact: David & Catherine May
Opening Times: Please phone for details.
Cat. Cost: None issued.
Specialities: Roses. Some varieties in short supply, please phone first.
Notes: Opening times vary according to season. Please telephone for details.

SSem **SEMPERVIVUMS BY POST**
Not open to the public
(E) sempervivumsbypost@gmail.com
(W) www.sempervivumsbypost.co.uk
Contact: Becky Scott
Opening Times: Not open, mail order only.
Min Mail Order UK: £15 + postage
Specialities: *Sempervivum*. A selection of cacti and other succulents.
Notes: Our nursery was established in 1981. In early 2018, we started a specialised internet shop to sell *Sempervivum* by post to anywhere in the UK. The response has been fantastic since then. We offer the best varieties, the best quality plants, at the best prices – plus a genuine first-class service.

SSFr **SOUTHERN FRUIT TREES** 🔖
The Old Grain Dryer Corner, Blackmoor, Hampshire, GU33 6BP
(T) (01420) 488822
(M) 07760 245524
(E) neil@southernfruittrees.co.uk
(W) www.southernfruittrees.co.uk
Contact: Neil Smith
Opening Times: 0900–1600 7 days, Nov–Apr. Webshop open all year.
Cat. Cost: Free.
Specialities: Over 200 varieties of fruit trees all grown in our Hampshire nursery, specialising in trained fruit including espalier, cordon and fan-trained stone fruit.
Notes: Wheelchair accessible.

SSien **SIENNA HOSTA**
Knap Hill Nursery, Barrs Lane, Knaphill, Surrey, GU21 2JW
(T) (01483) 663160
(E) nursery@siennahosta.co.uk
(W) www.siennahosta.co.uk
Contact: Ollie
Opening Times: Not open. Mail order only.
Specialities: *Hosta* growers with over 30 years' experience. Over 1000 varieties held within the collection with many available to order via our website. Availability may vary throughout the season.
Notes: Orders sent 1st class Royal Mail all year round. We aim to send out orders placed before 12pm Mon–Thu on the same day. Orders placed Fri–Sun will be sent on Mon.

SSta **STARBOROUGH NURSERY** 🔖
Starborough Road, Marsh Green, Edenbridge, Kent, TN8 5RB
(T) (01732) 865614
(E) starborough@hotmail.com
Contact: Sales
Opening Times: 0900–1600 Thu, Fri & Sat. Closed Jan, Jul & Aug or open by appt. only. Please phone first if travelling.
Specialities: Rare & unusual shrubs esp. *Daphne*, *Acer*, rhododendrons & azaleas, *Magnolia* & *Nyssa*.
Notes: Some plants only available in larger sizes or in small numbers and are not listed. Please request a supplementary list from the nursery. Arrangements can be made for collections from Cornwall. Deliveries can be made at cost. Planting & landscaping services available. Wheelchair accessible.

StAn **ST ANDREWS BOTANIC GARDEN**
Canongate, St Andrews, Fife, KY16 8RT
(T) (01334) 461200
(E) nursery@standrewsbotanic.org
(W) https://www.standrewsbotanic.org/
Contact: Peter Watson
Opening Times: 1000–1700 Mon–Fri Apr–Sep. 1000–1600 Mon–Fri Oct–Mar.
Specialities: Wide range of resilient, sustainable and bio-secure herbaceous plants and grasses. Grown and selected according to ecological principles and adapted to the local climate.
Notes: All of our plants are grown on site without heat, and are fully hardy. The nursery is 100% peat-free. Retail and wholesale. The plant sales area is fully wheelchair accessible, with café and toilet facilities. Beautiful 18-acre botanic garden with regular events.

SVen **VENTNOR BOTANIC GARDEN** 🔖
Undercliff Drive, Ventnor, Isle of Wight, PO38 1UL
(T) (01983) 855397

Ⓔ sales@botanic.co.uk
Ⓦ www.botanic.co.uk
Contact: Chris Kidd
Opening Times: 1000–1700 7 days (summer), 1000–1600 7 days (winter).
Cat. Cost: None issued.
Specialities: Coastal, drought-tolerant, Mediterranean & southern hemisphere plants. Rare & esoteric half-hardy trees, shrubs & perennials. National Plant Collections of hardy & half-hardy *Arecaceae* (Palms) and *Puya*.
Notes: Also sells wholesale. Wheelchair accessible.

SVic VICTORIANA NURSERY GARDENS
Challock, Ashford, Kent, TN25 4DG
Ⓣ (01233) 740529
Ⓔ help@victoriananursery.co.uk
Ⓦ www.victoriananursery.co.uk
Contact: Serena Shirley
Opening Times: Not open. Pre-arranged collections only.
Cat. Cost: Online only.
Specialities: Heritage & unusual vegetable plants, seeds, fruit trees & bushes. Specialist grower of chillies & tomatoes, with annual tasting days. Also 600+ varieties of *Fuchsia*.
Notes: This nursery is no longer open to the general public. Pre-arranged collections only. Also sells wholesale.

SWCr COOLINGS WYCH CROSS GARDEN CENTRE ♿
Colemans Hatch Road, Forest Row, East Sussex, RH18 5JW
Ⓣ (01342) 822705
Ⓔ wychcross@coolings.co.uk
Ⓦ www.coolings.co.uk/shop
Contact: Louise Kemp
Opening Times: 0900–1700 Mon–Sat Aug–Feb, 0900–1730 Mon–Sat Apr–Jul, 1000–1630 Sun.
Cat. Cost: Free.
Specialities: Specialises in roses. A wide selection of climbers and herbaceous plants.
Notes: Coffee shop on site. Outstanding views over the Ashdown Forest. Wheelchair accessible.

SWor WORLD GARDEN PLANTS
The Big Greenhouse, Abbotts Farm, Canada Road, West Wellow, Romsey, Hampshire, SO51 6DE
Ⓜ 07957 860157
Ⓔ jim@worldgardenplants.com
Ⓦ http://www.worldgardenplants.com
Contact: Jim Dawes
Opening Times: Visitors all year round by appt. only. See website. What3words soonest.grumble.race.
Specialities: Largest grower of bamboos plants in UK. Hedging & screening plants, climbers & evergreen plants all grown in our big greenhouse in the New Forest. We are moving our plants over to 100% recycled and recyclable pots.

WALES AND THE WEST

WAbe ABERCONWY NURSERY
Aberconwy Nursery, Glan Conwy, Conwy, LL28 5TL
Ⓣ (01492) 580875
Ⓔ enquiries@aberconwynursery.co.uk
Ⓦ www.aberconwynursery.co.uk
Contact: Tim Lever
Opening Times: 1000–1600 Tue–Sat mid-Mar–end Sep.
Cat. Cost: 2 × 2nd class.
Specialities: Alpines, including specialist varieties, esp. gentians, dionysias, dwarf *Dianthus*, *Primula*, *Saxifraga* & dwarf ericaceous plants. Some choice shrubs & woodland plants incl. smaller ferns.
Notes: Delivers to shows.

WBrk BROCKAMIN PLANTS ♿
Brockamin, Old Hills, Callow End, Worcestershire, WR2 4TQ
Ⓣ (01905) 830370
Ⓔ stone.brockamin@btinternet.com
Contact: Margaret Stone
Opening Times: By appt. only.
Specialities: National Plant Collections of *Pulmonaria* cvs, *Symphyotrichum novae-angliae*, *Geranium sanguineum*, *G. macrorrhizum* & *G. × cantabrigiense*. Plants available in small quantities only.
Notes: Wheelchair accessible.

WCAu CLAIRE AUSTIN HARDY PLANTS
White Hopton Farm, Wern Lane, Sarn, Newtown, Powys, SY16 4EN
Ⓣ (01686) 670342
Ⓔ enquiries@claireaustin-hardyplants.co.uk
Ⓦ www.claireaustin-hardyplants.co.uk
Contact: Claire Austin
Opening Times: Mail order only. Open by appt. for the NGS.
Cat. Cost: Free, UK only.

Specialities: *Paeonia*, *Iris*, *Hemerocallis* & hardy plants. National Plant Collections of Bearded *Iris*.

WCav CAVES FOLLY NURSERIES ♿
Evendine Lane, Colwall, Malvern, Worcestershire, WR13 6DX
Ⓣ (01684) 540631
Ⓜ 07918 649276
Ⓔ bridget@cavesfolly.com
Ⓦ www.cavesfolly.com
Contact: Bridget Evans
Opening Times: 1000–1600 Thu–Sat Mar–Oct.
Min Mail Order UK: £6
Cat. Cost: Free.
Specialities: Organically grown perennials and alpines. Plants for pollinators (member of The Saving Pollinators Assurance Scheme).
Notes: Nursery has grown plants in peat-free organic compost for over 35 years. Also soil association certified and members of the new Saving Pollinators Scheme run by The National Botanic Garden of Wales. Majority of plants grown from our own seed, division or cuttings. Also sells wholesale. Delivers to shows. Wheelchair accessible.

WCFE CHARLES F ELLIS
Oak Piece Nurseries, Stanway Road, Stanton, Nr Broadway, Worcestershire, WR12 7NQ
Ⓣ (01386) 584491
Ⓔ info@ellisplants.co.uk
Ⓦ www.ellisplants.co.uk
Contact: Charles Ellis
Opening Times: Nursery not open to visitors.
Min Mail Order UK: £15
Cat. Cost: None issued.
Specialities: Wide range of shrubs, conifers, climbers & perennials, some unusual. All available in small quantities only. A few specimen sizes (but not for mail order).

WCha CHARELLA GARDENS
Cheltenham Road, Broadway, Worcestershire, WR12 7LX
Ⓣ (01386) 859004
Ⓔ enquiries@charellagardens.co.uk
Ⓦ www.charellagardens.co.uk
Contact: Julie Carroll
Opening Times: 0900–1300 Mon–Fri.
Specialities: Bamboos, bay trees, acers and a wide selection of garden plants.
Notes: A family-run nursery in the heart of the Cotswolds.

WChS CHICKENSTREET
1–3 The Stanyards, Gobowen, Oswestry, Shropshire, SY11 4NG
Ⓣ (01691) 657178
Ⓔ enquiry@chickenstreet.co.uk
Ⓦ www.chickenstreet.co.uk
Contact: Jill Cawthray
Opening Times: Not open, mail order only.
Min Mail Order UK: £5.50
Cat. Cost: Online catalogue only.
Specialities: A good selection of grasses and easy care perennials that associate well in naturalistic plantings. Combinations for sunny, shady or boggy areas with emphasis on plants for pollinators and wildlife.
Notes: Plants are propagated by ourselves and therefore stock may vary throughout the year. Generally plants are only sent out during the growing season between early March and November. Delivers to shows.

WCor CORSESIDE NURSERY
Corseside Farm, Angle Road, Pembroke, Pembrokeshire, SA71 5AA
Ⓣ (01646) 641505
Ⓔ hello@corsesidenursery.com
Ⓦ www.corsesidenursery.com/
Contact: Rosie
Specialities: Succulents, hardy exotics and coastal hedging, in particular *Griselinia*.
Notes: A family-run boutique nursery specialising in succulents, hardy exotics and hardy coastal hedging. Unique gifts. Local delivery available in Pembrokeshire.

WCot COTSWOLD GARDEN FLOWERS
Sands Lane, Badsey, Evesham, Worcestershire, WR11 7EZ
Ⓣ (01386) 833849 (nursery) (01386) 422829 (mail order)
Ⓔ info@cgf.net
Ⓦ cotswoldgardenflowers.co.uk/
Contact: Edmund Brown
Opening Times: Please see website or call nursery.
Cat. Cost: Online only.
Specialities: A very wide range of easy to grow & unusual perennials & succulents.
Notes: Delivers to shows. Euro accepted. Limited wheelchair access.

WCra CRANESBILL NURSERY
17, Evesham Crescent, Mossley Estate, Bloxwich, Walsall, West Midlands, WS3 2SW

⊤ (01684) 770733
⊛ 07500 600205
⊜ gary@cranesbillnursery.com
⊛ www.cranesbillnursery.com
Contact: Gary Carroll
Opening Times: Not open, mail order only.
Cat. Cost: Free.
Specialities: Hardy geraniums, Approx 200 varieties in stock. Can supply large quantities with 6–8 weeks' notice. Please contact nursery for further details.
Notes: Cranesbill Nursery is the longest established UK specialist in hardy geraniums. Most of our stock is listed on the website when available, however we do also have limited stock of some unusual geraniums, so always ask. Collections by appt. only.

WCru CRÛG FARM PLANTS 🌿
Griffith's Crossing, Caernarfon, Gwynedd, LL55 1TU
⊤ (01248) 670232
⊛ 07774 980842
⊜ mailorder@crug-farm.co.uk/bleddyn@crug-farm.co.uk
⊛ www.mailorder.crug-farm.co.uk
Contact: B. and S. Wynn-Jones
Opening Times: 1000–1600 Mon–Fri by appt. all year except BH & National Holidays.
Cat. Cost: Online only.
Specialities: Mostly self, wild collected new introductions from Asia, Americas & southern Europe. Especially *Araliaceae*, *Asparagaceae*, shade tolerant perennials & shrubs. Unusual or rare trees, shrubs, herbaceous & bulbous. Many supplied bare-rooted when dormant.
Notes: Delivery by overnight carrier for UK. Delivers to shows. Wheelchair accessible.

WDib DIBLEYS NURSERIES 🌿
Llanelidan, Ruthin, Denbighshire, LL15 2LG
⊤ (01978) 790677
⊜ info@dibleys.com
⊛ www.dibleys.com
Contact: Gareth Dibley
Opening Times: 1000–1600 Mon–Fri Apr–Sep.
Cat. Cost: Free.
Specialities: *Streptocarpus*, *Columnea*, *Solenostemon*, *Saintpaulia* & other gesneriads & *Begonia*. National Plant Collections of *Streptocarpus*, *Saintpaulia* & *Petrocosmea*.
Notes: Also sells wholesale. Euro accepted. Delivers to shows. Wheelchair accessible.

WeWi WEST WALES WILLOWS
The Mill, Gwernogle, Carmarthen, Carmarthenshire, SA32 7SA
⊤ (01267) 202309
⊜ info@westwaleswillows.co.uk
⊛ www.WestWalesWillows.co.uk
Contact: Justine Burgess
Opening Times: Open by appt. only.
Specialities: National Collection Holder for *Salix* (Willow). Specialist grower of over 250 varieties of *Salix*. Sells living willow cuttings from Dec–Mar via mail order.
Notes: For details of open days and cultivation courses please see website.

WFar FARMYARD NURSERIES
Dol Llan Road, Llandysul, Carmarthenshire, SA44 4RL
⊤ (01559) 363389/(01267) 220259
⊜ sales@farmyardnurseries.co.uk
⊛ www.farmyardnurseries.co.uk
Contact: Richard Bramley
Opening Times: 0900–1700 7 days, excl. Xmas Day, Boxing Day & New Year's Day.
Min Mail Order UK: 3 plants
Cat. Cost: None issued.
Specialities: Huge range of home grown shrubs, herbaceous perennials, trees, climbers, alpines, conifers & bedding plants. National Collection of *Primula* sieboldii & *Sarracenia*. Specialise in *Hosta*, *Monarda*, *Begonia*, *Chrysanthemum*, *Impatiens*, *Salvia*.
Notes: Additionally sells from shop/yard in Carmarthen. Also sells wholesale. Partial wheelchair access (not garden or some areas of the nursery).

WGoo WILDEGOOSE NURSERY 🌿
The Walled Garden, Lower Millichope, Munslow, Craven Arms, Shropshire, SY7 9HE
⊤ (01584) 841890
⊛ 07798 628762
⊜ office@wildegoosenursery.co.uk
⊛ www.wildegoosenursery.co.uk
Contact: Laura Willgoss
Opening Times: Thu–Sat late Mar–Oct. Please see website for further details.
Cat. Cost: 1st class sae.
Specialities: *Viola*, incl. stock from Bouts Cottage Nursery. Herbaceous perennials & grasses. Some varieties propagated in small quantities.
Notes: Delivers to shows. Wheelchair accessible. Site is on a slope with gravel paths.

WGrf Hardy Eucalyptus
Grafton Nursery, Worcester Road, Grafton
Flyford, Worcester, Worcestershire,
WR7 4PW
Ⓣ (01905) 888098
Ⓜ 07307 413052
Ⓔ office@hardy-eucalyptus.com
Ⓦ www.hardy-eucalyptus.com
Contact: Hilary Collins
Opening Times: Not open, mail order or by appt. only.
Min Mail Order UK: £10
Min Mail Order EU: £35
Specialities: *Eucalyptus*.
Notes: Specialise in 70+ species and cultivars of *Eucalyptus* suitable for growing in UK gardens, incl. many smaller growing varieties ideal for modern town gardens. Also grow many species for floristry cut foliage and firewood/biomass production. Wholesale and Retail. Delivers to shows.

WGwG Gwynfor Growers
Gwynfor, Pontgarreg, Llangrannog, Llandysul, Sir Ceredigion, SA44 6AU
Ⓣ (01239) 654151
Ⓔ info@gwynfor.co.uk
Ⓦ www.gwynfor.co.uk
Contact: S. & A. Hipkin
Opening Times: Please see website for opening times.
Cat. Cost: Online only.
Specialities: National Plant Collection of *Salvia rosmarinus* cvs. Classic & contemporary plants grown organically & peat-free. Some plants available in small quantities only. Rarities propagated to order.
Notes: Plants also available at local farmers' markets, plant fairs & some NGS Open Gardens.

WHer The Herb Garden & Historical Plant Nursery
Frondeg, Gilfachreda, New Quay, Ceredigion, SA45 9SP
Ⓣ (01545) 580893
Ⓜ 07840 106956
Ⓔ corinnetremaine@gmail.com
Ⓦ www.historicalplants.co.uk
Contact: Corinne Tremaine
Opening Times: By appt. only.
Cat. Cost: Online only.
Specialities: Rare herbs, rare natives & wild flowers; rare, unusual & historical perennials, old roses, heritage pinks & Parma violets.

WHil Hillview Hardy Plants ♿
(off B4176), Worfield, Nr Bridgnorth, Shropshire, WV15 5NT
Ⓣ (01746) 716454
Ⓜ 07974 391608
Ⓔ hillview@onetel.net
Ⓦ www.hillviewhardyplants.com
Contact: Ingrid, John & Sarah Millington
Opening Times: 1000–1700 Mon–Sat, Mar–mid-Oct. At other times, please phone first.
Cat. Cost: Online only.
Specialities: Choice herbaceous perennials incl. *Acanthus, Albuca, Primula auricula, Eucomis, Ixia*. National Plant Collections of *Acanthus, Albuca* & *Primula auricula*.
Notes: Also sells wholesale. Delivers to shows. Wheelchair accessible.

WHnu Hedge Nursery Ltd
Ⓜ 07863 126719
Ⓦ https://www.hedgenursery.co.uk
Opening Times: Online only.
Specialities: Hedging plants.
Notes: Online hedging nursery supplying mainly bare-root hedging plants including native and evergreen varieties. Free delivery to UK mainland addresses on orders over £100 on smaller plants and £300 for taller. Please see website for further information.

WHoo Hoo House Nursery
Hoo House, Gloucester Road, Tewkesbury, Gloucestershire, GL20 7DA
Ⓣ (01684) 293389
Ⓔ nursery@hoohouse.co.uk
Ⓦ www.hoohouse.co.uk
Contact: Julie & Robin Ritchie
Opening Times: 1000–1700 Mon–Sat, 1100–1700 Sun Feb–Oct. Nov–Jan please phone for appointment.
Cat. Cost: 3 × 2nd class.
Specialities: Wide range of herbaceous & alpines grown peat-free. *Aster, Cyclamen, Geranium, Penstemon, Saxifraga* & many later-flowering varieties.

WHrl Harrells Hardy Plants
(office) 15 Coxlea Close, Evesham, Worcestershire, WR11 4JS
Ⓣ (01386) 443077
Ⓜ 07799 577120/07733 446606
Ⓔ mail@harrellshardyplants.co.uk
Ⓦ www.harrellshardyplants.co.uk
Contact: Liz Nicklin & Kate Phillips
Opening Times: By appt. only.

Cat. Cost: Online plant list.
Specialities: The nursery sells a wide range of hardy perennials esp. *Hemerocallis*.
Notes: Nursery located off Rudge Rd, Evesham. Please phone for directions or see website. Partial wheelchair access.

WHtc   **HUTCHINGS AND SON**
Badsey Lane, Knowle Hill, Evesham, Worcestershire, WR11 7EN
Ⓣ (01386) 834441
Ⓜ 07957 530964
Ⓔ enquiries@hutchingsandson.co.uk
Ⓦ www.hutchingsandson.co.uk
Contact: Helen and Matthew Hutchings
Opening Times: 0930–1600 Tue–Fri 1000–1600 Sat.
Cat. Cost: Online only.
Specialities: Trees and shrubs, including fruit trees and conifers. Stock a large variety of plants in small numbers. Large variety of *Trachycarpus fortuneii*.
Notes: Our sales display area is grassed and muddy when wet. Delivery within a 20 mile radius only. No mail order.

WIce   **ICE ALPINES** ♿
Lye Head Road, Bewdley, Worcestershire, DY12 2UW
Ⓣ (01299) 269219
Ⓔ icealpines@googlemail.com
Ⓦ www.icealpines.co.uk
Contact: Mark Lagomarsino
Opening Times: Not open, mail order only.
Min Mail Order EU: £18
Specialities: British grown alpine & rockery plants.
Notes: Delivers to shows. Wheelchair accessible.

WJek   **JEKKA'S** ♿
Shellards Lane, Alveston, Bristol, South Gloucestershire, BS35 3SY
Ⓣ (01454) 418788
Ⓔ sales@jekkas.com
Ⓦ www.jekkas.com
Contact: Jekka McVicar
Opening Times: Open on specific days only. Please check website or contact nursery for dates.
Min Mail Order UK: £10
Min Mail Order EU: £18
Cat. Cost: Online only.
Specialities: Specialist herb farm with Jekka's Herbetum containing over 400 culinary & medicinal herbs from all around the world.
Notes: Wheelchair accessible.

WJun   **ALAN'S JUNGLE PLANTS**
Ty'n-y-Brŵyn Bungalow, Coedkernew, Newport, NP10 8UD
Ⓜ 07774 377311
Ⓔ alansjungleplants@gmail.com
Contact: Alan Hemsley
Opening Times: Mail order. By appt. Apr–Oct inc. 1400–1700 Thu, 1400–1700 Sat, 1000–1600 Sun.
Specialities: Aroids, bananas, gingers. Hardy and half-hardy plants for the exotic and jungle effect including *Abutilon*, *Cestrum*, *Canna*, *Hedychium*, and *Salvia*.
Notes: We are an organic mail order nursery that specialises in plants for the exotic, jungle style. We stock a range of hardy and half-hardy plants as well as a few tender exotics. Visitors are welcome by appointment.

WJur   **JURASSICPLANTS NURSERIES LTD**
Waen Road, Waen, St Asaph, Denbighshire, LL17 0DY
Ⓜ 07909 100255
Ⓔ office@jurassicplants.co.uk
Ⓦ www.jurassicplants.co.uk
Contact: Dr Zoltan Hamori & Magdolna Hamori-Kovacs
Opening Times: Mail order only, but orders can be collected. Phone line open 0900–1700 Mon–Sat. Also contact by email, facebook or through our website.
Cat. Cost: Free.
Specialities: Rare & exotic fruit shrubs and trees, ornamental trees, conservatory plants, patio plants, bonsai subjects, bee friendly plants, wildlife friendly plants, unusual climbers.
Notes: Award winning, family run plant nursery, based in the UK, specialising in supplying hundreds of species of rare and exotic trees & shrubs, edibles, a good range of figs and pomegranates, bonsai starters and many more unusual plants. All plants grown on our site in the UK, in a fibre based potting compost. Gift vouchers available. Delivers to shows.

WKif   **KIFTSGATE COURT GARDENS** ♿
Kiftsgate Court, Chipping Camden, Gloucestershire, GL55 6LN
Ⓣ (01386) 438777
Ⓔ anne@kiftsgate.co.uk
Ⓦ www.kiftsgate.co.uk
Contact: Mrs J. Chambers
Opening Times: 1200–1800 Sun–Thu, May, Jun & Jul. 1400–1800 Sun–Thu, Aug. 1400–1800 Sun, Mon & Wed, Apr & Sep.

Cat. Cost: None issued.
Specialities: Small range of unusual plants.
Notes: Wheelchair accessible.

WKit KITCHEN GARDEN PLANT CENTRE
Ferndene, Strawberry Hill, Newent,
Gloucestershire, GL18 1LH
Ⓜ 07492 903 325/07492 903 325
Ⓔ enquiries@kitchengardenplantcentre.co.uk
Ⓦ www.kitchengardenplantcentre.co.uk
Contact: Neil Jones
Opening Times: By appt. only.
Specialities: Herbs, edibles.
Notes: Family growers of herbs and edible plants and seeds, selling online, at flower shows, food festivals and markets. Peat-free herbs, pesticide-free nursery.

WKor KORE WILD FRUIT NURSERY
Bridport House, Cilcennin, Lampeter,
Ceredigion, SA48 8RL
Ⓣ (01570) 470439
Ⓔ info@korewildfruitnursery.co.uk
Ⓦ www.korewildfruitnursery.co.uk
Contact: Coral Guppy
Opening Times: Mail order only.
Cat. Cost: Free.
Specialities: Range of mainly hardy trees, shrubs and perennials that produce edible fruit and some perennial veg. Unusual plants for indoors. Exotic and native species available.
Notes: Ideal for a range of uses, aspects and soil types. All plants propagated on site in 7cm pots and sold when 1 to 3 years old. Plants available all year round. Customers can arrange to collect.

WLav THE LAVENDER GARDEN
Ashcroft Nurseries, Nr Ozleworth, Kingscote,
Tetbury, Gloucestershire, GL8 8YF
Ⓣ (01453) 860356
Ⓜ 07837 582943
Ⓔ andrew007bullock@aol.com
Ⓦ www.thelavenderg.co.uk
Contact: Andrew Bullock
Opening Times: 1100–1600 Sat & Sun. Weekdays variable, please phone. 1st Nov–1stMar by appt. only.
Min Mail Order UK: £10 + p&p
Cat. Cost: Online only.
Specialities: *Lavandula*, *Buddleja*, plants to attract butterflies. Herbs, wildflowers. National Plant Collection of *Buddleja*.
Notes: Also sells wholesale. Delivers to shows. Limited wheelchair access.

WLov LOVEGROVES
The Old Chapel, Pendock, Gloucestershire,
GL19 3PG
Ⓣ (01531) 650918
Ⓜ 07973 331142
Ⓔ clare@plants-paradise.co.uk
Ⓦ www.plants-paradise.co.uk
Contact: Clare Lovegrove
Opening Times: By appt. only.
Cat. Cost: Available by email & website.
Specialities: Interesting selection of trees, shrubs, ferns and climbers; many of which are rare or unusual. All grown in peat-free compost.
Notes: Traditional plant nursery, producing an inspiring collection of desirable trees and shrubs grown in the UK. Nursery is only open by appointment – collection of plants by prior arrangement. Delivers to shows.

WMal MALCOLM ALLISON NURSERIES
79 Byron Road, St Mark's, Cheltenham,
Gloucestershire, GL51 7EY
Ⓣ (01242) 256349
Ⓜ 07817 730509
Ⓔ majallison2000@yahoo.com
Ⓦ www.malcolmallisonplants.com
Contact: Malcolm Allison
Opening Times: By appt. only.
Specialities: Drought tolerant perennials, cultivars of *Nerine*, *Sarniensis*, *Cistus* & *Halimium* species & cultivars.
Notes: Wide range of hardy and half-hardy herbaceous plants, many available only in small quantities.

WMAq MEREBROOK WATER PLANTS
Kingfisher Barn, Merebrook Farm, Hanley
Swan, Worcester, Worcestershire,
WR8 0DX
Ⓜ 07989 528647
Ⓔ hello@pondplants.co.uk
Ⓦ www.pondplants.co.uk
Contact: Biddi Kings
Opening Times: Not open. Mail order only.
Min Mail Order EU: £25
Cat. Cost: Online only.
Specialities: Hardy *Nymphaea*, Louisiana irises & other aquatic plants. International Waterlily & Water Gardening Soc. accredited collection.
Notes: Full range of pond plants including water lilies, marginal and deeper marginal plants, oxygenating plants, wetland and bog plants and moisture-loving plants.

WMat The Tree Shop at Frank P. Matthews Ltd. &
Berrington Court, Tenbury Wells, Worcestershire, WR15 8TH
T (01584) 812800
E thetreeshop@fpmatthews.co.uk
W www.frankpmatthews.com
Contact: Jack Williams
Opening Times: 0900–1700 Mon–Fri 0900–1600 Sat.
Cat. Cost: 4 × 1st class.
Specialities: Fruit & deciduous ornamental trees.
Notes: Also sells wholesale. Wheelchair accessible.

WMon National Plant Collection of Monarda &
Glyn Bach, Llangolman Road, Efailwen, Pembrokeshire, SA66 7JP
T (01994) 419104
M 07828 199303
E carole_whittaker@hotmail.com
W www.glynbachgardens.co.uk
Contact: Carole Whittaker
Opening Times: Open by appt. & May–Oct for collection of orders only.
Cat. Cost: Online only for our customers.
Specialities: National Plant Collection of *Monarda*. Limited stock available.
Notes: Gardens open under Plant Heritage and NGS by appt. (See website for details). Talks given. If travelling some distance please contact Glyn Bach first to check plant availability. Wheelchair accessible.

WMou Mount Pleasant Trees Ltd &
Rockhampton, Berkeley, Gloucestershire, GL13 9DU
T (01454) 260284
E info@mountpleasanttrees.com
W www.mountpleasanttrees.com
Contact: Tom Locke & Elizabeth Murphy
Opening Times: 0830–1630 Mon–Fri, 0830–1230 Sat, Oct–Apr.
Cat. Cost: Free.
Specialities: Wide range of trees for forestry, hedging, woodlands & gardens esp. *Populus, Salix, Tilia* & *Quercus*.
Notes: Mail order available for plants under 1m in height, quotes on request, p&p quoted on individual basis. Also sells wholesale. Wheelchair accessible.

WNHG New Hope Daylilies (formerly New Hope Gardens) &
Colebatch Farm, Colebatch, Nr Bishops Castle, Shropshire, SY9 5JY
M 07729 591479 (Liz)/07850 423081 (Fi)
E hello@newhopedaylilies.co.uk
W www.newhopedaylilies.co.uk
Contact: Liz Colbrook & Fiona Pidduck
Opening Times: By appointment only – see notes below and website for further information regarding open weekends.
Cat. Cost: See online shop for full product availability.
Specialities: American bred, British grown, *Hemerocallis*. Ships bare-rooted plants. Daylily plants are growing and for sale at New Hope Gardens, Colebatch Farm, Shropshire on open weekends.
Notes: We are a specialist nursery nestled in the gorgeous south Shropshire hills selling over 230 UK grown *Hemerocallis* cultivars. We ship 'bare-root' out of season and welcome visitors by appointment during prime blooming time (early to late summer). Open weekends during the summer. Refreshments available. Free parking onsite. Wheelchair accessible (site is level but no tarmac).

WNPC Newent Plant Centre &
Little Verzons Farm, Hereford Road, Ledbury, Herefordshire, HR8 2PZ
T (01531) 670121
E markmoir999@btinternet.com
W www.newentplantcentre.co.uk
Contact: Mark Moir
Opening Times: 0900–1700 Mon–Sat, 1000–1600 Sun.
Specialities: Extensive range of *Heuchera* & *Euphorbia*. Herbaceous perennials, climbers, shrubs, trees, alpines, herbs, roses & fruit.
Notes: Coffee shop & deli on site. Delivers to shows. Wheelchair accessible.

WOld Old Court Nurseries &
Colwall, Nr Malvern, Worcestershire, WR13 6QE
T (01684) 540416
M 07971 522891
E oldcourtnurseries@btinternet.com
W www.autumnasters.co.uk
Contact: Paul, Meriel or Helen Picton
Opening Times: 1100–1600 Thu–Sat Feb & Mar, 1100–1700 Wed–Sat Apr–end July,

1100–1700 Wed–Sun Aug, 1100–1700 7 days Sep–20th Oct.
Cat. Cost: Free.
Specialities: National Plant Collections of Michaelmas Daisies and Polypodiums (hardy cvs). Herbaceous perennials and tender succulents.
Notes: Mail order sent in spring only. Display garden open Feb–Oct, plus some early season open days. See website or contact nursery for further information. Wheelchair accessible.

WOrg WELSH ORGANIC WILD FLOWERS
Lower Pantgoida, Abergavennyy, NP7 8TH
Ⓜ 07515 881150
Ⓔ sally@welshorganicwildflowers.com
Ⓦ www.welshorganicwildflowers.com
Contact: Sally Jones
Opening Times: Mail order only, but sign up to our newsletter to receive notification of pop-up sales and open meadow days.
Specialities: Wildflowers. Plants grown from seed sourced from our organic farm in Wales.
Notes: A small family-run nursery on an organic farm certified by the Soil Association. All of our plants are grown in peat-free compost and are sold plastic-free. Our giant plugs are sold bare-root, and our pots are made from fully compostable coir fibre.

WPav PAVIOUR AND DAVIES PLANTS
The Poplar, Adforton, Craven Arms, Herefordshire, SY7 0NF
Ⓜ 07966 580812
Ⓔ markpaviour@gmail.com
Ⓦ www.paviouranddaviesplants.co.uk
Contact: Mark Paviour
Opening Times: Mon–Wed pm Apr–Aug. Other times by appt. only.
Cat. Cost: Online.
Specialities: Plants of Chilean and Argentinian origin together with a selection of unusual plants from Australasia. All plants propagated and grown on site. National Plant Collection of *Azara*. Some plants only available in small numbers.
Notes: Small arboretum open, groups by appointment. WC. Tea & coffee available. Order & collect.

WPGP PAN-GLOBAL PLANTS ♿
The Walled Garden, Frampton Court, Frampton-on-Severn, Gloucestershire, GL2 7EX
Ⓣ (01452) 741641
Ⓜ 07801 275138
Ⓔ info@panglobalplants.com
Ⓦ www.panglobalplants.com
Contact: Nick Macer
Opening Times: 1100–1700 Wed–Sun 1st Feb–31st Oct. Also B/hols. Closed 2nd Sun in Sep. Winter months by appt. please telephone first.
Min Mail Order UK: £25
Min Mail Order EU: £35
Cat. Cost: 4 × 1st class.
Specialities: Serious plantsman's nursery offering a wide selection of rare & desirable trees, shrubs, herbaceous, bamboos, exotics, climbers, ferns etc. Specialities incl. *Magnolia*, *Hydrangea*, *Tilia*, *Betula*, *Sorbus*, bamboo & *Agavaceae*.
Notes: Wheelchair accessible.

WPnP PENLAN PERENNIALS
Landre, Drefach, Llanybydder, Ceredigion, SA40 9YD
Ⓣ (01570) 480097
Ⓜ 07984 880241
Ⓔ info@penlanperennials.co.uk
Ⓦ www.penlanperennials.co.uk
Contact: Graham & Julie Moore
Opening Times: Open by appointment only.
Cat. Cost: Online only.
Specialities: Aquatic, marginal & bog plants. Shade-loving & woodland perennials, ferns, hardy geraniums & cottage garden plants, all grown in peat-free compost.
Notes: Mail order all year, next day delivery. Secure online web ordering. Also sells wholesale. Delivers to shows. Delivery within UK only.

WRBe ROSYBEE
Maypole, Monmouth, NP25 5QH
Ⓜ 07710 096734
Ⓔ rosi@rosybee.com
Ⓦ www.rosybee.com
Contact: Rosi Rollings
Opening Times: Not open except by appt. only.
Specialities: Plants for pollinators: mainly herbaceous perennials and sub-shrubs.
Notes: Small, independent nursery specialising in plants that attract pollinators. Also a research centre for plant/pollinator interactions.

WReH READYHEDGE LTD & HEDGEGROW LTD
Court Gate Nursery, Eckington, Pershore, Worcestershire, WR10 3BB
Ⓣ (01386) 750585
Ⓔ sales@readyhedgeltd.com

Ⓦ www.readyhedgeltd.com
Contact: Richard Gosling
Opening Times: 0800–1630 Mon–Thu, 0800–1530 Fri. Closed Sat & Sun.
Notes: Readyhedge are growers & suppliers of quality instant hedging and screening. Readyhedge Ltd is a wholesale nursery growing high quality instant hedging and screening plants for all landscaping projects. The Readyhedge trough range is grown in 1m troughs and is ready spaced for ease of planting.

WRjT RJ Trees and Hedging
Not open to the public
Ⓣ 01989 552028
Ⓔ enquiries@rjtreesandhedging.co.uk
Ⓦ www.rjtreesandhedging.co.uk
Contact: Ray Jenkins
Opening Times: Not open to the public. Telephone and online orders 0830–1630.
Specialities: Bare-root trees and hedging.
Notes: Although we are primarily a wholesale trade nursery, we do supply small orders though our website. Please contact us or see the website for further details. Peat-free.

WShi Shipton Bulbs
Y Felin, Henllan Amgoed, Whitland, Carmarthenshire, SA34 0SL
Ⓣ (01994) 240637
Ⓔ admin@shiptonbulbs.co.uk
Ⓦ www.shiptonbulbs.co.uk
Contact: John Shipton
Opening Times: By appt. only.
Cat. Cost: Sae.
Specialities: Native British bulbs. Bulbs & plants for naturalising.
Notes: Also sells wholesale.

WSpi Spinneywell Nursery
Spinneywell Farm, Waterlane, Oakridge, Stroud, Gloucestershire, GL6 7PH
Ⓜ 07209 133046
Ⓔ wendy@spinneywell.co.uk
Ⓦ www.plantproviders.co.uk
Contact: Wendy Asher
Opening Times: 0900–1700 Wed–Sat Mar–Oct, other times by appt. only. Please telephone first.
Min Mail Order UK: £10 + p&p
Min Mail Order EU: £30 + p&p
Cat. Cost: Online only.
Specialities: *Buxus*, *Daphne*, *Euphorbia*, ferns, grasses, *Hellebore*, hardy geraniums, unusual shrubs *Taxus* (yew) and topiary.
Notes: Plant sourcing service available. Mail order and organised collections/deliveries only. Open days & weekend events. Check website or contact nursery for details. Also sells wholesale.

WSSs Shropshire Sarracenias ♿
Beaufort, Coppice Drive, Wrockwardine Wood, Telford, Shropshire, TF2 7BP
Ⓣ (01952) 612452
Ⓔ mike@carnivorousplants.uk.com
Ⓦ www.carnivorousplants.uk.com
Contact: Mike King
Opening Times: By appt. only.
Cat. Cost: 2 × 1st class.
Specialities: *Sarracenia*. *Dionaea muscipula* & forms. Some stock available in small quantities only. National Plant Collections of *Sarracenia* & *Dionaea*.
Notes: Exports beyond EU. Delivers to shows. Euro accepted. Wheelchair accessible.

WSuV Sunnybank Vine Nursery (National Vine Collection)
Cwm Barn, King Street, Ewyas Harold, Rowlestone, Herefordshire, HR2 0EE
Ⓣ (01981) 240256
Ⓔ Sarah@sunnybankvines.co.uk
Ⓦ www.sunnybankvines.co.uk
Contact: Sarah Bell
Opening Times: Not open. Open day annually – see website for details.
Min Mail Order UK: £22 incl. p&p
Cat. Cost: Online only.
Specialities: Vines. National Plant Collection of *Vitis vinifera* (hardy, incl. dessert & wine). Small quantities of 60–70 varieties available as rooted plants, the entire collection usually available as bare wood cuttings for own propagation depending upon wood ripening this season.
Notes: Open day once a year advertised on both nursery & Plant Heritage websites.

WTho Thorncroft Clematis & Climbers Ltd
Rails End Nursery, Back Lane, Ashton-Under-Hill, Evesham, Worcestershire, WR11 7RG
Ⓣ (01953) 850407
Ⓔ sales@thorncroftclematis.co.uk
Ⓦ sales@thorncroftclematis.co.uk
Contact: Heather Carr

Opening Times: Mail order and collections only. Collections on a Friday year round, by appt. only.
Specialities: *Clematis* and Climbers.
Notes: We are a mail order clematis and climbers nursery offering year round mail order and collection from our nursery in picturesque Ashton-Under-Hill. Collection at Malvern Spring Show available.

WTor **TORTWORTH PLANTS LTD**
Old Lodge Farm, Tortworth, Wotton-under-Edge, Gloucestershire, GL12 8HF
Ⓣ (01454) 260020
Ⓔ info@tortworthplants.co.uk
Ⓦ www.tortworthplants.co.uk
Contact: Rebecca Flint or Tim Hancock
Opening Times: By appt. only.
Cat. Cost: Online or 2 × 1st for plant list.
Specialities: Herbaceous perennials & alpines, incl. the more unusual.
Notes: Also sells wholesale. Partial wheelchair access. Delivers to shows.

WTra **TRADESCANTIA HUB**
Ⓔ avery@tradescantia.uk
Ⓦ https://shop.tradescantia.uk/
Contact: Avery
Opening Times: Not open to the public.
Specialities: Tradescantia.
Notes: Independent researcher, *Tradescantia* specialist and collector. Provisional National Plant Collection holder for tropical *Tradescantia* cultivars. Propagate to order. Pesticide-free, and only use recycled or recyclable packaging. Plant list available online.

WTre **WALLED GARDEN TREBERFYDD**
Llangasty, Brecon, Powys, LD3 7PX
Ⓣ (01874) 730169
Ⓔ alison@walledgardentreberfydd.com
Ⓦ www.walledgardentreberfydd.com
Contact: Alison Sparshatt
Opening Times: 1100–1600 Wed–Sat Mar–Nov.
Cat. Cost: Online only.
Specialities: Unusual hardy plants, grown in Wales.
Notes: Beautiful plant nursery in an old walled garden, specialising in hardy plants grown in Wales which are structural, unusual, herbal or fragrant. Events & workshops throughout the year. Contact nursery for details.

WWct **WALCOT ORGANIC NURSERY**
Walcot Lane, Drakes Broughton, Pershore, Worcestershire, WR10 2AL
Ⓣ (01905) 841587
Ⓔ enquiries@walcotnursery.co.uk
Ⓦ walcotnursery.co.uk
Contact: Kevin O'Neill
Opening Times: Office open 0900–1700 Mon–Fri, 1000–1300 Sat Nov–Mar. Answer machine and emails checked year round. Visits are welcome Sep–Mar by arrangement.
Cat. Cost: Online or paper copy free of charge.
Specialities: Wide range of organic certified fruit trees suitable for outdoor growing in the UK. Apples, crab apples, pears, plums, gages, damsons, gages, cherries, quinces and medlars. Selection of rare local midlands varieties.
Notes: All fruit trees are grown on site and Soil Association certified. Collection from the nursery or delivery offered. Generally bare-rooted, so we can only supply when the trees are dormant. This is between late November and late March on a first-ordered, first arranged basis. We take advance orders from July onwards, and finish taking new orders in late March. We also have a small selection of containerised pre-trained espaliers that can be collected year round if they are in stock on our website. No delivery to EU, Northern Ireland, Isle of Man or Channel Isles.

ABROAD

XFar **FARMER GRACY LTD**
Bulb Trade Park 3, 2211 SW Noordwijkerhout, The Netherlands
Ⓣ 0330 808 7304
Ⓔ customercare@farmergracy.com
Ⓦ www.farmergracy.co.uk
Contact: Naomi Jones
Opening Times: Mail order only – online 24hrs.
Specialities: Flower bulbs and bare-root perennials.
Notes: Although the nursery headquarters is based in The Netherlands, they provide bulbs and perennials to customers both the UK and EU.

Nursery Index by Name

Nurseries that are included in the *RHS Plant Finder* for the first time this year (or have been reintroduced after a significant absence) are marked in **bold type**.

Full details of the nurseries will be found in **Nursery Details by Code** on page 780. For a key to the geographical codes, see the start of **Nurseries**.

Abbotsbury Sub-Tropical Gardens	CAbb
Aberconwy Nursery	WAbe
Abriachan Nurseries	GAbr
Acorn Trees and Shrubs	CAco
Adam's Apple Trees	**CAda**
Agroforestry Research Trust	CAgr
Akorn and Oake	SAko
Alan's Jungle Plants	**WJun**
Alchemy Ferns	NAlc
Angharad Pike Gardener and Plants	SAng
Architectural Plants	SArc
Ardcarne Garden Centre	IArd
Ardfearn Nursery	GArf
Arley Hall Nursery	MArl
Ashwood Nurseries Ltd	MAsh
Athelas Plants	SAth
Avondale Nursery	MAvo
Aylett Nurseries Ltd	LAyl
Babylon – The Nursery	SAdn
Bali-Hai Mail Order Nursery	IBal
Bamboo Giant	SBGi
Barcham Trees PLC	EBar
Barnes Nurseries	LBar
Barnsdale Gardens	MBNS
Barracott Plants	CBct
Bean Place Nursery	SBea
Beechbridge Plants	**SBeP**
Beeches Nursery	EBee
Beggar's Roost Plants	CBgR
Bennetts Water Gardens	CBen
Beth Chatto's Plants and Gardens	ECha
Bide-A-Wee Cottage Gardens	NBid
Big Plant Nursery	SBig
Binny Plants	GBin
Birkheads Secret Gardens & Nursery	NBir
Blackmoor Nurseries	SBmr
Blooming Wild Nursery	CBWd
Blue Nurseries Ltd	CBlu
Bluebell Arboretum & Nursery	MBlu
Bluebell Cottage Nursery	MBel
Boma Garden Centre	LBom
Bowden Hostas	CBdn
Bowhayes Trees	CBTr
Brackendale Nurseries	CBrac
Bressingham Gardens Nursery	EBlo
Bridge Nursery	MBrN
Brighton Plants	SBrt
Broadleigh Gardens	CBro
Brockamin Plants	WBrk
Brooklands Plants	CBrP
Brookside Nursery	MBros
Brownthwaite Hardy Plants	NBro
Buckingham Nurseries	LBuc
Bulbs.co.uk@Taylors Bulbs	ETay
Burncoose Nurseries	CBcs
Camellia Grove Nursery	SCam
Caths Garden Plants	NCth
Caves Folly Nurseries	WCav
CB Plants	CCBP
Champion Plants	CCps
Charella Gardens	WCha
Charles F Ellis	WCFE
Charleshurst Farm Nursery	SChF
Chestnut Nursery (Sheltered Work Opportunities Project)	CCht
Chew Valley Trees Ltd	CCVT
ChickenStreet	WChS
Chiltern Seeds Ltd	MCtn
Chrysanthemums Direct	MCms
Claire Austin Hardy Plants	WCAu
Cliff Bank Nursery	**NClf**
Coastal Hedging	CCoa
Coolings Wych Cross Garden Centre	SWCr
Corseside Nursery	WCor
Cornwall Plants	CoPl
Cotswold Garden Flowers	WCot
Cotswold Trees	**LCot**
Courtyard Planters	NCou
Craftyplants	NCft
Cranesbill Nursery	WCra
Crocus	LCro
Crûg Farm Plants	WCru

D'Arcy & Everest	EDAr	Hedging UK (Nurseries) Ltd	NHed
Delfland Nurseries Ltd	EDel	Hetty's Herbs and Plants	EHet
Desert to Jungle	CDTJ	Hill Close Gardens	MHCG
Dibleys Nurseries	WDib	Hill House Nursery Ltd	CHll
Dorset Perennials	CDor	Hillview Hardy Plants	WHil
Dorset Waterlily Company	**CLil**	Hintons Nursery	MHtn
Dove Cottage Nursery & Garden	NDov	Hollies Farm Plant Centre	MHol
Dryad Nursery	NDry	Home Farm Plants	LHom
Duchy of Cornwall	CDoC	Hoo House Nursery	WHoo
Dunlady Plants and Herbs	IDun	Hooksgreen Herbs	MHoo
E W King & Co. Ltd. (Kings Seeds)	EKin	Hortology Ltd	NHrt
Earthed Up!	**MEar**	Hutchings and Son	WHtc
East Northdown Nursery	SEND	Hydrangea Haven	SHyH
East of Eden Nursery	NEoE	Ice Alpines	WIce
Eastcroft Roses	**SEas**	**In the Garden Ltd**	**LInT**
Echium World	MEch	Iris of Sissinghurst	SIri
Edibleculture	SEdi	Irisesonline	EIri
Edrom Nurseries	GEdr	Ivy Hatch Plant Supplies	SIvy
Edulis	LEdu	Jacques Amand International Ltd	LAma
Eleplants Nursery	SEle	Jekka's	WJek
Elmlea Plants	GElm	Jemima's Garden	GJem
Elsworth Herbs	CEls	John Churcher	SChr
Elworthy Cottage Plants	CElw	John Cullen Gardens Ltd	ECul
Endsleigh Gardens Nursery	CEnd	Jo's Garden Enterprise	GJos
English Woodlands	SEWo	Junker's Nursery	CJun
Exclusive Plants Nursery	CExl	Jurassicplants Nurseries Ltd	WJur
Fairweather's Garden Centre	SFai	Keepers Nursery	SKee
Farmer Gracy Ltd	XFar	Kevock Garden Plants	GKev
Farmyard Nurseries	WFar	Kiftsgate Court Gardens	WKif
Firecrest Trees & Shrubs Nursery	EMac	Kinlochlaich Garden Plant Centre	GKin
Folium and Flos Plants Ltd	SFol	Kitchen Garden Plant Centre	WKit
Forde Abbey Nursery	CAby	Kits Nursery	CKit
Forest Edge Nurseries (The Heather Garden)	CFst	Knoll Gardens	CKno
Garden House Nursery	NGdn	Kore Wild Fruit Nursery	WKor
Glendoick Gardens Ltd	GGGa	Landford Trees	CLnd
Glenholme Herb Nursery	CGHo	Langthorns Plantery	ELan
Golden Hill Nurseries	SGol	Larch Cottage Nurseries	NLar
Goscote Nurseries Ltd	MGos	Leesa's not just Alpines	SLee
Great Dixter Nurseries	SDix	Lincolnshire Pond Plants Ltd	ELin
Green Island Gardens	EGrI	Little Brook Fuchsias	SLBF
Greenkoos	NGKo	Loder Plants	SLdr
Grenville Nurseries	EGren	Lodge Farm Plants & Wildflowers	MLod
Griselina "R" Us	CGri	Long Acre Plants	CLAP
Grow Tropicals Ltd	**NTro**	Long House Plants	ELon
Grow Wilder	CGwi	Lovegroves	WLov
Growild Nursery	GGro	Mac Pennys Nurseries	CMac
Gwynfor Growers	WGwG	Macplants	GMaP
Habitat Aid Ltd.	CHab	Madrona Nursery	SMad
Halls of Heddon	NHal	Majestic Trees	LMaj
Happy Houseplants	**EHap**	Malcolm Allison Nurseries	WMal
Hardy Eucalyptus	WGrf	Mallet Court Nursery	CMCN
Hardy's Cottage Garden Plants	SHar	Mandy Plants	EMdy
Harrells Hardy Plants	WHrl	Manor Farm Botanics	MVer
Hart Canna	SHaC	Marchants Hardy Plants	SMHy
Hartside Nursery Garden	NHar	Margery Fish Plant Nursery	CFis
Hedge Nursery Ltd	**WHnu**	Marshall's Malmaisons	EMal
HedgeXpress	MHed	Marwood Hill Gardens	CMHG
Hedging Plants Direct	EHeP	Mendip Bonsai Studio	CMen

Mendle Nursery	NMen	Primrose Cottage Nursery	MPri
Merebrook Water Plants	WMAq	Primrose Hall Peonies	LPmr
Merriments Gardens	SMrm	Proctors Nursery	MPro
Mickfield Hostas	EMic	Puddleplants	CPud
Middleton Nurseries	Midl	Quercus Garden Plants Ltd	GQue
Miles Japanese Maples	SMil	Quiet Corner Plants	NQui
Millais Nurseries	LMil	Rapkyns Nursery	SRkn
Millwood Plants	CMiW	RB Plants	EAri
Mintopia	MMen	ReadyHedge Ltd & Hedgegrow Ltd	WReH
Mires Beck Nursery	NMir	**Reuthe's – The Lost Gardens of Sevenoaks**	**SReu**
Moore and Moore Plants	EMor	Rewela Hostas	NRew
Morehavens	SMor	River Garden Nurseries	SRiv
Morlas Plants	MCor	**RJ Trees and Hedging**	**WRjT**
Morton Nurseries Ltd	MMrt	Rose Cottage Plants	ERCP
Mount Pleasant Trees Ltd	WMou	Roseland House Nursery	CRHN
Mucklestone Nurseries	MMuc	Rosie's Garden Plants	SRGP
National Plant Collection of Thalictrum	**MTha**	Rosybee	WRBe
National Plant Collection of Monarda	WMon	Rotherview Nursery	SRot
Natural Surroundings	NAts	Rumsey Gardens	SRms
New Hope Daylilies (Formerly New Hope Gardens)	WNHG	Ryal Nursery	NRya
		Seagate Nurseries	ESgI
New Wood Trees	CNWT	Seale Rose Garden	SSea
Newent Plant Centre	WNPC	Seaside Plants	CSde
Nightingale Nursery Ltd	SNig	Sempervivums By Post	SSem
Norfolk Herbs	ENfk	Shady Plants	ISha
Norfolk Lavender	ENor	Shipton Bulbs	WShi
Norfolk Snowdrops	**ENSn**	Shire Plants	LShi
Norwell Nurseries & Gardens	MNrw	Shropshire Sarracenias	WSSs
Old Court Nurseries	WOld	Shrubland Nurseries	EShb
Orange Pippin Ltd	NOra	Sienna Hosta	SSien
Orchard Nursery Plant Centre Ltd	SOrN	Southern Fruit Trees	SSFr
Packhorse Farm Nursery	MPkF	Southon Plants	LSou
Paddock Plants	SPad	Southwold Succulent Co.	ESuc
Pan-Global Plants	WPGP	Special Plants	CSpe
Papervale Trees	IPap	Spinneywell Nursery	WSpi
Paviour and Davies Plants	WPav	Spring Reach Nursery	LSRN
Peake Perennials	SPeP	**St Andrews Botanic Garden**	**StAn**
Pelham Plants	SPel	St Bridget Nurseries Ltd	CSBt
Penberth Plants	CPbh	Staddon Farm Nurseries	CSta
Penlan Perennials	WPnP	Starborough Nursery	SSta
Perry's Plants	NPer	Stillingfleet Lodge Nurseries	NSti
Peter Beales Roses	EBls	Stone Lane Gardens	CSto
Peter Nyssen Ltd	**NNys**	Stonyford Cottage Nursery	MSCN
Phedar Nursery	MPhe	Stotts Nursery	LSto
Phoenix Perennial Plants	SPhx	Straight Mile Nursery Gardens	ESMi
Piccolo Plants Nursery	CPic	Strete Gate Camellias	CSgt
Piecemeal Plants	MPie	Style Roses	ESty
Pippin Trees	NPip	Sue Proctor Plants	NSue
Plant Drop	**LDro**	Sunnybank Vine Nursery (National Vine Collection)	WSuV
Plantagogo.com	MPnt		
Plantbase	SPlb	Swallows Nursery & Plant Centre	MSwo
Plants, Shoots and Leaves	GPSL	Swines Meadow Farm Nursery	ESwi
Plants4Presents	SPre	Taylors Clematis Nursery	NTay
Pomona Fruits Ltd	EPom	**The Backyard Larder**	**NBac**
Pondfolk	EPfk	The Crocosmia Gardens	ECrc
Potash Nursery Ltd	EPts	The English Iris Company	EnIr
Potato House	GPoH	The Hardy Geranium Nursery	LHGe
Pottertons Nursery	EPot	The Hawthornes Nursery	NHaw

The Hebe Society (Selling on behalf of The Hebe Society)	SHeb	Trehane Nursery	CTrh
		Treseders Nursery	CTsd
The Herb Garden & Historical Plant Nursery	WHer	Trevor White Old Fashioned Roses	ETWh
		Triffids	CTtf
The Herb Nursery	MHer	Twelve Nunns	ENun
The Herbary	CHby	**Urban Jungle**	**EUrb**
The Lavender Garden	WLav	Ventnor Botanic Garden	SVen
The Little Green Plant Factory	NLit	Victoriana Nursery Gardens	SVic
The National Herb Centre	MNHC	Walcot Organic Nursery	WWct
The No Name Nursery	**SNoN**	Walled Garden Nursery	CWGN
The Norfolk Olive Tree Company	EOli	Walled Garden Treberfydd	WTre
The Palm Tree Company	NPlm	Waltham Herbs	EWhm
The Place for Plants	EPfP	Walworth Garden	LWaG
The Plant Centre at Hortus Loci	SHor	Water Garden Plants	EWat
The Plantsman's Preference	EPPr	Waterside Nursery	MWts
The Potted Garden Nursery	SPoG	Welsh Organic Wild Flowers	WOrg
The Potting Shed	IPot	West Acre Gardens	EWes
The Romantic Garden	ERom	West Wales Willows	WeWi
The Tree Shop at Frank P. Matthews Ltd.	WMat	Westcountry Nurseries (North Devon) Ltd	CWCL
The Walled Gardens of Cannington	CWal	Whitelea Nursery	MWht
The Water Garden	CWat	Wild But Rooted	CWRo
Thorncroft Clematis & Climbers Ltd	**WTHo**	Wildegoose Nursery	WGoo
Topiary Arts	LTop	Wildwood Plants	MWlw
Tor Garden Plants	CToG	**Willowbridge Plants Ltd**	**NWbg**
Tortworth Plants Ltd	WTor	Winrow Nurseries	CWnw
Tradescantia Hub	WTra	Wisley Plant Centre (RHS)	LRHS
Trecanna Nursery	CTca	Woodlands	EWld
Tree Peony Company	NTPC	Woottens of Wenhaston	EWoo
Tree2mydoor Ltd	**NTrD**	World Garden Plants	SWor

HERBS · BAY TREES · SALVIAS
SCENTED PELARGONIUMS

We specialise in growing naturally raised and peat-free plants on our wildlife rich nursery. Come and meet our friendly team or order online

www.norfolkherbs.co.uk
info@norfolkherbs.co.uk - 01362 860812

Blackberry Farm, Dillington, Dereham, NR19 2QD

Plants4Presents specialise in Delivering Plants as Gifts

Choose from a huge range of citrus trees, flowering plants, herbs and exotics delivered gift wrapped for birthdays, anniversaries and events throughout the year.

Plants4Presents
01825 721162
www.plants4presents.co.uk

SHEDFAST
QUICK DELIVERY ▸ FLEXIBLE LAYOUT ▸ STRONG ▸ UNBEATABLE VALUE

FAST DELIVERY

One Shed, Several Layouts

▸ **Tall Eaves (6'2")**
Higher headroom and more space.

▸ **Toughened Safety Glass**
Fixed toughened safety glass windows with PVC cills.

▸ **Modular Design**
Interchangeable panels, so you can position your doors or windows in the side or gable end.

▸ **Single Solid Timber Door**
Your door can be hinged on either the left or the right hand side. Comes complete with three heavy-duty hinges and lockable pad bolt.

▸ **12mm Shiplap Cladding**
Tongue and grooved shiplap cladding, factory treated in a premium protector treatment in a pleasant golden larch colour. 44x28 framework doubled up at every panel joint to heavy duty 56x44.

▸ **12mm Solid Timber Roof & Floor**
Manufactured from the finest North European redwood with robust trusses and high quality polyester backed black mineral roofing felt.

*some delivery restrictions may apply

Explore our extensive range of over **2000** greenhouses and garden buildings at one of our **34 nationwide branches** all open 7 days a week!
Visit www.greenhousepeople/display-sites to find your nearest display centre.

Index of Advertisers

A
Access Garden Products	30
Alpine Garden Society	4

B
Big Plant Nursery	32
BioBloom Soil Enricher	IFC

D
David Austin Roses	31
Dingle Nursery & Garden	31

G
Greenhouse People, The	IBC & 845

H
Hardy Plant Society	774

J
Jelitto Perennial Seeds	32

L
Lux Unique Limited	3

N
Norfolk Herbs	845

P
P de Jager & Sons Ltd	845
Peter Beales Roses	23

R
Plant Heritage	847
Plants4Presents	845
RHS Plants	6

S
Strulch	24
Swines Meadow Garden Centre	845

W
Winterling	31

For all advertising enquiries please contact:
Louise Bowering
T 01733 294679
E louisebowering@rhs.org.uk

Plant Heritage
CONSERVING THE DIVERSITY OF GARDEN PLANTS

Plant Heritage is working to conserve our garden plants for people to use and enjoy today and tomorrow.

HOW DO WE DO THIS?

The National Plant Collections® are at the heart of what we do – over 700 living plant libraries representing the diversity of our cultivated plants

Threatened Plants Programme – our research helps us identify plants at risk of disappearing so we can protect them

Plant Guardian® scheme – across the UK individuals are nurturing rare plants in their own house or garden

YOU CAN GET INVOLVED

Join us today to support our vital conservation work. As a member of Plant Heritage you can:

- receive our Directory, Journals and e-newsletters
- access our network of local groups
- attend talks, events, visits, plant sales
- receive hard-to-find plants in our annual Plant Exchange
- record your own rare plant by becoming a Plant Guardian

JOIN US: 01483 447540 | info@plantheritage.org.uk
WWW.PLANTHERITAGE.ORG.UK

Charity number 1004009/SC041785